THE WORLD OF CHILD LABOR

THE WORLD OF CHILD LABOR

AN HISTORICAL AND REGIONAL SURVEY

HUGH D. HINDMAN, EDITOR

M.E.Sharpe
Armonk, New York
London, England

Cover photos (top) courtesy of the Library of Congress, Lewis Wickes Hine National Child Labor Committee Collection; (bottom) courtesy Kristoffel Lieten

Library of Congress Cataloging-in-Publication Data

Hindman, Hugh D.
The world of child labor : an historical and regional survey / Hugh D. Hindman.
p. cm.
Includes bibliographical references and index.
ISBN 978-0-7656-1707-1 (cloth : alk. paper)
1. Child labor--History. 2. Child labor. I. Title.
HD6231.H56 2009
331.3'1--dc22 2008048167

Printed in the United States of America

The paper used in this publication meets the minimum requirements of
American National Standard for Information Sciences
Permanence of Paper for Printed Library Materials,
ANSI Z 39.48-1984.

∞

CW (c) 10 9 8 7 6 5 4 3 2 1

Publisher: Myron E. Sharpe
Vice President and Editorial Director: Patricia A. Kolb
Executive Editor: Lynn Taylor
Production Director: Carmen Chetti
Production Editor: Eileen Chetti
Editorial Assistant: Kathryn Corasaniti
Cover Design: Jesse Sanchez

Contents

PART 8: EAST ASIA AND THE PACIFIC

Editor and Contributors

Hugh D. Hindman is Professor of Labor and Human Resources at Appalachian State University. He received his undergraduate degree from the College of Wooster in 1972 and his Ph.D. in Labor and Human Resources from the Ohio State University in 1989. He is author of *Child Labor: An American History,* published in 2002 by M.E. Sharpe.

Laura S. Abrams, Ph.D., University of California, Los Angeles

A.A. Aderinto, Ph.D., Department of Sociology, University of Ibadan, Nigeria

Assefa Admassie, Director, Ethiopian Economic Policy Research Institute, Addis Ababa, Ethiopia

Marcos T. Aguila, Universidad Autónoma Metropolitana, Xochimilco, Mexico

Walter Alarcón Glasinovich, Director, Infancia y Desarrollo, Peru

Anita Amorim, International Labor Organization (ILO) – International Program for the Elimination of Child Labor (IPEC), Geneva

Leandro Feitosa Andrade, Professor of Psychology, Faculdades Metropolitanas Unidas (United Metropolitan Colleges), and Researcher, Carlos Chagas Foundation, Sao Paulo, Brazil

Shahid Ashraf, Professor, Department of Economics, Jamia Millia Islamia (Central University), New Delhi, India

Fatima Badry, American University of Sharjah, United Arab Emirates

Subrata Sankar Bagchi, Ph.D., Department of Anthropology, Bangabasi Evening College, Kolkata, India

Maureen Baker, Professor of Sociology, University of Auckland, New Zealand

Loretta E. Bass, Associate Professor, Sociology, University of Oklahoma, USA

Anastasiya Batykova, Institute of Sociology of RAS, Moscow

Tom Beck, Chief Curator, University of Maryland, Baltimore County, USA

Arjun Singh Bedi, Professor of Quantitative Economics, Institute of Social Studies, The Hague, Netherlands

Albert Berry, Professor Emeritus, Department of Economics, University of Toronto, Canada

Sharon Bessell, Senior Lecturer, Crawford School of Economics and Government, The Australian National University, Canberra, Australia

Mario Biggeri, Researcher, University of Florence, Italy

Jonathan Blagbrough, Forced Labour Programme Coordinator, Anti-Slavery International, London

Michel Bonnet, Former National Program Coordinator for Africa, International Labor Organization (ILO) – International Program for the Elimination of Child Labor (IPEC)

Michael Bourdillon, Professor Emeritus, Department of Sociology, University of Zimbabwe

Gabriella Breglia, Researcher, Understanding Children's Work (UCW) Project, University of Rome, Tor Vergata

Drusilla K. Brown, Associate Professor of Economics, Tufts University, USA

Enriqueta Camps, Professor of Economics, Pompeu Fabra University, Barcelona, Spain

Gail H. Corbett, teacher and author, Canada

Jennifer de Boer, Former Child Rights Policy Officer, Terre des Hommes, Netherlands

Afke De Groot, Research Associate, International Research on Working Children (IREWOC), Amsterdam

Albertine de Lange, MA, International Research on Working Children (IREWOC), Amsterdam

James DelRosso, Web Editor and Reference Assistant, Catherwood Library, Cornell University's School of Industrial and Labor Relations, USA

Yacouba Diallo, Statistical Information and Monitoring Programme on Child Labor (SIMPOC), International Labor Organization (ILO) – International Program for the Elimination of Child Labor (IPEC), Geneva

Alison Dilworth, Consultant to the Coalition to Stop the Use of Child Soldiers, London

George Dimock, Professor of Art History, University of North Carolina-Greensboro, USA

Onur Dinç, Ph.D., Assistant Professor, Girne American University, Turkish Republic of Northern Cyprus

Jaap E. Doek, Emeritus Professor of Family and Juvenile Law, Vrije Universiteit, Netherlands, and Chairperson UN Committee on the Rights of the Child (2001–2007), Amsterdam

Marcelo Justus dos Santos, Department of Economics, Ponta Grossa State University, Brazil

Mike Dottridge, Human Rights Consultant, Former Director of Anti-Slavery International, London

Leith L. Dunn, Senior Lecturer/Head, Centre for Gender and Development Studies, The University of the West Indies, Jamaica, and former Assistant Representative, UNFPA Caribbean Office

Martin Eaton, Ph.D., Reader in Human Geography, School of Environmental Sciences, University of Ulster, UK

Eric V. Edmonds, Department of Economics at Dartmouth College, Institute for the Study of Labor (IZA), and the National Bureau of Economic Research, USA

Patrick M. Emerson, Assistant Professor of Economics, Oregon State University, USA

Cennet Engin-Demir, Department of Educational Sciences, Middle East Technical University, Ankara, Turkey

Kristina Engwall, Ph.D., Institute for Future Studies, Stockholm, Sweden

Irving Epstein, Professor, Department of Educational Studies, Illinois Wesleyan University, USA

Guliz Erginsoy, Professor Dr., Department of Sociology, Mimar Sinan Fine Arts University, Istanbul, Turkey

Yakın Ertürk, UN Special Rapporteur on violence against women, its causes and consequences; Professor of Sociology, Middle East Technical University, Ankara, Turkey

Rosario M. Espino, Asian Institute of Management, Makati City, Philippines

Andres Pablo Falconer, Ashoka: Innovators for the Public, UK

Anaclaudia Gastal Fassa, M.D., Ph.D., Associate Professor, Department of Social Medicine, Federal University of Pelotas, Brazil

Andrea R. Ferro, Ph.D. candidate, Department of Economics at ESALQ, University of São Paulo, Brazil

Cármen Elisa Flórez, Senior Professor, Economics Department, Los Andes University, Colombia

Ken Fones-Wolf, Professor of History, West Virginia University, USA

Alec Fyfe, Senior Child Labor Specialist, International Labor Organization, Geneva

Nora Gaupp, Ph.D., Researcher at the German Youth Institute (DJI), Munich/Halle, Germany

Garance Genicot, Associate Professor, Economics, Georgetown University, USA

Boris B. Gorshkov, Assistant Professor of History, Auburn University, USA

Pedro Goulart, Institute of Social Studies, The Hague, and CISEP, ISEG, Technical University of Lisbon, Portugal

Richard Grabowski, Professor of Economics, Department of Economics, Southern Illinois University, USA

Jeanine Graham, Senior Lecturer in History, University of Waikato, New Zealand

Beverly Grier, Associate Professor of Government and International Relations, Clark University, USA

Lorenzo Guarcello, Researcher, Understanding

Children's Work (UCW) Project, University of Rome, Tor Vergata

Indrani Gupta, Professor, Institute of Economic Growth, Delhi, India

Hal Hansen, Departments of History and Economics, Suffolk University, Boston, USA

Risto F. Harma, formerly with Global March Against Child Labor, London

Harry Haue, Ph.D. (Philosophy), Associate Professor, University of Southern Denmark

Hasan Hawamdeh, Ph.D., Mu'tah University, Karak, Jordan

Gautam Hazarika, University of Texas at Brownsville, USA

Harry Hendrick, Associate Professor, Institute of History, University of Southern Denmark

Colin Heywood, Reader in Modern French History, University of Nottingham, UK

Diana Hincapié, Junior Researcher, Economics Department, Los Andes University, Colombia

Charu Lata Hogg, Consultant to the Coalition to Stop the Use of Child Soldiers, Chatham House, London

Joshua H. Howard, Croft Associate Professor of History and International Studies, University of Mississippi, USA

Reza Jalali, MHSA, Program Coordinator, Multicultural Student Affairs, University of Southern Maine, USA

Nancy Janovicek, Assistant Professor, Department of History, University of Calgary, Canada

Peter Jensen, Professor, Aarhus School of Business, University of Aarhus, Denmark

Zarina Jillani, Society for the Protection of the Rights of the Child (SPARC), Islamabad, Pakistan

Nicola Jones, Program Leader, Research and Policy in Development, Overseas Development Institute, UK

Atsuko Fujino Kakinami, Kyoto Sangyo University, Japan

Grace Kao, Director, Asian American Studies Program, Associate Professor of Sociology, Department of Sociology and Population Studies Center, University of Pennsylvania, USA

Ana Lúcia Kassouf, Professor, Department of Economics, University of São Paulo/ESALQ, Brazil

Bal Kumar KC, Ph.D., Professor and Executive Head, Central Department of Population Studies, Tribhuvan University, Kathmandu, Nepal

Timothy Kelly, Associate Professor of History, Saint Vincent College, USA

Wilma King, Strickland Professor of History, University of Missouri, USA

Andrew B. Kipnis, Research School of Pacific and Asian Studies, The Australian National University

Peter Kirby, Ph.D., Lecturer in Economic History, Department of History, University of Manchester, UK

Yuko Kitada, Ph.D., The Australian National University, Canberra

Felicia Marie Knaul, Senior Economist, Mexican Health Foundation, Mexico City

Esin Konanç, Ph.D., Professor Eastern Mediterranean University, Turkish Republic of Northern Cyprus

Ethel V. Kosminsky, Professor of Sociology, Social Sciences Graduate Program, São Paulo State University (UNESP)–Marília, and Researcher, CNPq, Brazil

Esin Kuntay, Ph.D., Professor, Department of Sociology, Mimar Sinan Fine Arts University, Istanbul, Turkey

Elizabeth Anne Kuznesof, Professor of History, University of Kansas, USA

Laura L. Leavitt, Human Resources and Labor Relations Librarian, School of Labor and Industrial Relations, Michigan State University, USA

Alysa Levene, Ph.D., Senior Lecturer in Early Modern History, Oxford Brookes University, UK

David Levine, Professor, Ontario Institute for Studies in Education, University of Toronto, Canada

Susan Levine, Ph.D., Lecturer, Department of Social Anthropology, University of Cape Town, South Africa

Deborah Levison, Associate Professor, Hubert H. Humphrey Institute of Public Affairs, University of Minnesota, USA

G.K. Lieten, Professor of Child Labour Studies at the International Institute of Social History and at the University of Amsterdam; Director, International Research on Working Children (IREWOC), Amsterdam

Kriste Lindenmeyer, Professor of History, University of Maryland, Baltimore County, USA

Sofia Lundberg, Centre for Regional Science at Umeå University (Cerum), Sweden

Scott Lyon, Researcher, Understanding Children's Work (UCW) Project, University of Rome, Tor Vergata

Mary Lyons-Barrett, Ph.D., University of Nebraska at Omaha, USA

Carmen Madrinan, Executive Director, End Child Prostitution, Child Pornography, and Trafficking of Children for Sexual Purposes International (ECPAT), Bangkok, Thailand

David Maidment, OBE, Co-Chair, Consortium for Street Children, Founder and Chairman, Railway Children, Children's Rights Advisor, Amnesty International UK

Reid Maki, Children in the Fields Campaign Director, Association of Farmworker Opportunity Programs, USA

Valeriy A. Mansurov, Institute of Sociology of RAS, Moscow

Richard Marcoux, Professor, Université Laval, Québec City, Canada

Pirjo Markkola, Professor, Åbo Akademi University, Adjunct Professor, University of Tampere, Finland

Zoë Marriage, Lecturer in Development Studies, School of Oriental and African Studies, London, UK

Pietro Masina, Associate Professor of International Political Economy, University of Naples—L'Orientale, Italy

Stan Meuwese, Retired Director, Defence for Children International, Netherlands

Joan Meznar, Professor of History, Eastern Connecticut State University, USA

Arup Mitra, Institute of Economic Growth, Delhi University, India

Phil Mizen, Department of Sociology, University of Warwick, UK

Heidi Morrison, Ph.D. candidate, University of California at Santa Barbara, USA

Jeylan T. Mortimer, Professor, Department of Sociology, University of Minnesota, USA

William E. Myers, Department of Human and Community Development, University of California, Davis, USA

Nguyen Van Chinh, Hanoi National University, Vietnam

Adelaja Odutola Odukoya, Department of Political Science, University of Lagos, Nigeria

Julia E. Offiong, Librarian, George Meany Memorial Archives Library, National Labor College, USA

Opolot Okia, Assistant Professor of History, Winthrop University, USA

Oris de Oliveira, Professor of Law, University of São Paulo, Brazil

Harold Olofson, Professor of Anthropology, University of San Carlos, Cebu City, Philippines

Lars Olsson, Professor of History at Växjö University, Sweden

Tom O'Neill, Ph.D., Department of Child and Youth Studies, Brock University, Canada

Nadine Osseiran, International Labor Organization (ILO) – International Program for the Elimination of Child Labor (IPEC), Geneva

Maria-Carmen Pantea, International Policy Fellowship, Open Society Institute and "Babes Bolyai" University, Romania

Jon Pedersen, Research Director, Fafo Institute for Applied International Studies, Norway

Felipe Peralta, Associate Professor, School of Social Work, New Mexico State University, USA

Elizabeth Perry, Head Librarian (retired), Centre for Industrial Relations, University of Toronto, Canada

Adrienne Pine, Professor of Anthropology, The American University in Cairo, Egypt

Maja Pleic, Mexican Health Foundation, Mexico City, and University of Toronto, Canada

Karen A. Porter, PhD, Associate Professor of Anthropology, Hanover College, USA

Dave Pretty, Assistant Professor of History, Winthrop University, USA

Munir Quddus, Dean and Professor of Economics, Prairie View A&M University, USA

Marjatta Rahikainen, Associate Professor in Social History, University of Helsinki, Finland

Usha Ramanathan, Honorary Fellow, Centre for the Study of Developing Societies, New Delhi, India

Ranjan Ray, Department of Economics, Monash University, Australia

Birgit Reissig, MA, Researcher at the German Youth Institute (DJI), Munich/Halle, Germany

Shirleene Robinson, Ph.D., Assistant Professor, Bond University, Gold Coast, Australia

Furio C. Rosati, Coordinator and Professor of Economics, Understanding Children's Work (UCW) Project, University of Rome, Tor Vergata

Heike Roschanski, Anthropological Researcher, International Research on Working Children (IREWOC), Amsterdam

Fúlvia Rosemberg, Professor of Social Psychology, Pontifical Catholic University of São Paulo, and Researcher, Carlos Chagas Foundation, Brazil

Abhra Roy, Kennesaw State University, USA

Thomas Max Safley, Professor of History, University of Pennsylvania, USA

Chris Sakellariou, Economics, Humanities and Social Sciences, Nanyang Technological University, Singapore

Bengt Sandin, Department of Child Studies, University of Linköping. Sweden

Mahir Saul, Associate Professor, University of Illinois, USA

Bernard Schlemmer, Sociologist, Senior Researcher, IRD, France

Deborah J. Schmidle, Social Sciences Librarian, Olin Library, Cornell University, USA

Peter Scholliers, Professor of History, Vrije Universiteit Brussel, Belgium

Ellen Schrumpf, Professor in Childhood Research and Modern Norwegian History, University of Trondheim, NTNU, Norway

Sharmistha Self, Assistant Professor, Department of Economics, Missouri State University, USA

Luis Serra, Ph.D., Center for Sociocultural Analysis, Central American University, Nicaragua

Heather Shore, Senior Lecturer in Social and Cultural History, Leeds Metropolitan University, UK

Mirela Shuteriqi, Advocacy and Legal Officer for Southeastern Europe, Terre des Hommes, Albania

Jan Skrobanek, Ph.D., Researcher at the German Youth Institute (DJI), Munich/Halle, Germany

Cor Smit, Ph.D., independent historian, The Netherlands

Ingrid Söderlind, Ph.D., Institute for Futures Studies, Stockholm, Sweden

Chivy Sok, Co-Director of the Women's Institute for Leadership Development (WILD) for Human Rights, USA

Tone Sommerfelt, Research Fellow, Department of Social Anthropology, University of Oslo, Norway

André Portela Souza, São Paulo School of Economics, Getúlio Vargas Foundation, Brazil

Nick Spencer, Emeritus Professor of Child Health, School of Health and Social Studies, University of Warwick, UK

Jeremy Staff, Assistant Professor, Department of Sociology, Pennsylvania State University, USA

Peter N. Stearns, Provost and Professor of History, George Mason University, USA

Govind Subedi, Lecturer, Central Department of Population Studies, Tribhuvan University, Kathmandu, Nepal

Shurlee Swain, Associate Professor, Reader in History, Australian Catholic University, and Senior Research Fellow, Department of History, University of Melbourne, Australia

Jerome Teelucksingh, Ph.D., University of the West Indies at St. Augustine, Trinidad and Tobago

Indrasari Tjandraningsih, AKATIGA–Center for Social Analysis, Bandung, Indonesia

Jeppe Toensberg, PhD, City Archivist of the Lyngby-Taarbaek Municipal Archives "Byhistorisk Samling," Denmark

Saadia Toor, Assistant Professor, Dept. of Sociology, Anthropology, and Social Work, College of Staten Island, City University of New York, USA

Mariano E. Torres B., Benemérita Universidad Autónoma de Puebla, Mexico

Roger A. Tsafack Nanfosso, Research in Applied Microeconomics, Faculty of Economics and Management, University of Yaoundé II, Cameroon

Nona Tsotseria, MD, MPPM, Doctoral Student, Muskie School of Public Service, University of Southern Maine, USA

Catherine Turner, Child Labour Programme Coordinator, Anti-Slavery International, London

Carolyn Tuttle, Betty Jane Schultz Hollender Professor of Economics, Lake Forest College, USA

Cristina Valdivia, Researcher Understanding Children's Work (UCW) Project, University of Rome, Tor Vergata

Marten van den Berge, M.A., Researcher, International Research on Working Children (IREWOC), Amsterdam

Elise van Nederveen Meerkerk, Ph.D., International Institute of Social History, Amsterdam

Mirellise Vazquez, Senior Policy Advisor, Christian Children's Fund, Washington, DC, USA

Nicola Verdon, Ph.D., University of Sussex, UK

Martin Verlet, Professor, University Paris I and Paris VII, Social Anthropologist, IRD, France

Eddy Joshua Walakira, Makerere University, Kampala, Uganda

Janet Wamsley, Researcher, Economics and Contracts Department, International Brotherhood of Teamsters, USA

David H. Wegman, M.D., M.Sc., Dean and Professor, School of Health and Environment, University of Massachusetts Lowell, USA

Ben White, Professor of Rural Sociology, International Institute of Social Studies, The Hague

Tassew Woldehanna, Department of Economics, Addis Ababa University, Ethiopia

Ryan Womack, Business and Economics Librarian, Rutgers University, USA

Chantana Banpasirichote Wungaeo, Associate Professor, Ph.D., Director of the International Development Studies Program, Faculty of Political Science, Chulalongkorn University, Thailand

Anna Yakovleva, Ph.D. (Sociology), Executive Director of Regional Public Organization of Social Projects in Sphere of Populations' Well-Being "Stellit," and Representative of Russian Alliance "Prevention of Commercial Sexual Exploitation of Children," Russia

Acknowledgments

Division of labor plays an important role in creating the child labor problem. Likewise, division of labor was essential to the completion of this volume on child labor. There are so many—literally several hundred—who contributed in ways large and small that I cannot possibly thank them all here. But there are some who must be thanked.

First, I must thank the 190 authors and co-authors who submitted entries for this volume. Since their names appear in the pages that follow, I won't repeat them here. It has been an enormous privilege to have worked with them. They represent many of the leading writers, thinkers, and doers on child labor and related issues in the world. They are busy doing important work, and I am humbled that they thought enough of my project to take the time to share their knowledge. I have not met most of the authors face-to-face, and for many of them English is a second or even third language. Yet I feel I've gotten to know each author, at least a little.

If division of labor plays a crucial role in creating both the child labor problem and this volume, so does technology. I am amazed that my authors and I have been able to assemble this volume almost entirely through e-mail correspondence. While technology greatly facilitates virtual human interaction, I look forward to meeting many of my authors face-to-face at some time in the future.

Next I must thank the editorial board. They are:

Constance Finlay, *Director (retired), Carey Library, School of Management and Labor Relations, Rutgers University*

Frank Hagemann, *Coordinator, Statistical Information and Monitoring Program on Child Labor (SIMPOC), International Program on the Elimination of Child Labor (IPEC), International Labor Organization*

Colin Heywood, *Reader in Modern French History, University of Nottingham*

G.K. Lieten, *Professor of Child Labor Studies at the International Institute of Social History and the University of Amsterdam; Director of the International Research on Working Children (IREWOC) Foundation*

Furio C. Rosati, *Understanding Children's Work (UCW) Project Coordinator and Professor of Economics, University of Rome, Tor Vergata*

Deborah J. Schmidle, *Social Sciences Librarian, Olin Library, Cornell University*

This editorial board is truly an exceptional group. While each member contributed in different ways, each made important contributions. Collectively, they helped to identify potential topics and authors for those topics. Later, they reviewed many of the essays submitted and made numerous suggestions regarding substance, style, and fit. They facilitated access to contacts, data, and data sources, and assisted with a variety of ancillary tasks. Over the duration of the project, at least two have earned promotions, at least one has married, at least one has relocated, and all have continued to publish and otherwise maintain active and productive professional lives in addition to their contributions to this volume. I am honored to have been associated with them.

While each member of the editorial board contributed substantially, none should be held responsible for any shortcomings, perceived or real, in the volume. That responsibility is mine. Editorial board members served in their individual capacities, out of a personal and professional commitment to the issue of child labor, and views expressed in this volume should not be imputed to their employing organizations. Particularly, Frank Hagemann, SIMPOC coordinator at ILO-IPEC, and Furio Rosati, of the UCW Project, served out of a long-standing personal commitment to make the best available data on child labor as widely accessible as possible, and not in their official capacities. Nor were they responsible for the selection of articles or the views expressed in them. Obviously, this volume is in no way a product of either the ILO or the UCW Project.

My colleagues and students at Appalachian State University have provided support in a variety of ways. Over the course of the project, I was the beneficiary of the capable assistance of graduate students, first Aaron Brooks, then Jeannie Barrett, and finally Nicole Jean Derballa. I hope each of you recognizes some of your work in the final product. Many of my faculty colleagues assisted with the project along the way. Mentioning just one by name is not intended to slight the many others who could be mentioned, but let me single out one to receive the thanks owed to many. Historian and Emeritus Professor Michael J. Moore, longtime editor of the British studies journal *Albion*, helped to conceptualize the project, identified potential authors throughout the far-flung and former British Empire, and assisted in other ways he probably does not realize. Numerous Appalachian librarians provided instrumental support to the project, both on the front end in conceptualizing and mapping out the work, and on the back end, in the fact- and reference-checking processes; they were masterful in locating often very obscure sources. My departmental colleagues have long provided an intellectual climate conducive to taking risks on long-range projects such as this. More instrumentally, they approved my sabbatical semester and covered my courses while I was out editing essays. Thanks to all.

Throughout the project, my principal contact at M.E. Sharpe was Lynn Taylor, executive editor for economics. I have been tremendously impressed with the team of professionals the publisher put to work on the volume. Each was highly competent and, considering the size and scope of the project, incredibly easy to work with. From Lynn Taylor to editorial coordinators Nicole Cirino and Katie Corasaniti, to Jean Mooney, who composed the index, to production editor Eileen Chetti, to managing editor Angela Piliouras, everyone who touched the project left a beneficial imprint. I would also like to thank Patricia Kolb, editorial director, for believing in the project.

Finally, on a personal level, I would like to thank my wife and best friend, Brenda. She is my most reliable "sounding board" on what matters, and she enhanced this project in more ways than anyone can know. I am deeply humbled that she considers the many hours I spent holed up in my "cave" an actual deprivation. If this book had a dedication, it would be to her. Thanks again, Babe.

Abbreviations

ADB	Asian Development Bank
ALO	Arab Labor Organization
ANPPCAN	African Network for the Prevention and Protection Against Child Abuse and Neglect (Kenya)
APIS	Annual Poverty Indicator Survey (Philippines)
ATSDR	Agency for Toxic Substances and Disease Register, U.S. Department of Health and Human Services
AU	African Union
BGMEA	Bangladesh Garment Manufacturers and Exporters Association
CEDAW	United Nations Convention on the Elimination of all Forms of Discrimination Against Women
CEDC	Children in Especially Difficult Circumstances (UNICEF)
CHILD	Children Helping Innocent Laborers Democratically
CLPRA	Child Labor Prohibition and Regulation Act (India)
CMDA	Calcutta Metropolitan Development Authority
CRC	Convention on the Rights of the Child (UN)
CRIN	Child Rights Information Network (UK)
CSC	Consortium for Street Children
CWA	Child Workers in Asia
CWIN	Child Workers in Nepal (NGO)
DCI	Defence for Children International
ECA	Employment of Children Act (Pakistan)
ECPAT	End Child Prostitution, Child Pornography, and Trafficking of Children for Sexual Purposes International (formerly End Child Prostitution in Asian Tourism)
EFA	Education for All (UN initiative)
ENDA	Environment and Development Action (Dakar)
FLSA	Fair Labor Standards Act (U.S.)
GCE	Global Campaign for Education
GDP	gross domestic product
GMACL	Global March Against Child Labor
HDI	human development index
HRW	Human Rights Watch
ILO	International Labor Organization
IMF	International Monetary Fund
INEI	Instituto Nacional de Estadística e Informática
IPC	Instituto Pró Criança/Pro-Child Institute label (Brazil)
IPEC	International Program for the Elimination of Child Labor (ILO)
IREWOC	International Research on Working Children Foundation
ISPCAN	International Society for Prevention of Child Abuse and Neglect
IWF	Internet Watch Foundation (UK)
KAPOW	Kids and the Power of Work
MAEJT	Mouvement Africain des Enfants et Jeunes Travailleurs/African Children and Young Workers' Movement (Dakar)

MANTHOC	Movimiento de Adolescentes y Niños Trabajadores Hijos de Obreros Cristianos (Bolivia)
MDGs	Millennium Development Goals (UN)
MICS	Multiple Indicator Cluster Survey
MNNATSOP	Movimiento Nacional de Niños, Niñas y Adolescentes Trabajadores Organizados de Peru
MOLACNATS	Latin American and Caribbean Movement of Working Children and Adolescents
MOU	Memorandum of Understanding
NATRAS	Movement of Working Children and Adolescents (Nicaragua)
NCL	National Consumers League (U.S.)
NCLC	National Child Labor Committee (U.S.)
NCHR	National Coalition for Haitian Rights
NGO	nongovernmental organization
NIOSH	National Institute for Occupational Safety and Health (U.S.)
NRA	National Recovery Act (U.S.)
NRC	National Research Council, Institute of Medicine
NSPCC	National Society for the Prevention of Cruelty to Children (UK)
NYSPCC	New York Society for the Prevention of Cruelty to Children
OECD	Organization for Economic Cooperation and Development
OHCHR	Office of the UN's High Commissioner for Human Rights
PEAC	Programa Empresa Amiga da Criança/Child-Friendly Company Program Label (Brazil)
PEL	permissible exposure limits
PETI	Programa de Erradicacao do Trabalho Infantil/Child Labor Eradication Program (Brazil)
PISA	OECD's Program for International Student Assessment
PLA	Plantation Labour Act (India)
PPP	purchasing power parity
PRSP	Poverty Reduction Strategy Paper
RA	rapid assessment (methodology)
SACCS	South Asian Coalition on Child Servitude
SAGE	schooling for age variable
SAP	structural adjustment program
SIMPOC	Statistical Information and Monitoring Program on Child Labor (ILO-IPEC)
SPARC	Society for the Protection of the Rights of the Child (Pakistan)
ST	scheduled tribes (India)
TBP	Time Bound Program (IPEC)
TDRI	Thailand Development and Research Institute
TP	Triangular Paradigm of human development
TRDP	Thardeep Rural Development Program (Pakistan)
UCW Project	Understanding Children's Work Project
UNAIDS	Joint United Nations Program on HIV/AIDS
UN CRC	United Nations Convention on the Rights of the Child
UNDP	United Nations Development Program
UNICEF	United Nations Children's Fund
UNESCO	United Nations Educational, Scientific, and Cultural Organization
USAID	United States Agency for International Development
VLSS	Vietnam Living Standards Survey
WACAP	West Africa Cocoa/Commercial Agricultural Program
WHO	World Health Organization

Editor's Introduction: Child Labor in Global and Historical Perspective

Hugh D. Hindman, Professor of Labor and Human Resources, Appalachian State University

Child labor is a problem of immense social and economic proportions throughout the developing world. While there are encouraging trends in a number of nations—Brazil, Mexico, Turkey, and Vietnam, to name a few—child labor rates remain persistently high in much of the world. Millions of children are stuck in absolutely intolerable situations, and many millions more are forced by necessity or circumstance to work too much, at too young an age, robbed of both their childhoods and their futures.

But this is nothing new. Historically, in the now developed nations of the world, millions of children once worked in mines, mills, factories, farms, and city streets, often in situations strikingly similar to those observed in the developing world today. Developed nations that took several generations to come to grips with their own child labor problems are now impatiently pressing the developing world for immediate and rapid progress.

But there is one important new feature of today's global child labor situation—a genuine global movement is under way to do away with it. With its roots in the histories of the developed nations, the movement began to coalesce in the late 1970s and early 1980s, picked up steam in 1989 with the adoption of the UN Convention on the Rights of the Child, gained enormous institutional capacity in 1992 with the creation of the International Labor Organization's International Program on the Elimination of Child Labor (IPEC), and has snowballed since.

Today, activists and nongovernmental organizations (NGOs) have been mobilized and are on the ground in nearly every region of the world. Governments at all levels have been put on notice regarding their duties to their youngest citizens—that if they seek a better future for their citizens, it starts with the children—and many are responding. There has been a burgeoning of scholarship on child labor that is generating important insights into causes, consequences, and cures. Donors, both public and private, from wealthier nations are stepping up their efforts to provide local parties, both public and private, with strengthened capacity to engage the problem. Citizens and consumers the world over are becoming increasingly aware of the problem. And employers are becoming increasingly aware that if they desire access to markets beyond the local, they must clean up their acts.

If history is any guide, once such a movement is fully under way against it, child labor will ultimately prove unsustainable. Certainly progress against child labor will be uneven—some nations will lead, but others will lag. Certainly there will be setbacks along the way, especially in the face of political and economic instability. Certainly some aspects of the problem will prove more stubbornly resistant to reform than others. Certainly the ultimate global accommodation to the child labor problem will not be as complete as many people hope it will. And certainly many children will continue to be killed, maimed, stunted, and enfeebled in the meantime. But just as certainly, the worst abuses of child labor will one day be a thing of the past, perhaps within the lifetime of most readers of this encyclopedia.

Structure of the Encyclopedia

If child labor is a global problem, then it deserves global treatment. Thus, we open with a section on the world as a whole, and then proceed to address child labor in each and every region of the world. Part 1 addresses child labor in broad global terms. After a brief note on measuring child labor, we begin with theoretical perspectives. While many academic disciplines have contributed to the literature on child labor, three in particular stand out: economics, social science (especially sociology and anthropology), and history. We then provide a broad overview of the history of the developed nations. In examining this history, we quickly discover that each has gone through a "dirty phase" of development involving heavy use of child labor. A series of essays under the heading "Coming to Terms with Child Labor" depicts some of the means by which developed nations struggled to come to grips with child labor. Turning to the developing world, Part 1 first presents a series of essays on the worst forms of child labor, covering several illustrative sectors, including activities considered "hazardous" and those categorized as "unconditional" worst forms. After a series of policy-oriented essays, the part concludes with a series of essays on action against child labor, addressing many of the key actors, institutions, and initiatives at the forefront of the global struggle against child labor.

After Part 1, the encyclopedia moves, part by part, to each major region of the world, from sub-Saharan Africa to Latin America and the Caribbean, to North America, to Europe, to North Africa and the Middle East, to Central and South Asia, and finally to East Asia and the Pacific. In the developing regions, coverage emphasizes the contemporary state of affairs on child labor. For many developing nations, we provide a statistical overview based on the latest data available (see the next essay, "Editor's Note: Measuring Child Labor"). Some historical coverage is also provided for developing regions and nations, often highlighting the effects of colonialism on child labor. In the developed regions of the world, coverage emphasizes the historical conditions of working children. As with other historical accounts of child labor, Britain is heavily represented, but so are many other developed nations, both on the European continent and elsewhere. Some coverage in the developed nations is reserved for contemporary issues, where a number of authors point to a puzzling reemergence of child labor among their own youth in recent years (did it reemerge, or has it been there all along, unnoticed?).

The essays are, broadly speaking, one of two types: *country overviews* or *thematic essays*. Country overviews form the core of the encyclopedia, presenting a summary of the child labor situation in a particular country, or occasionally an overview of a larger region. Country overviews may be historical in content, especially for developed nations, contemporary in content, especially for developing nations, or both. Thematic essays address more specific facets of the child labor problem, such as industries and occupations in which children commonly work, or other issues related to child labor, such as education, child welfare policy, or law, and often highlight significant initiatives against child labor.

Authors, Disciplines, and Viewpoints

The authors of the essays presented in this volume represent an impressive array of academics, researchers, activists, and policy makers distributed over a wide array of backgrounds and disciplines. Readers with only a passing familiarity with the literature on child labor will recognize several authors who are among the most venerated names in the field, and whose work spans multiple decades, beginning before child labor became a popular issue. Readers who are already thoroughly familiar with the literature on child labor will spot many names they do not recognize. We feel privileged to present the work of many bright young scholars and activists, several of whom are just beginning to make an important mark on the field, or are destined to do so in the future.

The encyclopedia includes 222 original essays by 190 authors and coauthors. Each author summarizes what is known about his or her assigned topic and provides readers with pointers to further sources on the topic. Authors approached their tasks in different ways. Some synthesized existing literature and research, often emphasizing their own previous or ongoing work. But there is also a considerable amount of original research included in this volume. Many authors present new research, results, or theses not previously published.

We imposed no definitional constraints on our authors regarding just what constitutes "child labor." Consequently, a range of perspectives are reflected in the essays that follow. In fact, many authors found it unnecessary to define the construct at all. Many authors implicitly or explicitly acknowledge a distinction between "child work," which may be benign or beneficial, and "child labor," which is harmful. But there is great variation in where different authors draw the line between harmful and not harmful. Some consider most work of children, especially very young children, as at least potentially harmful. Others see most work as, on balance, benign or beneficial, especially if it enables families to meet essential needs, and even if the work is performed under difficult circumstances. A number of authors articulated or relied on operational definitions derived from ILO Conventions 138 (on minimum age) and 182 (on worst forms of child labor), or derived from national laws and customs.

Similarly, we imposed no doctrinal constraints on the perspectives authors brought to bear on their topics beyond these: (1) We did apply a filter to ensure that perspectives were "legitimate," in the sense that they are shared by other respected figures in the field; and (2) regardless of perspective, each author was expected to competently address his or her assigned topic. While many authors, even among the activists, are quite dispassionate in their presentation, choosing to elucidate "just the facts," many other authors are quite impassioned in their presentation. And there is certainly plenty of space for passion in discussions of child labor.

The disciplines represented in this volume are extremely diverse, introducing inherently diverse perspectives. Among economists, there are those from neoclassical, neoliberal schools of thought and those from Marxist schools of thought. Among historians, there are economic historians, social historians, labor historians, and historians of childhood. There are anthropologists, sociologists, political scientists, demographers, educationalists, child development specialists, child health specialists, and varieties of public policy specialists. Each discipline brings a valuable and unique perspective to the debate. Beyond disciplinary perspective, there are also political perspectives expressed in many essays. Some authors are proglobalization and some are antiglobalization, some are pro-Western and some are anti-Western, and some are politically to the left while others are politically to the right.

On the child labor question itself, there seem to be two main viewpoints, to oversimplify things considerably. The first, the "mainstream" viewpoint, posits child labor, however defined, as a bad thing—that it not only robs children of their childhoods and futures, but entraps whole populations, regions, and nations in cycles of poverty and underdevelopment—and so its abolition is sought, the sooner the better. More nuanced approaches recognize many difficulties on the path to abolition—that poverty-reduction strategies are critical to the effort; that schooling must be made both accessible and of adequate quality; that if efforts are not thoughtfully and carefully targeted, children can be made worse off; and that efforts need to be prioritized to those children in greatest need. Yet abolition remains the ultimate goal. In contrast, a minority viewpoint holds that there are many things worse than premature labor that can happen to children—war, disease, orphanhood, crushing poverty—and that as long as children's economic contributions remain essential for family and child survival, rather than seeking to abolish child labor, we should support children and enable them to find "decent work." Needless to say, these competing viewpoints lead to radically divergent policy prescriptions.

But the rich tapestry of viewpoints and perspectives presented in this volume should not obscure certain universal truths. First, child labor is, in every instance, a highly localized phenomenon—located in specific places and at specific times, and conditioned and shaped by local circumstances. That said, there are numerous patterns and commonalities that can be observed to operate across space and time, and not just on the big issues, such as the relationship between poverty and child labor, or that schooling is the great bulwark against child labor, because there are numerous exceptions to those patterns, but also on many other issues, such as commonalities in the types of work children perform across the globe and across time; commonalities in factors that increase vulnerability to child labor, such as orphanhood, minority status, land tenancy arrangements, and migration patterns; commonalities in the types of production processes, employment relationships, and payment systems operating where large numbers of children are found working; and commonalities across time and space in the kinds of initiatives that can be successful, or unsuccessful, in finally coming to grips with child labor.

Editor's Note: Measuring Child Labor

Hugh D. Hindman, Professor of Labor and Human Resources, Appalachian State University

For many developing countries, apart from essays addressing the situation in the country, we have included a map and one or two tables. The first table provides some summary indicators that have been shown to be related, often causally, to the problem of child labor. The second table provides a quantitative summary of child labor in the country.

Country Indicators

Ratifications

Has the country ratified the UN Convention on the Rights of the Child and ILO Conventions 138 (on minimum age for employment) and 182 (on worst forms of child labor)? These three together comprise the core global policy instruments arrayed against child labor. Of course, there are others addressing more specific aspects of the problem, such as trafficking of children, and there are additional policy statements providing guidance for interpretation and implementation. But these three are the core. They reflect, if only roughly, a country's commitment to combating child labor. They also provide a rough indicator of the country's own child labor laws, since ratification obliges the country to bring its laws into conformance with the conventions.

Human Development Index

The human development index (HDI), compiled and reported by the UN Development Program (UNDP), attempts to go beyond measures of material wealth, to assess "people's quality of life" in a given country (UNDP 2006, 263). It "is a composite index that measures the average achievements in a country in three basic dimensions of human development: a long and healthy life, as measured by life expectancy at birth; knowledge, as measured by the adult literacy rate and the combined gross enrolment ratio for primary, secondary and tertiary schools; and a decent standard of living, as measured by gross domestic product (GDP) per capita in purchasing power parity (PPP) US dollars" (UNDP 2006, 276). Many, but not all, of the indicators listed below are included in the HDI. We report both the country's index and its rank among 177 countries in the world (index/rank).

Human Capital Indicators

We report, where available, population growth rates, percentage of the population under age fifteen, total fertility rates, life expectancy, infant mortality rates (per thousand live births), and adult literacy rates. High fertility rates are almost invariably associated with high levels of child labor, and declining fertility rates are among the most reliable markers presaging a decline in child labor. High population growth rates and fertility rates, especially when coupled with relatively low life expectancy, yield a high proportion of children relative to the total population. The proportion of the population under age fifteen has important implications for child labor. As this proportion increases, it means the material wealth created by adult producers and providers must be spread across more children. Each child gets less, and, if it is not enough, children may be sent to work. As this proportion decreases, adults and parents can invest a larger share of the material wealth created in each child. Children are less likely to be required to work and more likely to go to school.

Schooling is considered by many to be the most

effective antidote to child labor (Weiner 1991). The adult literacy rate is the single most effective long-term outcome measure of the level of a country's education. It is known that better-educated (more literate) parents are less likely to send their children to work, and more likely to send their children to school, even after controlling for other variables associated with child labor. School enrollment rates are more closely and directly related to the current child labor situation and so are included with the child labor data below.

Economic Indicators

We report, where available, gross domestic product (GDP) per capita (in purchasing power parity U.S. dollars), GDP growth rate, proportion of the population below the poverty line, and the Gini index. GDP per capita is the best single indicator of wealth or poverty in a nation, and when calculated in purchasing power parity, it enables broad comparisons between nations. GDP growth rate, especially when examined in conjunction with population growth rate, provides an indication of whether and how fast a country is improving its economic position. The proportion of the population below the poverty line is a useful indicator but does not enable comparison across countries, since each country draws its own poverty line. The Gini index is a commonly used measure of income inequality in a country, theoretically ranging from 0 to 100 (no country comes close to either 0 or 100). The higher the coefficient, the greater the inequality in the income distribution, and the lower the coefficient, the more equal the income distribution. Poverty is the most widely cited and most robust correlate of child labor in the economics literature. Thus, if one wants a single indicator of the likely current child labor situation in a country, GDP per capita is the statistic to examine. "[G]eneral economic development, equitably distributed" is then the policy prescription for eliminating child labor" (Grooteart and Kanbur 1995). Thus, to get an idea of the likely position of a country in the future, examine the GDP growth rate in conjunction with the Gini index. High growth rates and low Gini coefficients augur well for the future; low growth rates and high income inequality do not.

Where available, we report the labor force composition in the country by broad economic sectors—agriculture, industry, and services. We report this data more for descriptive purposes than for inferences that can be drawn from them about child labor. In the history of developed nations, the proportion of the labor force in nonagricultural work was a reliable indicator of the degree of industrialization. Moreover, as this proportion began to rise substantially—typically around the time it passed the 50 percent threshold—nations became aware that children were being drawn into mines, mills, and factories and began struggling to come to grips with the problem of industrial child labor. It is not clear the extent to which this historical pattern holds for today's developing nations.

Measuring Child Labor

When the International Program for the Elimination of Child Labor (IPEC) was created in 1992 to spearhead the International Labor Organization's (ILO) efforts against child labor, statistical data available to estimate child labor were limited to labor force surveys intended to capture adult economic activities. To illustrate the problem, in 1995, the ILO estimated that there were 73 million economically active children ten to fourteen years of age worldwide. Just one year later, based on special methodological surveys aimed specifically at child labor, the ILO estimated, "In the developing countries alone, there are at least 120 million children between the ages of 5 and 14 who are fully at work, and more than twice as many (or about 250 million) if those for whom work is a secondary activity are included" (ILO 1996, 8).

Finally, in 1998, the Statistical Information and Monitoring Program on Child Labor (SIMPOC) was launched as a part of ILO's IPEC to develop more rigorous quantitative and qualitative estimates of child labor. To provide quantitative estimates, SIMPOC has developed, and continues to refine, a series of child labor survey instruments. The most significant of these are household survey questionnaires, including a comprehensive stand-alone child labor survey, and a shorter version of essential questions that can be incorporated as a module into a larger survey, such as a labor force survey. By early 2008, sixty-two SIMPOC-assisted national child labor surveys had been conducted in fifty-six different countries.

Using results from the child labor surveys, SIMPOC developed two global estimates of child labor, in 2002 and 2006. The most recent global report estimates that there were 218 million child laborers worldwide in 2004, down from 245 million in 2000. In the five- to fourteen-year-old age-group, there were 191 million economically active children, of whom 166 million were considered child laborers and 74 million were engaged in hazardous work. Most working children (69 percent) are in agriculture, compared to only 9 percent in industry. The largest numbers of working children, 122 million, are in the Asia-Pacific region; the highest incidence of child labor is in sub-Saharan Africa, where 26.4 percent of children age five to fourteen years are economically active. For the first time, the ILO was able to report declining numbers and rates of working children, and especially children involved in hazardous work. The Latin American and Caribbean region has seen the most significant decline in child labor (SIMPOC 2006).

To provide qualitative estimates of child labor, SIMPOC relies on a variety of instruments, most prominent of which is its Rapid Assessment methodology. The Rapid Assessment methodology is designed to collect qualitative data from hard-to-reach populations whose activities are invisible or may be illegal. Thus, the Rapid Assessment approach has been extensively used to assess worst forms of child labor. Examples include children (mainly girls) working in domestic service in the homes of others; children (mainly girls) involved in commercial sexual exploitation; children working in isolated rural areas; children involved in illegal or illicit activities, such as drug trafficking; children who have been involuntarily trafficked; children working as bonded laborers; and children engaged in armed conflict, whether as part of rebel or government forces.

Today, the quantity, quality, and accessibility of data on and related to child labor are unprecedented in human history. SIMPOC has created a "Child Labor Statistics" Web site, where researchers can locate and obtain most of SIMPOC's methodological material, such as model survey instruments and manuals, as well as most of the survey reports produced in recent years. In addition to making available national surveys, a growing number of Rapid Assessments, which measure the difficult-to-measure child labor situations, are also available.

In December 2000, the three agencies with the most immediate interest in the problem, the International Labor Organization, UNICEF, and the World Bank, launched the Understanding Children's Work Project (UCW Project) to improve "research capacity" on child labor. In addition to conducting original research on important topics—the puzzle of idle children, the role of orphanhood and child labor, and many more—and coordinating country research reports, the UCW Project Web site makes a wealth of information available to researchers, including results of child labor surveys from more than seventy countries and extensive bibliographic materials.

Child Labor Tables

For many developed nations we include a table entitled "Child Activity Breakdown." These are summary tables compiled from the UCW Project's "Country Statistics," which, in most cases, report results from SIMPOC-assisted child labor surveys or survey modules. It is important to emphasize that we provide only simple summary tables. Readers are encouraged to consult the UCW-Project Web site for much more richly detailed data.

The tables first break children's activities down into four categories: economic activity only; school only; combining school and economic activity; and neither school nor economic activity. Where available, the proportion of children in each category is further broken down by gender and residence (urban versus rural). In many developing countries, substantial proportions of children engage in economic activity without attending school, but there are also substantial proportions that combine economic activity with schooling. A puzzling phenomenon, about which not enough is yet known, involves the children neither in school nor in economic activity. These are the so-called idle, or nowhere, children.

Economic activity includes "labor for the production of economic goods and services as defined by the United Nations System of National Accounts and Balances." As such, it includes "most production activities undertaken by children, whether for the market or not, paid or unpaid, part time or

Section 1. Understanding Child Labor

The Economic View of Child Labor

Patrick M. Emerson, Assistant Professor of Economics, Oregon State University

Though child labor has long been recognized as a common practice in developing countries (including the United States and Europe as late as the early twentieth century), only recently has it attracted the concentrated attention of economists. Thus the formal economic theory of child labor is relatively new. Though the term "child labor" references myriad activities and conditions, it is used fairly generically in the theoretical literature. It is important to note that there are many examples of abominable exploitation of children: bonded labor, prostitution, child soldiering or other extremely hazardous, unhealthy, or personally dehumanizing forms of child work. These have been termed "worst forms" of child labor by the International Labor Organization (ILO). No economist would ever defend these practices or try to justify their existence. However, the vast majority of child labor now practiced around the world does not fit these categories. For example, the single biggest sector of child labor is in agriculture—children who either work around family farms or work, often part-time, on other local farms. There are also many child laborers who do domestic work or who work in service industries or in office environments. In other words, child labor is a catchall term. It should be understood that its use in the theories described below, except when explicitly noted otherwise, is intended to exclude those "worst forms" of child labor. It is these other, more common, forms of child labor that give rise to questions that drive the theoretical literature: Why is it so prevalent, what are the forces driving child labor, what are the economic consequences of child labor, and what policies are most likely to help reduce child labor without harming children or families?

Little formal economic theory of child labor existed before the seminal work of Basu and Van in 1998. Most of the discussion and debate about child labor prior to their work focused on exploitative and harmful aspects of child labor and the industries and markets that utilize it. Child labor, as often viewed by those in industrialized, high-income countries, was a problem of demand. From this point of view, it was a natural conclusion that policy interventions such as bans on the importation of goods made with child labor were an appropriate response. This view failed to consider the supply side of the equation—it did not examine the motivation of families to send their children to work. Implicitly it assumed that families were simply exploiting their own children and that demand-side interventions would benefit those children. However, those who worried about the plight of poor families in low-income countries observed that these demand-side interventions could end up further impoverishing the very individuals they were intended to help. It is precisely in this context that the first formal economic theory on child labor arose.

Foundational Child Labor Theory

The first formal economic theory of child labor was introduced by Basu and Van (1998). Their theory starts with two essential observations that have become common in subsequent theory: one, that most families would prefer not to send their children to work; and two, that most families that do send their children to work do so out of dire necessity. In other words, Basu and Van focused not on the potentially exploitative employers, but on the decisions of families and, in so doing, focused on the supply of child labor rather than the demand. Basu and Van considered an economy where child labor can be substituted for adult labor in some fixed proportion because workers are paid according to their productivity (child labor is assumed to be less productive than adult labor, but children are also paid less). Firms are presumed to be indifferent on the question of child labor because they can obtain a given level of output for the same cost, regardless of the mix of children and adult workers. Initially, the model imposes no restrictions on employment of children—those are considered after the basic model is constructed. With these assumptions in place, the focus shifts to the supply side. There are a fixed number of (assumed identical) households and therefore a fixed number of potential adult and child workers in the economy. A household is assumed to be, solely for convenience, one adult and one child. All adults want to work full-time regardless of the prevailing wage. Additionally, all adults would prefer their children did not work. However, if the prevailing adult wage is too low for the adult to adequately provide for the family, adults will send their children to work to help supplement family income. Child work is assumed for simplicity to be an all-or-nothing choice—families cannot send their children to work part-time, though the results would still follow were this restriction relaxed.

From these assumptions the main result follows directly: If adult wages are high enough, all households will have enough income solely from the adults' earnings that they can afford to keep their children out of the labor pool. This decision also serves to ensure that wages remain high by restricting the supply of labor to the economy in general. However, if adult wages are too low, and the family cannot survive on adult income alone, households will be forced to send their children to work so that the children's wages can be added to those of the adults in order for the family to afford the minimum basic needs of the household. This decision also serves to ensure that wages remain low by increasing the supply of laborers in the economy.

One interesting result from this theory is immediately obvious. If all children were kept out of the labor market, this restriction in the supply of labor could force wages high enough to make them adequate for adults to provide the basic minimum needs of the household. But if all children were sent to work, the added supply of labor could depress prevailing wages enough that adult wages would not be enough to provide the minimum basic needs of the household. This is what is referred to as multiple equilibria. In this case, if an economy is in the low-wage, high-child-labor equilibrium, no one household can afford to pull its children out of the workforce. If all households pulled their children out at the same time, however, they would all be better off: Their children would not work, and adults could provide for the households' basic needs. From a policy perspective, what is important about this case is that, here, a ban on child labor could be a good thing for the households themselves if they are stuck in the high-child-labor equilibrium. By contrast, if wages are still below the poverty threshold even when all child laborers are withdrawn from the workforce, a ban on child labor could make households much worse off by condemning them to destitution.

One of the things that Basu and Van (1998) did not consider explicitly is the opportunity cost of working as a child, or what the child has to forgo in order to work. The most obvious opportunity cost is the ability to attend school (or curtailing the time available for school). Instead, Basu and Van used the simple assumption that households do not want their kids to work (which, of course, could be because of the missed education). Once one explicitly considers the educational opportunity cost of child labor, a dynamic implication becomes clear: A person who worked as a child will likely end up with a lower level of education than a person who did not work as a child, and this can impact the individual in adulthood. Two papers that take up this theme and expand on it are Baland and Robinson (2000) and Emerson and Souza (2003).

Dynamic Child Labor Theory

As a precursor to the fully dynamic models that followed, Baland and Robinson (2000) constructed a two-period static model in which there exists a trade-off between child labor and education. Child labor increases consumption in the first period through the added income, but hampers consumption in the second period though its detrimental effect on education. In this case, "positive" child labor arises due to the optimal solution to this trade-off. Child labor is "efficient" in an economic sense because families are maximizing their well-being and choosing positive amounts of child labor. However, the authors show that child labor can become inefficient if families who would like to are not able to borrow to invest in their children's education due to missing credit markets. In other words, families would choose no child labor if they could, but because they are not able to afford it in the first time period, they will resort to sending the children to work. This is true even though the additional income in the second period, from having an educated child, would easily justify the borrowing of the first period. Credit markets are discussed below.

Emerson and Souza (2003) built a fully dynamic model of child labor to show that the reduction in education on the part of children who work leads them to earn less as adults and be more likely to send their own children to work. This process can be repeated through generations, and thus families can get stuck in a "child labor trap." The mechanism through which this works is straightforward: If there is a positive correlation between education levels and adult incomes, then those children who worked and went to school part-time or did not go to school at all will end up poorer than those children who went to school full-time. Thus, it is more likely that adults who were child laborers will have to send their own children to work, and so families can get caught in a cycle of poverty and child labor. In addition, if returns to education vary with each additional year of schooling (or are "nonlinear," in economics jargon), then multiple equilibria can arise. At least one equilibrium will be characterized by low education, poverty, and high child labor (or a poverty-trap equilibrium), and another by high education and no child labor. If this is the case, then it can be possible to "shock" the economy out of the trap by, for example, banning child labor.

Rogers and Swinnerton (2004), presented a theory that is an extension of this basic framework. In their model, there is two-sided altruism, meaning that parents care about their children and their outcomes, and that children also care about their parents. So parents make educational investments for their children, and then children help provide for their elderly parents. On the surface the incentives are symmetric; adults invest heavily in education, ensuring that their children earn healthy incomes as adults and then can "repay" their parents for those investments by taking care of them in their old age. However, the authors showed that it is possible for situations to arise wherein parents get "too well-off," their children realize that they do not need help financially in their old age, and so parents, in response, curtail their investments in their children's education so that they can collect extra income from their children and save more for themselves for their old age.

Credit Constraints and Child Labor

One feature of all of these theories is an implicit assumption that credit is not available to these families, preventing them from borrowing to invest in their children. That credit is hard to obtain by poor families in low-income countries is a well-established empirical fact. However, there are a number of papers that explicitly model the credit market or deal with the issue of access to credit. Ranjan (2001) explicitly addressed credit market "imperfection" (meaning lack of access to credit) to show how child labor can arise as a direct consequence. In this model, parents who save (refrain from consumption) effectively leave a bequest to their children. However, they are not allowed to borrow against the future earnings of the child, nor is the child allowed to borrow to pay parents back for their investments in the child's education. Ranjan showed that income inequality can then be positively related to child labor, as low-productivity workers that earn less cannot afford to make large investments in the education (future productivity) of their children, while high-productivity workers can. Thus, high-productivity families continue to invest and get ever-more productive while low-productivity families remain low-productivity families.

Lack of access to credit by poor families begs a question: Are there ways in which a poor country can use fiscal policy to replicate a credit market to make these types of intergenerational transfers possible? Emerson and Knabb (2007a) suggested a variant of a pay-as-you-go social security program where the government transfers money from the current working population to the current elderly population. This reduces the need for families to save for retirement and thus frees up resources to invest in children's education and reduce or eliminate child labor. The authors showed that this type of transfer scheme could produce a Pareto improvement in the economy (meaning that no family would be left worse off and at least some would be better off). However, there arises a potential problem with this policy if citizens lack confidence in their government and do not believe that the government will follow through with the transfer once they reach old age. The effectiveness of the policy rests on the actions of families in anticipation of the transfer: Families must be confident that the transfer will be made in the future in order for them to invest in their children's education instead of saving for retirement. As low-income countries are often characterized by unstable governments and uncertain growth and national fiscal health, lack of confidence in the government's future promises may be quite common. This theory suggests that this type of instability and uncertainly may eliminate a whole host of government programs that could unambiguously improve the welfare of citizens.

Expectations and Child Labor

Emerson and Knabb (2007b) considered family decisions about how many children to have, how much to invest in their children's education, and whether to send their children to work, based on their expectations about how much investment in education would pay off in terms of the adult income of their children. An important feature of this model is that one's own education has an externality associated with it: The more educated people there are in an economy, the higher the return to one's own investment in schooling. This is because education makes you more productive, but how much so depends on how many other educated people there are to work with, and the type of higher-technology products you make will have a market only if there are a number of educated consumers to buy them. So herein lies the challenge: It is better for everyone if all families invest in education (and indeed all families would be better off in this case in the model), but it is not in the self-interest of a single family to invest in the education of their children if no other family does. So in this framework, Emerson and Knabb showed how expectations can play a pivotal role in eliminating child labor, limiting fertility, and increasing education. If all families believe, ex ante, that investments in education will pay off, then all families will invest and their beliefs will prove correct, ex post. However, if families are pessimistic about returns to investments in education, ex ante, they will limit their investments, and this will cause the returns on education to be low, and their pessimism will be confirmed, ex post. What is interesting in this theory is that policy interventions such as banning child labor and mandating education can eliminate the "pessimistic" equilibrium and, by forcing all households to educate their children, cause all families to "learn" that education has a high payoff.

Endogenous Fertility and Child Labor

One aspect that the Basu and Van theory does not address explicitly is how the number of children a family has determines, in part, whether the adult wage is sufficient for family survival, thus eliminating the need to send children to work (recall their simplifying assumption that a family is one adult and one child). The more children a family has, the higher the adult wage must be. The key point here is that, since children can help bring income into the household, poorer families may have an incentive to have more children, even though their presence may guarantee that they have to work. On aggregate, the increased supply of child labor can further depress market wages, making it more likely that adult wages will be insufficient to provide for families' basic needs. In essence, then, another type of child labor trap can arise from this endogenous fertility choice. Dessy (2000) explored this idea explicitly and examined policy interventions to address the issue. In this theory, adult wages may have to increase significantly in order for families to decide independently to reduce their fertility and keep children in school. However, a policy intervention that, for example, prohibits the use of children in the labor force, or makes education of children compulsory, could force families to have fewer children and escape the child labor fertility trap. This happens because adult wages do not have to be as high with fewer children in the household and because adult wages would likely rise with decreased labor supply as a result of this policy.

Hazan and Burdugo (2002) presented a very similar theory, but they went on to explore the presence of a "modern sector" that offers high productivity and higher wages and describes how technological progress can pull the economy out of the child labor fertility trap though improving adult wages.

Opportunity and Child Labor

As mentioned above, there is empirical evidence that income alone cannot fully explain the persistence of child labor across generations of a family. In that light, Emerson and Knabb (2006) proposed that another aspect of low-income countries can help explain the persistence of child labor. In this theory, the authors explored how differences in "opportunity" affect families' decisions to send children to work or to school. In this model, within the same economy, different families face different payoffs from education. This payoff differential can be the result of many things, for example, differential school quality, discrimination, or segmented labor markets (for instance, where rural children, even with education, might not have access to high-paying jobs). What this paper points out is that if this is the root cause of low investment in education and high child labor, then bans on child labor will hurt those very families that engage in it because those families are making optimal decisions based on the environment they face. To force those families to refrain from child labor or to force them to invest in schooling will be to make them worse off because the root cause of low investment in education has not changed. So it is this "opportunity" differential that is at the heart of the continuance of child labor through generations of a family, not income, per se.

Child Labor and Coordination Failures

Dessy and Pallage (2001) introduced an interesting theory of child labor that posits that investing in a child's education pays off if there are skill-intensive jobs available once education is complete. At the same time, firms' decisions to invest in technology and create skill-intensive jobs depend on having a population of skilled workers to fill those jobs. Thus a coordination problem can arise in an economy: It is in neither party's interest to invest in skills or technology unless the other does as well. In this instance, a ban on child labor can act as a coordination mechanism pushing families to send their children to school and ensuring that proper skill investments will be made and a modern, highly productive economy will develop.

Child Labor and Specialization

Up to this point, the models of child labor that have been described have either explicitly or implicitly assumed that all children would be treated equally. However, there is ample reason in economic theory (and in empirical evidence) to believe that families may instead practice specialization in the investments they make in their children. Quite simply, families may choose to invest in one child's education while sending another child to work. This theory was formally developed by Horowitz and Wang (2004); they demonstrated that if children are heterogeneous, it is often not efficient to invest in all of the children's educations equally. While this may sound a bit heartless, in fact, given the extreme poverty that many families face, it may be better for one child to become well educated and earn a high wage to support the family later rather than making a minimal investment in all children, leaving all of them unable to command a living wage.

Emerson and Souza (2008) explored a similar

theory in the context of potential child heterogeneity due to birth order. In this case there are two potential reasons for differential investments: one, differing abilities; and two, the fact that poverty and lack of access to credit can force earlier-born children into the workforce, while later-born siblings, with the assistance of the incomes that older siblings contribute to the family, can afford to be sent to school.

Trade and Child Labor

The theoretical link between trade and child labor is explored in Jafarey and Lahiri (2002). They demonstrated that the effect of trade sanctions on child labor may, in fact, increase child labor rather than reduce it. The authors assumed that in a low-income country, it is goods produced with unskilled labor (in which the country has a comparative advantage) that are exported. This unskilled sector also accounts for the child labor in the economy. Trade sanctions, therefore, affect the unskilled sector and thus child labor. At first blush it may seem that reducing the demand for unskilled goods through such sanctions will reduce child labor in that sector. However, a trade sanction can have other countervailing effects, including lowering the discounted present value of the wage premium from attending school, which, with restricted access to credit, can discourage investments in education. Thus, a trade sanction can actually increase child labor in the presence of imperfect credit markets.

Conclusion

Child labor remains a widespread and persistent economic reality for many children in low-income countries. And though much work has been done to understand better the economics of child labor, there is still much that remains to be discovered. Theory cannot exist in a vacuum, and the ongoing empirical research into the causes and consequences will have an enormous impact on the direction of child labor theory in the future. This is particularly true of empirical studies of the consequences of child labor, of which there is currently a dearth. Though almost every theoretical study of child labor posits a fairly rigid relationship between child work and diminished adult human capital, there is very little empirical evidence to support or refute this assumption. As we learn more empirical facts about real-world child labor, the economic theory of child labor should continue to progress to make sense of these facts. But we have already come very far in a few short years. While this essay is by no means comprehensive, taken as a whole, the studies discussed here represent a very large body of work in developing a very broad theory of child labor. The key factors in these models are poverty, the returns from education, the lack of access to credit, and the fertility choice. The consequences of child labor are poorly educated and impoverished children who may be forced to send their own children to work, a poorly educated and skilled workforce that may stunt the growth of the economy as a whole, and the potential for trade sanctions on the part of developed countries. It is clear from this received body of theory that the economic development implications of child labor are potentially huge and thus the need to understand the economics of child labor are equally large.

References and Further Reading

Baland, Jean-Marie, and James A. Robinson. "Is Child Labor Inefficient?" *Journal of Political Economy* 108:4 (2000): 663–79.

Basu, Kaushik. "Child Labor: Cause, Consequence, and Cure." *Journal of Economic Literature* 37:3 (1999): 1083–1119.

Basu, Kaushik. "On the Intriguing Relation Between Adult Wage and Child Labor." *Economic Journal* 110:462 (2000): 50–61.

Basu, Kaushik. "A Note on Multiple General Equilibria with Child Labour." *Economic Letters* 74:3 (2002): 301–8.

Basu, Kaushik. "Child Labor and the Law: Notes on Possible Pathologies." *Economic Letters* 87:99 (2005): 169–74.

Basu, Kaushik, and Pham Hoang Van. "The Economics of Child Labor." *American Economic Review* 88:3 (1998): 412–27.

Dessy, Sylvain. "A Defense of Compulsive Measures Against Child Labor." *Journal of Development Economics* 62:1 (2000): 261–75.

Dessy, Sylvain E., and Stéphane Pallage. "Child Labor and Coordination Failures." *Journal of Development Economics* 65:2 (2001): 469–76.

Dessy, Sylvain E., and Stéphane Pallage. "A Theory of

the Worst Forms of Child Labour." *Economic Journal* 115:500 (2005): 68–87.

Emerson, Patrick M., and Shawn D. Knabb. "Opportunity, Inequality and the Intergenerational Transmission of Child Labor." *Economica* 73:291 (2006): 413–34.

Emerson, Patrick M., and Shawn D. Knabb. "Fiscal Policy, Expectation Traps and Child Labor." *Economic Inquiry* 45:3 (2007a): 453–69.

Emerson, Patrick M., and Shawn D. Knabb. "Expectations, Child Labor and Economic Development" (Oregon State University Economics Department Working Paper, 2007b).

Emerson, Patrick M., and André Portela Souza. "Is There a Child Labor Trap? Inter-Generational Persistence of Child Labor in Brazil." *Economic Development and Cultural Change* 51:2 (2003): 375–98.

Emerson, Patrick M., and André Portela Souza. "Birth Order, Child Labor and School Attendance in Brazil." *World Development* 36:9 (2008): 1647–64.

Glomm, Gerhard. "Parental Choice of Human Capital Investment." *Journal of Development Economics* 53:1 (2007): 99–114.

Hazan, Moshe, and Binyamin Berdugo. "Child Labor, Fertility and Economic Growth." *Economic Journal* 112:482 (2002): 810–28.

Horowitz, Andrew, and Jian Wang. "Favorite Son? Specialized Child Laborers and Students in Poor LDC Households." *Journal of Development Economics* 73:2 (2004): 631–42.

Jafarey, Saqib, and Sajal Lahiri. "Will Trade Sanctions Reduce Child Labour? The Role of Credit Markets." *Journal of Development Economics* 68:1 (2002): 137–56.

Ranjan, Priya. "Credit Constraints and the Phenomenon of Child Labor." *Journal of Development Economics* 64:1 (2001): 81–102.

Rogers, Carol Ann, and Kenneth A. Swinnerton. "Does Child Labor Decrease When Parental Incomes Rise?" *Journal of Political Economy* 112:4 (2004): 939–46.

Social Science Views on Working Children

Ben White, Professor of Rural Sociology, International Institute of Social Studies, The Hague

This overview discusses sociological and anthropological perspectives on juvenile work as a social and cultural phenomenon. While there is no sociological or anthropological "theory of child labor" as such, there is much to be learned from the perspectives of sociology and anthropology. Better theoretical understanding of the employment and exploitation of children requires a cross-fertilization of these disciplinary perspectives with the interdisciplinary fields of childhood and youth studies on the one hand, and labor studies on the other.

Policy standpoints on the employment of children and young people are based, implicitly or explicitly, on models or theories of childhood and the proper place, if any, of work in children's lives and development (Myers 2001a). Good social science research on these issues goes beyond fact-finding to question existing ideas, models, and stereotypes, and to provide better understandings of situations, trends, and problems, which, in turn, can become the basis for action. In the case of young people and their involvement in work, this requires us to undertake a number of steps: first, to document the ways in which the lives and work experience of children and young people deviate from our common perceptions and normative models; second, to explore the ideas and assumptions that underlie those perceptions and models; third, to develop a set of key concepts for more realistic analysis; and finally, to arrive at an explicit standpoint or position linking theory to practice. These four steps, which we can summarize as "critique," "deconstruction," "theoretical work," and "standpoint" (Mayall 2001, 249–53), are all areas in which sociological and anthropological research (for brevity, hereafter simply "social sciences") has made, or can make, important contributions.

Working children often suffer discrimination, abuse, or harm in work relations. This problem is shared by other social groups: women, migrants, minorities, and individuals with disabilities. But it is only in the case of children that interventions aim to counter this problem by protecting them from work itself, rather than protecting them in work relations and promoting their rights as workers. Why do we think of child work situations differently from how we think of those involving adults? Do these ideas reflect a particular idea about childhood itself, whether factual (what is a child?) or normative (what is a good childhood?) (White 1994)?

What can the social sciences tell us about variations in children's work and work relations, between and within societies and over time? About the gendering of juvenile work? About the vulnerability and resilience of child workers? About the factors that make different kinds of work more or less harmful? About the compatibility or incompatibility of work and schooling? And about children's own views on these matters? Children's work, whether as social phenomenon or social problem, has only rarely been studied by social scientists as a subject of primary interest in itself. But social scientists have long been interested in child development, socialization, and education, as standard components of the comparative description and analysis of societies (Corsaro 2005). Originally circulated among colonial officials and anthropologists in the late nineteenth century, the handbook *Notes and Queries in Anthropology* recommends, "It should be noted at what age children are expected to work for the household or the community, and whether there is sex differentiation in this; whether children pick up their knowledge and skill casually or whether special training is given, and if so by whom" (Royal Anthropological Institute 1971, 103–4).

While studies of the social history of children's work in the North are now relatively abundant, comparable work on the global history of child work in developing countries is rare; Grier's (2006) detailed work on Rhodesia (Zimbabwe) is a rare example. Others have focused on specific aspects; Bass (2004) summarized work on sub-Saharan Africa, White (2002) on Indonesia. In studying children's work, anthropologists have focused on the cultural meaning of work, the familial or quasi-familial context of children's work relations, and the roles of work and school in children's socialization (Nieuwenhuys 1996). From the body of ethnographic work now available, we know something about comparative dimensions of children's work in different kinds of societies. But there are surprisingly few detailed ethnographic monographs focusing on contemporary child work; the best known are Reynolds (1991) on rural Zimbabwe, and Nieuwenhuys (1994) on rural southern India. For the kinds of problematic child work with which child labor legislation and intervention concern themselves, it is rare to find studies that go beyond fact-finding or economics to try to see how such work is experienced by children themselves, though some edited collections offer good comparative overviews (White 1982; Miljeteig et al. 1999; Lieten and White 2001; Schlemmer 2000; Hungerland et al. 2007). Ethnographic work on severely abusive or "worst forms" of child labor is hard to find; Montgomery's (2001) child-centered study of juvenile prostitution in Thailand is a rare exception.

Defining Childhood in Relation to Work and Exploitation

There is no universal definition of "child," and social science perspectives tend to expose further complexities rather than providing easy answers. Most legal and formal definitions use a simple age-based distinction. That is, in most UN definitions, children are between the ages of zero and seventeen years. However, chronological age is not a universally accepted basis for determining who is, or is not, a child, or who should, or should not, be treated as a child. No matter where the cut-off point is set, all simple, age-based, dichotomous distinctions between "child" (nonadult) and "adult" (nonchild) do violence to the realities of growing up. A "child" of seventeen years has more in common with an adult of eighteen (or twenty-five) years than with a child of seven years. Similar problems are evident in attempts to oppose harmless "child work" and harmful "child labor." Dichotomous (either/or) categories introduce an artificial binary opposition, misleading for both analytical and policy purposes, into what are in reality continua (White 1996; O'Connell Davidson 2005; Bourdillon 2006a).

While children are not a homogeneous group, they do share some features, for example, their dependence on others for survival in their early years, and gradual development of capacities that decrease their dependency; their lack of full legal standing; and some degree of age-based discrimination. Until quite recently, childhood studies were dominated by the idea that childhood is a "natural" rather than a "social" phenomenon, that growing up is a natural and inevitable process characterized by distinct, age-based stages in the development of cognitive and physical competences (see the work of developmental psychologists such as Jean Piaget, Lev Vygotsky, Erik Erikson, and others). Children's needs and problems were often defined in this way, as, for example, in G. Stanley Hall's (1904) theory of adolescence as a phase of "storm and stress." The sociology of childhood, in "socialization theory," paralleled these ideas but placed more emphasis on the role of child-rearing practices in the transformation of immature, dependent, irrational children into mature, competent, autonomous adults.

In the past two decades, however, all universalizing ideas of childhood have become the targets of criticism. Childhood dependence is only partly a natural phenomenon, and both the sequence and the timing of the development of specific competencies are highly dependent on cultural context (Rogoff 2003). These "new" social studies of childhood, though not all concepts are entirely new, have many implications for the way we think about work and learning in children's lives. In particular, the idea that childhood and youth are social or cultural constructions, already standard in anthropology since Margaret Mead's

(1928) pioneering critiques of Hall's theory of adolescence, is considered a hallmark of new approaches in the sociology of childhood (James and Prout 1997; James and James 2004). Other important theoretical windows on childhood are provided by recent work on childhood as generation and generational relationships (Alanen and Mayall 2001), and Liebel's (2004) "subject-oriented theory" of working children.

Varieties of Juvenile Work and Work Relations

Work has always been a part of the lives of most of the world's children. But comparison between societies and over time shows enormous variation in the nature and intensity of children's work, the contexts and relationships within which work is performed, and the social perception and valuation of children's work. Social science research on childhood and children's work is an important source for understanding this variation.

Child work in the modern world should not be seen as a relic or hangover from some primitive state, destined to disappear with modernization and economic development, for two reasons. First, it appears that the widespread involvement of children in economic activity is not a feature of preagricultural societies, but a relatively recent development in human social evolution. Second, while economic development and the spread of education may have put an end to full-time child employment in some countries, it has not removed children from the world of work, or from labor markets. The majority of children in developed societies such as the United Kingdom, the Netherlands, and the United States have some experience of regular involvement in part-time or seasonal labor markets before they reach the age of sixteen.

Archaeological work and studies of contemporary hunter-gatherer societies suggest that most preagricultural societies are relatively efficient in the ratio of food outputs to human energy inputs, and neither adults nor children (male or female) work as hard as they do in agricultural societies; children played a relatively minor role in economic activities until their teens. It is only with the development of settled agriculture, first appearing about 10,000 years ago and developing much later in some parts of the world, that we find work becoming part of the cultural definition of childhood: "[T]he most obvious change that agriculture brought was a reconsideration of children's utility in work. Much more clearly than in hunting and gathering societies, useful work became the core definition of childhood in most agricultural classes. . . . It also introduced a clearer tension into agricultural childhood than had been present in hunting and gathering. In order to get full value from child labour, families had to retain children's services until their mid- to late teens" (Stearns 2006, 11, 13).

Many features of contemporary childhood reflect the legacy of the thousands of years in which agriculture was the main activity of the majority of the world's population, and agricultural households provided the context in which most children grew up. This is reflected in mundane features like modern Western school calendars—our spring and summer holidays in the North reflect, not the attraction of vacationing in good weather, but the need for juvenile hands to help with agriculture's peak-season tasks of planting and harvesting. It is also reflected in basic features of intrahousehold relations. While gender-based status distinctions existed in hunter-gatherer societies, they were limited. Demands of agricultural work, however, promoted new kinds of gender differentiations among children; agricultural societies generally moved toward patriarchy in both gender and generational relations, and the need for parents to control their children's time is reflected in patterns of harsh discipline, and cultural emphasis on respect for the older generation, which are commonly seen in peasant societies worldwide (Stearns 2006).

Today, only a small fraction of the world's working children are involved in the export-manufacturing supply chains that excite the most interest and concern in international political and policy circles. The most common form of child work in developing countries remains unpaid work on a peasant farm or other family-based enterprise. Where anthropologists have studied time budgets in farm households, they have sometimes found children contributing more than half of all household productive labor (Reynolds 1991; White 1982).

Contexts and Relations of Work

Ethnographic studies of children's work have shown the huge variety, not only of task divisions between age cohorts and genders, but also of work relations. Not surprisingly, then, ethnographic work has been a major source of the criticism of universalist models of child development and the questioning of the general validity of European ideals of childhood (Mead 1928; Rogoff 2003; Corsaro 2005) and European norms regarding the place (or lack thereof) of work within childhood (Boyden et al. 1998). It has also been an important source of information on how children themselves perceive the work they do.

With the exception of a few classic examples, such as child labor in the early Industrial Revolution in parts of Europe and North America, the contribution of child work to the process of social reproduction and value creation has been relatively neglected, as was the case with women's work until the 1970s. Some early exceptions include the work of Schildkrout (1979), White (1982), Van Hear (1982), Morice (1982), and Standing (1982). Efforts to build a typology of the analytically most important categories of child work require further elaboration. A systematic typology would not only help us to place work situations and relationships by economic sector (agriculture, crafts, trade, manufactures, services) and paid or unpaid work, but should also include modes of recruitment (free or unfree) and payment (time rate or piece rate), location (at home or away from home), and status (dependent helper or autonomous agent). Like adults, child workers have historically been involved in a huge variety of work relations and labor regimes. These range from various forms of unfree labor (slavery, tributary, bonded, or indentured labor) to family-based petty commodity production and wage work. In colonial export crop production, children were involved in wage work of various kinds. While these were no doubt exploitative, there is evidence that children themselves often opted for wage work in preference to unpaid work as helpers in patriarchal peasant farms or other family enterprises (Grier 2006; White 2002).

Children remain involved in many different forms of work, and work relations can vary from complete subordination (whether in family, bonded labor, or wage relations) to relative autonomy. As examples of the latter, many children consider it a matter of pride to have been allocated one's own agricultural plot or livestock (Reynolds 1991; Liebel 2004). For children in especially difficult circumstances such as conflict, displacement, or abject familial poverty, access to an independent source of income or subsistence may be more attractive than "rescue," "protection," or placement in foster care. The prospect of gaining some control over their own lives in contexts where the world of adults has failed to protect or provision them can be self-affirming. To give a concrete example, here is what a thirteen-year-old Mozambican civil war orphan had to say about what he missed most during his period of traumatic bereavement, displacement, and "rescue" in a refugee camp: "The thing I hated most in Malawi was that I had no garden. I had no place where I could go and dig up my own food" (Gibbs 1994, 272).

Children's work is usually gendered, but in many societies, gender divisions are less strict among children than among adults. In academic studies, perhaps the most neglected form of child work in many societies, both poor and affluent, is domestic and caring work. Household chores and care of elderly or sick family members are often assigned to children, including those enrolled in school (Robson 2000). Paid domestic work in urban areas has also, both now and in the past, been one of the most common destinations of child migrants, and one of the last forms of child work to be regulated (Bourdillon 2006a; Camacho 1999; Jacquemin 2004).

While children's work contribution in the family is often seen as part of a household "survival strategy," access to unpaid labor of women, boys, and girls can also be a first step toward expansion and accumulation in small-scale enterprises, a process known as "endo-familial accumulation," which if successful may be followed by the hiring in of labor and the partial withdrawal of family members.

Both before and since the introduction of formal schooling, work has been an important vehicle for learning and preparation for adult livelihood responsibilities. This is particularly the case in family-based agriculture, crafts, and trades.

In many traditionally male crafts and trades, work-based learning is organized through the institution of apprenticeship, sometimes based on custom, sometimes on strict rules and entry barriers regulated by professional guilds or associations, and sometimes regulated and promoted by the modern state. Under certain conditions this becomes a kind of pseudo-apprenticeship, in which young workers are kept in a succession of underpaid apprenticeship contracts—often after having paid for entry in the first place—long after they have mastered the necessary skills (Morice 1982; Marguerat 2000; Garet 2000).

Work and School

Besides the elimination of those extreme or "worst forms" of labor in which a minority of the world's working children are involved, social policies regarding juvenile work have always had another objective: promotion of the historical shift from work to school as the principal activity of children. This becomes a policy issue only once formal education systems are in place, and when states and social consensus recognize children's right to an education. The relationship between work and education then takes a central place in often heated and polarized debates about child employment, with "abolitionists" urging the incompatibility of work among school-age children, and "regulationists" arguing that work has an appropriate place in the lives of schoolchildren. The social sciences potentially have much to contribute to these debates.

School is itself a form of work, as various sociologists have argued (Qvortrup 1995; 2001). School-work combinations, until quite recently, were actively promoted by various UN agencies, and it is not clear why they were quietly abandoned about a quarter century ago (Myers 2001a). In affluent countries, a few sociological studies have explored implications of the widespread phenomenon of school-work combinations (McKechnie and Hobbs 2001; Howieson et al. 2006). In the United States, where almost all adolescents engage in part-time paid work while attending secondary school, a landmark longitudinal study has followed the experiences of a sample of adolescents for more than fifteen years into adulthood (Mortimer 2003). The findings challenge conventional wisdom; the study found no evidence that work, even intensive work, significantly influenced time spent on schoolwork or school performance, and those boys and girls who held regular jobs in adolescence were more likely than others to settle quickly into career-oriented work. Unfortunately no such studies are available in developing-country contexts. In one important study of children's perspectives on their own working lives in Bangladesh, Ethiopia, the Philippines, and Central America, the majority of working children in all regions favored combining work with school, and simply did not see work and school as incompatible alternatives (Woodhead 1999; 2001).

Working Children as Objects, Subjects, and Agents

While we are now accustomed to seeing children as "legal subjects" in the sense that they possess and can claim rights of their own, in recent years many social scientists have argued that the Western view of childhood reduces children to the status of objects rather than social subjects, by structurally excluding them from the sphere of socially relevant work (Liebel 2004) or the production of value (Nieuwenhuys 1996; 1999). A parallel idea is found in Zelizer's (1985) image of the emotionally "priceless" and economically "useless" child of Western middle-class society, whose worth is seen not in terms of the child's activities but in the child's status as an object of affection.

Historical and contemporary work on children and youths as agents, rather than as passive beneficiaries or victims of adult decision making, has revealed weaknesses in common economics models in which household heads, or anthropomorphized "families," allocate the time of their children between school and work. Models of intrahousehold bargaining, negotiation, or "contracts" between generations come closer to reality. Social science research of the past two decades abundantly supports a view of children as capable of participating effectively in their own social and economic development, and manifesting "a level of responsibility, resilience and resourcefulness uncommon in adults" (Moore 2000, 544).

Individual agency is always constrained by

larger structures and forces. But even when engaged in what are internationally defined as "worst forms" of child labor, children often exercise agency and involve themselves in negotiations and decision making. This has been shown, for example, in recent work on the phenomenon of children's independent migration (Iversen 2002; Camacho 1999; Thorsen 2006), including migration into commercial sex work (O'Connell Davidson 2005; Montgomery 2001), all of which is automatically defined as "child trafficking" in international protocols when the migrant is under eighteen years of age.

The past two decades have seen some convergence between academic and political discourse on childhood. The notion of children as social subjects is implicit in the notion of children's rights as human rights, insofar as they go beyond rights to protection and provision and also embrace rights to participation, as established in the UN CRC. We thus need to understand children, including working children, as "people in their own right," and not merely as incompetent "part people" on a transition course to adulthood. We need to see them as members of communities, living within social structures, and thus as people with rights and obligations, located in specific, generational relationships to adults, characterized by varying degrees of subordination. We need to see children as a highly heterogeneous social group differentiated along lines of social class, gender, and ethnicity, as well as age.

This in turn has implications for the way we think about child work. We need to avoid simplistic, dichotomous "child-adult" distinctions, as well as crude distinctions between "good" child work and "bad" child labor. Universal standards are important but should not impose a single, quasi-universal model of "global childhood" that pathologizes those whose lives deviate from the model (Boyden, 1997). And we need to learn to listen to children. Many children in the North see their exclusion from socially relevant work as a questionable, unnecessary, and artificial prolongation of dependence (Liebel 2004), and studies of working children in both North and South have concluded that it is not only the need for cash that impels school-going children into labor markets.

Conclusion

Social science research on child work supports a balanced view of the place of work in the lives of children and young people, in which not all kinds of work are necessarily harmful and incompatible with access to good-quality education. Children themselves tend to articulate this view clearly. The challenge to conventional views of child labor is reflected also in the phenomenon, unheard of until a few years ago, of organized working children elaborating clear policy standpoints in their own national or international gatherings, as well in gatherings organized by adults. They include in their notions of normal, appropriate childhood the idea that, besides the right to good education and to protection from exploitation, children should have the right to work and to earn money, if they want to or if they need to (Invernezzi and Milne 2002; Miljeteig 2005; Swift 1999; Liebel 2004). A similar view is also part of "normal" childhoods in countries such as the Netherlands, the United Kingdom, and the United States, even if it is curiously neglected in normative models of Western childhood. The "child labor" problem thus becomes redefined as a problem, not of children's involvement in work as such, but of the abuse of children's capacity to work.

References and Further Reading

Alanen, Leena, and Berry Mayall, eds. *Conceptualizing Child-Adult Relations.* London: Routledge/Falmer, 2001.

Bass, Loretta. *Child Labor in Sub-Saharan Africa.* Boulder: Lynne Rienner, 2004.

Bourdillon, Michael. *Child Domestic Workers in Zimbabwe.* Harare: Weaver Press, 2006a.

Bourdillon, Michael. "Children and Work: A Review of Current Literature and Debates." *Development and Change* 37:6 (2006b): 1201–26.

Boyden, Jo. "Childhood and the Policy Makers: A Comparative Perspective on the Globalization of Childhood." In *Constructing and Reconstructing Childhood.* 2nd ed. London: Routledge/Falmer, 1997.

Boyden, Jo, Birgitta Ling, and William E. Myers. *What Works for Working Children.* Stockholm: UNICEF / Rädda Barnen, 1998.

Camacho, Agnes Z. "Family, Child Labour and Migration: Child Domestic Workers in Metro Manila." *Childhood* 6:1 (1999): 57–73.

Corsaro, William A. *The Sociology of Childhood.* 2nd ed. Thousand Oaks, CA: Pine Forge Press, 2005.

Garet, Bernard. "Apprenticeship in France: A Parallel Case in Industrialized Society." In *The Exploited Child,* ed. Bernard Schlemmer, 248–60. London: Zed Books, 2000.

Gibbs, S. "Post-war Social Reconstruction in Mozambique: Re-framing Children's Experience of Trauma and Healing." *Disasters* 18:3 (1994):268–76.

Grier, Beverly C. *Invisible Hands: Child Labor and the State in Colonial Zimbabwe.* Portsmouth, NH: Heinemann, 2006.

Hall, G. Stanley. *Adolescence: Its Psychology and Its Relations to Physiology, Anthropology, Sociology, Sex, Crime, Religion, and Education.* New York: D. Appleton, 1904.

Howieson, Cathy, Jim McKechnie, and Sheila Semple. *The Nature and Implications of the Part-time Employment of Secondary School Pupils.* Edinburgh: Scottish Executive Social Research, 2006.

Hungerland, Beatrice, Manfred Liebel, Brian Milne, and Anne Wihstutz, eds. *Working to Be Someone: Child Focused Research and Practice with Working Children.* London: Jessica Kingsley Publishers, 2007.

Invernizzi, Antonella, and Brian Milne. "Are Children Entitled to Contribute to International Policy Making? A Critical View of Children's Participation in the International Campaign for the Elimination of Child Labour." *International Journal of Children's Rights* 10 (2002): 403–31.

Iversen, Vegard. "Autonomy in Child Labour Migrants." *World Development* 30:5 (2002): 817–34.

Jacquemin, Mélanie Y. "Children's Domestic Work in Abidjan, Côte d'Ivoire: The *Petites Bonnes* Have the Floor." *Childhood* 11:3 (2004): 383–97.

James, Allison, and Adrian L. James. *Constructing Childhood: Theory, Policy and Social Practice.* Basingstoke: Palgrave Macmillan, 2004.

James, Allison, and Alan Prout, eds. *Constructing and Reconstructing Childhood.* 2nd ed. London: Routledge/Falmer, 1997.

Liebel, Manfred. *A Will of Their Own: Cross-cultural Perspectives on Working Children.* London: Zed Books, 2004.

Lieten, Kristoffel, and Ben White, eds. *Child Labour: Policy Options.* Amsterdam, Aksant, 2001.

Marguerat, Yves. "The Exploitation of Apprentices in Togo." In *The Exploited Child,* ed. Bernard Schlemmer, 239–47. London: Zed Books, 2000.

Mayall, Berry. "The Sociology of Childhood in Relation to Children's Rights." *International Journal of Children's Rights* 8 (2001): 243–59.

McKechnie, Jim, and Sandy Hobbs. "Work and Education: Are They Compatible for Children and Adolescents?" In *Hidden Hands: International Perspectives on Children's Work and Labour,* ed. P. Mizen, C. Pole, and A. Bolton, 9–23. London: Routledge/Falmer, 2001.

Mead, Margaret. *Coming of Age in Samoa.* New York: William Morrow, 1928.

Miljeteig, Per. "Childen's Democratic Rights: What We Can Learn from Young Workers Organizing Themselves." In *Children Taken Seriously in Theory, Policy and Practice,* ed. Jan Mason and Toby Fattore, 123–35. London: Jessica Kingsley, 2005.

Miljeteig, Per, Ben White, and Christopher Williams, eds. "Understanding Child Labour." Special issue, *Childhood* 6:1 (1999).

Montgomery, Heather. *Modern Babylon? Prostituting Children in Thailand.* New York: Berghahn Books, 2001.

Moore, Karen. "Supporting Children in Their Working Lives: Obstacles and Opportunities Within the International Policy Environment." *Journal of International Development* 12 (2000): 531–48.

Morice, Alain. "Underpaid Child Labour and Social Reproduction: Apprenticeship in Kaolack, Senegal." *Development and Change* 13:4 (1982): 515–26.

Mortimer, Jeylan T. *Working and Growing Up in America.* Cambridge, MA: Harvard University Press, 2003.

Myers, William E. "Can Children's Education and Work Be Reconciled?" *International Journal of Education Policy, Research, and Practice* 2:3 (2001a): 307–30.

Myers, William E. "Valuing Diverse Approaches to Child Labour." In *Child Labour: Policy Options,* ed. Kristoffel Lieten and Ben White, 27–48. Amsterdam: Akzant, 2001b.

Nieuwenhuys, Olga. *Children's Lifeworlds: Gender, Welfare and Labour in the Developing World.* London: Routledge, 1994.

Nieuwenhuys, Olga. "The Paradox of Child Labor and Anthropology." *Annual Review of Anthropology* 25 (1996): 237–51.

Nieuwenhuys, Olga. "The Paradox of the Competent Child and the Global Childhood Agenda." In *Modernity on a Shoestring: Dimensions of Globalization, Consumption and Development in Africa and Beyond,* ed. R. Fardon, W. van Binsbergen, and R. van Dijk, 33–48. Leiden: EIDOS, 1999.

O'Connell Davidson, Julia. *Children in the Global Sex Trade.* Cambridge: Polity Press, 2005.

Qvortrup, Jens. "From Useful to Useful: The Historical Continuity of Children's Constructive Participation." *Sociological Studies of Childhood* 7 (1995): 49–76.

Qvortrup, Jens. "School-work, Paid Work and the Changing Obligations of Childhood." In *Hidden Hands: International Perspectives on Children's Work and Labour,* ed. P. Mizen, C. Pole, and A. Bolton, 91–107. London: Routledge/Falmer, 2001.

Reynolds, Pamela. *Dance Civet Cat: Child Labour in the Zambesi Valley.* London: Zed Books, 1991.
Robson, Elsbeth N. A. "Young Carers in Southern Africa: Exploring Stories from Zimbabwean Secondary School Students." In *Children's Geographies: Playing, Living, Learning,* ed. S. Holloway and G. Valentine, 174–93. London: Routledge, 2000.
Rogoff, Barbara. *The Cultural Nature of Human Development.* Oxford: University Press, 2003.
Royal Anthropological Institute. *Notes and Queries on Anthropology.* 6th ed. 1874; London: Routledge and Kegan Paul, 1971.
Schildkrout, Enid. "Women's Work and Children's Work: Variations Among Moslems in Kano." In *Social Anthropology of Work,* ed. S. Wallman, 69–85. London: Academic Press, 1979.
Schlemmer, Bernard, ed. *The Exploited Child.* London: Zed Books, 2000.
Standing, Guy. "State Policy and Child Labour: Accumulation Versus Legitimation?" *Development and Change* 13:4 (1982): 611–31.
Stearns, Peter. *Childhood in World History.* New York: Routledge, 2006.
Swift, Anthony. *Working Children Get Organized: An Introduction to Working Children's Organizations.* London: International Save the Children Alliance, 1999.
Thorsen, Dorte. "Child Migrants in Transit: Strategies to Assert New Identities in Rural Burkina Faso." In *Navigating Youth, Generating Adulthood: Social Becoming in an African Context,* ed. C. Christiansen, M. Utas, and H. E. Vigh, 88–114. Uppsala: Nordiska Afrikainstitutet, 2006.
Van Hear, Nick. "Child Labour and the Development of Capitalist Agriculture in Ghana." *Development and Change* 13:4 (1982): 499–514.
White, Ben. "Child Labour and Population Growth in Rural Asia." *Development and Change* 13:4 (1982): 587–610.
White, Ben, ed. "Child Workers." Special issue, *Development and Change* 13:4 (1982).
White, Ben. "Children, Work and 'Child Labour': Changing Responses to the Employment of Children." *Development and Change* 25:4 (1994): 848–78.
White, Ben. "Globalization and the Child Labour Problem." *Journal of International Development* 8:6 (1996): 829–39.
White, Ben. "Constructing Child Labour: Attitudes to Juvenile Work in Indonesia, 1900–2000." In *Labour in Southeast Asia,* ed. Rebecca Elmhirst and Ratna Saptari, 77–105. London: RoutledgeCurzon, 2002.
Woodhead, Martin. "Combating Child Labour: Listen to What the Children Say." *Childhood* 6:1 (1999): 27–49.
Woodhead, Martin. "The Value of Work and School: A Study of Working Children's Perspectives." In *Child Labour: Policy Options,* ed. Kristoffel Lieten and Ben White, 103–16. Amsterdam: Aksant, 2001.
Zelizer, Viviana. *Pricing the Priceless Child: The Changing Social Value of Children.* New York: Basic Books, 1985.

A Brief Historiography of Child Labor

Colin Heywood, Reader in Modern French History, University of Nottingham

How have historians approached the subject of child labor over the past few decades? This essay gives an indication of the questions they have posed, their varying methodological stances, the type of primary source material they have consulted, and reasons why they have often come to very different conclusions. These historiographical matters underpin all of the contributions from historians to this encyclopedia. Much of the historical literature springs from the original debates provoked by child labor reform campaigns in Europe during the early nineteenth century. Reformers raised such issues as the impact of technological change on child labor in industry; motives of employers and parents in putting the young to work; the influence of industrial work on the health, education, and morals of children; and the desirability of state intervention. Historians, in turn, have taken these as a starting point, and diverged in their answers much as the interested parties did during the 1830s and 1840s. Some, like more radical reformers, have considered the early stages of industrialization disastrous for the welfare of child workers, while others have placed more confidence in the long-term process of wealth creation and technical progress inherent in economic development. Most have adopted the adult, or "top-down," perspective of reformers, employers, and administrators, but a few have followed British parliamentary inquiries in their efforts to hear what working children themselves had to say about their predicament. The majority have remained firmly wedded to a national perspective on child labor, heavily weighted toward the United Kingdom, the United States, and other countries in the West, but a minority have noted the international and global dimension to the phenomenon, evident during the nineteenth century as late developers copied legislation from the pioneers of industrialization. Of course, the march of time since the Industrial Revolution has added new perspectives for historians. Most in evidence was awareness that the late nineteenth and early twentieth centuries brought a decline of child labor in major industries in the West, such as textiles and mining. Nonetheless, the historiography on child labor continues to revolve around a few key questions that reappear in present-day debates among development economists and anthropologists.

Historians have generally used the term "child labor" as loosely as has the population at large. Far from being a neutral, technical description of an agreed set of human relations, it is rather "a rhetorical label that blends description with negative value judgments" (Ennew et al. 2005, 28). Much of the historiography concentrates on the employment of children as wage labor in the "formal" sector of mills, factories, and mines. It is debated whether the work of young people around a family farm or workshop should be described as "child labor." There is therefore the notion that one should distinguish between "child labor" and "child work," the former an onerous and exploitative form of employment for wages, the latter a satisfying and dignified contribution to the family economy. The distinction is easier to make in principle than in practice, given the range of circumstances in which children work. Although the most sensible approach might be to settle for a discussion of "children's work," and assessments of the harm and the benefits attributable to each job, this essay follows the convention among historians of talking of "child labor." For them, as for commentators in the nineteenth and twentieth centuries, this refers to the work done by children, variously defined by law in different countries as, say, under the age of fourteen, fifteen, or sixteen, with an implied critical stance (Ennew et al. 2005; Cunningham and Stromquist 2005).

"Crusades" for the Children: Campaigns for Child Labor Legislation

Where historical writing remains closest to the early debates between child labor reformers and their opponents is when it focuses on factory legislation. This is one of the oldest, yet most persistent strands in the historiography. Many countries, particularly in the West, have a long history to recount in this area. These studies range from early works on Britain, such as *A History of Factory Legislation,* by Hutchins and Harrison, first published in 1903, to more recent ones such as Weissbach (1989) on the French case or Ipsen (2006) on the Italian. Historians often bring some of the moral fervor of their forbears to these accounts. Moved by a left-wing distaste for unregulated capitalism, or some form of idealistic revulsion at the materialism of emerging industrial society, these historians tend to wax indignant at the plight of children in industry. The British historian E.P. Thompson famously proclaimed that "the exploitation of little children, on this scale and with this intensity, was one of the most shameful events in our history" (Thompson 1968, 384). Walter Trattner prefaced his history of the National Child Labor Committee with references to child labor as "one of the gravest social injustices in American life," an "evil" caused by prejudice, greed, and ignorance (Trattner 1970, 10–11). The twentieth century was doubtless propitious for such an approach, given widespread pride at the development of a welfare state in Western Europe, or at least a body of labor legislation elsewhere. Historical research in this field benefits from easy access to primary sources. Reformers frequently published their polemical works; debates in the legislature appeared in official publications; and the contributions of the administration remain preserved in national archives. Moreover, many historians feel at ease writing this type of social and political history, relying as it does on detailed empirical work in libraries and archives.

Obvious questions arising from this approach concern the background of those supporting and opposing child labor legislation, their motivation, and the experience of political elites in framing successive laws, strategies for enforcement, and the long-term impact of state intervention. At the risk of excessive schematization, one might suggest that a fairly consistent narrative emerges from this camp. It begins with the dragooning of large numbers of young people into textile mills, mines, and factories spawned by early industrialization, with new machinery making it possible to substitute women and children for adult male workers. Conditions in the workshops were grim, with the familiar tale of long hours to match the relentless pace of the machines, a damp and dusty environment, and a heartless disciplinary regime. Added spice comes from rumors of sexual promiscuity among the workers. A disparate group of reformers stepped forward at this point, to combat abuses with legislation, including hardheaded businessmen interested in maximizing profits, more philanthropically minded representatives of the landed gentry and professional classes, and, in the American case, leaders of organized labor. Gradually, by a process of trial and error, the state managed to curb some of the excesses of child labor, notably excluding younger age-groups from workshops, overcoming opposition from many industrialists and working-class parents in the process. Child labor thereby emerges as at its most abusive during the early, or "dirty," phase of industrialization, and gradually disappears in developed economies as the state manages to force children out of the workshops and into schools.

National histories bring out the different characteristics of these campaigns according to period and place. Britain, as the cradle of industrial civilization, produced the first, most intense, and most politically charged debate on child labor reform, which is reflected in its substantial historiography. Its historians could hardly avoid linking their researches to the long-running debate over the standard of living during the Industrial Revolution. Their line, that it required state intervention to rein in the excesses of industry in exploiting child labor, provided grist for the mill of the "pessimists." E.P. Thompson stands out as the doyen of this group. His *Making of the English Working Classes* emphasizes "a drastic increase in the intensity of exploitation of child labor between 1780 and 1840." It goes on to document efforts of working-class people themselves to improve conditions through their Short-Time Committee, the "veritable fury of passion which moved a few score northern professional men" to support child workers, and the violent opposition from mill owners and others (Thompson 1968, 366–84). There is now a well-documented case from historians of British child labor that industrialization brought an intensification of child labor, starting with the early "proto-industrial" phase and continuing with the establishment of the factory system. It emerges that textile industries above all relied heavily on children during early stages of development (Levine 1987; Horrell and Humphries 1999; Tuttle 1998).

Historians in other countries have revealed the particular socioeconomic and political influences on the reform campaigns. Even before the agreement on international standards from 1889 onward, a basic template for legislation emerged, as elites in each country learned from the experience of their neighbors (Caty 2002). Laws generally set minimum ages for work, graded hours according to age, banned night work, insisted on certain sanitary measures, and laid down a minimum of schooling. The French child labor law of 1841 was partly modeled on the British Factory Act of 1833 (Weissbach 1989; Heywood 1988). The first Italian law, passed in 1886, was spurred on by the fear of falling behind other modern, "civilized" nations in Europe (Ipsen 2006, 105). In the extreme case of African and Asian colonies, terms of the debate invariably favored employers—the farming and business interests of white settlers—in a way that was out of the question in Europe. In 1939, for example, leaders of the tea and tobacco companies in Nyasaland (Malawi) managed to have themselves specifically excluded from any legal restrictions on child labor (Chirwa 1993). Meanwhile, in the United States, historians have had to cope with the complication of intervention by numerous states producing a "crazy quilt of legislation" before a campaign to secure a federal child labor law finally succeeded with the Fair Labor Standards Act of 1938 (Hindman 2002, 85).

Demand for Child Labor: Employer Strategies and Technical Progress

The commonsense notion that increasing intervention by the state would provide a solution to the "problem" of child labor has by no means convinced all historians. It appears too narrow in its focus on humanitarianism and the political struggle over reform. Critics have argued that the decline of child labor in industry began before factory legislation made its impact. Clark Nardinelli led the way by demonstrating that in the British textile industries, child labor was already declining relative to adult labor before the 1833 Factory Act had the effect of levying a "tax" on it. Hence, the act "only speeded up the change" (Nardinelli 1980, 743). It is likely that child labor was experiencing a similar decline in France before the first law with any real "teeth" bit in the 1870s. In Japan, by the time the first child labor law came into force in 1916, the children under the age of twelve, whom it officially banned from work, had long disappeared from the factories. Likewise, in the United States, child labor was clearly on the way out when federal legislation finally appeared during the 1930s (Heywood 1988; Saito 1996; Hindman 2002; Moehling 1999). It was also the case that enforcement of the law in all countries was long hampered by a weak inspection system and the readiness of employers and workers to collude in cheating on a grand scale. Such considerations, after comparing the Asian and the European experiences, led Myron Weiner to make the persuasive argument that compulsory schooling was easier to enforce than factory legislation, and hence was the more decisive influence on the decline of child labor (Weiner 1991). Moreover, as Bengt Sandin noted in the Swedish case, efforts to remove children from the workshops were propelled by a change in values that redefined a "proper" childhood as one spent in school. "A child was in essence a schoolchild" (Sandin 1997, 17).

State intervention is likely to remain ineffectual if the underlying social conditions are unfavorable. This leads to questions on the workings of the market for child labor. Historians have asked why employers were interested in recruiting large numbers of child workers, why working-class families were willing to allow their young to enter the workshops, and when and why both parties changed their views. Finding evidence on these points is not easy. Historians have trawled through records left by official enquiries, social investigations, and child labor inspections, and, beyond these, quantitative sources such as census registers and lists of factory personnel. In contrast to earlier generations of historians, they have also applied economic theory to the history of child labor (Nardinelli 1990).

Whatever their views on the role of legislation, there is something of a consensus among historians that strong demand for child labor in a limited range of industries was a feature of the early stages of industrialization. In the textile industries of Europe, the United States, and Latin America, for example, historians have documented the relatively high percentage of juveniles and adolescents in the mills, as employers found the young suitable for work on the new machinery, and more willing than adults to submit to the discipline of large-scale production (Herdt 1996; Camps i Cura 1996; Galbi 1997; Kuznesof 1998; Tuttle 1999; Hindman 2002; Rahikainen 2004). Public authorities were generally supportive, particularly during the late eighteenth and early nineteenth centuries in Europe, as they worried more about poverty and idleness among the young than about excessive work. As Hugh Cunningham noted, the under- and unemployment of children appeared more of a problem than their employment in most towns and agricultural areas in England during this period (Cunningham 1991). Hence, authorities were often willing to supply children from institutions such as the workhouse in England, the *hôpitaux* in France—or, during the 1850s and 1860s, the orphanages of Rio de Janeiro and São Paulo in Brazil (Rose 1989; Kuznesof 1998). In the words of one survey, "orphans were in the vanguard of the early industrial labour force" (Horrell and Humphries 1999, 97). Carolyn Tuttle calculated that there was a rise in wages of children relative to those of adults in British textile industries between the 1830s and 1860, "supporting the hypothesis that the demand for child labor was increasing during this period" (Tuttle 1999, 132).

More contentious is the idea that in a maturing industrial economy, demand for child labor in industry would decline. There is an argument that, in the long run, technological change tended to reduce relative demand for child labor, by eliminating many of the little jobs in the factories. Clark Nardinelli cited the adoption of self-acting spinning mules in the cotton industry during the 1830s in Britain, which led to fewer broken threads and hence a fall in demand for young "piecers" (Nardinelli 1990). Peter Kirby demonstrated that innovations in underground haulage during the first half of the nineteenth century led to a decline in the proportion of young children employed in coal-mining areas of Britain (Kirby 1999). More generally, the later nineteenth century witnessed a renewed interest among employers in increasing labor productivity, and with a larger scale of machinery, speedups, and the rise of more science-based industries, they became reluctant to hire the young (Rahikainen 2004). Such reasoning can buttress the "optimistic" line on the Industrial Revolution, with the process of wealth creation and improvements in the factory system favoring child welfare. It harks back to claims made in official inquiries and polemical works on the "enlightened benevolence" of leading employers during the nineteenth century (Gray 1996, 121). Its proponents note that young children, under the age of ten, were rarely employed in the mills—a point now widely accepted. They also make the valid point that laws risked driving children into small, unregulated workshops, or depriving them of useful training and upsetting family budgets (Hutt 1954; Nardinelli 1980).

However, such a reassuring view of a laissez-faire economy, although symptomatic of the political climate of the late twentieth century, has attracted plenty of criticism. It is open to question how far new technology tended to reduce child labor. Per Bolin-Hort even disputed that the self-actor had this effect (Bolin-Hort 1989). Certain industries, notably glass manufacture, were notoriously reluctant to part with their youngest workers: During the 1890s, for example, demand for child workers in the glass factories of south-east France appears to have increased, leading to widespread recruitment of children from over the Italian border (Ipsen 2006). Moreover, if child labor did generally decline in factories during the late nineteenth century, it continued to flourish in the informal sector of the economy. Children shifted into casual employment in such areas as garment making, retailing, running errands, and selling newspapers. These jobs allowed them to combine work with school, giving the superficial impression that the problem of child labor had been solved (Lavalette 1994; 1999; Davin 1996; Schrumpf 1997). However, the resurgence of child labor during the late twentieth century in sweatshops and the service sector of the economy in various parts of Europe and North America counters any easy assumptions that the practice will disappear with modernization.

Even in Britain at the height of the Industrial Revolution, in 1851, agriculture was "by a long way the biggest provider of employment" for boys (Cunningham 1991, 143). Although generally ignored by contemporaries, the scandal of agricultural gangs excepted, historians have noted how agriculture's demand for child labor has proved remarkably persistent. Studies of European countries such as France, Spain, and Sweden reveal the school system's long battle to enforce regular attendance in rural areas during the nineteenth and twentieth centuries (Heywood 1988; Borrás Llop 2005; Sjöberg 1997). In a similar vein, American historians have highlighted agriculture as historically the largest employer of child labor, right down to the present day (Hindman 2006). Meanwhile, in certain African colonies, historians have described children as "invisible hands," because of the lack of documentation of their role on the farms. In colonial Swaziland, for example, children were mobilized in large numbers during the twentieth century to provide a low-cost solution to the problem of labor shortages on the commercial farms of white settler landlords (Grier 1994; Simelane 1998).

Supply of Child Labor: Family Structures and Family Budgets

Contemporary observers in the nineteenth century were inclined to blame parents as well as employers for the misfortunes of children working in industry, accusing them of greed and ignorance. Many historians have at least tacitly agreed with these elite views. However, it is also possible to argue that parents acted in the best interests of their offspring by sending them to work at a tender age. Clark Nardinelli urged that historians pay more attention to the economic reality underlying factory reform campaigns. He concluded that "under the conditions of the early industrial revolution, child labor may well have made children (and the family) better off" (Nardinelli 1990, 7). It is quite plausible to argue that, in a low-income economy, poor families had little choice in the matter. It would follow logically that as real incomes rose during the course of economic development, more and more families would be in a position to withdraw their children from the labor force and send them to school. Hence Nardinelli's conclusion that the decline in child labor in the West during the nineteenth and twentieth centuries was caused by the workings of the market rather than by factory legislation: "[T]echnological change reduced the demand for child labor and increasing income reduced the supply" (Nardinelli 1980, 750; 1990, 125; also Heywood 1981; Cunningham 2000).

Although the suggestion of a link between poverty and child labor runs like a red thread through the scholarly literature, the mechanistic assumption that rising incomes will produce a decline in child labor is not above criticism. Horrell and Humphries have discovered that in their sample of British households, a rise in the average real earnings of adult males from the mid-1830s onward was not accompanied by a decline in child participation rates, "cautioning against an overemphasis on income effects as an explanation of patterns in children's participation rates." Children themselves may have chosen to work because, for a while, their wages were increasing faster than those of adult males (Horrell and Humphries 1985, 503–4). Bolin-Hort has drawn attention to Lancashire cotton spinners in the late nineteenth and early twentieth centuries. Although a relatively well-paid group of workers, they remained stubbornly committed to the half-time system of child labor despite vehement criticism from education and trade union circles (Bolin-Hort 1989). There is also the line, articulated by Karl Marx among others, that large-scale employment of children served to depress the level of adult wages. For example, a study among late-nineteenth-century American families came to the conclusion that "much of the apparent gain to family income from child earnings was illusory; greater child earnings were almost wholly offset by lower earnings for the adult male" (Parsons and Goldin 1989, 657). Some way of jolting the economy into a new equilibrium, with high adult wages and no child labor, might then be preferable to the long haul of development under unregulated capitalism. Government intervention, in the form of a total ban on child labor, or better still, a minimum adult wage, might emerge as a more desirable policy option than those chosen in the nineteenth century: doing nothing or imposing partial bans (Basu 1999).

Historians concentrating on the supply side of the market for child labor generally take as their starting point the analysis of household strategies. This approach rests on economic models of decision making in the family and the insight that "families and households are the most fundamental decision-making units of the economy, determining a vast array of economic behavior"—including whether children should work or not (Goldin 1981, 277). With various surveys of household budgets and census data available as primary source material, the analysis of household strategies came to the fore in the 1970s and 1980s in the United States. Michael Haines, one of the first historians in this field of quantitative history, used the Commissioner of Labor Survey of 1889–90, which provided data on 8,544 families in the United States and five European countries (Haines 1979).

The method answers a number of questions, sometimes in a fairly predictable way. First, it is persuasive in exposing the pressures on poor families to send their children out to work, which, as Haines put it, "must temper our harsh judgments about the exploitation of children in the nineteenth and early twentieth century" (Haines 1979, 319). Nonetheless, there remains some doubt over how far the poor were obliged by low adult wages to seek employment for their children, and how far they chose to forgo education and leisure opportunities in favor of wages. A study of textile workers in 1888–90 emphasized "financial need, rather than greed" in explaining child labor, but also drew attention to the range of differences uncovered: "[I]n the Northeast, a third of the children in the highest income brackets were at work while a third of those in the lowest were still at school" (Holleran 1997; Angus and Mirel 1985, 139). Second, the method reveals the stark class dimension to child labor: A study of working-class families in Pittsburgh demonstrated that "a mere handful of middle- and upper-class boys began their life's work between the ages of 10 and 14, but 14 percent of the working-class boys and 39 percent of those with widowed mothers did so in 1880" (Kleinberg 1989, 179). Moreover, children whose father was unemployed, or children who were living apart from parents, were more likely to be working (Moehling 2004). Finally, the method was particularly illuminating in documenting such influences as age, sex, and ethnicity on children's participation rates. Analyzing data from Philadelphia in 1880, Claudia Goldin found that among white families, children of Irish and German immigrants were sent out to work more than their native-born counterparts (Goldin 1981). Boys were more likely than girls to work for wages outside the home, and older siblings were more likely to do so than younger brothers and sisters. There remains the drawback of this approach: that it struggles to go beyond the economic sphere, for as Angus and Mirel concluded, "these textile families continued to make decisions about what was best for themselves and their children on the basis of values that may never be plumbed by quantitative analysis" (Angus and Mirel 1985, 140).

Conclusion

This brief survey concentrates on the West European and American "core" rather than the "periphery" elsewhere, and on the modern rather than the medieval and early modern periods. It also highlights contrasting approaches to the subject, though these are not mutually exclusive. The range of experience revealed in the historiography, and the inevitable differences of interpretation among historians, mean that lessons from the past are not easy to discern. Most historians today are more skeptical about the effects of child labor legislation and compulsory schooling than earlier generations, without discounting their value entirely. They tend to see the intensification of child labor during early stages of industrialization as largely demand driven, and note the persistence of job opportunities in the informal sector during the twentieth century, even in wealthy capitalist societies. They have also begun to explore decision making within the family to understand why some families sent their children out to work and others opted for leisure or education, moving beyond simple motives such as greed or ignorance. What stands out is the protracted nature of the struggle to produce the modern phenomenon of what Viviana Zelizer famously described as the "economically 'worthless' but emotionally 'priceless' child" (Zelizer 1985, 3).

References and Further Reading

Angus, David L., and Jeffrey E. Mirel. "From Spellers to Spindles: Work-Force Entry by the Children of Textile Workers, 1888–90." *Social Science History* 9:2 (1985): 123–43.

Basu, Kaushik. "Child Labor: Cause, Consequence, and Cure, with Remarks on International Labor Standards." *Journal of Economic Literature* 37:3 (1999): 1083–1119.

Bolin-Hort, Per. *Work, Family and the State: Child Labour and the Organization of Production in the British Cotton Industry, 1780–1920.* Lund: Lund University Press, 1989.

Borrás Llop, Joé M. "Schooling and Child Farm Labour in Spain, circa 1880–1930." *Continuity and Change* 20:2 (2005): 385–406.

Camps i Cura, Enriqueta. "Family Strategies and Children's Work Patterns: Some Insights from Industrializing Catalonia, 1850–1920." In *Child Labour in Historical Perspective, 1800–*1985, ed. Hugh Cunningham and Pier Paolo Viazzo, 57–71. Florence: UNICEF, 1996.

Caty, Roland, ed. *Enfants au travail: Attitude des élites en Europe occidentale et méditerranéenne aux XIXe et XXe siècles.* Aix-en-Provence: Publications de l'Université de Provence, 2002.

Chirwa, Wiseman Chijere. "Child and Youth Labour on the Nysaland Plantations, 1890–1953." *Journal of Southern African Studies* 19:4 (1993): 662–80.

Cunningham, Hugh. "The Employment and Unemployment of Children in England, c.1680–1851." *Past and Present* 126 (1991): 115–50.

Cunningham, Hugh. "The Decline of Child Labour: Labour Markets and Family Economies in Europe and North America since 1830." *Economic History Review* 53:3 (2000): 409–28.

Cunningham, Hugh, and Shelton Stromquist. "Child Labor and the Rights of Children: Historical Patterns of Decline and Persistence." In *Child Labor and Human Rights,* ed. Burns H. Weston, 55–83. London: Lynne Rienner, 2005.

Davin, Anna. *Growing Up Poor: Home, School and Street in London 1870–1914.* London: Rivers Oram Press, 1996.

Ennew, Judith, William E. Myers, and Dominique Pierre Plateau. "Defining Child Labor as if Human Rights Really Matter." In *Child Labor and Human Rights,* ed. Burns H. Weston, 27–54. London: Lynne Rienner, 2005.

Galbi, Douglas A. "Child Labor and the Division of Labor in the Early English Cotton Mills." *Journal of Population Economics* 10 (1997): 357–75.

Goldin, Claudia. "Family Strategies and the Family Economy in the Late Nineteenth Century: The Role of Secondary Workers." In *Philadelphia: Work, Space, Family, and Group Experience in the Nineteenth Century,* ed. Theodore Hershberg, 277–310. New York: Oxford University Press, 1981.

Gray, Robert. *The Factory Question and Industrial England, 1830–1860.* Cambridge: Cambridge University Press, 1996.

Grier, Beverly. "Invisible Hands: The Political Economy of Child Labour in Colonial Zimbabwe, 1890–1930." *Journal of Southern African Studies* 20:1 (1994): 27–52.

Haines, Michael R. "Industrial Work and the Family Life Cycle, 1889–1890." *Research in Economic History* 4 (1979): 289–356.

Herdt, René de. "Child Labour in Belgium, 1800–1914." In *Child Labour in Historical Perspective, 1800–*1985, ed. Hugh Cunningham and Pier Paolo Viazzo, 23–39. Florence: UNICEF, 1996.

Heywood, Colin. "The Market for Child Labour in Nineteenth-Century France." *History* 66 (1981): 34–49.

Heywood, Colin. *Childhood in Nineteenth-Century France: Work, Health and Education Among the "classes populaires."* Cambridge: Cambridge University Press, 1988.

Hindman, Hugh D. *Child Labor: An American History.* Armonk, NY: M.E. Sharpe, 2002.

Hindman, Hugh D. "Unfinished Business: The Persistence of Child Labor in the US." *Employee Responsibilities and Rights Journal* 18 (2006): 125–31.

Holleran, Philip M. "Family Income and Child Labor in Carolina Cotton Mills." *Social Science History* 21:3 (1997): 297–320.

Horrell, Sara, and Jane Humphries. "'The Exploitation of Little Children': Child Labor and the Family Economy in the Industrial Revolution." *Explorations in Economic History* 32 (1985): 485–516.

Horrell, Sara, and Jane Humphries. "Child Labour and British Industrialization." In *A Thing of the Past,* ed. Michael Lavalette, 76–100. New York: St. Martin's Press, 1999.

Hutt, W.H. "The Factory System of the Early Nineteenth Century." In *Capitalism and the Historians,* ed. F.A. Hayeck, 160–188. London: Routledge, 1954.

Ipsen, Carl. *Italy in the Age of Pinocchio: Children and Danger in the Liberal Era.* New York: Palgrave Macmillan, 2006.

Kirby, Peter. "The Historic Viability of Child Labour and the Mines Act of 1842." In *A Thing of the Past? Child Labour in Britain in the Nineteenth and Twentieth Centuries,* ed. Michael Lavalette, 101–17. New York: St. Martin's Press, 1999.

Kleinberg, S.J. *The Shadow of the Mills: Working-Class Families in Pittsburgh, 1870–1907.* Pittsburgh: University of Pittsburgh Press, 1989.

Kuznesof, Elizabeth Anne. "The Puzzling Contradictions of Child Labor, Unemployment, and Education in Brazil." *Journal of Family History* 23:3 (1998): 225–39.

Lavalette, Michael. *Child Employment in the Capitalist Labour Market.* Aldershot: Avebury, 1994.

Lavalette, Michael. "The Changing Form of Child Labour *circa* 1880–1918." In *A Thing of the Past? Child Labour in Britain in the Nineteenth and Twentieth Centuries,* ed. Michael Lavalette, 118–38. New York: St. Martin's Press, 1999.

Levine, David. *Reproducing Families: The Political Economy of English Population History.* Cambridge: Cambridge University Press, 1987.

Moehling, Carolyn M. "State Child Labor Laws and the Decline of Child Labor." *Explorations in Economic History* 36 (1999): 72–106.

Moehling, Carolyn M. "Family Structure, School Attendance, and Child Labor in the American South in 1900 and 1910." *Explorations in Economic History* 41:1 (2004): 73–100.

Nardinelli, Clark. "Child Labor and the Factory Acts." *Journal of Economic History* 40:4 (1980): 739–55.

Nardinelli, Clark. *Child Labor and the Industrial Revolution.* Bloomington: Indiana University Press, 1990.

Parsons, Donald O., and Claudia Goldin. "Child Labor Among Late Nineteenth-Century American Families." *Economic Inquiry* 27 (1989): 637–59.

Rahikainen, Marjatta. *Centuries of Child Labour: European Experiences from the Seventeenth to the Twentieth Century.* Aldershot: Ashgate, 2004.

Rose, Mary B. "Social Policy and Business: Parish Apprenticeship and the Early Factory System 1750–1834." *Business History* 31:4 (1989): 5–32.

Saito, Osamu. "Children's Work, Industrialism and the Family Economy in Japan, 1872–1926." In *Child Labour in Historical Perspective, 1800*–1985, ed. Hugh Cunningham and Pier Paolo Viazzo, 73–90. Florence: UNICEF, 1996.

Sandin, Bengt. "'In the Large Factory Towns.' Child Labour Legislation, Child Labour and School Compulsion." In *Industrious Children,* ed. Ning de Coninck-Smith, Bengt Sandin, and Ellen Schrumpf, 17–46. Odense: Odense University Press, 1997.

Schrumpf, Ellen. "From Full-Time to Part-Time: Working Children in Norway from the Nineteenth to the Twentieth Century." In *Industrious Children,* ed. Ning de Coninck-Smith, Bengt Sandin, and Ellen Schrumpf, 47–78. Odense: Odense University Press, 1997.

Simelane, Hamilton Sipho. "Landlords, the State, and Child Labor in Colonial Swaziland, 1914–1947." *International Journal of African Historical Studies* 31:3 (1998): 571–93.

Sjöberg, Mats. "Working Rural Children, Herding, Child Labour and Childhood in the Swedish Rural Environment 1850–1950." In *Industrious Children,* ed. Ning de Coninck-Smith, Bengt Sandin, and Ellen Schrumpf, 106–28. Odense: Odense University Press, 1997.

Thompson, E.P. *The Making of the English Working Classes.* Harmondsworth: Penguin, 1968.

Trattner, Walter L. *Crusade for the Children: A History of the National Child Labor Committee and Child Labor Reform in America.* Chicago: Quadrangle Books, 1970.

Tuttle, Carolyn. "A Revival of the Pessimist View: Child Labor and the Industrial Revolution." *Research in Economic History* 18 (1998): 53–82.

Tuttle, Carolyn. *Hard at Work in Factories and Mines: The Economics of Child Labor During the British Industrial Revolution.* Boulder, CO: Westview Press, 1999.

Weiner, Myron. *The Child and the State in India: Child Labor and Education Policy in Comparative Perspective.* Princeton, NJ: Princeton University Press, 1991.

Weissbach, Lee Shai. *Child Labor Reform in Nineteenth-Century France: Assuring the Future Harvest.* Baton Rouge: Louisiana State University Press, 1989.

Zelizer, Viviana. *Pricing the Priceless Child: The Changing Social Value of Children.* New York: Basic Books, 1985.

Toward an Integrative Theory of Child Labor

G.K. Lieten, Professor of Child Labour Studies at the International Institute of Social History and at the University of Amsterdam; Director of International Research on Working Children (IREWOC)

In the long history of humankind, the organization of work and of social life has gone through various stages. It is only in the more recent period, that is, with the emergence of capitalism toward the late eighteenth century, that child labor emerged as a social phenomenon and a social problem. Alec Fyfe (1989, 28) has aptly stated, "Industrialization did not invent child work; it intensified and transformed it."

Two aspects were common features during most of the preindustrial stages. The first was the absence, by and large, of a division of labor. Clans, and later families, were engaged in basic economic activities such as hunting or agriculture. Labor was hardly differentiated, and children, through social rearing, gradually took on more and more tasks within that rather simple production structure. Early work was considered wholesome and was the only form of education. In later preindustrial periods, children who did not work on the land and who did not become roaming vagabonds lived and worked as apprentices with masters. The second aspect was that the undifferentiated labor process went hand in hand with low generation of surplus, or, as happened in feudal systems, with surplus that was ripped off by tributary powers. Survival demanded that all members of the household, including the children, contributed to the production of basic goods. The work was hard, but interspersed with seasonal periods of relative rest and recuperation, and it was done within a mutually supporting family system.

Both these aspects—the nondifferentiated labor processes and the struggle for survival at low levels of surplus generation—underwent drastic changes with the onset of capitalism. In the new production structure, starting with the Industrial Revolution in England around 1760, the work done by children underwent a qualitative change. For various reasons, the old anchorage of households in the land and in the community was lifted, and numerous families became footloose, looking for work with an employer. Children, who had worked with their parents in preindustrial times, continued to do so, but under dramatically changing circumstances.

Like the adults, children also became subservient to the dictates of the machinery, which meant year-round excessive hours in harmful and unhealthy environments. The production of goods, which had been for self-consumption or for barter trade, made way for the sale of labor power to an entrepreneur whose profit depended on the (at times inhuman) exploitation of children (and adults). Another important difference with the preindustrial period was the physical separation of children from their parents and the children's exposure to an environment where they were at the whims of other adults, their coercive demands, and their moral standards. Finally, there was an additional change in the lives of children. Classroom-based education, which was needed to prepare the newly emerging working class for more productive work, gradually became a norm of modern childhood, and, for the first time in history, a clear cleavage emerged between schoolchildren and working children. That norm has gradually been extended and now comprises all the children in the world. Since the achievement of universal basic education is the accepted aim, targeted by the Millennium Development Goals, no child can be allowed to exchange the school for the factory or the farm.

Child Labor

Child labor, the new phenomenon that emerged with the arrival of capitalism, was, for a very long time, fairly widespread in the industrializing countries. Historians have argued that the growth of capitalism thrived on the exploitation of children, just as it is argued that present-day globalization depends on child labor in developing countries. Other historians, however, have argued that the heavy concentration of children in some occupations, such as the textile mills, the street trades, and the household industries, was not exemplary for the entire economy. Work in agriculture may have provided fewer employment opportunities, except for the cropping season, and thus had a much lower incidence of child labor. Likewise, under conditions of globalization, child labor may occur less in the industrial sector, which uses modern production techniques and where trade union rights apply, than in agriculture, where wretched conditions keep families in premodern work relations.

Child labor, in earlier days and in present days, indeed was fairly widespread, but it became a problem for poor people and, above all, for people on the move. Households, driven from the land, roamed around in search of employment, within and across international borders. Children, like their parents, were torn asunder from protective structures and were made to work in dreadful circumstances. In the eighteenth and nineteenth centuries, the poor in the developing countries of those days (that is, the present developed countries) lived in outrageous conditions. Children were often employed from the age of six onward and were made to work in conditions of servitude for fourteen to sixteen hours a week. Hindman (2002) has appropriately referred to the phenomenon of young children working in agriculture and in the tenement industry in the United States as "infant labor." The high incidence and appalling conditions in some industries led to the emergence of an ethical and political movement against child labor.

The anti–child labor movement, in England roughly from the early nineteenth century, represented a new social consciousness and a change in ethics. It was a dramatic change because the welfare ethics of the previous period, lasting well into the century, had been to supply children from workhouses and orphanages to the new industrial mills, or to farmers in need of labor. Providing employment to children was considered an act of benevolence. When the massive influx of "free" child labor took over, to become the dominant form of child employment, the image of white slave children toiling in the mills aroused a public outcry and gave rise to the first official inquiries.

Regulation, however, was a tardy process. The same factors that still influence child labor practices in developing countries today were at work in those days and inhibited a quick solution. Parental poverty was the main cause and, as long as a comprehensive state-supported welfare system was not in place, the economic contribution of children remained necessary for the family's survival. Education for a long time had not been established as a norm for poor children, and the opportunity costs of not going to school were low. Governments were still very much under the dominance of entrepreneurial interests, and child labor legislation was opposed and obstructed. After the first meaningful legislation in England in 1833, restricting the work of children under the age of thirteen to seven hours a day, it took almost a century before the problem of child labor was finally solved in the developed countries.

Whereas child labor had a multitude of reinforcing causes (parental poverty, a perpetual child labor cycle embedded in social norms, family disorders, unproductive technologies requiring more labor input, gruesome employers, and others), the solution to child labor also had many triggering factors. Historians have followed different tracks. Some have questioned the importance of legislation, for example, on the grounds that the child labor acts, after a lengthy process, usually codified what already had become social practice. Legislation required a sufficiently strong government commitment to monitor and enforce, which was slow to materialize. Yet, legislation, by establishing a new convention, served as a point of reference and helped to lock in new social behaviors. Moreover, legislation was usually the outcome of various social movements, including the trade union movement and the education movement. The interaction of those movements led to the gradual decline of child labor in the developed world. Other historians have argued that the introduction of new technologies made the employment of children counterproductive. Since child labor had been associated with parental poverty, the gradual increase in wages, and the introduction of the family wage principle, where male household heads began to receive wages adequate to support the entire family, together with a decrease in family size, reduced the need for children to contribute to the household economy.

Although the different aspects may have combined in a dialectical process, once the threshold had been passed and a new concept of childhood had been accepted, the battle against child labor in the developed countries had been won. A new economic equilibrium based on decent adult wages and social support to children and the elderly had come in place of the old equilibrium. Herein lies an important lesson: Societies that critically relied on the use of child labor have managed to keep their economies going without having to take recourse in child labor. The transition to a new equilibrium signified a paradigmatic change, which involved different economic, cultural, and social practices.

Childhood

The trend toward compulsory and free education was an important aspect of the movement against child labor. Hendrick (1990), in his typologies of changing childhoods, has referred to the so-called evangelical child, a child to be rectified and to be guided into a settled society, characterized by order, obedience, and authority. The approach was a reaction to the debasement of the poor working-class child, or "the factory child," who had to work long hours in unhealthy conditions without access to education but with ample access to delinquency and vices.

Reclaiming children from early adulthood heralded the transformation of the working child into the school pupil. A child henceforth was to be treated as a person that was to be educated into becoming an obedient and disciplined citizen. The emerging nation-states required a unifying social, moral, and religious fabric. The classroom was essential in constructing such a "national childhood" for the benefit and orderliness of the nation. The "schoolchild," and later even the "welfare child," became the universal norm in Western countries, or, as Hendrick (1990, 55) summarized, "from the end of the [nineteenth] century a compulsory relationship between the family, the state, and public welfare services was legislated into practice."

The history of child labor and the construction of modern childhood in the developed countries have many similarities with conditions in the former colonial countries. As long as these countries were colonized by Western powers, child labor was not really on the political agenda, even though the ILO Conventions against child labor formally applied to the colonies as well. After independence, the former colonies became members of international organizations and started adhering to international customs and conventions. The role of the state in ensuring primary education and in banning child labor was included in those customs and conventions. The differences between former colonies and industrialized countries were that the policies had to be introduced within a much shorter time frame, and that legislation was normative rather than codifying: The state was to play a proactive role in a confrontation with tradition, low productivity, poverty, and the imposition of stringent legislation on unwilling employers.

The reasons that have been advanced for a ban on child labor in the developing countries were basically the same as those in Europe in the preceding century. So are the reasons that have been advanced for a more tolerant attitude toward child labor. One argument is that many families are so poor, and the contribution of children is so crucial that, in the absence of a social security system, physical survival would be threatened if the children stopped working. The incidence of child labor is highest in the poorest sections of the poorest countries. The other argument is that schools are typically dysfunctional, providing low-quality and nonrelevant teaching. The schools do not augment the prospects for a better life, and, according to this argument, the children will be better off if they get practical education through work.

The recent debate over eradication of child labor has included a dispute over the universality of childhood norms. Children in the West have been transformed from wage earners to economically useless but emotionally priceless objects. The cultural shift that took place shifted children out of the public domain into the private family domain, in which they were looked after, protected, and pampered. In the mainstream construction of childhood, children have henceforth been seen as individuals with an autonomy that should be safeguarded and fostered. An important trend in Western childhood studies is the assumption that culture and context in many developing countries are so dissimilar that a universal norm of childhood cannot possibly be imposed. The imposition of a universal standard would amount to "Western ethnocentricity." This has enabled scholars, for example Liebel (2004), to argue that child labor is not repugnant, but is actually embedded in local cultures, and should be respected.

Child Labor Statistics

Since those early days, and stretching into the present, there has been disagreement on the size and scope of the child labor problem. Child labor may have been abundant in specific industries—for example, the textile industries in early industrial England, or the plantations under the colonial system. But the focus of public attention and the investigative studies in those sectors may have led to a serious overstatement, by extrapolation, of the incidence of child labor in other industries. In earlier days as well in present days, concerned organizations, in order to get more public support for their case, may have inflated the numbers and the degree of exploitation.

Such "advocacy statistics," suggesting that child labor is an immense problem indeed, have helped to galvanize the world into action. They have come in handy for Western governments to argue for the inclusion of child labor as a social clause in international trade sanctions. The higher the child labor figures, the more likely it is that nimble and cheap fingers have been involved in production for export, and the more convincing the argument for trade policy initiatives banning child labor–tainted products. At the same time, exaggerated estimates have also helped to enlarge the resource base of child-focused organizations such as UNICEF, Save the Children, Plan International, and the World March, which, together with the ILO and national organizations, have become active players in the worldwide child labor initiatives in the 1990s and thereafter.

The ILO, in the late 1980s, estimated that 50 million children were economically active. That was probably an undercount, and when more surveys had been undertaken across the world, the figure for child labor below the age of fifteen was adjusted to 186 million in 2000 and 166 million in 2004. Different sets of figures are obtained when all economically active children are included (191 million), or only children in hazardous works (74 million). When the fifteen-year-old to seventeen-year-old age category is included, the magnitude of child labor and hazardous child labor is, respectively, 218 million and 126 million.

The statistics impose a serious challenge. It is not only a question of counting and aggregating, but even more so, of agreeing on a definition of what constitutes child labor. Different notions of the meaning of child work and labor have implications for the statistics. The ILO general secretary in his 1983 annual report even argued that figures "are not very meaningful. They may have dramatic effect but they do not offer a basis for policy. . . . They are also of a limited utility. In themselves, they tell us nothing about the nature of the work children are doing or the circumstances and conditions under which it is being done" (ILO 1983, 7). The statistics include many children who should not properly be considered child laborers. Employment—any contribution to the national accounting statistics—need not necessarily be conceived as child labor.

The figures on child labor may suffer from overcount, but they may also suffer from undercount. Generally, only work that can be captured by the national accounting statistics gets included in the statistics. This leaves the work done by children in the household unaccounted for. Ordinary household chores are not commonly a problem, but they become child labor when children, sometimes in the place of parents who are out at work, are tied to highly responsible and excessive household work, interfering with their schooling. From a child rights perspective, such work should be treated as child labor since it interferes with the rights of children as specified in the UN CRC. Likewise, children who engage in illegal work activities, including commercial sexual activities, illicit drug trading, or other unconditional worst forms of child labor, are not likely to be counted. Finally, the figures are likely to miss some children who work in various informal-sector street trades.

Work and Labor

A distinction should be made between child labor and child work. The concept of work should be used as the generic term and would refer to any type of physical (or mental) engagement done for any purpose. The concept of (child) labor, on the other hand, could better be restricted to the production of goods and services, including work in the household, that interferes with the normative development of children as defined in the UN CRC and that transgresses the ILO conventions on this issue.

Work, as such, can be located on a sliding scale from beneficial to bad. Millions of children legitimately undertake work, paid or unpaid, that is appropriate for their age and level of maturity. By doing so, they learn to take responsibility, and they gain skills and add to the family income, and thus, also to their own well-being. Article 3 of the CRC states that all rights should be applied in the best interest of the child. It is an important admission that involvement in work can have positive aspects.

How then to judge what is right and what is wrong? Article 32 of the CRC articulates a general case: "the right of the child to be protected from economic exploitation and from performing any work that is likely to be hazardous or to interfere with the child's education, or to be harmful to the child's health or physical, mental, spiritual, moral or social development." But Article 32 is not simply a general principle subject to the discretion of individual member states. It should be read in combination with the ILO conventions, and the CRC has actually called for such legislation. Clause 2 of Article 32 stipulates that governments shall take relevant measures such as the minimum age and the regulation of hours and conditions of employment. ILO Conventions 138 (on the minimum age) and 182 (on the worst forms of child labor) provide a general framework for national legislation. The conventions actually allow young children (from the age of twelve onward in developing countries and from thirteen onward in developed countries) to do light work for around two hours a day. The distinction between light work and work that is harmful, and therefore intolerable, was given firm shape with Convention 182 of 1999. It distinguishes hazardous work, which should not be undertaken by young people below the age of eighteen, harmful work, which no child under age fourteen should do, and light work, for which the age limit is twelve years in developing countries.

The term "child labor," unlike, for example, "female labor," should be treated as a single concept rather than as two separate words. It does not implicate all work done by children, but it is specific work done by children in a specific context with a specific duration and with a specific potentially harmful impact. Child labor needs to be defined, neither by the form of the labor relationship nor by the type of activity, but by the effect the activity has on the child. From the point of view of the child, it is immaterial whether the work can be counted as economically productive or not: Child labor is all work done by children, which prevents them from having a proper education and which is harmful to their normal development as children.

Policy Choices

Despite the caveats above, aggregate figures on child labor are probably not far off the mark. A more important problem related to the different manifestations of child work and child labor concerns the question of causes and solutions. The various solutions that have been proposed for tackling child labor derive from how the problem is characterized. But different mechanisms are associated with different forms of child deprivation, and misreading causes would lead to ill-targeted policies. If the concept of child labor is construed to include all children not attending school (which is clearly a trend among scholars and policy makers), then explanations for why child labor occurs will differ from the explanations offered when the concept of child labor is confined to children actually selling their labor power or having their labor power appropriated.

Causes and solutions are closely intertwined. In many cases, children work simply by default since schools in the vicinity are nonfunctioning, malfunctioning, or discriminating against certain groups of children, for example, girls, poor people, or ethnic minorities. Solutions in these cases are to be found in overhauling the school system. In contrast, when children have to work for a full day in order to earn indispensable income for the family, or to repay debts to a moneylender, solutions have to be found in overhauling labor relations and social security systems. Since child labor has often been a necessary evil for individual households, its abrupt eradication may have untoward consequences. The sudden dismissal of children from reasonably remunerated jobs can lead poor children into considerably more harmful professions, or into further economic misery.

Article 3 of the CRC has brought in a new mode of thinking on child labor. The article stipulates that all child-centered policies should have the "best interests of the child" as a primary consideration. One consequence of the centrality of the best interest of the child has been that, under extraordinary circumstances, the labor of individual children could be condoned. Such a principle could lead to arbitrary judgments about the nature of circumstances warranting continued child labor. A number of big players in the field, including both scholars and some well-known NGOs, have actually argued that children should have a "right to work" as long as it does not harm them, contributes to their survival, teaches them skills, and socializes them in cultural and artisanal traditions. UNICEF (2001, 20) also takes the position that an instant stop to child labor is not a viable option in most developing countries, and that attempts to stop children from working "usually degrade their situation further unless better alternatives are provided."

The nonworking child could indeed be worse off than the working child. The overall consensus, however, is that child labor has been an evil in the past and continues to be an evil in the present. In short, child labor is bad policy. It is bad economically since it keeps the wages of adult labor low and preempts a knowledge-based capacity building for economic development. It is bad socially since it fails to shield children from exploitation and misuse by adults and exposes the already vulnerable section of children to an unprotective environment. It is bad politically since it creates two classes of children, the schoolchildren and the labor children, who have different and unequal claims to social justice. It is bad culturally since it leaves a group of children unexposed to literacy and enlightened knowledge. Finally it is bad mentally and physically since it impairs the proper development of the children's bodies and brains.

These negative consequences of child labor will not combine in all cases—for example, a working child may grow up healthier than a poor nonworking child—but together they constitute a clear imperative: Child labor has a combination of causes, a variety of impairing consequences, and solutions along different tracks, but, in the best interest of all children and on grounds of justice and fairness, it ought to be eradicated.

References and Further Reading

Anker, Richard. "The Economics of Child Labour: A Framework for Measurement." *International Labour Review* 139:3 (2000): 257–80.

Bequele, Assefa, and Jo Boyden, eds. *Combating Child Labour.* Geneva: International Labor Organization, 1988.

Cunningham, Hugh. *Children and Childhood in Western Society Since 1500.* London: Longman, 1995.

Cunningham, Hugh, and Pier Paolo Viazzo, eds. *Child Labour in Historical Perspective, 1800–1985: Case Studies from Europe, Japan and Colombia.* Florence: UNICEF, 1996.

Fyfe, Alec. *Child Labour.* Cambridge: Polity Press, 1989.

Hendrick, Harry. "Constructions and Reconstructions of British Childhood: An Interpretative Survey, 1800 to the Present." In *Constructing and Reconstructing Childhood: Contemporary Issues in the Sociological Study of Childhood,* ed. Allison James and Alan Prout, 35–59. London: Falmer Press, 1990.

Hindman, Hugh D. *Child Labor: An American History.* Armonk, NY: M.E. Sharpe, 2002.

ILO. *Child Labour. Extract from the Report of the Director-General to the International Labour Conference, 69th Session.* Geneva: International Labour Office, 1983.

ILO. *Every Child Counts: New Global Estimates on Child Labour.* Geneva: International Labour Office, 2002.

James, Allison, Chris Jenks, and Alan Prout. *Theorising Childhood.* Cambridge: Polity Press, 1998.

Lavalette, Michael, ed. *A Thing of the Past? Child Labour in Britain in the Nineteenth and Twentieth Centuries.* Liverpool: Liverpool University Press, 1999.

Liebel, Manfred. *A Will of Their Own. Cross-Cultural*

Perspectives on Working Children. London: Zed Books, 2004.

Lieten, G.K. *Child Labour: Burning Questions.* Amsterdam: Aksant, 2005.

Lieten, G.K., and Ben White, eds. *Child Labour: Policy Perspectives.* Amsterdam: Aksant, 2001.

Mendelievich, Elias, ed. *Children at Work.* Geneva: International Labour Office, 1979.

Myers, William E., and Jo Boyden. *What Works for Working Children.* Stockholm: Rädda Barnan / UNICEF, 1998.

Rahikainen, Marjatta. *Centuries of Child Labour: European Experiences from the Seventeenth to the Twentieth Century.* Aldershot: Ashgate, 2004.

Rodgers, Gerry, and Guy Standing. *Child Work, Poverty and Underdevelopment.* Geneva: International Labour Office, 1981.

UNICEF. *Poverty and Children. Lessons of the 90s for Least Developed Countries.* New York: UNICEF, 2001.

Zelizer, Viviana. *Pricing the Priceless Child: The Changing Social Value of Children.* New York: Basic Books, 1985.

Section 2. More Developed Regions of the World

Periods of History: Childhood and Child Work, c. 1800–Present

Harry Hendrick, Associate Professor, Institute of History, University of Southern Denmark

To understand the evolution of attitudes toward working children, it is necessary to recognize that the potency of historically variable conceptions of "childhood" for changing forms of child employment (and child welfare in general), together with popular views of what constituted legitimate occupations, have always been linked to how adults socially constructed childhood as a stage of life. In a word, from time immemorial the realities of childhood and child labor have been inseparable from each other. Given the political and cultural importance of changing ideas about childhood, the focus in this essay is on providing a conceptual overview of the relevant continuities and discontinuities, rather than a descriptive account of the practices involved in child labor. As with much of the historiography of child labor, the account presented here is heavily weighted to British experience. Still, in its broad contours, it is generally applicable to much of Western society.

The Middle Ages

Older historical views of the Middle Ages held that the period had no concept of childhood, or at least that it had little or no understanding of the particular nature of children—that children were simply "little adults." After much debate, modern scholarship no longer believes this to be true. Instead, the medieval world is seen as having had a concept of childhood, but one whose particular conception differed from those that emerged during the Renaissance, the Reformation, and thereafter. Where child labor is concerned, given the predominance of agriculture, the prevalence of the family economy, and the absence of compulsory mass schooling, it follows that it was commonplace among all social groups. Employment opportunities were not confined to the countryside since young people also found work in towns, in aristocratic households, and in the church. Furthermore, it should be stressed that the entrance of children into the labor force was gradual (according to age and capability), both within the family and elsewhere, and that it was regarded as natural, occurring without comment. At that time, not only were children far more visible in communities than they are in modern societies, but also they were more involved in the comings and goings of daily life—however, to say that they were regarded as little adults would be to oversimplify medieval social relations.

Eighteenth and Nineteenth Centuries—Locke, Rousseau, the Romantics, and the Evangelicals

Although there were important changes in attitudes toward children brought about by humanism and the Protestant Reformation, not least the significance of their early years (ages one through seven) as a stage of social and religious education, it is generally agreed that the period stretching from the late seventeenth century to the 1890s witnessed several seminal social constructions of childhood, which would resonate throughout modernity, and that the laboring child figured prominently in those of the nineteenth century. From the adult standpoint the different and often overlapping understandings shared four main intentions: to identify the nature of childhood, to define a desirable state of childhood, to incorporate childhood into the philosophy of the meaning of life (humans and nature), and, increasingly important, to control children—the inhabitants of said childhood. As we shall see, these objectives were critical for the development of critiques of child labor.

With the publication of John Locke's *Some Thoughts Concerning Education* (1693), which attacked the notion of infant depravity and expressed a tentative interest in *understanding* children, the eighteenth century began a reassessment of children's nature. The principal architect of this process was Jean-Jacques Rousseau, author of *Emile* (1762), the most influential educational tract of the age. Rousseau captured the imagination of Europe with his validation of "nature" as he raged against what he saw as the forcing effects of conventional education in pushing children into adulthood. "Nature," he said, "wants children to be children before they are men." The importance of Rousseau was twofold: He revitalized the condition of childhood, portraying it as a foundational stage in life, as opposed to being merely a preparation for adulthood; and, in rejecting the Christian "fallen state," he freed children from the burden of original sin and, therefore, claimed for them an "innocent" nature. This proved to be a crucial assessment in succeeding decades, as critics of industrialization argued that children's nature was being corrupted through the brutalizing effects of factory work.

The natural child soon met up with the twin influences of the Romantic and Evangelical revivals at the end of the eighteenth and early nineteenth centuries, as well as the growing reality of child labor in factories and mines. For the Romantics, the child was pivotal for the desire to investigate the "self" and to protest against the perverse experiences of contemporary social and economic upheaval. The Romantics turned to children because they were in need of a new awareness and new psychological insights: They used the child figure to make their readers feel a truth rather than simply understand it. This construction of childhood, which demanded a dramatic curtailment of child labor, was integral to the political struggle among different social forces—religious, economic, political—over the direction and consequences of the Industrial Revolution.

In the early nineteenth century, however, optimistic perceptions of childhood found themselves pitted against the weight of Evangelical revival, with its belief in original sin and the need for redemption. In Evangelical hands, human nature was no longer "pleasing to the author of our Being." Parents were advised to teach their children that they were "sinful polluted creatures." However, in recognizing the importance of childhood as having its own nature, and as warranting investment of time, money, and concern, Evangelicals exercised a widespread influence throughout the nineteenth century in areas of child welfare reform, especially through the espousal of the Victorian middle-class "domestic ideal," which, in emphazising home, duty, love, family, and deference, promoted a domesticated childhood—one that was implicitly unwaged.

The Debate on the Factory Child

The growing use of child labor in factories and mines posed a number of problems for all the foregoing constructions of childhood, since, in different ways, it violated the child as natural, as pure, and as being in need of a familial and disciplined religious environment. No sooner was the factory system established than a debate arose as to the morality of using children in this capacity and the extent to which they were being economically exploited and having their health damaged. The campaign against industrial child labor (but not agricultural child labor) was long and complex and touched on a variety of issues in British society at the time, especially the political economy of "free" and "unfree" labor, antislavery, the meaning of "the natural order," and, at a time of industrial, social, and political turmoil, the reproduction of society itself.

By the 1830s, however, the fundamental categories of analysis had become "childhood-adulthood," and the substance of the argument concerning child nature was that it differed in kind from that of the adult. Hitherto, uncertainty had surrounded the age definition of childhood, but in 1833 the Royal Commission on the Employment of Children in Factories, which introduced the first effective Factory Act limiting children's working hours, declared age thirteen as being when "the period of childhood . . . ceases." This gave childhood a precise age limit. More important, it helped to establish a new construction of childhood in terms of qualifying children's freedom to labor, protecting them from exploitation, enforcing parental obligation, and legitimizing state intervention on their behalf. Furthermore, insofar as the debate about factory hours was also concerned with the nineteenth-century meaning of "progress," the childhood promoted by reformers was one that suited a civilized and Christian nation, the core of which was the patriarchal family, widely seen as integral to all forms of social stability.

Constructing the Schoolchild—Compulsory Mass Schooling

The social construction of childhood had progressed apace by the 1860s, but there remained a further and most significant development, which was inspired by middle-class ideals and supported by the respectable working class, namely, the introduction of compulsory mass schooling in the 1870s (however, among many social groups, school attendance for part of the week had been common long before this time).The degree to which compulsory schooling was responsible for ending, or at least significantly reducing the size of, the wage-earning child labor force is still debated since changes in technology and production processes are also held to have been influential. It was certainly the case that employment of children was much less common by the 1870s than it had been earlier in the century, and the amount of industrial work for younger children was negligible.

Broadly speaking, mass schooling made possible the imposition upon children of a number of features of what had come to be seen as the essence of childhood—a childhood, it should be noted, that was increasingly modeled on middle-class notions of familial relations as idealized in the mid-Victorian "domestic ideal." Many, but not all, of the natural/Romantic features of early-nineteenth-century childhood had been more or less lost sight of long before the 1870s insofar as they no longer protected children (particularly those of the so-called dangerous classes) against the intrusion of harsher and more self-serving adult designs. It is well-known that schools were seen as beacons of civilization whose primary objective, aside from academic learning, was to induct children into acceptable norms of behavior. The work of reforming "habits of order, punctuality, industry and self-respect," advised one moralist, must "begin with the young. . . . They are the depositories of our hopes and expectations" (cited in Hendrick 1997a, 45).

The significance of the school in the process of constructing childhood was that it in part created and in part consolidated a number of features that came to be accepted as natural. In other words, the school altered children's condition, molding it into a form that corresponded to a growing perception among adults of who children were and what childhood should be. Crucial to this understanding was the cultural acceptance of the inappropriateness of full-time wage-earning employment, not only because this offended the child's nature, but also because the school presented children as investments in the future: of economic competitiveness, of responsible parenthood, of military efficiency, and of the stability of the British Empire. Indeed, by the early 1900s, children were regarded as being "of the nation." Of course, what got lost in the making of the schoolchild was the fact that children worked at school. In school their labor was devoid of economic relevance, and was segregated into the classroom, away from the marketplace, with all this implied for their subordinate status.

The situation, however, was not as clearly defined as educationalists would have liked, for cultural and class-determined practices involving certain kinds of child labor continued. The part-time work of children (before and after school) surfaced as an issue (estimates varied between 150,000 and 600,000 children thus employed), as did that of 70,000 "half-timers," who were mainly employed in textiles. Child labor as such was not universally frowned upon for a certain amount of employment, either within the family economy or in wage-earning occupations; it was seen as helpful in encouraging the work ethic, maintaining discipline, and keeping older children off the streets. Nevertheless, alongside other child protection and welfare measures, such as school feeding and school medical inspection, infant welfare, and the prevention of cruelty, further legislation was passed in the early 1900s in an effort to restrict and inspect children's paid employment wherever possible. Despite the well-known fact that child labor continued, certainly in agriculture and the delivery trades, the passing of the 1918 Education Act (updated in the 1933 Children and Young Persons Act) made it appear that the child labor problem had been solved.

The Twentieth Century—Psychology and Welfare

By the early 1900s, the essential feature of modern childhood had been established: Children were no longer wage earners; children were school pupils. Childhood, as we know it, was institutionalized. This is not to say that there were no further significant developments. If the period from about 1860 to 1918 had seen children socially constructed through welfare concerns for their bodies, the interwar construction, much influenced by Freudianism, emphasized children's minds: emotions, fantasies, dreams, instincts, and habits. The "psychological child" was in large part the product of psychologists such as Cyril Burt (in his work on individual differences), the psychoanalyst and educationalist Susan Isaacs (in her work on children's emotional and social development), and the Child Guidance movement, which dealt with the "minor problems" of "normal" childhood. The principal concern was to produce children who were emotionally adjusted to their environment. Understandably, then, child labor—despite continuing among poor families during the Depression—did not figure in these constructions.

The experiences of the Second World War (1939–1945), in particular the evacuation process, provided social scientists and psychomedics with volumes of research material concerning family life, parent-child relations, and the social and psychological positioning of children in a variety of environments. But it was the creation of the classic welfare state between 1944 and 1948, through a series of innovative health and welfare acts, including the comprehensive Children Act of 1948, which consolidated the child as a welfare subject. The distinguishing feature of the 1948 act was that the newly established local child-care departments were to exercise their powers in such a way as to further the individual interests of the children over whom they had jurisdiction. This attention to children as people was a hallmark of seeing the child as "a citizen of a democracy, a citizen with rights" (cited in Hendrick 1997a, 56). There is a degree of hyperbole in this description, however, since children were, and are, denied full citizenship, being rather "citizens in waiting."

During this period, child labor was regarded as marginal and as beneficial in terms of providing young people with pocket money, a sense of responsibility, and a useful way of occupying their spare time. This view was challenged by a government report in the early 1970s, which maintained that before- and after-school labor had a deleterious effect on classroom concentration and attendance. However, despite proposed legislation, no action was taken. Further studies published in the 1980s and 1990s have all indicated that child labor is far more extensive than is commonly assumed, both in the proportions of employed children and in the range of occupations. Estimates of the percentage of children in part-time paid work vary between 35 and 43 percent. Although the UN Convention on the Rights of the Child calls for children to be given a "voice" in policy matters that concern them, this has not been the case in the United Kingdom in relation to employment policy.

The comforting myth underlying child labor in recent times is that it is confined to "children's jobs." In other words, it is the kind of work that is suitable for children. Of course, this begs the question: What is childhood? This reminds us that understandings of child labor are always associated with specific social constructions of childhood. For contemporary society, a key element in the perception of childhood is that children are defined through their school status. Such children, by definition, cannot be fully employed in wage labor. Those who are too young for school are identified through their vulnerability (however, it has to be remembered that an increasing number of young children are now being institutionally "schooled" through various "early years" programs). But it is not simply schooling that defines childhood and directs adult attitudes toward the wage labor of children. We should remember the Romantic inheritance, with its emphasis on childhood/nature, which was reinterpreted by psychoanalysis and child guidance in terms of a nature that was scientifically differentiated from adulthood, particularly with reference to the tasks that adults do. And no task is more central to "postmodern" adulthood than waged-work—it is a self-defining feature of our lives. Note how passionately it has been claimed by feminists in their pursuit of gender equality, and note also its political significance in the current restructuring of social welfare programs throughout Europe and North America.

Conclusion

Broadly speaking, it is possible to draw a number of conclusions about working children. First, since the early modern period, child labor has been a demand-driven rather than a supply-led phenomenon, which increased during the preindustrial period and accelerated rapidly with industrialization. But demand was not confined to private employers (and parents in home industries), since, abiding by the belief that the devil finds work for idle hands, throughout Europe, orphan and pauper children were put to work in orphanages and poor-law institutions. Second, while child labor has been more or less compulsory for children, it has been connected to the freedom adults have in choosing their work. Children, it seems got (and get) the jobs nobody else wanted. Third, child labor has always stood in relation to the lives of nonworking middle- and upper-class children, whose status so often required the exploitation of their social inferiors. Fourth, given that child labor was used extensively in those industries that pioneered industrial growth, it was indispensable for economic development.

"Child labor" reveals much of the ambivalence and many of the ambiguities that mark adult-child relations. By their exclusion from full-time employment, not only are children protected from economic exploitation and the rigors of jobs that undermine good health, and enabled to be educated, but also they are kept vulnerable, ignorant, economically dependent, and subject to comprehensive paternalism. Part-time wage labor before and after school is allowed to continue, and is often encouraged, because it serves a variety of adult needs (e.g., early-morning paper delivery and babysitting) and does not threaten the subordinate status of children. In contemporary Britain, and elsewhere, we are in the midst of a so-called crisis of childhood concerning obesity, mental health, leisure activities, truancy, antisocial behavior, classroom indiscipline, substance abuse, child-care costs, and consumerism. Only a "Supernanny," it seems, can save us. In such a climate, where the whiff of child hatred is so strong, for better or worse, child labor fails to register on the scale of our adult anxieties.

References and Further Reading

Cunningham, Hugh. *Children and Childhood in Western Society Since 1500.* Harlow: Pearson Education, 2005.

Hendrick, Harry. "Constructions and Reconstructions of British Childhood: 1800 to the Present." In *Constructing and Reconstructing Childhood*, ed. Allison James and Alan Prout, 34–62. London: Falmer Press, 1997a.

Hendrick, Harry. *Children, Childhood and English Society, 1880–1990.* Cambridge: Cambridge University Press, 1997b.

Hendrick, Harry. *Child Welfare: Historical Dimensions, Contemporary Debate.* Bristol: Policy Press, 2003.

Heywood, Colin. *A History of Childhood: Children and Childhood in the West from Medieval to Modern Times.* Cambridge: Polity Press, 2001.

Hopkins, Eric. *Childhood Transformed. Working-Class Children in Nineteenth-Century England.* Manchester: Manchester University Press, 1994.

Horn, Pamela. *Children's Work and Welfare, 1780–1880s.* Basingstoke: Macmillan, 1994.

Lavalette, Michael, ed. *A Thing of the Past? Child Labour in Britain in the Nineteenth and Twentieth Centuries.* Liverpool: Liverpool University Press, 1999.

Rahikainen, Marjatta. *Centuries of Child Labour: European Experiences from the Seventeenth to the Twentieth Century.* Aldershot: Ashgate, 2004.

Child Labor in the Industrial Revolution

Peter N. Stearns, Provost and Professor of History, George Mason University

The Industrial Revolution began in Britain in the late eighteenth century. By the early nineteenth century, industrialization was also under way in Western Europe and the United States. Japan and Russia launched industrial revolutions by the 1890s. By the late twentieth century most of the world's nations had developed significant industrial sectors, and other Pacific Rim countries had joined the ranks of outright industrializers. Furthermore, even during the initial decades of the Industrial Revolution, industrialization had impacts on traditional economies in many parts of the world. The Industrial Revolution, in other words, must be seen as a global process, though an uneven one.

The key features of the Industrial Revolution involved the application of fossil fuel (or water) power to the manufacturing process, with increasingly automatic mechanisms available to translate the new energy sources into spinning, weaving, metallurgy, and so on. The steam engine, first developed in a form applicable to manufacturing in the 1770s, was the core technological advance. New technologies greatly increased the productivity of individual workers, and greatly intensified the experience of work itself, mainly by accelerating the pace of operations. Accompanying new technology was the spread of the factory system, necessary to utilize new sources of power efficiently and also permitting a significant change in the organization of work. Factories, though initially small by modern standards, allowed an increasing specialization of labor. They also required more formal direction of workers, through shop rules and foremen. A key measure of advancing nineteenth-century industrialization was the rapid growth of cities: By 1850, 50 percent of the British population lived in cities, the first time this level of urbanization had occurred in human history.

From the start, the Industrial Revolution had a significant impact on child labor. Three preliminary points are essential. First, use of child labor varied significantly from one country to the next during the industrialization process. Second, industrialization affected child labor in agricultural regions as well as in the outright industrializers—an impact still important today. And finally, and most important, the long-run effects of industrialization often differed from the initial consequences; ultimately, the Industrial Revolution fundamentally altered the nature of childhood. A childhood defined in terms of work—the characteristic of agricultural economies everywhere—shifted to a childhood defined in terms of schooling. This massive historic change took a while to work out; indeed, many societies are still adjusting today. Early industrial developments might even point in a seemingly different direction, toward greater exploitation of child labor. But, as can be seen clearly in retrospect, there should be no mistaking the larger trend or its revolutionary consequences for children and adults alike. Indeed, early industrial conditions themselves encouraged new attitudes that made the labor of children seem increasingly unacceptable.

Great Britain

British industrialization depended heavily on the use of children in factories and mines. Estimates have ranged that children comprised up to 50 percent of the factory labor force, and 30 percent of the workforce in coal mines, by the early nineteenth century. Most of these workers were teenagers, but there was substantial utilization of young children as well—in a few cases as young as three, not uncommonly beginning at age five or six (Tuttle 1999).

Several factors explain this heavy reliance on children and adolescents. As the pioneers in industrialization, and facing substantial investments in novel technologies, many British factory owners were desperately eager to cut labor costs in order to maximize return on equipment. Children's wages, far lower than those of adults, seemed particularly attractive. British manufacturers sometimes imported crews of orphans and other vulnerable children, who had no other options and whose labor was particularly cheap. Furthermore, early industrial equipment, less sophisticated than what came later, provided many opportunities for young workers. Bobbin boys, to take one example, retied threads that broke on mechanical looms; their nimbleness and the small size of their fingers made them ideal, though at a cost of frequent accidents to the children themselves. Later generations of industrial equipment automated more of the processes children performed in the initial decades of industrialization (though historians continue to debate the extent of change). Early factory products quickly displaced rural manufacturing labor; rural spinners, particularly, could not compete with the prices of factory goods. Large numbers of workers were displaced as a result, including many children; not surprisingly, many became candidates for industrial employment. Adult workers themselves often sought jobs for their children. Some women workers urged employers to allow them to use their young children as helpers because they had no other way to take care of them. A variety of family considerations, and not just supplemental earnings, entered into the process. All this occurred in a context in which manufacturers and workers alike found child labor logical, given the centuries of precedent among peasants and craftspeople in the agricultural economy (Horrell and Humphries 1995).

Industrial conditions were novel, however, and novel attitudes were developing as well. Historians have debated the conditions of child workers in early British industrialization. There were clearly cases of dreadful abuse (and there would be in later industrializations as well), with high accident rates, whippings at the hands of adult workers, exhaustion amid low pay and inadequate food, and sexual exploitation. Some child labor, however, was less onerous. Many workers reported satisfaction that children could work with them and contribute earnings to the family economy (again, a new version of an established expectation that children would be economic assets). In some regions, concerns about child labor paled before concerns about its absence, as families in rural centers found it difficult to make ends meet. Clearly, child labor's impact varied from place to place. Horror stories were real in many textile factories and coal mines. But the picture they suggested was not uniformly applicable.

Fairly quickly, however, objections did surface to the use of children in industrial settings. Here, too, not surprisingly, Britain led the way. Three factors ultimately combined. First, factory work was obviously different from traditional work in several respects. It was more dangerous, and faster paced; its environment was less familiar, which may have increased opportunities for abuse. Second, the values of key portions of the rising middle class were also changing. New humanitarian sentiment called attention to problems that might previously have been ignored. Many middle-class families were themselves devoting increasing attention to education—which factory work obviously inhibited for the lower classes—and Enlightenment thinking more generally urged a new concern for the educability of children. Leading middle-class reformers soon emerged to galvanize campaigns for the limitation of child labor. For some, abuses of children formed a convenient target for more inchoate worries about the crudeness of the new, industrial economy. Finally, though gradually, many workers themselves turned against child labor. The focus was not on work itself, but on the extent to which children, in factories, were subject to adult discipline that was neither familial nor chosen by families. Working-class leaders also developed a rising stake in education, which could join them with middle-class reformers in urging labor limitations to permit school attendance.

These factors promoted increasing public debate about child labor, including a number of government hearings in the early decades of the nineteenth century. These hearings amplified a sense of exploitation and abuse. Many former child workers testified about the suffering they had endured. The most extensive hearings occurred in 1832, before the Sadler Commission. Michael Thomas Sadler was a Conservative philanthropist and member of Parliament who had been fighting for a blanket ten-hour limitation on the work of all children in the factories. His parliamentary committee set about to determine what actual conditions were, with encouragement to compare with more traditional agricultural uses of child labor. Testimony focused on the long hours and, even more, the lack of interruptions in factory work, with many meals taken on the fly. Workers who had labored twelve hours or more as children told of being whipped in order to stay alert. Reformers also made much of the fact that girls were as often mistreated as boys, in a society in which the middle classes were beginning to invest heavily in the idea of female delicacy. Several middle-class merchants who visited factories to buy goods testified about conditions that made their hearts "ready to bleed."[1] Lack of opportunity to attend school, even the Sunday schools that were beginning to spread in factory centers, formed another common theme. Child workers were also held to be far less moral than other children, because of the models of adult behavior they saw around them.

Hearings of this sort generated a great deal of indignation, as was intended. In addition to uncovering a host of real problems, from harsh discipline to frequent accidents and physical deformities, the accounts highlighted a few assumptions that might have been subjected to more critical scrutiny. Testimony showed a growing belief that children had a right to education—as one overseer of the poor put it before the Sadler Commission, the child workers "have been prevented from attaining that knowledge which children ought to have in the morning of life,"[2] without much recognition that this sentiment, however noble, was also untraditional. More revealing was the pervasive belief that children were far better treated in agricultural jobs, with no direct evidence, amid a clear sense of nostalgia for the good old days. The sense that factory work was particularly foul was a great goad to the unprecedented willingness to consider regulating the labor of children. But it would also long inhibit concern for children's work in general.

Opposition to reform surfaced as well in what was, for several decades, a heated running debate. While factory owners did not uniformly oppose regulation, many did, citing the need for low-cost labor, the benefits to training and to worker families, and the principle that property owners had a right to determine working conditions without interference. Many employers could not imagine how adult workers could function without child assistants, so that if the work of the latter were restricted, adults themselves would be hampered, at a cost to productivity, profit, and wages. Many workers doubtless worried about family earnings, though their opposition counted for less and was often exaggerated by self-interested middle-class opponents. There was some genuine sense, as well as convenient rhetoric, about the rights of parents to dispose of their children as they wished.

Nevertheless, as debate proceeded, it became increasingly clear that public sentiment was turning against the use of children in factories. It was this sentiment that began to create, through legislation as well as parental decisions, the historic shift away from work, and toward schooling, as the defining condition of childhood (Stearns 2006).

The first, and truly historic, piece of legislation to regulate child labor was the First Factory Act of 1802, which set maximum hours for children in factories at twelve and improved conditions in cotton mills. Fifteen subsequent child labor laws were issued in Britain during the nineteenth century. Generally—and this was a pattern repeated in later industrial revolutions—early laws imposed few actual restrictions and had even fewer teeth. Only gradually were actual factory inspections provided, with fines high enough to affect employer behavior. Early laws focused also on young children, not teenagers. Only later in the nineteenth century did legislation begin seriously to affect working conditions for children older than twelve. The early laws also differentiated strongly between factories and child labor in general. Exploitation of children in more traditional work settings not only persisted but might have increased. Desperate parents, barred from sending children to factories, might accept worse conditions elsewhere simply to sustain the family economy. Traditional employers, artisans, for example, often increased exploitation of children, partly because they were faced directly or indirectly with factory competition. Many crafts saw a reduction in customary durations of apprenticeship, with growing complaints that apprentices were also treated more as workers, and less as trainees.

It took time, in other words, for labor legislation to have its full impact on child labor in general. Nevertheless, by the 1830s in Britain, the worst factory abuse of children was in fact easing. Laws, public scrutiny, some sense of conscience among certain employers (particularly after the risks of industrial investment decreased a bit), and the increasing complexity of factory technology (which reduced the need for children) all combined to change children's role in the factory labor force. School attendance, correspondingly, began to rise within the working class. Gradually, child labor in general began to shrink and gradually limitations also extended to the lower teenage years.

It is revealing to note that child labor reform was really the first aspect of the Industrial Revolution to draw state interference, several decades before legislators turned to any regulation of safety conditions or even conditions for women workers. Actual problems of children in the factories, and the new visibility of these problems combined with the changing assumptions about the purposes of childhood to make child labor something of an exception to the government approach toward industry more generally. This was true in early industrial Britain, and it would be true in other parts of Europe and in the United States as well. Only gradually were the implications of child labor reform—that industry might not be suitably self-regulatory, that limits and inspections might apply to categories of adult workers as well—extended more broadly. For the nineteenth-century liberal, committed for the most part to a regime of laissez-faire, child labor and the attendant concern for education forced a modification of normal assumptions. Here, the British pattern provided a model for developments elsewhere.

Outside Britain

The extent of reliance on child labor in industrial revolutions after the British precedent was usually somewhat lower than in Britain itself, particularly where preadolescents were concerned. Every industrial revolution initially involved some child labor, and every case generated some examples of shocking abuse. There were, however, reasons for greater restraint. Later industrial revolutions used more sophisticated equipment, limiting the need for children from the start. In Germany and the United States, industrial revolutions also placed greater emphasis on heavy industry than on textiles, which also limited opportunities to employ children. Children were never extensively used in metallurgy. Several societies displayed earlier interest in mass education than had been true in early industrial Britain (which enacted compulsory schooling only in 1881—nine years later than even Japan). In the United States, northern states such as Massachusetts began passing obligatory school attendance laws by the 1830s, only a decade or two into the industrialization process; similar patterns developed in Germany, Belgium, and, only a bit later, in France (Heywood 2001).

The British example itself provided caution. By the time France began industrializing in the 1820s, Britain had already passed child labor laws. This generated an early impetus for reformers to urge that France follow suit. British reform was held up as a humanitarian standard. Additionally, in an atmosphere of great competitive anxiety, the fact that the world's industrial leader was already taking action reduced the viability of arguments that reform at home would place manufacturers as a cost disadvantage, though these concerns continued to surface. With the first child labor investigations in the 1830s, and with initial legislation in 1841, France moved a decade or two more quickly than Britain had in relation to its industrialization process. Prussia, with a first law in 1839, was even more advanced. When this relatively early reform action was combined with earlier mandatory schooling, the transformation of childhood, from work to schooling, proceeded more quickly, at least in the factory centers (Cunningham and Viazzo 1996).

Similar patterns occurred with Japanese industrialization later in the nineteenth century. Mandatory school attendance was introduced in principle in 1872, even before the country's industrial revolution itself was really under way. Of course, actual attendance fell short of goals for several years because of parental conservatism and the lack of adequate facilities, but still there was change. Japan would directly outlaw factory work for children under twelve in 1911—again, relatively early in the industrialization process. Russian legislation also occurred early, though enforcement and impact were more sporadic.

Later industrializations moved far more slowly where teenagers, as opposed to younger children, were concerned. Japanese industrialization, fairly advanced on the child labor front, long depended on extensive abuse of teenagers and young adults to provide cheap work in silk production and other industries where low wages were crucial to promote vital manufacturing exports. Into the twentieth century many rural families essentially sold teenage girls into work service amid deplorable conditions. Further industrial advance, a commitment to extend periods of schooling, and a reduction in reliance on low-wage textile sectors ultimately brought reform to this category of labor as well.

Even in the United States, the child labor debate continued for a surprisingly long time, cresting only after 1900. The National Child Labor Committee was established only in 1904, but then proceeded for several decades to mobilize public opinion and to generate legislation. Several factors entered into the protracted American discussion. Southern states, later to industrialize, relied on cheap wages to attract textiles and shoe manufacturing, and legislation was slow to come. Even in the north, work outside the factories continued to involve children, and high rates of immigration brought many families who persisted in finding children's work both natural and necessary. Sweatshops in industries such as the garment trades drew particular attention for their reliance on low-paid child labor, often amid long hours and unsafe conditions. Opportunities for employment for boys, in particular, proved particularly alluring as a source of support for the family economy; by the twentieth century it was clear that girls had fewer work opportunities and, in fact, in the working classes, were likely to stay longer in school than their brothers were. In 1910, 2 million children, or 18 percent of the total, were employed in the United States, even aside from farm labor.

This was the high point, however. After 1910, and with surprising speed, the combination of public pressure, legislation, and parental decisions about the advantages of schooling to the longer-run prosperity of children and families alike finally yielded a systematic pattern of change going well beyond the factories themselves. Even the younger teenage years began to be pulled into the process of transformation. By 1920 only 8 percent of all children under the age of fifteen worked in the United States, and by 1940 the figure had dropped to a mere 1 percent. There were a few anomalies: Newspapers, which had trumpeted the reform cause through the early decades of the twentieth century, fought hard for exemptions for newspaper delivery boys, and employment—many would argue, exploitation—of children continued in this venue for several more decades until the advantages of using adults with automobiles finally closed this legal loophole. Child actors were also exempted. But the basic revolution was complete, in the United States as in industrial Europe. A debate that had begun a century before, initially focused on factories alone, had succeeded in redefining the nature of childhood across the board (Mofford 1997).

Global Patterns

The Industrial Revolution has occurred in only some parts of the world, but it has had wide-ranging impact. Societies faced with increasing competition from industrial factories, but also pressed to increase production of foods or raw materials, might accelerate the use of children in compensation. The spread of indentured servitude, as a means of drawing workers from Asia to places like Latin America in the nineteenth century, often involved intense labor for children, as did migrant labor in agriculture in a number of regions. The million-plus indentured workers who traveled from places like India and China to Southeast Asia, Hawaii, and the Caribbean in the late nineteenth century, for work mainly in commercial agriculture, often included the involvement of whole families, and the same continues to apply to migrants in the United States today. The point is clear: In industrial economies proper, child labor uniformly declined at least after a few initial decades, but the opposite occurred in other parts of the world well into the twentieth century. This mixed result is historically important, and it continues to affect child labor patterns even today.

Marxist political movements played a crucial

role in limiting child labor, either early in the Industrial Revolution or even in advance of it. In Europe, Marx himself, and even more his colleague Friedrich Engels, held up abusive child labor in the factories as one of the most damning indictments of industrial capitalism. It was hardly surprising, then, that actual Marxist movements, once in power, worked quickly to reduce child labor. The Bolshevik government in Russia banned work for children under fourteen in 1917, and then established obligatory schooling two years later. Actual implementation was slower than the decrees, of course, but it did gradually occur, particularly in the factories and in the cities. Communist youth movements, to be sure, often stipulated some labor service after school—and this could involve serious work—but this was now a minor component of childhood, not a central feature. Similar patterns would emerge later as an early result of Communist success in places like China, Cuba, and Vietnam.

By the middle of the twentieth century, thanks to the example of industrial countries, human rights agitation, and the implications of political movements like communism, child labor began to decline in most places even as factory work spread more widely. From 1945 onward, United Nations and other human rights proclamations uniformly argued against work and for schooling as part of children's inalienable rights, and this pressure, along with more basic economic changes, clearly won results. In fact, urbanization and industrial growth now helped inhibit child labor—it was the traditional economic sectors that now raised greater questions. China's rapid industrial growth after 1978, for example, involved little or no child labor (though use of teenagers was another matter), thanks to legislation, inspection, and school requirements. Worldwide, only 28 percent of all children under fourteen were working in 1950, only 15 percent by 1990. Child labor was gone in industrial societies and diminishing rapidly elsewhere in favor of rapidly expanding schooling. Still, complexities remained. In South and Southeast Asia, by the 1990s, the number of child workers was actually rising, from 6 million to 9 million. Significantly, this increase occurred not in industry proper, but in more traditional sectors trying to cut labor costs to compete with factory output. Estimates suggest that no more than 5 percent of contemporary child labor occurs in actual factory settings or among the multinational corporations; here, the antilabor assumptions and the glare of global publicity deter abuse. Employers in small shops, and many hard-pressed parents, however, often continue to operate according to other assumptions (ILO 1996).

Conclusion

Industrialization unseated historic patterns of child labor. This did not occur uniformly, or right away, and the story is not over even today (partly because industrialization as a process remains incomplete on a global basis). But it did occur in the main. Industrial societies projected new models of childhood and new standards that were widely influential.

Like all historic changes, this one invites some subtle evaluation. Fifty years ago, with reform efforts still echoing, a history of the elimination of child labor would resound with triumph. And unquestionably, many children were relieved of great potential for abuse. Improvements in children's health and stature, though owing to many factors, undoubtedly reflected the elimination of premature work pressures—a pattern particularly visible in industrial societies but spread to other parts of the world as well.

Yet, without contesting important gains, certainly without urging that the clock be turned back, a broader perspective is now possible. In the first place, not surprisingly, the progressive elimination of child labor had broad consequences. Most obviously, families had to adjust from seeing children as economic assets to recognizing them as stark liabilities, as the absence of their earnings was compounded by the costs of sending them to school. Reduction of the birth rate was the only answer, and this occurred quickly in industrial countries. But birth-rate reduction could unsettle adults—what was the purpose of families if they could manage only a child or two?—and raised new questions about what children were worth. As a result, societies that trumpeted their deep concern for children, as U.S. reformers urged in the twentieth century, might in fact tolerate surprising neglect of children because of new doubts about purpose and utility. Uncertainties were compounded when the number of household chores available for children, and children's willingness to perform chores, also declined, another development that extended the decline of child labor in urban societies as the twentieth century wore on (Zelizer 1985).

Adult uncertainties aside, there were mixed results for children themselves. It has become apparent that many children like school less than they might have liked work. Some countries, like France, have modified school requirements to permit apprenticeship activity for people in their mid-teens who seem destined for blue-collar jobs. Still, alienation from school is a phenomenon that was not anticipated when reform goals focused on curtailing work. Even children who accept school may find it more difficult to relate their activities to larger purposes in life than when they worked directly alongside adults. In countries were schooling has replaced work most fully, such as Japan or the United States, issues of meaning, sometimes in unexpected ways, underscore the significance of the redefinition of childhood.

At least in the United States, the aspect of redefinition currently receiving greatest comment from child experts, including historians of childhood, involves the larger imagery of childhood that resulted from the campaigns against work. The zeal to remove children from work led many reformers to emphasize children's frailty and vulnerability, their need for protection in all settings, quite apart from work itself. The result, critics argue, has been a tendency to patronize and oversupervise children in ways that excessively complicate adult responsibilities and unduly detract from children's actual capacities. Here, of course, the argument is not for a return of child labor, but for a reconsideration of some of the arguments that flowed from the successful campaign.

Child labor was the social norm until recently; it still defines childhood in some settings and some parts of the world. The Industrial Revolution triggered a reconsideration of this norm, initially in the factories themselves and ultimately more widely. The results have been not only uneven, which is hardly surprising given the vast industrial differentials in the contemporary global economy, but also complex. Many societies, including some of the earliest industrializers, are still trying to refine the redefinition of childhood that resulted from reactions against work.

Notes

1. Great Britain. House of Commons, *Sessional Papers 1831–32*, Vol. 15, p. 18.
2. Ibid., p. 393.

References and Further Reading

Cunningham, Hugh, and Pier Paolo Viazzo, eds. *Child Labour in Historical Perspective, 1800–1985: Case Studies from Europe, Japan, and Colombia.* Florence: UNICEF, 1996.

Heywood, Colin. *A History of Childhood: Children and Childhood in the West from Medieval to Modern Times.* Cambridge: Polity Press, 2001.

Horrell, Sarah, and Jane Humphries. "The Exploitation of Little Children: Child Labor and the Family Economy in the Industrial Revolution." *Explorations in Economic History* 32:4 (1995): 485–516.

ILO. *Child Labor: Targeting the Intolerable.* Geneva: ILO, 1996.

Mofford, Juliet H. *Child Labor in America.* Carlisle, MA: Discovery Enterprises, 1997.

Stearns, Peter N. *Childhood in World History.* New York: Routledge, 2006.

Tuttle, Carolyn. *Hard at Work in Factories and Mines: The Economics of Child Labor During the British Industrial Revolution.* Boulder: Westview Press, 1999.

Zelizer, Viviana A. *Pricing the Priceless Child: The Changing Social Value of Children.* New York: Basic Books, 1985.

Coming to Terms with Child Labor

Hugh D. Hindman, Professor of Labor and Human Resources, Appalachian State University

All advanced industrialized nations have gone through a "dirty phase" involving heavy use of child labor in key industries, though some nations were considerably less dirty than others. Likewise, all advanced industrialized nations have, to a greater or lesser degree, come to terms with their child labor problems. In reaching their accommodation, certain policy instruments have formed the core response to the problem. Child labor laws and compulsory schooling policies were the mainstays, but a variety of child welfare policies and labor laws also played key roles in eradicating child labor.

Child Labor Law

Child labor law is one of the nearly universal public policy elements arrayed against child labor. Child labor law refers to that body of law that aims to draw a line of demarcation, however blurred or subject to interpretation, between childhood, on the one side, and the labor market on the other. Often the boundaries are expressed in terms of age, so these laws are often referred to as minimum-age legislation. Early child labor laws were aimed in particular at those new types of employment that accompanied industrialization. So, many of the first laws were called "factory acts." As child labor law developed, it also frequently included reference to other markers, such as night work, hazardous work, work underground, and excessive hours. The general pattern of development was to first prohibit employment of very young children in specific sectors such as factories and mines, and to regulate the hours of older children, often in conjunction with a schooling requirement. Over time, minimum ages were gradually increased, maximum hours were gradually reduced, and the law was extended to apply to additional economic sectors. The general pattern for mature child labor law in developed nations is also familiar. In the United States, for example, hazardous work is prohibited for all children under eighteen; minimum age for regular employment is sixteen; and fourteen- to sixteen-year-olds are permitted to engage in light work, for limited hours, that does not interfere with their schooling. As in many other developed nations, significant gaps remain permitting extensive work of children in some sectors, especially agriculture.

Britain, as the first industrializer, was the first to enact child labor legislation, but its halting, incremental approach meant that it was among the slowest to come to grips with child labor. While ineffective legislation was adopted as early as 1802, the Factory Act of 1833 was the first important turning point. The act prohibited employment of children under nine years of age; limited the work hours of children from nine through twelve years old to nine hours per day; limited the hours of "young persons" from thirteen to eighteen years old to twelve hours per day; and prohibited night work for all children under the age of eighteen. The act established several additional important precedents. For the first time, factory inspections were authorized for enforcement purposes, a feature that proved essential for effective legislation. Second, the act included a declaration that childhood ceased at age thirteen, establishing a clear line of demarcation between children and young people, and between young people and adults (those eighteen years and over). Finally, the act required that working children receive two hours of schooling per day. While this was an important affirmation of the role of education, the "part-time" schooling system it created slowed British progress on child labor by ensuring that children would remain available for work, a situation that continued until the Education Act of 1918 finally prohibited employment of school-age children.

The 1833 British Factory Act provided a template for other early industrializers on the continent of Europe, most notably Germany and France. Relatively early in their respective industrializations, Prussia enacted its first child labor law in 1839, modeled partly on the Factory Act, and France adopted its first child labor law in 1841, though it did not provide for factory inspectors until 1874 (Heywood 1988; Weissbach 1989). As other nations on the European periphery began to industrialize—in the Scandinavian north and the Mediterranean south—normative models of child labor legislation were readily available. By the 1890s, nearly every European nation had enacted child labor legislation (Rahikainnen 2004).

Among the earlier industrializers, the United States was the last to enact a sustainable national child labor law, adopting its Fair Labor Standards Act (FLSA) in 1938. But this was only because, until then, America's system of federalism precluded the national government's role in regulation of labor conditions. Thus, early child labor legislation was the province of state governments. By the time the FLSA was enacted, all states had already adopted child labor laws, most of which conformed to the standards of the FLSA.

In the United States, industrialization emerged first in the northeastern states. As early as 1813, Connecticut enacted a law requiring all factory children to receive instruction in reading, writing, and arithmetic. In 1842, Massachusetts passed a law limiting the work hours of children under age twelve to ten hours per day. The first minimum-age legislation was Pennsylvania's 1848 law establishing a twelve-year minimum age for work in textile factories. In 1867, Massachusetts established the nation's first system of factory inspection (Trattner 1970). With each step, surrounding states typically adopted similar laws, and there was gradual but steady progress in elevation of standards. By 1900, all industrialized states in the North had laws restricting child labor in, at least, mining and manufacturing.

In contrast, there were no child labor laws on the books in 1900 in the southern states, where industrialization did not begin in earnest until the 1880s. While early proposals for child labor legislation were strenuously resisted, creating the impression of a laggard South, southern states actually moved relatively quickly to adopt child labor laws. In 1903, four key southern states adopted a twelve-year minimum age for work in textiles, only one year after Britain adopted the same age standard. By 1916, all southern states but one had adopted a fourteen-year minimum-age standard (Hindman 2002).

While there is much debate over the causal role child labor laws played in reducing or eliminating child labor (Moehling 1999; Nardinelli 1980), there is little room for debate about their normative role in marking the boundaries between childhood and adulthood as well as the boundaries of "free" labor markets.

Universal and Compulsory Schooling

The second universal policy instrument arrayed against child labor is compulsory schooling. Many argue that compulsory schooling laws have been more important than child labor laws in eliminating child labor (Weiner 1991). Their profound importance in remaking both childhood and society as a whole is difficult to overstate.

Developments in child labor law and movements toward universal and compulsory schooling were inevitably intertwined. In some countries, child labor law led, and compulsory schooling law followed, as in Britain. In other countries, compulsory schooling law led, and child labor law followed, most notably in Germany and Japan (Fyfe 2007). But in all cases, the two essentially developed in tandem.

Child Welfare Policy

If child labor law and compulsory schooling were at the forefront of the policy response to child labor, a wide array of additional policies were inevitably brought into play. Child labor laws established the principal that the state has a duty to protect children. Compulsory schooling laws established the principle that the state has a duty to enhance the welfare of children. Together, they established the philosophical underpinnings and practical requirements for broader child welfare policies. If age-based child labor laws were to be enforced, systems of birth registration were required so age could be verified. Once children were compelled to attend school, their health, nutrition, and growth and development could be readily inspected.

Of particular importance were child welfare policies aimed at orphans. Orphans have, always and everywhere, been among the children most vulnerable to labor exploitation. Early policies almost invariably required orphans to work for their keep. Systems of institutional care commonly incorporated manufactories or outwork shops; early placement systems usually meant placement for work, in a variety of "apprenticeship" schemes. Gradually, over a long period, systems of residential care, foster care, and adoption emerged so that, today, orphans are no longer doubly punished for their orphanhood: punished first for having lost their parents, and punished second by being set to premature labor as a result.

Development of law and policy aimed at protecting children from abuse and neglect was also important. In this regard, what we today call the "unconditional worst forms" of child labor were generally not addressed as child labor problems, but as child welfare problems. When countries encountered "worst forms" problems, they were addressed through the criminal codes and not the child labor codes. The general pattern was to criminalize the conduct, and to establish programs to protect, prevent, and withdraw and rehabilitate children exposed to such abuses.

Today's developed nations vary greatly in the degree to which child welfare policies have developed. The most highly developed policies are found in the Nordic countries, where a rich mix of child and family allowances, health and nutrition programs, and early child-care programs operate (Christiansen et al. 2006; Hiilamo 2002). In comparison to the Nordic countries, child welfare policies in the United States would be considered only rudimentary, though they are far advanced in comparison to most of the developing world.

Labor Law

Child labor laws were usually the first state intervention into the workings of the labor market. Many employers and employer associations opposed child labor laws, not so much because they favored child labor, but because they feared child labor legislation would be the "entering wedge" for further state interventions in the labor market. Sure enough, additional interventions followed. Among them were some that, while not directed at child labor, had important implications for it.

Most nations adopted minimum-wage legislation and legislation regulating hours of work at a relatively early stage of industrial development. Such laws, in addition to their intended effects, have the effect of heightening management's concern over labor productivity. Each worker must produce enough per hour to justify payment of the minimum wage. Likewise, when management cannot simply add hours to the workday to achieve production goals, output per hour of work becomes critical. In management regimes driven by productivity concerns, employment of children came to be seen as a bad bargain. Similarly, most nations adopted various schemes of employer liability, workers' compensation insurance programs, or other workplace safety and health legislation. Since children injured themselves and others with greater frequency than adults, employment of children came to be seen as a bad risk.

Conclusion

While each nation struggled to come to grips with child labor on its own terms, after Britain, each nation could also learn from the experience of others. Thus, broad contours of the policy response—in child labor law, compulsory schooling, child welfare policy, and labor law—bore striking similarities from one nation to the next. In the process, as factory doors were closed to children and schoolhouse doors were opened, childhood itself was transformed.

References and Further Reading

Caty, Roland, ed. *Enfants au travail: Attitude des élites en Europe occidentale et méditerranéenne aux XIXe et XXe siècles.* Aix-en-Provence: Publications de l'Université de Provence, 2002.

Christiansen, N.F., K. Petersen, N. Edling, and Per

Haave, eds. *The Nordic Model of Welfare: A Historical Reappraisal.* Copenhagen: Museum Tusculanum Press, 2006.

Cunningham, Hugh, and Shelton Stromquist. "Child Labor and the Rights of Children: Historical Patterns of Decline and Persistence." In *Child Labor and Human Rights,* ed. Burns H. Weston, 55–83. London: Lynne Rienner, 2005.

Fyfe, Alec. *The Worldwide Movement Against Child Labour: Progress and Future Directions.* Geneva: International Labour Office, 2007.

Hendrick, Harry. *Child Welfare: Historical Dimensions, Contemporary Debate.* Bristol: Policy Press, 2003.

Heywood, Colin. *Childhood in Nineteenth-Century France: Work, Health and Education Among the "classes populaires."* Cambridge: Cambridge University Press, 1988.

Heywood, Colin. *A History of Childhood: Children and Childhood in the West from Medieval to Modern Times.* Cambridge: Polity Press, 2001.

Hiilamo, Heikki. *The Rise and Fall of Nordic Family Policy? Historical Development and Changes During the 1990s in Sweden and Finland.* Helsinki: National Research and Development Centre for Welfare and Health, 2002.

Hindman, Hugh D. *Child Labor: An American History.* Armonk, NY: M.E. Sharpe, 2002.

Hutchins, B.L., and Amy Harrison. *A History of Factory Legislation.* London: P.S. King and Son, 1903.

Kelley, Florence. *Some Ethical Gains Through Legislation.* New York: MacMillan, 1905.

Moehling, Carolyn M. "State Child Labor Laws and the Decline of Child Labor." *Explorations in Economic History* 36 (1999): 72–106.

Nardinelli, Clark. "Child Labor and the Factory Acts." *Journal of Economic History* 40:4 (1980): 739–55.

Rahikainen, Marjatta. *Centuries of Child Labour: European Experiences from the Seventeenth to the Twentieth Century.* Aldershot: Ashgate, 2004.

Trattner, Walter L. *Crusade for the Children: A History of the National Child Labor Committee and Child Labor Reform in America.* Chicago: Quadrangle Books, 1970.

Weiner, Myron. *The Child and the State in India: Child Labor and Educational Policy in Comparative Perspective.* Princeton, NJ: Princeton University Press, 1991.

Weissbach, Lee Shai. *Child Labor Reform in Nineteenth-Century France: Assuring the Future Harvest.* Baton Rouge: Louisiana State University Press, 1989.

Wennemo, Irene. *Sharing the Costs of Children: Studies on the Development of Family Support in the OECD Countries.* Stockholm: Swedish Institute for Social Research, 1994.

Coming to Terms with Child Labor: The Historical Role of Education

Alec Fyfe, Senior Child Labor Specialist, International Labor Organization

A Parable

> There once was a country that had a protracted debate for over 50 years about the desirability of introducing free and compulsory primary education. Millions of its children were out of school, many of them forced to work under highly exploitative conditions. Successive governments took the view that public education was beyond the means of the state. When the foundations of a national school system were finally laid, the results were extraordinary. Within a space of ten years, the number of children in state schools increased from fewer than 10,000 to over 1 million. Over the next ten years, enrollment doubled. And child labor declined dramatically. This country was England, during 20 years after the 1870 Education Act. (Watkins 2000, 195)

Learning from History: Education and Child Labor in the First Industrial Nations

Policy makers naturally look to the past in search of strategies for contemporary problems. What caused the decline of child labor in the first industrial nations? A number of interpretations have been put forward over the years, including changing economic circumstances and developments in technology. But many see the key factors as social in nature, particularly changes in society's attitude toward children and to childhood itself. Central to this interpretation is the emerging belief in the nineteenth century that children belong in school and not the workplace. Indeed, what was being asserted as part of a new notion of childhood is that children have rights and that it is the duty of the state to protect them (Cunningham 2001). Education, as the best work for children, is a central part of this new conception of childhood and the responsibility of the state toward children.

The American political scientist Myron Weiner has contended that all industrialized countries, at a certain stage in their development, have introduced compulsory education as a means of redefining childhood and combating child labor. According to Weiner, "Compulsory primary education is the policy instrument by which the state effectively removes children from the labor force" (Weiner 1991, 3). Though this policy varied considerably from country to country, it reflected the notion that universal education was a duty of the state.

This development was most evident in the first industrial nations in Europe, and was related to an important extent to the widening of democracy in general, and the rise of the labor movement in particular. Between 1840 and the 1880s, the population of Europe rose by 33 percent, but the number of children attending school increased by 145 percent (Hobsbawm 1989). Indeed, the period from 1870 to 1914 was, for most European countries, the age of the primary school. Germany took the lead in promoting compulsory education, and many countries such as England, France, and Japan were influenced by its example.

Germany

State-provided compulsory education is largely a German invention. The duty of the state to provide compulsory education was advocated by Martin Luther in 1530. In 1817 the Prussian state introduced compulsory education for all children between the ages of five and twelve. By 1837, more than 80 percent of children were enrolled in some form of elementary school. By 1871, school attendance was universal in Germany. This expansion in education went hand in hand with an official concern for child labor. A campaign against factory child labor started in the 1820s, with legislation following in 1839 mandating five hours of daily schooling for all factory children. In 1853, the minimum age for work was raised from nine to twelve, limiting the daily workday to six hours for children between the ages of twelve and fourteen, with three hours of compulsory education. The enforcement of compulsory education laws also reinforced child labor laws. By 1904, out of 9.2 million children under the age of fourteen, just 1.8 million were employed, only for a few hours and mostly in agriculture, and virtually all attended school. Germany, then, was among the most successful countries in ending child labor and in establishing compulsory education.

England

In contrast to Germany, England followed a more voluntary path, which delayed the introduction of a national system of education until 1870. But attempts to use voluntary means to promote education in the early nineteenth century were doomed to failure in the face of mass child labor. After all, there was little point in providing schools if there were no children to fill them. However, a start was made under the Factory Act of 1833, to reduce the working hours of children and provide nine- to eleven-year olds in textile mills two hours of schooling, six days a week. This system of part-time education was subsequently extended to other industries, but was intended, nevertheless, to enable children to remain in the labor force.

Though the principle of compulsory education had been established, without state funding, this proved a hollow victory. Though the 1840s and 1850s did see state funding of education steadily increase, there was still official opposition to compulsory education on the grounds of the necessity of child labor. It was the revival of the labor movement in the 1860s that provided the impetus behind a national campaign that led to the Elementary Education Act of 1870. Though the 1870 act did not impose compulsory education as such, it established local school boards that could do so. In 1871 the London School Board, for example, made education compulsory for all children up to the age of ten. Finally, in 1880, school boards were required to enforce compulsory education and parents could be fined for keeping their children out of school.

After 1870, education in England transitioned from a charity to a right upheld by the state. As in Germany, the enforcement of minimum working age and compulsory education laws became mutually reinforcing. After 1870, the problem of nonattendance diminished and, instead, there was greater public pressure for quality improvements to the education system. The sharpest decline in child labor in England occurred, therefore, between 1871 and 1881, when the state moved toward compulsory education. Compulsory education not only increased the number of children in school; it also edged up the minimum age for work. However, these interventions took time to have their full effect. Part-time education still meant that child labor was common in England well into the twentieth century. It was not until 1918 that the employment of school-age children was prohibited. And it was not until 1931 that child employment figures disappeared from the official census. Child labor elimination had taken the best part of a century to achieve in the first industrial nation.

The United States

The state of Massachusetts pioneered public education in the United States with laws passed in 1642 and 1647, first requiring parents to ensure education, and then requiring local towns to provide schools. However, before the Civil War, the notion of limited government prevented compulsory education from taking hold. After 1865, there was a growing public education movement across the states. Massachusetts again led the way with a law passed in 1876 prohibiting the employment of children under ten and requiring those between ten and fourteen to have attended school for at least twenty weeks in the previous year. A law passed by the state in 1878 required employers to have birth certificates and proof of school attendance on file for inspection.

By 1885, sixteen out of thirty-eight states had compulsory education laws, and by 1900, thirty-one states required school attendance from age eight to age fourteen. By 1918, the process had been completed. Enrollments exploded, with public schools opening at the rate of one every day between 1890 and 1918 (Faulkner 1971). As a consequence, child labor declined substantially after 1900, when compulsory education laws intersected with child labor laws. It was only in those southern states such as North and South Carolina, Georgia, and Alabama, which had neither compulsory schooling nor child labor laws until after 1900, that child labor continued to grow (Weiner 1991). By 1914, all but one state had minimum-age legislation linked, in most cases, to education requirements.

Japan

In Japan, the promotion of mass education became a central objective of state policy after 1868 as part of a deliberate "catching-up" modernization strategy. In 1886, Japan became the first non-Western country to make education compulsory. Between 1880 and 1900 primary school attendance doubled, and by 1910, 98 percent of six- to thirteen-year-olds were attending school. Enrollments soared after the late 1880s, when the central government began to subsidize compulsory education—from 1.3 million in 1873 to 5 million in 1903 (Saito 1996). Compulsory education was extended from four years to six years in 1907.

By time the time the first child labor legislation was introduced in 1911, Japan had achieved universal education. These combined measures, but particularly the promotion of universal education, meant that Japan, unlike the United States and many European countries, avoided a major child labor problem.

Historical Lessons in the Use of Education to Combat Child Labor

The historical record of the interplay of compulsory education and child labor is diverse, in terms of both countries and political circumstances that brought about change. What is constant is the notion that education is a duty of the state. Where the state was slow to act, political coalitions were critical in pressuring for compulsory education and child labor laws. In Europe, for example, the labor movement played such a strategic role.

Compulsory education and child labor laws proved mutually reinforcing. Indeed, child labor laws became enforceable only when children were required to attend school. Compulsory education laws and birth registration systems usually preceded child labor laws, and they proved less difficult to enforce than child labor laws. However, enforcing compulsory education laws was not an easy task in the first industrial nations. Historically, the state developed an apparatus for enforcement that combined teachers, social workers, truant officers, and school census takers. Good data, including school registers and birth registration, facilitated this process. Parents were less willing to bribe truant officers than employers were to bribe factory inspectors. In that sense school attendance was easier to enforce than child labor laws.

Moreover, education tended to be made compulsory when enrollment rates were already quite high. The task was to attract and retain the last 10 to 20 percent, hard-to-reach children. This was precisely the child population most likely to be working. Indeed, the reason England made education compulsory was to compel the remaining minority of children into school. Compulsory education was usually phased in, starting with the primary-age group. The minimum age for work and the minimum school-leaving age needed to be matched, as the ILO has recommended since 1921. If the age at which children are permitted to leave school is lower than the minimum age for work, children are likely to leave school to seek work.

The effective enforcement of compulsory education laws substantially reduced or eliminated child labor (Weiner 1991). Evidence from past experience appears to suggest that the tipping point for eliminating child labor occurs somewhere between the 10 and 20 percent child work participation rate. This is the point where compulsory education is much easier to achieve. This historic watershed in the decline of child labor in the first industrial nations appears to have occurred, in most cases, by around 1900, when the economic participation rate of children fell below 20 percent (ILO 2006). Compulsory education was a key factor in this historic transition.

References and Further Reading

Cunningham, Hugh. "Combating Child Labour: The British Experience." In *Child Labour in Historical Perspective—1800–1985: Case Studies from Europe, Japan and Colombia,* ed. Hugh Cunningham and P. Viazzo, 41–56. Florence: UNICEF, 1996.

Cunningham, Hugh. "The Rights of the Child and the Wrongs of Child Labour: An Historical Perspective." In *Child Labour: Policy Options,* ed. Kristoffel Lieten and Ben White, 13–26. Amsterdam: Aksant Academic Publishers, 2001.

Faulkner, Harold U. *A History of American Life: The Quest for Social Justice, 1898–1914.* Chicago: Quadrangle Books, 1971.

Hobsbawm, Eric. *The Age of Empire: 1875–1914.* London: Sphere Books, 1989.

International Labour Organization (ILO). *The End of Child Labour: Within Reach.* Geneva: ILO, 2006.

Saito, Osamu. "Children's Work: Industrialism and the Family Economy in Japan, 1872–1926." In *Child Labour in Historical Perspective—1800–1895: Case Studies from Europe, Japan and Colombia,* ed. Hugh Cunningham and P Viazzo, 73–90. Florence: UNICEF, 1996.

Watkins, Kevin. *Education Now: Break the Cycle of Poverty.* Oxford: Oxfam International, 2000.

Weiner, Myron. *The Child and the State in India: Child Labor and Educational Policy in Comparative Perspective.* Princeton, NJ: Princeton University Press, 1991.

Coming to Terms with Child Labor: History of Child Welfare

Bengt Sandin, Department of Child Studies, University of Linköping, Sweden

Child welfare as a concept originated during the nineteenth century partly as a critique of children's participation in the labor force. Certainly it had precursors, such as the establishment of foundling hospitals and early orphanages. As a concept that could be applied to children of all social classes, however, it was something novel, and as such it had multiple dimensions. It could refer to "child protection"—safeguarding children from corrupting or dangerous circumstances. It could also refer to uplift—using education, in particular, as an instrument of mental and moral improvement. In addition, it could refer to recognizing and meeting children's developmental needs. And in the late twentieth century, it could refer to promoting children's rights. One symbol of these changes was the emergence of the concept of the "best interests of the child" as a legal doctrine.

The Expansion of Child Labor: Family Care of Children

There are specific instances in history when child labor became visible in the eyes of social reformers. The detrimental effect of industrial labor on children's health became an issue when the number and concentration of children working under hazardous conditions made the health consequences obvious. As long as most children's work took place within households or on farms, it was not considered problematic. But when child labor in mines, on streets, and in factories and sweatshops expanded, reformers, who came to be known as "child savers," expressed alarm. During the nineteenth and early twentieth centuries, child labor was transformed from a fact of life into something that was defined as a social problem that needed to be addressed through state action and philanthropic organizations.

The discussion was not only about children's work, but about how the welfare of children was organized in relationship to the family. The family's apparent inability to care for the physical and moral well-being of their offspring worried reformers and philanthropists. Families dependent on child labor displayed traits that deviated from norms for family life that were being established in the nineteenth century. Generational and gender roles might be upset if adults were unemployed while the labor of children could be bought at a cheaper price. The work of children came into conflict with both the economic interest of adults and the understanding of the family, or the household, as the unit of care and creator of welfare for children. Reform movements were fed by a critique of the economic system that made child labor possible, both from the politically conservative and from the politically radical. Child labor in rural areas attracted less attention, though it was certainly very common. Rural family-oriented settings offered a context for the moral upbringing of children that made the use of children as workers appear less morally problematic. Children had traditionally participated in the work of family farms, and the breakthrough of agricultural capitalism from the eighteenth century made the work of children an asset to the laboring family.

Child Saving, Morals, and Child Welfare

The educational needs that reformers demanded for children were clearly aimed at improving the moral aspect of the care of children as well as their physical health. It was feared that working children would, as adults, be intellectually and morally hampered—a menace to society. It was held that working children might grow up in danger of becoming criminal and morally depraved. These aspects also underlined the arguments around the meaning of childhood as it appeared around the late nineteenth century. Working children came into conflict with the understanding of a good childhood, a period of emotional and physical growth under the protection of a family. Children working in family settings, or in small-scale crafts work, or even in manufacturing industries under adult supervision, were sometimes acceptable, but excessive use of children in the labor force became an upsetting phenomenon. But opinions were not unanimous. The effort to abolish child labor extended over many decades. This reflected not only opposition from employers, who exploited low-wage child laborers, but also from working-class parents, whose children's earnings helped make a crucial difference in the family's income. It also reflected a deep-seated ambivalence among many parents about the cultural value of work for children's development. Working-class culture entailed the notion that becoming an adult involved the formative experience of labor.

The prohibition of child labor also ran into conflict with important economic interests. Exceptions had to be made for industries or sectors dependent on child workers, such as the agricultural sector. Prohibition also reflects the role and organization of state power. In some nations with weak national regulatory power, prohibition came late in spite of a broad critique of the practices. In some cases, before legislation could be enacted, the technological level of industry had already made the use of child labor redundant. In Western Europe and the United States, the decline of child labor was due less to the enactment of statutes banning the practice, and more to technological change, which drastically reduced the need for bobbin girls and boys, messenger boys, and many other occupations.

Welfare and the Changing Meaning of Childhood

Working outside the confinement of the family and in public spheres could endanger the morals and behavior of children. Industrial labor, or work as street vendors or newsboys, was not compatible with the kind of normative understanding of childhood that became ingrained in Western experience during the late nineteenth century. Children's place was within the family or in an educational setting. This normative shift was the product of several factors, including changes in the nature and location of the work children performed; a romanticization of childhood innocence and a horror over juvenile precocity; a heightened emphasis on formal schooling; fears for children's health and physical and mental well-being; and the struggle to create a male family wage sufficient to support the entire household.

The creation of the program espousing education for all children represented an engagement in the care and welfare of children that marked Western experience. This is also expressed in legal codes. Much child labor legislation aimed at underpinning the commitment to mass education. During the early twentieth century, the presence of children working in the streets—as street vendors, newsboys, or delivery boys—was interpreted as disregard for the education that was offered, and raised concerns about children not under the surveillance of parents or guardians. As the understanding of what work children were allowed to do in the streets became more narrowly defined, it prompted discussions about delinquency and youth crime. Legal prohibitions on child labor had the effect of defining children as fundamentally different from adults. Childhood, increasingly, was defined in terms of play and schooling. Child labor was not consistent with the welfare of children.

Child protection laws aimed at making sure that children did not work and were taken care of properly by their parents. Foster parents were, for example, to make sure that children's educational and physical needs were tended to. There was also an increased commitment by states to regulate the behavior of children. The study of children and their development, care, and welfare became, in itself, a social movement in academic circles in the United States and Europe after the early years of the nineteenth century, and built an impressive body of scholarship. The Child Study Movement made important contributions to the development of social and behavioral sciences, and expanded knowledge of children's developmental needs.

The welfare issues driven by the use of children as workers cover a wide array of aspects, from the protection of their bodies and health, to education, morals, and behavior. The establishment of universal education provisions hampered the use of children as laborers, but it also had other effects. The development of education went hand in hand with increased interest in children's health, and mass education opened an avenue to inspect children to evaluate their development and health. Medical professions were able, through medical inspection in the schools and other health organizations, to observe the detrimental effects of children's social conditions and family life. In some countries these institutions became an integral part of the health commitments made by central governments.

It must be noted that obligatory schooling did not put an end to children's work. Some school systems were construed to make possible children's participation in the workforce, while others very intentionally tried to hinder such work. Success has varied depending on the social context. Children have nevertheless continued to combine schooling with domestic work done within the family.

The protection of children was initially directed at ensuring that children had certain rights, to education and healthy environments, for examples, thereby undermining children's use in the labor force. Expansion of mass education has, in some countries, brought about a questioning of the right of adults and professionals such as teachers to physically discipline children. This is a part of processes whereby children are granted certain universal rights to physical and intellectual integrity as individuals. International conventions have also marked a global commitment to such an understanding, in conflict with children's work in industrial and agricultural sectors, as well as their participation in an adult labor market as soldiers or sex workers. Conflicting images between children working in developing countries and in the industrial world today parallel the conflicting images of the early nineteenth century between working children and the notions of childhood that were established by child savers in Europe and the United States.

Globalization

The ascribing of rights to children under the UN Convention on the Rights of the Child reflects a critique of children doing the work of adults. In fact the convention tries to uphold a notion of childhood as a period in which children's lives are differently organized than in the adult world—dependent, growing, and cared for. In such an ideological frame, children ought not to do work as adults. At the same time, however, the understanding of children's work has been revaluated in some Western societies. Large numbers of teenage girls and boys have entered the workforce, balancing school with paid work. Further, some scholars claim that children's schooling must properly be regarded as work and rewarded as such. Children's acquisition of knowledge (and production of knowledge) in school is productive work as much as any work done in knowledge-based industries, and should be getting a reasonable pay.

Looking at children's work in this manner undermines the notion of differences between children and adults, and gives legitimacy to young people's participation in the workforce in different functions, protected by the same kind of welfare-protective measures as provided for the adults. The whole understanding of labor participation as a criterion for adulthood is contested. In recent years, the notion of children as different has eroded; the same social rights are attributed to children as to adults. In today's society, this creates an issue of how children's rights shall be negotiated between, on one hand, care and dependence, and on the other, adultlike independence and rights. This long-term shift involves a movement away from a view of middle-class children that emphasized their vulnerability and fragility, and a view of working-class children as precocious and undisciplined, to a newer view that emphasizes the similarity of children's needs across class lines.

References and Further Reading

Coninck-Smith, Ning de, Bengt Sandin, and Ellen Schrumpf, eds. *Industrious Children: Work and Childhood in the Nordic Countries 1850–1990.* Odense: Odense University Press, 1997.

Cooter, Roger, ed. *In the Name of the Child: Health and Welfare, 1880–1940.* London: Routledge, 1992.

Cunningham Hugh. *The Children of the Poor: Representations of Childhood Since the Seventeenth Century.* Oxford: Blackwell, 1991.

Cunningham, Hugh. *Children and Childhood in Western Society Since 1500.* London: Longman, 2005.

Dahlén, Marianne. *The Negotiable Child: The ILO Child Labour Campaign 1919–1973.* Uppsala: Uppsala University, 2007.

Engwall, Kristina, and Ingrid Söderlind, eds. *Children´s Work in Everyday Life.* Stockholm: Institute for Futures Studies, 2007.

Fass, Paula, ed. *Encyclopedia of Children and Childhood in History and Society.* New York: Macmillan Reference, 2004.

Hendrick, Harry. *Images of Youth: Age, Class, and the Male Youth Problem, 1880–1920.* Oxford: Clarendon, 1990.

Hendrick, Harry. *Child Welfare: Historical Dimensions, Contemporary Debates.* Bristol: Policy, 2003.

Heywood, Colin. *A History of Childhood: Children and Childhood in the West from Medieval to Modern Times.* Cambridge: Polity, 2001.

Hungerland, Beatrice, Manfred Liebel, Brian Milne, and Anne Wihstutz, eds. *Working to Be Someone: Child Focused Research and Practice with Working Children.* London: Jessica Kingsley Publishers, 2007.

Lindenmeyer, Kriste. *A Right to Childhood: The U.S. Children's Bureau and Child Welfare, 1912–46.* Urbana: University of Illinois Press, 1997.

Marshall, Dominique. "The Construction of Children as an Object of International Relations: The Declaration of Children's Rights and the Child Welfare Committee of League of Nations, 1900–1924." *International Journal of Children's Rights* 7 (1999): 103–47.

Mintz, Steven. *Huck's Raft: A History of American Childhood.* Cambridge, MA: Harvard University Press, 2004.

Qvortrup, Jens. *Studies in Modern Childhood: Society, Agency, Culture.* Basingstoke: Palgrave Macmillan, 2005.

Sandin, Bengt, and Gunilla Halldén, eds. *Barnets bästa: en antologi om barndomens innebörder och välfärdens organisering.* Brutus Östlings Förlag, Symposium, 2003.

Therborn, Göran. "Politics of Childhood: The Rights of Children in Modern Times." In *Families of Nations: Pattern of Public Policy in Western Democracies,* ed. F.G. Castles, 241–91. Aldershot: Dartmouth, 1993.

Zelizer, Viviana A. *Pricing the Priceless Child: The Changing Social Value of Children.* Princeton, NJ: Princeton University Press, 1994.

Coming to Terms with Child Labor: The Role of Technology

Carolyn Tuttle, Betty Jane Schultz Hollender Professor of Economics, Lake Forest College

Although children had worked for centuries, the demand for child labor created by the British Industrial Revolution was a new phenomenon. Both the nature (workplace, working conditions, and duties) and extent of child labor were dramatically different from what they had been in the past. A new class of workers, industrial workers, who "tended" or "operated" machines at various stages of the production process, came into being. They became cogs in the production process—separated from the final product, performing the same task repeatedly, supervised by a stranger, and restricted by a factory clock and a formal contract. Although many children still worked in the home and on the farm, "Help Wanted" notices on posters and in newspapers specifically asked for children for the mills. In contrast to home and farm, demand by factory and mine owners for child workers was different because children were hired as independent wage earners, they worked in the formal economy, and they performed tasks essential for the efficient operation of the factory or mine. Many scholars of child labor attribute this new demand to the technological innovations that accompanied the British Industrial Revolution. Others argue that it was due to children's low wages or docile nature.

Demand Versus Supply of Child Labor

Economists and economic historians use economic theory to evaluate the various explanations for child labor during industrialization. Using microeconomic models of the labor market, plausible causes of child labor can be classified as either supply induced or demand induced. The supply of child labor is modeled on the household economy, where parents make decisions about allocation of their child's time depending on the market wage rate, the value of leisure time, and nonlabor income.

Many development economists, economic historians (Anderson 1971; Medick 1976; Horrell and Humphries 1995), and international organizations such as the ILO, the UN, and UNICEF believe that most children in the world work because their families are poor. From their perspective, parents really have no choice but to send their children to work because, without their contribution, the family would starve. A few economic historians argue that a combination of parental abuse and greed drives children into the formal market to work because they receive better treatment from the supervisors than they do from their parents (Pinchbeck 1969; Pollock 1983; Nardinelli 1988). Social historians (Hammond and Hammond 1937; Pinchbeck and Hewitt 1973; Shorter 1975) claim that work is a normal phase of a child's development to becoming independent and self-sufficient. They maintain that the custom of sending children to work existed in Europe in the eighteenth and nineteenth centuries as it exists today in India, Asia, and Latin America. Any one of these factors—poverty, abuse and greed, or normal stage of development—would push children into the labor market from the supply side. The result would be increased employment of children and a decrease in the equilibrium nominal wage. The existence of mandatory schooling laws, however, would act as a drag on the supply of child labor, reducing employment of children while increasing their nominal wage.

Many other scholars argue that increases in demand, not supply, explain the increase in employment of children during industrialization. Demand for child labor is modeled using the competitive model of profit maximization by employers. Demand for labor is a derived demand depending on a fixed amount of capital (plant and equipment), price of the final product, and the existing level of technology. The majority of historians and economists believe that children are hired over adults because they are cheap (ILO 1996). This seems a compelling explanation because there is considerable evidence that firms, in order to maximize profits, seek out the cheapest workers. Historically, firms hired immigrants to minimize costs, and presently, firms outsource jobs to China and Mexico, where labor is cheap. But despite being compelling, it is not a convincing argument because children have always had the lowest relative wage in the labor market. This implies that children would always be in demand regardless of time, country, or industry. Since history has demonstrated that children are not working in all industries at all times, there must be more to the story. A few economic historians (Tuttle 1999; Berg 1991; Thompson 1966) argue that changes in technology must have made children more attractive to hire. They believe that children were particularly suited to the technological innovations that accompanied the Industrial Revolution.

The importance of the role of technological innovation as an explanation for the increase in child labor during the British Industrial Revolution has gained credibility among many well-known scholars. Several researchers have focused on the challenges to labor relations that were created by the new innovations (Bolin-Hort 1989; Pollard 1965). They claim that once the production process was divided into numerous steps and located under one roof, managers had difficulty recruiting and supervising adults to work in the factories and mines. Children were far easier to supervise than adults in the new industrial regime, where workers were subject to rules, discipline, and fines. Other scholars argue that it was the specific type of inventions that gave children the comparative advantage (Berg 1991; Thompson 1966; Tuttle 1999). Innovation changed the strength and skill requirements of spinning thread, weaving weft and warp, dressing metal ores, and transporting coal underground. This made it both profitable and productive to replace strong, skilled, more expensive adult male labor with weak, unskilled, cheaper child labor. Therefore, demand for child labor increased because division of labor and specialization increased the number of assistants needed, and technical innovations made it possible to replace costly skilled adults with cheap unskilled children. Any one of these factors—low wages, improved labor relations, or biased technological change—would pull children into the labor market from the demand side. The result would be increased employment of children along with an increase in the equilibrium nominal wage. Strict enforcement of existing child labor laws would act as an implicit tax on employers, decreasing demand for child labor. Although a consensus has not been reached on whether the increase in child labor during industrialization was supply induced or demand induced, recent evidence from Tuttle (1999) found rising wages of children relative to adults in British textiles from 1830 to 1860. This evidence supports the hypothesis that increasing employment of children during this period was caused by an increase in demand for child labor, not supply.

Technological Change and the Industrial Revolution

One of the defining features of the British Industrial Revolution was the impact of technological innovation on the manufacturing sector. The combination of automation, specialization, and mechanization dramatically changed the way many goods and services, from energy to earthenware, were made. Industrialists applied the principle of division of labor to production processes in textile, mining, paper, glass, and earthenware industries, thereby reducing the skill necessary for each task and increasing the number of tasks performed. As unskilled labor, children were very good at repetitive and monotonous tasks. Entrepreneurs explored how to replace animate with inanimate power to improve the continuity of production and quality of the product. As they moved from water power to steam power, machines no longer required brute strength to operate. Children, though smaller and weaker, were able to operate some machines as well as adults. The operation of other machines required small supple bodies or nimble fingers, which made children even more productive than adults. This child-intensive phase was followed by an adult-intensive phase as industrialization matured. As new machines were invented and existing machines perfected, the speed and complexity of production increased, requiring strong and skilled workers. The simple one-step jobs that had been created at the onset of industrialization were now performed by complex machines, eliminating the need for child labor. Therefore, technological change was a key factor contributing to both the increase of child labor at the onset of the Industrial Revolution and the decline in child labor during its mature phase.

Certain innovations favored the employment of children and young persons over adults in three ways. The first involved labor-intensive technology, which increased the demand for children as helpers. Application of the principle of the division of labor to production processes of making cloth and extracting coal and minerals increased the number of secondary workers. The second type of technological change that increased demand for child labor was the inventions that made it possible to replace adults with children. The technical innovations diluted either the skill or the strength required to efficiently operate machines such that children were as productive as adults. The third type of technological change favoring children was inventions and work situations that had special technical requirements. In this case, children actually had a comparative advantage in some situations and with certain machinery because they either had "nimble fingers" or could maneuver in tight spots.

In early stages of the Industrial Revolution, the technological change that occurred was not labor saving (Ashton 1948). Dividing the process of making cloth or extracting coal into many small steps created a plethora of jobs for children. Children assisted in every stage of the production of cotton, wool, and worsted and in three of the four stages of silk manufacture. During the preparation stage they were hired as "pickers" and "batters," while in the spinning stage they were employed as "piecers," "minders," and "doffers." As the water frame and mule were stacked, more and more "piecers" were needed to assist one adult spinner. In the final stage of production, children worked as "trimmers," "tenters," "darners," and "preemers." Similarly, in mining children (usually boys) could be found working in all stages except hewing. They worked underground as "trappers" controlling the passageways. Boys assisted the adult hewer by loading the carts with loose coal (as "fillers" and "putters") and transporting coal from the hewer to the main shaft (as "haulers," "pushers," "drawers," and "hurriers"). On the surface, many girls helped clean the coals (as "riddlers" or "pickers") or dress the metal ores (as "riddlers," "pickers," "cobbers," and "washers"). Labor-intensive production processes and technology increased the demand for child labor as secondary workers.

Rapid technological change in Britain's textile industry created an abundance of new machines, which led to a dramatic increase in exports of cotton, wool and worsted, and silk. Scholars of economic growth and technology have classified the new machines as "paleotechnic" or "macro" and "micro" inventions. Development literature of the 1930s dubbed certain types of innovation as "paleotechnic inventions" because the idea of the machine was to replace, rather than complement, the worker (Mumford 1934). Mumford described this era of scientific improvements as one where capital and labor became separate and distinct inputs such that machines did the work while unskilled labor operated the machines. This type of arrangement was in sharp contrast to both the past, where machinery was considered an extension of the skilled craftsman, and the present, where machinery is considered a robotic replication of the skilled craftsman. The early phase required mastery and rewarded originality, whereas the later phase requires sophisticated technical skills and rewards speed and uniformity.

More recent literature argues that innovation involves the subsequent diffusion and implementation of both macro and micro inventions. "Macro inventions" such as the steam engine, electricity, and the Internet are "dramatic new departures that opened entirely new technological avenues by hitting on something that was entirely novel and represented a discontinuous leap with the past" (Mokyr 1993, 18). These "macro inventions" permitted automation of production processes, which reduced the strength required to perform certain tasks. For example, application of Boulton and Watt's steam engine (1783) to the manufacture of textiles rapidly transformed the spinning and weaving processes. In 1790 the steam engine was used to power the mule. Thereafter, the number of factories containing Crompton's self-acting mule increased rapidly in urban areas. Consequently, the new technology increased the substitution of young weak child labor for older stronger adult male labor. Around this same time, Cartwright (1784) patented a power loom that could be operated by horses, waterwheels, or steam engines. Application of the steam engine to the power loom, however, diffused more slowly than the spinning inventions. By 1833 most cotton factories had converted and children were hired as "tenders" and "operators" of the power loom.

At the same time, several of the "micro inventions," which were "small, incremental improvements to known technologies" (Mokyr 1993, 18), replicated the hand motion of adults such that children were now able to operate the machines because no skill was necessary, merely placement of empty spools and removal of finished bobbins. As complements to the production process, children's tasks were essential in preserving the rapid and uninterrupted pace of the machinery. In the textile industry, small improvements to newly patented machinery often made it possible for children to become primary workers. Arkwright's water frame made it possible for child "piecers" instead of adult spinners to mind the machines. Cartwright's combing machine made it considerably easier to comb wool into slivers. This invention reduced the preparation time for worsted and substituted unskilled child helpers for skilled adult combers. Robert improved on Crompton's mule in 1829 by making it fully automatic such that children "minders" and "piecers" on the self-actor replaced adult spinners on the mule. Many more examples exist as adaptations of machinery invented for the production of cotton were made to the production of wool, worsted, and silk.

Although it was impossible to mechanize mining, several technical innovations increased demand for children both above- and belowground. For example, in the mining of coal, introduction of ponies underground allowed young boys to replace barrowmen pulling carts of coal through the tunnels. Introduction of cast-iron rail by John Curr in 1777 made it possible for children, instead of adults, to push and pull wagons full of coal underground. In addition, many small children were hired underground as "trappers" to open and shut the doors to improve ventilation once John Buddle introduced his system of triple shafts in 1790.

There are many examples of labor-specific technologies in both textiles and mining. Much of the early wooden machinery in mills stood very near to the ground and was ideally suited for children. The machines were so low that the backs of adults would have been severely injured after a day of stooping down to tie knots on the water frame or pull bobbins off the mule. The first invention in spinning was the spinning jenny by James Hargreaves in 1765. This spinning machine replicated the pulling and twisting motion of the spinning wheel and increased the number of threads that could be spun at one time. In its original form this machine was particularly suited for children because it had a horizontal wheel situated low to the ground. Rees' *Cyclopedia* claimed that "the awkward posture required to spin on them, was discouraging to grown up people, while they say, with a degree of surprise, children, from nine to twelve years of age, manage them with dexterity" (Ogden 1887, 97). In coal and metal mines children could maneuver in smaller openings and spaces in the underground tunnels, which often stood only three feet high (*British Parliamentary Papers* 1842[380] XV, 47–65). Children became essential because of their size and agility, which enabled them to perform work where adults simply could not fit or maneuver.

Thus, the innovations that occurred during the early stages of industrialization were biased toward the employment of children such that employers not only wanted to hire younger workers, but in some cases needed to hire children for their factories and mines. As the demand for child labor increased, children's role in production became essential to the growth of the industry. Industrialists needed, wanted, and had to hire child workers.

Technological change also played a role in the decline in child labor during the later part of the nineteenth century. Several contemporaries and economic historians argue that new technological advances in the textile and mining industries reduced the demand for children. Peter Gaskell, a factory owner, concluded that "every mechanical contrivance is, to do away with the necessity for human labour" (1836, 312) and T.J. Howell, a factory inspector, noted that the improvements in textile machinery (the carding machine, coupling and double-decking the self-actor, and the power loom) were displacing labor (*British Parliamentary Papers* 1842[410] XXII, 13). Several economic historians (Levine 1987; Mokyr 1993; Berg and Hudson 1992) argue that improvements in the spinning and weaving machinery gradually reduced the number of assistants and operators necessary per machine. Better-constructed machines broke fewer threads (the self-actor), and faster steam-powered machines increased the speed of production (the Northrop). The number of child "piecers" fell dramatically, and child operators were replaced by skilled adult men. Similarly, in mining, the installation of tramways made it possible for horses and engines, instead of young boys, to move loads of coal from the hewer to the shaft. In metal mining the processes of riddling, bucking, cobbing, and washing in the dressing process were mechanized, eliminating the need for girls and boys who had worked on the surface of copper mines performing these processes. In this mature capital-intensive phase of industrialization, many children's jobs became obsolete, while others became too difficult for children to perform. Initially, technological change led to a child labor–intensive phase of industrialization, while later its capital-intensive phase eliminated the need for child labor.

References and Further Reading

Anderson, Michael. *Family Structure in Nineteenth Century Lancashire.* Cambridge: Cambridge University Press, 1971.

Ashton, T.S. *The Industrial Revolution 1760–1830.* New York: Oxford University Press, 1948.

Berg, Maxine, ed. *Markets and Manufacture in Early Industrial Europe.* London: Routledge, 1991.

Berg, Maxine, and Pat Hudson. "Rehabilitating the Industrial Revolution." *Economic History Review,* 2nd series, 45 (1992): 25–50.

Bolin-Hort, Per. *Work, Family and the State: Child Labour and the Organization of Production in the British Cotton Industry.* Lund: Lund University Press, 1989.

British Parliamentary Papers, "Children's Employment (Mines)," Committee 1st report (Thomas Took and T. Southwood Smith), 1842, vol. 15, p. 380.

British Parliamentary Papers, *Factory Inspectors' Reports.* 1842, vol. 22, p. 410.

Gaskell, Peter. *Artisans and Machinery.* London: John W. Parker, West Strand, 1836.

Hammond, J.L., and Barbara Hammond. *Town Labourer.* New York: Doubleday Anchor, 1937.

Horrell, Sara, and Jane Humphries. "The Exploitation of Little Children: Child Labor and the Family Economy in the Industrial Revolution." *Explorations in Economic History* 32:4 (1995): 485–516.

ILO. *Child Labour: Targeting the Intolerable.* Geneva: International Labor Office, 1996.

Levine, David. *Reproducing Families: The Political Economy of English Population History.* Cambridge: Cambridge University Press, 1987.

Medick, Hans. "The Proto-Industrial Family Economy: The Structural Function of Household and Family During the Transition from Peasant Society to Industrial Capitalism." *Social History* 3 (1976): 291–315.

Mokyr, Joel. *The British Industrial Revolution.* Oxford: Westview Press, 1993.

Mumford, Lewis. *Technics and Civilization.* New York: Harcourt, Brace, 1934.

Nardinelli, Clark. "Were Children Exploited During the Industrial Revolution?" *Research in Economic History* 2 (1988): 243–76.

Ogden, James. "A Description of Manchester by a Native of the Town (1783)." In *English Historical Documents,* vol. 10, *1714–1783,* ed. D.B. Horn and Mary Ransome, 465–67, New York: Oxford University Press, 1969.

Pinchbeck, Ivy. *Women Workers and the Industrial Revolution 1750–1850.* London: Frank Cass, 1969.

Pinchbeck, Ivy, and Margaret Hewitt. *Children in English Society.* Vols. 1 and 2. London: Routledge and Kegan Paul, 1973.

Pollard, Sidney. *The Genesis of Modern Management.* Cambridge, MA: Harvard University Press, 1965.

Pollock, Linda. *Forgotten Children: Parent-Child Relations from 1500–1900.* New York: Cambridge University Press, 1983.

Rees, A. *The Cyclopaedia.* London: Longman and Rees, 1819.

Shorter, Edward. *The Making of the Modern Family.* New York: Basic Books, 1975.

Thompson, E.P. *The Making of the English Working Class.* New York: Vintage Books, 1966.

Tuttle, Carolyn. *Hard at Work in Factories and Mines: The Economics of Child Labor During the British Industrial Revolution.* Boulder: Westview Press, 1999.

Child Labor in the Developed Nations Today

Phil Mizen, Department of Sociology, University of Warwick

There is evidence that child work persists in the more developed industrialized countries of today, but this is a much underresearched topic. Data on work and employment among school-age children can be found for the industrial nations of the European Union, Australia, New Zealand, Japan, Canada, and the United States. Much of the accompanying literature is descriptive, although there has been considerable debate about the significance of high levels of child work in the United States and, to a lesser degree, the United Kingdom. The neglect of this topic is important since the persistence of child employment in developed nations belies aspirations to remove school-age children from the labor market; and because in some areas of the economy, children and young people still in full-time compulsory education continue to constitute a significant part of the workforce.

National standards for the employment of children in the developed nations generally conform to international conventions governing child labor, to which most of the developed nations are signatories. ILO Convention 138, in particular, prohibits entry to work before the minimum school-leaving age and, in no case, before the age of fifteen. Particularly important for children in developed nations are permissions to engage in "light work" from age thirteen. Light work is work deemed unlikely to interfere with a child's health, development, or education. Work done in schools is generally exempt from these limits, although vocational or apprentice training is limited to those age fourteen and over. ILO Convention 182 also limits hazardous work to those age eighteen and above.

ILO conventions set a baseline, which has been supplemented by more detailed national and supranational regulatory frameworks. Article 7 of the European Social Charter, for instance, guarantees children and young people protection against employment that poses a physical risk, threatens education, and is exploitative, and enshrines the right to a healthy childhood. Subsequent European Community directives have further limited child employment to age fifteen, raised the minimum age for light work to age fourteen, defined the times of day within which child employment is permissible, and set upper limits to hours worked during the school term and school vacations. In the United States, federal law restricts occupations open to those under eighteen years old, lists jobs deemed too hazardous for those under age sixteen, and limits the hours children can work during the school year. Some U.S. states impose additional limits relating to age, hours worked, and types of employment, such as door-to-door deliveries. In contrast, in New South Wales, Australia, children's employment is subject to only light regulation. New Zealand has failed to ratify a number of international conventions governing the employment of children under age sixteen.

Comparing the extent of child work across the developed nations today is difficult. Analysis is hampered by limits on available data, differences in measurement, and problems of definitional consistency. Variations in measurement account for part of the large disparities in employment rates among fifteen- to nineteen-year-olds in developed nations, evident in data from the OECD (Dorman 2001). Similarly, ILO data since 1980, showing the complete absence of employment among fourteen-year-olds in Western Europe, almost certainly reflects inadequacies of official intelligence. Nevertheless, data at the country level are more illuminating. For countries such as the United States and the United Kingdom, the availability of nationally representative data sets and accumulated research allows both reliable quantification and more detailed analysis. For others countries, such as France and Spain, data are both sparse and of limited value.

For industrial nations where data are more extensive, research confirms high levels of child work. In the United States, nearly half of all twelve-year-olds are in paid work, rising to almost two-thirds by age sixteen. The trend is also toward increasing numbers of teenagers in work. These figures include those working "freelance" (informal employment) and as "employees." Survey research from the United Kingdom also points to significant numbers of children working from age eleven onward, and that by the minimum school-leaving age of sixteen, between two-thirds and three-quarters of children have held a job (Mizen et al. 2001). Denmark and the Netherlands also display high levels of child employment, although data for both countries are less extensive. For Denmark, estimates suggest 7 percent of ten-year-olds work, the majority of children are working by age fifteen, and children age ten to seventeen show labor force participation rates of 40 percent (Frederiksen 1997). For the Netherlands, survey data suggest that around three-quarters of all thirteen- to seventeen-year-olds work for money.

Elsewhere among industrial nations, limits to data make assessment more problematic. Child employment in Japan is officially nonexistent. Neither Australia nor New Zealand collects statistics on the employment of children under fifteen (Smith and Wilson 2002), although school-based survey research points to high levels of paid employment among children age eleven to fourteen in New Zealand. For Canada, OECD data suggest that only one in three fifteen- to nineteen-year-olds are in paid employment, with more localized studies pointing to significantly higher rates of working (Hobbs and McKechnie 1997). Both France and Germany report low levels of school-age working, but again, for Germany, evidence from school-based surveys suggests significant levels of underreporting (Leibel 2004). In Portugal, estimates from civil-society organizations claim some 200,000 workers under age fourteen (Invernizzi 2005). Officially reported rates of working in Greece are low (Panagiotis and Goddard 2004). In Spain, two estimates place employment among those under sixteen at between 300,000 and 500,000, with 200,000 under fourteen working in the informal sector. In Italy, survey research suggests that around half a million six- to thirteen-year-olds are in paid work, with 400,000 workers age eleven to fourteen.

Typically, rates of economic activity among children increase with age, as does the nature of children's employment. Employment among younger children tends to be informal, perhaps working for neighbors and friends, usually on a casual basis. Younger children also tend to find work helping in family farms and businesses, and minding other children. Informal employment continues to be significant as children grow older, but increasing numbers also move into more structured employment involving regular working, structured hours, specified tasks, and predefined rates of pay. Data from the United Kingdom points to high levels of working among both boys and girls, although it is likely that boys enter the labor market at an earlier age. Further data from the United States shows that white children are significantly more likely to be employed than children classified as black or Hispanic (U.S. Department of Labor 2000). The reasons for this remain unclear, and detailed consideration of the relationship between paid employment and children from minority ethnic groups across the developed economies is conspicuously absent (Song 2001).

Data from the U.S. National Longitudinal Survey of Youth 1997 also shows that children living in households in the bottom income quartile (≤US$25,000) experience lower rates of paid employment. This finding is frequently invoked to assert that children's employment in industrial economies today demonstrates an inversion of both the historical record of these countries and the contemporary situation of developing economies, in which there exists a strong relationship between household poverty and higher prevalence of working children. Contemporary forms of child employment in industrial nations have, some claim, become divorced from pressures of poverty and material necessity. Thus, it is evidence of the enhanced capacity of relatively affluent children to make choices, and shows that school-age working has much value as a means to independence, work experience, and ultimately higher adult levels of pay (Hobbs and McKechnie

1997; U.S. Department of Labor 2000). For others, the claimed enhanced status of work in these children's lives raises more profound possibilities for the transformation of childhood itself (Leibel 2004).

The picture is less clear-cut, however. The 1997 Survey in the United States shows lower rates of working for the very poorest children, but the differences are only statistically significant for "freelance" (casual) working. Although children living in households in the highest income quartile (≥US$70,000) show marginally higher rates of participation across most categories of employment compared to middle income quartile groups, these differences are neither consistent nor statistically significant. Lower rates of working among the very poorest children are confirmed by research from the United Kingdom, although the differences are once again small (Middleton and Loumidis 2001). Equally significant are UK findings that children living in low-income households tend to work longer hours and are subject to comparatively lower hourly rates of pay. Reports of children contributing their earned income to family budgets are relatively rare. The vast majority of children working in most industrial economies no longer work to meet basic needs of themselves or their families; although this may still hold true for southern European nations. What is less clear is how questions of necessity and constraint have impacted upon work through the progressive monetization of children's lives.

Forms of child working vary from country to country, but some patterns seem to emerge. In northern European countries, North America, and Australasia most child employment is concentrated in the services (retail, distribution, catering), with employment in the trades (mining, construction, manufacturing) and agriculture (farm, forestry, fishing) accounting for a smaller but still significant proportions. Children in these countries tend to occupy jobs more commonly held by adults and, outside of employment in family-run enterprises, would seem to compete with adults for available work. In southern European countries, employment in the trades and agriculture appears more significant. In the south of Italy, for instance, children have been found working extensively in the construction and footwear industries, and as seasonal agricultural laborers. A similar picture also emerges for Greece. In Portugal, evidence points to a sizable proportion of working children employed in the economically important textile, apparel, and footwear industries. It has been suggested that, for southern European countries, the pattern of child employment resembles those more characteristic of the developing world (Dorman 2001; Council of Europe 1996).

Prevailing rates of pay for child workers are low. Where detailed data exists, as in the cases of the United States and United Kingdom, hourly rates of pay or their equivalent are significantly lower than hourly rates of pay stipulated by minimum-wage legislation. In neither the United States nor the United Kingdom are child workers under the age of sixteen covered by minimum-wage legislation, and evidence from both countries shows a downward trend in the real levels of pay for teenagers over the last quarter of the twentieth century (Mizen 2004; U.S. Department of Labor 2000). Children routinely work throughout the school year, and most children continue to work during school vacations. In the United States, a majority of fifteen-year-old working children are at work for more than fifteen hours per week, and most work throughout the calendar year. In the United Kingdom, studies suggest that working children average between eight and twelve hours each week at work (Hobbs and McKechnie 1997). Both countries place statutory limitations on the hours that school-age children can work, but there is evidence of widespread infringement.

Work that violates national labor standards, or fails to comply with national regulatory frameworks, indeed seems an endemic feature of children's employment across the industrial economies. The United States, alone among the developed economies, does not place a statutory requirement on the registration of school-age workers, but elsewhere, the majority of child workers go unregistered (Dorman 2001). In the United Kingdom, widespread ignorance, confusion, and failure of enforcement have resulted in the vast majority of children working without permits. Elsewhere, research from the Netherlands, Germany, Italy, Greece, and Japan suggests that because very large numbers of working children go unregistered, occupy jobs prohibited by law, or work outside of permitted hours, "the overwhelming majority of young workers are working illegally and even in the US illegality is widespread" (Dorman 2001, 34). Moreover, the nonreporting of child work through the failure of registration systems is a further significant factor depressing official estimates of the level of school-age employment.

Debate over the significance of working for children in developed nations has focused on its implications for education. Again, the research is most developed in the United States and the United Kingdom. In the United States, a subfield of study has been concerned with the psychosocial impact of teenage working, its costs and benefits, and the level and intensity at which these operate. There now seems to be a consensus that moderate levels of working (twenty or fewer hours per week) benefits working children, as measured in terms of the promotion of autonomy and self-reliance, independence from family, and developmental traits likely to produce competent and committed adult workers. For children less inclined to an academic education, paid work is also viewed as an important source of practical knowledge, work experience, and contact with employers. In contrast, high levels of working (more than twenty hours per week) are held to be deleterious, correlating with adolescent disorders such as lower academic test scores, truancy, early school dropout, substance misuse, delinquency, and occupational cynicism (Hansen et al. 2001). More recently, attention has turned to the implications of work of differing quality.

Among European researchers in particular there has been growing critique of the psychosocial approach. "Subject-oriented" scholars especially reject the view that children's employment represents a marker of adolescent development, or constitutes prefigurative episodes in children's socialization into normative patterns of working life. Rather, emphasis is placed on the significance of work in the present, and on children's own assessments of the place of work in their lives (James et al. 1998). Here work is held to involve conscious and meaningful choices on the part of children who have become freed from the determining force of necessity. Children are thus seen to value their employment not only because of the opportunities for income and consumption it allows, but also as a means of independence and freedom. Through work children derive considerable self-confidence, gain access to "adult" social worlds, enter new peer cultures, and accumulate practical skills and work experience. Much evidence points to children's enthusiasm for their jobs, pride in their productive roles, and satisfaction with their work-related accomplishments. At the same time, working children remain attentive to the limits of the work on offer and, in the main, see working as secondary to their education. For some, children's "protagonism" as workers represents a challenge to normative patterns of childhood that position children as a dependent and nonproductive subordinate social category (Leibel 2004).

These debates relate to "light work," but some children in industrial nations also undertake "worst forms" of child labor. The evidence of this is scarce; studies that highlight the problem are usually local in focus, and attempts at wider extrapolation remain problematic. Nevertheless, evidence from across the industrial nations points to the involvement of children in sex work, although the degree of involvement is difficult to gauge (Dorman 2001). It would nevertheless appear that child sex workers are a feature of most large urban areas across Europe and North America. It would seem that many children find their way into sex work having spent time previously living on the street (Mickelson 2000). Estimates of street children are notoriously problematic, but there is evidence from many European countries that a significant proportion of the large numbers of children who run away from home each year end up living on the street for a period of time (Panagiotis and Goddard 2004). Once on the street, children become more vulnerable to involvement in the sex industry, with estimates claiming that between one-fifth and one-third of boys and girls living on the street end up in some form of sex work (Dorman 2001). Associated factors seem to be extreme poverty, experience of residential care, family dissolution, and the failure of social services. Related to this, a further concern is the trafficking of children to the industrial nations. Evidence points to adults trafficking children from developing and "transitional" countries to the developed economies, either forcibly or under false pretences. Many of these children are trafficked into the sex industry, as forced labor, or as domestic servants.

References and Further Reading

Council of Europe. *Children and Work in Europe.* Strasbourg: Council of Europe Publishing, 1996.

Dorman, P. *Child Labor in the Developed Economies.* Geneva: ILO/IPEC, 2001.

Frederiksen, L. "Child and Youth Employment in Denmark: Comments on Children's Work from Their Own Perspective." *Childhood* 6:1 (1999): 101–12.

Hansen, D.M., J.T. Mortimer, and H. Kruger. "Adolescent Part-Time Employment in the United States and Germany: Diverse Outcomes, Contexts and Pathways." In *Hidden Hands: International Perspectives on Children's Work and Labor,* ed. P. Mizen, C. Pole, and A. Bolton, 121–38. London: Routledge-Falmer, 2001.

Hobbs, S., and J. McKechnie. *Child Employment in Britain.* London: Stationary Office, 1997.

Invernizzi, A. "Perspectives on Children's Work in the Algarve (Portugal) and Their Implications for Social Policy." *Critical Social Policy* 25:2 (2005): 198–222.

James, A., C. Jenks, and A. Prout. *Theorizing Childhood.* Cambridge: Polity Press, 1998.

Leibel, Manfred. *A Will of Their Own? Cross-Cultural Perspectives on Working Children.* London: Zed Books, 2004.

Mickelson, R., ed. *Children on the Streets of the Americas.* London: Routledge, 2000.

Middleton, S., and J. Loumidis. "Young People, Poverty and Part-Time Work." In *Hidden Hands: International Perspectives on Children's Work and Labor,* ed. P. Mizen, C. Pole, and A. Bolton, 24–36. London: Routledge-Falmer, 2001.

Mizen, Phil. *The Changing State of Youth.* Basingstoke: Palgrave, 2004.

Mizen, P., C. Pole, and A. Bolton, eds. *Hidden Hands: International Perspectives on Children's Work and Labor.* The Future of Childhood Series. London: Routledge-Falmer, 2001.

Panagiotis, A., and J. Goddard. "Street Children in Contemporary Greece." *Children and Society* 18:4 (2004): 299–311.

Smith, E., and L. Wilson. "The New Child Labor Problem: The Part-Time Student Workforce in Australia." *Australian Bulletin of Labor* 22:2 (2002): 120–37.

Song, M. "Chinese Children's Work Roles in Immigrant Adaptation." In *Hidden Hands: International Perspectives on Children's Work and Labor,* ed. P. Mizen, C. Pole, and A. Bolton, 55–69. London: Routledge-Falmer, 2001.

U.S. Department of Labor. *Report on the Youth Labor Force.* Washington, DC: U.S. Department of Labor, 2000.

Global Trade and Child Labor

Drusilla K. Brown, Associate Professor of Economics, Tufts University

Child labor has become the target of public scrutiny over the past two decades in part because of the increased visibility of the children producing goods for export. It is often argued that trade between high- and low-income countries increases demand for unskilled-labor-intensive goods, thereby generating new work opportunities for children in developing countries. This phenomenon would be particularly troubling if families were removing children from school in order to take advantage of employment opportunities created by international trade or foreign direct investment.

According to this line of argument, child wages and employment increase with foreign demand for export goods such as agricultural products, carpets, and soccer balls. Similarly, it has been argued that foreign investors may seek out markets with low wages generally, and especially those with an abundance of low-wage child workers. Trade may also increase the incidence of child labor by altering wages of unskilled workers. Child labor is most common in countries abundant in unskilled labor. Trade openness will bid up demand and wages for unskilled labor, and thereby lower the returns to education. Parents may respond by increasing work and reducing education investments in their children.

However, there may also be a counterbalancing income effect. International trade typically raises the wages of unskilled adults in developing countries. Such an increase in household income reduces the need for children's income and may enable parents to make investments in their children's schooling. That is, parents exposed to increased international trade will substitute away from child work toward education.

Cross-Country Empirical Evidence on Trade and the Demand for Child Labor

There are two types of evidence on whether or not globalization increases child employment. Cross-country studies find little correlation between the degree of trade exposure and child labor, while the evidence from individual country studies is mixed.

Cross-country studies typically look for a correlation between the incidence of child labor and measures of trade openness. For example, Cigno, Rosati, and Guarcello (2002) estimated the correlation between the incidence of child labor (or the rate of school nonattendance) and trade openness for the period 1980–1988. The analysis controls for other determinants of child labor such as real per capita income, health policy, and skill composition. The researchers found that trade openness is negatively correlated with child labor. The analysis, though, leaves open questions of causality. That is, do countries that are trade exposed have a lower incidence of child labor or do countries with low child labor trade more? Edmonds and Pavcnik (2006) were able to address this question by controlling for determinants of trade. They found that trade exposure reduces the incidence of child labor, arguing that household income is the principal channel through which trade deters child labor. Trade exposure increases household income, which in turn lowers the incidence of child labor.

Neumayer and de Soysa (2005) extended the results of Edmonds and Pavcnik to include foreign direct investment. Not only do countries open to trade have a lower incidence of child labor, but countries with a larger stock of foreign-owned capital also have fewer working children. Indeed, there is little empirical evidence that owners of capital are attracted to low-wage labor markets in which child labor is common. In fact, the opposite appears to be the case. Kucera (2002) found that child labor reduces human capital formation. The consequent scarcity of skilled labor is a deterrent to foreign investors (Braun 2006).

Case Studies on Trade Liberalization and Child Labor

While the cross-country studies find little effect of trade on child labor, individual country studies document a more subtle story. For example, Kruger (2004, 2006) observed that the mid-1990s boom in coffee prices increased market work among especially poor households in Nicaragua and Brazil. Children appear to have been withdrawn from school to take advantage of temporary employment opportunities created by the coffee boom. The negative impact on children and human capital formation, though, will be limited if the reduction in schooling is temporary.

Individual country studies also document considerable variation across demographic groups. For example, Edmonds and Pavcnik (2005) found that incidence of child labor depends on each family's asset portfolio. Between 1993 and 1998, Vietnam removed rice export restrictions, which had the effect of increasing the domestic price of rice by 29 percent. On balance, child labor declined following liberalization of the rice market by nine percentage points, but there was significant variation across demographic groups.

From a theoretical perspective, increasing returns to land and labor in rice production accompanying liberalization have an ambiguous impact on household decision making related to child work. On the one hand, adult wages in rice production will likely rise. The rise in wages of rural mothers may lead some families to draw their daughters out of school and into household production so that mothers are then free to engage in paid labor. The rise in wages of children working in the rice sector will also increase the opportunity cost of child leisure and schooling. Families for which these wage effects dominate may respond to the rise in the price of rice by increasing child labor. On the other hand, rising household wealth will reduce the need for children's earnings and may enable families to increase education investments in their children.

Edmonds and Pavcnik (2005) found that households with large and medium-sized landholdings reduced the amount of time their children worked, and increased leisure and schooling. The effect is particularly pronounced for older girls. However, children in families with small landholdings increased their supply of labor to the rice market. Trade increased the employment opportunities for these children. By contrast, the outcome for urban households was unambiguously negative. Such households have no assets that might appreciate with the increasing price of rice, but do suffer an increase in the price of an important part of their consumption. These families responded to the fall in real income by increasing the time their children spent working. A similar variety of responses to trade openness was observed by Edmonds, Pavcnik, and Topalova (2007) in their study of the impact of India's trade reforms during the 1990s. Child labor rises in those households negatively affected by the loss of trade protection.

Prohibiting Trade in Goods Produced by Children

Child welfare activists and organized labor in the West have often called for the prohibition of imports of goods produced by children. For example, the 1997 Sanders Amendment to the 1930 Tariff Act prohibits the United States from importing goods produced by indentured child labor. There are also implications for child labor in some regional and preferential trade arrangements. For example, provisions of the U.S. Generalized System of Preferences place considerable demands on beneficiaries of trade preferences. Developing country exporters are expected to adopt internationally recognized labor protections including rights to free association and collective bargaining, prohibition of forced labor and exploitative child labor, and acceptable conditions of work including minimum wages, maximum hours, and basic protections for health and safety. Failure to enforce labor protections may result in the suspension of tariff preferences.

Such prohibitions are justified both in terms of the potential positive impact on children and the perceived unfairness when adult workers in the West are required to compete with imports of goods produced by children. Indeed, Busse (2002) tested whether export of labor-intensive goods (textiles, clothing, footwear, toys) as a fraction of total exports is correlated with protections against child labor. He finds that weak protections against child labor are correlated with a country's comparative advantage in unskilled-labor-intensive goods.

There are some justifications for prohibiting child labor as a matter of domestic policy in developing nations. Basu and Van (1998) argued that the labor market in developing countries has two potential equilibria. The low-level equilibrium is characterized by low wages and heavy use of child labor. In the high-level equilibrium, adult wages reach a level at which families can afford to withdraw their children from the workforce. The high wages in the high-level equilibrium are made possible by the labor shortage created when children leave the workforce to attend school. Basu and Van argued that a ban on child labor will preclude the low-level equilibrium from emerging.

However, trade restrictions on goods produced by children may not address the core cause of child labor and thus may not be the best response. The weakness of a ban on imports of goods produced by children is neatly illustrated by Maskus and Holman (1996). They note that a prohibition against imports of goods produced by children, by reducing demand for such goods, will also lower the price. The subsequent fall in price will produce two potential outcomes for child workers. For those children who remain employed in the export sector, wages will decline. Others, of necessity, will move to other potentially less desirable employment. Indeed, reduced trade with countries in which child labor is common may have the counterintuitive effect of increasing child labor. Baland and Robinson (2000) laid much of the blame for inefficient child labor on capital market failures. Families lacking collateral may not be able to borrow the money necessary to educate their children. Any policy that reduces the income of families with working children will increase the time children spend working. In particular, trade sanctions imposed on countries with unacceptable levels of child labor will eliminate the income gains associated with free trade. The consequent decline in household income may further reduce the ability of households with working children to invest in schooling, thus increasing child time at work.

Inefficient child labor may also arise due to a coordination failure between households and firms (Dessy and Pallage 2001). Firms are reluctant to locate capital in markets that lack a supply of skilled labor, while parents are reluctant to educate their children if there are no jobs for skilled labor. In such a setting, laws that prohibit child labor and impose compulsory schooling can provide the needed signal to firms that the requisite supply of skilled workers will be forthcoming. Firms respond to the anticipated supply of skilled labor by installing the capital that, in turn, makes acquisition of the requisite human capital worthwhile for the family. However, international sanctions that prevent foreign capital from entering such markets will depress returns to skill, thus further reducing the incentive for families to make human capital investments in their children.

Child Labor–Free Product Labels

Product-labeling programs are an alternative to trade restrictions that leave the protection of working children to the workings of the market. Elliot and Freeman (2003) advanced the theoretical case for product labeling, and Hiscox and Smyth (2006) used field experiments to document consumers' willingness to pay for goods produced under humane conditions.

Certification programs relating to child labor are most active in monitoring hand-knotted-carpet producers in India, Nepal, and Pakistan, the leather footwear industry in Brazil, and the hand-stitched soccer-ball industry in Pakistan. Programs include the Jackciss carpet-weaving collective in Pakistan, begun in 1987, to certify that carpets are made exclusively by adult labor, and the Abrinq Foundation, established in 1990 with a certification program in the Brazilian footwear industry. Rugmark International is widely considered to be the most rigorous and well-known. Rugmark-certified manufacturers and distributors pay a fee, which is used to fund not only the certification operations, but also various services for children.

Though intuitively appealing, product labels are limited in their ability to accomplish their principle objective of improving working conditions for workers in a developing country. The weaknesses as regards child labor were drawn out by Basu, Chau, and Grote (2006). In a model with North-South trade, they found that product labels can help Western consumers identify products made with adult labor. However, this does not imply that working children are better off as a consequence. If consumers refuse to purchase unlabeled products, the South suffers deterioration in its trade, but the overall incidence of child labor is unaffected. Product labels help consumers sort themselves into those who want goods produced under humane conditions and those who do not care. This sorting, though, may not alter the incidence of inhumane labor practices. Brown (2006) showed that this sorting can create two groups of firms: One group produces labeled goods manufactured only with adult labor; the other group produces goods using a combination of child and adult labor. The adult-labor-only firms have a higher cost of production that must be covered by the labeling premium paid by socially conscious consumers. Working children are released from production of goods destined for socially conscious consumers. But in most underdeveloped economies, working children can be absorbed into other sectors. Thus, product labeling may alter the industry in which children and their parents work, but it may not affect the overall number of children working.

A more efficient outcome can be accomplished if labels emphasize, as Rugmark does, that some portion of the purchase price will be used to support child welfare services. Such "donation" labels are superior to "production-process" labels on efficiency grounds, and they ensure that at least a portion of the label premium inures to the benefit of the affected children.

The child labor–free industry has also been undermined by fraudulent labels. Some certification agencies claim to offer child labor–free goods but lack the record of detecting child employment attained by agencies such as Rugmark. Credibility has been more successfully achieved by multinationals with corporate codes of conduct prohibiting child workers in their vendor factories. Multinationals are highly motivated to establish and enforce minimum-age policies in their vendor factories for three reasons. First, the negative reputational effect that arises from the presence of children in vendor factories is severe. Second, child workers are unlikely to be able to produce the quality demanded by multinationals serving Western consumers. Third, establishing that a worker is at least eighteen years old is relatively straightforward. Corporate compliance officers typically require their suppliers to maintain personnel records documenting the age of each worker. Age is commonly established by the eruption of wisdom teeth.

Conclusion

Global trade is a fact of life that is here to stay. Consumers in rich nations may properly worry about purchasing goods made with child labor. But import bans, trade restrictions, or even product-labeling programs will not always improve conditions for children, even if they help consumers feel better about their purchases. If these initiatives are to be considered, there must first be a clear understanding of conditions in the local markets where children work.

References and Further Reading

Baland, Jean-Marie, and James A. Robinson. "Is Child Labor Inefficient?" *Journal of Political Economy* 108:4 (2000): 663–79.

Basu, Arnab K., Nancy H. Chau, and Ulrike Grote. "Guaranteed Manufactured Without Child Labor: The Economics of Consumer Boycotts, Trade Sanctions and Social Labeling." *Review of Development Economics* 10:3 (2006): 466–91.

Basu, Kaushik, and Pham Hoang Van. "The Economics of Child Labor." *American Economic Review* 88:3 (1998): 412–27.

Braun, Sebastian. "Core Labour Standards: Friends or Foe? The Case of Child Labour." *Weltwirtschaftliches Archiv* 127:4 (2006): 765–91.

Brown, Drusilla K. "Consumer Product Labels, Child Labor and Educational Attainment." *Berkely Electronic Journal of Economic Analysis and Policy* 5:1 (2006): article 23.

Busse, Matthias. "Comparative Advantage, Trade and Labour Standards." *Economics Bulletin* 6:2 (2002): 1–8.

Cigno, Alessandro, Furio C. Rosati, and Lorenzo Guarcello. "Does Globalization Increase Child Labor?" *World Development* 30:9 (2002): 1579–89.

Dessy, Sylvain E., and Stéphane Pallage. "Child Labor and Failures." *Journal of Development Economics* 65 (2001): 469–76.

Edmonds, Eric V. "Child Labor." In *Handbook of Development Economics*, vol. 4, ed. J. Strauss and T.P. Schultz. Amsterdam: North Holland, 2008.

Edmonds, Eric V., and Nina Pavcnik. "The Effect of Trade Liberalization on Child Labour." *Journal of International Economics* 65:2 (2005): 401–41.

Edmonds, Eric V., and Nina Pavcnik. "International Trade and Child Labor: Cross-Country Evidence." *Journal of International Economics* 68:1 (2006): 115–40.

Edmonds, Eric V., Nina Pavcnik, and Petia Topolova. "Trade Adjustment and Human Capital Investments: Evidence from Indian Tariff Reform." Working paper 12884, National Bureau of Economic Research, Cambridge, MA, 2007.

Elliott, Kimberly Ann, and Richard B. Freeman. *Can Labor Standards Improve Under Globalization?* Washington, DC: Institute for International Economics, 2003.

Hiscox, Michael J., and Nicholas F.B.Smyth. "Is There Consumer Demand for Improved Labor Standards? Evidence from Field Experiments in Social Labeling." Department of Government, Harvard University, Cambridge, MA, 2006.

Kruger, Diana. "Coffee Production Effects on Child Labor and Schooling in Rural Brazil." *Journal of Development Economics* 82 (2004): 448–63.

Kruger, Diana. "Child Labor and Schooling During a Coffee Sector Boom: Nicaragua 1993–1998." In *Trabajo infantial: teoría y evidencia desde Latinoamerica*, ed. L.F. Lopez-Calva. Mexico, D.F.: Fondo de Cultural Económica de México, 2006.

Kucera, David. "Core Labor Standards and Foreign Direct Investment." *International Labour Review* 141:1–2 (2002): 31–69.

Maskus, Keith. "Core Labor Standards: Trade Impacts and Implications for International Trade Policy." Washington, DC: World Bank, 1997.

Maskus, Keith, and Jill Holman. "The Economics of Child Labor Standards." Working paper 96-10, Department of Economics, University of Colorado, Boulder, 1996.

Neumayer, Eric, and Indra de Soysa. "Trade Openness, Foreign Direct Investment and Child Labor." *World Development* 33:1 (2005): 43–63.

Visual Representations of Child Labor in the West

George Dimock, Professor of Art History, University of North Carolina-Greensboro

In *The Making of the English Working Class,* E.P. Thompson quoted a passage from an 1842 investigation of children's employment in the coal mines regarding the astonishment of local middle-class professionals "when girls were brought half-naked out of the pits": "Mr. Holroyd, solicitor, and Mr. Brook, surgeon, practising in Stainland, were present, who confessed that, although living within a few miles, they could not have believed that such a system of unchristian cruelty could have existed." Child labor needed to be seen to be believed. At the same time, "[w]e forget how long abuses can continue 'unknown' until they are articulated: how people can look at misery and not notice it, until misery itself rebels" (Thompson 1963, 342).

Images of child labor possess a particular urgency and poignancy that have remained remarkably constant over time. Based on a Romantic appeal to the innocence and sanctity of childhood, they decry the economic exploitation of working-class children by industrial capitalism with an unequivocal moral force that remains a catalyst for political reform to the present day. Child labor, as an issue of political debate and social reform, finds its most characteristic and persuasive visual embodiments in photography, film, and video—those lens-based media that most authoritatively bear witness to empirical fact.

Documentary photography, as an aesthetic and social practice, and as a form of mass communication, received one of its earliest and most influential formulations in the work of Lewis Hine for the National Child Labor Committee (NCLC). Some 5,100 photographs made between 1908 and 1924 constituted compelling visual evidence of the pervasiveness and destructiveness of child labor in America in the early twentieth century.

Child labor figures only tangentially in older, more prestigious forms of visual imagery such as painting, drawing, and sculpture. Such representations inhabit a cultural realm in which aesthetic criteria and literary allusions all but eclipse the child worker as historical subject. Sir Joshua Reynolds's *Cupid as Link Boy* (1774), for instance, takes as its subject a familiar figure of eighteenth-century London nightlife whose job it was to light the way for more prosperous wayfarers. Yet as a "fancy picture"—a scene from everyday life transformed to serve an allegorical conceit—the boy's batlike wings, crude gesture, and phallic torch embody the theme of sexual conquest (Postle 1995).

In *Songs of Innocence and of Experience* (1794), William Blake lashed out in both word and image against the plight of the chimney sweep—the quintessential embodiment of abusive child labor in the formative stages of English industrialization. Yet in his two illuminated poems, both entitled "The Chimney Sweeper," the specificities of the children's circumstances are largely subsumed by the radical eccentricity of the poet's visionary Romanticism. So, too, with the pistol-brandishing street urchin who leads the way toward revolution in Delacroix's *Liberty Leading the People* (1830). Far from enacting the role of the oppressed child, he strides purposefully toward a victorious future wherein the glory of French painting and utopian republican values render superfluous the prospect of liberal reform.

Under the banner of Realism, Gustave Courbet's *The Stone Breakers* (1850) champions the historical presence and inherent dignity of a fifteen-year-old boy working alongside an old man "grown stiff with service and age," whose fate the boy is destined to share. They are engaged in the lowest, most backbreaking form of manual labor: pounding rocks into gravel for paving roads. The boy's stolid body turns away from the viewer as he strains to lift a basket filled with stones. His lack of a childhood constitutes the defining terms of his Sisyphean existence (Eisenman 1994). Manet's *Boy with Cherries* (1859), Renoir's *Two Little Circus Girls* (1879), and Degas's *Little Dancer Aged Fourteen* (1880), all represent children of the working class who will subsequently become the objects of child labor reform. Yet their cultural significance resides not in a social cause but rather in their radical contemporaneity, advocated by Charles Baudelaire, as a hallmark of the avant-garde.

Child labor figures prominently, if indirectly, in the photographic archives of Dr. Barnardo's Homes, a series of orphan asylums founded in London in 1870. Some 50,000 portraits, kept in albums along with case-history sheets, constitute a record of every child rescued from the streets. More controversially, Dr. Barnardo also created a collection of "before and after" photos attesting to the institution's transformative effects upon its charges—from vagrancy to gainful employment, from tattered malnutrition to well-clothed health, from listless pauperism to schooled literacy. In 1877 Barnardo lost a court case in which these photographs, used for publicity and fund-raising, were found guilty of "artistic fiction" in exaggerating the plight of particular children upon admission. Barnardo defended these images by claiming his intention of representing typologically "a *class* of children of whom many had been rescued" (Leggat 1999).

In their original context, Hine's child labor photographs were not intended to be either beautiful or important as pictures. In this they stand in stark contrast to the photographs of Alfred Stieglitz, Hine's contemporary, who devoted his career to championing photography as a fine art. Hine's photos provided empirical visual evidence for the widespread presence of children in the American workforce. Hine supplemented his camera work with meticulous captions and commentary characteristic of a social worker or investigative reporter. The specificity of information and depth of political analysis went far beyond the standards of what was to become known in subsequent decades as photojournalism.

Millie (about seven yrs. old) and Mary John (with the baby) eight years old. Both shuck oysters at the Alabama Canning Co. This is Mary's second year. She said, "I shucks six pots if I don't got the baby; two pots if I got him." (Many of the little ones, too young to work all the time, tend the baby when not working.) Location: Bayou La Batre, Alabama. February, 1911 *(Original caption; courtesy of the Library of Congress Prints and Photographs Division, National Child Labor Committee Collection, LC-DIG-nclc-00846)*

What makes Hine's NCLC archive so important and compelling is the quantity, variety, and quality of images combined with the specificity of information that accompanies them. Typically, a Hine caption will include the name and age of the child, date and location, NCLC catalogue number, task performed, hours worked, hourly or daily wage, length of employment, working conditions, family circumstances, availability of schooling, and fragments of verbatim testimony. A typical example is shown above.

Hine devoted immense efforts to his task, traveling for extended periods for more than a decade from Maine to Texas, gaining access to his subjects by courage, perseverance, stealth, and guile. The range of workplaces he photographed was extraordinary: mines, textile mills, commercial farms, factories of all kinds, canneries, glassworks, department stores, sweatshops, restaurants, bowl-

One of many exhibit panels created by the National Child Labor Committee using Lewis Hine photos. (*Courtesy of the Library of Congress Prints and Photographs Division, National Child Labor Committee Collection, LC-USZ62-46392*)

ing alleys, amusement parks, railroads, vegetable markets, theaters, fairgrounds, hospitals, schools, libraries, reformatories, juvenile courts, city streets, and tenement homes. Hine's images captured child labor practices in all their diversity and specificity even as they offered visual corroboration for many facets of the NCLC's argument for the abolition of child labor: namely that working-class children, like their middle-class counterparts, should go to school at taxpayers' expense rather than become "human junk" as a result of low-paying, repetitive, mind-numbing, dangerous, and debilitating wage labor.

Hine's photographs circulated in *Survey* magazine, a major reform publication, and in NCLC literature and posters. Their veracity and import were, at times, contested in the press by the conservative opposition (Dimock 1993). However, Hine's photographs did more than document the widespread existence of child labor. His candid and deeply empathetic portraits called attention to the child worker as a uniquely engaging and vulnerable individual with an immediacy and authority that no words could match. They allowed these children, and, by extension, all working-class children for whom these images served as metonyms, to be seen as emotionally priceless beings entitled to their fair share of the American dream (Zelizer 1985).

Hine's bulky cameras, both tripod and hand-held, with their relatively slow shutter speeds, necessitated a self-consciously posed image—one negotiated between photographer and the camera subject. So it is that these children, in most cases, have stopped whatever they were doing and looked

John Howell, An Indianapolis Newsboy Makes $.75 some days. Begins at 6 A.M., Sundays. (Lives at 215 W. Michigan St.) Location: Indianapolis, Indiana. August 1908 (*Original caption; courtesy of the Library of Congress Prints and Photographs Division, National Child Labor Committee Collection, LC-USZ62-53123*)

directly into the lens. Threatened by the forces of unbridled industrial capitalism, they stand in dire need of rescue through legislative means according to the values and expectations of an adult, reform-minded, middle-class electorate for whom these pictures were originally intended.

With the waning of child labor as a pressing political issue after the First World War, Hine's NCLC photographs lay dormant until "rediscovered" as part of the burgeoning interest and lucrative market in art photography in the 1970s. Hine's original activist agenda became assimilated to the aesthetics of American photographic modernism. The formal and conceptual terms established by Hine's work for the depiction of child labor have remained remarkably stable down to the present. Lens-based images convey the illusion of the viewer's direct, unmediated access to the subject of representation. Child labor is depicted as being economically exploitative, inhumane, and mentally and physically damaging. In the eyes of photographer and intended viewer alike, both of whom occupy economically and socially privileged positions, the child worker is seen to be trapped and in need of rescue. The child labor image induces feelings of guilt, pity, and moral outrage that find an outlet in an insistence upon political reform and relief funding that will "save" the child by way of the mitigation or abolition of child labor and the provision of educational opportunity in its stead.

The reality effect of social documentary challenges the distancing mechanisms of inattention and disavowal that protect the comfort levels of the middle-class viewer's psychic and political space. The polemical graphics of the editorial cartoon perform the more abstract and recondite task of rendering the argument against child labor visible in the most distilled and memorable terms possible. Wit, poignancy, and condensation are key attributes, as an explicitly ideological argument is staked out by way of words, symbols, and archetypes that coalesce into a melodramatic set piece. For example, in G.W. Rehse's *"Legislators! To the Rescue!"* (August 16, 1902), the chained and barefoot boy labeled "child labor" endlessly treads a waterwheel in order to supply power to "The Southern Cotton Industry" while a "New England Capitalist" guards the door, holding a rifle whose

G.W. Rehse, "Legislators! To the Rescue!" *St. Paul Pioneer Press* (August 16, 1902)

bullets are intended "For Philanthropists." The reception of such images tends to be pleasurable since they offer graphic virtuosity, fictive humor, and moral certainty as a welcome respite from the immediate sufferings of "real" children depicted in photography.

Until recently, the visual representation of child labor has taken the form of a historical romance—a narrative of a moral and political crisis successfully overcome in the course of enlightened Western development (Cunningham 1991). Hine's photographs often play a leading role in this story as the catalyst for the eradication of child labor. Yet the current economic and political forces of globalization have conspired to resurrect child labor, particularly in third-world nations, as a pressing social and moral issue. Lens-based representations of child workers have once again become the most legible and disturbing reminders of the contradictions and inequities plaguing economic development under capitalism.

Stolen Childhoods (2004), an eighty-five-minute documentary film by Len Morris and Robin Romano, updates Hine and, like David L. Parker's *Stolen Dreams* (1998), explores the moral and political dimensions of contemporary child labor. Narrated by Meryl Streep and featuring commentaries by prominent peace activists and human rights advocates, *Stolen Childhoods* documents child labor practices in eight countries including the United States. It shows migrant children working in pesticide-laden fields, young weavers chained to looms, boys forced to work on fishing platforms at sea, children scavenging city landfills, and young boys and girls working as bonded (slave) laborers in brick kilns and rock quarries.

While the film is governed by the same moral urgency and liberal faith that sustained Hine's NCLC work, images of child labor must now compete for attention in an instantaneous, digital world saturated with pictures that threaten to inure and desensitize by their sheer volume and ubiquity (Sontag 1977). A 2008 Google image search of "child labor" produced 540,000 items in 0.07 seconds. A YouTube search yielded 880 "child labor" videos. Yet the self-protective instinct of the viewer, what may look and feel like cynical indifference, coexists with unprecedented access to potentially empowering visual knowledge. To take but one example, Hine's entire NCLC archive is now unrestrictedly accessible and searchable online through the Prints and Photographs Division of the Library of Congress. The Internet offers the potential for organizing an international, democratic, real-time consensus concerning the problem of child labor, even as it generates an indiscriminate frenzy of competing voices and images.

Current representations of child labor are not immune to the mechanisms and dynamics of celebrity culture. Iqbal Masih, a Pakistani bonded-debt slave working as a carpet weaver from the age of four, was assassinated on Easter Sunday 1995 at age twelve for his world-renowned activism against child labor. Due to the abusive working conditions of his early years, Iqbal, at twelve, retained the body of a six-year-old. His diminutive size, appealing features, and winning smile, as captured in the international media, have become the most visible symbol for the plight of the child laborer. In 2000 he was the inaugural recipient of the World's Children's Prize for the Rights of the Child.

Born into Brothels is an American documentary film by Zana Briski and Ross Kauffman that won the 2005 Academy Award for Documentary Feature. The film features eight children living in Calcutta's red-light district who were given cameras and taught photography as an outgrowth of Briski's project of photographing their mothers. The sale of the children's photographs at prestigious Western art venues, including Sotheby's, is portrayed as offering them a chance of escape from prostitution by way of a boarding school education. The inherent attractiveness of these graceful, intelligent, and high-spirited children, combined with their exotic appeal and sexual endangerment as children of the brothel, operate to suppress the impulse to question the filmmakers' right to intervene so drastically in the lives of these children and their families.

In contemporary Western culture, the processes of image viewing, information assimilation, ethical debate, fund-raising, and political advocacy proceed instantaneously and continuously on multiple media platforms by way of the computer, digital technology, and the World Wide Web. For example, still photographs from the *Stolen Childhoods* project can be viewed and purchased online, with 10 percent of the purchase price going toward relief work. The illusion of visual immediacy coupled with a universal moral outrage against the violation of the inalienable rights of children creates an implicit demand that the problem of child labor be extricated from the more complex and intractable dynamics of international capitalism and local cultural practices so that it may be "solved" on humanitarian grounds by those privileged first-world viewers empowered to see, understand, and intervene. *Stolen Childhoods* includes U.S. Senator Tom Harkin's dire, media-savvy warning that child labor unchecked now constitutes a principal breeding ground for global terrorism.

The figure of the working child puts into question basic assumptions concerning human value and well-being. Lewis Hine's NCLC photos gave credibility and immediacy to that figure in such a way as to make child labor an urgent and deeply troubling political issue in the early decades of the twentieth century. A photographic image of a child worker is never "the thing itself" but always a social and historical construct whose tendentiousness, both in its making and in its reception, is part of the world in which children live and work (Szarkowski 1966; Sekula 1975).

Links to Illustrations Cited

Sir Joshua Reynolds. *Cupid as a Link Boy* (1774). Oil on canvas. Albright-Knox Art Gallery. http://www.abcgallery.com/R/reynolds/reynolds223.html.

Eugène Delacroix. *Liberty Leading the People (28 July 1830)* (1830). Oil on canvas. Louvre. http://www.abcgallery.com/D/delacroix/delacroix10.html.

Gustave Courbet. *The Stone Breakers* (1849; destroyed during World War II). Oil on canvas. http://faculty.etsu.edu/kortumr/HUMT2320/realism/htmdescriptionpages/stonebreakers.htm.

Edouard Manet. *The Boy with Cherries* (1859). Oil on canvas. Calouste Gulbenkian Foundation Museum. http://www.mystudios.com/manet/1850/manet-cherries-1859.html.

Pierre-Auguste Renoir. *Two Little Circus Girls* (1879). Oil on canvas. Art Institute of Chicago. http://www.abcgallery.com/R/renoir/renoir27.html.

Edgar Degas. *Little Dancer Aged Fourteen* (1880–1881, cast circa 1922). Bronze. Tate Museum. http://www.tate.org.uk/servlet/ViewWork?workid=3705.

Len Morris and Robin Romano. *Stolen Childhoods* (2004). http://www.stolenchildhoods.org/mt/index.php.

David L. Parker. *Stolen Dreams* (2001). Harvard School of Public Health Gallery. http://www.hsph.harvard.edu/gallery/.

Iqbal Masih. http://www.childrensworld.org/globalclassroom/page.html?pid=53.

Zana Briski and Ross Kauffman. *Born into Brothels: Calcutta'a Red Light Kids* (2004). http://www.hbo.com/docs/programs/born_into_brothels/index.html.

References and Further Reading

Blake, William. *Songs of Innocence and of Experience: Shewing the Two Contrary States of the Human Soul.* Princeton, NJ: William Blake Trust/Princeton University Press, 1991.

Blanchet, Therese. *Lost Innocence, Stolen Childhoods.* Dhaka: University Press Limited, 1996.

Brown, Marilyn. "Images of Childhood." In *Encyclopedia of Children and Childhood in History and Society,* ed. Paula S. Fass, 449–63. New York: Macmillan Reference USA, 2004.

Cunningham, Hugh. *The Children of the Poor: Representations of Childhood Since the Seventeenth Century.* Oxford: Basil Blackwell, 1991.

Dimock, George. "Children of the Mills: Re-Reading Lewis Hine's Child-Labour Photographs." *Oxford Art Journal* 16:2 (1993): 37–54.

Eisenman, Stephen F. *Nineteenth Century Art: A Critical History.* New York: Thames and Hudson, 1994.

Leggat, Robert. "Barnardo, Thomas." In *A History of Photography* (1999). http://www.rleggat.com/photohistory/index.html.

Parker, David L. *Stolen Dreams: Portraits of Working Children.* Minneapolis: Lerner Publications, 1998.

Postle, Martin. *Sir Joshua Reynolds: The Subject Pictures.* Cambridge: Cambridge University Press, 1995.

Sontag, Susan. *On Photography.* New York: Farrar, Straus and Giroux, 1977.

Sekula, Allan. "On the Invention of Photographic Meaning." *Artforum* 8:5 (1975): 36–45.

Szarkowski, John. *The Photographer's Eye.* New York: Museum of Modern Art, 1966.

Thompson, E.P. *The Making of the English Working Class.* London: Victor Gollancz, 1963.

Zelizer, Viviana A. *Pricing the Priceless Child: The Changing Social Value of Children.* New York: Basic Books, 1985.

Section 3. Less Developed Regions of the World

Worst Forms of Child Labor

Hugh D. Hindman, Professor of Labor and Human Resources, Appalachian State University

When the International Program for the Elimination of Child Labor (IPEC) was created in 1992 to spearhead the International Labor Organization's (ILO) efforts against child labor, the two principal policy instruments at its disposal were the ILO Minimum Age Convention 138, adopted in 1973, and the UN Convention on the Rights of the Child (CRC), adopted in 1989.

ILO Convention 138

Convention 138 takes an age-based approach, seeking to regulate the intensity of work (generally measured in hours) at various age thresholds. It requires ratifying nations "to pursue a national policy designed to ensure the effective abolition of child labour and to raise progressively the minimum age for admission to employment or work to a level consistent with the fullest physical and mental development of young persons" (Article 1). It provides that the minimum age for admission to employment "shall not be less than the age of completion of compulsory schooling and, in any case, shall not be less than 15 years" (Article 2[3]). A higher minimum age, eighteen years, is established for "work which by its nature or the circumstances in which it is carried out is likely to jeopardise the health, safety or morals of young persons" (Article 3[1]). Further, the convention provides that "[n]ational laws or regulations may permit the employment or work of persons 13 to 15 years of age on light work which is not likely to be harmful to their health or development; and not such as to prejudice their attendance at school" (Article 7[1a and b])

Convention 138 recognizes that some nations may not be able to immediately comply with its standards, so nations "whose economy and educational facilities are insufficiently developed" may initially establish the minimum age for regular work at fourteen, and the ages at which light work is permitted at twelve to fourteen. Further, nations "whose economy and administrative facilities are insufficiently developed" may initially exempt specified branches of economic activity from the scope of application of the convention. However, "mining and quarrying; manufacturing; construction; electricity, gas and water; sanitary services; transport, storage and communication; and plantations and other agricultural undertakings mainly producing for commercial purposes" cannot be exempted from application of the convention (Article.5[3]).

UN Convention on the Rights of the Child

In contrast to ILO Convention 138, the CRC takes a rights-based approach, defining a child as "every human being below the age of eighteen years" and articulating a wide array of fundamental rights of children, including "freedom of expression"; "freedom of thought, conscience and religion"; "freedom of association"; the right to "the highest attainable standard of health"; the right to "a standard of living adequate for the child's physical, mental, spiritual, moral and social development"; and the right to "rest and leisure, to engage in play and recreational activities appropriate to the age of the child." In short, children have the right to a childhood.

All of these rights are to be provided in accordance with the general principle that, in all matters concerning the child, "the best interests of the child shall be a primary consideration" (Article 3[1]). Further, children's right to participate in their own affairs is recognized. "State parties shall assure to the child who is capable of forming his or her own views the right to express those views freely in all matters affecting the child, the views of the child being given due weight in accordance with the age and maturity of the child" (Article 12[1]).

Of special relevance to the issue of child labor, the CRC recognizes the right of the child to an education directed to "[t]he development of the child's personality, talents and mental and physical abilities to their fullest potential" (Article 29[1] a). And the convention calls for making primary education free and compulsory for all children (Article 28[1a]). The convention addresses child labor more directly by recognizing "the right of the child to be protected from economic exploitation and from performing any work that is likely to be hazardous or to interfere with the child's education, or to be harmful to the child's health or physical, mental, spiritual, moral or social development" (Article 32[1]).

Further, the CRC calls for children to be protected from a variety of exploitative activities including use of children in trafficking of illicit drugs (Article 33); child sexual abuse including commercial sexual exploitation (Article 34); the abduction, sale, or trafficking of children for any purpose (Article 35); and the use of children in armed conflicts (Article 38). The convention calls for "measures to promote physical and psychological recovery and social reintegration" of children who have fallen victim to such exploitation (Article 39).

ILO Convention 182

In the 1990s, as IPEC began ramping up its efforts, it soon became apparent that the global child labor problem was so immense and so complex that it would be necessary to prioritize and target the "worst forms" of child labor for more immediate eradication. IPEC formally proposed adoption of a new convention in 1996, and Convention 182 was finally adopted at the International Labor Conference in June 1999.

Convention 182 commits ratifying nations to "take immediate and effective measures to secure the prohibition and elimination of the worst forms of child labour as a matter of urgency" (Article 1) and, in addition to removing children from worst forms of child labor, to provide for their rehabilitation and social reintegration.

Article 3 of the convention defines the worst forms of child labor as:

A. all forms of slavery or practices similar to slavery, such as the sale and trafficking of children, debt bondage and serfdom and forced or compulsory labour, including forced or compulsory recruitment of children for use in armed conflict;
B. the use, procuring or offering of a child for prostitution, for the production of pornography or for pornographic performances;
C. the use, procuring or offering of a child for illicit activities, in particular for the production and trafficking of drugs as defined in the relevant international treaties;
D. work which, by its nature or the circumstances in which it is carried out, is likely to harm the health, safety or morals of children.

Unconditional Worst Forms of Child Labor

Because the convention categorically condemns certain worst forms of child labor without qualification, it has become customary to refer to them as "unconditional worst forms of child labor." These include the sale and trafficking of children; children in forced and bonded labor; children in armed conflict; the commercial sexual exploitation of children in prostitution and pornography; and children in illicit activities such as drug trafficking. Most of these activities are also subject to other ILO or global human rights accords. In Recommendation 190, supplementing Convention 182, the ILO recommends that nations make these activities criminal offenses so that those responsible for involving children in them are subject to penal sanctions. Most nations have done so.

Partly because these activities are illegal, it is especially difficult to arrive at reliable estimates of the quantitative magnitude of unconditional worst forms of child labor. In 2002, IPEC attempted to do so, but cautioned that its figures were "minimum estimates, based on conservative calculations" (IPEC 2002, 25).

Trafficking of Children

IPEC estimated that about 1.2 million children are affected by trafficking. IPEC found that both boys and girls are trafficked to and from all regions of the world. Boys are most commonly trafficked for labor exploitation, especially in commercial farming, but also for forced labor in petty crimes and the drug trade. Girls are most commonly trafficked for commercial sexual exploitation or domestic service. Thus, most trafficked children end up in another unconditional worst form of child labor.

Children in Forced and Bonded Labor

After acknowledging "severe problems of quantification," IPEC estimated that 5.7 million children are in forced and bonded labor, the overwhelming majority of whom are in the Asia-Pacific region.

Children in Armed Conflict

IPEC estimated that about 300,000 children are involved in armed conflict at any given time in the world, with Africa and the Asia-Pacific regions accounting for the largest number of child soldiers. While boys clearly dominate, substantial numbers of girls are also involved.

Commercial Sexual Exploitation of Children in Prostitution and Pornography

IPEC estimated that about 1.8 million children are affected by commercial sexual exploitation, predominately girls, but many boys as well. All regions of the world are implicated. Unlike most other worst forms of child labor, which are mostly confined to developing nations, commercial exploitation of children is also prevalent and widespread in the developed industrialized economies, where about 420,000 children are affected.

Children in Illicit Activities

IPEC estimated that about 600,000 children are engaged in illicit activities, especially in drug production and trafficking. Like commercial sexual exploitation of children, this is a problem found in all regions of the world, including the more developed regions.

Hazardous Work

In contrast to the unconditional worst forms of child labor, which are categorically condemned, determining whether work, "by its nature or the circumstances in which it is carried out, is likely to harm the health, safety or morals of children"—or what has come to be referred to as simply "hazardous work"—entails an element of subjectivity. Convention 182 calls on ratifying nations to specify in their national laws or regulations those types of work considered hazardous. In determining hazardous types of work, Recommendation 190, supplementing the convention, urges that consideration be given to:

> A. work which exposes children to physical, psychological or sexual abuse;
> B. work underground, under water, at dangerous heights or in confined spaces;
> C. work with dangerous machinery, equipment and tools, or which involves the manual handling or transport of heavy loads;
> D. work in an unhealthy environment which may, for example, expose children to hazardous substances, agents or processes, or to temperatures, noise levels, or vibrations damaging to their health;
> E. work under particularly difficult conditions such as work for long hours or during the night or work where the child is unreasonably confined to the premises of the employer.

Since the convention leaves it to each nation to specify work it will treat as hazardous, there is no uniform "master list" that can be consulted to determine which activities are hazardous and which are not. Certain types of work, however, are nearly universally considered hazardous, such as work in mining or construction, or work with heavy machinery or exposure to pesticides. In mining and quarrying in particular, it is estimated that about 1 million children worldwide work in small-scale, informal-sector mines and quarries, and, unlike in other forms of hazardous work, this number may be growing (IPEC 2005). In 2006, IPEC estimated that about 126 million children were engaged in various types of hazardous work worldwide, 74 million in the five-year-old to fourteen-year-old age-group, and 52 million in the fifteen-year-old to seventeen-year-old age-group. Boys are more likely to be engaged in hazardous work than girls. While these numbers seem disturbingly large, it is important to note that, in the five-year-old to fourteen-year-old age-group, hazardous work declined by about one-third from IPEC's 2002 estimate, suggesting that targeting the worst forms of child labor for more immediate eradication may be paying off.

References and Further Reading

ILO. *Convention Concerning Minimum Age for Admission to Employment* (C138). Geneva: International Labor Conference, June 6, 1973.

ILO. *Convention Concerning the Prohibition and Immediate Action for the Elimination of the Worst Forms of Child Labour* (C182). Geneva: International Labor Conference, June 1, 1999.

ILO. *Eliminating the Worst Forms of Child Labour: A Practical Guide to ILO Convention No. 182. Handbook for Parliamentarians.* Geneva: International Labor Office, 2002.

ILO. *Girls in Mining: Research Findings from Ghana, Niger, Peru and the United Republic of Tanzania.* Geneva: ILO, Bureau for Gender Equality, International Program on the Elimination of Child Labor, 2007.

IPEC. *Every Child Counts: New Global Estimates on Child Labour.* Geneva: ILO-IPEC, 2002.

IPEC. *Eliminating Child Labour in Quarrying and Mining: Background Document to the World Day Against Child Labour, 2005.* Geneva: ILO-IPEC, 2005.

IPEC. *Global Child Labour Trends, 2000–2004.* Geneva: ILO-IPEC, 2006.

UN. *Convention on the Rights of the Child.* New York: United Nations, November 20, 1989.

Worst Forms of Child Labor: Agriculture

Alec Fyfe, Senior Child Labor Specialist, International Labor Organization

Agriculture is a complex and diverse economic sector and it is where most child labor is found. Unless a concerted effort is made to reduce agricultural child labor, it will be impossible to reach the global goal of the effective elimination of child labor, given that the vast majority of working children are toiling in fields and fisheries, not in factories. In fact, the number of children working in agriculture is nearly ten times the number involved in factory work. According to the global estimates of the ILO in 2006, nearly 70 percent of all child laborers, 130 million children under age fifteen, work in agriculture (ILO 2006). This situation is by no means confined to the developing world. Entire families of migrant laborers, as in the case of Mexican migrant workers in the United States, help plant and harvest the rich world's fruit and vegetables. In the United States, there are an estimated 300,000 children working in agriculture. They account for 8 percent of working children but suffered 40 percent of work-related fatalities. Children working on U.S. farms often work twelve-hour days and come from families of color—70 percent are Hispanic or other ethnic minorities (ILO 2002).

This basic fact about child labor is often ignored in favor of an urban and industrial image of the problem that has its origins in the nineteenth-century campaigns in the first industrial nations. But even during that period, most child labor in Europe and the United States was in agriculture, where it was taken for granted. This neglect of agricultural child labor, linked to an unquestioned assumption that children working on farms and in fisheries are at less risk than their urban counterparts, still prevails today and distorts our view of the problem. Millions of the world's child laborers in agriculture engage in hazardous work. Indeed, agriculture is, after construction and mining, the most dangerous sector in which to work at any age.

The family farm—that universal element in agriculture that is so bound up with culture and tradition—renders the work of children largely invisible, thereby making it difficult to acknowledge that children can be at risk in such a setting. The world over, children working on family farms, and in agricultural activities generally, are viewed as helping out and engaged in family solidarity. Moreover, such work is often seen as an important part of the child's socialization. Though this can be the case, it is important to penetrate below the surface and examine actual working conditions, many of which may well be hazardous, and the amount of time involved, particularly for girls, that is thereby lost to education.

These factors make agriculture a difficult sector in which to tackle child labor. Child labor regulation is much weaker in agriculture than in other sectors. However, it is precisely because of these factors—large numbers, hazardous work, lack of regulation, invisibility, and loss of education—that agriculture should be a priority sector for the elimination of child labor.

Children become agricultural workers at an early age. Until recently, most statistical surveys of child labor covered only those children age ten and above. However, many rural children begin work earlier. This is particularly the case for girls, who tend to start work at five, six, or seven years of age. In some countries, children under age ten are estimated to account for 20 percent of child labor in rural areas. The work children perform in agriculture is often invisible and unacknowledged because they assist their parents or relatives on the family farm, or they undertake piecework or work under a quota system on larger farms or plantations, often as part of a migrant workforce.

Types of Child Labor in Agriculture

Agriculture is a diverse economic sector comprised of a number of subsectors. It includes highly industrialized and mechanized commercial operations at one end of the spectrum and traditional small-scale, family-based subsistence farming at the other. However, this distinction is slowly eroding under commercial and globalization effects promoting export-oriented agriculture.

Children working in agriculture are engaged in all types of undertakings ranging from family farms to corporate-run farms, plantations, and agro-industrial complexes. At one end of the spectrum children may work with basic equipment, low levels of mechanization, and few agricultural inputs such as pesticides and fertilizers; at the other extreme, they may engage in intensive, highly organized, highly capitalized, commercial production systems. Risks increase where children are contracted to a third party outside the family, as in the case, for example, of labor contracted to commercial farms and plantations. In extreme cases, children may be victims of bonded labor or forced labor practices. Minorities and migrant workers are often the most vulnerable to exploitation. For example, the children of migrant workers are often classed as helpers, hired as part of a family unit by contractors or subcontractors, thus enabling farm and plantation owners to deny responsibility for underage workers. Children working in these commercial enterprises typically experience long and arduous working hours, little safety and health protection, and inadequate diet, rest, and education.

Hazardous Child Labor in Agriculture

Hazardous work is, by definition, one of the worst forms of child labor recognized under ILO Convention 182 on Worst Forms of Child Labor. There are many types of hazards and risks facing child laborers in agriculture, including mechanical, biological, physical, chemical, dust, ergonomic, welfare, hygiene, and psychological hazards, not to mention long hours of work and poor living conditions. Indeed, one of the distinguishing characteristics of agricultural work is that it is carried out in a rural environment where there is no clear boundary between working and living conditions. Moreover, children working in agriculture are susceptible to all the dangers faced by adult workers. However, these can affect child laborers more severely and have longer-lasting physical or psychological impact.

Children working in agriculture have greater vulnerability to particular hazards and their impacts. To begin with, hours of work tend to be extremely long, often from dawn to dusk, especially during the peak seasons of planting and harvesting. Much agricultural work is physically demanding and strenuous. Long and repeated standing, stooping, bending, and carrying of heavy loads can harm children's musculoskeletal development and may result in permanent disability. Children must often work in extreme temperatures, such as hot sun, or in cold and wet conditions, with little in the way of protection. Child laborers may use dangerous cutting tools such as machetes, knives, scythes, and sickles that lead to frequent and sometimes serious injuries. Children are at risk of being injured or killed by farm vehicles and heavy machinery. Tractor overturns are not uncommon and can be the cause of death in countries such as Australia and the United States, where children as young as seven years may be driving such vehicles. Many children also mix, load, and apply toxic pesticides. Many of these are poisonous, some are carcinogenic, and some may adversely affect brain function, behavior, and mental health. Children are often exposed to high levels of organic dust while harvesting crops or preparing feed for farm animals that can result in allergic respiratory diseases, such as occupational asthma and hypersensitivity pneumonia. Pastoral activities, such as herding and shepherding animals, can also bring the risk of injury and disease. Children in pastoral communities may spend many months in remote and isolated areas, vulnerable to attack from wild animals. Working barefoot in fields or around livestock also exposes children to cuts, bruises, thorn injuries, skin disorders, and infection with waterborne diseases, especially where the soil is wet and sticky, or deliberately flooded as in rice cultivation. Children are also vulnerable to snake and insect bites. Frequently, there is a lack of clean drinking water or decent washing or sanitation facilities.

For example, Human Rights Watch found children working in hazardous conditions on banana plantations in Ecuador. Children were exposed to toxic chemicals when they worked under fungicide-spraying airplanes and when directly applying postharvest pesticides in packing plants. Children used sharp tools, including knives, short, curved blades, and machetes, and they lacked potable water and sanitation facilities. Some boys were required to haul heavy loads of bananas from the fields to the packing plants, while some girls were subjected to sexual harassment. The average starting age for child workers was eleven, and the vast majority worked an average of thirteen hours a day. Such conditions were in violation of national and international law (Human Rights Watch 2002).

Strategies to Eliminate Hazardous Child Labor in Agriculture

As with other forms of child labor, any comprehensive response needs to strike a balance among actions aimed at prevention, withdrawal, and protection. Child labor cannot be tackled unless its eradication is linked to rural development and poverty-reduction efforts. In many instances, children in rural areas represent a plentiful source of cheap farm labor that can suppress adult wages and discourage technological improvement leading to productivity gains. Raising incomes of adult agricultural workers will, in the long term, reduce child labor by improving family incomes. At the same time, it is important to promote employment of youths who have attained the minimum age for work. The challenge is to attract youths to work in agriculture by improving training and employment conditions.

Improving legislation and enforcement has been the traditional response to child labor. Here the challenge is the extent to which agriculture appears exempt from normal regulation. Child labor laws—if they exist—are less stringently applied in agriculture than in other industries. Trade unions are also much weaker among rural workers, making the defense of labor rights more difficult to enforce.

Prevention is the most cost-effective approach in the long run, and requires an attack on poverty and poor education, which help feed the supply of children into the agricultural labor force. Microfinance and credit schemes such as the Grameen Bank of Bangladesh (winner of the 2006 Nobel Peace Prize) and other cooperative schemes are the types of responses that help forge social safety nets for the rural poor. Improvements in both the quantity and quality of education, particularly for girls, are another important part of the equation to prevent children from entering the labor force and to retain them in school. Part of the immediate response is to identify children in hazardous work and quickly get them into some form of education or skills training. In less extreme cases, protective measures can be put in place, such as improving occupational safety and health, while withdrawal strategies are pursued.

An important part of any child labor strategy is to mobilize all the key actors and have them respond on the basis of their comparative strengths. This means developing a partnership between government, which bears the prime responsibility to ensure the rights and welfare of children under national and international law, and civil society actors such as trade unions and NGOs, whose role, in part, is to keep reminding governments of this fact.

What Is Being Done to Tackle Hazardous Child Labor in Agriculture?

Given the relative neglect of agriculture in both child labor discourse and action, this remains an underdeveloped area of the global response to child labor. For example, agriculture accounts for less than 15 percent of the ILO's activity on child labor (ILO 2006). In 2006, the ILO began to stimulate a discussion with key global actors such as the UN Food and Agriculture Organization and the International Union of Food, Agricultural, Hotel, Restaurant, Catering, Tobacco and Allied

Workers Association with a view to responding to this anomaly. The focus on agriculture for the World Day against Child Labor in June 2007 helped advance this process—in particular, the agreement to adopt a follow-up action plan by the key global actors in agriculture.

There are a number of initiatives, particularly from the ILO, to build on. In 2002, the ILO initiated a pilot program in East Africa targeting the withdrawal and reintegration of children performing hazardous work in commercial agriculture. The Comagri project, active in Kenya, Malawi, Tanzania, Uganda, and Zambia had, by 2005, withdrawn 14,637 children from agricultural work, and 16,730 were prevented from entering the industry. Most of these children were either in school or had been given skills or grants to provide them with viable alternatives to hazardous work.

The ILO has also supported trade union action, particularly around the concept of child labor–free zones, under the slogan, "Make Your Farm a Child Labor–Free Zone." This campaign, promoting collective bargaining agreements and political statements, has been pioneered in Ghana, Malawi, South Africa, Uganda, and Zimbabwe, and has been built around developing trade union capacity to raise awareness of the issue. This has been paralleled at the national and international level by sector agreements in bananas, cocoa, coffee, cut flowers, and tobacco, following consumer pressure in developed countries for fair trade. This pressure has taken the form of a call for common codes and labeling schemes for certain products, as with bananas, coffee, and cocoa. In the case of tobacco, the response by the industry was to set up a foundation in 2002 sponsored by all the major industry stakeholders. The Foundation on the Elimination of Child Labor in Tobacco Growing develops independent research on conditions and levels of child labor and supports local projects and shares best practices and lessons learned. The foundation has developed projects in Malawi, the Philippines, Tanzania, and Uganda.

Starting in 2004–2005, employers' organizations in agriculture have also been active in supporting child labor surveys, for example, in Azerbaijan and Mali (cotton), Ethiopia (coffee and tea), Ghana (palm oil and rubber), Malawi (tea), Moldova (horticulture), Uganda (coffee), and Zimbabwe (tea). These fact-finding activities have been complemented with public awareness raising and political lobbying.

One of the great challenges facing the international movement against child labor is to find ways to overcome the widely perceived special status of agriculture and to penetrate its closed world. Indeed, it is these special factors, particularly the vast number of children working in the industry, many under hazardous conditions, that should make it a priority for action. The target of eliminating all worst forms of child labor by 2016 cannot be achieved without making the work of children in agriculture a central part of this campaign.

References and Further Reading

Human Rights Watch. *Tainted Harvest: Child Labor and Obstacles to Organizing on Ecuador's Banana Plantations.* New York: HRW, 2002.

Hurst, Peter. "Health and Child Labor in Agriculture." *Food and Nutrition Bulletin* 28:2 (June 2007): 364–71.

ILO. *Bitter Harvest: Child Labour in Agriculture.* Geneva: ILO, 2002.

ILO. *The End of Child Labour: Within Reach.* Geneva: ILO, 2006.

ILO. *Tackling Hazardous Child Labour in Agriculture: Guidance on Policy and Practice.* Geneva: ILO, 2006.

ILO. *Training Resource Pack on the Elimination of Hazardous Child Labour in Agriculture.* Geneva: ILO, 2006.

ILO. International Agricultural Partnership. *Harvest for the Future: Agriculture Without Child Labour.* World Day Against Child Labour, June 12, 2007.

Worst Forms of Child Labor: Child Domestic Labor

Jonathan Blagbrough, Forced Labour Programme Coordinator, Anti-Slavery International

Child domestic workers are persons under eighteen years of age who work in other people's households, doing domestic chores, caring for children, running errands, and helping their employers run their small businesses. Included in this group are children who "live in" and those who live separately from their employers, and children who are paid for their work as well as those who are not paid or receive in-kind benefits, such as food and shelter.

Children as young as seven years old are routinely pressed into domestic service. Although some children enter domestic labor in the hope of continuing their schooling, most are deprived of opportunities for education and are working in conditions that can be considered among the worst forms of child labor. Worldwide, the majority of child domestic workers are girls, and many have been trafficked, or are in debt bondage. Child domestic workers are isolated from their families and from opportunities to make friends—and are under the total control of employers whose primary concern is often not in their best interests as children.

Child domestic workers are large in numbers, yet they remain invisible and marginalized both economically and socially because of the myths that still surround their employment. While it is conventional to regard domestic work as a "safe" form of employment, in reality a wide range of abuses—including physical, verbal, and sexual violence—routinely accompanies this type of work.

The International Labor Organization (ILO) estimates that more girls under the age of sixteen are in domestic service than in any other category of work. Recent statistics from a number of countries show the numbers to be in the millions worldwide (ILO 2004). In addition, significant numbers of prepubescent and older boys are also engaged as domestic workers in many countries.

How and Why Do Children Become Domestic Workers?

Children become domestic workers primarily due to poverty, but also because the practice is seen as normal and, indeed, beneficial for girls who will one day become wives and mothers. Powerful and enduring myths surround the practice, which encourage it to continue. Parents believe, for example, that a daughter working for a wealthier family might bring opportunities for her and her family. It is also widely accepted that domestic work is less arduous than other kinds of labor and that work in the home offers a protective environment for girls and young children. Employers of child domestic workers, far from seeing themselves as exploiters, often consider that they are helping the child and her family by taking her in. In many cases employers believe that they are treating these children as "part of the family." Girls themselves also enter domestic service of their own volition, as this might be the only way that they have a chance of continuing their education.

In interviews with 450 current and former child domestic workers conducted by Anti-Slavery International and its partners in 2004, child domestic workers spoke of the many ways in which they were pushed and pulled into domestic service. The need to sustain themselves and their families due to poverty was commonly why children began in domestic service. In India, a number of children worked to repay loans. In Peru and the Philippines older children spoke of their decision to seek work in the city in order to pursue their education. A quarter of participants in Tanzania recounted that they were forced into domestic work, as family members had died due to HIV/AIDS and they had no reliable relatives to take care of them.

Often family problems were the catalyst for children to begin work. Family breakups and physical and sexual abuse in the children's own families were common causes, as were issues such as alcoholism. In India, several children cited alcoholic fathers as the reason they had left home to work in domestic service.

Children were also pulled into domestic service by siblings and friends already working as domestics, and because of employers' demands for younger workers. In Nepal children said that it was hard to continue working as a domestic worker above the legal minimum working age of fourteen, as employers had told them that older children are more trouble and are able to bargain for higher salaries and other rights.

Violence Against Child Domestic Workers

Concern about violence toward child domestic workers stems, not only from the work they do, but also from the situation they live and work in. Working away from home, often with very limited opportunities for family contact, the child is under the complete control of his or her employer. Child domestic workers in these situations routinely suffer a loss of freedom, identity, and self-esteem, and denial of schooling. Their isolated situation, coupled with their ambiguous role in the employers' household, makes them particularly vulnerable to physical, verbal, and sexual abuse. If and when violence does occur, their dependency on their employers for basic needs and their acceptance of the violence as an occupational hazard make them far less likely to report it.

There are broad similarities across regions with regard to the incidence and range of violence against child domestic workers, although differences exist in local manifestations of violence. For example, in some countries research has indicated that girls tend to suffer more from verbal abuse and boys more from physical violence. Verbal violence takes the form of name calling, insults, threats, obscene language, shouting, and screaming. Types of physical violence include beating, kicking, whipping, pinching, scalding, overwork, and denial of food. Sexual violence against child domestic workers is also widespread, including use of sexually explicit language, harassment, and rape.

Sexual abuse of child domestic workers is relatively common due to the children's vulnerability and isolation in the homes of their employers. For example, in Haiti, girl domestics are sometimes called *"la pou sa,"* a Creole term meaning "there for that." In other words, they are accepted sexual outlets for the men or boys of the household (National Coalition for Haitian Rights 2002).

In cases where girls become pregnant, they are often thrown out of the house and are forced to fend for themselves on the streets, since the shame of their situation makes it difficult for them to return home. Many families reject these "spoiled girls" because their behavior has brought dishonor to the family. In these instances, domestic work typically becomes a precursor for prostitution, as the girls and young women have few options available (Black and Blagbrough 1999). In Bangladesh, for example, an NGO interviewing children working in commercial sexual exploitation in Dhaka found that all of them had previously worked as child domestic workers and had been sexually abused by members of their employing family. Sexual abuse combined with working in conditions of servitude and the shame of their situation eventually forced them into a life of commercial sex work.

Traffickers of children into the sex trade routinely deceive children and their families about what will happen to them by promising them attractive jobs as domestic workers. In the Philippines, most of the children and young women trafficked to Manila from rural areas are assured jobs as domestic workers, but a significant number of them end up in the sex trade (Flores-Oebanda et al. 2001). In West Africa, where children are trafficked across borders to work as domestics, girls who are discarded or abused by employing families, and who have no means of returning home, often have little choice but to turn to prostitution as a means of survival in a foreign country.

Consequences for Child Domestic Workers

Aside from violence, child domestic workers are exposed to a variety of other household dangers. Hazardous household chemicals (such as cleaning fluids), kitchen knives, irons, boiling water, and unfamiliar household appliances have caused many child domestic workers serious injuries and even death—especially among younger children and those already exhausted from a full day's work. There are also likely to be long-term health impacts from chronic sleep deprivation and being "on call" twenty-four hours a day, as well as effects resulting from heavy tasks such as water collecting.

Concern about the impact of domestic work on children has tended to focus more on physical health than psychosocial well-being. However, when it comes to child domestic labor, understanding the psychosocial effects of child domestic work is vital to forming a comprehensive picture of their condition. In Kenya, one of the few field studies that specifically looked at the psychological impact found that child domestic workers experienced significantly more psychological problems than other children (both working and nonworking). Bed-wetting, insomnia, nightmares, frequent headaches, withdrawal, regressive behavior, premature aging, depression, and phobic reactions to their employers were found to be common (Bwibo and Onyango 1987).

In Indonesia, interviews with child domestic workers who have been working for a long time, or who began work at a young age, indicate that their self-esteem has been largely eroded. When asked about their future plans, many child domestic workers, unlike most other child workers, are unable to consider that they could do anything other than to continue life in domestic service (Blagbrough 1995).

The labels used to describe child domestic workers are important components in reinforcing their low self-esteem. In Haiti the term to describe child domestic workers, "*restavèks*" ("stay withs") has come to mean someone who is motherless or unwanted, and is often used as an insult to describe someone without a personality or a life of their own. Some employers routinely change the given name of child domestic workers, such as in Nepal. In the Philippines "*katulong*"—a term commonly used to describe domestic workers—has a derogatory connotation akin to "servant."

Why Are Child Domestic Workers So Abused and Exploited?

A number of factors conspire to make a child domestic worker particularly vulnerable to abuse and exploitation, and these relate mainly to the inequality of the relationship that the child has with members of the employing household. The worker is, after all, only a child, and, in most cases, a girl child at that. She is probably far from home. She is likely to be from a family of lower social class with fewer economic resources than the employing family. She may be of a different ethnic origin (one that is considered of lower status). She has likely been trafficked and will be in unfamiliar surroundings, without people she knows. In cases of cross-border trafficking, her illegal status puts her at even greater disadvantage.

Child domestic workers have reported that the daily experience of discrimination and their isolation in the employer's household are the most difficult part of their burden. Even if their relationship with members of the household is good, these relationships are not on equal terms. Their capacity to resist sexual advances or negotiate fair treatment is very limited, emotionally as well as practically, and there is little chance of their expressing desires and opinions with any expectation that they will be respected (Black and Blagbrough 1999).

Control is completely handed over to the employer because of the worker's live-in status, which is one of the reasons why child domestic labor can legitimately be considered a modern form of slavery. The child domestic worker has limited freedom of movement. She lives in her employer's house and is subject to the employer's rules. She is dependent upon her employer for her well-being and basic necessities. Commonly, child domestic workers are told not to leave the house by their employers, who frighten them with stories of what they will face on the outside. She may not have the resources to leave (even if she is paid, she may not handle her wages or have enough money to escape). While most employers do not take on child domestic workers with the express intention of committing violence, research from a number of regions indicates that employers take on child domestic workers because they perceive them to be more submissive and easier to control.

As parental substitutes, employers may feel at liberty to physically punish the child—especially as the interaction is in the private sphere. In societies where physical punishment of children is normal and acceptable, employers, as guardians, see themselves as having every right to hit or beat those children in their care. The ambiguity of the relationship of the child domestic worker to the employing family puts her in a legal vacuum. The child works but is not considered a worker. She lives with the family but is not considered a family member.

Attitudes of child domestic workers themselves with regard to violence are also important to consider. The child may expect or accept violence for various reasons: She may come from an abusive background herself; she is likely to feel a strong sense of duty to her parents to make the situation work out; she may see violence as an occupational hazard and accept it up to a certain point; she may see no alternatives to her situation; or she may simply be scared of the consequences of speaking up (Blagbrough 2003).

Conclusion

Child domestic workers are a uniquely vulnerable and violated group of child workers. While this group is large in numbers, their situation is easy to ignore because it is so widely accepted and because their exploitation takes place behind closed doors. A fundamental shift in attitude is needed if progress is to be made to protect children from exploitation of this kind. However, the social pressure and persuasion needed to effect such a social transformation is possible and is already well under way in many countries.

While international legal standards draw attention to child domestic labor, local regulation and enforcement often remain weak because the work takes place in the privacy of the employers' homes. While legislation by itself will not curb the practice, its existence is important—not only in terms of setting out minimum standards of protection, but also because it makes it easier to bring the issue out into the open.

It is easy to demonize employers of child domestic workers, but child domestic workers themselves tell us that the most effective form of protection for those who continue to work is to enlist the employers' cooperation. The practical result of alienating employers is that child domestic workers become harder to reach, and we are thereby less able to protect them.

Child workers themselves need to be involved as agents for change. Providing a platform from which children can articulate and express their views about their experiences is crucial to their personal development and their ability to "move on" and is one of the most effective forms of advocacy. Enabling older children to influence and operate services such as outreach and self-help organizations better ensures that the needs of child domestic workers will be met.

References and Further Reading

Black, Maggie. *Child Domestic Workers: A Handbook for Research and Action.* London: Anti-Slavery International, 1997.

Black, Maggie. *Child Domestic Workers—Finding a Voice: A Handbook on Advocacy.* London: Anti-Slavery International, 2002.

Black, Maggie. *Child Domestic Workers: A Handbook on Good Practice in Programme Interventions.* London: Anti-Slavery International, 2005.

Black, Maggie, and Jonathan Blagbrough. "Child Domestic Work." *Innocenti Digest* 5, UNICEF International Child Development Centre, Florence, 1999.

Blagbrough, Jonathan. *Child Domestic Work in Indonesia.* London: Anti-Slavery International, 1995.

Blagbrough, Jonathan. *Violence Against Child Domestic Workers.* Anti-Slavery International paper presented at Save the Children workshop, Thailand, September 2003.

Blanchet, T. *Lost Innocence, Stolen Childhoods.* Dhaka: University Press Limited, Save the Children Sweden, 1996.

Bwibo, N.O., and Philista Onyango. *Final Report of the Child Labour and Health Research.* Nairobi: University of Nairobi, 1987.

Flores-Oebanda, Cecilia, Roland Pacis, and Virgilio Montaño. *The Kasambahay—Child Domestic Work in the Philippines: A Living Experience.* Manila: ILO and Visayan Forum Foundation, 2001.

International Labor Organization. *Helping Hands or Shackled Lives? Understanding Child Domestic Labour and Responses to It.* Geneva: ILO, 2004.

National Coalition for Haitian Rights (NCHR). *Restavèk No More: Eliminating Child Slavery in Haiti.* New York: NCHR, 2002.

Worst Forms of Child Labor: Street Children and Street Trades

David Maidment OBE, Co-Chair, Consortium for Street Children, Founder and Chairman, Railway Children, Children's Rights Advisor, Amnesty International UK

Churchgate Railway Station, Mumbai. The six year old girl sits, lashing her back with a home-made whip. This is her street trade. Gullible tourists give generously, perhaps not realizing their donations will go, not to the young girl who has provoked their sympathy, but to the unscrupulous adult who is running her.

There are no "typical" street children. Numbers are notoriously difficult to assess—anything up to 120 million has been estimated by UNICEF. Children are found on the streets of developed and developing countries, many driven by events in their lives that cause them to see street life as preferable to other options. About 85 percent of street children are boys, but increasing numbers of girls are coming to the streets, often escaping abuse encountered when working as domestic servants. In a few countries a high percentage are girls. Most children first come onto the streets around the age of ten to twelve, but in certain countries, especially India, and those African countries ravaged by HIV/AIDS, it is not uncommon to find children as young as four or five, and seven- and eight-year-olds are typical.

In 1993, the Consortium for Street Children (CSC) undertook a simple risk assessment of being a street child. A "fault tree" identified root causes—being sent to the city to earn money for the family, then becoming detached from family contact; running away from physical or sexual abuse; being abandoned, neglected, or orphaned. These stem from family stresses and breakdowns, which are the consequences of extreme poverty, natural catastrophes, urban migration, civil conflicts, economic collapse, and HIV/AIDS. A simple "event tree" identified the immediate needs of a child thrust into the confusing and dangerous world of an unknown city—the need for food or money to buy food, the need for shelter, and the need for affection and the company of others—and the consequences to children in meeting these needs. A child's response is to survive, one day at a time.

Street-Living Children (Children of the Street)

Nongovernmental organization (NGO) members of the CSC estimate that 5 to 10 percent of street children in most cities are abandoned, orphaned, or runaway children with little or no contact with their families. For them, "family" consists of other street children loosely formed in gangs or small groups that often demonstrate considerable loyalty to their members. These children sleep where they can—in shop doorways, in covered bus and railway stations, under market stalls, in parks, and on beaches. Unless such children can find an NGO to provide food and shelter, they are dependent on their own efforts or those of other street children in their "family" to find food.

Such children gather where the possibility of casual labor exists. They seek out adults who can provide them with some activity in return for food and possibly some protection. Such activities include running errands; assisting at street vending; scavenging for refuse that can be sorted and recycled; or collecting empty water bottles, and then refilling and selling them. Many of these activities are dangerous, especially for younger children. They are exposed to road accident risks, darting into traffic to ply their trade. Indian street children cluster around railway stations, jumping on and off moving trains. They acquire seats for passengers, carry luggage and clean train compartments, and scavenge on the railway tracks, and many children are injured, some fatally. In a twelve-month period, one Indian NGO in Andhra Pradesh provided hospital and medical expenses for forty-eight of the 800 children it serves who were injured in road and rail accidents. A further risk is that children become dependent on adults for whom they operate. While some are sympathetic and protective, many adults exploit the children treating them as cheap and expendable labor, often reacting with violence if the children incur their temporary displeasure. Others—including older street youths who lead the gangs—may sexually abuse the younger children as the price for their protection—survival sex.

Children unable to earn money may resort to scavenging for leftover food in trains and trash cans, around restaurants, and in marketplaces. Children unable to work at all may resort to begging or become totally dependent on an exploitative adult or group of older children. In extreme cases, children get involved in illegal activities in order to survive. They may start by stealing trivial bits of food or money for food. They may get involved with a gang that forces them to steal more systematically, or get involved running errands for drug dealers, or, as a last resort, get involved in commercial sex activities. Interviews with 1,000 street children by a Mumbai NGO in 1993 found that the children identified a hierarchy of activities ranked by desirability, and they would resort to begging, stealing, drug-related activities, and sex selling—in that order—only if they could survive no other way.

These children, without some protective structure, are at constant risk of losing whatever cash or food they have managed to acquire. When children have money left over after meeting their immediate needs, they will frequently spend it on cheap entertainment or gamble it away. A nine-year-old in Ahmedabad Station in India, when asked how he stopped older boys from stealing his money, said, "I buy food and eat it straight away—they can't steal it from my belly." Children who have acquired money through illicit or informal trading activities often find they have to pay protection money, or provide sex in lieu of cash, to police or criminal gangs who would otherwise arrest them or beat them up.

Street-Working Children (Children on the Street)

The majority of street children spend their day on the street but return to their families at night. These include the children of street-living families, children who commute to city centers from the suburban slums, and the largest group, children from the city shantytowns and slums who remain in their neighborhoods and spend the day assisting their families to augment their income, often dropping out of school as a result.

Children of street-living families and slum children are heavily involved in activities such as scavenging for refuse that can be sold for recycling. Ragpicking is a variation of this activity that occupies many young children. The environment in which this activity takes place is particularly dangerous for children—the filth and open sewers, plus the dangers from infected items, expose these children to both chronic and acute diseases. Where no family breadwinner exists, or the adults are unemployed or sick, children are removed from schools to provide income for families. Children are employed in small factories, tea stalls, or petty vending activities, often for excessively long hours and for a pittance. These children, too, are frequently abused both sexually and physically as a result of failure to meet the performance required by their taskmasters. Children living on the street often cite a beating by someone for whom they worked, or from a father or stepfather, as the catalyst for their leaving home.

Children on the street are rarely supervised and are vulnerable to pressures detrimental to their health and morals. Seen as a nuisance by much of society, they have low self-worth, and they can be easy prey for unscrupulous adults who exploit or criminalize them. The children, or their parents, can be easily tricked into allowing them (or even selling them) into the commercial sex trade, or to be trafficked to other cities. They may be promised jobs in hotels, restaurants, bars, or private domestic work, only to learn, too late, that the promised job does not exist.

Children and youths who commute into city centers from slum suburbs undertake a wide variety of jobs—shoe shining, vending activities, collecting and reselling bottles and recyclable materials, windscreen washing, cleaning, and hotel and restaurant casual labor. Sometimes older children, adult criminals, or gang leaders organize territories for trading. In addition to regulating the activities of the children, they also carefully regulate their territories to prevent encroachment and competition from other children. Some children can earn sufficient income to spend on entertainment in addition to necessities, but they are operating at the margins of legality and under constant threat from adult operators and the police. In a situational analysis undertaken by the Railway Children NGO at the New Delhi railway station, where earning potential is unusually high, some children were found to be earning an average of Rs180 to Rs250 a day, more than many of the voluntary-sector workers seeking to help them. However, the children complained bitterly of police and gangster violence and the lack of facilities to help them escape from drug and alcohol addiction.

Consequences

Because the public's perception of street children is negative—they are seen as dirty, delinquent, at best a nuisance, at worst a danger, especially when in gangs—the children are at risk of abuse by those in authority who should be protecting them. Children are often rounded up by the police under laws against vagrancy or loitering. They are arrested on suspicion of committing petty crimes. Those children who are thought to have cash are susceptible to protection rackets from adult criminals, street gang leaders, and corrupt police, with threats of violence if they resist. Therefore, these children have little opportunity to save money, to find ways of bettering themselves, and to develop legitimate ways of getting themselves off the street. The risks the children take to earn any money, driven by their need to survive, and the environment in which they operate, means that many suffer injury and disease. As most street children have suffered rejection or abuse from their families and suffer further rejection from society, many form poor opinions of their own self-worth, which can make the temptation of criminal activities difficult to resist. When one considers all of the articles contained in the UN Convention on the Rights of the Child, street children are likely to have suffered violations of up to half of them.

Yet many street children survive these abuses. It is often the strongest children, physically and mentally, who decide to opt for the streets to avoid worse fates. There they learn to fend for themselves—they become resilient or they do not survive. They bond with others and develop loyalties and friendships. Many children demonstrate great potential, and there are many examples of street children who have shown academic or sporting prowess when their potential has been recognized and encouraged. These children develop, of necessity, powers of problem solving, and many become entrepreneurs in their own way, although too often on the margins of legality. At risk is their capacity to gain formal employment (after losing out on schooling) and to parent successfully (after insufficient or unhappy family experiences).

Conclusion

If neglect, rejection, and abuse persist, the experiences of children of the street and on the street can lead to extremes of antisocial behavior and negative consequences for society, such as the youth gang culture in parts of Central and South America, South Africa, and Eastern Europe, not to mention the costs of youth and adult penal systems everywhere. Society also suffers the loss of the contribution of these children as productive adults and the risk that they in turn will produce the next generation of street children.

Some international and national NGOs are working to support street children by offering educational and vocational training as well as welfare and health support systems, although the scale and complexities of the phenomenon are so great that comprehensive and thoughtfully targeted programs underpinned by governments are necessary to make wider use of the best practices developed by these NGOs. NGOs need to identify and support runaways and abandoned children early, before exploitation, abuse, and corruption seriously affect them. Family reintegration through child and family counseling at an early stage is important for many children who have become separated. Street girls face particular problems, which need to be explicitly researched and addressed. Governments need to support poor communities in a holistic way—adequate housing, health care, and income generation—as a preventative measure.

Banning all child labor could, in the short term, have a detrimental effect on street children, as alternative survival strategies may be far worse—begging, crime, sex selling. Older street children need emotional support in caring environments and training to enable their entrepreneurial skills to flourish in legitimate areas. They need encouragement to plan for their lives and opportunities to save their earned money safely through initiatives such as the children's bank movement. Police should be sensitized to the circumstances and rights of these children and trained to protect them, working in conjunction with NGOs. A priority for these children is the banning of activities that are most harmful and exploitative for children—and the vigorous implementation of such bans—and the protection of the children from those who force them to work excessive hours, deny their rights, or steal their meager earnings.

Notes

I wish to thank members past and present of the Consortium for Street Children (CSC), a UK-based umbrella organization consisting of forty-two NGOs supporting street children internationally, for sharing their experience and their suggestions. In particular, I put on record the contribution of Christian Harris, manager of CSC's International Resource Centre.

For further information on street children, please see the Consortium for Street Children Web site, http://www.streetchildren.org.uk.

References and Further Reading

Austin, S. "Child Labour and Child Participation: A Girl Child Perspective." *Child Workers in Asia* 16:2 (2000), 26–28. http://www.streetchildren.org.uk/reports/CWA%20Newsletter-Girl%20Child%20Workers.doc.

Barker, Gary, and Felicia Knaul. *Urban Girls: Empowerment in Especially Difficult Circumstances.* London: Intermediate Technology Publications and CSC, 1999.

Bhat, R., H. Joshi, and L. Visaria. *Children Without Childhood.* Ahmedabad: Ahmedabad Study Action Group, 2006. http://www.streetchildren.org.uk/reports/children%20without%20childhood%20(final).pdf.

Consortium for Street Children. *Child Labour in the Informal Urban Sector: From Individual Working Children to a National Plan.* London: CSC and Anti-Slavery International, 1999. http://www.streetchildren.org.uk/reports/CSC.ASI%20Child%20Labour%20Report.doc.

Frederick, J., and A. Tamang. "Asylums of Exploitation: Internally Displaced Children in the Worst Forms of Child Labour Due to the Armed Conflict in Nepal." Lausanne, Switzerland: Terre des Hommes Foundation, 2006, 50–52. http://www.streetchildren.org.uk/reports/tdh_f_sca06_asylums_of_exploitation[1].pdf.

Frew, K. "Vocational Training and Employment for Street Children." Ho Chi Minh City, Vietnam: Education for Development, 2003. http://www.streetchildren.org.uk/reports/Vocational%20Training%20and%20Employment%20for%20Street%20Children.pdf.

Gustafsson-Wright, E., and H. Pyne. "Gender Dimensions of Child Labor and Street Children in Brazil." World Bank Policy Research Paper 2897, Washington DC, October 2002.

UNICEF. "A Study on the Interface Between Orphanhood, Street Children and Child Labour in Namibia: Final Report." Windhoek, Namibia: UNICEF/Ministry of Women Affairs and Child Welfare, 2004.

Worst Forms of Child Labor: Commercial Sexual Exploitation of Children

Carmen Madrinan, Executive Director, ECPAT International

Commercial sexual exploitation of children is such an extreme violation and grave abuse of power exerted over a child that it should be considered a crime against humanity. These crimes are manifest in the form of child prostitution, child sex tourism, child pornography, and trafficking in children for sexual purposes. They may also include marriages where remuneration for access to children as sexual partners is involved. In all its forms, commercial sexual exploitation of children is a manifestation of power, greed, and inhumanity that represents an abdication of principles that recognize the inherent dignity of each human being.

The sexual exploitation of a child for profit, whether in cash or other form of consideration, embodies a planned and organized effort, whether on a small scale involving a few individuals, or on a large scale involving many people working in succession. Networks may operate locally or across national and international borders to profit from the demand for sex with children by abusers that may be within the child's own environment or located in distant places. In most instances, commercial sexual exploitation of children requires linkages among various persons involved as intermediaries in a process of entrapment and facilitation: local scouts, outside recruiting agents, drivers and transporters, innkeepers, complicit clerks, and others such as brothel owners and pimps. Often entrapment is facilitated by agents from the child's own local environment: neighbors, relatives, caretakers or other authorities, taxi drivers, or police. Each person plays a distinct role in the sequence that will result in the exploitation of the child: to deceive, lure, coerce, transport, falsify, negotiate, and provide the child to an adult for sex in exchange for cash, in-kind favor, or other form of consideration.

A child is defined by the UN Convention on the Rights of the Child (CRC) as any individual under the age of eighteen years. But the lack of common adherence to this definition in the legal and regulatory frameworks of many nations creates a gap that compromises the protection of children. Variances in legal definitions provide the space for people with a sexual interest in children to rationalize exploitation on the grounds that a child's entry to adulthood is determined relative to different social or cultural factors, as well as differences in the onset of physical maturity, usually associated with puberty. Research conducted by ECPAT International (End Child Prostitution, Child Pornography, and Trafficking of Children for Sexual Purposes) (2005a) and ILO-IPEC (2006) on dimensions of demand for sex with children demonstrate that such concepts insidiously shape the perceptions of exploiters and others in society, including children and adolescents. They create confusion and contradictions in how people conceptualize children's rights and their need for protection, which can result in tacit acceptance and tolerance of the presence of children in commercial sex, even though legislation may exist to criminalize such practices.

Demand for sex with children underpins and fuels a chain of crime and profit that ensures its perpetuation. Although it is difficult to quantify the number of sexually exploited children due to the clandestine nature of these crimes, ILO (2002) estimated that there are some 1.2 million children trafficked worldwide every year. While not all children are trafficked for commercial sex, many are (ECPAT 2004). In practice these crimes occur in specific areas of specific towns and cities, and within specific pockets of the population. Generally, those who facilitate sexual access to children have learned to identify and exploit the needs and vulnerabilities of children and families affected by social disintegration, insecurity and exclusion, limited livelihood opportunities, gender and ethnic discrimination, abuse and violence, displacement, social and political instability, and conflict. They know how to use legal loopholes and social gaps in the protection of children to act with impunity and to organize and profit from the sexual exploitation of children.

Prostitution of Children

The prostitution of children is one manifestation of the use of a child in sexual activities for remuneration or other consideration. Most often, it means an exploiter intermediary (pimp) who controls or oversees the child's activities and benefits from commercial transactions in which the child is made available for sexual purposes. Alternatively, abusers may negotiate an exchange directly with children for their own personal sexual benefit. The provision of children for sexual purposes may also be a medium of exchange between adults.

The prostitution of children is often organized in environments such as brothels, bars, clubs, and hotels, but it also takes place in private residences and on the street. It can involve individuals or groups working on a small scale or in large criminal networks. Children can be entrapped in prostitution as they seek to meet needs such as food, shelter, clothing, or drug dependency, or in exchange for physical or social safety on or off the street. They may also be prostituted in exchange for higher school grades, extra pocket money, or goods and favors otherwise out of their reach, for example, in tourist destinations where they may be groomed for exploitation with offers of gifts. In all cases, children exploited in prostitution are entrapped by complex social circumstances that render them vulnerable to agents who recognize and exploit these vulnerabilities. Prior violence or sexual abuse suffered in their immediate environment is a common example of circumstances that can lead to the prostitution of children.

Misunderstandings surrounding the term "child prostitution" have led to use of the term "commercial sexual exploitation of children," as the latter is a more encompassing description of the full range of commercial sexual violations perpetrated against children. Nevertheless, "child prostitution" remains in common usage even though "child prostitution" and "child prostitute" carry problematic connotations that can result in blaming the victims of these crimes. These constructions fail to make it clear that children cannot be expected to make an informed choice to prostitute themselves, as the act of prostituting the child, in every instance, is in fact carried out by another party.

Although international law clearly establishes that the element of choice does not apply to any form of adult sexual act with a child, references to "child prostitutes," particularly in the case of adolescent children, often carry negative connotations that negate the child's experience of force, exploitation, and physical and psychological harm inflicted through their entrapment in prostitution. In addition, public understanding of "prostitution" and "prostitute" worldwide has been shifting as a result of the introduction of the term "sex worker," intended to raise the perceived status and protection of the rights of adult women in prostitution. However, in relation to children, reference to "sex work" is wholly misleading and harmful, as it downplays the criminal exploitation of the child and can suggest that the child has somehow made a choice to follow a "profession" in "sex work." This is a rationale that exploiters often employ. In light of these concerns, any reference to "child prostitution" must provide an understanding that children are induced, tricked, and entrapped by vulnerabilities that others exploit to prostitute them.

Child Pornography

Article 34 of the UN CRC commits signatories to act to prevent "the exploitative use of children in pornographic performances and materials." A broader general definition of child pornography is provided in the CRC's Optional Protocol on the Sale of Children, Child Prostitution and Child Pornography (2000), which states that child pornography means any representation, by whatever means, of a child engaged in real or simulated explicit sexual activities, or any representation of the sexual parts of a child for primarily sexual purposes. The Council of Europe's Convention on

Cybercrime (2001) has added a more comprehensive definition, which also encompasses computer-generated images, relevant in the context of new technologies of the information society.

Essentially, pornographic depictions portray a child or children in a manner that is intended to aid sexual arousal and gratification. They may depict a child engaged in real or simulated explicit sexual activities, or lewdly depict parts of a child's body. Other pornographic images may not be sexually explicit but involve naked and sexualized images of children. Child pornography also includes the use of various media that allow for artificially created child pornography imagery, usually referred to as "pseudo–child pornography." This includes digitally created images and blended or "morphed" images of children. The term "pseudo" in this sense should be used warily because its synonymic link to "false" may downplay the exploitative significance of such imagery and normalize images of child sexual abuse under the pretext of it not being "real." Moreover, the use of "pseudo" can obfuscate the intent of such images, which is sexual arousal that can incite sexual exploitation of children (ECPAT 2005c). Reference to these kinds of composite, morphed, or digitally created images in the Convention on Cybercrime has strengthened the framework for protection of children.

Child pornography exploits children in many different ways. First, children who are physically forced, coerced, or tricked into making these images are directly sexually abused and exploited. Pornographic images of children are often copied multiple times and may remain in circulation for many years; thus, the victim continues to be subjected to humiliation long after the image has been made. Second, consumers who possess pornographic depictions of children, even though they may not directly participate in the abuse of the child depicted, use the images for their sexual gratification. These people are not necessarily pedophiles or preferential abusers; nevertheless, their demand and consumption of child pornography maintains the incentive to produce such material, thus furthering the abuse and exploitation of yet more children. Third, there is evidence that the use of child pornography does incite some people to sexually abuse other children. While previous studies have suggested that 30–40 percent of child pornography consumers have also sexually molested children, an unpublished U.S. government study of convicted Internet offenders found that 85 percent said they had committed acts of sexual abuse against minors (Sher and Carey 2007). Finally, it is common for child sexual abusers and exploiters to use pornographic materials to lower a child's inhibitions to entice or coerce them into engaging in inappropriate sexual behavior. The makers of child pornography also commonly use their products to intimidate and blackmail children used in making such material.

Distribution of child pornography via the Internet, whether for commercial gain or for sharing among people with a sexual interest in children, is growing rapidly as more child sex abusers are viewing, trading, downloading, and keeping online child pornography. In 2006, the UK's Internet Watch Foundation (IWF) confirmed 10,656 URLs as containing child sexual abuse content; 3,077 separate domains, just over half of which were commercial Web sites, accounted for these URLs; and 82.5 percent of the domains were hosted by servers in the United States and Russia (54.3 percent in the United States and 28.2 percent in Russia). Since 2003, the IWF has noted a trend in increasing severity of the abuse depicted in online images, and estimates that 80 percent of the victims are girls and 91 percent of the victims appear to be under twelve years of age (IWF 2006).

Child victims of the abuse depicted in child pornography live with the reality that their images will circulate on the Internet in perpetuity. In addition to the physical and psychological trauma, this form of sexual exploitation can cause depression, post-traumatic stress disorder, and unending fear of discovery and disclosure that in some cases has led to suicide (ECPAT 2005d). There is growing consensus that the term "child pornography" undermines the seriousness of the abuse and the nature and impact of these offenses. Thus, these sexual depictions of children are now more commonly referred to as "child abuse images."

Child Trafficking for Sexual Purposes

People can become victims of human trafficking when, seeking better alternatives to personal life situations, they are deceived or tricked with promises of work or other opportunities that are false and intended to entrap them in exploitative situations where they can be used by others for their benefit or profit.

The UN Protocol to Prevent, Suppress and Punish Trafficking in Persons, adopted in 2000, defines trafficking in children as "[t]he recruitment, transportation, transfer, harboring or receipt of a child for the purpose of exploitation," whether or not coercion, fraud, deception, or the giving or receiving of payments is involved; and the consent of the child is irrelevant.

Children are vulnerable to trafficking for many of the same reasons as adults. They may wish to escape social situations that provide them with few opportunities, or they may seek to fulfill social or educational aspirations out of reach in their own context, or they may want to escape abuse and violence. Children's relative lack of experience in assessing risks and consequences make them more susceptible to entrapment by exploiters. Children are recruited through various means, such as false promises of work in hotels or homes, or in the modeling and entertainment sectors. Once children are involved, the mechanisms by which they are kept in the control of traffickers for sexual and other forms of exploitation can include movement to another location within the same country or across country borders, placement in unfamiliar surroundings, social isolation, the use or threat of violence to the child or family members, forced indebtedness, removal of identity documents, and falsification of the child's identity.

Children of all ages can become victims of trafficking. Younger children are often trafficked for adoption, begging, use in petty crime, or child labor, while adolescents are more often trafficked for sexual exploitation (ECPAT 2007b). About 80 percent of the victims of human trafficking, the majority of whom are women and young girls, are trafficked into prostitution. The remaining 20 percent, who are mostly men and boys, face forced labor. Human trafficking is estimated to have a market value of US$32 billion, of which US$10 billion is derived from the initial "sale" of individuals and the remainder made through their exploitation (UNODC 2006).

Interventions Addressing Commercial Sexual Exploitation of Children

The CRC is the key international treaty that provides special protection for children. It establishes measures that are to be taken to protect the fundamental rights of children and embodies the basic minimum standards for child protection. As with all human rights, the rights of children are universal, interdependent, and indivisible. The interrelationships among the different dimensions of children's lives are delineated in the articles of the CRC, defined in rights that children are guaranteed, all in equal measure. Thus, when articulating frameworks for intervention to protect children from sexual exploitation, government bodies must link these measures to broader initiatives that ensure application of other rights of children, such as the right to family support, the right to education, the right to community and state care, and the right to be heard and participate. Recognizing that all rights are interdependent implies that, while measures to protect children from sexual exploitation must be specific and targeted, these interventions must form part of the broader effort and duty to guarantee all the rights of children. Practically, this means that the protection of children from commercial sexual exploitation must be part of a coherent effort that contributes in an integrated way to address the different dimensions (economic, legal, social, familial) and conditions (education, health) of children's lives. Where any of these rights are compromised, this exacerbates vulnerability of children to commercial sexual exploitation.

Prevention

Children of socially and economically marginal communities are significantly affected by lack of access to education, health care, and protection. The proportion of children living in poverty has increased in the last decade in countries across the economic spectrum, reflecting greater globalization of economies, accompanied by increased disparity, and lower government spending on social benefits. This means that the basic standards of living required for children's physical, spiritual, moral, and social development are beyond the reach of a growing number of families.

Thus, preventive measures need to be considered and developed in light of the socioeconomic shifts that have eroded the safety nets that buffered vulnerable families. Diagnostic processes that examine the context and underlying factors that make specific families, communities, and children vulnerable to exploiters are essential to ensure well-targeted and well-integrated interventions. Also essential are analyses of the modus operandi and strategies employed by child sex exploiters to attract and entrap children in determined contexts. As the methods of entrapment often involve offers of specific forms of employment and proposals for quick social or economic advancement that are perceived as credible, these specificities must be well understood to enable the development of locally relevant and effective responses.

Prevention work with children is particularly important to open channels for their participation, to increase their understanding about their rights, and to provide them with practical tools to enhance their own protection. Children's socioeconomic status is largely determined by that of their families. Thus, socioeconomic problems or social exclusion may have profound effects on children, driving them to search for ways to better their future opportunities. But, as children, even older children, have few formal channels for socioeconomic improvement, they can be more accepting of informal avenues, where they can be ensnared into commercial sexual exploitation.

Prevention work thus needs to be realized at multiple levels. ECPAT groups, for example, work with local communities to assess the ways and means through which sexual exploitation of children is constructed in the local context. Such information is used to develop awareness campaigns and to undertake direct counteraction. Mapping high-risk areas and groups, and identifying the actors and institutions responsible for the protection of children, can help secure their involvement in control and counteraction against these crimes. The result of such efforts may be formation and training of community watchdog committees that work in collaboration with law enforcement and social services; establishment of local systems of support and assistance to vulnerable families and children; local measures for reporting, assistance, and response; or increased data collection and analysis at local levels.

Work among children can involve the creation of discussion forums where an atmosphere of trust and openness is developed to promote sharing and support. Information related to sexual health, including measures for protection against sexual exploitation, can be shared in such groupings. These forums emphasize self-protective strategies that reinforce the sense of determination and control children have over their bodies. Links can be established with relevant institutions that have responsibility to protect and support children. Identification of children in high-risk or exploitative situations is made through these processes, and relevant steps are taken to work with children, their families, and other relevant social actors.

At the institutional level, initiatives may include multidisciplinary training to promote coordination among statutory institutions and NGOs working with children to develop a shared understanding regarding the causes, nature, and impact on children of commercial sexual exploitation. Such efforts bring together legal and judiciary personnel, social workers, police, health professionals, and others, to form strong linkages for sharing for information, referral, and other rights-based responses (ECPAT 2007a).

Protection

The adoption of international human rights instruments has triggered advances in legislative reform, which have strengthened legal protection against commercial sexual exploitation of children. Many new laws have been enacted to typify and criminalize all forms of commercial sexual exploitation of children, to punish perpetrators, and to protect children throughout the legal process. The harmonization of national laws with international legal instruments provides an essential framework. Thus, significant effort has been directed by ECPAT and other child rights organizations to ensure that nations take the required steps to apply international instruments in national law as mandated by their adoption and ratification.

Despite progress, ECPAT's monitoring work demonstrates that there is still a wide gap between enactment of laws and implementation of the legal and social measures needed for effective enforcement (ECPAT 2007b). Variations in definitions and understandings of commercial sexual exploitation continue to leave legal gaps that work against effective protection of children. For example, in many countries, pornography laws still refer to definitions of obscenity that identify a wide range of different images, only some of which may be illegal and related to child pornography, thus limiting law enforcement. Similarly, in some countries it is assumed that there is no legal basis for police intervention once children have reached the legal age of consent, which may be below eighteen. Harmonization of the definition of a child within all jurisdictions is thus critical for effective child protection.

Even where specific laws have been enacted to protect children, enforcement remains weak due to lack of socialization of the law among the judiciary, the various levels of law enforcement, and the relevant state institutions responsible for their implementation. In this regard, there is also a need to strengthen measures for criminal investigation to effectively prosecute offenders and to prevent revictimization of children. Among other things, this requires special training on evidence gathering specific to the different forms of commercial sexual exploitation. For example, trafficking in children poses particular challenges to investigation as it is generally a multijurisdictional crime (ECPAT 2006). Failure to properly identify clues, preserve evidence, or adequately prepare a case often compromises prosecution. Another challenge to effective protection of children is the financial and political influence that criminals exert over law enforcement and other power brokers, often allowing exploiters to act with impunity. And finally, there are still many countries where child victims of commercial sexual exploitation are treated as criminals.

Care of Child Survivors of Commercial Sexual Exploitation

The extreme physical, psychological, and emotional trauma that commercial sexual exploitation inflicts on children can have devastating consequences that affect their capacity to live full and meaningful lives. This type of child victimization can create fear, denial, helplessness, shame, and sometimes indoctrinated accommodation of the abuse. These factors present unique challenges for those providing care and support for the recovery of child victims. Children can develop various defense mechanisms to cope with these damaging experiences that may find expression through self-injurious or self-indulgent behavior, anger, aggression, or mental blocks. Child victims may reject offers of help or assistance despite the harm they experience, for fear of disclosure or reprisals, or due to a concern for the loss of independence or the unknown consequences of entering systems that have repeatedly failed them (ECPAT 2005b).

Children who have been victims of commercial sexual exploitation may be identified through various means. For example, a child victim may come to the attention of health services when being treated for sexually transmitted diseases, sexual assault, or other physical abuse injuries. Social services may be in contact with a child who is abusing illegal substances; or a child may enter the legal system for charges of prostitution. Therefore, all institutions and entities responsible for the welfare of children need knowledge and skills to be able to assess signs of sexual victimization in order to respond in ways that will protect the children's best interests. Few countries throughout the world have developed targeted awareness and training programs to orient personnel working with children on procedures for identification, assessment, and response to cases of commercial sexual exploitation.

Wider adoption of children's rights principles, and orientation and training on their application, for all levels of personnel involved in care and protection of children is needed to ensure that children are not revictimized by insensitive and harmful questioning, misplacement into programs that lack the capacity to address the harms experienced in commercial sexual exploitation, or providing care ill-suited for children and young people who have suffered commercial forms of sexual victimization (UNICEF 2006). At minimum, there is a need to impart an understanding of quality care standards among those assisting the recovery of victims of commercial sexual exploitation. Moreover, as institutionalization of child victims should be avoided, efforts to reunite and reintegrate the child safely within the family and community should begin immediately, with orientation, ongoing guidance, and follow-up to support the restitution of the rights of the child and to ensure recovery and social reintegration in the family and community.

Note

For further information on commercial sexual exploitation of children, please see the ECPAT Web site, http://www.ecpat.net/EI/Main/Front/index.asp.

References and Further Reading

ECPAT. *Joint East West Research on Trafficking in Children for Sexual Purposes in Europe: The Sending Countries.* Amsterdam: ECPAT Europe Law Enforcement Group, 2004.

ECPAT. *Mercancía sexual: cómo hemos creado la demanda para la explotación sexual comercial de niños, niñas y adolescentes en el Perú.* Bangkok: ECPAT International, 2005a.

ECPAT. *Psychosocial Rehabilitation of Children Who Have Been Commercially Sexually Exploited.* Bangkok: ECPAT International, 2005b.

ECPAT. *Semantics or Substance: Towards a Shared Understanding of Terminology Referring to the Sexual Abuse and Exploitation of Children.* Subgroup Against the Sexual Exploitation of Children, NGO Group for the Convention on the Rights of the Child, 2005c. http://www.ecpat.net/EI/About_CSEC/resources/pdf.asp?lang_id=20.

ECPAT. *Violence Against Children in Cyberspace.* Bangkok: ECPAT International, 2005d.

ECPAT. *Combating the Trafficking in Children for Sexual Purposes: Questions and Answers.* Amsterdam: ECPAT Europe Law Enforcement Group, 2006.

ECPAT. *Action Programme Against Trafficking in Minors for Sexual Purposes.* Bangkok: ECPAT International, 2007a.

ECPAT. *Global Monitoring Report on the Status of Action Against Commercial Sexual Exploitation of Children.* Bangkok: ECPAT International, 2007b.

ILO. *A Future Without Child Labor.* Geneva: ILO, 2002.

ILO-IPEC. *La demanda en la explotación sexual comercial del adolescente: estudio cualitativo en Sudamérica.* Lima: ILO, 2006.

Internet Watch Foundation (IWF). *Annual and Charity Report 2006.* Cambridge: IWF, 2006.

Sher, Julian, and Benedict Carey. "Debate on Child Pornography's Link to Molesting." *New York Times,* July 19, 2007.

UNICEF. *Guidelines on the Protection of Child Victims of Trafficking.* New York: UNICEF, 2006.

United Nations Office on Drug and Crime (UNODC). *Trafficking in Persons: Global Patterns.* Vienna, Austria: UNODC, April 2006.

Worst Forms of Child Labor: Children and War

Zoë Marriage, Lecturer in Development Studies, School of Oriental and African Studies

Croesus, the Lydian king who appears in Herodotus's *Histories,* remarks that in peace sons bury their fathers but in war fathers bury their sons (Herodotus *Histories* 1.87). This maxim captures the inversion of norms that accompanies war, and the essence of transition, destruction, and the reallocation of roles.

Children have always been involved in war. Like adults, they experience wars in many ways: as targets, indirect victims, bystanders, witnesses, and perpetrators of violence. War brings children new vulnerabilities: when they are displaced or forcibly recruited, or through the death of family members or the destruction of physical, economic, or political infrastructure. Depending on their age, gender, cultural background, and personal characteristics, children respond differently to wars, often assuming new identities and functions. Alongside the increased vulnerabilities, war can sometimes offer new opportunities.

A child is defined in international law as being any person under the age of eighteen years. This codification brings with it the assumption of biological, emotional, or psychological immaturity, and can also imply a degree of legal irresponsibility and cognitive irrationality. Notwithstanding this definition, childhood is more comprehensively understood as being socially rather than biologically constructed, and as such the impact of violent experiences depends on a number of factors, including the capacities of the children and the social understanding of childhood and child rearing (Boyden and de Berry 2004).

The portrayal of children as innocent and essentially passive victims of war has contemporary currency but has not always been the dominant interpretation. The American Civil War was fought largely by young people, and death in battle was seen to ennoble, rather than waste, a short life. In Europe and the United States, a shift has taken place over the last century, from the depiction of child combatants as heroic, to an interpretation that they are victims or demonic. This is linked to the discourse of human rights and humanitarianism that associates the military with criminality or deviance (Rosen 2005).

Wars disproportionately impact the young, and affect boys and girls differently; the effects are emotional and psychological as well as physical, economic, and political. How children survive depends largely on the labor opportunities that are available to them and the kinds of development these lead to.

The World Wars

During the First World War, the official age for recruitment into the armed forces across Europe was eighteen years, but in all countries involved in the conflict, younger children enlisted. In Britain, many children left school at fourteen, and there were an estimated 250,000 underage soldiers in the British army. Recruitment into the army brought release from poor living conditions at home, and the promise of an opportunity to see the world; it was also responsible for the deaths of many thousands of young soldiers.

The Second World War again saw a massive mobilization of children in Europe. In Germany, nearly 9 million under eighteen joined the Hitler Youth, inspired or coerced by Nazi ideology. At the outbreak of the War, many of these were pressed into active service. Their female counterparts also received new social responsibilities as members of the League of Young Girls, reproducing and nurturing the perceived purity of the German people.

Life for millions of Jewish, Gypsy, or handicapped children in Europe was also transformed by the Second World War, and up to 1.5 million of these children were killed by the Nazis. In occupied territories, Jewish children were at the forefront of the armed resistance, and those who joined partisan groups in the forests of Eastern Europe experienced survival rates that were higher than those for children who remained as civilians (Rosen 2005).

Elsewhere in Europe, the Second World War was a time in which traditional roles could be challenged, and many teenagers left school to find employment or join the military. Measures were introduced to protect younger children from war, the most notable of which was mass evacuation: In September 1939, hundreds of thousands of children were taken from British cities to the countryside in an effort to save the lives of a generation of children from the disruption and bombing caused by the war.

Legislation Protecting Children

At the end of the Second World War, the Geneva Conventions outlined a number of international agreements on the treatment of civilians during conflict, which, by implication, included the protection of children. The Additional Protocols of 1977 extended protection to victims of armed conflict, and as such had relevance for child soldiers. Notwithstanding these developments, UNICEF estimates that 2 million children died in armed conflict in the ten years preceding 1996 (Machal 1996).

The Rome Statute of 1988 made recruitment of children under fifteen years of age a war crime, and the following year the Convention on the Rights of the Child defined a child soldier as "any person under the age of eighteen who is part of any kind of regular or irregular armed force or any armed group in any capacity other than purely as family members." In 1999, the International Labor Organization (ILO) Convention on the Worst Forms of Child Labor (Convention 182) called for an end to children's participation in armed conflict, including ending their forced recruitment. The Optional Protocol, which came into force in 2002 and laid the foundations for the International Criminal Court in Sierra Leone, set eighteen as the minimum age for compulsory government recruitment, all recruitment into nongovernmental forces, and direct participation in combat.

The use of child soldiers has been denounced repeatedly in UN Security Council resolutions, and there is some evidence that there has been a decline in the use of children in governmental forces since 2001 (Coalition to Stop the Use of Child Soldiers 2004). In recent years, human rights organizations and aid agencies have promoted child demobilization and reintegration projects in a number of countries, including Sierra Leone, Sudan, and the Democratic Republic of the Congo. While legislation and the implementation of demobilization projects indicate some consolidation of an international position, they are not backed by robust political mechanisms for enforcement, and the use of child soldiers continues in many wars.

The ILO estimates that there are around 300,000 child soldiers fighting in thirty-six countries around the world. These children are serving as combatants, spies, camp followers, wives, porters, and minesweepers in regular troops, paramilitary, and opposition forces. In Palestine, children operate as suicide bombers. Children are widely considered to be relatively fearless and obedient and, as such, make good frontline fighters. The availability and portability of light weaponry mean that children are easily and cheaply armed, and are able to carry and operate guns, particularly automatic assault rifles, pistols, and handheld grenade launchers.

Contemporary War in Africa

The majority of contemporary warfare takes place in Africa, and around half the child soldiers in the world are serving in this region. The context for these wars is the post–Cold War dominance of neoliberalism in global politics and the fallout from the AIDS epidemic.

The end of the Cold War brought a decline in patronage offered by rich nations to leaders in developing countries. The financial impact of this has been offset by increased commercial opportunities granted by the rise of neoliberalism, which enables integration, however uneven, into the world economy through formal and informal trading routes. These economic activities are accompanied by decentralized configurations of political power, which are, in turn, reflected by patterns of decentralized violence manifested in intrastate wars with high proportions of civilian casualties.

Alongside these economic and political developments, AIDS has reshaped demographics over the past two decades. Sub-Saharan Africa has the highest regional incidence of AIDS, and particularly high seroprevalence rates are recorded in armed groups that are mobile, use commercial sex workers, and often do not practice safe sex. AIDS decreases life expectancy, placing greater responsibility on younger members of society in all forms of employment. In the light of the decentralized structures, this employment—including work as soldiers—is frequently informal and unprotected, may not afford a subsistence level of return, and regularly involves violence or other forms of abuse.

The influence of neoliberalism, experienced through structural adjustment and unequal labor conditions, and the AIDS epidemic, means that many people in sub-Saharan countries contend with dangerous levels of poverty irrespective of the onset of fighting. In Sierra Leone and the Democratic Republic of the Congo, for example, years of predatory government, repressive international interventions, and impoverishment placed many millions of children in a precarious situation before the start of the wars.

War exacerbates these conditions of poverty, through the further loss of assets, houses, and farmland, or through loss of public entitlements or market opportunities. Children are made homeless through war, can be internally displaced, or can become refugees in another country, all of which affect their labor opportunities. The death of parents and the destruction of social structures during war propel children into roles as breadwinners, often providing for other children. Child-headed households face particular obstacles in terms of land rights, access to education and health services, and legal protection.

Displacement either within a country or across borders is also closely associated with the informalization of politics and the economy. In countries at war in sub-Saharan Africa, the state's capacity is reduced and the market is unregulated. This leads to increased violence and coercion in trading arrangements, the most extreme form of which is abduction for recruitment, forced labor, or slavery. War gives cover for these practices, which often target young people: Boys are taken into agricultural work or mining; girls are more generally used for domestic chores or for sexual exploitation.

While coercion into armed groups can increase the vulnerability of children, it can, in other circumstances, improve their security, and an ILO study found that two-thirds of children fighting in wars in central Africa were volunteers (Dumas and de Cock 2003). For children born during a war, violent conflict is normal and militarization a familial and social expectation. Faced with violent conditions, children may use violence to protect themselves or promote their interests (Brett and Specht 2004).

Being a child implies that one is the child of someone, and when families are torn apart, armed groups can take the place of the biological parents and siblings. The imagery of patriarchy, easily adopted in hierarchical structures, can be interpreted variously by combatants and their commanders, and can play a part in reallocating responsibility for violence (Schafer 2004). The nature of voluntarism in joining an armed group is debatable, and choices are circumscribed by environmental conditions, but to an important degree many children make an informed decision to fight. In a similar vein, wars often increase children's vulnerability to sexual exploitation, but in other circumstances offer increased opportunity to challenge gender roles, as occurred in the Female Detachment of FRELIMO during the Mozambican war (West 2004).

Working with Violence

The combination of aggressive commercial interests in war, a declining life expectancy, and increased poverty has aggravated the impact of war on children, particularly in Africa. The conditions of war tend to make economic, political, and social transactions more violent, influencing the forms of commercial exchange and labor that children engage in. This leads to a heightened dependence on nonformal or subsistence work, which may be exploitative, demeaning, or dangerous. Loss of family capital or income can lead children to begging, stealing, prostitution, or violence—as individuals, or as members of gangs or armed groups.

In the process of making choices about their labor and survival, children are agents not only in their own futures, but in the social and political development of their communities. They are included in areas of life that might previously have been considered the reserve of adults. This means the increased risks that accompany wars surface, not only as vulnerabilities, but also as new ways of finding and attributing meaning to existence and violence, as new negotiations of social and political spheres, and lead ultimately to new realities fashioned by the processes of conflict.

References and Further Reading

Boyden, Jo, and Joanna de Berry, eds. *Children and Youth on the Front Line. Ethnography, Armed Conflict, and Displacement.* New York: Berghahn Books, 2004.

Brett, Rachel, and Irma Specht. *Young Soldiers: Why They Choose to Fight.* London: Lynne Rienner Publishers, 2004.

Coalition to Stop the Use of Child Soldiers. *Child Soldiers: Global Report 2004.* London: Coalition to Stop the Use of Child Soldiers, 2004.

Dumas, Laetitia, and Michaelle de Cock. *Wounded Childhood: The Use of Child Soldiers in Armed Conflict in Central Africa.* Geneva: ILO, 2003.

Herodotus. *The Histories.* Ed. Robin Waterfield. Oxford: Oxford University Press, 1998.

Machal, Graca. *Promotion and Protection of the Rights of Children. Impact of Armed Conflict on Children.* New York: UNICEF, 1996.

Rosen, David M. *Armies of the Young: Child Soldiers in War and Terrorism.* New Brunswick, NJ: Rutgers University Press, 2005.

Schafer, J. "The Use of Patriarchal Imagery in the Civil War in Mozambique and Its Implications for the Reintegration of Child Soldiers." In *Children and Youth on the Front Line: Ethnography, Armed Conflict, and Displacement,* ed. J. Boyden and J. de Berry, 87–104. New York: Berghahn Books, 2004.

West, H.G. "Girls with Guns. Narrating the Experience of War of FRELIMO's 'Female Detachment.'" In *Children and Youth on the Front Line: Ethnography, Armed Conflict, and Displacement,* ed. J. Boyden and J. de Berry, 105–29. New York: Berghahn Books, 2004.

Worst Forms of Child Labor: Child Bonded Labor

Garance Genicot, Associate Professor, Economics, Georgetown University

Bonded labor—also known as debt bondage or peonage—designates the practice of pledging labor as payment or collateral on a debt. Child bonded labor refers to situations where a child's labor services are offered in exchange for a loan. In some cases, the labor of the child alone, or of the entire family, is directly offered. In other cases, bondage is intergenerational: Once a parent is no longer able to work, debts are passed down from parent to child.

Bonded labor has been widespread since ancient times and has flourished at various periods in most countries. Aristotle himself described the situation of debt bondsmen in Athens. Similarly, various form of voluntary slavery and bonded labor existed in Rome of the antiquity and in Ptolemaic Egypt. In Judaic law, a distinction was made between chattel and debt slaves (Ennew 1981). Perhaps less well-known is the extent to which these institutions persist in more recent times. A report of the Temporary Slavery Commission of the League of Nations in 1925 provides evidence of bonded labor in South America and the Philippines and indicates that the practice was widespread all over Africa and Asia (MacMunn 1974). The presence of bonded labor was reported in Indonesia, the Philippines, Malaysia, Siam, Burma, colonial Laos and Cambodia (Lasker 1950), and Ethiopia and Sudan (Ennew 1981).

Bonded labor is outlawed by the 1956 UN Supplementary Convention on the Abolition of Slavery, the Slave Trade, and Institutions and Practices Similar to Slavery, and most countries have passed their own bans. However, it is estimated that millions of people are still held in bonded labor around the world, including 15 million children in India alone (Human Rights Watch/Asia 1996).

At the origin of bonded labor lies a loan that a family takes from an employer (often to repay another loan or to pay for food, health care, a wedding, or a funeral). Having no other asset, the family may pledge the labor of some of its members—adults or children—to the employer-cum-lender in exchange for the loan. The debts tend to be modest. In India, for instance, they average from Rs500 to Rs7,500 for bonded child labor, depending on the industry and the age and skill of the child (Human Rights Watch/Asia 1996). These family members are then forced to work until the debt is paid off with their wages. Employers generally charge very high interest rates, pay low wages, deduct payments for equipment used, charge fines for faulty work, and sometimes take advantage of the debtor's illiteracy and lack of basic math skills. As a result, in many cases the debt actually increases instead of decreases as the family member works. If it is not repaid, the debt is transferred to the debtors' descendants, continuing the cycle. Working conditions are typically difficult. Children employed as bonded laborers work long hours over many years, in some cases in dangerous occupations.

The existence and persistence of child bonded labor raises many questions. Indeed, this institution combines many elements that have been banned by governments around the world: child labor, bonded labor, and inheritability of net debt.

Voluntary Slavery

In the case of debt bondage, a tenant or debtor voluntarily places him- or herself or his or her child in a position of servitude. Many observers find the voluntary nature of this choice puzzling and disturbing. Most countries have banned the long-term pledge of labor services including bonded labor and contract labor.[1] Supporters of a ban on voluntary servitude often use paternalistic arguments. They argue that people cannot foresee the consequences of their choices and that if they did, families would not opt for debt bondage. In this view, banning bonded labor prevents costly "mistakes."

However, in regions where bonded labor is prevalent, one would expect that families have a reasonable idea of what to expect. Evidence suggests that in many situations, bonded laborers might be better off than they would be as free workers.[2] There are numerous accounts of freed bonded laborers returning into bondage (Kloosterboer 1960; Bales 2002). To be sure, there may be different types of employers, some worse than others, and some information asymmetry such that families do not know beforehand which type of employer-cum-lender they are dealing with (Rogers and Swinnerton 2008), but a rational individual who became a bonded laborer must have preferred bondage ex ante among his available options.

That these arrangements can be voluntary should not be surprising. After all, these labor relationships typically concern very poor workers whose set of opportunities is so limited that such contracts may well represent their best option. Moreover, by the voluntary nature of these arrangements, it is not always clear whether banning them, or better enforcing an existing ban, would result in an improvement or a deterioration of workers' welfare.

It is easy to see why in some situations a ban could actually harm the very people it tries to help. Bonded labor can sometimes permit Pareto-improving transactions that would not otherwise occur. For assetless individuals, pledging their labor could be the only way to obtain much-needed loans. For instance, debt bondage is pervasive in human smuggling. Illegal immigrants frequently borrow large amounts from their smuggler to cover smuggling fees. Then they have to work for a friend or relative of the smuggler, often in "sweatshops," and are sometimes imprisoned until their debt is repaid (Kyle and Koslowski 2001). Without such arrangements, many of these migrations would never occur. In another example, Bardhan (1983) showed why "tied-labor agreements" can provide risk-averse laborers with insurance against wide swings in income due to fluctuations in demand for their service, and ensure landlords of cheap labor during peak seasons. Mukherjee and Ray (1995) provided an explanation for why tied-labor agreements can coexist with a large pool of large casual laborers (who are worse off than the tied laborers). Finally, in a case study of child bonded labor in brick kilns in Tamil Nadu, Bhukuth (2005) showed how bondage enables employers to guarantee a given labor supply from rural areas in exchange for advance payment for the workers.

However, banning bonded labor might not make families worse off, even if bondage is the best option for some assetless families. In a world where markets are incomplete, it is well-known that restrictions on contracting can be welfare improving. This is because the set of options available is not exogenous, and banning bonded labor could alter the options available to families or even trigger new ones. For instance, Genicot (2002) showed how the mere existence, or even potential existence, of bonded labor contracts can prevent the development of welfare-enhancing credit opportunities. Other potential lenders are deterred from lending to assetless borrowers who might simply default and enter into debt bondage. Hence, a ban on bonded labor could make assetless families better off by stimulating development of new credit opportunities. Basu (2003) provided another argument why banning some forms of labor contracts can be welfare improving for the workers. Even if one bonded labor contract would benefit both sides, a large number of them can affect labor market conditions, in particular wages, in a way that makes all laborers (bonded or not) worse off. In this case again, a ban on bonded labor would improve the welfare of families. Finally, if bonded labor allows employers to effectively collude on low wages, a ban could be beneficial (Conning and Kevane 2006).

Hence, whether enforcing a ban on bonded labor would help bonded laborers and families susceptible to debt bondage is likely to depend on the specific context. Notice that the fact that a contract is voluntary does not mean that it is not exploitative. In the spirit of Basu (1986), Hirshleifer (1991), and Bardhan (1991), a contract is exploitative when one party uses power to strategically affect alternatives available to the other party, so that the latter has no better choice than to agree upon a contract very advantageous to the first party. Genicot (2002) and Genicot and Ray (2006) characterized settings in which bonded labor arrangements are exploitative in this sense. This concept of exploitation is captured by a judgment of the Supreme Court of India in a bonded labor trial: "Any factor which deprives a person of a choice of alternative and compels him to adopt one particular course of action may properly be regarded as 'force' and if labor or services is compelled as a result of such 'force' it would be 'forced labor.'"[3]

Child Bonded Labor

Additional issues arise in the case of child bonded labor. Child bondage has two possible origins. Sometimes a child's labor is directly pledged as a security for a loan. Allowing other family members to be responsible for repayment of a debt can clearly improve credit access, and is often used informally or formally. For instance, La Ferrara (2003) showed how incentives to default are lower for community members who can expect retaliation on their offspring. During the borrower's life, depositing a child, or a wife, with a creditor as security for repayment of debt seems a common practice in many regions of the world. Even the Code of Hammurabi (1795–1750 B.C.E.) in ancient Mesopotamia explicitly allowed pledging a family member for up to three years (Harris 2002). South Asia is often cited as the region where child bonded labor is most prevalent. But use of children as "debtor-pawns"—children given as household servants by debtors—is also well documented in the history of Western Africa (Falola and Lovejoy 1994).

In other situations, the condition of bonded laborer is intergenerationally transmitted to the child after the death of a parent. This raises interesting questions of the inheritability of debt. Among different societies in the past, children have been responsible for their parents' debt at their death. Clauses 9–11 of the Magna Carta suggest that parental debt was inheritable in feudal England. In contrast, nowadays, children are no longer legally responsible for debts contracted by their parents that exceed the value of their estate.

That a parent can use his or her child as collateral, as in the case of child bonded labor, raises serious questions. Even when parents are fully altruistic toward their children, allowing this practice could make not just the child but the entire household worse off. Moreover, all parents do not always act in the best interests of their children, in which case, allowing parents to pledge their children's labor would be clearly undesirable. In contrast to the "voluntary" servitude of adult debt bondage, child bonded labor is, at least from the perspective of the child, clearly involuntary. Finally, passing debts from parents to children reinforces the intergenerational transmission of inequality, and can have long-term consequences for the society and its income distribution.

Conclusion

This essay argues that the welfare effect of stricter enforcement of laws against bonded labor and child bonded labor is ambiguous. There is no guarantee that it will actually help the potential bonded laborers and their families. Far from suggesting inaction, this conclusion calls for more, but different, action from governments and nongovernmental organizations. Providing alternatives for bonded child laborers and their families is crucial in fighting this practice. In particular, it is essential to provide poor families with alternative sources of small-scale consumption loans. The rapid development of microcredit organizations that provide small loans is certainly encouraging, although microcredit loans are given mainly for production purposes. Recent initiatives in providing poor households with micro–insurance products—mainly life and health insurance—could go a long way in reducing household vulnerability to moneylenders and bondage. In addition, such policies should be complemented with investments in education and vocational training for these children. Raising the opportunity cost of child labor should further discourage it. Only when enforcement efforts are complemented by these policies, can we be confident that they will be beneficial.

Notes

1. "Contract labor" refers to the practice in which a laborer commits to work for a specific employer for one or several years, but can choose freely whether to renew the contract at expiration. The practice is illegal in most countries, but exceptions exist, for example, in military service in the United States.

2. Describing bonded labor relationships in South India in 1825, Lumsden wrote in a letter, "I believe the [debt] slaves to be more comfortable than the free portion of their respective castes." Half a century later this statement was unequivocally repeated: "Hali [bonded laborers] are still, as a rule, better off than those of their clan who are nominally free labourers" (*Gazetteer of the Bombay Presidency: Gujarat*, vol. 2 [Bombay: Surat and Broach, 1877], 201). More than a century later, Jan Breman wrote, "[I]nstead of wishing to terminate the relation as soon as they could, both parties aimed at continuing it as long as possible" (Breman 1993, 59).

3. Supreme Court of India's judgment dated September 18, 1982, in *Peoples Union for Democratic Rights and Others v. Union of India and Others* (WP 8143 of 1981).

References and Further Reading

Bales, Kevin. "The Social Psychology of Modern Slavery." *Scientific American*, April 2002.

Bardhan, Pranab K. "Wages and Unemployment in a Poor Agrarian Economy: A Theoretical and Empirical Analysis." *Journal of Political Economy* 87:3 (1979): 479–500.

Bardhan, Pranab K. "Labor-Tying in a Poor Agrarian Economy: A Theoretical and Empirical Analysis." *Quarterly Journal of Economics* 98:3 (1983): 501–14.

Bardhan, Pranab K. "On the Concept of Power in Economics." *Economics and Politics* 3 (1991): 265–77.

Basu, Kaushik. "One Kind of Power." *Oxford Economic Papers* 38 (1986): 259–82.

Basu, Kaushik. "The Economics and Law of Sexual Harassment in the Workplace." *Journal of Economic Perspectives* 17 (2003): 141–57.

Breman, Jan. *Beyond Patronage and Exploitation: Changing Agrarian Relations in South Gujarat*. Delhi: Oxford University Press, 1993.

Bhukuth, Augendra. "Child Labour and Debt Bondage: A Case Study of Brick Kiln Workers in Southeast India." *Journal of Asian and African Studies* 40:4 (2005): 287–302.

Conning, Jonathan H., and Michael Kevane. "Freedom, Servitude and Voluntary Labor." In *The Ethics and Economics of Slave Redemption*, ed. K.A. Appiah and M. Bunzl, 108–140. Princeton, NJ: Princeton University Press, 2007.

Edmonds, Eric, and Sharma Salil. "Institutional Influences on Human Capital Accumulation: Micro Evidence from Children Vulnerable to Bondage." Working Paper, Department of Economics, Dartmouth College, November 2006. http://www.dartmouth.edu/%7Eeedmonds/kamaiya.pdf.

Ennew, Judith. *Debt Bondage: A Survey*. Human Rights Series Report 4. London: Anti-Slavery Society, 1981.

Falola, Toyin, and Paul E. Lovejoy, eds. *Pawnship in Africa: Debt Bondage in Historical Perspective*. Boulder, CO: Westview Press, 1994.

Genicot, Garance. "Bonded Labor and Serfdom: A Paradox of Voluntary Choice." *Journal of Development Economics* 67:1 (2002): 101–27.

Genicot, Garance, and Debraj Ray. "Contracts and Externalities: How Things Fall Apart." *Journal of Economic Theory* 131:1 (2006): 71–100.

Government of India. "Bonded Labour System Abolition Act" (1976). In *Bonded Labor in India*, ed. Manjari Dingwaney, R. Vidyasagar, and Anil Chaudhary, 41–44. New Delhi: Rural Labour Cell, 1986.

Harris, Edward M. "Did Solon Abolish Debt-Bondage?" *Classical Quarterly* 52:2 (2002): 415–30.

Hershleifer, Jack. "Paradox of Power." *Economics and Politics* 3:3 (1991): 177–200.

Human Rights Watch/Asia. *The Small Hands of Slavery: Bonded Child Labor in India*. New York: Human Rights Watch, 1996.

Kloosterboer, Willemina. *Involuntary Labour Since the Abolition of Slavery: A Survey of Compulsory Labour Throughout the World*. Leiden: E.J. Brill, 1960.

Kyle, David, and Rey Koslowski, eds. *Global Human Smuggling: Comparative Perspectives*. Baltimore: Johns Hopkins University Press, 2001.

La Ferrara, Eliana. "Kin Groups and Reciprocity: A Model of Credit Transactions in Ghana." *American Economic Review* 93:5 (2003): 1730–51.

Lasker, Bruno. *Human Bondage in South-East Asia*. Chapel Hill: University of North Carolina Press, 1950.

MacMunn, George Fletcher. *Slavery Through the Ages*. 1938. Reprint, Salt Lake City, UT: E.P. Publishing, 1974.

Mukherjee, Anindita, and Debraj Ray. "Labor Tying." *Journal of Development Economics* 47:2 (1995): 207–39.

Rogers, Carol, and Kenneth A. Swinnerton. "A Theory of Exploitative Child Labor." *Oxford Economic Papers* 60:1 (2008): 20–41.

The Puzzle of "Idle" Children, neither in School nor Performing Economic Activity

Mario Biggeri, Researcher, University of Florence; **Lorenzo Guarcello,** Researcher, UCW Project; **Scott Lyon,** Researcher, UCW Project; and **Furio C. Rosati,** UCW Project Coordinator and Professor of Economics, University of Rome, Tor Vergata

Data sets from developing countries that provide information on children's activities consistently show a significant group of "idle" children, who neither attend school nor participate in economic activity. Idle children constitute an important policy concern—they are not only denied schooling but are also the category of children most at risk for becoming part of the child labor force when households are exposed to individual or collective shocks. Reaching this group is therefore important to achieving both Education for All and the elimination of child labor.

While considerable research attention has been accorded to child laborers, the often large group of children absent from both school and economic activity has been the subject of very little research. Data from six countries—Brazil, Cameroon, Guatemala, Nepal, Turkey, and Yemen—were analyzed in an attempt to address this research gap. This essay is intended as an initial contribution to a broader discussion concerning the extent and characteristics of this overlooked group of children.

The proportion of children left out of both school and economic activity varies significantly across the six countries studied. Exclusion from school and economic activity is most common in Yemen and Cameroon, accounting for one-third and one-fourth, respectively, of seven- to fourteen-year-olds. It is least common in Brazil and Turkey, where only around one in twenty children are neither in school nor economically active. But even in these latter two countries, the absolute number of children in this group is significant: 0.6 million children between the ages of seven and fourteen in Turkey, and 1.1 million in Brazil.

Reasons for Absence from School and Economic Activity

What might explain this large group of children left out of both school and economic activity? A number of possibilities exist. First and most obviously, these children might not go to school or work in economic activities because they are needed at home to perform chores. Another possibility is that they are simply unemployed, wanting to work in economic activity but unable to find a job. A third possibility is that they are chronically ill or disabled. These possibilities are explored in turn.

Household chores such as water collection or caring for younger siblings, which are technically noneconomic activities, constitute a major time burden for only a small proportion of idle children. Less than one-half of idle children in Cameroon, and less than one-fifth in the other five countries, put in four or more hours each day on household chores. Moreover, many economically active children and students also perform chores at home, suggesting that responsibility for household chores may not play a central role in exclusion from school and economic activity.

Unemployment appears to play an important role in idleness only in Turkey, the one middle-income country examined. More than one-quarter of all idle Turkish children are actively seeking work. In Brazil, Guatemala, Nepal, and Yemen, however, the inability to find a place in the labor market appears to play a smaller role. Job seekers in these countries account for fewer than one in ten idle children.

The possibility that children's absence from economic activity or school is dictated by health is also only partially supported by the data. About one in ten idle children in Brazil, Turkey, and Yemen, and a slightly higher proportion in Nepal, suffers from chronic illness or disability. Among economically active children and children attending school, by comparison, levels of chronic illness and disability are much lower in all countries. Data on reported chronic illness and disability must be interpreted with caution since questions relating to child health are not standardized across surveys.

Taken together, household chores, unemployment, and chronic illness or disability can account for some of the idle children, but by no means the entire group. Indeed, only in Turkey do these three possibilities account for at least half of all idle children. In Nepal, they account for only about one-fifth of children not in school or economic activity, and in Guatemala, Brazil, and Yemen for fewer than one-third of idle children. What, then, are these remaining children doing?

Accounting for the "Unexplained" Portion of Idle Children

One possibility is that these children are actually economically active or in school, but the household surveys failed to capture them due to reporting error or omission. Such errors or omissions could arise for several reasons. Parents may falsely report their children as being idle instead of working, for example, because work by children is forbidden or because their children are engaged in illegal or dangerous activities. Alternatively, parents may misinterpret the survey question, and report children as idle because they were not working at the time of the interview, although they may work during other periods. Parents may report their children as being out of school when in fact they are in some form of nonformal or informal schooling.

Another possibility is that these children are indeed idle in the full sense of the word, engaged only in leisure activities. Such an outcome might be optimal for households where there are high costs to access education and work, on the one hand, and low returns to work and education, on the other. These circumstances could arise in areas where schools are difficult to access or too expensive and where labor markets are slack and work possibilities are available only at some distance from the residence.

The degree to which this unexplained portion of the group of nonworking, nonstudying children reflects involvement only in leisure, on the one hand, or unreported economic activity or schooling, on the other, requires further investigation. In particular, it is important to assess how the structure of survey questionnaires or the amount of "probing" influences the estimate of idle children. In addition, detailed econometric analyses of the determinants of children's activities would help to clarify whether the data are consistent with the hypothesis that children are really idle.

References and Further Reading

Biggeri, Mario, Lorenzo Guarcello, Scott Lyon, and Furio C. Rosati. "The Puzzle of 'Idle' Children: Neither in School nor Performing Economic Activity. Evidence from Six Countries." Understanding Children's Work Project Working Paper Series, October 2003.

UCW Project. *Understanding Children's Work in Guatemala.* Understanding Children's Work Project Country Report Series, March 2003.

UCW Project. *Understanding Children's Work in Yemen.* Understanding Children's Work Project Country Report Series, March 2003.

UCW Project. *Understanding Children's Work in Nepal.* Understanding Children's Work Project Country Report Series, July 2003.

Child Labor Policy for Developing Nations

Deborah Levison, Associate Professor, Hubert H. Humphrey Institute of Public Affairs, University of Minnesota

Adults, especially those in agenda-setting and program-implementation positions, have the potential to profoundly affect the lives of working children. Their attitudes regarding child labor depend on both their understanding of the issues and their broader agendas. Their actions are greatly influenced by the social norms, economies, and political institutions of their countries. This essay summarizes explicit and implicit policies directed toward child workers in developing nations, as well as some of the factors underlying their effectiveness, with the caveat that generalizations rarely describe any one country or situation completely accurately.

Policy Levels and Types

Child labor policy has multiple levels. At the most global level, there are international conventions, the most important of which are ILO Conventions 138 (Minimum Age) and 182 (Worst Forms) and the UN Convention on the Rights of the Child (CRC). When nations become signatories to these instruments, they agree to bring national laws and practices into alignment. There is no way, however, to enforce international conventions in any given country, even if that country is a signatory to the conventions (Bachman 2005). Between international conventions and national policies, another category of interventions is policies promulgated by industrialized countries with the intent of abolishing child labor in the export sectors of developing nations. In an infamous case, proposed legislation in the United States resulted in the layoff of thousands of child workers in Bangladesh's garment industry in 1993–1994, with many of the laid-off children moving into even more hazardous jobs (Bissell 2004).

At the national level, child labor laws typically forbid children from holding specific types of jobs or performing certain tasks that are deemed hazardous. Laws may impose procedural requirements on children, parents, and employers. For example, child workers are often required to obtain work permits from a governmental organization, and permits are awarded only if children and their employers meet particular criteria. Many child labor policies are, explicitly or implicitly, at the level of the regional (state or provincial) government or the local (municipal or city or town) authorities. For example, city officials may encourage police to arrest children caught working on city streets.

Other policies affect child labor indirectly, but possibly more effectively, than child labor legislation. Legislation may affect child labor indirectly by making school attendance mandatory for children of specific ages, by providing funding to agencies that implement social insurance or protection programs for children, by reducing family poverty, or by affecting the structure of labor markets. For example, Weiner (1991) advocated compulsory education as the best mechanism for moving children out of the labor force in India. He takes this position in part because school attendance is much easier to enforce than child labor laws. Mexico's conditional cash-transfer program *Progresa* (renamed *Oportunidades*), which rewards poor families with cash for children's school attendance, not only leads to increased school attendance, but also decreases the likelihood that children work in the labor force (Skoufias and Parker 2001). The premise is that if children's earnings can be replaced, poor families will feel able to reduce their labor force work. Through education, the cycle of poverty will be broken, reducing child labor in the next generation.

The *Progresa* social experiment has had a great influence on antipoverty programs in Latin America and elsewhere. Much of the work that children do is not, however, incompatible with school. In Latin America more children combine work and school than work without going to school, especially at younger ages. The evidence remains mixed as to whether combining work and school is generally helpful or generally harmful. Certainly children who work long hours cannot do much studying, and they may be too tired to learn well at school. Policies address this issue by limiting the number of hours that children may work per day or per week, or by prohibiting work after a certain hour of night. Such policies, however, are often directed only to the formal sector, where relatively few children work.

Legal Criteria for Addressing Child Labor

Some types of work are considered so deleterious to child well-being that these "worst forms" are completely illegal for children (and often adults) in most countries. As specified by ILO Convention 182, these are any work taking place under conditions of slavery or bonded labor; work in prostitution or pornography production; and involvement in illicit activities, such as drug trafficking. Other hazardous types of work are specified on a country-by-country basis. Sectors of the economy may also be ruled out for work by children: Any job related to mining, for example, is frequently precluded.

Aside from "worst forms," age is the primary criterion used in policies of all sorts for deciding whether work should be acceptable or not for young people. Although children develop at different rates, age provides one way for adults to generalize about physical, emotional, intellectual, and social aspects of development in order to provide rules about the acceptability of particular tasks at particular ages. Labor force work, except in family enterprises, is usually ruled out for children under the age of twelve. Work that is considered hazardous to adults is generally illegal for those under age eighteen. Between the ages of twelve and eighteen, age is often used to determine whether particular jobs or tasks are legal, or how many hours children may work. Bourdillon, Myers, and White (forthcoming) criticized the minimum-age criterion as currently implemented: They argued that it drives child labor underground, thereby failing to protect exploited children, while also interfering with useful child-rearing practices that involve nonharmful child work.

Policies also tend to target work that is considered "economic activity" or "labor force work," and ignore or exempt other work, including household chores. It may seem odd to use criteria created by statisticians for purposes of national accounting and determining gross domestic product, yet the idea that work in the labor force is fundamentally different from other work has taken firm root in industrialized societies over the past century or so. Work is counted if it is in paid employment or in self-employment, including unpaid family labor provided it makes "an important contribution to the total consumption of the household" (ILO 2000, 25). Work that is not counted typically includes tasks fundamental to family reproduction: caring labor, including child care and tending the disabled, ill, and elderly; meal preparation and cooking; cleaning and washing clothes; sewing; repairs of various sorts; and running errands. Levison (2000, 129) argued that "the belief that it is desirable to exclude children from 'real work' (which is paid) but reasonable to require them to undertake unpaid work is a reflection of children's relative lack of power rather than a reflection of systematic evidence about how best to promote children's well-being."

Whether work takes place in a family context is another widespread criterion. Most legislation, even in industrialized countries, exempts children's labor force work in family enterprises from regulation. From a political perspective, this is not surprising. Until the last century, the majority of people lived and worked on farms, and the idea of farm children not working would have been startling. Other children work in family restaurants, shops, and various other kinds of nonfarm enterprises. The idea that child labor is acceptable if it takes place under the supervision of parents or other relatives is, today, understood to mean that kin will make sure that no harm comes to working children. That this assumption is belied by evidence about child abuse has not affected the use of this criterion.

An assumption underlying all child labor policies is that adults will provide for children who are not allowed to provide for themselves. One criterion that is not taken into account, but perhaps should be, is whether or not children actually have an adult to provide and care for them. Child labor policies target all affected children, regardless of their alternatives. Some children, however, have few alternatives that will allow them to survive. Many AIDS orphans do not have adults to provide and care for them; instead they work to support themselves and their siblings. Bass (2004) questioned why it is acceptable for children to do unpaid work for family enterprises, or earn a little pocket money doing labor force work, but it is not acceptable for the most disadvantaged children to work for basic necessities.

Implementation and Enforcement

Once policy is formulated, issues of implementation and enforcement need to be addressed. Authorities may decree that children should work only if they have permits, or that employers using children to do hazardous work should be fined. Whether or not these things happen depends on complex institutional, social, and economic relationships. First, authorities must allocate enough resources to the appropriate agencies to allow them to carry out their assigned tasks, and the agencies must be reasonably competent. Labor inspectors cannot inspect far-flung rural work sites if they do not have functioning vehicles. There must be sufficient staff. In Peru, for example, in 2005 the Ministry of Labor had only 170 labor inspectors, and 120 of them worked in Lima. They carried out approximately 1,000 inspections per year, focusing on the formal sector (Schmidt 2005). But Peru has an estimated 659,046 formal sector enterprises and 1,903,586 informal sector enterprises. The labor inspectorate clearly could not possibly meet its responsibilities. An ILO (1998) report lists additional impediments to implementation: lack of training for inspectors; laws that do not apply to the informal sector, where many children work; and inspectors' lack of motivation, among others.

Second, the governmental and judicial systems must function at an adequate level. If national or state authorities add more tasks to the workload of already overworked and underpaid bureaucrats, will they do as they have been ordered, or will they ignore the mandate? If employers are fined by the labor ministry, will the fine actually be collected? If employers contest fines in court, will they be acquitted because the judge is "in the pocket" of local businesses? When systems are dysfunctional, people learn that it is not worthwhile to try to enforce child labor policies, as they make enemies and do not attain their objectives.

Labor inspectors face substantial resistance to enforcement of child labor policies. Resistance comes, first, from those who gain from child labor, including employers, purchasers of cheap services, and parents. Second, other people believe that children's work is advantageous for the children and their families, especially when the families are very poor. Inspectors themselves may believe this. Third, children themselves sometimes want to be able to work and earn money, though under reasonable conditions, as asserted by various organizations of working children (Bourdillon 2005).

The design and targeting of policies also has important implications for their effectiveness. A well-designed and targeted policy affects the people it is intended to reach, in the desired ways. In many cases of problematic targeting, the most vulnerable children may not benefit from social welfare because benefits instead go to children from better-off families. In the Brazilian PETI program (Programa de Erradicação do Trabalho Infantil or Child Labor Eradication Program), benefits were provided for children working in targeted industries, but nontargeted children may have actually entered hazardous employment in order to become eligible for PETI support. Another infamous case relates to India's Factories Act of 1948, which targeted work establishments above certain size thresholds for abolition of child labor. The act backfired: Children were instead employed in small sweatshops that were hard to find and impossible to monitor (Weiner 1991).

What Is Different about Developing Nations?

Developing nations tend to differ from industrialized nations, not so much with respect to international agreements or national laws limiting child labor, but more with respect to implementation and enforcement. Industrialized nations arrived at their current positions on child labor over decades of economic, social, and political change. Today's positions would not seem natural to people of earlier eras. In the United States, "reformers' plans . . . sometimes provoked open resistance and often met with noncompliance" (Macleod 1998, xii). There were often serious challenges to legal limitations on the use of child labor and to the institution of universal primary and secondary education that eventually became widely accepted. There is evidence that child labor laws followed changes in social norms and typical behavior, rather than vice versa (Moehling 1999).

Child labor policy in developing nations has been enormously influenced by these nations' positions in the world. Most achieved statehood following independence from a colonial power. Today's governing "elites," those adults in agenda-setting or program-implementation positions, are often relatively wealthy or from historically privileged families. These elites often have a strong desire to be on an equal footing with the global North. Because many have earned university or graduate degrees in Europe or North America, they are keenly aware of European and American norms and values, including those concerning childhood. This may help to explain why the governments of so many poor countries have ratified international conventions with strong limitations on child labor, even while child work remains widely acceptable among their populations.

Developing nations that have ratified child labor conventions have generally followed through on their commitments to bring national legislation into alignment with the conventions. In most cases, however, countries have been extremely reluctant to enforce such legislation. Different researchers have addressed the intent of legislators in such cases. Boyden, Ling, and Myers (1998, 183) wrote that "states often address social issues by legal means, not because the questions involved are best resolved that way, but because making laws is what they can do. Even in puzzling or complicated situations . . . they often find it convenient to legislate national or international laws to at least signal their concern and good faith, or sometimes just to express hope for an eventual solution."

Others are more cynical. Bass (2004, 62) described child labor laws driven by international conventions as "little more than window dressing for debt-ridden countries eager to please Western donors."

When the majority of a country's population does not find most forms of child labor to be undesirable, or considers them unavoidable, there will be little public pressure to fund labor inspections and child labor programs. Pressure is more likely to come from activist groups from industrialized countries, using the threat of trade restrictions to force action on the part of a reluctant government or employer. Alternatively, NGOs may build upon legal frameworks concerning child labor when formulating programs and advocacy plans for child workers, street children, and vulnerable children in general (Wiseberg 2005).

In many cases, it is not simply that legislation and mandates are not enforced; often, they are unenforceable. To clarify this distinction, when Nicaraguan labor inspectors cannot enforce child labor laws in rural areas because they lack adequate transportation, legislation is not enforced because of a political decision to limit funding to the labor inspectorate. In contrast, when an entire Indian village colludes to make sure that carpet-knotting children are never caught working, legislation is not enforceable.

Policy Approaches to Child Labor: The Abolition-to-Regulation Spectrum

Policies may differ substantially in their approaches to child labor. Advocates in industrialized countries often speak of "abolishing" child labor in developing nations, and ILO Convention 138 takes an age-based abolitionist position. Others point out that children have worked side by side with adults for centuries and, even today, the high prevalence of youth employment in industrialized countries is evidence that work is not always bad for children.

Many argue that there is a "continuum from the least to the most tolerable forms of work" (Pierik and Houwerzijl 2006, 202) and thus child labor should be regulated, not abolished. Nieuwenhuys (2005: 176), an anthropologist, has gone further, arguing that in many societies, children need to work to "prove their worth and their ability to make what is invested in them profitable, acquiring thereby their place in the order of intergenerational reciprocal obligations." Some policies thus attempt to distinguish between work that is harmful for children, and work that is benign or even helpful with respect to child development or social roles. ILO Convention 182, addressing "worst forms" of child labor, takes this approach, leaving it to individual countries to make many of the decisions about what work is "hazardous" for children.

Even where clear consensus emerges with regard to policy preferences, there often remain concerns about policy implementation. Sometimes what seems morally right may not be practical. When laws make child labor illegal, police tend to treat child workers as criminals instead of protecting them. When child labor is illegal, children's work tends to be hidden from public view, and wages are likely to be lower since children cannot compete openly. Opponents of abolitionist policies argue that when work is legal, it can be regulated; when it is illegal, regulation is impossible and conditions of work are likely to be much worse. Countries have struggled with this issue. White (1994, 870) described how "the government of Indonesia finds itself torn between the desire on the one hand to recognize and address the problem of child labour, and on the other hand to downplay or even deny the existence of the problem . . . because of the threat of international sanctions."

Conclusion

Boyden, Ling, and Myers (1998, 331) argued that "much of the conventional wisdom regarding how to protect children against workplace abuse" in both rich and poor countries "is founded in myth rather than fact." They went on to assert, "To a surprising extent, policy-makers, programme-planners, and child advocates promoting actions they assume to be good for children simply do not know what they are doing." The need to adopt national legislation that is consistent with international conventions has driven *de jure* policy in developing nations. Because this legislation has come from a top-down rather than a bottom-up process, its effectiveness in making positive change has been limited. Instead, laws focused on child labor often backfire, hurting child workers; they do not generally ameliorate the living conditions that lead families to find children's work essential, and they typically do not find ways to make enforcement actually work in local contexts. Laws may, however, have symbolic value, and the recent proliferation of NGOs includes many that draw upon child labor standards established in law.

Prerequisites for effective child labor policy include a social awareness of differences between adults and children, and a general agreement on the benefits of a period of education for children, as well as reform movements to improve conditions of work for vulnerable children. Legislation must provide clear guidelines, banning child labor in some situations while regulating it in others. Programs intended to implement legislation, including providing alternatives for the very poor, are essential. Resources and mechanisms for enforcing legislation at multiple levels (national, state or province, and local) are needed, including adequate training of inspectors and other community workers, and prosecution of offenders, with conviction a real possibility. Complementary laws, programs, and funding should aim to provide desirable alternatives to work for children, mainly in the form of education of reasonably high quality.

Everything is interconnected. If legislation specifies minimum ages for work, then a means of accurately determining ages is required, such as a system of birth registration, combined with identity cards or birth certificates. Also required are systems that support children who do not have adult support, such as orphans. To pay for the support for orphans without requiring orphans to work for their own support, a country needs a system of taxation, with little enough corruption that people are willing to pay taxes, and so forth. An integrated policy framework reaches far beyond child labor legislation. An effective policy framework is based on knowledge, not simply good intentions.

References and Further Reading

Bachman, Sarah L. "Translating Standards into Practice: Confronting Transnational Barriers." In *Child Labor and Human Rights: Making Children Matter,* ed. Burns H. Weston, 117–41. Boulder: Lynne Rienner, 2005.

Bass, Loretta E. *Child Labor in Sub-Saharan Africa.* Boulder: Lynne Rienner, 2004.

Bissell, Susan. "Incentives to Education and Child Labour Elimination: A Case Study in Bangladesh." In *Small Hands in South Asia: Child Labour in Perspective,* ed. G.K. Lieten, Ravi Srivastava, and Sukhadeo Thorat, 268–89. New Delhi: Manohar Publishers, 2004.

Bourdillon, Michael. "Translating Standards into Practice: Confronting Local Barriers." In *Child Labor and Human Rights: Making Children Matter,* ed. Burns H. Weston, 143–66. Boulder: Lynne Rienner, 2005.

Bourdillon, Michael, Bill Myers, and Ben White. "Reassessing Minimum-Age Standards for Children's Work." *International Journal of Sociology and Social Policy* (forthcoming 2009).

Boyden, Jo, Birgitta Ling, and William Myers. *What Works for Working Children.* Florence: Radda Barnen and UNICEF, 1998.

Humphries, Jane. "Child Labor: Lessons from the Historical Experience of Today's Industrial Economies." *World Bank Economic Review* 17:2 (2003): 175–96.

ILO. *Documento no. 75: trabajo infantil en los países Andinos: Bolivia, Colombia, Ecuador, Perú y Venezuela.* Working Paper. Lima: ILO/IPEC, 1998.

ILO. *Current International Recommendations on Labour Statistics—2000 Edition.* Geneva: International Labour Office, 2000.

Levison, Deborah. "Children as Economic Agents." *Feminist Economics* 6:1 (2000): 125–34.

Macleod, David I. *The Age of the Child: Children in America 1890–1920.* New York: Twayne Publishers and Prentice Hall International, 1998.

Moehling, Carolyn. "State Child Labor Laws and the Decline of Child Labor." *Explorations in Economic History* 36 (1999): 72–106.

Nieuwenhuys, Olga. "The Wealth of Children: Reconsidering the Child Labour Debate." In *Studies in Modern Childhood, Society, Agency, Culture,* ed. Jens Qvortrup, 167-83. Basingstoke: Palgrave MacMillan, 2005.

OECD. *Combating Child Labour: A Review of Policies.* Paris: OECD, 2003.

Pierik, Ronald, and Mijke Houwerzijl. "Western Policies on Child Labor Abroad." *Ethics and International Affairs* 20:2 (2006): 193–218.

Schmidt, Caterina. *Child Domestic Work in Peru. A Question of Political Will?* Master's diss., Institute of Development, Policy and Management, University of Antwerp, Belgium, 2005.

Skoufias, Emmanuel, and Susan W. Parker. "Conditional Cash Transfers and Their Impact on Child Work and School Enrollment: Evidence from the PROGRESA program in Mexico." *Economia* 2:1 (2001): 45–96.

Weiner, Myron. *The Child and the State in India: Child Labor and Education Policy in Comparative Perspective.* Princeton, NJ: Princeton University Press, 1991.

White, Ben. "Children, Work and 'Child Labour': Changing Responses to the Employment of Children." *Development and Change* 25 (1994): 849–78.

Wiseberg, Laurie S. "Nongovernmental Organizations in the Struggle Against Child Labor." In *Child Labor and Human Rights: Making Children Matter,* ed. Burns H. Weston, 343–76. Boulder: Lynne Rienner, 2005.

Education and Child Labor: A Global Perspective

Ranjan Ray, Department of Economics, Monash University

Notwithstanding centuries of social and economic progress, child labor continues to pose a significant problem in several parts of the world. Much of the recent concern over child labor stems from the belief that it has a detrimental effect on human capital formation. Kanbargi and Kulkarni (1991), Psacharopoulos (1997), Patrinos and Psacharopoulos (1997), Jensen and Nielsen (1997), Ravallion and Wodon (2000), Ray (2000a, 2000b, 2000c, 2004), Ray and Lancaster (2005), Heady (2003), Rosati and Rossi (2003), Gunnarsson et al. (2006) are part of a large body of literature that provides evidence on the trade-off between child labor and child schooling. While the evidence on the link between household poverty and child labor is, at best, a weak one (Addison et al. 1997; Ray 2000a, 2000b), the literature is near unanimous on the harmful effects of a child's employment on her or his learning outcomes.

This essay seeks to bring together the international evidence on the interaction between education and child labor. The global perspective of this paper is useful in highlighting the common features that hold universally and the distinctive characteristics that are unique to a country or a region. The policy importance of this topic is immense since, by impeding the child's intellectual and physical development, child labor has both microconsequences for the child and his or her family, and macroconsequences for the nation and the wider international community. While the lack of human capital formation condemns the child and her or his successors to an intergenerational cycle of child labor (Emerson and Souza 2003), the resulting lack of a skilled workforce may lead to a state of perpetual economic backwardness and underdevelopment. The literature is near unanimous on the positive role that rising adult education levels can play in reducing child labor and enhancing child schooling. These findings point to the need to devise comprehensive strategies that promote adult educational levels and social awareness, and increase the school enrollment rates of children.

Regional Heterogeneity in Child Employment

Though the term "child labor" is used in a regionally neutral sense, there are wider regional variations that need to be recognized for policy interventions to be effective. Table 1 presents a breakdown of the world's population of economically active children by three age-groups: five to nine years, ten to fourteen years, and fifteen to seventeen years. The corresponding statistics of the two worst-performing regions, namely, Asia-Pacific and sub-Saharan Africa, are also presented for comparison. The increase in the child labor participation rate with age is much faster in the Asia-Pacific region than in sub-Saharan Africa. Commentators that have remarked that child participation rates in sub-Saharan Africa are the highest in the world have overlooked the disaggregated picture, especially of children in the higher age-group (fifteen to seventeen years). In the context of the theme of this essay, Table 1 suggests that the cost that child labor entails on the child's education is felt by the younger children (five to nine years) in sub-Saharan Africa and by the older children (fifteen to seventeen years) in the Asian countries. Ray (2004) provided a further discussion of the regional variation in child labor and reported

Table 1

Estimates of Economically Active Children Age 5–17 Years, in Asia-Pacific and Sub-Saharan Africa, 2000 (by age-group)

Age-group and region	Number of children (millions)	Participation rate (%)	Regional share of child workers (%)	Regional share of child population (%)
5–9 Years				
Asia-Pacific	40.9	12.3	54.64	54.99
Sub-Saharan Africa	20.9	23.6	28.55	14.55
Total (World)	73.2	12.0	n.a.	n.a.
10–14 Years				
Asia-Pacific	87.3	26.5	63.35	55.01
Sub-Saharan Africa	27.1	21.5	19.67	13.03
Total (World)	137.8	23.0	n.a.	n.a.
15–17 Years				
Asia-Pacific	86.9	48.4	61.94	54.07
Sub-Saharan Africa	18.1	35.0	12.90	12.14
Total (World)	140.3	42.3	n.a.	n.a.

Source: ILO 2002.
Note: n.a., not applicable.

that the nature, magnitude, and decline in child labor over time vary sharply among Asian countries. For example, East Asia now has little child labor; however, child labor continues to have a significant presence in South Asia and in parts of Southeast Asia.

Cross-Country Comparisons of the Child's Choice Between Schooling and Employment

Table 2 compares school enrollment rates and combinations of schooling and employment of children in the age-group twelve to fourteen years, in a select group of countries based on surveys conducted by the Statistical Information and Monitoring Program on Child Labor (SIMPOC) of the International Labor Organization (ILO). While Sri Lanka stands out among the developing countries for its outstanding success in school enrollment, there does not appear to be much variation in the aggregate school enrollment rates of this group of countries. However, there is considerable variation among these countries on the choice a child makes among the four possible combinations of work and schooling. For example, children in Asian countries, especially Cambodia and Sri Lanka, are more successful in combining schooling with employment than children elsewhere. However, Cambodia has the lowest percentage of children in the most preferred "in school but don't work" category. If one adopts the corresponding rates of Portuguese children in this category as a developed-country benchmark for the other countries in Table 2 to emulate, then they still have a long way to go in getting their older children involved in education exclusively without the distraction of employment. Children in Cambodia and the Philippines record higher participation rates in the least preferred "not in school but work" category than children from other countries. Since children in this category are among the most disadvantaged, suffering the ill effects of child labor without enjoying any of the benefits of education, they cry out for immediate and targeted policy intervention.

Evidence regarding the influence of various household and child attributes on the child's choice among the four possible outcomes is provided in Table 3, which compares marginal probabilities among three countries located on different continents. In all these countries, household poverty moves the child away from schooling to employment, while an increase in the education level of the adult female in the household helps in keeping the child exclusively in school without

Table 2

Cross-Country Comparison of Children's Choice Between Schooling and Work

	Belize		Cambodia		Namibia		Panama		Philippines		Portugal		Sri Lanka	
Variable	Boys	Girls	Boys	Girls	Boys	Girls	Boys	Girls	Boys	Girls	Boys	Girls	Boys	Girls
School Enrollment Rate	91	88	89	85	83	89	88	90	89	92	98	98	94	95
Percentage of children who are:														
In school, but don't work	72.0	79.7	30.9	28.5	73.3	79.6	81.0	87.9	70.4	79.6	95.2	96.1	65.5	77.3
In school and work	18.6	7.7	57.7	56.6	9.8	9.4	6.8	1.7	18.4	12.0	3.2	1.9	28.5	18.1
Neither in school nor in work	3.8	9.5	2.4	2.6	11.5	8.8	5.5	9.1	4.3	5.4	1.0	1.4	2.6	2.9
Not in school but work	5.1	2.6	9.0	12.3	5.5	2.3	6.7	1.4	7.0	2.9	0.6	0.6	3.4	1.7%

Source: Ray and Lancaster 2005.

Table 3

Marginal Probabilities for a Selection of Variables

	Peru				Pakistan				Ghana			
Variable	School Only	Both School and Work	Neither School nor Work	Work Only	School Only	Both School and Work	Neither School nor Work	Work Only	School Only	Both School and Work	Neither School nor Work	Work Only
AGE	0.0212	0.0735	–0.0887	–0.0060	0.0275	0.0412	–0.1173	0.0486	0.0518	0.1137	–0.2168	0.0513
GIRL	0.0797	–0.1029	0.0321	–0.0089	–0.2363	–0.0754	0.2858	0.0259	–0.1159	–0.0449	0.1344	0.0264
URBAN	0.2733	–0.2587	–0.0028	–0.0118	0.2029	–0.0412	–0.1055	–0.0562	0.0493	–0.0026	–0.0102	–0.0364
NCHILD	–0.0100	0.0060	0.0040	0.0000	–0.0061	0.0002	0.0035	0.0024	–0.0033	0.0037	–0.0003	–0.0001
NADULT	0.0105	–0.0148	0.0041	0.0002	0.0246	–0.0019	–0.0036	–0.0190	–0.0178	–0.0065	0.0206	0.0037
FHH	–0.0007	–0.0050	–0.0055	0.0112	–0.0468	0.0207	0.0154	0.0107	0.0652	–0.0206	–0.0071	–0.0375
HEADAGE	–0.0010	–0.0001	0.0009	0.0002	–0.0012	–0.0001	0.0007	0.0006	–0.0002	0.0006	–0.0006	0.0001
MAXFEMED	0.0064	–0.0045	–0.0002	–0.0017	0.0283	–0.0009	–0.0104	–0.0169	0.0373	0.0062	–0.0333	–0.0103
POV	–0.0385	–0.0006	0.0364	0.0027	–0.1144	–0.0225	0.0890	0.0479	–0.1494	0.0224	0.0790	0.0481

Source: Maitra and Ray 2002.

Notes: *AGE,* age of child; *GIRL,* girl/boy; *URBAN,* urban/rural; *NCHILD,* number of children in the household; *NADULT,* number of adults in the household; *FHH,* female-headed household; *HEADAGE,* age of the household head; *MAXFEMED,* education level of the most educated adult female in the household; *POV,* household poverty: 1, poor; 0, otherwise.

any involvement in employment. The magnitude of the effect of rising household poverty in pushing children to the labor market without any schooling enrollment, that is, to the least preferred "not in school but work" category, is much lower in Peru[1] than in Pakistan or Ghana. In all the three countries, the urban child is more likely to be in the "in school but don't work" category than the rural child. In contrast, the rural child is more likely to combine schooling with employment than the urban child. This may reflect the nature of child work in the urban areas along with the greater distances, compared to the rural areas, between schools and workplaces. This calls for a need to locate schools near workplaces in the urban areas. In Peru and Pakistan, but not in Ghana, a child from a female-headed household is less likely to be exclusively in school with no work involvement than a child from a male-headed household.

The discussion so far has revolved around the snapshot of a child's selection of a particular schooling/employment combination at a point in time. Vietnam experienced one of the largest reductions in child labor anywhere in the 1990s and has, therefore, attracted considerable attention (Edmonds and Turk 2004). Table 4 shows how the Vietnamese child's choice among the four possible outcomes has changed over the period 1992–1993 to 1997–1998. Table 4 shows that, for each of the three principal ethnic communities and for Vietnam as a whole, there has been a sharp increase in the percentage of children who are in school with no work involvement. A closer examination of the figures shows that much of this increase has come from the categories, "in school and work," and "neither in school nor in work," each of which registered large declines over this period, 1992–1993 to 1997–1998. Note, however, that the percentage of children in the least preferred category, "not in school but work," did not show any downward movement at the All Vietnam level. This aggregate picture hides significant ethnic differences with the minority Tay and Chinese children, especially the Tay girls, abandoning full-time work involvement to move toward exclusive school enrollment, a feature that is not shared by children from the majority Kinh community.

Examples of the effects of ethnic or other differences on child education and child labor arise in other countries as well. For example, Ray (2000c, Tables 5–7) provided Indian evidence that suggests that children from backward classes experience substantially less schooling and record higher child employment rates than the rest of the population. In devising policies to promote child welfare, authorities need to recognize such ethnic and class differences in the key indicators of education and child labor in order to make the interventions effective. Another significant finding of this Indian study is that child laborers exhibit substantially lower levels of general education than children who are attending school. This points to the cost that child labor entails on the child's education, a topic to which we turn in the following section.

The Consequences of Child Labor for Child Education

Child labor, especially beyond an "acceptable level," has a potentially damaging impact on the child's intellectual and physical development. While much of the earlier literature concentrated on the determinants of child labor, several recent studies have examined the educational effects of child employment. Figures 1 and 2 from Ray and Lancaster (2005) provide evidence of the adverse impact of child labor on the child's learning opportunities. Figure 1 shows the relationship between study time and child ages for nonworking and working children in Sri Lanka. The mean study time of working children falls below that of nonworking children at around the age of eleven years. The decline in the graph of the working children accelerates over the twelve- to fourteen-year age-group so that, by the time children reach the school-leaving age, a large gap has opened up between the mean study times of nonworking and those of working children. Figure 2 shows, for Cambodia, the percentages of working and nonworking children in the various age-groups who can read and write. The cost of child work is again evident in the lead that nonworking children enjoy over working children in the twelve- to fourteen-year age-group in regard to reading and writing. To put the prima facie evidence on the cost of child labor to child education beyond reasonable doubt, Figure 3 plots, for working and nonworking children in Vietnam, the relationship between the "schooling for age" variable (SAGE) and the child age from the 1997–1998 Vietnam Living Standards Survey (VLSS), where

$$SAGE = \left(\frac{\text{Years of Schooling}}{\text{Age} - \text{School Entry Age}} \right) \times 100$$

Clearly, for older children age eleven years and above, the school performance variable, SAGE, is unambiguously lower for working children. A common feature of these graphs is that, for younger children, especially those in the age-group seven to nine years, working children do not necessarily experience inferior learning opportunities compared to those enjoyed by nonworking children. The explanation possibly lies in the fact that, in the younger age-groups, the nature and intensity of the work are not as harmful to the child's education as is the case in the older age-groups. This feature needs to be kept in mind in devising policies that allow a limited amount of work, in recognition of the fact that in countries such as Pakistan many households are heavily reliant on child labor earnings to stay above the poverty line (Ray 2000b, Table 4).

Figures 1–3, while pointing to the adverse impact of child labor on the child's education, do not give any quantitative guidance on the marginal cost of the child labor hour since they do not control for the other characteristics. An attempt to do so was made in Ray and Lancaster (2005) that used SIMPOC data from a number of countries to estimate the impact of child labor hours on the child's schooling, measured by SAGE, taking into account the simultaneity of SAGE and child labor in the estimation. The exercise, which was performed on data sets involving children in the age-group twelve to fourteen years, sought to answer the question: Is there a threshold of (weekly) hours of work for twelve- to fourteen-year-olds below which school attendance and performance are not adversely affected? The policy importance of this question stems from Article 7 of the ILO's Minimum Age Convention, 1973 (Convention 138), which stipulates that "light work" may be permitted for children from the age of twelve or thirteen provided it does not "prejudice their attendance at school . . . or their capacity to benefit

Figure 1 Relationship Between Mean Study Time and Child Ages in Sri Lanka

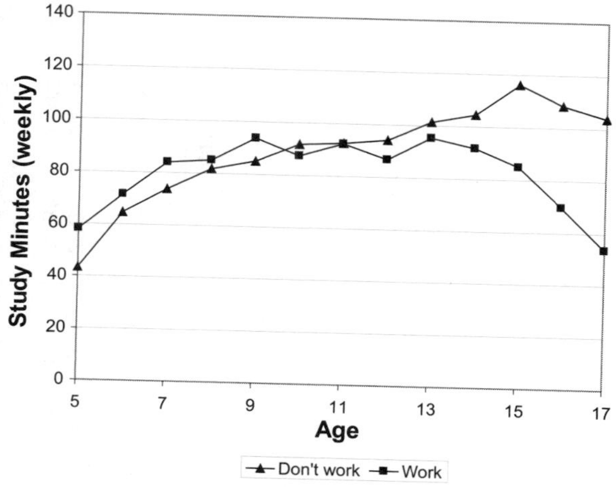

Source: Ray and Lancaster 2005.

Figure 2. Relationship Between the Percentage of Children Who Can Read/Write and Child Ages in Cambodia

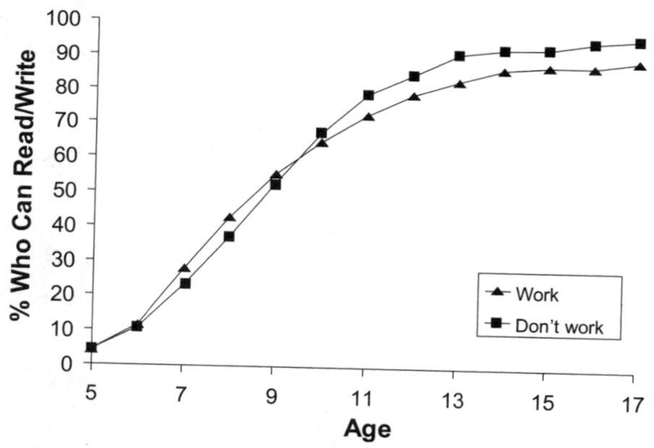

Source: Ray and Lancaster 2005.

Figure 3. Relationship Between Average School Performance and Child Ages in Vietnam

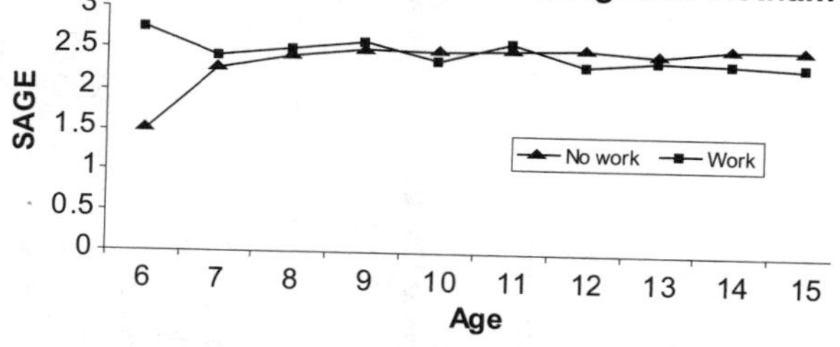

Source: Author's calculations based on the Vietnam Living Standards Survey, 1997–1998 data set.

Note: SAGE, schooling for age.

Table 4

Vietnamese Children's Choice Between Schooling and Work

1992–1993	Kinh			Tay			Chinese			All Vietnam		
Percentage of children who are:	Boys	Girls	Overall	Boys	Girls	Overall	Boys	Girls	Overall	Boys	Girls	Overall
In school, but don't work	40.16	28.35	34.30	38.71	25.42	32.23	66.10	43.48	56.19	38.53	26.73	32.70
In school and work	45.14	57.45	51.25	41.94	49.15	45.45	16.95	41.30	27.62	42.81	55.03	48.85
Neither in school nor in work	11.02	10.12	10.57	16.13	15.25	15.70	11.86	8.70	10.48	13.46	11.52	12.50
Not in school but work	3.69	4.08	3.88	3.23	10.17	6.61	5.08	6.52	5.71	5.20	6.71	5.95

1997–1998												
Percentage of children who are:	Boys	Girls	Overall	Boys	Girls	Overall	Boys	Girls	Overall	Boys	Girls	Overall
In school, but don't work	72.41	70.75	71.60	54.55	64.06	59.23	83.33	85.29	84.29	68.93	68.09	68.52
In school and work	16.29	14.88	15.60	34.85	28.13	31.54	2.78	5.88	4.29	18.36	15.47	16.95
Neither in school nor in work	6.21	8.38	7.27	9.09	6.25	7.69	11.11	5.88	8.57	7.19	9.02	8.08
Not in school but work	5.09	5.99	5.53	1.52	1.56	1.54	2.78	2.94	2.86	5.53	7.42	6.45

Source: Author's calculations from the Vietnam Living Standards Survey, 1992–1993, and Vietnam Living Standards Survey, 1997–1998 data sets.

from the instruction received." The central message of the Ray and Lancaster (2005) study is that children's work, even in limited amounts, does adversely affect child learning, when one controls for other characteristics. The marginal impact of child work was generally found to be more detrimental to the learning experience of girls than of boys. A significant exception was provided by the Sri Lankan evidence, which suggested that a child in the age-group twelve to fourteen years can work up to twelve to fifteen hours a week without suffering a decline in her or his school attendance rate or in the overall duration of her or his schooling. Even in Sri Lanka, however, the child's school performance deteriorates sharply beyond the threshold.

Policy Initiatives to Reduce Child Labor and Promote Child Schooling

Widespread appreciation of the potentially harmful consequences of child labor, both for the child and for society at large, has triggered concerted international actions to eliminate child labor. A central theme in many of these interventions has been an attempt, via legislation such as compulsory schooling, or incentives such as school enrollment subsidies, to keep children in school and away from work. For example, the midday school meal program in India, which dates back to 1925, was formally relaunched as the National Programme for Nutritional Support to Primary Education (NPNSE) on August 15, 1995, by the government of India to enhance the nutritional status of children and boost the universalization of primary education by encouraging economically disadvantaged families to send their children to school and ensure that they attend regularly. The Food for Education program in rural Bangladesh aims to keep the children of poor rural families in school by providing households with free food rations so long as they send their children to primary schools.

The role of incentives in promoting schooling cannot be overstated, though their effect in reducing child labor is less clear. For example, in a study of the effects of the Food-for-Education program in rural Bangladesh, Ravallion and Wodon (2000) found that the program had a greater effect in increasing schooling than in reducing child labor. This may, however, be a statistical artifact since many of the rural children who were encouraged by the program to attend school were previously involved in domestic duties and were not counted as "child labor."

The recognition that schooling is an effective strategy to combat child labor has prompted the Europe-based campaign "Stop child labour: School is the best place to work."[2] Another example of an NGO activity that gives primacy to schooling in efforts to combat child labor is that of the MV Foundation, based in the South Indian state of Andhra Pradesh. This foundation has been working with community groups, parents, employers, and government officials in an effort to remove children from work and enroll them in schooling. The success of the MV Foundation's efforts is evident from the fact that nearly 420,000 children have been enrolled and retained in schools, more than 4,000 bonded laborers have been released, and 168 villages in Andhra Pradesh are now child labor free in the space of ten years.

Ultimately, the most effective strategy for dealing with child labor has to concentrate on the household itself. There is near unanimity in the literature on the positive role that increasing education levels of the adults in the household can play in promoting child schooling and reducing child labor. Decisions on the child's schooling and work involvement are made by the adults, not by the children themselves. As Basu and Ray (2002) observed in their empirical study on Nepalese child labor, the nature of intrahousehold decision making has a significant influence on the extent of involvement of children from that household in child labor. The Basu and Ray (2002) study draws attention to the need to educate both the adult male and the adult female, not just one or the other, since a household where both spouses have an equal say in decision making shows the least involvement in child labor. More generally, the link between adult education levels and intrahousehold decision making, on the one hand, and the outcomes on child education and child labor, on the other hand, has opened up a variety of possible strategies for combating child labor. Such strategies are likely to be more effective than simple legislation banning child labor.

Conclusion

This brief and partial review, from an economist's viewpoint, shows that there is a two-way relationship between child education and child labor. The evidence presented here suggests that child labor impedes the child's learning, thereby constraining her or his intellectual development. The resulting lack of human capital formation condemns the child and the child's family to an intergenerational cycle of child labor and poverty and impedes social and economic progress of the country. Compulsory schooling, and incentives to attend school simultaneously help in reducing the child's work involvement and enhancing the child's human capital development.

Notes

I am grateful to Vinod Mishra for his help with some of the calculations reported in this paper. The work on this paper was partially supported by a grant from the Australian Research Council.

1. See Ray (2000a, 2000b) for a more detailed comparison of the labor market participation, work hours, and schooling experience between Pakistani and Peruvian children.

2. See the campaign's Web site, www.schoolisthe bestplacetowork.org, for details on worldwide efforts to propagate and implement the view that "school is the best place to work."

References and Further Reading

Addison, T., S. Bhalotra, F. Coulter, and C. Heady. "Child Labour in Pakistan and Ghana: A Comparative Study." Mimeograph, Centre for Development Studies, University of Bath, UK, 1997.

Basu, K., and R. Ray. "The Collective Model of the Household and an Unexpected Implication for Child Labour: Hypothesis and an Empirical Test." Policy Research Working Paper WPS2813, World Bank, Washington, DC, 2002. http://www.econ.worldbank.org/.

Edmonds, E., and C. Turk. "Child Labour in Transition in Vietnam." In *Economic Growth, Poverty and Household Welfare in Vietnam,* ed. P. Glewwe, N. Agrawal, and D. Dollar. Washington, DC: World Bank, 2004.

Emerson, P., and A.P. Souza. "Is There a Child Labour Trap? Intergenerational Persistence of Child Labour in Brazil." *Economic Development and Cultural Change* 51:2 (2003): 375–98.

Gunnarsson, V., P.F. Orazem, and M.A. Sanchez. "Child Labour and School Achievement in Latin America." *World Bank Economic Review* 20:1 (2006): 31–54.

Heady, C. "The Effect of Child Labour on Learning Achievement." *World Development* 31:2 (2003): 385–98.

ILO. *Every Child Counts: New Global Estimates on Child Labour.* Geneva: ILO, 2002.

Jensen, P., and H.S. Nielsen. "Child Labour or School Attendance: Evidence from Zambia." *Journal of Population Economics* 10:4 (1997): 407–24.

Kanbargi, R., and P.M. Kulkarni. "Child Work, Schooling and Fertility in Rural Karnataka, India." In *Child Labour in the Indian Subcontinent,* ed. R. Kanbargi, 125–63. Thousand Oaks, CA: Sage, 1991.

Maitra, P., and R. Ray. "The Joint Estimation of Child Participation in Schooling and Employment: Comparative Evidence from Three Continents." *Oxford Development Studies* 30:1 (2002): 41–62.

Patrinos, H.A., and G. Psacharopoulos. "Family Size, Schooling and Child Labour in Peru: An Empirical Analysis." *Journal of Population Economics* 10:4 (1997): 387–406.

Psacharopoulos, G. "Child Labour Versus Educational Attainment: Some Evidence from Latin America." *Journal of Population Economics* 10:4 (1997): 377–86.

Ravallion, M., and Q. Wodon. "Does Child Labour Displace Schooling? Evidence on Behavioural Responses to an Enrolment Subsidy." *Economic Journal* 110:462 (2000): C158–C175.

Ray, R. "Analysis of Child Labour in Peru and Pakistan: A Comparative Study." *Journal of Population Economics* 13:1 (2000a): 3–19.

Ray, R. "Child Labour, Child Schooling and Their Interaction with Adult Labour: Empirical Evidence for Peru and Pakistan." *World Bank Economic Review* 14:2 (2000b): 347–67.

Ray, R. "Poverty, Household Size and Child Welfare in India." *Economic and Political Weekly* 35:39 (2000c): 3511–20.

Ray, R. "The Determinants of Child Labour and Child Schooling in Ghana." *Journal of African Economies* 11:4 (2003): 561–90.

Ray, R. "Child Labour: A Survey of Selected Asian Countries." *Asian-Pacific Economic Literature* 18:2 (2004): 1–18.

Ray, R., and G. Lancaster. "The Impact of Children's Work on Schooling: Multi-Country Evidence." *International Labour Review* 144:2 (2005): 189–210.

Rosati, F.C., and M. Rossi. "Children's Working Hours and School Enrolment: Evidence from Pakistan and Nicaragua." *World Bank Economic Review* 17:2 (2003): 283–95.

Special Health Risks of Child Labor

Anaclaudia Gastal Fassa, MD, PhD, Associate Professor, Department of Social Medicine, Federal University of Pelotas; and **David H. Wegman,** MD, MSc, Dean and Professor, School of Health and Environment, University of Massachusetts Lowell

[P]ound for pound of body weight, children drink more water, eat more food, and breathe more air than adults [and] in some instances, children are less able than adults to detoxify chemicals and are thus more vulnerable.

—ATSDR 1997, 41

Characteristics That Make Young People More Susceptible to Work Hazards

Children and adolescents undergo a process of growth and development, and consequently, they have particular anatomical, physiological, and psychological characteristics associated with age that might make them more susceptible than adults to work hazards. Organs and systems are not mature at birth; they grow at a variable pace from birth to adolescence, and in certain periods they experience rapid growth and development. Since organs and tissues mature at different rates, effects of exposures are likely to be different at different stages of development. Moreover, children who begin work at an early age have many more years to develop illness than adults engaged in the same work (ATSDR 1997; Forastieri 2002).

Because of their rapid growth, younger children have a higher metabolic rate and oxygen consumption than adults, and therefore a greater intake of air per unit of body weight. They breathe faster and more deeply than adults and may have an increased absorption of fumes, gases, and particles. For infants, the immature development of their kidneys may result in poor ability to excrete chemical metabolites. There is also a concern that for child workers of low socioeconomic status, there may be a problem of malnutrition that can increase the impact of toxic exposures on child health (ATSDR 1997; Forastieri 2002).

During adolescence, growth in several body systems (e.g., renal excretion and size of alveoli in pulmonary system) is slowed. However, two systems that change a great deal are the endocrine system, which undergoes significant development during puberty, and the musculoskeletal system, which experiences an adolescent growth spurt. Moreover, effects in the brain that lead to altered learning capacities may have more serious implications in children and adolescents during this intense learning period (NRC 1998).

In addition to biological development, adolescents need at least as much sleep as younger children. Evidence suggests that the circadian rhythm is altered during adolescence, making children in this age-group stay awake later. Because of the need to rise early for school (or work), adolescents often experience midafternoon sleepiness. This has been seen to occur even in youngsters who have had enough sleep, and certainly could be exacerbated in those who get fewer hours of sleep than necessary. Having a job during the school week might contribute to further decreasing the amount of sleep an adolescent gets, resulting in increased fatigue (NRC 1998; Carskadon 1990).

Adolescents are not emotionally mature and may be more susceptible to peer influence. Their abilities to recognize and assess potential risks and to make decisions about them are still developing, and, therefore, they are very prone to take risks. Moreover, children and teen workers are intrinsically inexperienced, which can increase their exposure to several hazards (NRC 1998; NIOSH 1997).

Increased Susceptibility to Hazards

There are few epidemiological studies evaluating differences between children and adults in susceptibility to toxic substances and other hazards. However, studies of young workers and of children exposed to air pollutants in their living environment suggest that some important differences might exist (Bequele and Myers 1995).

Toxic Exposures (Hazardous Substances)

Some epidemiological studies have shown that children are more susceptible than adults to lead exposure. At the same level of exposure, children tend to absorb higher amounts of lead than adults do, and they exhibit more severe toxicity at lower levels of exposure; for example, they are more liable to develop irreversible neurological complications (Bequele and Myers 1995; Ide and Parker 2005; ATSDR 2005a, 2005b).

Evidence on age-related susceptibility to benzene is not clear (ATSDR 2005a, 2005b). Children have higher activity levels and ventilation than adults, which could increase the inhalation of this agent in situations where exposure is possible. Moreover, age-related differences in benzene metabolism could lead to higher susceptibility. However, there is no study confirming this hypothesis. One study showed that among 365 adult workers exposed to benzene, the youngest group (eighteen- to twenty-one-year-olds) had the highest number of workers affected and those with worst hematological changes induced by benzene, as compared with the twenty-two- to twenty-five-year-old and twenty-six- to thirty-five-year-old age-groups (Bequele and Myers 1995).

Some authors suggest that children and adolescents could also be more vulnerable to asbestos and ionizing radiation (Forastieri 2002; Bequele and Myers 1995; WHO 1987). These hypotheses are based on the fact that children and adolescents experience rapid cell growth and could be particularly vulnerable to potential carcinogens. Moreover, diseases with long latency are of particular concern because children have more future years of life than adults and, thus, more time to develop chronic diseases related to early exposures. However, direct evidence for this hypothesis is not available (NRC 1998; ATSDR 1999, 2001).

The endocrine system may also be an important target for toxicants, particularly during adolescence, altering the hormonal balance or its feedback loops, and having negative effects on sexual maturation (ATSDR 1997; NRC 1998). There is a need for studies comparing childhood and adult susceptibility to potential harmful effects of toxic substances. Moreover, consequences of exposure to combinations of chemicals, as well as to the new synthetic chemicals that are being developed every year, are not fully known (ATSDR 1997; Forastieri 2002). Most children and teens in the world who work are active in agriculture, where there is good reason to be concerned about their exposure to pesticides.

Heat and Noise Exposure

Children have lower heat tolerance than adults and therefore are subject to higher risk of heat stress at work. This is due to the fact that children's sweat glands are still developing, and high temperature will cause an increase in oxygen consumption in children before it will in a healthy adult. In addition, as children grow, muscular activity plays a more important role than in adults with respect to temperature-related oxygen consumption (Forastieri 2002; NRC 1998; Tucker 2000). Heat stress is particularly important in agriculture.

Some authors suggest that young workers are also more susceptible to induced hearing loss than adults (Forastieri 2002; Bequele and Myers 1995). However, despite the developmental characteristics giving rise to this concern, evidence from studies, either at work or in the general environment, is very scant. Higher susceptibility to noise among youths, therefore, is not conclusive (WHO 2002).

Ergonomic Hazards

Children and adolescents, like adults, can be exposed to repetitive motion, high force, and awkward posture at work. Although little research has focused on children and adolescents, long-term consequences of work-related musculoskeletal disorders, such as carpal tunnel syndrome, tendonitis, and back strain, are of concern, as any impact on the musculoskeletal system will affect children over a longer life span (NRC 1998).

Adolescents are at particularly high risk of injury to ligaments and to bone growth plates. Adolescence is a period of rapid growth. Between ten and twenty years of age, they will acquire 15 to 20 percent of their height, and half of it will be gained during a two-year growth spurt. Injuries to growth plates can result in various osteochondroses (localized bone tissue death), some of which can have long-term consequences, such as limbs of unequal length (Forastieri 2002; NRC 1998).

In contrast to exposures discussed previously, much more is known about the comparative risk of work-related injuries between children and adults. Several epidemiological studies point to higher rates of fatal and nonfatal injuries among child workers (Forastieri 2002; NRC 1998; Erlich et al. 2004). Data from the National Center for Health Statistics, taking into account the intensity of work, showed that the injury rate per full-time equivalent (FTE) workers in children was almost double that of adults (4.9 per 100 FTE in fifteen- to seventeen-year-olds and 2.8 per 100 FTE in adults sixteen years old and older). There is also evidence of interaction effects between age and job stressors, such as inexperience, that result in higher rates of injuries for adolescents (Mueller et al. 1987).

The studies also indicated higher rates of injury-related disability among young workers when compared to adults (NRC 1998). A study using workers compensation system records found that, for any job category, injuries in children tend to be more serious and require surgical intervention more frequently than do those in adults. Construction, manufacturing, and agriculture were highlighted as industries that resulted in a proportionally higher risk of severe injuries (Erlich et al. 2004). The higher risk of work injuries among children and adolescents could be related to inexperience; inappropriate assessment of potential risks; the desire to demonstrate responsibility and independence by accepting risky tasks; or fatigue and sleepiness due to the double burden of school and work or the sleep needs of adolescence (NRC 1998).

Mismatches Between Size of Young People and the Tools They Use

Generally, machinery, equipment, tools, and workstations have been designed for adult use. Mismatches between younger workers' size and the equipment they use might increase the risk of fatigue, injuries, and musculoskeletal problems (Forastieri 2002; NRC 1998; NIOSH 1997). One study by the Consumer Product Safety Commission has shown that young, short, and lightweight operators of ride-on mowers were more likely than others to be injured (CPSC 1993). This association raises concerns about the operation of other machinery by children and adolescents.

Personal protective equipment (PPE) is also designed for adult use. There is a likelihood that such PPE will prove to be oversized for child laborers and might not provide proper protection. Moreover, if it does not fit at all, which often happens with children, they might either work without it or use alternatives that do not provide real protection (Forastieri 2002). In both situations, young workers would be more vulnerable to the exposures that should be prevented by the PPE. The need to use PPE indicates the presence of hazardous exposures, which should alert responsible parties to evaluate the appropriateness of the work for young workers.

Permissible Exposure Limits

Throughout the world, permissible exposure limits (PEL) are based on reference studies in adults, mainly males. Due to the uncertainty about how differently susceptible children and adolescents are to most of the exposures, it would be prudent to assume that children will have greater susceptibility than adults. One suggestion is that wherever PELs for children and adolescents are provided, these should be equivalent to those established for the public (Forastieri 2002).

Conclusion

The lack of scientific evidence that addresses the susceptibility of youths to the wide range of risks that exist in their places of work is striking. Despite the lack of direct evidence, there is good reason to believe that the theoretical bases for higher susceptibility to most exposures, grounded in physical or emotional development, is important. Certainly, in most situations, children and adolescents will have at least the same susceptibility to occupational exposures as adults. But there are several areas where developmental biology suggests the likelihood that children's susceptibility to work exposures will be higher than for adults. A priority should be placed on studying and understanding these relationships so that proper precautionary actions can be planned. In the meanwhile, the need for children and adolescents to have higher levels of protection at work is strongly supported. Special health risks should be taken into consideration when prioritizing definitions of work appropriate for adolescents and in enforcement of minimum-age regulations.

References and Further Reading

Agency for Toxic Substances and Disease Register (ATSDR). *Healthy Children—Toxic Environment.* Atlanta, GA: U.S. Department of Health and Human Services, Public Health Service, 1997, 41.

ATSDR. *Toxicological Profile for Ionizing Radiation (Draft for Public Comment).* Atlanta, GA: U.S. Department of Health and Human Services, Public Health Service, 1999, 16–17.

ATSDR. *Toxicological Profile for Asbestos (Draft for Public Comment).* Atlanta, GA: U.S. Department of Health and Human Services, Public Health Service, 2001, 101–5.

ATSDR. *Toxicological Profile for Benzene (Draft for Public Comment).* Atlanta, GA: U.S. Department of Health and Human Services, Public Health Service, 2005a, 206–8.

ATSDR. *Toxicological Profile for Lead (Draft for Public Comment).* Atlanta, GA: U.S. Department of Health and Human Services, Public Health Service, 2005b, 41.

Bequele, A., and W.E. Myers. *First Things First in Child Labour: Eliminating Work Detrimental to Children.* Geneva: ILO/IPEC, 1995.

Carskadon, M.A. "Patterns of Sleep and Sleepiness in Adolescents." *Pediatrician* 17:1 (1990): 5–12.

Consumer Product Safety Commission. "Ride-on Mower Hazard Analysis (1987–1990)." Washington, DC: U.S. Consumer Product Safety Commission, Division of Hazard Analysis, Directorate for Epidemiology, National Injury Information Clearinghouse. Unpublished data, 1993.

Ehrlich, P.F., W.T. McClellan, J.C. Hemkamp, S.S. Islam, and A.M. Ducatman. "Understanding Work-Related Injuries in Children: A Perspective in West Virginia Using the State-Managed Workers' Compensation System." *Journal of Pediatric Surgery* 39:5 (2004): 768–72.

Forastieri, V. *Children at Work: Health and Safety Risks.* 2nd ed. Geneva: ILO/IPEC, 2002.

Ide, L.S., and D.L. Parker. "Hazardous Child Labor: Lead and Neurocognitive Development." *Public Health Report* 120:6 (2005): 607–12.

Mueller, B.A., D.L. Mohr, J.C. Rice, and D.I. Clemmer. "Factors Affecting Individual Injury Experience Among Petroleum Drilling Workers." *Journal of Occupational Medicine* 29:2 (1987): 126–31.

National Institute for Occupational Safety and Health (NIOSH). *Child Labor Research Needs: Report of the Child Labor Research Group.* Cincinnati, OH: Publications Dissemination, Education and Information Division, NIOSH, 1997.

National Research Council—Institute of Medicine (NRC). *Protecting Youth at Work: Health, Safety, and Development of Working Children and Adolescents in the United States.* Washington, DC: National Academy Press, 1998.

Tucker, L. *Fingers to the Bone: United States Failure to Protect Child Farmworkers.* Washington, DC: Human Rights Watch, 2000.

WHO. *Technical Meeting on Exposure-Response Relationship of Noise on Health.* Bonn: World Health Organization—Regional Office for Europe and European Center for Environment and Health, 2002, 199.

WHO Study Group. *Children at Work: Special Health Risks.* WHO Technical Report Series 756. Geneva: World Health Organization, 1987.

Section 4. Action Against Child Labor

The United Nations and UNICEF

Alec Fyfe, Senior Child Labor Specialist, International Labor Organization

Child labor is a multifaceted problem requiring a variety of interventions, both social and economic. The mandate of the United Nations to promote social and economic development and human rights necessarily means that it has a systemwide concern for child labor. Though the ILO may have the lead responsibility within the UN system for child labor, other agencies have a key role to play if underlying factors that give rise to child labor are to be addressed. Indeed, this has long been recognized by the ILO itself, which has argued for closer cooperation among the various agencies of the UN system so that its full force can be brought to bear, for example, on poverty reduction, education, and children's rights. This requires the active engagement of appropriate agencies of the UN system, including UNICEF, UNESCO, WHO, and the World Bank. UNICEF is viewed as particularly critical because of its mandate to protect and promote the welfare and rights of all children.

The key challenge is to streamline and better integrate the UN's response to child labor so as to deploy to maximum effect the comparative advantages of the various agencies and to avoid wasteful duplication and unnecessary competition. This is part and parcel of increasing pressure from governments for UN reform that was given new impetus by the *Report of the Secretary-General's High-Level Panel* (UN 2006). A less fragmented UN system that delivers "as one" would provide the framework for a more effective response.

In particular, it would enable a better integration of child labor elimination into UN-sponsored development initiatives, especially the Millennium Development Goals (MDGs) and Education for All (EFA), adopted in 2000 and 1990, respectively.

United Nations Children's Fund (UNICEF)

UNICEF was established in 1946, initially on a temporary emergency basis, as a response to child welfare concerns in war-torn Europe, but in the early 1950s this mandate became widened to include the developing world. Over the years, UNICEF has become the most publicly recognized and supported UN agency, and it is one of the most field based. These two characteristics—broad public support and an extensive network of field operations—mean that UNICEF is well positioned to contribute to child labor elimination efforts.

However, for much of its early history UNICEF showed little interest in child labor (Cunningham 2001). During the 1980s, UNICEF's strategic focus was predominately on child survival issues related to the first five years of life, rather than child development and children's rights. From the mid-1980s, child rights concerns gradually gained in profile within UNICEF, especially with the adoption of a policy on "Children in Especially Difficult Circumstances" (CEDC) that included street and working children. In fact, much of UNICEF's involvement with child labor at the time, and into the early 1990s, came through a focus on street children, especially in Latin America and, more specifically, Brazil.

It was not until 1994 that UNICEF began to formulate a global policy on child labor in response to the growing international interest in the problem and the impact of the rapid ratification of the UN Convention on the Rights of the Child (CRC), adopted in 1989. UNICEF began to give more attention to child protection issues, as they were now called, as a consequence of reviewing its position on CEDC in 1996. In the same year, UNICEF decided to devote its flagship publication, *The State of the World's Children* (UNICEF 1997), to the problem of child labor.

Through a series of consultations and initiatives during 1995–1997, UNICEF began to define its comparative advantage in child labor. It was recognized that UNICEF brought considerable strengths via its extensive country presence; capacity to work across sectors; ability to partner NGOs and support social mobilization efforts; and, not least, its work in support of basic education. Moreover, from its experiences in promoting child survival in the mid- to late 1980s, UNICEF had learned that setting quantifiable, time-bound goals is an important means of galvanizing global effort on behalf of children.

During the 1990s, UNICEF became a respected international leader in education. UNICEF was one of the sponsors of the EFA conference held at Jomtien, Thailand, in 1990, and its follow-up in Dakar, Senegal, in 2000. Following Dakar, thirteen agencies formed the UN Girls' Education Initiative under the leadership of UNICEF. This recognition and leadership in basic education gives UNICEF an important entry point in global efforts against child labor.

Starting in 2002, UNICEF made child protection one of five organizational priorities. This move was reaffirmed in UNICEF's corporate plan for 2006–2009, in which child labor features as part of both its basic education and child protection strategies. UNICEF views child labor as an issue that needs to be integrated within all of its appropriate programs spanning child rights advocacy, education, and health. During the period 1998–2002, UNICEF piloted a program called "Education as a Preventive Strategy Against Child Labor" as a means of promoting this concept.

UNICEF has, in particular, developed the concept of the protective environment as central to its approach to child labor and other child protection issues. Building a protective environment for children involves many elements, from government commitment to children's rights to providing services for recovery and reintegration of child victims of exploitation and abuse.

UNICEF also played an important role in facilitating the 2002 Special Session of the United Nations General Assembly on Children. The special session provided a new focus on child labor within the broader context of international cooperation. A key outcome was the agreement that child labor needed to be mainstreamed into national poverty eradication and development efforts, especially in policies and programs dealing with health, education, employment, and social protection.

UNICEF also has a special role in supporting the supervisory machinery of the CRC. In addition to examining country reports, the CRC also holds annual one-day discussions, called "Days of General Discussions," on designated topics. In 1993, economic exploitation was chosen. UNICEF was also given the lead role in supporting the UN Study on Violence against Children, which was reported to the General Assembly in October 2006, and which had a dedicated chapter on the workplace.

Finally, UNICEF has been an important partner in various interagency initiatives, most notably, the memorandum of understanding project in Bangladesh with the ILO and the Bangladesh Garment Manufacturers Association (1997); the Understanding Children's Work research project with ILO and the World Bank (2000); and the Global Child Labor and EFA Task Force with ILO, UNESCO, the United Nations Development Program, and the World Bank (2005). Though these interagency initiatives have high transaction costs in terms of consultation and planning, they send the right message that cooperation and coordination are preferable to going it alone—and they represent the future of how the UN system should do business.

United Nations Educational, Scientific, and Cultural Organization (UNESCO)

UNESCO made some early contributions to child labor. At the Fourteenth International Conference on Public Education, held in Geneva in July 1951, under the auspices of UNESCO, a recommendation was adopted affirming the interrelationship between compulsory education and child labor elimination. In 1989, both UNESCO and UNICEF collaborated on a digest on child labor and education in India and Southeast Asia. UNESCO's main contribution to child labor efforts after 1990 was its leadership of the EFA movement. However, the explicit link between the EFA goal and child labor elimination lay dormant until after the Dakar conference in 2000. Since 2005, however, UNESCO has joined the interagency Global Task Force on EFA and Child Labor, and its 2006 monitoring report on EFA acknowledged the linkage with the goal of child labor elimination.

World Health Organization (WHO)

WHO collaborated with the ILO in the 1980s on hazardous child labor, a collaboration that was not revived until 2002. By 2003, WHO collaborating centers in occupational health had identified child labor as a priority area. WHO produced a training resource on child labor in 2006 and has included the issue in child health campaigns.

The World Bank

The World Bank is the newest major actor on the international child labor scene. In the run-up to the Oslo International Child Labor Conference in 1997, the bank began to formulate a child labor policy. In the following year it produced a position paper and launched its Global Child Labor Program. The bank has been an active partner with the Understanding Children's Work Project, reflecting its comparative advantage in child labor research, albeit largely from an economics perspective. Individual researchers attached to the bank have made important contributions to the literature since the early 1990s. The World Bank views child labor, not from a rights perspective, but from an economic standpoint, stressing the role of household decision making and the role child labor plays in perpetuating poverty. However, there is a question about how far its research and policy stances penetrate its mainstream lending activities, policy dialogues with governments, and steerage of global development mechanisms such as the MDGs, Poverty Reduction Strategy Papers, Fast-Track Initiative, and support of EFA.

The Global Compact

At the World Economic Forum, Davos, on January 31, 1999, UN secretary-general Kofi Annan challenged world business leaders to adopt a Global Compact and to embrace and uphold nine universal principles in their corporate practices. Principle 5 calls for the effective abolition of child labor. The Global Compact is not a regulatory instrument, nor a code of conduct, but a means of promoting core ILO labor standards within the business community. Those corporations that sign on to the Global Compact are asked to post, at least once a year, on their Web sites, concrete steps they have taken to act on any of the now ten principles (an "anticorruption" principle was adopted in 2004) along with the lessons they have learned from doing so. The Global Compact shows the UN tapping into the growing movement of corporate social responsibility that has been stimulated, in no small measure, by the issue of child labor in supply chains.

The Millennium Development Goals

At the Millennium Assembly, which took place at the UN in September 2000, the largest ever gathering of world leaders adopted the "Millennium Declaration," setting forth a series of quantifiable and time-bound goals (to 2015) to reduce poverty, disease, and deprivation. There are eight MDGs and eighteen targets to achieve sustainable development for the world's poorest people. Though child labor does not appear explicitly in the MDGs, there are strong linkages between child labor and many of the MDGs, for example, poverty reduction (MDG 1); education for all (MDG 2); gender equality (MDG 3); combating HIV/AIDS (MDG 6); and a global partnership for development (MDG 8), including decent work for youths (ILO 2006, 56).

The MDGs, Poverty Reduction Strategies, and EFA have become the major potential vehicles for the worldwide movement against child labor. The major challenge in the coming years for the global effort against child labor is to better integrate child labor elimination into these dominant development frameworks at national and international levels.

References and Further Reading

Cunningham, Hugh. "The Rights of the Child and the Wrongs of Child Labour: An Historical Perspective." In *Child Labour: Policy Options,* ed. Kristoffel Lieten and Ben White, 13–26. Amsterdam: Aksant Academic, 2001.

Fyfe, Alec. *The Worldwide Movement Against Child Labor: Progress and Future Directions.* Geneva: ILO, 2007.

ILO. *The End of Child Labour: Within Reach.* Geneva: ILO, 2006.

Pinheiro, Paulo. *World Report on Violence Against Children.* Geneva: UN, 2006.

Tzannatos, Zafris, and Peter Fallon. *Child Labor: Issues and Directions for the World Bank.* Washington, DC: World Bank, 1998.

UN. *Delivering as One: Report of the Secretary-General's High-Level Panel.* New York: UN, 2006.

UNICEF. *The State of the World's Children.* New York: Oxford University Press, 1997.

Millennium Development Goals

Professor Jaap E. Doek, Emeritus Professor of Family and Juvenile Law, Vrije Universiteit, and Chairperson, UN Committee on the Rights of the Child (2001–2007)

At the dawn of a new millennium, heads of state and government adopted the United Nations Millennium Declaration. This declaration contains what became known as the eight Millennium Development Goals (MDGs):

MDG 1. Eradicate extreme poverty and hunger.
MDG 2. Achieve universal primary education.
MDG 3. Promote gender equality and empower women.
MDG 4. Reduce child mortality.
MDG 5. Improve maternal health.
MDG 6. Combat HIV/AIDS, malaria and other diseases.
MDG 7. Ensure environmental sustainabililty.
MDG 8. Develop a global partnership for development.

The efforts to prevent and eliminate child labor can contribute to the achievement of these goals. The linkages between combating child labor and the first, second, and sixth Millennium Development Goals are the most obvious, but there are other connections as well. Further, these linkages are not a simple one-on-one matter between specific MDGs and child labor. There is a complex system of interrelations that connect efforts to reduce poverty, increase completion of primary education, combat HIV/AIDS, and prevent and eliminate child labor. Achievements in one area, for example, poverty, often have an impact in other areas, such as education, child labor, and health care (child mortality and maternal health).

To avoid the possible misunderstanding that combating child labor is mainly a tool in achieving MDGs, it is important to emphasize that it is a human rights imperative. Article 32 of the Convention on the Rights of the Child (CRC) says, "State Parties recognize the right of the child to be protected from economic exploitation and from performing any work that is likely to be hazardous or to interfere with the child's education or to be harmful to the child's . . . development." Section 2 of this article requires that state parties take a variety of measures to ensure that this right is implemented. ILO Conventions 138 and 182 confirm and elaborate the human rights approach to combating child labor. The protection provided in Article 32 of the CRC is a right for all children on the state party's territory, without discrimination of any kind (Article 2 of the CRC). In this regard it should be noted—as confirmed by various studies—that children most vulnerable to economic exploitation often belong to groups subject to discrimination, such as ethnic minorities, indigenous and tribal peoples, low and poor socioeconomic class or caste members, and groups living in remote areas.

The CRC has been ratified by 193 states (out of the 195 that exist) and it is therefore almost universally applicable to all children in the world. Combating child labor, providing education for all, and eradication of poverty are not only important for economic reasons. The MDGs are relevant for all children, and are not just morally binding, but can be firmly based in the CRC, and are therefore meant to respect and implement the fundamental human rights of children (and all other human beings).

Reduction of Extreme Poverty and Child Labor

The link between poverty and child labor runs both ways. On the one hand, child labor contributes to a continuation of poverty; on the other hand, poverty is a major cause of the continuation of child labor. This vicious circle can be broken only if effective measures are taken to reduce and eliminate extreme forms of poverty. It goes beyond the scope of this contribution to give a full description of the many and complex aspects of poverty reduction. In his book *The End of Poverty*, Jeffrey D. Sachs gave a full picture of these many aspects and provided a compelling blueprint for eliminating extreme poverty, affecting about 1 billion people, by 2025.

In the Monterrey Consensus of 2002, the international community has committed itself to various measures to achieve the first MDG, such as urging "all developed countries that have not done so to make concrete efforts towards the goal of 0.7 percent of gross national product (GNP) to official development assistance" (UN 2002, repeating a similar commitment made at the Rio Summit of 1992). One of the measures introduced in recent years in many developing countries is the development and implementation of Poverty Reduction Strategy Papers (PRSPs) in cooperation with the IMF and the World Bank. The PRSP contains the country's goals, targets, policies, and strategies to reduce poverty and is meant to give coherence to the country's efforts to fight poverty and to provide a framework for official debt relief. But an explicit concern—and related measures—with the elimination of child labor is often missing in the PRSPs. A review by the World Bank in 2005 showed that, of the seventy countries that have prepared a PRSP, only twelve paid specific attention to child labor.

In the coming years, more targeted measures are needed to mainstream elimination of child labor in the poverty-reduction strategies. The ILO is active in this regard, reporting that a growing number of countries, such as Bangladesh, Chad, Honduras, Pakistan, Senegal, and Tanzania, have taken steps to incorporate child labor indicators in the monitoring of their poverty-reduction policies. Furthermore, it is important and encouraging that many PRSPs emphasize agriculture and rural development given the fact that most working children are involved in agricultural activities.

In conclusion, in order to make progress on the elimination of child labor, the PRSPs must incorporate measures to that effect, and the countries that have developed these strategies should be provided with the foreign assistance needed for their implementation instead of being forced to work with a fixed budget set by donors. Unfortunately, as Jeffrey D. Sachs illustrated, poverty-reduction programs are chronically underfunded compared with what is needed to achieve the MDGs.

Primary Education for All and Child Labor

The link between the second MD—to ensure that all boys and girls complete a full course of primary schooling—and the elimination of child labor is quite obvious and, as with poverty, the link runs both ways. For many years the movement for Education for All (EFA) and the one for the elimination of child labor were segregated worlds running in parallel, but with little interconnection. In recent years, however, there has been a growing recognition of the interconnection at the international and national levels, and cooperation among such agencies as the ILO, UNESCO, UNICEF, and the World Bank is growing.

However, the link is not that simple, as more children in education means fewer child workers. A comprehensive and integrated policy is required to achieve the second MDG and at the same time to eliminate child labor. Measures in the area of education should improve not only the availability and accessibility, with special attention for girls and other groups of children subject to discrimination, but also the quality of education. For many countries, this will require a significant increase in investments in education. Many countries are incorporating measures to expand the number of schools, and to improve accessibility and quality of education, along with various income-transfer programs, into their PRSPs. Allocations of at least 6 percent of gross national product (GNP) are required to meet the minimum international standard. Priority should be given to primary education (for example, 50 percent of the total allocation), along with proper investment in secondary and higher education. In addition, specific measures such as income-transfer programs should be taken to compensate for the loss of income from child labor, but with the condition that school-age children do attend school.

Furthermore, primary education must be free, in compliance with Article 28, Part 1, of the CRC. But the abolition of school fees should come with measures to compensate for the schools' loss of income. Failure to do this can result in hidden fees imposed by teachers, or very large class sizes and a lack of teachers, impacting the quality of education and resulting in high dropout rates. But even completion of primary schooling does not automatically result in the elimination of child labor. In many countries, compulsory (primary) education ends between the ages of twelve and fourteen. However, the minimum age for admission to employment under ILO Convention 138 is fifteen years. It is therefore important to harmonize the age for the end of compulsory education with the minimum age for labor, as is regularly recommended by the UN Committee on the Rights of the Child.

Special attention should be given to children who combine work and education. The ILO estimated in 2002 that close to half of working children also attend school. Studies do indicate some differences between working children and nonworking children in terms of less regular attendance and more tardiness and tiredness. Careful assessment is needed of the impact of hours worked per day and the nature of children's work on educational performance.

A recent study by ILO/IPEC found that the elimination of child labor and its replacement by universal primary education (for the six- to fifteen-year-old age-group), will yield enormous economic benefits. It estimated the global costs over the period 2001 to 2020 at US$760 billion, whereas the total benefits accruing during that period would amount US$5,106 billion. This means that the benefits exceed the costs by a ratio of 6.7 to 1. Regional differences are highest in North Africa and the Middle East (8.4 to 1), and lowest in sub-Saharan Africa (5.2 to 1). In short, if the international community—in particular the rich donor countries—is serious about its commitment to achieve universal primary education for all boys and girls, the investment necessary should not be a problem given its internal rate of return of 43.8 percent.

HIV/AIDS and Child Labor

Between HIV/AIDS and child labor there again is a two-way link. A series of ILO/IPEC rapid assessments of child labor in sub-Saharan Africa confirm that children who are severely affected by HIV/AIDS are most likely to be in the worst forms of child labor. For instance, in Zambia the pandemic has increased the child labor force by as much as 24 to 30 percent. At the same time, information indicates that victims of the worst forms of child labor, such as sexual exploitation, trafficking, and domestic labor, are at significant risk to be infected with HIV/AIDS.

Programs addressing these forms of child labor should and do pay special attention to avoiding or preventing these risks. In doing so they contribute to halting the spread of HIV/AIDS and to reversing it (MGD 6). ILO/IPEC is developing various actions to integrate into its programs for the elimination of child labor focused attention on the risks and implications of HIV/AIDS for working children, including educational and awareness-raising campaigns. Of course, combating child labor is only one tool to reduce the number of children at risk for HIV/AIDS. Much more is needed, and we know by now that education is the key social vaccine against this pandemic. In particular, improving education for girls reduces their risk of HIV/AIDS.

Some Final Observations on MDGs and Child Labor

The previous remarks on the links between the prevention and elimination of child labor and achieving the MDGs provide just an illustrative snapshot. For instance, combating child labor can also contribute to the promotion of gender equality (MDG 3) and the reduction of incidences of other major diseases. There are also links with developing a global partnership for development (MDG 8). A global partnership to combat child labor has been developing and growing in strength. The ILO/IPEC is developing a movement that involves other UN agencies (UNESCO, UNICEF, WHO, World Bank), employers' organizations, trade unions, the donor community, nongovernmental organizations (at the national and international level), the media, and, last but not least, the children themselves. It is this international movement for the elimination of child labor that can significantly contribute to the achievement of the millennium development goals.

References and Further Reading

Alston, Philip, and Mary Robinson. *Human Rights and Development: Towards Mutual Reinforcement.* Oxford: Oxford University Press, 2005, "Part C. Child Labor and Access to Education."

Betcherman, Gordon, Jean Fares, Amy Luinstra, and Robert Prouty. *Child Labour, Education, and Children's Rights.* Social Protection Discussion Paper, Series 0412, World Bank, Washington, DC, July 2004.

Fyfe, Alec. "Child Labour and Education: Revisiting the Policy Debate," in *Child Labour: Policy Options,* ed. Kristoffel Lieten and Ben White, 67–84. Amsterdam: Aksant Academic Publishers, 2001.

ILO. *Investing in Every Child: An Economic Study of the Costs and Benefit of Eliminating Child Labor.* Geneva: ILO/IPEC, December 2003.

ILO. *The End of Child Labor: Within Reach.* Global Report under the Follow-Up to the ILO Declaration on Fundamental Principles and Rights at Work 2006. International Labor Conference, 95th Session, 2006, Report 1B.

Lieten, G.K., ed. *The Child Labour Problem, Issues and Solutions.* Amsterdam: IREWOC/DCI, 2004.

Rau, Bill. *Combating Child Labor and HIV/AIDS in Sub-Saharan Africa. A Review of Policies, Programs and Projects in South-Africa, the United Republic of Tanzania and Zambia to Identify Good Practices.* Geneva: ILO/IPEC, July 2002.

Sachs, Jeffrey D. *The End of Poverty: Economic Possibilities for Our Time.* New York: Penguin, 2005.

UN. *Report on the International Conference on Financing for Development: Monterrey, Mexico, 18–22 March 2002.* New York: United Nations, 2002.

UNESCO. *EFA Global Monitoring Report 2005: Education for All: The Quality Imperative.* Paris: UNESCO, 2004.

UNICEF. *Medium Term Strategic Plan (MTSP), 2006–2009: Investing in Children: The UNICEF Contribution to Poverty Reduction and the Millennium Summit Agenda.* New York: UNICEF, July 2005.

World Bank. *A Sourcebook for Poverty Reduction Strategies.* Washington, DC: World Bank, July 2004.

World Bank. *Going to School/Going to Work: A Report on Treatment of Child Labor and EFA in World Bank Projects and Policy Documents.* Washington, DC: World Bank, 2005.

International Labor Organization (ILO) and the International Program for the Elimination of Child Labor (IPEC)

G.K. Lieten, Professor of Child Labour Studies at the International Institute of Social History and at the University of Amsterdam; Director of International Research on Working Children (IREWOC)

The International Labor Organization (ILO) is the paramount supranational organization to put in place international consensus on policies in regard to child labor. The ILO, headquartered in Geneva, came into existence in 1919 as part of the peace treaty at the end of World War I. It is a tripartite organization in which national representatives from governments, trade union federations, and employers' organizations in the member countries are represented as equal partners. It thus has a fairly democratic representation of the different stakeholders in the field of labor relations. The so-called conventions on specific labor standards and labor rights and their accompanying recommendations, which are adopted at regular intervals, have formed the basis for labor legislation by member states after their national governments have ratified the conventions. The ILO has in place supervisory procedures, which help to assure that member states introduce a proper legislative framework and introduce proper measures to ensure that legislation is implemented.

Most of the work of the ILO focuses on various aspects of adult labor, which are now being covered by the motto "Decent Work." Child labor, however, right from its inception, has also been on the agenda. Prior to the existence of the ILO, a diplomatic conference at Berne, Switzerland, in 1913 had already adopted a convention prohibiting the employment of young persons in industry during the night. The peace conference at the end of World War I included as one of the major tasks of the ILO "the abolition of child labor and the imposition of such limitations on the labor of young persons as shall permit the continuation of their education and assure their proper physical development" (Thomas 1931, 143). The wording was quite similar to Clause 32 on child labor in the UN Convention on the Rights of the Child of 1989.

The first session of the annual ILO conference was held in Washington in 1919, although the United States had not ratified the peace treaty and took specific exception to the labor clause in the treaty (Johnston 1924). At this first session, representatives from thirty-nine nations fixed the minimum age for employment of children in industry at fourteen years, and prohibited night work for children under eighteen. The impact of these conventions was minimal. By the early 1930s, eighteen countries had ratified the minimum-age convention. Half of these countries already had similar national legislation in place before 1919: Belgium, Bulgaria, Czechoslovakia, Denmark, Great Britain, Ireland, Greece, Switzerland, and Yugoslavia. In the list of other countries that ratified (Chili, Cuba, Estonia, Japan, Latvia, Luxemburg, the Netherlands, Poland, and Romania), some of the major industrialized countries were missing. Albert Thomas, the ILO secretary-general, later lamented that "the convention did not aim high enough, and that the ratification involved practically no change in national custom even where that custom was quite unsatisfactory" (Thomas 1931, 143).

The age limit, which was set at fourteen, was a compromise. Some countries, using the physical and mental immaturity of the child as the basic argument, had pleaded for sixteen as the cutoff. The problem, however, was that many countries had compulsory education only up to a lesser age, and many children would then be left in a void: no longer in school and not allowed to work. This consideration would pop up again at the 1973 Minimum Age Convention, which set different age levels depending on the length of education. The first ILO convention actually made an exception for Japan and India, which were not expected to catch up with the more advanced school-leaving age.

Ratification of the 1919 convention proceeded slowly, and the policy throughout the long period up to 1973, when a new convention covering the entire economy was adopted, was to develop instruments that applied only to specific sectors. Many countries that could not yet accede to legislation against all forms of child labor could nevertheless be expected to collaborate in measures relating to specific sectors in which child labor was prevalent and could not be tolerated. This approach has similarities with Convention 182, on worst forms of child labor, which would be developed in 1999. Separate conventions fixed the same minimum age (fourteen) for maritime work and agricultural work. The latter, although it allowed many exceptions, attracted very few ratifying nations. Some of the worst abuses of child labor were known to exist outside the fields covered by the separate conventions, and, in 1932, a convention forbidding employment in small workshops, shops, and hotels was added. An exception was made for light work for a maximum of two hours a day outside school hours by children over the age of twelve. Beginning with the revised minimum-age convention on shipping in 1936, the minimum age was raised to fifteen. That age limit thereafter would become the norm.

In 1973, the annual International Labor Conference agreed on Convention 138 (the Minimum Age Convention for Admission to Employment). Convention 138 incorporated many of the provisions and exceptions of the earlier conventions. It was decided that the time had come, as stated in the preamble, for a new convention to "gradually replace the existing ones applicable to limited economic sectors, with a view to achieving the total abolition of child labor." The insertion of the word "gradually" implied that countries initially could choose to abide by the earlier sectoral conventions, and that governments, together with international aid agencies, could work toward the eradication of poverty and underdevelopment, which were regarded as constituting the basic cause of child labor, and which also needed to be eradicated gradually.

Convention 138 constructed three age categories. In the youngest category (six to twelve years old), work was prohibited except for light work in family undertakings and work in the household, including domestic work. In the thirteen- to fourteen-year-old category, only light work was allowed, outside school hours, for fewer than fourteen hours a week and not straining the physical and mental maturity of the child. In the category of adolescents (age fifteen and above), regular work was permissible, but not in sectors that could become injurious to health, such as the mining or chemical industries.

The convention conceded that not all countries had the same level of development, and so, distinctions should be made in the minimum age for developed countries and for countries that had insufficiently developed economic and educational systems. The age at which light work could start was lowered to twelve in developing countries (unless they decided otherwise) and the minimum age for full employment was fourteen instead of fifteen. Recommendation 146, which was a sequel to Convention 138, states that the objective of member states should be to raise the minimum age to sixteen. Article 2 of the convention requires that the minimum age shall not be less than the age of completion of compulsory schooling. Linking child labor to education is an important feature of the convention and allows for both upward and downward adjustments: lower age limits when children leave the school system earlier, and higher limits when compulsory school-leaving age is revised upward.

In addition to the age exception, Convention 138 allowed countries that were administratively or economically less developed to exclude certain sectors, except for mining, transport, construction, electricity, plantations, and manufacturing. Legislation in many developing countries thus excludes certain sectors and certain types of undertaking, such as those with a small workforce, from their child labor legislation. The convention allowed governments to exclude certain types of work, even in the six- to eleven-year-old category, such as work in family undertakings, as long as it is not dangerous to the child and does not interfere with schooling. Work in the household also remained excluded from the definition of child labor. If the ILO had not made provisions for these exceptions, consensus on the new convention, and its rapid ratification, would have been in jeopardy. The ILO has to follow a middle course between a codifying convention that merely restates the legal code in specific countries, as happened with the 1919 convention, and a normative convention that imposes a more radical code on countries that are lagging.

Convention 138 was also important for the inclusive meaning that it gave to child labor. Child labor was essentially restricted to productive work, that is, all economic activities regardless of employment status. The practice in many countries, until then, was that only wage work falling under a formal employment relationship was covered by legislation and that self-employment, work within the informal sector, and work within the family were not covered. The new convention, by including the nonwage sector, went a long way in covering most working children, since the majority of child laborers are actually in nonwage employment.

Following the Year of the Child, set by the UN in 1979, the ILO Committee of Experts examined the impact of Convention 138 through the first general survey on child labor. The committee made it clear that not every kind of activity should be considered inappropriate and should not be forbidden. Child labor should be considered as work that calls for greater physical and mental capacities than children of a particular age normally possess, or work that interferes with their educational development. Since poverty and underdevelopment are the major reasons for child labor, the problem should not be considered in isolation, and solutions should be found in the general improvement of economic conditions and educational infrastructure. The committee therefore also warned that "the fact that they do work must be faced, and their work must be progressively restricted and regulated" (Swepston 1982, 579). That vision had been basic to ILO's policies and would continue to be so.

In 1990, with an initial financial injection by Germany, the International Program on the Elimination of Child Labor (IPEC) was set up. Within a couple of years, IPEC became the biggest division within the ILO. It combined project work with an elaborate scheme of countrywise statistical surveys and specific sector studies on child labor. Together with SIMPOC (Statistical Information and Monitoring Program on Child Labor) and relying on data provided by World Bank studies, IPEC authored a number of important studies on child labor, its extent, its cause, and its solutions.

Against a background of growing concern that certain forms of child labor are so grave and inhumane that they can no longer be tolerated, a consensus emerged in the 1990s that the highest priority should be given to eliminating these worst forms of child labor. It was further agreed that visible results should be achieved within a short time frame, rather than in some indefinite future, and that a concerted program of action should be launched in order to achieve rapid results: "Giving priority to combating the worst forms of child labor is simply a matter of doing first things first. It provides an entry point to promote and facilitate further action to attain the ultimate goal" (ILO 2002, 21).

In 1999, after years of deliberation on the exact wording, Convention 182 on Elimination of the Worst Forms of Child Labor was adopted. After restating that poverty was the main cause of child labor, and that the long-term solution lies in sustained and equitable economic progress, Article 3 identified different types of worst forms: the unconditional worst forms—slave labor, bonded labor, prostitution, participants in armed conflicts, and illicit traders, totaling 8 million children—and the hazardous forms: "work which, by its nature or the circumstances in which it is carried out, is likely to harm the health, safety or morals of children."

Within a short period of time, Convention 182 was ratified by a majority of member states. In its aftermath, ratification of Convention 138 also started accelerating. By the middle of 2007, 165 countries had ratified Convention 182 and 150 countries had ratified Convention 138. The progress in finding a consensus on an international agenda was remarkable, and accordingly, the 2006 International Labor Conference has called for appropriate time-bound measures, parallel to the Millennium Development Goals, which would allow for the elimination of the worst forms of child labor by 2016.

Like previous conventions, Convention 182 allowed for flexible interpretation. The "worst forms" industries are to be determined by national laws or regulations, after consultation with the organizations of employers and workers concerned. Since the ILO does not have coercive powers, the interpretation and the implementation of worst-forms policy is to be negotiated at the national level. Formally, each country decides on the proper reading of the "worst forms." The strength of the convention is its focus on an action program that distinguishes the worst forms of child labor from other forms of work done by children that do not have obvious and tangible harmful effects. Interpretation and implementation are subject to national consensus, but the important role of the ILO lies in its prudent fostering of a new consensus on what is to be understood as decent work. Child labor is integral to that approach, and an international norm on what is tolerable in childhood, and what is not, has clearly been reached.

References and Further Reading

Gibberd, Kathleen. *ILO: Unregarded Revolution.* London: Dent and Sons, 1937.

ILO. *Child Labor: Targeting the Intolerable.* Geneva: International Labor Office, 1996.

ILO. *A Future Without Child Labor: Global Report Under the Follow-up to the ILO Declaration on Fundamental Principles and Rights of Work.* Geneva: International Labor Office, International Labor Conference 90th Session, Report I(B), 2002.

ILO. *The End of Child Labor Within Reach.* Geneva: ILO, 95th Session, Report I(B), 2006.

IPEC. *Investing in Every Child: An Economic Study of the Costs and Benefits of Eliminating Child Labor.* Geneva: ILO/IPEC, 2004.

Johnston, G.A. *International Social Progress. The Work of the International Labour Organisation of the League of Nations.* London: Allen and Unwin, 1924.

Lieten, G.K. "Child Labor: What Happened to the Worst Forms?" *Economic and Political Weekly* 61:2 (2006): 102–7.

Swepston, Lee. "Child Labor: Its Regulation by ILO Standards and National Legislation." *International Labor Review* 121:5 (1982): 577–93.

Thomas, Albert. *The International Labor Organisation: The First Decade.* London: George Allen and Unwin, 1931.

The Role of Nongovernmental Organizations

Mike Dottridge, Human Rights Consultant, Former Director of Anti-Slavery International

At the time the International Labor Organization (ILO) adopted Convention 138 (Minimum Age) in 1973, very few nongovernmental organizations (NGOs) were involved in activities concerning working children. In contrast, by the time the next ILO convention on child labor was adopted a quarter century later, in 1999, many hundreds of NGOs were protesting about child labor or assisting working children, and NGOs had organized a vast protest march that brought working children into the very hall in Geneva where the International Labor Conference was meeting.

Between the 1970s and early years of the twenty-first century, NGOs around the world became involved in a wide range of initiatives to address child labor at the local, national, and international levels. Most were motivated by a sense of outrage at what they saw happening to working children, particularly in the streets, fields, and workshops of developing countries, but their ideas about what response was appropriate varied enormously. Some felt they should pursue a goal of stopping any children below a specific minimum age from entering the world of work (usually the age of fourteen or fifteen). Many felt that some forms of exploitation were more unacceptable than others and focused their efforts on eliminating these. Yet others felt their role was to support working children and provide them with specific services, such as nonformal education. Some gave priority to supporting working children by insisting that all their rights be respected—not just their right to be free from economic exploitation, but also their rights to freedom of expression and freedom of association. This encouraged some adolescent workers to form associations of their own, virtual trade unions, which called for labor rights for adolescent or child workers.

For much of the past twenty years, disagreements among NGOs over the most appropriate objectives and strategies to pursue have been divisive. These disagreements have often taken the form of rivalries between prominent personalities running NGOs. The disagreements put some NGOs at loggerheads with other institutions responding to child labor, both intergovernmental organizations, such as the ILO, and trade union organizations, such as the International Confederation of Free Trade Unions. Even so, the various activities of NGOs have all had a substantial impact.

NGOs and the UN Convention on the Rights of the Child

During the 1980s, a number of NGOs concerned about children's human rights lobbied governments and the United Nations to adopt the Convention on the Rights of the Child (CRC), and worked to influence its provisions. The convention was eventually adopted in 1989. Prominent among these NGOs was Save the Children, an alliance of independent charities based in Europe and North America, each of which organizes or funds projects concerned with children around the world, including children experiencing exploitation or abuse. Also prominent was Defence for Children International, a Geneva-based NGO established especially to coordinate NGO efforts related to debates over the new convention. These debates took place principally in Geneva.

While provisions of the convention were being discussed, activists in South and Southeast Asia urged that the predicament of child workers should be properly addressed in the new convention. This led to the creation in 1986 of a regional network of Asian NGOs, Child Workers in Asia (CWA). CWA drew on the experience of individual NGOs in Asia to influence the contents of the new convention and tried to ensure that the voices of child workers were heard during the debates.

Regional NGO Activism

While discussions about the draft UN convention were going on, other NGOs were focusing their energy on efforts to eradicate specific forms of child exploitation and abuse. In South Asia, activists involved in a campaign against debt bondage during the 1970s and 1980s in India (and in the late 1980s in Pakistan) strategically shifted their focus from adult bonded laborers to child bonded laborers in order to increase their impact (Anti-Slavery Society 1991). Debt bondage, a practice akin to slavery and prohibited by UN convention, involves individuals who accept a loan pledging their labor in repayment. Children become involved when a parent or relative accepting a loan pledges the labor of the child to work off the loan, or when a child inherits a debt from one of his or her parents. In 1989 the Bandhua Mukti Morcha (BMM), or Bonded Liberation Front, in India joined forces with NGOs in Nepal and Pakistan to form the South Asian Coalition on Child Servitude (SACCS), a regional organization to campaign against bonded child labor. While these NGOs were committed to ending all forms of bonded child labor, much of their initial focus was on children engaged in making hand-knotted carpets for export, a new industry developed in India from the 1970s (Anti-Slavery Society 1988).

In Southeast Asia, activists were focusing attention on tourists paying for sex with adolescent girls in Thailand and elsewhere. A widely supported campaign, End Child Prostitution in Asian Tourism (ECPAT), was transformed in the mid-1990s into an international NGO campaigning to stop the commercial sexual exploitation of children by anyone (not just tourists) anywhere in the world. ECPAT played a key role in international conferences held in 1996 and 2001 to promote efforts to stop the commercial sexual exploitation of children, and eventually changed its name to End Child Prostitution, Child Pornography and the Trafficking of Children for Sexual Purposes.

In sub-Saharan Africa, the form of exploitation that attracted NGO attention was the recruitment of children as soldiers (often young children below the age of fifteen). Although this use of children was initially highlighted in Uganda when the insurgent army under the command of Yoweri Museveni took control of the country in 1986, it did not galvanize NGOs throughout Africa into action until the 1990s, under the impetus of conflicts in both West Africa (Liberia and Sierra Leone) and Central Africa (Congo, formerly known as Zaire).

In Latin America, the initial focus on working children took an altogether different form. As a reaction to working children being excluded from trade unions, NGOs supporting what came to be called "child participation" helped working children set up organizations of their own to articulate their views about what measures would or would not be helpful to them as workers. In most cases these workers were adolescents rather than younger children. In Peru, the Movimiento de Adolescentes y Niños Trabajadores, Hijos de Obreros Cristianos (Movement of Adolescent and Child Workers Who Are Children of Christian Workers) spearheaded this movement.

Meanwhile, at the international level, a London-based NGO, Anti-Slavery International, took the lead in the early 1990s in focusing attention on children working as domestic servants, one of the largest single sectors of child employment where the vast majority of workers were girls. Its initial focus was in West Africa, but as the decade progressed, many other NGOs focused attention on this form of employment, where the relative "invisibility" of the child workers had led to them being ignored by previous efforts to tackle child labor.

Child Labor in Export Sectors: NGO Alliances with Trade Unions

By the early 1990s, NGOs in India were working closely with their counterparts in Europe, especially Germany, on a campaign involving children making hand-knotted carpets for export. The focus was initially on bonded children, but the difficulty in distinguishing between these and other children working on carpet looms moved the focus to all children working on carpets illegally, that is to say, children age thirteen or younger. The resulting coalition stopped short of calling for a boycott on imports of Indian or South Asian carpets and instead urged importers to offer a guarantee that their carpets had not been made with the illegal use of children.

When actors in the United States became involved in 1992, the strategy changed. The limelight shifted to Bangladesh and the employment of adolescent girls in factories producing garments for export. At the time, about 1 million women were working in the industry; alongside them were between 50,000 and 75,000 children under age fourteen, mainly girls (UNICEF 1997). This time, however, it was not NGOs in the region that developed the strategy, but trade unions based in the United States and a U.S.-based NGO, the International Labor Rights Fund, working closely with U.S. senator Tom Harkin. Senator Harkin's proposal that imports made by child workers should be not be allowed into the United States precipitated a panic among Bangladesh employers, who summarily dismissed thousands of girls. The unexpected loss of the girls' income caused major difficulties for many households, leading some children to resort to much more hazardous forms of work. This campaign was criticized by NGOs that argued this could not possibly be in the children's best interests. They asserted that it was dangerous for any child labor campaigns to focus on child workers in export sectors, because of the high risk of summary dismissals. This put the NGOs into direct conflict with trade unions in North America and Europe, which wanted such campaigns precisely because the use of cheap child workers was enabling businesses across the developing world to produce items more cheaply than those in the industrialized countries, where union members were losing their jobs.

Arguments about the appropriateness of product boycotts led to a split in India's campaign against bonded child labor. Two of the BMM's leaders held differing views. Swami Agnivesh, who argued that making the import of products conditional on respect for labor rights was simply a cover for Western protectionism, kept the BMM name, while Kailash Satyarthi, who advocated closer links with campaigners in the United States, appropriated the name of SACCS for a new campaign against all forms of child labor in India.

The issue of children in export production was highlighted again in a 1996 campaign about children stitching soccer balls and producing other sporting goods in Pakistan. Both NGOs and trade unions focused public attention on products being imported into Europe or North America whose manufacture involved large numbers of children. Meanwhile, other NGOs were documenting the harm caused to children by such campaigns, arguing that they were not in the children's best interests and consequently violated one of the fundamental principles of the UN's CRC—Article 3.1, "In all actions concerning children . . . the best interests of the child shall be a primary consideration."

The focus on child workers in export sectors led to a spate of initiatives to label goods as "child labor free." Some of these initiatives were driven by companies importing goods from countries with high levels of child labor, while others involved NGOs. SACCS and its partner NGOs in Europe and North America supported the establishment of a special "Rugmark" label to guarantee that certain exported carpets had not been manufactured by children under the age of fourteen and promoted the sale of labeled carpets (Sharma et al. 2000). The scheme started in India and later spread to other countries. In time, the commitment of certain businesses to preventing the employment of children in their supply chains allowed NGOs to become involved in monitoring these commitments, along with the other commitments made by the same businesses to ensuring corporate social responsibility.

1989 Onward: NGOs Promoting General Child Rights

Once the UN CRC was adopted in 1989, many of the NGOs that had influenced its provisions focused their attention on promoting the general framework established by the convention. They felt the convention set out a framework that encouraged respect for children's rights in general, and that it was more important to implement this than to focus on violations of particular articles of the convention, such as Article 32, banning the economic exploitation of children. The framework was intended to help resolve contradictions between competing rights and also between the obligations to allow children to exercise their rights, on the one hand, and the obligation of governmental authorities to protect children, on the other. Chief among the convention's generic provisions were two highlighted by NGOs such as Save the Children: "the principle that the best interests of the child should always be a prime consideration in actions concerning children (article 3); and children's right to express their views on matters affecting them and to have these taken into account in accordance with their age and maturity (article 12)." Such NGOs argued that when trade unions and other NGOs denounced the involvement of children in stitching soccer balls in Pakistan, they were not taking either of these provisions into account. Consequently, in the late 1990s, Save the Children focused its efforts in Pakistan on trying to remedy the harm experienced by children who were dismissed from their jobs, by providing them with suitable alternatives. In 2003, the Save the Children Alliance (representing Save the Children organizations in twenty-nine countries) adopted a policy statement that reflected these principles: "Most forms of work have both good and bad elements, and for this reason, can be both harmful and beneficial to children's development and well-being. Therefore, we accept neither blanket bans of all child work, nor an approach which unequivocally promotes children's work. We believe that different responses are appropriate for different forms of work and for different working children" (International Save the Children Alliance 2003).

Bridging the Gaps: The International Working Group on Child Labor and the International Conferences of 1997

In an effort to confront the contradictions in the approach of different NGOs to the issue of child labor, an International Working Group on Child Labor was established in 1992. It published thirty-five country reports, four regional reports, and a final report in 1998 entitled *Working Children: Reconsidering the Debates.* Under the chairmanship of Nandana Reddy of Concerned for Working Children, an Indian NGO, the working group published a working paper entitled "Have We Asked the Children?" This coincided with the first of two major international conferences held in 1997 on the issue of child labor, and resulted in bringing eight working children from three continents to attend and speak at the conference hosted in Amsterdam by the government of the Netherlands. This focus on the participation of working children alienated some NGOs that wanted priority to be given to eliminating specific forms of exploitation.

The two international conferences in 1997, one in Amsterdam and the other in Oslo, provided opportunities for governments, trade unions, and employers' organizations to say what they thought ought to be done about the increasing numbers of working children in developing countries and to try and build consensus. They were also an opportunity for NGOs to present their findings, to confer with one another, and to influence the international agenda. The outcome of the conferences paved the way for the preparation of the ILO's Convention on the Worst Forms of Child Labor (Convention 182), adopted in June 1999.

The two conferences also resulted in a plan for a campaign that became the Global March Against Child Labor. The march took place between January and June 1998, starting in three separate places (the Philippines, Brazil, and South Africa), and culminated in Geneva on the eve of the first round of discussions about the ILO's new convention. The Global March was supported by both NGOs and trade unions, and consisted of both working children and other activists traveling from country to country to highlight the abuse experienced by working children. They called both for an intensification of efforts to put an end to child labor and for more investment in education (the campaign's slogan was "From Exploitation to Education"). The task of organizing the Global March was given to SACCS of India, which already had experience in organizing long-distance protest marches. Following the march, SACCS and some other supporters opted to keep the Global March in existence, in effect turning the one-off campaign into a permanent NGO with substantial backing from Western-based trade unions.

NGO Activity After the Adoption of ILO Convention 182

Following adoption of ILO Convention 182, many NGOs focused their attention on children in the worst forms of child labor and promoted the new convention. Another consequence of the two 1997 international conferences was increased monetary support for the ILO's International Program for the Elimination of Child Labor (IPEC). More NGOs than ever were becoming service providers to IPEC, carrying out parts of its program, financed by donors such as the government of Germany and the U.S. Department of Labor. However, initial expectations that the new focus on worst forms of child labor would allow efforts to address a more limited and manageable number of children were soon shown to be wrong. The ILO estimated that many tens of millions of children were involved in worst forms. This persuaded some donor governments and NGOs to refocus their efforts on more narrowly defined groups, such as children who were being trafficked (either for commercial sexual exploitation or into various forms of forced labor).

Since 1999 NGOs have continued with a wide range of initiatives concerning working children. The level of infighting between some NGOs and Western-based trade unions has diminished. Reports denouncing the unacceptable involvement of child workers in a range of sectors and countries are still published regularly, but the emphasis on exporting industries has largely been abandoned for several reasons: Multinational companies can no longer afford to ignore labor conditions in their supply chains; many NGOs have recognized the harm such publicity can inflict on working children; and international trade union bodies no longer depend on "name and shame" publicity to persuade multinationals to improve labor conditions.

Many of the NGOs once involved primarily in advocacy and protests have moved their focus onto campaigns for education and better provision of schooling. Kailash Satyarthi, the SACCS and Global March leader, for example, was elected chairperson of a Global Campaign for Education, a coalition of NGOs working in education. The noise and energy that had been channeled into protests against child labor in the late 1990s were subsequently redirected into positive campaigning for more and better schools, bringing them new allies such as UNICEF and Oxfam International.

Among the most notorious worst forms of child labor—such as commercial sexual exploitation, bonded labor, and the recruitment of children as soldiers—none has yet disappeared. NGOs, often working in coalitions, continue to channel their efforts into both publicity about them and efforts to bring them to an end. Human rights NGOs in particular, such as Amnesty International and Human Rights Watch, have kept their focus narrow, either joining coalitions to end these worst forms or putting the limelight on restricted groups of children, such as bonded children working in India's silk industry (Human Rights Watch 2003).

Editor's Note

At the risk of leaving out NGOs that are doing important work in the area of child labor, what follows is a list of major NGOs with programs that are global in scope and missions that relate directly to child labor. A sampling of other NGOs with regional and local scope is provided in later essays throughout this volume.

Anti-Slavery International (www.antislavery.org)
Child Rights Information Network (www.crin.org)
Coalition to Stop the Use of Child Soldiers (www.child-soldiers.org)
Consortium for Street Children (www.streetchildren.org.uk)
Defence for Children International (www.dci-is.org)
ECPAT International (www.ecpat.net)
Global March Against Child Labour (www.globalmarch.org)
Human Rights Watch (www.hrw.org)
International Federation Terre des Hommes (www.terredeshommes.org)
International Save the Children Alliance (www.savethechildren.net)

References and Further Reading

Anti-Slavery Society. *A Pattern of Slavery: India's Carpet Boys*. Child Labor Series 9. London: Anti-Slavery Society, 1988.

Anti-Slavery Society. *Children in Bondage. Slaves of the Subcontinent*. Child Labor Series 10. London: Anti-Slavery Society, 1991.

Human Rights Watch. *Small Change: Bonded Child Labor in India's Silk Industry*. New York: Human Rights Watch, 2003.

International Save the Children Alliance. *Save the Children's Position on Children and Work*. London: International Save the Children Alliance, 2003.

McKechnie, Jim, and Sandy Hobbs, eds. "Working Children: Reconsidering the Debates, Report of the International Working Group on Child Labour." *International Journal of Children's Rights* 7:1 (1999): 91–98.

Sharma, Alakh N., Rajeev Sharma, and Nikhil Raj. "The Impact of Social Labeling on Child Labour in India's Carpet Industry." ILO/IPEC Working Paper, Institute for Human Development, New Delhi, 2000.

UNICEF. *The State of the World's Children 1997—Focus on Child Labour*. New York: Oxford University Press, 1997.

The Role of Trade Unions

Alec Fyfe, Senior Child Labor Specialist, International Labor Organization

Trade unions have played a historic role in combating child labor. In the latter part of the nineteenth century, trade unions were part of broad social movements in Europe and the United States calling for the abolition of child labor through domestic and international legislation. Following a number of national efforts to restrict child labor—as, for example, in Britain and Germany in the 1830s—the first International Workers Congress, held at Geneva in September 1866, called for an international effort to regulate child labor and promote compulsory education.

Trade unions played a key role in setting up the International Labor Organization (ILO) in 1919, and the subsequent adoption of international labor standards regulating child labor, starting with the adoption of Convention 5 on the Minimum Age for Industrial Employment, and culminating in Convention 182 on the Worst Forms of Child Labor in 1999. As one of the three constituents in the tripartite structure of the ILO, along with employer associations and governments, trade unions have historically used the organization as a platform to promote their campaigns against child labor.

The trade union movement took up the child labor challenge once again in the 1980s and early 1990s and helped push child labor toward the top of the international policy agenda. For trade unions, both in Europe and in the United States, the entry point was the increased use of child labor in export industries supplying goods to their domestic markets. Here the labor movement was particularly influential in promoting consumer and political reaction to conditions in certain export industries in developing countries, ranging from garments, to carpets, to sporting goods, to cocoa. This issue, perhaps more than any other, gave child labor an unprecedented international profile in the mid- to late 1990s.

What Do Trade Unions Bring to Child Labor Action?

To begin with, trade unions have a strong vested interest in combating child labor. Child labor flies in the face of their fundamental objectives of more jobs and rights at work. Child labor is seen as a major impediment to opportunities for adult workers to take home a decent living wage and to organize in the workplace. Conversely, providing adult workers with decent wages and freedom to organize is likely to put a stop to child labor.

As mass membership and vertically integrated organizations, linking the local with the global, trade unions bring considerable potential to the worldwide movement against child labor. Sector unions are strategically placed to work at the grassroots level, combating child labor in specific industries. National trade union centers are better placed to support these industry-specific campaigns through their convening role, and also to act in policy areas with governments. At the international level, bodies such as the International Trade Union Confederation, formed in November 2006, and the Global Union Federations, which represent sector-based trade unions in agriculture, mining, and textiles, can support national trade union centers and lobby within global policy debates such as the design and implementation of Poverty Reduction Strategies and Education for All.

Trade unions have been most effective in

their efforts against child labor when they have been part of wider social movements fighting for democracy and social justice. This was the case at the end of the nineteenth century in Europe and the United States, as it was a century later in countries as diverse as Brazil, South Africa, and the transition economies of central and eastern Europe. The most effective role trade unions can play within these broader social movements is to be true to their own goals as workers' organizations fighting for more jobs, increased wages, and improved working conditions.

Collective bargaining is one of the main strategies adopted by trade unions in combating child labor. Likewise, campaigning and lobbying are second nature to trade unions, and they have more than 150 years of experience in targeting child labor. Today, trade unions can lobby governments for changes in public policy and spending—in education, for example—that are organic and sustainable responses to child labor. Additionally, trade unions are at the forefront of campaigns for respect of international standards, such as ILO conventions, that governments have ratified..

Types of Engagement by Trade Unions

Trade unions have a broad range of engagements on the child labor problem. Key among these are lobbying and campaigning; sector alliances; monitoring; support to working children; networking with others; and research and resource mobilization.

Lobbying and campaigning are key activities of trade unions fighting child labor. In Tanzania, for example, the Conservation Hotels and Allied Workers' Union has been active against child domestic labor since 1996, and passed a resolution in 2004 to earmark 25 percent of its resources to tackling this neglected issue. In Kenya, the Union of Domestics, Hotels, Educational Institutions, Hospitals and Allied Union has been campaigning against child domestic labor since 2000. The union has also lobbied the government to ratify ILO Convention 182. In Peru, the Domestic Workers Union successfully lobbied for new legislation, adopted in June 2003, that regulated the sector. The campaign included daily radio programs broadcast across the country. Leading trade unions in Mexico, in May 2006, initiated a call for a National Commission on Child Labor. In Honduras, in 2004, it was trade union representatives who successfully lobbied for the inclusion of child labor in the national Poverty Reduction Strategy. The ratification of ILO Minimum Age Convention 138 by Pakistan in 2006 was the result, in part, of lobbying by the national Pakistan Workers' Federation. In July 2006, teachers' trade unions in Albania achieved a new collective agreement with the Ministry of Education and Science that commits the central and regional education administration to engage in child labor elimination activities.

Trade unions have played an active role in a variety of sector alliances involving child labor that emerged from the mid-1990s onward. It was the labor movement in the United States that prompted the first of these in the Bangladesh garment industry with the signing of a memorandum of understanding in July 1995. This project served as an important model, and its major lessons have been applied subsequently in other export sectors, for example, in soccerball stitching (1997), tobacco (1999), cocoa (2001), and small-scale mining (2005). One important model to have emerged is the Foundation on the Elimination of Child Labor in Tobacco Growing. Founded in 2002, the foundation is industry funded, but has on its board the International Union of Food, Agricultural, Hotel, Restaurant, Catering, Tobacco and Allied Workers' Associations. The ILO initiative, launched in 2005, to eliminate child labor from small-scale mining in ten years is also supported by the International Federation of Chemical, Energy, Mine and General Workers' Union.

Trade unions have traditionally played a watchdog role monitoring and exposing child labor. For example, in the Donetsk region of the Ukraine, the Independent Trade Union of Miners of Ukraine first identified child labor in informal mines and carried out support work for a network of community inspectors. In Nigeria, industrial unions in footwear, rubber, and leather have established monitoring committees against the worst forms of child labor. In the Philippines, the Trade Union Congress has included child labor monitoring in its collective bargaining agreements, and also supports a national initiative called "Sagip-Batang Manggagawa" (Rescue Child Laborers).

Direct support to working children is the most immediate and tangible response to the problem of child labor, and it is not surprising, therefore, that this is an area that has also attracted the involvement of trade unions. Typically this action involves trade unions engaging in education and training activities for working children. In Nepal, trade unions have been involved in developing apprenticeship programs. In other countries, trade unions have supported the establishment of nonformal education programs.

Child labor elimination is a collective endeavor in which broad social networks are important. In Brazil, trade unions are part of a national forum for developing child labor policy and action. There are twenty-seven states that provide networking opportunities for trade unions to link up with other key actors on child labor. Often, as in the case of the Indian state of Andhra Pradesh, trade unions have to first form their own internal coalitions before they can join broader social alliances. In 2001, the six major unions in Andhra Pradesh joined together for the first time to work on one issue together—child labor. The ILO facilitated this coming together of the trade unions as a first step in becoming part of a wider coalition including other civil society partners.

Trade unions have an important role in conducting research on child labor that makes use of their workplace expertise and labor rights concerns. Trade unions can either sponsor research themselves or participate in the research of others. For example, trade unions have contributed to ILO-sponsored Rapid Assessment studies in recent years into the worst forms of child labor. In Sri Lanka, representatives of the national trade union both administered questionnaires in a study of child domestic labor and opened doors for researchers.

Trade unions have also provided resource support to child labor elimination efforts. The Italian Partners Initiative, launched in 1998, brought together Italian trade unions and employers to finance ILO child labor activities in Bangladesh, Nepal, and Pakistan. Trade unions in Japan have supported ILO public education efforts in Albania, Cambodia, Indonesia, and Nepal.

Challenges Facing Trade Unions

The capacity of trade unions to respond to the child labor problem depends on their level of organization. The priority of all trade unions is to strengthen and extend collective bargaining. However, child labor is strong where trade unions are weak. Most child labor is found in the informal economy, particularly agriculture, where trade union organization is limited. Challenges facing trade unions in maximizing their potential as child labor actors can be highlighted in terms of the "four Cs": capacity, commitment, coherence, and cooperation.

Trade unions face a particular set of capacity constraints in responding to child labor in the rural and urban informal economy, as these are typically nontraditional sectors for trade union mobilization. Organizing workers in the informal economy presents major challenges, including legal constraints to organizing young workers who are over the legal minimum age but have not yet reached eighteen years of age. Furthermore, trade unions, unlike many nongovernmental organizations (NGOs), are not single-issue organizations, but have a range of concerns. Child labor may appear, therefore, as one of a host of concerns, if at all.

There is a long way to go, therefore, in convincing many trade unions that combating child labor, particularly in the informal economy, is a way of building effective trade union structures for the future—that the issue of child labor is an important vehicle to promote their objectives and is an entry point into the informal economy. Part of this awareness raising has to do with trade unions' special role, and the need to avoid duplicating the efforts of others, especially NGOs. Generally speaking, providing direct support services to working children and their families, attractive as it might appear, falls outside the comparative advantage of trade unions. Finally, forming alliances with actors outside (sadly, in many instances, also inside) the labor movement remains a considerable challenge.

Trade unions are indispensable in the struggle against child labor as part of a vigorous civil society movement. However, trade unions need to deepen and widen their commitment to the elimination of child labor by coming to terms with the central challenges relating to their capacity, particularly in the growing informal economy, where most child labor is found.

References and Further Reading

Fyfe, Alec, and Michele Jankanish. *Trade Unions and Child Labour: A Guide to Action.* Geneva: ILO, 1997.

ILO. *Trade Unions and Child Labour.* Geneva: ILO, 2000.

ILO. *The End of Child Labour: Within Reach.* Geneva: ILO, 2006.

ILO. *The Role of Employers' and Workers' Organizations in Combating Child Labour.* Geneva: ILO, 2006.

Organization of Working Children

William E. Myers, Department of Human and Community Development,
University of California, Davis

In recent decades, one of the more interesting developments in national and international action addressing child labor has been the widespread emergence of working children's own collective voice. Their participation has been organized both informally in response to particular situations and formally for sustained action over time. There is nothing new about working children's organization in their defense, or even their leadership of labor actions that include adults. Protests, strikes, and other forms of organization undertaken by working children to promote change in employment conditions have been traced at least as far back as the 1830s (Liebel 2004). What is new today is the prominence of working children's movements and the increasing degree to which they are recognized and encouraged by many agencies and experts, but not always from a labor perspective. In fact, perhaps most active supporters of working children's organization today invest in it primarily as a vehicle of children's welfare, development, and human rights, citing as the most pertinent policy framework the UN Convention on the Rights of the Child (CRC) rather than an ILO labor convention. This shifting perspective has engendered widespread controversy, there being no necessary reason why judgments about working children's organization from the standpoint of child development, health, education, protection, or socialization should apply the same values and criteria as does analysis from a labor perspective. Diversity both breeds and enriches the debate (Myers 2001).

Informal Organization

Working children having some autonomy and contact with other young workers have been self-organizing in their own defense since early in the industrialization of Europe and North America (Liebel 2004; Nasaw 1996). They continue to be so today. For example, "street children" in developing countries, urban self-employed working children who may or may not also be homeless, commonly affiliate in informal groups to share shelter and other resources. They also seek company and moral support, protection against the bullying of other children, and extortion from predatory adults such as petty criminals, exploitative employers, and violent or corrupt authorities. Some also engage in altruistic activities benefiting others. The relationships in these peer groups can help provide children's lives with meaning, order, self-efficacy, and resilience they do not get from adult society (Aptekar 1988). The self-organization of working children has through its history raised ambivalent reactions. When American child newspaper sellers mobilized a hundred years ago to protect their economic interests and to pressure city authorities to grant their legitimacy, their resourceful actions stirred trepidation and admiration from the public, grudging acceptance from authorities, and consternation and resistance from adult activists campaigning for the elimination of child labor. Working children's own initiatives meet similar mixed reactions today.

It is not clear how prevalent these initiatives are, in what regions they are most common, or what proportion of working children participates in them where they are present. It does appear that the phenomenon is overwhelmingly urban, even though most working children are rural, and that only a small percentage of the world's working children are engaged in the sorts of occupations in which self-organization is practical.

Working children often become informally organized by others, often from charitable, religious, or government programs. Such programs typically gather working children together in locations near their workplaces to converse with them collectively and to develop feelings and practices of solidarity among them. Since the early 1970s this approach has expanded worldwide to the point that it has become a standard social work method for approaching and serving children working in the streets and other accessible workplaces. Older youth and adults are routinely recruited and trained (as either volunteers or paid employees) to work as "street educators" who establish contact with working children in or near their workplaces, befriend and organize them into groups based on location or occupation, and then address their problems, both personal and occupational, through group discussion and activity, developing working children's solidarity, awareness, and problem-solving skills in the process. In the dynamics of such groups, working children typically identify common work-related problems and address them through concerted action, such as consultation with employers and public authorities, usually with the support of adults working with them. In various places, programs using this informal organization approach have been reported to be effective in protecting working children, promoting their psychosocial development, and even in catalyzing social change (Swift 1997). Programs of this type usually arise from concerns and ideological perspectives that differ substantially from the labor discourse informing most national and international child labor policy. Therefore, organizations assisting working children to organize tend to see issues very differently from those who, regarding the world from a traditional child labor framework, believe children should not be working at all, let alone be organized (Myers 2001).

Formal Organization of Working Children

In various parts of the world, organizations of working children have been formalized as unions or other types of structured associations. Many of these organizations seem to have originally evolved from programs of informal organization; others have been formed directly (Swift 1999). In some cases, formalization has simply channeled children's own organizing efforts into structures that adults consider more socially appropriate. For example, in some American cities of the early twentieth century, local governments established official councils of working children to maintain justice and order, replacing through peaceful due process the violence children frequently employed against one another to maintain hierarchy and order in the street (Nasaw 1996). Recent decades have witnessed a trend toward not only the formalization of working children's organizations but also their national, regional, and global networking in what are commonly termed "movements." These movements have been vocal in presenting working children's ideas to an international public, where they have been an increasingly visible presence (Miljeteig 2000; Swift 1999; Boyden et al. 1998). In the words of a senior UNICEF observer, "Working children, with their organizations and networks, have today entered the public stage of discourse on child labor and have come increasingly to be recognized as key social actors to be taken into serious account in policies and interventions on child labor" (Karunan 2005, 304).

While the day-to-day activities of formalized working children's organizations may be run by children, overall guidance is generally in partnership with adults (Miljeteig 2000). As one researcher on working children's participation noted, "[T]he dominant framework of children's participation that generally promotes autonomous decision-making processes whereby adults are only facilitators or supporters appears to be unable to deal with many children's experiences in normal life contexts. Inclusion of adults around them is also required" (Invernizzi 2007). Few countries allow minors to register and be responsible for legal entities, so adults almost always have to assume a sponsoring role. Since child workers are transitory—they soon grow up—adult sponsors also have a major role in ensuring organizational continuity. Many working children's organizations have worked out rules guiding the relationships between adults and children so as to maintain functional decision-making independence for youngsters within overall organizational parameters overseen by responsible adults. The most important issues are discussed between children and adults and resolved through dialogue. Children's own governance activity is usually structured democratically, with regularly elected officers and spokespersons.

Issues of Current Debate

Competence: Are Children Competent to Represent Themselves Collectively?

Some question whether children are capable of understanding their collective situation well enough to recognize and defend their own interests. Popular concepts of childhood that inform most child labor policy stress children's innocence and vulnerability, and presume that adults should make the important protective decisions concerning them. Contemporary social science views children very differently, however, and places more emphasis on children's competence and participation in their own protection and development. Of course, children are both competent in some respects and vulnerable in others, and much of the debate is about how to honor children's abilities without exceeding them. Human rights law through the CRC assumes some level of child competence according to age and makes children's participation in decisions concerning them a matter of obligation for all ratifying states. Working children's movements have, with partial success, asserted their right to have a voice in the formulation of national and international policies governing child work. In this they have met resistance from government, trade unions, and other actors insisting that policy decisions are beyond children's competence and that working children's organizations have no special right to participate in them. Field research into what working children know and understand about their situation (Woodhead 1998) clearly favors claims of sufficient competence made by working children's organizations, but the politics of this dispute have yet to play out. How those politics are eventually resolved may determine the future advocacy influence of working children's organizations.

Legitimacy: Should Children Have the Right to Organize?

Not everyone believes, as do most working children's organizations, that child workers should be able to join existing trade unions or establish their own. National ministries of labor, mainstream trade unions, and the ILO are among those inclined to believe that children who are not legal workers (those below the legal minimum age for employment, for instance) should not have workers' rights of representation (Ennew et al. 2005). In fact, working children's organizations have arisen partly in response to the refusal of trade unions to admit children working "illegally" as members, regardless of their actual work history. Some working children's organizations and their allies point out that the right to organize is a recognized basic human right extended to all functioning workers without exception, a claim difficult to deny. In fact, achievement of that right in practice is on at least one recently suggested human rights agenda for addressing child labor (Weston 2005). Some also claim, rather more controversially, that children have a human right to engage in voluntary work that is nonexploitative and safe and that does not deny them an education. That claim is important because it suggests that child labor policies violating children's right to work if they so wish could not be used as a pretext to impede children from joining or organizing trade unions.

Inclusiveness and Authenticity: Who Is Represented?

It is widely observed that autonomous and mobile child workers, such as those in street trades, are easier and more likely to be organized than are young workers shut away in factories, shops, farms, or homes. That has raised questions about whether working children's organizations represent only children from a very narrow range of occupations, and are therefore not qualified to represent working children beyond their own specific membership. However, it is now becoming clear that some programs and organizations have found ways to successfully organize children even from difficult environments. There is little indication that the general viewpoints of children from similar backgrounds vary greatly by occupation, although field research on this point is needed.

Some worry that the adult partners in working children's organizations may unduly manipulate or otherwise influence children's thinking to the point that opinions expressed by children are in fact those of adults. The slight existing research into this issue does not confirm the charge of manipulation (Tolfree 1998), but the fact remains that caring adults who assist working children often present attractive positive models that children wish to emulate. It would be naive to suggest that the viewpoints of such adults do not influence children. What is important is that adults make a special effort to ensure that children represent themselves authentically and are able to dissent from adult views free of pressure. The major working children's organizations and movements go to considerable effort to prepare their adult workers to skillfully maintain a respectful, nonexploitative relationship with the young people. That said, a general confounding of adult with youthful voices is far from unusual, especially in the media. Various working children's movements and organizations produce a variety of publications and audiovisuals, some clearly the work of children with adult facilitation, but others obviously by adults and voicing primarily adult concerns and priorities. These sometimes claim to articulate and elaborate working children's own views when, to the casual observer, that would appear unlikely. While there is nothing wrong with adults writing and filming in support of children, or in projects shared with children, the credibility of working children's organizations and advocacy could benefit from more conscientious identification of voice, authorship, and attribution of ideas and opinions.

Influence: What Social Space Can Working Children's Organizations Fill?

Recent international meetings of working children's organizations reveal that, in many places, working children's organizations feel that their voice and social space is shrinking. As international agencies, national governments, and other donors pour investments into the "elimination of child labor" through policies based entirely on adult assumptions and objectives, and without responsible consultation with working children, results sometimes prove catastrophic for working children and their families. It is often working children's organizations who call attention to such problems, and they report that as bearers of inconvenient bad tidings they tend to be ignored and rejected by the ILO, national labor ministries, trade unions, and others working from a labor perspective. This may help account for the drift of working children's organizations, and activist and institutional support for them, away from a labor-oriented identity and toward a more amenable home in human rights, education, child development, child protection, and other policy areas that regard children more comprehensively and sympathetically and that are more open to their participation.

References and Further Reading

Aptekar, Lewis. *Street Children of Cali.* Durham: Duke University Press, 1988.

Boyden, Jo, Birgitta Ling, and William E. Myers. *What Works for Working Children.* Stockholm: Radda Barnen, 1998.

Ennew, Judith, William E. Myers, and Dominique Pierre Plateau. "Defining Child Labor As If Human Rights Really Matter." In *Child Labor and Human Rights: Making Children Matter,* ed. Burns H. Weston, 27–54. Boulder: Lynne Rienner Publishers, 2005.

Invernizzi, Antonella. "Children's Work as 'Participation': Thoughts on Ethnographic Data in Lima and the Algarve." In *Working to Be Someone: Child Focused Research and Practice with Working Children,* ed. Beatrice Hungerland, Manfred Liebel, Brian Milne, and Anne Wihstutz, 135–44. London: Jessica Kingsley Publishers, 2007.

Karunan, Victor P. "Working Children as Change Makers: Perspectives from the South." In *Human Rights: Making Children Matter,* ed. Burns H. Weston, 293–317. Boulder: Lynne Rienner Publishers, 2005.

Liebel, Manfred. *A Will of Their Own: Cross-Cultural Perspectives on Working Children.* London: Zed Books, 2004.

Miljeteig, Per. *Creating Partnerships with Working Children and Youth.* Social Protection Discussion Paper Series. Washington, DC: World Bank, 2000.

Myers, William E. "Valuing Diverse Approaches to Child Labour." In *Child Labour: Policy Options*, ed. Kristoffel Lieten and Ben White, 27–48. Amsterdam: Aksant Academic Publishers, 2001.

Nasaw, David. *Children of the City at Work and at Play.* New York: Oxford University Press, 1996.

Swift, Anthony. *Children for Social Change: Education for Citizenship of Street and Working Children in Brazil.* Nottingham: Educational Heretics Press, 1997.

Swift, Anthony. *Working Children Get Organized.* London: International Save the Children Alliance, 1999.

Tolfree, David. *Old Enough to Work, Old Enough to Have a Say: Different Approaches to Supporting Working Children.* Stockholm: Save the Children, Sweden, 1998.

Weston, Burns H. "Bringing Human Rights to Child Labor: Guiding Principles and Call to Action." In *Child Labor and Human Rights: Making Children Matter,* ed. Burns H. Weston, 427–36. Boulder: Lynne Rienner Publishers, 2005.

Woodhead, Martin. *Children's Perspectives on Their Working Lives.* Stockholm: Radda Barnen, 1998.

The Economics of Consumer Actions Against Products with Child Labor Content

Eric V. Edmonds, Department of Economics at Dartmouth College, Institute for the Study of Labor (IZA), and the National Bureau of Economic Research

Public opinion polls in high-income countries regularly document near universal condemnation of child labor in low-income countries. Calls for consumer boycotts against products with child labor content are ubiquitous in America's universities, but the consequences of such boycotts require examination. Can consumer boycotts and product-labeling campaigns against products with child labor content make affected children better off?

The problem is that restrictions on choice are generally not welfare improving. If children, or children's agents, can freely choose between two options (say, jobs or school, or job A or job B), they choose what they perceive to be their best option. Thus, their preferences are revealed by the choices they make. If the most attractive job is eliminated, what will the children do? If nothing happens to eliminate the factors that cause children to work, they switch to a less preferred job, perhaps for less income or in worse conditions.

This essay examines this revealed-preference argument. The argument relies on several assumptions: The agent making decisions about the child has the child's best interest at heart; there is free choice over activities at the time of employment, and full information about all the amenities associated with the choices open to the child; the restriction imposed is effective in eliminating the preferred job; and the restriction does not otherwise alter the options available to the child, nor does it fundamentally alter the factors that cause children to work in the first place. This essay examines these assumptions in detail.

Why Do Children Work?

Sadly, there is child abuse and neglect in the world. However, systematic abuse and neglect cannot explain why more than 200 million of the world's children work today. Abuse and neglect as principal causes of child labor would imply that child labor is not responsive to changes in the broader economic environment. Hundreds of studies document exactly the opposite—whether and how a poor child works is extremely sensitive to a wide variety of economic factors (Edmonds 2007). Broadly speaking, children work because it is the best use of their time that their families can afford.

Sometimes Working Is the Best Option Available to the Child

How can work be the best use of child time when wages are low? Low wages paid to children are often cited as evidence of exploitation and coercion in child labor markets. However, in a competitive labor market, workers are paid according to their productivity, or, more precisely, the value of their labor's marginal product. Children are often involved in the production of low-value products, and children are often not especially productive workers. The most detailed case study we have on child productivity in manufacturing focuses on the hand-knotted carpet industry in India (Levison et al. 1998). In this industry, adults and children tend to work on the same types of carpets. Children were found to be 21 percent less productive than adults, where productivity was measured in square inches knotted per hour. A profit-maximizing firm must pay less productive workers less money.

The fact that children work despite low observable wages is often referenced to suggest that only uncaring parents send their children to work. But not everyone considers a few cents a small amount. Fifty cents per day might seem trivial to many, but fifty cents is at least a 50 percent increase in income to the billion or so people living on less than a dollar a day. Even if wages are low, often the alternative uses of child time are not attractive. In many developing countries, access to schooling is a serious problem. Even when it is available, school quality is sometimes deplorable. Chaudhury et al. (2006) documented that fewer than one in four teachers were present in Ugandan schools during random visits on school days. The *Public Report on Basic Education in India* (Probe Team 1999) documented that nearly 90 percent of rural primary schools lacked a working toilet and that class sizes in many states would exceed 100 students per classroom if all of the students attended.

Often, Children Work Even Though It Is Not the Best Use of Their Time

Poverty is a strong correlate of child labor. Three-fourths of the cross-country differences in economic activity rates of children can be explained by variation in living standards (Edmonds and Pavcnik 2005). Within-country studies often find a similarly strong association between poverty and child labor, and between improving living standards and declining child labor. In Vietnam during the 1990s, 80 percent of the decline in market work of children in families living near the poverty line can be explained by improving living standards (Edmonds 2005); and more than half of India's decline in child labor in the 1980s and 1990s can be explained by falling poverty (Edmonds et al. 2007). Sometimes economic growth is associated with additional earning opportunities for children as wages increase. However, consistently, when economic growth is accompanied by poverty reduction, child labor declines rapidly. This evidence strongly suggests that children often work because of factors related to poverty rather than it being the best use of their time. When incomes rise, families quickly move their children out of work.

Are Children Free to Choose and Leave Employers?

Children are often not free to make their own decisions about how they spend their time, and this can present difficulties in evaluating the welfare consequences of child labor or its elimination. Most parents are trying to do what is best for their children. Rogers and Swinnerton (2008) emphasize that parents can be misinformed about the child's working conditions and may agree to allow a child to leave home for work, when if they were fully informed they would not. In a normal job, workers quit if the working conditions are not sufficiently compensated. Children, especially those living away from home, might have more difficulty leaving. Caring parents that allow their children to leave home for work want to be confident that the child will be protected and supervised in his or her destination. If the employer has taken on this responsibility, he or she may feel that preventing the child from leaving the job is in the child's best interests. Moreover, an estimated 5.7 million children are bonded, a portion of their wages having been paid in advance of their departure from home. Given the possibility of forced or bonded labor, anyone concerned with child welfare should consider whether the child can freely leave the job before applying the revealed-preference argument. That said, most working children are not bonded, and a concerned consumer cannot assume that they are without additional evidence.

The Economics of Restrictions on Employment

Product boycotts and product-labeling campaigns aim to restrict the involvement of children in specific types of employment. In product boycotts, consumers choose not to buy certain products that are known to have a child labor component. Labeling campaigns reduce the informational costs to the consumer associated with knowing what products to boycott by certifying some producers of a given good as "child labor free." Boycotts have the potential to lead to product-labeling campaigns that can lead to differentiated products (produced with or without child labor), or, if universal and effective, boycotts could completely eliminate jobs for children in a particular industry. The former scenario, that creates differentiated products, is the more likely outcome.

What Happens When the Target of Consumer Action Is a Small Share of Local Employment?

When a job is a free choice, as is typically the case, the welfare consequences of restrictions on employment depend on how important the job is in the relevant labor market. Most often, child and adult wages are set in local labor markets. When the affected export-oriented job is a small fraction of the local labor market, the likely effects of employment restrictions for child and adult wages are small. Nothing happens to any of the reasons why children work, and the sole effect of the action against child employment in the targeted job is to cause children to change employers. When individuals are free to make decisions about employment and jobs, restrictions on children in one job cause them to switch to other, less preferred jobs, according to the revealed-preference argument.

Baland and Duprez (2007) emphasized that both consumer demand for the label (or willingness to boycott), and the label's availability influence the impact of consumer action on child welfare. Suppose the label is accessible freely to all qualifying employers, consumer demand for the label is a small part of the total market demand, and adult and child workers can perform the same tasks. In that case, the labeling campaign may have little effect on wages or child labor rates. Adults replace children in the export sector and children replace adults producing for the home market or other markets where there is no labeling premium. This reshuffling of workers may not be beneficial to children if they are now more isolated from their parents or other adults, but the net effect on child labor caused by this displacement can be minimal.

What Happens When the Target of Consumer Action Is a Large Share of Local Employment?

In an alternative scenario, the affected employment is a large enough share of the local labor market to have a substantive effect on the employment opportunities open to children. With fewer jobs available, but the same number of children willing to work, child wages should decline. Basu et al. (2006) emphasized that wages can also decline if labeling campaigns induce consumers to buy fewer products overall. The consequences of lower wages for children depend on why the children are working. Suppose children work because it is the best use of their time in the sense that wages are valued more highly than other uses of child time. Lower wages should mean fewer children working in wage employment. Children switch to their next best alternative, such as other forms of work or even schooling. The child's family is made worse off by the decline in income. But it is possible that, if the family's interest diverges from the child's best interest, or if the family is not as well informed as the consumer about the child's best interest, the child can be made better off by this change in activity.

Typically, however, children are not working because their wages are so high. Rather, they work because of poverty. Reduced employment opportunities do not eliminate this motive for work. Children then switch to other, less preferred jobs. Moreover, when poverty is the motive for work, lower wages can increase child labor, as existing workers have to spend more time to earn the same income, and additional children, previously supported by working children, have to start working (Basu and Zarghamee 2006).

Efforts to punish products with child labor content, when substantive enough to affect local labor markets, can also change the types of jobs available. For example, Davies (2005) emphasized that labeling campaigns can create a profitable niche for adult-labor-only firms, which, in turn, can create an analogous, profitable niche for low-price child-labor-only firms. Not only can child wages be depressed, but rather than working by a parent's side, children end up working away from parents and adults, perhaps in situations where working conditions are more difficult to observe.

When Can Consumer Action Make Families Better Off?

Another possibility arises if employers shift from child to adult labor as a result of consumer action.

When the child-labor-free label is valuable and not available to all firms, adult wages can increase in labor markets that produce the child-labor-free product. This increase in wages to adults will reduce the number of working children through reducing poverty. This optimistic scenario has a formal articulation within economics in Basu and Van (1998). It presumes that the affected employer or industry is large enough that the increases in adult wages will eliminate poverty motives for work. Thus, in even the best of scenarios, the effect of consumer boycotts on child labor supply depends on local conditions.

Implication for Consumers

The main implication is that information about local economic conditions is critical for inferring whether consumer action can improve the welfare of working children. The educated consumer should understand why children are working in a given job, what will happen to local labor markets in the absence of child labor in the target industry, and what other options are available to the children affected by consumer action. When destitution drives children to work, preventing the employment of children may do nothing other than drive children and their families further into poverty.

There are several cases where, with complete information, it is possible to justify consumer action as likely to improve child welfare. When children are bonded, coerced, or somehow unable to change jobs, then it is easier to assert that their work does not reflect revealed preference. When the individual taking the consumer action has better information about what is best for the child than the child's caretaker, the case for consumer action is stronger. Finally, there may be cases where the presence of children in the labor market depresses adult wages so that children have to work. That is, without children in the labor market, adult wages would be high enough to eliminate child labor supply. Of course, without proper consideration of the context of child labor, the danger is that consumer action against products with child labor content may just punish the poorest in the world for being poor. Consumer actions can hurt exactly the people they are aimed to help.

So what options does this leave the concerned consumer? One policy option is to improve the conditions in which children work rather than to prevent children from working. Freeman (1998) argued that the enforcement of labor standards may address many of the concerns raised by consumer activists. To the extent that labor standards raise the costs of labor, however, they may create many of the deleterious effects associated with consumer boycotts. But it is possible that implementation of basic standards may have a minimal impact on labor costs while significantly improving the working conditions of children. A second policy option is to work toward eliminating the reasons why children work. If the ire that fuels consumer boycotts could be redirected toward persistent support for poverty relief and schooling improvements, it might be possible to attain a world where child labor was rare rather than pervasive.

References and Further Reading

Baland, J., and C. Duprez. "Are Fair Trade Labels Effective Against Child Labor?" Working paper 144, Bureau for Research and Economic Analysis of Development, 2007.

Basu, A., N. Chau, and U. Grote. "Guaranteed Manufactured Without Child Labor: The Economics of Consumer Boycotts, Social Labeling, and Trade Sanctions." *Review of Development Economics* 10 (2006): 466–91.

Basu, K., and P.H. Van. "The Economics of Child Labor." *American Economic Review* 88 (1998): 412–27.

Basu, K., and H. Zarghamee. "Is Product Boycott a Good Idea for Controlling Child Labor?" Unpublished paper, Cornell University, Ithaca, NY, 2007.

Chaudhury, N., J. Hammer, M. Kremer, K. Muralidharan, and F.H. Rogers. "Missing in Action: Teacher and Health Worker Absence in Developing Countries." *Journal of Economic Perspectives* 20:1 (2006): 91–116.

Davies, Ronald B. "Abstinence from Child Labor and Profit Seeking." *Journal of Development Economics* 76:1 (2005): 251–63.

Edmonds, E. "Does Child Labor Decline with Improving Economic Status?" *Journal of Human Resources* 40 (2005): 77–99.

Edmonds, E. "Child Labor." In *Handbook of Development Economics,* vol. 4, ed. T.P. Schultz and J. Strauss. Amsterdam: Elsevier, 2007.

Edmonds, E., and N. Pavcnik. "Child Labor in the Global Economy." *Journal of Economic Perspectives* 19 (2005): 199–220.

Edmonds, E., N. Pavcnik, and P. Topalova. "Trade Adjustment and Human Capital Investments: Evidence from Indian Tariff Reform." Working paper 12884, National Bureau of Economic Research, 2007.

Freeman, R. "What Role for Labor Standards in the Global Economy?" Paper presented at the UN Expert Meeting on Policy Perspectives on International Economics and Social Justice, Pocantico, New York, November 13, 1998.

Levison, D., R. Anker, S. Ashraf, and S. Barge. "Is Child Labor Really Necessary in India's Carpet Industry?" In *Economics of Child Labor in Hazardous Industries in India,* ed. R. Anker, S. Barge, S. Rajagopal, and M.P. Joseph. New Delhi: Hindustan Publishers, 1998.

Probe Team. *Public Report on Basic Education in India.* New Delhi: Oxford University Press, 1999.

Rogers, C., and K. Swinnerton. "A Theory of Exploitative Child Labor." *Oxford Economic Papers* 60:1 (2008): 20–41.

Global March Against Child Labor

Risto F. Harma, formerly with Global March Against Child Labor

The origins of Global March Against Child Labor (GMACL), as an event and an ongoing NGO coalition and movement, are to be found in a confluence of factors that came together to make the 1990s the decade of child development (White 2005). While child labor had first come to public attention in developed nations during the nineteenth century, child labor in the developing world had to gain its own recognition as a major social and economic problem. In the 1990s key elements of the confluence that made the GMACL possible were: (1) the realization by activists in developing countries that their local-level interventions lacked critical mass to instigate irresistible pressure for large-scale action, (2) supernational measures, for example, the creation and adoption of the 1989 UN Convention on the Rights of the Child (CRC), (3) the shift in thinking whereby human development problems began to be analyzed in human rights terms (Weston 2005), and (4) the concomitant increase in public awareness in developed countries about child labor in terms of imported consumer goods, and about development issues in general.

Origins of Global March Against Child Labor

To be clear, GMACL was literally a march, or trek, of child laborers and development activists across Africa, Asia, the Americas, and Europe. It was comprised of NGO, trade union, and employers' groups from 108 countries, in total more than 1,400 member organizations (currently GMACL has more than 2,000 in 144 countries). The march set off in three groups from Manila, São Paulo, and Cape Town, and covered fifty-six countries. It culminated in Geneva on June 17, 1998, with march participants addressing the ILO conference on Convention 182 on Elimination of the Worst Forms of Child Labor. As the ILO records, "There was a core group of some 200 child and adult marchers, many of whom were or had been child laborers themselves."

Kailash Satyarthi, the founder and chairperson of the South Asian Coalition on Child Servitude (SACCS), founded in 1980 (in Hindi, Bachpan Bachao Andolan), had the idea for the march. Support for the GMACL was cemented among NGOs and trade unions at the November 1997 Oslo International Conference on Child Labor. Marches were an awareness-raising campaigning tool that Satyarthi had used previously for SACCS in India, as the only means of reaching layers of society where reading is not an embedded social activity and where electricity shortages make electronic media less than a mass phenomenon. The GMACL was not the first attempt by Satyarthi to take international action; however, the need for a global march came as a realization that regional and niche international action (for example, consumer boycotts) was not effective enough at raising mass awareness among the general public and in high-level policy-making circles. Previously, niche international action had been applied by SACCS in the case of the rug-making industry in South Asia. This brought about Rugmark in 1994, the label attached to rugs made without the use of child labor. The rug issue and initiative also marked the entry of Western public opinion into the momentum-building process against child labor (Wiseberg 2005). Satyarthi observed, "Ninety-seven to 98 percent of carpets are exported to western consumers, and demand is rising rapidly. Thus, we decided to focus on the consumer market. . . . The only success we have seen has been through consumer pressure. It was only after our consumer campaign that the industry even admitted the problem of child labour existed" (Satyarthi 1994, 25). Simultaneously, other events began increasing the profile of child labor, including bringing to bear U.S. political and economic power: The threat of the proposed Harkin Bill (the Child Labor Deterrence Act) in 1992, to ban child labor imports, famously frightened Bangladeshi garment manufacturers into firing their child employees; the mandate by the U.S. Senate in 1994 that the Department of Labor produce annual reports on international child labor; initiatives by students at U.S. universities against clothing produced in exploitative conditions and sold by university shops. Elsewhere, the International Confederation of Free Trade Unions launched the International Trade Union Campaign Against Child Labor, said to be "one of the most far reaching child labor campaigns in decades" (Wiseberg 2005), which brought the ILO to the 1997 Oslo Conference on Child Labor. The Oslo conference acted as a stimulus not only for research collaboration among the ILO, UNICEF, and the World Bank through creation of the Understanding Children's Work (UCW) Project, but for the GMACL itself.

While consumer product campaigns and the engagement of established international organizations were important tactical victories that demonstrated international concern over child labor, a strategic approach was required if child labor was to gain traction as an issue in the societies in which it exists. Hence, with the field of Western public opinion partially prepared, and with the attention of policy makers engaged, the existence of a global movement of NGOs and their allies, if successful, would act to channel global advocacy power to the grassroots where child labor exists. This is how GMACL set out to achieve action on child labor.

Immediate Outcome and Longer-Run Impact

In order to have long-run impact, GMACL moved from an awareness-raising event to an office-based NGO, and adopted high-level policy advocacy with the World Bank, bilateral donors, and the UN; it joined other NGO coalitions with shared interests, for example, the Global Campaign for Education (GCE), while continuing to participate in innovative events, such as the Children's World Congresses on child labor (2004 and 2005); the South Asian March Against Child Trafficking (2007); and specific campaigns including the FIFA World Cup Campaign (2002 and 2006) and Fair Chocolate for the World (2002).

Attempting to quantify the effectiveness of GMACL's efforts, or that of any advocacy organization, is difficult. There are three areas that GMACL focuses on: (1) general public awareness, (2) policy change (mainstreaming of child labor into all development policy), and (3) tangible living-standards improvements for children (rehabilitation of child laborers, elimination of child labor starting with the worst forms, an education system worthy of the name).

Concerning the first of these, GMACL's effect on public awareness is somewhat difficult to assess, as there have been a plethora of actors focusing on children's well-being, with each benefiting from awareness raised by other's campaigns; what is clear is that together they have established child labor as an issue.

The second is easier to assess: Clear success has been achieved in getting child labor and the rights-based approach to child development recognized by high-level policy makers. GMACL has been very important in pushing child labor into the most influential development policy circles, for example, the World Bank. The U.S. government's Department of State reports regularly on trafficking, while its Department of Labor has a permanent child labor section. GMACL's most notable high-level success with policy change has been linking child labor with the Education for All (EFA) campaign through its involvement with the EFA High Level Group, and through Satyarthi's role with the GCE. The GCE and GMACL have a direct consultative role on the EFA Global Monitoring Report editorial board at UNESCO, and GMACL is also a part of the UNESCO Working Group on EFA.

In 2003, Satyarthi founded and launched the Triangular Paradigm (TP) of human development. The TP idea has wide-ranging implications: TP takes the view that in order to achieve success with poverty, education, or child labor, all three must be tackled jointly. This involves embedding the linkages of the three in development policy, programs, and national education systems, and represents the operational and advocacy equivalent of Amartya Sen's "capabilities" approach to human development (Sen 1987; 1999). One focus is to complete the operationalization of the TP by including it in Poverty Reduction Strategy Papers (PRSP). The core ideas of the TP are policy coherence, coordinated program interventions, and mainstreaming of child labor and education in poverty policy and programs, and vice versa (White 2005). This is a significant success, given that for some time, policy incoherence, and duplication among major development organizations have been the norm, and little has been done to address child labor (Fukasaku and Trzeciak-Duval 2005; Stryker 2001). This has been due to the often highly politicized nature of bilateral development organizations' assistance. Until recently, these organizations have had more measurable success in promoting forces inimical to development through their often poor program design, and uncritical and politicized support for financially corrupt and administratively inept governments. This has helped lead to debt crises (in the 1980s and 1990s), the undermining of democratic institutions, and assisting civil war, corruption, ineffective governance, and ineffective aid. The TP also marks a break with traditional criticize-and-embarrass NGO tactics, by injecting properly thought-out ideas into the most strategic areas. Therefore, if comprehensively applied, the TP will have wide-ranging impact. The TP is now established with an annual roundtable meeting to allow direct consultation among GMACL, UNESCO, ILO, UNICEF, and the World Bank. At the 2005 TP roundtable meeting, the Global Task Force on Child Labor and Education was launched to implement the TP.

Finally, concerning the third area, the ultimate goal of improving children's lives, it is perhaps too early to judge whether this has been a success or failure for GMACL, as it takes time for governments to change policy and to set up and reform programs and services. The assessment will be based on whether more children attend school regularly and receive quality education; whether health indicators improve; and whether significantly fewer children work in the worst forms of child labor and weekly hours in economic activity and own household work are significantly reduced. In the end, it may be unrealistic to judge GMACL on this measure, as multiple actors will ultimately have been involved. It is, however, at least worth noting that the ILO's most recent global estimate of child labor was published with the title *The End of Child Labor: Within Reach* (ILO 2006).

Note

For further information on the Global March Against Child Labor, please see the GMACL Web site, http://www.globalmarch.org/.

References and Further Reading

Fukasaku, Kiichiro, and Alexandra Trzeciak-Duval. "Policy Coherence of OECD Countries Matters: Evidence from East Asia." Policy Insights 4. Paris: Organization for Economic Cooperation and Development (OECD), 2005.

GMACL. "The Triangular Paradigm." http://www.globalmarch.org/aboutus/triangularparadigm.php.

GMACL and Save the Children Foundation. *Worst Forms of Child Labour Report, 2005.* http://www.globalmarch.org/child_labour/index.php#05.

ILO. *The End of Child Labor: Within Reach.* Ninety-fifth Session, 2006, Report I(B). Geneva: ILO/IPEC, 2006.

Pincus, Jonathan R., and Jeffrey A. Winters, eds. *Reinventing the World Bank.* Ithaca, NY: Cornell University Press, 2002.

Satyarthi, Kailish. "The Tragedy of Child Labor: An Interview with Kailash Satyarthi." *Multinational Monitor* 15:10 (October 1994): 24–26.

Sen, Amartya. *Commodities and Capabilities.* New Delhi: Oxford University Press India, 1987.

Sen, Amartya. *Development as Freedom.* Oxford: Oxford University Press, 1999.

Stryker, J. Dirck. "Common Diagnostic Framework for Poverty Reduction." In *Negotiating Poverty: New Directions, Renewed Debate,* ed. N. Middleton, P. O'Keefe, and R. Visser, 75–88. London: Pluto Press, 2001.

Understanding Children's Work, An Inter-Agency Research Cooperation Project on Child Labour

UNESCO. *Education for All: 2006 Global Monitoring Report.* Paris: UNESCO, 2006.

Weston, Burns H., ed. *Child Labor and Human Rights: Making Children Matter.* Boulder, CO: Lynne Rienner, 2005.

White, Ben. "Shifting Positions on Child Labor: The Views and Practice of Intergovernmental Organizations." In *Child Labor and Human Rights: Making Children Matter,* ed. B.H. Weston, 319–42. Boulder, CO: Lynne Rienner, 2005.

Wiseberg, Laurie S. "Nongovernemtal Organizations in the Struggle Against Child Labor." In *Child Labor and Human Rights: Making Children Matter,* ed. B.H. Weston, 343–77. Boulder, CO: Lynne Rienner, 2005.

Part 2
Sub-Saharan Africa

Section 1. Introduction

Child Labor in Postcolonial Africa

Michel Bonnet, Former National Program Coordinator for Africa, ILO-IPEC (Translated by Lucie Maguire)

"Africa is the only continent where the proportion of the population in poverty is growing. Consequently, Africa is far off track in meeting the millennium development goals" (ILO 2006). This statement by the director general of the ILO, delivered to the International Labor Conference of June 2006, sums up the situation of child labor in postcolonial Africa to this day, and likely for decades to come.

The principal cause of child labor, though by no means the only one, is poverty. It is a constant observed across the world that when poverty increases in a population, in order to survive, the hardest-hit families require all of their members, even the youngest, to contribute economically. Apart from a brief improvement in the 1960s, the fifty years since African independence have seen deterioration in the population's living and working conditions. We have lost count of the number of conferences and reports by international institutions that, decade after decade, have sounded the alarm in a bid to halt what has been called "Africa's decline." The most exhaustive of these reports is without doubt the 464-page document presented to the G8 summit in Gleneagles in July 2005 (Commission for Africa 2005). The problem of Africa was deemed sufficiently serious to merit an entire chapter in the global report on child labor presented to the International Labor Conference in June 2006. We must not forget that Africa's population doubles every twenty-five years and that children under age fifteen represent 44 percent of that population. Africa is the continent with the highest number of working children as a percentage of the child population, exceeding 50 percent in some regions.

In fact, the evolution of the problem of child labor in Africa is directly dependent on two factors that are external to the continent—first, economic pressure: Debt-repayment mechanisms and price fixing of raw materials on world markets mean that Africa is deprived of a significant part of its riches to the benefit of rich countries; the African states are thus constrained to reduce spending on those areas that have little short-term economic benefit—education and health—which are precisely those which have the greatest impact on children's lives. The second factor is cultural pressure: Adoption of the UN Convention on the Rights of the Child in 1989 imposed on Africa a "worldview" of the child and, more specifically, an abolitionist position on child labor, in an era in which independence might have enabled Africans to revive their traditional concepts of the relationship between children and adults, in particular, the place accorded within education to contributions by even the youngest of children to the community's economic activities.

The impact of international pressure is particularly strong with regard to child labor. Policies and action plans, not to mention financial resources, generally come from abroad. With the adoption and application of ILO Convention 182 on worst forms of child labor, international pressure has been responsible, since 1999, for setting new action priorities that, in the case of Africa, are likely to have an impact on only the fringes of the child labor problem.

Children's Areas of Activity

As the population of African countries is generally rural, three-quarters of working children are in rural environments. We should differentiate between children working in commercial agriculture and those working with their families. Commercial agriculture is the sector that receives most media attention, even though it probably employs less than 10 percent of the total number of working children. It takes the form mainly of specialist plantations growing, depending on the country, cocoa, coffee, tea, tobacco, sugar cane, rubber, sisal, vanilla, and flowers. The main danger facing children on these plantations derives from the massive use of chemicals, particularly pesticides. The children usually live on the plantation with their families. It is difficult, if not impossible, for parents to refuse to allow their children to work. Schools are often built near the edges of plantations, and children have to work before and after school hours; this is very tiring and hampers their development. In recent years there has been increased demand for child workers to replace adults affected by HIV/AIDS.

Outside of commercial agriculture, within the family context, the greatest hardships endured by children are the result of working conditions rather than economic exploitation as such. They are permanently exposed to the vagaries of the weather and to attacks by insects, reptiles, and even wild animals; they use archaic tools to work with hard soil and often have to travel long distances, especially to collect water. Solitude is an additional burden for children whose job it is to tend livestock. Surveys show that children who have migrated to towns and cities to work as vendors or shoe cleaners, and in similar small trades (and who are of such concern to public opinion) have no wish to return to their villages, where, from their point of view, life is much more difficult. Pressure from international markets, particularly since the 1980s, has led families to change their agricultural production away from crops for local consumption to export crops. More and more children working with their parents on family land, producing small amounts of fruit or vegetables on a daily basis, now find their lives regulated by the schedules of collection trucks.

Although it concerns only a minority of children, work in the urban environment gains more media attention than work in rural areas and is the preferred target of most humanitarian action plans. The employment of children in large industrial enterprises is exceptional in Africa. Working children in urban environments can be divided into two categories: child servants and children in small trades. Even more than on other continents, domestic work is carried out by girls, sometimes very young (less than ten years old). There is now a considerable flow of children from the countryside into the towns; this is increasingly organized and often crosses national boundaries so that international cooperation has become necessary to control the traffic. Young housemaids are all the more at the mercy of their employers because they are isolated within a family and therefore cannot be monitored. The second category of urban working children is in small trades. As the most visible child workers, these street children are seldom involved in production in the strict sense. Instead, they provide various services in more or less mobile businesses that are highly specialized and flexible enough to respond rapidly to customer demand. A survey in Yaoundé (Cameroon) identified 121 different small trades involving children (Fodouop 1991). These children are to be found in every kind of small business, and their activities are sometimes not far removed from begging.

HIV/AIDS is having an enormous impact on children and their work. Child prostitution is continually growing, especially in coastal towns, where sex tourism is rife. Several million African children are either carriers of the virus themselves or have been orphaned by it. Orphan-headed households are becoming increasingly common. As victims of discrimination, most of these children have no choice but to seek work, whatever the conditions, in order to survive.

The growing use of child soldiers has become a major problem. Child soldiers are one of the cankers on the face of postcolonial Africa, and one that spread rapidly in the 1980s. It was not until the year 2000 that the United Nations began to take the problem seriously (UN 2000). Traumatizing military experience is a handicap that makes it extremely difficult for children to be reintegrated into society.

One form of child labor that should be distinguished from those discussed previously is the work of apprentices. Traditional apprenticeships (in crafts and small businesses) represent one of Africa's riches. Family relationships continue during the apprenticeship so that it becomes a continuation of the child's education, with the added benefits, on the one hand, of providing a stepping-stone to a job and, on the other, of acting as a process of socialization. There are exceptions to the rule, and in some cases the apprentices' terms of employment continue long after the end of adolescence; however, traditional apprenticeships are one of the pillars of the informal economy by which the population manages to survive despite crushing poverty.

Policies and Action Plans

It has taken decades for political decision makers and public opinion to start paying sufficient attention to the problem of child labor. For many years, it has to be said, denunciations of child exploitation focused, on the one hand, on what were considered to be exceptional cases that would disappear as development progressed and emanated, on the other, from those same Western countries whose pillage of the continent's resources was actually the cause of much child labor. As a result, such denunciations tended to fall on deaf ears. Child labor became worthy of attention in official circles only with the adoption in 1989 of the UN Convention on the Rights of the Child, and with the ILO's launch of the International Program on the Elimination of Child Labor (IPEC) in 1992. Meeting in Cairo in April 1993, the working commission of the Organization of African Unity (OAU), now the African Union (AU), adopted a report by the secretary-general of the OAU on child labor in Africa—a first (see Bonnet 1993, note 13). Since then, the movement has accelerated at all levels through numerous regional, subregional, and national meetings, and cooperation has gradually spread among the major UN institutions concerned with child-related issues and the IMF and the World Bank. The Millennium Development Goals adopted by 189 countries at the Millennium Summit in September 2000 set the standard for such programs.

Most African countries have ratified both Convention 138 on minimum age and Convention 182 on worst forms of child labor. The most important international program dealing with child labor, IPEC is at the forefront of efforts to combat the problem in Africa. IPEC is more and more in demand by governments wishing to develop or support their own policies and action plans. Its current priorities, as set out at the 2006 International Labor Conference, are to improve understanding of child labor issues by improving data collection and developing indicators with which to analyze that data; to support the development in individual countries of a policy framework for action plans, with particular emphasis on integrating the problem of child labor into programs implemented by other international institutions; and finally, to give priority to all measures that facilitate children's education, considered the primary instrument for sustainable action.

Of the plethora of NGOs active in the area of child labor, two deserve particular attention. Originating in Africa, they have both achieved international status. The African Network for the Prevention and Protection Against Child Abuse and Neglect (ANPPCAN) was formed in Nigeria in 1986. With its headquarters currently in Nairobi (Kenya), it operates in eleven African countries and has active contacts in around ten more. The organization does not specialize in child labor, as each country sets its own priorities, but the issue is always part of its field of activities. ANPPCAN prioritizes research, advocacy, training, education, and participatory approaches. The Mouvement Africain des Enfants et Jeunes Travailleurs, or MAEJT (African Children and Young Workers' Movement), was established in 1994 and is based in Dakar (Senegal). It operates in twenty African countries, bringing together some 400 groups representing 30,000 working children. Active mainly in urban environments, it works with housemaids, vendors, apprentices, and independent children and young workers in the streets and markets. It promotes the protagonism or agency of the children themselves, as a way of stimulating the development of social policies; what sets it apart from other NGOs is that it allows the children to make their own decisions and to represent themselves, even when invited to meetings at national and international levels. The movement maintains close links with similar organizations in Asia and Latin America.

References and Further Reading

Admassie, Assefa. "Explaining the High Incidence of Child Labour in Sub-Saharan Africa." *African Development Review* 14:2 (2002): 251–75.

African Network for the Prevention and Protection against Child Abuse and Neglect (ANPPCAN). http://www.anppcan.org.

Bass, Loretta E. *Child Labor in Sub-Saharan Africa*. Boulder, CO: Lynne Rienner, 2004.

Bonnet, Michel. "Child Labor in Africa." *International Labor Review* 132:3 (1993): 371–89.

Commission for Africa. *Our Common Interest: Report of the Commission for Africa*. March 2005. http://www.commissionforafrica.org/english/report/introduction.html.

Fodouop, Kegne. *Les petits métiers de la rue et l'emploi: le cas de Yaoundé.* Yaoundé: Editions Sopecam, 1991.

ILO. *A Future Without Child Labor*. Geneva, International Labor Office, 2002.

ILO. *Wounded Childhood: The Use of Children in Armed Conflict in Central Africa.* Geneva: ILO-IPEC, 2003.

ILO. *The End of Child Labor: Within Reach*. Global Report, International Labor Conference 2006. Report 1(B). Geneva: International Labor Office, 2006.

Kielland, Anne, and Mauriza Tovo. *Children at Work: Child Labor Practices in Africa.* Boulder, CO: Lynne Rienner, 2006.

Mouvement Africain des Enfants et Jeunes Travailleurs (MAEJT) (African Children and Young Workers' Movement). http://eja.enda.sn.

Rau, Bill. *Combatting Child Labour and HIV/AIDS in Sub-Saharan Africa*. Geneva: ILO-IPEC, 2002.

UN. *Optional Protocol to the Convention on the Rights of the Child on the Involvement of Children in Armed Conflict.* New York: United Nations, 2000.

Child Labor in Colonial Africa

Beverly Grier, Associate Professor of Government and International Relations, Clark University

When Europeans colonized South Africa in the mid-seventeenth century and the rest of the continent at the end of the nineteenth century, they found societies in which children—prepubescent and pubescent boys and girls—were an integral part of the labor force. Alongside adults, children were engaged in farming, herding, trading, hunting, mining, manufacturing, and even fighting in military organizations. Most of the children were free, but a significant percentage of them were not free. Some were slaves who had been captured in wars and raids or purchased on the market. Some were pawns (debt servants) whose labor services had secured loans for their parents in time of need. The development of colonial economies moved forward on this precolonial foundation, incorporating the labor of children, both free and unfree, kin and nonkin, into the production of goods for a rapidly industrializing Europe.

In those parts of the continent where a permanent European population did not settle and, therefore, where African peasants retained control of the land—West Africa and Central Africa—children's labor became essential to the production and transportation of peasant crops produced for export and for consumption in emerging urban centers. Taxation, forced crop production, the desire to take advantage of new markets, and the rapid displacement of locally manufactured goods such as farm implements and cloth by cheaper European imports were among the factors that gave rise to a massive expansion of indigenous crops, such as oil palm, cotton, groundnuts, and rubber, and of introduced crops such as cocoa, coffee, and tea in colonies such as the Gold Coast (Ghana), Nigeria, Senegal, Côte d'Ivoire, Belgian Congo, Uganda, and parts of Tanganyika. The increased demand for labor was met, in part, by the intensification of the lineage- and family-based age and gender division of labor, with adult and adolescent males clearing new forests for the planting of crops, and women, adolescent girls, and younger boys and girls planting, weeding, harvesting, and processing the crops. Families headloaded crops to markets or sold their crops to middlemen traders, who, in turn, used adults (very often women) and children as porters to carry crops to the coast and to carry imported goods such as cloth, sugar, flour, and farm implements back to village markets in the interior.

In the initial years of colonial rule, the increased demand for labor in peasant-dominated Africa was also met by expanding the use of unfree labor, largely children and adolescents. British, French, Portuguese, and Belgian colonial authorities were reluctant to stop the continuing traffic in humans, or to free known slave populations, in part because of the cheap labor these groups provided to the growing export-crop economy. They feared jeopardizing their new political alliances with chiefs who raided neighbors and trafficked in children. They were also wary of the social dislocation that was likely to result from the emancipation of large numbers of previously enslaved men, women, and children. Thus, for one or two decades into the twentieth century, raiding continued in the hinterland of the Côte d'Ivoire, the Gold Coast, Nigeria, and the Belgian Congo, among other colonies, with captives being transported in small groups and sold in the cash-crop-growing areas. Even more than in the precolonial era, children were the predominate victims of this trafficking, particularly after colonial states made concerted efforts to suppress the trade. This was so because children were easier than adults to capture, transport, control, and assimilate into new lives as servile laborers. They had longer productive lives ahead of them than did adults. Moreover, they were easy to disguise as adoptees, wards, and child brides of traffickers and farmers. As during the precolonial period, trafficked girls were the most highly desired because of their double reproductive value: They were not only farm laborers and porters but potential wives and reproducers of the labor force.

Pawning also increased as the demand for agricultural and commercial labor grew. In the southern part of the Gold Coast and Nigeria, for example, where cocoa was grown for export, peasant farmers pawned their unmarried daughters or (in matrilineal systems) nieces for cash to buy land, or in exchange for cash advances given by traders before the harvest. Wealthy peasant farmers and traders (often the same people) acted as creditors, using female child and adolescent pawns to expand their own cash-crop production and trading and to expand the family labor force through marriage. Boys continued to be pawned as well. Parents in southern Nigeria "apprenticed" them, in exchange for money, to bead makers, leather workers, smiths, weavers, and butchers, while they "apprenticed" girls to female potters. As in the precolonial era, pawning often occurred in times of hardship, when drought, famine, political instability, or warfare reduced food security. Male guardians also pawned children to raise money to pay fines levied by chiefs or to acquire additional wives or prestigious new titles. The colonial political economy brought with it new needs, wants, and hardships, thereby reinforcing and strengthening the practice of pawning children: taxes, school fees, wildly fluctuating world prices for export crops in the short term, and worldwide depressions that sent export crops into steep decline over the long term. By the end of the Second World War, pawning began to decline, due to official suppression in British West Africa, the use of land as collateral for loans from local lenders, the emergence of new sources of loan capital (cooperative societies, banks, and ethnic welfare associations), and the increasing insecurity of child pawns, many of whom resisted being pawned by running away.

Child workers, particularly boys, also worked in the growing towns, cities, and mining centers of peasant Africa. Many migrated with their parents to the cities, while, in time, others were town born. Many migrated on their own, with the permission of their parents, but many others left without permission, fleeing the intensification of work in cash-crop farming, the authority and control of parents, or the prospect of living out their lives as pawns or in an arranged marriage with an older man. In town, they worked in mining (usually aboveground), as domestic servants to Europeans and fellow Africans, and as shop assistants. However, most (including girls) found employment in the growing informal economies of the cities, working as hawkers and as assistants to traders, craftspeople, and other entrepreneurs. Those who lived on their own in town were the forerunners of today's street children. They survived through legal and illegal means, including theft, gambling, and commercial sex. In most colonies, rates of "juvenile delinquency" increased as the numbers of children in town grew and as colonial authorities looked for ways to control the legions of "vagabonds," "ruffians," and "urchins." While colonial authorities may have called it delinquency, such behavior can also be seen as agency—the desire of young people to shape their own childhoods and young adulthoods beyond adult control.

In those parts of sub-Saharan Africa where Europeans settled permanently and in large numbers—much of eastern and southern Africa—child labor was just as integral to expanding colonial economies. However, because of the deeper penetration of capitalist relations of production, some of the forms child labor took were different from those in peasant Africa. The oldest of these settler colonies was South Africa, whose original settlement at Cape Town was established by the Dutch in 1652. The slaves that were imported from West Africa and the Dutch East Indies were primarily adults, but the children of the slave women, like their mothers, were also slaves. They were used as laborers in agriculture, wine making, herding, and domestic service. The settlers subjugated the indigenous Cape Khoi population, incorporating them as quasi-servile labor on their farms and in town. Khoi children, like their parents, were bonded laborers who were not free to move away from the farm. As settlers moved eastward and northward from the cape, they subjugated the indigenous Bantu-speaking peoples, incorporating entire families, who, as labor tenants, were required to work for the new landowners in exchange for continued access to land. Settlers also conducted commando raids on independent African communities with the explicit purpose of capturing children, who were brought back and sold or incorporated on farms as bonded "apprentices." When the British took control of the Cape Colony after 1800, they abolished slavery but introduced a system of apprenticeship whereby orphaned or abandoned children, or children whose parents signed contracts for them, could be bonded to white farmers until the age of eighteen or twenty. British farmers used the labor of African children from "reserves" that were established after most of the land was set aside exclusively for white ownership. When diamonds and gold were discovered in the 1860s and 1880s, respectively, the rapid urbanization of South Africa ensued. Boys were recruited from within South Africa and from neighboring colonies (particularly Mozambique) to work in above- and belowground mining operations and as domestic servants in all-male compounds. Growing rural poverty on the reserves, resistance to parental authority, and resistance to landlords on labor tenant farms drove many children, male and female, to the towns, where, as in peasant Africa, they worked in the formal and informal sectors and by their wits on the streets.

South Africa's patterns of child labor acquisition and use were replicated in other settler colonies as these were established in eastern and southern Africa (most notably, Kenya, Southern Rhodesia [Zimbabwe], and Southwest Africa [Namibia]) after 1890. Child labor was on the wane in Britain and the rest of Europe, but laws and policies were devised in many colonies to allow and encourage boys and girls under the age of fourteen to leave home and work for wages. In Kenya, Northern Rhodesia (Zambia), and Nyasaland (Malawi), governments allowed boys to be recruited and transported far from home, including to neighboring territories. Though children in these colonies were prohibited from working in certain industries and at night, they were allowed to sign their own labor contracts and were subject to penalties for contract violations.

Though European missionaries were often critical of settlers' use of child labor, arguing that African children should be in school, they also made use of child labor. Government grants-in-aid required that mission schools teach Africans "industrial" skills for part of the day. Under this guise and without pay, students were put to work growing food crops for the staff and students, and for sale in town. Male students made furniture, while female students did needlework. The proceeds from the sale of crops and craftwork were used to support the missions and extend their evangelical and educational work to other parts of the colony. Female mission students also cleaned and cooked for the European staff. Some missions were accused of being more interested in making a profit from unpaid student labor than in educating students. Students in South Africa and colonial Zimbabwe protested unpaid manual work by boycotting classes and refusing to work. Part-time schooling, such as that which developed on mission stations, was used as a model for "farm schools" on white farms in South Africa, Southern Rhodesia, Nyasaland, and Kenya. Children who lived with their parents, or who were recruited to work and live on these farms without their parents, attended school for "free" for part of the day and worked at reduced wages during the remaining part of the day. Some farm schools closed down completely during the busy agricultural season so the students could be turned out to work full-time.

The history of child labor in Africa during the colonial period underscores several points. First, children were not "extra" hands, useful to employers only when adult labor was in short supply. Children were sought after in their own right because they had qualities adults did not appear to have: They were considered cheaper, easier to control, more adaptable, and, with their "nimble" fingers, better at handling certain crops such as tea, tobacco, and cotton. Second, through tax, pass, and labor laws, colonial governments played an important role in facilitating child labor. Finally, children were not passive victims of adults, be they parents, masters, settlers, or colonial officials. Rather, they found ways to resist adult authority over them and their labor. In subtle and not-so-subtle ways, they helped to construct their own childhoods.

References and Further Reading

Anti-Slavery Society. *Child Labour in South Africa. A General Review.* Child Labour Series 7. London: Anti-Slavery Society, 1983.

Glaser, Clive. *Bo-Tsotsi: The Youth Gangs of Soweto, 1935–1976.* Portsmouth, NH: Heinemann, 2000.

Grier, Beverly. *Invisible Hands: Child Labor and the State in Colonial Zimbabwe.* Portsmouth, NH: Heinemann, 2005.

Jeeves, Alan H., and Jonathan Crush, eds. *White Farms, Black Labor: The State and Agrarian Change in Southern Africa, 1910–1950.* Portsmouth, NH: Heinemann, 1997.

Lovejoy, Paul E., and Toyin Falola, eds. *Pawnship, Slavery, and Colonialism in Africa.* Trenton, NJ: Africa World Press, 2003.

Miers, Suzanne, and Richard Roberts, eds. *The End of Slavery in Africa.* Madison: University of Wisconsin Press, 1988.

Summers, Carol. *Colonial Lessons: Africans' Education in Southern Rhodesia, 1918–1940.* Portsmouth, NH: Heinemann, 2002.

Van Hear, Nick. "Child Labour and the Development of Capitalist Agriculture in Ghana." *Development and Change* 13 (1982): 499–514.

HIV/AIDS and Child Labor in Sub-Saharan Africa

Anita Amorim and **Nadine Osseiran**, International Labor Organization (ILO)–International Program for the Elimination of Child Labor (IPEC)

The Joint United Nations Program on HIV/AIDS (UNAIDS) estimated that 39.5 million people worldwide are living with HIV/AIDS, of whom 63 percent are in sub-Saharan Africa (UNAIDS 2006). The epidemic has forced many children who are HIV positive, orphaned, or affected by the virus to enter the labor market prematurely. In 2005, UNAIDS estimated 15 million children under eighteen years of age were orphans as a result of AIDS, more than 12 million of them in sub-Saharan Africa. The relationship between poverty and HIV/AIDS is bidirectional. Poverty contributes to increased risk of HIV infection. In turn, HIV infection becomes a major financial and asset drain on households, communities, businesses, and countries, leading to growing and intensification of poverty.

Children Affected by HIV/AIDS

HIV/AIDS infects mostly adult members of the household, who are likely to be breadwinners. Often, when an adult family member falls ill or dies, one or more children are sent away to extended family members to ensure they are cared for. However, as the number of orphans grows, and the number of potential caregivers shrinks, traditional coping mechanisms are stretched to their breaking points. If children remain at home, the oldest child is often forced to become head of the household. Households headed by orphans are becoming increasingly common in countries where the AIDS epidemic is prevalent.

In some countries in Africa, up to 10 percent of all children orphaned by HIV/AIDS are heads of households and caring for siblings, especially in eastern and southern Africa. Child-headed households exist because there are no relatives left to care for the children, or remaining relatives are too overburdened or sick to adequately care for the children they have inherited. This is a new phenomenon brought on by the HIV/AIDS pandemic. Many children who become household heads have little option but to seek work to support themselves and their siblings. Stories exist of older children earning cash to keep younger siblings in school, but continued schooling for any of the children in these households is problematic. In the longer term, orphans face increased risk of stunting and malnourishment, which jeopardizes their ability to contribute to society in adulthood.

Orphans experience deep trauma from the harrowing experience of seeing a parent suffering in the final stages of an HIV-related death. They may not be able to replace the love, attention, and affection they received from their parents. They are in urgent need of counseling. There is also need for counseling before the parent dies. Parents need help to talk with their children about the fact that they may die very soon. Children need help to face up to the real possibility that their parents or other loved ones may die.

Zambia is experiencing one of the worst HIV/AIDS epidemics in the world. HIV infection is currently estimated at 17 percent in persons between fifteen and forty-nine years old (UNAIDS 2006). Moreover, life expectancy, which stood at fifty-four years in the not-too-distant past, has plummeted to thirty-seven and is projected to decline in the coming decade to just over thirty. Following inexorably in the wake of the epidemic is growth in the number of orphans. It is estimated that in 2005, 710,000 children were orphans due to AIDS (UNAIDS 2006). More than 7 percent of Zambia's 1,905,000 households were without any adult member in 2001 (Kelly 2001).

The death of an adult family member can have a serious impact on household and caring structures for surviving children. In Zimbabwe, where HIV/AIDS prevalence reached 20 percent in 2005, two-thirds of households in which a female adult died dissolved, leaving the children to be raised by relatives, usually grandmothers (Mutangadura 2000). The emergence of households headed by siblings is an indication that the extended family is under stress (Foster et al. 1995). In western Tanzania, many relatives refuse to take responsibility for orphaned children. Grandparents are most likely to take in orphans, but they are also particularly likely to be poor and unable to offer substantive material support. This increasing inability of relatives to provide for orphaned children may be symptomatic of change in the concept of family. Under economic pressures, related to a combination of recession and unemployment, drought, and HIV/AIDS, family responsibilities are increasingly confined to nuclear rather than extended relations (Tibajiuka and Kaijage 1995).

In patrilineal societies, women widowed by HIV/AIDS and their children risk losing household assets and claims to land or livestock. Even where legal agreements provide for inheritance of assets, cultural practices may take precedent. Thus, children orphaned by HIV/AIDS often have no assets to bring to caretakers, to pay for education, or to begin their own lives.

HIV/AIDS has a direct impact on children's participation in the workforce. Children enter or increase their participation in the workforce to compensate for changes in household earnings. In this context, these children commonly contribute about 20–25 percent of family income. The impact on the household begins as soon as a member of the household starts to suffer from HIV-related illnesses. Even before one or both parents die of an HIV-related illness, pressures on the household may result in children increasing their workload, either within the household, or by taking on work outside the household, or both. The more prolonged the HIV-related illness, the more dramatic the cuts in household income. To supplement these economic losses, children may be withdrawn from school or told to work, or both.

Many children orphaned by HIV/AIDS find work in the informal sector, such as petty trade and services. Initially, most children seek work patterned on their parents' experiences. Children whose parents worked on a commercial agricultural estate are likely to find employment on the estate. Many informal-sector jobs are in urban areas. The presence of children on the street, and their need for money, food, shelter, and companionship, all increase the chances of being exposed to HIV infection. They may be drawn into casual sexual relationships or commercial sexual exploitation, or they may use drugs or alcohol, which increase risky behaviors and exposure to HIV. Thus, the impact of HIV/AIDS can go full circle, from affecting a child, to infecting a child.

Children Who Are HIV Positive

Many children have become HIV positive and are living with the virus. These children may also be AIDS orphans, who have contracted the virus from their mother, or through child labor. There are various forms of child labor where children are at risk of HIV infection, such as commercial sexual exploitation, or child labor where children are victims of sexual abuse or are exposed to substance abuse. As regards commercial sexual exploitation, unfortunately, in sub-Saharan Africa, an increasing number of adults are seeking children for commercial sex because of the perception that there is less danger of infection. There is also a common myth that younger girls can "disinfect" an HIV-positive person. Commercial sexual exploitation subjects children to one of the most intolerable forms of child labor.

There are a number of reasons why children may be drawn into commercial sexual exploitation. An ILO-IPEC Rapid Assessment in Tanzania suggested that, in addition to poverty, lack of education, limited alternative employment opportunities for youth, and orphanhood (whether due to AIDS or other causes) contributed significantly to the likelihood of children becoming prostitutes. The study revealed that the majority became engaged in prostitution at early ages, some as young as ten to thirteen years. Health care was a problem since the girls did not understand their bodies' changes at that age. About 10 percent of respondents interviewed were found to be sick with signs of HIV/AIDS. These girls had been on the street for more than five years, and all had children. The findings disclosed that 68 percent of respondents indicated that clients refuse the use of condoms.

Gender inequalities are a major driving force behind the HIV/AIDS epidemic. Female children are most vulnerable to HIV/AIDS due to their ascribed family and societal roles. Girls are more likely to be victims of commercial sexual exploitation, which poses great risks, as girls are often forced to have unprotected sex with multiple partners. Women in the fifteen- to forty-nine-year-old age-group represent 43 percent of all new HIV infections. Sociocultural environments unfavorable to women contribute to their vulnerability. A variety of factors, such as low social and economic status, lack of education among girls, and certain types of exploitative working sectors, increase the vulnerability of women and girls to HIV/AIDS. Social norms and different attributes and roles that societies assign to women deny them knowledge of sexual health practices and prevent them from controlling their bodies or deciding the terms on which they have sex. Compounding women's vulnerability is their limited access to economic opportunities and autonomy, and the multiple household and community roles with which they are burdened. Reversing the spread of HIV/AIDS therefore demands that women's rights be realized and that women be empowered in all spheres of life. The need for gender equality has been recognized in the ILO Code of Practice on HIV/AIDS and the World of Work (2001) and in the Resolution on Women, the Girl Child and HIV/AIDS adopted by the UN Commission on the Status of Women (March 2006).

Traditionally, in many eastern and southern African countries, boys were expected to leave school and begin work earlier than girls. Thus, education levels for women could exceed those of men. This, however, is not the case when gender is linked to HIV/AIDS and child labor. Increasing economic pressure due to HIV/AIDS, and the loss of a major income earner, tend to make poor families take their daughters out of school, rather than their sons. The value of girls' labor exceeds the returns parents expect from educating their daughters. This impedes the goal of making progress toward gender equality through education. This tendency is further exacerbated by AIDS, as girls are seen to have a high capability of providing care for infected family members.

While the female child must be targeted to increase education levels for survival and protection, the male child must also be educated to arrive at more favorable behaviors toward women. Socioeconomic inequalities play out in cultural and social patterns that define male prerogatives. Added to these are the prerogatives that come with having income to spend on sex. Whether children are exploited in the sex industry, or secondary school are girls enticed by consumer goods, they are subject to the wealth that men can use to gain sexual advantage. A study in Kenya found that one important reason for high infection rates among girls is the frequency of sexual intercourse with older men. "Sugar daddies" induce young, impressionable, and inexperienced girls with cash, consumer goods, and supposed status.

HIV/AIDS and Education

Studies suggest that the death of a parent diminishes the chance of a child attending school by half. Orphans who continue attending school spend less time in school than they did prior to losing a parent. Many orphans are unable to pay school fees, and many children never complete basic schooling. Case studies do, however, show that most orphans would be willing to continue school if given the chance. UNICEF estimated that only 65 percent of schoolchildren enrolled in South African schools between 1990 and 1995 reached grade five, representing a dropout rate of 35 percent. Compulsory education to grade nine, or fifteen years of age, is only a relatively recent phenomenon in South Africa with the passing of the South African Schools Act. Data from the 2000–2001 child labor survey in Tanzania suggest that 4.1 million out of an estimated 10.2 million children age five to fourteen years are not attending school, and that nearly 4 million of these were engaged in either economic activities or housekeeping.

Education is crucial to national development, income growth, and labor productivity. But HIV/AIDS is playing havoc with education systems. It impacts both the availability and use of schooling. Those children who survive to school age may not be able to afford school fees and books, lack parental care, face hunger and emotional distress, and may have to work or care for sick parents. HIV/AIDS is reducing the number of children in school because sick parents are taking their children, especially girls, out of school. Orphans are not attending school since households are becoming more reliant on child labor and the economic contribution children can make. The increased costs of care for HIV/AIDS-affected family members are reducing family ability to meet even modest educational expenses.

On the supply side, the disease is constraining the ability to provide educational services, with high levels of morbidity and mortality among teachers. UNICEF has estimated that in 1999 alone 860,000 children in sub-Saharan Africa lost their teachers to AIDS. In many rural areas of southern Africa, the regular income of teachers gives them a fairly high and secure socioeconomic status. Some male teachers use their status and income to obtain sex with schoolchildren and women of less secure means in surrounding communities. Thus, teachers have, on average, higher HIV/AIDS prevalence rates than the general population (Kelly 1999). In Zambia, data show that the rate of teacher deaths doubled from 1996 to 1998, from 680 in 1996 to 1,300 in the first ten months of 1998. The number of teachers who died in 1998 was more than one-fifth of the number estimated to be HIV positive. While one cannot attribute all of these deaths to AIDS, the 1998 teacher deaths represented a mortality rate of thirty-nine per thousand, about 70 percent higher than the mortality rate in the general population. For the education system, the 1998 deaths were equivalent to the loss of about two-thirds of the annual output of newly trained teachers from all training institutions combined.

Teachers constitute the largest single educational expense. But since they cannot be severed from service while they are ill, the system must carry a large number of nonproductive persons. In addition, the mortality of so many young qualified teachers represents a great national loss in terms of their earlier training at public expense. Teachers are also deeply personally affected by the incidence of HIV/AIDS among their relatives and colleagues. Though this is a major cause of concern, they receive little support. The unresolved HIV-related stresses that teachers experience, in the classroom and at home, need to be acknowledged in initial and ongoing teacher training. Recognizing the magnitude of this personal problem, the Zambian Ministry of Education has proposed to introduce HIV/AIDS counseling for teachers and other education personnel and to integrate HIV/AIDS awareness into its in-service training programs.

There is evidence that the role of the school is changing because of HIV/AIDS. Traditionally, there were very high expectations that schools would educate the whole child across the broad spectrum of the intellectual, social, moral, aesthetic, cultural, physical, and spiritual domains. In practice, most schools find this impossible. Instead, they concentrate on only a few of these areas, and give the greatest emphasis in their curriculum to intellectual development. But the intrusion of HIV/AIDS necessitates psychological support for children from affected families. Teachers find that they are increasingly being called upon to counsel their pupils to help them deal with the stresses arising from HIV/AIDS in their families.

The impact of HIV/AIDS on the education sector is not altogether straightforward. At one level, evidence is emerging that education remains virtually the only "vaccine" currently available for warding off HIV infection. Beyond the early stages of the AIDS pandemic, education reduces the risk of HIV since better-educated persons expose themselves less to the risk of infection. Providing more extensive and better-quality education, even if not dealing directly with reproductive health and AIDS education, is likely to make a population less vulnerable to HIV infection. The education sector represents an existing infrastructure to be used as a channel for promoting HIV/AIDS education. Teachers need to be appropriately trained for the successful integration of life skills and AIDS education.

Initiatives to Address HIV/AIDS and Child Labor

Numerous communities, NGOs, and some national programs have emerged to address children affected by HIV/AIDS, but very few of these address the socioeconomic factors driving the pandemic. Most of the programs are already overwhelmed by the magnitude of the problem. There are a handful of programs to improve work opportunities for youth affected by HIV/AIDS. Some vocational training programs, usually targeted to boys, have incorporated HIV/AIDS information, but they rarely address male sexual norms and associated behaviors. There are experiments in southern Africa with microsavings and microcredit initiatives to help cover education expenses of children orphaned by HIV/AIDS, and to include such children in small-business financing. Some community groups in Uganda and South Africa, for example, use informal savings programs to help pay for school fees for orphaned children. Some long-established programs, such as the AIDS Service Organization (TASO) in Uganda, are working with HIV-positive parents to help them make arrangements for their children for when death comes. Several governments in Africa have instituted reductions or elimination of school fees for orphaned children.

Many children whose parents died of HIV/AIDS visit this primary school of the Kiwohede (Kiota Women's Health and Development) Center in Dar es Salaam, Tanzania (pictured in October 2003). As a partner of the IPEC program of the ILO, this NGO is actively involved in gender promotion, health, and child development. It has launched vocational training and readaptation centers for young girls withdrawn from prostitution. *(© International Labor Organization / M. Crozet)*

The ILO, through its International Program on the Elimination of Child Labour, has been addressing the issue of child labor and HIV/AIDS since 2001. It has carried out studies in sub-Saharan Africa on the linkages between child labor, in particular its worst forms, and HIV/AIDS. In 2003, a plan of action was elaborated during a subregional tripartite workshop in Lusaka leading to an ILO-IPEC pilot project on HIV-induced child labor, called Combating and Preventing HIV/AIDS-Induced Child Labour in Sub-Saharan Africa. It was a three-year project that began implementation in 2004 and focused on Uganda and Zambia. The project developed models for preventing and combating child labor by assisting HIV/AIDS-affected boys and girls. Tools developed in Uganda and Zambia are to be disseminated and replicated in South Africa, Tanzania, Ghana, Madagascar, Kenya, Senegal, Malawi, and Cameroon.

Working with and building the capacity of national partner organizations in Uganda and Zambia, the project has developed community-based models for preventing HIV/AIDS-affected boys and girls from entering child labor and dropping out of school, and for withdrawing those children already engaged in worst forms of child labor. This model integrates HIV-affected children into education or vocational training, offering them rehabilitation, provision of scholastic materials, health and psychosocial counseling, and reintegration into communities. To ensure sustainability, the project has set up community structures and social protection schemes for HIV/AIDS-affected families. The most successful social protection mechanisms are income-generating activities and savings schemes. In addition to working directly with governments, the project is working with employers' and workers' organizations in both countries to raise awareness and conduct training on the issues of HIV/AIDS and child labor. It is also developing tools for policy makers and program planners to deal with HIV/AIDS and child labor issues and facilitate replication of best practices in the subregion.

So far, the project has directly impacted more than 5,000 HIV/AIDS-affected boys and girls in Uganda and Zambia, and more than 500 HIV-affected families have benefited from income-generating activities or are participating in savings schemes. The project has supported the governments in Uganda and Zambia to mainstream HIV/AIDS into their draft national child labor policies and programs. Uganda's National Child Labor Policy was adopted in November 2006, and implementation of the policy will impact more than 1.5 million HIV/AIDS-affected boys and girls.

HIV/AIDS and the Future of Child Labor

What does HIV/AIDS portend for the future of child labor? Demographic changes resulting from HIV/AIDS have mixed implications. The deaths of millions of working adults in the eighteen- to forty-five-year-old age-group will leave vast gaps in the labor force over the next two decades. Will there be greater demand for younger people to fill these gaps? The prevailing demand-side reasons for using children in the workforce will continue, but it is unclear whether children will fill places formerly held by adults. As noted, the pandemic has increased demand for younger children within the sex industry. HIV/AIDS is placing millions of children in situations where they are likely to have to work more and at an earlier age, and often without the benefits of adequate education or training, than has been the case for most children in the past. Thus, both demand and supply factors are increasing.

The estimated 50 million children orphaned by HIV/AIDS who will be around over the next two decades will enter the workforce with many disadvantages: gaps in education, limited technical skills, psychological problems associated with the trauma of a lost parent, lack of social structure to guide effective decision making, and the stigma and discrimination surrounding people affected by HIV/AIDS. They will not be the first choices for hire by formal-sector employers. In countries heavily impacted by HIV/AIDS and with fragile economies, the prospects for nonhazardous employment for children are not good. In Zimbabwe, for example, young people are already the most affected by unemployment. The ILO (1999) observed, "The impact of HIV/AIDS has affected the highly qualified people and, therefore, affecting the supply of labor and obviously deepening the skills shortages which are already existing dealing a big blow on competitiveness."

Bill Rau (2002) has pointed out that, although the labor force will not grow as fast as it has in the past, given the influence of HIV/AIDS, the implications for all forms of child labor are likely to be mixed. With tens of thousands of children affected by HIV/AIDS unable to gain quality education or training, there is only limited likelihood they will be able to step into positions vacated by employees infected by HIV/AIDS. Also, as business productivity, competitiveness, and profitability are compromised by HIV/AIDS in the workforce, those businesses will be less able to hire new employees, resulting in reduced tax revenues that might be used for training and employment creation. Zimbabwe's "poor economic performance," argued the World Bank (2000), "has also led to decreased [public] spending on the social sectors, just at the time when the services are most needed."

A similar situation exists in South Africa. One-third of African men and nearly half of African women are unemployed. The country has lost more than half a million formal-sector jobs in the past decade. Since 1994, almost 10 percent of nonagricultural jobs have disappeared, and people are turning to low-income, insecure, informal-sector work. For children affected by HIV/AIDS, or at risk of infection, the labor market does not offer much hope for achieving economic security. So too Kenyan employers, including those in small-scale agriculture, are unable to absorb a growing labor force, and the employment gap was particularly vast for young people, and even worse for school dropouts, a situation that describes many children affected by HIV/AIDS.

Conclusion

The HIV pandemic in sub-Saharan Africa is the crisis of a generation. The response must continue to expand and improve on all fronts as rapidly as possible. It is widely acknowledged that the most promising long-term channel to stopping AIDS is prevention of the spread of HIV. However, even in countries where HIV infection rates are on the decline, AIDS-related illnesses and deaths remain high, and will for many years to come. While prevention offers the hope of stopping AIDS, the lives of this generation's children, and those of the next, depend on the protection that society can offer them from the vulnerabilities inherent in the condition.

Responsibility for establishing and operating effective social protection mechanisms lies with the whole of society. The response must come from the formal and informal, private and public sectors, combining their strengths under the supervision of a central coordinating authority. Psychosocial support is one essential element, generally conducted by NGOs and informal initiatives reliant on indigenous knowledge, self-help groups, and voluntarism. While there is strong interest from international and national providers, there is a need to harmonize efforts and improve coordination in order to maximize the impact of these programs.

Ultimately, the solution to HIV/AIDS-induced child labor will depend largely on the efforts to prevent HIV/AIDS infection and death, effective management of the poverty induced by the epidemic, and mitigation strategies to address the girls and boys already affected. All stakeholders (governments, social partners, NGOs, international organizations, communities, donors, households, and individuals) will have to undertake a series of responses while working in a coordinated manner toward common objectives. For the global society, the key to breaking through and putting a stop to the spread of HIV/AIDS is knowledge and communication. In response to this, ILO-IPEC has produced the "special SCREAM module" on HIV/AIDS to raise awareness among young people about HIV/AIDS issues and the vulnerabilities and dangers that they present for children. It capitalizes on a range of participatory, expressive, and fun techniques that connect with the minds of young people to provide a broad and deep level of understanding of HIV/AIDS and child labor issues.

Note

This article reflects opinions of the authors only and not those of the ILO.

References and Further Reading

Africa Youth Alliance. Alliance with African Youth for Reproductive Health and HIV/AIDS. http://www.ayaonline.org/index.htm.

Ayiedo, M.A. "From Single Parents to Child-Headed Households: The Case of Children Orphaned by AIDS in Kisumu and Siaya [Kenya] Districts," Study Paper 7. UN Development Program, New York, 1998.

Beijuka, J.K. *A Study on the Revolving Fund/Credit Schemes—Final Report.* Kampala, Uganda: UNDP Micro-Projects Programme to Combat AIDS, 1994.

Forsythe, Steven, and Bill Rau, eds. *AIDS in Kenya.* Washington, DC: Family Health International, 1996.

Foster, G., R. Shakespeare, F. Chinemana, H. Jackson, S. Gregson, C. Marange, and S. Mashumba. "Orphan Prevalence and Extended Family Care in a Peri-Urban Community in Zimbabwe." *AIDS Care* 7:1 (1995): 3–18.

Hargreaves, James R., and Judith R. Glynn. "Educational Attainment and HIV-1 Infection in Developing Countries: A Systematic Review." *Tropical Medicine and International Health* 7:6 (2002): 489–98.

ILO. *National Child Labour Survey Country Report Zimbabwe 1999.* Geneva: ILO, 1999.

ILO. *An ILO Code of Practice on HIV/AIDS and the World of Work.* Geneva: International Labor Office, 2001.

ILO. *HIV/AIDS and Work: Global Estimates, Impact on Children and Youth, and Response.* Geneva: International Labor Organization, 2006.

ILO-IPEC Series on Child Labor and HIV/AIDS in Sub-Saharan Africa:

Combating Child Labour and HIV/AIDS in Sub-Saharan Africa (Bill Rau), 2002.

Educational Perspectives on the Impact of the HIV/AIDS Pandemic on Child Labour in Uganda, 2004.

Enhancing Social Protection to Alleviate HIV/AIDS Induced Child Labour: Experiences from Uganda, 2007.

HIV/AIDS and Child Labour in South Africa: A Rapid Assessment, 2003.

HIV/AIDS and Child Labour in Sub-Saharan Africa: A Synthesis Report (Bill Rau), 2003.

HIV/AIDS and Child Labour in the United Republic of Tanzania: A Rapid Assessment, 2003.

HIV/AIDS and Child Labour in Zambia: A Rapid Assessment, 2002.

HIV/AIDS and Child Labour in Zimbabwe: A Rapid Assessment, 2002.

Policy Paper on Educational Perspectives Related to the Impact of HIV/AIDS on Child Labour in Zambia, 2006.

Policy Paper on Educational Perspectives Related to the Impact of the HIV-AIDS Pandemic on Child Labour in Malawi (Bright Sibale), 2005.

Report of the Thematic Study on Child Labour and HIV/AIDS in Uganda. Ministry of Gender, Labour and Social Development, 2004.

Training Manual on Child Labour and HIV/AIDS: A Publication Under the ILO-IPEC Project: Combating and Preventing HIV/AIDS-Induced Child Labour in Sub Saharan Africa: A Pilot Action in Uganda and Zambia, 2006.

ILO-IPEC. *SCREAM: A Special Module on HIV/AIDS and Child Labour.* Geneva: International Labor Office, 2007.

Kelly, M.J. "The Impact of HIV/AIDS on Schooling in Zambia." Paper presented at the International Conference on AIDS and STDs in Africa, Lusaka, September 1999.

Kelly, M.J. "Challenging the Challenger: Understanding and Expanding the Response of Universities in Africa to HIV/AIDS." Synthesis Report for the Working Group on Higher Education, Association for the Development of Education in Africa, March 2001.

Mutangadura, G. "Household Welfare Impacts of Mortality of Adult Females in Zimbabwe." Paper presented at the AIDS and Economics Symposium, Durban, July 2000.

Rau, Bill. "The Politics of Civil Society in Confronting HIV/AIDS." *International Affairs* 82:2 (2006): 285–95.

Rugalema, G. "It Is Not Only the Loss of Labor: HIV/AIDS, Loss of Household Assets and Household Livelihood in Bukoba District, Tanzania." In *AIDS and African Smallholder Agriculture*, ed. G. Mutangadura, H. Jackson, and D. Mukurazita. Harare, Zimbabwe: SAFAIDS, 1999.

Tibajiuka, A., and F. Kaijage. "Patterns and Processes of Social Exclusion in Tanzania." In *Social Exclusion, Rhetoric, Reality, Responses*, ed. G.C. Rodgers, C. Gore, and J. Figueiredo, 187–200. Geneva / New York: ILO-UNDP, 1995.

UNAIDS. *Force for Change: World AIDS Campaign with Young People.* Geneva: Joint UN Program on HIV/AIDS, 1998.

UNAIDS. *AIDS in Africa: Three Scenarios to 2025.* Geneva: Joint UN Program on HIV/AIDS, 2005.

UNAIDS. *Report on the Global AIDS Epidemic, 2006.* Geneva: Joint UN Program on HIV/AIDS, 2006.

UNICEF, UNAIDS, and USAID. *Children on the Brink 2004: A Joint Report of New Orphan Estimates and a Framework for Action.* Washington, DC: USAID, 2004.

UNICEF. *Child Workers in the Shadow of AIDS: Listening to the Children.* Nairobi: UNICEF, 2001.

UNICEF. *Africa's Orphaned and Vulnerable Generations: Children Affected by AIDS.* Geneva: UNICEF, 2006.

World Bank. "Zimbabwe-Multi-Sectoral AIDS Project." Report PID9727. World Bank, Washington, DC, 2000.

Influence of Orphanhood on Children's Schooling and Labor: Evidence from Sub-Saharan Africa

Lorenzo Guarcello, Researcher, Understanding Children's Work (UCW) Project; **Scott Lyon,** Researcher, UCW Project; **Furio C. Rosati,** UCW Project Coordinator and Professor of Economics, University of Rome, Tor Vergata; and **Cristina Valdivia,** Researcher, UCW Project

A full understanding of child vulnerability in sub-Saharan Africa is not possible without an examination of its links with the region's orphan crisis. AIDS orphans number some 12 million in the region (UNAIDS/WHO 2006), and for every child orphaned by AIDS, another is caring for a sick relative or is affected by the disease in some other way. The worst off are forced onto the street, where they become involved in prostitution or other harmful and exploitative forms of work.

Although these general facts are clear, little research exists that sheds light on the concrete links between orphanhood and child labor. A study aimed at addressing this gap examined orphanhood as a factor in child labor and schooling decisions using household survey data from ten sub-Saharan African countries (Angola, Burundi, Central African Republic, Côte d'Ivoire, Gambia, Kenya, Lesotho, Senegal, Swaziland, and Zambia).

Orphanhood as a Determinant of Child Labor and Schooling Decisions

Econometric evidence (based on the estimated probability of working as a function of a set of household and individual characteristics) indicates that becoming an orphan makes it less likely that a child has the opportunity to attend school and more likely that a child is exposed to the hardships of work. The size and significance of these effects varies considerably across the ten countries analyzed, but in only one—Lesotho—does orphanhood appear to have no significant effect on either work involvement or school attendance.

Loss of parents particularly affects a child's chances of attending school. The death of both parents significantly reduces the likelihood that a child attends school full-time in all countries except Lesotho, while the death of one parent significantly reduces the probability of school attendance in all countries except Gambia and Lesotho. The size of the effect is, in many cases, very large. In Gambia, for example, becoming a double orphan reduces the probability of full-time school attendance by 21 percentage points, in Burundi by 14 percentage points, and in Angola, Côte d'Ivoire, and Kenya by around 10 percentage points.

The effect of parental death on children's work involvement is less consistent across the countries analyzed. Becoming a double orphan significantly increases the risk of work involvement in five of the countries, but has an insignificant effect in the other five. The effect of orphanhood on work is strongest in the Central African Republic and Côte d'Ivoire. Becoming a double orphan in the Central African Republic and Côte d'Ivoire raises the risk of work exposure by six and eight percentage points, respectively; becoming a single orphan in these two countries raises the likelihood of work involvement by four and five percentage points, respectively.

Orphanhood also appears to have an important effect on the likelihood of a child being inactive, that is, not in school, not economically active, and not spending significant amounts of time on household chores. Indeed, parental death has a greater effect on inactivity than on work in many of the countries. This result suggests that children are frequently forced out of school by parental death, but that not all of these dropouts are forced into work. While some move into economic activity or spend greater time on household chores, others remain at home, outside of economic activity and school, presumably inactive.

Reasons for the apparent link between orphanhood and inactivity are not immediately clear and merit further investigation. It may be that some families take their children from school upon the death of a breadwinner because they are no longer able to afford school costs, but that the children are not needed for productive activities. Another more worrying possibility is that this residual "inactive" category reflects orphans' move into unreported worst forms of work. Household heads are unlikely to acknowledge to survey interviewers the involvement of their child household members in dangerous or morally repugnant forms of work, and could instead simply report them as inactive.

The econometric evidence does not show a consistent pattern of poor orphans being more vulnerable to work than nonpoor orphans. In four of the countries analyzed, poor children were found to face a considerably higher risk than nonpoor children of work exposure upon becoming orphans. But in the remaining countries, household income levels were found to have either inconsistent or small effects on the vulnerability of orphans to work. This argues for caution in using targeted income transfers as a policy prescription for reducing work among poor orphans.

Conclusion

The study takes the existing literature on the AIDS orphan phenomenon a step further by demonstrating a clear causal link between orphanhood, on the one hand, and child labor and school dropouts, on the other. The study also indicates that social protection and schooling policies need to be designed considering the specific country situation, as the magnitude and significance of the effects of orphanhood on schooling and work, and patterns of movement from school to work, vary greatly from country to country.

Additional information is needed in a number of areas to further understanding of the relationship between orphanhood and child labor. Information is needed on the relationship of the orphan to the household head, for example, and the effect of this on the risk of work exposure, as a basis for justifying extended-family-based care solutions for orphans. Better information on orphans not living in households, who are most at risk of involvement in worst forms of child labor and who are least likely to be reached by schools and other state institutions, will be essential to identifying policy alternatives for this group.

Incorporating questions relating to orphanhood status and care arrangements into standard household survey instruments is a necessary first step in filling information gaps on orphanhood and vulnerability. The UNICEF Multiple Indicator Cluster Survey (MICS) is currently the only such survey instrument containing a component relating to orphanhood, but questions on orphanhood are being added to other planned surveys. Analysis of this new evidence will help provide a more complete picture of orphans' vulnerability to child labor and school dropout.

References and Further Reading

Guarcello, Lorenzo, Scott Lyon, Furio C. Rosati, and Cristina Valdivia. "Influence of Orphanhood on Children's Schooling and Labour: Evidence from Sub Saharan Africa." UCW Working Papers, Understanding Children's Work Project, October 2004.

Guarcello, Lorenzo, Scott Lyon, and Furio C. Rosati. "Orphanhood and Child Vulnerability." Country reports for Burundi, Côte d'Ivoire, Malawi, Senegal, and Zambia. UCW Project and Children and Youth Section, World Bank, September 2004.

Joint United Nations Programme on HIV/AIDS / World Health Organization (UNAIDS-WHO). *AIDS Epidemic Update.* Geneva: UNAIDS, December 2006.

Children's Work Among Traditional Healers in Africa

Eddy Joshua Walakira, Lecturer and Consultant, Makerere University, Kampala, Uganda

While children's participation in activities such as agriculture, mining, manufacturing, construction, commercial sex, armed conflict, and slavery have been well documented in sub-Saharan Africa, there has been little specific mention of their participation in traditional medicine, which is a large and growing sector in Africa, and where children are actively involved.

Owing to limited access to allopathic care, up to 80 percent of the population in sub-Saharan Africa utilize traditional medicine to meet their health needs (WHO 2002). In countries such as Uganda, the ratio of traditional doctors to the population stands at 1 to 400, compared to less than one allopathic doctor for every 18,000 in the population (Ministry of Health 2006). People often consult traditional healers, the specialists in traditional medicine, when they are unable to access modern health care, or when care in modern health facilities fails to remedy a prolonged health condition.

Traditional healers often use herbal remedies, minerals, and animal parts to treat ailments (medication therapies). Those who rely exclusively on the use of herbs are called herbalists. The majority, however, up to 60 percent, as Reynolds (1996) showed in Zimbabwe, use spirit mediums (spiritualists), combining medication therapies with spiritual therapies. Elements of spiritual therapies include the use of healing rituals involving divination, ancestor worship, magic, or witchcraft. The use of manual therapies and acupuncture is not common.

As there are many peoples and diverse cultures in Africa, so too there are many varied expressions of beliefs. Notwithstanding this diversity, there are commonalities running through most traditional beliefs tied to one or more of the following features: (1) the conception of a supreme god who is all-powerful; (2) a belief in the presence of gods, spirits, or supernatural beings in space, on the earth, or under the earth; (3) the worship of ancestors or their spirits; and (4) consecrated human beings who mediate between living persons and the world of energetic spirit beings.

These features of traditional beliefs are manifest among the Shona of Zimbabwe, the Azande of Zaire, the Yoruba of Nigeria, the Baganda of Uganda, the Akan of Ghana and Côte d'Ivoire, and the Xhosa and Zulu Nguni speakers in southern Africa, among others. The Yoruba of Nigeria, for example, worship the orishas, the 201 gods who inhabit the earth (*Aye*), but also believe in the supreme being (*Olodumare*), who inhabits the sky (*Orun*), and beings of the underworld (*Ile*), the place of the dead (Olupona 2004). Alembi (2003) gave an account of ancestor worship in his case study of Wellington Masatia Tambwa, a traditional healer from Kenya. He uses herbs and ancestral spirits that sometimes appear as frames of fire, bushes, and huge snakes. Similarly, Turner (2006) gave a narrative of Muchoma, an herbalist and diviner of the Ndembu people in Zambia, and how four spirits from the grave afflicted him with the sickness (*Kayombu*) that precedes the call to become a doctor and diviner. Now he treats diseases of the heart and lungs and imparts a teaching spirit.

The Work of Children in Medication Therapies

The most visible work of children in traditional medication therapies is in the areas of collecting, processing, storing, and dispensing herbal medi-

Boys gathering medicinal leaves from a garden in Uganda's Rakai District. (*Photo by Eddy J. Walakira*)

cations. Accordingly, children go into the bush during the learning phase and participate in the identification of medicinal plants, as well as the harvesting of the relevant parts. When considered independent or ready, they can be sent out to collect and harvest on their own. The harvesting normally involves plucking leaves, flowers, and fruits, and sapping liquids from plants through piercing or cutting (Bukuluki et al. 2007). It also includes cutting the stem, barks, and roots, and sometimes uprooting the whole plant, or cutting or breaking the shoots off a plant. Some of the harvesting methods may harm plant species at risk of extinction.

During processing of herbal medicines, children do the bulk of the work, sometimes assisted by relatives. Herbal collections from the bush or garden are sun dried or boiled, depending on the purpose or urgency of need. During sun drying, children spread herbs on any locally available material such as a tarpaulin (*tundubali*), old iron sheets, or mats, among the Baganda herbalists in Uganda (Walakira 2007). Children grind herbs using a pestle and mortar, quite a laborious exercise. They sieve or filter herbs (*Kuwewa*), and pack the medicine in tins or plastic bags. Boiled extracts are packed in cans before distribution to clients.

Children are responsible for regularly cleaning storage cans and other stores where unprocessed and processed medications are kept. They collect the firewood for boiling herbs and participate in dispensing the medications following instructions of the healers. When clients are unable to collect medicine from the healer, children are sent to deliver it to the clients. Children also participate in maintaining the gardens of medicinal plants if healers happen to have them.

Children participating in herbal work acquire traditional skills relevant for meeting basic household health needs. They learn to identify medicinal plants, and master various harvesting practices, reproduction of plants, processing, preservation, packaging, and costing. At a more advanced level, they acquire knowledge about appropriate prescriptions for some ailments. To many children, the work supports their livelihood and education, provides career prospects, and can be a source of self-esteem when it improves their welfare and social status.

Nonetheless, this work is not devoid of harm. Children regularly experience injuries and pains in the hands and chest, associated with pounding herbs. Cuts and sprains are also common, leading to loss of school days. Exposure to dust resulting from grinding herbs, and risks associated with going into the bush to look for herbs, are common experiences (Walakira 2007). While these hazards present a challenge, appropriate regulation might bring this work into the category of "light work," approved by the ILO for children twelve to fourteen years of age, provided it does not harm the children, it does not exceed fourteen hours per week, and it is performed under the supervision of a parent or guardian for purposes of training or learning.

The Role of Children in Ritual Healing Activities

At the center of traditional African beliefs are rituals of sacrifice and offerings to appease the spirits, dispel misfortune, remove guilt, and pacify the spirit world. Some are conducted to initiate children and adults into the healing profession, normally having been preceded by prolonged illness. Green (1989) confirmed this among the female diviner mediums in Swaziland (*Sangomas*), including Zulu *Sangomas* of South Africa, who are called or coerced into their profession by an illness sent by an ancestor.

Children participate in rituals as helpers, curious observers, and enthusiastic participants. Reynolds (1996) noted that among the Shona community in Zimbabwe a child as young as nine years of age starts to work with a traditional healer, spending most of her time in the healer's company. The child is expected to help not only in collection of herbs, but also during sessions, including those in which the healer is possessed. While possessed, the healer's actions and behavior are directed by a spirit that invades his body. The healer may also enter a trance, when possession leads to loss of consciousness and the healer's spirit is considered to have departed the body to perform an activity in the spirit world. In these situations, the child interprets to the healer what has transpired, and also participates in dispensing medicine.

As curious observers and enthusiastic participants, children are attracted to the aesthetics involved in ritual worship. There is usually much dancing, singing, and feasting. These rituals have been described as works of art performed for the spirits (Kremser 2004; Turner 2004). Children participate in these activities, many of which are carried out during the night, and find them quite entertaining (Walakira 2007). However, beyond the fun, these are experiences that affect the social, psychological, and physical health of children, and are a cause for concern.

Many children participating in rituals are being prepared to enter the healing profession. This ensures continuity of the healing traditions and the use of spirit mediums alongside medications. However, little is known or understood about just how well children are prepared to handle spiritual powers, and how safe they can be. While children's participation in rituals can bring excitement, it is also associated with regular loss of sleep, and exposure to substances including alcohol and drugs—some of which act as catalysts for possession. There are additional hazards. At the core of rituals of sacrifice is the shedding of blood to please the supernatural force—a god, spirit, or ghost, or spirits or divinities of earth and water (Levinson 2005). Children, being the most vulnerable, have often fallen victims to ritual murders. Further, some practices of healers, like voodoo, a combination of magic and witchcraft, expose children to danger. The labeling of healers as witches often translates into social stigma that haunts children and can result into persecution. In the Democratic Republic of Congo, children accused of witchcraft face abuse from parents, communities, and the places where they are sent for the exorcising of demons (Human Rights Watch 2006). The mob justice that communities often apply to healers described as witches often does not spare the children serving as their helpers.

Conclusion

It is high time that public engagement with traditional healers be given special consideration because of the children who are participating in their activities. The regulation of the healers' activities needs to be given priority so as to explore ways of knowing more about what part children play in their work and how they can be protected against its associated hazards.

References and Further Reading

Alembi, Ezekiel. "The Calling and Work of Wellington Masatia Tambwa. A Traditional Healer from Bunyore, Kenya." *Journal of Folklore* 24 (2003):78–90.

Bukuluki, Paul, Eddy Joshua Walakira, and Bukenya Ziraba. *Conservation of Medicinal Plants Through Sustainable Harvesting Practices Among Herbalists: The Case of Mbale and Kampala Districts, Uganda.* Kampala: Makerere University, 2007.

Green, C. "Mystical Black Power: The Calling to Diviner Mediumship in Southern Africa." In *Women as Healers: Cross-Cultural Perspectives*, ed. C.S. McCain, 186–200. New Brunswick, NJ: Rutgers University Press, 1989.

Human Rights Watch. "What Future? Street Children in the Democratic Republic of Congo." *Human Rights Watch* 18:2 (2006).

Kremser, Manfred. "Afro-Caribbean Religions." In *Encyclopedia of Religious Rites, Rituals and Festivals: Religion and Society, A Berkshire Reference Work*, ed. F.A. Salamone, 22–26. New York: Routledge, 2004.

Levinson, David. "Sacrifice and Offerings." In *Encyclopedia of Religious Rites, Rituals and Festivals. Religion and Society, A Berkshire Reference Work*, ed. F.A. Salamone, 379–80. New York: Routledge, 2004.

Ministry of Health. *Policy on Traditional and Complementary Medicine (Final Draft).* Kampala: Ministry of Health, Republic of Uganda, 2006.

Olupona, Jacob K. "Owner of Day and Regulator of the Universe: Ifa Divination and Healing among the Yoruba of South Western Nigeria." In *Divination and Healing: Potent Vision,* ed. M. Winkelman and P.M. Peek, 103–17. Tucson: University of Arizona Press, 2004.

Reynolds, Pamela. *Traditional Healers and Childhood in Zimbabwe.* Athens: Ohio University Press, 1996.

Turner, Edith. *Among the Healers: Stories of Spiritual and Ritual Healing Around the World.* Westport, CT: Praeger, 2006.

Walakira, Eddy Joshua. "Children Working with Healers in Uganda: Are They Safe?" Paper presented at the Symposium on Social and Cultural Anthropology, Institute for Social and Cultural Anthropology, University of Vienna, April 26–27, 2007.

WHO. *WHO Traditional Medicine Strategy 2002–2005.* Geneva: WHO, 2002.

Child Labor Unions in Africa

G.K. Lieten, Professor of Child Labour Studies at the International Institute of Social History and at the University of Amsterdam; Director of International Research on Working Children (IREWOC)

One approach to the problem of child labor aims at ameliorating the conditions of work rather than abolishing child labor itself. One way to achieve this is the organization of trade unions by and for children. The Mouvement Africain des Enfants et Jeunes Travailleurs (MAEJT; also, African Movement of Working Children and Youths [AMWCY]), with its headquarters in Senegal, together with Movimiento de Adolescentes y Niños Trabajadores Hijos de Obreros Cristianos (MANTHOC) and Movimiento Nacional de Niños, Niñas y Adolescentes Trabajadores Organizados de Perú (MNNATSOP), in Peru, are among the earliest and best-known organizations in this field (Tolfree 1998; Swift 1999; Groves 2004).

The MAEJT has been active since the early 1990s. It has contributed in a significant way to international debates on child rights and the protection of working children. It maintains a network of child-run groups in various countries in Africa. Although the running of the organization is formally done by young adolescents, overall management and technical backstopping is in the hands of an adult NGO, Environment and Development Action (ENDA) Jeunesse. ENDA was set up in Dakar, Senegal, in 1985, in response to emerging issues of child neglect, particularly in regard to street children and housemaids. ENDA reached out to these children in need and provided them with a more structured organization. Gradually, starting with the inclusion of housemaids, a wider selection of children was included in the protection network: not only children living on the streets, but also those engaged in economic activities on the streets and in workshops.

ENDA, with its central management infrastructure in Dakar, aims to instruct and organize the children so that they can fight for their basic rights. Up to around 1990, the approach had been to act and decide on behalf of, and with, the children. It was then decided, in the wake of the adoption of the UN Convention on the Rights of the Child (CRC), with its emphasis on child rights and participation, that ENDA would opt for children's protagonism (support for child-led action, that is, not the child participating in adult actions, but adults supporting the children in their own initiatives). Accordingly, the MAEJT was created in 1994 at a meeting in which delegates of working children from five African countries participated. In the following years, according to claims of the organization, hundreds of local groups from some twenty countries have joined the movement. The movement has expanded from Francophone Africa into English-speaking and Portuguese-speaking Africa, although its organizational setup in the latter groups of countries remains weak (Nimbona and Lieten 2007a).

The working children themselves are said to have created their own African charter of child rights at the first meeting in Bouake, Côte d'Ivoire, in 1994 (Bamba Diaw et al. 2001). The twelve children present at the meeting constructed a list of twelve rights, which included the right to be respected, the right of organization, the right to be able to read and write, the right to learn a profession, the right to be listened to, the right to equitable justice, and the right to do light and limited work. Most of these rights are aligned with the CRC, but with a few modifications. The MAEJT agrees with the right to education in the CRC, but stresses that education should be more pragmatic, in line with the actual lives of children, who are often working and who need more vocational training. The MAEJT stresses that education is different from schooling in the sense that it is a much broader term. It wants literacy courses that can be combined with children's work (in classes that allow them to have parallel activities, thus, after the working day is over).

Particularly the assertion of a right to work seems to deviate from the general concept of childhood rights as contained in the CRC and ILO conventions. The international conventions have been important, leaders of ENDA argue, but they have also appropriated the rights of children. African children have reappropriated their rights by rebuilding them through their own experience so as to integrate them with their immediate effects on everyday life. Laws should take into consideration the capacities of children rather than their age, and a minimum-age regulation, in the view of ENDA, actually means that children are not allowed to work for their survival.

Boys and girls in a local area can register with a grassroots group (*groupe de base*) and then become "card-holding members" upon payment of a small card fee and a monthly contribution. The group process is supposed to increase participation, cohesion, and mutual understanding, but in practice the viability of a group depends to a great extent on the paid monitors. In most cases, local groups have boys and girls belonging to different professions. This means that the groups actually function more as social interest groups rather than trade union organizations with members of a specific professional background fighting for improvements within their profession. According to ENDA, MAEJT-Dakar, for example, is said to have twenty-three *groupes de base* and a membership of 1,653, which is far less than the number of children in need in Dakar (estimated at 400,000). There does not seem to be an active search for children in need, nor does there seem to be an active policy to establish more *groupes de base*. The most recent groups to be formed were made up of school dropouts who are not actually child laborers and who may have joined the organization in order to receive "formation" (vocational training).

The policy of ENDA management is to stimulate a participative approach that leaves the initiative with the children. With children in the driver's seat, adults must learn to listen to and understand the children. Through its publications and the organization of public events, with children in the forefront, the MAEJT is presented as an authentic organization by working children with a high degree of autonomy. In practice, however, the organization is run with a top-down approach. ENDA continues to play a decisive role in the functioning of the MAEJT, but officially it is stressed that the children manage the organization themselves and that ENDA is only a technical support structure. This structure provides a number of mechanisms that help the children in building up expertise and guide them in "sensibilization" campaigns and in lobbying with national authorities and international organizations. The African Training Programme (ATP) organizes workshops that last several weeks and that provide training to selected children who are brought in from different countries. It has offered courses on participative research and action, income-generating activities, communication techniques, and alternative education.

The children who sit on the committees and attend the meetings appear to be well trained in the ideology of the movement, and usually agree with the suggestions and strategies proposed by the adults in ENDA. They belong to a limited set of members with a good command of French or English and with an assertive personality. The delegates are typically older than the common child laborer, and no longer work. Downward reporting to the grassroots groups is usually absent, and the much-reported MAEJT view on child rights and child labor have been found to be at loggerheads with ideas among the membership at large. In a survey of 150 members of the movement in Burkina Faso and Togo, the right to education, the right to respect, and the right to equitable justice came clearly at the top of preferences. On the contrary, the right to work (that is, light and nonexploitative work) was hardly ever considered as a basic right. The members surveyed said that they were compelled to work in order to survive. It was dire poverty that left them no choice between work and nonwork, but it was clearly not a "right" that children should enjoy (Nimbona and Lieten 2007b).

The interest of many members is not so much

the improvement in labor conditions, but the acquisition of technical skill for self-employment. The MAEJT aims to provide two basic services to its members: (1) training courses and literacy education and (2) provision of small loans. The loans should enable those youths who have successfully completed the training and literacy courses to start up an individually owned income-generating business. As such, becoming a member of the organization is an attractive proposition.

The local training courses are heavily oriented to tailoring. Occasionally, classes are given on health care and disease prevention, accounting, organizational skills, and hairdressing. This type of training attracts more girls than boys. Given the nature of its activities and its support facilities, the MAEJT probably attracts the more enterprising youths who, with a vision to developing technical skills, enroll in the ENDA training programs. The members of the *groupes de base* are usually neither the neediest nor the poorest, but the "easy-to-help" girls who have decided to discontinue their studies and start an independent business as a dressmaker or a hairdresser. The MAEJT thus appears to be attracting young adolescents who already are, in some way, helping themselves. Children and adolescents find their way to the organization rather than the organizations getting into the poor neighborhoods and soliciting the invisible and vulnerable working children. Its activities are akin to those of a vocational training institute and micro-credit institute for upwardly mobile adolescents. The activities and interventions cannot possibly be classified as those of an organization fighting for the interests of child laborers.

The majority of the boys and girls, it appears, do not work, or work mainly in their own households. Some other boys and girls are active in petty-trade activities, such as the sale of cosmetic products, clothes, or fruit, or are just roaming the streets. They do not work long hours, if they work at all, and have sufficient time for skills training. The assertion that the MAEJT is a representative organization of child laborers thus is not accurate. ENDA actually works with a concept of child labor that includes all types of work. The term "working children and youths," as it is used by the MAEJT, involves the following two definitions: A working child (*enfant travailleur*) is a person under the age of eighteen for whom the daily principal activity is work; a working youth (*jeune travailleur*) is between nineteen and thirty years of age. The average age of the members covered in a survey in Senegal was 17.8 years. Most of the members were neither children nor laborers (Nimbona and Lieten 2007b).

It therefore appears that many of the "working children and youths" do not fall into the category of child laborer according to ILO norms. The consequence of this is that, although working children as well as nonworking children are in the movement, the worst forms of child labor fail to be targeted. The work done by the children is, by and large, harmless. This may explain why the organization takes an ideological stand in favor of the right to work.

References and Further Reading

Bamba Diaw, C.A., P.M. Coulibaly, and F. Terenzio. *L'approche d'ENDA Tiers Monde dans le soutien aux enfants travailleurs au Sénégal et en Afrique.* Dakar: ENDA Jeunesse Action, 2001.

ENDA Tiers Monde. *WCY Face the Challenge.* Annual News Bulletin of the African Movement of Working Children and Youths (AMWCY), 2003.

Groves, Leslie. *Good Practice in Working Children's Participation: A Case Study for Senegal.* London: Save the Children, 2004.

Nimbona, Godefroid, and Kristoffel Lieten. *Child Labour Organisations in Eastern Africa Still in the Making.* Amsterdam: IREWOC, 2007a.

Nimbona, Godefroid, and Kristoffel Lieten. *Child Labour Unions, MAEJT Senegal.* Amsterdam: IREWOC, 2007b.

Swift, Anthony. *Working Children Get Organized: An Introduction to Working Children's Organizations.* London: International Save the Children Alliance, 1999.

Tolfree, David. *Old Enough to Work, Old Enough to Have a Say: A Different Approach to Supporting Working Children.* Stockholm: Rädda Barnen, 1998.

SECTION 2. WESTERN AFRICA

Trafficking for Labor Exploitation in West and Central Africa

Albertine de Lange, MA, International Research on Working Children (IREWOC)

Until recently, the term "child trafficking" was mainly associated with the commercial sexual exploitation of children. With the adoption of the UN Protocol to Prevent, Suppress and Punish Trafficking in Persons, Especially Women and Children in 2000, however, the term "trafficking" has increasingly been interpreted to include the recruitment, transportation, transfer, and harboring of a child for labor exploitation, as in, for example, domestic service, industry, or agriculture. The protocol states, "[E]xploitation shall include, at a minimum, . . . forced labour or services, slavery or practices similar to slavery, or servitude" (Article 3a).

Child trafficking for labor purposes is a form of child labor migration that is criminalized in international law. It is often used as a synonym for child slavery. Whereas child labor migration involves all minors who move away from home to work, the term "child trafficking" refers to those cases whereby children are recruited, moved, or harbored by people who have the intention of exploiting them, or the intention of delivering them into the control of someone else who will exploit them.

West and Central Africa have long traditions of child fosterage, of placement of children with relatives for work, and of normal labor migration practices. Some definitions of child trafficking attempt to distinguish these traditional practices, which may not be exploitative, by regarding the conclusion of a transaction and the intervention of an intermediary as prerequisites of trafficking (ILO-IPEC 2001). But the definition most commonly used today, derived from the UN Protocol to Prevent, Suppress and Punish Trafficking in Persons (UN 2000) does not quite make this distinction as there is no mention of conclusion of transactions or intervention of intermediaries. Still, it is generally agreed that the term "trafficking" implies that there has to be some form of movement or transfer by people who intend to exploit the child (Human Rights Watch 2003). Furthermore, in the case of children it is agreed that even those who have consented to their recruitment or employment can be called victims of trafficking because children can be more easily coerced into doing as they are told.

Even though child slavery, the sale of children, and child trafficking are not new phenomena in West Africa (Piot 1996; Van Hear 1982), the issue of children being recruited in one West African country or region to work in another became a matter of international concern in the second half of the 1990s, when journalists and NGOs reported the exploitation and abuse of children from Mali and Burkina Faso in Côte d'Ivoire. Children were found to be subject to labor market transactions by middlemen, and the conditions they were working in were such that this came to be referred to as child slavery and child trafficking. Children working in the cocoa sector received considerable attention, set off by a 2000 British television documentary. Reports of a ship called the *Etireno* carrying "slave children," which disappeared between Benin and Gabon, further put the spotlight on child trafficking in the region. In 1999, IPEC launched a project entitled LUTRENA ("Combating the Trafficking in Children for Labour Exploitation in West and Central Africa"). Programs were set up in Benin, Burkina Faso, Cameroon, Côte d'Ivoire, Gabon, Ghana, Mali, Nigeria, and Togo to combat the trafficking of children, both within countries and across borders.

Some weaknesses in the conceptualization of child trafficking and its application in the field have been identified. It has been observed that the current policy emphasis on trafficked children may constitute a self-imposed need to find such children, which could result in child migrants falsely being treated as trafficked children (Whitehead and Hashim 2005). In the context of West African traditions, using too broad a definition of child trafficking carries the risk of rendering all labor migration practices criminal, even those that may be harmless to the child (Castle and Diarra 2003; Dottridge 2004).

Characteristics of Child Trafficking for Labor Exploitation in West Africa

In West Africa, child trafficking for labor exploitation has different manifestations. Parents do hand their children over to employers, but it is often the child who decides to leave the home for work. A child can be recruited by an intermediary or directly by the employer. Recruiters may be strangers, relatives, or even peers who have already made the journey before. Recruiters make arrangements with either the parents or the child. Outright kidnapping of children is less common. Trafficked children can be recruited from their home village, or from other settings such as on the streets in cities to which they have migrated. Professional trafficking networks exist, but in many cases the recruitment and transportation occurs through informal, unorganized networks. The practice of offering the labor of children as payment for debt is not widespread in the region, but some cases have been reported from Benin and Ghana (ILO-IPEC 2001; UNICEF 2004).

A child can move or be moved to a nearby village, to a different region, or to a different country. Cross-border trafficking has received more attention than trafficking within country borders, yet children transported across borders are not necessarily treated more harshly. Research suggests that, partly because of the artificial nature of many national borders in Africa, the question of whether a border is crossed does not necessarily determine the degree of risk a child is running (de Lange 2006). The majority of children in West Africa are trafficked locally or regionally, but networks of trafficking from West Africa to Europe and to the Middle East have also been reported.

Trafficked children are exploited in various sectors: domestic service, agriculture, mining, street or market vending, and begging. A common type of trafficking among girls is recruitment into domestic service in private households, where they work as child minders, maids, cooks, or cleaners. As in many sectors, distinctions among trafficking, child fostering, and placement with relatives are not always clear, but in some cases it is clear these girls are trafficking victims. Girls also work in bars or as porters, carrying heavy loads on their heads. Many trafficked boys work in agriculture cultivating cocoa, coffee, cotton, rubber, fruits, or vegetables. Exploitation of children can take place on large plantations, but also on small family farms, which children cannot leave if they want to. Children, especially boys below roughly thirteen years old, are also recruited to herd animals. Mining and quarrying are additional sectors that sometimes use trafficking to recruit labor. Trafficked boys girls and boys work in street vending and market selling. They can be found selling water, fruits, or items such as phone cards, in markets or bus stations.

The time a child spends away from home may be a few months or years. Some children never return home. They may work on short assignments or on an annual contract basis, or they may be held captive where they work. Children are usually lured away with promises of money or material rewards, but these are often empty promises. While some children stay with their employers voluntarily, despite long working hours or other forms of abuse, others are forced to stay through violence, threat, or simply because they lack money to travel home. They often have to repay the costs of their recruitment or pay for food and lodging; payments to the children may be deferred for months or years, which can be a way to control the children's movement. Promised payments are often in kind: kitchen utensils, a sewing machine or clothing, a radio, or a bicycle. Some children are trafficked more than once.

Parents' role in trafficking varies. While in some cases they hand over their children to recruiters, in other cases they may oppose it, or not even be aware of the departure of their children. In some cases, parents are paid for the services of their child, yet cases have been reported where parents paid intermediaries for the placement of the child.

Reported Cases of Child Trafficking

The familiarity with the term "trafficking," the degree of action undertaken, and the data available on its occurrence vary considerably among different countries in the region. While in Burkina Faso, Togo, Benin, and Mali, for example, anti-child-trafficking measures have been implemented at different levels, the concept seems hardly known in Sierra Leone (Surtees 2005). Estimating the scale of the problem is difficult. Available figures are usually based on governmental and NGO records of intercepted children and hence leave out those children who are not stopped during the trafficking process (ILO-IPEC 2001). Moreover, reported figures often include child labor migrants who are not necessarily trafficking victims.

The recruitment, movement, or harboring of children for exploitative work occurs in many areas and in many directions in the West African region. Some trafficking routes have been identified by NGOs and governments, yet these patterns are under constant change, and it is likely that many routes remain undocumented. Côte d'Ivoire, Nigeria, and Gabon are generally recognized as destination countries, whereas the Sahel countries as well as Togo and Benin are considered major "sending states." Research shows, however, that many countries are countries of both origin and destination (UNICEF 2004).

Well-known child-trafficking routes in the region include Mali and Burkina Faso to Côte d'Ivoire (for work in agriculture) and Benin and Togo to Nigeria and Gabon, mainly for domestic work (Dottridge 2004). Another trafficking route of considerable scale is from Benin to stone quarries in Nigeria (Terre de Hommes 2006). In Sierra Leone, recruitment of children for work on plantations in Guinea and Côte d'Ivoire has been documented (Surtees 2005). Other cases identified over the last few years include trafficking of Ghanaian boys as young as four into fishery, and recruitment of young boys for work in horticulture and cotton production within Burkina Faso.

Causes

The root causes of child trafficking are complex and often interrelated. Causes should be analyzed on both the supply side and the demand side. The desire to earn income, for the household or the child, often plays an important role in the parents' decision to send a child away or in the child's decision to leave. For girls there may be a desire to earn items needed for marriage, toiletries, and clothing. Boys are often lured away by the prospect of status symbols such as a radio, bicycle, or clothing. For both sexes, saving money for education can be a pull factor. The financial needs of the parents or the households play a role in many cases, especially when parents are financially compensated for the child's departure and employment.

Research has repeatedly indicated that incentives for children and parents are not merely financial. A desire for autonomy and adventure among youth has been mentioned as contributing to child labor migration and sometimes trafficking. The migration of young boys, which sometimes turns into trafficking, has been characterized as a "rite of passage" into adulthood (Castle and Diarra 2003). On the demand side, commercialization of agriculture and low prices of agricultural commodities can be discerned as contributing factors. In Burkina Faso, for example, increased cotton production set in motion recruitment of children from other areas, which in some cases resulted in situations resembling forced labor (de Lange 2006). Exploitation of child migrants in the cocoa sector in Côte d'Ivoire has been related to declining cocoa prices (Anti-Slavery International 2004).

Several factors have been identified to explain

why the practice has become so common in certain West African areas. Traditions of child fostering, or placement of children with relatives for work, have been said to create a climate in which child labor and child trafficking could easily develop. In some cases, placement with relatives leads to labor exploitation and hence trafficking. The long-standing tradition of labor migration is also said to contribute to child trafficking, as traffickers often use existing migration networks. But the question remains why migration turns into trafficking and why the age of migrants seems to have fallen in some areas. In addition, low levels of education also contribute to the availability of children for traffickers, even though it has been observed that school-going children are also at risk of being trafficked. Weak governance and porous borders are considered additional factors facilitating the practice.

Policy Responses and Legislation

African commitment to combat trafficking, abduction, and sale of children is found in the African Charter on the Rights of the Child (1990). The African Union reaffirmed its commitment to combat trafficking in 2002, when it identified elimination of trafficking as an operational priority. An important West African initiative is the Declaration and the Plan of Action adopted by the Economic Community of West African States in 2001 and the Plan of Action adopted in Libreville in 2000, containing strategies to fight against exploitative labor in West and Central Africa. Even though most anti-trafficking laws focus mainly on commercial sexual exploitation, an increasing number of countries are adopting laws that target trafficking for labor exploitation. Among them are Mali, Burkina Faso, Senegal, and Nigeria. In some countries, these laws have resulted in the interception of intermediaries or employers traveling with children, as well children migrating for work by themselves. In addition, intercountry agreements have been signed to combat transborder trafficking of children and facilitate their repatriation. In 2000, Mali and Côte d'Ivoire signed a cooperation agreement on combating transborder trafficking of children. Other West African agreements include one between Benin and Côte d'Ivoire and a repatriation agreement among Togo, Ghana, Benin, and Nigeria. In several countries, local vigilance committees have been set up to identify vulnerable children and track potential traffickers. Programs addressing child trafficking in the region focus largely on border control, and interception and repatriation of children, yet it has been reported that many children leave again soon after their repatriation. Sensitization to the risks attached to child migration is another important feature of programs, yet the effectiveness of such campaigns to fundamentally modify underlying ways of thinking has been questioned (Terre des Hommes 2006)

References and Further Reading

Anti-Slavery International. *The Cocoa Industry: A History of Exploitation.* London: Anti-Slavery International, 2004.

Castle, Sarah, and Aisse Diarra. *The International Migration of Young Malians: Tradition, Necessity or Rite de Passage?* London: School of Hygiene and Tropical Medicine, 2003.

De Lange, Albertine. *"Going to Kompienga": A Study on Child Labour Migration and Trafficking in Burkina Faso's South-Eastern Cotton Sector.* Amsterdam: IREWOC, 2006.

Dottridge, Mike. *Kids as Commodities? Child Trafficking and What to Do About It.* Lausanne, Switzerland: International Federation Terre des Hommes, 2004.

Human Rights Watch. *Borderline Slavery: Child Trafficking in Togo.* New York: Human Rights Watch, 2003.

ILO-IPEC. *Combating Trafficking in Children for Labour Exploitation in West and Central Africa. Synthesis Report. Based on Studies of Benin, Burkina Faso, Cameroon, Côte d'Ivoire, Gabon, Ghana, Mali, Nigeria and Togo.* Geneva: ILO-IPEC, 2001.

Piot, Charles. "Of Slaves and the Gift: Kabre Sale of Kin During the Era of the Slave Trade." *Journal of African History* 37:1 (1996): 31–49.

Riisoen, Kari Hauge, Anne Hatloy and Lise Bjerkan. *Travel to Uncertainty: A Study of Child Relocation in Burkina Faso, Ghana and Mali.* Oslo: Fafo Research Program on Trafficking and Child Labour, 2004.

Save the Children Canada. *Children Still in the Chocolate Trade: The Buying, Selling and Toiling of West African Child Workers in the Multi-Billion Dollar Industry.* Canada: Save the Children, 2003.

Surtees, Rebecca. *Child Trafficking in Sierra Leone.* New York: UNICEF, 2005.

Terre des Hommes. *Little Hands of the Stone Quarries: Investigation of Child Trafficking Between Benin and Nigeria.* Benin: Terre des Hommes, 2006.

UNICEF. *Child Trafficking in West Africa: Policy Responses.* Florence: UNICEF Innocenti Research Center, 2002.

UNICEF. *Trafficking in Human Beings, Especially Women and Children, in Africa.* Florence: UNICEF Innocenti Research Center, 2004.

UN. *UN Protocol to Prevent, Suppress and Punish Trafficking in Persons, Especially Women and Children, Supplementing the United Nations Convention Against Trans-National Organised Crime.* New York: United Nations, 2000.

Van Hear, Nick. "Child Labour and the Development of Agriculture in Ghana." *Community and Change* 13 (1982): 499–514.

Whitehead, Ann, and Iman Hashim. *Children and Migration: Background Paper for DFID Migration Team.* London: Department for International Development, 2005.

Koranic Schools and Child Labor in West Africa

Mahir Saul, Associate Professor, University of Illinois

"Koranic school" is the name given to a traditional educational institution in West Africa. Parents entrust their boys, around the age of ten, to a teacher for an extended period of training. The number of pupils in a given school ranges from a handful to a hundred or more for ambitious teachers in highly populated areas. The agreement between parent and teacher is conventional and informal. The pupil becomes a member of the teacher's household, and eats and sleeps in his compound, and the teacher acts as guardian and disciplinarian. Typically the parents live far away and, even when they do not, communicate with their child infrequently. The arrangement is therefore similar to fosterage. The pupil works on the teacher's farm or contributes to the teacher's upkeep in other ways. Where girls are admitted, they remain a minority and live with their parents. Koranic schools have existed in parts of West Africa for at least 300 years.

Koranic Education

Although government schools have been gaining ground in urban centers, Koranic schools abound in many parts of West Africa, and may claim a larger total of pupils than official schools. Besides fundamentals of religious practice, the scholastic program of Koranic schools centers on the Arabic text of the Koran. Reading exercises start with the opening chapter ("Fatihah"), then proceed, in reverse order, from the shortest chapters, at the end, to the longer chapters, at the beginning. A pupil first works on texts written out for him on his writing board by a more advanced student, but by successive iterations he improves his enunciation and practices writing, finally mastering reading and writing the text of the Koran. A public ceremony marks the completion of this course, after which the pupil returns to the custody of his parents.

The ideal is to commit the entire Koran to memory, which can take up to ten years. In many contemporary situations this is an unrealistic aim, and most pupils memorize only a small number of verses used in prayers or repeated with great frequency. After graduation, a small minority continues to an advanced level—the vernacular exegesis of the Arabic text, and then the Islamic sciences: jurisprudence, theology, and Arabic grammar, often under another teacher elsewhere. The pupils are not organized into grades, although they typically stand at different levels. Pupils receive their assignments individually, but they take their lessons and study together. A young scholar can serve as general assistant to the teacher, and more experienced pupils train and drill the beginners.

The teacher does not receive fees but expects a gift at graduation—often a sheep—in order for parents to redeem their son. When parents are unable to meet this obligation, the pupil takes a leave to work for wages and obtain his release by paying from his savings. Graduates may also remain indebted to their former teacher, bring him periodic gifts, and eventually entrust one of their sons as a pupil, renewing the dependency for another generation. Notions of the pupil as indentured servant linger in many areas.

The Pupils' Work

Throughout the year, pupils fetch firewood for cooking and heating, draw water, take grain to the mill, and work on construction and repairs. But what patterns the pulse of education most importantly is the agricultural calendar. Pupils participate in clearing new fields, felling and burning brush and trees, and cleaning and stubbing the farms. After the onset of the rains (in May or June in the West African savanna, depending on latitude) they spend most of their daytime on farming tasks: plowing, sowing, weeding, watching the fields against pests, and the harvests. Then they can apply themselves to their studies only after dark. Generally this is done in the blaze of a bonfire, the symbol of these schools, which is said to bring blessings on the community and defend the pupils on Judgment Day.

Today, rural Koranic schools count among the largest farming enterprises thanks to stable labor force of pupils, but historically this has not always been the case. In precolonial times, the pupils were children of a literate elite who spent relatively little time farming. Instead, slaves shouldered most of the burden of production. After emancipation, Koranic schools changed character; they recruited among the former slaves, using the arrangement to perpetuate ties of servitude. With growing urban demand for foodstuffs, today's Koranic school farm assumes yet another character. Whereas the household basis of much agricultural production in the savanna limits farmers' ability to expand production, the steady supply of pupil labor allows enterprising teacher-farmers to augment production beyond the level needed to provision their own crowded household. In Burkina Faso, some city-based Koranic teachers relocate their schools to a village for the rainy season to operate large farms and sell a good portion of their crops for profit. Koranic school pupils can provide a source of wage labor when the teacher contracts them out to soliciting farmers. While participating in farm work, Koranic pupils receive agricultural training and become agents in the diffusion of new production techniques and seed varieties.

The nutrition and well-being of the pupils is a much-discussed topic. Traditionally well-wishers in the community earned religious merit by supplementing the livelihood of the pupils with food and cash gifts. Despite this collective subsidy, Koranic pupils suffer hardship on top of severe discipline, but this condition is also proffered as necessary for spiritual and educational growth. Nonetheless, the pupils' plight in the hands of unscrupulous teachers provokes widespread criticism, especially in urban areas, where, for lack of farms, the pupils depend on charity to a large extent. A ubiquitous sight in many cities, small groups of Koranic pupils hold telltale empty red tomato-paste cans and beg for a dollop of dinner or a few coins. Newspapers denounce the practice and officials make pronouncements, albeit ineffectively. In the 1990s, UNICEF joined the fray with a campaign on behalf of Koranic pupils, arousing other humanitarian nongovernmental organizations to activity, but also stirring criticisms of hasty judgment and excessive zeal.

Koranic schools cannot be discussed only in terms of labor or farming; they draw sustenance from aspirations for salvation, religious education, and the desire to belong to social networks. Many wish for their reform, though, and indications exist that a host of factors, from growing formal school capacity, including Islamic private schools, to agricultural development, are shrinking the number of Koranic schools and bringing about an amelioration of their conditions.

References and Further Reading

Brenner, Louis. *Controlling Knowledge: Religion, Power and Schooling in a West African Muslim Society.* Bloomington: Indiana University Press, 2001.

Cruise O'Brian, Donal. *The Mourids of Senegal: The Political and Economic Organization of an Islamic Brotherhood.* Oxford: Clarendon, 1971.

Perry, Donna L. "Muslim Child Disciples, Global Civil Society, and Children's Rights in Senegal: The Discourse of Strategic Structuralism." *Anthropological Quarterly* 77:1 (2004): 47–86.

Sanneh, Lamin. *The Crown and the Turban: Muslims and West African Pluralism.* Boulder, CO: Westview, 1997.

Saul, Mahir. "The Quranic School Farm and Child Labour in Upper Volta." *Africa* 54:2 (1984): 71–87.

Burkina Faso

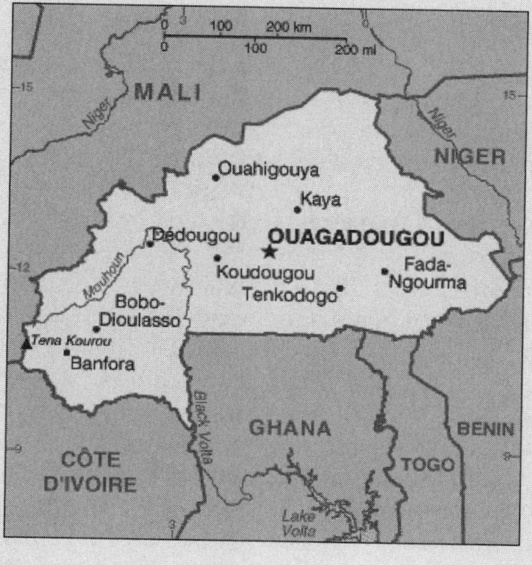

BURKINA FASO			
	CRC	C 138	C 182
Ratifications	Y	Y	Y
Human Development Index/Rank	0.342/174		
Human Capital			
Population Growth Rate	3%		
% Population 0–14	46.8%		
Total Fertility Rate	6.47		
Life Expectancy	48.85		
Infant Mortality Rate	91.35		
Literacy Rate	26.6%		
Economic			
GDP/Capita	$1,300		
GDP Growth %	5.2%		
% Poverty	45%		
Gini Index	48.2		
Labor Force Composition			
% Agriculture	90%		
% Industry and Services	10%		

CHILD ACTIVITY BREAKDOWN, BY SEX AND RESIDENCE

RESIDENCE	Percentage of children in the relevant age-group[a]							
	Economic activity only		School only		Combining school and economic activity		Neither in school nor in economic activity	
	Male	Female	Male	Female	Male	Female	Male	Female
Urban	10.2	10.8	67.2	62.3	0.3	0.6	22.4	26.2
Rural	51.5	54.1	23.2	15.6	1.0	0.5	24.3	29.8
Total	45.5	47.1	29.6	23.1	0.9	0.6	24.0	29.2

Source: Burkina Faso, Enquête sur les Conditions de Vies de Ménages, 2003 (see UCW Project Web site, http://www.ucw-project.org, country statistics).

Note: [a]Children age 5 to 14.

Child Labor in Burkina Faso

Albertine de Lange, MA, International Research on Working Children (IREWOC)

Burkina Faso is a landlocked country with approximately 14 million inhabitants. Farming is the main source of income for 90 percent of its inhabitants, and the manufacturing and service sectors are weakly developed. It is among the least developed countries in the world. School enrollment rates are around 40 percent for primary and 12 percent for secondary school (UNDP 2006), with a strong underrepresentation of girls. The climate ranges from arid in the north to semihumid in the southwest. Cotton is the main export product. Conditions for agriculture are far from favorable in most parts of the country. Rainfall is unreliable and the soil is often poor. Poor households commonly have diverse sources of livelihood to achieve food security in adverse conditions, including labor migration to neighboring countries.

Burkina has signed and ratified the UN Convention on the Rights of the Child, ILO Conventions 138 and 182, and the African Charter of Rights and Welfare of the Child. It is currently in the process of identifying subsectors that use worst forms of child labor. The minimum age for admission to work is fixed at fifteen. IPEC has been active in the country since 1999, and the Ministry of Labor recently set up a child labor section.

Children in Burkina Faso perform a range of economic and domestic activities. According to UNICEF estimates, 57 percent of children between five and fourteen years of age are engaged in child labor, which is among the highest rates in the world (UNICEF 2004). As in most African countries, work performed by children is mainly family controlled, on family farms, in the household, or in a family business (Andvig 2001; Kielland and Tovo 2006). Most children who are employed as paid laborers have temporarily left their home village (Yaro and Sawadogo 2005; CERFODES 2005). Especially in rural areas, work intensity varies with the calendar. The agricultural season, from June to October, is very busy; the long dry season involves few agricultural activities.

Family-Controlled Activities

In rural areas, children from about the age of four start herding goats and sheep. Girls this age are often expected to look after younger siblings while their mothers work the fields. Fetching things from neighbors is another task frequently assigned to young children. After the age of six, girls' responsibilities in the household typically increase. They sweep the yard, fetch buckets of water from the communal tap, well, pump, or lake, and do dishes and laundry. One of the most time-consuming tasks for girls (and women) is the pounding of grains with large wooden pestles in stone mortars. Mechanized mills can be used for this, but the costs are too high for poor families. Girls also assist their mothers in cooking. Learning to prepare the national staple dish, *to* (thick porridge), is an important part of the education of girls. Another task rural girls, and boys to a lesser extent, perform is collecting firewood in the bush. Women and girls also gather shea nuts (*noix de karite*) for processing into shea butter for sale or home use.

Boys and girls are expected and needed to work in the family fields, which produce food for the family's consumption and sometimes cash crops. Initially, children's tasks are mainly directed at developing skills, but boys and girls age ten and above are expected to contribute considerably. By the age of fourteen, they are expected to be full contributors to the work. They are engaged in all stages of production: plowing, sowing, weeding, and harvesting. Few families have animal-drawn plows, so most work is done with small hoes.

Children, both boys and girls, often have their own farming plots where they grow groundnuts, rice, or other crops (de Lange 2006; Thorsen 2005). Children usually spend their earned money on personal needs such as clothing or school supplies. In some villages, children and young people form cooperatives. They cultivate a certain plot, then divide their earnings or deposit them into a communal account.

Cattle rearing is an important economic activity in which children play an important role, especially in the northern regions of Burkina Faso. In the rainy season, when crops need to be protected, cattle are herded by boys from about the age of ten. Cattle often roam unguarded during the dry season, but some farmers prefer their cattle to be herded in the dry season as well, to prevent theft. Boys herd alone or in pairs; within families, rotation systems exist to give children a rest. Herding is rarely done by adults, though young men herd among some semipastoralist groups, such as the Fulani. The responsibility of herders is great, as cattle are the family's bank account. The work can be dangerous at times; children encounter wild animals and snakes, as well as the occasional aggressive farmer whose crops the cattle may have destroyed.

School holidays generally coincide with the farming season, which means that these agropastoralist activities do not entirely explain low school attendance figures in the country. Schoolchildren work the fields or guard animals during summer holidays. The fact that cattle are increasingly being herded in the dry season, however, poses a problem for schooling. Domestic chores are performed year-round and, together with culture and gender-related factors, often create obstacles to a girl's education. Primary school schedules take up the whole day, five days a week, and sending all girls to school would mean a heavy additional workload for adult women in rural households.

Petty Trade

Many children are involved in petty trade on streets, in markets, and in bus stations. In cities, this may include children who have migrated from villages and who work for patrons. In rural areas this trade is often done from home. Children sell snacks, drinks, or food from plates on their heads or from stalls. In markets boys are found pushing carts loaded with merchandise. They often work for their parents or other relatives, or earn pocket money by carrying out small tasks for covillagers or traders. In villages and cities alike, children can be observed working as assistants in stores, often for a relative, and often for long hours.

Apprenticeship Arrangements

Though not as common as in some other African countries, learning a trade is often seen as an important way to get diversified income for uneducated youths and those who have dropped out of school. These trades can include tailoring or hairdressing for girls. Boys commonly apprentice with carpenters, smiths, bicycle mechanics, masons, or welders. Even though apprenticeships can be successful strategies to prevent child labor, abuse of apprentices occurs. Children work long hours and are usually not paid; in fact, often they are required to pay their teachers a fee. The quality of their training varies greatly and is highly dependent on the skills of the patron.

Children's Relocation for Work in Domestic Service and Agriculture

Child labor in Burkina Faso must be understood in relation to child labor migration and child trafficking since most children leave home to engage in paid labor. A study found that in 2002, 165,000 children between six and seventeen years old had migrated for work. Child migration within Burkina Faso has steadily increased (Kielland and Sanogo 2002; Yaro and Sawadogo 2005).

First, there are girls who leave their villages to work as domestic servants in urban centers, for relatives or strangers. In the most positive cases, a girl (or her parents) has made an agreement with a host family to stay with them because better educational opportunities are available, in exchange for some help in the household or babysitting. In a worst-case scenario, a girl ends up with people who abuse her mentally, physically, or sexually and make her work long hours (Terre des Hommes 2003). Girls who have migrated often follow a more or less fixed career path. After a few years in domestic service, the step is often made to waitressing jobs in restaurants and bars, where they are often confronted with implicit offers of money in exchange for sexual services.

Second, farms in the countryside and in neighboring countries attract many male child migrants. Cotton areas in the south, as well as the irrigated garden plots scattered around the country, are popular destinations for boys in search of work. Farmers and middlemen in search of children come to villages with promises of a bicycle or money for a year's work. Some children leave independently and go to relatives or meet farmers on the way. The work is hard and children are often paid less than promised or nothing at all. Large quantities of pesticides used in cotton farming pose another threat to children (de Lange 2006). On the irrigated garden plots, children are usually promised a third of the profit, but in cases of crop failure, children earn nothing. Children often eat and sleep next to the gardens, alone or with their colleagues.

Serious cases of abuse have been reported, and the government and NGOs have set up interventions to stop children from leaving home in search of work. Their focus is mostly on prevention, interception, and repatriation, rather than improving working conditions. Eradicating the practice is complicated, as migration has evolved into a rite of passage for young persons (de Lange 2006; Thorsen 2005).

A stone cutter near Ouagadougou, Burkina Faso. *(Photo by Kristoffel Lieten, 2004, courtesy of IREWOC Foundation)*

Mining and Quarrying

Many children, including child migrants, work in gold mining and stone quarrying. The country hosts many unregulated open mines that attract all types of people in search of money. Working in the mines is heavy and dangerous (Yaro and Sawadogo 2005; CERFODES 2005). Children can be engaged in a variety of activities; they descend into the shafts, use chemicals, or crush minerals with heavy tools. Problems have been recognized in this sector since the late 1990s, but despite a number of interventions, they continue. Several NGOs are now setting up programs to address these practices.

Muslim Clerics

Another prominent group of child laborers are the Koranic students, or Talibés, who can be seen throughout the country begging for food or money. They are Muslim boys placed with Koranic teachers (*marabous*) by their parents for several years to receive religious education. They are commonly expected to beg for a religious tax for their teachers and to learn to be humble (Risoen et al. 2003; Kielland and Tovo 2006). Apart from begging, the boys also engage in other economic activities for their teachers, such as farming. As in other forms of child work, conditions vary depending on the employer. UNICEF has categorized Talibés as one of the most vulnerable groups of African children.

Causes

Several, often interrelated, circumstances should be taken into account when attempting to understand the high prevalence of child labor in Burkina Faso. First, the country's low level of development and extreme poverty make household and farm work very labor intensive, especially for rural inhabitants, who constitute more than 80 percent of the population. Remote water sources, lack of electricity, and low levels of technology mean that all hands are needed.

Second, the problem of child labor should be understood in the context of persistently poor-quality schools and insufficient access to education. Work can be an impediment to education, causing some children to forfeit their education completely, and others to limit their study time. However, there are also large numbers of children engaged in economic or domestic activities because education is considered too expensive, too far away, or too ineffectual.

Third, attitudes about childhood and work influence the use of child labor, but would probably not lead to exploitative child labor if circumstances were more favorable. Learning how to farm or how to prepare food are considered indispensable parts of a child's upbringing. Most children feel a strong responsibility to lessen their parents' burden, to contribute to the family's income and subsistence, and to cater to their own personal needs, such as clothing. Children often justify their labor activities with remarks such as "I cannot sit down and watch my father work on the field in the sun; that's impossible," or "I cannot make my mother do all the work alone." Further, some adults see certain jobs as more suitable for children than for adult men. A grown man herding goats or sheep is likely to be laughed at or pitied. Some parents say that physical or mental suffering prepares children well for the harsh life on the savanna, where laziness is considered a major vice. The fact that they did the annoying jobs when they were young is often used to justify assigning these jobs to their own young ones.

The reasons for child labor outside the family realm, generally involving migration, include factors in addition to those mentioned above. Research suggests that child labor migration is not always a last resort and that the child's own agency plays a major role (de Lange 2006; Kielland and Sanogo 2002). The decision to migrate for work can be an escape from domestic responsibilities or can result from a desire for autonomy and adventure, as well as money for personal items (Terre des Hommes 2003; Thorsen 2005). Forces on the demand side should be taken into account as well. Commercialization of agriculture, low levels of technology, urbanization, and low commodity prices, as well as certain ideas about children and work, all add to the demand for young laborers.

References and Further Reading

Andvig, Jens. "Family-Controlled Child Labour in Sub-Saharan Africa—A Survey of Research." Social Protection Discussion Papers 0122. World Bank, Washington, DC, 2001.

CERFODES. *Étude de base sur la lutte contre le trafic et les pires formes de travail des enfants dans la région est du Burkina.* Ouagadougou, Burkina Faso: Centre d'Études, de Recherches et de Formation pour le Développement Économique et Social, 2005.

De Lange, Albertine. *Going to Kompienga: A Study on Child Labour Migration and Trafficking in Burkina Faso's South-Eastern Cotton Sector.* Amsterdam: IREWOC, 2006.

Kielland, Anne, and Ibrahim Sanogo. "Burkina Faso: Child Labour Migration from Rural Areas: The Magnitude and Determinants." World Bank, Washington, DC, and Terre des Hommes, Geneva, Switzerland, 2002.

Kielland, Anne, and Maurizia Tovo. *Children at Work: Child Labor Practices in Africa.* London: Lynne Rienner, 2006.

Riisoen, Kari Hauge, Anne Hatloy, and Lise Bjerkan. *Travel to Uncertainty: A Study of Child Relocation in Burkina Faso, Ghana and Mali.* Oslo: Fafo Research Program on Trafficking and Child Labour, 2004.

Terre des Hommes. *Les filles domestiques au Burkina Faso: Traite ou migration? Analyse de migration laborieuse des enfants de la province du Sourou au Burkina Faso.* Lausanne: Fondation Terre des Hommes, 2003.

Thorsen, Dorte. "Child Migrants in Transit: Strategies to Become Adult in Rural Burkina Faso." Paper presented at the conference Childhoods 2005, Oslo, June 29–July 3, 2005.

UNICEF. *The State of the World's Children: Children Under Threat.* New York: UNICEF, 2004.

UNDP. *The Human Development Report 2006.* New York: UNDP, 2006.

Yaro, Yacouba, and Alamissa Sawadogo. *Étude de base sur le trafic et les pires formes de travail des enfants dans la région sud-ouest du Burkina.* Ouagadougou, Burkina Faso: Centre d'Études, de Recherches et de Formation pour le Développement Économique et Social, 2005.

Côte d'Ivoire

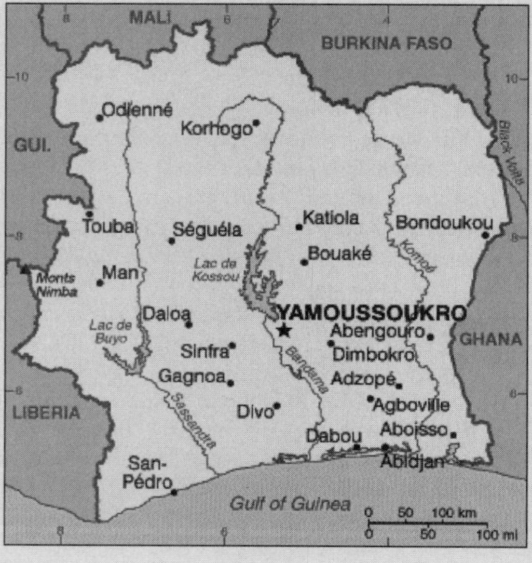

CÔTE D'IVOIRE			
	CRC	C 138	C 182
Ratifications	Y	Y	Y
Human Development Index/Rank	0.421/164		
Human Capital			
Population Growth Rate	2.03%		
% Population 0–14	40.8%		
Total Fertility Rate	4.5		
Life Expectancy	48.82		
Infant Mortality Rate	89.11		
Literacy Rate	50.9%		
Economic			
GDP/Capita	$1,600		
GDP Growth %	1.2%		
% Poverty	37%		
Gini Index	45.2		
Labor Force Composition			
% Agriculture	68%		
% Industry	NA		
% Services	NA		

CHILD ACTIVITY BREAKDOWN, BY SEX AND RESIDENCE

RESIDENCE	Percentage of children in the relevant age-group[a]									
	Economic activity only		School only		Combining school and economic activity		Neither in school nor in economic activity		Child labor[b]	
	Male	Female	Male	Female	Male	Female	Male	Female	Male	Female
Urban	7.2	12.2	56.4	46.6	13.7	12.1	22.7	29.1	n/av	n/av
Rural	24.6	29.3	23.6	22.7	28.4	18.5	23.4	29.6	n/av	n/av
Total	18.4	22.2	35.3	32.6	23.1	15.8	23.1	29.3	36.2	34.2

Source: Côte d'Ivoire, Multiple Indicator Cluster Survey 3, 2006 (see UCW Project Web site, http://www.ucw-project .org, country statistics).

Notes: [a]Children age 5 to 14. [b]Estimate includes (a) children under age 12 engaged in economic activities, (b) children age 12–14 engaged in excessive economic activities (more than 14 hours per week), and (c) children under age 15 engaged in excessive household chores (at least 28 hours per week). Estimate does not account for children engaged in hazardous work or other unconditional "worst forms" of child labor.

Children's Work, Child Domestic Labor, and Child Trafficking in Côte d'Ivoire

Yacouba Diallo, Statistical Information and Monitoring Programme on Child Labor (SIMPOC), International Program on the Elimination of Child Labor (IPEC), International Labor Organization

This essay first presents a broad overview of the nature and prevalence of children's work in Côte d'Ivoire. Then it examines two especially problematic and often interrelated aspects of child labor in the country: child domestic labor and child trafficking. While there are numerous other forms of child labor in Côte d'Ivoire that are hazardous or likely to harm the health, safety, or morals of children, child domestic labor and child trafficking are particularly difficult to track largely due to their informal nature and the fact that they occur in private and hidden spaces.

Prevalence and Nature of Children's Work

Côte d'Ivoire ratified ILO Convention 138 on minimum age and Convention 182 on the worst forms of child labor in 2003. The minimum age for admission to work is fourteen years old. In national laws, there is no explicit provision limiting engagement to light work only, but the legislation provides specific conditions, such as limits on working hours and the prohibition of night work. There is also a list of hazardous work, the types of work determined to be likely to harm the health, safety, or morals of children. The legal age for entrance to public school is six years. In spite of this legislative framework, several studies have documented the phenomenon of child labor in Côte d'Ivoire.

However, reliable data on children's work in Côte d'Ivoire remain limited. While earlier surveys have been conducted, the most recent and complete picture of children's work can be derived from examining a combination of two household surveys: a 2005 child labor survey (SIMPOC) and the living standards measurement survey conducted in 2002 (LSMS). Côte d'Ivoire's National Institute of Statistics conducted the child labor survey using the framework provided by SIMPOC, the statistical information and monitoring program of IPEC. It was a stand-alone survey, based on 4,440 households, intended to collect information on economic and noneconomic activities of boys and girls, ages five to seventeen years. It would seem to be the best source of information. Unfortunately, due to the conflict in Côte d'Ivoire that began in September 2002, the survey covers only the areas of the country under control of the government authorities, representing nearly 80 percent of the population.

While not quite as current, the 2002 LSMS survey has the advantage that it covers the entire country. It was based on a nationally representative sample of 10,800 households and yields a wide variety of data in areas such as education, employment, health, expenditure, and consumption that together help shed light on children's activities. Unfortunately, since it was not designed specifically for quantifying the child labor phenomenon, it does not probe into sufficient detail to capture all aspects of children's activities and occupations, especially those aspects that are "hidden." Thus, the LSMS 2002 figures may be considered to underestimate the magnitude of children's work. While both surveys have limitations, examining them together provides a good overview of children's work.

Conceptually, "child labor" is a narrower concept than "children's work," "working children," or "economically active children," comprising the harmful subset of children's work that needs to be abolished. The 2005 SIMPOC child labor survey, however, reveals that, based on national laws and standard definitions of child labor (Hagemann et al. 2006), 95 percent of working children in Côte d'Ivoire are child laborers. Thus, in the case of Côte d'Ivoire, "economically active children" is a good proxy for "child labor."

Results of the LSMS 2002 survey indicate that 305,536 males (14.2 percent) and 313,317 females (15.3 percent), or a total of 618,853 of children ages six to fourteen (14.7 percent) are working. In contrast, results of the 2005 SIMPOC child labor survey indicate that almost 20 percent of children ages six to fourteen are economically active. Children's work appears to be primarily a rural phenomenon in Côte d'Ivoire. According to LSMS 2002, 21.4 percent of rural children worked, against 4.5 percent of urban children.

Further, the LSMS 2002 survey shows 93.9 percent of working children, approximately 581,000 (13.8 percent of children ages six to fourteen), participate in the labor force without attending school. Among children ages six to fourteen, those who are economically active are less likely to attend school than those who are not (6.1 percent vs. 61.7 percent). The percentage of children combining school and work is negligible, and fully one-quarter of children are reported as apparently idle, neither working nor attending school. It is possible that the survey overestimates the proportion of children reported as idle, as some of these children may be involved in housework (household chores) or in some activity contributing to household welfare.

The proportion of working children varies significantly by region. Overall, it is highest in the North compared to other regions. Prevalence is 37.2, 11.2, and 43.4 percent, respectively, in the North, the Northeast, and the Northwest. The proportion of children working is lowest in Abidjan (2.6 percent), the country's largest city. The proportion also varies by ethnic group. The proportion of working children is most prevalent among children belonging to the Voltaïque ethnic group (27.2 percent). It is lowest among children belonging to the Krou ethnic group (4 percent). Prevalence is much higher than the national average among foreign children: 23.4 percent among children from Burkina Faso, and 19.3 percent among children from Ghana. According to previous studies, wherever they come from, migrant workers are always disadvantaged in terms of pay and social protection.

An overwhelming majority of working children ages six to fourteen are employed as unpaid family workers (91 percent of boys and 93 percent of girls). Relatively few working children are self-employed or work for wages. Among working children, almost nine out of ten are employed in the agricultural sector, only 2.2 percent are employed in the industrial sector, and the remaining 9.4 percent are employed in the services sector. One-quarter of working children are engaged in cocoa (17 percent) and coffee (8 percent) plantations. Sometimes, they work alongside their families in carrying out numerous tasks for task-based or piece-rated remuneration. Studies on child labor in agriculture have highlighted the long hours of work, meager wages, and dangerous conditions in which children work. As in most countries, girls are less likely to be employed in the agricultural sector and more likely to be domestic workers.

Characteristics of Child Domestic Labor

In the context of Côte d'Ivoire, the term "child domestic" implies diverse situations. Strictly speaking, whatever the child's relationship to the head of household, it means a child carrying out any form of domestic chores, such as preparation of meals, hanging out the wash, mowing the lawn, babysitting younger children, or feeding the chickens. In a broad sense, it is a child who is doing economic and noneconomic work in a household. Many children in the country do housework, both for other households for payment in cash and kind, and within their own households, unpaid, by participating in chores.

It is important to distinguish between "household chores" or "housework," performed in one's own household, which is considered nonmarket and noneconomic work, and "child domestic labor" which refers to situations where children less than eighteen years of age are engaged to perform domestic tasks in the home of a third party or employer, and is therefore considered economic activity (ILO-IPEC 2007). This section focuses on child domestic labor.

Conceptual and Historical Framework

Historically, from the colonial period to now, child domestic labor has taken different forms and includes trafficking or work that by its nature or the circumstances in which it is carried out is hazardous and likely harms the health, safety, or morals of children. Also historically, there have been three waves of the phenomenon of domestic labor in Côte d'Ivoire. From the colonial period to the 1970s, domestics were mostly mature girls, the majority from two sociolinguistic areas of the country: Abron-Koulango and Baoulé. Most were illiterate and from poor households. Then, during the 1980s, increasing numbers of children became involved in domestic labor due to exclusion from school. Contrary to the earlier domestics, these children were not from any specific rural areas of the country. Finally, in the 1990s, the phenomenon of child domestic labor became extensive, with the development of employment agencies and increasing numbers of children excluded from schools.

There are several more or less pejorative terms used to describe domestic servants in Côte d'Ivoire. For instance, "boy" is a person in charge of household chores in another family. In common usage, this term is more pejorative since it presumes this person to be illiterate and ignorant. Contrary to that, the terms "employee of house," "maid," and "servant" apply to persons more or less educated who are in charge of domestic service in another family. However, from a sociological point of view, there is no difference between these concepts in the sense that they cover a similar reality. Further, according to anthropologists, the lexicon "boy" or "servant" did not exist in traditional societies in Côte d'Ivoire. In other words, these terms entered the local vocabulary only with colonialism, which started in 1893 (Bureau International Catholique de l'Enfance 1999).

Involvement in Child Domestic Labor: Descriptive Evidence

What do we know about child domestic workers in Côte d'Ivoire? The 2005 SIMPOC child labor survey included a section on child domestic labor. The survey shows that there were about 50,000 children between the ages of six and fourteen years doing domestic work on a full-time basis outside the homes of their biological parents in the regions covered by the survey. These children account for about 2.2 percent of all children ages six to fourteen years old. They perform a variety of tasks: 76.4 percent cook and set and serve tables; 69.9 percent shop for personal and household goods; 87.4 percent do washing; 87.9 percent care for textiles; 13.2 percent repair personal and household goods; 43.1 percent collect wood and water; and 23.8 percent babysit.

Generally, girls are more involved than boys in domestic work (52.1 percent against 47.9 percent). While child labor in Côte d'Ivoire is mostly a rural phenomenon, child domestic labor is more heavily concentrated in the cities: 51.1 percent of child domestic workers are in urban areas and 48.9 percent are in rural areas. Almost one-third of child domestic workers are in Abidjan. Four percent of children are combining domestic work and some form of nondomestic economic work. In the regions covered by the survey, only 5.5 percent of child domestic workers originated from outside Côte d'Ivoire.

Studies highlight the difficult working conditions of child domestic workers: long and tiring working days, handling dangerous items such as knives, insufficient or inadequate food and accommodation, and degrading treatment. Half of the children work twenty hours per week or more. Only 2 percent of child domestics are paid for their work. Many do not receive the wages they have been promised. For others, the employment arrangements do not involve the exchange of money. One main concern regarding child domestic workers concerns their schooling. Data show that 21.5 percent of child domestic workers have never attended school.

There is a strong correlation between child-fostering arrangements and child domestic labor. More than 90 percent of children in domestic work are relatives of the head of the household in which they work. This means that many child domestics have been given by parents or guardians to another person to be fostered, but in reality the child becomes an unpaid servant for the host family. Child fostering is a temporary and reversible transfer of child-rearing responsibilities to people other than the natural parents. In most countries in sub-Saharan Africa it is common to see natural parents sending their children to relatives. The phenomenon is more diffused in Côte d'Ivoire. Traditionally, the institution of fostering has favored the movement of children to the houses of relatives, where they become domestic workers. In this way, the distinction between child placement and child domestic employment is sometimes hard to pin down. However, some child domestic workers are recruited through recruitment agents or have sought out a placement on their own initiative. In addition, children may be trafficked for domestic labor.

Child Trafficking

It has been reported that children are being trafficked for domestic labor, agriculture, the informal sector, and mining in Côte d'Ivoire. The trafficking of children, internally between different regions of the country, or across national borders, is linked with the demand for cheap, malleable, and docile labor in sectors where the working conditions violate the human rights of the children.

Human trafficking is a multifaceted phenomenon that has been analyzed from a variety of perspectives. The UN Protocol to Prevent, Suppress, and Punish Trafficking in Persons, the so-called Palermo Protocol, adopted in 2000, defines human trafficking as "[t]he recruitment, transportation, transfer, harboring or receipt of persons [. . .] for the purpose of exploitation." In the case of children, the protocol is clear that such transactions are to be considered trafficking even if no coercion, fraud, or deception is involved, and that the consent of the child is irrelevant.

Since 1998, reports of child trafficking for work on cocoa farms in Côte d'Ivoire have been issued by foreign governments, international agencies, NGOs, and the media. Previous studies assumed that weak commodity markets forced farmers to cut costs by reducing expenditures and increasing the use of children instead of adult labor from neighboring countries. The issue assumes particular importance because Côte d'Ivoire is the largest cocoa producer in the world, with 40 percent of global cocoa production.

In 2002, a study of child labor on some 1,500 cocoa-producing farms in Cameroon, Côte d'Ivoire, Ghana, and Nigeria was carried out by the Sustainable Tree Crops Program of the International Institute of Tropical Agriculture in cooperation with IPEC. It found that children were engaged in hazardous tasks on cocoa farms in Côte d'Ivoire. There was evidence that a number of child workers may have been trafficked for cocoa work from outside the cocoa-growing areas. The majority of children came from impoverished countries such as Burkina Faso, Mali, and Togo, while the rest came from Côte d'Ivoire, mainly Baoulé children originating from the Yamoussoukro-Bouaké area, or children from northern ethnic groups such as the Senoufo and Lobi.

In most cases, a third-party intermediary was involved in the recruitment process, and there was no written agreement or contract of employment between the farmer and the child. Parents often sell their children in the belief they will find work and send earnings home. Most of the children earned subsistence wages, and one-third of children reported that their earnings were paid either to a family member or to the recruiter who had brought them to the work site. The majority of the children had never been to school. The most frequent reason given for agreeing to leave home with the intermediary recruiter was the promise of a better life.

Further, recent evidence shows that there is also trafficking of children to Côte d'Ivoire by labor intermediaries for work in mining and the informal sector. The children work on average ten hours per day. The recruitment process and origins of the children are similar to those in cocoa-growing areas.

Trafficked children are often not free to leave their place of employment should they so wish. Many children trafficked for work in agriculture, domestic labor, mining, and the informal sector may be held in debt bondage by their employer, or to repay fees to the recruiter for being trafficked. Recent evidence suggests that, since the political crisis that began in 2002, trafficking of children to Côte d'Ivoire from neighboring countries by labor intermediaries is less prevalent compared to the earlier period.

Conclusion

The characteristics of child labor are multiple and multifaceted. As in most African countries, the majority of working children are found in agriculture, where they work alongside their families. Girls are less likely to be employed in the agricultural sector and more likely to be domestic workers. Housework is one of the most common and traditional forms of child labor in Côte d'Ivoire. Children working as child minders, maids, cooks, cleaners, and general household helpers are a familiar sight. As long as these activities do not interfere with the children's education and health, they can be positive experiences. They help children learn basic skills in preparation for their future. In situations such as these, children do not need to be protected from their sociofamilial obligations. However, in developing countries, the domestic workload required to support daily life can be extremely heavy. As demand for domestic workers grows, their supply also becomes more organized, based on family networks, recruitment agents, and occasionally traffickers.

The long hours of work, meager wages, and dangerous conditions in which many children work compromise the human development and future productivity of this rising generation of workers. One of the pillars of sustainable development and growth is investment in human resources, with investment in education foremost on the list.

References and Further Reading

Bureau International Catholique de l'Enfance. *Les petites bonnes à Abidjan.* Paris: Bureau International Catholique de l'Enfance, 1999.

Bureau International du Travail. *La traite des enfants aux fins d'exploitation de leur travail dans les mines d'or d'Issia–Côte d'Ivoire.* Dakar: IPEC-LUTRENA, 2005.

Bureau International du Travail. *La traite des enfants aux fins d'exploitation de leur travail dans le secteur informel à Abidjan–Côte d'Ivoire.* Dakar: IPEC-LUTRENA, 2005.

Bureau International du Travail–United Nations High Commissioner for Refugees. *L'exploitation des enfants dans le contexte de la crise militaire, social et politique en Côte d'Ivoire: situation particulière dans les zones d'accueil des déplacés et des réfugiés.* Dakar: IPEC-LUTRENA, 2006.

Centre d'Études Prospectives et Appliquées sur les Politiques Sociales et les Systèmes de Sécurité Sociale, International Institute of Tropical Agriculture. *Étude communautaire sur le travail des enfants dans les plantations de cacao en Côte d'Ivoire.* Abidjan: Centre d'Études Prospectives et Appliquées sur les Politiques Sociales et les Systèmes de Sécurité Sociale, International Institute of Tropical Agriculture, 2002.

Centre d'Études Prospectives et Appliquées sur les Politiques Sociales et les Systèmes de Sécurité Sociale, International Institute of Tropical Agriculture. *Les pratiques de travail dans les plantations de cacao en Côte d'Ivoire.* Abidjan: Centre d'Études Prospectives et Appliquées sur les Politiques Sociales et les Systèmes de Sécurité Sociale, International Institute of Tropical Agriculture, 2002.

Diallo, Y. *Les enfants et leur participation au marché du travail en Côte d'Ivoire.* PhD diss. Université Montesquieu Bordeaux IV, 2001.

Hagemann, F., Y. Diallo, A. Etienne, and F. Mehran. *Global Child Labour Trends 2000 to 2004.* Geneva: ILO-IPEC/SIMPOC, 2006.

ILO-IPEC. *Children's Non-Market Activities and Child Labour Measurement: A Discussion Based on Household Survey Data.* Geneva: ILO-IPEC/SIMPOC, 2007.

Jacquemin, M. "Children's Domestic Work in Abidjan, Côte D'Ivoire: The Petites Bonnes have the Floor." *Childhood* 11:3 (2004): 383–97.

Sustainable Tree Crops Program, International Institute of Tropical Agriculture. *Child Labor in the Cocoa Sector of West Africa: A Synthesis of Findings in Cameroon, Côte d'Ivoire, Ghana, and Nigeria.* Abidjan: Sustainable Tree Crops Program, International Institute of Tropical Agriculture, 2002.

UNICEF. *Recherche sur l'élaboration des stratégies pour abolir le trafic des enfants à des fins d'exploitation économique en Afrique de l'Ouest et du Centre.* Rapport de la Côte d'Ivoire. Abidjan: UNICEF, 2001.

Gambia

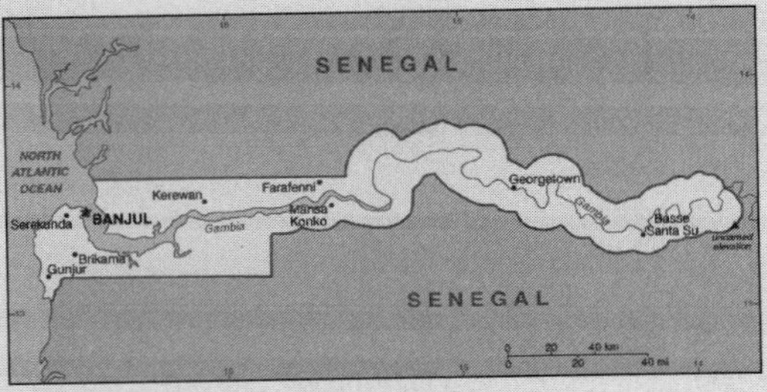

GAMBIA			
	CRC	C 138	C 182
Ratifications	Y	Y	Y
Human Development Index/Rank	0.479/155		
Human Capital			
Population Growth Rate	2.84%		
% Population 0–14	44.3%		
Total Fertility Rate	5.3		
Life Expectancy	54.14		
Infant Mortality Rate	71.58		
Literacy Rate	40.1%		
Economic			
GDP/Capita	$2,000		
GDP Growth %	5%		
% Poverty	NA		
Gini Index	—		
Labor Force Composition			
% Agriculture	75%		
% Industry	19%		
% Services	6%		

CHILD ACTIVITY, BY SEX AND AGE

Age in years	Percentage of children in the relevant age-group[a]									
	Economic activity only		School only		Combining school and economic activity		Neither in school nor in economic activity		Child labor[b]	
	Male	Female	Male	Female	Male	Female	Male	Female	Male	Female
Urban	2.7	6.6	67.6	53.6	13.2	24.6	16.5	15.2	n/av	n/av
Rural	12.3	20.5	38.0	27.7	22.2	29.9	27.5	21.9	n/av	n/av
Total	9.2	15.8	47.6	36.6	19.3	28.1	23.9	19.6	20.4	28.7

Source: Gambia, Multiple Indicator Cluster Survey 3, 2005 (see UCW Project Web site, http://www.ucw-project.org, country statistics).

Notes: [a]Children age 5 to 14. [b]Estimate includes (a) children under age 12 engaged in economic activities, (b) children age 12–14 engaged in excessive economic activities (more than 14 hours per week), and (c) children under age 15 engaged in excessive household chores (at least 28 hours per week). Estimate does not account for children engaged in hazardous work or other unconditional "worst forms" of child labor.

Ghana

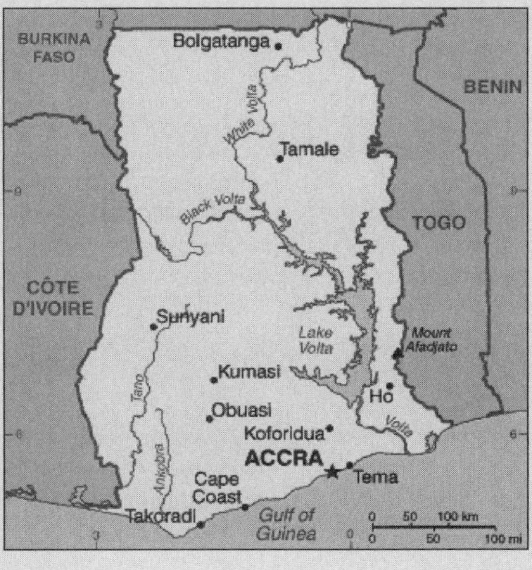

GHANA	CRC	C 138	C 182
Ratifications	Y	N	Y
Human Development Index/Rank	0.532/136		
Human Capital			
Population Growth Rate	2.07%		
% Population 0–14	38.8%		
Total Fertility Rate	3.99		
Life Expectancy	58.87		
Infant Mortality Rate	55.02		
Literacy Rate	74.8%		
Economic			
GDP/Capita	$2,600		
GDP Growth %	5.7%		
% Poverty	31.4%		
Gini Index	30		
Labor Force Composition			
% Agriculture	60%		
% Industry	15%		
% Services	25%		

CHILD ACTIVITY BREAKDOWN, BY SEX AND RESIDENCE

RESIDENCE	Percentage of children in the relevant age-group[a]									
	Economic activity only		School only		Combining school and economic activity		Neither in school nor in economic activity		Child labor[b]	
	Male	Female	Male	Female	Male	Female	Male	Female	Male	Female
Urban	1.7	3.7	87.2	80.9	6.3	9.4	4.7	6.1	n/av	n/av
Rural	13.0	12.2	53.3	54.1	20.1	18.7	13.5	15.1	n/av	n/av
Total	9.1	8.9	65.0	64.4	15.3	15.1	10.5	11.6	26.0	25.5

Source: Ghana, Child Labour Survey, 2000 (see UCW Project Web site, http://www.ucw-project.org, country statistics).
Notes: [a]Children age 5 to 14. [b]Estimate includes (a) children under age 12 engaged in economic activities, (b) children age 12–14 engaged in excessive economic activities (more than 14 hours per week), and (c) children under age 15 engaged in excessive household chores (at least 28 hours per week). Estimate does not account for children engaged in hazardous work or other unconditional "worst forms" of child labor.

Child Labor in Ghana

Martin Verlet, Professor, University Paris I and Paris VII, Social Anthropologist, IRD (France)

The development of child labor is a recent phenomenon in Ghana, occurring within the last three decades. A basic distinction is drawn between two childhood realities: (1) domestic activities within the household economy that contribute to the socialization of children and their initiation to productive life and (2) child labor per se, which is crude exploitation of the juvenile labor force. The trend in child labor has accelerated since 1983 because of the implementation of structural adjustment programs (SAPs), inspired by the IMF and the World Bank, which deregulated and depressed the labor market. The recent extension of child labor is concomitant with the crisis of households and the redistribution of social and economic roles within those households.

Girl in northwest Ghana preparing millet porridge, Ghana 2006. *(Photo by Albertine de Lange courtesy of IREWOC Foundation)*

Genesis of the Phenomenon

In traditional societies, domestic activities of children were usual. Girls helped their mothers in domestic duties, fetching water or collecting firewood. The boys, as young as six years old, were required to look after the goats and protect the crops against birds or other predators. The production of foodstuffs was aimed at the consumption of the household. From the age of ten, boys participated in farming activities. The initiation was gradual, the work corresponding to the age of the child. The activities were considered to contribute to the integration of the children within the domestic community, to their socialization, and to their initiation to productive life. Child work supplemented the labor of the domestic unit and was not exploitative.

The expansion of trade and the market economy provoked the introduction of child labor. Girls were mobilized more intensively in domestic duties. They had to carry loads of goods to the market and to assist the women in their business. They were asked to run itinerant selling. Boys were engaged more precociously in arduous farming activities. A large degree of exploitation was introduced. The gap between child work (socialization, apprenticeship) and child labor (abuse, exploitation) narrowed. Exploitation of children now permeates the domestic units.

During the three last decades, a new generation of laboring children emerged. The phenomenon is a result of the correlation between the deregulation of the labor market and "domestic deregulation."

Clearer still is the correlation between both of these processes and the general spread of child labor. "Domestic deregulation" refers to the breakup of family units combined with the increasing fragility and destabilization of households, which has been gathering pace and becoming more serious under the impact of policies of liberalization through structural adjustment. The loss of the authority of the man, who ceases to be considered the head of the family, and the economic marginalization and exclusion of the wage earner because of unemployment, confers new responsibilities on the women. Economic and social roles within the domestic units are reshaped. This is especially the case in monoparental households (40 percent of them). Child labor becomes necessary to the survival of the domestic unit. Children are dragooned into a ruined labor market. Severely exploited, they are transformed into juvenile proletarians.

The Scope of the Phenomenon

In Ghana, child labor is less systematic and oppressive than in many other developing nations. The phenomenon may be less visible in Ghana, but it is increasing rapidly. Presently, around 420,000 children are victims of child labor. Eighty percent of child labor is located in the main urban centers, and 20 percent is in the rural areas. Most of the laboring children originated from the poor and deprived urban suburbs: Accra (Adenta, Madina, Labadi, Sabon Zongo, Nima), Tema (Ashaiman), Kumasi, Sekondi-Takoradi, and Tamale. They are employed in furniture factories (Kumasi) and garment workshops (Kumasi, Accra). Apprenticeship is the most common mode of exploitation of children's labor. In the cities there are thousands of child street workers. In the main markets (Agbobleshie, Timber Market, Dagomba Market in Accra, Ashaiman in Tema, Kejetia in Kumasi, Mankessim, Nkawkaw, and Techiman), boy and girl porters (*kaya-kaya*) carry heavy loads of goods for the traders or the customers. On the Atlantic seashore, around the Volta Lake, along the rivers (Black Volta, White Volta, Oti, Tano, Pra), young children work in the fishing settlements. In the Volta Region, girls (*trokosi*) fall into servitude, constrained to bonded labor, because of the indebtedness of their parents. Young children are also used as laborers on the rice and cotton mechanized farms in the Upper West, Upper East, and Northern regions.

Putting the Children to Work

The best-known forms of child labor are a manifestation of the household crisis. Some children decide to look for work of their own accord. More often than not, the parents encourage and broker their admission into the world of work. A father or his brother might arrange and pay for an apprenticeship, standing surety with an employer. Or he may place his child with a relative, friend, or acquaintance to work as a servant or assistant. But the women are the ones who play the key role in putting young children to work. This generally applies first to the girls, as they are easier to remove from school than boys. Young girls are frequently left in charge of the day-to-day running of the household while their mothers are at work. They are more systematically and consistently drawn into moneymaking activities where they increase the labor power of their mothers or female relatives, usually in petty retailing or street vending.

As a rule, girls are kept close to the household, within its protection. Boys, on the contrary, are more likely to find themselves in a working environment separated from the home. The woman's action and influence are once again the decisive factors in boys' admission to employment. As soon as a boy leaves school, she will watch over him, often putting up the capital he needs to start a lucrative business of his own. Children's earnings help to boost the household; the money is regularly handed over to the woman, who decides how it will be used and distributed.

The household's role in the mechanics of premature employment is not to be ignored. First, it shows how economic exploitation is rooted in, if not initiated by, the household. The fact that a child enters employment via family channels lends a domestic feel to working relations, giving them a veneer of kinship. An employer can then adopt a pseudoparental role on the grounds that his authority comes from the parents, from the child's own environment. This domestic veneer can serve as a mask for exploitation.

The Types of Work

Whenever the issue of child labor crops up in Ghana, it immediately evokes images of street children. Yet the street child is merely the visible side of a far-reaching phenomenon. There are other, more common, more excessive forms of exploitation. Those linked to apprenticeship are well-known. Those at the core are more difficult to recognize. Some working environments are simply ignored. The types of work differ by gender. The majority of the boys are employed in two sectors: services (40 percent) and production. The girls are mainly engaged in domestic activities (30 percent) and services (45 percent).

Analysis of working environments reveals the complicated, varied, and shifting connections between family relations and exploitation-based relations. A number of major types of working environments can be differentiated. The first type are those that have strong connections with the household, when an adult member of the household uses the residence as a base for sales, repairs, or processing of services, and the child helps with the work itself or, more commonly, concentrates on selling the goods outside the residence. A second type involves clearer divisions between the household and working life, where work is performed in shops, hairdressing salons, workshops (clothing, repairs, garages), and apprenticeships. Another type also making use of domestication, but featuring a clear break from the household, is represented by work in factories or on building sites. Large numbers of children can be found working in such places as furniture factories or industrial bakeries. The employer will have hired the children in his hometown or neighboring villages, with the parents' consent. The children live full-time on the premises and can therefore be made to work nights if need be. They may spend five to seven years at the factory before the employer decides to send them back home.

Yet another type is comprised of working environments created away from and independently of the household, where the network of connections leading to recruitment is based not on kinship, but on acquaintances, affinities, and peer groups. They are largely male dominated and include several subtypes: the queue (attracting hordes of child street vendors on the busiest thoroughfares); the team (a specialized working environment where children monopolize recruitment); the gang (the *kaya-kaya* porters, for instance, living full-time in certain marketplaces); vagrancy (totally autonomous children of no fixed abode, with no family ties); and exile (especially girls who migrate to the Côte d'Ivoire and Nigeria, often totally losing touch with their families).

Far from resolving the household financial crisis, the vast range of child labor types seen in the various working environments can, in some cases, serve to deepen it. Far from mitigating domestic deregulation and household instability, child labor can actually fuel it.

The Modes of Exploitation

Analysis should look beyond the notion of "domestication" of exploitative relations, as it contaminates only one segment of the spectrum of working environments. Two complementary, yet possibly more crucial aspects of the working relationship and its conversion into exploitation can be described through the dialectics of goodwill and willingness, leading to "serviceability" and the state of being "ruthlessly serviceable."

The exploitative relationship builds a constant tension between two poles: goodwill and willingness. The dialectic between the two is, of course, rooted in and cultivated by the domestication of the working relationship. They demonstrate the asymmetry between the position of the master and the condition of the working child. The master's goodwill gives him the power to do what he will. His desires, his needs and moods, govern the wages, set the working hours, assign the tasks, and influence the quality of the relationship. Willingness means the availability, the obedience expected from a child. Vulnerable children seeking protection and support see themselves bound to remain meek, ever present, and ever willing. Their labor power is malleable, flexible. The polarization of goodwill and willingness is both line of force and field of live current. Although rarely breaking into open confrontation, children have several forms of resistance, evasion, and retaliation available and simmering below the surface.

An inventory of the types of work done by

children reveals that child work is highly concentrated in the services sector. Even when it is production work, the form of working relationship will often be disguised as services. As such, there is a sort of slide from the legal to the prohibited, from the licit to the illicit, and, commonly, from one job to another. Child labor puts children in the position of general service suppliers. With the small groups of *kaya-kaya* porters living in the marketplaces, for example, supply and demand of general services can range from carrying loads to sexual intercourse. Sometimes the same sort of crossover can be observed in hairdressing salons, sewing shops or, more commonly, in chop bars.

Child workers "enter service," a term formerly applied to domestic servants, and become dependent and available. It may be tempting to describe it as "servile labor," but "servile" has the drawback of being linked to the state of slavery and serfdom. So, consider use of the term "serviceable" a way to describe a personal, transitory condition of dependence and submissiveness, which, in many cases, forces children into a general system of service supply and demand. It can be said that children prematurely sucked into working and exploitative relations are fated to become "ruthlessly serviceable." Such is their lot.

Conclusion

Two brief comments conclude this analysis. The first concerns making children subservient versus autonomous; the second, how they see their future. Children sent to work for the sake of their much-needed earnings are placed in a position of household protectors, breadwinners. They are cast in the role of lessening the effect of domestic poverty by the women, their mothers in particular. When they become partially responsible for the reproduction and survival of the household, their bonds with their mothers are deeper. At the same time, the children, made to work in an environment away from home, are likely to take their distance and to gain an illusory autonomy. Entrepreneurs without an enterprise, proletarians without wages, and "ruthlessly serviceable," all Ghanian boys harbor the same dream for the future: exile.

References and Further Reading

Apt Van Ham, N., E.Q. Blavo, and S.K. Opoku. *Street Children in Accra. A Survey Report.* Legon: University of Ghana, Department of Sociology, 1992.

Ardafio-Schandorf, E., ed. *Family and Development in Ghana.* Accra: Ghana University Press, 1994.

Goody, Esther. *Parenthood and Social Reproduction: Fostering and Occupational Roles in West Africa.* Cambridge: Cambridge University Press, 1982.

Mensah-Bonsu, H., and C. Dowuona-Hammond, eds. *The Rights of the Child in Ghana: Perspective.* Accra: Woeli, 1994.

Robertson, C.C. *Sharing the Same Bowl: A Socio-economic History of Women and Class in Accra.* Bloomington: Indiana University Press, 1984.

Schildkrout, E. "Children's Work Reconsidered." *International Social Science Journal* 32:3 (1980): 479–490.

Twumasi, P.A., ed. *Children and Women in Ghana: A Situation Analysis.* Accra: UNICEF, 1990.

Van Hear, Nick. "Child Labour and the Development of Capitalist Agriculture in Ghana." *Development and Change* 13 (1982): 499–514.

Verlet, Martin. "Grandir à Nima: Dérégulation domestique et mise au travail des enfants." *Travail Capital et Société* 27:2 (1994): 162–190.

Verlet, Martin. *Grandir à Nima (Ghana). Les figures du travail dans un fauborg populaire d'Accra.* Paris: Karthala, 2005.

Guinea-Bissau

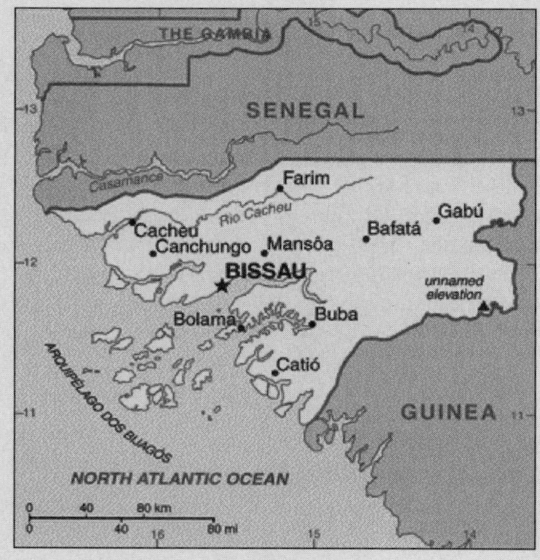

GUINEA-BISSAU			
	CRC	C 138	C 182
Ratifications	Y	N	N
Human Development Index/Rank	0.349/173		
Human Capital			
Population Growth Rate	2.07%		
% Population 0–14	41.4%		
Total Fertility Rate	4.86		
Life Expectancy	46.87		
Infant Mortality Rate	105.21		
Literacy Rate	42.4%		
Economic			
GDP/Capita	$900		
GDP Growth %	2.9%		
% Poverty	NA		
Gini Index	—		
Labor Force Composition			
% Agriculture	82%		
% Industry and Services	18%		

CHILD ACTIVITY BREAKDOWN, BY SEX AND RESIDENCE

RESIDENCE	Percentage of children in the relevant age-group[a]									
	Economic activity only		School only		Combining school and economic activity		Neither in school nor in economic activity		Child labor[b]	
	Male	Female	Male	Female	Male	Female	Male	Female	Male	Female
Urban	13.1	15.3	44.3	40.8	24.8	22.8	17.8	21.0	n/av	n/av
Rural	58.6	66.0	4.2	2.6	20.6	14.3	16.6	17.1	n/av	n/av
Total	42.5	46.5	18.4	17.3	22.1	17.6	17.0	18.6	53.9	54.0

Source: Guinea Bissau, Multiple Indicator Cluster Survey 2, 2000 (see UCW Project Web site, http://www.ucw-project.org, country statistics).

Notes: [a]Children age 5 to 14. [b]Estimate includes (a) children under age 12 engaged in economic activities, (b) children age 12–14 engaged in excessive economic activities (more than 14 hours per week), and (c) children under age 15 engaged in excessive household chores (at least 28 hours per week). Estimate does not account for children engaged in hazardous work or other unconditional "worst forms" of child labor.

Mali

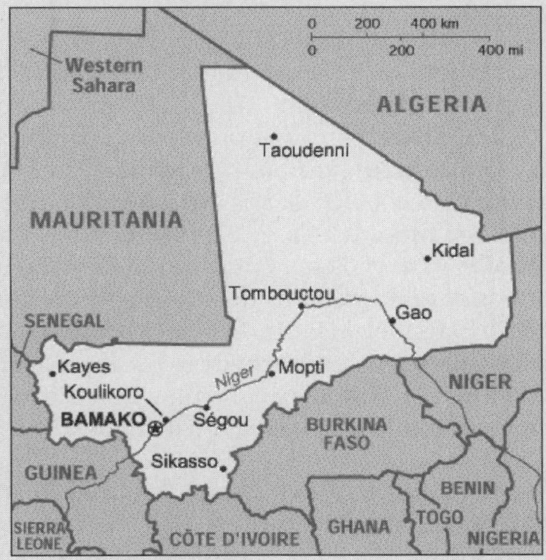

MALI			
	CRC	C 138	C 182
Ratifications	Y	Y	Y
Human Development Index/Rank	0.338/175		
Human Capital			
Population Growth Rate	2.63%		
% Population 0–14	48.2%		
Total Fertility Rate	7.42		
Life Expectancy	49		
Infant Mortality Rate	107.58		
Literacy Rate	46.4%		
Economic			
GDP/Capita	$1,200		
GDP Growth %	5.1%		
% Poverty	64%		
Gini Index	50.5		
Labor Force Composition			
% Agriculture	80%		
% Industry and Services	20%		

CHILD ACTIVITY BREAKDOWN, BY SEX AND RESIDENCE

RESIDENCE	Percentage of children in the relevant age-group[a]									
	Economic activity only		School only		Combining school and economic activity		Neither in school nor in economic activity		Child labor[b]	
	Male	Female	Male	Female	Male	Female	Male	Female	Male	Female
Urban	25.2	30.8	36.2	25.7	27.7	32.8	10.8	10.6	n/av	n/av
Rural	42.7	44.5	13.4	11.3	28.5	21.5	15.4	22.7	n/av	n/av
Total	37.4	40.1	20.3	16.0	28.2	25.2	14.0	18.8	65.23	67.95

Source: Mali, Enqueête National sur le Travail des Enfants, 2005 (see UCW Project Web site, http://www.ucw-project.org, country statistics).

Notes: [a]Children age 5 to 14. [b]Estimate includes (a) children under age 12 engaged in economic activities, (b) children age 12–14 engaged in excessive economic activities (more than 14 hours per week), and (c) children under age 15 engaged in excessive household chores (at least 28 hours per week). Estimate does not account for children engaged in hazardous work or other unconditional "worst forms" of child labor.

Child Labor in Mali

Richard Marcoux, Professor, Université Laval, Québec City, Canada

In 2000, Mali ratified ILO Convention 182, condemning the worst forms of child labor, and then, two years later, signed ILO Convention 138 regarding the minimum age of employment, set at fifteen years. Though we may celebrate the first event, as it signals a commitment by Malian public powers to join an emerging international consensus on child welfare, we must not lose sight of the fact that in Convention 138 the term "employment" is in no way synonymous with "labor" as defined by most African societies, and, therefore, in Mali as elsewhere, we find the following paradox: There are few children who are employed but many children who work!

How might we understand this paradox? There has been little published research on child labor in Mali. Unlike India or Egypt, Mali does not have the kind of industrial infrastructure that, if children were employed, would attract the attention of investigators. Mali is a huge rural country whose economic strongholds are based in self-subsistence agriculture, primarily supported by family production methods. Does this mean that young Malians do not work? Quite the contrary. One has only to stroll through Bamako's working-class neighborhoods, or one of Mali's villages, to see children carrying out many kinds of work: selling ice or peanuts, transporting goods, producing crafts, repairing all sorts of things, and collecting water or wood. One should also walk past the yards of houses, which, in both the city and the country, are like beehives, with the young and not so young busily going about their various tasks. For Malian societies, children's contribution is simply part of the socialization process, and Malians have a hard time understanding that this socialization process, which has always helped to shape tomorrow's men and women, should be subject to condemnation.

Three distinct groups of working children, ages eight to fourteen, can be identified in Mali. Starting with a fairly classic definition of work, the first are those who are considered to be "economically active." The second group is made up of children who are considered to be "inactive" but who nonetheless perform tasks as part of their families' self-subsistence activities. The third group is composed of students, many of whom combine going to school with production activities.

What Is the Primary Activity of Children in Mali?

What do the children of Mali do every day? Census accounts of the primary activity of children place them in one of three broad categories: school, work, and a residual category of children considered to be "inactive." As we will see, these categories prove to be empirically inadequate. First are those who self-identify as students. After major investments in the education sector, the proportion of eight- to fourteen-year-olds in school climbed from 20 percent in 1975 to 31 percent in 2000. But more than two-thirds of young Malians ages eight to fourteen still did not attend school at the beginning of the new millennium. However, the proportion of children of this age-group who identified as working has remained stable over time at around 40 percent. The expansion of formal education has had the most significant effect on the residual category, children who are considered "inactive." The proportion of children who are inactive fell from 42 percent to 31 percent from 1975 to 2000 and has continued to decline in recent years.

Next, consider the group described as "economically active," which, for the past thirty years, has included about 40 percent of young Malians from eight to fourteen years old. Economic activity of children is more common in the country than in the city: In rural areas, nearly half of eight- to fourteen-year-olds work, compared to 14 percent in urban areas. More than 80 percent self-identify as family helpers. A little more than 17 percent of working children declare an activity in which they have independent status. These proportions are similar for boys and girls and for rural and urban areas. Less than 1 percent of child laborers say that they receive salaries. But 15 percent of young workers in urban settings receive salaries, reflecting the importance of the domestic work performed by "little maids" in Malian cities. Overall, the primary activity of 94 percent of young Malian laborers is in agriculture and husbandry, while 2 percent fall under crafts production, and 4 percent under sales and services. In short, child laborers in Mali work mainly within the family and in the agricultural sector.

Invisible Workers Who Do Not Strike

Census data identified two large and relatively homogenous groups of children: students and workers. One residual population that is relatively significant (more than 30 percent of children in 2000) includes children who do not go to school and who declared no primary activity. Should we consider that these children perform no productive activities? It has already been shown that this category includes children who carry out many different production activities that are undetected by the criteria previously used in administrative statistics (Marcoux 1994). For example, these activities include various household chores, keeping small livestock, and child care. Similar to many women who self-identify as "homemakers" and who are therefore declared inactive, children of this group are actually dedicated to an array of productive tasks. In order to better define this reality, research conducted in 2000 in Mali created a category of activity called "child at home." This grouped children who did only household work and who made up more than 30 percent of the sample studied (Marcoux et al. 2006). Surprisingly, 97 percent of children who self-identified as neither employed nor in school fell into the category of "child at home." Qualitative research led to estimates that these children's domestic activities often take up six or seven hours of work a day. Failure to acknowledge the importance of household work in daily life obscures a large portion of the productive activities of women and children. As sociologist Agnès Barrère-Maurisson aptly pointed out, domestic work "is only noticed when it isn't done" (Barrère-Maurisson 1992, 93).

Students at School and at Work After School

Like other children, schoolchildren participate in household subsistence activities. Of course, by dedicating more than thirty hours a week to educational activities, students' participation in production activities will certainly be less that that of children who do not go to school. A study of the extracurricular activities of schoolchildren in Bamako, Mali's capital city, examined four distinct activities that children perform outside of school: collecting water, participating in maintenance work, preparing meals, and doing commercial activities (Marcoux et al. 1999).

Fewer than 20 percent of households in Bamako have indoor plumbing. Starting in the first year of elementary school, collecting water is a task performed by one out of every four girls and one out of every ten boys. Increasing feminization of this activity occurs throughout the school career: The proportion of girls who carry water increases in higher grades, while it decreases for boys. At the end of elementary school, fewer than 5 percent of male students take care of water collection, while 40 percent of their female counterparts are responsible for this task. Schoolchildren's contribution to maintenance work and to meal preparation also follows this trend, marking a major gender division. At the end of elementary school, more than half of girls participate in maintenance work, and nearly three-quarters prepare meals after school, while fewer than 5 percent of boys do these same tasks. Finally, sales and other commercial activities are, in fact, quite marginal in students' lives. Only one out of twenty students say they participate in this type of activity. Some children engage in commercial sales activity before the fourth grade, after which the numbers progressively decline.

Conclusion

Even though Mali ratified the major international conventions on child labor, many children below the age of fifteen still work. However, the type of work and the environment in which it is performed in no way resemble the child labor in eighteenth-century British factories, or what we might see in some newly industrialized countries today. Indeed, in Mali, children work almost exclusively to contribute to their families' production activities. The primary activity of economically active children, estimated to number nearly 1 million and, since 1976, representing nearly 40 percent of children, is of an agropastoral nature performed with other family members. The children previously considered inactive by official statistics have been shown to contribute significantly to the household performing tasks that keep them busy for an average of six hours per day. Finally, even school does not exempt children from having to contribute to household tasks. In the morning before school, after school, and even during lunch breaks, many schoolchildren can be found in line waiting under a hot sun at the pump or spring so that they can return home with a few liters of water. The increase in school attendance observed in Mali since the beginning of the 1990s does not seem to have reduced families' expectations that children should contribute to household subsistence activities.

Overall, children in Mali often fulfill the need for unskilled, but essential, household labor. Child welfare organizations continue to play a major role in slowing the shameful exploitation of many children. But, as Rodgers and Standing pointed out, "'exploitation' is perhaps a word we abuse" (1981, 36). While acknowledging that there are indeed cases of clearly condemnable child abuse in Mali, according to the best available data, it is difficult to consider most child labor as the kind of exploitation condemned by welfare organizations once we take into consideration the work reality of the vast majority of children in Mali. Actions that could encourage a reduction or a lightening of children's economic activities—and probably, in consequence, an increase in school enrollment rates, which are currently among the lowest in the world—must necessarily take into consideration the various elements of the family dynamic, within which child labor in Mali is performed.

References and Further Reading

Barrère-Maurisson, Marie-Agnès. *La division familiale du travail.* Paris: Presses Universitaires de France, 1992.

Marcoux, Richard. "Invisible Workers Who Do Not Strike: A Reflection on Child Labor in Urban Mali" (Des inactifs qui ne chôment pas: une réflexion sur le travail des enfants en milieu urbain au Mali), *Labour Capital and Society/Travail Capital et Société* 27:2 (1994): 296–319.

Marcoux, Richard, Mouhamadou Gueye, and Mamadou Kani Konate. "Environnement familial, itinéraires scolaires et travail des enfants au Mali." *Enfants d'aujourd'hui. Diversité des contextes, pluralité des parcours* 11:2 (2006): 961–73.

Marcoux, Richard, Cécile-Marie Zoungrana, Joël Tokindang, and Mamadou Kani Konate. "Le travail des enfants." In *Population et société au Mali,* ed. Ph. Bocquier and T. Diarra, 177–90. Paris: L'Harmattan, 1999.

Rodgers, G., and G. Standing. "Le rôle économique des enfants dans les pays à faible revenu." *Revue internationale du travail* 120:1 (1981): 35–55.

Niger

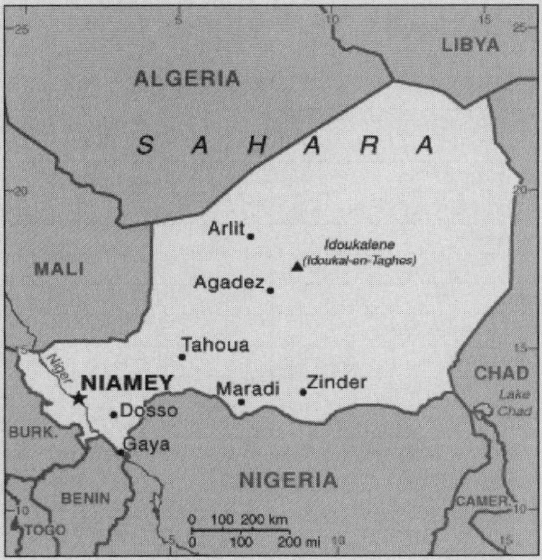

NIGER			
	CRC	C 138	C 182
Ratifications	Y	Y	Y
Human Development Index/Rank	0.311/177		
Human Capital			
Population Growth Rate	2.90%		
% Population 0–14	46.9%		
Total Fertility Rate	7.37		
Life Expectancy	44.03		
Infant Mortality Rate	116.83		
Literacy Rate	17.6%		
Economic			
GDP/capita	$1,000		
GDP Growth %	3.5%		
% Poverty	63%		
Gini Index	50.5		
Labor Force Composition			
% Agriculture	90%		
% Industry	6%		
% Services	4%		

CHILD ACTIVITY BREAKDOWN, BY SEX AND RESIDENCE

RESIDENCE	Percentage of children in the relevant age-group[a]									
	Economic activity only		School only		Combining school and economic activity		Neither in school nor in economic activity		Child labor[b]	
	Male	Female	Male	Female	Male	Female	Male	Female	Male	Female
Urban	18.6	19.0	31.3	33.1	31.8	27.0	18.3	21.0	n/av	n/av
Rural	50.3	51.7	6.7	6.7	25.4	11.9	17.6	29.8	n/av	n/av
Total	45.3	46.3	10.5	11.0	26.4	14.3	17.7	28.3	68.3	63.2

Source: Niger, Multiple Indicator Cluster Survey 2, 2000 (see UCW Project Web site, http://www.ucw-project.org, country statistics).

Notes: [a]Children age 5 to 14. [b]Estimate includes (a) children under age 12 engaged in economic activities, (b) children age 12–14 engaged in excessive economic activities (more than 14 hours per week), and (c) children under age 15 engaged in excessive household chores (at least 28 hours per week). Estimate does not account for children engaged in hazardous work or other unconditional "worst forms" of child labor.

Nigeria

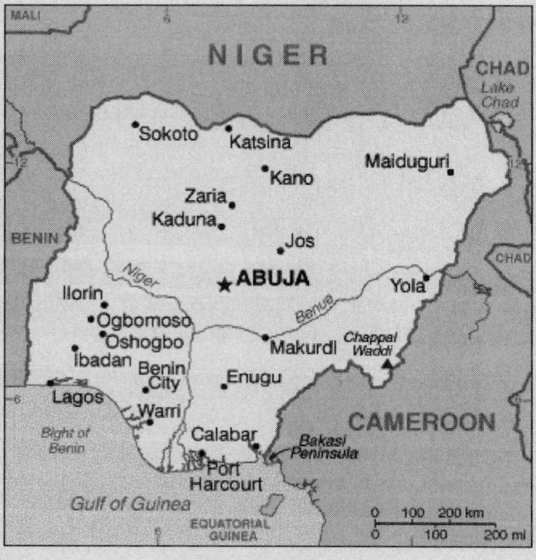

NIGERIA			
	CRC	C 138	C 182
Ratifications	Y	Y	Y
Human Development Index/ Rank	0.448/159		
Human Capital			
Population Growth Rate	2.38%		
% Population 0–14	42.2%		
Total Fertility Rate	5.45		
Life Expectancy	47.44		
Infant Mortality Rate	95.52		
Literacy Rate	68%		
Economic			
GDP/Capita	$1,400		
GDP Growth %	5.3%		
% Poverty	60%		
Gini Index	50.6		
Labor Force Composition			
% Agriculture	70%		
% Industry	10%		
% Services	20%		

Child Labor in Nigeria

Risto F. Harma, formerly with Global March Against Child Labour

Nigeria is Africa's most populous nation, with a population of 140 million. It is an oil-rich country, but much of its oil revenues have been squandered due to corruption, mismanagement, political instability, and inadequate infrastructure. Income inequality is extremely high and poverty remains widespread, especially in the subsistence agriculture sector, which has failed to keep pace with population growth. Roughly 70 percent of the labor force is in agriculture, but the sector generates only 17 percent of the country's gross domestic product.

Children's Economic Activities and Schooling

There are 31 million children from five to fourteen years of age in Nigeria, and 38 million from five to seventeen. A child labor survey was conducted in 2001 by ILO-IPEC and Nigeria's Federal Office of Statistics, and is reported on in detail by Okpukpara and Odurukwe (2006). Table 1 provides a summary of children's activities by age and gender.

Roughly 30 percent of children age five to fourteen are engaged in economic activities, but most of them work in combination with schooling. Only 4 percent of boys, and 3 percent of girls, engage in economic activities without attending school. More than 90 percent of Nigerian children are in school, and the proportions of boys and girls are roughly equal. Overall, 4 percent of children are "idle," neither in school nor engaged in economic activity, but this is confined to very young children. By age ten, nearly all children are in school, or working, or both. About 14 percent of children are already economically active by age five. Economic activity rates increase steadily by age until, by age fourteen, 35 percent are working. Boys are slightly more likely to work without going to school, while girls are slightly more likely to combine schooling and work.

In urban areas, nearly all (97 percent) of children are in school, but even in rural areas, where most of the children reside, school attendance is about 90 percent. Children in rural areas are considerably more likely to combine schooling with work. The high rates of school attendance may be somewhat misleading, especially for children who combine school with work, and should not be taken at face value. Fully 65 percent of working students report missing at least one day of school per week as a result of their economic activities, and 25 percent report missing four days per week. In the poorer and more rural northern parts of the country, most children's work is unpaid and connected with agriculture. In the less poor, more urban, southern parts of the country, children's work is more likely to be paid.

Poverty is certainly a factor in determining both economic activities and school attendance of children, but not as strong a factor as one might expect. The likelihood of attending school without working increases as household income increases, but even among the poorest quintile of households, roughly 60 percent of children attend school without working. Likewise, the likelihood of working without attending school, or being idle, is highest in the poorest households, but the likelihood of combining schooling with work is nearly constant at 25 percent across all income levels.

Child Labor

While the 2001 survey is called a "child labor survey," it does not actually calculate child labor, instead emphasizing children's economic activities. Measuring economic activities of children does

Table 1

Child Activity Breakdown, by Age and Gender

	Percentage of children of the relevant age							
	Economic activity only		School only		Combining school and economic activity		Neither in school nor in economic activity	
Age	Male	Female	Male	Female	Male	Female	Male	Female
5	3	2	63	62	11	12	22	25
6	3	2	72	67	17	21	8	10
7	4	2	68	72	25	24	3	2
8	3	2	70	67	25	28	1	3
9	5	2	69	69	25	28	1	1
10	5	3	64	64	30	32	1	1
11	5	2	68	66	30	36	0	0
12	4	3	64	65	31	32	0	0
13	5	3	63	67	31	30	1	0
14	5	4	65	64	29	31	0	1
Total	4	3	67	66	25	27	4	4

Source: Okpukpara and Odurukwe (2006), 7.

not distinguish between work that might be beneficial, or at least benign, and work that is likely to be harmful—that is, child labor. According to ILO-IPEC (2002), economic activities by children under age twelve may be presumed to be harmful. But light work for children age twelve to fourteen may not be harmful, so long as hours are limited and do not interfere with schooling. The ILO establishes the cutoff for light economic activities for children age twelve to fourteen at fourteen hours per week.

But household chores are not counted as economic activities even though they may also be light and benign, or heavy and harmful. Most Nigerian children perform household chores, such as carrying water and firewood, cooking, and caring for younger siblings. Many children perform these activities in addition to their schooling and economic activities. The ILO considers twenty-eight or more hours per week for children age five to fourteen to be excessive and, thus, constituting child labor.

Through an examination of the data from the 2001 child labor survey concerning ages and hours of economic activities, and hours of household chores, it can be estimated that 2,941,888 children age five to fourteen years of age in Nigeria are engaged in child labor (author's calculations). This represents 9.5 percent of the children in this age-group. While the numbers of child laborers are substantial, this is a much more conservative estimate than, for example, UNICEF's estimate that 39 percent of children age five to fourteen, or roughly 12 million, are child laborers.

Worst Forms of Child Labor

The estimate that 9.5 percent of Nigerian children are engaged in child labor should be taken as a lower-bound estimate. First, it does not identify those who are engaged in hazardous work (including children age fifteen to seventeen in hazardous work). Second, and even more important, it does not account for children in unconditional worst forms of child labor. Nigeria has problems, especially, with forced labor of children, trafficking in children for purposes of labor or sexual exploitation, and other commercial sexual exploitation of children.

Within the country, girls are forced into work

as domestic servants, often under the guise of the traditional cultural practice of fosterage, and in prostitution. Boys are engaged in forced begging for religious teachers, especially in the northern part of the country, and are also engaged in forced labor in mining, in stone quarries, and on cocoa and rubber plantations. Children are trafficked within Nigeria, from other African countries into Nigeria, and from Nigeria to other countries in Africa and beyond.

Especially troubling is the trafficking of children, mostly girls but also some boys, for purposes of commercial sexual exploitation. This is all the more disturbing when set in the context of the HIV/AIDS epidemic. Prostitution is ubiquitous in Nigerian society. Nigerian prostitution ranges from street prostitutes, which include many young girls, to parents offering their girls, to students and women involved in regular client networks through referral. Noncommercial versions of prostitution, based on traditional cultural norms of "gift giving" in sexual relationships, have now evolved into a purely economic activity. Hence, women are said to have, not clients, but "boyfriends," who provide them with goods, shelter, and money. The presence of European and North American workers in Nigeria's oil industry has made prostitution, including child prostitution, much more lucrative (Leach et al. 2003). In addition to prostitution, the Internet is of increasing significance as a forum for the production and dissemination of child pornography.

An estimated 2.9 million Nigerians are infected with HIV/AIDS, roughly 4 percent of the population. Children may be both affected and infected by HIV/AIDS. Already, it is estimated that there are more than a million AIDS orphans who have lost at least one parent. Orphan-headed households are a growing phenomenon. AIDS is a factor pushing children out of schools and into the labor force. Child prostitutes are also vulnerable to infection. Married men's tendency to maintain multiple sexual partners, and the longstanding cultural belief, which predates HIV/AIDS, that sex with children rejuvenates men, is today exacerbated by men seeking younger sexual partners and prostitutes in the belief that they will be free of HIV/AIDS.

In addition to internal and regional trafficking, substantial numbers of Nigerian women and girls are trafficked to other countries for purposes of commercial sexual exploitation or forced domestic service. Many are trafficked to Europe, especially Italy, but also France, Spain, the Netherlands, Belgium, Austria, and Norway. Some are trafficked to North Africa or Saudi Arabia, and smaller numbers are trafficked to the United States for purposes of domestic servitude or commercial sexual exploitation.

Future Trend of Nigerian Child Labor

Nigeria is projected to experience high population growth into the future—the population will stop growing only in year 2150, having reached 500 million (PRB 1990). With highly unequal economic growth, deepening poverty among the already poor, a government seemingly unable to deliver improvements in all types of infrastructure, and the social and economic devastation associated with the HIV/AIDS epidemic reinforced by the already high degree of social acquiescence to prostitution, it is difficult to be optimistic about the future of child labor in Nigeria. Unless these trends are reversed, increasing child labor, especially in its worst forms, is likely. A reasonable conclusion is for child labor to worsen, particularly in prostitution, domestic work, and forced labor across a range of industries, along with a concomitant rise in trafficking.

References and Further Reading

ECPAT International. Newsletters, Africa and the Middle East: Commercial Sexual Exploitation of Children (CSEC) 34 (March 1, 2001). http://www.ecpat.net/eng/Ecpat_inter/IRC/articles.asp?articleID=5&NewsID=5.

Hodges, Anthony. *Children's and Women's Rights in Nigeria: A Wake-up Call, Situation Assessment and Analysis 2001*. Lagos: UNICEF and the Nigeria National Planning Commission, 2001.

"Human Traffickers from Nigeria: Nigeria's Other Export." Economist, April 22, 2004.

International Confederation of Free Trade Unions (ICFTU). "Internationally Recognised Core Labour Standards in Nigeria, Report for the WTO General Council Review of the Trade Policies of Nigeria." Geneva, May 11 and 13, 2005. http://www.icftu.org/www/pdf/clsnigeriareport2005.pdf.

ILO-IPEC. Every Child Counts: The New Global Estimates on Child Labour. Geneva: ILO-IPEC, 2002.

ILO-IPEC. Combating the Trafficking of Children for Labour Exploitation in West and Central Africa (Phase II). Project document RAF/01/P53. Geneva: ILO-IPEC, 2001.

Leach, Fiona, Vivian Fiscian, Esme Kadzamira, Eve Lemani, and Pamela Machakanja. *An Investigative Study of the Abuse of Girls in African Schools.* Education Paper Series. London: Department for International Development (DFID), 2003.

Okpukpara, Benjamin Chiedozie, and Ngozi Odurukwe. "Incidence and Determinants of Child Labour in Nigeria: Implications for Poverty Alleviation." Research paper 156, African Economic Research Consortium, Nairobi. 2006. http://www.sarpn.org.za/documents/d0002214/index.php.

Pannell, Ian. "Trafficking Nightmare for Nigerian Children." British Broadcasting Corporation (BBC) PM Programme, January 10, 2001. http://news.bbc.co.uk/2/hi/africa/841928.stm.

Population Reference Bureau (PRB). World Population: Fundamentals of Growth. Washington, DC: Population Reference Bureau, 1990.

UNICEF. "Information by Country, West and Central Africa: At a Glance: Nigeria, Statistics, 2006." http://www.unicef.org/infobycountry/nigeria_statistics.html#30.

U.S. Department of Labor. The Department of Labor's 2005 Findings on the Worst Forms of Child Labor, Nigeria. Washington, DC: Bureau of International Labor Affairs, 2006, 360–65.

U.S. Department of State. Trafficking in Persons Report 2007, Nigeria. Washington, DC: U.S. Department of State, 2007, 160–61.

World Bank. *Taking Action for Poverty Reduction in Sub-Saharan Africa.* Development in Practice Series. Washington, DC: World Bank, 1996.

Children in Street Trading in Nigeria

A.A. Aderinto, PhD, Senior Lecturer, Department of Sociology, University of Ibadan, Nigeria

There are no precise estimates of the number of children involved in street trading in Nigeria. National labor force data exclude children, and, even if they were included, informal-sector workers are undercounted. In spite of the scarcity of data, there is no contention about the soaring number of children involved in street trading in Nigeria. Anecdotal reports from most Nigerian cities suggest an increasing number of these children.

In the streets, children are engaged in all manner of economic activities, including load carrying, bus conducting, water fetching, scavenging, hawking and vending, begging, and prostitution. A worrisome development is the increasing number of children who leave their homes to stay permanently on the streets, living under bridges, in motor parks, or in empty buildings (Aderinto 2000). Hazards associated with street trading are immense, including physical exertion, road accidents, contamination of cuts and sores because of walking barefoot, recruitment into gangs, use of psychoactive drugs (mainly among boys), assault, and vulnerability to ritual killings.

Many street traders, even those not engaged in prostitution, are victims of sexual abuse. Street traders are often exposed to early initiation into sex. Among girls, this may result in pregnancy followed by illegal abortion, single parenthood, or baby abandonment. Among commercial sex workers, the risk of AIDS is high, with HIV seroprevalence rates in prostitutes estimated at 34 percent (Federal Office of Statistics 2001).

Reasons for Street Trading

Children involved in street trading can be found in both urban and rural areas, though different reasons account for their involvement. In rural areas, street trading by children is seen as a positive development in the process of maturation, and is generally regarded as nonexploitative. Such children, it is argued, develop to be economically independent early in life, and their thinking capacity is enhanced (Oloko 1986). In urban areas, where the phenomenon of children in street trading appears in its clearest manifestations, the practice is seen as arising from Nigeria's dismal socioeconomic development (Adesioye 1993). The poor socioeconomic situation has made it difficult for parents to meet the needs of their families, so children are used as street traders to augment the family income (Oloko 1993). The impact of this is more intense in large families (Aderinto and Okunola 1998) than in small ones. Given the early age at which children get involved in street trading and the prevalence of the practice among those most affected, such children tend to believe that their work is normal and acceptable.

Beyond factors that push children into street trading, pull factors such as the development of friendly relations on the streets, and the possibility of making some extra income for themselves, sustain children in their work (Aderinto 2000).

Street-Trading Children and Education

Two broad categories of children involved in street trading can be observed. The first, which tallies with the assumed socialization function of street trading, involves children who trade at specific times of the day, early in the morning before school and late in the afternoon after school. For these children, street trading is not disruptive of education, and therefore is acceptable. The second category involves street trading during school hours among children who have dropped out of school due to either poverty or persistent failure in school. This is the most common pattern, as more than 90 percent of street-trading children do not attend school (Federal Office of Statistics 2001).

There is an important gender dimension to child street trading also. While boys comprise the vast majority of street traders, girls are less likely to be in school, are more likely to be on the streets during school hours, and tend to work longer hours than boys. Because of the patriarchal nature of Nigerian culture, female children are considered subordinate to their male counterparts. When decisions about whom to send to school arise, if funds are inadequate, girls lose out. Female children often marry earlier than male children in Nigerian culture, and street trading is thought to provide a form of early socialization.

Efforts at Combating Street Trading

Because of the adverse effects of street trading on children, steps have been taken to curb the practice. Rights of children are enshrined in the Constitution of the Federal Republic of Nigeria, and the country is signatory to numerous international instruments aimed at curbing child labor. More specifically, the Children and Young Persons Act prohibits street trading by children in most states of the country. Recent efforts, such at the Universal Basic Education Board, aim at retaining children in school and discouraging their parents from engaging them in street trading. Unfortunately, despite these efforts at curbing the incidence of children in street trading and its associated hazards, the practice has gone unabated.

References and Further Reading

Aderinto, A.A., and R.A. Okunola. "Push, Pull and Sustaining Factors of Child Labour in Nigeria." *Ife Psychologia* 6:1 (1998): 173–184.

Aderinto, A.A. "Social Correlates and Coping Measures of Street-Children: A Comparative Study of Street and Non-Street Children in South-Western Nigeria." *Child Abuse and Neglect* 24:9 (2000): 1199–1213.

Adesioye, M. "Child Abuse via Street Hawking." *Daily Times,* June 28, 1993.

Federal Office of Statistics. *Report on National Modular Child Labour Survey, Nigeria, 2000/2001.* Lagos, Nigeria: Federal Office of Statistics, 2001.

Oloko, Beatrice A. "Children's Domestic Work Versus Economic Work and School Achievement." *Proceedings of the First International Workshop on Child Abuse in Africa,* 1–9. Enugu, Nigeria: African Network for the Prevention and Protection Against Child Abuse and Neglect, 1986.

Oloko, Beatrice A. "Children's Street Work in Urban Nigeria as Adaptation and Maladaptation to Changing Socioeconomic Circumstances." *International Journal of Behavioral Development* 16:3 (1993): 465–482.

Child Labor in Nigeria: Historical Perspective

Adelaja Odutola Odukoya, Assistant Lecturer, Department of Political Science, University of Lagos

Nigerians, like other African people, love children profoundly, with almost a maniacal zeal. Hence, having many children is very popular. The love of children has both sociocultural and political-economy dimensions. Socioculturally, children are seen as gifts from God, as jewels, the essence of the consummation of matrimonies. According to the Yoruba, one of the three largest ethnic groups in the country, children are *omo la so*, protective cover of parental nakedness. Couples without children are perceived as incomplete. In a political-economy sense, children are economic assets, a basis for material wealth, possession, and power, as they provide additional labor power for increased productivity. This economic dimension of child love finds cultural currency in proverbs and idiomatic expressions. For instance, the Yoruba say, "*Eni omo sin lo bi mo.*" This statement has connotations that vary depending on the accent placed on the operative word *sin,* that is, "bury" or "serve." Socioculturally, the statement implies that it is only those who live to be buried by their children who can claim to have children. However, the political-economy dimension implies that children are morally and culturally obligated to serve their parents. This finds concurrence in another Yoruba proverb, "*Bi okete ba da gba, omu omo re ni yio mu,*" that is, "When a rabbit is of age, it naturally depends on its offspring for survival."

Children are seen as social insurance against future uncertainty, especially in the context of subsistence food production under a feudalist mode of social organization. This, therefore, forms the contextual basis of the historical analysis of the trajectory of child labor in Nigeria. It explains the lack of cultural revulsion and consequent historical pervasiveness of child labor in the precolonial Nigeria political economy all through the colonial and postcolonial dependent capitalist political economies.

Dimensions of Child Labor: A Historical Reconstruction

The idea of child labor in Nigeria is a contemporary one. In fact, most Nigerians still consider advocacy against child labor as a sort of colonial mentality. Two factors can be said to be accountable for this situation. Work occupies a central position in Nigerian culture. The Yoruba say, "*Ise ni ogun ise,*" that is, "Hard work is the only antidote for poverty," and also, "*Ise kii pa niyan,*" meaning "Hard work does not kill." A collectivist orientation, occupational training for skill acquisition, and socialization of children into the culture of responsible citizenry, sense of community, and obedience and respect were culturally at the core of children's involvement in work in traditional Nigerian societies. For these reasons, Oloko (2003) argued that exclusion of children from work was not in the interests of society, as it portends negative and dysfunctional implications for the integration of children.

Child labor in Nigeria has its own unique and particularistic geography. Certain forms of child labor are predominant in certain geographical locations in the country, in tandem with the specific fauna, occupational imperatives, and cultural or religious orientations of those areas. In this regard, while cattle rearing and Almajeria child labor were specific to northern Nigeria, child pawning and bonded labor were found more in eastern and western regions. These geographical typologies of child labor are not to be taken as rigid and specific characteristics of particular geographical locations to the total exclusion of other areas. On the contrary, different forms of child labor exist in varying degrees, dimensions, and intensities all over Nigeria.

Agricultural Child Labor

The traditional Nigerian society was agrarian. Since the household was the primary economic unit, and labor commoditization was most rudimentary, family labor, including children, was the primary labor force for agriculture all over Nigeria. This was partly responsible for the very high procreation rate among Nigerians in the nineteenth and early twentieth centuries, as more children within a household meant more hands available for farm work. In fact, the number of a man's children had a bearing on his prosperity and wealth. Children seven years of age and older were involved in farm work for long hours daily. These children worked under harsh tropical weather conditions using dangerous implements. Expectedly, schooling in most cases was out of the question. In this regard, Otite (1990, 16) noted, "In the past, as now, a child is a blessing, another hand, an addition to the human capital in the process of survival and social inter-dependence."

Under the *gandu* farming practice, a Hausa patriarchal institution that was supposedly voluntary and mutually beneficial, a married son worked under his father in agricultural production on the father's farm. The married son, and his entire family including his children, worked four days a week on the father's farm during farming season, in return for food supplies (Hill 1990).

Another variant of agricultural child labor, specific to the north, was the Fulani nomadic pastoralist practices in cattle rearing. The totality of Fulani existence centered on the cattle complex, and was in fact defined by it. A Fulani without his cattle was considered useless and empty. The initiation of children into the pastoralist agrarian culture from very young ages was a normal practice, despite the attendant risks, dangers, and health and developmental implications for the growth and well-being of the children. Both Fulani boys and girls were involved in the cattle affairs. Boys acted as herd boys, and girls were used as dairy maids. According to van Raay (1990, 52), "[A]t the age of 7 a boy is normally considered strong enough to spend all day with the herd and it is not uncommon for an eight year old to take a herd for grazing on his own." Cattle rearing entailed trekking several hundreds of kilometers south in search of green vegetation and fodder. As a result of the insecure life, perpetual wandering, and exposure to nature, the Fulani children were highly disadvantaged in terms of life chances and opportunities for social and educational development compared to their peers in other parts of the country.

In both the western and eastern parts of the country, children provided cheap labor for production of both subsistence food and cash crops. Given the abundant rainfall in these two parts of the country, children tended to be engaged on the farm all year-round. When education was introduced during colonialism, children still went to farm with their parents after school, during the weekends, and especially during holidays. Children worked not only to support family production and survival, but in some cases to raise the money for their education.

The migrant Igbira farmers, known for their dexterity as waged farmhands, also used the services of their children for cultivation of large acreages (Udo 1990). The cocoa boom during the colonial era in western Nigeria, coupled with the absence of a local landless class, engendered a high demand for labor, which was filled by the Igbira and their children. Painfully, children that were supposed to be in school were used for work on cocoa farms in the Ife and Ondo cocoa-producing regions. The practice of farm apprenticeship was another form of child labor that was common among Abakaliki migrant farmers in the East. These apprentices doubled as both farm assistants and domestic workers.

Street Trading

Trading is one of the nonagrarian occupations of Nigerian rural economies. Prior to the introduction of cowries as legal tender, Nigerians exchanged goods and services under a barter economy, which often involved child traders hawking wares. Isamah and Okunola (2003) reported attempts dating to the 1920s and 1930s to stop the practice of child hawking.

A variant of *gandu* farming in northern Nigeria was *fatauci*, a trading equivalent. The *fatauci gandu* was a form of long-distance trading, under which a son followed the father on trading journeys (Otite 1990). Given the absence of modern means of transportation, *fatauci* constituted very serious and strenuous labor engagements for children involved in this form of trading. Child trading in the north found cultural legitimacy in practices of wife seclusion. Women kept in harems were forbidden to appear in public. Hence, women depended on children for marketing their wares. The profitability of the business of women in seclusion has been traced directly to the efficiency and resourcefulness of child traders (Oloko 2003).

Domestic Servitude

Child exploitation within the household was a common practice all over Nigeria. Historically, domestic servitude predated colonialism and urbanization. For instance, Fulani pastoralists were known for the use of household help. Under this practice, Fulani women bring their unmarried sisters or nieces to assist them in carrying out domestic chores (van Raay 1990). In the west and the east, children lived with relatives who were wealthy or known for discipline. In some situations, children were sent to live with master craftsmen. Poverty was a major reason for children in domestic servitude.

Urbanization and increasing employment opportunities for women in both the public and private sectors, especially after independence, led to increased demand for domestic help. Children were taken from villages to the cities to serve as domestic servants in return for opportunities for education and sometimes to acquire occupational skills. In most cases, the children were subjected to very hard, long, and gruesome labor. These children, unlike the children of their benefactors, were often poorly fed, mistreated, and, in case of girls, sexually violated. The commoditization, commercialization, and marketization of household help resulted in the development of trafficking of children from the hinterlands of Calabar, Badagry, Saki, Oyo, and Iseyin to work as domestic servants in the cities. Trafficked children were often exploited by the middlemen who brought them to the cities from the villages. Those who were sent to live with craftsmen in order to learn a trade or acquire skills also served as domestic hands and ran all sorts errands for the wives of their masters.

Pawns and Bonded Labor

Pawning was a pre-nineteenth-century financial practice involving the pledging of human labor as security for loans. Pawning was very common in the eastern and western parts of Nigeria. Children were often pledged or pawned and consequently worked for the creditors until the final liquidation of the loan. The work of the child served as payment of the interest elements on the loan. Pawning was given different nomenclatures all over Nigeria: Yoruba, *iwofa*; Efik/Ibibio, *ubion*; Igbo, *igba ibe*; Edo, *iyoha*; Ijaw, *pagi* (Lovejoy and Richardson 2003, 31).

This category of child labor was the most vicious and inhumane in the history of child labor in Nigeria. Calamity underscored pawnship, as nobody willingly agreed to subject him- or herself or his or her children to unmitigated bondage, oppression, servitude, and exploitation (Oroge 2003; Lovejoy and Falola 2003). Children constituted the largest population of pawns. They were often used for the totality of their childhood, as it took a very long time to settle loans. In fact, in cases of pawning of girls, parents often lack incentives to pay back the loan on time, unlike in the cases of boy pawns, who were considered more useful for labor on their parents' farms.

Falola (2003, 389) provided a number of justifications for pawning among the Yoruba. "Culture provided the ideology to legitimize it, because: (a) it was better to borrow than to steal; (b) children were obliged to help their parents, and pawnship was one of the ways of doing so; (c) it was more honorable to raise money through pawnship than to renege on the social payments involved in funeral rites, bride wealth, and other obligations."

Children were pawned by their parents, guardians, or other relatives. They were admitted into pawnship from very young ages: boys from age eight, girls much younger. Preference for girl pawns was due to their low resistance, as well as the possibility of liquidating the loan if the girls were sexually violated by the creditor or any member of his family. In such cases, the girls were a sort of sexual bait (Falola 2003). Unlike the practice in other areas, in the Edo region, girls that were pawned rendered sexual services. Pawning was therefore conterminous with child marriage (Usuanlele 2003).

Pawning of children in order to acquire occupational skills in *lantana* bead making, leather works, weaving, or pottery was very popular in the Ilorin Emirate (O'Hear 2003). Additional reasons for pawning were to inculcate discipline, hard work, and diligence in a child. Among the Nembe, religious, customary, and vocational reasons were factors responsible for pawning (Alagoa and Okorobia 2003). For instance, apprentices who were unable to pay for their training pawned themselves or were pawned by their parents in lieu of training fees, or for the acquisition of tools after completion of training. Among the Igbo, children were pawned to pay for the education of other siblings (Ekechi 2003).

Militarization of juvenile pawns began in Ibadan in southwest Nigeria. Under the *baba-ni-nma* system, which originated during the Ijaye war, parents in financial difficulty pawned their children to warlords. These war chiefs often took the children to war fronts for practical training in warfare. Of the 400 children that went to the Kiriji war of 1880 with Balogun Ajayi and Ogboriefon as *baba-ni-nma,* none came back (Byfield 2003).

Child Begging

Child begging is a very old cultural and religious practice in most parts of Nigeria. Children were often sent out by their parents, guardians, or caregivers to beg for alms. In some cases, children acted as aids to adult beggars who were (or who pretended to be) blind. In some parts of the country, women hired children from their parents as begging baits for unsuspecting members of the public. The parents got paid for the children's service. Among the Yoruba, *ibeji* (twins) begging was a religiously based practice. As part of traditional religious obligations, mothers of *ibeji* were often required to dance around town with the twins begging for alms. It was believed that failure to do this would lead to the death of the twins.

In the northern cities of Kano, Kaduna, Zaria, Yola, and Funtua, child begging was not just pervasive, but institutionalized. The most common form of child beggar was the *almajiria* street beggar. Though this practice was generally perceived as a product of Islamic religion, this was not quite true. The *almajiri* were children put in the care of ulamas for purposes of obtaining Koranic education. Parents were often too poor to pay for the cost of such education, and with no other way to provide for their welfare, the ulamas used them as farm labor and child beggars in order to provide for the upkeep of both the ulamas and the children.

Child Marriage

Child marriage was, and still is, a pervasive phenomenon in northern Nigeria and, to a lesser degree, in other parts of the country. The absence of a minimum age for marriage and low concern for education of girls were propitious factors in aid of child marriage. Since matrimony was considered the ultimate destination of the female child, every effort to accelerate her arrival at this traditionally ordained destination was considered merely the march of destiny. It is therefore not surprising that child marriage was not an issue that was considered properly treated along with the issue of child labor. This is, however, a faulty position. The female child in marriage not only forfeited her innocence and youth; she performed sexual services for her husband and undertook sundry domestic chores such as cooking, laundry, cleaning, and farming, along with other functions of motherhood twenty-four hours a day.

Conclusion

The culturally engrained love of children by Nigerians was, sadly, not a sufficient militating factor against the incidence of child labor in the history of the country. On the contrary, cultural imperatives to ensure children's social integration, sense of responsibility and community affinity, discipline, parental support, and other socially desirable norms associated with child work were overorchestrated such that child work and training transformed into child labor in a seamless and unmanaged way. The net effects of these practices were stunted development, exploitation, and social maladjustment of children. These conditions ultimately compromised both the childhood and the adulthood of these unfortunate children subjected to child labor.

References and Further Reading

Alagoa, E.J., and A.M. Okorobia. "Pawning in Nembe, Niger Delta." In *Pawnship, Slavery, and Colonialism in Africa*, ed. P. Lovejoy and T. Falola, 97–107. Trenton, NJ: Africa World Press, 2003.

Byfield, J. "Pawns and Politics: The Pawnship Debate in Western Nigeria." *Pawnship, Slavery, and Colonialism in Africa*, ed. P. Lovejoy and T. Falola, 356–86. Trenton, NJ: Africa World Press, 2003.

Ekechi, F.K. "Pawnship in Igbo Society." In *Pawnship, Slavery, and Colonialism in Africa*, ed. P. Lovejoy and T. Falola, 165–86. Trenton, NJ: Africa World Press, 2003.

Falola, T. "Pawnship in Colonial Southwestern Nigeria." In *Pawnship, Slavery, and Colonialism in Africa*, ed. P. Lovejoy and T. Falola, 387–408. Trenton, NJ: Africa World Press, 2003.

Hill, P. "Fathers and Sons in Gandu." In *Readings in Nigerian Rural Society and Rural Economy*, ed. O. Otite and C. Okali, 48–84. Ibadan: Heinemann Educational Books (Nigeria), 1990.

Isamah, A.N., and R.A. Okunola. "Family Life Under Economic Adjustment: The Rise of Child Bread Winners." In *Money Struggles and City Life*, ed. J.I. Guyer, L. Denzer, and A. Agbaje, 63–75. Lagos: BookBuilders, 2003.

Lovejoy, P., and T. Falola. "Pawning in Historical Perspective." In *Pawnship, Slavery, and Colonialism in Africa*, ed. P. Lovejoy and T. Falola, 1–26. Trenton, NJ: Africa World Press, 2003.

Lovejoy, P.E., and D. Richardson. "The Business of Slaving: Pawnship in Western Africa, c. 1600–1810." In *Pawnship, Slavery, and Colonialism in Africa*, ed. P. Lovejoy and T. Falola, 27–51. Trenton, NJ: Africa World Press, 2003.

O'Hear, A. "Pawning in the Emirate of Ilorin." In *Pawnship, Slavery, and Colonialism in Africa*, ed. P. Lovejoy and T. Falola, 137–64. Trenton, NJ: Africa World Press, 2003.

Oloko, Sarah B.A. "Child Work and Child Labour in Nigeria: Continuities and Transformation." Inaugural Lecture Series, University of Lagos, April 16, 2003.

Oroge, E.A. "Iwofa: An Historical Survey of the Yoruba Institution of Indenture." In *Pawnship, Slavery, and Colonialism in Africa*, ed. P. Lovejoy and T. Falola, 324–56. Trenton, NJ: Africa World Press, 2003.

Osoro, E. J. "Producer Prices and Rural Economic Activity: A Case Study of Two Itak Villages in the South-Eastern State of Nigeria." In *Readings in Nigerian Rural Society and Rural Economy*, O. Otite and C. Okali, 185–200. Ibadan: Heinemann Educational Books (Nigeria), 1990.

Otite, O. "Rural Nigeria." In *Readings in Nigerian Rural Society and Rural Economy*, ed. O. Otite and C. Okali, 13–22. Ibadan: Heinemann Educational Books (Nigeria), 1990.

Udo, R.K. "Farming Activities of Migrant Farmers." In *Readings in Nigerian Rural Society and Rural Economy*, ed. O. Otite and C. Okali, 200–211. Ibadan: Heinemann Educational Books (Nigeria), 1990.

Usuanele, Uyilawa. "Pawnship in Edo Society: From Benin Kingdom to Benin Province Under Colonial Rule." In *Pawnship, Slavery, and Colonialism in Africa*, ed. P. Lovejoy and T. Falola, 225-37. Trenton, NJ: Africa World Press, 2003.

Van Raay, Hans G.T. "Fulani Pastoralists and Cattle." In *Readings in Nigerian Rural Society and Rural Economy*, ed. O. Otite and C. Okali, 49–84. Ibadan: Heinemann Educational Books (Nigeria), 1990.

Senegal

SENEGAL			
	CRC	C 138	C 182
Ratifications	Y	Y	Y
Human Development Index/Rank	0.460/156		
Human Capital			
Population Growth Rate	2.65%		
% Population 0–14	42%		
Total Fertility Rate	5		
Life Expectancy	56.69		
Infant Mortality Rate	60.15		
Literacy Rate	40.2%		
Economic			
GDP/Capita	$1,800		
GDP Growth %	4.9%		
% Poverty	54%		
Gini Index	41.3		
Labor Force Composition			
% Agriculture	77%		
% Industry and Services	23%		

CHILD ACTIVITY BREAKDOWN, BY SEX AND RESIDENCE

RESIDENCE	Percentage of children in the relevant age-group[a]									
	Economic activity only		School only		Combining school and economic activity		Neither in school nor in economic activity		Child labor[b]	
	Male	Female	Male	Female	Male	Female	Male	Female	Male	Female
Urban	3.5	2.9	66.7	67.6	2.5	1.3	27.3	28.1	n/av	n/av
Rural	17.5	9.1	30.2	36.2	10.2	4.8	42.1	50.0	n/av	n/av
Total	12.8	7.0	42.5	46.8	7.6	3.6	37.1	42.6	18.0	17.1

Source: Senegal, Enquête Nationale sur le Travail des Enfants, 2005 (see UCW Project Web site, http://www.ucw-project.org, country statistics).

Notes: [a]Children age 5 to 14. [b]Estimate includes (a) children under age 12 engaged in economic activities, (b) children age 12–14 engaged in excessive economic activities (more than 14 hours per week), and (c) children under age 15 engaged in excessive household chores (at least 28 hours per week). Estimate does not account for children engaged in hazardous work or other unconditional "worst forms" of child labor.

Child Labor in Senegal: Contemporary and Historical Perspective

Loretta E. Bass, Associate Professor, Sociology, University of Oklahoma

Currently in Senegal, about 28 percent of children age ten to fourteen years work. While child labor is a problem, the situation is much better today than it was in 1980, when 43 percent of Senegalese children age ten to fourteen years were estimated to be working (World Bank 2001). This decline of 15 percentage points over roughly twenty years indicates marked improvement in the situation for Senegalese children, and is examined in relation to the economy, the educational context, gender expectations, and current child labor legislation.

Boys weaving on the street corner, Dakar, Senegal, April 2005. *(Photo by Godefroid Nimbona courtesy of IREWOC Foundation)*

The Economy

The developing economy sets the backdrop for child labor in Senegal, where average per capita annual income is $1,800. This amounts to less than $5 per day per person in real income at the local level. Even though the economy has grown considerably, the informal sector—or untaxed, unregulated, unprotected work—continues to serve as a pull factor for child labor. Nearly 60 percent of the urban population is employed in the informal sector (Sene 1993). Further, case studies on women's and children's work show that, although a few women attain professional, clerical, and factory work, most opportunities for women and children lie in the informal sector. The large informal economy in Senegal influences occupational opportunities for all Senegalese workers, but in particular for women and children.

It is also necessary to consider children's work in relation to the economic benefit their households receive from children's labor. Bass (1997) focused on the types of occupations children hold, and what these occupations mean for the child and the household. A job where one primarily learns a craft is different from a job where one sells, because these two jobs offer different earning potential, working conditions, and training. Some households are able to secure only short-term opportunities with limited training potential, whereas other households place their children in positions with long-term opportunities for training that is more in-depth and specialized. Different households seek different opportunities for their children in the market, based on the economic resources and needs of their households. If a household has more economic and social resources, it is likely to place a child in an apprenticeship position. With less money, households harness social resources in order to create opportunities for their children in the labor market.

The Educational System

The Senegalese public school system is modeled after the French system, where there are six levels of primary school and the language of instruction is French. The first primary schools were opened by the French colonial government in 1903 for African children in urban areas and in 1930 for a sprinkling of African children in rural areas (de Benoist 1982). Students followed the six-level course of study in order to attain the *certificat d'études primaires élémentaires*, or primary school certificate. After completing the elementary school certificate, those students could then attend a teacher's training program or study in an *école primaire supérieure*. Better students from an *école primaire supérieure* were then admitted to high school, or *école normale*. These first urban students became instructors in primary schools and clerical workers for the colonial government.

It was not until 1944 that the French colonial government made a formal commitment to education for all children in what became the independent country of Senegal in 1960. By 1965 only 1 percent of the population was literate (Gellar 1982). Today, about 40 percent of the Senegalese population is literate. Official governmental statistics show that 87.6 percent of children are enrolled in primary school, while 26.4 percent of children are enrolled in secondary school. Schools are unevenly distributed throughout the country. Children in urban areas have more educational options and free time than children in rural areas, and therefore are more likely to attend school. Educational data show the unequal distribution of children's educational access; more than 70 percent of children in the more urban Dakar and Ziguinchor regions were enrolled in school, compared with the more rural regions of Tambacounda and Diourbel, where less than 25 percent of children were enrolled (Republic of Senegal 1992). Two factors explain this uneven education outcome: the higher dropout rates for rural children and the lack of secondary schools in rural areas.

Data from a national survey of child market workers show that a slight majority, 55 percent, of children working in markets have had some formal schooling (Bass 1997). This suggests that parents of child workers value formal schooling for their children. Of the child market workers who attended primary school, most children quit school during the sixth year, generally at age eleven or twelve, which is typical of the quitting pattern for all children in Senegal (Republic of Senegal 1993). The sixth year of primary school is critical, because children take an exam at this grade level to determine whether they receive the primary school certificate and merit a place in a secondary school. These exams are extremely competitive. In the 1995–96 school year, just 40 percent of all sixth-year students from private and public schools who took the primary school certificate exam passed. Earning a seat in a secondary school is even more competitive. During the same test cycle, 22 percent of the children who took the secondary school placement exam passed. While good students are likely to attain the primary school certificate, only the best students will earn a place in secondary school. The pass rate for the secondary school placement exam reached its high in 1980 when 29 percent of those who took the exam passed. In 1990, the pass rate slid to 25 percent, and the pass rate fell again between 1990 and 1995 to 22.4 percent (Association for the Development of African Education 1995). Parents want their children to continue in school, and their children therefore take and retake these exams. Some children take the last level of primary school several times before reaching the age limit of fifteen, further adding to teachers' burden to educate already large classes.

Cultural expectations also influence the schooling rates of children differently across ethnic groups. National statistics show that Dioula and Mandinka children are better educated than other ethnic groups (Ndiaye et al. 1994). Similarly, survey data of child market workers (Bass 1997) found that 27 percent of Dioula child market workers had attended the last year of primary school, whereas just 22 percent of Wolof, 20 percent of Poular, and 19 percent of Sereer children had attended the last year.

One main reason for quitting school in Senegal is the high cost of education. Public schools do not charge tuition, but the student's family must furnish books, paper, and pencils at an estimated cost of about CFAF10,000, or US$20, per year. This sum can be an obstacle when considering the average number of children per Senegalese woman is five. Consequently, many children share books with a sibling, cousin, or even neighbor. Parents committed to an Islamic education spend about CFAF3,000 (about US$6) per month to school a child. Thus, parents of modest means are willing to pay for an Islamic education. Parents committed to a formal French-style education must pay CFAF17,500 (about US$35) per month at the local French primary school run by Catholic nuns in the neighborhood of the market. In addition to cost, the opportunity cost the household incurs by the loss of the child's earnings is a factor. Education is one commodity that can be purchased by a household. But the household can purchase other commodities in education's place.

Bonnet (1993) has argued that many parents prefer child labor over formal public education to educate and prepare their children for the future. Interview data lend some support to this assertion, especially among child workers who have never attended formal school (Bass 1997). Parents may prefer market-work training because it is more applicable to a career or because they are financially unable to invest in formal education for their children. However, cultural expectations also help explain why parents value market work. Many parents do not entertain formal schooling as an option because they never attended school. If the father can teach his son how to do carpentry or market selling, and a mother can teach her daughter selling or house cleaning, formal schooling is not always viewed as the way to prepare their children for adult careers.

Overall, parents prepare their children for adult life in an environment of an expensive private school system and an inadequate public school system. The impact of this larger educational context varies by region (Geller 1982), by ethnic group (Creevey 1992; Bass 2004), by parents' economic resources, and by gender.

Gender as a Social Structure That Frames Child Labor

Gender stratification adds to our understanding of children's work in Senegal because both work and social lives are separated by sex. This sex-stratification process draws on African and Islamic patriarchal traditions, and offers boys higher status and more opportunity than girls. When Islam spread to West Africa, it reinforced the patriarchal values of the traditional Wolof, Sereer, and Toucouleur ethnic groups (Callaway and Creevey 1994). Before Islam, both the Sereer and the Wolof had a mixture of matrilineal and patrilineal systems (Diop 1985).

This gender stratification is supported by Senegalese culture. Men have more power and prestige than women in their interpersonal relations, households, and work. This hierarchy of male over female is reproduced in childhood socialization, as girls are socialized differently than boys. Wolof boys are taught to be decision makers, while Wolof girls are taught to be obedient and submissive, and are instructed that their future lies in marriage to men who will treat them well and provide them with the social and economic status they desire (Diop 1985). Girls do housework, cook, and care for younger children at an early age, generally five or six. Boys help with some household tasks, such as carrying water or charcoal, until age twelve, but they are never required to sweep and cook. In addition, studies of Senegalese child market workers show that girls are less likely than boys to receive any formal education (Bass 1997). Of the total population of school-age Senegalese children, boys (58 percent) outnumber girls (42 percent) in primary school (Republic of Senegal 1993).

The work of boys and girls is valued differently. In terms of work opportunities, Bass (1997) found that boys have better access to full-time market positions such as apprenticeships because they have fewer household responsibilities than girls. Girls and women tend to enter selling positions with more flexible hours. Jobs thought appropriate for girls allow them to do their housework now and when they are older. In this way, girls train for a career that will not interfere with their expected roles as housewives and mothers. In contrast, boys are expected to take apprenticeships and enter well-established sales work that will allow them to support their future families.

Legislation

Most child labor in Senegal is visible and tolerated by the authorities, even though there is a basic minimum age of fourteen for work in all sectors.

For seasonal and light work there is a minimum age of twelve, with the consent of the parents and for a maximum of seven to ten hours per day. Labor inspectors are authorized to remove children from work not proportional to their development. The code provides, "[T]he child may not be kept in employment thus recognized that is above his strength and must be assigned suitable employment" (Republic of Senegal 1992). Additionally, a child has the right to a minimum of eleven consecutive hours of relaxation between any two days of work. The child should also be allowed twenty-four hours of consecutive rest once a week.

While the legislation prohibits children from performing difficult types of work, it does not deal with the kinds of work most children perform, work in family-run businesses, in rural settings, or in informal-sector positions such as domestic work, ambulatory sellers, and apprentices. The Senegalese example repeats the two-pronged approach used by Europe in the nineteenth century to curb child labor by prohibiting factory work and fighting illiteracy through a national system of education. In Europe, many nonfactory-work activities were left untouched by legislation (Fyfe 1989; Weiner 1991). Therefore, work that is connected with household production, such as keeping house, babysitting, working as a maid, selling in the street, running errands, and assisting adult family members, was not mentioned in the legislation. In Senegal, this same pattern exists of not questioning work activities that are deemed necessary for the livelihood of the family. Seventy percent of children sampled in a national survey of Senegalese child market workers were found to labor with parents or extended-family members; many child market sellers discussed their work in terms of "my mother's stall" (Bass 1997). Their work is exempted from protective legislation.

Legislation exists to regulate industry- or factory-based work for children, but parents manage children's work on the household level. Their work is considered essential to household production and household economic survival in many cases, and is acceptable and considered to have educational value. Current legislation is therefore irrelevant as an enforcement mechanism for most of the child labor that exists in Senegal, because most children work in informal-sector positions outside the definition of regulated child labor.

Conclusion

Child labor in Senegal remains a prominent social issue. The ailing Senegalese economy shares an important relationship to Senegalese households that view the work of children as fundamental to the sustenance of the household. Child labor persists because there is a large informal sector economy to absorb it. If the economy continues to improve, child labor will continue to diminish as it has in the last few decades. Insufficient education, sex segregation of the workplace, and inadequate legislation also help explain Senegal's unique experience with child labor. Children's work is considered an extension of household economic strategy. This explains why parents may choose work over schooling for their children, why some children in a family are schooled while others are not, and why much child labor remains invisible and unregulated by legislation.

References and Further Reading

Association for the Development of African Education. *Education in Africa*. CD-ROM. Washington, DC: U.S. Agency for International Development, 1995.

Bass, Loretta E. "Child Labor in Urban Markets of Senegal." Diss., University of Connecticut, 1997.

Bass, Loretta E. *Child Labor in Africa*. Boulder, CO: Lynne Rienner, 2004.

De Benoist, Joseph Roger. *L'Afrique Occidentale Française de 1944 à 1960*. Dakar: Les Nouvelles Éditions Africaines, 1982.

Bonnet, Michel. "Le travail des enfants en Afrique." BIT/ILO publication of the Séminaire sous-régional sur l'abolition du travail des enfants et l'amélioration de la condition des enfants qui travaillent, 1993.

Callaway, Barbara, and Lucy Creevey. *The Heritage of Islam: Women, Religion, and Politics in West Africa*. Boulder, CO: Lynne Rienner, 1994.

Creevey, Lucy. "The Sword and the Veil." Manuscript. University of Connecticut, Storrs, 1992.

Diop, Abdoulaye-Bara. *La famille Wolof*. Paris: Karthala, 1985.

Fyfe, Alec. *Child Labour*. Cambridge: Polity Press, 1989.

Gellar, Sheldon. *Senegal: An African Nation Between Islam and the West*. Boulder: Westview Press, 1982.

Glenn, Evelyn Nakano. "From Servitude to Service Work: Historical Continuities in the Racial Division of Paid Reproductive Labor." *Journal of Women in Culture and Society* 18:1 (1992).

Ndiaye, Salif, Papa Demba Diouf, and Mohamed Ayad. *Enquête démographique et de santé au Sénégal.* EDS II 1992–93. Dakar: Ministère de l'Économie, des Finances et du Plan, 1994.

Republic of Senegal. *Situation économique. Édition 89–90.* Dakar: Ministère de l'Économie et des Finances, Direction de la Statistique, Bureau Informatique, 1992.

Republic of Senegal. *Dimensions Sociales de l'Adjustement.* Dakar: Ministère de l'Économie et des Finances et du Plan, Direction de la Prevision et de la Statistique, Bureau Informatique, 1993.

Sene, Soce. *Le travail des enfants au Sénégal "Cas des apprentis."* Dakar: Government of Senegal and UNICEF-ILO, 1993.

UNICEF. *Analyse de la situation de l'enfant et de la femme au Sénégal.* Dakar: Government of Senegal and UNICEF, 1995.

Weiner, Myron. "Suffer the Children." *Far Eastern Economic Review* 151 (February 1991): 26–27.

World Bank. *World Development Indicators 2001.* Washington, DC: World Bank, 2001.

Sierra Leone

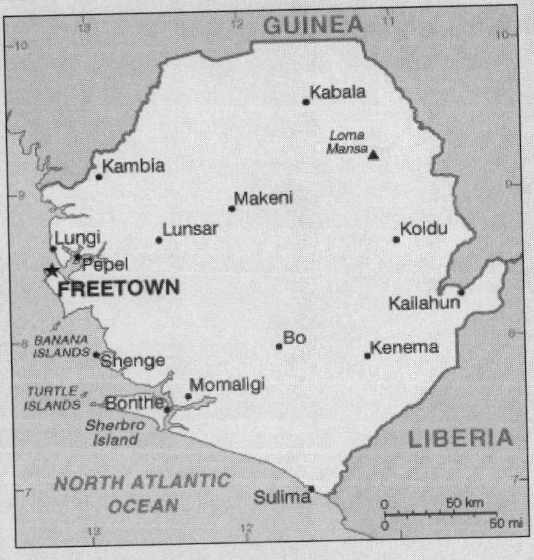

SIERRA LEONE	CRC	C 138	C 182
Ratifications	Y	N	N
Human Development Index/Rank	0.335/176		
Human Capital			
Population Growth Rate	2.29%		
% Population 0–14	44.8%		
Total Fertility Rate	6.01		
Life Expectancy	40.58		
Infant Mortality Rate	158.27		
Literacy Rate	29.6%		
Economic			
GDP/Capita	$900		
GDP Growth %	6.8%		
% Poverty	68%		
Gini Index	62.9		

CHILD ACTIVITY BREAKDOWN, BY SEX AND RESIDENCE

RESIDENCE	Percentage of children in the relevant age-group[a]									
	Economic activity only		School only		Combining school and economic activity		Neither in school nor in economic activity		Child labor[b]	
	Male	Female	Male	Female	Male	Female	Male	Female	Male	Female
Urban	4.5	6.4	52.6	52.1	35.7	32.1	7.2	9.4	n/av	n/av
Rural	25.5	27.2	20.5	19.8	40.7	39.4	13.3	13.6	n/av	n/av
Total	19.7	20.8	29.4	29.7	39.3	37.2	11.7	12.3	48.8	47.7

Source: Sierra Leone, Multiple Indicator Cluster Survey 3, 2005 (see UCW Project Web site, http://www.ucw-project.org, country statistics).

Notes: [a]Children age 5 to 14. [b]Estimate includes (a) children under age 12 engaged in economic activities, (b) children age 12–14 engaged in excessive economic activities (more than 14 hours per week), and (c) children under age 15 engaged in excessive household chores (at least 28 hours per week). Estimate does not account for children engaged in hazardous work or other unconditional "worst forms" of child labor.

Togo

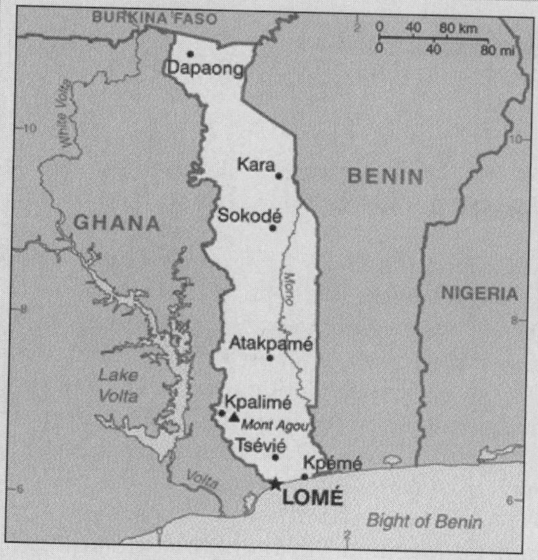

TOGO			
	CRC	C 138	C 182
Ratifications	Y	Y	Y
Human Development Index/Rank	0.495/147		
Human Capital			
Population Growth Rate	2.72%		
% Population 0–14	42%		
Total Fertility Rate	4.9		
Life Expectancy	57.86		
Infant Mortality Rate	59.12		
Literacy Rate	60.9%		
Economic			
GDP/Capita	$1,700		
GDP Growth %	3%		
% Poverty	32%		
Gini Index	—		
Labor Force Composition			
% Agriculture	65%		
% Industry	5%		
% Services	30%		

CHILD ACTIVITY BREAKDOWN, BY SEX AND RESIDENCE

RESIDENCE	Percentage of children in the relevant age-group[a]									
	Economic activity only		School only		Combining school and economic activity		Neither in school nor in economic activity		Child labor[b]	
	Male	Female	Male	Female	Male	Female	Male	Female	Male	Female
Urban	7.5	15.1	39.7	32.5	43.8	37.6	9.0	14.9	n/av	n/av
Rural	23.1	29.9	12.3	11.8	48.3	38.5	16.3	19.8	n/av	n/av
Total	18.8	25.1	19.9	18.5	47.1	38.2	14.3	18.2	61.3	59.6

Source: Togo, Multiple Indicator Cluster Survey 2, 2000 (see UCW Project Web site, http://www.ucw-project.org, country statistics).

Notes: [a]Children age 5 to 14. [b]Estimate includes (a) children under age 12 engaged in economic activities, (b) children age 12–14 engaged in excessive economic activities (more than 14 hours per week), and (c) children under age 15 engaged in excessive household chores (at least 28 hours per week). Estimate does not account for children engaged in hazardous work or other unconditional "worst forms" of child labor.

SECTION 3. MIDDLE AFRICA

Child Soldiers in the Great Lakes Region of Africa

Alison Dilworth, Consultant to the Coalition to Stop the Use of Child Soldiers

Forced or compulsory recruitment of children under the age of eighteen for use in armed conflict is considered a worst form of child labor under ILO Convention 182. However, the widespread and systematic use of children has been a disturbing feature of conflicts in Burundi, Democratic Republic of the Congo, and Uganda, where tens of thousands under eighteen years of age have been used as fighters, porters, or domestic servants, or for sexual purposes.

By 2006, significant progress had been made toward ending internal and regional conflict, and the demobilization of many of these children was under way. However, challenges to building a durable peace are enormous and, given the fragility of regional peace processes and challenges faced by disarmament, demobilization, and reintegration programs, former child soldiers are vulnerable to rerecruitment. Should peace hold, there remain enormous challenges for the successful reintegration of child soldiers.

Years of poverty, discrimination, and a context of impunity have undoubtedly facilitated recruitment of children. While many were abducted and forced into child soldiering, others joined "voluntarily," sometimes to avenge the killing of family members or violence against their communities, or because joining was perceived to provide access to protection, clothes, and money. Propaganda and peer or parental pressure have also been factors behind recruitment. Addressing the reasons why children in the Great Lakes joined armed forces and groups will be key to preventing further recruitment.

Regional Use of Child Soldiers

Burundi

Burundi's ten-year civil war ended finally in November 2003 with the entry of the main armed group, the Conseil National pour la Défense de la Démocratie–Forces pour la Défense de la Démocratie (CNDD-FDD [Nkruunziza]), into transitional government institutions and the reform of the government security forces. Sporadic armed conflict continued between government armed forces and the one remaining armed political group, Forces Nationales de Libération (FNL), in western provinces. Formal negotiations between the new government and the FNL led to a fragile cease-fire agreement in September 2006.

With the reform of the security forces, recruitment of children officially ended, and all under age eighteen were officially demobilized. However, the government is yet to pass legislation raising the age of recruitment to eighteen.

Despite condemning the use of child soldiers by the FNL since coming to power, the government continues to use captured FNL child soldiers for intelligence purposes, and at least forty children were among hundreds of civilians arbitrarily arrested and detained since August 2005 on suspicion of providing assistance, such as food or water, to the FNL. Charged with belonging to an armed group, none have been tried. At least until September 2006, the FNL was reported to continue to recruit, sometimes by force, and use child soldiers.

Democratic Republic of the Congo

From 1996, Democratic Republic of the Congo (DRC) government forces and numerous armed groups, some of which were heavily backed by Rwanda and Uganda, fought for political, military, and economic supremacy in eastern DRC. The signing of a Global and All-Inclusive Peace Agreement in December 2002 led to a significant reduction of the fighting. By mid-2003, both Rwanda and Uganda had officially pulled out of DRC. A fragile transition process led to elections in 2006. However, several armed factions remain openly suspicious of, or hostile to, the peace process. Security in eastern DRC, such as it is, continues to depend mainly on a UN peacekeeping force.

Recruitment and use of children is reported to have significantly declined from mid-2005, in part due to the lessening of conflict as well as implementation of a disarmament, demobilization, and reintegration program for children. Significantly, in May 2005, the chief of staff of the Congolese armed forces (FARDC) issued clear written orders to all FARDC units prohibiting the recruitment or use of children under age eighteen. Some FARDC brigades, however, continue to include children.

New recruitment and rerecruitment continues to be reported, particularly in eastern DRC, by dissident and nonaligned armed groups, with new child recruits reportedly forced to recruit other children. Several Burundian, Rwandese, and Ugandan armed groups remain active or hold bases in the DRC, posing a risk to regional security. All include children in their ranks.

Rwanda

During its participation in the DRC conflict, Rwandese armed forces recruited children in both Rwanda and DRC, forcing children as young as eight into their forces. The Rwandese government directly supported and largely controlled some armed political groups active in the DRC conflict, including the Rassemblement Congolais pour la Démocratie–Goma (RCD-Goma). All made extensive use of child soldiers.

There are no current confirmed reports of the use of child soldiers by Rwandese government forces. Several Rwandese armed groups based in the DRC, whose members include former members of the former Rwandese army and the Hutu Interahamwe militia, which carried out the 1994 genocide, continue to use child soldiers.

Uganda

Uganda reportedly withdrew the last of its troops from DRC in May 2003. They included children recruited to local defense units, which, although intended to provide security for local villages or camps, are reported to have been active in both DRC and the Sudan, as well as fighting with government armed forces against the Lords Resistance Army (LRA) in northern Uganda. The government also heavily backed several armed groups in DRC, which included a high proportion of children in their ranks, including the Union des Patriotes Congolais.

Improved relations between Uganda and Sudan, the formation of a new "government of national unity" in Sudan, followed the signature of a "comprehensive peace agreement" in Sudan in January 2005. The indictment of LRA leaders by the International Criminal Court on charges of war crimes and crimes against humanity, including enslavement, rape, murder, and child enlistment, also appeared to have been a factor motivating peace negotiations to restart between the Ugandan government and the LRA. Following talks mediated by the government of southern Sudan, where the LRA maintains bases, the government of Uganda and the LRA signed an agreement on the cessation of hostilities in August 2006, offering some hope that an end to the twenty-year war might be in sight. However, by October, the process appeared to be faltering. While the International Criminal Court indictments are believed to have been persuasive in bringing LRA leaders to the negotiating table, fear of arrest and prosecution appears to be affecting the progress of the talks.

There are no reports of widespread use of child soldiers by government forces. Some under the age of eighteen continue to be recruited into the armed forces and the local defence units, through nonrigorous application of national legislation, inadequate birth registration, and failure to verify the age of recruits.

The LRA has depended significantly on child

soldiers. LRA child soldiers, some as young as five, have been abducted from their families, and forced to kill other children, family members, and other civilians, as well as taking part in raids. The LRA also abducted large numbers of girls, forcing them mainly into sexual slavery, as well as into combat duties. Many of these girls have had children born and raised in the LRA.

According to UNICEF estimates, by 2004, some 20,000 children had been abducted by the LRA in the course of the conflict, and an estimated 20,000 children, known as night commuters, slept away from their homes each night in nearby towns to avoid abduction. From January 2006, due to increased security, the numbers of child night commuters began to drop and were estimated in August to be approximately 7,650. In September 2006, the LRA stated that it would release 1,500 noncombatant women and children it was holding captive.

Disarmament, Demobilization, and Reintegration

Current Disarmament, Demobilization, and Reintegration (DDR) programs in Burundi and DRC are multiagency programs, involving a wide range of government and nongovernmental actors, and are supported financially by the World Bank and the Multi-Country Demobilization and Reintegration Program (MDRP), a multi-donor trust fund. The programs face huge challenges, not least because of ongoing conflict in DRC, and the sheer numbers of children involved, as well as logistical difficulties and security constraints in family tracing and repatriation. Ensuring long-term reintegration in a context of economic collapse, and the huge post-conflict challenges of reestablishing the rule of law, will require sustained international support.

Burundi

Demobilization of child soldiers from government forces, and all but one of Burundi's armed groups, was complete by mid-2006, with a total of 3,015 child soldiers demobilized. Many child soldiers had reached the age of majority by the end of the conflict and were demobilized as adults. A high proportion of the government Peace Guards militia, for example, had previously been child soldiers with armed political groups. By June 2006, more than 17,000 Peace Guards had been demobilized.

The program involved the participation of a range of ministries as well as national and international nongovernmental organizations and agencies. The process generally appears to have been well received. However, issues likely to cause serious future problems were identified. They include a lack of focus on the prevention of rerecruitment, problems arising from the treatment of battle-hardened eighteen-year-olds as children rather than adults, and a lack of long-term reintegration strategies.

Signature of a cease-fire agreement with the FNL in September 2006 paved the way for further demobilization of child soldiers. In June 2006, some 400 FNL combatants, captured and detained by government forces, had already been assembled at a "welcome center" in the north of the country in anticipation of DDR. They included at least twenty-five child soldiers. Representatives of the UN mission in Burundi, partners of the government's demobilization program, and the World Bank have asked the government to clarify the status of FNL child combatants, including those in detention, so that they can prepare for their demobilization.

Democratic Republic of the Congo

By July 2006, more than 19,000 child soldiers were reported by the DRC National DDR Commission to have been released from armed forces and groups through official programs, but thousands more were reported to have simply returned to civilian life. Some 11,000 children were reportedly still with armed forces or groups, or otherwise unaccounted for, including a high proportion of girls.

The DDR program faces serious challenges, including reaching children in nonaligned groups, addressing the particular problems faced by girls, and effectively implementing the social and economic activities crucial to reintegration. The high-profile arrest of several commanders guilty of recruiting children under the age of fifteen has had the unintended effect of slowing the release of children by other commanders fearful of arrest.

Although a DDR program including repatriation exists for foreign armed groups operating in DRC, no mechanism exists under the program for the release and reintegration of large numbers of Congolese child soldiers attached to these groups.

Uganda

No specific country DDR program exists in Uganda. However an official program entitled the Repatriation, Rehabilitation, Resettlement and Reintegration of Reporters project was established in the context of the Amnesty and Suppression of Terrorism Act of January 2000. It aimed to offer immunity and resettlement packages to all 15,300 ex-combatants from the LRA and other armed groups who surrendered their weapons. The program was launched in May 2005, and by August 2006, 11,851 "reporters" of an estimated 15,310 target number had received resettlement packages. The project did not appear to address the special needs of child soldiers.

Demobilization of Girl Child Soldiers

Although the current DDR programs in Burundi and the DRC are based on a broad definition of "child soldiers" to include all children involved with fighting forces, rather than only those engaged in fighting or using a weapon, the majority of participants have been males used in active combat. This in part appears due to the difficulties in successfully identifying girl combatants.

While the number of girls who took part in the Burundi conflict is not confirmed, they are known to have performed a number of roles, including active combatant, sexual slave, spy, cook, and other noncombat laborer. However, fewer than fifty girl soldiers had been demobilized by June 2006. The number of girl soldiers likely to be eligible for demobilization from the FNL is not known.

In DRC, some 12,500 girls are estimated to have been associated with armed forces or groups—around 40 percent of the estimated child soldiers. However, of the 19,000 child soldiers demobilized in DRC, only some 2,900 were girls. Many girl soldiers in DRC are known to have been used as sex slaves, to have been repeatedly raped, and to have conceived—all of which carry strong stigma in the DRC. Few have access to medical care. Some are thought to have missed DDR programs because they were wrongly perceived to be dependents of male combatants, while others may have simply left the fighting forces in an attempt to avoid stigma.

International and National Law

The governments of Burundi, the DRC, Rwanda, and Uganda have ratified some of the applicable international and regional standards protecting children from involvement in armed conflict. They include ILO Convention 182 and the UN Convention on the Rights of the Child (CRC), which prohibits recruitment or use in armed conflict of children under the age of fifteen. The optional protocol to the CRC on the involvement of children in armed conflict prohibits the recruitment or use in direct hostilities of children under the age of eighteen. DRC, Rwanda, and Uganda have ratified the optional protocol; Burundi is a signatory but has yet to fully ratify it. Burundi, DRC, and Uganda have all ratified the Rome Statute of the International Criminal Court, which defines the recruitment and use of children under age fifteen as a war crime.

Stated government policy in all countries has set the minimum military recruitment age at eighteen years. This is supported by legislation in the DRC, Uganda, and Rwanda. Legislation punishing and preventing the crime of genocide and crimes against humanity, passed in Burundi in May 2003, classifies the recruitment of children under the age of fifteen as a war crime and provides for the death penalty for those found guilty.

However, the governments have yet to fully implement the principles and spirit of international standards and their own legislation.

An End to Impunity for Those Committing Crimes Under International Law

The International Criminal Court has begun to address the issue of child soldiering in the Great Lakes. In July 2005, arrest warrants were issued for five senior leaders of the LRA on charges of crimes against humanity and war crimes, including murder, rape, enslavement, and forced enlisting of children. In March 2006, Thomas Lubanga, leader of the armed group the Union des Patriotes Congolais, was arrested and transferred to the International Criminal Court in The Hague on charges of committing war crimes, including "enlisting and conscripting children under the age of fifteen and using them to participate actively in hostilities."

One person has been prosecuted in the DRC on charges related to the recruitment of children into the armed forces. Jean-Pierre Biyoya, former commander of an armed group and a major in the new Congolese armed forces, was sentenced to death for the illegal arrest and detention of children. His sentence was later reduced to five years' imprisonment.

These developments, although significant, remain exceptional, and there is little evidence of progress in national courts in confronting and providing redress for grave and systematic human rights abuses committed during the region's conflicts, including the prosecution of child recruiters. Without substantial reform and international assistance, and, importantly, the commitment of national governments, the justice systems of Burundi, DRC, and Uganda will be unable to tackle the issue of child recruitment effectively.

References and Further Reading

Amnesty International. *Burundi: Child Soldiers—The Challenge of Demobilization.* AFR 16/011/2004, March 2004. http://web.amnesty.org/library/Index/ENGAFR160112004?open&of=ENG-2AF.

Amnesty International. *DRC: Children at War, Creating Hope for the Future.* AFR 62/017/2006, October 2006. http://web.amnesty.org/library/Index/ENGAFR620172006?open&of=ENG-2AF.

Annan, Jeannie, Christopher Blattman, and Roger Horton. *The State of Youth and Youth Protection in Northern Uganda: Findings from the Survey for War-Affected Youth.* Report for UNICEF Uganda, 2006. http://www.sway-uganda.org/SWAY.Phase1.FinalReport.pdf.

Coalition to Stop the Use of Child Soldiers. *Child Soldiers Global Report 2004.* http://www.child-soldiers.org/document_get.php?id=966.

Human Rights Watch. *Stolen Children: Abduction and Recruitment in Northern Uganda.* New York: Human Rights Watch, March 2003. http://hrw.org/reports/2003/uganda0303/uganda0403.pdf.

Human Rights Watch. *A Long Way from Home: FNL Child Soldiers in Burundi.* New York: Human Rights Watch, June 2006. http://hrw.org/backgrounder/africa/burundi0606/.

International Crisis Group. *Peace in Northern Uganda?* Africa ICG Briefing 41, September 2006. http://www.crisisgroup.org/home/index.cfm?id=4374&1=1.

International Labor Organization. *Wounded Childhood: The Use of Children in Armed Conflict in Central Africa.* Geneva: ILO-IPEC, 2003.

United Nations. *Concluding Observations of the Committee on the Rights of the Child (Uganda).* CRC/C/15/Add.270, September 30, 2005.

United Nations. *Report of the Secretary-General on Children and Armed Conflict in the Democratic Republic of Congo.* S/2006/389, June 13, 2006.

United Nations. *Seventh Report of the Secretary-General on the United Nations Operation in Burundi.* S/2006/429, June 21, 2006.

United Nations. *Report of the Secretary-General on the Sudan.* S/2006/728, September 12, 2006.

Angola

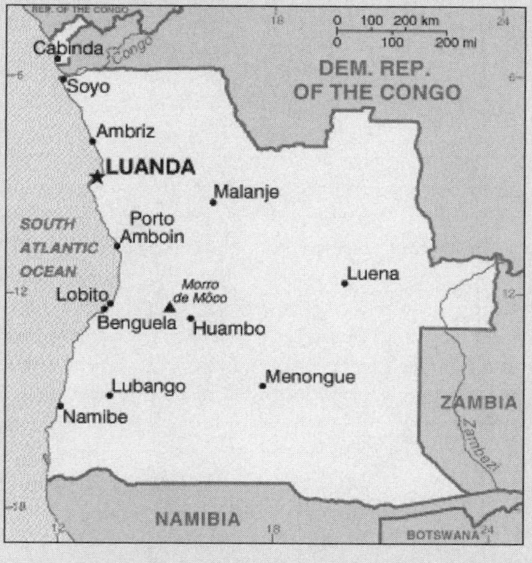

ANGOLA			
	CRC	C 138	C 182
Ratifications	Y	Y	Y
Human Development Index/Rank	0.439/161		
Human Capital			
Population Growth Rate	2.45%		
% Population 0–14	43.7%		
Total Fertility Rate	6.35		
Life Expectancy	38.62		
Infant Mortality Rate	185.36		
Literacy Rate	66.8%		
Economic			
GDP/Capita	$4,300		
GDP Growth %	14%		
% Poverty	70%		
Gini Index	—		
Labor Force Composition			
% Agriculture	85%		
% Industry and Services	15%		

CHILD ACTIVITY BREAKDOWN, BY SEX AND RESIDENCE

RESIDENCE	Percentage of children in the relevant age-group[a]									
	Economic activity only		School only		Combining school and economic activity		Neither in school nor in economic activity		Child labor[b]	
	Male	Female	Male	Female	Male	Female	Male	Female	Male	Female
Urban	5.2	5.9	56.2	52.3	14.5	15.7	24.2	26.2	n/av	n/av
Rural	12.3	14.3	31.0	31.0	27.5	22.3	29.2	32.4	n/av	n/av
Total[c]	7.2	8.3	48.8	46.1	18.3	17.6	25.6	28.0	21.5	24.2

Source: Angola, Multiple Indicator Cluster Survey 2, 2001 (see UCW Project Web site, http://www.ucw-project.org, country statistics).

Notes: [a]Children age 5 to 14. [b]Estimate includes (a) children under age 12 engaged in economic activities, (b) children age 12–14 engaged in excessive economic activities (more than 14 hours per week), and (c) children under age 15 engaged in excessive household chores (at least 28 hours per week). Estimate does not account for children engaged in hazardous work or other unconditional "worst forms" of child labor. [c]The totals, that is, urban and rural combined, represent what can be described as Angola-Secured Territory but not the nation as a whole.

Cameroon

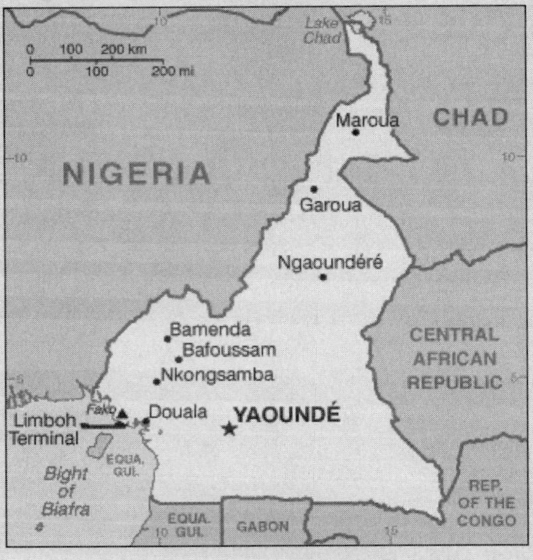

CAMEROON			
	CRC	C 138	C 182
Ratifications	Y	Y	Y
Human Development Index/Rank	0.506/144		
Human Capital			
Population Growth Rate	2.04%		
% Population 0–14	41.2%		
Total Fertility Rate	4.39		
Life Expectancy	51.16		
Infant Mortality Rate	63.52		
Literacy Rate	79%		
Economic			
GDP/Capita	$2,400		
GDP Growth %	4.1%		
% Poverty	48%		
Gini Index	44.6		
Labor Force Composition			
% Agriculture	70%		
% Industry	13%		
% Services	17%		

CHILD ACTIVITY BREAKDOWN, BY SEX AND RESIDENCE

RESIDENCE	Percentage of children in the relevant age-group[a]									
	Economic activity only		School only		Combining school and economic activity		Neither in school nor in economic activity		Child labor[b]	
	Male	Female	Male	Female	Male	Female	Male	Female	Male	Female
Urban	1.3	1.8	90.4	89.0	2.1	1.7	6.2	7.5	n/av	n/av
Rural	9.1	14.8	74.9	66.1	10.7	10.1	5.4	9.0	n/av	n/av
Total	6.5	10.2	79.9	74.1	7.9	7.2	5.6	8.5	51.0	50.4

Source: Cameroon, Enquête Camerounaise Auprès des Ménages II, 2001 (see UCW Project Web site, http://www.ucw-project.org, country statistics).

Notes: [a]Children age 10 to 14. [b]Estimate includes (a) children under age 12 engaged in economic activities, (b) children age 12–14 engaged in excessive economic activities (more than 14 hours per week), and (c) children under age 15 engaged in excessive household chores (at least 28 hours per week). Estimate does not account for children engaged in hazardous work or other unconditional "worst forms" of child labor.

Child Labor in Cameroon

Roger A. Tsafack Nanfosso, Researcher in Applied Microeconomics, Faculty of Economics and Management, University of Yaoundé II, Cameroon

There is a clear consensus nowadays that "child work" and "child labor" are not necessarily the same. The first phenomenon refers to any form of economic activity performed by a child, whether paid or unpaid, legal or illegal, in the formal or informal sector. By contrast, "child labor" refers only to negative or undesirable forms of work that should be eliminated in accordance with ILO Conventions 138 and 182. From these definitions child labor in Cameroon is defined accordingly, covering all kinds of work that prevents a child under the age of fifteen from attending or participating in school or that is performed under hazardous (health, physical, intellectual, mental, or moral) or exploitative conditions.

The objective of this essay is to present the reality of child labor in Cameroon by focusing on the extent of the phenomenon, the major causes, and policies designed to fight child labor.

Table 1

Child Involvement in Economic Activity, by Age and Sex

Age in years	Percentage of children in the relevant age-group[a] Male	Female	Total
10	17.2	14.0	15.6
11	8.9	16.0	12.5
12	15.0	21.9	18.4
13	13.7	16.3	14.9
14	16.9	18.3	17.6
Total 10–14	14.5	17.4	15.9

Source: NIS (2001).

Note: [a]Independent of school attendance status.

Overview

Estimates of child labor in Cameroon vary widely depending on the sample, the methodology, the design of the questionnaire, and the sources. The most conservative estimates come from Cameroon's National Institute of Statistics (NIS), which estimates that 15.9 percent of children ten to fourteen years of age are engaged in economic activities (see Table 1) (NIS 2001). In 1997, the ILO projected that by the year 2000 there would be 430,000 economically active ten- to fourteen-year-olds, representing 23 percent of this age-group (ILO 1997). But a 2001 ILO study estimated that there were 610,000 child workers at that time (ILO 2001). In contrast, in 2000, UNICEF's Multiple Indicator Cluster Survey estimated that 58.1 percent of children five to fourteen years of age were working, but that only 5 percent worked for wages. Among those children who performed domestic tasks, who are not counted as economically active in the ILO and National Institute of Statistics surveys, 11 percent worked for more than four hours per day (MINEFI 2000). The most extreme estimate suggested that 64 percent of children were economically active (Biggeri et al. 2003).

Table 2 illustrates the occupational dispersion of children in the country's economic activities. The government estimates that 88.2 percent of child labor occurs in agriculture, particularly on tea, cocoa, banana, and rubber plantations. In rural areas, 22.2 percent of children ten to fourteen years of age are economically active; in urban areas, 3.5 percent are economically active. In addition to agriculture, children are engaged in all manner of economic activities, including domestic service,

Table 2

Sector of Child Economic Activity, by Sex

	As percentage of children in economic activity[a]						
Sex	Agriculture	Manufacturing	Mining	Construction	Wholesale and retail trade	Transport	Other
Male	90.42	1.85	0.00	0.26	4.17	0.90	2.39
Female	86.32	2.32	0.48	0.00	8.84	0.00	2.05
Total	88.21	2.10	0.26	0.12	6.68	0.42	2.21

Source: NIS (2001).
Note: [a]Children age 10 to 14.

exploitative apprenticeship positions, selling at the market, and working on urban streets as beggars, hawkers (of cooked food or household articles), thieves, truck pushers, mechanics, car washers, or prostitutes (female and male). Kegne Foudouop (1991) has identified no less than 121 jobs involving children in the capital city of Yaoundé.

Two particularly disturbing forms of child labor found in Cameroon are child slavery and trafficking of children. Child slavery occurs especially in the Rey Bouba Division of North Province, where, in some cases, parents offer their young girls to the chief as gifts. The Ministry of Social Affairs has also reported that children in some large rural families are "loaned" to work as domestic servants, vendors, prostitutes, or babysitters in urban areas in exchange for monetary compensation (U.S. Department of Labor 2007). Trafficking of children is also widespread, and the country is involved as a source, in transit, and as a destination. A study by the ILO (2001, 11) revealed that trafficking accounted for as much as 84 percent of child labor, or approximately 530,000 of an estimated 610,000 working children. The majority of victims are trafficked within the country. Other source countries include Nigeria, Benin, Niger, Chad, Congo, Togo, and Central African Republic (see also U.S. Department of State, 2006, chap. 4).

Child Labor Determinants

In Cameroon, like in many other African countries, the causes of child labor are now well documented. A recent study by Tsafack and Ntamack (2005), implementing a fieldwork survey and using standard econometric estimation models to check the determinants of child labor in Yaoundé, found that poverty, education, residence and quality of life, and size of family powerfully explain child labor.

Poverty

The implementation of structural adjustment policies in Cameroon abolished numerous subsidies and induced much formal-sector retrenchment, which resulted in many firm closures and wage reductions. This increased unemployment increased the number of dependants, poor city dwellers, and peasants (Tsafack and Mama 2000). As poverty rates rose, families were increasingly involved in informal, irregular, and marginal wage-earning activities. In 1997, for example, 85 percent of the active population was working in the informal sector and only 15 percent in the formal sector (ILO 2001, 5). Aiming to supplement family income, or simply to survive, growing numbers of children were engaged in manual labor (Amin 1994). Tsafack and Ntamack (2005) showed that economic activity of the parents, especially mothers, clearly reduces (almost eliminates) child labor; in turn, child labor is boosted by their joblessness.

Education

The country's structural adjustment policies have limited state expenditures on social welfare programs, restricted the budget for primary education, and increased the illiteracy rate. Moreover, a long-standing gender-based disparity is reflected in lower enrollment rates for girls than boys in primary school, and higher rates of illiteracy among women. In the nation's major cities of Yaoundé, Douala, and Bamenda, estimates are that 40 percent of employed children were female, 7 percent were less than twelve years of age, and 60 percent had dropped out of primary schools (U.S. Department of State 2001). Tsafack and Ntamack (2005) demonstrated multiple links between education and child labor. The higher the level of parents' education (especially mothers'), the more children are away from work. In addition, education of children themselves reduces (almost eliminates) their probability of working, as does the education of their brothers or sisters.

Residence and Quality of Life

Child labor is greater in rural than in urban areas. Besides the fact that most of the population is rural, this is due, in part, to the lack of access to proper roads, medical facilities, education, drinking water, and electricity in rural areas (ILO 2001, 6). In towns, children who reside with both parents are unlikely to work, but for children who live outside the family compound, the probability of work is high. In the same vein, children living in shantytowns exhibit a high probability of working compared to those in luxurious suburbs.

Family Composition

Large families, rivalry among spouses in polygamous arrangements, and large numbers of siblings are strong catalysts for child labor. The chances that children will work increase if they have a brother or sister at work. In addition, the eldest child is four times more likely to be exposed to work than younger brothers and sisters. Finally, orphans (by single or both parents) are more likely to work than other children.

Fighting the Phenomenon

Given the evidence presented here, child labor is somewhat alarming in Cameroon. The government is now well aware of the phenomenon, thanks to international organizations and the actions of local NGOs. Many policies have been implemented to address the problem on three fronts, namely, prosecution, protection, and prevention (U.S. Department of State 2001, 2006).

Prosecution

Cameroon's penal code outlaws kidnapping of minors and kidnapping involving fraud and violence; it criminalizes slavery and forbids prostitution of children, corruption of youth, child abuse, and forced marriages. In December 2005 Cameroon enacted a statute prohibiting child trafficking. The government has also been considering a child protection code and has created an antitrafficking vice squad within the National Office of Interpol. Twelve traffickers of children were arrested in 2005, and one was deported to the United States. In addition, with the support of the U.S. Department of State, Cameroon is participating in an ILO-designed program to strengthen antitrafficking legislation and train law enforcement and judicial officials in antitrafficking strategies.

Protection

Cameroon's labor code sets the minimum age for employment at fourteen years and prohibits forced labor. Conditions of work for domestics are stipulated in a 1968 decree, and a 1969 decree sets fourteen as the minimum age for entering an apprenticeship. It also forbids a tutor, when single, to lodge an apprentice in his or her house.

In 2005, the government collaborated with the ILO on a U.S.-funded project to remove 1,200 children from cocoa plantations and provide them with schooling or skills training. Since 2004, Cameroon has recruited at least fifty-eight inspectors responsible for investigating child labor. There are 318 youth centers that give children an opportunity to develop their creativity and provide vocational training. On the occasion of the celebration of World Day for Safety and Health at Work (April 28, 2006), Alice Ouedrago, the subregional director of the ILO in Yaoundé, said that the West Africa Cocoa/Commercial Agricultural Project (WACAP) had successfully withdrawn 300 children from cocoa farming in the Centre Province, 250 in the Northwest, and 259 in the Southwest.

Prevention

Cameroon ratified ILO Conventions 138 and 182 on August 13, 2001, and June 5, 2002, respectively. Education is free and compulsory through the age of fourteen years. Three ministries are now in charge of education: the Ministry of Basic Education, the Ministry of Technical and Secondary Education, and the Ministry of Higher Education. National family planning is being implemented to sensitize people about the optimal family size. A National Strategic Plan Against Child Trafficking was to have been finalized in 2006, but has not yet been adopted. In 2004, Cameroon launched a program called Education for All Week and signed a protocol of agreement to eradicate child labor with the ILO. To amplify the need to combat exploitative child labor, Cameroon participated in various child labor awareness-raising activities including the ILO's World Day Against Child Labor, Red Card Against Child Labor Initiative, and the UN's Day of the African Child. The government is working with UNICEF on the Child-Friendly, Girl-Friendly Schools initiative to support quality education and to increase enrollment of girls in nonformal basic education settings. Finally, national legislation is based on the principle of equal pay for equal work without discrimination on the basis of age, making employment of children less attractive.

Conclusion

Child labor in Cameroon is increasingly worrying given the number of children involved, the types of work they are involved in, the existing slavery, and the country's position in the flow of trafficking. Child labor is due to many factors, including poverty, low level of education (both of parents and of children), residence and quality of life, and the size of family. Thanks to the growing awareness of the phenomenon and the aid of the international community, the government is implementing, with some success, many policies to address this problem with the three-part approach of prosecution, prevention, and protection.

References and Further Reading

Amin, Aloysius Ajab. "The Socio-Economic Impact of Child Labour in Cameroon." *LABOUR Capital and Society/TRAVAIL Capital et Société* 27:2 (1994): 234–48.

Biggeri, Mario, Lorenzo Guarcello, Scott Lyon, and Furio C. Rosati. "The Puzzle of "Idle" Children: Neither in School nor Performing Economic Activity: Evidence from Six countries." Working papers, Understanding Children's Work Project, October 2003.

Fodouop, Kegne. *Les petits métiers de la rue et l'emploi: le cas de Yaoundé.* Yaoundé: Editions Sopecam, 1991.

ILO. Bureau of Statistics. "Economically Active Population 1950–2010." STAT Working Paper, Geneva, 1997.

ILO. *Combating Trafficking in Children for Labour Exploitation in West and Central Africa: Synthesis Report Based on Studies of Benin, Burkina Faso, Cameroon, Côte d'Ivoire, Gabon, Ghana, Mali, Nigeria and Togo.* Geneva: IPEC, 2001.

Ministère de l'Économie et des Finances (MINEFI). *Enquête à indicateurs multiples (MICS) au Cameroun: rapport principal.* Yaoundé: MINEFI, 2000.

National Institute of Statistics (NIS). *Enquête Camerounaise auprès des ménages.* ECAM II. Yaoundé: NIS, 2001.

Tsafack Nanfosso, Roger, and Touna Mama. "Ajustement structurel et désindustrialisation au Cameroun." In *Qui contribue à la désindustrialisation des régions fragilisées?* ed. Alexandra Sagarra, 185–230. Neuchâtel: CEDIMES-CRD: Centre de Recherche sur le Développement, Université de Neuchâtel, 2000.

Tsafack Nanfosso, Roger, and Simon Song Ntamack. "Child Labour in Yaoundé—Cameroon: Some Lessons Drawn from a Survey on Children." *Journal of Economics and Business (Proceedings of the Faculty of Economics of Rijeka)* 23:2 (2005): 195–216.

U.S. Department of Labor. "Cameroon." In *2006 Findings on the Worst Forms of Child Labor,* 80-3. Washington, DC: Bureau of International Labor Affairs, 2007.

U.S. Department of State. *Country Reports on Human Rights Practices 2000.* Washington, DC: U.S. Department of State, February 2001.

U.S. Department of State. *Victims of Trafficking and Violence Protection Act of 2000: Trafficking in the Persons Report.* Washington, DC: U.S. Department of State, 2006.

Central African Republic

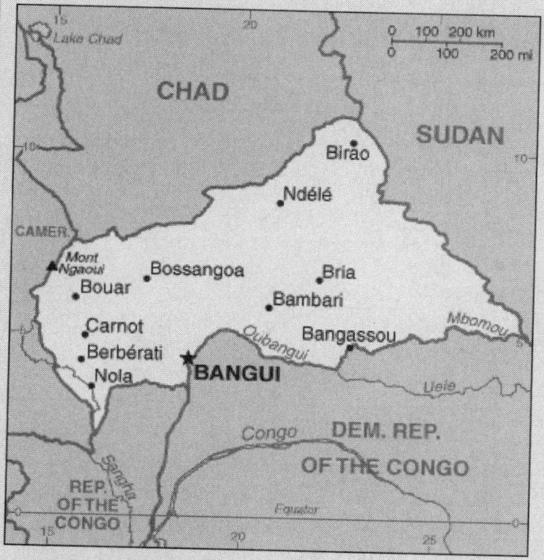

CENTRAL AFRICAN REPUBLIC			
	CRC	C 138	C 182
Ratifications	Y	Y	Y
Human Development Index/Rank	0.353/172		
Human Capital			
Population Growth Rate	1.53%		
% Population 0-14	41.9%		
Total Fertility Rate	4.41		
Life Expectancy	43.54		
Infant Mortality Rate	85.63		
Literacy Rate	51%		
Economic			
GDP/Capita	$1,100		
GDP Growth %	3%		
% Poverty	NA		
Gini Index	61.3		

CHILD ACTIVITY BREAKDOWN, BY SEX AND RESIDENCE

RESIDENCE	Percentage of children in the relevant age-group[a]									
	Economic activity only		School only		Combining school and economic activity		Neither in school nor in economic activity		Child labor[b]	
	Male	Female	Male	Female	Male	Female	Male	Female	Male	Female
Urban	18.4	21.9	28.7	25.5	28.6	28.1	24.2	24.5	n/av	n/av
Rural	42.6	52.4	7.6	6.3	26.9	17.5	22.9	23.8	n/av	n/av
Total	33.3	40.5	15.7	13.8	27.6	21.6	23.4	24.0	54.1	57.3

Source: Central African Republic, Multiple Indicator Cluster Survey 2, 2000 (see UCW Project Web site, http://www.ucw-project.org, country statistics).

Notes: [a]Children age 5 to 14. [b]Estimate includes (a) children under age 12 engaged in economic activities, (b) children age 12–14 engaged in excessive economic activities (more than 14 hours per week), and (c) children under age 15 engaged in excessive household chores (at least 28 hours per week). Estimate does not account for children engaged in hazardous work or other unconditional "worst forms" of child labor.

Chad

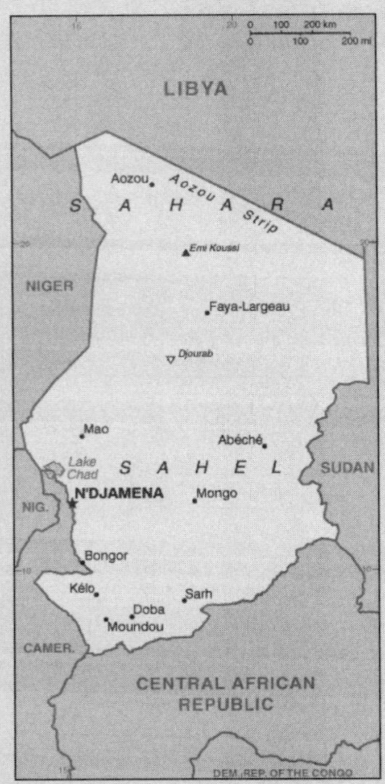

CHAD			
	CRC	C 138	C 182
Ratifications	Y	Y	Y
Human Development Index/Rank	0.368/171		
Human Capital			
Population Growth Rate	2.93%		
% Population 0–14	47.9%		
Total Fertility Rate	6.25		
Life Expectancy	47.52		
Infant Mortality Rate	91.45		
Literacy Rate	47.5%		
Economic			
GDP/Capita	$1,500		
GDP Growth %	7%		
% Poverty	80%		
Gini Index	—		
Labor Force Composition			
% Agriculture	80%		
% Industry and Services	20%		

CHILD ACTIVITY BREAKDOWN, BY SEX AND RESIDENCE

RESIDENCE	Percentage of children in the relevant age-group[a]									
	Economic activity only		School only		Combining school and economic activity		Neither in school nor in economic activity		Child labor[b]	
	Male	Female	Male	Female	Male	Female	Male	Female	Male	Female
Urban	11.2	13.0	44.0	38.4	23.6	18.0	21.1	30.6	n/av	n/av
Rural	37.6	42.1	12.2	11.7	28.4	16.1	22.1	30.1	n/av	n/av
Total	32.3	36.6	18.3	16.8	27.5	16.5	21.9	30.2	53.8	50.8

Source: Chad, Demographic and Health Survey, 2004 (see UCW Project Web site, http://www.ucw-project.org, country statistics).

Notes: [a]Children age 6 to 14 [b]Estimate includes (a) children under age 12 engaged in economic activities, (b) children age 12–14 engaged in excessive economic activities (more than 14 hours per week), and (c) children under age 15 engaged in excessive household chores (at least 28 hours per week). Estimate does not account for children engaged in hazardous work or other unconditional "worst forms" of child labor.

SECTION 4.
EASTERN AFRICA

Burundi

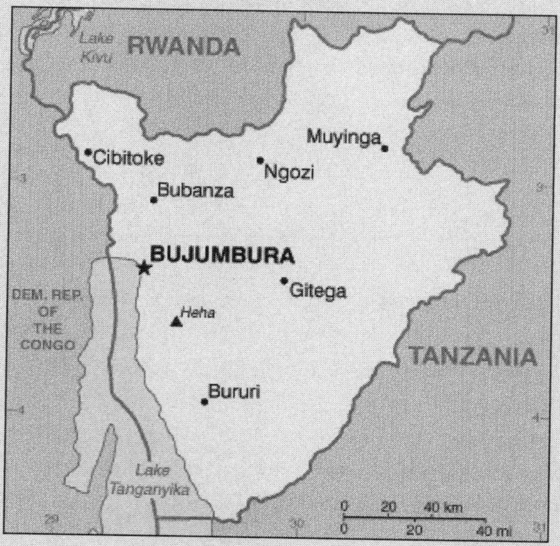

BURUNDI			
	CRC	C 138	C 182
Ratifications	Y	Y	Y
Human Development Index/Rank	0.384/169		
Human Capital			
Population Growth Rate	3.7%		
% Population 0–14	46.3%		
Total Fertility Rate	6.55		
Life Expectancy	50.81		
Infant Mortality Rate	63.13		
Literacy Rate	51.6%		
Economic			
GDP/Capita	$700		
GDP Growth %	5%		
% Poverty	68%		
Gini Index	33.3		
Labor Force Composition			
% Agriculture	93.6%		
% Industry	2.3%		
% Services	4.1%		

CHILD ACTIVITY BREAKDOWN, BY SEX AND RESIDENCE

RESIDENCE	Percentage of children in the relevant age-group[a]									
	Economic activity only		School only		Combining school and economic activity		Neither in school nor in economic activity		Child labor[b]	
	Male	Female	Male	Female	Male	Female	Male	Female	Male	Female
Urban	8.0	5.3	54.2	59.9	11.3	6.8	26.4	28.0	n/av	n/av
Rural	16.0	17.1	25.2	25.3	17.1	14.1	41.7	43.5	n/av	n/av
Total	15.4	16.4	27.2	27.4	16.7	13.6	40.6	42.5	25.9	23.6

Source: Burundi, Multiple Indicator Cluster Survey 2, 2000 (see UCW Project Web site, http://www.ucw-project.org, country statistics).

Notes: [a]Children age 5 to 14. [b]Estimate includes (a) children under age 12 engaged in economic activities, (b) children age 12–14 engaged in excessive economic activities (more than 14 hours per week), and (c) children under age 15 engaged in excessive household chores (at least 28 hours per week). Estimate does not account for children engaged in hazardous work or other unconditional "worst forms" of child labor.

Ethiopia

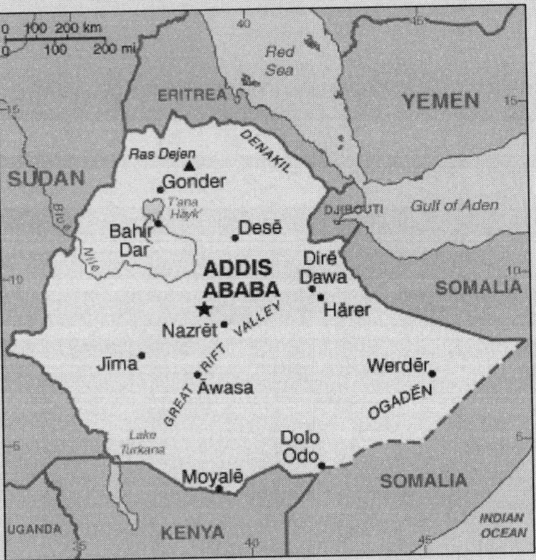

ETHIOPIA	CRC	C 138	C 182
Ratifications	Y	Y	Y
Human Development Index/Rank	0.371/170		
Human Capital			
Population Growth Rate	2.31%		
% Population 0–14	43.7%		
Total Fertility Rate	5.22		
Life Expectancy	49.03		
Infant Mortality Rate	93.62		
Literacy Rate	42.7%		
Economic			
GDP/Capita	$1,000		
GDP Growth %	9.6%		
% Poverty	38.7%		
Gini Index	30		
Labor Force Composition			
% Agriculture	80%		
% Industry	8%		
% Services	12%		

CHILD ACTIVITY BREAKDOWN, BY SEX AND RESIDENCE

RESIDENCE	Percentage of children in the relevant age-group[a]									
	Economic activity only		School only		Combining school and economic activity		Neither in school nor in economic activity		Child labor[b]	
	Male	Female	Male	Female	Male	Female	Male	Female	Male	Female
Urban	3.1	3.1	60.0	60.0	9.8	6.8	27.1	30.1	n/av	n/av
Rural	46.4	35.0	7.9	10.7	17.6	11.3	28.1	43.0	n/av	n/av
Total	41.4	30.9	13.9	17.1	16.7	10.7	28.0	41.3	58.9	45.8

Source: Ethiopia, National Labour Force Survey, 2005 (see UCW Project Web site, http://www.ucw-project.org, country statistics).

Notes: [a]Children age 5 to 14. [b]Estimate includes (a) children under age 12 engaged in economic activities, (b) children age 12–14 engaged in excessive economic activities (more than 14 hours per week), and (c) children under age 15 engaged in excessive household chores (at least 28 hours per week). Estimate does not account for children engaged in hazardous work or other unconditional "worst forms" of child labor.

Child Labor in Ethiopia: Overview and Policy Challenges

Tassew Woldehanna, Assistant Professor, Department of Economics, Addis Ababa University; and **Nicola Jones,** Program Leader, Research and Policy in Development, Overseas Development Institute, UK

According to the 2001 Ethiopian Central Statistics Authority's (CSA 2002) national child labor survey, 52 percent of all Ethiopian children are involved in some form of productive or household work, spending on average thirty-three hours per week on work activities. Despite these disturbing figures, a content analysis of Ethiopia's first- and second-generation Poverty Reduction Strategy Papers reveals that child labor is not referred to as a significant social problem (Jones et al. 2005; Heidel 2004).

The 2001 CSA child labor survey has provided nationally representative data on the distribution of child labor in rural and urban areas as well as by age category (Table 1). The report estimates that approximately 52 percent and 78 percent of children were engaged in productive and housekeeping activities, respectively. Girls engaged more in housekeeping activities while boys are involved in productive activities. The participation rate in productive activities was 62 percent for boys and 42 percent for girls. For housekeeping activities, this figure was 22 percent for boys and 44 percent for girls. In rural areas, children are more frequently engaged in productive activities than in housekeeping activities, whereas in urban areas children are more involved in housekeeping activities than in productive activities.

The average working hours of children involved in productive activities are thirty-three hours per week. One-third of children involved in productive activities work more than forty hours per week. This intensity of work is higher for boys (thirty-six hours) than for girls (thirty-three hours) in rural areas, whereas in urban areas it is higher for girls (thirty-one hours) than for boys (twenty-eight hours). The survey also revealed that 35.6 percent of children involved in domestic activities work for three to four hours per day.

Of the working children, about 88 percent are involved in elementary occupations, namely, street vending, shoe shining, messenger service, elementary agriculture, mining, construction, manufacturing, and transport. The participation rate of five- to nine-year-old children in elementary occupations is higher than that of ten- to fourteen-year-old and fifteen- to seventeen-year-old children, indicating that younger children are more likely to be involved in low-paying activities. The participation rate of working girls in elementary occupations is slightly lower than that of working boys in both rural and urban areas. Service-provider employees, combined with shop and market staff, account for approximately 26 percent of urban working children, with girls (28 percent) participating more than boys (23 percent).

Children's involvement in work is a major obstacle to children's school attendance. The 2004 CSA Welfare Monitoring Survey indicated that children's involvement in paid and unpaid productive and domestic activities constituted the most important reason for children's dropouts from primary and secondary school. According to the CSA child labor survey report (CSA 2002), of the children attending school, only 3.9 percent are not involved in any household and productive activities. Some 61.9 percent are involved in both sets of activities, while a further 17.8 percent and 16.4 percent are involved

Table 1

Distribution of Working Status of Children Age 5–17 In 2001 (In Percent)

	Housekeeping activities only	Productive activities only	Housekeeping and productive activities	Not working	Total
National					
Total	33.3	7.4	44.7	14.6	100
Male	22.8	11.7	50.3	15.2	100
Female	44.3	2.9	39.0	13.8	100
Urban					
Total	59.1	4.5	14.3	22.1	100
Male	53.0	4.0	15.8	27.2	100
Female	64.5	4.9	12.9	17.7	100
Rural					
Total	29.4	7.8	49.4	13.4	100
Male	18.6	12.8	55.1	13.5	100
Female	40.9	2.5	43.4	13.2	100
By Age					
5–9	35.3	6.0	32.9	25.8	100
10–14	32.9	7.6	54.8	4.7	100
15–17	28.6	10.7	56.8	3.9	100

Source: CSA (2002).

in productive activities and housekeeping activities, respectively. Throughout Ethiopia, 39 percent start working at age five. The proportion of children who started working at the age of five is higher for rural children (41 percent) than for urban children (22 percent). The reason why rural children start working at an earlier age is due to children assisting parents in farm activities and herding livestock.

Children's involvement in productive and household activities does affect their schooling. Children may be late or absent for class, or they may spend less time studying and doing homework. Among children who were attending school and involved in work, about 39 percent responded that their work had affected their schooling. This figure is 29 percent for urban children and 42 percent for rural children. There is no significant difference between male (39 percent) and female (38 percent) children in this regard. Given the substantial gender differences, with girls engaged in housekeeping activities and boys engaged in productive activities, we can assume that the negative effect on schooling is similar for both productive and housekeeping activities.

Surprisingly, child labor is positively correlated with parents' wealth. Participation of children in economic activity increases with increasing wealth, reaching its maximum at Br100–300 per month and declining thereafter. These results are especially remarkable when this relationship is decomposed into rural and urban areas. In urban areas, participation in economic activity declines as the household's level of wealth increases. In a nutshell, the result for urban areas indicates that child labor is the result of poverty, as expected. But the trend is the reverse for rural areas: There is a positive relationship between the level of wealth and the participation rate in economic activity (child labor), indicating the kind of wealth paradox that has been observed in Pakistan and Ghana (Bhalotra and Heady 2003).

Key Reasons for Children's Involvement in Work

Understanding why children work is complex, as multiple interlinked child-, household-, and community-level factors are at play. In addition, cultural understandings of childhood and children's roles in the family play a critical role. With more than 80 percent of the Ethiopian population involved in subsistence agriculture, and 39 percent living below the national poverty line, it is perhaps not surprising that children are routinely expected to contribute to the household. As one respondent of the Young Lives Project noted, "In the village no one eats without working. There is always something to be done by children as early as 3 years of age and sometimes even at the age of 2. If a boy is above 3, tending sheep and cattle is his job. Girls of the same age help in household chores such as making coffee and gathering firewood."

Herding in Yabello, Ethiopia, 2006. *(Photo by Heike Roschanski courtesy of IREWOC Foundation)*

Child-Level Factors

Although the literature has paid greater attention to boys' labor contributions (Cockburn 2001), in Ethiopia child labor is widespread among all children—boys and girls, urban and rural residents. Children's own agency also plays a role in their decisions to work. While interviews with children underscore the time and energy commitment involved in daily work activities, a number emphasized that they felt a duty to help, even at the cost of their education, given their family's poverty status.

Household-Level Factors

Household factors are especially important determinants of child labor. Factors such as wealth or poverty, family assets, parental education, and family social capital shape decisions regarding children's time use in important ways. Although family poverty is frequently linked with child labor, research suggests that the relationship is more complex and, in Ethiopia (mainly in rural areas), follows an inverted U-curve pattern after controlling for other factors. That is, an initial increase in wealth raised the likelihood that children combined schooling and work (e.g., helping to tend more livestock or assisting in petty businesses), but that work activity declined after peaking at a certain level of wealth (Woldehanna et al. 2005).

Ownership of productive assets such as land and livestock is linked to children's involvement in work. Greater asset holdings may allow households to forgo the income child work brings, but absent perfect labor markets, land and livestock ownership can also have the opposite effect on child schooling and child labor, which is the more likely case in Ethiopia. Owners of larger land plots and more livestock who are not able to hire labor often use their children's labor instead of sending them to school. This was found to be particularly prevalent in northern Ethiopia, where ownership of animals is traditionally viewed as a status symbol in addition to its economic value. Although land ownership often necessitates child involvement in labor activities, it also provides greater economic security than that enjoyed by families compelled to rent or sell their land due to natural disasters and financial strains. Such families are often forced to migrate in search of low-paying off-farm work, or to send their children to work on construction sites or to sell food in the vicinity of places selling alcohol (simultaneously increasing the risk of sexual harassment, abuse, and exploitation), or to allow their children, particularly their daughters, to be trafficked to Arab countries.

If households do not have access to credit, evidence suggests that they will rely on their children's labor. An interesting implication is that relieving household liquidity problems may reduce child labor and increase child schooling. However, it is also important to point out that because credit is commonly given to families to purchase additional livestock, the impact on children can be negative, as it puts additional pressure on them to be involved in herding activities.

The likelihood of children, especially boys, being involved in work is closely linked to area-wide and idiosyncratic economic shocks that affect households. In times of crisis, such as drought or the death of the breadwinner, households rely on their children to supplement household income. In some cases, particularly in northern Ethiopia, children often substituted for their parents in food-for-work programs, for which the household received payment in grain, oil, or cash. Similarly, in the coffee-producing areas of Jimma and Awassa, a number of respondents emphasized the problem of school dropouts and rising child labor rates when coffee prices fell in the late 1990s.

Parental education levels impact children's involvement in labor activities: The father's education tends to be correlated with less child labor, whereas, somewhat surprisingly, children with better-educated mothers (in both male- and female-headed households) were more likely to be engaged in work. One possible explanation could be that better-educated women are more likely to be involved in paid activities outside the house and, thus, in the absence of widely available child-care facilities, need to rely on their children to help manage the execution of their domestic and caring responsibilities. It should also be noted that parental commitment to education should not be underestimated. Many uneducated parents are eager for their children to receive an education so that they will have better life opportunities than themselves.

Social capital—formal and informal relationships within the community—may help improve child schooling and reduce children's engagement in labor activities through the following channels: communication and the reduction of information asymmetries; raising awareness about the importance of schooling and problems associated with child labor; and its complementary effect on governmental efforts to increase educational access and encourage enrollment. Recent research suggests that Ethiopian mothers' involvement in community groups was associated with lower child labor levels, suggesting that group membership may play a facilitating role in promoting the value of children's education. By contrast, research suggests a link between the number of organizations from which a household receives social support and higher rates of child labor. One plausible explanation is because social support is commonly provided in the form of food-for-work programs. These programs typically involve children working alongside their parents to complete, for example, construction or terracing work, increasing the likelihood that children combine work and education (Woldehanna et al. 2005).

Community-Level Factors

Proximity to school is a significant factor in shaping household decisions about children's time use. As distance to school increases, children tend to choose schooling or labor only, whereas when schools are closer to children's homes, they are more likely to combine both education and work activities. One important advantage of closer schools is linked to cost savings. Not only do parents spend less on transportation, but they also avoid costs of accommodation and food for children who live outside the family home during the week to attend school. The positive association between schooling and school availability is particularly strong for girls, as parents had been reluctant to send their daughters to distant schools (particularly in rural areas) primarily because of safety concerns. Sexual assault and marriage abduction, leading to a loss of family honor, represent serious fears for many Ethiopian parents.

Policy Challenges

In order to tackle the widespread problem of child labor in Ethiopia, due consideration to the intra-household allocation of resources and responsibilities is urgently needed national poverty-reduction strategies are developed.

Child-Targeted Policies

One possible solution for offsetting education costs incurred by parents is cash transfers to promote child schooling in higher grades rather than food-for-work programs, which typically involve children in work. Developing employment training programs for secondary school students that would enhance future job and income prospects could also provide incentives to continue to invest in education. Similarly, in order to support girls' education, and to reduce their work and caring burden, existing affirmative action programs for girls involving extra tuition and local government employment quotas need to be scaled up.

Household-Targeted Policies

The negative income effects of reducing child labor and increasing child schooling could be offset if credit measures enabled the poor to substitute hired labor for child labor. In addition, long-term credit programs targeted specifically at covering educational expenses could be implemented if cash transfers are either unavailable or insufficient.

Labor-saving policy improvements should focus on modernizing farming and household technologies to reduce children's, especially girls', substitution in such work. This could include improved access to water, increased usage of herbicides to reduce demand for weeding, introducing modern stoves that reduce the need for time-consuming fuel-wood collection, and introducing simple farm technology such as better plows. Rationalizing livestock-raising practices would reduce the involvement of children. Options include indoor livestock farming, community-shared livestock herding where households pool resources to care for livestock, as well as community-level, rather than household-level, fodder production.

Implementation of subsidized community child-care arrangements or preschool services could relieve older children of substituting for their mothers' care work. While such services have been included in the second phase of the national poverty-reduction strategy, initial research suggests that coverage is still very limited (Dercon et al. 2005).

Community-Level Policies

Recent governmental efforts to mobilize communities to tackle low school enrollment and dropout rates have had a positive influence on community attitudes toward education. In particular, efforts by the government-affiliated women's associations to enforce the child marriage ban have been remarkable.

Development of fuel-saving mechanisms and alternative energy sources not only would alleviate pressures on children but also would also protect the environment, as Ethiopia is facing widespread deforestation and soil erosion. Other infrastructure improvements that would reduce children's work burdens include reducing the distance to water sources by constructing wells and piped water sources in all villages, and developing better public transport systems to reduce children's involvement in taking pack animals to market. Better transport would also reduce the amount of time caregivers involved in petty trade need to be away from home.

School-Targeted Policies

Because of the importance of school proximity in encouraging greater education enrollment and less child work, improving school availability in rural areas constitutes an urgent policy imperative. Steps should also be taken to develop more flexible school schedules and curricula that allow rural children to be absent during peak times in the agriculture calendar, which is when many children, especially boys, drop out either temporarily or permanently. Children's need to earn money to support their education costs could be minimized by providing families with credit for education purposes. Safer alternative income-generating strategies for children in impoverished families who have to rely on child labor could be developed. This could include supervised, paid training or apprenticeships that contribute to reducing future poverty through marketable skills.

National Poverty-Reduction Policies

Given that children's involvement in labor activities is likely to remain a reality, in at least the short to medium term, in many poor communities, it is important that the annual implementation plans of Ethiopia's 2006–10 national poverty-reduction strategy (known as PASDEP) pay specific attention to child labor. One initiative currently being debated is the development of child labor guidelines to raise awareness about the potential negative effects of both paid and unpaid work. International best practices suggest that such guidelines need to be carefully designed to preclude children being compelled to take up more exploitative work as employers eliminate more easily regulated child labor opportunities. Such guidelines should also address the involvement of children in food-for-work schemes as substitutes for adult labor, and highlight the risks of promoting labor-intensive agricultural subsistence.

References and Further Reading

Bhalotra, Sonia, and Christopher Heady. "Child Farm Labour: The Wealth Paradox." *World Bank Economic Review* 17:2 (2003):197–227.

Central Statistical Authority (CSA). "Ethiopia Child Labor Survey 2001." *Statistical Bulletin 262.* Addis Ababa: CSA, 2002.

CSA. "Welfare Monitoring Survey 2004: Analytical Report." *Statistical Bulletin 339-A.* Addis Ababa: CSA, June 2004.

Cockburn, J. *Child Labour Versus Education: Poverty Constraint or Income Opportunity?* Oxford: Centre for the Study for African Economies (CSAE), Oxford University, 2001.

Dercon, Stefan, John Hoddinott, and Tassew Woldehanna. "Shocks and Consumption in 15 Ethiopian Villages, 1999–2004." *Journal of African Economies* 14:4 (2005): 559–85.

Heidel, K. *Poverty Reduction Strategy Papers: Blind to the Rights of the (Working) Child?* Duisburg: Werkstatt Okonomie, 2004.

Jones, Nicola, with Bekele Tefera, and Tassew Woldehanna. "Research, Policy Engagement and Practice: Reflections on Efforts to Mainstream Children into Ethiopia's Second National Poverty Reduction Strategy." Young Lives Working Paper 21. Young Lives Project, Save the Children UK, London, 2005.

Woldehanna, Tassew, Bekele Tefera, Nicola Jones, and Alebel Bayrau. "Child Labour, Gender Inequality and Rural/Urban Disparities: How Can Ethiopia's National Development Strategies Be Revised to Address Negative Spill-Over Impacts on Child Education and Well-Being?" Young Lives Working Paper 20. Young Lives Project, Save the Children UK, London, 2005.

Attending School, Learning, and Child Work in Ethiopia

Arjun Singh Bedi, Professor of Quantitative Economics, Institute of Social Studies, The Hague, Netherlands; and **Assefa Admassie,** Director, Ethiopian Economic Policy Research Institute, Addis Ababa, Ethiopia

Apart from the most egregious types of work, which no doubt harm a child, there may be a wide range of activities carried out by children, especially in rural areas, which may not harm their overall development. Before labeling all types of work as child labor it is important to identify the potentially different effects of various types of work activities that children perform. Although the highest incidence of child labor is found in sub-Saharan Africa, studies of child labor on the continent are limited and sketchy. This essay uses detailed data on time-use patterns of children to provide an idea of the links between child labor and education in rural Ethiopia. In particular, it is concerned with the effect of the number of hours and the type of work done by children on their school attendance and reading and writing ability.

Background Information

Ethiopia is the second-largest country in sub-Saharan Africa, with an estimated population of more than 60 million. It is one of the world's least developed nations, and agriculture is the mainstay of its economy (Admassie 2002). In terms of labor laws, a reading of the Ethiopian constitution and current legislative measures on child labor shows that Ethiopia follows international standards and gives consideration to the rights and the welfare of the child. However, these labor laws focus mainly on the manufacturing sector and disregard the rural economy. Ethiopian labor law does not make any reference to the problem of child labor in the agricultural sector, and it appears that agricultural and household employment are exempt from such laws. Thus, a majority of national economic activity falls outside the protection of the labor code, as it consists of small-scale and subsistence farming.

Data

The data used for this essay are drawn from the fifth round of a rural survey that was conducted during the 1999–2000 crop season in eighteen peasant associations. The survey sites are located in four major regional national states. These four regions include more than 90 percent of the country's population and account for a similar proportion of economic output. Data were collected from 1,680 households. Detailed information on the time-use patterns of all children in the age-group four to fifteen years in the seven days preceding the survey was collected. Household heads were asked to provide information on the hours spent by children on farming, child care, carrying out domestic chores, fetching wood or water, and herding. The survey yields a sample of 3,043 children between four and fifteen years of age on whom we have complete information.

Patterns of Work

The data allow construction of a detailed portrait of the work activities of children (Admassie and

Bedi 2008). About 75 percent of all children in rural Ethiopia participate in work activities. On average a child spends around four hours a day on work activities. There are no differences in participation rates or the mean number of total hours worked across genders. Children as young as four years of age have a 21 percent participation rate and work for about five hours a week. Work activities increase with age and show a concave pattern. By the age of eleven, work participation reaches a peak of 91 percent, and weekly hours of work reach a peak of about forty-one at the age of fourteen.

While total time spent on work activities does not differ by gender, a breakdown of work activities by five different types of work reveals considerable differences. Boys spend more than 50 percent of their total hours of work on herding and 10–15 percent of their time on activities such as farm work, fetching water or wood, and other domestic tasks. Girls, as may be expected, spend considerable time on domestic tasks (about 33 percent of their total work time) followed by around 23–24 percent of their time on fetching wood or water and herding, respectively.

Schooling and Learning

School participation rates, at about 44 percent, are quite low. There are clear differences across gender, with 47 percent of boys attending while the corresponding figure is 41 percent for girls. Gender differences in the probability of attending school emerge between the ages of nine and ten and remain steady at about 7–10 percentage points until children reach the age of fifteen. Patterns in children's reading and writing ability are very similar to the patterns of school participation. About 40 percent of children are able to read and write. While 43 percent of boys are able to read and write, the corresponding figure for girls is about 36 percent. There is a gap (4 percent) between school participation and the ability to read and write, which implies that not all those who attend school acquire the ability to read and write. Apart from this gap, the age-specific patterns are similar, suggesting that school attendance and reading and writing ability may be treated synonymously.

Figure 1 Probability of Attending School Conditioned on Hours of Work (per week)

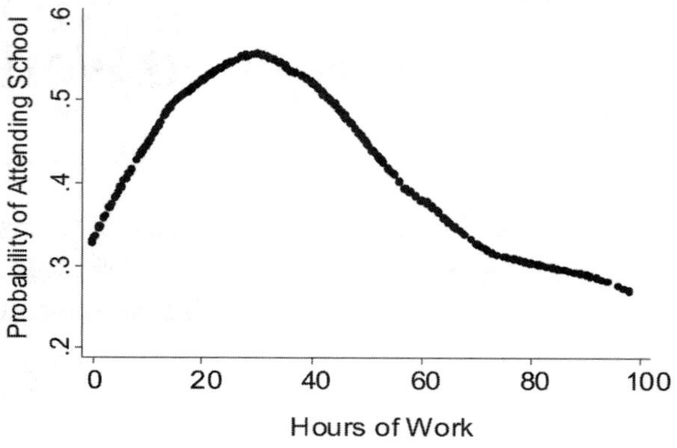

Work Participation, Schooling, and Learning

Figure 1 is a graphic exploration of the relationship between school attendance and hours of work, presenting estimates of the probability of attending school conditioned on the total number of hours of work per week. The figure shows that there is a nonlinear relationship between the probability of attending school and hours of work. Until about thirty hours of work, school participation and working are positively related, but beyond that peak there is a negative relationship between the two variables. The same pattern prevails for the probability that a child can read and write. These patterns suggest that it is only beyond a certain number of hours of work that the labor contribution of children begins to hinder school attendance.

A formal statistical analysis supports the pattern displayed in Figure 1. There is a clear nonlinear relationship between hours of work and school attendance. Initially, there is a positive relationship between hours of work and school attendance. Gradually, this positive effect declines, and, beyond a certain threshold, additional work effort is associated with declining school participation and learning. According to our estimates, the inflection point occurs between sixteen and twenty-two hours of work for reading and writing ability and between twenty-four and thirty-one hours of work for school attendance. The nonlinear relationship and different thresholds suggest that work effort of about two hours a day does not interfere with school or the formal human capital development of a child. Beyond this threshold, between a daily workload of two to three hours a day, the school performance of a child may be expected to suffer. A workload of more than three hours a day may be expected to hinder school performance and school attendance.

Estimates of the relationship between school attendance and various types of work activity show some clear-cut patterns. The clearest effect is that herding activities and school attendance are unequivocally incompatible. There is a negative and approximately linear relationship between hours of work spent on herding and schooling. The effect of farm work is nonlinear, similar to the overall effect of hours of work. Up to a certain threshold, there is a positive relationship, which gradually becomes negative. This effect is far clearer for boys than for girls. For the total sample, the effect of child-care work activities on school attendance is negative. Once again, the effect is pronounced for boys and not very clear for girls. For other types of work activities, effects on schooling are not very distinct. Domestic work and schooling appear to be uncorrelated, while there appears to be a positive link between schooling and fetching wood and water.

While the effect of different types of work requires more careful scrutiny, what is clear is that with 60 percent of children working more than sixteen hours per week, the formal human capital development of a majority of Ethiopian children is hindered.

References and Further Reading

Admassie, Assefa. "Allocation of Children's Time Endowment Between Schooling and Work in Rural Ethiopia." Discussion Papers on Development Policy 44, University of Bonn, Center for Development Research, 2002. http://www.zef.de/fileadmin/webfiles/downloads/zef_dp/ZEF-DP44.PDF.

Admassie, Assefa, and Arjun Bedi. "Attending School, Reading, Writing and Child Work in Rural Ethiopia." In *Economic Reforms in Developing Countries: Reach, Range, Reason*, ed. J. Fanelli and L. Squire, 185–225. Cheltenham, UK: Edward Elgar, 2008.

Cockburn, John. "Income Contributions of Child Work in Rural Ethiopia." Working paper 117, University of Laval, Quebec, 2001. http://www.crefa.ecn.ulaval.ca/cahier/0117.pdf.

Kenya

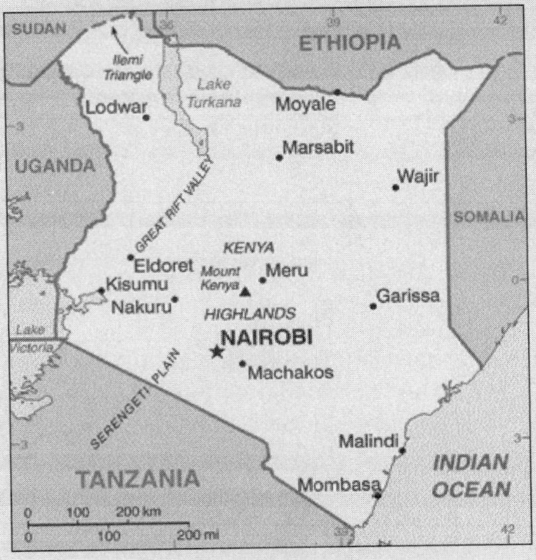

KENYA			
	CRC	C 138	C 182
Ratifications	Y	Y	Y
Human Development Index/Rank	0.491/152		
Human Capital			
Population Growth Rate	2.57%		
% Population 0–14	42.6%		
Total Fertility Rate	4.91		
Life Expectancy	48.93		
Infant Mortality Rate	59.26		
Literacy Rate	85.1%		
Economic			
GDP/Capita	$1,200		
GDP Growth %	5.5%		
% Poverty	50%		
Gini Index	44.5		
Labor Force Composition			
% Agriculture	75%		
% Industry and Services	25%		

CHILD ACTIVITY BREAKDOWN, BY SEX AND RESIDENCE

RESIDENCE	Percentage of children in the relevant age-group[a]									
	Economic activity only		School only		Combining school and economic activity		Neither in school nor in economic activity		Child labor[b]	
	Male	Female	Male	Female	Male	Female	Male	Female	Male	Female
Urban	0.9	2.8	76.9	78.2	4.2	3.8	18.0	15.3	n/av	n/av
Rural	6.4	5.9	46.1	51.6	37.2	32.1	10.2	10.4	n/av	n/av
Total	5.5	5.4	51.3	56.0	31.7	27.5	11.5	11.2	27.3	26.3

Source: Kenya, Multiple Indicator Cluster Survey 2, 2000 (see UCW Project Web site, http://www.ucw-project.org, country statistics).

Notes: [a]Children age 6 to 14. [b]Estimate includes (a) children under age 12 engaged in economic activities, (b) children age 12–14 engaged in excessive economic activities (more than 14 hours per week), and (c) children under age 15 engaged in excessive household chores (at least 28 hours per week). Estimate does not account for children engaged in hazardous work or other unconditional "worst forms" of child labor.

Child Labor in Kenya

Janet Wamsley, Researcher, Economics and Contracts Department,
International Brotherhood of Teamsters

The nation of Kenya is located in East Africa. It is bordered by Ethiopia to the north, Somalia and the Indian Ocean to the east, Tanzania to the south, and Uganda and the Sudan to the west. Its geographic area is 224,080 square miles, which is approximately the size of the state of Texas. Kenya has a population of 36.9 million and a gross domestic product of US$455 per capita. The Kenyan population is very young. Life expectancy at birth is 55.3 years. Of the 37.9 million people, 15.5 million are under fifteen years of age. The majority, 23.1 million people, live in rural areas, and the remaining 14.8 million live in urban areas.

In 2000, it was estimated that 83.2 percent of Kenyan children six to fourteen years of age attended school, though 29.6 percent were working while attending school, 5.4 percent worked but did not attend school, and 11.4 percent neither worked nor attended school. When broken down by gender, approximately the same proportions of boys and girls attend school, but boys are somewhat more likely to combine school and work activity: 31.7 percent of males and 27.5 percent of females combined school and work. The breakdown by residence indicates that rural children are more likely to work than urban children, even though they attend school at approximately the same rates: 34.7 percent of rural children combine work and school, compared to only 4 percent of urban children who combine the two activities. Further, 6.2 percent of rural children were engaged in economic activity without attending school, compared with only 1.8 percent of urban children. However, urban children were more likely to be idle, neither working nor attending school, than rural children (16.7 percent and 10.3 percent, respectively).

The overwhelming majority, 82.6 percent, of working children were involved in agricultural work. Approximately 76 percent of girls who worked were involved in agricultural work, with 10 percent in health and social work, and approximately 10 percent in domestic work. Some 87.2 percent of boys were involved in agricultural work, with boys also involved in mining, fishing, manufacturing, and construction. Most working children, 86 percent, were unpaid family workers, with only 12 percent working as paid employees. Other work done by children includes quarrying soapstone, mining sand throughout the country, and mining gold in western Kenya.

Of children working in agriculture, approximately 34 percent were working in commercial agriculture settings, such as rice, coffee, and sugar plantations, as well as smaller-scale farming operations of sisal, tea, corn, wheat, and pineapples. During peak seasons, children make up nearly half of the workforce on sugar estates, and between 50 and 60 percent of the workforce on coffee plantations. The remaining 23.6 percent of children in agricultural activity work in subsistence agriculture, laboring to produce food for their families or communities.

Many girls, some as young as ten years of age, participate in domestic work outside their own households. They often receive little or no pay, and isolation from their families can lead to psychological, sexual, or physical abuse. In urban areas, children also wash cars, sell goods on the street, and collect and sell waste materials for money. Some children in Kenya are involved in some of the worst forms of child labor. Reliable data is difficult to gather due to the illegal nature of the use of children in prostitution, pornography, the drug trade, and trafficking. But street children may be involved in these illegal trades in order to survive.

Children in Kenya work for a variety of reasons. Nearly 73 percent of working children contribute at least 20 percent of the family's total income. In cases where parents are AIDS victims, children sometimes work while grandparents raise the family. If grandparents or other relatives are not available, children may move into the streets, or older children may act as heads of households to support younger siblings.

Kenya is committed to eliminating child labor. The Employment Act of 1976 prohibits employment of children—defined as individuals who are under sixteen years of age—in any "industrial undertaking," including mines or quarries, factories, construction sites, or transportation of passengers or goods. Permitted activities for children include agricultural work—the type of work reported for the majority of working children—and work in family businesses. Rules for employing children, established under the act, outline procedures for employing children, specify hours of work, and detail record-keeping requirements for employers. The law also provides for fines and other penalties for breaking the rules. The rules apply to all instances of child labor other than apprenticeships. Wages of apprentices, indentured learners, and children under the age of eighteen are governed by the Regulations of Wages and Conditions of Employment Act. As a result of amendments to the labor statutes in 1990, the Ministry of Labor's health and safety inspectors may issue citations to employers for practices or activities that involve risk of serious personal injuries. The number of factory inspections has increased significantly since 1992.

Kenya has also ratified the key international conventions concerning child labor. ILO Convention 138 on the minimum age for employment was ratified on April 9, 1979, and ILO Convention 182 on the worst forms of child labor was ratified on May 7, 2001. Convention 138 sets the age of twelve as appropriate for light work that does not interfere with a child's education, but specifies eighteen as the minimum age for hazardous work. Convention 182 defines the worst forms of child labor and was intended to make elimination of the worst forms a matter of urgency, while keeping the long-term goal of eliminating child labor altogether. These two conventions detail specific articles of the UN Convention on the Rights of the Child, which the UN General Assembly adopted in 1989, and which Kenya ratified in 1990.

The government of Kenya sees education as a means for both reducing poverty and eliminating child labor. Primary school tuition fees were eliminated in 1982, and the government set a goal of universal primary school education by 2015. Policy makers in Kenya concluded that replacing child labor with education will provide social and personal benefits that cannot be measured in economic terms. In addition, the economic benefits of eliminating child labor will outweigh the costs of financing primary school education. Therefore, the government has concluded that this goal is clearly in the interest of the both the nation and its citizens.

References and Further Reading

Buchmann, Claudia. "Family Structure, Parental Perceptions, and Child Labor in Kenya: What Factors Determine Who Is Enrolled in School?" *Social Forces* 78:4 (2000): 1349–78.

IMF. *Kenya: Poverty Reduction Strategy Annual Progress Report—2003/2004.* IMF Country Report 07/158. Washington, DC: International Monetary Fund, 2007.

Kulundo Manda, Damiano, Paul Kieti Kimalu, Nancy N. Nafula, Diana Njeri Kimani, Robert K. Nyaga, John Mutwii Mutua, Germano Mwabu, and Mwangi S. Kumenyi. *Costs and Benefits of Eliminating Child Labor in Kenya.* Geneva: ILO-IPEC and Kenya Institute for Public Policy Research and Analysis, 2005.

Suda, Collette A. "The Invisible Child Worker in Kenya: The Intersection of Poverty, Legislation and Culture." *Nordic Journal of African Studies* 10:2 (2001): 163–75.

U.S. Department of Labor. "Kenya." In *The Department of Labor's 2006 Findings on the Worst Forms of Child Labor*, 268–72. Washington, DC: Department of Labor, Bureau of International Labor Affairs, 2007.

U.S. Department of Labor. "Kenya." In *Advancing the Campaign Against Child Labor: Efforts at the Country Level*, 143–50. Washington, DC: Department of Labor, Bureau of International Labor Affairs, 2002.

Children and Forced Labor in Colonial Kenya

Opolot Okia, Assistant Professor of History, Winthrop University

In Kenya, the historical roots of child labor originate in the political and economic needs of the colonial state, and the demands of settler accumulation. Kenya was colonized by the British from 1895 to 1963. In 1903 European settlers were encouraged to settle in Kenya to help stimulate the export sector. Many of the settlers who moved to Kenya were poorly capitalized and required state intervention to procure cheap African labor to work on their plantations and farms. As a result, Africans began engaging in migratory labor patterns that influenced the development of child labor.

To stimulate Africans into the labor market, the state instituted hut and poll taxes that had to be paid in cash. To meet tax requirements or for their own personal needs, many Africans were driven into wage employment. The development of tea, coffee, pyrethrum, and sisal plantations by European settlers stimulated a demand for African labor.

Initially, children would accompany parents to help them work on plantations, or they would sometimes be paid a small wage themselves. However, with the growth of the export sector after the 1930s, child labor became more systematic, particularly in agriculture. By the 1940s, when child labor peaked at about 20 percent of the workforce, child laborers were working more formally, either on thirty-day labor contracts, as daily casuals, on plantations, or as domestic servants. Most children were employed about four months out of the year. After the 1940s and up to independence in 1963, the incidence of child labor in agriculture declined, but this was counterbalanced by the rise in employment of children as house servants.

The work of children was governed by the Employment of Women, Young Persons and Children Ordinance, which was modeled on similar colonial legislation from Southern Rhodesia. Children as young as ten could be employed in contract work for light labor with parental consent. Children under twelve could not be employed in industrial labor, and children under fourteen could not be employed in mines or in hazardous work. After children entered into labor contracts, they came under the Masters and Servant Ordinance, governing employment of African laborers. Racist thinking also buttressed the institution of African child labor. European settlers believed that African children developed faster than European children and, hence, were performing labor more consistent with their biological status. This attitude encouraged light regulation of the labor of children.

The development of a forced labor regime in Kenya also fostered child labor. Not only were the colony's settlers impoverished, but the colonial state itself was also poor and required cheap African labor for the development of infrastructure. The state used different forms of forced labor with varying degrees of effect upon children. The Native Authority Ordinance of 1912 allowed colonial chiefs to call out forced labor for so-called communal purposes. According to the law, only able-bodied men were liable to be called out for up to six days a quarter, or twenty-four days a year, to work. Legally, the work was supposed to cover making or maintaining watercourses, footpaths, light bridges or dams, or other work constructed for the benefit of the local community. This work was deemed a traditional communal obligation and was supposed to be a continuation of traditional duties Africans would have owed to their chief or ruler in precolonial times. Communal forced labor was unpaid but, theoretically, performed in the interests of the local community. It was not intended for the construction of heavy bridges, large roads, and railroads, but that is exactly what it came to be used for.

Estimates of the number of people called out for communal labor range as high as 15,000 people per year. Forced labor affected mainly the Kikuyu, Luo, and Luyia peoples in the Central and Nyanza provinces. Central Province was located in the middle highland area of Kenya, whereas Nyanza Province was located in the Lake Victoria Basin in western Kenya. Although the Native Authority Ordinance, which governed forced labor, applied only to able-bodied men, children and young women were found in high numbers on communal road projects. Reasons for the coercion of child labor were varied. On the one hand, forced labor affected mainly poor households. Communal forced labor was highly exploitative and placed a heavy burden upon impoverished peasants. Wealthy peasants or salaried individuals could buy their way out of the labor requirement or were exempt. Consequently, the burden fell hardest upon poor households, which made more marginal members of the household vulnerable to coercion. In some cases, men would send their children or wives as substitutes.

The practices of migrant labor also influenced child coerced labor. In many locations, children were coerced as laborers because the population of able-bodied males was already working elsewhere for Europeans. The haphazard nature of labor recruitment also influenced the decision to use children. In some cases, the call for coerced labor came so abruptly that only children and young women were available for work. Manipulation of customary practice also played a role. Technically, it was illegal for children under the age of fourteen to be forced to work. However, it was deemed acceptable to allow children to work in place of their parents for the good of the community. Part of the reason for the pervasiveness of child labor on communal labor projects, then, was that it was seen by colonial authorities as a continuation of traditional duties.

Many children on communal forced-labor details were employed on tedious roadwork, which involved cutting grass or maintenance and helping with building camps. They could also be forced to work on sisal, tea, cotton, and coffee plantations. One of the problems with coerced juvenile labor was the increased opportunity for sexual abuse. Due to the distance of the work site from their home villages, when coerced child laborers were forced to stay away overnight, they were more vulnerable to sexual harassment from guards or overseers. In some cases young girls on forced-labor details were raped by tribal retainers or became pregnant after being coerced to work.

The incidence of child labor in Africa is high due to the impact of poverty. During the colonial period the conditions that fostered child labor were similar. The structures of the colonial economy created a demand for unskilled low-wage workers. The undercapitalized settler sector coupled with the demands of an impoverished state nourished an economic system that relied, in part, upon child labor.

References and Further Reading

Andvig, Jens C. "An Essay on Child Labor in Sub-Saharan Africa: A Bargaining Approach." NUPI Working Paper Series 613, Norwegian Institute of International Affairs, Oslo, 2000.

Clayton, Anthony, and Donald Savage. *Government and Labour in Kenya 1895–1963.* London. Frank Cass, 1974.

Dilley, Marjorie. *British Policy in Kenya Colony.* 2nd ed. New York: Barnes and Noble, 1966.

Federation of Kenya Employers. *Child Labour in Commercial Agriculture in Kenya.* Nairobi: Federation of Kenya Employers, 1996.

Okia, Opolot. "Forced Child Labor in Kenya, 1920–1930." Paper presented at Child Labour's Global Past, international conference of the International Institute of Social History, Amsterdam, November 15–17, 2006.

Onyango, Philista, and Diane Kayongo-Male. "Child Labour and Health." *Proceedings of the First National Workshop on Child Labour and Health.* Nairobi: Acme Press, 1983.

Oyuga, Benson Odera, Collette Suda, and Afia Mugambi. *A Study of Action Against Child Labour in Kenya.* Nairobi: ILO-IPEC, 1997.

Stichter, Sharon. *Migrant Labour in Kenya: Capitalism and African Response.* London: Longman, 1982.

Van Zwanenberg, R.M.A. *Colonial Capitalism and Labor in Kenya.* Nairobi: East African Literature Bureau, 1975.

Zeleza, Paul. "Labor Coercion and Migration. In *Forced Labor and Migration*, ed. Abebe Zageye and Shubi Shero. New York: Hans Zell Publishers, 1989.

Madagascar

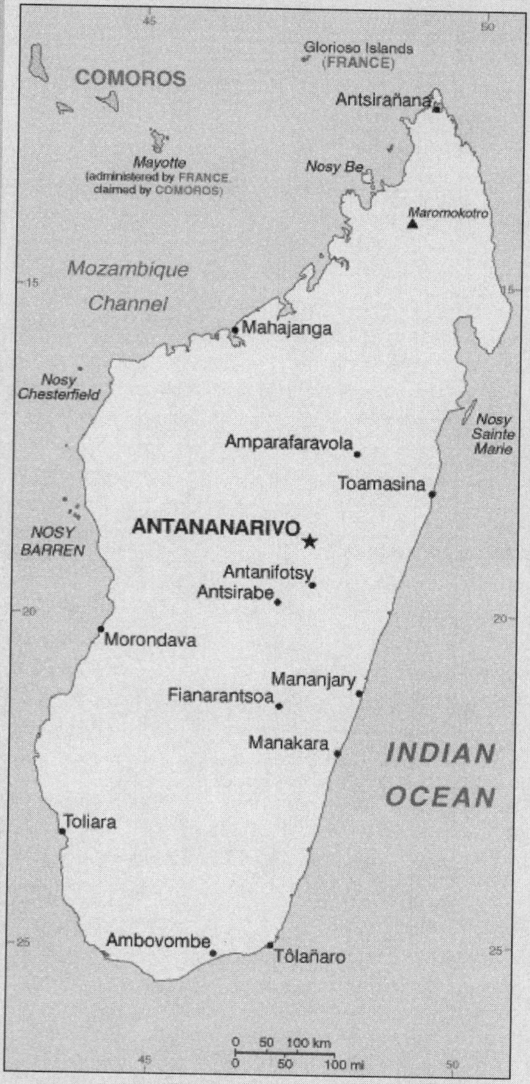

MADAGASCAR			
	CRC	C 138	C 182
Ratifications	Y	Y	Y
Human Development Index/Rank	0.509/143		
Human Capital			
Population Growth Rate	3.03%		
% Population 0–14	44.8%		
Total Fertility Rate	5.62		
Life Expectancy	57.34		
Infant Mortality Rate	75.21		
Literacy Rate	68.9%		
Economic			
GDP/Capita	$900		
GDP Growth %	5.5%		
% Poverty	50%		
Gini Index	47.5		
Labor Force Composition			
% Agriculture	26.9%		
% Industry	16.5%		
% Services	56.6%		

Malawi

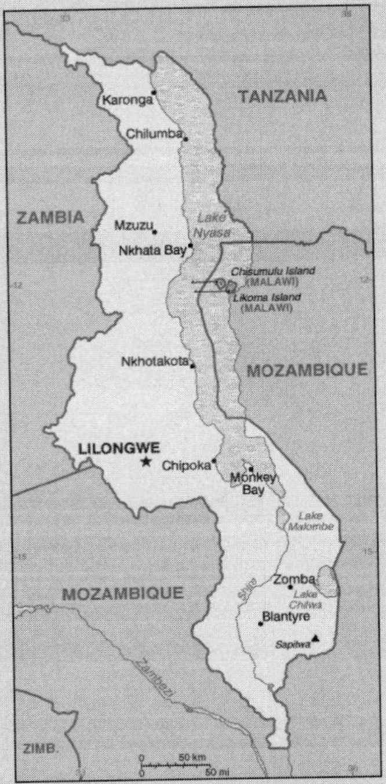

MALAWI			
	CRC	C 138	C 182
Ratifications	Y	Y	Y
Human Development Index/Rank	0.400/166		
Human Capital			
Population Growth Rate	2.38%		
% Population 0–14	46.5%		
Total Fertility Rate	5.92		
Life Expectancy	41.7		
Infant Mortality Rate	94.37		
Literacy Rate	62.7%		
Economic			
GDP/Capita	$600		
GDP Growth %	7%		
% Poverty	53%		
Gini Index	50.3		
Labor Force Composition			
% Agriculture	90%		
% Industry and Services	10%		

CHILD ACTIVITY BREAKDOWN, BY SEX AND RESIDENCE

RESIDENCE	Percentage of children in the relevant age-group[a]									
	Economic activity only		School only		Combining school and economic activity		Neither in school nor in economic activity		Child labor[b]	
	Male	Female	Male	Female	Male	Female	Male	Female	Male	Female
Urban	1.7	2.1	73.7	73.1	14.7	12.9	10.0	11.9	n/av	n/av
Rural	6.6	5.7	39.1	45.6	34.9	31.4	19.3	17.3	n/av	n/av
Total	5.9	5.2	44.2	49.5	32.0	28.8	17.9	16.5	24.5	23.1

Source: Malawi, Demographic and Health Survey 2004 (see UCW Project Web site, http://www.ucw-project.org, country statistics).

Notes: [a]Children age 5 to 14. [b]Estimate includes (a) children under age 12 engaged in economic activities, (b) children age 12–14 engaged in excessive economic activities (more than 14 hours per week), and (c) children under age 15 engaged in excessive household chores (at least 28 hours per week). Estimate does not account for children engaged in hazardous work or other unconditional "worst forms" of child labor.

Rwanda

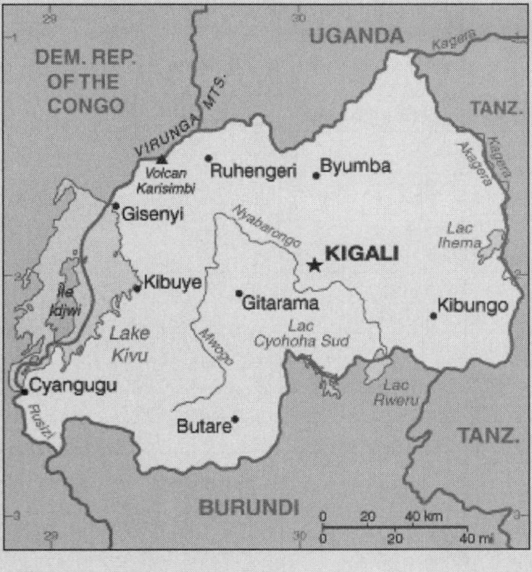

RWANDA			
	CRC	C 138	C 182
Ratifications	Y	Y	Y
Human Development Index/Rank	0.450/158		
Human Capital			
Population Growth Rate	2.77%		
% Population 0–14	41.9%		
Total Fertility Rate	5.37		
Life Expectancy	48.99		
Infant Mortality Rate	85.27		
Literacy Rate	70.4%		
Economic			
GDP/Capita	$1,600		
GDP Growth %	5.8%		
% Poverty	60%		
Gini Index	28.9		
Labor Force Composition			
% Agriculture	90%		
% Industry and Services	10%		

CHILD ACTIVITY BREAKDOWN, BY SEX AND RESIDENCE

RESIDENCE	Percentage of children in the relevant age-group[a]									
	Economic activity only		School only		Combining school and economic activity		Neither in school nor in economic activity		Child labor[b]	
	Male	Female	Male	Female	Male	Female	Male	Female	Male	Female
Urban	3.1	3.4	62.0	56.8	9.4	9.9	25.5	29.9	n/av	n/av
Rural	9.3	8.8	31.9	36.0	23.4	18.1	35.4	37.1	n/av	n/av
Total	8.5	8.1	35.7	38.7	21.6	17.0	34.2	36.1	34.5	33.9

Source: Rwanda, Multiple Indicator Cluster Survey 2, 2000 (see UCW Project Web site, http://www.ucw-project.org, country statistics).

Notes: [a]Children age 5 to 14. [b]Estimate includes (a) children under age 12 engaged in economic activities, (b) children age 12–14 engaged in excessive economic activities (more than 14 hours per week), and (c) children under age 15 engaged in excessive household chores (at least 28 hours per week). Estimate does not account for children engaged in hazardous work or other unconditional "worst forms" of child labor.

Tanzania

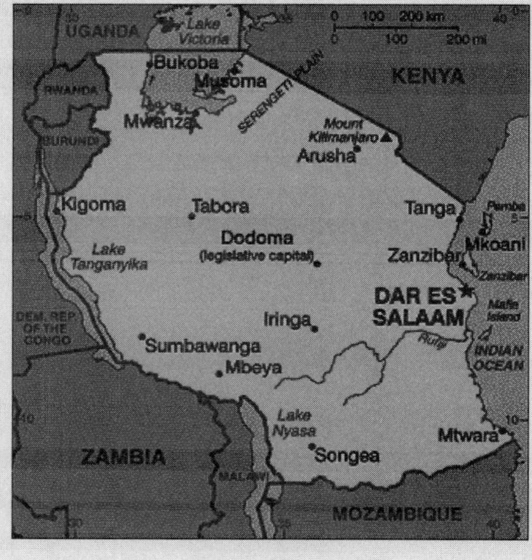

TANZANIA			
	CRC	C 138	C 182
Ratifications	Y	Y	Y
Human Development Index/Rank	0.430/162		
Human Capital			
Population Growth Rate	2.09%		
% Population 0–14	43.9%		
Total Fertility Rate	4.77		
Life Expectancy	50.71		
Infant Mortality Rate	71.69		
Literacy Rate	78.2%		
Economic			
GDP/Capita	$800		
GDP Growth %	5.8%		
% Poverty	36%		
Gini Index	38.2		
Labor Force Composition			
% Agriculture	80%		
% Industry and Services	20%		

CHILD ACTIVITY BREAKDOWN, BY SEX AND RESIDENCE

RESIDENCE	Percentage of children in the relevant age-group[a]									
	Economic activity only		School only		Combining school and economic activity		Neither in school nor in economic activity		Child labor[b]	
	Male	Female	Male	Female	Male	Female	Male	Female	Male	Female
Urban	3.8	2.5	61.9	64.8	8.5	10.9	25.8	21.8	n/av	n/av
Rural	20.3	17.4	29.1	32.1	21.8	22.7	28.7	27.8	n/av	n/av
Total	17.0	14.3	35.7	38.9	19.2	20.3	28.2	26.5	22.9	20.6

Source: United Republic of Tanzania, Integrated Labour Force and Child Labour Survey, 2000–2001 (see UCW Project Web site, http://www.ucw-project.org, country statistics).

Notes: [a]Children age 5 to 14. [b]Estimate includes (a) children under age 12 engaged in economic activities and (b) children age 12–14 engaged in excessive economic activities (more than 14 hours per week). Estimate does not account for children engaged in excessive household chores, hazardous work, or other unconditional "worst forms" of child labor.

Child Labor in Tanzania

Karen A. Porter, PhD, Associate Professor of Anthropology, Hanover College

Renowned for geographical, ecological, and cultural diversity and postcolonial stability, Tanzania is located in East Africa and bordered by the Indian Ocean, Mozambique, Malawi, Zambia, Democratic Republic of Congo, Burundi, Rwanda, Uganda, and Kenya. Coastal plains become inland plateaus from which highlands ascend in the north and in the south. Mount Kilimanjaro is the highest point in Africa, and Lakes Victoria, Tanganyika, and Nyasa shape the western border. Climate varies from tropical along the coast to temperate in the highlands.

Germany declared the area a protectorate in 1885. By 1919, Tanganyika was a United Kingdom League of Nations Mandate. Independence in 1961, followed by the union of the islands of Zanzibar and Pemba to Tanganyika in 1964, created the United Republic of Tanzania. The transition from a one-party state under the Chama Cha Mapinduzi to a multiparty state in 1995 was peaceful.

Tanzania is home to 35 million people and 127 ethnic groups, and like many other countries of the global South, 44 percent of its population is age fourteen or younger. The median age is 17.7 years. Males have a life expectancy at birth of forty-nine years, and women fifty-two. According to 2003 estimates, 8.8 percent of the population has HIV/AIDS, making Tanzania one of the nations hardest hit by this deadly disease.

Tanzania's majority population is African, with Asian, European, and Arab minorities. Thirty percent of the mainland population is Christian, 35 percent practice indigenous religions, and 35 percent is Muslim. On the coastal mainland and Indian Ocean islands, 97 percent of the population is Muslim. Arabic is widely spoken in Zanzibar, Kiswahili is the official language of Tanzania, and English is the language of commerce, administration, and higher education. According to the 2002 census, nearly 70 percent of the population age fifteen and older can read and write Kiswahili, English, or Arabic, though literate men outnumber literate women by approximately 15 percent.

Ranked one of the poorest and least developed countries in the world, Tanzania struggles, with 36 percent of its people below the poverty line. Though only 4.23 percent of Tanzania's land is arable, the economy is heavily agrarian. Agricultural products make up almost half of GDP and 85 percent of exports, and more than 80 percent of the workforce performs rural labor. Cash crops include cotton, coffee, cashews, pyrethrum, sisal, tea, tobacco, and ornamental flowers. Light manufacturing and agricultural processing also contribute to the economy, as do fisheries and, most significantly in recent years, gemstone and other mining operations.

Tanzania was food self-sufficient and exported surpluses until the late 1970s. But as an energy importer, it was devastated by the oil crisis, the collapse of commodity prices, drought, the breakup of the East African Community, and the Uganda war. Although Tanzania attempted to develop on its own terms since independence, using concepts and practices of African family-hood (*Ujamaa*), it changed directions in the mid-1980s to respond to regional and global pressures. By the mid-1990s, Tanzania accepted IMF and World Bank structural adjustment programs (SAPs). Tanzania privatized state-owned enterprises, removed staple-crop subsidies, rescheduled foreign debts, devalued currency, cut allocations to health, education, and other public sectors, drastically curtailed public service employment, and permitted goods to be imported from previously eschewed South Africa and Western countries. Supporters characterize the changes as economic advancement, evidenced by economic growth, a reduced rate of inflation, increased privatization, and substantially greater outputs of minerals, particularly gold. Critics note that life for the majority has gotten much harder, especially for children.

History of Child Labor

In hunting and gathering societies, such as the Sandawe and Hadzabe, children learn about the environment, survival skills, and key social networks, though few contribute to family or band food supply. In agricultural, pastoral, or mixed-economy societies such as the Bena, Maasai, and Pare, children also learn critical skills while adding significantly to food stores. Broadly speaking, socialization shaped by reverence and respect for authority, age, and hierarchy brings children into the adult world of work by age five. As they grow, children acquire additional responsibilities subject to gender, age, birth order, and the strengths and weaknesses of particular family and kin-group structures. Contributing to household economic sustenance builds pride and helps children secure social position and future security (Porter 1996). Children's work is widely accepted as part of childhood.

Child harvesting and drying coconut before taking it to market, October 2003, Tanzania. *(© International Labor Organization / M. Crozet)*

Eighty percent of the Tanzanian population works in the countryside in smallholder agriculture. Women are the principal farmers and grow food crops on plots averaging 0.9–3.0 hectares each, using hand hoes and other basic tools. Both boys and girls labor on family and kin-group farms. Children are responsible for other laborious and time-consuming tasks. Girls perform child care, food processing, cooking, cleaning, washing, and gathering water and wood for fuel. Indeed, female gender is the most predictable determinant of natural resource collection (Andvig et al. 2001). Boys' work is more episodic: herding or stall feeding cattle, clearing and preparing fields for cultivation, running errands, building, and other tasks.

In coastal zones and in Zanzibar, male children may beg because it instills humility and discipline while also enabling adults to give alms, one of the five pillars of Islam, as a way to worship. Children earn individual and household money by running errands and selling cooked food and other items for mothers and married adult women who live in seclusion.

Colonial Christian rule transformed children's work lives by demanding African labor on monocrop plantations dedicated to coffee, tea, and cotton production. When adult men migrated, subsistence production fell to women and children, dramatically increasing their work responsibilities. German missionaries recorded how children involved in plantation agriculture were paid much less than adults (Kimambo 1991). This pattern continued under the British, facilitating the expansion of the colonial economy (Rwegoshora 1997).

Child Labor in the Tanzanian Context Today

Like adults, children do not escape the cultural and social constraints of their environments. In Tanzania, 3.4 million out of 12.1 million children under age eighteen work regularly. Tanzania ratified ILO Convention 138 (on minimum age) in 1998 and Convention 182 (on worst forms of child labor) in 2001. Children under eighteen years are prohibited from working in hazardous conditions and may work in industries only between 6 A.M. and 6 P.M. Twelve- to fifteen-year-olds may be employed on a daily wage basis, but must have parental permission and return to their guardian's residence at night. Overall, formal employment opportunities are few in Tanzania, and most adults and children work in the informal sector, including rural agriculture, or the shadow economy, which is not regulated by the government.

There is a strong correlation between women's income and children's welfare (Fratkin and Smith 1995). Women and children's time-intensive labor as food producers and processors is unremunerated. One in three rural children work, compared to one in ten in urban settings. When both income-generating activities and household work are accounted for, rural people work longer hours than urbanites, women more than men, and girls at every age have heavier work burdens than boys, making their labor more central and less expendable to rural households. When thirteen- to fifteen-year-old boys are in school, the household loses twenty-five hours of work per week; for girls of the same age the figure is thirty-seven hours per week (Andvig et al. 2001).

Poverty is usually identified as the root cause of child labor. But poverty includes more than income earned; it includes "time," which contextualizes labor by recognizing how "the burden of competing claims on individuals' time lead[s], in many instances, to increased work intensity and to tradeoffs among various tasks. . . . The poor substitutability of labor allocation in non-market work" makes females *time poor*, and unable to pursue income-generating activities (Andvig et al. 2001, 16–17), even though national statistics suggest they are untapped labor. Time use is central to the relationship between poverty and child labor.

Children's time is shaped by structural factors that marginalize many families. For example, privatization required under SAPs compels families to pay for school uniforms, books, and supplies, making education prohibitively expensive. Many children then turn to early employment. Overall declining educational standards, the threat of HIV/AIDS and other infectious diseases, and ever-more numerous orphans and child-headed households exemplify the challenging context in which many Tanzanian children live.

Commercial Agriculture

The seasonal nature of agriculture creates both labor shortages and underemployment at different times of the year, underscoring the hardships faced by rural dwellers who seek cash to meet an ever-widening range of needs. Most child laborers work on commercial tea, coffee, sisal, sugar, cotton, tobacco, pyrethrum, and flower plantations, and while they constitute one-third of the labor force, they are paid half the adult wage.

Sisal and tobacco work are especially hazardous, but overall, children in rural work tend to have protection and support from family members. In Zanzibar, boys fish, process fish, deep-sea dive, and farm seaweed to earn money. These often dangerous activities are categorized by the ILO as hazardous child labor. There are far fewer employment opportunities in rural areas than urban areas, and children find themselves drawn to cities and towns with hopes for the future that are seldom realized.

Urban Labor

The urban population in Tanzania is estimated to be 26 percent; of that, children under age fifteen years make up 46 percent of the total population. Children below age fifteen constitute about half the workforce in the urban informal sector, despite national laws. They scavenge, ragpick, beg, sell newspapers, hawk a variety of products, do piecework manufacturing, work as barmaids, street vendors, car washers, shoe shiners, cart pushers, carpenters, auto repair mechanics in garages, and perform virtually any other income-generating task they can.

Some urban children have chosen life on the street. Others have had no choice. Many come from impoverished areas such as Singida, Dodoma, and Mtwara. Some work after school to contribute to family income (Tripp 1997), and still others work for themselves. Most are involved in informal-sector activities. While many children "of" the streets have no home or social protection, most children "on" the streets return at night to quarters shared with families, caretakers, or peers (May 1996). On the streets, children develop cognitive skills and the art of persuasion, while also weaving social safety nets that provide love, continuity, and a sense of belonging, while helping them cope with the dangers of street life. Children on and of the street face police brutality; refugee children and those in conflict with the law are especially vulnerable to abuse and exploitation.

Domestic Labor, Sex Work, and Trafficking

Children learn early to understand themselves as members of broad social networks, and spend time serving others through their labor. In the context of child labor, however, socialization practices may turn ominous. The urban domestic laborer is one of the most exploited, and girls are far more vulnerable than boys. Most domestic laborers are between nine and seventeen years old and female. Few have been schooled, even at the primary level. Many are lured to towns and cities by older men who promise opportunities to study while working to support themselves or supplement their family's income. Most are bitterly disappointed to find that they are treated, not as family, even when they are kin, but as servants—even slaves—who must work for a pittance if anything at all. The instance of such abuse has risen since the mid-1990s as labor becomes disembedded from socialization and as hardships increase. Domestic laborers bear heavy burdens with long hours, rising before dawn and going to bed after the family, having no day of rest, no vacation, no job security, and few if any rights. Many are physically and sexually abused.

Indeed, 25 percent of child prostitutes are former domestic servants, and many have few social skills, and little guidance, love, affection, or care. Some have histories of drug abuse and criminal records. Though the government criminalizes child prostitution and child pornography, research conducted by the Tanzania Media Women Association shows that entrenched networks are difficult to dismantle. Since major customers are big businessmen, bureaucrats from public and private sectors, policemen, tourists, and foreigners, as well as common men, motivation to curtail child sexual abuse is often conflicted.

The trafficking of children abets proliferation of child sex work. Both boys and girls sent initially to labor on farms, in mines, or as domestics become sex workers. The ILO has reported that Tanzanian girls are trafficked to South Africa, Oman, Saudi Arabia, the United Kingdom, and other Middle Eastern and European countries, and that children from neighboring countries are trafficked through Tanzania to other destinations. In Zanzibar, hotels sponsor girls as maids who then become prostitutes. The Tanzanian government has yet to outlaw either internal or external trafficking.

Mining

The mining industry booms as the government invites foreign investments. The Tanzanian government projects that the mining sector will contribute 10 percent of GDP by 2025, up from 2.3 percent in 2008. Yet most export earnings, and more than 50 percent of Tanzania's gemstone production, derive from small-scale mining operations. Eighty percent of that work falls outside any legal or regulatory framework, and children are heavily involved. The sector burgeons even though the "workplace fatality rate [is] up to 90 times higher than in industrialized countries' mines" (ILO 1999).

Children labor in stone quarries, where they work without shoes or proper tools. Boys in low-paid, high-risk, seasonal labor in gold and gemstone mines, such as Mererani, are dubbed "snakeboys" because they can enter and maneuver in narrow, poorly constructed shafts more easily than adults. They also break rocks with hammers, scavenge for materials, wash, sieve, fill sacks, transport ore on their heads or in carts, and run errands for adults, and by twelve years of age, do the same work as adult males though they are paid far less. Subjected to earsplitting noise, excessive heat, dust, harmful gases, and inadequately ventilated mines, boys develop numerous physical and respiratory ailments, especially silicosis and tuberculosis, and psychological problems. The work environment is vulnerable to flooding, cave-ins, and rock falls.

Protagonists argue that because small-scale mining operations are closely linked to economic development, particularly in rural sectors, they offer employment that can slow rural-urban migration, help people maintain links to the land, contribute significantly to foreign exchange earnings, and bring valued resources into the market. Detractors note that much of the work is clandestine, underreported, and hazardous, and functions without clearly articulated worker rights and responsibilities. Many argue that mining communities pose great threats to children and other workers because of overcrowding, inadequate sanitation, exposure to silica dust, mercury poisoning, and contamination of home water supplies.

Policy Perspectives and Practices

The government of Tanzania has taken important steps to address the issue of child labor, particularly in its worst forms, including ratifying ILO conventions, dovetailing national and international working-age standards, and forging collaborations with various nongovernmental organizations. For example, the government adopted the Yokohama Global Commitment in 2001 to help protect children from sexual exploitation. With ILO assistance and U.S. Department of Labor funds, groups such as the Timebound Program work to rehabilitate child prostitutes and provide them with educational opportunities. Street children may find refuge in centers operated by NGOs such as DogoDogo in Dar es Salaam, Kuleana in Mwanza, Tuamaini Centre in Dodoma, the Social Welfare Centre in Morogoro, and the Iringa Development of Youth, Disabled and Children Care in Iringa. The Amani Children's Home, founded by local Tanzanians in 2001, rescues children from child abuse and neglect. The Kwetu Centre helps rehabilitate prostitutes and drug-addicted children. And TAPAC (Tanzania Parliamentarians AIDS Coalition), formed in 2001, addresses discrimination against children and adults infected with HIV/AIDS. Many of these organizations operate with support from the government to provide children with meals, medical care, and training opportunities. The Tanzania Federation of Trade Unions, for example, fights for better and safer working conditions for children on tobacco, tea, and other plantations. Tanzania Women Lawyers Association networks with IPEC to raise awareness, protect rights, and give free legal aid to domestic servants and prostitutes.

Conclusion

One Tanzanian interviewee recently observed, "[I]n the 1970s we didn't have child labour; the country had good policies, egalitarian policies, which benefited all people—the rich and the poor." Today, however, "policies facilitating the regeneration of classes" widen the gap between the haves and have-nots (Kadonya et al. 2002, 54, 57). The need for knowledge of historical, political, socioeconomic, and cultural contexts that produce child labor remains urgent.

Steps that could be taken to deal with child labor include consolidating laws, escalating law enforcement, improving inspector training and site inspection, and developing and strengthening partnerships with industries, labor groups, and international organizations. Caution is in order, however. Public awareness and subsequent responses have been known to worsen children's working conditions by driving operations underground. Unaccompanied by structural transformation that mitigates the clash between visible markets and invisible household economies, however, such changes are unlikely to eliminate child labor in Tanzania.

References and Further Reading

Andvig, Jens, Sudharshan Canagarajah, and Anne Kielland. "Issues in Child Labor in Africa." Working Paper Series, Human Development Sector, Africa Region, World Bank, Washington, DC, September 2001.

Bass, Loretta E. *Child Labor in Sub-Saharan Africa.* Boulder, CO: Lynne Rienner, 2004.

Blackden, C. Mark, and Quentin Wodon, eds. "Gender, Time Use, and Poverty in Sub-Saharan Africa." World Bank Working Paper 73, World Bank, Washington, DC, 2006.

Fratkin, E., and K. Smith. "Labor, Livestock, and Land: The Organization of Pastoral Production." In *African Pastoralist Systems: An Integrated Approach,* ed. E. Fratkin, K.A. Galvin, and E.A. Roth, 91–112. Boulder, CO: Lynne Rienner, 1994.

Harsch, Ernest. "Child Labour Rooted in Africa's Poverty: Campaigns Launched Against Traffickers and Abusive Work." In "Protecting Africa's Children," special feature, *Africa Recovery* 15:3 (2001): 14–17. http://www.un.org/ecosocdev/geninfo/afrec/vol15no3/153chil4.htm.

ILO. *Social and Labour Issues in Small-Scale Mines. Report for Discussion at the Tripartite Meeting on Social and Labour Issues in Small-Scale Mines.* Geneva: ILO, 1999.

Kadonya, C., M. Mahidi, and S. Mtwana. *Tanzania Child Labour in the Informal Sector. A Rapid Assessment.* Geneva: International Labour Office, January 2002.

Kapinga, Theofrida A. "Action Against Child Labour in Tanzania." *Finnish Institute of Occupational Health. African Newsletter* (2000): 48–51. http://www.ttl.fi/Internet/English/Information/Electronic+journals/African+Newsletter/2000–02/07.htm

Kielland, Anne, and Maurizia Tovo. *Children at Work: Child Labor Practices in Africa.* Boulder, CO: Lynne Rienner, 2006.

Kimambo, Isaria. *Penetration and Protest in Tanzania: The Impact of the World Economy on the Pare, 1860–1960.* Athens, OH: James Currey, 1991.

Kimaryo, Michael, and Ron Pouwels. "An African Perspective: Child Domestic Workers in Tanzania." *Child Workers in Asia CWA Newsletter* 15:2 (May–August 1999).

May, Ann. "Handshops and Hope: Young Street Vendors in Dar es Salaam, Tanzania." In "On the Backs of Children: Children and Work in Africa," ed. Karen A. Porter. Special issue, *The Anthropology of Work Review* 17:1–2 (Summer–Fall 1996): 25–34.

Mayombo, Alakok. "Children Drawn into Sex Trade." Harare, Zimbabwe: Inter Press Third World News Agency (IPS), 1998.

Mehra-Kerpleman, Kiran. "Finding Ways to Fight Child Labour in Tanzania." *World of Work* 28 (February 1999).

Porter, Karen A. "The Agency of Children, Work and Social Change in the South Pare Mountains, Tanzania." In "On the Backs of Children: Children and Work in Africa," ed. Karen A. Porter. Special issue, *The Anthropology of Work Review* 17:1–2 (Summer–Fall 1996): 8–19.

Rwegoshora, H. *A Country Study Towards a Best Practice Guide on Sustainable Action Against Child Labour for Policy Makers: The Case of Tanzania.* Dar es Salaam: ILO, 1997.

Tripp, Aili. *Changing the Rules: The Politics of Liberalization and the Urban Informal Economy in Tanzania.* Berkeley: University of California Press, 1997.

United Republic of Tanzania. National Web site. http://www.tanzania.go.tz.

Uganda

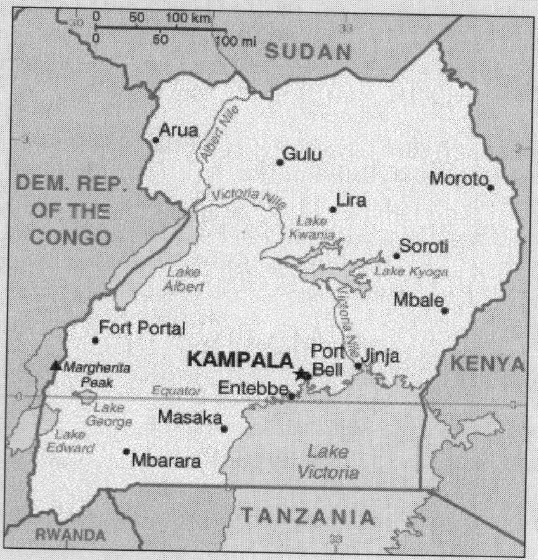

UGANDA	CRC	C 138	C 182
Ratifications	Y	Y	Y
Human Development Index/Rank	0.502/145		
Human Capital			
Population Growth Rate	3.57%		
% Population 0–14	50.2%		
Total Fertility Rate	6.84		
Life Expectancy	51.75		
Infant Mortality Rate	67.22		
Literacy Rate	69.9%		
Economic			
GDP/Capita	$1,800		
GDP Growth %	5%		
% Poverty	35%		
Gini Index	43		
Labor Force Composition			
% Agriculture	82%		
% Industry	5%		
% Services	13%		

CHILD ACTIVITY BREAKDOWN, BY SEX AND RESIDENCE

RESIDENCE	Percentage of children in the relevant age-group[a]									
	Economic activity only		School only		Combining school and economic activity		Neither in school nor in economic activity		Child Labor[b]	
	Male	Female	Male	Female	Male	Female	Male	Female	Male	Female
Urban	1.6	1.3	78.1	79.9	11.9	10.4	8.4	8.4	n/av	n/av
Rural	2.9	2.6	51.7	53.5	32.4	30.1	13.0	13.8	n/av	n/av
Total	2.8	2.4	55.1	57.1	29.8	27.5	12.4	13.0	24.9	27.0

Source: Uganda, Uganda National Household Survey, 2005–2006 (see UCW Project Web site, http://www.ucw-project.org, country statistics).

Notes: [a]Children age 5 to 14. [b]Estimate includes (a) children under age 12 engaged in economic activities and (b) children age 12–14 engaged in excessive economic activities (more than 14 hours per week), and (c) children under age 15 engaged in excessive household chores (at least 28 hours per week). Estimate does not account for children engaged in hazardous work or other unconditional "worst forms" of child labor.

Child Labor in Uganda

Eddy Joshua Walakira, Lecturer and Consultant, Makerere University, Kampala, Uganda

In 2002, Uganda's population stood at 24.4 million and had grown at a rate of 3.3 percent per year since 1991 (UBOS 2005). Children below eighteen years of age constitute 56 percent of the population. Those between the ages of five and seventeen account for more than 36 percent of the population. Higher population growth, coupled with deteriorating terms of trade, HIV/AIDS, and the incessant civil war in northern Uganda, has contributed significantly to high levels of poverty. Thirty-five percent of the population is in absolute poverty. Nonetheless, higher levels of GDP growth, averaging 5–6 percent over the last two decades, have sharply reduced the absolute poor from 56 percent to the present 35 percent (Ministry of Finance, Planning and Economic Development 2003). Per capita income stands at US$1,800 per year.

Legal Provisions

Uganda's Employment Act, adopted in 1997 and amended in 2000, prohibits the employment of children younger than twelve years of age. Up to this age, children are expected to be at school. Between ages twelve and fifteen years, the act allows children to participate in light work, which may be prescribed by the Ministry of Gender, Labor and Social Development (MGLSD), consisting of domestic work performed under parental supervision for purposes of training or learning. The laws overlook light work children do before age twelve, which may be positive for their development. Children below age sixteen cannot be admitted into work considered hazardous, as provided for under the Uganda constitution. However, forms of hazardous work specified under the Employment Act represent only a handful of hazardous work situations, mainly in industry. Despite the existence of laws, there are glaring gaps that have made their enforcement difficult. These include limited awareness of the laws among employers, law enforcement agencies, and children and their parents; limited resources to enforce the laws; and lack of alternatives for children who are working.

Uganda has already ratified most international conventions aimed at fighting child labor and protecting the rights of children.

Table 1

Uganda's Ratifications of International Conventions Related to Child Labor

August 1990	United Nations Convention on the Rights of the Child, 1989
May 2002	Optional Protocol to the CRC (CRC-OP-AC) on the Involvement of Children in Armed Conflict
August 2002	Optional Protocol to the CRC on the Sale of Children, Child Prostitution, and Child Pornography
June 1963	ILO Convention 29 on Forced Labor, 1932
June 1963	ILO Convention 105 on the Abolition of Forced Labor, 1957
June 1967	ILO Convention 123 on Minimum Age (Underground Work), 1965
March 2003	ILO Convention 138 on Minimum Age of Employment, 1973
June 2001	ILO Convention 182 on the Elimination of the Worst Forms of Child Labor, 1999

Magnitude of the Problem

Despite facing a ballooning problem of child labor, much of the available data in Uganda does

Table 2

Sector of Child Economic Activity, by Sex

Sex	As percentage of children in economic activity[a]						
	Agriculture	Manufacturing	Mining	Construction	Wholesale and retail trade	Transport	Other
Male	90.42	1.85	0.00	0.26	4.17	0.90	2.39
Female	86.32	2.32	0.48	0.00	8.84	0.00	2.05
Total	88.21	2.10	0.26	0.12	6.68	0.42	2.21

Source: NIS (2001).

Note: [a]Children age 10 to 14.

not clearly distinguish between "child work" and "child labor." This is because definitive parameters sharply distinguishing between harmful and non-harmful forms work are not in place. As a result, there is a tendency among some actors to consider all work children do as constituting child labor, even forms of work that are benign. Following ILO Convention 182, child labor is considered work by those younger than age eighteen that exposes them to physical, psychological, social, or moral harm. But not all work by children is considered harmful.

At the turn of the millennium, the Uganda Bureau of Statistics (UBOS) estimated that 2.7 million children from age five to age seventeen were working, out of a total population of 7.9 million children (UBOS 2001). Interestingly, children between the ages of ten and fourteen years had the highest work activity rates; 1.46 million children, more than 46 percent of the 3.16 million children in this age-group, were working. Children age from five to nine years of age and from fifteen to seventeen years of age have work activity rates of about 23 percent and 30 percent, respectively. More girls (26 percent) than boys (21 percent) are at work among children between the ages of five and nine, while in the upper age bracket of fifteen to seventeen years of age, more boys are at work (33 percent) than girls (27 percent). By implication, girls start work earlier than boys, but fewer can hold on to work as they grow, risking unemployment and greater vulnerability.

Several more specific studies have been undertaken distinguishing between working children and those considered to be in child labor. In the urban informal sector, nearly all working children (98 percent) are considered child laborers; 78 percent have left school and 61 percent are orphans (Walakira 2004). In a study of child labor in HIV/AIDS-affected communities, 72 percent of children were found to be working, and 87 percent of those working were found to be in child labor (Walakira et al. 2005). Another study by MGLSD (2004b) found that 11 percent of more than 1,200 children surveyed were involved in sex work. Other studies have examined worst forms of child labor, including children in armed conflict and cross-border trade (MGLSD 2004c, 2004d); children in commercial agriculture (Kyomuhendo et al. 2004); and child labor in the construction sector (Federation of Uganda Employers 2001).

Activities in Which Children Are Involved

Children work in numerous occupations in Uganda. In agriculture, on both plantation farms and subsistence farms, children work picking, weeding, spraying, and drying tea, coffee, and cocoa in central, western, and eastern parts of the country; they tend animals mainly in pastoral communities in western and northeastern Uganda. Children work in factories, industries, mining, and fishing. They engage in street work and informal-sector activities such as motor mechanics in garages, bar maiding, waitressing, hawking, luggage carrying, and scavenging. Some are involved in sex work and pornographic activities (Walakira 2002).

Trafficking of children and their involvement in illicit activities, recruitment of children for armed conflict for use as child soldiers, and child slavery and bonded labor are not uncommon.

The Ministry of Gender Labour and Social Development showed that 20,000 children were abducted between 1990 and 2001 in conflict areas in Uganda. A good number were recruited as child soldiers. Only 5,000 out of the 20,000 returned to their communities (MGLSD 2004e). Fewer and fewer children will face the risk of abduction. For example, out of 337 people who returned to Uganda after a series of peace agreements, only 157 were children (UNICEF 2001).

Causes of Child Labor

Poverty has been singled out as the major reason why children work. Thirty-five percent of Ugandans live in absolute poverty, and of the absolute poor, 62 percent are children younger than age eighteen (UBOS 2003). The high level of child poverty forces children into child labor to help support their families. A related view is that not only does poverty cause child labor, but child labor also causes poverty and hampers development by driving wages down.

HIV/AIDS has exacerbated the situation by creating a generation of orphans. More than 1 million people are reported to have died in Uganda since the advent of HIV/AIDS in the early 1980s (UNDP 2002). Nearly 2 million children have been orphaned to HIV/AIDS and related diseases (Hunter 2000). Increasing child labor has been linked to the growing incidence of orphanhood, owing to the fact that children are forced to work to support themselves when their parents die or are ailing (UNICEF 2001).

Insecurity in northern Uganda has contributed to trafficking and abduction of children from homes and schools to work as child soldiers, slaves, or sex objects. Other factors have been mentioned as contributing to child labor. Structural inequalities based on gender, caste, class, religion, and disability may lead to exclusion from school and limited employment prospects. Lack of access to good-quality and relevant education, different ways of bringing up children, and the desire of children themselves for work are factors. Finally, some cite child work as an important form of learning.

Conclusion

In addition to promulgation of child labor laws, Uganda has endeavored to eliminate child labor through the introduction of universal primary education policy in 1997 and universal secondary education policy in 2007, and implementation of the Poverty Eradication Action Plan. Other efforts include increasing access to skills training, strengthening enforcement at local levels, increasing awareness about existing laws, and working to pacify war-affected areas in northern Uganda. Civil society agencies have played an instrumental role in supporting government efforts to implement the programs. While child labor remains a problem, attempts to fight it are likely to pay off in the long term.

References and Further Reading

African Network for the Protection Against Child Abuse and Neglect. *Innocence at Stake—A Situation Analysis of Child Abuse in Uganda.* Kampala: African Network for the Protection against Child Abuse and Neglect, 2003.

Federation of Uganda Employers. *Child Labour Within the Construction Sector in Uganda.* Kampala: Federation of Uganda Employers and International Labour Office, 2001.

Hunter, S. *Reshaping Societies: HIV/AIDS and Social Change.* New York: Hudson Run Press, 2000.

Kyomuhendo, Swizen, Rose Ssenabulya, M. Matovu, and Joseph Kiwanuka. *Rapid Assessment on the Nature, Prevalence, and Other Dynamics of Child Labour Within the Coffee Agricultural Sector in Uganda: Employers' Perspective.* Kampala: Federation of Uganda Employers, 2004.

Ministry of Finance, Planning and Economic Development. *Uganda's Progress in Attaining the PEAP Targets—in the Context of the Millennium Development Goals.* Kampala: Ministry of Finance, Planning and Economic Development, 2003.

Ministry of Gender, Labor and Social Development (MGLSD). *Child Labour and the Urban Informal Sector in Uganda.* Kampala: MGLSD and ILO-IPEC, 2004a.

MGLSD. *Report of the Sectoral Study on Child Labour and Commercial Sex Exploitation of Children in Uganda.* Kampala: MGLSD and ILO-IPEC, 2004b.

MGLSD. *Thematic Study of Children and Armed Conflict in Uganda.* Kampala: MGLSD and ILO-IPEC, 2004c.

MGLSD. *Sectoral Study on Child Labour and Cross-Border Trade in Uganda.* Kampala: MGLSD and ILO-IPEC, 2004d.

MGLSD. *National Strategic Programme Plan of Interventions for Orphans and Other Vulnerable Children. Fiscal Year 2005/6–2009/10.* Kampala: MGLSD, 2004e.

MGLSD. *Economic Study on Child Labour Wages and Productivity in the Fishing and Construction Sectors in Uganda.* Kampala: MGLSD and ILO, 2005.

Save the Children. *The Silent Majority: Child Poverty in Uganda.* London: Save the Children UK, 2002.

Uganda Bureau of Statistics (UBOS). *Child Labour in Uganda: A Report Based on the 2000/2001 Demographic and Health Survey.* Entebbe: UBOS, ILO-IPEC, and MGLSD, 2001.

UBOS. *Uganda Household Survey 2002/2003: Report on the Labour Force Survey.* Entebbe: UBOS, 2003.

UBOS. *The 2002 Uganda Population and Housing Census Main Report.* Entebbe: UBOS, 2005.

UNICEF. *Child Workers in the Shadow of AIDS.* New York: United Nations Children Fund, 2001.

UNDP. *Uganda Human Development Report 2002: The Challenge of HIV/AIDS: Maintaining the Momentum.* Kampala: United Nations Development Programme, 2002.

Walakira, Eddy Joshua. "Worst Forms of Child Labour: An Investigation into Commercial and Sex Exploitation of Children in Uganda." *MAWAZO* 8 (June 2002): 46–55.

Walakira Eddy Joshua. "Child Labour in Uganda's Urban Informal Sector: The Perceptions and Work Practices of Employers." *Abuja Journal of Sociology* 2:1 (2004): 67–80.

Walakira, Eddy Joshua, Julius Omona, Jimrex Byamugisha, and Goretti Nakabugo. *Child Labour and Situation of Education for Children in HIV/AIDS Affected Communities in Uganda.* Kampala: Academy for Educational Development, World Vision, International Rescue Committee, and U.S. Department of Labor, 2005.

Zambia

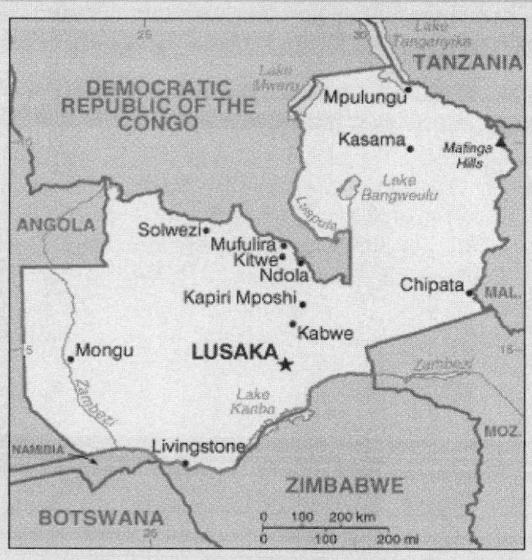

ZAMBIA			
	CRC	C 138	C 182
Ratifications	Y	Y	Y
Human Development Index/Rank	0.407/165		
Human Capital			
Population Growth Rate	1.66%		
% Population 0–14	45.7%		
Total Fertility Rate	5.31		
Life Expectancy	38.44		
Infant Mortality Rate	100.71		
Literacy Rate	80.6%		
Economic			
GDP/Capita	$1,000		
GDP Growth %	6%		
% Poverty	86%		
Gini Index	52.6		
Labor Force Composition			
% Agriculture	85%		
% Industry	6%		
% Services	9%		

CHILD ACTIVITY BREAKDOWN, BY SEX AND RESIDENCE

RESIDENCE	Percentage of children in the relevant age-group[a]									
	Economic activity only		School only		Combining school and economic activity		Neither in school nor in economic activity		Child labor[b]	
	Male	Female	Male	Female	Male	Female	Male	Female	Male	Female
Urban	2.6	1.7	67.3	68.0	8.5	7.8	21.6	22.5	n/av	n/av
Rural	20.4	18.4	18.6	19.5	39.4	39.2	21.5	23.0	n/av	n/av
Total	14.6	13.0	34.6	35.2	29.3	29.0	21.6	22.8	39.3	37.2

Source: Zambia, Labour Force Survey, 2005 (see UCW Project Web site, http://www.ucw-project.org, country statistics).
Notes: [a]Children age 5 to 14. [b]Estimate includes (a) children under age 12 engaged in economic activities and (b) children age 12–14 engaged in excessive economic activities (more than 14 hours per week). Estimate does not account for children engaged in excessive household chores, hazardous work, or other unconditional "worst forms" of child labor.

Child Labor in Zambia

Peter Jensen, Professor, Aarhus School of Business, University of Aarhus

Zambia has experienced an economic decline for more than three decades. This has generated severe and pervasive poverty, thereby creating fertile conditions for child labor. Despite this, Zambia's policy of providing universal primary education to all children has enabled it to keep school attendance rates relatively high and the incidence of child labor relatively low, compared with many other sub-Saharan African countries.

After independence in 1964, the Zambian economy was heavily dependent on copper mining and related industries. The oil crisis in the 1970s, combined with falling demand for copper and inadequate economic policy, led to a strong economic decline, with GDP per capita falling almost 3 percent annually for at least two decades. Together with rapid labor-force growth, decreasing public expenditures on education, and increasing private costs of schooling, these economic developments created circumstances where many Zambian households may have seen child labor as a necessary way to fight poverty. During the early 2000s, the economy has recovered slightly, with a moderate pace of expansion.

The Extent and Nature of Child Labor in Zambia

The most recent surveys of child labor in Zambia are from the late 1990s: a World Bank Priority Survey conducted in 1998 and an ILO Child Labor Survey conducted in 1999. Blunch et al. (2005) concluded that the two surveys yield similar results about the extent and nature of child labor and schooling. Earlier surveys are also available. Jensen and Nielsen (1997) reported results from a World Bank Priority Survey conducted in 1993; and Admassie (2002) relied on data from the ILO for a number of African countries in the first half of the 1990s.

The incidence of child labor is relatively moderate in Zambia. Estimates from the late 1990s show around 10 percent of children age five to fourteen years working, with almost one-quarter of them both working and going to school. Other surveys have previously estimated the same general magnitude of incidence for the first half of the 1990s: A little more than 12 percent of children age seven to eighteen years work (Jensen and Nielsen 1997), and around 16–17 percent of children age ten to fourteen years work (Admassie 2002). These figures show that Zambia differs from many other sub-Saharan African countries, since many children attend school and relatively few work.

The structure of child labor in Zambia is similar to that in many other sub-Saharan African countries. Children from poor households are more likely to be active in child labor than are children from better-off households. Child labor incidence rises with age, such that more child workers are found among the older children than among very young children. More girls than boys are occupied in housework, and more boys than girls are occupied in occupations outside the home. In contrast to the situation in many other African countries, girls and boys in Zambia have the same tendency to work and nearly the same school attendance rate. Earlier surveys have indicated that slightly more boys than girls go to school because girls drop out earlier than boys (Jensen and Nielsen 1997).

Child labor is much more common in rural areas than in urban areas. In particular, the Western, Northern, Eastern, and Southern provinces of Zambia are characterized by widespread use of child labor, with the incidence of child labor being highest in the Western Province. More than 90 percent of all working children are found in the agricultural sector, and most children are working in subsistence farming as unpaid family workers. Younger children are almost exclusively employed in subsistence farming, whereas older children are more likely to be employed outside subsistence farming. Other occupations for child workers include street vending, quarrying and stone breaking, digging wells and garbage pits, domestic services, small-scale manufacturing, and prostitution.

Since many of the jobs performed by child workers take place in hazardous environments, the children might be expected to experience health problems. The health impact of child labor is inherently difficult to measure, but results of recent surveys seem to indicate that working children are no worse off than other children (Blunch et al. 2005). However, these results may reflect that the healthiest children are selected for work or that health consequences may not reveal themselves until later in the children's lives.

Child Labor and School Attendance

One of the most detrimental effects of child labor is its influence on school attendance, through which it may reduce investment in human capital and thereby cause future economic growth to suffer. Hence, it is important to consider the relationship between child labor and school attendance. This relationship has been well researched for Zambia (Jensen and Nielsen 1997; Nielsen 2001), partly due to the fact that adequate data have been available.

School attendance is higher in Zambia than in many other sub-Saharan African countries. In addition, the intergenerational transmission of education in Zambia appears to be rather strong, in the sense that the educational attainment of the household head is a strong factor behind school attendance and child labor. School attendance is highest, and child labor is correspondingly lower, when the head of household is an educated person (with at least a secondary education). It is also remarkable that even though many poor parents may have found it too expensive to send their children to school, this does not necessarily lead to more child labor. In fact, a substantial fraction of children are neither in school nor working. In recent surveys, as many as around 36 percent of children age five to fourteen years fall in this category.

Jensen and Nielsen (1997) performed an empirical analysis of the determinants of school attendance and child labor in Zambia. The analysis was based on a household survey that allowed unobserved household effects to be taken into account. Results suggested that both economic and sociological factors were important determinants for the choice between school attendance and child labor. The empirical analysis identified poverty as a main factor behind child labor. In addition, the analysis revealed that low quality of education and imperfect capital markets were driving forces behind many parents' decision to keep their children out of school.

Nielsen (2001) performed a cost-benefit analysis taking into account the economic gains and losses of child labor. The trade-off analyzed is whether a household should let a child work and earn money now, or attend school and thereby increase potential future earnings. Estimating returns to human capital and income from child labor, the cost-benefit analysis predicts a total loss of 1–2 percentage points in annual growth from using child labor instead of sending the children to school. It is calculated as an aggregate loss to the Zambian economy, meaning that the GDP could have grown by an additional 1–2 percent annually. This is a substantial loss given that the Zambian economy has experienced long periods of economic decline.

Main Factors Behind Child Labor in Zambia

Several studies have found support for the hypothesis that poverty forces households to keep their children away from school (Jensen and Nielsen 1997). However, this positive relation between poverty and child labor appears to be weaker in Zambia than in other countries (Nielsen 2001). Empirical analysis for the case of Zambia shows that while poverty is an important determinant of child labor and school attendance, other factors are at least as important. One important factor is the high degree of urbanization in Zambia, one of the most urbanized countries of sub-Saharan Africa, with heavily urbanized provinces of Lusaka and the Copperbelt. Since child labor is predominantly a rural phenomenon, this helps to explain why Zambia is among the sub-Saharan African countries with the lowest incidence of child labor. Another factor is community-related effects. These might include school quality, traditions, norms, and credit availability. A weaker relationship between poverty and child labor would help explain why the incidence of child labor is relatively low in Zambia, despite the serious economic difficulties the country has experienced. These findings should be taken into consideration when designing policies and programs aimed at reducing child labor. Poverty reduction may have an effect, but other policies may be more effective, especially since general poverty-reduction policies may be a very expensive way to reduce child labor.

Relation Between HIV/AIDS and Child Labor

Another important factor behind child labor in Zambia is the HIV/AIDS epidemic. Zambia is one of the countries in southern Africa with the highest HIV/AIDS infection rates—the UN estimates that at least one in five adults in Zambia has HIV or AIDS. Furthermore, the HIV/AIDS epidemic has caused Zambia to experience a significant decline in life expectancy. Hence, Zambia currently has a very high prevalence of HIV/AIDS and a very low life expectancy.

An ILO (2002) report assessed the impact of HIV/AIDS on child labor in Zambia. Stating that poverty and HIV/AIDS are intimately linked as preconditions for child labor, the report concluded that HIV/AIDS is responsible for increasing child labor force participation up to 30 percent. One of the mechanisms behind the increase in the child labor force is that parents or guardians have died, thereby forcing children out to work, often in hazardous and low-paid jobs. At the same time, these child workers do not attend school, typically because no one is able to pay for them. An increasing number of children may also be acting as household heads in child-headed households. This age-inappropriate role may prevent them from both market work and going to school. The report also found that commercial sexual exploitation was common among older children. Hence, HIV/AIDS has clearly worsened the situation, and policies and programs aimed at reducing child labor need to take this into account along with more traditionally recognized aspects such as poverty and school costs.

References and Further Reading

Admassie, Assefa. "Explaining the High Incidence of Child Labour in Sub-Saharan Africa." *African Development Review* 14 (2002): 251–75.

Blunch, Niels-Hugo, Admit Dar, Lorenzo Guarcello, Scott Lyon, Amy Ritualo, and Furio C. Rosati. "Child Work in Zambia: A Comparative Study of Survey Instruments." *International Labour Review* 144 (2005): 211–35.

ILO. *HIV/AIDS and Child Labour in Zambia: A Rapid Assessment.* IPEC report 5. Geneva: ILO-IPEC, 2002.

Jensen, Peter, and Helena Skyt Nielsen. "Child Labour or School Attendance? Evidence from Zambia." *Journal of Population Economics* 10 (1997): 407–24.

Nielsen, Helena Skyt. "Child Labor and Schooling in Zambia." In *Child Labor and Schooling in Africa: A Case Study of Ghana, Tanzania, Côte d'Ivoire and Zambia,* ed. S. Canagarajah and H.S. Nielsen, 123–52. Washington, DC: World Bank, 2001.

Zimbabwe

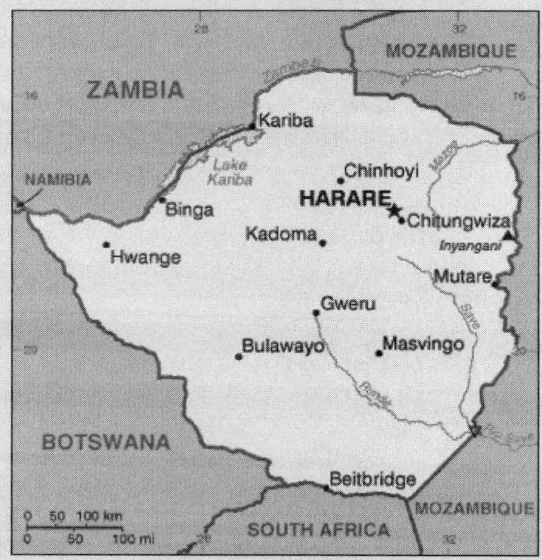

ZIMBABWE			
	CRC	C 138	C 182
Ratifications	Y	Y	Y
Human Development Index/Rank	0.491/151		
Human Capital			
Population Growth Rate	0.56%		
% Population 0–14	37.2%		
Total Fertility Rate	3.08		
Life Expectancy	39.5		
Infant Mortality Rate	51.12		
Literacy Rate	90.7%		
Economic			
GDP/Capita	$2,000		
GDP Growth %	–4.4%		
% Poverty	80%		
Gini Index	56.8		
Labor Force Composition			
% Agriculture	66%		
% Industry	10%		
% Services	24%		

CHILD ACTIVITY BREAKDOWN, BY AGE AND SEX								
Age in years	Percentage of children in the relevant age-group							
	Economic activity only		School only		Combining school and economic activity		Neither in school nor in economic activity	
	Male	Female	Male	Female	Male	Female	Male	Female
Total 5–14	1.6	1.8	72.2	70.8	10.0	11.7	16.2	15.7

Source: Zimbabwe, Labor Force Survey, 1999 (see UCW Project Web site, http://www.ucw-project.org, country statistics).

Working Children in Zimbabwe

Michael Bourdillon, Professor Emeritus, Department of Sociology, University of Zimbabwe

Most people in Zimbabwe see work as integral to growing up in a community. Young children start to help with household chores, such as cleaning, caring for infants, and, in the rural areas, collecting water and fuel and helping with the family farm and livestock (Reynolds 1991). This is how children learn responsibility and grow to full membership in their families and communities. The issue is not whether children should work, but what and how much work is appropriate for them at different ages. Many consider moves to abolish child labor as a foreign imposition, inappropriate to Zimbabwean conditions and culture.

Children and adolescents in Zimbabwe perform a wide range of work, from household chores to light income-generating activities to hard and sometimes abusive employment (Bourdillon 2000). The boundaries between beneficial and harmful work are not always clear. Unpaid work in the home can be integral to a child's socialization, but it can also be heavy and impede the child's social and physical development. Employment can be abusive, but it can also be benign and help children in a variety of ways, including paying for their schooling.

Background

In 1997, the Zimbabwe government amended its Labour Relations Act to forbid the employment of children under twelve, while those age twelve to seventeen were permitted to perform light work a maximum of six hours a day during school holidays. In 1999, Zimbabwe ratified ILO Convention 138 on minimum age for entry to employment and raised the minimum age to fifteen. In 2000, Zimbabwe ratified ILO Convention 182 on worst forms of child labor. The minimum-age legislation is occasionally enforced, but is widely considered inappropriate and frequently breached. Child domestic workers have suggested twelve as a reasonable minimum age for this kind of employment. Child employees are not effectively protected by these minimum-age laws.

Since much of children's work is hidden, sometimes not even acknowledged, it is difficult to provide accurate statistics on its scale and extent. A survey in June 2004 (Government of Zimbabwe 2006) showed 32 percent of Zimbabwean children age fifteen to seventeen engaged in "economic activities" in the previous year, with just under half of these working at the time of the survey. Sixteen percent of children age five to fourteen were engaged in economic activities at least three hours a day, with 82 percent of these also attending school. An additional 4.5 percent age five to seventeen were working five or more hours a day in household work, the majority of these also attending school. The survey underestimates the full contribution of children's economic activities because it was conducted at a time of year when little work is performed in rain-fed family agriculture, the sector that engages most rural children.

In 2006, the economic inflation rate in Zimbabwe rose to more than 1,000 percent, the increase partly related to the disruption of commercial agriculture by land reform. Less than 25 percent of the potential labor force was formally employed. In 2003, an estimated 41 percent of the population was below the age of fifteen, and more than 55 percent under age eighteen. The census of 2002 showed close to 50,000 child-headed households, a number that is increasing due to the AIDS epidemic, with many more households effectively run by children on behalf of incapacitated adults. In mid-2006, life expectancy was estimated at around thirty-five years of age. As the economy of the country became harsher and more unstable, children could no longer expect full adult support. The contributions of children have become increasingly essential to family economies, often because there is no able adult in the household. These children need protection and support, but it does not usually help them or their families to impede them from earning. Working children frequently complain about their conditions of work; rarely do they want to be prevented from working.

Domestic Work

As in most societies, the most common and earliest form of work for children is helping with household chores, which starts as playful imitation. For the most part such work helps children to grow in competence and confidence, but a number of problems can arise, and may be exacerbated by the country's economic situation.

One problem is the gendered nature of household work. Many chores are considered girls' work, including caring for younger children, cleaning, cooking, and carrying water (though any of these chores may fall on boys in the absence of girls). Young girls may be left with very little time for leisure or creative activities, although such tasks as caring for infants can be combined with play.

In rural areas, children can be required to carry heavy weights, such as firewood or containers of water, which may damage their physical growth. Where there are many adults in an extended family and few children capable of helping, the children can be overburdened with demands from the adults. Adults often regard a number of chores as inappropriate for adults, and sometimes do not notice the burden that these may impose on children.

When members of the family are seriously ill, a frequent occurrence in Zimbabwe when they succumb to AIDS, the caring work of children, added to household chores, may amount to full-time activity, leaving no time for school, leisure, or socializing with peers. Sometimes a child is withdrawn from school to care for an ailing relative.

When parents die or are incapacitated, older children may be left responsible for caring for younger siblings and running the household. Not infrequently, older children are left with similar responsibilities when parents are away seeking employment and income; this happens even in middle-class families when parents seek to earn hard currency outside the country. Children complain of responsibilities inappropriate for their age in looking after the home and children in the absence of adults.

As children reach adolescence, and sometimes sooner, they may spend time living with extended family members, where they continue to perform household work. Ideally, this enables children to move beyond the confines of their natal home and learn responsibility to the extended family. It may give them more secure nutrition and better educational opportunities. However, children are sometimes distributed to where adults need or want help with household work, irrespective of the children's interests. Thus, certain adults obtain cheap household labor; in some cases a fictitious kinship relationship conceals exploitative employment outside the family. When wealthy kin claim to help poorer children, these children may be called upon to perform chores at any time in the day or night, and receive little if any compensation. These children may relieve wealthy children of household chores, freeing them for leisure and school. Working for kin is sometimes harsher than formal employment (Bourdillon 2006).

Many children benefit from part-time domestic employment. They learn valuable domestic skills and may be able to contribute to stretched family budgets or even their own school expenses. Such employment may enable older girls to escape harsh rural life and gain some independence from problems such as pressure for early marriage. However, tens of thousands of child domestic workers work for long hours and low pay. They often have poor living conditions, are given little opportunity to maintain contact with their families, are frequently insulted, and sometimes are physically and even sexually abused.

Farm Work

Roughly 65 percent of Zimbabwe's population is rural, and the most common economic activity of rural children is working on small family farms and tending to family livestock. Such activities are an integral part of rural family life. Herding livestock or guarding fields, normally tasks for boys, allow for cooperation with peers and play, but can also interfere with schooling. Herding can extend to handling draft animals hired out to neighbors, and consequently long hours of intense work. Agricultural work can be heavy, especially in the peak season, and can interfere with school attendance and schoolwork. Interference with schooling tends to be exacerbated when the family is producing for the market in addition to producing for its own consumption. Children living with kin or others, often because they are orphaned, may be required to work in the fields of their guardians for no pay; such children might be relieved by paid employment.

Agricultural work, even within families, can involve contact with pesticides and other chemicals particularly dangerous to children. At all levels of agriculture, children risk injury from work with dangerous implements or insufficient protective clothing. Families with few or no resources of their own have to work for others. Such work often involves children as well as adults in contract labor in small- or large-scale agriculture. This may be relatively benign for the children, or it may deprive them of the chance to go to school.

Children of commercial farm workers are sometimes required by the farm owner to work during peak seasons. Frequently, they work on a voluntary basis during school holidays or on weekends to earn money for school and other expenses. On some commercial farms, children under contract to work on the farm attend farm schools. The quality of schooling provided and amount of work demanded vary. In spite of the harsh life these schools impose, some are much in demand by children and their families as a way to access quality secondary education and earn income besides, allowing many to break out of poverty.

With many people in the country desperate and homeless, and the system of commercial agriculture disrupted by land reform, some families accept a place to stay and some food from new farm owners in exchange for their labor. Such exploitation affects adults and children alike.

Informal Sector

When parents make a living through informal trade, children often help out, sometimes at the expense of schoolwork, and sometimes because they are excluded from school by its expense. Street children and others may also trade on their own account, or find other ways of earning in the cities, by such entrepreneurial activities as parking and guarding cars, carrying loads for bus passengers, running errands, and polishing shoes. They may also trade for others on commission. Some children take on work in informal manufacturing or repair work, often producing little income from long hours of work. Conditions of work are frequently unsafe and unhealthy.

Girls on the street find it virtually impossible to survive without prostituting themselves, a lethal occupation in the context of HIV/AIDS. In addition to income, a sexual partner may be able to provide protection (Bourdillon and Rurevo 2003). Street boys also frequently earn extra income through sex, with both men and women. Off the streets, sex provides a quick and tempting way of acquiring cash or patronage for poor children, especially girls. Street children and other urban children may learn to earn extra income through pickpocketing and shoplifting, and may easily become involved in gangs that survive through burglary and other forms of thieving. They may be involved in the trade of such drugs as marijuana and glue.

Particularly dangerous for children is their involvement in small-scale mining in the informal sector, where the work is hard, tunnels are small and insecure, wages are low, and there is no opportunity for schooling (Save the Children UK 2000). Children involved in such work have asked for employment in large, formal mines, where conditions and pay are much better. Mining, however, is categorized as a worst form of child labor, so work in the better-organized mines in the formal sector is illegal.

Children are also involved in carrying goods smuggled across borders in remote areas, often at night. Children also cross borders to work and earn. In the past, many children crossed from Mozambique into Zimbabwe for better earning opportunities. Now more frequently children cross from Zimbabwe to South Africa for such opportunities, where they risk abuse and gross exploitation, along with summary repatriation to the nearest border post.

Conclusion

Of necessity, many children are involved in household work and economic activities. Some of this work is hazardous, and often the hours and nature of the work impede progress at school. Few of the issues raised here are exclusive to Zimbabwe, but the extent of children's work is both a result and a symptom of severe social and economic problems in Zimbabwean society. Work for the children is often their solution to greater problems: It is a means of survival, and often of education. To prevent children from working would be to remove the means chosen by children and their families for coping, and is unlikely to improve their quality of life. We need rather to find ways to support and protect children in their work while we try to resolve the problems that drive them to work.

References and Further Reading

Bourdillon, Michael. *Child Domestic Workers in Zimbabwe.* Harare, Zimbabwe: Weaver Press, 2006.

Bourdillon, Michael, ed. *Earning a Life: Working Children in Zimbabwe.* Harare, Zimbabwe: Weaver Press, 2000.

Bourdillon, Michael, and Rumbidzai Rurevo. *Girls on the Street.* Harare, Zimbabwe: Weaver Press, 2003.

Government of Zimbabwe. *Child Labour Report, 2004.* Harare, Zimbabwe: Central Statistics Office, 2006.

Reynolds, Pamela. *Dance Civet Cat: Child Labour in the Zambezi Valley.* Harare, Zimbabwe: Baobab Books, 1991.

Save the Children UK. *A Situational Analysis of Children in the Informal Mining Sector in Mutorashanga and Shamva.* Harare, Zimbabwe: Save the Children UK, 2000.

Child Labor in Colonial Zimbabwe

Beverly Grier, Associate Professor of Government and International Relations, Clark University

Child labor was integral to the economy of colonial Zimbabwe (formerly Southern Rhodesia). Prepubescent and pubescent boys and girls were engaged to grow tobacco, tea, coffee, cotton, sugar, and maize, and herd cattle on farms owned by European—largely British—settlers. They worked in mines, including the mica and asbestos mines, where "piccaninnies," as they were called, formed a significant minority, if not the majority, of the workers. They worked as domestic servants in the rural and urban households of settlers. They also worked as domestic servants for African urbanites and were hired directly by mining companies to cook and clean for African workers housed in all-male compounds. As early as 1898, mining companies and white farmers had established wage rates for piccaninnies, setting them at half the rate of adult African wages. Child labor was so much a part of the assumptions of colonial officials that government advertisements to prospective settlers boasted of the young age at which Africans began to work and their usefulness to employers.

The colonial government was instrumental in encouraging male children and adolescents to leave home to work for settlers. In the early 1900s, a state-subsidized recruiting organization signed up piccaninnies as well as adult males and transported them to employers in various parts of the colony. Professional recruiting of local Africans was halted by 1906, but another state-subsidized recruiting organization was set up to recruit boys, adolescent males, and adults in neighboring Mozambique, Nyasaland (Malawi), and Northern Rhodesia (Zambia). To encourage local Africans to enter the migrant labor force without being recruited, the colonial government imposed taxes on African males over "the apparent age of fourteen" and allowed them to sign their own labor contracts. Officials made a practice of issuing "underage" passes to seek work and labor contracts to boys who were younger than fourteen. Under the 1926 Native Juveniles Employment Act, these extralegal passes and contracts for children were given legal status. Henceforward, children were liable to penal sanctions (whipping for boys) if they deserted employers, behaved in an insolent manner, or destroyed or neglected employers' property. By teaching child workers to respect contracts and the authority of employers and the state, the colonial government was attempting to socialize child workers into their future role as adult laborers.

Prior to the 1920s, many children, especially boys, left home to search for work in response to taxes, conflicts with fathers, and a desire to earn money of their own. In the early years, fathers sent their young sons out to earn tax money and to help them buy cattle, farm implements, and other items that would enhance agricultural production. This was the era of peasant expansion, when African farmers intensified the labor of their wives and children to meet the growing demand for food in the colony's urban centers. However, not all boys left home with parental permission. Many fled their fathers' authority and increased labor demands. Many other boys rebelled against the authority of fathers who lived on settler-owned farms as labor tenants. In the early years, as settlers claimed African land, they allowed African family heads to remain on the land and farm a small plot if they supplied the farmer with the labor of their wives and unmarried children. If landlords paid wages at all, they paid them to the family head. Children fled such farms to earn their own wages on other farms or in the cities. Finally, many boys left home, with or without parental permission, to earn cash to buy European clothing and other imported goods. Acquiring a pass, even an "under-age" pass, and going out to work for wages became a rite of passage for many boys and adolescent males, as they struggled with their fathers over their labor and its fruits.

By the early 1920s, conditions had begun to change radically for peasant farmers. More whites took up land, squeezing peasants onto "reserves," and imposing onerous labor conditions on tenants. Growing rural poverty, combined with drought and postwar inflation, led to a massive exodus of male children and adolescents from the reserves and tenant labor farms. Increasingly, girls followed suit, fleeing the intensification of their labor, debt servitude (pawning), and arranged marriages to older men. Many of the boys signed contracts with white farmers but deserted their jobs routinely. Others went to the towns and cities, where they lived by their wits in the informal sector. Called "hooligans" and "vagabonds" by officials and settlers, these forerunners of today's street children engaged in theft, housebreaking, assault, gambling, beer brewing, and commercial sex.

The 1920s marked a turning point in the history of child labor in colonial Zimbabwe. Officials and settlers, experiencing a boom in agricultural production coupled with severe labor shortages, found themselves in the midst of a crisis of control over unemployed urban boys and child workers. Farmers pressed the state to indenture or apprentice to white employers, for three to five years, the large numbers of undisciplined young workers and the "army of *piccaninnies*" on the streets of the colony's towns. The outcome of this pressure was the aforementioned Native Juveniles Employment Act of 1926, which, in addition to legalizing passes and labor contracts for children and punishing child workers for breach of contract, empowered officials to remove unemployed and unattached children from the streets and forcibly contract them to private employers for six months. The law contained few penalties for employers and no specific prohibitions on the kind of work children could be forced to do. Called a "child slavery" law by many missionaries and liberal white critics in both the colony and England, the forced contracts provision was rarely enforced.

As white farmers moved from labor tenancies to wage labor in the 1920s, they increasingly employed women and children from the reserves as casual or seasonal labor. They also sought to attract entire families to reside permanently on their farms as wage laborers. To attract families, including children, they increasingly used the device of the "farm school," a primary school on the farm that catered to farm workers' children. Farm schools were often poor in quality and opened and closed according to the farm schedule. The largest farm schools were those on the estates of the Rhodesia Tea Company, which, by the mid-1950s, employed more than 1,600 children and adolescents who worked part-time on the farm for nominal wages and attended the company's schools part-time "for free." These part-time schools were modeled after schools on mission stations that benefited financially from the unpaid labor of their students.

From the mid-1960s to the late 1970s, children continued to work on farms for white employers and in towns and cities. During this period, large numbers fled across the borders into independent Zambia and Mozambique to join nationalist guerrillas fighting for independence. In the refugee and military camps, they continued to serve as a source of labor, growing food, cooking, cleaning, and, in some cases, fighting as child and adolescent soldiers.

References and Further Reading

Grier, Beverly. "Invisible Hands: The Political Economy of Child Labour in Colonial Zimbabwe, 1890–1930." *Journal of Southern African Studies* 1 (1994): 27–52.

Grier, Beverly. *Invisible Hands: Child Labor and the State in Colonial Zimbabwe.* Portsmouth, NH: Heinemann, 2006.

Section 5. Southern Africa

Lesotho

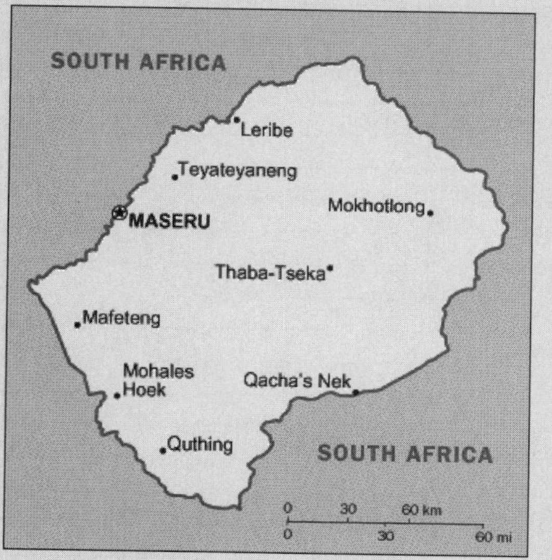

LESOTHO	CRC	C 138	C 182
Ratifications	Y	Y	Y
Human Development Index/Rank	0.494/149		
Human Capital			
Population Growth Rate	–0.46%		
% Population 0–14	36.8%		
Total Fertility Rate	3.28		
Life Expectancy	34.4		
Infant Mortality Rate	87.24		
Literacy Rate	84.8%		
Economic			
GDP/Capita	$2,600		
GDP Growth %	1.7%		
% Poverty	49%		
Gini Index	63.2		
Labor Force Composition			
% Agriculture	86%		
% Industry and Services	14%		

CHILD ACTIVITY BREAKDOWN, BY SEX AND RESIDENCE

RESIDENCE	Percentage of children in the relevant age-group[a]									
	Economic activity only		School only		Combining school and economic activity		Neither in school nor in economic activity		Child labor[b]	
	Male	Female	Male	Female	Male	Female	Male	Female	Male	Female
Urban	3.3	2.3	66.5	64.5	19.9	20.9	10.2	12.3	n/av	n/av
Rural	9.0	3.5	51.5	61.4	24.2	21.9	15.3	13.2	n/av	n/av
Total	7.9	3.3	54.4	62.0	23.4	21.7	14.4	13.1	12.7	11.7

Source: Lesotho, Multiple Indicator Cluster Survey 2, 2000 (see UCW Project Web site, http://www.ucw-project.org, country statistics).

Notes: [a]Children age 5 to 14. [b]Estimate includes (a) children under age 12 engaged in economic activities, (b) children age 12–14 engaged in excessive economic activities (more than 14 hours per week), and (c) children under age 15 engaged in excessive household chores (at least 28 hours per week). Estimate does not account for children engaged in hazardous work or other unconditional "worst forms" of child labor.

Namibia

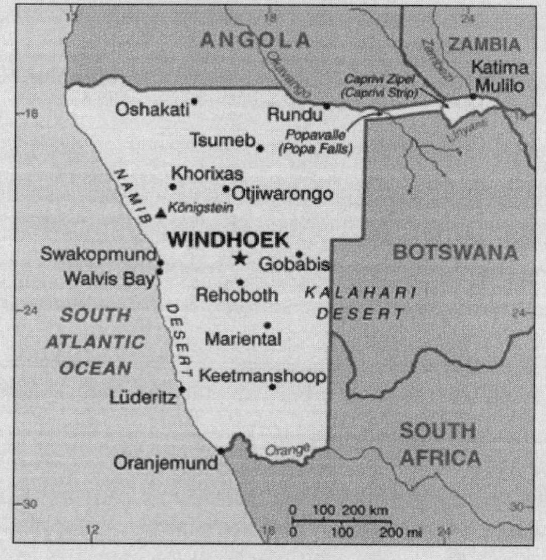

NAMIBIA			
	CRC	C 138	C 182
Ratifications	Y	Y	Y
Human Development Index/Rank	0.626/125		
Human Capital			
Population Growth Rate	0.59%		
% Population 0–14	38.2%		
Total Fertility Rate	3.06		
Life Expectancy	43.39		
Infant Mortality Rate	48.1		
Literacy Rate	84%		
Economic			
GDP/Capita	$7,400		
GDP Growth %	4.1%		
% Poverty	55.8%		
Gini Index	70.7		
Labor Force Composition			
% Agriculture	47%		
% Industry	20%		
% Services	33%		

CHILD ACTIVITY BREAKDOWN, BY SEX AND RESIDENCE

RESIDENCE	Percentage of children in the relevant age-group[a]									
	Economic activity only		School only		Combining school and economic activity		Neither in school nor in economic activity		Child labor[b]	
	Male	Female	Male	Female	Male	Female	Male	Female	Male	Female
Urban	0.1	0.1	95.2	95.1	1.1	0.6	3.5	4.2	n/av	n/av
Rural	1.5	3.2	73.1	68.3	18.4	19.8	7.0	8.7	n/av	n/av
Total	**1.1**	**2.2**	**80.2**	**77.2**	**12.8**	**13.4**	**5.9**	**7.2**	**11.9**	**14.6**

Source: Namibia, Namibia Child Activities Survey, 1999 (see UCW Project Web site, http://www.ucw-project.org, country statistics).

Notes: [a]Children age 6 to 14. [b]Estimate includes (a) children under age 12 engaged in economic activities and (b) children 12–14 engaged in excessive economic activities (more than 14 hours per week). Estimate does not account for children engaged in excessive household chores, hazardous work, or other unconditional "worst forms" of child labor.

South Africa

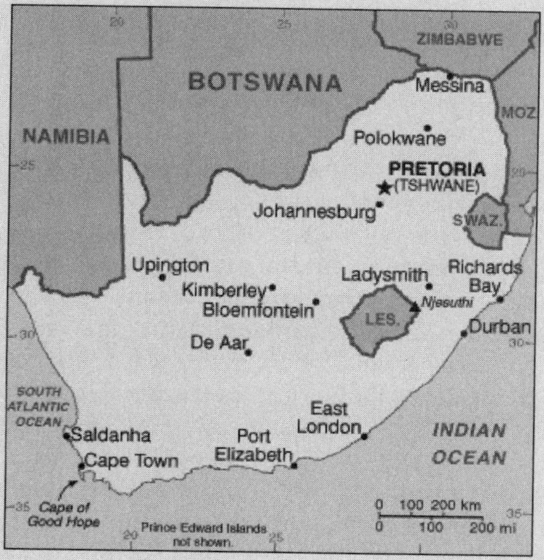

SOUTH AFRICA			
	CRC	C 138	C 182
Ratifications	Y	Y	Y
Human Development Index/Rank	0.653/121		
Human Capital			
Population Growth Rate	–0.46%		
% Population 0–14	29.1%		
Total Fertility Rate	2.16		
Life Expectancy	42.45		
Infant Mortality Rate	59.44		
Literacy Rate	86.4%		
Economic			
GDP/Capita	$13,000		
GDP Growth %	4.5%		
% Poverty	50%		
Gini Index	59.3		
Labor Force Composition			
% Agriculture	30%		
% Industry	25%		
% Services	45%		

Mapping Children's Work in South African History

Susan Levine, PhD, Lecturer, Department of Social Anthropology, University of Cape Town

The current South African constitution states that a child's best interests are of paramount importance in every matter concerning the child. Every child, defined as a person under age eighteen, has the right to protection against maltreatment, neglect, abuse, and degradation. Children are also protected by law from exploitative labor practices. They are not required or permitted to perform work that places the child's well-being at risk.

Due to the deepening of childhood poverty in postapartheid South Africa, the law that aims to protect children from exploitation in the labor force has proved untenable. In contexts of extreme poverty, children often regard work as beneficial, and policy makers are currently identifying perceived benefits of child labor, including earning money and meeting the family's basic needs. These benefits need to be carefully weighed against any harm of such work to children's health, development, and emotional well-being. An expanding definition of child rights is being considered in relation to social scientific research that indicates a deepening of poverty among children who are unable to support themselves due to protective laws that make child labor illegal. This conundrum lies at the heart of the child labor debate in South Africa.

Situating the current historical juncture in the context of the history of child labor in South Africa, this essay suggests that, while great strides have been made since the end of apartheid in 1994, the historical inequalities that underpin child labor persist into the present.

Child Slavery in South Africa

In his historical work on the political economy of child labor in South Africa, anthropologist Bernard Magubane has argued that child slavery in Africa was not an invention of the colonists, but rather the continuation of practices that date far back in history (Magubane 1988). In South Africa, child slavery dates back to the first large oceanic slave trade engineered by the Dutch East India Company in 1658. Within ten years of the founding of the Cape refreshment station in 1652, slaves were recruited from Angola, Dahomey in West Africa, Madagascar, and Mozambique. Children were also imported as slaves. Robert Shell, the leading expert on the history of slavery at the Cape of Good Hope has argued that Dutch slave owners justified child slavery by suggesting the benefits of work and discipline for child development in the colonies (Shell 1994). Jan van Riebeeck, an employee of the Dutch East India Company, and the first chief of the victualing station at the Cape of Good Hope, abducted 250 children from a Portuguese Angolan ship off the Brazilian coast. He transported them to South Africa, where they were sold as slaves. In his diary, van Riebeeck congratulated himself for saving the boys from the "dangerous hulk" that was the Portuguese ship (Shell 1994, 78). In this sense, slave traders imagined themselves as saviors of black children who would otherwise have remained "primitive." Indeed, the assistance of six-year-old African boys and girls during the early years of Dutch occupation of the Cape was arranged "in order to secure lasting and permanent good in the adoption of civilized habits and the acquisition of knowledge of useful trades, as well as the knowledge of the principles and practice of agriculture, and also with a view to check the roving habits of the natives" (Magubane 1983, 24) Jan van Riebeeck highlights this ethos in his diary:

> 17 April [1658] This morning beautiful, clear weather. We have begun to make preparations for the establishment of a school for the Company's Angolan slave children from the *Amersvoort*. . . . [S]chool will be held in the morning and afternoon . . . teaching them correct Dutch language. To animate their lessons and to make them really hear the Christian prayers each slave should be given a small glass [*croesjen* or *kroesje*, a mug or cup] of brandy and two inches of tobacco, etc. A register must be established and names should be given to those who do not have any names. . . . Within a few days, these slaves will be brought under a proper sense of discipline and become decent people. (Shell 1994, 79)

This essay sheds light on the roots of three forms of child labor control that took hold in the colonial period. The first relates to the role of farm schools, which were established to control child labor in commercial agriculture. Until 1994, when the current national school calendar was implemented, the farm schools prepared students only for an agricultural life, and thus aided in the reproduction of child and adult farm labor (Grier 2006). The second relates to the use of liquor as a form of labor control on farms. Liquor was used as payment, a system that is now known as the dop system (Scully 1992). The third relates to the deployment of Christian missionaries to bring "civilization" to the natives in the colony.

With the abolition of slavery in 1838, new measures of control were required to harness the labor of children, including the unpaid apprenticeship of Khoisan children. Between 1812 and 1823, 3,933 Khoisan children were born, and, of these, 2,295 were apprenticed (Boddington 1983). Their "employers" were expected to provide adequate food and clothing and to ensure instruction in the principles of Christianity. In addition to religious instruction, children were taught agricultural skills. The 1812 proclamation that allowed these apprenticeships was extended, in 1819, to include the apprenticeship of orphans. In 1842, the Masters and Servants Act further secured access to children's labor. Boddington wrote, "Farmers gained access to labor through the apprenticeship of 'destitute' children. . . . The provisions regarding these child apprentices were particularly paternalistic. . . . The contract stated that the apprentices 'shall faithfully and honestly serve and obey his master'; the master in turn was to provide, apart from maintenance and clothing, education and religious instruction (Boddington 1983, 144).

In addition to apprenticeship, the taking of child captives was another way to secure child labor after slavery. Trapido wrote:

> Since slavery was forbidden under the treaty by which Boer independence was acknowledged by Britain, republican law created a façade which forbade both the condition of the totally unfree laborer and the sale or barter of such. Since no very great distance was put between the slave's community of origin and his place of enslavement, deracination was achieved by the seizure of children rather than adults. These children were deemed to be orphans—very often slave raiding ensured that they became orphans. . . . Although the law forbade their sale, compensation for their keep could be claimed if they were handed on to new masters (Trapido 1976, 2–3)

The work that child captives performed did not differ significantly from the work children of the household were expected to do, but while the latter would inherit the role of "madams" and "masters," the former were destined to become adult servants (Trapido 1976).

Another form of disinheritance was manifest in the 1913 Native Land Act, which allocated 13 percent of South African land to the black South African majority. The rest of the land, including seaports, fertile agricultural land, and mineral beds, was reserved for the privileged white minority (Mbeki 1964). The Pass Law, which prohibited black people from being in South Africa without a valid pass, was also introduced in 1913, with the effect that black people could not purchase land, and their contracts as sharecroppers and independent farmers were dismissed. Magubane has made the point that "the setting aside of the African reservations as communities unequally integrated into the South African social and economic life had to be done in such a way that Africans would be unable to satisfy their barest needs" (Magubane 1979, 123). Forced to live in underresourced areas, black people became dependent on migrant wage labor. Thus, the 1913 Natives Land Act laid the foundation for the centrality of migrant labor in South Africa's political economy. Poverty in the reserves forced men, children, women, and the elderly into the migrant labor economy. Children also participated in family subsistence strategies in the newly developed "homelands." They contributed to agricultural work, cared for infants, cooked, and cleaned. Parents preferred their children to contribute to the household income "rather than wasting their time at school" due to the inferiority of black schools and the shortage of jobs for school leavers (Glaser 2000, 31).

Child Labor in the Mining Industry

In the early 1900s child labor was so common that in both Southern Rhodesia and South Africa, "picannin" wages were entered in the mines' annual reports. By 1920, half of the labor force in South Africa's asbestos and mica mines were children, while the other half were men over the age of seventy (van Onselen 1976). Mica and asbestos mine managers paid low wages to the aged and the very young as a means to compete with more lucrative mining industries. Young boys were recruited by gold and diamond miners as domestic servants. Known as "mine wives," boys accompanied men from the rural reserves to the mines, where they stayed on to provide emotional and sexual support (Levine 1999; Moodie 1992; van Onselen 1976). This social practice began in the early 1900s, when Rhodesian boys performed domestic tasks for adult mine workers. These boys received pocket money in exchange for cleaning, cooking, and washing clothes for their "husbands." They also formed sexual relationships with their "husbands."

At first critical of the mine-wife system, management later encouraged these "marriages" because they found that men spent more money at the mines for their "brides" than they sent home to the rural areas. One miner interviewed by Moodie said that it was a waste to send money back to his wife: "That's somehow a loss of money. I mean, she does not even wash your vest, while with these boys it was better because evenings were for legs" (1992, 126). Moodie has argued that these young boys, in their attempt to combat childhood poverty, delayed full proletarianization and secured for themselves a niche that was preferable to the work that children did underground in the mica and asbestos mines.

Girls' Domestic Work

In precolonial society, girls in African villages assisted their mothers with domestic tasks. Delius wrote about Pedi girls, "From an early age girls helped with child care in the *kgoro*. They also learned how to maintain the mud walls of the courtyards and the dung floors of the huts. They were taught to identify and gather wild foods. Girls spent long hours grinding corn, and fetching water and kindling wood. As they grew older they did more and more work in the fields, initially assisting with weeding but subsequently also helping with planting and harvesting" (Delius 1996, 28). Young girls also assisted their mothers with waged domestic and agricultural work. Thus, childhood roles were shaped by the particular construction of childhood along lines of race and class during the colonial and apartheid eras.

Cecil Rhodes, who became prime minister of the Cape Colony in 1890, declared, "The Native is to be treated as a child and denied the franchise" (Magubane 1988, 63). Frantz Fanon interpreted this double life when he wrote, "The black man has two dimensions. One with his fellows, the other with the white man" (1967, 17). The slippery nature of this double life is reflected by the fact that while black adults were registered by the state as minors, their wages reflected their differential status from children, who were paid "picaninn" wages. Children were thus superexploited in relation to the already exploited adult labor force. The following Xhosa poem captures this historical tendency:

> How can I live in this world?
> Oh, what can I do? It is so dark ahead of me
> Mother and father do not want us
> They sell us to thugs . . .
> (Translation of children's poem cited in Reynolds 1989, 73)

In 1953, Hendrik Verwoerd, then the minister of native affairs, and later South Africa's prime minister, proposed and implemented the Bantu Education Act. This act enforced the link between the educational system devised for black children and the labor requirements of the state. Verwoerd introduced the bill as follows: "When I have control of Native education I will reform it so that the natives will be taught from childhood to realize that equality with Europeans is not for them. . . . What is the use of teaching a Bantu child mathematics when it cannot use it in practice? . . . Education must train and teach people in accordance with their opportunities in life" (quoted in Tatum 1982, 18).

Regarding the system of Bantu education, Jonathan Hyslop argued, "The educational policies of the state during that decade were above all an attempt to respond to the crisis of reproduction of the labor force . . . [because] . . . the urban workforce was not providing sufficient numbers with the education required for semi-skilled labor in the expanding factories" (Hyslop 1988, 394). The De Villiers Commission of 1948 concluded that "for their present stage of development [Africans] profit much more from practical subjects than from academic subjects" (quoted in Hyslop 1988, 398).

Bantu education perpetuated feelings of inferiority among black children by foregrounding their "primitive nature" as the reason for their natural disposition for particular forms of labor. Steve Biko addressed the psychological effects of such domination: "It sometimes looks obvious here that the great plan is to keep the black people thoroughly intimidated and to perpetuate the 'super-race' image of the white man, if not intellectually, at least in terms of force" (Biko 1978, 76). Grooming black children for lives of servitude was part of an effort to perpetuate a hegemonic "superrace." A pillar of apartheid, Bantu education underpinned the state's ideology of race and class domination. While the Bantu Education Act no longer organizes education in South Africa, the crisis in the education sector continues to underprepare black students for lives outside of menial labor.

Conclusion

South Africa has been identified as one among several nations having especially high numbers of working children whose labor is hidden or entrenched. There is a tendency to regard child labor as an aberration of capitalist social relations, rather than a fundamental feature of it. But the structural inequalities in South African history that gave rise to particular forms of child labor in the country have not been erased after apartheid. In many instances, poverty has deepened along with unemployment, the HIV/AIDS pandemic, and the restructuring of social grants in the postapartheid neoliberal age. Since 2003, with greater adherence by farmers to laws that prohibit child labor, children's ability to work as a means of survival has given way to informal and illegal occupations, notably sex work and drug selling. Future work in this area must consider the unintended consequences of making child labor illegal in the context of deep structural inequalities that persist in postapartheid South Africa.

References and Further Reading

Biko, Steve. *I Write What I Like.* South Africa: Raven Press, 1978.

Boddington, Erica. "Domestic Service: Changing Relations of Class Domination, 1841–1948: A Focus on Cape Town." Thesis, University of Cape Town, 1983.

Burman, Sandra, and Pamela Reynolds, eds. *Growing Up in a Divided Society: The Contexts of Childhood in South Africa.* Johannesburg: Raven Press, 1986.

Delius, Peter. *A Lion Amongst the Cattle: Reconstruction and Resistance in the Northern Transvaal.* Johannesburg: Heinemann, 1996.

Fanon, Frantz. *Black Skin White Masks.* New York: Grove Press, 1967.

Gailey, Christine Ward. "Rethinking Child Labor in an Age of Capitalist Restructuring." *Critique of Anthropology* 19:2 (1999): 115–19.

Glaser, Clive. *Bo-Tsotsi: The Youth Gangs of Soweto, 1935–1976.* Cape Town: David Phillip, 2000.

Grier, Beverly. "Invisible Hands: The Political Economy of Child Labour in Colonial Zimbabwe, 1890–1930." *Journal of Southern African Studies* 1 (1994): 27–52.

Grier, Beverly. *Invisible Hands: Child Labor and the State in Colonial Zimbabwe.* Portsmouth, NH: Heinemann, 2006.

Hansen, Karen Tranberg. *Distant Companions.* Ithaca, NY: Cornell University Press, 1989.

Hyslop, Jonathan. "School Student Movements and State Education Policy: 1972–87." In *Popular Struggles in South Africa*, ed. William Cobbett and Robin Cohen, 183–209. Trenton, NJ: Africa World Press, 1988.

Levine, Susan. "Bittersweet Harvest: Children, Work and the Global March Against Child Labor in the Post-Apartheid State." *Critique of Anthropology* 19:2 (1999): 139–55.

Levine, Susan. "In the Shadow of the Vine: Child Labor in South Africa." PhD thesis, Temple University, 2000.

Levine, Susan. "The 'Piccaninny Wage': An Historical Overview of the Persistence of Structural Inequality and Child Labour in South Africa." *Anthropology Southern Africa* 29:3–4 (2006): 122–31.

Magubane, Bernard. *The Political Economy of Race and Class in South Africa.* London: Monthly Review Press, 1979.

Magubane, Bernard. "Imperialism and the Making of the South African Working Class." In *Proletarianization and Class Struggle in Africa,* ed. Bernard Magubane and Nzongola-Ntalaja, 19–56. San Francisco: Synthesis Publications, 1983.

Magubane, Bernard. *Whither South Africa?* Johannesburg: Africa World Press, 1988.

Mbeki, Govan. *South Africa: The Peasants Revolt.* Baltimore: Penguin African Library, 1964.

Molobi, Eric. "From Bantu Education to People's Education." In *Popular Struggles in South Africa*, ed. William Cobbett and Robin Cohen, 155–62. Trenton, NJ: Africa World Press, 1988.

Moodie, Dunbar. "Mine Culture and Miners' Identity on the South African Gold Mines." In *Town and Countryside in the Transvaal*, ed. Belinda Bozzoli, 176–97. Johannesburg: Raven Press, 1983.

Moodie, Dunbar. *Going for Gold: Men, Mines, and Migration.* Berkeley: University of California Press, 1992.

Reynolds, Pamela. *Childhood in Crossroads.* Cape Town: David Philip, 1989.

Scully, Pamela. "Liquor and Labor in the Western Cape, 1870–1900." In *Liquor and Labor in Southern Africa*, ed. Jonathan Crush and Charles Ambler, 56–77. Athens: Ohio University Press, 1992.

Shell, Robert C.H. *Children of Bondage.* Witwatersrand, South Africa: Witwatersrand University Press, 1994.

Tatum, Lyle. *South Africa: Challenge and Hope.* Philadelphia: Hill and Wang, 1982.

Trapido, Stanley. "The Long Apprenticeship: Captivity in the Trans-Vaal, 1843–1841." Paper presented at the Conference on Southern African Labour History, University of Witswatersrand, April 10, 1976.

Van Onselen, Charles. *Chibaro: African Mine Labour in Southern Rhodesia, 1900–1933.* London: Pluto Press, 1976.

Wolpe, Harrold. *Race, Class, and the Apartheid State.* Trenton, NJ: Africa World Press, 1998.

Swaziland

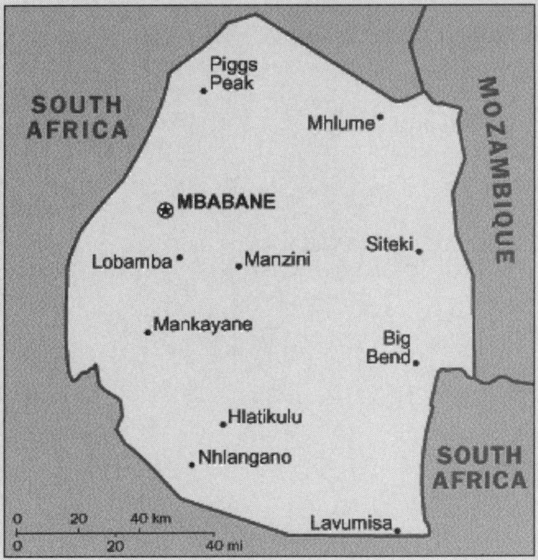

SWAZILAND			
	CRC	C 138	C 182
Ratifications	Y	Y	Y
Human Development Index/Rank	0.500/146		
Human Capital			
Population Growth Rate	–0.34%		
% Population 0–14	40.3%		
Total Fertility Rate	3.43		
Life Expectancy	32.23		
Infant Mortality Rate	70.66		
Literacy Rate	81.6%		
Economic			
GDP/Capita	$5,500		
GDP Growth %	2%		
% Poverty	69%		
Gini Index	—		

CHILD ACTIVITY BREAKDOWN, BY SEX AND RESIDENCE

RESIDENCE	Percentage of children in the relevant age-group[a]									
	Economic activity only		School only		Combining school and economic activity		Neither in school nor in economic activity		Child labor[b]	
	Male	Female	Male	Female	Male	Female	Male	Female	Male	Female
Urban	1.2	2.2	74.7	74.4	14.4	14.0	9.8	9.5	n/av	n/av
Rural	1.6	1.6	70.1	71.7	7.4	7.3	20.8	19.4	n/av	n/av
Total	**1.6**	**1.7**	**70.7**	**72.1**	**8.2**	**8.3**	**19.5**	**17.9**	**9.2**	**9.5**

Source: Swaziland, Multiple Indicator Cluster Survey 2, 2000 (see UCW Project Web site, http://www.ucw-project.org, country statistics).

Notes: [a]Children age 5 to 14. [b]Estimate includes (a) children under age 12 engaged in economic activities, (b) children age 12–14 engaged in excessive economic activities (more than 14 hours per week), and (c) children under age 15 engaged in excessive household chores (at least 28 hours per week). Estimate does not account for children engaged in hazardous work or other unconditional "worst forms" of child labor.

Part 3
Latin America and Carribean

SECTION 1. INTRODUCTION

Child Labor in Latin America

Walter Alarcón Glasinovich, Director, Infancia y Desarrollo

Child labor in Latin America is a symptom of the historical accumulation of exclusion and inequity. Despite the limitations of current international statistics on child labor, this essay attempts to provide an account of the evolution and present state of the labor situation of boys and girls in Latin America. A panoramic approach such as this has the advantage of presenting an image of the region as a whole. Inevitably, however, it has the disadvantage of obscuring unique characteristics of some countries.

Historical Background

Just as the concept of childhood as a stage of protection and special care began to form in Europe, Latin American boys and girls in European colonies were condemned, along with the adult population, to servitude and slavery (Pedraza-Gómez 2004). Historian Pablo Macera (1985) stated that during colonial times "the galleries of the Potosí mines and the lands of the Spanish encomiendas concealed thousands of working children; children whose names have been lost in the dark anonymity of a horrible genocide." Thousands or millions of boys and girls were reduced to the condition of slaves. As Aguirre (2005) stated, "The domestic slaves included men and women. . . . We also find domestic slaves within all age spectrums, from very young children, mainly the children of the female slaves who served in the same house, to very old people."

As a result of colonial domination, from the beginning of the sixteenth century to the beginning of the nineteenth century, the social structure in Latin America was radically pyramidal and exclusive. At the wide base were millions of indigenous and black men and women.

In spite of political independence, which occurred during the first decades of the nineteenth century, there were few significant changes in the economic and social structure. Slavery was progressively eliminated, but servitude was maintained. The economic structure persisted, sustained on agricultural production and mining exploitation, principally aimed at the international market. Along with this, the indigenous majorities remained linked to a peasant economy of self-subsistence. The few cities that existed at the time were administrative and political centers with economies based on craft production, services, and trade. Among the indigenous peasant families, the work of boys and girls was an integral part of daily life and was socially accepted. In countries such as Bolivia, Peru, and Mexico, the majority of peasants lived in indigenous communities. Another sector of peasants worked with their families on large estates of propertied landowners, under semifeudal production relationships.

From the beginning of the republican period, the classic liberal model was adopted by the states and adapted to the Latin American context. Toward the last third of the nineteenth century, in the small urban centers, besides craft production, the first manufacturing industries began to appear. Since the initial impulse of industrial capitalism in Latin

America, child labor has been present. Gilberto Harris (2002), in research on Chile, reported the extensive use of child labor at the beginning of industrialization. Chilean children worked from the age of twelve years in textile factories and tanneries and with tobacco, matches, soaps, and other products:

> In the half agricultural and half mining Chile of the XIX Century, women and children performed an important role as cheap labor in the process of "early industrialization." . . . The Nacional de Tipos factory "employed almost in its totality children within the ages of 12 to 16 years"; the factory that manufactured tobacco from Valparaiso, employed in 1877, 60 to 70 workers "in its majority child orphans from the Casa de San Vicente de Paul"; . . . the coat factory of J.E. Ramirez, located in La Calera, employed mainly women and children ages 12 to 14 years; . . . the Fundicion de Carlos Klein, employed children that moved machines and wrapped percussion caps. (Harris 2002, 121, 127)[1]

In 1907, Argentina promulgated the first law that regulated child labor in Latin America. Rapidly other countries of the region would follow the same path. However, this legislation, in fact, was more symbolic than effective. Since the first decades of the twentieth century, particularly after the crisis of 1929, the import substitution model, as an alternative to the classic liberal model, was progressively assumed in Latin America. In the middle of the twentieth century this model became widespread in nearly all the countries of Latin America. In this new stage of economic life, the state became the engine of the modernization process.

Trends in the Evolution of Child Labor: 1950–1990

Table 1 is interesting because it shows the labor evolution of boys and girls between the ages of ten and fourteen from 1950 until 1990. In the case of Latin America and the Caribbean, there has been a consistent trend of decreasing child labor from 1950 to 1990. It must be noted, however, that the percentage decrease of child labor in Latin America is, comparatively, less than that observed in other

Table 1

Economically Active Population, 10–14 Years Old, 1950–1990 (as % of age-group)

Geographical area	1950	1960	1970	1980	1990
Africa	38.4	35.9	33.1	31.0	27.9
Asia	36.1	32.3	28.4	23.4	15.2
Latin America and the Caribbean	19.4	16.5	14.6	12.6	11.2
North America, Western Europe, and Australia	6.6	3.8	2.1	0.5	0.1
Total	27.6	24.8	22.3	19.9	14.7

Source: Bulletin of Labour Statistics 1995, I–IV, International Labour Office, from Gunnarsson et al. 2005.

poor regions throughout the world. Decomposing the trend reveals that, between 1950 and 1970, child labor in Latin America declined more vigorously than it did in subsequent decades. From 1950 to 1970, the labor force participation rate of boys and girls declined from 19.4 to 14.6 percent. Beginning in 1980, however, the declining trend stalled, and from 1980 to 1990, the child labor rate dropped very little, from 12.6 to 11.2 percent.

What were the elements that produced this moderate decrease in child labor in Latin America from 1950 to 1990? A first matter to emphasize is the process of economic modernization, and the processes of urbanization and migration that appear to be entwined. In Latin America, agricultural activities have been losing relative influence in their contribution to gross domestic product in favor of the industrial and service sectors. These changes in the structure of production imply progressive alterations in the labor market structure, where the economically active population in agricultural activities declined from 55 percent in 1950 to 32 percent in 1980 (Weller 1998).

On the one hand, this modernization of the productive structure and labor markets, along with the decrease in the total volume of the rural population, created conditions that would begin to explain the decrease in child labor over the long term. On the other hand, the inability of the modern sector to create employment at the same pace as demographic growth caused the formation and expansion of the so-called informal sector. In Latin America, the economic modernization processes maintained certain traditional agrarian features, fostering a growing participation in microenterprises and self-employment in the informal sectors of the cities. It is precisely these conditions that help to explain why the decrease in child labor has not been as marked as in other regions experiencing economic modernization. In other words, the type of modernization in Latin America produced economic patterns that, due to their low productivity and reliance on less advanced technologies, allow the continued participation of child labor.

Related to the economic modernization are the processes of urbanization and migration toward the thriving cities. At the beginning of the twentieth century, only 25 percent of the entire Latin American population lived in cities. By 1950, the urban population had grown to 42 percent. This trend has continued gradually to the point that, today, it is estimated that 75 percent of the Latin American population lives in urban areas.

At a cultural level, urbanization implies a gradual process of diffusion of modern conceptions of the meaning and roles of childhood, where childhood would be assumed essentially as a phase of school attendance and human capital formation. To be sure, traces of traditional rural cultural roots of the social meaning of childhood remain, but they are no longer hegemonic. Similarly, as the urbanization processes matured, they were accompanied by changes in the composition of families. Gradually, a trend toward families with fewer children began to consolidate.

Urbanization also created closer proximity and easier access to public educational services. The expansion of school enrollment that followed is a crucial factor that helps to explain the declining trend in child labor since the middle of the twentieth century. In countries of Latin America and the Caribbean, by the year 1960, the net school enrollment rate for children between six and eleven years old was 58 percent. Since then, the primary school enrollment rate has increased consistently, reaching 88 percent in 1992 (Schiefelbein 1996), and climbing to 96 percent by the year 2001. In spite of these achievements, however, it is estimated that 2.5 million primary school age boys and girls remain outside of the educational system (Burnett 2006). While the increase in the school enrollment rate helps to explain the long-run decline in child labor, the continuing deficit of educational coverage is of vital importance in explaining the moderate character of this decline.

As noted previously, the declining trend of child labor in Latin America stalled in the 1980s. The decade of the 1980s witnessed an economic recession in Latin America. Between 1945 and 1980, the historic annual growth rate of gross domestic product in Latin America averaged 5.5 percent (Ocampo 2001). This fell to an average of 0.9 percent in the decade of 1980s. Debt crisis and the beginnings of economic restructuring toward a neoliberal design immediately produced important consequences. Employment in the modern formal sector of the economy fell, and the informal sector experienced exponential growth, producing absolute instability in the labor market. Unemployment grew and real incomes fell, exacerbating an already unequal distribution of income. These unfavorable economic conditions, since the middle of the 1980s, prevented further decline of child labor, and, more important, this economic deterioration created conditions that would later lead to an increase in child labor.

Thus, from a long-term perspective, the special characteristics of peripheral capitalism, and what this entails in terms of the persistence of traditional agrarian structures and significant maintenance of the urban informal sector, the inequality of national income distribution, and the subsequent extended poverty, coupled with the lack of a genuine universal education system, mainly in rural areas, in spite of the gains in school enrollment, comprise a set of substantive factors that explain the stalling of a more consistent decline of child labor trends.

Current Situation of Child Labor in Latin America

Table 2 presents the participation rates of girls, boys, and adolescents ages five to seventeen years in the labor force for the year 2000. Note that the economic activity rate for ten- to fourteen-year-olds is estimated at 22 percent, compared to the estimate of 11.2 percent for the year 1990 (in Table 1). While there are methodological divergences that may account for some of the increase, it appears that the long-term trend in declining child labor, which stalled in the 1980s, was actually reversed

Table 2

Latin America and the Caribbean, 2000: Distribution of the Economically Active Population by Age-Group

	Economically active population		
Age ranges	EAP total (in millions)	Activity rate	Percent distribution
5–9 Years	5.8	11	21
10–14 Years	11.6	22	42
15–17 Years	10.3	35	37
Total	27.7	20	100

Source: Based on information from ILO 2002.

Table 3

Latin America and the Caribbean, 2005: Harmful and Nonharmful Child and Adolescent Labor

	5–17 years	5–14 years	15–17 years
Population in Economic Activities (in millions)[a]	19.7	9.8	9.9
Total in Harmful Labor (in millions)	12.6	8.5[b]	4.2[c]
Percent in Harmful Labor	64.0	86.7	42.4
Percent in Nonharmful Labor	36.0	13.3	57.6

Source: Author's calculations based on information from Sauma 2005.

[a]This category includes all harmful and nonharmful labor participation of girls, boys, and adolescents.

[b]This number includes boys and girls between the ages of 5 and 14 years who work under the legal minimum age in each country (68%) and those involved in the worst forms of child labor (32%).

[c]This number includes all adolescents between 15 and 17 years of age registered in worst forms of child labor according to the definition in ILO Convention 182.

between 1990 and 2000, and that children's activity rates have increased by roughly 10 percent.

Table 2 reveals the obvious fact that the labor activity rate increases with age: 11 percent of boys and girls five to nine years old were economically active; 22 percent of those ten to fourteen; reaching 35 percent among fifteen- to seventeen-year-old adolescents. However, it is important to emphasize that fully 63 percent of the minors who worked in Latin America and the Caribbean are between the ages of five and fourteen years old. In this context, it must be remembered that laws in the region prohibit labor force participation of boys and girls until they turn fourteen years of age. Even in countries such as Ecuador and Chile, the minimum age for work is fifteen years old, while in Brazil the minimum is sixteen years of age. It is quite a dramatic development that Latin America entered the twenty-first century with 17.4 percent of boys and girls fourteen years of age and younger registered as workers.

Further, the majority of these children work in occupations, environments, or conditions that are harmful for their well-being. Table 3 provides information regarding the involvement of Latin American boys, girls, and adolescents in both harmful and nonharmful work situations in the year 2005. It should be noted that the information presented in Table 3 is not rigorously comparable to the information presented in Table 2, due to the coverage of the involved countries and the technical treatment of the data. But it does provide clear information about the distribution of harmful and nonharmful work.

In general, practically two-thirds (64 percent) of the total of boys, girls, and adolescents who work in Latin America do so in harmful labor or in work that is otherwise inappropriate for their age. A significant proportion work at ages that do not correspond to those stipulated in national laws; others openly perform work that is harmful to their health, safety, or morals; still others engage in especially egregious forms of work, including subordination to chains of sexual exploitation and other illicit activities. This is the cruel reality of child labor in Latin America and the Caribbean. In our region, child labor is just another way of slowly taking away the lives of our boys and girls, and it is one more expression of the failure of the governments to exercise authority and take responsibility on matters of childhood. Some people argue that child labor should be a right of the poor. But to argue for such a right, given the widespread prevalence of children in harmful work situations throughout Latin America, is to argue against the best interests of the children. Harmful work is not a right, but for many poor families it is an unpleasant reality.

According to Table 3, youngest children appear to be in the worst situation: 87 percent of the total of working boys and girls between the ages of five and fourteen years old are dedicated to labor that hurts their possibilities for present and future development. Only 13 percent work in a job with protected conditions. On the one hand, of this 87 percent, 5.8 million (68 percent of the total) are boys and girls who work at an age that is younger than what is legally permitted in their home country. They work in both urban and rural areas that may be quite different economic and sociocultural spaces. It is essential to have more information about this group. For example, many of these boys and girls from rural areas, while working under the legal minimum age, may be working in traditional peasant self-subsistence family economies. While these children and their families may live in difficult economic conditions, labor participation by boys and girls in traditional rural economies may provide a necessary space for the process of learning, development of abilities, practical knowledge, and socialization in cultural contexts. Their work is absolutely different from the work performed by children in modern and urban contexts.

On the other hand, it is pertinent to point out that, in the year 2005, of the 8.5 million boys and girls between the ages of five and fourteen years old that worked in Latin America, 2.7 million (32 percent of the total) were involved in activities incorporated under the "worst forms" of child labor. In other words, they worked in occupations and conditions the world has deemed humanly unacceptable. When we add in the 4.2 million adolescents fifteen to seventeen years of age in similar situations, nearly 7 million children throughout Latin America and the Caribbean were engaged in "worst forms" of child labor.

The Future of Child Labor in Latin America and the Caribbean

The ILO's most recent global estimate of child labor suggests that Latin America and the Caribbean was the most successful region in the world in reducing child labor between the years 2000 and 2004. The numbers of economically active children from five to fourteen years old decreased in the region from 17.4 million in 2000 to 5.7 million in 2004, and the economic activity rates similarly declined from 16.1 to 5.1 percent (ILO 2006).

However, using statistics published by the ILO itself, this essay has examined how child labor decreased moderately from 1950 until 1990, and then increased by the year 2000. We pointed out that this increase was a social expression of the high rates of poverty and inadequate social policies in the context of economic restructuring. Was this increase in child labor only a temporary growth that is diminishing as Latin American economies gain strength and achieve a better redistribution of income? Or is the recent decline in child labor the temporary phenomenon?

Region-wide numbers are very useful for assembling global estimates, but they can hide divergent realities among the countries in the region. It is important to remember that Latin America and the Caribbean are constituted by extremely diverse countries.

In fact, most of the decline in child labor reported by the ILO is confined to two countries—Brazil and Mexico. These are the two most populous countries in the region, and the two countries that represent the largest absolute number of child laborers in Latin America and the Caribbean. And despite their success in reducing child labor, in the year 2005, Brazil and Mexico accounted for 44 percent of the region's child labor between five and fourteen years old, and in these same countries were concentrated half of the region's child labor in their "worst forms" (Sauma 2005).

Brazil and Mexico have been able to reduce their rates of child labor mainly through programs of conditional income transfers that have been consistently carried out since the 1990s. These programs, which provide income to poor families conditioned on their sending their children to school, tend to strengthen human capital, essentially through school attendance, and seem to be an essential tool, at least in the short and medium term, in the fight against child labor. Based on the accomplishments of these two countries, one might optimistically conclude that other Latin America and the Caribbean countries could attain similar success in the decrease or elimination of child labor by emulating these conditional cash transfer programs. Unfortunately, at the present time in many other countries of the region, the problem of boys and girls who work not only subsists, but has increased.

All evidence suggests that the elimination of child labor demands sustained economic growth, social policies aimed at the redistribution of wealth, changes in public culture in the sense of becoming aware of the risks of child labor, and governments committed to enforcing childhood protection laws. Along the way, programs such as conditional cash transfers aimed at working boys and girls and their families can help to alleviate the situation, but in the long term, what is essential are public policies that aim toward growth with equity.

Note

1. Translation from the original Spanish: "En el Chile mitad agrícola, mitad minero del siglo XIX, mujeres y niños desempeñaron un importante papel como mano de obra barata en el proceso de la 'temprana industrialización.' . . . [F]ábrica Nacional de Tipos que 'ocupaba casi en su totalidad niños de 12 a 16 años'; fábrica elaboradora de tabaco de Valparaíso, ocupando en 1877 60 a 70 operarios 'en su mayoría niños huérfanos de la Casa de San Vicente de Paul'; . . . Fábrica de sacos de J.E. Ramírez, ubicada en la Calera, ocupando fundamentalmente mujeres y niños entre los 12 y 14 años; . . . la Fundición de Carlos Klein, ocupando a niños que movían máquinas y envolver fulminantes."

References and Further Reading

Alarcón, W. *De la explotación a la esperanza: ensayos sobre trabajo infantil en América Latina.* Madrid: Ed. Proyecto Solidario, 2006.

Aguirre, C. *Breve historia de la esclavitud en el Perú: una herida que no deja de sangrar.* Lima: Fondo Editorial del Congreso del Perú, 2005.

Burnett, N., coord. *Informe de seguimiento de la EPT en el mundo—educación para todos: la alfabetización un factor vital.* Paris: UNESCO, 2006.

Gunnarsson, V., P. Orazem, and G. Sedlacek. *Changing Patterns of Child Labour Around the World Since 1950: The Roles of Income Growth, Parental Literacy and Agriculture.* Washington, DC: World Bank, 2005.

Harris, G. "La importancia de mujeres y niños en la 'cultura del vapor' en la sociedad porteña chilena: 1850–1905." *Revista del archivo histórico de Viña del Mar* 4 (2002): 121–29.

ILO. *The End of Child Labor: Within Reach.* Coord. F. Hagemann. Geneva: ILO-IPEC, 2006.

ILO. *Every Child Counts: New Global Estimates on Child Labour.* Coord. F. Hagemann. Geneva: ILO-IPEC, 2002.

Macera, P. *Historia del Peru 2.* Lima: Ed. Bruño, 1985.

Ocampo, J.A., coord. *Construir equidad desde la infancia y la adolescencia en Iberoamérica.* Santiago de Chile: CEPAL-UNICEF-SECIB, 2001.

Pedraza-Gómez, Z. "Child Workers and the Cultural Perception of Childhood." Paper presented at the international symposium What Does Work Mean to Children? Theoretical Approaches and International Empirical Reports, Berlin, April 12–17, 2004.

Sauma, P. *Construir futuro, invertir en la infancia: estudio económico de los costos y beneficios de erradicar el trabajo infantil en Iberoamérica.* San José: IPEC/OIT, 2005.

Schiefelbein, E., coord. *Situación educativa de América Latina y el Caribe 1980–1994.* Santiago de Chile: UNESCO, 1996.

Weller, J. *Los mercados laborales en América Latina: su evolución en el largo plazo y sus tendencias recientes.* Santiago de Chile: CEPAL, 1998.

History of Childhood and Child Labor in Latin America

Elizabeth Anne Kuznesof, Professor of History, University of Kansas

In Latin America, the concept of child and adolescent labor includes a broad range of activities that have had varying meanings since the time of conquest. Children under age twenty constituted from 30 to 50 percent of the population of Latin America in the eighteenth and nineteenth centuries, and they make up more than 50 percent of the population today. Historically, nonelite child labor has been a normal part of the domestic economy throughout Latin America, and continues to be so today, particularly in rural areas. For this reason, it is important to differentiate labor that is harmful to children from work that might be viewed as educational and as that might transmit skills. Also, for the popular classes, work has been given priority over formal education, such that school absenteeism is extremely common. The acceptance of child labor as normal and even positive is clearly associated with the history of the family and childhood in Latin America.

From a historical and legal perspective, the family in Latin America is consistently represented as the fundamental unit of society, and as a patriarchal institution, based on monogamous marriage, and focused on reproduction. However, colonial Spanish and Portuguese legal codes considered the care and nurturing of children private functions, falling into the corporate sphere of the family, so that "legitimate" children were seldom mentioned in law. This vision has been retained from the sixteenth to the twenty-first century in spite of the remarkable diversity in family and household forms that have existed in Latin America. The "legitimate" family can be seen as the codification of an elite world vision, concerned with paternal power, the legitimacy of offspring, and the regulation of family wealth.

The remarkable fact is that the majority of children born in Latin America since 1492 were not born in "legal" families. Between 30 and 60 percent of free births were illegitimate in most Latin American countries between the sixteenth and the end of the nineteenth centuries. For slaves illegitimacy was much higher. Children that appear in historical documents were predominantly abandoned and orphaned children, or children contracted out as apprentices, inducted into the military, or caught up in the criminal justice system. Thus, in both the law and the historical record, children have been seen as marginal in one way or another, and often in need of social control by some institution.

Definition of Childhood in Latin America

The very definition of childhood in Latin America evolved over time as clerics and legislators defined the duties and responsibilities of parents and children toward one another, and the responsibilities of the state toward children. In the colonial period, focus was on parental obligations toward children up to age seven, the age of reason. The period from birth to age three was designated "infancy" and was distinguished by the child being sustained by human milk. In the period from age four to age seven, the father was responsible for providing sustenance. Education, in the sense of learning obedience, manners, and prayers, was emphasized. From age four the child was taken to mass. The father had the legal right of *patria potestad,* which included the obligations to feed, clothe, discipline, educate, select occupations, and sanction marital plans of children. In return, children were to obey parents and work without wages. To have a legal heir, fathers had to acknowledge paternity; otherwise, single mothers had to support children alone, though mothers were denied the legal rights of *patria potestad.* Fathers who felt little obligation to children existed at all levels. During the colonial period, orphaned children were usually the responsibility of grandparents or their parents' siblings. Abandoned children were estimated to constitute between 10 and 25 percent of births in the eighteenth and nineteenth centuries, and often died from exposure.

From age seven, children were seen as having reason and were morally responsible for their acts. Children were required to study, work, confess, and follow the rituals of Catholicism. Girls were expected to be modest. At age seven little boys could go to primary school or work for a salary in somebody's house while they learned a skill or profession. Little girls at that age began to help with domestic tasks, learned to sew and embroider, and very rarely might learn to read and write from a cleric or teacher. Until age ten children could not be legally punished for crimes. Families assumed any penalties for crimes committed by their children. After age ten girls and boys had to sleep separately. According to colonial law, girls could be married at age twelve, boys at fourteen.

After age seven children's labor was believed to have value. Judges in Brazil emphasized the right of orphaned children from age seven to receive a salary from a tutor, and not to be exploited for free labor. However, there was no real discussion about what kind of work was appropriate for that age, or how many hours children should work. Slave children might be introduced to light tasks from the age of five or six. While no formal education was offered to slave children, it was not unusual for slave boys to be put into apprenticeships, or for slave girls to become domestic laborers on the plantation, or even be rented out to other households. In the colonial period, work was clearly integral to the lives of all children in Latin America, except the most elite.

The Nineteenth Century

In the late eighteenth and early nineteenth centuries, elite discourse emphasized an ethic of protection of children, including adolescents, citing their fragility and innocence, as well as the importance of education (Szuchman 1988). Early republican governments and beneficent societies began to assist abandoned children through orphanages and poorhouses. In Mexico, poor families would sometimes "abandon" a child for weeks or months at an orphanage, and then reclaim the child when the family had more resources. For older children, orphanages often functioned as workhouses where children remained until they were sent out for foster care, often as servants.

Child labor was common in the nineteenth century. For example, an 1831 census for Minas Gerais, Brazil, revealed that, by the age of ten, 20 percent of children (including free, freed, and slaves) listed occupations; 44 percent of children ages thirteen and fourteen listed occupations. Agricultural work was the most common occupation for boys, while girls mostly were domestics or worked in textiles. Fairly young slave children might even be sold away from parents and kinfolk to work.

Emergence of the concept of adolescence, and a specific focus on how children ages twelve through nineteen should be treated, were linked to dramatic economic and social developments in late-nineteenth-century Latin America. These changes extended life expectancy and created expanded employment opportunities dependent on longer schooling. For example, the substantial sector of service occupations that developed in increasingly urbanized communities was an important source of new employment, particularly for children and women.

By the late nineteenth century, discourse emphasizing education as a means to foster civic responsibility was displaced by a growing penal consciousness intent on the prevention and punishment of crime. An ideology focused on children's protection was transformed into a preoccupation with order and social control. Nineteenth-century legislation very often targeted abandoned or orphaned children, since unruly vagrant youths were seen as potentially dangerous to society. In Brazil and Chile, the "child" began to be referred to as a "minor," with the latter term carrying an implication of danger and a tendency toward crime. Brazilian criminal codes of 1830 and 1890 emphasized the moral responsibility of children between the ages of seven and fourteen regarding consciousness of right and wrong and the ability to appreciate consequences for their acts. Children who understood their crimes could be jailed as adults rather than in juvenile facilities.

Until the first decades of the twentieth century, the definition of education was essentially identical with that of work. Much education took the form of apprenticeship or some kind of specific job. In Peru, boys from age eight to age twenty-five, of all ethnicities, were educated in this manner; most entered apprenticeship between ages eleven and fourteen (Premo 2005). For adolescents in the lower classes, this education was often provided through a kind of child circulation, in which young people from poorer families were sent to serve in the homes or businesses of more elite families.

The persistence of high child mortality in the late nineteenth and early twentieth centuries returned public attention to questions of child protection. Legislators refocused on childhood as "the key to the future." Intellectuals spoke of "investing in children," arguing that protecting children protected society. By the early twentieth century, efforts were made to limit the types and hours of labor for children under age fourteen, and to specifically reinforce formal education for children.

The Twentieth and Twenty-first Centuries

In Brazil and Chile, special juvenile justice systems were created in the 1920s to deal with minors. Although legislators wished to rehabilitate delinquent children, they did not make education a priority because they saw education as a dangerous weapon. It was recognized, however, that education could be an antidote for criminality; a minimal education was desirable to make minors into useful workers. Legislators debated the challenge of creating an educated population that would also be docile and hardworking. Because the laws focused on marginal children, legislators did not consider developing a national policy of quality education accessible to all. Children remained at the margins of social policy, still seen as a threat to law and order.

Brazilian laws in 1988 and 1990 changed at least the rhetoric of Brazil's approach to children, with guarantees for the protection of child and adolescent rights and a dignified life. In philosophical terms this implied that children had ceased to be viewed as a danger to society and the object of state intervention, and instead would be seen as subjects and citizens with rights to be defended. The epidemic of abandoned street children in urban Latin America since 1950 has received international attention from human rights agencies focused on issues from child abuse to child labor and education. The movie *Pixote: The Law of the Weakest* (1980) internationalized the idea that millions of poor and homeless Brazilian children live in the streets by violent means, and are themselves abused and murdered by police and death squads. Scholars from Brazil, Venezuela, Mexico, and other countries in Latin America have concluded that this problem results from insufficient resources at home—nowhere to sleep, not enough to eat, no money to pay for necessities. The streets of the wealthy are a resource-rich environment where children can effectively find money and food to take home to their families. Reformers often see mandatory education as a solution to the situation of street children. However, according to Tobias Hecht, such a policy could "threaten the position of poor urban children within the home . . . and make the home less viable." (Hecht 1998, 198) The majority of so-called street children are working in the street to bring resources to their families.

Mandatory schooling for children ages seven to fourteen was instituted in most of Latin America in the first decades of the twentieth century, though social control of an otherwise disruptive population was a major incentive. While school attendance and literacy have improved in most countries, child labor continues to compete actively with schooling. Families with minimal incomes often view the salaries of children as vital to family survival strategies. Many Latin American countries have implicitly or explicitly attempted to accommodate schooling with work. National labor codes in Chile, Peru, and Mexico have avoided the question of whether or not child labor necessarily conflicts with schooling. While children under age fourteen are theoretically prohibited from most employment, recent empirical studies make clear their significant labor contribution in the informal sector all over Latin America. Child laborers are most common in rural agricultural areas and include children age five and older. Work by children under twelve years old is widespread: in Guatemala, Ecuador, Peru, and Colombia, 16 to 27 percent of child workers are under age twelve (Salazar and Glasinovich 1999). Observers in several Latin American countries argue that childhood, as a stage of life, is denied to a large proportion of their children; however, it might be more accurate to say that the childhood experienced by poor children is distinct from that experienced by the elite.

References and Further Reading

Del Priore, Mary, ed. *Historia da crianca no Brasil.* São Paulo: Contexto, 1991.

Hecht, Tobias. *At Home in the Street: Street Children of Northeast Brazil.* Cambridge: Cambridge University Press, 1998.

Hecht, Tobias, ed. *Minor Omissions: Children in Latin American History and Society.* Madison: University of Wisconsin Press, 2002.

Kuznesof, Elizabeth A. "The House, the Street, Global Society: Latin American Families and Childhood in the 21st Century," in "Globalization and Childhood," special issue, *Journal of Social History* (June 2005): 859–72.

Lipsett-Rivera, Sonya, guest ed. "Children in the History of Latin America." Special issue, *Journal of Family History* 23:3 (July 1998).

Post, David. *Children's Work, Schooling and Welfare in Latin America.* Boulder, CO: Westview Press, 2001.

Premo, Bianca. *Children of the Father King: Youth, Authority and Legal Minority in Colonial Lima.* Chapel Hill: University of North Carolina Press, 2005.

Salazar, Maria Cristina, and Walter Alarcon Glasinovich, eds. *Child Work and Education: Five Case Studies from Latin America.* Ashgate: UNICEF, 1999.

Szuchman, Mark. *Order, Family and Community in Buenos Aires, 1810–1860.* Stanford, CA: Stanford University Press, 1988.

Child Labor and Education in Latin America

Mirellise Vazquez, Senior Policy Advisor, Christian Children's Fund

About half of the working children in Latin America do not attend school. Many are unable to attend school because there are no schools nearby, or because they cannot afford school fees and other school costs, or because they have no choice but to work in order to contribute to their families' survival. The other half of working children combine school and work, often attending school without adequate food or sleep, or with insufficient time to study or prepare homework. They complete fewer years of schooling and tend to drop out at younger ages than do those who do not work. By not attending school, or by attending for only short periods of time, working children do not gain many of the skills they need to obtain stable and more highly remunerated employment as adults, and therefore perpetuate the cycle of poverty and child labor.

Education in Latin America

Secular public schools were first established in Central America in the early 1800s. Throughout the region, enrollment in public elementary education increased from 10 percent in 1848 to 20 percent in 1854 (Institute for Research in History 1984). In the period between 1870 and 1910, the growth of export economies allowed for education to become more public and available throughout Latin America. By World War I, though universal education was widely viewed as important in achieving social justice and economic growth, few countries had even a 10 percent literacy rate (Clayton and Conniff 1999). As a result, many of the populist governments of the early 1900s began to make primary school compulsory. In most countries in the region, education became constitutionally guaranteed. More recently, most Latin American countries have pledged to extend compulsory education to eight or ten years.

Unfortunately, the 1980s brought severe downturns to the economies of Latin America, resulting in reduced social and educational expenditures. While this "lost decade" had negative effects on the lives of the poor and vulnerable, out of it arose a human rights rationale for participation in the educational system (Post 2002). Thus, in the 1990s, recognizing the need for reform and greater inclusion, the educational systems in Latin America were opened to NGOs, parents' associations, and other members of civil society, on the basis of a shared consensus that education should be a national and regional priority. Countries have also started devolving power to parents, teachers, schools, and local communities—transferring resources and authority from a centralized ministry of education to local actors (PREAL 2006).

Today, in most Latin American countries, basic education is free and compulsory, and governments have committed to making basic education available to as many children as possible. "There is a broad regional consensus that improving the quantity and quality of education is vital for economic development, to reduce Latin America's disfiguring inequalities, and to create stable democracies" ("Education in Latin America" 2002).

In general, school infrastructure is sufficient, though improvements could always be made. The percentage of children entering and completing primary school has increased dramatically over the past ten years. However, basic education often excludes early-childhood education and secondary school. Thus, it is no surprise that preschool and secondary school enrollment rates in Latin America are below those in other regions (PREAL 2006). In countries where early-childhood programs are being implemented, they have reduced the rate of malnutrition and stunting. These programs also contribute to children's school readiness and have decreased the likelihood of these children entering into hazardous work activities. Most recently, Chile has made early-childhood development a national priority. This commitment has led to new national policies, an expansion in the provision of services, increased attention to quality, and increased government financial support (UNESCO 2006).

Gaps in the Latin American Education Sector

Latin America is the region with the world's highest levels of income inequality, with the rich holding most of the region's financial resources and the poor becoming more excluded from society. At least four out of ten children in Latin America and the Caribbean under age nine (approximately 43 million) live on less than $2 a day. Low income is a major deterrent to primary school participation. Children of primary school age from the poorest households in developing countries are three times more likely to be out of primary school than those from the wealthiest households. In addition, 77 percent of children who are not in school come from the poorest 60 percent of households. This disparity is even greater in Latin America and the Caribbean, where this figure jumps to 84 percent (UNICEF 2005).

While Latin American countries are investing more in education and access has improved, resulting in more children attending school, the overall quality of education remains poor. Students in the region consistently score near the bottom on international test comparisons. In addition, over the past ten years, the gap in literacy between countries in Latin America and those in other regions of the world has widened. School completion rates are low and repetition is high. Fewer than 83 percent of first-grade students reach the last grade in most countries in Latin America and the Caribbean. In some countries, only 10 percent of students graduate from the sixth grade without repeating a grade. Many children drop out of school altogether. Young workers in the region enter the labor force with fewer years of education than workers in other regions of the world. In Latin America, children attend school an average of 5.4 years. Indigenous, rural, and poor urban students particularly suffer from unequal access to quality education. They remain at the fringes of public school systems, often leaving school early and learning less than other children (PREAL 2006; USAID 2005).

Teachers in the region continue to be poorly trained, managed, and compensated, leaving them unable to meet the needs of their students. Many teachers have not finished secondary school, are ill prepared, and have insufficient materials and support in the classroom (USAID 2005). In some Latin American countries, due to an insufficient number of teachers, students attend school for only a few hours each day ("Education in Latin America" 2002). This approach allows for two or three shifts of students in one classroom each day. While this shift approach may allow more children to receive some schooling, it significantly reduces the amount of classroom and instruction time each student receives.

While many Latin American countries have made progress in providing basic primary education to children, the region lags in the provision of preschool and other early-childhood-development programs. Most countries in Latin America offer only one or two years of pre-primary education within the formal education system. Other forms of early childhood education, however, especially for children under three, fall under a variety of government ministries, making neglect of this age-group more likely (UNESCO 2006). The region also lags in provision of secondary and vocational schooling for older children. Many school systems in the region are ill equipped to address the learning needs of youths who are often vulnerable to idleness, exploitative labor, and crime. A significant challenge for many countries remains providing youths with access to lower and upper secondary education or vocational training opportunities (World Bank 2006).

Another barrier to education facing poor, rural, and indigenous children especially is the lack of a birth certificate. Approximately 2 million newborn babies in Latin America and the Caribbean go unregistered every year. Without proper birth registration and documentation, these children are often denied access to education, making them more vulnerable to, among other risks, premature work (UNICEF 2006).

Child Labor and Education: Mexico and Brazil

According to the ILO, child labor is decreasing in Latin America and the Caribbean. Two countries that stand out in contributing significantly to this decline are Mexico and Brazil. It is no coincidence that these two countries have been rigorously implementing conditional transfer-for-education programs (Bolsa Familia in Brazil and PROGRESA/Oportunidades in Mexico) aimed at enrolling more poor and marginalized children in school and improving the health of families. Conditional transfer-for-education programs provide funds to targeted households (primarily very poor families) on the condition that these funds are invested in the education of their children (Morley and Coady 2003). Cash transfers are provided directly to mothers, enabling them to pay school fees for their children, buy food and school supplies, and pay for health-care visits for the family. The Inter-American Bank and the World Bank are providing financial support to these programs (UNICEF 2004).

While there is much debate as to whether these cash-transfer programs improve the quality of education or are sustainable, the programs have increased the number of children enrolled in primary and secondary school by reducing costs associated with enrollment and attendance. The programs have also reduced dropout rates and improved access to health-care services (UNICEF 2004). They have also reduced child labor (Souza 2006). Today, other countries in the region are implementing or planning to begin similar programs.

Addressing Quality of Education in Latin America

While many countries in Latin America have focused on increasing access to education, many are also working to address the quality of education. For example, several countries are implementing incentive strategies for teachers: Bolivia has increased salaries for teachers in rural areas; Chile and Mexico have introduced performance-based incentive systems; El Salvador and Honduras have decentralized and implemented school-based management policies, allowing teachers a greater say in decisions regarding their schools; Brazil provides incentives to all state governments to hire and train additional teachers. In addition, several countries have introduced shorter training programs and now stress on-the-job training, in order to increase the number of teachers and link training to the real world of teaching (UNESCO 2006).

However, much more work is needed to improve the quality of education, especially for children outside of the school system or with special needs, including working children. In most Latin American countries, teachers lack the training and support needed to understand the issue of child labor and are unprepared for the challenges of teaching children who combine school and work. In addition, many schools lack guidance counselors or social workers, who are often better trained to address the psychosocial needs of working children.

Combating Child Labor Through Education

Improving children's access to basic education often reduces the likelihood of children engaging in hazardous or exploitative work. Thus, investments in the education of children, especially working children, are essential to any nation's social and economic development. Educated children are more likely to enter adulthood better able to make positive decisions, earn an income, and lead healthier and more productive lives. As a result, their communities and countries enjoy higher standards of living (U.S. Department of Labor 2006).

In Latin America, in order to truly combat child labor through education and to maximize financial and human resources, the following actions are needed: increased government and private sector investments in education, including early-childhood, primary, secondary, vocational, and literacy programs; minimizing or abolishing school fees and other, often prohibitive, costs associated with schooling; implementing longer school days so children spend more time in the classroom; increased investments in after-school programs as a means to both combat child labor and improve learning and retention; greater outreach and support to poor, rural, and indigenous children so they too may attend school; birth registration of all children so that parents are able to enroll children in school; increased coordination between efforts to combat child labor and efforts to promote basic education; greater recognition that child labor is an education issue and that many working children do not attend school; including child laborers as a target group in national education and poverty reduction strategies; increasing school-attendance monitoring and following up on absenteeism and dropouts; increased decentralization of the education system, allowing communities to be more involved in decision making; greater teacher training on child labor and the distinct needs of working children; and greater emphasis and financial resources allocated to improving the quality of education. Only by improving access to quality primary and secondary education for all children in Latin America will child labor be significantly reduced over the long term.

References and Further Reading

Clayton, Lawrence, and Michael Conniff. *A History of Modern Latin America.* Fort Worth, TX: Harcourt Brace College Humanities, 1999.

"Education in Latin America: Cramming Them In. More Latin Americans Are Being Educated but Not Well." *Economist*, May 9, 2002.

Institute for Research in History. *History of Education.* New York: Haworth Press, 1984.

Morley, Samuel, and David Coady. *From Social Assistance to Social Development: Targeted Education Subsidies in Developing Countries.* Washington, DC: Center for Global Development, International Food Policy Research Institute, 2003.

PREAL (Partnership for Educational Revitalization in the Americas). *Quantity Without Quality: A Report Card in Education in Latin America.* 2006. http://www.preal.org/.

Post, David. *Children's Work, Schooling, and Welfare in Latin America.* Boulder, CO: Westview Press, 2002.

Souza, André Portela. "Fighting Long-Run Poverty in Brazil: Are Conditional Cash Transfer Programs Making a Difference?" March 2006. http://www.webmeets.com/files/papers/LACEA-LAMES/2006/521/preal_bolsa_escola_Mar_2006.pdf.

UNESCO. *Early Childhood Care and Education: Education for All Global Monitoring Report, 2007.* Paris: UNESCO, 2006.

UNICEF. *The State of the World's Children 2005: Childhood Under Threat.* New York: UNICEF, 2004.

UNICEF. *The State of the World's Children 2006: Excluded and Invisible.* New York: UNICEF, 2005.

UNICEF. "UNICEF, Organization of American States and Inter-American Development Bank Launch Initiative to Grant Official Identity to Millions of Unregistered Children." Press release, August 8, 2006. http://www.unicef.org/media/media_35255.html.

USAID. "Education in Latin America and the Caribbean." Washington, DC: USAID, 2005. http://www.usaid.gov/locations/latin_america_caribbean/issues/education_issue.html.

U.S. Department of Labor, *2005 Findings on the Worst Forms of Child Labor.* Washington, DC: U.S. Department of Labor, 2006. http://www.dol.gov/ilab/media/reports/iclp/tda2005/tda2005.pdf.

World Bank. *World Development Report 2007: Development and the Next Generation.* Washington, DC: World Bank, September 16, 2006.

Children's Social Movements in Latin America

Marten van den Berge, MA, Researcher, Foundation for International Research on Working Children (IREWOC), Amsterdam

Within the field of child labor there exists a long and extensive discussion on what child labor actually entails and what its causes are. Different views and interpretations have led to different opinions on how to deal with the phenomena in practice. Across the diverse range of views on child labor activism, one important school of thought holds that, to improve their conditions, working children have to be organized into children's social movements: movements run exclusively by and for working children themselves.

Latin America has the longest history of these movements. The Peruvian Movement of Working Children and Adolescent Children from Christian Working Class Families (MANTHOC; Movimiento de Adolescentes y Niños Trabajadores Hijos de Obreros Cristianos), established in 1976, was the first working children's movement in the world. Soon other countries on the continent followed, and nowadays most Latin American countries have their own working children's movements. The movements boast thousands of child members and claim numerous successes in improving the working and living conditions of children and their families. They are seen as an example by similar movements that have appeared on other continents.

Ideology

One of the remarkable aspects of the Latin American working children's movements is their stance on child labor, which, in essence, defends children's right to work. Two basic arguments are used to support this point of view. First, work is believed to have beneficial and creative elements, which are able to teach children things that schools may not offer them, such as a sense of independence and certain skills, and which help them to develop their personalities. Second, work is considered to be inevitable because it provides the children and their families with the necessary income to meet their basic needs. The movements therefore strongly oppose the elimination of child labor as advocated by the International Labor Organization (ILO). Instead they are of the opinion that the focus should be on the amelioration of the conditions under which children work. In order to improve these conditions, the movements intend to give children the opportunity to negotiate the terms of their own labor. In the Latin American context, this stance toward child labor is ideologically classified as *regulacionistas.*

Equally characteristic of the Latin American children's social movements is the emphasis they lay on the rights that concern children's participation in society. Their criticism is that these rights, which are included in the UN Convention on the Rights of the Child, are not being sufficiently demanded or protected. The movements insist that children are not regarded as "beneficiaries of the goodwill of adults or the institutions created by them, but as independent individuals that can judge and design their lives themselves and can give something to society" (Liebel 2003, 36).[1] This idea of participation in the Latin American context is referred to as *protagonismo.* By emphasizing children's *protagonismo,* the movements "oppose the idea of a childhood that is tamed, obedient and exclusive, in favor of a new concept that considers children to be social subjects with the capacity to participate in society and to transform it" (Liebel 2000, 211).[2] Stimulating *protagonismo* will eventually end the hierarchical relationship between children and adults and readjust adult culture (Cussiánovich 1997).

These ideological stances are subscribed to by national and continental coordinating committees of the movements. Members of the movements at the local level, however, do not always fall in line with these positions, and some local chapters are reported to belong to opposing ideological camps. Thus, the ideological rhetoric employed at higher levels of the movement sometimes appears to be a poor reflection of how grassroots members think (van den Berge 2005).

Levels of Organization

The children's movements on the Latin American continent operate at various organizational levels. A basic distinction can be made between the spontaneous local forms of self-organization, on the one hand, and formal organizations at higher levels, on the other hand. Whereas the former often originate from initiatives of children themselves, the latter are usually initiated by social movements and NGOs of adults and youngsters, which advocate the rights and demands of the children, and that organize children on a national level (Liebel 2000). These national movements function as umbrella organizations that bring together diverse groups of children, varying from local groups of self-organized children to adult-led children's groups of internationally operating NGOs.

Of all the national movements in Latin America, MANTHOC and MNNATSOP (in Peru) and NATRAS (in Nicaragua) have the best organizational structures. Together the movements form the Latin American and Caribbean Movement of Working Children and Adolescents (MOLACNATS). At the international level, MOLACNATS has sent various delegates to the International Meetings of Working Children's Movements, which have been held in Kundapur, India (1996), and Berlin, Germany (2004).

Organizational Structure and Performance

Children join the movement at the local level in one of three ways: through special recruitment drives, through use of provided support services, or through peer group information. Once they join they are entitled to fully participate in the movement's democratic procedures and to play a role in the different levels of organization. Groups at the local, regional, and national levels are required to choose their representatives and leadership. Studies conducted in Peru and Bolivia have shown that some elected representatives, at higher organizational levels, are not actually representative of the members of local groups; the elected delegates are usually adolescents who no longer work, or who have barely worked before. This results in resentment among members of the grassroots groups, and social distance between local members and elected representatives. These feelings are reinforced when delegates, once they move into levels of national coordination, fail to communicate properly with the grassroots groups they originated from (van den Berge 2005).

Members are guided by adults during all activities and procedures. In theory, the adults simply act as consultants, who respect the children and help them articulate their interests and set up the organizational structures. In this capacity they are referred to as *facilitadores* (intermediaries) or *colaboradores* (collaborators) (Liebel 2000, 57). However, in only a few countries do the national children's movements have an autonomous existence. The movements are often part of, and legally and financially dependent on, supporting adult NGOs (Liebel 2000). Furthermore, adults have a significant influence on decision-making processes, sometimes directly overruling the children. Indirectly, the children are influenced in their decision making by adults through the information they receive. This information is often ideologically biased, as children are educated to perceive child labor issues from a *regulationista* perspective, with other points of view being excluded (van den Berge 2007b). Children have, however, been reported to sometimes question this adult influence. In addition, they do value the relationships with adults inside the movements, as they are taken seriously and treated respectfully by them, and because they are playful and make life more enjoyable (Swift 1999; van den Berge 2005).

Members

The majority of the members come from the poorer socioeconomic segments of society. Many of these children migrated with their families from the countryside to the city, or were born in the city as children of migrants. They usually live in city slums. Most of the members are active in the informal sector, working in the streets, in the markets, and in other public spaces, but also as domestic servants of rich families. Because of this focus on urban street trades, which is very much the domain of boys, girls as well as children from rural areas are underrepresented in the organizations. Evaluations also show that the organizations have difficulties in reaching the most needy and vulnerable child laborers. Most of the members are occupied with light tasks for only a few hours a day, usually within the family realm or in self-employment (Chacaltana 1998; van den Berge 2005). Most members are between twelve and eighteen years old. However, in some national children's movements, for example, in Bolivia, there are also members above the age of eighteen. The number of adolescents generally outweighs the number of younger children.

Impact

The impact of participation on the children within the movements can be measured at various levels. The first level concerns children's activities within the organization. Children are involved in the decision-making processes within the organization and, as such, feel respected and responsible. In addition, the movements fulfill important affective needs. They offer a social space where children can meet and form new friendships. Children also value the respect gained from, and friendships made with, adults inside the movements (Swift 1999). In some cases the movement functions as a "substitute family" and provides a safer and more caring environment than the one found at home. Last, through various activities, children develop skills such as assertiveness, voicing their opinions, and speaking in public, which in turn have a positive effect on their self-respect (van den Berge 2007b).

The movements also manage to effect changes on a broader scale, and influence the children's working and living conditions. Self-organization has provided some children with increased resilience, enabling them to face temporary setbacks in their family situations as well as in their working conditions. For example, studies carried out in Peru and Bolivia identified groups that had set up saving systems with which children were able to buy necessary protective materials for the workplace. Resilience is also improved by the children's rights education offered by the organizations. Knowledge of these rights gives some children the confidence to stand up to abusive employers, customers, or police. However, these improvements are limited to children whose conditions were not so bad initially. Children in the most difficult working conditions are the least able to effect changes in their working conditions (van den Berge 2007a, 2007b). The severe poverty of these children and their families leads many to endure exploitation and abuse rather than to stand up for their rights and risk losing their vital income. Moreover, children who live in extreme poverty and who work in the worst conditions do not have the time to invest in the movements, and if they do, they are tired and therefore less able to profit from the benefits that participation in the movements can offer them.

By regarding the children as social subjects, the movements have influenced national laws on child labor as well as NGO policy and media coverage regarding child participation (Swift 1999; Liebel 2000, 2003). More instrumentally, children get direct material benefits from the various services offered by the organizations. In Peru and Bolivia the children and their parents consider this one of the most important aspects of the movements (van den Berge 2007a, 2007b). The inexpensive lunch services are attractive to poor children. The nonformal education offered is a valuable complement to the sometimes poor quality of the formal public school system. The different employment projects offer opportunities to gain working experience and to earn additional income. Lastly, the dormitories in the movements' shelters are a great "pull" factor for many children (van den Berge 2007a, 2007b).

Conclusion

The working children's social movements in Latin America can, on the whole, be credited with effecting positive changes in self-esteem and in the working and living conditions of many children. In addition, they fulfill affective needs and should be credited with supplying opportunities for participation and for providing highly valued services to this specific segment of deprived children. Unfortunately, the movements have a limited impact on the most vulnerable children in society. These children are significantly more difficult to reach and, when they do succeed in becoming members, are the least likely to benefit from what the movements have to offer them.

Notes

1. Translation by van den Berge; original text: "Se ven no sólo como beneficiarioso como objeto de la Buena voluntad o del amparo de los adultos o de las instituciones creadas por éstos, sino como individuos independientes, que son capaces de juzgar y deseñar su propia vida y pueden aportar algo a la sociedad."

2. Translation by van den Berge; original text: "manifestamos una vision que contradice la idea de una infacia domesticada, obiente y excluida, en favor de un Nuevo concepto que considera al niño y a la niña como sujetos socials con la capacidad de participar y de transformarla."

References and Further Reading

Alarcón, Walter. "Enfoques de políticas entorno al trabajo de niños y adolecentes en América Latina." *Realidad & Utopia* 1:1 (1996).

Chacaltana, J. "Estudio de caso de Manthoc, un movimiento de niños y niñas trabajadores en Peru." In *Si puedo trabajar . . . también puedo opinar: diferentes enfoques a los niños y niñas trabajadores,* ed. David Tolfree. Estocolmo: Rädda Branen, 1998.

Cussiánovich, A. "Del olvido a una emergente visibilidad social de la organización de los NATs en América Latina." In *Niñas trabajadores: protagonismo y actoría social.* Lima: IFEJANT, 1997.

Cussiánovich, A. *Algunas premisas para la reflexión y las práticas socials con niños y adolescents trabajadores.* Lima: Rädda Barnen, 1997.

Domic Ruiz, J. *Ninos trabajadores: la emergencia de nuevos actors social.* La Paz: PIEB, 1999.

IFEJANT. *Niñas trabajadores. protagonismo y actoría social.* Lima: IFEJANT, 1997.

Liebel, Manfred. *Protagonismo infantil: movimientos de ninos trabajadores en America Latina.* Managua: Editores Nuevas Nicaragua, 1994.

Liebel, Manfred. *La otra infancia: niñez trabajadora y acción social.* Lima: IFEJANT, 2000.

Liebel, Manfred. *Infancia y trabajo.* Lima: IFEJANT, 2003.

Liebel, Manfred, B. Overwien, and A. Recknagel, eds. *Working Children's Protagonism: Social Movements and Empowerment in Latin America, Africa and India.* Frankfurt am Main: IKO, 2001.

Schibotto, Giani. *Niños trabajadores: construyendo una identidad.* Lima: MANTHOC, 1990.

Swift, Anthony. *Working Children Get Organized. An Introduction to Working Children's Organizations.* London: Save the Children, 1999.

Van den Berge, Marten P. "El Movimiento de NATs in Bolivia and Peru." In *Studying Child Labour: Policy Implications of Child-Centred Research,* ed S. Zweegers. Amsterdam: IREWOC, 2005.

Van den Berge, Marten P. *Working Children's Movements in Bolivia.* Amsterdam: IREWOC, 2007a.

Van den Berge, Marten P. *Working Children's Movements in Peru.* Amsterdam: IREWOC, 2007b.

National Organizations of Working Children in Latin America

Argentina: Argentinean Movement of Working Children and Adolescents

Bolivia: Union of Bolivian Working Children and Adolescents (UNATsBO) (www.shinealight.org/spanish/UNATSBo.html)

Chile: Movement of Chilean Working Children and Adolescents (MOCHINATs)

Colombia: Organization of Working Children and Adolescents of Colombia (ONATsCOL) (http://www.onatscol.org/)

Guatemala: NATS GUATEMALA: Guatemalan Movement of Working Children and Adolescents (MONATsGUA)

Nicaragua: Movement of Working Children and Adolescents (NATRAS)

Paraguay: National Coordinator of Working Children and Adolescents (CONNATs)

Peru: Peruvian Movement of Working Children and Adolescents Children from Christian Working Class Families (MANTHOC) (www.manthocperu.org)

National Peruvian Movement of Organized Working Children and Adolescents (MNNATSOP)

Venezuela: Children's Action Movement (MOANI) Venezuela

National Coordination of Working Children and Adolescents (CORENATs)

Section 2. South America

Worst Forms of Child Labor in the Andes Region

Marten van den Berge, MA, Researcher, Foundation for International Research on Working Children (IREWOC), Amsterdam

The Andes is a mountain range forming a continuous chain of highland throughout South America. It extends over seven countries, from the south of Argentina, through Chile, Bolivia, Peru, Ecuador, Colombia, and Venezuela, and into the Caribbean Sea. The Andes is more than 4,400 miles long and has an average height of about 13,000 feet. Because it covers such a large area, the climate in the Andes varies greatly, depending on location, altitude, and proximity to the sea. The most populated section of the Andes is called the altiplano (high plain), where the Andes is at its widest (up to 300 miles). The altiplano occupies parts of Peru, Bolivia, and Chile and has an average altitude of 11,000 feet. The central Andes was the cradle of the famous Inca civilization. Nowadays the region is mainly inhabited by Quechua- and Aymara-speaking people.

People of the Andes make their living in agriculture, cattle breeding, mining, tourism, and the informal sector. There are various mining centers, some as high as 17,500 feet. Most of the tourism is concentrated around Lake Titicaca. There are a number of large cities in the altiplano, such as La Paz, El Alto, Puno, and Cusco, where people work in all kinds of economic sectors. Children participate in most of these economic sectors; some do so under very difficult and hazardous conditions, with mining one of the most notorious examples.

Children in Mining: Geography and Numbers

The mining industry of the Andes is one of the most important in the world. Child labor has been reported in several mines, but particularly in the small-scale artisan mining centers (*mineria artesanal*). This is because the production methods used here are more labor-intensive than in the large-scale industrial mines (UNICEF-ILO 2004b). In addition, large-scale mining corporations are more vulnerable to international public scrutiny, and they have better security; thus, child labor is more likely to be effectively controlled.

Child labor has been reported in small-scale artisan mines of several Andes areas, but mainly in Bolivia, Colombia, Ecuador, and Peru (see Table 1). The types of mines that children work in depend on the countries and regions. In Ecuador and Peru children work mainly in gold mines. In Bolivia children have been found working in gold, silver, tin, lead, and zinc mines. In Colombia children work in gold, silver, tin, and coal mines, as well as emerald and clay mines. Estimates on the number of children involved in mining vary greatly, from a low of 2,100 in Ecuador to a high of 200,000 in Colombia. In Bolivia, the estimated 3,800 constitute 10 percent of the workforce in Bolivian mining (UNICEF-ILO 2004b). In total, it is estimated that more than 250,000 children perform labor activities related to mining in the Andes.

These numbers, however, vary according to time of year and geographical region. The number of children involved in mining increases significantly during school vacations. The number of children involved, especially adolescents, also depends on the agricultural schedule, with more adolescents coming to work in the mines outside the harvesting and sowing seasons. Child labor,

Table 1

Children in Mining in the Andes Region

Country	Mining centers and minerals	Estimated number of children	Source
Bolivia	Child labor has been found in the mining centers of Huanuni and Antequera (department of Oruro), and Siglo XX, Cerro Rico, Chorolque, and Colquechaca (department of Potosi). These are silver, zinc, and tin mines. In the department of La Paz children are working in the gold mines of Tipuani.	3,800	UNICEF-ILO 2004
Colombia	Child labor has been found in the gold mines of the municipalities of Nariño (Los Andes and La Llanada) and two municipalities of Chocó (Condoto and Istmina); in the emerald mines of three municipalities of Boyacá (Maripí, Muzo, and San Pablo de Borbur); in the coal mines of seven municipalities of the department of Boyacá (Tasco, Socha, Sogamoso, Paipa, Corrales, Mongua, and Tópaga) and five municipalities of the department of Antioquia (Amagá, Angelópolis, Fredonia, Venecia, and Titiribí). Child labor has been found in clay exploitation in one municipality of Cundinamarca (Nemocón).	200,000	Dialogos 2005; ILO-IPEC 2001
Ecuador	Children have been reported to be working in the gold mines of Bella Rica, Chinapintza, Zaruma-Portovelo, San Gerardo, and Nambija.	2,100	ILO-IPEC 2002
Peru	Children have been found working in the mines of La Rinconada, Cerro Lunar, and Ancoccala in the Puno district, Huaypetuhe and alongside the river Madre de Dios (Madre de Dios department), Pataz (in the department of Libertad), and between Nazca and Ocoña, where there are more than forty different mining locations, of which the most important are Saramarca (department of Ica, province of Palpa) and Tulín (province of Nazca), in Ayacucho: Huanca (province of Lucanas), Santa Filomena, San Luis (Jaquí), and Relave, and in Arequipa: Mollehuaca, Eugenia, and the Cerro Rico (province of Caravelí).	50,000	ILO-IPEC 2001

in some regions, notably around the Potosi area in Bolivia, is currently on the rise because of the increasing price of minerals.

Children in Mining: The Activities and Hazards

The specific hazards of child labor in mining depend to a large extent on whether the activities children perform are in the mining shafts or outside the mines. Inside the mines, children assist adults with drilling and perforating stone, or with preparing dynamite. Children can also be involved with operating mine carts, or, in the absence of carts, they may be expected to carry the minerals out on their backs. These tasks are mainly carried out by male adolescents. The hazards of working inside the mines include injuries from falling stones or from falling into deep shafts, lung disease caused by inhaling dust particles or poisonous gases released in explosions, damage to hearing by loud explosions and drills, and bone deformities from carrying heavy burdens.

The majority of girls and younger children work outside the mining shafts. Their activities include grinding minerals by means of a grinding mill (*quimbalete*), crushing stones with a hammer (*chancar*), looking for minerals among the debris that has been deposited outside the mine (*pallaqueo*), treating the minerals with toxic washings, wrapping the minerals, selling the minerals, guarding the mining tools, and cooking dinner and washing clothes for the mine workers. In gold mines (in Tipuani, for example) children participate primarily in the *barranquilleo*: a chemical process during which minerals are treated with mercury to extract the gold. In larger mines, like the Cerro Rico in Potosi, Bolivia, some children

Adolescents adding mercury to minerals to extract gold in Santa Filomena, Peru, 2007. *(Photo by Laura Baas courtesy of IREWOC Foundation)*

conduct guided tours for tourists in the mine shafts and sell them minerals. The specific tasks children and adolescents perform largely depend on the particularities of the mines.

When grinding minerals with the *quimbalete,* children run the risk of crushing their hands and feet in the mill. This work is heavy manual labor; thus, children risk muscle and bone deformations. Shattering rocks with a hammer can lead to broken fingers or eye injuries from stray shards. Treatment of the minerals is one of the most dangerous tasks children perform: Simply inhaling these chemicals (such as xanthate and mercury) is extremely dangerous and can lead to acute and chronic organ diseases. Girls also report sexual harassment as a hazard in this male-dominated environment. The hazards of the workplace are intensified by the lack of official state security, such as police.

Agriculture

Agriculture is an important economic sector in the Andes, especially in the region of the altiplano. Agriculture in the Andes is dominated by small-scale farming because of an absence of fertile ground for large plantations. Quinoa, maize, potatoes, broad beans, barley, tobacco, cotton, and coffee are the main crops. Coca has been grown there for centuries and has a fundamental place in Andean culture. Animals are reared (cows, sheep, pigs, chickens, llamas, and alpacas) for the production of wool and meat.

Children participate in several different activities of small-scale farming, such as sowing, harvesting, weeding, and milking, herding, feeding, and caring for cattle. These activities depend on gender and age. Girls mainly care for the cattle (feeding, milking, herding), whereas boys are more involved in sowing and harvesting (UNICEF and INE 2004). Young children help their parents on the land for a few hours per week, but this intensifies as children get older.

In several Andean countries there is a general belief that the tasks children perform in small-scale, family-based farming are not harmful. The activities are seen as part of the socialization process; teaching children traditional knowledge (of production) and values of respect, solidarity, and reciprocity. Andean families, therefore, generally do not categorize these activities as child labor, but rather as *yanapakuy* (Quechua for "helping") (Galvez and Jaramillo 2002). It is estimated that 92.1 percent of children in Peru in the age-group six to thirteen years old (almost 1 million), perform agricultural activities with their parents (INEI-ILO 2001). In Bolivia, on the altiplano, this percentage is as high as 98.8 for children below age eighteen (UNICEF 2004). Although it is believed that the activities children perform in small-scale farming are less harmful than those performed on plantations, studies do show that in traditional subsistence farming, the amounts of chemicals used are on the increase, as is the length of time that children work (Van Damme 2002). Most of these children do, however, combine education with their agricultural tasks.

Child Labor in the Cities

Several large cities are located in the Andes mountain range, including La Paz and El Alto (Bolivia), Puno and Cusco (Peru), Quito (Ecuador), and Bogotá (Colombia). Large numbers of children have been reported to be working in these cities, mostly as independent entrepreneurs or in a familial context. Children and adolescents work in a variety of activities, mainly as shoe shiners, car washers, and street and market sellers, in restaurants and hotels, and as bus attendants, market porters, domestic servants, and store assistants (UNICEF and INE 2004). Most of the younger children are accompanied by a family member. Boys generally perform heavy manual labor or work independently in public spaces. Girls mainly work in markets (alongside a family member) or as domestic workers. Domestic labor is considered a hazardous form of child labor; these children are particularly vulnerable for abuse since there is a lack of protection and control. Other jobs, such as those performed at night, those that involve potential contact with alcohol, and those that are carried out near busy traffic, are also considered to be dangerous forms of child labor.

Child prostitution, which is an illegal, unconditionally hazardous form of child labor, can also be found in all major cities: 360 adolescents were reported to be involved in prostitution in the cities of La Paz and El Alto (UNICEF-ILO 2004a); 400 child victims of prostitution were reported in the city of Cusco (CODENI 2002); in Quito, Ecuador, 2,000 girls are sexually exploited; and in Bogotá, Colombia, ECPAT has estimated that there are more than 10,000 girls and nearly 1,000 boys exploited as child prostitutes. Research in Bolivia has shown that the children involved in this sector often originate from surrounding rural areas; they are pushed out by rural poverty and attracted by stories of easy money in the cities (UNICEF-ILO 2004b). Child trafficking also occurs in the Andes region: Bolivian children are trafficked from La Paz and Oruro to sweatshops in Buenos Aires (DNI 2001; Bastia 2005); girls also have reportedly been trafficked from La Paz and El Alto to work for commercial sexual exploitation in the mining center of La Rinconada ("Menores bolivianas prostituidas en Perú" 2007).

Armed Conflict

A specific worst form of child labor found in the Andes region is the involvement of children in the armed conflict in Colombia, which has lasted more than forty years. As many as 14,000 children have been recruited on both sides of the conflict—some into armed opposition groups and others into government-backed paramilitaries (CSUCS 2004). While there are no reports of children serving in the regular Colombian army, the army sometimes uses children as informants, and is often present when children undergo paramilitary training, where it is reported that beatings are common.

The children are used in combat, as messengers, to carry supplies, and to lay mines. Most are trained in the use of automatic weapons and explosives. While some children are forcibly recruited, especially into opposition groups, most children are volunteers. The promise of regular pay is cited as a primary motive for joining the paramilitaries (Human Rights Watch 2003). In the armed opposition groups, women and children comprise a large proportion of the total force. The government of Colombia, in cooperation with NGOs, has established a disarmament, demobilization, and reintegration program. Since 1999, approximately 1,200 former child soldiers have taken part in these programs. This represents roughly 10 percent of all child soldiers.

Government and NGO Policy

All the Andean countries have ratified the UN Convention on the Rights of the Child and ILO Conventions 138 and 182. In addition, all the countries have specific national laws setting minimum ages for work, and defining rules for the protection of minors against dangerous, unhealthy, and physically taxing work. Official state policy in all countries is geared toward the eradication of child labor.

There are many NGOs working on child labor in the Andes. Most of them, however, focus on child labor in the urban areas. There are some NGOs working with children in mining areas, but it appears that the more remote the mine, the less NGO activity there is. For example, dozens of NGOs are active in the relatively accessible mining area of the Cerro Rico in Potosi, Bolivia, but only two NGOs are active in La Rinconada, Peru. There is almost no NGO activity concerning working children in agriculture. This is surprising, as most of the working children in the Andes work in rural areas. This might be because the activities these children perform are relatively less harmful, and that children are dispersed over wide areas and not concentrated, as is the case in cities and mining centers.

The objectives of the different NGO projects vary from improving the working conditions of child laborers (*regulacionista*) to the total abolition of all child labor (*abolicionista).* There is a striking lack of collaboration between NGOs from these ideological camps (van den Berge 2005). However, while there seem to be unbridgeable differences on an ideological level, these differences become blurred in the field. Reality often forces the organizations to compromise, especially regarding worst forms of child labor: All NGOs strive for their eradication.

References and Further Reading

Bastia, Tania. "Child Trafficking or Teenage Migration? Bolivian Migrants in Argentina." *International Migration* 43:4 (2005): 58–89.

CODENI. *Interrogantes que preocupan.* Cusco, Peru: CODENI and Save the Children Sweden, 2002.

CSUCS. *Child Soldiers Global Report 2004: Colombia.* London: Coalition to Stop the Use of Child Soldiers, 2004. http://www.child-soldiers.org/document/get?id=820.

Dialogos. "Especial sobre trabajo infantil." *Publicacion del instituto Colombiano de bienestar de la familia* 19 (July 2005).

DNI. *La necesidad: nos hace cómplices? Tráfico de niños, niñas y adolecentes con fines de explotacion laboral en Bolivia.* Cochabamba: DNI-Bolivia, 2001.

ECPAT International (End Child Prostitution, Child Pornography and Trafficking of Children for Sexual Purposes). http://www.ecpat.com.

Galvez, N., and E. Jaramillo. *Los niños trabajadores del Perú.* Lima, Peru: Universidad Nacional Mayor de San Marcos, 2002.

Human Rights Watch. *You'll Learn Not to Cry: Child Combatants in Colombia.* London: Human Rights Watch, 2003.

ILO-IPEC. *Estudio nacional sobre el trabajo infantil en la mineria artesanal: niños que trabajan en la mineria de oro en el Perú.* Lima: ILO-IPEC, 2001.

ILO-IPEC. *Diagnostico sobre el trabajo infantil en el sector minero artesanal en Colombia: estudios y estadisticas.* Lima: ILO-IPEC, 2002.

ILO-IPEC. *Imperdonable: estudio sobre la explotacion sexual commercial de la infancia y adolcencia en Perú: Cajamarca, Iquitos, Cusco y Lima.* Lima: ILO-IPEC, 2007.

INEI-ILO. *Vision del trabajo infantil y adolecente en el Perú, 2001.* Lima: INEI, 2001.

"Menores bolivianas prostituidas en Perú." *La Prenza* (Lima), April 23, 2007.

UNICEF-ILO. *La niñez clausurada.* La Paz: UNICEF Bolivia, 2004a.

UNICEF-ILO. *Buscando la luz al funal del tunnel: niños, niñas y adolecentes en la mineria artesanal en Bolivia.* La Paz: UNICEF Bolivia, 2004b.

UNICEF and INE. *Trabajo infantil en Bolivia: caracteristicas y condiciones: una realidad que no les corresponde.* La Paz: UNICEF Bolivia, 2004.

Van Damme, P. "Disponibilidad, uso y calidad de los recursos hídricos en Bolivia." Summit on Sustainable Development, Johannesburg, August 26–September 4, 2002.

Van den Berge, Marten. "El Movimiento de NATs in Bolivia and Peru." In *Studying Child Labour: Policy Implications of Child-Centred Research,* ed. S. Zweegers, 9–14. Amsterdam: IREWOC, 2005.

Bolivia

BOLIVIA	CRC	C 138	C 182
Ratifications	Y	Y	Y
Human Development Index/Rank	0.692/115		
Human Capital			
Population Growth Rate	1.45%		
% Population 0–14	35%		
Total Fertility Rate	2.85		
Life Expectancy	65.84		
Infant Mortality Rate	51.77		
Literacy Rate	87.2%		
Economic			
GDP/Capita	$3,000		
GDP Growth %	3.3%		
% Poverty	64%		
Gini Index	60.6		

CHILD ACTIVITY BREAKDOWN, BY SEX AND RESIDENCE

RESIDENCE	Percentage of children in the relevant age-group[a]									
	Economic activity only		School only		Combining school and economic activity		Neither in school nor in economic activity		Child labor[b]	
	Male	Female	Male	Female	Male	Female	Male	Female	Male	Female
Urban	0.0	0.9	91.7	91.7	5.8	5.1	2.6	2.3	n/av	n/av
Rural	3.7	3.6	50.5	56.3	44.4	36.5	1.3	3.6	n/av	n/av
Total	1.6	2.0	74.1	77.1	22.3	18.2	2.0	2.8	20.2	16.7

Source: Bolivia, Encuesta Continua de Hogares, 2005 (See UCW Project Web site, http://www.ucw-project.org, country statistics).
Notes: [a]Children age 7 to 14. [b]Estimate includes (a) children under age 12 engaged in economic activities, and (b) children age 12–14 engaged in excessive economic activities (more than 14 hours per week). Estimate does not account for children engaged in excessive household chores, hazardous work, or other unconditional "worst forms" of child labor.

Child Labor in Bolivia

Marten van den Berge, MA, Researcher, Foundation for International Research on Working Children (IREWOC), Amsterdam

Child labor in Bolivia is a controversial subject. The statistics vary greatly and the discussion of definitions, causes, and solutions is diverse. It is also a subject that has mobilized many actors; various government commissions are working on the theme, special laws and policies have been formulated, numerous NGOs are implementing various projects, and the international development community has shown its interest and concern.

Child Labor in Bolivia: The Actors

Policies and laws of the Bolivian state are directed toward abolition of child labor. Laws regulating child labor can be found in the Bolivian constitution, the General Labor Law, and the Children and Adolescents Code. These laws set the minimum age for employment at fourteen and define rules for the protection of minors against dangerous, unhealthy, and physically taxing work. The Bolivian government signed the UN Convention on the Rights of the Child in 1990, ILO Convention 138 (minimum age) in 1997, and ILO Convention 182 (worst forms of child labor) in 1999. Besides preparing the legislative framework to combat child labor, the Bolivian government also established the National Ombudsman for Children and Adolescents, to which anyone can report children's rights violations, including incidences of child labor. Additionally, under the responsibility of the Ministry of Labor, the National Commission for the Eradication of Child Labor was created. Despite all these governmental efforts, several thousands of children are still working under dangerous circumstances. A gap clearly exists between the legal framework and implementation.

Besides the government, dozens of NGOs are also involved with child labor. Their goals vary from improving the working conditions of child laborers (*regulacionista stance*) to the total abolition of all child labor (*abolicionista stance*). Despite the clear-cut ideological differences, in practice NGOs implement a wide range of projects with a variety of objectives, regardless of their ideology (van den Berge 2004). All actors appear to be more involved with the visible forms of child labor, such as the children working on the streets, than with less visible children in sectors such as prostitution and domestic work, or with child laborers in remote areas (mining or plantation work).

Child Labor in Bolivia: The Numbers

Estimates of the numbers of children working in Bolivia vary greatly from study to study (UCW 2004). An estimate made by UNICEF in 2004 claimed that 313,500 children were engaged in economic activities; that is approximately 10 percent of all economically active people in Bolivia and 10 percent of all children younger than eighteen years old. Furthermore, UNICEF reported that the majority of all working children are boys. However, this apparent gender gap could be explained by the fact that domestic activities, performed primarily by girls, are excluded from statistics on economic activities. This exclusion indicates an underestimate of the real number of child laborers (UNICEF and INE 2004).

Child Labor in Rural Areas

The activities of child laborers in Bolivia are somewhat region specific. In rural areas, children are incorporated into various economic activities at a very early age. The total number of children working in agriculture is almost 100,000, approximately one-third of the total number of child laborers (UNICEF and INE 2004). The precise activities of child laborers in rural areas depend on whether the work is performed in small-scale farming or on plantations.

Small-Scale Farming

Small farmers comprise 90 percent of the people working in the countryside (Oostra and Malaver 2003). Subsistence family farming is particularly present in the Bolivian highlands (around La Paz and Potosi), where there is an absence of fertile ground for large plantations. Some farmers produce a small surplus, which is sold in local markets. In the highlands, farmers cultivate crops such as quinoa, potatoes, broad beans, and barley; some farmers raise stock (cows, sheep, pigs, chickens, llamas, and alpacas). Subsistence farming also exists in the valleys and lowlands; farmers there grow potatoes, manioc, maize, rice, cacao, quinoa, peanuts, bananas, coffee, and tea; they also breed cattle.

Children participate in sowing and harvesting, weeding, milking, herding, feeding, and caring for cattle. The nature of their activities depends on gender and age. Girls generally care for the cattle (feeding, milking, herding). Boys are more involved in sowing and harvesting (UNICEF and INE 2004). Younger children help their parents on the land for a few hours per week; this labor intensifies as children get older. Although it is generally believed that childrens' activities in subsistence farming are less harmful than comparable activities on plantations, studies show that the amounts of chemicals used in traditional subsistence farming are on the increase, as are the lengths of time children work (Van Damme 2002).

Medium-Size and Large Plantations

Child laborers can also be found on medium-size and large plantations, primarily sugarcane and cotton plantations in the regions of Tarija and Santa Cruz. Plantation work is mainly performed by migrant laborers during harvesting season. It is estimated that between May and November, approximately 35,500 people, among them 10,000 children, leave their homes to work and live on the plantations (ILO-UNICEF 2004). Not all of these children actually work on the plantation; some simply join their parents so as to not be left at home alone. However, living conditions can be extreme. Often, there is lack of running water, sanitary services, and medical care. Furthermore, by living away from home for long periods, the children miss out on their education.

Although plantation work involves comparably fewer children than small-scale farming, the nature of the work is potentially more dangerous, as it is commercial and export oriented and involves excessive use of pesticides and chemicals (UNICEF and INE 2004). ILO-IPEC and ILO-UNICEF studies on these sectors report the arduous working conditions of children on sugarcane plantations in Santa Cruz, with children complaining about infections, snakebites, and injuries resulting from the use of machetes (ILO-IPEC 2002; ILO-UNICEF 2004).

Brazil Nut Sector

Child laborers can also be found in the Brazil-nut sector, located in the department of Beni, near the city of Riberalta. Migrant labor is involved in this sector too; it mobilizes 31,000 people a year (Durango 2005). As on the plantations, children accompany their parents when migrating and therefore miss out on schooling. During their stay they risk diseases such as malaria and diarrhea, are bitten by snakes or spiders, and are frequently injured by falling nuts or by machetes (Durango 2005; Baas 2006). The children who assist their parents are mostly involved with collecting, cutting, and carrying the nuts; they are generally active from 5 A.M. to 6 P.M. Children as young as eight have been found harvesting the nuts.

Mining

Rural activities, although mainly agricultural, also include mining. The number of children working in mining fluctuates according to school vacations, during which more children participate in mine-related activities. Estimates vary greatly, but ILO-IPEC has calculated that approximately 13,500

Fourteen-year-old boy entering the mine, Bolivia, 2007. *(Photo by Anna Ensing courtesy of IREWOC Foundation)*

children are involved in mining (ILO-IPEC 2001). With a recent rise in the price of minerals, more children have been reported working in mining. The majority of children (77 percent) work in family-based, small-scale mines concentrated in the altiplano; 13 percent in the departments of La Paz, Oruro, and Potosi; and 10 percent of the children working in mines were found in valley and tropical areas of Bolivia (UNICEF and INE 2004).

Girls and the youngest children are mostly involved in cooking dinner for the workers, washing their clothes, watching over the mining tools, and looking for minerals among the waste material that has been deposited outside the mine (*pallaqueo*). Some children, though, are also involved in extremely dangerous activities such as working with explosives or chemicals, and washing and grinding minerals. In general, only boys enter the mines and work in the grinding mills that are used to crush the minerals (*quimbalete*). Girls also mention sexual harassment as a hazard in this male-dominated environment.

Child Labor in Urban Centers

A small percentage of children living in urban areas perform agricultural activities. Many families that have migrated from rural to urban areas still have productive parcels of land. The children of these families often work on the land during harvest and sowing seasons, which is reported to negatively influence their school achievements (van den Berge 2004). This process is especially familiar in El Alto, the poor suburb of La Paz, where many migrant families from the countryside live.

The majority of child laborers in urban areas, however, work in the secondary (industry and construction) and tertiary (service) sectors (UNICEF and INE 2004). The service sector includes numerous occupations: shoe shiners, car washers, street and market sellers, restaurants and hotel workers, bus attendants, market porters, store assistants, and others. Most of these children work either as independent entrepreneurs or in a familial context. Younger children often work accompanied by a family member. A gender analysis shows that boys are more likely to perform heavy manual labor (working in garages and as porters on markets) or work independently in public spaces. Girls mainly work on markets (alongside a family member) or as domestic workers.

A small percentage of the work performed by children in the service sector falls into the category of worst forms of child labor, such as prostitution and selling liquor. Domestic labor is also often in this category. Approximately 33,000 children are involved in domestic labor, of which 32,000 are girls (UNICEF and INE 2004). These children are exposed to all kinds of abuse due to the lack of protection and control found in this sector. Children working on the streets are also extremely vulnerable, especially at night. This work exposes children to theft, violence (verbal and physical), and sexual abuse, and has a serious moral impact on children, as they are exposed to crime, drugs, and alcohol abuse.

The secondary sector entails mainly small-scale industry and construction work. Many children work in food production (bakeries, for example), retail, metal mechanics (such as soldering), woodwork, and cobbling. Conditions of this work may put a burden on children, as they often involve nighttime work (especially in baking), chemicals, and dangerous equipment, and frequently require physical strength. Again, a gender division is evident, with more girls working in retail and more boys in construction, mechanics, and food production. Approximately 75 percent of children working in the tertiary and secondary sectors can be found in the economic centers of La Paz, Cochabamba, and Santa Cruz.

Causes of Child Labor

Several interrelated factors explain why children in Bolivia work. One of the main causes, especially of the hazardous forms of child labor, is poverty. Numerous studies indicate a direct correlation between increasing levels of poverty and increasing numbers of family members involved in economic activities (UNDP 2002). It is also interesting that many children themselves take the initiative to work; working can be seen as a form of child agency in reaction to poverty (IREWOC 2005).

Child labor is also related to the poor situation of the Bolivian school system. Access and quality can be substandard, and the number of secondary schools is limited, especially in the countryside. This may explain why children in the countryside become involved in economic activities at very early ages. However, children in the cities also drop out of school and engage in economic activities due to the poor quality of education, or because they fail to see the relevance of education for their lives and prospects (van den Berge 2004).

Cultural norms concerning childhood and child labor also play a role. In Andes culture, the child is seen as part of a family and a broader community that is responsible for protecting the child. The child, in turn, is expected to perform certain activities for the common good. These activities may include certain labor tasks, depending on the child's age and capacity. Certain forms of child labor are thus seen as an important part of a child's integration into the community while simultaneously securing the community's continuity. Working is part of the socialization process, teaching children traditional knowledge (of production) and values of solidarity and reciprocity (UNDP 2002). However, it is also important to realize that a worsening household economic situation has transformed this custom from an activity in which children work according to their age and capacity to a situation of exploitation and abuse in an attempt to secure family survival.

References and Further Reading

Baas, L. "Bolivian Kids in Brasil Nuts: Possibilities for HIVOS to Contribute to the Eradication of Child Labour in the Brasil Nut Sector of Northern Bolivia." Master's thesis, Radboud University Nijmegen, 2006.

Durango, J. *Trabajo infantil en la zafra de la castaña en Bolivia: una sistematizacion.* La Paz: Prodeli, 2005.

ILO-IPEC. *Projecto para la prevension y la eliminacion progresiva en la mineria artesanal en Sud America: estudio de caso.* Bolivia: ILO-IPEC, 2001.

ILO-IPEC. *Bolivia. Child Labour on Sugarcane Plantations: A Rapid Evaluation.* Lima, Peru: IPEC-Sud-America, 2002.

ILO-UNICEF. *Caña dulce, vida amarga.* La Paz: ILO-UNICEF, 2004.

IREWOC. *Children as Agents in Development.* Amsterdam: IREWOC Foundation, 2005.

Oostra, M., and L. Malaver. *Bolivia: mensen-politiek-economie-cultuur-milieu.* Amsterdam: KIT Publishers, 2003.

UNICEF and INE. *Trabajo infantil en Bolivia: caracteristicas y condiciones: una realidad que no les corresponde.* La Paz, Bolivia: UNICEF, 2004.

UCW. *Child Labour in Bolivia: A Comparison of Estimates from MECOVI and MICS Survey Instruments.* Rome: UCW Project, 2004.

UNDP. *Informe de desarrollo humano en Bolivia.* La Paz: UNDP, 2002.

Van Damme, P. "Disponibilidad, uso y calidad de los recursos hídricos en Bolivia." Summit on Sustainable Development, Johannesburg, August 26–September 4, 2002.

Van den Berge, Marten. "Child Agency in Bolivia." In *Working Children Around the World: Child Rights and Child Reality*, ed. G.K. Lieten. New Delhi: Institute for Human Development, 2004.

Brazil

BRAZIL			
	CRC	C 138	C 182
Ratifications	Y	Y	Y
Human Development Index/Rank	0.792/69		
Human Capital			
Population Growth Rate	1.04%		
% Population 0–14	25.8%		
Total Fertility Rate	1.91		
Life Expectancy	71.97		
Infant Mortality Rate	28.6		
Literacy Rate	86.4%		
Economic			
GDP/Capita	$8,600		
GDP Growth %	2.8%		
% Poverty	31%		
Gini Index	56.7		
Labor Force Composition			
% Agriculture	20%		
% Industry	14%		
% Services	66%		

CHILD ACTIVITY BREAKDOWN, BY SEX AND RESIDENCE

RESIDENCE	Percentage of children in the relevant age-group[a]									
	Economic activity only		School only		Combining school and economic activity		Neither in school nor in economic activity		Child labor[b]	
	Male	Female	Male	Female	Male	Female	Male	Female	Male	Female
Urban	0.3	0.2	91.0	93.3	3.6	1.9	5.1	4.5	n/av	n/av
Rural	1.8	0.5	68.4	81.7	20.5	9.6	9.2	8.2	n/av	n/av
Total	0.6	0.2	86.3	91.0	7.1	3.4	6.0	5.3	5.9	2.5

Source: Brazil, Pesquisa Nacional por Amostra de Domicilios, 2004 (See UCW Project Web site, http://www.ucw-project.org, country statistics).
Notes: [a]Children age 5 to 14. [b]Estimate includes (a) children under age 12 engaged in economic activities and (b) children age 12–14 engaged in excessive economic activities (more than 14 hours per week). Estimate does not account for children engaged in excessive household chores, hazardous work, or other unconditional "worst forms" of child labor.

Recent History of Child Labor in Brazil

Ethel V. Kosminsky, Professor of Sociology, Social Sciences Graduate Program, São Paulo State University (UNESP)–Marília, and Researcher, CNPq

In any discussion of childhood labor in Brazil, it is necessary to first describe Brazilian society, a profoundly unequal society in terms of social class, race, gender, and cultural opportunity, which contributes to unequal access to the benefits of citizenship. Brazilian society is also stratified by age: Adults have the political and economic power to control the entire society (Pereira de Queiroz 1976). Poor children in this society, especially black and female children, occupy an inferior position.

To understand how this inequality and its correlated violence came to be, we need to examine Brazil's history. Brazil embraced more than four centuries of slavery and was the last country in the Americas to make slavery illegal, in 1888. Slave children were considered property and could be taken to the owner's house as a "toy" for the white children (Freyre 1987). Slave boys in the cities were used as *moleques de recado,* or messengers. Slave girls were raised as *crias da casa,* "girls of the house," who had to help with all household chores.

However, the abolition of slavery did not improve the freedmen's social conditions. Many freed slaves in the Northeast went to Salvador and Recife looking for work. Women sold food on the streets, washed laundry, and worked as housemaids. Men could only find work doing small chores. Blacks leaving the São Paulo coffee plantations for the city faced competition from Italian immigrants (Fernandes 1965).

The Beginning of Child Labor in São Paulo Factories

The Division of Statistics and Archives of São Paulo State showed that, in 1894, adolescents and children represented roughly 25 percent of the workers in four major textile factories. This proportion increased by 1912 to approximately 30 percent, and by 1919 to 40 percent (Moura 1982). Many women, adolescents, and children worked in the textile industry, in food processing, and in hat, cigar, and shoe factories. In glass factories, adolescents and children worked near furnaces as glass blowers. In match factories and paint factories, and in paper, firework, beverage, and furniture plants, child labor represented a small but significant part of the workforce. Not all children worked in the factories; some sold newspapers on the street, and others shined shoes.

The workday was long, extending through the evening, even for children. Children and adolescents received poor care within the factories, and bosses maintained discipline through spanking. Factories were not healthy environments, and the lack of hygiene led to an increase in diseases such as tuberculosis. Accidents were common, some fatal, because of the long hours, the lack of safety procedures, and the workers' youthfulness.

Federal Decree 1313 of 1891 was the most important attempt to administer adolescent and child labor until 1920. It stated that only children over the age of twelve could work in factories. However, it allowed the textile industry to employ children between eight and twelve years of age as apprentices. Between 1890 and 1920, the policy of the São Paulo State Department of Labor permitted children to work in factories. The lack of schools meant that children of working parents had to be on their own, a situation that often led them to the streets, where they committed small robberies. As juvenile delinquency started to be seen as a result of idleness, the elite began demanding that children and adolescents be employed in factories or even institutionalized.

Recent Data on Child Labor in Brazil

To understand child labor in Brazil and the public policy related to it, it is necessary to understand the social inequalities in the country. In 2006, Brazil's Human Development Index ranked it sixty-ninth in social and economic indicators among the 177 countries and territories studied. Among Latin American countries, thirteen nations showed more improvement than Brazil, including Mexico, Cuba, and Chile. Although Brazil still holds the tenth-highest income inequality among 126 countries contributing information, it is no longer the most unequal in Latin America, having been overcome by Bolivia and Colombia (Góis and Constantino 2006).

Brazil's Constitutional Amendment 20 (December 15, 1998) raised the minimum legal age for entering the labor market from fourteen to sixteen years old. This law reinforced the Child and Adolescent Statute of 1990 (Estatuto da Criança e do Adolescente), which had allowed adolescents to work from the ages of fourteen to sixteen years old, since work was combined with learning. Thus, child and adolescent labor between the ages of five and thirteen is prohibited according to the Brazilian constitution.

In 2003 in Brazil, 5.1 million children and adolescents between five and seventeen years of age were working, although that number has been diminishing. Nonetheless, this still shows the existing social inequalities in the country, especially for the 1.3 million children from five to thirteen years old who were still working, a number close to the entire population of the Brazilian state of Tocantins. Forty-two percent of the total number of children and adolescents working in the country were in the Northeast region; 33.5 percent of them (700,000 children) were between five and thirteen years old. Moreover, among 270,000 working children from five to nine years old in the Northeast, almost 80 percent worked in agriculture

The socioeconomic characteristics of children and adolescents who work show their precarious living conditions. Children and adolescents between ten and seventeen years old received income that represented 17 percent of their family's total income. In rural areas this proportion increased to 21.5 percent. In the Southeast, 25 percent of working children contributed more than 30 percent of the total family income. In comparison, in Amazonas State, located in the North region, working children contributed 42 percent of total family income.

Therefore, child labor within the family is still very important to total family income and affects the family's social and economic situation. Almost half of the children working in Brazil lived in families whose per capita family income is less than or equal to one-half of the legal monthly minimum wage. In the Northeast region, 73.3 percent of working children lived in families whose income is less than or equal to one-half the minimum wage. Living conditions for children and adolescents in the Northeast region were more precarious than for those living in the Southeast region, independent of what kind of work they had been doing. Another important indicator related to the severity of child labor: 38 percent of working children and adolescents did not receive any payment for their work. In the ten- to fifteen-year-old age-group, this proportion was even bigger (53.2 percent), and it reached 64.8 percent in the Northeast region.

The proportion of children and adolescents who work without attending school has been diminishing in recent years, dropping to 3.4 percent in 2003. The proportion that work and attend school also diminished, from 15.3 to 13.9 percent from 2003 to 2004. As a result, there was a 2 percent increase in the proportion of children and adolescents who attended school without working. The Northeast and South regions presented the highest proportions of children and adolescents who worked (including those who only worked and those who both worked and attended school), around 22.5 percent in the Northeast and 20.3 percent in the South.

The effects of working go beyond simply abandoning school: 67 percent of children and adolescents between ten and seventeen years of age who were working and attending school at the same time were below the normal grade level for their age. The rate of school attendance is sensitive to the labor market. For those working, school attendance reached 81 percent of the population between five and seventeen years old, and for those who were not working, the rate was higher, reaching 92 percent. Although working children and adolescents were concentrated in the Northeast region, the worst school attendance was observed in the South region, at 79.1 percent. In the rural Southeast region, school attendance was 72.7 percent.

In 2003, the proportion of working children and adolescents who could be classified as employees, domestic servants, or unpaid workers fell, while the category of self-employed workers increased from 6.7 to 7.4 percent. Unpaid work is characteristic of the Northeast region, reaching 64.8 percent of the children and adolescents between ten and fifteen years old, although domestic service included 17.6 percent of this Northeast age-group. In the age-group between sixteen and seventeen, more than 50 percent of the working population worked as paid employees.

Most children and adolescents from ten to seventeen years of age who were working started their activity in the labor market at an early age. In Brazil's rural areas, of the 1.8 million working children and adolescents from ten to seventeen years old, 37.6 percent started working before the age of ten. The highest proportions were observed in the Piaui (67.1 percent) and Paraiba (51.7 percent) states. In contrast, in urban areas, children and adolescents entered the labor market at a later age. In 2003, 33.1 percent of working children and adolescents started their employment between the ages of fifteen and seventeen. The increase of almost 1 percent of this rate in relation to 2002 showed that children and adolescents were kept longer in school, postponing their entrance to the labor market.

Regarding the distribution of working children and adolescents according to their place of work, there were no significant changes compared to the earlier year. Working in stores or workshops, and in the employer's house, diminished a little, while there was a small increase in the number of people working in their own homes. This increase was noticed principally in the Southeast, where the percentage of self-employed workers rose from 4.1 to 5.8 percent in 2003. Also significant is the high proportion of children working on the streets of the Recife metropolitan region (26.3 percent). In the North region of the country, the proportion of children working on the streets reached 13.3 percent in the ten- to fifteen-year-old age category.

The Child Labor Eradication Program (PETI)

In the 1990s, the Child Labor Eradication Program (PETI, Programa de Erradicação do Trabalho Infantil) assumed the role of retrieving children between the ages of seven and fifteen from the "worst forms" of labor—work considered dangerous, difficult, exhausting, unhealthy, and degrading. With the support of the ILO and UNICEF, and through an agreement with the federal government, individual states, and municipalities, PETI has given priority to the areas where child labor had been widely used. In 2000, the program helped 140,000 children and adolescents in the country; in 2002 this number grew to 810,769 children living in 2,590 different municipalities throughout the nation (Carvalho 2004).

PETI has given priority to families whose income is only one-half the monthly minimum wage, a group living under extremely poor conditions. The program offers financial aid to the families so that their children can stop working. Each child who lives in a rural area receives R$25 monthly, and each urban child, living in municipalities with more than 250,000 inhabitants, receives R$40 per month. Families have to send their children to schools regularly and to after-school classes, which are called *jornada ampliada*. Municipalities are responsible for coordinating the *jornada*, and they receive R$20 per month for each child or adolescent from the federal government to hire staff and provide adequate space and material. Besides a healthy lunch and snack, the *jornada* staff helps children with their homework and provides cultural and sporting activities. Children and adolescents now receive these grants for up to four years. The program has expanded to include retrieving children who performed activities such as collecting material to be resold as scrap, selling things on the streets and the open markets, working on cotton plantations, collecting cigar leaves, coffee beans, and oranges, and making china in workshops and bricks in kilns.

It is difficult to evaluate PETI's results in all the municipalities where it has been in effect. However, case studies reveal some problems, such as insufficient grant money and delays by the federal government in sending money to the municipalities. The municipalities do not give enough financial support to the after-school program and have allowed politics to affect administration of the system. The public school system is independent of the after-school classes, although they should be working together on behalf of the children. The after-school classes suffer from poorly qualified monitors and inadequate locations.

However, PETI has contributed to improvements in children's nutrition and their school attendance, as well as taking them out of the labor market. It has also reduced the school dropout rate and helped children advance to the next grade rather than being left behind to repeat the same school year again. The children PETI was able to remove from dangerous and degraded labor conditions have been allowed to remain at school and have access to leisure and cultural activities. Besides this, PETI stresses the importance of preventing children from working at younger ages and fighting the myth that labor is the destiny of poor children.

Although PETI attempts to focus on the worst forms of child labor, it ignores some occupations that are also harmful. Besides this, it does not enroll enough working children. Unfortunately, PETI is not able to significantly change the living conditions of poor children and adolescents. Whatever they have gained in nutrition and social and cultural stimuli, their school learning is restricted and temporary. When PETI begins helping children and adolescents, they have all too often begun school at a late age. This late start is a result of the low quality of the public schools, which do not motivate students to continue attending. When students reach the age limit of the PETI grant, most of them are not able to finish grammar school. After PETI, few continue attending school, as they have to work to ensure their family's survival. Therefore, they continue on the same path to low levels of schooling and limited job opportunities. Inevitably, they become part of the same cycle of poverty that their parents have experienced.

Re-creating Child Labor in Brazil

Globalization has allowed employers to seek out cheap labor all over the world, and this policy encourages child labor in peripheral countries such as Brazil. Although Brazil's law and public policy oppose child labor, it has not been eliminated, even with the help of the ILO and UNICEF, the support of communal organizations and labor unions, and the help of the Catholic Church. For example, in Limeira, located about ninety miles from São Paulo, approximately 6,000 children and adolescents up to the age of seventeen, out of a total of 30,800 students attending public schools, work with their mothers and siblings at home assembling costume jewelry for 450 small jewelry companies. Almost 33,000 people work illegally as outsourced labor for larger companies, resulting in a profit of US$220 million in Brazil in 2006 (60 percent coming from Limeira). Research conducted by the Universidade Metodista de Piracicaba (UNIMEP, Methodist University of Piracicaba) found that repetitive labor tasks afflicted the children's arms and hands. Workers receive very little money, only R$5 for 1,000 pieces of assembled jewelry (Tonocci 2006).

Large multinational and national companies alike subcontract with smaller companies, which in turn hire families to assemble products in their own homes. Similar supply chains also exist in the agricultural industry. A giant multinational food-processing company located in Goiás State, in the Center-West region of the nation, transforms fresh tomatoes into tomato sauce. In the 1990s this multinational, working with the Employer Association of Food Industry and the Regional Division of Labor of Goiás State (DRT), signed an agreement, ostensibly to eradicate child labor from its supply chain. The agreement was based both on Brazilian law that forbids employment of children and adolescents under the age of fourteen, and on the maxim "A country that does not care for its children has no future." The DRT inspects the tomatoes used in the production process and provides a list of those small farmers who do not meet the requirements of the agreement to the multinational corporation and to the employer association. In this way, both the multinational corporation and the employer union are able to say that if there is any exploitation of child labor, the responsibility rests with the producers of the raw materials, that is, with the small rural farmers. These rural producers are then inspected, and if they are found to have violated the law, their contracts are terminated (Marin 2006).

This was the strategy used by the industry in order to avoid complications involving the use of child labor. By placing child labor only in agricultural production, at the origins of the supply chain, the multinational corporation freed itself of any responsibility for exploitation of children and shifted the responsibility to the agricultural producers. However, agricultural production is the weakest link in the supply chain. Agro-industries determine the prices of the raw materials paid to rural producers. This price sets the budget, which includes all of the producer's labor costs. Agro-industries want adequate quality and quantity of raw materials at low prices so that they can compete in national and international markets. So the prices paid for agricultural products are low. As a result, the agricultural producers earn little money, and the only way to survive is to reduce their own labor expenses. Finally, parents find themselves in the weakest part of this supply chain, needing the support of their children in order to complete the work profitably.

Whenever there are prohibitive measures against child labor, children are soon sent to other services, often receiving even lower pay for work in unhealthy and dangerous conditions. Thus, wealth continues to concentrate in the hands of the large industries, while poverty remains the condition endured by families forced to exploit the labor of their own children.

References and Further Reading

Carneiro, Ana Gilka Duarte. "Erradicação do trabalho infantil: estudo de políticas públicas contra a exploração da mão-de-obra infantil em Curitiba." Master's thesis, Sociology Graduate Program, Paraná Federal University, 2002.

Carvalho, Inaiá Maria Moreira de. "Algumas lições do programa de erradiação do trabalho infantil." *São Paulo em perspectiva* 18:4 (2004): 50–61.

Fernandes, Florestan. *A integração do negro na sociedade de classes.* São Paulo: Dominus Editora, 1965.

Freyre, Gilberto. *Casa-grande & senzala: formação da família Brasileira sob o regime da economia patriarcal.* 25th ed. Rio de Janeiro: José Olympio Editora, 1987 [1933].

Góis, Antônio, and Luciana Constantino. "IDH do Brasil melhora, mas o país cai uma posição em ranking da ONU." *Folha de São Paulo,* November 10, 2006.

Marin, Joel Orlando Bevilaqua. *Trabalho infantil: necessidade, valor e exclusão social.* Brasília: Plano Editora, Goiânia, Editora UFG, 2006.

Moura, Esmeralda Blanco B. de. *Mulheres e menores no trabalho industrial: os fatores sexo e idade na dinâmica do capital.* Petrópolis: Vozes, 1982.

Pereira de Queiroz, Maria Isaura. "Educação como uma forma de colonialismo." *Ciência e cultura* 28:12 (1976): 1433–71.

Tonocchi, Mário. "Produção de jóias em limeira emprega 6 mil crianças e jovens." *O estado de São Paulo,* December 12, 2006, A14.

Child Street Vendors in Brazil

Ana Lúcia Kassouf, Professor, and **Andrea R. Ferro,** PhD Student,
Department of Economics at ESALQ, University of São Paulo

Working on the streets is considered one of the worst forms of child labor, mainly due to a greater exposure of children to traffic accidents, drugs, violence, criminal activities, prostitution, and other health and moral dangers. Children and adolescents spend long hours on the streets selling goods, cleaning cars, polishing shoes, or performing for drivers stopped at red lights, which can result in fatigue, malnutrition, motor vehicle injuries, sexually transmitted diseases, unwanted pregnancy, and drug addiction. Brazilian legislation regarding child labor is very strict, prohibiting children below the age of sixteen from working and establishing eighteen years old as the minimum age for hazardous work, which includes street vending.

In Brazil, the Brazilian Geographical and Statistical Institute (IBGE) undertakes an annual national household survey that collects information on children working from the age of five. The survey considers any person a worker who performs any paid or unpaid activity at least one hour per week, with the exception of household tasks. According to the Brazilian National Household Survey (PNAD) from 2005, out of almost 5.5 million working children in Brazil, there are 270,090 children and adolescents from five to seventeen years old working on the streets of Brazil. Therefore, among the five- to seventeen-year-old population in the country, 12.2 percent are working, and among them 5 percent are performing activities on the streets, mainly selling candies and other goods (52 percent), polishing shoes, guarding cars or delivering papers (33 percent), and collecting recyclable materials (15 percent). Since this was a household survey, however, the data exclude children who are also living on the streets.

Working on the streets, especially as a street vendor, requires a demand for the products being sold, and so this work is concentrated in large metropolitan areas. Cities such as São Paulo, Rio de Janeiro, Bahia, Fortaleza, Recife, Belém do Pará, Porto Alegre, Belo Horizonte, and Curitiba have the highest numbers of children working on streets. The great majority of those children are boys, about 80 percent, as compared to the percentage of boys among children working in other economic activities (63 percent). This may reflect the notion that girls are more vulnerable than boys on the streets (which does not mean that boys are not at risk).

Children and adolescents work on average twenty-four hours a week, but 21 percent of them spend more than forty hours a week working on the streets. Since many children work from sunrise to long after sunset peddling anything of value, there is not much time left for school. The result is that 20 percent of the seven- to seventeen-year-old children that are working do not go to school, compared to only 6 percent of those not working who do not attend school. Legislation in Brazil mandates nine years of schooling (from age six to age fourteen), but a large number of children are not in the right grade for their age. For example, it is common to find a seventeen-year-old in primary school.

The loss of education caused by having to work long hours at an early age, has the effect of limiting employment opportunities to unskilled, low-paid jobs, locking the child into a repetition of the cycle of poverty that the child's parents experienced. There is, therefore, a trade-off between added current household income obtained through the work of the child and foregone future income of the child as a result of the reduction in earning capacity caused by disruption to the child's education.

Families' per capita income in households where children work on the streets is less than US$80 per month. Because they are very poor, any money received by the children represents a large percentage of their family's income. In 34 percent of the families, earnings from five- to seventeen-year-olds working on the streets account for more than 20 percent of the family's income; for 13 percent of the families, the contribution is more than 40 percent of the family's income. In those families, income generated by working children is crucial to their survival and, unless those families are assisted, banning child labor could exacerbate poverty. Along with a policy to ban child labor, it is necessary to assist the families through social or income-transfer programs.

In the last decade, Brazilian policy makers at the municipal, state, and federal levels instituted social programs that paid poor families cash stipends conditional on their children's school attendance, medical care, and nutritional status. These social programs include the Programa de Erradicação do Trabalho Infantil (PETI; program to eradicate child labor) and Bolsa-Escola (school scholarship program), which was incorporated in 2004 into a national comprehensive welfare program, the Bolsa-Familia program, an income-transfer program for poor families with a monthly per capita income of up to R$100 (less than US$50). Because children working on the streets live in poor households, a large proportion of their families participate in income-transfer programs. Considering that they are poor and more dependent on governmental help, children and their parents accept work on the streets in order to meet basic family consumption needs, even knowing it is a harmful situation.

Conclusion

The dangers imposed on children working on the streets require their immediate removal from these activities and further prevention from being lured into unsafe situations again. Important policies to eradicate these worst forms of child labor include sensitizing public opinion, reintegrating children into the school system, improving the school system, and providing subsidies and income support for families.

References and Further Reading

Groves, Leslie, and David Johnson. "Education for All? Transforming Educational Provision for the Inclusion of Street Children in Brazil." *Oxford Studies in Comparative Education* 10:2 (2000): 157–73.

Mickelson, Roslyn Arlin. *Children on the Streets of the Americas: Homelessness, Education, and Globalization in the United States, Brazil, and Cuba.* New York: Routledge, 2000.

Swift, Anthony. *Children for Social Change: Education for Citizenship of Street and Working Children in Brazil.* Nottingham: Educational Heretics Press, 1997.

Prostitution and Commercial Sexual Exploitation of Children and Adolescents in Brazil

Leandro Feitosa Andrade, Professor of Psychology, Faculdades Metropolitanas Unidas (United Metropolitan Colleges), and Researcher, Carlos Chagas Foundation; and **Fúlvia Rosemberg,** Professor of Social Psychology, Pontifical Catholic University of São Paulo, and Researcher, Carlos Chagas Foundation

Conceptually, child prostitution in Brazil has come to be treated as "the commercial sexual exploitation of children and young people." This expression is considered to broaden the concept to include modalities other than sexual practice, such as pornography, sexual tourism, and traffic for sexual commerce. Moreover, the expression focuses on the exploiter, thus reducing the stigma and discrimination against children and adolescents.

Before the 1990s, the issue of commercial sexual exploitation of young people appeared only sporadically in academic writing, specialized production (by public and private nonacademic institutions), and the media. Only beginning in 1992 did the issue gain emphasis, especially as a result of a newspaper campaign against "slavery" of children and adolescents in the mining areas of the northern region of Brazil. A guesstimate of 500,000 Brazilian girls and adolescents in prostitution came to be widely cited and uncritically disseminated by the media. But the sources, criteria, and procedures to sustain this "estimate" have never been located or publicized, and it has been discarded by academics and official agencies, who agree that these number are fictitious, employed as a rhetorical artifice in discourses of denunciation. However, the "estimate" is still circulating in the national and international media.

These fictitious "estimates" are just one of the sensationalist strategies that have characterized the rhetoric around sexual exploitation of adolescents in Brazil in recent decades. The goal of denouncement, which has oriented governmental, activist, academic, and media discourse, has contributed to a lack of reflective rigor, which not only has generated a new subcategory for identification of poor children and adolescents, but also has been converted into the ideological equivalent of a range of experiences of young people and their families: sexual abuse, adolescent pregnancy, sexual permissiveness, violence, and family neglect. One notes, especially in media production, that the theme of child and adolescent prostitution appears alongside a strong stigmatization of poor children and their families, the invasion of their privacy through exposing their identities, and the production and reproduction of a depreciated representation—a "lost childhood"—with a compromised past and without alternatives for the future.

Sexual exploitation of children and adolescents in Brazil, despite the emphasis on specific processes, has been interpreted as an expression of economic inequalities associated with poverty in a social context marked by unequal relations of gender, race, and age. Generally, the explanations rely on the social status of the exploited children and adolescents, and studies that focus on the exploiters and their psychological processes are few and far between.

Thanks to social mobilization, the issue entered the public policy agenda, where it was the subject of two congressional inquiries (1993 and 2003), stimulating the development of programs, projects, and academic production, as well as the creation of specialized institutions. Thus, since the 1990s, the commercial sexual exploitation of children and adolescents has been included on the agendas of governmental and nongovernmental agencies in Brazil, in both discourse and practice.

The following are the main activities for combating the sexual exploitation of children and adolescents in contemporary Brazil: the National Campaign to Combat Child and Adolescent Sexual Exploitation; the appearance in 1993 of the News Agency on Children's Rights (ANDI); the Seminar Against Sexual Exploitation of Children and Adolescents in the Americas, held in 1996; a phone service to receive complaints, known as the National System for Combating Child and Adolescent Sexual Abuse and Exploitation, which has been functioning since 1997 under the coordination of the Brazilian Multi-Professional Association for the Protection of Children and Adolescents (ABRAPIA); the dissemination of the Study on Traffic of Women, Children and Adolescents for Commercial Sexual Exploitation (PESTRAF), under the responsibility of the Center for Reference, Study and Action on Children and Adolescents (CECRIA), which mapped national and international routes of trafficking of children, adolescents, and adult women for purposes of sexual commerce; the discussion and dissemination of the National Plan to Confront Sexual Violence Against Children and Young Adults (in 2002), in which 130 agencies under the coordination of the Ministry of Justice participated; the creation of the Sentinel Program, the Program to Combat Sexual Abuse and Exploitation of Children and Adolescents, linked to the Program of the Ministry for Social Assistance and Promotion, created in 2000 to serve abused or sexually exploited children and their families; the organization of campaigns against sexual tourism (1997) by the Brazilian Tourism Agency (EMBRATUR) with support from the World Tourism Organization, especially in the tourist regions of northeast Brazil; initiation of broad actions by the federal police under the government of Luiz Inácio Lula da Silva (2002–2006), in partnership with state police and the identification and imprisonment of owners of nightclubs where adolescents were found in situations of prostitution, one of them known as Operation Tamar; the alteration of an article in the *Statute on Children and Adolescents* (the national law declaring the rights of children and adolescents), in 2003, making pedophilia on the Internet explicitly a crime, and the dissemination by governmental and nongovernmental agencies of the Campaign Against Child Pornography on the Internet; the mapping by the federal highway police, which, in 2005, identified 844 points along Brazilian highways where there was sexual exploitation of children and adolescents.

References and Further Reading

Andrade, Leandro Feitosa. *Child Prostitution in the Media: Stigmatization and Ideology.* São Paulo: EDUC, 2004.

Rosemberg, Fúlvia, and Leandro Feitosa Andrade. "Ruthless Rhetoric: Child and Youth Prostitution in Brazil." *Childhood* 6:1 (1999): 113–31.

Special Health Risks to Child Workers in Brazil

Anaclaudia Gastal Fassa, MD, PhD, Associate Professor, Department of Social Medicine, Federal University of Pelotas; and **David H. Wegman,** MD, MSc, Dean and Professor, School of Health and Environment, University of Massachusetts Lowell

Brazil has a large number of working children, representing 7 percent of the total workforce. The most recent estimates indicate that there are 3.5 million employed under the age of sixteen (young child workers) and 2 million employed sixteen- and seventeen-year-olds (older child workers) (Instituto Brasileiro de Geografia e Estatística 2003). The health risks associated with working children are best understood by looking at where the majority work.

Hazardous Occupations That Employ More Than 10 Percent of Working Children

Three sectors employ 60 percent of all child laborers in Brazil. The largest number of children work in agriculture, an estimated 2.4 million children. This population is 38 percent of all child workers and an even higher proportion of child workers under age fifteen (50 percent). Children work most commonly with sisal, cotton, coffee, sugarcane, and tobacco, as well as tending cattle and cutting trees. Agriculture is well recognized throughout the world as one of the highest-risk sectors for all ages. Work in agriculture often requires long hours and involves a number of hazardous activities, including substantial risk of work-related injuries as well as exposure to chemicals, mainly pesticides. Around 5 percent of rural child workers are involved in poultry work, an activity with high exposure to dust and high risk for respiratory problems (Schwartzman and Schwartzman 2004; Fassa 2003; Faria et al. 2006). Other important hazards in agriculture include exposure to extreme temperatures (mainly heat), strenuous physical work, noise, and several general environmental conditions such as unsafe transportation and poor field sanitation (Fassa 2003).

The second-largest sector, domestic service, employs 11.5 percent of child workers but accounts for one-third of all working girls (Schwartzman and Schwartzman 2004). There are few epidemiological studies of this occupation, even among adults. One study estimated that 36.5 percent of those workers between six and seventeen years of age perform weekly shifts of forty hours or more (Facchini et al. 2003). Another study showed increased risk of musculoskeletal pain, specifically back pain, among child domestic workers compared with nonworkers and workers in retail (Fassa et al. 2005). Santana et al. (2003) studied domestic workers of all ages and found a 7.3 percent annual incidence of work-related injuries compared with 4.5 percent among other occupations. However, among child domestic laborers fifteen to seventeen years old, the annual incidence was 25 percent. Thirty-two percent of domestic workers lived in their employers' houses. Young domestic workers who live with an employer are likely to be disconnected from their own families and more vulnerable to moral and sexual abuse.

The third most important sector is manufacturing, where more than 10 percent of child workers are employed. Among these, more than one-quarter work in the food, textile, and footwear industries (Schwartzman and Schwartzman 2004). Other manufactures that employ some children, but that are very hazardous, include pottery and brick making; paper, plastic, and rubber; glass; leather; and metallurgy (Kassouf 2004). Many children working in manufacturing jobs are located in small or home-based workshops, including a number that are subcontractors to medium-size or large enterprises (U.S. Department of Labor 1998). Child workers in manufacturing face high risk of work-related injuries, ergonomic hazards (with awkward postures, repetitive and monotonous work, and heavy physical work), and exposure to noise and chemicals (solvents, dyes, and sodas, among others) (Fassa 2003). One study in Brazil showed that child workers in manufacturing reported 70 percent more back pain than nonworkers (Fassa et al. 2005).

Hazardous Occupations That Employ Approximately 4 Percent of Working Children

Several other sectors employ fewer child workers but are quite hazardous. The construction sector employs mainly boys and presents a high risk of work-related injuries. No Brazilian data on injuries exist, but in the United States this sector presents high fatality rates among youths mainly due to falls and electrocution (Kisner and Fosbroke 1994). Construction workers are also exposed to ergonomic hazards such as heavy physical work, awkward postures, and repetitive work (Fassa et al. 2005). Moreover, children and adolescents in construction can be exposed to noise, as well as asbestos, lead, cement, solvents, and other chemical substances (Fassa 2003). The informal sector of street workers presents high risk of traffic accidents. Children doing this work are also more exposed to violence and could suffer physical or sexual abuse, or could be lured to drugs, prostitution, or criminal activities (Fassa 2003). Those employed as cooks handle unsafe tools and machinery, such as slicing machines and hot grease, posing substantial risk of accidents. They too are exposed to ergonomic hazards (Forastieri 2002). Finally, work in auto-repair garages and gas stations expose youths to unsafe tools and machinery, and to several chemical substances such as solvents, benzene, and carbon monoxide (Fassa 2003).

Hazardous Occupations That Employ Between 1 and 2.5 Percent of Working Children

While this last category includes a small proportion of the child workforce, jobs in these sectors carry substantial risks. Warehouse workers handle heavy loads with unsafe machinery and very low training for the job, presenting a high risk of injuries and musculoskeletal problems. Those in the needle trades use unsafe machinery in an awkward posture, resulting in musculoskeletal problems and work-related injuries. This work is also characterized by visual stress associated, at least, with chronic eye irritation (Kassouf 2004). Last, work as a joiner includes exposure to unsafe tools and machinery, wood dust, asbestos, heavy physical work, repetitive work, and several chemical substances such as formaldehyde, pesticides, and glue, presenting risk of work-related injuries, cancer, and musculoskeletal and respiratory problems (Fassa 2005).

There is even a small proportion of child laborers (1 percent) working in mining. They are mainly located in the North and Northeastern regions of Brazil (Kassouf 2004). This is considered one of the most hazardous occupations, particularly due to its high risk of fatal injuries. Children in this occupation can be engaged in underground work, exposed to falling objects, unsafe tools and machinery, heavy loads, noise, harmful dusts, gas, fumes, carbon monoxide, and other chemicals, depending on the activity (e.g., mercury in gold mining). Moreover, they often are exposed to poor sanitation and inadequate nutrition. Some children are employed far from their homes and end up suffering physical or sexual abuse or are caught in a bonded labor situation (Fassa 2003).

Unconditional Worst Forms of Child Labor in Brazil

There are no official statistics on unconditional worst forms of child labor in Brazil. More than half a million children and teens are estimated to be subject to commercial sexual exploitation in Brazil; 95 percent of them are girls. This problem is mainly in the North, Northeastern, and Center-West regions of the country. In addition to being exposed to drugs and physical, moral, and sexual abuse, these children are at high risk of sexually transmitted diseases such as AIDS as well as unwanted pregnancy (Fassa 2003).

There are also a small number of children and adolescents involved in illegal activity such as robbery and drug trafficking. In Rio de Janeiro, NGOs estimate that about 5,000 children work for drug traffickers, and most of them are armed. These children are mainly exposed to drugs and to physical and moral abuse (Dowdney 2003). Most desperate of all are the estimated 20,000 to 40,000 people, many of them children, subjected to practices similar to slavery. These individuals are concentrated in agriculture, charcoal mining, crab picking in swamps, domestic services, and commercial sexual exploitation ("Trabalho escravo no Brasil" 2004; Couto 2005; Camara 2006).

Conclusion

Public opinion about child labor is changing slowly, and 77 percent of youths already believe that the best age to start to work is after age sixteen (Andrade 2006). Brazil has recently initiated a number of governmental actions to deal with the problem, including Child Labor Eradication Programs providing scholarships to those children that stop working and keep going to school, as well as other focal programs (U.S. Department of Labor 1998). These actions have led to a 7 percentage point reduction in economically active children between 1992 and 2001. The action against slavery has also been strong. From 1995 to 2004, 10,000 workers were released from such exploitation by work inspectors. This important work, however, has generated violent reaction, and four work inspectors were killed in 2003 ("Trabalho escravo no Brasil" 2004).

References and Further Reading

Andrade, J. *Pesquisa mostra que jovem está mais consciente sobre prejuízos do trabalho infantil.* Vol. 2006. Brasília: Radiobras, 2006.

Camara, E.B. "Emprego doméstico: casos revelam exploração." BBCBrasil.com, 2006.

Couto, L. *Paraibanos são levados para catar caranguejo no RN.* Brasília: Câmara dos Deputados—DETAG Sessão: 018.3.52.0, 2005.

Dowdney, L. *Crianças do tráfico: um estudo de caso de crianças em violência armada organizada no Rio de Janeiro.* Rio de Janeiro: Sete Letras, 2003.

Facchini, L.A., A.G. Fassa, M.M. Dall'Agnol, M.dF. Maia, and D.C. Christiani. "Individuals at Risk: The Case of Child Labor," in *Global Inequalities at Work*, ed. Jo Heymann. New York: Oxford, 2003.

Faria, N.M., L.A. Facchini, A.G. Fassa, and E. Tomasi. "Farming Work, Dust Exposure and Respiratory Symptoms Among Farmers." *Revista de saude publica* 40:5 (2006).

Fassa, A.G. *Health Benefits of Eliminating Child Labour.* Geneva: ILO-IPEC, 2003.

Fassa, A.G. "Matriz de trabalho infantil perigoso (anexo 1)." *Trabalho infantil: diretrizes para atenção integral de crianças e adolescentes economicamente ativos.* Normas e Manuais Técnicos. Brasília: Ministério da Saúde, 2005, 36–73.

Fassa, A.G., L.A. Facchini, M.M. Dall'agnol, and D.C. Christiani. "Child Labor and Musculoskeletal Disorders: The Pelotas (Brazil) Epidemiological Survey." *Public Health Reports* 120 (2005): 665–73.

Forastieri, V. *Children at Work: Health and Safety Risks.* 2nd ed. Geneva: ILO-IPEC, 2002.

Instituto Brasileiro de Geografia e Estatística. *Pesquisa nacional por amostra de domicílios: trabalho infantil 2001.* Rio de Janeiro: Instituto Brasileiro de Geografia e Estatística, 2003.

Kassouf, A.L., coord. *O Brasil e o trabalho infantil do século 21.* Brasília: Organização Internacional do Trabalho—Programa Internacional para a Eliminação do Trabalho Infantil–IPEC, 2004.

Kisner, S.M., and D.E. Fosbroke. "Injury Hazards in the Construction Industry." *Journal of Occupational Medicine* 36:2 (1994): 137–43.

Santana, V.S., A.M. de Amorim, R. Oliveira, S. Xavier, J. Iriart, and L. Belitardo. "Housemaids and Non-Fatal Occupational Injuries." *Revista de saude publica* 37:1 (2003): 65–74.

Schwartzman, S., and F. Schwartzman. *Tendências do trabalho infantil no Brasil entre 1992 e 2002.* Brasília: Organización Internacional del Trabajo, 2004.

"Trabalho escravo no Brasil." *Observatório social* 6 (2004).

U.S. Department of Labor. *By the Sweat and Toil of Children.* Vol. 5, *Efforts to Eliminate Child Labor.* Child Labor Series. Washington, DC: U.S. Department of Labor, Bureau of International Labor Affairs, 1998.

The Intergenerational Persistence of Child Labor in Brazil

André Portela Souza, São Paulo School of Economics, Getúlio Vargas Foundation, Brazil

The intergenerational persistence of child labor refers to the possibility of child labor spanning successive generations within a family. Empirical evidence exists on the topic. Wahba (2006), in a study of Egypt in 1988, and Emerson and Souza (2003), in a study of Brazil in 1996, found the same empirical regularity: Children whose parents were child laborers are more likely to be child laborers themselves. This regularity can be observed in more recent data for Brazil. Table 1 shows the incidence of child labor among ten- to fourteen-year-olds and the child labor status of the head of their households for 2005.

Table 1

Child Labor Incidence: Brazil, 2005 (in percent)

		Household head was child laborer?	
Child is child laborer?	Total	No	Yes
No	89.8	95.9	87.0
Yes	10.2	4.2	13.0
Total	100	31.3	68.7

Source: Brazilian Household Survey, 2005 (Pesquisa Nacional por Amostra de Domicílios, Instituto Brasileiro de Geografia e Estatística), and author's calculations.

Table 1 shows that of all ten- to fourteen-year-old children in Brazil in 2005, 10.2 percent were child laborers. The last row of Table 1 shows that 68.7 percent of household heads started to work at age fourteen or younger. Interestingly, of all children that live in households where the head was a child laborer, 13 percent work in the labor market. However, of all children that live in a household where the head was not a child laborer, only 4.2 percent work in the labor market. That is, a child in a household headed by a former child laborer is more than four times more likely to be a child laborer than a child that lives in a household where the head was not a child laborer. This empirical regularity is the intergenerational persistence of child labor.

What mechanisms underlie this regularity? One possible underlying mechanism is what has come to be known as the "child labor trap." Many economic studies suggest that child labor is both a result of, and a strategy to avoid, household poverty. In this sense, the income generated by child labor may be viewed as a solution to poverty's crushing effects. However, if there is a trade-off between child labor and human capital formation, as many studies also suggest, using child labor to avoid poverty can cause it to persist through generations of families (Basu 1999; Emerson and Souza 2003; Emerson and Knabb 2006). The argument can be summarized briefly: Children who work either do not attend school, or devote less time to their schooling, than children who do not work. They accumulate less human capital (not to mention that premature work can directly harm physical and psychological abilities). Since human capital is directly linked to earnings potential in the labor market, former child workers are more likely to remain poor as adults, and, thus, are more likely to rely on the labor supply of their own children to make ends meet. This is the child labor trap.

An alternative explanation of the underlying mechanism causing intergenerational persistence of child labor involves social norms and preferences. Parents who worked as children may simply send their children to work because they believe that early work imparts important qualities in

Figure 1 **Probability of a 12-Year-Old Male Child Working**

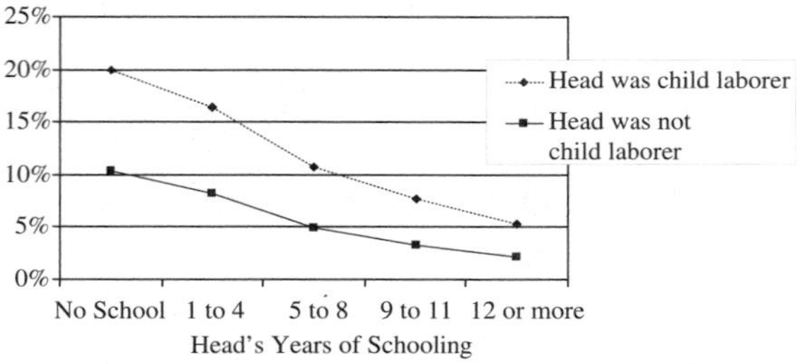

children. That is, having been a child laborer, the parent might be likely to hold more positive values and attitudes toward child labor (Basu 1999; Lopez-Calva 2003).

Disentangling the relative importance of these two possible explanations remains an open challenge. There is evidence that both arguments have some validity. Figure 1 updates the findings of Emerson and Souza (2003) using the 2005 PNAD (Brazilian household survey). The figure presents the probability that a twelve-year-old male child works as a function of the educational attainment of the head of the household.

First, as found by Emerson and Souza (2003), the probability of the child working decreases as the household head's schooling increases. Higher education is associated with higher permanent income. It is shown elsewhere (Emerson and Souza 2007) that being a child laborer is associated with lower education and lower earnings when one becomes an adult. Altogether, this evidence is consistent with the child labor trap. Individuals who worked as children have lower education and earnings, and thus their children will have higher probabilities of being child laborers (compared to individuals who did not work as children and have higher education and earnings as adults).

However, Figure 1 also shows that, controlling for education (and income), children from households headed by a former child laborer have a higher probability of being child laborers (compared to children from households with a head who did not work as a child). Indeed, these children are two times more likely to be child laborers once other factors are controlled. This is true for all levels of education. This result suggests that there are other factors, over and beyond wealth, income, and education, that explain the intergenerational persistence of child labor. This evidence is consistent with the explanation that social norms and preferences are the underlying mechanism of intergenerational persistence of child labor.

These results pose challenges for policy makers. If child labor is indeed primarily a result of familial poverty, a more challenging policy problem is presented. Banning child labor could have quite harmful effects (Basu and Van 1998) and should be undertaken only with the utmost caution. If, however, poverty is only a small part of the story, and social norms or parental preferences are the major factors, policy solutions such as absolute bans on child labor may be more effective.

References and Further Reading

Basu, Kaushik. "Child Labor: Cause, Consequence, and Cure, with Remarks on International Labor Standards." *Journal of Economic Literature* 37:3 (1999): 1083–1119.

Basu, Kaushik, and Pham Hoang Van. "The Economics of Child Labor." *American Economic Review* 88:3 (1998): 412–27.

Emerson, Patrick, and Shawn Knabb. "Opportunity, Inequality and the Intergenerational Transmission of Child Labor." *Economica* 73:291 (2006): 413–34.

Emerson, Patrick, and André Portela Souza. "Is There a Child Labor Trap? Intergenerational Persistence of Child Labor in Brazil." *Economic Development and Cultural Change* 51:2 (2003): 375–97.

Emerson, Patrick, and André Portela Souza. "Is Child Labor Harmful? The Impact of Working Earlier in Life on Adult Earnings." Mimeo, São Paulo School of Economics, Getúlio Vargas Foundation, 2007.

Lopez-Calva, Luis. "Social Norms, Coordination and Policy Issues in the Fight Against Child Labor." In *International Labor Standards: History, Theory, and Policy Options*, ed. K. Basu, H. Horn, L. Roman, and J. Shapiro, 256–70. Malden, MA: Blackwell, 2003.

Wahba, Jackie. "The Influence of Market Wages and Parental History on Child Labour and Schooling in Egypt." *Journal of Population Economics* 19:4 (2006): 823–52.

Child Labor Labeling in Brazil

Andres Pablo Falconer, Ashoka: Innovators for the Public

Brazil has awakened to the problem of child labor. Before the 1990s, the issue ranked low on the social agenda. Child labor was often not only tolerated, but encouraged, as a solution to poverty and juvenile delinquency. Work was contrasted with idleness rather than with schooling, play, and adequate child care. With the reestablishment of constitutional democracy and enactment of child protection laws in the 1980s, children's rights were given priority, and understood as a shared responsibility of families, government, and society as a whole. A surge of civil society activity, as well as a growing movement for corporate social responsibility, has inspired innovative programs and instruments beyond the traditional state-driven command-and-control policies. It was against this backdrop that child labor came under the spotlight, with new instruments, such as social labeling, designed to address the issue.

A social label typically involves utilization of a mark or logo on product packaging or advertising to demonstrate compliance of the product or its manufacturer with specific social standards. The label is usually conferred by an organization (NGO, business or labor association, certification agency) that sets standards and establishes compliance mechanisms. Labeling entered the scene in Brazil in the mid-1990s, when Fundação Abrinq, a renowned children's rights NGO with origins in the business sector, introduced the Programa Empresa Amiga da Criança (Child-Friendly Company Program), or PEAC, label. This later inspired other initiatives, such as the Pro-Criança (Pro-Child), or IPC, label of the Instituto Pró-Criança, and Fundação SEMEAR, both in the footwear industry. While international examples of labeling—such as fair-trade, eco-friendly, organic, or quality-certification labels—were not new, this type of instrument was unheard of in Brazil, and only recently has become widespread.

Comparing the PEAC and IPC Labels

Comparison between two labeling programs, the Empresa Amiga da Criança and Pró-Criança, reveals contrasting circumstances in which labeling has been applied, and highlights labeling's potential strengths and weaknesses.

The PEAC label came about as one of a range of innovative programs devised by the Abrinq Foundation for the protection and promotion of children's rights. The label is conferred on companies that voluntarily comply with ten standards regarding children's rights, including important protections against child labor. Beyond labeling, through its advocacy campaigns PEAC has targeted specific sectors that employ children, such as agribusiness (oranges, sugar, sisal), extraction (charcoal), and industry (leather footwear). Unlike many labels, the PEAC program was not a corporate reaction to perceived child labor problems within its own ranks, nor was it a response to threats of sanctions from domestic or international consumer markets. Rather, it resulted from the visionary strategy of the foundation's leadership to bring visibility to the issue of child labor and children's rights, and to provide a means for socially responsible businesses to be recognized and benefit from consumer preference. Taking advantage of its strong support within the business sector, its labeled products can be seen on a wide range of products in the domestic market.

In sharp contrast, the IPC label was a busi-

Table 1

PEAC Label Companies Commit To:

Not employing children under sixteen years of age, except as apprentices, who must be at least fourteen.
Respecting youth workers, not employing them in nocturnal, dangerous, or unhealthy activities.
Alerting their suppliers, preferably through contractual means, that occurrence of child labor may lead to the interruption of commercial relations.
Offering child care to working parents.
Ensuring that employees enroll their underage children in school.
Encouraging and supporting prenatal care of pregnant employees.
Encouraging and offering adequate conditions for breastfeeding of employees' infants.
Supporting employees in obtaining proper documentation for their infants.
Investing a stipulated minimum in non-employee-related activities for the benefit of children.
Contributing to children and youth rights funds.

ness response to a flagrant situation of child labor within a specific sector: the leather footwear industry. In this competitive export-oriented industry, extensive use of child labor has been documented. Children have been found to participate in production processes such as stitching and gluing in sweatshop conditions, often in small workshops or domestic production settings. Reports of child labor brought strong international repercussions, including threats of sanctions by importing countries. One particular city, Franca, a major shoe-manufacturing hub, with large industrial plants and thousands of small workshops, was caught in the whirlwind. While the initial reaction of the industry was to rebut the accusations as a disguised form of northern protectionism, in association with "unpatriotic" labor unions, it quickly recognized the need to address the issue directly. In this context, and with the support of the Abrinq Foundation, the IPC label was born.

Unlike the PEAC label, which makes claims about an accredited company's "child-friendly" policies and practices, the IPC label makes claims about the product—that it was not made with child labor. This claim is backed not only by a written commitment, but also by independent audits that cover not only factories, but also outsourced suppliers. Whether the footwear industry's newfound interest in children's rights is sincere, its chosen strategy proved effective in addressing the issue of child labor.

While the PEAC labeling program inspired the IPC label, they differ significantly in design, implementation, and motivation. Over the years, PEAC has moved beyond the mere notion of a child labor label, has eschewed certification, and has become a more general children's rights program with strong brand recognition. IPC has invested in systematizing its experience and replicating it in other footwear-producing regions, in association with national and local trade associations.

Strengths and Weaknesses of Labeling Programs

Child labor labels present an ambitious promise. They attempt to harness the forces of the market to remove children from inappropriate work. At their best, labels are instruments that reward companies' good social practices, certify and monitor continued good behavior, and offer consumers a powerful opportunity to act, providing information that can influence purchasing decisions, and increasing awareness about issues of child labor and children's rights.

But labeling schemes have their limitations and have not been found to work in all circumstances. While the voluntary nature of labeling is considered a strength, it also means that industries and firms with no record of child labor are more likely to opt in; conversely, those that may rely on child labor are unlikely to adhere. Further, the higher the standards and the more rigorous the monitoring, the less likely the labeling programs are to be embraced. Consumer behavior is also voluntary. Labels assume the existence of informed and socially conscious consumers rationally preferring child-labor-free products. But there are multiple factors affecting consumer behavior—price, quality, brand value—and large amounts of information competing for consumers' attention. Even among the growing minority of socially conscious consumers, child labor labels must contend for allegiance against other social and environmental claims—organic, recyclable, charitable.

There is also a divide between domestic and international markets. International pressure played a large role in raising the issue of child labor in Brazil, and international consumers are often more demanding in their social standards for products. However, Brazilian social labels have been designed with the domestic consumer in mind, and are not marketed internationally. Export-oriented firms and foreign buyers tend to have their own independent certification and labeling schemes, often lacking on-the-ground expertise and commitment to improving conditions for children. The resulting lack of synergy leads to less than optimal results both in consumer outreach and in benefits to children.

Finally, labeling schemes are not effective in addressing all forms of child labor. While some have demonstrated the capacity to find "invisible" child labor by following the supply chain back to small, domestic workshops, many other forms of child labor remain invisible. Quantitatively, most child labor occurs in activities distant from modern competitive markets. These include most types of domestic work and subsistence agriculture. Further, labels cannot reach many of the unconditional worst forms of child labor.

Conclusion

Labeling of products is an innovative example of a market-driven instrument to achieve a public objective. By attempting to harness the energy of markets, through positive and negative incentives, it offers an alternative to traditional, and often ineffective, enforcement strategies. The experience of Brazilian social labels offers insight into the strengths and limitations of such instruments. The economic rationale, by itself, has proved insufficient to exert a meaningful impact on child labor. However, when labeling programs are taken holistically, their results can be seen in a different light. Social labels are widely recognized among specialists in Brazil as an important element in obtaining public support for the eradication of child labor and the promotion of children's rights.

Obviously, there is no single magic-bullet solution to address the complex issue of child labor. Mobilizing public opinion, targeting specific sectors, building the capacity of state and civil society institutions, and providing solutions for poor families with children are all important elements of a successful strategy. The case of Brazil is illustrative of the growing market for certified products. Whether for bona fide interest, to avoid negative repercussions, or to gain a market edge, labeling is being increasingly adopted by business. Especially for its potential to unite diverse interests for a common cause, and within the broader policy environment, labeling has a key role to play.

References and Further Reading

CEATS/FIA/University of São Paulo. "Social Labeling Against Child Labour: Brazilian Experiences." Working paper, ILO-IPEC, 2000.

Abrinq Foundation. http://www.fundabrinq.org.br/.

Development of Child Labor Law in Brazil

Oris de Oliveira, Professor of Law, University of São Paulo

In the past years, the ILO has been striving through IPEC to eliminate child labor throughout the world, focusing on countries where the phenomenon is more prevalent and more severe—among them, Brazil. Brazil adhered to IPEC in 1992 when child labor started to be the object of governmental and nongovernmental programs seeking its causes and bringing about the means to eliminate it, a difficult task in a country of continental proportions with major social and economic disparities. Children and adolescents were always a part of the economically active population. It is important to know how effective or ineffective juridical norms have been in the face of social reality.

Years 1500 to 1890

Brazil was a Portuguese colony from 1500, the date of its "discovery," to 1822. In the first four centuries until 1888, agrarian production based on slave labor prevailed. The imperial regime lasted from 1822 to 1889; in 1889 the federative republic was proclaimed. During the period of slavery, children from the age of eight were deemed fit to work and were allowed to be bought and sold. When slaves were imported, there was a preference for children since they adapted to work more easily, had a longer life expectancy, and were more docile (Florentino 1995).

The only laws in this period pertained to free children. One permitted a person below twenty-one years of age to enter into contracts with parental consent. Another permitted free children in the cities to enter medieval-style guilds (abolished in 1824). The scarcity of specific norms at the time is explained by the cultural acceptance of child labor, combined with the unwillingness of the liberal spirit to legally interfere in work relations.

Years 1890 to 1930

There were scattered industries prior to 1890. But beginning that year, a substantial growth in the industrial sector took place. Hand in hand with industries came internal migration, population increase in the largest cities, and adult unemployment—factors that gave rise to a child population that either lived or spent hours in the streets. One of the solutions to "rescue" the "abandoned and criminal children" was to introduce them to work as a social and disciplinary containment mechanism. A large number of children started working at the age of ten, in twelve-hour shifts, with wages lower than those of adults, and no concern for working conditions. There were countless cases of five- and six-year-old boys and girls working twelve-hour shifts in the textile industry (Foot and Leonardi 1982).

In 1891, Decree 1313 became the first law regulating child and adolescent work in industry, with its application restricted to the capital city. The main points included a minimum age of twelve for employment, with the exception of textile-factory apprentices, where the minimum age was eight. Females twelve to fifteen years old and males twelve to fourteen years old were limited to no more than seven hours per day with breaks every four hours; fourteen- and fifteen-year-olds were barred from working more than nine hours. In textile factories, eight- to ten–year-olds accepted for "apprenticeship" were allowed to work three hours with a half-hour break; ten- to twelve-year-olds, four hours with one-hour breaks. The law contained norms on hygiene and medicine, forbidding the handling of health-hazardous products in industrial facilities, and called for the institution of permanent inspection.

In the states of the federation, working conditions were regulated by the sanitation codes, which designated the minimum hiring age (twelve and later fourteen years of age), as well as banning unhealthy and dangerous work. Inspection was the responsibility of the sanitation inspector.

Several contemporary authors confirmed that Decree 1313 and the sanitation codes were not effective—one of the reasons pointed out was the lack of inspection (Moraes 1905; Barbosa 1951; Brito 1929; Bastos Tavares 1910). The inefficacy of Decree 1313 and the sanitary codes is further confirmed by the prevalence of child labor, especially in the textile industry, in the period between 1890 and 1920. Despite lower wages than adults were paid, there was no reduction in children's workday, and many had to cope with tuberculosis contracted on the job (Moura 1982).

In the 1920s, attention turned to poverty, delinquency, the abandonment of children, and, most of all, the children wandering the streets. This provided the opportunity for promulgation of several hygiene, health, and aid policies, norms that were consolidated in the Minors' Code of 1927, geared toward the "abandoned and criminal child" (Article 1). Among the provisions on work or minors, the basic minimum age for employment was kept at twelve years of age, but higher minimums were established for certain categories: fourteen years of age for elementary school dropouts; fourteen years of age in workshops of milling and manufacturing plants, shipyards, quarries, mines, or any underground work; and eighteen years of age for work that was dangerous, unhealthy, painful, or harmful to life and morality. A maximum workday of six hours was established, also requiring a break of at least one hour. The code also had work-related provisions aimed at children on the streets. A minimum age of fourteen was established for work in the streets by males; eighteen years of age was the minimum established for single females. Detailed conditions were also established for participation in theatrical shows and acrobatics in the streets.

The 1927 code was repeatedly criticized by business entities because of the minimum employment age and the six-hour workday. They claimed that certain jobs could be carried out only by children. It was also alleged that, because of the scarcity of schools, children would rather spend their time in the streets than be forced to work in the factories (Moraes 1980).

Years 1930 to 1990

As of 1930, there was an industrial upsurge accompanied by internal migration and population increase in the more industrialized urban centers, which enabled widespread employment of adult woman and child labor. Academic studies of the period began to investigate the social reality of child labor—its national, regional, and sectoral dimensions, and relationships with living conditions and with education. But concern over the situation did not go beyond the academic environment.

As a result of the 1930 internal revolution, government policies favorable to state intervention began to prevail, through numerous laws and administrative actions regulating the employment relationship—including children and young people. In the period from 1932 to 1988, the minimum age for admission to employment or work was altered several times: Between 1932 and 1967, it was fourteen years of age; in 1967 it was lowered to twelve years of age; and in 1988 it was set back to fourteen years of age, where it remained until 2000. Several features of the law remained constant throughout this period: Young persons under eighteen years of age could not work during the night or be involved in any type of employment or work that, by its nature or the circumstances in which it was carried out, was likely to jeopardize their health, safety, or morals. Notably, in the Consolidation of Labor Laws, young persons began to have all the rights of adult employees—for instance, vacations, weekly rest, compensation for unjustified firings—as long as the basic child labor laws were adhered to.

Brazil ratified, without any conflict between the international and national norms, most of the important ILO conventions pertaining to child labor, including: C5, Minimum Age (Industry) Convention (1919), ratified in 1934; C6, Night Work of Young Persons (Industry) Convention (1919), ratified in 1934; C16, Medical Examination of Young Persons (Sea) Convention (1921), ratified in 1936; C58, Minimum Age (Sea) Convention (Revised) (1936), ratified in 1938; and C124, Medical Examination of Young Persons (Underground Work) Convention (1965), ratified in 1970.

Years 1990 to 2007

Brazil's adhesion to IPEC in 1992 began a new phase in the approach to child labor, involving governmental and nongovernmental entities, labor unions, and employers in seeking the elimination of child labor. With the support of ILO and UNICEF, numerous studies on child labor were carried out detailing its relationship with a variety of factors such as the economic situation of families, school attendance and performance, inadequate labor inspection, occupational health, and cultural acceptance.

In 2000, Brazil ratified ILO Convention 182 (worst forms of child labor). In 2000, there was an effective change in the minimum age for employment, which is now set at sixteen years of age, with provision for adolescents of fourteen years of age engaging in light work as apprentices in a company. Finally, in 2001, Brazil ratified ILO Convention 138 (minimum age). After ratification of ILO Convention 182, governmental and nongovernmental programs have given priority to actions that seek elimination of the "worst forms" of child labor. In the executive branch, the Department of Labor, and in the judicial branch, the Public Prosecution Service, have been maintaining vigorous inspection and enforcement efforts, respectively. The granting of scholarships, always conditioned on school attendance, has been a major success in the prevention of child labor. Scholarships are benefiting more than a million children between nine and fifteen years of age from poor families. By 1999, school enrollment reached 96 percent of children in the seven- to fourteen-year-old age-group (ILO 2006).

The actions promoted by IPEC, and undertaken by various groups within Brazil, have had a dramatic effect on the elimination of child labor, as is confirmed by the ILO-IPEC report *The End of Child Labor: Within Reach:* "[T]he rate of activity of the 10 to 17 age-group underwent a reduction of 36.4 percent from 1992 to 2004 from 7,579,126 to 4,814,612. The decline was even more prominent in the 5 to 9 age group, which fell by 60.9 percent during the same period. In 1992, a total of 636,248 children worked, in comparison to 248,594 in 2004" (ILO 2006, 24).

Conclusion

In hindsight, it is evident that there have not been a lot of changes in Brazil's norms on minimum age, but, with the exception of the period from 1967 to 1988, there is a clear trend toward progressive elevation: In 1927 it was set at twelve; in 1932 it was elevated to fourteen; in 1967, in the only retrograde legislation, the age was reduced to twelve; it was finally restored to fourteen in 1988; then it was raised again to sixteen in 2000. In contrast, one can note the constancy in the ban on unhealthy and unsafe work, harmful to morality. There is also a constant disconnect between juridical norms that seek to protect children and social reality, which shows constant, abundant, and not infrequent predatory use of child labor, with economic interests prevailing over child protection.

Since 1992, when child labor began to be the object of serious programs and actions, Brazil has made great strides in dramatically reducing child labor. But substantial problems remain. It will be a difficult challenge for years to come, to continue the fight to finally eliminate child labor, in both absolute and relative terms, especially while many of the complex factors that condition child labor persist.

It should be recognized that Brazil has adopted policies that are fully in line with the commitments it assumed when ratifying the ILO conventions, because it "pursues a national policy designed to ensure the effective abolition of child labour and to progressively raise the minimum age for admission to employment or work to a level consistent with the fullest physical and mental development of young persons" (Article 1, ILO Convention 138 [minimum age]), and "takes immediate and effective measures to secure the prohibition and elimination of the worst forms of child labour as a matter of urgency" (Article 1, ILO Convention 182 [worst forms of child labor]).

References and Further Reading

Barbosa, Ruy. *A questão social e política no Brasil.* Rio de Janeiro: Organização Simões, 1951.

Bastos Tavares, José. *Legislação operária sobre acidentes mecânicos e proteção à infância operária.* Rio de Janeiro: H. Garnier Editor, 1910.

Brito, Lemos. *As leis de menores no Brasil: paginas de critica e de doutrina.* Rio de Janeiro: Ed. F. Briquete, 1929.

Chahad, José Paulo, and Ruben Cervini, eds. *Crise e infância no Brasil O impacto de políticas de ajustamento econômico.* São Paulo: IPE-USP, 1988.

Fausto, Ayrton, and Ruben Cervini, eds. *O trabalho e a rua: crianças e adolescentes no Brasil urbano dos anos 80.* São Paulo: Editora Cortez, 1991.

Florentino, Manolo. *Em costas negras: uma história do tráfico atlântico de escravos entre a África e o Rio de Janeiro, séculos XVIII e XIX.* Rio de Janeiro: Arquivo Nacional, 1995.

Foot, Francisco, and Victor Leonardi. *História da indústria no Brasil: da origem aos anos 20.* São Paulo, Global Editora, 1982.

Moraes Filho, Evaristo. *Apontamentos de direito operário.* Rio de Janeiro: Imprensa Nacional, 1905.

Moraes Filho, Evaristo, ed. *Idéias sociais de Jorge Street.* Rio de Janeiro: Senado Federal, 1980.

Moura, Esmeralda Blanco. *Mulheres e menores no trabalho industrial. os fatores sexo e idade na dinâmica do capital.* Petrópolis: Vozes, 1982.

Oliveira Oris. *O trabalho da criança e do adolescente.* São Paulo: Editora Ltr., 1994.

Organização Internacional do Trabalho-OIT (ILO). *O fim do trabalho infantil: um objetivo ao nosso alcance* [The end of child labor: within reach]. Geneva: ILO, 2006.

Rizzini, Irene. *A criança e a lei no Brasil: revisando a história (1822–2000).* Rio de Janeiro: UNICEF-CESP/USU, 2002.

Salazar, Maria Cristina. *O trabalho infantil nas atividades perigosas.* Brasília: OIT, 1993.

The History of Child Labor in Brazil

Ana Lúcia Kassouf, Department of Economics, University of São Paulo/ESALQ; and
Marcelo Justus dos Santos, Department of Economics, Ponta Grossa State University

Different forms of labor—whether light or heavy, visible or invisible, legal or illegal, poorly remunerated or even nonremunerated, free or slave—have been part of the history of poor children in Brazil since the country was discovered in 1500.

The constitutions of 1934, 1937, and 1946 set the minimum working age at fourteen years. However, in 1967, during the military dictatorship, that minimum age was lowered to twelve. This situation was reviewed only in the 1988 constitution, which prohibited dangerous forms of labor for children under eighteen, and any other form of labor for children under fourteen. Currently, thanks to a constitutional amendment passed in December 1998, the minimum working age is sixteen years. Notwithstanding advances made in regulation and eradication of child labor in Brazil, studies show that the number of working children and adolescents is still high. Data from the 2005 Brazilian National Household Survey (PNAD) indicate 3 million working children between the ages of five and fifteen. This figure accounts for almost 8 percent of children in this age-group, in spite of the sharp decrease that occurred in the second half of the 1990s. In 1992, for example, the number of working children neared 5.5 million, or 15 percent of the population between the ages of five and fifteen. These statistics do not include those working in illegal activities such as prostitution and drug trafficking, or those performing household tasks.

The first reports of child labor in Brazil appeared in indigenous societies during the country's colonization and later during nearly four centuries of black slavery, when the children of slaves engaged in tasks that extended far beyond their physical limits. The abolition of slavery led to an increase in demand for child labor as a result of the industrialization process that started in the late nineteenth century, and which is similar to the experience of other countries in terms of child labor. In 1890, 15 percent of all people employed in industries in São Paulo were children and adolescents. In that same year, according to the Department of Statistics and Archives of São Paulo, child labor accounted for one-fourth of the labor force in the textile industry. Twenty years later, that figure had increased to 30 percent. In 1919, data from the State Labor Department showed that 37 percent of all textile workers were children and adolescents. In the state capital the percentage was as high as 40.

Nowadays, 97 percent of children are in school. Brazil has several laws prohibiting child labor, social programs transferring income to poor families, and a society mobilizing to eradicate child labor. What, then, causes children to work today? To answer this question we have recovered historical elements of child labor in Brazil, its origins, features, and consequences, as well as its relation with the current exploitation of child labor.

The Origins of Child Labor in Brazil

Brazil was "officially" discovered in 1500 and has been populated by the Portuguese since 1530. The first reports of child labor date to the days when men, women, and boys and girls ventured toward the Land of Santa Cruz on sixteenth-century Portuguese vessels (Ramos 2004). At that time, fifteen-year-old girls were regarded as fit for marriage and nine-year-old boys as suitable for work. The replacement of adult labor with child labor became indispensable for sea adventures. A list of payments to the crew of a Portuguese vessel shows that approximately 22 percent of the workers were minors, thus demonstrating the importance of children to transoceanic adventures (Barcellos 1989). Although the issue then was not the exploitation of Brazilian children, it did show that the labor of poor children and adolescents was regarded as something normal by the Portuguese and, later on, by other Europeans who came to Brazil during the long immigration period that started in the nineteenth century and became more intense in the mid-twentieth century.

Officially, child labor in Brazil was first registered among indigenous children. According to Ferreira (2001), children helped adults extract *pau-brasil* (the native Brazilian tree) and build the first villages early in the sixteenth century. In the woods they looked for honey, turtle eggs, and products of animal origin, hunted birds, carried meat and weapons to the village, and scared birds away from crops in the preharvest period. Despite the fact that these tasks were undeniably pleasant to children, they marked the beginning of child labor in colonial Brazil. Although children already had responsibilities alongside the adults, the arrival of Portuguese settlers led to a qualitative and quantitative change (ILO 2003).

In Brazil, the first organization to use child labor was probably the navy. After the country's independence, the navy recruited children trained by the Apprentice Sailor Companies (Companhias de Aprendizes Marinheiros) and subsequently sent them to fight in the Paraguay War, which lasted from 1864 to 1870 and was contested between the Triple Alliance (Brazil, Argentina, and Uruguay) and Paraguay (Venâncio 2004). Examination of naval medical files from the Paraguay war (kept in the national archives) reveals that many children between the ages of nine and twelve fought in the war and at least 600 children in that age-group were in the fields, rivers, and seas where the battles took place. Data reported by Souza (1996) indicate that, in 1868, 1,470 minors were enlisted in the Brazilian navy. Venâncio (2004) has shown that sailor boys helped with the sails and loaded weapons with cartridges and gunpowder, serving as "cannon fodders," a task that often exceeded their physical limits.

Child labor was also registered during the nearly four centuries of slavery in Brazil, when children of slaves were assigned tasks that far exceeded their physical capacity. Several studies show that the children of slaves worked as hard as their parents in sugarcane plantations and sugar production. For slaveholders, the work of these children meant an increase in the price of slaves in their adult lives, as they would have acquired skills that were valued in the slave market (ILO 2001).

Although child labor in Brazil started in indigenous societies and was used heavily during slavery, it was only with the rise of industrialization, when many children and adolescents were precociously pushed into the labor market, that child labor was considered a socioeconomic problem. This is because, in indigenous communities, at least before the arrival of settlers, child labor was not characterized as exploitation but rather reflected cultural norms. Furthermore, during slavery, children and their parents were left with no option. After 1888, when the abolition of slavery led to an increase in demand for free labor, child and adolescent labor began to be heavily used by capitalists. Notwithstanding specific legislation on the matter, child labor is still highly used in Brazil today.

Child Labor and Brazil's Industrialization

Brazil's experience with industrialization was very much like that of other countries where the exploitation of children in factories occurred on a grand scale (Dulles 1977). Brazil's growing industrialization in the early twentieth century can be characterized as a period of great demand for child labor, mainly because the work of minors was not regulated and cost less than adult labor. For Rizzini (1997), the only reasons for regulating child labor were to prevent excesses and to better prepare children for work through professional institutes and schools. According to Campos (2001), those institutions were established based on the belief, inherited from the British, that idleness is the main source of evil and industry is the main virtue.

There are reports that, as early as the 1840s, emerging industries employed many children between the ages of five and twelve, most of whom came from charitable institutions and orphanages, to work in the textile industry for up to twelve hours per day (Dulles 1977). Foot and Leonardi (1982) report the case of an 1865 textile factory located in Parati, in the state of Rio de Janeiro, in which approximately 64 percent of the labor force was made up of children.

It is common knowledge that the working class of São Paulo was formed mainly by immigrants, many of whom were children and adolescents. They were joined by waves of migrants encouraged by the urbanization triggered by industrialization. By the mid-1870s, the number of ads published by industries recruiting children to work—mainly in the textile sector—began to multiply in the São Paulo press (Moura 1982). To industrialists, the work of children and adolescents represented a reduction in costs and a labor force trained from an early age. Moura (1982) has stated that the work of children and adolescents in that period was a reflection of the low standard of living of working families, which were subject to low salaries and a high cost of living. All existing reports indicate that minors worked in the worst possible conditions. Precarious working conditions included poor meals, unhealthy environment, authoritarian labor relations, long working hours, and high incidence of diseases such as tuberculosis, which was incurable in those days (Rizzini 2004).

In 1890, 25 percent of the labor force in the textile sector in São Paulo was made up of children and adolescents, according to data from the Department of Statistics and Archives of the State of São Paulo. Nonetheless, the first regulation on child labor in the factories of São Paulo—which was actually a provision included in the sanitary code rather than the labor law—was passed in 1894. The code set the minimum age for admission of children to employment in factories at ten and prohibited night work for children under eighteen. Sixteen years later, participation of children had reached 30 percent, and, according to the state labor department, it had increased to 40 percent by 1919 (ILO 2001). Many very young children were included. In 1912, approximately 4 percent of the textile labor force was made up of children under twelve years of age, and 28 percent were between the ages of twelve and sixteen (Rizzini 2004).

Famous capitalists of those days claimed that the reason employers hired children and adolescents to work in their shops and factories was because their parents wanted them to work and that, in spite of the inconvenience to employers, it was better for them to be working than to be exposed to the dangers of the streets (Faleiros 1995). Statements such as these may reflect the mind-set of capitalists of the period, but they contradict two more direct motives for exploitation of child and adolescent labor: its low relative cost and the opportunity to keep adult wages low. Due to market forces, the recruitment of child and adolescent labor pushed the wages of adult workers down. The real interest of capitalists in the period was to keep overall wages low. Children were paid less than adults, even for the same jobs. In the textile industry, for example, the average wage of a child worker was approximately one-third that of an adult worker (Faleiros 1995). It was only in 1908 that the country woke up to the situation, as can be seen by newspaper accounts of the period, according to which there were thousands of children working in factories, whereas thousands of young and strong men were unemployed (Moura 2004).

New opportunities for using child and adolescent labor in cities emerged alongside the country's growing industrialization, mainly as a result of the increasing urbanization. The problem was not only the increase in the number of working children, but also the emergence of new forms of child labor, especially in informal activities such as peddling, shoe shining, and selling or delivering newspapers on the streets, as well as activities regarded as totally deplorable: prostitution and drug trafficking. The emergence of new job opportunities for children certainly encouraged the migration of many families from rural to urban areas, where they saw opportunities for all members of the family. This rural exodus, as we know, contributed to further aggravating certain social problems such as misery, poverty, violence, and criminality. In 1920, a census carried out by the General Directorate of Statistics for the State of São Paulo concluded that, in the state of São Paulo as a whole, 7 percent of the labor force hired by the secondary sector was made up of children and adolescents (Moura 1982; Faleiros 1995).

There were many strikes during the country's intense industrialization period. The long lists of demands negotiated with the industrialists often included the reduction of working hours for minors, an increase in their wages, and, many times, attempts to eradicate child labor. For these reasons, the first laws regulating child and adolescent labor were probably the result of long battles fought by adult workers, who sought to protect not only the children, but also their own jobs and salaries.

The history of Brazil shows that until a little over a century ago children had no rights to protect themselves from the exploitation of employers. A major decree in 1891 proposed to regulate the work of children employed in factories of the federal capital, but the law was never complied with (Campos 2001). In 1912, sixty-eight labor organizations met during the Fourth Brazilian Workers' Congress held in Rio de Janeiro to establish the Brazilian Labor Confederation, an entity that fought for regulations limiting the working hours of children under fourteen, as well as for other labor regulations (Dulles 1977). In 1917, the industrial sector came to a halt due to the strike of thousands of workers, who set up a Workers' Advocacy Committee to negotiate with the capitalists. Their demands included the full elimination of night work for women and children under the age of eighteen and elimination of employment for children under age fourteen in factories in the city of São Paulo. However, no effective results were achieved as regards child labor. In that same year, workers of the América Fabril textile company, located in Rio de Janeiro, went on strike to demand, among other things, school for working children. In 1919, the workers of São Paulo scored their first major victory by succeeding in passing a law that prohibited work for children under the age of fourteen (Dulles 1977). Campos (2001) has pointed out that, in spite of the advances made in the regulation of child labor, such as the Law on Industrial Accidents of 1919, the Minors Code was not published until 1927. Among other things, the code sought to organize different forms of labor, set a minimum age for work at fourteen, establish a working day of six hours, and prohibit night work for minors.

References and Further Reading

Adorno, Sérgio. "Criança: a lei e a cidadania." In *A criança no Brasil hoje: desafio para o terceiro milênio,* ed. Irene Rizzini, 101–12. Rio de Janeiro: Santa Úrsula, 1993.

Barcellos, C. *Construções de naus em Lisboa e Goa para a carreira da Índia no começo do século XVII.* Reprint, Lisbon: Central Library of the Portuguese Navy, 1989.

Campos, Herculano Ricardo. *Pobreza e trabalho infantil sob o capitalismo.* Doctoral thesis, Universidade Federal do Rio Grande do Norte, Natal, 2001.

Dulles, John W.F. *Anarquistas e comunistas no Brasil, 1900–1935.* Rio de Janeiro: Nova Fronteira, 1977.

Faleiros, Vicente de Paula. "Infância e processo político no Brasil." In *A arte de governar crianças: A história das políticas sociais, da legislação e da assistência à infância no Brasil,* ed. Francisco Pilotti and Irene Rizzini, 47–98. Rio de Janeiro: Santa Úrsula, 1995.

Ferreira, Eleanor Stange. *Trabalho infantil: história e situação atual.* Canoas: ULBRA, 2001.

Foot, Francisco Hardman, and Victor Leonardi. *História da indústria e do trabalho no Brasil: das origens aos anos vinte.* São Paulo: Global, 1982.

ILO. *Combatendo o trabalho infantil: guia para educadores.* Brasília: ILO-IPEC, 2001.

ILO. *Boas práticas de combate ao trabalho infantil: os 10 anos do IPEC no Brasil.* Brasília: ILO-IPEC, 2003.

Kassouf, A.L., and M.J. Santos. "Child Labour in Brazil: More than 500 Years of National Shame." Paper presented at the conference Child Labour's Global Past (1650–2000), International Institute for Social History, Amsterdam, November 15–17, 2006.

Moura, Esmeralda Blanco B. de. *Mulheres e menores no trabalho industrial: os fatores sexo e idade na dinâmica do capital.* Petrópolis: Vozes, 1982.

Moura, Esmeralda Blanco B. de. "Crianças operárias na recém-industrializada São Paulo." In *História das crianças no Brasil,* ed. Mary Del Priore, 231–58. São Paulo: Contexto, 2004.

Pires, Julio Manuel. "O trabalho infantil na legislação Brasileira." In *IV encontro nacional de estudos do trabalho.* São Paulo: Anais da Associação Brasileira de Estudos do Trabalho (ABET), 1995.

Ramos, Fábio Pestana. "A história trágico-marítima das crianças nas embarcações Portuguesas do século XVI." In *História das crianças no Brasil,* ed. Mary Del Priore, 19–54. São Paulo: Contexto, 2004.

Rizzini, Irma. "Principais temas abordados pela literatura especializada sobre infância e adolescência: séculos XIX e XX." In *Olhares sobre a criança no Brasil: séculos XIX e XX,* ed. Irene Rizzini, 39–77. Rio de Janeiro: USU/AMAIS, 1997.

Rizzini, Irma. "Pequenos trabalhadores do Brasil." In *História das crianças no Brasil,* ed. Mary Del Priore, 377–406. São Paulo: Contexto, 2004.

Sousa, Jorge Prata de. *Escravidão ou morte: os escravos Brasileiros na guerra do Paraguai.* Rio de Janeiro: Mauad, 1996.

Venâncio, Renato Pinto. "Os aprendizes da guerra." In *História das crianças no Brasil,* ed. Mary Del Priore, 192–210. São Paulo: Contexto, 2004.

Orphans and the Transition from Slave to Free Labor in Northeast Brazil

Joan Meznar, Professor of History, Eastern Connecticut State University

Nineteenth-century Brazilian society was divided between laborers and the propertied class. Those who owned property, it was understood, possessed a vested interest in maintaining order and thereby protecting their property. Those who were destitute would be less likely to threaten property holders if they were kept occupied with work. This concern with labor and property was clearly expressed in inheritance laws dealing with orphans, for although designed primarily to protect the interests of the propertied class, they also contemplated the children of the poor. In order to minimize social upheaval, the law recognized that orphans who claimed no inheritance must be raised to accept the importance of work. It therefore established that orphans (including those children who had lost only one parent) should be placed under the care of appropriate guardians who would either protect the inheritance of their wards or ensure that poor children were properly occupied with work. The law further determined that guardians of orphans who inherited no property should deposit a yearly stipend (*soldada*) into a special fund beginning when the wards turned seven and continuing until their twenty-first birthday. Upon becoming adults, orphans would redeem their accumulated stipends (with accrued interest) and begin life independently.

While the property provisions of inheritance laws were scrupulously observed, those governing destitute orphans were largely ignored for much of the nineteenth century. In the 1860s, however, circumstances came together that eventually prompted honoring the law. During the preceding decade, a large number of slaves had been sold from the languishing sugar fields of the northeast to the prospering coffee plantations in the south. Strict enforcement of the prohibition against importing slaves from Africa after 1850 spurred this interprovincial slave trade. When civil war broke out in the United States, demand for cotton from northeast Brazil skyrocketed as owners of British textile mills, cut off from U.S. cotton, turned to Brazil to help fill the gap. As cotton revenues for northeastern Brazilian farmers increased, so did demand for wardships of poor orphans, as slaves were no longer available. In fact, demand for these children grew to such an extent that bidding wars were sometimes set off as prospective guardians increased their stipend offers in order to get custody of healthy young boys.

In this context, mothers' control over their children changed significantly. The laws governing orphans were clear: Widows who led "honorable" lives were to retain custody of their children, although they were not exempt from depositing the *soldada* into municipal coffers. The new demand for labor, however, brought a spate of accusations against the moral character of destitute widows. Those deemed promiscuous, dishonest, or otherwise incapable of raising orderly citizens lost their children, often to strangers. Widows who owned no property then sought out the protection of more powerful men in their communities who would vouch for their integrity. Even when allowed to keep their children, respectable widows had to find bondsmen who would guarantee payment of the yearly stipend. Poor women, therefore, had to conform to the moral and social expectations of the community if they hoped to keep the company of their children (and the benefit of their labor). Widows who felt particularly at risk of losing their children to strangers sometimes asked friends or relatives to become legal guardians of very young children, before they aroused the interest of those looking for inexpensive laborers.

Besides highlighting the vulnerability of poor women, the Brazilian system of guardianship also stunted the emergence of wage labor in northeast Brazil. In the absence of slaves, using orphans for agricultural labor seemed to make economic sense. There was no initial outlay of capital, the stipend was a small fraction of the price of a slave, and guardianship could be revoked should the child become ill, run away, or refuse to work. Wards might work for many years before becoming eligible to withdraw their accumulated *soldadas* upon reaching the age of twenty-one. In the precarious environment of northeast Brazil, furthermore, those funds could easily disappear from one year to the next. In any case, a significant group of teenage laborers had no access to wages and could not, therefore, participate in a consumer society.

Not surprisingly, orphans (and their surviving parent or other relatives) sometimes complained of abuse by court-appointed guardians. Workdays must have been long, and there was little incentive for guardians to invest in the health or education of their wards. In one case, the aunt of a fourteen-year-old orphan who had been assigned to a guardian complained to the judge that poor orphans were not destined by law to become slaves of the powerful. She also accused orphans' judges of rewarding political supporters in the community with the labor of wards.

When Brazil's short-lived cotton boom busted in the 1870s, demand for orphan wards disappeared. Between 1877 and 1879, northeast Brazil suffered one of the worst droughts in its history. As refugees streamed from the now barren backlands into coastal cities, town treasuries were depleted and funds in the orphans' coffers disappeared. Government authorities, desperate to find work for so many displaced citizens, encouraged many northeasterners to relocate to the Amazon region, where those who did not succumb to malaria eked out a living tapping rubber trees. Ten years later, however, when slavery was abolished in 1888, demand for orphan wards spiked once again. This time, it was the children of recently freed unmarried slave women who were most in demand.

As slavery declined and eventually disappeared in Brazil, orphans became a plausible alternative to African laborers. Laws already in place allowed landowners to appropriate the labor of poor children. Instead of moving toward a wage-labor system, northeastern Brazilians clung to an old model that, while familiar, failed to provide the foundation for a new type of economic growth.

References and Further Reading

Lewin, Linda. "Natural and Spurious Children in Brazilian Inheritance Law from Colony to Empire: A Methodological Essay. *The Americas* 48:3 (1992): 351–96.

Meznar, Joan. "Orphans and the Transition from Slave to Free Labor in Northeast Brazil: The Case of the Campina Grande, 1850–1888." *Journal of Social History* 27:3 (Spring 1994): 499–515.

Chile

CHILE			
	CRC	C 138	C 182
Ratifications	Y	Y	Y
Human Development Index/Rank	.859/38		
Human Capital			
Population Growth Rate	0.9%		
% Population 0–14	24.1%		
Total Fertility Rate	1.97		
Life Expectancy	76.96		
Infant Mortality Rate	8.36%		
Literacy Rate	95.7%		
Economic			
GDP/Capita	$14,400		
GDP Growth %	5.2%		
% Poverty	18.2%		
Gini Index	54.9		
Labor Force Composition			
% GDP Agriculture	13.6%		
% GDP Industry	23.4%		
% GDP Services	63.0%		

CHILD ACTIVITY BREAKDOWN, BY SEX AND RESIDENCE

RESIDENCE	Percentage of children in the relevant age-group[a]									
	Economic activity only		School only		Combining school and economic activity		Neither in school nor in economic activity		Child labor[b]	
	Male	Female	Male	Female	Male	Female	Male	Female	Male	Female
Urban	0.1	0.1	94.2	95.0	3.6	2.4	2.1	2.5	n/av	n/av
Rural	0.8	0.0	87.3	93.6	7.6	3.0	4.2	3.3	n/av	n/av
Total	0.2	0.1	93.3	94.8	4.2	2.5	2.4	2.6	3.4	2.4

Source: Chile, Encuesta Nacional Sobre las Actividades de Ninos y Adolescentes, 2003 (see UCW Project Web site, http://www.ucw-project.org, country statistics).
Notes: [a]Children age 5 to 14. [b]Estimate includes (a) children under age 12 engaged in economic activities, (b) children age 12–14 engaged in excessive economic activities (more than 14 hours per week), and (c) children under age 15 engaged in excessive household chores (at least 28 hours per week). Estimate does not account for children engaged in hazardous work or other unconditional "worst forms" of child labor.

Colombia

COLOMBIA			
	CRC	C 138	C 182
Ratifications	Y	Y	Y
Human Development Index/Rank	0.790/70		
Human Capital			
Population Growth Rate	1.46%		
% Population 0–14	30.3%		
Total Fertility Rate	2.54		
Life Expectancy	71.99		
Infant Mortality Rate	20.35		
Literacy Rate	92.5%		
Economic			
GDP/Capita	$8,400		
GDP Growth %	5.4%		
% Poverty	49.2%		
Gini Index	53.8		
Labor Force Composition			
% Agriculture	22.7%		
% Industry	18.7%		
% Services	58.5%		

CHILD ACTIVITY BREAKDOWN, BY SEX AND RESIDENCE

RESIDENCE	Percentage of children in the relevant age-group[a]									
	Economic activity only		School only		Combining school and economic activity		Neither in school nor in economic activity		Child labor[b]	
	Male	Female	Male	Female	Male	Female	Male	Female	Male	Female
Urban	0.8	0.2	91.7	96.4	1.8	0.9	5.7	2.6	n/av	n/av
Rural	5.3	1.2	77.9	87.0	8.7	2.7	8.1	9.2	n/av	n/av
Total	1.9	0.4	88.4	94.2	3.5	1.3	6.3	4.1	4.5	2.6

Source: Colombia, Demographic and Health Survey, 2005 (see UCW Project Web site, http://www.ucw-project.org, country statistics).

Notes: [a]Children age 6 to 14. [b]Estimate includes (a) children under age 12 engaged in economic activities, (b) children age 12–14 engaged in excessive economic activities (more than 14 hours per week), and (c) children under age 15 engaged in excessive household chores (at least 28 hours per week). Estimate does not account for children engaged in hazardous work or other unconditional "worst forms" of child labor.

Child Labor in Colombia

Cármen Elisa Flórez, Senior Professor, Economics Department, Los Andes University; and **Diana Hincapié,** Junior Researcher, Economics Department, Los Andes University

According to the Child Labor National Survey of 2001 (DANE 2001), a total of 1,752,000 Colombian children were in the labor force. Among those, 1,568,000 were working and 184,000 were unemployed. If we add in those children who performed household chores, nearly 2,261,000 children were working. Although child labor is not a new issue in Colombia, it has received more attention in recent decades for several reasons. First, child labor is strongly negatively linked to household socioeconomic status—it is mainly a problem for poor families. Second, working and studying seem to be mutually exclusive activities among Colombian children (Flórez and Mendez 1996). Under this condition, working implies giving up human capital formation for the child. Third, as they do in most developing countries, many children in Colombia work under harmful conditions. They work more than the permitted hours, for low pay, and sometimes in what are considered "worst forms" of child labor.

Given the number of working children and the conditions of their work, in 1995 the Colombian government initiated a national program, supported by ILO, to prevent labor-force participation among children younger than fourteen years of age, and to give attention to working children fourteen to seventeen years old (Flórez et al. 1995). However, prevention of child labor is not easy. There is a trade-off between benefits in the short run and benefits in the long run. Studies indicate that one of the main causes of child labor is poverty. Poor households need to send children to work in order to increase household income. Bernal and Cárdenas (2006) have estimated that working children between fifteen and seventeen years old, in the poorest quintile of Colombian families, contribute about half of total household income. So, elimination of child work could have negative consequences for both the household's and the children's well-being in the short run. On the contrary, when child work reduces school attendance and human capital accumulation, it has negative consequences in the long run, leading working children to reproduce household poverty conditions.

The Conceptualization and Measurement of Child Labor

A child is considered to be working who participates in any productive activity, with or without payment, for at least one hour a week, excluding work done in the child's own household (DANE 2001). Many children are responsible for household chores, in some cases for many hours per week. To take the activities of these children into account, some authors have proposed an "extended child labor definition" that includes household work exceeding a certain numbers of hours (Flórez et al. 1995). Flórez and Méndez (1996) considered twenty hours or more per week as the threshold for considering household tasks as child labor. Others use fifteen hours per week (DANE 2001). But all agree that this extended definition is important for a complete understanding of the characteristics of child labor in Colombia.

Most studies of child labor in Colombia are based on household surveys. There are two main problems with this type of data. First, most surveys are designed to measure adult labor. Labor market participation is measured through questions about the main activity performed the week before the survey. Adults normally work for fixed periods of time, so it could be expected that a "reference week" captures real participation rates. The same assumption cannot be made for children. There are some activities that are considered work when carried out by adults but are considered just "help" when done by children (Flórez et al. 1995). Surveys normally ask about typical adult occupations, and they do not even ask about younger children (under age ten). Second, because of legal restrictions on hiring children, household members interviewed may hide children's labor market participation, making it difficult to count working children (Salazar 1994). As a consequence, traditional labor force participation rates normally underestimate child labor.

Additionally, most household surveys are cross-sectional data; that is, the surveys are taken at a given moment of time, and do not follow individuals over time. This makes it difficult to identify consequences of child labor, such as whether working children are giving up education because of work (Bernal and Cárdenas 2006), or whether they are being affected physically by their work (Hincapié 2006).

Child Employment Rates

In 2001, 14.5 percent of children five to seventeen years old, one out of every seven kids, were working in the labor market, excluding household chores (DANE 2001). Trends in child labor are difficult to discern, but some studies indicate a decrease in labor force participation rates between 1992 and 2001 for children over age twelve, in both rural and urban areas under both the traditional and the extended definitions of child labor (Flórez and Méndez 1996; DANE 2001). For younger children, however, studies suggest there was an increase in participation rates for children between ten and eleven years old between 1996 and 2006 (DANE 2001). Thus, in spite of the governmental program to prevent child labor, which was initiated in 1995, it seems that there has not been a significant overall decrease in child labor.

Child employment is higher in rural than in urban areas, a factor that is related to higher poverty and less access to education in rural than in urban areas. Poverty in Colombia is high in rural areas, and children suffer the consequences of this condition, which makes them more vulnerable to joining the labor force early. Low household income leads to fewer possibilities to attend school, and also to greater possibility of having parents whose jobs require children to labor with them (such as agricultural work, where having children picking crops or helping taking care of cattle or other animals is common) (Salazar 1990).

Figure 1 **Child employment rates by age and area of residence, 2001**

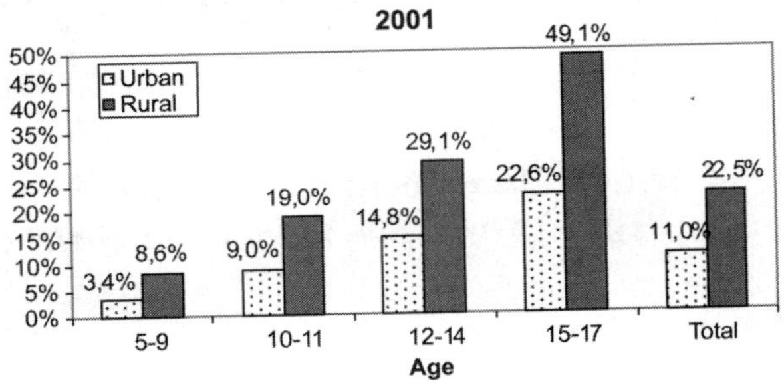

Source: DANE 2001.

In 2001, the proportion of children working in rural areas was more than double the proportion of children working in urban areas (Figure 1). More than 20 percent of rural children work. Among rural youths fifteen to seventeen years of age, almost half participate in the labor market. In urban areas less than one-fourth do so.

As expected, labor participation rates increase with age. Among children from five to nine years of age, 5 percent were working, but that proportion increases to almost 30 percent among those fifteen to seventeen years old (Figure 1; Table 1). In urban areas, 22.6 percent of children fifteen to seventeen years old work, which is almost seven times the participation rate for the smaller children (five to nine years old). In rural areas, the participation rate for youths (fifteen to seventeen) is about six times the rate for children five to nine years of age.

Evidence also indicates clear differences in working patterns by gender: Boys have higher employment rates (Table 1). In 2001, about one-fifth of boys fifteen to seventeen years old worked, while less than one-tenth of girls did so. In all age-groups, boys' employment rates more than double girls' rates. This gender bias could be related to the fact that child labor is mainly rural labor, where boys

Table 1

Child Employment Rates by Age and Gender (Traditional Definition), 2001 (in percent)

Age	Boys	Girls	Total
5–9 years	6.8	3.3	5.1
10–11 years	16.5	7.4	12.1
12–14 years	25.9	12.1	19.0
15–17 years	40.2	18.2	29.9
Total	19.7	8.9	14.5

Source: DANE 2001.

Table 2

Child Employment Rates by Age and Gender, Including Household Work, 2001 (in percent)

Age	Boys	Girls	Total
5–9 years	73.8	88.4	79.3
10–11 years	77.3	95.8	82.8
12–14 years	74.2	85.9	77.9
15–17 years	63.7	81.1	68.7
Total	70.1	85.6	74.8

Source: Bernal and Cárdenas 2006, based on DANE 2001.

play an important role in agricultural activities. The story is completely different when household chores are included. As Table 2 indicates, when household work is included in the definition of work, girls' employment rates are greater than boys' for all age-groups. Measured in this way, 85.6 percent of girls work as compared to 70 percent of boys.

Child labor in Colombia, as in many other countries, is most prominent in poor households, where the need for greater income induces parents to send their children to the labor market (Flórez et al. 1995). Table 3 shows employment rates in 2005 for children six to seventeen years of age, by household wealth quintile. Employment rates clearly decrease as wealth increases. Whereas in the poorest households nearly one out of six children work, in the richest households only one out of twenty-five children do. Thus, there is a strong social gradient on child labor. This result confirms the hypothesis of child labor being related to the socioeconomic status of the household. The social gradient is even stronger

Table 3

Child Employment Rates by Wealth Index Quintiles, 2005 (in percent)

Quintile	Traditional definition	Extended definition
Poorest	16.8	25.2
Poorer	10.2	15.9
Middle	7.4	11.3
Richer	4.9	8.5
Richest	4.0	5.8
Total	9.2	14.1

Source: Author's calculations using *Colombia: Demographic and Health Survey* (Bogotá: Profamilia, 2005).

when household chores are included in the definition of child work. In this case, the poorest households have a child employment rate of 25.2 percent, nearly five times the rate in the richest households.

Occupation

Child labor is concentrated in two branches of activities: agriculture and commerce. In 2001, almost 70 percent of working children were occupied in those two branches. In urban areas, more than 50 percent of working children were working in commerce, whereas in rural areas 70 percent were occupied in agriculture (DANE 2001). Most of the working children—37 percent of boys and 46 percent of girls—work as family workers without payment. More boys (40 percent) worked as paid workers than girls (21 percent). A higher proportion of girls are engaged as domestic servants (12 percent) than boys (0.5 percent). Given the occupations children are engaged in, their payment is low. More than half of the working children did not receive any payment for their work, and half of those who work for payment received less than one-fourth of the minimum wage (Bernal and Cárdenas 2006).

Law and Reality of Child Work

Until 2006, Colombian legislation (the child code—Código del Menor, 1989), prohibited work by children under twelve years of age and restricted the

Table 4

Hours Worked by Age, 2001 (in percent)

Hours	Age: 5–9 years	10–11 years	12–14 years	15–17 years	Total
Less than 10 hours	55.1	47.2	31.8	20.4	32.3
10–24 hours	28.5	37.4	30.8	25	28.8
25–48 hours	14.4	12.1	19.6	32.1	23.2
More than 48 hours	1.9	3.4	17.8	22.5	15.7
Total	100	100	100	100	100

Source: Bernal and Cárdenas 2006, based on DANE 2001.

number of hours that older children could work to a maximum of twenty-four hours per week for children twelve to thirteen years old; thirty-six hours per week for children fourteen to fifteen years old; and forty-eight hours per week for children sixteen to seventeen years old. In 2006, a new child code was issued in Colombia prohibiting any work for children less than fifteen years of age.

Reality is different from the conditions implied by the law. In 2001, 5 percent of children five to nine years of age and 12 percent of those ten to eleven years old were working in spite of the law (Bernal and Cárdenas 2006). Although nearly half of them were working less than ten hours per week, none of them should be working according to the law. Similarly, the law forbids all children from working more than forty-eight hours per week. However, as Table 4 shows, this restriction is not followed at all: 22.5 percent of working children fifteen to seventeen years old exceed that limit of hours, while 17.8 percent of children twelve to fourteen years of age do so. Exceeding the legal number of hours of work has negative consequences for children, exposing them to health risks and other dangers, and increasing the probability that they abandon school in order to work.

Very young children working in spite of the law, and youths working hours in excess of those permitted by law, are not new in Colombia. On the contrary, the situation has improved from the previous decade, perhaps as a consequence of the governmental program to prevent child labor. For example, in 1992, boys twelve to thirteen years old worked an average of just under thirty-eight hours per week, while girls worked thirty-nine hours. Boys fourteen to fifteen years old worked an average of just under forty-three hours per week, while girls worked about forty-four and a half hours (Flórez et al. 1995).

In spite of the negative effect of a long working day on child's health and human capital accumulation, more working hours might also imply a larger income for the child's household. Table 5 shows the contribution of working children to household income in the poorest households, and in the whole population. The contribution of children under age ten is, at most, 5 percent of household income in the poorest households. On average, children ten to fourteen years old contribute almost 10 percent of household income, but the contribution is larger in the poorest households, where income brought in by children represents one-fourth of household income. The contribution to household income is largest among working youths (fifteen to seventeen years of age) living in households from the poorest quintile. They contribute more than half of household income.

Table 5

Contribution of Working Children to Household Income, 2003 (in percent)

Age	Total	Poorest quintile
5–9 years	4.2	5
10–14 years	9.7	24.9
15–17 years	20.4	52.1

Source: Bernal and Cárdenas 2006.

Table 6

School Attendance and Child Labor by Age and Definition of Labor, 2005 (in percent)

	Traditional definition				Extended definition			
Age	At school and at work	At school but not at work	Not at school; at work	Neither at school nor at work	At school and at work	At school but not at work	Not at school; at work	Neither at school nor at work
6–9 years	1.2	92.3	0.2	6.3	2	91.5	0,2	6.3
10–11 years	3.5	91.2	0.7	4.6	6.0	88.6	1.0	4.3
12–13 years	5.2	86.4	2.6	5.8	9.1	82.4	3.8	4.7
14–15 years	7.2	74.7	8.2	10.0	12.9	69.0	11.0	7.1
16–17 years	8.8	52.9	17.3	21.0	13.5	48.3	24.2	14.1
Total	4.5	82.0	4.7	8.8	7.5	78.9	6.5	7.0

Source: Authors' calculations based on *Colombia: Demographic and Health Survey* (Bogotá: Profamilia, 2005).

Working and Schooling

In the short run, children's work contributes to household income. In the long run, it may imply lower future income because of a negative effect on school attendance and human capital accumulation. This latter effect depends on how compatible schooling and work are. Table 6 shows the combinations of school attendance and work, by age and work definition. Here, the extended definition follows Flórez and Méndez (1996), meaning at least twenty hours of household chores per week.

Using the traditional definition, results indicate that most children are attending school and are not involved in any working activity. This is especially true for younger children: More than 90 percent only go to school. This is consistent with the fact that governmental policies are focused on having the biggest impact on school attendance among those under age ten. Also, as mentioned previously, children at this age are forbidden to work. For children ten to thirteen years old, the proportion of working children attending school is larger than the proportion of working children that do not study. In contrast, among children sixteen to seventeen years of age, 17.3 percent work but do not attend school. Because sacrificing human capital formation is considered one of the worst consequences of child labor, special attention should be paid to this age-group, where more working children are abandoning school.

The percentage of children in each age range, and in the total, who study and work at the same time increases from 4.5 percent under the traditional definition to 7.5 percent under the extended definition. This is so because household chores are more flexible and can be more easily combined with school attendance. Nevertheless, patterns by age hold, as in the case of the traditional work definition.

Not working and not studying become important as children get older. More than one-fifth of youths (sixteen to seventeen years old) do not attend school and do not work either (Table 6). They may be unemployed, disabled, or simply idle.

Conclusion

In spite of the fact that child work is a complex issue to define and measure, several studies have addressed the problem in Colombia. They indicate that youth labor has been decreasing in the country, maybe as a consequence of the government program launched in 1995 to prevent child labor. However, results are not so positive for younger children. By 2001, 14.5 percent of children five to seventeen years of age were working. Compared to other Latin American countries, Colombia is not a country with especially high child labor force participation rates, but it is not a country with especially low rates either. Although legal regulations prohibit child labor among young children and limit the number of working hours among youths, there is evidence of substantial amounts of work by children in violation of the limits imposed by law.

Child labor is higher in rural than in urban areas, increases with age, is closely related to socioeconomic status, is concentrated in agriculture and commerce, and is mainly unremunerated or low paying. In spite of these conditions, working children make important contributions to household income and household well-being in the short run. However, an important proportion of children drop out of school to work as they get older. This has negative consequences for children's human capital accumulation and future income. Social public policy should emphasize actions toward preventing school dropout and child labor at the same time that they support poor households with income programs.

References and Further Reading

Bernal, Raquel, and Mauricio Cárdenas. "Trabajo infantil en Colombia." Working paper, Northwestern University and Fedesarrollo, January 2006.

DANE. *Encuesta nacional de trabajo infantil: análisis de los resultados de la encuesta sobre caracterización de la población entre 5 y 17 años en Colombia*. Bogotá: Departamento Administrativo Nacional de Estadística y OIT-IPEC, 2001.

Flórez, Cármen Elisa, and Regina Méndez. *Niñas, niños y jóvenes trabajadores en Colombia 1996*. Bogotá: CEDE-Universidad de Los Andes, OIT, AECI, IPEC, and Tercer Mundo Editores, 1996.

Flórez, Cármen Elisa, Regina Méndez, and Felicia Knaul. *Niños y jóvenes: cuántos y dónde trabajan*. Bogotá: Ministerio de Trabajo y Seguridad Social, CEDE-Universidad de Los Andes, and Tercer Mundo Editores, 1995.

Hincapié, Diana. "El trabajo infanto-juvenil y el estado nutricional de los menores colombianos." Master's thesis, Universidad de Los Andes, 2006.

ILO. *Convenio sobre la prohibición de las peores formas de trabajo infantil y de la acción inmediata para su eliminación*. Geneva: ILO, 1999.

Salazar, Maria Cristina. *Niños y jóvenes trabajadores: buscando un futuro mejor*. Bogotá: Universidad Nacional de Colombia, 1990.

Salazar, Maria Cristina. "Retos y alternativas: el trabajo de menores en áreas urbanas y rurales de Colombia." In *Programa nacional de acción a favor de la infancia: memorias del seminario interinstitucional sobre el menor trabajador en Colombia*, ed. DNP-UNICEF. Bogotá: Trazo, 1994.

Ecuador

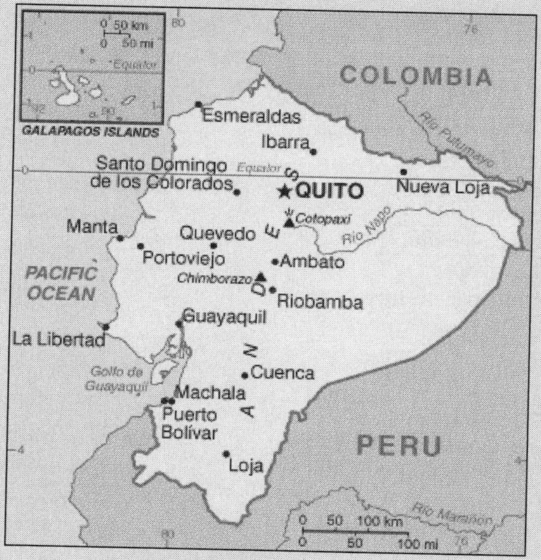

ECUADOR			
	CRC	C 138	C 182
Ratifications	Y	Y	Y
Human Development Index/Rank	0.765/83		
Human Capital			
Population Growth Rate	1.5%		
% Population 0–14	33%		
Total Fertility Rate	2.68		
Life Expectancy	76.42		
Infant Mortality Rate	22.87		
Literacy Rate	92.5%		
Economic			
GDP/Capita	$4,500		
GDP Growth %	3.6%		
% Poverty	41%		
Gini Index	42		
Labor Force Composition			
% Agriculture	8%		
% Industry	24%		
% Services	68%		

CHILD ACTIVITY BREAKDOWN, BY SEX AND RESIDENCE

RESIDENCE	Percentage of children in the relevant age-group[a]									
	Economic activity only		School only		Combining school and economic activity		Neither in school nor in economic activity		Child labor[b]	
	Male	Female	Male	Female	Male	Female	Male	Female	Male	Female
Urban	1.2	0.6	90.8	92.8	3.8	2.6	4.2	4.0	n/av	n/av
Rural	7.4	4.1	66.8	73.6	17.4	11.5	8.4	10.9	n/av	n/av
Total	3.6	1.9	81.6	85.6	9.0	5.9	5.8	6.5	11.9	12.8

Source: Ecuador, Encuesta de Empleo, Desempleo, Subempleo y Empleo Infantil, 2004 (see UCW Project Web site, http://www.ucw-project.org, country statistics).

Notes: [a]Children age 5 to 14. [b]Estimate includes (a) children under age 12 engaged in economic activities, (b) children age 12–14 engaged in excessive economic activities (more than 14 hours per week), and (c) children under age 15 engaged in excessive household chores (at least 28 hours per week). Estimate does not account for children engaged in hazardous work or other unconditional "worst forms" of child labor.

Guyana

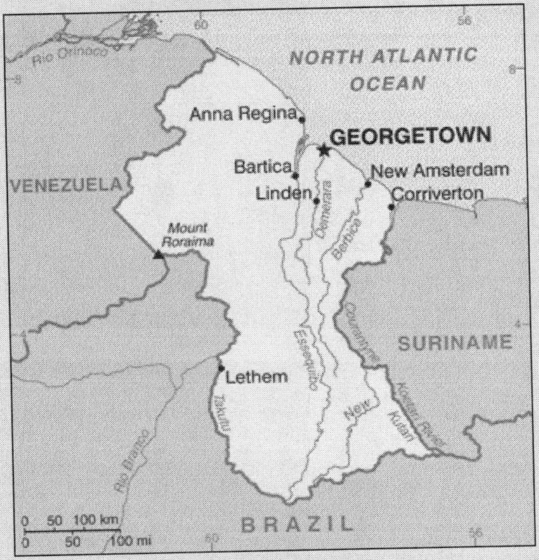

GUYANA	CRC	C 138	C 182
Ratifications	Y	Y	Y
Human Development Index/Rank	0.725/103		
Human Capital			
Population Growth Rate	0.25%		
% Population 0–14	26.2%		
Total Fertility Rate	2.04		
Life Expectancy	65.86		
Infant Mortality Rate	32.19		
Literacy Rate	98.8%		
Economic			
GDP/Capita	$4,700		
GDP Growth %	3.2%		
% Poverty	NA		
Gini Index	—		

CHILD ACTIVITY BREAKDOWN, BY SEX AND RESIDENCE

RESIDENCE	Percentage of children in the relevant age-group[a]									
	Economic activity only		School only		Combining school and economic activity		Neither in school nor in economic activity		Child labor[b]	
	Male	Female	Male	Female	Male	Female	Male	Female	Male	Female
Urban	0.4	0.0	76.6	77.7	21.5	20.6	1.5	1.7	n/av	n/av
Rural	2.1	1.2	65.2	71.9	29.3	23.9	3.4	3.0	n/av	n/av
Total	1.6	0.9	68.3	73.5	27.1	23.0	2.9	2.7	20.8	20.8

Source: Guyana, Multiple Indicator Cluster Survey 2, 2000 (see UCW Project Web site, http://www.ucw-project.org, country statistics).
Notes: [a]Children age 5 to 14. [b]Estimate includes (a) children under age 12 engaged in economic activities, (b) children age 12–14 engaged in excessive economic activities (more than 14 hours per week), and (c) children under age 15 engaged in excessive household chores (at least 28 hours per week). Estimate does not account for children engaged in hazardous work or other unconditional "worst forms" of child labor.

Paraguay

PARAGUAY			
	CRC	C 138	C 182
Ratifications	Y	Y	Y
Human Development Index/Rank	0.757/91		
Human Capital			
Population Growth Rate	2.42%		
% Population 0–14	37.2%		
Total Fertility Rate	3.84		
Life Expectancy	75.34		
Infant Mortality Rate	26.45		
Literacy Rate	94%		
Economic			
GDP/Capita	$4,700		
GDP Growth %	4%		
% Poverty	32%		
Gini Index	56.8%		
Labor Force Composition			
% Agriculture	45%		
% Industry	NA		
% Services	NA		

CHILD ACTIVITY BREAKDOWN, BY SEX AND RESIDENCE

RESIDENCE	Percentage of children in the relevant age-group[a]									
	Economic activity only		School only		Combining school and economic activity		Neither in school nor in economic activity		Child labor[b]	
	Male	Female	Male	Female	Male	Female	Male	Female	Male	Female
Urban	1.3	0.6	83.7	89.9	8.3	4.4	6.7	5.0	n/av	n/av
Rural	4.5	2.3	68.7	80.6	16.9	5.4	9.9	11.7	n/av	n/av
Total	2.9	1.4	76.4	85.5	12.5	4.9	8.3	8.2	16.8	12.2

Source: Paraguay, Encuesta Permanente de Hogares, 2004 (see UCW Project Web site, http://www.ucw-project.org, country statistics).

Notes: [a]Children age 5 to 14. [b]Estimate includes (a) children under age 12 engaged in economic activities, (b) children age 12–14 engaged in excessive economic activities (more than 14 hours per week), and (c) children under age 15 engaged in excessive household chores (at least 28 hours per week). Estimate does not account for children engaged in hazardous work or other unconditional "worst forms" of child labor.

Peru

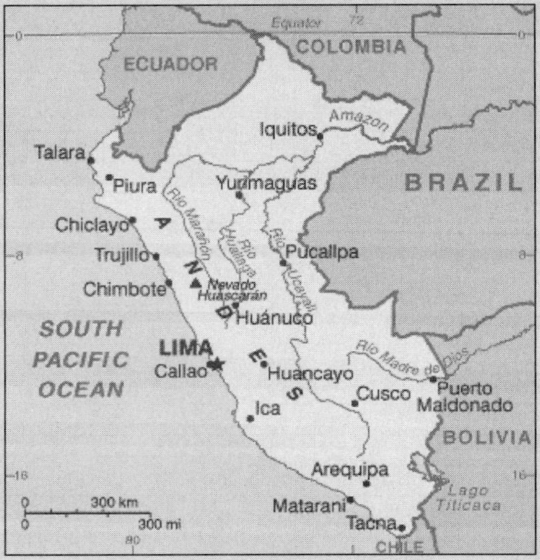

PERU			
	CRC	C 138	C 182
Ratifications	Y	Y	Y
Human Development Index/Rank	0.767/82		
Human Capital			
Population Growth Rate	1.29%		
% Population 0–14	30.3%		
Total Fertility Rate	2.46		
Life Expectancy	70.14		
Infant Mortality Rate	29.96		
Literacy Rate	87.7%		
Economic			
GDP/Capita	$6,400		
GDP Growth %	6.5%		
% Poverty	54%		
Gini Index	49.8		
Labor Force Composition			
% Agriculture	9%		
% Industry	18%		
% Services	73%		

CHILD ACTIVITY BREAKDOWN, BY SEX AND RESIDENCE

RESIDENCE	Percentage of children in the relevant age-group[a]									
	Economic activity only		School only		Combining school and economic activity		Neither in school nor in economic activity		Child labor[b]	
	Male	Female	Male	Female	Male	Female	Male	Female	Male	Female
Urban	0.7	0.5	90.9	91.6	7.7	7.1	0.8	0.8	n/av	n/av
Rural	1.6	1.8	52.5	60.4	44.3	36.2	1.6	1.6	n/av	n/av
Total	1.0	1.1	75.0	78.4	22.9	19.4	1.1	1.1	20.1	18.7

Source: Peru, Encuesta Nacional de Hogares Sobra Medición de Niveles de Vida, 2000 (see UCW Project Web site, http://www.ucw-project.org, country statistics).
Notes: [a]Children age 6 to 14. [b]Estimate includes (a) children under age 12 engaged in economic activities, (b) children age 12–14 engaged in excessive economic activities (more than 14 hours per week), and (c) children under age 15 engaged in excessive household chores (at least 28 hours per week). Estimate does not account for children engaged in hazardous work or other unconditional "worst forms" of child labor.

Venezuela

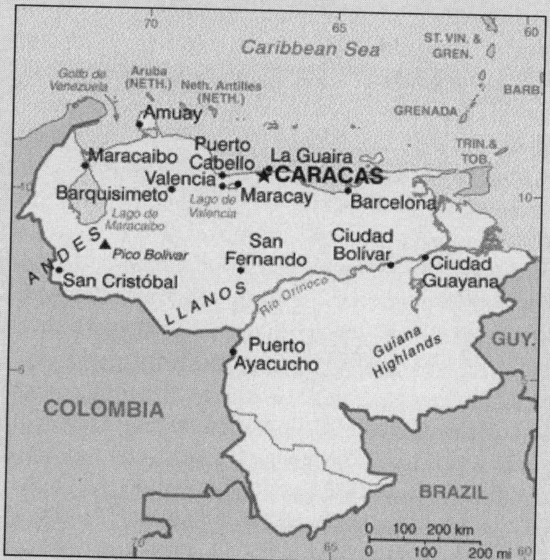

VENEZUELA			
	CRC	C 138	C 182
Ratifications	Y	Y	Y
Human Development Index/Rank	0.784/72		
Human Capital			
Population Growth Rate	1.49		
% Population 0–14	31.6%		
Total Fertility Rate	2.55		
Life Expectancy	73.28		
Infant Mortality Rate	22.52		
Literacy Rate	93.4		
Economic			
GDP/Capita	$6,900		
GDP Growth %	8.8%		
% Poverty	37.9%		
Gini Index	49.1		
Labor Force Composition			
% Agriculture	13%		
% Industry	23%		
% Services	64%		

CHILD ACTIVITY BREAKDOWN, BY AGE AND SEX

Age in years	Percentage of children in the relevant age-group									
	Economic activity only		School only		Combining school and economic activity		Neither in school nor in economic activity		Child labor[a]	
	Male	Female	Male	Female	Male	Female	Male	Female	Male	Female
Total 10–14	2.2	0.4	90.0	93.7	4.8	3.2	3.0	2.7	5.9	2.6

Source: Venezuela, Encuesta de Hogares por Muestreo—2005 second semester, 2005 (See UCW Project Web site, http://www.ucw-project.org, country statistics).
Notes: [a]Estimate includes (a) children under age 12 engaged in economic activities and (b) children age 12–14 engaged in excessive economic activities (more than 14 hours per week). Estimate does not account for children engaged in excessive household chores, hazardous work, or other unconditional "worst forms" of child labor.

Section 3. Central America

Belize

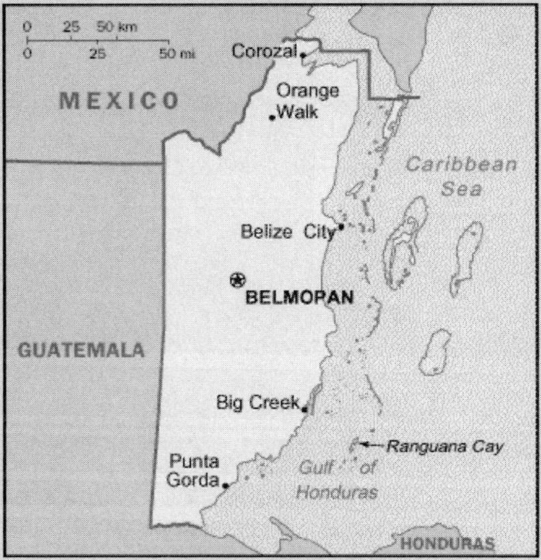

BELIZE			
	CRC	C 138	C 182
Ratifications	Y	Y	Y
Human Development Index/Rank	0.751/95		
Human Capital			
Population Growth Rate	2.31%		
% Population 0–14	39.5%		
Total Fertility Rate	3.6		
Life Expectancy	68.3		
Infant Mortality Rate	24.89		
Literacy Rate	94.1%		
Economic			
GDP/Capita	$8,400		
GDP Growth %	3.5%		
% Poverty	33.5%		
Gini Index	—		
Labor Force Composition			
% Agriculture	22.5%		
% Industry	15.2%		
% Services	62.3%		

CHILD ACTIVITY BREAKDOWN, BY SEX AND RESIDENCE

RESIDENCE	Percentage of children in the relevant age-group[a]									
	Economic activity only		School only		Combining school and economic activity		Neither in school nor in economic activity		Child labor[b]	
	Male	Female	Male	Female	Male	Female	Male	Female	Male	Female
Urban	0.5	0.5	91.0	94.1	4.1	1.6	4.4	3.8	n/av	n/av
Rural	1.6	1.1	83.8	85.2	8.8	5.3	5.8	8.3	n/av	n/av
Total	1.2	0.8	86.7	89.1	6.9	3.7	5.2	6.4	39.0	41.6

Source: Belize, Child Activity Survey 2001 (see UCW Project Web site, http://www.ucw-project.org, country statistics).
Notes: [a]Children age 5 to 14. [b]Estimate includes (a) children under age 12 engaged in economic activities, (b) children age 12–14 engaged in excessive economic activities (more than 14 hours per week), and (c) children under age 15 engaged in excessive household chores (at least 28 hours per week). Estimate does not account for children engaged in hazardous work or other unconditional "worst forms" of child labor.

Costa Rica

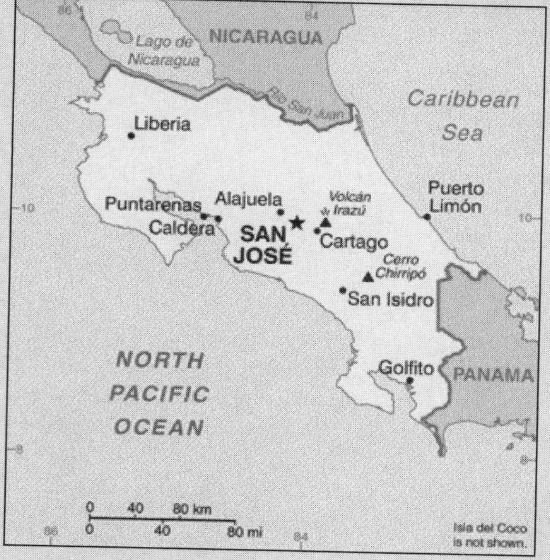

COSTA RICA	CRC	C 138	C 182
Ratifications	Y	Y	Y
Human Development Index/Rank	0.841/48		
Human Capital			
Population Growth Rate	1.45%		
% Population 0–14	28.3%		
Total Fertility Rate	2.24		
Life Expectancy	77.02		
Infant Mortality Rate	9.7		
Literacy Rate	96%		
Economic			
GDP/Capita	$12,000		
GDP Growth %	4.7%		
% Poverty	18%		
Gini Index	46.5		
Labor Force Composition			
% Agriculture	20%		
% Industry	22%		
% Services	58%		

CHILD ACTIVITY BREAKDOWN, BY SEX AND RESIDENCE

RESIDENCE	Percentage of children in the relevant age-group[a]									
	Economic activity only		School only		Combining school and economic activity		Neither in school nor in economic activity		Child labor[b]	
	Male	Female	Male	Female	Male	Female	Male	Female	Male	Female
Urban	0.6	0.1	89.7	92.4	3.2	1.2	6.5	6.4	n/av	n/av
Rural	3.6	0.9	76.1	82.3	10.1	4.5	10.2	12.3	n/av	n/av
Total	2.0	0.5	83.5	87.7	6.4	2.7	8.2	9.1	6.0	3.4

Source: Costa Rica, Encuesta de Hogares de Propositos Multiples, 2002 (see UCW Project Web site, http://www.ucw-project.org, country statistics).

Notes: [a]Children age 5 to 14. [b]Estimate includes (a) children under age 12 engaged in economic activities, (b) children age 12–14 engaged in excessive economic activities (more than 14 hours per week), and (c) children under age 15 engaged in excessive household chores (at least 28 hours per week). Estimate does not account for children engaged in hazardous work or other unconditional "worst forms" of child labor.

El Salvador

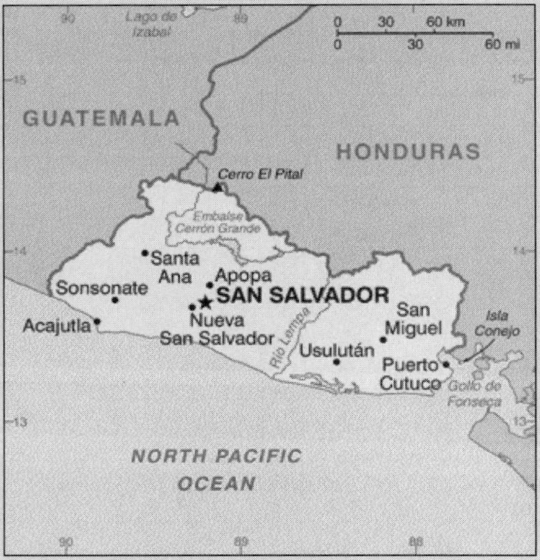

EL SALVADOR	CRC	C 138	C 182
Ratifications	Y	Y	Y
Human Development Index/Rank	0.729/101		
Human Capital			
Population Growth Rate	1.72%		
% Population 0–14	36.3%		
Total Fertility Rate	3.12		
Life Expectancy	71.49		
Infant Mortality Rate	24.39		
Literacy Rate	80.2%		
Economic			
GDP/Capita	$4,900		
GDP Growth %	4.2%		
% Poverty	35.2%		
Gini Index	52.5		
Labor Force Composition			
% Agriculture	17.1%		
% Industry	17.1%		
% Services	65.8%		

CHILD ACTIVITY BREAKDOWN, BY SEX AND RESIDENCE

RESIDENCE	Percentage of children in the relevant age-group[a]									
	Economic activity only		School only		Combining school and economic activity		Neither in school nor in economic activity		Child labor[b]	
	Male	Female	Male	Female	Male	Female	Male	Female	Male	Female
Urban	0.7	0.6	78.8	79.6	6.1	6.4	14.4	13.4	n/av	n/av
Rural	6.6	0.5	58.1	70.9	14.9	5.4	20.4	23.2	n/av	n/av
Total	3.4	0.6	69.1	75.6	10.3	5.9	17.2	17.9	8.7	3.5

Source: El Salvador, Enquesta de Hogares de Propositos Multiples, 2003 (see UCW Project Web site, http://www.ucw-project.org, country statistics).

Notes: [a]Children age 5 to 14. [b]Estimate includes (a) children under age 12 engaged in economic activities and (b) children age 12–14 engaged in excessive economic activities (more than 14 hours per week). Estimate does not account for children engaged in excessive household chores, hazardous work, or other unconditional "worst forms" of child labor.

Child Labor in El Salvador

Lorenzo Guarcello, Gabriella Breglia, and **Scott Lyon,** Researchers,
Understanding Children's Work (UCW) Project

This essay provides an overview of the child labor phenomenon in its various dimensions—its extent, its nature, and its causes and consequences—in El Salvador. It is drawn from a detailed interagency report on child labor developed by the UCW Project in 2003.

Extent of Children's Work

Children's work, defined as any form of economic activity performed by children, is not uncommon in El Salvador. Some 109,000 children between the ages of five and fourteen years, about 7 percent of total children in this age-group, are engaged in work (all figures are for the 2001 reference year). Actual numbers of child workers are likely higher, as this estimate does not include children in so-called unconditional worst forms of child labor or children performing noneconomic activities.

The other children in the five- to fourteen-year-old age-group either are full-time students (75 percent) or are reportedly involved in neither work nor school (18 percent). This latter group of children requires further investigation, but it stands to reason that many from this group are in reality performing functions that contribute in some way to household welfare, that is, either working or doing household chores. Those who are indeed inactive can be even more disadvantaged than their working counterparts, benefiting neither from schooling nor from the learning-by-doing that some forms of work offer.

The prevalence of children in work varies substantially by sex, age, and residence. The work prevalence of male five- to fourteen-year-olds is more than twice that of female five- to fourteen-year-olds. This gender gap in work prevalence is primarily the result of boys' greater involvement in rural (mostly agricultural) work; the difference in work prevalence by sex in urban areas is quite small. Children's involvement in work increases with age, a likely reflection both of the higher opportunity costs of school in terms of earnings forgone as a child gets older, and of the more limited schooling opportunities at the higher grades. Children's work is mainly a rural phenomenon in El Salvador. The prevalence of children's work in rural areas is almost twice that of urban areas; rural child workers make up almost three-fourths of total child workers. Children's work rates also vary somewhat by region. The highest concentrations of child workers are found, not coincidentally, in the regions of the country that also feature the highest levels of poverty. Children's involvement in work is lowest in the region with the lowest level of poverty.

The performance of household chores is also very common among Salvadoran children. Around 950,000 children from five to fourteen years of age—39 percent of this age-group—perform household chores. Of these, around 22,000 (2 percent) also perform economic activities, and around 69,000 (7 percent) also both perform economic activities and attend school. But for most children, household chores constitute a relatively minor daily activity—those performing chores do so for an average of only about one hour per day. Only 2 percent spend an average of more than four hours per day on these tasks.

Characteristics of Children's Work

The agriculture sector accounts for the largest share of child workers. More than half of working children (53 percent) are found in this sector, with most of the remainder either in the retail trade (22 percent) or manufacturing (15 percent). But these totals mask important differences by residence and sex. Agricultural work predominates in rural areas, but work in retail trade and manufacturing is most important in urban areas. Girls are much less likely than boys to work in agriculture, but much more likely than boys to be involved in retail trade, manufacturing, private household work, and the hotel and restaurant industry.

Children's work is concentrated primarily in the informal economy, and specifically in non-waged work in family micro-enterprises. Some 78 percent of working children work for their families and not for wages. Family work is most important in the agriculture sector, accounting for 85 percent of total child workers, but also predominates in manufacturing and the retail trade, the other two main employers of children in the country. Again, there are some differences by sex. Girls are much more likely to work as domestics, and more likely to work as permanent wage earners, and to be self-employed. Boys are more likely to be temporary wage earners. Family work, however, predominates for both boys and girls.

Children's work in El Salvador is characterized by very long working hours. Children put in an average of twenty-six hours of work per week, with little variation by sex or residence. Working children who do not go to school put in the longest hours—an average of thirty-six hours per week. But even those who also attend school put in a twenty-two-hour workweek on average, with obvious consequences for the time and energy they have for study. Children in two sectors—mining and private household work—put in much longer average workweeks (fifty-four and forty-eight hours, respectively) than their counterparts in other sectors.

Available evidence suggests that children can face hazardous conditions in many of the sectors in which they work. Around 16 percent of working children report operating hazardous tools, equipment, or machinery, while less than 7 percent report using some form of protective equipment. Fisheries, the fireworks industry, refuse dumps, and sugarcane fields are among the work sectors or settings identified as being especially hazardous to children in El Salvador.

Working children appear disadvantaged in terms of their ability to attend school. About 71 percent of working children go to school compared to 81 percent of nonworking children. The ability of working children to attend school appears to depend somewhat on the type of work in which they are engaged. Of the three main sectors employing children, school attendance is lowest in agriculture (65 percent), followed by the retail trade (73 percent) and manufacturing (76 percent). The relationship between work and school performance has not been investigated in the El Salvador context, but evidence from elsewhere suggests that school performance declines appreciably with additional hours worked.

Determinants of Children's Work and Schooling

As most children (excluding those who live on their own) exercise little control over their time allocations, determining why children work requires investigating why parents choose to engage their children in work rather than sending them to school or leaving them idle at home. A multivariate analysis making use of household survey data points to a number of factors influencing parents' decisions concerning children's time use.

Age and Sex

Parents in El Salvador are more likely to involve their male children in work. With household income, parents' education, and other relevant factors held constant, boys are more likely to work full-time (1 percentage point) and to work while attending school (3 percentage points) than girls. Girls, however, are more likely than boys to attend school (4 percentage points). The analysis shows that the probability of a child working increases with age. The available information is insufficient to provide a precise idea of the magnitude of the two most probable reasons for this, that is, the rising opportunity cost of schooling with the age of the child, and the lack of access to schooling at the postprimary level.

Poverty

Work prevalence among children from extremely poor households (9 percent) is almost one third higher than work prevalence among nonpoor children (6 percent). Work prevalence falls and school attendance rises progressively as household income goes up, but the income effect is relatively weak. For example, an increase in income of about 10 percent has only negligible effects on the probability that a child goes to work. This indicates that relatively small changes in income are not likely to produce a significant effect on the decision to work or attend school. Interventions aimed at reducing child labor and increasing school attendance based on income transfers are not likely to produce substantial changes, unless the size of the transfer is large.

Education of the Head of the Household

Work is more common among those children whose head of household has no education, and declines progressively as the educational level of the household head rises. These relationships are likely at least partially the product of a disguised income effect; that is, household heads with higher levels of education are also likely to have higher levels of income, and therefore less need to involve their children in work. However, the relationship between the education of the head of household and child work prevalence holds even when controlling for income. A possible explanation of these findings is that more educated parents might have a better knowledge of the returns to education, or be in a position to help their children exploit the earning potential acquired through education.

Household Structure

Children from households with more young children are less likely to study and are more likely to be inactive. Controlling for other factors, each additional child age zero to four years decreases the probability that a school-age child will attend school by 4 percentage points, and increases the probability that a school-age child is neither working nor studying by 3 percentage points. The effect of an additional young child on the likelihood of children working, however, is negligible. Probably they stay at home to look after their siblings if the parents are working.

Basic Services

About 40 percent of the households surveyed do not have access to public water systems, although about 80 percent of households surveyed do have access to electricity. Both indicators of basic services have a strong impact on the probability that children go to school. Children from households with access to public water are 5 percentage points more likely to study and 4.3 percentage points less likely to be neither working nor studying. The same picture appears in relation to the availability of electricity. Both indicators of infrastructure availability show a significant but negligible negative relationship with the probability of working.

Children's work is a complex phenomenon, however, and the factors mentioned previously clearly represent only a partial list of determinants. Better data and more in-depth analysis are needed for a more complete understanding of why children become involved in work. Information on school quality, access to credit markets, and social protection schemes is especially needed. Better qualitative analyses of factors such as parental attitudes and cultural traditions are also necessary. The demand for child workers, not considered in household surveys, is another area that needs to be better understood. The unique circumstances causing children's involvement in unconditional worst forms of child labor, also not captured by traditional household surveys, is an area requiring particular research attention.

Reference and Further Reading

UCW Project and ILO-IPEC. *Entendiendo el trabajo infantil en El Salvador.* Geneva: ILO-IPEC, 2003. http://www.ucw-project.org/.

Guatemala

GUATEMALA			
	CRC	C 138	C 182
Ratifications	Y	Y	Y
Human Development Index/Rank	0.673/118		
Human Capital			
Population Growth Rate	2.27%		
% Population 0–14	41.1%		
Total Fertility Rate	3.82		
Life Expectancy	69.38		
Infant Mortality Rate	30.94		
Literacy Rate	70.6%		
Economic			
GDP/Capita	$4,900		
GDP Growth %	4.6%		
% Poverty	56.2%		
Gini Index	59.9		
Labor Force Composition			
% Agriculture	50%		
% Industry	15%		
% Services	35%		

CHILD ACTIVITY BREAKDOWN, BY SEX AND RESIDENCE

RESIDENCE	Percentage of children in the relevant age-group[a]									
	Economic activity only		School only		Combining school and economic activity		Neither in school nor in economic activity		Child labor[b]	
	Male	Female	Male	Female	Male	Female	Male	Female	Male	Female
Urban	4.8	3.0	77.5	80.2	9.4	5.7	8.3	11.1	n/av	n/av
Rural	8.5	3.7	60.2	67.4	20.2	8.0	11.0	20.9	n/av	n/av
Total	7.1	3.4	67.0	72.6	16.0	7.1	9.9	16.9	20.3	8.3

Source: Guatemala, Encuesta Nacional Sobre Empleo e Ingresos, 2004 (see UCW Project Web site, http://www.ucw-project.org, country statistics).
Notes: [a]Children age 7 to 14. [b]Estimate includes (a) children under age 12 engaged in economic activities and (b) children age 12–14 engaged in excessive economic activities (more than 14 hours per week). Estimate does not account for children engaged in excessive household chores, hazardous work, or other unconditional "worst forms" of child labor.

Child Labor in Guatemala

Lorenzo Guarcello, Gabriella Breglia, and **Scott Lyon,** Researchers,
Understanding Children's Work (UCW) Project

This essay provides an overview of the child labor phenomenon in its various dimensions—its extent, its nature, and its causes and consequences—in Guatemala. It is drawn from a detailed interagency report on child labor developed by the UCW Project in 2003.

Extent of Children's Work

Children's work, defined as any form of economic activity performed by children, is very common in Guatemala. Some 507,000 children age seven to fourteen years old, one-fifth of total children in this age-group, are engaged in work (all estimates relate to the 2000 reference year). The other children in the seven- to fourteen-year-old age-group either are full-time students (62 percent) or are reportedly involved in neither work nor school (18 percent). This latter group of children requires further investigation, but it stands to reason that many are in reality performing functions that contribute in some way to household welfare, that is, either working or doing household chores. Those who are indeed inactive can be even more disadvantaged than their working counterparts, benefiting neither from schooling nor from the learning-by-doing that some forms of work offer.

The prevalence of children in work varies substantially by sex, age, ethnicity, and residence. The work prevalence of male seven- to fourteen-year-olds is almost twice that of female seven- to fourteen-year-olds, and the work prevalence of indigenous children almost twice that of nonindigenous children. Work prevalence is highest among older children, but the absolute number of very young Guatemalan children engaged in work is nonetheless significant. Some 206,000 children age five to eleven years old are economically active. These very young working children are the most vulnerable to workplace abuses, and most at risk of work-related ill health or injury. Children's work is mainly a rural phenomenon: The prevalence of children in work in rural areas is almost twice that of urban areas, and rural child workers make up three-fourths of total child workers.

The prevalence of children in work appears to be rising in Guatemala. The latest national employment survey, in 2002, estimated that 23 percent of children were involved in work. This compares with a 20 percent estimate generated by a 2000 survey, an estimate of 14 percent from 1998–99, and an estimate of 8 percent from the 1994 population census. However, differences in survey methodologies mean that caution must be exercised before reading too much into comparisons of these survey results.

The performance of household chores is also very common among Guatemalan children. Around 300,000 children age seven to fourteen years old—12 percent of this age-group—perform household chores for at least four hours per day. The proportion of female seven- to fourteen-year-olds performing household chores is more than triple that of male seven- to fourteen-year-olds. This underscores the fact that work prevalence alone is a misleading indicator of girls' total involvement in activities that are not related to school or to leisure. Indeed, when work is defined to also include household chores for at least four hours per day, girls and boys work in equal proportion.

Characteristics of Children's Work

Two out of three Guatemalan working children are found in the agricultural sector and work for their

Ten-year-old girl picking coffee in Guatemala, 2007. *(Photo by Luisa Quiroz Moreno courtesy of IREWOC Foundation)*

families without wages. But the type of work children perform appears to depend to an important extent on their sex. Boys tend to work on the farm (three-fourths of them), with commercial activities coming a distant second (10 percent), while girls' activities are more evenly spread among agricultural work (40 percent), commerce (28 percent), manufacturing (20 percent), and personal services (12 percent).

Children's work in Guatemala is characterized by very long working hours, leaving children little time for study or play. Working children put in an average of forty-seven hours of work per week, considerably more than full-time adult workers in the industrial world. Working children who do not go to school put in the longest hours—an average of fifty-eight hours per week—but even those who also attend school put in a forty-hour workweek on average. Household chores also eat into children's time for play and study. Children performing household chores do so for an average of forty hours per week.

Available evidence suggests that children can face hazardous conditions in many of the sectors in which they work:

Domestic service in private homes: Child domestic servants, almost all girls, must work extremely long hours; reports of threats, beatings, harassment, and even sexual abuse are not uncommon; benefits are not paid, and vacations or sick days generally are nonexistent. Less than one-third are able to attend school.

Firecracker production: The production of firecrackers is probably the most dangerous occupation in which Guatemalan children are involved. Children as young as six, mostly boys, insert fuses into firecrackers and perform other related tasks requiring a great deal of concentration to avoid accidents (for example, if the "wheel" holding the firecrackers in which children insert fuses falls, it explodes). As a result, accidents are not uncommon, causing severe burns and sometimes even the death of children.

Agricultural work: Children in the agricultural sector frequently endure long working days under a hot sun, carrying heavy loads, and risking cuts from sharp knives. Injuries such as fractures, cuts, loss of eyesight, and loss of limbs are not uncommon, not to mention death from disease, malnutrition, and injury.

Mining and quarrying: Children work in the mining and refining of lime. They often lift and crush heavy rocks, putting them in danger of bone fractures, burns, and respiratory ailments, as well as landslides. Many work in slavery-like conditions to pay off debt for their parents. They face serious health hazards, including lung and skin disease, deformation, blindness, and loss of limbs.

Garbage picking: Children are found in the garbage dumps of urban areas picking through and collecting items that can be recycled or reused. According to an ILO-IPEC Rapid Assessment, some 82 percent sustain cuts or other injuries; 56 percent suffer burning eyes as a result of gas released by the decomposing garbage; and 40 percent experience headaches from sun exposure.

Unconditional worst forms of child labor are also found in Guatemala. The UN special rapporteur on the sale of children, child commercial sexual exploitation, and child pornography cites information received from authorities and social workers that suggests that commercial sexual exploitation of children exists on a significant scale in a variety of localities. Guatemala is both a source for and a destination of trafficked children, although the total extent of child trafficking in the country is not known. The government indicates that the number of street children has increased in recent years. Estimates of their total numbers range from 3,500 to 8,000, but precise estimates are impossible because of the fluid and mobile nature of the street population.

Consequences of Children's Work

Work appears to interfere with children's ability to attend school. About 62 percent of working children attend school compared to 78 percent of nonworking children. Child workers complete only about half the total number of years of schooling of their nonworking counterparts. Of the four sectors employing the largest number children, school attendance is lowest (41 percent) in the health and personal services sector, where the largest proportion of child workers are female servants in private homes. Work interferes with girls' schooling more than boys' schooling in all but the manufacturing sector. And for working children who do go to school, work reduces the time they have for their studies and is a frequent reported cause of absenteeism, undoubtedly affecting their ability to derive educational benefit from schooling.

Available data do not indicate a clear negative relationship between children's work and child health. The prevalence of health problems is almost the same for children who work full-time, children who are full-time students, and children who neither work nor attend school, at around 22 percent. Only children who combine school and work have a slightly higher prevalence of health problems (27 percent). Nutritional status, as measured by the body mass index (BMI), is actually slightly better for children who work than for those who are full-time students. But these findings are likely the product of measurement problems encountered when attempting to look at the work-health relationship.

Determinants of Children's Work and Schooling

As most children (excluding those who live on their own) exercise little control over their time allocations, determining why children work requires investigating why parents choose to engage their children in work rather than sending them to school or leaving them idle at home. A multivariate analysis making use of household survey data points to a number of factors influencing parents' decisions concerning children's time use.

Gender. Boys are more likely to work full-time (3 percentage points) and to work while attending school (10 percentage points) than girls. Girls, however, are more likely than boys to be neither attending school nor working (7 percentage points), and therefore presumably involved in household chores.

Ethnicity. Indigenous children are 9 percentage points more likely to work, and 8 percentage points less likely to attend school full-time, than their nonindigenous counterparts.

Poverty. Work prevalence falls and school attendance rises progressively as household income goes up, but the effect is relatively weak. For example, an increase in income of about 10 percent has only negligible effects on the probability that a child goes to work. This indicates that relatively small changes in income are not likely to produce a significant effect on the decision to work or attend school. Interventions aimed at reducing work by children and increasing school attendance based on income transfers are not likely to produce substantial changes, unless the size of the transfer is large.

Mothers' educational status. A mother having no education increases the likelihood that a child works by 5 percentage points, and decreases the likelihood that a child attends school by 18 percentage points.

Household composition. Each additional adult in a household increases the probability of a child attending school full-time by 3 percentage points. Each additional child age zero to six years increases the probability that a child will be working and studying by 1.5 percentage points.

Exposure to collective shocks. Children from households exposed to collective shocks are 4 percentage points more likely to work (either attending school or not) and 2 percentage points less likely to attend school only.

Exposure to individual shocks. Children who belong to a household that has suffered from an individual shock are about 5 percentage points more likely to be working.

Credit rationing. Children belonging to credit-rationed households are 7 percentage points less likely to attend school than children from nonrationed households. Children from credit-rationed households are more likely to be idle (about 6 percentage points) and to work full-time.

Health insurance. Children from households where at least one member is covered by health insurance are 4.5 percentage points less likely to work. Likewise, children from households with a member covered by health insurance are 4.5 percentage points more likely to attend school.

Children's work is a complex phenomenon, however, and the factors mentioned previously clearly represent only a partial list of determinants. Better data and more in-depth analysis are needed for a more complete understanding of why children become involved in work. Information on availability of infrastructure, school quality, access to credit markets, and social protection schemes is especially needed. Better qualitative analyses of factors such as parental attitudes and cultural traditions are also necessary. The demand for child workers, not considered in household surveys, is another area that needs to be better understood. The unique circumstances causing children's involvement in unconditional worst forms of child labor, also not captured by traditional household surveys, is an area requiring particular research attention.

References and Further Reading

Rosati, Furio C., and R. Straub. "Does Work During Childhood Affect Adult's Health? An Analysis for Guatemala." Understanding Children's Work Project Working Paper Series, UCW Project, Rome, February 2006.

UCW Project. *Understanding Children's Work in Guatemala.* Rome: Understanding Children's Work (UCW) Project, University of Rome, Tor Vegata, 2003. http://www.ucw-project.org/.

Honduras

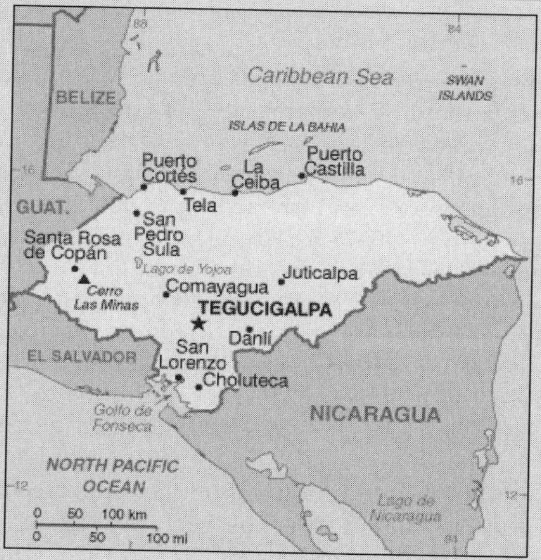

HONDURAS			
	CRC	C 138	C 182
Ratifications	Y	Y	Y
Human Development Index/Rank	0.683/117		
Human Capital			
Population Growth Rate	2.16%		
% Population 0–14	39.9%		
Total Fertility Rate	3.59		
Life Expectancy	69.33		
Infant Mortality Rate	25.82		
Literacy Rate	76.2%		
Economic			
GDP/Capita	$3,000		
GDP Growth %	5.2%		
% Poverty	53%		
Gini Index	55		
Labor Force Composition			
% Agriculture	34%		
% Industry	23%		
% Services	43%		

CHILD ACTIVITY BREAKDOWN, BY SEX AND RESIDENCE

RESIDENCE	Percentage of children in the relevant age-group[a]									
	Economic activity only		School only		Combining school and economic activity		Neither in school nor in economic activity		Child labor[b]	
	Male	Female	Male	Female	Male	Female	Male	Female	Male	Female
Urban	1.4	1.1	88.4	89.8	2.2	1.6	8.0	7.6	n/av	n/av
Rural	6.1	1.0	74.1	80.5	5.1	1.6	14.7	17.0	n/av	n/av
Total	4.2	1.0	79.7	84.1	4.0	1.6	12.0	13.3	6.8	2.1

Source: Honduras, Encuesta Permanente de Hogares de Propósitos Múltiples, 2004 (see UCW Project Web site, http://www.ucw-project.org, country statistics).
Notes: [a]Children age 5 to 14. [b]Estimate includes (a) children under age 12 engaged in economic activities, (b) children age 12–14 engaged in excessive economic activities (more than 14 hours per week), and (c) children under age 15 engaged in excessive household chores (at least 28 hours per week). Estimate does not account for children engaged in hazardous work or other unconditional "worst forms" of child labor.

Child Labor in Honduras

Adrienne Pine, Professor of Anthropology, American University in Cairo

A 2002 survey by Honduras's National Statistics Institute (INE), supported by ILO-IPEC, estimated that 356,241 boys and girls between the ages of five and seventeen (15.4 percent of the population in that age-group), and 123,195 between the ages of five and fourteen, worked in economic activities in Honduras. According to the survey, the percentage of children and adolescents engaged in economic activities was higher among males (22.3 percent) than among females (8.2 percent) and increased with age. It was also higher in rural areas (18.6 percent) than in urban areas (11.1 percent). The average length of the workweek for children was 35.9 hours and was significantly longer in the service sector. Child laborers were more likely to be working for their families than otherwise, and the majority of working children (56.2 percent) were occupied in agriculture, forestry, hunting, and fishing. The legal daily minimum wage ranges from L68 (US$3.58) to L107 (US$5.63) in Honduras, and child laborers are concentrated in the lowest-wage regions and sectors. However, most child laborers, especially those working for their families, worked without remuneration (ILO-IPEC 2003).

There are presently very few employers in the highly visible maquiladora industry (export-processing textile factories) who knowingly hire underage workers. But this has not always been the case. In 1994, Lesly Rodriguez, a fifteen-year-old who had been working for two years in a maquiladora sewing clothing for the Liz Claiborne line, traveled to the United States with members of the National Labor Committee (NLC) to give testimony at a congressional hearing about the work conditions she and her colleagues faced. Lesly told of being prohibited from attending school, of working extremely long hours, of being denied bathroom and meal breaks, of humiliating treatment by her superiors, of young women being forced to take pregnancy tests and birth control pills, of blatant union busting on the part of management, and of earning a weekly salary equivalent to US$21.50. At the time of Lesly's testimony, 2 percent of the Honduran maquiladora workforce was twelve to thirteen years of age and 11 percent was fourteen to fifteen, according to results of a survey of women maquiladora workers conducted by the Honduran Committee for the Defense of Human Rights (CODEH). As a result of the intensely negative international publicity around Lesly's testimony, and following a second visit to the United States by Lesly and underage maquiladora worker Wendy Diaz in 1996, which targeted television personality Kathie Lee Gifford because her Wal-Mart clothing line was manufactured using underage labor, maquiladora owners ceased hiring children to work in their factories. Lesly, Wendy, and the NLC were joined by various student, labor, and religious organizations in both Honduras and the United States in pressuring the industry to take this stance. Despite what some in government and industry have suggested, this was not a result of voluntary industrial codes of conduct; rather, it stemmed directly from the threat of lost revenue. Unfortunately, while children are no longer employed on a large scale in maquiladoras, other working conditions have improved little. And although maquiladoras today rarely hire workers under age eighteen, many young women use borrowed identity cards to obtain employment in these factories, which provide better salaries than other jobs requiring a minimal education. Additionally, in some factories workers are encouraged to take work home to complete their quotas;

in those cases family members, often children, are called upon to help.

In part because of the availability of maquiladora work to young women, middle-class Hondurans complain that it is hard to find servants. This has led to increased hiring of younger girls, many of whom migrate from rural areas to urban centers to engage in domestic work, where, without their usual support networks, they are in a position of added vulnerability. More than 18,000 persons between the ages of five and seventeen were domestic workers in 2002 (ILO-IPEC 2003).

In 1998, Hurricane Mitch exacerbated nearly every preexisting social problem, including child labor, in Honduras, as poverty, homelessness, and a tattered national infrastructure forced many children to abandon school for work even earlier than they might have otherwise. Several years later, IPEC, working with the Ministry of Labor, identified the worst forms of child labor in the country as commercial sexual exploitation (particularly in North Coast tourist areas), fireworks production, offshore diving from boats in commercial lobster fishing, limestone quarrying and other mining, garbage-dump picking, melon and other commercial agriculture production involving the handling of pesticides, woodcutting in sawmills, and construction activities (ILO-IPEC 2001).

Child Labor Law in Honduras

Although its application is largely ineffective, child labor law in Honduras is clearly designed to protect youths, who make up the majority of Honduras's population. In 1996, six years after ratifying the UN Convention on the Rights of the Child, the Honduran congress passed the Code of Childhood and Adolescence. This law expands protections afforded to children in Honduras's 1982 constitution. In May 2001 the Honduran congress ratified ILO Convention 182 on the worst forms of child labor, which became law a month later, outlining specific activities prohibited for children and adolescents and sanctions for employers who violate these rules and regulations.

The legal working age in Honduras is considered to be eighteen, though younger children are permitted to work under a variety of circumstances. Youths between the ages of sixteen and eighteen can work, but no longer than six-hour days, and no later that 8 P.M. Children under eighteen are prohibited from working in hazardous conditions, including undersea fishing, garbage work, and work that exposes them to vehicular traffic, though limited exceptions can be made on a case-by-case basis for sixteen- to eighteen-year-olds. Further, children under eighteen are prohibited from work that "affects their morality," including labor in brothels and other places where alcohol is served; also prohibited is their paid participation in pornographic, snuff, and crime movie scenes.

Children fourteen to fifteen years of age are permitted to work, up to four hours daily, but not at night. However, parents or a legal guardian must request permission from the labor ministry, and the ministry is required to perform a home study to assess the economic necessity for the child to work. An employer who hires a fourteen- to fifteen-year-old must certify that the child has finished or is finishing the required compulsory schooling. Children under fourteen years of age are prohibited from working, even with parental permission.

Employers with more than twenty school-age children on their farm, ranch, or business facility must provide a location for a school. While schooling is compulsory only to age fourteen, adolescents above age fourteen who have not completed their secondary schooling are considered to be school-age. Persons who violate the law are subject to fines between L5,000 and L25,000 (roughly between US$265 and US$1,323). The fine is to be doubled upon on the second infraction, but not raised above the latter amount. Prison sentences of three to five years are possible for individuals who allow children to work illegally.

Why Are the Children Working?

Honduran children work for a number of interrelated reasons, among them economic necessity, lack of educational opportunities, an atmosphere of violence that severely limits their options, government inaction, the profit interests of large industry, and neoliberal policies fomented by international lending institutions.

Income distribution in Honduras is similar to that in the United States—dramatically unequal. In

2002, the wealthiest income quintile of Hondurans earned 55.6 percent of the national income share, whereas the poorest quintile earned only 3.9 percent (Hammill et al. 2005). However, in absolute numbers, Hondurans are much poorer than their northern neighbors, with an average per capita GDP estimated by the World Bank to be US$1,771 and by the United Nations Development Programme US$2,876. Because of poverty, families depend on their children's labor for subsistence, and when children all too frequently find themselves homeless, they must depend on themselves.

The vast majority of Honduran children are poor, and poor children are much less likely than those with sufficient means to finish their education. Additionally, Honduras's educational infrastructure is not adequate to comply with the constitutional mandate that all children between ages seven and fourteen be in school. According to the NGO Social Watch, in 2004, more than 50 percent of secondary school students were in poorly regulated private schools, which have a greater number of teachers than state schools and are more expensive (Kennedy et al. 2004). The public schools are supposed to be free, but parents are required to pay for uniforms, supplies, and fees. Further, strikes and other disruptions are a common occurrence, as Honduran teachers are regularly forced to go without pay and work under very poor conditions. In 2002, 26.9 percent of children between the ages of five and seventeen did not attend school (43.9 percent in rural areas), and only 44.8 percent of adolescents between the ages of fifteen and seventeen attended school (ILO-IPEC 2003). Lack of access to education serves the dual purpose of freeing children up for labor and preventing them from access to good jobs in the present and future. Even for high school graduates, good jobs are scarce, a fact that provides an added disincentive for children to remain in school.

Children's options are further limited by an atmosphere of violence, which takes many different forms. About 4,000 cases of child abuse and maltreatment are reported every year (UN CRC 2007). Domestic violence is the primary factor influencing children to leave home, which usually represents the end of their formal education. Children living on the streets, whose numbers the Honduran government estimated to be 20,000 in 2006, only half of whom had shelter, are especially vulnerable to abuse and exploitation in sex work and human trafficking. In 2003, the NGO Casa Alianza found 10,000 children being prostituted in twenty cities in Honduras.

Children with and without homes confront extreme street violence, which comes not only from highly publicized gangs, but also from agents of the state who in recent years have committed hundreds of extrajudicial murders with impunity (Jahangir 2002). Casa Alianza reported that between January 1998 and November 2006, 1,193 children and adolescents had been murdered. The organization's report notes that "the majority of murdered youths were at just the right age for their educational-vocational formation, and nonetheless their lives were cut short without the opportunity to forge a better future for themselves and their families"(Casa Alianza 2006, 5). The extrajudicial killings affect even those who have not lost immediate family members and friends by creating an atmosphere of fear, an atmosphere in which people do not trust the police and state to protect them. This fear is felt especially among weaker members of society, the poor and the young, who are less likely to report their own labor exploitation to officials whom they do not trust.

Young people have little reason to look to their government for solutions. Despite numerous declarations and initiatives over the years, money from USAID and NGOs, assistance from the ILO, ultimatums from the World Bank, and private industry "partnerships" with government to reduce child labor, Honduras has failed to make a dent in the problem. As the U.S. State Department reported in 2006, "Government measures had minimal impact on diminishing child labor in light of extreme poverty, famine conditions in rural areas, and a lack of jobs for school graduates" (U.S. Department of State 2006). For while the Honduran government announces plans to combat child labor, it understaffs its Ministry of Labor, whose inspectors are already too often beholden to private industry, and weakens labor protections in compliance with the restructuring mandates of the World Bank's Heavily Indebted Poor Countries initiative. While the government announces its intent to crack down on human rights abuses, it closes offices of its National Human Rights Commission and ignores findings of independent human rights agencies. While the government claims that children's education is a priority, it fails to strengthen the internal tax base necessary to fund education, thereby encouraging privatization of the educational system. Along with liberalization of labor protections, the government's educational policy has also been aligned with World Bank and IMF demands. Honduras's acquiescence to the demands of such donors has not, however, meant that the latter have kept their end of the bargain; debt relief has been slow in coming and education remains woefully underfunded (Burdett and Jensen 2004).

Perhaps the most important reason why Honduran children work is that capitalism demands it. It would be inappropriate to blame parents, teachers, or any aspect of Honduran culture for this widespread problem when private industry is so eager to hire underage workers, despite high unemployment rates among the legal workforce. Children are attractive workers in Honduras, as elsewhere, precisely because of their increased vulnerability and lower cost to employers. As long as this advantage is greater than the risk of employing children, Honduran employers will seek children as workers. Similarly, private industry is complicit in underfunding the school system through its resistance to paying taxes. In this same way, despite the fact that the maquiladora industry no longer employs children on a large scale, it continues to contribute to the problem of child labor in Honduras. Because of tax exemptions and other privileges enjoyed by export industries, thanks to neoliberal policies promoted by the World Bank, the IMF, and the U.S. Caribbean Basin Initiative, maquiladoras disproportionately contribute to the underfunding of the Honduran educational system, public infrastructure, and effective enforcement of labor laws, all of which in turn lead to higher rates of child labor.

References and Further Reading

Bacon, David. "The Human Price of a T-shirt." August 13, 1995. http://dbacon.igc.org/Latin%20America/1995humanprice.html.

Burdett, Mauricio Diaz, and Soren Kirk Jensen. "Honduras: Pushed to the Edge." Paper presented at the spring meetings of the IMF and the World Bank, Washington, DC, April 2004.

Casa Alianza. *Análisis mensual sobre problemáticas de la niñez hondureña.* Tegucigalpa: Casa Alianza, 2006.

Hammill, Matthew, and Economic Commission for Latin America and the Caribbean (CEPAL). *Income Inequality in Central America, Dominican Republic and Mexico: Assessing the Importance of Individuals and Household Characteristics.* México: CEPAL, 2005.

Honduras, Government of. "Código de la niñez y la adolescencia: decreto no. 73–96." *Diario ofical la gaceta,* no. 28,053, September 5, 1996.

ILO-IPEC. *Plan de acción nacional para la erradicación gradual y progresiva del trabajo infantil en Honduras: fase 1 2001–2006 erradicación de las peores formas de trabajo infantil.* Honduras: ILO-IPEC, 2001.

ILO-IPEC. *An In-Depth Analysis of Child Labor and Poverty in Honduras.* San José, Costa Rica: ILO-IPEC, 2003.

Jahangir, Asma, and United Nations. *Civil and Political Rights, Including the Question of Disappearances and Summary Executions.* Ed. Commission on Human Rights, 27. New York: Economic and Social Council, UN, 2002.

Kennedy, Mirta, Suyapa Martínez, Ana María Ferrera, Filadelfo Martínez, and Centro de Estudios de la Mujer (CEM-H). "An Insecure and Corrupt Model." In *Social Watch Country by Country Report.* Montevideo, Uruguay: Third World Institute, 2004.

UN CRC. *Consideration of Reports Submitted by States Parties under Article 44 of the Convention: Concluding Observations: Honduras.* New York: United Nations Committee on the Rights of the Child, 2007.

U.S. Department of Labor. *The Apparel Industry and Codes of Conduct: A Solution to the International Child Labor Problem?* Washington, DC: Department of Labor, Bureau of International Labor Affairs, 1996.

U.S. Department of Labor. *Honduras: Incidence and Nature of Child Labor.* Washington, DC: Department of Labor, Bureau of International Labor Affairs, 2007. http://www.dol.gov/ilab/media/reports/iclp/tda2004/honduras.htm.

U.S. Department of State. "Honduras." In *Country Human Rights Reports.* Washington, DC: Department of State, 2006. http://www.state.gov/g/drl/rls/hrrpt/2006/78896.htm.

Mexico

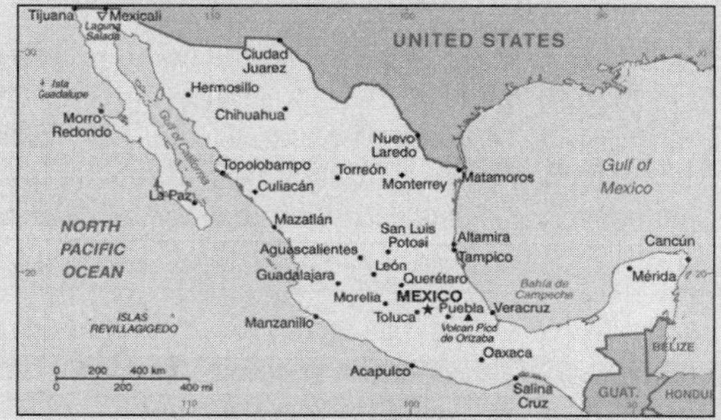

MEXICO			
	CRC	C 138	C 182
Ratifications	Y	N	Y
Human Development Index/Rank	0.821/53		
Human Capital			
Population Growth Rate	1.16%		
% Population 0–14	30.6%		
Total Fertility Rate	2.42		
Life Expectancy	75.41		
Infant Mortality Rate	20.26		
Literacy Rate	92.2%		
Economic			
GDP/Capita	$10,600		
GDP Growth %	4.5%		
% Poverty	40%		
Gini Index	54.6		
Labor Force Composition			
% Agriculture	18%		
% Industry	24%		
% Services	58%		

Table 1 MEXICAN CHILDREN AGE 12–14 ENGAGED IN ECONOMIC WORK, IN SCHOOLING, AND IN BOTH, BY GENDER (percent)

Year	1992	1994	1996	1998	2000	2002	2004	2005	2006
School—Total	81.79	82.06	83.83	84.8	88.85	88.85	91.17	90.81	92.4
School—Boys	83.93	83.95	86.89	87.1	88.71	90.05	91.59	92.13	91.97
School—Girls	79.65	80.15	80.76	82.5	88.97	87.64	90.74	89.48	92.83
Economic Work—Total	10.07	11.79	14.74	15.15	10.7	13.02	8.98	10.45	11.13
Economic Work—Boys	16.38	18.66	20.01	19.3	15.78	15.8	12.26	13.13	15.29
Economic Work—Girls	3.75	4.91	9.46	11	5.61	10.23	5.69	7.75	6.96
School but Not Economic Work—Total	78.4	76.51	75.78	75.25	81.82	80.76	85.29	83.69	84.38
School but Not Economic Work—Boys	78.42	75.08	76.07	74.8	78.14	79.95	83.5	82.87	81.05
School but Not Economic Work—Girls	78.38	77.93	75.49	75.7	85.49	81.56	87.08	84.51	87.71
Economic Work Only—Total	6.68	6.24	6.69	5.6	3.67	4.93	3.1	3.33	3.11
Economic Work Only—Boys	10.87	9.79	9.19	7	5.21	5.7	4.17	3.87	4.37
Economic Work Only—Girls	2.48	2.69	4.19	4.2	2.13	4.15	2.03	2.78	1.84
Combine Economic Work and School—Total	3.39	5.55	8.05	9.55	7.03	8.09	5.88	7.12	8.02
Combine Economic Work and School—Boys	5.51	8.87	10.82	12.3	10.57	10.1	8.09	9.26	10.92
Combine Economic Work and School—Girls	1.27	2.22	5.27	6.8	3.48	6.08	3.66	4.97	5.12
Neither Work nor School—Total	11.54	11.71	9.49	9.55	7.5	6.23	5.75	5.87	4.49
Neither Work nor School—Boys	5.2	6.25	3.92	5.8	6.09	4.24	4.25	4	3.66
Neither Work nor School—Girls	17.87	17.16	15.05	13.3	8.9	8.21	7.24	7.73	5.32

Source: Authors' estimations based on data from the Encuesta Nacional de Ingresos y Gastos de los Hogares (Mexico City: Instituto Nacional de Estadística y Geografía (INEGI), 1992–2006).

Child Labor in Mexico

Maja Pleic, Mexican Health Foundation and University of Toronto;
Felicia Marie Knaul, Senior Economist, Mexican Health Foundation; and
Albert Berry, Professor Emeritus, Department of Economics, University of Toronto

Article 123 of the Mexican constitution prohibits the work of individuals under the age of fourteen, and work exceeding six hours per day for individuals between fourteen and sixteen. Mexico has committed itself to the struggle against child labor by signing ILO Convention 182 on elimination of the "worst forms" of child labor. Notwithstanding these legal efforts, child labor is still common in Mexico, particularly among the poorest and most vulnerable populations.

The term "child labor" is a blanket phrase covering a wide spectrum of activities in which children find themselves, and an equally wide range of associated risks and benefits. On one hand, a fourteen-year-old boy working ten hours a week as a grocery packer earning money for lunch can gain positive work experience, build social capital, and perhaps even be encouraged to stay in school. On the other hand, a twelve-year-old girl working more than forty hours a week taking care of younger siblings and doing household chores would not even show up in most child labor statistics. Yet her investment in the household, while benefiting the family in the short run, is putting her at high risk of dropping out of school and handicapping her future earning potential in the long run.

The seriousness of child labor as a social problem depends on the age of the child, the type of work, the number of hours worked, and the conditions of work. It is also necessary to take into account the effects of work on the child's schooling and physical, mental, and social development. Based on these criteria, a spectrum of child labor emerges with such extreme forms as prostitution and work with heavy machinery at one end, and less damaging (if damaging at all) forms such as helping on the family farm after school at the other end. The most vulnerable groups in Mexico are domestic workers outside their own homes, children of agricultural day laborers (*jornaleros*), and the indigenous. Each of these groups has a higher than average incidence of child labor and also works under more severe conditions for lower pay. Children in these groups are also at greater than average risk for dropping out of school.

Causes of Child Labor

As is true almost everywhere, child labor in Mexico is almost exclusively a phenomenon of poorer income groups. The majority of working children do so because the family needs the additional income, or does not have enough income to hire salaried help (DIF et al. 2004). The Instituto Nacional de Estadistica, Geografia e Informatica (INEGI) has reported that 22 percent of working children cited the former reason and 51 percent the latter (INEGI 2004).

Several other determinants of the incidence of child labor stand out. Children living with a more educated household head are less likely to work and more likely to attend school; they are also less likely to mix school and work (INEGI 2004; Knaul 2001; Levison et al. 2001). Having a mother present in the house also has a positive relationship with children staying in school and out of the workforce. With the mother outside of the home, both boys and girls act as substitutes for the mother's work inside the home, though the effect is more pronounced for girls (Levison et al. 2001). The likelihood of a child working increases with family size (INEGI 2000). Also, the presence of a very young child (age zero to nine years) creates more work in the household and decreases the likelihood that older children will specialize in schooling or that they will not work (Levison et al. 2001). As might be expected, child labor is more likely in indigenous than in nonindigenous households, and indigenous children have a higher workforce participation rate than the national average.

Levels, Types of Work, and Trends by Age and Gender

As of 2002 in Mexico, there were 1.5 million children between the ages of six and fourteen engaged in economic activity, defined as work for at least an hour a week in the labor market, with or without pay (INEGI 2004). This is a labor force participation rate of 7.1 percent (10.0 percent for boys and 4.1 percent for girls). But these rates reflect only "economic activity" and thus miss a large and hidden population of children, mostly girls, who work in their homes as domestic workers. Using a more inclusive definition, which incorporates domestic work of fifteen hours per week or more, INEGI finds that the prevalence of child labor more than doubles to 3.3 million children. This reveals a much higher child labor participation rate of 15.7 percent (16.0 percent for girls and 15.4 percent for boys). In this essay, we use "child labor" to refer to the broad definition, which includes domestic work, and refer to the narrow definition as "economic work."

Trends in Child Labor

INEGI's figures suggest that child labor (broad definition) has decreased from 3.6 million child workers in 1995 to 3.3 million in 2002, though the descent has not been a smooth one. Our own analyses of economic work for children age twelve to fourteen (narrow definition) suggests a less marked decline, with the participation rate for boys falling from 16.39 percent in 1992 to 15.29 percent in 2006, while that for girls actually increased from 3.75 in 1992 to 6.97 percent in 2006 (see Table 1 and Figures 1a and 1b). A sharp spike in female economic work in 1996, most likely a result of the macroeconomic crisis in late 1994, which had a negative impact on household incomes, almost doubled girls' participation from 4.91 percent in 1994 to 9.46 percent in 1996. The boys' participation rate shows a much smaller increase, from 18.66 percent to 20 percent, suggesting that the pressure on families to find other sources of income pushed girls into the labor force more often than boys. For both genders the period 1992–96 saw sharp increases in the share that combined work with school. Over the period 1992–2006, the share working

Figures 1a and 1b. Mexican Children Age 12–14 Engaged in Economic Work, in Schooling, and in Both, by Gender (percent)

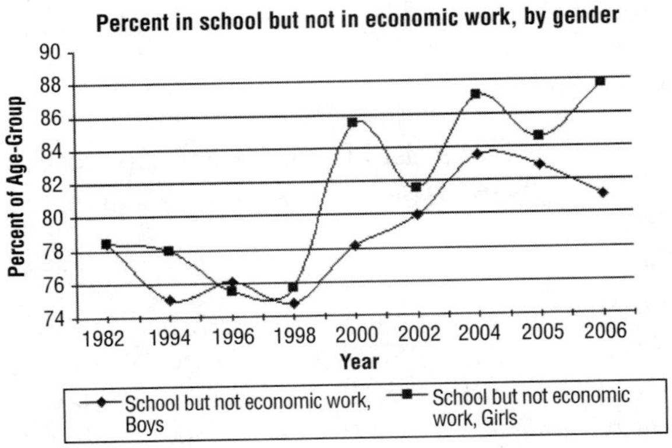

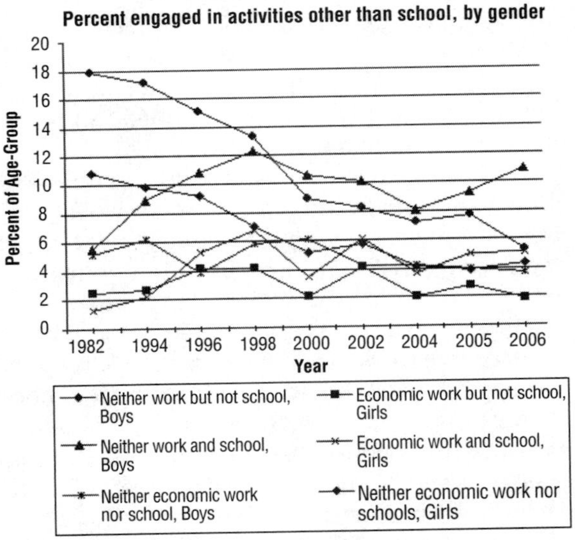

Source: Authors' estimations based on data from the Encuesta Nacional de Ingresos y Gastos de los Hogares (Mexico City: Instituto Nacional de Estadística y Geografía, 1992–2006).

showed no net change (at around 15 percent), but there was a significant substitution of about 5 percent away from work only to combining work and school. The chronology was similar for girls, with a significant decline in those only working after 1996, and no significant change in those combining work and school. The period as a whole, though, saw a net increase in children working. Regarding school attendance, there was a drop over 1992–96 for both genders in the share attending school without working, then a subsequent increase, much more marked for girls (75.5 percent to 87.7 percent in 2006). The share combining school and work rose sharply during the macroeconomic crisis around 1994, causing the share going to school to rise throughout, for boys from about 84 percent in 1992 to about 92 percent in 2006, and for girls from 79.5 percent to about 93 percent. This rapid rise in schooling of girls reflected a dramatic drop in the share of girls neither in school nor engaged in economic work (17.9 percent to 5.3 percent). Since these data do not include domestic work, this may reflect that, over time, girls have been less engaged in the types of domestic work that prevent their going to school (Levison et al. 2001).

Composition of Child Labor

A large share (48.2 percent) of child economic work in Mexico takes place in agriculture and fishing, where children usually work alongside their families. Other major categories include manual production workers or their assistants (20.5 percent), salespeople (14.2 percent), service workers (11.0 percent), and domestic workers outside of the home (4.3 percent) (INEGI 2004). The composition of activities varies by gender. Boys are much more likely to work in fishing and agriculture (56.8 percent vs. 26.8 percent for girls), while more girls are in sales (35.8 percent vs. 14.3 percent for boys) and domestic work outside of the home (12.9 percent vs. 0.9 percent for boys). The frequency of work increases with age. Of all working children under age fifteen, 8.7 percent are between the ages of six and eight, 23.9 percent are between the ages of nine and eleven, and 67.4 percent are between the ages of twelve and fourteen (INEGI 2000).

Domestic Work

Though often accepted as a less problematic form of child labor, or simply as socially acceptable household chores, recent studies suggest that domestic work is especially incompatible with school attendance (Knaul 1995, 2001; Levison et al. 2001) In 2002, there were 1.8 million children working more than fifteen hours per week in their own homes, and 77,744 working in the homes of others (INEGI 2004). While child economic work has been on the decline, domestic work has proven much more resistant to change. Perhaps due to its hidden nature, social acceptance, and the difficulty of policy targeting, child domestic work has decreased only modestly in absolute terms since 1995 (INEGI 2004). As a result, the share of all child workers so engaged rose from 43 percent in that year to 54 percent in 2002.

Of all children involved in economic work, 71.6 percent are boys and 28.4 percent are girls. In contrast, of all domestic workers, 67.9 percent are girls while 32.1 percent are boys (INEGI 2004). As a consequence, excluding such work from consideration not only leads to seriously underestimating the real prevalence of child labor, but also gender biases the results. With domestic labor included, the apparent gender gap in child labor disappears, with about half of child workers being female (INEGI 2004).

A particularly vulnerable, but largely unrecognized subgroup of domestic workers are those who work in the homes of third parties. Data for 1999 suggest that 84,969 children (or 4.3 percent) in economic work were domestic workers outside the home. However, there is reason to believe that this number is an underestimate. Often this arrangement reflects the fact that families cannot afford to take care of their children themselves; many children working in these circumstances receive no remuneration beyond food and board. This group is especially susceptible to maltreatment, physical abuse, or sexual abuse, as well as being at extremely high risk of dropping out of school.

Indigenous Population at Risk

The indigenous people of Mexico, as in the Latin American region as a whole, suffer a high incidence of poverty. With more than 12 million people and about 13 percent of the total population, Mexico has the largest indigenous population in Latin America (Bando et al. 2004). Indigenous children are a group at particular risk. They are more likely to work than other children; in 1997, the last year for which data are available, their labor force participation rate, at 35.9 percent, was almost double the national rate (INEGI 1997). They also tend to start working at a younger age. Almost a quarter of indigenous children age six to eleven were already working. They also work longer hours, for lower pay, and in more difficult situations. Indigenous families, in particular, use their children as substitutes for hired help in agriculture and fishing; 79.2 percent of indigenous child laborers said they worked because the family did not have money to contract workers. As a result, the vast majority of these children (93.1 percent) receive no remuneration for their work (INEGI 1997). An especially hazardous form of child labor, predominantly found in the indigenous population, involves the children of *jornaleros* (day laborers).

Children of *Jornaleros*

Agricultural day laborers are a heterogeneous population in Mexico, comprised of low-income mestizos and indigenous, migrants and locals, and men, women, and children of all ages who work on large fruit and vegetable farms. About half are migrant laborers, mostly indigenous people from the poorer southern states who migrate seasonally to the farms of the northern states. Children often accompany their parents into the work as young as four or five years of age. They work under the same physically demanding conditions and long hours as their parents, often earning an equal wage (SEDESOL and UNICEF 2006). Malnutrition, illiteracy, and low school attendance characterize this population. The nature of their work and lifestyle makes it difficult to know exactly how many agricultural day laborers there are, how many migrate annually, and how many children are with them, but it is estimated that 374,000 children and youths between the ages of six and fourteen work as agricultural day laborers and that youths under age seventeen account for 27 percent of the agricultural workforce (Cos-Montiel 2001).

A survey of migrant agricultural workers in twenty-three regions of Mexico, conducted in 1998, found 128,081 migrant agricultural day laborers. Of these migrants, 28,651 were children between the ages of six and fourteen, of which 16,478 worked. In many cases children are paid the same as adults, as in tomato picking, where children's small hands are highly productive. Because there are often more children working than adults, they may become the principal income earners of the family. In 44 percent of the families studied, children brought in half or more of the family income. Often, even with the children working, the income earned is only enough to sustain the family on a day-to-day basis, and there is no possibility for savings (SEDESOL and UNICEF 2006).

Among seasonal migrant workers, 58 percent migrate with their families. Of these families, 27 percent come from Guerrero, 15 percent from Oaxaca, and 9 percent from Puebla (SEDESOL and UNICEF 2006). The principal destinations of these families are central and northern Sinaloa and the San Quintin Valley (Valle de San Quintin) in Baja, California. The children normally migrate with the family for lack of a place to leave them, though more often than not, the children also take part in the work. By the age of ten, 65.5 percent of migrant children work with their parents, and by the ages of thirteen and fourteen, nearly 90 percent are incorporated into the work. In Sinaloa, the principal location for migrant agricultural workers in Mexico, the numbers of child day laborers have decreased significantly, from 12,149 in 1998 to approximately 5,000 in 2005. Still, there is evidence of the cycle of poverty being passed on through generations in migrant families. In 46 percent of migrant families with child workers, the parents themselves began working as children between the ages of six and fourteen. Roughly 75 percent started migrating seasonally before the age of eighteen (SEDESOL and UNICEF 2006).

Urban Informal Child Labor

For many, the most visible form of child labor in Mexico is that of children and youths who work in the streets and public spaces of large cities and slums. Urban informal child workers are a diverse group whose work comprises activities of varying risks and benefits. Their work includes selling merchandise on streets and in markets; street entertainment; begging; services such as squeegeeing; and other types of informal work such as bagging in supermarkets for tips. The greatest concentration of urban child labor is found in Mexico City, where a survey found 14,322 urban informal workers under the age of eighteen in 1999 (GDF et al. 1999). A more recent survey of the 107 largest cities (excluding Mexico City) estimated there were 94,795 workers under the age of eighteen in 2002, a decline of 17.2 percent from a survey conducted in 1997 (DIF et al. 2004). The majority (65.2 percent) were boys; 37.2 percent were between fourteen and seventeen years old, a striking 52.1 percent were between six and thirteen years of age; and 10.7 percent were under age six. This youngest group is made up generally of children who accompany their parents to work, usually as street vendors or street entertainers. There is a misconception that parents who work on the streets take their young children with them to exploit the "pity factor"; however, surveys found that 70 percent of parents report not having anywhere to leave the child. The indigenous population is especially overrepresented in the under-six age-group. In Mexico City, although indigenous people represent only 1.3 percent of the population, 20 percent of child workers under age six are indigenous (GDF et al. 1999).

Urban child labor takes place not only within a family context but principally for the family. Contrary to popular belief, 92 percent of urban informal child workers live with at least one parent, 61 percent live with both, and only 2 percent live on the streets (DIF et al. 2002). With the exception of this latter group, the principal reason for working is to "help the family." Working children pay for necessities such as food and clothing, as well as personal goods that their parents may not be able to afford. Of urban youth workers, 27 percent reported giving all their earnings to the family, 60 percent said "some earnings" went to the family, and only 14 percent indicated that none did. In Mexico City, 30 percent work as baggers in supermarkets; 23 percent are street vendors; 10 percent work with the family in public markets; 4 percent are squeegee kids; and the remaining 14 percent engage in miscellaneous activities including washing and taking care of cars. Half of informal urban child laborers work only for tips, and only 14 percent are salaried workers. On average, these informal workers receive daily tips equivalent to twice the daily minimum wage. Packagers, who have the highest quality of life and education, receive on average 3.8 times the daily minimum wage. Most of these urban child workers also attend school (64 percent); 74 percent work five days or more per week, and the average work day is 6.3 hours (DIF et al. 2004).

A particularly hazardous and well-hidden form of child labor in Mexico is the commercial sexual exploitation of children, which includes the use of children in prostitution, sexual trafficking, pornography, and sex tourism. A recent study of the top six tourist cities estimates that there are 16,000 child sex workers in Mexico (Azaola 2000). However, the lack of information on this topic and its hidden nature means that the real number is likely to be much higher.

Education

One of child labor's worrisome impacts is on the educational attainment of children from lower-income families. This now constitutes one of the major sources of continuing income inequality in Mexico. Overall, considerable advances have occurred over time: Average years of schooling for adults over age fifteen has risen from 2.6 years in 1960 to 8.1 years in 2005, and the literacy rate for children eight to fourteen years of age increased from 66 percent to 96.6 percent in 2005 (INEGI 2005). But children in lower-income families lag well behind these averages, partly because poverty pushes many out of education and into the workforce. Children who work are less likely to stay in school than their nonworking peers. And the greater the household's need for additional income or for unpaid help at home, the less it invests in children's education (Bando et al. 2004; Knaul 2001). The older the child, the greater the contribution to family income, household production, and child care; thus, the opportunity cost of a child's going to school increases with age, heightening the incentive to drop out. While 8.7 percent of working children between the ages of six and eleven do not attend school, this rate rises to 33.7 percent for youths age twelve to fourteen (INEGI 2000).

Specific groups at particular risk of dropping out of school to specialize in work include domestic workers outside of the home, indigenous children, and children of day laborers (*jornaleros*). Of the 13.5 percent of female child workers between the ages of twelve and fourteen who perform domestic work outside their home, only 37.1 percent attend school, compared to the national average of 89.0 percent. Such low attendance likely reflects both the nature of the work and the circumstances that impel the child to undertake it. Not only is the work ill paid, but the nature of the work (cleaning, preparing meals, and child-care) is not easily compatible with regular school attendance. By the ages of fifteen to seventeen, only 5.3 percent of these domestic workers remain in school (INEGI 2002). Indigenous children who work are also more likely to be prevented from school attendance: 18.7 percent of indigenous children between the ages of nine and fourteen work, and only 60.6 percent of them also study (INEGI 2004). *Jornaleros,* mostly indigenous, are the group most at risk of not completing school. By following in their parents' footsteps, *jornaleros,* like many child workers, are risking future income and helping to perpetuate a cycle of poverty and child labor.

Though significant barriers to educational attainment remain, the continued improvement over 1992–2006 is reassuring. While the aggregate figures do not prove causation, the trends suggest that economic work has been a decreasing barrier to children's education and that combining it with schooling may have helped about 10 percent of boys and a somewhat smaller share of girls to continue in school.

PROGRESA/Oportunidades

Introduced in 1997, PROGRESA/Oportunidades is an important antipoverty program that pays families a monthly rate that increases with the child's age, to keep their children enrolled in school. There is evidence that the PROGRESA/Oportunidades program has improved the situation of indigenous children. A recent study found that the incidence of child labor in indigenous households fell by 8 percent between 1997 and 2000 after enrolment in the PROGRESA program. Further, the group specifically targeted by PROGRESA/Oportunidades showed a 25.5 percent decline after implementation of the program, and the program had a greater impact on indigenous children who did not speak Spanish than it did on bilingual or Spanish-speaking children. While indigenous children were more likely than others to work in 1997, in 1999, after involvement in the program, such children were less likely to work than nonindigenous children (Bando et al. 2004). The program also decreased the education gap between indigenous children and those who speak Spanish or are bilingual. Results show that boys are 15 to 25 percent less likely to participate in paid work after enrollment in the program. Similarly, researchers found girls to be 10 percent less likely to participate in domestic work (Parker and Skoufias 2000).

References and Further Reading

Azaola, Elena. *Infancia robada: niños y niñas victimas de explotacion sexual en Mexico.* Mexico: UNICEF, Sistema Nacional para el Desarrollo Integral de la Familia and Centro de Investigaciones y Estudios Superiores en Antropología Social, 2000.

Bando, Rosangela G., Luis F. Lopez-Calva, and Harry A. Patrinos. "Child Labour, School Attendance, and Indigenous Households: Evidence from Mexico." Working paper, Understanding Children's Work (UCW) Project, 2004.

Cos-Montiel, Francisco. "Sirviendo las mesas del mundo: las niñas y los niños jornaleros agricolas en Mexico." In *La infancia vulnerable en Mexico en un mundo globalizado,* ed. Norma del Rio Lugo. Mexico: UAM-UNICEF, 2001.

DIF, PNUFID, and UNICEF. *Estudio de niñas, niños y adolescentes trabajadores en 100 ciudades.* Mexico: Sistema Nacional para el Desarrollo Integral de la Familia, Programa de las Naciones Unidas para la Fiscalización Internacional de Drogas, and UNICEF, 2002.

DIF, PNUFID, and UNICEF. *Estudio en cien ciudades de niñas, niños, y adolescentes trabajadores: Mexico, 2002–2003.* Mexico: Sistema Nacional para el Desarrollo Integral de la Familia, Programa de las Naciones Unidas para la Fiscalización Internacional de Drogas, and UNICEF, 2004.

GDF, DIF-DF, and UNICEF. *Niños, niñas y jóvenes trabajadores en el distrito federal.* Mexico: Gobierno del Distrito Federal, Sistema Nacional para el Desarrollo Integral de la Familia Distrito Federal, and UNICEF, 1999.

INEGI. *Encuesta nacional de empleo en zonas indígenas, 1997.* Aguascalientes: Instituto Nacional de Estadìstica, Geografía e Informàtica, 1997.

INEGI. *Módulo de empleo infantil 1999.* Aguascalientes: Instituto Nacional de Estadística, Geografía e Informática, 2000.

INEGI. *Encuesta nacional de empleo 2001.* Aguascalientes: Instituto Nacional de Estadística, Geografía e Informática, 2002.

INEGI. *El trabajo infantil en México 1995–2002.* Auascalientes: Instituto Nacional de Estadística, Geografía e Informática, 2004.

INEGI. *Conteo de población y vivienda 2005.* Aguascalientes: Instituto Nacional de Estadìstica, Geografía e Informàtica, 2005.

Knaul, Felicia M. *Young Workers, Street Life and Gender: The Effect of Education and Work Experience on Earnings in Colombia.* PhD thesis, Harvard University, 1995.

Knaul, Felicia M. *The Impact of Child Labor and School Dropout on Human Capital: Gender Differences in Mexico.* Washington, DC: World Bank, 2001.

Levison Deborah, Karine S. Moe, and Felicia M. Knaul. "Youth Education and Work in Mexico." *World Development* 29:1 (2001): 167–88.

Parker Susan, and Emmanuel Skoufias. *The Impact of PROGRESA on Work, Leisure and Time Allocation.* Washington, DC: International Food Policy Research Institute, 2000.

PRONIM. *Evaluacion externa 2005.* Oaxaca de Juarez: Programa Educación Primaria para Niños y Ninas Migrantes, 2006.

Ramirez-Jordan, Marcela. "Situación de vulnerabilidad de las niñas y niños migrantes en Mexico." In *La infancia vulnerable de Mexico en un mundo globalizado,* ed. Norma del Rio Lugo. Mexico: AUM-UNICEF, 2000.

Robles Berlanga, F. "El trabajo infantil urbano informal en la ciudad de México." *Revista Mexicana del trabajo* 2 (2000): 116–18.

SEDESOL and PRONJAG. *Jornaleros agricolas.* Mexico: Secretaría de Desarrollo Social and Programa Nacional con Jornaleros Agricolas, 2001.

SEDESOL and UNICEF. *Diagnostico sobre la condicion de las niños y niñas migrantes internos, hijos de jornaleros agrícolas.* Mexico: Secretaría de Desarrollo Social and UNICEF, 2006.

Street Children in Mexico

Felipe Peralta, Associate Professor, School of Social Work, New Mexico State University

UNICEF estimates there are more than 100 million children who live and work on the streets in the developing world. Latin America is home to 40 million street children (Ferguson 2004). In Mexico, at least 1.5 million children live and work on the streets as part of the informal economy. Mexico City has more than 650,000 children, with no legal protection, working and living on the streets. The greatest increase in the number of street children in Mexico in the last two decades has been experienced in cities along the U.S.-Mexico border. Street children in such cities as Tijuana, Sonora, Nuevo Laredo, and Ciudad Juárez have become a major social problem for local authorities.

Street children are defined as minors who earn their living working on the streets, or as children who reside on the streets full- or part-time. Most research on this topic suggests that street-working children are more likely to come from impoverished families who reside in disadvantaged neighborhoods (Ferguson 2004). Thus, a street child is one who depends on the streets for part or total survival (Bárcena 1990). Mexico has more than 90 million residents, with 47 percent under the age of eighteen and 40 percent living in poverty.

Street Children in Mexico

Street children in Mexico share many similarities with their counterparts in other Latin American countries. They are disproportionately male, tend to come from poor homes, are on the street primarily to earn income, are more likely to be truant, come from large families, and report a history of physical abuse. In the last decade, there has been a significant increase in the number of girls living and working on the streets. Young females have migrated from the countryside to large urban centers looking for employment. There are already a significant number of young women who have given birth to children and started street families (Magazine 2003).

Economic conditions in Mexico have greatly increased the number of street children. In 1994, the value of the peso was reduced by almost 50 percent, which created an economic recession that adversely affected families. Two-thirds of working Mexicans earn between $3 and $6 a day. The majority of families need $18 a day to meet basic needs. According to a report by the Mexican Collective in Support of Children, 17 percent live in extreme poverty. Budget cuts at the level of city government, inspired by neoliberal political-economic reform, have eliminated most social programs for low-income families and street children (Magazine 2003).

Types of Street Children

A series of comprehensive studies of street children in two important urban centers in Mexico identified three distinct types of street children. Ciudad Juárez is located in the farthest northern region of the country, across the border from El Paso, Texas. This city has doubled its population in the last twenty years with migrants from all parts of the country attracted by the maquiladora industry (population 1.31 million as reported by the 2005 census). The other urban center studied is Mexico City, located in the central region of the country with a population of more than 20 million (2005 census). The three types of street children identified were the independent street workers, the family street workers, and the children of the street. These distinctions are very important because each category displays different types of work, different relations with parents, different relations to governmental authorities, and different needs.

Independent Street Workers

The independent street workers are the largest group, comprising more than 50 percent of the street children in Mexico. The majority of these children attend school on a regular basis. Most of them live with their parents and work to supplement the household income. The majority of the children work selling items in the streets such as candy, seeds (semillas), or toys. Major problems in this group are the significant reports of child abuse by their parents and arrests by local officials.

Family Street Workers

Children in the family-street-worker category make up more than 30 percent of the children working and living in the streets of Mexico. These children work in the streets with their parents, or they work with siblings and have daily contact with their parents. In this category, girls play a significant role. Most commonly, family workers sell food or candy to pedestrians. In most cases the parents prepared the food items at home for sale on the streets by their children. There are also a number of children who are musicians, dancers, and other street performers. In this group only a handful of children attend school. One major problem with this group is the long hours worked. Children worked after midnight on a regular basis.

Children of the Street

While this group represents less than 20 percent of street children, children of the street are extremely vulnerable because the streets have become more than a workplace. Most of these children have very little contact with their parents and sleep on the streets on a full-time basis. These children do not attend school, and there is significant involvement in youth gangs, substance abuse, and youth institutions. Most of them have been arrested and have major psychological problems. Much of their work involves illegal activities such as stealing and prostitution.

Under the best circumstances, life on the street is difficult and often perilous. Children in such circumstances receive little or no adult supervision or protection. They are exposed to the hazards of their physical and social environments, thereby facing the risks of being victimized by adults or other youngsters. Few perceive public officials as their protectors. Instead, children rely on other children and street adults for protection. This has resulted in violence against children. Half of the children interviewed reported a traumatic experience while working the streets. Most commonly they referred to being beaten, being mugged, and having their money and goods stolen. There is also a significant increase in sexual attacks on children throughout the country.

References and Further Reading

Bárcena, A. "Niños de la calle: Una nueva raza dulce de acero y de cristal." *Infancia* 3 (1990):1–3.

Ferguson, K. "Measuring and Indigenizing Social Capital in Relation to Children's Street Work in Mexico: The Role of Culture in Shaping Social Capital Indicators." *Journal of Sociology and Social Welfare* 31:4 (2004): 81–103.

Lusk, M.W. "Street Children Programs in Latin America." *Journal of Sociology and Social Welfare* 16 (1989): 55–77.

Lusk, M.W., F. Peralta, and G.W. Vest. "Street Children of Juarez: A Field Study." *International Social Work* 32:4 (1989): 289–302.

Magazine, Roger. "Action, Personhood and the Gift Economy Among So-Called Street Children in Mexico City." *Social Anthropology* 11:3 (2003): 303–18.

Peralta, Felipe. "Children of the Streets of Mexico." *Children and Youth Services Review* 14:3–4 (1992): 347–62.

Trussell, R. "The Children's Streets: An Ethnographic Study of Street Children in Ciudad Juárez, Mexico." *International Social Work* 42:2 (1999): 189–99.

PROGRESA/Oportunidades: Mexico's School Stipend Program

Abhra Roy, Kennesaw State University

One of the central policy issues plaguing developing countries is the incidence of child labor. A higher incidence of child labor often goes hand in hand with lower levels of educational attainment and thereby adversely affects human capital accumulation. As a result, governments and other international bodies have been in search of ways to reduce child labor. Among such endeavors, PROGRESA stands out because of its innovative structure and its effect on educational attainment and child labor.

To design policies to curb the incidence of child labor in an effective way, it is imperative to understand the major causes of child labor. One important factor highlighted in the literature that affects the incidence of child labor is poverty and lack of household assets. Basu and Van (1998) have shown that heads of households send their children to work, not because they prefer child work, but because of poverty. Once household income rises above a certain threshold, the same households stop sending their children to work. Further, if parents could borrow against the future earnings of their children, they could afford to send them to school to acquire the human capital necessary to earn high wages as adults. But poor parents typically lack this capacity to borrow.

In this sense, children act as an insurance mechanism by which households transfer income from the future to the present by having the children work. This precipitates low levels of human capital attainment among children and often adversely affects their health. Poor households are also subject to various adverse shocks such as droughts, floods, earthquakes, loss of employment for the head of household, and health shocks, all of which tend to increase child work. In this vein, by relying on conditional cash transfers, PROGRESA aims at mitigating the adverse effect of these income shocks and the lack of insurance and borrowing alternatives on household decisions regarding school enrollment and child labor.

The Structure of PROGRESA

PROGRESA was introduced in 1998 in rural localities of Mexico. The program targeted 506 communities in 10,000 villages that were deemed eligible based on selected criteria such as degree of poverty (measured by the "index of marginalization") and proximity to certain basic structures such as health centers and schools. Of the eligible communities, 186 were randomly selected to serve as a control group but were included in the program after two years. The program targeted three areas: education, health, and nutrition, of which education received the largest impetus.

The program provided cash transfers to mothers for keeping their children at school. The educational subsidy was paid to mothers bimonthly if their children attended school regularly. Subsidies started when children reached the third grade and continued until they reached the ninth grade. The amount of cash transfer increased with the level of education and was slightly higher for girls than for boys. In 1998, bimonthly school subsidies ranged from 130 pesos for children attending the third grade up to 420 pesos for boys and 480 pesos for girls attending the ninth grade. In 1999, the subsidies were increased to 160 pesos for children attending the third grade and 530 for boys and

610 for girls attending the ninth grade. In addition to the bimonthly subsidies, the household also received a lump-sum subsidy for buying school supplies.

The program also provided nutritional support to mothers who enrolled their children for growth and development checkups and also attended courses on hygiene, nutrition, and contraceptive use. The nutritional component was 190 pesos per month in 1998 and 250 pesos per month in 1999, which represented about 8–10 percent of household income.

The Effect of PROGRESA on Education and Child Labor

PROGRESA's most important contribution has been to increase school enrollment, attendance, and educational attainment among children in rural households. Keeping the causes of child labor and the structure of the program in mind, it is worthwhile to note the effectiveness of the program. The lump-sum payment and health benefits create incentives for household to enroll children in school by raising the opportunity cost of not enrolling. Attanasio, Meghir, and Santiago (2005) reported that school enrollment increased on average by 3 percent after program implementation among boys between six and seventeen years of age, the effect being much greater for older boys.

The bimonthly stipend paid to households for regular attendance creates incentives for parents to keep children in school. As a result, school attendance rose on average about 1–7 percent after PROGRESA was implemented. The effect on attendance rates has been particularly pronounced in the older cohorts. Nonattendance decreases about 1 percentage point for children age eight years to about 7 percent for children age fourteen years or older. Further, school dropout rates fell substantially because of monetary benefits the family received by keeping children in school. Finally, cash transfers contingent on satisfactory progress to the next grade level (after two tries) have substantially improved educational attainment in children, measured in terms of progression to the next grade.

It is interesting to note, however, that although the program has made substantial improvements in terms of school attendance, reduced dropout rates, and progression through grades, its impact on child labor has been modest. De Janvry, Finan, Sadoulet, and Vakis (2006) suggested that this may be because schooling and child work are not incompatible with each other, especially when school days are short. It is also noteworthy that a large percentage of children remain out of school and yet do not work. The percentage of children neither in school nor working ranges is about 11 percent for eight-year-olds and about 30 percent for fifteen-year-olds. Roy (2006) explained why one may observe education subsidies to have little or no impact on the incidence of child labor, while they unambiguously improve educational attainment. He showed that the fixed and variable components of the subsidy have opposite effects on child labor, which could result in a negligible net effect.

The program may also suffer from selection bias. At the outset, PROGRESA selected households based on certain criteria such as proximity of schools and health centers and the index of marginalization. It may be argued that households in such areas are not among the poorest, and therefore their subjective notion about education may be quite different from that of even poorer families. As a result, these families may be more responsive to changes in education policies.

Conclusion

Despite some drawbacks, PROGRESA has been very effective in increasing educational attainment among the rural poor in Mexico. The conditional cash transfers have acted as a safety net for educational attainment for children who would have dropped out of school otherwise. This helps current and future generations avoid the long-term consequences of lack of education on human capital accumulation. It has also been successful, at least in some degree, in preventing the use of children as a risk-coping instrument by increasing the opportunity cost of not attending school.

References and Further Reading

Attanasio, O., C. Meghir, and A. Santiago. "Education Choices in Mexico: Using a Structural Model and a Randomized Experiment to Evaluate Progresa." Economics Working Paper EWP0501, Institute for Fiscal Studies, London, 2006.

Basu, K., and P.H. Van. "The Economics of Child Labor." *American Economic Review* 88 (1988): 412–27.

De Janvry, A., F. Finan, E. Sadoulet, and R. Vakis. "Can Conditional Cash Transfers Serve as Safety Nets in Keeping Children at School and from Working When Exposed to Shocks?" *Journal of Development Economics* 79:2 (2005): 349–73.

Ranjan, P. "Credit Constraint and the Phenomenon of Child Labor." *Journal of Development Economics* 64 (2001): 81–102.

Roy, A. "Educational Attainment and Child Labor: Do Subsidies Work?" Working paper, Kennesaw State University, 2006.

Impact of Temporary Labor Migration on Schooling Among Mexican Children

Grace Kao, Director, Asian American Studies Program, Associate Professor of Sociology, Department of Sociology and Population Studies Center, University of Pennsylvania

Temporary labor migration is one of the primary means through which residents in poor countries generate cash income. Remitted earnings help migrant households purchase capital goods such as houses, land, vehicles, appliances, and so forth, which in turn raise their standard of living and provide them with some socioeconomic mobility (Massey et al. 1987). This is true of almost all international (and domestic) labor migrants and helps to justify their long absences from home. It is certainly the case for Mexicans, for whom, in some communities, migration to the United States is almost a way of life.

One of adult migrants' primary motivations is to provide their children with a higher standard of living and better socioeconomic opportunities. But the likely impact of temporary labor migration on children's educational and work outcomes is not obvious. On the one hand, parents' labor migration has significant psychological costs for youths and can be stressful for all family members. Children may suffer from lack of parental supervision. Moreover, children may have to assume more adult responsibilities in the home, which can compete with academic concerns. Finally, if children believe that labor migration can offer better economic opportunities than staying in school, they may aspire to become migrants rather than invest in education. This may be especially true in countries where the actual return for education is less than the return for international labor migration. For the vast majority of Mexicans who migrate to the United States, their placement in unskilled occupations is not dependent on their years of schooling. Agricultural workers are not rewarded for educational experience. If these jobs are the only ones that Mexican youths believe are available, it becomes irrational for youths who hope to migrate to the United States to stay in school.

On the other hand, cash income from temporary labor migration by family members and youths can provide the means to pay for school fees and to offer the household in Mexico a higher standard of living. It may also help to lessen the odds that children have to work outside of the household (Kandel and Kao 1999).

Empirical Study

My colleague William Kandel and I investigated the link between temporary labor migration and schooling by surveying 7,620 students in grades 6 through 12 in schools in the western Mexican state of Zacatecas during the 1995–96 academic year (Kandel and Kao 1999, 2001). It is important to note that these data were collected just after a devaluation of the peso that led to a Mexican financial crisis. Zacatecas has a population of approximately 1.4 million, and has historically served as a primary source of migrants to the United States relative to other Mexican states (Durand et al. 1999). Specifically, the sites focused on were Zacatecas, the state capital, and Jerez. The former is the largest city in the state, while the latter serves as a commercial center to its surrounding rural areas. The areas sampled lie in a part of the state that offers important educational and employment opportunities. Thus, residents witness firsthand the options of local employment, which requires educational investments, as opposed to migration to the United States.

The survey included detailed measures of the migration histories of students' families. In addition, information about the time students spent on studying, part-time work, and domestic chores was collected, along with data on how students felt about any extended absence of their fathers. We focused on children's academic performance in school, their educational aspirations, and their aspirations to migrate to the United States.

Our analyses suggest that family migration history was positively associated with aspirations to migrate to the United States. In other words, the more that youths are surrounded by frequent migrant trips, the more likely youths hope to migrate themselves at a later date. In addition, family migration history was negatively associated with aspirations to attend university. It is clear that aspirations to migrate to the United States make college aspirations somewhat irrational. If other adults migrate to the United States to perform low-skilled jobs, then there is no reason for youths to increase their educational attainment.

However, family migration history was positively associated with current grades at school. Migration increases the wealth of the family and makes it less likely for youths to have to work—hence they are better equipped to achieve in school. In contrast, children who had themselves migrated on a tourist visa had higher educational aspirations. Long-term migration of youths had no effect on their academic achievement.

Overall, family migration seems to have mixed consequences for children's academic performance. Migration offers an attractive alternative to higher education but makes it possible for children to earn higher grades in school. In other words, children may be more likely to persist in school and remain out of the workforce; hence, in the short term, family migration positively affects educational attainment, but in the long term, it hurts educational aspirations.

References and Further Reading

Durand, Jorge, Douglas S. Massey, and Fernando Charvet. "The Changing Geography of Mexican Immigration to the United States: 1910–1996." *Social Science Quarterly* 81:1 (2000): 1–15.

Kandel, William, and Grace Kao. "Shifting Orientations: How U.S. Labor Migration Affects Children's Aspirations in Mexican Migrant Communities." *Social Science Quarterly* 81:1 (2000): 16–32.

Kandel, William, and Grace Kao. "The Impact of Temporary Labor Migration on Mexican Students' Academic Aspirations and Performance." *International Migration Review* 35:3 (2001), 1205–31.

Massey, Douglas, Rafael Alarcón, Jorge Durand, and Humberto González. *Return to Aztlan.* Berkeley: University of California, 1987.

History of Child Labor in Mexico

Marcos T. Aguila, Universidad Autónoma Metropolitana, Xochimilco; and
Mariano E. Torres B., Benemérita Universidad Autónoma de Puebla

The history of Mexico can be divided into several periods, including the pre-Columbian period; the period of the viceroys up to the time of the Porfiriato; the Porfiriato itself, which refers to the presidency of General Porfirio Díaz, who remained the central figure in power from 1876 to 1910; the Mexican Revolution and its consequences; and finally the crisis linked to the opening of the economy and the signing of the North American Free Trade Agreement in 1994.

The idea of identifying child labor as a particular form of work performed by children is relatively modern. In Mexico, jurisdictional acknowledgment and efforts to protect the work of minors go back only to the second decade of the twentieth century as a result of the deep social revolution of 1910–20, which was derived from the abuses that characterized economic modernization during the Porfiriato.

Yet, much earlier, during the late Classic period of civilizations that occupied the Mesoamerican region (fourteenth and fifteenth centuries), children's participation in the division of family work was simply an aspect of the social reproduction of groups, castes, and social classes. Children were considered young adults, not only in the old period before the arrival of the Spaniards in America, but also during the period of the viceroys (*virreinato*). The family lifestyle of the original occupants of what is now Mexico was tough. Bound by agricultural production and the obligatory payment of dues, children contributed to household tasks, participated in construction of public buildings, and produced food, clothes, and handcrafts. The division of work operated in accordance with their physical capacity. Neither school nor play occupied any considerable role in the lives of children except in the case of the offspring of higher classes belonging to the Teotihuacán, Mexica, and Mayan imperial families. For them, the ecclesiastical and military hierarchy focused on religious and artistic education and physical exercise for combat.

The viceroyalty of New Spain, which emerged after the fall of Mexico-Tenochtitlán, was established based on the institutions and power structures of the Castilian monarchy. After the Spanish conquest, imported Spanish customs did not modify the obligation of children of the poorer classes to work, and possibly intensified it, especially with respect to the exploitation of mining concerns, or *reales de minas,* where the Spaniards concentrated their major efforts on the production of silver.

After complaints made by Fray Bartolomé de las Casas regarding the inhumane treatment of the indigenous people by the Spaniards, "new laws" were promulgated in 1543. A new rule of law and system of segregation was established, named the República de Indios and the República de Españoles. The system required the indigenous peoples to work as tributary subjects to the king of Castilla under a legal and fiscal scheme different from that applied to Spaniards. Under this system, male subjects were obliged to pay a tribute to the king as of their fourteenth year. Thus, from that young age they had to work in order to earn enough to pay tribute to the crown.

That was the legal beginning of the separation of the servant (*mozo*) from the landowner and tax payer (*tributario*), which also spelled the beginning of Spanish dominion over the old Mexica Empire. But the legal age for males to work meant nothing to those working without pay. These young servants worked in the fields as shepherds, carrying objects from the house to the fields and back, collecting fuel or wild fruits, and participating in the preparation of land for planting and harvesting crops. In urban labor, children contributed as helpers in various construction projects. Little girls had specific tasks within the family economy too. One of their more frequent functions was to work as babysitters for their younger brothers and sisters. These girls were known as *pilmama* or *chichihua*. They also had to work in other domestic tasks such as food preparation. Beginning approximately at the age of seven, children were the typical petty helpers or *mandaderos*.

According to the Catholic Church at the time, the age of majority for boys was fourteen and for girls twelve. This meant from that age they could marry and form an independent household, and assume responsibilities for earning a livelihood. During the viceroyalty, indigenous families lived in nuclear households. Once married, the new couple established their own home, even if it was near parents or other family members. The Spaniards and mestizos lived in extended families of up to three generations, along with perhaps some godchildren or other guests. Some households headed by those with greater financial wherewithal, such as artisans, often took in children known as godchildren (*ahijados* or *arrimados*) so they could be educated. In return, the children had an obligation to do domestic chores in the owner's house.

The types of work performed by children depended on the local economy. In areas with silver mines, silver being the principal export from New Spain, many tasks were available for children. Mining was heavy work. Extraction of minerals was done by cutting the rock with round iron bars. This was the job of the *barretero*, who always had a servant of ten to twelve years old to hold the lamp, collect the loose stones, or take the iron bar to be sharpened. Another child, called the *cuñero*, broke smaller pieces of rock with wooden planks to get to the silver. There was also a need for child servants to carry the multiple instruments and collect the obtained mineral.

In cities such as Querétaro, Puebla, and Mexico, there were a variety of artisan workshops where child servants worked as helpers, assistants to the artisan, and apprentices, from the age of seven years. There are no specific data on the number of children in specific jobs in this period, but their importance is recognized by indirect references. For example, in 1788, in a census of the city of Mexico, there were 1,806 child apprentices, who represented 18 percent of the almost 10,000 listed workers.

The royal regulations (*ordenanzas*) prohibited mulattos and indigenous peoples from becoming artisans, but never dispensed of their services as apprentices. Overseers and supervisors provided food rations but established limits on salaries, always below those of white or criollo personnel. In 1579, a regulation specified that every indigenous person should receive "18 tortillas, fourteen tamales and meat two or three times a week and on other days and during lent, beans, *chiles*, and habas." Because the regulation required that the indigenes receive "the necessary maintenance," obligatory rations of food were established three times daily and a fine of fifty pesos was levied if this was not fulfilled. Later, in 1769, another proclamation, signed by José de Gálvez, indicated the diverse means of paying workers in accordance with occupation. To the miners working with iron bars or similar labor, payment would be seven pesos a month, and "every week they would receive two bags of corn, a half quarter of fresh meat or a quarter of jerked beef whether they were married or single." The muleteers and minors would be paid five pesos in coins, but "if they were Indians less than 18 years old . . . they would enjoy similar rations but only four pesos in coins." Racial, gender, and age discrimination was constant in the viceroyalty period.

The Nineteenth Century

During the nineteenth century, besides an overwhelming presence in rural areas, another sphere of importance for child labor was artisan work in the cities, where thousands of little boys and girls worked as apprentices. According to an "industrial" census in Mexico City in 1879, of all those employed in factories and workshops, 28 percent were women, 13 percent children, and 59 percent men. Children might enter factories and workshops as early as age twelve for boys and thirteen for girls, but usually only adolescents were listed officially as having an occupation. In rural towns and villages, many children worked in artisan workshops, small factories, or home-based production. In Jiquipan, a town in the state of Michoacán in the west of Mexico, testimonies were obtained regarding the daily life of artisan families. A certain Samuel Santillán, born in 1919, remembered how, as a member of a family dedicated to the weaving of shawls, "[w]e learned there with my dad, we were born, as they say, 'in wool' underneath the looms." In the same town, Viviana Novoa, a contemporary of his, reported that since she was eight years old she "sewed shawls" (*rebozos*) and passed some on to her sister of six. Other girls worked directly in the workshops and worked twelve-hour shifts from six in the morning.

In the early textile factories, since 1870, single adolescent girls worked in weaving, and young boys and girls were utilized in maintenance and cleaning of tools and machines, workshops, and living quarters. An investigation of the principal textile factories in the capital city found that the percentage of working children was between 10 and 14 percent. In the Miraflores factory, for example, there were 60 children, 80 women, and 290 men. This workforce composition could change depending on the branch of manufacturing and services, but the presence of children was constant. Thus, after a detailed study of official sources from Mexico City, Thompson (1992) concluded that, "[g]enerally speaking, the majority of the households during the 1880s were composed of roughly equal ratios of wage and market incomes provided by men, women and children." The prevalence of extremely low wages during the Porfirian ancien régime required an increased number of income providers in poor households.

Mining was a special case. The techniques in mining changed very little between the period of the viceroys and the beginning of the nineteenth century, when the first Mexican republic was established. Engineer Pedro Castera (1987) described child labor in the mines at the end of the century: "They are called *morrongos* in the mines, those boys who enter the town or workers' gatherings, and those who also work in less tiring jobs, for example, leading the way illuminating the streets for the bosses, guiding the work and the day-laborers, bringing and taking candles, irons, water, etc. etc.; they are expedient, light, vivacious, bold and arrogant." In spite of the fact that mechanical winches existed, and the refining had evolved from amalgamation to the use of cyanide, child labor continued to be widespread. Their work was not considered tiring and dangerous: "They know the mine like their house with all the exits and entrances, canyons and wells, galleries, rests, hiding places and mounts of rubble. If the light goes off, they work in the dark, by touch." These tiny workers earned the respect of the other workers in the mines and, in certain situations, they were not looked upon as children: "If a woman is hit by one of the iron workers, the child defends her, he shouts at the worker, insults him and looks for someone else to help him defend her; sometimes they fight among themselves; *I learn to become a man,* they answer when asked why they fight. They are annoyed when they are called toys or children. *I am small but strong* is the reply." Still, their conditions of life were often brutal. Many were orphans and most were providing for other family members. Such was their career: "They are *morrongos* up until the age of twelve, young day-laborers up to the age of fifteen, workers and miners later on, and bosses in their old age." But many did not make it to old age. Castera concluded: "It's not necessary to state that three quarters of these youths fall ill to anemia, to the excess of work before reaching the age of twenty. When one of them dies the others smile and murmur: Better off, now he won't get so tired, he is with *Tata* God" (Castera 1987).[1]

During the time of the Porfiriato, there was a surge in the mining of other industrial products, such as copper and coal, which were added to the production of precious metals extracted from the old *reales de minas.* The new mining industry received important foreign investments and combined antiquated methods of work based on the intensification of physical labor with new modern machinery and more efficient techniques of extraction, refining, and commercialization. Child labor in the mines diminished but did not disappear entirely, hidden under the disguise of helpers.

Regulations dating from 1912 indicated, "It is forbidden to hire children under twelve in the subterranean and open sky mines. Those individuals of ages 12 to 18 will be assigned jobs in proportion with their strength." However, companies operating in regions distant from urban centers never took these dispositions seriously. In the Real del Monte and Pachuca Company, for example, a policy in 1926 admitted to accepting, as helpers, workers "from the age of 16," but indicated a preference for those "having been employed previously" and who had not been dismissed for disciplinary reasons.

The Mexican Revolution and Beyond

The Mexican Revolution limited the excesses of the Porfiriato. Between 1910 and 1920, Mexico went through one of the most profound social revolutions of the twentieth century. The basic component of the armed uprising was agrarian, as suggested by the slogan "Land and Freedom." Nevertheless, the revolution also had an important urban and industrial component, especially in the resistance of textile workers to the authoritarian policies of businessmen toward the end of the Porfiriato and the first two decades of the twentieth century. The Mexican Revolution represented a reaction to the abuses of a runaway capitalist system that had created the first great wave of industrialization. Hence, Mexico experienced not only an agrarian revolution that questioned the extensive concentration of landownership (*latifundio*) but also a parallel revolution disputing for control over the processes of industrial work at the workshop level. Workers demanded not only better labor conditions and more pay, but also a direct involvement in hiring and firing as well as the elimination of bad treatment by overseers. Abolition of child labor was simply an addendum to this atmosphere of insubordination.

As early as July of 1906, in its manifesto, the Mexican Liberal Party, led by Ricardo and Enrique Flores Magón, had set among their goals the limitation of the working day to eight hours, the establishment of a minimum wage according to the regions of the country, and "the absolute prohibition of the employment of minors less than fourteen years old." The legal process against child labor began with the elaboration of military decrees of revolutionary factions in some states of the republic such as Veracruz, which later contributed to the approval of the progressive political constitution of 1917, and the first federal labor law, promulgated in 1931.

Shortly after the revolution was consolidated, a new challenge confronted the postrevolutionary leaders in the form of the Great Depression of 1929. The Depression delayed the implementation of the revolutionary legislation but in the end opened the door to the radicalization of the Nationalist president Lázaro Cárdenas. Utilizing the existing pressure from below, Cárdenas set up ambitious plans of social reform, especially in the areas of education and union organization, and he extended community land (*ejidal*) ownership, expropriated oil interests, and, above all, put an end to the worst abuses of industrial authoritarianism. Not only did this reduce the liberal excesses of the Porfirian ancien régime; it also brought about a reduction of the presence of both women and children in the labor market. Expectations of better standards of living were created among the popular classes. The basic family structure of the Porfirian period was modified by and partially substituted with "the new proletarian household" accompanied by a "proletarian domesticity" (Thompson 1992). In the 1880s, households were rather small, averaging 3.6 members. By the 1930s, the average household size in Mexico City had grown to 5.2 members. After real wages began to rise during the post–World War II boom, wage earners could support far more unpaid household members than during the ancien régime. As a result, fewer children and mothers were forced to work. At the same time, efforts in the field of primary education began to yield fruit. More children were attending school rather than working, at least in the urban areas.

Sustained economic and social progress continued through the period of "stabilizing development" (roughly the 1950s through the 1970s), which some optimistic contemporaries called the "Mexican Miracle." This is not to say that Mexico eliminated child labor, however. It is important to note that child labor remained prominent in the rural areas, and especially with respect to the internal and external migratory phenomenon involving migrant day laborers (*jornaleros*), who harvested diverse crops such as strawberries, tomatoes, oranges, chiles, and cotton in areas of northern Mexico and the southern United States.

Mexico's economy began encountering difficulties with the crisis of Latin American foreign debt in the 1980s, with its subsequent high inflation, and continuing through the signing of the North American Free Trade Agreement in the middle of the 1990s. Economic liberalization brought about a structural fall in the standards of living of the poorer population, forcing families to incorporate more of their members into the struggle to obtain income. More children began to leave school earlier to work. Child labor, already common in the rural areas, also emerged in the informal sectors of urban areas. All of this has brought about a return to a family structure that reduces its size and multiplies its working members at a reduced wage scale, a situation notoriously similar to the reality of the old Porfiriato. Thus, toward the end of the year 2000, the percentage of working children in households with less than five persons was 14.3, and in households of seven and eight members it reached a surprising 21.4 percent. The ancien régime appears to have been resuscitated.

Note

1. Translations of Castera (1987) quotations by the authors.

References and Further Reading

Alberro, Solange. "Familia y trabajo en la Nueva España: las ambigüedades del tema." In *O trabalho mestico: maneiras de pensar e formas de viver, seculos XVI a XIX*, ed. Eduardo Franca Paiva and Carla Maria Junho Anastasia, 513–25. São Paulo: Annablume Editora, 2002.

Bernard, Carmen. "Las representaciones del trabajo en el mundo Hispanoamericano: de la infamia a la honra." In *O trabalho mestico: maneiras de pensar e formas de viver, seculos XVI a XIX*, ed. Eduardo Franca Paiva and Carla Maria Junho Anastasia, 393–411. São Paulo: Annablume Editora, 2002.

Bortz, Jeffery. "The Revolution, the Labor Regime, and Conditions of Work in the Cotton Textile Industry in Mexico, 1910–1927." *Journal of Latin American Studies* 32:3 (2000): 671–703.

Bortz, Jeffery. "The Legal and Contractual Limits to Private Property Rights in Mexican Industry During the Revolution." In *The Mexican Economy, 1870–1930: Essays on the Economic History of Institutions, Revolution, and Growth*, ed. Jeffrey Bortz and Stephen Haber. Palo Alto, CA: Stanford University Press, 2002.

Bortz, Jeffrey, and Marcos Aguila. "Earning a Living: A History of Real Wage Studies in XXth Century Mexico." *Latin American Research Review* 41:2 (2006): 112–38.

Casas, Fray Bartolomé de las. *Brevísima relación de la destrucción de las Indias, colegida por el obispo don Fray Bartolomé de las casas o causas de la orden de Santo Domingo.* Seville: En casa de Sebastian Trugillo, 1552.

Castera, Pedro. *Las minas y los mineros.* Mexico City: Coordinación de Humanidades, Universidad Nacional Autónoma de México, 1987.

Castillo Troncoso, Alberto del. *Conceptos. imágenes y representaciones de la niñez en la ciudad de México, 1880–1920.* Mexico City: Colegio de Mexico-Instituto Mora, 2006.

Flores Clair, Eduardo. *Conflictos de trabajo de una empresa minera: Real del Monte y Pachuca, 1872–1877.* Mexico City: Instituto Nacional de Antropología e Historia, 1991.

López Miramonte, Alvaro. *Las minas de Nueva España en 1753.* Mexico City: Instituto Nacional de Antropología e Historia, 1975.

López Miramonte, Alvaro, and Cristina Urrutia De Stebelski, eds. *Las minas de Nueva España en 1774.* Mexico City: Instituto Nacional de Antropología e Historia, 1980.

Necoechea Gracia, Gerardo. "Los jóvenes a la vuelta del siglo." In *Historias de los jóvenes en Mexico: su presencia en el siglo XX*, ed. José Antonio Pérez Islas and Maritza Urteaga Castro-Pozo. México City: Instituto Mexicano de la Juventud y Archivo General de la Nación, 2004.

Pérez Toledo, Sonia. *Los hijos del trabajo: los artesanos de la ciudad de Mexico, 1780–1853.* México City: Colegio de México, Centro de Estudios Históricos, Universidad Autónoma Metropolitana Iztapalapa, 1996.

Thompson, Lanny. "Artisans, Marginals, and Proletarians: The Households of the Popular Classes in Mexico City, 1876–1950." In *Five Centuries of Mexican History*, Vol. 2, ed. Virginia Guedea and Jaime E. Rodriguez O. México City: Instituto Mora and University of California at Irvine, 1992.

Trujillo Bolio, Mario. *Operarios fabriles en el valle de México (1864–1884): espacio, trabajo, protesta y cultura obrera.* México City: Colegio de México, Centro de Investigaciones y Estudios Superiores en Antropología Social, 1997.

Nicaragua

NICARAGUA			
	CRC	C 138	C 182
Ratifications	Y	Y	Y
Human Development Index/Rank	0.698/112		
Human Capital			
Population Growth Rate	1.85%		
% Population 0–14	35.5%		
Total Fertility Rate	2.69		
Life Expectancy	70.92		
Infant Mortality Rate	27.14		
Literacy Rate	67.5%		
Economic			
GDP/Capita	$3,000		
GDP Growth %	3.7%		
% Poverty	48%		
Gini Index	55.1		
Labor Force Composition			
% Agriculture	29%		
% Industry	19%		
% Services	52%		

CHILD ACTIVITY BREAKDOWN, BY SEX AND RESIDENCE

RESIDENCE	Percentage of children in the relevant age-group[a]									
	Economic activity only		School only		Combining school and economic activity		Neither in school nor in economic activity		Child labor[b]	
	Male	Female	Male	Female	Male	Female	Male	Female	Male	Female
Urban	1.9	0.4	85.2	90.1	3.5	2.2	9.4	7.3	n/av	n/av
Rural	7.1	0.7	63.8	78.6	14.0	3.1	15.1	17.6	n/av	n/av
Total	4.6	0.6	74.2	84.3	8.9	2.6	12.3	12.5	11.9	2.5

Source: Nicaragua, Encuesta Nacional de Hogares sobre Medicion de Nivel de Vida, 2005 (see UCW Project Web site, http://www.ucw-project.org, country statistics).
Notes: [a]Children age 5 to 14. [b]Estimate includes (a) children under age 12 engaged in economic activities, and (b) children age 12–14 engaged in excessive economic activities (more than 14 hours per week). Estimate does not account for children engaged in excessive household chores, hazardous work, or other unconditional "worst forms" of child labor.

Child Labor in Nicaragua

Luis Serra, PhD, Center for Sociocultural Analysis, Central American University, Nicaragua

The demographic structure of Nicaragua is like a pyramid with a wide base, where children and adolescents under nineteen years of age constitute 49 percent of the total population. Children are one of the poorest social groups in Nicaragua; 60 percent live under the poverty line and 20 percent in extreme poverty. In everyday life, poverty means that children and adolescents are undernourished and lack clothing and school equipment. They live in overcrowded shacks, they are put to work, and they do not have enough time for study, recreation, and rest. The transition from childhood to adulthood is often very short, since adolescents have to work full-time and have early sexual relations. Lacking sexual education and access to family-planning methods, they become young parents; 30 percent of births are from women younger than eighteen years old.

Every year some 800,000 children and adolescents remain out of the formal educational system, 19 percent at the primary level and 63 percent at the secondary level. Only 25 percent of children entering elementary school manage to graduate. Concerning health, the rate of child mortality is 31 for 100 live births; 25 percent of children present chronic malnutrition; and 36 percent were not legally registered at birth. It is estimated that one-fourth of children and adolescents live in situations of risk as a result of abandonment, dangerous work conditions, violence, abuse and sexual exploitation, addiction to drugs, and street gangs. Poverty, emigration, interpersonal violence, and the irresponsibility of many parents contribute to family disintegration and lack of proper attention to children. It is estimated that 40 percent of the million Nicaraguans who emigrated to Costa Rica and the United States are children and adolescents (PNUD 2005).

In Nicaraguan society, opportunities for children and adolescents are differentiated according to family economic, social, and educational resources. Children from the high and middle social classes enjoy satisfactory material and educational conditions, while the majority of children and adolescents who live in poverty have limited opportunities for growth and development since the state invests very little in public programs that favor the development of children.

Legal Framework on Child Labor

During the last decade, Nicaragua has made important advances in legislation and public policies for the benefit of children and adolescents based on a human rights approach. The government has ratified the UN Convention on the Rights of the Child, along with ILO Conventions 29 (forced labor), 138 (minimum age of employment), and 182 (elimination of the worst forms of child labor). Article 84 of the constitution establishes that "[c]hild labor is forbidden in those jobs that may damage their normal development or their access to education. Children and adolescents shall be protected against any sort of social and economic exploitation." A Code of Childhood and Adolescence was approved in 1998. The minimum age for most work in Nicaragua is set at fourteen.

The major official institution that addresses issues of children and adolescents is the National Council for Integral Attention to Childhood and Adolescence, but there is also a National Commission for the Prevention and Eradication of Child Labor, coordinated by the Ministry of Labor (MITRAB) and supported by international agencies and private institutions. State institutions together with NGOs have elaborated a National Policy for Integral Protection of Children and Adolescents, a Plan for Prevention of Juvenile Violence, and a National Plan for the Prevention and Eradication of Child Labor. There is a State Defender of Childhood and Adolescent Human Rights, and there are specialized offices in many police stations for cases of violations of women's and children's rights.

Nevertheless, there is a gap between legal regulation and social reality due to several factors: the prevalence of "adultist" and authoritarian attitudes, the increasing poverty of the population, the reduction of state social investments, and the limited effectiveness of state institutions in charge of implementing children's rights. However, it is necessary to emphasize the work of multiple civil society organizations in promoting the rights of children and adolescents, extending their opportunities for development, and lobbying for public policies.

Situation of Child Labor

Historically, in rural Nicaragua, child labor was considered to be a learning activity and a traditional obligation in peasant families, based on intergenerational solidarity and survival strategies. Even today children are in high demand in many agricultural tasks, such as cutting coffee and peanuts. In addition, the rural emigration of poor families to the cities has facilitated the child labor found today in the informal urban sectors, where children and adolescents are found working as street sellers, garbage collectors, package carriers, and even in prostitution linked to the increase of tourism and truck transportation with Central America.

The national survey on child and adolescent labor conducted by the Ministry of Labor in 2005 shows a total of 238,827 children and adolescents working, which represents 13.4 percent of the population from five to seventeen years of age (MITRAB 2006a). In recent years there has been a small decrease in labor among children under fourteen years of age, but an increase in work among adolescents age fifteen to seventeen years. In 2005 one-third (36 percent) of working children were under fourteen years of age, that is, under the minimum legal age for employment. Two-thirds of working children and adolescents were located in rural areas, while one-third were in urban zones. This distribution shows the weight of peasant family traditions in the rural environment, where 44 percent of the national population lives. As for the situation of child and adolescent labor by age, Table 1 shows that child labor increases parallel to the increase in age, as is common in other countries.

Table 1

Distribution of Working Children and Adolescents by Age

Age	Population	Children working	%
5–9	693,677	18,817	2.71
10–14	703,201	96,912	13.78
15–17	382,727	123,099	32.16
Total	1,779,605	238,827	13.42

Sources: MITRAB 2006a; Population Census 2005; INEC 2006.

The main economic activities that children and adolescents are involved in are in agriculture, beginning as early as age five. Second, they work in commercial activities, followed by manufacturing industries, and then by the social and personal services where girls predominate, as shown in Table 2.

Table 2

Distribution of Working Children and Adolescents by Activity and Sex

Economic activity	Number	%	% Males	% Females
Agriculture, forestry, and fishing	135,133	56.6	68.4	27.9
Commerce, restaurants, hotels	51,546	21.6	15.0	37.5
Manufacturing	23,758	9.9	7.5	16.0
Social and personal services	19,124	8.0	4.0	17.6
Building	4,652	1.9	2.7	0.2
Transport and communications	3,223	1.3	1.8	0.3
Others	1,752	0.6	0.6	0.5
Total	238,827	100	100	100

Source: MITRAB 2006a.

The informal sector, where many of the children and adolescents work, is characterized by high risk and exploitation, and many children have suffered wounds and illnesses at work sites. Given the quantity and the dispersion of the small businesses of the informal sector, it is difficult for state institutions to control child labor. According to the Ministry of Labor, of the businesses inspected in 2005, almost half of them (45.8 percent) had children or adolescents working, and 25 percent had children under fourteen years of age working. It is estimated that 80 percent of the tasks carried out by children and adolescents would be considered among the "worst forms of child labor." Nevertheless the majority of children and adolescents and their parents are not conscious of the risks they face (MITRAB 2006b).

Almost two-thirds (62 percent) of working children and adolescents are under the command of relatives who do not give them any payment, just one-third (32 percent) are paid, and 6 percent work on their own. Of those who earn wages, 43 percent receive less than US$1 a day, 35 percent get between US$1 and US$2 per day, and only 23 percent earn more than US$2 daily. Most of that income is distributed among purchases of clothing, food, and education expenses, and as contributions to household expenses. Two-thirds of working children and adolescents work more than five hours per day, and 11 percent work at night. The exploitation of girls and adolescents working in domestic services, who labor from ten to twelve hours daily in exchange for food, shelter, and low wages, has been noted (MITRAB 2006a).

Most children and adolescents carry out household tasks such us cleaning, washing dishes and clothes, ironing, getting firewood and water, going to the store, cooking, babysitting brothers and sisters, and taking care of the garden. These tasks increase in intensity with family poverty, and with the age and gender of the children. Since women do most housework according to the traditional sexual division of labor, girls are expected to perform a disproportionate share of domestic chores in preparation for their adult role, while boys perform more tasks in public spaces.

Conditions and Effects of Child Labor

At first glance, the incorporation of child labor constitutes a survival strategy used by families living in poverty. However the ILO (ILO-IPEC 2003) cites three sets of factors that contribute to the expansion of child labor in Nicaragua: immediate factors such as extreme poverty or abandonment by parents; underlying conditions such as families with many children, the authoritarian culture, and the scarcity of employment and income-generating activities; and structural factors such as the economic crisis, neoliberal policies, the low state social budget, and uneven distribution of incomes and resources.

The consequences of child labor are observed in high rates of school dropouts, low academic performance, undernourishment, chronic illnesses, and psychological traumas, all of which damage the personal and social development of children and adolescents. In Nicaragua, 12 percent of working children and adolescents are illiterate, and just 57 percent attend school. Those who do not attend school say that the main reasons are lack of economic resources, the need to work, little interest, and the lack of a nearby school.

Perceptions of Children and Parents on Child Labor

Several researchers of Latin American children and youths propose to include working children's and adolescents' vision of their situation, as Manfred Liebel has indicated: "To approach the issue of child labor from a subject-oriented perspective means to understand working children as 'social actors,' who contribute to the conservation and development of human life and the society in which they live, and they deserve social recognition for it" (Liebel 2003, 24).[1]

Since 1992, there has been a movement of working children and adolescents (NATRAS) formed by members of different organizations with support of NGOs. Through NATRAS, children and adolescents demand their right to work in healthy environments with just payment, as well as their rights to education and recreation, and they oppose proposals to eradicate all forms of child work. This network of organizations has contributed to public awareness of children's rights and to the problem of child labor and has generated spaces for participation and training of children and adolescents.

When children and adolescents are asked why they work, they pinpoint their contribution to family expenses, the purchase of personal goods, learning a skill, and obedience to their parents (MITRAB 2006a). Other studies suggest that children and adolescents feel a family obligation to do household chores and like to help their families. Nevertheless, some girls criticize their heavy workload, which limits their possibility for study and recreation. Children and adolescents working for income expressed three distinct positions: One group said that they should not work outside their households since they should study and there are many dangers in the street; another group thought they should work to help their parents, to earn money, and to avoid becoming beggars; and a third group considered that small children should not work outside the home, but adolescents may work and at the same time should study (Castillo and Serra 2003).

The vision of parents of working children and adolescents is differentiated according to socioeconomic class and educational level. On one hand, parents from lower classes and limited education think that children and adolescents should work in the labor market to learn skills and to contribute economically to family expenses. On the other hand, upper and middle classes with college education think that children and adolescents should prioritize their education before engaging in work. However, most parents from different backgrounds agree that children and adolescents should contribute to the performance of household chores.

Most parents probably agree that "[w]ork in and of itself is not necessarily damaging to the development of children. The issue is to determine at what point the work is too much for what a child of a certain age is able to handle, both physically and mentally. The problem arises when work impedes the development of other potential strengths the child has, not only intellectually and academically at school, but also in terms of their participation in other groups, social contexts and activities" (Pineda and Guerra 1998, 5).

Challenges for the Future

To gradually eliminate the worst forms of child labor in Nicaragua and to foster the development of children and adolescents, and of society, basic challenges must be overcome: to reduce the level of poverty and extreme poverty that affects 46 percent of Nicaraguan families; to implement legal norms and public policies on child labor, which implies budget allocation, political will, and interinstitutional coordination; to promote communication programs for parents and adults on children's rights; to offer special educational programs for working children and adolescents; and to promote their participation in cultural and social activities.

Note

1. Translation by Serra; original text: "Tratar de acercarse el tema del trabajo infantil desde una perspectiva orientada en el sujeto significa entender a los niños y niñas tabajadores como 'actores sociales,' que mediante su trabajo contibuyen a la conservación y al desarollo de la vida humana y de la sociedad en la que viven, y que merecen reconocimiento social por ello."

References and Further Reading

Castillo, M., and L. Serra. *La niñez y la adolescencia en Nicaragua: perspectivas de desarrollo.* Managua: UCA-Plan Internacional, 2003.

Duran, Sonia. *Retrospectiva del trabajo infantil en Nicaragua.* Managua: Save the Children Noruega, 2003.

ILO-IPEC. *Estudio a profundidad del trabajo infantil y adolescente en Nicaragua.* Managua: La Prensa, 2003.

INEC (Instituto Nicaragüense de Estadisticas y Censos). *Censo de población y vivienda* 2005. Managua: INEC, 2006.

Liebel, Manfred. *Infancia y trabajo.* Lima: IFEJANT, 2003.

MITRAB (Ministerio del Trabajo). *Encuesta nacional de trabajo infantil 2005.* Managua: MITRAB, 2006a.

MITRAB (Ministerio del Trabajo). *Estadisticas sociolaborales 2005.* Managua: MITRAB, 2006b.

Ortega, M., and L. Serra. *Estilos de crianza en Nicaragua.* Managua: CASC-UCA-PROMUNDO–Save the Children, 2006.

Pineda, Gustavo, and B.R. Guerra. *How Children See Their World: An Exploratory Study.* Managua: IMPRIMATUR, 1998.

PNUD (Programa Naciones Unidas para el Desarrollo). *Informe desarrollo humano de Nicaragua 2005.* Managua: PNUD, 2005.

Powel, Carlos. *Trabajo de niños y niñas . . . responsabilidad de adultos.* Managua: Save the Children Noruega, 2005.

Panama

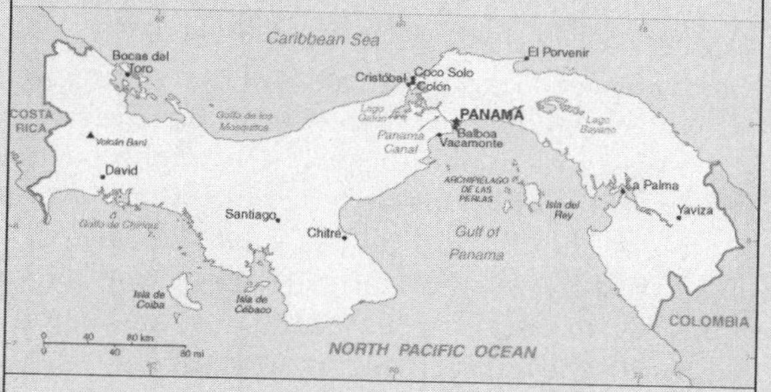

PANAMA			
	CRC	C 138	C 182
Ratifications	Y	Y	Y
Human Development Index/Rank	0.809/58		
Human Capital			
Population Growth Rate	1.56%		
% Population 0–14	30%		
Total Fertility Rate	2.66		
Life Expectancy	75.19		
Infant Mortality Rate	15.96		
Literacy Rate	92.6		
Economic			
GDP/Capita	$7,900		
GDP Growth %	6.3%		
% Poverty	37%		
Gini Index	56.4		
Labor Force Composition			
% Agriculture	20.8%		
% Industry	18%		
% Services	61.2%		

CHILD ACTIVITY BREAKDOWN, BY SEX AND RESIDENCE

RESIDENCE	Percentage of children in the relevant age-group[a]									
	Economic activity only		School only		Combining school and economic activity		Neither in school nor in economic activity		Child labor[b]	
	Male	Female	Male	Female	Male	Female	Male	Female	Male	Female
Urban	0.5	0.2	92.0	93.2	1.5	0.7	6.0	5.9	n/av	n/av
Rural	3.8	0.6	76.9	81.4	5.4	1.0	13.9	17.0	n/av	n/av
Total	2.0	0.4	85.2	88.0	3.2	0.8	9.5	10.8	4.7	1.8

Source: Panama, Encuesta del Trabajo Infantil, 2000 (see UCW Project Web site, http://www.ucw-project.org, country statistics).

Notes: [a]Children age 5 to 14. [b]Estimate includes (a) children under age 12 engaged in economic activities, (b) children age 12–14 engaged in excessive economic activities (more than 14 hours per week), and (c) children under age 15 engaged in excessive household chores (at least 28 hours per week). Estimate does not account for children engaged in hazardous work or other unconditional "worst forms" of child labor.

SECTION 4. CARIBBEAN

Child Slaves on West Indies Sugar Plantations

Jerome Teelucksingh, PhD, University of the West Indies

The traditional historiography of slavery in the Caribbean, with its emphasis on the rebellions and revolts that were common throughout the region, focuses overwhelmingly on the experiences of the adult slaves. Slave uprisings were often harshly suppressed by the plantocracy, causing many slave children to lose one or both parents. But the experience of child slaves themselves, because they were generally excluded by their parents from participation in the rebellions and revolts, remains largely "invisible" in the slavery historiography. This essay seeks to redress this imbalance by investigating the pivotal contributions and presence of child slaves in the West Indies. Despite their absence from the historical record, throughout the period of slavery, children played pivotal roles in the daily operation of the estates, roles that were undervalued by plantation owners.

Natural Increase Versus Immigration

The absence of complete and reliable statistics makes it difficult to accurately assess the number of children who survived the trip from Africa to the Caribbean. The hardships of the Middle Passage and grueling demands of the plantation meant that physically strong and healthy adult slaves would have been preferred to children, but the records suggest that children nevertheless comprised a noteworthy component of the transported slaves. Overall, children formed 14 percent of slave cargoes to the British West Indies from 1673 to 1725, and between 7 and 14 percent of those transported to the region from 1791 to 1798. The feeling among the West Indian plantocracy in the eighteenth century was that it was better to buy than to breed. Almost one-third of all the slaves imported into the West Indies, including children, died within a three-year period of seasoning or socialization. As a result, the value of survivors doubled.

Child slaves were not cheap, and in the years prior to abolition, the cost of young slaves increased. Illustrative prices from around 1803 to 1805 include the following: On Grenada on the Duquesne Estate in the parish of St. Mark, a little "negro girl" was sold for £100; Mary Louise, a ten-year-old girl, sold for £140, and Rose, a seventeen-year-old female slave, sold for £170 (approximately $10,000 to $17,000 in today's prices). Despite their high costs, child slaves were a significant asset to the estate. The monetary value placed on children strongly suggests that they were neither easily disposable nor easily replaceable.

Slave Children's Labor

Although a few slave children were selected as domestic servants, the vast majority were employed in the fields. In both the British and French Caribbean, the plantation labor force was organized into gangs that were stratified by gender and age. Depending on the size of the estate and the number of slaves, a plantation might have from one to four gangs. Children under five were generally considered by planters as too young to work. From age five until they were old enough to be assigned to a gang, they would typically accompany their mothers to the fields and perform light work. These young children were often referred to as "basket children," since each child usually carried a basket. Their task was to collect cane trash from around the mill, pull out weeds, feed animals, and perform other light labor.

Most of the children from eight to thirteen, and all of the smallest and weakest children, occasionally as young as four, were placed in the lowest gang—a third or fourth gang—and would work their way up to the first gang as they grew in age, size, and strength. This gang was variously referred to as the "pickaninny," "hogmeat," "little," "grass," or "pot" gang and worked under the supervision of an elderly female slave. The size of these gangs was often fairly large. For example, the third gang on one sugar plantation in Saint-Domingue included 64 children of a total of 249 slaves. On the Lowther's Estate in Barbados in 1774, the 45 "grass gang" children represented 30 percent of the slave workforce.

As early as age nine or eleven, promising workers might be promoted to second gang, where they would serve as "meat pickers" and would gradually adjust to more arduous work regimes. More valued than members of the third gang, their duties included land clearance after cultivation, and serving as cane carriers, water assistants, and mill attendants.

The strongest adult female and male slaves belonged to the first gang. Their workload entailed planting and reaping the cane and growing food crops. In Saint-Domingue, on the Breda Plantation, for example, slaves who attained the age of seventeen entered the first gang.

Infant and Child Mortality

It is difficult to ascertain with real precision the health of infants because children between the ages of one and three often went unrecorded by planters, both to reduce their taxes and to avoid accusations of cruelty that might result from infant deaths. Thus, up to 50 percent of children's deaths on Jamaican plantations in the eighteenth century might have gone unrecorded. Even where children were included in plantation records, there was often no allusion to the condition of their health.

Despite the incomplete records, it is known that infant mortality rates were high among slave children. For example, half of the children born in Barbados during two decades (1730s and 1740s) died from nutrition-related diseases before they were one week old. In Trinidad, there was also a high mortality rate among infants. More than a third of slave children died before their first birthday, and fewer than half attained five years of age. A slave born between 1813 and 1816 lived an average of only seventeen years. During childbirth, there was a high risk of infection, as midwives delivered babies in unsanitary slave quarters.

For those who survived infancy, slave child mortality remained high in part due to poor sanitation and in part due to poor nutrition. Many planters failed to provide proper toilets. When toilets were provided, they were usually situated in poorly drained flatland. Slave children and adults walked and worked in feces-contaminated soil and stagnant water, which attracted disease-carrying mosquitoes and flies. As a result of these unhygienic conditions, dysentery, worms, whooping cough, malaria, yaws, diarrhea, and tetanus (lockjaw) contributed to the high child mortality rate.

On the plantations, food was allocated through an allowance system based on the tasks performed and the ages of the slaves. This meant that physically stronger slaves were given more food than slaves who were ill, old slaves, nursing mothers, and children. Usually, children between one and five years old were given a one-third allowance of food. Boys and girls between five and ten years old received a one-half allowance, and children ages ten to fifteen and invalids received two-thirds of the allowance. As a result of this food rationing, it was no surprise that the children were often malnourished. Marasmus, a severe form of malnutrition caused by a protein-deficient diet, was common.

The combination of poor sanitation and poor diet meant that deaths usually exceeded births on the Caribbean plantations. It was a testament to the hardiness and the survival mechanisms imbued in those few slave children who survived into adulthood.

Child Care and Welfare

Throughout the West Indies, planters were concerned with profit maximization. For many, this meant that the provision of better housing, a proper hospital, a nursery, or other amenities was not a priority. They saw this kind of expenditure as an extra allocation of capital to projects that that did not contribute directly to profits. Some, however, recognized the value of certain paternalistic investments in children. The children, especially the youngest ones, were treated with a certain amount of consideration by many planters.

Traditionally, superannuated women and those with disabilities served as surrogate mothers for unweaned children. These nannies cared for children who were too young to work and were returned to their mothers at night. The children were generally treated well by the kind nannies so that many children became more attached to their nannies than to their mothers. In some West Indian colonies, nurseries were built in which elderly women cared for the infants. By the late eighteenth century, hospitals or sick houses had been built on the majority of estates. Slaves benefited from biweekly or weekly visits by a medical doctor. In spite of this, however, mortality rates for mothers and children continued to be high.

Cruelty toward children was not widespread in the West Indies. To illustrate, in Demerara and Essequibo in British Guiana, during the first half of 1828, of more than 10,000 reported cases of neglect and cruelty among the colony's 62,000 slaves, there were only ten reported cases involving children. As a result of this relatively good treatment, few children rebelled openly against slavery. Some engaged in theft or arson, a classic form of protest. Children were also often involved in maroonage, where groups of runaway slaves established their own permanent communities. For infants, maroonage was involuntary—their mothers took them with them when they fled. However, some older children fled alone. For example, in Grenada, Kitty, a twelve-year-old slave girl, ran away in February 1815, as did sixteen-year-old Mary (nicknamed Monkey) in September 1821.

Of all the British West Indian colonies, it was only in Barbados that planters made any systematic effort to provide education for slave children. Most masters believed that formal education would result in the slaves being unsuitable for or resistant to plantation labor. Despite these limitations, there were occasional instances of paternalistic treatment that extended to education. For instance, in the eighteenth century on the Gabrielle Plantation in French Guiana, Marie-Rose gave religious instruction to the young slaves. But the absence of educational and recreational facilities on most plantations made work the only viable life activity for slave children.

Conclusion

Slavery finally came to an end with the passage of the Emancipation Bill in 1833. The British government paid £20 million in compensation to the planters. All child slaves under six years of age on August 1, 1834, were to be freed immediately. In the British West Indies 88,306 children under age six were freed.

References and Further Reading

Bush, Barbara. *Slave Women in Caribbean Society 1650–1838.* London: James Currey, 1990.

Bush-Slimani, Barbara. "Hard Labour: Women, Childbirth and Resistance in British Caribbean Slave Societies." *History Workshop—A Journal of Socialist and Feminist Historians* 36 (1993): 83–99.

Higman, B.W. "The Slave Family and Household in the British West Indies, 1800–1834." *Journal of Interdisciplinary History* 6 (1975): 261–87.

Higman, B.W. *Slave Population and Economy in Jamaica, 1807–1834.* Cambridge: Cambridge University Press, 1976.

Jabour, A. "Slave Health and Health Care in the British Caribbean: Profits, Racism and the Failure of Amelioration in Trinidad and British Guiana, 1824–1834." *Journal of Caribbean History* 28:1 (1994): 1–26.

John, A.M. *The Plantation Slaves of Trinidad, 1783–1816: A Mathematical and Demographic Enquiry.* Cambridge: Cambridge University Press, 1988.

Mason, K. "Demography, Disease and Medical Care in Caribbean Slave Societies." *Bulletin of Latin American Research* 5:1 (1986): 109–19.

Poyen de Sainte-Marie, M. *De l'exploitation des sucreries ou conseil d'un vieux planteur aux jeunes agriculteurs des colonies.* Basse-Terre: Imprimerie de la Republique, 1792.

Dominican Republic

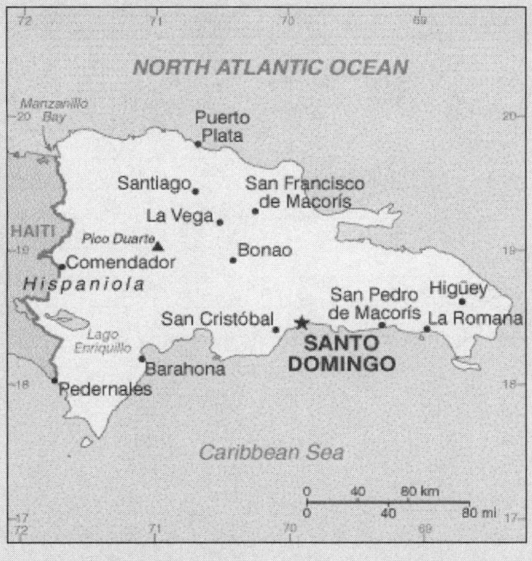

DOMINICAN REPUBLIC			
	CRC	C 138	C 182
Ratifications	Y	Y	Y
Human Development Index/Rank	0.751/94		
Human Capital			
Population Growth Rate	1.47%		
% Population 0–14	32.6%		
Total Fertility Rate	2.83		
Life Expectancy	71.73		
Infant Mortality Rate	28.25		
Literacy Rate	84.7%		
Economic			
GDP/Capita	$8,000		
GDP Growth %	7.2%		
% Poverty	25%		
Gini Index	47.4		
Labor Force Composition			
% Agriculture	17%		
% Industry	24.3%		
% Services	58.7%		

CHILD ACTIVITY BREAKDOWN, BY SEX AND RESIDENCE

RESIDENCE	Percentage of children in the relevant age-group[a]									
	Economic activity only		School only		Combining school and economic activity		Neither in school nor in economic activity		Child labor[b]	
	Male	Female	Male	Female	Male	Female	Male	Female	Male	Female
Urban	1.1	0.3	84.0	88.0	9.9	6.8	5.0	4.9	n/av	n/av
Rural	1.2	0.5	76.9	86.9	16.2	7.0	5.6	5.6	n/av	n/av
Total	1.2	0.4	80.9	87.5	12.7	6.9	5.3	5.2	11.2	6.9

Source: Dominican Republic, Multiple Indicator Cluster Survey 2, 2000 (see UCW Project Web site, http://www.ucw-project.org, country statistics).

Notes: [a]Children age 5 to 14. [b]Estimate includes (a) children under age 12 engaged in economic activities, (b) children age 12–14 engaged in excessive economic activities (more than 14 hours per week), and (c) children under age 15 engaged in excessive household chores (at least 28 hours per week). Estimate does not account for children engaged in hazardous work or other unconditional "worst forms" of child labor.

Haiti

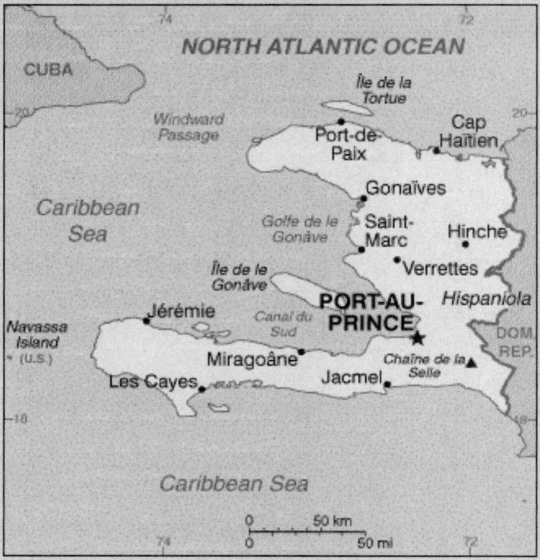

HAITI			
	CRC	C 138	C 182
Ratifications	Y	N	N
Human Development Index/Rank	0.482/154		
Human Capital			
Population Growth Rate	2.45%		
% Population 0–14	42.1%		
Total Fertility Rate	4.86		
Life Expectancy	57.03		
Infant Mortality Rate	63.83		
Literacy Rate	52.9%		
Economic			
GDP/Capita	$1,800		
GDP Growth %	1.8%		
% Poverty	80%		
Gini Index	—		
Labor Force Composition			
% Agriculture	66%		
% Industry	9%		
% Services	25%		

CHILD ACTIVITY BREAKDOWN, BY SEX AND RESIDENCE

RESIDENCE	Percentage of children in the relevant age-group[a]									
	Economic activity only		School only		Combining school and economic activity		Neither in school nor in economic activity		Child labor[b]	
	Male	Female	Male	Female	Male	Female	Male	Female	Male	Female
Urban	2.6	1.8	77.1	74.2	14.3	15.2	6.0	8.8	n/av	n/av
Rural	8.8	6.1	43.9	52.7	31.0	25.8	16.2	15.5	n/av	n/av
Total	6.8	4.4	54.6	60.8	25.7	21.8	12.9	13.0	21.9	19.2

Source: Haiti, Demographic and Health Survey, 2005–6 (see UCW Project Web site, http://www.ucw-project.org, country statistics).

Notes: [a]Children age 5 to 14. [b]Estimate includes (a) children under age 12 engaged in economic activities, (b) children age 12–14 engaged in excessive economic activities (more than 14 hours per week), and (c) children under age 15 engaged in excessive household chores (at least 28 hours per week). Estimate does not account for children engaged in hazardous work or other unconditional "worst forms" of child labor.

Child Labor in Haiti

Tone Sommerfelt, Research Fellow, Department of Social Anthropology, University of Oslo; and **Jon Pedersen,** Research Director, Fafo Institute for Applied International Studies

Child labor in Haiti is dominated by participation in domestic work, petty commerce, and agriculture. Few children work in the small, formal industrial sector. Outside of homes, children work in marketplaces and stalls, taking part in crafts and sales, and boys in particular are involved in carrying and loading goods. In the urban centers, children who shine shoes and clean car windows are especially visible. Some of the children who live in the streets try to live from begging, and some are forcibly recruited into prostitution or into armed gangs (Bernier and Ponticq 1999; UNICEF 2006; UNICEF Haïti 1996).

Much of children's work involves assistance to parents and kin, in housework and on small family plots. In order to contribute to the livelihood of the family, children are expected to participate in economic activities from an early age. Children are also placed in other homes where they work for their upkeep. This work away from parental homes makes up a considerable proportion of child domestic labor. Striking in the Haitian case, however, is the degree to which children are present in the labor market. Data from the Haiti Living Conditions Survey (HLCS) in 2001 show that, of children age ten to fourteen, 4 percent were registered as employed. Of those age fifteen to seventeen, 8 percent were employed. While most societies do not have much unemployment for children, 4 percent of the ten- to fourteen-year-olds and 12 percent of the fifteen- to seventeen-year-olds were registered as unemployed, that is, actively seeking and being available for work. Thus, children appear to be present in the labor market in large numbers, and in larger numbers than the labor market can absorb. Unemployment among child workers must be seen in the context of high unemployment for young adult workers (at 26 percent of the entire eighteen- to twenty-four-year-old group, or 56 percent of the labor force members) (findings derived from the HLCS 2001; see IHSI 2003, 2005). Moreover, children's economic activities reflect severe economic conditions, Haiti being the poorest country in the Western Hemisphere.

Child Labor, Gender, and Urban-Rural Divisions

The economic sectors in which Haitian children work differ markedly according to gender and area of residence. Boys in urban areas divide their time principally between agricultural tasks and trade, and to some extent domestic work. In rural areas they work nearly exclusively in agriculture. Girls in urban areas are employed in petty commerce and domestic work, whereas in rural areas they work to a large extent in agriculture and to a lesser extent in petty commerce. Agricultural work, among both boys and girls, is somewhat less frequent in the north and northeast regions.

The large plantations in Haiti were broken up in the nineteenth century, and today there are almost no large landowners (Sletten and Egset 2004). The majority of farms are owned and cultivated by farmers themselves, and some plots are sharecropped. Plots are small. Children's agricultural field labor mostly takes place in these family-owned plots. In irrigated areas with high demand for agricultural labor, some teenagers are reported to work for wages. Haitian children are also trafficked to the Dominican Republic to work on plantations there (Smucker and Murray 2004).

Most children's work is not paid. In the HLCS in 2001 it was found that only 13 percent of children considered employed work for wages; one-third are self-employed; the majority, 54 percent, work for family enterprises. If domestic work—difficult to register in a labor force survey—is included, the proportion of wage work would be even lower (findings derive from the HLCS; see IHSI 2003, 2005).

Children in Haiti carry out a substantial amount of work within the household. According to one study (Sommerfelt 2002), the average (median) hours worked per week for seven- to eight-year-olds is two, increasing to nine for thirteen- to fourteen-year-olds, and eleven for fifteen- to seventeen-year-olds. An important dimension of children's work in Haiti is the distinction between children who live with one or both parents and children who live without their parents (19 percent of children age five to seventeen years). Children who live away from their parents and who are engaged in domestic work are sometimes referred to as *restavèk* in Creole, deriving from the French terms for "living" (*rester*) and "with" (*avec*). The term illustrates the blurry distinction between fosterage arrangements and child labor, as it is not always clear whether a child's work constitutes the primary motivation for its being fostered or this is simply regarded as a natural part of the issue of fosterage as a whole (Sommerfelt 2002). Locally, the term evokes the kinds of tasks that these children are assigned: washing and cleaning, fetching water, and running errands (IPSOFA 1998). But the term has also come to carry negative connotations about underprivileged children and servitude and slavery (Cadet 1998).

Several estimates of the extent of child domestic labor in Haiti exist, but a precise determination is nearly impossible due to problems of estimating the total child population and due to the fact that all children, regardless of whether they live with or away from their parents, may be engaged in heavy workloads and may or may not be enrolled in education or follow normal school progression. The various estimates of child domestic laborers are recounted in a recent report (Smucker and Murray 2004).

Based on data from the HLCS from 2001, the number of child domestics was estimated at 173,000, or 8.2 percent of the child population age five to seventeen years old. Nearly 60 percent of these children are girls. In absolute numbers, the majority live in rural areas, as two-thirds of the Haitian population is rural. Relatively speaking, child domestics make up about the same proportion of the population in urban and rural areas, but in the urban centers, the share of girls is higher (72 percent) than in rural areas, where boys and girls are more equally distributed (Pedersen and Hatløy 2002).

Poverty, Inequality, and Education

Haitian society is highly stratified, and hierarchy is a pervasive aspect of social relations. The use of children in petty commerce and domestic and agricultural work forms part of social and economic hierarchies, in the sense that employers secure their own benefit at working children's expense. With respect to children's domestic labor in homes other than their own, children are sent to homes with higher average incomes than those of their original households. Parents introduce children to work as a response to a desperate economic situation. Many parents convey hopes of upward social mobility as a result of their children obtaining skills, contacts, and education through their work. Adults who employ children, on the other hand, are represented as assisting parents in a difficult situation (Sommerfelt et al. 2002).

Practices of child placement for domestic and agricultural work have been described in literature from Haiti by several earlier writers (Herskovits 1937; Simpson 1941; Bastien 1961). In 1830, Mackenzie described godparenthood as a means for Haitian landowners to procure young laborers in agricultural fields. More recently, attempts have been made to explain child domesticity in Haiti, and abuse of children, with reference to the history of slavery, referring current practices to an alleged "Haitian mentality" or "culture of violence." Myths "about what is wrong with Haiti and Haitians . . . appear with surprising regularity" (Farmer 1994, 349), and analysis too often merely conforms to these myths rather than undertaking serious efforts to understand the complex social, economic, and political structures of which child relocation practices and child labor are a part. In this context, it is important to note that exploitation of children's labor does not mimic relations between the most privileged classes and the poor, as children's labor is employed by all layers of the population, including the urban poor. (For an analysis of the distribution of child domestics according to the receiving households' income levels, see Sommerfelt et al. 2002.) Indeed, it has been argued that the practice of placing children in domesticity was uncommon until the twentieth century, when it developed as a response to the difficult conditions of the rural population, and is less a part of the heritage from colonial times, slavery, or the nineteenth century (Haïti Solidarité Internationale 2001).

Conventions and Child Labor Laws

The Haitian Labor Code of 1984 set the minimum age for children's domestic labor at twelve years (Article 341), for apprenticeship at fourteen years (Article 73), and for work in all other sectors (industrial, agricultural, and commercial) at fifteen years (Government of Haiti 1984). Legislation adopted by the Haitian government in 2003 made trafficking illegal and repealed provisions in the labor code of 1984 that permitted child domestic labor (U.S. Department of Labor 2005).

Neither ILO Convention 138 concerning minimum age for admission to employment, nor Convention 182, against worst forms of child labor, have been ratified by Haiti. Though the Convention on the Rights of the Child was ratified in 1994, little progress has been made in its implementation. Monitoring systems of children's rights are weak, in part due to lack of resources. An unstable political situation and prolonged parliamentary and financial crises have weakened the potential of political initiatives and limited programmatic activities aimed at combating internal trafficking of children.

References and Further Reading

Bastien, Rémy. "Haitian Rural Family Organization." *Working Papers in Caribbean Social Organization: Social and Economic Studies* 10:4 (1961): 478–510.

Bernier, Martine, and Françoise Ponticq. *Planification d'interventions utilisant les modes d'organisation sociale et économique des enfants et des jeunes vivant et travaillant dans les rues en Haïti et entre autre, de ceux et celles vivant de la prostitution.* Haiti: Unité de Recherche sur les Enfants en Situation Difficile (URESD), Université Quisqueya, 1999.

Cadet, Jean-Robert. *Restavec: From Haitian Slave Child to Middle-Class American.* Austin: Texas University Press, 1998.

Farmer, Paul. *The Uses of Haiti.* Monroe, ME: Common Courage Press, 1994.

Government of Haiti. "Décret du 24 février 1984 actualisant le code du travail du 12 septembre 1961." 1984. http://www.ilo.org/dyn/natlex/docs/WEBTEXT/135/64790/F61HTI01.htm.

Haïti Solidarité Internationale. *Étude sur les fondements de la pratique de la domesticité des enfants en Haïti.* Port-au-Prince: United Nations Development Program, 2001.

Herskovits, Melville J. *Life in a Haitian Valley.* New York: Knopf, 1937.

IHSI (Institut Haïtien de Statistique et d'Informatique). *Enquête sur les conditions de vie en Haïti (ECVH 2001).* Vol. 1. Port-au-Prince: IHSI, Fafo, and UNDP, 2003.

IHSI (Institut Haïtien de Statistique et d'Informatique). *Enquête sur les conditions de vie en Haïti (ECVH 2001).* Vol. 2. Port-au-Prince: IHSI, Fafo, and PNUD, 2005.

IPSOFA (Institut Psycho-Social de la Famille). *Restavek: la domesticité juvénile en Haïti.* Port-au-Prince, IPSOFA, 1998.

Mackenzie, Charles. *Notes on Haiti. Made During a Residence in that Republic.* Vol. 1. London: H. Colburn and R. Bentley, 1830.

Pedersen, Jon, and Anne Hatløy. "Extent and Demographic Characteristics of Haitian Child Domesticity." In *Child Domestic Labour in Haiti: Characteristics, Contexts and Organisation of Children's Residence, Relocation and Work,* ed. Tone Sommerfelt, 32–43. Oslo: Fafo, 2002.

Simpson, George Eaton. "Haiti's Social Structure." *American Sociological Review* 6 (1941): 640–49.

Sletten, Pål, and Willy Egset. *Poverty in Haiti.* Fafo-paper 31. Oslo: Fafo, 2004.

Smucker, Glenn R., and Gerald F. Murray. *The Uses of Children: A Study of Trafficking in Haitian Children.* Port-au-Prince: USAID–Haiti Mission, 2004.

Sommerfelt, Tone. "Characteristics, Definitions, and Arrangements of Children's Residence and Child Domesticity in Haiti." In *Child Domestic Labour in Haiti: Characteristics, Contexts and Organisation of Children's Residence, Relocation and Work,* ed. Tone Sommerfelt, 20–31. Oslo: Fafo, 2002.

Sommerfelt, Tone, ed. *Child Domestic Labour in Haiti: Characteristics, Contexts and Organisation of Children's*

Residence, Relocation and Work. Report to UNICEF, ILO, Save the Children UK, and Save the Children Canada. Oslo: Fafo Institute for Applied Social Science, 2002.

Sommerfelt, Tone, Jon Pedersen, and Anne Hatløy. "The Social Context: Households, Kinship and Social Inequality." In *Child Domestic Labour in Haiti: Characteristics, Contexts and Organisation of Children's Residence, Relocation and Work,* ed. Tone Sommerfelt, 64–90. Oslo: Fafo, 2002.

UNICEF. "Child Alert Haiti." *Child Alert* 2 (March 2006). http://www.unicef.org/childalert/haiti/.

UNICEF Haïti. *Les enfants d'Haïti en situation particulièrement difficile (un état de la question).* Port-au-Prince: UNICEF Haïti, 1996.

U.S. Department of Labor. "Haiti." In *The Department of Labor's 2004 Findings on the Worst Forms of Child Labor.* Washington, DC: Bureau of International Labor Affairs, 2005. http://www.dol.gov/ilab/media/reports/iclp/tda2004/haiti.htm.

Jamaica

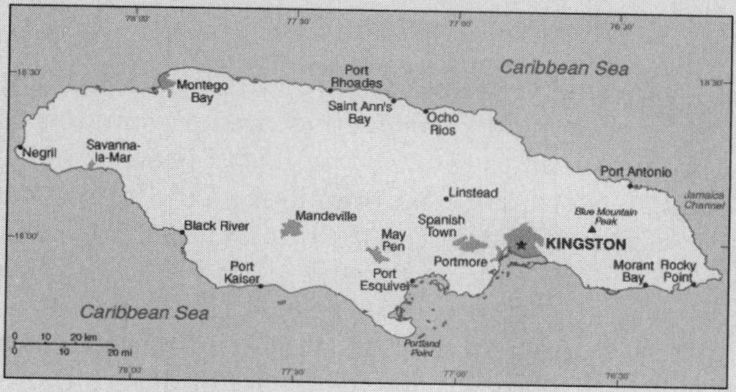

JAMAICA			
	CRC	C 138	C 182
Ratifications	Y	Y	Y
Human Development Index/Rank	0.724/104		
Human Capital			
Population Growth Rate	0.8%		
% Population 0–14	33.1%		
Total Fertility Rate	2.41		
Life Expectancy	73.24		
Infant Mortality Rate	15.98		
Literacy Rate	87.9%		
Economic			
GDP/Capita	$4,600		
GDP Growth %	2.7%		
% Poverty	14.8%		
Gini Index	38.1		
Labor Force Composition			
% Agriculture	18.1%		
% Industry	17.3%		
% Services	64.6%		

CHILD ACTIVITY BREAKDOWN, BY AGE AND SEX

RESIDENCE	Percentage of children in the relevant age-group[a]									
	Economic activity only		School only		Combining school and economic activity		Neither in school nor in economic activity		Child labor[b]	
	Male	Female	Male	Female	Male	Female	Male	Female	Male	Female
Urban	0.4	0.2	91.1	92.4	8.1	6.9	0.3	0.5	n/av	n/av
Rural	0.2	0.0	87.3	90.2	10.8	7.4	1.7	2.4	n/av	n/av
Total	0.3	0.1	89.5	91.4	9.3	7.1	0.9	1.4	6.8	5.6

Source: Jamaica, Multiple Indicator Cluster Survey 3, 2005 (see UCW Project Web site, http://www.ucw-project.org, country statistics).

Notes: [a] Children age 5 to 14. [b] Estimate includes (a) children under age 12 engaged in economic activities, (b) children age 12–14 engaged in excessive economic activities (more than 14 hours per week), and (c) children under age 15 engaged in excessive household chores (at least 28 hours per week). Estimate does not account for children engaged in hazardous work or other unconditional "worst forms" of child labor.

Child Labor in Jamaica

Leith L. Dunn, Senior Lecturer/Head, Centre for Gender and Development Studies, University of the West Indies, Jamaica, and former Assistant Representative, UNFPA Caribbean Office

This essay provides a synthesis of relevant child labor laws and conventions ratified by the government of Jamaica and an overview of research studies on child labor in that country. Readers will gain insight into the child labor situation in a small developing country in the Caribbean, whose experiences are rarely included in global reports. The essay concludes with policy recommendations, and identifies future research and advocacy needs to promote a future without child labor.

Child Labor and Human Rights

Jamaica has a well-developed human rights framework from which to support academic research, advocacy, and policies to eliminate child labor. The country has ratified the UN Convention on the Rights of the Child, the United Nations Convention on the Elimination of all Forms of Discrimination Against Women, and ILO Conventions 138 (minimum age for work) and 182 (elimination of worst forms of child labor). The nation's Child Care and Protection Act (2005) provides comprehensive coverage to protect the rights of children including the right to not be engaged in child labor.

Research on Child Labor in Jamaica

One of the earliest studies on child labor in Jamaica identified children working in markets or agriculture, or involved in domestic work (Ennew and Young 1981). In 1994 UNICEF and the Statistical Institute of Jamaica estimated that some 23,000 children age six to sixteen years were working in farming, growing marijuana, street vending, newspaper delivery, carpentry and mechanics' workshops, domestic service, and prostitution. The same year, the state party report (government of Jamaica) to the UN Committee on the Rights of the Child estimated that the number of children who live and work on the streets had increased from fifty in 1984 to 2,500 in 1994. Accurate estimates of the true extent of child labor are difficult to establish, as many work activities are underground, are concentrated in the informal sector, and operate in private domestic spaces. Several studies have documented widespread problems of commercial exploitation of children in Jamaica (Crawford Brown 1996; Williams 1999, 2000).

Jamaica's National Child Labor Program

Jamaica's child labor program for research and advocacy was established in 2000, pursuant to a memorandum of understanding executed by the Jamaican government and ILO-IPEC. It was part of the global campaign to ratify ILO Convention 182 on the worst forms of child labor. As a result, a series of research studies and program interventions were initiated involving partnerships among government, civil society groups, academia, and international agencies.

In 2000, the ILO commissioned a Rapid Assessment to study the situation of children in prostitution (Dunn 2001). The RA methodology is designed to collect qualitative data from hard-to-reach populations whose activities are invisible or may be illegal. The study confirmed that Jamaica has serious problems in the commercial sexual exploitation of its children. Based on other information revealed in the RA, the ILO then commissioned three baseline studies in three key sectors: the informal sector, tourism, and fishing.

Cooke (2002) conducted the study of the informal sector and identified 1,220 children involved in five categories of child labor: children who live and work on the street (22.1 percent); children who work on the street and live elsewhere (24.6 percent); domestic or agricultural helpers (41 percent); sexually exploited children (4.1 percent); and children who are commercial or industrial employees (8.2 percent). The average age of entry to child labor was ten, but some begin as early as five years of age. A clear gender division of labor was evident. Among the group of children working as domestic and agricultural helpers, more than 60 percent were girls, and among the group of sexually exploited children, girls dominated (87.5 percent). The research showed that approximately one-quarter of the children lived in rural areas and came to urban centers to work; they also comprised the majority of children who were sexually exploited.

Wint and Madden (2002) studied the situation of child labor in tourism. They found an estimated 800 children (44 percent boys and 56 percent girls) eight to eighteen years of age who were involved in child labor. Most children worked as street vendors, making and selling paper bags, and selling sweets and other snacks and chewing gum, garlic, bread and scallions, fruit juice, matches, lighters, and haberdashery for shop owners. Children as young as six to eight years were used to transport drugs locally and some children fourteen to eighteen years of age (mostly girls) were given passports and visas to transport drugs internationally. There were also reports that children eleven to twelve years of age were used to transport guns.

Degazon-Johnson and Associates (2002) conducted the study of child labor in fishing villages. This study revealed the irregular attendance of an estimated 25–37 percent of the children in fishing communities. Based on school attendance records, the study estimated that 2,000 children age six to seventeen years old could be involved in child labor. Of note, twelve-year-old boys, in their final year of primary schooling, exhibited high dropout rates. Not surprisingly, males comprised the majority of child laborers, but it was also recognized that girls were involved in hidden forms of child labor. In the fishing industry, children's work activities ranged from cleaning boats to dumping garbage to diving to set pots and retrieve fishing nets. Children were expected to dive to dangerous depths without protective gear. Other potential risks to children in fishing communities were associated with small fishing boats being used in the drug trade between Latin America and the United States. Home communities close to seaports made them difficult to police.

A report synthesizing the results of the three sectoral studies noted that the combined studies had estimated more than 4,000 child workers (D'Souza 2001). Most of these children worked part-time, combining school and work. But others worked long hours—up to seventeen hours per day—and many traveled across the island for work, taking advantage of job opportunities in tourist resort towns and urban centers. Factors contributing to child labor included poverty and the need to survive; family disintegration resulting from death, abandonment, or migration of parents; trauma of child abuse; school abandonment; peer pressure; social norms that tolerate child labor; and inadequate law enforcement. Consequences included risks to health, loss of human dignity, and unfulfilled aspirations. The synthesis report concluded that children wanted to attend school and gain work skills to get better jobs. Among the recommendations were to provide parenting counseling, revise the school curriculum to equip secondary school graduates with basic skills for the labor market, reintegrate street children by using residential centers, or train street educators to keep in touch with working children. One of the main lessons highlighted was the importance of multisector partnerships and the importance of involving working children in the process of policy development and programs (D'Souza 2001).

A few years later, Fox (2004) conducted a youth activity survey that provided updated quantitative data. Fox cautiously estimated that some 2.2 percent of children five to seventeen years of age (approximately 16,240) were involved in some form of economic activity in 2002, down from the 1994 estimate of 23,000. Another 21,000 children 10 years of age and older were identified who were neither working nor attending school. Most were in rural areas where employment opportunities were low.

Of the 16,240 economically active children, Fox estimated that 7,500 were engaged in "child labor" as defined by the ILO—that is, work that was excessive, harmful, or otherwise inappropriate for their age. The 7,500 child laborers were found "in areas of concentration across the island," mainly urban centers. The report also identified an important subgroup of child laborers not normally identified by household surveys. Approximately 6 percent of the child laborers were girls engaged in domestic housework for excessive hours. This supports earlier findings by Evans (1999) who reported that 13 percent of adolescents were hindered in their schoolwork because of excessive household chores. It also may help to explain why girls have been underrepresented in earlier quantitative surveys.

From Research to Action

While research laid the foundation for Jamaica's successful National Child Labor Program, the program is not all about research. Other key action elements of the program included an aggressive public education media campaign; a campaign to ratify ILO Conventions 138 and 182 (ratified in 2004); promulgation and enactment of national legislation (the Child Care and Protection Act, passed in 2005) and the appointment of a children's advocate in 2006 to monitor abuses and protect the rights of children; funding of NGO programs to prevent child labor and rehabilitate and reintegrate children and families at high risk of child labor in targeted communities in home, school, and community, and through family support; and provision of training for labor inspectors, policy makers, trade unions, and employers to improve monitoring and evaluation. On completion of the ILO project, political commitment to the problem of child labor was demonstrated by institutionalizing the national program within the Ministry of Labor and Social Security.

A number of programs have been established aimed at prevention, protection, and rehabilitation. Among these was a USAID-funded program entitled Uplifting Adolescents, providing health services, literacy, and skills training for school dropouts. The Possibility Programme for Street Children, an urban outreach program of the St Andrew Parish Church in Kingston and the government of Jamaica, supports working children and their families but needs consistent funding to expand its programs to eliminate child labor. The LEAP Center caters to inner-city boys who dropped out of school. The Sam Sharpe Teachers College supports literacy skills and school guidance programs. Children First (in St. Catherine) and the Western Society for the Upliftment of Children (in Montego Bay) include public education, alternative popular education, skills training, counseling, HIV/AIDS and environmental awareness, culture, and child rights. The National Initiative for Street Children, which predates the ILO interventions, targets children nine to fifteen years of age and provides food, remedial instruction, and vocational training for young Kingston-based street children.

Future Needs

To achieve a future without child labor, policy recommendations must promote parenting-education programs, provide microbusiness opportunities for parents, and support school-community partnerships. These will facilitate the return of some working children to the formal education system. The National Poverty Reduction Program must also target interventions to families in the poorest quintile of the population. Multisector partnerships have proven effective in providing services to child workers and their families and should be continued. Priority areas for collaboration include academic multidisciplinary research to fill remaining gaps; and partnerships with the National Child Labor Program and National HIV/AIDS Program, as sexually exploited children are at increased risk of contracting the virus.

Future research needs include both qualitative and quantitative studies to provide data on the scope, characteristics, and impact of child labor. Priorities include the situation of boys and girls involved in drug trafficking, human trafficking, child soldiers (in gangs), and child domestic workers. This research must be gender sensitive to clarify the different experiences of boys and girls across specific sectors in both public and private work spaces. Production and dissemination of data must continue to guide policy, advocacy, legal reform, planning, and programming. Coherent policies and programs will have a positive impact on national development as well as the Millennium Development Goals and targets. They can also reduce the risk of human trafficking, the risk of HIV/AIDS infection, and, eventually, eliminate child labor in the Jamaica.

References and Further Reading

Cooke, Ruel. *Baseline Survey on Child Labour: Informal Sector Work in Spanish Town, Jamaica.* Kingston: Government of Jamaica, 2002.

Crawford Brown, Claudette. "Child Prostitution and Pornography in Jamaica: A Brief Summary of the Issues." Paper prepared for the Department of Sociology and Social Work at the University of the West Indies, Kingston, 1996.

Degazon-Johnson and Associates. *Baseline Survey on the Fishing Areas of Rocky Point and Old Harbour Bay.* Kingston: Government of Jamaica, 2002.

D'Souza, Asha. *Preliminary Assessment of the Worst Forms of Child Labour in Jamaica—Summary Report of Base-Line Survey Conducted in 2001.* Kingston: ILO-IPEC, 2001.

Dunn, Leith. *Jamaica: Children in Prostitution: A Rapid Assessment.* Geneva: ILO-IPEC, 2001.

Ennew, Judith, and Pansy Young. *Child Labour in Jamaica.* Caribbean Labour Series 6. London: Anti-Slavery Society, 1981.

Evans, Hyacinth. *Gender and Achievement in Secondary Education in Jamaica.* Kingston: Planning Institute of Jamaica, 1999.

Fox, Kristin. *Jamaica Youth Activity Survey 2002.* Kingston: ILO-IPEC and Statistical Institute of Jamaica, 2004.

Jamaica, Government of. *Evaluation Report on National Child Labour Programme, ILO/IPEC.* Kingston: Government of Jamaica, 2004.

Ruddock, Thalia. *Child Labour in Jamaica.* Kingston: UNICEF and Statistical Institute of Jamaica, 1994.

Williams, Sian. *Sexual Violence and Exploitation of Children in Latin America and the Caribbean: The Case of Jamaica.* Kingston: Caribbean Child Development Centre, University of the West Indies, 1999.

Williams, Sian. "The Mighty Influence of Long Custom and Practice: Sexual Exploitation of Children for Cash and Goods in Jamaica." Paper presented at the Symposium on the Rights of the Child Caribbean Experience, Barbados, March 2000.

Wint, Eleanor, and Frances Madden. *Baseline Survey of Child Labour in Tourism Locations of Montego Bay and Negril.* Kingston: Government of Jamaica, 2002.

Commercial Sexual Exploitation of Children in Jamaica

Leith L. Dunn, Senior Lecturer/Head, Centre for Gender and Development Studies, University of the West Indies, and former Assistant Representative, UNFPA Caribbean Office

Like many poor nations that serve as tourist destinations for citizens of wealthier nations, Jamaica has been wrestling with a serious problem. Commercial sexual exploitation of children violates children's basic human rights, deprives them of access to basic needs, and increases their risk of exposure to violence, sexually transmitted disease, and unplanned pregnancy. It also undermines moral values, self-esteem, and self-worth, and limits children's ability to achieve life goals.

Previous Research

Jamaica's lucrative tourism industry presents both prospects and challenges for the people of Jamaica. Prospects are obvious, including the substantial national revenue generated and the direct and indirect employment opportunities for thousands of citizens. But the challenges are daunting, including the sexual exploitation of children in the country's informal sex tourism industry (Dunn and Dunn 1999, 2002).

Several studies provide insight into children's involvement in commercial sex work (Williams 1999, 2000; Campbell et al. 1999). Girls as young as fourteen are recruited to work as dancers in adult entertainment clubs. Williams describes the weekly "auctions" held in a bus park in a rural town to recruit young girls. There, some 150–200 girls and women competed for the interests of the men buying services and businessmen seeking to employ dancers. Starting as go-go dancers, girls may progress to exotic and pornographic dancing, and on to other forms of commercial sex work. Transactional sex between a child and an adult in exchange for goods or money becomes a survival strategy for the children and their parents, providing food for the family, children's school fees, and day-to-day financial support.

ILO Rapid Assessment on Children in Prostitution in Jamaica

In 2001, an ILO-commissioned Rapid Assessment on children in prostitution in Jamaica was published (Dunn 2001). The research objectives were to produce qualitative data describing the character, causes, and consequences of the involvement of children in prostitution and to provide recommendations for policy. The study used the ILO-UNICEF Rapid Assessment methodology, which is designed to collect qualitative data from hard-to-research populations whose activities are invisible and may be illegal. Using participatory methods and what is known as a nonrandom, "snowball" sampling method, 269 people provided data through interviews, focus groups, and direct observations. Thirty-five locations across seven parishes were sampled, including urban, rural, inner-city, suburban, and tourist locations. Approximately half the persons sampled were adults and half were children.

The study found that, while both sexes are at risk, girls were far more likely to be commercially sexually exploited and tended to experience more extreme forms of exploitation. Girls were generally involved in various forms of heterosexual relations and in pornography. Sexual exploitation of boys was mainly through homosexual contacts, with sex exchanged for money, material goods, and desired lifestyles. Older heterosexual women sometimes sexually exploited boys.

The most common categories of sexually exploited children and sexual exploitation of children were identified.

Street Children

Mostly boys, twelve to seventeen years of age, exchanged sex for basic economic survival. Many were from very poor families, suffered severe economic and social deprivation, and either attended school sporadically or not at all. Risk factors were lack of familial or institutional protection, which increased their vulnerability and also served as a "push" factor for living on the streets. Children in this category were among the most severely exploited. These children engaged in many types of deviant behavior to support themselves and survive on the streets; for some of the boys, this included sexually exploitative relationships with homosexual males in exchange for basic food, clothing, or token gifts. Consequences for these children included emotional trauma, sexually transmitted infections including HIV/AIDS, and physical violence from clients and peers. Engaging in homosexual activities not only increases risk and vulnerability, but because it operates in a secretive and invisible culture, it also tends to socially isolate the boys. Homophobia further isolates them, limiting access to support and rehabilitation. Campbell and Campbell (2001) have highlighted the importance of peer support, especially for male sex workers who have sex with men.

Sex for Gain

Children in this category, mostly girls ten to seventeen years of age, exchanged sex for money, food, and goods, in brothels, bars, massage parlors, go-go dancing clubs, and fishing communities. Their clients were both local and foreign males across several social classes. Again, weak familial and institutional structures emerged as pathways to the children engaging in sex for gain. In some cases children carry out these activities with the knowledge of their parents; some children even reported that their mothers were their pimps and managers, though this kind of parental involvement is not the norm. Like their adult counterparts involved in commercial sex work, the children had access to short-stay hotels and brothels. Some children operated from their homes and had regular clients as well as visitors. Like adult sex workers, the children performed various kinds of sexual activities, charging their clients varying rates in accordance with the activities they performed. Some children also acted as escorts for local and foreign clients.

Exotic Dancing / Go-Go Dancing

Many children, nearly all of them girls, are employed as go-go dancers, some of whom are recruited through weekly auctions in rural communities. Physical beauty and light skin color were considered to afford better opportunities for being invited to dance. The girls, like older dancers, are expected to be very good dancers and to be proficient with the pole around which they dance. They are also expected to wear tight, exotic clothes. Female relatives commonly introduced children into the industry and acted as their guardians. Among the contributory factors were not only economic need, but also greed and the desire to purchase expensive materials because of peer pressure.

Seasonal Tourism Sex

Children, mainly girls from thirteen to eighteen years of age, provided sexual services to tourists (e.g., college students on spring break), especially in resort towns such as Montego Bay and Negril. Children's increased involvement in sex work peaked in periods such as spring break. Some tourists pay to engage in sex with locals; children were also hired to work private parties. It was reported that European men, in particular, seek out local children, as they are seen as "black and exotic." Sex was exchanged for money to meet both wants (desired items and lifestyles) and needs (basic living expenses and education expenses).

Pornographic Productions

Children, mainly girls from thirteen to eighteen years of age, were involved in sex videos or photographs, live sex shows, and exotic dancing. Pornographic movies are difficult to police because of the secretive nature of these activities. In one reported case, a white adult male had enticed a young girl to become his prospective bride, but then exploited her by making and showing pornographic movies of their lovemaking, unbeknownst to her.

Massage Parlors

Girls from fifteen to eighteen years of age are forced to provide sex to clients as a condition of their employment. Recruited to work in massage parlors, this group of exclusively young educated females were forced to provide sex and fulfill the fantasies of their clients, who were mainly businessmen and professionals. Challenges encountered in identifying the scope and extent of exploitation in this subsector relate to difficulties in ascertaining the number of establishments because of the clandestine manner in which they operate, which encourages exploitation. Aggressive advertising of massage parlors was also noted.

"Sugar Daddy Girls" and "Chapses"

These are schoolgirls and schoolboys who receive security, education, and protection from older males and females in exchange for sex. This was the largest group of children involved in prostitution or related activities. Most of this form of sexual exploitation takes place behind closed doors in the homes of the adults, and sometimes in the children's own homes, or other places of safety. "Sugar daddies" (older males) exploit young girls by paying school fees and providing financial support to the child and her family in exchange for sex. Older women also exploit young school boys ("chapses"). The boys are entertained, taken to and picked up from school, sometimes in luxury vehicles, and taken on holidays. Some families are aware of the sexual abuse but receive the financial rewards nevertheless.

Causes and Consequences

While poverty was an important factor contributing to the commercial sexual exploitation of children, other factors were identified. These included informal tourism contacts, poor parenting practices, incidence of family violence, distorted values, lack of respect for the rights of children (especially girls), gender inequality, and peer influence. Children whose parents or guardians were very poor, who were abused or neglected, who were living and working on the streets, and whose parents had migrated or were living in state institutions were found to be at the greatest risk of exploitation. Among the consequences were low levels of educational attendance, low completion rates, and high dropout rates. The study showed that some children traded sex to get money for school fees, uniforms, books, or graduation expenses. Their involvement in sex-related activities reduced their ability to take advantage of the education opportunities available. Sex work interfered with completing homework, participation in school activities, and ability to concentrate in school because of fatigue and lack of sleep.

Conclusion

Publication of the Rapid Assessment led the U.S. State Department to downgrade Jamaica's standing in its Trafficking in Persons report. This could have subjected Jamaica to U.S. trade sanctions. In response, the government of Jamaica implemented an innovative and aggressive advocacy program aimed at reducing commercial sexual exploitation of children. This included enhanced public awareness and stronger legislation for violations. A range of public and private sector and civil society programs were implemented to address the problem. Following the Jamaican government's quick introduction of measures to reduce commercial sexual exploitation of children, the U.S. State Department returned Jamaica to its previous grade, and trade sanctions were averted. Further, the Rapid Assessment was the first major research component of what would become Jamaica's successful National Child Labor Program aimed not only at commercial sexual exploitation but also at other worst forms of child labor.

Jamaica is far from eliminating the commercial sexual exploitation of its children. But the people are now more aware of the problem, laws and policies have been enacted, training and sensitization have been provided for labor inspectors and other groups, the government's attention has been captured, and the capacity of Jamaica's civil society institutions has been strengthened.

References and Further Reading

Campbell, Penelope, and Ann Marie Campbell. *HIV/AIDS Prevention and Education for Commercial Sex Workers in Jamaica: An Exploratory Study and Need Assessment.* Report prepared for the National HIV/STI Prevention and Control Programme. Kingston: Ministry of Health, 2001.

Campbell, Shirley, Althea Perkins, and Patricia Mohammed. "Come to Jamaica and Feel Alright." In *Sun, Sex and Gold: Tourism and Sex Work in the Caribbean,* ed. Kamala Kempadoo. Oxford: Rowman and Littlefield, 1999.

Crawford-Brown, Claudette. *Children, Prostitution and Pornography in Jamaica, Brief Summary of the Situation.* Mimeo, Department of Sociology and Social Work, University of the West Indies, Kingston, 1996.

Dunn, Hopeton S., and Leith Dunn. *Jamaican Attitudes to Tourism.* Kingston: Jamaica Tourist Board, 1999.

Dunn, Hopeton S., and Leith Dunn. *People and Tourism: Issues and Attitudes in the Jamaican Hospitality Industry.* Kingston: Arawak Publications, 2002.

Dunn, Leith. *Jamaica: Children in Prostitution in Jamaica: A Rapid Assessment.* Geneva: ILO-IPEC, 2001.

ILO-UNICEF. *Manual on Child Labour Rapid Assessment Methodology.* Geneva: ILO-UNICEF, 2005.

U.S. Department of State, *Trafficking in Persons Report.* Washington, DC: U.S. Department of State, various years. http://www.state.gov/g/tip/rls/tiprpt/.

Williams, Sian. *Sexual Violence and Exploitation of Children in Latin America and the Caribbean: The Case of Jamaica.* Kingston: Caribbean Child Development Centre, University of the West Indies, 1999.

Williams, Sian. "The Mighty Influence of Long Custom and Practice: Sexual Exploitation of Children for Cash and Goods in Jamaica." Paper presented at the Symposium on the Rights of the Child and the Caribbean Experience, Barbados, March 13–15, 2000.

Wint, Eleanor, and Frances Madden. *Baseline Survey of Child Labour in Tourism Locations of Montego Bay and Negril.* Kingston: Government of Jamaica, 2002.

Part 4
North America

SECTION 1. CANADA

Child Labor in Canada

Nancy Janovicek, Assistant Professor, Department of History, University of Calgary

Canadian children have always worked, but urbanization and industrialization changed the patterns of child labor as well as the opportunities that it offered. In agricultural communities, parents expected children to work to develop the family farm, and in exchange children could expect to inherit the farm or to have their parents pay for their education. Many daughters from farm families and working-class urban families worked as domestic servants to contribute to the family economy. In the preindustrial period, many parents established their sons in an apprenticeship to ensure that they would be trained in a craft. Industrialization undermined the apprenticeship system in many sectors, and children entered factories as unskilled workers. The decline of apprenticeship instigated middle-class social reformers and labor leaders to question the usefulness of children's labor.

These new patterns of children's work coincided with the adoption of the modern conception of children as dependent and vulnerable to corrupting influences. In the mid-nineteenth century, social reformers began to argue that factories were an immoral and dangerous environment for children, and pressed for legislation to ban factories from hiring children under the age of fourteen. Children's advocates were also concerned that working-class families did not provide a suitable environment for children, and believed that schools would better prepare children to become productive citizens. Parents and labor leaders shared middle-class school promoters' enthusiasm for universal education, but many working-class families simply could not afford to educate their children. Federal and provincial governments were more influenced by manufacturers' arguments about the need for cheap labor in order to remain competitive with other nations than they were by reformers' demand for legislation to protect children. Moreover, since education and labor legislation were provincial responsibilities, Canadian policy to regulate child labor and to establish schools developed in a piecemeal manner. Ultimately, the needs of working-class families, rather than legislation, determined whether or not families sent their youngest members to work.

The Impact of Industrialization and Urbanization on Children's Work

Canada experienced an industrial revolution between the late 1840s and the 1890s. Industrial development was concentrated in the large urban centers in Quebec and Ontario, in particular Montreal, Toronto, and Hamilton. Industrial expansion in the Maritime provinces was short-lived due to the absence of a diverse resource base, lack of investment in New Brunswick and Nova Scotia, and a small population, which was drawn to the factories in Boston. The fur trade continued to be the foundation of economic development in Western Canada until the 1870s and 1880s, when the federal government began to promote agricultural development on the prairies. Economic policy fostered industrial development primarily in Ontario and Quebec. In 1878, the Conservative government, led by John A. Macdonald, adopted an economic policy, commonly called the National Policy, based on high tariffs to stimulate manufacturing in central Canada, immigration to promote agricultural development in Western Canada, and the completion of a transcontinental railway to facilitate trade among the provinces. Though the policy unfolded in a haphazard manner, the number of factories in central Canada increased significantly as a result of tariff policy. In addition, the late nineteenth century witnessed the consolidation of small factories and increased mechanization in many industries. Industrial development in central Ontario stimulated growth in coal production in Nova Scotia, British Columbia, New Brunswick, Alberta, and Saskatchewan. This growth increased demand for boys to operate ventilation doors, lead horses, and fill wagons. In 1866, about 450 boys worked in coal mines; by the early twentieth century more than 1,200 boys were employed in coal production. Hiring boys for unskilled jobs was much more common in Eastern Canada than it was in Western Canada because British Columbia colliers relied on Chinese men as a cheap source of labor rather than miners' sons.

The majority of Canadians lived in rural areas until 1921, and thus, the majority of children who worked (often without pay) were employed in the agricultural sector. Rural depopulation began in the 1870s and 1880s, when agricultural crises and the decrease of available arable land compelled many families to move to the cities to work in factories. Migration to industrial centers fundamentally altered family economies. In cities, families could no longer produce most of their own food and clothing and relied on waged labor to purchase necessities. Making ends meet became increasingly difficult for many families because mechanization undercut the negotiating power of skilled craftsmen. Most working-class families relied on a combination of wages earned by the male head of the household and children. In families headed by a skilled worker, children's work provided stability, but in families in which the main breadwinner was an unskilled worker, children's wages were vital to survival. Children of widows and deserted women, or from families in which the father was not able to work, were most likely to enter factories at a very young age.

Mechanization of the labor process introduced tasks that did not require heavy lifting or specialized knowledge, thus making it possible to hire women and children as unskilled workers. Cigar making and textiles and clothing were the primary sites of children's labor, but a significant number of children also worked in printing, basket making, brick making, glass making, woodwork, and broom and brush making. Most children entered factories when they were twelve years old, but it was not unusual to find children as young as eight years old running errands and cleaning up. The average workday was ten to twelve hours. Factory owners employed children at low wages in order to maximize profits. In Montreal cigar factories in the 1880s, boys earned $1 a week during their first year, and their earnings increased by $1 in the next two years. Girls earned less than boys. These wages were reduced by penalties for lateness, talking, and other conduct that managers deemed unruly. In addition to fines, managers and foremen used corporal punishment to discipline young workers for disobedience and slow work. In testimony recorded in the *Report of the Royal Commission on the Relations of Labour and Capital* (1889), children reported cruel and severe beatings. Managers denied excessive punishment and defended their actions by insisting that they should have the same right to punish children as parents and schoolmasters.

Nineteenth-century factories were dangerous, unhealthy places, and social reformers worried about the health of youthful workers. It was common for children to suffer debilitating injuries on the job. If families sued, they were not likely to win meaningful compensation because the common-law precedent of "modified liability" put the onus on the worker to prove the employer was aware of unsafe work conditions. The Ontario Workers' Compensation Injuries Act (1886) changed the definition of liability so employers could no longer argue that they were not aware of dangerous conditions. As a result of the legislation, injured employees were more successful in the courts, but settlements were not generous. When fourteen-year-old Adam Moore lost his arm on the job, the judge overruled a jury decision in his favor, arguing that he was old enough to be capable of understanding the dangers of his job. Moore won an appeal, but the judge awarded him only $500. A contributory insurance scheme was not in place in Ontario until 1914, leaving families with little support to care for disabled children.

Not all children worked in factories. The clothing and textile industries relied on contracting out, and many girls worked with their mothers in homes converted into sweatshops. Sweated labor paid less because the wages were based on piecework, and fierce competition and long workdays drove wages down. An 1896 study on the sweating system in Canada reported that children often worked more than sixty hours per week. Working conditions in home sweatshops were as bad as those in factories, and these children were even more vulnerable to exploitation because they were not protected by labor legislation. Many boys were engaged in street trades such as polishing shoes and selling newspapers and other small wares. These boys had more autonomy than young factory workers, but because they were so visible, they also attracted the attention of middle-class child savers, who were concerned that the rough street culture and lack of proper supervision would turn these children into irresponsible and unproductive adults. Reformers also worried that young women would be lured into prostitution. In 1913, Ontario passed legislation that prohibited boys under the age of twelve and girls under the age of sixteen from any street trade after 10 P.M.

Factory Acts

The decline of the apprenticeship system instigated the campaign to ban child labor in the 1830s and 1840s. National labor groups, such as the Trades and Labour Congress (1883) and the Knights of Labor (1898) passed resolutions to ban children under the age of fourteen from factory work. Labor leaders' primary concern was that children's labor would undercut men's wages, but they also shared middle-class reformers' concerns about the impact of dangerous factory conditions on children's health. Anglo-Saxon Protestant reformers were particularly worried about girls and young women's reproductive health. Their concerns were connected to fears of "race suicide" that were fueled by increasing immigration rates, the declining birthrates of Anglo-Saxon women, and high infant mortality rates.

Parliament considered regulation of child labor in 1879, 1880, and 1882 but did not pass legislation. Government officials were unsympathetic to the difficulties working-class families faced. The Royal Commission on Mills and Factories (1882) recommended legislation banning child labor but blamed parents' laziness and greed rather than low wages for the extent of child labor. The Canadian Manufacturers' Association convinced politicians that banning child labor would make it difficult to compete with nations that allowed factories to employ children at low wages. Jurisdiction also prevented federal action since the provinces were responsible for labor legislation.

Ontario passed the Factories' Act in 1884, which went into effect in 1886, and the Quebec Manufacturing Act became law in 1885. Both provinces made it illegal to hire boys under twelve and girls under fourteen, though the Quebec legislation included a provision that made it possible to hire younger children if parents produced a special work certificate. Children could not work longer than ten hours per day, and Ontario set a maximum of sixty hours per week. The acts applied only to establishments with more than twenty workers; thus, the smaller firms that tended to rely on child labor because of intense competition could still hire young children. Piecework conducted in private homes was explicitly excluded from the legislation. Both acts included measures to improve ventilation, sanitation, and safety in the factories. The legislation was ineffective because there were only three inspectors in Ontario, and they tended to be more sympathetic to manufacturers than to workers' grievances, and Quebec did not hire factory inspectors until 1888. In that same year, however, Quebec amended its legislation to cover factories with fewer than twenty employees, and to ban employment of all children under age fourteen. Ontario increased the minimum age for boys working in factories to fourteen in 1875, and extended the legislation to include factories with more than five employees in 1886.

Even though more children worked in the 1890s than in previous decades, the proportion of children working for wages began to decrease in the 1880s. In 1881, children made up 8.2 percent of the workforce; in 1891 they made up 6.4 percent; and in 1901, only 3.5 percent of the workforce was under age fourteen. The decrease in the importance of child labor had less to do with restrictive legislation than it did with immigration, which introduced a new source of cheap labor, and the consolidation of industries, which stabilized markets and made children's work less necessary. By the 1890s, men were more likely to find steady work that paid wages that enabled families to survive without the wages of its youngest members.

Education Policy

Politicians began to debate establishment of a free school system in the 1840s, but it was not until the 1890s that some provinces introduced legislation that made school attendance compulsory up to the age of fourteen. Early school reform attempted to accommodate children's work schedules, but with the rise of the child-saving movement in the 1880s, school promoters began to argue that children would benefit from the moral environment of the schools. Municipalities hired truancy officers to attempt to regulate legislation that made school attendance compulsory for children up to age fourteen. By the late nineteenth century, factory inspectors opposed child labor and began to press for measures to enforce mandatory education because they were concerned about illiteracy. In 1907, the Quebec legislature made a literacy test compulsory for fourteen-year-old children who began to work in a factory, and obliged fourteen- to sixteen-year-old workers who could not read or write to attend night school after a ten-hour workday. The 1907 *Report on Child Labour* argued that education should replace labor. By 1905, every province except Quebec had legislation that made school attendance compulsory for children between the ages of seven and fourteen. Quebec passed the Compulsory Education Act in 1943.

Although the majority of children were enrolled in school by the 1870s, few attended school regularly. Provinces passed legislation that gave municipalities the right to levy funds to finance schools, but parents still paid for books and school fees in most jurisdictions well into the twentieth century. These added costs made school attendance unaffordable for many, and in the poorest families, parents could not afford the boots and warm clothing that their children needed to attend school in the winter. Municipalities would waive school fees to encourage school attendance, but most parents were reluctant to accept this due to the stigma associated with public relief. Working-class parents wanted their children to have access to education and protested overcrowded schools and lack of resources. They were supported by labor leaders who believed that working-class children had a right to education, and protested government measures, such as the half-day education, that tried to accommodate education and work patterns.

Availability of work and the needs of working-class families determined whether or not children attended school instead of working. Patterns of school attendance varied in different cities, but children were more likely to attend school during economic slumps, when there was little work available. By the early twentieth century, more families had enough earning power to send their children to school, and most working-class families recognized that education would improve their children's standard of living. Provincial governments began to increase the minimum school-leaving age to sixteen after the First World War.

The wars and the Depression introduced new discourses about young people as the cornerstone of modern prosperity and industrial development. Sociologists and political economists argued that young people were leaving school early to take dead-end jobs. In 1919, the federal government introduced the Technical Education Act to encourage provinces to develop technical education and modern apprenticeship programs. Some inroads were made at the provincial level, but the Great Depression put experiments with the modern, state-managed apprenticeship system on hold. During both world wars, adolescents played an important role in helping employers cope with labor shortages, but teenage workers could not find employment during the Depression of the 1930s. The federal government instructed the Canadian Youth Commission to investigate the impact of unemployment on young people, and it concluded that war and high unemployment had created a demoralized generation. It urged the federal government to take responsibility for full employment and to develop programs to train young people for meaningful work.

After the Second World War, children's advocates adopted the language of universal children's rights. Politicians argued that all children had a right to education to improve their opportunities, and that all children under the age of sixteen should be guaranteed a minimum standard of living. The federal government passed the Family Allowances Act in 1945, the first universal social welfare program in Canada. Under the legislation, all parents received a monthly stipend until their children reached age sixteen; the payment was based on the age of the children and the size of the family. The act gave the federal government more control in working-class parents' decisions about their children's labor because children had to attend school in order for the parents to be eligible for the program.

The majority of teenagers over the age of sixteen continued to work in postwar Canada, but in part-time jobs after school rather than as full-time workers. Experts argued that after-school work instilled discipline and character in teenagers; thus, even upper-middle-class teens were encouraged to find part-time jobs. Generally children worked for pocket money, but it was still common for children to contribute some of their earnings to the family economy, particularly in immigrant families. Emphasis on education and the relative prosperity of the postwar era extended children's dependence on the family to the age of sixteen, but entering the labor market as a full-time worker remained the rite of passage to adulthood in modern Canada.

References and Further Reading

Bradbury, Bettina. *Working Families: Age, Gender, and Daily Survival in Industrializing Montreal.* Kingston: McGill-Queen's University Press, 1993.

Bullen, John. "Hidden Workers: Child Labour and the Family Economy in Late-Nineteenth Century Urban Ontario." *Labour/Le Travail* 18 (Fall 1986): 163–87.

Comacchio, Cynthi. *The Dominion of Youth: Adolescence and the Making of Modern Canada, 1920–1950.* Waterloo: Wilfrid Laurier University Press, 2006.

Copp, Terry. *The Anatomy of Poverty: The Condition of the Working Class in Montreal, 1897–1929.* Toronto: McClelland and Stewart, 1974.

Davey, Ian. "The Rhythm of Work and the Rhythm of School." In *Egerton Ryerson and His Times: Essays on the History of Education,* ed. A. Chaiton and N. McDonald, 221–53. Toronto: Macmillan, 1978.

Gaffield, Chad. "Children, Schooling, and Family Reproduction in Nineteenth-Century Ontario." *Canadian Historical Review* 72:2 (1991): 157–91.

Hurl, Lorna F. "Restricting Child Factory Labour in Late Nineteenth Century Ontario." *Labour/Le Travail* 21 (Spring 1988): 87–121.

MacIntosh, Robert. *Boys in the Pits: Child Labour in Coal Mines.* Montreal: McGill-Queen's University Press, 2000.

Marshall, Dominique. *The Social Origins of the Welfare State: Quebec Families, Compulsory Education, and Family Allowances, 1940–1960.* Translated by Nicola Doone Danby. Waterloo: Wilfrid Laurier University Press, 2006.

Piva, Michael J. "The Workmen's Compensation Movement in Ontario." *Ontario History* 39 (1975): 39–56.

Prentice, Alison. *The School Promoters: Education and Social Class in Mid-Nineteenth Century Upper Canada.* Toronto: University of Toronto Press, 2004.

Royal Commisstion on the Relations of Labour and Capital. *Report of the Royal Commission on the Relations of Labour and Capital in Canada.* Ottawa: Royal Commission, 1889.

Sutherland, Neil. "'We Always Had Things to Do': The Paid and Unpaid Work of Anglophone Children Between the 1920s and the 1960s." *Labour/Le Travail* 25 (Spring 1990): 105–41.

Children in Canadian Mining

Elizabeth Perry, former Head Librarian, Centre for Industrial Relations,
University of Toronto, Canada

Coal mining in Canada began in the early nineteenth century in shallow mines in Nova Scotia. By the confederation of the nation in 1867, approximately 4,000 workers were employed in much deeper, steam-powered mines, chiefly in the province of Nova Scotia and on Vancouver Island in the province of British Columbia. Smaller coal mines also existed in the provinces of New Brunswick, Alberta, and Saskatchewan and the interior of British Columbia, but Nova Scotia alone accounted for more than half of Canada's coal production until 1910 and employed by far the greatest number of workers. In 1866, approximately 450 boys worked in coal mines across Canada; by 1890 the number had grown to approximately 1,000, reaching its peak at 1,200 boys employed in the first decade of the twentieth century.

"Pit boys," as the young workers were known, were employed in the coal mines of Nova Scotia and, to a lesser extent, Vancouver Island. Mine owners in these large, technologically advanced collieries recruited experienced coal miners from northern England, southern Wales, and Scotland. These men brought with them a traditional belief in their right as craftsmen to control entry into their trade, and a traditional practice whereby miners contracted directly with mine owners. Each miner would hire, supervise, and train his sons or young male relatives in a family-based apprenticeship system that simultaneously controlled access to mining jobs and ensured employment and income for his own family. Initially, the experienced miner was valued for his ability to recognize danger in the mine and for his mastery of techniques required to produce large, unbroken pieces of coal. His wage premium and autonomy were gradually diminished, especially as the market for smaller, coking coal expanded and a supply of inexperienced, transient, and seasonal workers became available.

While mine owners contested the miners' authority to control entry to the apprenticeship system, they continued to hire boys because they were the cheapest source of unskilled labor available. In the mines at Sydney, Nova Scotia, boys constituted 24.7 percent of the labor force in 1866, 27.6 percent in 1876, and 26.9 percent in 1886. Generation after generation worked in the mine; entering work was an accepted rite of passage for a boy, and endowed him with higher status in his family and community. The passage of the Nova Scotia Mines Act in 1873 prohibited employment of boys under the age of ten, and of any females; it also restricted hours of work to ten per day and sixty per week for children under the age of sixteen, and fifty-four hours per week for children under age thirteen. By 1891, following a submission from the miners' union, the Provincial Workmen's Association, and in spite of resistance from mine operators, the Mines Act was amended; no boy was to work underground unless he had reached age twelve and was able to read, write, and count. The province also passed education laws, beginning in 1883, promoting compulsory school attendance, although it was not until 1915 in urban areas and 1923 in rural mining communities that school attendance was made compulsory for children between the ages of six and sixteen.

In British Columbia, the Mines Act of 1877 prohibited boys under the age of twelve from working in the mines, and required that mine operators obtain special permission to hire boys under the age of fourteen. Boys from fourteen to sixteen years old were restricted to working six hours per day and five days per week. The act was amended in 1883 to allow full-time work for boys age fourteen years and older. Not only was child labor protection stronger in British Columbia than in Nova Scotia, but it was more rigorously enforced and paired with more restrictive education legislation. By 1876, all children ages seven to twelve were required to attend school for at least six months of the year. Further, in the mines on Vancouver Island, boys' access to mining jobs was undermined by a plentiful supply of Asian laborers willing to work at or below a boy's wages. Chinese were first employed in 1867; by the 1870s they worked underground as unskilled laborers, and in 1883, Chinese strikebreakers were employed underground as miners. Miners and their protective associations conducted strikes and lobbied for legislation to exclude Chinese from the mines, but they were unsuccessful. As a result, pit boys never represented more than 5.2 percent of the mine labor force on Vancouver Island (in 1896), and by 1914, only fifty-two boys were employed (2.2 percent of the labor force).

Working Conditions for Boys

Most pit boys were from thirteen to sixteen years of age, with younger boys performing less physically demanding tasks. The workday began at six or seven in the morning, and might extend for ten hours, although the hours were dictated by the activities of the day. Boys could be employed on the mine surface as "tally boys," helping to record the amount of coal each miner sent to the surface; driving and tending horses or mules; operating pumps; dumping coal cars on the wharf; or as "pickers," picking out any impurities as the coal passed on a conveyor belt. Underground, the youngest and smallest worked in the dark as "trappers" or "door-boys," opening doors to allow the passage of miners, horses, and wagons, and closing the doors after them to maintain the underground ventilation system. Older, stronger boys would drive the horses used to haul cut coal to the surface, or work "at the bords" as helpers to the miners cutting coal at the coal face. This most physically demanding job was essential preparation if the boy was to graduate to the highest-paying position as a miner, customarily around age eighteen. A strong sense of camaraderie among boys, combined with a precocious sense of independence, led to frequent protests by "boys committees." In the mines of Nova Scotia between 1880 and 1926, evidence exists of forty-seven strikes by boys (independent of adults)—usually over pay, hours of work, discipline, or changes to job duties.

By the end of the nineteenth century, technological advances and mechanization in the mine reduced the need for unskilled labor and put a premium on education, a combination that redirected boys from the mines to the schools. Early twentieth-century social opinion had shifted to the view that child labor was detrimental to a child's moral, intellectual, and physical health. As miners' incomes improved and social programs such as pensions and insurance developed, there was less financial need for children to contribute to the family income. And finally, a general decline in demand for coal after World War I reduced employment levels in the mines. Mine owners and unions reached agreements that preference in hiring should go to married men and family breadwinners. By the 1930s, boys were gone from Canada's coal mines.

References and Further Reading

Kealey, Gregory, ed. *Canada Investigates Industrialism: The Royal Commission on the Relations of Labor and Capital, 1889.* Toronto: University of Toronto Press, 1973.

McIntosh, Robert. *Boys in the Pits: Child Labour in Coal Mines.* Montreal: McGill-Queen's University Press, 2000.

Sutherland, Neil. *Childhood in English Canadian Society: Framing the Twentieth Century Consensus.* Waterloo, Ontario: Wilfrid Laurier University Press, 2000.

Nation Builders: Orphans in the Canadian Wilderness

Gail H. Corbett, teacher and author

From the early nineteenth century to the commencement of World War II, the British and Canadian governments cosponsored child emigrant programs whereby British pauper children served as indentured laborers in Canada's rapidly evolving agrarian society. As early as 1825, the concept of transplanting homeless pauper children from Great Britain to the colonies was advanced by members of the Canada Company, who suggested that the pauper population be employed as indentured laborers to assist retired British military men in their colonial agricultural ventures. By 1830, the Children's Friend Society of London had sent pauper children to Canada, placing them on farms between Montreal and Niagara Falls.

Britain viewed Canada as a prime destination for all emigrants, including pauper children. If orphaned and destitute children were left on the streets of Great Britain, the poverty cycle would be repeated. If they were transplanted, both Britain and Canada would prosper. Child emigration was viewed as benefiting the child, the motherland, and the developing country. Emigration provided homeless children with a place to live, to work, and to eventually raise their own families. It provided agricultural and domestic laborers for growing nations as well as relieving Britain of its increasing pauper population.

Emergence of the Barnardo Emigration Program

The Industrial Revolution in Britain did not initially increase general prosperity among working-class families. As the poor poured into Britain's great evolving cities, overpopulation and unemployment created a class of pauper children who took to the streets seeking food and sustenance. As these "street arabs" filled the cities, the motherland turned its eyes toward emigration, toward the ever-expanding and fertile lands of the colonies, as a solution to poverty. By the 1850s, Lord Shaftesbury had filled his "Ragged Schools," yet thousands of destitute urchins still slept in alleys and on rooftops. Shaftesbury agreed that agricultural situations for England's street children would benefit both the motherland and the emerging colonies.

In the 1860s, propelled by Canada's crying need for agricultural labor, and supported by Lord Shaftesbury's emigration policies, feminist Maria Rye and Annie MacPherson, a Quaker, spearheaded organized child emigration to Canada. Within a few years, numerous child emigration agencies surfaced, among them Fagan's Homes, Middlemore Homes, and National Children's Homes, but the most successful program was founded by Dr. Thomas Barnardo. Known by some as a child emancipator, this idealistic young medical student started a school for the poor in a donkey shed in east London, soon had the support of England's charitable wealthy, and eventually the patronage of Queen Victoria.

Barnardo was aware of criticism of using Canada's virgin soil as the great dumping ground for Britain's urchins, but it was clear to him that "[w]e in England, with our 470 inhabitants to the square mile, were choking, elbowing, starving each in the struggle for existence: the British colonies were crying out for men to till their soil" (Barnardo 1889). He echoed the sentiments of many on the multiple benefits of child emigration:

> Well planned and wisely conducted child-emigration especially to Canada, contains within

> its bosom the truest solution to some of the mother country's most perplexing problems, and the supply of our Colonies' most urgent needs. . . . First, it relieves the over-crowded centres of city life and the congested labor markets. Second, it supplies what the colonies are most in want of, an increase of the English speaking population. Third, it confers upon the children themselves unspeakable blessings. The change at the young and formative period of their lives gives to each child whose character is good, and who is successfully absorbed into the colonial population, such an immediate prospect of an independent existence upon a higher plain as hardly could have been imagined as within its reach. (Barnardo 1889)

By 1868, Barnardo was convinced that child emigration was the only answer to Britain's crowded streets and poverty and carefully proceeded with a child emigration plan. In the autumn of 1882, he finally launched the first shipload of Barnardo boys, bound for Canada. When they arrived in Canada they were inspected by federal and provincial agents and distributed into Ontario's rural districts. In 1883, the first party of Barnardo girls entered Canada and were received at Peterborough, Ontario, and Niagara Falls.

By the 1900s, child emigration was in full swing. Barnardo children filled the steerage compartments of Britain's major steamships: the Corinthian, the Melita, the Parisian, and the Sardinian. The Allan Line was considered part and parcel of the Barnardo emigration machinery. Four parties of children sailed each year. Four hundred children could be transported at one crossing. The total cost per child from London to Canada was less than the cost of one year's boarding-out in England.

While orphaned and pauper children were also sent to Australia and South Africa, Canada was the principal destination for emigrating children because it was the nearest British colony. Canada's weather was temperate and the demand for settlers insatiable. Only the "flower of the flock" was selected. Each child was to be sound in body and mind, and educated in the rudiments of a plain English education. Boys would have some training in agriculture, girls in domestic science. Children applying for the Canada List were assembled at the great export emporium, Stepney Causeway, where they were lectured and outfitted for the great Canadian adventure. Doris Frayne, who emigrated to Canada in 1915, recalled being told:

> You are going to a new country and you are British subjects and you are to show the people in Canada that you are a good subject. It is your duty to prove yourself to the Canadians, especially to the Canadian government because it was they who are interested in having young people come out. If you don't do well the government will not have that class of young person come over. It is your life. You know what is right and wrong. (Doris Frayne, quoted in Corbett 2002, 97)

Major points of entry into Canada were St. John; New Brunswick; Halifax; Nova Scotia; Portland, Maine; and Point Levis, Quebec. Here, children boarded a train called the Barnardo Special, provided by the Grand Trunk Railway. This iron artery carried thousands of children into Ontario's agricultural heartland. Farmers could apply for a Barnardo child in advance of their arrival. These children would be dropped off at the appointed train stations throughout the province. Children not preregistered for farms were taken to receiving and distribution homes at Belleville, Peterborough, Niagara Falls, Ontario, or even Winnipeg, Manitoba, where Barnardo had secured an 8,900-acre industrial farm. From these homes, children were placed on Canadian farms, where they were expected to work in exchange for board. It was Barnardo policy that each child emigrant should receive board, clothing, and an allowance for labor performed. This allowance was to be deposited by the farmer in the Canadian Imperial Bank of Commerce. Children who "fell on good soil" would receive a stipend every month. This money could be withdrawn at the end of their indenture, when boys reached eighteen and girls reached twenty-one.

Barnardo Children in Canada

While a number of criticisms of the Barnardo program surfaced over the years, for many children placed on Canadian farms, emigration was a true blessing: "I was really lucky to have a farm home where I was treated as a son, although I was never officially adopted. I worked on the farm with my employer until I was married and then I bought the farm from the kind family where I had spent my first five years in Canada" (Walter Longyear, quoted in Corbett 2002, 108).

In spite of the ups and downs encountered by tens of thousands of child emigrants to Canada, the success rate was very high. In 1893, Canada's high commissioner to London, Sir Charles Tupper, stated, "I am happy to bear testimony to the great and good work of Dr. Thomas Barnardo," and Sir John Carling, minister of agriculture, claimed that 98 percent of Barnardo child emigrants placed in Canada had been successful.

Life on Canadian farms was challenging. The farms were miles apart. Emigrant children were isolated. Canadian weather and customs were all foreign to the little immigrants and the farm workload was heavy. While Barnardo cautioned, "To over work and make a drudge of little boys or girls of ten or eleven would be a wrong to be condemned," there was no question that the children were expected to work. They were, in fact, indentured laborers, boys until eighteen, girls until twenty-one. But work from an early age was the norm, and childhood consisted of a very brief time span. As early as five or six years of age, children of the laboring poor were expected to earn their keep and secure a few extra pence for the family pocket. Children were considered little adults and expected to do their share of work. The sooner they began work, the sooner everyone could benefit. This work ethic existed in both rural and urban communities, in the Old World and in the New.

As the child emigrants grew older and prospered, they were encouraged to invite their British families to immigrate to Canada. In 1903, *Ups and Downs,* the official Barnardo magazine, urged Barnardo boys to save up money for the passage of mothers, sisters, and brothers. Barnardo staff would be happy to look the family up and assist with their emigration to Canada. Once grown, many emigrants stayed in the same rural areas to which they had emigrated, married, raised their own families, and, as Barnardo observed, "[a]ttached to the land, making two potatoes grow where one grew before, and contributing in this way to the wealth of the country." Some moved on to employment in the cities:

> I landed at my Canadian farm. I had turned 14 on the way over and felt I was ready for work. We were briefed on the style of life in Canada. One point I remember quite well was that when a farmer speaks, he may seem harsh and not to get upset, that is their way of life. My farm family was very good and saw that I got lots to eat and attend Sunday School. When WWII broke out, I joined the Navy. I finished with the service, removed the cash I had in my Barnardo Account and moved on. (Jim Inwards, quoted in Corbett 2002, 118)

While many Barnardo children thrived, many were maltreated and abused, leading even to death. Some children ran away, as in the case of film star Wallace Ford, who ran out of Canada and into Hollywood fame. In order to provide some child protection, Barnardo hired personnel to periodically visit the children in their farm placements. One criticism of the program, however, was its sometimes less than adequate monitoring. Some children were removed from unsuitable situations, but others were not:

> At the age of 14, I was sent to various farms as a domestic. Farm jobs were not to my liking. There was always some man trying to make advances towards me. So being a strong minded girl I told the Home visitor I would not work on a farm. This caused me some uncomfortable treatment but finally I was given a place in a small Canadian village which seemed quite normal except for the occasional snobbery because I was a Barnardo girl. But I learned how to protect myself. I was a born leader and became involved in the church. . . . I never advertised my connection, no body likes to be a "Home Child," but I am grateful to Barnardos for bringing me to Canada. (Ethel Lewis, quoted in Corbett 2002, 109)

Another criticism, one that surfaced early in the program, was that some children were taken from Britain without parental knowledge or consent. In 1890, the Custody of the Children's Act, referred to as the Barnardo Act, explicitly granted parish authorities permission to send children to the colonies without the consent of their parents.

From Sea to Sea

By 1912 there was not an accessible part of the Dominion of Canada where Barnardo boys and girls were not to be found. Older boys and girls were now fathers and mothers, some owning their own homes and farms and bringing in more child emigrants to work on the land, and to build their own life. Their descendants entered all walks of life: medicine, teaching, politics, theology, and many trades. They rose from orphans in the wilderness to nation builders extraordinaire.

By World War I, child emigration to Canada had slowed to a trickle, and the last Barnardo child emigrated to Canada on July 8, 1939. In March 2000, the British Home Children mail list was created to help descendents with genealogical research. To date there are estimated to be more than 4 million Canadian descendants searching for their British child emigration roots. This does not include the thousands of child emigrants who were adopted by Canadian families. Many Canadians will never know that their forebears were child emigrants, orphans in the wilderness. Today we consider these child emigrants to be among Canada's most courageous nation builders.

References and Further Reading

Barnardo, T.J. *Something Attempted, Something Gained.* London: William Clowes and Son, 1889.

Batt, John H. *Dr. Barnardo, Foster Father of No-body's Children.* London: SW Partridge, 1904.

Bready, J.Wesley. *Dr Barnardo, Physician, Pioneer, Prophet.* London: Allen and Unwin, 1930.

Corbett, Gail H. *Nation Builders: Barnardo Children in Canada.* 4th ed. Toronto: Dundurn Press, 2002.

Harrison, Phyllis. *The Home Children.* Winnipeg: Watson and Dwyer, 1979.

Mayhew, Henry. *London Labour and the London Poor.* New York: Dover Publications, 1968.

Morton, W.L. *Manitoba: A History.* Toronto: University of Toronto Press, 1967.

Neuman, A.R. *Dr. Barnardo.* London: Constable, 1914.

Parr, Joy. *Labouring Children: British Immigrant Apprentices to Canada, 1869–1924.* London: Croom Helm, 1980.

Pinchbeck, Ivy. *Children in English Society.* London: Routledge and Kegan-Paul, 1973.

Scott, Carolyn. *Ever Open Door.* London: Lutterworth, 1972.

Sutherland, Neil. *Children in English Canadian Society.* Toronto: University of Toronto Press, 1976.

Wagner, Gillian. *Barnardo.* London: Weidenfeld and Nicolson, 1979.

Evolution of Child Welfare Policy in Canada

Maureen Baker, Professor of Sociology, University of Auckland, New Zealand

Policies and programs relating to the welfare and well-being of children in Canada have evolved along with changes in children's value to parents, the social circumstances of parenthood and childhood, and new ideas about children's rights. From the nineteenth to the twentieth century, children's economic contributions to households and their potential to support parents in old age became less important with urbanization, compulsory education, and the development of old-age pensions. Redefinitions of motherhood also influenced childhood, particularly ideologies that focused on the mother's natural duty to support the health and well-being of her child and to raise "quality" children. The value of children was further enhanced by new government programs focusing on children's welfare and rights rather than simply their discipline and education. The economic utility of children was gradually replaced by the idea that government should invest in children for the good of the nation.

In the eighteenth century, both English common law and Quebec civil law expected parents to maintain, protect, and educate their children, giving them nearly absolute authority over their offspring. However, controversies about the growth of unsupervised and destitute children that accompanied urban expansion forced governments in the late nineteenth century to create laws to protect children and intervene in families with parenting problems (Bala and Clarke 1981). Parental authority was eroding. By the 1960s, the concept of the "best interests of the child" became a guiding principle to justify state intervention in cases of neglect, delinquency, or custody disputes. Eventually, child welfare reformers, backed by the United Nations, argued that children should be granted most of the same legal rights as adults, though many see this as more lip service than action.

The evolution of children's rights for those born outside legal marriage is particularly evident. Well into the twentieth century, such children were considered illegitimate because they had no legal father, which meant that they took their mother's name, were not entitled to paternal support or inheritance, and were socially denigrated. Child advocates, especially in the 1960s, argued that children should not be punished for their parents' behavior. The concept of illegitimacy was gradually removed from laws. All children were granted similar rights, and lone mothers were supported by provincial welfare benefits. After the 1980s, governments tightened the enforcement of paternal child support and provided legal advocacy for children involved in family disputes or disruptions.

This essay focuses on three areas of child welfare in Canada: child protection, the right to education and child care, and state income support.

Child Protection Policies

Daytime supervision of children became a political issue in the 1880s when the number of truant and delinquent children began to increase in industrialized towns. Children were often left to their own devices while parents worked, but orphans and children in trouble with the law were placed in children's homes run by charities. Social reform groups urged governments to create protective legislation for these children as well as to safeguard the public from juvenile delinquents.

In early Canadian policy, local governments were expected to administer and fund welfare programs, including operating industrial and reformatory schools to house and educate children who were abused, orphaned, or delinquent. In 1891, the first Children's Aid Society was established in Canada, and by 1893, reformers persuaded the Ontario legislature to enact the Children's Protection Act to mandate these societies to remove abused or problem children from parents and become their legal guardians. The development of child protection agencies and legislation demonstrated state concern for children's well-being but also signaled that parents no longer held absolute authority over them.

Abused, neglected, or delinquent children were removed from their families and placed in institutions providing basic care, education, work skills, and moral training. Over the years, however, professionals came to believe that these institutions failed to provide adequate love and stimulation. Also, residential institutions proved costly and presented disciplinary challenges for care workers. The Toronto Children's Aid Society began to place children in private foster homes whenever possible, so they could grow up in a family. In addition, children's institutions became less prevalent in Ontario after 1920, although many still operated in other provinces.

Canada also received an influx of poor, homeless, and orphaned children who were brought to the colony from overcrowded British cities. British philanthropist Thomas Barnardo organized the emigration of more than 25,000 children to Canada between 1882 and 1915 (Corbett 1981). Child emigration agencies argued that they were offering the opportunity to grow up in healthier environments, but they were also providing colonial families with cheap labor. Public controversy eventually brought the orphan emigration project to an end. Some of the children had been placed in British institutions for temporary care, and then sent to Canada without the consent of their parents. Many child emigrants subsequently lost contact with birth families and spent years searching for parents and siblings. Also, agencies could not always find suitable foster families and many children were left in orphanages. Some foster families overworked or abused children in their care.

Modern child welfare policy and practice emerged in the 1960s with the professionalization of social work. The state began to encourage more impoverished parents to care for children at home, offering them income support and professional advice about budgeting and child rearing. New family casework procedures were developed, and social service workers were held to higher educational standards. The state also regulated existing children's homes and screened potential foster and adoptive parents, or mandated private agencies to do so. Family interventions were managed by new guidelines, such as the "principle of least intrusion" and "family preservation" (Krane 2003). Some jurisdictions provided their own protection programs (such as Quebec), while others mandated private agencies to offer services (such as Ontario).

By the 1970s, fewer children were placed in orphanages, and more were supported at home, or sent to foster homes, with small government subsidies. Foster care was seen as a temporary solution, permitting children to retain contact with their birth families while receiving care in a stable and disciplined environment. The state also attempted to ensure that foster and adoptive homes were suitable, which usually meant that they contained two healthy parents living in a stable marriage with adequate income. Eventually, foster parents became harder to find, as female employment rates and child-rearing costs increased. Social workers began encouraging extended family members, including grandparents, to care for children when parents could no longer manage. This trend to kin care was justified by preserving families and providing cultural continuity for children.

Despite increased support, reported cases of child abuse and neglect continue to rise, indicating either an increase in abuse or more effective reporting. Initially authorities focused on physical abuse, but attention turned to sexual abuse when 1980s research found that the percentage of adults who had been victimized as children was much higher than previously thought. Community leaders continue to search for new ways to identify potential abusers before incidents occur, and to deal effectively with perpetrators. However, allegations remain difficult to verify because they are often made decades after the incident, with few witnesses.

Indigenous and minority-group children continue to be overrepresented among child welfare caseloads in Canada (Baker 2001). By the 1970s, the former practice of keeping indigenous children in state-regulated residential schools, or having them adopted by white families, fell into disrepute. Today, kin care is preferred because it keeps children in their cultural community. However, studies reveal that kin caregivers typically receive less government support than nonrelated foster parents, and concepts of suitable parents and standards of care are less rigorously applied. This suggests that the current practice of placing children with extended family is based as much on cost cutting as on child welfare principles (Connolly 2003).

Measures to prevent and control abuse in Canada today also include appointment of children's ombudspersons, integration of home-visiting services, establishment of help lines and child-abuse registers, and close monitoring of at-risk children. Social reformers continue to argue that strategies must also address economic circumstances because parents living in impoverished, overcrowded, and stressed conditions are more likely to be charged with abuse. Yet public support for children and families is seldom adequate when the public also demands lower taxes.

Educational Rights and State Support for Child Care

Before 1900, educational opportunities for most children were limited. Both churches and governments supported schools, but attendance rates were low, schools in poor areas were underfunded, and education was not seen as a human right (Bradbury 2005). Hard work and physical strength, especially among the poor, were valued more than formal schooling and high culture. Children of the rich were educated in private schools or by tutors.

The movement for compulsory education arose from not only child-oriented reformers, but also employers demanding a skilled labor force. The Canadian constitution established that the provinces were responsible for education, and legislation varied by province. In Ontario, compulsory education laws were developed in 1871 requiring parents to send children to school from age six to sixteen years (Gaffield 1990). But not all parents supported regular attendance when they needed their children's labor. Low-income parents could seek permission to remove their children from school at twelve or fourteen years if they needed their earnings or assistance at home. In fact, most parents could not afford to have their children complete secondary school until after World War II, and university was reserved for rich families and scholarly sons.

In 1951, only 48 percent of Canadians over fifteen years old had completed a primary education, and only 2 percent were university graduates. But with increased funding and attention to issues of access and equity, educational attainment increased. Today 90 percent of Canadians have more than a primary education, and more than 15 percent have a university degree (Wotherspoon 2004). Schools may have become larger and more bureaucratic, but new programs have increased educational attainment for girls and children from low-income or minority families. Governments have subsidized student loans and offered more bursaries and scholarships, encouraging students to remain in school longer. Today Canadians are among the best-educated citizens in the world.

As with education, Canadian child-care policies and programs evolved over time and were, at times, controversial. In Europe, public kindergartens and nursery schools had been established in the 1880s, and European educators traveled to the colonies promoting their ideas. Canada's first public kindergarten opened in Ontario in 1883 (Sutherland 1976), but it was not until the 1920s that they became more socially acceptable. McGill University and the University of Toronto established nurseries for preschool children in 1925 as part of their child-study programs (Strong-Boag 1982). Although the McGill experiment lasted only until 1930, the University of Toronto continued and became the model for settlement house and church nurseries for welfare children.

Debate from the 1930s to the 1950s over mothers working outside the home was inextricably tied to child-care policy. As researchers emphasized the importance of maternal bonding and postwar studies showed that European orphans became intellectually and emotionally disadvantaged, a new term—"maternal deprivation"—entered the lexicon, suggesting that employed mothers somehow damaged their children when they left them with substitute care providers (Swift 1995). Many believed that nursery schools would encourage married mothers to compete with male breadwinners, leading to divorce and male unemployment (Pierson 1977). Others argued, however, that some children, especially those from poorer families, needed a head start for primary school.

Opposition to married women's employment abated during the Second World War when women's labor was needed. The Canadian government revised the Income Tax Act to allow husbands to claim their wives as dependants regardless of women's earnings, and federal cost sharing was offered to provinces providing day-care centers for children of mothers working in war industries, later extended to all employed women. Yet only Quebec and Ontario took up this offer, and the nurseries closed after the war (Pierson 1977).

By the 1950s, a play-center movement grew in popularity. Noncompulsory kindergarten programs expanded into the elementary school system in provinces such as Ontario, offering half-day enrichment programs for five-year-olds. Educational theories in the 1960s emphasized creative play, and more private preschools were developed. In 1966, the Canadian government began to subsidize the cost of provincial child-care programs for families in need through the Canada Assistance Plan, and in 1971 started offering tax deductions for the child care of employed parents.

Throughout the 1970s and 1980s, as maternal employment rates increased, advocates pressed for national standards and increased subsidies. A national child-care program was attempted, but floundered over jurisdictional and funding disputes. When federal and provincial funding arrangements were renegotiated in 1996, Quebec extended subsidized child care to all families regardless of financial need and dramatically reduced the cost. However, demand for public child care continues to increase across Canada with welfare-to-work programs and increasing numbers of two-earner families. Nevertheless, debate continues over issues of affordability, quality, and funding of child-care programs.

Income Support for Parents

Before the early twentieth century, parents were expected to support their own children, and local municipalities seldom assisted, forcing some to rely on charity and others to send their children to work. Government allowances were first paid to low-income mothers with dependent children in Manitoba in 1916, but only for women deemed "morally upright" (Armitage 2003). After the development of income taxes in 1918, and the hardships of the Depression of the 1930s, both federal and provincial governments became more able and willing to help support family income.

Unemployment insurance was first paid in 1941, after years of debate and a constitutional amendment. Fathers were still expected to provide most family support through their earnings, but in 1945 the federal government began paying family allowances to mothers regardless of household income. The idea behind universal child allowances was that raising children was an expectation of citizenship, providing future workers, consumers, and taxpayers for the nation. For decades, governments and interest groups argued about whether the state should enable low-income mothers to earn a living by subsidizing public child care, or whether they should be paid a pension to care for children at home.

Throughout the 1960s, provincial inequalities in social assistance payments and social services encouraged the federal government to share these costs. From 1966 to 1996, the Canada Assistance Plan matched provincial funding, but the federal government also subsidized provincial health-care programs, expanded eligibility for unemployment insurance, raised the level of child benefits and old-age pensions, and developed a student loan program. In the 1970s, divorce, unemployment, and living costs increased, expanding the need for state income support, but by the 1980s conservative governments became concerned about rising public expenditures.

In 1989, the United Nations adopted the Convention on the Rights of the Child as a binding international agreement. Prime Minister Brian Mulroney promised, before both the United Nations and Canada's Parliament, to seek an end to child poverty by the year 2000 (Baker 1995), but throughout the 1990s, the federal government tightened access to unemployment insurance and reduced transfers for social programs, encouraging the provincial governments to make program cuts.

The tightening of welfare payments, rising living costs relative to earnings, and increases in mother-led families meant that child poverty would continue. In fact, throughout the 1990s, Canadian child poverty rates remained persistently high. More mothers were employed and child benefits were raised, but fewer fathers held full-time jobs, more children lived in mother-led families, and eligibility for income support was tightened. Poverty rates are highest when children live with one parent who depends on income support, and in these households 89.7 percent of Canadian children live in poverty (when poverty is defined as household income less than 50 percent of the national median, after taxes and government transfers) (OECD 2005).

Considerable research shows that children from impoverished families experience a higher risk of negative outcomes such as health issues, learning problems, early school leaving, premarital pregnancy, delinquency, and excessive premature work. Early school leavers are more likely to experience unemployment and low income throughout their lives, as well as other personal and family problems. Researchers have demonstrated that preventing child poverty would be less costly to the state than dealing with the long-term consequences.

Conclusion

Over the past century, Canadian children have gained more rights and access to protective services. Governments now focus on preserving family units by offering professional services and income support, or encouraging extended family to care for children when necessary. As divorce and separation rates increase, governments have tightened enforcement procedures for parental child support, but they also provide more opportunities for contact between children and nonresident parents (mainly fathers). Not only have children gained new rights as citizens, but the state has also assisted them in exercising these rights.

The state continues to subsidize child-care spaces for low-income families, although the demand for employment-related care continues to rise with greater expectations that parents will provide the basic necessities for their children through their earnings. While state involvement in family life has increased considerably since 1900, the welfare of many Canadian children continues to be threatened by low household incomes, inadequate family time, and unstable parental relationships.

References and Further Reading

Armitage, Andrew. *Social Welfare in Canada.* 4th ed. New York: Oxford University Press, 2003.

Baker, Maureen. *Canadian Family Policies: Cross-National Comparisons.* Toronto: University of Toronto Press, 1995.

Baker, Maureen. *Families, Labour and Love.* Sydney: Allen and Unwin; Vancouver: UBC Press, 2001.

Bala, Nicholas, and Kenneth L. Clarke. *The Child and the Law.* Toronto: McGraw-Hill Ryerson, 1981.

Bradbury, Bettina. "Social, Economic, and Cultural Origins of Contemporary Families." In *Families: Changing Trends in Canada,* 5th ed., ed. M. Baker, 71–98. Toronto: McGraw-Hill Ryerson, 2005.

Connolly, Marie. *Kinship Care—A Selected Literature Review.* Paper prepared for the Department of Child Youth and Family Services, Wellington, New Zealand, 2003.

Corbett, Gail H. *Barnardo Children in Canada.* Peterborough, Ont.: Woodland Publishing, 1981.

Gaffield, Chad. "The Social and Economic Origins of Contemporary Families." In *Families: Changing Trends in Canada,* 2nd ed., ed. M. Baker, 23-40. Toronto: McGraw-Hill Ryerson, 1990.

Krane, Julia. *What's Mother Got to Do with It? Protecting Children from Sexual Abuse.* Toronto: University of Toronto Press, 2003.

Organization for Economic Cooperation and Development. *Society at a Glance: OECD Social Indicators.* Paris: OECD, 2005.

Pierson, Ruth. "Women's Emancipation and the Recruitment of Women into the Labour Force in World War II." In *The Neglected Majority: Essays in Canadian Women's History,* ed. S.M. Trofimenkoff and A. Prentice, 125–45. Toronto: McClelland and Stewart, 1977.

Strong-Boag, Veronica. "Intruders in the Nursery: Childcare Professionals Reshape the Years One to Five, 1920–1940." In *Childhood and Family in Canadian History,* ed. J. Parr, 160–78. Toronto: McClelland and Stewart, 1982.

Sutherland, Neil. *Children in English-Canadian Society: Framing the Twentieth Century Consensus.* Toronto: University of Toronto Press, 1976.

Swift, Karen. *Manufacturing "Bad Mothers"? A Critical Perspective on Child Neglect.* Toronto: University of Toronto Press, 1995.

Wotherspoon, Terry. "Education." In *Sociology,* ed. L. Tepperman and J. Curtis, 186–212. Toronto: Oxford University Press, 2004.

SECTION 2. UNITED STATES

History of Child Labor

The Work of Enslaved Children in the United States

Wilma King, Strickland Professor of History, University of Missouri

Although priceless to their parents, enslaved children were economically worthless to owners until they entered the world of work. Owners or employees classified them as fractional hands—one-quarter, one-half, or three-quarter hands—until they performed chores ordinarily expected of able-bodied adults. The value of children's work was inestimable in actual dollars but could not be overlooked. Examples abound: One slaveholder observed the work of her six-year-old house servant and wrote, "You have no idea how useful she is. . . . I could hardly get along without her."[1] In 1859 the Wake County, North Carolina, planter Alonzo T. Mial noted that it was "mostly women and small boys and girls" who produced a bountiful crop. Physical development, intellectual maturation, and endurance were more significant than chronological age in determining when children began toiling in homes, in mills, in shops, in fields, or on docks.

According to the Texan Jacob Branch, "Us chillen start to work soon's us could toddle. First us gather firewood." In all probability Branch was referring to gathering wood chips or kindling used in igniting fires but not gathering much heavier cordwood. That he began working at an early age is of greater significance than the weight of the wood he fetched. Like Branch, Mingo White claimed that he too began working at an early age. "I weren't nothing but a child endurin' slavery," he said, "but I had to work the same as any man." White's comment suggests that he was young chronologically but sufficiently mature physically to complete more meaningful jobs than picking up wood chips or gathering twigs. That enslaved children began working at early ages is undisputed; however, Frederick Douglass added depth when he wrote, "We were worked in all weather. It was never too hot or too cold; it could never rain, blow hail, or snow, too hard for us to work in the field." According to the slave-born autobiographer, "Work, work, work, was scarcely more the order of the day than of the night." The needs of persons who owned or hired slaves determined which chores they completed and when.

The jobs performed at the earliest ages, as mentioned by Branch, were associated with domestic tasks or housewifery. Domestic work included food preparation and preservation, cleaning and maintaining living quarters, and caring for children. Other responsibilities involved laundering and repairing wearing apparel, household linens, and bedding. Housewifery required the care of poultry and livestock in addition to manufacturing clothes and household items such as soap and candles.

Finally, services performed by valets and nursemaids were also domestic work. Personal services for owners or others included a wide variety of chores ranging from removing seeds from watermelons, to combing hair, massaging feet, rocking cradles, and emptying chamber pots. Children also waved fans to shoo flies away from dining tables and to reduce the body temperature of owners or others. The South Carolina planter

Charles Manigault arranged for a small boy to perform a special service for a Mr. Venters. The child was to "run with his umbrella and great coat in case he should be caught by rain in the field." Regardless of the mundane nature of many such jobs, they were for the comfort and convenience of owners, employees, or others without regard for age or gender of the worker.

Enslaved children were often obliged to cater to and obey white children sometimes younger than themselves. Slave-owning parents established standards of behavior and expectations to guide relationships between enslaved and slaveholding children. When Lu's owner introduced her to the "young mistress" in Juniper County, Mississippi, the nonplussed eleven-year-old stared at the infant in her mother's arms and said, "I don't see no young mistress, that's a baby." Despite her tender age, the "young mistress" occupied a power position in relationship to the enslaved girl and would eventually command Lu's labor at will. Consider Louella Williams's position. She was responsible for seeing that "Miss Lucy" wore a sunbonnet while outside. As the child played and shook the bonnet from her head, Williams, who was somewhat older, ran to pick up and place the bonnet on Lucy's head again. On the one hand, Williams's job held the potential for a long-lasting relationship with her "little mistress." On the other hand, one misstep on Williams's part resulting in an injury or worse for "Miss Lucy" would incur the owner's wrath or worse.

Fortunately for Ralph, a child inherited by a younger child, Charles L.C. Minor, in 1808 or 1809, there were no serious missteps in more than two decades of bondage. Charles remembered Ralph as a "playmate and nurse." Not a "nurse" in the medical tradition, Ralph was Charles's companion as well as babysitter and caregiver. After the boys matured, Ralph did not remain a body servant. Instead he became an artisan. He apparently hired his own time and gave Charles a portion of the wages. In 1832, Charles Minor emancipated Ralph and urged him to emigrate to Liberia as protection against re-enslavement. With the stroke of a pen, Charles L.C. Minor severed the master-slave relationship and liberated Ralph, who could now own his own person and was free to enjoy all wages earned as a skilled laborer.

Domestic Pursuits

Unlike Ralph, most girls and boys were not personal servants, but performed domestic work nonetheless. They assisted with preparing foods and laundering clothes, two of the most arduous household responsibilities. Gastronomic creations and plain meals that pleased and satisfied owners or others required experience and skill beyond the ken of children. Certainly there were exceptions. As an enslaved child in a small New York household, Isabella Van Wagenen, better known as Sojourner Truth, fulfilled cooking responsibilities. She failed to please her owners, but it was not because she was inept. Instead, a young white servant in the household ruined the food deliberately as a way of causing trouble for Isabella (Gilbert 1850).

Food preparation involved gathering produce and shelling, peeling, or washing it. If meat, poultry, or fish were served, it required dressing, plucking, or scaling. Afterward, it was necessary to haul water, chop wood, and build the fire. Once the food was ready, servants carted it from the kitchen into the main house. Later, they cleared the table, put leftover food away, and washed dishes and utensils. Over time, selected servants gained necessary on-the-job training and skills to assume the full responsibilities of a cook. In the meantime, boys and girls too young to assume greater responsibilities elsewhere helped cooks by picking and shelling legumes, shucking corn, plucking chickens, dressing game, chopping wood, toting water, building fires, and minding pots.

Laundering clothes, like cooking, required experience and skill beyond the abilities of young children. Nevertheless, boys and girls assisted washerwomen, who laundered clothes one day and ironed them the next. One weekly wash for an average-size family required at least fifty gallons, or four hundred pounds, of water. Children hauled water from nearby rivers, creeks, or wells. They also gathered wood and built fires to heat water for washing or boiling clothes. Thereafter, they assisted with scrubbing, rinsing, wringing, and hanging clothes out to dry. Once clothes dried, sorting and folding them was an easy task. By contrast, the ironing of fine linens or special garments required careful attention to heating metal flatirons over a fire until they reached the right temperature for smoothing out wrinkles without damaging fabrics. No thoughtful adult would thrust such responsibility upon children who lacked the skill to perfect it.

Less precise attention was needed for scouring floors, polishing furniture, spinning thread, gathering eggs, milking cows, churning butter, and feeding poultry or livestock. All were tasks that enslaved children in households of the urban North or rural South could complete.

Agricultural Pursuits

Many boys and girls worked in gangs on plantations in the Upper South where tobacco and hemp were the cash crops. In the Lower South, children learned from older women and men in their work gangs how to pick cotton, cut sugarcane, and harvest indigo. Those living along the South Carolina and Georgia coast cultivated rice under the "task system," which required completion of specific daily jobs, after which workers were free to spend the remainder of the day as they chose. Neither the task system nor gang labor was used on northern farms, where enslaved children helped in cultivating subsistence crops or cash crops such as wheat or corn.

Few gender distinctions existed in agricultural pursuits, but it was readily assumed that plowing was a man's job. In actuality, the size of the household and the owner's needs determined who did or did not plow fields. One former slave said, "Mama plowed wid three horses." She asked, "Ain't dat somp'n?" and appeared more intrigued by the number of animals used than by the fact that the woman "worked like a man." Another former slave commented, "[I] thought women was 'sposed to work 'long wid men, I did" (Perdue et al. 1976, 292). Indeed, many enslaved males and females, without regard for age, worked together and shared a mean sort of equality. Both were exploited.

Some farm boys were reportedly eager to become plow hands, a sign of manhood. Not only did boys who plowed "like men" receive more food, commensurate with their responsibilities; they also received pants. Ordinarily, young enslaved children dressed in a one-piece garment called a shift if donned by a girl and a shirt if worn by a boy. Trousers eliminated any embarrassment caused by wearing shirts too short to hide the nakedness of rapidly growing adolescent boys.

Regardless of the chores performed or clothing worn, parents and others taught boys and girls the value of mutual cooperation in the workplace. A former slave remembered hearing the warning, "Keep yo' eye on de sun, / See how she run, / Don't let her catch you with your work undone." The disappearance of the sun signaled the end of the day, when tallies were taken and punishments meted out if laborers fell short of standard requirements. Slaves assisted with chores or did whatever was necessary to ward off chastisements at nightfall.

Coopers, carpenters, wheelwrights, blacksmiths, and other skilled workers did not end their days with the same trepidations as field hands. The craft skills set artisans apart from the amorphous mass of slaves and created more options for managing their own time. Once they satisfied financial obligations to owners, craftsmen used any remaining money for personal needs or desires, including their liberty. Youngsters acquired craft skills through apprenticeships or by working with others in more casual settings; however, girls did not become artisans. Childbearing and rearing were key factors preventing access to trades for female slaves, since craft work, unlike chopping cotton or suckling tobacco, could not be completed by a substitute worker. The work of skilled female slaves was associated with domestic or housewifery chores. Furthermore, pregnant or lactating cooks, laundresses, spinners, weavers, and seamstresses continued work as usual.

Aside from the traditional domestic, agricultural, and skilled jobs of enslaved children, a wide variety of other work, such as industrial work and cleaning chimneys, was completed by young children. In industrial work, traditional housewifery skills were adaptable beyond private homes. The southern textile industry did not rival the New England industry until after the Civil War; however, cotton mills existed in the antebellum South, and it was not unusual to find enslaved women and children working in the industry. The rising cost of slaves explains the paucity of chattel in southern textile mills after 1850. Mill operators found it more cost effective to hire white women and children than to buy slaves.

In both the North and South, young boys worked as chimney sweeps. They crawled into cramped spaces and maneuvered into small zigzag, sometimes warm, chimneys with scrapers to remove soot from flues. Once they reached the rooftop, they reversed the climb and collected the debris at the bottom. They worked under harsh, even brutal, conditions. Those who conquered their fear of heights were still subjected to injuries from falling or scraping their bodies against the rough mortar. Sores and bruises were marks of the trade. An advertisement for a runaway called York noted that he had "a scar under, or nearly under his left temple like unto a burn." Ordinarily, chimney sweeps wore nothing more than underwear and a stocking cap covering their faces with small openings for their eyes. This was little protection from the hazards of fire, tar, and smoke. According to the ad, York's "hair wool [was] cut short, and full of soot" (Hodges and Brown 1994, 229). A study of chimney sweeps in New York describes their working conditions:

> Soot collected over the sweeps from head to toe. Eventually their bodies became calloused with scar tissue from lacerations, and their skin developed an armorlike leathery texture. Sweeps also had a tendency to develop "cancer of the scrotum" from infections caused by imbedded soot . . . [and] Soot lodged under the eyelids, causing infections and leaving the taletell "red-rimmed eye." Finally, there was enormous danger of consumption, or tuberculosis, from soot in the boys' lungs. (Gilje and Rock 1999, 275)

Scholars will never know if York associated his physically challenging job with its potential health risks and wanted no part of it. Apparently, he hated the job and his legal status left him without the option of choosing where and when he worked. His reproof of both kindled the desire to liberate himself from the job and slavery.

Summary

Opinions about the chores children performed varied. The Virginia-born Julia Frazer "liked dustin' best," especially her owner's library where she fingered through books containing illustrations of "Injuns and kings and queens wid reefs on dey heads." It was not so much the job that she enjoyed as the residual benefits—the library books. As a child Cornelius Garner realized that his owner liked "his ho'sses looking fine." As a result, "I made hit my business to keep dem ho'sses looking spic and span." The owner noticed "dat I was inrested in his ho'sses," Green recalled, and he "kept me sorta close 'round de house." Green may have enjoyed grooming the horses, but it is clear that he, like Frazer, appreciated the residual benefits.

By contrast, the slave-born Jabob Stroyer's autobiography includes no pleasant memories of his varied work as a child. He wrote about the overseer whipping him severely for ignoring orders to report to the cotton field rather than the carpenter's shop, the boy's preference. Stroyer worked in the fields several weeks but returned to the carpenter's shop and received another punishment for ignoring orders. Stroyer's owner envisioned that the boy would become a jockey. However, Stroyer was not agile and suffered a beating each time he fell from a horse. The floggings continued over time but were less severe once Stroyer came under the supervision of a different trainer.

The chores discussed above were for the benefit of owners or others rather than the enslaved boy's or girl's family. Once the children completed work outside their owners' homes, there were responsibilities to fulfill for their parents or other kin. To be sure, many experiences and skills were transferable from one situation to another in slavery or freedom. Even a cursory look at the historical data shows that enslaved girls and boys made large contributions to the nation's economic growth. Their work was static only in the sense that they were destined to toil as soon as they were useful, and continued to toil until they were useless.

Note

1. Except where other sources are cited, all quoted material is from Wilma King, *Stolen Childhood* (1995).

References and Further Readings

Blassingame, John W., ed. *Slave Testimony: Two Centuries of Letters, Speeches, Interviews and Autobiographies.* Baton Rouge: Louisiana State University Press, 1977.

Gilbert, Olive. *Narrative of Sojourner Truth: A Northern Slave, Emancipated from Bodily Servitude by the State of New York, in 1828.* Boston: Printed for the author, 1850.

Gilje, Paul A., and Howard B. Rock. "'Sweep O! Sweep O!': African-American Chimney Sweeps and Citizenship in the New Nation." In *A Question of Manhood: A Reader in US Black Men's History and Masculinity,* vol. 1, ed. Darlene Clark Hine and Earnestine Jenkins, 274–301. Bloomington: University of Indiana Press, 1999.

Hodges, Graham Russell, and Alan Edward Brown, eds. *"Pretends to Be Free": Runaway Slave Advertisements from Colonial and Revolutionary New York and New Jersey.* New York: Garland Publishing, 1994.

Jones, Norrece T., Jr. *Born a Child of Freedom, Yet a Slave: Mechanisms of Control and Strategies of Resistance in Antebellum South Carolina.* Hanover: Wesleyan University Press, 1990.

Joyner, Charles W. *Down by the Riverside: A South Carolina Community.* Urbana: University of Illinois Press, 1984.

King, Wilma. *Stolen Childhood: Slave Youth in Nineteenth-Century America.* Bloomington: Indiana University Press, 1995.

King, Wilma. "Within the Professional Household: Slave Children in the Antebellum South." *Historian* 59 (Spring 1997): 523–40.

Landers, E.M., Jr. "Slave Labor in South Carolina Cotton Mills." *Journal of Negro History* 38 (April 1953): 161–73.

Owens, Leslie Howard. *This Species of Property: Slave Life and Culture in the Old South.* New York: Oxford University Press, 1977.

Perdue, Charles L., Jr., Thomas E. Barden, and Robert K. Phillips, eds. *Weevils in the Wheat: Interviews with Virginia Ex-Slaves.* Charlottesville: University Press of Virginia, 1976.

Orphan Trains

Laura L. Leavitt, Human Resources and Labor Relations Librarian, School of Labor and Industrial Relations, Michigan State University

In the mid-nineteenth century, metropolitan areas on the East Coast of the United States were growing very rapidly due to increased immigration and industrialization. As a result, housing shortages, unemployment, and poverty were commonplace, and thousands of children were abandoned on the streets, forced to fend for themselves. The New York City chief of police estimated in an 1848–1849 report that 10,000 vagrant children roamed the streets of New York at a time when the total population of the city was approximately 500,000. Many of these children engaged in criminal activity to survive, and it was reported that four-fifths of felony charges in New York City in 1852 were against minors. Churches and other charitable organizations were ill equipped to deal with the number of children that needed help, and many social reformers demanded that something be done. One strategy employed by charitable groups to alleviate the situation involved the placement of orphaned children from large eastern cities with western and midwestern families. The practice also served to provide labor to the rural and agricultural communities in which the children were placed. Western states were expanding rapidly and suffering from labor shortages. There was a high demand for farm hands and domestic help in particular, and this was work for which children were viewed to be particularly well suited. This system of permanent relocation of orphaned children from large urban centers to rural communities became known as "placing out" and the trains that transported the children as "orphan trains."

Charles Loring Brace was a social reformer and Christian minister devoted to improving the lives of poor children in New York City. In his role as secretary of the New York Children's Aid Society, he is credited with developing the system of placing out in the United States that later became the model for other organizations. He believed that all children, regardless of their station in life, were inherently good and redeemable. He also believed that for many poor children in urban areas, their ultimate salvation lay in removing them from the evils of the city and placing them in good Christian homes in the country. Here the children could learn self-sufficiency and the value of hard work as well as receive moral training through a Christian upbringing. In 1860, several years after he had initiated this "emigration plan," Brace wrote a pamphlet entitled *The Best Method of Disposing of Our Pauper and Vagrant Children.* In his concluding remarks, he wrote, "The country is interested in this, as well as the city; for not only would these children, if left in vice and poverty, curse the whole nation, but, moreover, we by sending them out, are supplying the greatest and sorest need in American families, *a permanent labor,* educated in the habits of the house" (emphasis in original). Many other people agreed with Brace, as it is estimated that from 1854, when the system of placing out began, through the last placement in 1929, between 100,000 and 300,000 children had been placed on orphan trains and relocated.

There were several larger forces at work that led to the emergence of placing out in the United States in the mid-nineteenth century. Westward expansion of the railroads made the transport of large groups of children a more manageable venture. There were also evangelical forces afoot that demanded that good Christians assist their less fortunate brethren. This, combined with a changing view of children as inherently good, and capable of redemption if placed in the right environment, contributed to the emergence of an increased focus on helping poor children. The West also represented the best of America to many people. It was believed to be a place where anyone with a pioneering spirit could succeed, regardless of their beginnings, if they were only willing to work hard. It logically followed that it would also be a great place for children to learn lessons of hard work and self-sufficiency.

As time passed and social conditions changed, criticisms of orphan trains and placing out began to emerge. One criticism stemmed from the fact that many of the children sent west were not in fact orphans and had at least one living parent. Despite this, the New York Children's Aid Society and other organizations discouraged children from maintaining contact with their original families. There was also a great deal of concern about lax screening of families and about the less-than-thorough follow-up of placements. Some individuals in the receiving communities also felt that the eastern cities were intentionally dumping their undesirables on them. It was expressed that the orphans brought with them myriad problems that would only result in criminal behavior or poverty once they reached adulthood. Furthermore, as cities such as Chicago and Cincinnati began to grow in the West, so too did their social ills. Faced with growing numbers of their own urban poor, many thought it more prudent to devote their attention to those who needed their help locally as opposed to helping children from the likes of New York City, Boston, and Philadelphia.

The way in which these placements were conducted often led to a sense of rootlessness and despair in the orphans themselves. This is recounted in a number of personal stories shared by orphan-train riders later in their lives. There were many instances in which the placed child was treated as one of the family, but there were also situations in which the children were abused, exploited, and treated like servants. As the orphan-train children grew older and tried to reconnect with their original families, many found it difficult if not impossible to do so. Many children's names were changed when they moved west, while other children bounced around from family to family. Perhaps as a result, several orphan-train riders created the Orphan Train Heritage Society to help people understand their personal stories and to help find any surviving family members.

Several factors led to the ultimate demise of orphan trains and the end of placing out in 1929. By the early twentieth century, views had changed on how best to manage the welfare of children, and the goal of most rehabilitative efforts was to keep a family together regardless of socioeconomic status. Social work was also becoming professionalized, and many of those prominent in the new field were critical of the placing-out system and of the informal methods used to relocate children. There was also a growing tide of opposition to child labor in the United States. States enacted legislation putting limits on child labor and mandating that every child be afforded a minimal level of education. Both served to make child labor a less attractive alternative to filling any labor shortages that might have existed.

References and Further Reading

Brace, Charles Loring. *The Best Method of Disposing of Our Pauper and Vagrant Children.* New York: Wynkoop, Hallenbeck and Thomas, 1859.

Holt, Marilyn Irvin. *The Orphan Trains: Placing Out in America.* Lincoln: University of Nebraska Press, 1992.

Liebl, Janet. *Ties That Bind: The Orphan Train Story in Minnesota.* Marshall, MN: Southwest State University Press, 1994.

Marks, Frances E., and Patricia J. Young. *Tears on Paper: The History and Life Stories of the Orphan Train Riders.* Bella Vista, AR: PJ Young, 1990.

History of Children in U.S. Coal Mining

Julia E. Offiong, Librarian, George Meany Memorial Archives Library, National Labor College

Owen Lovejoy of the National Child Labor Committee noted that American coal mining, in contrast to coal mining in England of a hundred years earlier, started on a "higher plane." Whereas in England, a large proportion of the underground workforce was women and girls, in America, it started with "little boys" (Lovejoy 1911). Boys as young as ten years old commonly worked in both anthracite and bituminous coal mining.

Anthracite coal, or hard coal, is credited with igniting the Industrial Revolution in the United States (Miller and Sharpless 1985). Mined in a concentrated region of northeastern Pennsylvania, in close proximity to the major cities of Philadelphia and New York, it became the preferred commercial and residential heating fuel, and the preferred fuel for the railroads, which came to own or control 95 percent of anthracite coal production. Bituminous coal, or soft coal, was mined throughout a widely dispersed geographic swath comprising roughly half the eastern United States. It was preferred, for its coking properties, by the newly emerging steel industry, and by the electrical power plants that were beginning to dot the industrial landscape by the late nineteenth and early twentieth centuries.

In Pennsylvania alone, in 1902, the Department of Mines estimated that 27,393 boys under sixteen years of age worked in the mines, and as many as 13,000 worked in the anthracite breakers (Derickson 1993; Hindman 2002). Most were immigrants or sons of immigrants. Their birth records were often incomplete, making it difficult to determine their ages. The law prohibited employment of children under age twelve aboveground in anthracite, and under age sixteen belowground. In bituminous mining, children as young as twelve were permitted to accompany their fathers to the coal face underground. Enforcement of the law was ineffective in both branches of mining.

Lewis Hine photograph and original caption. "View of the Ewen Breaker of the Pa. Coal Co. The dust was so dense at times as to obscure the view. This dust penetrated the utmost recesses of the boy's lungs. A kind of slave-driver sometimes stands over the boys, prodding or kicking them into obedience. S. Pittston, Pa., 01/10/1911." (*Courtesy of the National Archives and Records Administration, College Park, MD, National Child Labor Committee photographs taken by Lewis Hine series, NWDNS-102-LH-1938*)

In bituminous mining, the youngest boys worked at the coal face, serving as loaders and general assistants for their fathers. In anthracite, the youngest boys were "breaker boys." After extraction, anthracite was put through the revolving cylinders of the coal breaker for processing. It was broken into little pieces and passed through screens for sorting. The process culminated with the work of the breaker boys, who handpicked and discarded pieces of slate and other debris. They were "seated on ladders beside the chutes, bent over all day long, their backs were round, their chests narrow. Cut, broken, and crushed fingers were common. If their attention wandered, they were struck across the knuckles by the long stick of the 'breaker boss.'" Mother Jones, "the Miner's Angel," observed, "The fingers of the little boys bled onto the coal" (Atkinson 1978, 115).

After a few years in their entry-level positions, boys in both anthracite and bituminous mining might begin a progression up the career ladder of mining. Some became "nippers" or "door-boys," opening and closing doors that served as the mine's ventilation system. Many became drivers, hauling the loaded cars from the coal face to the tipple or breaker. In some mines the boys were assisted by mules; in others they relied solely on their own muscle. This work, in turn, had its own division of labor. "Spragging," which was considered the most dangerous job of all, involved the use of a heavy wooden prop to wedge under the wheel or in the spokes, to prevent the coal cars from rolling away. Runaway cars posed extreme danger to all underground, and sudden deaths were not uncommon. Finally, when the boys became adults, they could assume positions as miners or other skilled workers in or around the mine.

Runaway cars, roof falls, and gas explosions posed danger for everyone underground, but it was estimated that boys were three times more likely to be injured than adult men. Aboveground, breaker boys occasionally slipped into the coal chutes and were buried alive. There were additional dangers associated with both anthracite and bituminous coal mining. The boys inhaled coal dust throughout the course of their ten- to twelve-hour workday. Whether they began their careers at the coal face in bituminous mining, or in the coal breaker in anthracite, the youngest boys worked at the point in the mining process where exposure to mineral dust was the most suffocating. It was not surprising that they often developed health complications by the time they were ten. The weakening of their respiratory systems was almost unavoidable and they became susceptible to lung disease in their later years. "Miner's asthma," common among adult miners, with its estimated fifteen-year latency period, almost certainly began to develop when most were mere boys (Derickson 1993).

Ultimately, the career ladder in coal mining was circular. As adult miners became worn-out and used up, whether through physical or respiratory disability, many concluded their career where it began: in bituminous coal, loading coal at the coal face; in anthracite, back in the breaker. "As the strength of the victims of miners' asthma faded, they retrace their steps on the job ladder. Some gradually went back to being a miner's helper, then a door tender, and finally, old and decrepit, a slate picker again" (Derickson 1993, 102). As one old miner told a government investigator in 1919, "You begin at the breaker, and you end at the breaker, broken yourself" (U.S. Children's Bureau 1922, 9). Ironically, the tendency of miners to decline in their middle years helped to perpetuate both supply and demand for child labor. When adult men could no longer work, their only recourse was to send their sons to the mine. Likewise, as men left the mines in their middle years, the mines demanded a continuous supply of fresh labor.

References and Further Reading

Atkinson, Linda. *Mother Jones: The Most Dangerous Woman in America.* New York: Crown Publishers, 1978.

Derickson, Alan. "Occupational Disease and Career Trajectory in Hard Coal, 1870–1930." *Industrial Relations* 32:1 (1993): 94–110.

Hindman, Hugh D. *Child Labor: An American History.* Armonk, NY: M.E. Sharpe, 2002.

Lovejoy, Owen R. "The Coal Mines of Pennsylvania." *Annals of the American Academy of Political and Social Science* (July 1911): 133–38.

Miller, Donald L., and Richard E. Sharpless. *The Kingdom of Coal: Work, Enterprise, and Ethnic Communities in the Mine Fields.* Philadelphia: University of Pennsylvania Press, 1985.

Roy, Andrew. *A History of the Coal Miners of the United States: From the Development of the Mines to the Close of the Anthracite Strike of 1902.* Westport, CT: Greenwood Press, 1905.

U.S. Children's Bureau. *Child Labor and the Welfare of Children in an Anthracite Coal-Mining District.* Bureau Publication 106. Washington, DC: U.S. Government Printing Office, 1922.

U.S. Children's Bureau. *Child Labor and the Welfare of Children in a Bituminous Coal-Mining District.* Bureau Publication 117. Washington, DC: U.S. Government Printing Office, 1923.

Child Labor in the American Glass Industry

Ken Fones-Wolf, Professor of History, West Virginia University

The Early Industrial Glasshouse

Although glass manufacture was one of the enterprises established at Jamestown before 1610, Americans imported the majority of their windows, bottles, and tableware until well into the nineteenth century. The glasshouses that existed in the preindustrial era were small shops in which mostly German-trained craftsmen made a wide variety of items with the help of apprentices and perhaps a journeyman or two. Located in rural areas where forests could supply the wood used as furnace fuel, glassworks conformed to an irregular production schedule that alternated hours of inactivity waiting for the batch to melt in clay pots with by bursts of hard, hot labor. Child labor was present from the outset, but at first the children (mostly the sons or nephews of the master craftsmen), as apprentices, gained a profitable trade.

Young apprentices learned the mysteries of the craft incrementally over a number of years that might begin as soon as they were physically capable of performing useful tasks. Training began with gathering the right amount of hot glass on the end of the blowpipe and learning to give it a rudimentary shape (marver) by rolling the gob on a flat piece of stone or marble. Gradually, the apprentice learned to crack the item off the end of the pipe when the craftsman was finished and later to begin inflating the gob by blowing into the pipe. All the while, however, the young boys performed a range of tasks necessary to keep the glassworks functioning—shoveling sand, cleaning tools, carrying finished items to the annealing oven, and anything else required by the master craftsman. By the age of seventeen or eighteen, apprentices had learned most of what their master could teach them and were expected to "go on the tramp" to pick up the additional skills that would enable them to become well-rounded master craftsmen. This meant working as journeymen for masters in other glasshouses until they were ready to run their own shops. Thus, child labor, while hard work, had tangible rewards.

The industrialization of glassmaking, beginning in the 1820s, changed that. Increasingly, glasshouses specialized in the items they made, limiting the range of skills they required of craftsmen. Specialization gave a routine to production that put a premium on speed above craft. Greater changes followed with the development of molds and presses that enabled men of lesser skills to make bottles, tumblers, or bowls. Molds enabled the glassblowers to more quickly give the form and standard size to the items they made. Presses took this a step further; by applying a plunger to a mold, the presser merely cut off a glob of molten glass from a "punty" provided by a gatherer, let it drop into the mold, and then pressed it. The main skill was knowing the appropriate amount of glass for each of the molds.

This early industrialization drastically altered the nature of child labor. Production teams by mid-century included gatherers, "snapping-up" boys, who took the item out of the mold to a finisher, and "carrying-out" boys, who were responsible for taking the finished item to the annealing oven. Most distressing to many observers were the "mold boys," who sat at the feet of the glass blower in a squat, cramped position, closing and opening the molds for hours at a time. The teams (or shops, as they were called) operated in factories that had

Lewis Hine photograph and original caption. "Glass blower and mold boy. Boy has 4 1/2 hours of this at a stretch; then an hour's rest and 4 1/2 more: cramped position. —Day shift one week: night shift next. Grafton, W. Va., 10/1908." (*Courtesy of the National Archives and Records Administration, College Park MD, National Child Labor Committee photographs taken by Lewis Hine series, NWDNS-102-LH-151*)

furnaces capable of holding eight pots and melting more than 1,000 pounds of glass per day. Thus, actual glass making took place somewhat removed from the furnaces and relied on growing numbers of boys darting past one another carrying molten or finished glass to the next stage of the process. By 1860, the industry had expanded to 9,000 workers, probably one-quarter of whom were under age sixteen.

As the teams became larger and more specialized, glassworkers had fewer skills to pass on to their children, but more work that needed to be done if they were to meet production quotas. Consequently, blowers, pressers, and finishers wanted more boys, but fewer sons, for their team. Glasshouses increasingly hired children from outside the glassmaking fraternity for jobs that did not lead to craftsman status. Working for one's father or uncle might provide some protection against physical abuse, but the employment of growing numbers of children with no family connections lessened inhibitions against verbal and corporal punishment. Since the blowers' and pressers' earnings depended on production, the temptations to abuse were rife.

Technology, Industry Expansion, and the Modern Glass Factory

The decades bracketing the turn of the century witnessed a revolution in glass manufacturing that made it a particular target of child labor reformers. The earliest changes involved fuel. The switch from charcoal to coal caused the industry to move from its centers in the rural northeast regions to the Old Northwest. Then, in the 1880s, the industry turned to natural gas to fuel the new furnaces and the tanks that allowed the batch to be melted continuously. Almost overnight, glass factories relocated to an extensive natural gas field that stretched from rural northwestern Pennsylvania in an arc that dipped to include much of West Virginia before sweeping up through Ohio and Indiana. Equally important, the gas-fueled furnaces and the continuous tanks ballooned the scale of production. New factories in window glass, for example, doubled in size. Window manufacture, however, employed few children—the work simply required too much strength. But bottles and tableware factories also increased in size, and the larger scale meant that production teams were even farther from the tank, necessitating more help. Some critics complained that young boys might be on their feet for hours at a time, logging as many as twenty miles in a day's work. Moreover, these advances coincided with a period of expansion that allowed American manufacturers to capture a growing share of the domestic market. By 1900, the glass industry employed nearly 46,000 adult workers and more than 7,000 children.

New scales of production compounded problems, and observers worried that the glass industry provided major hazards to children. Most of the boys (there were some girls under fifteen who worked in washing, wrapping, and packing small glassware) worked near the furnace rooms where the temperature of molten glass reached 2,500 degrees Fahrenheit. The thermometer routinely ranged between 100 and 130 degrees in the factories, so hot that they often closed during the peak of summer. Heat prostration, headaches, and exhaustion were not uncommon in warm weather. In the winter months, boys working in the heat took breaks outside in the cold. Complaints included stiff necks, pneumonia, rheumatism, and other throat and lung ailments. Throughout the year, the fumes and dust in the factory damaged tracheal passages, and furnace glare caused eye trouble. Cuts from broken glass, burns from hot tools and molten glass, and skin irritations caused most of the grumbling, but tuberculosis was also a familiar glasshouse malady.

The continuous tank added the new problem of night work. Production in the modern factories moved toward three shifts, meaning that boys were needed for a night shift that began at five in the evening and stopped at three in the morning. Night work intensified the temperature variations between the factory and the outside, and it also increased the likelihood of accidents as tired youths tried to adapt to new routines. In addition, there was the problem of transportation. Many of the young boys did not have older relatives traveling with them to and from the factory. Since streetcars rarely ran in the early hours of the morning when the night shift was finishing, boys had the option of taking a nap in the hot, dusty factory until the cars began running or walking home in the cold night air in sweaty clothes.

Finally, there was the problem of abuse by the craftsmen. One glassworker who began work at age thirteen recalled, in 1910, "You know what I got when I first went into the glasshouse? A kick in the ass. I dropped a piece of glass; dropped a tumbler I was carrying over." When I went back, "the presser cracked me over the head with his scissors." Another remembered that he was whacked with a fork for gathering too much glass for the mold and allowing it to go to waste. When child labor became less a path to learning the mysteries of the craft and more just low-paid labor, blowers and pressers refused to allow their own children to enter the factory at an early age. Hiring youths from hard-pressed new immigrant groups offered the children less protection from the wrath of craftsmen paid by the piece. In one case, two Slavic coal miners met a cruel glassworker at the plant gate after the night shift and made him pay for abusing their young kinsman. At other times, physical punishment elicited the involvement of the local courts.

Getting Children Out of the Glasshouse

Critics of child labor in the glass industry received a boost from the early investigations of Florence Kelley when she was state factory inspector for Illinois in the 1890s. Illinois soon passed a pioneering law against child labor, targeting particularly night work in factories, due to her awareness of glass manufacturing. Kelley lost her position in Illinois but kept up her attack on child labor in the National Consumers League and the National Child Labor Committee (NCLC). Recalling her earlier work, the NCLC undertook a follow-up investigation in 1904 to examine the impact of the new law. What they found was shocking. Company officials and glassworkers routinely hid children from investigators or sent them home when an inspection was pending. Although employers and unionized workers might fight over a number of issues, when it came to child labor, they were in general agreement. Neither side wanted to substitute other potential sources of cheap labor—women, African Americans, or new immigrants. Manufacturers testified to the U.S. Industrial Commission that "it is almost impossible to do without the small boy in carrying the work over from the presser to the finisher . . . , carrying it to the reheating furnace, and to be tempered." Glass Bottle Blowers president Denis Hayes was unfazed. He recalled going to work at age twelve; many began at age nine.

Only slowly did company-union unity on child labor disappear, making the reformers' task difficult. Even the photographs of Lewis Hine in yet another NCLC investigation did little to alter the situation. In New Jersey, efforts to ban night work for children under sixteen failed five times before 1910; a Pennsylvania statute exempted the glass industry from restrictions on night work; and West Virginia would not bar children from night work until 1919. Furthermore, as the earlier Illinois investigations had demonstrated, laws alone could not halt the practice. A 1918 investigation of Ohio glass factories discovered that many children continued to toil in small tableware factories, and a 1926 survey by the Pennsylvania State Department of Labor learned that nearly 40 percent of the state's glass factories employed children under age sixteen.

Although advancing technology in the 1880s had worsened conditions for children, advances after 1900, combined with state laws, slowly eradicated the problem. Semiautomatic and automatic machines transformed the production process in bottles and in some parts of tableware, the areas of the industry where nearly all of the children worked. Machine-made bottles, tumblers, and lamp chimneys dispensed with the mold boys, and gatherers and conveyors in the most modern factories did away with the need for carrying-over and snapping-up boys. As early as 1905, children declined from 15.5 percent to 10.1 percent of the industry workforce. When inventor and industrialist Michael Owens opened his modern bottle factory in Fairmont, West Virginia, in 1910, he claimed that his production process had virtually ended the need for humans. There was much hyperbole in Owens's statement, but the truth was that the industry was transforming the production process that relied on both skilled union members and the children who helped them to maintain production quotas. In the end, where mass-production technologies could cut labor costs, children disappeared; in those marginal factories producing small items for a market niche, child labor would linger until federal laws finally forced change.

References and Further Reading

Child Labor: Report of the Subcommittee on Child Labor. New York: White House Conference on Child Health and Protection, 1932.

Fones-Wolf, Ken. *Glass Towns: Industry, Labor and Political Economy in Appalachia, 1890–1930s.* Urbana: University of Illinois Press, 2007.

Hindman, Hugh D. *Child Labor: An American History.* Armonk, NY: M.E. Sharpe, 2002.

Spargo, John. *The Bitter Cry of the Children.* New York: Macmillan Company, 1916.

Trattner, Walter I. *Crusade for the Children: A History of the National Child Labor Committee and Child Labor Reform in America.* Chicago: Quadrangle Books, 1970.

U.S. Industrial Commission. Report on the Relations and Conditions of Capital and Labor Employed in Manufactures and General Business. Vol. 7. Washington: Government Printing Office, 1901.

Zembala, Dennis. "Machines in the Glasshouse: The Transformation of Work in the Glass Industry, 1820–1915." Ph.D. diss., George Washington University, 1984.

Child Labor in American Textiles

Hugh D. Hindman, Professor of Labor and Human Resources, Appalachian State University

The American textile industry originated in the northeastern New England states. In 1789, Samuel Slater established the first cotton textile factory using modern technology in Pawtucket, Rhode Island. Slater's original workforce consisted entirely of mothers and their children. His provision of housing and payment of a single wage to the head of the family created a distinctive labor regime, heavily reliant on child labor, that came to be known as the "Rhode Island model" (Tucker 1984).

An alternative model emerged in the early 1800s in and around Lowell, Massachusetts, where the first truly large-scale factories in America were built. There, the "boardinghouse system" was used to recruit "Yankee farm girls" from surrounding rural areas. Most of these girls were from sixteen years of age into their early twenties. Very few young children were employed in the Lowell mills. While the girls worked long hours, living conditions in the boardinghouses were reasonably pleasant, equipped as they were with amenities like libraries and pianos and chaperoned by middle-aged matrons. The boardinghouse system flourished into the 1850s, even winning praise from Charles Dickens for its industrialization on a higher, kinder, gentler plane (Dublin 1979).

Ultimately, however, the boardinghouse system proved unsustainable. When competitive pressures forced wage cuts, many Yankee farm girls went back to the farm, and replacements became harder to recruit. In the 1840s, mills began recruiting Irish immigrants who were arriving in America in large numbers to escape the potato famine in their homeland. When competitive pressures forced further wage cuts, Irish families, having nowhere else to go, sent their children to the mills. Thus, as Yankee farm girls gave way to Irish immigrants, the boardinghouse system gave way to the Rhode Island system of family wages and mill villages (Gitelman 1967).

The Southern Cotton Textile Industry

Prior to the American Civil War (1861–1865), there were only a few scattered mills in the South. A mill-building boom began in the 1880s that, by the early twentieth century, came to rival New England's dominance in the industry. In 1870, when New England still dominated, 14.5 percent, or 13,767 members, of its workforce were children under age sixteen. In the same year, in southern cotton mills, children constituted 23 percent of the workforce, but the number of working children was only 2,343. By 1905, the proportion of the New England workforce under sixteen had fallen to 6 percent (9,385 children). In the South, the workforce remained 23 percent children. But now the numbers were no longer trivial. In the Carolinas, Georgia, and Alabama alone, it was estimated that there were 62,000 children under fourteen working in the mills. Only 30 percent of the entire workforce was over twenty-one, and 75 percent of the spinners were under fourteen (Hindman 2002).

Mill Village and Family Wage

Borrowing from northern experience, but adding substantially to it, the southern cotton textile industry worked out the most highly evolved forms of the Rhode Island system of mill villages and family wages. Mill owners recruited whole families from the mountains of southern Appalachia and the rural Piedmont with promises of work in the mill and a house in the mill village. The mill villages provided housing for most or all of their employees. Most villages also provided a store, a church, and a school, all of which were owned and financed by the mill. Many mills went well beyond these minimums to provide an extensive array of social welfare programs from medical care to gardens and libraries; economic institutions from banks to funeral parlors; and all the services expected of a municipal government from law enforcement to fire protection to streets and sewage.

The mill village, and whatever amenities it provided, represented a gain in material standard of living for those families who migrated in from the mountains and surrounding farms. But is also fostered a fierce dependency on the mill. Once in the mill village, there was often no going back. Few families were ever able to return to the mountains or farms. Many families sold their rural property in the process of moving to the mills. Many others carried substantial debt as a result of their move. Once the move was made, the mill controlled everything, including the villagers.

If the mill village imposed a fierce dependency of the family on the mill, it also, in turn, imposed a fierce dependency of the mill on the labor of village children. Mill villages entailed a considerable capital investment, often equal to or greater than the investment in the mill itself. Further, as little or no work was conducted in the homes, it was largely a nonproductive capital investment. Mill owners had a strong incentive to spread the cost of the mill village over as many workers as possible. Once families were in the mill villages, their young children comprised a captive group of recruits to replenish the workforce. Specific arrangements varied from village to village. Some required at least one worker for the mill for every room of housing provided. Others required at least three workers per house. The so-called Pelzer Contract, associated with South Carolina's Pelzer "show mills" was a popular model. Under this arrangement, the mill contracted with the head of the household for the labor of the entire family. The contract provided that children under twelve, but at least five years old, were required to attend the mill school every day it was in session, and that children twelve and over were required to work in the mill, unless released from work by the superintendent. In this way, a new cohort of workers would be introduced to the mills each year.

But it was not just the mill owners that demanded the labor of children. Parents, too, would insist that their children be hired and would provide false statements of age if necessary. "They argued that if they raised the children to the age of ten or twelve they should begin to get money back on their investment. If the children went to school they would probably marry before going to work and the parent would lose all he had spent" (Davidson 1939, 110). Many workers fell into debt to company stores, banks, hospitals, funeral parlors, and other profit centers, and this debt further encouraged families to offer up their children.

Thus, households and mill owners alike had strong incentives to get as many of the children as possible to work as early as possible. Similarly, large families with more available or potential hands had stronger incentives to go to the mills, and mills had strong incentives to recruit large families.

Training the Workforce of the Future: The Helper System

By the time the children came of age for regular work in the mill, they were already well socialized into the regimen of the mill and well trained in many of the work processes. The helper system enabled the mill to gain production from very young children and to train the workforce of the future while disavowing a direct employment relationship. The character of the training and socialization of very young children was conditioned on the presence or absence of a mill school. Where there was no mill school, many families had few alternatives but to bring the children to work. It was the only readily available source of child care and enabled parents to keep the children under parental supervision. Under this informal arrangement, the youngest children played more than they worked. As they gained familiarity with the mill, they were expected to contribute to production by helping their parents in simple ways.

Where a mill school was present, the socialization and training program of the helper system could be coordinated and integrated with the educational program of the mill. One famous practice was that of "dinner toting," a practice that interrupted school in the middle of the day so children could carry dinners to their parents and older siblings in the mill. While their elders ate, the children helped out by sweeping, cleaning, or tending their parents' machines. Many schools observed that, as children approached the age for regular work in the mill, they did not return from their dinner-toting mission for the afternoon session of school.

Children did more than help out and train for their roles in replenishing the labor supply. They also served as a reserve labor supply, helping the mill accommodate fluctuations in production schedules and product demand. Many schoolteachers commented on how enrollment and attendance plummeted when there was a call to the mill. It should be noted that whatever schooling children may have received in the lower grades, most were gone to the mill by the time they would have reached the upper grades. In most mill schools, the upper grades were reserved for the sons and daughters of management.

Spinners and Doffers—Girls at Work and Boys at Play

Children in the mills tended to be concentrated in certain occupations and rare in others. For example, few young children worked as weavers, and virtually none worked as loom fixers. Children were concentrated in the spinning rooms of the mills to the extent that, in some mills, the spinning room was referred to as the Children's Department. The children most commonly worked as spinners, doffers, and sweepers. Boys generally started as doffers and sweepers, but some progressed to spinning after gaining experience. Girls were more likely to start out as spinners.

Doffing involved replacing full bobbins, filled by the spinners, with empty ones. It was intermittent work, involving relatively short bursts of high activity, with extended pauses for rest (or play) in between. At the required moments, the doffers invaded the mill and changed over every bobbin on every spindle as quickly as possible so that spinning could commence again. In mills with more modern machinery, which usually stood taller than earlier designs, boys often had to climb onto the spinning frames to replace the bobbins.

Lewis Hine photograph and original caption. "Boy from Loray Mill. 'Been at it right smart two years.' Gastonia, N.C., 11/08/1908." (*Courtesy of the National Archives and Records Administration, College Park MD, National Child Labor Committee photographs taken by Lewis Hine series, NWDNS-102-LH-248*)

In some mills, doffers doubled as sweepers, sweeping up cotton lint in between the doffing runs. In larger mills, doffing and sweeping were more likely to be distinct occupations. After the doffing was completed, doffers could often leave the mill for hours at a time, remaining close enough to be called when needed. One mill superintendent commented, "[T]he doffer boys played base ball, went swimming, and at least once, for a considerable period of time, played cards. Their actual working hours were about four hours each day" (quoted in Hindman 2002, 161–62). Doffers were often able to play, on company time, more hours than they worked.

In contrast to doffing, spinning was real, continuous work. Spinning cotton into yarn involved tending spinning frames. Each frame contained several spindles, each with its own bobbin to be filled. Spinners tended as many frames as their skill and competence enabled them to tend. They were usually paid on a piece rate based on the number or weight of the bobbins they filled. Much of the work involved "piecing up," or tying together broken pieces of yarn. It was considered light work in that it did not require great physical strength. But it did require endurance, constant attention, nearly continuous movement, fine-motor dexterity, and if not great skill, at least a knack for accommodating to the pace of the work process.

Lewis Hine photograph and original caption. "Rhodes Mfg. Co. Spinner. A moment's glimpse of the outer world. Said she was 11 years old. Been working over a year. Lincolnton, N.C., 11/11/1908." (*Courtesy of the National Archives and Records Administration, College Park MD, National Child Labor Committee photographs taken by Lewis Hine series, NWDNS-102-LH-249*)

When performed for ten, eleven, or twelve hours per day, work as a spinner was quite physically and mentally demanding.

Spinners did get the opportunity to take breaks from time to time during the workday. When they got caught up on their work—when they were all "pieced up"—they could rest momentarily, though being caught up too much of the time only indicated a readiness to tend a greater number of frames. More significantly, when the boys were called in to doff the bobbins, the spinners could enjoy a short break from their work.

Southern Textiles and the Child Labor Reform Movement

In many ways and for many reasons, southern cotton textiles became the major battleground on which the social, political, and economic war over child labor in America was fought. By the time a national movement to abolish child labor had come into being, as embodied in the National Child Labor Committee (NCLC), founded in 1904, child labor had already declined substantially in northern textile mills, but the number of children in southern mills was still growing. Of all industries, southern textiles received the most attention from the NCLC. In turn, southern mill owners reacted to protect their competitive advantage in cheap child labor.

Child labor reform in the South was complicated by issues of schooling. Unlike the North and most of the Midwest, where compulsory schooling laws long predated child labor reform efforts, in the South, while each state had begun to provide at least some public support for schooling, none had yet required schooling for all children or provided for anything approximating universal availability. In the North, the movement for compulsory and universal schooling preceded the period of greatest agitation for child labor reform; in the South the movements for compulsory schooling and child labor reform were coincident.

Mill owners were able to use concerns about schooling to forestall child labor legislation. They insisted that compulsory schooling must be established before the question of child labor legislation could be addressed. Mill interests argued that if children neither worked nor attended school, but instead remained idle, it would breed "a dangerous class of loafers and budding criminals" (quoted in Hindman 2002, 178). For their part, reformers played on racial prejudices, warning of the racial degeneration of children of "pure Anglo-Saxon stock," dissipated by premature work in the cotton mills, in contrast to African Americans, who were eagerly seeking education for their children (Sallee 2004).

One individual in particular, David Clark, publisher of the *Southern Textile Bulletin,* did more to delay federal child labor legislation in America than any other single person. When Congress enacted laws in 1916 and again in 1919 intended to abolish child labor from mining and manufacturing, Clark personally arranged the cases that resulted in the Supreme Court declaring the laws unconstitutional. When America debated the proposed Child Labor Amendment to the Constitution in the 1920s, Clark went so far as to create a Farmers' States Rights League to organize opposition to the amendment throughout rural America.

In the end, however, southern textile interests were finally able to play a positive and decisive role in child labor reform. In 1933, the Cotton Textile Code was the first industry code adopted under the National Industrial Recovery Act. Southern textile manufacturers wanted to ensure that the code established a low minimum wage and weak provisions regarding unions. So, as a bargaining ploy, they offered a "startling proposal" to set the minimum age for employment at sixteen. This was well above the prevailing standard for the industry. At the time there were only four states with a sixteen-year minimum age for factory work, none of them in the South. But with the adoption of the Cotton Textile Code, and the other industry codes that followed, sixteen rapidly became the new national standard for factory work, a standard that remains in place today (Hindman 2002, 83).

References and Further Reading

Davidson, Elizabeth H. *Child Labor Legislation in the Southern Textile States.* Chapel Hill: University of North Carolina Press, 1939.

Dublin, Thomas. *Women at Work: The Transformation of Work and Community in Lowell, Massachusetts, 1826–1850.* New York: Columbia University Press, 1979.

Freze, Gary R. "Poor Girls Who Might Otherwise Be Wretched: The Origins of Paternalism in North Carolina's Mills, 1836–1880." In *Hanging by a Thread: Social Change in Southern Textiles,* ed. Jeffrey Leiter, Michael D. Schulman, and Rhonda Zigraff, 21–32. Ithaca, NY: ILR Press, 1991.

Gitelman, Howard M. "The Waltham System and the Coming of the Irish." *Labor History* 8 (Fall 1967): 227–53.

Hall, Jacquelyn Dowd, James Leloudis, Robert Korstad, Mary Murphy, LuAnn Jones, and Christopher Daly. *Like a Family: The Making of a Southern Cotton Mill World.* New York: Norton, 1987.

Hindman, Hugh D. *Child Labor: An American History.* Armonk, NY: M.E. Sharpe, 2002.

Holleran, Philip M. "Family Income and Child Labor in Carolina Cotton Mills." *Social Science History* 21:3 (1997): 297–320.

McHugh, Cathy L. *Mill Family: The Labor System in the Southern Cotton Textile Industry, 1880–1915.* New York: Oxford University Press, 1988.

Mitchell, Broadus. *The Rise of the Cotton Mills in the South.* Baltimore: Johns Hopkins University Press, 1921.

Sallee, Shelley. *The Whiteness of Child Labor Reform in the New South.* Athens: University of Georgia Press, 2004.

Tucker, Barbara M. *Samuel Slater and the Origins of the American Textile Industry, 1790–1860.* Ithaca, NY: Cornell University Press, 1984.

Ware, Caroline. *The Early New England Cotton Manufacture: A Study in Industrial Beginnings.* Boston: Houghton-Mifflin, 1931.

Woodward, C. Vann. *The Origins of the New South, 1877–1913.* Baton Rouge: Louisiana State University Press, 1951.

Child Labor in Commercialized Agriculture, 1890–1966

Mary Lyons-Barrett, PhD, University of Nebraska at Omaha

Agriculture has always been the largest child-employing sector in America, and remains so today. This essay examines patterns of child labor in commercial agriculture, especially through the period when child labor in other industries came to be regulated, in an effort to provide some insight into why agriculture escaped similar regulation.

The Rise of Commercial Agriculture in America

Prior to the American Civil War (1861–1865) there were two contrasting "blueprints" of agrarian economy. First, there were the small, freehold farms of New England and the Midwest, producing crops and livestock for household subsistence and trade in local markets. In contrast, commercial agriculture prevailed in the plantation South, producing cash crops for distant markets, and relying on slave labor (Chen 1995).

In the decades following the Civil War, aided by technological advances in commercialized canning, irrigation systems, and refrigerated rail cars, the commercial agricultural model grew in most agricultural regions of the country. The increase in one-crop farms, patterned after the bonanza wheat farms of the 1860s, evolved into large industrial or factory farms. The labor needs for these one-crop farms varied. Some crops, such as sugar beets or cotton, required workers who would be available at various stages of the crop cycle and so required a labor force that would remain on the land throughout the growing cycle. Other crops, including many fruits and vegetables, required a large labor force for only a short period, usually for the harvest, which might extend into processing and canning. This seasonal demand was most often met by migrant workers who would show up at the proper time and move on, often to the next crop, when the harvest was complete.

In the South, though slavery was abolished, the plantation system was not. Former slaves and their descendants provided much of the labor force, continuing to work the plantations as sharecroppers or tenant farmers. Beginning around World War I, and continuing through the Great Depression and World War II, many blacks left the plantations and migrated North or to the cities so that, today, very few blacks remain in agriculture.

In the rest of the country, immigrants and their children comprised the bulk of the commercial agricultural labor force. For immigrants who came to America after the best farmland had been distributed under the Homestead Act of 1862, the notion of working as laborers in agriculture was an alternative to working in urban sweatshops. New immigrants—Italians and Poles on the East Coast, Russian-Germans in the Midwest, and Mexicans on the West Coast—gravitated to these one-crop industrial farms with their children. It was a means of establishing an economic foothold in America. However, getting ahead often meant sacrificing schooling for at least one generation of children.

Geographically, there were three majority migratory streams in commercial agriculture—the East Coast stream, the West Coast stream, and the midcontinental stream, which ran from the Great Lakes to the Rio Grande and encompassed the Rockies. On the East Coast truck farms of Maryland, Delaware, and New Jersey, they worked in potatoes, strawberries, sweet corn, snap beans, tomatoes, cucumbers, and onions. In Massachusetts and Maine, they worked in the bogs picking cranberries. On the West Coast, children worked

Lewis Hine photograph and original caption. "All these children five years, six years, seven years, nine years and two a little older, were picking cotton on H.M. Lane's farm Bells, Tex. Only one adult, an aunt was picking. Father was plowing. Edith five years, . . . picks all day. 'Hughie' six years old, girl, picks all day. Alton, seven years old, picks fifty pounds a day. Ruth, nine years old, picks seventy-five pounds a day. Rob and Lee are about ten or eleven years old. The very young children like to pick, but before long they detest it. Sun is hot, hours long, bags heavy. Location: Bells, Texas. September 1913." (*Courtesy of the Library of Congress Prints and Photographs Division, National Child Labor Committee Collection, LC-USZ62–63802*)

Lewis Hine photograph and original caption. "Seven-year-old Alex Reiber topping. He said, 'I hooked me knee with the beet-knife, but I jest went on a-workin'.' Location: Sterling [vicinity], Colorado / Photo by Hine, Oct 23/15." (*Courtesy of the Library of Congress Prints and Photographs Division, National Child Labor Committee Collection, LC-USZ62–100669*)

in sugar beets, potatoes, hops, figs, raisin grapes, walnuts, melons, olives, and peas. Part of the Midcontinental stream included work in hops, sugar beets, onions, and by the 1930s, cotton. In the Rockies, Plains states, and Great Lakes area including Michigan and Minnesota, families of many nationalities worked with their children in the cultivation of sugar beets.

Work Performed by Children

Most work in commercial agriculture was paid on some variation of a piece rate. Payment was based on the number of cotton bales produced in a season, or the number of cartons filled with berries in a day. Payment for the entire family's output was usually made to the household head. The system of payment created incentives for parents to put children to work as young as possible, for long hours of work, and favored large families with many children.

In migrant labor camps, children of all ages accompanied their parents to the fields. Infants and children too young to work might be put under the care of a nursing mother or older girl, but as soon as the children were old enough to contribute, they were put to simple tasks. In addition to the economic incentives, this was a practical way to provide adult supervision of the youngsters.

Children worked wherever handwork that did not require adult strength or endurance was involved. Because of their size, children were especially well adapted to the many "stoop labor" tasks. Most common was harvesting, but children were often involved in hulling and shucking, planting, weeding and hoeing, topping, and carrying loaded containers to central collection points.

In the onion marshes of Ohio and the cranberry bogs of Massachusetts and New Jersey, children worked on hands and knees on damp ground, plagued by mosquitoes. In cotton, children harvested bolls in sweltering heat from sunup to sundown. In sugar beets, children topped beets (removed foliage) with sharp knives and pulled the heavy beets from the soil by hand. In California picking figs, hops, and raisin grapes was sticky work that drew lots of insects.

Early Reform Efforts

Agrarian romanticism is deeply imprinted in the American psyche, and its imprint carries over to the work of children in agriculture, creating one of the major impediments to reform. The image of rosy-cheeked children assisting their parents with chores on the family farm is rooted in ideals of the Jeffersonian agrarian republic but bears little resemblance to the reality of children working as day laborers for large commercial growers. When a reform movement emerged in the 1890s to eliminate child labor from mines, mills, and factories, child labor in agriculture was largely ignored. Some early reformers accepted the romanticized version of agricultural work, distinguishing work on the farm, which had produced many strong, robust men, from industrial child labor. Well-known child labor critic John Spargo said that there was an "immense difference between the dust-laden air of a factory and the pure air of a farm," and public health workers touted "fresh air" as a remedy for tuberculosis.

In 1904 the National Child Labor Committee (NCLC) was formed. From the beginning, the NCLC was concerned about children in commercial agriculture. Attacking child labor in agriculture as "factory work without the factory roof," the committee was ultimately unable to overcome the aura of romantic charm associated with work in the fields. Lewis Hine, conducting the NCLC's first investigation of agricultural child labor, cautioned, "We have met everywhere the universal feeling that there is nothing harmful in outdoor work for children, no matter how young" (Hindman 2002). In the end, years of "intensive field work failed to achieve anything more than confirmation of already known facts to which nobody listened" (Trattner 1970, 153).

By the early twentieth century, most states had rudimentary child labor laws restricting industrial child labor, but none of these laws extended to agriculture. Compulsory schooling laws had some effect but often exempted children from attending school during peak periods, granting beet, apple, or tobacco vacations to ensure that children would be available for the local harvest. Further, early compulsory schooling laws had no effect on migrant children.

Early federal child labor laws were found unconstitutional, but they would not have regulated child labor in agriculture anyway (except in canneries, which were classed as factories). Sometimes federal policy actively encouraged child labor in agriculture. During World War I, severe labor shortages in agriculture, exacerbated by restrictions on immigration from many Eastern and Southern European countries and the great migration of African Americans out of agricultural work in the South to take defense industry jobs in northern cities, led growers to turn to children and Mexican immigrants for their labor needs. Enforcement of state child labor laws was relaxed, and schools let children out to help harvest. A new federal agency was created, the U.S. Boys Working Reserve, to match growers with boys ages sixteen to twenty-one, and Junior Reserves for boys fourteen to sixteen years old.

During the 1920s, because previous federal child labor laws had been found unconstitutional, reformers sought to amend the Constitution to explicitly permit Congress to regulate child labor. Unlike earlier federal laws, the proposed constitutional amendment would have clearly allowed Congress to regulate child labor in agriculture. When the amendment went to the states for ratification, farm groups such as the American Farm Bureau Federation and the Grange voiced their opposition to the amendment. The amendment ultimately failed after it had stalled in many rural-controlled state legislatures.

Depression-Era Reform Efforts

The Great Depression fueled concern over child labor in both industry and agriculture as the American public saw how working children depressed adult wages and took jobs from adults. In agriculture, the Okie children working as migrant farm workers in California due to the Dust Bowl in the Midwest gave child agricultural workers a native-born face. Yet when federal child labor regulations were codified in the Fair Labor Standards Act (FLSA) of 1938, agriculture was exempted with very little debate. In fact, agriculture, along with domestic service, was exempted from every piece of Franklin Roosevelt's New Deal labor legislation. These were the two sectors in which most African Americans worked, and southern Democrats, who controlled a majority of committee chairmanships and leadership positions in every New Deal Congress, were committed to maintaining the "plantation system" (Linder 1987).

Child labor did come under federal regulation in one agricultural sector during the Depression—sugar beets. Major companies comprising the "Sugar Trust" had transformed agriculture in the South Platte Valley in Colorado and the North Platte Valley in Nebraska into one where the owner of the land and tiller of the soil were not one and the same. Between 1891 and 1893, some 200 Russian-German families were brought to Lincoln, Nebraska, and then transported by train to western Nebraska to work in the sugar-beet fields. The sugar companies sponsored the train service to bring the families to the fields and even provided a semblance of housing, though often that meant an old chicken coop, a tent, or an abandoned railroad car. There, entire families, including very young children, toiled raising and harvesting beets for some of the most profitable commercial agricultural enterprises in the nation. When Congress enacted the Sugar Act of 1937, it made receipt of federal sugar subsidies contingent on agreement not to employ children.

World War II and Beyond

In spite of the publication of John Steinbeck's *Grapes of Wrath* in 1939, the plight of migrant farmworkers faded into the background as the United States entered World War II and many of the Okies joined the military or left agriculture to work in defense industries. Wartime labor shortages in agriculture once again prompted Congress to establish an emergency worker program for nonfarm youths, more than a million of whom supported the war effort by working on the nation's farms. Congress also established the *bracero* (migrant worker) program with Mexico to recruit Mexican labor. While the *bracero* program, which lasted until 1964, was aimed at recruiting adult men, it also increased both child labor and illegal immigration. Since World War II, people of Mexican origin have dominated the U.S. agricultural workforce. Meanwhile, in 1949, Congress amended the FLSA to prohibit children under sixteen from working in agriculture during school hours.

Significant amendments to the FLSA were adopted in 1966 as the culmination of several trends. First, child labor had declined by the mid-1950s in key agricultural sectors, notably cotton and sugar beets, as a result of mechanization. Second was a renewed interest in the problems of migrant workers, heightened by the CBS news documentary *Harvest of Shame* aired the day after Thanksgiving, 1960. The third trend was the unionization of agricultural workers, through the efforts of Cesar Chavez and Dolores Huerta, into the United Farm Workers Association. Chavez did not condemn child labor in the early 1960s because he knew that too many parents were dependent on the wages of their children, but he realized that if the parents belonged to the union, they would in time see their own wages rise and want their children in school. The 1966 amendments prohibited children under sixteen from performing "hazardous" work in agriculture and extended the federal minimum wage to most of agriculture. Finally, in 1974, the FLSA was amended to provide minimum ages for work in agriculture, but these minimums remain far less stringent than those applied to other industries.

References and Further Reading

Chen, Jim. "Of Agriculture's First Disobedience and Its Fruit." *Vanderbilt Law Review* 48 (1995): 1261–1332.

Chute, Charles L. "The Cost of the Cranberry Sauce." *Survey* 27 (December 1911): 1281–84.

Hendrickson, Kent. "The Sugar Beet Laborer and the Federal Government: An Episode in the History of the Great Plains in the 1930s." *Great Plains Journal* 3 (Spring 1964): 44–59.

Hindman, Hugh D. *Child Labor: An American History.* Armonk, NY: M.E. Sharpe, 2002.

Linder, Marc. "Farm Workers and the Fair Labor Standards Act: Racial Discrimination in the New Deal." *Texas Law Review* 65 (1987): 1335–93.

Lyons-Barrett, Mary. *Child Labor in Commercialized Agriculture, 1890–1966.* PhD diss., University of Nebraska, Lincoln, 2002.

May, William John, Jr. *The Great Western Sugarlands: The History of the Great Western Sugar Company and the Economic Development of the Great Plains.* New York: Garland Publishing, 1989.

Spargo, John. *The Bitter Cry of the Children.* New York: Macmillan, 1906.

Trattner, Walter. *Crusade for the Children: A History of the National Child Labor Committee and Child Labor Reform in America.* Chicago: Quadrangle Books, 1970.

Evolution of U.S. Child Labor Policy

Hugh D. Hindman, Professor of Labor and Human Resources, Appalachian State University

Child labor law is a nearly universal component of public policy arrayed against child labor. Yet, a prominent theme in economic history is that law matters little in the prevalence of child labor. State child labor laws are given little credit for the reduction of child labor in early-twentieth-century America (Brown et al. 1992; Moehling 1999). Likewise, compulsory schooling laws are given little credit for either increasing school enrollment or decreasing child labor (Landes and Solomon 1972; Angrist and Krueger 1991; Margo and Finegan 1996). Finally, there is abundant evidence that, in spite of our laws, widespread and persistent violations occur (Kruze and Mahony 2000).

Under the American system of federalism, the federal government was precluded from regulating employment relationships until 1937. The Tenth Amendment of the Constitution reserved all rights not specifically elucidated to the otherwise sovereign states. There was an ongoing tension between the Commerce Clause, which authorized Congress to regulate interstate commerce, and the Tenth Amendment. Until 1937, the U.S. Supreme Court held consistently that Congress could regulate only commerce itself, and not conditions under which goods and services entered the channels of commerce. Thus, regulation of working conditions generally, and child labor in particular, remained the province of state legislatures.

Owing to these republican features of the Constitution, U.S. history before 1937 may be especially informative for child labor in the world today. We established ourselves as a republic of sovereign states, each of which was responsible for regulating its own internal affairs. At the same time, however, the sovereign states were becoming increasingly integrated into a strong national economy, where each state was in competition with the others. In certain respects, the United States of the years before 1937 represents in microcosm the world of today, in which sovereign nations struggle to come to grips with their own child labor problems in the larger context of an increasingly integrated global economy.

Evolution of State Law Before 1906

Before the twentieth century there was no national reform movement and no federal role on the question of child labor. Early reform efforts took place at the state level on a state-by-state basis. Well into the twentieth century, while the question of whether there should be a federal role in child labor was debated, many of the most important advances continued to originate in the sovereign states. What emerged was a crazy quilt of legislation where state standards varied considerably. The situation permitted and engendered the worst sorts of sectionalism—of the "race to the bottom" sort where "the worse inevitably checks the progress of the better" (Kelley 1905, 103). But there was also real progress through this process of gradualism. It was a patchwork not merely in the sense that each state had its own unique standards, but also in the sense that patches were continually being stitched on top of patches. Within each state, legislation evolved and, generally, with this evolution came progress. States also tended to emulate similarly situated states so that a steady upward harmonization of standards occurred over time. More progressive states, usually but not always the more heavily industrialized, led, and less progressive states followed. "While every legislature followed a separate course, there was a tendency for the less progressive states to follow the lead of the more progressive and in time to narrow the gap between them. This was due to the gradual diffusion of ideas and the growth of regional and national reform groups" (Nelson 1975, 123).

From the beginning, development of child labor legislation and schooling legislation were equally intertwined. "Although distinct from the movement for public education, it came hand in hand with it, and the success of one was accompanied or followed by that of the other" (Davidson 1939). In some areas, schooling legislation and child labor legislation came about simultaneously. In other areas schooling legislation came first and child labor legislation followed.

In much of the North, concern for schooling provided the leading impetus. Tax-supported systems of free public education were established in most northern industrial states in the 1830s and 1840s. Schooling was not yet compulsory and in more remote areas was not widely available, but it was valued. The first regulatory concession sought by working people was the opportunity to send their children to school. Children who worked too many hours could not properly attend to their studies, and so the first child labor laws provided restrictions on hours. It is important to note that these laws were an attempt not so much to reduce or eliminate child labor, but to redirect some portion of that labor to schooling.

By 1900, all of the industrialized states of the North had statutes restricting child labor in mining and manufacturing. Though age standards varied, and they were enforced (or not enforced) with varying degrees of vigor, at least there were laws on the books. Most common were restrictions on working hours of children. By 1900 most northern industrial states had adopted the ten-hour day and sixty-hour week as the legal maximum for women and children. Several states specified minimum ages, and most incorporated rudimentary compulsory schooling provisions.

The South lagged behind the North considerably, both in development of industry and in enactment of progressive child labor legislation. Before 1900, there had been laws in a few southern states, a legacy of the Knights of Labor, but these had been repealed. In 1900 none of the southern states had effective child labor legislation on the books. Around the turn of the century, however, several southern states began considering legislative restrictions on child labor. In 1903 Alabama and both Carolinas passed laws prohibiting the work of children under twelve (with some exceptions for hardship). A few progressive southern governors attempted to push for educational reforms.

Legislative standards meant little without effective compliance and enforcement provisions. Many early laws contained loopholes that essentially nullified their intent. For example, many of the ten-hour laws adopted by northern states in the 1850s contained exceptions for those working under "special contracts." Thus, employers could offer employment on condition that the hours provisions could be exceeded at will, and the employee's choice was to take it or leave it. Many of the first minimum-age laws, especially in the south, contained "hardship exemptions," permitting younger children to work if helping to support a widowed mother, disabled father, or otherwise indigent families, thereby encouraging claims of indigence. Other laws required no proof of age, but rather only a parent's oath, thereby encouraging perjury. Still others prohibited only "employment" of children, but not necessarily all productive work. So if children were kept off the payroll, they could still be required to help. Finally, under many laws, employers were liable only for "knowing" violations, thereby rewarding employer ignorance. Even good laws could be rendered ineffective through ineffectual inspection and enforcement regimes. While some employers and parents would voluntarily comply with the law, others would have to be forced to comply. Florence Kelley argued that "compulsion incarnate" in the position of the factory inspector or school truant officer was the necessary adjunct of legislative standards. She proposed three "objective tests" of effective enforcement of child labor laws: presence of children in school; actual prosecutions of violators; and public and published records of the enforcement agencies (Kelley 1907).

Reformers also found that they had to address a wide array of issues beyond child labor and schooling, from widows' pensions to maintenance of birth records. Often overlooked in accounts of child labor reform was the influence of developments such the emergence of employer liability and workers' compensation laws. Throughout the nineteenth century, employers could escape liability for disabling or fatal workplace accidents through the contributory negligence theory when the employee's own negligence contributed to the accident. In the early twentieth century, courts began holding that employers could not plead contributory negligence when children under the legal age were injured. Some courts held, even in the absence of a legal minimum age, that the contributory negligence defense could not be used in cases involving children under a certain age (Davidson 1939). When most states adopted some form of worker compensation system between 1910 and 1920, the risks associated with hiring children were magnified. Children posed higher risks of accident and injury (both to themselves and to others with whom they worked), so employers who agreed not to hire children could often qualify for lower insurance premiums.

Evolution of Federal Law

A superficial reading of the legislative history of federal child labor legislation would seem to support the conclusion that law matters little, that it was belated and, ultimately, that it was unnecessary. The United States' first serious attempt at federal legislation, the Beveridge Bill of 1906, went nowhere. It was nearly a decade before another bill received serious consideration. The Keating-Owen Act, banning interstate commerce in goods produced by children, was enacted in 1916 but was found unconstitutional. A second attempt—the Child Labor Tax Act of 1918, imposing a 10 percent excise tax on child-made goods—was also found unconstitutional. In the mid-twenties, Congress recommended a constitutional amendment to the states, but it too failed. Industry codes developed under the 1933 National Recovery Act addressed child labor, but just as these codes were being put into effect, the NRA was found unconstitutional. The Fair Labor Standards Act (FLSA) of 1938 was the United States' first enduring federal child labor legislation. By the time it was enacted, however, child labor had largely been relegated to the past.

While it is true that the FLSA merely codified prevailing practices long since achieved, the earlier legislative efforts had important normative influences on development of child labor policy throughout the nation. Even though it had no legal force, the Beveridge Bill established the first federal standard in 1906. While the evolutionary history of federal child labor law is rich and complex, the evolution of the U.S. national standard on child labor was deceptively simple. The federal standard came about in three discrete steps. The years 1906, 1916, and 1933 stand out as watershed dates.

The Beveridge Bill called for a fourteen-year minimum age in mining and manufacturing and limited the hours of fourteen- to sixteen-year-olds to eight per day. This became the de facto federal standard that prevailed for a decade. The failure to enact the Beveridge Bill also led directly to the creation of the Children's Bureau in 1912 and the commissioning of a massive study of child labor by the Labor Bureau (authorized in 1906 and completed from 1910 to 1913). The second movement in the national standard came in 1916. The Keating-Owen Act adopted the basic framework of the Beveridge Bill but elevated the minimum age in mining to sixteen and prohibited night work in manufacturing by those fourteen to sixteen years of age. Before Keating-Owen, only nine states had laws that measured up to its standards. Between 1916 and 1933, most states came into substantial conformity with the federal standard, but only four states went on to establish higher standards. In 1933, the federal age standard was elevated again. Codes developed under the NRA contained child labor provisions for numerous industries and occupations. The most important change in the standard was elevation of the minimum age for most industries and occupations from fourteen years of age to sixteen. In addition, a variety of exceptions were carved out for specific industries and occupations. The NRA standard rapidly became the norm for states to emulate. Nowhere is this normative effect illustrated more clearly than when North Carolina, which had led resistance to child labor regulation for so long, adopted the sixteen-year standard after the NRA was invalidated (Johnson 1935; Davidson 1939; Wood 1968). When the Fair Labor Standards Act was finally enacted in 1938, the child labor provisions of the NRA codes provided the template. Child labor provisions of the

FLSA have been amended relatively few times (for example, agriculture was not addressed until 1974) so that today's regulatory scheme can be traced, in large measure, directly to the NRA codes.

It is also important to note that the Keating-Owen Act and the Child Labor Tax Act were the law of the land for short but important periods before they were invalidated by the Supreme Court. Keating-Owen was in effect for nearly a year, until June 1918. After the law was found unconstitutional, its provisions were imposed by executive order, as a wartime measure, on federal contractors. The Child Labor Tax Act was effective from April 1919 until May 1922, just over three full years. Many employers adjusted to operating without children during this period and found no need to go back to hiring children when permitted.

U.S. Child Labor Law Today

Child labor in mining, manufacturing, and most other hazardous industrial sectors has been effectively abolished. Retail and many services now serve to socialize youth fourteen to sixteen years of age into work, but hours are regulated so as not to interfere with schooling. While many American children work from young ages, and while violations of the law are numerous, the vast majority of American children grow up without experiencing child labor.

The United States remains vulnerable to child labor problems in sectors not originally regulated by the FLSA, in the street trades, in industrial homework, and especially in agriculture. First, as industrial child labor began to wane, child labor in the street trades boomed. Most prominent were the newsboys. The news media, which generally supported child labor reform, reacted to protect its franchise in newsboys. They were not employees of the papers; they were independent businessmen—little merchants. Newsboy exemptions were incorporated in the FLSA that permit related activities. American children remain vulnerable to a variety of street-selling scams, sometimes organized under the guise of charity. Second, in a variety of industries, but especially in the garment trades, homework systems were an integral aspect of the larger sweating system. But regulating homework was tantamount to regulating private conduct performed in the sanctity of the home, and is especially difficult to enforce.

The United States remains vulnerable to the reemergence of sweatshops on domestic soil, especially in traditional child-employing industries such as the garment trade. Further, as American business continues to globalize, it risks encountering sweating sectors in other nations that are rife with labor abuses, including the use of child labor.

Finally, agriculture represents the clearest failure of American child labor policy. Agriculture was not covered under the FLSA until 1974. Today standards remain far below those considered minimally acceptable in other sectors. The minimum age for employment in agriculture is twelve, and there are no restrictions on hours. There are hundreds of thousands of children under sixteen working as hired agricultural laborers. Compulsory schooling laws may be better enforced today, though among migratory populations this cannot be ensured, but even where they are enforced, it often means only a six-hour break in a workday that would otherwise run to twelve or fourteen hours.

References and Further Reading

Angrist, Joshua, and Alan Krueger. "Does Compulsory School Attendance Affect Schooling and Attendance?" *Quarterly Journal of Economics* 106 (1991): 979–1014.

Brown, Martin, Jens Christiansen, and Peter Philips. "The Decline of Child Labor in the U.S. Fruit and Vegetable Canning Industry: Law or Economics?" *Business History Review* 66 (Winter 1992): 723–70.

Davidson, Elizabeth H. *Child Labor Legislation in the Southern Textile States.* Chapel Hill: University of North Carolina Press, 1939.

Ensign, Forest. *Compulsory School Attendance and Child Labor.* Iowa City: Athens Press, 1921.

Hindman, Hugh D. *Child Labor: An American History.* Armonk, NY: M.E. Sharpe, 2002.

Johnson, Elizabeth Sands. "Child Labor Legislation." In *History of Labor in the United States, 1896–1932,* ed. John R. Commons. Vol. 4, *Labor Legislation,* 450–56, ed. Elizabeth Brandeis. New York: MacMillan, 1935.

Kelley, Florence. *Some Ethical Gains Through Legislation.* New York: MacMillan, 1905.

Kelley, Florence. "Obstacles to the Enforcement of Child

Labor Legislation." *Annals of the American Academy of Political and Social Science* (January 1907): 50–56.

Kruze, Douglas L., and Douglas Mahony. "Illegal Child Labor in the United States: Prevalence and Characteristics." *Industrial and Labor Relations Review* 54:1 (2000): 17–40.

Landes, William M., and Lewis C. Solomon. "Compulsory Schooling Legislation: An Economic Analysis of Law and Social Change in the Nineteenth Century." *Journal of Economic History* 22 (1972): 54–91.

Margo, Robert A., and T. Aldrich Finegan. "Compulsory Schooling Legislation and School Attendance in Turn-of-the-Century America: A 'Natural Experiment' Approach." *Economic Letters* 53 (1996): 103–10.

Moehling, Carolyn M. "State Child Labor Laws and the Decline of Child Labor." *Explorations in Economic History* 36 (1999): 72–106.

Nelson, Daniel. *Managers and Workers: Origins of the New Factory System in the United States—1880–1920.* Madison: University of Wisconsin Press, 1975.

Ogburn, William F. *Progress and Uniformity in Child-Labor Legislation: A Study in Statistical Measurement.* New York: Columbia University Press, 1912.

Steinhilber, August W., and Carl J. Sokolowski. *State Laws on Compulsory Attendance.* Washington, DC: U.S. Department of Health, Education and Welfare, 1966.

Wood, Stephen B. *Constitutional Politics in the Progressive Era: Child Labor and the Law.* Chicago: University of Chicago Press, 1968.

Florence Kelley and the National Consumers League

Laura S. Abrams, PhD, University of California, Los Angeles

Florence Kelley (1859–1932), a notable Progressive Era social reformer, spearheaded the movement to abolish child labor in the United States. Kelley was an avowed socialist and a lawyer who advanced from her work as the first Illinois factory inspector and resident at Chicago's Hull House to head the National Consumers League (NCL). Kelley channeled her outrage over unregulated factory conditions into historically significant legislative victories on behalf of children, women, and the laboring class in industrial America.

Kelley was born in 1859 in Philadelphia to a Republican congressman, William Kelley, and her mother, Caroline Bartram-Bonsall. She graduated from Cornell University in 1882 and proceeded to study law and government at the University of Zurich. There she joined the Socialist Democratic Party and married a socialist medical student, Lazare Wishnewetzky, with whom she bore three children. In 1890, the family settled in the United States. Shortly thereafter, she left her husband and children and joined a flourishing generation of educated women reformers at Chicago's famed Hull House.

Female social reformers of the late nineteenth century spearheaded the public movement to regulate factory conditions for all workers. As part of a prevailing maternalist ideology that touted women's unique caring capacity, they focused specific attention on protecting women and children. Along with her progressive-minded colleagues, Kelley pioneered the use of scientific data to justify legislative reforms. Her first field study entailed an intensive survey of child labor in the square mile surrounding Hull House, where she discovered alarmingly high rates of children who were working in home or factory industries. This research led the Illinois legislature to pass its first law prohibiting employment of children under the age of fourteen. Kelley was then appointed by then Illinois governor John Peter Altgeld as the state's first factory inspector. During this time she also earned a law degree from Northwestern University.

In 1899, Kelley moved to New York to become the leader of the newly formed National Consumers League and the head of the New York Child Labor Committee. The NCL is an advocacy organization modeled after a similar movement in England, whose mission is to promote a fair and safe marketplace for workers and consumers. Among other initial goals, the NCL worked for the abolition of child labor.

In its early years, the NCL and Kelley used creative strategies to garner public attention to the issue of child labor. They pioneered the use of consumer boycotts to promote fair labor standards and safe workplaces. In a forerunner to today's social labeling programs, the NCL implemented its white-label program to designate products that were manufactured under fair and safe working conditions and, significantly, without child labor. The NCL's consumer advocacy movement spread across the country with the formation of league branches in many urban centers.

Kelley's passion for social justice extended beyond her concern to abolish child labor. As the NCL's power grew, it moved beyond tactics such as consumer boycotts and protests to influential legislative and legal work. Kelley worked with future Supreme Court Justice Louis Brandeis to prepare the landmark 1908 Supreme Court case *Mueller v. Oregon,* which established the constitutionality of a ten-hour-maximum workday for women. Kelley and the NCL also played a key role in passage of the landmark 1921 Sheppard-Towner Act, aimed at reducing infant and maternal mortality by authorizing federal aid to states for maternity, child health, and welfare programs. The NCL also influenced state legislation, drafting the first minimum-wage law in Massachusetts, and lobbied for improved child labor and compulsory education laws.

Throughout her life, Florence Kelley participated in numerous organizations and supported socialism, women's suffrage, and African American civil rights. She helped to form the National Association for the Advancement of Colored People and she was a member of the Women's International League for Peace and Freedom. She also authored several books. Kelley's fervent passion for social change and justice led to concrete legislative reforms that improved the lives of working-class children, women, and families. She died in 1932 at the age of seventy-four.

After Florence Kelley passed away, a new generation of women leaders took charge of the NCL, including Lucy Randoph Mason and Mary Dublin. The Great Depression and its associated public disenchantment with the free market led to massive government intervention into the social welfare of U.S. citizens. Roosevelt's New Deal ideology thus provided unprecedented opportunity for the NCL to advance its causes on a national scale. The organization played a major role in lobbying for the Fair Labor Standards Act of 1938, which provided the first enduring federal regulation of child labor. Historian Landon Starr has argued that contrary to the popular belief that the heyday of the NCL was the Kelley years, some of the most important work of the NCL was accomplished in the 1930s as a result of the more open political climate. Indeed, the NCL exercised its relationship with the Roosevelt administration to advocate for national health insurance and improved food- and drug-safety laws, among other federal programs and regulations.

Today the NCL continues to be a largely female-headed advocacy organization that has remained a steadfast opponent of child labor. It continues to push for improved child labor laws and monitors compliance. One recent priority deals with global child labor, seeking to assure that U.S. consumers do not unwittingly purchase goods produced by children in global factories of U.S. companies. Another priority seeks to protect migrant farmworker children by strengthening the Fair Labor Standards Act so that standards in agriculture are harmonized with the higher standards for other industries.

References and Further Reading

Goldmark, Josephine. *Impatient Crusader: The Life of Florence Kelley.* Urbana: University of Illinois Press, 1953.

Kelley, Florence. *Some Ethical Gains Through Legislation.* New York: Macmillan, 1905.

Kelley, Florence. *Modern Industry in Relation to the Family, Health, Education, Morality.* New York: Longmans Green, 1914.

Sklar, Kathryn Kish. *Florence Kelley and the Nation's Work.* New Haven, CT: Yale University Press, 1995.

Storrs, Landon R.Y. *Civilizing Capitalism: The National Consumers' League, Women's Activism, and Labor Standards in the New Deal Era.* Chapel Hill: University of North Carolina Press, 2000.

National Child Labor Committee

James DelRosso, Web Editor and Reference Assistant, Catherwood Library, Cornell University's School of Industrial and Labor Relations

For more than a century, the National Child Labor Committee (NCLC) has battled the exploitation of children in the name of productivity and commerce. While the success of this effort can be measured in the numerous legal restrictions currently placed on children's labor, the NCLC continues to promote education of both children and the general public, many of whom are unaware of how prevalent child labor remains, especially among communities such as migrant farmworkers.

The NCLC was founded in 1904 through an alliance between southern child labor activist Edgar Gardner Murphy and the New York Child Labor Committee as a result of Murphy's desire to engage the problem of child labor on a national level. Since such broad-based action had never before been attempted, the committee spent its first years in a primarily investigative role, gathering evidence to argue that the practice of child labor—although supported by businesses, parents, and even the children themselves—should be abolished. These investigators laid the foundation for the NCLC's later victories; the photographs of one of the investigators, Lewis W. Hine, would put a face on child labor that was impossible for the United States to ignore; these photographs remain the archetypal images of the practice to this day.

Even as the committee began to leverage its findings into legislative action, disagreements rooted in the previous century's regional conflicts began to take their toll on the organization. Murphy and southern moderates departed the organization after it endorsed federal child labor legislation, and a series of popular publications that focused exclusively on alleged abuses in the South's textile industry kept them away. The NCLC became an organization of northern progressives pursuing recognition and legislative action at a federal level; a goal that was achieved in 1907, when the committee was officially incorporated by an act of Congress. Five years later, a Children's Bureau was established in the U.S. Department of Commerce and Labor, concrete evidence of the committee's success at the federal level.

On September 1, 1916, President Woodrow Wilson signed into law the Keating-Owen Act, which would have heavily regulated or outright abolished many common forms of child labor. However, what seemed to be a major victory for the NCLC would prove to be short-lived. The following August, one month before the law would take effect, a lawsuit funded by the Executive Committee of Southern Cotton Manufacturers challenged its constitutionality. The challenge would prove successful. In the summer of 1918, the Supreme Court ruled that federal regulation of child labor was unconstitutional. When this precedent served to invalidate the Child Labor Tax Act three years later, the committee embraced new tactics. One, an attempt to amend the Constitution to ban child labor, would prove fruitless. But parallel efforts to gain passage for state laws proved far more successful.

During the Great Depression of the 1930s, Franklin D. Roosevelt's New Deal heralded the arrival of a federal government far more willing to regulate businesses on the local level. While Roosevelt's National Industrial Recovery Act would eventually be overturned by the Supreme Court, its provisions—primarily the Cotton Textile Code—remained in force, amounting to a de facto increase of the minimum working age to sixteen almost everywhere in the country. Passage of the 1938 Fair Labor Standards Act (FLSA) was lauded as a triumph for the NCLC, but many of its regulations merely codified existing practices and it left child agricultural workers completely unregulated. The committee's efforts to bring these children, especially migrant workers, whose plight was immortalized by John Steinbeck in *The Grapes of Wrath* (1939), under the protection of federal legislation were frustrated by the onset of World War II, but not abandoned. Preventing the exploitation of young migrant workers remains one of the NCLC's highest priorities to this day.

In addition to helping migrant workers, the postwar NCLC has focused on improving education, both to provide children with a viable alternative to work and to better prepare them for the workplace they will eventually enter. The committee has been a driving force in legislation such as the Manpower Development and Training Act, the Economic Opportunity Act, and the Vocational Education Act, and organizations such as the National Youth Employment Coalition. Today's NCLC pursues its goals of educating children and preventing their exploitation, improving opportunities for children of migrant farmworkers, and increasing public awareness of the current state of child labor through programs such as the Lewis Hine Awards for Service to Children and Youth and KAPOW (Kids and the Power of Work).

References and Further Reading

Hindman, Hugh D. *Child Labor: An American History.* Armonk, NY: M.E. Sharpe, 2002.

National Child Labor Committee. http://www.nationalchildlabor.org/index.html.

Trattner, Walter I. *Crusade for the Children: A History of the National Child Labor Committee and Child Labor in America.* Chicago: Quadrangle Books, 1970.

Felix Adler

James DelRosso, Web Editor and Reference Assistant, Catherwood Library, Cornell University's School of Industrial and Labor Relations

Remembered primarily as the founder of the Ethical Culture movement, Felix Adler dedicated his life to realizing his vision of a humanity that lived rightly, by a morality that was both fiercely independent and deeply progressive. For the final three decades of his life, this dedication included efforts to end the exploitation of working children, the legacy of which can still be seen today.

Born in 1851, in Alzey, Germany, Adler immigrated to the United States six years later with his father, Samuel Adler, and the rest of his family. The elder Adler was the latest in a long line of rabbis, and the vanguard of Reform Judaism, sent to introduce the movement's innovations to the Temple Emanu-El in New York City, then the wealthiest Jewish congregation in the New World.

Adler grew up amidst an environment of modernism and the reevaluation of long-held tradition; his first sermon on his return from studying the rabbinate at the University of Heidelberg boldly challenged the congregation to go even further than the Reform they had thus far adopted, calling on them to forsake their traditional religious and cultural identity, and instead "embrace in one great moral state the whole family of men" (quoted in Radest 1969, 17). The resultant controversy indicated to Adler that his beliefs were too distinct from those of the temple's congregation, and he therefore declined to continue his ministry.

After two years at Cornell University teaching Hebrew and Oriental literature, Adler returned to New York City and founded the Society for Ethical Culture, the group he would be most associated with throughout his life. The society would be the culmination and the vehicle for Adler's philosophy, and made him a hub of sorts within the growing community of New York progressives.

While the philosophy of Ethical Culture mandated concern for the welfare of children, education, and the strength of the family, Adler's official involvement with the movement to eradicate child labor came in 1903, when he became a founding member of the New York Child Labor Committee. The next year, Rev. Edgar Gardner Murphy, whose Alabama Child Labor Committee had been the nation's first such organization, approached Adler to propose an organization to address the exploitation of children in the workforce on a national level; Adler agreed and became the first chair of the National Child Labor Committee.

By this time, Adler was a professor at Columbia University. This position in the academy, in conjunction with the important role played by his Society for Ethical Culture, allowed the nascent NCLC to enlist some of the nation's most influential progressives (not to mention its most generous philanthropists) among its first members and contributors. After the departure of Murphy's southern faction from the committee in 1906, the organization became firmly entrenched in New York's potent progressive community, and was incorporated by an act of Congress the following year. Adler's early support helped lay the foundation for the movement's later victories, despite mixed success and setbacks during his lifetime. In his eulogy for Adler in 1933, John L. Elliott of the Society for Ethical Culture cited Adler's commitment to making childhood a time of happiness and learning; five years later, the passage of the Fair Labor Standards Act would help bring that dream closer to reality.

References and Further Reading

"Dr. Felix Adler Dies in 82d Year." *New York Times*, April 26, 1933, 15.

"Eulogies Are Paid to Dr. Felix Adler." *New York Times*, April 28, 1933, 17.

Radest, Howard B. *Toward Common Ground: The Story of the Ethical Societies in the United States*. New York: Ungar, 1969.

Edgar Gardner Murphy

James DelRosso, Web Editor and Reference Assistant, Catherwood Library, Cornell University's School of Industrial and Labor Relations

Edgar Gardner Murphy was one of the most influential voices of Southern progressivism in the United States during the early twentieth century. Born in 1869 and raised in the poverty of the Reconstruction South, Murphy became a practicing Episcopalian priest in 1893. He was a founding member of the National Child Labor Committee, and served in numerous organizations dedicated to social justice.

Murphy's initial forays into activism occurred during his time in the ministry, targeting first racism, and then the terrible conditions that afflicted the working poor, regardless of race or creed. He became involved in the fight to end child labor after he witnessed its destructive effects on the communities he ministered to in Alabama. After several unsuccessful years spent lobbying for child labor legislation, Murphy enlisted the aid of activists with whom he had served on the Conference on Race Relations to form the Alabama Child Labor Committee in 1901. The first organization of its kind, the Alabama Child Labor Committee engaged in a program of education that not only covered Alabama, but also reached north to New England to address the owners of many of the southern factories that employed children.

Murphy expressed his dedication to the eradication of child labor everywhere in America in his 1903 address to the National Conference on Charities and Corrections in Atlanta. Simply and directly titled "Child Labor Is a National Problem," this speech drew the praise of many northern progressives who were similarly eager to address the problem of child labor on the national level. One of these progressives, Felix Adler, invited Murphy to New York for a series of discussions and speeches on the matter. This collaboration would culminate in the creation of the National Child Labor Committee in 1904. As the committee's first secretary, Murphy put an early emphasis on the investigation and documentation that would later allow the NCLC to arouse public sentiment against child labor. He also helped draft the committee's constitution, which would facilitate the NCLC's incorporation by Congress three years later.

Unfortunately, 1907 would also mark a parting of the ways between Murphy and the NCLC. His enthusiasm for a national organization that focused on changing state laws was not shared by many others in the NCLC. They favored federal legislation and threw their support behind Senator Albert Beveridge, who proposed a bill that would have banned the interstate commerce of goods produced by child labor. Murphy felt such a law would decimate public opposition to child labor, especially in a South that still thought of the federal government in terms of Reconstruction, and thus would be devastating to the cause. Despite requests that he stay with the committee even in opposition, Murphy tendered his resignation on January 13, 1907. Murphy's opposition contributed to the bill's eventual failure, and when invited to rejoin the NCLC in 1908, he was too ill to accept.

The chronic illness that claimed Murphy's life in 1913 restricted his efforts to eradicate child labor after leaving the NCLC, but his legacy was realized in the continued efforts to sway the American public to the cause, which have by and large succeeded.

References and Further Reading

Bailey, Hugh C. *Edgar Gardner Murphy: Gentle Progressive.* Coral Gables, FL: University of Miami Press, 1968.

Murphy, Edgar Gardner. *Problems of the Present South: A Discussion of Certain of the Educational, Industrial and Political Issues in the Southern States.* New York: Macmillan, 1904.

Lewis Wickes Hine

Tom Beck, Chief Curator, University of Maryland, Baltimore County

The extensive photographic survey of child labor made by Lewis Hine during the early twentieth century provided reform groups and the public with visual evidence of the negative impact that work had on children. Hine's photographs helped mobilize society against child labor, while providing an extensive record of working children.

Born on September 26, 1874, to Douglas Hull Hine, a Civil War veteran, and Sarah Hayes Hine, an educator, in Oshkosh, Wisconsin, Hine grew up living above the family business, Hine's Coffee-House and Restaurant. Tragedy struck in 1892, the year Hine graduated from high school, when his father was killed in an accident. That year, Hine found work at an upholstery factory, but it closed three years later during a depression. Long periods of unemployment were punctuated by sporadic work splitting wood, delivering packages, and selling water filters door-to-door. He finally found steady employment as a janitor for a local bank, a position that eventually allowed him to move into various clerical jobs at the bank.

Hine met Frank Manny, head of experimental education at Oshkosh's State Normal School, in 1899, and Manny hired him as a part-time school clerk and personal secretary. The next year, Manny arranged for Hine to work and study pedagogy at the Chicago Institute and to enroll at the University of Chicago that fall. Hine's teachers included such leading advocates of progressive education as John Dewey and Ella Flagg Young. In 1901, Manny became superintendent of New York's Ethical Culture School, an institution founded by German-Jewish immigrant Felix Adler to educate working-class children. Adler propounded that moral principles need not be taught as religious dogma so much as concern for others. Manny hired Hine to teach elementary science at the school.

In 1904, Manny saw the need for a photographic record of school activities, and asked Hine to fill the job. Manny also requested that Hine photograph some of the thousands of immigrants arriving daily at Ellis Island, so students would learn equal regard for these immigrants as they had already learned for the Pilgrims who landed at Plymouth Rock three hundred years earlier. The contemporary immigrants were mostly workers coming to the United States in search of a better life, and Hine typically endowed the images with great respect and dignity. That momentous year, he began teaching photography and returned to Oshkosh to marry Sara Rich. In 1905, Hine completed a master's degree in pedagogy at New York University.

While attending the Columbia University School of Social Work in 1904, Hine met Paul Kellogg and, through him, other influential people in the social welfare community. Kellogg was assistant editor of *Charities,* a nationally distributed social welfare magazine, and Hine suggested to him in 1906 that the use of photographs in the magazine would be advantageous. Beginning in 1907, Hine photographed not only for the magazine, but also for the National Child Labor Committee (NCLC). He finally resigned his teaching position in 1908 to work full-time as a photographer for the NCLC, and later noted that he was "merely changing his educational efforts from the schoolroom to the world."

The NCLC was an outgrowth of increasing national concern for the abuses endured by children who worked long hours for low wages in mines, mills, and factories across the United States. The reform-minded members of the NCLC sought stricter laws and better enforcement to protect child laborers from employers who claimed that they needed the cheap and plentiful supply of child workers to bring their products profitably to the marketplace. Among its founders was Felix Adler, who hired Hine even though he was not convinced the photographer had the required broad sociological outlook. Hine's work for the NCLC from 1908 to 1918 surely refuted Adler's skepticism, as the photographer documented horrific child labor conditions during the many thousands of miles he traveled from Maine to Texas. Among the famous images that Hine made were those of little spinners, breaker boys, and cigar makers.

Frequent among Hine's subjects were newsies and mill workers. Newsies began selling newspapers on city streets during predawn hours and were often still working when theatergoers bought the last editions late at night to read the postperformance reviews. If newsies went to school at all, they worked before classes as well as afterward, when homework might have been the focus of their attention. Cotton-mill workers, like newsies and other child laborers, rose before dawn and returned home at dusk or later. For their ten- or twelve-hour workdays, they were paid between 15 and 30 cents. Hine often gained access to the mills by saying that he was sent to photograph the machinery. Then he would make sure that child workers were at their posts when the pictures were made. He would surreptitiously estimate the ages of his child subjects by noting their heights relative to his vest buttons. When unsuccessful in gaining access to mills, he waited outside until the child laborers arrived, left for the day, or took their lunch breaks. The photographs were published in newspapers and magazines, as well as mounted on posters for NCLC conventions.

Hine left the NCLC to photograph American Red Cross activities in Europe during World War I but still worked for the NCLC off and on between 1921 and 1934. He had become an independent, freelance photographer whose clients were foundations, consumer groups, unions, and government agencies. From 1930 to 1931, he was the official photographer for the construction of New York's Empire State Building, a job that allowed him to show workers as heroes rather than slaves as in the child labor photographs. His child labor photographs have proven to be his most important work, because they document irrefutably the difficult circumstances suffered by young workers. These more than 7,000 images are the most extensive known photographic record of child labor and are a standard against which to measure the toil of children into the distant future. Hine died on November 3, 1940, in Hastings-on-Hudson, New York.

References and Further Reading

Dimock, George, ed. *Priceless Children: American Photographs, 1890–1925: Child Labor and the Pictorialist Ideal.* Greensboro, NC: Weatherspoon Art Museum, 2001.

Kaplan, Daile, ed. *Photo Story: Selected Letters and Photographs of Lewis W. Hine.* Washington, DC: Smithsonian Institution Press, 1992.

Rosenblum, Walter, with Naomi Rosenblum and Alan Trachtenberg. *America and Lewis Hine: Photographs 1904–1940.* New York: Aperture, 1977.

The U.S. Children's Bureau

Kriste Lindenmeyer, Professor of History, University of Maryland, Baltimore County

On April 8, 1912, President William Howard Taft signed into law legislation creating the U.S. Children's Bureau in the federal Department of Commerce and Labor. It moved to the newly created Department of Labor in 1913. The U.S. Children's Bureau was the first federal-level agency in the world focused on a nation's youngest citizens. In the United States, it was a clear reflection of progressive reform. Endorsed by the National Child Labor Committee as early as 1905, the U.S. Children's Bureau was instructed by Congress to "investigate and report . . . upon all matters pertaining to the welfare of children and child life among all classes" of Americans.

While hindsight suggests that passage of the measure establishing the agency was inevitable, it took many years of lobbying before the U.S. Children's Bureau became a reality. The proposal's close connection to the controversial anti–child labor movement hindered its progress. At the time, several states had moved to restrict children's employment, but there was not yet adequate support for similar federal laws, and many business and other groups strongly opposed federal legislation. Supporters of the Children's Bureau could not afford for it to be seen as a backdoor attempt to regulate child labor at the federal level. To overcome this hurdle, women reformers and organizations supporting the bureau argued that the agency's broad agenda included issues for the "whole child," not just those related to labor. In recognition of the importance of women's efforts to establish the agency, President Taft named Julia C. Lathrop the Children's Bureau's first chief. This made Lathrop the first woman to head a federal bureau in the United States, seven years before women obtained national suffrage.

Opening the agency's doors with a tiny budget of only $25,640, Lathrop devised a plan to use female volunteers along with her small staff. She also initially avoided the controversial issue of child labor by focusing on saving babies' lives. Studies showed that despite the United States' position as the world's most modern industrial economy, its infant mortality rate ranked twelve out of twenty comparable nations. The bureau's work also showed that child poverty was the single most important indicator of child health. The bureau called for improved public sanitation, education for mothers about how to protect and improve infant and child health, and the use of mandatory birth certificates to help authorities identify newborns who might be in need of public health services.

While the bureau's efforts to improve infant health were popular in their own right, many of these activities were also aimed, at least indirectly, at restricting child labor. For example, by highlighting the links between poverty and poor living conditions for many children who also worked for wages, the bureau also demonstrated the links between poverty and child labor. Similarly, the anti–child labor movement had learned that passage of minimum-age laws alone was not sufficient to end the employment of children. Government-mandated birth certificates were necessary to verify children's ages. The call for mandatory birth certificates was a roundabout way to connect the bureau's popular infant health work to the more controversial anti–child labor movement. Government-mandated birth certificates made it difficult for parents or employers to lie about a child's age.

When Congress passed the nation's first child

labor regulations under the Keating-Owen Act in 1916, it gave the U.S. Children's Bureau responsibility for enforcing the new law. The act barred goods produced by children under fourteen years of age from interstate commerce, but the U.S. Supreme Court's 1918 *Hammer v. Dagenhart* decision declared the act unconstitutional before it went into effect. Over the next two decades the bureau and its supporters continued to advocate for federal regulation of child labor, finally achieving lasting success in 1938 with the passage of the Fair Labor Standards Act. During World War II the bureau further expanded its reach by administering the nation's first federal health insurance program, the Emergency Maternity and Infant Care Act, offered to the wives and newborns of enlisted men in the U.S. military.

Despite the optimism surrounding its first decades of work, since the end of World War II, the Children's Bureau has served as little more than a low-level clearinghouse for information. The U.S. Children's Bureau survived a governmental reorganization in 1946, but just barely. Symbolic of its reduced influence and authority, the agency lost the "U.S." designation along with the administration of funded programs and regulatory responsibilities. The reasoning for the change, argued President Harry Truman's White House, was a government reorganization based on function rather than constituency. Consequently, America's children lost a powerful advocate and had a much weakened voice in the federal government to speak on their behalf.

References and Further Reading

Ladd-Taylor, Molly. *Raising Baby the Government Way: Mothers' Letters to the Children's Bureau, 1915–1932.* New Brunswick, NJ: Rutgers University Press, 1986.

Ladd-Taylor, Molly. *Mother-Work: Women, Child Welfare, and the State, 1890–1930.* Urbana: University of Illinois Press, 1994.

Lindenmeyer, Kriste. *"A Right to Childhood": The U.S. Children's Bureau and Child Welfare, 1912–1946.* Urbana: University of Illinois Press, 1997.

Muncy, Robyn. *Creating a Female Dominion in American Reform, 1890–1935.* New York: Oxford University Press, 1991.

Trattner, Walter I. *Crusade for Children: A History of the National Child Labor Committee and Child Labor Reform in America.* Chicago: Quadrangle Books, 1970.

Child Labor and the United States Today

Children in the Fields: America's Hidden Child Labor Problem

Reid Maki, Children in the Fields Campaign Director, Association of Farmworker Opportunity Programs

> Sweat beads down Sergio's face as he toils in a south Texas onion field. He picks onions with the skill and pace of an adult, yet he is only ten years old. Sergio wears a sleeveless shirt and shorts, and the May sun scorches his skin. His bare feet sink into the hot earth, exposing him to harmful pesticides that have been sprayed on the soil. A Band-Aid falls off his sweaty finger, revealing a gash where Sergio had cut himself earlier with his razor-sharp scissors, used for trimming the onion stalks. He has been working in the fields since age seven. (Hess 2007, 3)

Most Americans would be surprised to learn that the field described above is not in a third world country. It is located in Batesville, Texas. Sergio, who was found working in May 2003, is one of an estimated half million children and teens who toil in the fields each year in the United States, supplementing their families' incomes. Many U.S. farmworkers are not paid a living wage and must pool the resources of all family members to survive.

Federal data from 2000–2001 reveal that the average annual income for individuals in farmwork (including nonfarm income) was only $10,000–$12,499. Researchers found that 30 percent of farmworkers interviewed lived below the federal poverty line. As family size increased, so did poverty. Half of the families with six mouths to feed were below the poverty line.

In addition to low wages, agriculture increases the likelihood of child labor by paying for the harvesting of certain crops by piece rates or the quantity picked. The more you pick, the faster you pick, the more you earn. If a farmworker has four children helping him harvest fruit, he can pick more fruit in a shorter time, earning more money for the family. For this reason, agricultural child labor is focused on such crops as onions, cherries, berries and other similar fruits and vegetables.

Counting the number of children working in U.S. agriculture is difficult. Most children work under their parents' Social Security numbers and do not appear officially as "hired farmworkers." However, in 1998, the General Accounting Office (GAO), now called the Government Accountability Office, estimated the number of children working in U.S. fields at 300,000. That same year, the National Agricultural Workers Survey estimated the number of hired farmworkers between the ages of twelve and seventeen at 431,000. An unknown, but significant, number who are under twelve also work in the fields, like Sergio.

An estimated 85 percent of migrant and seasonal farmworkers—the workers who typically hand harvest fruits and vegetables in the United States—are racial minorities. They are predominantly Latino, from Mexico or Central America, or are U.S. residents from Mexican American families. Informal field research conducted between 2003 and 2005 by the Association of Farmworker Opportunity Programs, a coalition of organizations providing services to farmworker families, suggests that half or more of the children who harvest fruits and vegetables were born in the United States and are U.S. citizens. An increasing number of immigrant youths between the ages of fourteen and seventeen are migrating to the United States from Mexico and Central America to perform farm labor without the protection of their immediate families. A 1997 Department of Labor report estimated that there were 55,000 of these "unaccompanied minors" working in the United States.

Field Work and Migration Present Educational and Health Risks

Long hours in the field make it difficult to succeed in school. Children often go to school exhausted. Migrant children often change school districts two, three, or more times a year, disrupting their schooling. Frequently, they are placed in class levels that are either too high or too low. Many farmworker students miss the end and the beginning of the school year because of summers spent migrating. When they return to their home school district, they are asked to perform extra schoolwork to catch up. For many, it is a daunting task. Unfortunately, little systematic research has assessed the impact of migration and child labor on the educational outcomes of farmworker youths. A federally funded study in the 1980s found that high school graduation rates of farmworker youths were only 49 percent. Many farmworker advocates, however, believe that the school dropout rate is much higher. Anecdotally, educators from schools in migrant communities cite dropout rates as high as 80 percent.

Farmwork also presents significant health risks to children. Children account for about 20 percent of all farm fatalities (although many of those killed are helping their parents on family farms). According to the GAO in 1998, more than 100,000 children and teens are injured on farms each year. Farmworkers regularly work in fields treated with pesticides, some of which are known carcinogens. Child farmworkers are exposed to the same pesticide levels as adults, so likely face a far greater health risk. In March 2003, the U.S. Environmental Protection Agency (EPA) estimated that children between the ages of three and fifteen may experience at least three times the cancer threat that adults face from the same chemicals. Yet, the agency has not established additional protections for working children under the Worker Protection Standard, the body of regulations that limits farmworkers' exposure to recently sprayed fields. Working children are less likely to wear clothing that protects them from pesticides—or the sun—and more likely to work in bare feet than are adult farmworkers.

Many farmworker families bring young children to the fields because of the lack of child-care options. The children play in the fields or perform light work-related tasks like bringing their parents sacks or containers for harvesting fruits. These young children are exposed to dangers from farm tools and machinery and the possibility of being run over by farmworkers' cars and trucks.

Federal Laws Treat Children Working in Agriculture Differently

Gaps in U.S. labor law allow farmworker children to work at younger ages and in more dangerous tasks than children who work in other industries. It is legal for a child of twelve to perform backbreaking harvest work under a broiling sun, but that same child cannot be paid to work in an air-conditioned office. These differences exist for no sound reason. The children are victims of the myth of the agrarian idyll—that farms are safe, nurturing places. In fact, according to government statistics, agricultural work is usually ranked along with mining and construction as one of the three most dangerous occupations in America.

The Fair Labor Standards Act (FLSA) of 1938 contains America's federal child labor laws. It established sixteen as the minimum age for regular employment in most industries; children age fourteen and over can perform light work that does not interfere with schooling (no more than three hours per day or eighteen hours per week while school is in session). The original FLSA exempted agriculture altogether, so for many years there were no restrictions on child labor in agriculture at all. It was not until 1974 that the FLSA was amended to include minimum ages in agriculture. Today, children of fourteen (twelve if accompanied by a parent or with parental consent) can work unlimited hours in agriculture. Thus, a fifteen-year-old may work only eighteen hours per week at McDonald's, but a twelve-year-old might work fifty or more hours per week in the fields. Current federal law also allows teenagers age sixteen and seventeen working in agriculture to perform tasks—driving a forklift, for example—classified by the government as "hazardous." In other industries, workers must be eighteen to perform these hazardous tasks.

Since 2001, farmworker advocacy groups have been attempting to amend the child labor provisions of the FLSA and end the double standard that allows agricultural child laborers to be treated differently. Although legislation to end the agricultural exemptions has been introduced in Congress several times this decade, the bills have yet to make it to a vote. When this legislation is eventually enacted, child labor in American agriculture may finally come to an end.

In the absence of comprehensive protection from federal laws, farmworker advocates continue to seek increased protection for children in agriculture by urging states to tighten their own child labor laws. Advocates are also pushing for increased enforcement of existing protections and for additional resources, such as child care, which farmworkers often cannot find or afford. Farmworker advocates also continue to press for additional federal resources. After-school and summer-school programs have been successful in helping farmworker children succeed academically. However, the federal government has cut back programs that help tutor and mentor farmworker children, ending a successful farmworker youth program in 2004.

References and Further Reading

Association of Farmworker Opportunity Programs. http://www.afop.org/.

Head Start Bureau. *Descriptive Study of Seasonal Farmworker Families.* Washington, DC: U.S. Department of Health and Human Services, September 2001.

Hess, Benjamin. *Children in the Fields: An American Problem.* Washington, DC: Association of Farmworker Opportunity Programs, 2007.

Tucker, Lee. *Fingers to the Bone: United States Failure to Protect Child Farmworkers.* Washington, DC: Human Rights Watch, 2000.

U.S. Department of Labor. *Findings from the National Agricultural Workers Survey, 1997–1998: A Demographic and Employment Profile of United States Farm Workers.* Washington, DC: U.S. Department of Labor, 2000.

U.S. Department of Labor. *Findings from the National Agricultural Workers Survey, 2001–2002: A Demographic and Employment Profile of United States Farm Workers.* Washington, DC: U.S. Department of Labor, 2005.

U.S. General Accounting Office [now General Accountability Office]. *Child Labor in Agriculture: Characteristics and Legality of Work.* GAO/HEHS-98–112R. Washington, DC: U.S. General Accounting Office, 1998.

Twenty-First-Century Adolescence in America

Jeremy Staff, Assistant Professor, Department of Sociology, Pennsylvania State University; and
Jeylan T. Mortimer, Professor, Department of Sociology, University of Minnesota

Among recent cohorts of youths in the United States, increasing numbers are postponing marriage and parenthood and continuing their formal education into young adulthood (Arnett 2004). The once typical transition from school to work is changing as young people frequently combine school with paid work or return to full-time schooling after periods of full-time work. The sharing of work and school begins in early adolescence and translates into a substantial history of employment by the time of school completion.

The combination of work and school during adolescence has caught the attention of sociologists, economists, and developmental psychologists, who debate the potential short- and longer-term consequences of early work experiences for social development and attainment. One view is that paid work during adolescence draws young people from school and promotes behaviors that interfere with achievement and positive adjustment. An alternative view is that paid work during adolescence fosters good work habits, dependability, responsibility, and occupational values, as well as encourages skill development through on-the-job training. In particular, early work experience can help youths navigate the largely unstructured school-to-work transition in the United States, especially with the increasing difficultly young people have in making occupational choices. A third view is that any consequences of early paid work may be spurious due to preexisting individual differences in ability, motivation, ambition, and perseverance.

In this essay we address three key issues regarding teenage employment in the United States: (1) Does teenage work affect achievement? (2) Does teenage work affect social development? and (3) How do gender, race, and family background affect early work experiences? We begin with a brief review of the scope of teenage employment in the United States.

Scope of Teenage Labor in the United States

Most young people in the United States hold paid jobs as teenagers. An estimated 80 to 90 percent are formally employed at some point during the high school period (U.S. Department of Labor 2000). The likelihood of employment, as well as the intensity of paid work (average hours), increases each year of high school, in part because federal and state legislation targets oppressive child labor through age, hour, and safety restrictions on employment of minors. For most youths, employment prior to the age of sixteen is informal—girls typically work as babysitters and boys perform yard maintenance activities.

While school is in session, fifteen-year-old youths average approximately eleven hours of work per week, and seventeen-year-old youths average nearly eighteen hours of paid work per week. The majority of youths (62 percent) are employed in the retail sector of the economy (in department stores, grocery stores, restaurants, and retail stores) and approximately one-quarter of working teenagers are employed in the service sector (in education, recreation, health services, and private households). Most young people work in restaurants and grocery stores. Stock handler and grocery bagger are the most common jobs for boys, while girls are most likely to work as cashiers. However, these jobs account for only 13 percent of employed boys and 25 percent of working girls, which suggests considerable diversity in the early work experiences of contemporary teenagers.

Early Work Experiences and Socioeconomic Attainment

A long-standing critique of teenage employment is that paid work disrupts academic performance and limits time for school-related activities (Greenberger and Steinberg 1986). One concern is that paid work during adolescence limits time that could be spent participating in extracurricular sports and various academic clubs and organizations that provide important opportunities for young people to learn and explore potential interests. Paid work may also detract from school-related activities, such as getting help from teachers, completing homework, and studying for examinations. Research shows that although work status in adolescence is unrelated to school performance, youths who work intensively (more than twenty hours of paid work per week during the school year) report fewer hours of homework, lower grade point averages and standardized test scores, and a greater likelihood of high school dropout than youths who do not work or who limit their hours. Intensive work hours during adolescence have been shown to reduce the likelihood of postsecondary school attendance and receipt of a college degree.

Proponents of youth work contend that when youths limit the hours they spend in paid work, they are able to effectively balance their commitments to school, to family, and to their jobs, while at the same time acquiring workplace skills and resources that may help them make good choices in selecting future careers. Paid work during adolescence may also promote attachment to and success in school if it encourages time-management skills and enables young people to practice what they are learning in school. Some scholars find that moderate work hours (twenty hours or less per week) can benefit socioeconomic achievement. Moderate work hours do not limit time for homework and extracurricular activities, and even increase involvement in school activities, grade point averages, the likelihood of high school completion, and wages in young adulthood. Moderate work hours over the duration of high school increase the likelihood of a four-year college degree, especially for youths who display limited educational promise at the onset of high school (Staff and Mortimer 2007).

Relationships between early work experience and achievement may also be spurious. When students have little interest in school, and when their achievement is poor, they may choose to work, or invest more time in employment, than youths who have greater success in school (Bachman and Schulenberg 1993). Youths with limited ability may avoid both work and school during teenage years, as low intelligence scores and limited reading skills in adolescence predict both school dropout and poor labor market outcomes in young adulthood. More able youths may invest in both school and work during the transition to adulthood, thereby maximizing their human capital acquisition through school, on-the-job training, and other workplace knowledge.

In summary, these studies suggest that the relationship between teenage work hours and socioeconomic attainment is curvilinear—limited hours benefit achievement while excessive involvement in early work is detrimental. An understudied area in research on teenage employment is what constitutes a "good" job during adolescence. Past studies overwhelmingly focus on hours of work and devote very little attention to different types of jobs and qualities of work experience. Conditions of youth work appear to vary substantially across important dimensions such as its provision of external and internal rewards, its stressful features, and its compatibility with school (Mortimer 2003), yet only a handful of studies have investigated the socioeconomic consequences of work quality or even job type. Because young people work in many different types of jobs, and certainly some of these jobs are better than others, the predictive power of different qualities and types of jobs for socioeconomic attainment has received insufficient attention.

Early Work Experiences and Social Development

Given the importance of adolescent experiences for developmental trajectories over the life course, debates extend to the short- and longer-term effects of teenage work on behavioral and social adjustment. One view is that paid work helps young people build character and develop a positive work ethic. For instance, adolescent employment has been associated with self-reported dependability, personal responsibility, and self-confidence, especially for young people whose earnings contribute to the economic needs of their families. Other studies have emphasized the positive developmental consequences of paid work by exposing teenagers to new challenges, promoting valuable coping skills, building status among peers, and helping young people solidify their occupational values (Mortimer 2003).

However, paid work may unnecessarily place teenagers at risk for social and behavioral maladjustment. A long-standing critique of teenage employment is that it not only limits time for school work and other extracurricular activities, but also may potentially jeopardize the moratorium youths need to explore new identities and interests free from demands of the adult world. Critics of youth work argue that most adolescent jobs, especially those in fast-food restaurants and retail settings, do not provide opportunities for adult mentorship because many are supervised by peers approximately the same age as their subordinates. Thus, young workers may take on adult responsibilities before they have adequate coping skills, engendering a pseudomaturity, or precocious maturity, characterized by more adultlike methods of managing stress, including use of alcohol and illicit substances. The concentration of young people in industries with higher-than-average rates of workplace injury, as well as in occupations characterized by limited on-the-job training, worker discretion, and security, can heighten the risk of injury to social development.

If paid work is too intensive, teenagers may not participate in extracurricular activities in the arts, sports, and various academic clubs and organizations that provide important opportunities for youths to explore interests and values and that have been shown to foster positive adjustment in high school and young adulthood. As youths work more hours, their participation in extracurricular sports decreases. Declining participation in extracurricular athletics may potentially undermine a healthy lifestyle, even though sports offer little protection from alcohol and drug use. Consistent with this point of view, Bachman and Schulenberg (1993) found that long hours of work are associated with unhealthy lifestyles (such as less sleep and exercise and a greater frequency of skipping breakfast). Youths who work long hours may also have less flexibility in their work schedules compared to those who work fewer hours. As such, not only does work reduce their capacity to engage in sports and other extracurricular activities, but they may also become more attracted to less structured, unsupervised, and potentially deviant activities outside the workplace. Youths who spend long hours on the job are more likely to go to parties and bars and to ride around in cars for fun than are their peers working fewer hours; these are activities that increase the likelihood of delinquency and substance use. Employment may also provide teenagers financial resources—money for gas and car payments—and autonomy from parental supervision, for example, when they work late in the evening away from home, that enable more unstructured socializing. Indeed, much evidence suggests that those who work more than twenty hours per week are more likely to engage in delinquency and substance use.

Again, little research has addressed whether the quality of the work matters for delinquency and other health-risk behaviors. Teenage work that is high quality may provide an additional avenue to material success. Early work experiences may support identities that are unfavorable to deviance and favorable to conventional work, especially when adolescents are employed in contexts that connect them to family and school. Moreover, some research finds that jobs that do not compromise the student role appear to inhibit deviance, net of work hours, prior deviance, and self-selection processes (Staff and Uggen 2003).

Paid work and engagement in health-risk behaviors may also constitute a syndrome of early adultlike identity formation and pseudomaturity. Youths who have less involvement and success in conventional adolescent activities—such as going to school and participating in extracurricular sports, clubs, and organizations—are more likely to invest themselves in paid work and to prefer work over school. Moreover, prior engagement in delinquency, such as drinking, having sex, using drugs, and school misconduct, may predispose some youths to enter work environments that offer fewer social constraints on these behaviors than do school and family. Thus, some contend that delinquency precedes involvement in work and any observed association between paid work and deviance are spurious, related to preexisting differences among individuals. For instance, ninth graders with higher rates of substance use, school-related deviance, and law violations report greater work hours in subsequent years of high school. Once these individual differences are considered, recent analyses find that the effects of intensive work hours on substance abuse, delinquency, and school-related misconduct diminish to statistical nonsignificance (Paternoster et al. 2003).

In summary, prior investigations of the social, psychological, and developmental consequences of teenage work have overwhelmingly focused on the hours of work, although some studies suggest that the quality of the job may be more predictive. Furthermore, we know very little about whether different work experiences have lasting impressions on social and behavioral change. The longer-term consequences of work experiences for health, well-being, and social development deserve further attention.

Sociodemographic Variation in Early Work Experiences

Age, gender, race and ethnicity, and socioeconomic background influence the onset, intensity, duration, and earnings of paid workers during adolescence. For instance, girls tend to work at an earlier age than boys, but boys typically average more hours of paid work, especially in later years of high school. White youths are nearly twice as likely as African American and Hispanic youths to work during the school year, although African American and Hispanic teenagers average three to five additional hours of employment during the school year when they are employed (U.S. Department of Labor 2000). Family socioeconomic background influences the age of labor market entry and the intensity of employment. Youths in lower-income households are less likely to hold jobs at younger ages. However, many youths in poor urban neighborhoods face a limited and competitive job market. In families reporting annual income less than $27,300, only 16.5 percent of fifteen- to seventeen-year-olds were employed, almost half the rate of employment for teenagers in families reporting higher annual household income. Although youths from lower socioeconomic backgrounds are less likely to be employed, they average more hours when they are employed than their more advantaged peers.

Because the decision about whether to work, and how much to work, reflects the young person's background and prospects for the future—defined by gender, race, and socioeconomic background—some studies suggest that the effects of teenage work hours are conditional on these preexisting individual characteristics. For instance, long work hours may not be as harmful for those youths who come from more disadvantaged backgrounds (who are also likely to need to work more hours). Lee and Staff (2007) found that the effect of intensive work hours on high school dropout was conditional on socioeconomic disadvantage, educational promise, and other preexisting characteristics. Using propensity score methods to control for observable differences among individuals, the authors found that long hours on the job did not encourage high school dropout among youths who had especially high or low probabilities of intensive work. The effect of teenage work on school dropout was conditional on the young person's propensity to work long hours on the job.

Despite the evidence regarding these conditional effects, little research has documented whether boys and girls, Whites, African Americans, and Hispanics, and youths from more or less advantaged backgrounds follow distinct work careers (involving movement between different types of jobs and hours of work) during adolescence. Though there is substantial variation in the employment behavior of adult workers across these dimensions, it is important to document how sociodemographic characteristics affect whether teenagers work, what kinds of jobs they hold, and how much they work, and how these patterns change during high school. Furthermore, little research has specified why certain demographic characteristics are likely to condition the effects of teenage work on achievement and social development.

One possible reason why the effects of work hours are conditioned by socioeconomic background is that the context of employment is different for poor and rich youths. Youths from poor families may need to work long hours to support their families (Entwisle et al. 2000). Employment can help poor youths pay for educational expenses such as field trips, transportation, and lab fees. Furthermore, whereas many youths in poor neighborhoods face a restricted and very competitive labor market, youths in more prosperous areas may find a labor market characterized by an abundance of lower-level retail and service jobs. More advantaged youths may have little stake in their jobs with the numerous opportunities to lose and regain work. Another possible reason why certain background characteristics may condition the effects of employment is that gender, race and ethnicity, and socioeconomic status are known to affect the timing and ordering of other life transitions as well.

Against this backdrop, it is important to specify conditions under which the effects of teenage work hours on socioeconomic achievement and social development vary by gender, race and ethnicity, and socioeconomic background. Not only could the meaning of intensive versus moderate work hours be different for more or less advantaged youths, but the quality of these early work experiences may also differ. Furthermore, it is important to specify why gender, race and ethnicity, and socioeconomic background may condition the effects of teenage work on adjustment and attainment. Is it because the context of work is different? More research is needed on these issues.

Conclusion

For many youths in the United States, paid work begins at an early age, involves a considerable time commitment during the school year, and predominates in industries and occupations with higher than average rates of workplace injury. Evidence suggests that highly intensive work is associated with lower school achievement and higher rates of delinquency and substance abuse. When work is limited, allowing balance among employment, school, and other activities, work does not appear to have these negative consequences. Nonetheless, debates surround teenage work in the United States: Does it have a causal effect on achievement and adjustment? Alternatively, do patterns of work, school, and leisure activities result from prior orientations and behaviors? In coming to terms with this seemingly contradictory literature, it is important to recognize that adolescent agency influences work and school activities, as well as time use more generally. The decisions about whether to work in adolescence and how much to work reflect the young person's social location and prospects for the future—defined by gender, race, parental education, early educational promise, and the adolescent's prior involvement in problematic or deviant behaviors.

References and Further Reading

Arnett, Jeffrey J. *Emerging Adulthood: The Winding Road from the Late Teens Through the Twenties.* Oxford: Oxford University Press, 2004.

Bachman, Jerald G., and John E. Schulenberg. "How Part-time Work Intensity Relates to Drug Use, Problem Behavior, Time Use, and Satisfaction Among High School Seniors: Are These Consequences or Merely Correlates?" *Developmental Psychology* 29 (1993): 220–35.

Entwisle, Doris R., Karl L. Alexander, and Linda Steffel Olson. "Early Work Histories of Urban Youth." *American Sociological Review* 65 (2000): 279–97.

Greenberger, Ellen, and Laurence D. Steinberg. *When Teenagers Work: The Psychological and Social Costs of Teenage Employment.* New York: Basic Books, 1986.

Lee, Jennifer C., and Jeremy Staff. "When Work Matters: The Varying Impact of Adolescent Work Intensity on High School Drop-out." *Sociology of Education* 80:2 (2007): 158–78.

Mortimer, Jeylan T. *Working and Growing Up in America.* Cambridge, MA: Harvard University Press, 2003.

National Research Council. Committee on the Health and Safety Implications of Child Labor. *Protecting Youth at Work: Health, Safety, and Development of Working Children and Adolescents in the United States.* Washington, DC: National Academy Press, 1998.

Paternoster, Raymond, Shawn Bushway, Robert Brame, and Robert Apel. "The Effect of Teenage Employment on Delinquency and Problem Behaviors." *Social Forces* 82 (2003): 297–336.

Staff, Jeremy, and Jeylan T. Mortimer. "Educational and Work Strategies from Adolescence to Early Adulthood: Consequences for Educational Attainment." *Social Forces* 85 (2007): 1169–94.

Staff, Jeremy, and Christopher Uggen. "The Fruits of Good Work: Early Work Experiences and Adolescent Deviance." *Journal of Research in Crime and Delinquency* 40 (2003): 263–90.

U.S. Department of Labor. *Report on the Youth Labor Force.* Washington, DC: U.S. Government Printing Office, 2000.

American Students' Activism Against Global Child Labor

Chivy Sok, Codirector of the Women's Institute for Leadership Development (WILD) for Human Rights

Ending global child labor is one of the most challenging human rights tasks of our time. American students, with dedicated teachers who have been able to use the child labor issue to motivate student learning, have joined the global fight and are using their classroom lessons to change themselves and the world around them. This is a story of three groups of students who were motivated to find solutions to make their world a better place.

Thinking Globally and Acting Locally: Monroe High Students Take Child Labor Concerns to Their Officials

"Children as young as 6 years old are taken from their homes and put into factories to stitch soccer balls while making a meager 60 cents a day. If I was in that situation, I would want someone to help me," said seventeen-year-old Joseph Jung, speaking to the Los Angeles County Board of Supervisors in 1997 (Helfand 1997). Jung was one of the many students in Mark Elinson's International Relations course at the James Monroe High Law and Government Magnet School. He and his classmates took their classroom lessons about child labor, organized, and helped changed policies in their communities.

In 1996, child labor in the soccer ball industry made headlines around the world as NGOs and investigative journalists exposed Pakistani children laboring to produce soccer balls bound for North American and European markets. Elinson knew that he had found an issue that would capture student interest and quickly integrated it into his curriculum. "The child labor project was integral to my International Relations class. It was not an isolated unit, but the students worked on the project periodically throughout the semester. I used the project to illustrate a variety of international relations concepts: treaties, sovereignty, globalization, protocols, etc."[1]

Elinson's first group of students began their advocacy work where they thought they could have the most direct impact. The Los Angeles School District purchases approximately 800 soccer balls per year. For these students, there is a direct connection between their athletic activities and abusive child labor. So, they took their research to members of the Los Angeles Board of Education. The board responded favorably, unanimously adopting a resolution "[t]hat the District only purchase products that have been certified as having been manufactured without the illegal use of child labor." As a result, contractors who conduct business with the Los Angeles School District were subject to the district's Sweat-Free Procurement Policy, which prohibits child labor. If contractors were found to be in violation of the policy's purchasing principles, a number of actions could be taken, including contract cancellation and vendor debarment.

The following year, another group of Elinson's students, inspired by their classmates' success, decided to go one step further. They took their concerns straight to the county of Los Angeles Board of Supervisors. The county purchases approximately 400–500 soccer balls per year for use in recreational facilities and juvenile halls. Joseph Jung and classmates Gazell Javantash and Brenda Linares took the lead to research child labor in the soccer ball industry in Pakistan. They searched the Internet and reviewed news clippings and reports from human rights organizations. Using this research material, they prepared packets for each county supervisor. The students were then invited to make a presentation to the board of supervisors. At the board's December 9, 1997, meeting, Jung and his classmates urged each supervisor to support the worldwide effort to end abusive child labor in the soccer ball industry. Shortly after the students' address, the board of supervisors unanimously adopted a resolution instructing the directors of Internal Services and Parks and Recreation to ensure that balls sold to the county were not made by children in violation of the ILO's minimum-age convention, and that each vendor determine the country of origin for each soccer ball.

The decision by the Los Angeles county supervisors to use their purchasing policy to help end child labor is representative of a larger movement in the United States where students, including those at universities across the country, were working to pressure their schools to adopt similar practices. The 1990s was a pivotal decade for student activists like those in Elinson's class. Through education, grassroots organizing, and advocacy, these young activists succeeded in pushing for purchasing policies that prohibited the use of child labor.

Impact on Students

Students have learned valuable life skills. Some continue to work on issues related to child labor. After graduating from college, Zarah informed Elinson, "Now I am currently in San Francisco and involved in a non-profit organization called Global Exchange where one of their goals is to promote fair-trade and promoting socially conscious products, such as products that are sweatshop free and even chocolate made without child labor!" Amy, another former student, wrote to Elinson to let him know that she was graduating from law school and would have an article published in the *American Criminal Law Review* (Messigian 2006). Her article is a direct outgrowth of her research in Elinson's class. "My article is on a law targeting American child sex tourists, which has been an on-going interest of mine since taking International Law in high school." Alisha, another alumna, went on to the University of California, Berkeley, graduating with a double major in political science and African American studies. Her e-mail illustrates the lifelong impact that a teacher can have:

> Thinking back on the choices that I made during my undergraduate career, choosing activism and community service over typical recreational activities, and the perspective that I had in investigating American History for the truth of what had happened, I realized was rooted in the experiences that I had in your class; the way that you taught us to look beyond what is given to us, and that we could play a role in changing the way that the world [works], and making history. . . . [T]hank you for doing more than you had to. I will make every effort, as the woman that I have become, to do the same for all.

Kids' Campaign to Build a School for Iqbal: How Broad Meadows Middle School Students Changed Their World

Ron Adams, a language arts teacher at Broad Meadows Middle School in Quincy, Massachusetts, is passionate about teaching and believes that every single individual, especially young students, can make a positive difference in their world.

Meeting Iqbal Masih

In 1994, twelve-year-old Iqbal Masih, a former child slave from Pakistan, was flown to Boston to receive the Reebok Youth in Action award. Iqbal's parents sold him to a carpet factory owner for the equivalent of US$12 at age four. He was a slave until, at the age of ten, he managed to escape with the help of a local NGO. After his escape, Iqbal became intensely outspoken about slavery in the carpet industry. He traveled throughout Europe and the United States waging a campaign that, in a very short period, helped to raise the visibility of child labor and changed carpet industry practices.

During his trip to Boston, Iqbal wanted to see an American classroom. Adams's class was selected because he had been introducing human rights and the history of child labor in his classroom. Adams recalls the day his students met the famous child activist. "Iqbal's visit changed everything at our school. Students were immediately shocked.

. . . It was as if a modern day Oliver Twist was in our classroom." Iqbal sat before the students, his feet dangling from the chair because he was not tall enough for them to reach the floor. Years of malnutrition, forced labor, and lack of exercise and sunlight had stunted his growth, making him appear physically smaller than Adams's students who were the same age. Iqbal told his American peers about his years enslaved in a Pakistani carpet factory, forced to work all day and given very little to eat. He told them of the beatings he endured because he made some weaving mistakes. Amanda Loos, twelve, was jolted by his presentation. "He was brave enough to sit in front of all these people he didn't even know and tell us his story about how he had escaped bonded labor. He said one thing that really got to me. He said that the carpet owners told the children that Americans are the ones making them do this" (A Kids' Campaign for Freedom 1997).

Broad Meadows students were inspired by Iqbal's passion for justice and were moved to get involved. They asked Iqbal what he would like them to do to help his cause. Iqbal suggested that they educate others about what is going on in Pakistan. He also shared his dream of building a world in which every child can be free and educated (American Federation of Teachers 2000). Adams's students responded immediately. They wrote letters and visited carpet stores to ask questions about how the rugs sold in their communities were made. Some store managers became annoyed and called the principal to complain. In response, the principal said, "What exactly are these kids doing? They're asking you a question. I'll never stop students from asking questions" (A Kids' Campaign for Freedom 1997).

A Bullet Can't Kill a Dream

In April 1995, a few months after Iqbal's visit, Broad Meadows students received news that the Pakistani child activist who had inspired them was shot dead while riding a bicycle in his village in Pakistan. To date, no one has been held accountable for Iqbal Masih's murder. Adams's students were extremely saddened and angry. "All of a sudden, writing letters didn't seem enough" (American Federation of Teachers 2000). What more could a group of seventh-grade students in an American suburb do?

The Monday after news about Iqbal broke, between twenty and thirty students gathered at their school to brainstorm actions they might take to honor the boy who touched their lives. Loos remembered that Iqbal's dream was to build a world where all kids are free and educated. "Why don't we build a school in Pakistan?" (A Kids' Campaign for Freedom 1997). With twenty years of teaching experience, Adams knew not to say no immediately. He sent them home with an assignment. "Okay, all right, you guys go home tonight, write a letter about your idea, and you can send it to the school" (A Kids' Campaign for Freedom 1997). Overnight, they developed an action plan for the Kids' Campaign to Build a School for Iqbal.

The campaign's plan was simple: Ask each person they connect with to donate $12. This amount was chosen because Iqbal was sold into slavery for the equivalent of $12 and was killed when he was twelve years old. It was small, but it was a strong symbol of the person they wanted to honor. To initiate the Kids' Campaign, the students reached out to other middle schools, their parents, and their parents' workplaces. Checks and in-kind donations started coming in from many sources. The students organized bake sales and car washes, sold lemonade and Popsicles, and solicited donations from friends, parents, community members, and anyone willing to help. Word spread rapidly across their community and later across the nation. In-kind donations, such as 5,000 envelopes and Rice Krispies treats for volunteers, arrived at school. A retired woman donated typing services. Mirror Image and Amnesty International teamed up to develop a campaign Web site to help reach a wider community. Support also came from high-profile celebrities, including Peter Gabriel and Michael Stipe.

In two years the Kids' Campaign engaged students from fifty U.S. States and twenty-two nations and collectively raised $143,000. The students partnered with SUDHAAR, a small Pakistani NGO, to build the school. In February 1997, A School for Iqbal was opened in Kasur City and served 278 of the poorest working children between four and twelve years old. The campaign did not stop there. Students continued to raise money and worked with SUDHAAR to start a microcredit program to enable families to buy back the children they had sold into bonded labor. Today, Quincy students' efforts remain ongoing. They endeavor to create an educational project every year in Iqbal's memory. Along with six other U.S. schools, they cofounded a school-building campaign called Operation Day's Work-USA (ODW). Since 1999, student members of ODW successfully established, renovated, or reopened schools for children at risk of becoming child laborers in Rwanda, Ethiopia, Nepal, Bangladesh, Vietnam, El Salvador, and Haiti.

Learning Life Skills

Through the campaign, students learned valuable life skills usually not taught in American classrooms. For example, after funds were raised, they had to figure out how to build a school in a foreign country they had never visited. With Adams's help, the students turned to Senator Edward Kennedy, who approached Pakistan's prime minister to secure permission. "We welcome your project," was the official response (Adams 2006). Then the students had to develop a grant-making process to select a Pakistani-based organization to implement their plan. In the process, they learned how to develop a request for proposals, develop selection criteria, conduct proposal reviews, and make selection decisions. In addition, students developed public education and outreach skills; and several students became quite gifted public speakers through numerous speaking engagements, including one at the Harvard Forum sponsored by Harvard University's Graduate School of Education.

Iowa City's Outstanding Youth Citizens: Elementary School Students Join the Global Fight Against Child Labor

"A good citizen is a dreamer, a goal-setter. Someone who can imagine a way to make their school, city, state, country, or world a better place to live in, and finds a way to make it a reality," said eleven-year-old Zoe Grueskin, recipient of the Iowa City 2003 Outstanding Youth Citizenship Award (Sok and Quintero 2004). Grueskin's acceptance speech embodies the spirit and commitment of Hoover Elementary School students, who decided to help make their world a better place. She is one of the many students of Marlene Johnson's sixth-grade social studies classes who have been studying about child labor. Johnson found it easy to teach child labor without disturbing the standard curriculum:

> Integration of child labor into the classroom was an easy focus for me, since I have been interested in human rights issues for over 40 years. The material enriches the present day curriculum, by simple overlapping of subject matter. If one is discussing civil war, ancient cultures, community activities in any village in the world, making cloth, tending sheep, picking coffee beans, fishing, and etc., children and behavior towards children is always involved.

Johnson's students learned about the types of work that American children performed during the Industrial Revolution. When her students understood aspects of the past, Johnson brought them to the present by providing stories of contemporary child labor such as a boy working on a banana plantation in Ecuador or a girl making bricks in Pakistan. Consequently, they understood that these child laborers were no longer faces in distant lands but kids their age. Once this connection was established, her students were driven to help solve this problem.

Across the city, students of Alisa Meggitt at Lucas Elementary School were also introduced to child labor by a guest speaker. Lucas sixth graders, like Hoover students, were surprised to learn about child labor for the first time. That same week, they approached Meggitt about starting an after-school club to work on the issue. In November 2003, Children Helping Innocent Laborers Democratically (CHILD) was born and Lucas students went to work.

Youth Activists Take Child Labor Concerns to Officials

CHILD members took their awareness-raising campaign to their churches, local libraries, bookstores, and any community gathering they were able to attend. They also went to their city council and persuaded them to adopt a proclamation on child labor. Then they secured the mayor's permission to help launch their Purple Ribbon campaign to raise citywide awareness. The mayor allowed them to tie purple ribbons to city vehicles—police cars and bicycles, fire trucks, and garbage collection trucks—to help raise the visibility of their message. Their next target was the Iowa State Senate. During their visit to participate in the Open Legislative Forum in Des Moines, CHILD members wanted to know if Iowa's procurement policy ensures that no state funds were used to purchase products made by children. "The Senators were stunned and looked at each other for answers. But they didn't have any," said Meggitt, who observed her students practicing democracy.

Youth Activists Contribute to National Conference

In the spring of 2004, Meggitt and Johnson introduced the two student groups to each other. The students concluded that CHILD's mission was representative of their collective commitment and that it would be more effective to merge the two groups. Around this time, the University of Iowa was planning a national conference on child labor for American educators. Since the conference was about providing tools, resources, and expertise on child labor to enable educators to integrate the materials in their classrooms, the organizing committee decided to include these young activists who had already demonstrated that they could make a difference.

In July 2004, American educators and activists listened in amazement as twelve-year-old Spencer Lundquist delivered the opening address at the conference:

> I was shocked, then saddened to learn that 246 million children are working in horrible conditions rather than going to school. Then I felt anger rippling through my body. I began to see everything around me in a different perspective. I began to question everything. The things that I am wearing—where do they come from? The things I am consuming—bananas, sugar, chocolate—how did they end up here? What about the soccer balls that I kick? The rugs that I walk on? How is my life related to this issue that I was introduced to in Mrs. Meggitt's 6th grade Social Studies? (Lundquist 2004)

This drawing, by then twelve-year-old Spencer Lundquist, won the T-shirt design contest at the Child Labor World Congress in Florence in 2003. *(Image courtesy of the Child Labor Coalition of the National Consumers League)*

The educators were captivated by the passionate, articulate, and well-prepared youth panelists who spoke eloquently about their experiences in learning about child labor and their activism. In the evening, participants were treated to a vignette staged by CHILD members to evoke images of children being abducted and forced to become child soldiers. While the conference participants appreciated learning from the "experts," it was the youth activists who inspired them. For these educators, it was a unique experience to see children being fully integrated into the process.

Iowa City youth activists made substantial contributions to the global fight against child labor. In the process of learning and organizing, they became more empowered citizens. Meggitt summed it up best:

> The students were empowered in many capacities: as students, as citizens, as humans and as peer children. Struggling students were empowered through "desire-based learning" whereby they were challenged to conduct academic exercises in the course of helping others

> . . . not just as mindless, meaningless exercise. They read, researched, wrote, spoke publicly, persuaded others, problem-solved, networked, worked in teams and learned new technologies in the process.

Seth Saeugling, eleven, also a recipient of the Outstanding Youth Citizenship Award, shared his thoughts at the award ceremony. "Being a good citizen to me means making a difference in our world. Our world is a place where people need our help. We cannot abandon this fact, we cannot turn our backs on the desperate people who are crying for help" (Sok and Quintero 2004). Seth and other CHILD members did not abandon the fact when they learned about child labor. They directly confronted it and made sure that they played a part in helping to eliminate child labor. A group of ordinary students became extraordinary citizens because two teachers decided to introduce child labor into their classrooms.

Conclusion

Kailash Satyarthi, organizer of the Global March Against Child Labor, is hopeful about ending child labor because of youth activism. In a keynote address at the 2004 child labor conference, he shared his observation: "I see the emergence of youth leaders all across the world. They are the real leaders. They are [our] hope" (Erb 2004).

Note

1. Except where other sources are cited, quoted material is from e-mail correspondence, survey responses, and other notes on file with the author.

References and Further Reading

American Federation of Teachers. *Lost Futures: The Problem of Child Labor.* Washington, DC: American Federation of Teachers, 2000.

Adams, Ron. "A School for Iqbal." *FACES Magazine* 22:8 (April 2006): 24–26.

Bachman, S.L. "A Stitch in Time." *Los Angeles Times Magazine,* September 16, 2001, 10–15.

Coleman, Sandy. "Child's Death Stirs Another Crusade." *Boston Globe,* March 2, 2001, B1.

Erb, Christina. "Driven to Help Humanity." *The Gazette* (Cedar Rapids), July 3, 2004, 1D.

Erb, Christina. "Respected Child Labor Activists Speak at Conference." *The Gazette* (Cedar Rapids), July 29, 2004, 4D.

Helfand, Duke. "Students Press L.A. Supervisors to Join Fight Against Child Labor." *Los Angeles Times,* December 9, 1997, B1.

"A Kids' Campaign for Freedom." *New Designs for Youth Development* 13:1 (Winter 1997).

A Kids Campaign to Build a School for Iqbal. http://www.mirrorimage.com/iqbal/.

Lundquist, Spencer. "Student Opening Address." Teaching About Global Child Labor Conference, University of Iowa, Iowa City, July 26, 2004.

Messigian, Amy. "Love's Labour's Lost: Michael Lewis Clark's Constitutional Challenge of 18 U.S.C. 2423(C)." *American Criminal Law Review* 43 (Summer 2006).

Morales, Leslie Anderson. "Teacher's Guide for FACES: Child Labor." *FACES Teachers' Guides,* April 2006. http://www.cobblestonepub.com/resources/fac0604t.html.

Reed, Jennifer. *Elizabeth Bloomer: Child Labor Activist.* Farmington Hills, MI: KidHaven Press, 2007.

Shuppy, Annie. "Activism Isn't Child's Play." *Daily Iowan* (Iowa City), April 22, 2004.

Sok, Chivy, and Buffy Quintero. "Transforming Effects." *International Accents* (Iowa City) (Spring–Summer 2004): 8–16.

Part 5
Europe

Section 1. Introduction

Europe: An Introduction and Overview

Colin Heywood, Reader in Modern French History, University of Nottingham

Europe was where child labor first erupted as an emotive issue for political debate during the eighteenth and nineteenth centuries. It was where the shock of the new for many influential observers of early industrial society included the spectacle of young children working to the intensive rhythms imposed by the machine and the factory system. And it is where the employment of children first ceased to be an obscure practice, buried in the villages and the popular neighborhoods of the towns, to become a matter for government intervention. Of course, it was not long before employers in other parts of the world began to dragoon children into textile mills and other industrial establishments. The cotton mills of the United States gave an early hint that the practice of employing child labor in industry was easily exported. At the same time, one should not exaggerate the pace of industrialization and the consequent upheavals in the labor market during this period. Even within Europe, the so-called Industrial Revolution was slow to move from a core of nations in the West during the late eighteenth and early nineteenth centuries, notably Britain, Belgium, and France, to a periphery in Scandinavia and the southern and eastern parts of the continent. If the story of the exploitation of child labor in industry has traditionally focused on the British case—not unreasonably, given its status as the cradle of industrial civilization—there remains plenty to be said about what happened to working children in "follower" nations (Rahakainen 2004). Moreover, it is important to emphasize that work in agriculture and the service sector remained the predominant forms of employment for children in much of Europe well into the twentieth century. The highly moralistic tone adopted by early historians of child labor, focusing on horror stories from the mills and the coal mines recounted by ardent reformers, has gradually given way to a more balanced view, noting the benefits as well as the costs of work for the young, and the variety of jobs available to them.

What struck early commentators on child labor in Europe was the impact of power-driven machinery on the composition of the labor force. In the famous words of Karl Marx: "In so far as machinery dispenses with muscular power, it becomes a means for employing workers of slight muscular strength, or whose bodily development is incomplete, but whose limbs are all the more supple. The labour of women and children was therefore the first result of the capitalist application of machinery!" (Marx 1976, 517).

Some dreamed of a future society where industrial work could for the most part be left to women and children, as the machines provided a series of undemanding jobs. Others depicted a nightmarish scenario of families torn asunder and frail bodies subjected to the relentless rhythms of the machine. There followed a highly charged debate on the impact of the new industrial civilization on child welfare, and the pros and cons of legislative intervention. Apologists for the factory system talked of children flourishing with the light "gymnastics" of their work, while their opponents thundered over slavery, torture, and the degeneration of the race. Historians have since pondered whether the rise of early proto-industrial forms in the countryside might have been as important as the factory system in transforming the work of children. They have tried to gauge as accurately as possible the extent to which women and children did actually invade the shop floor during the nineteenth century—concluding in various national contexts that it was confined to a few branches of industry. They have also set out to measure the impact of child labor at successive stages of economic development on child mortality and health, on literacy and school attendance. They have drawn attention to the declining role of children in key industries such as textiles and mining from the late nineteenth century onward in Europe. Finally, they have become wary of writing off child labor as a relic of the past (e.g., Lavalette 1999; Cunningham and Stromquist 2005). Evidence from the traditional core during the late twentieth century, in the sweatshops of east London, for example, as well as from more recently developing nations on the periphery, such as Portugal and Turkey, indicates that the practice continues in certain sectors of the economy. Employers, parents, and even children themselves can in some circumstances continue to feel the lure of an early start to working life for the poor.

References and Further Reading

Cunningham, Hugh, and Shelton Stromquist. "Child Labor and the Rights of Children: Historical Patterns of Decline and Persistence." In *Child Labor and Human Rights,* ed. Burns H. Weston, 55–83. London: Lynne Rienner, 2005.

Lavalette, Michael, ed. *A Thing of the Past? Child Labour in Britain in the Nineteenth and Twentieth Centuries.* New York: St. Martin's Press, 1999.

Marx, Karl. *Capital: A Critique of Political Economy.* Vol. 1. Transl. Ben Fowkes. Harmondsworth: Penguin, 1976.

Rahikainen, Marjatta. *Centuries of Child Labour: European Experiences from the Seventeenth to the Twentieth Century.* Aldershot: Ashgate, 2004.

European Proto-Industrialization

David Levine, Professor, Ontario Institute for Studies in Education, University of Toronto

During the protracted transition from peasant agriculture to urban-based "machinofacture," the plebeian family's organization of production and consumption was in an unstable equilibrium. Maintaining a balance between hands that produced and mouths to be fed was a precarious act. Whether they were peasants, urban proletarians, or craftsmen, the slightest hint of adversity could destabilize the family unit enough to drive it into poverty and destitution, from which escape was difficult.

The European population grew from about 65 million in 1500 to around 127.5 million in 1750, reaching almost 300 million in 1900. Most of this increase occurred as a result of a widening social pyramid whose base increased far faster than its upper segments. Furthermore, during rapid population growth, populations get younger as the age pyramid thickens at its base. Before 1750 most proletarianization was the result of downward mobility from the peasantry into the ranks of the poor—the vagrants, the migratory laborers, and the unskilled who made up the lumpen proletariat—who comprised the majority of the urban population and a very substantial minority of country dwellers. After 1750, this trajectory of social decline was supplemented by a massive increase in a new kind of lateral mobility, as the rural industrial sector experienced dramatic growth. Cottagers and dwarf-holders, who made up a huge proportion of the northwest European population, found that their tenuous hold on the land was terminated when the products of the first phase of the Industrial Revolution destroyed the income supplements they derived from proto-industry.

Population increased after 1750 in response to falling levels of mortality and gently rising levels of fertility. The rise in fertility rates was itself remarkable because, all else remaining equal, it would be expected that fertility rates would decline in response to declining mortality. But all else was not equal. What is now known as the "demographic revolution" may have stemmed from declining mortality rates, but this new state of affairs released uncontrollable forces when unexpected levels of survival combined with earlier marriage and skyrocketing illegitimacy rates. Increased longevity is especially significant to the birth rate because even small changes in mortality and birth rates, when compounded over several generations, have profound implications.

The changing tempo of daily life during the demographic revolution affected family formation strategies. The older world of family farming and family workshop production was not lost for everyone, although the success of the few was predicated on the failure of the many. The majority of that population was forced to migrate—socially or physically—and to establish wholly new routines. In consequence, new ways of social life were simultaneously created and abandoned. Cottagers first became wage earners and then lost their purchase on the land altogether. The value of women's and children's labor was initially enhanced during the proto-industrial phase of rural industrialization, and then radically depreciated. In handicraft cottage industry, women and children supplied hands (i.e., labor) that were subsequently marginalized by the emerging political economy of urban and industrial capitalism. In moving toward the patriarchal breadwinner economy, in which a male household head commanded both economic and moral authority over the family, the social standing of those who were neither patriarchs nor breadwinners was jeopardized. While individual families struggled desperately against these larger historical forces, it is possible to understand their demographic behavior only if we conceive it as one of a series of coping maneuvers within the calculus of conscious choice.

The explosive demographic implications of cottage industrialization were as much the result of more frequent marriages, by more people, as of earlier and more fertile ones. In addition, the dynamic of rural industrialization permitted married couples to stay together, whereas earlier, marriages were constantly being fragmented—and wives and children deserted—because the plebeian family's economic base was both flimsy and subject to cyclical strains. The rural cottage economy, therefore, formed a large population reserve from which people were siphoned out of the rural economy. Whereas before 1750, delayed marriage and permanent celibacy had acted as a "prudential check" on population growth, as Thomas Robert Malthus postulated, afterward boom times meant more frequent and earlier marriage as well as a decline in celibacy.

Extensive labor migration had long been a feature of the pastoral economies in upland areas in England where servants in husbandry often changed employers and settlements on an annual basis. Yet, absolute levels of population growth did not reflect the actual momentum of demographic change in these areas. In fact, they seem to have suffered net losses as a result of individual-level migration between agricultural and proto-industrial cottages.

In the preindustrial demographic-economic system of reproduction, about three-fifths of all families had an inheriting son, while another fifth had an inheriting daughter, which meant that about one-fifth of all niches in the landed economy became vacant each generation. Urbanization, with its filthy environment breeding microorganisms so lethal to babies, partially counterbalanced the broader improvements in life expectancy. Overall, however, mortality rates dropped, and it is probable that improvements in infant, child, and adult health were especially significant in the rural environment. Married couples remained intact and continued to reproduce for longer periods of time, while a higher proportion of children reached adulthood and marrying age.

These trends raise some pertinent questions: Why, when rising life expectancy yielded more survivors, did they produce so many children over and above replacement rates? How were these additional children to find their way in a world that was already overcrowded? How were new economic niches created? Were such niches in agriculture, industry, or service sectors? There were other effects that resulted from this shift in the mortality schedule. Most significantly, the age pyramid rapidly broadened at its base as enhanced child survival combined with the diminishing chance of marital breakup to swell the lower age-groups at the end of the eighteenth century. Generations followed one another more quickly, contributing to the maintenance of high fertility rates.

Something else was at work in maintaining high levels of age-specific fertility. Marginal groups—such as noninheriting children—felt the full force of the implications of population growth, as over the course of three generations the number of niches remained the same but the population increased exponentially. Villagers who were over and above replacement could either wait in the hopes of marrying into a niche or they could emigrate—that is, they could move socially down or physically out of their native land. This second alternative had been the reality presented to generations of their predecessors for whom noninheritance meant downward social mobility and demographic death.

For a time, however, cottage industry was a godsend for these noninheriting, marginal people; the luckiest ones could even find a way to subsidize the formation of a new household without having to leave their native hearth. The less lucky ones could move to the villages, towns, and cities where proto-industry was located; once there, they could support themselves with income derived from their labor, and with common rights, keep a cow, a pig, some chickens, fruit trees, and even a small vegetable garden. Thus, a large segment of the population experienced what have been called "lifetime moves" into the proletariat. While their actions may have consisted of efforts to retain control over the means of production, they were swimming against a powerful historical current that ultimately pulled most of them down into the ranks of the proletariat. This occurred with astonishing frequency in the period of the classic Industrial Revolution—between 1775 and 1850—as the population in the countryside thickened. If boom times were like a siphon sucking population out of their rural cottages, then proto-industrial communities were like sponges in their ability to soak up these footloose extras.

What about those who stayed behind? In what ways were their lives and the lives of their children altered by the outlet provided by rural, proto-industrialization? The opportunity to export noninheriting children relaxed the pressure on resources the exporting regions would have experienced. Parents with additional, noninheriting children had the knowledge that their offspring could relocate. Proto-industry acted not only as a magnet, then, attracting migrants, but also as an insurance policy in perpetuating the reproduction of those who would become migrants.

In addition to absorbing excess population, rural industry also provided a source of ready cash for children who would eventually inherit but were required to wait for a niche to open. Children who were to inherit the family farm or household were available as a source of income while waiting. Indeed, most had spent time as living-in servants in husbandry during the long wait between puberty and marriage and inheritance. The prevalence of annual service for cash wages in the rural economy came into direct competition with more attractive, better-paid opportunities in proto-industrial households.

Cash earned in proto-industry was a kind of income transfer to the cottage economy: It gave some the opportunity to buy into an available, vacated niche; it gave others money to purchase the consumer products and the capital goods being produced more cheaply in an age of early industrialization; cottagers in proto-industrial communities could generate further supplemental income by taking in wage-earning lodgers; and it provided a valuable infusion of funds into a sector that was notoriously undercapitalized. Dwarf-holdings multiplied, households became workshops—at some stages of the family cycle there were almost as many hands earning money as there were mouths consuming its income. Intensive cultivation and new crops—especially the potato—along with a more vigorous division of labor in the tertiary sector combined to make it possible for the land to fill up to the point of supersaturation. Therefore, rural industrial communities provided both an outlet for, and a stimulus to, this demographic dynamic in those villages that were the source of migrants. Consequently, the countryside filled up quickly. It could not continue, and it didn't.

If rural industrialization and population increase were the most prominent features of the countryside in the period after 1750, then deindustrialization and depopulation typified the countryside in the middle half of the nineteenth century—from 1825 to 1875. The respiration of the countryside inhaled the majority of marginally propertied peasants and exhaled landless proletarians. By the mid-nineteenth century, forces holding villagers to their land were in tatters. Many tried to stay, but more left in despair. The second half of the century also witnessed unprecedented levels of migration, both external—millions left Europe—and internal—continental urbanization proceeded furiously to catch up with British levels, where 40 percent lived in six large conurbations by 1881. Together, the demographic revolution and the Industrial Revolution wreaked disaster on an overstretched peasantry clinging to proto-industry as a supplement to their subdivided holdings, undermining the continued viability of the family farm.

The family production unit's reliance on its own labor merely served to expose its unsustainability when the terms of trade swung violently against it in the mid-nineteenth century. For the social classes who experienced this violence, this is what was revolutionary about the Industrial Revolution. The significance of simple, repetitive tasks by which women and children had contributed to the domestic economy of the peasant household—most notably, spinning—inexorably declined in the face of competition from emerging "machinofacture." The mechanization of spinning in the last decade of the eighteenth century effectively demolished this cottage industry at the moment when population growth was creating increasing stress on the income of semiproletarian households. Compounding this decline, women and children were further marginalized in the world of work by the increased emphasis on gender roles and age-stratified activities in this emerging domestic economy. The ideology of domesticity provided the key entry point for the new culture of breadwinning respectability, as work was reclassified as a masculine endeavor, and masculinity, in turn, was judged by the harmony of domestic discipline and its respectable independence. Accordingly, observers of the time worried that the natural character of rural, proletarian women was threatened by masculine work. Such women would not only be unsexed but also socially deranged since they would be indisposed to a woman's proper duties at home. Powerful as this prescription proved to be, it was irrelevant to the lives of working women, who had never conformed to bourgeois expectations, nor given "femininity" priority over family subsistence needs. Similarly, the romanticization of childhood and youthful innocence brutally conflicted with the reality of long hours of drudgery and minuscule wages—a situation that Charles Dickens experienced directly in his time in a blacking workshop, a time that was so horrible that the great Victorian novelist was haunted by its memories for the rest of his life.

Proletarians' high fertility during the early era of industrialization was incomprehensible to the bourgeoisie, who considered the additional children mouths to feed. The working class, however, considered them hands to work and insure the family against the ill luck of any particular member. In England as well as in France, the moral economy of the proletarian family was cited by social policy makers and reformers as evidence of deficient moral education. The organization of national social systems during the later nineteenth century provided the historical context in which the revolution in the family was keynoted by the decline in fertility. It was both an innovation and an adjustment, not only responding to broad changes in social organization, but also representing one of the primary ways in which men and women acted to make their own history.

References and Further Reading

Almquist, Eric L. "Pre-Famine Ireland and the Theory of European Proto-Industrialization: Evidence from the 1841 Census." *Journal of Economic History* 39:3 (1979): 699–718.

Almquist, Eric L. "Labour Specialization and the Irish Economy in 1841: An Aggregate Occupational Analysis." *Economic History Review,* 2nd ser. 36 (1984): 506–17.

Anderson, Michael. *Family Structure in Nineteenth Century Lancashire.* Cambridge: Cambridge University Press, 1971.

Cobbett, William. *Cottage Economy.* Oxford: Oxford University Press, 1979 [1822].

Collins, Brenda. "Proto-Industrialization and Pre-Famine Emigration." *Social History* 7 (1982): 127–46.

Goldstone, Jack. *Revolution and Rebellion in the Early Modern World.* Berkeley: University of California Press, 1991.

Hufton, Olwen. *The Poor Eighteenth-Century France.* Oxford: Oxford University Press, 1974.

Levine, David. *Family Formation in an Age of Nascent Capitalism.* New York: Academic Press, 1977.

Levine, David. *Reproducing Families: The Political Economy of English Population History.* Cambridge: Cambridge University Press, 1987.

Lynch, Katherine A. *Family, Class and Ideology in Early Industrial France.* Madison: University of Wisconsin Press, 1988.

Malthus, Thomas Robert. *An Essay on the Principle of Population.* London: J. Johnson, 1798.

Mendels, Franklin. "Proto-Industrialization: The First Phase of the Process of Industrialization." *Journal of Economic History* 32 (1972): 241–61.

Reay, Barry. *Microhistories.* Cambridge: Cambridge University Press, 1996.

Sharpe, Pamela. *Adapting to Capitalism. Working Women in the English Economy, 1700–1850.* London: Macmillan Press, 1996.

Tilly, Charles. "Demographic Origins of the European Proletariat." In *Proletarianization and Family History,* ed. D. Levine, 1–85. Orlando: Academic Press, 1984.

Wrigley, E.A. "Fertility Strategy for the Individual and the Group." In *Historical Studies of Changing Fertility,* ed. C. Tilly, 135–54. Princeton, NJ: Princeton University Press, 1978.

European Industrialization and Child Labor

Marjatta Rahikainen, Associate Professor of Social History, University of Helsinki

The return of paid child labor in affluent Western societies in the last few decades of the twentieth century has put historical child labor in a new perspective, and received ideas have been challenged. At the same time, the persistence of extensive child labor in developing countries brought about instructive comparisons between past and present. Today child labor is a topical and debated issue in historical writing.

This is related not only to present-day child labor but also to changes in historical writing itself. First, after Philippe Ariès's seminal volume, *Centuries of Childhood: A Social History of Family Life,* numerous studies on the history of children and childhood in different parts of Europe have been published. Thanks to them we now know much more about children's work and labor in the past than was known just a couple of decades ago. Second, novel approaches to the past (e.g., family history, history from below, and oral history) have made children's work and labor visible in rural and urban households, in charitable and disciplinary institutions, in urban trades, and in the street. Yet systematic information on historical child labor in different parts of Europe is either nonexistent or scarce. Numerical data are seldom available prior to the mid-nineteenth century, and even thereafter it is the exception rather than the rule to have reliable time-series data on different kinds of child labor.

In Mines, Mills, and Factories

Broadly speaking, European industrialization, urbanization, and the emergence of consumer society proceeded together. Looking at Europe as a whole, the transformation called the Industrial Revolution took about two centuries. Its opening is usually traced to late-eighteenth-century Britain, and it was brought to conclusion in the European periphery during the post-1945 period of economic growth. At that time even among the latecomers to capitalist development, the proportion of the economically active population in agriculture and forestry fell below that in mining and manufacturing, or below the latter and service trades put together—whereupon industrialization gave way to the transformation called deindustrialization. In Western Europe, industrial child labor seemed a thing of the past, until reports on child labor in sweatshops and subcontracted home industries started to accumulate in the 1980s. Today industrial child labor appears to be far from a closed story ("Children and Work in Europe" 1996; "The Influx of Young People" 1957).

Factory children were a product of the first Industrial Revolution, but they had their early modern predecessors. From the sixteenth century, orphanages were transformed into workhouses for children, taking manufactories for their model. Industrial child labor as we now understand it may be said to have come into being with the early manufactories. Unlike traditional craft production, manufactories applied division of labor, and this enabled them to use cheap, unskilled workers, such as women and children. However, working conditions in early manufactories and textile mills were often so dreadful that people avoided them, preferring industrial homework, even if it was more poorly paid. Difficulties in recruiting workers led early industrialists to use unfree labor, such as children from orphanages in the west and serf children in the east. Children in the early mills grew accustomed to monotonous work and long confinement, and thus were transformed into industrial wage workers. Eventually, manufactured goods undermined traditional crafts, and the status of apprentices deteriorated into a cheap juvenile labor force, not unlike factory children (Chassagne 1998; Tugan-Baranovsky 1970 [1907]).

Mining went through a parallel development. During the early modern centuries, coal mining changed in Britain from craftsmanlike by employment of free husbandmen into full-time wage work in dark and dangerous subterranean collieries, after which those who had a choice began to avoid it. Subsequently, wage-earning coal miners resorted for assistance to their own children, who from an early age grew accustomed to hard work in dark pits. Though child labor in British coal mines became notorious, children worked in mining (coal, iron, salt, even mercury) in other parts of Europe too.

The first Industrial Revolution, whose champion was the textile industry, was characterized by the use of child labor. In contrast, the leading sectors of the second Industrial Revolution, such as the electricity and chemical industries, employed few children. Industrial child labor was concentrated in a relatively limited number of sectors. In nineteenth-century Europe, textiles were almost everywhere the largest industrial employer of children, especially girls, while other sectors employing significant numbers of children varied from one country to the next. In the late nineteenth century they included clothing, hosiery and footwear, tobacco, food and drink, pottery, brick making and glass, printing trade and traditional papermaking, metal and machinery, matches, wood and furniture, building and construction, and, in some countries, sawmills. Long working days and tiresome night shifts meant that factory children had little time and energy for school, though some efforts to combine factory work and elementary education were made during the nineteenth century.

Boys and girls at night work in mills, and half-naked in mines, gave rise in Britain to moral concern resulting in the first laws regulating child labor. Other countries followed suit, stipulating minimum ages for industrial work—in the first half of the nineteenth century usually eight to nine years, and in the second half ten to twelve years. By 1890 almost every European state had enacted such laws. Their role in the decline of industrial child labor has been debated ever since (Borrás Llop 1996; Caty 2002; de Coninck-Smith, Sandin, and Schrumpf 1997; Humphries 2003; Tuttle 1999).

Although quantitative evidence is sparse, it seems that across Europe the trend in industrial child labor turned downward during the last quarter of the nineteenth century. Approached from the perspective of supply, customary explanations for the decline of industrial child labor include child labor laws, preference for school attendance and compulsory education, and rising living standards. If approached from the perspective of demand, the decline indicated that the economic rationale of industrial child labor must have eroded. Industrial child labor failed when its productivity and profitability were challenged by increasing competition during the long depression of the late nineteenth century, and definitely with the breakthrough of fatigue and productivity studies associated with scientific management, or Taylorism, and its assembly lines. Children, with their nimble fingers, were cheap, flexible, and energetic, but they grew tired sooner than adults, and despite factory discipline and corporal punishments, often proved unfocused workers. Children were the first group of manufacturing workers to be rationalized away (Heywood 1988; Nardinelli 1990; Olsson 1980; Rahikainen 2004).

In the Countryside

In the early nineteenth century, after the Napoleonic Wars, the European countryside was still an incongruous patchwork, from market-oriented family farming in the west to serfdom in the east, and from transhumant cattle breeding in the south to slash-and-burn cultivation in the north. Half a century later, the agricultural depression and cheap grain in the international market left no region untouched. A shift from cereals to more profitable products was generally accomplished, but even so, young people increasingly left the country. World War I devastated the countryside in parts of continental Europe, and during the interwar period, agricultural policies tended to uphold outdated rural institutions. After World War II, the remnants of the old order largely disappeared, and unprofitable smallholdings were abandoned. This accelerated an exodus from the countryside.

The commercialization of rural life progressed with industrialization. The countryside attracted early industrialists because of the availability of energy, raw materials, and cheap labor, especially women and children. Increasing demand for consumer goods and manufacturers' quest for cheap labor led to an extension of putting-out work, or outwork, in rural households, while new factory-made consumer goods increased incentives for acquiring cash. This has been characterized as "the industrious revolution." It kept peasant children busy with, for example, straw plaiting, lace making, embroidery, spinning, reeling, and spooling (Kriedte, Medick, and Schlumbohm 1993; Ogilvie 1986).

In general the agricultural revolution increased the demand for cheap seasonal labor. In the south, vine growing and silkworm breeding required the labor of all household members, old and young, while in Europe at large, the shift to animal husbandry and dairy farming increased the need for herding, a task that often fell to children. In many areas farmers took advantage of foundlings and parish pauper children, or employed (with or without pay) children of tenants, farm laborers, and underlings. By the same token, children of humble folk traveled long distances hoping to be hired by farmers. Although labor-saving machines began to spread in the late nineteenth century, labor-intensive practices, and therewith child labor, continued on undercapitalized farms (Rahikainen 2004; Uhlig 1978).

Children's jobs changed with age but seem to have been rather similar across Europe. First jobs included minding younger children, tending sheep and poultry, and acting as crow scarers. Slightly older children were involved in clearing stones, weeding, fruit and potato picking, helping at the harvest, root-crop hoeing, and herding cattle. Around the age of ten to twelve, boys began to focus on men's work, such as working with horses and field work; girls, on women's work, such as domestic chores, milking, and textiles. Children's workload also varied by social status. Substantial farmers had no need to set their children to work, save to train them in skills matching their social status. In middle-size farms, the families' own children contributed according to their capacity, and occasionally more if times were hard and they had to substitute for hired labor, though eventually children's school attendance took priority over farm work. Moreover, the family's own children could be spared by employing nonfamily children, who were often set to work in excess, even being deprived of school attendance. On smallholdings, children's labor remained crucial, to the detriment of children's schooling (Borrás Llop 1996; Cunningham 1990; Heywood 1988; Schlumbohm 1994).

In Urban Settings

In 1800 Europe was still predominantly rural. In the majority of countries only one in ten, and in the most urbanized countries about three in ten, lived in urban areas. By 1900, Western Europe was largely urbanized and in the rest of Europe urbanization was under way. Nineteenth-century migrants from the countryside left behind a partly self-sufficient rural economy and faced, in the cities, a fully commercialized urban economy. To children this brought an imperative and an opportunity to earn hard cash.

Among urban newcomers, the most vulnerable ones were that minority of children who came to the city without their parents. From south to north there were middlemen who traveled around the impoverished countryside and mountain villages and purchased children from credulous parents. Once in the city, children either were sold to low-market craftsmen or were set to beg on the street or to act as entertainers to whom passersby would give money that was collected by their masters. Inventive working-class children had discovered varied (but in a European perspective, surprisingly similar) ways to make money by taking advantage of the purchasing power of urban consumers. Children performed small services, girls cleaned people's homes, and boys carried shopping baskets and polished shoes. Children sold newspapers and small goods such as cigarettes, candy, shoe laces, postcards, and haberdashery. However, the authorities took a stern view of children who busied themselves in public places day and night, suspecting them of vagrancy, beggary, and petty crimes. Boys and girls encountered on the street were often sentenced to reformatories, and boys also to agricultural colonies, where hard manual work was expected to mold them into steady workers (Heywood 1988; Rahikainen 2004; Zucchi 1992).

In the nineteenth century, the open urban labor market for children comprised many kinds of jobs. Girls found short-term, poorly paid sewing jobs in dressmakers' workshops, but it was probably more common to be hired as nursemaids and maids-of-all-work. Boys found jobs in delivery and distribution and as hands in workshops. Boys and girls were hired as shop assistants and to run errands and deliver newspapers, flowers, bread, and milk. Most of the urban service jobs had the advantage that they could be performed before and after school hours. Thus, in the urban economy it was possible to combine school and work, even if this may have taken its toll on children.

Industrial cities offered factory work too, even though by the late nineteenth century mechanization and automation were making child labor redundant in many sectors. Nonetheless, industrial child labor continued in small, sweated workshops and urban home industries as long as various assembly jobs and routine manual piecework were done as subcontracted outwork. Such work was so poorly paid that it took many long hours before the daily bread was earned; thus, it could become truly tedious to children and led to overwork (Borrás Llop 1996; Papathanassiou 1999).

Work and School

Today elementary education is seen as an investment in human capital and children's futures. In primary school all children learn reading, writing, and basic arithmetic that will enable them to pursue more advanced studies. Two centuries ago, elementary education for children of lower social strata was not understood as an investment that would promote economic growth. Consequently, in institutional education, more attention was given to disciplining children than to nurturing their intellectual and learning potential. Parents in lower social strata were also skeptical of schooling because it would not improve their children's economic prospects, and the path beyond primary-level schooling was blocked. Thus, it appeared rational to parents to keep children working rather than attending school.

Before the mid-nineteenth century, in most of the European countryside (there were exceptions), primary schools were few and far between, were of poor quality, and offered a curriculum that included plenty of religion but little proper literacy or arithmetic. Primary school laws often ignored the fact that children's labor was needed in the agricultural high season, and this tended to alienate peasant children from school. In urban areas, primary schools were seen more favorably by lower social groups, but schools characterized as pauper schools and industrial schools carried a stigma. For many working children, factory schools offered an option for learning basic literacy, even though fees may have taken quite a proportion of their wages. In the course of the nineteenth century more and better primary schools were established, and the practical value of literacy and basic arithmetic became obvious. Starting in the third quarter of the nineteenth century, school attendance improved in most of Europe, usually in urban areas first, and later in the countryside, while industrial child labor began to decline (De Herdt 1996; Eklof 1986; Caty 2002; Papathanassiou 1999).

The introduction of compulsory primary education is one of the explanations commonly offered for the decline in child labor. Yet this line of reasoning has its problems. First, in many European countries it seems to be a matter of convention (or dispute) which one of the many school laws should be considered to have introduced compulsory education. Second, its introduction often came in stages and did not always take place simultaneously for rural and urban areas, or for boys and girls. Moreover, the implementation of compulsory education took so long that it is difficult to tell when it actually was effectively achieved. Finally, there were countries where school attendance was high even without compulsory education and countries where industrial child labor declined before compulsory education.

After World War II, all or almost all children in Europe went to school for at least some years, and paid child labor largely appeared a bygone phase. Nobody would have believed that toward the end of the twentieth century child labor would again expand and that school-age boys and girls might end up in drug traffic and prostitution ("Children and Work in Europe" 1996; Lavalette 1994; Mizen, Pole, and Bolton 2001).

Conclusion

Notwithstanding the differences in children's work and labor across Europe, children's jobs display many similarities over time and place: Typically they were time-consuming and required relatively little skill or training, and were usually so poorly remunerated (the pay might be nothing but meals) that adults avoided them. As workers, children were energetic and flexible and quick to grasp an opportunity, but they were less steady and had less stamina than adults. The extent to which children substituted for adult labor remains a debated issue, but during industrialization, the phrase "women and children" figured so often that evidently contemporaries saw these two groups as having more in common as workers than did men and children.

In present-day historical writing, children's work and labor are often related to family economy and, in the period of industrialization, to education. Current interpretations differ in many respects from those of contemporaries. As regards urban children trying to make money in public places, the moral alarm that always used to come first has given way to survival stories of young city dwellers, whereas agricultural child labor that was seldom of any concern to contemporaries now includes stories of exploited nonfamily child labor. Conversely, industrial child labor is today as controversial as it was in the nineteenth century—some see it approvingly while others are critical of it—and even now the British experience figures large in the discussion.

In a broad European perspective, changes in child labor were connected with major processes conveniently called the Industrial Revolution, agricultural revolution, and consumer revolution. Although cultural, social, and institutional factors modify the forms it takes, child labor appears, essentially, as an economic phenomenon. Despite the sentimental rhetoric in nineteenth-century pamphlets on industrial child labor, contemporary reformists seem to have been quite clear that what was at stake in child labor laws was international competition.

Today a standard explanation for "why the West grew rich" is that the labor force left the low-productive agriculture for more-productive manufacturing industries and further for service trades. In fact, European child labor followed the very same path: from agriculture to industry and then to consumer services—and this is where children earn their first wages today.

References and Further Reading

Ariès, Philippe. *Centuries of Childhood: A Social History of Family Life.* Translated from the French by Robert Baldick. London: Jonathan Cape, 1962.

Borrás Llop, José María. "Zagales, pinches, gamenes . . . aproximaciones al trabajo infantil." In *Historia de la infancia en la España contemporánea 1834–1936,* ed. José María Borrás Llop, 227–309. Madrid: Ministerio de Trabajo y Asuntos Sociales and Fundación German Sánches Ruipérez, 1996.

Caty, Roland, ed. *Enfants au travail: attitudes des élites en Europe occidentale et Méditerranéenne aux XIX et XXe siècles.* Aix-en-Provence: Publications de l'Université de Provence, 2002.

Chassagne, Serge. "Le travail des enfants au XVIIIe et XIXe siècles." In *Histoire de l'enfance en occident.* Vol. 2, *Du XVIIIe siècle à nos jours,* ed. Egle Becchi and Dominique Julia, 224–72. Paris: Éditions du Seuil, 1998.

Council of Europe. *Children and Work in Europe: Steering Committee for Employment and Labour Report, 1994–95.* Strasbourg: CE Publishing, 1996.

Cunningham, Hugh. "The Employment and Unemployment of Children in England c. 1680–1851." *Past and Present* 126 (1990): 115–50.

De Coninck-Smith, Ning, Bengt Sandin, and Ellen Schrumpf, eds. *Industrious Children: Work and Childhood in the Nordic Countries 1850–1990.* Odense: Odense University Press, 1997.

De Herdt, René. "Child Labour in Belgium 1800–1914." In *Child Labour in Historical Perspective 1800–1985: Case Studies from Europe, Japan and Colombia,* ed. Hugh Cunningham and Pier Paolo Viazzo, 23–39. Florence: UNICEF International Child Development Center and Instituto degli Innocenti, 1996.

Eklof, Ben. *Russian Peasant Schools: Officialdom, Village Culture, and Popular Pedagogy, 1861–1914.* Berkeley: University of California Press, 1986.

Heywood, Colin. *Childhood in Nineteenth-Century France: Work, Health and Education Among the Classes Populaires.* Cambridge: Cambridge University Press, 1988.

Humphries, Jane. "At What Cost Was Pre-eminence Purchased? Child Labour and the First Industrial Revolution." In *Experiencing Wages: Social and Cultural Aspects of Wage Forms in Europe Since 1500,* ed. Peter

Scholliers and Leonard Schwarz, 251–68. New York: Berghahn Books, 2003.

"The Influx of Young People into the Employment Market in Western and Northern Europe." *International Labour Review* 75 (1957): 335–53.

Kriedte, Peter, Hans Medick, and Jürgen Schlumbohm. "Proto-industrialization Revisited: Demography, Social Structure, and Modern Domestic Industry." *Continuity and Change* 8:2 (1993): 217–52.

Lavalette, Michael. *Child Employment in the Capitalist Labour Market.* Averbury: Aldershot, 1994.

Mizen, Phillip, Christopher Pole, and Angela Bolton, eds. *Hidden Hands: International Perspectives on Children's Work and Labour.* London: RoutledgeFalmer, 2001.

Nardinelli, Clark. *Child Labor and the Industrial Revolution.* Bloomington: Indiana University Press, 1990.

Ogilvie, Sheilagh. "Coming of Age in a Corporate Society: Capitalism, Pietism and Family Authority in Rural Württemberg, 1590–1740." *Continuity and Change* 1:3 (1986): 279–331.

Olsson, Lars. *Då barn var lönsamma: om arbetsdelning, barnarbete och teknologiska förändringar i några svenska industrier under 1800- och början av 1900-talet.* Stockholm: Tidens Förlag, 1980.

Papathanassiou, Maria. *Zwischen Arbeit, Spiel und Schule: Die ökonomische Funktion der Kinder ärmerer Schichten in Österreich 1880–1939.* Vienna: Verlag für Geschichte und Politik and R. Oldenbourg, 1999.

Rahikainen, Marjatta. *Centuries of Child Labour: European Experiences from the Seventeenth to the Twentieth Century.* Aldershot: Ashgate, 2004.

Schlumbohm, Jürgen. *Lebensläufe, Familien, Höfe: Die Bauern und Heuerleute des Osnabrückischen Kirchspiels Belm in proto-industrieller Zeit, 1650–1860.* Göttingen: Vandenhoeck and Ruprecht, 1994.

Tugan-Baranovsky, Mikhail I. *The Russian Factory in the Nineteenth Century.* Homewood, IL: Richard D. Irwin, 1970 [1907].

Tuttle, Carolyn. *Hard at Work in Factories and Mines: The Economics of Child Labor During the British Industrial Revolution.* Boulder, CO: Westview Press, 1999.

Uhlig, Otto. *Die Schwabenkinder aus Tirol und Voralberg.* Innsbruck: Universitätsverlag Wagner and Konrad Theiss Verlag, 1978.

Zucchi, J.E. *The Little Slaves of the Harp: Italian Child Street Musicians in Nineteenth-Century Paris, London, and New York.* Montreal: McGill-Queen's University Press, 1992.

History of Education in Europe: Schooling and Child Labor in Europe Since the Reformation

Harry Haue, PhD, Associate Professor, University of Southern Denmark

In the traditional European agricultural society, most production took place on farms, in shops, and in homes. Child labor had two objectives: socialization and production. No one questioned the father's duty to introduce his son to work at an early age in the stable, the field, or the shop. Likewise, the mother was expected to educate her daughter in the different branches of housework. Children were conceived as both a blessing and a gain, and large families were the norm. In the last part of the eighteenth century, industrialization offered new outlets for child labor. Many children from the poorer parts of society had to work in the new industries: boys in the coal mines and girls in the textile factories. However, during the nineteenth and twentieth centuries, mandatory schooling, coupled with state regulations forbidding children from participating in many aspects of industrial production, made it difficult for children to work. The state and the school had taken the children away from the family and from crude industrial work. Generally children were still regarded as a blessing, but no longer a gain insofar as their contribution to the family economy was reduced. In the late twentieth century, the service and knowledge economy gave children new options on the labor market. Beginning in the 1950s, children from the age of thirteen became teenagers and gradually liberated themselves from the traditional embedded dependence on the family. They entered the age of puberty earlier than their parents and grandparents did, and mercantile forces spotted them as a special target group of consumers. Today's thirteen- to fifteen-year-old youngsters are a new group of children who are able to combine schooling and paid work in the knowledge economy, independent of the economic situation of their parents. This economy offers many flexible jobs that can be managed without damage to the children's health or schoolwork. Perhaps, on the contrary, it can give them experiences to use in their lessons. Now, again, children can be both a blessing and gain. The combination of schooling and a reasonable amount of paid work can be seen as an appropriate part of socialization to an adult life in a complex and changing world.

This broad sketch of the development of education in Europe omits many variations from country to country, from sparsely populated Iceland to the metropolises of France, England, and Germany, and from church-based schools in Greece, Italy, and Spain to the state or municipality-organized schools of Scandinavia. But during half a millennium, all European countries underwent the transformation from traditional agricultural societies to knowledge economies.

The Traditional Society

Martin Luther's introduction of a personal and individual religious life in the first half of the sixteenth century had a very substantial impact on both schooling and child labor. In order to know the gospel it was necessary to read it, and therefore all congregations were obliged to teach children at least how to read. The children's lessons began in the church after the Sunday service, with the sexton as their teacher. Of course both boys and girls were taught, as all mankind should have access to salvation. This was the beginning of the establishment of general education in Europe. If children were to be educated, it meant taking them away from work, which in turn resulted in a reduction of child labor. For more than two centuries discussion ensued as to the appropriate balance between private and public instruction. The church and the state wanted to occupy more of children's time, not only to educate them, but also to make them humble subjects. Luther's recommendations were clear: "Thou shallst send them to school for them to hear and learn what they must believe. It's a big sin to keep them away from school" (Luther 1652). In sparsely populated areas such as northern Scandinavia, parents themselves were expected to teach their children, and the church was to ensure that this was done. Another of Luther's recommendations was that children should help their parents and obey them; if they did not, they should be punished by rod and stick (Luther 1652). Soon the Catholic parts of Europe answered the challenge from Luther and formed a system of Jesuit schools. John Amos Comenius (1592–1670), the Bohemian Protestant educationist, gave the school a central place in children's lives. Two hundred years later, Immanuel Kant (1724–1804) recognized that schooling was imperative; otherwise, children would learn not only the good manners of their parents, but their bad behaviors as well.

The Lutheran tradition told generations that duty, work, and obedience were the cornerstone of all upbringing and education. In contrast to this were the writings of French philosopher Jean Jacques Rousseau (1712–78). In his paradigmatic book *Émile* (1762), he argued that from nature children were good, and if they did not behave accordingly, it was due to bad upbringing. Children ought to be brought up in freedom. Rousseau's theories were practiced only in small idealistic circles, but in the long run they became influential and challenged the Lutheran tradition. Nowadays more European parents identify themselves with the principles of Rousseau than with those of Luther; this change must be seen in relation to the different character of child labor today.

The Industrial Society

One consequence of the expansion of schooling in the nineteenth century was that children had less time for paid work. The age of enlightenment inspired landowners and governments to focus on the education of the masses. At the same time, a new way of production was invented, namely industry, which on the one hand presupposed some schooling, and on the other hand created a new division of labor that made room for children's work. "There was a drastic increase in the intensity of exploitation of child labor between 1780 and 1840, and every historian knows that this is so." Thus wrote the British historian E.P. Thompson in his famous book *The Making of the English Working Class* (366). We know of those children's fate from literature, such as the novels of Charles Dickens. These famously exposed the cruelty of child labor in industrial England, as he himself had experienced it as a child, while contributing to the livelihood of his family. In *Oliver Twist* (1838) he made the cruel side of child labor a part of world literature by describing the orphan's progress from the workhouse to the criminal slums of London. The Danish author Hans Christian Andersen wrote the famous fairy tale *The Little Match Girl* (1845) which in a sentimental yet realistic way stressed the relation between poverty and child labor.

The development of the textile industry had a great impact on child labor. In traditional society children had worked together with their parents and grandparents. Therefore, it was convenient for factory owners to hire the whole families, with all the advantages this method offered in the way of discipline and efficiency. But technological development intensified child labor. In 1824, the self-acting mule was invented. This machine was operated by one adult and up to nine assistants, often children. The next technological innovation was the power loom, which outdid hand-loom workers because it could be operated by a child. By 1828, only 23 percent of the textile workforce in England consisted of adult males. The rest were women and children because they were cheaper and put up less resistance.

The Factory Act of 1833 was aimed at the textile mills, especially where girls were engaged. Working time for children from eleven to thirteen years of age was restricted to forty-eight hours a week, or no more than twelve hours in one day; the children were to have an hour and a half for meals, and they should attend school for at least two hours a day. Much of the work of children was never documented, but the 1833 act introduced inspection by government officials, and their reports were used in the First Report of the Children's Employment Commissioners in 1863. The inspectors had interviewed children and produced material for the parliamentary debate on child labor. In 1835, 15 percent of the workers in the cotton industry were boys and 12 percent were girls under the age of thirteen. The corresponding figures in 1870 were 12 and 7 percent.

The School and Children's Working Conditions

During the nineteenth century, most European countries passed laws to limit child labor. One indicator of the degree of enforcement was the percentage of illiterates in society. In the 1870s, 17 percent of bridegrooms in England were illiterate, and as for conscripts, 18 percent in France were illiterate, as were 6 percent in Switzerland, 52 percent in Italy, 63 percent in Spain, and 79 percent in Russia. Germany, Sweden, and Denmark had fewer than 3 percent illiterate. British historian J.H. Hobsbawm came to the conclusion that there was a close relation between high literacy and the level of a country's industrial technology. Regulation of factory labor for children was passed in all European countries as soon as the consequences of unhealthy child labor became a political topic.

In Denmark, for example, the first regulation came in 1873. Thereafter it was prohibited for children under ten years to work in factories, and children were not allowed to work more than six and a half hours per day, including a half-hour break. In 1901 the working age was increased to twelve years and the maximum hours per day reduced to six. The maximum distance allowed between work and school was ninety minutes on foot. An investigation in 1908 concluded that every third schoolboy and every fourth schoolgirl had paid work up to four hours a day. For each decade the regulations grew stricter, and also included children's paid work outside the factory. One of the main arguments favoring such legislation was put forth by the school system. The chief educational officer in Copenhagen wrote in 1916, "The school system opposes in principle children carrying out paid work before school starts, because the children arrive exhausted for their educational work which should be their main occupation" (Coninck-Smith, Sandin, and Schrumpf 1997, 129). The regulations were supposed to apply only to children's work in towns and not to agriculture, fisheries, and maritime work or to work in private homes. Both trade unions and the teachers' organization were eager to reduce child labor, and it was the teachers' job to register the child as absent and the reason for it. Beginning in 1814, a period of seven years of schooling was mandatory in Denmark, and in case of absence because of work, parents had to pay a fine. Some municipalities engaged a person as supervisor of schoolchildren's paid work as part of school policy. Gradually the half-day school in the cities was made a full-day obligation, which had a decisive limiting effect on child labor.

In Norway the same tendency can be seen. In 1875, children worked in industries related to agriculture, tobacco, and glass production. By 1912, boys had become distributors of newspapers and girls worked in domestic service. In the late nineteenth century, children's paid work had been an important supplement to the family economy. In a textile town in Spain, children's contributions amounted to nearly half of the family income. In 1910 in France, children's paid work accounted for only 10 percent. The growth in real wages made it possible for the head of the family to be the single provider, and the paid work of the children lost some of its original purpose.

The international labor conference in Washington in 1919 adopted the first international convention on the minimum age for work in industrial enterprises, and many European countries ratified the convention. One of the most important results was the prohibition of children's work during school hours. In Norway the number of days in school increased by 50 percent from 1880 to 1914. However, in the countryside in most of Europe, the half-day school continued into the 1950s, and therefore much child labor occurred, including milking, herding, collecting potatoes, and cleaning nets in the fishing communities. Nonetheless, the tendency in the twentieth century was for the state and especially the school to expropriate the children from the family without compensation. In the 1950s schooling was extended from seven to nine years in the most advanced industrialized countries of Europe for mainly two reasons: a high-technology society depends on better-educated employees, and the income of the parents had reached a level that made them able to feed their thirteen- to fifteen-year-olds at home.

Teenagers in a Knowledge Economy

New conditions for children in early puberty made them a target group for advertisers, who offered them special clothing, bicycles, motorbikes, radios, and amusements. They even got a new name—now they are called "teenagers." In spite of obligatory full-day schooling for at least nine years, this new group of teenagers wanted to earn money. High-tech society had many jobs suited for thirteen- to fifteen-year-olds, especially service occupations such as newsboys, babysitters, and assistants in supermarkets and cinemas. The European Union accepts children's right to work from the age of thirteen under specific conditions. A 1994 directive demands that employers make sure that all employees are at least thirteen years of age, and that employees from thirteen to fifteen years of age perform only light work for a maximum of two hours a day.

Research in modern Germany has shown that about half of all pupils between thirteen and fifteen years of age have paid jobs (Ingenhorst 2001). Similar figures are confirmed by a 2005 Danish survey, which shows that 48 percent of boys and 44 percent of girls between thirteen and fifteen years of age have paid work, often ten hours a week, and that teenagers from more wealthy families are the most eager to work. The reasons why they take up paid work vary, but the main reason is children's desire to separate themselves from the parental home and to generate independent forms of social existence. Two-thirds of young teenagers regard money as the most important reason for working, as it enables them to buy attractive items such as mobile phones, television sets, and brand-name clothing. Paid work gives children a feeling of recognition in the adult world. Children who have work experience tend to have greater feelings of independence and self-confidence compared to children with no work experience. This, in turn, is good for their schooling. Since the 1960s, inspired by Jean Piaget and others, many European countries have developed constructivist pedagogies. The pupils can therefore use their work experiences in the classroom and be better prepared to function in a complex knowledge economy.

Half a Millennium—Schooling and Child Labor

When considering the relationship between education and child labor, it is important to focus on three modes of production: traditional agrarian society, industrialization, and the postindustrial knowledge society. In agrarian society children were seen as a gain insofar as they could contribute to the livelihood of the family. Consequently the birth rate was high, and it remained high during the first century of industrialization. On the one hand, the new industrial system of production created a place for child labor; on the other hand, industrial society had to give priority to schooling and education. Children therefore had to attend an all-day school, and the state's demand for more schooling expropriated the latent productivity of children, permitting only limited contributions to the family economy. That might be one of the reasons for the low birth rate in Europe during the twentieth century. In the knowledge economy that developed in the later part of the twentieth century, children sought paid work not to sustain the family economy, but solely because they wanted to be independent of the family and to gain experiences from the world outside the school. During half a millennium, the conditions of child labor have changed, and the school played an important role in this process—both for purposes of socialization and as a political tool to reform society.

References and Further Reading

Coninck-Smith, Ning de, Bengt Sandin, and Ellen Schrumpf, eds. *Industrious Children: Work and Childhood in the Nordic Countries, 1850–1990.* Odense, Denmark: Odense University Press 1997.

Haue, Harry. "Education Europe." In *Children and Childhood: In History and Society,* ed. P. Fass, 302–7. New York: Thompson and Gale, 2004.

Hobsbawm, J.H. *The Age of Capita 1848–1875.* London: Abacus, 1977.

Ingenhorst, Heinz. "Child Labor in the Federal Republic of Germany." In *Hidden Hands: International Perspectives on Children's Work and Labor,* ed. Phillip Mizen,

Christopher Pole, and Angela Bolton, 139–48. London: RoutledgeFalmer, 2001.

Luther, Martin. *Tischreden (Dr. Martin Luther's divine discourses at his table, &c., which in his life time he held with divers learned men . . . collected first together by Antonius Lauterbach, and afterward disposed into certain common-places by John Aurifaber; translated out of the High Germane into the English tongue by Henrie Bell).* London: William Du-gard, 1652.

Mizen, Phillip, Christopher Pole, and Angela Bolton, eds. *Hidden Hands: International Perspectives on Children's Work and Labor.* London: RoutledgeFalmer, 2001.

Qvortrup, Jens. "School-Work, Paid Work and the Changing Obligations of Childhood." In *Hidden Hands: International Perspectives on Children's Work and Labor,* ed. Phillip Mizen, Christopher Pole, and Angela Bolton, 91–107. London: RoutledgeFalmer, 2001.

Schrumpf, Ellen. "Child Labor in the West." In *Children and Childhood: In History and Society,* ed. P. Fass, 159–62. New York: Thompson and Gale, 2001.

Thompson, E.P. *The Making of the English Working Class.* London: Penguin Books, 1963.

Thomson, David. *England in the Nineteenth Century 1815–1914.* Pelican History of England, Vol. 8. London: Penguin Books, 1972.

Apprenticeship Practices in Europe

Hal Hansen, Departments of History and Economics, Suffolk University

Apprenticeship is a form of child labor that combines learning with work. Unlike an employment contract, it involves a lengthy indenture that was once seven years or longer. In its modern form, however, apprenticeship lasts only three to four years, entails systematic training, is often accompanied by part-time schooling, and generally leads to formal occupational certification. In several European countries, it constitutes an educational alternative to secondary schooling.

At its core, apprenticeship is an arrangement in which apprentices exchange unpaid labor for training. Ideally, training is heavily concentrated during the initial stages, when apprentices know little and have everything to learn. The costs of training and support (or wages) during this initial period of low productivity are recouped by the trainer in the final stages of the contract, when apprentices' productivity exceeds their cost.

Due to the nature of the exchange, however, moral hazard threatens at every turn. Historically, two problems grew over time. In the absence of regulation, masters limited training, assigned apprentices easy-to-learn, repetitive tasks, and exploited them as cheap labor. For their part, apprentices abrogated their indentures and absconded once they had acquired salable skills, thus depriving trainers of returns on their investments.

These problems came to a head in the leading industrial nations around 1900, the result of a steeply rising demand for skilled labor that accompanied the second Industrial Revolution. Desperate for competent manpower, firms in the rapidly expanding skill-using metalworking, machinery, and electrical branches began poaching older apprentices from training firms. Since training did not pay under these conditions, trainers increasingly switched to poaching—resulting in a global decline in the production of skills.

This training dilemma elicited several responses. In the United States, apprenticeship effectively disappeared as Americans moved to full-time schooling for prospective white-collar employees, and on-the-job learning and skill-minimizing mass-production strategies for most blue-collar workers. Europeans found these strategies less available due to the size of their markets, their comparative advantage in skill-using customized and small-batch manufacturing, and competition from American mass producers. Yet each country responded differently, since demand for training and the social-institutional resources available for regulating it varied. Despite large differences in effectiveness, nearly all European societies now make apprenticeship an important part of their education and employment policies.

Historic Origins

Apprenticeship traces its origins to the household economies of medieval Europe. It was an urban version of the more common service, a parallel, mostly rural practice in which training was secondary. Both practices extended the family model of social hierarchy and organization to extrafamilial members of the household. Both also functioned to redistribute underutilized labor from families unable to employ fully their children's labor to households needing more hands. Since food, clothing, and heat consumed most family resources, transferring a child to the care of others represented significant financial relief. For the vast majority of servants and apprentices, this economic incentive stood foremost in their parents' decision to indenture them. Similarly, public authorities bonded out orphans and indigent children as a means of public relief.

Throughout most of the medieval and early modern periods, two types of apprenticeship coexisted. The first, practiced in rural villages and towns, closely resembled service. Artisans of modest means indentured their children as much for economic relief as for training. Skill acquisition resulted from observation, imitation, and work, supplemented by informal instruction during the sporadic work lulls that characterized early craft labor. Although masters pledged to instruct their charges in a trade, they often withheld crucial trade secrets to prevent future competition. In the absence of guild regulation or influential parents, apprentice exploitation was widespread.

A second, predominantly instructional type of apprenticeship originated in the elite urban guilds of the Middle Ages. Though this is the ideal often represented in the literature, it was far less common than its rural counterpart. Prominent merchants, professionals, and artisans placed their sons in the tutelage of a guild brother or associate to socialize and train them in a profession—often, though not always, the father's. Economic relief was secondary in these placements. Guild oversight and influential parents protected the interests of the young, generally assuring them of good training.

Guilds exercised strict oversight for two reasons. Because they maintained high standards, good training reduced exposure to competition from less-skilled, nonsanctioned producers, especially as cottage industry spread. Moreover, rigorous training helped guildsmen maintain prices by restricting entry into the trades and, thus, labor supply. However, when training became too restrictive, government officials and influential consumers generally acted to weaken guild authority.

Widely practiced, apprenticeship was far from universal. Young women commonly entered domestic service but were apprenticed only in female-dominated crafts such as embroidery or silk weaving. Eldest sons in primogeniture-practicing agricultural regions rarely left the households they stood to inherit. Further, families seldom indentured their children in areas where cottage industry or viniculture thrived. By pooling the labor of the household, families were able to employ children at home.

Whatever its particular form, apprenticeship shared three characteristics. First, it involved both educational and economic components, though the relative weight of each varied across time, space, and social class. Second, regardless of the emphasis placed on instruction, most learning occurred inductively through work. Apprentices acquired knowledge and skill as children do language: by observing, imitating, practicing, and interacting with experienced practitioners. Third, apprentices learned more than technical skills and work discipline; apprenticeship socialized them to their community's norms and behaviors. Thus, the master served a public function, one in which both the guild and the community had vested interests.

Modern Development

As household economies of early modern Europe gave way to early industry and the separation of work from home, economically motivated apprenticeships lost their appeal. Like service, they transitioned relatively quickly into simple wage relationships. These offered everyone something desirable. Wages released the young from onerous, constant surveillance, eliminated household chores, limited work hours, and permitted them to change employers when they wished. Wages permitted parents to keep their older children at home by pooling incomes. Masters benefited too, for as households became homes separated from shops and offices, they grew into private spaces in which saucy apprentices proved intrusive. Finally, wage relations allowed small producers to hire and fire child labor as needed, in place of lengthy indentures.

Training suffered, though the young continued to learn inductively through work. However, the growing division of labor accompanying nineteenth-century industrialization restricted the range of work to which young workers were exposed. In response to this and a rising demand for skills beginning in the 1880s, large skill-using firms built elaborate in-house corporation schools organized around industrial apprenticeships. Once rival firms began poaching apprentices, however, training firms found it difficult to justify the expense.

Two forms of regulation proved essential to addressing these problems. First, it was necessary to compel apprentices to serve out their indentures. Without this, firms refused to make investments in training workshops, instructors, and wages, since these costs could be recouped only at the end of the apprentices' term. In return, apprentices needed assurance that their training would be rigorous and broad. This meant forcing trainers to provide strictly instructional tasks when no paying work was available. Apprentices needed wide-ranging, general skills in order for their training to have value on the labor market.

Pioneers of modern, systematic apprenticeships, Germans devised a comprehensive testing and certification system that addressed both problems. By standardizing the certification process and instituting rigorous written and practical examinations, certificates developed an economic value Germans institutionalized in law. Thus, the certification required to practice any of several hundred licensed occupations forced apprentices to complete their indentures. Certification also compelled them to work hard at mastering the knowledge and skills requisite for passing their occupational exams, a process that engendered both technical skill and broader intellectual capacities.

Furthermore, the certification process disciplined training firms by providing authorities with an easy way to evaluate their programs. If too many apprentices failed their exams, trainers risked losing their authorization to train and found it hard to recruit apprentices. Authorization required highly trained, licensed masters to oversee instruction and inspection to ensure that training shops, factories, and offices were properly equipped. Finally, the certifying exams imposed a methodical, rigorous curriculum on trainers, one they were not at liberty to ignore.

Although conventional wisdom has been that modern apprenticeship is a relatively straightforward outgrowth of traditional practice, the effort to regulate, modernize, and systematize it was enormous. Most societies failed, for as the economic functions of apprenticeship waned with the rise of wage labor, its educational role grew, escalating moral hazard and its costs. In Germany, a legally distinct craft (*Handwerk*) sector proved instrumental in regulating and modernizing the practice around 1900, creating a model that diffused to industrial and service sectors in the 1930s and 1940s. Three factors contributed to this outcome. First, the crafts predominated in smaller, slower-growing communities, where the economic functions of apprenticeship persisted longest, giving these areas more time to adapt apprenticeship to new conditions. Second, *Handwerk*'s dependence on skilled manpower reinforced demand for apprentice training since it could neither substitute a division of labor and machines for skill nor build elaborate company schools. Finally, the legally distinct status of *Handwerk* in Germany allowed it to develop a regulatory framework that the industrial and service sectors would have fought, had they also been subject to it.

Apprenticeship in Europe Today

Nowhere is apprenticeship more influential than in Germany, where it remains a fixture in the nation's economic and educational systems. Two-thirds of each German cohort undertake an apprenticeship in one of 356 licensed occupations—from hairdressing and auto mechanics to banking, accounting, and engineering. Within the so-called dual system, apprentices spend three to four days per week in private training firms and another day or two per week in a vocational school. Occupational content, testing standards, apprentice pay, length of indentures, and other details of the system are negotiated by organized groups of employers and unions with state oversight. In an effort to tie training to the communities of practice for which it trains, Germans intentionally divorced their training system from academic schools. Educational officials serve as consultants but lack the power to subordinate vocational education and training to the interests of the academic system, a development that has weakened vocational programs in other countries.

Apprenticeship evolved quite differently in England, where early large-city urbanization and industrial development quickly undercut the economic basis of apprenticeship. Lacking a separate legal environment in which to operate, the craft sector declined relatively quickly and grew organizationally weak. Parliament finally abolished the seven-year apprenticeship as an occupational prerequisite in 1814. Thereafter, craft unions took the lead in organizing apprenticeships, particularly in the building, metalworking, and engineering trades. However, in contrast to Germany, where training constituted a joint economic strategy of labor and capital, employers and unions in the United Kingdom contested its control. Further, a series of apprentice strikes in the twentieth century progressively drove up apprentice wages to the point where employers gradually abandoned training. Since 1994, the government has attempted to revive apprenticeship and extend it into the service sector. However, lacking strong employer support and suffering from low status in comparison with academic degrees, the future of apprenticeship in the United Kingdom remains uncertain.

In France, the Revolution undercut apprenticeship by abolishing all associational bodies mediating between the state and its citizens, including guilds. Absent these intermediate institutions, apprentices widely suffered exploitation by employers, while skill-using sectors of the economy experienced chronic labor shortages. The French government responded with school-based initiatives: a system of technical schools that trained highly skilled workers, foremen, and skilled technicians for industrial concerns; and lycées *professionnels* that prepared lower-status shop-floor and clerical workers. This two-tier, school-based vocational education system worked relatively well until de Gaulle's modernization policies extended general schooling to age sixteen, expanded the baccalaureate degree, and fostered a proliferation of engineering and commercial colleges. These developments undermined the value, status, and desirability of vocational certificates, which became terminal credentials for weak students with limited choices. Because of this, French policy makers have recently embraced apprenticeship as a preferable alternative. The French, however, still lack strong mediating institutions and struggle to win employer cooperation.

Several European nations have made apprenticeship a central part of their education and employment policies: Germany, Switzerland, Austria, and, to a lesser extent, Luxembourg, Denmark, and Ireland. Others, resembling England and France, have been less successful and, thus, made school-based vocational training a bigger part of the training mix: the Netherlands, Sweden, Italy, Spain, and Portugal.

Why the continuing interest in apprenticeship? An educated, skilled workforce is essential and widely trumpeted, especially for sustaining a high-employment, high-wage economy. Other educational advantages of apprenticeship, however, are often overlooked. First, in contrast to book learning, apprenticeship offers a natural means of acquiring knowledge and skill, establishes context and utility on the spot, and, thus, supplies meaning and motivation that are often absent in schools. Second, it instills more than technical knowledge and general intellectual skills; it socializes and disciplines in ways that schools find hard to do. This results from a real-world hierarchy of age, experience, and authority that peer-dominated school cultures generally lack. Third, it transfers the cost of learning from the individual—in the form of tuition and lost earnings—to the firm and provides a modest wage. Finally, it eases the school-to-work transition that most schools regard as beyond their mission and means, a transition particularly problematic for youth from families without social capital or connections. In sum, it appears to enhance social and educational justice.

Like all social practices, however, apprenticeship is far from perfect. It is not appropriate for all kinds of learning. Most daunting, it is notoriously difficult to regulate in ways that render it educational, economically valuable, and equitable to all parties involved. Nor is it easy to determine at what age students' educational paths should diverge or how to create second-chance ports of entry from vocational into academic tracks, and vice versa. However, compared with American-style comprehensive, school-based, winner-take-all educational systems—which most European nations have tried and found wanting—its ongoing appeal is easy to understand.

References and Further Reading

Ainley, Patrick, and Helen Rainbird, eds. *Apprenticeship: Toward a New Paradigm of Learning. The Future of Education from 14+*. London: Kogan Page, 1999.

Epstein, Stephan R. "Craft Guilds, Apprenticeship and Technological Change in Preindustrial Europe." *Journal of Economic History* 58 (1998): 684–713.

Hajnal, John. "European Marriage Patterns in Perspective." In *Population in History: Essays in Historical Demography,* ed. D.V. Glass and David E. Eversley. London: E. Arnold, 1965.

Hansen, Hal. "Caps and Gowns: Historical Reflections on the Institutions That Shaped Learning for and at Work in Germany and the United States, 1800–1945." PhD diss., University of Wisconsin–Madison, 1997.

Kaplan, Steven L. "L'apprentissage au XVIIIe siècle: le cas de Paris." *Revue d'histoire moderne et contemporaine* 40 (1993): 436–79.

Land, Joan. *Apprenticeship in England, 1600–1914.* London: UCL Press, 1996.

Lenger, Friedrich. *Sozialgeschichte der deutschen Handwerker seit 1800.* Frankfurt: Suhrkamp, 1988.

Mitterauer, Michael. *Sozialgeschichte der Jugend.* Frankfurt: Suhrkamp, 1986.

Quenson, Emmanuel. *L'école d'apprentissage Renault, 1919–1989.* Paris: CNRS Editions, 2001.

Rinneberg, Karl-Jürgen. *Das betriebliche Ausbildungswesen in der Zeit der industriellen Umgestaltung Deutschlands.* Cologne: Böhlau Verlag, 1985.

Church and Child Labor—Catholicism

Timothy Kelly, Associate Professor of History, Saint Vincent College

The Catholic Church has only recently turned its formal gaze to issues of child labor. Any discussion of Catholicism and child labor therefore must be rooted beyond official church pronouncements in a focus on church practices or even the experiences of Catholic children, parents, and employers. Here too the evidence is not so rich, though one can attempt an interpretation. It was not until the West underwent the Industrial Revolution that issues connected to child labor emerged in Catholic public discourse, and even then it remained muted compared to the more prominent place that adult labor held in that arena.

The Early Church

The church had no clear theology of work in its early centuries, let alone a theology of child labor. Robert Marcus (1960) tells us that early Christian writings had many admonitions to work hard and avoid idleness, but these did not stand apart from the broader culture. As with others in the Roman Empire, Christian childhood was short and children joined the labor force as soon as they were able.

Augustine's writings mark the first significant development of a theology of work, and this focused on adults. Augustine saw work both as a means of human development and as a way of distinguishing humans from the rest of creation. In his view, work was to be seen as a calling, a way for adults to mature further in their growth. Work was to have dignity and distinguished humans from other animals who did not labor in the same way. His theology focused on adult work, however, not that of children.

The church did not confront child labor per se until the Western world began to see childhood as a separate stage of human life. Hugh Cunningham (1995) credits Erasmus with pushing Catholics to see childhood as a separate yet crucial period for successful adulthood. He urged fathers to take special interest in young sons, age one to seven, and in their proper development. This focus helped to spur a shift in Catholic views of childhood between 1500 and 1700 and the development of a Catholic advice literature that placed a growing emphasis on the family as the location of affectionate emotions. Though Protestants adopted this view earlier than Catholics, all shared the perspective by 1700.

Unique to Catholicism was a growing child-rearing institutional presence that came to rival the family. Catholic schools mitigated, and in the case of orphanages, replaced entirely, the influence of parents in shaping Catholic childhood. The Jesuits were especially critical to the development of boarding schools in the late 1600s and 1700s. Though established as places of education, these institutions regularly put their charges to tasks designed both to develop the child and to generate the income needed to sustain the institution itself.

Industrial Revolution

The Roman Catholic Church began to confront labor issues more substantively during the Industrial Revolution. The first significant papal pronouncement on work came late in the industrialization period, with Pope Leo XIII's 1891 *Rerum Novarum: The Condition of Labor.* Most historians identify this papal encyclical as the wellspring for all subsequent Catholic social teaching on economic issues. Leo XIII released his document after more than a century of industrial development, though, and Catholics negotiated their engagement as workers and employers for this period in the absence of formal instruction from Rome.

Early factory owners prized children's labor and sought to utilize it regularly. Parents and others worried about factory work's impact on children's health and moral character, though, and often expressed reservations about both the physical and moral threats that factories posed. For their part, factory owners struggled with ways to keep their charges on task for extended periods. Colin Heywood (1989) tells of one strategy that French employers used to satisfy both sets of concerns beginning in the 1830s. French factory owners hired nuns to supervise children in mills, especially silk mills. The nuns used moral suasion and corporal punishment to keep children attentive to their tasks and, in this way, imbued the children with both Catholic ideals of deference to authority and a capitalist work ethic.

There is little evidence of a peculiarly Catholic concern for children's rights through the emergence of the Industrial Revolution. Catholicism did not mitigate employers' urge to exploit children's labor, nor did it ensure quality working conditions, just wages, or fair treatment generally. The late-nineteenth-century concern about child labor in Western countries, which resulted in regulations and child labor legislation, did not derive from church-driven moral arguments, though the Catholic Church did later join calls for such protections. It came instead from broader cultural changes in the definition of childhood and from technological advancements that allowed factory owners to reduce their dependence on children.

Initially, the Catholic Church seems rather to have worked against government impulses to regulate or outlaw child labor for two reasons. The first is the general suspicion that church officials had for the liberal state, and especially for its reach into realms that church officials saw as more appropriately under the purview of parents. Church officials were especially concerned about the growing support for socialism in Western nations, and specifically opposed any ideology that saw classes in conflict with one another or that threatened private property. At the same time, church officials worried about the exploitive nature of unchecked capitalism, especially as it rewarded those who successfully exploited adult and child workers. Church officials privileged a family model in which fathers headed households; mothers ranked below fathers and cared for children, who were lowest of all. Fathers determined when their children would work in this structure.

Second, the church had a number of institutions that depended on child labor for their survival. As governments moved to ban or regulate child labor, the church sought special exemptions for their orphanages, schools, and children's homes. In some cases, children in Catholic institutions worked extremely hard under harsh conditions. The twentieth-century Magdalene homes in Ireland provide a good example. Girls and young women who had reached puberty and were deemed by their families or other authority figures to have transgressed the bounds of acceptable sexual behavior were sent to these institutions both to prevent them from scandalizing the community and to ensure that they atoned for their alleged transgressions. Some of these young women might have become pregnant out of wedlock, or were thought to be sexually promiscuous, or were deemed to be too interested in sex. In the Magdalene homes they were confined to the grounds by high walls and locked doors, and they took in laundry to support the homes. The girls worked twelve-hour days, six days each week, every week of the year, for no pay, under the supervision of nuns.

Though the Vatican remained silent on child labor through the early decades of the Industrial Revolution, other Catholic voices did emerge in opposition to it. Most notably, Bishop von Ketteler of Mayence, Germany, argued that child labor was "a monstrous cruelty of our times, a cruelty committed against the child by the spirit of the age and the selfishness of parents" (McQuade 1938, 30). In early-nineteenth-century France, laymen led the critique, especially Paul Alban Villeneuve-Bargemont. In Austria, Catholic bishops and priests assisted in passing legislation to restrict children's work to eleven hours a day in 1890. The Italian archbishop (and later Pope Leo XIII) of Perugia penned a pastoral letter that asked, "And does not the sight of poor children, shut up in factories, where in the midst of premature toil, consumption awaits them—does not this sight provoke words of burning indignation from every generous soul, and oblige Governments and Parliaments to make laws that can serve as a check to this inhuman traffic?"

The official Catholic voice on child labor finally

came at the nineteenth century's end. Pope Leo XIII decried the excesses of industrial capitalism in 1891 when he issued *Rerum Novarum: On the Condition of Labor.* This papal encyclical seems to embrace employers' prerogatives as it reiterates the church's condemnation of socialism and its insistence on the centrality of the right to private property. It also asserts workers' rights to dignity, just wages, time off from work for religion and family, and safe working conditions. In its insistence on the right to private property, the letter asserts that children belong to their fathers rather than to the factory or the state. Later, the letter maintains that children should not be placed in "workshops and factories until their bodies and minds are sufficiently mature." Pope Leo XIII also sought to shield children from work "which is suitable for a strong man." The assumption throughout the letter is that children above a certain age—usually seven or eight years old—will work, and that the work should respect their dignity and not endanger their development. The papal encyclical on the condition of labor devotes only one-half of one of its forty-five sections to child labor, though, and even this "Child Labor" section focuses mostly on adult female labor. Still, subsequent Catholic positions on child labor grew from the foundation of workers' rights contained within this encyclical.

Pius XI issued *Quadragesimo Anno* on *Rerum Novarum*'s fortieth anniversary. He also asserted that "it is wrong to abuse the tender years of children" by putting them to hard labor. He did stipulate, however, that in addition to the fathers' wages, "it is indeed proper that the rest of the family contribute according to their power toward the common maintenance." He shared the assumption that children would work, and that their work should be limited by their weaker physical and intellectual abilities. By the time Paul VI wrote his eightieth-anniversary letter in 1971 (*Octogesimo Adveniens*), and John Paul II wrote the ninetieth-anniversary letter (*Laborem Exercens: On Human Work*) and the hundredth-anniversary letter (*Centesimus Annus: On the Hundredth Anniversary of Rerum Novarum*), even the meager direct mention of child labor present in the earlier encyclicals had disappeared.

It appears that, as child labor diminished in Western nations, largely as the result of labor legislation and compulsory school attendance laws, the formal discussion of child labor in Catholic social teaching lessened as well. The formal Catholic focus on child labor reemerged in the discussion of third world experiences and in the broader context of children's rights. As the Vatican turned its attention to Africa and Asia in the later twentieth century, it saw the survival of these nations to be rooted in the health, education, and welfare of children. Pope John Paul II praised diplomats who worked to stress "the effort against the exploitation of child labor," and the Vatican supports United Nations efforts to protect children's rights. Yet even in recent years the Vatican has refrained from identifying specific children's rights, and from endorsing an outright ban on child labor.

References and Further Reading

Cunningham, Hugh. *Children and Childhood in Western Society Since 1500.* New York: Longman, 1995.

Heywood, Colin. "The Catholic Church and the Formation of the Industrial Labour Force in Nineteenth Century France." *European History Quarterly* 19 (1989): 509–33.

Heywood, Colin. *A History of Childhood: Children and Childhood in the West from Medieval to Modern Times.* Malden, MA: Polity Press, 2001.

Hinsdale, Mary Ann. "'Infinite Openness to the Infinite': Karl Rahner's Contribution to Modern Catholic Thought on the Child." In *The Child in Christian Thought,* ed. Marcia J. Buage. Grand Rapids, MI: William B. Eerdman's Publishing, 2001.

Humphries, Steve, dir. *Sex in a Cold Climate.* Video documentary. 1997.

John Paul II. *Laborem Exercens.* Encyclical. 1981.

Leo XIII. *Rerum Novarum.* Encyclical. 1891.

Marcus, Robert A. "Work and Worker in Early Christianity." In *Work: An Inquiry into Christian Thought and Practice,* ed. John M. Todd. Baltimore: Hilicon Press, 1960.

McQuade, Vincent A. *The American Catholic Attitude on Child Labor Since 1891: A Study of the Formation and Development of a Catholic Attitude on a Specific Social Question.* Washington, DC: Catholic University of America, 1938.

O'Brien, David J., and Thomas A. Shannon. *Catholic Social Thought: The Documentary Heritage.* New York: Orbis Books, 1992.

Osiek, Carolyn. "Family Matters." In *Christian Origins: A People's History of Christianity.* Vol. 1, ed. Richard A. Horsley. Minneapolis, MN: Fortress Press, 2005.

Ryan, John A., and Joseph Husslein. *The Church and Labor.* New York: Macmillan, 1920.

Todd, John M., ed. *Work: An Inquiry into Christian Thought and Practice.* Baltimore: Hilicon Press, 1960.

Church and Child Labor—Protestant Reformation

Thomas Max Safley, Professor of History, University of Pennsylvania

The Protestant Reformation, here broadly understood as the movement for religious and social renewal that began in the early sixteenth century, had no direct effect on child labor. Church leaders ignored the uncompensated employment of children, whether in the customary activity of household chores, schoolwork, and agricultural tasks, or in the systematic exploitation of workshop and factory. Child labor was an unremarked commonplace in agriculture and manufacturing long before the Industrial Revolution, as historians such as E.P. Thompson have noted; the increased intensity of industrial exploitation, beginning in the late eighteenth century, and the humanitarian campaigns for industrial reform, led by such men as Lord Shaftesbury, recast it as a social evil.

Yet, the Reformation had indirect effects. First, Protestant preaching and publishing on marriage and the family cast the household as a unit of economy as well as of authority and emotion, thus legitimating child labor as a domestic resource. Second, Protestant reforms gave the state responsibility for social programs, including poor relief, that had once been within the jurisdiction of the church, thus promoting work as a fundament of child education and discipline. Third, Protestant institutions helped inspire the first public debate about child labor and its ill effects, thus presaging by nearly a century those debates and reforms that culminated, for example, in the British "Factory Acts." Finally, though Protestant reforms promoted child labor in a number of ways, none of those ways were intrinsic or limited to Protestantism, thus revealing child labor to have been a constant of preindustrial society.

Protestant preachers viewed the family as a community, a group of people united by common authority, common values, and common goals. They uniformly insisted on the responsibility of the paterfamilias—the husband, father, or master—to govern the other members of the household—wife, children, and servants—by instructing them in right behavior, correcting their occasional errors, providing for their material needs, and directing their productive labors. Especially in economic terms, the family constituted a clear hierarchy, in which the husband instructed his wife in all matters pertaining to housekeeping. She, in turn, oversaw the servants and trained the children in the performance of all tasks essential to the household. Servants and children alike were enjoined to avoid idleness and accept correction. In the eyes of Protestant divines, work was the activity that seemed to define the family most clearly. As a shared activity, leading to a shared prosperity, it constituted the wellspring of affection between husband and wife and among parents and children. Those reformers who wrote most frequently on the family—Cyriacus Spangenberg, Johannes Coler, and Paul Rebhun, to name but a few—spoke regularly of the abiding love born of a common enterprise. Nor was affection the only consequence. Acculturation and integration occurred in the context of labors shared, arising from a precise division of labor that extended from the household to the field or shop. Such a division of labor encouraged, so it was thought, order, obedience, industry, and diligence, preparing the young for eventual entrance into the world as self-sufficient laborers.

None of this was original; Protestant reformers drew from other, older sources. The Bible urged fathers and mothers to love and discipline their children, processes that included work *expressis verbis.* Roman clergy, such as St. Bernard of Clairvaux and the Pseudo-Bernard of the fifteenth century, wrote explicitly of child labor as a natural, essential, and legitimate household resource. Household and workshop were theoretically and spatially contiguous. Children had a moral as well as material duty to labor. Quite apart from their eventual socialization, the family's survival depended on it. Indeed, they could hardly avoid it. The fields might begin right at a peasant's door; the loom might stand in the weaver's living room. Therein lies a source of confusion from the postmodern perspective. It was inconceivable that children, especially among peasant and artisanal families in a preindustrial, subsistence economy, would not work.

Child labor moved beyond the protected space of household and workshop, where it had long been an accepted aspect of domesticity, and became a social issue with the welfare reforms that began in the late fifteenth century and continued throughout the early modern period. This process was coincident with but not contingent on the Protestant Reformation. Structural changes in agriculture and manufacturing rendered an increasing proportion of the European population susceptible to natural and human disasters. The poor flowed onto the roads and into the towns of Europe, becoming an ever-more pressing and persistent problem. Institutions and authorities came to distinguish among types of poverty, according to its various causes and consequences. The categories of deserving and undeserving attained a new relevancy. It was generally understood that the undeserving—those criminals and charlatans whose poverty was a matter of choice rather than need—should receive no assistance. The deserving—those whose poverty was permanent, such as orphans, cripples, and widows, and those whose poverty was temporary, such as the unemployed or sick—suffered through no fault or choice of their own. A welter of ecclesiastical, municipal, and familial charities, many which had existed long before the Reformation, struggled to succor them, and states struggled with issues of legal jurisdiction and rational organization.

Protestant polities were not alone in promoting reforms to address the rising tide of impoverishment; Catholic authorities in Italy, Spain, and France also reviewed, renewed, and rationalized the various organs of poor relief within their boundaries. Where the Reformation took hold, however, municipal and regional governments acquired autonomy from their ecclesiastical overlords and jurisdiction over their local churches. Secular authorities took direct charge of defining policies and relieving poverty. Beginning in the 1520s Protestant poor laws gave a new coherence to poor relief, distinguishing various kinds of assistance and developing specialized institutions to deliver them, all under the control of central administrations. Work was a centerpiece of these new laws. The poor were to be rendered productive, both to inculcate a habitus of self-sufficient industry and to relieve the strain on available resources. Only the truly unfit would receive alms; the able-bodied—men and women, adults and children—would be set to work. Again, it must be emphasized that the implementation of work as remedy was not uniquely Protestant. The Spanish humanist Juan Luis Vives, a Catholic, wrote the first and most influential tract on the relief of poverty through work. Catholic as well as Protestant authorities recognized the disciplinary and fiscal advantages of work and built it into their various reforms of poor relief.

What amounted to widespread efforts not only to relieve but also to monitor and discipline the poor did not focus exclusively on children. The young were not statistically important in the tide of misery that seemed to spread over Europe in the early modern period, but they attracted particular attention from Protestant and Catholic authorities. They were particularly visible among the growing population of poor people, crowding public plazas and church doorways; magistrates and officers reported their piping voices and ragged appearance among the beggars, importuning the well-to-do. They were particularly deserving of assistance; orphans, meaning parentless and abandoned children, were considered among the traditional poor, who received alms without question. They were particularly interesting to authorities; the administrators of poor relief understood that children might be more readily disciplined to lives of self-sufficient productivity than adults. They were not yet set in an immoral idleness. Thus, they were particularly well suited to regimes of work; their productivity might cover some or all of the costs of their poor relief and at the same time discipline them to lives of labor, free of poverty.

Protestant and Catholic authorities recognized at roughly the same time that so-called total or centralizing institutions constituted the ideal means to create such supposedly salutary work regimes. Across Europe varieties of poorhouses, workhouses, and orphanages arose, in which children might be sheltered and schooled. Indeed, the pace of construction quickened over the course of the seventeenth and into the eighteenth century. Within four walls, the young could be protected from the hardships of the world, provided with the basic necessities of life, monitored in their moral, intellectual, and physical development, and compelled to work in a regular, persistent manner. Catholics and Protestants alike believed that children might well be expected to grow into upright, productive, self-sufficient subjects and Christians under such ideal circumstances.

The children admitted to these institutions had to be in good health and of sufficient age to walk and obey. In brief, they had to possess all the physical and mental capacities to perform simple labor. Once admitted, they were uniformly clothed and fed. Their daily routines were fully regulated, and that regulation shows considerable uniformity across countries and confessions. The children rose, dressed, and attended morning worship. After a modest breakfast, they went to school or to work. These activities might occur intra muros or extra muros, though most institutions displayed over time a tendency to keep their charges within the walls. After the midday meal, which was usually the principal meal of the day, they returned to work and continued a variety of labors until the evening meal. Tasks might be gender or age specific and usually varied from household chores to industrial labor. Production for use or sale could cover the full spectrum of goods, the book printing of the *Franckesche stiftung* in Halle being a noteworthy example, but children seem most often to have engaged in spinning or weaving textiles. Whether they performed industrial labor within the institution or wage labor in artisanal workshops, as was arranged for Augsburg's Protestant and Catholic orphans, poor children worked relentlessly, an exercise in time and work discipline before the factory. Nor did that discipline cease when these children left the supposedly sheltered environment of the institution. In the case of Augsburg's Lutheran and Catholic orphanages, for example, administrators helped to arrange apprenticeships and other positions for their charges at some point between the ages of thirteen and eighteen years. They provided a variety of services beyond education and training—subsidies, clothing, lodging, health care, and replacement—to employee and employer alike that reduced the transaction and opportunity costs of employment. Thus, these institutions not only prepared children for labor but also promoted the use of child labor. Confession made not the least difference; Christian churches and church-affiliated institutions contributed to the spread of child labor beyond the household.

The emphasis on labor remained the same, whether proclaimed by Protestant or Catholic authorities, whether applied to the family or exercised in poor relief. Children were expected to labor as soon as they were physically capable. That labor was viewed as a good for two fundamental reasons: First, it contributed positively to the moral development of the individual; second, it contributed positively to the material success of the family or institution. Yet, neither all work nor all children are the same. Uncompensated labor, performed in the context of a family's household or enterprise, occupied a different social place and possessed a different moral valence—whether rightly or wrongly—from compensated labor, undertaken for the sake of one's own self-sufficiency. The former served as a preparation for the latter and was carried out for different ends and subject to different authorities. The child of four or five years who began to assist his or her parents in their work possessed different capacities from the child of fourteen or fifteen years who entered a stranger's workshop or household to labor at a trade. The definitions of "labor" and of "child" seem to have changed over the course of the early modern period.

The widespread assumption that children should and would labor, especially in the industrial context of early workhouses or orphanages, which had gone unchallenged through the sixteenth and seventeenth centuries, came under open attack in the so-called Orphanage Dispute, which spread across central Europe in the second half of the eighteenth century. Again, the role of Protestantism was contingent rather than constitutive. The dispute seems to have found its focus in Protestant polities and Protestant institutions, though Catholics were also affected. The lack of consistent records before the late eighteenth century—to say nothing of differences in local circumstance and policy—makes comparisons difficult, but such fragments as exist suggest that most of those institutions, charged with the care of parentless children, did little or nothing to ensure the present well-being or future self-sufficiency of their charges. There were notable exceptions to this observation, but the evidence seemed unequivocal and provoked a violent controversy. States and communities had responded to the growing number of impoverished, parentless children by founding centralized institutions often attached to manufactories, intended to be both cost-effective and socially useful. Because of the frequent confluence of conflicting functions, however, in which child care was combined with poor relief and criminal justice, these institutions placed children in very real danger. Their opponents pointed to a series of grave, widespread problems: high mortality; proximity to adult offenders; neglect of education; emphasis on heavy, deleterious industrial labor. Children were not allowed to be children; they were denied the proper setting and training. Scholars have yet to identify convincingly the sources for such supposedly new concepts of childhood as a biological phase and a social construct distinct from adulthood and requiring, therefore, its own particular circumstances, but most assume some affiliation with the novel ideas of Jean-Jacques Rousseau. Opponents of orphanages echoed his sentiments when they argued that these problems could best be resolved by closing such institutions and transferring the children wholesale to the care of foster families. These families would provide healthier environments, appropriate labor, regular education, and improved socialization, rendering their charges economically independent and socially integrated at less cost. These claims resulted in the widespread dissolution of orphanages and a general movement to fostering in the late eighteenth century.

The Protestant Reformation did little to alter child labor, largely contenting itself with advancing traditional arguments and practices under new legitimations. Changes in poor relief that coincided with the Reformation but were not limited to Protestantism had the effect, however, of moving child labor outside the household and workshop and associating it directly and publicly not merely with notions of industry but also with the goals of efficiency and cost-effectiveness. That the results resembled industrial exploitation before the Industrial Revolution—and prompted analogous calls for reform—comes as no surprise.

References and Further Reading

Denman, R.D., and Olive Jocelyn Dunlop. *English Apprenticeship and Child Labor: A History.* London: T.F. Unwin, 1912.

Gavitt, Philip. *Charity and Children in Renaissance Florence: The Ospedale degli Innocenti, 1410–1536.* Ann Arbor: University of Michigan Press, 1990.

Hufton, Olwen H. *The Poor of Eighteenth Century France: 1750–1789.* Oxford: Clarendon Press, 1974.

Hunecke, Volker. *Die Findelkinder von Mailand. Kindsaussetzung und aussetzende Eltern vom 17 bis zum 19. Jahrhundert.* Stuttgart: Klett-Cotta, 1987.

Safley, Thomas Max. *Charity and Economy in the Orphanages of Early Modern Augsburg.* Boston: Humanities Press, 1997.

Safley, Thomas Max. *Children of the Laboring Poor: Expectation and Experience Among the Orphans of Early Modern Augsburg.* Leiden: Brill Academic Publishers, 2005.

Sonenscher, Michael. *Work and Wages: Natural Law, Politics and the Eighteenth-Century French Trades.* Cambridge: Cambridge University Press, 1989.

Stier, Bernhard. *Fürsorge und Disziplinierung im Zeitalter des Absolutismus. Das Pforzheimer Zucht- und Waisenhaus und die badische Sozialpolitik im 18. Jahrhundert.* Sigmaringen: Thorbecke Verlag, 1988.

Sträter, Udo, and Josef N. Neumann, eds. *Waisenhäuser in der Frühen Neuzeit.* Stuttgart: Fritz Steiner Verlag, 2004.

Thompson, Edward P. *The Making of the English Working Class.* New York: Vintage Books, 1966.

Section 2. United Kingdom

History of Child Labor in Britain

Peter Kirby, PhD, Lecturer in Economic History, Department of History, University of Manchester

Britain was the first state to regard the industrial employment of children as a serious social problem. The growth of new industries that characterized the Industrial Revolution (ca. 1760–1850) led to unprecedented opportunities for child workers. Early government and private investigations into child labor tended to focus on occupations such as coal mining and factory work, in which children were thought to be at risk of exploitation or poor working conditions. For much of the twentieth century, moreover, historical discussions about child labor were overshadowed by a dispute over living standards during industrialization. Condemnation of child labor on moral grounds owed much to early works on the development of the factory, which portrayed living standards during industrialization as extremely poor, and historians of the Left argued that industrialization had led to the abuse of child workers on an unprecedented scale. Such approaches established children's employment as a socially negative aspect of British economic growth. Other historians took a more "optimistic" view of child labor, stressing that many of the views of the pessimists were based on a small number of examples of ill-treatment and poor conditions and, therefore, ignored the wider picture of children's employment. Although it has been common among historians to imply that child labor during British industrialization was concentrated in large industrial processes, the major surviving national statistics suggest that large industries were never the predominant site of child employment.

Numbers and Occupations

When the first large-scale information on occupations became available in the middle of the nineteenth century, only 30 percent of English and Welsh children ten to fourteen years of age were actually recorded as having a job. The employment of very young children was exceptional; fewer than 2 percent of five- to nine-year-old children were recorded with an occupation. Traditional forms of production remained dominant, and most working children were in agricultural, workshop, or domestic production: 52 percent of ten- to fourteen-year-old males were in agricultural, workshop, or handicraft occupations (compared with 15 percent in large factories), while 70 percent of females in the same age-group were employed in agriculture, handicrafts, or domestic service (compared with 24 percent in factories).

Agriculture was the single most important occupation for male children until the late nineteenth century and accounted for 35 percent of the total number of occupied male children between the ages of ten and fourteen. The scale of agricultural production remained small and, despite notable increases in productivity, by the mid-nineteenth century, a third of farmers did not employ any laborers and relied mainly on family labor. Between the late seventeenth and the mid-nineteenth century, in areas of the country that had undergone enclosure of land, enlargement of farms, and intensification of production, many of the older forms of labor contract (under which

Table 1

Occupations of Employed British Children Age 10–14, 1851 (in percent)

	England and Wales		Scotland	
	Males	Females	Males	Females
Agriculture, animals, and fisheries	34.6	21.6	33.3	28.7
Workshops and handicrafts	17.3	23.0	18.3	16.9
Factory	15.4	24.1	21.6	31.5
Transport and communications	11.4	1.1	7.5	1.1
Mines and quarries	8.8	0.8	8.7	0.1
Indefinite occupation	3.9	0.3	1.7	0.1
Building	3.1	0.0	1.9	0.0
Retail, foodstuffs, and hostelries	2.7	3.5	4.6	2.0
Domestic service	1.8	25.3	1.1	19.2
Professional, clerical, and local government	0.9	0.4	1.3	0.3
Armed forces	0.2	0.0	0.0	0.0

Source: Kirby 2003, table 3.1, p. 52.

working children would "live-in" with farmers' families) suffered substantial decline. There was a shift to greater reliance on adult "outdoor" wage labor, while the work of children became increasingly casualized. By the middle of the nineteenth century, although child employment in agriculture had fallen significantly, those children who remained had become wage laborers. In areas of intense production, such as East Anglia, menial field work such as weeding and spreading manure was frequently subcontracted to gangs of mixed child and female casual laborers under the direction of middlemen, or "gang masters." Such gangs, though relatively uncommon in the agrarian sector as a whole, offered the poorest pay, the longest hours, and the worst working conditions. Overall, there was a steady decline during the eighteenth and nineteenth centuries in the incidence of child labor in British agriculture.

Structural changes in British agriculture were crucial in releasing labor for the burgeoning workshop and handicraft sector of eighteenth- and nineteenth-century Britain. This diverse sector consisted mainly of small-scale domestic units in which small manufacturers (often male heads of household) found a ready labor supply among members of their own families. The family labor supply was bolstered by a population increase of more than 300 percent between 1750 and 1850, which resulted in a more youthful labor force. By the middle of the nineteenth century, the manufacturing sector remained reliant upon an enormous variety of small units of production. Even in the modern cotton-manufacturing sector, more than half of manufacturers employed fewer than twenty people, and a great deal of production was carried out on inexpensive hand-powered machinery. Among the most important employers of boys were shoemakers, silk workers, tailors, hose and stocking manufacturers, and blacksmiths, while the most common workshop employments for girls were silk workers, lace makers, straw plaiters, glovers, and hose and stocking manufacturers.

The workshop and handicraft sectors also contained the widest range of skill requirements, ranging from highly skilled crafts such as blacksmithing and engine making to largely unskilled occupations such as basket weaving and straw plaiting. Skilled apprenticeships had existed in law as far back as the later sixteenth century within the Statute of Artificers (1563), which laid down specific criteria under which apprenticeships were to be conducted. Among the statute's major provisions were a minimum term of training of seven years and the provision of a formal, legally binding contract (or "indenture") between the master and apprentice. Statutory regulation of apprenticeship came under attack by political economists during the later eighteenth and early nineteenth centuries. In an age of laissez-faire, formal statutory labor contracts seemed increasingly anachronistic and were antithetical to ideas about individual liberty. By 1814, the apprenticeship clauses were abolished by Parliament, and, thereafter, only highly skilled sectors were able to justify the continuation of formal indentured apprenticeships. By the middle of the nineteenth century, males had become much more prominent than females in the statistics of skilled occupations. During the Industrial Revolution, females tended to become concentrated in less-skilled areas, and by 1850 occupations such as factory textiles (especially cotton weaving) and domestic service were becoming increasingly common for girls. Given the limited occupational expectations imposed on women by an essentially patriarchal society, such occupations permitted females to maximize their earning capacity between adolescence and marriage.

One of the major features of traditional accounts of child labor during British industrialization is an emphasis on the employment of orphan apprentices in the early textiles factories. Although numerically few, these children often lived in the worst conditions, experienced the longest hours of work, and were placed at greater risk of accidents. Local parish authorities had a duty to care for orphans, but some of them were anxious to bind such children as unskilled apprentices at early ages in order to relieve the parish of the financial burden of support. A pauper child might cost four pounds a year to support in a workhouse, but could be bound permanently to an outside worker by the provision of a set of clothes and a one-off premium paid to the new master. The binding of pauper children became more intense from the second half of the eighteenth century, at a time when population increase and rising rural poverty increased the financial burden on parishes. Some London parishes bound in excess of 90 percent of their pauper apprentices outside of the parish, and between the 1760s and 1811, the number of London children apprenticed more than doubled. Parish apprentices featured prominently in contemporary accounts of ill-treatment and dangerous working conditions. On completion of their terms of apprenticeship, pauper children often had to compete for employment with the children of operatives, and many would be forced to seek employment elsewhere. One contemporary observed in 1817 that very few girls were kept on when their terms of apprenticeship expired, "but too often, such truly unfortunate young Women, disperse themselves over the Country . . . and at no distant periods, are passed home to Parishes they were apprenticed in" (quoted in Pinchbeck 1930, 183–84). The practice of binding parish children to factory work declined during the first two decades of the nineteenth century, partly due to a shift toward urban manufacture (which removed the labor-supply problems associated with remote rural water-powered mills) and partly due to rising living standards, which meant that the costs of keeping apprentices rose considerably. From the 1830s, the English Poor Law authorities became increasingly hostile to the principle of parish apprenticeships, and by the 1840s the system survived in only a few districts.

Urban Child Labor

One of the major features of the Industrial Revolution period in Britain was the rapid rate of urbanization. By 1851, the English urban population outnumbered rural dwellers. Urbanization has traditionally been seen as intensifying many of the problems of child workers. Works of Henry Mayhew and others on the London labor market, for example, discuss the working conditions of chimney sweeps, crossing sweepers, and child street traders. Recent research has suggested that the incidence of child labor in the major conurbations was actually exceedingly low compared with that in the rest of the country. In London, for example, employment of both boys and girls in the ten-to-fourteen age-group was about half that in the rest of England and Wales. Large conurbations also contained higher levels of casual child employment, with portering and errand running forming 45 percent of occupied males from age ten to age fourteen. Domestic service accounted for nearly 60 percent of female employment in the same age-group. Hence, prospects for urban children obtaining employment that might lead to a "proper" adult job declined substantially throughout the nineteenth century, and by the end of the century, child employment in urban districts had become heavily concentrated in menial occupations. While the employment of females in domestic service increased substantially in the latter part of the nineteenth century, the prospects for skilled employment among urban boys continued to decline, leading to a perceived "boy labour problem," which preoccupied social commentators toward the close of the nineteenth century—by which time 54 percent of London male school leavers became "errand boys, shop boys, or van boys" and three quarters of Glaswegian male school leavers entered into unskilled jobs (Tawney 1909).

The Industrial Revolution was founded upon the growth of overseas trade and the spread of textiles manufacture, as well as the expansion of the coal industry. A major feature in the development of eighteenth- and nineteenth-century urban society was the growth of major manufacturing centers and trading ports of the north of England. Compared with other areas of employment, child labor in these sectors was relatively small. For example, the number of boys occupied in coal and cotton combined in 1841 was estimated to be around 86,000, compared with 187,000 in agriculture and domestic service. Nonetheless, the new industrial sectors tended to attract child labor rather rapidly, and children formed a highly visible part of the new, more centralized, factory and mine labor force. In textiles, during the late eighteenth century, domestic spinning was giving way to factory spinning. Though the decline of domestic spinning resulted in some unemployment among women and children, the growing complexity and labor intensity of the new spinning factories multiplied the opportunities for children to work alongside adult operatives in ancillary tasks such as carding, piecing, and scavenging. In 1816, only 18 percent of the cotton labor force were adult males. Factory work was not susceptible to seasonal influences or poor weather, and its low labor intensity relative to agriculture made it popular among parents seeking work for their children.

The coal industry also recruited children in large numbers and employed them in specific tasks: chiefly underground haulage and ventilation work (underground trapdoor operators), as well as sorting coal at the pit bank. It has been estimated that child workers in the coalfields of the early 1840s formed about 10 to 13 percent of the mining labor force (approximately 15,000–20,000 children). Historians long thought that technological advancement in coal mining during the first half of the nineteenth century had led to an increase in the proportions of employed children, but subsequent research has proven that coal districts using more primitive technologies employed the largest proportions of children.

The textiles and coal-mining industries both came under legislative scrutiny in the early nineteenth century. By 1833, the first major factory act sought to regulate child factory labor, though it is doubtful whether the act was very successful, and it has even been suggested that the numbers of children in factories increased in the decades after the legislation was passed. The Coal Mines Act of 1842 was hampered by similar problems of implementation. The failure of legislation to be implemented effectively has led historians to explain the later decline of child labor in industrial employments in terms of technological change and rising real incomes. In cotton spinning, there was initial heavy demand for children in picking and carding in the late eighteenth century. This was followed by mechanization of many preparatory processes, and it is thought that by the 1830s, most children had become concentrated in menial piecing jobs, which declined in importance as spinning machinery became more reliable and produced fewer broken threads. It is far from clear whether improvements in machinery actually did lead to a decline in the numbers of children required to work with mule spinners, because employment statistics drawn from factory inspectors' reports are notoriously difficult to interpret.

Poverty

Orthodox historical accounts of child labor in Britain have tended to focus almost exclusively on changes in demand for child labor from various production sectors, and have overlooked the importance of wider social and demographic factors. Between 1750 and 1851, the number of persons in England and Wales increased from about 5.8 million to 16.7 million, and in Scotland from 1.2 million to 2.9 million. These major changes in the size of the population in the eighteenth and nineteenth centuries resulted in a much more youthful age structure, higher levels of child dependency, and worsening household poverty. In 1661, the children represented 29 percent of the population as a whole, but by 1821 that proportion had risen to 39 percent. These factors certainly affected parents' decisions about whether or not to send their children to work. Poor families living on a subsistence income were often forced into exploiting the labor of their own children. The children of single-parent households, especially, were prone to being put to work at early ages in order for their families to gain from their marginal earnings (the offspring of widows, especially, were susceptible to early working). Hence, child labor during the Industrial Revolution can be interpreted as a systemic problem of poverty that was intensified by structured child dependency.

Public policy changes also influenced the likelihood that children would work. The deteriorating economic situation in the later eighteenth century intensified problems of poverty, particularly in rural districts where only limited welfare payments were available. The later reform of the English Poor Law in 1834 further intensified poverty by aiming to remove the right to welfare payments from adults who were physically able to perform work. These policies led to greater labor-market participation among children from poor families.

Conclusion

The extent of child labor during the British Industrial Revolution was a product of growing demand from industrial sectors, unfavorable demographic conditions, and the relative poverty of families. Most child labor was concentrated in the ten- to fifteen-year-old age-group, while the employment of very young children was associated with only the very poorest, such as single-parent households and children in the care of local welfare agencies. Even at the high point of the Industrial Revolution, most child laborers worked in "traditional" sectors (agriculture, small-scale workshop manufacture, and a variety of services). The labor of children was valued in early textile mills and in coal mining, but demand from large industries was short-lived as increasingly complex industrial workplaces, changes in industrial location, and rising real wages led progressively to a falling demand for child labor in the British economy as a whole.

References and Further Reading

Cunningham, Hugh. "The Employment and Unemployment of Children in England c.1680–1851." *Past and Present* 126 (1990): 115–50.

Cunningham, Hugh. "Combating Child Labour: The British Experience." In *Child Labour in Historical Perspective, 1800–1985: Case Studies from Europe, Japan and Colombia,* ed. H. Cunningham and P.P. Viazzo, 41–56. Florence: UNICEF, 1996.

Hair, Paul. "Children in Society, 1850–1980." In *Population and Society in Britain, 1850–1980,* ed. T. Barker and M. Drake, 34–61. New York: New York University Press, 1982.

Hopkins, Eric. *Childhood Transformed: Working-Class Children in Nineteenth-Century England.* Manchester: Manchester University Press, 1994.

Horn, Pamela. *Children's Work and Welfare, 1780–1880s.* Cambridge: Cambridge University Press, 1995.

Horrell, Sara, and Jane Humphries. "'The Exploitation of Little Children': Child Labor and the Family Economy in the Industrial Revolution." *Explorations in Economic History* 32:4 (1995): 485–516.

Kirby, Peter. *Child Labour in Britain, 1750–1870.* London: Palgrave Macmillan, 2003.

Kirby, Peter. "A Brief Statistical Sketch of the Child Labour Market in Mid-Nineteenth Century London." *Continuity and Change* 20:2 (2005a): 229–45.

Kirby, Peter. "How Many Children Were 'Unemployed' in Eighteenth and Nineteenth-Century England?" *Past and Present* 187 (2005b): 187–202.

Nardinelli, Clark. *Child Labor and the Industrial Revolution.* Bloomington: Indiana University Press, 1990.

Pinchbeck, Ivy. *Women Workers and the Industrial Revolution, 1750–1850.* London: G. Routledge and Sons, 1930.

Rose, Mary B. "Social Policy and Business: Parish Apprenticeship and the Early Factory System, 1750–1834." *Business History* 31:4 (1989): 5–32.

Tawney, Richard H. "The Economics of Boy Labour." *Economic Journal* 19 (1909): 517–37.

Pauper Apprenticeship in England

Alysa Levene, PhD, Senior Lecturer in Early Modern History, Oxford Brookes University

Pauper children formed a specific subsection of the wider apprentice group in England: They were bound out by the parish or a charity rather than their families. Pauper apprentices had come under the authority of another body because of their poverty, although many had parents who were still living. Similarly, many privately bound children came from quite poor families, but the two groups are considered very different from each other in significant regards. This has perpetuated a dichotomy between private and pauper apprenticeship that is perhaps overdrawn, particularly at the lower social levels. There has also been a focus in the literature on the eighteenth and nineteenth centuries at the expense of earlier periods. Nonetheless, there are some long-standing distinctions between pauper and private apprentices that made their work prospects, supervision, and legal framework distinctive, especially over the period up to the passing of the Poor Law Amendment Act in 1834.

One of the most important distinctions was the supporting legal background. Parish and charity officials responsible for apprenticing pauper children were, like parents, bound by the terms of the 1563 Statute of Artificers. They had the same requirements to draw up properly stamped and witnessed indentures. Parish officials were further guided by the late Tudor and Elizabethan vagrancy and poor laws, which empowered them to put poor or vagrant children of both sexes to work, against both the parents' and the master's wishes if necessary (George 1965; Snell 1985; Lane 1996; Slack 1990). Although it is unclear how often these powers were invoked where either party was unwilling, they brought an aspect of social control into pauper apprenticeship, which could be contentious (Hindle 2004). Further legal provisions were added to the corpus of apprenticeship law over time; for example, the eighteenth century gave apprentices some recourse in cases of bad treatment, while the 1802 Health and Morals of Apprentices Act and the 1816 Factory Act laid down (largely unsupervised) minimum standards for factory conditions for London paupers (Lane 1996).

The aims of pauper apprenticeship were to provide training, employment, and social stability for poor children. Apprenticeship also gave the individual legal rights to poor relief in the future; serving even part of an indentured term granted a settlement in the parish. Some historians have highlighted how parish officials could be eager to bind pauper apprentices to masters and mistresses in other parishes, to avoid this ongoing responsibility (Dunlop and Denman 1912; George 1965). The settlement aspect of pauper apprenticeship was so important, however, that it may have helped keep the institution alive longer than its private equivalent, which seems to have been dying off by the mid-eighteenth century (Snell 1985; Dunlop and Denman 1912). Apprenticing pauper children was also cheaper than keeping them in a workhouse, which may have contributed to their young average age at binding: approximately twelve years old rather than the more usual thirteen to fourteen for privately bound apprentices (Levene 2007; Snell 1985). It is also a distinctive feature of the system that girls were bound out as frequently as boys, probably to give them a settlement and to ensure respectable employment (Snell 1985; Levene 2007; Simonton 1991). Pauper children bound either by parishes or by charities such as the London Foundling Hospital tended, however, to be priced out of the most desirable occupations by high premiums, and are generally characterized as supplying a workforce for impoverished and overstocked trades such as stocking making, watchmaking, and later, chimney sweeping and factory manufacture (Lane 1996; George 1965; Rose 1989; Levene 2007). They also rarely engaged with the mechanisms of city companies or the freedoms of the city, since they were often younger than the terms of those companies allowed, and frequently worked outside the boundaries of the old cities.

Local studies of pauper apprenticeship have largely confirmed these broad characterizations of employment type, but have highlighted that it was not uniformly accurate. Pauper apprentices served in a wide range of geographically distinctive trades and manufactures. Children in Birmingham and Manchester, for example, rarely traveled to factory employment elsewhere, instead serving the needs of local, often small-scale industry such as carpet making or metalworking. Smaller towns and rural areas frequently placed their pauper children with local masters, although those in the Midlands and the industrialized northwest took advantage of local industry to place children in factories (Honeyman 2007; Lane 1996; Crompton 1997; Sharpe 1991). Similarly, London's pauper apprentices went into local, small-unit manufacture at least as frequently as to northern textile mills (Levene 2007; Honeyman 2007). The geographical mobility of large groups of pauper apprentices, particularly to late-eighteenth- and early-nineteenth-century water-powered textile mills, has been one of the most frequently mentioned aspects in the literature (Lane 1996; George 1965). The likelihood of a child being assigned to a particular trade or location, however, probably depended on the inclinations and opportunities of different parish officials, and also on the state of local employment. Some towns provided a vibrant enough labor market that parish and charity officials did not need to place their children far from home; others did not.

Although the dominance of pauper child factory labor may have been overstressed in the literature, it cannot be denied that it was a feature of early industrialization. Factory owners were often eager to take on pauper children since they were easily transportable and relatively cheap, and might not have family nearby to interfere with hours and conditions of work. Parishes from many cities and rural areas entered into agreements with factory industrialists, which accounted for large numbers of children. Some London parishes such as St. Pancras, St. Clement Danes, and St. Leonard Shoreditch sent hundreds of children to Lancashire and Yorkshire from the late eighteenth century through the early nineteenth century, supporting the growth of several factories (Levene 2007; Rose 1989; Honeyman 2007). Other parishes did not engage in this sort of placement, either because they had an existing network of employment opportunities, or because they feared that it was not good for the children's health and prospects (Rose 1989; Levene 2007).

Poor work conditions have featured heavily in the literature on children's work and industrialization, although the main nineteenth-century campaign to reform factory labor was focused on waged children rather than apprentices. The 1816 Factory Act set out minimum ages for pauper apprentices, and maximum distances they could be sent to masters, which should have, at least theoretically, curtailed some of the most exploitative aspects of their employment (Lane 1996; Dunlop and Denman 1912). Factories were not unique in offering opportunities for exploitation, however, although one author has suggested that pauper factory apprentices may have been particularly vulnerable to corporal punishment since they had no waged incentive to increase their productivity (Nardinelli 1982). This might also hold true for apprentices in nonfactory trade and manufacture, however, sometimes exacerbated by lax supervision by parish and charity officials, the poor state of many trades used for pauper apprentices, and their particularly young age at binding. Pauper apprentices do appear in court records in cases of mistreatment, and in cases brought by masters for bad behavior (George 1965). Detailed research has suggested that some parishes and charities were relatively assiduous at checking on their children's situations; however, others were undoubtedly neglectful (Honeyman 2007). Expectations for training and prospects are particularly difficult to establish for pauper apprentices, as their indentures often failed to specify exactly what they were to learn. This was particularly true for girls, who might be more likely to be trained in domestic service by the master's wife than in the master's own trade (Levene 2007). The types of trades pauper apprentices were bound to did not necessarily bring many opportunities for advancement: An eighteenth-century manual of trades disparaged apprenticeships in retail, for example, which was a common source of employment for poor children (Campbell 1969 [1747]). The young average age at binding makes it unlikely that these children were assigned to very skilled tasks, at least initially, but they were expected to be able to earn their own living by the end of their term. As with privately bound apprentices, little is known of completion rates or final occupational profiles.

Pauper apprentices thus formed a distinctive subgroup of the wider class, especially with regard to their legal framework, and the greater likelihood that they would be bound to poor trades with little supervision. Recent work, however, has highlighted the variation among pauper apprentices, and stresses that some may have been little different from the lower tiers of privately bound children. Some officials were careful in their choice of placements, and took the supervision of their children seriously. Many also followed local and individual priorities in choosing the location and typology of apprenticeships, making pauper apprentices as a group more varied than was previously assumed.

References and Further Reading

Andrew, Donna. *Philanthropy and Police: London Charity in the Eighteenth Century.* Princeton, NJ: Princeton University Press, 1989.

Campbell, R. *The London Tradesman.* Newton Abbot: David and Charles, 1969 [1747].

Crompton, Frank. *Workhouse Children: Infant and Child Paupers Under the Worcestershire Poor Law, 1780–1871.* Stroud: Sutton, 1997.

Cunningham, Hugh. *The Children of the Poor: Representations of Childhood Since the Seventeenth Century.* Oxford: Blackwell, 1991.

Dunlop, J., and R.D. Denman. *English Apprenticeship and Child Labour: A History.* London: T.F. Unwin, 1912.

George, M. Dorothy. *London Life in the Eighteenth Century.* Harmondsworth: Penguin, 1965.

Hindle, Steve. "'Waste' Children? Pauper Apprenticeship Under the Elizabethan Poor Laws, c. 1598–1697." In *Women, Work and Wages in England, 1600–1850,* ed. P. Lane, N. Raven, and K.D.M. Snell, 15–46. Woodbridge: Boydell Press, 2004.

Honeyman, Katrina. *Child Workers in England, 1780–1820: Parish Apprentices and the Making of the Early Industrial Labour Force.* Aldershot: Ashgate, 2007.

Lane, Joan. *Apprenticeship in England, 1600–1914.* London: UCL Press, 1996.

Levene, Alysa. "Pauper Apprenticeship and the Old Poor Law in London: Feeding the Industrial Economy?" Paper presented at the Annual Conference of the Economic History Society, University of Exeter, Devon, UK, March 30–April 1, 2007.

Nardinelli, Clark. "Corporal Punishment and Children's Wages in Nineteenth-Century Britain." *Explorations in Economic History* 19 (1982): 283–95.

Rose, M.B. "Social Policy and Business: Parish Apprenticeship and the Early Factory System, 1750–1834." *Business History* 31:4 (1989): 5–32.

Sharpe, Pamela. "Poor Children as Apprentices in Colyton, 1598–1830." *Continuity and Change* 6:2 (1991): 253–70.

Simonton, Deborah. "Apprenticeship: Training and Gender in Eighteenth-Century England." In *Markets and Manufacture in Early Industrial Europe,* ed. Maxine Berg, 227–58. London: Routledge, 1991.

Slack, Paul. *The English Poor Law, 1531–1782.* Basingstoke: Palgrave Macmillan, 1990.

Snell, K.D.M. *Annals of the Labouring Poor: Social Change and Agrarian England, 1660–1900.* Cambridge: Cambridge University Press, 1985.

History of Child Labor in Coal Mining in Britain

Peter Kirby, PhD, Lecturer in Economic History, Department of History, University of Manchester

The employment of children in British coal mines has long been an iconic symbol of the worst social effects of early industrial capitalism. The image of the exploited coal-mining child looms large in the historical imagination. Anecdotal accounts of small children working underground in narrow coal seams while suffering physical abuse at the hands of cruel masters support a general perception that the employment of children underground was an unqualified social evil. Popular historical accounts of social conditions during the Industrial Revolution treat coal-mining children as the subjects of an innately abusive environment, and evidence drawn from contemporary social commentary—the reports of government inquiries—supports a profoundly pessimistic viewpoint. By contrast, the social and economic context of child labor in coal mines still remains largely overlooked as a subject of serious historical research.

Children had worked in connection with coal mining for almost as long as records exist. The increased output of coal during the Industrial Revolution, however, led to a growth in the size of collieries and a larger proportion of the population working in coal mining. State interest in the conditions of child workers in British coal mining began in earnest in 1840 when the Children's Employment Commission investigated reports from the factory inspectors about poor underground working conditions. The commission was set up at the behest of the prominent philanthropist Lord Ashley. Four commissioners and eighteen district subcommissioners were appointed, and the final report of the commission, together with its appendixes, was published in 1842. The evidence of the commission remains the preeminent source on the employment of children in nineteenth-century coal mining. The report focused on three main themes: the early ages at which children were employed, the working conditions of child workers, and the moral dangers that were presumed to arise from the employment of women and children underground.

Ages, Conditions, and Moral Dangers

It has been common for historians to claim that coal-mining children commenced work at very early ages, but contemporary survey evidence suggests that they commenced at about the same ages as children in other occupations. A sample of people in several occupations (coal mining, farming, pottery, and worsted factories) taken in 1841 showed an average age at starting work of 8.86 years, while miners commenced at 8.61 years. Most children in the nineteenth-century British coal-mining industry worked in the underground haulage sector. They carried or dragged baskets or boxes of coal or pushed wheeled trolleys along the underground levels, from where the coal had been cut from the face by the adult miners, to the shaft from whence it would be transported to the surface. A lesser number of much younger children worked as trapdoor operators: These were concentrated in the technologically more advanced coal districts, where the workings were more extensive and where ventilation systems were necessary to purge the mines of the explosive and poisonous gases that tended to accumulate in the workings. Some children were also employed in ancillary work such as carrying water and leading horses. Most of the children employed belowground in British coal mines were boys, though there was a significant minority of young girls working in some coal districts (notably in Lancashire, West Yorkshire, and parts of Scotland).

The process of coal production had an important effect on the proportions of children employed, and also on the types of work that children performed. The large increases in coal production that fueled the Industrial Revolution were achieved by the employment of more adult male miners at the face, and more children in haulage (where most children were employed), and by advances in underground transportation. Almost all substantial improvements in coal production in the nineteenth century occurred in the underground haulage sector, mainly through the increased use of rails and horse-drawn trolleys, as well as more efficient machine haulage. However, not all coal districts employed new technology. In West Yorkshire and in parts of Lancashire, where coal seams were thin, the use of many forms of underground mechanical conveyance was impractical, and haulage was only possible by the employment of small children as underground haulers. By contrast, where thicker seams existed, coal could be removed from the coal face more quickly and efficiently because a greater roof space enabled more efficient haulage technology and allowed physically larger workers to gain access to the seams of coal. In the northeast, for example, where seams might average between four and five feet, underground haulage was performed by older workers and by pit ponies. Improvements in haulage technology led to a relative decline in the proportions of employed children in the haulage sector. In districts such as Durham, especially, ponies were increasingly substituted for children at the coal face. This meant that there were profound differences in the age structure of the industry in different districts. In the advanced districts of Northumberland and North Durham, only 13 percent of the labor force in 1841 were below thirteen years of age, while in a sample of primitive small pits in West Yorkshire the comparable figure was 25 percent. Hence, low levels of technological development in mining tended to harbor a larger proportion of child workers. There was also a close relationship between the degree of capital investment and technological advancement in coal districts and the ages at which children started work. In the haulage sector, the average age at starting work in advanced collieries in the northeast of England was nearly eleven, while, by comparison, children in the relatively primitive Yorkshire coal district commenced at just over eight years.

The second-most common child occupation in nineteenth-century coal mining involved the operation of underground trapdoors. With the opening of more extensive collieries in the early nineteenth century, previously inaccessible seams were brought into production. The larger and more extensive coal workings were at greater risk of accidents as a result of accumulations of explosive methane gas (known as "fire-damp") or a suffocating mixture of carbon dioxide and nitrogen (known as "choke-damp"). These dangers were countered by complex methods of purging dangerous gases from the mines. Underground haulage roads were stopped by trapdoors manned by children; these trapdoors, when opened, would allow the passage of coal tubs, but they needed to be closed immediately afterward to maintain the direction of the ventilation currents. Despite the simplicity of their work, the young "trappers" were charged with a huge responsibility for safety. Trappers would sometimes leave their doors ajar, or fall asleep in the warm, dark atmosphere of the mine, and fail to attend their doors: This sometimes led to explosions. By the third and fourth decades of the nineteenth century, a general perception had emerged among northeast managers that inattentive younger children were responsible for pit explosions, and many coal-mine managers and engineers campaigned for the exclusion of very young children from ventilation operations on the grounds of safety.

A further problem identified by the commission of 1842 was that of moral decline among the mining population. It was argued that the employment of women and children in a brutalizing underground environment led to sexual immorality. The pages of the Children's Employment Commission report contain many references to illicit sexual intercourse among miners, as well as numerous illustrations of male miners working naked underground. The alleged instances of underground impropriety added support to calls for legislation to prohibit the employment of women and young children underground. Lord Ashley stated in a speech in the House of Lords that young female coal miners "commonly work quite naked down to the waist, and are dressed—as far as they are dressed at all—in a loose pair of trousers . . . In many of the collieries the adult colliers, whom these girls serve, work perfectly naked." There were vociferous protests at the time from miners and colliery managers who doubted the veracity of such evidence and argued that the miners' lack of clothing resulted not from any decline in moral standards but from the effects of much higher temperatures generally experienced when working underground at the coal face.

The Report of the Children's Employment Commission of 1842 formed the basis for the first and most important legislative reform of child labor in coal mining. The Mines Act of the same year prohibited the employment underground of all females and of boys below the age of ten years. The Act excluded the youngest and least reliable workers, especially the young "trappers" working in ventilation systems. Hence, the most important effect of the Act was almost certainly to reduce the incidence of mine explosions caused by an interruption of underground ventilation. The Act was never properly implemented on a national scale however: only a single inspector was appointed to inspect all British and Irish mines and there is no evidence to suggest that the Inspector ever entered a coal mine. The state budget for mines inspection was also very small and the legislation failed to give powers to magistrates to summon witnesses in prosecutions under the Act: it was therefore almost impossible to enforce the legislation effectively. Nineteenth-century legislation (in 1850, 1855, 1860, and 1862) attempted further regulation with regard to coal-mine safety, but largely overlooked the issue of child labor.

Conclusion

There was a decline in the proportion of very young children employed in coal mining in the first half of the nineteenth century. This was due primarily to an increase in the efficiency of underground haulage systems, and by the desire to improve underground safety. Attempts by the state to regulate child labor in mines were successful only where it was in the interests of employers to enforce the legislation. Marginal coal districts were afforded virtual immunity from inspection or prosecution under the Coal Mines Act, and, apart from some minor clauses regarding the ages at which young people could operate winding machinery, the Act failed to deal adequately with the harsh working conditions complained of in government inquiries. It remained legal for children aged ten to work underground until the 1870s.

References and Further Reading

Benson, John. *British Coalminers in the Nineteenth Century: A Social History.* Dublin: Gill and Macmillan, 1980.

Church, Roy. *The History of the British Coal Industry, Vol. 3, 1830–1913, Victorian Pre-Eminence.* Oxford: Clarendon Press, 1986.

Commission for Inquiring into the Employment and Condition of Children in Mines and Manufactories, First Report of the Commissioners (P.P. 1842, XV); *Appendix to First Report of the Commissioners, Part I* (P.P. 1842, XVI); *Appendix to First Report of the Commissioners, Part II* (P.P. 1842, XVII).

Cooper, Anthony Ashley. *Speeches of the Earl of Shaftesbury upon Subjects Relating to the Claims and Interests of the Labouring Class.* London: Chapman and Hall, 1868 (repr.; Shannon: Irish University Press, 1971).

Hair, Paul Edward Hedley. *The Social History of the British Coalminers, 1800–1845.* Oxford DPhil thesis, Oxford, 1955.

Heeson, Alan. "The Coal Mines Act of 1842, Social Reform, and Social Control." *Historical Journal* 24:1 (1981): 69–88.

Heeson, Alan. "The Northern Coal-Owners and the Opposition to the Coal Mines Act of 1842." *International Review of Social History* 25 (1980).

Kirby, Peter. "The Historic Viability of Child Labour and the Mines Act of 1842." In *A Thing of the Past? Child Labour in Britain in the Nineteenth and Twentieth Centuries,* ed. M. Lavalette. Liverpool: Liverpool University Press, 1999.

Kirby, Peter. *Aspects of the Employment of Children in the British Coalmining Industry, 1800–1872.* PhD thesis, Sheffield, 1995.

Lewis, Brian. *Coal Mining in the Eighteenth and Nineteenth Centuries.* Harlow: Longman, 1971.

MacDonagh, O. "Coal Mines Regulation, the First Decade, 1842–1852." In *Ideas and Institutions of Victorian Britain: Essays in Honour of George Kitson Clark,* ed. R. Robson. London: Bell, 1967.

Taylor, Arthur J. "Labour Productivity and Technological Innovation in the British Coal Industry, 1850–1914." *Economic History Review* 14:1 (1961): 48–70.

Tuttle, Carolyn. *Hard at Work in Factories and Mines: The Economics of Child Labor During the British Industrial Revolution.* Boulder, CO: Westview Press, 1999.

Child Labor in the United Kingdom—Textiles

Carolyn Tuttle, Betty Jane Shultz Hollender Professor of Economics, Lake Forest College

Child labor did not begin in the textile industry of Great Britain, but it has become the symbol of Great Britain's Industrial Revolution. Nearly every scholar of child labor has familiarized him- or herself with the extensive employment of children in the cotton textile mills during the British Industrial Revolution. Although children had been working for centuries, this was the first time children worked in the formal sector and were hired as independent laborers. Unlike for their work in the home, on the farm, or in cottage industry, children signed contracts, worked set hours, and were supervised by a stranger. The nature of child labor changed dramatically, as did the significance of their contribution. On the farm, in the home, and even in many cottage industries, the family worked together to maximize production and income. In the factory, many children worked apart from their families. They worked with other children and were pushed by an overseer to maximize production. Their pay, however small, usually made up one-third of the family's income and often meant the difference between survival and starvation. Therefore, this symbol—the factory child—reflected a new, highly visible contributor to the family and the economy.

The changes in child labor that occurred in the textile industry during the British Industrial Revolution created quite a controversy among politicians, industrialists, leaders of the Factory Movement, humanitarians, and families. Those who opposed these changes believed that child labor in the textile mills of Great Britain symbolized the evil consequences of industrialization. The debate is still unsettled and the legacy of child labor in textile factories lives on in many developing countries in the twenty-first century.

Child Labor Debate

Opposition between the views of the "Pessimists" and those of the "Optimists" on the plight of child labor began as a debate on the floor of Parliament in 1802 and continues today. Although the debate started over how many hours children should work, it has continued to the present day over whether conditions in the factories were actually worse than they were in the home or on the farm. Contemporary writers of the eighteenth century such as Charles Dickens, Elizabeth Gaskell, and Frances Trollope wrote about horrible living and working conditions of poor and working-class children in their novels. The term "dark Satanic mills" was introduced by H.J. Hobsbawn and was subsequently used by the Pessimists to depict the exploitation of children. Pessimists such as Leonard Horner (1840), Karl Marx (1909), E.P. Thompson (1966), and Arnold Toynbee (1884) decried the exploitation of children hired as young as five and six years of age to work twelve to sixteen hours a day, six days a week, without a break for meals. Children toiled in hot, stuffy factories breathing in the cotton flue that hung in the air, to earn as little as four shillings each. To substantiate these claims, sympathizers in Parliament established a commission to collect evidence from the textile factories. The Factory Commission produced the "The Blue Books," or "Sadler Reports," by interviewing children, parents, overseers, factory owners, and doctors on the conditions of employment in textile factories. Testimony revealed a considerable amount of abuse: Children were beaten, had their ears torn off, and were kicked if they talked, fell asleep, or were too slow.

In contrast, Optimists claimed that the Pessimists exaggerated the extent and conditions under which children worked. Optimists (Ashton 1948; Hammond and Hammond 1920; Ure 1835) believed that "The Blue Books" were biased because they had been prepared by members of Parliament who were in favor of passing prohibitive child labor legislation. Rather than represent the "typical case," they argued that factory inspectors focused on the worst examples of abuses to make the strongest case for Parliament. Optimists believed that working conditions in the factories were no worse than those that had existed for centuries in the home and that wages were much better. The only consensus between Optimists and Pessimists was the acknowledgment that large numbers of children did work in the textile mills during the British Industrial Revolution.

The Rise and Fall of Child Labor in Textiles

The textile industry was the leading industry of the British Industrial Revolution. Children were employed in cotton, wool, worsted, flax, and silk factories located in the northern cities of Manchester, Bolton, Lancashire, and Bradford. Cotton dominated the industry beginning in 1815, and the cotton mill became the preeminent model of the factory system. Most of the technological innovation in spinning and weaving first occurred in cotton, and then spread to other textiles. Many scholars believe it was these innovations, Arkwright's water frame, Robert's self-acting mule, and Cartwright's power loom, that increased the employment of children. The fact that hundreds of thousands of children worked in the British textile mills from 1816 to 1870 has been well documented in the literature (Chapman 1904; Kirby 2003; Nardinelli 1990; Tuttle 1999). Freudenberger, Mather, and Nardinelli (1984) found that more than half of the labor force in cotton factories in 1818 consisted of children under nineteen years of age. In 1833, "[T]here were, for example, 4,000 children in the mills in Manchester, 1,600 in Stockport, 1,500 in Bolton and 1,300 in Hyde" (Cruickshank 1981, 51). Nardinelli (1990) gives aggregate figures for the number of children employed in textile mills in 1835 at 56,000 and 1838 at 33,000. Using factory inspectors' reports from 1835 to 1850, Tuttle (1999) shows that children under the age of eighteen comprised close to 50 percent of the workforce in cotton, wool, worsted, flax, and silk mills. Kirby (2003) identifies "factory" as the second-most popular occupation in 1851 for children from age ten to age fourteen, with 15.4 percent of males and 24.1 percent of females working in textile factories despite years of prohibitive child labor laws. Overall, the employment of children increased from 1818 through 1833, with a peak sometime between 1835 and 1840, after which the number of children in textile factories declined. The use of child labor in British textile factories, however, did not totally disappear. Chapman shows that in 1870 still 15 percent of the workforces in cotton factories were children under the age of eighteen.

The Jobs Children Performed

Many industrialists and overseers felt that the employment of children was necessary to the efficient operation of their factories. When asked how a reduction in hours to ten would impact his mill, Peter Gaskell replied, "This economy consists of a series of operations which the child performs an essential part. There is mutual dependence of the entire labourers one upon the other, and if the children who are employed principally by the spinner are dismissed, his work ceases, and the mill is at a stand still" (1836, 168). Children were employed in textile factories as both assistants and primary operatives. In the process of spinning, small children were "piecers," "sweepers," and "doffers." All three worked on the water frame and common mule, the piecers using their tiny, nimble fingers to tie knots when the thread broke and the sweepers picking up the waste cotton flue under the machine. Doffers were typically young boys who replaced full bobbins with empty ones all day long. The machines reduced the number of skilled workers necessary and increased the number of assistants. In the woolen industry, small children who filled these jobs were called "pieceners," "cleaners," and "fillers." Once the mule was automated (powered by steam), older children replaced adults as "spinners" and "minders" on the water frame and self-actor. The same substitution of children for adults occurred in the process of weaving. The old hand loom required strength and skill to operate, but the new power loom did not. Consequently, older children became "weavers" in cotton mills and "winders" and "warpers" in wool mills.

Children performed these tasks ten to twelve hours a day, six days a week. Most of the jobs, except for sweepers, required children to stand on their feet all day. As the spinning and weaving machines were perfected, children had to work faster and faster to keep up. There were no safety apparatuses on the machines, so accidents were not uncommon. There is a plethora of testimony in "The Blue Books" of children losing fingers, hands, and hair while working in textile mills. There is also testimony by doctors who examined the mill children and found some of them suffering from knock-knees, curved spines, respiratory illnesses, and malnutrition. Critics of the factory system argued that these ailments were the result of the poor working conditions inside the factory and the fact that children never saw the light of day during their childhood. Supporters, however, believed that these illnesses were merely the result of growing up poor.

Conclusion: The Importance of Child Labor in Textiles

During the British Industrial Revolution, children toiled away their childhoods in textile factories. There is still considerable debate about the conditions in the factories relative to cottage industries, but there is consensus that child labor contributed much to the success of the textile industry. From the initial small wooden mills in rural villages near rivers to the large brick factories in urban centers, children comprised from one-third to one-half of the factories' workforce. In a few exceptional cases, children made up the entire workforce, except for a few female or male supervisors. It was no secret that hundreds of thousands of children toiled over spinning frames and weaving machines for ten to twelve hours a day, six days a week, for wages that were roughly one-third an adult male's wage. Most poor and working-class parents felt that they had no choice but to send their sons and daughters to work, and factory owners were eager to hire children because they were cheaper and more docile than adults. The rest of society was more conflicted about this new industrial workforce. The Optimists were convinced that this work was good for the children (prevented idleness), their families (supplemented income), and the country (increased competitiveness). The Pessimists, however, argued that the physical and intellectual costs of employing (and not educating) "the country's future" outweighed the immediate financial benefit to the family and firm. As the Pessimists gained ground in Parliament, a number of child labor laws were drafted and passed. Despite gallant efforts beginning with the First Factory Act of 1802, it was not until the Regulation of Child Labor Law in 1833 that enforcement was established. Many scholars argue that the laws did not have much impact on reducing child labor, which continued, albeit at lower levels, until the late nineteenth century.

References and Further Reading

Ashton, T.S. *The Industrial Revolution 1760–1830.* New York: Oxford University Press, 1948.

Chapman, S.J. *The Lancashire Cotton Industry.* Manchester: Manchester University Press, 1904.

Cruickshank, Marjorie. *Children and Industry.* Manchester: Manchester University Press, 1981.

Freudenberger, Hermann, Francis J. Mather, and Clark Nardinelli. "A New Look at the Early Factory Labor Force." *Journal Economic History* 44 (1984): 1085–90.

Gaskell, Peter. *Artisans and Machinery.* London: John W. Parker, 1836.

Hammond, J.L., and Barbara Hammond. *The Skilled Labourer, 1760–1832.* London: Longmans, Green and Company, 1920.

Hobsbawn, H.J. *Labouring Men.* New York: Anchor Books, 1964.

Horner, Leonard. *On the Employment of Children in Factories and Other Works in the United Kingdom and in Some Foreign Countries.* London: Bancks and Co., 1840.

Kirby, Peter. *Child Labour in Britain, 1750–1870.* London: Palgrave MacMillan, 2003.

Marx, Karl. *Capital.* Vol. 1. Chicago: Charles H. Kerr and Company, 1909.

Nardinelli, Clark. *Child Labor and the Industrial Revolution.* Bloomington: Indiana University Press, 1990.

Thompson, E.P. *The Making of the English Working Class.* New York: Vintage Books, 1966.

Toynbee, Arnold. *Toynbee's Industrial Revolution: A Reprint of Lectures on the Industrial Revolution.* New York: David and Charles, 1884.

Tuttle, Carolyn. *Hard at Work in Factories and Mines: The Economics of Child Labor During the Industrial Revolution.* Boulder, CO: Westview Press, 1999.

Ure, Andrew. *The Philosophy of Manufactures.* London: Charles Knight, 1835.

Child Work in Agriculture in Britain

Nicola Verdon, PhD, University of Sussex

Agriculture was a key child-employing sector in the British economy in the eighteenth century and remained so even at the height of the Industrial Revolution in the nineteenth. The types and amount of agricultural labor performed by children were influenced by a number of factors, including the age and gender of the child, the pattern of agricultural production in a particular region, and the size of the farm. Changing economic fortunes of the agricultural sector also had a decisive impact. The child labor market was highly localized, and patterns of work and wages could vary significantly among villages and counties, let alone among England, Scotland, and Wales.

Child Labor in the Late Eighteenth Century

In the late eighteenth century, child labor in British agriculture broadly fell into three categories: day labor, farm service, and family labor. Young children were employed by the day by farmers to perform a range of casual and seasonal tasks suitable to their age, gender, and physical strength. These included bird minding; stone picking; planting, picking, and gathering crops such as potatoes, turnips, and beans; tenting (minding animals such as cows, sheep, horses, and pigs); weeding; hop picking; and fruit picking. Children also took part in hay making and harvest, usually working as part of a family team. Boys could earn up to 16 pence a day in Scotland and areas of northern England, girls around 6 to 12 pence. In southern English counties, day rates were lower, at around 4 to 6 pence a day. In early adolescence many children left home to be hired as servants on farms. Farm service was an almost universal form of hiring in early modern Britain, forming a bridge between childhood and adulthood. Boys and girls employed as farm servants typically left home between the ages of ten and fourteen, were hired on a contract (usually a year, although there were some regional variations), and were housed and fed in the farmhouse. This ensured that they were readily available for year-round work. Female servants' work centered on the farmhouse, dairy, and farmyard, while boys were trained in field work and animal work. Boy servants in England in the late eighteenth century received between 1 and 3 guineas a year (£1.1s to £3.3s), while girls were paid between £1 and £2.10s. In lowland Scotland, young plowboys were paid around £5 a year and female servants around half this (Devine 1984; Kussmaul 1981). The final category of child workers in agriculture was the family laborer, the sons and daughters of farmers whose unpaid work was vital to the maintenance of small farms across the country.

Agriculture During the Industrial Revolution

There is much debate among historians about what happened to the level of child labor in British agriculture during the period of the Industrial Revolution. Agriculture underwent profound structural changes in the late eighteenth and early nineteenth century. Parliamentary enclosure, the enlargement of farms, and a shift to arable production (particularly wheat) enabled farmers to maximize profits during the Napoleonic War era. This transformation was regional, felt most strongly in southern and eastern areas of England and Scotland. Arable agriculture demanded seasonal inputs of day labor, and this shift, along with the introduction of new, heavy hand technology such as the scythe, is seen by many as reducing demand for both resident farm servants (particularly in southern areas of England) and child labor on farms in general. The evidence, however, is contradictory. Recent research has suggested that farm service was an adaptable form of hiring and persisted much later than was previously thought, meaning that service remained a life-cycle experience for teenage boys and girls in many areas of southern and midland England well into the nineteenth century, as well as remaining dominant in northern counties of England and throughout most of Scotland and Wales (Kussmaul 1981; Allen 1992; Howkins and Verdon 2008).

Evidence from printed literature and farm account books also shows that demand for child day labor actually grew in some areas at the turn of the nineteenth century as increased arable output and more extensive cultivation of new crops promoted the use of cheap day labor of children (and women) for certain tasks. Introduction of innovations in agriculture such as drill husbandry (sowing seeds in small furrows), dibbling (sowing seeds by making small holes in the soil), hoeing, and weeding aided the production of crops and also provided employment for women and children who could easily be taught such tasks. One commentator called for all farmers to drill all their turnips "as well as pease and beans, as the hoeing may be then done by the women and children." Another argued that dibbling wheat by hand gave "helpful and satisfactory occupation, and means of subsistence, to thousands of women and children, *at the dead seasons* of the year, when there is a general want of employment" (Pinchbeck 1981, 58–59; emphasis added). Moreover, although some areas witnessed profound changes in the nature of agricultural production, Britain overwhelmingly remained a nation of small family-run farms. In the mid-nineteenth century, two-thirds of farms in England and Wales, and 80 percent in Scotland, were less than 100 acres and continued to rely overwhelmingly on family labor with the input of seasonal workers employed on a casual basis.

Child Agricultural Labor, 1850–1914

It is difficult to estimate child labor market participation in British agriculture prior to the introduction of more reliable census data in the mid-nineteenth century. From the data reproduced in Table 1, we can gain a clearer overview of the age and gender of child employment in England, Wales, and Scotland between 1851 and 1901. In 1851, at the height of the Industrial Revolution, agriculture remained by far the largest occupational sector for boys, accounting for just under 35 percent of employed boys age ten to fourteen in England and Wales, and 33 percent in Scotland. The largest proportion of male child agricultural workers were relatives of farmers, followed by farm servants and agricultural laborers. For girls in the same age-group, agricultural work was less common. In England and Wales, more girls worked in domestic service, factory work, and handicrafts, but only factory work employed more girls than agriculture in Scotland (Kirby 2003).

By the middle of the nineteenth century, child agricultural labor in Britain was performed mostly by children over the age of ten, usually working a ten-hour day in summer, and from light to dark in winter. Although there were concerns that very young children were being exploited by farmers, especially in areas of eastern England where the notorious "gang" system aroused the consternation of Victorian observers, in fact few boys and even fewer girls below the age of ten were hired to perform agricultural work. A parliamentary commission in the late 1860s found little evidence of employment of children under the age of ten in day work. It was explained that "[s]peaking generally, farmers are adverse, except in cases of absolute necessity, to employing very young children, and they consider that their labour is the most expensive of the farm, as they require constant watching and are apt to interrupt other workers" (British Parliamentary Papers 1870, Report by Mr. J.H. Tremenheere, 96). Boys and girls were reported as entering farm service between the ages of twelve and fourteen, although in Scotland and Wales, younger boys were hired during the summer months and returned to school in the winter. Many observers in the mid-nineteenth century believed that agricultural employment was not harmful to boys if "the hours are not too long, or the work too hard," and it gave a boy "a good training for his future career" (British Parliamentary Papers 1867–68, Report by Hon. E. Stanhope, 79).

Table 1

Child Employment in British Agriculture, 1851–1901

	England and Wales					Scotland				
	Male			Female		Male			Female	
	Agricultural laborers	Shepherds	Farm servants	Agricultural laborers	Farm servants	Agricultural laborers	Shepherds	Farm servants	Agricultural laborers	Farm ser-vants
1851										
5–9	5,463	53	451	261	193	81	7	147	33	68
10–14	73,054	1,020	25,667	2,703	10,085	3,575	155	7,251	1,084	2,423
1861										
5–9	6,996	207	447	256	20	43	2	132	36	45
10–14	81,434	2,060	27,853	3,161	2,645	3,243	158	7,106	694	1,410
1871										
5–9	3,212	31	144	107	17	15	8	56	6	11
10–14	71,417	1,271	21,942	2,069	1,984	3,021	115	5,884	1,101	1,699
1881										
5–14	67,054	941		2,054		5,652	130		2,196	
1891										
10–14	63,268	886		1,340		5,896	190		977	
1901										
	37,613	950		385		3,642	117		752	

Sources: PP 1851, LXXXVIII, Ages and Occupations, vol. 1 (1852–53); PP 1861, LIII, Abstracts of Ages, Occupations and Birthplaces of People, vol. 2 (1863); PP 1861, Census of Scotland, II, (1864); PP 1871, LXXI, Ages, Civil Condition, Occupations, and Birthplaces, vol. 3 (1873); PP LXXIII, Census of Scotland (1873); PP 1881, LXXX, Ages, Condition as to Marriage, Occupations and Birthplaces, vol. 3 (1883); PP II Census of Scotland (1883); PP 1891, CVI, Ages, Condition as to Marriage, Occupations and Birthplaces, vol. 3 (1893–94); PP, 1891, CVIII, Census of Scotland (1893–94); PP 1901, CVIII, Ages, Condition as to Marriage, Occupations, and Birthplaces, vol. 1 (1904).

Notes: After 1871, agricultural laborers and farm servants were classified together. In 1891 the age-group 5 to 9 was removed, as technically the employment of children under the age of 10 was now illegal under the 1880 Education Act.

The utility of child wages to the family economy of the rural poor was also obvious from evidence given to the commissioners by working men and women. A laborers' wife in Wales explained, "I have four children, and I cannot afford to lose the small earnings of the children by sending them to school. My boy of 10 years old goes to work in the fields. I know it is a good thing to have learning, but still the sixpences are a great help" (British Parliamentary Papers 1870, Report by Hon. E.B. Portman, 9).

After peaking in the mid-nineteenth century, census figures reveal an inexorable decline in child labor in agriculture. Why did this happen? There are several reasons. First, after the early 1870s, British agriculture entered a period of prolonged depression. Farmers attempted to economize by dispensing with nonessential labor, and along with the increased use of agricultural machinery, this eroded the need for casual child workers. Moreover, after the 1860s there were a series of legislative attempts to curtail child employment in agriculture. The 1867 Gangs Act and 1873 Agricultural Children's Act were designed to prevent employment of very young children in public gangs, though their effectiveness was probably negligible. More successful were a series of Education Acts (1870, 1876, 1880, 1891, and 1893), which gradually introduced universal elementary education in England and Wales, and raised the minimum school-leaving age to eleven by the end of the century. Thus, both the demand for and the supply of child labor in agriculture had declined considerably by the beginning of the twentieth century, and legislative change had effectively pushed up the age of the typical agricultural worker. In the 1890s, it was claimed that boys in midland England "seldom go to work before they are 12 or 13, except in harvest" (British Parliamentary Papers 1893–94, Report by William Bear on Nottinghamshire, 106).

Conclusion

Although the census suggests the inexorable decline of child workers on farms in Britain during the second half of the nineteenth century, child labor did not disappear from British agriculture as the First World War approached. Small family-run farms continued to be worked by the sons and daughters of farmers. These family members remain the "unknown" workforce of British farming, absent from data sources as their labor was unpaid and not subject to government inquiry. Farm service continued to be an integral part of the hiring system in many parts of Britain into the twentieth century, employing young adolescent boys and girls. Attendance books show the absence of children from school, demonstrating continued regional seasonal demand for child day labor in agriculture even in the late nineteenth and early twentieth century. Intermittent child earnings also continued to be vital to the households of rural families. Arthur Tweedy, a farm worker born in North Yorkshire in 1900, was sent out to work in order to contribute to family income. Although his early working life on the farm took place in the twentieth century, the sentiment of his memoirs could be applied to any of the previous 120 years: "Most parents were anxious to get their children off to work to earn their own living. Being a rural area there was not much choice of jobs: it was chiefly farming and we were sent farming whether it was to our interest or not. . . . I was compelled to leave school and go to a farm place before I was 14 years old simply because my father could not afford to keep us all on the very low wages he received" (Tweedy 1973, 3).

References and Further Reading

Allen, Robert C. *Enclosure and the Yeoman.* Oxford: Oxford University Press, 1992.

British Parliamentary Papers. 1867–68, 1868–69, 1870. First to Fourth Reports from the Commissioners on the Employment of Children, Young Persons, and Women in Agriculture.

British Parliamentary Papers. 1893–94. Royal Commission on Labour: The Agricultural Labour.

Devine, T.M., ed. *Farm Servants and Labour in Lowland Scotland, 1770–1914.* Edinburgh: John Donald Publishers, 1984.

Horn, Pamela. *The Victorian Country Child.* Kineton, UK: Roundwood Press, 1974.

Howkins, Alun, and Nicola Verdon. "Adaptable and Sustainable? Male Farm Service and the Agricultural Labour Force in Midland and Southern England, c.1850–1925." *Economic History Review* 61:2 (2008) 467–95.

Kirby, Peter. *Child Labour in Britain, 1750–1870.* Basingstoke: Macmillan, 2003.

Kitteringham, Jennie. "Country Work Girls in Nineteenth-Century England." In *Village Life and Labour,* ed. R. Samuel, 73–138. London: Routledge, 1975.

Kussmaul, Ann. *Servants in Husbandry in Early Modern England.* Cambridge: Cambridge University Press, 1981.

Pinchbeck, Ivy. *Women Workers and the Industrial Revolution, 1750–1850.* London: Virago, 1981.

Reay, Barry. *Rural Englands.* Basingstoke: Macmillan, 2004.

Tweedy, Arthur. "Recollections of a Farm Worker: Part 1." *Bulletin of the Cleveland and Teesside Local History Society* 21 (Summer 1973): 1–6.

Verdon, Nicola. "The Employment of Women and Children in Agriculture: A Reassessment of Agricultural Gangs in Nineteenth-Century Norfolk." *Agricultural History Review* 49 (2001): 41–55.

Verdon, Nicola. "The Rural Labour Market in the Early Nineteenth Century: Women's and Children's Employment, Family Income, and the 1834 Poor Law Report." *Economic History Review* 55:2 (2002): 299–323.

Street Children and Street Trades in the United Kingdom

Heather Shore, Senior Lecturer in Social and Cultural History, Leeds Metropolitan University

While child labor in the United Kingdom has a history of both continuity and change, there is little doubt that the nineteenth century remains something of a watershed in terms of the fusing of public and state concerns about child workers. In this period, the state increasingly intervened with a raft of legislation aimed at both protecting the child within the workplace and, increasingly, removing the child from the workplace. The great thrust of this legislation (particularly the Factory Acts passed between 1819 and 1874) was focused on those children who were the most visible sufferers of industrializing society, the textile workers. Parliament's gaze also turned to the problem of children in agriculture in the 1843 Select Committee on the Employment of Women and Children in Agriculture. The child factory worker has, in many ways, become a cultural icon in the trope of Victoriana that sees the relentless industrialization of Britain's northern and midland counties as representing a peak in child cruelty, and a turning point in changing attitudes to child welfare. Children involved in the street trades of Victorian Britain were not subject to the same state "interference." Nevertheless, changing social, cultural, and political attitudes toward working-class children were to dramatically shape the experience of street trades and street children.

From the early nineteenth century, contemporary commentators turned their attention to the problem of the street child. Children who worked in the urban streets were often rolled together with delinquent children, who, by the 1830s and 1840s, were a target for social and criminal justice reformers. Throughout the middle decades of the century, street children were seen as objects to be rescued from the potential corruption of delinquency. The line between street children and delinquent children was thin; both were regarded as precocious and threateningly independent. As Anna Davin has pointed out, "Street children were highly visible. Boys and girls emerged from slum courts and rookeries to scratch a living in busy streets and public places—wherever work, charity or pickings might be available" (Davin 1996, 161–62). What to do with children once they were rescued would prove more of a problem to the child savers, who resorted to institutional forms of control to remove vulnerable children from the contaminating families and streets that they occupied. While the rhetoric of child saving focused on the disorderliness and putative criminality of street children, working-class children on the street were much more likely to be engaged in a variety of legitimate street trades.

Child Street Trades

While historians know a great deal about the nature of child labor in manufacturing and industry, the range of urban street trades that children were involved in is much more difficult to quantify. Most of our knowledge about street trade is based on nineteenth-century London, particularly through the work of mid-nineteenth-century ethnographer and social journalist Henry Mayhew. The streets were a highly casualized, informal, and irregular market for children's work. Peter Kirby has argued that much of the work of urban children was unrecorded and unspecified in official listings. Juvenile delinquents awaiting transportation on the *Euryalus* hulk between 1835 and 1837 give some insight into this market. For example, fifteen-year-old Francis Boucher had a donkey and cart, which he used for street selling; another fifteen-year-old, William Cook, sold apples from a basket on the street; John Darvill, a fourteen-year-old, collected wood shavings and sawdust to sell to bakers for three or four pence (Shore 1999). Street-trading children could be resourceful, often selling or reselling goods they had scavenged or bought at a lower price. For instance, cat and dog meat was bought from the local knackers' yard to be resold on the street (Kirby 2003). Children also worked as delivery and errand boys, hawkers and costermongers, scavengers, crossing sweepers, mudlarks, and entertainers.

The costermonger was a street seller of fruit or vegetables and would later evolve into the iconographical barrow boy of the London markets. However, young children were unlikely to be costermongers, given the initial financial outlay involved in buying a cart to trade from and fresh goods to trade with. Nevertheless, juvenile costermongers were subject to considerable scrutiny by Henry Mayhew, who tended to conform to the prevailing stereotype that saw a link, even if unproven, between costermongering and delinquency. The child crossing sweeper was immortalized by Charles Dickens in his portrayal of Jo in *Bleak House* (1853), and also in the 1858 painting by William Powell Frith (RA), *The Crossing Sweeper*. The mudlarks scavenged from the river. The prolific social investigator James Greenwood devoted a chapter to the "gleaners of the Thames Bank" in his 1867 publication, *Unsentimental Journeys*, describing the mudlark in essentially Dickensian terms: "A RAGGED, tailless coat, minus the sleeves, buttoned over a shirtless back, a wonderful collection of materials and colours fashioned somewhat to the shape of trousers, and descending as low as the knees, with a pair of brown mud hose—said hose renewed at every tide, the new pair more often than not put on over the old—completes the costume of the mud-lark" (Greenwood 1867, chap. 20).

The Extent of Child Street Trading

Child street traders were highly visible in Victorian and Edwardian social rhetoric, but largely invisible in terms of any serious attempts to quantify their numbers. Drawing on the 1851 census, Peter Kirby found that London contained 27 percent of the English and Welsh total of messengers and porters between ten and fourteen years of age (Kirby 2003). Indeed, Kirby pointed out that for England and Wales as a whole, "Nearly a third of the total of male porters, errand boys, car-men, carriers, carters, and draymen . . . were aged below twenty" (Kirby 2005, 236). However, the census has its limits for the enumeration of child street trades. Classification of children's street trading was not undertaken in the 1851 census, which contained no separate category for street vendors (Kirby 2005). Consequently, much of our knowledge about child street traders is derived from qualitative and often impressionistic sources such as the work of nineteenth-century social investigators and journalists Henry Mayhew and James Greenwood. While child street traders in the nineteenth century were not subject to the regulation that covered other child occupations (the Factory and Mines acts), increasingly, a range of state-led strategies, revolving around child protection and the use of institutions, would be used to restrict child employment. Moreover, by the early twentieth century, a range of child protection legislation evolved that, at least implicitly, addressed issues of child street trading.

The State and the Street Child

The government had formally intervened to protect child workers from the early nineteenth century. Yet, for children who worked on the streets, regulation came more slowly and with much less visibility. A combination of public- and private-sector initiatives from the late 1870s began to regulate street children and the street trades in which they were engaged. Social legislation dealing with education, sanitation, and public health meant that working-class families were to be subject to greater scrutiny and regulation. For example, the education acts (1870, 1876, 1881) targeted truancy, the police targeted street children, and the National Societies for the Prevention of Cruelty to Children, set up from 1883, increasingly intervened between the family and the child (Davin 1996). The Prevention of Cruelty to Children Acts, passed in 1889 and amended in 1894, explicitly addressed child street trading (Hopkins 1994).

In many ways there was a sea change in attitudes toward street children, who became increasingly recast as neglected and in need of protection, rather than as semidelinquent urchins. One way of dealing with street children was removal. For those children who did not have families, or whose families were deemed morally unfit, a range of institutions came into play (Cunningham 1995). The prevalence of child emigration at this time, which sent child delinquents and children of the poor out to the colonies, was seen as a way of rescuing and reforming neglected children. Ironically, the great majority were sent into some form of child labor in domestic service or agriculture. From the mid-nineteenth century, under the guise of the Children's Friend Society and later organizations such as Dr. Barnardo's orphan homes, children were sent to Western Australia, Canada, New York State, and the African Cape. According to Cunningham (1995), 80,000 children were "emigrated" from Britain to Canada between 1870 and 1914. Despite this raft of intervention and child saving, child street traders were rarely specifically targeted as a group in danger. Nevertheless, emphasis on education, child neglect, and child rescue created a climate in which child street traders would become subject to scrutiny from the 1890s.

The 1903 Employment of Children Act

Inquiries were initiated culminating in the *Report of the Departmental Committee on the Employment of Children Act, 1903*. An inquiry into children's wages in 1899 uncovered large numbers of children who combined paid work with school attendance. This resulted in the 1901 Committee on the Employment of School Children, which recommended regulation, but not prohibition, of children's street trading, noting that around twenty hours a week of light work could be beneficial to children. More regulations were put into place by the Employment of Children Act, which was passed in 1903. This act was the first to focus narrowly on what it described as the "urgent" question of street trading, defining it to include "the hawking of newspapers, matches, flowers, and other articles, playing, singing and performing for profit, shoe-blacking or any other like occupation, carried on in streets and public places" (Dearle 1910, 488). The law enabled local bylaws to regulate child street traders under eleven, and night work between 9 P.M. and 6 A.M. for boys under fourteen and girls under sixteen. A 1910 committee was formed to review the effectiveness of the act and to push toward full prohibition of child street trading, which it saw as essentially a town problem and a moral problem: "The Committee speaks forcibly, but justly, of the evils of the system. It exposes the youthful trader to many moral evils and to the habits of the gutter" (Dearle 1910, 490). A Child Labour Committee was appointed in 1912 to draw up a report on child labor in the United Kingdom and to address those occupations not covered by the Factory and Mines acts. Ultimately, the permissive nature of the 1903 act meant that, despite the committee's concerns, full prohibition of child street trading was never achieved. Moreover, the very casual and urban nature of the market undermined attempts to enforce bylaws.

By 1914, a substantial debate about the "boy labour problem" began to overshadow the problem of street trading. The question of what to do with Edwardian working-class lads was becoming increasingly urgent in light of the national efficiency debate in the prewar period, and would dominate debate about working youths for much of the interwar period as well (Childs 1990; Springhall 1986). Ultimately, the child street trader was part of a hidden economy. Despite the collision of social reform and child rescue, it proved more difficult to control and regulate the street. Eric Hopkins stated that by 1900, "[f]ull-time child labour under the age of twelve had largely ceased to exist" (1994, 232). Nevertheless, as he pointed out, the pervasiveness of illegal, part-time, and casual child labor would continue during the twentieth century, often supported by working-class parents who needed the extra income, and by children who continued to work alongside their schooling (Hopkins 1994).

References and Further Reading

Assael, Brenda. "'Music in the Air': Noise, Performers and the Contest over the Streets of the Mid-century Metropolis." In *The Streets of London: From the Great Fire to the Great Stink*, ed. T. Hitchcock and H. Shore, 183–97, London: Rivers Oram, 2003.

Childs, Michael J. "Boy Labour in Late Victorian and Edwardian England and the Remaking of the Working Class." *Journal of Social History* 23:4 (1990): 783–802.

Cunningham, Hugh. *Children and Childhood in Western Society Since 1500*. Harlow: Longman, 1995.

Davin, Anna. *Growing Up Poor: Home, School and Street in London, 1870–1914*. London: Rivers Oram, 1996.

Dearle, N.B. "Report of the Departmental Committee on the Employment of Children Act, 1903." *Economic Journal* 20:79 (1910): 487–92.

Fowler, David. *The First Teenagers: The Lifestyle of Young Wage-Earners in Inter-War Britain*. London: Woburn, 1995.

Greenwood, James. *Unsentimental Journeys; or Byways of the Modern Babylon*. London: Ward Lock, 1867. http://www.victorianlondon.org/publications/unsentimental-20.htm.

Hilton, Matthew. "'Tabs,' 'Fags' and the 'Boy Labour Problem' in Late Victorian and Edwardian England." *Journal of Social History* 28 (1995): 587–607.

Hopkins, Eric. *Childhood Transformed: Working-Class Children in Nineteenth-Century England*. Manchester: Manchester University Press, 1994.

Jackson, Louise A. "Children of the Streets: Rescue, Reform and the Family in Leeds, 1850–1914." *Family and Community History* 3:2 (2000): 135–46.

King, Peter. "The Rise of Juvenile Delinquency in England 1780–1840: Changing Patterns of Perception and Prosecution." *Past and Present* 160 (1998): 116–66.

Kirby, Peter. *Child Labour in Britain, 1750–1870*. Basingstoke: Macmillan, 2003.

Kirby, Peter. "A Brief Statistical Sketch of the Child Labour Market in Mid-Nineteenth Century London." *Continuity and Change* 20:2 (2005): 229–45.

Manton, Jo. *Mary Carpenter and the Children of the Streets*. London: Heinemann, 1976.

Mayhew, Henry. *London Labour and the London Poor*. Vol. 1. London: Woodfall, 1851.

Purves, Gladstone Dougal. *Mudlarks and Ragged Schools: Lord Shaftesbury and the Working Children*. London: H.A. Humphrey, 1968.

Ramsland, John. "Juvenile Streetsellers and Traders." *East London Record* 16 (1993): 9–13.

Shore, Heather. *Artful Dodgers: Juvenile Crime in Early Nineteenth Century London*. Woodbridge: Boydell Press, 1999.

Springhall, John. *Coming of Age: Adolescence in Britain, 1860–1960*. Dublin: Gill and Macmillan, 1986.

Weinberger, Barbara. "Policing Juveniles: Delinquency in Late Nineteenth- and Early Twentieth-Century Manchester." *Criminal Justice History* 14 (1993): 43–55.

Yeo, Eileen Jane. "'The Boy Is the Father of the Man': Moral Panic over Working-Class Youth, 1850 to the Present." *Labour History Review* 69:2 (2004): 185–99.

Zucchi, John, E. *The Little Slaves of the Harp: Italian Child Street Musicians in Nineteenth-Century Paris, London, and New York*. Canada: McGill-Queen's University Press, 1992.

Chimney Sweep—Cultural Icon

Heather Shore, Senior Lecturer in Social and Cultural History, Leeds Metropolitan University

The historical child worker is an object of some tension, in both contemporary and historical descriptions. For the generation of middle-class and elite Victorians who engaged the thorny issue of child labor, these children were a curious and even repellent mixture of innocence and experience, displaying a precocity that set them apart from their own newly idealized and romanticized children. The chimney sweep was perhaps the most iconographical of these most worrisome childhoods. Encapsulating so many elements of the tension that underlay Victorian charity and philanthropy, the boy chimney sweep was, on the one hand, a suitable object for compassion and rescue. On the other, he was dirty, wretched, almost inhuman; moreover, he was a child who crossed the boundary from the street to the home.

The climbing boy had long been a part of British laboring history, as we know from early apprenticeship indentures to chimney sweeps. However, it was from the late eighteenth century that the climbing boy became an object of concern, when Master Sweep David Porter presented a petition for the better regulation of chimney sweeps, with the act of 1788 fixing eight as the minimum age for a climbing boy (Cullingford 2000). In 1834 and 1840, further attempts were made to regulate and restrict children in the chimney-sweeping trade. However, it was the campaign of 1864, publicly led by Lord Shaftesbury, that finally culminated in the 1875 Chimney Sweeping Act that effectively put an end to the use of children in the trade.

In the hundred or so years during which the campaign to reform and regulate the trade unfolded, the climbing boy emerged as an iconographical figure in eighteenth- and nineteenth-century literature, lore, and art. Thus, the chimney sweep was immortalized in literary form in the work of Blake, Lamb, and Dickens. William Blake included verses on the chimney sweep in both his *Songs of Innocence* (1789) and *Songs of Experience* (1794); Charles Lamb wrote his essay "In Praise of Chimney-Sweeps" in 1822; Charles Dickens wrote about child sweeps in *Sketches by Boz* (1836) and apprenticed Oliver to Mr. Gamfield, in *Oliver Twist* (1837–1838). However, perhaps most significant was the 1863 publication of Charles Kingsley's *The Water Babies,* a thinly veiled attack on forced child labor. Appropriately, Kingsley made his central character, Tom, a chimney sweep. This immensely popular children's novel was arguably instrumental in increasing public support for Lord Shaftesbury's campaign. The plight of the sweep Tom did much to engage the sympathies of the Victorian reading public: "He cried when he had to climb the dark flues, rubbing his poor knees and elbows raw; and when the soot got into his eyes, which it did every day in the week; and when his master beat him, which he did every day in the week; and when he had not enough to eat, which happened every day in the week likewise" (Strange 1982, 125).

Chimney sweeping was only one of the occupations in which children were involved that attracted the attentions of Victorian social reformers. However, the public sympathy for the soot-faced little boy, whose "experiences" were portrayed not only in parliamentary debate and political pamphlet, but by the Victorian public's favorite authors and artists, ensured his place as a cultural icon of Victorian Britain.

References and Further Reading

Cullingford, Benita. *British Chimney Sweeps: Five Centuries of Chimney Sweeping.* Chicago: New Amsterdam Books, 2000.

Phillips, George Lewis. *England's Climbing Boys: A History of the Long Struggle to Abolish Child Labor in Chimney-sweeping.* Boston: Harvard Graduate School of Business Administration, 1949.

Newey, Katherine. "Climbing Boys and Factory Girls: Popular Melodramas of Working Life." *Journal of Victorian Culture* 5:1 (2000): 28–44.

Strange, Kathleen H. *The Climbing Boys: A Study of Sweeps' Apprentices, 1773–1875.* London: Allison and Busby, 1982.

Wallace, Jo-Anne. "De-scribing 'The Water Babies': 'The Child' in Post-colonial Theory." In *De-scribing Empire: Post-colonialism and Textuality,* ed. C. Tiffin and A. Lawson, 171–84. London: Routledge, 1994.

Anthony Ashley-Cooper, Seventh Earl of Shaftesbury

Deborah J. Schmidle, Social Sciences Librarian, Olin Library, Cornell University

Anthony Ashley-Cooper, seventh Earl of Shaftesbury (1801–1885), was a leading proponent of social reform in Victorian Britain, particularly in the areas of factory legislation and child labor. As the grandson of the fourth Duke of Marlborough and the eldest son of and heir to Cropley Ashley-Cooper, sixth Earl of Shaftesbury, Ashley was born into great privilege. Educated at Harrow and Christ Church, Oxford, he was a devoted evangelical Christian.

Ashley's interest in philanthropy and social reform were initially formed shortly after his election as a Tory to the House of Commons in 1826, where he served on the Select Committee on Pauper Lunatics in the County of Middlesex and on Lunatic Asylums.

His crusade for child labor reform began in 1833. Michael Sadler, a Tory member of Parliament from Yorkshire, was a strong advocate for the limitation of children's working hours, introducing a Ten Hours Bill into the House of Commons in 1831 and serving as chair of a select committee that produced the seminal report on the working conditions of factory children in Victorian England. When Sadler was not reelected in 1832, Ashley was urged to take up the former parliamentarian's charge. Though Ashley initially had little interest in the subject of factory reform and knew the task was a controversial one that involved long hours with no guarantee of professional or financial gain, he felt the challenge was a calling from God that could not be ignored.

An unlikely champion of the factory reform movement, Ashley would nonetheless go on to embrace his charge with a single-minded tenacity. In 1840, he assisted in the establishment of the Children's Employment Commission. Over the next twenty years, Ashley was the driving force behind significant pieces of legislation, including the Coal Mines Act of 1842 (barring children under thirteen years of age from working underground); the Lunacy Act of 1845; the Factory Act of 1847 (initially the Ten Hour Bill, it limited the workday for children under eighteen years of age to ten hours per day); and the Factory Act of 1850 (which redefined the workday to limit working hours for children to between 6 A.M. and 6 P.M. in the summer and between 7 A.M. and 7 P.M. in the winter). In addition to these efforts, Ashley (who succeeded his father as seventh Earl of Shaftesbury in 1851) championed the cause of education for working-class children, by helping form the Ragged Schools Union in 1844. Ashley remained devotedly involved with this endeavor through the rest of his life, acting as chairman and president for more than forty years.

Despite his political achievements, Ashley battled depression, financial hardship, and family problems through much of his life. Though ill health and physical pain plagued his final years, he remained actively involved in advocating for the poor and found continued comfort in his Christian faith.

Upon his death on October 1, 1885, the government honored his life with a funeral service in Westminster Abbey. Perhaps the greatest testimony to his achievements, however, consisted of the crowds of factory workers, flower girls, and other working-class citizens who lined the streets around Westminster Abbey to pay their respects to a man who worked so tirelessly on their behalf.

References and Further Reading

Battiscombe, Georgina. *Shaftesbury: A Biography of the Seventh Earl, 1801–1885.* London: Constable, 1974.

Finlayson, Geoffrey B.A.M. *The Seventh Earl of Shaftesbury, 1801–1885.* London: Eyre Methuen, 1981.

National Society for the Prevention of Cruelty to Children

Deborah Schmidle, Social Sciences Librarian, Olin Library, Cornell University

The National Society for the Prevention of Cruelty to Children (NSPCC) is the United Kingdom's leading charity in child protection and welfare. Originally established in July 1884 under the name the London Society for the Prevention of Cruelty to Children, it drew upon the experience of similar, older organizations to deal with protecting the rights of children, including securing legislation that mandated a minimum age for children street traders.

In 1881, Liverpool banker Thomas Agnew visited the New York Society for the Prevention of Cruelty to Children (NYSPCC), the first officially established child protective agency in the world. The NYSPCC had been incorporated only six years earlier, with the goal "to rescue little children from the cruelty and demoralization which neglect, abandonment and improper treatment engender; . . . [and] to aid by all lawful means in the enforcement of the laws intended for their protection and benefit." Agnew regarded the work of the NYSPCC so highly that he subsequently established, in 1883, the Liverpool Society for the Prevention of Cruelty to Children. The following year, the London Society for the Prevention of Cruelty to Children was formed with assistance from Agnew. The society's officials included Lord Shaftesbury, Reverend Benjamin Waugh, and Reverend Edward Rudolf.

Over the next five years, the society established more than thirty aid committees across England, Scotland, and Wales. These committees were responsible for securing (through donations and subscriptions) the funds necessary to establish inspectors who investigated reports of child abuse and neglect. In 1889, the society was renamed the National Society for the Prevention of Cruelty to Children, and Queen Victoria became the NSPCC's patron.

In addition to raising funds for the establishment of inspectors, one of the main goals of the NSPCC was to raise public and government awareness about the poverty and abuse that plagued many of London's children. To this end, the NSPCC was actively involved in lobbying Parliament to approve legislation regarding child protection. The Children's Charter (the first Act of Parliament that sought protective rights for children regarding cruelty) was enacted in 1889. Subsequent legislation (the 1904 Prevention of Cruelty Act) provided NSPCC inspectors with the power to remove children from abusive home settings. By the turn of the century, the NSPCC had nearly 165 inspectors and had assisted more than 1 million children.

In the 1920s the mission of the NSPCC broadened to include addressing problems associated with nutrition and living conditions. During the Second World War, the NSPCC worked for fair treatment of child evacuees and other child protection issues. Following the war, the organization was involved with the Curtis Committee, which made recommendations regarding the protection of children in foster homes. The latter half of the twentieth century saw the NSPCC develop advice bureaus for families in need, including family and child therapy. Playgroups for at-risk children were also formed, and twenty-four-hour telephone help lines were established.

Today, the NSPCC continues to be the United Kingdom's leading charity in child protection, with 180 child protection teams providing support for England, Wales, Northern Ireland, and the Channel Islands.

References and Further Reading

National Society for the Prevention of Cruelty to Children. http://www.nspcc.org.uk.

New York Society for the Prevention of Cruelty to Children. http://www.nyspcc.org/.

Rose, Lionel. *The Erosion of Childhood: Child Oppression in Britain 1860–1918.* London: Routledge, 1991.

Child Work and Child Labor in the United Kingdom Today

Phil Mizen, Department of Sociology, University of Warwick

Paid employment among children before they have reached the minimum school-leaving age is a majority experience in the United Kingdom today. Research findings from each region—Wales, Scotland, England, and Northern Ireland—consistently underline the pervasive presence of school-age working and allow important insights into its form and nature. Debate has emerged around the significance of work for children. Concerns about the consequences of working for children's education and welfare have been incorporated into studies of the relationship between work and adolescent development. "Subject-oriented" approaches have also explored the meaning and significance that children attach to their work, and to the relationship between employment and childhood more generally.

This renewed interest in children's work and labor in the United Kingdom is itself rooted in broader economic and social changes. The "rediscovery" of child employment in the early 1970s occurred in the context of deepening anxieties over the sustainability of postwar affluence and, especially, the capacity of education to deliver the human capital and skills deemed necessary for economic and social modernization (Mizen 2004). Evidence that compulsory secondary education and raising the minimum school-leaving age had not removed children completely from the labor market fed into broader concerns about the failure of the education system to harness the untapped pool of working-class talent. High levels of child employment continued to be noted in a series of official reports throughout the postwar period, but it was not until the government-commissioned Davies report (1972) that "out of school" work became the object of systematic inquiry.

Post-Davies research findings were produced by trades unions, children's rights organizations (O'Donnell and White 1998), and a growing number of academic researchers (Finn 1984). Often driven by the need for audit, these studies sought to establish reliable estimates of the extent of child working, clearer categorization of the jobs held, the effectiveness of the regulatory framework, and the duration of hours worked, levels of remuneration, and incidences of mishap or accident. By the end of the twentieth century, this renewed interest had developed into a body of evidence that emphatically underscored the pervasive presence of school-age working in the United Kingdom: "[T]here is evidence that *employment is a majority experience* for children. The onus is on anyone who wishes to suggest that child employment in Britain is trivial or marginal to present evidence that this is indeed the case" (Hobbs, Lindsay, and McKechnie 1996, 16; emphasis in original).

Between one-third and one-half of school-age children in the United Kingdom are in paid employment at any one time, and between two-thirds and three-quarters of children hold down a paid job before they reach the minimum school-leaving age of sixteen. Further, it is apparent that the experience of working is dominated by recruitment into semiskilled or unskilled jobs, usually in the lower echelons of the service sector, or, much less frequently, into labor-intensive forms of petty manufacturing or the building trades (Hibbett and Beatson 1995). Children typically find work undertaking door-to-door sales or deliveries, serving in shops and cafes, preparing food, washing up or waiting tables in restaurants and take-out food establishments, cleaning offices and homes, or caring for children for pay for family or friends

(Mizen, Bolton, and Pole 1999). Less typical is employment in light assembly work or laboring on unregulated construction sites. Children usually organize their work around the requirements of full-time schooling, and hours of employment average between eight and ten per week. Rates of pay tend to be low, and minor work-related accidents are commonplace, but reports of serious health and safety problems are rare. The entry of boys into paid employment at an earlier age than girls gives way to approximately equal rates of participation by the mid-teenage years. Attention to the implications of ethnicity for school-age working remains a conspicuous absence in the research literature (Song 2001).

It is also the case that the vast majority of children working in the United Kingdom today are employed illegally. Many children are recruited into work before the minimum age of thirteen, undertake jobs outside the light work designated as appropriate, or are required to work hours not permitted by legislation. Possession of a permit to work is also a rarity. Recent research has further underlined the ineffectiveness of legislation and highlights extensive confusion in local government understanding of the national legislative framework regulating children's employment, together with major inconsistencies in implementation (Trades Union Congress / National Society for the Prevention of Cruelty to Children 2004).

With the progressive accumulation of research findings, marked shifts in thinking have occurred. Earlier government interest has not been maintained, and this is justified by the view that children's work involves largely harmless pursuit of odd jobs for a little extra pocket money. The enmity that has historically characterized the attitude of trade unions and children's rights' organizations to school-age working has also undergone notable qualification, and both types of organization now willingly entertain the prospect that paid employment may constitute a valuable childhood experience—subject, of course, to appropriate oversight and regulation (Trades Union Congress 1997).

Changes in attitudes are also evident within academic debate. Universal condemnation of children's employment is rare, and attention is now directed more toward judging the implications of specific modes and patterns of work on working children. Following methods mapped out in the United States, one approach has sought to model the costs and benefits of working, conditioned on level and intensity of work, for children's psychosocial development. The conclusion is that moderate levels of work in relatively benign forms of employment have positive associations with a range of developmental indicators such as cognitive ability, formation of self, separation from the family, and capacity for autonomous action. In the United Kingdom, particular emphasis is given to the positive correlation between this type of employment and higher levels of school attendance, enhanced performance in public examinations, and continued participation in education beyond the minimum school-leaving age (Hobbs and McKechnie 1997). Conversely, excessive hours spent working in poor-quality or exploitative forms of employment are associated with indicators of psychosocial disorder, such as substance misuse, delinquency, and lack of respect for authority. Again for the United Kingdom, much is made of associations between such work experiences and lower levels of school attendance, poorer examination performance, and higher levels of early school dropout.

Other researchers reject such psychosocial models in favor of a subject-oriented approach. Rather than viewing employment in terms of its developmental significance—of what children are destined to become in the future—emphasis is placed on children's own understandings of work in the present. Here it is asserted that the decision to work represents a conscious choice, and that children possess rational assessments of their work and its import to their lives. Children value their employment not only as a source of income and a means to consume, but also as a way of deriving self-confidence and independence, accessing adult social worlds, participating socially with peers, and accumulating valuable work experience. It is also clear that working children take considerable pride in their productive contributions and their capacity to assume a degree of responsibility for their own social reproduction. Alongside this, working children remain attentive to the limits of their work. While asserting their right to work, working children clearly understand the absence of appropriate regulation, low wages, poor or inconsistent work quality, and their vulnerability to exploitation. Taken in sum, these findings suggest that children are enthusiastic, competent, and realistic workers capable of making significant productive contributions. In some examples, working is viewed as evidence of children's growing subjectivity and productivity, and the possibility that through work children can challenge, even transcend, Western models of a passive and dependent childhood (Liebel 2004).

Central to the subject-oriented position is a view of work and employment born of children's choices. Accordingly, it rests on a view of childhood in affluent societies like the United Kingdom as, in the main, divorced from imperatives of absolute material need and the corresponding necessity to labor. Participation in work is thus positioned as increasingly disarticulated from the requirements of physical subsistence for either children themselves or their families. Evidence does indeed suggest that children from all income groups work in similar proportions and that rates of working may be higher for children living in more affluent areas (Hobbs and McKechnie 1997). Suggested reasons for this include the disadvantages accruing to children from lower-income groups due to their relative immobility, more-restricted social networks, and the higher value placed on work experience by middle-class parents. Nevertheless, important sources of constraint remain. A significant minority of children report using their earned income to relieve the family budget, or report placing their earnings directly at the service of the family (O'Donnell and White 1998). Such considerations seem especially acute for children living in families in receipt of state welfare benefits (Middleton and Loumidis 2001). Furthermore, issues of constraint have also been raised in relation to the progressive monetization of children's lives (Mizen, Bolton, and Pole 1999). For children in the United Kingdom, access to money has become a progressively more important prerequisite for inclusion in many of those "normal" routines of childhood, so that employment may be a progressively important means for children to secure their participation (Mizen, Pole, and. Bolton 2001).

References and Further Reading

Davies, E. "Work Out of School." *Education* 19 (November 1972): i–iv.

Finn, D. "Leaving School and Growing Up: Work Experience in the Juvenile Labor Market." In *Schooling for the Dole? The New Vocationalism,* ed. I. Bates, J. Clarke, P. Cohen, D. Finn, R. Moore, and P. Willis, 17–64. Basingstoke: Macmillan, 1984.

Hibbett, A., and M. Beatson. "Young People at Work." *Employment Gazette* (April 1995): 169–77.

Hobbs, Sandra, and James KcKechnie. *Child Employment in Britain.* London: Stationary Office, 1997.

Hobbs, S., S. Lindsay, and J. McKechnie. "The Extent of Child Employment in Britain." *British Journal of Education and Work* 9:1 (1996): 5–18.

Liebel, Manfred. *A Will of Their Own? Cross Cultural Perspectives on Working Children.* London: Zed Books, 2004.

Middleton, S., and J. Loumidis. "Young People, Poverty and Part-Time Work." In *Hidden Hands: International Perspectives on Children's Work and Labour,* ed. P. Mizen, C. Pole, and A. Bolton, 24–36. London: RoutledgeFalmer, 2001.

Mizen, Phil. *The Changing State of Youth.* Basingstoke: Palgrave, 2004.

Mizen, P., A. Bolton, and C. Pole. "School Age Workers: The Paid Employment of Children in Britain." *Work, Employment and Society* 13:3 (1999): 423–38.

Mizen P., C. Pole, and A. Bolton. "Why Be a School Age Worker?" In *Hidden Hands: International Perspectives on Children's Work and Labour,* ed. P. Mizen, C. Pole, and A. Bolton, 37–54. The Future of Childhood Series. London: RoutledgeFalmer, 2001.

O'Donnell, C., and L. White. *Invisible Hands: Child Employment in North Tyneside.* London: Low Pay Unit, 1998.

Song, M. "Chinese Children's Work Roles in Immigrant Adaptation." In *Hidden Hands: International Perspectives on Children's Work and Labour,* ed. P. Mizen, C. Pole, and A. Bolton, 55–69. London: RoutledgeFalmer, 2001.

Trades Union Congress. *Working Classes: A TUC Report on School Age Labour in England and Wales.* London: Trades Union Congress, 1997.

Trades Union Congress / National Society for the Prevention of Cruelty to Children. *Dazed and Confused: The Complicated Picture of Child Employment.* London: Trades Union Congress / National Society for the Prevention of Cruelty to Children, February 2004.

SECTION 3. NORTHERN EUROPE

History of Child Labor in the Nordic Countries

Ellen Schrumpf, Professor in Childhood Research and Modern Norwegian History, University of Trondheim, NTNU

Most children in the Nordic countries have always worked. In preindustrial times children in peasant and fishery households worked with their parents as soon as they could make themselves useful. By their work children contributed to the livelihood of the family.

While "child work" is considered to be unpaid work within or outside the household, "child labor" is here defined as wage work carried out by children below fifteen years. Historically, by age fifteen most Nordic children had finished school, had attained confirmation and taken their First Communion, and were expected to take part in the workforce like adults. The economic contribution from working children was part of a family's breadwinning strategy. Generally, the children's contribution depended on gender; boys carried out wage work to a larger extent than girls. Girls, however, contributed substantially to the family's livelihood by unpaid work in the household, or they worked as domestic servants in other households. Children's contributions depended on physical strength as well.

The fact that children were economic agents and contributed to the family economy affected the power relations within working-class families. As children grew up, they began work, and their wages gradually increased; simultaneously the father grew older and got less pay. Working children had an empowered position in the family, and the changing age composition of family members meant changing power relations. Since both women and children contributed to the family's livelihood, the working-class family differed from the bourgeois family, in which the father, as the only breadwinner, controlled the resources.

Historians' Treatment of Child Labor

Although children have carried out a variety of types of work, historical research in the Nordic countries has focused primarily on industrial child labor in the nineteenth century. The one-sided focus on industrial child labor is partly a consequence of circumstances concerning historical sources. While child labor in agriculture and fishing was considered to be natural and good for the child, industrial child labor soon became the subject of public concern. Governmental committees were established in all the Nordic countries, except Iceland, at the end of the nineteenth century with the aim to investigate the extent of industrial child labor. Hence, there is a wealth of historical data on industrial child labor. At the same time, the focus on industrial child labor has to do with the epistemological tendency to perceive history as continuous progress from an unenlightened and uncivilized past, and to view the past and present as fundamentally different. Within that perspective, industrial child labor stands out as an example of a distant and brutal past, in contrast to the present, which represents the peak of historical progress.

Among the Nordic countries, historical research on child labor has been carried out most extensively in Sweden. Two explanations of why industrial child labor first increased and then decreased have dominated among historians since World War II. First, the progress of humanitarian ideas and legislation against child labor has been considered decisive. Second, economic motivations—financial needs of poor families, need for profit among manufacturers—as well as technological changes have been ascribed vital importance. In a comparative study of child labor in Swedish and Finnish industry, Per Schybergson (1974) concluded that the use of child labor in Finland was comparatively higher in the early industrial years, 1850–1862. The high level of child labor in Finnish industry was, in Marxist terms, caused by the free float of market forces (Schybergson 1974). The Norwegian historian Edvard Bull (1953) also ascribed decisive importance to the economic conditions in the market as well as in the working families for the supply and demand of child labor. In general, scholars have focused on economic, social, and political structures, and on historical discontinuity rather than continuity.

More recently, however, the new social and cultural history has opened another understanding of child labor in the Nordic countries. In the new cultural history, working families and children moved to the center of attention and became agents and subjects in their own lives. The mentality of working-class families turned out to be essential in the studies of child labor (de Coninck-Smith, Sandin, and Schrumpf 1997).

In Swedish research, the expansion of obligatory elementary school was interpreted as an expression of cultural modernization and as part of a social control strategy. Together the two historical factors explain why child labor decreased and faded out. From a working-class perspective, and based on oral history sources, mentality studies became central in the interpretation of Finnish child labor, which was widespread in the textile industry in Tampere in the 1860s and 1870s. Furthermore, we have had to rethink our history of Danish child labor: Around the turn of the nineteenth century, milk boys participated in the strikes of adult working colleagues in Copenhagen, and working boys were active in the trade union movement. The Danish tobacco industry experienced a wave of children striking. In Norwegian historical research, child labor has been found to be a common part of growing up in urban and rural settings during the nineteenth century. Work was educational in traditional Norwegian childhood (Schrumpf 1997).

According to the cultural perspective, child labor was not understood as one-dimensional economic exploitation. In a historical and cultural context, children at work appeared as useful and important agents in families and the local community. Children's economic contribution was substantial and influenced their own and their families' lives and well-being. Still, the cultural perspective acknowledges the importance of social, economic, and political structures, and recognizes structural influence on children's everyday lives.

Child Labor in the Nordic Countries

Generally, the industrial breakthrough can be dated to the 1870s in Denmark, Sweden, and Norway, and some years later in Finland. Huge factories in the textile and consumer goods industries, as well as in the iron and lumber industry, characterized the breakthrough. Iceland, however, ran her own course. The growth of the fishing sector in the late nineteenth century is regarded as the industrial breakthrough in Iceland, when fisheries were industrialized and steam trawlers displaced the old small-scale fishing fleet. In Iceland the shift to major industrialization took place after 1880 with large-scale mechanization of the fisheries during the period 1910–30.

Industrial child labor increased in the Nordic countries during the first phase of industrialization. In 1875, a total of 4,306 children below fourteen years of age were employed in Swedish industries with more than 1,000 workers. Children's share of the Swedish workforce was 5.5 percent that year. In Finland children below fifteen years of age accounted for 17 percent—2,200 in numbers—of the total industrial workforce in 1870, and decreased to 8 percent in 1883. In Norwegian industry 3,000 children below fourteen years of age worked in 1875, accounting for 7 percent of the total industrial workforce. Here, industrial child labor had increased by 60 percent from 1870 to 1875. In Finland, Sweden, and Norway, children were most intensively employed in the tobacco, match, glass, and textile industries. For instance, 97.5 percent of all child laborers worked in such industries in Finland in 1870.

Contemporary child labor was first and foremost perceived as a working-class problem located in urban settings and large factory towns. While politicians and professional groups such as teachers and physicians considered child labor in agriculture to be healthy for children, they regarded working in polluted and unsanitary environments in the cities harmful to children. Additionally, the fact that children in factories worked together with strangers of both sexes was considered morally dubious.

Beyond industry, child labor in agriculture was widespread in the Nordic countries. In Norway, for instance, 50 percent of child laborers in 1891 worked in agriculture, cattle breeding, and fisheries. In the cities, children worked in trades other than industry; they delivered goods and messages, sold newspapers, worked in domestic service, and had casual work in loading berths and shipyards. According to Danish statistics, one out of three boys and one out of four girls in the cities had wage work. In the rural districts, one out of three boys and one out of five girls worked for pay in 1908. Boys had factory work, carried goods, and worked as shepherds and helpers for adult workers. Girls did the cleaning, milked cows, and did the weeding.

Accordingly, industrial child labor amounted to just a small part of the total. Moreover, it was a fact that industrial child labor in factories was often less enervating than alternative work outside the factories in paid or unpaid employment. Child laborers employed in factories had generally better pay, the workday was regulated, and working tasks were easier than in agricultural work. Still, industrial child labor was the main subject of public concern.

Child Labor Legislation

Industrial child labor decreased in the Nordic countries except Iceland after the 1870s. Paradoxically, child labor became a political and social issue at the same time as the decline was already a fact. Governmental committees were established to prepare legislation with the aim to regulate or abolish child labor in factories. Two motives for legal actions against child labor were predominant in the Nordic debate: concerns over children's health and concerns over school attendance. Accordingly, factory acts in general demanded medical certificates from minor workers and made it mandatory to have completed primary school.

Campaigns against industrial child labor took an ideological turn concerning the well-being of both children and nations. The two were considered to be interrelated; children were the future of the nations, crucial in the era of nation building. In this respect it became improper for them to spend their formative years working in unhealthy conditions.

There were similarities and differences in socioeconomic structures and political cultures in the north. The differences appeared in the child labor debates as well. In Denmark, Norway, Sweden, and Finland, the debates concerning child labor restrictions were dominated by negative connotations. During the last decades of the nineteenth century, Finland, Sweden, Denmark, and Norway all adopted legislation that introduced specific minimum ages for children who worked in industry. Working hours were restricted for children above the minimum age, and work at night was forbidden for children below eighteen years.

Denmark was the first country to pass the Regulation of Factory Labour Act in 1873. According to the law, child labor in factories was banned for children younger than ten years of age, and children between ten and fourteen were not allowed to work longer than six and a half hours per day, or to work at night. In 1901 the Factory Act was made stricter as the minimum work age was increased to twelve years and the maximum working hours reduced to six hours per day. The employer was obliged to obtain a certificate of age from a physician. The regulations were supposed to apply to children's work only in towns and not in agriculture, forestry, horticulture, fisheries, and maritime work. In 1913 schoolchildren were banned from factories and ten years was established as the minimum age for hazardous work in agriculture. By that time, however, children had already disappeared from the factories. The 1925 act determined fourteen years to be the new minimum age—not only for industrial work but also for craft and transport—and in 1975 restrictions on child labor in agriculture were passed.

As Denmark was the first Nordic country to adopt legal restrictions on child labor, it used English factory laws as models. Later on, the Nordic countries elaborated a common legal frame from which the Nordic welfare state gradually developed. There were, however, socioeconomic and cultural differences among the five countries that found their ways into the laws on child labor.

In contrast to Denmark, Sweden had restrictions regarding admission of children to the guilds, dating from the seventeenth century. Children had to be ten or twelve years old to be taken on as apprentices in the guilds. According to the ordinance, master craftsmen were responsible for the moral development of their employees and to ensure that they had a reasonable knowledge of the catechism. A Factory and Craft Ordinance from 1846 decreed that no one under twelve could be taken on as apprentice, factory worker, or craft worker. Minors, who fell short of the minimum requirements specified by the Elementary School Code of 1842, were to be given instruction at times decided by the employer. Night work was prohibited for children under twelve in 1852.

Without government inspection, however, the legislation was inadequate, and in 1881 the Swedish Minority Ordinance was passed. Children under twelve were prohibited from working in factories, while children between twelve and fourteen had their hours restricted to six hours per day. Young workers between fourteen and eighteen years were allowed to work ten hours per day. Children employed by factories, craftsmen, and other tradesmen were obliged to have instruction in school at times directed by the school council, and certain minimum knowledge from elementary school was required. Inspections by health authorities were established to keep children who suffered from diseases or physical weakness out of the factories. Legal offenses were punished by fines. In 1900 the 1881 law was replaced by another law, which embraced all industrial enterprises: sawmills, dairies, mills, and breweries, in addition to the factories.

Finland had legal restrictions regarding factory work from the 1860s and 1870s. In 1868, night work for children below eighteen years was forbidden in factories, and children younger than twelve years were not allowed to work longer than six hours per day. In 1879, children below twelve were not allowed to work in factories unless a doctor or guardian could guarantee that the health of the child was not at risk. For children younger than fifteen, the workday was restricted to eight hours (Schybergson 1974). The Labour Protection Act of 1889 ordered that minor workers under fifteen years of age who had not completed the primary school curriculum had to be provided with at least twelve hours a week of schooling.

In Norway, a clause in the School Act of 1860 instructed employers to take responsibility for child laborers' school attendance. The clause was considered to be of little importance, however. The Factory Act of 1892 prohibited industrial work for children younger than twelve years; children between twelve and fourteen years were allowed to work six hours a day; and work at night for young people between fourteen and eighteen was prohibited. The act made the employers responsible for the young workers' completion of elementary school.

A common aspect of the factory acts in all Nordic countries, except Iceland, is obvious: Children's health and school attendance were of great importance. As a consequence of legislation and political debates during the nation-building era, a modern concept of childhood emerged in the north. Children's place was defined to be outside the economic and public sphere, and within the private family and school. Elementary school became compulsory and was extended to seven years in the Nordic countries. In the twentieth century child labor was no longer perceived as belonging to the concept of a proper childhood.

Iceland, however, was an exception in this picture. A child protection law was not passed until 1947. According to this law, the employment of adolescents below the age of fifteen in factories was prohibited. In Iceland, child labor had positive connotations. The dominant seasonal fishing industry in Icelandic commercial structure, combined with a social recognition of the benefits of child labor, influenced the political debate as well as the school calendar far into the twentieth century. It was generally accepted that the school year was adjusted to the commercial demands for children's work in the fisheries. In all larger townships in Iceland, so-called work-schools have been operating since the economic depression of the 1930s. Schoolchildren from thirteen to fifteen years of age were provided with work during the summer. The pedagogical theory of the work-schools was also institutionalized in summer work camps and school gardens for younger pupils. Children were an important reserve labor force in the highly seasonal labor market. At the end of the twentieth century the Icelandic school system was still organized in accordance with the need to do seasonal work (Gardarsdóttir 1997).

Conclusion

Until the age of industrialization, children's participation at work was considered to be best for children in terms of social, economic, and cultural abilities. According to the Lutheran ethics, which had a strong hold on Nordic mentality, work was morally elevating. Child labor could be harmful, however, and the most harmful conditions existed in the match and tobacco industries. Harmful labor was also found in agricultural work as well as in fisheries, where drowning accidents were frequent. Economic need in working-class families and the need for profit among manufacturers were important driving forces behind child labor. The history of child labor is a complex historical phenomenon, however, in which the mentality of working-class families and local cultures were also of vital importance.

Protections from harmful environments were gradually implemented in industrial life in the Nordic countries, often as a result of labor movement campaigns. For children, the abolition of harmful work was absolute and meant an end to industrial child labor. Children were no longer considered to be workers. The debate about child labor legislation had actual and cultural consequences. Legislation and discursive changes shaped the modern Nordic child as a schoolchild and not a child laborer. Child labor—at least full-time industrial labor—decreased and faded out in the Nordic countries.

References and Further Reading

Bull, Edvard. "Barnearbeid i norsk industri." *Nordsik Tidsskrift* 1 (1953).

Olsson, Lars. *Då barn var lönsamma.* Stockholm: Tiden förlag, 1980.

De Coninck-Smith, Ning, Bengt Sandin, and Ellen Schrumpf, eds. *Industrious Children: Work and Childhood in the Nordic Countries 1850–1990.* Odense: Odense University Press, 1997.

Gardarsdóttir, Ólöf. "Working Children in Urban Iceland 1930–1990: Ideology of Work, Work-Schools and Gender Relations in Modern Iceland." In *Industrious Children: Work and Childhood in the Nordic Countries 1850–1990,* ed. N. de Coninck-Smith, B. Sandin, and E. Schrumpf, 160–85. Odense: Odense University Press, 1997.

Schrumpf, Ellen: *Barnearbeid–plikt eller privilegium.* Oslo: Institutt for Humanistiske Fag, 1997.

Schybergson, Per. "Barn-och kvinnearbete i Finlands fabrikindustri vid mitten av 1800-talet." *Historisk tidskrift för Finland* (1974): 3–17.

Family Policy in the Nordic Countries

Pirjo Markkola, Professor, Åbo Akademi University, and
Adjunct Professor, University of Tampere

Family policy as a social policy targeted to families with children is an essential part of welfare policies in the Nordic countries, where family policy is understood to consist of public, tax-financed measures to improve the living conditions of families with children. Compulsory schooling and child labor legislation increase the economic burden on parents by reducing the possibilities for children to earn their own living, thus creating a social need for measures in the field of family policy. In brief, as a result of the development of Nordic family policy, principles of encouraging the education of children and waged work of both parents have become dominant in the latter part of the twentieth century. However, during the last century, the formation and implementation of these principles took shape in differing ways. Moreover, there have been and still are some differences among the five Nordic countries (Denmark, Finland, Iceland, Norway, and Sweden).

In the Nordic context, family policy usually consists of family legislation, public social services, and income transfers to families. The concept of family policy is a relatively recent construction deriving from the postwar period, but active policies to support families with children have been developed since the 1930s, and some measures related to child welfare can be traced to the end of the nineteenth century (Ohlander 1991). Population policy in the 1930s put families with children on the public policy agenda. New directions in active family policies were sought during the postwar period. The introduction of child allowances in the late 1940s can be seen as an important turning point in the Nordic version of modern family policy.

Population Policy

A crucial turning point in the development of family policy took place in the 1930s when the question of population policy became a burning issue, particularly in Sweden. Declining birth rates and signs of conscious family planning suggested that living conditions were not considered satisfactory by working-class families. The Swedish debate on population policy was stimulated by Alva and Gunnar Myrdal's influential book *Kris i befolkningsfrågan* (Crisis in the population question), published in 1934. In the field of social policy, the debate led to wide-ranging policy measures aimed at higher nativity by supporting future mothers and poor families with children. At the same time, the voluntary nature of parenthood was emphasized and the distribution of contraceptive methods was liberalized in Sweden.

One concrete result of the concern for population policy was establishment of a Swedish population committee in 1935 to study reasons for declining birth rates. The committee proposed several measures to ease child care, both in terms of family economy and in practice. Among proposed measures were tax reductions, improvements in reproductive health, mothers' pensions, public housing loans, and public financial aid to children's day care and summer camps. "More children and of better quality" became an explicit goal of the Swedish population policy (Kälvemark 1980).

Concern for falling birth rates was topical in Denmark, Finland, and Norway as well. In Denmark and Finland, population committees were established and population policy was initiated. In Denmark, the focus was on the welfare of mothers and children. Likewise, the work of the

Finnish committee resulted in improved maternal welfare during World War II; moreover, means-tested maternity grants were paid to mothers, and marriage loans were introduced. In Norway, the Swedish recommendations were discussed thoroughly in the public debate on the economy of poor families (Christiansen and Petersen 2001; Hiilamo 2002; Haavet 2006). Population policy directed the Nordic attempts to reduce the poverty of families with children.

Child Allowances

World War II affected families with children by increasing poverty, forcing politicians to address problems in the fields of housing, schooling, and health care, among others. In the late 1940s, universal child allowance systems were introduced in the Nordic countries. As the most significant family policy measures of the postwar period, they expressed a general conception of public responsibility for the living conditions of all children. The major argument for child allowances to provide equal opportunities for families with children was based on social justice. The aim was to create horizontal justice and horizontal equality across income categories, not only to support needy families.

Child allowances were launched in 1946 in Norway, Denmark, and Iceland and in 1948 in Sweden and Finland. In Norway, allowances were paid to each family with more than one child; however, single mothers received payment beginning with the first child. In Sweden and Finland, each child was entitled to an allowance. Previous Finnish reform in 1943 had made families with more than three children eligible for means-tested family benefits. Danish reform in 1946 introduced means-tested child allowances, which were made universal in 1961 and again became means-tested in the 1970s. The Icelandic allowances were first paid for the fourth child in the family, but from 1963 they were paid for all children. Child allowances were usually paid for children under the age of sixteen or seventeen (Seip and Ibsen 1991; Wennemo 1994; Lundberg and Åmark 2001; Haavet 2006; Eydal and Ólafsson 2006). In comparison to the other Nordic countries, Finnish family-policy benefits formed the largest proportion of national income. In addition to child allowances and means-tested family allowances, school attendance allowances and family housing allowances were paid (Hiilamo 2002). In each Nordic country, child allowances are paid directly to mothers. As cash benefits, child allowances diminished the need for children's earned income and strengthened the ideal that children were to attend school instead of working.

Education and Labor

Public primary schools were introduced in the nineteenth century in Nordic countries. However, demand for child labor in agriculture continued to delimit the scope of schooling. Until the 1950s, part-time schools were common in rural areas, and the Nordic Factory Acts did not cover agricultural work. It was not until the late 1940s that agriculture was included in Swedish labor legislation. In Denmark, legislation on occupational safety and health was expanded to cover agriculture in 1954. Only the introduction of full-time schools in rural areas established the idea of schools as children's primary workplaces (Sjöberg 1997; de Coninck-Smith 1997).

From the 1960s onward, Nordic family policy has been motivated by principles of equality and effectiveness. Modern societies demand a highly qualified labor force; therefore, it is considered the responsibility of society to invest in education that lasts longer than early mandatory schooling. Welfare policies encouraged parents to keep their children in school. Family policy, together with school reforms, has promoted children's education and defined schools as the proper sphere for children. Until the 1950s, most Finnish children finished their mandatory education by the age of thirteen; the new school act in 1957 extended the age to sixteen years. In Norway, correspondingly, mandatory education in the early 1950s lasted seven years, from age seven to age fourteen. In the 1960s compulsory school was expanded to nine years, extending to age sixteen (Frønes 1997; Telhaug, Mediås, and Aasen 2006).

Secondary schooling has also expanded in the Nordic countries. In the early 1970s almost half of the Norwegian age-group sixteen to seventeen was entering the labor market as workers or apprentices. It was not until the 1980s and 1990s that the vast majority of youth spent their days in secondary or vocational schools (Frønes 1997). Since 2000 in Sweden, secondary education is strongly encouraged. Unemployed youths under the age of twenty without a high school diploma now receive remarkably lower unemployment benefits than youths with a diploma. Further, municipalities are required to offer special school-to-work programs for young people (Arnesen and Lundahl 2006). Finland and Denmark have also emphasized that young people should stay in school. Children are encouraged to study, while both parents are encouraged to work.

Iceland, however, lags behind other Nordic countries in welfare policy. Industriousness of children and a common acceptance of child labor have been important features in Icelandic culture and society. During a three-month-long summer vacation, work-schools are organized for fourteen- to sixteen-year-old schoolchildren to carry out manual labor. Moreover, until the 1990s, Icelandic children came of age at sixteen. The ratification of the UN CRC in 1992 led to legislative changes in 1997 that established eighteen as the age of legal competence (Gardarsdóttir 1997; Jonsson 2001; Eydal and Ólafsson 2006).

Parents at Work

One explicit goal of Nordic family policy is to further gender equality. From the early 1960s, a central feature has been the promotion of women's employment. Since 1965, Swedish family policy has been directed toward the dual-earner model, in which both parents were to engage in paid labor. Separate taxation for married couples was made mandatory in Sweden in 1971; in Finland, similar reform took place in 1976, and in Denmark in 1983. Norwegian tax laws allowed separate taxation since 1959, but joint taxation for spouses is still possible (Leira 1992; Ellingsaeter 1998). Although one of the explicit objectives of the Nordic welfare policy has been full employment and a high rate of labor force participation for adults, children are excluded from this principle. Their role is that of a dependent family member. In this context, child labor became rather insignificant.

One distinctively Nordic feature of family policy is the development of parental benefits: paid maternity, paternity, and parental leaves. Fathers were entitled to parental benefits in the 1970s in Finland, Sweden, and Norway and in the 1980s in Denmark and Iceland (Leira 2002; Eydal and Ólafsson 2006). Various cash benefits contribute both directly and indirectly to the family economy. While child allowances ease the economic burden of families with children, parental insurance encourages both parents to stay at work by guaranteeing them paid leaves of absence upon the birth of a child.

Moreover, public child-care services ease parents' return to work after parental leaves. Public day care was made mandatory in most of the Nordic countries in the 1970s. In Finland, an alternative to public day care introduced in the 1980s is the child home care allowances paid for children less than three years old who are not in public day-care institutions. Norway has also introduced benefits to support parental care in the home or private child-care arrangements (Leira 2002). The introduction of a subjective right to day care further strengthens the idea that both parents are responsible for the maintenance of their children. It also encourages single mothers and divorced mothers of small children to stay at work. With an established position at work, women can better maintain their children and relieve them from working.

References and Further Reading

Arnesen, Anne-Lise, and Lisbeth Lundahl. "Still Social and Democratic? Inclusive Education Policies in the Nordic Welfare States." *Scandinavian Journal of Educational Research* 50:3 (July 2006): 285–300.

Christiansen, Niels Finn, and Klaus Petersen. "The Dynamics of Social Solidarity: The Danish Welfare State, 1900–2000." *Scandinavian Journal of History* 26:3 (2001): 177–96.

De Coninck-Smith, Ning. "The Struggle for the Child's Time—At All Times: School and Children's Work in Town and Country in Denmark from 1900 to the 1960s." In *Industrious Children: Work and Childhood in the Nordic Countries 1850–1990,* ed. N. de Coninck-Smith, B. Sandin, and E. Schrumpf, 129–59. Odense: Odense University Press, 1997.

Ellingsaeter, Anne Lise. "Dual Breadwinner Societies: Provider Models in the Scandinavian Welfare States." *Acta Sociologica* 41 (1998): 59–73.

Eydal, Gudný Björk, and Stefán Ólafsson. "Family Policy in Iceland: An Overview." Unpublished paper, University of Iceland, 2006. http://www.hi.is/~olafsson/familypolicyiniceland.doc.

Frønes, Ivar. "The Transformation of Childhood: Children and Families in Postwar Norway." *Acta Sociologica* 40 (1997): 17–30.

Gardarsdóttir, Ólöf. "Working Children in Urban Iceland 1930–1990: Ideology of Work, Work-Schools and Gender Relations in Modern Iceland." In *Industrious Children: Work and Childhood in the Nordic Countries 1850–1990,* ed. N. de Coninck-Smith, B. Sandin, and E. Schrumpf, 160–85. Odense: Odense University Press, 1997.

Haavet, Inger Elisabeth. "Milk, Mothers and Marriage: Family Policy Formation in Norway and Its Neighbouring Countries in the Twentieth Century." In *The Nordic Model of Welfare: A Historical Reappraisal,* ed. N.F. Christiansen, K. Petersen, N. Edling, and Per Haave, 189–214. Copenhagen: Museum Tusculanum Press, 2006.

Hiilamo, Heikki. *The Rise and Fall of Nordic Family Policy? Historical Development and Changes During the 1990s in Sweden and Finland.* Helsinki: National Research and Development Centre for Welfare and Health, 2002.

Hiilamo, Heikki. "Changing Family Policy in Sweden and Finland During the 1990s." *Social Policy and Administration* 38:1 (February 2004): 21–40.

Jonsson, Gudmundur. "The Icelandic Welfare State in the Twentieth Century." *Scandinavian Journal of History* 26:3 (2001): 249–67.

Kälvemark (Ohlander), Ann-Sofie. *More Children of Better Quality? Aspects of Swedish Population Policy in the 1930s.* Uppsala: Almquist and Wiksell, 1980.

Leira, Arnlaug. *Welfare States and Working Mothers: The Scandinavian Experience.* Cambridge: Cambridge University Press, 1992.

Leira, Arnlaug. "Updating the 'Gender Contract'? Childcare Reforms in the Nordic Countries in the 1990s." *NORA* 10:2 (2002): 81–89.

Lundberg, Urban, and Klas Åmark. "Social Rights and Social Security: The Swedish Welfare State, 1900–2000." *Scandinavian Journal of History* 26:3 (2001): 157–76.

Ohlander, Ann-Sofie. "The Invisible Child? The Struggle for a Social Democratic Family Policy in Sweden, 1900–1960s." In *Maternity and Gender Policies: Women and the Rise of the European Welfare States 1880s–1950s,* ed. G. Bock and P. Thane, 60–72. London: Routledge, 1991.

Seip, Anne-Lise, and Hilde Ibsen. "Family Welfare, Which Policy? Norway's Road to Child Allowances." In *Maternity and Gender Policies: Women and the Rise of the European Welfare States 1880s–1950s,* ed. G. Bock and P. Thane, 40–59. London: Routledge, 1991.

Sjöberg, Mats. "Working Rural Children: Herding, Child Labour and Childhood in the Swedish Rural Environment 1850–1950." In *Industrious Children: Work and Childhood in the Nordic Countries 1850–1990,* ed. N. de Coninck-Smith, B. Sandin, and E. Schrumpf, 106–28. Odense: Odense University Press, 1997.

Telhaug, Alfred Oftedal, Odd Asbjørn Mediås, and Petter Aasen. "The Nordic Model in Education: Education as Part of the Political System in the Last 50 Years." *Scandinavian Journal of Educational Research* 50:3 (July 2006): 245–83.

Wennemo, Irene. *Sharing the Costs of Children: Studies on the Development of Family Support in the OECD Countries.* Stockholm: Swedish Institute for Social Research, 1994.

Denmark

Child Labor in the Danish Textile Industry

Jeppe Toensberg, PhD, City Archivist of the Lyngby-Taarbaek Municipal Archives, "Byhistorisk Samling," Denmark

Until 1913, the Danish textile industry employed children as young as twelve years of age. From then on, children below fourteen years of age were not allowed to work in factories, even though they could still work just as hard in agriculture or in their families. In Denmark, the term "child" or "children" refers to those zero to thirteen years of age, whereas those fourteen to seventeen years old were called "young ones" or "young people." After children had made their confirmation and left school at thirteen or fourteen years of age, they were, in principle, adults. As workers in industry, however, they were to be protected until they reached eighteen years of age. Today, young people below eighteen years of age are not allowed to work with dangerous machines or hazardous substances. If the work is harmless, however, young people from fifteen years of age are allowed to do it, even in factories. Schoolchildren from thirteen years of age are allowed to do "light work" two hours a day after school, even in factories.

The Early Industrial Period in Denmark, 1800–1850

Next to the tobacco industry, textiles employed the largest number of Danish factory children. In this industry, child labor was found particularly in woolen cloth production. Children mostly worked in spinning and spooling yarn. Spinning of wool has always been common in Denmark. Cotton was spun during the Napoleonic War, but after the war English yarn was imported for all cotton weaving. It was not until the 1890s that cotton spinning was taken up again, and the city of Vejle became "the Danish Manchester."

The cloth factory of Johan Carl Modeweg, established in Copenhagen in 1810, provides a good illustration of Danish cloth production in the years 1800–1850. In 1819 he employed ninety-one adults and fifty children, and in 1829 this number had grown to 200 people, of whom forty-four boys were placed there by the poor-law authorities. In 1832, J.C. Modeweg moved his factory from Copenhagen to Brede to get waterpower. In a description of the work process at the Brede Cloth Factory in 1835, it is mentioned that fastening slivers of wool to the spindles on spinning machines was done by children. In the 1840 census, at least twenty-five children are mentioned as workers in the factory. The girls and the small boys (eight to ten years old) spooled yarn, whereas the older boys (eleven to thirteen years of age) were employed at the cutting machines.

Stories about abuse of children in the factories are generally not reported from Denmark. Danish industrialization began only in about 1800, and in 1814 compulsory school attendance was introduced. This shows that children were regarded as valuable, and the school authorities would protest if children were prevented from going to school. Nevertheless, during the first half of the 1800s, Denmark has its stories of misery and exploitation of children in other sectors of the textile industry. In lace production in southern Jutland, girls as young as five or six years of age were making lace in their own homes. They worked sixteen hours a day, and the sedentary labor was unhealthy and spoiled their eyesight. Many became blind early in life. The lace-making girls were also "excused" from school, except for religious lessons given by their supervisors in lace making.

The 1855 Factory Census

During the previous two centuries, poor-law authorities had systematically educated workhouse children in spinning and weaving to enable them to earn a living. So child labor in textiles was considered quite natural, and many children were employed in the early textile industry. After 1850, however, the children's share diminished steadily up to the abolition of industrial child labor in 1913. Already in the 1850s the number of children working in the factories was much smaller than it had been before 1850. Probably the revolutionary events of 1848 and the appearance of socialism in Europe played a part in the change of attitudes toward child labor in industry.

According to the first Danish factory census of 1855, thirty cloth factories employed 1,127 persons, and thirty-one cotton-weaving factories employed 1,147 persons. The cloth factories employed 182 children below fifteen years of age (111 boys and 71 girls), but the cotton-weaving factories employed only fifty-two children (twenty-five boys and twenty-seven girls). Children comprised 10.3 percent of the workforce in the textile industry, though some of them may have been fourteen years old, and therefore would have been considered adults.

The Factory Laws of 1873 and Later

Criticism of child labor in factories resulted in laws aimed at restricting and later abolishing child labor, requiring that children be discharged from school before they could be employed in a factory. The first Danish factory law, passed in 1873 with inspiration from Britain and Sweden, required factory children to be at least ten years old, and they were allowed to work only half the day. Because of this restriction, the child workers in a factory were often divided into two shifts, one working in the morning and the other in the afternoon. This required the schools to offer both morning and afternoon classes. In 1899, Copenhagen and most Danish market towns had schools with classes both in the morning and in the afternoon. Very large factories, for example, Brede, might have their own schools.

Table 1

Protection of Children and Young People Working in Factories (and in Other Sectors Since 1954)

Year	Children (Under 14 Years)	Young People (14–17 Years)
1873	10 years old, 6½ hours a day	12 hours a day
1901	12 years old, 6 hours a day	10 hours a day
1913	(Forbidden)	
1922	(Forbidden)	10 hours a day
1954	2 hours a day (Errand boys only)	10 hours a day
1975	2 hours a day "light work" (14 and under)	15–17 years old, 10 hours a day
1996	13–14 years, 2 hours a day "light work" (7 hours a day on nonschool days)	15–17 years old, 8 hours a day

After 1873, the still-growing demands for child protection resulted in new factory laws that generally had become more restrictive. Table 1 shows the evolution of Danish child labor law since 1873.

Table 2 depicts trends in employment of children and young people in the Danish textile industry relative to their employment in industry as a whole. The table shows an obvious decline in employment of children through 1913, accompanied by a slight increase in employment of young people. Proportionally, more children, but fewer young people, were employed in textiles than in industry as a whole. But even though children's share of the workforce was diminishing from about 1850, numerically the number of child workers rose until about 1900. After 1913, young people's share of the textile workforce stabilized at a level lower than their participation in industry as a whole. It should be noted, however, that young people are still employed in the Danish textile industry today.

Children's Jobs in Textile Factories

The jobs done by children differed slightly from factory to factory. In 1866, Brede Cloth Factory employed fifty-five men, eighty-five women, and thirty children. This was the year the factory got self-acting spinning machines, probably the first self-actors in Denmark, and it was noticed that a self-actor could

Table 2

Children and Young People in the Workforce of the Danish Textile Industry (and in Total Danish Industry), 1855–2006

	Children (Under 14 Years)				Young People (14–17 Years)			
Year	Children in Textiles	% of Textile Workforce	Children in Industry	% of Total Workforce	Young People in Textiles	% of Textile Workforce	Young People in Industry	% of Total Workforce
1855	234	10.3						
1872	366	7.0	2763	6.4				
1897	651	5.2	4672	2.6	1019	8.1	26,555	15.1
1906	374	2.6	2566	1.2	1215	8.5	26,993	13.1
1914	126	0.9	1261	0.5	1278	8.9	30,311	13.0
1925					606	5.4	37,177	13.8
1935					852	5.1	29,335	9.2
1948					714	3.0	26,460	7.8
1965					990	5.1	34,812	7.5
1981					1646	9.3	54,108	11.2
1997					692	7.4	42,407	9.5
2006					313	5.5	22,478	6.1

Sources: Danmarks Statistik, Factory Census 1855; Ole Hyldtoft, Teknologiske forandringer i dansk industri 1870–1896, 1996, Table A.7 (1872); Danmarks Statistik, Census of Manufacturing, Distribution and Other Industries (Statistical Department, 1897–1948); Danmarks Statistik, Folke- og boligtællingen 1965; Danmarks Statistik, Statistikbanken (1981, 1997, 2006).

Notes: (1) The presence of children in 1914 is because the 1913 factory law allowed children already employed when the law was created to continue; (2) beginning in 1981, "young people" are defined as wage and salary earners 13–19 years of age.

Twelve-year-old "sweeping-boys" at Brede Cloth Factory 1912. The boys had left the factory just for a moment to be photographed, and two of them had not taken the time to put their shoes on. At this time children could be employed at the factory even though their parents were not. (Author's note: The second boy from the right—with the *x* above his head—gave me this photo in 1981.) *(Photo courtesy of Byhistorisk Samling, Lyngby-Taarbæk)*

be operated by a ten-year-old boy. A description from 1871 says that children at that time actually did operate machines, which was unusual in comparison with other branches of industry. Even though, since 1889, children were not allowed to operate machines by themselves, they continued to work at machines in the textile industry right up to 1913.

In Brede, the boys worked mostly in spinning. They replaced pirns on the self-actors' long rows of spindles, they tied broken threads, and they swept the floor under the machines to remove and reuse fallen wool fibers. Because of this work, the boys were called "sweeping boys." Thereafter they brought cops, that is, pirns with yarn reeled on, to the spooling and weaving departments, and they took with them empty pirns, which they made ready for the spinner. The girls worked mostly in the weaving department. They spooled yarn and replaced empty bobbins with full ones on the warping machines. Therefore, the girls were called "spooling girls." They might also assist the weavers.

In 1840, in the Usserod Cloth Factory, north of Copenhagen, thirteen men and seven women did the spinning, helped by fifty-seven children. In 1872 the factory employed seventy-four men, fifty-two women, and twenty-two children. The twelve boys did "laying on, reeling and cleaning of cards." Laying on meant laying wool on the feeding belt in the carding machines. The ten girls did "reeling, hasping, bobbining, cutting and laying on" (Gjerlev and Rosted 1948).

As a general rule, the jobs done by children were so easy that adults could not do them better, and children were much cheaper than adults. A half-timer earned 15 percent of an adult worker's wage, so even though two children were necessary to fill a working day, the work was done for 30 percent of the adult wage. Thus, the factory owners had good reason for continuing to use child labor. For the children, factory work was attractive because the wages were good compared with other work, such as in agriculture. The children were engaged directly by the factory, and not as family helpers. The jobs they did were not done by other adult workers, and it has been said that if the boys decided to go on strike, it would have stopped the whole factory. Even though the general public disapproved of child labor in industry, parents wanted the children to continue to work because they contributed substantially to family income.

Nevertheless, the factory laws of 1873 and 1901 restricted child labor in the textile industry, and the 1913 law forbade it. So the factory owners had to learn to do the manufacturing without children. They did this by mechanizing the processes carried out by children, if possible, or they let the second-cheapest portion of the labor force carry out these processes. In the textile industry, both alternatives seem to have been pursued.

Why Did Child Labor Stop?

It has been argued that child labor had already become obsolete for technical reasons when the 1913 law was passed. This may have been true for the girls because of better spinning and spooling machines, but the spinning boys continued working right up to the end, and young men took over the boys' work after 1913. There may have been other reasons for passing the factory laws, such as children's health. Nevertheless, when debating the 1913 bill in the Danish Parliament, supporters did not mention health, but instead pointed out the claims of the schools on children's time.

At that time, factories and factory work were still new elements in the Danish labor market, and so they invited legislation. The much more widespread domestic and agricultural child labor was deep-rooted and was accepted as natural, and no one thought of legislating it. In this case, it was only the claims of the schools that gradually forced the children from work and into the schools. Even today, when young people less than eighteen years of age are prevented from dangerous work, exemptions can be granted to young people sixteen or even fifteen years of age in agriculture or domestic enterprises. It is here we find the strongest tradition of child labor in Denmark.

References and Further Reading

Christensen, Joergen Peter. *Fabriksarbejdere og funktionaerer 1870–1972* [Factory workers and employees 1870–1972]. Odense, Denmark: Odense Universitetsforlag, 2002.

de Coninck-Smith, Ning, Bengt Sandin, and Ellen Schrumpf, eds. *Industrious Children: Work and Childhood in the Nordic Countries 1850–1990.* Odense, Denmark: Odense University Press, 1997.

Egsmose, Lisbeth. *Arbejderbeskyttelse gennem hundrede år* [Labor protection during one hundred years]. Copenhagen: Copenhagen University, 1980.

Gjerlev, Aage Richter, and H.C. Rosted. *Den militaere klaedefabrik 1849–1949* [The military cloth factory of Usseroed 1849–1949]. Copenhagen: Den Militære klædefabrik, 1948.

Hyldtoft, Ole. *Teknologiske forandringer i dansk industri 1870–1896* [Technology changes in the Danish industry 1870–1896]. Odense, Denmark: Odense Universitetsforlag, 1996.

Nielsen, Axel, ed. *Industriens historie i Danmark* [History of Danish industry]. Copenhagen: I Kommission hos G.E.C. Gad, 1943–44. Vols. 1–3: 1–2 (esp. Vol. 2, pp. 225–28; Vol. 3, pp. 157–75).

Nygaard, Sven-Peter. *Boern og unges arbejde* [Child and young people labor today]. 4th ed. Copenhagen: DA Forlag, 2006.

Toensberg, Jeppe. "Boernearbejde i dansk tekstilindustri [Child labor in the Danish textile industry]." *Arbejderhistorie* 3 (1997): 33–50.

Toensberg, Jeppe. *Brede Klædefabrik* [Brede cloth factory] (English summary). Aarhus, Denmark: Erhvervsarkivets Forskningsfond, 2004.

Finland

History of Child Labor in Finland

Marjatta Rahikainen, Associate Professor of Social History, University of Helsinki

Today Finland is an affluent consumer society, with a well-educated population and a relatively equal income distribution. This is, however, a very recent development. The postwar baby-boom generation was born in a semiagricultural country with a low average educational level and widespread poverty. Childhood was commonly characterized by austerity and hard work on the family farm.

In the nineteenth century, Finland was a poor, agricultural country, whose competitive advantage came from low labor costs. Under such circumstances child labor never caused much moral concern. Authorities welcomed employment opportunities for children in the first cotton mills, because that would keep pauper children from burdening the parish, and lawmakers spoke of "children's right to factory work." Agricultural labor was considered ideal for children. In the nineteenth century, pauper children were placed out to work on farms; in the early twentieth century, delinquent urban children were sentenced to work in agricultural reformatories (Rahikainen 1995, 2001a, 2002a).

Finland was a latecomer in terms of compulsory primary education too. The Primary School Act of 1866 did not include compulsory education, but did encourage development of public primary schools. From the 1880s, urban working-class children generally attended primary school for a few years, but nine out of ten children still lived in the countryside, where primary schools only slowly replaced short-term instruction by ambulatory teachers. Not until 1921 was compulsory education introduced in Finland, and not until World War II did all rural children attend primary school.

Agricultural Child Labor

Child labor in the Finnish countryside generally involved the same kinds of jobs as elsewhere in Europe: Children ran errands, minded younger children, carried water, fetched and chopped firewood, picked stones, herded first sheep and then cows, weeded, helped in hay making, picked berries, and harvested potatoes. Children became part of their rural household's workforce gradually as they grew in strength; starting out, their activities were half play. Yet much of the traditional farm work remained too heavy for them, for instance, in slash-and-burn cultivation children were of no use. Some forms of rural child labor that were common elsewhere were rare in Finland. There are no stories of rural children burdened with exhausting work in putting-out production (outwork), because this type of proto-industrial system was never widespread in the Finnish countryside. Rural families were, on average, not "burdened with children" and the poor had the smallest families. Only in the late nineteenth century, declining infant mortality and emergence of a monetary economy brought with them one generation of larger families (Kaukiainen 1978; Korkiakangas 1990; Moring 1993; Rahikainen 2004; Waris 1995).

Some children left home to work on other farms, but it is not possible to say how common this practice was. In agricultural Finland, authorities were not interested in registering this phenomenon (in legal terms, children were those under fifteen years of age). It seems that children were often hired over the summer for herding, but they seldom left home permanently before confirmation and First Communion which usually took place around the age of fifteen. Anecdotal information suggests that children of the landless were not much in demand in the rural labor market before the commercialization of agriculture, which commenced in earnest in Finland only after the great famine of 1867–1868. After that, there is much information on boys and girls of the landless population who left home around the age of ten for work with landholding farmers. Children were generally hired for lodging and board only, boys to work at herding and helping in field and forest work, girls to mind infants and do other female jobs. By 1950 nonfamily child labor had become very rare.

In Finland's northern latitudes, the high season for agricultural work lasted for about three months and the outdoor grazing season about five months. There were virtually no opportunity costs if, during the winter months, children were engaged in learning basic reading skills and repeating Luther's Small Catechism—few children learned more than that before the coming of primary schools. Even the primary schools allowed for child labor in agriculture. The summer vacation lasted a full three months, and truancy because of work was tolerated, albeit grudgingly. Until the 1950s, rural primary schools were permitted to have a shorter school year and more limited curriculum than urban schools (Abrahams 1991; Myllyntaus 1990; Rahikainen 2007; Tuomaala 2004).

Industrial Child Labor

Industrial child labor in Finland appears a practice imported from abroad, as children were used in similar work as elsewhere. The first Finnish children employed in manufacturing are found in early seventeenth-century Stockholm, in the great *barnhus,* a combined orphanage and canvas and broadcloth manufactory. The first textile machines were imported in 1800 from England by a woolen manufactory that was in all respects a copy of its larger English models, including its use of child labor. Large-scale industrial child labor came into being in Finland with the first cotton mill, which was promoted by a Scotsman. He established an orphanage that provided his mill with workers, in addition to hired children. This cotton mill grew into the largest single employer of children in nineteenth-century Finland. Its employment policy was copied by other textile mills, all of which were, like the first one, established and supervised by foreigners. In 1870, the largest establishments in the tobacco, cotton, woolen, and match industries were owned by foreign-born men, and all employed large numbers of children. Other industries employing substantial numbers of children were sawmills, machinery, brickworks, and glassworks (Rahikainen 2001b, 2004).

As long as deep poverty ruled in the Finnish countryside, many children migrated alone to work in mills and factories. Larger mills established dormitories for such children, while other lone child migrants lodged in crowded working-class homes. Children hired by large cotton mills were considered lucky, because they had bread every day. Yet the wages of first-generation factory children were so trifling that they were just enough for their own basic subsistence. In Finland factory children were hired and paid directly by the employer or his agent. The system of parents or spinners subcontracting child assistants was never used. Usually children started in the mills when they were about twelve years old. Children younger than ten were very seldom employed. The law made masters responsible for ensuring that their workforce had basic reading skills, so many industrialists provided child workers with elementary instruction.

Child workers in cotton mills behaved like children. The youngest girls living in the dormitory of a large cotton mill were remembered for taking their dolls with them to work, and at times forgetting to tend their machines because they secretly nursed the dolls. Boys in another large cotton mill amused themselves by climbing up supporting pillars. Boys ran along the corridors when cotton was good enough that they did not have to tend to broken yarns. They could also get into mischief, for example, by erasing production numbers posted near the machines, and of course boys fought with one another. Fines were the most common punishment, but management also resorted to corporal punishment. Childish carelessness made children vulnerable to accidents (Rahikainen 2002b).

Second-generation factory children were very different from their predecessors, the half-starving children from the destitute countryside. In the early twentieth century, urban working-class children skillfully bid up their wages by switching from one employer to another. Many of them were eager to start earning money as soon as possible, and some even pressed their parents to let them drop out of primary school. These factory children had been born in urban working-class families and had grown up with a wage-labor mentality.

In the Finnish case, neither factory laws nor school laws seem to explain the decline of industrial child labor. Children's share of the industrial labor force reached its peak at about 25 percent and declined during the long depression of the late nineteenth century. By 1890, when the first Labor Protection Act came into force, children's share was less than 4 percent. Although children's share of the rapidly growing industrial labor force was trifling after 1900, their numbers continued to rise and fall following business cycles and even rose back to the turn-of-the-century level during World War II (Markkola 1997; Rahikainen 2001a).

Children in Service Trades

Up to World War II, service trades in Finland were largely concentrated in urban areas and market towns. There is hardly any trace of children in urban service trades before the mid-nineteenth century. There was no tradition of children as domestic servants in Finland, but presumably pauper girls placed out in upper-class and bourgeois homes were set to work as servants. In the nineteenth century, municipal authorities usually placed pauper children and child beggars in private households because experience with institutional care had been disappointing. In 1850 in Helsinki, the capital, one-third of welfare children were placed in urban households, the rest in the surrounding countryside.

Urbanization in Finland took off during the 1870s at a period when industrialization was also accelerating. Country children seem to have adjusted surprisingly smoothly to the urban economy. Like their counterparts elsewhere in Europe, working-class children in Finnish cities at the turn of the twentieth century were occupied out of school hours with hawking, running errands, delivering newspapers and flowers, collecting rags, bottles, metal scrap, and bones for dealers, and entertaining passersby.

Worker autobiographies suggest that boys and girls themselves thought that earning some coins in these ways was within their rights, whereas the authorities and respectable citizens saw a moral risk in children's presence in streets and public places. However, since idleness was considered even worse, charitable associations organized employment for working-class children out of school hours in "workhouses for children." Child-welfare authorities argued that at the age of twelve or thirteen, after leaving school, boys should find industrial work and girls should go into service. Even service jobs in public places were preferable to idleness and relying on poor relief. After the civil war of 1918, when many worker families lost their providers, municipal authorities in Helsinki licensed the Young Men's Christian Association to subcontract poor boys for shoe polishing (Pulma 1985; Rahikainen 2002a, 2004).

When paid child labor returned in the 1980s to a more affluent Finland, children's jobs often appeared as updated versions of the ways children earned money in streets and public places a century ago. At that time the children's work aroused much condemnation; today the children are seen as providing acceptable consumer services.

Conclusion

Child labor in Finland was associated with international markets. Before the nineteenth century, Finnish children in manufactories worked for the benefit of the Swedish navy and army. In the nineteenth century Finland was a part of the Russian Empire, and the foreigners, whose textile mills employed the majority of factory children, all saw their most lucrative market in Russia. In the late nineteenth century the lumber industry grew into Finland's leading export industry; thus, economic expansion in England and the European continent always indicated more seasonal child labor in Finnish sawmills.

After the revolutionary unrest of 1917 and 1918, a great land reform was implemented in Finland. Rather perversely, the result was that Finland became a country of tiny, unprofitable family farms. The economic rationale lay in the fact that these farms provided labor for the forestry industry. In winter smallholders' sons followed their fathers to logging sites, and in summer they and their sisters weeded potato and sugar-beet fields. As soon as the postwar baby-boom generation reached working age, they abandoned this hard-pressed life that offered no prospects. They left their villages for wage work in cities and in Sweden—and thus joined the ongoing international labor migration.

References and Further Reading

Abrahams, Ray. *A Place of Their Own: Family Farming in Eastern Finland.* Cambridge: Cambridge University Press, 1991.

Kaukiainen, Yrjö. "Variations in Fertility in Nineteenth Century Finland: Lohja Parish." In *Chance and Change: Social and Economic Studies in Historical Demography in the Baltic Area,* ed. Sune Åkerman, Hans Christian Johansen, and David Gaunt, 212–18. Odense: Odense University Press, 1978.

Korkiakangas, Pirjo. "Work and Play in the Lives of Country Children." *Ethnologia Scandinavica* 20 (1990): 85–93.

Markkola, Pirjo. "'God Wouldn't Send a Child into the World Without a Crust of Bread': Child Labour as Part of Working-Class Family Economy in Finland 1890–1920." In *Industrious Children: Work and Childhood in the Nordic Countries 1850–1990,* ed. Ning de Coninck-Smith, Bengt Sandin, and Ellen Schrumpf, 79–105. Odense: Odense University Press, 1997.

Moring, Beatrice. "Household and Family in Finnish Coastal Societies 1635–1895." *Journal of Family History* 18:4 (1993): 395–414.

Myllyntaus, Timo. "Education in the Making of Modern Finland." In *Education and Economic Development Since the Industrial Revolution,* ed. Gabriel Tortella, 153–71. València: Generalitat Valenciana, 1990.

Pulma, Panu. "The Riksdag, the State Bureaucracy and the Administration of Hospitals in Eighteenth-Century Sweden." *Scandinavian Journal of History* 10:2 (1985): 119–41.

Rahikainen, Marjatta. "The Fading of Compulsory Labour: The Displacement of Work by Hobbies in the Reformatory Schools of Twentieth-Century Finland." *Scandinavian Economic History Review* 43:2 (1995): 251–62.

Rahikainen, Marjatta. "Children and 'the Right to Factory Work': Child Labour Legislation in Nineteenth-Century Finland." *Scandinavian Economic History Review* 46:1 (2001a): 41–62.

Rahikainen, Marjatta. "Historical and Present-Day Child Labour: Is There a Gap or a Bridge Between Them?" *Continuity and Change* 16:1 (2001b): 137–55.

Rahikainen, Marjatta. "Compulsory Child Labour: Parish Paupers as Indentured Servants in Finland, c. 1810–1920." *Rural History* 36:2 (2002a): 163–78.

Rahikainen, Marjatta. "First-Generation Factory Children: Child Labour in Textile Manufacturing in Nineteenth-Century Finland." *Scandinavian Economic History Review* 50:2 (2002b): 71–95.

Rahikainen, Marjatta. *Centuries of Child Labour: European Experiences from the Seventeenth to the Eighteenth Centuries.* Aldershot: Ashgate, 2004.

Rahikainen, Marjatta. "Children Educating Children: Young Girls as Nursemaids in Sweden and Finland." *Paedagogica Historica* 43:4 (2007): 589–602.

Tuomaala, Saara. "How Does a Shepherd's Life Story Become a Patriotic Song? Narrating Rural Childhood of the 1920s and 1930s in Finland." In *History and Change,* ed. Anu Lahtinen and Kirsi Vainio-Korhonen, 57–77. Helsinki: SKS/Finnish Literature Society, 2004.

Waris, Elina. "The Extended Family in the Finnish Karelia: The Family System in Ruokolahti 1750–1850." *Scandinavian Journal of History* 20:2 (1995): 109–28.

Sweden

History of Child Labor in Sweden

Lars Olsson, Professor of History, Växjö University, Sweden

In peasant society, children were put to work according to age and gender as far back in history as we have knowledge. Normally, children were put to work at the age of six or seven, performing the simplest chores in agriculture, cattle tending, dairy farming, and cloth making. As they grew, their work became an increasingly important part of the family economy, as they reduced the number of hired hands required by both freeholders and tenant farmers. Gradually, boys and girls in peasant society did heavier and more advanced work and were trained to learn men's and women's work so they could run a farm household when they reached maturity. Parents and older sisters and brothers supervised their work and taught them.

Where feudal labor relations existed in parts of Sweden from the late thirteenth until the early twentieth century, peasant children also contributed by their work to the feudal fee the tenant farmer paid the landlord. The work of girls in dairy farming was especially important in that context, although it is totally hidden in available historical sources. Children of freeholders, in contrast, helped to produce value that was, in part, turned into taxes.

Precapitalist Urban Child Labor and Artisan Apprentices

In urban precapitalist and preindustrial societies, children of poor families provided for themselves by begging or even stealing. We know little about these poor children, only that local authorities in larger cites such as Stockholm worried about their way of living. Efforts were made in the late 1600s to remove them from the streets by putting them in schools for poor children, where they could be controlled and given food. In the 1700s, some children were put to work in rasping and spinning houses. Some urban children, mostly boys, worked for craftsmen as apprentices. According to Swedish guild legislation from 1720, boys could be apprenticed at the age of fourteen. That regulation effectively refutes nineteenth-century arguments by employers in glassmaking that children had to start working at very young ages to become skilled workers. Still, the main aim of apprenticeship was to develop journeymen, who later expected and were expected to become masters. In many respects, there were great similarities between peasant society and the craft system: Children started performing simple tasks and were gradually put to harder and more complicated operations according to the ruling system.

Proletarianization, Proto-Industrialization, and Child Labor

In the second half of the eighteenth century, a vital change was initiated in Sweden. To oversimplify: Peasants were gradually transformed into two new social classes—farmers and proletarians who had no property other than their labor to sell. In the nineteenth century, as farmers developed into a class for itself, their children were sent to schools instead of being put to work. Many farmers employed boys and girls of proletarian families on an annual or seasonal basis. Religious confirmation, gradually reintroduced in Protestant Sweden around 1800, became a *rite de passage.* At the age of thirteen or fourteen, proletarian and peasant children alike left their homes to work for those who would employ them. In practice, however, poor children were sent to work for farmers earlier than that. Often boys had to sleep in barns, while girls got a small space close to the kitchen so they could easily be available for housework early in the morning and late in the evening. Authorities sent orphans from the cities to foster parents in the countryside. Sometimes those foster parents acted out of philanthropic motives, but often they took in children only to get cheap labor.

In the late 1700s, capitalists organized market-oriented production of nonagrarian goods in rural households. Most of the work consisted of spinning, knitting, and weaving of textiles, which was done on seasonal basis, when there was less agricultural work to be done. Every member of the household was involved in that work, including children. When organized by farmers, proletarian children contributed to the profits not only of the capitalist, but also of the farmer who hired them. Some proletarian households, however, focused on their own home industrial work for their living.

Industrial Capitalism and Child Labor

Development of manufactures in Sweden first happened in tobacco and glassmaking, where a few large-scale male work units were organized as factories in the eighteenth century. Family-based textile spinning and weaving began to be reorganized into textile manufactures in the late 1700s. However, the number of factories did not expand significantly until the 1830s, when industrial child labor also increased to great importance.

One of the fundamentals of industrial capitalism and the factory system was the division of labor. Adam Smith formulated a theory of its importance for capital accumulation, but in Sweden, no less than Carl von Linné made observations about the division of labor in tobacco spinning as early as 1741. The division of labor is also crucial for understanding child labor in the rise of industrial capitalism. The logic is simple. Since children could perform the simplest work operations, often as helping hands for skilled workers, the possibilities of exploiting children in manufactures depended on the ability of the managers to divide work into many simple operations. Those possibilities varied among manufactures, which is why the exploitation of children also varied considerably. Most children were employed in the making of glass and tobacco products, textiles, and, later, matches, where children younger than fifteen comprised around half of all workers (Table 1). Later, and to a lesser degree, children were exploited in the brick and stone industry, sawmills, lumberyards, and paper (pulp) mills (Table 2).

Child labor peaked in the middle of the nineteenth century. After 1860, both the number and proportion of child workers decreased in three of the manufacturing sectors where children had been of greatest importance, while children remained important in glassmaking long into the twentieth century. The average age of entry in tobacco and match-making factories was raised significantly between the early 1860s and the late 1870s: from 12.3 years of age to 13.6 in tobacco, and from 13.1 to 14.3 in match making. Consequently, in 1863, Statistics Sweden replaced the registration of children below the age of fifteen with registration of work by youngsters below age eighteen. Still, industrial child labor would exist for many years to come, although to a much lesser extent than up to the 1860s.

To summarize the use of child labor in early industrial capitalism, it is necessary only to quote a memorial to capitalist and politician Frans Suell of Malmö: "He was always thinking of the increase of his own capital, and he founded a lot of industries, where old and young women and children were employed, and where all of them out of their work ability could either fully earn their living costs or, at least, partly contribute to them by a smaller income. . . . After his death especially the tobacco factory declined, where hundreds of children had a small but daily earning, so that they were prevented from begging but instead were used to hard work" (Olsson 1980, 102).

Thus, children contributed to providing for themselves and their families, although Suell acknowledges he did not pay the full cost of reproduction of the child labor force. Further, industrial child labor prevented poor children from begging. With capitalism, the force of able-bodied children should not be wasted begging, but rather should be put into the service of capitalists. Finally, cheap and wage-depressing child labor contributed to the accumulation of capital. Indeed, it was an important basis for mechanization and further development of industrial capitalism in Sweden. Kockum Shipyard in Malmö and the world-leading Swedish Match Inc. were developed out of large profits from child labor.

Child Labor Legislation

Industrial child labor was already regulated by 1720, when an employer could employ children from the ages of ten to twelve. Since local authorities super-

Table 1 Number of Child Workers and Children as a Percentage of the Workforce in Glass Workshops, and Tobacco, Cotton, and Match Factories in Sweden, 1830–1891

	Glass		Tobacco		Cotton		Matches	
1830	151	25.6%	164	23.6%	n/av	n/av	n/av	n/av
1835	172	33.5%	249	35.8%	(231)	41.4%	n/av	n/av
1840	137	28.1%	260	31.1%	569	63.3%	n/av	n/av
1845	169	30.9%	387	39.1%	507	46.1%	99	84.6%
1850	273	34.3%	404	35.8%	733	33.0%	133	46.3%
1855	317	31.2%	570	32.6%	(608)	28.6%	177	37.0%
1860	304	28.1%	478	25.4%	(1,026)	26.6%	461	43.9%
1875	( )	32.2%	( )	15.5%	(317)	19.4%	( )	17.7%
1891	375	20.8%	178	3.1%	(384)	12.3%	556	12.0%

Sources: Kommerskollegii arkiv. Årsberättelser [Annual reports] 1830, 1835, 1840, 1845, 1850, 1855, 1860. Fabriker [Factories]. Riksarkivet; *1875 års barnarbetskommittés arkiv* [National Archive]; *1891 års revisionskommittés arkiv* [National Archive].

Note: ( ) means that there are no total figures available.

vised enforcement of the labor legislation, however, and many capitalists were engaged in local politics, employers often supervised themselves. Consequently, men such as Suell could employ boys in their tobacco factories at the age of seven, and boys and girls as young as six in their clothing factories, without risk of prosecution. Later, when enforcement of labor legislation became more independent of the employers, illegally working children were hidden when the inspector arrived, and put back to work again when he left.

With the abolition of the guild system in 1846, child labor was once again regulated for artisan shops and factories. No employer was permitted to employ children younger than twelve. Intensified debate in Parliament in the 1850s resulted in the first state investigation of industrial labor relations in Sweden, focusing on child labor (Table 2). New legislation was enacted in 1881. Industrial work for children ages twelve and thirteen was limited to six hours a day, and to ten hours for youngsters fourteen to seventeen. However, in 1883, exceptions were carved out for sawmills, lumberyards, and mining, industries where demand for child labor remained strong.

A second investigation in 1891 was followed by new legislation in 1900, which extended regulation to sawmills, lumberyards, and mines, exempted from the 1883 law, as well as to agrobusiness. However, the age limit for the ten-hour workday was lowered to thirteen, and other exceptions were made for sawmills and mining. Further legislation came about in 1912 providing, for the first time, supervision by a state institution. Also for the first time, labor legislation was gendered, as boys were permitted to enter industrial work (at thirteen) at a younger age than girls (fourteen). Exceptions were made for glass mills such as Kosta and Boda, where children of twelve still could be legally exploited. The ten-hour-per-day limit was retained for boys age thirteen and girls of fourteen. In 1949, after the Social Democratic political takeover in the 1930s, none younger than fourteen were allowed to do any paid work, and for industrial work the minimum age was fifteen. For mining, the minimum age was eighteen, and for the first time, agriculture and service work were included in child labor legislation.

From Child Labor to Youth Unemployment

As shown, industrial child labor was of great importance for capital accumulation in the early phase of industrial capitalism in Sweden. Its decline from around 1860 was, however, not caused by legislation. Early legislation did not make child labor illegal, but only regulated it. Fully enforceable legislation was not introduced until child labor was of less interest to industrial capitalists. Further, it should be noted that the work of youngsters from fifteen to eighteen, which was not regulated, also decreased significantly in branches like match and tobacco making, from between a fourth and a third of all workers at the turn of the century to 2 to 4 percent in the 1930s.

The main reason for the decline of industrial child labor, and the increasing difficulty for youngsters to be employed in former child-intensive branches, was that managers of the most expansive plants changed the work organization. New machinery was introduced, and machine constructors were charged with mechanizing manual work. This

Table 2 All Workers and Child Labor in Selected Industries in Sweden in 1875

	All workers		Children under 14		% Children
Industry	Men	Women	Boys	Girls	
Glass	1,675	67	335	22	20.5
Matches	2,160	1,885	374	280	16.2
Tobacco	1,695	1,561	248	142	12.0
Cotton and linen spinning	2,736	6,013	382	417	9.1
Paper (pulp)	2,628	989	118	86	5.6
Brick and porcelain	2,785	488	155	22	5.4
Sawmill work	9,000	665	375	110	5.0
Cloth making	2,054	1,942	145	54	5.0
Stonecutting	1,465	13	70	1	4.8
Ironworks	14,533	298	374	44	2.8
Carpentry shops	1,708	8	46	2	2.8
Iron mines	3,218	147	49	13	1.8
Engineering shops	10,491	15	132	n/av	1.3
Breweries	878	128	4	n/av	0.4
All branches	64,566	15,726	3,113	1,293	5.5

Source: Betänkande angående minderårigas antagande och användande i fabrik, handtverk och annan handtering afgifvet af dertill af Kongli. Maj:t förordnade Kommitterade. (Stockholm: Haggström, 1877), table 3, pp. 143–49.

movement followed the same logic that originally gave rise to child labor in factory work. Simple work operations were deemed fit for children, but these same simple operations were also the easiest to mechanize. Changed work organization in match making in the 1860s and 1870s followed this pattern. In cigar making, even skilled work was mechanized, and starting in the early 1860s managers replaced work teams of skilled men and children with female machine operators. It was not only the ambition to increase profits, but also a desire to reduce the influence of skilled workers, that guided the managers in changing industrial work. The process was accelerated by a dramatic monopolization of both match making and cigar making in the early twentieth century.

The decline of industrial child labor in expanding urban settings gradually created another social problem—proletarian children did not work. Even if some children were still employed in smaller, less-advanced factories and, increasingly, as errand boys, public opinion and authorities complained about the idleness of proletarian children, who were seen as threats to the social order of bourgeois society.

In 1882, at the same time industrial child labor was regulated by law, school reform was introduced saying that every child should attend school for six years. Through the twentieth century, compulsory schooling was gradually expanded into seven, eight, and nine years. Since the early 1960s, education has regulated the daily lives of children in Sweden up to the age of sixteen. Only seasonal child labor remained in agriculture, until farmers could do without child workers due to mechanization and chemicalization of agriculture. As late as the 1950s, children could be freed from school for a week in October to pick potatoes on the family farm, or to work as hired hands on neighboring farms. Some children continued to help their parents weed, hoe, and harvest sugar beets into the 1960s. Today, only a marginal number of children work to earn money by selling Christmas magazines or distributing advertisements. A few children, mostly of immigrants, help their parents clean private and public buildings in the evenings.

References and Further Reading

Edgren, Lars. *Lärling—Gesäll—Mästare. Hantverk och hantverkare i Malmö 1750–1847.* Lund: Dialogos, 1987.

Göransson, Anita. *Från familj till fabrik. Teknik, arbetsdelning och skiktning i svenska fabriker 1830–1877.* Lund: Arkiv, 1988.

Linné, Carl von. *Öländska och gotländska resan år 1741.* Stockholm: Wahlström and Widstrand, 1977.

Nyström, Per. *Stadsindustriens arbetare före 1800.* Stockholm: Tiden, 1955.

Olsson, Lars. *Då barn var lönsamma. Om arbetsdelning, barnarbete och teknologiska förändringar i några svenska industrier under 1800-talet och början av 1900-talet.* Stockholm: Tiden, 1980 (repr., Lund: Morgonrodnad 1995, 1999).

Sandin, Bengt. *Hemmet, gatan, fabriken eller skolan. Folkundervisning och barnuppfostran i svenska städer 1600–1850.* Lund: Arkiv, 1986.

Financial Incentives in Child Auctions in Nineteenth-Century Sweden

Sofia Lundberg, Centre for Regional Science at Umeå University (Cerum), Sweden

During the nineteenth century, auctions were held on a regular basis in Sweden for the purpose of allocating to foster parents children who were either orphaned, or abandoned, or unable to stay with their biological parents for social or financial reasons. Public auctions were used to establish the monetary compensation paid to the foster parent for taking a boarded-out child. Bids placed by prospective foster parents reflected the compensation they demanded from the local Public Assistance Board (PAB; sometimes referred to as the municipal Poor Relief Committee). Different parties to the auctions had differing financial motives. For the local PAB, struggling with scarce resources in its capacity as provider of poor relief and supervisor of foster care, allocation of foster parents by auction was considered more cost-effective and offered children more tolerable living conditions than institutional care. For poor parents who gave up one or more children, the motive was to reduce the size of the family and thereby improve the family's existence (Engberg 2004). Finally, regarding motives underlying the decision of foster parents to bid for and raise a child, Lundberg (2000) provided evidence that boarded-out children served as cheap labor in foster parents' households.

The Child Auctions

The local PAB was the authority with responsibility to provide for children up to the age of fifteen who could not stay with their biological parents and who lacked relatives or other social networks who could provide for them.[1] Children came under the jurisdiction of the PAB for a variety of reasons: They had been abandoned by one or both parents; one or both of their parents had died; or financial or social problems had arisen (Montgomery 1951). Children put up for auction were present at the auction so prospective foster parents could judge the children's qualities (Ejdestam 1969; Engberg 2004). Prospective foster parents bid openly against one another, and the lowest bidder was contracted and paid by the local PAB. Bids reflected the annual costs anticipated for raising a foster child. Children were usually auctioned one by one, but sometimes siblings were auctioned for a unit price. The contract signed by the local PAB and the foster parent (usually the male household head) specified the child's right to education and a Christian upbringing. There is evidence that (in theory at least) the foster parent was supervised so that the child would be treated properly (Wawrinsky 1896; Engberg 2004). Field data from child auctions in Northern Sweden indicate that some children remained with the same foster family until the age of fifteen, while others were contracted to new foster parents one or more times.

From a societal perspective, it was efficient to use auctions to match foster parents and boarded-out children and to determine the level of compensation. The practice bears many similarities to the way public procurement is organized today (Lundberg 2005, 2006). The local PAB applied a cost-minimizing mechanism, for the more bidders there were, the more aggressive the bidding would be. Engberg (2004) noted that organizers, when faced with only a small number of prospective foster parents, interrupted and postponed the auction for fear of facing demand for excessively high levels of compensation.

Financials Incentives

The biological family, the foster parent, and the local PAB each had a financial motive for taking part in the child auctions. From the perspective of the biological family, the vast majority of boarded-out children came from families in non-property-owning classes and large widowed households. These families often put more than one child up for auction, and in general, it was intermediate children who were selected. Infants, toddlers, and older children were considered less attractive to prospective foster parents (Engberg 2004). The first two age categories were of little use: They could not contribute to the housework and, at the same time, demanded care. Older children were of more value to the foster family even if they consumed more of the household's resources. Other characteristics of the child, such as gender and health, could also reflect the child's abilities to contribute in the foster home.

The prospective foster parents also had financial incentives at stake in taking on a boarded-out child. Harsh circumstances characterized Sweden at this time, and any analysis of the financial incentives underlying these auctions must consider that the marginal value of compensation to a foster parent might differ depending on social status. Empirical research from 601 child auctions held during the nineteenth century in three municipalities in northern Sweden supports the conclusion that financial incentives were linked to the foster parent's socioeconomic status (Bergman and Lundberg 1998; Lundberg 2000). Farmers preferred older children and also preferred boys to girls. That agrarian households preferred older children, especially boys, is not surprising since there are lots of chores (some of them hard work) on farms that children can manage, and the self-subsistent agrarian households had lower living costs compared to urban households.

While farmers may have preferred boys, on average, other foster parents bid more aggressively for girls. Thus, foster parents were willing to accept a lower level of compensation for a girl than for a boy. Why was that? It could be that work performed by girls was more highly valued. Or it could be that, while the tasks performed by girls differed from those performed by boys, they were considered of equal value, but the girls consumed less of the household's resources.

Foster parents categorized as crofters (tenant farmers) and unskilled workers, probably living on the margin, demanded more compensation than wealthier foster parents. The money paid for the foster child was a welcome contribution to the family budget. Another group of foster parents who welcomed this contribution and demanded a higher level of compensation relative to others was unmarried upper-class women. Their financial motive probably had its origin in the fact that they were forced to support themselves, yet finding a job during this period was not easy for an unmarried woman.

Bidding for children with some kind of health problem, for example, if the child was deaf or disabled, was less aggressive. The outcome was a higher compensation level for boarding these children. They could not contribute to the household to the same extent as a healthy child, and they also required more care.

In 212 of the cases studied, the child was re-auctioned. Research indicates that foster parents with incomplete information about the ability of re-auctioned children compensated for this risk by demanding a higher payment from the local PAB (Bergman and Lundberg 1998; Lundberg 2000).

Conclusion

Child auctions were held on a regular basis in Sweden during the nineteenth century. The purpose of the auctions was to match boarded-out children with foster parents. The bid placed by the prospective foster parent was the annual compensation that the foster parent demanded from the organizer of these auctions, the local Public Assistance Board. The lowest bidder won and was assigned the child. The foster parent had a financial incentive for undertaking to care for a boarded-out child. Less compensation was demanded when qualities made the child capable of performing housework or other chores around the farm or the workshop. Although the auction might be considered a callous mechanism for finding foster homes for needy children, it should be judged according to the circumstances of the time. Child auctions were prohibited by law in Sweden in 1918, but the question of financial motives still has relevance. Though the circumstances are different, Swedish authorities still pay foster parents to care for children who cannot remain with their biological parents.

Note

1. In Stockholm, the Out-Placement Bureau managed the assignment of foster parents on behalf of the Poor Relief Committee (Sköld 2006).

References and Further Reading

Bergman Mats A., and Sofia Lundberg. "Auctioned and Re-auctioned Children in 19th Century Sweden, in The Economics of Child Auctions in 19th Century Sweden." *Umeå Economic Studies* 468 (1998).

Ejdestam, Julius. *De fattigas Sverige.* Stockholm: Rabén and Sjögren, 1969.

Engberg, Elisabeth. "Boarded Out by Auction: Poor Children and Their Families in Nineteenth-Century Northern Sweden." *Continuity and Change* 19:3 (2004): 431–57.

Lundberg, Sofia. "Child Auctions in 19th Century Sweden: An Analysis of Price Differences." *Journal of Human Resources* 35:2 (2000): 279–98.

Lundberg, Sofia. "Restrictions on Competition in Municipal Competitive Procurement in Sweden." *International Advances in Economic Research* 11:3 (2005): 353–66.

Lundberg, Sofia. "Auction Formats and Award Rules in Swedish Procurement Auctions." *Rivista di Politica Economica* 96:1–2 (2006): 91–116.

Montgomery, Arthur. *Svensk socialpolitik under 1800-talet* (in Swedish). Stockholm: KF:s bokförlag, 1951.

Sköld, Johanna. *Fosterbarnsindustri eller människokärlek. Barn, familjer och utackorderingsbyrån i Stockholm 1890–1925.* PhD thesis (in Swedish with English summary). Stockholm Studies in Economic History 49, Acta Universitatis Stockholmiensis, 2006.

Wawrinsky, Rich. *Barnavården och särskilt fosterbarnsvården i äldre och nyare tid.* Stockholm: Isaac Marcus' Boktr.-Aktiebolag, 1896.

Child Work and Child Labor in Sweden Today

Kristina Engwall, PhD, and **Ingrid Söderlind,** PhD, Institute for Futures Studies, Stockholm

Education is a decisive factor in determining children's work opportunities. Since 1971, it has been compulsory for all Swedish children to attend school for nine years, from age seven to age sixteen. Most of them go on to attend three more years of voluntary, upper-secondary college-preparatory school. In practice, few Swedes seek full-time employment before the age of nineteen.

Labor law also imposes restrictions. In Sweden, children under the age of thirteen can perform only light yard work, berry picking, and selling, for example, Christmas magazines. Few such jobs are available in the labor market. With respect to children over the age of thirteen, special rules apply for thirteen- to fifteen-year-olds and for sixteen- to eighteen-year-olds. In principle, children who have reached the age of sixteen can take various types of jobs, except for those involving hazardous chemicals, heavy lifting, or dangerous machinery. In addition, they are not allowed to work at night.

Our knowledge concerning the extent to which children are currently working, and in what contexts, is limited. In terms of government policy, child labor issues have not played a major role in recent decades; the focus has been on expanding the educational system, and on the transition between education and work. Official labor market statistics include both full-time and part-time work, but the lower age limit used in the statistics accords with the provisions of Swedish school law, and therefore only workers over the age of sixteen are factored in. From a statistical point of view, age rather than actual involvement in work determines who is considered in the labor force. Information about young people must be sought elsewhere.

It is also apparent that labor market statistics do not always include those who work for just a few hours a week, or for short periods of time. According to the labor statistics for 2000, approximately 30 percent of young people from age sixteen to age nineteen had some tie to the labor market. The figures differ when young people themselves are surveyed in other contexts. One study conducted in 1999 showed that 60 percent of the sixteen- to seventeen-year-olds surveyed had private income from work. Although the data are not entirely comparable, they do point to the difficulty of incorporating information about jobs that are being done on the fringes of the work covered by the official statistics.

Other studies in which children were asked about their free time and finances indicate that children under the age of sixteen are also working. For example, in the early 2000s, 22 percent of senior-level pupils indicated that they had had jobs the previous summer. In addition, children with summer jobs are increasingly likely to be from well-off families rather than from families with unemployed or low-income parents—in contrast with earlier times.

When compared with data from the 1970s and 1980s, the numbers indicate that fewer and fewer young people are gainfully employed. Adults are now doing many part-time jobs previously done by young people, such as delivering newspapers and handing out advertisements. Employers are preferring to hire people who have reached the age of eighteen.

Child Labor Market in the Twenty-first Century

There are, however, some areas in which employment among young people is on the rise, such as the entertainment industry. Under Swedish labor law, it is possible for those under the age of thirteen to obtain exemptions in order to work as movie extras, models, or actors. One study conducted concerning requests for such exemptions indicated that there was a noticeable increase in the number of applications for permission to take part in theatrical plays, films, and TV between 1990 and 2000. Stricter application of the law may have contributed to this increase, but the entertainment industry does appear to have a greater need for children in its productions. Even though many children under the age of sixteen are working regularly, they are not covered by the provisions of the Swedish collective agreements, which apply only to adults.

Sales represents another area where an increase can be seen. Sweden has a long-standing tradition of children earning money for themselves by selling Christmas magazines. However, cases in which children who are members of athletic associations performing certain sales tasks for their associations represent a recent development. These associations typically order goods that the children then sell, a practice known as commission sales. The children earn no money for themselves, with all the profit going to the association. Even though many children devote massive amounts of time to such sales, and even though such sales represent many hundreds of millions of Swedish kroner, such work leaves behind no traces in the official records.

Children Working in the Home

The dominant trend in the formal labor market is toward diminishing participation by children, but the situation is more complex when it comes to work being done within the household. A study from 2000 indicates that children from age ten to age eighteen spend an average of one to two hours a week on household chores. Children do spend less time on household chores than adults, but when asked to compare with their own teenage experiences, many parents acknowledged that their children were currently doing more than they themselves had done. Set chores within families are more common. Nearly all parents in Sweden are gainfully employed, and it is likely that the higher rate of gainful employment among women has contributed to this change. Strong convictions among parents that children should pitch in at home, together with changing attitudes regarding gender and generational issues, also likely play a part.

In summary, we see that Swedish children are being pushed away from the formal labor market. It is difficult for anyone under the age of eighteen to find a paying job. However, children are active in other arenas. Many are assuming more responsibility at home than their parents did at the same age, and many are devoting time to collecting money for various activities. The way in which we define work is therefore a key issue.

References and Further Reading

Children's Living Conditions. Report no. 110. Stockholm: Statistics Sweden, 2005 (English summary).

Engwall, Kristina, and Ingrid Söderlind, eds. *Children's Work in Everyday Life.* Stockholm: Institute for Futures Studies, 2007.

Statistics Sweden. http://www.scb.se.

SECTION 4. WESTERN EUROPE

Belgium

Child Labor in Belgium

Peter Scholliers, Professor of History, Vrije Universiteit Brussel

As in other European nations up to the early twentieth century, children in Belgium were extensively performing agricultural labor, working in workshops or modern factories, aiding with vending, or doing other paid and unpaid labor. Perhaps surprisingly, this history of child labor in Belgium has yet to be studied systematically. Child labor appears in general histories of labor in Belgium as a secondary point of attention. More consideration is to be found in studies that deal with compulsory education. All of these studies rely on inquiries that were conducted since the 1840s, and consequently emphasize the second half of the nineteenth century, which was characterized by the harshest of working conditions in both traditional and modern industries.

Classifications and Definitions, Censuses and Inquiries

As a consequence of the contemporaries' attention, information about child labor in mines and modern factories is much more abundant than information about child labor in agriculture or services, which remains highly invisible. Therefore, public debates and, hence, legislation were almost exclusively oriented toward industry. Child labor was viewed and classified differently according to activity. If child labor was condemned in mines, child labor in stores or orphanages was praised for educational reasons.

The industrial census of 1846, the first comprehensive census in Belgium including all industrial workers, separates various age-groups, starting below nine years, and moving to the cohorts of nine to twelve, twelve to sixteen, and above sixteen years. The latter category was labeled "adults." The 1880 census included three categories: below fourteen, from fourteen to sixteen, and above sixteen, while the 1896 census contained five categories: below twelve, twelve to fourteen, fourteen to sixteen, sixteen to twenty-one, and above twenty-one. This implies that work of children below nine years was habitual around 1850, but not sufficiently significant to be counted in the second half of the century. Likewise, up to 1880 a sixteen-year-old was viewed as an adult, whereas in the 1890s, a separate cohort (sixteen to twenty-one) was introduced, creating a group of young adults.

In 1843 a large-scale inquiry was conducted to investigate general working conditions and, particularly, the work of children, with the aim to submit a bill to regulate child labor. The proposal included a general prohibition on industrial work by children younger than ten years (which, since 1813, was the case for underground work in mines), limitation of work by children between ten and fourteen years of age to six and a half hours per day, and by children between fourteen and eighteen years of age to ten and a half hours per day. This bill was never introduced, but it helps to sharpen the definition of child labor, with a clear hierarchy of what was to be morally rejected (work by children younger than ten years of age), accepted to a certain extent (work by children between ten and fourteen years of age), and generally approved (work by children older than fourteen years of age).

In 1859, a new bill was drafted that foresaw the prohibition of work below the age of twelve, limitation to twelve hours per day for children between twelve and eighteen, and no limitation for adult workers. Once more, this bill was not introduced in Parliament. Again in 1872, a new proposition was launched that foresaw the prohibition of mine labor by boys below fourteen and girls below fifteen years. After long investigations and debates, a bill was introduced in 1884 that would have prohibited work in mines for boys below twelve and for girls below fourteen years. Social outburst in 1886 led to the installation of an investigation committee that heard social observers and representatives of employers, workers, and unions. This led to the 1889 bill, which was enacted into law. It prohibited the labor of children below twelve years, limited children between twelve and sixteen to twelve hours per day, and forbade work on Sunday for boys younger than fifteen and girls younger than twenty-one. Finally, accompanying the 1914 bill on compulsory school attendance, a bill was passed that prohibited industrial work by children younger than fourteen years. Thus, in Belgium, legal limitations on industrial labor for children were introduced very late when compared to other West European countries, and propositions foresaw a gradual increasing of the age for limitation of child labor (below ten in the 1840s, below twelve in the 1850s, and below fourteen in the 1900s).

Dispersal of Child Labor Since 1800

Inquiries and censuses provide information about the presence of child labor in Belgian industry since the 1800s. In the Ghent industry in 1817, for example, children up to sixteen years of age accounted for 20 percent of total employment. The first nationwide census was conducted in 1846. Table 1 summarizes its results, and compares them with those of the 1896 census (age categories were harmonized). The censuses underestimated the presence of children in industry, because enterprises provided false information out of concern for public image.

Table 1

Child Labor in Belgium According to the Censuses of 1846 And 1896, Boys and Girls, All Industries

	1846		1896	
Age	Number	%	Number	%
Below 12	6,300	6.7	439	0.06
12 to 16	45,374	14.4	75,708	11.3
Above 16	248,457	78.9	595.449	88.7
Total	314,842	100	671,596	100

Sources: Industrial Census, 1846, p. 530; Industrial Census 1896, vol. 7, p. 391.

Table 2

Labor of Children Below Age 16 in Some Belgian Industries, Boys and Girls, According to the Censuses of 1846 and 1880 (percentage of total employment)

Industry	1846	1880
Sugar	30	22
Cotton	27	17
Ceramics	25	28
Mining	22	17
Glass	18	22
Iron	7	16

Source: Industrial Census 1880, vol. 1, p. 70.

According to the industrial censuses, the labor of children below twelve vanished in the course of the nineteenth century. Proportionally, the labor of boys and girls between twelve and sixteen diminished too (14.4 to 11.3 percent of total industrial employment). The share of children below sixteen years fell from 21.1 percent in 1846 to 11.4 percent in 1896. The partial census of 1880 (some industries were not considered) registered that 16.4 percent of the total workforce was below sixteen years of age, thus indicating the continuing decline of child labor prior to the 1889 bill. Yet, the census compared data from 1846 and 1880 and noted contradictory developments, as shown in Table 2.

Between 1846 and 1880, while child labor was in general decline and had decreased in several key industries, it continued to increase in other important industries, including ceramics, glass, and iron. Differences in child labor among industries remained important up to 1914, which is valid also for differences between girls and boys. In 1846, 14.8 percent of the total male workforce was younger than sixteen, but no less than 42.5 percent of the female workers were younger than sixteen. This much higher proportion of girls remained in the 1896 census, with 8.9 percent of the male workforce younger than age sixteen, but 23.3 percent of the female workforce younger than age sixteen.

Working and Living Conditions

Working hours for children did not differ from the factories' general working time, meaning that work lasted about twelve to thirteen hours per day around 1850 and ten hours per day around 1900. Frequently, children fell asleep during work. Working conditions were often rough; children were beaten and punished in order to teach them regularity, tidiness, and, indeed, skills. In some cases, adult workers directly hired and supervised children (as in textiles), without interference by factory owners. Small children not only assisted adults, but some could perform independent work (mostly transportation of semifinished goods).

Long working hours and demanding efforts led to bad health conditions and deformity of the body. Children who worked in textile mills in Ghent were shorter and lighter than children of the same age going to school; children dipping matchsticks in phosphor, and children employed by tobacco workshops suffered from breathing problems. Moreover, all children employed full-time lacked basic education. In 1843, 51 percent of army recruits could not read or write. By 1880 this figure had fallen to 22 percent, and by 1914 to 8 percent.

The industrial censuses provide general information on children's wages. In 1846, children below sixteen years earned 0.46 francs per day, women above sixteen earned 0.71 francs, and men above sixteen earned 1.49 francs. That is, women's daily wage averaged half of the adult male wage, and children's daily wage reached one-third of it. In 1896, children below sixteen received on average 1.18 francs per day; men above sixteen earned 3.26 francs per day. Between 1846 and 1896 children's wages grew 2.5 times; adult wages only 2.2 times. Wages differed highly according to the children's age, as shown by the example of the Ghent textile factories.

Children's contribution to family income fluctuated according to their age and type of work, and to the general income level of the household (in particular the wage of the father). For example, in Ghent circa 1900, textile households took advantage of child labor much more than did families of artisans or metalworkers. Throughout the family life cycle, labor by living-in children of all ages remained higher in textile families than in households headed by artisans or metalworkers. In general, when children were around ten they contributed less than 2 percent to total family income of working-class households, but as the family aged, children around fifteen years contributed up to 10 percent of total household income.

The Public Debate over Child Labor

The debates surrounding public inquiries and proposed legislation reveal the contemporaries' conflicting points of view with regard to child labor. In spite of the increasing age for what was seen as child labor, arguments remained largely the same throughout the nineteenth century. Proponents of prohibition of child labor developed their arguments around four axes: health, social and moral order, technological progress, and children's rights. Physicians' reports of the 1840s showed the generally weaker health of laboring children vis-à-vis schoolchildren of the same age. Hence, labor for children should be prohibited until growth was "secured." Second, the modern factory, with rude relationships, shouting and quarreling, promiscuity, and occasional drinking and fighting, was not the right environment for children. In order to keep them away from crime and drunkenness, children should learn moral values in school. Third, technological progress had led to a lesser need for young workers but a much greater need for schooled laborers; hence the need to restrict child labor in factories and, subsequently, provide for compulsory school attendance. Fourth, child labor should be a matter not only for employers, families, and the state, but also for children's rights proper, which were articulated for the first time in the 1860s by the Ligue de l'Enseignement (Education league).

These arguments were fiercely and, up to 1889, successfully combated by opponents of any limitation on child labor. Five axes underpinned their argument, which hardly dealt with the arguments of proponents of prohibition. First, wages would rise, leading to harsher competition and more unemployment, which would put the working class into misery. Limiting the (very adaptable) labor of children would boost wage costs in two ways: The long-term pressure on the general wage level would disappear, and the adults' pay would rise. Second, limitations on child labor would mean a radical intervention in the entrepreneurs' freedom, which was in total disagreement with all economic principles. Third, paternal authority would be undermined, which would attack the very basis of society—the family. Fourth, children's wages were a crucial part of the total family income, and taking them away would plunge the working class into misery. Besides, most working-class families preferred that children work for a wage. Fifth, child labor provided children not only with a wage, but also with an education. As in past times, experience on the work floor was of great value in forming well-trained workers. Moreover, such training also permitted children to get used to discipline, regularity, and tidiness, which were important moral values beyond the factory doors.

A large majority of entrepreneurs and members of Parliament embraced the economic arguments of the opponents of child labor legislation. When, in 1889, a bill was finally passed, it did not mean that economic arguments were weaker; it simply meant that children below twelve had become very rare in industrial factories, and that power relations, both in and out Parliament, were now in favor of the prohibition of child labor below the age of twelve.

References and Further Reading

De Herdt, René. "Child Labour in Belgium: 1800–1914." In *Child Labour in Historical Perspective, 1800–1985: Case Studies from Europe, Japan and Colombia,* ed. H. Cunningham and P.P. Viazzo, 23–39. Florence: UNICEF and Instituto degli Innocenti, 1996.

Gubin, Eliane. "Elites, patronat, travail des enfants et obligation scolaire en Belgique avant 1914." In *Enfants au travail: attitudes des élites en Europe occidentale et Méditerranéenne aux XIXe et XXe siècles,* ed. R. Caty, 235–52. Aix-en-Provence: Publication de l'Université de Provence, 2002.

Loriaux, Florence. *Enfants-machines: histoire du travail des enfants en Belgique aux XIXe et XXe siècles.* Brussels: CARHOP, 2000.

Scholliers, Étienne. "De kinderarbeid, de leerplicht en de burgerij (1843–1871)." In *Onderwijs, opvoeding en maatschappij in de 19de en 20ste eeuw,* ed. M. Depaepe and M. D'Hoker, 175–84. Leuven–Amserfoort: Acco, 1987.

Van den Eeckhout, Patricia. "Family Income of Ghent Working-Class Families Circa 1900." *Journal of Family History* 18:2 (1993): 87–110.

Child Labor in the Ghent Cotton Mills, Nineteenth Century

Peter Scholliers, Professor of History, Vrije Universiteit Brussel

Ghent is considered one of the first industrial cities of continental Europe. The modern cotton industry appeared in Ghent (province of East Flanders, Belgium) in the 1790s, with the setting up of semiautomatic printing mills. These developed into fully mechanical spinning (1800s) and weaving mills (1820s). By 1830 a workforce of some 10,000 people was employed in about fifty factories that produced mainly coarse yarn and cloth. Both numbers fluctuated highly according to business cycles and technological innovations, but the number of approximately 10,000 workers was reached again in the 1900s. The mills tended toward vertical integration (spinning plus weaving), although spinning remained the city's main activity. Also, these factories tended toward concentration: The ten biggest accounted for 53 percent of total cotton employment in 1830, and 77 percent in 1890.

After a short period of high wages during the booming 1820s, wage costs became a central concern to mill owners. One tactic to lower this cost was to enlist cheap and docile workers, and hence, many women entered the cotton mills. This permitted them to contribute to the family budget. In the Ghent cotton mills, women accounted for about 35 percent of the total employment up to the 1870s, but for almost 50 percent up to 1914. Cheap labor also was the main drive for enlisting children.

Registering Children at Work

Industrial censuses and private estimations provide an indication of the trend in employment of children in the cotton workforce (child labor has been underestimated for various reasons). Table 1 summarizes the outcome. It should be noted that industrial censuses used the following age classification: below nine years, between nine and twelve years, between twelve and sixteen years, and above sixteen years.

Both categories together reached almost 30 percent of total employment in the first half of the century, but they decreased gradually to one-tenth of total employment in the 1900s. This meant that a constant group of some 1,500 boys and girls below age sixteen worked in the city's cotton mills in the nineteenth century. The 1846 census registered 2.3 percent of children younger than nine years old, and the 1860 inquiry recorded 0.8 percent of very young children, but this group was absent from other censuses and inquiries. Technical changes led to diminishing work for children below age twelve. For example, self-acting mules required fewer young workers than mule jennies did.

The share of children between twelve and sixteen years of age rose into the 1880s but dropped thereafter. Generally, more young boys (below age fourteen) were present than young girls, but in the age cohort between fourteen and sixteen years of age, many more girls were present than boys, implying that girls entered the labor market slightly later than boys, but when they did, they appeared in greater numbers. Overall, women had shorter careers than men in this industry.

Most of these children were born in Ghent and lived with their parents in poor lodgings in the immediate neighborhood of the cotton mills. Beginning in the 1870s, with the emergence of suburban working-class districts and, later, the development of public transport, workers came from more remote places, and dwelled at greater distances from the city's mills in somewhat more comfortable dwellings. Workers in the weaving section lived in more remote places. Overall,

Table 1

Registered Child Labor (Both Boys and Girls) in the Ghent Cotton Mills (percentage of total employment)

Year	Below 12	Between 12 and 16
1817	13	16
1846	10	14
1860	4	n/av
1880	0	19
1896	0	16
1900	0	11

Source: Scholliers 1996, 93–94.

Table 2

Age of Boys and Girls, and Their Wages, 1899

Age	Male, francs per week	Male, percentage of adult average	Female, francs per week	Female, percentage of adult average
13	4.07	22	4.85	35
14	5.75	31	5.08	37
15	6.65	36	6.13	45
16	7.42	40	6.93	50
17	8.31	44	8.48	62
18	10.28	55	8.97	65
19	10.68	57	9.88	72
20	12.09	65	11.52	84
21	13.92	75	11.98	88
21–50	18.66	100	13.66	100

Source: Varlez 1901, annex 42.

however, they originated from Ghent and the surrounding villages. Often, their parents or other relatives brought them along to get a job; cotton mills' personnel records show numerous family networks. Working under the supervision of a relative did not make life easier in the mill, for these children were often brutally treated.

Children on the Work Floor

Children under age twelve were found in all divisions of the cotton mill up to the 1860s. Some performed a helper's task, like the piecers who assisted the spinners working at a mule jenny or, later, at a self-actor; both were male. Eventually, the piecers would become spinners. Others had a proper job, like young girls carrying yarn between various frames; they were not helping particular categories of workers, but would eventually start at the drawing frame or another machine in the preparatory division of spinning. Between the ages of twelve and sixteen, working without being subject to the direct control of an adult (i.e., independently) became more important, and both girls and boys performed weavers' tasks, while other girls started work in the preparatory division of spinning.

In the course of the nineteenth century, the average age of the workforce rose. This was not only because younger children disappeared from the cotton mills, but also because intrafactory mobility became blocked due to fewer job opportunities. This prevented, for example, young piecers from becoming spinners, and, hence, the gradually increasing average age of both piecers and spinners, and the near impossibility for a boy of twelve to start work as a piecer in the last decades before the Great War.

Children had the same work schedules and working hours as adults. Throughout the century, the weaving division worked more irregularly but longer than the spinning section (which could produce for stocks and thus operated more regularly). In the first half of the nineteenth century, an ordinary day lasted for thirteen hours of effective work and fifteen hours of presence (three breaks were allowed). At six days per week, this amounted to seventy-eight hours of work per week. Night work was exceptional. In 1880, the average workweek had diminished to seventy-two hours, and in 1900 to sixty-six hours. In 1889, a bill had been passed that limited the duration of women's and children's work to twelve hours per day.

All children were paid a wage either directly or indirectly. If they were assisting their mother or father, and their pay was part of a collective wage earned by the parent (for example, pay for one task, to be divided between two to three workers, as at a spinning mule), they would generally receive no money. If they were working for non-kin or doing independent work, they would be given their own wage. An inquiry among almost 2,000 male and female Ghent cotton workers in 1899 showed a close bond between age and wage. The boys' wages rose by 14 percent per year between the ages of thirteen and twenty-one, while the girls' wages rose by 10 percent. The rhythm of increase is shown in Table 2.

At thirteen, boys' weekly wage lay below that of girls, but the wage of the former rose more rapidly than that of the latter (by 3.4 and 2.4 percent per year, respectively), which left boys with higher wages than girls of the same age. At age nineteen, boys earned almost 60 percent of the average wage of an adult male worker, but girls then had already obtained nearly three-quarters of the average wage of an adult female worker. All in all, the strict, almost universal, hierarchy of wages appears, with male workers at the top, female adult workers earning about three-quarters of the male wage, and children (of both sexes) earning about one-third of the male wage.

The fact that the Ghent cotton mills employed many women and children was seen as influencing the general wage level of the industry. Wages of adult male workers in the Ghent cotton mills lay below the average wage of such workers elsewhere in Belgium. As a result of lower male wage levels, children and especially women contributed highly to the family income of Ghent cotton workers, more than in other industrial centers of Belgium. Around 1900, all living-in children (disregarding age) contributed 20 percent to total family income of Ghent cotton workers, which was slightly below the national average. This is explained by the fact that wages in Ghent were low, and by the fact that mothers contributed significantly more to the Ghent family budget than mothers in other parts of the country.

The proportion of the children's contribution to the family budget fluctuated according to the family life cycle. In the beginning of the life cycle, about 5 percent of children between six and ten years old worked for a wage (which, then, was prohibited by law), contributing about 3 percent to total household income. In mature families, about 70 percent of children (between twelve and eighteen years) performed paid labor, and they contributed about 40 percent to the total household income. The contribution of children to the budget of "cotton families" was directly linked to the mother's income, which, in turn, was influenced by her husband's (generally moderate) wage.

Child Labor Discussed and Limited, but Utilized

The participation of child labor in factories was investigated and discussed since the 1830s, but it was not until 1889 that a bill was passed limiting child labor in Belgian industry. Ghent industrialists were particularly active in the debates, generally advocating prohibiting child labor below twelve years. In 1859, for example, the association of Ghent employers proposed to prohibit the labor of all children below the age of twelve, as well as to limit the work of girls below the age of eighteen to a maximum of twelve hours per day. Actually, the contemporary state of Ghent textile mills was already in line with both measures. In Parliament, arguments against the prohibition were that children could learn a job, that they contributed to the family income, that the wage cost in the mills remained under control, and that a bill would affect the employers' freedom. Such arguments were formulated well into the 1880s, when the bill was finally passed.

Children below twelve years of age disappeared from the cotton mills after the 1860s, but the number of children between twelve and sixteen rose. This was directly linked to control of the mills' wage bill. The employment of boys and girls from the age of twelve onward was hardly discussed in legislative debates, and the wages of this group of workers generally reached 30 to 40 percent of the adult wage. Further, technological and organizational changes since the 1860s enabled nearly identical quantity and quality of work by all workers. Hence, employment of boys and girls between twelve and sixteen grew. Some factories developed specific employment policies that were aimed at the systematic enlistment of the cheapest workforce—that is, young girls—even after the share of young girls started to diminish in most factories after 1880. One cotton mill expanded the number of girls below the age of nineteen from 13.2 percent of the total workforce in the 1840s to 41.1 percent in the 1900s. These factories could not invest in new machinery, nor could they move to the surrounding countryside to lower the wage bill. Hence, they developed this particular low-wage strategy.

The number of boys and girls between twelve and sixteen in the Ghent cotton mills fell gradually in the first half of the twentieth century. In the 1920s the mills did not use workers younger than fifteen. Ongoing technological innovations, the introduction of compulsory school attendance in

1914, with effects in the early 1920s, and the pressure of unions and other progressive forces led to the gradual diminishing of work of youngsters below age sixteen.

References and Further Reading

De Neve, Mieke. "Kinderarbeid van omstreeks 1800 tot 1914." *Tijdschrift voor Industriële Cultuur* 10:1 (1992): 4–45.

Scholliers, Peter. *Wages, Manufacturers and Workers in the Nineteenth-Century Factory: The Voortman Cotton Mill in Ghent.* Oxford: Berg Publishers, 1996.

Van den Eeckhout, Patricia. "Family Income of Ghent Working-Class Families circa 1900." *Journal of Family History* 18:2 (1993): 87–110.

Varlez, Louis. *Les salaires dans l'industrie gantoise. I. Industrie cotonnière.* Brussels: Office du Travail–Lebègue, 1901.

France

France: A Historical Overview

Colin Heywood, Reader in Modern French History, University of Nottingham

France was one of a small group of countries that embarked early on the path to industrialization during the eighteenth and early nineteenth centuries. It had its share of spinning mills, coal mines, ironworks, and other manifestations of modern industrial society—not least the widespread employment of "child labor" as conventionally understood during the Industrial Revolution. Yet her gradual, unobtrusive path to industrialization meant that small-scale forms of industry in town and countryside proved exceptionally resilient. Throughout the nineteenth century, as much as nine-tenths of French industry took the form of a *fabrique collective* (collective works), a form of production in which specialized firms of varying sizes came together to manufacture a particular product. Well-known examples include the silk industry of Lyon and the fine furniture trade of the Faubourg St.-Antoine in Paris. Beyond that, there was the persistence of a large agricultural sector in France. As late as the 1940s, up to a third of the French labor force remained on traditional, often marginal farms. The upshot was that children were employed in numerous types of work, whose impact on their health, education, and moral welfare varied considerably. Campaigns to regulate or abolish child labor during the nineteenth and twentieth centuries struggled to come to terms with these circumstances. It was one thing to enforce a law covering a relatively limited number of factories, quite another to inspect a myriad of small workshops in a city such as Paris or Lyon.

Child Labor in the Textile Mills

The conventional story of *le travail des enfants* (child labor) begins with the borrowing of new British technologies for spinning cotton and other fibers during the late eighteenth century. James Milne, one of the first renegade workers to smuggle new inventions from Lancashire to France, supported his bid for government funding during the 1780s by emphasizing the potential for employing the previously unemployable on his textile machinery, including "very small children." Some of the early mills mobilized child labor on a large scale. Nine-tenths of the labor force at the Foxlow mill in Orléans in 1790 were boys and girls between five and sixteen, or widowed and infirm women. The Perret spinning mill at Neuville, in the Lyonnais, occupied forty-two women and ninety young girls in 1783 (Chassagne 1991, 193–94).

The association of the first generation of textile mills with the employment of marginal elements in the labor force encouraged a further parallel with British experience: the drafting of *enfants assistés* (pauper apprentices) onto the shop floor. Charitable institutions in France had a long tradition of placing orphaned and abandoned children on farms or in workshops to help give them a start in life. The turbulent period of revolution and war during the 1790s swelled the ranks of such children, providing the new breed of industrial entrepreneurs with one solution to a tricky problem: tempting workers into the unfamiliar conditions of the factory system. The unfortunate children became, in effect, forced labor. A decree of 1796 allowed employers to bid for batches of *enfants assistés* to take on as apprentices. The hard-pressed administration was relieved of the need to pay for their upkeep, and the employers benefited from the long-term contracts imposed on them. Cotton spinners Bernard Delaître and Antoine Noël, for example, requested a contingent of 120 such girls age ten to fourteen, arguing that labor was difficult to recruit in their rural area of the Seine-et-Oise *département*. Their contract revealed that the girls had to remain with the firm until they were twenty-one, and any who tried to escape were liable to be arrested and returned to the mill.[1]

The 1790s set the pattern for the routine employment of children in French textile mills. Contemporaries soon came to perceive child labor as an issue associated with the factory system. The Alsatian industrialist and reformer Jean-Jacques Bourcart wrote in his pamphlet *Du travail des jeunes ouvriers dans les manufactures, usines ou ateliers* (1840), "It is in industrial establishments where power-driven machinery necessitates the work of children beside adults, and especially in all types of mechanized spinning mills and similar workshops, that the harmful effects of excessive child labor have been particularly noted." There was some justification for this particular social construction of child labor. Factory children in manufacturing regions such as Normandy and Alsace were conspicuous by their numbers on the streets around the mills. Investigations into conditions in the textile industry during the 1830s by Dr. Louis Villermé produced a number of distressing—and eminently quotable—images of child workers. Of those in Alsace, he wrote, "All pale, nervous, slow in their movements, quiet at their games, they present an outward appearance of misery, of suffering, of dejection, that contrasts with the rosy color, the plumpness, the petulance and all the signs of glowing health that one notices in children of the same age each time that he leaves a manufacturing area to enter an agricultural canton" (Weissbach 1989, 49). The long working hours and noxious atmosphere that Villermé and other social investigators uncovered in the early mills are well-known. During the 1830s, for example, the spinning mills emerged as the most exacting branch of industry for children, who routinely worked from five in the morning until eight o'clock at night. An official survey of child labor in 1837 noted that in some towns, such as Mulhouse and Rouen, children might start work at the age of five or six—though in others ten or twelve was common.

An industrial inquiry of 1839–1845, in principle focused on larger enterprises, found that of the 1.2 million workers covered, 143,665 (12.1 percent) were children under sixteen years of age. More than two-thirds of these young people were employed in the textile industries. Certain branches relied heavily on juvenile employees. Above all, in spinning and calico printing, children accounted for between a quarter and a third of the labor force. Otherwise, it was only in a few sections of metalworking trades, ceramics, and papermaking that children formed a sizable proportion of the total (Heywood 1988, 104–6). Children were therefore of some importance to industry, though by the 1840s most acted merely as assistants to adult workers.

Children in the Smaller Workshops and on the Land

All the attention devoted to the drama of children dragooned into the new textile mills brings the risk for historians of overlooking the far larger cohorts who worked in the informal sector of manufacturing or on family farms. Many of these were hidden from view in the backstreets of big cities or deep in the countryside, making it difficult to estimate the numbers involved. The first inquiry into child labor in France in 1837, organized by the Ministry of Commerce, showed little interest in them, beginning as it did with the question, "From what age are children received into the factories?" Yet a summary of the findings of the inquiry by the Bureau des Manufactures noted that, whereas large workshops were relatively common in England, workers in France were generally more isolated.

The rapid spread of cottage industries in the countryside, linked to international markets by merchant-manufacturers in the towns, drew large numbers of children into a grueling work regime. In the Pays de Caux area of Normandy, for example, the number of handloom weavers shot up from around 20,000 in 1780 to 110,000 in 1848. Young children in weaving families prepared bobbins for the weavers' shuttles, while older ones, from the age of ten or eleven, learned to weave (Gullickson 1986, 108–9). In the cutlery industry of the Auvergne, centered on the town of Thiers, family workshops for ten to fifteen miles around straddled mountain streams that turned wheels for sharpening and polishing. In 1880 a child labor inspector reported that the children spent the summer watching over livestock in the surrounding hills, and the winter polishing in the workshops. Marie-Catherine Gardez, in *Mémé Santerre* (1975), left a vivid account of life as a child worker in one such cottage industry: linen weaving in the Pas-de-Calais. She recalled how, during the 1900s, she started work on the handloom when she was still too short to reach the pedals without special wooden blocks, and put in an eighteen-hour day like the other villagers around her.

Meanwhile, "sweatshops" in the towns occupied another small army of child workers in conditions that often appalled contemporary observers. In Lyon, for example, there were approximately 17,000 handlooms for weaving silk by the middle of the nineteenth century, and a further 12,000 in the *faubourgs*. The looms were dispersed in a myriad of small workshops. The children of the *canuts,* as the silk weavers were known, began when they were very small winding bobbins, then from the age of nine to fourteen worked as *lanceurs,* throwing the shuttle on the larger looms. Most of the work was quite light, but the fourteen-hour day of the weavers was, to say the least, tiring for the young. Once again, an autobiographical account of life for a child worker in a sweatshop provides compelling evidence of the strains and stresses involved. Norbert Truquin described in his *Mémoires et aventures d'un prolétaire à travers la révolution* (1888) the experience of working from the age of seven in a wool comber's shop in Reims during the 1840s. He recalled trying to stay awake during a working day that lasted from four in the morning until ten at night, to avoid the blows of his master. His job was to hold a strand of wool tightly in his hands and pick out any impurities with his teeth.

The most numerous group of child workers was presumably those employed on the land, particularly the small family farms of the peasantry, given that three-quarters of the French population still lived in a village in 1851. However, contemporaries tended to consider farm work a healthy outdoor activity for the young rather than an abuse. Children were physically unsuitable for most jobs in the fields, so they took on little tasks such as looking after infants, fetching water, and, above all, *la garde des bestiaux*: keeping an eye on the family's livestock. Shepherding was sometimes a lonely occupation, with long hours exposed to the elements, but it was often possible to meet up with other young people and play games. The eighteenth-century writer Rétif de la Bretonne depicted his character Monsieur Nicolas volunteering to look after the family's flock of sheep, even though he was from a wealthy enough background to spare him such tasks, purely for the sociability involved. Once they had taken their First Communion, usually in their early teens during the eighteenth and nineteenth centuries, the young peasants were ready to move on to more arduous work beside adults in the fields, or, in the case of females, around the home.

The Child Labor Reform Campaign

The first group of reformers in France were themselves employers of child labor, from the Industrial Society of Mulhouse. Their main concern was the future quality of their workers. They had no objections to child labor per se, seeking rather to curb abuses appearing in the new factory system. Cotton spinner Jean-Jacques Bourcart effectively launched the campaign in 1827 with a famous speech that depicted children working in the mills as feeble, illiterate, and morally debased. He proposed following the British model of factory legislation, with the emphasis on improving the health and education of the workers. During the 1830s the Académie des Sciences Morales et Politiques joined the fray. Its leading light in this field, Dr. Villermé, took a different perspective. His extensive investigations into the conditions of workers in textile towns led him to assert that industrial employers were victimizing some of the weakest and most vulnerable members of society. He wrote that children were already subject to the "debauchery and thriftlessness" of their parents. His most pressing concern was the mingling of the sexes in the workshops, notably at night. It followed that one of the principal recommendations of his monumental *Tableau de l'état physique et moral des ouvriers* (1840) was a law to ensure the separation of males and females in the factories. Villermé also assembled evidence to show that industrial employment was destroying the health of children, though he went no further than to demand a limitation on the hours that they could work. He listed such afflictions as lung disease among cotton workers and bandy legs among children operating the drawstrings on silk weaving looms. He and other reformers made extensive use of military conscription records to argue that manufacturing areas struggled more than agricultural ones to meet their quotas for men fit enough to serve.

The 1837 inquiry on child labor revealed business interests to be divided on the issue of reform. Supporters of factory legislation in Mulhouse and a few other towns faced opposition from their counterparts elsewhere, especially in Lille. The latter group denied that conditions in France made it necessary for the state to intervene in the labor market as it had in Britain. They warned that poor families depended on income from their children, and that French firms would risk succumbing to foreign competition if their liberty was curtailed. The French reform campaign was notable for remaining firmly confined to polemics among members of the upper strata of society. In contrast to Britain, the government made no effort to find out what workers thought about the issue, nor was there any pressure from below from organized labor. The polarized nature of French politics at this period came into play here, with the labor movement heavily repressed after the revolutionary upheavals of the early 1830s. Successive ministers of commerce during this period proved lukewarm on the matter. However, the persistence of the reformers eventually produced the Child Labor Law of March 22, 1841. The law followed a pattern already well established by the earlier British factory acts. It graded working hours, allowing children age eight to twelve years no more than eight hours of work a day, those age twelve to sixteen no more than twelve hours. It banned night work for those under thirteen. No less important, it insisted on some education for working children until the age of twelve.

The Decline of Child Labor

Measuring the decline in child labor during the nineteenth and twentieth centuries proves difficult in the French case, above all because the census did not publish data on the age distribution of the economically active population until 1896. Evidence suggests that there was a growing reluctance to employ children among larger industrial enterprises during the second half of the nineteenth century, but the withdrawal of the young from work in smaller workshops and on the land was a more protracted process. In some areas, the mid-nineteenth century brought a decrease in the proportion of children under sixteen employed in the factories. In the spinning mills of the Seine-Inférieure *département,* for example, their share of the labor force fell from over a quarter to less than a fifth between 1840 and 1870, and in the weaving sheds, from one-fifth to one-tenth. Moreover, if reports of child labor inspectors are at all reliable, the 1870s and 1880s witnessed a steady elimination of the youngest children, those under twelve, from the workshops. In the domestic workshops and family farms, the scope for skimping on the education of children, or at least of expecting work before and after school, prolonged the employment of children until the First World War, and beyond.

Historians have diverged in their explanations for the decline in child labor. The most obvious explanation, and indeed the one routinely proffered by French historians, is the gradual tightening of child labor legislation over the long term. Thus, the 1841 law is written off as a virtual dead letter, notably on account of its ineffectual system of inspection by voluntary, unpaid commissions. A new law would not appear until 1874. At least its willingness to cover all workshops, rather than those with only twenty or more workers, and its network of sixteen paid inspectors, gave it some teeth. The next law, passed in 1892, took decisive steps in raising the minimum working age to thirteen, and in requiring an inspector in each *département* to support the existing divisional inspectors. However, this line of argument has its drawbacks. Above all, it can do little to explain any decline in child labor before the 1870s, and it underestimates the difficulties of enforcing such legislation in the face of widespread cheating and the sheer number of small workshops in the towns. The divisional inspector based in Lyon noted in 1880 that he had 12,000 small workshops to visit in the city alone, not to mention those in Saint-Étienne and Grenoble.

A very different explanation is to assert that the onward march of industrialization itself encouraged the withdrawal of children from the workshops. A growing scale of machinery and an interest in raising the productivity of labor arguably caused employers to become disillusioned with child workers. In the calico-printing industry of Alsace, for example, the replacement of hand printing by machinery with rollers made the child *tireurs* redundant. During the 1880s, an inspector in Lyon attributed a reduction in employment of children to "the incessant perfecting of mechanisms which tend increasingly to be substituted for labor." Meanwhile, rising real wages from the 1850s onward made it rational for parents to invest in the education of their children instead of expecting them to bring in income. This is all very well, but the sweatshops that flourished beside the factories, even in the twenty-first century, rather dent the optimistic perspective of this explanation. Moreover, even quite well-paid groups of workers, such as those in the glassworks, proved remarkably attached to the practice of child labor during the late nineteenth and early twentieth centuries.

Finally, one explanation points to the influence of a secular change in attitudes toward childhood. People began to think it was wrong to expect children to work, and that a "proper" childhood allowed time for schooling and play. The influence of an Enlightenment thinker such as Jean-Jacques Rousseau, or the Romantic poets, was at first confined to the educated elite. Peasants, in particular, remained committed to the notion that one should learn to be a farmer *sur le tas* (on the job), and even in the mid-twentieth century often feared that schooling would uproot the young from the land. All the same, it was during the nineteenth century that the French population demonstrated a growing appetite for primary schooling. Measuring school attendance in this period is a hazardous business, but statistics do at least indicate a precocious start to primary schooling early in the century, followed by a massive boost during the 1850s, and regular increases after that. If education, in a sense, welled up from below in French society, the state played a supportive role, encouraging much of the infrastructure with the Guizot Law of 1833, and local authorities pitched in with funding for free places. Hence, most children were receiving some schooling by the time the Ferry Laws of the 1880s made it free, and compulsory to the age of thirteen, or twelve if one had passed the *certificat d'études.*

Note

1. French National Archives (series on commerce and industry) 2458, Paris.

References and Further Reading

Caty, Roland, ed. *Enfants au travail: attitude des élites en Europe occidentale et méditerranéenne aux XIXe et XXe siècles.* Aix-en-Provence: Publications de l'Université de Provence, 2002.

Chassagne, Serge. *Le coton et ses patrons: France, 1760–1840.* Paris: Éditions de l'École des Hautes Études en Sciences Sociales, 1991.

Chassagne, Serge. "Le travail des enfants aux XVIIIe et XIXe siècles." In *Histoire de l'enfance en Occident.* Vol. 2, *Du XVIIIe siècle à nos jours,* ed. Egle Becchi and Dominique Julia, 224–72. Paris: Seuil, 1998.

Furet, François, and Jacques Ozouf. *Reading and Writing: Literacy in France from Calvin to Jules Ferry.* Cambridge: Cambridge University Press, 1982.

Gullickson, Gay L. *Spinners and Weavers of Auffay: Rural Industry and the Sexual Division of Labor in a French Village, 1750–1850.* Cambridge: Cambridge University Press, 1986.

Heywood, Colin. *Childhood in Nineteenth-Century France: Work, Health and Education Among the "Classes Populaires."* Cambridge: Cambridge University Press, 1988.

Traugott, Mark, ed. *The French Worker: Autobiographies from the Early Industrial Era.* Berkeley: University of California Press, 1993.

Weissbach, Lee Shai. *Child Labor Reform in Nineteenth-Century France: Assuring the Future Harvest.* Baton Rouge: Louisiana State University Press, 1989.

Germany

History of Child Labor in Germany: An Overview

Thomas Max Safley, Professor of History, University of Pennsylvania

Children have always labored. This bald statement is true in Germany, as it is elsewhere. Problems arise, however, with regard to the definition of terms, specifically of "children" and "labor." What exactly is a child? In premodern Europe, a number of ages, ranging from as young as seven to as old as sixteen, might mark the transition from child to youth or adult, the age at which people might reasonably be expected to contribute, partially or entirely, to their own keep. It is worth noting that all these ages would be seen, today, as stages of childhood, thus arrogating to the concept of child labor the employment of what were then considered adults. For purposes of this essay, "children" are taken broadly to mean persons who had not yet received First Communion, which occurred as a rule between the ages of fourteen and sixteen, and was often taken to mark the point at which a young person was physically and spiritually ready to labor. What is labor? Children labored from a tender age within the parental household—a social and economic reality of premodern Europe—in ways that ceased to be the case as household and workplace became physically separated in the course of industrialization. Whereas such labor could have economic value, reducing the costs of production and increasing the earnings of the family, it rarely took the form of paid employment. Tasks appropriate to the physical and mental abilities of children were seen as integral to their training and rearing, and the setting of these tasks formed an integral part of every parent's responsibility. For purposes of this essay, "labor" refers to the compensated work of children, whether hired, institutionalized, indentured, or kept, outside the parental household.

Thus understood, child labor may well have been not only a social reality, but even a daily commonplace, in premodern Germany. Much anecdotal evidence exists to suggest as much: The laboring child appears variously in folk traditions, householder literature, moral tracts, and craft ordinances. Unfortunately, none of these sources provides the necessary quantitative data to make possible measurement and comparison over time. It is, therefore, impossible to know with certainty, though it seems highly likely, that the resort to child labor expanded during the early modern period, becoming more intensive and systematic as states and elites promoted labor as a discipline to be exercised and children as a resource to be mobilized.

Because the majority of Germany's population engaged in rural occupations until the nineteenth century, any consideration of child labor should begin in the countryside. Peasant children usually entered the labor force by performing agricultural chores, domestic service, or proto-industrial employment. Where adults were unwilling or unable to labor, children often took their place, performing such tasks as were appropriate to their physical and mental abilities. The agricultural revolution of the late seventeenth and eighteenth centuries contributed to this process as the drive to increase crop production while reducing labor costs encouraged reliance on child labor. Livestock herding, for example, though traditionally an adult employment, came to be viewed as a suitable job for children. With the enclosure of common lands in Upper Swabia, the number and size of livestock herds increased, raising demand for herders. A seasonal traffic in child labor (*Schwabenkinder*) emerged to meet this demand. Boys between the ages of seven and seventeen walked every spring from the regions of Tyrol and Vorarlberg to work summers as herders for peasants over the border in Swabia. By 1796 the number of juvenile migrants had risen as high as 700, with informal hiring fairs in cities such as Kempten. It remained an established practice well into the nineteenth century. Nor was such labor always voluntary on the parts of parents and children. The compulsory placement of orphaned, abandoned, or destitute children has a long history in Germany. Authorities and institutions placed poor children in households, whether through private indenture (*Kostkinder*) or public auction.

The transformation of agriculture and the variety of agricultural employments created new forms of child labor and many opportunities for child exploitation. Domestic service was another common employment of children in rural Germany from the Middle Ages into the modern era, though the evidence is equivocal. In Bavaria, for example, the role of children in domestic service may have increased during the early modern period, the result of unwillingness on the part of adults to perform it. In Westphalia, however, it appears that children under the age of fourteen were seldom sent away from the parental household, and tended to live with their parents beyond the age of service. Many parents refused to expose their children to the bad treatment, poor food, and low wages that were too often characteristic of indentured service and domestic labor.

For many rural children in Germany, there was labor to be had within the parental household. Proto-industry or cottage industry, understood as traditionally organized market-oriented manufacturing, tended to increase the labor performed by children. In a widely cited article, Hans Medick argued that child labor "which both in its intensity and duration went far beyond that of the corresponding labor of farm peasants' households, was in fact a vital necessity for the rural cottage workers' families," to the point that the material existence of the proto-industrial family depended on child labor as the "capital of the poor man." Nearly all textile-producing regions of Germany saw similar developments. Children labored alongside their parents. Often they performed ancillary tasks, such as spinning yarns, winding spools, or threading looms. In many places, they entered directly into the production process. In and around Krefeld, for example, children made lace as putting-out work.

As with rural work, where the lack of specific information makes generalization difficult, the same can be said of child labor in penal or charitable institutions. Compulsory industrial work in orphanages and workhouses appears to have been an innovation of early modern Europe. In many parts of Europe, Germany included, the number of poor increased from the fifteenth century, a result of structural changes in the labor market: high unemployment, declining wages, and population growth. City and state authorities responded with regulations that prohibited begging and required labor. Rather than succored with alms at great expense to the community and its elite, the poor were to be made self-sufficient: The able would be required to work for their sustenance; the young would be accustomed to work for their self-sufficiency. In prisons, workhouses, and orphanages, children past early infancy and adults were compelled to work. The work they performed most often involved textile and clothing production, especially spinning. Such institutions proliferated in Germany from the late seventeenth century onward, but the doctrine of educating and acclimating poor children to lives of labor gained currency far earlier, as demonstrated by the orphanages of Augsburg. The orphans of Augsburg were subjected to a rigid time discipline that governed their movements through each day of the week. With a certain amount of time given over to study—in principle, each child should learn to read, write, and reckon—the majority of each day was spent in purposeful labor, assisting orphanage servants in the entire range of housekeeping tasks. Never themselves sites of industrial production, the orphanages nonetheless exposed their charges to the rigors of productive labor by placing them temporarily as wage laborers in the city's households and workshops and, thus, allowing them to earn a part of their keep, to learn the basic tasks of a craft, and to acquire the ability and inclination to labor. Needy orphans were to become self-supporting workers. In the course of time, usually by the age of sixteen, Augsburg's orphans were placed in households and workshops to make them productive and self-sufficient. They were also indentured to those new industrial forms that began to emerge in the seventeenth and eighteenth centuries: putting-out industries, large manufactories, and, eventually, machine technologies. As a result, children and youths became more prominent in the labor forces of Augsburg and elsewhere. Yet, the resort to child labor seems to have lagged behind in Germany compared to other more rapidly industrializing nations or regions. Perhaps due to their late industrialization, German manufactories made relatively little use of child labor, except in textile production. That said, early modern German authorities and elites, like their peers elsewhere in Europe, did not hesitate to use child labor in households, workshops, and manufactories—anywhere adults were unwilling or unable to work.

The resort to child labor increased with the Industrial Revolution. Two factors seem to have determined the presence of children in mills: availability and cost. As has been argued for Britain, poor children were often the only available labor force that could be compelled to work in the new factories. Adults, accustomed to other technologies and organizations, simply refused the new systems and new ways. Likewise, the costs of child labor were assumed to be lower than those of adult labor. Textile producers especially attempted to cut costs by employing women and children, the unskilled and dependent. Only the advent of new, more sensitive means of accounting for productivity revealed the reality that child labor resulted in lower productivity and lower profitability and encouraged, therefore, a turn to cost-cutting alternatives. Child labor remained common in Germany until the 1880s, perhaps because the majority of German laborers worked in technologically less-advanced industries. The textile industry offers an example. Most German industrial establishments were small, employing fewer than ten persons and producing labor-intensive consumer goods. Though by no means unknown, large textile factories were still rare in Germany at the turn of the twentieth century. The dominance of handicraft-type firms may explain both their lower labor productivity and their continued reliance on child labor. More-efficient production processes, characterized by automated spinning and weaving, obviated the need for cheap labor in the 1920s and 1930s, but the use of child labor persisted in textiles, as it did in the more artisanal industries of glass, brick, and pottery manufacturing. Industrial tradition may explain, in part, the reluctance to abandon child labor, even when its use was no longer economically rational. Another explanation resides in the simple fact that most labor reformers did not object to it. They wished to regulate it, not to abolish it. The 1903 German Child Labor Act, for example, limited only the work time for children, age twelve and over, during the school year. That child labor was abandoned during the late nineteenth and twentieth centuries, in Germany as elsewhere, had to do not with outraged moral censure but rather with new forms of production and exploitation.

Though the lack of reliable statistical data renders nearly all conclusions suspect, a few generalities seem warranted. Child labor appears to have been a social and economic reality throughout history in Germany. Its full extent and intensity cannot finally be determined. Changes in the employment of children can be linked to the supply of adult labor; children entered those industries or sectors where adults were unavailable or uneconomical. All evidence indicates that child labor increased from the late fifteenth to the early twentieth century, the result of changing market conditions that placed a premium on increased productivity and decreased costs. These conditions were accompanied by an ethos—by no means new in itself—of work as a social and moral good. Child labor was abandoned not because it came to be viewed as immoral, but rather because it ceased to be economical.

References and Further Reading

Braun, Rudolf. *Industrialization and Everyday Life.* Cambridge: Cambridge University Press, 1990.

Büttner, Christian, and Aurel Ende, eds. *Jahrbuch der Kindheit 1: Kinderleben in Geschichte und Gegenwart.* Basel: Beltz Verlag, 1984.

Herzig, Arno. "Kinderarbeit in Deutschland in Manufaktur und Proto-Fabrik (1750–1850)." *Archiv für Sozialgeschichte* 13 (1983): 311–75.

Hoppe, Ruth, ed. *Geschichte der Kinderarbeit in Deutschland 1750–1939.* Vol. 2. Berlin: Verlag Neues Leben, 1958.

Kreidte, Peter, Hans Medick, and Jürgen Schlumbohm. *Industrialization Before Industrialization: Rural Industry in the Genesis of Capitalism.* Cambridge: Cambridge University Press, 1981.

Kuczynski, Jürgen. *Geschichte der Kinderarbeit in Deutschland 1750–1939.* Vol. 1. Berlin: Verlag Neues Leben, 1958.
Lenger, Friedrich. *Sozialgeschichte der deutschen Handwerker seit 1800.* Frankfurt: Suhrkamp, 1988.
Medick, Hans. "The Proto-Industrial Family Economy: The Structural Functions of Household and Family During the Transition from Peasant Society to Industrial Capitalism." *Social History* 1:3 (1976): 291–315.
Medick, Hans. *Weben und Überleben in Laichingen, 1650–1900.* Göttingen: Vandenhoeck and Ruprecht, 1997.
Ogilvie, Sheilagh. "Coming of Age in a Corporate Society: Capitalism, Pietism and Family Authority in Rural Württemberg, 1590–1740." *Continuity and Change* 1:3 (1986): 279–331.
Pollock, Linda. *Forgotten Children: Parent-Child Relations from 1500 to 1800.* Cambridge: Cambridge University Press, 1983.
Rahikainen, Marjatta. *Centuries of Child Labour: European Experiences from the Seventeenth to the Twentieth Century.* Aldershot: Ashgate, 2004.
Rinneberg, Karl-Jürgen. *Das betriebliche Ausbildungswesen in der Zeit der industriellen Umgestaltung Deutschlands.* Cologne: Böhlau Verlag, 1985.
Ruppert, W., ed. *Die Arbeiter: Lebensformen, Alltag und Kultur von Frühindustrialisierung zum "Wirtschaftswunder."* Munich: Verlag C.H. Beck, 1986.
Safley, Thomas Max. *Charity and Economy in the Orphanages of Early Modern Augsburg.* Boston: Humanities Press, 1997.
Safley, Thomas Max. *Children of the Laboring Poor: Expectation and Experience Among the Orphans of Early Modern Augsburg.* Leiden: Brill Academic Publishers, 2005.
Schlumbohm, Jürgen. *Lebensläufe, Familien, Höfe: Die Bauern und Heuerleute des Osnabrückischen Kirchspiels Belm in proto-industrieller Zeit, 1650–1860.* Göttingen: Vandenhoeck and Ruprecht, 1994.
Stier, Bernhard. *Fürsorge und Disziplinierung im Zeitalter des Absolutismus. Das Pforzheimer Zucht- und Waisenhaus und die badische Sozialpolitik im 18. Jahrhundert.* Sigmaringen: Thorbecke Verlag, 1988.
Sträter, Udo, and Josef N. Neumann, eds. *Waisenhäuser in der Frühen Neuzeit.* Stuttgart: Fritz Steiner Verlag, 2004.
Tenfelde, Klaus, ed. *Arbeit und Arbeitserfahrung in der Geschichte.* Göttingen: Vandenhoeck and Ruprecht, 1986.
Uhlig, Otto. *Die Schwabenkinder aus Tirol und Voralberg.* Innsbruck: Universitätsverlag Wagner and Konrad Theiss Verlag, 1978.

New Risks and New Opportunities in School-to-Work Transition: The Transformation of the German Apprenticeship System

Jan Skrobanek, PhD, **Birgit Reissig,** MA, and **Nora Gaupp,** PhD, Researchers at the German Youth Institute (DJI), Munich/Halle

In nearly all industrialized countries, young people increasingly face rapid changes in vocational training and employment. They have to adapt themselves more and more quickly to changing requirements with regard to qualification, employment, and ways of acquiring qualifications needed for employment, and have to develop strategies for dealing with these requirements in a productive way (Blossfeld et al. 2005). The reasons for the rapid changes in job preconditions lie in increasing internationalization of markets, increasing competition between industrial sites and companies, the associated up-and-down dynamics of working conditions and the organization of work processes, and the increasing importance of the Internet. These developments have strong direct and indirect impacts on the transition into the adult world for the younger generation (Shavit and Müller 1998).

Against the background of these driving forces, a fundamental structural change has taken place in the developed Western societies that is opening up new opportunities for these societies and their members, but also exposing them to risks. In the past, risks such as unemployment, illness, or inability to work were largely cushioned by social security systems. However, particularly in the strongly industrialized nations, the challenge of coping with these risks is now increasingly being left to individuals themselves, presupposing that they have access to the necessary resources. The costs and risks of structural developments are being individualized and thus left to people's own responsibility. Mills and Blossfeld (2005, 6) argued, "Increasing uncertainty about economic and social developments is therefore a definite feature of globalization in advanced economies."

One aspect of society that is severely affected by these developments is the transition from school to employment. There is now a consensus that the developments described above are in fact taking place, and that qualification standards are now playing a much more decisive role in the ability of industrial societies to compete internationally. At the same time, however, there is considerable confusion about the effects of these changes on existing qualification structures and on vocational standards in each country.

The German apprenticeship system traditionally has been considered an effective approach to securing school-to-work transition for the majority of school leavers as well as providing qualified candidates to fill a large variety of positions in the labor force. As training takes place in enterprises, its relevance to the current and future requirements of the labor market seem to be guaranteed. In addition, the apprenticeship system traditionally has provided training and employment opportunities for adolescents who have completed only nine or ten years of compulsory general schooling. Will this system be able to continue to fulfil this function in a global economy?

School, Training, and Work in Germany: General Trends

Three factors are of particular interest for providing insights into the educational and training system in

Germany and setting it in relation to other countries: expenditure on education, participation in education, and levels of education achieved. The National Education Report (Konsortium Bildungsberichterstattung 2006) states that educational expenditure increased by 6.2 percent to €135.2 billion between 1995 and 2003. Although this expenditure represents a decline in relation to gross domestic product, due to demographic changes, more funds were actually available per person receiving education in 2003 than in 1995. The largest proportion of educational expenditure goes into the field of general schooling (36 percent). Large amounts also go into the apprenticeship system (10 percent) and vocational schooling (7 percent). Overall, expenditure on education in Germany is slightly above the average for all OECD countries.

Currently, nearly two-thirds of the population under the age of thirty in Germany are attending educational institutions; this corresponds to 20 percent of the total population. The level of participation in education has increased continuously over the past thirty years, and is currently above the international average. This is mainly due to the well-developed vocational education system, in which vocational schools have become more important in recent years as a supplement to the apprenticeship system. Like the level of participation in education, the level of education in Germany has also markedly risen in recent years, as can be measured by the educational qualifications obtained. For example, among those now age thirty to thirty-five, the proportion with only lower secondary school (*Hauptschule*) certificates has fallen, and the proportion with university entrance diplomas (*Abitur*) has steadily increased. The level of education has also become markedly closer between the genders; the proportion of girls with university entrance qualifications is now higher than that of boys.

As people's lives and opportunities to attain better careers and positions in Germany are largely arranged around education, great importance is attached to diplomas and certificates (Müller and Shavit 1998). In their effort to achieve a qualitatively better status in the labor market, young people with poor school-leaving certificates, or without certificates, are thus often left empty-handed in comparison with those who have a better schooling and educational background (Solga 2005). In addition to the competition for status positions in the labor market between young people with better or poorer educational certificates, features of social structure play an important part in the distribution of opportunities. For example, there are significant regional disparities in Germany, mainly involving the differential between east and west.

The Special Case of the Tripartite School System

Although most school systems in Western Europe moved, between 1960 and 1980, to comprehensive structures with integrated schooling of the younger generation at the lower secondary level (up to grades nine or ten), the majority of German states continue to stream pupils into different types of secondary school after only four years of common elementary education. The different levels of secondary schooling consist of the lower secondary school (*Hauptschule*), in which compulsory education is completed after a total of nine or ten years; the middle school (*Realschule*), in which schooling is completed after a total of ten years; and the high school (*Gymnasium*), in which pupils are prepared for university entrance, involving a total of twelve or thirteen years of schooling. International observers tend to be puzzled by the survival of traditional educational structures that so obviously appear to lead to unequal access to further education and opportunities in the labor market.

Particularly because of the results of the OECD's international PISA (Program for International Student Assessment) study, which compared the competencies of fifteen-year-olds in the years 2000 and 2003, controversy over the future of the tripartite school system has, once again, arisen in Germany (PISA-Konsortium 2001). The results of PISA showed that sociocultural characteristics of the family of origin had a decisive influence on the competencies of fifteen-years-olds, thus underlining the high degree of social selectivity involved in the tripartite school system. In addition, the results showed that a substantial proportion of pupils completed their school careers much later in comparison with other countries, as a result of starting school later and repeating years. Finally, the authors of the German PISA study predicted that up to one-fourth of the age-group would find it difficult to meet the qualification requirements of the labor market due to an insufficient acquisition of competencies in literacy, mathematics, and the natural sciences.

The German Apprenticeship System

The Federal Republic of Germany (as well as Austria and Switzerland) has a school-to-work transition system that is unique throughout the world. The key institution in the German system is vocational education and training in apprenticeships (Müller, Steinmann, and Ell 1998). The apprenticeship system—paradigmatic for the German vocational training system—is strongly standardized and divided into vocational segments. The system's characteristic is that most of the vocational training provided takes place within enterprises, on the basis of a contractual relationship between apprentice and enterprise. While in many other European countries (particularly in Western Europe), access to skilled employment is obtained through vocational training in secondary schools, Germany's apprenticeship system traditionally has provided school leavers, who have completed compulsory education, with high-quality vocational training in enterprises. The system has provided access to this type of training at an early age and enabled its graduates to obtain attractive positions in the labor market at a younger age than their peers in other European countries. Comparatively low unemployment rates for young persons in Germany (particularly in comparison with countries in which vocational training takes place in schools) appear to prove the point that the apprenticeship system partly compensates for the potential disadvantages of early streaming of pupils and provides a relatively fast school-to-work transition for school leavers who have completed only compulsory general schooling.

Nevertheless, the functioning of this apprenticeship system is endangered by an increasing scarcity of training positions within the system (Figure 1). During the last seventeen years, the number of training positions within the apprenticeship system in Germany has declined by more than one-third, while the number of pupils leaving the general school system each year has increased continually since 1992 (Granato and Ulrich 2006). In 1992, 721,800 young persons began an apprenticeship. In 2005 that number was down to 562,800. The entry rate into the apprenticeship system fell from just under 80 percent in the early 1990s to below 60 percent by 2005. Causal factors include the increasing number of school leavers, an increasing number of applicants for apprenticeships, who, having failed to obtain a position in previous years, repeat their efforts in the following years, and the falling numbers of training positions being offered.

Figure 1 **Development of Participation in Vocational Training in Germany from 1992 to 2004–5 (as a percentage of school leavers)**

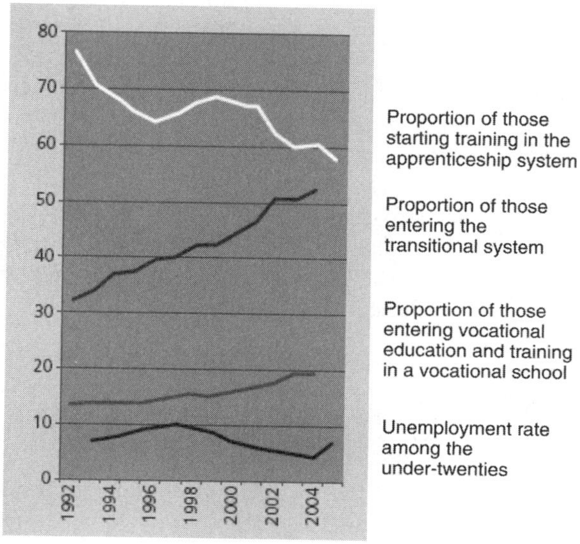

Source: Granato and Ulrich 2006, 35.

Expansion of the Transitional System Between School and Regular Vocational Training in an Apprenticeship

To compensate for the shortage of training positions in the apprenticeship system, there has been a substantial expansion of training schemes that were established between general education and regular vocational training. These training schemes, installed in vocational schools and charities, provide basic vocational training or preparation for regular training ("vocational preparation"), but do not lead to any formal vocational-training certificate. In 2006, the first National Education Report (Konsortium Bildungsberichterstattung 2006, 80) introduced the term "transitional system" for this new and expanding type of training activity between schools and apprenticeships. The report described the expansion of the transitional system that had taken place during the previous fifteen years as "possibly the most momentous and problematic structural shift" in the system of vocational education and training in Germany. The expansion of vocational preparation, installed to support the apprenticeship system as a key institution of school-to-work transition, has become an indicator of its erosion.

Effects on Young Persons' Transitions from School to Vocational Training

The expansion of the transitional system has had effects on the paths taken by young women and men in the transition from school to training and work. The general trend is an extension of the transition process: This involves increasingly longer periods of searching, more frequent participation in schemes of vocational preparation, and greater problems in subsequently converting these experiences into vocational qualifications or formal training. Transitions from school to work have become destabilized.

The German literature on transitional paths from school to employment for adolescents and young adults is voluminous. The studies unanimously show that there is a close connection between (low) educational levels achieved in general education and increased risks of unemployment (Shavit and Müller 1998). In addition, the studies provide evidence that generally the apprenticeship system reduces transition problems for those entering the employment market. However, employment risks are particularly high for persons who have completed only compulsory general education, and who, after general schooling, continued through the transitional system. If they are unable to take up and complete regular vocational training after that, they are likely to face precarious employment careers.

Though they are at a disadvantage compared to school leavers who manage to start an apprenticeship immediately, young persons may, under certain circumstances, improve their educational situation in the transitional system. Those who entered without a school diploma, but who managed to complete the transitional system, are more likely to continue through regular vocational education and training and to gain access to stable employment. However, there is also evidence that the chances of switching from the transitional system to regular training or employment decline the longer a young person is situated in that system. Despite this evidence, however, it is unclear under what circumstances the expanding transitional system in general, and schemes of vocational preparation in particular, improve training and employment opportunities or increase risks of exclusion from regular training and employment.

Young People from the Lower Secondary Schools—Losers or Winners in the Trend Toward Destandardization of the Transition Process?

Graduates from the lower secondary schools (*Hauptschule*) constitute the group of adolescents that is particularly affected by the process of destandardization of school-to-work transition in Germany. Adolescents who have completed only compulsory schooling bear a higher risk of ending up without any regular vocational training, of becoming unemployed, of having nonstandard work and employment conditions, or of following fragmented and interrupted working careers (Hammer 2003; Scherer 2001).

Despite the trends toward structural transformation of the transition phase, and the associated risk of a deterioration in opportunities for training and employment among adolescents with poor formal qualifications, there is also evidence that those affected find ways of dealing with this difficult situation productively (Braun 2006). In spite of poor initial chances, many of these adolescents are extremely flexible and try to achieve their goals—usually regular vocational training in an apprenticeship—by exploring a wide variety of detours through the transitional system.

Data from a national survey—the first to provide this extent of coverage—on school-to-work careers of educationally disadvantaged young people (see Figure 2) show that the majority of

Figure 2 **Educational and Training Paths Taken by Lower Secondary School Leavers**

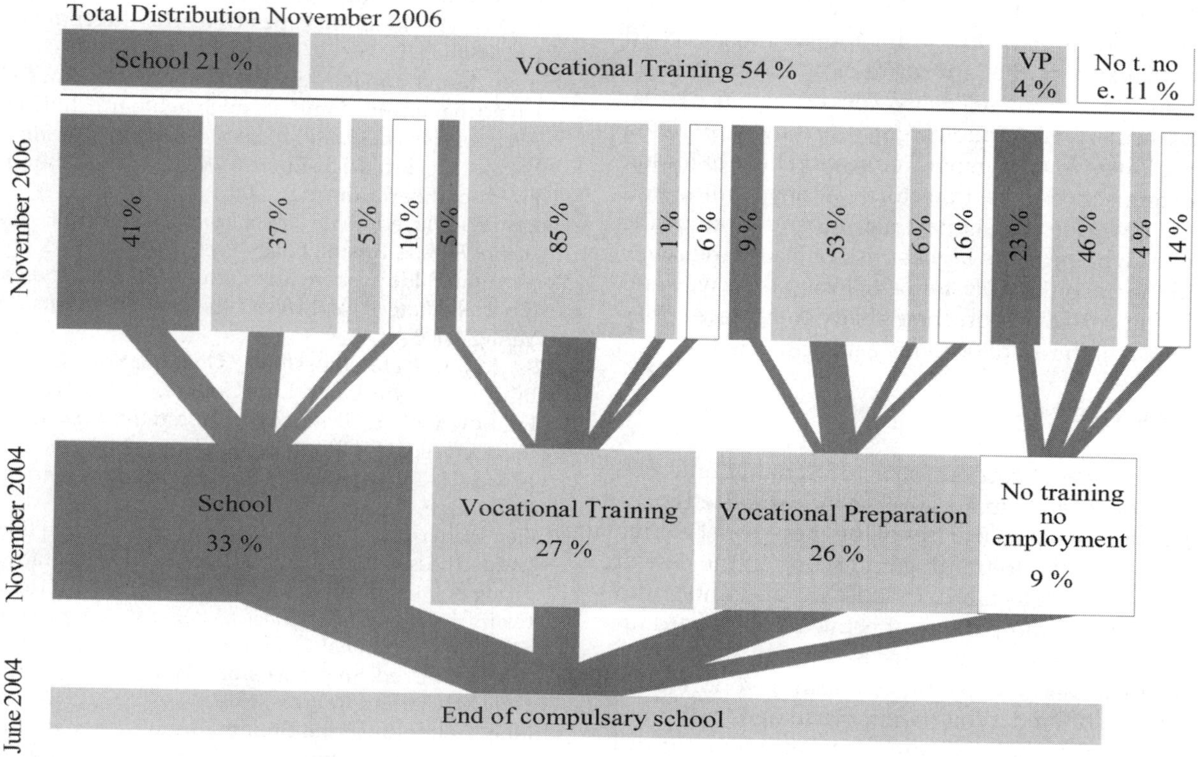

Source: DJI Ubergangspanel. © DJI 2006.
Notes: N = 1,522; VP = Vocational Preparation; No t. no e. = No training, no employment.

graduates from the lower secondary schools, using a wide variety of strategies, stopovers, and detours, do ultimately succeed in obtaining one of the coveted training places in the apprenticeship system (Reissig et al. 2006).

Only just over a quarter of the young people investigated were able to start an apprenticeship immediately after the end of compulsory schooling. The largest group, representing one-third, continued to attend school, either to repeat school-leaving examinations or to obtain better diplomas. Approximately a quarter went into schemes of vocational preparation in order to improve their qualifications for starting an apprenticeship, or at least to bridge the time until taking up an apprenticeship. A relatively small group, approximately one in ten, were neither in school, nor in the transitional system, nor in regular vocational training—that is, they were unemployed. Two years later, just over half of the young people had entered regular vocational training. One in five was continuing to attend school. In all, 80 percent of these young people continued to be in school, in the transitional system, or in regular training. The number of young people with neither training nor work remained at a constant level of 10 percent. In addition, there was an annual increase in the proportion of adolescents who had given up on education and training and had turned to unskilled labor.

What are our conclusions about the effects of an erosion of the apprenticeship system and the expansion of the transitional system on school-to-work transitions of adolescents from the lower secondary school? Our first conclusion is that the tripartite school system and the apprenticeship system no longer provide fast access to vocational training and skilled employment, but rather force young people to go through a period of difficult decision making, with uncertain outcomes, in a transitional system that, in the long run, provides access to vocational training for the majority and severe risks of exclusion for the rest. The second conclusion is that the transitional system lacks transparency and reliability. The consequence is that particularly those adolescents who have completed the lowest level of general education have to master extremely complex trajectories if they want to find their way into vocational training. And these are the ones who bear the highest risk of losing their way in the transitional system—of losing their way and losing confidence in their ability to achieve. They bear a high risk of becoming marginalized.

Prospects

The dynamic process of structural change enforced by globalization in the Western industrialized countries is leading to changes in the transitional regime from school into training and work. In the case of Germany, the facts are obvious: The apprenticeship system as a comparably effective route toward integration into employment is severely affected. Its ability to integrate young people into working society has suffered. While twenty years ago an apprenticeship was the way from school into training and then into employment, a many-faceted transitional system has been established, and it is still difficult to determine whether the trend this represents will lead to integration or failure to integrate.

This question particularly affects adolescents with poor starting conditions who, due to the changes in the labor market and the resulting risks, are threatened with exclusion, marginalization, and failure to integrate. Despite this, these young people—contradicting various prejudices in society—are often (against the background of their usually poor resources) highly motivated to find ways and means of integrating themselves into society. For the industrialized societies, recognizing this as a potential resource represents one of the central challenges for the future.

References and Further Reading

Blossfeld, Hans-Peter, Erik Klijzing, Melinda Mills, and Karin Kurz. eds. *Globalization, Uncertainty and Youth in Society.* London: Routledge, 2005.

Braun, Frank. "School-to-Work Transitions of Disadvantaged Youth: Competences and Transition Patterns." ICOVET-Background Paper. Deutsches Jugendinstitut, Munich, 2006.

Granato, Mona, and Joachim Gerd Ulrich. "Also was soll ich noch machen, damit die mich nehmen?" In *Kompetenzen stärken, Qualifikationen verbessern, Potentiale nutzen,* ed. Friedrich-Ebert-Stiftung, 32–50. Bonn: Friedrich-Ebert-Stiftung, 2006.

Hammer, Torild, ed. *Youth Unemployment and Social Exclusion in Europe.* Bristol: Policy Press, 2003.

Konsortium Bildungsberichterstattung. *Bundesbildungsbericht. Bildung in Deutschland.* Bielefeld: Bertelsmann Verlag, 2006.

Mills, M., and H.P. Blossfeld. "Gobalization, Uncertainty and the Early Life Course: A Theoretical Framework." In *Globalization, Uncertainty and Youth in Society*, ed. H.P. Blossfeld, E. Klizing, M. Mills, and K. Kurz, 1–24. Advances in Sociology Series. London: Routledge, 2005.

Müller, Walter, and Yossi Shavit. "The Institutional Embeddedness of Stratification Process: A Comparative Study of Qualifications and Occupations in Thirteen Countries." In *From School to Work: A Comparative Study of Educational Qualifications and Occupational Destinations,* ed. Shavit Yossi and Walter Müller, 1–48. Oxford: Clarendon Press, 1998.

Müller, Walter, Susanne Steinmann, and Renate Ell. "Education and Labour Market Entry in Germany." In *From School to Work: A Comparative Study of Educational Qualifications and Occupational Destinations,* ed. Shavit Yossi and Walter Müller, 143–88. Oxford: Clarendon Press, 1998.

PISA-Konsortium, Germany. *PISA 2000: Basiskompetenzen von Schülerinnen und Schülern im internationalen Vergleich.* Opladen: Leske and Budrich, 2001.

Reissig, Birgit, Nora Gaupp, Irene Hofmann-Lun, and Tilly Lex. *Schule und dann? Schwierige Übergänge von der Schule in die Berufsausbildung.* Munich: Deutsches Jugendinstitut, Forschungsschwerpunkt Übergänge in Arbeit, 2006.

Scherer, Stefani. "Early Career Patterns: A Comparison of Great Britain and West Germany." *European Sociological Review* 17 (2001): 119–44.

Shavit, Yossi, and Walter Müller, eds. *From School to Work: A Comparative Study of Educational Qualifications and Occupational Destinations.* Oxford: Clarendon Press, 1998.

Solga, Heike. *Ohne Abschluss in die Bildungsgesellschaft. Die Erwerbschancen gering qualifizierter Personen aus soziologischer und ökonomischer Perspektive.* Opladen: Verlag Barbara Budrich, 2005.

The Netherlands

Child Labor in the Netherlands During Proto- and Early Industrialization

Elise van Nederveen Meerkerk, PhD, International Institute of Social History, Amsterdam

For a long time, historians have defined child labor as a "social problem" of industrialization. Technological change, shifts in the organization of production, and the rise of capitalism brought about a large demand for child workers in the transitional phase to industrial society. However, in recent years it has been acknowledged that child labor was just as prevalent in preindustrial societies as in industrial societies. Presumably, this applied especially to the northern Netherlands, which experienced spectacular economic growth in the seventeenth century. Although the Dutch miracle of preindustrial economic growth is usually attributed to the country's remarkable commercial activities, it has recently been stressed that the growth of the industrial sector (such as textiles, shipbuilding, and pipe making) and changes in the agricultural sector were equally important factors leading to Dutch prosperity. Notably, in labor-intensive export industries, there was a large demand for cheap child laborers. However, industrialization in the Netherlands occurred relatively late in the nineteenth century (from the late 1860s), which might also have affected child labor in specific ways.

Despite these interesting characteristics, literature about child labor in the Netherlands is scarce. For the period of industrialization, there have been a few publications, but recent literature for the earlier period is virtually nonexistent. In order to provide a first long-term overview, this essay addresses the occurrence of child labor in the preindustrial and industrializing Dutch economy. The aim of this essay is twofold. On the one hand, it provides factual information about child labor before and in the early stages of industrialization. How many child workers were there? In what branches were they present? How much did the experiences of boys and girls vary? On the other hand, the essay assesses the extent to which there was continuity or change in the history of child labor before and during the process of industrialization. This last question is particularly interesting since effective child labor legislation and compulsory education were implemented only when industrialization in the Netherlands had already taken place, toward the end of the nineteenth century.

Preindustrial and Proto-Industrial Child Labor

It is difficult to trace exactly how many children worked in the preindustrial Netherlands. There are almost no quantitative data on child labor for the period before 1850, and unpaid labor, especially, was hardly ever recorded. Nevertheless, we may assume that many children worked in agriculture, either for wages or helping their parents. A rare early-nineteenth-century census from the proto-industrial town of Tilburg (about 10,000 inhabitants), which does record employment of children, shows only 2.4 percent of the children working in the agricultural sector. However, occupations of farmers' children are mentioned less frequently than occupations of children whose parents worked in other sectors. This is probably because helping parents on the farm was so ubiquitous that it was not worth mentioning to census administrators. This is confirmed by the fact that occupations of farmers' children who did nonagricultural work (mainly spinning) were indeed registered.

We can say more about the qualitative aspects of children's agricultural work in the preindustrial period. Normally, children started working when they were eight or nine years old, usually performing lighter tasks such as planting, weeding, raking, and tending animals. In typical dairy regions, they also milked cows and made cheese from the age of nine. When children, and especially boys, got older, they performed heavier duties, such as plowing and transporting manure. The older girls increasingly performed household chores, either for their parents or as live-in servants.

Most data on preindustrial child labor concerns work in the crafts and the less traditional "early capitalist" organized proto-industries. Already in the early-seventeenth-century Dutch republic, several export industries, such as textiles and pipe making, required large numbers of cheap laborers. In the textile center of Leiden, thousands of children were recorded to have been spinning, carding, and weaving. Also in other towns, large numbers of poor children were found working in various branches of industry including textiles, button making, and pin making.

Children also worked in traditional crafts while receiving an apprenticeship. This primarily involved boys above a certain age (twelve to fourteen years old), whereas younger boys, and girls of all ages, were found in the lower-skilled segments of the industrial labor market. Thus, for boys, the range of occupations widened in their early teens, whereas most girls remained working in either the textile or garment industry. The same pattern is visible in early-nineteenth-century Tilburg, where boys and girls under twelve did mostly the same work (spinning), while experiences diverged for both sexes above this age: girls spun or sewed, and boys started to work as weavers, dry shearers, shoemakers, or carpenters.

In the preindustrial service sector we also find a distinct division of labor. Many boys worked in the transport sector, for instance, in shipping, both for the East India Company and in inland shipping. Girls, in contrast, were more likely to work in domestic service. Although exact numbers are not known, it appears that the phenomenon of children working as servants grew during the eighteenth century. Regarding children in other services, such as retailing, even less is known. It is probable that many children whose parents owned small businesses helped in the shop or in the marketplace, but they hardly ever appear in the historical sources.

The traditional literature assumes that child labor in the Netherlands increased dramatically between 1820 and 1870. However, this is mainly derived from sources on children working in industry. Of course, industrialization brought significant changes in the characteristics of child labor, but it is questionable whether industrialization significantly changed the scale on which children were working.

On the Eve of Industrialization

For the nineteenth century, there are two complete population registrations, recording the occupations of all Dutch inhabitants in 1849, before large-scale industrialization occurred, and in 1899, when the transformation to an industrial society was more or less completed. Although there are problems with this source material, it does give a rough impression of minimum numbers of children working, and of changes between 1850 and 1900. Interestingly, the first serious attempts to fight child labor in the Netherlands date from this era. In 1874, the first law against the work of children was issued, but this Van Houten law merely restricted child labor in industry for children below the age of twelve. Investigating shifts in the actual number of working children in the second half of the century may give some evidence of the effectiveness of this legislation.

In 1849, children formed almost 5 percent of the total working population; about 7 percent of all children under age sixteen had an occupational registration. Of these working children, 15.6 percent were younger than twelve years old. Figure 1 illustrates the subdivision of working children by sector. The majority worked in agriculture, although there were differences according to sex and age. About a third worked in industry, the textile industry being the largest branch, with 7 percent of all working children. A quarter worked in the service sector, mostly in domestic service, although for boys older than twelve, trade and transport were also relatively important. It is striking that the majority of children under twelve, both boys (37.7 percent) and girls (57.8 percent) worked in domestic services. These figures enable us to quantify what effect the Van Houten law against child labor might have had. While Samuel van Houten initially wanted to take measures against child labor much further, the law eventually implemented

Figure 1 **The Work of Children Under Age 16 in the Netherlands by Sector, 1849 and 1899**

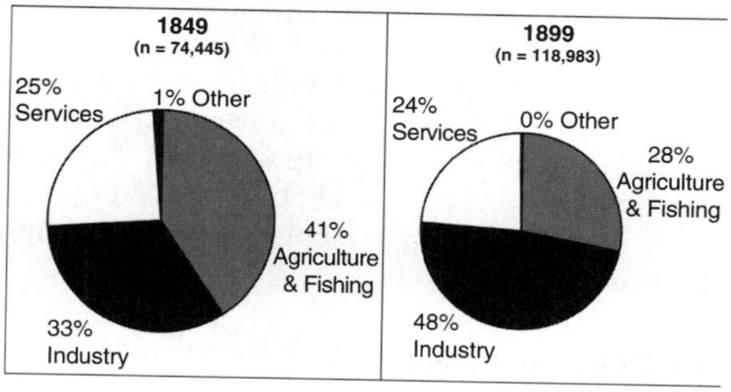

in 1874 forbade only the work of children under twelve, notably excluding agricultural work and domestic service. Remarkably, in 1849, 70 percent of all registered working children younger than twelve were active in precisely these branches. Thus, the law would affect only some 5 percent of all working children, or 0.5 percent of all children (working and nonworking) under twelve.

In 1850, as in the seventeenth and eighteenth centuries, there was a rather rigid gender division of labor. Boys of all ages had many more employment opportunities than girls. For one thing, girls were highly overrepresented in one occupation: almost 39 percent of girls under sixteen worked as domestic servants. Furthermore, in the industrial sector, girls were confined mostly to textile and garment production, whereas there was a wide range of occupations for boys to choose from. While textiles and garment production were also important for boys, many of them worked in leather, woodworking, metalworking, construction, or food industries. Unfortunately, data on agricultural work are insufficiently specified to see whether there were large gender differences in this sector. We do see more boys present in branches where girls are virtually absent, such as forestry and horticulture. Also, in the service sector, far more boys, especially older ones, were employed in transport and retail trade than girls.

The Transition to an Industrial Society

There were surely fluctuations in the occurrence of child labor between 1849 and 1899 due to changes in economic trends leading to changes in demand for child labor. However, it is possible to make a comprehensive comparison only of the whole Dutch labor market between these two separate years. By 1899, large shifts had occurred in the occupational structure, suggesting that industrialization indeed had led to great changes in the work children did. Now industry was the largest sector, employing almost half of all children under sixteen. Although a considerable share of the children still did agricultural work, this sector had diminished to less than 30 percent. These are surely effects of industrialization. However, rather than a spectacular rise in child labor due to industrialization, instead the effect was rather modest: Children now formed slightly more than 6 percent of the total labor force (compared to 5 percent in 1849). Moreover, the number of working children as a percentage of all children decreased from 7 percent in 1849 to 6 percent in 1899.

The 1874 legislation may have had an effect, because it was precisely the proportion of working children under twelve that had decreased. Furthermore, compared to fifty years earlier, more young children from all social classes had access to general education. Strikingly, among twelve- to fifteen-year-olds, the percentage of boys working had risen substantially, while the percentage for girls stayed about the same. A demographic transition in the late nineteenth century may have played a role. The share of children under sixteen in the total population had risen from 35 to 39 percent, and, compared to 1849, the group of children age twelve to fifteen had grown the most. Thus, legislation and demographic changes reinforced each other, resulting in decreased labor market participation of children under twelve, notably in industry, while at the same time, children over twelve were becoming more active in the Dutch labor market.

Although there remained differences between boys and girls, the variety of work opportunities for girls older than twelve increased with industrialization. Although their share in textiles and garment production was still the largest, in 1899 they appear in larger numbers in the earthenware, food, and many other industries, including the newly emerging electric lightbulb industry. Other branches of industry employed teenage girls on a larger scale due to increasing factory production and the accompanying process of deskilling. Nevertheless, domestic service was still by far the largest category of employment for girls, and it was even more important than it had been fifty years earlier: In 1899 almost half of all girls under sixteen worked as domestic servants. In contrast, almost no boys worked in domestic service, which in 1849 had been of quite some importance especially for younger boys. This might be, in part, a matter of registration differences. Probably, a lot of young male domestic servants worked on farms in 1849, and half a century later they were listed as agricultural laborers. The fact that this was not the case for girls, however, shows the different attitude of administrators in the valuation of male and female labor, even with regard to the youngest workers.

Conclusion

Before, during, and after industrialization, large numbers of boys and girls were active in the Dutch labor market. However, during the industrialization process, although dependency rates went up, the occurrence of child labor, especially among younger children, decreased. This was partly due to legislation, but probably demographic changes following industrialization also played a role, leading to a larger share of working children older than twelve in this period. The character of children's work also changed: More children, especially over the age of twelve, started working in the industrial sector, whereas their official numbers in agriculture declined. Nevertheless, experiences for boys and girls varied quite a lot, and although industrialization brought about some changes in the gendered division of labor, it did not alter this division fundamentally.

References and Further Reading

Nederveen Meerkerk, Elise van, and Ariadne Schmidt. "Between Wage Labor and Vocation: Child Labor in Dutch Urban Industry, 1600–1800." *Journal of Social History* 41:3 (2008): 717–36.

Noordegraaf, Leo, and Jan Luiten van Zanden. "Early Modern Economic Growth and the Standard of Living: Did Labour Benefit from Holland's Golden Age?" In *A Miracle Mirrored: The Dutch Republic in European Perspective,* ed. Karel Davids and Jan Lucassen, 410–37. Cambridge: Cambridge University Press, 1995.

Vries, Jan de, and Ad van der Woude. *The First Modern Economy: Success, Failure, and Perseverance of the Dutch Economy, 1500–1815.* Cambridge: Cambridge University Press, 1997.

White, Ben. *Children, Work and "Child Labour": Changing Responses to the Employment of Children.* The Hague: Institute of Social Studies, 1994.

Work, Education, and Discipline: Attitudes Toward Child Labor in the Netherlands, 1500 to 1875

Cor Smit, PhD, Independent Historian

In 1874 the Van Houten law restricted children laboring in factories in the Netherlands to a minimum age of twelve years. This law ended a discussion that had started in the 1830s, but it could not be the final word on child labor legislation. The Van Houten law simply was too limited and inadequate. This essay gives the history leading up to this law but also sketches the attitudes toward child labor from the sixteenth century to the 1870s. While the story of legislation might be connected to that of industrialization, the history of child labor starts much earlier.

The Sixteenth and Seventeenth Centuries

Little is known about medieval concepts of children and work in the Netherlands, but it is clear that children were supposed to assist their parents in their work. When old enough, some could get an apprenticeship. When industry developed in towns, relations could turn into actual wage relations, with children involved through their parents. But urban regulations, and notices concerning play and vandalism from the fifteenth and early sixteenth centuries, suggest that working-class children did not work full-time. Also, in the late fifteenth century, children remained exempt from bans on begging.

In the sixteenth century, new regulations banned begging by children, and pressed them to learn to work. The end of the sixteenth century witnessed the birth of the workhouses and houses of correction, used to combat petty crime and pauperism far into the nineteenth century. The fight against pauperism—a daily nuisance, even a threat, and at the same time a financial burden on the well-to-do—is one of the main threads in the history of Dutch social policy. Poor children were as much subjected to this fight as adults. Educating and disciplining them to work, getting them off the streets, and getting a nice profit from it went hand in hand.

The exploitation of children grew when the Dutch economy flourished in the seventeenth century, especially in the towns. Manufacturers hired children from orphanages. Generally these deals included some arrangements for training. This apparent concern for working children was not confined to orphans. The ruling bourgeois elite seemed to feel uneasy about exploitation, so regulations were issued to maintain the temporary and instructive character of apprenticeship. Manufacturers were told that children should learn to read and write (everyone had to be able to read the Bible to be a decent citizen). Sometimes maximum working hours were set. The town of Leiden, by then the largest producer of woolen fabrics in Europe, even employed supervisors and schoolteachers to verify that children were not made to beg, could go to school, received a reasonable wage, and were not mistreated by their employers. It is not clear how effective these measures were. Sometimes, when business was poor, adult workers tried to limit child labor, fearing for their jobs. They referred to the old regulations on apprenticeship, claiming that employers circumvented these.

So, from the sixteenth century onward, working by children was considered a virtue. Children could be forced to work when their parents were poor, or when they were orphans, but children were not simply seen as small adults; childhood was a distinct phase. Until twelve or fourteen years of age, they were to be protected and to get some schooling. Children should not be exploited, but trained. Still, in contrast to these values, exploitation was abundant.

The Eighteenth and Early Nineteenth Centuries

In the eighteenth century attitudes concerning children and child labor were changing as the ideas of the Enlightenment, stressing education and the importance of childhood, found their way into the Netherlands. Equally important was the long decline of Dutch industry, especially in the towns of its most important province, Holland. In the second half of the eighteenth century, unemployment reached enormous levels, pauperism grew, and working-class family life was breaking down.

The bourgeoisie responded in several ways. New ideals of family life were formulated, stressing the role of the mother as educator and caretaker and the father as breadwinner. Better education would counter poverty, strengthen civil life and morality, and benefit industry. It was only during the Batavian Republic and the French domination (1795–1813), however, that these ideas could be implemented as public policy. This period saw a national reform of education (1806) that created a new group of professional teachers who would later play an important role in child labor reform. Also during this period, many constraints on industry were removed, giving manufacturers more freedom in handling their workers.

At the same time, the virtue of work was stressed like never before. The policy to put paupers and their children to work intensified, and the number of state and private work institutions grew steadily. More than before, child labor was ideologically sanctified as beneficial for the working classes, educationally sound, and important in the fight against pauperism. This would be the dominant line of thought about child labor into the 1840s. The only protective legislation for children introduced in this period was the Miners' Act of 1813, which was imposed by a foreign ruler, Napoleon. The different responses to economic problems and the threat of social disintegration were sometimes at odds, in particular the stress on formal education and pressing poor children to work. Also, the new morality, with its emphasis on family life, could conflict with child labor.

In the 1830s the first critical notes were heard. Some local authorities, people involved with education, Roman Catholic priests, and academics expressed their concerns. They worried about education, morality, and the quality of future working-class housewives. In response, the Dutch government started an investigation in 1840–41, and some regional governors advised introduction of legislation similar to Prussia's 1839 child labor law. However, nothing was done. At the national level people were more concerned with reforming the Dutch state into a parliamentary democracy. When this succeeded in 1848, the orthodox Liberal position on state intervention triumphed too. Reduction of legislation and other impediments to industry were on the agenda; social legislation was out of the question.

Politics, Religion, and Education

After 1848, the sociopolitical landscape of the Netherlands changed. A process of gradual segmentation started, known as *verzuiling* (literally "pillarization"), in which people were organized along lines of their religious convictions in every aspect of life: trade unions, culture, press, even leisure activities. This process was started by orthodox Protestants and the Roman Catholic clergy around 1850, reached its zenith in the 1910s to 1950s, and faded away in the late 1960s. The antithesis between religious and nonreligious groups (Liberals, Socialists) was an important element of Dutch political and social life.

Orthodox Protestants (called antirevolutionaries) were essentially patriarchal, stressing the authority of the king, the father of the family, and the employer, who would beneficially rule their subjects. This implied responsibility for the well-being of minors, which gave this middle-class party a social note. This social note can also be found in the Roman Catholic emancipation movement. Moreover, stressing Catholic identity and morality also meant that many clergymen tried to keep children out of factories and larger establishments until their religious training was finished with the First Communion, around the age of eleven.

To both orthodox Protestants and Catholics, control over education was essential for raising children according to their principles and for building their own group identity. They demanded equal financing of their own private schools, which led to a long "school struggle" (*schoolstrijd*). Support for state-sponsored public schools, against these private religious schools, was the main item that united the Liberals, who actually were an amalgam of hard-core noninterventionists, social reformers, and conservatives. Fearing nonreligious state education, both antirevolutionaries and Catholic clergy opposed compulsory education, an idea raised by professional teachers and some Liberals in the 1850s and 1860s. The antirevolutionaries also opposed compulsory education because it would infringe on the authority of fathers. This patriarchal point of view was shared by many others, including many Liberals.

Though increasingly divided along religious lines, the bourgeoisie was united in their concerns about the lower classes: the unremitting poverty and the dangers this presented to society, the apparent unfitness of the lower classes, the inadequate reproductive capacities of working-class family life. The second half of the nineteenth century witnessed a process of disciplining the lower classes into a more civilized way of life. This included a growing interest in children and their education. Working-class children had to be saved from idleness, vandalism, and criminality. Now education was increasingly seen as the most important remedy against pauperism. In the eyes of a growing number of people of all denominations, child labor contradicted education, was wearing out the working class, and sustained pauperism.

The Long Way to Legislation

In the 1850s, concerns about child labor were increasingly expressed from different sides. Schoolteachers were among the first to sound the alarm. Conservative philanthropists worried because of falling school attendance, morality, and the physical condition of the nation. Professional physicians emphasized the negative effects on health of modern industry, especially on women and children. In the end, even some industrialists questioned whether child labor was in the long-term interest of industry. So, the surging movement against child labor was a patchwork of interests and ideologies, finding one another in a proposal to introduce the English part-time system: not abolishing child labor altogether, but combining six hours of work a day with six hours of school.

As a response to growing public pressure, in 1861 the government decided to investigate child labor again. But when the report by engineer A.A.C. de Vries Robbé pleaded for legislation, it was set aside by the Liberal government, which was unwilling to interfere with industry. The movement grew in volume, and numerous petitions were sent by organizations of teachers, physicians, philanthropists, and many others, including Twente and Leiden industrialists. This could not be neglected and, in 1863, a special state committee was installed. It took six years before this committee finished its report. Only chairman De Vries Robbé pleaded for introducing the half-time system again. The majority of the committee—most of them loyal supporters of J.R. Thorbecke, the Liberal leader who had brought parliamentary democracy to the Netherlands—advised the introduction of compulsory education. Without a parliamentary majority supporting the proposal, however, Thorbecke saw no reason to create a new law.

Concerns about the broader "social question" grew, though. Young Liberals conferred with Liberal trade unionists, looking for ways to defuse growing tensions between the classes. Child labor would be the first issue to tackle. For growing numbers of Liberals, protective legislation for children (and women) was acceptable, because they were *personae miserabiles,* not free agents. In 1873 the young Liberal Samuel van Houten brought his own bill to Parliament. This included a ban on all child labor before the age of ten, a part-time system of school and work for ten- to twelve-year-olds, and compulsory education until the age of thirteen.

Many reformers wanted to stretch protection to fifteen or even sixteen years, including the Liberal trade union that organized the first big Dutch working-class demonstration when the bill was discussed in Parliament. Conservatives, religious politicians, the agricultural lobby, and many industrialists, however, opposed the proposition or parts of it. By an overwhelming majority, all elements of compulsory education were voted away, including the part-time system. Exceptions to the ban on child labor were made for agriculture and household and personal services. That kind of work was said to be harmless, even salutary. Thus, greatly amputated, the bill was passed. While criticizing the law for its many inadequacies, reformers saw it as an important first step to regulate labor, particularly of all children up to age sixteen and of women.

Conclusion

Fear of pauperism and the working class was a powerful driver in shaping Dutch attitudes toward child labor. From the sixteenth to the middle of the nineteenth century, it provided a motive to force children of the poor to work. In the nineteenth century, education became the new panacea to battle threats of poverty, and industrial child labor now was seen as perpetuating pauperism. Education was seen as a means of social control and discipline when applied to the lower classes. Compulsory schooling, however, could not win the day in the nineteenth century because it conflicted with concepts of patriarchal authority and the interests of religious groups, for whom education was important in controlling their rank and file.

From the sixteenth century, working was considered to be good for children, a virtue, but children had to be protected from exploitation at the same time. This idea of protection, however, could hardly be effective when prospering seventeenth-century industry demanded masses of cheap labor, and it was forgotten when a long depression called for measures against spreading pauperism. Emphasis on the virtues of work turned into a justification for exploitation, an attitude that reigned from the eighteenth far into the nineteenth century. Finally, the concept of protection returned.

The child labor reform movement was a strange amalgam of conservatives, progressive Liberals, and clergymen. Professional groups like teachers and physicians played a leading role in mobilizing public opinion, joined by many philanthropic and social organizations rooted in the broad bourgeoisie. Some industrialists joined the movement, too, but business interests also produced the fiercest opposition to reform. To them, resistance to any state intervention with business was an important drive. As a result of all these conflicting ideologies and interests, the eventual law on child labor was a highly unsatisfactory one, but still an important milestone.

Finally, the movement against child labor can be seen as part of a broader process of "civilizing" or disciplining the working class. In this process the reconstruction of childhood was linked with a reconstruction of working-class family life according to late-eighteenth-century ideals—the male breadwinner, the mother taking care of daily and generational reproduction, and the children being properly educated at home and in school.

References and Further Reading

Damsma, Dirk. *Familieband: geschiedenis van het gezin in Nederland.* Utrecht: Kosmos–Z&K Uitgevers, 1999.

Peeters, Harry, Lène Dresen-Coenders, and Ton Brandenbarg, eds. *Vijf eeuwen gezinsleven: liefde, huwelijk en opvoeding in Nederland.* Nijmegen, Netherlands: SUN, 1988.

Swaan, Abram de. *In Care of the State: Health Care, Education and Welfare in Europe and the USA in the Modern Era.* Cambridge: Polity Press, 1988.

Veld, Theo. *Volksonderwijs en leerplicht: een historisch sociologisch onderzoek naar het ontstaan van de Nederlandse leerplicht, 1860–1900.* Delft: Eburon, 1987.

Vleggeert, J.C. *Kinderarbeid in Nederland 1500–1874: van berusting tot beperking.* Assen, Netherlands: Van Gorcum, 1964.

Development of Child Labor Policy in the Netherlands Since 1874

Stan Meuwese, Retired Director, Defence for Children International—The Netherlands

Today, Dutch children are at school and not at work; child labor is not an issue on the political agenda in the Netherlands. In Dutch eyes, child labor is perceived as a phenomenon of the past, the nineteenth century, and of elsewhere, the poor countries in the South. Enforcement of compulsory education remains a problem, where according to existing law, a youngster who is not attending school can be brought to court for committing a misdemeanor. Youth unemployment, the mirror image of child labor, is seen by many as a serious social problem. People are more worried about young people living in idleness than about children who are working.

Today, economic aspects are very important in the pattern of living of young persons. To have money has become an important aspect in the socialization process of today's youth. Young persons between twelve and twenty years of age have become a target market for the products and services of companies and institutions. Parents, employers, and the government are giving more and more financial responsibilities to young persons, starting at a very young age. They are getting pocket money to buy clothes and traveling money from their parents, and many young people are earning money doing jobs and holiday work of all sorts.

Van Houten's "Little Law"

As the Netherlands began to be increasingly industrialized after the 1860s, discussion arose over the issue of child labor, influenced by the theories of the French philosopher Jean-Jacques Rousseau on childhood and the development of children. The novelist J.J. Cremer published an emotional book titled *Factory Children, a Supplication, but Not for Money* in 1863, and people such as the industrialist Le Poole of Leiden and the medical doctor S. Coronel began agitating for child labor reform.

This led to a first-draft proposal for a child labor law, introduced by the young, liberal, anticlerical, neo-Malthusian member of Parliament Samuel van Houten in 1874. In his proposal, labor of children below the age of twelve was forbidden, with exceptions for the agricultural and domestic sectors. Van Houten defended his proposal, not by reference to the awful conditions of working children, but with an appeal to improve the functioning of the free enterprise system. A well-educated labor force was a precondition for a strong Dutch economy; illiterate and weak children were a threat to the competitive position of the Netherlands.

Van Houten also proposed that municipal authorities be authorized to establish systems of compulsory education, but this part of his draft law was not adopted because of strong opposition from the churches. They objected because they believed that the proposal would force children to go to state schools and because, in their view, it was the church that should take responsibility to improve the working conditions of children, not the state. This long political and social debate—called the "school dispute"—over the respective roles of the state and the church in educational matters lasted to the end of World War I, when a historic compromise was reached. The socialistic party accepted equal financing for state and private religious schools, and the Christian political parties accepted voting rights for every citizen.

Van Houten's child labor law is considered the starting point of the Dutch legal system for social security. It was a breakthrough for the role of the state in economic and social development. In Dutch, the law is called "*het kinderwetje* Van Houten," which means Van Houten's little law, of course because the law is about children, but also because the law contains no more than five articles.

Step-by-Step

We can divide the social and legal developments on child labor since Van Houten's law roughly into six periods. In this scheme, the main legal developments are related to the prohibition of child labor and the extension of compulsory education. This scheme makes clear how both developments, in combination and step-by-step, took children out of the workplace and brought them to school.

The first phase starts with the introduction of Van Houten's child labor law and ends just after World War I, which politically and socially affected the Netherlands even if it was not one of the belligerents. In this period the foundations of both legal systems were laid: the legal prohibition of child labor and, in 1901, the introduction of compulsory education.

In the first years after World War I, there was an optimistic view and space for new developments. A new child labor law was adopted elevating the minimum age to fourteen, financing was equalized between state schools and private religious schools, and compulsory education was extended to seven years. In the years of the Great Depression, before World War II, there was much more concern about youth unemployment than about child labor.

The first decade after World War II was a period of restoration and a literal rebuilding of the Dutch society. Youth were urgently called upon to devote themselves to the reconstruction of the Netherlands. The minimum age for employment was raised to fifteen for boys, and sixteen for girls, and new educational policy extended compulsory education to eight years. The baby boom resulted in more emphasis on quantity than quality of educational provisions.

The end of the sixties and the beginning of the seventies brought a tendency for modernization of the education systems. Many policy papers and research reports were written, and many pilot projects were launched. The Compulsory Education Act of 1900 was overhauled, and compulsory education was extended at a rather quick pace. Part-time compulsory education was introduced to make a combination of part-time schooling and part-time work possible. On the international level, the first child labor convention was introduced.

From the mid-1970s through the 1980s, education was considered one of the most important factors in social change and the democratization of society. There was much emphasis on keeping youngsters in school longer to give them a better starting position in society. Compulsory education was extended to ten and then eleven years. At the same time, a rather high youth unemployment rate was an indication that the position on the labor market for youngsters without full vocational training was difficult.

With the adoption of the UN Convention on the Rights of the Child in 1989, children came to be seen as fellow citizens who were entitled to human rights. It was the government that was responsible for the implementation of the rights of children. The history of eradication of child labor in the Netherlands is the story of a combination of prohibitive child labor law, as part of the social security system, and compulsory schooling law, as part of the educational system, that brought working children from the factory to the classroom over the course of about a century—step-by-step—first out of the formal mechanized industries, and later also from the domestic and agricultural sectors.

Current Child Labor Law

The existing regulations on the labor of minors are formulated in the Youth Statute of 1981, which was based on the Labor Act 1919. A distinction is made between a "child" and a "young laborer." In the terminology of the Labor Act, combined with the Compulsory Education Act, a child is a person below the age of fifteen who is subject to compulsory education. The law contains a nearly absolute prohibition on labor of children below the age of thirteen years. There are additional provisions regulating the labor of children and young laborers between the ages of thirteen and eighteen.

The concept of labor, as defined in the civil code, exists where a labor agreement contains the following three elements: labor, payment, and subordination. In the Labor Act, however, the defini-

Table 1

Development of Dutch Child Labor Policy and Law Since 1874: A Timeline

Phase I—1874–1919: The Basis of Child Protection	
1874	Van Houten´s child labor law: no child labor below the age of 12 years, with the exception of domestic, personal, and agricultural services
1878	A new education law established for the purpose of improving the quality of education: one of the articles forbids more than 100 children in a classroom
1886	Report of the Dutch Parliament about the functioning of Van Houten's child labor law: a report full of horrible details about the working conditions of children, especially in china factories
1889	A new labor act: no child labor below the age of 12; no night work and no Sunday work below the age of 16 years; and 11 hours (including 1 hour for rest) as the maximum working hours a day; no night work from 7 P.M. to 5 A.M.; a prohibition of hazardous labor; the same limitations for women; a labor inspectorate (with 3 inspectors for the whole country) established
1900	A set of the child protection laws are adopted (entered into force in 1905): a special juvenile justice system for minors (penal law); limitations on parental authority in case of serious neglect of the child (civil law); and an act to organize the child protection system
1901	Adoption of the Compulsory Education Act: six years of compulsory education between the ages of 7 and 12
1911	A new labor act: no labor by children under the age of 13 years; special protection for children from 13 to 17 years of age
Phase II—1919–1947: The Interbellum—Further Developments	
1919	A new labor law: no labor by children under the age of 14 years; special protection for children from 14 to 18 years of age
1920	Financial equal rights for state education and private education (based on religious denomination)
1921	Compulsory education extended to 7 years
1924	Compulsory education reduced to 6 years (related to budget cuts)
1928	Restoration of 7 years of compulsory education
1942	Compulsory education extended to 8 years (during the German occupation, to enable students to learn the German language)
Phase III—1947–1969: Restoration	
1947	Return to 7 years of compulsory education
1950	Compulsory education extended to 8 years
1960	No labor of children under the age of 15 years
1965	No labor of girls under the age of 16 years; conditional prohibition for 14-year-old boys with one day a week for education
Phase IV—1969–1975: Modernization	
1969	Modernization of the Compulsory Education Act of 1901
1970	No labor of boys under the age of 16 years
1971	Full compulsory education of 8 years (5 days a week) plus partial compulsory education of 1 year (one day a week)
1973	Full compulsory education of 8 years (5 days a week) plus partial compulsory education of 2 years (one day a week)
	Adoption of ILO Convention 138 concerning minimum age for admission to employment
1974	Full compulsory education of 9 years (5 days a week) plus partial compulsory education of 2 years (1 year of two days a week and 1 year of one day a week)
Phase V—1975–1989: Democratization	
1975	Full compulsory education of 10 years (5 days a week) plus partial compulsory education of 1 year (two days a week)
1981	Modernization of the Youth Statute based on the Labor Act of 1919
1985	Merger of kindergarten (for toddlers of 4 and 5 years) and primary school for children of 6 to 12 years into one new primary school for children from 4 to 12 years, which led to a still existing system of compulsory education of 11 years plus 1 year of partial compulsory education of two days a week
Phase VI—1989 to Present: Introduction of Children's Rights	
1994	Modernization of the Compulsory Education Act of 1969; children, along with their parents, face legal sanctions for failing to fulfill the legal obligation to attend school
1995	New legislation on the status of juvenile employees
	Ratification of the UN Convention on the Rights of the Child by the Netherlands
2007	New legislation on labor of young persons; youngsters of 13 and 14 years are allowed to work 7 hours a day on Saturday (and school holidays)
	New legislation extending compulsory education to the age of 18, unless a youngster obtains a "start qualification," that is, a certificate for vocational training

tion is wider: "all work in an enterprise," and later jurisprudence formulated it thus: "[L]abor is every performance that requires any efforts of body and mind." Domestic work, that is, helping the parents in the household, is the major exemption from the definition of labor.

There are numerous exceptions in the law, and it is very difficult for young persons to know exactly whether they are allowed to work or not. Employers are better informed about the regulations applicable for their own sectors. For example, children under age thirteen, including very young children, are permitted to work on a limited basis performing in theater plays, fashion shows, commercials, and television shows.

Children thirteen and fourteen years of age are permitted to work two hours per day on school days between 7 A.M. and 7 P.M. They may work seven hours on Saturdays, and seven hours per day during school holidays, but no more than five days in succession and no more than four weeks a year. Types of work permitted include babysitting, washing cars, delivery of advertising flyers and papers, domestic labor in a family, light work in shops, light labor in agriculture, and light work in the recreational industry (at a riding school, a camp ground, a playground, a bowling center, or a museum). Types of work explicitly prohibited include working in a factory plant, working with machinery, working with dangerous or toxic materials, lifting goods of more than twenty-two pounds, working as a cashier in a shop, loading and unloading vans, and serving at a restaurant. Similar restrictions apply to children fifteen years of age, except that they may work eight hours per day on weekends and during school holidays.

For young laborers sixteen and seventeen years of age, the basic rule is that a young person is allowed to work so long as compulsory schooling is no longer applicable. Since eleven years of full-time schooling, plus one year of part-time schooling, are compulsory, this means that a person of sixteen years is allowed to work for three days a week, and a person of seventeen years for five days a week. The maximum workday is nine hours (school hours are considered to be working, so three hours for work remain after six hours at school), and night work between 11 P.M. and 6 A.M. is prohibited. Young laborers are permitted to perform any type of work, but hazardous work, such as work with dangerous machines, heavy lifting, work in a slaughterhouse, or work with toxic commodities, must be performed under the guidance of an adult.

References and Further Reading

Meuwese, Stan, Sharon Detrick, and Sjaak Jansen, eds. *100 Years of Child Protection*. Nijmegen, Netherlands: Wolf Legal Publishers, 2007.

White, Ben. "Children, Work and 'Child Labour': Changing Responses to the Employment of Children." *Development and Change* 25 (1994): 849–78.

Newspaper Delivery in the Netherlands

Stan Meuwese, Retired Director, Defence for Children International—The Netherlands

Newspaper delivery is one of the most common jobs performed by young persons in the Netherlands, especially boys. In 1994, the youth organization of the National Federation of Christian Trade Unions, CNV Jongeren, researched the situation of young persons who deliver newspapers. They were concerned about the growing number of complaints from young persons about their working conditions and their legal position. The goal of CNV Jongeren is to improve the legal position of young people who deliver newspapers through a collective labor agreement that lays down their rights and duties. CNV Jongeren also wants the Dutch Supreme Court to review one of its verdicts from 1957, in which the court decided that persons who deliver newspapers do not need a collective agreement because they are not working within a "regular" working relationship, but rather according to an "agreement to do a few services."

To find out how the persons who deliver newspapers think about a collective agreement, CNV Jongeren developed a survey and distributed it on a large scale. The survey showed that most of the young persons delivering newspapers were at least fifteen years old, but that 18 percent were under the age of fifteen. Visits to the places where papers are distributed showed that the work very often starts before 5 A.M. Dutch law allows young persons from the age of fifteen onward to do light forms of work but forbids them from working after 7 P.M. or before 6 A.M. Thus, it was concluded that the law was being violated on a large scale.

Most of the survey respondents reported that they have to find a replacement when they are ill or when they are going on vacation. In many cases they have to transfer their payment to the person who is replacing them. This situation makes it very easy for young persons who deliver newspapers to hand their work over to younger brothers and sisters, or other young persons under the age of fifteen, who are officially not allowed to do this work.

In 2000, questions concerning young people delivering newspapers resurfaced when the European Committee of Social Rights raised a question for the Netherlands regarding working hours and rest periods for minors. Pursuant to the European Social Charter, school-age children are not allowed to work to the extent that they cannot fully benefit from their education.

The Dutch Ministry of Social Affairs and Employment asked the Institute for Applied Social Science Nijmegen to conduct a survey to answer the question: What is the impact of delivering morning papers on the school achievements of fifteen-year-old paperboys and girls? Recent data from CEBUCO, the newspapers' marketing association, indicated that there were approximately 3,400 fifteen-year-olds delivering morning papers. For the survey there were three groups of respondents: 804 paperboys and girls, 915 pupils age fifteen or sixteen who do not deliver morning papers, and 81 teachers of the paperboys and girls. Results of the survey were published in 2004.

The survey found no indications that having a paper route has a negative effect on the school achievements of fifteen-year-olds. There was no difference in advancement and grades. Paperboys and girls attend the same level of education as their peers. The physical and psychological fitness of pupils with a paper route is better in all aspects than that of their peers. They feel better rested and they are able to focus better. Furthermore, it seems that they have more ambition and are more enterprising than their peers. They also enjoy going to school more than pupils in the comparison sample. According to their teachers, paperboys and girls are more ambitious and enterprising than their peers in the comparison sample. They want to achieve something in life by working hard, even more than children in the comparison sample.

SECTION 5. SOUTHERN EUROPE

Albania

Exploitation of Albanian Children in Greece

Mirela Shuteriqi, Advocacy and Legal Officer for Southeastern Europe, Terre des Hommes

Our knowledge of the situation of Albanian children exploited for labor purposes in Greece is based on the work of two not-for-profit organizations: Terre des Hommes Foundation in Lausanne, Switzerland, and a Greek organization, the Association for the Social Support of Youth. By working within the frame of the Transnational Action Against Child Trafficking project, their aim has been to counter the exploitation of Albanian children in Greece and within Albania by establishing and enhancing the child protection environment in both countries.

The Fall of Communism

When communism fell in 1992, Albania became the most isolated country in Europe. The country had an underdeveloped economy with very poor infrastructure. There was a strong desire to democratize political life and liberalize markets, but no experience in doing so. The first democratic governments in Albania failed to find a balance between market liberalization and social measures. As a result, many families were reduced to extreme poverty. While particular groups, such as the Roma, suffered from social exclusion even during communism, after its fall, a larger part of the population experienced the phenomenon and with heavier consequences.

Economic crisis was accompanied by institutional and social transformations. Due to the lack of democratic traditions, Albania needed time to replace old institutions with new democratic ones. The institutional vacuum was accompanied by a vacuum of common norms and values. Relations of the individual within the family and society, and toward the state, which had seemed self-evident in the past, were strongly put into question.

Due to their age, dependence on adults, and need for stability, children suffered most from these phenomena. Large-scale poverty and unemployment made their parents hopeless about the future. Economic factors played a role in the increased rate of family disruption and domestic violence. For many families, migration, either across the border or internally, was the only solution. Migrating abroad, in particular to the neighboring European Union countries of Greece and Italy, was most attractive for many Albanians. Because of their isolation during communism, Albanian perceptions of Greece and Italy were based on television images. Both adults and children were convinced that, once they were abroad, many new opportunities would be available to them. The desperation of many families was exploited by criminal individuals and organizations offering possibilities to immigrate illegally. A new phenomenon appeared in Albania. Parents of families experiencing poverty, social problems, and exclusion were lured into allowing their children to accompany a trafficker, convinced that, once abroad, not only would the child have a better life, but the family back in Albania would profit as well. The children would be moved to Greece illegally across the mountains of the border areas, where they would have to walk for days under constant threats from the trafficker and with the fear of facing either Albanian or Greek police.

Exploitation in Greece

In Greece, the children would be placed at traffic lights, where they would beg, sell tissues, flowers, and religious icons, or wash windshields. Gradually they were told to move to bars and restaurants, where, in addition to selling activities, they would be forced to perform entertainment activities, such as playing musical instruments. They were constantly observed by their traffickers while working, and were instructed to provide either no information or false information if approached. The children, poorly dressed and looking unhealthy, raised feelings of compassion in Greek citizens, who would give money or buy products sold by the children. As stated by one Albanian child exploited on the streets of Greece, "[D]uring the winter we had to wear light clothes to provoke pity among the Greeks and encourage them to give money" (Philippe and Tournecuillert 2003, 22). This, together with the long hours worked by the children, would bring high profits to the traffickers. The children were cheap—accommodation and food were provided in minimum quantity and quality, and, in most cases, no profits were shared with the parents in Albania. In order to ensure their full obedience, physical and psychological force was exercised on the children.

Social workers seeking to assist the children have reported on various forms of ill-treatment. In the first investigations conducted in Greece by Terre des Hommes, forms of physical ill-treatment described by children themselves included cigarette burns on the body, blows, verbal abuse, or the obligation to swallow a solution of shampoo to make the child ill. When necessary, exploiters reminded the children they were there to help the family back in Albania. Cases of children detained and deported back to Albania by Greek police were used by the exploiters to demonstrate to the children what would happen if they failed to obey. For the exploiters, few risks were involved: The Albanian institutions were weak, and the Greeks were generally unaware or unprepared to address the problem. Estimated numbers of Albanian children trafficked to Greece by the end of the 1990s would reach the thousands (Philippe and Tournecuillert 2003).

Measures Undertaken

The first civil society initiatives to address the problem involved efforts to raise awareness in both countries. Steps were taken to identify vulnerable communities in Albania, where parents and children were informed about the exploitation children suffered in Greece. In Greece, awareness-raising activities targeted the demand side by demonstrating to the general public how giving money to the children contributed to the establishment of a profitable market that was exploited by third parties against the interests and well-being of the children.

Great efforts were invested in increasing the awareness of governments in both Albania and Greece. Positive results were achieved in assisting some children, exploited in the streets of Greece, to liberate themselves and willingly return to Albania. Their stories constituted evidence the authorities in both countries could not ignore. The presence of the problem was recognized, and state institutions commenced to intervene.

State intervention, in both Albania and Greece, has emphasized criminalization of the phenomenon. The movement of children across the border, followed by their exploitation for begging and other labor purposes, is defined by both Albanian and Greek criminal legislation as trafficking. A number of cases have been prosecuted, resulting in severe sentences against the perpetrators. Media reporting on these cases has also contributed to raising the awareness of children and their parents. However, this criminal approach, alone, has proved insufficient to eliminate the problem. Even though the trafficking of Albanian children to Greece for begging and forced labor has decreased, it still exists (Pippidou, Shuteriqi, and Stoecklin 2006).

Evolution of the Phenomenon

With the decrease in trafficking of Albanian children by third parties, the nature of the phenomenon has changed. Now most of the Albanian children exploited in the streets of Greece are accompanied by at least one of their parents. As long as poverty, social exclusion, poor education, and lack of opportunities continue in Albania, families will continue to seek a better life abroad. In addition, some children migrate on their own. Some older children, mainly fifteen to eighteen years old, arrive in Greece to seek employment in agriculture or the construction sector. Little information is available on their numbers and working conditions. Other children depart illegally from Albania, seeking to join parents who are already residing in Greece.

Even though their parents are also living in Greece, many Albanian children still work or beg in the streets (though begging has diminished). The majority sell tissues or small items (small icons, pins and small toys, or decorations for mobile phones), or play a musical instrument. Their merchandise changes according to the current fashion. In most cases, the children look healthier and are better dressed than those working in the streets in times past. Their behavior is also different. The children show less fear, and their attitude toward their customers is professional (Pippidou, Shuteriqi, and Stoecklin 2006).

For some Albanian families living in Greece, income from child labor is the only income they can access. After entering the country illegally, parents discover that few employment opportunities are available to them. Low levels of education, few professional skills, and the lack of a residence permit all hinder efforts to find employment. In addition, most do not master the language and, instead of support, they face racism in many settings. Even when they find employment, it is often short-term, hard work for low pay. Moreover, in many families, only the father seeks employment, while the role of the mother is confined to the home. Often, when children are very young, the mother begs with them, and later on, the children are left to beg or work in the streets alone or with their siblings. In all these cases, income derived from begging or child labor is considered necessary by the family.

Few social programs in Greece target these communities seeking to ease their poverty or to improve the family environment and support the children's development. As a result, successes remain limited. One program in Thessaloniki—a Transnational Action Against Child Trafficking project—has succeeded in integrating Albanian children into school. However, after finishing school in the morning, the majority of these children still work in the streets in the afternoon and evening. Full elimination of their exploitation demands regulating their resident status and guaranteeing employment for their parents.

The Roma

Many of the Albanian families in Greece are Roma. This fact presents another obstacle to their employment, whether in Albania or Greece. The Roma presence in both countries dates back several centuries. Throughout most of this period, this group has suffered discrimination and social exclusion. Today, antidiscrimination laws are in force in both Greece and Albania, but their implementation by public and private structures is very weak. Very few programs aim at fighting social exclusion or promoting economic growth of the Roma population. Most initiatives have remained mainly on paper.

As result, the Roma continue to suffer from poverty, illiteracy or very low levels of education, lack of shelter, and limited access to resources and services. The Roma are often mistreated by authorities in both countries, especially at the local level. Greece has, on occasion, been subject to international criticism for its policy toward Roma who are Greek citizens (United Nations 2004). The situation of Roma who migrate to Greece from Albania is much worse (Minority Rights Group International 2005).

To resist the discrimination suffered throughout the centuries, the Roma continue to follow age-old traditions and family institutions, including early marriage and subordination of women and children. The majority of Roma, in both Albania and Greece, distrust the authorities and undervalue some common societal institutions, including child protection institutions. Child labor is tolerated among the Roma and, in a number of cases, parents, either in Greece or in Albania, do not even seek employment. The easy solution for them is child labor.

Addressing the Phenomenon: Conclusion

Political will, accompanied by structural adjustments and adequate resources, is necessary to fully eliminate the exploitation of Albanian children in Greece. Some improvements have already occurred. The number of Albanian children trafficked to Greece has decreased. Most of these children are no longer subject to third-party exploitation and live with at least one of their biological parents. Some of them are even attending school.

However, the children continue to work long hours in the streets, in conditions that seriously endanger their health and development. There exist few prospects for substantially improving their situation as long as parents lack sustainable employment and resources. This would require the legalization of their residence status. Greek social and development policies should be extended to include Albanian migrants living there.

In addition, the extremely restrictive immigration policies applied by Greece have proven to be ineffective. They do not correspond to the labor market situation in Greece, but feed instead the need for forced and exploitative labor. In Albania, more realistic information on the nature of job opportunities abroad should be available. Internally, coherent and concrete steps should be undertaken to fight poverty, enhance education, create job opportunities, and improve the social protection net.

Specific attention in both Albania and Greece should be paid to the Roma. Concrete measures and resources should be invested in ensuring their access to rights and services. Registration of the Roma population to ensure their adequate sheltering and employment are first priorities. Roma themselves should become part of the decision-making process. As long as the Roma remain socially excluded, there will be no open and constructive dialogue on the role of children and women within the community. Strong commitment of the community remains a necessary precondition to address child labor and exploitation.

References and Further Reading

Dottridge, Mike. *Kids as Commodities? Child Trafficking and What to Do About It.* Geneva: Terre des Hommes, 2004.

Kane, June. *Child Trafficking—The People Involved: A Synthesis of Findings from Albania, Moldova, Romania and Ukraine.* Geneva: ILO-IPEC, 2005.

Minority Rights Group International. *Roma Poverty and the Roma National Strategies: The Cases of Albania, Greece and Serbia.* London: Minority Rights Group International, 2005.

Philippe, Pierre, and Vincent Tournecuillert. *The Trafficking of Albanian Children in Greece.* Geneva: Terre des Hommes, 2003.

Pippidou, Dimitra, Mirela Shuteriqi, and Daniel Stoecklin. *Transnational Protection of Children: The Case of Albania and Greece.* Tirana, Albania: Terre des Hommes and ARSIS, 2006.

Rinne, Cia. "The Situation of the Roma in Greece." *KURI Journal* 1:6 (2002). http://www.domresearchcenter.com/journal/16/index.html.

Stoecklin, Daniel, and Vincent Tournecuillert. *Child Trafficking in South-eastern Europe: The Development of Good Practices to Protect Albanian Children.* Lausanne: Terre des Hommes and Ndihme per Femijet, 2004.

United Nations. *Final Conclusions on the Initial Report of Greece.* Geneva: UN Committee on Economic, Social and Cultural Rights, 2004.

Bosnia and Herzegovina

CHILD ACTIVITY BREAKDOWN, BY SEX AND RESIDENCE

	Percentage of children in the relevant age-group[a]									
	Economic activity only		School only		Combining school and economic activity		Neither in school nor in economic activity		Child labor[b]	
RESIDENCE	**Male**	**Female**	**Male**	**Female**	**Male**	**Female**	**Male**	**Female**	**Male**	**Female**
Urban	0.1	0.5	79.7	80.2	4.9	4.2	15.3	15.2	n/av	n/av
Rural	0.4	0.1	71.5	73.6	12.1	9.4	16.0	16.9	n/av	n/av
Total	0.3	0.2	74.4	75.8	9.6	7.7	15.8	16.3	6.6	3.9

Source: Bosnia and Herzegovina, Multiple Indicator Cluster Survey 3, 2006 (see UCW Project Web site, http://www.ucw-project.org, country statistics).

Notes: [a]Children age 5 to 14. [b]Estimate includes (a) children under age 12 engaged in economic activities, (b) children age 12–14 engaged in excessive economic activities (more than 14 hours per week), and (c) children under age 15 engaged in excessive household chores (at least 28 hours per week). Estimate does not account for children engaged in hazardous work or other unconditional "worst forms" of child labor.

Portugal

History of Child Labor in Portugal

Pedro Goulart, Institute of Social Studies, The Hague, and CISEP, ISEG, Technical University of Lisbon

Children have contributed to the labor force in Portugal for many centuries. For example, in the sixteenth century children were an important part of ships' crews in the merchant marine (Kassouf and Santos 2006). However, historical data suggest that twentieth-century Portugal witnessed much of the kind of change experienced earlier by other European countries. Interestingly, the sectors of work have not changed much: Children were employed mostly in agriculture, textiles, clothing and footwear, civil construction, commerce, lodging and restaurants, and domestic service.

Early Accounts of Child Labor

Legislation on child labor was adopted later in Portugal than other European countries, being first promulgated only in 1891. Campinho (1995) attributes the need to regulate child labor in Portugal, after centuries of "natural" work contribution by children, to rising urban social unrest. The minimum working age was set at twelve years, with some exceptions. However, by 1898 it was clear that the practice of child labor continued illegally, especially in industrial centers far from Lisbon. Both sexes worked from the age of seven for up to ten hours per day, or four hours per night (Cardoso 2001).

In spite of the slow development of industry during the nineteenth century (Reis 1993), and even acknowledging the underreporting of children's work, industrial surveys suggest an increase in the number of working minors under sixteen years of age from 1852 to 1881. The number of minors in industry almost doubled, even if their share in the labor force decreased from 25 to 7 percent. Most children (50–55 percent) worked in the weaving industry, while others were apprentices to locksmiths and carpenters. The fireworks industry was the most child intensive, with minors representing 63 percent of the labor force. In public works (1883–1884), the salary ratio between male adults and children was approximately two to one, while children were paid about the same as women. However, the bulk of child labor was in agricultural and domestic work, which, unfortunately for historians, was poorly documented.

Child Labor During the Dictatorship

A military coup in 1926 led to an extremely conservative dictatorship, which idolized a rural and a very modest life and would run the country until 1974.[1] In the first years, industrialization was slowed down, leading to economic stagnation and the strengthening of rural interest lobbies (Mónica 1978). Eventually the government felt the need to promote economic reforms in order to legitimize the regime and allowed a few families to build what became powerful economic groups. By 1971, 0.4 percent of companies held 53 percent of the capital (Williams 1992).

Until 1950

Child work was perceived favorably when performed within the household or in a rural setting, as opposed to "cruel" industrial working conditions (Mónica 1978). Following a period of capitalist penetration between 1870 and 1913 (Reis 1993), by 1940 industrialization had made considerable progress, and the number of working children increased accordingly (see Table 1). Industrial labor

Table 1

Youngsters in the Most Relevant Sectors, 1940 and 1950

	10–14 years				15–19 years			
	Boys	Girls	Total	Rate	Boys	Girls	Total	Rate
Sectors								
Industry								
1940	10,864	6,151	17,015	2.1%	43,555	24,737	68,292	9.1%
1950[a]	17,549[b]	7,622[b]	25,171[b]	5.1%[b]	81,903	35,969	117,872	14.5%
Agriculture								
1940	63,816	17,970	81,786	10.2%	152,598	34,535	187,133	25.0%
1950	65,238[b]	13,948[b]	79,186[b]	16.1%[b]	164,793	38,228	203,021	25.0%
Domestic services[c]								
1940	10,460	243,079	253,539	31.6%	15,584	273,751	289,335	38.7%
1950	4,325[b]	183,279[b]	187,604[b]	38.1%[b]	8,401	295,623	304,024	37.5%

Source: Goulart and Bedi 2006.

Note: Rate is the incidence rate in the respective age-group. [a]The figure is underestimated, as in 1950 it refers only to the 12–14 age-group. [b]Includes the minors in the extractive industry. [c]There is not a homogeneous definition of domestic service between the 1940 and 1950 censuses. See Goulart and Bedi 2006 for details.

continued increasing, and the number of working minors skyrocketed after 1950.

By 1950, twelve- to fourteen-year-olds had a significant participation rate, while fifteen- to nineteen-year-olds were considered regular workers in most industries. The gender composition was fairly evenly mixed for twelve- to nineteen-year-olds, but faded away as girls started to marry. Tobacco, shoes and clothes, and textile industries employed proportionally more girls, while construction, metals and machines, and furniture took on more boys. The earnings of minors remained lower than those of adults, and the difference may even have widened, while reportedly children worked more days than adults on average. In the glass industry, minors were three times more likely than adults to be injured in an industrial accident, and they were two to four times more likely to lose working days through incapacity.

In spite of industry's increasing share of the economy, most children continued working in agriculture and domestic service. In agriculture, working children ten to fourteen years of age were three times more numerous than their industrial counterparts, while those fifteen to nineteen years of age were twice as numerous (see Table 1). Furthermore, most of the 93,636 ten- to fourteen-year-old boys and the 63,393 fifteen- to nineteen-year-old boys reported as unpaid workers in 1950 were probably employed in agriculture. As for domestic service, this occupied ten times more children ten to fourteen years of age and two and a half times more fifteen- to nineteen-year-olds than industry, whereas the pay was very often in meals. By 1950, up to 81.5 percent of twelve- to fourteen-year-olds worked; 16.1 percent of twelve- to fourteen-year-olds worked in agriculture, 38.1 percent worked in domestic service, 5.1 percent worked in industry, and the rest in other activities. The increase in child labor during the 1940–1950 period was part of the formalization of the labor market with its accompanying intensification of labor use.

Small land ownership and land inheritance from parents to children characterized the northern region, while in the southern region children were less dependent on parents (rarely working under parental supervision or inheriting land). By 1940, small plots in the northern region were associated with higher child labor rates (Mónica 1978). Even today, the traditional sector prevails in different forms and the informal economy is more important in the northern regions. Technology is at a low level, and most production units (farms, industries, or other companies) have failed to upgrade the process and the product, and to move

Figure 1 **Child Labor Incidence Rate**

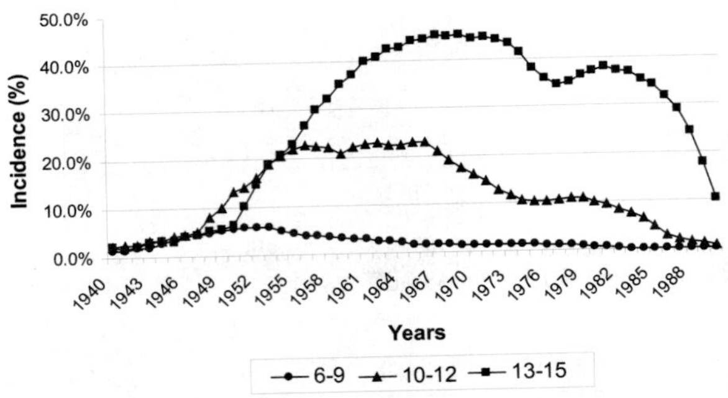

Source: Goulart and Bedi 2006.
Note: The first 10–15 years and the last years of the studied period are less reliable due to few observations.

away from low-skill and labor-intensive work processes. These remain favorable conditions for the persistence of child labor.

1950 to 1974

Figure 1 depicts an estimation of children's economic activity rates for specific age-groups over the second half of the twentieth century. Working children below the age of six were only a residual throughout the period. The next age-group (six- to nine-year-olds) reached its peak in 1951 and after then decreased, which may be related to educational reforms in 1952.

The increase in the employment of youngsters over ten years of age seems to track the growing demand for labor in general, reflecting the decline of a family-based economy and the penetration of capitalism. This does not mean that the total burden of child's work had increased, but that work within the household had been substituted by work outside the household. The increase coincides with the regime's downplaying of the role of education or even perceiving it as a threat. Mónica (1978) suggests that the opportunity cost of education was high while the perceived utility of school learning was low. The rationale was that the family could not afford to spare children's earnings and there was no room for upward mobility in the regime's rigid social structure: "[I]n an illiterate society, ignorance does not constitute . . . a disadvantage; and it is also not a stigma because illiteracy is the rule, not the exception." Not surprisingly, by 1950 the literacy rate in Portugal continued to diverge from that of the rest of Western Europe (Candeias 2004). This period also witnessed a strong rural migration. Estimates set emigration figures at more than 1.7 million Portuguese from the 1950s to 1974, approximately 20 percent of the population (Valério 2001). This may have induced a substitution of child labor for that of adults.

The work participation rate of youngsters ten to twelve years of age did not diverge much from that of the older age-group until it peaked in 1956 and stabilized thereafter. This coincided with the extension of compulsory schooling from three to four years for boys. The law acknowledged that "the main difficulty in the efficient compliance of this measure is the economic condition of those tutors for which the work of their children represents a precious help, that only with hard sacrifice can be dispensed" (Carvalho 1986).[2] In 1950 the juvenile unemployment rate was lower than the adult rate, hinting at a high demand for child labor. By 1960, however, youth unemployment was double the rate for the workforce as a whole, and by 1970 it was triple. Unsurprisingly, labor of ten- to twelve-year-olds started to decrease after 1966 with only a small interruption in 1977–1980.

As for working youngsters thirteen to fifteen years of age, there was a sharp increase after 1950, which might have had several causes: the stagnation of the working population from 1951 to 1962 and the decrease thereafter, which resulted in a scarcity of labor; the increased demand for labor following accelerated industrialization during the 1950s and 1960s; and the delayed entry into the labor market of children that in earlier generations would have started working before the age of thirteen. After 1961, the rate of increase slowed down; it ended in 1969. This coincided with raising the minimum working age to fourteen, while education expenditures began an ascending trend after 1968. This was also the last year agriculture employed more workers than did industry.

High economic growth rates characterized the 1950–1973 period, accompanying the post–World War II boom. Initially, simple technology encouraged child labor. The introduction of more complex technology requiring skilled labor contributed to a decrease in child labor and higher youth unemployment rates. Productivity gains were larger in the services sector (Valério 2001). In the late 1960s, when the aging dictator Salazar literally fell from his chair, the ruling elite made a final effort to promote reforms to allow the regime to survive, but it was already too late. A colonial war that exhausted the country, international isolation, and civil discontent prepared the ground for the fall of the regime, and the oil price shock of 1974 delivered the final blow.

Developments Since 1974

After 1974, when the overthrow of Salazar's successor brought the dictatorship to an end, political changes broke through the international isolation and led to Portugal's increasing integration with Europe. A generally unskilled and cheap labor force favored specialization in labor-intensive and low-skill sectors. In education, the philosophy was transformed into one of supporting the training of the population, which promoted higher enrollment rates, availability of pre-primary school, and more accessible higher education. In particular, after Portugal joined the European Union in 1986, compliance with its norms led to an increase in compulsory education from six to nine years of schooling, and the education budget steadily increased.

From 1974 to 1977 child labor decreased, but there followed a growth spurt from 1977 until 1981. Silva (1991) suggests that the second oil crisis, coupled with restrictive governmental policies coordinated with the IMF, increased both child poverty and child labor around 1980. For example, expenditures on welfare more than tripled after 1974, but peaked in 1979, and declined thereafter until 1982. This increase in child labor also reflected the new openness to Europe following the 1973 agreement, leading once again to specialization in low-skill, labor-intensive activities for comparative advantage. Subcontracting from European companies increased. For some regions this represented an economic boom, and small, medium-size, and family enterprises tended to use child labor to compete, even if seasonally or temporarily (Williams 1992).

In terms of gender, the cohort born in 1973–1977 seems to have benefited from a change in mentality concerning education, favoring equal opportunities for males and females. Curiously, this cohort is also the first in which more girls than boys declared they started working between the ages of thirteen and fifteen. This inflection may be related to increased participation of women in the labor market, or to changes in the importance of some industries or patterns of subcontracting (Eaton and Pereira da Silva 1998).

However, the sharp drop in child labor in one generation was deemed insufficient in a now more progressive society. In the 1980s and 1990s, denunciations of child labor by unions and Catholic organizations were frequent and paved the way for EU and government interventions. The generation born under parliamentary democracy has been the beneficiary of pre-primary school, nine years of compulsory education, and additional benefits such as milk provided in school (Silva 1991). In addition to strengthening attitudes toward learning, other attitudes toward schools have emerged. For example, school has come to be seen, quite simply, as the place where children stay, whereas previously parents often had to take children with them to work.

The long-term trend depicted in Figure 1 is largely demand driven. However, factors other than demand have been decisive for specific turning points. There are key moments that seem to be associated with policy issues such as education and labor laws, especially when accounting for the cumulative effects of education for future generations. Children whose fathers started working before the age of twelve are up to three times more likely to work than others, and children of mothers who started working early are four times more likely to do so. Children of poorly educated parents have more than five times the probability of working than children with better-educated parents.

Conclusion

Before 1970 and during the early part of the 1970s, the labor force participation of children (up to the age of fifteen) may have been as high as 45 percent. However, with the evolution of the economic structure and the end of the dictatorship in 1974, Portugal witnessed a sharp decline in child labor.

Table 2.

Evolution of Net Child Labor Outside of the Household

Period	Characteristics
Pre-1950	Typical case of premarket introduction
Until mid-1960s	Child participation in the labor market increases with the growing economy and industrialization
Mid-1960s to 1970s	Decrease with the change in economic structure and the expansion of education; the agony of the regime, urbanization, and the rise of a middle class also played a role
Late 1970s to early 1980s	Spurt with growing dynamics due to openness and specialization in labor-intensive activities; recessive policy also played a role
Mid-1980s and 1990s	Trend in reduction of demand for child labor returns; further reduction with entrance in European Union and increasing investment and interest in education
Present day	In spite of detriment to the children involved, reduced to a minority

Source: Goulart and Bedi 2006.

Notes: Net child labor comprises subphenomena with different, sometimes contradictory, evolutions. The increasing role of formal economy may artificially inflate the numbers of children considered working. Informal and family work may lead to underreported work, especially in historical contexts.

Table 2 summarizes the evolution of child labor in Portugal.

Notes

This essay draws heavily on Goulart and Bedi (2006). The author thanks Tiago Mata, Arjun Bedi, Hugh Hindman, and Catarina Grilo, as well as Hugh Cunningham, Colin Heywood, and other participants at the Child Labour's Global Past (1500–2000) Conference for helpful comments.

1. The philosophy was summed up in the mottos "God, Fatherland, and Family." In a famous movie song of that time, a "typical" Portuguese sang, "[I am] poor but honored / Owing to Providence the grace of being born poor." Some significant views in the regime's early years by its supporters: "The most beautiful, stronger and healthier part of the Portuguese soul resides in these 75 per cent of illiterate" (Virginia de Castro e Almeida, writer, 1927); "Portugal does not need schools" (João Ameal, writer and historian). See Mónica (1978), Carvalho (2001), and Henriques Carneiro (2003).

2. Translation by the author.

References and Further Reading

Campinho, Alberto. *Regime jurídico do contrato de trabalho de menores.* Braga: Editora Correio do Minho, 1995.

Candeias, António, ed. *Alfabetização e escola em Portugal nos séculos XIX e XX: os censos e as estatísticas.* Textos de Educação. Lisbon: Fundação Calouste Gulbenkian, 2004.

Cardoso, Manuel Pereira. "O caso Português: quantificação, caracterização do trabalho infantil e medidas adoptadas no combate à sua exploração." In *Actas da conferência internacional políticas de combate à exploração do trabalho infantil na Europa.* Vol. 1, 171–76. MTS/PETI. Lisbon: PETI, 2001.

Carvalho, Rómulo de. *História do ensino em Portugal: desde a fundação da nacionalidade até ao fim do regime de Salazar-Caetano.* Lisbon: Fundação Calouste Gulbenkian, 1986.

Eaton, Martin, and Carlos Pereira da Silva. "Portuguese Child Labour: Manufacturing for Change or Continuing Exploitation in the Textiles Industry." *Childhood* 5:3 (1998): 325–43.

Goulart, Pedro, and Arjun Singh Bedi. "History and Determinants of Child Labour in Portugal." Child Labour's Global Past (1500–2000) Conference. Amsterdam, November 15–17, 2006.

Henriques Carneiro, A. *Evolução e controlo do ensino em Portugal.* Textos de Educação. Lisbon: Fundação Calouste Gulbenkian, 2003.

Kassouf, Ana Lúcia, and Marcelo Justus dos Santos. "Child Labor in Brazil: More Than 500 Years of National Shame." Child Labour's Global Past (1500–2000) Conference. Amsterdam, November 15–17, 2006.

Mónica, Maria Filomena. *Educação e sociedade no Portugal de Salazar. A escola Salazarista de 1926–1939.* Lisbon: Editorial Presença, 1978. Translation from an Oxford PhD thesis.

Reis, Jaime. *O atraso económico Português, 1850–1930.* Lisbon: Imprensa Nacional Casa da Moeda, 1993.

Silva, Manuela. *A pobreza infantil em Portugal.* Lisbon: UNICEF, 1991.

Valério, Nuno, ed. *Estatísticas históricas Portuguesas.* Lisboa: INE, 2001.

Williams, Suzanne. *Child Workers in Portugal.* London: Anti-Slavery International, 1992.

Child Labor in Portugal Today

Martin Eaton, PhD, Reader in Human Geography, School of Environmental Sciences, University of Ulster; and **Pedro Goulart,** Institute of Social Studies, The Hague, and CISEP, ISEG, Technical University of Lisbon

The use of children as a source of labor is an enduring, difficult, and damaging issue in Portugal. Trade union concerns, public debate, and political pressure from the European Union in the 1990s led to calls for investigation. As a result, the most recent authoritative estimate suggested that around 4 percent of Portuguese children between the ages of six and fifteen were working (ILO 2002). This amounted to 49,000 child workers in Portugal in 2001. While child work is engaged by a small minority, in many regional centers the importance of child workers is heightened. Indeed, despite its illegality, in many small towns of northern and central Portugal child laborers continue to underpin local economies. At the micro scale, therefore, the issue is an ongoing cause for concern.

Between 1998 and 2001, surveys suggested an increase in attendance at school and a decrease in children working outside the household, results that were corroborated by intensified inspections by the Portuguese Labor Inspectorate. However, these declines were offset by increases in children working within the domestic household sphere. While some new forms of child labor in theater, fashion modeling, and advertising have emerged (Pereira 2004), most labor is still of a traditional form, and in spite of claims that it has disappeared, the problem endures (Sarmento 2004). The spread of small and medium-size businesses is often portrayed as an extension of the small, local farming, land-ownership pattern and follows a similar rationale. Both situations have utilized child labor. As a result, Portuguese child workers are common in the agricultural, civil construction, manufacturing, and commercial sectors (Sistema de Informação Estatísticas Sobre Trabalho Infantil 2003). These workers, invariably encouraged by family circumstances, can be found in locations as diverse as smallholdings, factories, marketplaces, cafes, restaurants, hotels, and circuses. Often only the lucky ones get paid. Many cut short their hours of school attendance, while others absent themselves completely.

More recently, the work of children in the household sphere has grown in importance. Informal arrangements have exploited a loophole in Portuguese labor legislation linked to subcontracting. It is not illegal, for example, for children to undertake piecework in private homes. So, many small firms in textiles, clothing, and footwear subcontract work into private homes. The real scale of this type of child labor is unknown and difficult to control.

Street children are found mostly in Lisbon and number around 2,500 (Cecchetti 1998). In extreme cases, their work activities can extend into criminality such as prostitution or the exploitation of minors in pornographic literature or as drug couriers. Their presence is officially recognized and has led to the establishment of an important private welfare organization, the Instituto de Apoio à Criança (Child Support Institute), aimed at defending the rights of children and alleviating suffering (Instituto de Apoio à Criança 2006).

Child labor often occurs in circumstances where much of the population is either complacent or actively in favor of it. Local conditions are such that child labor is now culturally determined and work is often considered more valuable than education or leisure. Barroso (2001), a representative of CAP (the large and medium landowner's association), for example, argued that working would "avoid the [children] wandering and having nothing to do, [allowing them] better spending of money, [rather than] gaining addictions, which the State spends millions in preventing [with limited success]."[1] His words echo the findings of Villaverde Cabral et al. (1995), who claimed that 42 percent of Portuguese believe child labor is acceptable in certain circumstances. It is not surprising that the authorities have struggled to alter engrained attitudes, ones that have prevailed in peripheral areas of the country long used to surviving on their own devices.

Key determinants of child labor include, on the supply side, chronic poverty among families (Invernizzi 2005) and, on the demand side, work opportunities in many of the rural, semirural, and partially industrialized areas of the country (Chagas Lopes and Goulart 2005). Both the low value placed on education and the perception of high opportunity costs associated with the loss of children's income often make working in the home preferable to gaining an education. While in the short term, the household may benefit from them earning money, in the longer term these youngsters' ambitions are being impeded. Entering the job market at too early an age has a detrimental impact on children's abilities to gain qualifications, proceed to higher education, and ultimately, to improve Portugal's human resource base (ILO 2002).

Contemporary initiatives aimed at alleviating child labor are embodied in Portugal's Programa para Prevenção e Eliminação da Exploração do Trabalho Infantil (PETI—Programme for the Prevention and Elimination of the Exploitation of Child Labor). Established in 2004, and utilizing the slogan "Our Work Is to Study," this government-sponsored organization was charged with altering the "intolerable" exploitation of those minors in work, as well as rectifying the tendencies for some to abandon their schooling early. Significantly, PETI was not compelled to eradicate child labor, but rather was expected to influence the poor conditions under which children were working such that their life experiences could be improved. This assumption that it is better to improve what exists rather than try to eradicate a working pattern that has been utilized by many families for generations now lies at the heart of the organization's mission. In spite of its members' commitment, it is clearly a task that may bring only limited success in a time of rapid change but enduring backwardness and entrenched attitudes.

In conclusion, while child labor has decreased in Portugal, it has not been eliminated. In spite of a declining trend since the 1990s, the debate still persists. Financial expediency and the practical reality for some children having to abandon education early in order to work and earn money often outweigh the moral and idealistic objections raised by concerned parties. Indeed, unless local communities, including industrialists, trade union activists, educationalists, parents, and politicians come together to alter the structural characteristics that promote the use of child labor, some localized Portuguese economies will continue to take advantage of minors and the cheap, productive capacity that they offer.

Notes

For more information on Portugal's program to eliminate child labor, see Programa para Prevenção e Eliminação da Exploração do Trabalho Infantil, http://www.peti.gov.pt/default.asp.

1. Translation by the author.

References and Further Reading

Barroso, José Luis. "O papel dos parceiros sociais e da sociedade civil no combate à exploração do trabalho infantil, em Portugal" [The role of social partners and civil society in combating the exploitation of the child worker, in Portugal]. In *Actas da conferência internacional políticas de combate à exploração do trabalho infantil na Europa*. Vol. 1, MTS/PETI, 237–42. Lisboa: PETI, 2001.

Chagas Lopes, Margarida, and Pedro Goulart. *Educação e trabalho infantil em Portugal* [Education and child work in Portugal]. Lisboa: Ministério do Trabalho e da Solidariedade Social, 2005.

Cecchetti, Roberta. *Living on the Edges, Children Who Work in Europe: From Exploitation to Participation.* Brussels: European Forum for Child Welfare, 1998.

Instituto de Apoio à Criança. At the Service of the Child/Youth in Portugal. http://www.iacrianca.pt.

ILO. *O trabalho infantil limita as ambições profissionais dos jovens* [Child work impedes the professional ambitions of youngsters]. Geneva: ILO, 2002.

Invernizzi, Antonella. "Perspectives on Children's Work in the Algarve (Portugal) and Their Implications for Social Policy." *Critical Social Policy* 25:2 (2005): 198–222.

Pereira, Inês. *Caracterização das actividades dos menores em espetáculos, moda e publicidade* [Characterization of activities of minors in shows, fashion and advertising]. Lisboa: SIETI, MSST, 2004.

Sarmento, Manuel Jacinto. *O trabalho infantil na sociedade Portuguesa: 1998–2003* [Child work in Portuguese society: 1998–2003]. Braga: Instituto de Estudos da Criança da Universidade do Minho, 2004.

Sistema de Informação Estatísticas Sobre Trabalho Infantil. *Tipificação das situações do trabalho dos menores* [Classification of the work situations of minors]. Lisboa: Sistema de Informação Estatísticas Sobre Trabalho Infantil, 2003.

Villaverde Cabral, Manuel. "Equidade social, estado providência e sistema fiscal: atitudes e percepções da população Portuguesa (1991–1994)" [Social equity, state provision and the tax system: attitudes and perceptions of the Portuguese population, 1991–1994]. *Revista sociologia—Problemas e práticas* 17 (1995): 9–34.

Child Labor in Portuguese Textiles

Martin Eaton, PhD, Reader in Human Geography, School of Environmental Sciences, University of Ulster

The use of young children to provide a source of manual labor for Portugal's economic development process continues to be a sensitive issue. In June 2006, the Spanish-owned fashion-retailing company Zara became embroiled in controversy. A report in the Portuguese magazine *Expresso* alleged that one of its suppliers was paying young children €20 a day to make shoes bearing the company's brand name. Journalists highlighted the cases of Carlitos, eleven, and Miguel, fourteen, who worked in their family home to hand sew the interiors of up to fifty pairs of shoes a day. A subcontracting firm based in Felgueiras, a small, economically depressed town close to Oporto in northwest Portugal, was accused of offering the boys miserable levels of pay in return for high rates of productivity. This case swiftly reignited debate over the role of child labor in the textiles, clothing, and footwear industries of Portugal and brought into relief some anomalies in the country's labor legislation.

Portugal has struggled to derive accurate information on an issue that, by its clandestine nature, does not lend itself to rigorous investigation (Ministério do Trabalho e Solidariedade 1999). The broadcast of several documentary television programs in the 1990s helped raise the issue into public consciousness. In so doing it precipitated a series of academic surveys, and speculation that up to 200,000 child laborers were at work (Pestana 2003). However, the most recent authoritative estimate, in 2001, determined a figure of 49,000 child laborers (ILO 2002). While agriculture (particularly in the smallholding, family-plot sectors) accounts for the largest proportion (around one-half) of child labor in Portugal, it is in manufacturing where the issue is most hotly debated. According to the ILO (2002) some 13 percent of child workers were found employed illegally in the secondary sector, and in turn, almost 4 percent of those were working in the textiles, clothing, and footwear industries. The number of children working directly in factories has fallen since the turn of the millennium, but a crude calculation suggests that there were still almost 1,900 children at work stitching clothes, making knitwear, and assembling shoes.

The geographical distribution of working minors illustrates the localized nature of the textiles industry and its concentration in the northwest of the country around Braga and Oporto, and in the central eastern interior of Guarda and Castelo Branco. As the scale of analysis becomes smaller, the influence of child labor becomes more important. Indeed, in many mono-industrial towns such as Felgueiras, the textiles, clothing, and footwear factories may provide the only source of locally available jobs for adults and children alike.

Employment of this type reflects the internationalization of Portugal's economy (especially since accession to the European Union in 1986) and was fueled by the country's comparatively cheap labor costs. This factor favored those traditional, labor-intensive, and low-skilled sectors of industry, where the advantages of using cheap child workers could be exploited. Faced with competitive strains imposed by joining the Single European Market, Portugal received considerable funds to modernize the sector. While many textiles, clothing, and footwear firms invested in new machinery or upgraded the quality of their products, some businesspeople preferred to cut labor costs further. Entrepreneurs took advantage of employing perhaps ten children for the equivalent of one adult worker's wage, but gaining ten times the productivity from their collective inputs

(Eaton and Pereira da Silva 1998). The flexibility afforded by these illegal child laborers, and the fact that they were not required to register for social welfare or national insurance contributions, meant that factory owners were in an advantageous position. Many earned comfortable livings and demonstrated considerable purchasing power to the extent that Felgueiras has the second-highest concentration of ownership of Ferraris (behind Monaco) in Western Europe. At the same time, many of the child workers continued to operate in precarious, sometimes even dangerous working conditions (Sistema de Informação Estatísticas Sobre Trabalho Infantil 2003), with little recourse to health and safety protection.

Ironically, these arrangements gave many local economies a resilient nature. In the face of the economic recession affecting Portugal since 2000, such local labor market arrangements have enabled many regional economies in semirural, semi-industrialized parts of the country to survive the downturn. Moreover, several multinational and domestic companies have now subcontracted out their production, as international textiles tariffs have decreased, thus increasing the role of small businesses in this deeply rooted sector. Consequently, for many poverty-stricken families, the only way to generate much-needed income was through the industrious efforts of their children. This often came at the expense of school attainment and helped contribute to the ongoing cycle of poverty now found in these areas (Goulart and Bedi 2005).

Returning to the case of Zara, the retailer's parent company, Inditex, based in Madrid, investigated the allegations made against it. In a recurring theme, the company found no evidence of children at work in its subcontracting firm. Given the press coverage and the likelihood that evidence of children working would have been removed, it appears that little has changed. Indeed, technically, the engagement of Carlitos and Miguel to sew shoes is not an offense under current Portuguese labor legislation. Working for piece rates while in a private home is a perfectly legal activity. Not surprisingly, therefore, this newer form of child labor has proliferated. Even in the more traditional setting where children worked in small factories, denial of its existence is still common. Detection of child laborers is rare, especially as it is not always evident where the household starts and the factory stops in these small enterprises. Between 1996 and 2000, Portugal's Labor Inspectorate was able to detect a total of 845 child laborers in more than 20,000 factory visits. Corruption and complicity within local communities continues, prosecutions of exposed employers are scarce, and deterrents such as fines are largely ineffective.

In conclusion, industrialists in the textiles, clothing, and footwear sectors continue to offer employment to minors, often with the tacit approval of parents and almost invariably with low levels of pay. As long as the practical and financial benefits to local communities outweigh the moral indignation that periodically surfaces among trade unions, social associations, politicians, and the general public, it is likely that allegations like those that ensnared Zara will continue to emerge in Portugal.

References and Further Reading

Eaton, Martin, and Carlos Pereira da Silva. "Portuguese Child Labour: Manufacturing for Change or Continuing Exploitation in the Textiles Industry?" *Childhood: A Global Journal of Child Research* 5:3 (1998): 325–43.

Goulart, Pedro, and Arjun S. Bedi. "Child Labor and Educational Success in Portugal." ISS Working Paper 142. Institute of Social Studies, The Hague, 2005.

ILO. *O trabalho infantil limita as ambições profissionais dos jovens* [Child work impedes the professional ambitions of youngsters]. Geneva: ILO, 2002.

Ministério do Trabalho e Solidariedade. *Inquírito a caracterização social dos agregados familiares com menores em idade escolar* [Survey on the social makeup of households with children of school age]. Lisboa: Ministério do Trabalho e Solidariedade, 1999.

Pestana, Catalina. "Combate a exploração do trabalho infantil" [Combating the exploitation of the child worker]. *Janus* (2003). http://www.janusonline.pt/2003/2003_1_4_6.html.

Sistema de Informação Estatísticas Sobre Trabalho Infantil. *Tipificação das situações do trabalho dos menores* [Classification of the work situations of minors]. Lisboa: Sistema de Informação Estatísticas Sobre Trabalho Infantil, 2003.

Spain

Children's Work in Spanish Textiles During the Nineteenth and Twentieth Centuries

Enriqueta Camps, Professor of Economics, Pompeu Fabra University

This essay deals with industrial Spain, and more specifically the Spanish textile industry. This fact implicitly limits the geographical focus to Catalonia, in the northeast of the Iberian Peninsula. Since the seventeenth century, Catalonia has been the most dynamic Spanish region for manufacturing, especially textiles, and mercantile activities. During the second half of the nineteenth century, coal mining and iron and steel industries emerged in the northwest of Spain, in the Basque Country and Asturias regions, but these industries never made extensive use of children. While this essay focuses on Catalonian textiles, Spanish historiography has highlighted children's work in a variety of other industries, including agriculture (Borras Llop 1999, 2002), lace making and personal services (Sarasúa 1998), the Galician canning industry (Muñoz-Abeledo 2003), and tobacco manufacturing (Galvez-Muñoz 2000).

Why Were Children Working in Nineteenth-Century Spanish Textile Factories?

Meager living standards and high levels of exposure of women and children to paid production were a matter of concern to Spanish political authorities. The Comision de Reformas Sociales (Commission of social reform) and Instituto de Reformas Sociales (Institute of social reform) were created in the late nineteenth century with the aim of removing women and children from paid work, or at least from the most dangerous and unhealthy economic activities. Nonetheless, this regulation proved to be very unefective (Borras Llop 1999). In a country such as Spain, with very low levels of social capital, both employers and working-class families were ready to defy the law in order to defend their economic interests. In the social reformers' inspection reports, reliable information was difficult to obtain because women and children were often hidden when the inspectors were present. Before the advent of the welfare state in the post-Franco years, state resources to deal with social welfare were very scarce. Therefore, in spite of the fact that the economic and cultural elites regarded women's and children's work as damaging, the state was unable to effectively control the real conditions of work for laboring children.

Instead, the structure of earnings and expenditures over the life course of men and women in a labor market with low wages put pressure on families to employ all the labor resources at their disposal, including children and women. In such a situation, it was unlikely that any state would be able to successfully eliminate children's work, since it represented a basic economic resource for the household. Even a government rich in financial resources would have been hard-pressed to remove children from economic activity.

There is a common misconception that, in the past, families had large numbers of children because they could use their labor to profit from their meager wages. It may be true, in some historical contexts, that inheritance laws led to family arrangements where children, once grown, provided financial support and care of their parents when they grew old. But the idea that the main reason to conceive children was to profit from their labor is erroneous. It has been shown that children were not financial assets in nineteenth-century England (Williamson 1990) or in poor countries today (Mueller 1976). Nor were children financial assets in industrializing Catalonia (Camps 1996).

Figure 1 **Balance of the Family Budget (Current Incomes – Current Expenditures) by Age of Household Head**

Figure 1 simulates the balance of the family budget (income minus expenditures) for the year 1890 in the town of Sabadell, referred to by contemporary citizens as "Catalan Manchester." Based on estimates of household expenditures, and using existing wage rates for adult males, adult females, and children, the figure depicts the net contribution to the household budget of all three (adult males, adult females, and children) based on the age of the head of the household. Notice the current deficit contributed by children over most of the course of the family life cycle. Sons and daughters began to positively contribute to the family budget only when they became adults residing with their parents. It is clear that children were an economic burden, even when they attended school only before the age of ten (on average, for one and a half years), and were then employed in factories. Precisely because of the high financial costs the family faced in rearing children, all family members had to work in order to secure economic subsistence.

Women, too, yielded very poor economic returns to the family over most of the course of the family life cycle. Females generally worked before marriage and as young mothers. But when the first child reached working age, the child replaced their mother in the workforce. In fact, the wages of children were very similar to those of women. In other words, a working child represented the same financial input to the family budget as the

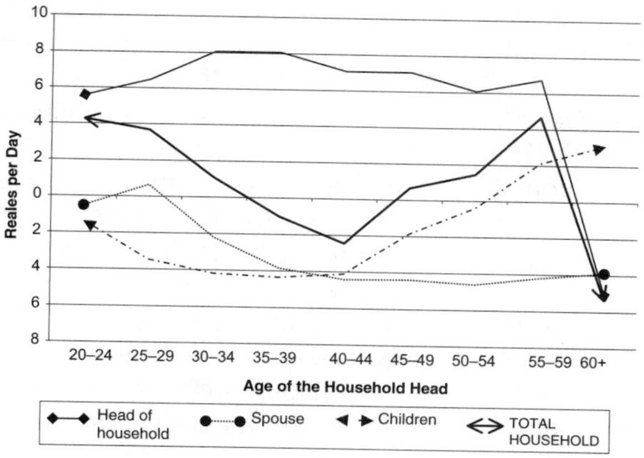

mother, and therefore, in nineteenth-century Spanish textiles, women and children were nearly perfect substitutes.

In the case of Spanish textiles, where families exerted only limited control over fertility, and where children represented an economic burden, the inadequacy of household incomes relative to expenditures normally implied that all children had to undertake paid work in industrial activities after the age of seven to ten. Otherwise, the family could not cover the very basic expenditures of the household. Notice in Figure 1 that even when the family made full use of its labor resources, including women and children, the household went through two periods of the family cycle in which current expenditures were higher than current incomes, and therefore the household had a current deficit. The first of these periods occurred when the household head was between the ages of thirty-five and forty-five and the birth of successive children who were still economically inactive raised family expenditures. The second period occurred after the household head reached the age of sixty, the beginning of his period of inactivity. To face these deficits the family made use of all its human resources, including children, and the final financial balance from this allocation of family labor time was a very modest savings capacity of the household at the end of the family life cycle.

In Catalonia, obedience to inheritance laws implied that the first-born male inherited the family property, even if it was very modest. In exchange, he had to take care of his parents when they were growing old. These wealth transfers were agreed on at the moment of marriage. Parents on both sides were explicit about their contribution to supporting the newly created couple and, in return, the son and daughter-in-law agreed to their obligations to the parents. This is why, in Catalonia, children were, in the long term, a financial asset to sustain the elderly. In fact, however, for the long period before children arrived at adulthood, having children represented a net drain on the family's resources.

Since children had to work from very young ages, they could not attend school. During the nineteenth century, the Spanish social reform authorities explicitly recommended school from age six to age nine. Under the economic circumstances confronting families, though, it is obvious that education could not be made mandatory. Ultimately, public authorities were unable to remove children from paid economic activities. Unfortunately, this had a very high opportunity cost for Spain in the lack of educational investments in children. The consequences of this included very low literacy levels throughout Spain, but also in industrializing Catalonia. Well into the twentieth century, less than half of all Spanish adults were literate (Nuñez 1992).

When and Why Were Children Removed from the Labor Force?

From the wage structure according to age and gender presented in Camps (1996), the marginal financial contribution of a child was equivalent to that of the mother, and children and women were perfect substitutes for each other. In the Catalan textile sector, the wage levels of women twenty-five to thirty years of age were very similar to the wage levels of a boy or a girl of age ten. As long as this remained the case, it made economic sense for children to replace their mothers in the labor market as soon as they were able. This point is important for understanding the reasons why Catalan working families were able to remove children from the labor force.

The exogenous factor that triggered a number of changes was a series of specific human capital policies pursued during the first third of the twentieth century that were designed to improve the economic condition of adult women in the rural textile factories of the Catalan region. These policies yielded important increases in the labor productivity of women, which boosted their hourly wages. In contrast to the historical stagnation of women's real wages, from 1900 to 1936 the hourly real wage of women increased by 80 percent (Llonch 2004). The average wages of women remained lower than those of men, but their situation had improved considerably. In the second half of the nineteenth century, the gender wage gap (women's wage / men's wage) in Sabadell was placed around 50 percent. By 1925 the gender gap had improved to 64.6 percent. It now made economic sense for mothers to remain in the workforce, since they could earn more than their children.

The increasing value of women's paid work, in turn, raised the opportunity cost of their unpaid work of childbearing and child rearing (Camps 2006). As a result, couples sharply reduced fertility. By 1930, fertility rates had dropped below the replacement rate (Cabre 1999). This reduction in the quantity of children made possible an increase of their quality as families began to invest in their education.

Nonetheless, in a backward country like Spain, the incentives to invest in formal education were not yet very high. In Sabadell in 1925, the "literacy premium" remained very low, particularly for girls. Literate male workers earned only 15 percent more than illiterate workers, while in the case of women the marginal literacy premium was only 1.6 percent. Therefore, the incentives to study provided by this industrial society were very low. This is an additional reason why parents of boys, and especially girls, did not invest in their formal education until the period after World War I.

Conclusion

The main reason for the persistence of children in the labor force in the nineteenth century was the inadequacy of the family structure of incomes and expenditures by age and gender, coupled with the very small economic incentives for investment in education provided by Spanish society. The first fact implied that, other things being equal, families had to employ all their labor resources in paid production, including children. Even in this situation, in which children began to provide earnings to the family from the age of ten, the savings capacity of the family was very low. This meant that at times of economic crisis or social distress, or because a wage earner was afflicted by illness and could not contribute as an active wage earner to the family, working-class families could fall below the primary poverty line. In addition, parents had very low incentives to invest in the education of their children, particularly girls. The economic returns to education were very low and, in average terms, did not compensate for the economic contribution made by children to the household in the short run.

This situation changed only by means of social policies promoting the increase of women's labor productivity and real wages through their specific human capital investment. The increase in the value of women's work had an impact on the family's preferences in labor allocation. It shifted women's activity from unpaid (including child rearing and childbearing) to paid activities. As a result of this set of phenomena, Catalan fertility declined to levels below replacement rates by the 1930s. The increase in the educational level of women meant that families could begin to make a rational-choice calculation in their decision making regarding quantity and quality of children. Lower fertility rates meant the family could begin to invest in the education of their children. This is why children up to the age of fourteen were removed from the labor force during the first third of the twentieth century.

References and Further Reading

Borderias, Cristina. "La transición de la actividad femenina en el mercado de trabajo Barcelonés (1856–1930): teoría social y realidad historica en el sistema estadístico moderno." In *Eficiencia o privilegios? Mujeres y hombres en el mercado de trabajo,* ed. L. Galvez and C. Sarasua, 241–76. Alicante: Publicaciones de la Universidad de Alicante, 2003.

Borras Llop, José Maria. "El trabajo infantil en la industria Barcelonesa segun el censo obrero de 1905." *Historia Social* 33 (1999): 25–48.

Borras Llop, José Maria. "El trabajo infantil en el mundo rural español, 1849-1936: ge´nero, edades y ocupaciones." In *El nivel de vida en la España rural,* ed. José Miguel Martinez Carrion, 373–413. Alicante: Publicaciones de la Universidad de Alicante, 2002.

Cabre, Anna. *El sistema Català de reproducció.* Barcelona: Proa, 1999.

Camps, Enriqueta. "Family Strategies and Children's Work Patterns: Some Insights from Industrializing Catalonia, 1850–1920." In *Child Labour in Historical Perspective, 1800–1985,* ed. H. Cunningham and P.P Viazzo, 57–72. Florence: UNICEF, 1996.

Camps, Enriqueta. *La formación del mercado de trabajo industrial en la Cataluña del siglo XIX.* Madrid: Ministerio de Trabajo y Seguridad Social, 1995.

Camps, Enriqueta. "The Rise and Decline of Children's Labor Participation Levels During the Early Stages of Industrialization: Catalonia (1850–1925)." Barcelona Economics Working Papers Series 51, Barcelona Graduate School of Economics, 2003.

Camps, Enriqueta. "Wage Structures and Family Economies in the Catalan Textile Industry in an Age of Nascent Capitalism." *Continuity and Change* 19:2 (2004): 265–81.

Camps, Enriqueta. "Poverty and Children's Work in Spain and Latin America: Some Preliminary Remarks." Barcelona Economics Working Paper Series 225, Barcelona Graduate School of Economics, 2006.

Cerdà, Ildefons. "Monografía estadística de la clase obrera de Barcelona en 1856." In *Teoría general de la urbanización y aplicación de sus principios y doctrinas a la reforma y ensanche de Barcelona.* Madrid: Imprenta Española, 1867, vol. 2, 556-700.

Galvez-Muñoz, Lina. *Compañía arrendataria de tabacos, 1887–1945.* Madrid: Cambio Teconológico y Empleo Femenino, LID Editorial Empresarial, 2000.

Llonch, Montserrat. "La feminització del treball textil a Catalunya (1891–1959)." In *Treball textil a la Catalunya contemporania,* ed. M. Llonch, 77–93. Lleida: Editorial Pages, 2004.

Mueller, Eva. "The Economic Value of Children in Peasant Agriculture." In *Population and Development: The Search for Selective Interventions,* ed. Ronald Ridker, 98–153. Baltimore: Johns Hopkins University Press, 1976.

Muñoz-Abeledo, M. Luisa. "Hombre, mujeres y latas: la segmentación laboral en la industria de conservas de pescado." In *Eficiencia o privilegios? Mujeres y hombres en el mercado de trabajo,* ed. L. Galvez and C. Sarasúa, 279–306. Alicante: Publicaciones de la Universidad de Alicante, 2003.

Nuñez, Clara E. *Laq fuente de la riqueza: educacion y desarrollo económico en la España contemporanea.* Madrid: Alianza, 1992.

Sarasúa, Carmen. "Understanding Intra-Family Inequalities: The Montes de Pas, Spain, 1700–1900." *History of the Family: An International Quarterly* 3:2 (1998): 173–97.

Williamson, Jeffrey G. *Coping with City Growth.* Oxford: Oxford University Press, 1990.

Section 6. Eastern Europe

Romania

Child Labor in Romania

Maria-Carmen Pantea, International Policy Fellowship, Open Society Institute, and "Babes Bolyai" University, Romania

As in other Eastern European countries, most of the working children in Romania combine limited school attendance with rather irregular work, often in agriculture. For the most part, child labor passes as an invisible social issue with little public recognition (unlike the case for street children, who attract much attention). Child labor is rarely addressed as a cause for school dropouts or for low educational performance. However, in spite of the low level of concern, child labor is an emerging phenomenon in today's Romania, whose total population of children (five to seventeen years of age) is now approximately 4 million.

History of Child Labor During Communism

Under communism child labor was regarded as an external problem. The issue was highly politicized and there was no attempt to denounce it as a social problem in Romania. On the one hand, it was considered a typical phenomenon in the ghettos of capitalist metropolitan areas and, thus, a consequence of capitalist economic polarization. On the other hand, it was considered a racial problem of less-developed countries in the third world, thus further confirming the value of the communist system. Child labor was, by no means, understood as a phenomenon taking place in Romania.

However, children did work during communism. Starting from fifth grade (eleven years old), all had to participate in seasonal work (usually harvest) at least two weeks annually. In the countryside, this period was usually extended, and rural schools undertook agricultural projects of their own. Involvement of children in agriculture was a practical need in response to labor shortages in rural areas after forced industrialization (Ghinararu 2004).

Children's perceptions about their work during communism were ambivalent. On the one hand, they enjoyed the time out, as a temporary alternative to the formal demands of schooling. On the other hand, there were many aspects that situated their work at the border of exploitation. They always worked long hours at manual tasks that were often tiresome and unrewarding. Secure transportation to the fields was not always provided. For children above age fifteen, working camps were arranged in order to make the work more efficient. Apart from the work organized through school, children from the countryside also worked with their parents at the so-called cooperatives or in the household. Still, as ownership of land and animals was limited, the need for children's contributions was not very great inside the households.

General Context at Present

Since 1989, Romania has endured a slow and difficult economic transition characterized by land retrocession, but also increased poverty, unemployment, and an informal economy. Subsistence agriculture, external labor migration, and dependence on state benefits became temporary solutions for poverty for a large segment of the population. Due to high rates of poverty and exclusion, Roma children and children living in the countryside are those most likely to enter into child labor. According to official data, the Roma minority accounts for 2.5 percent of the total population, and children are one of its largest groups. Despite social policies encouraging school attendance, Roma enrollment in primary and secondary education is still lower than the national rate by 25 percent and 30 percent, respectively.

Particularly relevant are the increased economic discrepancies between urban and rural areas (where 46.3 percent of the children live). Up to the age of fourteen, children from rural areas can attend schools locally. After this age, they have to continue their education in the cities. Many cannot afford the related costs. According to the Ministry of Education, in 2005, 39 percent of fouteen-year-old children from the countryside (more boys than girls) discontinued their education. Under these circumstances, for many children, the age of fourteen becomes the doorway to adulthood and to entry into labor.

Child Labor in Its Current Policy and Legal Framework

Romania has ratified all relevant ILO Conventions and IPEC has been active in the country since 2000. There is also a National Plan of Action for the Elimination of Child Labor and a National Steering Committee to supervise its implementation. As a matter of urgency, both IPEC and the National Plan for Action tend to focus on the worst forms of child labor.

However, there are legislative inconsistencies that reduce the institutional capacity to monitor and eliminate child labor. Contrary to ILO Convention 138, the Romanian Labor Code applies only to persons employed on the basis of a labor contract, and there is no minimum age for admission to unpaid employment. Consequently, labor inspectors do not have the authority to examine children's work inside the household. Another discrepancy is that the minimum age for entry into employment (fifteen), is lower than the age for completion of compulsory education (sixteen).

Reviews of the national legislation and programs carried out are contradictory. On the one hand, according to the Romanian Ministry of Labor, Social Solidarity and Family (2004), Romania's progress "was the basis for the country's nomination as the focal point for all ILO-IPEC programs carried out in Eastern Europe during 2004–2007." On the other hand, the International Confederation of Free Trade Unions (2005) and U.S. Department of State (2004) denounce the lax enforcement of child labor legislation and the poorly defined roles of agencies that enforce child labor laws.

Incidence and Forms of Child Labor at Present

Estimates of the incidence of child labor are controversial. They vary from 70,690 children according to the National Institute of Statistics up to 300,000 according to unofficial economic estimates adopted by the International Confederation of Free Trade Unions. There are limitations on the analysis of official statistics, as definitions applied are somewhat different than the international ones. For instance, the National Institute of Statistics does not include a category that corresponds to "worst forms of child labor." Instead, it created a new category of "children who perform hard activities," with a narrower meaning than the ILO's conception of worst forms.

According to the National Institute of Statistics, between 2.1 and 3.7 percent of all children are economically active. Almost 90 percent of economically active children are working in agriculture, 5 percent in industry and construction, and 3 percent in trade, hotels, and restaurants. Half of the economically active children are considered to be "child laborers." More than 90 percent of them are from rural areas, and more than 60 percent of child laborers are boys (National Institute of Statistics and ILO 2003).

Whereas most children work for their own households, those from disadvantaged regions, those from deprived families, and many Roma children have scarce resources for work in their own homes. Under these circumstances, they are more likely to look for daily or temporary work outside. Alternatively, many of them form a distinct category of "idle children," who are neither in school nor working, but are exposed to the risks of entering worst forms of child labor.

In extreme situations, they may be rented out by their parents for work, or may enter internal or external child trafficking.

In recent years, there has been major social and political concern for children involved in external migration (for labor, prostitution, or small criminal activities). In 2003, a total of 1,034 unaccompanied children were repatriated to Romania from twenty-five European countries. Many of them, especially those between fifteen and seventeen years old, were victims of trafficking. The external trafficking of girls for sexual exploitation is a phenomenon that has acquired increased visibility (Ghinararu and van der Linden 2004).

The link between child labor and migration is manifold. Apart from the issue of migrant children, there is also a less-documented problem of children left home by emigrating parents. While many parents are working abroad, an increasing number of children are left home to provide for themselves. Despite recent adoption of a process for registering migrant parents and the adults left responsible for the children, most of these situations remain undocumented. Even if the household financial situation is improved by parental migration, this puts a tremendous burden on the children, especially the girls, who have to care for their siblings and to run the household.

Children working in the cities perform a variety of jobs: collection of recyclable materials, street trading, loading and unloading products in local markets. Even if street children occupy a very small fraction of the child labor phenomenon as a whole, due to its higher visibility, they have attracted more political and social interest. The problem of street children, whose number is estimated at 2,000, tends to take over the meaning of child labor in urban areas. Most programs in the area of child labor are intended for street children, but even if many street children do work, the connection with child labor is rarely made.

Reasons Child Labor Exists

Of working children from both cities and countryside, 59.9 percent declared that the main reason for working is to help their families (National Institute of Statistics and ILO 2003). If the high rates of poverty in Romania today might be considered a powerful reason for child labor, it is still problematic whether poverty alone is generating this phenomenon. Only 8.1 percent (especially boys) said they work because they need money. In only 3 percent of the cases does the survival of the children's households depend on their labor (National Institute of Statistics and ILO 2003). Moreover, it is a matter of debate whether the highest incidence of child labor is in fact in the poorest regions (northeast and south), given the scarcity of work opportunities there.

Other structural economic dysfunctions may be responsible. One such condition is the system of subsistence agriculture, with the household as the core production unit, which is characterized by low productivity, low mechanization, and a high level of informal work (Ghinararu 2004). In such a context, child labor appears as a family need, an economic demand, and often a social expectation.

During the transition from communism, many unemployed parents remained less exposed to the principles of the new labor market and isolated from the world where education matters (Ghinararu 2004). Many parents are skeptical about the value of education for their children. Stories of success through education have become extremely rare in rural and poor communities. Under these circumstances, the practice of more work and less education is reinforced as the best preparation for life.

A qualitative study undertaken in the poorest regions revealed that at least 66 percent of parents believe it is good for their children (both girls and boys) to undertake as many tasks as possible in the household. Children also internalized the working expectations of their families: At least 70 percent think it is normal for them to work. The gender distribution is significant: Most families tend to maintain girls in school longer than boys, who can be involved in agricultural work at an earlier age (Stativa 2002).

Conclusion

In January 2007, Romania joined the European Union. Following its obligations to meet EU standards in child protection, there are reasons to hope there will be more programs addressing child labor. Combating child labor remains a realistic aim. In economic terms, the reorganization of means for agricultural production, the increase in the living standards of families with more children, and an enhanced link between education and labor market may be practical tools. However, a refined understanding of economic means of combating child labor must incorporate the social dimension of the phenomenon. The economic perspective needs to consider the power of social models, the gender, generational, and ethnic dimensions of child labor in Romania today.

Note

Research supported by the Open Society Institute, with the contribution of the International Policy Fellowships of OSI-Budapest.

References and Further Reading

Ghinararu, Catalin. *Child Labour in Romania: Discussion Paper.* Bucharest, Romania: RO MEDIA Publishing House, 2004.

Ghinararu, Catalin, and Mariska N.J. van der Linden. *Trafficking of Migrant Workers from Romania: Issues of Labour and Sexual Exploitation.* Geneva: International Labour Office, 2004.

International Confederation of Free Trade Unions. "Internationally-Recognised Core Labor Standards in Romania, Report for the WTO General Council Review of the Trade Policies of Romania." Geneva, 2005.

National Institute of Statistics and ILO. *Ancheta asupra activitatii copiilor: raport national.* Bucharest, 2003.

Pantea, Maria-Carmen. *Combating Roma Child Labor Through Education in Romania: Challenges and the Need for Child Centered Roma Policies.* Budapest: Open Society Institute, 2007. http://www.policy.hu/pantea/Files/Pantea%20Policy%20Paper.pdf.

Romanian Ministry of Labor, Social Solidarity and Family, Press Office. Press release, February 18, 2004.

Stativa, Ecaterina. *Baseline Survey on Rural Child Labour in Five Selected Counties in Romania.* Bucharest: Institute for Mother and Child Protection, 2002.

U.S. Department of State, Bureau of Democracy, Human Rights, and Labor. "Romania. Country Reports on Human Rights Practices—2003." February 25, 2004. http://www.state.gov/g/drl/rls/hrrpt/2003/27860.htm.

Russia

History of Child Labor in Imperial Russia

Boris B. Gorshkov, Assistant Professor of History, Auburn University

Child labor left a significant mark on Russia's industrialization during the late nineteenth century. Children comprised about 15 percent of the industrial labor force, ranging from 0 to 40 percent in individual mills and factories. Most working children came from rural families, while a few were lower-class urban dwellers or inmates of orphanages and foundling homes. Industries employed children for various unskilled auxiliary tasks, and sometimes for tasks normally done by adults. In textile production, they carried bobbins and spindles, cleaned equipment and floors, and on occasion worked as spinners, weavers, or dyers. In mining, they fueled lamps and carried equipment inside the mines. Children received wages at one-third of the lowest adult wage rate. The workday of many children lasted for twelve or more hours. Writings of late-nineteenth-century Russian authors captured the grim realities of child factory labor.

Traditional Society

Children's involvement in productive labor in Russia was hardly a consequence of industrialization. Traditionally, children had worked in the countryside in agriculture and the cottage industry. The upbringing and education of children existed within the context of the real productive activity of the family. The use of children in production had been a common practice aimed at apprenticing children and preparing them for adult responsibilities. Most lower-social-class families in Russia viewed the early initiation of children into productive work appropriate to their age and ability as a form of education. The broad popular acceptance of child labor in the countryside was reflected in an old Russian custom of calling children according to the labor they performed. Boys engaged in helping to plow or harrow were called "plowboys" (*pakholki*); girls were called "nanny-girls" or "mentor-girls" (*nianka, pestunia*).

In the countryside, the types of work assignments children performed differed according to age, gender, and strength, and depended on the local economy. Initiation into productive work for both boys and girls usually started at the age of five or six. To initiate very young children into productive activity, parents developed various treats and rewards, or assigned simple tasks in the form of play. Many games and recreational activities children engaged in between the ages of six and fourteen imitated adult occupational and social activities. Boys engaged in work traditionally fulfilled by male peasants—helping to sow, thresh, and spread manure. Girls helped mothers in maintaining the household, caring for children, raking, strewing, and reaping. Depending on the province, boys and girls also learned various crafts and worked in cottage industries. As they grew up and gained more strength and ability, children were assigned greater responsibilities and taught more complicated tasks. By the age of eighteen, children were considered to be full workers and assigned full labor duty.

Was there exploitation of child labor in the countryside before the Industrial Revolution? This question provokes highly contradictory responses from historians of child labor. The extent of exploitation depended on the specific time and place in which the child lived. In small nuclear families and in families with no adult males, child labor might prove to be more economically significant and the labor burden placed on children therefore heavier than in extended families. Furthermore, capitalization of the rural economy in Russia during the nineteenth century as the market economy intensified may also have led to an increasing labor burden on children in some families.

Nevertheless, the purpose and nature of children's involvement in productive activities in the Russian countryside were not for the sake of profit or the value of children's labor. Historians of child labor suggest that children's productivity in agriculture was usually low and greatly lagged behind their consumption until children attained the age of thirteen or fifteen. The same was true for the nonagricultural sector of the rural economy. Most evidence suggests, therefore, that parents in the countryside engaged their children in productive work primarily for the purpose of teaching and apprenticing children. Moreover, children were given work tasks according to their gender, physical strength, and abilities, and they worked under the supervision of their parents or other adult members of the family. Thus, the ultimate goal of child productive activities in the countryside was to prepare children for adult life, to help them become full functioning members of the family and community. Perhaps the term "child labor" is inappropriate for young children's involvement in production in the countryside. Instead, it was for peasant families a form of schooling, education, or apprenticeship. Children were taught what they would be expected to do when they became adults.

The state corresponded to the popular perception that children's participation in productive labor served as an education and preparation for adult life. Apprenticeship of children had long been a legally established practice. During the eighteenth century, with the goal of having children learn a craft or gain a professional education, the state sanctioned sending many ten-year-old urban and rural children, including inmates of orphanages and foundling homes, to state and manorial factories. Alongside apprenticeship, or even instead of it, state and manorial factories sometimes employed children as auxiliary workers. During the first half of the nineteenth century, the state undertook some timid measures to restrict child labor. An 1845 decree prohibited night work for children under the age of twelve, though without any significant provision for enforcement.

Industrialization

During the second half of the nineteenth century, as industrialization intensified in Russia, production switched from the family and the household to mechanized factories where work practices involving child and family labor received wide acceptance. The rapid growth of the industrial economy during the second half of the nineteenth century, coupled with mechanization and technological innovation, created massive demand for semiskilled and unskilled industrial workers, including those underage.

Existing statistics on industrial labor suggest that in the early 1880s, 49,581 (9.2 percent) of 540,794 factory workers in some 2,792 surveyed factories were children fifteen years of age and under. The overwhelming majority of child workers (30,171, or 60.9 percent) engaged in textile production and, particularly, in the cotton industry (18,826, or 38 percent). Many children also worked in mines and metallurgical plants (7,667, or 16 percent) and in the food-processing industry (6,458, or 13 percent). Children also worked in food and organic materials (animal skins and bones) processing mills. The data from individual textile factories suggest that children performed various auxiliary tasks, which included piecing together broken threads, setting up bobbins, and sorting; some even worked as weavers. The workday lasted for twelve hours (two six-hour shifts). The working week consisted of five and a half days.

The number of girls of age fifteen and below was significantly lower than the number of boys of the same ages. In Moscow's factories, for instance, out of 1,756 children of age fifteen and under 1,451 (82.6 percent) were boys and only 314 (17.4 percent) girls. For children sixteen years and older, the proportions of boys and girls are closer. In Vladimir Province, men comprised 63.7 and women 36.3 percent of the province's workers. Most girls remained in the countryside. Others left to work in various domestic services. Many of those who remained in villages engaged in cottage industries in addition to their numerous household and agricultural activities. For all its personal, social, and economic significance, none of this labor appeared in statistics.

Why did so many children enter the factory

labor force during industrialization? Why did industries employ children? Before industrialization, children's productive activities had been broadly accepted as a means of preparing children for adult life, and such factors were crucial in influencing children's factory employment during industrialization. However, industrialization itself produced new economic and social realities that spurred industrial child labor. On the one hand, dramatic economic and social changes in the countryside during the second half of the nineteenth century, including acceleration of the market economy, rapid growth of the rural population, and the decline of traditional extended families, created a ready supply of labor. On the other hand, rapidly growing industries created massive demand for wage labor. These factors, complemented by the wide popular acceptance of child productive labor, along with the absence of any efficient child labor regulations in private factories, made children an easily available and often desirable source of labor for late-nineteenth-century industrialization.

Health and Welfare of Factory Children

The new industrial environment had a strong negative impact on the health of working children. Unlike work in traditional agriculture and cottage industry, labor in the new mechanized factories subjected children to the rapid pace of machinery and exposed them to moving belts, shifting parts, intense heat, high noise levels, and hazardous conditions associated with dust and chemicals. In addition to numerous illnesses, factory children were more prone to work-related injuries than adult workers. According to data from the Sokolovsk Cotton Mill in Vladimir Province, central Russia, during 1881–1882, of 165 registered accidents, eighty-seven (53 percent) occurred among working children, whereas children accounted for only about 11 percent of factory workers. About 16 percent of the employed children experienced accidents, as opposed to less than 3 percent of adult workers. Most accidents involved cuts, wounds, and fractures of arms, fingers, and legs. The most frequent accidents happened among children who pieced thread and set up bobbins. About 37 percent of accidents in the spinning shop were associated with setting up bobbins.

Various state commissions and local governments also reported that the highest number of work-related injuries occurred among child workers. Medical and police reports, for instance, illustrate that the most common work-related accidents involved hand and limb injuries to children. According to government officials, a similar pattern of child injuries existed in Moscow and its province, confirming that children were more vulnerable to injuries than adult workers. A St. Petersburg government factory commission set up in 1859 also reported that the highest number of work-related accidents occurred to children. The commission found that in one given period, there were 148 accidents with "serious consequences" that required a physician's attention. Children fourteen and under incurred forty-eight of these accidents, and children fifteen and sixteen incurred twenty-eight accidents, for a total of seventy-six. This compares to only seventy-two accidents among adults, even though the number of adult workers greatly exceeded the number of children. Work-related accidents also caused deaths. For example, according to police records, in the Guk factory in St. Petersburg, two to four children died annually.

Most contemporaries attributed the ill health among factory children to their physical immaturity and to hazardous conditions in factories. They suggested that labor in mechanized factories and the high pace of new machines required greater energy from working children than they possessed. Overall, rates of work-related accidents were highest in textile (cotton-spinning) factories and in metallurgical plants, both industries with high levels of mechanization.

What were the causes of frequent industrial injuries among children? Recent medical studies shed significant light on differences between adults and children as regards physical condition and mental abilities. For example, one study finds that eye movements of preschool children differ from the eye movements of adults, a factor that limits children's ability to acquire adequate visual information (Kowler and Martins 1982). One may imagine the significant impact this factor would have had, especially when children were working with high-speed mechanized equipment. Alongside the impact of incomplete physical development, another explanation for high rates of work-related accidents among children can be found in recent research about neurology and developmental psychology. This research emphasizes stages of development of the human brain, which in turn produce different patterns of behavior and responses to environment. Children cannot think in abstract terms (Sugarman 1986; Hetherington, Lerner, and Perlmutter 1988; Paterson et al. 2006). Thus, children's behavior and responses to the factory environment and machines were dissimilar to those of adult workers. Below a certain age, children and young adults fail to project the consequences of their actions. Medical research suggests that humans reach complete cerebral maturity only by the age of twenty-one. In turn, conditions of brain immaturity and low ability to coordinate attention would have increased the incidence of work-related injuries among working children.

Emergence of Child Labor Regulation

The decline of working children's health and physical condition produced concern among many statesmen and public figures about its potential consequences for the security and well-being of the empire. At this point the state began to take the issue of children's engagement in productive labor seriously and generated an important discussion of industrial labor among state officials, industrialists, lawyers, and academicians. During the 1860s and 1870s, the government organized commissions to inspect labor conditions in factories and review existing labor legislation. These commissions produced legislative proposals concerning the employment, welfare, and health of working children, which were subsequently discussed in provincial governments (*zemstvos*) and industrialists' associations.

Most state- and local-level bureaucrats supported state involvement and legislative measures to restrict children's factory employment. They were the first ones to observe and mediate workers' complaints. As members of the ruling class, they believed it was their paternalistic and humanitarian duty to protect working children. In contrast, most employers opposed the proposed restrictions. They argued that without the input of children, factory work could not be conducted successfully. Some contemporaries associated children's factory employment with the poor economic conditions of working families and emphasized the material benefits that children's wage labor brought these families. Legislative initiatives and the debates about child labor laws continued during the 1870s.

From the 1870s on, various periodicals began to publish regular articles on the working and living conditions of working children. These publications exposed to public view child labor and conditions among children in industry. Educated society had previously been largely unaware of these matters. Many publications now devoted whole issues to child rearing, children's upbringing, and children's health and education. Most of these articles portrayed child labor as an evil practice that must be outlawed. Childhood had always been a subject of Russian literature, but during the second half of the nineteenth century, themes of childhood and children were especially prominent in literary publications. Many authors exposed and, in effect, denounced abuses against children employed in factories, workshops, and domestic service. The public discussion of the whole issue of childhood produced an environment and an important foundation for the introduction and enforcement of child labor laws in the late imperial period.

In 1882, the state council abolished employment of children under the age of twelve and limited the workday for juveniles from twelve to fifteen years of age to eight hours (no more than four consecutive hours). The law also banned night and Sunday work, and employment in "harmful industries," and introduced the factory inspectorate to supervise implementation of the regulations. An 1884 law called for mandatory schooling for all children employed in industries, requiring children to complete a one-year curriculum at a public school or its equivalent. Additional laws in 1885 and 1886 prohibited night work for children under the age of seventeen, and for women in the cotton, linen, and wool industries, and in mills that processed mixed fibers considered harmful to workers.

How did the child labor law affect labor conditions for children working in industries? To be sure, the laws of 1882, 1884, and 1885 initially regulated child labor only in private businesses, and only those that used certain kinds of technology and employed at least sixteen workers. The laws applied only to European Russia. Although they affected hundreds of thousands of children, the laws did not address labor in agriculture, domestic services, and small artisan workshops, which also employed many children. The labor of children working in agriculture, where work was usually supervised by adult family members, and in domestic services still remained entirely unregulated and unprotected. Furthermore, after the introduction of the 1882 law, many children under the age of twelve from poor families in all likelihood shifted to agriculture and domestic services out of sheer necessity.

Regardless of these shortcomings, during the three decades before World War I the employment of children in industry gradually declined. The records of factory inspectors show a notable decline of children's industrial employment after the implementation of the 1882 law. For example, before 1883, children accounted for 10 percent of industrial workers in Vladimir Province, a textile center in central Russia. By 1885 the number of children employed there dropped to 3.8 percent. In general, in 1884, employed children accounted for 15 percent of Russia's industrial workers. In 1913, 1.6 percent of industrial workers were children between the ages of twelve and fifteen and 8.9 percent were youths from fifteen to seventeen. It is clear that the employment of children below fifteen in industries was disappearing in late czarist Russia.

References and Further Reading

Gorshkov, Boris B. "Factory Children: An Overview of Child Industrial Labor and Laws in Imperial Russia, 1840–1914." In *New Labor History: Worker Experiences and Identity in Russia, 1840–1918,* ed. Michael Melancon and Alice K. Pate, 9–33. Bloomington, IN: Slavica Publishers, 2002.

Hetherington, E. Mavis, Richard M. Lerner, and Marion Perlmutter, eds. *Child Development in Life-span Perspective.* Hillsdale, NJ: Lawrence Erlbaum Associates, 1988.

Kowler, Eileen, and Albert Martins. "Eye Movements of Preschool Children." *Science,* New Series 215 (February 19, 1982): 997–99.

Paterson, Sarah V., Sabine Heim, Jennifer Thomas Friedman, Naseem Choudhury, and April A. Benasich. "Development of Structure and Function in the Infant Brain: Implications for Cognition, Language, and Social Behaviour." *Neuroscience and Biobehavioral Reviews* 30:3 (2006): 1087–1105.

Sugarman, Leonie. *Life-span Development: Concept, Theories and Interventions.* New York: Methuen, 1986.

Zelnik, Reginald E. *Labor and Society in Tsarist Russia: The Factory Workers of St. Petersburg.* Stanford, CA: Stanford University Press, 1971.

Zelnik, Reginald E. *Law and Disorder on the Narova River: The Kreenholm Strike of 1872.* Berkeley: University of California Press, 1995.

Child Labor in the Russian Textile Industry

Dave Pretty, Assistant Professor of History, Winthrop University

As in most industrializing nations, textile production was the motor that drove Russian industrialization, and child labor was an important component of the textile workforce from the beginning. Its role grew as mechanization reduced the skills and strength necessary to manufacture cloth. However, the growth of civil society and medical research on industrial environments spurred the generally effective state regulation of child and adolescent labor in the textile workforce that lasted through the late imperial and Soviet periods. Although child labor has become a matter of increasing concern in the post-Soviet era, the collapse of the Russian textile industry in the face of international competition has rendered the use of children and adolescents in this sector moot.

Child Labor in Textiles During Serfdom (to 1861)

In traditional Russian society, until the mid-1800s, all levels of society, including the state, accepted age-appropriate amounts of child labor as not only acceptable, but also desirable. This general approval of child labor held firm as factory textile production slowly increased in Russia during the 1700s.

Domestic production of linen and wool had long been a major activity of Russian peasants, especially in the less agriculturally productive provinces of north-central Russia. Even before Peter the Great, some rural regions had come to specialize in textile production; by the 1660s, Ivanovo possessed a nationwide reputation for linen production, and only one-eighth of the village's population still engaged in agriculture.

This cottage industry was supplemented in the late 1600s and 1700s by factories. From the beginning child labor played an important role in factory textile production. In 1739, 2.8 percent of the main state wool factory's workforce were eleven years or younger, and another 9.7 percent were between twelve and fourteen. At another state woolen factory in 1797, about 40 percent of workers were children or adolescents. At the major linen factory in Yaroslavl in 1813, 37 percent were children or adolescents; most were younger than seven, though these numbers may include children who did not work but were included on the factory rolls with their parents.

The cotton industry became the most dynamic branch of textiles, and was also the sector in which freely hired labor dominated. In 1859, children age fourteen or younger constituted 7.5 percent of cotton-spinning-mill workers in St. Petersburg, and 12.5 percent of those in weaving and finishing mills; for all industry in textile-dominated Moscow Province they made up 15.2 percent. These data may understate the number, for during mid-century, weaving was primarily a cottage industry of women and children.

Traditional attitudes approving child labor as beneficial and even necessary initially carried over to factories. One inspector's criticism in 1811 of a state textile mill resulted in a decree that the male children of peasants ascribed to that mill must be apprenticed by age twelve. Factory apprenticeships were often used as social welfare for orphans and poor children. These beliefs were premised, however, on the assumption that children performed labor consonant with their growth and development.

Changing Attitudes in the Reform Era

Such attitudes began to break down as industry grew in importance, as the first signs of a labor movement emerged, as the Great Reforms of the 1860s produced the critical mass of independent professionals and print media for "public opinion" to emerge, and as government inquiries revealed the actual state of factory child labor and the effects it had on children.

The first law regulating child labor in private industry, in 1845, resulted directly from an 1843 textile strike during which many serf children were found working eleven-hour days for no pay. Investigators found that more than 2,000 children fourteen or younger worked in thirty-three textile mills. They worked twelve-hour days on both day and night shifts. As a result, the government prohibited factory work between midnight and 6 A.M. for children under twelve. The law contained no penalties, however, and was generally evaded.

In 1859, the government began a major review of labor conditions in the factories of St. Petersburg and discovered that in half the city's cotton mills children between eight and fourteen worked night shifts, while other mills expected fourteen-hour days from children as well as adults. Physical violence against child workers by overseers was apparently so common that it occurred twice in front of inspectors. Such abuses prompted discussion within the government and increasingly in the press about the need to regulate child labor.

Child Labor in Textiles During the Postreform Era

By the end of the 1870s, 13 percent of workers in Moscow textile mills were younger than fifteen, and 16.5 percent in St. Petersburg textile mills were between ten and fifteen. Scattered data from the 1870s from larger mills outside the two metropolises indicate that often half the workforce consisted of children and juveniles under eighteen. In 1883 a comprehensive survey of Russian industry found that 12.7 percent of employees in textile factories were fifteen or younger, with the largest proportions in cotton spinning (21 percent) and wool spinning (31.2 percent). Most industrial workers started as children; as late as 1899, after fifteen years of government regulation, a survey of local peasants working in factories around the cotton center of Ivanovo found that more than half had become factory workers before their sixteenth birthday.

Soviet historiography emphasized that factories utilized child labor because, as industrial processes became mechanized and deskilled, children could be paid less than adults. While this factor was important, factory owners also had other motives. Children were often more accepting and understanding of new technology, with fewer preconceptions about the work process; in some cases, owners preferred children because they had no craft identity. Industrialists also valued their agility, dexterity, and smaller stature in such tasks as piecing threads and doffing bobbins.

Traditional explanations for child labor stressed the progressive impoverishment of the Russian peasantry in the postreform era that compelled families to migrate to the cities, where the high cost of living forced as many members as possible to earn a wage. However, evidence also suggests that those peasant families that adapted best to market conditions diversified, participating simultaneously in agricultural and industrial sectors. Evidence from the Ivanovo region shows that factory families that sowed the most land also did quite well in the factories.

One reason cotton-spinning mills had such a high proportion of child labor is that thread was produced, not by individuals, but teams in which a skilled adult spinner hired and supervised one or two minors who performed such dangerous tasks as piecing broken threads and doffing bobbins, both of which required close contact with moving machinery. In weaving sheds, children put the warp through the reeds or worked on spooling and winding machines; some operated their own looms. Some of the most dangerous jobs were in cotton-printing plants, in which children worked in overheated drying and starching drums, or with the harmful chemicals in dyes. In all divisions, children performed errands and cleaned machines that were usually still moving. Children were more prone to industrial accidents than adults; at one mill in the 1880s, 16 percent of children suffered an accident as opposed to 2.7 percent of adult workers. Working hours were generally the same as for adults, ranging from twelve to fifteen hours, six days a week, but wages were much lower. In 1885, in the Moscow region, children in all industries made just over a third of an adult male's salary; by 1908, children and adolescents in Moscow Province textile factories made about half the adult male salary.

State Regulation of Child Labor

The commissions established to examine child labor in 1859 made a series of recommendations in 1862, but industrialists successfully resisted the proposed legislation on grounds that limiting child and adolescent work would disrupt the entire industrial process, since so many children worked in teams with adults. Another round of commissions and legislative proposals followed in the 1870s. Although these efforts also failed, they swayed both state and public opinion toward the eventual adoption of wide-ranging labor legislation.

The first major legislation regulating labor was enacted in 1882. Children younger than twelve could no longer work in factories; those under sixteen could not work more than eight hours a day, or more than four hours consecutively, or at night, and were required to have at least three hours a day to attend school. An 1884 law mandated a year of school for workers between twelve and fifteen. An 1885 law extend the prohibition on night work to all who were not yet seventeen.

The effects of the legislation on employment of children in textiles were dramatic. By the mid-1890s, those under eighteen comprised only 17 percent of the textile workforce, a mere fraction of which was younger than fifteen. In cotton textiles in 1913, only 1.1 percent of workers were younger than fifteen, and 8.9 percent were fifteen to seventeen. While inspectors continued to find numerous violations, in general the late imperial labor laws were successful in controlling and mitigating the worst abuses of child labor.

Textile Child Labor in War and Revolution

The outbreak of the First World War increased demand for child labor, as adult males were drafted into the army. On the eve of the revolution, adolescents comprised 14 percent of the textile workforce. By this time both adults and minors in textiles were usually women; in 1917, one Moscow textile factory was known for hiring only girls who had recently migrated from the countryside. By late 1915, protective labor legislation had been abrogated and night work and longer hours were generally permitted. Longer hours and decreasing experience led to teenagers experiencing twice as many accidents in 1915 as their proportion of the workforce. Conditions throughout Russia worsened as the empire's economic and political structures proved incapable of waging total war while also supplying its cities with food or its factories with raw materials. Female textile workers demanding bread began a general strike in Petrograd in March 1917 that quickly turned into a revolution. It is not clear how many of these women were minors, nor is it clear how many adolescent textile workers participated actively in the events that unfolded between the overthrow of the monarchy in March and the Bolshevik seizure of power in November. Provincial textile workers supported the Bolsheviks and the transfer of power to the soviets of worker deputies earlier than most workers, yet no leaders of Moscow's very active youth organizations seem to have been textile workers.

From the Bolshevik Revolution to Stalin's Revolution

Between the end of 1917 and the end of 1920, the new regime fought a vicious civil war to remain in power. The economy collapsed and textile production dropped precipitously, to 5 percent of 1913 levels. One of the first decrees of the new government prohibited employment of children under fourteen, and limited those between fourteen and eighteen to six hours a day; no one under sixteen could work nights, nor could anyone under eighteen work overtime. However, despite working fewer hours, adolescents were to receive a full day's pay. Beginning in 1919, the minimum age for employment was raised to fifteen, and the maximum teenage workday was lowered to four hours. Despite the collapse in production, however, the mobilization of millions of young men for military service produced intense pressure on factory managers to bend these rules. In 1918, 3 percent of the cotton textile workforce were fifteen or younger; and 8 percent were sixteen or seventeen. A 1919 survey of textile factories found that 95 percent of adolescent employees worked substantially longer than four hours a day.

After the Communist victory, large enterprises, including textile factories, remained state controlled but were expected to make a profit. This New Economic Policy would remain in effect until the end of the decade. One consequence of the war's end was massive adolescent unemployment, as millions of demobilized soldiers returned to civilian life. In textiles, between July 1921 and July 1922 the proportion of adolescent labor fell from 8.7 percent to 4.9 percent. To counteract this trend, quotas for adolescent labor were promulgated. In textiles this was 8 percent of the workforce, which was never met; the percentage of adolescents in cotton textiles fell from 11.1 percent in 1918 to 3.1 percent in mid-1929. Managers were not eager to hire adolescents because they could not work a full day but were supposed to receive a full day's pay. Another reason for this decrease may have been the growing attractiveness of other trades: Boys especially preferred the higher pay and greater educational opportunities of metal factories. The 1922 labor code set a minimum age of fourteen for wage labor, while those between fourteen and sixteen could work only with government permission in cases of economic need. Those younger than sixteen could not work more than four hours a day, sixteen- and seventeen-year-olds could not work more than six hours, and no one younger than eighteen could perform night work. Adolescents still had to be paid the same daily wage as adults. Violations continued, however; in 1923, one survey found that 7.7 percent of adolescent textile workers labored more than the permissible six hours, while 4.2 percent (12.5 percent in woolens) filled job descriptions officially labeled as too dangerous for them. A greater frustration was the differential between adult and adolescent wages. According to one 1926 report, adolescent textile workers made only half the adult wage, primarily because they filled mostly lower-paid positions.

Child Labor in Textiles Under Stalin

By 1927, Soviet industry had returned to its 1913 capacity; further growth would be more expensive, however. During the next two years, Joseph Stalin and the Soviet leadership took a series of decisions that led to the First Five-Year Plan. Adolescents, dissatisfied with their low pay and status, supported the First Five-Year Plan; young textile workers began the "shock brigade" movement in 1928 to try to shake up the shop-floor hierarchy. However, the First Five-Year Plan also marked the end of textiles' domination of Russian industry. The aim of the period was to not to make goods with machines, but to make machines that made machines; the steelworker, not the weaver, would become the archetypal hero. As Soviet industrial production more than doubled, the textile industry's share of production fell from 30 percent to 18 percent between 1927 and 1930. Consequently, while the overall economy saw sizable growth in adolescent labor, the proportion of textile workers under age twenty-three grew only from approximately 26 percent to 29 percent in 1926–1933. For industry as a whole, the same figure rose from 25 percent to 41 percent between 1930 and 1933.

The continued growth of Soviet industry through the 1930s necessitated an increased use of child labor, most notably through the institution of a state labor reserve system in 1940. Young men between fourteen and seventeen were recruited for trade schools, much of which was on-the-job training. However, few of these conscripts were utilized in textiles. Russia's entry in the war in June 1941 increased the use of child and adolescent labor, often voluntarily; in late 1941, 300,000 schoolchildren age twelve to fifteen volunteered for factory labor. These children were more likely to go into textiles because of the heavy recruitment of experienced workers into war industries. Volunteers were not the only new workers: In September 1942, teenage girls were included in the state labor reserve system. For all industries, the percentage of workers under eighteen rose from 6 percent to 15 percent in 1939–1942. The labor reserve system became more important immediately after the war, as the regime attempted to recover quickly from economic devastation in conditions of demographic catastrophe; however, only a fraction—5.1 percent in 1947—of these labor conscripts went into textiles. Nonetheless, in 1947, 19.8 percent of textiles workers were under twenty.

Child Labor in Textiles in Post-Stalin Russia

The maturation of the planned economy under Khrushchev and Brezhnev became the regime's legitimating principle, including the promise of full employment; this disguised unemployment reduced the need to utilize child labor. A new labor code in 1955 returned to the basics of 1922, including stricter age restrictions, one month's paid leave, a ban on night work, and a shorter workday at a full day's wage. While this gave most factory directors an incentive to not hire adolescent workers, the situation was different in textiles, where wages seriously lagged behind those of other sectors. Even the most skilled weaver did not earn as much as semiskilled metalworkers. By 1966, Leningrad textile factories could not fill all the spaces in their training schools and had to hire more schoolchildren and retirees to fill available jobs. Textile factory training schools became a conduit for rural youth to avoid strict residence restrictions and move to the city. By the 1970s, no textile job description appeared anywhere in the responses to a poll on which professions Leningrad schoolchildren considered attractive.

The gradual reintroduction of market mechanisms under Gorbachev led to contradictory responses. With all state compulsion lifted, some factory directors stopped hiring untrained adolescents altogether, while others—including those in the textile center of Ivanovo—had to hire even more rural girls to replace employees fleeing for the more lucrative and burgeoning private sector.

The collapse of the Soviet Union, and the abrupt opening of the Russian economy to the global market in 1991–1992, devastated the Russian textile industry. By 2000, textile production and employment had fallen to less than 20 percent of their late Soviet numbers. Even as child labor in Russia has become a greater concern, it seems to have become a moot point in textiles. Indeed, recent studies of Russian child labor make no mention of factory labor, as children themselves see more hope for profit and advancement in street *biznes*, both legal and illegal.

References and Further Reading

Chase, William J. *Workers, Society, and the Soviet State: Labor and Life in Moscow, 1918–1929.* Urbana: University of Illinois Press, 1987.

Filtzer, Donald. *Soviet Workers and Stalinist Industrialization: The Formation of Modern Soviet Production Relations, 1928–1941.* London: Pluto Press, 1986.

Filtzer, Donald. *Soviet Workers and De-Stalinization: The Consolidation of the Modern System of Production Relations, 1953–1964.* Cambridge: Cambridge University Press, 1992.

Filtzer, Donald. *Soviet Workers and the Collapse of Perestroika: The Soviet Labour Process and Gorbachev's Reforms, 1985–1991.* Cambridge: Cambridge University Press, 1994.

Filtzer, Donald. *Soviet Workers and Late Stalinism: Labour and the Restoration of the Stalinist System after World War II.* Cambridge: Cambridge University Press, 2002.

Gorshkov, Boris. "Factory Children: Child Industrial Labor in Imperial Russia, 1780–1914." PhD diss., Auburn University, 2006.

Ward, Chris. *Russia's Cotton Workers and the New Economic Policy: Shop-Floor Culture and State Policy 1921–1929.* Cambridge: Cambridge University Press, 1990.

Children in Sex Trades in Russia

Anna Yakovleva, PhD, Executive Director of Regional Public Organization of Social Projects in Sphere of Populations' Well-Being "Stellit," and Representative of Russian Alliance Prevention of Commercial Sexual Exploitation of Children, Russia

The problem of children in sex trades in Russia has never been the subject of regular scientific research. As a result there are no reliable statistical data characterizing the situation in the country, and some historical periods are blind spots in the history of the phenomenon. However, one can form a general picture of the problem, both its historical and modern aspects, based on indirect historical sources, expert data, and results of the few local studies.

Imperial Period

There is little factual information about children in sex trades in Russia before the time of Peter I in the eighteenth century, but historical sources about life and morals of the time point to large-scale debauchery, including child sexual abuse. However, no data is available about the commercial basis of such cases. The first reference to children in sex trades appears in the criminal code of 1846. The reason was the widespread sexual exploitation of minor boys and girls of lower social strata. Medical-police committees established in those years to regulate prostitution set the minimum age for girl sex workers at seventeen years.

Nevertheless, the child sex trade was widespread in St. Petersburg and other large cities. The share of minors among prostitutes under surveillance was about 2 percent (Sokolov 1921). However, a large portion of girl sex workers became prostitutes before the "established" age: more than half before they were eighteen, and one-fourth before they were sixteen (Kuznetsov 1871). Official reports contained data about the considerable number of rap parlors (off-grade brothels), where underage girls of unknown origin, or those sold by parents or so-called middlewomen (Fedorov 1897), were kept. There are also reports of girls of nine to fourteen years of age getting syphilis as a result of the sex trade. The high profitability of the child sex trades gave rise to a special kind of fraud—manufacture of forged documents for minors stating an older age (Bentovin 1994). Regional and international trafficking of children for the sex trade was also common (Stites 1978). The problem had such a wide scope that a special corrections institution was established in St. Petersburg for girls who were sex-trade victims, and in 1909 the official age for working in rap parlors was raised to twenty-one years.

Revolutionary Period (1918–1930)

The revolutionary changes of 1917 and the subsequent five years of the civil war changed the social image of Russia dramatically. The traditional form of child sex trade in brothels was preserved into the 1920s only in the White movement centers (Omsk, Rostov, Vladivostok). In 1919, an interdepartmental commission on prostitution control was established at the People's Committee of Social Security. The commission proposed wide-ranging measures of economic and social support for women and children involved in prostitution (provision of medical services, improvement of general education level, professional training, employment). The commission on juvenile delinquency, created in 1921, was directly involved in control of child homelessness and, consequently, the child sex trade. However, the scale of these measures was insufficient for solving the problem against the background of the social and economic difficulties of the postwar period. At the time, there were 7 million homeless children in Soviet Russia (Madison 1968). They were involved in beggary, theft, and prostitution. From 60 to 88 percent of minor girls detained for offences in 1920–1921 were selling sex services (Sokolov 1921).

Communist Period (1931–1990)

In the 1930s all social problems in Soviet Russia were managed by repressive measures. Homeless children were forcibly placed in orphanages organized on prison principles. Sex trade organizers, like other criminals, were relocated to specialized workers' settlements. This began the period of official suppression of social phenomena related to sex trades, violence, drug addiction, and crime. Still, the sex trades were widely used to attract currency through the "Torgsin" system created in the 1930s, which was aimed at foreigners and the hotel sector of the economy (Golosenko and Golod 1998; Lebina and Shkarovsky 1994). However, nothing points directly to the involvement of children.

Around the Second World War, child homelessness, starvation, and devastation aggravated the problem of child sex trades. It is known that brothels were organized for soldiers and officers in occupied territories of the Soviet Union, and that minor girls were forcibly kept in them. The difficult problems of the postwar decade laid the foundation for growth in the sex trades in the 1960–1980s "thaw" period. The main supply of prostitutes were single mothers and underprivileged girls, including many who came from rural areas to large cities to study or in search of a job. There were also secret brothels for representatives of the political and economic elite where minors were used. Alongside hotel and "mobile" (on call through taxi drivers) prostitution, in the late 1970s there appeared the so-called shoulder prostitutes—young girls traveling with long-distance drivers in exchange for sexual services. There are some documented cases of mentally disordered children brought up in specialized asylums being involved in the sex trade (Gurvich et al. 2003). In 1987, every twentieth prostitute in Russia was under eighteen. Although there was no official acknowledgment of a problem of children in the sex trades, the criminal code provided for punishment for getting minors involved in prostitution.

Postcommunist Period (after 1991)

The perestroika period (1985–1991) leading to the reorganization of the Soviet Union (1991) was accompanied by political and socioeconomic changes that were major factors in the growth of the child sex trade in the present period of Russian history. The transition to a market economy caused a sharp increase in poverty and unemployment. At least 30 percent of Russians were recognized as poor. Increased numbers of families were unable to provide proper maintenance and upbringing for their children. As a result, cases of termination of parental rights and withdrawal of children from families doubled from 1997 (24,400) to 2001 (48,200). The number of orphans and children without parental support (so-called social orphans) also keeps growing, from 658,200 in 1999 to 700,000 in 2002. This has promoted the appearance of a large number of street children. In 2002, official estimates of the number of street children in Russia ranged from 1 million to between 3 million and 4 million.

The life of children in the street is connected with criminal activity—fraud, theft, abuse of toxic substances and drugs, and sex trades. However, only a small number of cases come to the attention of law enforcement. For example, from 1998 to 2002 there were only 3,007 documented crimes in Russia involving minors in antisocial actions. However, other estimates reveal large numbers of street children involved in illegal sex trades. In 1993, more than 1,000 children in Moscow were involved in prostitution; in 2000, in Primorsky territory, the share of minors among apprehended prostitutes was 25 percent (Erokhina and Buryak 2003); independent researchers estimate the share of minors among street prostitutes in St. Petersberg was at least 30 percent in 2000, and about 50 percent of street prostitutes were involved in sex trades before they were eighteen (Gurvich et al. 2001). On the whole, in 1996 alone, every eighth prostitute in Russia was under eighteen, and in the capitals (Moscow and St. Petersburg) it was every fifth prostitute.

Another factor in the commercial sexual exploitation of children in contemporary Russia is the liberalization of the norms of sexual behavior in the transition from the Soviet era, characterized by privacy of sexual life and low sexual culture, to active promotion of the idea of sexual delight. This process paralleled the stabilization of social life and the beginnings of economic growth in the 2000s, which resulted in the abrupt formation of demand for sexual services of various kinds—from striptease shows and telephone sex to nontraditional kinds of sexual practices. As a result, the range of sex trades involving children expanded considerably.

Today, minor girls and boys are used both in various kinds of prostitution (street, hotel, on call, in clubs, and in brothels) and in pornography. In the northwest region alone, about 6 percent of young men and 3 percent of young women have rendered paid sexual services, most often acting in pornographic films (Gurvich et al. 2001). According to Interpol data, in 2005 there were at least seventeen studios producing pornographic materials involving children in St. Petersburg (the most active center of child pornography in Russia). Pornography is produced using both girls and boys, sometimes as young as eight or ten, more commonly thirteen or fourteen. Children are recruited from among street children or from those brought from other regions of Russia. Most of this child pornography is placed on the Internet and is oriented toward foreign users.

Another concern is trafficking of children for sex use. Children are brought to Russia from less trouble-free countries (Moldova, Belorussia, Ukraine, Kazakhstan). In 2001 alone, there were 500 registered cases of children exported from Moldova to Russia. From Russia, children are exported to countries of Western Europe and the Middle East. There is also trafficking of children from less economically developed and rural regions of central Russia, the Ural Mountains, and Siberia to the capitals (Moscow and St. Petersburg) and large industrial centers. Various schemes are used to traffic children, from use of forged passports to falsification of school exchange-program documents to "commercial adoption" and "surrogate maternity."

To improve the position of children, Russia has and ratified a number of international conventions, including most of the important conventions dealing with sexual exploitation of children. However, at the state level there is little evidence of the practical application of measures necessary to fulfill the obligations specified in these conventions. Legal control of child sex trades is addressed in a series of articles of the criminal code, the Code of Administrative Offences, as well as the federal law of 1998 On Basic Guarantees of the Rights of the Child in the Russian Federation. Again, however, most of these articles (especially criminal ones) have not been applied in practice.

Efforts to prevent commercial sexual exploitation of children and to provide help to victims are being carried out with financial support from international organizations, including ECPAT, UNICEF, and the World Childhood Foundation. State agencies dealing with child and social welfare are active within the framework of these programs. A promising direction in the development of practices and programs aimed at countering commercial sexual exploitation of children is development and introduction of mechanisms for identifying vulnerable children and providing rehabilitation services to child victims.

Conclusion

The problem of the child sex trade in Russia is expressly related to socioeconomic factors. Analysis of the problem in historical context shows that the major reasons for aggravation of the problem in periods of social change and economic slump are the social vulnerability of children, child homelessness, and neglect. In contrast, periods of social stability and economic growth are characterized by increasing demand for sexual services, including those using children. Children in sex jobs are concentrated in metropolitan centers and large industrial cities, while less-developed regions are suppliers of children for the sex industry.

Involvement of children in sex trades has always been prosecuted in Russia. The attitude of society and the state to sex jobs has always been negative and morally condemnatory (even in the short period when prostitution was regulated and surveilled prostitutes were under strict medical-police control). It appears that because of the moral condemnation of the sex trades, even more so when involving children, there has never been a clearly manifested affirmative approach to its solution on the part of state authorities in Russian history. It is likely to be the basic reason for lack of a system of countering commercial sexual exploitation of children within the framework of state policy even at the present stage.

References and Further Reading

Ball, Alan M. *And Now My Soul Is Hardened: Abandoned Children in Soviet Russia, 1918–1930*. Berkeley: University of California Press, 1994.

Bentovin, Boris. "Selling Her Body." In *History of Prostitution: E. Fuks, M. Kuznetsov, B. Bentovin*. St. Petersburg: Firma "Brask," 1994.

Erokhina, Ludmila D., and M.Y. Buryak. *Women and Children Trade for Sexual Exploitation in the Social and Criminological Perspective*. Moscow: Profobrazovanie, 2003.

Fedorov, A.I. *An Essay on Medical-Police Surveillance over Prostitution in Petersburg*. St. Petersburg, 1897.

Golosenko, I.A., and S.I. Golod. *Sociological Studies of Prostitution in Russia: History and State-of-the-Art*. St. Petersburg: Petropolis, 1998.

Gurvich, I.N., V. Rusakova, T. Pyshkina, and A.A. Yakovleva. *The Commercial Sexual Exploitation of Children in St.Petersburg and North-West Russia*. Denmark: Save the Children, 2001.

Gurvich, I.N., M.M. Rusakova, A.A. Yakovleva, and T.T. Pyshkina. *Commercial Sexual Exploitation of Minors in Saint Petersburg in the Mirror of Sociology*, ed. V. Koslovsky, 412–43. Saint Petersburg: M.M. Kovalevsky Sociological Society, 2003.

Kuznetsov, Mikhail. "Prostitution and Syphilis in Russia" (1871). In *History of Prostitution: E. Fuks, M. Kuznetsov, B. Bentovin*. St. Petersburg: Firma "Brask," 1994.

Lebina, Natalia B., and M.V. Shkarovsky. *Prostitution in Petersburg: 40-ies of XIX Century–40-ies of XX Century*. Moscow: Progress-Akademii, 1994.

Madison, Bernice. *Social Welfare in the Soviet Union*. Stanford, CA: Stanford University Press, 1968.

Russian Federation. *Report on Implementation of the Convention on the Rights of the Child by the Russian Federation*. Moscow, 2005. http://www.omct.org/pdf/cc/2005/report/report_children_russia_eng.pdf.

Sokolov, B. *Save the Children! About Children in Soviet Russia*. Prague, 1921.

Stites, Richard. *Female Liberation Movement in Russia: Feminism, Nihilism and Bolshevism, 1860–1930*. Princeton, NJ: Princeton University Press, 1978.

Position of Children and Child Labor in Russia Today

Valeriy A. Mansurov and **Anastasiya Batykova,** Institute of Sociology of RAS, Moscow

In the twentieth century, Russia lived through a series of dramatic cataclysms that had a significant impact on the position of children in the country. Prior to the revolution of 1917 and the Bolsheviks coming to power, child labor in czarist Russia was permitted starting from the age of eight. Children in cities worked in factories and plants, in service, and elsewhere. But as Russia was an agricultural country and the major part of the population lived in rural areas, child labor was used primarily in agriculture.

In the first days of Soviet power, from October to December of 1917, the Council of People's Commissars issued several decrees aimed at improving the condition of children. In 1919, the program adopted at the Eighth Congress of the Russian Communist Party (Bolshevik Party) called for providing all students with food, clothing, and books at the expense of the state. Child labor was also prohibited up to the age of sixteen and, until eighteen, was limited to six hours per day.

One of the gravest problems of the time was orphanhood and child homelessness. Before the Great October Socialist Revolution of 1917, there already were tens of thousands of orphans and children with only one parent who had lost their families at the fronts of World War I. Hundreds of thousands more orphaned, disadvantaged, and homeless children appeared as a result of the bloody civil war (1918–20) and the subsequent years of ruined economy, epidemics, and famine. Mass child homelessness was recorded in the historic memory of the nation as a peculiar symbol of the 1920s.

By the mid-1930s, the state managed to eliminate child homelessness. Virtually all orphaned, disadvantaged, and homeless children were placed under state supervision in orphanages and specialized child-care institutions. However, hardly had they grown up and graduated school when the country was engulfed in another, even bloodier war (1941–45), which created many thousands of newly orphaned children. Thus, the distressful period of mass orphanhood lasted for many years more.

More recently, other factors are related to orphanhood, such as natural disasters and production and transport accidents causing premature death of parents. The number of disadvantaged children is growing as parents are deprived of parental rights due to alcoholism, immoral lifestyles, mothers refusing to nurture and support their children, and growing numbers of single and underage mothers. There is a new term, "social orphanhood," which means orphanhood when the parents are alive. The share of such children in hostel institutions today totals about 95 percent.

During the years of Soviet power, Russia saw the establishment of free health care and education, and various measures aimed at the protection of maternity and childhood were adopted. For example, working mothers, families with many children, and needy and incomplete families were paid allowances; some preschool and school-age children were provided full social security; and a system of mass summer recreation for children and teenagers was established. However, the noble concept of providing equal opportunities for life and development of all children was never implemented in full.

The collapse of the Soviet Union in late 1991, and the start of reforms in political, social, and economic spheres of independent Russia, along with the transition to a market economy, while positive in many respects, were hard blows for socially vulnerable groups of the population. The state of crisis in Russian society and the related decline in living standards were exacerbated by the decrease in the level of social protection for children.

Current Position of Children in Russia: General Trends

A question regularly debated in the media and in scientific publications concerns which of two institutions—the family or the school—should bear the primary responsibility for nurturing the younger generation. In the current situation, families are dealing with a more significant problem, mere survival, which forces education into the background. Families with children constitute the largest group, 53.4 percent, of the poor. Poverty is closely related to family size. Families with one to two children are more than twice as likely as childless families to be in poverty. In families with three or more children, especially in families consisting of several generations, the poverty level is almost 2.8 times the average level countrywide. The birth of a second child in a complete family increases the poverty risk to 50 percent (Konygina and Dmitrieva 2007). Families with one parent, or "incomplete" families, as they are dubbed in Russia, experience higher levels of poverty than families with two parents ("complete" families) of the same family size.

Just as family financial conditions have shifted focus from nurturing children to survival, fiscal austerity has also caused schools to reduce their nurturing activities to focus on their primary function of giving children knowledge. Meanwhile, the position of youths in terms of utilizing the right to education worsens along with decreasing living standards. As of 2004 about 11,900 children did not have even elementary education, and 1,300 students were excluded from school for misbehavior (Gogoleva 2004). According to polls, more than 50 percent of enterprise managers feel that qualifications of graduates from basic and specialized secondary education institutions had clearly decreased within the past decade, and only 10 percent of managers point to an improved level of training (Kovaleva 2005).

Weakened societal concern about children's socialization has led to a number of unfavorable social effects, including increasing social disadaptation of children, which shows in a wide range of deviant behavior patterns (early alcohol and drug abuse, prostitution, and other immoral or illegal behavior); early maternity and increased numbers of illegitimate children; renewal of child homelessness as a social phenomenon, aggravated by social orphanhood; new categories of children living in especially grave conditions, such as refugee children; and increasing rates of juvenile and adolescent crime, along with growing numbers of child victims of criminal assault, exploitation, and sexual violence.

Child Labor in Modern Russia

Juvenile labor is not a new phenomenon in Russia, but early employment has come to be seen as an acute social problem only relatively recently. Perestroika, the transition from a planned to a market economy, and economic, social, and political reforms have altered the customary foundations of life and brought about significant changes in value systems. New social institutions have been created and old ones have disappeared. Previously child labor (excluding domestic work) took place mostly in organized and officially approved forms, while now spheres of activities where an official hiring procedure is not required, and often is not desirable, have grown.

What was a highly formal process has become highly informal. Formal placement offices, which also performed pedagogical functions, have been replaced by unofficial employment channels, where both the employer and the employee pursue financial advantages, or are guided by personal relations. One problem with weakly institutionalized labor markets is related to poor distribution of information regarding vacant positions. For this reason, the main intermediaries for teenagers searching for work are their relatives, friends, and acquaintances. Lack of information also contributes to children remaining in the informal sector, as it is much easier to use the channels of job search already tried. A poll among employers in Moscow showed that in very few cases (8.7 percent) do employers actively recruit children. In most cases (65.4 percent), children approach employers and

Young girls from Moldavia employed on a demolition site, Podolsky district, Moscow region. Photographic mission to Russian Federation, September 22–29, 2006. *(© International Labor Organization / M. Crozet)*

ask for work themselves; sometimes they are brought by their parents or relatives (19.7 percent) (MOT 2002).

One clearly negative aspect of informal employment of Russian youths is the fact that they lose their special position guaranteed by the law, which prohibits employing minors in night work, Sunday work, hazardous work such as work performed underground, and regulates their hours so as not to interfere with their schooling. Further, it leaves children vulnerable to violation of their rights by the employer. For the large number of children working in the Russian streets, their labor is not subject to protection, and can lead to most harmful consequences for health, and is sometimes connected with explicit criminal practices.

In spite of the disadvantages, children see a number of advantages associated with informal employment. One advantage is that informal employment generally pays better. Under the widespread "gray" salary systems, informal employment is more advantageous in terms of income earned by children for almost all types of work (Borisova et al. 2001). Another factor that attracts Russian youths to the informal sector is easy access. Entering this market is possible for children of any age and does not require any bureaucratic procedures, such as health certification. Moreover, informal employment usually allows flexible work hours, which makes it possible for a student to combine work and classes. While labor law officially prohibits children working on the weekend, this restriction is easily circumvented in informal employment.

Another advantage of the informal sector is the possibility for children to set up their own lines of business. One in every five teenagers in Moscow spends leisure time on gambling, and for some of them this has become a permanent source of income (Scheglova, Vasil'eva, and Kochnev 2001). New types of children's businesses develop, ranging from sale and resale of Dendy cartridges (unauthorized Nintendo game cartridges) and creating computer games to cleaning sales stands and offices, posting advertisements, and black-market leasing of fashionable clothing.

How Russian Children View Their Work

According to Solodova and Kharchenko (2001), Russian youths, as economic agents, possess the personal and social resources that are in demand today, including the necessary system of values, a sense of self-efficacy regarding their capacity to influence their situation, and a reasonable conformism—that is, a readiness to meet the requirements of the labor market. Unlike their parents, they have no paternalistic expectations, and they are accepting of social inequality, without which it is not easy to get a job outside the governmental sector. The nature of their involvement in economic activities and differences in patterns of economic behavior are determined, not so much by their level of satisfaction with their personal financial position or by their assessment of the financial position of the family, but more by the social and psychological peculiarities of the prevailing value system related to their attitude to wealth. This dominant value largely determines the different character of economic activities of young people—initiated or organized, regular or one-time, constructive or deconstructive, as pastime or related to financial considerations. Thus, one of the major motives for the involvement of teenagers in labor activities is "the wish to have a high income, lots of money, to become rich" (Solodova and Kharchenko 2001).

Clearly, children are sensitive and responsive to the changes in the society's value system. Still, the widespread opinion that children have adopted one-dimensional commercial ideals since the collapse of socialism should not be overstated. For example, research by Korzheva conducted among senior school students asked, "Would you like to be rich?" While a substantial majority responded affirmatively to this aspiration, a substantial minority of students expressed indifference to becoming rich (Korzheva 1995). Further, by the late 1990s, there were indications of trends toward postmaterialistic values—the value of labor as a means of self-realization increased, skills and professionalism became of greater importance, and instrumental attitudes to work weakened (Chuprov and Zubok 2000). Yet wealth remains a dominant value orientation that is a strong differentiating factor of not only perception but also behavior regarding work.

Some sociologists distinguish between major and secondary causes of early employment. Major causes include family illness, parents' incapacity to work, and low material welfare. Secondary causes include lack of pocket money and children's striving for entertainment and enjoyment (Pronina 2000). Scheglova, Vasil'eva, and Kochnev (2001) solicited responses from children regarding the causes for the involvement in labor activities. Based on responses, the authors constructed a hierarchy of motives for working. Having pocket money to spend on one's personal needs was first on the list. Relatively few children said they work because "parents earn little." Some noted they "don't want to beg" for money from their parents. A strong second motive was the wish to show one's independence. Only a few respondents named "interesting work" as a motive for job search. Considerable differences between the children from poor and those from well-to-do families were observed. Children from well-to-do families are more likely to strive to get a job, are more apt to pick their own job, and tend to make more demands. The needy children agree to anything in order to get money. They are more likely to perform adult jobs or to be engaged in criminal activities (Scheglova, Vasil'eva, and Kochnev 2001).

Research conducted by Breeva found that 37 percent of students were working. More than 80 percent said they worked to be independent and have their own money, 30 percent wanted to save start-up capital, and only 10 percent said they were helping their families and viewed this as a way to prepare for adult life. When asked what criteria guided their choice of employment, 46.7 percent cited pay, 20 percent said work should be interesting, and 20.5 percent said work should combine pay with interest. Only 6.7 percent cited that work should not interfere with studies (Breeva 1999).

For the most part, teenagers make their own decisions about work. Breeva notes that it is not only children from poor families that work. Some are from well-to-do families, have loving parents, but dream about becoming rich by any means (Breeva 1999). The predominantly voluntary nature of child labor in Russia is observed for senior school students, among whom only 6 percent have to work under the pressure of parents or other people (Borisova et al. 2001). In a situation where financial inequality among disadvantaged people is fixed in their perception, and where the possibility that children will inherit the poverty of their parents is very high, such economic behavior appears to be one of the possible versions of children's projecting their own alternative future.

Sociological surveys of children may show the image teenagers want to create rather than the actual factors for their behavior in the labor market. However, surveys of employers confirm much of this information and provide additional insights as well. From a survey of employers in Moscow, employers believe that 47.3 percent of children who work do so because of their wish to have pocket money. About one in six children are seen to be working to help parents or other family members, and one in four are seen as having to work to support themselves. About one-third of working children are from well-to-do families. A similar survey of employers in St. Petersburg shows several things in common with the Moscow survey—that most working children cannot be classified as those who have to work in order to survive, and that a large proportion simply want to earn a bit of pocket money for everyday expenses. However, there were also some differences. Larger proportions of children were seen as working to give financial support to their families. And, unlike in the Moscow survey, employers in the northern capital are of the opinion that about 8 percent of children are involved in labor activities to earn money for drugs (MOT 2000).

Employers were asked about the value of work for children. Their main reason in favor of early work is the fact that children start learning the value of money as they earn it from their own efforts. Children gain income not by beggary or theft but by their work. This was the opinion expressed by more than two-thirds of the employers interviewed (69.1 percent). Thus, employers say industriousness is implanted in children and they get accustomed to work and are not idle. Moreover, they are constantly under the supervision of adults, which is also important.

As anywhere in the world, in Russia the work performed by the minors is usually of a low-skilled and low-paid character. In certain cases this work is connected with different risks and health threats. Regardless, many children and employers see this as an important first step in acquiring material well-being in Russia's increasingly open and competitive labor markets.

References and Further Reading

Borisova, L.G., G.S. Solodova, O.P. Fadeeva, and I.I. Kharchenko. *Neformal nyi sektor: ekonomicheskoe povedenie detei i vzroslykh.* Novosibirsk: Novosibirskii Gos. Universitet, 2001.

Breeva, E.B. *Deti v sovremennom obschestve.* Moscow: Editorial URSS, 1999.

Chuprov, V.I., and U.A. Zubok. *Molodezh' v obschestvennom vosproizvodstve: problemy i perspektivy.* Moscow: Rossiiskaia Akademiia Nauk, ISPI, 2000.

Dement'eva, I.F. *Socializaciya detey v sem'e: teorii, faktory, modeli.* Moscow: Rossiiskaia Akademiia Nauk, In-t Sotsiologii, 2004.

Gogoleva, A.V. *Besprizornost': social'no-psihologicheskie i pedagogicheskie aspekty.* Moscow: Voronezh, 2004.

Konygina, N., and O. Dmitrieva. "Bednye deti bogatyh roditeley." *Rossijskaja gazeta* (March 9, 2007).

Korzheva, E.M. "Adaptaciya podrostkov k rynochnym otnosheniyam." *Sociologicheskiy zhurnal* 2 (1995): 141–51.

Kovaleva, N. "Ekonomika obrazovaniya Rossii: itogi monitoringa." *Narodnoe obrazovanie* 10:33 (2005).

MOT. *Analiz polozheniya rabotayuschih ulichnyh detey v Sankt-Peterburge.* St. Petersburg: Byuro Mezhdunarodnoy Organizacii Truda, 2000.

MOT. *Uglublenniy analiz polozheniya rabotayuschih ulichnyh detey v Moskve.* Moscow: Byuro Mezhdunarodnoy Organizacii Truda, 2002.

Pronina, E.I. "Prichiny detskoy zanyatosti v Moskve." *Sociologicheskie issledovaniya* 1 (2000): 117–18.

Scheglova, S.N., N.V. Vasil'eva, and S.V. Kochnev. *Prava rebenka na zaschitu ot ekonomicheskoy ekspluatacii: sociologicheskiy analiz.* Moscow: Socium, 2001.

Solodova, G.S., and I.I. Kharchenko. "Formirovanie ekonomicheskogo soznaniya vypusknikov obscheobrazovatel'noy shkoly." *Sociologicheskie issledovaniya* 9 (2001): 89–95.

Zhuravleva, I.V. *Zdorov'e podrostkov: sociologicheskiy analiz.* Moscow: Rossiiskaia akademiia nauk, In-t sotsiologii, 2002.

Part 6
North Africa and Middle East

Section 1. North Africa

History of Child Labor in North Africa

Heidi Morrison, PhD Candidate, University of California at Santa Barbara

Over the course of the twentieth century, the North African countries of Algeria, Libya, Morocco, and Tunisia have depended predominately on agriculture. Whether in the hands of colonizers or North Africans themselves, organizational factors relating to cultivating the land have had serious repercussions for the living and working conditions of children. The traditional institution linking landowners and agricultural workers throughout much of the North African region was the *khammessat,* a verbal contract between the landowner and the head of an agricultural household (the *khammès*). The landowner provided the draft animals, seeds, and agricultural implements, and the *khammès* provided the labor and assumed full responsibility for the crop outcome. *Khammès* were remunerated by being given a proportion of the crop, in principle, one-fifth, called the *khoms.* Since the *khammès* could not afford to hire labor, in order to maximize the *khoms* they engaged the whole family, wife and children, in the work. *Khammès* and their families typically worked seven days per week (except holy days and funerals), and historically, if they tried to leave they could be imprisoned or forced to return to work. The *khammessat* predated the colonial period but proved a flexible enough institution that it continued through colonization and into the postindependence period, though it has by now undergone considerable reform in most countries.

For the first half of the twentieth century, nearly all child labor legislation in North Africa was geared toward nonagricultural and nondomestic child workers, while nearly all child workers were in agriculture or domestic service. During the second half of the twentieth century, all of the North African countries ratified ILO Conventions 138 (minimum age) and 182 (worst forms of child labor), and increasing proportions of children are attending school. However, many children still work in agriculture and, accompanying the postindependence shift toward urbanization, increasing numbers of children are working as street vendors, as domestic servants, and in handicraft industries.

References and Further Reading

Arab Labor Organization. "Child Labor in Libya: A Passing Phenomenon or an Endless Reality?" [in Arabic]. Loose-leaf study. Arab Labor Organization, Libya, 2002.

Arab Labor Organization. "National Meeting on Child Labor in the Arab World" [in Arabic]. Loose-leaf study. Algerian Ministry of Work and Social Security, Algiers, April 2002.

Arab Childhood and Development Council. *The Phenomenon of Child Labor in the Arab World* [in Arabic]. Cairo: Arab Childhood and Development Council, 1998.

International Labor Office. *Labour Survey of North Africa.* Geneva: La Tribune de Genève, 1960.

Algeria

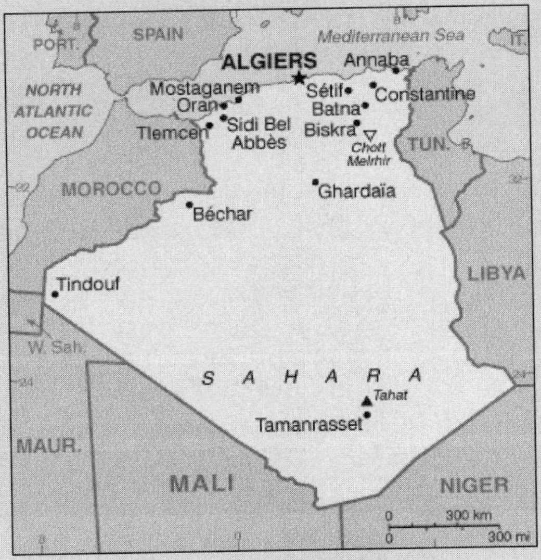

Algeria			
	CRC	C 138	C 182
Ratifications	Y	Y	Y
Human Development Index/Rank	0.728/102		
Human Capital			
Population Growth Rate	1.22%		
% Population 0–14	27.2%		
Total Fertility Rate	1.86		
Life Expectancy	73.52		
Infant Mortality Rate	28.78		
Literacy Rate	70%		
Economic			
GDP/Capita	$7,700		
GDP Growth %	5.6%		
% Poverty	25%		
Gini Index	35.3		
Labor Force Composition			
% Agriculture	14%		
% Industry	13.4%		
% Services	72.6%		

History of Child Labor in Algeria

Heidi Morrison, PhD Candidate, University of California at Santa Barbara

French colonization of Algeria began in 1830. By the beginning of the twentieth century, large-scale French settlers had seized and held most of the irrigated land, which was worked by either poor European settlers or landless Algerian peasant families. The landowners adopted the *khammessat* system of sharecropping, in which the landowner provided the draft animals, seeds, and farm implements and the worker (the *khammès*) provided the labor in exchange for a one-fifth share of the crop (the *khoms*). This made for a grueling work regime for the children. The *khammès* engaged the whole family in the farm work, and since the landowner did not pay for supplementary work, they were all virtually forced laborers. Children were expected to help out from a very young age, and as they grew older, both the nature and extent of their contributions increased. As a result of this economic system, as well as French discriminatory practices in social welfare funding, most Algerian children were not enrolled in schools. At the turn of the century, more than five times as much money was spent on European children's education in Algeria than on Algerian children's education, and less than 5 percent of Algerian children were in school.

By the mid-twentieth century, Algeria's economy remained predominately agricultural. An ILO survey in 1960 stated that three-quarters of the economically active Algerian population were engaged in traditional agriculture, while the rest worked on their own account or for wages in commerce, industry, mining, transport, and services. The role of children had changed slightly from its early twentieth-century form, due to changes in the *khammessat*. A growing trend toward urbanization made the *khammès* more sought after and, thus, contributed to an improvement in their situation. The *khammessat* was transformed by an official decree in 1956, which declared that the landowner may get no more than one-half of the total crop and *khammès* may not be required to provide additional labor. However, dispensing with family labor in the *khammès'* contract did not necessarily improve the welfare of children, because in Algeria there were no regulations covering the minimum age of admission to employment in agriculture. Financial incentives remain for *khammès* to work their children. UNESCO statistics on education show that from 1950 to 1954, only 19 percent of Algerian children between the ages of five and fourteen were enrolled in schools.

The only Algerian child workers who experienced any real protection by the mid-twentieth century were those employed in nonagricultural and nondomestic sectors. The Labor Code amendments of 1956 set the minimum age for employment outside agriculture and domestic service at thirteen. The code provided young workers and apprentices under eighteen years of age more favorable provisions for holiday than it did male adults. For example, the annual holiday for adults was calculated at one and a half working days for every month, as opposed to two for children. However, other protections for children in nonagricultural sectors were limited. The minimum age at which children could join trade unions was set at sixteen, and the minimum wage applied only to workers over eighteen years of age.

In the years following Algerian independence in 1962, the government nationalized French estates and intensified agricultural production. The Labor Code set the minimum age for employment at sixteen and prohibited the recruitment of children for employment without the consent of a parent or legal guardian. From 1992 until 2002, Algeria was under military rule and plagued by civil violence. In late 1992, Algeria ratified the UN Convention on the Rights of the Child. In 1999, the government enacted an order calling for the formation of a national committee to investigate the protection of children and to propose judicial procedures. A report issued by the Ministry of Work and Social Security in 2002, on the occasion of an Arab Labor Organization (ALO) conference in Casablanca on the status of child labor in the Arab world, claims that the situation of working children in Algeria is not worrisome and there are no known cases of exploitation or mistreatment of children who work. The report also claims that girls and boys under nineteen years of age do not work together at night. The U.S. State Department reported in 2003 that many Algerian children work in small workshops, family farms, and informal trade and that the minimum-age standard is not enforced in the agricultural and domestic sectors. The U.S. Department of Labor reports that commercial sexual exploitation in Algeria is a problem, including some reports of girls being kidnapped to work for terrorist groups. UNICEF has no statistics on the current percentage of working children in Algeria. However, UNICEF reports that the adult literacy rate in Algeria between 2000 and 2004 was 70 percent and the net primary school enrollment for 2000–2005 was 97 percent.

References and Further Reading

Ageron, Charles-Robert. *Modern Algeria: A History from 1830 to the Present.* Trenton, NJ: Africa World Press, 1991.

Arab Childhood and Development Council. *The Phenomenon of Child Labor in the Arab World* [in Arabic]. Cairo: Arab Childhood and Development Council, 1998.

Arab Labor Organization. "National Meeting on Child Labor in the Arab World" [in Arabic]. Loose-leaf study. Algerian Ministry of Work and Social Security, Algiers, April 2002.

International Labor Organization. *Labour Survey of North Africa.* Geneva: La Tribune de Genève, 1960.

Libya

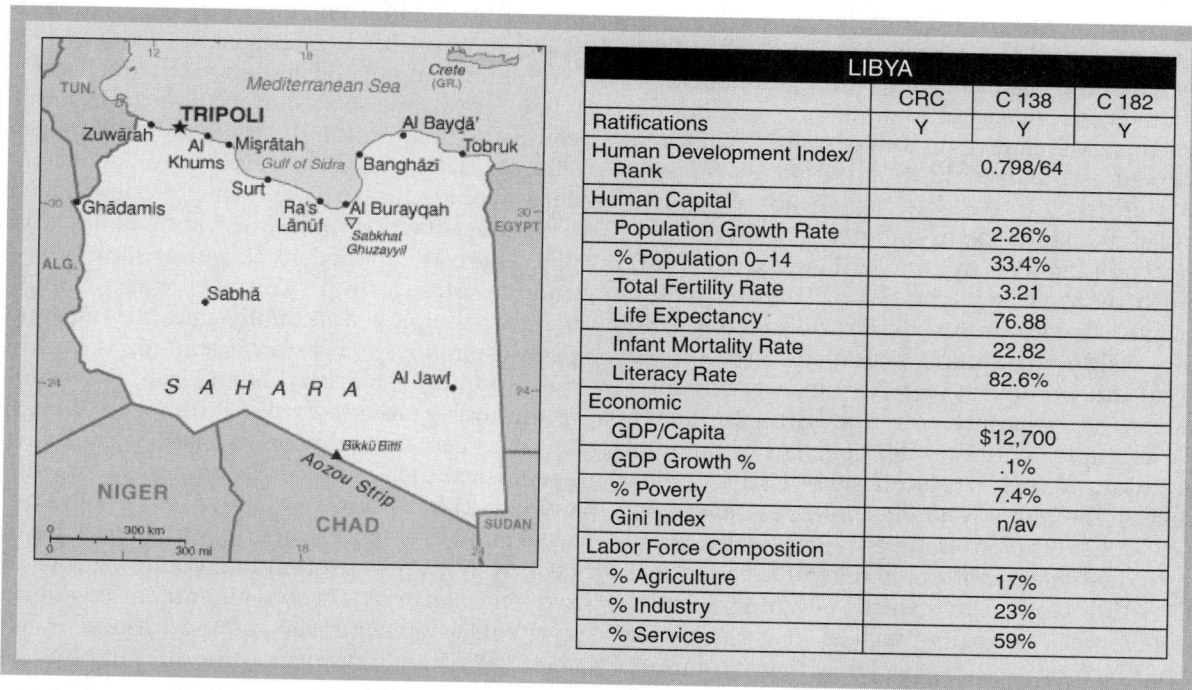

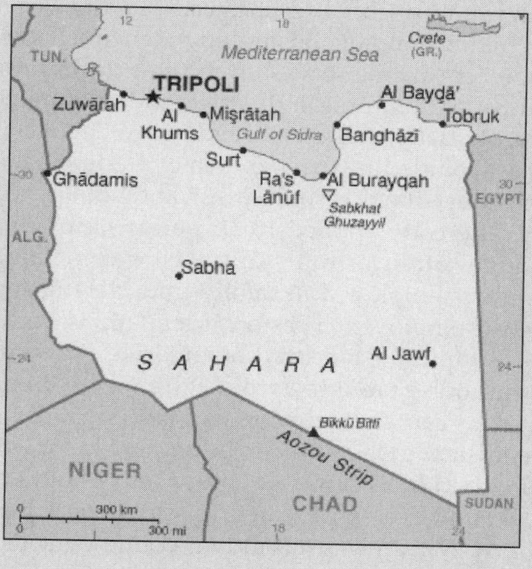

LIBYA			
	CRC	C 138	C 182
Ratifications	Y	Y	Y
Human Development Index/ Rank	0.798/64		
Human Capital			
Population Growth Rate	2.26%		
% Population 0–14	33.4%		
Total Fertility Rate	3.21		
Life Expectancy	76.88		
Infant Mortality Rate	22.82		
Literacy Rate	82.6%		
Economic			
GDP/Capita	$12,700		
GDP Growth %	.1%		
% Poverty	7.4%		
Gini Index	n/av		
Labor Force Composition			
% Agriculture	17%		
% Industry	23%		
% Services	59%		

History of Child Labor in Libya

Heidi Morrison, PhD Candidate, University of California at Santa Barbara

Libya entered the twentieth century with a nomadic population that emigrated for long periods of time and was divided into small groups for watering, pasturing, and rearing camels. Some nomads practiced cultivation, growing barley, wheat, figs, and olives as rain permitted. Children worked as they would in any nomadic society, meaning they worked both as a means of survival and as an expression of communal solidarity.

The Italian occupation of Libya (1911–1951) did little to change the basic structure of the Libyan economy, other than making a few land concessions to Italian capitalists. At the time of its independence in 1951, Libya remained a subsistence economy with low education levels. For example, in 1955, only 8 percent of the total population had attended school (ILO 1960). During the years following independence, the Libyan government initiated vocational training for industry, agriculture, handicrafts, commerce, and office work. The material taught in primary schools was essentially practical so as to give it a direct bearing on the social life of the community. In rural areas, the elementary school was the basis for all training in agriculture. For children in urban areas, there were increased facilities for training craftsmen. The Muslim Arts and Crafts School, founded in Tripoli by the Turkish administration in the late nineteenth century, still provided training for young boys and girls in a variety of crafts. In the mid-1950s, the federal government created a handicraft center in Tripoli for graduates of primary schools, and a small carpentry center for girls was set up in Benghazi. In 1952 the ILO, in cooperation with the Libyan Ministry of Education, took over full administration of the Tripoli Technical and Commercial Training Center, which began to offer training in car maintenance, electrical fitting, plumbing, welding, and bookkeeping to students with primary school certificates.

In this changing postindependence economy, where government was attempting to improve youths' agricultural, industrial, and commercial labor skills, there also emerged a set of labor standards, codified in the 1957 Labor Code, dealing with hours of work, weekly rest, and holiday with pay. The code applied to all persons employed under written or oral contracts, except family members employed in family undertakings and persons employed in pastoral occupations, both of which typically consisted of children. Provisions of the code geared toward children were limited to urban centers and were as follows: Under no circumstance was a child to be employed for work more than five hours per day or thirty hours per week, and the employment of children at night (10 P.M.–5 A.M.) was forbidden; young persons of sixteen years or older could enter themselves into apprenticeship contracts; and persons under sixteen years had to produce certificates of physical fitness for employment. The trade union movement in Libya started developing only when the country became independent. There was no minimum age for joining trade unions, but unions were prohibited by law from representing agricultural workers and domestic servants, economic sectors highly occupied by children.

Since the 1967 military coup by Muammar al-Gadhafi, there have been changes that have affected the types of labor children are engaged in, as well as the standards protecting them. In 1958, petroleum was discovered in Libya, and in 1972–1973 the government nationalized foreign petroleum firms operating in the country. Today, oil products continue to generate a substantial percentage of the country's income, despite the massive water-development project, called "The Great Manmade River," intended to increase arable land for cultivation. It is difficult to determine where child workers fit into today's oil-centered economy due to a dearth of studies on the issue since Libya's estrangement with Western nations in the 1980s. However, a 2002 Arab Labor Organization (ALO) study on child labor in Libya claims that, while it is difficult to think that child labor exists in Libya due to its high standard of living, strict laws, and social welfare system, child labor does exist, especially in the cities. According to the study, the most important forms of child labor in Libya are helping in family housework; helping in family agriculture; pushing carts (called *baroata*) of vegetables and fruit to the markets of Benghazi and Tarabulus; selling food, sweets, drinks, small goods, and cigarettes in the main streets; and sitting in public centers to sell shaving razors and women's beauty products. Sometimes the police catch these child street workers and they disappear only to reappear in other parts of the city. The study notes that children in Libya do not work in factories or industries and, because Libya is a socialist Islamic society, it is highly unlikely that children are selling drugs or involved in prostitution. One of the main factors contributing to child labor, according to the ALO study, is that Libyan culture has become controlled by "material success," which has resulted in a push by families to send their kids to work and social pressure to copy the new clothes and toys of others. Fathers give preferential treatment to sons based on who brings home the most money. The study also points to social fragmentation as a cause of child labor, claiming that because the extended family no longer cares for the child, the child must be sent out to work.

During the years of Gadhafi's rule, the Libyan Arab Republic enacted two national child labor laws. In 1972, the Libyan Ministry of Labor issued an order setting forth the industries in which it was prohibited to employ young persons under the age of eighteen. In 1997, the Children's Protection Act defined a child as a person under sixteen years of age, provided that education be compulsory for children, and prohibited child labor except when in training and with their consent.

References and Further Reading

Arab Childhood and Development Council. *The Phenomenon of Child Labor in the Arab World* [in Arabic]. Cairo: Arab Childhood and Development Council, 1998.

Arab Labor Organization. "Child Labor in Libya: A Passing Phenomenon or an Endless Reality?" [in Arabic]. Loose-leaf study. Libya, 2002.

International Labor Organization. *Labour Survey of North Africa.* Geneva: La Tribune de Genève, 1960.

Wright, John. *Libya: A Modern History.* Baltimore, MD: John Hopkins University Press, 1982.

Morocco

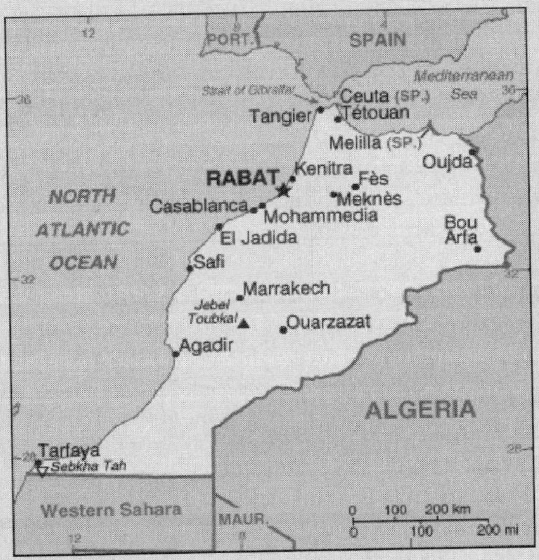

MOROCCO			
	CRC	C 138	C 182
Ratifications	Y	Y	Y
Human Development Index/Rank	0.640/123		
Human Capital			
Population Growth Rate	1.55%		
% Population 0–14	31.6%		
Total Fertility Rate	2.68		
Life Expectancy	70.94		
Infant Mortality Rate	40.24		
Literacy Rate	51.7%		
Economic			
GDP/Capita	$4,400		
GDP Growth %	6.7%		
% Poverty	19%		
Gini Index	40		
Labor Force Composition			
% Agriculture	40%		
% Industry	15%		
% Services	45%		

CHILD ACTIVITY BREAKDOWN, BY SEX AND RESIDENCE

RESIDENCE	Percentage of children in the relevant age-group[a]							
	Economic activity only		School only		Combining school and economic activity		Neither in school nor in economic activity	
	Male	Female	Male	Female	Male	Female	Male	Female
Urban	4.5	2.1	90.2	85.7	0.4	0.0	5.0	12.1
Rural	19.4	21.9	66.6	41.7	2.1	0.9	11.8	35.4
Total	12.2	12.3	78.0	63.0	1.3	0.5	8.5	24.1

Source: Morocco, Enquête Nationale sur les Niveaux de Vie des Ménages, 1998–1999 (see UCW Project Web site, http://www.ucw-project.org, country statistics).

Note: [a]Children age 7 to 14.

History of Child Labor in Morocco

Heidi Morrison, PhD Candidate, University of California at Santa Barbara

For the first half of the twentieth century, the French controlled the Moroccan economy, which was based on agriculture (cereals, fruits, olives) and, to a much lesser extent, on mining (phosphates) and handicrafts. With the onset of the French protectorate in 1912 came the ill-fated idea of making cultivation in Morocco like that in California. A few French settlers became very wealthy, while the majority of Moroccans became poor. Moroccan children worked in agriculture either as unpaid family workers under the *khammessat* sharecropping institution, or independently as paid wage laborers. Before independence in 1956, the only legislation protecting child workers in agriculture was a minimum-wage law passed in 1952. The minimum wage in agriculture was fixed at 18 piasters a day for men and 10 for women and children. However, there was no minimum age set for entry into employment in agriculture, and the minimum wage would not reach unpaid family labor under the *khammessat.* Boys of school age in rural areas were given agricultural training to increase their knowledge of agricultural subjects and to maintain the atmosphere of rural life in the schools.

In the period before independence, children working in mines were protected, at least in principle, by an order issued in 1927. This order contained a complete list of the types of work in underground tunnels in which employment of young persons between twelve and sixteen years of age was allowed: These included sorting, loading ore, shunting and hauling of trucks, looking after and opening and closing ventilation doors, manipulation of hand-operated fans, and other minor jobs that were not beyond the strength of young persons. Supervision of this labor law was undertaken by public officials. Unfortunately, immediately before and after independence, there was a sharp decline in the number of inspectors due to the departure of French officials. Despite these protections for children in the mines, an organized system of recruiting continued to put children at risk. A system utilizing prison labor had been outlawed in 1929. Local qadis enforced a system of forced labor, and organized systems for recruiting workers, including child workers, persisted into the 1950s. Morocco is the only territory in North Africa whose pre-independence recruiting systems were comparable to those observed in East, Southern, and Central Africa for years.

During the years of the French protectorate, the French took a large interest in preserving and promoting the quality of local handicraft trades. For example, exhibitions were organized in Morocco and France, and a number of publications on Moroccan arts were produced. In 1919 the government introduced an official stamp guaranteeing the quality and origin of Moroccan carpets. In the 1940s, it was estimated that 11.5 percent of the artisans in Morocco were apprentices (ILO 1960). The 1940s and 1950s saw the adoption of several decrees concerning the type of work children and women could do in artisan and industrial sectors; however, these decrees were largely cosmetic. This was a period in Moroccan history when the Moroccan government was very concerned with its image of modernity, and enacted laws more for their appearance than for the sake of actual fulfillment of individuals' rights (Pennell 2000).

The condition of child workers in postindependence Morocco was shaped by unsuccessful state economic plans and a monarchy that displayed a lack of respect for human rights. By 1973, almost two decades after independence, foreign land had been expropriated, but the Moroccan landlords were indistinguishable from the former French ones. In 1978, the ratio in income between the top 5 percent of the population and the bottom 50 percent was 1:12. In the 1980s and 1990s, with rural depopulation and urbanization, more children began to work in cities; however, 1999 census data from Morocco report that the majority of economically active children, 88.6 percent, still lived in rural areas. Children working in the nonagricultural sector were most often employed in rug factories or as domestic servants (*petites bonnes*). An Arab Labor Organization report on child labor in Morocco found that children in rug factories worked between sixty and seventy-two hours per week, and the majority of them were very young girls. In 1989–1990, 39 percent of the girl workers in a particular Fez rug industry were between five and eight years of age, and 61 percent were between the ages of nine and eleven (Pennell 2000).

A new king in 1999 led many citizens and activists to be hopeful about increased human rights protections. The debate on child labor in Morocco has become more politically acceptable, due to the will of Moroccan authorities to respect international human rights accords such as the UN Convention on the Rights of the Child. A new labor law went into effect in 2004, raising the minimum age of employment from twelve to fifteen and prohibiting children under the age of sixteen from working more than ten hours per day.

In 2002, the ALO estimated that 15.1 percent of Moroccan children work (Pennell 2000). The U.S. Department of Labor reports that girls and boys working as domestic servants and street vendors are increasingly targeted in child sex tourism, particularly in Casablanca and Marrakech. Also, children are "rented" out by their parents to other adults to beg. UNICEF found that, by the early twenty-first century, the adult literacy rate in Morocco was 52 percent and net primary school enrolment was 86 percent.

References and Further Reading

Arab Childhood and Development Council. *The Phenomenon of Child Labor in the Arab World* [in Arabic]. Cairo: Arab Childhood and Development Council, 1998.

International Labor Office. *Labour Survey of North Africa.* Geneva: La Tribune de Genève, 1960.

Pennell, C.R. *Morocco Since 1830: A History.* New York: New York University Press, 2000.

Morocco: Why Children Go to Work Instead of School

Bernard Schlemmer, Sociologist, Senior Researcher, IRD, France (Translated by Philip Dresner)

The situation in Morocco exemplifies why "child labor" must be considered not as a single, isolated issue, but as part of a complex, overall social and economic growth and development policy. The fate of Moroccan children hinges on three common yet highly discriminating and mutually reinforcing factors: gender, the rural-urban divide, and education. Official policy has evolved from one of ignoring the issue to one of acknowledgment and targeted policies to address it, aligned with the abolitionist stances of the ILO and UNICEF. Notwithstanding deep changes in Moroccan society, the nature of children's work is still tied to cultural perceptions of the status of children, with the obligation to be obedient, submissive, and respectful toward hierarchical structures, and with the widespread violence underlying social relations.

The Current Situation

All children whose work activities impinge on their rights—the "rights of the child"—should be counted as child workers, including those whose right to education is sacrificed in favor of long hours of domestic labor. Although this may seem self-evident, statistical surveys rarely make the distinction. Official labor-force statistics break down into three categories: employed, unemployed, and out of the labor force. While the first includes children age seven and over, the second only starts counting at fifteen years, and the under-fifteens unable to go either to school or to work fall—like housewives—into the third category. So while child domestic servants are classed as employed, the Labor Force Survey does not regard the many more children doing exactly the same kind of work for their own families as part of the workforce. The 2000 Labor Force Survey, in its *module enfant* section—the first ever survey to take account of domestic labor—found that 56.6 percent of fourteen-year-olds worked more than two hours per day in their own households, and that, on average, they worked twenty hours per week (Direction de la Statistique 2000). In classing many child workers as out of the labor force, official sources fail to convey the contribution they make to the Moroccan economy and, indeed, exactly how many of them there are.

The *module enfant* section of the Labor Force Survey puts the number of working children at 600,000, or 11 percent of their age-group. Some serious academic researchers, using a broader definition of child workers, rightly reckon that figure to be well short of the mark. According to Lahlou (2002) and Guessous (2002), for instance, there may be up to twice as many. But they base their figures on the number of out-of-school children, which may be equally misleading, resulting in both an overstatement—because not all out-of-school children are working—and an understatement—some go to school and to work. The fact is that researchers have had to rely on just two sources of regularly updated data: the annual Labor Force Survey and school enrollment statistics.

Regarding school enrollment, UNESCO (2005) showed clear progress in the field of compulsory education, with a primary net enrollment ratio of 89.6 percent. But this is relatively mediocre compared to other countries with a similar per capita GDP. Furthermore, the Moroccan net enrollment ratio exaggerates significantly the number of in-school children. Government education officials admit that "nearly one in three children aged

9–15 years is out of school" (Secrétariat d'État 2005, 11).

Morocco's problems in education are accentuated by gender discrimination, especially in rural areas, where four times as many girls are out of school as boys (Secrétariat d'État 2005). Rural areas are also home to 88 percent of the country's working children. But it is hard to tell the exact extent of gender discrimination as far as child labor is concerned, because while 85 percent of rural working children are classed as "family workers" (Baghagha 2002), this category focuses mainly on male farmhands and tends to neglect the girls confined to domestic chores.

Children account for a quarter of the migrants fleeing poverty-stricken rural areas for the city (El Aoufi and Bensaid 2005). Some have ended up joining the most socially excluded group of all—street children, a minority of whom are city born—but many have capitalized on the greater access to education and jobs found in urban areas. In urban areas, boys tend to outnumber girls in the formal-sector child labor force; and fewer girls in the city remain confined to "invisible" domestic labor, with more of them either going to school or into formal-sector jobs, mainly as maids or carpet and clothing trade workers.

Geopolitical disparities are further enhanced by a vicious circle that sees the bulk of investment plowed into the vast coastal plain known as "useful Morocco," and rendering many isolated rural areas, already blighted by deep poverty, even more marginalized and poverty-stricken due to migration from the land (Abdelkhalek 2006). Hence, the Labor Force Survey finding that fewer than 10 percent of children in "useful Morocco" were working in 2001, versus between 13.7 and 15.5 percent elsewhere, does not seem an awfully big difference until one considers that the figures do not include out-of-the-labor-force girls, who are far more numerous in the school-deprived parts of "non-useful" Morocco. Progress in addressing such disparities is slow but steady.

Economic and Social Policy

Until fairly recently, child labor was a taboo subject in Morocco, broached by none but a handful of bold intellectuals, and field surveys were out of the question. Attitudes began slowly to change as the country ratified the UN Convention on the Rights of the Child in 1993, followed by the establishment of a national children's rights watchdog group chaired by Princess Lalla Meryem in 1995. ILO Convention 138 concerning the minimum age for admission to employment was ratified in 1999, and Convention 182 on the elimination of the worst forms of child labor was ratified in 2000. Morocco's new labor code, introduced in 2003, includes a ban on employing any child less than fifteen years of age—the recently established compulsory school-leaving age—and no longer allows employers to pay lower wages to younger workers. The new code does not, however, cover the informal sector, traditional crafts, or domestic and family work, where the employment age and conditions of work depend entirely on the goodwill of the employer.

All this paved the way for NGOs and others to conduct and publish surveys—beginning with case studies and purely descriptive observations, then moving on to efforts to root out the causes—and led to a program of action launched in 2001 by the government of Morocco and ILO-IPEC, which evolved into a partnership with UNICEF and the World Bank. Other government actions, especially in the field of nonformal education, have also drawn support from a host of NGOs. But most of the latter are small-scale, dispersed, and confined to addressing isolated, localized aspects of this complex issue (Gouzi 2002).

The kingdom of Morocco long believed that economic development alone would be enough to bring an end to poverty, and that the most extreme or unjust situations could be remedied merely by providing a "social safety net" of indemnities, support services, school canteens, and so on (Zouiten 2006). Unfortunately, the basic welfare benefits came to be enjoyed by just "15% or so of the population, and not those that needed them most" (El Harras 2006). Coherent human development policy began to emerge only in 1996 thanks to significant funding from the World Bank—albeit with "good governance" strings attached. Social dialogue was then encouraged, and efforts to combat poverty were, for the first time, declared a "national priority." This was followed by a series of reforms in the fields of education (under the 1999

Education Charter), labor (with the 2003 code), and social welfare (ongoing).

Sadly, the intended effects of the laws are too often undermined and obstructed by the need to "compete with other forms of social control [such as] corruption, favoritism, pirating and unfair competition" (El Bacha 2006). Meanwhile, the ambiguous—neither public nor private—new institutions established by the palace and the government may be supplying services to the poor merely to be shown "helping the needy" in the media (Catusse 2005a, 2005b). Morocco has far to go before it can match the human development index of the other countries to which it compares itself. According to a World Bank survey on poverty in Morocco (cited in Gouzi 2002), the returns on most current social programs (in health, education, social security) are limited and of benefit mainly to higher- and middle-income groups rather than the poor.

In retrospect, Moroccan education policies seem geared to closing the enrollment gap, with successive government efforts to bolster the system and to boost student flows. As far as the youngsters left out of the education system are concerned, especially since implementation of the structural adjustment plan (1983), the solution has been to tailor education supply to the demands of the labor market. The vocational training reforms launched in 1984, however, smacked of that same "headlong dash of a system struggling in vain to remedy the shortcomings in basic education" (Zouggari 2006). Enrollment in vocational training did indeed skyrocket, but job opportunities remained just as scarce, and little over 50 percent of graduates managed to find work in 2001 (El Yacoubi and Benkerroum 2006). The reforms failed to achieve their purpose because the courses ended up being of benefit mainly to those with a better school education (Gérard and Chaouai 2006). Jobs could have been created through "informal" apprenticeship in the crafts industry, but until 2001 the government regarded that sector as sociocultural heritage to be safeguarded rather than as an exploitable economic asset (Chikhaoui 2006).

Meanwhile, the nonformal education policies, first developed in 1997, reflect official resignation to the fact that effective compulsory schooling was impossible to achieve in the short term; that child labor in fact existed; and that an alternative was needed to school education. The task "seems enormous compared to the means allocated" (Lamarkbi 2004), and the results so far leave much to be desired (only 141,525 children enrolled by 2004). But the aim is still to "guarantee education for every child who has dropped out of—or never been to—school by the year 2010," especially young girls in rural areas (Secrétariat d'État 2005).

Ironically, except in the case of postgraduates, the lower a person's level of school education these days, the greater their chances of finding work (Gérard and Chaouai 2006).

Social Integration and Participation

Traditional Moroccan society is governed by the principle of authority, with its own social welfare structures based on group solidarity and, moreover, mutual loyalty between hierarchical superiors—from the family head to the head of state—and their dependents. Within this framework, children are expected to contribute to the family economy within a rigid division of labor. But the traditional order is being transformed by economic changes. "Mutual support used to amount to a safety net protecting individuals and families from the worst. The disintegration of the old social frameworks, and the breakdown and individualization of the family unit have largely deprived society of such safeguards" (Zouiten 2006).

The transmission of values has, to some extent, shifted from the family to the classroom. Yet it continues, in rural areas especially, to promote respect for one's superiors, rote learning rather than comprehension, and reproduction of the model instead of critical thinking. Even asking a question is a threat to the hierarchical order. Things are changing, of course, and this image of school hardly reflects the situation in big-city neighborhoods. But the paternalistic model still has great resonance: "[S]ociety used to—and, indeed, still does—regard physical violence as a bona fide pedagogical argument" (Guessous 2002, 192). Despite much progress, violence and coercion continue to prevail not just in schools but in social relations as a whole (Schlemmer 2006a).

School used to be regarded as the best route to social mobility, in the days when qualifications meant access to much-coveted public-sector posts. But those posts are harder to come by today, and low enrollment in school stems not just from undersupply but also from faltering demand. Most working children see school, not so much as a right, but as an obligation they have managed to dodge (Schlemmer and Gérard 2004).

Moroccan child labor surveys rightly argue that its elimination hinges on access for all children to school. But they also present school as the only road to successful social and professional integration. This, however, is debatable, as working-class families know only too well. Research in Fes from 2000 to 2004 (Schlemmer 2006b, 2007) found that not going to school does not necessarily mean being condemned to a social or professional wilderness. A university degree or PhD does, of course, guarantee access to jobs beyond the reach of anyone excluded from school as a child; a bachelor's degree remains a safeguard against total failure; and secondary school studies improve one's chances of successful social and professional integration. Those chances may well be hampered by a failure to complete or even reach junior high school. Some do manage nonetheless to achieve success, and even bona fide social mobility, especially through apprenticeship in traditional crafts industries, where a school education tends to be more of a handicap than an advantage (Gérard 2005).

School can be useful, of course, but only if one stays on at least until the end of primary education. Recent doubts about the benefits of schooling stem not just from traditional perceptions of boys in economic activities and girls in home economics, but also from a rational economic calculation: Poorer parents simply cannot afford to risk banking on returns from investment in schooling at a time when a diploma no longer secures instant access to public-sector jobs.

Opinions may differ on subjects such as poverty reduction and income inequality, but none can deny the ever-growing intensity of economic pressures on the working population. Indeed, it has even surpassed that of the violence in social relations, which appears to be dwindling as society continues to modernize. Employers faced with increased competition, in a country where labor-code compliance is far from absolute, all too often opt for the easy solution: the comparative advantages to be gained in paying low wages. Hence the continuing use of child labor, especially in the textile and clothing sectors (El Aoufi and Bensaid 2005); in the crafts industry, where apprenticeship is seen increasingly as a means of cutting labor costs (Mejjati Alami 2006); and in agriculture, where farmers who once put their children to work as part of a traditional socialization process are now compelled to do so with a view to generating income.

Working children are almost completely helpless in the presence of an employer. In a nutshell, "child workers are usually young, assigned to menial and hazardous tasks, unprotected, underpaid, if at all, and highly malleable in terms of how long and when they work. Their legal position is, as a rule, precarious: no contracts, working well beyond the statutory hours, and no welfare benefits" (Mejjati Alami 2006).

Doctrine and Pragmatism

What must be done to improve the situation? The solutions are well known: education for all children, especially girls, not least in isolated, rural areas; better-quality teaching; providing isolated areas with basic infrastructure—more girls would be enrolled if schools had proper washrooms; effective law enforcement—labor inspectors are powerless to defend the rights of formal-sector adult workers, never mind children; combating poverty; and social policy development, while at the same time remaining globally competitive. So the solutions are well known; it is their complexity that is vexing.

Pressure from international organizations has forced Morocco to face up to these problems. But is pushing for an immediate end to child labor the solution? As long as school is not seen as the sole road to adulthood, children will continue going to work. Is it right to impose school as the one and only option? In creating a nonformal education department, the government has shown its awareness of the gulf between the law and real-life circumstances. But to bring itself further into line with the declared goals of the ILO, it has just "decreed" the enrollment of all children up to and beyond the age of fifteen. Meanwhile, if children have to work, yet are forbidden to do so, who will defend them, and on what legal grounds? Self-organization might be the only solution for working children, but the chances of that happening in Morocco are slim.

References and Further Reading

Abdelkhalek, Touhami. "La pauvreté au Maroc." In *Cinquante ans de développement humain au Maroc et perspectives pour 2025* (Pauvreté et Facteurs d'Exclusion). Rabat: Royaume du Maroc, 2006, 7–55.

Baghagha, Layachi. *Comprendre le travail des enfants au Maroc: aspects statistiques.* Florence: UCW Project, 2002. http://www.ucw-project.org/pdf/publications/moroc_aspect_statistique.pdf.

Catusse, Myriam. "Les réinventions du social dans le Maroc 'ajusté.'" *Revue des mondes Musulmans et de la Méditerranée,* ed. Elizabeth Longuenesse, Myriam Catusse, and Blandine Destremeau, 105–6. Aix-en Provence, MMSH-IREMAM, Edisud, 2005a.

Catusse, Myriam. "Le travail et la question sociale au Maghreb et au Moyen-Orient." *Revue des mondes Musulmans et de la Méditerranée,* ed. Elizabeth Longuenesse, Myriam Catusse, and Blandine Destremeau, 221–46. Aix-en Provence, MMSH-IREMAM, Edisud, 2005b.

Chikhaoui, Said. "Politiques publiques de l'artisanat: esquisse d' un bilan." In *Cinquante ans de développement humain au Maroc et perspectives pour 2025* (Dimensions Culturelles, Artistiques et Spirituelles). Rabat: Royaume du Maroc, 2006, 7–30.

Direction de la Statistique. "Enquête nationale sur l'emploi." Haut Commissariat au Plan, Royaume du Maroc, 2000.

El Aoufi, Noureddine, and Mohamed Bensaid. *Chômage et employabilité des jeunes au Maroc.* Cahiers de la stratégie de l'emploi. ILO, Genève, 2005–2006.

El Bacha, Farid. "Rapport sur l'état d'avancement de la construction d' un cadre juridique du développement humain et des processus de réformes legislative et réglementaires lies à l'encouragement du développement général et humain en particulier." In *Cinquante ans de développement humain au Maroc et perspectives pour 2025* (Gouvernance et Développement Participatif). Rabat: Royaume du Maroc, 2006, 303–28.

El Harras, Mokhtar. "Les solidarités sociales au Maroc: évolution et état actuel." In *Cinquante ans de développement humain au Maroc et perspectives pour 2025* (Société, Famille, Femmes et Jeunesse). Rabat: Royaume du Maroc, 2006, 45–60.

El Yacoubi, Driss, and Mohamed Benkerroum. "La formation professionelle au Maroc: éléments d'analyse des réformes et des résultats des cinquante ans d'indépendence." In *Cinquante ans de développement humain au Maroc et perspectives pour 2025* (Systèmes Éducatifs, Savoir, Technologies et Innovation). Rabat: Royaume du Maroc, 2006, 245–82.

Gérard, Étienne. "Apprentissage et scolarisation en milieu artisanal marocain. Des savoirs qui s'imposent et s'opposent." *Cahiers de la recherche sur l'éducation et les savoirs* 4 (2005): 163–86.

Gérard, Étienne, and Abdeltif Chaouai. "Entre formation et savoir, des articulations socialement différenciées." In *Savoirs, insertion et globalisation—vu du Maghreb,* ed. Étienne Gérard, 77–108. Paris: Publisud, 2006.

Gouzi, A. Berrada. *Comprendre le travail des enfants au Maroc: aspects économiques.* Understanding Children's Work Project Working Paper Series. UCW Project, Florence, March 2002. http:// http://www.ucw-project.org/pdf/publications/standard_economic_normative.pdf.

Guessous, Chakib. *L'exploitation de l'innocence—le travail des enfants au Maroc.* Casablanca: EDDIF, 2002.

Lahlou, Mehdi. "Le travail des enfants au Maroc. Cadre macro-économique et social et données de base." Paper presented at the international symposium Enfants d'Aujourd'hui: Diversité des Contextes, Pluralités des Parcours. Dakar, December 10–13, 2002.

Lamarkbi, Nadia. *Education non formelle au Maroc: lorsque l'état s'en mêle.* Paris: Université Paris I, 2004.

Mejjati Alami, Rajaa. "Le secteur informel au Maroc." In *Cinquante ans de développement humain au Maroc et perspectives pour 2025* (Croissance Économique et Développement Humain). Rabat: Royaume du Maroc, 2006, 419–53.

Royaume du Maroc. *Cinquante ans de développement humain au Maroc et perspectives pour 2025,* 2006. http://www.rdh50.ma/Fr/index.asp.

Schlemmer, Bernard. "Violence sociale et violence économique dans la vie des enfants travailleurs." In *Les enfants travailleurs—repenser l'enfance,* ed. M. Bonnet et al., 39–58. Lausanne: Editions Page 2, 2006a.

Schlemmer, Bernard. "L'école ou le travail, une alternative?—le cas des enfants d'âge scolaire de familles populaires dans la ville de Fès." In *Savoirs, insertion et globalisation—illustrations par le Maghreb,* ed. Étienne Gérard, 55–76. Paris: Publisud, 2006b.

Schlemmer, Bernard. "Working Children in Fez (Morocco). Relationship Between Knowledge and Strategies for Social and Professional Integration." In *"Working to Be Someone": Child Focussed Research and Practice with Working Children,* ed. Beatrice Hungerland, Manfred Liebel, Brian Milne, and Anne Wihstutz, 109–16. London: Jessica Kingsley Publishers, 2007.

Schlemmer, Bernard, and Étienne Gérard. "Le rapport à l'école dans les milieux populaires de Fès." Paper presented at Actes du Colloque: Le Droit à l'École—

Quelle Effectivité au Nord et au Sud? Ouagadougou, Burkina Faso, March 9–12, 2004.

Secrétariat d'État auprès du Ministre de l'Éducation Nationale, de l'Enseignement Supérieur, de la Formation des Cadres et de la Recherche Scientifique, Chargé de l'Alphabétisation et de l'Éducation non Formelle. "Stratégie d'alphabétisation et d'éducation non formelle." Ministère de l'Éducation Nationale, Royaume du Maroc, 2005.

UNESCO. *Education for All: Literacy for Life (Education for All Global Monitoring Report 2006).* Paris: UNESCO, 2005.

Understanding Children's Work Project. "Understanding Children's Work in Morocco." UCW Project, Florence, 2003. http://www.ucw-project.org/pdf/publications/report_morocco_draft.pdf.

Zouggari, Ahmed. "La formation professionelle de 1842 à la charte d'éducation et de formation." In *Cinquante ans de développement humain au Maroc et perspectives pour 2025* (Systèmes Éducatifs, Savoir, Technologies et Innovation). Rabat: Royaume du Maroc, 2006, 283–308.

Zouiten, Mounir. "Les systèmes de solidarité et les politiques d'integration sociale." In *Cinquante ans de développement humain au Maroc et perspectives pour 2025* (Pauvreté et Facteurs d'Exclusion Sociale). Rabat: Royaume du Maroc, 2006, 119–49.

The Pyjama Trail Affair: A Case Study in Child Labor

Fatima Badry, American University of Sharjah

The events of the "Pyjama Trail Affair" occurred in late 1995 and early 1996 in Meknes, Morocco, but the implications of these events transcend their time and place (Badry-Zalami et al. 1998). This essay provides a brief chronology of the Pyjama Trail events and analyzes the responsibility of the stakeholders and the impact their actions had on young female workers in the export textile industry in Morocco.

Around 100 girls between twelve and fifteen, employed under contracts of apprenticeship in Sicome, a textile factory working exclusively for the export market, were summarily dismissed from their jobs as a result of media attention around the issue of child labor. In the course of an investigation of allegations of mislabeling garments by Desmond & Sons, one of the suppliers of the British multinational retailer Marks & Spencer, TV investigative reporters from the British television program *World in Action* stumbled on the much more sensational issue of young girls working in the factory and producing pyjamas for the UK market. The reporters notified Marks & Spencer that, during their visit to the factory, where they had posed as potential buyers, they had noticed that many of the girl workers on the floor appeared to be underage. Soon afterward, the Sicome management fired all workers below the age of fifteen to protect its contract. Following these dismissals, the International Working Group on Child Labor carried out a case study to determine why these young girls were working rather than attending school; what their working conditions were, and how they compared with conditions elsewhere in the region; what the impact on the working girls and their families was, and how their needs could be met; and finally, who was responsible (Badry-Zalami et al. 1998).

The study adopted a qualitative approach based on ethnographic observations, discussions with residents of the neighborhoods of the former Sicome workers, and interviews of a sample of twelve dismissed girls and their families. The girls' statements during the interviews suggest that their experiences were common and shared by most workers.

The girls had all been hired by Sicome under apprenticeship contracts. Under Moroccan labor law, apprenticeship contracts can be offered to minor unskilled workers, with the goal of teaching them a trade or skill. The apprenticeship contract must be endorsed by the parent or guardian and the employer and approved by the labor inspector. Apprenticeship has a long tradition in Morocco. Where formal education is not accessible to all, especially girls, and is no guarantee of a good job, many parents see apprenticeship as the best way to teach their children a valuable trade or skill. The apprenticeship contract stipulates several conditions aimed at protecting the young worker from exploitation and abuse by the master (*m'allem*).

The girls' accounts of their period of employment at the Sicome factory revealed that they had been systematically exploited. Many of the regulations pertaining to apprentices had been routinely violated. They received no training, worked for long hours standing up all day, were paid wages lower than those specified in their contracts, received no overtime pay, and had no health benefits. Despite these harsh conditions, the girls had considered themselves to be lucky to have a job in the textile industry. In their community, working in the factory was perceived as a privilege compared to other jobs available, such as domestic work. They all blamed the foreigners for the unexpected loss of their jobs and hoped for another factory job in the future.

In order to understand these girls' reactions to their firing from exploitative employment, we must examine the cultural and economic context that led them to work in the first place. Morocco has a very high rate of illiteracy, with wide gaps based on gender and between urban and rural populations. Countrywide literacy rates are estimated at 64 percent among men, but only 39 percent among women, and female literacy in rural areas is only 10 percent. These girls were aware of their limited choices. Not only were they deprived of schooling compared to boys, but also their only options outside of factory work were to be domestic servants or to stay home doing housework and engaging in handicraft production. They considered working in the factory prestigious because the pay was higher and the working hours ended when the workday ended.

None of the girls mentioned return to school as an option. They knew that their long absence from schooling prevented them from being reinstated into the inflexible formal educational system; nor were the government-run vocational training centers open to them. Sewing and embroidery training programs were not attractive to them because they did not prepare participants for paid jobs outside the home. Unlike their mothers, these girls did not consider marriage an obvious alternative. The unemployed young men in the neighborhood could not offer the financial stability traditionally linked to marriage. Moreover, since many of the mothers had been abandoned by their husbands, the girls felt responsible and protective of their mothers.

Paradoxically, although they were well aware of the exploitative conditions they endured in the factory, they regretted losing their jobs. Work at the factory offered several advantages. It was a form of liberation, an escape from the home and the often oppressive constraints of the family. It opened the possibility of a secure long-term job in the formal sector, which the educational system no longer guaranteed. Their income gave them power within the family that was usually reserved for sons. It also gave them a degree of financial independence. In short, factory work heightened their self-esteem and accorded them respect within the family and community.

The economic impact of the dismissals was strongly felt by the girls and their families. In some cases, the girls' income had been a vital part of the household's revenue, and its loss meant families had to make significant adjustments. For example, one of the girls' families had to leave their house because her mother's job as a janitor in a café could cover only their living expenses. The rent had been paid with the girl's Sicome salary. As a result, the whole family moved in with the grandmother, who was already sharing a one-room apartment with two other divorced daughters and a grandson. Other families had taken out loans to pay for water installation or to build houses. They had relied on their daughter's monthly income to repay these loans. The issue of debt repayment was particularly crucial for families living in neighborhoods that were developed as part of the government's slum relocation program. In these areas, shacks had been converted into houses by families who had taken out loans. Their daughters' dismissals put them in a precarious situation.

The Pyjama Trail Affair ended up potentially harming not only the young girls in the Sicome factory but also all those in similar socioeconomic backgrounds. Some girls did find employment, but as domestic workers. Others got married, and one became involved in prostitution. The foreign intervention, instead of eliminating exploitation, put the girls to work once again, but for longer hours, very little pay, nonexistent training, and no security. It also effectively closed off employment in the export sector to all apprentices under fifteen who are excluded from the formal education system, who are unable to access good-quality training programs, and whose only option is work. Exclusion from the formal sector leads to a shift to the informal, less visible, and potentially more exploitative sectors of the economy.

Conclusion

The Pyjama Trail Affair had no winners, least of all the girls. But the impact on the foreign players in this affair, both the media and Marks & Spencer, was also mixed. *World in Action* may have succeeded in getting a good story that gave Marks & Spencer a black eye, but in the end it lost an expensive and protracted libel case. As a result of the false labeling allegations, Desmond & Sons lost its contracts with Marks & Spencer, and eventually, Marks & Spencer pulled out of Sicome altogether. Both sets of foreign actors were concerned with their image in Europe and had little thought to how their actions affected the young female laborers in Morocco; no concern was manifested over the possible negative consequences of the summary firings of the girls. Locally, the firings produced a muted response from the government, trade unions, and the press, all of whom were more concerned with repercussions the affair would have on the textile industry.

Interventions for working children should aim to improve their quality of life. This requires not just focusing narrowly on work-related exploitation, but broadening the approach to encompass the wider exploitation faced by girls such as those involved in the Pyjama Trail Affair. This case also demonstrates that assessing the impact of interventions on children should not be left to chance. Mechanisms need to be established to monitor interventions to ensure that actions taken have positive consequences for the group they set out to benefit.

Reference and Further Reading

Badry-Zalami, Fatima, Nandana Reddy, Margaret A. Lynch, and Claire Feinstein. *Forgotten on the Pyjama Trail: A Case Study of Young Garment Workers in Meknes (Morocco) Dismissed from Their Jobs Following Media Attention.* International Working Group on Child Labour Reports. Amsterdam: Defence for Children International, 1998.

Small Maids in Morocco

Tone Sommerfelt, Research Fellow, Department of Social Anthropology, University of Oslo

Household work in urban Moroccan homes is to a large extent performed by paid maids. It has been estimated that between 66,000 and 88,000 of these housemaids are girls age five to fifteen years, who make up 2.3 to 3 percent of the total number of girls in this age-group. The "small maid"—referred to as *petite bonne* in French or simply as "maid," *khadēma,* in Arabic—thus constitutes a significant proportion of the child labor complex in Morocco, outnumbering girls in urban areas who work outside of private homes (see Pedersen 2001; numbers based on population figures from 1999).

Young Girls as Employees

The small maids perform household tasks, like washing and cleaning, taking care of children, and running errands. They live in their employers' homes, and contact with their own parents is limited. Young girls' labor as maids in Morocco is locally defined as work, not as "caretaking" (as is often done farther south on the African continent). Correspondingly, many who employ girls make a point of emphasizing that girls are hired for work and are not "daughters of the house." Generally, little maids are not included in the family life of their employers, and relationships between young maids and employers fill primarily one function: that of work (Sommerfelt 2001). In this sense, these employment relationships bear no resemblance to adoption, which is rare in Arab countries, where kinship ideology emphasizes blood relations as grounds for identity and rights within families (Bargach 2002).

In spite of the fact that the domestic service of small maids is discussed in terms of wage labor and employment, terms of work are vague and are not discussed when parents and employers meet. Salary, however, is determined upon the girl's appointment. In a study from 1996, the majority of the small maids interviewed earned less than 300 dirhams per month (equivalent to about US$35 at the time). In the majority of cases, the salary is given directly to the parents (Ligue Marocaine pour la Protection de l'Enfance and UNICEF 1996). Arguments over remuneration occur, as expenses for medical and dental care (and occasionally gifts) are regularly deducted from salaries. In general, small maids do not attend school, though a few centers in urban areas offer evening classes (Sommerfelt 2001).

For many of the girls, parents' monthly visits to collect their daughters' salaries are the only occasions for parental contact. Some of the little maids are allowed to visit their families for special occasions. In a study carried out by Fafo and Save the Children UK from 2000 to 2001 (Sommerfelt 2001), parents described the ideal employer as one that ensures their daughter's welfare, providing her with food and clothes, and refrains from beating. Parents also expect employers to ensure that their daughters are kept under surveillance, preventing them from "running around" (also implying engagement in premarital sex). From the girls' point of view, however, this may be experienced as entrapment in their employer's house, and it limits their social network. Parents have few possibilities of checking on their daughters' well-being, and abuse of little maids, including sexual abuse, is slowly becoming a subject of public discussion.

Small maids are, by and large, an urban phenomenon, and the young maids make up more than 5 percent of the population of girls in urban areas (Pedersen 2001). The vast majority come from rural areas, and some from suburban areas (i.e., the urban outskirts). For rural families, placing daughters as maids is a response to a desperate economic situation. Daughters' incomes contribute significantly to the parents' household income. The gender structures in this response to poverty are clear. Girls are sent to work as maids because housework is a female domain. Boys are given priority for education, and when they do work, it is mostly in nondomestic settings, and they generally stay with kin. Husbands and employers alike often represent it as inappropriate for adult women to work as maids. By the same token, small maids' employment is often ended when they grow older; the presence of young, unmarried women in the employer's home is seen as morally problematic, or indecent, in relation to sons of the house (Sommerfelt 2001).

Recruitment

The small maids are recruited through informal middlemen (*samsar, samsara*), that is, men and women who travel between town and countryside in search of maids. Occasionally, young maids themselves recruit relatives from their home areas as a means of extending their own social network. Recruitment processes appear to take the shape of "chain migration." Rural girls (above ten years of age) occasionally claim to want to join their sisters to work in towns, imagining urban centers as places of opportunity. This facilitates the recruitment of young girls into potentially abusive labor relationships.

Lately, the use of middlemen that charge a onetime fee upon the girl's appointment seems to be more common (Sommerfelt 2001). Such middlemen profit economically from regularly placing girls with new employers. In fear of losing maids to new employers, and worrying about maids' loyalties to outsiders, employers respond by curtailing the social network of the little maids that work for them. Even though young maids may use middlemen to help them out of difficult circumstances, this further commercialization of young girls' labor hinders development of long-term relationships between employer and maid and further impairs parents' bonds with their daughters.

References and Further Reading

Bargach, Jamila. *Orphans of Islam: Family, Abandonment, and Secret Adoption in Morocco.* Lanham: Rowman and Littlefield, 2002.

Belarbi, Aïcha. *Situation de la petite fille au Maroc.* Rabat: Association Marocaine de Soutien à l'UNICEF, 1992.

Ligue Marocaine pour la Protection de l'Enfance and UNICEF. *Journée d'étude et de reflexion sur les petites filles "bonnes" travaillant dans les familles.* Rabat: Ligue Marocaine pour la Protection de l'Enfance and UNICEF, 1996.

Pedersen, Jon. "The Demography of Petites Bonnes in Morocco." In *Domestic Child Labour in Morocco: An Analysis of the Parties Involved in Relationships to "Petites Bonnes,"* ed. Tone Sommerfelt, 15–20. Oslo: FAFO Institute for Applied International Studies and Save the Children UK, 2001.

Sommerfelt, Tone, ed. *Domestic Child Labour in Morocco: An Analysis of the Parties Involved in Relationships to "Petites Bonnes."* Oslo: FAFO Institute for Applied International Studies and Save the Children UK, 2001.

Tunisia

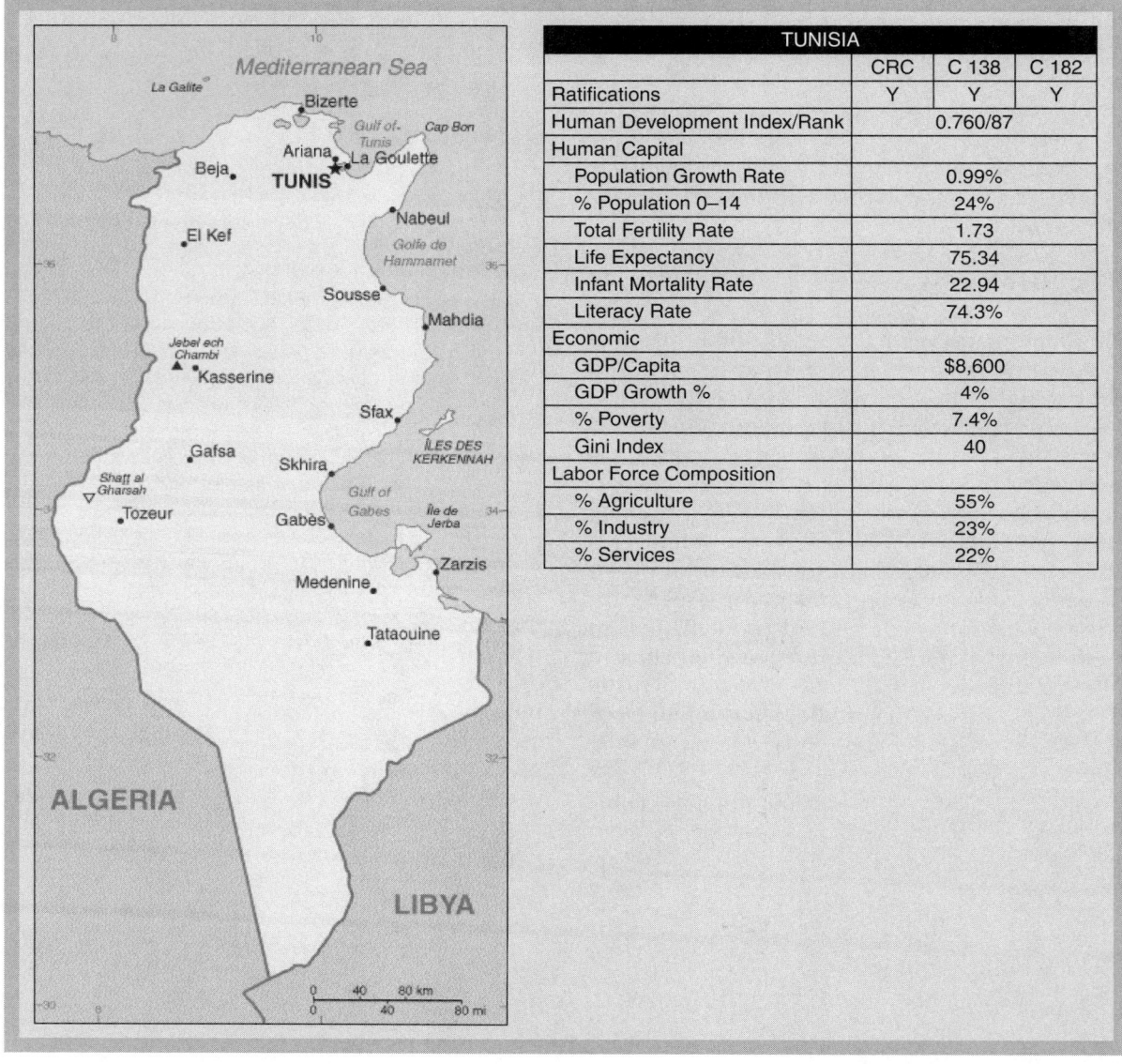

TUNISIA			
	CRC	C 138	C 182
Ratifications	Y	Y	Y
Human Development Index/Rank	0.760/87		
Human Capital			
Population Growth Rate	0.99%		
% Population 0–14	24%		
Total Fertility Rate	1.73		
Life Expectancy	75.34		
Infant Mortality Rate	22.94		
Literacy Rate	74.3%		
Economic			
GDP/Capita	$8,600		
GDP Growth %	4%		
% Poverty	7.4%		
Gini Index	40		
Labor Force Composition			
% Agriculture	55%		
% Industry	23%		
% Services	22%		

History of Child Labor in Tunisia

Heidi Morrison, PhD Candidate, University of California at Santa Barbara

Similar to those of its North African neighbors, the economy of Tunisia for the first part of the twentieth century was based on agriculture, in addition to livestock and fisheries. French colonization of Tunisia began in 1881. Subsequently, state land was sold to colonists at low prices and European settlers used modern techniques and large-scale farming to cultivate the land. The majority of the Tunisian population engaged in raising cereals by traditional means, cultivating olive trees and date palms and tending flocks. The *khammessat* was the prevalent form of association practiced by the landowners, which meant that children worked alongside their parents as unpaid family laborers. The age of admission to employment in Tunisia was twelve, and, unlike in the rest of North Africa, the minimum-age rule covered agricultural workers. In Tunisia the labor inspector had the right to insist on children under the age of twelve being discharged if the work in which they were engaged was too heavy for them.

Industry in Tunisia developed slowly in the first half of the twentieth century due to a shortage of technicians and skilled labor along with the French industrialists' unwillingness to finance ventures in Tunisia. Local workshops and handicrafts products included textiles (silk, tarbooshes, and carpets), leather goods, footwear, mats, pottery, and jewelry. The first comprehensive decree regulating the situation of young apprentices in the handicraft workshops came in 1956; it controlled contracts of apprenticeship and established a Vocational Training Council that made recommendations concerning training of apprentices and young workers.

After independence in 1956, Tunisia used law and legal reform, to a much greater degree than its North African neighbors, as instruments of social change and development. Habib Bourguiba ruled Tunisia for thirty-one years, during which time he repressed Islamic fundamentalism, established rights for women, and envisioned a Tunisian republic. When Bourguiba came into office, one of his first moves was to change the Islamic laws of personal status, and this included raising the age of marriage for girls to seventeen, and abolishing polygamy and requiring women's consent for marriage and repudiation. Zine El Abidine Ben Ali overthrew and replaced Bourguiba in 1986 but changed little in the existing system. Protection for child workers in Tunisia has generally come under the form of national legislation bearing on children's rights in general. For example, in 1995 the Tunisian government adopted a Child Protection Code, which protects children from abuse and

Young boy making shoes, Tunisia, 1996. *(© International Labor Organization / J.M. Derrien)*

exploitation, including at work. UNICEF reported that, by the early twenty-first century, primary school enrollment was 97 percent for boys and 98 percent for girls, and the adult literacy rate was 74 percent. The U.S. Department of Labor reported that only an estimated 2.1 percent of Tunisian children between the ages of five and fifteen years were working in 2000.

References and Further Reading

Arab Childhood and Development Council. *The Phenomenon of Child Labor in the Arab World* [in Arabic]. Cairo: Arab Childhood and Development Council, 1998.

International Labor Office. *Labour Survey of North Africa.* Geneva: La Tribune de Genève, 1960.

SECTION 2. MIDDLE EAST

Azerbaijan

AZERBAIJAN			
	CRC	C 138	C 182
Ratifications	Y	Y	Y
Human Development Index/Rank	0.736/99		
Human Capital			
Population Growth Rate	0.66%		
% Population 0–14	24.6%		
Total Fertility Rate	2.46		
Life Expectancy	63.85		
Infant Mortality Rate	79		
Literacy Rate	98.8		
Economic			
GDP/Capita	$7,300		
GDP Growth %	32.5%		
% Poverty	49%		
Gini Index	36.5		
Labor Force Composition			
% Agriculture	41%		
% Industry	7%		
% Services	52%		

CHILD ACTIVITY BREAKDOWN, BY SEX AND RESIDENCE

RESIDENCE	Percentage of children in the relevant age-group[a]									
	Economic activity only		School only		Combining school and economic activity		Neither in school nor in economic activity		Child labor[b]	
	Male	Female	Male	Female	Male	Female	Male	Female	Male	Female
Urban	0.6	0.4	75.3	77.3	4.8	3.0	19.2	19.3	n/av	n/av
Rural	1.2	0.8	63.4	69.3	14.6	9.0	20.8	20.9	n/av	n/av
Total	0.9	0.6	69.4	73.5	9.7	5.8	20.0	20.1	10.7	10.1

Source: Azerbaijan, Multiple Indicator Cluster Survey 2, 2000 (see UCW Project Web site, http://ucw-project.org, country statistics).

Notes: [a]Children age 5 to 14. [b]Estimate includes (a) children under age 12 engaged in economic activities, (b) children age 12–14 engaged in excessive economic activities (more than 14 hours per week), and (c) children under age 15 engaged in excessive household chores (at least 28 hours per week). Estimate does not account for children engaged in hazardous work or other unconditional "worst forms" of child labor.

Child Labor in Azerbaijan

Ryan Womack, Business and Economics Librarian, Rutgers University

Azerbaijan—named the "Land of Fire" since ancient times for its petroleum deposits—is a country of 8.5 million people, located in the Caucasus, and bordered by Armenia, Georgia, Iran, Russia, and the Caspian Sea. The Azeri-majority autonomous republic of Nakhchivan is part of Azerbaijan but is physically separated from the rest of the country by Armenia. Although quite mountainous, Azerbaijan contains the largest amount of agricultural land in the Caucasus. As a developing and transition economy that has not yet emerged from the lower-middle-income level, Azerbaijan still struggles to reduce the use of child labor in the agricultural sector of its economy, while growth in the petroleum sector has not produced widespread benefits for the majority of the population.

Crossroads and Conflict

The culture of Azerbaijan is ancient, having absorbed Islam from the Arabs in the seventh century, its language from the Turko-Mongol conquests of the tenth to twelfth centuries, and Shi'ism from the Persian Empire in the sixteenth century. The Russian empire conquered the territory of present-day Azerbaijan from 1805 to 1828, leaving two-thirds of former Azeri lands within the borders of today's Iran. After a brief period of autonomy from 1918 to 1920, Azerbaijan was incorporated into the Soviet Union. Since declaring independence in 1991, Azerbaijan has been unable to maintain the positive legacy of the Soviets in education and health, and is burdened by their legacy of environmental pollution and outdated industry. Since 1993, the political leadership of the country has been in the hands of the Aliyev family, first Heydar Aliyev, then his son Ilham.

According to the latest census, in 1999, the population is more than 90 percent Azeri, with the second-largest ethnic group being Lezghins, or Dagestani, at just over 2 percent. Ethnicity does not appear to play a role in the incidence of child labor, although Islamic traditions of parental authority over children are thought to make it easier for parents to send their children to work (ASK 2005). The population is more than 80 percent Muslim. The age profile of the population is still young, although the share of people age zero to fourteen has declined from 34 percent in 1995 to 24.6 percent in 2008. The urban and rural populations are roughly equal.

Between 1988 and 1994, Azerbaijan fought with neighboring Armenia over the Nagorno-Karabakh region of Azerbaijan, which has a majority Armenian population. Currently, Armenia occupies Nagorno-Karabakh and several provinces to its west, although Azerbaijan still claims sovereignty over this territory. More than 1 million persons have been internally displaced by the conflict, and this population struggles to find adequate employment and income. Uncertainty over the conflict's resolution inhibits economic growth in the region.

Oil Growth and Social Stagnation

Azerbaijan suffered during the transition from its socialist past, showing increases in child poverty and deteriorating health conditions through the 1990s. Inefficient state-owned enterprises in the public utility and transportation sectors are still a drag on the economy. Although income is slowly increasing, the World Bank classifies the country in the lower-middle-income tier, with a gross domestic product per capita of $7,300.

The economy's bright spot is the oil sector, driving an overall economic growth rate of 32 percent in 2006. Oil is booming, and the completion of the Baku-Tbilisi-Ceyhan pipeline in 2006 secures these gains (ADB 2007). Oil accounts for more than 90 percent of Azerbaijan's exports, and for 98 percent of its foreign direct investment. But oil is not a labor-intensive industry, and has in many cases led to increased corruption rather than increased living standards. According to Political Risk Services, "Like most developing countries cursed with an abundance of oil, governance in Azerbaijan is basically a criminal conspiracy between a self-perpetuating political hierarchy and a business elite who own or control the bulk of the country's wealth" (Political Risk Services 2006, 13). Rising oil prices also run the risk of higher inflation, already at 11 percent in 2007. Price controls have already been imposed in the agricultural sector. Oil is unlikely to provide secure and well-paid employment to large numbers, and may adversely impact the rest of the economy.

The agricultural sector, which accounts for much of the child labor, has been declining in output. Lack of investment and maintenance in the mechanized agriculture of Soviet times has led to increased use of manual labor methods, even as output declines. Cotton is the largest cash crop, followed by tobacco and tea.

The official unemployment rate is under 2 percent, but international organizations estimate the actual rate to be 10 to 20 percent or more. Many workers in the industrial sector, often highly skilled, remain unemployed or underemployed, putting downward pressure on wages. According to the 2003 Household Budget Survey, 44.7 percent of the total population lived in poverty on less than $36.50 per month, and 9.6 percent lived in extreme poverty on less than $25.50 per month (ADB 2005). Clearly, a sufficient and stable income is not available to large segments of the population.

The erosion in income and weakening public provision of child care, health care, and education have led to greater insecurity for women and children. For example, the rate of child mortality through age five is the highest among the former Soviet states, at 105 per 1,000 births (UNICEF 2004). Although education is officially universal and compulsory, actual attendance rates at the secondary level are well under 90 percent and are worse for girls and in rural areas (ADB 2005). All of these factors increase the pressures on poor families to put their children to work.

Children Working to Support Their Families

The nationwide rate of child labor has been estimated at 11 percent, and although official Azeri statistics do not track child labor, the government has recognized it as a significant problem. A most interesting survey of attitudes and experiences with child labor was conducted by the National Confederation of the Entrepreneurs Organizations of Azerbaijan Republic, known by its acronym ASK. More than 180 children, 180 parents, 180 employers, and 60 educators were interviewed in eight cotton-growing provinces of Azerbaijan (ASK 2005).

According to the survey, more than 80 percent of both parents and children agree that children are put to work out of financial necessity. The earnings of the families studied averaged about $40 per month, and the parents reported that they would not require their children to work if the family could earn about $100 per month. By comparison, the poverty line in Azerbaijan is defined as 250,000 manat per month, or about $54. Most of the working children reported that they had no gas heat or sewer access at home, but they did live with their families.

The average child worked just over thirty hours per week, ranging from a high of almost thirty-seven hours per week for girls age five to fifteen to a low of just over twenty-six and a half hours per week for boys age five to fifteen. For older boys and girls, the pattern is reversed, as boys seek more paid employment, while girls begin to do more domestic work. Reflecting the family nature of children's work in Azerbaijan, 52 percent of the sample gave all of their earnings to their parents, and another 32 percent gave part of their earnings to the family.

Perhaps surprisingly, employers had a negative opinion of child labor and felt that it harmed children's education and health. They did not view children as effective workers, but they used child labor because of a lack of alternatives.

In Azerbaijan's rural regions, there is a vicious circle in which poverty, lack of financial support for the educational system, lack of interest in education, lack of employment opportunities for educated workers, and the resulting pressure for both children and parents to seek work in the fields all reinforce one another. Those able-bodied adults who do achieve the requisite skills flee to the city for better working conditions, leaving employers no choice but to use child labor (ASK 2006).

Trafficking and Street Children

Trafficking of women and girls from Azerbaijan has been documented. Most Azerbaijani victims were trafficked for sexual exploitation to countries such as Turkey, Russia, Iran, Pakistan, Germany, and states in the Persian Gulf. The U.S. State Department classifies Azerbaijan as a tier 2 trafficker, since current enforcement measures are inadequate to stem trafficking. There are also reports of children being trafficked internally for begging (U.S. Department of State 2007).

Roughly 20 percent of children age five to fourteen do not attend school. Some are working to support their families, others may be refugees or internally displaced children, and others are street children, who are at particular risk for labor exploitation in drug and sex trafficking. Reports of organ trafficking have also surfaced (BBC News 2004).

Legislation

Azerbaijan has signed and ratified most of the major international conventions on child labor. In addition to the UN Convention on the Rights of the Child and ILO Conventions 138 and 182, Azerbaijan has ratified the Protocol to Prevent, Suppress and Punish Trafficking in Persons, the Optional Protocol to the Convention on the Rights of the Child on the Sale of Children, Child Prostitution and Child Pornography, the Optional Protocol to the Convention on the Rights of the Child in Armed Conflict, ILO Convention 29 on forced labor, and ILO Convention 105 on abolition of forced labor.

In addition, legislation of the Republic of Azerbaijan prohibits work of children under fourteen, and fourteen- to fifteen-year-olds can work only with parental permission. Children under sixteen are prohibited from working more than twenty-four hours per week, and sixteen- to eighteen-year-olds can work no more than thirty-six hours per week (ASK 2005). However, these laws are rarely enforced in the agricultural sector, where the bulk of nondomestic child labor occurs.

The government supports the goals of IPEC and has taken steps to raise awareness. The activities of the ASK also include educational programs on the problem of child labor in cooperation with the ILO. The first phase of anti–child labor activities concentrated on the cotton sector, while the next phase will target tobacco and tea plantations, where child labor is common. There are no formal obstacles to the reduction of child labor in Azerbaijan, and advances continue to be made. For example, in May 2007, school-age children were prohibited from working as conductors on the bus system.

Economic Progress Required

In addition to legislation, Azerbaijan must commit to greater enforcement of laws on child labor and trafficking. The cooperation of the ASK is an indication that business attitudes are not an obstacle to the reduction of child labor. But more progress on the economic front is needed—basic education, health, and job opportunities in Azerbaijan are stagnant, pushing families on the margin to depend on child labor. It has been found that once compulsory education extends through age fourteen and annual incomes rise over $500, child labor rates begin to decline rapidly (ILO 2006). As the agricultural sector is reformed, and as incomes gradually rise across all segments of society, including the poorest, the use of child labor in Azerbaijan should begin to decline.

References and Further Reading

Asian Development Bank (ADB). *Azerbaijan: Country Gender Assessment.* Manila: ADB, 2005. http://www.adb.org/Documents/Reports/Country-Gender-Assessments/cga-aze.pdf.

Asian Development Bank (ADB). "Azerbaijan." *Asian Development Outlook 2007: Growth Amid Change.* Manila: ADB, 2007, 108–13. http://www.adb.org/Documents/Books/ADO/2007/AZE.pdf.

Azərbaycan Respublikası Sahibkarlar (İşəgötürənlər) Təşkilatları Milli Konfederasiyası (National Confederation of the Entrepreneurs [Employers'] Organizations of Azerbaijan Republic) (ASK). "Study on Child Labour on Cotton Plantations in 8 Regions of Azerbaijan." ASK, Baku, Azerbaijan, 2005. http://www.ask.org.az/docs/study_on_child_labour.doc.

Azərbaycan Respublikası Sahibkarlar (İşəgötürənlər) Təşkilatları Milli Konfederasiyası (National Confederation of the Entrepreneurs [Employers'] Organizations of Azerbaijan Republic) (ASK). "Project Progress." ASK, Baku, Azerbaijan, 2006. http://www.ask.org.az/en/p_progress.

BBC News. "Azerbaijan Probes Child-Organ Traffickers." February 23, 2004. http://news.bbc.co.uk/2/hi/europe/3513439.stm.

ILO. The *End of Child Labour: Within Reach.* Geneva: ILO, 2006.

Political Risk Services. *Azerbaijan Country Risk Forecast.* Syracuse, NY: Political Risk Services, 2006.

UNDP. *2006—Living Conditions in the Azerbaijan Republic.* Baku, Azerbaijan: UNDP, 2006. http://www.un-az.org/doc/AzerbaijanRCAR_2006_e.pdf.

UNICEF. *Progress for Children: A Child Survival Report Card.* New York: UNICEF, 2004. http://www.unicef.org/publications/files/29652L01Eng.pdf.

UNICEF Azerbaijan. "Azerbaijan—The Children." http://www.unicef.org/azerbaijan/index.html.

U.S. Department of State. *2006 Trafficking in Persons Report.* Washington: U.S. Department of State, 2006. http://www.state.gov/documents/organization/66086.pdf.

Egypt

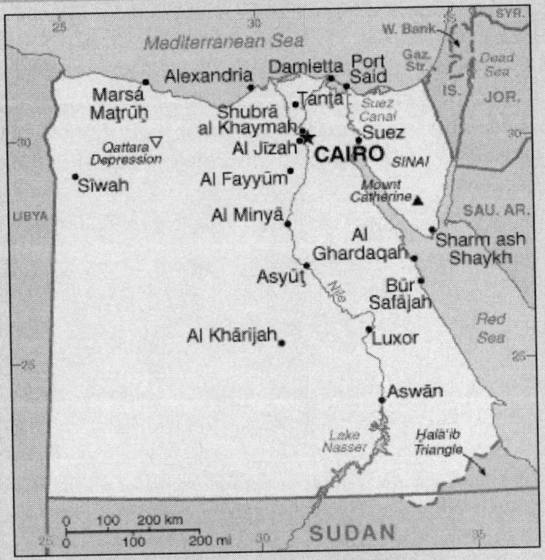

EGYPT			
	CRC	C 138	C 182
Ratifications	Y	Y	Y
Human Development Index/Rank	0.702/111		
Human Capital			
Population Growth Rate	1.75%		
% Population 0–14	32.6%		
Total Fertility Rate	2.83		
Life Expectancy	71.29		
Infant Mortality Rate	31.33		
Literacy Rate	57.7		
Economic			
GDP/Capita	$4,200		
GDP Growth %	5.7%		
% Poverty	20%		
Gini Index	34.4		
Labor Force Composition			
% Agriculture	32%		
% Industry	17%		
% Services	51%		

CHILD ACTIVITY BREAKDOWN, BY SEX AND RESIDENCE

RESIDENCE	Percentage of children in the relevant age-group[a]									
	Economic activity only		School only		Combining school and economic activity		Neither in school nor in economic activity		Child labor[b]	
	Male	Female	Male	Female	Male	Female	Male	Female	Male	Female
Urban	1.1	0.3	87.1	87.4	1.8	0.7	10.0	11.6	n/av	n/av
Rural	2.1	2.1	71.5	76.0	11.3	3.4	15.0	18.6	n/av	n/av
Total	**1.8**	**1.4**	**77.4**	**80.4**	**7.7**	**2.3**	**13.1**	**15.9**	**7.7**	**5.2**

Source: Egypt, Demographic and Health Survey, 2005 (see UCW Project Web site, http://www.ucw-project.org, country statistics).

Notes: [a]Children age 5 to 14. [b]Estimate includes (a) children under age 12 engaged in economic activities, (b) children age 12–14 engaged in excessive economic activities (more than 14 hours per week), and (c) children under age 15 engaged in excessive household chores (at least 28 hours per week). Estimate does not account for children engaged in hazardous work or other unconditional "worst forms" of child labor.

Child Labor in Egypt

Heidi Morrison, PhD Candidate, University of California at Santa Barbara

For the first half of the twentieth century, Egypt was essentially dependent on agriculture. The agricultural system employed was that of the Ottoman Land Code of 1858. The code's main legal categories for dividing the land were: *mulk* lands (lands over which the owner had full control); *miri* lands (lands that were state domains that could be taxed directly by the occupiers of the country); and *wafq* lands (lands dedicated to religious or charitable purposes). In order to understand the role of child labor in agricultural production, it is necessary to look at the arrangements made between landowners and those who were actually responsible for cultivating the land, since these arrangements largely determined the standard of living of the farm families involved. *Fellaheen* is the named used to refer to peasant agricultural workers in Egypt.

The larger landowners in Egypt had two methods of exploiting their property. The majority chose to divide the land into small units suitable for family farming on a rental basis (year contracts or less). Others chose to exploit the land themselves with the aid of machinery and paid labor. Under the rental system, the paying tenant was far from being his own master since the owner fixed crop rotation and harvesting dates and retained control of the water. After the tenant paid for the land usage, he was left with between one-fifth and one-half the value of the crop, if all he supplied was his labor and that of his family.

Most laborers in Egypt were not part of a rental system, but instead were casual laborers recruited by contractors who directed their work in cotton and sugarcane harvesting, digging canals, and repairing roads. This system was known as *tarhila.* In many cases the employer contracted with the head of the group of workers to pay a certain sum in accordance with the quantity produced. Payment was made to the leader, who was then responsible for distributing the earnings to the workers. There are accounts of this practice as early as 1932, whereby girls recruited to work in ginning factories saw their wages paid to their recruiters, who frequently retained a substantial portion of their small earnings (ILO 1960).

The large landowners who employed children in Egypt were primarily British (until the end of the occupation in 1923) and local elites. Labor historian Ellis Goldberg claimed that, during the period 1880–1950, the labor of children was the single largest input in the production of the country's cotton. Children were used especially for picking, eliminating insect infestations, and working in some ginning operations. Overall the labor of boys accounted for nearly 35 percent of the total labor requirement for the major Egyptian crops, and most of them were employed in cotton (Goldberg 2004). Children were employed because their wages were cheap, and child labor was Egypt's comparative advantage in the global market. Egyptian cotton was produced as a labor-intensive good in an economy with abundant labor, as opposed to a capital-intensive good in an economy with abundant capital that could invest in mechanization of production (Goldberg 2004).

Because child labor was Egypt's comparative advantage, meager investments were made in education of children. During the British occupation of Egypt, from 1882 to 1923, demand for the labor of children and the acquisition of literacy were inversely related. In 1910, about 3.4 percent of the state budget was spent on public education, and 90 percent of the pupils in the elementary school were boys (Goldberg 2004). Money invested in education by British occupiers, particularly after completion of the Aswan Dam in 1902, was largely directed toward establishing courses of study to improve the efficiency of the *fellaheen.* Although expenditures on education in the postindependence era increased, students attended only half-day sessions in order to leave them available for work. Usually children attended school for only two to three years.

For the first half of the twentieth century, there was little recourse for child laborers through labor unions. The first trade union organization was set up in the beginning of the twentieth century, and by 1911 there were eleven unions with 7,000 members. In 1919 the government officially recognized labor unions by setting up a central committee of conciliation, and in 1942 the government recognized freedom of association in trade unions. Despite the legal recognition of trade unions, agricultural workers were not covered by the laws, and the minimum age for joining trade unions was fifteen years.

There was also little protection for child laborers in the law. The earliest protective legislation, enacted in 1909 and prohibiting the employment of children below the age of nine in certain industries, was widely acknowledged to be completely ineffective (Beinin 1998). The first Labor Office was set up in Egypt in 1930, but its main function was formulation of legislation and settlement of disputes in matters relating to the trade union movement. After an ILO mission to Egypt in 1932, a law was promulgated in 1933 to regulate the employment of children. The ILO report observed boys and girls under the age of ten being paid low wages in traditional handicraft workshops and factories (Butler 1932). The 1933 law established twelve years as the minimum age for employment, but children over nine years of age could work in certain industries (including textiles, carpet weaving, and furniture) upon production of a certificate of physical fitness. This was the first law regulating child work enacted since 1909, but it fell short of necessary protection (Beinin 1998). The law was largely ignored and inadequately enforced, as the Labor Office employed only five inspectors and one clerk to cover all of Egypt.

It was not until the 1952 revolutionary government of Gamal Abdel Nasser that the structure of the economic system in Egypt changed. The main effect of the agrarian reform of 1952 was to shatter the economic power of the royal family and the landed elite connected to it. Seventy thousand former tenants or permanent laborers were given land of their own, in the hopes that an increase in rural incomes would increase demand for the industrial goods being produced as part of the newly adopted import-substitution model of development. Little scholarship has been conducted on the effects of land redistribution on the phenomenon of child labor, but it is clear that Egypt remained a country whose workforce was primarily agricultural and whose economy was still dominated by the price of cotton exports. About 75 percent of the total population was engaged in agriculture. The other main avenues of employment included manufacturing, commerce, services, transport, construction, mining, and quarrying. Only 30 percent of persons engaged in agriculture were wage earners; the rest were unpaid family workers (ILO 1960). Due to their abject poverty and small individual holdings, the *fellaheen* continued to use traditional tools such as the hoe and threshing sledges pulled by camels and donkeys.

The main changes that took place for child laborers in the postrevolutionary period were related to legislation in the industrial sector of the economy. The labor movement's campaign for more jobs for adult men had the indirect effect of decreasing the training period during which children could work without pay. The first real labor legislation for children came in the form of a 1959 Labor Law which fixed the minimum age for employment at twelve, with no exceptions, and some industries in which the minimum age was set at fifteen or seventeen. Additionally, this law limited young persons under the age of fifteen to six hours of work per day, prohibited work for more than four hours without a break, and prohibited work at night and overtime. The law specified maximum weights on carrying loads, and provided for apprenticeships in certain occupations such as spinning, weaving, and knitting. Children would apprentice for a certain period under a foreman, after which they were be given a certificate stating that they could work without supervision. The law required posting the regulations in all workplaces and required registration of all those who supervised or recruited juveniles. This law was not applicable to agricultural workers or to persons working in home workshops in which members of the family were employed.

School attendance rates remained low in the postrevolutionary era, and school attendance was still not mandatory. In 1955, 9 percent of the total population was in schools, and in 1958, 12.5 percent was (ILO 1960). The largest growth in school attendance occurred in urban Egypt, where the new labor law discouraged hiring children in large factories. Demand for skilled workers constantly increased as a result of the departure of foreign specialists and the adoption of economic development schemes. As a result, vocational training systems emerged in urban areas. Education in agriculture and rural handicrafts continued to occupy a prominent part of the school curricula in rural areas. One form of vocational training adopted by the government came in the form of land settlement projects, in which the government selected families, after medical, social, and psychological screening, to live in villages on reclaimed land. Men and women received vocational training, children went to school, and everything was disciplined and organized.

Following the reign of Nasser came the economic liberalization period of Anwar el-Sadat, from 1970 to 1981, and then the combined statist, private-investment reign of Hosni Mubarak, from 1981 to the present. Throughout these two periods, child labor decreased in the formal sector, but children remain in the labor market to the present day. Education became mandatory through the ninth grade in 1991. A 1997 national survey estimated that some 1.7 million Egyptian children age six to fourteen worked in paid and unpaid labor (Human Rights Watch 2003). UNICEF found that many youths enter the workforce at age fourteen, at the end of compulsory schooling. Children work in agriculture, the quarry industry, and handicrafts, and as street vendors. Within the agricultural sector, more than 1 million children between the ages of seven and twelve are hired each year to take part in cotton pest management (Human Rights Watch 2001).

Despite the fact that, since the 1980s, Egypt has passed national laws against child labor and has been signatory to international human rights accords, child rights abuses have persisted. Egypt's most comprehensive law setting limits on child labor was enacted in 1996. Under this Child Law, children under fifteen are not allowed to work, but the law allows a minimum age of twelve for seasonal agricultural work. The law regulates working hours and mandates safe working conditions for those between the ages of fifteen and seventeen, but because many children do not work in the formal sector, the law does not affect them. Egypt has not yet signed ILO Convention 182 on elimination of worst forms of child labor.

References and Further Reading

Beinin, Joel, and Zachary Lockman. *Workers on the Nile.* Cairo: American University in Cairo Press, 1998.

Butler, H.B. *Report on Labor Conditions in Egypt with Suggestions for Future Social Legislation.* Cairo: Government Press, 1932.

Goldberg, Ellis. *Trade, Reputation, and Child Labor in Twentieth-Century Egypt.* New York: Palgrave Macmillan, 2004.

Human Rights Watch. "Charged with Being Children: Egyptian Police Abuse of Children in Need of Protection." New York: Human Rights Watch 15:1 (February 2003).

Human Rights Watch. "Underage and Underprotected." New York: Human Rights Watch 13:1 (January 2001).

International Labor Organization. *Labor Survey of North Africa.* Geneva: La Tribune de Genève, 1960.

Georgia

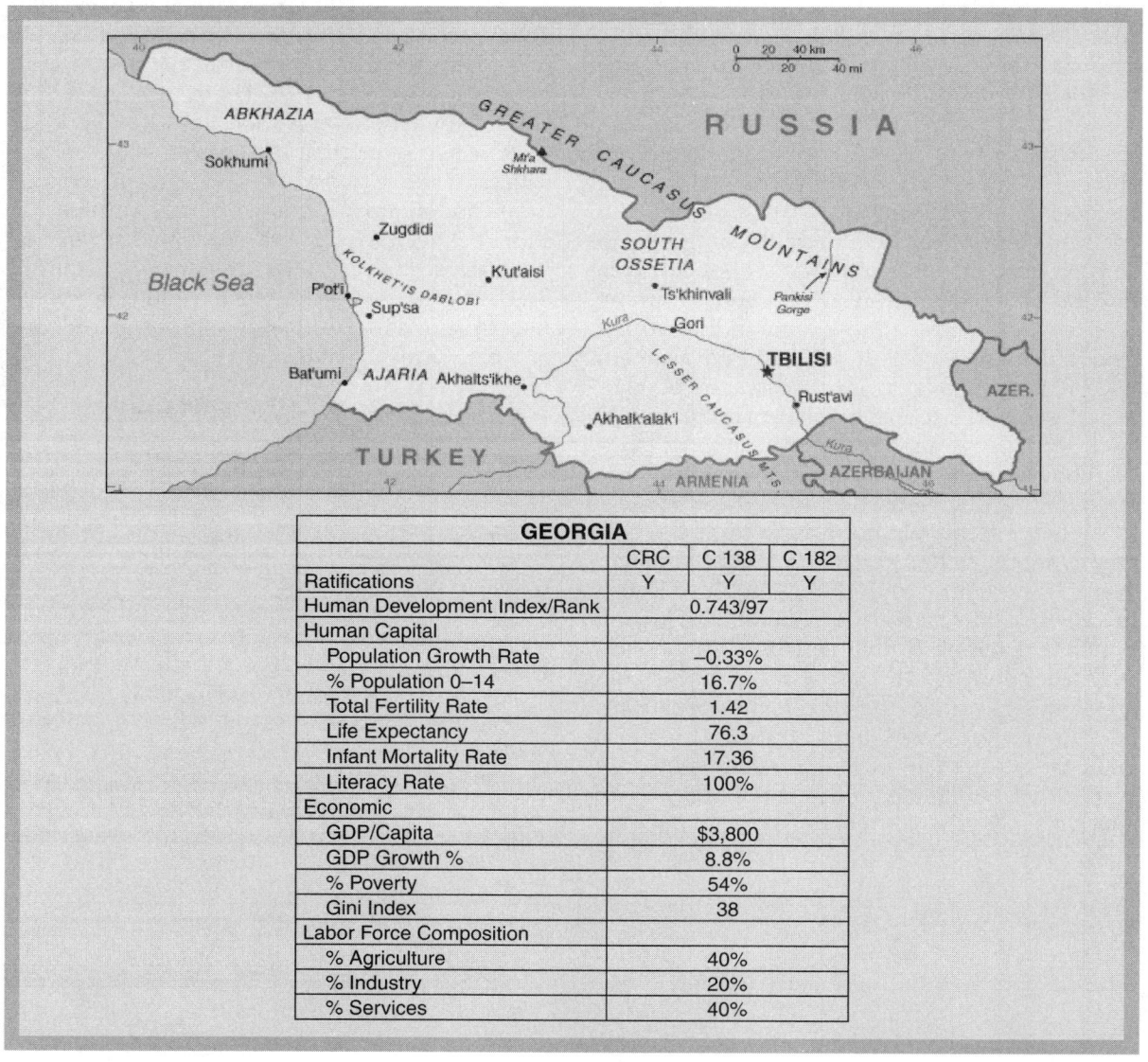

GEORGIA			
	CRC	C 138	C 182
Ratifications	Y	Y	Y
Human Development Index/Rank	0.743/97		
Human Capital			
Population Growth Rate	–0.33%		
% Population 0–14	16.7%		
Total Fertility Rate	1.42		
Life Expectancy	76.3		
Infant Mortality Rate	17.36		
Literacy Rate	100%		
Economic			
GDP/Capita	$3,800		
GDP Growth %	8.8%		
% Poverty	54%		
Gini Index	38		
Labor Force Composition			
% Agriculture	40%		
% Industry	20%		
% Services	40%		

Child Labor in Georgia

Nona Tsotseria, MD, MPPM, Doctoral Student, Muskie School of Public Service, University of Southern Maine

Georgia, the country of the Golden Fleece, with spectacular nature, smart and beautiful people, and the aspiration to knowledge, education, and intelligence, should not be troubled with issues such as child labor. But, as a former Soviet republic, surviving the cataclysms of the transition to independence, and building a new economic system, Georgia was struck by poverty. Child labor in Georgia appears on a scale and in a form that make it not considered a serious problem. It is one of the symptoms of the overall poverty in the country, however, and the main remedy for it is the economic development of the country, to which Georgia has been committed since the Rose Revolution of November 2003.

Geographic Location and Population of Georgia

Georgia is located on the east shore of the Black Sea. In the north, Georgia is crowned by the Caucasus Mountains. Its territory, comprised of 27,000 square miles, includes a great diversity of nature, with glaciers in the north, deserts in the east, and subtropical gardens in the west. Georgia's mostly mild climate and fertile soil were the basis for the development of agriculture. In the Georgian language, the name of the country is "Sakartvelo." According to one analysis, the word "Georgia" derived from the ancient Persian "Gurj" or "Gorg," meaning "gorgeous." Another version suggests that Georgia was so named by the Greeks on account of its agricultural resources, since "Georgia" means "farming" in Greek.

Georgia has celebrated 3,000 years of statehood and 2,000 years of Christianity, and is a country with a rich culture and history and a very distinct alphabet, language, and literature. It was not easy to preserve independence and identity being surrounded and invaded by great empires, starting from Romans and Byzantines and followed by Arabs, Mongols, Persians, Turks, and Russians. Today Georgians comprise 83.8 percent of the Georgian population of 4.6 million. Other ethnic groups include Russians, Armenians, Azeri, Ossetians, and Abkhazs. Orthodox Christians comprise 83.9 percent of the population, Muslims 9.9 percent, and Armenian Apostolic 3.9 percent. The capital, Tbilisi, is a modern city with a rich history, and is the political, cultural, and economic center of the country. One-third of the whole population lives in Tbilisi.

Political and Socioeconomic Situation in Georgia

On April 9, 1991, Georgia gained its independence from the Soviet Union, but the process of rebuilding Georgia as an independent country was not easy. A military putsch against the first president was followed by a civil war in 1991–1992, and the exile of more than 300,000 Georgians from Abkhazia and South Ossetia, which dragged the country into poverty. The country began to recover in 1994–1996, but the global economic crisis of 1997 and the corruption of the Georgian government not only prevented further recovery but also worsened the situation. Finally, in November 2003, the Rose Revolution overthrew the corrupt government of President Eduard Shevardnadze. The new president, Mikhail Saakashvili, promised to eradicate corruption and has been quite successful in this fight. These positive developments, however, have been insufficient to eradicate poverty. According to recent data, 54 percent of the population lives below the poverty line, in a country where 30 percent of the population has higher education and technical qualifications. The official unemployment rate is 12.6 percent, but this might be understated. According to law, any farmer owning at least one hectare of agricultural land is defined as self-employed, but income from this land is not substantial. Thus, the rural employment rate artificially decreases the national unemployment rate (Labbate and Jamburia 2004). In 2006 the national minimum wage for public employees increased to $67.11 (115 lari), but when the official minimum subsistence level for a single person is $67.69 (116 lari), it is not surprising that many people with higher education still live in poverty.

History of Child Labor in Georgia

Georgia's recent history can be divided into three periods: the pre-Soviet period, the Soviet period (1921–1991), and the period after independence in 1991. Before the Soviet period, only children of noble and wealthy families were able to receive education. Other children had to work from early ages in order to support their families. Since Georgia was an agrarian country, most children worked in agriculture. Today's elderly people, who experienced childhood in the early 1920s, talk with delight about possibilities the Soviet system brought for them. Education was not only affordable; it was mandatory, and parents could not prevent children from going to school. The Soviet system improved the well-being of those in poverty. The well-being and education of children was at the top of the Soviet agenda, and the literacy rate reached 100 percent. Within the Soviet Union, Georgia had the highest proportion of its population with higher and technical education. Children were socially protected. Education and health care were constitutional rights. Child labor was not an issue. The government was the only official employer, and it could not violate its own laws. Age and conditions of employment for minors were defined in the Labor Code of the Soviet Republic of Georgia. Children were allowed to work at the age of sixteen, and their workday was shorter than that of adults (Tsotseria 2004). There were cases where children in rural settings were helping in family farming, but this did not jeopardize their health or education. If there were families who could not provide care for their children, the government became the guardian for these children.

Child Labor Today

The transition from Soviet Georgia to independent Georgia has been a painful process, and, after more than fifteen years, it is still under way. In the early 1990s, superinflation reduced the savings of the majority of the population to zero. The salaries of the employed population dropped to as low as $2 to $5 per month. Almost the whole population of Georgia was dragged into poverty. The situation of internally displaced people from Abkhazia and South Ossetia, who lost houses, savings, and health, was even more severe. Until the government managed to organize support for them, people survived solely with the support of relatives and friends, who themselves were in a desperate situation.

This turmoil triggered the reemergence of child labor in Georgia. In order to survive, many children in rural areas had to devote more time to work on family farms. In the cities, children started to sell ice cream and beverages, newspapers and cigarettes, and worked in gas stations and cafés. The phenomena of street children and child prostitutes emerged. High unemployment forced adults, many of them women, to seek job opportunities abroad. The children took the responsibilities of household care under supervision of grandparents or other relatives. Many children orphaned during wars became breadwinners for their families.

The most recent comprehensive data on child labor in Georgia are based on a survey implemented by the State Department of Statistics of Georgia with technical and financial assistance from the ILO in 1999–2000 (Labbate and Jamburia 2004). According to the survey, 21.48 percent of children perform economic activities for at least one hour per week. About half of these children are involved in work considered unacceptable for their age. The work these children are performing is helping in family plots in rural areas. Of all children engaged in economic activity, most work helping the family and only about 9 percent receive monetary payment for their services. Many children (44.23 percent) are involved in noneconomic domestic activities involving family chores such as washing, cooking, and looking after family members who are old or in need of care. In the rural regions, 38.9 percent of children are involved in economic activities, comprising 77.25 percent of the national total. Urban children account 61.8 percent of all children involved in noneconomic activities. More boys are engaged in economic activities, while girls dominate in noneconomic domestic activities.

Children's work in family businesses is not seen as a serious problem; it is considered life-skill training, and children are not prevented from education and their health does not suffer. The major child labor concerns are expressed about street children and prostitutes. There are more than 4,000 street children registered in Georgia. In addition to state-owned orphanages and children's shelters, private organizations, NGOs, the Georgian Orthodox Church, and other religious charitable organizations have organized support for street children, but the problem persists. Official data do not exist about child prostitutes, but their number has increased in parallel with economic hardships (UNICEF 2000). The criminal code of Georgia addresses issues concerning trafficking and prostitution of minors.

Laws Regulating Child Labor

According to the Georgian Code of Labor, the minimum employment age is sixteen, but children of age fourteen and fifteen can work with parental consent. Working hours for children under eighteen are shorter, and these children are prohibited from unhealthy and underground work. The official entity responsible for enforcement of child labor laws is the Ministry of Labor, Health and Social Affairs. In addition, the National Public Defender's Office has been working since 1996 to ensure protection of human rights and the rights of children. Georgia acceded to the UN Convention on the Rights of the Child in 1994, and adopted ILO Convention 138 (minimum age) in 1996 and ILO Convention 182 (worst forms of child labor) in 2002.

Future of the Issue

Child labor in Georgia is a symptom of the poverty that struck the country due to local and global political and economic cataclysms. For people from developed countries it is difficult to understand why smart, well-educated, hardworking people living in a fertile country such as Georgia are in poverty. It is painful when physicians cannot support their families and are forced to work as babysitters in foreign countries to guarantee the existence of their families in Georgia. The new generation of children has witnessed the devaluation of education. Government mismanagement and corruption, and economic and military pressure from powerful neighbors, produced economic crises, which are more severe for countries in transition. The government that came after the Rose Revolution promised to lead the country to prosperity, but the misdeeds of the prior fifteen years are not easy to overcome. It will take time. Georgians, with their intelligence and aspiration to education, should succeed in this journey. When jobs for adults are created, health care and education are affordable, and education is valued, the child labor problem will lose its importance. Georgia should have prosperous families and happy children.

In its assessment of Georgia, the U.S. Department of State observed that "with high unemployment resulting in a large pool of adults workers willing to work for low wages, child labor was uncommon in the country" (U.S. Department of State 2007, 25). It would be more appropriate to assert that, with high employment for adults, child labor will be not issue at all.

Conclusion

Historically, Georgians highly appreciate education and intelligence. A Greek epic poem, *The Argonautica,* written by Apollonius Rhodius in the third century B.C.E., tells the myth of the voyage of the Argonauts to retrieve the Golden Fleece, the symbol of knowledge and wisdom, from the land of Colchis, which is now West Georgia. Colchis was a powerful country and Colchians' knowledge in medicine, gold processing, and pharmacy was unsurpassed in the world. Inspired by its rich historical background, Georgia should be able to overcome current its difficulties. Child labor, a persistent problem, even if it is not as serious as in many other countries, will cease to be an issue in a prosperous Georgia. The only way to success is the hard work of all Georgians.

References and Further Reading

Apollonius Rhodius. *The Argonautica.* New York: Macmillan, 1912 [ca. 200 B.C.E.].

Chilashvili, L., and N. Lomouri. "A Brief History of Georgia: The Eternal Crossroads." In *National Treasures of Georgia,* ed. Ori O. Soltes, 30–38. London: Philip Wilson Publishers, 1999.

Gogishvili, T. "Trends of Child and Family Well-Being in Georgia." Background paper prepared for *Regional Monitoring Report No 8: A Decade of Transition.* Florence: UNICEF Innocenti Research Centre, 2001.

Labbate, Gabriel, and Levan Jamburia. *Child Labour in Georgia.* Tbilisi: International Labor Organization and State Department of Statistics of Georgia, 2004.

Soltes, O. "The Eternal Crossroads." In *National Treasures of Georgia,* ed. Ori O. Soltes, 18–29. London: Philip Wilson Publishers, 1999.

Tsotseria, N. "Georgia." In *Child Labor: A Global View,* ed. C.L. Schmitz, E.K. Traver, and Desi Larsen, 69–77. Westport, CT: Greenwood Publishing Group, 2004.

UNDP. *Millennium Development Goals in Georgia: Progress Report for 2004–2005.* Tbilisi: United Nations Development Programme, 2005. http://undp.org.ge/new/files/24_136_229587_mdg.pr.eng.pdf.

UNICEF. *National Report on Follow-up to the World Summit for Children: Georgia: December 2000.* New York: UNICEF, 2000.

U.S. Department of State. "Georgia." *Country Reports on Human Right Practices—2006.* Washington, DC: U.S. Department of State, 2007. http://www.state.gov/g/drl/rls/hrrpt/2006/78813.htm.

Iran

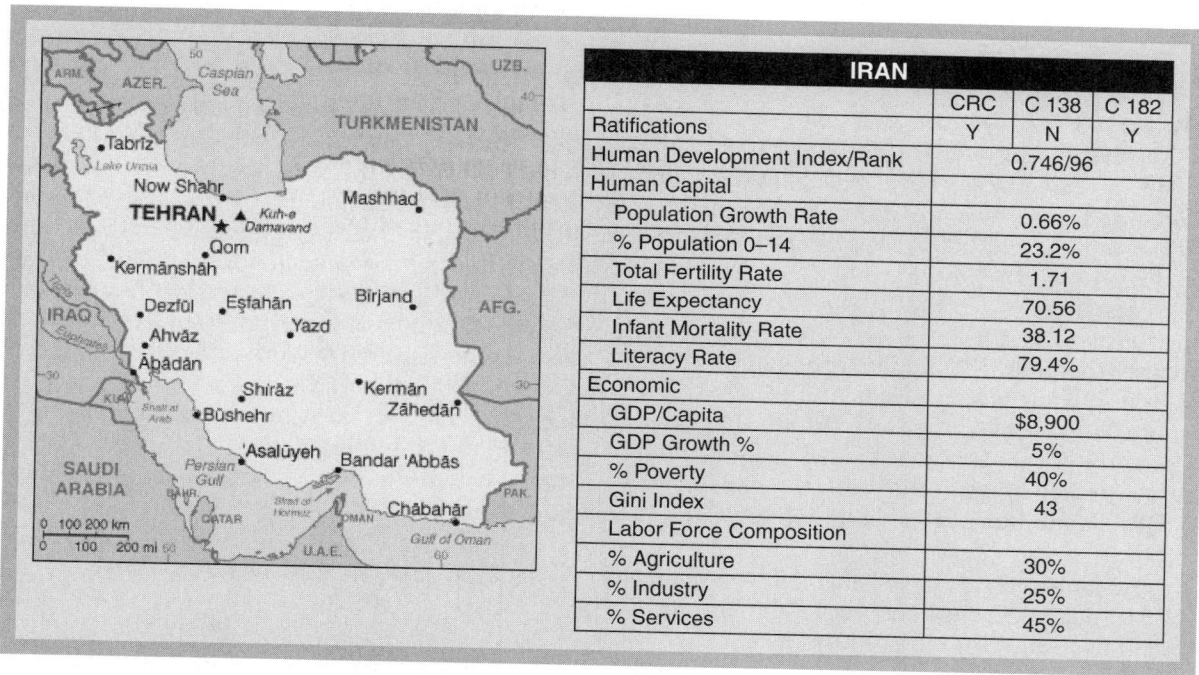

IRAN			
	CRC	C 138	C 182
Ratifications	Y	N	Y
Human Development Index/Rank	0.746/96		
Human Capital			
Population Growth Rate	0.66%		
% Population 0–14	23.2%		
Total Fertility Rate	1.71		
Life Expectancy	70.56		
Infant Mortality Rate	38.12		
Literacy Rate	79.4%		
Economic			
GDP/Capita	$8,900		
GDP Growth %	5%		
% Poverty	40%		
Gini Index	43		
Labor Force Composition			
% Agriculture	30%		
% Industry	25%		
% Services	45%		

Child Labor in Iran

Reza Jalali, MHSA, Program Coordinator, Multicultural Student Affairs, University of Southern Maine

As an oil-rich country, Iran enjoys a relatively high standard of living and has a highly educated and skilled workforce. Due to its oil production, Iran has become the second-largest economy in the region. High oil prices have enabled Iran to amass some $40 billion in foreign exchange reserves. Iranian society is Westernized and open to change. Despite its modernity and national wealth, the issue of child labor remains a serious social problem in today's Iran. According to some, "more than one million Iranian children live below a poverty line of $1 and $2 a day income, while approximately 14 percent work to contribute to family income and meet schooling costs" ("Uprooting Child Labor" 2005).

Iranian society is ambivalent on the question of child labor. On the one hand, social stigma attaches to children working outside the home. On the other hand, child labor has been a long-established tradition (Jalali 2004). Historically, work is recognized as a natural part of a child's upbringing and a necessary preparation for adulthood. In today's Iran, with unprecedented new poverty in both rural and urban centers, one of the many strategies that poor and low-income families use to survive economically and improve their living conditions is by looking to children as a source of additional income for the household.

Historical Traditions

Even though children working for wages carries social stigma, exploitation of children has been accepted by Iranian society. Historically, wealthy families sent their children to religious and private schools, but poor families needed their children to work. In keeping with Islamic tradition, Iranians tend to protect girls when it comes to work outside the home. For that reason, boys are more likely to work than girls of the same age. In most cases, sons worked outside the home to earn wages or apprenticed to learn a craft. Daughters, in contrast, were sent to work as servants in houses of the wealthy. Traditionally, sons were expected to inherit careers from their fathers or to continue family businesses and so were required to work alongside their elders to learn the craft and the business. Similarly, girls were expected to learn homemaking skills from their mothers and extended family members, or through work as domestic laborers in wealthy households.

Contemporary Child Labor in Iran

According to unofficial sources, there are 1.8 million children from nine to eighteen years of age working in Iran. In 1996, the ILO estimated that there were 368,000 economically active children: 237,900 boys and 130,100 girls, from age ten to age fourteen. In 2005, the number of economically active children changed to 335,000. The number of boys increased to 244,000, but the number of girls dropped to 91,000 (ILO 2005). While most child workers are Iranians, there are some Afghan and Iraqi children from the refugee communities as well.

Keeping to tradition, children from poor families begin working in the informal sector, such as agriculture and household help, as soon as they are physically able. Some work as seasonal hands on farms, others in manufacturing, or after school, while many work long hours to the exclusion of education and recreation. Children working on the streets in large and small cities are especially problematic. Jalali (2004) noted that children are employed in occupations such as rug making, carpet weaving, textile work, mining, auto repairs, masonry, glass (window) making, foundry, construction, chemical production, heater manufacturing, coal sales, and food business, and in stores.

Causal Factors

Poverty and economic distress are the primary causes of child labor in Iran. High unemployment (unofficially at 16 percent nationally), forces many low-income and poor families to depend on additional income generated by their children's wages. Children's rights advocates in Iran estimate that children contribute 25 percent of total family income in poor families (Shahabi 2002). In some cases children are forced to work as a result of parental death, disability, or illness. Absence of a public safety net for the poor exacerbates the problem.

Other factors include the mass migration of people from rural parts of the country to settle in the cities. Responding to the promise of prosperity due to oil wealth, large numbers of Iranian farmers left their traditional village lives and migrated to the cities seeking economic opportunities. Jalali (2004, 117–18) observed, "The mass migration of these unskilled and mostly uneducated newcomers looking for jobs in factories and the service industry opened a new chapter in the social life of Iran." A related factor is the presence of a large non-Iranian refugee population from neighboring Afghanistan and Iraq in cities across Iran. Due to the Iran-Iraq War, and the long-standing conflicts in neighboring Afghanistan and Iraq, millions of foreign refugees and Iranians living in border regions were forced to flee to urban centers in search of safety and employment. With the higher standard of living in the cities, and absence of affordable housing due to lack of planning by local municipalities, communities of slum dwellers were created on the outskirts of the cities. Thus, large-scale urban poverty, unknown until recently, has become a reality in Iran (Jalali 2004).

Legal Framework

Iran's modern system of government emerged in the late nineteenth century, spawning a number of social reforms, including mandatory education. For the first time, Iranian families were encouraged to send their children to school. These educational reforms, however, did not reach the poor and those living in rural regions. As a result, many families continued to have their children work (Jalali 2004). Recently, the Islamic Republic of Iran has made serious efforts to create better access to education for all. The constitution guarantees free education for all citizens up to secondary school (International Bureau for Children's Rights 2007).

The 1958 Labor Law, approved by the National Consultative Assembly (Majlis), which functioned as the lower parliament during the shah of Iran's era, prohibited employment of children below twelve years of age, except in family workshops. The law prohibits employment of women and minors in hard labor or night work. This law and similar laws, however, were never fully implemented. For the most part, employers were simply told to avoid employing children below twelve years of age, but no regulations were issued, and the problem was not taken seriously.

After the Islamic revolution and the end of the Iran-Iraq War, due to the internal displacement of a large number of Iranians, there was an increase in the number of street children. With the increase came pressure from children's advocates seeking new laws to protect the rights of children. Soon the Expediency Council (a council of religious experts and elders with political power) agreed to intervene. The council raised the minimum age for employment from twelve to fifteen years and stipulated fines for violators. Today, the minimum age for most employment is fifteen, except in agriculture, where the minimum is twelve.

Problem Areas

Carpet Weavers

In both ancient and modern Iran, girls and boys as young as seven have worked long hours in hand-knotted carpet-making workshops. They weave the expensive "Persian carpets" that are known internationally for high quality, design, and beauty. Persian carpets are Iran's second-largest export, next to crude oil. Children are hired to weave because their small hands are said to make smaller knots, creating more delicate carpets of higher value. Another reason for hiring children is the added incentive of paying a lower salary to child workers.

In most cases, children work in family-owned rug-making workshops set up within family compounds. Other children are "rented" from their parents for substantial sums of money. Middlemen scour poor sections of towns and villages, recruiting children from families willing to send them away to work. The children work long hours, in some cases for years, in order to pay off the middleman's rent. Some rug-weaving workshops are licensed, but many are not. Licensed workshops, subject to regular governmental inspection, offer better protection for working children, generally hiring only children who are old enough to work legally. Though the Iranian government strongly discourages the use of children below fifteen, tens of thousands of unlicensed workshops continue to hire children as young as ten to weave carpets (Jalali 2004).

Children as Soldiers

During Iran-Iraq War of the 1980s, Iran was accused by international agencies of using children as soldiers. The Iranian government denied the charges, asserting, "The minimum employment age for the armed forces for the purpose of receiving military training is 16 years and the minimum age of employment for the Police Forces is 17" (Coalition to Stop the Use of Child Soldiers 2004). Yet there is enough evidence to suggest that children as young as ten were drafted by the Basij, the voluntary army. "According to critics of the Islamic Republic, the children were sent to the front as waves of human shields to stop the advancing Iraqi Army" (Jalali 2004, 120). In addition, the Revolutionary Guard Corps, a voluntary counterrevolutionary force, has many members younger than eighteen years of age (International Bureau for Children's Rights 2007).

Street Children

There has been an increase in the number of street children in large cities across Iran. According to government reports made to the UN Committee on the Rights of the Child, there were fewer than 60,000 street children in the country. Others estimated the number of street children close to 200,000 (Aminmansour 2004). Primary factors include the internal displacement of a large number of Iranians and non-Iranian refugees. It is important to note that most street children in Iran are not homeless. They live with their families, using the streets as a place to generate income, peddling goods from flowers to drugs and offering services such as shoe shining and car cleaning (Jalali 2004). These children do not have access to health care or rehabilitation services for physical, sexual, or substance abuse (International Bureau for Children's Rights 2007).

Refugee Children

The general poverty experienced by displaced foreign refugees, mostly from Afghanistan but also from Iraq, forces refugee families to send their children to work. "Throughout Iran, the children of Afghan and Iraqi refugees join other street children to peddle, selling newspapers, chewing gums, flowers, and even drugs and banned alcohol" (Jalali 2004, 119). In 2001, according to child advocates, 65 percent of street children in Tehran were refugee children (Ghanbari 2002). Though many of these children, born in refugee camps in Iran and elsewhere, lack the national identity cards required to attend public schools, poverty is believed to be the primary cause for sending the children to work rather than to school.

Household Help

Historically, having a young person work as household help is an embedded practice of upper-class families in Iran. Many children from poor families are engaged in this work, some as young as eight years old. They have long working hours, with very little opportunity for rest. Some are victims of verbal, physical, and sexual abuse and may be exposed to hazards while doing heavy household work. Children working as household help, hidden from the public eye, are the most invisible child laborers.

Conclusion

More effective enforcement of existing child labor laws, aggressive efforts to expand access to education, along with the increasing numbers of women joining the job market and the decreasing rate of population growth, have contributed to a decrease in demand for child labor in Iran.

References and Further Reading

Aminmansour, Morteza. "Street Children, Women Trafficking in Iran." *Persian Journal,* December 21, 2004.

Coalition to Stop the Use of Child Soldiers. *Child Soldiers Global Report 2004* (Iran). http://www.child-soldiers.org/document/get?id=943.

Ghanbari, V. "Street Children or Child Labor?" *Khorasaan,* May 21, 2002, 11.

International Bureau for Children's Rights. *Making Children's Rights Work: Country Profile on Iran (Draft).* Montreal: International Bureau for Children's Rights, 2007. http://www.ibcr.org/Publications/CRC/Draft_CP_Asia/IranPDF.pdf.

International Labor Organization. *Yearbook of Labour Statistics.* Geneva: ILO, 2005.

Jalali, Reza. "Iran." In *Child Labor: A Global View,* ed. Cathryne L. Schmitz, Elizabeth KimJin Traver, and Desi Larson, 113–22. Westport, CT: Greenwood Press, 2004.

Shahabi, Soraya. "This Deplorable Condition Is Not the Doomed Fate of Children." Children First: International Campaign for Children's Rights, 2002. http://www.childrenfirstinternational.org/article/fade.htm.

"Uprooting Child Labor." *Iran Daily,* February 8, 2005. http://iran-daily.com/1383/2210/html/panorama.htm#43380.

Iraq

IRAQ	CRC	C 138	C 182
Ratifications	Y	Y	Y
Human Development Index/Rank	n/av		
Human Capital			
Population Growth Rate	2.66%		
% Population 0–14	39.7%		
Total Fertility Rate	4.18		
Life Expectancy	69.01		
Infant Mortality Rate	48.64		
Literacy Rate	40.4%		
Economic			
GDP/Capita	$2,900		
GDP Growth %	2.4%		
% Poverty	n/av		
Gini Index	n/av		

CHILD ACTIVITY BREAKDOWN, BY SEX AND RESIDENCE

RESIDENCE	Percentage of children in the relevant age-group[a]									
	Economic activity only		School only		Combining school and economic activity		Neither in school nor in economic activity		Child labor[b]	
	Male	Female	Male	Female	Male	Female	Male	Female	Male	Female
Urban	2.7	0.9	71.6	70.5	7.0	2.3	18.7	26.2	n/av	n/av
Rural	6.2	10.0	53.7	42.1	16.5	8.7	23.5	39.3	n/av	n/av
Total	4.2	4.7	64.3	58.8	10.9	5.0	20.6	31.6	12.1	9.2

Source: Iraq, Multiple Indicator Cluster Survey 3, 2006 (see UCW Project Web site, http://www.ucw-project.org, country statistics).

Notes: [a]Children age 5 to 14. [b]Estimate includes (a) children under age 12 engaged in economic activities, (b) children age 12–14 engaged in excessive economic activities (more than 14 hours per week), and (c) children under age 15 engaged in excessive household chores (at least 28 hours per week). Estimate does not account for children engaged in hazardous work or other unconditional "worst forms" of child labor.

Jordan

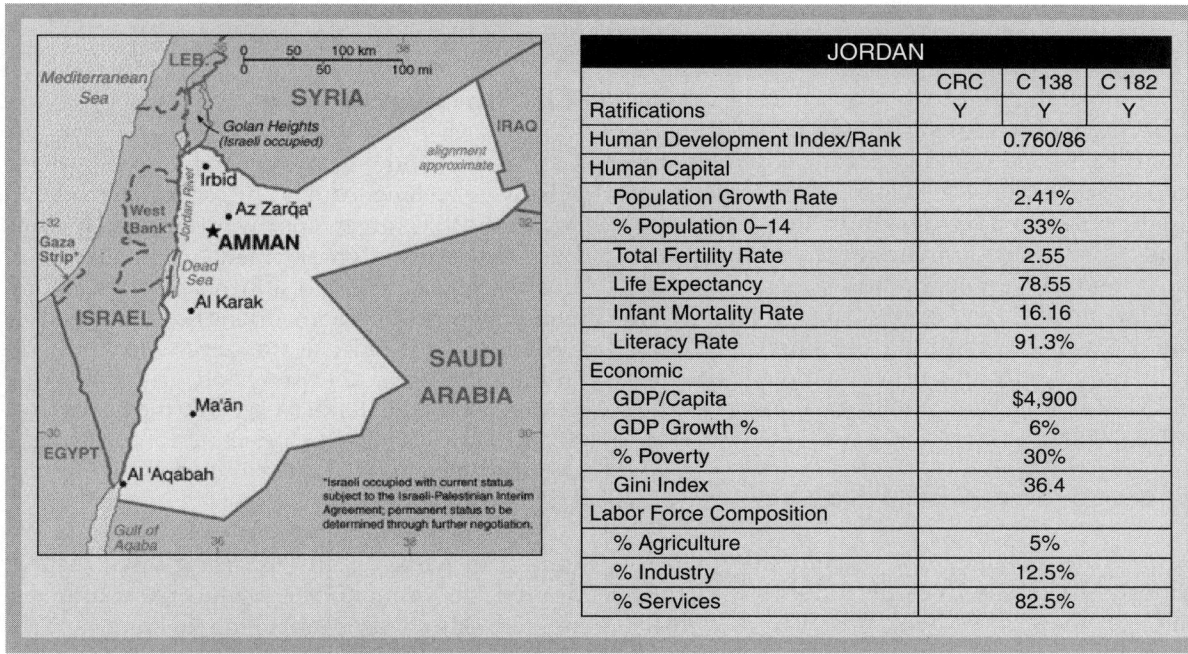

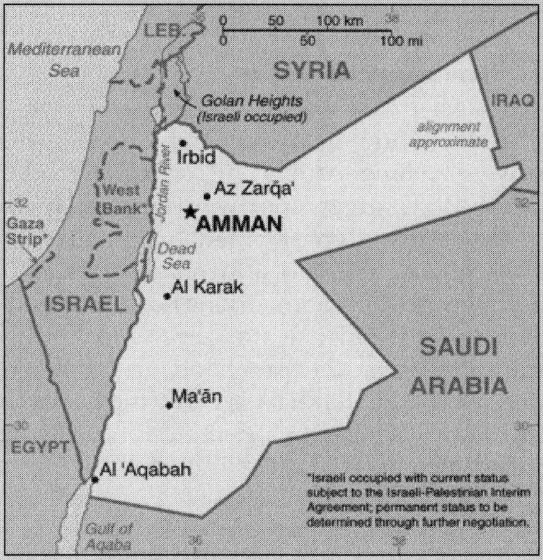

JORDAN			
	CRC	C 138	C 182
Ratifications	Y	Y	Y
Human Development Index/Rank	0.760/86		
Human Capital			
Population Growth Rate	2.41%		
% Population 0–14	33%		
Total Fertility Rate	2.55		
Life Expectancy	78.55		
Infant Mortality Rate	16.16		
Literacy Rate	91.3%		
Economic			
GDP/Capita	$4,900		
GDP Growth %	6%		
% Poverty	30%		
Gini Index	36.4		
Labor Force Composition			
% Agriculture	5%		
% Industry	12.5%		
% Services	82.5%		

Child Labor and Child Growth in Jordan

Nick Spencer, Emeritus Professor of Child Health, School of Health and Social Studies, University of Warwick; and **Hasan Hawamdeh,** PhD, Mu'tah University, Karak, Jordan

The impact of child labor on child health has been widely debated. Growth in childhood is a marker of health and general well-being, and the excessive physical demands of some types of labor may impair growth in the developing child. This essay summarizes the findings of a study undertaken in three Jordanian areas (Irbid, Jarash, and the North Jordan Valley) in the mid-1990s that examined the impact of child labor on growth and other markers of health and well-being (Hawamdeh and Spencer 2002, 2003a, 2003b).

Growth and Child Labor

Despite the global extent of child labor and its importance in the lives of children and their families, there have been relatively few studies of its impact on child growth. Those studies that have been undertaken have reached conflicting conclusions. Gross, Landfried, and Herman (1996) reported on a study in Jakarta showing that working children grew better than their nonworking peers. Nuwayhid et al. (2005) found no differences in growth between working and nonworking boys in Lebanon. By contrast, studies from India (Satayanaranaya et al. 1986) and Israel (Ellen and Janice 1994) suggest that working children are at increased risk of impaired growth.

A major problem in interpreting the effect of child labor on growth is distinguishing the effects of work from the effects of poverty. Poverty is a major driver of child labor in most countries. Inadequate measures of family social and material circumstances render many studies of the impact of child labor impossible to interpret.

The Jordan Study

In brief, 135 working boys age ten to sixteen years, who were no longer attending school, were identified in the three areas. They were engaged in three different forms of employment—agricultural, industrial, and service or commercial sectors. A comparison group of 405 nonworking boys, matched for age and area of residence, was selected from schools in the three areas. Each boy and his family were interviewed and standard growth measurements taken. Full household sociodemographic data were obtained. Heights of mothers and nonworking male siblings of the working boys were also obtained.

The methodology enabled us to study the impact of work on growth using three distinct approaches: comparing growth of working and nonworking children (adjusting for household sociodemographic factors) (Hawamdeh and Spencer 2003b), comparing growth of working boys and their nonworking male siblings (adjusting for age) (Hawamdeh and Spencer 2002), and examining effects of work-related factors on the growth of the working boys (Hawamdeh and Spencer 2003a).

Findings of the Jordan Study

As expected, the working boys in the study came from poorer homes than their nonworking peers. Twenty-three percent of working boys lived in households with a per capita income less than 20 Jordanian dinars (JD) per month, compared with 8.4 percent of nonworking boys. Among working boys, 57 percent of their households were headed by unskilled workers compared with 40 percent among nonworking boys.

When the height of working boys was compared to the height of nonworking boys, adjusting for a range of sociodemographic factors including the child's smoking status, working boys were found to be significantly shorter (Hawamdeh and Spencer 2003b). We estimated that the difference in height accounted for by working was approximately 2.08 inches (5.3 centimeters).

The finding that work among these boys had a negative impact on their growth was confirmed in the study comparing their heights to those of their nonworking male siblings (Hawamdeh and Spencer 2002). Out of the sample of 135, 103 working boys had nonworking male siblings on whom data were available. Adjusting for age, working boys were significantly shorter than their nonworking siblings. The use of nonworking siblings to test the impact of work on growth is particularly valuable as it reduces the potential confounding effects of socioeconomic or familial genetic factors.

Collection of detailed information about work-related variables from the boys enabled us to study the effects of work duration, child's monthly income from work, type of work, and a range of other variables on their growth (Hawamdeh and Spencer 2003a). The findings suggest that longer duration of working and low monthly income were associated with a detrimental effect on growth in height, independent of maternal height, age, and household per capita income.

Discussion and Conclusions

As indicated previously, published studies are divided in their conclusions on the impact of child labor on growth. Our studies, using a robust methodology, enabled us to confidently conclude that, among these Jordanian boys working in three distinct types of work environments, work is detrimental to their growth in height. Further, we were able to show that long duration of working and low remuneration were particular features of child labor in the Jordanian context that increased the adverse impact on growth. The findings have a plausible physiological explanation in that additional nutrients are required to undertake higher levels of physical activity associated with work, especially during critical periods for growth such as puberty. As much of the child's income is likely absorbed into the household income, this may leave insufficient income to make up the nutritional deficit, even if all is spent on additional calories.

The extent to which our findings can be generalized to all working children is open to debate. It is likely that the particular economic situation of Jordan as a middle-income country ensures that few children suffer severe levels of malnutrition, unlike those in many poorer countries. In poorer countries, where many working children are street children, the additional nutritional advantage that might accrue to working children from independent income might compensate for the additional energy consumption associated with working. It is also important to note that girls were not included in our study and it is not possible to generalize from these findings to working girls.

The findings from our study indicate the need for robust methodologies in examining the impact of child labor on growth and suggest that growth impairment might be one of the important adverse health consequences of child labor.

References and Further Reading

Ellen, F., and W. Janice. "Walk-Through Surveys of Child Labor." *American Journal of Industrial Medicine* 26 (1994): 803–7.

Gross, R., B. Landfried, and S. Herman. "Height and Weight as a Reflection of the Nutritional Situation of School-Aged Children Working and Living in the Streets." *Social Science and Medicine* 43 (1996): 453–58.

Hawamdeh, H., and N. Spencer. "Growth of Working Boys in Jordan: A Cross-Sectional Survey Using Non-Working Male Siblings as Comparison." *Childcare, Health and Development* 28 (2002): 47–49.

Hawamdeh, H., and N. Spencer. "Effect of Work-Related Variables on Growth Among Working Boys in Jordan." *Journal of Epidemiology and Community Health* 57 (2003a): 154–58.

Hawamdeh, H., and N. Spencer. "The Effects of Work on the Growth of Jordanian Boys." *Childcare, Health and Development* 29 (2003b): 167–72.

Nuwayhid, I.A., J. Usta, M. Makarem, A. Khudr, and A. El-Zein. "Health of Children Working in Small Urban Industrial Shops." *Occupational and Environmental Medicine* 62 (2005): 86–94.

Satayanarayana K., K.T. Prasanna, and R.B.S. Narasinga. "Effect of Early Childhood Undernutrition and Child Labour on Growth and Adult Nutritional Status of Rural Indian Boys Around Hyderabad." *Human Nutrition: Clinical Nutrition* 40 (1986): 131–39.

Kuwait

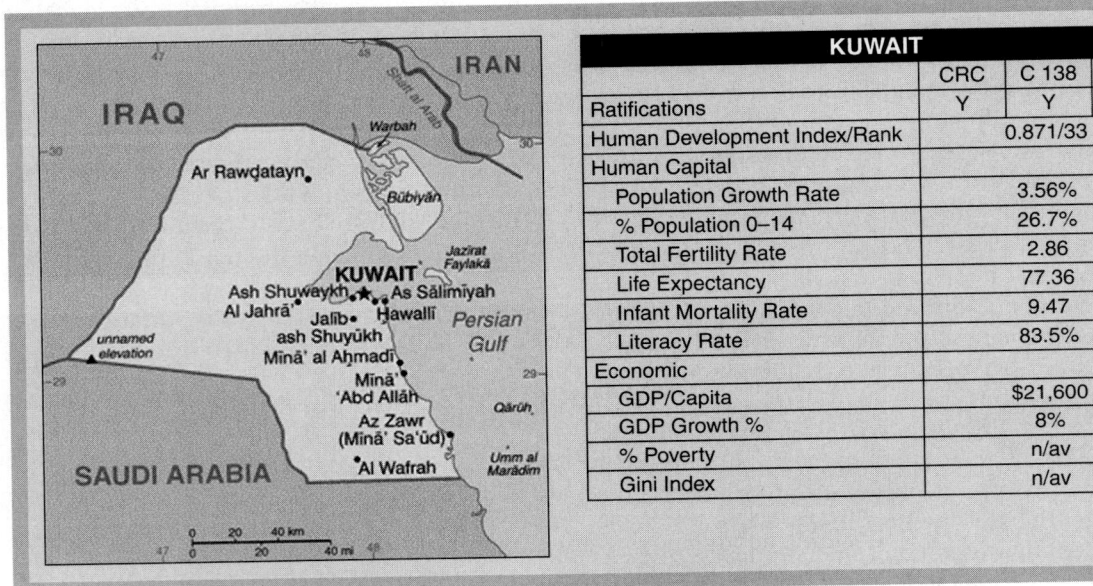

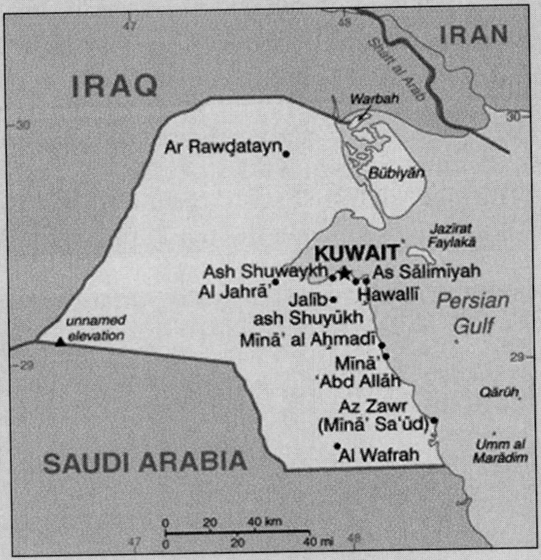

KUWAIT			
	CRC	C 138	C 182
Ratifications	Y	Y	Y
Human Development Index/Rank	0.871/33		
Human Capital			
Population Growth Rate	3.56%		
% Population 0–14	26.7%		
Total Fertility Rate	2.86		
Life Expectancy	77.36		
Infant Mortality Rate	9.47		
Literacy Rate	83.5%		
Economic			
GDP/Capita	$21,600		
GDP Growth %	8%		
% Poverty	n/av		
Gini Index	n/av		

Selling Girls in Kuwait

Tom O'Neill, PhD, Department of Child and Youth Studies, Brock University

One of the hallmarks of the postindustrial world order is transnational migration, the significant movement of peoples from the underdeveloped world to the developed to find employment. At the outset of the twenty-first century, this no longer exclusively means migration to Europe, Australasia, or North America; the global economy has created many new opportunities in East and Southeast Asia, as well as in the affluent Persian Gulf States. Remittances sent by guest workers working abroad to their families in India, Pakistan, Indonesia, the Philippines, and Nepal are an increasingly important component of household income, and a significant boon to the national economy (Seddon et al. 2002). Households deciding about labor allocation take these new opportunities into account, and thus women and children are being sent abroad in growing numbers to meet household needs at home.

One area in which there has been substantial growth for young transnational female labor is domestic service. In the Persian Gulf, in particular, generous state subsidies to families for child care and an abundance of, and market for, visas for foreign workers have brought tens of thousands of women from Sri Lanka, India, Pakistan, and Nepal to work as domestic servants who cook, clean, and provide child care for their employers. This has inspired an international outcry over the exploitation and abuse of these women that is too often grounded in racist and sexist assumptions rather than in the actual experience of these workers. A case of fifteen young Tamang women from Nepal who traveled to Kuwait provides one example (O'Neill 2001).

Nepal is something of a latecomer to the transnational labor market. Toward the end of the 1990s, manpower agencies advertising opportunities in the Persian Gulf began to open in Kathmandu, and word spread that there was an excellent opportunity to make a lot of money working in the Persian Gulf. Much of this was menial labor for young males, but a few Nepalese women found employment as domestic servants in places like Kuwait and Dubai. In November of 1998 one of these women, Kani Sherpa, from the Sindhupalchok region just north of Kathmandu, committed suicide in Kuwait after being abused by her Arab employers (as reported by IRIN 2006). Though the official story is that she took her own life after being informed that she would be arrested as an illegal alien, the media in Kathmandu portrayed her death as murder, and people demanded action to protect Nepalese women. The government banned all females from working abroad, and a very strict watch was placed at Tribhuvan International Airport for women leaving for the Persian Gulf.

That same month, fifteen young women from Sindhupalchok were preparing to travel to the Persian Gulf to be employed as domestic servants. As they could no longer legally leave the country for that purpose, the network that was smuggling them out of the country mounted an elaborate scheme by which the girls would be bused to Bodh Gaya, the town on the Indian border that was then celebrating the 2,500-year anniversary of the Buddha's birth. From there they would cross the border on foot and proceed to New Delhi, from whence they would embark to Kuwait. In order to clear the way for their passage, the broker who was organizing, and profiting from, their employment arranged for falsified passports and visas that showed each girl to be twenty-one years of age, when their true ages ranged from sixteen to eighteen. The girls intended to work in Kuwait for two years, remitting money to their families at home. The broker, of course, took a substantial fee for his services, and the families had to arrange for a substantial cash deposit to pay for his services.

Before the buses left for Kathmandu, the police interceded. The broker and fellow *dacoits* (bandits), as they were dubbed in the Kathmandu media, were arrested, and the fifteen girls were "rescued" by Maiti Nepal, a prominent Nepalese NGO active in protecting Nepalese girls from the brothels of Mumbai. Noting that girls from Sindhupalchok are also trafficked regularly to these brothels, the media reported that the fifteen girls on their way to the Persian Gulf were being "sold" for morally suspect reasons to suspicious Arabs who were said to be capable of most anything. In many people's imaginations, these reasons included prostitution and sexual abuse, and the fact that these girls were underage only amplified these fears. The broker and the trafficking network he ran were charged, and the girls were eventually released to the same families who had attempted to send them abroad in the first place.

Significantly, most of these girls did eventually get to Kuwait, or Dubai, where they worked for two years and sent a substantial amount of money home to their families. They did so illegally, once again, as Nepal's policy did not change until 2003, when feminist groups and others argued that the policy was unnecessarily restrictive and discriminatory. The overwhelming desire of families for more affluence and stability, and the overwhelming desire of these young women to be good daughters and provide for their parents, meant that neither laws nor policies, nor even the cautionary tale of the death of Kani Sherpa, could deter them. The criminal network not only corrupted officials and extorted funds from families to traffic these girls to Kuwait; it put them at significant risk for other forms of abuse because of the illegal, and thus invisible, nature of their employment. Ironically, the same policy that was intended to protect young women put them at greater risk. Allowing women to travel legally to the Persian Gulf has lowered that risk; it has also acknowledged that young women are not merely objects for protection, but rather active agents that are capable of making decisions in their own best interests, as well as their family's best interests.

References and Further Reading

IRIN. "NEPAL: Domestic Workers Abroad Need Protection—Activists." UN Office for the Coordination of Humanitarian Affairs. Integrated Regional Information Networks, Humanitarian News and Analysis. August 23, 2006. http://www.irinnews.org/Report.aspx?ReportId=60499.

O'Neill, Tom. "Selling Girls in Kuwait: Domestic Labour Migration and Trafficking Discourse in Nepal." *Anthropologica* 5:2 (2001): 153–64.

Seddon, D., J. Adhikari, and G. Gurung. "Foreign Labour Migration and the Remittance Economy of Nepal." *Critical Asian Studies* 34:1 (2002): 19–40.

Turkey

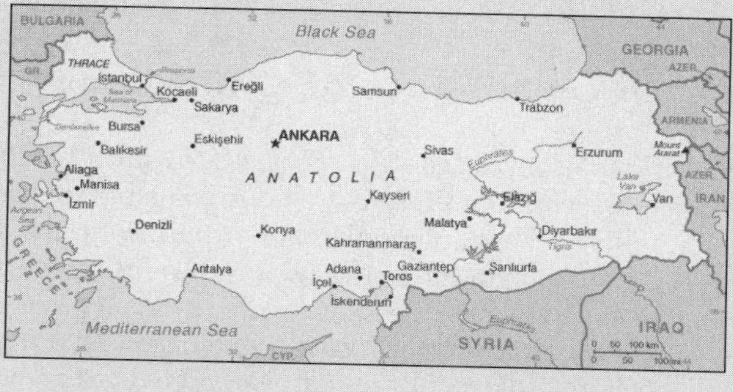

TURKEY			
	CRC	C 138	C 182
Ratifications	Y	Y	Y
Human Development Index/Rank	0.757/92		
Human Capital			
Population Growth Rate	1.04%		
% Population 0–14	24.9%		
Total Fertility Rate	1.89		
Life Expectancy	72.88		
Infant Mortality Rate	38.33		
Literacy Rate	86.5%		
Economic			
GDP/Capita	$8,900		
GDP Growth %	5.2%		
% Poverty	20%		
Gini Index	42		
Labor Force Composition			
% Agriculture	35.9%		
% Industry	22.8%		
% Services	41.2		

CHILD ACTIVITY BREAKDOWN, BY SEX AND RESIDENCE

RESIDENCE	Percentage of children in the relevant age-group[a]									
	Economic activity only		School only		Combining school and economic activity		Neither in school nor in economic activity		Child labor[b]	
	Male	Female	Male	Female	Male	Female	Male	Female	Male	Female
Urban	2.2	0.9	91.5	87.0	0.5	0.1	5.8	12.1	n/av	n/av
Rural	4.5	4.8	85.7	80.1	3.5	2.5	6.3	12.5	n/av	n/av
Total	3.1	2.5	89.2	84.2	1.7	1.1	6.0	12.3	4.2	5.5

Source: Turkey, Labor Force Survey, 1999 (see UCW Project Web site, http://www.ucw-project.org, country statistics).
Notes: [a]Children age 6 to 14. [b]Estimate includes (a) children under age 12 engaged in economic activities, (b) children age 12–14 engaged in excessive economic activities (more than 14 hours per week), and (c) children under age 15 engaged in excessive household chores (at least 28 hours per week). Estimate does not account for children engaged in hazardous work or other unconditional "worst forms" of child labor.

Child Labor in Turkey

Yakın Ertürk, UN Special Rapporteur on Violence Against Women, Its Causes and Consequences; Professor of Sociology, Middle East Technical University, Ankara

Child labor in Turkey, although on the decline, continues to be a concern. Children work on the streets; in agriculture as regular or seasonal migrant labor; in small establishments as apprentices and blue-collar workers; in the service and entertainment sectors; and in the home. Despite its prevalence, consideration of child labor as a public policy issue is relatively new. The adoption, by the government, of the ILO Program on the Elimination of Child Labor (IPEC) in 1992 has been instrumental in prioritization of the problem.

The Eighth Five-Year Development Plan (2000–2005) commits the government to respond to emerging challenges arising from child labor, combat its root causes, ensure full implementation of eight-year compulsory education, and take necessary institutional and legislative measures to fully comply with international commitments.

Turkey is party to a number of international treaties and conventions; in addition to the UN Convention on the Rights of the Child and ILO Conventions 138 (minimum age) and 182 (elimination of worst forms), Turkey has ratified the UN Convention on the Elimination of All Forms of Discrimination Against Women and other important instruments. There is also a growing civil society in the country, contributing to a public discourse that is increasingly sensitive to the rights of children and human rights protection in general.

All these factors combined give Turkey an edge in combating child labor. Since the adoption of IPEC, impressive progress has been achieved in building national capacity, in raising awareness, in building research capacity through creation of a database on the subject, and in creating an enabling environment to effectively address child labor.

Determinants of Child Labor

Within the context of household survival strategies, children present a readily available resource whose labor can supplement or be substituted for adult labor, in the home or outside, and can be exchanged for cash, goods, services, or debt repayment within or outside the formal market. Declining levels of household security and poverty provide a particularly fertile ground for compelling families to rely on the labor of their children in making ends meet. Dayıoğlu (2006) found that, because the incidence of child labor is higher among households that are asset poor, as opposed to being income poor, more children may be pushed to the labor market during major economic downturns, when household assets shrink. Under such circumstances, children's access to schooling may be constrained. While household resource base is a primary determinant of the use of child labor, its attributes are determined at the intersections of gender, age, and sectoral systems.

In order to capture the full range of child labor in Turkey, which has a relatively large agricultural and informal sector, it is important to recognize "work" as a dynamic process that changes in scope and value according to changing socioeconomic conditions. Particularly where livelihoods are marginal to the labor market—as in subsistence production or the informal sector—the demarcation between domestic and nondomestic spheres and notions of work and nonwork are ambiguous. At this juncture, child labor is an essential component of household survival, and their productive and reproductive activities, remunerated or not, need to be factored into the work outputs of children.

A focus on unpaid and paid, reproductive and productive work, whether home based or performed outside the home, therefore, helps capture the wide range of activities boys and girls are involved in. Exclusion of nonmarket activities from the analysis results in loss of information that has direct bearing on work and schooling outcomes of children, particularly of girls.

Comprehensive research from a gender perspective, with emphasis on sex- and age-disaggregated data, has been insufficient. In partial response to this gap in our knowledge, Ertürk and Dayıoğlu (2004) found that, sectoral factors held constant, sexual division of labor largely determines how child labor is used. Reproductive responsibilities, whether performed in or outside the home, are disproportionately assigned to girls. This reproductive work of women and girls is both essential for family sustenance and irreplaceable. While allocation of the labor of younger girls may be more flexible, with increasing age there is greater conformity to patriarchal sex-segregated work structure in all sectors. Consequently, all female members of the household may be called on to contribute to household work to maximize family sustenance.

Furthermore, because female labor is considered to have low opportunity cost, it has the flexibility of sporadically engaging in productive and labor-intensive tasks that have low returns. Male labor, which is socially less flexible, tends toward higher-opportunity jobs. While the labor of younger boys shows similar flexibility to that of girls, higher value is attached to their education. On the whole, however, male children stand at higher risk of labor market employment (Dayıoğlu 2006).

Despite some deviations, child labor patterns correspond to the established sex-based division of labor. Child labor becomes a viable option, particularly in the absence of "suitable" employment opportunities for adult men, or when there are sociocultural constraints on adult women. Hence, child labor reduces the pressure on adult labor, frees them—particularly women—to engage in other activities that contribute to the improvement of family sustenance (Ertürk and Dayıoğlu 2004).

Profile and Patterns of Child Labor

The 2004 Regulations on the Principles of Child and Youth Work establish the legal working age in Turkey at fifteen. Among fifteen- to seventeen-year-olds attending school, they may work up to two hours a day and ten hours a week during the semester, and seven hours a day and thirty-five hours a week during vacation time. Children fifteen and above who do not go to school may not work more than eight hours a day and forty hours a week.

In 1994 and 1999 the Turkish Statistical Institute launched child labor surveys as modules in the October round of the Household Labor Force Survey. While the age-group covered in the 1994 survey was six to fourteen, the 1999 survey covered children six to seventeen. These surveys were initiated to develop a nationwide database on working children that includes sectoral employment, work conditions, socioeconomic and demographic characteristics of the households of working children, and their expectations. The 1999 survey revealed that the vast majority of working children work out of need. While 38.4 percent of the children indicated that they work to contribute to family income, 19.8 percent to assist in family economic activities, and 15.9 percent due to family requirement, only 10.4 percent said they work in order to attain a career.

The child labor module was repeated in the 2006 Household Labor Force Survey, and while the number of questions was reduced and there are other inconsistencies that limit comparability, this provides the most recent information on the subject. The Child Labor Survey includes two categories of working children: employed persons (those who are engaged in economic activity with or without pay) and persons engaged in domestic chores. According to the 2006 survey, of the 16,264,000 children in the six-to-seventeen age-group, close to a million (958,000) are engaged in "economic" activity, which amounts to a child employment rate of 5.9 percent, of which 66 percent are male. A further 43.1 percent are engaged in domestic chores, and 51.0 percent are not engaged in any form of work. Of the children who are employed, 40.9 percent work in agriculture. While 53 percent of the employed earn wages, 2.7 percent are self-employed, and the remaining 43.8 percent work as unpaid household labor.

The percentage of children engaged in economic activity has shown a steady decline from

15.2 percent in 1994 to 10.3 percent in 1999 to 5.9 percent in 2006. Downward trends are also observed in both urban and rural localities, although much sharper in the latter, where the rates are 23.3, 16.9, and 7.9 percent, compared to 7.8, 5.3, and 4.6 percent in urban areas. By gender, 9.6 percent of boys and 6.3 percent of girls in rural areas are economically active; in urban areas, 6.6 percent of boys and 2.5 percent of girls are economically active. The systematic decline in employment of children over the three survey periods can be attributed to three factors: raising compulsory education from five to eight years; recent education campaigns, particularly targeting girls; and reduced demand for child labor due to growing public awareness of the need to combat the problem.

The figures for children engaged in domestic chores, on the other hand, show an increase over time. While 28.3 percent of children in 1999 were found to be engaged in domestic chores, the figure for 2006 is 43.1 percent. When considered by sex, 41.8 percent of girls and 15.1 percent of boys in 1999, and 53.1 percent of girls and 33.1 percent of boys in 2006, reported that they do domestic chores. Overall, in 2006 girls comprised 61 percent of those engaged in domestic chores. Due to measurement discrepancies, the data for domestic chores across time are dubious. While the first two surveys had a single question on whether the child is engaged in domestic chores or not, in 2006 children were asked to respond separately to an itemized list of chores.

It is important to note that the nature of girls' work in Turkey is significantly different from the work done by boys. Girls' work can be characterized as less visible and lower in value. However, unlike in countries where girls are engaged in hazardous occupations, sold or contracted as bonded labor, and trafficked as prostitutes, in Turkey girls are less likely to be subjected to these forms of abuse and exploitation due to the observance of female seclusion. Yet, these very cultural taboos that act to protect girls may also act to disguise such practices. Recent media reports have drawn attention to worrying incidents of exploitation, particularly of little girls, in child pornography. Such reports and anecdotal evidence need to be examined with diligence. The available data fall short of capturing such vulnerabilities. Another area of concern is the situation of children who work on the street, and the seasonal migrant workers. Analysts have referred to these children as the "new actors of new poverty" (Hoşgör and Çameli 2007). These children are denied their basic citizenship rights and encounter extreme forms of abuse and exploitation that go unregulated.

Interplay Between Schooling and Work Outputs of Children

In contrast to the decrease in child employment, school attendance has shown an increase from 75.4 percent in 1994 to 79.1 percent in 1999 to 84.7 percent in 2006. The data for boys is 80.2, 83.4, and 87.5 percent, and for girls 70.3, 74.9, and 81.9 percent. Similar trends are observed in urban and rural areas. In urban areas during the three consecutive survey periods, school attendance increased from 81.4 to 82.5 to 87.2 percent, as compared to 68.6 to 74.6 to 79.9 percent in rural areas. While girls' school attendance shows an overall improvement, the gender gap in schooling continues to favor boys in both localities.

Although education is often seen as a panacea for child labor, the data are not so clear. While the increase in a child's schooling is accompanied by a decrease in formal employment, this is not the case with domestic chores. The percentage of children attending school who are employed dropped from 3.1 percent in 1999 to 2.2 percent in 2006, but over the same period the percentage of schoolchildren who engaged in domestic chores increased from 27.1 percent to 42.8 percent. Girls, at older ages, are more likely to combine domestic chores and schooling. For example, 75.2 percent of the fifteen- to seventeen-year-old girls going to school reported that they are engaged in domestic chores, compared to 46.7 percent of girls six to fourteen years old. In contrast, older boys tend toward economic activity that entails long hours. However, when economic and domestic activities are considered together, the gender gap in hours of work becomes negligible (Ertürk and Dayıoğlu 2004).

Research globally shows that children's schooling is positively affected by both parental education and household income. It is also well documented that household-based establishments increase the likelihood of the employment of children, particularly of girls. In such cases, children generally combine household work and schooling. While the gender gap at all levels of schooling in Turkey is closing, prioritization of the education of boys continues to be a commonly upheld value for families.

Increasing compulsory education to eight years in 1997, and the recent campaigns to promote education, have contributed to higher enrollment rates, especially for girls, and have helped to keep them in school longer. However, due to gender biases, girls are at risk of being taken out of school at age fourteen, which marks the end of compulsory education, and at age sixteen, which roughly corresponds to the age of marriage.[1]

In Turkey, there are two types of nonformal education: community education centers and vocational and apprenticeship training centers. The former offers training in conventional women's activities with little or no economic returns, and the latter are coed schools organized around typical male occupations. These pose further bottlenecks in girls' education, as neither type of school offers educational opportunities that can contribute toward enhancing girls' job opportunities in the labor market.

Conclusion

Since 1992, many programs have been launched to remove children from hazardous work, improve work conditions where children continue to work, and use education as a vehicle to keep children out of employment and in school (Ertürk and Dayıoğlu 2004). These contributed to reducing children's formal employment levels. Similar outcomes in children's engagement in domestic chores, however, have not been realized. This is mainly due to the fact that the domestic sphere is less receptive to policy interventions, while at the same time, more responsive to the privatization and the increased flexibility of work that has accompanied global restructuring.

Although figures for domestic chores show a distinct increase for both sexes, there is need for qualitative research to ascertain the actual impact these tasks have on school performance. In this regard, integrating a gender perspective into the analysis at all levels can help in better capturing the link between market and household sectors, and the shifts that take place between the two, as well as the gender-blind aspects of time allocation for human capital development and the production of goods and services. Such analyses at the macro, meso, and micro levels can reveal how the positions of boys and girls are differentially constructed and how their experience of work and schooling are determined (Ertürk and Dayıoğlu 2004). Gender analysis complements sex-disaggregated data, which is essential for formulating intervention strategies and developing indicators for monitoring change.

There is also a need to monitor more closely the impact of the adoption of ILO Convention 182 on worst forms of child labor to ensure that its implementation does not render other forms of child labor invisible or deemed acceptable.

While increasing access to education must be an integral component of a program to combat child labor, in the final analysis its eradication depends on three conditions: first, a systematic improvement of macroeconomic variables that affect household resources, and just distribution of goods and services; second, women's empowerment and social, economic, political, and legal equality; and third, a strong commitment to human rights at the societal and governmental levels that recognizes every child's right to live a childhood free of all forms of violence, abuse, and exploitation and that nourishes children's potential and capabilities, thus increasing their adulthood options.

Note

1. The 2002 reformed Civil Code increased the age of marriage from fifteen to seventeen. In remote areas, girls may be married off at younger ages by religious marriage. This not only prevents them from going to school but also leaves them without any legal protection, as their marriage is not officially recognized.

References and Further Reading

Dayıoğlu, M. "The Impact of Household Income on Child Labour in Urban Turkey." *Journal of Development Studies* 42:6 (2006): 953.

Ertürk, Y., and M. Dayıoğlu. *Gender, Education and Child Labour in Turkey*. Geneva: ILO, 2004.

Hoşgör, Ayşe Gündüz, and Tuba Çameli. Untitled needs assessment report (in Turkish) submitted to UNICEF on campaign for population registry. Ankara, 2007.

Legal Protection of Working Children in Turkey

Esin Konanç, PhD, Professor, Eastern Mediterranean University (TRNC); and
Onur Dinç, PhD, Assistant Professor, Girne American University (TRNC)

In developing countries, most working children are deprived of education and healthy development. They often work in environments hazardous to their physical, psychological, social, and moral development. In Turkey, as in other countries, there are many laws, including the Labor Act, General Health Act, Vocational Training Act, Primary Education Act, and Act of Contracts, which include provisions to protect working children from exploitation and to prevent child employment in early age. In addition, the Turkish Parliament has ratified key international accords pertaining to child labor, including the UN Convention on the Rights of the Child and ILO Conventions 138 (on minimum age for employment) and 182 (on elimination of worst forms of child labor). According to the Turkish Constitution, once ratified, they became part of national legislation. Therefore, after ratification, the Turkish Parliament revised national child labor legislation in order to eliminate contradictions between international instruments and the relevant Turkish acts.

However, there remain significant gaps in Turkey's legislative scheme. For instance, the Labor Act does not cover all types of workplaces where substantial numbers of children work. Workplaces not covered under the law include those employing fewer than fifty employees in agricultural and forestry work; any construction work related to agriculture that falls within the family economy; handicraft work performed at home by members of the family or close relatives; domestic services; apprenticeships; and small handicrafts and tradesmen establishments employing three or fewer employees. Likewise, the Vocational Training Act covers only those workplaces specified by the Vocational Training Board where "candidate apprentices" and "apprentices" are trained.

The many children working in workplaces not covered by law, including children working on the streets, do not benefit from legal protection. Hence, these children are more susceptible to all kinds of abuse (Zeytinoiglu 2001). Lack of adequate provisions aimed to protect working children cause children to work at early ages, often in environments hazardous to their health, and contribute to frequent dropping out from school (*Report on Child Labor in Turkey* 1999).

Minimum Age for Admission to Employment

The Labor Act, Vocational Training Act, General Health Act, and Primary Education Act all regulate minimum ages for admission to employment in some work. The Labor Act prohibits employment of children under fifteen and provides that children under eighteen are not allowed to work in any type of work that is determined by regulation as hazardous to their health, development, or education (more specifically, children under eighteen cannot be employed in underwater or underground work such as mines, cable laying, sewerage, and tunnel construction). Further, children who have not completed the age of sixteen cannot be employed in arduous or dangerous work. A regulation of the Ministry of Labor and Social Security specifies the categories of work deemed to be arduous or dangerous in which only children older than age sixteen may be employed.

However, children fourteen or fifteen years of age who have completed primary education may be employed in light work that is not likely to be harmful to their physical, intellectual, and moral development and does not interfere with school attendance.

In contrast, the Vocational Training Act allows employment of children who are fourteen years of age or older and have completed compulsory education as "candidate apprentices," to prepare them for vocational education during work. This act also allows employment of children who have reached the age of fourteen as "apprentices," provided that they finish primary education (eight years of compulsory schooling) and that their health is appropriate for the conditions of work in which they will be trained. Both "candidate apprentices" and "apprentices" are considered by this law to be "students," and they are not included in the number of workers of the workplace.

Another law that provides minimum age for admission to work is the General Health Act. According to this act, children under eighteen cannot be employed in cafés, nightclubs, casinos, and public baths.

Regulation of Hours of Work

Like minimum age, hours and times of day minors may work are regulated by several acts. According to the Labor Act, children who have completed their compulsory education and do not continue with further education may not work more than seven hours a day and thirty-five hours a week. For children above age fifteen, working hours may increase to eight hours a day and forty hours a week. For children who attend school, working hours may not exceed two hours a day and ten hours a week during school days. On days when there is no school and during summer vacation, working hours for these children are the same as those for children who do not attend school.

There are also limits on the time of day when children can work. The Labor Act prohibits employment of children under age eighteen in industrial work on night shifts (from 8 P.M. to 6 A.M.). But this restriction on night work covers only children in industrial work. This gap is partly compensated by the General Health Act, which prohibits employment of children between the ages of twelve and sixteen at night in all sectors. Therefore, children between the ages of sixteen and eighteen who work in nonindustrial sectors are not protected by prohibition of work at night.

Working Conditions of Children

International instruments and national laws require that workplace conditions not be harmful to workers' health and regulate the responsibilities of employers concerning workplace health and safety. As children's health is more vulnerable, conditions of work should be more carefully set. Taking this into consideration, the Turkish Labor Act contains detailed provisions on workplace safety and health. According to the act, employers should take all necessary measures and maintain all essential means to ensure occupational health and safety in their establishments. In addition, employers must inspect measures taken for occupational health and work safety in the establishment; inform the employees about occupational risks and measures that must be taken against these risks; inform employees of their legal rights and their obligation to observe all the measures taken to protect occupational health and safety; provide employees the necessary training on occupational health and safety; and provide health examination of all employees who work at night. If defects exist in the installations and arrangements of the workplace, in the working methods and conditions, or in the machinery and equipment that endanger the lives of employees, operations shall be stopped partly or completely, or the establishment itself shall be closed until the danger is eliminated.

These measures reduce the exploitation of working children, but it is also necessary to determine the suitability of the job to the child's health and development. To this effect, the Labor Act contains a detailed article related to health examinations of working children. According to this article, before being admitted to any employment, children from age fourteen to age eighteen should be examined by an authorized medical practitioner or health service. After this examination, the medical practitioner or health service, taking into consideration the nature and conditions of the work, reports whether the child is physically fit for the job to be performed. Until they have completed the age of eighteen, employees shall be subject to medical examinations at least every six months.

Rights of Working Children

The Vocational Training Act regulates wages to be paid to working children. The terms of payment should be determined in the apprenticeship contract and the wage to be paid cannot be less than 30 percent of the minimum wage. As the actual minimum wage determined by the Minimum Wage Fixing Board is 419 Turkish liras (US$322), the minimum wage for candidate apprentices and apprentices is 127 Liras (US$96). This amount is so low that many Turkish children forego apprenticeships, preferring to work on the street (Konanç 1992).

The Vocational Training Act also provides that candidate apprentices and apprentices are to receive one month of annual leave with pay. In addition, all provisions of the Labor Act related to the paid weekly rest day, national and public holidays, and annual leave with pay apply also to the children who work in workplaces covered by this act.

If children fall victim to work-related accidents or occupational illness, the responsibility lies with the employer. The provisions of Social Insurance Act (SIA) related to work accidents and occupational illness apply to children who work in workplaces covered by the Labor Act and the Vocational Training Act.

Work and Education

The UN Convention on the Rights of the Child requires protection from work that is likely to interfere with education and requires appropriate measures to encourage regular school attendance and reduction of school dropout rates. Further, ILO Convention 182 requires state parties to ensure access to free basic education for all children removed from worst forms of child labor. Turkish laws contain articles to meet these requirements. According to the Turkish Constitution and the Primary Education Act, basic education is compulsory for all Turkish citizens and is free in state schools. The Labor Act, the Primary Education Act, and the Vocational Training Act all prohibit employment of children of compulsory education age (six to fourteen years old) and those who have not completed compulsory education. However, the Primary Education Act provides some exceptions to this rule, permitting children to work in domestic chores or help with the harvest, and the Labor Act allows employment of schoolchildren if their working hours do not exceed two hours a day and ten hours a week. However, parents who fail to enroll their children in school and employers who employ children who have not completed primary education and are still of compulsory schooling age are both subject to punishment.

The Vocational Training Act regulates the academic and vocational education of children. According to this act, candidate apprentices and apprentices are to be trained eight hours a week in workplaces or in vocational training high schools specified by the Vocational Training Board. The curriculum of this training should contain theoretical and practical aspects, which should be mutually complementary. In addition to this, there must be at least one master vocational trainer in workplaces where candidate apprentices and apprentices are employed.

Worst Forms of Child Labor

The Turkish legal system provides many dispositions aimed at preventing what are considered to be worst forms of child labor.

Protection of Children from Practices Similar to Slavery

Until recent years in Turkey, there was a practice that could be considered similar to slavery. It was common for female children to be given to rich families to do domestic work. These children were not adopted. The wealthy families were not acting as foster parents. They did not take in these children for protection, upbringing, or education. They took them in to do housework. This practice disappeared after court rulings that compensation should be paid by these wealthy families to the child domestic workers. Another practice that has been made illegal is the hiring out of children, generally by parents or relatives, for seasonal or other temporary jobs.

Protection of Children from Prostitution and Pornography

A new Turkish Criminal Code that came into force in 2004 provides detailed provisions on child prostitution and child pornography. It stipulates that anyone who uses, procures, or offers a child for prostitution should be punished by imprisonment and a judicial fine. If this crime is committed by close relatives, custodians, or persons who have power over the child (such as the employer), the punishment is increased by half. Child pornography is also prohibited by the same code. The person who uses a child in the production of pornographic material is subject to imprisonment and a fine. In spite of these provisions, child prostitution and pornography have shown an increase in recent years due to overall economic deterioration, increasing inequality in income distribution, easy access to Internet facilities, and abuse of children in families resulting in their forsaking the home (Polat 2006).

Protection of Children from Use in Illicit Activities and in Production and Trafficking of Drugs

According to the Turkish Criminal Code, any person who instigates or uses children to commit crime of any kind, or in the production and trafficking of drugs, should be punished by imprisonment and a judicial fine.

Protection of Children from Work Hazardous to Health and Safety

As noted above, the Labor Act prohibits employment of children who have not completed the age of sixteen in arduous and dangerous work. The Arduous and Dangerous Work Regulation enumerates these types of jobs and also depicts the types of jobs in which children above age sixteen can work, provided that they have the requisite health certificate showing their fitness for such a job.

Conclusion

In the Turkish Legal system, provisions protecting working children are scattered in various laws. The existing laws do not cover all working children. Furthermore, existing provisions are not always effectively implemented due to rapid urbanization, inequality in income distribution, high unemployment rate, and unfavorable educational conditions and facilities, along with lack of coordination among the institutions responsible for working children and insufficient inspection of workplaces. The Turkish laws concerning child labor still need improvement.

References and Further Reading

Hodgkin, R., and P. Newell. Implementation Handbook for the Convention on the Rights of Child. Geneva: UNICEF, 2002.

Konanç, E. Korunmaya muhtaç kent cocukları [Urban children needing protection]. Istanbul: Frederic Ebert Foundation,1992.

Konanç, E. "Child Protection System in Turkey." In *Child Protection Systems in Europe*. London: NSPCC Publisher, 1992.

Konanç, E. "Child Abuse in Turkish Legal System," In *Proceedings of the International Society for Prevention of Child Abuse and Neglect*. Toronto: ISPCAN, 1994.

Polat, O. "Çocukların cinsel sömürüsü" [Sexual abuse of children]. 2006. http://www.sokakcocuklari.net.

Report on Child Labor in Turkey. Ankara: State Institute of Statistics of the Republic of Turkey, 1999.

Zeytinoğlu, Sezen. Çalışan çocukların istismarı ve ihmali [Abuse and neglect of working children]. İzmir: Ege Üniversitesi Yayını, no. 113, 2001.

Primary Education and Child Labor in Turkey

Cennet Engin-Demir, Assistant Professor, Department of Educational Sciences, Middle East Technical University

Education—particularly high-quality, universal, free, and compulsory primary education—is recognized as one of the key tools for combating child labor in developing countries. This essay focuses on the role of primary education in the elimination of child labor in Turkey.

Primary Education in Turkey: Structure and Goals

The Turkish formal education system includes preschool and primary, secondary, and higher education institutions. Prior to 1997, formal education was built on a 5-3-3 system comprised of five years of compulsory elementary schooling, three years of junior high school, and three years of senior high school. With the Education Act of 1997, the Turkish government extended primary education from five to eight years, combining elementary and junior high school into a unified program of compulsory basic education for all children between six and fourteen years of age.

As mandated by Article 42 of the Constitution of the Republic of Turkey, "Primary education is compulsory for all citizens regardless of sex and free of charge at public schools." The purpose of primary education is to ensure that every Turkish child acquires the basic knowledge, skills, and behaviors necessary to become a good citizen; is raised in line with national concepts of morality; and is prepared for life and for the next education level in line with his or her interests and skills (MONE 1995). In the 2005–2006 academic year, the gross enrollment rate in primary education was estimated to be 95.59 percent (98.83 percent for males and 92.24 percent for females) (State Institute of Statistics 2006).

Primary Education and Child Labor

The extension of compulsory schooling from five to eight years in 1997 has two implications of direct relevance to child labor in Turkey: First, children will remain in school for an additional three years, thus potentially delaying their participation in the labor market; and second, children will be channeled into vocational technical education at a later age, increasing their future prospects and enhancing their ability to make informed life choices (Ertürk and Dayıoğlu 2004).

To expand and improve existing educational facilities to meet its responsibility of providing formal education to all children between the ages of six and fourteen, the Ministry of Education (MONE) developed the Basic Education Project in 1996. Implemented with World Bank support, the Basic Education Project also clearly states that child labor is a key issue on the Turkish education agenda.

In collaboration with governmental, nongovernmental, and international organizations, the MONE has developed a number of projects to promote the full implementation of the new education act and address the issue of child labor in the educational system. Working closely with ILO-IPEC, the MONE implemented an action program aimed at increasing the attendance, retention, and performance rates of working children in the primary education system. The project targeted children combining work and school as well as children attending school but at risk of entering work. It combined direct support to children with institutional capacity building to ensure that the MONE General Directorate of Primary Education has a sound understanding of the problem of child labor and education. Within this framework, a core group of thirty trainers was formed to act as a catalyst for change within the education system, and a project-coordination unit was set up within MONE to monitor the project. Low-achieving students and potential dropouts were identified through in-depth research. They were provided with educational and psychological support to optimize their school achievement and prevent them from dropping out. Families were provided with educational support, counseling, and information on accessing social welfare and vocational training services. School personnel and inspectors were also trained on child labor as part of awareness-raising activities.

The MONE has incorporated its regional primary boarding schools (RPBSs) and provincial primary pension schools (PPPSs) into the Basic Education Project as well as efforts to eliminate worst forms of child labor, especially street work and seasonal agricultural work. RPBSs and PPPSs are particularly effective in combating child labor because children enrolled in these schools reside there for the course of the academic year, effectively preventing them from working during the school term. The regulated nature of RPBSs and PPPSs provides an ideal environment to prevent dropping out, and the cost of school expenses, uniforms, books, materials, food, and lodging are incurred by the state, thus reducing the burden on poor families and providing them with strong incentives to enroll their children.

In cooperation with Turkey's three largest trade unions, MONE developed a project aimed at removing children between six and fourteen years of age from work on the streets and placing them, as well as children considered at risk of dropping out, in either an RPBS or PPPS. The targeted children were closely monitored in terms of attendance, adaptation, and academic achievement. The success of this program prompted the MONE to commit to establishing additional boarding schools in urban areas.

Another ongoing pilot project developed in cooperation with the ILO enrolls children employed as seasonal labor in harvesting cotton in either an RPBS or a nearby primary school and provides them with free transportation, school uniforms, and school supplies. A similar project aimed at increasing access to basic and vocational education for children employed in seasonal agricultural work was recently initiated in six provinces by MONE, in cooperation with the Turkish Ministry of Labor and with financing from the U.S. Department of Labor.

Two other projects designed to address specific shortcomings of the Turkish education system have had particular impact on the situation of working children. The first project aimed to partially eliminate the financial burden that may inhibit the school attendance of children from poor families by providing them with school supplies and ensuring that free textbooks are distributed in all public primary schools. The second project, the Child-Friendly School project developed jointly by the MONE and UNICEF, was based on the assumption that low-quality schooling contributes to higher dropout rates and thus more children engaging in economic activity. The project aimed to improve the quality of instruction by revising the primary school curriculum to increase its relevance to the daily lives of children. An additional nationwide project conducted jointly by MONE and UNICEF in 2005 secured the enrollment of 62,000 girls in primary school.

Conclusion

Between 1994 and 1999, the percent of children six to fourteen years of age engaged in economic activity in Turkey dropped dramatically from 8.5 percent to 4.2 percent (State Institute of Statistics 2002). This improvement can be attributed to the extension of compulsory education, an increase in the legal working age, and stricter implementation of the Education Act. The negative relationship found between schooling and work (Dayıoğlu 2005) and the experiences gained through MONE Action Programs to combat child labor suggest that children need to be kept in school longer. This can be achieved by providing incentives to families, increasing education for girls, and raising the quality of schooling and the relevance of the curriculum to children's lives and future employment opportunities. Additional learning-support programs can also be provided to increase the performance rates of primary school children, thereby preventing them from dropping out of school, and to reintegrate dropouts into the education system.

References and Further Reading

Aksit, Bahattin, Nuray Karancı, and Ayse Gunduz-Hosgor. *Turkey, Working Children in Three Metropolitan Cities: A Rapid Assessment.* Geneva: ILO-IPEC, 2002.

Dayıoğlu, Meltem. "Patterns of Change in Child Labor and Schooling in Turkey: The Impact of Compulsory Schooling." *Oxford Development Studies* 33:2 (2005): 231–46.

Ertürk, Yakin, and Meltem Dayıoğlu. *Gender, Education and Child Labor in Turkey.* Geneva: ILO, 2002.

ILO-IPEC. *Education as an Intervention Strategy to Eliminate and Prevent Child Labor: Consolidated Good Practices of the IPEC.* Geneva: ILO-IPEC, 2006.

Ministry of Education (MONE). *Ilkögretim Programı* [The primary education curriculum]. Ankara: Milli Egitim Basimevi, 1995.

State Institute of Statistics. *Child Labor, 1999.* Ankara: State Institute of Statistics, 2002.

State Institute of Statistics. "Schooling Ratio by Level of Education." 2006. http://www.tuik.gov.tr/PreIstatistikTablo.do?istab_id=102.

Sexual Exploitation of the Girl Child: Juvenile Commercial Sex Workers in Istanbul

Esin Kuntay, Professor Dr., Department of Sociology, Mimar Sinan Fine Arts University; and **Guliz Erginsoy,** Professor Dr., Department of Sociology, Mimar Sinan Fine Arts University

A girl child commercial sex worker is someone under the age of eighteen who is sexually exploited and used for sexual activities in exchange for money and goods. The concept of "sex work" is used in a general sense; it can be perceived as a job done in return for payment in cash or in kind. The term does not indicate the degree of exploitation, but whereas it involves both a commercial element and violence, it is considered a worst form of child labor under ILO Convention 182 and is often described as a contemporary form of slavery (Szanton-Blanc 1994).

Turkey is a state party to the UN Conventions on the Rights of the Child. The CRC obliges state parties to undertake every caution to protect children from all forms of sexual exploitation and abuse, including prostitution and involvement in pornography. As a first step in combatting child commercial sex work, a sociological study, sponsored by UNICEF, was undertaken (Kuntay and Erginsoy 1998, 2005). The basic aim of the study was to find out the mechanisms underlying the institution of juvenile sex work in Istanbul and eventually to play a guiding role in starting a shelter home to function as a refuge center for sexually abused girls. The primary objectives of the research were to highlight life stories of girl child sex workers, to determine causes of the problem, to reveal the risks of being involved in sex work, and to raise awareness among decision makers and the public about the sexual exploitation of children in order to gain cooperation of public authorities and NGOs in starting a first-aid center for girl child sex workers.

Research on a Sensitive Topic: Methodology

Conducting research on such a sensitive topic as child commercial sexual exploitation is not an easy matter. The target population was girls below the age of eighteen involved in commercial sex work who were apprehended by police vice squads and taken to the moral bureau of the Istanbul Police Headquarters. Survey participants consisted of thirty girls between the ages of fourteen and eighteen. Participants in research on sensitive topics may have great anxiety about being stigmatized, which may cause them to refrain from participation (Raymond 1994). Taking this into consideration, interviewers used extra time to explain the purpose of the survey and gain the confidence of participants, assuring them that the interviewers were neither members of the police force nor members of the media. Anonymity was guaranteed. The research method required adaptation of qualitative and grounded theoretical approaches. In-depth interviews of between three and one-half to five hours were conducted, and with the permission of the participants, the narratives were audio-recorded. Participants were given the mobile phone numbers of the interviewers to enable contact in case of need. This made possible further contact and enabled interviewers to fill in the gaps in previous narrations.

An in-depth interview questionnaire was constructed covering closed- and open-ended questions. Four hundred twenty-six questions explored the following fields: existing household conditions, demographic characteristics, origin and migration, history of absconding, types of abuse, sex experience, opinion about sex work, religion and belief, crime history, other jobs, initiation into prostitution, abortion, child marriage, unmarried motherhood, prostitution of other female family members, mediators (pimps), intoxicating substance abuse, smoking, places and locations of prostitution, clients, exploitation in the production of pornography, human trafficking, health status, relations with the police and media, leisure time, daily routine, future aspirations, and opinions about a refuge center. At the end of the interviews, descriptions of the physical appearence and any injuries or damage on the body were documented.

Causes of Girl Child Sex Work

The most remarkable aspect of the research findings was the similarity of the life stories and the conditions confronting girl child sex workers (Kuntay and Erginsoy 1998, 2005). The social dynamics emphasized in the research included family life and abuse during childhood, the bond between the concepts of honor and virginity in a patriarchal household along with the associated gender dimensions and hierarchies, and social attitutes toward prostitution.

Girl child sex work is a complex phenomenon, and multiple factors lie in its origin. At the foundation for initiation into commercial sex work lies the unguided presence of the child on the streets. Negative conditions force the child out of the family. Broken family structure, disintegration of the relations between its members, domestic violence (emotional, physical, or sexual), intoxicating substance abuse, and pressure imposed by social and cultural norms binding together the concept of honor and virginity are among the main factors forcing the girl child away from the family circle. The study found that 76.70 percent of the girl participants are from broken families. Only 23.30 percent live in nuclear families with their biological parents (Kuntay and Erginsoy 1998, 2005). Even where girls live with their families, this does not necessarily indicate a peaceful atmosphere. Alcohol and drug addiction (especially of the father), severe conflict between parents, disputes, and events of violence indicated that family bonds have disintegrated to a great extent.

When the child is forced to step out of the family circle and is left unguided and uncontrolled, she becomes easy prey. Unqualified for a job, she can be tricked, lured, or forced into sex work for survival purposes. The narratives revealed that the youngest person initiated into sex work was eleven. The child's vulnerability exposes her to the exploitation of crime organizations trafficking and marketing women, children, and drugs. The basic types of commercial sex work include working in discos, bars, and dance halls as a belly dancer or singer, in massage parlors or being sent to a client's house on call, and hitchhiking, which is the most dangerous of all as hitchhikers are subjected to great risks.

Consequences of Commercial Sex Work During Childhood

Commercial sex work has effects on the girl child's identity, which manifest as low self-esteem, absence of self-confidence, loss of liveliness, and self-hatred. Its impacts on the health condition of the exploited child include a deeply rooted trauma, headaches and pains in the joints, heavy coughing, insomnia, fungus in the feet and vagina, sexually transmitted infections, intoxicating substance addiction, and self-mutilation.

Chemical substance abuse is a way of dealing with the tensions and stress of working in the illegal market. Among the drugs most frequently consumed are amphetamines purchased from the underground market. Addiction severely damages the girl child's health status. Another health risk among girl child sex workers is the prevalent behavior of self mutilation. Clinical studies associate childhood trauma with self-injuring behavior (Miller 1994), findings replicated in this study. It is common for girls, often under the influence of tranquilizers, to administer self-inflicted wounds, mostly on the arms and wrists, by means of various tools of incision such as broken glass, razor blades, pocketknives, or tin cans. Self-mutilating behavior is performed for self-revenge at a moment of intense nervousness, and under the influence of feelings of shame, guilt, self-blame, and estrangement. There is a common belief among the girl child sex workers that self-injury will have a soothing effect and help release their tensions (Kuntay and Erginsoy 1998, 2005).

Prevention and Rehabilitation

The first step to abolish and prevent sex work, or to rehabilitate sexually abused children, is to accept existance of the phenomenon of child sexual exploitation. Joint effort and coordination by statutory and nongovernmental bodies is essential to counter the sexual abuse of minors. In Turkey, only women twenty-one years old and above may work legally as sex workers in specified zones. Mandatory licencing and periodic health checkups are compulsory. In spite of the fact that the sex work of a girl child is illegal, considering her vulnerability and unwillingness to be engaged in sexual activities, she is entitled to be treated not as an offender, but as a victim in need of protection. Although many factors may render a child vulnerable to people with bad intentions, where there is demand, a child can be forced to supply sexual service. The perpetrator is the exploiter and offender; thus, he is the one who should be held legally responsible. Within the framework of the New Turkish Criminal Code that came into force in 2005, parents, mediators, guardians, and caretakers responsible for offering a child into prostitution face more severe penalties. It is of vital importance that the client be judged among perpetrators and regarded as the enabler of child prostitution. In fact, the Optional Protocol on the Sale of Children, Child Prostitution and Child Pornography of the UN CRC, which was ratified by Turkey in 2002, requires that state parties criminalize and prosecute perpetrators. The convention also requests that children who are the victims of child prostitution be treated humanely, that their rights be respected, and that their rehabilitation and reintegration into society be considered.

This research is one of the unique examples in its field in documenting the sensitive problems of girl child sex workers, activating authorities to draw up social policy, and providing a solid rationale for the realization of the establishment of a refuge house. The first refuge center established in Istanbul during 2001 serves as a first-aid center, meeting the immediate needs of the girl child sex worker. A second center was established recently as a long-term institution providing support for the girls with the aim of helping them find alternative means of livelihood and achieving their integration into society. Both institutions are run by the State Ministry Responsible for Women's and Children's Issues and function under the auspices of the provincial government.

References and Further Reading

Kuntay, Esin, and Guliz Erginsoy. *Teenage Female Sex Work in Istanbul Metropolitan Area.* Istanbul: UNICEF, 1998.

Kuntay, Esin, and Guliz Erginsoy. *Istanbul'da on sekiz yaşından küçük ticari 'seks işçisi' kız cocuklar.* Istanbul: Bağlam Yayınları, 2005.

Miller, Dusty. *Women Who Hurt Themselves: A Book of Hope and Understanding.* New York: Basic Books, 1994.

Raymond, M. Lee. *Doing Research on Sensitive Topics.* London: Sage Publications, 1995.

Szanton-Blanc, Cristina. *Urban Children in Distress: Global Predicaments and Innovative Strategies.* Langhorne, PA: Gorden and Breach Science Publishers; Florence: UNICEF International Child Development Center, 1994.

United Arab Emirates

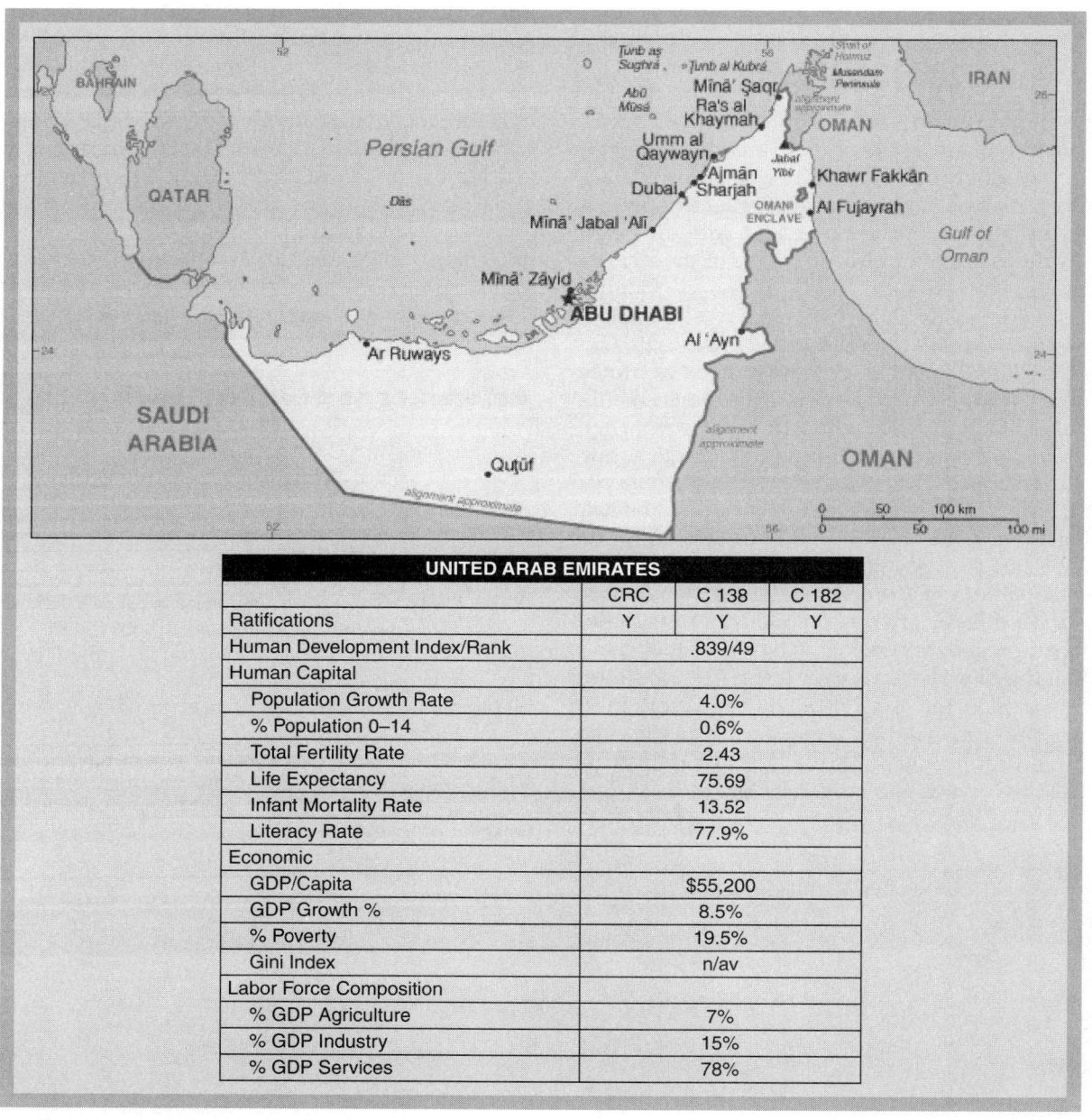

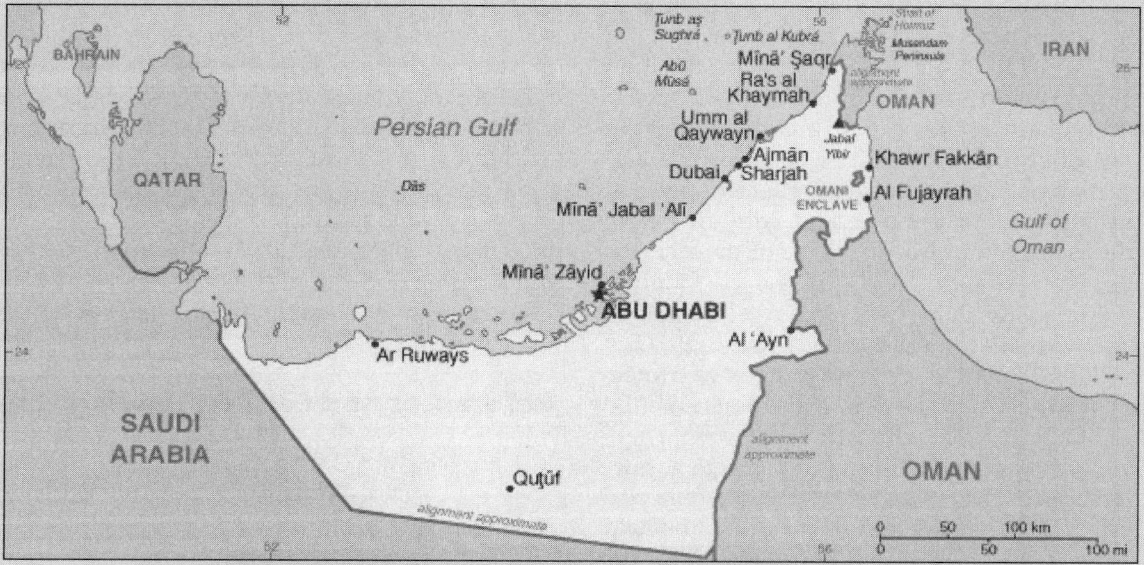

UNITED ARAB EMIRATES			
	CRC	C 138	C 182
Ratifications	Y	Y	Y
Human Development Index/Rank	.839/49		
Human Capital			
Population Growth Rate	4.0%		
% Population 0–14	0.6%		
Total Fertility Rate	2.43		
Life Expectancy	75.69		
Infant Mortality Rate	13.52		
Literacy Rate	77.9%		
Economic			
GDP/Capita	$55,200		
GDP Growth %	8.5%		
% Poverty	19.5%		
Gini Index	n/av		
Labor Force Composition			
% GDP Agriculture	7%		
% GDP Industry	15%		
% GDP Services	78%		

Children Trafficked to Gulf States for Use as Camel Jockeys

Catherine Turner, Child Labour Programme Coordinator, Anti-Slavery International

Camels hold a uniquely honored place in Gulf societies. Camels' strength, endurance, and ability to withstand the harsh desert conditions of the Arabian Peninsula have been central to these traditionally nomadic communities' economic, social, and cultural well-being for hundreds of years. As a result, camel racing has been a much-enjoyed sport over the centuries. Originally it was not a regulated sport, but just a chance for local communities to celebrate together and for riders to display their skills. The oil boom of the 1970s brought huge wealth to the region along with rapid socioeconomic changes, and camel racing was not untouched by this process. Races became more competitive and the stakes rose. Like top racehorses, the fastest camels could change hands for huge sums of money. Camels were bred smaller to increase their chances of winning, and so camel owners sought smaller, and younger, jockeys.

Since the 1990s, Anti-Slavery International has been aware of children being trafficked from countries such as Bangladesh, Pakistan, and Sudan for use as camel jockeys in the United Arab Emirates (UAE) and other Gulf states, such as Qatar and Kuwait. The children can be as young as four or five years old when they are taken from their homes, and can stay in the Gulf for up to ten years before being sent home again. Until very recently, children raced quite openly at the main camel-racing tracks such as Nad al Sheba in Dubai, and exercised camels nearby. Major races in the UAE were broadcast on national TV and attended by hundreds of people, including the country's elite. Tourists visiting the tracks as part of their holiday may well have seen the children riding camels dressed in their racing silks, and not thought twice about it, unaware that the children were trafficked and living in harsh conditions in camel camps.

Life as a Child Camel Jockey

Testimonies of boys who have returned from the Gulf, gathered by Anti-Slavery International's partner NGOs between 2003 and 2006, reveal much about life in the camel camps. These statements have not been published. Camel racing is extremely dangerous; a fall can result in serious injury or death. When not racing, the children spend every day, from early until late, cleaning, feeding, and exercising the camels. They usually sleep in the camps near the camels. Most children are separated from their parents. As they are taken far from home, where the people, language, and culture are largely unknown to them, they are completely dependent on their employers. Some children are abused, beaten for making mistakes or deprived of food to keep them light so the camels can run faster. There have also been cases of children subjected to electric shocks to keep them small (Asghar, Farhat, and Niaz 2006). Very few have even an afternoon off during the week to rest; none go to school or have any form of education during their time in the camps.

Children have been abducted to supply this trade; others are lured by traffickers with promises of a better life away from parents, who are struggling to support their families; some are even taken by their own parents—parents who have perhaps themselves found work in the Gulf, but were encouraged to bring any young children of camel-racing age along; sometimes this can be an explicit part of the parents' employment deal. Child camel jockeys come from just a few areas known to be especially

Only owners get money or prizes for winning; the children get nothing. *(© CDP / Anti-Slavery International)*

vulnerable to this form of trafficking. They tend to be particularly poor areas, such as Cox's Bazaar in Bangladesh. Others have established links with Gulf states, notably Rahim Yar Khan in the Southern Punjab of Pakistan, which is a favorite hunting area for rich sheikhs, or have a camel-riding tradition themselves, for example, among the Rashaida tribe of Kassala in Eastern Sudan.

Children commonly "earn" in the region of 500 dirhams (US$135) per month, but are unlikely to see anything more than a few dirhams' tip as a reward if they should win a race. Their income usually goes to the trafficker. Even if the trafficker has made a deal with the parents to send money home, in many cases the parents are deceived and receive hardly anything at all. When they return home, many boys have lasting physical disabilities from falls or ill-treatment, or suffer from various forms of mental or psychological trauma. These, combined with their lack of schooling, greatly inhibit their chances later in life.

International Protest

Human rights groups, including Anti-Slavery International, began campaigning on behalf of the child camel jockeys in the late 1990s. During the early stages, the Gulf states refused to acknowledge that a problem even existed. For example, the UAE appeared before the International Labor Conference in June 2000 and referred to "isolated events . . . [which] were unsubstantiated as they were based on hearsay" (International Labor Conference 2000, 83). So, Anti-Slavery International decided to invigorate its approach to the issue in 2002. Together with NGO partners in Bangladesh, Pakistan, and Sudan, Anti-Slavery International gathered more evidence, mobilized media attention, particularly in the United States and Europe, and continued to raise the issue in international forums, such as the UN and the ILO. By 2003, governments in the Gulf states acknowledged that they had a limited problem, and the UAE even agreed to an official fact-finding mission by representatives of the ILO to help resolve the issue (International Labor Conference 2003, 13).

Finally, in 2004, Anti-Slavery International raised the matter directly with the U.S. government's Office for Monitoring of Trafficking in Persons in the State Department. Anti-Slavery International compiled extensive photographic evidence gathered in January 2004 depicting children in races and exercising camels openly in Dubai (Anti-Slavery International 2004). In June 2005 the department's *Trafficking in Persons Report* reclassified Kuwait, Qatar, Saudi Arabia, and the UAE from tier 2 to tier 3, which carries the threat of U.S. trade sanctions (U.S. Department of State 2005).

The Response of Governments in the Gulf States

The campaign culminated in the introduction of new legislation and rules across the Gulf in the early summer of 2005. The UAE, which had been the most high-profile case, prohibited the use of children under the age of eighteen years as camel jockeys in July 2005. By law, offenders face up to three years in prison and fines of at least 50,000 dirhams (US$13,600). This law was preceded in May 2005 by a similar law banning use of those under eighteen in Qatar, and measures adopted in Kuwait through ministerial decree in June 2005 outlawing the use of minors under eighteen in camel racing. All three countries also announced the trial and use of robots for public racing events in the forthcoming racing season, which typically runs from October to March each year.

The UAE took this a step further. In May 2005, the government signed a memorandum of understanding with UNICEF to rescue and repatriate an estimated 3,000 child camel jockeys, 93 percent of whom were under ten years of age. The UAE also agreed to provide $2.7 million to help the "return and re-integration" of child camel jockeys to their home countries (UNICEF 2006a). In December 2006, the UAE government announced the extension of its agreement with UNICEF until May 2009 and the allocation of a further US$9 million to include compensation and rehabilitation services for former camel jockeys who returned home, but were not part of the original repatriation and rehabilitation program (UNICEF 2006b).

A Problem Solved?

The new laws and the UAE-UNICEF repatriation agreement were undoubtedly landmark events, and demonstrate that the negative publicity generated had a considerable effect on the UAE and other Gulf states. The initial repatriation program officially ended in the spring of 2006 and was pronounced a complete success. This sense was echoed by various bodies, as noted in the UN's *World Report on Violence Against Children,* which cited the UAE's latest law and repatriation program as an example of the successful enforcement of child labor standards (UN 2006). However, information gathered systematically by Anti-Slavery International's partners over 2006 and 2007 indicates that although the problem is likely to have diminished, it would be premature at this stage to claim that the trafficking and use of children for camel racing has been eradicated altogether.

As of March 2006, when the repatriations were officially completed, UNICEF reported that 1,071 boys in total had been formally repatriated to their countries of origin. This figure was subsequently revised upward to 1,075 (UNICEF 2006a). The UNICEF figures broke down as follows: 573 from Pakistan, 316 from Bangladesh, 157 from Sudan, 18 from Mauritania, and 7 from Eritrea. Even allowing for the many children who returned by other means, and so were not included in the official figures, this total is far below the UAE's own estimate of 3,000 child camel jockeys in the country. The number of children formally repatriated should have been much higher to justify confidence that most children are being sent back and not simply hidden or retrafficked across borders. Moreover, those children who did not return through official channels were, at the time, not eligible for the UNICEF-UAE-sponsored rehabilitation and compensation packages. Despite new laws being introduced in other Gulf states, formal repatriation programs along the lines of the UAE-UNICEF scheme have not been introduced in neighboring countries. To be fully effective, and to prevent children from simply being trafficked across borders, there needs to be a regionwide response in practice as well as law.

There are other issues of concern. Anti-Slavery International's partner NGO in Bangladesh, the Bangladesh National Women Lawyers' Association, received nineteen boys into its care, who returned to Bangladesh in September 2006. Its NGO partner in Pakistan, the Democratic Commission for Human Development, interviewed seven boys in October 2006, who had returned between July and September 2006. In both cases, these boys returned after the repatriation program had officially ended. The Democratic Commission for Human Development's interviews also revealed that there were some, although not racing, who were still working in stables and tending camels in the UAE. For example, they informed Anti-Slavery International about a high-profile case of a father who found out that his then five-year-old son was working as a camel jockey in the UAE. He had been seeking his son's return since 2003, but when the repatriation program lapsed, the child was still missing. The Bangladesh National Women Lawyers' Association is also aware of 431 additional children who are missing, among whom only twelve have been traced and rescued, though it cannot be known with certainty how many of these were working as camel jockeys.

Finally, Anti-Slavery International has received two separate reliable eyewitness accounts of groups of child camel jockeys seen exercising camels in the UAE, once in January 2006, and then, more worryingly, in June 2006, after the repatriation program had officially ended.

The UAE's Track Record

Despite the regular reports from 1997 to 2005 documenting the use of very young children as camel jockeys, and despite protests by the UAE government that it was a limited problem, the use of young children as camel jockeys has actually been illegal in the UAE for decades. For example, employment of any child under the age of fifteen had been prohibited since 1980 under the Federal Labor Code; the UAE's independent Camel Jockey Association had a rule since the early 1990s that using children younger than fourteen or lighter than ninety-nine pounds (45 kilograms) as camel jockeys was prohibited; and in July 2002, Sheikh Hamdan bin Zayed Al Nahyan, chairman of the Emirates Camel Racing Association and minister for foreign affairs, promulgated an order prohibiting children under fifteen or weighing less than ninety-nine pounds (45 kilograms) from being employed in camel racing.

It is to be hoped that the most recent measures will be effectively implemented and enforced this time. The UAE government reported to the ILO Committee of Experts in 2006 that "it envisages training the police and other relevant bodies on child rights as laid down in international conventions" (ILO 2006, 227). The government should ensure that this training take place as a matter of priority. This is especially pertinent in light of a documentary broadcast by the Australian Broadcasting Corporation on February 25, 2003, which showed police escorting very young camel jockeys to a bus. The police were more concerned with stopping the film crew than apprehending anyone involved in the races, despite laws and regulations in force at the time prohibiting the use of children under fifteen years of age as camel jockeys.

Strengthening Action in Countries of Origin

Many positive steps have been taken by governments, UNICEF, and NGOs in the countries to which these boys returned to prevent further child trafficking. For example, in 2004, the Bangladeshi government created a national Trafficking Monitoring Cell, and more recently a dedicated camel-jockey task force, which opened up new avenues for consultation and for putting pressure on the government to act. The Sudanese Ministry of the Interior put in place new airport checks, which have proved an effective measure in preventing new trafficking cases. Youths require a certificate to demonstrate that they are eighteen years old to qualify for an exit visa. Airport authorities now have a right to stop anyone holding these certificates if the age is in doubt. The Pakistani government created the Child Protection and Welfare Bureau as the lead agency to handle repatriations to Pakistan. They also established three rehabilitation centers in Multan, Alipur, and Rahim Yar Khan, where most of the boys originated.

There have been some activities at the community level too. For example, the Bangladesh National Women Lawyers' Association began setting up community care committees in 2005. Made up of key figures in the local communities, they decide on child trafficking prevention and protection measures appropriate to each community. They were tasked with tracking and reporting on local incidences of trafficking or missing children, liaising with their local administrations, and general awareness raising in the community. To date, seventy community care committees have been established in nineteen districts.

However, despite laudable initiatives such as these, little has fundamentally changed in the communities of origin. The repatriation program was announced in May 2005, and the first boys were returned home just a month later, allowing the receiving countries very little time to prepare for their arrival. Furthermore, the compensation arrangements that were promised for those who participated in the formal repatriation scheme have not been forthcoming in all cases.

Throughout 2005 and 2006, Anti-Slavery International's NGO partners conducted a total of 106 interviews with repatriated boys soon after they had returned home, with 101 follow-up interviews some four to ten months later. The results indicated the vast majority of children were pleased to be back home with their families and did not want to return to camel racing. This is despite the fact that their families' financial insecurity, which had been a key factor in their being taken away in the first place, had not improved in the meantime. All had missed out on their education while away, and on return either did not go back to school, being by then of legal working age, or were only beginning to catch up on their schooling. So none had promising long-term prospects. Not all of them were confident that their families would never send them back to the Gulf.

Much more needs to be done in these communities to combat general poverty and to challenge prevailing attitudes among some community members who still hold the view that sending children away is a viable way of contributing to the family's survival. This is essential to prevent other children from being trafficked to camel camps in the Gulf or into other forms of exploitation. More could be done to enlist the support of development agencies operating in these regions. Gulf states could also use some of the tremendous wealth at their disposal to help revitalize these areas and thereby help to redress some of the damage caused.

Conclusion

There is reason to believe that the recruitment of children for this form of trafficking has been greatly reduced. Many boys have returned home, and their testimonies indicate that, while their families still face the same struggles to survive that pushed the children away in the first place, and these children now have to face additional problems on their return, the vast majority of officially and unofficially repatriated boys are pleased to be back home. There is also far greater awareness of the problem at local, national, and international levels than had been the case before 2003. This should form a good basis for improving the situation in the future of former camel jockeys, children at risk of this form of trafficking, and, hopefully, other boys who may still be racing camels or working in camel camps in the Gulf.

A number of concerns have been noted, however, that indicate that it is too early to say that the practice of trafficking children to the Gulf for use as camel jockeys has stopped altogether. There are also numerous challenges still to face to ensure that the children who have returned are provided with a smoother transition back into life with their families and their communities of origin, and that no more children are trafficked into this or other forms of exploitation. International pressure must continue to be put on the Gulf states to be sure that the latest round of laws and measures are effectively implemented this time, and that the states live up to their responsibilities to protect all children who find themselves in their jurisdiction, regardless of their country of origin.

References and Further Reading

Anti-Slavery International. "Child Camel Jockeys in the UAE." Photograph gallery, 2004. http://www.antislavery.org/homepage/resources/cameljockeysgallery/gallery.htm.

Anti-Slavery International. "Trafficking and Forced Labour of Children in the Gulf Region." Submission to the United Nations Commission on Human Rights, June 2005. http://www.antislavery.org/archive/submission/submission2005-cameljockeys.htm.

Asghar, Syed Mehmood, Sabir Farhat, and Shereen Niaz. *Camel Jockeys of Rahimyar Khan.* Stockholm: Save the Children Sweden, 2006.

International Labor Conference. "Report of the International Labour Conference Committee on the Application of Standards (Part Two) Observations and Information Concerning Particular Countries." ILO, Geneva, June 2000. http://www.ilo.org/public/english/standards/relm/ilc/ilc89/pdf/pr-19–2.pdf.

International Labor Conference. "Report of the International Labour Conference Committee on the Application of Standards (Part Two) Observations and Information Concerning Particular Countries." ILO, Geneva, June 2003. http://www.ilo.org/public/english/standards/relm/ilc/ilc91/pdf/pr-24p2.pdf.

International Labour Organization, "Report of the Committee of Experts on the Application of Conventions and Recommendations (Report III [Part 1A]) General Report and Observations Concerning Particular Countries." ILO, Geneva, March 2006. http://www.ilo.org/public/english/standards/relm/ilc/ilc95/pdf/rep-iii-1a.pdf.

Krane, J. "Child Jockeys Eliminated from Camel Racing in UAE, Say Government, UNICEF." Associated Press, December 17, 2006.

UNICEF. *Starting Over: Children Return Home from Camel Racing.* Dubai: UNICEF Gulf Area Office, 2006a.

UNICEF. "UAE Commits $9 Million to Help Former Camel Jockeys." Press release. UNICEF, New York, December 18, 2006b. http://www.unicef.org/media/media_37798.html.

United Nations. *World Report on Violence Against Children.* Geneva: UN, 2006.

U.S. Department of State. *2005 Trafficking in Persons Report.* Washington, DC: U.S. Department of State, 2005. http://www.state.gov/documents/organization/47255.pdf.

Yemen

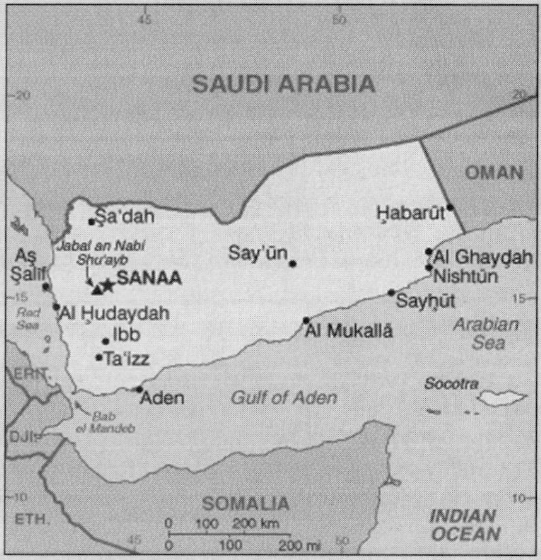

YEMEN			
	CRC	C 138	C 182
Ratifications	Y	Y	Y
Human Development Index/Rank	0.492/150		
Human Capital			
Population Growth Rate	3.46		
% Population 0–14	46.3%		
Total Fertility Rate	6.49		
Life Expectancy	62.52		
Infant Mortality Rate	57.88		
Literacy Rate	50.2%		
Economic			
GDP/Capita	$900		
GDP Growth %	3.2%		
% Poverty	45.2%		
Gini Index	33.4		

CHILD ACTIVITY BREAKDOWN, BY SEX AND RESIDENCE

RESIDENCE	Percentage of children in the relevant age-group[a]							
	Economic activity only		School only		Combining school and economic activity		Neither in school nor in economic activity	
	Male	Female	Male	Female	Male	Female	Male	Female
Urban	1.1	1.5	73.8	78.6	0.6	2.5	24.5	17.5
Rural	13.9	6.1	27.3	57.7	2.4	7.4	56.4	28.7
Total	10.8	5.0	38.4	62.6	2.0	6.3	48.8	26.1

Source: Yemen, National Poverty Phenomenon Survey, 1999 (see UCW Project Web site, http://www.ucw-project.org, country statistics).

Notes: [a]Children age 5 to 14.

Child Labor in Yemen

Lorenzo Guarcello, Gabriella Breglia, and **Scott Lyon,** Researchers,
Understanding Children's Work (UCW) Project

This summary paper provides an overview of the child labor phenomenon in its various dimensions—its extent, its nature, and its causes and consequences—in Yemen. It is drawn from a detailed interagency report on child labor developed by the UCW Project in 2003.

Extent of Children's Work

An estimated 700,000 children age six to fourteen years, 12 percent of this age-group, are engaged in work (all figures refer to the 1999 reference year), where work is defined as any form of economic activity. Actual numbers of child workers are likely higher, as this estimate does not include children in so-called unconditional worst forms of child labor or children performing noneconomic activities.

A large portion (37 percent) of the remaining children in the six-to-fourteen age-group are reported neither involved in work nor attending school. This group requires further investigation, but it stands to reason that many are in reality also performing functions that contribute in some way to household welfare, that is, either work or household chores. The children from this group who are indeed idle can be even more disadvantaged than their working counterparts, benefiting neither from schooling nor from the learning-by-doing that some forms of work offer.

Girls are more likely than boys to be involved in work and are much less likely than boys to attend school. Girls are also almost twice as likely as boys to be reported as inactive, some in reality performing unreported work or household chores. Work prevalence is highest among older children, but the absolute number of very young Yemeni children engaged in work is nonetheless significant. Some 120,000 children six to eight years of age are economically active. These very young working children are the most vulnerable to workplace abuses, and most at risk of work-related ill health or injury. Children's work is overwhelmingly rural: The prevalence of children involved in work in rural areas is more than five times that of children in urban areas; rural child workers account for 94 percent of total child workers.

Characteristics of Children's Work

The overwhelming majority of Yemeni working children are found in the agriculture sector. Ninety-two percent of total working children ten to fourteen years of age, or, in absolute terms, 440,000 of the total 475,000 working children in this age-group, are involved in farm work. This, however, is primarily a reflection of work by children in rural areas, where 95 percent of working children are involved in agriculture. Children working in urban areas are more evenly spread among agriculture (42 percent), commerce (35 percent), and other sectors (17 percent). The work performed by children varies somewhat by sex. Working girls are more likely to be involved in agriculture, but much less likely to be involved in commerce, than their male counterparts, with the differences particularly pronounced in urban areas.

Most—87 percent—of working children work for their families and not for wages. Family work is especially important in the agriculture sector, where it accounts for more than nine out of ten working children. It is less important in commerce, the only other sector employing significant numbers of children. In the commerce sector, about half of children work for their families, with the remainder divided roughly equally between wage earners and the self-employed. Again, some differences exist by sex. Boys are slightly less likely than girls to work for their families, and more likely than girls to be wage earners or self-employed. The proportion of children, both boys and girls, working as apprentices is marginal.

Working children in Yemen put in very long hours. Working children put in an average of almost thirty-eight and a half hours of work per week, that is, almost as much as full-time adult workers in the industrial world. Thirteen- and fourteen-year-old working children put in the longest hours (about forty and a half hours per week), but even six- and seven-year-old working children put in a thirty-four-hour workweek on average. Working children who also attend school work an average of thirty-five hours per week, fewer than their out-of-school counterparts, but still undoubtedly too many to be able to effectively perform in school. There is only a slight variation in hours worked by sector.

Available evidence suggests that children can face hazardous conditions in many of the sectors in which they work. Work-related hazards encountered by children include the following:

Agriculture: chemicals from the use of pesticides, lengthy exposure to extreme cold and heat, handling heavy agricultural equipment, and carrying heavy loads

Construction: chemical toxins, handling paints

Car repair workshops: respiratory problems from inhaling fumes, physical injuries, burns, electrocution

Stonecutting and quarry work: lifting and crushing heavy rocks

Machine welding: lead poisoning, extreme heat

Restaurants: sexual abuse

Consequences of Children's Work

School attendance is very low among working children, limiting their prospects for securing more gainful employment in the future. Only about one-third (36 percent) of ten- to fourteen-year-old working children attend school, compared to 58 percent of their nonworking counterparts. Attendance is especially low for working girls—just 14 percent of them go to school. The ability to attend school appears to depend somewhat on the sector of work. Less than 25 percent of children in private household work attend school, for example, compared to more than 60 percent of children in commerce. For working children that do manage to attend school also, work reduces the time (and presumably the energy) they have to study. The relationship between work and school performance has not been investigated in the Yemeni context, but evidence from elsewhere suggests that school performance declines appreciably with additional hours worked.

Working children do not report significantly more health problems than children attending school or inactive children. Around 12.5 percent of full-time working children reportedly experienced health problems compared to 11.2 percent of full-time students and 12.3 percent of children involved in no activities. Reported ill health was slightly higher for children combining school and work, at 13.7 percent. But these findings are likely the product of measurement problems encountered when attempting to look at the work-health relationship.

Determinants of Children's Work and Schooling

As most children (excluding those who live on their own) exercise little control over their time allocations, determining why children work requires investigating why parents choose to engage their children in work rather than sending them to school or leaving them idle at home. A multivariate analysis making use of household survey data points to a number of factors influencing parents' decisions concerning children's time use.

Gender

Parents' decisions concerning whether to involve their children in school or work appear strongly influenced by gender in Yemen. Holding constant household income, parents' education, and other relevant factors, girls are more likely to work full-time (by 5 percentage points) and much less likely to study full-time (25 percentage points), than boys. Girls are also much more likely than boys to be reported as idle (23 percentage points), a category that can reflect unreported work or involvement in household chores.

Age

The analysis shows that the probability of a child working increases with age. The available information is insufficient to provide a precise idea of the relative importance of the two most probable reasons for this, that is, the rising opportunity cost of schooling with the age of the child, or the lack of access to schooling at the postprimary level.

School Availability

The presence of a basic cycle school in a village increases the likelihood of school enrollment by almost 4 percentage points. The increase in enrollment, however, comes primarily from the group of children previously inactive; the presence of a basic cycle school appears to have only a relatively small effect on parents' decision to involve their children in work. The effect of a Koranic school in a village also increases enrollment by about 4 percentage points, while the effect of a secondary school in a village is slightly larger, increasing enrollment by almost 5 percentage points. The presence of a secondary school reduces, in almost equal measure, the proportion of children working and the proportion that are idle, suggesting that these schools attract children who otherwise would have left the school system to either start work or remain idle.

Water Availability

Access to a public water network has a dramatic effect on schooling, increasing the likelihood of enrollment by 9 percentage points for all children, and by more than 11 percentage points for girls. This is not surprising in view of studies showing that children, and particularly girls, from villages without access to a public water network must spend a considerable amount of time each day fetching water, limiting the time and energy they have for attending school. Most of the increase in enrollment comes from the group of children neither working nor attending school, rather than from the group of working children, suggesting that many reportedly idle children in fact perform household chores such as water collection. Access to a public water network makes it almost 7 percentage points less likely that a child is idle, but only about 3 percentage points less likely that a child is working. Reducing time spent on wood collection also makes it more likely that a child attends school.

Poverty

Work prevalence falls and school attendance rises progressively as household income goes up, but the income effect is relatively weak. For example, an increase in income of 10 percent has only negligible effects on the probability that a child goes to work. This indicates that relatively small changes in income are not likely to produce a significant effect on the decision to work or attend school. Interventions aimed at reducing work by children and increasing school attendance based on income transfers are not likely to produce substantial changes, unless the size of the transfer is large.

Parents' Educational Status

Work prevalence is highest among children whose parents have no education, and falls progressively as parents' education level rises. School attendance and parents' education, however, are positively related. These relationships are likely at least partially the product of a disguised income effect; that is, parents with higher levels of education are also likely to have higher levels of income, and therefore less need to involve their children in work. However, the relationship between parents' education and children's work prevalence holds even when controlling for income, although the effect is relatively small. Holding income constant, children of educated fathers are 5 percentage points more likely to study full-time and 0.5 percentage points less likely to work, than children of illiterate fathers. Children of educated mothers are 2 percentage points more likely to attend school, and 1 percentage point less likely to work, than children of illiterate mothers. Another possible explanation is that more educated parents might have a better knowledge of the returns to education, or be in a position to help their children exploit the earning potential acquired through education.

Household Structure

Children from households with more adults, and therefore more available potential earners, are less likely to work and more likely to attend school. Less than 1 percent of children from households with one to three members are involved in work, compared to 44 percent of those from households with seven to nine members. Children from households with more young children, and therefore more dependent mouths to feed, in contrast, are more likely to work, although the effect is relatively small. Controlling for other factors, each additional child age zero to five years increases the probability that a child works by 0.5 percentage points, and reduces the probability that a child goes to school by about 1 percentage point.

References and Further Reading

UCW Project. *Understanding Children's Work in Yemen.* Rome: Understanding Children's Work Project, University of Rome "Tor Vegata," 2003. http://www.ucw-project.org/.

Guarcello, Lorenzo, and Scott Lyon. "Children's Work and Water Access in Yemen." Understanding Children's Work Project Working Paper Series, Rome, April 2003.

Part 7
Central and South Asia

SECTION 1.
CENTRAL ASIA

Kazakhstan

KAZAKHSTAN			
	CRC	C 138	C 182
Ratifications	Y	Y	Y
Human Development Index/Rank	0.774/79		
Human Capital			
Population Growth Rate	.35%		
% Population 0–14	22.5%		
Total Fertility Rate	1.89		
Life Expectancy	67.22		
Infant Mortality Rate	27.41		
Literacy Rate	98.4%		
Economic			
GDP/Capita	$9,100		
GDP Growth %	8.5%		
% Poverty	19%		
Gini Index	31.5		
Labor Force Composition			
% Agriculture	20%		
% Industry	30%		
% Services	50%		

CHILD ACTIVITY BREAKDOWN, BY SEX AND RESIDENCE

RESIDENCE	Percentage of children in the relevant age-group[a]									
	Economic activity only		School only		Combining school and economic activity		Neither in school nor in economic activity		Child labor[b]	
	Male	Female	Male	Female	Male	Female	Male	Female	Male	Female
Urban	0.1	0.3	87.7	88.2	3.5	2.5	8.8	9.0	n/av	n/av
Rural	0	0	85.7	88.9	4.0	2.3	10.2	8.8	n/av	n/av
Total	0.1	0.2	86.7	88.6	3.7	2.4	9.5	8.9	2.4	2.1

Source: Kazakhstan, Multiple Indicator Cluster Survey 3, 2006 (see UCW-Project Web site, http://www.ucw-project.org, country statistics).

Notes: [a]Children age 5 to 14. [b]Estimate includes (a) children under age 12 engaged in economic activities, (b) children age 12–14 engaged in excessive economic activities (more than 14 hours per week), and (c) children under age 15 engaged in excessive household chores (at least 28 hours per week). Estimate does not account for children engaged in hazardous work or other unconditional "worst forms" of child labor.

Child Labor in Kazakhstan

Ryan Womack, Business and Economics Librarian, Rutgers University

Many people had not heard of Kazakhstan until the appearance of the film *Borat,* whose eponymous lead depicted his purported homeland as an economically backward haven of bizarre customs, which have little basis in the reality of Kazakh life. In fact, Kazakhstan is the most economically advanced of the Central Asian republics that declared independence from the Soviet Union in 1991. Because Kazakhstan is a magnet for growth in a relatively undeveloped region, some of its child labor problems result from its prosperity. To meet rising demand, migrant workers, including children, are trafficked into the country for labor and sexual exploitation.

Kazakhstan's large landmass is composed mostly of steppe and desert, and it is one of the least densely populated countries in the world, with roughly 15 million people inhabiting an area comparable to that of India. While the ethnic Kazakh population descends from nomadic Turkic and Mongol tribes of the Golden Horde, its northern region has long-standing ties to Russia and received a large influx of ethnic Russian farmers during Khrushchev's Virgin Lands campaign. The Caspian Sea region, including the cities of Atyrau and Aktau, is the center of the oil industry. Separated from the north by a large band of steppe, the cities of southern Kazakhstan, such as Almaty and Shymkent, have closer ties to the other Central Asian countries of Uzbekistan, Kyrgyzstan, Turkmenistan, and, to a lesser extent, Tajikistan. Before the breakup of the Soviet Union, the ethnic Russian population was larger than the Kazakh population, but the emigration of Russians since 1991 and the higher birth rates of Kazakhs have made Kazakhs the majority once again.

During the Soviet period, Kazakhstan developed several major industrial centers that were closely and rigidly linked to the centrally planned economy. Many of these industries had difficulties during the transition period and were privatized in a corrupt and inefficient manner in the 1990s. The economy contracted throughout the 1990s during this difficult adjustment. Another legacy of the Soviet period is severe environmental pollution in the Aral and Semey regions, which has harmed children's health.

Oil Fuels Rapid Growth

More recently, the tapping of the Caspian's large oil reserves, with concomitant Western investment, has led to explosive growth. The real GDP has grown by 8 to 10 percent annually since 2002 and is projected to continue that rate of growth (Asian Development Bank 2007). Gross national income per capita rose from $1,270 in 2000 to $2,940 in 2005.

Oil wealth has made Kazakhstan the economic star of the region, generating high-wage jobs in oil, finance, and associated sectors. The money flowing into the economy has created an associated demand for construction and domestic labor that attracts migrant workers, particularly from neighboring Uzbekistan and Kyrgyzstan. Not all segments of Kazakh society have kept pace, however. Agriculture remains backward, and the broken families, poverty, and alcohol abuse generated by the traumas of transition have consequences for child labor. Although poverty is decreasing, roughly 20 percent of the population still earns less than the subsistence minimum.

The education, health, and social services of the Soviet period crumbled in the 1990s and still have not been fully restored. For example, Kazakhstan is one of only eleven countries in which child mortality for children under age five has increased since 1990 (UNICEF 2004). Political power and its spoils have been tightly controlled by President Nursultan Nazarbayev since independence. It remains to be seen whether the country's oil wealth will be used to improve the basic social infrastructure and to provide benefits to the lower rungs of society (Pomfret 2006).

Child Labor in Agriculture and Services

There are few reliable statistics on the prevalence of child labor in Kazakhstan. It appears to be a persistent presence in many sectors. Large numbers of children work in the fields on cotton and tobacco farms in the south of the country, although not on the same scale as in neighboring Uzbekistan. One recent study used surveys and interviews with the children themselves to document the prevalence of child labor and the conditions confronting working children in the agricultural sectors of tobacco and cotton (ILO-IPEC 2006). The use of child labor has a direct impact on child development: In the rural south, school attendance and test results are much lower than the national average. A particularly intractable problem is the prevalence of parents who use their own children's labor on family farms, which authorities have little ability or authority to change.

In the cities, children's work is decreasing, but they have been found loading freight, making deliveries, washing cars, working at gas stations, and begging (U.S. Department of Labor 2006). Small family shops often run on child labor. The parent-proprietors often view school as a waste of time for their own children, who instead spend their days learning the family trade. When small businesses hire nonfamily children, it is usually to keep costs down. About 30 percent of these child workers earn 400–500 tenge per day, amounting to less than US$4. Others, without documents or relatives to protect them, are cheated of their wages entirely (Aladina 2007).

Migrant Workers and Trafficking

There is a large flow of migrant workers into Kazakhstan from the poorer neighboring countries of Uzbekistan, Kyrgyzstan, and Tajikistan, attracted by relatively plentiful work opportunities. The government began to register migrant workers in 2006 and to expel unregistered workers in 2007. These measures have been incompletely implemented, and many businesses still hire illegal workers (Dosybieva 2007). Although the exact number of children in these sectors is unknown, migrants work in the same agricultural and service jobs where Kazakh child workers are present. While many workers come voluntarily, others are recruited through deceptive or coercive means. Exploitation via passport confiscation, beatings, and debt bondage is common. There have been reports of parents selling teenage children at the border for between 1,500 and 2,000 tenge, approximately US$10 (Kelly 2005).

Sex trafficking is another significant problem in Kazakhstan, and the government's ineffectual efforts to control trafficking have led to its placement on the State Department's Tier 2 Watch List since 2002. Although antitrafficking legislation is in place, only one trafficker was prosecuted in 2006 (U.S. Department of State 2007a). Teenage girls are a particular target for trafficking from Kazakhstan to other countries (U.S. Department of Labor 2006). Destination countries include Israel, Korea, Pakistan, Russia, Turkey, the United Arab Emirates, and Western Europe. Both girls and boys are trafficked into Kazakhstan from Turkmenistan and Kyrgyzstan for commercial sexual exploitation (U.S. Department of State 2007a). Although the number of children trafficked in this manner is unknown, Kazakh police records show that one in three street prostitutes is underage. There is a significant trade in boys that remains largely underground (Babakulov et al. 2004).

The disadvantaged in society are particularly vulnerable to such exploitation, including the poor, residents of rural areas, and orphans. Family breakdown due to the stresses of the transition period has left many children without adequate support from their parents. There is also a large orphan population in Kazakhstan. Many are legally adopted: 755 Kazakh orphans were adopted by U.S. citizens in 2005 (U.S. Department of Homeland Security 2006). Others are vulnerable to recruiters' deceptive tactics, which lure them into bondage (Baituova 2005). Parents also sell their children directly for labor and sexual exploitation (ECPAT International 2004). Organized crime, in combination with corrupt police and government officials, plays a large role in both labor and sex trafficking in Kazakhstan.

Legislation and Remedies

Kazakhstan has signed and ratified many of the major international conventions on child labor, including the UN Convention on the Rights of the Child and ILO Conventions 138 and 182. Although Kazakhstan has not ratified the ILO's Protocol to Prevent, Suppress and Punish Trafficking in Persons, it has passed its own version of antitrafficking legislation. In addition, Kazakhstan has signed and ratified the following international conventions: the Optional Protocol to the Convention on the Rights of the Child on the Sale of Children, Child Prostitution and Child Pornography; the Optional Protocol to the Convention on the Rights of the Child in Armed Conflict; ILO Convention 29 on Forced Labor; and ILO Convention 105 on Abolition of Forced Labor. Officially, the minimum age for employment is sixteen years, although children between fourteen and sixteen years of age are permitted to work in nonhazardous jobs, with parental permission.

Lack of coordination among government bodies, insufficient resources for enforcement, and entrenched corruption are all factors working against implementation of Kazakhstan's current laws against trafficking and child labor. However, in the first nine months of 2006, the Ministry of Labor reported ninety-four criminal cases involving child labor (U.S. Department of State 2007b). ILO-IPEC operates the Central Asian portion of its program out of an office in Almaty. This three-year program, part of which is an active public awareness and education campaign, began activities in Kazakhstan in 2005. Clearly Kazakhstan has begun to take steps to reform child labor practices.

Kazakhstan's continuing economic growth will lift wages and household income and should reduce both the supply and demand for child labor. The country's desire to move into the ranks of more-developed nations will bring political pressure to bear on the enforcement of labor and trafficking legislation. However, the prospects for reform of government corruption are dimmer in the current authoritarian climate under Nazarbayev. The government must also rebuild a stronger social safety net to protect those segments of society that are not participating in the boom. Another concern is the generally declining status of women in Central Asia. As women get less education and fewer high-level employment opportunities, social progress for future generations of children is harmed. The volume of external migration and trafficking into Kazakhstan will also depend on the relative poverty or progress of neighboring states such as Uzbekistan and Kyrgyzstan. Currently, Kazakhstan acquiesces in allowing trafficking and labor abuses, but it has the opportunity and ability to choose the path of progress against child labor and exploitation in the years ahead.

References and Further Reading

Aladina, Tatyana. "Украденное детство" [Stolen childhood]. *Express-K*, April 20, 2007. http://www.express-k.kz/show_article.php?art_id=8502.

Asian Development Bank. "Kazakhstan." *Asian Development Outlook 2007: Growth amid Change.* Manila: Asian Development Bank, 2007, 113–16. http://www.adb.org/Documents/Books/ADO/2007/KAZ.pdf.

Babakulov, Ulughbek, Natalia Domagalskaya, Elena Lyanskaya, Alla Pyatibratova, Roman Sadanov, Asel Sagynbaeva, Leila Saralaeva, and Nargis Zokirova. "Lost Children of Central Asia." Institute of War and Peace Reporting, January 19, 2004. http://iwpr.net/?p=rca&s=f&o=177649&apc_state=henirca2004.

Baituova, Gaziza. "Kazakh Women Sold as Sex Slaves." Institute for War and Peace Reporting, June 2, 2005. http://www.iwpr.net/?s=f&o=245442&p=wpr&1=EN&apc_state=hena-sex%20slaves_2______publish_date_1_10_compact.

Dosybieva, Olga. "Kazakstan: Migrant Workers Face Deportation." Institute for War and Peace Reporting, January 23, 2007. http://www.iwpr.net/?p=rca&s=f&o=328709&apc_state=henirca200701.

ECPAT International. *Analysis of Commercial Sexual Exploitation of Children (CSEC) and Institutions Combating CSEC in Kazakhstan.* Bangkok: ECPAT, 2004. http://www.ecpat.net/eng/Ecpat_inter/projects/monitoring/kazakhstan/PDF/2004_ECPAT_Kazakh_research_ENG.pdf.

ILO-IPEC. "Child Labour in Tobacco and Cotton Growing in Kazakhstan: Rapid Assessment Report." Almaty: ILO-IPEC, 2006.

Kelly, Liz. *Fertile Fields: Trafficking in Persons in Central Asia.* Vienna: International Organization for Migration, 2005. http://www.iom.int/jahia/webdav/site/myjahiasite/shared/shared/mainsite/published_docs/books/fertile_fields.pdf.

Pomfret, Richard. *The Central Asian Economies Since Independence.* Princeton, NJ: Princeton University Press, 2006.

UNICEF. *Progress for Children: A Child Survival Report Card.* New York: UNICEF, 2004. http://www.unicef.org/publications/files/29652L01Eng.pdf.

U.S. Department of Homeland Security. *Yearbook of Immigration Statistics 2005.* Washington, DC: U.S. Department of Homeland Security, 2006. http://www.dhs.gov/xlibrary/assets/statistics/yearbook/2005/OIS_2005_Yearbook.pdf.

U.S. Department of Labor. "Kazakhstan: Incidence and Nature of Child Labor." *The Department of Labor's 2005 Findings on the Worst Forms of Child Labor.* Washington, DC: U.S. Department of Labor, Bureau of International Labor Affairs, 2006, 265–68. http://www.dol.gov/ilab/media/reports/iclp/tda2005/tda2005.pdf.

U.S. Department of State. *2007 Trafficking in Persons Report.* Washington, DC: U.S. Department of State, 2007a. http://www.state.gov/documents/organization/82902.pdf.

———. "Kazakhstan." *2006 Country Reports on Human Rights Practices.* Washington, DC: U.S. Department of State, Bureau of Democracy, Human Rights, and Labor, March 6, 2007b. http://www.state.gov/g/drl/rls/hrrpt/2006/78820.htm.

Uzbekistan

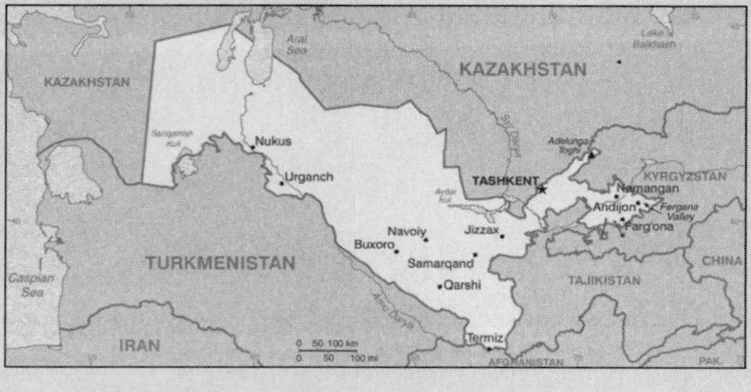

UZBEKISTAN			
	CRC	C 138	C 182
Ratifications	Y	N	N
Human Development Index/Rank	0.696/113		
Human Capital			
Population Growth Rate	1.73%		
% Population 0–14	32.4%		
Total Fertility Rate	2.88		
Life Expectancy	64.98		
Infant Mortality Rate	68.89		
Literacy Rate	99.3%		
Economic			
GDP/Capita	$2,000		
GDP Growth %	6.8%		
% Poverty	33%		
Gini Index	26.8		
Labor Force Composition			
% Agriculture	44%		
% Industry	20%		
% Services	36%		

CHILD ACTIVITY BREAKDOWN, BY SEX AND RESIDENCE

RESIDENCE	Percentage of children in the relevant age-group[a]									
	Economic activity only		School only		Combining school and economic activity		Neither in school nor in economic activity		Child labor[b]	
	Male	Female	Male	Female	Male	Female	Male	Female	Male	Female
Urban	0.1	0.2	82.2	82.0	5.9	5.6	11.9	12.3	n/av	n/av
Rural	0.1	0.2	79.1	79.0	3.7	3.3	17.1	17.5	n/av	n/av
Total	0.1	0.2	80.0	79.9	4.3	3.9	15.6	16.0	2.0	1.8

Source: Uzbekistan, Multiple Indicator Cluster Survey 3, 2006 (see UCW Project Web site, http://www.ucw-project.org, country statistics).

Notes: [a]Children age 5 to 14. [b]Estimate includes (a) children under age 12 engaged in economic activities, (b) children age 12–14 engaged in excessive economic activities (more than 14 hours per week), and (c) children under age 15 engaged in excessive household chores (at least 28 hours per week). Estimate does not account for children engaged in hazardous work or other unconditional "worst forms" of child labor.

SECTION 2. SOUTH ASIA

Rural Child Labor in South Asia

Afke De Groot, Research Associate,
International Research on Working Children (IREWOC) Foundation

Although child labor force participation is highest in Sub-Saharan Africa, Asia contains the largest number of child workers. In South Asia, the ILO estimates that, of 300 million children in the age-group of five- to fourteen-year-olds, 21.6 million are working (ILO 2004). According to UNICEF, 15 percent of boys and 14 percent of girls in the age-group of five- to fourteen-year-olds are involved in child labor activities (UNICEF 2005). Since the 1980s, child labor figures have shown a secular decline, but the reduction has been uneven (Ray 2004; Chaudhri, Nyland, and O'Rourke 2004). In some areas, in the wake of armed conflicts, the vulnerability of children, especially girls, has increased, and in those areas (northern Sri Lanka, Nepal, northeastern India, and northern Pakistan), trafficking and child labor may have increased (ILO 2004). In India the decrease in labor market participation rates of children age ten to fourteen years was from 29 percent in 1950 to 11 percent in 2000. Within the country, however, wide differences exist: The province of Kerala has the lowest incidence of rural child labor (0.7 percent); Andhra Pradesh (25 percent), Rajasthan (16 percent), and Karnataka (15 percent) have much higher incidences of rural child labor. Throughout South Asia child labor remains a serious issue, especially in Nepal and Bangladesh, with a labor market participation rate in 1999 of 29 percent in Bangladesh and 43 percent in Nepal for children age ten to fourteen (World Bank 2001). Child labor is less rampant in Sri Lanka.

Table 1 provides rough indications of the differences between countries and of the longitudinal trends. Care has to be taken in interpreting the data as there are significant variations in the estimates of child labor in the subcontinent and the figures in Table 1 are generally understood to underestimate child labor. One of the reasons has to do with the problem of defining child labor (Lieten, Srivastava, and Thorat 2004; Lieten 2005). The concept of "nowhere children" is especially crucial in discussing rural child labor: It relates to the millions of children who are not enrolled in school and who are not enumerated as "economically active" in the periodic census or labor surveys. The focus on economic activities, however, has the disadvantage of missing many children who may work invisibly in the household or in the informal sector of the economy. In rural areas, many children work as "unseen hands—unpaid and unacknowledged—that facilitate the work of adult men and women" and who "must be classed as child workers, whether or not they are formally recognized as child laborers" (Ramachandran and Massün 2002, 1).

Table 1

Incidence of Child Labor in South Asia, 1950–2000
(children age 10–14 years)

	1950	1960	1970	1980	1990	2000
Bangladesh	37	36	35	34	31	27
India	29	26	24	21	16	11
Nepal	68	66	57	49	41	38
Pakistan	14	15	15	15	13	12
Sri Lanka	12	7	4	3	2	2

Source: Chaudhri, Nyland, and O'Rourke 2004, 76.

Girls in the cottonseed fields in Andhra Pradesh, India, 2004. *(Photo by Kristoffel Lieten courtesy of IREWOC Foundation)*

Where Children in South Asia Work

International interest in child labor in South Asia was generated by gruesome stories of young children working in industrial sectors that often had export linkages: carpets, diamonds, and fireworks in India; sporting goods in Pakistan; garments in Bangladesh; tourism in Sri Lanka; and carpets in Nepal. However, in all countries throughout South Asia child labor is largely a rural phenomenon. In the countryside, it is common to find children working in agriculture, animal husbandry, the household industry, and household works.

In a number of cases, children are found working under bondage, which can be considered a form of temporary slavery (Bales 2004). In India and Pakistan, as well as in Bangladesh and Nepal, bonded labor is most prevalent in agriculture, but children are also found working under bondage in brick kilns, the bidi (cigarette) industry, rice mills, lock making, leather tanneries, and handloom and carpet weaving. Bonded labor in India and Pakistan can be attributed to the caste system as well as to the remnants of the feudal land system. In the colonial past, big landlords, the *zamindars*, could continue to treat the people on their domain, including the children, as a servant class to be exploited at whim. After independence in 1947, governments in the respective countries introduced a series of land reforms and other measures to improve the position of the downtrodden families of landless laborers and small tenants, but in a number of rural districts, the feudal powers of many landlords remained intact. Landless people were often pulled into the system of bondage due to debts caused by loans needed to meet daily living expenses. The system remains rampant in many provinces in Pakistan and Nepal and in the rural districts of northern and eastern India. It captures whole families in a double bind as children are sent to work to repay debts and thus are unable to escape the cycle of poverty.

Besides the forms of agricultural labor that occur under bondage, most agricultural production in South Asia is in family-based farms where children work as part of the division of labor within the household (Lieten, Srivastava, and Thorat 2004). Family-based labor is commonplace in rural South Asia. Some of this child labor may not be detrimental since it involves fairly light work for only a couple of hours a day, sometimes in combination with schooling. In some cases children help out their fathers on the land. In other cases children take care of the cows, buffalo, camels, goats, or sheep, spending whole days with the animals, which can enable parents to work elsewhere.

Young children are frequently engaged as agricultural laborers outside the household. Rural child labor in the agricultural sector is found on cottonseed farms, on tea plantations, and in the cultivation of tea, sugarcane, tobacco, rice, wheat, and other cash crops. Other children take care of the cattle of well-to-do individuals. For these children it is not possible to attend school regularly.

More generally, the work done by children in rural areas of the subcontinent is not the main reason why they do not attend school. Instead, it is the malfunctioning system of education—bad teaching, bad infrastructure, distant schools, and financial constraints—that is more often the reason children do not enroll in school or drop out at a young age. When they drop out, children normally become engaged in some form of work, but this is more out of need to occupy their time than out of necessity. The problem of child labor in rural areas is thus intrinsically linked to the absence of high-quality universal primary education as a binding norm.

While boys outnumber girls among the "economically active," it is especially girls who are required to help out their mothers in the household with domestic chores (Ray 2004). It is common for girl children in rural areas to shoulder domestic chores such as taking care of younger siblings, cooking, and cleaning so the mother is free to do wage work. Girls also join their mothers when they do domestic work in other households.

Work by children in the countryside, especially in agriculture, is often defended with such notions as tradition, skill formation, and family solidarity. However, hazardous forms of child labor in rural areas deserve special attention, since children are often required to work long hours or may be exposed to toxins. The majority of children in Pakistan who are working under hazardous conditions are found in the agricultural sector (ILO 2004). Hazardous forms of child labor also occur in many industries that usually are located in rural areas: brick making, stone quarrying, and the carpet industry.

Some 80 percent of child labor in South Asia occurs in rural areas, but in addition, much of the child labor occurring in urban areas is also associated with the poverty and inequality in rural areas: In urban areas many child laborers are migrants from villages (Kanbargi 1991). Labor migration of children from rural areas in South Asia occurs in various forms. Within countries, children migrate from rural to urban areas to work in the domestic sector or to work in roadside restaurants and shops. Children from rural areas are also trafficked across borders within South Asia (for example, girls are trafficked from rural areas of Bangladesh and Nepal to brothels in Indian cities) or to other parts of the world such as the Middle East and Southeast Asia.

Why Children in Rural South Asia Work

Much has been written about why children in South Asia are pulled into child labor. Economists and others have examined the roles of many variables but are divided on their relative importance. Most authors agree that child labor is generated by poor economic circumstances (Ramachandran and Massün 2002; Cigno and Rosati 2004; Chakraborty and Lieten 2004). Sending children to work is a necessity in the struggle for survival, especially since, with notable exceptions in India and Sri Lanka, social security systems are lacking in most of South Asia. Often, poor economic conditions are intensified by family crisis, such as illness, death, or disappearance of one or both parents. Ray (2004) argues, however, that household economic status seldom has a great impact on the labor force participation rate or labor hours of children. Since there are many poor families whose children are not working, and since some families in better economic conditions do require their own children to work, it is necessary to consider other factors. Some argue that sending children to work is a rational decision by parents, rooted in cultural beliefs (Weiner 1991). Factors pertaining to community and family background such as ethnicity and caste can also play a role. There is a correlation between illiteracy of mothers and child labor (Ray 2004), but it is difficult to separate out the effects of other variables such as poverty and landlessness. Finally, it remains true that a large number of offspring is positively correlated with child labor.

References and Further Reading

Bales, Kevin. *Disposable People: New Slavery in the Global Economy.* Berkeley: University of California Press, 2004.

Chakraborty, Sudip, and G.K. Lieten. "What Do Child Labourers Do? Details of a Rural District in Northeast India." In *Working Children Around the World: Child Rights and Child Reality,* ed. G.K. Lieten, 140–57. New Delhi: Institute for Human Development, 2004.

Chaudhri, D.P., Chris Nyland, and A. O'Rourke. "Child Poverty and Gender Bias in Education in South Asia: Human Capital or Human Rights?" In *Small Hands in South Asia: Child Labour in Perspective,* ed. G.K. Lieten,

Ravi Srivastava, and Sukhadeo Thorat, 61–92. New Delhi: Manohar, 2004.

Cigno, Alessandro, and Furio C. Rosati. "Child Labour, Education, Fertility, and Survival: An Analysis of Linkages in Rural India." In *Small Hands in South Asia: Child Labour in Perspective,* ed. G.K. Lieten, Ravi Srivastava, and Sukhadeo Thorat, 111–26. New Delhi: Manohar, 2004.

Gulrajani, Mohini. "Child Labour and the Export Sector in the Indian Carpet Industry." In *The Exploited Child,* ed. Bernard Schlemmer, 51–66. London: Zed Books, 2000.

ILO. *Child Labour in South Asia: Bangladesh, India, Nepal, Pakistan, Sri Lanka.* Geneva: ILO-IPEC, 2004.

———. *Global Child Labour Trends 2000 to 2004.* Geneva: ILO-IPEC, 2006.

Kanbargi, Ramesh. *Child Labour in the Indian Subcontinent: Dimensions and Implications.* New Delhi: Sage Publications, 1991.

Lieten, G.K. "Child Labour and Work: Numbers, from the General to the Specific." *Indian Journal of Labour Economics* 48:1 (2005): 29–46.

Lieten, G.K., Ravi Srivastava, and Sukhadeo Thorat, eds. *Small Hands in South Asia: Child Labour in Perspective.* New Delhi: Manohar, 2004.

Ramachandran, Nira, and Lionel Massün. *Coming to Grips with Rural Child Work.* New Delhi: Institute for Human Development, 2002.

Ray, Ranjan. "Child Labour: A Survey of Selected Asian Countries." *Asian-Pacific Economic Literature* 18:2 (2004): 1–18.

UNICEF. *The State of the World's Children 2006: Excluded and Invisible.* New York: UNICEF, 2005.

Weiner, Myron. *The Child and the State in India.* Delhi: Oxford University Press, 1991.

World Bank. *Attacking Poverty: World Development Report 2000/2001.* Washington, DC: Oxford University Press, 2001.

Bangladesh

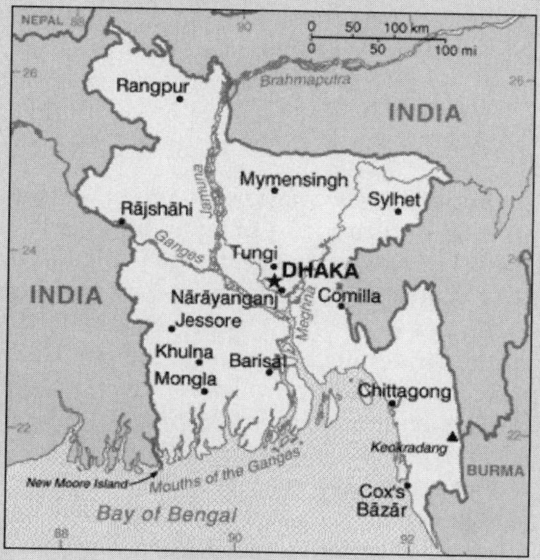

BANGLADESH			
	CRC	C 138	C 182
Ratifications	Y	N	Y
Human Development Index/Rank	0.530/137		
Human Capital			
Population Growth Rate	2.09%		
% Population 0–14	32.9%		
Total Fertility Rate	3.11		
Life Expectancy	62.46		
Infant Mortality Rate	60.83		
Literacy Rate	43.1%		
Economic			
GDP/Capita	$2,200		
GDP Growth %	6.1%		
% Poverty	45%		
Gini Index	31.8		
Labor Force Composition			
% Agriculture	63%		
% Industry	11%		
% Services	26%		

CHILD ACTIVITY BREAKDOWN, BY SEX AND RESIDENCE

RESIDENCE	Percentage of children in the relevant age-group[a]									
	Economic activity only		School only		Combining school and economic activity		Neither in school nor in economic activity		Child labor[b]	
	Male	Female	Male	Female	Male	Female	Male	Female	Male	Female
Urban	7.8	2.8	68.7	75.9	7.7	2.5	15.8	18.9	n/av	n/av
Rural	8.6	1.4	58.9	75.7	14.9	4.3	17.6	18.7	n/av	n/av
Tribal	7.1	6.0	56.9	65.8	18.8	8.5	17.3	19.7	n/av	n/av
Total	8.4	1.8	61.5	75.6	13.0	3.8	17.1	18.8	17.5	8.1

Source: Bangladesh, Multiple Indicator Cluster Survey 3, 2006 (see UCW Project Web site, http://www.ucw-project.org, country statistics).

Notes: [a]Children age 5 to 14. [b]Estimate includes (a) children under age 12 engaged in economic activities and (b) children age 12–14 engaged in excessive economic activities (more than 14 hours per week) and (c) children under age 15 engaged in excessive household chores (at least 28 hours per week). Estimate does not account for children engaged in hazardous work or other unconditional "worst forms" of child labor.

Bangladeshi Garment Industry: From the Harkin Bill to the Bangladesh Garment Manufacturers and Exporters Association

Munir Quddus, Dean and Professor of Economics, Prairie View A&M University

Widespread use of underage workers (child labor) in the modern industrial sector is one of the most vexing and tragic symptoms of poverty in the twenty-first-century global economy. As advanced economies integrate with poor economies in an attempt to take advantage of global markets, the use of child labor may rise. For example, according to Kailash Satyarthi, in the 1980s and 1990s there was a large increase in child servitude in the export-oriented industries of India, Pakistan, Nepal, and Sri Lanka (Satyarthi 1994). In the Indian carpet-export industry, with $300 million in sales, there were 300,000 child workers compared to 100,000 a decade earlier when the industry had $100 million in sales.

The Ready-made Garment Industry in Bangladesh

The garment industry in Bangladesh is an excellent case study of how changes in global manufacturing have opened up opportunities for developing nations to benefit from participation in the global economy. The Bangladesh apparel-export sector is usually traced to a 1979 agreement between the South Korea multinational Daewoo and Desh Garments of Bangladesh, and has grown to an $8 billion manufacturing and export industry employing close to 2 million workers, 90 percent of whom are women. Many foreign firms operate in the export-promotion zones, and others operate outside these special tax-free zones. Many local firms work with foreign partners through joint ownership, production, or marketing agreements. The industry exports apparel to Japan and European markets, but the United States is its biggest customer. The success of the garment-export industry has been one of the most significant catalysts for social and economic change in the country and has impacted the society beyond the immediate and visible economic and financial benefits. With more than 1 million women employed in semiskilled and skilled jobs, it is easy to see why.

However, success has attracted unwelcome attention, particularly from labor unions in the United States, where employment in textiles has suffered due to imports from low-income nations such as Bangladesh. Their concern over impending expiration of import quotas in 2005 resulted in legislative and public relations efforts to slow apparel imports. In this campaign, an early and easy target was Bangladesh's ready-made garment industry. Reporters from mainstream American media, including top television networks, investigated garment factories in Bangladesh, documenting the presence of child labor. When their reports were aired in America, the resulting public outcry forced major American apparel importers to modify their buying patterns. Wal-Mart and Levi-Strauss, among others, canceled orders and imposed a set of guidelines on factory owners that explicitly prohibited the use of underage workers. American labor unions, the media, local and international NGOs, and even the American ambassador to Bangladesh actively pressured the industry to eliminate the use of child labor.

The Harkin Bill and the Memorandum of Understanding

In the United States, Iowa Democratic senator Tom Harkin is perhaps the most well-known advocate of anti–child labor and antisweatshop legislation. Through a combination of actions, including authoring the famous Child Labor Deterrence Act, he has put great pressure on exporters in developing nations that use child labor. The Child Labor Deterrence Act, initially introduced to Congress in 1992, would prohibit the importation of products produced by child labor and includes civil and criminal penalties for companies and nations that employ underage workers. Some believe that Senator Harkin's legislation, requiring the Department of Commerce to identify nations where child labor is used in factories, was partly inspired by the efforts of American unions.

In response to the intense media scrutiny and political pressure, thousands of children were summarily dismissed from garment factories in Bangladesh. Local press reports indicated that many former garment workers ended up on the streets, engaged in hard labor such as stone breaking at construction sites, or worse.

In 1995, under continuing pressure, the Bangladesh Garment Manufacturers and Exporters Association (BGMEA), the industry's trade organization, agreed to sign a Memorandum of Understanding (MOU) with the ILO and UNICEF. According to the MOU, the industry agreed to work quickly to eliminate all underage workers from the factories. A joint BGMEA-ILO-UNICEF survey for identification of child labor in the garment factories of Bangladesh was completed in 1995. All export-oriented garment factories were visited, and 10,546 child workers below the age of fourteen were identified. The children were placed in special schools paid for by the industry association (with a monthly stipend of $6). The first industry-supported school opened on January 31, 1996, and by April 30, 1998, some 353 schools for the released child laborers were functioning in different parts of Dhaka, Narayanganj, Chittagong, Gazipur, and Khulna. Eventually, 9,743 former child workers were enrolled in school, and seven schools added skill-building training to their curricula. The training programs help child labor students to supplement their income. The intent was to gradually extend the program to other schools. Within a year the industry demonstrated that it was completely free of underage workers.

Views of Entrepreneurs

From 1993 to 1995, after the Harkin Bill was introduced, but before the MOU had been executed, a group of forty apparel entrepreneurs were interviewed on several aspects of their business, including the child labor issue. Some of their views, both on the hiring of children and on the pressure felt from the Harkin Bill, are summarized below. Certainly, many of their views are self-serving; occasionally they are based on false information. However, there is also much merit to many of their views. They help us to understand the political economy of this important issue. To effectively deal with problems in this industry, and especially the issue of child labor, it is important to understand the culture and the mind-set of the employers.

On the Hiring of Children

Entrepreneurs usually do not want to employ underage workers since there is little cost advantage. Many workers in garment factories are single mothers, in great need of gainful employment to support their families. In any hiring practice, they should receive preference. The income earned by the mother would directly assist in the development of the children in the family. The children come with their mothers since there are no day-care facilities available. Managers faced with pleas from mothers usually relent and allow them to bring their children to the job. The children initially do various chores but gradually become more skilled.

While the environment in the garment factory may not be ideal, entrepreneurs insist that it is far better than the alternatives. The factories are relatively clean and safe, and food is available. It is much better than the shanties where these children would be left unattended otherwise. A very common view is that the alternative for these young workers is almost certainly not going to be attending school. Many of the girls, if not in the factory, would be in danger of ending up as prostitutes or otherwise abused in the streets. Hiring them and allowing them to work in the factory is actually preventing child abuse.

Some view the garment factories as a sort of school for the children—the only form of school available for most of them. They go with their relatives and spend the day learning a useful trade. It is not the traditional school where reading and writing is taught, but a place of learning skills nevertheless. Denying them access to the factory classroom, while not ensuring that alternate traditional schools are available, borders on abetting child abuse.

Certain factory owners argue that the whole notion of exploitation of children—that they are given only unproductive jobs and are paid low wages—is a misconception. There is considerable vertical mobility. They start at the bottom, as unskilled helpers, often as thread cutters, at a low salary in apprenticeship positions (allowed by international law). As they learn and mature, they become semi-operators and often full operators. For many of these workers, learning is self-directed—they take advantage of an idle machine to practice. Many of them progress to become skilled workers commanding high salaries. With significant competition for skilled workers, they can readily bargain with their employers as they gain skills.

As employees, children have some advantages over the adult workers; they are enthusiastic, motivated, and deft and have fewer learning constraints than their parents have. They do not have the distractions that go with being a housewife and mother; consequently, they learn faster, and many firms pay them an adult salary or higher depending on their skills. Thus, an underage worker is not necessarily cheaper than an adult worker, or less productive for that matter.

Several factory owners pointed out that even if a manager wants to exclude all underage workers, it is difficult to accomplish. For most Bangladeshis, there is no birth certificate to determine age. With many workers suffering from malnutrition, it is difficult to distinguish between a fourteen-year-old worker and a sixteen-year-old worker simply by physical appearance. How can the employer be penalized for hiring an underage worker? If there are penalties, there will be widespread discrimination on the basis of age against younger workers and workers of smaller physique. If the manager insists on birth certificates, it will be easy for workers to submit false certificates. Finally, factory owners argued that they should not be held responsible for employing child laborers, since it is the supervisors and salaried managers who actually hire and deal with the workers. In a poor society, there is a strong incentive for hiring managers to employ people who are personally known to them and their relatives.

Finally, one factory owner expressed a sentiment shared by others: "We should let this generation work so that their children are able to go to schools. We need to be more concerned with the children of the child workers instead of the child workers of this generation." In other words, working children may not be a good thing, but given the poverty and the opportunity, future generations would be better off if we allow the sacrifices of the present generation.

Views on the Harkin Bill

Most local garment entrepreneurs believe Bangladesh was unfairly singled out and penalized on this issue because of political considerations in the United States. Some believe it is not only American organized labor but also competing nations that are interested in stopping Bangladesh from becoming a major power in the global apparel market. In interviews with factory owners and managerial staff, the view that Bangladesh is a victim of international conspiracy takes several forms.

They believe the American position is politically motivated. The United States has seldom shown interest in the welfare of Bangladeshi children. Even now, the United States is not concerned with children outside the garment sector. Labor unions in the United States are raising this issue to protect their jobs, even at the expense of American consumers. They should realize that, with or without child labor, Bangladesh has a comparative advantage in apparel manufacturing. A businesswoman who frequently travels to the United States noted that American society has enough problems with its own children—exposure to violence, drugs, sex. Should not this great caretaker of children take care of its own before worrying about children in other countries? Forcing other nations to conform to U.S. standards is no less than interfering in the internal affairs of other countries.

Most garment-factory owners believe that Bangladesh has been unfairly singled out. Bangladesh is not much different from India, Pakistan, Sri Lanka, or Burma in using young children in apparel production. Why was Bangladesh labeled as the worst case of child labor abuse? For example, India employs many children in apparel production, but because they use the so-called tailor-shop system of garment production, the children remain unseen, whereas in Bangladesh the children are in the view of the news cameras. Wal-Mart is shifting its buying from Bangladesh to Burma because of child labor concerns, despite the disastrous human rights record of the Burmese military regime. Why are the American public, labor unions, and buyers such as Wal-Mart not equally concerned about human rights abuses in Burma?

Garment entrepreneurs, including factory owners who are highly educated and frequently travel overseas, believe different versions of conspiracy theories regarding the issue of child labor. One version is that other competing apparel-producing countries are seeking to undermine this dynamic industry in Bangladesh using the American government and labor unions to do so. For example, if China systematically denies its people basic civil rights, employs prison labor extensively, and has a terrible human rights record, it should also be forced by political and economic means to submit to the same international laws. But successive American presidents have failed to deny most-favored-nation status to China. Why? China is in a position to retaliate and hurt American businesses. Humanitarian sentiments of U.S. lawmakers extend only to nations such as Bangladesh that are too small or poor to effectively resist or retaliate. There is a double standard at work here. It is not fair to single out struggling poor nations such as Bangladesh and look the other way when it comes to bigger, more powerful nations such as China.

Some entrepreneurs wonder where such strong-arm tactics will stop. Today Americans insist on not using child labor in the garment industry and threaten taking their business elsewhere. Tomorrow they may find child labor in the shrimp sector or even in public construction projects. Under the threat of stopping all foreign aid, will they make Bangladesh stop using underage workers in road building? There are fourteen charters in the ILO list, and Bangladesh is a signatory to all of them, whereas many developed countries have not signed them all.

One owner, commenting on the hypocrisy of the whole affair, noted that developed-country consumers and producers are busy exploiting the poor and unskilled workers of the world. The only reason they buy from Bangladesh is because it is one of the cheapest sources of good-quality apparel. This is certainly because skilled labor is cheap and even exploited. Why is there no concern about the thousands of adults who work two shifts, who are forced to work overtime to ensure the timely delivery of their product, and who are paid a fraction of the wages earned by workers in developed countries? What is the validity of the moral outrage of American business when it is taking full advantage of poverty in other nations?

Conclusion

Ultimately, the Harkin Bill never became law, but the pressure it created forced the BGMEA to enter into the MOU with the ILO and UNICEF. Senator Harkin visited Bangladesh and was impressed by the efforts of the industry to deal with its child labor problems. He declared that the industry had successfully dealt with the problem, which has improved the international image of the industry. Even though the Bangladesh garment industry was somewhat unfairly singled out on this issue in the foreign media, it took strong measures to protect its position. Whatever the numbers were before the MOU, the present employment of young workers is much smaller. Moreover, the apparel industry in Bangladesh retains its 30 percent cost advantage over other low-cost producers such China and India, even without the employment of child workers.

Note

I am grateful to Salim Rashid for his help in related research. The comments received from William Vetter and Cathy Preston helped to improve the essay. This essay draws upon an article by the author published in the *Journal of Asian Business* (1999).

References and Further Reading

Bangladesh Garment Manufacturers and Exporters Association. http://www.bgmea.com.bd/.

Quddus, Munir. "Apparel Exports from Bangladesh." In *Development Issues of Bangladesh,* ed. Ashraf Ali, M. Faizul Islam, and Ruhul Kuddus. Dhaka: University Press Limited, 1996a.

Quddus, Munir. "Apparel Exports from Bangladesh: Brilliant Entrepreneurship or Spurious Success?" *Journal of Asian Business* 12:4 (Winter 1996b): 51–70.

Quddus, Munir. "Child Labor and Global Business: Lessons from the Apparel Industry of Bangladesh." *Journal of Asian Business* 15:4 (1999): 81–91.

Quddus, Munir, and Salim Rashid. *Entrepreneurs and Economic Development: The Remarkable Story of Garment Exports from Bangladesh.* Dhaka: University Press Limited, 1999.

Satyarthi, Kailash. "The Tragedy of Child Labor: An Interview." *Multinational Monitor* 16:10 (October 1994). http://multinationalmonitor.org/hyper/issues/1994/10/mm1094_07.html.

Timm, Richard W. *Forty Years in Bangladesh: Memoirs of Father Timm.* Dhaka: Caritas, Bangladesh, 1995.

UNICEF and ILO. *Addressing Child Labour in the Bangladesh Garment Industry, 1995–2001: A Synthesis of UNICEF and ILO Evaluations Studies of the Bangladesh Garment Sector Projects.* New York and Geneva: UNICEF and ILO, 2004.

India

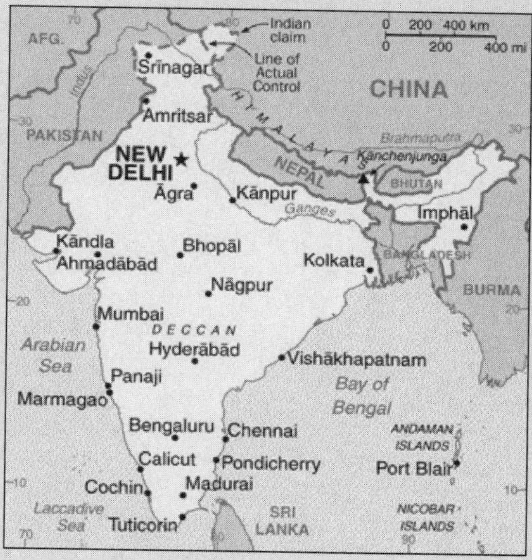

INDIA			
	CRC	C 138	C 182
Ratifications	Y	N	N
Human Development Index/Rank	0.611/126		
Human Capital			
Population Growth Rate	1.61%		
% Population 0–14	31.8%		
Total Fertility Rate	2.81		
Life Expectancy	68.59		
Infant Mortality Rate	34.61		
Literacy Rate	59.5%		
Economic			
GDP/Capita	$3,700		
GDP Growth %	8.5%		
% Poverty	25%		
Gini Index	32.5		
Labor Force Composition			
% Agriculture	60%		
% Industry	12%		
% Services	28%		

CHILD ACTIVITY BREAKDOWN, BY SEX AND RESIDENCE

RESIDENCE	Percentage of children in the relevant age-group[a]									
	Economic activity only		School only		Combining school and economic activity		Neither in school nor in economic activity		Child labor[b]	
	Male	Female	Male	Female	Male	Female	Male	Female	Male	Female
Urban	3.9	2.1	74.7	77.1	8.6	6.4	12.7	14.4	n/av	n/av
Rural	5.0	5.3	66.8	65.1	12.2	7.9	15.9	21.8	n/av	n/av
Total	4.7	4.5	69.0	68.2	11.3	7.5	15.1	19.8	12.5	12.8

Source: India, Demographic and Health Survey, 2005–6 (See UCW Project Web site, http://www.ucw-project.org, country statistics).

Notes: [a]Children age 6 to 14. [b]Estimate includes (a) children under age 12 engaged in economic activities, (b) children age 12–14 engaged in excessive economic activities (more than 14 hours per week), and (c) children under age 15 engaged in excessive household chores (at least 28 hours per week). Estimate does not account for children engaged in hazardous work or other unconditional "worst forms" of child labor.

Economic History of Modern India

Sharmistha Self, Department of Economics, Missouri State University

Discussion of the economic history of modern India generally begins after India gained independence in 1947. This is because there is a general belief that India, prior to colonization, was an extremely backward economy. There are other interpretations of India's economic condition prior to colonization, however. In addition to the view that precolonial India was poor and underdeveloped, there is a second view that at least the southern region of India was thriving economically with flourishing agricultural production. India was a major exporter of textiles in the precolonial period, with the Indian subcontinent accounting for a quarter of world manufacturing output as early as 1750 (Bairoch 1993).

The impact of colonization on India's economy has several different interpretations as well (Grabowski, Self, and Shields 2007). Some have argued that arrival of the English spelled doom for the Indian people and led to the deindustrialization of India. A second version contends that India underwent deindustrialization prior to British colonization due to the collapse of the Mughal Empire, which drove down grain productivity, pushed up nominal wages, and hurt India's competitiveness in terms of manufactured textiles. The second stage of deindustrialization occurred after the British invasion, as Indian manufactures could not compete with advances in production in England. There is yet a third interpretation of colonial experience. According to this view, colonization brought with it the foundations for a modern India, which was enhanced by investments in improving India's infrastructure as well as through the establishment of, and improvements in, the institutions necessary for economic growth.

Thus, there is much debate about India's economic condition prior to and during colonization. However, regardless of the different interpretations, what one can say with certainty is that at the end of the colonization process, India was a very poor country.

India gained its independence from British rule in 1947. Along with independence came partition of the country, as India was divided into India and Pakistan along religious and communal lines. Domestic problems India inherited included an influx of Hindu refugees from Pakistan, the integration of the princely states into the new political structure, and controversies associated with reorganization of the states on a linguistic basis. On the economic front, at the time of independence, Indian per capita income was very low (US$95 in 1974 prices).

One of the main priorities of political leaders after independence was achieving economic growth. During that period, the world witnessed how the Soviet Union transformed itself economically as well as militarily. India's development strategies were greatly influenced by the Soviet model. This was evident in the implementation of centrally conducted five-year plans. India's first prime minister, Jawaharlal Nehru, set up a Planning Commission and launched three successive five-year plans. The emphasis was on heavy industry and a turning away from the market and the private sector in favor of a dominant role for the state. Each plan period laid out the priorities, plans, and objectives for the following years. The first five-year plan was launched in 1951. Even though development strategies have changed over the years, the five-year plans have continued. India is currently on its eleventh five-year plan (2007–2012).

The strategy of development Nehru utilized was that of industrialization through import substitution. This involved various forms of trade barriers to protect development of new domestic industries, which were expected to replace imports. Tariffs were imposed on foreign imports, along with government control of foreign exchange policy, to discourage import of consumer goods and encourage import of capital goods. The result of such manipulation was often an overvalued exchange rate. Allocation of resources was also controlled to a large extent by the state using the issuance of licenses and contracts as a means of controlling funds available for investment purposes. The important role of licenses during this time is evident from the nickname "license raj" (rule of licenses) that has been attributed to this period of India's history.

India's growth was modest in the first few decades following independence. There were some successes but several setbacks as well. While the 1960s saw an increase in agricultural productivity from the green revolution, benefits were localized in a few northern states, and much of the rest of the country did not initially benefit. Nehru worked toward India gaining self-sufficiency in food, and while there were successes such as the green revolution, the country also suffered several famines during this period. Additionally, the economy was hit hard by the oil crisis of 1973. On the political side, India was torn by political unrest both internally and externally. India fought a war with Pakistan in 1965, and then again in 1971. The early 1970s also saw India carrying out its first nuclear explosion. Troubles with China continued to escalate as well. The economic and political situation created the perfect atmosphere for corruption to prevail. At the center, the government was embroiled in all sorts of corruption charges, and the trickling down of this corruption along the political and economic chain was apparent. Additionally, the country was dragged down by its nonperforming new industries. Last, but definitely not least, the country's manipulation of the exchange rate led to rapidly falling exports and an eventual balance-of-payments crisis.

It needs to be remembered that Nehru inherited a country that was limping at best. In spite of the troubles the country faced, Nehru also brought about sweeping changes. The moderate growth experienced during Nehru's time appeared remarkable in comparison to the years prior to India's independence. India's economy grew three times faster during the 1950s and 1960s than during British rule (Thakur 1997). Nehru was succeeded by his daughter, Indira Gandhi, who served as prime minister for fifteen years and was, in turn, succeeded by her son Rajiv Gandhi. Both Indira Gandhi and Rajiv Gandhi were assassinated (Indira Gandhi in 1984 and Rajiv Gandhi in 1991) by radical factions within the country.

Between 1950 and 1980, savings rose from 10 to 25 percent of GDP, while growth rates for GDP (real) and per capita GDP were 3.7 percent and 1.5 percent, respectively (DeLong 2003). The 1980s saw a marked difference in political attitude toward business and business leaders. There appeared to be a softening of attitude and an encouraging tone toward the private sector. In order to promote private industry, the country undertook various reforms and deregulation of industries. Additionally, there was a push toward promotion and rationalization of the tax structure. While all these changes were taking place economically, the country was also facing political upheaval and political unrest. This contributed to an atmosphere of political instability, which seemed to contrast with the efforts to encourage industrial growth.

There was a marked change in India's growth experience since the 1980s. From 1985 to 1990 India's real GDP growth rate rose to 5.6 percent. The dollar value of exports also showed marked improvement, increasing 14 percent annually. There is significant disagreement among economists regarding the real source of economic growth during this period. While some argue that it was a result of an attitudinal shift toward promoting business and exports, others argue that it was a result of freeing up the market. While the growth rate was encouraging, it was neither stable nor long-lived. It appears that India's economic growth was more borrowed than homegrown. India's spending patterns caused a budget deficit that led to a fiscal crisis of such proportion that, by 1991, India was on the verge of bankruptcy. India's political problems also continued relentlessly throughout this period. Thus, while the country was facing an economic crisis, it was also dealing with political crises, both internal and external, especially with regard to its neighbor Pakistan.

The country witnessed some sweeping economic changes during the 1990s by moving toward a policy of radical liberalization. The country put emphasis on export-led growth along with increased foreign direct investment to reduce its trade deficits. The result of these reforms was remarkable growth in exports and annual average growth rates of real GDP and GDP per capita of 6.24 percent and 4.4 percent, respectively. India has continued on the path of economic reform and growth established in the early 1990s. There has been deregulation in infrastructure and greater emphasis placed on public and private partnerships. Industries that have been deregulated include the telecom sector, electricity, individual port operations, and the hydrocarbon sector.

In the last decade, labor markets all over the world, especially in developed countries have been forced to contend with the emerging global impact of India's information technology industry. India's strength lies in an educated and English-speaking workforce that is willing to work for lower wages than their Western counterparts. This has resulted in hundreds of thousands of jobs being outsourced to India due to a "huge supply of cheap brain workers" ("The World Is My Oyster" 2006). Initially, most of the jobs outsourced were low-tech, low-skill jobs. However, in recent years, the move has been toward jobs that require higher levels of skill and jobs in areas other than information technology. This has made it possible for India to earn millions of dollars. India's per capita GDP in 2006 was $3,700, and real GDP grew at a remarkable rate of 8.5 percent.

The last decade has seen sweeping changes in India on multiple fronts, ranging from gaining nuclear status (along with its neighbor Pakistan) to a move toward reform and liberalization; from improved political relations and friendlier negotiations with Pakistan (with whom it has fought three wars) to a move toward the creation of special economic zones similar to China's; and from crossing the 1 billion mark in population to becoming a formidable supplier of services and information technology to the rest of the world. However, it needs to be understood that the political situation in India takes center stage in determining which and to what degree these changes will be successful.

It appears that India is headed in the right direction economically. In fact, India seems a unique case, where the country has skipped a stage of development and moved ahead. Typically, as countries develop, they export labor-intensive products and import capital-intensive products. A move to the service sector generally comes at a later stage of development. In India's case, it seems to have skipped over the exportation of labor-intensive products (though it did some of that, too) and moved on to the service-oriented economy. This has been fueled mainly by India's prowess in information technology.

What cannot be ignored in all the good news about the economy is that growth has come at a cost—mainly increased poverty and inequality. Some of this is linked to conditions that have prevailed in India for centuries. Traditionally, India has been an agricultural and rural economy. It has been plagued by dependence on agriculture, poor infrastructure, overpopulation, and a caste system. Additionally, achieving compulsory education has been a challenge. All these factors have created several related problems such as high levels of unemployment and underemployment, poverty, inequality, and child labor. Some of these problems have diminished with economic growth, but they have not been eradicated and they continue to prevent the economy from enjoying the full fruit of its success.

The traditional Indian economy has been dominated by agriculture. At the time of independence, agriculture accounted for 50 percent of India's GDP and provided about 70 percent of the country's employment. The twenty-first century has seen a marked reduction in dependence on agriculture and a structural shift toward industry and services. GDP composition by sector in 2005 shows that agriculture accounted for 19.9 percent, industry 19.3 percent, and services 60.7 percent. A falling share of GDP, coupled with increased production, implies that Indian agriculture has experienced a significant increase in total factor productivity.

At the time of independence, India inherited an educational system that was characterized by imbalance both between and within regions.

The literacy rate in 1947 was a mere 14 percent. The Indian government resolved to provide free education to all up to the age of fourteen by 1960. However, there were clear inconsistencies between goals and actions, and the date was constantly moved back. The most recent decade has seen the most remarkable progress in education so far, though the level of success was not evenly distributed. The 2001 census claimed that the male literacy rate stood at 75.85 percent; the rate was 54.16 for females. Moreover, most states had achieved at least 60 percent literacy for males and 50 percent literacy for females.

Gender bias in education is quite obvious. This gender bias in education permeates employment and other socioeconomic aspects of the economy. The most common areas of gender bias are evident in the labor market, in education, and in the household. South Asia is one region in the world where the natural ratio of women to men is severely distorted. In the late 1980s, Amartya Sen coined the term "missing women" to describe the great numbers of women in the world who are literally not alive due to discrimination. According to 1991 census figures in India, it was estimated there were 927 women for every 1,000 men, while the ratio worldwide is 106 women for every 100 men.

Other problems the economy faces include population pressure, unemployment, and underemployment. It is now well-known that India and China are the only two countries in the world that have crossed the 1 billion population mark. What sets India apart is that one will find 16.7 percent of the world's population living on 2.4 percent of the world's surface area. The tenth five-year plan in India projected a decline in population growth rate to below 2 percent per annum by the end of the plan period. Given India's demographic characteristics, the current labor force has been growing at a rate of 2.5 percent annually, but employment has been growing at only 2.3 percent. While India's economic growth in the last decade implies the creation of additional jobs, it remains a daunting task to tackle the predictions for unemployment. It was expected that the overall open unemployment rate would fall from 1.9 percent in 1996–1997 to 1.47 percent by 2007.

Related to the problems of population pressure and unemployment are poverty and inequality. Poverty has been a chronic problem for the South Asian region in general, and India in particular, for a very long time. Estimates in the late 1970s put the number of Indians living in poverty at 300 million, or nearly 50 percent of the population. Poverty was reduced during the 1980s, but slower economic growth and higher inflation in 1990 and 1991 reversed this trend. In 1991, it was estimated that 332 million people, or 38 percent of the population, lived below the poverty line. Poverty rates in India have varied among regions and among Indian states. According to Deaton and Drèze (2002), regional disparities in poverty increased in the 1990s, with southern and western regions doing much better than northern and eastern regions. As late as 2005, it was estimated that a quarter of India's population lived below the poverty line.

With globalization and India's rapid economic progress in recent years, one can expect incomes to rise and poverty to be reduced. Policy makers in India have accepted this as a priority, but they seem to have overlooked or ignored the issue of inequality. According to Jha (2000) India's postreform period has seen a sharp rise in inequality and only a marginal decline in poverty. This has diminished the poverty-reducing potential of higher growth. Additionally, one finds a widening regional inequality as well as inequality among Indian states.

Finally, another problem that plagues India is child labor. Child labor has a long history in South Asia and continues to be a pervasive problem in India. Estimates range between 60 million and 115 million working children in India—the highest number in the world (Human Rights Watch 1996). India undertook initiatives to reduce child labor during British rule and continued to champion the cause following independence and into the present. While the efforts have had some success, child labor remains a pervasive problem in the country. The government's child labor policies try to reduce and restrict the employment of children, but they cannot change the demand for child labor. Given India's recent economic success, coupled with better technology, increases in employment, and per capita income, one can expect that the demand for child labor will also see a downward trend in coming years.

Boy carrying hides in the leather industry in Kolkata, 2005. *(Photo by Kristoffel Lieten courtesy of IREWOC Foundation)*

Thus, India represents a mixed bag—there clearly have been some signs of success, especially in the last decade. However, some problems persist. Some of these problems have economic roots, some have social or cultural roots, and others have roots so complicated that one cannot separate the economic from the social and cultural aspects. The economic progress of India has definitely been a major accomplishment. With improved education and income, one can expect that foundations for better-quality institutions will be established and strengthened, which, in turn, will bring about further growth and development.

References and Further Reading

Bairoch, Paul. *Economics and World History: Myths and Paradoxes.* New York: Harvester Wheatsheaf, 1993.

Deaton, Angus, and Jean Drèze. "Poverty and Inequality in India: A Reexamination." Centre for Development Economics, working paper 107, Delhi School of Economics, New Delhi, 2002.

DeLong, Bradford. "India Since Independence: An Analytic Growth Narrative." In *In Search of Prosperity: Analytic Narratives on Economic Growth,* ed. D. Rodrik. Princeton, NJ: Princeton University Press, 2003.

"The World Is My Oyster." *Economist,* October 5, 2007.

Grabowski, Richard, Sharmistha Self, and Michael Shields. *Economic Development: A Regional, Institutional, and Historical Approach.* Armonk, NY: M.E. Sharpe, 2007.

Human Rights Watch. *The Small Hands of Slavery—Bonded Child Labor in India.* New York: Human Rights Watch, 1996.

Jha, Raghabendra. "Reducing Poverty and Inequality in India: Has Liberalization Helped?" Working paper 204, UNU World Institute for Development Economics Research, Helsinki, Finland, 2000.

Thakur, Ramesh. "India in the World: Neither Rich, Powerful, nor Principled." *Foreign Affairs* (July–August 1997).

Evolution of the Law on Child Labor in India

Usha Ramanathan, Honorary Fellow, Centre for the Study of Developing Societies

Early Child Labor Legislation

Acknowledgment of child labor as a distinct constituent of the workforce has been on India's statute book since at least 1881. The Factories Act of 1881 set the minimum age of employment at seven years, with a maximum of nine hours of work per day. The act also outlawed the "double employment" of child workers in two factories on the same day. In 1891 the Factories Act was amended, increasing the minimum age for employment in a factory to nine years. In 1911, the act was again amended to prohibit the employment of children in certain dangerous processes. The device of a "certificate of fitness" was introduced. This has survived to the present, where a certifying surgeon is entrusted with assessing whether a "young person has completed his 14th year, that he has attained the prescribed physical standards and he is fit for such work."[1]

In 1922, it was ILO Convention 5 that prompted raising the minimum age in the Factories Act to fifteen years and restricting working hours for child workers to six hours with a half-hour break after four and a half hours. In 1901, the Mines Act prohibited the employment of a child under twelve years in any mine where the conditions were dangerous to their health and safety. Employment of children was restricted to open-cast mines with a depth of less than twenty feet.

Reporting in 1929, the Royal Commission on Labour, under the chairmanship of John Henry Whitley, had a significant impact on the recognition and legislative treatment of child labor. It reported widespread prevalence of child labor in a range of industries including carpet, bidi, textile, match, and plantations. A series of laws followed. The Indian Ports Act of 1931 set twelve years as the minimum age for handling goods in ports. The Tea Districts Emigrant Labour Act of 1932 provided that no child below sixteen years be employed, or allowed to migrate, unless accompanied by parents. The Factories Act of 1934 prohibited children below twelve years from being employed in factories and restricted work to five hours a day for children between twelve and fifteen. The Mines Act, in 1935, raised the minimum age to fifteen years and required a certificate of fitness for children between fifteen and seventeen years.

The Children (Pledging of Labour) Act, passed into law in 1933, is the first acknowledgment of the problem of child bondage. Enacted because "it is expedient to prohibit the making of agreements to pledge the labour of children, and the employment of children whose labour has been pledged,"[2] the act defines a child as a person under the age of fifteen. While declaring that an agreement to pledge the labor of a child shall be void, it prescribes punishment for parents or guardians who make an agreement to pledge the labor of a child and for any person who makes such an agreement with the parent or guardian. Punishment may also attach to one who knowingly employs a child bound by such an agreement. This act of 1933 survives, virtually unchanged, leaving even the minuscule penalties of Rs. 50 to Rs. 200 for the various breaches unamended.

1938 to 1986

In 1938, the Employment of Children Act was the first enactment squarely addressing the issue of child labor. This followed from the twenty-third session of the International Labor Conference, held in 1937, which adopted a special article exclusively on India, recommending that children below thirteen years be prohibited from work in certain categories of employment. The 1938 act set the minimum age of employment in certain industries at fifteen and in the transport of goods on docks and wharves at fourteen.

In 1950, the Constitution of India was promulgated. Article 24 reads, "No child below the age of 14 years shall be employed to work in any factory or mine or engaged in any other hazardous employment." This is considered a Fundamental Right, guaranteed in part 3 of the constitution. Part 4 sets out nonjusticiable Directive Principles of State Policy. These include directives that "the tender age of child are not abused and that citizens are not forced by economic necessity to enter avocations unsuited to their age and strength"; "that children are given opportunities and facilities to develop in a healthy manner and in conditions of freedom and dignity and that childhood and youth are protected against exploitation and against moral and material abandonment"; and that the state shall endeavor to provide "free and compulsory education for all children until they complete the age of 14 years" within ten years. In 1993, many years after the ten-year period had elapsed, the supreme court, in a landmark decision, declared free education to age fourteen to be a Fundamental Right.[3] In 2002, the constitution was amended to reflect the supreme court's judicial declaration. Article 21-A reads, "Right to Education. The state shall provide free and compulsory education to all children of the age of 6–14 years in such manner as the state may, by law, determine." This was accompanied by the inclusion of Article 51-A(k), which makes it "the duty of every citizen of India . . . (k) who is a parent or guardian to provide opportunities for education to his child or, as the case may be, ward of the age of 6 and 14 years."

Despite the existence of the Employment of Child Act of 1938, the Labour Investigation Committee (1944–1946), also known as the Rege Committee after its chairperson, found that child labor was extensive in bidi making, carpet weaving, glass, and other small-scale industries. There were references particularly to the match industry in South India, the cement industry in Rajasthan, the spinning industry in Cochin, and carpet weaving in Kashmir. The committee found children in large numbers on plantations, "mainly due to the fact that recruitment is on a family basis." In the case of tea, the committee estimated, "children form about 15% of the total number of workers in Assam; 20% in Bengal and about 10% in South India. In the case of coffee and rubber, their proportion is 10% and 4% respectively for India as a whole." In 1969, the National Commission of Labour, chaired by Justice P.B. Gajendragadkar, observed that child labor was "noticed mostly in agriculture, plantations and shops."[4]

In the meantime, the Factories Act of 1948 prohibited a child under fourteen from working in a factory and required that a child between fourteen and fifteen years be given a certificate of fitness before being employed. The Plantations Labour Act of 1951 prohibited the employment of children below twelve, and adolescents between the ages of twelve and eighteen were required to obtain a certificate of fitness. Both laws prohibited night work for children. The Mines Act of 1952, and especially since 1984, has categorically rejected the employment of persons below the age of eighteen years, with the exception of apprentices under the Apprentices Act of 1961, or other trainees under proper supervision who may be as young as sixteen years. The Merchant Shipping Act of 1958 prohibits employment of children under fourteen. The Motor Transport Workers Act of 1961 prohibits employment of children below fifteen "in any capacity in any motor transport undertaking." The Apprentices Act of 1961 disqualifies a person less than fourteen years from being engaged as an apprentice.

The tobacco industry, where child labor has been rampant and the handling and inhalation of tobacco have been recognized as hazardous, was drawn into the law in 1966, in the Beedi and Cigar Workers (Conditions of Employment) Act. The act prohibits the employment of children under fourteen in any industrial premises, and "young persons" between fourteen and eighteen years were not to be engaged in work except between 6 A.M. and 7 P.M. A significant exception placed "self-employed persons in private dwelling houses" outside the purview of the act. This provision expressly allowed the "assistance of the members of his family living with him in such dwelling house and dependent on him." This provision, along with the practice of subcontracting to "outworkers" who are paid piece rates for the finished product, has kept a space open for children to be engaged in bidi manufacture.

The Trade Unions Act of 1926 restricts the right of membership to a trade union to persons who have attained the age of fifteen, and it disqualifies a member from becoming an officer of a union if they have not reached the age of eighteen. In the 1990s, these provisions were challenged, unsuccessfully, in the Delhi High Court by Butterflies, a nongovernmental organization working among street and working children.

The Bonded Labour System (Abolition) Act of 1976 was a response to a customary system of usury under which a debtor or his descendants or dependents have to work for little or no wages in order to extinguish the debt. The 1976 act abolishes the bonded labor system and extinguishes the liability to repay bonded debt. Identification, release, and rehabilitation of the bonded laborers forms the nucleus of the 1976 act. In the 1980s, the supreme court also struck at the practice of bonded labor.[5]

1986 Forward

In 1979, the Gurupadaswamy Committee on Child Labour reported on the status of child labor. The committee noted flagrant violations of the laws, difficulties in regulation, the paucity of prosecution, and the meagerness of penalties prescribed. It recommended a law that would adopt uniformity in defining the child, with regulation of hours of work and conditions of work, and identification of areas of employment where child labor would be prohibited. In 1986, as a prelude to the Child Labour (Prohibition and Regulation) Act, the Sanat Mehta Committee was set up, which reiterated the recommendations of the Gurupadaswamy Committee.

The Child Labor (Prohibition and Regulation) Act (CLPRA) of 1986 prohibits employment of children in a scheduled list of occupations and a scheduled list of processes. The act carves out an important exception where children are permitted to work in any workshop where the process is carried on by the occupier with the aid of his family. This exception made for work within the family has been criticized as providing a loophole through which many law breakers escape. A Child Labour Technical Advisory Committee has been tasked with advising the central government on additions to the list of prohibited occupations and processes. When enacted in 1986, the schedule concentrated on occupations and processes considered hazardous. The list grew from five to thirteen occupations and from eleven to fifty-seven processes between1986 and 1999. The act provides for the regulation of child labor in those occupations and processes where it is not prohibited. The experience with regulation has not been encouraging, with few prosecutions, fewer convictions, and mild penalties when imposed, which are unlikely to act as a deterrent.

India ratified the UN Convention on the Rights of the Child in December 1992 with a declaration that it would not be "practical immediately to prescribe minimum age for admission to each and every area of employment in India." This helps to explain why India has not signed and ratified ILO Conventions 138 and 182. The First Periodic Report to the Committee on the Rights of the Child, however, adverted to an assurance that the prime minister had given in 1994, in his speech on Independence Day, that child labor would be abolished in five years and to a scheme for the Elimination of Child Labour in Hazardous Industries that was intended to be "implemented intensively in states and regions where employment of child in hazardous industries is maximum."

The 1986 act aimed to achieve uniformity in the definition of child labor, prescribing a uniform age of fourteen years in the definition of a child. In pursuing the objective of uniformity, the 1986 act actually reduced the minimum age for employment in merchant shipping and motor transport from fifteen to fourteen years. Further, the act repealed the prohibition of child labor on plantations. In 2001, the act was amended to restore the minimum age of fifteen in merchant shipping and motor transport and to restore the prohibition of child labor on plantations.

Extension of the law to what had been considered nonhazardous work was initiated by the National Human Rights Commission. Reports of exploitation and abuse of child domestic servants in the homes where they are employed recur with regularity. In 1997 and again in 1999, the National Human Rights Commission urged administrators of the central government, as well as states and union territories, to prohibit government employees from hiring children below fourteen years as domestic help. Subsequently, the central government and many state governments did bring in a change in their rules. Finally, in October 2006, this ban reached beyond government servants when "domestic workers or servants" were added to the list of prohibited occupations in the CLPRA. A companion entry addressed another arena where child labor abounds: "Dhabas (roadside eateries), restaurants, hotels, motels, tea shops, resorts, spas or other recreational centres" are also prohibited venues for employing child labor since October 2006.

The Role of Public Interest Litigation

Public interest litigation has contributed significantly to the development of the law concerning child labor. For example, children under fourteen were found to be among the migrant workers and contract laborers engaged in construction work for the Asian Games. In 1982, the case was taken to the supreme court by a democratic rights organization.[6] The court found that, at the time, construction was not on the list of prohibited occupations for children. Drawing on the constitutional injunction against children being in hazardous employment, the court held: "There can be no doubt that notwithstanding the absence of specification of construction industry in the schedule to Employment of Children Act 1938, no child below 14 years can be employed in construction work and the Union of India as also every State Government must ensure that this constitutional mandate is not violated in any part of the country." In 1983, the court reiterated this position when a case concerning child laborers working on a hydroelectric project was brought before it.[7] The prohibition of child labor in the building and construction industry was included in the CLPRA when it was enacted in 1986.

Employing children in the manufacture of matches, explosives, and fireworks has been prohibited since 1938. Yet child labor has been rampant in these industries. Explosions and accidents are common, and it was one such incident that led the supreme court to require a liability insurance scheme be put in place that would cover the risk of accidents, providing compensation where risk is not averted.[8] This formula was repeated in a public interest litigation concerning the tobacco industry.[9] Unfortunately, there was a certain regression in the court's judgment relating to the match factories in Sivakasi in Tamil Nadu, when it permitted children to be employed in match factories in the process of packing, considering this to be a nonhazardous aspect of an otherwise hazardous industry.

In 1996, there was a discernible change of mood in the supreme court when confronted with the issue of child labor. A survey had identified eighteen child laborers in electroplating units in Delhi. The court ordered substantial fines against employers as penalties for employing the children. This was followed by a "Public Notice to Employers Employing Child Labour" in the New Delhi edition of a national daily on November 25, 1996, where the names and addresses of 230 employers, the names of the children they employed, and the amounts of the proposed penalties were published. The employers included shops, mechanic garages, and tea stalls, which were, at that time, not on the prohibited list in the 1986 act. Confronted by this judicial approach, the formality of the law had to give way to the court's appreciation of what would have been the impact of curtailing the practice of employing child labor.

On December 10, 1996, a three-judge bench of the supreme court revisited the issue of child labor in Sivakasi fireworks factories and issued a landmark decision. The court had before it the report of a committee of advocates set up to investigate the employment of children in Sivakasi. This committee was constituted following an accident in a fireworks factory in which thirty-nine people had died. Acknowledging the poverty that characterized child labor and the possibility that compulsory education may be the answer to the problem, the court ordered the offending employer to pay compensation of Rs. 20,000 for each child in their employ. This sum would be deposited in a Child Labour Rehabilitation–cum–Welfare Fund, interest from which was to be used only for the concerned child. Further, given the constitutional directive that the state has to help realize the "right to work," the court considered whether the state may have an obligation to ensure that when a child is withdrawn from work, an adult in the child's family is provided employment. Yet, given the large number of child workers, this could strain the resources of the state. Instead, where it is not possible to provide alternative employment to an adult, the court ordered that a "contribution/grant . . . of Rs.5000 for each child employed in a factory or mine or in any other hazardous employment" be deposited in the Rehabilitation Fund by the government. The child should then be withdrawn from employment and assisted by the Rs. 25,000 fund or the Rs. 20,000 and alternative employment. Assistance was to be halted if the child was not sent to school. As for nonhazardous jobs, the court charged the inspector under the 1986 act with ensuring that children did not work longer than four to six hours a day and that they received "education at least for two hours each day." The "entire cost of education is (to be) borne by the employer." This landmark decision had the effect of placing child labor squarely on the state's agenda.

Conclusion

In 2003, the government of India, by resolution, adopted a National Charter for Children that includes a clause concerning protection of children from economic exploitation and from performing tasks hazardous to their well-being: "The state shall move towards a total ban of all forms of child labour." In 2005, India enacted the Commissions for Protection of Child Rights Act. The preamble to the 2005 act invokes the 2003 charter along with the UN Convention on the Rights of the Child and the document titled "A World Fit for Children," which emanated from the UN General Assembly Special Session on Children held in May 2002. This act came into effect on January 20, 2006, and the commission has been set up and a chairperson appointed. The first chairperson, Shantha Sinha, is founder of the M.V. Foundation, a child rights organization working for the protection of children and the abolition of child labor.

Law and policy have begun to veer toward formal abolition of child labor since the "right to education" was declared a fundamental right by the supreme court in 1993 and the prime minister's statement in 1994. There has been a spurt of activity intended to give content to the right to education for all persons between the ages of six and fourteen years, and a link has been forged in law and policy between child labor and school going. The question of whether all work done by children should fall within the definition of child labor has been resolved by presuming all children out of school as labor-force constituents. The practice of employment of child labor has not yet shown any discernible decline, though. The route to enforcing the ban on all forms of child labor is still being chalked out.

Notes

1. S.69(2)(a), Factories Act, 1948.
2. S.2, Children (Pledging of Labour) Act, 1933.
3. *J.P. Unnikrishnan v. State of Andhra Pradesh* (1993) 1 SCC 645.
4. *Report of the National Commission of Labour* (1969) at 34.
5. See, for example, *Bandhua Mukti Morcha v. Union of India* (1984) 3 SCC 161.
6. *PUDR v. Union of India AIR* (1982) Supreme Court 1480.
7. *Labourers Working on Salal Hydro Project v. State of Jammu and Kashmir* (1983) 2 SCC 181 at 191.
8. *M.C. Mehta v. State of Tamil Nadu* (1991) 1 SCC 283.
9. *Rajangam, Secretary, District Beedi Workers Union v. State of Tamil Nadu* (1992) 1 SCC 221.

Children in India's Carpet Industry

Shahid Ashraf, Professor, Department of Economics,
Jamia Millia Islamia (Central University), New Delhi

Child labor in India's carpet industry is a complex phenomenon that has been compounded by social and cultural factors encouraging the continuity of trade and skill in particular castes or communities. Most of the work performed by children is also performed by adults, and most children work side by side with adult laborers. Children possess no irreplaceable skills for this work and could be replaced by adults since many adults are already doing this work, but the situation is complicated by a fragmented and informal industrial structure that relies extensively on subcontracting. This has important implications for policy on child labor. One has to be very clear and specific about the specialized types of enterprises under consideration and, within enterprise type, about the specific activities performed, since the concentration of child labor and its attendant health hazards differ quite markedly across work activities and enterprise types.

In 1986, the Child Labour (Prohibition and Regulation) Act prohibited the employment of children below the age of fourteen in specific occupations and processes, but the act permits employment of children in family enterprises, even in hazardous situations. The argument is that children are less likely to be exploited as part of family labor, but this policy promotes the creation of a subcontracting network of small family-based enterprises and, thereby, actually encourages the continuation of child labor.

The Indian carpet industry is centered largely in the states of Uttar Pradesh, Rajasthan, Kashmir, and Bihar. The industry has few large businesses and consists mostly of small family enterprises. The export market includes woolen, silk, and synthetic carpets, but around 90–95 percent of exports are woolen carpets. These woolen carpets are the Persian hand-knotted pile carpets and are generally woven in the southeastern districts of Uttar Pradesh. In 2005–6, the total value of carpet exports was US$623.4 million. In the 1990s, the largest export destination was Germany, followed by the United States, but the trend has reversed and now the United States is the largest importer of Indian carpets. The issue of child labor in the carpet industry acquired prominence in the 1990s in discussions on the relationship between international trade and labor standards in the context of the World Trade Organization.

Organizational Structure of the Carpet Industry

The exporter is the prime figure around whom the overall organizational structure of the carpet industry revolves. He is the link between foreign importers and local contractors. Local contractors, in turn, are the link between the exporter and the loom owners and weavers. The weavers are at the bottom of the hierarchy. They are paid the least and their work is the most monotonous, requiring them to sit for hours in a fixed position. Adult weavers are paid so little that they are forced to bring their children, or the children of relatives, to weave with them. About 80 percent of weavers are illiterate, and it is very rare for a weaver to complete primary education. About half are low-caste Hindus, and 20 percent are Muslims. The low-caste Hindus face barriers to upward mobility, with no aspirations beyond that of a weaver. The rigid caste system tacitly encourages low-caste parents to send their children to work at an early age.

The carpet industry has developed a large and

informal contracting and subcontracting network. Weaving is given out by the exporters through the contractors to the loom owners, who in turn hire additional weavers. Wage payments are made on a piece-rate basis depending on the quality of the carpet. Of the initial piece rate, contractors take a 20 percent commission. Wages are not paid daily or weekly. Contractors receive payments from exporters as advances equaling the total expected weaving charges. Contractors subsequently loan small amounts to the weavers during emergency or festivities, with deductions subsequently made against the weaving payments. On completion of the carpet, the balance amount is received by the weavers from the contractors.

Weaving is a misnomer for Persian carpets, as the process consists of tying a knot of woolen yarn to a cotton thread, cutting it with a sharp, curved knife, and repeating. The quality of carpets depends on the knots per square inch, the motifs and intricacies of design, as well as the number of colors used. It is sometimes said that children are hired because their "nimble fingers" enable them to tie more knots per square inch, thus improving the quality of the carpets. This is not true. The process requires strong fingers, particularly for high-quality carpets, and the best weavers tend to be between eighteen and thirty-five years of age. Children are more liable to cut their fingers while cutting the woolen thread after tying the knot in higher-quality carpets. For the carpet industry, the nimble-fingers argument is merely another excuse for employing children, thereby also maintaining a pool of trained weavers for the future.

A six-foot-by-three-foot carpet may take four to six months to complete. Generally, two to five weavers work together on a single carpet, each being responsible for a horizontal area of eighteen to thirty inches. The weaving has to be done together by all the weavers so the vertical level woven does not vary. Variations due to a weaver being absent reduce the overall quality of the carpet. Quality-conscious exporters insist that all weavers weave together or not at all. Thus, the absence of a single weaver could stop the weaving for that particular day. Children tend to be more pliable and less likely to be absent than adult weavers. Therefore, loom owners prefer a mix of both adult and child weavers to meet quality standards and delivery deadlines.

Female weavers are rare in the carpet industry. Carpet weaving is a male-dominated activity, where two or more weavers sit together in close physical proximity to each other. The loom sheds are usually part of the loom owners' houses, and loom owners hire the weavers. For a woman to go to somebody else's house to work is not socially acceptable in rural India. Cultural sensitivity requires that women not mix with men other than those in the immediate family. Encouraging women weavers would require women-only loom sheds and the formation of women's cooperatives.

Child Labor Elimination

Campaigns for the elimination of child labor in the Indian carpet industry have been controversial. Statements on the number and percentage of child weavers have not always been properly substantiated. Estimates of child labor in the industry range from 4 percent to 80 percent of the workforce. More reasonable and careful statistical methods, however, estimate child labor in the range of 8 percent to 30 percent of total workers in the carpet industry. The sensitization component of these campaigns has been largely successful in promoting awareness that child labor is bad for the individual, the society, and the nation. This awareness has trickled down to the villages.

Education has been put forward as the key to the elimination of child labor. NGOs have made efforts to promote education and have set up schools at the primary level, but beyond primary school it becomes difficult for children to continue formal education because the schools are located far from their homes. The opportunity cost of schooling is actually quite low, even among very poor rural households. Poverty, as a limiting factor, is highly overrated. Parents do want their children to be educated, and the willingness of parents to bear the costs (school fees, uniform, and books, as well as foregone earnings) may depend crucially on the quality of the schooling the children obtain. A large pool of children who are not attending school becomes a large group from which child labor can be recruited.

Among nonlegislative measures to eliminate child labor from carpet making, social labeling programs such as Kaleen and Rugmark are important strategies. These initiatives include prohibiting child labor in the production of carpets and providing for the rehabilitation of child workers, along with attempts to improve and enforce fair working conditions. Inspection and monitoring of carpet weaving is also an important aspect of social-labeling initiatives. Kaleen is the social-labeling initiative of the Carpet Export Promotion Council, established by the Ministry of Textiles. The council has more than 2,300 members, and membership is mandatory for all carpet exporters. Members commit that no child labor will be employed on their premises. Violators are subject to cancellation of export privileges or other punitive action. The council has also created a Child Welfare Fund. The Rugmark brand was initiated by the Indo German Export Promotion Project along with several NGOs. The Rugmark label guarantees the importers that the carpet has been manufactured or exported by a company that has voluntarily committed itself to work without children.

The weakest aspect of the anti–child labor campaign is in providing alternatives for child workers. Children who have been rescued from loom sheds and sent back to their villages often have no viable alternatives for their betterment. There is a limit to the number of tailors, carpenters, and electricians that can get regular employment in rural areas. Thus, even when rescued children are trained in these vocations, they often return to carpet weaving. Follow-up investigations on rescued children have revealed that most have returned to weaving, either by going back to where they worked before or by getting looms set up in their villages.

The fight against child labor should involve the cooperation of the local self-government units at the village level, called *panchayats*. Given the complexities of rural India, the *panchayats* may turn out to be an effective instrument at the grassroots level. A constitutional amendment enhancing their administrative and financial powers puts them in a position to respond to the issue of child labor at the village level, where it is really needed. Pressure should be put on the Indian government to reorganize the worker-owner relationship in the carpet industry, to improve law enforcement with regard to labor standards, and to improve access to schools and other basic infrastructure.

References and Further Reading

Anker, Richard, Sandhya Barge, Shahid Ashraf, and Deborah Levison. "Economics of Child Labour in India's Carpet Industry." In *Economics of Child Labour in Hazardous Industries of India,* ed. Richard Anker, Sandhya Barge, M.P. Joseph, and Shobhita Rajagopal. Baroda, India: Centre for Operations Research and Training (CORT), 1998.

Ashraf, Shahid. "Children Labourers Without Alternatives." *International Politics and Society* 3 (2001): 303–9.

———. "The Elimination of Child Labour in the Carpet Belt of North India: Possible NGO and Trade Union Strategies." In *Against Child Labour: Indian and International Dimensions and Strategies,* ed. Klauss Voll. New Delhi: Mosaic Books, 1998.

Drèze, Jean, and Amartya Sen. *Indian Development: Selected Regional Perspectives*. New Delhi: Oxford University Press, 1997.

Levision, Deborah, Richard Anker, Shahid Ashraf, and Sandhya Barge. "Is Child Labour Really Necessary in India's Carpet Industry?" In *Economics of Child Labour in Hazardous Industries of India,* ed. Richard Anker, Sandhya Barge, M.P. Joseph, and Shobhita Rajagopal. Baroda, India: Centre for Operations Research and Training (CORT), 1998.

Lieten, G K. "Child Labour in India: Disentangling Essence and Solutions." *Economic and Political Weekly*, December 28, 2002.

———. "Child Labour: What Happened to the Worst Forms?" *Economic and Political Weekly*, January 14, 2006.

Mishra, Lakhsmidhar. *Child Labour in India*. New Delhi: Oxford University Press, 2000.

Thorat, Sukhade, and Nidhi Sadana. "Magnitude, Determinants and Activities of Child Labour in Rural India." Paper presented at the Conference of Child Labour in South Asia, New Delhi, October 15–17, 2001.

Weiner, Myron. "Child Labour in India: Political Agenda." *Economic and Political Weekly*, November 9, 1996.

Children in India's Glass Industry

Shahid Ashraf, Professor, Department of Economics,
Jamia Millia Islamia (Central University), New Delhi

The glass bangles industry is concentrated in and around the city of Ferozabad near Agra in the state of Uttar Pradesh. Development of the glass industry started around 1910. The industry in Ferozabad, which is centered in factories—large establishments with tall chimneys—uses primitive technology, with coal as the main fuel in the furnaces, leading to high levels of pollution. Initially the glass industry was not included in the Child Labour Act of 1986, but it has been listed among occupations hazardous to children since 1993. A range of glass products are produced in India, including domestic wares, scientific and laboratory wares, glass chandeliers, and glass bangles, a traditional Indian accessory worn especially during marriage ceremonies. Glass bangles have a symbolic significance in the cultural system of India. During festivals and marriage ceremonies, bangles are worn by all females, whether Hindu or Muslim.

Child labor is concentrated mainly in the production of glass bangles, rather than the glass industry as a whole. The glass sector producing bangles has a complex production structure, with work divided into many separate activities. Much of the work is done through subcontracting to small, informal-sector enterprises. The different production steps are performed by a specified manufacturing unit under subcontract, involving piece-rate systems of payment. It is important to understand the subcontracting industrial structure because working conditions, pay rates, and use of child labor vary among the stages of production. Estimates of child labor vary from 10 percent to 50 percent of the workforce, depending on the stage of production and the type of work.

Production Process, Wages, and Child Labor

At the factory level, the first stage of making bangles is done at the furnace by a team consisting of nearly twenty-five people, with each assigned a specific activity. Molten glass on a long rod is softened and transformed into a thin wire, which is subsequently rolled into a springlike spiral on a small rotating rod. The members of this team of twenty-five have specialized skills, and strong adults are employed at this stage. Within this team there are a few children, whose job is to carry rods to different team members. The skilled team members enjoy the highest wage levels in the glass-bangles production chain, ranging from US$2 to US$4 per day and linked to their productivity. This springlike spiral of glass is cut across, leaving individual open glass rings, with the ends on top of each other. These rings are counted, tied, and sent to smaller informal enterprises for further processing, where child labor generally occurs.

The glass rings are straightened by girls and women. The work is performed in their houses very early in the morning for three or four hours each day, before household work is started. Small kerosene burners are kept in a closed room, with no ventilation, so that the flame does not move, and as a result, the girls and women inhale the poisonous smoke. The side of the bangle opposite the cut is held near the flame, and the glass is softened just enough so the two sides of the cut can be pushed together to line up in preparation for joining. The daily piece rate for this work amounts to less than US$1.

Once the bangles have been straightened, they are sent to the joining units. The cut in the bangles is joined together in small rooms, also equipped with kerosene burners. Again, ventilation in the room is poor so that the flames remain steady. Male children and adults work side by side earning a daily piece rate in the range of US$1–$2.

The glass bangles are fragile after the joining stage and must be hardened. The hardening units are small furnaces housed in small thatched structures. Each furnace requires a team of 3–4 male persons, at least one of them a child. The bangles are laid on metal trays and baked (hardened) for around five minutes. The daily piece rate ranges from US$1 to US$2.

After the bangles have been hardened, workers etch intricate designs onto them by holding them against a spinning wheel with abrasive ridges. Generally, male adults work on these small cutting units, earning a daily piece rate of around US$2. Hardened bangles are sent for coloring, either before or after the designs have been cut. The chemical colors, toxic in nature, are applied either by small brushes or by hand. The coloring of bangles by hand is generally done by young girls. The daily piece rate for coloring ranges from US$1 to US$3.

The participation of child labor varies a great deal by type of enterprise and activity. In the case of straightening, young girls and women work in a closed room, exposed to smoke from kerosene burners. Both joining and cutting involve long hours of sitting in one cramped position. Coloring has a toxic impact on the girls, as chemical-based colors stick to their hands and are difficult to remove. When they are asked, the girls proudly say they are saving money for their marriage. The irony is that after some years of this work, many are afflicted with tuberculosis. Pollution levels are high, and respiratory problems, throat problems, and burns are common. Ferozabad has a tuberculosis hospital, where young men and women are admitted as patients after some years of working in these manufacturing units.

References and Further Reading

Barge, Sandhya, and Shahid Ashraf. "Child Labour in Glass-Bangles Industry of Ferozabad Uttar Pradesh: An Economic Analysis." In *Economics of Child Labour in Hazardous Industries of India,* ed. Richard Anker, Sandhya Barge, M.P. Joseph, and Shobhita Rajagopal. Baroda, India: Centre for Operations Research and Training (CORT), 1998.

Burra, Neera. *Born to Work: Child Labour in India.* New Delhi: University Press, 1995.

Lieten, G.K. "Child Labour: What Happened to the Worst Forms?" *Economic and Political Weekly,* January 14, 2006.

Children in India's Tea Industry

Shahid Ashraf, Professor, Department of Economics,
Jamia Millia Islamia (Central University), New Delhi

The tea industry in India is confined to four states: Assam and West Bengal in the northeast, and Kerala and Tamil Nadu in the south. Tea is made from the young leaves and leaf buds of the tea bush. The cultivation of tea in India began in 1834, with the planting of wild tea found growing in Assam. India and China are the world's largest tea producers. India's tea exports were estimated at Rs.17.31 billion in 2006. Major export destinations are Russia, the United Arab Emirates, the United States, the United Kingdom, and Germany. There were an estimated 129,027 tea estates in India in 2006, nearly all of them small holdings of less than ten hectares of land. These small holders typically sell their output to middlemen, to other larger plantations, or to tea factories.

Child labor in the tea industry is concentrated on tea plantations where tea is grown and plucked, and not in the factories where tea is processed and packed for sale. The Child Labour Act of 1986 does not mention work on tea plantations as an occupation hazardous to the health of children. The Plantation Labour Act (PLA) of 1954 defines three categories of workers: adults are those over age eighteen; adolescents are fourteen to eighteen years of age; and children are those twelve to fourteen years of age. Accordingly, the act permits children to work. Proposals to amend the Plantation Labour Act to restrict the employment of children below the age of fourteen were introduced in Parliament in 1991. Plantation employers voluntarily agreed not to engage child labor after 1998, but during peak plucking season this law has generally been violated.

Plantation and Labor

Tea plantations need large areas of land and a large labor force. 1.27 million workers are employed as permanent, temporary, or casual labor on the plantations. Of this number, around 50 percent are women, and 5 to 10 percent are children, though no reliable estimates of child labor on tea plantations have been undertaken. Among permanent workers, child labor is minimal. Children are mainly needed for temporary work during peak plucking season. The peak plucking season is from June to September in North India. In South India the crop is harvested from December to March.

In colonial India, plantation workers were brought from tribal regions to work in the tea estates, which were largely owned by the British. These tribal workers remained unskilled, and their children were made to help their parents to augment the family income. Though the workers have usually been affiliated with trade unions, their economic status has not improved.

With scarce employment opportunities in the plantation regions, workers are forced to bring their children to work, rather than sending them to school. Plantation owners also encourage family-based employment as it saves on recruitment and housing costs. Plantation owners are required to provide small single-room dwellings to plantation workers. So, a family of five needs one unit of housing, whereas five workers from five different families need five units of housing. Most plantation workers live in unhygienic conditions within the tea estates.

Unlike other agricultural operations, tea plantations are considered to be part of industry. The employment conditions of plantation workers are protected just like those of industrial workers. Casual workers receive the same wages as regular workers, but they are not entitled to any benefits. For example, casual women workers have no maternity benefits, and their children cannot study in the plantation schools. Employers are required to provide free primary schools within the plantation area, but only if there are twenty-five or more children in the age-group six to twelve in the plantation.

Workers are needed in the field for plucking, weeding, pesticide spraying, pruning, clearing the garden, and making pits for new saplings. Plucking and weeding are generally done by women and their daughters. Tea plucking is a tough job and is physically debilitating. The heavy baskets workers carry concentrate the weight on the head and neck, leading to severe back pain. Generally, women bring their daughters to help them with plucking. This initiation subsequently leads the girls to work on the tea estates when they are grown. Spraying of pesticides in the tea gardens is done by male adolescents and children, leading to exposure to toxic materials.

Work begins at sunrise. Working hours for adults are limited to no more than eight hours per day for a six-day week. Adolescent and child workers are limited to no more than four and a half hours per day for a six-day week. Wages are of three kinds. Workers are paid a time-rated wage (daily wage) and a price-rated wage (extra leaf price) and are given food grains at subsidized rates. All three together constitute the minimum wage. The total minimum wage ranges from US 50 cents to US$1.50 per day.

Conclusion

Child labor is a moral outrage to human dignity. Many children in poor families are sent to work without getting an opportunity to educate themselves and learn skills. Child labor has been prevalent in different industries for historical reasons, as parents passed on traditional skills to their children, but on tea plantations the reasons seem to be the low wages received by adult workers and the lack of other viable employment opportunities.

References and Further Reading

Bhowmik, Sharit K., Virginius Xaxa, and M.A. Alam. *Tea Plantation Labour in India.* New Delhi: Friedrich Ebert Stiftung, 1996.

Joseph, M.P., and Shahid Ashraf. Background paper. National Consultation with Trade Unions for Developing Projects on the Elimination of Child Labour in India. ILO-IPEC, New Delhi, 1998.

Proceedings of the Workshop on Elimination of Child Labour in Tea Plantations Area in West Bengal. Labour Department, Government of West Bengal, with ILO (IPEC), February 21–22, 1997.

Children of Kolkata Slums

Subrata Sankar Bagchi, PhD, Department of Anthropology,
Bangabasi Evening College, Kolkata, India

Like many other decolonized third world cities, Kolkata (formerly Calcutta), India, is densely dotted with slum settlements. In one category of slums, *bustees,* the residents construct permanent buildings, which are later authorized by the government. In *jhupris,* another category of slums, the housing is in much worse condition because residents of the settlements lack both security of tenure and basic infrastructure. Kolkata Metropolitan Development Authority (erstwhile Calcutta Metropolitan Development Authority [CMDA]) data show that there are 2,011 registered and about 3,500 unregistered slums in Kolkata (CMDA 1993), which house 1.5 million people, or 32.5 percent of the total Kolkata population. The slums of Kolkata stand as the mark of desperation of those with no other option but to shelter themselves in overcrowded conditions with little prospect of having a safe water supply, hygienic waste disposal facilities, or adequate ventilation. They face the possibility of endemic diseases in the settlement area, with grossly insufficient municipal services and an inadequate primary health-care system with little or no affordable secondary and tertiary referral curative facilities. Absence of skills to work in the formal economy compels an overwhelming number of people in these slums to be absorbed in work in the so-called informal sector of the economy. In most cases, family income is less than US$1 per day (Kar et al. 1997).

Children in Kolkata Slums

The situation is equally precarious for the nearly half million children residing in the Kolkata slums. Very few children come from literate families; only 100,000 of nearly 1.5 million people in the slums are literate. Education takes a backseat, as children are sent to work because of their families' need for their financial contribution, to help in the family business, or because of their own need to make money for survival. The spiraling poverty and lack of interest in education compel parents in these slums (particularly in the unregistered slums) to release the overwhelming proportion of their children into the ruthless labor market (Bagchi 2006).

Children and Work in Kolkata Slums

The children from the slums of Kolkata generally start working at seven or eight years of age, and they work strenuously for more than eight hours a day, six to seven days a week, with little or no rest during their working hours. They work in a wide variety of settings. Some work in family businesses, and others are self-employed in the informal economy. Some are domestic helpers or workers in roadside food stalls and restaurants. Children work as waste pickers, porters, van and rickshaw pullers, bidi (cigarette) rollers, shoe shiners, and paper-packet makers. Many slum children in Kolkata work as beggars. Some are engaged as apprentices in various skilled work such as garage work, cooking, or construction. Much of this work is hazardous, exposing children to noxious gases, harmful chemicals, tobacco, dangerous flames, dog bites, and other accidents that are sometimes fatal. Very few workplaces have any facility for hazard prevention, self-protection, first aid, or even toilets. The children often have to walk a long way to and from their workplaces because they cannot afford any other mode of transport.

In return for their daily ordeal, many children

earn pitiable amounts—US 25 cents per day or less. Children working as apprentices often receive no money at all; their employers provide only meals as remuneration for their work. In other cases where children themselves are not paid, an adult family member may receive their wages. In most cases where children are paid, they contribute nearly the entire amount of their earnings to their families to support the household budget. These children frequently receive harsh treatment from their employers or adult colleagues in their workplaces. However, in spite of harsh treatment, it is surprising to note that the overwhelming majority of these working children do not leave their jobs unless they are compelled to do so.

Inside Their Lives

Bagchi (2006) recorded observations of perceptions of various parties regarding child labor in Kolkata. Children recognize that their families' financial inability to continue their schooling is the main reason they work. Parents tend to cite the family's financial inability to pay for schooling, or they maintain that apprenticeship to a skilled and lucrative job is a better prospect than schooling for their children. Most employers say that they employ children in their establishments only to help the families. Most of these working children consider their lives to be very harsh, but they have somehow accepted it as their destiny. They also tend to be optimistic about their future, for example, expecting that they might earn more money to support their families.

Toward a Vicious Cycle?

Promulgation of laws against child labor has proved to be counterproductive for the working children in Kolkata slums. Recent measures, such as the 2006 ban on children working as domestic servants and in roadside eateries (*dhabas*), have only worsened the child labor situation in Kolkata by increasing surreptitious employment of children in informal establishments, or by bringing about the outright firing of children. Without any rehabilitation, this may leave the children and their parents no alternative but to beg in the streets. In response to the forces of globalization, the government has hardened its stance on child labor, but it seems completely oblivious to the actual fallout of more restrictive measures on the lives of children and their families in a third world city such as Kolkata.

References and Further Reading

Bagchi, Subrata Sankar. "Child Labor in Kolkata." *Asian Anthropology* 5 (2006): 131–44.

———. "Social Dynamics of the Marginalisation of Population and Child Labour in Calcutta." PhD thesis, University of Calcutta, 2006.

CMDA. *Kolkata Slum Improvement Project 1991–92.* Kolkata: CMDA, 1993.

Kar, Kamal, with S.N. Datta, S. Goswami, et al. *Participatory Impact Assessment, Kolkata Slum Improvement Project.* New Delhi: Calcutta Metropolitan Development Authority, Department for International Development, 1997.

Children of Delhi Slums

Arup Mitra, Institute of Economic Growth, Delhi University

The work of street children has bothered social scientists a great deal. Children participate in economic activities, however petty the work may be, to augment household income. This is one reason why large household size and high fertility rate are seen as assets by poor households. From society's point of view, however, this means poor human capital formation and perpetuation of poverty. School enrollment conflicts directly with the short-term interest of low-income households. Hence, government initiatives in the form of compensatory schemes are necessary to demotivate households from sending their children into the labor market. The exemption of children from school fees, free midday meals, and free supplies and study materials are some measures that can motivate households to send children to school. Notwithstanding government initiatives to ban child labor, the phenomenon is prevalent and school dropout rates are quite high.

The conventional distinction between economic and noneconomic activities is quite unsatisfactory for both the analysis and the measurement of child activity patterns in slum environments (Rodgers and Standing 1981). Children may be engaged in more than one activity at a time, combining work and school; their work may be intermittent, or they may change activities frequently; they may or may not be paid for their work; or they may share a workload with adults or a family labor force.

Because the construct *child labor* is so imperfectly measured by *economic activities,* some authors have used indirect evidence, drawing inferences from indicators related to education and poverty. For example, Gupta and Mitra (1997) estimated child labor in Delhi slums, based on education criteria, at about 34 percent; based on poverty criteria, the estimate ranged up to 65 percent. Education criteria include illiteracy, low enrollments, and high dropout rates. However, education criteria may underestimate child labor because a large percentage of slum children are neither in school nor reported to be working. Regarding poverty, households engaged in casual employment in the low-productivity tertiary sector are the major suppliers of child labor. They are characterized by high fertility rates, large numbers of children, and high incidence of poverty. Households with their principal earners engaged in manufacturing are less likely to send their children to earn an income because industrial wages are higher than are those for other activities. Among child workers, early starters usually earn less and put in longer hours than late starters. Early starting is not associated with the acquisition of skills, job specialization, and the type of work experience and other factors that contribute to higher incomes (Swaminathan 1997).

Another aspect of the problem of child labor in slums is the relationship of households to political parties. When households take up residence on public land, affiliation with a political party is seen as way of legitimizing their encroachment on public land as well as securing their entitlement to basic amenities. But in the long run this process perpetuates dependence on political parties and traps low-income households permanently in a low equilibrium of poverty, illiteracy, and poor health. In such a situation, child labor remains endemic. The role of civil society is important to create awareness among low- income households to overcome the greed of short-term gains at the cost of long-term prospects for upward mobility.

Because extreme poverty compels children to work, antipoverty schemes and other income-generating opportunities are important for reducing the incidence of child labor, rather than conceiving its eradication entirely in terms of compulsory education (Weiner 1996). The state must provide economic incentives to compensate at least part of the cost of rearing and educating the child, that is, a part of the income that might have been earned in the labor market. Otherwise, households often make deliberate efforts to conceal the fact that their children are participating in the labor market. Another effective policy is to introduce vocational training courses in the educational system. The formal education system does not encourage parents to send their children to schools, as it does not help them find jobs in the formal sector. In fact, it is seen as a pure waste of time and effort. Vocational-training courses can enhance prospects for future income-earning opportunities.

References and Further Reading

Gupta, I., and Arup Mitra. "Child Labour: A Profile of Delhi Slums." *Indian Journal of Labour Economics* 40:4 (1997).

Rodgers, Gerry, and Guy Standing. *Child Work, Poverty and Underemployment.* Geneva: ILO, 1981.

Swaminathan, M. "Do Child Workers Acquire Specialised Skills? A Case Study of Teenage Workers in Bhavnagar." *Indian Journal of Labour Economics* 40:4 (1997).

Weiner, Myron. "Child Labour in India: Putting Compulsory Primary Education on the Political Agenda." *Economic and Political Weekly* 31:45–46 (1996).

Working Children's Unions in India

Heike Roschanski, Anthropological Researcher,
International Research on Working Children (IREWOC) Foundation

Inspired by the 1989 UN Convention on the Rights of the Child (CRC), a rights-oriented and "child centered approach to child labor" (Karunan 2005, 294) has become an increasingly accepted concept in India. A rights-oriented and child-centered approach to child labor entails a strong emphasis on the active involvement of children themselves and a focus on children's perspective on their working lives, their perceptions of problems, as well as their capacities to find solutions. Within the broad spectrum of organizations working on the issue of child labor in India, working children's organizations form a small but distinctive group, aiming to take "child-centeredness" further than other organizations by giving children a central role in all aspects of project planning and implementation.

Working children's movements emerged in Latin America in the 1970s and have grown into national networks in several countries, most notably Peru and Bolivia. In India, the first working children's organizations were formed more recently, in the early 1990s. Among the first organizations were Bhima Sangha from the southern state of Karnataka and the Bal Mazdoor Union, which is active in the capital, Delhi. In 1996, the first international meeting of working children's organizations took place in Kundapur, Karnataka, hosted by the Concerned for Working Children and Bhima Sangha. During this meeting, representatives from children's organizations from Africa, Latin America, and Asia came together for the first time and drafted the "Kundapur Declaration" outlining their viewpoints and demands. The meeting in Kundapur was followed by a series of similar events in different countries, and more declarations emerged out of those events during the following years, including the "Dakar Declaration" of 1998 and the "Berlin Declaration" of 2004.

Ideology

Working children's organizations, while not to be confused with trade unions, focus on the working lives of children and their identity as working children. Instead of focusing on welfare measures, the organizations demand that working children be acknowledged as a group that possesses rights, and that in order to create lasting change, children must be given the space to voice their own opinions and develop their own initiatives. The organizations do not call for unconditional eradication of child labor, at least not in the short term; rather, they call for more control, regulation, and protection within their work sphere. One of the main arguments brought forth by working children's organizations in favor of regulation, or a gradual approach toward the eradication of child labor, is the belief that children and their families often do not have a choice and that the income of children is essential to the survival of the family and the children themselves. From this point of view, the abolition of child labor would violate the child's right to earn a livelihood, while it also tends to criminalize working children without offering feasible alternatives and is therefore not in the best interest of the child. Work is seen as a legitimate strategy of children to respond to the challenges and hardships they face in their daily lives. The Berlin Declaration of 2004 asserts, "In our lives our work allows us to resist with dignity the economic, political and suppressing model that criminalizes and excludes us and continues to worsen the living conditions of ourselves, our families and our communities."

The organizations make a practical distinction between child work and child labor, the first being tolerated and to some degree supported, the second being regarded as undesirable or even intolerable. However, as *harmfulness* is a relative and poorly defined concept, there is also some disagreement about the kind of work deemed acceptable for children. As a consequence, some organizations accept the fact that children below the age of fourteen may have to make substantial contributions to their families and should therefore be supported and strengthened within their work environment, even if this environment is potentially harmful. Others, such as Hasiru Sangha (supported by the Association for Promotion of Social Action), firmly defend the position that a child below the age of fourteen needs to be educated and should not be engaged in any work that obstructs full-time formal education.

Structure

Working children's organizations are said to be set up by children and for children, according to their own needs and priorities. In practice, the children's organizations are frequently born out of programs and activities conducted by NGOs (Miljeteig 2000). The children's organizations consequently remain, to differing degrees, embedded in the wider program of the supporting NGOs. Some claim to function as autonomous organizations, receiving support and advice only when they need it, while others are acknowledged by their supporting NGOs as being part of their program, albeit a part that offers children a high degree of participation. The activities of the children's organizations either overlap or are complemented by those provided by the adult organizations. The support received from adults is often substantial, and adult educators or facilitators are involved in most of the children's activities, ranging from supervision to planning and running activities.

Working children's organizations in India mainly function on a local level, usually in one city. The only organization with a regional network is Bhima Sangha, which operates in different parts of the state of Karnataka. All organizations operate local chapters or groups, which form the core of the children's organizations. These local chapters consist of an average of ten to twenty children living or working in the same area. Due to the local or regional character of the respective organizations, there is little or no formal hierarchy among the groups. The regular members of the groups are usually also those who represent the groups at larger meetings. The contact and cooperation between local groups varies but is mostly limited to monthly or bimonthly meetings.

The National Movement of Working Children was officially founded in 1999 as a federation of working children's organizations in India; most members are situated in the southern part of India. The cooperation between the organizations is loose because of both distance and language barriers, as well as differing priorities of their supporting organizations. The regular activities of the National Movement of Working Children consist mainly of meetings twice per year, where information and experiences are shared among members. Among the achievements of the movement was the production of an alternative CRC report, published in 1998. This "Working Children's Report" was prepared by Bhima Sangha, Mahashakti Sangha (Tamil Nadu), and Soshu Panchayat (Orissa) and presented before the Committee on the Rights of the Child in Geneva. A second "Alternate Report" was compiled with the aid of representatives of Indranush Sangam, Vidiyal Vanavil Sangham, Ele Nakshatra, Hasiru Sangha, and Bhima Sangha and submitted to the Committee on the Rights of the Child in 2003.

The Members

None of the Indian working children's organizations have formal membership criteria, and all are principally open to children between the ages of six and eighteen. The target groups are working children, but *work* is defined broadly and differently by the respective organizations. The Bal Mazdoor Union, for example, is open to any street and working child, although there are rules regarding conduct. Another children's organization is open to working children as well as former working children; yet another organization is flexible in the admission of children and does not restrict membership to children whose main activity is work; part-time work and even smaller contributions to the household qualify a child as a "working child." In general, active members of all organizations are rarely younger than ten to twelve years old and are mostly aged between twelve and sixteen. In theory, membership ceases when the age of eighteen is passed, but some members subsequently become facilitators or take on other responsibilities within the NGO's wider program.

Occupation and economic activities of the members differ by organization, as each works with a specific target group. Most are self-employed and work irregular hours. Common activities include rag picking and street vending, as well as work in tea stalls or restaurants. The street-based membership consists mainly of boys. Other organizations or chapters attract girls working part-time as domestic workers, or children working in the construction sector. Children working full-time and for an employer are the exception among the active members. This is mainly due to the fact that their work does not leave them sufficient time and energy to attend meetings and other activities. Child laborers, that is, those working excessive hours or under conditions deemed harmful or detrimental to their development, tend to be among the children who are not reached and often not even systematically targeted by the organizations. As a consequence, those children actively involved in the organizations tend to be working part-time, are often going to school (frequently sponsored by supporting NGOs), and are sometimes not working at all.

Recruitment of children into the organizations takes place through different channels: through the services provided by the supporting NGOs; through contact with social workers and other staff members of these NGOs; and through hearsay from other children. As membership is not strictly formalized, the size of the organizations is difficult to determine and is based on estimates. Bhima Sangha, the biggest working children's organization in India, claims to have a membership ranging between 13,000 and 20,000. The much smaller but very vocal Bal Mazdoor Union counts between 500 and 1,000 children as members. Another working children's organization, Hasiru Sangha, also has a membership of around 500 children.

Child Rights

Besides dealing with child labor and the working conditions of their members, working children's organizations and their supporting NGOs also set out to claim children's rights on a broader scale. Some of these rights, as defined in the UN CRC, are central to understanding the organizations and their programs and activities. Key among those rights are the right to participation, the right to freedom of association and assembly, and the right to education. The right to participation is set out in a cluster of articles in the CRC. Article 12 states that "State Parties shall assure to the child who is capable of forming his or her own views the right to express those views freely in all matters affecting the child, the views of the child being given due weight in accordance with the age and maturity of the child." The right to participation also extends to the work sphere: "In addition to protective legislation and procedures to prevent exploitation of children in employment (article 32), under article 12, respect is required for the views of the child, and in any judicial or administrative proceedings relating to employment of children, the child has the right to be heard" (UNICEF 2002).

The "child's right to the freedom of association and peaceful assembly" (Article 15) has been leveraged to legitimize the existence of children's organizations. For example, the Bal Mazdoor Union tried to register with the Registrar of Trade Unions. Their application was rejected on the grounds that no person below the age of fifteen can be a member of a union or form a union according to the Trade Union Act of 1925. The organization then filed a petition in the Delhi High Court, which was dismissed on the grounds that children cannot enter into contracts with adults. While the attempt to officially register the organization failed and the issue has since been shelved, the exercise of the right of association and assembly has helped to create an important social dimension to the children's organizations. The local groups provide social spaces where children can meet peers, make friends, play, and feel safe.

The right to education features high on the organizations' agenda, but work and education are not viewed as being necessarily incompatible. The NGOs supporting the children's organizations frequently run or support education programs, ranging from nonformal education provided to children in afternoon or evening hours to government-accredited schooling programs and sponsorships for children to attend government schools. Education is seen as a right, but the respective organizations take different positions on whether education should be exclusively full-time formal education, or whether the education schedule should be adjusted to the needs of working children. The latter refers to evening classes, providing children with the opportunity to study after they are finished working.

Activities

Regular meetings are the core activities of the children's groups. Local chapters meet at fixed intervals, usually weekly, to discuss various issues and plan activities. This takes place on the initiative of both the children themselves and their adult facilitators. Issues discussed are sometimes related to the children's work sphere, a child's personal problems, or problems in the community where the children live. More often, however, the meetings are used to plan or follow up on other activities, such as cultural or sporting events or meetings on a higher level. Some activities are directly aimed at improving working conditions of the members but are not treated as a priority by the organizations. This is because the members are often self-employed, the nature of their work leaves little space for adjustment, or their bargaining power is too weak. Where improvements have been achieved, it often involves the payment of outstanding wages or securing alternative employment.

Children's organizations are also involved in various lobbying and advocacy activities, on local, regional, national, and even international levels. Examples include theater groups staging plays to educate communities, door-to-door information campaigns, production of printed publications, and participation in public meetings. Activities that take place beyond the local level are largely initiated by the supporting NGOs, and only a small number of children participate in them. Differentiation between activities initiated and run by children and those initiated and run by adults cannot always be clearly made.

A Right to Work?

Part of the controversy around working children's organizations stems from the perception that, by demanding a "right to work," they are actually promoting, or at least condoning, child labor. The right to work, however, is not expressed by all working children's organizations to the same extent. The degree to which labor market participation is deemed acceptable differs from organization to organization, and none of the organizations demands a right to work that is exploitative by nature. In general, the types of work defended by the organizations do not contradict provisions of ILO Conventions 138 and 182 or the UN CRC.

Conclusion

The members of working children's organizations are vulnerable children, not only as working children but also as generally deprived children. This vulnerability is the result of their general socioeconomic background, rather than mainly a consequence of their engagement in "economic activities." The strength of working children's organizations lies foremost in the following aspects: the provision of a safe and stimulating environment that enables children to interact and to learn; the stimulation of children's participation in their own affairs; the mobilization of communities and the drawing of attention to social problems; and pressure on authorities to address structural problems that cause and perpetuate child labor.

References and Further Reading

"Berlin Declaration." Adopted by representatives of the Movement of Working Children and Youths of Africa, Latin America, and Asia at their meeting in Berlin, Germany, 2004.

Boyden, Jo, Birgitta Ling, and William E. Myers. *What Works for Working Children.* Stockholm: UNICEF / Rädda Barnen, 1998.

Butterflies Programme with Street and Working Children. http://www.butterflieschildrights.org/home.asp.

———. *In Search of Fair Play: Street and Working Children Speak About Their Rights.* New Delhi: Mosaic Books, 2001.

———. *Annual Report 2003–2004.* New Delhi, 2004.

Concerned for Working Children. http://www.workingchild.org/.

———. *Work We Can and Cannot Do, by the Children of Balkur.* Bangalore: Concerned for Working Children, 1999.

———. *Annual Report 2003.* Bangalore: Concerned for Working Children, 2003.

"Dakar Declaration." Adopted by representatives of the Movement of Working Children and Youths of Africa, Latin America, and Asia at their meeting in Dakar, Senegal, 1998.

IREWOC. *Studying Child Labour: Policy Implications of Child-Centred Research.* Amsterdam: IREWOC Foundation, 2005.

Karunan, Victor P. "Working Children as Change Makers: Perspectives from the South." In *Child Labour and Human Rights: Making Children Matter,* ed. Burns H. Weston. Boulder, CO: Lynne Rienner, 2005.

Kundapur Declaration. Adopted at the First Meeting of Working Children, Kundapur, India, November 27–December 9, 1996.

Liebel, Manfred. *A Will of Their Own: Cross-Cultural Perspectives on Working Children.* London: Zed Books, 2004.

Liebel, Manfred, B. Overwien, and A. Recknagel, eds. *Working Children's Protagonism: Social Movements and Empowerment in Latin America, Africa and India.* Frankfurt: IKO–Verlag fuer Interkulturelle Kommunikation, 2001.

Lieten, G.K., Ravi Srivastav, and Thorat Sukhadeo, eds. *Small Hands in South Asia: Child Labour in Perspective.* Manohar, Delhi: IDPAD, 2004.

Lieten, G.K., and Ben White, eds. *Child Labour: Policy Options.* Amsterdam: Aksant, 2001.

Miljeteig, Per. *Creating Partnerships with Working Children and Youths.* Washington, DC: World Bank Social Protection Discussion Paper Series, 2000.

Mishra, Lakshmidhar. *Child Labour in India.* New Delhi: Oxford University Press, 2000.

National Movement of Working Children. *The Alternate Report.* Bangalore, India, July 2003.

Reddy, N., and Kavita Ratna. *A Journey in Children's Participation.* Bangalore: Concerned for Working Children, 2002.

Roschanski, Heike. "Working Children's Organisations in India." In *Working Children: Unionisation and Participation,* ed. Marten van den Berge, Godefroid Nimbona, and Heike Roschanski. Amsterdam: IREWOC Foundation, 2007.

Swift, A. *Working Children Get Organised: An Introduction to Working Children's Organisations.* London: Save the Children Alliance, 1999.

UNICEF. *Implementation Handbook for the Convention on the Rights of the Child.* New York: UNICEF, 2002.

Child Labor and HIV and AIDS in India

Indrani Gupta, Professor, Institute of Economic Growth, Delhi

The two-way link between child labor and HIV/AIDS has only recently become an important component of the discourse on the epidemic, with international organizations, NGOs, and national governments increasingly starting to emphasize the need for more innovative policies to tackle the issue of child labor in the context of the AIDS epidemic (ILO 2003; Le Breton and Brusati 2001).

The consensus on the links between AIDS and child labor can be summarized in three points. First, poverty forces children into various kinds of labor, exposing them to a wide range of vulnerabilities, which in turn lead to the likelihood of contracting HIV. Second, HIV and AIDS lead to a deepening of poverty through significant socioeconomic impact at the household level, forcing children to replace adults as primary wage earners and caregivers. Third, HIV and AIDS render significant numbers of children orphaned and homeless, forcing them to earn a livelihood and depriving them of education and a normal childhood.

These three links indicate that HIV and AIDS can increase the incidence of child labor, and the presence of a large pool of vulnerable child workers has the potential of deepening the epidemic. Preventing child labor can, therefore, act as both prevention and mitigation strategies in the context of the HIV/AIDS epidemic, and prevention of HIV among children can reduce the incidence of child labor. Organizations such as the ILO now clearly recognize that "poverty leads to child labor and vice-versa. Not only does HIV/AIDS add a tragic dimension to this vicious circle; it also makes the poverty–child labor link more difficult to break by exacerbating the root causes of child labor and adding strongly to the supply of child laborers. As a consequence of the losses in human resources due to the pandemic, inter-generation solidarity—of adults caring for children, sending them to school and ensuring the future of society—disintegrates" (ILO 2003).

Child Labor in India

National estimates of child labor in India have been under some debate and discussion in the recent past, with many arguing that estimates may not reflect the true state of affairs. The two major official sources of data on child employment, the National Sample Survey and the census, derive child labor estimates from the age-wise distribution of workers. Census estimates indicate 12.5 million working children between the ages of five and fourteen in 2001, whereas the National Sample Survey estimates the number to be 10 million. The estimates ignore children working in various unpaid activities, including household activities, as well as children who neither attend school nor do paid work or obvious household chores. The estimates also do not include activities such as prostitution, begging, or smuggling, which, though they may generate income, are not conventionally considered economic activities (National Sample Survey Organisation 2005).

The NGO Child Rights and You recently estimated that there might be as many as 16.5 million working children in India, including those who perform domestic chores. In addition, the National Sample Survey data indicate that there are about 46 million children in the category "others" who neither work nor do any domestic chores, and who do not attend school. These children are potentially vulnerable to child abuse, exploitation, and labor. It is thus estimated that the number of child laborers in India could range from 60 million to 100 million (Child Rights and You India 2007; Mukherjee et al. 2006).

HIV and AIDS in India

The AIDS epidemic affects children in two principal ways. First, there are children *infected* by HIV through one of the following routes: mother-to-child transmission, sexual abuse, child prostitution and child marriages, infected blood, and injecting drug use. Second, there are children *affected* by HIV: This includes children orphaned by the epidemic and children who take on the role of caregivers. Clearly, the two categories have large overlaps, with infected children also taking on the role of caregivers and becoming orphans, and vice versa.

Currently, there are no firm estimates available on any of these categories in India. Child marriage is still widely practiced in many parts of the country. Some reports indicate that more than one-third of all brides in India are below the legal age of eighteen (Chopra 2006). Very little data exist on the prevalence or consequences of child marriages, but in the context of both child labor and HIV, child marriage is a phenomenon that cannot be ignored. Similarly, estimates of the number of children contracting HIV through infected mothers or through injecting drug use or infected blood are not only unavailable but also often not included in discussions of HIV and AIDS.

Globally, UNAIDS estimates that 5 million children have been infected with the HIV virus and some 15 million children under age eighteen have lost one or both parents to AIDS. Some sources put the number of HIV-infected children in India at 2 million and the number of infected children born every year at 56,700 (Menon 2007). The source of infection is not available. As for orphans, World Bank estimates suggest that the number of children in India orphaned by AIDS is approaching 2 million, which places India at the top of the list in terms of AIDS orphans. The proportion of orphaned children is expected to double in the next five years and remain exceptionally high until 2020 or 2030. According to UN estimates, there are approximately 35 million orphans in India, from AIDS and other causes, with an orphan being defined as a child under age eighteen who has lost one or both parents (UNAIDS, UNICEF, and USAID 2004). In the absence of other more recent or official estimates, these numbers indicate that AIDS orphans comprise about 6 percent of all orphans in India.

AIDS orphans have been reported to have a plight worse than other orphans due to discrimination and stigma. Many of these orphans may be infected themselves, making their situation worse. To the number of AIDS orphans should be added other AIDS-affected children, who have turned into caregivers and principal wage earners in their families but whose parents are still alive. However, no estimates are available on how many nonorphan children are affected in a year due to parents' illnesses. These children have a plight very similar to that of the AIDS orphans.

Few organizations cater to the needs of these orphans or other AIDS-affected children, who are likely to join the visible or invisible child labor force. The status of the girl child is an important issue. Many studies show that in a time of crisis, the girl child is more likely to be withdrawn from school than the boy child, especially in their roles as caregivers (Rau 2002). Girls, and sometimes boys, without parents, who take care of themselves and their siblings, are also targets of sexual abuse and violence. Save the Children (2006) has been documenting this phenomenon in India, pointing to child domestic work as an especially important concern in this context, since many such children are targets of abuse. They also reported that 40 percent of commercial sex workers in India are girls below eighteen years of age; that much sexual abuse takes place at home and is perpetrated by a known person; and that disabled children and mentally challenged girls are at greater risk of sexual abuse than other girls (Save the Children 2006).

Policy Response

Many argue that HIV- and AIDS-infected and affected children are nearly invisible in the Indian government's policy response. "Children affected by HIV/AIDS are being discriminated against in education and health services, denied care by orphanages, and pushed onto the streets and into the worst forms of child labor. Gender discrimination makes girls more vulnerable to HIV transmission and makes it more difficult for them to get care. Many children, especially the most vulnerable, as well as the professionals who care for them, are not getting the information about HIV they need to protect themselves or to combat discrimination" (Human Rights Watch 2004).

The various legal and administrative laws and regulations on child labor in India remain inadequate to address the special case of HIV- and AIDS-infected and affected children, who form a significant part of the vulnerable children in the country. Currently, the Indian Child Labor (Prohibition and Regulation) Act (1986) prohibits employment of children below fourteen years of age in certain specified hazardous occupations and processes and regulates working conditions in others. A 2006 amendment to the Child Labor Act states that action can be taken against anyone who employs children under age fourteen in domestic work in homes or hotels. The National Policy on Child Labor also mentions the need to focus on general developmental programs benefiting child laborers and their families. Specific interventions have been launched in 250 districts of high-child-labor prevalence in the country. In addition, twenty-one districts have been covered under INDUS, a scheme for rehabilitation of child laborers in cooperation with the U.S. Department of Labor. For the districts that are not covered under these schemes, the government provides funds directly to NGOs under a grants-in-aid scheme for running special schools for rehabilitation of child laborers.

While these schemes and plans seem good, the fact remains that India has rampant child labor exploitation, indicating that the policies have not been able to address the issue in a significant way. The existing provisos are weak enough to ensure that all children who are being forced to work to earn a livelihood will not be covered; it is therefore very unlikely that the special case of HIV- and AIDS-affected children will be addressed without further policy changes.

The AIDS epidemic in India is likely to increase the phenomenon of child labor; at the same time, the presence of a large pool of vulnerable children is likely to increase the pool of infected children in the country. In the coming years, India is likely to see an increasing number of AIDS-affected children, even if the epidemic itself tapers off among adults. The twin phenomena of vulnerability and HIV in such large numbers makes India a unique case in the world. In the absence of comprehensive policies to address both child labor and HIV/AIDS, it is unlikely that the country will see improvements in the situation in coming years. The need for a multipronged, multisectoral, and holistic approach from all those engaged in either of these issues is urgently required. Anything less than this would render the set of current policies and statements on child welfare merely lip service.

References and Further Reading

Child Rights and You India. "Concept Paper on Child Labour in India." Presented at an Operations Meeting on Child Labor Estimation, Delhi, March 26–27, 2007.

Chopra, Anuj. "India Tackles Child Marriages." *Christian Science Monitor,* May 24, 2006. http://www.csmonitor.com/2006/0524/p06s02-wosc.html.

Human Rights Watch. *Future Forsaken: Abuses Against Children Affected by HIV/AIDS in India.* New York: Human Rights Watch, 2004. http://hrw.org/reports/2004/india0704/FutureForsaken.pdf.

ILO. *Facts on the HIV/AIDS Crisis and Child Labour.* Geneva: ILO/IPEC, 2003.

Le Breton, Sarah, and Annalisa Brusati. *Child Labor and HIV/AIDS: Exploring the Interface I. A Brief Overview of Recent Literature, Research and Organizational Commitment.* London: Save the Children UK, 2001.

Menon, Jaya. "3 Months On, Drugs for HIV+ Kids Run Short." *Indian Express,* February 13, 2007. http://www.indianexpress.com/story/23161.html.

Mukherjee, S.P., Ratan Khasnabis, Dipankar Coondoo, Pradip Maiti, and Sharmistha Banerjee. *Draft Report on the Project of Centre for Studies in Economic Appraisal.* Kolkata: CSEA in partnership with Child Rights and You, Mumbai, 2006.

National Sample Survey Organisation. *Employment and Unemployment Situation in India. NSS 60th Round (January 2004–June 2004).* Report 506 (60/10/1), 2005.

Rau, Bill. *Combating Child Labour and HIV/AIDS in Sub-Saharan Africa.* Geneva: ILO/IPEC, 2002.

Save the Children. *Abuse Among Child Domestic Workers: A Research Study in West Bengal.* Kolkata: Save the Children UK, 2006. http://www.savethechildren.org.uk/en/docs/abuse_amongst_Child_Domestic_Workers_in_India.pdf.

UNAIDS, UNICEF, and USAID. *Children on the Brink 2004: A Joint Report of New Orphan Estimates and a Framework for Action.* Washington, DC: USAID, 2004. http://www.unicef.org/publications/files/cob_layout6–013.pdf.

Education and Child Labor in India

Sharmistha Self, Department of Economics, Missouri State University

India is a country where the problems of child labor and universal education continue to pose serious difficulties. Estimates from the 2001 Census of India (which shows wide variations between states) indicate that there are about 12.6 million children in employment in India. This is a marked increase from the 1991 census, which reported this number to be 11.28 million. The numbers officially reported could be greatly underestimating the real numbers. This trend of increasing child labor is perplexing in a country experiencing remarkable economic growth over the same period. Traditionally, policy makers and economists have blamed poverty as one of the primary causes of child labor. If this is indeed true, then India represents an anomaly.

The government of India has been tackling the issue of child labor for several decades, but it remains a daunting task given the sheer magnitude of the problem. As early as 1933, the Indian government enacted the first child labor law, which has been followed by nine separate additional laws. It ought to be obvious that child labor laws alone cannot cure this problem. One essential solution is that of making education compulsory and accessible to all. One cannot discuss child labor without looking at education. Clearly child labor and education are substitutes. When children are at work they miss out on their education; and when children are in school, they are not working. Numerous studies have shown high correlation between schooling and child labor, but an alternative argument urges that the two are complementary; children have to work to provide the income to enable them to go to school (Siddiqi and Patrinos 1995). Regardless of whether child labor and education are substitutes or complements, it is important to recognize that in countries where education is not compulsory, decisions regarding schooling or work lie mainly in the hands of parents. If children are perceived as a source of income, parents need some assurance regarding the returns to education before they are willing to forgo income to send their children to school. Thus, factors such as parents' education (Tienda 1979), family income (Ilon and Moock 1991), the established role for females (Bequele and Boyden 1988; Lahiri and Self 2007), and order of birth (Patrinos and Psacharopoulos 1993), all come into play.

Unless there is an effort at making education compulsory, accessible, and affordable to all, especially the poor and those living in remote and rural areas, any policy aimed at reducing child labor is unlikely to succeed. This is particularly important for India. According to the 2002 census, literacy stands at 65.38 percent overall, with 75.85 percent of males and 54.16 percent of females being literate. This is an impressive increase over the 1991 census, which showed an overall literacy rate of 40.8 percent (World Bank 1995). However, India's overall literacy rate lags far behind those of other developing countries such as China (72.6 percent), Sri Lanka (86.1 percent), and Indonesia (74.1 percent). These numbers are, of course, averages for the entire country. One state in India that has proven to be an exception to the rule, and a success in both increasing schooling and combating child labor, is the state of Kerala. Kerala's emphasis on primary education resulted in a dropout rate close to zero and a literacy rate of 94 percent for males and 86 percent for females (World Bank 1995). Further, Kerala's child labor force participation rate was as low as 1.9 percent as early as 1971, compared to the Indian average of 7.1 percent at the same time

(Weiner 1991). Kerala also ranks among the highest in terms of per capita GDP and growth.

Somewhat curiously, despite improvement in literacy rates, the number of children in the labor force continues to increase. There are some important implications here. First, the government's education policy needs to be strengthened and made more effective. Dropout rates of 35 percent for males and 39 percent for females (government of India cited in World Bank 1995) are unacceptable and spell doom for the success of policy. Primary or elementary education is especially important, particularly for an agricultural country such as India (Self and Grabowski 2004). Second, education policy and child labor policy cannot be formulated independently from each other, as has been the case in the past. In recent years the Indian government has tried to align and coordinate its education policy with its child labor policy. The introduction of nonformal education into its education policy was designed to provide education to children that work. However, nonformal education has been criticized for making it easier and more acceptable for people to send their children to work (Sinha 1996). Providing education and elimination of poverty are certainly important, but they are targeting mainly the supply of child labor. One also needs to understand factors that explain demand for child labor in India to understand the problem in its entirety.

An in-depth look at the distribution of child labor reveals that this is a problem mainly in the rural sector of the economy. According to India's embassy to the United States, "Children under fourteen constitute around 3.6% of the total labor force in India. Of these children, nine out of every ten work in their own rural family settings. Nearly 85% are engaged in traditional agricultural activities. Less than 9% work in manufacturing, services and repairs. Only about 0.8% work in factories." Factors commonly used to explain child labor are, among others, poverty, the substitutability of adult and child labor, especially in agriculture, differences in adult and child labor, labor-intensive technology, and low returns to education or lack of understanding about the returns to education. The rural agricultural sector is much poorer than the more advanced industrial sector, which is clear from the lower per capita GDP in the more rural states (Bihar, Madhya Pradesh, Assam, West Bengal) as compared to the more industrial states (Gujarat, Maharashtra, Karnataka). Moreover, traditionally the rural sector in India has used low-level, labor-intensive technology where adult and child labor could be easily substituted. Additionally, schools in rural areas are often inaccessible and come at a cost in lost wages, which many cannot afford. Rural schools in India have traditionally been notorious for functioning improperly, with problems ranging from lack of a school building to lack of trained teachers, and from very high student-teacher ratios to lack of books and other teaching aids. Finally, lack of job opportunities upon completion of schooling adds to the unattractiveness of schools to parents.

Agricultural technology develops in three stages as a country develops (Majumdar, Dolui, and Banerjee 2001). First is the land-using stage, when land usage increases faster than labor. Second is the labor-using stage, when agricultural employment increases faster than cultivated land. The third stage is critical. The capital-using stage is when capital accumulation and technology overcome the forces of diminishing returns. Once this technological progress takes place, adult and child labor become imperfect substitutes. Moreover, this stage, which is more productive and yields greater income, also requires greater skill and knowledge, which increase returns to education. Thus, it makes children's education more lucrative for parents while making children redundant as laborers. Using data from the Green Revolution period in India, this outcome has been confirmed by Foster and Rosenzweig (1996). In addition, since adults are more productive, it implies an increase in family earnings, which eliminates poverty as a reason for sending children to work (Basu and Tzannatos 2006). Thus, one can expect to find a reduction in child labor and an increase in education when a country enters this stage of development in agriculture.

So, how does one explain the observed spike in child labor in a country such as India, where the agricultural sector, along with the rest of the economy, is experiencing improvements in technology? Using the state of West Bengal as a case study, Majumdar, Dolui, and Banerjee (2001) argue that the division of labor that comes about with better technology also creates certain small jobs that require little to no skill and are perfect for children, who would work at a much lower wage than adults would. During initial phases of technological improvement, the technology is not efficiently implemented, leading to suboptimal use of resources, which leads to increases in production costs and the hiring of children to reduce costs. Thus, as a country moves up the technological ladder, one can expect to see an increase in child labor and thereafter a drop as the technology is fine-tuned and properly implemented. While it may be true that technological progress ultimately leads to a reduction in child labor, it may take some time and may make the situation worse before it gets better.

Another explanation for the demand for child labor is the difference in child wages and adult wages. Children not only work for lower wages; they have a low reservation wage as well. Thus, hiring adults comes with a premium that employers have to pay for no additional gain in marginal revenue. As long as adult labor and child labor are substitutable, it makes no sense to any rational employer to hire an adult if he or she can get by with a child. Additionally, any increase in adult wages will make child labor even more attractive. The only way this wage differential can be battled from the demand side would be by creating an atmosphere where adult and child labor are not substitutable, by increasing the opportunity cost of child labor by increasing returns to education and through correctly framed and enforced child labor legislation, which would make it costly for employers to hire children. On the supply side, an increase in income would make it unnecessary for children to work, while correctly framed and enforced education legislation would prevent parents from taking children out of school.

After looking at the nature and causes of child labor and problems of universal education in India, one finds overwhelming evidence in support of technological advance. This needs to be accompanied by more affordable and accessible education and not necessarily a movement toward an immediate and complete abolition of child labor, though that has to remain the ultimate goal. On the demand side, technological progress would tackle the problem by creating a mismatch between adult and child labor (though this may happen gradually and make the situation worse before it gets better). Technological progress would also increase the returns to education as labor productivity increases with increased skill levels. Additionally, increases in productivity lead to increased demand for jobs and employment opportunities. On the supply side, technological progress would lead to increased wages and decreased poverty. All of this along with properly coordinated education and child labor policy ought to help the country extricate itself from the high-child-labor, low-education trap.

References and Further Reading

Basu, Kaushik, and Zafiris Tzannatos. "The Global Child Labor Problem: What Do We Know and What Can We Do?" *World Bank Economic Review* 17:2 (2006): 147–73.

Bequele, Assefa, and Jo Boyden. "Working Children: Current Trends and Policy Responses." *International Labor Review* 127:2 (1988): 153–71.

Embassy of India. "Child Labor in India." Washington, DC. http://www.indianembassy.org/policy/Child_Labor/childlabor.htm.

Foster, A.D., and M.R. Rosenzweig. "Technical Change and Human Capital Returns and Investments: Evidence from the Green Revolution." *American Economic Review* 86:4 (1996): 931–53.

Ilon, L., and P. Moock. "School Attributes, Household Characteristics and Demand for Schooling: A Case Study of Rural Peru." *International Review of Education* 37:4 (1991): 429–52.

Lahiri, Sajal, and Sharmistha Self. "Gender Bias in Education: The Role of Inter-Household Externality, Dowry and Other Social Institutions." *Review of Development Economics* 11:4 (2007): 591–606.

Majumdar, P., D. K. Dolui, and H. K. Banerjee. "Agricultural Modernization, Child Labour and Fertility: Rural West Bengal, India." Paper presented at the International Union for the Scientific Study of Population, 26th IUSSP General Population Conference, Salvador, Brazil, August 18–24, 2001.

Patrinos, Harry A., and George Psacharopoulos. "Schooling and Non-Schooling Activities of Peruvian Youth: Indigenous Background, Family Composition and Child Labor." *International Journal of Educational Development* 15:1 (1993): 47–60.

Self, Sharmistha, and Richard Grabowski. "Does Education at All Levels Cause Growth? India, A Case Study." *Economics of Education Review* 23 (2004): 47–55.

Siddiqi, F., and H.A. Patrinos. "Child Labor: Issues, Causes and Interventions." Human Resources Development and Operations Policy, Working Paper 56. Washington, DC: World Bank, 1995.

Sinha, Shantha. "Child Labor and Education Policy in India." *Administrator* 16 (1996): 17–29.

Tienda, M. "Economic Activity of Children in Peru: Labor Force Behavior in Rural and Urban Contexts." *Rural Sociology* 44 (1979): 370–91.

Weiner, Myron. *The Child and the State in India.* Princeton, NJ: Princeton University Press, 1991.

World Bank. *Economic Developments in India: Achievements and Challenges.* Washington, DC: World Bank, 1995.

Challenges for Tribal Schooling in India

Afke De Groot, Research Associate,
International Research on Working Children (IREWOC) Foundation

Scheduled Tribes are tribal communities and groups within these communities that are identified as such by the Indian Constitution. India nowadays counts 573 such Scheduled Tribes (STs), constituting 8 percent of the Indian population. Scheduled Tribes are often referred to as *adivasi* (original inhabitant) communities. In its constitution, India commits itself "to promote the educational and economic interests of . . . the scheduled tribes and shall protect them from social injustice and all forms of exploitation" (Article 46). This article looks at problems related to the education of Scheduled Tribes in India.

It is mainly in the northeastern states of India where Scheduled Tribes constitute majorities (see Table 1). Other states with a significant percentage of STs are Chhattisgarh, Gujarat, Jharkand, Lakshadweep, Madhya Pradesh, Orissa, and Rajasthan. The percentage of illiterates among the ST population is higher than the percentage in the total population. In India as a whole, the ST literacy rate of 47.1 percent falls well below the national average of 64.8 percent. Female education and literacy deserve special attention: Whereas the female literacy rate in India is 53.7 percent, among ST communities the female literacy rate is 34.8 percent.

There has been significant improvement in the school enrollment of ST children, especially of tribal girls. Nearly all tribal children attend at least some school (Kabeer 2003). The major problems with tribal schooling in India are irregular attendance, low achievement in school, and lack of retention (Govinda 2002). Dropout rates among tribal children are equal to those of children from other marginalized groups such as Scheduled Caste (*dalit-*) communities but much higher than those of other social groups in both rural and urban areas (Thorat 1999).

Table 1

States with Large Scheduled Tribes (ST) Populations: ST Population and Illiteracy

State/Union Territory	% ST of Total Population	% Illiterates of ST Population	% Illiterates of Total Population
Arunachal Pradesh	64.2	60.06	55.85
Assam	12.4	47.91	47.42
Chhattisgarh	31.8	57.28	46.37
Dadra and Nagar Haveli	62.2	67.41	52.88
Gujarat	14.8	60.65	41.13
Jharkand	26.3	67.00	56.29
Lakshadweep	94.5	27.25	26.33
Madhya Pradesh	20.3	67.66	47.65
Manipur	34.2	43.38	39.52
Meghalaya	85.9	51.50	50.07
Mizoram	94.5	25.41	25.56
Nagaland	89.1	43.70	43.10
Orissa	22.1	69.21	46.10
Rajasthan	12.6	65.05	50.98
Sikkim	20.6	42.41	41.14
Tripura	31.1	52.78	36.79

Source: Census of India, 2001.

Disparities within and between different ST communities should not be overlooked (Govinda 2002). Within tribal communities, the education of girls deserves extra care. Among ST communities, tribes differ from one another in terms of economic and social standards, and thus the extent to which their children attend school. Generally speaking, however, ST communities are among the most marginalized within Indian society, and children from ST communities are likely to be extremely vulnerable (Kabeer 2003).

Why Are Tribal Children Out of School?

A major reason that explains why many children from ST communities perform poorly in school or drop out eventually is their seasonal absence from school due to work. Means of subsistence of ST communities are mainly agriculture and wage labor, and children are expected to help out in the household. Also, many *adivasis* are caught in debt bondage (Larsen 2003). According to a NSSO survey in 1993–1994, 7.2 percent of all children aged five to fourteen were working. Among ST communities, however, the percentage is much higher, as 12.8 percent of the children were working (Nambissan 2003). This high incidence of child labor among children from Scheduled Tribes has a negative impact on their ability to go to school. Especially during peak agricultural and cotton-picking seasons, children are absent from school because they either have to help their parents in the field or have to stay home to take care of younger siblings and perform other household chores so both parents can work in the field. Seasonal migration of households in search of work keeps children out of school as well.

A large proportion of tribal children who drop out of school are not involved in regular work (Kabeer 2003). Thus, there are other important reasons why many ST children are out of school. One of them relates to access to schools. The majority of tribal communities live in remote and inaccessible areas of India. Since many tribal communities are small, it is a challenge for the government to provide a school within walking distance of every household. The road leading to the school might be an uneasy one, with a forest, hills, or rivers to be crossed (Govinda 2002; Kabeer 2003).

Further, when a school is located in an area predominated by upper castes, caste-based discrimination might cause inhibitions for lower-caste children going to school. Discrimination exists within the schools as well. This becomes apparent from school practices, from seating arrangements in the classroom, and from teachers' remarks (Kabeer 2003). According to the 1999 Public Report on Basic Education, teachers are still predominantly recruited from upper castes. In the classroom this might create a social distance between teachers and pupils and lead to tribal children fearing teachers. These situations do not encourage children to achieve in school and can lead to irregular attendance and eventually to dropout. Gautam (2003) addresses the positive influence of using local teachers. Changing teachers' perceptions about tribal children is important: "Teachers must be sensitized to the cultural and behavioral strengths of tribal children and motivated to do their best for them in school" (Gautam 2003, 7). A study in several tribal villages in seven states indicates that school participation in tribal areas increases when schoolteachers are accepted by the local community (Jha and Jhingran 2005).

The curriculum used in government schools is often not congruent with tribal cultures, which leads to alienation of ST households from the schools. In particular, the denial of tribal languages in schools is seen as one of the major reasons why children from ST communities are underachieving in school and often drop out. Tribal communities often have their own language and mathematics and their own way of dealing with life issues, which are different from what is taught in school. Sinha (2005) argues that using the dominant language of the state might lead to feelings of inferiority among tribal children and feelings of alienation from their language and culture. Article 350 of the Constitution of India allows the mother tongue to be used as the medium of instruction in school. However, this may not happen in practice as many tribal communities are not aware of their rights. Schools in tribal areas usually use the regional language, which can lead to a lack of interest in studying, poor results, and eventually withdrawal from school (Nambissan 2003). Another explanation for alienation from the school environment is that in most ST communities, there is little sense of ownership or participation among parents when it comes to the school. This can be the result of social dynamics in a village or of lack of time or interest on the part of the parents themselves.

Data indicate that children are often sent to school for a few years until they reach an age at which they can help out in the household. Incentives such as scholarships and tuition waivers make it more affordable for families to send their children to school or to keep them there. Education remains expensive for poor households, however, and many of these incentives are poorly implemented and do not reach all the children. In addition, costs for notebooks, stationery, and transportation add further to the expenses of education.

As the statistics show, throughout India tribal communities have grown more aware of the importance of sending their children to school, which is why most children attend at least some years. However, there are still obstacles to overcome before all children from these communities are able to complete their primary education.

References and Further Reading

Gautam, Vinoba. "Education of Tribal Children in India and the Issue of Medium of Instruction: A Janshala Experience." 2003. http://www.sil.org/asia/ldc/parallel_papers/vinoba_gautam.pdf.

Govinda, R., ed. *India Education Report: A Profile of Basic Education.* New Delhi: Oxford University Press, 2002.

Jha, Jyotsna, and Dhir Jhingran. *Elementary Education for the Poorest and Other Deprived Groups.* New Delhi: Manohar Publishers, 2005.

Kabeer, Naila, Geetha B. Nambissan, and Ramya Subrahmanian, eds. *Child Labour and the Right to Education in South Asia: Needs Versus Rights?* New Delhi: Sage Publications, 2003.

Larsen, Peter Bille. *Indigenous and Tribal Children: Assessing Child Labour and Education Challenges.* Geneva: ILO-IPEC / COOP INDISCO, 2003.

Nambissan, Geetha B. "Social Exclusion, Children's Work and Education: A View from the Margins." In *Child Labour and the Right to Education in South Asia. Needs Versus Rights?* ed. Naila Kabeer, Geetha B. Nambissan, and Ramya Subrahmanian, 109–42. New Delhi: Sage Publications, 2003.

National Sample Survey Organisation. "Economic Activities and School Attendance by Children of India." Report 412. Fifth Quinquennial Survey NSS 50th Round, 1993–1994. New National Sample Survey Organisation, Department of Statistics, Government of India, Delhi, 1997.

PROBE Team. *Public Report on Basic Education.* New Delhi: Oxford University Press, 1999.

Sinha, Smita. "Linguistic Human Rights in Tribal Education in Orissa." *Language in India: Strength for Today and Bright Hope for Tomorrow* 5:5 (May 2005).

Thorat, Sukhadeo K. "Poverty, Caste and Child Labour in India: The Plight of Dalit and Adivasi Children." In *Against Child Labour: Indian and International Dimensions and Strategies,* ed. Klaus Voll, 154–75. New Delhi: Mosaic Books, 1999.

Voll, Klaus, ed. *Against Child Labour: Indian and International Dimensions and Strategies.* New Delhi: Mosaic Books, 1999.

Nepal

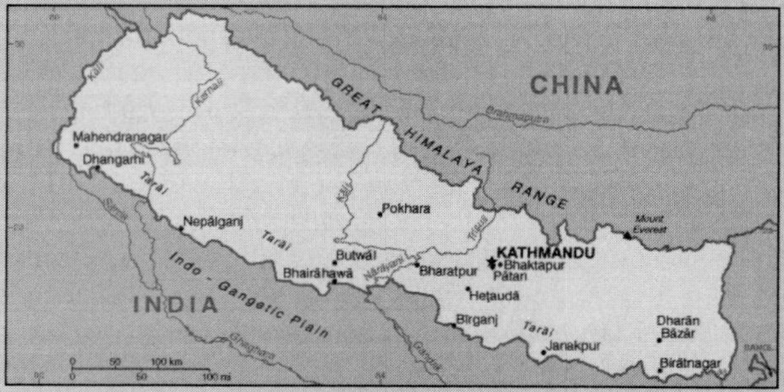

NEPAL			
	CRC	C 138	C 182
Ratifications	Y	Y	Y
Human Development Index/Rank	0.527/138		
Human Capital			
Population Growth Rate	2.13%		
% Population 0–14	38.3%		
Total Fertility Rate	4.01		
Life Expectancy	60.56		
Infant Mortality Rate	63.66		
Literacy Rate	48.6%		
Economic			
GDP/Capita	$1,500		
GDP Growth %	2.4%		
% Poverty	31%		
Gini Index	37.7		
Labor Force Composition			
% Agriculture	76%		
% Industry	6%		
% Services	18%		

CHILD ACTIVITY BREAKDOWN, BY SEX AND RESIDENCE

Percentage of children in the relevant age-group[a]

RESIDENCE	Economic activity only		School only		Combining school and economic activity		Neither in school nor in economic activity		Child labor[b]	
	Male	Female	Male	Female	Male	Female	Male	Female	Male	Female
Urban	3.4	6.5	76.0	69.0	13.4	13.7	7.2	10.8	n/av	n/av
Rural	9.0	22.3	46.9	33.7	28.8	24.5	15.4	19.5	n/av	n/av
Total	8.4	20.6	50.1	37.5	27.0	23.4	14.5	18.5	30.1	40.8

Source: Nepal, Nepal Labour Force Survey 1998–1999 (see UCW Project Web site, http://ucw-project.org, country statistics).

Notes: [a]Children age 5 to 14. [b]Estimate includes (a) children under age 12 engaged in economic activities, (b) children age 12–14 engaged in excessive economic activities (more than 14 hours per week), and (c) children under age 15 engaged in excessive household chores (at least 28 hours per week). Estimate does not account for children engaged in hazardous work or other unconditional "worst forms" of child labor.

Child Labor in Nepal

Bal Kumar KC, Professor and Executive Head, Central Department of Population Studies, Tribhuvan University, Kathmandu

The child labor situation in Nepal has been worsening despite increasing attention focused on eliminating worst forms of child labor through the Time Bound Program (TBP) of the ILO's International Program for the Elimination of Child Labor (IPEC), which was launched in 1995. IPEC in Nepal aimed to eliminate the worst forms of child labor by 2009 and all forms of child labor by 2014, ahead of reaching the Millennium Development Goals (MDGs) by 2016. The timing of IPEC's objectives was set to coincide with Nepal's National Master Plan for the Elimination of Child Labour (ILO 2006). Because of eleven years of Maoist insurgency and political instability, which have increased the number of displaced and exploited children, many development programs had to be delayed or postponed. Consequently, the most recent phase of the IPEC TBP ended in 2006 with no extension. The situation of child laborers in Nepal may further deteriorate with the closure of the IPEC TBP and the Nepal government's other political priorities.

The problem of child labor in Nepal is related to the country's prevailing socioeconomic structure and level of economic and social development. Nepal's Human Development Index ranks 138 out 177 countries in the world. The national poverty line is estimated at 30.9 percent of the total population of about 27 million. Nepal ranks 68 out of 102 developing countries in the Human Poverty Index. The total fertility rate stands at 4.01 children per woman of reproductive age. Of the total population, 38.3 percent are under fifteen years of age. Child labor not only originates from poverty; it also increases poverty by exerting negative effects on the country's labor market and education system.

Much research on child labor in Nepal has been conducted in the last decade. Even though statistics generated through such research have been useful, they are not necessarily uniform. This essay summarizes the most salient features of the child labor situation in Nepal.

Collecting firewood in Nepal, June 2007. *(Photo by Afke De Groot courtesy of IREWOC Foundation)*

Definition of Child Work and Child Labor

Child work includes activities that are not necessarily harmful and may contribute to healthy child development, such as light household chores with some learning value. *Child labor* consists of all types of work performed by children up to the age of eighteen that is damaging to the children's health or physical, mental, intellectual, moral, or social development. It is exploitative and deprives children of education and rights to survival, development, protection, and participation.

The UN Convention on the Rights of the Child (CRC) defines a child to be a person below the age of eighteen. Article 20 of the Constitution of Nepal prohibits employment of minors in any factory or mine or other hazardous work. The Civil Service Act (1975) prohibits government employment of anyone younger than sixteen years of age. In the Labour Act (1992), a child is defined as a person younger than fourteen years of age and is not to be engaged in the work of any enterprise, whereas a minor is defined as a person younger than eighteen years of age. The Child Prohibition and Regulation Act (1999) prohibits children younger than fourteen years of age to work in any establishment.

Table 1

Distribution of the Estimated Child Population by Age and Sex and Place of Residence

Categories	Suwal, KC, and Adhikari 1997		Central Bureau of Statistics 1999	
Child Population (5–14 Years)	6,225,000		4,860,000	
% of Total Population		29.3%		25.4%
Males	3,202,000	(51.4%)	2,480,000	(51.0%)
Females	3,024,000	(48.6%)	2,380,000	(49.0%)
5–9 Years	3,403,000	(54.7%)	2,437,000	(50.1%)
10–14 Years	2,822,000	(45.3%)	2,423,000	(49.9%)
Urban	520,000	(8.4%)	540,000	(11.1%)
Rural	5,795,000	(91.6%)	4,320,000	(88.9%)

Sources: Suwal, KC, and Adhikari 1997; Central Bureau of Statistics 1999.

Magnitude of Child Population and Working Children in Nepal

Suwal, KC, and Adhikari (1997) estimated that there are 6.2 million children between the ages of five and fourteen years in Nepal (Table 1). This comprised 29.3 percent of the total population of the country. Male and female children constituted 3.2 million and 3 million, respectively, with a sex ratio of 106. About 92 percent of children lived in rural areas. The Central Bureau of Statistics (1999) estimated that there are 4.9 million children in Nepal constituting 25.4 percent of the total population, with a sex ratio of 104.

Many of the statistics on child labor in Nepal are not comparable due to different sample sizes, absence of estimates of child labor incidence, and the time of the survey. The Central Bureau of Statistics (2004) reported that, of the total child population five to fourteen years of age, 55.3 percent were attending school without working, 20.6 percent were attending school and working, 10.8 percent were working and not attending school, and 13.3 percent were neither in school nor working. Based on the National Living Standards Survey of 2003–2004, the ILO (2006) estimated that there were 1.83 million working children, about 1 million of whom were considered child laborers. To present the clearest picture possible, this essay uses data from *Child Labour Situation in Nepal* (Suwal, KC, and Adhikari 1997), which was derived from the *Employment Situation in Nepal* (KC et al. 1997).

Of the total estimated 6.2 million children, 2.6 million (41.6 percent) were working irrespective of school attendance, 2.3 million (36.7 percent) were attending school without working, and 0.93 million (15 percent) were idle (Figure 1). Of the total estimated working children, 1.6 million (25.5 percent of children) were working and attending school and 1 million (16.1 percent of children) were working without attending school. Of the total number of children who were working and attending school, 987,000 (15.9 percent of children) were involved in economic activities, and 597,000 (9.6 percent of children) were involved in noneconomic activities. Of those involved in economic activities, only 124,000 (2 percent of children) were in paid activities, and 864,000 (13.9 percent of children) were in unpaid activities. Similarly, of the children who were working only, without attending school, 673,000 (10.3 percent of children) were involved in economic activities and 331,000 (5.3 percent of children) were involved in noneconomic activities. Of those involved in economic activities, 155,000 (2.5 percent of children) were in paid activities, whereas 519,000 (8.3 percent of children) were in unpaid activities.

Figure 1

Magnitude of Children's Activities in Nepal

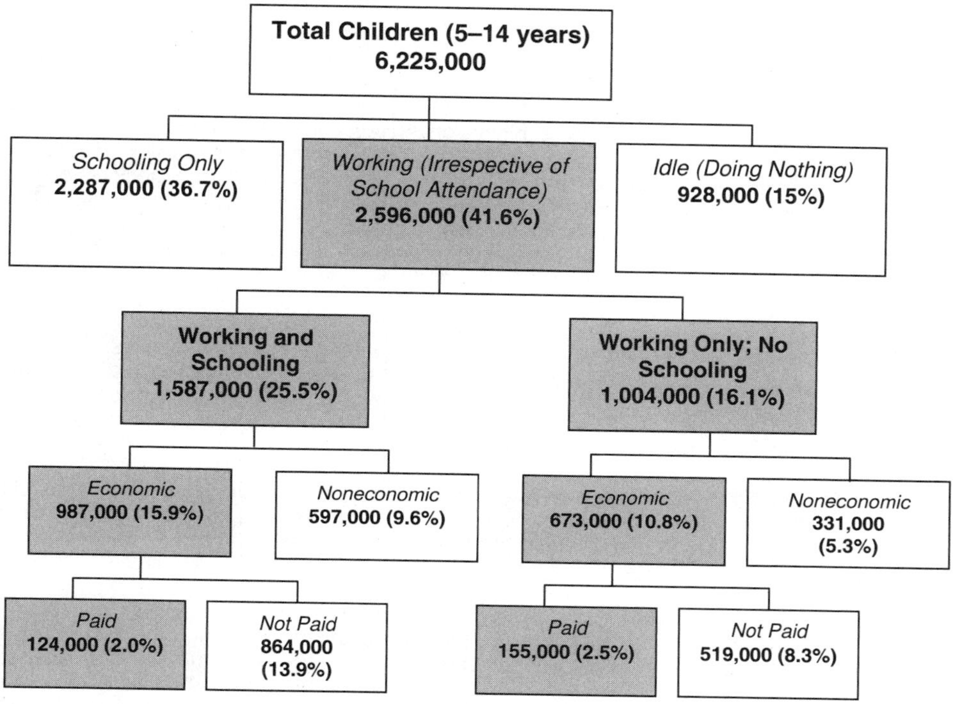

Source: Suwal, KC, and Adhikari 1997, 27.

The total number of economically active children, whether paid or not, including those who attend school (1 million) and those who do not (0.7 million) is 1.7 million. Counting only those who are paid as wage laborers, those attending school number 124,000, and those not attending school number 155,000, for a total of 279,000. This figure has sometimes been misrepresented as the best estimate of the number of child laborers in Nepal.

Economically Active Children

Of Nepalese children, 26.7 percent, or 1.7 million, are considered to be economically active (KC and Shakya 1999). About 28 percent of boys were economically active compared to 26 percent of girls. Children in the ten- to fourteen-year-old age-group had an economic participation rate of 40.8 percent, while the participation rate for the five- to nine-year-old age-group was 12.5 percent. Of the economically active children, 40.4 percent did not attend school. A much higher proportion of girls performed economic work without going to school (56.1 percent) as compared to boys (27.1 percent). Only 278,000 (16.7 percent) of the economically active children were in paid activities. About 18 percent of the economically active children age ten to fourteen were in paid activities. The figure for children age five to nine was about 13 percent.

In urban areas, about 27 percent of the economically active children were in paid activities, whereas in rural areas, only 16 percent of the economically active children were in paid activities. Of the economically active children, 1.4 million (83.4 percent) worked fourteen hours or more per week (two hours or more per day). About 88 percent of the economically active girls worked fourteen hours or more per week, compared to 80 percent of boys. About 35 percent and 22 percent of the

Table 2

Economically Active Children by Occupation

Occupation	Number of Children (% of Economically Active Children)	Activities and Sectors
Agricultural Workers	1,576,000 (94.8%)	*Agriculture:* plantation of sugarcane, tea, tobacco, millet, and maize; rice farming, grass cutting, weeding, irrigation, plowing, harvesting, portering, horticulture, and nursery. *Animal husbandry:* livestock grazing, fodder collection and milking cows/buffalo, poultry farming, fishing. *Domestic workers:* fetching water, collecting fuels and fodder, caring for younger siblings, working in the kitchen and cleaning, washing the dishes and doing the laundry, cutting and collecting firewood
General Technical Workers	14,000 (0.8%)	Auto mechanics, bicycle repair, carpentry, plumbers, grill welding, tailoring, and electroplating; activities related to cutting machines, activities carried out underground, underwater, or at high altitudes, and electrical or painting work at heights; activities related to production and distribution of hydroelectricity, solar energy, wind energy, coal, oil and natural gas, biogas, and other sources of energy
Sales Workers	7,000 (0.4%)	Selling of sweets, working in teashops and in restaurants and bars, wholesale/retail shops, storage assistant, mobile traders, newspaper vending/delivery, street hawkers, footpath vendors, fruit sellers, tea suppliers, and hosiery goods sellers
Service Workers	28,000 (1.6%)	Child prostitution, massage parlors, cabin restaurants and dance bars; girls trafficked for prostitution and pornography, drug peddling, children in armed conflicts, domestic workers/caretakers for fetching water, taking care of younger siblings, cleaning, kitchen work, collecting fuel/fodder, cooking, washing, and customer service in hotels, motels, restaurants, and teashops; garbage collection and processing, street sweeping, portering for short distances in urban areas and long distances in rural areas; activities related to laundry service, barber, watchman and security guard, petrol pump attendant, shoe shiner, ticket selling in cinema halls, circus performer, street acrobats, and beggars, washing cars, buses, and trucks; working in casino, rafting, trekking, cable car, and golf course; ragpickers, beggars, street singers, shoe shiners/makers, drug addicts, and criminals
Production Workers	13,000 (0.8%)	*Factory workers:* carpet factories such as weaving/dyeing, knitting, tailoring, washing and printing of garment, textile and handloom garments/textiles, handicrafts, printing press, welding, confectionery, bread making, making matches, pottery and brick kilns. *Agrofood production and processing:* rice mills, tea, sugarcane, marijuana, tobacco, beverages, confectionery, bakery, cement production and packing; production of soap, pulp, paper, pencil/slate, pesticides, lubricating oil, production and sales of explosives and inflammables like matches, beer/alcohol, bitumen, photo processing and activities involving chemicals; working in slaughterhouse, cold storage, leather tannery, candle production, plastic bags and shoes. *Traditional family artisans:* carpentry, carving, painting, Thanka painting, metal/wooden handicrafts, jewelry
Construction and Transportation Workers	26,000 (1.6%)	*Construction:* construction of houses, bridges, and sewage systems, road/building, rock breaking, stone and slate quarries, and coal mines, extraction, processing and distribution of minerals, oil, and natural gas. *Transportation:* conductors, ticket collectors on buses and tempos and microvans, rickshaw and cart pullers

Source: Suwal, KC, and Adhikari 1997.

Table 3

Estimates of the Worst Forms of Child Labor from Rapid Assessments and Baseline Surveys

Target Group	Estimate from Rapid Assessment Surveys (RAS)	Estimate from Baseline Surveys (BLS)
Children in Bonded Labor	17,152 (Sharma et al. 2001b)	17,466 (Sharma and Sharma 2004)
Child Ragpickers	3,965 (KC et al. 2001c)	3,695 (Mukherjee and Central Department of Population Studies 2003)
Short-Distance Child Porters	3,825 (KC et al. 2001a)	5,682 (Catalla and Mukherjee 2003)
Long-Distance Child Porters	42,204 (KC et al. 2001a)	106,696 (Catalla and Mukherjee 2003)
Child Domestic Workers	55,655 (Sharma et al. 2001a)	51,340 (Sharma et al. 2006)
Children in the Carpet Sector	7,689 (KC et al. 2002)	n/av
Girls Trafficking for Prostitution	12,000 (KC et al. 2001c)	n/av
Children in Stone Quarries	32,000 (Sainju 2002)	n/av
Children in Coal Mines	115 (Rapti Awareness Rural Association 1999)	1,650 (Department of Mines and Geology 2005)
Children in Brick Kilns	1,993 (BISCONS 1998)	

economically active girls and boys, respectively, worked forty-two hours or more per week.

Suwal, KC, and Adhikari (1997) identified six major occupational groups of economically active children (Table 2). By far, the largest group were involved in agriculture-related work (94.8 percent, or 1.58 million children). Other occupational groups identified included general technical workers, sales workers, service workers, production workers, and construction and transportation workers.

Worst Forms of Child Labor in Nepal

Economic activity measures often fail to distinguish between child work, which may be beneficial, and child labor, which is clearly harmful. The ILO has commissioned numerous Rapid Assessment Surveys (RAS) and Baseline Surveys (BLS) of various worst forms of child labor in Nepal (Table 3). Worst forms estimated include children in bonded labor, ragpickers, short- and long-distance porters, child domestic workers, children in the carpet sector, girls trafficked for prostitution, and children in stone quarries, coal mines, and brick kilns. These studies alone estimate anywhere from 172,013 to 244,796 children working in clearly harmful, worst forms of child labor.

Each of these worst forms of child labor comes with its associated hazards. For instance, porters face physical danger by carrying heavy loads on their backs. Sometimes the load is more than their body weight. A short-distance porter earns Rs. 96 per day compared to Rs. 71 earned per day by long-distance porters. In both cases, girls earn less than boys, and younger children (ten to fourteen years) earn less than older children (fifteen to seventeen years) (KC et al. 2001a).

For ragpickers, 88 percent of whom are boys, the work itself is very unhealthy. Rags are found at the riverside and dumping sites. These children work and play with dirt and wastes. They are exposed to wounds and injuries from broken glass and sharp tins. They are vulnerable to a variety of skin and respiratory diseases, including tuberculosis. For this work, ragpickers receive Rs. 87 per day.

More than 27 percent of domestic child laborers (Sharma et al. 2001b) and 33 percent of bonded child laborers (Sharma et al. 2001a) encountered accidents during work, mostly cuts and burns. About 53 percent of the domestic child workers are not paid at all; about 40 percent are paid less than Rs. 4,000 per year.

Of the sex workers in Nepal, 20 percent are under age sixteen. KC et al. (2001c) estimated that 12,000 girl children were trafficked to India every year for commercial sexual exploitation. Trafficking in girls for prostitution in Nepal has long been associated with poverty, social exclusion, and exploitation of certain disadvantaged ethnic groups.

Conclusion

The high figures for both economically active children and children involved in the worst forms of child labor in Nepal may seem provocative, but the figures are no more provocative than the situation in which too many children are working. Children in Nepal are involved too young in doing work inappropriate for their age. Their working conditions are often hazardous, with considerable physical, mental, and emotional stress. Working children are forced to work for long hours, often at night, for low wages. It violates their basic human rights to survival with dignity and prohibits them from pursuing educational opportunities, so vital for the development of the country.

References and Further Reading

BISCONS. *Child Labour in Brick Kilns of the Kathmandu Valley, a Rapid Assessment.* Kathmandu: BISCONS, 1998.

Catalla, Rebecca F., and Sanjukta Mukherjee. *Child Porters in Nepal: A Report on the 2002 Baseline Survey.* Bangkok: ILO-IPEC, 2003.

Central Bureau of Statistics. *Report on the Nepal Labour Force Survey.* Kathmandu: Central Bureau of Statistics, 1999.

Central Bureau of Statistics. *Nepal Living Standards Survey 2003/04.* 2 vols. Kathmandu: Central Bureau of Statistics, 2004.

Department of Mines and Geology. *Child Labour in the Mines of Nepal.* Kathmandu: Department of Mines and Geology, 2005.

Gillgan, Brian. *Child Labour in Nepal: An Analysis of the Determinants of Child Labour in Nepal, the Policy Environment and Response.* Understanding Children's Work (UCW): An Inter-Agency Research Cooperation Project on Chid Labor, 2003.

Gurung, Yogendra B. "Nature, Extent and Forms of Child Labour in Nepal." *Nepal Population Journal* 11:10 (2004): 17–43.

ILO. *Combating the Worst Forms of Child Labour in Nepal: An Update on Facts and Figures, Achievements and Challenges within the Seven Sectors Covered by the IPEC, Nepal Core TBP Project.* Kathmandu: ILO-IPEC, 2006.

KC, Bal K., and Keshav P. Adhikari. "Labour Market Dynamics and Child Porters: The Nepalese Context." *Nepal Population Journal* 11:10 (2004): 5–16.

KC, Bal K., Keshav P. Adhikari, Yogendra B. Gurung, and Govind Subedi. *Nepal, Situation of Child Porters: A Rapid Assessment, Investigating the Worst Forms of Child Labor, No. 6.* Geneva: ILO-IPEC, 2001a.

KC, Bal K., Yogendra B. Gurung, Keshav P. Adhikari, and Govind Subedi. *Nepal, Situation of Child Ragpickers: A Rapid Assessment, Investigating the Worst Forms of Child Labor, No. 4.* Geneva: ILO-IPEC, 2001b.

KC, Bal K., and Dhanendra Shakya. "The Nature and Magnitude of Working Children in Nepal." *Nepal Population Journal* 8:7 (1999): 1–32.

KC, Bal K., Govind Subedi, Yogendra B. Gurung, and Keshav P. Adhikari. *Nepal, Trafficking in Girls with Special Reference to Prostitution: A Rapid Assessment, Investigating the Worst Forms of Child Labor, No. 2.* Geneva: ILO-IPEC, 2001c.

KC, Bal K., Govind Subedi, Yogendra B. Gurung, Keshav P. Adhikari, and Dhanendra V. Shakya. *Child Labour in Carpet Industries in Kathmandu Valley: A Rapid Assessment.* Kathmandu: ILO-IPEC, 2002.

KC, Bal K., Parthibeswor P. Timilsina, Pitamber Rawal, Rudra P. Gautam, Keshav P. Adhikari, Bidhan Acharya, and Bhim R. Suwal. *Employment Situation in Nepal.* Kathmandu: Central Department Population Studies, Tribhuvan University, 1997.

Mukherjee, Sanjukta, and Central Department of Population Studies. *Child Ragpickers in Nepal: A Report on the 2002–2003 Baseline Survey.* Bangkok: ILO-IPEC, 2003.

Pradhan, Gauri. "An Overview of the Child Labour Problem in Nepal." In *Child Labour in Nepal.* Vol. 1. Kathmandu: ILO-IPEC, 1995.

Rapti Awareness Rural Association. *Child Labour in Coal Mines, A Study Conducted in Dang and Rolpa Districts of Nepal.* Kathmandu: Rapti Awareness Rural Association, 1999.

Sainju, Bijaya. *Child Labour in Stone Quarries.* Kathmandu: CONCERN-Nepal, 2002.

Sharma, Shiva, Bijendra Basnyat, and Ganesh G.C. *Nepal, Bonded Child Labour Among Child Workers of the Kamaiya System: A Rapid Assessment, Investigating the Worst Forms of Child Labor, No. 5.* Geneva: ILO-IPEC, 2001a.

Sharma, Shiva, and Ram Sharma. *Socio-economic Information on Ex-Kamaiyas of Nepal, Dang, Banke, Bardia, Kailali and Kanchanpur.* Kathmandu: National Labour Academy, 2004.

Sharma, Shiva, and Ram Sharma, in collaboration with Rebecca F. Catalla, Tap Catalla, Jr., and Sanjukta Mukherjee. *Child Domestic Workers in Nepal: A Report on the 2003 Baseline Survey.* Kathmandu: ILO-IPEC, 2006.

Sharma, Shiva, Manasa Thakurathi, Krishna Sapkota, Bishnu Devkota, and Brahma Rimal. *Nepal, Situation of Domestic Child Labourers in Kathmandu: A Rapid Assessment, Investigating the Worst Forms of Child Labor, No. 3.* Geneva: ILO-IPEC, 2001b.

Shrestha, Binod, and Casper Edmond. *Child Labour Situation in Nepal: Status Paper.* Kathmandu: ILO-IPEC, 2002.

Suwal, Bhim R., Bal K. KC, and Keshav P. Adhikari. *Child Labour Situation in Nepal.* Kathmandu: Central Department of Population Studies, Tribhuvan University, 1997.

Child Labor in the Tibeto-Nepalese Carpet Industry

Tom O'Neill, PhD, Department of Child and Youth Studies, Brock University

The image of the carpet-weaving child is one of the most ubiquitous and widely disseminated examples of child labor as a direct product of an inequitable global economy. Forced to work in appalling conditions that put physical, mental, spiritual, and moral development at great risk, the child carpet weavers figure prominently in international efforts to eradicate child labor in South Asia. In Nepal, the plight of the exploited child carpet weaver has become inexorably associated with Tibetan carpet production, which, despite its claims to cultural authenticity, is a very recent industry that has grown from emerging international markets. Despite efforts to eradicate illegal child labor from the industry, sustained suspicion that the industry exploits children continues to haunt it, and its impact on the industry is felt at all levels.

There is little doubt that child labor played an important part in the formative years of the industry as it grew from a cottage industry that employed a handful of Tibetan refugees in the 1960s into Nepal's largest foreign-exchange earner in the early 1990s and the employer of hundreds of thousands of people. The actual number of child workers remains a mystery, however. In 1992 the Nepalese child-protection NGO Child Workers in Nepal (CWIN 1993) estimated that fully one-half of the 300,000 workers employed by the industry were under eighteen years of age. However, a 1994 estimate by USAID put the number of all workers at 108,000, and fieldwork conducted in 1995 resulted in an estimate between 80,000 and 90,000 (O'Neill 2004). CWIN's estimate was thus exaggerated, perhaps intentionally, to counter the government of Nepal's equally implausible claim that only 11 percent of the weaving force was underage prior to state intervention, which reduced the level to less than 1 percent by 1994 (O'Neill 2004).

Anyone walking through the streets and alleyways in the Kathmandu Valley in the early 1990s would have understood that claim to be spurious, as many children could be plainly seen weaving carpets in dark, crowded, and filthy red-brick sheds. As they sat on wooden planks beneath metal looms, their hands could be seen repeatedly knotting wool around a metal rod, wool dust and cigarette smoke filling the air. Their lives, according to reports, were being broken by persistent illness, undernourishment, harsh physical discipline, and sexual abuse; they were separated from their families and alone in a hostile environment, cheated of education and even of the earnings that should rightfully have been theirs. They were being trafficked from the less-developed mountainous and lowland regions that surround Kathmandu, lured by the enticements of work and life in the big city, sold to labor contractors by their destitute families, and tricked or even kidnapped by contractors looking for a cheap and docile labor force to feed the growing industry. These reports made sensational reading that outraged child protectionists around the world, earning the industry international opprobrium (Sattaur 1993; NSAC 1998).

The problem with such representations of child carpet weaving was that little effort was made to put them into context. As carpet exports exploded in the early 1990s, the demand for weaving labor grew proportionately. Numerous entrepreneurs and would-be entrepreneurs, many with little or no experience in carpet weaving, set up factories of all sizes to try to capitalize on global demand. Thousands of migrants moved to the Kathmandu

Valley, some in families or groups of contracted workers, while others came alone to earn a wage that far exceeded what they could earn in their villages, though it fell far short of what other workers in the Kathmandu Valley earned. Unquestionably, abuses occurred during this exodus, and probably continue today, although on a much-reduced scale. But the image of the child carpet weaver, particularly the image of the very young child forced through debt bondage or other forms of domination to weave carpets, is not consistent with the experience of most young carpet weavers in the industry, either then or now.

As a signatory to the UN Convention on the Rights of the Child (CRC), Nepal is committed to enforcing Article 32, which protects children from exploitation and hazardous work, and under which it must set minimum ages and hours of work for young workers, as well as penalties for violation of its laws. In 1994, the government of Nepal established new minimum ages and conditions for carpet-weaving work, and the Department of Labour was charged with enforcement. Children under the age of fourteen were to be protected from carpet work, and those between fourteen and sixteen could work a maximum of thirty-six hours a week. Many carpet factories, fearing fines or closure, released child weavers from employment unless they could prove themselves to be the minimum age. It is debatable whether this was in the best interests of many child weavers, who were forced onto the street and left to their own resources; nevertheless, the state and the carpet industry, anxious to protect their reputations and halt a decline in exports that some attributed to the child labor controversy, had acted (Cross, Sharma, and Shrestha 2001).

Weaver Exploitation

Protection of children from labor exploitation is one the most important objectives of the CRC, particularly when labor is detrimental to their physical, psychological, or social development. All wage labor, of course, can be considered exploitative, but the salient question regarding carpet weavers is whether they are free to submit themselves, knowingly and instrumentally, to that exploitation. Children are broadly conceived as incompetent or incapable of making such critical decisions and require protection from the adverse consequences of these decisions.

Carpet weavers have been routinely and systematically exploited by the middlemen and labor contractors who organize weaving labor for carpet manufacturers. These middlemen are often referred to as *naike* by outsiders, which roughly means "gang leaders." People within the industry simply refer to them as *thekadaar,* or "contractors," who bring laborers to employers. This ethnosemantic distinction is an important indication of how people outside the industry understand the labor contractor as a principal culprit in the exploitation of weavers, particularly child weavers. Typically, a new weaver working for the first time will work under a *thekadaar,* who exacts a hefty portion of the weaver's wage as payment for training, brokering employment, and supervising the weaving. Weavers begin with a three- to six-month apprenticeship period during which they are not paid at all but are provided only food and general care by the *thekadaar,* who, of course, often pays more attention to his or her own profit than to the welfare of the weaver. After the apprenticeship period, the *thekadaar* continues to retain a portion of the weaver's wage, which can be as high as 50 percent. In practice, most weavers choose to end their association with the *thekadaar* once they have gained enough training and move to another factory on their own or with friends to work for their full wage; younger children, however, stay with their *thekadaar* for a much longer period of time, as they are less capable of managing on their own.

Contracted weavers, regardless of age, often work beside other weavers who are essentially self-employed. Payment to carpet weavers, uniformly across the industry, is by piece rate, and autonomous weavers receive payment for each square meter of carpet they weave, payable when the entire carpet is completed. A trained weaver can complete one square meter of carpet every three to four days, depending on the complexity of the design and the grade of carpet. Carpet weaving is a basic skill that most weavers acquire quickly, and with only this basic training they can potentially find work on their own. There is plenty of opportunity for this; most factories experience a high rate of turnover as weavers leave for better wages elsewhere or retire from the work entirely when they get older.

In addition, the widespread practice of granting salary advances (*peskii*) to weavers subsidizes this instability. This form of informal credit, which is expected by most weavers at some point, provides much-needed cash to meet immediate needs between wage payments. Many young weavers complain that some carpet manufacturers cheat them by continuing deductions for repayment long after the loan has been repaid. Young, uneducated weavers are unable to calculate for themselves what they owe and incapable of keeping track of their repayments. Debt bondage, a South Asian practice that has been associated with the industry in the past, is not at all widespread, but debt from salary advances sometimes ties weavers to manufacturers and prevents them from finding work of their own choosing (O'Neill 2004).

Despite the sensational accounts of child carpet weavers that dominated the news in past decades, most young carpet weavers were victimized by the more banal realities of working for wages in a global industry that relied on cheap labor and by the everyday pressures of living in overcrowded, unhealthy conditions. Children are clearly ill prepared to work under those conditions, and one of Nepal's greatest challenges is to provide meaningful alternatives for them.

The Decline of the Industry

As carpet exports began a slow decline in 1996, so too did demand for weaving labor. By the late 1990s the heady days of Nepal's carpet boom were long over, and experienced and skilled weavers were preferred by most carpet manufacturers. Even during the heyday of the carpet boom, manufacturers preferred older, more vigorous weavers who could perform the physically demanding Tibetan weaving method; children who were less developed were used despite their lack of stamina and ability to pay sufficient attention to design templates. The advent of the Rugmark program in 1996 did much to continue pressure on manufacturers not to hire children, and robust efforts by trade unions to organize weavers in the larger factories also discouraged child labor. Children and young people still try to find work in factories, but it is questionable now whether this is due to outward forms of oppression or bondage or to individual and household subsistence strategies. Causes of the decline in carpet production are debatable, but one potential reason is the persistent claim that Tibeto-Nepalese carpets are being woven by children. Whatever the reasons, the economic conditions that led to the widespread exploitation of child laborers in the last decade have changed; what has not changed as much is the child labor "brand" that the industry has so regrettably acquired.

References and Further Reading

Cross, J.J., M. Sharma, and S. Shrestha. "Weaving Carpets, Weaving Lives: Childhood and Ethnicity in Downtown Kathmandu." *International Journal of Anthropology* 16:2–3 (2001): 153–59.

CWIN. *Misery Behind the Looms*. Kathmandu: Child Workers in Nepal Concerned Centre, 1993.

NSAC. *Nepal Human Development Report 1998*. Kathmandu: Nepal South Asia Centre, 1998.

O'Neill, Tom. "Weaving Wages, Indebtedness and Remittances in the Nepalese Carpet Industry." *Human Organization* 62:2 (2004): 211–20.

Sattaur, O. "Child Labour in Nepal." *Anti Slavery International, no.* 13, Child Labour Series, 1993.

Social Labeling Programs in Nepal's Carpet Industry

Tom O'Neill, PhD, Department of Child and Youth Studies, Brock University

Social labeling is becoming an increasingly important way of educating consumers about the products they obtain on the global market. Labels that mark products as union made, fair trade, and environmentally sustainable are now commonly seen on many products to ensure consumers that the products they purchase meet a range of ethical standards (Hilowitz 1997). Social labels that mark products as "child labor free" have also emerged as important tools for establishing ethical standards for many products available on the global market so that Western consumers can be reassured that children have not been involved in their production. One of these programs, Rugmark, has become centrally important to the carpet-making industries in India, Pakistan, and Nepal.

The Rugmark labeling program began in Nepal in 1996 in response to persistent reports about the exploitation of children in the Nepali carpet industry. The program assists the Nepali government in its efforts to comply with its commitments to the UN Convention on the Rights of the Child (CRC), as well as ILO Convention 138 (minimum age), which it signed in 1996. Previously, the cash-strapped Nepali government could devote minimal resources to regulating the industry. In 1994, for example, the Department of Labour had only two inspectors available to inspect more than 1,500 carpet factories in the Kathmandu Valley (O'Neill 2003).

Rugmark is a voluntary program funded by participating carpet manufacturers and importers who pay the program a percentage of their carpet profits. Participating manufacturers must submit to unannounced visits by a team of Rugmark inspectors, who view every aspect of production, then identify and remove underage workers. Inspectors visit not only major carpet factories and the subcontractors that supply carpets to them, but also other small subcontracting factories when it is suspected they are supplying carpets to a participating manufacturer. Attempts are made to reunite children removed from factories with their families, where they are assisted to remain in school, and Rugmark also subsidizes many children so they can attend school or other occupational programs in Kathmandu.

As a result of the program, Western carpet consumers can be assured that the carpets they buy have not been made with child labor. There are, however, several concerns that people inside the industry have with the program. First, though ostensibly a voluntary program, most carpet manufacturers have little choice but to participate, as their carpets would be suspected of being made with child labor, even if they were not. Currently, about 70 percent of all carpets manufactured in Nepal bear the Rugmark label, including those made by the top producers in the country (O'Neill 2005). As Rugmark certifies carpets as child labor free, it also brands the entire industry as one that would exploit child labor should the program ever end. Second, by taking on a labor regulation role that should properly belong to the national government, the program tends to obviate the need for government regulatory activity. Since the program is focused only on the issue of minimum-age compliance, other issues can be neglected that affect all workers, such as fair wages and working conditions, or health and safety standards. The government of Nepal should address these other issues, but to date it has been distracted from this task.

References and Further Reading

Hilowitz, Janet. "Social Labelling to Combat Child Labour: Some Considerations." *International Labour Review* 136:2 (1997): 215–32.

O'Neill, Tom. "Anti-Child Labour Rhetoric, Child Protection, and Young Carpet Weavers in Kathmandu, Nepal." *Journal of Youth Studies* 6:4 (2003): 411–31.

O'Neill, Tom. "Labour Standard Regulation and the Modernization of Small-Scale Carpet Production in Kathmandu, Nepal." In *Petty Capitalists and Globalization: Flexibility, Entrepreneurship, and Economic Development*, ed. Alan Smart and Josephine Smart, 201–25. Albany: State University of New York Press, 2005.

Rugmark Foundation. http://www.rugmark.org.

Trafficking of Child Workers in Nepal

Govind Subedi, Lecturer, Central Department of Population Studies,
Tribhuvan University, Kathmandu

The history of trafficking of child workers in Nepal is fundamentally associated with Nepal's patriarchal and feudal social structure. There are instances of internal trafficking of girls before and during the autocratic Rana regime (1847–1951). Beautiful girls were recruited in the Kathmandu Palaces as housemaids. When the Rana regime collapsed in 1951, some Rana families fled to India, accompanied by their housemaids, who were brought along for luxury and sexual pleasure. Eventually, these housemaids ended up in Indian brothels. Later, they opened their own brothels and started recruiting girls from their place of origin. This process was fully established in the 1960s. Criminal links between Indian and Nepali traffickers were well established by the 1970s, and the trafficking increased tremendously as a profitable business in the 1980s (Pradhan 1996; Sangroula 2001). Traffickers' networks extended from the village to the palace level as the Panchayat regime (1960–1989), the partyless political system led by the king, became more corrupt, unaccountable, and tyrannical.

Magnitude of Trafficking: A Gray Area

There are no reliable data on the number of trafficked children, places of origin and destination, and purposes of trafficking. The magnitude of trafficking is, thus, speculative and is often estimated with reference to brothel-based prostitution in India. Studies provide numbers of girls and women trafficked to India, but they fail to explain the methodology on how the figures have been derived. These guesstimates range from 80,000 to 200,000. One study suggests that 12,000 children below eighteen years of age are trafficked annually to India for sexual exploitation, and that nearly 40 percent of them are below the age of fourteen years (KC et al. 2001).

Process of Trafficking

The problem of trafficking has become widespread in the country. Officially, thirty-nine out of seventy-five districts have been identified as trafficking-prone districts. Almost all caste and ethnic groups come under the threat of trafficking. The caste and ethnic composition of trafficked victims largely tallies with caste and ethnic composition of the traffickers (Office of the National Reporter on Trafficking 2007). Trafficking occurs through a multitude of routes across the open border between Nepal and India. There are only twenty-six legal border-crossing points along the entire border, but there are hundreds of unofficial points where interception either by the security forces or by NGOs is virtually impossible. Trafficking takes place mostly in networks of traffickers, extending from villages to working places or urban areas to points of destination. Eighty-six percent of traffickers operate in a group (Daywalka Foundation and Center for Research on Environment Health and Population Activities 2007). The traffickers adopt various methods to lure children, ranging from "good promises" to coercion, force, and threats.

Children are trafficked for sexual exploitation, labor exploitation, and entertainments. Each of these has both internal and cross-border trafficking dimensions. With regard to internal trafficking for sexual exploitation, one-fifth of the surveyed 440 female sex workers in the Kathmandu Valley are children (Suwal and Amatya 2002) and at least 14 percent of the 110 surveyed street children in the valley are victims of trafficking (Subedi 2002). In the labor sector, such as the embroidery industry in Mumbai, employers prefer to employ Nepalese boys over Indian adults because the eyes of the boys are very sharp, the children can work longer hours, their wage is far lower than that of the adults, and they are easier to exploit than Indians (Women's Rehabilitation Centre 2002). In the entertainment sector, a large number of children, especially girls, are trafficked to India for circus performance. They are trafficked at the age range of ten to twelve years (Child Workers in Nepal Concerned Centre 2006a).

Contributing Factors to Trafficking in Children

No single factor explains the trafficking phenomenon. Various studies show that trafficking occurs in a complex web of causation (Institute for Development Studies and United Nations Development Fund for Women 2004). The often-cited causes of trafficking at the individual level are domestic violence, child vulnerability, gender discrimination, forced marriage, divorce, separation, and stigmatization from incest and rape. At the household level, illiteracy, poverty, unemployment, and cultural and religious practices such as the *deuki* system (offering young girls to gods and goddesses in the Hindu temples in western Nepal) are important causes of trafficking.

In addition, there are two broader processes that have led to an increase in trafficking. They include growth in the carpet industry (from the early 1990s) and armed conflict (1996–2006). The growth of the carpet industry has had both positive and negative impacts on Nepalese society. While the industry emerged as the country's largest foreign export industry and has provided employment to about 300,000 people (Child Workers in Nepal Concerned Centre 1993), it has also led to high demand for child labor. Children constitute about half of the workforce in the carpet industry. Further, the industry became a transit center for trafficking of children. While girls were mainly trafficked for sexual exploitation, boys were trafficked to Indian carpet factories. One study indicated that there were more than 25,000 Nepali child laborers in different carpet factories in India in the early 1990s (Women's Rehabilitation Centre 2002).

Another, broader process leading to increased trafficking is the armed conflict between the Maoists and the state. The conflict has increased both internal and cross-border trafficking in children. The internal trafficking has been mainly reported for prostitution in the Kathmandu Valley, the highway headways, and border towns (Rana 2005; Rai 2005; Child Workers in Nepal Concerned Centre 2006b). Some argue, though, that most girls enter prostitution not because they are forced but because they have no alternatives for survival (Frederick 1998; Terre des Hommes 2003; Hausner 2005). The cross-border trafficking is reported for both sexual exploitation and labor exploitation in India (Center for Children Welfare Board 2004).

Conclusion

The problem of trafficking in children is no longer confined to a specific ethnic group and a limited catchment area as it was fifteen or twenty years ago. Yet *dalit* (untouchable) children are most vulnerable to trafficking because of their poor socioeconomic condition. The vulnerability to trafficking has also increased with the growth and diversification of foreign labor migration. Gulf nations are increasingly becoming destination countries for sexual exploitation. Internal trafficking of teenage girls has been on the rise mainly because of the long-term adverse impact of armed conflict on girls' lives and an increase in the commodification of children, especially girls, in cabin restaurants, in beauty parlors, and on the streets in urban areas of Nepal. As child trafficking is a complex problem, effectively combating it requires simultaneous prevention, prosecution, and protection measures.

References and Further Reading

Center for Children Welfare Board. *An Increasing Wave: Migration of Nepalese Children to India in the Context of Nepal's Armed Conflict.* Kathmandu: Center for Children Welfare Board and the Save the Children Alliance, 2005.

Child Workers in Nepal Concerned Centre. *Misery Behind the Looms: Child Laborers in Carpet Industry.* Kathmandu: Child Workers in Nepal Concerned Centre, 1993.

———. "Assessments of Worst Forms of Child Labor in CWIN-Plan Nepal Working Districts (Morang, Sunsari and Makwanpur)." Research report, Child Workers in Nepal Concerned Centre, Kathmandu, 2006a.

———. "A Study on Impact of Armed Conflict on Adolescent Girls in Nepal: Narratives of Adolescent Girls from Morang, Kathmandu, Makwanpur, Salyan and Banke Districts." Research report. Child Workers in Nepal Concerned Centre, Kathmandu, 2006b.

Daywalka Foundation and Center for Research on Environment Health and Population Activities. *A Study on Male Trafficker Prisoners with Special Reference to Human Trafficking in Kathmandu Valley.* Kathmandu: Daywalka Foundation and Center for Research on Environment Health and Population Activities, 2007.

Frederick, John. "Deconstructing Gita." *Himal SouthAsian* 11:10 (October 1998).

Hausner, Sondra L. *The Movement of Women: Migration, Trafficking, and Prostitution in the Context of Nepal's Armed Conflict.* Kathmandu: Save the Children, USA, 2005.

Institute for Development Studies and United Nations Development Fund for Women. *Status and Dimensions of Trafficking within Nepalese Context.* Kathamndu: Institute for Development Studies and United Nations Development Fund for Women, 2004.

KC, Bal Kumar, Govind Subedi, Yogendra Bahadur Gurung, and Keshab Prasad Adhikari. *Nepal: Trafficking in Girls with Special Reference to Prostitution: A Rapid Assessment.* Geneva: ILO-IPEC, 2001.

Office of the National Reporter on Trafficking. *Trafficking in Persons Especially on Women and Children in Nepal, National Report 2006.* Kathmandu: Office of the National Reporter on Trafficking, National Human Rights Commission, 2007.

Pradhan, Gauri. *Back Home from Brothels.* Kathmandu: Child Workers in Nepal Concerned Centre, 1996.

Rai, Deep Ranjani. *A Pilot Survey on Internally Displaced Persons in Kathmandu and Birendranagar.* Kathmandu: South Asia Forum for Human Rights, 2005.

Rana, Pinky Singh. *Impact of Armed Conflict Pushing Girls and Women into Sexual Abuse and Sex Trade.* Kathmandu: Save the Children Norway, 2005.

Sangroula, Yuabaraj. *Trafficking of Girls and Women in Nepal: Building a Community Surveillance System for Prevention.* Kathmandu: Kathmandu School of Law, 2001.

Subedi, Govind. *Trafficking and Sexual Abuse Among Street Children in Kathmandu.* Kathmandu: ILO-IPEC and Trafficking in Children South Asia, 2002.

———. *Institutions, Gender Relations and Poverty in Nepal.* PhD thesis, Jawaharlal Nehru University, New Delhi, 2007.

Suwal, Bhim Raj, and Tulsa Lata Amatya. *Internal Trafficking Among Children and Youth Engaged in Prostitution in Nepal.* Kathmandu: ILO-IPEC and Trafficking in Children South Asia, 2002.

Terre des Hommes. *Child Trafficking in Nepal: An Assessment of the Present Situation.* Kathmandu: Terre des Hommes, 2003.

Women's Rehabilitation Centre. *Cross Border Trafficking of Boys.* Kathmandu: Women's Rehabilitation Centre, ILO-IPEC, and Trafficking in Children South-Asia, 2002.

The Recruitment and Use of Children in Nepal's Armed Conflict

Charu Lata Hogg, Consultant to the Coalition to Stop the Use of Child Soldiers

Forced or compulsory recruitment of children below the age of eighteen for use in armed conflict is considered a worst form of child labor under ILO Convention 182. In Nepal, children have been recruited and used in various ways by both the opposition Communist Party of Nepal–Maoist (CPN-M) and government forces. Since the eruption of armed conflict in 1996, the Maoists have abducted hundreds of children for political indoctrination programs, and some are thought to have remained in the group. Government forces have reportedly used children as spies and messengers, and some children suspected of being Maoist sympathizers have been detained or killed. Since May 2006, the CPN-M has engaged in talks with an alliance of national political parties, and a cease-fire has remained in place. However, recruitment of children—whether forced or voluntary—has continued in violation of international children's rights principles and instruments, which both sides have pledged to respect. In the event of a resumption of hostilities, children remain at risk of being used to participate in the armed conflict.

Context

The CPN-M launched an armed insurgency in 1996 in the underdeveloped western districts of Rolpa and Rukum. A state of emergency was declared in November 2001, and numerous attempts at peace talks were made throughout 2002 and 2003. In February 2005, King Gyanendra declared a state of emergency and took direct power. Hundreds of people were arrested, and clashes between Maoists and security forces increased. The Maoists declared a four-month unilateral cease-fire in September 2005, which the government did not reciprocate. In November 2005, the parties—known as the Seven Party Alliance (SPA)—and the Maoists signed a twelve-point agreement that formalized the Maoist offer to enter a multiparty political system. A four-day strike called by the SPA on April 7, 2006, swelled into a nationwide protest by hundred of thousands of Nepalis. On April 24, King Gyanendra agreed to reinstate parliament to protect multiparty democracy and restore peace. On May 4, Maoist rebels welcomed a government cease-fire offer and said they were ready to enter peace talks. In April 2006 the Maoists pledged to respect the rights of children and said that no one below the age of eighteen would be recruited into its forces. Around 13,000 people have been killed in the civil war, with 8,000 civilian deaths reported since November 2001.

National Recruitment Laws

There is no provision for conscription in Nepal, including during war or national emergency, and there are no known plans for its introduction, as volunteers fulfill recruitment quotas (Horeman and Stolwijk 1998). According to government information, the 1962 Royal Army New Recruitment Rules require recruits to be at least eighteen years old. However, the 1971 Young Boys' Recruitment and Conditions of Service Rules state that boys must be between fifteen and eighteen years old to be recruited.[1] The government has stated that "young Nepalese men could enlist from the age of 15 years in order to follow military training, but nobody under 18 years of age could be recruited into the army."[2]

Children's Involvement in Government Forces

The government has denied that children under eighteen are involved in the armed forces, but reports indicate that twelve- to sixteen-year-olds may have been used as spies, couriers, and messengers throughout the course of the conflict. Children who have left the CPN-M or who have surrendered to the security forces risk detention. The situation of children accused of being associated with CPN-M who were arrested by security forces before the cease-fire was of concern, especially those detained under the Terrorism and Disruptive Activities (Control and Punishment) Ordinance (TADO) without judicial oversight. Most were thought to have been released after the change of government in April 2006. Some had been detained for long periods beyond the limits of the law; and some were arrested when they were below the age of sixteen—the definition of a child under Nepal's Children's Act 1992.

In 2005, the UN Committee on the Rights of the Child urged the government to review its legislation and policies to ensure full implementation of juvenile justice standards and norms, to amend or repeal the TADO, and to develop appropriate measures for children affected by conflict. In particular, it recommended the criminalization of abduction, recruitment, and use of children for military purposes, and the establishment of a rule of engagement for the security forces with regard to children.

Children in the CPN-M and the People's Liberation Army

With no systematic monitoring, there are no exact figures on the numbers of children recruited or used by the CPN-M and its armed wing, the People's Liberation Army (PLA). The Maoists have continued to deny using children for military purposes. However, the UN's Office of the High Commissioner of Human Rights (OHCHR), has confirmed the presence of numerous children in the PLA, as well as the use of children as combatants before the cease-fire. Other information clearly suggests that significant numbers of children are in CPN-M cultural groups and militias and may also be used for military purposes—as messengers or informants. The OHCHR reported in October 2006 that up to fifty children—including some as young as twelve years old—had been taken from their families since the April 2006 cease-fire declaration to take part in PLA and militia activities.

Life for children with the CPN-M appears to be harsh, although most children have reported being fairly treated with little or no gender discrimination. Some girls have reported sexual abuse, but few complaints are made openly for fear of social ostracism. Some cases of beatings and harsh punishments, including hard labor, have been reported, particularly by children who tried to escape. While some children volunteer to join the CPN-M, inspired by its political ideology or for personal reasons, most are coerced into joining. Those who volunteer often have specific reasons: experience of harassment by the Nepalese Army (formerly the Royal Nepalese Army), loss of home or family members, displacement, or revenge against rape or other human rights violations against a family member. Apart from forcibly removing children from schools, the Maoists use other strategies to gain recruits, conducting door-to-door campaigns and organizing cultural programs in villages to encourage children to join.

Both international and national NGOs in Nepal have initiated programs to care for children released by parties to the conflict, captured children, or those who have simply left the ranks of the armed forces or the PLA. Some children have been provided with temporary shelter; those who have been illegally detained have been given legal assistance. Family tracing and negotiations with the parties concerned have also been carried out to allow for the safe return of children to their families. In April 2006, the CPN-M made a Statement of Commitment to Human Rights and Humanitarian Principles, which included the statement that "the rights of children will be respected" and no one below the age of eighteen would be recruited into the PLA. In August, the CPN-M leadership agreed to allow child protection agencies carrying out assessment missions to gather information and plan the process of returning children to their families. However, reports of child recruitment have continued, and efforts to secure the release of children from the PLA have not always been successful.

Hostilities ceased in April when there was a change of government, but peace talks have yet to result in a comprehensive agreement on the government or on troops and arms management. Such an agreement could have a major impact in reducing children's involvement in the armed conflict and preventing their future recruitment. In the meantime, the release of children recruited or used in the armed conflict should not depend on a peace agreement and should be sought unconditionally and at all times.

Notes

1. Initial report of Nepal to UN Committee on the Rights of the Child, UN Doc. CRC/C/3/Add.34, May 10, 1995.

2. UN Committee on the Rights of the Child, Consideration of the Initial Report of Nepal, UN Doc. CRC/C/SR.302, June 24, 1996.

References and Further Reading

Coalition to Stop the Use of Child Soldiers. "Child Soldiers Global Report 2004 (Nepal)." http://www.child-soldiers.org/document_get.php?id=861.

Horeman, Bart, and Marc Stolwijk. *Refusing to Bear Arms: A World Survey of Conscription and Conscientious Objection to Military Service.* London: War Resisters International, 1998. http://www.wri-irg.org/co/rtba.

Pakistan

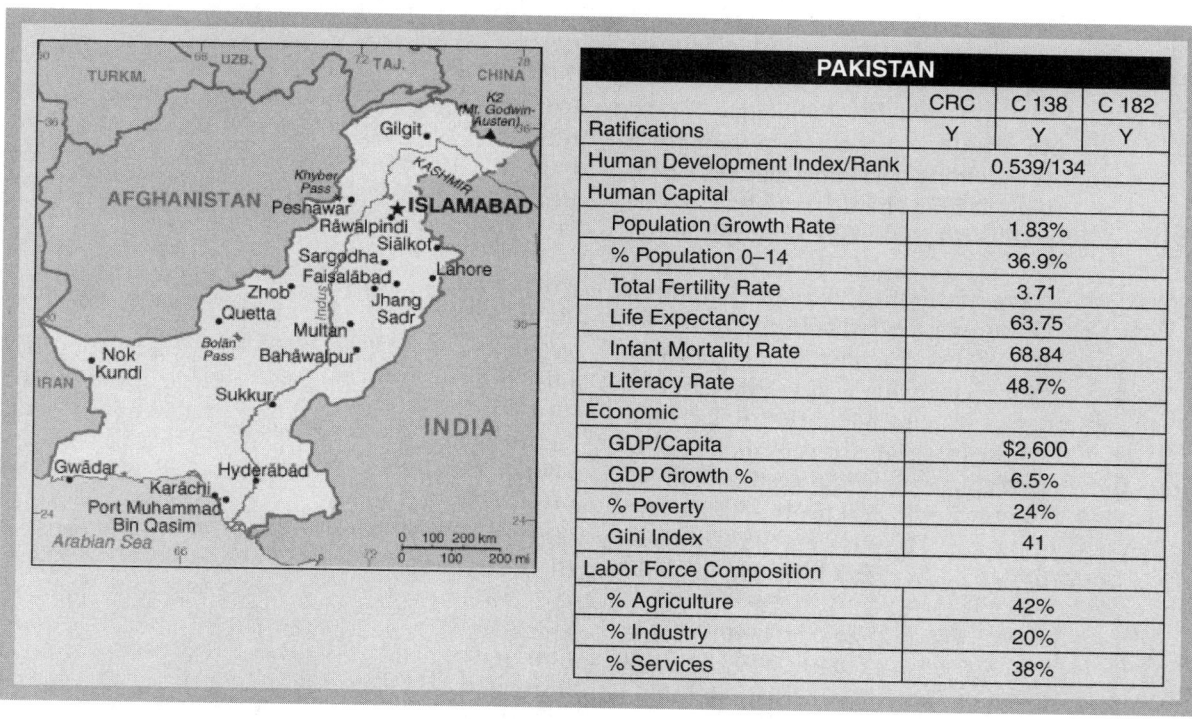

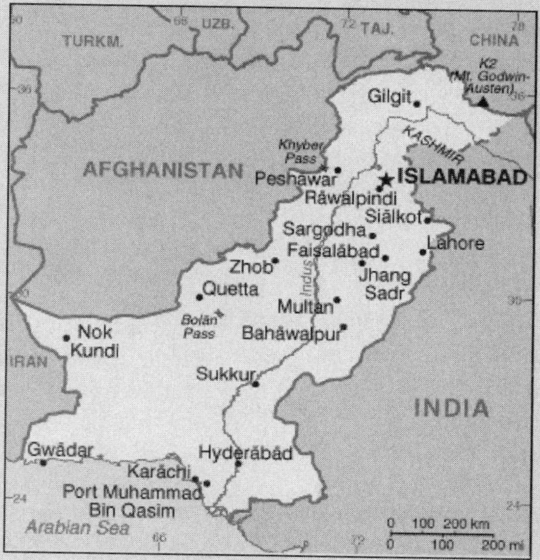

PAKISTAN			
	CRC	C 138	C 182
Ratifications	Y	Y	Y
Human Development Index/Rank	0.539/134		
Human Capital			
Population Growth Rate	1.83%		
% Population 0–14	36.9%		
Total Fertility Rate	3.71		
Life Expectancy	63.75		
Infant Mortality Rate	68.84		
Literacy Rate	48.7%		
Economic			
GDP/Capita	$2,600		
GDP Growth %	6.5%		
% Poverty	24%		
Gini Index	41		
Labor Force Composition			
% Agriculture	42%		
% Industry	20%		
% Services	38%		

Child Labor in Pakistan

Zarina Jillani, Society for the Protection of the Rights of the Child (SPARC), Islamabad

The issue of child labor in Pakistan received exposure in the 1990s, triggered by images of young children stitching soccer balls in the major industrial city of Sialkot. The international media coverage of poor working conditions and young children employed by major factories that supply world-class soccer balls to major international sporting-goods companies provoked outrage by Western consumers. More concrete threats came in the form of the Harkin Bill, which called for ban on imports of goods in which child labor had been used at any stage of manufacturing; the Sanders Amendment, which prohibits importation of products made with forced or indentured labor; and petitions filed against Pakistan by the AFL-CIO on the allegation of widespread incidence of child labor and bonded labor.

Pakistan, which initially denied the seriousness of the issue, was compelled to change its position to one of reluctant acceptance. The threats of boycotts of Pakistani goods, particularly major export goods, prompted manufacturers, the government, and leading international organizations to search for solutions to the problem of child labor. In 1994 the government of Pakistan signed a Memorandum of Understanding with the ILO initiating a national program for the elimination of child labor within the framework of the International Program on the Elimination of Child Labor (IPEC). Since then, Pakistan has ratified ILO Conventions 182 and 138, relating to worst forms of child labor and minimum age for employment, respectively. These provide the basis for undertaking interventions for elimination of child labor and, more important, for international monitoring of child labor practices in the country.

The launch of IPEC in Pakistan was followed by a national survey in 1996 to find out the magnitude of the child labor problem. A number of small, medium, and large interventions to address the priority issues of child labor in the country were also launched thereafter.

The Statistics

According to the 1996 National Child Labor Survey, there were 3.3 million child laborers in the country, roughly 8 percent of the 40 million children in the five- to fourteen-year-old age-group. Nongovernmental organizations and independent experts challenge the survey results and consider the figure of 3.3 million an underestimation, first because it failed to account for more than 20 million children who were out of school at the time and second because it omitted a number of sectors where child labor is quite common. They estimate the number of child laborers in the country to be anywhere from 8 million to 10 million.

The National Child Labor Survey is now more than ten years old. There has been no follow-up survey, and it is difficult to assess the current situation of child laborers in the country, or for that matter, the impact of the interventions undertaken to address the problem during the past decade. The survey, nonetheless, gave a broad picture of the nature, extent, and causes of child labor in the country and provided a basis for further action.

According to the survey, approximately 67 percent of the total child labor force was engaged in occupations relating to agriculture; around 11 percent in the manufacturing sector; 9 percent in wholesale, retail trade, and hotels; 8 percent in community, social, and personal services; 3 percent in transport, storage, and communication; and just

Table 1

Child Laborers in Pakistan, 1996

Provinces/	All Areas			Rural			Urban		
Age-Groups	Total	Boys	Girls	Total	Boys	Girls	Total	Boys	Girls
Pakistan	3,313,420	2,431,992	881,428	2,945,675	2,110,358	835,317	367,745	321,634	46,111
5–9	573,084	333,656	239,428	536,145	302,694	233,451	36,939	30,962	5,977
10–14	2,740,336	2,098,336	642,000	2,409,530	1,807,664	601,866	330,806	290,672	40,134
Punjab	1,943,305	1,414,787	528,518	1,704,577	1,212,330	492,247	238,728	202,457	36,271
5–9	217,817	147,836	69,981	192,973	127,710	65,263	24,844	20,126	4,718
10–14	1,725,488	1,266,951	458,537	1,511,604	1,084,620	426,984	213,884	182,331	31,553
Sindh	298,303	273,350	24,953	208,783	190,798	17,985	89,520	82,552	6,968
5–9	30,099	27,938	2,161	21,995	20,680	1,315	8,104	7,258	846
10–14	268,204	245,412	22,792	186,788	170,118	16,670	81,416	75,294	6,122
NWFP	1,058,089	730,471	327,618	1,021,147	696,207	324,940	36,942	34,264	2,678
5–9	323,201	155,915	167,286	319,375	152,502	166,873	3,826	3,413	413
10–14	734,888	574,556	160,332	701,772	543,705	158,067	33,116	30,851	2,265
Balochisan	13,723	13,384	339	11,168	11,023	145	2,555	2,361	194
5–9	1,967	1,967	n/av	1,802	1,802	n/av	165	165	n/av
10–14	11,756	11,417	339	9,366	9,221	145	2,390	2,196	194

Source: National Federal Bureau of Statistics, 1996 Survey on Child Labor.

under 2 percent in the construction sector. Approximately 70 percent of these children worked as unpaid family helpers, mostly in rural areas. Female child workers were one-fourth of the total child labor population.

The survey shows that 46 percent of the children worked more than thirty-six hours a week, and 13 percent worked more than fifty-six hours a week. About 33 percent of the employed children had been through the formal system of education. The family profile of child laborers shows a low income and large family size, with an average of eight household members. The main reasons given by parents and guardians for letting their children work included assisting in household enterprise and supplementing household income.

Sectors

Child labor in Pakistan, ranging from light work to more serious and hazardous work, exists in a number of sectors with varying degrees of prevalence. Most child labor is in the informal sector, mainly agriculture and domestic labor, areas that are outside the scope of national child labor legislation. Child labor is also found in many manufacturing processes and industries in contravention of child labor laws.

In rural areas, children are mainly engaged in unpaid farm work. They assist their families throughout the year, and more so during the sowing and harvesting seasons. Their activities include looking after animals, collecting firewood, fetching water from distant sources, spreading fertilizers, and spraying insecticides. In these chores girls take on a disproportionate share of the total workload, and their added responsibilities include domestic work, cooking, taking care of younger siblings, and tending to and keeping the house clean.

In urban settings, children are employed in more diversified occupations. The most well-known sectors are the soccer-ball-stitching industry, the carpet industry, surgical instruments, brick kilns, auto repair workshops, and the glass-bangle industry. Children are also employed in occupations such as loading and unloading of goods and fishing and in settings such as hotels, restaurants, and shops. They are also self-employed as shoe polishers, ragpickers (sorting out refuse and recycling), street vendors, and car washers. In many of the manufacturing sectors, children work in home-based workshops, getting material supplied to their homes by middlemen or subcontractors. This has created a large informal sector within the formal sector.

Less visible, but more important in terms of numbers, are children working as domestic servants and those suffering under a system of bonded labor. According to a study on child domestic labor, every fourth house in an urban setting employs child domestic workers. With more women working outside their homes and a rising trend toward nuclear families, there is increasing demand for cheap and safe domestic help. Supply-side factors include poverty and lack of educational and skill-development opportunities. Domestic work can be considered an entry-level job, as it requires little training or skills, and for many families it is the only way to supplement household incomes and at the same time feed and clothe their children in an environment they consider relatively safe.

Because child domestic work is outside the scope of national child labor legislation, the working conditions, including working hours, salary, recreational time, and days off, are almost entirely dictated by the employers. The ages of domestic child workers range from six to eighteen years, the majority being in the eleven- to fourteen-year-old age-group, and almost a third in the six- to ten-year-old age-group. These workers are often expected to perform multiple duties and in many cases work for ten to fourteen hours a day. Some children may not get even a weekly day off; others, once a month or only during religious festivals. The salary can range from US$10–$30 a month. Some work for only room and board and occasional financial help during emergencies.

Children in Pakistan also suffer under a system of bonded labor. Bonded labor, also called debt bondage, is a form of slavery in which poor workers take loans, instead of wages, in exchange for their work, and pledge themselves or members of their family to work until the loan is paid off. More often than not the loan cannot be paid back due to exorbitant interest rates, so the debt passes from one generation to the next. Bonded labor is common in brick kilns, carpet weaving, agriculture, fisheries, and stone and brick crushing. In the case of children, their bondage can be a result of a loan taken out by a parent or guardian, who then provides the child to work off the debt. This kind of bondage also features in the internal trafficking of children from rural to urban areas. A child may also be part of a family that is bonded and is expected to work along with the family to pay off the loan.

Causes of Child Labor

Widespread poverty and the country's weak education system are widely accepted as the major reasons behind the child labor problem. However, sociocultural practices, the legislative framework, and patterns of social and economic development also contribute to and determine the forms of child labor.

Pakistan is a low-income country with a population over 157 million, growing at a rate of 2.2 percent per year. At least a quarter of the population lives below the poverty line, and a much larger portion live in precarious economic conditions where the slightest crisis can push them into poverty. State social safety nets, or welfare mechanisms, are arbitrary and inadequate, and in times of economic stress, ineffective. For many poor families, children—especially sons—are considered the most reliable support system: the underlying linkage between dependence on child labor and high fertility rates. Poverty and the desire for imparting skills to their children influence parents in favor of child labor.

Almost 45 percent of the country's population is below eighteen years of age, with more than 50 million children in the five- to eighteen-year-old age-group. Educational opportunities for this expanding pool of children have been limited at best. The adult literacy rate is 50 percent, and the net primary school attendance rate is 56 percent. It is estimated that 50 percent of children drop out before completing five years of primary schooling. Government expenditure on education has remained at or below 2 percent of the total central government expenditure. Almost 90 percent of this is spent on salaries; the rest is spent on providing educational inputs. Even these scarce allocations are not properly utilized due to poor management, bureaucratic inefficiencies, and corruption. Pakistan has yet to make even primary education up to grade five compulsory or free. Laws have been developed for this purpose but are not enforced. The majority of child laborers are in the ten- to fourteen-year-old age-group. In order to have an impact on them, there is a need to extend compulsory education up to the secondary level, something not foreseeable in the near future.

Pakistan's education system also reflects deep class divisions, where opportunities are determined by social origin or economic status. The public versus private, and Urdu versus English, divides are the hallmarks of the country's education system. On the one hand, the system produces elitist leaders, hailing from rich private schools with marketable English-language skills and quality education; on the other hand, the system produces a vast disillusioned majority with questionable skills and competencies.

The public education system, especially in the rural areas, where more than 60 percent of the population lives, is characterized by poor-quality education, dilapidated school structures, shortage of trained and motivated teachers, and lack of teaching materials. In addition, corporal punishment, a standard disciplinary feature of the education system, is one of the main reasons for high dropout rates. Many families prefer the present value of a child's income as opposed to the future value of education, which for many is uncertain at best. An irrelevant and outdated curriculum is a major factor behind the current disillusionment with the education system. On-the-job training is widely seen as better preparation for the future than schooling.

Child labor has widespread social acceptance in Pakistan. Employing children is still considered a form of "social service" among families and businesses and is widely considered as vital to the survival of poor families. While much of this acceptability comes from lack of alternatives or social safety nets, traditional notions and patterns of social hierarchy also play a significant role. Pakistani society is still dominated by feudal culture, especially in the rural areas, where the lives of ordinary people and the patterns of social development are generally controlled by powerful landlords. Even in urban areas, socioeconomic status is a major determining factor in social intercourse. Domestic and bonded labor, two of the more insidious forms of child labor, are directly linked to this mind-set.

The patterns of socioeconomic development have encouraged rural-to-urban migration. While the rural areas are marked by poor development, infrastructure, and employment opportunities, Pakistan's major cities are rapidly growing urban centers, attracting rural migrants from across the country in search of livelihoods. But the growing urban slums offer little in terms of sustainable livelihoods. Many migrants find employment in low-income and highly insecure occupations in the informal sector, where the use of child labor to generate a minimum income for household survival becomes a critical factor.

Child Labor Law

The widespread prevalence of child labor is also due to the legitimacy it derives from a legislative framework that is more regulatory than prohibitive, lacks substance and scale, and is poorly enforced. The Employment of Children Act, the major law governing child labor, prohibits employment of children under fourteen years of age in certain occupations, regulates the conditions of work in others, and exempts certain establishments from the provisions banning or regulating child labor. The law does not apply to a large number of sectors where child labor is most common. It leaves out child domestic labor, children working in agriculture, self-employed children, street vendors, and children working in family enterprises.

The exemption of family-run establishments, and small establishments where ten or fewer people are working, from the prohibitive or regulatory provisions of the law are exploited by employers. In urban and semi-urban areas, most of the working children are employed in small-scale, unregistered establishments, where the employers can easily evade the legislative protections granted to working children with respect to hazardous occupations and working hours. Child labor therefore continues to thrive in the large informal sector

Cleaning the hands after toiling with lubricants, Karachi, 2005. *(Photo by Kristoffel Lieten courtesy of IREWOC Foundation)*

by means of the contract system, under which children are employees of a contractor while actually performing work for larger industries in the formal sector.

Weak enforcement of the law is an indication of the lack of importance the government attaches to the child labor issue. The Employment of Children Act calls for appointment of specialized child labor inspectors to monitor the implementation of the law, but the inspection system is almost nonexistent. No specialized inspectors have been appointed in the past sixteen years, and regular labor inspectors are expected to do the job. Trends in recent years show an alarming decrease in labor inspections. In Sindh, for example, there has been not a single inspection since 2004; in the province of Balochistan no data is available; and in Punjab the number of inspections has gone down drastically since 2003. Under the Punjab Industrial Policy of 2003, inspections by the labor department have been stopped, and a self-declaration system for labor inspection has been introduced, which virtually gives a free hand to employers to do anything to safeguard their interests. This has made it almost impossible for labor inspectors to check labor law violations.

Action Against Child Labor

Another important reason for the persistence of child labor is the approach taken to tackle the problem. In practice, attempts to address child labor rely on a variety of programs and projects, funded mainly by international donors and involving millions of dollars but benefiting only a few thousand children. The sustainability of these projects remains doubtful. Even the more well-known and celebrated ones have been criticized for flawed design, poor implementation and monitoring, and an exorbitant cost-benefit ratio.

The National Policy and Plan of Action is the main government program to combat child labor. Approved in 2000, its main objectives are progressive elimination of child labor from all economic sectors; immediate withdrawal of children from worst forms of child labor; preventing entry of underage children into the labor market through universalization of primary education and family empowerment; and rehabilitation of working children through nonformal education, prevocational training, and skill development. The main intervention under this plan thus far has been the establishment of the National Center for Rehabilitation of Child Laborers, which provides nonformal education and financial incentives to children and families. The concept and its application are widely criticized. Enrollment criteria in these centers are regularly flouted, and the compensatory scheme has encouraged parents of nonworking children to withdraw their children from regular schools and enroll them in these centers. The sustainability and the high costs of running this program are additional issues that point to the inherently flawed concept. The program is currently running 146 schools but serves only a few hundred children.

In 2003 the government of Pakistan joined with IPEC to launch a Time Bound Program as a follow-up to ratification of ILO Convention 182 on elimination of worst forms of child labor. The four-year program has financial support from the U.S. Department of Labor and directly targets an estimated 11,800 children working in six identified hazardous sectors: glass-bangle making, surgical-instruments manufacturing, tanneries, coal mining, scavenging, and deep-sea fishing and seafood processing. The program aims to address non-formal education, vocational and skills training, and awareness of occupational safety and health issues in seven targeted districts across the four provinces of Pakistan. The upstream interventions under this project have yielded only one result so far, which is the expansion and notification of the list of hazardous child labor.

Conclusion

Despite the attention given to child labor in recent years, a visible difference in its prevalence has yet to be seen. Its persistence stems directly from a lack of political commitment and a flawed approach to its solution. In order to move forward, there is a need to go beyond the "project approach" and address the issue at the macrolevel by introducing free and compulsory education, linking school-leaving age to the minimum age of entry into the workforce, and introducing child labor laws that extend to all sectors. At an even more fundamental level, the societal value system, underpinned by principles of equality and fairness, and carried forward by a universal system of quality education, must be introduced so that children of all social classes have access to equal opportunities.

References and Further Reading

Aftab, Ahmed M. "Child Labor in Pakistan: A Study of the Lahore Area." *Child Welfare* 70:2 (1991): 261–67.

Ray, Ranjan. "Analysis of Child Labour in Peru and Pakistan: A Comparative Study." *Journal of Population Economics* 13 (2000): 3–20.

Society for the Protection of the Rights of the Child. http://www.sparcpk.org/.

———. *Fading Light: A Study on Child Trafficking.* Islamabad: Society for the Protection of the Rights of the Child, 2006.

———. *The State of Pakistan's Children 2006.* Islamabad: Society for the Protection of the Rights of the Child, 2006.

Toor, Saadia. "Child Labor in Pakistan: Coming of Age in the New World Order." *Annals of the American Academy of Political and Social Science* 575 (May 2001): 194–224.

Child Work and Schooling Costs in Pakistan

Arjun Singh Bedi, Institute of Social Studies, The Hague, Netherlands;
and **Gautam Hazarika,** University of Texas at Brownsville

A conventional argument in the child labor debate is that improving access to school is an effective way to reduce the labor force participation of children. It is argued that schooling competes with economic activity in the use of children's time, and enhanced access to schools, interpretable as reduction in schooling costs, may raise school attendance at the expense of child labor. This entry draws a distinction between child labor within the household (intrahousehold) and child work in the labor market (extrahousehold) and examines the separate effects of schooling costs on these two types of labor in rural Pakistan.

Background

In official surveys, a child is considered to be economically active if he or she worked at least one hour during the reference week as a paid employee, was self-employed, or worked as an unpaid family member on a family farm or nonfarm enterprise. A child who did not have a job but was seeking one is treated as unemployed. Following accepted definitions, the sum of employed and unemployed children constitutes the child labor force. Child participation in domestic work in their own households is not treated as labor. Various international agencies and local sources have estimated that Pakistan has between 3.3 million and 10 million child workers (a labor force participation rate of 8–20 percent). The estimates span a wide range depending on the definition of child work (Burki and Fasih 1998; Hyder 1998).

Intra- and Extrahousehold Labor

Work activities of children can be categorized into three broad types: work in the labor market for a wage, unpaid work on the family farm or enterprise, and unpaid domestic work. Some authors have recast this trichotomy of child work into a dichotomy consisting of work outside and work within the household (Bequelle and Boyden 1988). Holding that work by children is child labor only if it is exploitative, they have argued that work within the household does not constitute child labor. Work on a family farm or other family enterprise, or in a household domestic capacity, provides on-the-job training, equips a child with essential skills that may not be learned elsewhere, and enhances the self-esteem of the child. Since work within the household is typically executed under the guidance and supervision of parents, it is deemed not to be exploitative. According to this view, only work that involves an employee-employer relationship and that is remunerated in cash or kind constitutes child labor.

While work outside and within the household may be different, the view that work undertaken in the context of the household is not child labor needs to be subjected to scrutiny. Given that the majority of child work in rural areas consists of household chores and unpaid work on family farms, accepting a narrow definition of child labor that focuses on an employer-employee relationship may lead to the erroneous conclusion that the problem of child labor in rural areas is marginal.

While there are disagreements about the type of work that falls under the rubric of child labor, it is potentially important to distinguish between work done within the household and work done outside it. Such a distinction is desirable particularly because parents may view the two types of children's work as different. If the two types of child labor are indeed viewed differently by parents, it is possible that they will exhibit differing sensitivities to policy interventions designed to curb child labor. If extrahousehold work is motivated primarily by a need to augment household income, parents may be responsive to income subsidies or reductions in schooling costs. If, on the other hand, work within the household is viewed as essential training that cannot be acquired elsewhere, parents may not be as responsive to such economic stimuli. Consistent with this argument, this essay draws a distinction between intra- and extrahousehold labor and examines the effect of school costs on these two different types of labor.

Data and Patterns of Work

The analysis is based on data from the 1991 Pakistan Integrated Household Survey (PIHS). The survey covered 4,800 households in 300 communities divided equally between rural and urban areas. Since work by children younger than age ten is unreported in the PIHS and workers older than fourteen are generally not considered child laborers, the analysis is performed on a sample of 1,900 ten- to fourteen-year-old children drawn from among the survey's rural respondents. Excluding domestic work, the labor force participation rate of ten- to fourteen-year-old children in rural Pakistan was approximately 28 percent in 1990–1991. The rates for boys and girls in rural Pakistan were similar (28 percent versus 29 percent). When the definition of child labor is expanded to include domestic work, these figures alter dramatically. The overall labor force participation rate increases to 55 percent while the rate for girls climbs to 86 percent. The steep increase in the labor force participation rate of girls is due to the fact that only females in the PIHS were asked about household domestic work. The survey presumes, not unreasonably in the context of rural Pakistan, that household domestic work is the exclusive domain of girls and women. Total time at work (including domestic work) is about fourteen hours a week, with females (twenty-one hours) working considerably longer than males (eight hours). This is largely due to their substantial contribution to household chores. Exclusion of domestic tasks from the concept of work reduces the duration of the work week to seven hours, with males working eight hours and females working about five hours. Thus, when domestic work is excluded from the definition of work, children's time at work appears modest.

School costs are measured by three variables. The first of these is the direct cost of primary schooling. For middle and secondary schools, measures of direct costs are not available. So, to capture one aspect of cost, we used distance to the closest middle and secondary schools. In addition to school-cost reduction, policies to reduce child labor can emphasize improvement in school inputs (quality). While measures with direct bearing on student achievement are not available, we explored potential school input effects by including three measures that capture the quality of local school infrastructure: the proportion of area primary schools supplied with water, the proportion supplied with electricity, and the proportion with walls made of permanent material.

School Costs, Child Labor, and Schooling

Although the primary aim is to explore the differential effect of schooling costs on extrahousehold and intrahousehold labor supply, in order to facilitate comparisons with the existing literature, the discussion begins by eschewing the distinction between these two types of child labor (for detailed results, see Hazarika and Bedi 2003).

Total Child Labor Supply

The three measures of schooling costs are positively related to child labor supply decisions. However, it is only the direct cost of primary schooling that has a substantial impact. The three school infrastructure measures also appear to play a role, with access to water playing the most important role. Separate estimates for boys and girls reveal similar patterns. The main conclusion is that, when there is no distinction drawn between intrahousehold and extrahousehold child labor, consistent with conventional wisdom, reduction in the cost of schooling and improvements in its quality would lead to a reduction in children's labor supply in rural Pakistan.

Extrahousehold Child Labor Supply

In a similar vein, turning to work done outside the household, it is found that the direct costs of primary schooling and the costs of postprimary schooling as measured by distance to the closest school are positively related to hours of work. There is some evidence that improvements in school infrastructure, as measured by the proportion of area primary schools supplied with water, would reduce the extrahousehold child labor supply. In sum, there appears to be a strong link between schooling-related variables and extrahousehold child labor supply, which may be construed as evidence of the substitutability of children's schooling and work.

Intrahousehold Child Labor Supply

In contrast, examination of the link between work within the household and schooling-related variables provides a different picture. Schooling-related variables are not related to the intrahousehold labor supply of children. The gender-wise estimates indicate that, for boys and girls, schooling cost and input variables do not have a bearing on intrahousehold labor supply. Hence, while schooling costs and extrahousehold child labor supply appear positively and significantly correlated, schooling-related variables are generally insignificant correlates of the intrahousehold labor supply of children, leading to a much less sanguine conclusion about the substitutability of children's schooling and work.

Schooling

Almost 61 percent of our sample has attended school, but there are stark differences across gender. While 80 percent of boys have attended school at some stage, the corresponding figure for girls is 39 percent. For the full sample, the three school-cost variables have the expected negative signs. The variables are individually and jointly statistically significant at conventional levels. The gender-specific estimates show that this finding is mainly attributable to the behavior of girls, in that a reduction of primary schooling costs would increase the probability of a girl's school attendance while having no discernible effect on the school attendance decisions of boys.

Conclusion

The ILO considers improvement in access to schools and school quality to be the most effective way of reducing child labor in less developed countries. Improvement in access to schools, interpretable as a reduction in schooling costs, is expected to raise school attendance at the expense of child labor. Given that the child labor force consists mainly of unpaid family workers, this essay examined whether work by rural Pakistani children in household production (intrahousehold child labor) responds differently to changes in schooling costs than work in the labor market (extrahousehold child labor).

Our analysis indicates that schooling costs and extrahousehold child labor supply are positively related. However, the intrahousehold labor supply of children is unresponsive to changes in schooling costs, suggesting that parents distinguish between these two types of child labor. It seems that while parents consider children's extrahousehold labor and schooling to be substitutes, they view intrahousehold child labor differently. The relative insensitivity of intrahousehold child labor to changes in schooling costs might arise if parents perceived that the benefits from such labor consist of more than increases in household consumption. For example, parents may hold that participation in household production will lead to their children accumulating skills that may not be acquired at school. Regardless of the reasons, our findings indicate that intrahousehold child labor and schooling are not substitutes in rural Pakistan.

References and Further Reading

Alderman, H., J.R. Behrman, D.R. Ross, and R. Sabot. "Decomposing the Gender Gap in Cognitive Skills in a Poor Rural Economy." *Journal of Human Resources* 31:1 (1996): 229–54.

Bequelle, A., and J. Boyden, eds. *Combating Child Labour.* Geneva: ILO, 1988.

Burki, A.A., and T. Fasih. "Households' Non-Leisure Time Allocation for Children and Determinants of Child Labour in Punjab, Pakistan." *Pakistan Development Review* 37:4 (1998): 899–914.

Hazarika, G., and A. Bedi. "Schooling Costs and Child Work in Rural Pakistan." *Journal of Development Studies* 39:5 (2003): 29–64.

Hyder, N.S. "Child Labour in Pakistan: Problems, Policies and Programmes." *Asia-Pacific Development Journal* 5:1 (1998): 121–32.

Ray, R. "Analysis of Child Labour in Peru and Pakistan: A Comparative Study." *Journal of Population Economics* 13:1 (2000): 3–19.

Child Labor Policy and Legislation in Pakistan

Zarina Jillani, Society for the Protection of the Rights of the Child (SPARC), Islamabad

The legal and regulatory environment relating to child labor in Pakistan consists of constitutional provisions, various laws and policies, and international commitments, including ratification of core ILO conventions and the UN Convention on the Rights of the Child. There is no blanket prohibition on child labor in the country. Legislative bans on child labor extend to specific occupations, and major sectors that employ child labor are outside the scope of any of these laws.

The Constitution of Pakistan

The constitution of Pakistan explicitly forbids slavery, prohibits forced labor and trafficking in human beings, and bars employment of children under age fourteen in factories, mines, and "other hazardous employment," though the latter term is not defined. In addition, the constitution makes it a Principle of Policy of the State of Pakistan to protect the child; to remove illiteracy and provide free and compulsory education within the minimum possible period; and to make provision for securing just and humane conditions of work, ensuring that children and women are not employed in vocations unsuited to their age or sex.

The Employment of Children Act of 1991

The Employment of Children Act (ECA) is the country's major national law regarding child labor. It defines a child as a person who has not completed his or her fourteenth year of age. The ECA prohibits the employment of children in certain occupations, regulates their conditions of work in others, and exempts certain establishments from the provisions banning or regulating child labor.

Key Provisions of the Constitution

Article 11(1)	Slavery is nonexistent and forbidden and no law shall permit or facilitate its introduction into Pakistan in any form.
Article 11(2)	All forms of forced labor and traffic in human beings are prohibited.
Article 11(3)	No child below the age of fourteen years shall be engaged in any factory or mine or any other hazardous employment.

Employment of children is prohibited in specific occupations and processes that are listed in the ECA's schedule. The federal government is empowered to add any occupation or process to the schedule. In 2005, following ratification of ILO Convention 182, the original list was revised to include a total of thirty-four hazardous forms of child labor.

The ECA regulates working children's hours and periods of work, weekly holidays, and health and safety in those establishments that are not listed in the schedule of prohibited occupations and processes. These regulations apply to various establishments, including shops, commercial establishments, workshops, residential hotels, and restaurants.

Total daily hours for children cannot exceed seven, inclusive of the interval for rest and time spent in waiting for work on any day. It is obligatory for employers to give children an interval of at least one hour for rest after they have worked more than three hours. In addition, children cannot work between 7 P.M. and 8 A.M. and cannot work overtime. Children also cannot work in an establishment on a day in which they have already worked in another establishment. Finally, every

2005 Revised Schedule of Banned Hazardous Occupations and Processes
Work inside underground mines and aboveground quarries including blasting and assisting in blasting
Work with power-driven cutting machinery such as saws, shears, and guillotines and agricultural machines, thrashers, and fodder-cutting machines
Work with live electrical wires over fifty volts
All operations related to leather-tanning processes, for example, soaking, dehairing, liming, chrome tanning, deliming, pickling, defleshing, and ink application
Mixing and manufacture of pesticides and insecticides, and fumigation
Sandblasting and other work involving exposure to free silica
Work with exposure to all toxic, explosive, and carcinogenic chemicals, for example, asbestos, benzene, ammonia, chlorine, sulfur dioxide, hydrogen sulfide, sulfuric acid, hydrochloric acid, nitric acid, caustic soda, phosphorus, benzidene dyes, isocyanates, carbon tetrachloride, carbon disulphide, epoxy resins, formaldehyde, metal fumes, heavy metals such as nickel, mercury chromium, lead, arsenic, beryllium, and fiberglass
Work with exposure to cement dust in the cement industry
Work with exposure to coal dust
Manufacture and sale of fireworks and explosives
Work at sites where LPG and CNG is filled in cylinders
Work on glass and metal furnaces and in glass-bangles manufacturing
Work in the cloth-weaving, printing, dyeing and finishing sections
Work inside sewer pipelines, pits, and storage tanks
Stone crushing
Lifting and carrying of heavy weights (15 kilograms and above), especially in the transportation industry
Carpet weaving
Working two meters or more above the floor
All scavenging, including hospital waste
Tobacco processing, including *niswar* and bidi making
Deep-sea fishing, commercial fishing, and processing of fish and seafood
Sheep casing and wool industry
Ship breaking
Surgical-instrument manufacturing especially in vendors' workshops
Spice grinding
Work in boiler houses
Work in cinemas, minicinemas, and cybercafes
Mica cutting and splitting
Shellas manufacturing
Soap manufacture
Wool cleaning
Building and construction industry
Manufacture of slate pencils, including packing
Manufacture of products from agate

working child is required to be given a whole day of holiday every week.

Whoever employs any child or permits any child to work in contravention of the ECA risks imprisonment for a term extending up to one year, a fine of up to Rs. 20,000, or both. Repetition of the offense is punishable by imprisonment for a term extending up to two years but not lasting less than six months. The penalty provisions contained in the ECA override penalty provisions of the earlier Factories Act, Mines Act, and Shops and Establishments Ordinance.

The ECA contains a number of important exemptions. Its provisions do not apply to a large number of sectors where child labor is most common. It leaves out child domestic labor, children working in agriculture, self-employed children, street vendors, and children working in family enterprises. Employers and subcontractors often exploit this provision, as they can always use the defense that the child laborer is only assisting adult family members in the establishment.

Other Important National Laws

Prior to the ECA in 1991, there were already a number of laws that address child labor in specific sectors. The first of these were the Mines Act and the Merchant Shipping Act, both adopted in 1923. The

Mines Act forbids employment of children under fourteen in a belowground mine. It also requires children under the age of eighteen to provide a certificate of fitness granted by a qualified medical practitioner. Under the Merchant Shipping Act, no child below fourteen years of age is to be engaged or carried to sea to work in any capacity on any ship registered in Pakistan or on any foreign ship. Exceptions are provided for a ship on which all persons employed are members of one family, or where the child is employed for nominal wages and is in the charge of his father or other adult male close relative.

A few years later, the Factories Act of 1934 was adopted. It contains a chapter with special provisions for adolescents and children. Under this law no child under fourteen is allowed to work in a factory. *Factory* is defined as "any premises, whereon ten or more workers are working, and in any part of which a manufacturing process is being carried on." An establishment that employs fewer than ten people would not be considered a factory, and it could then employ children. In 1961, the Road Transport Workers Ordinance was adopted, governing conditions of employment of road transport workers. It is the only law at present that prohibits employment of children below the age of eighteen and fixes the minimum age for employment of drivers at twenty-one years.

Finally, in 1969, the Shops and Establishments Ordinance was adopted, prohibiting employment of children under fourteen in any establishment. The term *establishment* is defined to mean a shop, commercial establishment, industrial establishment, private dispensary, maternity home, hotel, restaurant, cinema, theater, circus, or other place of public entertainment. That same year, a similar West Pakistan Shops and Establishments Ordinance was adopted that grants the provincial government some latitude in identifying prohibited establishments.

Since the ECA in 1991, Pakistan has enacted several important laws aimed at curbing human rights abuses that often involve child labor. In 1992, the Bonded Labor System (Abolition) Act was adopted. The law does not specifically target child bonded labor, but it does cover children trapped in bondage, and its proper enforcement can free a large number of children from bondage. The act declares all customs, traditions, practices, contracts, or agreements concerning bonded labor to be void and inoperative. Any obligations of the bonded laborer to repay any bonded debt were canceled. Penalties for violating this law include imprisonment from two to five years, a fine of Rs. 50,000, or both. A fund for rehabilitation of bonded laborers has also been established, with an initial amount of Rs.100 million.

The Prevention and Control of Human Trafficking Ordinance of 2002 applies to all children and youths less than eighteen years of age. According to the ordinance, human trafficking means recruiting, buying, or selling a person, with or without consent, by use of coercion or abduction or by giving payment or share for such person's transportation, for exploitative entertainment. It defines exploitative entertainment as all activities in connection with human sports or sexual practices. The Ordinance prescribes seven to fourteen years of imprisonment for perpetrators, depending on the degree of involvement in trafficking.

International Obligations and National Policy on Child Labor

Pakistan has ratified all major international instruments relating to children. It ratified the UN Convention on the Rights of the Child in 1990 and ILO Conventions 182 and 138 in 2001 and 2006, respectively. Once they ratify a convention, state parties are expected to make changes in their national laws to conform to international standards. In the case of Pakistan, an act of Parliament is required to incorporate these international standards into national laws. So far, there has been little progress in this respect.

However, in 2000, the government of Pakistan approved the National Policy and Plan of Action. This policy for the elimination of child labor, administered principally by the Federal Ministry of Labor, focuses on awareness raising and community mobilization; withdrawal of children from worst forms of child labor and provision for their rehabilitation through education and vocational training; situation analysis and development of a child labor database; law enforcement; capacity building of relevant ministries and departments; enhancing education and skills-training opportunities for children; empowerment of poor families, and promoting coordination with social partners. Provincial labor and manpower departments act as special resource centers. Workers' organizations, employers' organizations, and NGOs are involved in advocacy, awareness raising and community mobilization, and the rehabilitation of child workers. Finally, following ratification of ILO Convention 182 in 2001, a Time Bound Program, with technical assistance and financial support from IPEC, was launched to eliminate worst forms of child labor in certain sectors, targeting approximately 11,000 children.

References and Further Reading

Jillani, Anees. *Child Labor: The Legal Aspects.* Islamabad: Society for the Protection of the Rights of the Child, 1998.

Jillani, Anees, and Zarina Jillani. *Child Rights in Pakistan.* Islamabad: Society for the Protection of the Rights of the Child, 2000.

Child Labor in Pakistan's Export Industries

Saadia Toor, Assistant Professor, Department of Sociology, Anthropology, and Social Work, College of Staten Island, City University of New York

Child labor became a hotly contested issue in the international arena in the 1990s. In the United States, this was initiated by the 1995 Harkin Bill, which sought to impose trade sanctions on countries that used child labor. Pakistan first hit international headlines around this time through Iqbal Masih, a former child carpet weaver who had been freed from indenture by the efforts of the Bonded Labour Liberation Front. Iqbal soon became the front's international face and a popular international media figure, giving talks on child labor across the world. He was killed on Easter Sunday in 1995, almost certainly by the carpet mafia in Pakistan, because of the negative press that he had brought to the industry. Iqbal was posthumously awarded the World's Children's Prize for the Rights of the Child in 2000.

The focus on child labor in Pakistan eventually turned to the manufacture of soccer balls. Pakistan—in particular the area around the town of Sialkot in Punjab—produces 80 percent of the world's soccer balls, which used to be predominantly stitched by children. Northern trade unions first brought the issue to light around the time of the European Soccer Championship in 1996, and again as the 1998 World Cup drew near. The media exposure served to increase consumer awareness in the north about the conditions under which goods consumed in the north were produced. The fact that the controversy involved children was instrumental in building the consumer campaign, which quickly caught on in schools and colleges across the United States.

Multinational corporations generally respond to demands of consumer advocates in the North through improved public relations ("greenwashing"). Often this does not go beyond launching a new ad campaign that presents the corporation in a better, more responsible, and altogether benevolent light. Alternatively, in this age of fly-by-night capital, where it is easy for multinationals to pack up and leave undesirable areas for greener pastures, they simply move on from the source of the problem, hoping that media attention will fade. Sometimes, however, the corporation concerned cannot in fact run away, or the media attention is so severe and unremitting that it finds itself in the unpleasant position of actually having to do something about the problem. This is what happened in the case of the soccer ball controversy in Pakistan, given the timing of the unprecedented media attention and Pakistan's near monopoly on the production of soccer balls. Thus, sports industry giants such as Nike and Adidas, among others, were forced to address the issue, or at least be perceived to be doing so.

The Sialkot Initiative

The fallout from all this was the signing of the Atlanta Agreement on February 14, 1997, so named because it was signed in Atlanta, Georgia. This was the first multistakeholder agreement of its kind, involving the ILO, the Sialkot Chamber of Commerce and Industry, and UNICEF. The Atlanta Agreement resulted in the establishment of the Project to Eliminate Child Labour in the Soccer Ball Industry in Pakistan, better known as the Sialkot Initiative to end child labor in the soccer ball industry. Partners included domestic and international NGOs such as Save the Children Fund (UK) and Bunyad (Pakistan), the All Pakistan Federation of Trade Unions, the Fédération Internationale de Football Association (FIFA), the World Federation of Sporting Goods Industries, the U.S. Department of Labor, and the government of Pakistan. Under the agreement, international sporting goods brands agreed to procure only soccer balls produced by manufacturers who had signed on to participate in the project, thus indicating their commitment to ending child labor. Other initiatives included various types of independent monitoring and development of child-free labels for various products, such as Rugmark for carpets.

More than a decade later, and after many debates over this issue at the international level, it is worthwhile to step back and assess the current situation in Pakistan. The Sialkot Initiative is a much-touted success story, and it has been successful in achieving limited goals, but it is necessary to temper the laudatory discourse around the project because its use as a model is limited to export industries. It is no coincidence that these initiatives were taken in export industries, which are important to domestic and international stakeholders such as multinational corporations, domestic capitalists, and governments. It is unlikely that the kind of cooperation between multiple levels and types of stakeholders that the Sialkot Initiative enjoys would be possible in an industry that produces only for the domestic market. Neither multinational nor domestic corporations have any real interest in improving the condition of ordinary Pakistanis or their children. Nor does the government of Pakistan, and even if it did, it would probably not have the capacity to do so. In any case, it is instructive to note the extent to which the Sialkot Initiative has been successful, because it is being used as a model internationally, as well as for other industries in Pakistan.

The project itself had two components: a Prevention and Monitoring Program and a Social Protection Program. Under the former, the first step was to move manufacture out of private households and into registered stitching centers, where it could be monitored. The crucial work of monitoring was initially carried out by ILO-IPEC, which already had an office in Pakistan. In 2002, the Sialkot Chamber of Commerce and Industry, with help from ILO-IPEC, established the Independent Monitoring Association for Child Labour. This monitoring association officially took over in March 2003 and is currently responsible for overseeing the monitoring of soccer ball production in Sialkot. ILO-IPEC concluded its formal participation in the project in 2004.

On the surface, the Social Protection Program seems to recognize the structural factors that contributed to child labor, including poverty, lack of alternative income-generating options, lack of good educational opportunities, and entrenched community attitudes. The problem, however, is that these are all ultimately linked to domestic and international structures and processes that are not identified or addressed. By all accounts, the project has been largely successful in meeting its limited goals. Children have been removed from stitching centers, and many have been enrolled in institutions of formal and nonformal education. ILO-IPEC reports that 10,572 children have been educated through 255 nonformal education centers, and 5,838 of these were mainstreamed into the formal education system. The Sialkot district government now spends 70 percent of its budget on education and has passed a resolution making Sialkot a child-labor-free zone (ILO-IPEC 2004).

In the wake of a massive media campaign around the time of the 2002 World Cup in which FIFA was exposed as having ignored its own code of conduct with regard to sourcing child-labor-free sports equipment, not surprisingly, the 2002 World Cup was dedicated to the children of the world. As a result, FIFA entered into a partnership with the ILO on a "Give a Red Card to Child Labour" campaign. In 2006, FIFA inaugurated a new "sports module" to be added to the Sialkot Initiative. The idea was that children should be moved from making soccer balls to playing with them as a formal part of their schooling. The much-hyped inauguration was to be the symbolic kickoff for the 2006 World Cup.

Of late, however, questions over the efficacy of monitoring in the Sialkot soccer ball industry have reemerged, in part, no doubt, from Nike's decision to discontinue sourcing soccer balls from Sialkot after two children were discovered working in the home of a subcontractor in May 2006. Nike did not renew its contract with Saga Sports, which alone accounts for $33 million of the industry's $210 million total and employs 5,000 stitchers. In response, the government of Pakistan recently held a "tripartite" workshop to address concerns voiced by stakeholders in the Sialkot Initiative.

The Independent Monitoring Association for Child Labour oversees compliance at Sialkot's 3,000 soccer-ball-stitching centers, and it relies on production taking place in these centralized stitching centers. It is impossible for monitoring to be successful when contractors and subcontractors simply move farther away from the city and from surveillance. Further, removing children from soccer ball production does not solve the problem of child labor. Without the resolution of the underlying structural problems of poverty and limited employment opportunities for adults, children often simply move into another industry or into informal labor. For example, in Sialkot, many children removed from soccer ball production ended up working for the surgical-instruments industry, highlighting the limitations of a sectoral approach to the child labor issue. Sialkot is one of the world's top producers of high-precision scalpels, forceps, and retractors, producing 100 million instruments a year and employing more than 2,000 instrument makers. This issue may be addressed by expansion of the Sialkot Initiative to the surgical instruments industry (Greimel 2006).

The Thardeep Rural Development Program

The Thardeep Rural Development Program (TRDP) is a development NGO based in the desert region of Sindh, where it has, over the years, worked with various village communities to set up Para Development Committees and Village Development Committees through which various microcredit, income-generating, and savings schemes are administered. Increased international pressure on child labor in export industries brought to light the fact of children working in the carpet industry in Thar. This led to the decision by TRDP to launch a sector-specific intervention in collaboration with Save the Children (UK) and RAASTA, a local development consultancy.

Carpet weaving is not indigenous to the Thar area. It was started as a cottage industry in the 1950s by the government, as part of the Sindh Small Industries initiative. Carpets from Thar became well-known in the international market and an important source of income for Thari people. Eventually, the government carpet-making units disappeared and were replaced by private ones controlled by moneylenders, traders, and middlemen in an extremely exploitative system. The carpet industry is not formally registered with the government of Sindh's Labour Department, which puts it outside the purview of most labor legislation. When rains fail in the desert, as they often do, people have no choice but to take loans from moneylenders at exorbitant rates. Since they are structurally unable to pay these back, they are forced to work on carpet looms, taking their children with them. Of carpet-weaving families, 98 percent were indebted, and 47 percent of the children of these families were involved in weaving. Needless to say, these children are exploited economically, and their health suffers from the long hours of work, sitting at looms in areas with poor lighting and ventilation. They are vulnerable to sexual exploitation as well. Reports of fever, poor eyesight, coughs, body aches, tuberculosis, and injuries to hands are common. Ironically, conditions were worse for children working at home than for those working in workshops.

TRDP has been tackling this issue for more than a decade, beginning with a survey identifying problems in the carpet industry, then a comprehensive research phase from 1997 to 1999, then a two-year pilot project, as a result of which eighty-one families were freed from debt and began to send their children to school. Demand grew at the community level for replication of the project, which TRDP addressed by initiating a major Child Rights Protection Project, which is now being expanded to other villages in the Thar region.

The first part of TRDP's initiative involved enabling families to pay off their debts to their contractors. The project provided loans to indebted carpet-weaving families with children under fourteen who were involved in weaving and for whom the loom was the main source of income. The loan came with conditions: The money could be used only to pay off the debt; the loom had to be placed in an open, well-ventilated area; and children must be removed from labor and sent to school. Strict monitoring had to be conducted by the local committees to ensure compliance, since weavers would occasionally remove their own children from the loom but hire others, or remove their children from the loom and send them to work elsewhere. TRDP worked hard at addressing these and other problems.

Ensuring that the project was successful also involved addressing other structural issues. It was found, for example, that when removed from work, children did not want to go to school because they did not like the school experience. In Pakistan, teaching in a government school is an ill-paid and therefore low-status position. In remote areas, many government schools lack teachers altogether. TRDP addressed this by partnering with a private teacher-training institute to train twenty local primary school teachers as "master trainers" in new child-friendly and context-sensitive pedagogical techniques, so that they can actually make school interesting and useful for the children. These master trainers then went on to train 355 other teachers. TRDP also had to start a pickup and drop-off service to ensure that teachers made it to school regularly. Children's organizations have also been created that mobilize children, help them gain confidence, especially through savings and credit schemes, and help them network among themselves. Children involved in these organizations are already showing signs of progress in personal development and increased self-confidence.

The project has proved to be successful because TRDP was already embedded within the communities and because it addressed the issue of child labor in a multidimensional fashion. It removed weaver families from the debt cycle and released them from a relationship of dependency on middlemen by helping them access the market themselves—taking orders directly and controlling the supply of carpets to the market collectively. In order to address the issue of occasional recessions in the carpet market, TRDP set up vocational training centers that introduced alternative sources of income generation and helped weavers market their carpets in the urban centers. The area in which the project started is being converted into an artisanal village. No doubt because of the importance of carpets as an export product, and because of pressure from the ILO and other agencies, the project has had a lot of cooperation from the government; it has strong links with the Labour Department and various district governments, as well as the Export Promotion Bureau. This has contributed to the success and sustainability of the initiative.

However, the fact that the project would not have worked if TRDP had not fixed existing institutions (schools) and established new ones (weaver cooperatives) is sobering. The public education system in Pakistan is suffering from extreme neglect for many reasons, and no initiative—public or private—committed to the rights of children will be successful unless this problem is addressed. However, placing the responsibility for fixing the schools on the nonprofit or private sector is not a strategy that will work in the long run and for the majority of Pakistan's poor.

Conclusion

Homilies about "poverty traps" and "vicious cycles" between child labor and poverty are glibly trotted out by everyone, from international agencies such as the ILO and the World Bank to domestic NGOs and governments. The governments of developing countries are exhorted to "do something" about child labor and poverty—ratify ILO treaties, succumb to monitoring. Poverty-reduction strategies and papers are de rigeur, and Millennium Development Goals are the order of the day. The government of Pakistan, under pressure from international public opinion and international institutions such as the ILO and the World Bank, announced its National Policy and Plan of Action in 2000 to combat child labor and remove children from the most hazardous industries and ultimately from all sectors of the economy. Yet no one seems willing or able to question where this poverty comes from and why, despite more than half a century of development efforts, it persists and, in the case of Pakistan, has gotten worse. Pakistan has gone from decreasing poverty in the 1970s and 1980s to a sharp increase in poverty beginning in the 1990s. This can be traced in large part to the initiation of a new comprehensive IMF-enforced structural adjustment package in 1987–1988. Overall, this package of policies has resulted in a situation in Pakistan where "[g]rowth rates have fallen, poverty has increased, unemployment has grown and opportunities for labour have diminished" (Zaidi 2006, 5).

Analysts and labor activists have long argued that paying a fairer wage to workers in export industries, in addition to alleviating poverty, might help allay the problem of child labor as well, since the latter is correlated with low adult wages in a vicious cycle. For example, Sialkot suppliers are paid $2 for forceps that eventually fetch more than $60 when sold to a hospital in North America. However, given that this differential lies at the heart of the current global system of free trade, it is unlikely that it will be addressed anytime soon, and certainly not through the aegis of international agencies such as the World Bank or even the ILO.

References and Further Reading

Crawford, Sheena. "Impact Assessment of the SC-UK/Thardeep Rural Development Programme, Project on Child Labour in the Carpet Industry of Thar Desert." Report to Save the Children UK, December 2000.

Deeplai, Hamid. *Dawn of Hope: Protection of Rights of Working Children in Carpet Industry of Thar.* Sindh, Pakistan: Thardeep Rural Development Programme, 2003.

Greimel, Hans. "Program Tackles Child Labor in Pakistan." *Washington Post*/Associated Press, December 14, 2006.

ILO-IPEC. *From Stitching to School: Elimination of Child Labour in the Soccer Ball Industry in Pakistan.* Geneva: International Labor Organization, 2004.

Sialkot Initiative, 2007. Report on the Government of Pakistan–ILO Tripartite Workshop. Islamabad, Pakistan, February 21–22, 2007. http://home.scci.com.pk/Sialkot_Initiative_2007.pdf.

TRDP. *Blooming Colours, Wilted Children.* Sindh, Pakistan: Thardeep Rural Development Programme / RAASTA / Save the Children, 1999.

———. *Weaving Bridges: Protection of Rights of Working Children in the Carpet Industry of Thar.* Sindh, Pakistan: Thardeep Rural Development Programme, 2005.

———. *Innocent Childhood with Miserable Atmosphere: A Rapid Assessment.* Sindh, Pakistan: Thardeep Rural Development Programme, 2007.

Thardeep Rural Development Programme. http://www.thardeep.org/.

Zaidi, S. Akbar. "Globalisation in Pakistan: The Impact on the Economy and on Labour." Paper presented at the panel sponsored by the South Asia Alliance for Poverty Eradication, SAAPE, at the Asian Social Forum, Hyderabad, India, January 3, 2003.

Sri Lanka

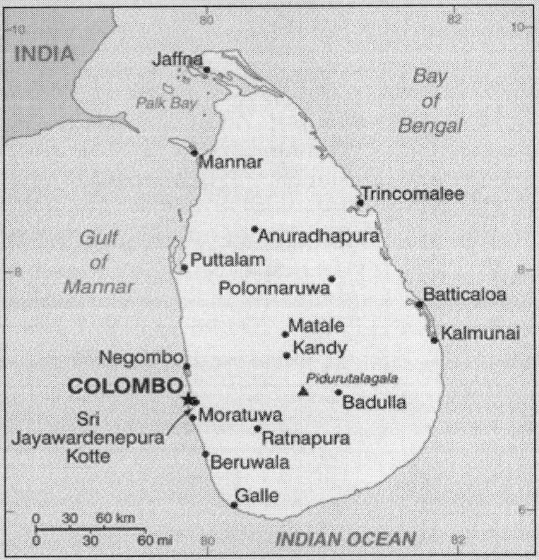

SRI LANKA	CRC	C 138	C 182
Ratifications	Y	Y	Y
Human Development Index/Rank	0.755/93		
Human Capital			
Population Growth Rate	0.98%		
% Population 0–14	24.3%		
Total Fertility Rate	2.05		
Life Expectancy	74.8		
Infant Mortality Rate	19.45		
Literacy Rate	92.3%		
Economic			
GDP/Capita	$4,600		
GDP Growth %	6.3%		
% Poverty	22%		
Gini Index	50		
Labor Force Composition			
% Agriculture	34.3%		
% Industry	25.3%		
% Services	40.4%		

CHILD ACTIVITY BREAKDOWN, BY AGE AND SEX

Age in years	Percentage of children in the relevant age-group									
	Economic activity only		School only		Combining school and economic activity		Neither in school nor in economic activity		Child labor[a]	
	Male	Female	Male	Female	Male	Female	Male	Female	Male	Female
Total 5–14	1.0	0.5	80.0	86.2	16.9	11.3	2.1	2.0	9.4	6.9

Source: Sri Lanka, Child Activity Survey 1999 (see UCW Project Web site, http://www.ucw-project.org, country statistics).
Notes: [a]Estimate includes (a) children under age 12 engaged in economic activities, (b) children age 12–14 engaged in excessive economic activities (more than 14 hours per week), and (c) children under age 15 engaged in excessive household chores (at least 28 hours per week). Estimate does not account for children engaged in hazardous work or other unconditional "worst forms" of child labor.

Forcible Recruitment of Children in Sri Lanka

Charu Lata Hogg, Consultant to the Coalition to Stop the Use of Child Soldiers

Forced or compulsory recruitment of children below the age of eighteen for use in armed conflict is considered a worst form of child labor under ILO Convention 182. In Sri Lanka, the armed opposition group, the Liberation Tigers of Tamil Eelam (LTTE), has forcibly recruited and used children throughout the civil war, which began in 1983. While there have been no reports of children being recruited and used by government forces, the use of children in at least one government-backed paramilitary force was reported in 2001. In 2006, children were known to have been forcibly recruited by an armed group that broke away from the LTTE in April 2004. Some of the children were recruited in the vicinity of government forces, suggesting at least some acquiescence on their part.

Context

Tensions between Sri Lanka's Sinhalese majority and the LTTE, a group seeking an independent homeland for the minority Tamil population in the northeast of the country, erupted in violence in 1983. By the mid-1980s, the LTTE had established itself as the most powerful armed group in the northeast, quickly gaining control of territory. By 1989, the LTTE was effectively governing significant portions of north and east Sri Lanka, collecting "taxes" and administering an informal justice and police system.

A formal cease-fire agreement between the government and the LTTE was signed with Norwegian government facilitation in February 2002, and a Sri Lanka Monitoring Mission of representatives of five Nordic countries was set up to monitor its implementation. Although the cease-fire agreement technically remains in force, peace talks have, for all intents and purposes, broken down since the two sides met in Geneva in February 2006. Beginning in early 2006, military activity intensified, which has given rise to grave violations of international humanitarian and human rights law, including killings of civilians, enforced disappearances, and persistent attacks on civilian targets. More than 200,000 civilians were displaced between April and October 2006 in the war-torn northeast of the country.

National Recruitment Laws

The government has stated that there is no compulsory, forced, or coerced recruitment into the national armed forces; recruitment is solely on a voluntary basis; and the minimum age for recruitment into the armed forces is eighteen. There is no evidence of recruitment of children below the age of eighteen in the Sri Lankan armed forces. According to the 1985 Mobilization and Supplementary Forces Act, the National Cadet Corps is open to those over age sixteen. It provides premilitary and civil training to students, but cadets cannot be called to active service and are not members of the armed forces. Under domestic law, the definition of a child is anyone below the age of eighteen, and child abuse includes all acts of sexual violence against, trafficking in, and cruelty to children. The law prohibits the use of children in exploitative labor or illegal activities.

Child Recruitment in the LTTE

The LTTE has recruited and used children as soldiers—some as young as nine—throughout the civil war (Amnesty International 1998), although in recent years the average age of children when recruited has been fifteen (UNICEF 2004). The LTTE reportedly began recruiting large numbers of women and children after declaring war against the 100,000-strong Indian Peace Keeping Force in October 1987. Initially, children are used as guards, cooks, and helpers, and then as messengers and spies. They are gradually inducted into the fighting forces, initially in battlefield-support functions, and later in active combat. A typical unit of children is trained for four months in the jungle. All links between the children and their families are broken, and discipline is strict.

Many children have been recruited through a "quota" system, whereby the LTTE orders families to hand over a child to them. A "handing-over" ceremony is often carried out, with each family bringing a child to a designated place in the village or town. Other children are simply abducted from their homes, while returning from school in both government and LTTE-controlled territories, and at public events such as temple festivals. Child-recruitment drives appear to follow a cyclical pattern, depending on the level of international scrutiny, and forced recruitment has been used if families fail to contribute their "quota." Many families are known to flee to safer places to save their children from the LTTE (Manoharan 2003). LTTE child recruitment decreased from mid-2005, but UNICEF continued to report an average of fifty cases a month during the first half of 2006. The LTTE reportedly continued to recruit children in August and September 2006 in LTTE-controlled areas.

In July 2003, the government and the LTTE signed an Action Plan, developed with UNICEF, to address the needs of war-affected children in the north and east. The plan included provision for children to be released from the LTTE ranks. The LTTE has formally released more than 1,400 child soldiers to UNICEF since signing the plan. In addition, some 2,500 children have run away or were returned to their homes or to the LTTE's Northeastern Secretariat on Human Rights. A further 1,800 children returned home following the disbanding of the eastern command, led by Colonel Karuna, in March 2004. This was followed, however, by a major recruitment drive as the LTTE sought to reestablish control of the east (Human Rights Watch 2004).

According to UNICEF, by August 2006 at least 1,545 cases of child recruitment were outstanding with the LTTE. Of these, 902 children were underage when recruited but are now over eighteen. While some have probably returned home, others are thought to remain in the ranks of the LTTE, and recruitment has continued.

Child Recruitment by Paramilitaries

The government-linked paramilitary People's Liberation Organization of Tamil Eelam reportedly recruited children as young as twelve in the Vavuniya area in northern Sri Lanka in early 2001, but such recruitment appears to have stopped after the February 2002 cease-fire agreement.

Forced Recruitment by the Karuna Armed Group

From early 2006, reports emerged of forced recruitment by the Karuna group, which broke away from the LTTE in March 2004. UNICEF said it had documented thirty cases in June, and by August the total had reached 118, although the actual figure was believed to be higher. Those recruited included male youths as young as fifteen. They are frequently forced into white vans without license plates, often in the vicinity of government forces. The recruits are then taken to Karuna camps (often close to army camps) after passing through military checkpoints. Police appear to have taken little, if any, action on cases reported to them. As a state party to the Optional Protocol to the Convention on the Rights of the Child on the involvement of children in armed conflict, the government has a legal obligation to end child recruitment into armed groups, to investigate individual cases, and to prosecute suspected recruiters.

Conclusion

Despite its stated commitment to ending the practice, the LTTE has continued its practice of child recruitment. International initiatives, ranging from constructive engagement to public condemnation and targeted measures against the group, have had limited impact. For its part, the government has been harshly critical of the LTTE's use of child soldiers but has yet to take action to stop abductions by the Karuna group—some of which have been reported to the police or have taken place in the vicinity of government forces.

Child recruitment is occurring against a background of widespread human rights violations in Sri Lanka's war-torn north and eastern regions. Neither government forces nor the LTTE has acted to protect civilians, and when violations are reported, both sides trade accusations and counteraccusations rather than taking steps to halt the violence. As military activities intensified during the latter months of 2006, children remained vulnerable to forced recruitment by both the LTTE and the Karuna group. In a context of escalating hostilities, children in armed forces and groups risk being used in combat and may face injury or death during military operations.

References and Further Reading

Amnesty International. *Children in South Asia: Securing Their Rights.* London: Amnesty International, 1998. http://web.amnesty.org/library/index/engASA040011998.

Coalition to Stop the Use of Child Soldiers. "Child Soldiers Global Report 2004 (Sri Lanka)." http://www.child-soldiers.org/document_get.php?id=878.

Human Rights Watch. *Living in Fear: Child Soldiers and the Tamil Tigers in Sri Lanka.* New York: Human Rights Watch, 2004. http://hrw.org/reports/2004/srilanka1104/srilanka1104.pdf.

Manoharan, N. "Child Soldiers—III: Baby Brigades of the LTTE." *Peace and Conflict* 6:10 (2003).

UNICEF. "Action Plan for Children Affected by War: Progress Report 2003." UNICEF, 2004. http://www.unicef.org/french/emerg/files/Progress_Report_2003.pdf.

Part 8

East Asia and the Pacific

SECTION 1.
EAST ASIA

China

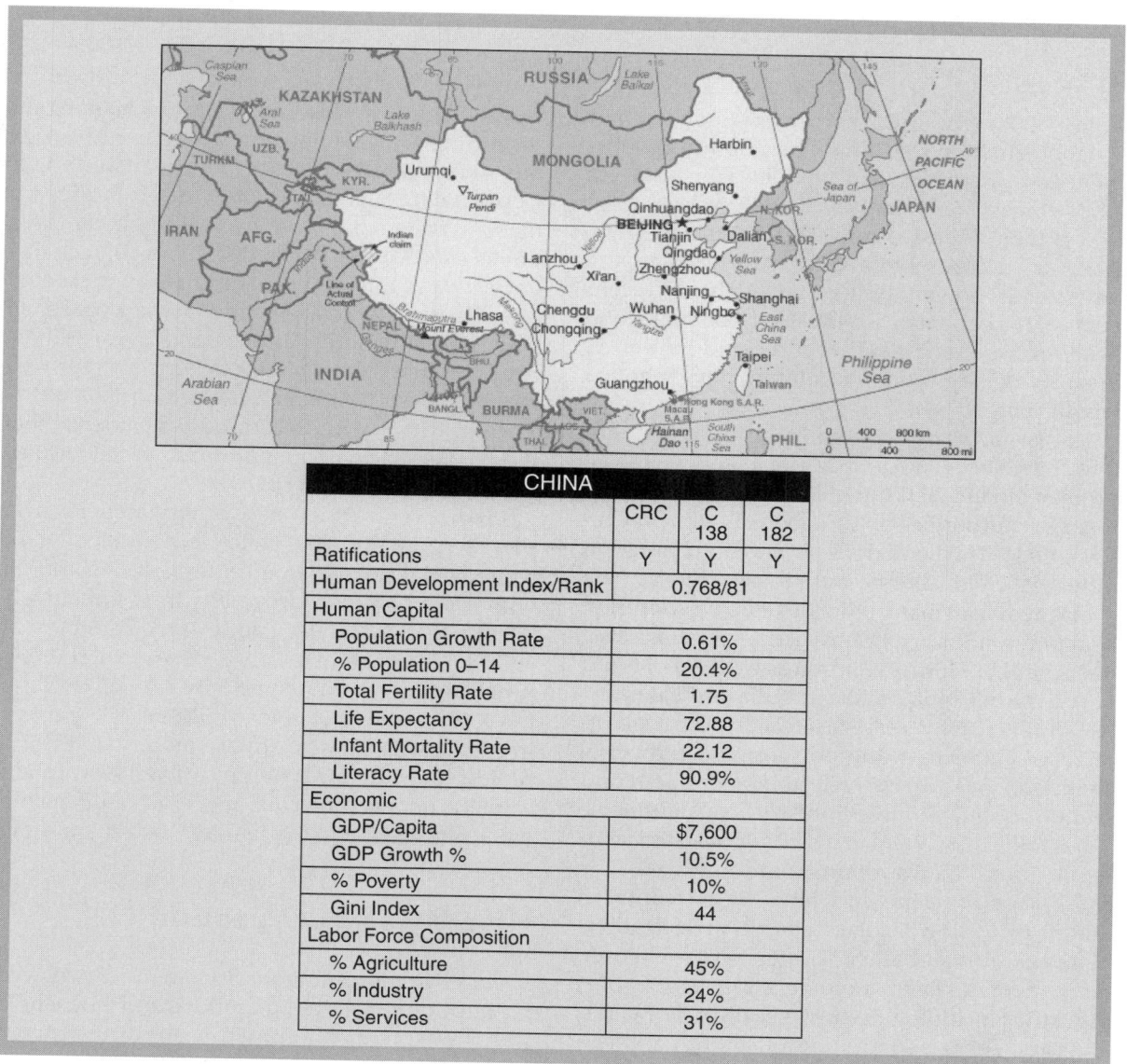

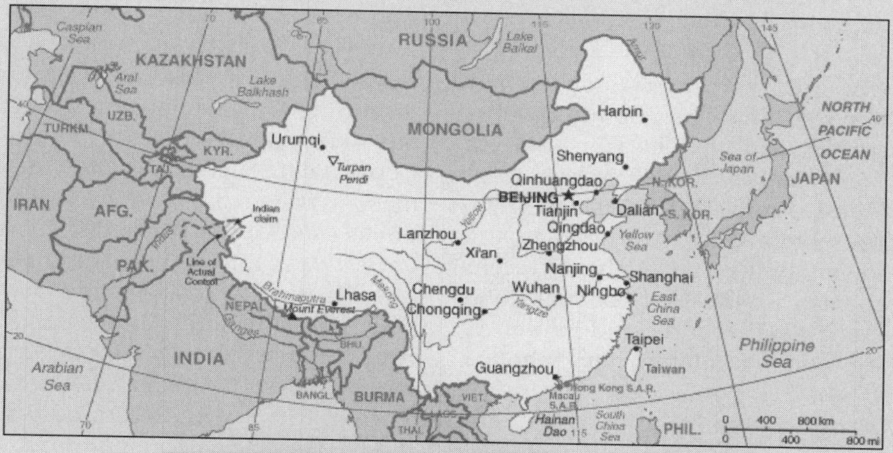

CHINA			
	CRC	C 138	C 182
Ratifications	Y	Y	Y
Human Development Index/Rank	0.768/81		
Human Capital			
Population Growth Rate	0.61%		
% Population 0–14	20.4%		
Total Fertility Rate	1.75		
Life Expectancy	72.88		
Infant Mortality Rate	22.12		
Literacy Rate	90.9%		
Economic			
GDP/Capita	$7,600		
GDP Growth %	10.5%		
% Poverty	10%		
Gini Index	44		
Labor Force Composition			
% Agriculture	45%		
% Industry	24%		
% Services	31%		

Child Labor in China: An Overview

G.K. Lieten, Professor of Child Labour Studies at the International Institute of Social History and at the University of Amsterdam, and Director of IREWOC; and **Hugh D. Hindman**, Professor of Labor and Human Resources, Appalachian State University

Little is known with certainty about the child labor situation in China. The Chinese government does not publish data on child labor—indeed, labor statistics are treated as state secrets—and others have found it difficult to obtain permission for such research. China studies scholars have published very little on child labor in recent years. Consequently, we must rely on anecdotal evidence, sporadic news reports, and inference, making inquiry more speculative than scholars would prefer.

Most authorities seem to be in agreement that child labor is not a widespread and pervasive problem. In her 2001 book, Anita Chan, one of the foremost authorities on the labor situation in China, noted, "The book does not have a chapter on industrial child labor because this is a less serious problem than in many other developing countries. In a country the size of China, it does of course exist in pockets, but hiring children as wage labor is not pervasive in China, unlike in India and Pakistan" (Chan 2001, 225). As early as 1994, the U.S. Department of Labor took the position that industrial child labor was a relatively minor problem and that no specific Chinese industry was identifiable as a significant violator of international child labor regulations: "News reports alluding to possible child labor problems in China are anecdotal in nature, providing details on specific investigations of factory fires and other disasters where children were present. These involve a range of export industries including garments/textiles, fireworks, and toys. There is some anecdotal information on child labor in the footwear, electronics, handicrafts (including artificial flowers), and gun industries, but supporting evidence is not available" (U.S. Department of Labor 1994, 36). Further, the department's *Findings on the Worst Forms of Child Labor,* published each year since 2002, has never included an entry on China. Finally, the International Labor Organization, in its 2006 report on the global child labor situation, notes, "In the past 25 years, China has taken more people out of poverty and enrolled more children in school than any other country. There is thus strong circumstantial evidence that this has also had a dramatic impact on child labour in China" (ILO 2006, 11).

However, numerous China watchers infer persistent and growing child labor problems, particularly in export-oriented enterprises. Moreover, with a population as large as China's, relatively small problems may include large numbers of children in absolute terms. For example, the ILO projected the economic activity rate of children ten to fourteen years old would be 7.86 percent in the year 2000, a relatively modest rate for a rapidly developing economy (ILO 1996). In absolute numbers, however, this equals 9.2 million working children in the ten- to fourteen-year-old age-group alone.

Historical Background

Children in prerevolutionary China always played an important role in agriculture and household industry. Many families throughout imperial

China were kept in conditions of serfdom by local landlords and warlords. Children were required to work on the family land or to do corvée for the feudal lords. Education was restricted to the culturally sophisticated gentry class of mandarins, which excluded the vast majority of Chinese children. By the end of the nineteenth century, when one out of ten Chinese, mainly adult males, was thought to be an opium addict, pressure on the labor power of children increased.

Children were a normal component of the labor force, particularly in the coastal cities, which had been leased out to colonial powers, and where modern factories, particularly textile factories, attracted a cheap migrant labor force. The Child Labour Commission in the early twentieth century noted horrifying abuses of young children in Shanghai and other treaty ports. It noted that the widespread abuse of children was as bad as in the heyday of early industrialization in England, and that children of five normally worked fourteen hours a days seven days a week. Many of these were indentured laborers, brought in from the remote countryside, where large families and extreme poverty went hand in hand.

The Communist revolution largely succeeded because of the unfathomable immiseration and the loathsome degree of exploitation of the people, including young children. Not much is known of the role assigned to children in the immediate postrevolutionary decades. The Communist Party, led by Mao Zedong, which came to power and established the People's Republic of China in 1947, was ideologically opposed to child labor, but the practice continued for many decades. According to official statistics, gross enrollment in primary school in 1960 was almost universal, which, if taken at face value, would suggest that child labor had diminished among very young children. The problem of school dropouts, however, remained. As late as 1995, only 86 percent of pupils reached grade five. The ILO estimated that 48 percent of children from ten to fourteen years old were economically active in 1950 (ILO 1996).

Economic Takeoff

The nature and context of China's dramatic economic growth over the last decades of the twentieth century, judging from the experiences of other developing and developed nations, would seem to have provided fertile ground for the exploitation of its most vulnerable people. An export-led growth strategy fueled by foreign investment, reliant on simple manufacturing technologies in its early phases, and coupled with severe rural-urban income disparities and a massive migration of population from the rural hinterlands to the eastern and southern coastal cities, is a formula for economic growth that almost guarantees extensive use of child labor.

Both Epstein (1993) and the U.S. Department of Labor (1994) cite numerous examples of child labor abuses that received attention in the Chinese press in the late 1980s, especially in rural areas, in the special economic zones, and in the Pearl River Delta area in Guangdong Province. The reports included cases of trafficking of women and children for labor exploitation. Calling the development strategy "commodity socialism," Epstein concluded that "foreign investment is contributing directly to the creation of Dickensian working conditions for children in China, reminiscent of the worst abuses of child labor common to Western European settings during the late eighteenth and early nineteenth centuries" (Epstein 1993, 231).

In July 1988, China's Ministry of Labor estimated that child laborers accounted for 10 percent of all workers in county township and town enterprises, and as much as 20 percent of all workers in some of these enterprises (Foreign Broadcast Information Service 1988). Much of the evidence of child labor was derived from data from the large special economic zone of Shenzen in southern China. It was reported in 1988 that forty-four of 206 foreign-owned companies in Shenzen employed children under sixteen years of age. These adverse reports may have sensitized public officials into a more proactive policy against child labor. In the mid-1990s, the Asian-American Free Labor Institute (1994) reported that, at least in large urban factories, underage employment did not occur on a mass basis but that violations continued in subcontracting factories.

China's One-Child Policy

China's one-child family-planning policies were put in place at the front end of the great economic takeoff. There is little doubt that these policies provided a countervailing demographic force that kept growth-induced child labor at lower levels than they might have been. Historically, declining fertility rates are among the clearest markers presaging declining child labor. A small number of offspring reduces the supply of child laborers. Since there are fewer mouths to feed, even poor parents have more resources to invest in the development of each child. In China, parents are unlikely to send their "little emperors" to work. Good education has become a general aspirational norm, and parents are willing to endure privation if need be to get their children some education.

The government implements a rigorous one-child policy in the urban areas. In the rural areas, the implementation is less rigorous. Local policies may allow for two children, especially when the first child is a daughter. Today, children below the age of fifteen form only 20 percent of the entire population, which is quite low in comparison with most developing countries. Women's net fertility rate is only 1.75.

Policy Framework

While negligent or corrupt local bureaucracy may hamper implementation of national legislation, China's legislative framework is among the more thorough of the developing countries. The age limit for employment has been put at a high level. In earlier legislation, employment was prohibited before completing nine years of education. A new labor law, prohibiting the employment of children under age sixteen, was published in 1994. Counterfeit ID cards were often found falsifying children's ages, so a new law, promulgated in 2002, in addition to banning child labor below the age of sixteen years, imposed fines for employers and put the onus on the employing companies to check workers' ages.

China ratified the UN Convention on the Rights of the Child as early as 1992. The government ratified ILO Conventions 138 and 182 in 1999 and 2002, respectively. Both the ILO Committee of Experts and the UN Child Rights Committee have been satisfied with the progress made and with the implementation reports. More attention has been asked for street children, children of migrants, and trafficked children.

China's Compulsory Education Law mandates nine years of education for all children. Primary school encompasses six years, and junior middle school three years. Since children generally enter primary school at age six, they usually graduate from middle school at age fifteen or sixteen, so that the end of compulsory schooling is closely harmonized with the minimum age for employment.

Twenty-First-Century China

Much of the information on the current situation of child labor in China is anecdotal in nature, often based on news reports referring to local occurrences that may not reflect conditions in the rest of the country. Further, many news reports are highly unreliable, making it difficult to discern the truth. The following report provides an example: "When news of the Shanxi brickyard slavery scandal broke in early June 2007, Chinese media reports claimed nearly a thousand children had been abducted into forced labor. Following a massive police crackdown and the rescue of hundreds of slave laborers, the number of rescued children was put at between 51 and 109. Shanxi provincial governments officials subsequently claimed the actual figure was 12, and, after a monthlong investigation, on 16 July, stated without further elaboration that only six of the rescued workers were actually children" (China Labour Bulletin 2007, 3).

Overall, today, it appears that there are very few children under sixteen employed as regular workers (*zhengshi de gugong*) in state-owned enterprises or in the large factories in the export-processing zones. It also appears that child labor among very young children, under twelve years of age, is rare, though many youngsters work as household helpers (*jiating banggong*). But there are substantial numbers of children thirteen, fourteen, and fifteen years of age working in a variety of low-level service positions and in labor-intensive industries including textiles, clothing, and footwear, electronics, plastics, small coal mines, brickyards, luggage and toy manufacturing, and the food and beverage industry. They are mostly rural children. Most of their employers are individual workshop owners or owners of small private enterprises, and most of their workplaces are small to medium-size establishments (China Labour Bulletin 2007).

For years, juvenile laborers from poorer regions of China have been drawn to the rapidly developing southern and coastal areas looking for work. In recent years, the poor wages and harsh working conditions have led to worker protests and a subsequent labor shortage in the region. Under conditions of labor shortages, many smaller firms and backwater subcontracting firms are dipping into the pool of younger workers as replacement labor (*tidai laodongli*). In June 2006, the state-controlled media reported that the Ministry of Justice and the Ministry of Labor and Social Security were intensifying their efforts "to fight illegal employment of child laborers," indicating that the government may be growing increasingly concerned about the problems of child labor (Congressional-Executive Committee on China 2006, 69).

Another concern involves the subcontracting networks for cheap small-scale products. These networks fan out from the larger factories to subcontracting workshops and often extend into rural homes. At each step backward in the subcontracting supply chain, the likelihood of child labor increases. When the subcontracting networks reach into homes, production is usually compensated on a piece-rate basis, and children often work alongside their mothers to maximize production. Such practices were quite common in coastal and southern provinces in the past, for example, in villages in Guangdong Province in the late 1980s, before Guangdong villagers became prosperous. With the growing prosperity in those provinces, the subcontracting may have moved farther inland to poorer provinces.

Trafficking of underage children and trafficking of children as forced laborers (*nugong*), though not widespread, have also been documented. In 2000, Chinese media reported that eighty-four children had been kidnapped from southern Fuizhou Province to work in coastal cities assembling Christmas lights. Many of these workplaces are illegal and are allowed to operate with the tacit agreement of local officials, who work hand in glove with the entrepreneurs. Rural-to-urban migration patterns create vulnerabilities to trafficking for either labor or sexual exploitation, or for begging in the megacities. Particularly in the southern region, around Yunan Province, close to the borders with Thailand, Myanmar, and Vietnam, trafficking of girls has been a serious problem. This is one aspect of child labor the Chinese government is greatly concerned about. The only formal program ILO-IPEC has operating in China is on the trafficking issue. The kidnapping of children may not be widespread, but the cases are shocking.

A thirteen-year-old boy selling flowers late at night, Xian, China, April 2007. *(Photo by Kristoffel Lieten courtesy of IREWOC Foundation)*

Children working on the streets as itinerant traders, porters, and restaurant assistants are not as visible as in many other developing countries. In some instances, rural parents cooperate and allow children to travel to the cities with a labor middleman. A 2004 report notes that some parents "rent" their children to flower sellers. The children work selling flowers for fourteen hours per day. They have strict sales quotas to meet and are subject to abuse if they fall short (American Center for International Labor Solidarity 2004). Another report documents school dropouts from You County in Hunan Province taken to Beijing,

Guangzhou, Shenzhen, Wuhan, and coastal cities in Zhejiang and Fujian provinces for flower selling (China Labour Bulletin 2005). They generally ply their trade at night, from sundown until before dawn, to better evade city authorities, who might detain or expel them.

Finally, there are certainly a great many children working in agriculture, but this is not a serious child labor problem in China. Nearly all of these children go to school, and their work is almost completely composed of doing tasks for their parents on their family's own farm holdings. These small family holdings were formed when the collective fields were divided among families in the early 1980s. China lacks the large-scale latifundias and export-oriented plantations that in Africa and Latin America tend to be a source of child labor.

Education and Child Labor

Although education is generally considered the great bulwark against child labor, an ironic situation has emerged in China, where the education system actually contributes to many of the worst child labor abuses in the country. There are two important dimensions to this problem: the problem of middle school dropouts and the situation of work-study students (*qingong jianxue*).

Education through nine years is compulsory: six years of primary school and three years of middle school. But high school and university education is competitive, available to the few who successfully pass required entrance exams. "China's educational goals, especially in middle and high school, have long been shaped by a heavily exam-oriented system in which the educational needs of the majority take second place to those of an aspiring elite" (China Labour Bulletin 2007, 29). While China has essentially achieved universal primary education, and nearly all students go on to enter middle school, many do not complete it. Students who are performing poorly and see little chance of gaining entrance to high school often drop out. The cost of school fees and the opportunity cost of foregone earnings are not seen to be worth staying to complete middle school. While official statistics place the middle school dropout rate at 2.49 percent, independent sources place it in the 30 to 40 percent range in many poorer rural areas. It is these middle school dropouts who comprise the core of China's illegal child labor workforce.

The ILO (2006, 13) notes that "China has achieved universal education at a lower cost than most other countries" and attributes this to slower population growth and market reforms. Another way to look at it is that China did it on the cheap. Costs of education are borne mainly by local governments. Parents value education highly and will sacrifice to ensure that their children receive education. Especially in rural areas, however, schools are underfunded, tuition and fees are high, and teacher pay is low (indeed, teachers sometimes go without pay). In order to be able to sustain operation of the schools, fund-raising in the form of industrial production is often pursued through work-study programs. Also known as "labor skills classes," "education practice labor," or "social practice activities," these programs date to a Maoist past, when China still had the commune system, and remain a common feature in the educational curriculum. Work-study programs take one of three forms. First, children may spend part of their school day, or time after school, engaged in industrial production in the school itself. Second, in areas not too geographically distant from industrial areas, subcontracting of outwork production into rural homes is common (for example, plastic flowers or cheap toys). Third, groups of schoolchildren migrate to industrial zones during periods of school vacations to work in the factories, often under the supervision of their schoolteachers.

Many of the media reports of child labor in China, the same reports that lead some commentators to conclude that child labor is on the rise, are, in fact, illustrations of the abuses of the work-study program. A few of many examples include the following:

- The 2001 explosion at a fireworks workshop in Fanglin Village in Jiangxi Province, where sixty primary school children and three teachers were killed. The area surrounding Fanglin is a center for fireworks production (Pomfret and Pan 2001). Despite the adverse publicity, the arrangement continues, though it is not clear on what scale and how much of the work is carried on in schools.
- A 2005 China Central Television exposé that

uncovered several hundreds children as young as thirteen working summer "apprenticeships" in a variety of toy factories in Dongguan, Guangdong Province. Most had migrated from rural areas and typically worked ten hours per day (Chueng and Welford 2005).

• A 2005 Radio Free Asia report of more than 100,000 Uyghur children from the far western province of Xinjiang taken out of school every September and October for the annual cotton harvest (IHLO 2007). Students from cities are required to participate from the third grade and up; students from rural areas are required to participate from the first grade and up. They rise at 6 A.M. and work until dark. After the initial report, rules on work-study were tightened up. Older students continue to pick cotton, but younger students now pick hops (Congressional-Executive Committee on China 2008).

• A November 2006 report of 240 "student apprentices" fourteen and fifteen years old, who had been recruited through an arrangement with their teachers at a school in Shaanxi Province to work in a joint-venture electronics factory in Shenzhen in southern China. The students thought they were going for the summer, but many were still there well into the fall. "The students' families owe money to the school for tuition and school fees, and so the schools send students to factories" (IHLO 2007, 7).

• In a recent study of four companies producing gadgets for the Olympic Games, child labor was found in one Taiwan-invested factory in Dongguan in southern China. Twenty children below the age of sixteen years (5 percent of the labor force) were found to be working excessively long days stacking notebooks into packing cartons. They had migrated with their working parents during the winter break from school. Some children had been contracted on school premises to come and work during the school holidays. They said that they had been brought to the factory in order to pay their school fees (PlayFair 2007).

Conclusion

It appears that China launched its export-led economic takeoff with little thought to the implications for child labor. Consequently, substantial child labor ensued, held in check only by China's one-child policies. By the twenty-first century, however, child labor appears to have been dramatically reduced owing to a variety of factors including reductions in fertility, dramatic reductions in poverty, and the government's sensitivity to foreign consumers' sensibilities. Pockets of child labor remain, fueled by a number of persistent problems, not least involving inadequacies in the educational system. However, contrary to the views of a number of commentators, we do not believe that child labor is currently increasing in China.

References and Further Reading

American Center for International Labor Solidarity. *The Struggle for Worker Rights in China.* Washington, DC: American Center for International Labor Solidarity, 2004.

Asian-American Free Labor Institute. *Child Labor in China.* Washington, DC: Asian-American Free Labor Institute, 1994.

Chan, Anita. *China's Workers Under Assault: The Exploitation of Labor in a Globalizing Economy.* Armonk, NY: M.E. Sharpe, 2001.

Cheung, Dennis, and Richard Welford. "Is Child Labour on the Increase in China?" *CSR-Asia Weekly* 1:45 (September 11, 2005): 2–4.

China Labour Bulletin. "An Investigation into the Phenomenon of Rural Children Selling Flowers in Chinese Cities." *China Labour Bulletin* (Hong Kong), June 10, 2005.

———. *Small Hands: A Survey Report on Child Labour in China.* Research report 3. Hong Kong: China Labour Bulletin, 2007.

Congressional-Executive Committee on China. *Annual Report 2006.* Washington, DC: Congressional-Executive Committee on China, 2006.

———. "Work-Study Programs Using Child Labor Continue in Xinjiang." Congressional-Executive Committee on China, Washington, DC, January 11, 2008.

Epstein, Irving. "Child Labor and Basic Education Provision in China." *International Journal of Educational Development* 13:3 (1993): 227–38.

Fong, Vanessa. *Only Hope: Coming of Age Under China's One-Child Policy.* Stanford, CA: Stanford University Press, 2004.

Foreign Broadcast Information Service. "Renmin Ribao Urges Banning Child Labor." CHI-88-136. Washington, DC: U.S. Government Printing Office, July 15, 1988, 29–30.

IHLO. *Child Labour and "Work Experience" in China—The*

Blurred Lines of Illegality. Hong Kong: Hong Kong Liaison Office of the international trade union movement, August 2007. http://www.ihlo.org/LRC/W/020807.html.

ILO. *Economically Active Population, 1950–2010.* 4th ed. Geneva: ILO, 1996.

———. *The End of Child Labor: Within Reach.* Geneva: ILO, 2006.

PlayFair. *No Medal for the Olympics on Labour Rights.* PlayFair 2008, June 2007. http://www.playfair2008.org/docs/playfair_2008-report.pdf.

Pomfret, John, and Philip P. Pan. "Blast Kills 37 Students in China." *Washington Post,* March 8 2001, A1.

U.S. Department of Labor. *By the Sweat and Toil of Children: The Use of Child Labor in American Imports.* Washington, DC: U.S. Department of Labor, 1994.

Education in the People's Republic of China

Andrew B. Kipnis, Research School of Pacific and Asian Studies, Australian National University

By early 2007, the education system of the People's Republic of China (PRC) included nine years of compulsory education—six years of primary school followed by three years of junior middle school. According to official statistics available from the Ministry of Education, in 2003, 98.7 percent of primary school–aged children were enrolled in primary school, more than 95 percent of primary school graduates enrolled in junior middle school, and 92 percent of those who enrolled in junior middle school graduated. In urban China and the wealthier parts of rural China, primary school is usually preceded by three years of preschool and followed by three years of either academic or vocational senior middle school, so in these places the majority of children attend school for at least fifteen years. Nationwide, perhaps half of Chinese children are able to attend these noncompulsory forms of schooling. In addition, graduates of academic senior middle schools may go on to various forms of tertiary education, including various technical diplomas, regular four-year undergraduate programs in almost every conceivable academic discipline, and, eventually, a wide variety of masters and doctoral programs. Places for university students have been expanding rapidly since the turn of the century, and in 2005 almost 20 percent of university-aged students were enrolled in some form of tertiary education (Bai 2006).

Fees for schools in China are high in relation to average incomes. Even public primary and junior middle schools charge some fees, while tuition for university is extremely high. Fees for public senior middle schools and preschools are between these extremes. China is also a highly stratified society, and there are great gaps in the levels of educational opportunity between the poorer and wealthier parts of the country, as well as between rural and urban areas. In poorer areas school fees are often higher than in more wealthy areas, as local governments cannot raise the tax revenues necessary to run the schools. In some impoverished areas, examples of teachers taking their students to factories during summer vacations, or running factories with student labor inside of schools, have been discovered (Cheung and Welford 2005).

No introduction to the Chinese education system could be complete without some discussion of the "examination mania" that dominates the lives of most Chinese secondary school students. Desire to attend university is nearly universal and, for students enrolled at academic senior middle schools, competition is keen. In the relatively wealthy area of rural Shandong, about 80 percent of children now attend academic senior middle school. Except for mealtimes and brief breaks, these students attend classes or study halls from 6 A.M. until after 10 P.M., seven days a week, for almost the entire year. Though there are breaks for summer and winter vacation, students are given copious amounts of homework to complete during these breaks. For students in years nine and twelve (just before the entrance exams for senior middle school and university), special class sessions are run during these "holidays." Throughout the year students continually face a barrage of tests and assignments to prepare them for entrance exams to the next level of schooling. Teachers are judged primarily on the exam results of their students (Kipnis 2001).

The intensity of competition to attend university and the resultant exam mania in the schools has been influenced by both the birth control policy and the recent history of spatial inequality in China. For most of the Deng era (1980s and early 1990s), rural students could be assigned urban jobs and receive urban household registrations if they graduated from a tertiary institution. While graduation from a tertiary institution no longer guarantees urban household registration, it still increases the chances of obtaining this privilege. A spatial inequality, in which residents of urban areas receive more valuable citizenship rights than do residents of rural areas, and an education system that grants mobility to rural people within this hierarchy have been defining features of the process of urbanization in China over the past thirty years. As the birth control policy limited urban couples to one child and rural couples to one or two, the extent of parental investment in their children's educational success has increased. Parents of several children generally lack the time, money, and energy to focus on a given child's education the way the parents of single children do (Fong 2005).

Variations in Educational Opportunity and Experiences

Until recently, schools in China have been locally funded, resulting in great differences between more and less wealthy areas. In addition, structural differences between urban and rural China as well as geographic and ethnic differences between regions have led to different patterns of schooling in different areas of China. In rural areas, secondary schools (both junior and senior) are often boarding schools located in towns and county seats. Depending on the geography and the transportation resources in a given area, these schools can be located at quite a distance from students' home villages. Some rural citizens and many educators believe that this arrangement has advantages in that students' study habits can be strictly disciplined in such a setting. In Shandong Province, some urban parents actually pay extra fees to send their child to a rural secondary school precisely because they believe the strict discipline will give their child an edge in the university entrance exam.

In large urban areas there are populations of migrant workers from rural areas, and the education of migrant worker children has been a tricky issue. Until recently, such children were rejected by local public schools, and many unofficial private schools for the children of migrant workers emerged. Though poorly equipped, these schools oriented themselves toward migrant worker children and were often better able to address the problems of such children than the local public schools. As a consequence, though local urban schools are now required by law to accept the children of migrant workers, many migrant worker children prefer the private migrant worker schools. The education environment for migrant worker children is currently evolving very rapidly.

Universities are generally located in urban areas, and this gives urban students an advantage in the race for university admittance. Urban areas reserve the largest quotas of university places for local students, with the result that rural students must achieve much higher test scores to get into the same level of university. Even at major national universities, such as Peking University, it is much easier to gain admittance if you are a Beijing student than if you are a student from a rural area.

There has been a substantial push from the central government for local governments to build high-quality schools, and most rural counties have at least one well-equipped senior middle school. However, while some wealthier rural counties have now invested in good schools at all levels, in poorer rural counties there are likely to be many impoverished schools at the primary and junior secondary levels. At least until very recently, such schools often faced a triple disadvantage. First, because the county governments have few tax resources, they do not invest much in schools and have often attempted to fund education by charging illegally high fees. Second, parents themselves are impoverished and thus even less able to pay school fees than parents from wealthier areas. Finally, because the birth control policy is not even officially a one-child policy in most rural areas, and because the policy is often enforced less strictly in relatively impoverished areas, poor rural parents have to pay the school fees for two, three, or even more children.

Recent Reform to the Chinese Education System

The central government of the PRC is now undertaking four major types of reforms to the education system: more equitable distribution of resources, rural school consolidation, "education for quality," and improved vocational education.

The government is beginning to take measures to reduce some of the inequality among students from different parts of the country. First, it has demanded that children of migrant workers be allowed to attend schools in the districts where their parents work and live. While this policy may not make much difference in the largest cities, where children of migrant workers feel uncomfortable in local schools, in some smaller cities this policy has had a positive impact. Second, the central government announced (in December 2006) that it has budgeted money to abolish school fees for 150 million of its poorest rural residents. The plan is to use a combination of central government and provincial government money to fund the education system of impoverished counties. How well this new system of school funding will work has yet to be seen.

In rural areas, the central government has pushed for consolidation of primary schools. In the past, almost every village had its own primary school. Now in some areas of the countryside there are only one or two primary schools per township, that is, one or two primary schools for perhaps forty villages. Children at these schools may be served by school buses, may ride their bikes to school, or may be taken by their parents. Two official reasons exist behind these changes. First, because of the birth control policy, the number of school-age children is declining. Second, the government wishes to centralize rural schools so that each school has better equipment and facilities, employs more specialized teachers, and is easier to administer. The reactions of parents and students have been mixed. In areas of the country with better transportation infrastructure, reactions are more positive. In those parts of the country where long school commutes are inconvenient, however, loss of the local village school can force rural women to spend significant periods of time taking their children to school (Kipnis 2006a).

"Education for Quality" is the slogan given to nationally mandated education reform. Originally, the slogan came from a group of education researchers concerned with the exam mania in China's education system. They argued that rather than an education system oriented to passing exams, China should institute an education system oriented to improving the "quality" of the population. They managed to have "Education for Quality" (*suzhi jiaoyu*) inscribed as the guiding slogan for China's education law in 1999. The result has been that almost all proposals for education reform are labeled as education for quality, no matter how contradictory. Though many changes have been made to national, provincial, and local school curricula, teaching methods, and equipment under these reforms, the exam mania of China's education system has not declined. More attention is paid, however, to exposing students to a diverse curriculum. Some educators argue that cramming for exams is not necessarily in contradiction with the goal of improving the quality of the population, as long as the exams are structured in the proper manner (Kipnis 2001; 2006b).

Finally, there has been a push to improve China's vocational education. The emphasis on academic success in China has led many families to disparage vocational education, seeing it as a last resort to be undertaken only after failure in the regular academic track. With the recent increase in university enrollments, however, there has been a rapid increase in the number of university graduates on the job market. Given China's rapidly expanding manufacturing economy, in many parts of China there is a significantly higher unemployment rate among university graduates than among vocational school graduates. Central and provincial governments are reacting by trying both to devote more resources to vocational education and to convince parents that vocational schools offer a viable alternative to more academic ones. As with other recent reforms, it is too early to know how successful this push will be.

Conclusion

In many parts of China, the resources and energy devoted to the pursuit of academic excellence are breathtaking. At the same time, the uneven distribution of educational resources has prevented many students from receiving the education they desire. Recent reforms to equalize access to education in China are a step in the right direction, though only time will tell if they succeed.

References and Further Reading

Bai, Limin. "Graduate Unemployment: Dilemmas and Challenges in China's Move to Mass Higher Education." *China Quarterly* 185 (2006):128–44.

Cheung, Dennis, and Richard Welford. "Is Child Labour on the Increase in China?" *CSR Asia Weekly* 1:45 (2005): 2–4.

Fong, Vanessa. *Only Hope: Coming of Age Under China's One-Child Policy.* Stanford: Stanford University Press, 2005.

Kipnis, Andrew B. "The Disturbing Educational Discipline of 'Peasants.'" *China Journal* 46 (2001):1–24.

———. "School Consolidation in Rural China." *Development Bulletin* 70 (2006a): 123–25.

———. "Suzhi: A Keyword Approach." *China Quarterly* 186 (2006b): 295–313.

People's Republic of China, Ministry of Education. http://www.moe.edu.cn.

History of Child Labor in China

Joshua H. Howard, Croft Associate Professor of History and International Studies, University of Mississippi

The phenomenon of child labor has a long history in China. Children traditionally participated in agricultural and household work and, by the Tang dynasty (618–907 C.E.), they assumed apprenticeships outside the home in such skills as bricklaying and weaving. Yet consciousness of child labor and its manifestation in language are of recent origin, dating to the late nineteenth century, when China began to industrialize. An early reference to the term *child labor* (*tong gong*) can be found in an 1886 document describing women and children packing matchboxes. After 1895, rapid growth of British and Japanese textile mills in China's treaty ports, particularly Shanghai, intensified the use of child labor. Although both foreigners and Chinese employed children, legal privileges and tax advantages accorded to foreign enterprises, coupled with their higher capitalization and greater technical and management experience, may have motivated Chinese employers to hire more children to gain a competitive advantage. Child labor seems to have peaked by the late 1920s, when it became a target of Marxist intellectuals and Christian reformers intent on achieving social justice and strengthening China by exposing its societal evils. The following description conveys the strong moralistic condemnation of the practice:

> In rural districts ten and twelve year old boys can be seen coming up out of the mouths of primitive mines, straining at loads of coal attached by rope to their shoulders, providing cheaper labor than animals or machinery. Hundreds of pasty-faced young girls trudge home in the gray dawn of the Shanghai morning after twelve or fourteen hours on the night shift in the cotton mills. Little children, fortunately not so many in recent years, may be seen in the silk filatures, hardly tall enough to reach the basins at which they stand dipping the silk cocoons in boiling water, their fingers a horrid sight, the atmosphere in the room so humid and the odor so fetid that fainting is not uncommon. (Wagner 1938, 29)

Just as child labor served critics of capitalism, its abolition and the promotion of childhood development were linked to Chinese nationalism. One reformer argued, "[O]nly by having the growth of sound children can we have a healthy citizenry and only with a healthy citizenry can we have a healthy nation. If we desire our society's advancement, a strong and wealthy nation, and a revitalized people, we must protect children's welfare" (Liu 1936, 10).

Both poverty and population pressure perpetuated child labor during China's Republican era (1911–1949). Public schooling was lacking for many of the more than 40 million children of school age in the early 1930s. "There are fewer than 1,500 middle schools in the entire country, which means that there is only one middle school for every 300,000 Chinese" (Lowe 1933, 105). Thus child labor became a strategy for economic survival. Low wages earned by adults forced parents to push their children into employment to earn supplemental income. Parents, too, viewed the factory as a safer haven for children than if they were left to roam the streets. This perspective contributed to a vicious cycle, since workers did not correlate child labor with depressed adult wages, which in turn encouraged child labor.

It remains difficult to pinpoint the extent of child labor owing to the relatively late development of statistical surveys, widespread only by the

1920s, and the different standards used to tabulate the number of child laborers. Government surveys usually underrepresented the extent of child labor by restricting themselves to factories employing more than thirty workers, thereby ignoring numerous children employed in small-scale factories, sweatshops, handicraft industries, home factories, and shops. Some surveys even omitted the category for child labor as the Nationalist government sought to make a good impression on international bodies such as the ILO.

As China's industrial and financial capital, Shanghai was a magnet for working children. In 1899, some 7,000 children and 20,000 women formed the majority of Shanghai's total factory workforce of 34,500 (Smith 2002). Shanghai's early industrialization was geared toward textiles, which employed predominantly women and children. By 1924 the Shanghai Municipal Council's Child Labor Commission found 173,272 children employed by the 275 factories surveyed: some 105,921 girls and 44,741 boys between twelve and sixteen years of age; 18,135 girls and 4,475 boys under the age of twelve (Li 1925). Nationwide, the 1930 Ministry of Industry survey of 799,912 workers employed in twenty-eight cities and nine provinces showed that roughly 7 percent were children. These figures, however, should be treated as low estimates. The textile industry, for instance, employed 41,794 children, or 8.4 percent of 497,420 workers (Wagner 1938). A survey of 222,000 factory workers in Shanghai found that as many as 21 percent of those engaged in silk reeling were children. In machine industries, 24 percent of the total 7,635 employees were children (Stuart and Fang 1930).

More children were employed in southern provinces, such as Guangdong, Jiangsu, and Zhejiang, where light industries and labor-intensive jobs were dominant. Women and girls were concentrated in silk reeling and weaving, cotton spinning and weaving, embroidery, hosiery, knitting, pottery, and furniture making. One important exception to this regional distribution was the northern seaport city of Tianjin, where numerous boy laborers wove silk and cotton, spun cotton, and wove carpets. Up to a fifth of the workforce in Tianjin industries were children, more than double the rate in Shanghai. Unlike Shanghai industrialists, who consciously replaced men with allegedly more docile female employees in the wake of the nationalist class-inflected labor movement of the mid-1920s, Tianjin textile owners continued to employ boys and adult males. Women in North China were more constrained to the home, so most rural migrants to Tianjin were male, further skewing the city's population imbalance.

A division of labor based on sex largely shaped the basic types of child labor. Boys dominated apprenticeships and resided in the shops, small workshops, laundries, or factories, where they learned their trade or skill. Girls worked with their mothers in home industries, were sold and employed as domestic workers and sex workers, or accompanied their mothers or went alone to do simple tasks as piece workers or factory hands. The contracting out of jobs to hundreds of thousands of women and their children developed on the periphery of China's treaty-port cities where foreign capital and export firms were concentrated. Production of embroidery, lace work, hairnets, and matchboxes depended on contractors, who distributed materials to farmhouses and paid extremely low wages by the piece. Mother and child, for instance, made 2,000 matchboxes per day during the nonfarming season, earning enough to pay for their food. By the turn of the century, women and girls also sought employment in workshops as casual piece workers, filling matchboxes, winding yarn, sewing soldiers' uniforms, and so forth.

Women employed in manufacturing plants often preferred their children's presence to leaving them home alone; thus, children entered the factories as babies and by the age of five began assisting their mothers. Workshops during night shifts resembled makeshift dormitories. "Walking through these dimly lit mill-rooms one sees baskets containing children, sleeping or awake, between the whirring, clacking machines. Sometimes a tot of two or three sits cheerfully playing with cotton waste in the aisles through which the foreman guides the visitor. Girls a little older help their mothers tend the rows of spindles, and the deftness of five-year-old fingers is amazing" (Gannett 1927, 19). Conditions in silk filatures were little different. "Here are mothers working with nursing babies lying on the floor beside them or strapped to their backs. The children learn to work as soon as they are able to walk" (Finch 1925, 761).

Although employers regarded children as cheap labor, paying them a third to one-half the wages of male adults, both workers and employers viewed the presence of young children in the factory as an opportunity for informal on-the-job training. As one former mill hand recalled, "When I was ten years old, the workshop buildings were being erected. I often went with people to the compound in order to play there, and by playing around I just learned [the job]. At the age of thirteen I entered the factory to work in the spinning room" (Köll 2003, 113). Interviews with 200 former mill hands indicate that approximately two-thirds entered the workforce before the age of thirteen (Mu and Yan 1994). Children learned a variety of skills. At the age of five, children wound yarn or pasted or filled matchboxes. In the cotton mills, most children worked in the spinning departments, where ten-year-old girls helped with doffing and spinning. Hand-reeling rooms in modern cotton mills employed children almost exclusively, to the extent that they "have more the appearance of over crowded elementary school rooms than of factories" (Orchard 1935, 577). In the silk filatures, children as young as six years of age stood for five to six hours at a stretch over basins of near-boiling water, where they beat and brushed cocoons to free the silk filament for reeling. As one factory inspector described a Shanghai filature: "Tiny children stood for an eleven-hour day, soaked to the skin in a steamy atmosphere, their fingers blanched to the knuckles and their bodies swaying from one tired foot to the other, kept at their task by a stern overseer who did not hesitate to beat those whose attention wandered" (Perry 1993, 170).

Contract Labor System

Adolescent girls were typically employed in silk filatures and cotton mills after being bought and sold through the contract labor system. According to one observer, "Often the children are brought in from the country by a contractor, who follows disaster like vultures and pays starving parents about a dollar a month for a contract which amounts to slavery; the girls live for years in his compound, eating his food, or in the factories, eating factory rice, working sometimes fifteen or sixteen hours a day, and often sleeping on the floor beneath their machines" (Gannett 1927, 19). British industrialists in Shanghai may have first adopted this recruiting system to avoid linguistic barriers in recruiting workers. By the late 1920s, the notorious Green Gang had cornered the cotton-mill labor market with the encouragement of mill owners seeking a more pliant workforce after the heated labor battles of the mid-1920s. Agents recruited girls from impoverished rural families north of the Yangzi River, paying ten to thirty dollars to the parents for at least three years of their child's labor. Contractors often hired out children to cotton-mill foremen who would guarantee a post in the mill and take 20 to 30 percent of the children's wages. The remainder would go to the contractor. Contract workers shared the same arduous twelve-hour shifts as other mill hands, but their isolation and total dependence on the contractor for room and board made them vulnerable to physical and sexual abuse (Honig 1986). Until the outbreak of the Anti-Japanese War, the contract labor system flourished in Shanghai under the Green Gang's domination. Although the contract labor system persisted until 1949, managers in Shanghai and elsewhere increasingly turned to mill agents to recruit teenage girls and adopted training programs to wield more direct control over the workforce. Under this system, teenage girls assumed apprenticeships of up to two years before being hired as full-time wage-earning workers.

Apprenticeships

Apprenticeships had traditionally been the preserve of boys and male adolescents, functioning to disseminate trade education and provide poor children with a livelihood in the handicraft sector, partially mechanized industries, and provision shops. Under contract for periods of more than three years, the apprentice was taught a skill that, in theory, would guarantee employment in the particular trade. Masters would also provide apprentices a nominal payment to cover room and board. Conditions were onerous, with working hours lasting up to fourteen per day.

By the 1920s, the customary guild apprenticeship had devolved into a thinly disguised form of cheap child labor, since employers no longer guaranteed future employment after completion of the contract. In Tianjin and Beijing, the number of apprentices working as handloom weavers, hosiery knitters, glassmakers, mat weavers, and carpet makers far exceeded that of regular workers, making it difficult to receive the necessary training to become a journeyman. Observers of Beijing carpet factories concluded that this form of apprenticeship "does not give them a trade which they can ply, nor does it make them in any way independent. It is a 'blind alley' job in every way. At present it can certainly be called nothing less than indentured child labor" (Lowe 1933, 25).

Although it is difficult to quantify, reports from the mid-1930s suggest an increased use of apprentices in industries transitioning from workshop to factory. Unpaid apprentices produced consumer goods ranging from thermos flasks to rubber goods. By the early 1940s, China employed an estimated 20 million to 30 million apprentices. "In the interior cities, almost every third person you meet on the street is an apprentice, or some one who has gone through the system" (Liao 1948, 91). Although more than 19 million children were enrolled in schools during 1942, the remaining 80 million youths looked to farming or employment in commerce, handicrafts, or industry. Apprenticeships continued to offer the hope of technical training, given the continued inadequacy of the education system, particularly for rural children.

Protective Legislation

Impetus for legislation to protect children derived from introduction of the modern factory system as well as intensification of the older industrial regime. Foreign influence also played an important role in the movement to eliminate child labor. The first proposal for child labor legislation was brought to the attention of Chinese authorities as a result of the International Labor Conference in 1919. Under pressure from the ILO, the Peking government adopted a provisional Factory Law in 1923, which called for prohibiting employment of girls under age twelve and boys under age ten, but the law remained a dead letter without provisions for enforcement. At the prodding of the YWCA and the Federation of Women's Boards of Foreign Missions, the Municipal Council of the International Settlement of Shanghai established a Child Labor Commission, whose 1924 report recommended prohibiting employment of children under ten years of age, rising to twelve years within four years of the implementation of such regulations. However moderate, these recommendations failed to become law, derailed by an insufficient quorum of international settlement ratepayers. Subsequent efforts by the Shanghai Municipal Council to pass regulations, however well intentioned, were perceived as an attempt to extend foreign power and jurisdiction over Chinese lives and were duly rejected (Chesneaux 1968).

The first industrial legislation with national scope was the 1929 Factory Law, revised in 1932. The law prohibited employment of children under the age of fourteen in any factory, although children from twelve to fourteen years old who were already employed before the law was promulgated could continue to work. In a departure from previous legislation, the Factory Law redefined children as those between fourteen and sixteen years of age and permitted them to be employed only for light work. Night work would be abolished for children and the workday limited to eight hours. The Factory Law also regulated apprenticeships, mandating that no more than a third of a factory's regular workforce be apprentices, imposed a minimum age of thirteen for apprenticeships, restricted the work day to eight hours, and stipulated that apprentices be supplied with room, board, medical care, and an allowance for incidentals (Wagner 1938).

These laws were more easily promulgated than enforced. The Nationalist government postponed key provisions, for instance, waiting until 1936 to enforce the prohibition of night work for women and children. The absence of a factory inspection system, and birth or health certificates needed to register the ages of children, made enforcement all the more difficult. Moreover, the Factory Law did not apply to factories with fewer than thirty employees, thus providing no protection measures where they were most needed. Both employers and workers voiced opposition to the Factory Law. If schooling was not mandatory, free, or widespread, it was inevitable that workers would bemoan the loss of their children's jobs and income. Some employers argued that they would be forced to dismiss thousands of workers in order to enforce the law; others maintained the legislation unfairly targeted Chinese businesses because extraterritoriality meant the regulations would not be enforced among foreign concerns.

Whether promulgated by Nationalists or Communists (the latter adopted a labor code in 1930 that prohibited employment of children under the age of fourteen), protective legislation marked an important shift in how the state conceived of child labor. The very definition of the child became more expansive by raising the benchmark from twelve to sixteen years of age. Increased awareness of the child coincided with Nationalist government efforts to popularize education, thus providing an alternative to child labor. The relative paucity of wartime documentation (1937–1949) decrying child labor as morally repugnant suggests that child labor was less pervasive. While the proportion of children in the factory workforce in wartime Nationalist China remained steady at about 8 percent, in absolute numbers the roughly 20,000 children employed mark a sharp reduction from fifteen years earlier (Epstein 1949). Similar trends are apparent in surveys of Shanghai's factory workers. Children comprised 3.6 percent of the roughly 150,000 workers surveyed in 1946. A 1948 survey of various industries found only 418 children employed in cotton mills (Liu and Tang 2002). Only Tianjin witnessed a resurgence of child labor during the war. By 1946, nearly 100,000 children were employed, as employers looked to children as an abundant and docile labor supply during the Japanese occupation (Hershatter 1986).

Overall, the reduced demand for child labor may have been a consequence of the growing importance of the state-owned heavy industrial sector, which increased demand for skilled male labor and forced managers to adhere more closely to industrial legislation. Moreover, modern factories' demand for skilled labor stemming from technological advances, such as the introduction of central boiler systems in silk filatures, may have rendered child labor uneconomical and contributed to its decline during the 1930s.

Despite progressive laws, a weakened central government embattled in the Anti-Japanese War from 1937 to 1945, and then a civil war against the Communists, thwarted enforcement of protective legislation across the country. Moreover, the public outcry that had contributed to these laws dissipated during the Anti-Japanese War. The issue of child labor became subsumed under a broader patriotic discourse to the extent that public criticism of child labor as a social ill became muted while children were encouraged to work (albeit not in factory labor) as a form of participation in China's resistance against Japan. In sum, not until after the 1949 Revolution, when a reunified China under Communist control began to address the structural reasons underlying child labor, impede rural to urban migration, and popularize education in both rural and urban areas, did the numbers of child laborers significantly recede.

References and Further Reading

Chesneaux, Jean. *The Chinese Labor Movement 1919–1927.* Stanford, CA: Stanford University Press, 1968.

Epstein, Israel. *Notes on Labor Problems in Nationalist China.* New York: Institute of Pacific Relations, 1949.

Finch, Percival. "Battle Against Child Labor in China." *Current History Magazine* (August 1925): 761.

Gannett, Lewis S. *Young China.* New York: The Nation, 1927.

Hershatter, Gail. *Workers of Tianjin, 1900–1949.* Stanford, CA: Stanford University Press, 1986.

Honig, Emily. *Sisters and Strangers: Women in the Shanghai Cotton Mills, 1919–1949.* Stanford, CA: Stanford University Press, 1986.

Köll, Elisabeth. *From Cotton Mill to Business Empire: The Emergence of Regional Enterprises in Modern China.* Cambridge, MA: Harvard University Asia Center, 2003.

"Labor Conditions and Labor Regulations in China." *International Labor Review* 10:12 (December 1924): 4.

Li Dazhao. "Shanghai de tonggong wenti" [Shanghai's child labor problem]. *Zhongguo Gongren* 4 (April 1925): 516.

Liao T'ai-ch'u. "The Apprentices in Chengtu During and After the War." *Yenching Journal of Social Studies* 4:1 (August 1948): 91, 99.

Liu Mingda and Tang Yuliang, eds. *Zhongguo jindai gongren jieji he gongren yundong* [Modern China's working class and labor movement]. Vol. 13. Beijing: Zhonggong Zhongyang Dangxiao Chubanshe, 2002.

Liu Shuncheng. "Xiandai Zhongguo tonggong wenti" [Child labor in modern China]. *Laogong Yuekan* 5:10 (October 1936): 10.

Lowe, Chuan-hua. *Facing Labor Issues in China.* Shanghai: China Institute of Pacific Relations, 1933. Repr., Washington, DC: University Publications of America, 1977.

Mu Xuan and Yan Xuexi, eds. *Dasheng shachang gongren shenghuo de diaocha (1899–1949)* [Investigation of the life of workers in the Dasheng spinning mills, 1899–1949]. Nanjing: Jiangsu Renmin Chubanshe, 1994.

Orchard, Dorothy J. "Man-Power in China" *Political Science Quarterly* 50:4 (December 1935): 561–83.

Perry, Elizabeth J. *Shanghai on Strike: The Politics of Chinese Labor.* Stanford, CA: Stanford University Press, 1993.

Plum, Colette M. "Unlikely Heirs: War Orphans During the Second Sino-Japanese War, 1937–1945." PhD diss., Stanford University, 2007.

Smith, S.A. *Like Cattle and Horses: Nationalism and Labor in Shanghai, 1895–1927.* Durham, NC: Duke University Press, 2002.

Stuart, Maxwell, and Fu-an Fang. "A Statistical Study of Labor and Industry in China." *Chinese Economic Journal* 7 (October 1930): 1099.

Wagner, Augusta. *Labor Legislation in China.* Peking: Yenching University, 1938. Repr., New York: Garland Publishing, 1980.

History of Chinese Education

Irving Epstein, Professor, Department of Educational Studies, Illinois Wesleyan University

Education has traditionally been associated with many of the basic principles that governed different currents of traditional Chinese thought. As eclectic and diverse as those currents were, they all affirmed the importance of learning as a key process in fostering self-cultivation and moral improvement. Not simply a moral imperative for the individual, education was also viewed as a social necessity, as a means of promoting social cohesiveness and good governance. In China's case, the growth of formal education preceded economic industrialization and centralization of the power of the state. Because the importance of education preceded such developments, its significance was continually apparent in every aspect of Chinese life, including family, gender relations, class formation and conflict, and state governance, prior to China's modernization. Traditional and contemporary attitudes toward child labor thus must be viewed within a historical context where the importance of learning, from an ideological perspective, was widely acknowledged and rarely questioned, even during preindustrial eras. In time, however, the ways in which this ideal was implemented belied the universalism of its orientation.

Confucianism became prominent during the first century B.C.E., even as it competed with Buddhism and Taoism for widespread social influence through the first eight centuries of the common era (Lee 2000). Together the three traditions shared a belief in the importance of moral perfectibility, to be accomplished through learning. Thus, early Confucian academies resembled Buddhist monasteries in their emphasis on personal discipline and their isolation from external social influences. Qu Xi (1120–1200 C.E.), father of neo-Confucianism, specifically argued that one should become one with what one was learning and offered detailed prescriptions on how to study that were followed in the academies he and his followers established. A basic tenet that all Confucians shared was the belief that demonstration of individual concern for moral behavior was a precondition to creating social harmony (Lee 2000). It is thus understandable why the world's first attempt at meritocratic governance occurred during the Han dynasty (206 B.C.E.–220 C.E.), and was nationalized during the Northern and Southern Song dynasties (420–588 C.E.). Written civil service examinations were implemented during the Sui (580–618 C.E.) and Tang dynasties (618–907 C.E.) Imposition of an examination system had the effect of ensuring preservation of Confucianism as a state ideology; early forms of civil service recruitment included both oral and written evaluations of moral suitability, commitment to filial piety, and knowledge of Confucian classics. When a more formalized examination system was established, ability to memorize classical texts was assessed. Creation of a meritocratic system that rewarded talent, as opposed to inherited aristocratic privilege, as a condition for providing public service to the emperor and his state, was one of the great social achievements of Chinese civilization.

But by the eighteen and nineteenth centuries, the system's effectiveness was seriously compromised through corruption and ossification. In truth, the examination system was never meant to provide for mass education but instead served the state's purpose of staffing its bureaucracy by recruiting loyal officials from the gentry. The examinations themselves, with emphasis on the importance of memorizing Confucian classical texts, demonstrating expertise in calligraphy, and expressing facility in classical Mandarin, required successful applicants to use cultural capital that could most readily be acquired through family status. The privileging of classical and formal learning above that of practical and vocational training was an intrinsic characteristic of the system, as mental labor was valued over the physical. At the same time, the promise of upward mobility, no matter how unlikely to be fulfilled, promoted widespread loyalty to the state and, more generally, to Confucian ideological orthodoxy. Thus, while examinations were held at county, prefecture, and provincial levels, one had to acquire a basic level of literacy prior to beginning the study of Confucian texts. State academies established at the county level and above, for purposes of preparing prospective examination candidates, required students to have acquired basic literacy skills prior to enrollment. Thus, educational provision became closely related to family status and standing (Elman 1991; Pepper 1996). At the preacademy level, if one's family had resources, one would be privately tutored. For those less fortunate, public charity and clan schools were funded by wealthy local elites and officials. Their curricula consisted of lower and upper levels, with an emphasis on memorization of characters and primary texts at the lower level and rudimentary training in the classics at the upper level (Leung 1994). The total number of successful examination candidates was determined through a quota system that became severely compromised during the nineteenth century, as affluent candidate families were able to purchase the designations formally awarded to successful candidates, overtly blurring distinctions between academic achievement and family connections and financial resources.

Not surprisingly, traditional Chinese notions of childhood also were directly influenced by Confucian ideals, with their emphasis on the importance of patriarchy, filial piety, a respect for ancestral authority, and reciprocity of obligation between child and parent. The gendered nature of family life led to valuing boys over girls; boys could be counted on to provide for parents' sustenance in old age; girls, who traditionally married into their husband's families, would not be in a position to do so. Instances of female infanticide repeatedly occurred throughout Chinese history (Kinney 1995), and educational provision mirrored this gender preference, as girls were never allowed to sit for civil service examinations. At most, 2 to 10 percent of the female population was literate by the end of the nineteenth century (Rawski 1979).

Between 1901 and 1905, educational reformers attempted to introduce a public schooling system based on the Japanese model, and the government abolished the civil service examination system in 1905 (Pepper 1996). With the dissolution of the empire in 1911, reformers looked to Western models, including that of the United States, for solutions in modernizing a broken educational system. Their efforts were part of a larger effort on the part of Chinese intellectuals, who sought to quickly modernize their country, which they recognized had fallen behind the Western powers and Japan by the beginning of the twentieth century. The uncritical embrace of the West by these intellectuals and social critics was at variance with their late-nineteenth-century predecessors, who thought it both possible and desirable to merge Western scientific knowledge with traditional Chinese learning. But with the advent of the May Fourth Movement and the ensuing nationalism it generated, disillusioned students and intellectuals understood that the uncritical borrowing of Western educational models failed to provide for China's needs. Mass education was never universally implemented; provisions for schooling were fragmented and often restricted to urban areas. Much of the educational borrowing that did occur reinforced traditionally elitist notions of learning, albeit within Western frameworks. Thus, notable efforts by reformers such as James Yen, who started the Chinese Association for the Promotion of Popular Education in 1923, and Tao Xingzhi, who established a mass education program in the countryside after 1923, ultimately proved unsuccessful (Pepper 1996). Instead, it was those espousing a Marxist alternative that merged traditional Chinese sensibilities with modernist orientations, including a respect for historical context and the immutable nature of historical progress, a faith in the efficacy of human agency to overcome systematic material oppression, and a belief in the importance of control over one's labor in determining personal and collective identity, that found resonance among the Chinese peasantry. These beliefs were translated into educational terms during the Yan'an mass education experiment, during the late 1930s and 1940s.

After Mao Zedong was forced to lead his Chinese Communist followers on the Long March, escaping from Nationalist forces and settling in the Northwest (1934–1935), Mao established his base in Yan'an and, in so doing, created mass education programs, attempting to combat peasant illiteracy. From 1938 to 1942, educators emphasized Soviet educational models whereby standardized and centralized regulatory control was stressed at the expense of expanding delivery of basic educational services. By 1942, Mao embarked on a rectification campaign, and from 1943 through 1947, radical educational reform was implemented, including school expansion, provision for work-study and evening schools, and local community input into the curriculum (Pepper 1996).

The tensions between those who favored elitist and bureaucratic party control of political affairs and those who espoused Mao's own belief in the importance of encouraging mass popular support were part of a larger ideological conflict. Failure to resolve these tensions not only characterized the first seventeen years of the People's Republic but culminated in the Cultural Revolution (1966–1976). During the Great Leap Forward (1958–1959), for example, the number of work-study schools in rural areas dramatically increased; but in the ensuing years prior to the Cultural Revolution, a two-tiered system became institutionalized, with the *minban* (work-study) model becoming a second-rate alternative to its formal, academic counterpart (Barendson 1964).

Outstanding features of educational reform during the Cultural Revolution included implementation of mass education through extension of the middle school to rural areas, albeit on the basis of local funding, an emphasis on integrating basic literacy skills with productive labor, and creating overtly politicized yet practical and less formalistic academic curricula relevant to local community needs. These reforms, as well as efforts to send urban middle school graduates to the countryside to assist in rural development, represented a perspective that associated the importance of engaging in manual labor with expression of one's commitment to the Chinese Revolution. The fact that they never succeeded in permanently transforming the character of the Chinese educational system can be attributed to problems of implementation, their lack of support among educational professionals and intransigent elites, and the threats they posed to entrenched interests, who considered their prospects for social mobility threatened by broadening the base of the educational pyramid.

In the early years of the post-Mao era, national university entrance examinations, eliminated in the year immediately prior to the Cultural Revolution, were reinitiated—provincially administered in 1977 and nationally operated as of 1978. Both schools and universities were subject to external reputational ranking that partially determined funding, based on candidates' examination performance (Rosen 1985). When vocational programs were initiated for non–university bound students, their popularity suffered due to their disparate status.

Other political, social, and economic reforms of the 1980s significantly influence educational provision within the People's Republic. Adoption of the one-child family policy in 1979 and of market reforms such as the rural responsibility system in the 1980s, which effectively ended communal agricultural arrangements, placed increasing pressure on rural peasant children to support family farming as opposed to staying in school. Diminution of local political authority resulted in less local school funding; continued imposition of school fees charged to peasant parents served as a disincentive for keeping children in school. In response to such pressures, in 1986, a nine-year compulsory education law was implemented and, as of 2002, according to the Chinese Ministry of Education, 90 percent of the country's inhabited regions were in compliance with its provisions. Within those regions, 98.5 percent of the relevant population was enrolled in primary school. As impressive as these statistics appear, they do not address dropout or illiteracy trends, which disproportionately affect girls and women.

By the 1990s, the tyranny of the market and globalization pressures that accompanied economic expansion had an increasingly important effect in changing the character of rural Chinese life, including rural education. From 1993 to 2003, China's "floating" or migrant population doubled from 70 million to 140 million people, as rural workers moved to provincial cities and coastal provinces in search of temporary work. As more and more family members left their farms to pursue urban work, rural villages have found it increasingly difficult to support local schooling. Pressures placed on children and youth to assist in supplementing family income have resulted in many joining the floating population in pursuit of menial labor in wealthier cities and regions targeted for foreign investment. At the same time, as much of the floating population resides illegally in urban centers, without the ability to obtain official residence permits, children and youths have few opportunities to continue their schooling. Dickensian labor conditions to which young girls particularly were subjected in the Pearl River Delta and special economic zones in Guangdong Province, reported during the late 1980s and early 1990s (Epstein 1993), have proliferated dramatically over the past two decades, as the effects of unregulated global capitalism have taken their toll throughout the country. Educational reform efforts have thus failed to immunize the children of China's poor from these effects.

Throughout China's history, education has been valued as a vehicle for promoting orthodox Confucian values and, during the twentieth century, as a means of preserving the core values of Chinese Marxism. However, the government's inability to provide basic equality of educational opportunity for all or even most of its citizenry has been a historical constant, regardless of ideological dispositions or political orientations. Even as late as the early years of republican rule, reported instances of female infanticide and child bondage among China's poor proliferated. Reports of their occurrence continue to surface, albeit only occasionally, even today. Thus, the child labor abuses that have marked the late twentieth and twenty-first centuries not only bring to mind the historical legacy of oppression for which educational provision was unable to provide remediation but remind us that the power of global capitalism can be as pernicious as some of the worst practices of China's past.

References and Further Reading

Barendsen, Robert. *Half-Work Half-Study Schools in Communist China: Recent Experiments with Self-Supporting Educational Institutions.* Washington, DC: U.S. Department of Health, Education, and Welfare, 1964.

Elman, Benjamin. "Political, Social and Cultural Reproduction via Civil Service Examinations in Late Imperial China." *Journal of Asian Studies* 50:1 (1991): 7–28.

Epstein, Irving, ed. *Chinese Education: Problems, Policies, and Prospects.* New York: Garland Publishing, 1991.

———. "Child Labor and Basic Education Provision in China." *International Journal of Educational Development* 13:3 (1993): 227–38.

Kinney, Anne, ed. *Chinese Views of Childhood.* Honolulu: University of Hawaii, 1995.

Lee, Thomas H.C. *Education in Traditional China: A History.* Leiden: Brill, 2000.

Leung, A. "Elementary Education in the Lower Yangtze Region in the Seventeenth and Eighteenth Centuries." In *Education and Society in Late Imperial China, 1600–1900,* ed. B. Elman and A. Woodside. Berkeley: University of California Press, 1994.

Pepper, Suzanne. *Radicalism and Education Reform in Twentieth Century China.* New York: Cambridge University Press, 1996.

Rawski, Evelyn. *Education and Popular Literacy in Ch'ing China.* Ann Arbor: University of Michigan Press, 1979.

Rosen, S. "Recentralization, Decentralization, and Rationalization: Deng Xiaoping's Bifurcated Educational Policy." *Modern China* 11:3 (1985): 301–46.

Japan

History of Child Labor in Japan

Atsuko Fujino Kakinami, Kyoto Sangyo University

The view that "children are treasures" is typical in Japan, seen in the mid-sixth-century poetry of Yamanoue no Okura. Some researchers have suggested that Japan's industrialization did not lead to as extensive use of child labor as in the British cotton-spinning industry. Saito emphasizes that the main factor behind the smaller number of child laborers in Japan was unique family values (Saito 1997). In fact, however, there are very few studies focused on child labor in Japan.

Nevertheless, the history of trafficking and sexual exploitation of children in Japan is quite long and deeply rooted. Destitute families were officially permitted to sell their daughters as prostitutes to licensed brothels in the Edo era (1603–1867). In the Meiji era, many girls from poor peasant families became cheap laborers in factories in industries such as silk reeling and spinning. Despite rapid modernization, their employment conditions remained primitive, and their recruitment was no more than a form of human trafficking. Many such girls endured sexual abuse in the workplace. Japan still confronts problems of commercial and sexual exploitation of children domestically and internationally. Thus, the child labor problem in Japan can be considered a gender problem, and the tendency has been to examine the child labor problem within studies on female labor or gender.

Periods in Japanese history are generally defined as follows. The medieval age refers to the period before the start of the Edo era in 1603; the early-modern age refers to the Edo era (1603–1867); and the modern age refers to the period after the Meiji Restoration in 1868.

Child Labor Before the Modern Age

Descriptions of slavery and human trafficking appear in the year A.D. 712 in the *Kojiki* (the oldest history book in Japan). Another source is *Sanshō dayū,* Ōgai Mori's famous 1915 novel based on the narrative literature of the late Kamakura era (ca. 1185–1333). In this story, a bailiff named Sanshō dayū buys kidnapped children and forces them to work as slaves. There are many other stories written on the kidnapping and trafficking of children in the medieval age. It was perceived as an everyday occurrence and an inevitable misfortune for some children. Trafficking of children was systematized in this period (Maki 1971).

As Japan began to trade with Portugal in the late sixteenth century, more and more children were exported abroad as soldiers or slaves (Maki 1971). The Edo government strictly prohibited acts of human trafficking and slavery, regarding them as capital crimes. Nevertheless, the Edo government permitted girls from poor families to be sold into prostitution as *yūjo.* This practice was even regulated by law in 1733 (Yamamoto 1983). As a result, it became socially acceptable for parents to sell their daughters because of poverty. Behind this approval was a system of licensed prostitution. The Edo government permitted prostitution in licensed prostitution districts called *yūkaku* in order to maintain social order and to obtain tax revenue.

Prostitutes were employed as apprentices like merchants. Working prostitutes were usually between fourteen and twenty-seven years old. Girls sold into the prostitution industry were only four or five years old. At first, they worked for senior prostitutes as servants until they became fledging prostitutes, called *kamuro.* Their apprenticeships were quite different from those in other industries, as no conditions of employment were specified in their contracts. Anything was possible, even being treated as slaves. They were constantly exposed to disease and violence (Sone 2003).

In the late Edo era, many farmers confronted extremely difficult economic conditions. Under these circumstances, abortion and infanticide became widespread, and female babies were sacrificed. The number of male babies clearly exceeded that of female babies, especially in the Tōhoku region, where living standards were quite low (Ochiai 1994). In contrast, there was little infanticide in areas where people could sell daughters as *yūjo* (Inoue 1967).

Besides prostitutes, many daughters of poor families worked as nursemaids, or *komori,* during the early-modern age. Before the early-modern age, *komori* was merely a family duty left to older siblings while parents were working in the fields. Luis Frois, who came to Japan as a Portuguese missionary in the sixteenth century, noted that young Japanese girls were carrying babies on their backs almost all the time (Frois 1991). By the late eighteenth century, the practice of hiring young girls as *komori* emerged and continued until the early twentieth century (Akamatsu 1994; Akasaka 2006). Most *komori* were contracted for a specified period, typically three, five, or ten years. Their parents received money and rice at the beginning of the contract periods. Sending their daughters away to work as *komori* also meant a reduction in the number of mouths to feed at home. Girls began working as *komori* at the ages of five or six (Tamanoi 1991).

The life of a *komori* can be glimpsed in the *komori* songs. There are numerous traditional lullabies in Japan, most of which are purely for the sake of making a baby sleep or cradling a crying baby. Yet, others are by and for *komori* themselves and embody their own emotions and thoughts. Even today, their anger, resignation, and longing for their hometowns are apparent in their lullabies.

In the late Edo era, markets for physical commodities developed rapidly. As a result, successful merchants and rich farmers emerged and swelled the demand for female *komori.* With the start of the Meiji era, many *komori* were absorbed into the factory labor force with the rapid modernization of industries. In other cases, they became prostitutes after having worked as *komori* during their girlhoods. Akamatsu points out that female workers' songs in the spinning factories have characteristics in common with *komori* songs and concludes that they shared the same social background (Akamatsu 1994).

Child Labor in the Modern Age: Early Industrialization

After the Meiji Restoration in 1868, Japan was released from its feudal system, enabling people to choose their occupations freely. With this liberalization, a modern economy began to grow, and Japan experienced its industrial revolution. Modern industries created huge employment opportunities for low-wage workers. Moreover, both abortion and infanticide were banned in 1869. Consequently, the birth rate rose and the bias against female babies disappeared. These conditions were factors that led to the existence of child wage-earning laborers.

There are two main studies on child labor during Japan's early industrialization. One is the 1899 book titled *Nihon no kasō shakai* (Lower classes of Japan) by Gennosuke Yokoyama (Yokoyama 1949). It was based on reports on the work and lives of members of the lower classes in the late nineteenth century. The other study is a 1903 book titled *Shokkō jijō* (Factory workers' conditions), containing surveys of factories in all industries in Japan conducted around 1900 by the Ministry of Agriculture and Commerce (Nōshōmushō 1998).

These two studies show that many child laborers were in factories doing such tasks as making matches, weaving rugs, and reeling and spinning silk. Yokoyama (1949) reported that there were many more child laborers in the match and rug factories than in any others. In a chapter of *Shokkō jijō,* there are surveys of fourteen match factories in the Kansai region from 1900 to 1902 and of rug-weaving factories in Osaka in 1900. According to the surveys, 40 percent of the 5,330 employees in the match industry were children under fourteen, and 50.7 percent of the 9,014 employees in the rug industry were under fourteen (Nōshōmushō 1998).

These factories were often built in the slums of Kobe and Osaka, as they required masses of cheap laborers, and accordingly, all family members in these districts could work in the factories. Making matches was unskilled work: Male workers coating match heads with chemicals were paid daily wages; however, the majority of workers were paid by the piece. For that reason, children could easily participate in match-making work after school. For the same reason, 75 percent of all employees were female. According to the survey, many seven- or eight-year-olds were in the match factories. The survey reported there were 194 child laborers (62 males, 132 females) under the age of ten but pointed out that there were, in reality, more than that. Furthermore, girls accounted for 74 percent of child laborers under fourteen.

Conditions in the rug industry were quite similar. Owing to the simplicity of the work, there were many child laborers. Children under the age of ten accounted for 10 percent of all employees, and the youngest children were six or seven years old. No doubt their tasks were simple, but they worked as much as a twelve-hour day. Again, girls accounted for 73 percent of child laborers under fourteen.

In the silk-reeling industry, mechanization was relatively slow because most companies were small. However, the volumes of silk exported were enormous. The total number of workers in factories with more than ten employees had already reached 100,781 in 1898 (Nōshōmushō 1998). The silk-reeling industry had more workers than any other industry at the beginning of industrialization. In the spinning industry, on the other hand, the number of workers gradually increased with rapid mechanization. Despite such differences between the two industries, both had an important role in the industrialization of Japan from the late nineteenth century to the early twentieth century (Nishinarita 1988). According to the *Kojō yōran* (General survey of factories), in 1902 women constituted 92.2 percent of the silk-reeling workforce and 77.5 percent of the spinning workforce (Gonse 1972). These female workers were mainly from poor peasant families who had left their villages for work in factories. As the Industrial Revolution came late to Japan, the industry was able to introduce the latest ring-spinning machine, requiring little physical strength or skill. This allowed for massive employment of low-paid female workers.

A survey of sixteen spinning factories in the Kansai region revealed that half of the 27,472 employees were women under the age of twenty. The proportion of children under age fourteen was 10.2 percent, and it is reported that there were quite a few children under the age of ten. In contrast, there were few children under the age of ten in the silk-reeling factories. According to a survey of 205 factories in Nagano in 1898, the proportion of children under fourteen among the 13,620 employees was 14.7 percent, the majority female (Nōshōmushō 1998).

Saito concluded that the reason why these leading industries employed juvenile labor, but not many school-age children, was because Japanese people desire to preserve the family unit. In Japan family ties are very strong. Mothers or older children in families participated in the labor force first, and young children started to work only in cases regarded as a "vital necessity" (Saito 1996, 1997). This interpretation, however, does not take gender differences into consideration. In most cases, girls rather than boys were forced to go out to work. The Meiji civil code gave male household members—such as the father and the first son—authority to maintain the family system. The discrepancy in birth rate disappeared because of the family policy of the Meiji government. Therefore, there would have been a household labor surplus in girls. Even in the match and rug industries, where all family members could work, the proportion of female child laborers was much higher than that of males. Another reason why there were few young child laborers is that the majority of these factories had dormitory systems. It would have been difficult for very young children to live independently in the dormitories, so girls who had reached a certain age went out to work in the factories in order to support the family and to reduce the number of mouths to feed in the household.

Some authors overestimate the influence of early universal education on child labor in Japan. The Meiji government announced the establishment of universal education in 1872. However, in 1903, 41.5 percent of girls in the spinning and silk-reeling industry had no education, and 50.4 percent had dropped out of primary school

(Nōshōmushō 1998). The purpose of education for girls was different than for boys. Girls were imbued with women's roles in the family (Miyoshi 2000). Thus, it was more important for girls to sacrifice themselves for the sake of their families than to become well educated. Therefore, not only poverty but also the low status of women were crucial determinants for children going out to work. In fact, of the total of 20,115 children under fourteen in major industries in 1902, 15,790 were girls (Gonse 1972). The number of working girls was almost three times that of boys.

The girls' working conditions were harsh. They were subjected to cruelties including sexual abuse. Their conditions are documented at length in *Shokkō jijō* (Nōshōmushō 1998). Also, in 1925, Wakizo Hosoi published *Jokō aishi* (The pitiful history of female factory workers), which included a detailed record of work and life in the Japanese spinning industry for females (Hosoi 1954). In 1977, Shigemi Yamamoto published *Aa, Nomugi tōge: aru seishi kōjo aishi* (Ah, Nomugi pass: the pitiful history of some female silk workers), based on interviews of several hundred former workers in the silk-reeling factories (Yamamoto 1977). Finally, E. Patricia Tsurumi (1990) provides a wealth of information in English in her study on factory girls in the thread mills of Meiji Japan.

In the spinning industry, unlike silk reeling, double shifts were adopted for the sake of efficiency. Employees occasionally worked all night, and conditions were so severe that a large number of the girls died of tuberculosis. According to Osamu Ishihara's (1970) study, of 80,000 girls who returned home one year, 13,000 had tuberculosis. While there was no double shift in the silk-reeling industry, the girls worked at least thirteen hours a day and seventeen or eighteen hours during busy periods. Nevertheless, in both industries, wages were quite low. In the late nineteenth century, girls' wages were lower than those in India, and just half of the wages for Japanese men (Nishinarita 1988). The girls could not easily escape from such dreadful conditions. They were bound by the employment contract between their employers and their fathers. In many cases, parents in the countryside had received a large advance loan against their daughters' future earnings. The girls were victims of debt bondage.

Children were employed in other industries, including glassmaking, iron manufacturing (mainly shipbuilding), and printing industries. According to a survey in 1899, there were relatively more boys in the glass industry, though still quite a few girls. In a factory in Tokyo, 83 out of 180 male employees were children under fourteen. In the glass factories in Osaka, 1,390 out of 3,423 male workers were children under fourteen. In the iron industry, only 6 percent of workers were children, and these were boys. In the printing industry, 15 percent were children under fourteen, and boys were the overwhelming majority (Nōshōmushō 1998).

Boys aimed at becoming skilled workers during their apprenticeships in these industries. During their probationary period they received no payment. They were given only the basic necessities such as food and clothing, and nothing more than a small allowance. However, their working conditions were better than those of the girls in the spinning and silk-reeling factories. Labor unions had already been established in some companies in the iron and printing industries. Furthermore, the children were not recruited by force or deception and were not bound to their employers (Murakami 1986).

Child Labor After Enforcement of the First Factory Law

A bill to protect the rights of women and children was first put on the national agenda in 1887. The Diet, however, did not pass this bill until 1911, and the Factory Law was not enforced until 1916. The 1911 law had several problems. First, it prohibited children under the age of twelve from working as a general principle, but those older than ten were allowed to work as long as their tasks were simple and easy. Therefore, industries might employ children even before they had completed compulsory education, as the law also permitted employment of such children provided that they could either study at the workplace or commute to a primary school nearby. Further, the law was applicable only to factories with fifteen employees or more.

Was the 1911 Factory Law effective in reducing the number of child workers? Some argue that the law merely forced them to work in worse situations outside the law's jurisdiction. A survey conducted in 1919 shows that the national total of employed workers under twelve years old was around 70,000. A large proportion of children were engaged as *komori*. Four times as many girls as boys were *komori*. It is conceivable that girls were forced to change jobs to those where the Factory Law did not apply (Tanaka 1967). In fact, many primary schools began *komori* classes, where children studied while nursing younger children (Ishii 1992).

Silk-reeling factories with a large number of girls under age twelve set up primary schools on their premises. It was, however, virtually impossible for those girls to manage their work and study. They either had to study during the day and work the night shift, or vice versa. The true reason behind such in-house schools was for factories to secure the necessary number of laborers during busy periods. They attracted school-age girls by advertising the existence of a school on the premises (Hosoi 1954).

During the Shōwa era (1926–1989), the whole country went through an unprecedented economic crisis called the Shōwa Depression in 1931, following the Great Depression. The number of wage-earning workers drastically dropped, and unemployment increased. In agriculture, poverty among farmers became a severe problem after the poor harvests and cold-weather damage of 1931 and 1934. This resulted in an increase in families selling daughters into prostitution (Yamashita 2001). The system of licensed brothels dating back to the Edo period spread across the country during the Meiji era. Repeated protests to abolish prostitution did not succeed until after World War II.

Postwar Child Labor

Immediately after World War II, it became common to see children who had lost at least one parent during the war polishing shoes or selling newspapers on street corners. The government reacted quickly to problems of street children and introduced a string of bills that eventually led to enforcement of the Child Welfare Law in 1947.

In early December 1948, newspapers began reporting the trafficking of war orphans. For example, the *Mainichi* newspaper reported in February 1949 that eleven brokers dealing in human trafficking had been turned over to the Public Prosecutor's Office. The paper reported they had sold 103 children—most were age thirteen or fourteen—and had received payments in advance. According to an official report issued by the Bureau for Women and Children of the Ministry of Labor for 1948–1949, 70 percent of the victims were under eighteen, and fourteen- to sixteen-year-olds were most prevalent. Most had been sold to wealthy farming families to work in agriculture (Ohara Institute of Social Research 1952).

Despite these reports, human trafficking continued and the number of related arrests increased. Data from the Metropolitan Police Department show that, in 1956, there were 15,595 arrests connected to human trafficking, of which 2,107 cases were under eighteen (2,072 females) and 98 were under fourteen (67 females). The majority were women who ended up in commercial sex industries (Ohara Institute of Social Research 1958). Not surprisingly, about half of those arrested said they had sold themselves because of poverty. As a result of this social phenomenon, the Diet enacted the Law for the Prevention of Prostitution.

During the rapid economic growth of the 1960s, the rate of domestic human trafficking decreased rapidly. However, a new problem has come to light in the sex industry since the 1980s: the importation of women, including minor girls, from countries such as the Philippines, Thailand, and Colombia into Japan for employment as prostitutes (Yoshida and Japan Network Against Trafficking in Persons 2004).

The connection between poverty and prostitution has become less obvious in recent years, but different types of sexual exploitation of children are increasing. Delinquents involved in sexual activities are becoming younger, and girls under eighteen are sometimes lured into prostitution through so-called *enjo kōsai* (assisting dates online). Moreover, cases in which Japanese males have been involved in child prostitution in other countries have increased. These problems led to the enforcement of the Law for Child Prostitution and Pornography in 2002. In light of globalization, human trafficking has been increasing internationally. Twenty-first-century problems of child labor in Japan are particularly noticeable in terms of commercial sexual exploitation. As a result of international criticism, the government started to tackle human-trafficking problems in 2000 and aims to eradicate them.

Conclusion

In Japan, the view that "children are treasures" has been common for generations. Moreover, the people's desire to preserve the family was strengthened by the strategies of the Meiji government. However, there has been a gender gap. Some argue that the numbers of child laborers in early industrial Japan was not significant in comparison to other industrializing nations. Yet, many girls have been involved in child labor throughout Japan's history. Importantly, the practice of buying girls from poor families was already common through the Edo-era licensed-prostitution system. Such a gender-biased view helped to justify the harsh conditions of the factory girls later. There are some important similarities among *kamuro* (prostitutes), *komori* (nursemaids), and factory girls from this historical perspective. The persistence of a gender-biased view appears to be closely linked to contemporary Japanese problems of human trafficking and commercial sexual exploitation of children. These gender problems are intrinsically related to child labor in Japan.

References and Further Reading

Akamatsu, Keisuke. *Minyō waika no minzokugaku* [Folklore of folksongs]. Tokyo: Akashi Shoten, 1994.

Akasaka, Norio. *Komori uta no tanjō* [The birth of lullabies]. Tokyo: Kōdansha Gakujutsu Bunko, 2006.

Frois, Luis. *Yōroppa bunka to nihon bunka* [European culture and Japanese culture]. Trans. Okada Akio. Tokyo: Iwanami Shoten, 1991.

Gonse, Tomohiko. "Jidō rōdō no jitsujō to jidō hogo no shisō: kōjohō seiritsu katei no dankai ni oite" [The reality of child labor and the idea of child protection: the process of the enforcement of factory law]. *Kindaishi Kenkyū* [Modern history studies] 16 (1972): 16–25.

Hosoi, Wakizo. *Jokō aishi* [The pitiful history of female factory workers]. Tokyo: Iwanami Shoten, 1954; first ed., 1925.

Inoue, Kiyoshi. *Shinpan nihon no joseishi* [The history of women in Japan, new ed.]. Tokyo: Sanitsu Shobo, 1967.

Ishii, Shōji. *Kindai no jidō rōdō to yakan shogakkō* [Child labor and night school in the modern age]. Tokyo: Akashi Shoten, 1992.

Ishihara, Osamu. "Jokō to kekkaku" [Female factory workers and tuberculosis]. In *Jokō to kekkaku* [Female factory workers and tuberculosis], ed. Kagoyama Takashi. Tokyo: Kōseikan, 1970.

Maki, Hidemasa. *Jinshin baibai* [Human trafficking]. Tokyo: Iwanami Shoten, 1971.

Miyoshi, Nobuhiro. *Nihon no josei to sangyō kyōiku* [Japanese women and industrial education]. Tokyo: Toshindo, 2000.

Murakami, Nobuhiko. *Meiji joseishi: onna no shokugyō* [The history of women in the Meiji era: women's occupations]. Tokyo: Rironsha, 1986.

Nishinarita, Yutaka. *Kinsei nihon rōshi kankeishi* [The history of labor relations in the early modern age in Japan]. Tokyo: Tokyo University Press, 1988.

Nōshōmushō [Ministry of Agriculture and Commerce] *Shokkō jijō* [Factory workers' conditions]. Vols. 1–3. Corrected and ed. Inumaru Giichi. Tokyo: Iwanami Shoten, 1998; first ed., 1903.

Ochiai, Emiko. "Kinsei matsu ni okeru mabiki to shussan" [Infanticide and births toward the end of the early modern age]. In *Nihon no jendā shi* [Japan's gender history], vol. 1, ed. Wakita Haruko and Suzan Hanley. Tokyo: Tokyo University Press, 1994.

Ohara Institute of Social Research. *Nihon rōdō nenkan* [Japanese labor yearbook]. Vol. 24. 1952.

———. *Nihon rōdō nenkan* [Japanese labor yearbook]. Vol. 30. 1958.

Saito, Osamu. "Children's Work, Industrialism and the Family Economy in Japan." In *Child Labour in Historical Perspective 1800–1985: Case Studies from Europe, Japan and Colombia*, ed. Hugh Cunningham and Pier Paolo Viazzo, 73–90. Italy: UNICEF International Child Development Centre, 1996.

———. "Rekishi no naka no jidō rōdō: Yōroppa, Nippon, Koronbia" [Child labor in history: case studies in Europe, Japan and Colombia]. In *Hikakushi no enkinhō* [Perspectives in the history of comparative studies], ed. Osamu Saito, 217–39. Tokyo: NTT Shuppan, 1997.

Sone, Hiromi. *Shōfu to kinsei shakai* [Prostitutes in early modern society]. Tokyo: Yoshikawa Kōbunkan, 2003.

Tamanoi, Mariko Asano. "Songs as Weapons: The Culture and History of *Komori* (Nursemaids) in Modern Japan." *Journal of Asian Studies* 50:4 (1991): 793–817.

Tanaka, Katsufumi. "Jidō rōdō to kyōiku: toku ni 1911 nen no kōjohō no sekō wo megutte" [Child labor and education: with respect to the application of the 1911 Factory Law]. *Kyōiku Shakaigaku Kenkyū* [Sociological education studies] 22 (1967): 148–61.

Tsurumi, E. Patricia. *Factory Girls: Women in the Thread Mills of Meiji Japan.* Princeton, NJ: Princeton University Press, 1990.

Yamamoto, Shigemi. *Aa, Nomugi tōge: aru seishi kōjo aishi* [Ah, Nomugi pass: the pitiful history of some female silk workers]. Tokyo: Kadokawa Bunko, 1977.

Yamamoto, Shunichi. *Nihon koushoshi* [Japan's history of licensed prostitution]. Tokyo: Chuohouki Shuppan, 1983.

Yamashita, Fumio. *Shōwa Tōhoku daikyōsaku* [The harvest failure of Tōhoku region in the Shōwa era]. Tokyo: Mumeisha Shuppan, 2001.

Yokoyama, Gennosuke. *Nihon no kasō shakai* [Lower classes in Japanese society]. Tokyo: Iwanami Shoten, 1949; first ed., 1899.

Yoshida, Yoko, and Japan Network Against Trafficking in Persons, eds. *Jinshin baibai wo nakusu tame ni* [In order to eliminate human trafficking]. Tokyo: Akashi Shoten, 2004.

Education and Child Labor in Japan

Richard Grabowski, Professor of Economics, Department of Economics, Southern Illinois University; and **Sharmistha Self,** Assistant Professor, Department of Economics, Missouri State University

It was estimated that as of 2000 there were 186 million child laborers worldwide (Basu and Tzannatos 2006). This is a problem of stunning proportions, but it is not a new problem. Historically, child labor has accompanied the industrialization process in a number of countries that are today highly developed. Thus, in trying to understand the forces giving rise to child labor, and to develop policies to reduce it, an examination of historical experience would seem to be useful. This short essay analyzes Japanese experience with child labor, paying particular attention to the impact of education. Given that Japan is the only non-Western nation to industrialize, it is of great interest to analyze its child labor experience. The main problem is the limited amount of historical data available. Perhaps the best discussion of Japanese experience using country data is presented in Saito's (1996) work.

Japanese history is often divided into the Tokugawa period (1600–1867) and the Meiji period (1868–1912). It is the beginning of the Meiji period, 1868, that is usually taken as the starting point for industrialization or modern economic growth in Japan. The first factory laws aimed at regulating child labor were not passed until 1911, and they came into effect in 1916. Employment of children under twelve was prohibited, and by 1926 night work was also eliminated and twelve-hour workdays for children under fifteen came into being. However, some scholars believe that by that time most children were already out of the factories and in schools. In 1872, educational ordinances issued by the Meiji government announced the establishment of universal education. By 1879, four years of schooling were compulsory, and by 1900 all school fees were abolished. As of 1911, according to Nardinelli (1990), 98 percent of children between the ages of six and thirteen were in school. This would seem to indicate that child labor was in rapid decline prior to enactment of laws aimed at regulating this activity.

Saito's work provides evidence from investigations conducted by the Industry Department of the Ministry of Agriculture and Commerce. These investigations covered only factories with ten operatives or more in 1899, while in 1904 and 1914 they covered factories of five operatives or more. The data measured the proportion of the labor force made up of children, with children being defined by several different age spans. The results indicate that there were very few children under twelve, male or female, employed in any of these three years. There was a larger role played by children twelve to fourteen. The data indicate that males made up 6 percent of the labor force in 1899, 3 percent in 1909, and 3 percent in 1914. Rates for females were twice as high. This indicates a declining usage of twelve- to fourteen-year-old children as industrialization proceeded.

Since most modern manufacturing occurs in larger firms, Saito breaks down the data by size of firm. There is no discernible pattern for males in terms of the percent of the labor force. However, for twelve- to fourteen-year-old females a pattern does emerge. The percentage of the labor force made up of twelve- to fourteen-year-old females rises with the size of establishment (from 13 percent to 17 percent in 1899, and from 6 percent to 10 percent in 1909). However, by 1914 this pattern disappeared and the percentage of twelve- to fourteen-year-old females employed declined for the larger establishments.

The expansion of manufacturing in the early Meiji period was dominated by cotton spinning and silk reeling. The proportion of males and females twelve to fourteen years of age employed in these industries in 1900 were 9 percent (male) and 12 percent (female) in cotton spinning and 4 percent (male) and 10 percent (female) in silk reeling. Thus, female laborers twelve to fourteen years of age did play a significant role, although children under twelve (whether male or female) did not. However, female employment (twelve- to fourteen-year-olds) in more traditional manufacturing such as rug weaving, rope braiding, and paper products was higher. Thus, the expansion of modern manufacturing did not seem to employ an extremely high percentage of twelve- to fourteen-year-old females, especially in comparison with more traditional manufacturing activities.

Saito also examined data from a census taken in 1879 in the Yamanashi Prefecture. It provides data on children's age-specific activity rates by single years. Age profiles of workforce participation indicate that few children entered the labor force before the age of eleven. The proportion working was slightly over 10 percent by age eleven for both sexes, rising to reach 90 percent by age fifteen. Saito designates this as "late starting" in the labor force. The average age that both males and females entered the labor force was around thirteen years. Thus, the evidence shows that while industrialization in Japan found increasing employment of juveniles, it did not come with increased child labor practices.

This experience seems to have been very different from that of England and other European nations. Saito explores the idea that perhaps this difference was due to the effects of education, noting the educational reforms of the Meiji government in the 1870s. Cunningham and Viazzo (1996) point out that simply passing laws relating to compulsory education would not be effective if parents needed to be convinced about the returns to educating their children. Clearly, parents in Japan must have been convinced. Saito points out that by 1905 the proportion of male children enrolled in school approached 98 percent. The interesting point is that as early as 1875 the enrollment rate was already 51 percent, while a substantially higher proportion of children could already read and write (Saito 1996). This latter fact is puzzling in that it implies that a significant amount of literacy existed prior to the Meiji educational reforms. According to Dore (1965) the literacy and school-attendance rates in Japan prior to the Meiji period (at the end of the Tokugawa period) were far higher than those for most European countries at that time.

For commoners the most important educational institution was the *terakoya,* a form of schooling that was completely unregulated by the government. These schools accepted both boys and girls. Usually children entered at the age of six or seven and continued their education until age ten to thirteen. The teaching concentrated on reading, writing, and calculation. Reliable statistics on these schools are very limited. However, it appears that in the late Tokugawa period, there were 1,200 of these schools around Edo (modern-day Tokyo) and the total number in the country was in excess of 15,000. What is also important is that most of these schools were supported by fees and private donations. "It was increasingly recognized by the people themselves that the sacrifice of money and time for education was economically worthwhile" (Kobayashi 1965, 293–94).

How is one to explain the Japanese experience with child labor? First, consider some fundamentals of economic theory. Assume that child schooling is a leisure good, implying that as incomes (in particular wages) rise, families choose to remove children from the labor force and enter them in school. Next, assume that child and adult labor are substitutes, subject to an adult equivalency correction. Now consider a rural agricultural economy of the kind that existed in the late Tokugawa period in Japan. Agriculture, especially in developing countries, is typified by low-level, labor-intensive technology where adult and child labor can be easily substituted. If demand for labor is very low, wages are low and families need their children to work if the family is to generate a subsistence income. As the demand for labor grows and wages rise, eventually incomes will be high enough that families can choose to remove children from the labor market (Basu and Tzannatos 2006). Demand for labor in agriculture depends on a number of factors, the most important of which is likely to be technological change. Improving technology is likely to increase demand for labor, both directly and indirectly. Similarly, improving technology is also likely to influence the attractiveness of education for children. Because of the enhanced skills required and higher wages provided by improved technology, future returns from education rise, fewer children will enter the job market, and more will enter school. Utilizing data drawn from the green-revolution period in India, Foster and Rosenzweig (1996) have found that technological change had a significant positive effect on returns to education.

By applying this economic theory to the late Tokugawa period (1700s), a meaningful explanation can be provided for the peculiar experience of Japan during the Meiji period with respect to child labor. The Tokugawa period has often been portrayed as a time of extreme poverty, involving the exploitation of the peasantry and stagnation and famine in the countryside. However, in recent decades a new view of this period, especially the latter part, has emerged.

Beginning in the latter part of the 1600s and the early part of the 1700s, a long process of slow but appreciable agricultural growth began to occur. Given the slow growth of the population, this agricultural growth resulted in a rise in output per person (Hanley and Yamamura 1972). The increase in output was, according to Smith (1973), substantially captured by the farmers themselves. The result of this slow rise in income was an expansion in demand for nonagricultural goods. Thus, proto-manufacturing and handicraft activities grew in response such that, by the mid-eighteenth century, many farmers were involved in nonagricultural activities and employment. As a result, specialization and the division of labor resulted in a process of economic growth with productivity slowly increasing. Thus by the end of the Tokugawa period peasant farmers were far better off than they had been previously (Hauser 1983). Similar conclusions have been drawn, in an indirect way, by Ramseyer (1995). Ramseyer's study focused on relationships among Japanese urban workers, peasant employment contracts, and parental control over working-age children for the period 1600 to the mid-eighteenth century. In the process of trying to ascertain determinants of parental control over children, Ramseyer found that there was a marked decline in the hiring of children for long-term employment. In terms of the change in employment patterns, he concluded that the reason was the development of a large nonagricultural labor market in Japan during that period.

If the theory discussed earlier is applied to this experience, a number of explanations concerning child labor in Japan can be developed. The economic growth experienced raised demand for labor in a Japan that was rapidly becoming commercialized, and this, in turn, raised the standard of living of peasant farmers. The rising wage rates and increased opportunities for employment lessened the family's dependence on child labor. Additionally, the technological innovation that occurred in late Tokugawa Japan increased the return to education. This, along with changing family values in favor of education, resulted in the reduction of child labor practices in early-modern Meiji Japan.

References and Further Reading

Basu, Kaushik, and Zafiris Tzannatos. "The Global Child Labor Problem: What Do We Know and What Can We Do?" *World Bank Economic Review* 17:2 (2006): 147–73.

Cunningham, Hugh, and Paolo Viazzo, ed. *Child Labour in Historical Perspective 1800–1985: Case Studies from Europe, Japan, and Colombia.* Italy: UNICEF International Child Development Center, 1996.

Dore, R.P. *Education in Tokugawa Japan.* Berkeley: University of California Press, 1965.

Foster, A.D., and M.R. Rosenzweig. "Technical Change and Human Capital Returns and Investments: Evidence from the Green Revolution." *American Economic Review* 86:4 (2006): 931–53.

Hanley, S., and K. Yamamura. *Economic and Demographic Change in Preindustrial Japan, 1600–1868.* Princeton, NJ: Princeton University Press, 1972.

Hauser, W. "Some Misconceptions About the Economic History of Tokugawa Japan." *History Teacher* 16:4 (1983): 569–83.

Kobayashi, T. "Tokugawa Education as a Foundation of Modern Education in Japan." *Comparative Education Review* 9:3 (1965): 288–302.

Nardinelli, Clark. *Child Labor and the Industrial Revolution.* Bloomington: Indiana University Press, 1990.

Ramseyer, Mark, J. "The Market for Children: Evidence from Early Modern Japan." *Journal of Law, Economics, and Organization* 11:1 (1995): 127–49.

Saito, O. "Children's Work, Industrialism and the Family Economy in Japan: 1872–1926." In *Child Labor in Historical Perspective 1800–1985: Case Studies from Europe, Japan and Colombia,* ed. H. Cunningham and P.O. Viazzo, 73–90. Florence: UNICEF International Child Development Centre, 1996.

Smith, T.C. "Premodern Economic Growth: Japan and the West." *Past and Present* 60:1 (1973): 127–69.

Mongolia

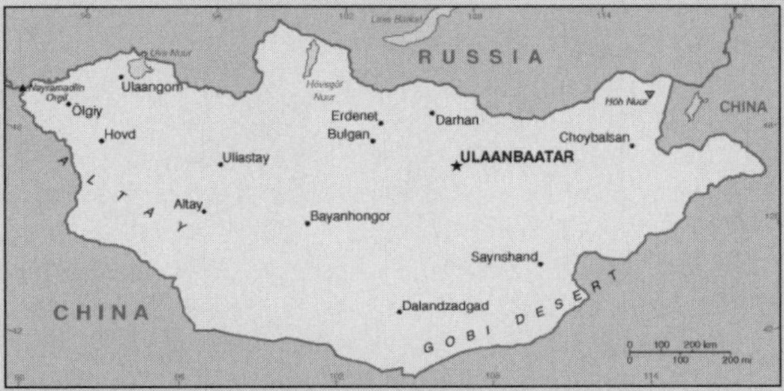

MONGOLIA			
	CRC	C 138	C 182
Ratifications	Y	Y	Y
Human Development Index/Rank	0.691/116		
Human Capital			
Population Growth Rate	1.46%		
% Population 0–14	27.9%		
Total Fertility Rate	2.25		
Life Expectancy	64.89		
Infant Mortality Rate	52.12		
Literacy Rate	97.8%		
Economic			
GDP/Capita	$2,000		
GDP Growth %	7.5%		
% Poverty	36.1%		
Gini Index	44		
Labor Force Composition			
% Agriculture	39.9%		
% Industry	31.4%		
% Services	28.7%		

CHILD ACTIVITY BREAKDOWN, BY SEX AND RESIDENCE

RESIDENCE	Percentage of children in the relevant age-group[a]									
	Economic activity only		School only		Combining school and economic activity		Neither in school nor in economic activity		Child labor[b]	
	Male	Female	Male	Female	Male	Female	Male	Female	Male	Female
Urban	0.3	0.2	85.7	88.2	4.6	3.4	9.4	8.1	n/av	n/av
Rural	5.0	2.5	63.9	71.1	16.5	13.6	14.5	12.7	n/av	n/av
Total	2.6	1.3	75.3	79.8	10.3	8.5	11.8	10.4	18.9	17.4

Source: Mongolia, Multiple Indicator Cluster Survey, 2005 (see UCW Project Web site, http://www.ucw-project.org, country statistics).

Notes: [a]Children age 5 to 14. [b]Estimate includes (a) children under age 12 engaged in economic activities, (b) children age 12–14 engaged in excessive economic activities (more than 14 hours per week), and (c) children under age 15 engaged in excessive household chores (at least 28 hours per week). Estimate does not account for children engaged in hazardous work or other unconditional "worst forms" of child labor.

Section 2. Southeast Asia

Cambodia

CAMBODIA			
	CRC	C 138	C 182
Ratifications	Y	Y	Y
Human Development Index/Rank	0.583/129		
Human Capital			
Population Growth Rate	1.78%		
% Population 0–14	35.6%		
Total Fertility Rate	3.37		
Life Expectancy	59.29		
Infant Mortality Rate	68.78		
Literacy Rate	73.6		
Economic			
GDP/Capita	$2,600		
GDP Growth %	13.4%		
% Poverty	40%		
Gini Index	40		
Labor Force Composition			
% Agriculture	75%		
% Industry	n/av		
% Services	n/av		

CHILD ACTIVITY BREAKDOWN, BY SEX AND RESIDENCE

RESIDENCE	Percentage of children in the relevant age-group[a]									
	Economic activity only		School only		Combining school and economic activity		Neither in school nor in economic activity		Child labor[b]	
	Male	Female	Male	Female	Male	Female	Male	Female	Male	Female
Urban	5.3	6.3	48.4	46.6	28.4	29.3	17.9	17.8	n/av	n/av
Rural	8.8	9.7	29.8	30.5	38.7	37.0	22.7	22.9	n/av	n/av
Total	**8.2**	**9.0**	**33.2**	**33.5**	**36.8**	**35.6**	**21.9**	**22.0**	**39.2**	**38.1**

Source: Cambodia, Cambodia Child Labour Survey, 2001 (see UCW Project Web site, http://www.ucw-project.org, country statistics).

Notes: [a]Children age 5 to 14. [b]Estimate includes (a) children under age 12 engaged in economic activities, (b) children age 12–14 engaged in excessive economic activities (more than 14 hours per week), and (c) children under age 15 engaged in excessive household chores (at least 28 hours per week). Estimate does not account for children engaged in hazardous work or other unconditional "worst forms" of child labor.

Child Labor in Cambodia

Lorenzo Guarcello, Gabriella Breglia, and **Scott Lyon,** Researchers,
Understanding Children's Work (UCW) Project

This essay provides an overview of the child labor phenomenon in its various dimensions—its extent, its nature, and its causes and consequences—in Cambodia. It is drawn from two detailed interagency reports on child labor developed by the UCW Project.

Extent of Children's Work

Child involvement in economic activity is widespread in Cambodia. In all, an estimated 52 percent of seven- to fourteen-year-olds—more than 1.4 million children in absolute terms—are economically active (all figures are for the 2001 reference year)—a very high percentage relative to other countries with similar levels of income. There is evidence that child economic activity has fallen and school enrollment increased since 2001, but data comparability issues make it difficult to assess trends in children's work with any degree of confidence.

Involvement in economic activity starts very early and rises sharply with age, inducing late school entry and early school dropout. About 16 percent of children are already economically active at age six years, and more than half of all children are economically active by the age of ten years. By the age of fifteen, the share of children working in economic activity surpasses that of children attending school. School enrollment, in contrast, peaks at 91 percent at age eleven years; thereafter, attendance declines as children begin leaving school and working exclusively. The proportion of children studying exclusively, unhindered by the exigencies of work, peaks at the age of nine, at 49 percent.

An even larger proportion of children are engaged in noneconomic productive activities, specifically housework. An estimated 79 percent of seven- to fourteen-year-olds were engaged in housework activities on a regular basis each week in 2001. Housework tends to start earlier than economic activity but is performed much less intensively. One of every two children performs double duty, that is, is involved in both housework and economic activity each week.

Child Involvement in Child Labor

Children's involvement in child labor—a legal concept reflecting the subset of work that is injurious, negative, or undesirable to children—is also very high. More than 750,000 economically active children are below the absolute minimum working age of twelve years. Additionally, 500,000 (twelve- to fourteen-year-old) children engage in nonlight economic activity that is more intensive than permitted for this age-group. More than 250,000 children age fifteen to seventeen years work in one of the seven (of sixteen) nationally identified hazardous sectors for which data are available, or are working forty-three or more hours per week. Putting these groups together yields an estimate of almost 1.5 million seven- to seventeen-year-olds in child labor, 40 percent of this age-group. It should be stressed that this is a lower-bound estimate, as it does not include involvement in nine of the sixteen nationally identified hazardous sectors, nor involvement in unconditional worst forms of work. Limited evidence from Rapid Assessment Surveys and other sources suggests that while children in unconditional worst forms constitute a small proportion of total child laborers, their numbers are by no means negligible.

Characteristics of Children's Work

Most economically active children are found on farms and work for their families. Three-quarters of economically active children are in the agriculture sector, compared to only 15 percent in commerce, 5 percent in manufacturing, and 2 percent in services. About 90 percent of economically active children work for their families as unpaid labor. Most of the remaining economically active children work as casual day laborers (7 percent). Very few economically active children (less than 2 percent) work as paid employees in formal entities, the only category currently covered by the provisions on child labor in the Cambodia Labor Law.

For the few children who report earnings, daily earnings (in-cash and in-kind) are far from inconsequential for families. On average, children earn about $1 per day, accounting for 28 percent of total household labor income. Using the child wage as an imperfect measure of the opportunity cost of schooling, and comparing it with direct schooling cost estimates, it clearly stands as the most important component of the total cost of schooling, and thus the most important cost barrier for the schooling of poor children.

Work is typically very time intensive for children. Economically active children age seven to fourteen years perform an average of almost twenty-two hours of economic activity each week. The subgroup that combines economic activity and schooling puts in a slightly shorter average workweek of twenty hours in economic activity. This is still only a little less than the twenty-three and a half hours spent on average studying each week. The total work burden of economically active children rises markedly when the noneconomic activity that these children perform is also considered. Noneconomic activity adds an average of eight hours per week to the total work burden of economically active seven- to fourteen-year-olds, bringing total average weekly working hours to almost thirty-one.

A very high proportion of economically active children face work-related hazards and dangers. Adults interviewed as part of a 2001 household survey reported considering "some aspects of their child(ren)'s work risky or dangerous" in almost two out of three cases (61 percent). Many working children also appear to have less workplace protection than their adult counterparts; half of children not using safety equipment indicate that others performing similar work did benefit from such equipment.

Impact of Children's Work

Children's work is a key factor behind the two most important and interrelated challenges to the basic education system in Cambodia: late school entry and substantial dropout starting in the upper primary grades. An empirical model investigating the impact of work on schooling indicates that school enrollment and work activities are negatively related, particularly school enrollment and economic activity. The relation between school enrollment and economic activity becomes more negative with age, particularly among girls. This indicates that the trade-off or degree of substitution between school participation and economic activity increases as the child gets older, and that this trend is especially pronounced among girls. Estimation results also suggest that work delays school entry (or prevents it altogether), which in turn reduces the probability of completing primary school.

Additional empirical analysis shows that child work has a significant detrimental effect on learning achievement, as measured by literacy and numeracy test scores. Among fourth graders, working every day before going to school reduces both literacy and numeracy test scores by 9 percentage points, even when controlling for possible differences in school quality.

The incidence of work-related illness and injury is very high among Cambodian working children, underscoring that children's work is often hazardous in nature. Adults interviewed for the 2001 survey indicated that almost half of working children in Cambodia have suffered some form of work-related ill health at some time. Regression results indicate that the probability of suffering work-related ill health decreases with the age of the child, underscoring that workplaces are especially hazardous for younger children. Girls are about 2 percentage points less likely than boys to suffer ill health, suggesting underlying differences in the nature of work tasks performed by boys and girls.

Regression results also indicate that both work intensity and work sector exert a significant effect on the probability of negative health outcomes. Each hour of work performed during a week adds an additional 0.3 percentage points to the probability of falling ill. The risk of ill health due to work varies dramatically by sector. Cambodian children working in agriculture, for example, are 12 percentage points more likely to suffer injuries than those working in manufacturing. In order to face the same injury risk across sectors, children would need to log substantially different amounts of working hours. This is a key finding, as it points to a need to consider both work sector and work intensity as primary criteria for hazardous work.

Determinants of Children's Work and Schooling

Most families cite economic motives in explaining the decision to send their children to work. Either family poverty or the need to supplement family income is given as the primary motive in the case of three out of every four working children. Children's work does not appear to play a role in helping families afford children's schooling. Less than 1 percent of respondents cite schooling costs as the reason for their children working, and similarly small proportions indicate that cessation of work would force a child to leave school. It is interesting to note that, given a choice—that is, in the absence of financial constraints—two-thirds of household heads would choose to involve their children in some form of education.

The findings of a multivariate analysis point to a number of additional factors influencing household decisions to involve children in work or school: (1) household income or wealth negatively affects child labor supply; (2) exposure to early childhood education reduces child labor supply; (3) presence of preschool-age children reduces school attendance, especially of girls; (4) school availability reduces children's work involvement and increases enrollment; (5) school quality helps working children to remain in school; (6) presence of parents' associations increases school attendance and retention and reduces child work; (7) parents' education, especially mothers' education, reduces child labor supply; (8) possession of productive assets in agriculture is positively related to the child labor supply; (9) children who are offspring of the household head are less likely to work; (10) non-Khmer children are more likely to work; and (11) female-headed households are more likely to send children to work than to school.

National Response to Child Labor

Cambodia has made a number of important legal commitments in the area of child labor, but important ambiguities and gaps in legislation relating to child labor remain. Of particular concern, the Cambodia Labor Law has not been extended to informal-sector enterprises or settings, where the overwhelming majority of child laborers are concentrated. The law also does not specifically define what constitutes child labor in terms of type of work, conditions of work, and work hazards. The enforcement of child labor laws is another major challenge facing the government. By its own admission, the government currently does not have the capacity to properly enforce and monitor laws relating to child labor.

Cambodia's national development plans are highlighted in the second Socio-Economic Development Plan, the National Poverty Reduction Strategy, the 2003 Cambodian Millennium Development Goals, the Rectangular Strategy, and the National Strategic Development Plan 2006–2010. Of these, the Cambodian Millennium Development Goals and National Poverty Reduction Strategy documents contain specific child labor reduction targets. The Cambodian Millennium Development Goals document targets a reduction in the proportion of five- to seventeen-year-old working children from 16.5 percent in 1999 to 13 percent in 2005, 10.6 percent in 2010, and 8 percent in 2015. The National Poverty Reduction Strategy targeted a reduction of labor force participation of children aged ten to fourteen years from 8.3 percent in 1999 to 5.3 percent in 2005.

References and Further Reading

Cruz, A., and L. Ratana. *Understanding Children's Work in Cambodia: Mapping and Costing Current Programmes Targeting the Worst Forms of Child Labour*. Rome: Understanding Children's Work (UCW) Project, University of Rome, Tor Vergata, 2007.

UCW Project. *Children's Work in Cambodia: A Challenge for Growth and Poverty Reduction*. Rome: Understanding Children's Work (UCW) Project, University of Rome, Tor Vergata, 2006.

Indonesia

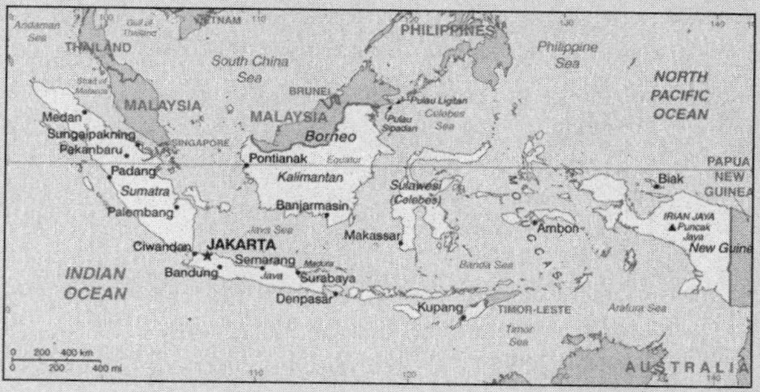

INDONESIA			
	CRC	C 138	C 182
Ratifications	Y	Y	Y
Human Development Index/Rank	0.711/108		
Human Capital			
Population Growth Rate	1.21%		
% Population 0–14	28.7%		
Total Fertility Rate	2.38		
Life Expectancy	70.16		
Infant Mortality Rate	32.14		
Literacy Rate	87.9%		
Economic			
GDP/Capita	$3,800		
GDP Growth %	5.4%		
% Poverty	17.8%		
Gini Index	34.8		
Labor Force Composition			
% Agriculture	43.3%		
% Industry	18%		
% Services	38.7%		

CHILD ACTIVITY BREAKDOWN, BY SEX AND RESIDENCE

RESIDENCE	Percentage of children in the relevant age-group[a]									
	Economic activity only		School only		Combining school and economic activity		Neither in school nor in economic activity		Child labor[b]	
	Male	Female	Male	Female	Male	Female	Male	Female	Male	Female
Urban	0.8	1.3	77.5	78.4	3.8	4.2	17.8	16.0	n/av	n/av
Rural	2.2	2.4	69.9	70.9	6.7	6.4	21.1	20.3	n/av	n/av
Total	**1.7**	**1.9**	**73.0**	**74.1**	**5.5**	**5.5**	**19.8**	**18.5**	**4.0**	**4.5**

Source: Indonesia, Indonesia Family Life Survey—third wave, 2000 (see UCW Project Web site, http://www.ucw-project.org, country statistics).
Notes: [a]Children age 7 to 14. [b]Estimate includes (a) children under age 12 engaged in economic activities and (b) children age 12–14 engaged in excessive economic activities (more than 14 hours per week). Estimate does not account for children engaged in excessive household chores, hazardous work, or other unconditional "worst forms" of child labor.

Child Labor in Indonesia

Sharon Bessell, Senior Lecturer, Crawford School of Economics and Government, Australian National University

Child labor remains an important social problem in Indonesia, but its incidence has diminished over the past several decades. In 2000, the ILO estimated that approximately 1,685,000 children between the ages of ten and fourteen were employed. This represents 7.8 percent of that age-group. Of those children who work, approximately 729,000 are girls and 955,000 are boys. Both census and labor force data from Indonesia suggest that child labor slowly but steadily decreased over the period 1971 to 2000. According to population-census data, 13 percent of children age ten to fourteen were employed in 1971. In 1980, that percentage had declined to 10.9 and by 1990 to 9.5. Over that thirty-year period, the employment of boys was consistently higher than that of girls. That picture changes, however, if unpaid work within the family in included.

The Impact of the 1997 Economic Crisis on Child Labor

In 1997 Indonesia experienced a massive financial shock as the value of the rupiah plunged, inflation skyrocketed, and foreign capital was withdrawn. The financial crisis in turn triggered social, economic, and political crises, ultimately leading to the demise of the New Order regime after three decades of authoritarian rule. In 1998 Indonesia experienced a 14 percent contraction in total GDP (Soesastro and Basri 1998). Real wages dropped between 30 and 50 percent in 1999 (Manning 2000). Against this backdrop, there were grave concerns about the impact on the incidence of child labor, as many families adopted emergency coping strategies in the face of spiraling costs for basic commodities.

According to labor force survey data, the proportion of children age ten to fourteen in waged employment increased from approximately 7 to 8 percent from 1997 to 1998. By 1999, the figure returned to 7 percent (Suryahadi, Priyambada, and Sumarto 2005). Children's employment actually fell in most sectors in 1998 but increased in agriculture (Manning 2000). Children's work—already most common in the informal and agricultural sectors prior to 1997—underwent further informalization in the wake of the crisis. The most visible consequence was the increase in children working on the streets of large cities, particularly on the most populous island of Java.

The Nature of Children's Work

Suryahadi, Priyambada, and Sumarto's study of child labor in Indonesia indicates that more than 90 percent of working children in Indonesia are between ten and fourteen years of age, with the largest proportion aged thirteen or fourteen. The incidence of child labor among five- to seven-year-olds is less than 1 percent, and among eight- and nine-year-olds around 2 percent (Suryahadi, Priyambada, and Sumarto 2005). There is no evidence to suggest that child labor is common among very young children.

Labor force survey data consistently show higher percentages of children engaged in economic activity in rural areas than in urban areas. In 1999, 9.64 percent of children in rural areas were working in paid employment. In urban areas, the percentage was 3.12 percent. Survey data also reveal that the number of hours worked by children is consistently and considerably higher in urban areas. In 2000, approximately 64 percent of working children in rural areas worked less than thirty-five hours a week, with 37 percent working between ten and twenty-four hours per week. Approximately 36 percent of working children in rural areas worked more than thirty-five hours per week, with 5.3 percent working more than fifty-five hours per week. In urban areas, in contrast, working children tend to work long hours. In 2000, only 32 percent of working children in urban centers worked less than thirty-five hours per week. Approximately 68 percent worked more than thirty-five hours per week, with approximately 28 percent working more than fifty-five hours per week.

Not surprisingly, given the concentration of child labor in rural areas, the majority of working children are engaged in agriculture. Labor force surveys from the late 1990s into the early 2000s consistently indicate that approximately two-thirds of working children are employed in the agricultural sector. The percentage of working children employed in agriculture varies across Indonesia, from a low of 61 percent in Kalimantan to a high of 85.2 percent in Sulawesi (Manning 2000). However, everywhere across the archipelago, agriculture is the main source of children's employment.

The vast majority of children's work is undertaken in small-scale and largely unregulated enterprises, which are often family owned or operated. The employment of children in large-scale, formal-sector enterprises is relatively uncommon in Indonesia. A comparatively small proportion of children work in manufacturing—a sector that tends to attract greatest attention, particularly from outside Indonesia. Those who do work in manufacturing tend to be engaged in small-scale enterprises (Manning 2000).

The Worst Forms of Child Labor

While many children work in conditions that are characterized by exploitation and hazard, slavery and bondage are not usual characteristics of child labor in Indonesia. The only documented form of systematic forced labor is the involvement of children (almost exclusively boys) in offshore fishing platforms (known as *jermal*). The *jermal* are most common in North Sumatra. Boys live and work on the platforms, sometimes for several months at a time, without adequate food, shelter, or health care. In some cases, boys are not permitted to leave the *jermal* until another child is found to replace them (Pardeon 1995). The shocking conditions that children are exposed to on the *jermal* have resulted in considerable media, public, and political attention both from within Indonesia and abroad.

While it is extremely difficult to establish numbers, recent reports indicate that commercial sexual exploitation is a problem in parts of Indonesia. A study of the commercial sexual exploitation of children in Central and West Java found two similarities among children engaged in prostitution (UNICEF 2004b). First, of the thirty child prostitutes involved in the study, all came from disadvantaged families. Second, the children's parents relied heavily on them for income and for the maintenance and well-being of the family. Rather than contributing to family income, these children were often responsible for it. An IPEC study (2004a) found a more mixed picture in terms of the socioeconomic background of sexually exploited children, with some middle-class children involved in the sex industry. The study also found that a significant proportion of children contributed significantly to their family's well-being, although parents often denied knowledge of the nature of their children's work.

A far more common form of child labor—potentially highly exploitative and subject to abuse—is domestic service. The employment of children as *pembantu* (household helpers), often in a live-in capacity, is a culturally accepted practice in Indonesia. Providing employment of this type to a "needy" child is often considered an act of benevolence. As studies in Indonesia and elsewhere have shown (Blagbrough 1995), the hidden nature of domestic service—particularly in live-in situations—makes children extremely vulnerable and regulation is difficult. Because the practice of employing child domestics is culturally and socially acceptable across Indonesia, the problem of child domestic service has been largely ignored by both government and nongovernmental organizations until very recently.

Why Do Children Work?

In a diverse, multiethnic archipelago such as Indonesia, there is no simple response to the question of why children work. Children work for a range of complex and often interrelated reasons. Poverty is an important contributing factor, with children most likely to enter the workforce prematurely when there are multiple risk factors at play. A study of children's work in East Java (UNICEF 2004a) identified family and community attitudes as critical in determining children's entry into the workforce. Importantly, attitudes toward children's work vary across individual families and from one location (often one village, or social grouping within a village) to the next. Parents' level of education is also an important contributing factor, with children of parents with a primary school education or less most likely to work (Suryahadi, Priyambada, and Sumarto 2005). Other factors, such as distance to school and current employment prospects, are also important (Daliyo, Guest, and Tirtosudarmo 1998).

Family Expectations

The concept of mutual cooperation (*gotong royong*) underpins Indonesian social life and has been used by policy makers, particularly during the authoritarian New Order period (1966–1998), as an important instrument in shaping the nation's social fabric. Ideas of cooperation and reciprocity extend into family life, whereby all able members make a contribution. Children's contribution may be in the form of paid work outside the household or unpaid work within the household. Unpaid work generally takes the form of agricultural work or work in the informal sector as part of the family unit. Here children are not paid individually, but their contribution is important in enhancing overall family income. A second form of work that children undertake is domestic work within the home (including the care of younger siblings or relatives) so as to free adults (usually women) to undertake paid work. In low-income households, these activities are the norm for children and are rarely questioned. In middle-class and wealthy households, particularly in urban centers, childhood is very different, with children's lives dominated by school and often out-of-school-hours tutorials.

Educational Quality and Children's Experience of School

During the New Order period, the expansion of primary school education was a policy priority, with considerable success in terms of increasing enrollment figures. In 1970, primary school enrollment stood at 58 percent. By 2006, more than 90 percent of children age seven to twelve were enrolled in school, with little discrepancy between boys and girls (SMERU 2005). Primary school became an expected and normalized part of children's lives.

Children's relationship with primary school is, however, often complex and difficult. Children often express a desire to attend school, seeing it as an appropriate part of childhood. However, there is often considerable ambivalence. For many children, school can be a hostile environment. Children unable to afford "voluntary" fees, uniforms, and school supplies can face humiliation at the hands of some teachers. The following extract exemplifies an experience that is not uncommon:

> When asked about school, A (aged 11) initially said "No, I no longer go to school. Why not? I must be lazy." We then talked a lot about what he does now and how it compares to being at school. A drew some pictures as we talked. He had liked some aspects of school, but found others difficult to deal with. "I often felt embarrassed. When I didn't wear shoes, the teacher pointed to my feet, and said 'this is not the way to come to school. This is bad for everyone. You must wear shoes.' I had to stand at the front—other children laughed. These things often happened. Then I no longer wanted to feel embarrassed. I stopped [going to school]." (Author's field notes, Jakarta, August 1995)

The emphasis placed on correct shoes and uniforms by school authorities—and the inability of some families to afford them—was a recurring theme among children interviewed in the mid- to late 1990s. Dropping out of school—or attending irregularly—was one of the few strategies children could employ in the face of humiliation and hostile treatment.

Other dimensions of school also come into play in determining whether children remain in school, particularly beyond late primary school. The relationship between school and future opportunities is an ambivalent one for many low-income families. While parents and children may hope that schooling will provide greater opportunities, they are often aware that these hopes may not be fulfilled. While there has been an admirable increase in the numbers of children engaged in the education system, quality remains a serious issue. In many cases, the view that schooling does not provide a pathway to greater employment opportunities is well-founded. The standard of schooling available to children from low-income families is a particular concern, often exacerbated in rural and remote areas. Teachers are often poorly trained, have no opportunity for in-service training, and work without professional support. While the consequences for the quality of education are readily apparent, there are also consequences for children's educational experience. Without training and support, classroom discipline is often grounded in punishment, in some cases quite violent forms of punishment (Beazley et al. 2006).

Thus, the inadequacies of formal school and the negative experiences of some children contribute to their exiting the education system. While school is often presented as the preferred alternative to work, it is necessary to question the nature and quality of schooling that is on offer.

Financial Pressures

Poverty is a significant contributing factor to children's involvement in the labor force. In Indonesia, poverty rates declined dramatically during the two decades prior to the economic crisis of 1997. In 1976, the percentage of households living in absolute poverty stood at 40 percent; by 1996 that figure had declined to 11 percent (Betke 2001). During that period, the percentage of average household spending on food decreased from 77 percent to 55 percent, indicating an improvement in overall social welfare.

Despite the improvement in household income and welfare status over a period of three decades, a large proportion of the population is just above the official poverty line. For low-income families in particular, the costs of school remain a significant burden. National socioeconomic survey data show that among the poorest 20 percent of households, the cost of education per student accounts for 10 percent of total household expenditure at the primary school level, rising to 18.5 percent in junior secondary school and 28.4 percent in senior secondary school (Bappenas 2005). These data suggest three likely outcomes. First, children leave school prematurely due to financial pressures. Second, children work in order to help finance their own schooling. Third, some children within a household enter the workforce in order to finance the education of siblings. Across Indonesia, each of these scenarios plays out. Thus, rather than school and work being incompatible, some children enter the workforce in order to make school a viable option.

Children's Choices

Children in Indonesia often work in situations that present dangers to their immediate and long-term health. They commonly work long hours (often the same hours as adults) and generally receive low wages. While not all work is characterised by danger or exploitation, much is. Nevertheless, it is important to recognize that some children choose to work. Research with girls working in factories on the periphery of Jakarta in the mid- to late 1990s revealed that children often made the decision to work. The other choices open to these girls were often limited, and none offered a childhood characterized by play, recreation, and learning. Within the options available to them, the girls often saw work as offering the greatest benefits, as the following quote indicates: "I send some money home to my family in the village. That helps them. It is good for me, for how they think of me—I am helping. I send some money home and I keep some. I spend the money I keep on lipstick and snacks. Sometimes I go to the cinema. I didn't do that at home [in the village], there was no money" (author's field notes, Jakarta, May 1996).

While working children often contribute at least part of their income to their families, it is not unusual for children in Indonesia to keep some of the money they earn. In a study of children's work in East Java in 2002–2003, children commonly say that a main reason for working is to have money for themselves (UNICEF 2004a). While working children often have extremely limited choices, many do exercise agency and make choices within a heavily constrained environment. While children's work should not be romanticized, it would also be inaccurate to assume that all working children are hapless victims.

In interviews and group discussions with girls aged twelve to fourteen working in pesticide factories, some girls indicated that working provided the opportunity to make or at least contribute to other decisions about their lives. Several girls said that working had two important consequences for them. First, it meant that they could delay marriage, and second, they felt more confident that they would have some input into the choice of a husband. In a social context where early marriage was not uncommon, this is an unexpected and arguably beneficial aspect of child labor.

Indonesia's Child Labor Policy Framework

International concern has been a key factor in shaping Indonesia's response to child labor over time. In the early 1990s, the government of Indonesia entered into discussions with the ILO on the subject of child labor. The ILO was in the process of establishing the International Program for the Elimination of Child Labour (IPEC), with Indonesia invited to be among the first cohort of countries to be included in the program. After lengthy negotiations, Indonesia joined IPEC in 1992.

The establishment of IPEC resulted in unprecedented attention directed toward child labor, from both within the country and beyond. In particular, the number of nongovernmental organizations increased markedly, in large part due to the funding provided by IPEC to child labor–focused organizations. Following ratification of the key ILO conventions on child labor, the Indonesian government developed a National Plan of Action on the Elimination of the Worst forms of Child Labor. The plan identifies thirteen forms of child labor to be addressed immediately through a time-bound program, with the aim of ending children's involvement within twenty years. The forms of child labor targeted through the plan are prostitution, mining, pearl diving, construction, offshore fishing (*jermal*), scavenging, the production and use of explosives, domestic work, cottage industries, plantation agriculture, logging, and work with hazardous chemicals. The plan was formalized through a presidential decree and represents the most comprehensive approach to child labor to have been adopted in Indonesia. Gaps remain in Indonesia's child labor policy framework. Nevertheless, the child labor policy framework is stronger now than at any time in Indonesia's history.

Conclusion

With official data suggesting that less than 8 percent of children age ten to fourteen are engaged in employment, child labor remains a social problem in Indonesia—but one that is declining. Through the National Plan of Action, the government of Indonesia has adopted a clear—and welcome—focus on the especially egregious forms of child labor. Yet, despite a stronger policy focus on child labor in recent years, many children continue to work without adequate protection or support.

References and Further Reading

Bappenas. "Strategi nasional penanggulangan kemiskinan" [National poverty eradication strategy]. Jakarta: Bappenas Poverty Reduction Committee, 2005.

Beazley, Harriot, Sharon Bessell, Judith Ennew, and Roxana Waterson. *What Children Say: Results of Comparative Research on the Physical and Emotional Punishment of Children in Southeast Asia and the Pacific, 2005.* Bangkok: Save the Children Sweden, 2006.

Bessell, Sharon. "The Politics of Child Labour in Indonesia: Global Trends and Domestic Policy." *Pacific Affairs* 72:3 (1999): 353–71.

Betke, Friedhelm. *The "Family-in-Focus" Approach: Developing Policy-Oriented Monitoring and Analysis of Human Development in Indonesia.* Innocenti working paper 83. Florence: UNICEF, 2001.

Blagbrough, Jonathon. *Child Domestic Work in Indonesia: A Preliminary Situation Analysis.* London: Anti-Slavery Society, 1995.

Daliyo, Marion May, Philip Guest, and Riwanto Tirtosudarmo. "Pekerja anak dan perencanaan pendidikan di Nusa Tenggara Barat dan Nusa Tenggara Timur" [Working children and education planning in East West Nusa Tenggara and East Nusa Tenggara]. Policy paper 7. LIPI, Jakarta, 1998.

IPEC. *Child Labour in the Informal Mining Sector in East Kalimantan: A Rapid Assessment.* Jakarta: ILO-IPEC, 2004a.

———. *Child Trafficking for Prostitution in Jakarta and West Java: A Rapid Assessment.* Jakarta: ILO-IPEC, 2004b.

Manning, Chris. "The Economic Crisis and Child Labour in Indonesia." ILO-IPEC working paper, ILO-IPEC, Geneva, 2000.

Pardeon, Sutrisno. "Children in Hazardous Work in the Informal Sector in Indonesia." Working paper, Atma Jaya Research Centre, Jakarta, 1995.

SMERU. "The Implementation of the School Operational Assistance (BOS) Program 2005." *SMERU Newsletter* 19 (July–September 2005).

Soesastro, Hadi, and M. Chatib Basri. "Survey of Recent Economic Developments." *Bulletin of Indonesian Economic Studies* 34:1 (1998): 3–54.

Suryahadi, Asep, Agus Priyambada, and Surdarno Sumarto. "Poverty, School and Work: Children During the Economic Crisis in Indonesia." *Development and Change* 36:2 (2005): 351–73.

UNICEF. *Kondisi dan situasi pekerja anak pada beberapa sektor di Tulungagung dan Probolinggo, Jawa Timur* [The condition and situation of working children in several sectors in Tulungagung and Probolingo, East Java]. Jakarta: UNICEF, 2004a.

UNICEF. *Participatory Research on Commercial Sexual Exploitation of Children in Surakarta (Central Java) and Indramayu (West Java), Indonesia.* Jakarta: UNICEF, 2004b.

Child Labor in Subcontracting Sectors of Indonesia's Garment and Footwear Industries

Indrasari Tjandraningsih, AKATIGA—Center for Social Analysis, Bandung, Indonesia

The garment and footwear industries in Indonesia are major sectors in the employment of children under fifteen years of age. Nevertheless, studies indicate that child labor is concentrated in small and home-based workshops where the product orientation is to the domestic market and the production system is based on subcontracting to household production units (the "putting-out" system) (IPEC 2003; IHS 2002; Irwanto et al. 1995; Haryadi and Tjandraningsih 1995).

The garment and footwear industries in Indonesia consist of home-based and small-, medium-, and large-scale industry, with a wide range of product diversification and market orientation. The Central Statistical Bureau establishes categories of industrial scale based on the number of employees involved. Home-based and small industry involve up to nineteen employees; medium-scale industry involves twenty to ninety-nine employees; and large-scale industry involves more than 100 employees. Interdependency among production units of various sizes is created through the mechanism of subcontracting—a production relationship between a firm as principal and another firm as subcontractor, where the principal places an order to the subcontractor. Subcontracting takes two forms: industrial subcontracting, when a firm places an order with another firm for manufacture of parts to be incorporated into a product, and commercial subcontracting, when a subcontractor firm manufactures a finished product for the principal (Dicken 1989).

Small and home-based workshops, where most children are employed, usually cluster in certain geographic areas, thus creating small industrial centers. The product market orientation of small and home-based enterprises aims mostly at the domestic market, though a small number also intend their products for the export market. Large- and medium-scale enterprises are usually export oriented, subcontracting for branded products of multinational corporations (Tjandraningsih 1991).

While the legal minimum age for work in manufacturing is fifteen, in the garment and footwear sectors one can easily find younger children working, with no legal sanctions whatsoever for these violations. Some children receive their own wages, working on a piece-rate basis. Others are unpaid members of a family-based workforce. Girls are more heavily involved in the garment industry, sewing, trimming clothes lining, placing the tag, folding, ironing, and packing. This work is usually performed in the living room of the employer's house or in the girl's own house. Boys dominate in the footwear industry (Thamrin 1991; IPEC 2004). The work varies from placing the sole to tracing the sole pattern to finishing and packing. This work is usually performed in a workshop dedicated to footwear production. In both sectors, children perform the same work as adults. Girls do women's jobs, while boys do men's jobs. In the garment industry, children receive the same rate of pay as adults. In footwear, children usually start out as assistants or apprentices to adult workers and receive lower rates of pay than adults.

For school-age children, the work in both industries is conducted after school for four to five hours per day, with one day off per week. The children who do not attend school work full-time, eight hours per day. Overtime is common, however, frequently resulting in children working late into the evening. In Tasikmalaya, West Java, for example, children living in their employer's house usually do additional work in the evening while waiting for bedtime, thus working three to four additional hours per day. Further, during peak season, overtime until midnight or later is also common in order to fill orders.

Work in the garment industry is relatively safe in comparison to work in the footwear industry, which uses more chemicals, particularly the pungent glue that often causes headaches. In addition, the use of blades, scissors, and other cutting utensils creates an occupational hazard. IPEC found that the main hazard for children in footwear comes from the adhesive material (glue) and its solvents. A burn hazard also exists from the process of joining the upper and the sole of the shoe using an open stovetop fire. IPEC also found that spasm of the hand muscles, headache, cough, and skin irritation were common health conditions among children of the industry (IPEC 2004).

As the industry creates clusters and centers of subcontractors, children's involvement in the industry is largely an environmental factor. For example, Cibaduyut is a small industrial footwear center well known in West Java, one of the densely populated provinces in Indonesia. Several local villages support the industry, and most of the villagers work as shoemakers. In almost every household, the whole family works in shoe making, some working in other people's workshops, and some bringing work home through the putting-out system. Under such circumstances, working from an early age becomes common, being part of the socialization process. Parents rarely forbid their children to work. Instead, they often encourage it. Children who are not working become unusual. The children consider working as a way to earn money, and as an arena for playing and socialization with friends.

References and Further Reading

Dicken, Peter. *Global Shift: Industrial Change in a Turbulent World.* London: Harper and Row, 1986.

Haryadi, Dedi, and Indrasari Tjandraningsih. *Buruh anak dan dinamika industri kecil* [Child workers and the dynamics of small industry]. Bandung: AKATIGA, 1995.

IHS. *Women and Children in Home-Based Industry.* Jakarta: IHS, 2002.

IPEC. *Pekerja anak di industri sepatu informal di Jawa Barat: sebuah kajian cepat* [Child workers in informal footwear industry in West Java: a rapid assessment]. Jakarta: ILO-IPEC, 2004.

Irwanto, S.R. Pardoen, S. Sitohang, et.al. *Child Workers in Three Metropolitan Cities: Jakarta, Surabaya, Medan.* Jakarta: UNICEF and Atma Jaya, 1995.

Thamrin, Juni, ed. *Organisasi produksi dan ketenagakerjaan pada industri kecil sepatu: studi kasus Cibaduyut, Bandung* [Production organization and employment in the small-scale footwear industry: a case study of Cibaduyut, Bandung]. Bandung: ISS-ITB-IPB, 1991.

Tjandraningsih, Indrasari, ed. *Tenaga kerja pedesaan pada industri besar sepatu olahraga untuk ekspor: studi kasus Tangerang dan Bogor* [Rural workers in the large-scale export sports-shoe industry: case study of Tangerang and Bogor districts]. Bandung: ISS-ITB-IPB, 1991.

Children and Work in Indonesia: Historical Overview

Ben White, Institute of Social Studies, The Hague

While aspects of Indonesian colonial childhood and child work are sometimes mentioned in the work of social and economic historians (often alongside women's work), Indonesian childhood has not yet been the subject of a dedicated historical study based on primary sources. This makes comparison with other countries and regions difficult. Nevertheless, available evidence suggests that while child labor was present in Indonesian colonial export production, it did not play as important or indispensable role as that which historians have documented in colonial African countries.

Childhood and Child Work in the Nineteenth Century

Frequent references in local officials' reports from the early nineteenth century suggest that children participated in productive work from a very early age, even five or six years old, in such tasks as agricultural work, guarding fields against birds and other pests, looking after livestock, and household chores; by their early teens, they were fully engaged in work. The tax burden on peasants placed heavy demands on the labor of both landed and landless households, and the work contributed by children was an important dimension of household survival (Elson 1994).

The colonial system of forced cultivation introduced in 1830 required peasants, as a condition of access to land on which to grow their own crops, to provide part of their land or labor for the cultivation of export crops to be delivered against fixed prices. Like household-based contract farming everywhere, such arrangements place great pressure on the labor of all household members. Children, alongside women and men, were widely involved, not only in household chores and subsistence production, but also in the expanding export-crop sector, in such crops as indigo, cochineal, coffee, tea, cinnamon, tobacco, and sugarcane. They also were frequently used to replace parents or patrons in forced-labor obligations (Elson 1994). Large landless groups who traveled as seasonal migrants throughout Java, following the harvest seasons of different crops, often traveled as families, and men, women, and children earned a wage; children's wages were generally on a par with women's wages (at about 60–80 percent of the rate for adult men). It was common for households with larger landholdings to take in the children of landless and marginal-peasant households as live-in hired servants, who received food and clothes for their labor (Boomgaard 1989; White 1982; Elson 1994).

As far as labor obligations to community and state were concerned, the boundary line between *child* and *adult* seems to have been around fourteen years. Many boys and girls below this age, however, were already married, and access to juvenile labor was one of the reasons for this. We cannot tell how much work interfered (or possibly was combined) with children's other needs for rest and play. Since very few children attended school, work was the main medium for learning life skills.

The rapid expansion of large-scale plantations in the later nineteenth century brought new patterns of wage employment. The labor force was drawn primarily from Java's landless, recruited as coolie contract workers to Sumatra and on shorter-term arrangements in Java. The labor inputs of children were a common but not always essential feature. Both native and European enterprises employed children on a large scale. In general, the workday for children was reported as being the same as that for adults (most commonly between eight and ten hours), and children's wages were generally about one-half those of adult men, and 65–75 percent of those of adult women. In rural crafts and small industries, children were commonly employed both as family helpers and for wages. The very low earnings in this sector—much less than prevailing agricultural wage rates—meant that all family members, including children, had to participate in production in order to attain a survival income for the household. In the plantation regions of Sumatra and other islands, however, reports of the Labour Inspectorate do not mention any child workers (White 2004).

The employment of children was not considered a social issue in Indonesia before World War I. Child employment (including wage employment) was unregulated, considered desirable, and unaffected by international developments, despite the emergence of social concern and legislation on these issues in the Netherlands itself.

The general view that work was a natural or desirable element in children's lives is not surprising if we recall that at the beginning of the twentieth century only about one in 200 native children attended formal school of any kind. It was not until the so-called ethical policy and the gradual establishment of village schools from 1907 onward that villagers in most regions had any prospect of access to education. Even by the 1930s, only about one-third of native children went to primary school. They attended these schools for only three years, and for only two and a half hours each day, which therefore did not interfere greatly with their capacity to work, although it may have reduced their involvement in various kinds of full-time work away from home.

Regulating Childhood and Child Employment in the Late Colonial Period

Late-colonial (from the 1920s onward) interventions in child employment highlight the absurdities of legislation establishing minimum ages for admission to employment based on European concerns about child labor in factories. In a context where education was not compulsory, where most children did not go to school (and where those who did left school by age ten), and where only a tiny fraction of child employment was factory labor, imposition of European standards was patently misguided.

As a signatory to the Treaty of Versailles, the government of the Netherlands was obliged to apply ILO Convention 5 (1919) to its colonial possessions as well as at home. This was the ILO's original minimum-age convention, establishing fourteen as the minimum age for industrial employment. The convention was intended to apply only to industry (thus excluding the agriculture, trade, and service sectors), reflecting the tendency in Europe and North America to associate the child labor problem with factories and urban industries.

The colonial Labour Office circulated an inquiry on the feasibility of applying the ILO convention (with the minimum age reduced from fourteen to twelve years) to various departmental heads, regional and district authorities, and a number of employers' organizations representing the main export crops. A new ordinance was formally adopted in 1925. The sugarcane employers' association had already preempted the new ordinance by prohibiting employment of children under twelve in sugar factories. In fact, the sugar industry did make extensive use of juvenile labor, but not in its factories (which were covered by the convention). Rather, children were employed in the fields (which were not covered), in such tasks as fertilizing, planting, watering, and weeding. One year after the ban, the sugar association's 138 factories reported using 14.4 million person-days of so-called half-adult labor, as much as 23 percent of all hired labor-days in some districts.

In the tobacco belt of Besuki (East Java) about 5,000 children were at work, almost entirely girls. They worked from six in the morning until five or five-thirty in the evening in both drying and packing sheds, particularly the latter, fetching and carrying bundles of tobacco leaf to the sorting and stacking women, and bringing the sorted bundles to the weighing scales and packing chests. The tobacco industry's objections to the new ordinance were overcome by formulating the definition of *workplace* in such a way that the mainly open drying sheds were not included, with the consequence that some of the largest concentrations of child employment in export production (in field work and in the drying sheds) would be left undisturbed.

It was also decided to redefine *nighttime* from the convention's original "rest-period of 11 consecutive hours, which includes the hours between 10 pm and 5 am" to a period of only seven hours between 10 P.M. and 5 A.M. *Childhood* itself was redefined by lowering the minimum age from fourteen to twelve years, in spite of the fact that in the Netherlands, the minimum age had just been raised to fourteen in the new Labour Law of 1919. No attempt was made to shift the convention's industrial focus to the conditions of Indonesia's overwhelmingly agrarian economy. The new ordinance was not intended to keep children away from the world of work, from agricultural production, or even from earning money, and certainly not intended to push children into school—which is hardly mentioned in debates and discussions of this period—but only to exclude them from the world of "industry" and large-scale, formal-sector agroprocessing in enclosed buildings.

In the 1930s, the Labour Office was quite active in investigating and prosecuting violations of the new ordinance. The most commonly prosecuted enterprises were (in descending order of frequency): batik workshops, tobacco sorting and processing, kapok processing, textile weaving, rice or maize milling, tea processing, ground-nut sorting, tapioca making, and coffee roasting, with smaller numbers of prosecutions in bakeries, leather tanneries, cotton sizing, copper beating, mosquito coils, floor tiles, fireworks, can factories, copra drying, printing shops, glassworks, hat weaving, *kerupuk* making, cooking oil, cigarette papers, and tofu processing (White 2004).

In the plantation enterprises outside Java, it was reported that child employment was limited to light garden and field work, for a few hours only, such as picking caterpillars and collecting seeds. Similarly, on tobacco farms, children were employed stringing up tobacco leaves in the drying sheds. We should not assume too readily that child labor was an important or necessary element in all labor-intensive agricultural or industrial enterprises producing for the market. In most districts of West Java, for example, the Labour Office's detailed report on the hand-rolled cigarette industry found no child workers under twelve at all.

The 1925 ordinance remained in force without changes for more than twenty years. In the late 1940s, various developments in labor legislation in a newly independent Indonesia left the legal status of child workers in a state of some confusion. Most observers agree that, formally speaking, the amended 1925 ordinance is the regulation that remained in force in independent Indonesia until a new Labour Law was introduced in 1987. The question is mainly academic, however, since not a single case was prosecuted after independence.

Child Work and Education in Independent Indonesia

During the past half century, since independence, the lives of Indonesian children have changed in many ways. "Childhood" itself has become extended and redefined through a combination of raising the age of marriage, the rapid spread of primary and junior secondary education, and correspondingly changed patterns of involvement in work for most children, both boys and girls. For the first three decades after independence, the child labor problem as such was given little if any attention by the government or the labor movement, although sporadic reports appeared in the media. No efforts were made to resolve the lack of clarity in the law surrounding child employment, nor were any employers prosecuted for employing underage children.

Much greater efforts were directed to rapidly extending access to primary and secondary school. Dramatic growth in access to education meant that by the mid-1980s, even before the introduction of compulsory education in 1984, more than 90 percent of boys and girls age seven to twelve, and just under 70 percent of girls and just over 70 percent of boys between thirteen and fifteen years of age were already attending school. By the end of the twentieth century, attendance had risen to 96 percent in the seven- to twelve-year-old age-group, and 79 percent among those age thirteen to fifteen (Oey-Gardiner 2000).

The great majority of Indonesia's working children are, thus, school-going children involved in part-time work. School attendance, though occupying only four to five hours per day in the first six years, places limits on the kinds of work available to children, and of course restricts employment to a part-time activity (White and Tjandraningsih 1998).

A good example is given by East Java's tobacco industry. Today's tobacco companies still make widespread use of child labor, but all the children attend school for at least some years. Many, particularly girls, begin working in the drying or sorting sheds before they are twelve years old, but the majority combine this with school attendance, working four hours or less on school days. Also in contrast to earlier times, child workers generally earn their own wages, although some give part or all to their parents (Tjandraningsih and Anarita 2002).

References and Further Reading

Bessell, Sharon. "The Politics of Child Labour in Indonesia: Global Trends and Domestic Policy." *Pacific Affairs* 72:3 (1999): 353–71.

Boomgaard, Peter. *Children of the Colonial State: Population Growth and Economic Development in Java 1795–1880.* Amsterdam: Free University Press, 1989.

Elson, Robert. *Village Java Under the Cultivation System 1830–1870.* Sydney: Allen and Unwin, 1994.

Hardjono, J. "The Effect of the Economic Crisis on Working Children in West Java." In *Indonesia in Transition: Social Aspects of Reform and Crisis,* ed. C. Manning and P. van Diermen, 164–83. Singapore: Institute of Southeast Asian Studies, 2000.

Oey-Gardiner, M. "Schooling in a Decentralized Indonesia: New Approaches to Access and Decision-Making." *Bulletin of Indonesian Economic Studies* 36:3 (2000): 127–34.

Tjandraningsih, Indrasari, and Popon Anarita. *Pekerja anak di perkebunan tembakau* [Child workers in tobacco plantations]. Bandung, Indonesia: AKATIGA, 2002.

White, Ben. "Child Labour and Population Growth in Rural Asia." *Development and Change* 13 (1982): 587–610.

———. "Constructing Child Labour: Attitudes to Juvenile Work in Indonesia, 1900–2000." In *Labour in Southeast Asia: Local Processes in a Globalised World,* ed. R. Elmhirst and R. Saptari, 77–105. London: Routledge, 2004.

White, Ben, and Indrasari Tjandraningsih. *Child Workers in Indonesia.* Bandung, Indonesia: AKATIGA/International Working Group on Child Labour, 1998.

Development of Child Labor Policy in Indonesia

Indrasari Tjandraningsih, AKATIGA—Center for Social Analysis, Bandung, Indonesia

The issue of child labor poses a dilemma for the government of Indonesia. For many years the government wished to ignore the problem and did not officially acknowledge the existence of child labor. But, as Indonesia was a developing country, the existence of child labor was inevitable. Eventually, largely in response to international pressure, the government acknowledged the problem and created a policy framework to address child labor. However, the government's continuing ambivalence toward child labor as a policy issue is manifest in its inconsistent and weak enforcement of the child labor laws.

Early Legislation

In 1925, during Indonesia's colonial period, an ordinance was adopted prohibiting children under twelve from industrial work, but the law applied only to mining and manufacturing and workplaces such as factories, leaving most child labor in Indonesia's largely agrarian economy unregulated. Shortly after Indonesia's independence in 1945, the child labor ordinance was amended in ways that confused as much as it clarified the legal status of working children. Agricultural work, household domestic work, and work within the scope of a family enterprise remained unregulated, but the actual state of the law mattered little, as there was virtually no enforcement for some forty years.

In 1987, the Ministry of Manpower issued a Ministerial Regulation on Protection for Children Who Are Forced to Work. The regulation, issued in part to attract more investment, was considered controversial. The main thrust of the regulation was to permit employment of children under age fourteen in work situations considered to be appropriate, in order to enable those in difficult socioeconomic circumstances to contribute support to the livelihood of themselves and their families. The regulation also provided protective safeguards, limiting work to no more than four hours per day, prohibiting night work, ensuring appropriate remuneration, and requiring compliance with the Compulsory Education Program, which had been established in 1984.

IPEC and the National Plan of Action

In the 1980s and early 1990s, as global awareness of child labor increased, Indonesia came under trade pressure to reform its child labor policies. Facing the threat of trade sanctions for numerous violations of labor rights, including substantial use of child labor, Indonesia moved to adopt minimum-age regulations in its export sectors (Bessel 1995).

Also in the early 1990s, the ILO was in the process of establishing its International Program on the Elimination of Child Labor (IPEC). The ILO invited Indonesia to be in the first cohort of nations to join IPEC; Indonesia joined in 1992. The adoption of IPEC brought increased attention and resources to the problem of child labor. NGOs and other civil society institutions oriented to children's issues flourished. National conferences on child labor have been held regularly since 1993. Labor inspectors are now trained in monitoring child labor (White and Tjandraningsih 1998).

Joining IPEC not only influenced attitudes; it also shaped various concrete policy developments. One condition of joining IPEC was that Indonesia was expected to ratify ILO Convention 138

Children learning at school thanks to the International Programme on Child Labour (ILO-IPEC), Indonesia, 2005. (© *International labor Organization / T. Falise*)

(minimum age). This proved to be a controversial proposal, and the convention was not ratified until 1999, establishing finally and with clarity a legal minimum age of fourteen in Indonesia.

Another important policy development brought about as a result of joining IPEC was the adoption of the National Action Plan on Child Labor. As IPEC shifted its vision from elimination of all child labor to a more realistic goal prioritizing the elimination of forms of labor especially dangerous for children, ILO Convention 182 (elimination of worst forms of child labor) was adopted. Indonesia ratified the convention in 2000. Following ratification, presidential decrees in 2001 and 2002 established both a National Action Committee for the Elimination of Worst Forms of Child Labor—comprised of government officials, academics, and representatives of the military, labor unions, business associations, NGOs, and press organizations—and a National Action Plan on the Elimination of Worst Forms of Child Labor, respectively. The National Action Plan commits Indonesia to protecting child workers under eighteen years of age. Previously, regulations extended only to children up to age fourteen.

The final public policy piece is the 2003 law establishing fifteen as the minimum age for work but providing exceptions for those between thirteen and fifteen years of age doing simple jobs that do not interfere with their health or their physical, mental, or social development. Employment of thirteen- to fifteen-year-old children requires written parental permission and limits working hours to three per day so as not to interfere with school. This law explicitly prohibits employment of children in worst forms, including prostitution and pornography, drug trading, slavery, and other jobs that might endanger children's health, safety, or morals.

Additional policies that support Indonesia's child labor policies include the Compulsory Education Program, established in 1984 to encourage each child to enter school, the Child Welfare Law to ensure children's welfare, and the 2002 Child Protection Law, which, among other things, protects children from economic exploitation. Ratification of the UN Convention on the Rights of the Child (CRC) was followed by the formation of child protection institutions in six provinces to provide protection and generate public awareness and understanding of children's rights. Members of these institutions include government, NGOs, academics, businesspeople, and religious figures (Yohannes 1997).

Evaluation of Indonesia's Child Labor Policy

While Indonesia's policy framework for child labor appears, on the surface, quite adequate, problems of implementation and enforcement reveal the government's continuing ambivalence toward child labor. The political willingness of government to commit to strict and consistent implementation and enforcement of existing policies depends heavily on the monitoring efforts of civil society, NGOs, and the international world. Because external pressure drives so much of Indonesia's child labor policy, the frame of mind, formulation of the problem, and problem-solving methods are much influenced by international trends (Bessel 1999). In this sense, Indonesia, as a developing country, has become an object of international society in accepting and adopting the international community's views and policies about child labor problems. Unfortunately, genuinely localized and adequately contextualized policy has yet to be formulated.

Another factor hindering the effectiveness of child labor policies is the influence of other macropolicies. For example, economic and industrialization policies giving more freedom of capital movement, conversion of land use, opening of industrial estates, and conglomeration and monopoly contribute to the process of the proletarianization of society, thus increasing the likelihood of child labor (Tjandraningsih 1997). Similarly, failure to integrate child labor policy into the larger framework of national development policy means that many of the underlying causes of child labor remain unaddressed. For example, Indonesia is consistent with the CRC in acknowledging that children have both the right to obtain education and the right to work, by providing compulsory schooling while permitting children to work for three to four hours after school, but these policies do not address the economic hardship that causes children to work, so limiting their work to three to four hours means that for many their wages will no longer be sufficient.

References and Further Reading

Bessel, Sharon. "The Political Dynamics of Child Labour in Indonesia." Working paper 93, Centre of Southeast Asian Studies, Monash University, Clayton, Australia, 1995.

———. "The Politics of Child Labour in Indonesia: Global Trends and Domestic Policy." *Pacific Affairs* 72:3 (1999): 353–71.

Tjandraningsih, Indrasari. *Persepsi LSM terhadap kebijakan tentang anak* [NGO perception on child's policy]. Paper presented in the Preliminary Survey on Vulnerable Children, organized by the Bureau of Central Statistics and UNICEF, Bandung, Indonesia, 1997.

White, Ben, and Indrasari Tjandraningsih. *Child Workers in Indonesia.* Bandung, Indonesia: AKATIGA/International Working Group on Child Labour, 1998.

Yohannes, Ferry. *Rancangan perlindungan anak* [Draft on child protection]. Paper presented in the Preliminary Survey on Vulnerable Children, organized by the Bureau of Central Statistics and UNICEF, Bandung, Indonesia, 1997.

Myanmar

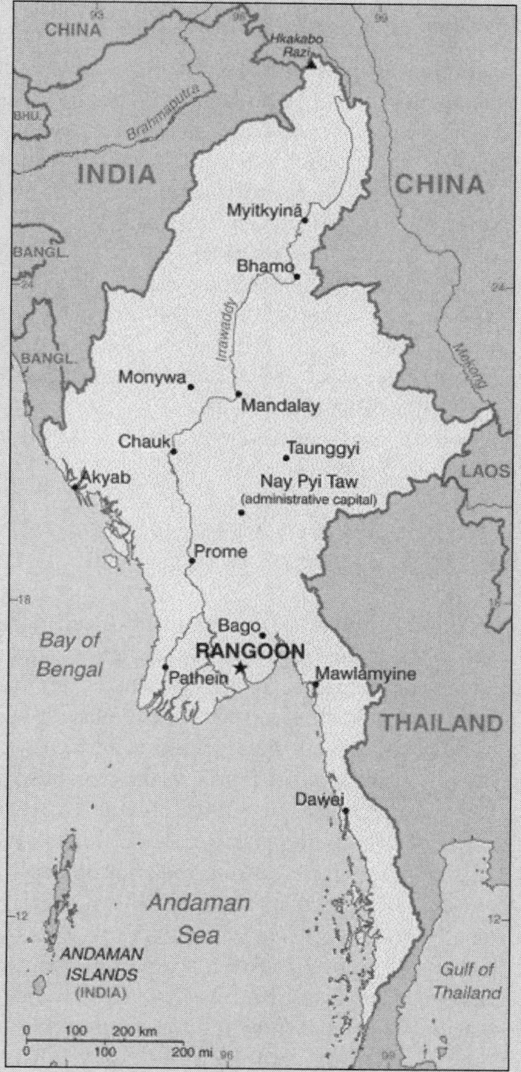

MYANMAR			
	CRC	C 138	C 182
Ratifications	Y	N	N
Human Development Index/ Rank	0.581/130		
Human Capital			
Population Growth Rate	0.82%		
% Population 0–14	26.1%		
Total Fertility Rate	1.95		
Life Expectancy	62.49		
Infant Mortality Rate	50.68		
Literacy Rate	85.3%		
Economic			
GDP/Capita	$1,800		
GDP Growth %	2.6%		
% Poverty	25%		
Gini Index	n/av		
Labor Force Composition			
% Agriculture	70%		
% Industry	7%		
% Services	23%		

Child Soldiers in Myanmar

Research staff at the Coalition to Stop the Use of Child Soldiers, Director Victoria Forbes Adam

Forced or compulsory recruitment of children below the age of eighteen for use in armed conflict is considered a worst form of child labor under ILO Convention 182. In Myanmar thousands of children remain in the *tatmadaw* (army) as internal armed conflict continues in some areas of the country. Although cease-fire agreements remain in force between the government and fifteen ethnic-minority-based armed groups, the *tatmadaw* and several other ethnic-minority armed groups, most notably the Shan State Army–South, the Karen National Union, and the Karenni National Progressive Party, continue to engage in battles in the eastern part of the country.

Context

Armed conflict broke out almost immediately after Myanmar gained independence from the United Kingdom in 1948, as groups representing various ethnic minorities took up arms against the central Burma authorities in a struggle for independence or greater autonomy.

The State Peace and Development Council (the military government) has ruled by decree since the constitution was abrogated in 1988. Armed conflict continues to affect millions of people, hundreds of thousands of whom have become internally displaced or have sought asylum in neighboring countries, including former child soldiers.

National Recruitment Laws

Under the 1993 Child Law, aimed at the protection and care of children, a "child" is anyone under the age of sixteen, and a "youth" is anyone over sixteen and below eighteen. The law defines penalties for offenses including the abuse and torture of children, and states that "employing or permitting a child to perform work which is hazardous to the life of the child or which may cause disease to the child or which is harmful to the child's moral character" is punishable by imprisonment of up to six months or a fine, or both.

In a letter to the UN Security Council in January 2004, the government stated that recruitment of child soldiers is prohibited by the Myanmar Defence Services Act of 1947 and that War Office Council instruction 13/73 of January 1974 stipulates that a person cannot enlist with the armed forces until the age of eighteen.

Child Recruitment and Deployment

Independent monitors have only limited access to areas of ongoing conflict. Nevertheless, recent credible reports indicate that the *tatmadaw* continues to forcibly recruit children as young as twelve on a regular basis. They are subjected to ill-treatment and harsh living conditions, characterized by overcrowding and inadequate food and medical care. *Tatmadaw* recruiters target poor children, who often cannot afford to attend school, in public places such as train and bus stations. Children are often promised good salaries or are otherwise deceived, or they are threatened with imprisonment if they do not obey recruiters. They are instructed to fill out forms and to state that their age is eighteen; they are then sent to training centers, where they undergo a harsh physical regime. Afterward, they serve as guards or servants, carry supplies to the front line, act as minesweepers, or are forced to engage in combat with armed political groups.

Armed Political Groups

Almost all armed political groups have recruited and used child soldiers, and in mid-2006 a reliable source estimated that there were 4,000 in various groups. In July 2006, the Karen National Union chairman stated that their armed wing had not recruited any child soldiers since 2000 but also said that a few local commanders may still recruit them in contravention of orders from superiors. The Karenni National Progressive Party reported that any minors attempting to enlist would be sent to school. In August 2006, it was reported that there were fewer than fifty child soldiers in the Karen National Union and Karenni National Progressive Party combined. In July of the same year the Shan State Army–South leadership also claimed they do not use child soldiers, although other sources state that children continue to serve in their armed wing. Some cease-fire groups also reportedly use child soldiers.

Developments at the National and International Levels

In January 2004, the government informed the UN Security Council that it had established a new Committee for the Prevention of the Recruitment of Minors for Military Service, comprising State Peace and Development Council members and other officials. The government also said it had invited the special representative of the UN secretary-general for children and armed conflict to visit Myanmar. A visit planned for 2003 was postponed following the deterioration of the human rights situation and mass arrests of pro democracy activists, and the visit has not yet taken place. The State Peace and Development Council secretary-1 reassured the committee in August 2006 that, because of the cooperation of UNICEF and the UN, there were very few cases of recruiting minors for military service, although some units unknowingly accepted minors who lied about their age; however, when parents came to look for their children, the units return them to their parents.

Myanmar is a state party to the UN Convention on the Rights of the Child and submitted its second periodic report to the Committee on the Rights of the Child, which considered it at its session in May 2004. In the committee's concluding observations, it expressed extreme concern about the use of children under age fifteen by both the *tatmadaw* and armed groups. As part of its longstanding efforts to help eliminate state-imposed forced labor of civilians, the ILO Liaison Office in Myanmar has raised cases of forcible recruitment of children into the *tatmadaw* with the government. In December 2005, the UN General Assembly adopted its most recent resolution on the situation of human rights in Myanmar, expressing grave concern over the continued use of child soldiers, among other human rights violations.

At a July 2006 UN Security Council meeting, the Myanmar government delegation stated that they had drawn up "an action plan that included protection of children's rights, prevention measures, promoting public awareness and coordinating with UNICEF."[1] The plan reportedly outlines procedures for discharging soldiers found to be under eighteen, including vocational training, other educational options, and income support. However, there is no information available about concrete measures the State Peace and Development Council has taken in this regard, including any official disarmament, demobilization, and reintegration programs for child soldiers in Myanmar or neighboring countries.

Conclusion

The *tatmadaw* continues to recruit and deploy children despite its stated public commitment to end the practice. The UN and its member states, including the UN Security Council, the General Assembly, and the Human Rights Commission, have repeatedly expressed concern about child soldiers in Myanmar. Moreover, international and regional nongovernmental organizations have conducted research and reported widely on their plight.

Note

1. Security Council Reiterates Commitment to Address Impact of Armed Conflict on Children, Determination to Implement Landmark 2005 Resolution 1612, UN Security Council 5494th Meeting, July 25, 2006. http://www.unis.unvienna.org/unis/pressrels/2006/sc8784.html.

Reference and Further Reading

Coalition to Stop the Use of Child Soldiers. "Child Soldiers Global Report 2008 (Myanmar)." http://www.childsoldiersglobalreport.org/content/myanmar.

Philippines

PHILIPPINES			
	CRC	C 138	C 182
Ratifications	Y	Y	Y
Human Development Index/Rank	0.763/84		
Human Capital			
Population Growth Rate	1.76%		
% Population 0–14	34.5%		
Total Fertility Rate	3.05		
Life Expectancy	70.51		
Infant Mortality Rate	22.12		
Literacy Rate	92.6%		
Economic			
GDP/Capita	$5,000		
GDP Growth %	5.4%		
% Poverty	40%		
Gini Index	46.1		
Labor Force Composition			
% Agriculture	36%		
% Industry	15%		
% Services	49%		

CHILD ACTIVITY BREAKDOWN, BY SEX AND RESIDENCE

RESIDENCE	Percentage of children in the relevant age-group[a]: Economic activity only		School only		Combining school and economic activity		Neither in school nor in economic activity		Child labor[b]	
	Male	Female	Male	Female	Male	Female	Male	Female	Male	Female
Urban	1.2	0.5	84.0	86.2	6.5	5.2	8.3	8.0	n/av	n/av
Rural	3.5	1.0	68.7	77.5	14.4	9.5	13.4	12.0	n/av	n/av
Total	2.5	0.8	75.4	81.4	10.9	7.6	11.2	10.2	7.8	4.8

Source: Philippines, Labour Force Survey, 2001 (see UCW Project Web site, http://www.ucw-project.org, country statistics).
Notes: [a]Children age 5 to 14. [b]Estimate includes (a) children under age 12 engaged in economic activities, (b) children age 12–14 engaged in excessive economic activities (more than 14 hours per week), and (c) children under age 15 engaged in excessive household chores (at least 28 hours per week). Estimate does not account for children engaged in hazardous work or other unconditional "worst forms" of child labor.

Education and Child Labor in the Philippines

Chris Sakellariou, Economics, Humanities and Social Sciences,
Nanyang Technological University, Singapore

The Philippines has free public education at the primary and secondary levels. Education is compulsory to grade six. Still, only 88 percent of children in the under-twelve age-group, and 83 percent of children in the six- to seventeen-year-old age-group, were enrolled in 1999, and an even smaller percentage actually attended. Many of these children eventually drop out. School enrollment has increased moderately compared to a decade earlier, when 82 percent of children under twelve attended school.

This essay provides new evidence on determinants of the decision of whether to send a child to school or to work. Using the 1999 Annual Poverty Indicator Survey (APIS), a large, nationally representative survey of Philippine households and their members, I examine information on different indicators related to poverty and the socioeconomic profile of families, along with other information relating to their living conditions.

Schooling and Child Work

In a sample of children six to fifteen years of age (47,770 observations), about 86 percent of children were attending school and not working, 3.4 percent were combining school and work, and 2.3 percent were working and not attending school. The remaining 9.1 percent were neither in school nor working, and about 50 percent of them were in the six- to eight-year-old age bracket. Children's contribution to household income in the Philippines is substantial. On average, a child worker contributed nearly 7 percent to household income in both urban and rural areas. This is only the child's direct, monetary contribution; it does not include his or her indirect contribution to household tasks, which allows mothers to engage in paid work.

Comparison of the evidence from the 1999 APIS with evidence from a decade earlier (Sakellariou and Lall 2000) shows that, in spite of modest improvements in school enrollment, the overall incidence of child labor for children in the ten- to seventeen-year-old age-group (the age-group used in the earlier study) in the Philippines is roughly unchanged, at a little over 12 percent. This finding is somewhat surprising in light of declining poverty rates in the Philippines. Poverty estimates declined from 40.6 percent at the beginning of the 1990s to 32.1 percent in 1994, with updated estimates showing further reductions in 1997 (Balisacan 1999). One would expect that reductions in poverty would have been matched by lower child labor incidence rates.

Poverty and Schooling

Poverty may be the most important determinant of school attendance versus work activity. Because of insufficient family income, the household may be compelled to keep children away from school. Poverty may inhibit schooling either because poor families cannot afford the cost of schooling or because they cannot afford the loss of children's income.

The link between poverty and child labor is well established in many studies (Grootaert and Patrinos 1999; Blunch and Verner 2000), though some argue that it is overstated (Nielson 1998; Canagarajah and Coulombe 1997; Sasaki and Temesgen 1999). Estimates from the 1999 APIS of the effect of poverty on child schooling provide conclusive evidence in support of a link: Children from poor households (lowest decile) are much less likely to enroll in school (by 3.4 percentage points). While the effect of poverty on school attendance is clear, its effect on labor market participation is not as clear. Children from poor households are more likely to work, but the magnitude of this effect is rather small.

Cost of Schooling

From a human-capital perspective, the decision about child school attendance is based on a cost-benefit calculus, given the available alternatives (for example, work). That is, the decision is affected by the perceived return on investing in a child's education in comparison to investing in other assets. High direct and indirect costs of education, in relation to family income, lower the perceived returns to children's education. Where public education is free, as it is in the Philippines, direct costs are minimal, but there may remain significant indirect costs. One important indirect cost is captured in the distance from the home to the local school. The 1999 APIS yields conclusive results on the effect of a long commute to school on school attendance. A long distance to school has a detrimental effect on school attendance and increases the probability that the child will work either with or without schooling.

Family Characteristics and Schooling

In the Philippines, boys are significantly more likely to work than girls, and the probability of girls attending school without working is significantly higher than that for boys. The latter finding is not a common one in the international literature. The opposite has been found for Egypt (Wahba 2005), Ghana (Blunch and Verner 2000), Côte d'Ivoire (Grootaert 1999), and others, where boys are more likely to attend school than girls. This effect is particularly strong in rural areas, where girls have a 7.5 percent higher probability than boys of attending school without working. This gender bias leads to a gender imbalance in acquisition of education between men and women. APIS data on adults eighteen to sixty-five years of age indicate that men have on average 9.8 years of schooling, compared to 10.2 years for women. Furthermore, 16 percent of women have completed university education compared to 11 percent of men.

Fathers' education has a strong effect on both schooling and work decisions. Having a better-educated father increases the probability of the child attending school and decreases the probability of combining school and work as well as the probability of work without schooling. The effect of higher education of mothers is of similar nature but less pronounced. Children in households headed by women are less likely to attend school and more likely to work, suggesting that the dominant effect is the lack of resources in such households.

Empirical evidence suggests that the effect of household size on child labor depends on a combination of factors such as family culture; sibling sex, age, and activities; and birth order of children. For example, DeGraff, Bilsborrow, and Herrin (1993) reported that in the Philippines, the relationship between household size and child work depends on the sex and birth order of the child. The presence of older siblings decreases the likelihood of paid work by a child (suggesting a substitution effect). However, no such effect was found in the case of domestic work.

Family Assets and Schooling

The expected effects of the household owning a family business or agricultural land are ambiguous. On the one hand, one might expect that ownership of a family business or a farm would increase the probability of schooling and decrease the probability of working for wages because of an income effect. On the other hand, one might expect asset ownership to increase the probability of the child working in the family business or farm, where legal restrictions on child labor are scant, which might interfere with schooling. Evidence from the 1999 APIS reveals that ownership of a small family business or farm has a detrimental effect of on school enrollment and child labor in the Philippines. Having a self-employed father increases the probability of working without schooling, especially in rural areas and for boys. Of those who worked and did not attend school, about 50 percent worked without pay on a family-operated farm or business. Of those who combined school and work, 80 percent worked without pay on a family-operated farm or business. The effect of fathers' self-employment decreases the probability of school enrollment and increases the probability of combining school and work as well as working without attending school.

Policy Implications

A number of results in this study can be discussed in a policy context. The first relates to the link connecting poverty, schooling, and child labor. While the effect of poverty on school attendance is clear, its effect on labor market participation is rather small and not always statistically significant. Poor households can be the target of policy intervention. The need for intervention is underlined by the observation that over the 1990s the incidence of child work in the Philippines has remained about the same, despite reductions in the incidence of poverty over the same period.

Recent results based on theoretical models (Basu and Van 1998; Dessy 2000; Ranjan 1999, among others) provide useful clues as to appropriate policy interventions. These results suggest that simply banning child labor in poor countries may not produce the intended results, especially when a ban can be enforced only in the formal sector. This could reduce the well-being of children by forcing them to work in the informal sector under worse work conditions than existed in the formal sector. Making education compulsory is a preferred alternative. Even under free and universal access to education, without compulsory education laws, an underdevelopment trap with high incidence of child labor and low human capital formation may ensue. Once education is made compulsory, possible consequences of imperfect enforcement of the compulsory schooling laws are of particular importance. Bellettini and Berti Ceroni (2004) find that imperfect enforcement of compulsory schooling laws may lead to multiple-equilibria underdevelopment traps and adverse welfare effects on households. Finally, low parental incomes in combination with lack of access to credit markets can inhibit school attendance and generate child labor.

Any policy designed to reduce the problem of child labor by increasing school enrollments will be expensive and cannot be implemented with the existing budget allocations. Funding from international organizations is essential; however, on the domestic front, education budgets need to be increased, even considering the scarcity of funds that the government of a developing economy such as the Philippines faces.

References and Further Reading

Balisacan, A.M. "Poverty Profile in the Philippines: An Update and Re-examination of Evidence in the Wake of the Asian Crisis." Working paper, School of Economics, University of the Philippines Diliman, Quezon City, 1999.

Basu, Kaushik, and Pham Hoang Van. "The Economics of Child Labor." *American Economic Review* 88 (1998): 412–27.

Bellettini, Giorgio, and Carlotta Berti Ceroni. "Compulsory Schooling Laws and the Cure for Child Labour." *Bulletin of Economic Research* 56:3 (2004): 227–39.

Blunch, Niels-Hugo, and Dorte Verner. "Revisiting the Link Between Poverty and Child Labour: The Ghanaian Experience." Centre for Labour and Social Research, Department of Economics, Aarhus School of Business, Aarhus, Denmark, 2000.

Canagarajah, S., and H. Coulombe. "Child Labour and Schooling in Ghana." Policy Research Working Paper 1844, World Bank, Washington, DC, 1997.

DeGraff, D., and R. Bilsborrow. "Children's School Enrolment and Time at Work in the Philippines." *Journal of Developing Areas* 37:1 (2003): 127–58.

DeGraff, D., R. Bilsborrow, and A. Herrin. "The Implications of High Fertility for Children's Time Use in the Philippines." In *Fertility, Family Size and Structure—Consequences for Families and Children. Proceedings of a Population Council Seminar,* ed. C.B. Lloyd. New York: Population Council, 1993.

Dessy, Sylvain. "A Defence of Compulsory Measures Against Child Labour." *Journal of Development Economics* 62 (2000): 261–75.

Grootaert, Christiaan. "Child Labour in Côte d'Ivoire." In *The Policy Analysis of Child Labour: A Comparative Study,* ed. C. Grootaert and H. Patrinos, 23–62. New York: St. Martin's Press, 1999.

Grootaert, Christiaan, and H.A. Patrinos. "Policies to Reduce Child Labour." In *The Policy Analysis of Child Labour: A Comparative Study,* ed. C. Grootaert and H. Patrinos, 151–62. New York: St. Martin's Press, 1999.

Institute for Labour Studies. "Comprehensive Study on Child Labour in the Philippines." Monograph series 1, Institute for Labour Studies, Manila, Philippines, 1994.

Nielsen, Helena. "Child Labour and School Attendance: Two Joint Decisions." Working paper 98-15, Centre for Labour and Social Research, Department of Economics, Aarhus School of Business, Aarhus, Denmark, 1998.

Ranjan, Priya. "An Economic Analysis of Child Labour." *Economics Letters* 64 (1999): 99–105.

Sakellariou, Chris, and Ashish Lall. "Child Labour in the Philippines." *Asian Economic Journal* 14 (2000): 233–53.

Sasaki, Masaru, and Tilahun Temesgen. "Children in Different Activities: Child Labour and Schooling in Peru." Draft, World Bank, Washington, DC, 1999.

Wahba, Jackline. "The Influence of Market Wages and Parental History on Child Labour and Schooling in Egypt." Institute for the Study of Labour (IZA) Bonn 1771, September 2005.

Child Labor on Sugarcane Plantations in the Philippines

Jennifer de Boer, Former Child Rights Policy Officer, Terre des Hommes, Netherlands

Sugarcane provides an income to more than 6 percent of the Philippine people. It is one of the main commercial crops of the archipelago and had an export value of $70 million in 2005. Cane is grown mainly on the Visayan Islands and Mindanao, and production is manual. It is estimated that 60,000 to 200,000 children between five and eighteen years of age work in sugarcane fields (Apit 2002). Their working conditions vary from light work to exploitation. With agriculture and fishing being the sectors where the bulk of working children can be found, sugarcane alone is responsible for 1.5 to 5 percent of all Filipino child workers.

Sugarcane was already being grown on the Philippine islands before the Spanish arrived in the sixteenth century. However, it was not until colonial rule that cane sugar became a commercial agricultural product (Apit 2002). Nowadays most sugarcane is produced on big commercial haciendas owned by powerful families, mostly of Spanish descent. Workers are hired on a seasonal or daily basis, and pay is low (Hortelana 2004). Accommodations for the workers and their families are provided on the hacienda. Children of the sugarcane workers are thus an accessible workforce that can be hired during the busy seasons of planting, weeding, and harvesting. They are pushed into the fields by family poverty, dependency on the hacienda for income, and high costs of education. At the same time, they are pulled by the demand for simple manual labor and uncritical laborers. As the Philippine sugar sector has a history of violent trade union activity, plantation owners prefer children workers since they cannot be trade union members. Another pull factor is the opinion of plantation owners and middlemen that they are doing the children and their families a favor by letting them work and earn money (De Boer 2005).

Children's Involvement

Children from the age of six are involved in clearing fields, planting, weeding, and fertilizing. Older children are also involved in the hard labor of harvesting. Often, they work long hours (from 6 A.M. to 5 P.M.) under the hot sun. Although parents protect their children from the harmful work of spraying pesticides, the children work in or near recently sprayed fields, thus inhaling and touching pesticides (De Boer 2005). Remuneration for the work is low: in 2006, 30 pesos (US$.65) for weeding 100 meters (about 110 yards) of cane, which takes a child two days; 100 pesos (US$2.12) for every ton of cane that is cut. The official minimum wage for plantation work in the Visayan Islands in 2006 was 158 pesos (US$3.35) a day.

As sugarcane production is highly seasonal, children's work on the plantations varies from not working at all to doing light work to being exploited through hazardous labor. Although the work they do is not always onerous, the children do experience negative effects from working in the fields. Working prevents them from attending classes regularly, from doing homework, and sometimes from going to school altogether. When at work, children risk overheating, exhaustion, cuts from the tools and from the sharp cane leaves, insect bites, and pesticide poisoning, resulting in 60 percent of the children involved in agricultural work (including sugarcane) reporting health problems, according to the Labor Force Survey of 2001. All these factors jeopardize children's health in the short term, as well as their possibilities later in life, reinforcing a vicious circle of poverty and exploitation.

Legal Framework

Philippine law does not allow children under the age of fifteen to work, with the exception of four hours of work per day under the supervision of parents, on condition that this work does not harm education, life, safety, health, morals, or development of the child. Further, children under the age of eighteen are not allowed to perform hazardous tasks, such as work underwater, in noisy surroundings, or with poisonous substances (Republic Act 9231; Republic of the Philippines 2003). In the ILO-IPEC-supported Time-Bound Program on the Elimination of the Worst Forms of Child Labor in 2002, working on sugarcane plantations was specifically categorized as a worst form of child labor. This implies that children under the age of eighteen are not to be employed in sugarcane work.

Despite these legal provisions, child labor is still rampant in the sector. Labor inspections fail to disclose child labor in the sugarcane fields for several reasons. One is lack of a sufficient number of inspectors, resulting in poor-quality inspections because the available inspectors can check only the books of the sugarcane enterprises. This leaves a lot of room to "hide" working children. Another reason is the incorrect perception of agricultural work as "family business," in which the government does not wish to interfere (De Boer 2005).

Although the Philippine government is slowly recognizing the child labor problem in the haciendas, positive outcomes for working children can be achieved only when reforms reduce both pull and push factors and are combined with a good system of labor inspection. The present situation on the commercial sugarcane plantations puts too many children at risk, jeopardizing their development and their future.

References and Further Reading

Apit, A. *Child Labor in the Sugar Plantations: A Cursory Assessment.* Manila: DOLE, 2002.

De Boer, Jennifer. *Sweet Hazards: Child Labor on Sugarcane Plantations in the Philippines.* Den Haag: Terre des Hommes Netherlands, 2005.

De Vries, Saul. *Child Labor in Agriculture: Causes, Condition and Consequences. The Case of Sta. Fe and Ormoc, Leyte.* Manila: Institute of Labor Studies, 2001.

Garcia-Dungo, Nanette. "Post-Crisis Development in the Sugar Hacienda and the Participation of Women in the Labor Force: The Case of Negros." In *Population, Human Resources and Development,* ed. Alejandro N. Herrin, 976–89. Quezon City: University of the Philippines, 1994.

Hortelana, Clara Mae. "Don't Pass Sugar Crisis Burden to Us: Workers." *SunStarBacolod,* February 11, 2004.

Republic of the Philippines. *An Act Providing for the Elimination of the Worst Forms of Child Labor and Affording Stronger Protection for the Working Child* (Republic Act 9231), 2003. http://www.lawphil.net/statutes/repacts/ra2003/ra_9231_2003.html.

Rollolazo, Mildred G., and Luisa C. Logan. *An In-Depth Study on the Situation of Child Labor in the Agricultural Sector.* Manila: Department of Labor and Employment, 2004.

Child Domestic Work in the Philippines

Yuko Kitada, PhD, The Australian National University

Invisible behind the walls of private homes, child domestic workers are vulnerable to abuse. The Philippines has initiated innovative programs to make this potentially very hazardous work safe for children. It was also in the Philippines that the world's first association of child domestic workers was founded.

The Plight of Child Domestic Workers

Hiring domestic workers is a common practice not only among the upper class but also in middle-class households. According to the 1995 labor force survey by the National Statistics Office, 301,701 domestic workers were nineteen years old or younger, but the actual number of child domestic workers today is estimated to be more than three times that figure (Flores-Oebanda, Pacis, and Alcantara 2004).

There are both female and male child domestic workers, but the vast majority are female, as housework is considered to be more feminine than masculine. In the face of economic hardship, some families, especially in the rural areas, are willing to let their children work as domestics in the provincial cities or Manila in exchange for money (advance payment or salary), or for the children's education plus room and board. Children themselves often take up such work willingly, as they aspire to get educational opportunities in the urban centers while they work. Many regard working as domestics their only chance to go to school. However, once within the compound of a private home, away from their friends and families, children are easily taken advantage of. They are on duty twenty-four hours a day, and some do not receive the education, pay, holiday, food, or bed that they were promised. Worse still, some children are subjected to psychological, physical, and sexual abuse (Flores-Oebanda, Pacis, and Montaño 2001).

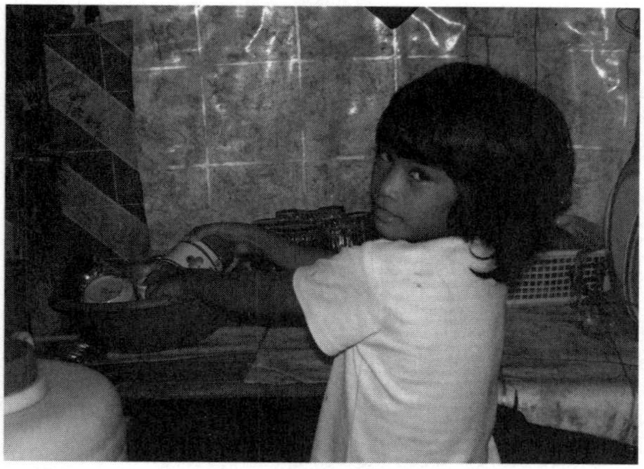

Helping hand: A girl-child in Bacolod, Philippines, misses out on primary school at an early age. She works as domestic help to earn some money and to gain some experience before deciding to migrate to the city later. In the Philippines, there are an estimated 1 million domestic workers, according to the Visayan Forum, an NGO that has been lobbying for a law to protect these children. *(Photo by Roland Pacis courtesy of the Visayan Forum)*

Is Child Domestic Work Really Safe?

Culturally, children are brought up with the belief that they have *utang na loob* (a debt of gratitude) toward their parents for being born and raised. Therefore, it follows that children should help their parents in any way they can, especially in difficult situations such as poverty. While there are children who are forced into work, other children actively look for work to help their families. Leaving home to work as domestics elsewhere helps the family financially in two ways: by contributing to family income and by reducing the number of mouths that need to be fed (Camacho 1999). As domestic work is seen as an accessible and appropriate job for females, sometimes children seek a part-time job as domestic help at a better-off family in their own neighborhood, combined with schooling (Kitada 2005). In these situations where children live with their own families and work close to home as part-time domestic workers, children's social contacts can quickly intervene in the event of mistreatment. However, when children work as live-in domestic workers in families other than their own, they are extremely vulnerable to abuse. They are isolated from sources of help, and their welfare is completely dependent on the employing family, whose first concern is not the well-being of the child (Blagbrough and Glynn 1999).

Visayan Forum Foundation's Work on Child Domestic Workers and Child Trafficking

Visayan Forum Foundation is a Filipino NGO supporting children and their families in the informal sector since 1991. Since 1995, they have been advocating for the rights and safety of child domestic workers, with an expanding network of program partners. Recognizing that the practice of hiring domestic workers, with its roots in slavery, will not disappear overnight, Visayan Forum's strategy is to create a social environment where domestic workers are properly accounted for and can live with dignity.

Visayan Forum reaches out to child domestic workers where they can be found. If given a day off, usually on Sundays, child domestic workers often go out to the parks. Visayan Forum conducts regular outreach activities in such places to talk to the workers and disseminate support information. In 1995, Visayan Forum organized the child domestic workers into an association called SUMAPI (Samahan at Ugnayan ng mga Manggagawang Pantahanan sa Pilipinas, or Association and Linkage of Domestic Workers in the Philippines). Today, with around 8,000 members and local chapters all around the country, SUMAPI connects child domestic workers with their peers, who are otherwise isolated in their respective employers' houses. Visayan Forum and volunteers from SUMAPI continue to reach more child domestic workers, conduct resiliency-building seminars, and offer psychosocial support as well as social activities. Local parishes and schools have joined in the movement to support child domestic workers, raising awareness within local communities and establishing night schools to address their needs.

Child domestic work has links with child trafficking. Children are often trafficked by recruiters whose promises often involve deception, whether it is about the conditions, type, or exact location of work. Visayan Forum established support houses in domestic ports, with the cooperation of the Philippine Port Authority and other governmental departments, to intercept those being trafficked. At these port halfway houses, children are given shelter and protection, legal support, and referral to trusted partner organizations for further services. Some are repatriated, while others go on to work, but with a telephone hotline number for them to call if they need help in the future.

Visayan Forum and its partners identified a gap between existing national laws for domestic workers and the reality of child domestic workers. In order to accord humane treatment to child domestic workers, they have been campaigning for the enactment of a new national law, Batas Kasambahay. The law aims to set minimum working conditions and provide social protection measures, such as increased minimum wage and membership in the national social security system and health insurance scheme.

Conclusion

The Philippines is one country where there is in-depth documentation of the plight of child domestic workers and where some cutting-edge work is under way to address this potentially very harmful form of child labor. Visayan Forum Foundation, with its many partners, has been the leading organization in this area of work in the Philippines.

References and Further Reading

Blagbrough, Jonathan, and Edmund Glynn. "Child Domestic Workers: Characteristics of the Modern Slave and Approaches to Ending Such Exploitation." *Childhood* 6:1 (1999): 51–56.

Camacho, Agnes Zenaida V. "Family, Child Labour and Migration: Child Domestic Workers in Metro Manila." *Childhood* 6:1 (1999): 57–73.

Flores-Oebanda, Ma. Cecilia, Roland Romeo R. Pacis, and Virgilio P. Montaño. *The Kasambahay—Child Domestic Work in the Philippines: A Living Experience.* Manila: Visayan Forum Foundation and International Labour Office, 2001.

Flores-Oebanda, Ma. Cecilia, Roland R. Pacis, and Jerome A. Alcantara. *Reaching Out Beyond Closed Doors: A Primer on Child Domestic Labor in the Philippines.* Manila: Visayan Forum Foundation, 2004.

Kitada, Yuko. *Earning Childhood in Manila, Philippines: Working Children's Agency in Their Everyday Life.* PhD diss., Australian National University, 2005.

Visayan Forum Foundation. http://www.visayanforum.org.

Children in Muro-Ami Fishing

Harold Olofson, Professor of Anthropology, University of San Carlos, Cebu City, Philippines

Muro-ami fishing technology originated in the 1930s with Okinawan migrant fisherfolk who came to fish in the central Philippines. After the Second World War, a Filipino family in southern Cebu Island began to recruit large numbers of impoverished upland farmers and coastal fishermen to make up the crews of vessels owned by a shipping company based in Manila. By the 1980s their expeditions were known to include hundreds of easily taught, apparently fearless, but often badly treated children. Crews were taken far from their home in southern Cebu for ten months of each year (Olofson, Cañizares, and Jose 2000).

Muro-ami is sometimes wrongly described as "deep-sea fishing" when in fact it is designed as a relatively near-shore operation conducted on coral reefs. To understand the risks to which children are exposed in *muro-ami,* it is necessary to understand the design and setting of the net and how fish are driven into it. The net is a large cone-shaped bag, open at the wide end, and is set to face a mild current, which naturally carries fish into the net. The bottom of the net lies on the sea floor, down eighty feet or more. While the net is set to collect fish, two wing panels are opened wide to direct the fish into the net. The wing panels are closed just before the net is pulled up.

Some children work as divers. Their job is to keep the net open, to prevent it from snagging on coral, and to untie the ropes holding the wing panels before the net is pulled up. The children free dive, wearing only homemade goggles, shirt, and pants, without air tank and fins. They must learn to conserve energy, to be aware of elapsed time, and to ascend gradually so as to avoid life-threatening decompression sickness. As if the current and panels were not enough, the fish must be "scared" into the net. This is done by a ring of swimmers, usually boys aged twelve to fourteen, sometimes numbering as many as 350. Each boy is on the surface, holding a "scare line" to which a stone is tied. Colored nylon or plastic strips are tied to the line every two feet. The swimmers bounce the stones on the sea floor, creating noise and vibrations that drive the fish into the net. Bouncing stones can cause considerable reef damage. Should a scare line and its stone lodge in the reef, the swimmer must either dive to retrieve them, replace the materials later, or be fined for their loss. The swimmers begin in a semicircle at one end of the reef and swim toward the opening of the net. The object is to clean the reef of nearly its entire fish population.

This process is dangerous for the divers and swimmers. New recruits must learn to jiggle the heavy scare line up and down to make the stones bounce. Every time the stone is lifted, the swimmer sinks underwater but must struggle up again to prevent the stone from sticking in the reef. This process takes a fatiguing month to learn, sometimes just after the upland children have learned to swim. The stones, as they fall, come very close to the heads of the divers below. Those working to untie the side panels or to free a snagged net or scare line might wound themselves and invite shark attack. All of these "plain soldiers," as they are called, are wary of being stabbed by needlefish.

After the net is pulled up, the fish are loaded into skiffs, taken to the mother boat, and sorted into tubs, where nothing is wasted, not even the smallest fish. After having worked at up to ten settings of the net and at sorting for twelve to fourteen hours, children may then be assigned to sew, repair, and dye the nets, by this time in poor light (Olofson and Tiukinhoy 1992).

Ostensibly, swimmers and divers are paid a share of the profit, but allowances are commonly provided to the laborer's family, which are then deducted from the child's pay. Further deductions for disciplinary fines, medical care, repairs to scare lines, and other supplies mean that a *muro-ami* child is never able to understand how the amount of his ultimate share is determined. Shares of the laborers have declined historically for reasons that are unclear.

Other fears and problems face the *muro-ami* child. Overcrowded and wet living conditions may cause illness. Common illnesses include kidney infections, chest pains, fever, vomiting blood, hepatitis, typhoid fever, stomach cramps, and headaches, along with hunger and fatigue (Olofson, Cañizares, and Jose 2000). Sick children who refuse to swim may have their pay deducted or may be subject to blows to the head from the manager of the fishing crew (his recruiter) (Abregana 1999). Each vessel has a physician, but consultations and prescribed treatments are deducted from the patient's pay. Other hardships reported by children include anxiety over sharks, inadequate food (children are given corn grits and low-quality fish and may be driven to eat a newly caught fish raw), dangerous work and Herculean tasks (being forced to swim during typhoons), and unsanitary living conditions (Olofson, Cañizares, and Jose 2000). Divers are praised when they bleed from the ears for the first time after a deep dive, and when this happens, the barrel of water from which the workers must drink is often tainted by blood. Children occasionally drown (Abregana 1999) or die from other causes. There is a cemetery for *muro-ami* children on the station island of Talampulan in the Calamianes.

In a survey of *muro-ami* laborers taken in the towns of origin, Olofson, Cañizares, and Jose (2000) found that 58 percent had first entered *muro-ami* before age eighteen. Among the most worrisome things for the child is the realization that he has been far removed from the safety of his family. He must tread carefully, for example, in dealing with bullies. The maestro, or recruiter and master, is often from the recruit's home village and may even be a relative.

Release of a documentary film, *Coral Triangle* (Carey 1988), along with discovery of the cemetery for *muro-ami* boys, brought public attention and international pressure, resulting in a temporary ban on *muro-ami* fishing in 1989. After the ban, the Bureau of Fisheries and Aquatic Resources designed an improved form of *muro-ami* to eliminate reef damage. Named *pa-aling* or *otoshi-ami,* it involves the use of compressors and hoses distributed from boats to scare fish into the net by using bubbles. This even more efficiently cleans the reef of its fish. There is still a place for swimmers and divers to manage the hoses and the net, and if these workers are children, they may be hidden in barrels when inspectors sail near. Abregana (1999) spoke to a child who was almost drowned when a hose got wrapped around his arms. Because of the expense of compressed air, ships may revert to use of the old-style scare lines and weights when the *muro-ami* vessel is well out of sight of observers.

A recent attempt to interview informants about *pa-aling* in southern Cebu could find none. It is not clear whether laborers and their families simply failed to identify themselves as *pa-aling* families, or whether fisherfolk have become disenchanted with *muro-ami.* It was concluded that they have become "invisible" (Remedio, Amadora-Nolasco, and Alburo 2004). It is clear that the fishing companies have lost influence over rural families and have lost political power in the region.

The *pa-aling* companies are, however, still recruiting on Negros Island, which neighbors Cebu. From time to time newspapers report on recruits running away from their ships in Palawan (they are referred to as "jumpers"). Shocked by conditions that Cebuans have come to expect, they seek refuge with local mayors. Some are underage and allege that recruiters lied about how much they would earn. They are taken on a *muro-ami* vessel to Navotas, in Metro-Manila, until their families reimburse their initial credit and any outstanding debts to the recruiting company. It is not difficult to see why *muro-ami* is coming to be seen by rural families as a form of slavery.

References and Further Reading

Abregana, Betty C. "Labor Force Participation of Children in Selected Fishing Villages in Negros Oriental." *Silliman Journal* 40:1 (1999): 48–94.

Carey, Lenora, producer. *Coral Triangle.* London: BBC and Television Trust for the Environment, 1988.

Hall, Howard. "Muro-Ami." California: The Ocean Channel, nd. http://www.ocean.com/resource.asp?resourceid=2237&catid=43&%2010cationid=1.

ILO-IPEC. *Children in Pa-aling and Kubkub Fishing Expeditions: An Assessment Report for the Deep-Sea and Fishing Sector Studies.* Cebu City: University of San Carlos and ILO-IPEC, 2002.

Olofson, Harold, Bernie Cañizares, and Farah de Jose. "A People in Travail I: Labor Relations History of Veteran Muro-ami Fisherfolk in the Central Philippines." *Philippine Quarterly of Culture and Society* 28 (2000): 224–62.

Olofson, Harold, and Araceli Tiukinhoy. "'Plain Soldiers': Muro-Ami Fishing in Cebu." *Philippine Studies* 40:1 (1992): 35–52.

Pomeroy, Robert S. "The Role of Women and Children in Small Scale Fishing Households: A Case Study in Matalom, Leyte, Philippines." *Philippine Quarterly of Culture and Society* 15:4 (1981): 353–60.

Remedio, Elizabeth M., Fiscalina Amadora-Nolasco, and René E. Alburo. *Children in Pyrotechnics, Deep-Sea Fishing, Sugarcane Plantations and Commercial Sex: A Baseline Survey in Selected Cities and Municipalities in the Province of Cebu.* Cebu City: University of San Carlos Social Science Research Center and ILO-IPEC, 2004.

Children in the Philippine Gold-Mining Industry

Rosario M. Espino, Asian Institute of Management, Makati City, Philippines

Emmanuel, age sixteen, was a Filipino child laborer who started working in the mining areas of Paracale, a town in Camarines Norte Province in the Philippines, at age ten. At the time of his interview, he was part of a group of more than ten miners working on a site in a small village. He had just surfaced from an underground tunnel ten feet deep, where he had been for almost three hours in search of gold ore. "I had to come up to the surface to breathe some fresh air," he says. He had an hour to rest before he could be ready for another plunge into the tunnel. Since he had a lean frame, it was easy for him to fit into the hole, barely three feet in diameter, and he was light enough for others to lift him out. A rope connected to the surface was tied around his waist. He would just pull the rope to signal to his colleagues when he wanted to come up to the surface or to indicate an emergency.

Emmanuel was out of school and did not seem to have any intention of pursuing formal studies, as his earnings from mining contributed significantly to the family income. His biggest haul was 10,000 pesos (US$220) for two weeks of backbreaking tunneling and digging to extract gold ore from the mines. However, the flow of income was erratic since the mining did not always yield chunks of the high-grade gold ore that brought in relatively huge sums of money.

Emmanuel is just one of thousands of child laborers in the Philippine gold-mining industry, where they have been a significant part of the labor force since the 1980s. Engaged mainly in small-scale mining, many of these child laborers, male and female, age seven to seventeen years, are found in the mining areas of Camarines Norte, a province with one of the highest incidences of the worst forms of child labor in the country.

Child Labor in Small-Scale Mining in the Philippines

A 2001 survey conducted by the National Statistics Office of the Philippines reported that 4 million out of 24 million five- to seventeen-year-old Filipino children, or one out of six children, were working. About 2.4 million of these children were involved in hazardous work (ILO-IPEC and ASIADEV 2003). The same National Statistics Office survey reported that the mining and quarrying sector employed an estimated 17,980 five- to seventeen-year-old children, who were subjected to daily health hazards such as noise, high temperature and humidity, inadequate illumination, slipping and falling, exposure to dust and chemicals, and absence of protective work gear.

Small-scale mining in the Philippines is predominantly a family business, where a family or group of families pool resources to find gold or other precious metals. They work known mineral deposits or excavated mining areas abandoned by bigger mining companies. In many cases, small-scale mining areas are found within large mining concessions granted to large multinational companies or their local affiliates, under various forms of cosharing and ownership arrangements.

Child laborers are usually found in gold-rush mining communities, where the location of activities shifts from one area to another depending on the volume and quality of gold ore present. The child miners and their families live transiently, remaining in one mining community until the site is considered to be emptied and it is time to move on to another deposit, where gold ore is rumored to be abundant.

The average child laborer in small-scale mining

is male, is between fifteen and seventeen years of age but began working at age ten or even earlier, is a school dropout, and has an annual income of 36,614 pesos (US$776), which constitutes 30 percent of the total family income (Philippine Rural Reconstruction Movement 1998).

Small-Scale Mining Methods

Small-scale gold mining employs a variety of methods to extract gold, including the compressor system, tunneling and sinking, open-cast mining, and panning and sluicing. Each of these methods poses different levels of danger to the life and limb of child miners.

The compressor system is an underwater-mining method and is considered the most dangerous (Ponciano and Espino 2000). Child miners plunge into a well-like shaft approximately 12 inches (30 centimeters) wide and about thirty to fifty feet (ten to fifteen meters) deep. The shaft may be vertical or it may be a sloping passageway leading to the surface. The miners wear no protective gear except for crude goggles for their eyes and cotton for their ears to prevent water from entering. A diesel-driven compressor that pumps oxygen into the miner's mouth through a hose serves as his breathing apparatus. The miner is made to stay inside the murky pit, with zero visibility, for up to eight hours to extract soil possibly containing gold bits. The miner works in a squatting position, anchoring himself with elbows and knees pressed against the walls. He uses a spade or shovel to extract the soil from the well and places the soil in a sack tied around his waist. He usually stays underwater for three to five hours before surfacing to take a break.

Tunneling and sinking are regular activities undertaken by miners. This is the method used by the boy miner Emmanuel described earlier. The miners work as a team, divided into the tunneling group, which digs holes horizontally, and the sinking group, which digs holes vertically to maximize the exploration of the mining site for gold ore.

Open-cast mining is considered the easiest and least dangerous method of extracting gold and is sometimes used during the rainy season, when rocks are washed down from the mountains to the riverbanks. Child laborers and their families simply gather the rocks and break them into smaller pieces in the hope of finding gold inside. However, this method has been found to yield the least amount of gold and is thus seldom used.

Gold panning is the most common method used by mining households. Miners use a pan to separate gold bits from the soil with the aid of the chemical mercury. In sluicing, miners pass water through a long, sloping trough with grooves at the bottom to separate the gold from gravel or sand.

Issues and Challenges in Child Labor in Small-Scale Mining

Since small-scale mines in the Philippines are generally unregistered and, in this sense, illegal as formal business undertakings, they are also unregulated when it comes to application of occupational safety and health protection measures and child labor laws. Along with commercial agriculture and construction, mining is considered one of the three most dangerous industries for children to work in. Child laborers in small-scale mining are at great risk of death, severe injury, or suffering from serious work-related health problems. Many injuries and health problems may result in permanent disability that may not become apparent until the child worker becomes an adult. Because their bodies and minds are growing and developing, child laborers are at greater risk of getting injured or falling seriously ill than adult workers (ILO-IPEC 2005).

Children in the Philippine gold-mining industry are marginalized, isolated from mainstream society, and deprived of education and a normal childhood as a consequence of their work. Further, while income derived from the small-scale mining activities of child laborers is able to put food on their families' tables, the income is highly irregular and so actually offers minimal economic returns that are barely enough to sustain the quality of life of their families and the communities in which they live.

References and Further Reading

ILO-IPEC. *Eliminating Child Labour in Mining and Quarrying: Background Document (World Day Against Child Labor).* Geneva: ILO-IPEC, 2005.

ILO-IPEC and ASIADEV. *In Search for the Pot of Gold: A Case Study of the Experiences of the ILO-IPEC Program on the Elimination of Child Labor in Small Mining Communities in the Province of Camarines Norte, Philippines.* Manila: ILO-IPEC and Asia Development Bank, 2003.

Philippine Rural Reconstruction Movement. *Report on Camarines Norte.* Quezon City: Philippine Rural Reconstruction Movement, 1998.

Ponciano, Ronnie C., and Cherie M. Espino. "The Philippine Rural Reconstruction Movement's Community-Based Intervention to Combat Child Labour in Small-Scale Gold Mining Communities in Camarines Norte, Philippines." *United Nations Centre for Regional Development Publications: Regional Development Dialogue* 21:2 (2000): 119–30.

The Role of NGOs in the Philippines

Yuko Kitada, PhD, The Australian National University

The Philippines is known for its active civil society with roots in the political history of the country. There are numerous NGOs and people's organizations focusing on various issues of societal concern. Child labor is no exception. There are several local NGOs tackling problems associated with child labor and street children, as well as child abuse, as these terms are often used synonymously.

Civil Society in the Philippines: History and Overview

The beginnings of civil society in the Philippines can be traced to the nineteenth century during Spanish colonization. Alongside the proto-NGOs of Spanish colonial welfare associations and Roman Catholic parish organizations, there were also quasi-religious peasant protest movements and secret antichurch organizations such as the Masons. Ever since, there have been various civil organizations, as well as movements of people in resistance to authority, throughout subsequent American and Japanese occupations. It was, however, the lack of democracy and prevalent human rights abuses during the fifteen years of President Ferdinand Marcos's dictatorship that nurtured the vibrant civil society found in the Philippines today. During the Marcos era, civil organizations had to go underground, but after Marcos was ousted in 1986 by the peaceful protest of citizens, known as People Power, NGOs flourished, eager to build a democratic society. In 1986, there were 27,100 NGOs registered as nonstock and nonprofit organizations with the Philippines Securities and Exchange Commission. By 1992, the number increased to 50,800 (Racelis 2000). Some NGOs were founded by foreign clergies committed to working with and for the Filipinos. With this climate for NGOs and a democratic society, Filipino people readily responded to such initiatives and carried forward the activities of the NGOs after the founders retired.

Toward the year 2000, the number of NGOs in the Philippines was estimated to be anywhere between 60,000 and 95,000. Even though only about 5,000 to 7,000 of them are grassroots NGOs aiming to empower the poor and disadvantaged (the rest address more middle-class interests), the role and energy of these grassroots NGOs in building a more equitable and democratic society are far from negligible. Since 1986, foreign donors have recognized that grassroots NGOs in the Philippines could deliver aid directly and efficiently to those who need it most. Subsequently, funding poured directly into Filipino NGOs, contributing to the growth in their numbers and operational capacities. The NGOs focused on women, indigenous peoples, the environment, rural farmers, the urban poor, and children (Racelis 2000).

Child Labor NGOs in the Philippines

In the Philippines, child labor is addressed within the broader aim of protecting children from abuse. This is because the gravest ills of child labor are thought to be not that children are working but that children are often subjected to exploitation in various work situations. Therefore, Filipino NGOs known to address problems of child labor often focus on street children (both children *on* the street and children *of* the street), abandoned or neglected children, exploited children such as those in forced prostitution, and children working in various sectors. In fact, in the Philippines, *child labor* is often understood to be synonymous with *child abuse*, and the work of these child labor NGOs focuses on removing children from hazardous situations and assisting in their rehabilitation. Child labor NGOs also engage in creating safe and caring communities for children, recognizing that to reduce child labor, the environment and living conditions that surround children need to be improved.

The child-focused activities of NGOs include rescuing operations, offering shelter for rescued children, referring children to appropriate partner agencies and organizations including legal services, assisting in children's recovery by providing counseling and psychosocial support, and conducting resiliency-building seminars for children. NGOs also provide social and leisure activities for children, including workshops for artistic and expressive activities, such as acting in plays, which allows children to see their plight objectively and to advocate for their own cause. Some of the NGOs use a peer-to-peer approach in their work, where former street children (or working children or abused children) reach out to current street children, being their mentors and informing them of programs, services, and help available to them.

Activities of the NGOs to create a supportive environment for children center on building family and local community. This is done through awareness-raising activities in the community on issues of child abuse and child labor, but also through skills training for livelihood and administering microfinance and savings programs. There are also programs to improve community health and schemes to provide scholarships and other financial assistance in emergencies such as bereavement or loss of house in a fire or to cover medical costs.

In order to implement these activities in local communities, NGOs' strategy is to help the people help themselves. NGOs engage in community organizing. They provide training for adult members of the community to create and manage a "people's organization." With the help and training provided by NGOs, the local people are empowered to organize themselves, voice their needs more effectively, and manage the programs with a sense of ownership. NGOs have focused on empowering women in community organizing, but more recently, there has been an awareness that men need to be fully engaged in order to make a fundamental change in the power structure in the community. After establishing a people's organization, the NGO works hand in hand as its partner in advocacy and implementing programs. Therefore, child labor NGOs in the Philippines, like other grassroots NGOs in the country, can also be considered community-development organizations.

NGO-Government Collaboration

NGOs recognize that child labor is part of the larger problem of poverty and unequal distribution of resources and political power in society. With their main sources of funding coming from abroad or from individual citizens (Quebral 2004), Filipino NGOs can operate independently of major power holders in the Philippines, be it the government or other interest groups. However, NGOs not only foster empowerment of the disadvantaged in a country where political power has traditionally been concentrated in the hands of a few. Many NGOs manage to collaborate with the government successfully.

As signatory to the major international conventions on child labor, the Philippine government has made a pledge to act on child labor issues. Many NGOs join in this endeavor, working in partnership with governmental departments and agencies. Where the national government does not have the financial or human resources necessary to reach all the sections of the society in need of help and services, NGOs can fill this gap. NGOs operate at the grassroots level and connect the needy with governmental services and programs.

Conclusion

NGOs complement government's work by filling gaps in services and delivering assistance where it is most needed, but that is just a result of NGO activities and not their primary purpose. NGOs in the Philippines are primarily the platform for the action of ordinary citizens in a society where political power is largely monopolized by a few. The work of NGOs, including their collaboration with government, can be understood as the citizens' direct participation in creating a society in which they want to live.

References and Further Reading

Quebral, Marianne G. "Nongovernmental Organizations and Fundraising: Why People Equals Power." *New Directions for Philanthropic Fundraising* 46 (Winter 2004): 77–90.

Racelis, Mary. "New Visions and Strong Actions: Civil Society in the Philippines." In *Funding Virtue: Civil Society Aid and Democracy Promotion,* ed. Marina Ottaway and Thomas Carothers, 159–87. Washington, DC: Carnegie Endowment for International Peace, 2000.

Some Important Child-Oriented Philippine NGOs and Their Web Sites

Bahay Tuluyan: Program for Empowerment of Abused and Exploited Street Children. http://www.geocities.com/bahaytuluyan.

ChildHope Asia: An International Movement on Behalf of Street Children. http://www.childhope.org.ph.

Community Organizers Multiversity. http://www.comultiversity.org.ph.

Educational Research and Development Assistance (ERDA) Foundation. http://www.erdafoundation.org.

People's Recovery, Empowerment and Development Assistance (PREDA) Foundation. http://www.preda.org.

Visayan Forum Foundation. http://www.visayanforum.org.

Thailand

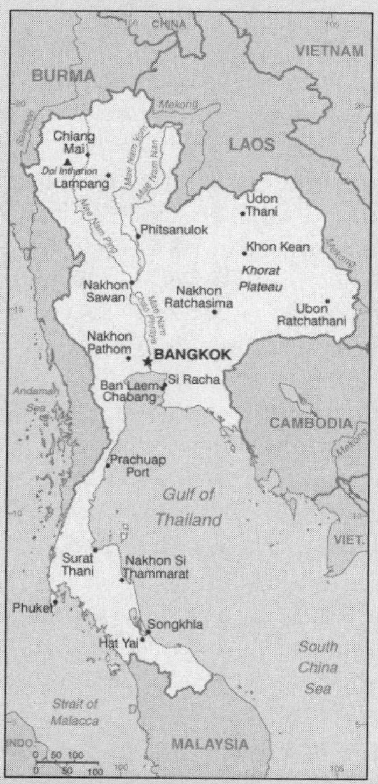

THAILAND			
	CRC	C 138	C 182
Ratifications	Y	Y	Y
Human Development Index/Rank	0.784/74		
Human Capital			
Population Growth Rate	0.66%		
% Population 0–14	21.6%		
Total Fertility Rate	1.64		
Life Expectancy	72.55		
Infant Mortality Rate	18.85		
Literacy Rate	92.6%		
Economic			
GDP/Capita	$9,100		
GDP Growth %	4.8%		
% Poverty	10%		
Gini Index	51.1		
Labor Force Composition			
% Agriculture	49%		
% Industry	14%		
% Services	37%		

CHILD ACTIVITY BREAKDOWN, BY SEX AND RESIDENCE

RESIDENCE	Percentage of children in the relevant age-group[a]									
	Economic activity only		School only		Combining school and economic activity		Neither in school nor in economic activity		Child labor[b]	
	Male	Female	Male	Female	Male	Female	Male	Female	Male	Female
Urban	0.5	0.3	85.4	86.2	11.6	11.3	2.5	2.2	n/av	n/av
Rural	0.7	0.5	82.8	83.5	13.2	12.4	3.3	3.5	n/av	n/av
Total	0.7	0.5	83.5	84.2	12.8	12.1	3.1	3.2	8.4	8.2

Source: Thailand, Multiple Indicator Cluster Survey 3, 2005–2006 (see UCW-Project Web site, http://www.ucw-project.org, country statistics).

Notes: [a]Children age 5 to 14. [b]Estimate includes (a) children under age 12 engaged in economic activities, (b) children age 12–14 engaged in excessive economic activities (more than 14 hours per week), and (c) children under age 15 engaged in excessive household chores (at least 28 hours per week). Estimate does not account for children engaged in hazardous work or other unconditional "worst forms" of child labor.

Child Labor in Thailand

Chantana Banpasirichote Wungaeo, Associate Professor, Director of the International Development Studies Program, Faculty of Political Science, Chulalongkorn University

Over the past thirty or forty years, child labor in Thailand has changed with the country's social and economic development. The issue first became known in Thailand when the Department of Labour published the first survey report on Women and Child Labour in 1968. At that time, the participation of children in the labor force was seen as part of the policy of employment promotion during a period of economic stagnation (Chantana 1995). Although the presence of working children in Thai society was not unusual thirty years ago, seeing children leaving their homes to seek a full-time job elsewhere was considered a new social phenomenon. The public perception of working children changed subsequently due to the shocking reality brought to public attention by a well-known BBC documentary entitled *One Way Ticket to Hualampong* (the central train station in Bangkok) in 1981. That was, perhaps, the beginning of the child labor industry, whereby child labor recruitment became a profitable business. Children working in the household economy had to be differentiated from child laborers employed by enterprises and earning their wages independently from their families. The migration of child laborers from rural to urban areas, particularly Bangkok, was a dominant trend during the 1970s and 1980s. In the 1970s, poverty was widely believed to be the primary cause of child labor migration. Child brokers, in the name of job placement, were the key driver in facilitating child migration for work. Exploitation in the process of job placement was the major issue.

The boom in child labor was observed during the period of high economic growth in the late 1980s. A labor force survey in 1988 indicated that one out of every four children from eleven to fourteen years old was employed (Chantana 1992). The economic growth signified Thailand as a newly industrialized country, with a remarkable expansion of its export sector. This growth, however, has not resulted in adequate development of social welfare for children and families. On the contrary, it has created a wider social and economic gap. The compulsory education that was started in 1980 could keep children in school for only six years (until the age of thirteen). Children not continuing to secondary school became active in the labor market. In this situation, poverty was no longer an important factor causing child labor. The expansion of urban labor markets naturally attracted children from the rural communities. Seeking an opportunity to work was considered a choice rather than an alternative compelled by destitution.

Problems of child labor during the boom period were defined in the context of social exclusion. Pressing issues, apart from the minimum age, were working conditions, hazardous work, and the limited participation and development of child laborers. Since child laborers have gone through a decade of migration, they have established social networks for job placement and learned how to lend one another a hand. As a result, the role of child brokers has declined. In addition, problems of child labor have been recognized by the efforts of NGOs and international organizations in social campaigns and policy advocacy. Child laborers sought to be integrated into the larger economy; in that process, they have ironically been excluded by the rationale of the market itself and weak social service institutions.

Changing Trends

The latest assessment of child labor by the Thailand Development and Research Institute (TDRI)

indicates that the number of children in the labor market has decreased constantly over the past fifteen years, particularly after the boom. A sharp decrease was detected during 1993–1996, when the economy changed its nature from manufacturing to capital investment. Possible explanations include the decreasing population in the eleven- to seventeen-year-old age-group and the implementation of a universal education policy in 1990, which increased opportunities for children to stay in school for nine years, until age fifteen (Nipon et al. 2001). There have also been some changes on the demand side, where higher technology now plays a greater role in competitive advantage, resulting in the need for more-qualified workers with secondary and high school education. Children in the new economic setting aim for factory work rather than small enterprises.

Education that responds to the labor market seems to be the most important variable in the declining trend of Thai children in the labor market. The TDRI report estimates that the number of children between thirteen and seventeen years old in school has increased 1.8 times, from 2.43 million in 1984 to 4.30 million in 2000. As a result, the number of child laborers age thirteen to seventeen decreased from 3.37 million in 1987 to 1.04 million in 2000, an average decrease of 4.5 percent each year. The decrease in the rural areas was greater than in urban areas (Nipon et al. 2001). By 2004, the estimate of child laborers was down to 334,207. Boys comprise 60 percent of child laborers and girls 40 percent (Ministry of Labour 2005). It is unfortunate that, since 1995, labor statistics have excluded children under thirteen years old because the law defines child labor by the minimum age of thirteen years. Children younger than thirteen years old were not counted regardless of their working status. The official statistics therefore do not reflect the full reality of child labor.

Despite decreasing numbers, studies confirm that child labor can still be found since there are still children who have no choice. This applies particularly in urban areas, where job opportunities are higher. So, children from poor families in the urban areas are still engaged in job activities, despite the expansion of universal education (Nipon et al. 2001). It is true that fewer children from rural areas are migrating to the cities. Needing seed money as well as good social connections to get a job, very poor families find it difficult to support their children to come to work in the city.

Vic, thirteen years old, is employed as a mason at US$3 per day to rebuild this restaurant for tourists that looks over Kamala Beach. Phuket, Thailand, January 2007. *(© International Labor Organization / M. Crozet)*

Immigrant Child Labor

In the early 1990s, nongovernmental organizations such as the Foundation for Child Development started reporting cases of child laborers from neighboring countries found in Bangkok and provincial towns along the Thai-Myanmar and Thai-Cambodia borders. By 2000, the foundation's emergency home for child laborers, which rescues and assists 200–250 children per year, reported that it was assisting more immigrant children from neighboring countries than Thai children. The migrant labor of Thai children is no longer the dominant theme; it has gradually shifted to immigrant child labor from the neighboring countries of Myanmar, Laos, and Cambodia.

Until recently, Thailand did not have a system for keeping track of immigrant labor, let alone immigrant child labor. Registration of illegal immigrant laborers from neighboring countries was not initiated until 2003, after a countrywide debate on legalizing immigrant laborers. A research report by the Foundation for Child Development estimates that 20 percent of the immigrants are child laborers. It is astonishing that, in 2004, the number of children below fifteen years reported to the registration office was 93,082. Specifically, twelve- to fourteen-year-old children who are likely to be hired in small enterprises numbered 15,944 (Khemporn et al. 2006). These estimates do not include those who did not report to the registration office. If all immigrants reported, it is believed the numbers could be double the current estimate.

While child labor among Thai children has been decreasing constantly as children's aspirations shift to more skilled work in larger factories, immigrant child labor has taken on the unskilled work in fisheries, domestic work, construction, small manufacturing enterprises, street vending, local restaurants, and plantation agriculture. Immigrant children are more vulnerable due to their lack of legal status. Many therefore become victims, falling into child trafficking and being traded into illegal types of work, such as begging and prostitution.

Worst Forms of Child Labor

Thailand has gone through debates on child labor ranging from an early phase in which it denied the existence of the problem to advocating for the elimination of child labor, to applying a minimum age, to defending children's right to development, to campaigning against the worst forms of child labor. Thailand has attempted to transcend this issue by, first, accepting the truth about the exploitation of children, and second, trying to solve it, of course with interventions from many organizations—national and international, government and nongovernmental. However, the problem could not be solved immediately due to the fact that child laborers and their families share the same destiny. It has been accepted that some children of poor families will have to work, but only within acceptable standards. Child brokers have been strictly prohibited. The minimum age has been enforced and adjusted from twelve to thirteen and then fifteen years. Hazardous forms of work have been identified, including deep-sea fishing, mining, late-night work, and sex-related services. The most difficult and the most important issue facing Thailand today is child trafficking.

Restrictions on child labor have been adopted as intermediate measures because child labor cannot be completely eliminated within the present social and economic conditions. Thailand ratified ILO Convention 182 on elimination of the worst forms of child labor in 2001. In 2006, the faculty of social administration at Thammasat University conducted a sample survey to assess the worst forms of child labor in the country. The results revealed that traditional forms of bonded labor and slavery are not clearly practiced and are hardly reported. The remaining severe problems are concentrated in the use of children in illegal activities such as drug trafficking, pornography, and prostitution. However, concerned parties have not been able to reach a consensus on the magnitude of the problem, holding different estimates of the numbers (Surapon and Saksri 2006). It is also unfortunate to find that a considerable number of child laborers under fifteen years old (34.5 percent of the samples) still fall into the categories of agricultural workers and beggars (Surapon and Saksri 2006). Although the use of children in dangerous forms of work (sweatshops or small factories) has been declining, child laborers continue to be treated as second-class labor compared to male adult workers. Their wages, working hours, workplace environments, work shifts, and opportunities for personal development are not well protected, particularly in those types of work that are difficult to regulate, such as domestic work, subcontracted work, and home work. This situation is tolerated because the implementation of general labor standards remains problematic. Perhaps the most effective interventions so far are the expansion of universal education and the flexible access to nonformal education for child laborers.

Thailand has gone through its most difficult problems with child labor over the past twenty-five to thirty years and has progressed to a more acceptable condition. This is attributed more to the changing course of the economy and investment in education than to the enforcement of child labor regulations. It is depressing to recognize, however, that the improvement of child labor incidence among Thai children occurs at the cost of the suffering of immigrant child laborers. Because child rights are not confined by nationalities or territories, the protection of child laborers in Thailand is not yet accomplished. The concerted efforts of nongovernmental organizations, as well as the presence of international organizations, have always been a critical factor for policy innovation. Regional mechanisms to tackle child trafficking, including agreements between the government and civil society organizations, and bilateral agreements between Thailand and neighboring countries, are a significant step toward the protection of child rights in Thailand, but significant results reversing the trend have yet to be seen.

References and Further Reading

Chantana Banpasirichote Wungaeo. *The Study of Situations and Policies on Disadvantaged Children and Youth: Child Labour.* Bangkok: Chulalongkorn University Social Research Institute, 1992.

Chantana Banpasirichote. *A Comprehensive Report on the Situation of Child Labour in Thailand.* Bangkok: ILO-IPEC, 1995.

Chantana Banpasirichote and Amara Pongsapich. *Child Workers in Hazardous Works in Thailand.* Bangkok: Chulalongkorn University Social Research Institute, 1992.

Khemporn Wiroonrapan, et al. *A Research Report on Guidelines for the Protection Assistance and Development of Immigrant Child Labour in Thailand.* Submitted to the National Health Foundation. Bangkok: Foundation for Child Development, 2006.

Ministry of Labor. *The Study of Child Labour in Thailand.* Bangkok: Ministry of Labour, Department of Labour Protection and Welfare, 2005.

Nipon Puapongsakorn, et al. *A Research Report on the Situation and Trends of Child Labour in Thailand and Impacts on Their Future Opportunities.* Submitted to the Permanent Secretary Office, Minister of Social Welfare and Labour. Bangkok: Thailand Research and Development Institute, 2001.

Surapon Patanwanich and Saksri Boribanbanpotket. *A Research Report on the Situation Analysis of the Worst Form of Child Labour in Thailand.* Submitted to ILO-IPEC. Bangkok: Faculty of Social Administration, Thammasat University, 2006.

Vietnam

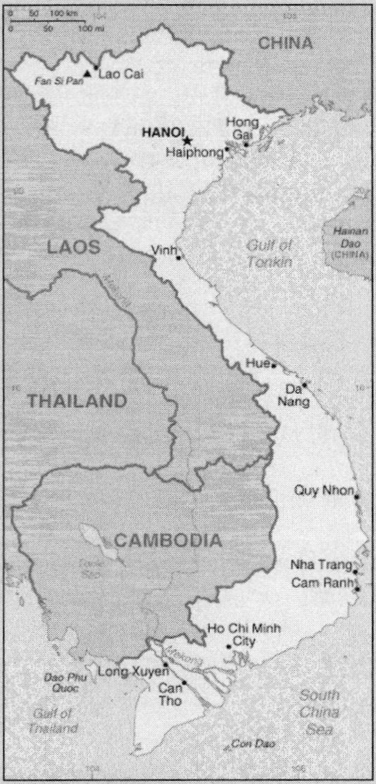

VIETNAM			
	CRC	C 138	C 182
Ratifications	Y	Y	Y
Human Development Index/Rank	0.709/109		
Human Capital			
Population Growth Rate	1%		
% Population 0–14	26.3%		
Total Fertility Rate	1.89		
Life Expectancy	71.07		
Infant Mortality Rate	24.37		
Literacy Rate	90.3%		
Economic			
GDP/Capita	$3,100		
GDP Growth %	7.8%		
% Poverty	19.5%		
Gini Index	36.1		
Labor Force Composition			
% Agriculture	56.8%		
% Industry	37%		
% Services	6.2%		

CHILD ACTIVITY BREAKDOWN, BY SEX AND RESIDENCE

RESIDENCE	Percentage of children in the relevant age-group[a]									
	Economic activity only		School only		Combining school and economic activity		Neither in school nor in economic activity		Child labor[b]	
	Male	Female	Male	Female	Male	Female	Male	Female	Male	Female
Urban	0.8	0.8	92.0	87.6	6.0	9.1	1.2	2.5	n/av	n/av
Rural	2.1	2.9	75.2	75.4	18.6	17.5	4.0	4.2	n/av	n/av
Total	1.9	2.5	78.7	77.9	16.0	15.8	3.4	3.8	15.3	16.4

Source: Vietnam, Multiple Indicator Cluster Survey 3, 2006 (see UCW Project Web site, http://www.ucw-project.org, country statistics).

Notes: [a]Children age 5 to 14. [b]Estimate includes (a) children under age 12 engaged in economic activities, (b) children age 12–14 engaged in excessive economic activities (more than 14 hours per week), and (c) children under age 15 engaged in excessive household chores (at least 28 hours per week). Estimate does not account for children engaged in hazardous work or other unconditional "worst forms" of child labor.

Social Transformation and Children's Work in Vietnam

Nguyen Van Chinh, Hanoi National University, Vietnam

Before market-oriented economic reform, which began in the mid-1980s, Vietnam's economy was built on socialism's ideal principles of planning and collectivization. The 1990s were viewed as a turning point in the course of economic reform, when the command economy was replaced by a multisectored and open economy. Since the 1990s, the country's annual economic growth rate has remained stable between 7 and 8 percent. Successful economic reform has contributed to improving social welfare and household income. Hunger and starvation have decreased substantially, but poverty remains the most challenging problem. Poverty has increased in rural and mountainous areas, especially among ethnic minorities. At the same time, income inequality and the gap between the rich and the poor has widened dramatically. Social views and values have also changed. Under the socialist subsidized economy, ideas of private enrichment were abolished. Nowadays, under the market economy, money is highly appreciated and the rich are respected. In addition, social services such as health and education, which once were considered the responsibility of the state, have now returned to the responsibility of individual families. As the people's belief in the lofty ideals of socialism collapsed, the desire to restore traditional social values and hierarchical order has been revived.

While studies tend to emphasize poverty and low household income as direct causes for child labor, it is important to recognize that elements of social structure, such as the hierarchical order, moral values, and the conception of children's position and roles in families and society, are among the factors influencing their entrance into the labor market.

Opening scallops in the harbor of Mui Né, Vietnam, 2002. (© *International Labor Organization / P. Deloche*)

Children's Work

Before the 1990s, child labor in Vietnam was not a priority issue. National statistics rarely paid attention to child labor. Since the 1990s, censuses and living standards surveys have asked questions about the participation of children younger than fifteen years of age in economic activities. Most of the recent analyses on child labor in Vietnam used information from the general censuses of 1989 and 1999 (TCTK 2002) and the living standards surveys of 1993, 1998, and 2002 (O'Donnell, Van Doorslaer, and Rosati 2003; Edmonds and Turk 2002; Liu 2000; Vo and Trinh 2005).

Tables 1 and 2 summarize findings from the general censuses and the Vietnam Living Standard Surveys (VLSS), respectively. Table 1 reports results from the 1989 and 1999 censuses. In 1989, the census indicated that 22.9 percent of children aged thirteen and fourteen were working in stable

Table 1

Work Participation Rates of Children Age 13–14, 1989 and 1999, by Censuses (in percent)

	1989			1999		
	All	Male	Female	All	Male	Female
Age 13–14	22.9	19.8	26.3	15.8	13.9	17.8
Urban	5.3	5.3	5.4	7.1	7.0	7.3
Rural	26.8	23.0	30.9	17.9	15.6	20.4

Source: TCTK [General Statistical Office] 2002, Tables 6.1 and 6.2, 87–88.

Table 2

Work Participation Rates of Children Age 6–15, 1993 and 1998, by Vietnam Living Standard Surveys (in percent)

	1993			1998		
Indicators	All	Male	Female	All	Male	Female
All	33.95	33.17	34.76	24.99	25.22	24.75
Urban	16.30	15.99	16.60	6.87	6.35	7.39
Rural	37.47	36.46	38.52	28.76	29.03	28.46
Age 6–11	17.82	n/av	n/av	10.51	n/av	n/av
Age 12–15	61.26	n/av	n/av	44.17	n/av	n/av

Source: O'Donnell, Doorslaer, and Rosati 2003, Table 1, 29.

employment situations. Ten years later, the 1999 census indicated that the relevant rate was 15.8 percent (TCTK 2002). Table 2 reports results from the VLSS surveys of 1993 and 1998. In 1993, 33.95 percent of children from six to fifteen years old were working. By 1998, that figure had fallen to 24.99 percent. The data reflected in these tables cover the period when Vietnam was shifting from a command to a market-oriented economy. Though they used different age-groups and different criteria, they reveal an unmistakable trend in declining rates of child-labor-force participation.

Female children, in both urban and rural areas, tend to participate in work at roughly the same rates as male children. In all periods, labor force participation rates are substantially higher in rural areas than in urban areas. One discrepancy between census data and VLSS data is that the censuses showed an increasing trend in the rate of working children in urban areas, from 5.3 percent (1989) to 7.1 percent (1999), whereas the VLSS showed the rate of working children in urban areas to be decreasing, from 16.3 percent (1993) to 6.87 percent (1998). This difference might result from the surveys' use of different criteria and definitions.

The surveys also point out meaningful differences in children's participation in economic activities in different regions of the country. Liu (2000, 3) analyzed economic activities of children from six to fifteen years of age based on the 1992–1993 VLSS and came to the conclusion that "children in the North are more likely to work in either paid or unpaid work than their peers in the South." However, statistics for the thirteen- to fourteen-year-old age-group in the 1999 census show a contrary tendency: The northwest mountainous area and the Mekong River Delta (in the South) have the highest rates of working children. Between 26 and 27 percent of children in these areas worked steadily for more than twelve months before the date of the survey. The 1999 census also found a clear gender difference in the northern mountainous area: Nearly 37 percent of female children work, while the rate for male children rate was just 19 percent. This difference was not significant in the southern areas (TCTK 2002).

There are a number of problems with the census and VLSS data. First, the organizations that compiled them do not specialize in child labor. In addition to their use of different criteria, definitions, and age-groups, they tend to miss many forms of child labor. They do not capture the work of children who live outside their families and work in the informal sector, which may involve earning activities in street, prostitution, and other risky and illegal forms of work. Nor do they count as economic activity household chores, tasks that adults consider light work and a form of socialization and that children might consider hard and boring work. Another group of child workers not adequately captured by the quantitative statistics are apprentices. A significant number of children work as apprentices in handicraft workshops and cottage industries, which developed rapidly in rural areas after the economic reform. Most of these children work without payment and spend several years as apprentices. Using child apprentices is a trick bosses use to increase profit, and it is obviously a form of child labor abuse.

Up to 92.35 percent of working children helped their parents with farming, production, and housework. Only 3.25 percent children worked for wages. Working children in urban areas were more likely to be paid than working children in rural areas, about 8.4 percent and 2.9 percent, respectively. Similarly, male children were more likely to be in paid work than female children, 3.75 and 2.68 percent, respectively. Vietnamese children begin to participate in economic activities at a very young age. By the age of five, about 7 percent of children spent more than nine hours per week participating in housework to help their parents. Female children did more housework than male children.

Overall, the child labor situation in Vietnam differs from the popular perception that depicts child labor as a form of abuse at the hands of parents and greedy bosses. The fact that most children participate in productive household work at a very young age is seen by many Vietnamese people as promoting the children's socialization and development of responsibility. Still, the children's conception of this kind of work is different from that of adults. In their opinion, housework is not a light task, and if they had the right to choose, they would take the paid work to help their parents.

The most important summary finding from the collection of surveys is the sharp decline in the rate of children's participation in economic activities over the past decade. According to analysts, "the transition to market economy has helped improve living conditions and increase the rate of children going to schools, that leads to the reduction of their participation in the labor force" (TCTK 2002, 86).[1] Amazed at these findings, foreign researchers have also found that the increased income of rice-farming households, resulting from the liberalization of the economy, has led to the decreasing rate of children working. Their studies (Edmonds and Turk 2002; Edmonds and Pavcnik 2003) suggest that "households appear to take advantage of higher income after the rice price increase to reduce child labor despite increased earning opportunities for children." However, this simple explanation seems unconvincing, given the fact that the Mekong River Delta, the largest rice-exporting region in Vietnam, is home to more than one-fourth of the children who work full-time, a rate much higher than in other regions of the country. In reality, child labor is a complex matter. Children's work is but a component of social construction; it should not be understood in terms of economics alone. Further emphasis needs to be placed on local cultural perceptions of childhood, child work, and child education.

Despite the lower rate of child labor in Vietnam, the nature and social relations of economic activities that involve children have changed. Prior to the market-oriented economy, almost all children worked in their own households to support their families, under family members' guidance and protection. More recent data indicate an increasingly popular trend of children seeking paid jobs outside the household in the new context of the multisectored economy. This changes the nature of working relations in fundamental ways. What used to be a form of socialization under the guidance of parents has been replaced by a relationship with an owner or employer, and children work for wages while the owner works for profit. The transformation of the economic system has also brought about a wider range of employment options for children. If most children previously worked in the agricultural sector, now they tend to move far from home to be engaged in paid employment in private workshops and households. It is clear that children working in the market economy are more vulnerable than they were before. To study the nature of their economic activities, therefore, we need more qualitative analysis in addition to quantitative approaches.

Finally, up to the present day, there have been no official surveys of the worst forms of child labor in Vietnam. However, there have been Rapid Assessments of the situation of children earning their living in the streets, especially of those working as prostitutes. While there are no statistics on the exact number of children working as prostitutes, the available evidence indicates that the number of children participating in prostitution has increased consistently since 1989. According to a 2002 ILO-IPEC Rapid Assessment, approximately 5 to 20 percent of the prostitutes in Vietnam's four largest cities were children, depending on the geographical area. For example, the rate in southern areas is higher than that in northern areas. Poverty, broken families, and other social problems are considered the main reasons for children to participate in prostitution (Le Bach Duong 2002).

Children's Education

Vietnam is known for its age-old history of education and tradition of veneration for educational ethics. After the country gained independence from the French in 1945, the colonial education system was banned and socialism-based education was designed to uplift the society. The Vietnamese Communist Party considered children's education a national mission, not a family's duty. Thanks to the education policy being practiced nationwide for decades, the literacy rate was 91 percent in 2002. This was a great achievement for public education in Vietnam, where the poverty rate was still very high. Socialist education, however, has undergone a severe crisis since the country shifted to a market-oriented economy. The state did not maintain free education as a social benefit. Instead, the burden of school fees is now shouldered by individual households.

There is a close relationship between children's school attendance and the changing economic system. In the late 1980s and early 1990s, school attendance rates fell while school dropout rates rose, hovering between 12 to 14 percent at primary school and 24 to 29 percent at the secondary level (Ministry of Education and Training 1994). In 1993, 16.7 percent of children under the age of twelve had dropped out of school; the dropout rate accelerated to 28.2 percent at the age of thirteen; 46.7 percent at fourteen; and 58.6 percent at fifteen. By age sixteen, 71.0 percent had dropped out. The problem has been gradually addressed. By the year 2002, the dropout rate had been slashed to 6 percent at the age of twelve and to 35.2 percent at age sixteen These indicators of improvement in school attendance are seen in the context of a stable market economy and changes in parents' awareness of the value of education. However, the dropout rate of girls tends to be higher than that of boys of the same age and grade, despite a small improvement in recent years. In 1993, the dropout rate of twelve-year-old girls stood at 23.6 percent, while that of boys of the same age was only 9 percent. By the age of sixteen, girls' dropout rate swelled to 79 percent compared to 63 percent for boys. By 2002, girls' dropout rate had declined and "the gap between girls' and boys' drop-out rates was only 4.3%" (Vo and Trinh 2005, 27). These gender differences are closely linked to the male-oriented structure of the family. Traditionally, married girls leave their parents' home to reside with the husband's family. This practice encourages parents to give more opportunities to boys for higher education if they cannot afford to ensure equal education for both boys and girls.

Moreover, post-economic-renewal social classifications can have an impact on school enrollment rates and trigger education inequality. During 1992–1993, the literacy rate was reported to be relatively equal among different income groups. Only five years later, statistics indicated that illiteracy tended to be more prominent in lower income groups and ethnic minorities. Further, school enrollment rates (see Table 3) show that rates of primary school enrollment are approximately equal across all segments of society. But enrollments of poor children and ethnic minorities in secondary school are far lower than those in other groups. Even though secondary school enrollment gener-

Table 3

School Enrollment Rate of Children Between 1993 and 2002 (in percent)

Indicators	Primary			Lower Secondary			Upper Secondary		
	1993	1998	2002	1993	1998	2002	1993	1998	2002
All	86.7	91.4	90.1	30.1	61.7	72.1	7.2	28.6	41.8
Poorest	72.0	81.9	84.5	12.0	33.6	53.8	1.1	4.5	17.1
Near Poorest	87.0	93.2	90.3	16.6	53.0	71.3	1.6	13.3	34.1
Middle	90.8	94.6	91.9	28.8	65.5	77.6	2.6	20.7	42.6
Near Richest	93.5	96.0	93.7	38.4	71.8	78.8	7.7	36.4	53.0
Richest	95.9	96.4	95.3	55.0	91.0	85.8	20.9	64.3	67.2
Urban	96.6	95.5	94.1	48.5	80.3	80.8	17.3	54.5	59.2
Rural	84.4	90.6	89.2	26.3	57.9	69.9	4.7	22.6	37.7
Ethnic Kinh and Chinese	90.6	93.3	92.1	33.6	66.2	75.9	7.9	31.9	45.2
Ethnic Minority	63.8	82.2	80.0	6.6	36.5	48.0	2.1	8.1	19.3

Source: Vo and Trinh 2005, 24.

ally increased from 1993 to 2002, poor and ethnic minority children remain far behind.

The low enrollment rate of poor and ethnic minority children in secondary education has been attributed to school fees and the need for children's labor contribution to the household economy. At the primary level, education is both compulsory and free. At upper levels, tuition and other expenditures often create a burden for poor families. According to calculations made by Vo and Trinh (2005, 31), "during 1993 and 2002, the cost of schooling for a child increased by 126.3% while per capita expenditure increased just by 67%." Apart from unaffordable education expenditures, children out of school often spend much more time working for their household (including chores and productive activities) in comparison with those attending school. For example, in 1993, at the age of twelve, a schoolchild spent 800 hours per year, on average, helping the family, while an out-of-school child worked for 1,397 hours per year, on average. There is also a marked gender difference, in which schoolgirls worked for 780 hours per year, on average, compared to 1,411 hours per year for girls out of school. By 2002, hours worked in domestic activities by schoolchildren had been cut in half, but hours worked in domestic activities remained relatively high for children out of school.

It is undeniable that the state has made an effort to add budget allocations for education since the economic reform and the removal of the free education system. The budget for education, in proportion to the total state budget expenditure, increased from 9 percent in 1993 to 12 percent in 2001 and 15 percent in 2005. This state disbursement, however, was mainly for payment of teacher salaries. Other payments for education, such as fundamental construction, teaching equipment, curriculum building, and textbooks, occupied less than 20 percent of the total annual budget for education. This poses the great challenge for the national education system to reach its goal of renovation and enhancement.

Conclusion

Market-oriented economic reform has been the greatest impetus for social change in Vietnam over the last decade of the twentieth century. This has influenced nearly all aspects of life and social values. Dramatic reductions in poverty rates have been accompanied by decreasing rates of child-labor-force participation and escalating rates of school attendance. There is no doubt that stable economic growth and rising household income are major forces helping to curb child labor. Economic factors, however, are not the only agents spurring change. Others, such as changes in the conception of children's position and value in family and society, the improvement of the education system, and reinforcement of legal commitments to ensure children's rights, have also played an essential part.

Although there is a declining trend in child labor, the number of children age six to fourteen engaged in economic activity remains high. Further, the nature of child employment has become more complicated and difficult to control. Under the collective economy, almost all children had the advantage of working under the protection of family members or social bodies. After the shift to a market economy, the window of employment opportunities for children in private and informal sectors opened. A number of children have begun to search for outside paid jobs. The increasing movement of rural children to urban areas to earn their living on the streets, as domestic servants, or in prostitution has set off the alarm bells warning of the increasing complexity of child labor under a market economy. It can be predicted that the rate of child labor will continue to decrease in coming decades, but the number of children working for wages, and those in worst forms of child labor, could be on the rise. Consequently, the unresolved matter of child labor in Vietnam will continue to be a huge challenge for development and prosperity in the next decades.

Note

1. Translation by the author.

References and Further Reading

Edmonds, E., and N. Pavcnik. *Does Globalization Increase Child Labor? Evidence from Vietnam.* Working paper 8760, National Bureau of Economic Research, Cambridge, MA, 2003.

Edmonds, E., and C. Turk. *Child Labor in Transition in Vietnam.* Hanoi: World Bank, 2002.

Le Bach Duong, ed. *Vietnam: Children in Prostitution in Hanoi, Hai Phong, Ho Chi Minh City and Can Tho: A Rapid Assessment.* Hanoi: ILO-IPEC, 2002.

Liu, A.Y.C. "Children at Work: Do Regions Matter and Why? A Case Study in Vietnam." Working paper 00-2. Asia Pacific Press at the Australia National University, Canberra, 2000.

Ministry of Education and Training. "Nghiên cứu giáo dục" [Educational studies], no. 3 (1994).

O'Donnell, O., E. Van Doorslaer, and F. Rosati. "Health Effects of Children's Work: Evidence from Vietnam." Understanding Children's Work Project Working Paper Series, Rome, April 2003.

TCTK [General Statistical Office]. *Tổng điều tra dân số và nhà ở Việt Nam 1999: chuyên khảo về lao động và việc làm tại Việt Nam* [The 1999 census: issues of labor and employment in Vietnam]. Hanoi: Thống kê, 2002.

Vo Tri Thanh and Quang Long Trinh. "Can Vietnam Achieve One of Its Millennium Development Goals? An Analysis of Schooling Dropouts of Children." Working paper 776, William Davidson Institute, Ann Arbor, MI, June 2005.

Street Children in Vietnam

Pietro Masina, Associate Professor of International Political Economy, University of Naples–L'Orientale

After a century of colonial rule and decades of war, Vietnam was finally at peace in April 1975. The war legacy was heavy. The little infrastructure that existed in the country had been destroyed or had deteriorated. The economy had been distorted through dependence on foreign aid, the dislocation of people, and the channeling of industrial and agricultural production to military purposes. Society was divided and traumatized. Poverty was widespread and so deep that the country faced famine during bad harvesting years. The invasion of Cambodia (to remove the Pol Pot regime) and the tragedy of the boat people in 1979 left the country internationally isolated and largely dependent on Soviet support for survival.

Against this backdrop, Vietnam started a process of economic reform that was officially sanctioned in December 1986 under the name of *doi moi* (renovation). This reform process consisted of a progressive convergence toward a market economy (but with key guidance functions left to the state) and closer integration into the world economy. The reforms created important results in economic growth and even more important results in poverty reduction. From 1993 to 2004 the number of households living below the national poverty line fell from almost 60 percent to below 20 percent—no other country in the world managed to do better in such a short period of time.

To understand the reality of street children in Vietnam, it is important to keep in mind the country context. On the one hand, Vietnam is a poor country facing mechanisms of social exclusion typical of other developing nations. On the other hand, Vietnam is a country in which economic transition is substantially successful in creating broad-based improvement in living conditions in both urban and rural areas. Thus, the movement of young rural people to urban areas is a result of push factors (poverty, lack of opportunities) and pull factors (existing or imagined opportunities in major urban centers).

The term *street children* is used to cover a rather wide array of conditions, ranging from teenagers working in the urban informal sector to abandoned young children. While these different conditions cannot be easily categorized, it is important to distinguish among cases in terms of both the problems the children face and the policies that should be implemented to shelter them.

One very large group of street children is represented by young peasants migrating to urban areas for seasonal or temporary engagement in the informal sector. Many teenage girls move to towns as nannies, street fruit vendors, waiters, or shop assistants. Teenage boys typically work as shoe shiners, newspapers sellers, peddlers, or market haulers. Their work in the urban informal sector is part of the livelihood strategy of their rural family, often contributing to securing basic needs for very poor households. In some cases, temporary migration may allow small savings to be remitted back to the village. These young migrants tend to move back to their home villages once they approach the age for marriage—their life in town is too marginal to make the prospect of a permanent migration concrete or appealing. Further, some activities such as shoe shining are reported to yield decent, if irregular, income but are socially acceptable only for teenagers. These young people are defined as street children because they often literally live and work on the street. Their youth and unfamiliarity with the urban context may expose them to dangers and risks. Although they often have a caring family back in the village, in their life in town they are vulnerable.

A second group of street children is represented by young children who have lost the protection of their families. Poverty is a contributing factor, but often not the main reason, in forcing these children onto the street. Many children report stories of broken families and abuse. Among the different patterns emerging through interviews, two are particularly recurrent: a widowed mother abandons her children to search for a new husband (since a wife will normally live with her husband's family, she would not be allowed to take her children with her); a widowed father marries a second time and the new wife manages to expel the children born during the first marriage.

The condition of vulnerability faced by these children is particularly dramatic. Not only do they face the dangers of living on the street, but they also suffer trauma deriving from their family history. Although life on the street in Vietnam is safer and less violent than life in many other developing countries, these children may be manipulated by criminal groups, exposed to drugs, or even sexually exploited—these risks are more apparent in Ho Chi Minh City than in Hanoi or smaller towns.

A third group of street children is represented by children moving to town with migrant parents, particularly migrant mothers, with informal occupations such as garbage collection for recycling. Very young children collecting garbage can be met in the markets of major towns, often wandering around in small groups. These children are normally far from parental protection and supervision for large parts of the day, even at very young ages, and are therefore exposed to severe risks.

The major success of the Vietnamese reform process—poverty reduction—implies an improvement in conditions for those still living below the poverty line. This improvement in conditions also affects street children, who can access food and shelter, sharing rented rooms with other migrants in private houses, more easily than was possible ten or twenty years earlier.

Formal safety nets and policy measures in support of street children are still limited and rudimentary. Besides a lack of resources, an insufficient targeting of measures prevents adequate interventions. At the same time, the flexibility of many local authorities in accepting unregistered children into the local schools contributes to reducing the social exclusion and the vulnerability of many migrant and street children.

Reference and Further Reading

Gallina, Andrea, and Pietro Masina. "Street Children in Vietnam: An Inquiry into the Roots of Poverty and Survival Livelihood Strategies." Federico Caffé Centre, Department of Social Sciences, Roskilde University, 2002.

SECTION 3. OCEANIA

Australia

Development of Child Welfare Policy in Australia

Shurlee Swain, Associate Professor, Reader in History, Australian Catholic University, and Senior Research Fellow, Department of History, University of Melbourne

Child welfare policy constituted one of the three principal legislative controls on child labor in Australia. Intersecting with education and labor laws, it functioned to progressively remove most children of settler or European descent from paid employment. No such protection was offered to indigenous children, who, until the late twentieth century, were subject to a child-removal program designed to separate them from the "idle" ways of their parents and transform them into domestic and rural laborers.

Training Children in the Principles of Morality and Industry

In the early Australian colonies (New South Wales, established 1788; Van Diemen's Land—later Tasmania—established 1803; Western Australia, established 1829; South Australia, established 1836; Victoria, separated from New South Wales in 1851; and Queensland, separated from New South Wales in 1859), the authorities were more concerned with rendering poor children productive than with providing them with access to an idealized concept of childhood. The first public provision for neglected children was institutional, designed to train them "in the principles of morality and industry" (Ramsland 1986, 2) before apprenticing them out. As the colonial economies were primarily agricultural, most apprentices found work as domestic servants or rural laborers. Pauper apprenticeships were given legal authority in 1834 when the New South Wales governor gazetted "An Act for Apprenticing the Children of the Male and Female Orphan Schools, and Other Poor Children in the Colony of New South Wales" (Ramsland 1986). South Australia passed similar legislation in 1842 and four years later established a Children's Apprenticeship Board to act as legal guardian for all apprenticed children (Davey 1956). In the Swan River Colony (later Western Australia) a similar ordinance, introduced in 1845, gave magistrates the power to indenture poor children with parental consent "if that parent was living in the colony," in order "that they [the children] earn their keep and not become a charge on the state" (Hetherington 2002, 25). Parents, however, were not always in the colony because, to overcome a chronic labor shortage, the colony had accepted orphans sent as migrants by the English Society for the Encouragement of Juvenile Emigration and boys sent out from the Parkhurst prison, all of whom were apprenticed under the new ordinance (Hetherington 2002).

In response to the population growth that followed the gold rushes of the 1850s, these early provisions in relation to settler children were codified in the first series of colonial child welfare laws. Beginning with Victoria in 1864, each of the now self-governing colonies passed legislation establishing variously named state children's departments, which were charged with constructing and administering industrial schools on the English model.

Children neglected or abandoned by their parents could be removed to such institutions, initially for terms of up to seven years, and later until the age of eighteen. The goal of such legislation was to train children for, rather than protect them from, labor, and the old apprenticeship system survived, with children leaving the institutions for employment from the ages of twelve to fourteen (Jaggs 1986; Ramsland 1986; Reekie and Wilson 1996; Swain 1998; van Krieken 1991). A growing distaste for the barracks-like conditions, high death rates, and increasing cost of institutional care led most colonies to introduce boarding-out schemes from the 1870s. While the family-like atmosphere of such care was welcomed, work remained central. As future citizens and workers, state children were expected to assist their foster parents in productive labor and continued to be apprenticed at the end of their formal schooling (Murray 1999).

Although this legislation was not racially specific, it was applied primarily to children of settler descent. In the wake of invasion and dispossession, Aboriginal communities were dramatically disrupted; adults and children died as a result of starvation, disease, and frontier violence. Those children who did survive were quickly absorbed into the settler workforce, particularly on the large pastoral properties that now occupied their land. Without even the minimal protection provided by the existing apprenticeship legislation, indigenous children were employed for "keep" rather than wages and subject to no official inspection. Many had become completely detached from their parents and communities as well. Yet, when calls came for reform of the child welfare legislation in order to free juveniles from exploitative labor, no voices were raised on behalf of Aboriginal child workers (Hetherington 2002; Robinson 2002).

Reconstituting Child Workers as Victims

The calls for reform came from urban child savers, most of whom drew their inspiration from the Children's Charter passed in the United Kingdom in 1889. The charter was the result of lobbying by the National Society for the Prevention of Cruelty for Children, branches of which were soon to appear in the Australian colonies (Scott and Swain 2002). Four of the eight categories of abused children identified in the charter involved employment. Child workers, previously seen as valiant supporters of poor families, were reconstituted as victims of lazy and avaricious parents. Child hawkers working out of doors in all weather, children employed in "unwholesome, degrading, unlawful, or immoral callings," whose "powers" were "overtaxed" or whose "hours of labour [were] unreasonably prolonged," and those found begging on the streets were now seen as being in need of care, and the state was given the power to remove them from their parents in order to provide them with such protection (Behlmer 1982, 64).

Legislation passed in Australian colonies (which became states of the new Commonwealth of Australia following federation in 1901) encoded this new understanding of childhood. Although there were some parliamentarians who argued that the milder climate caused colonial children to mature earlier and rendered street trading less dangerous, child protection legislation passed in the period 1890–1911 targeted several categories of child employment for state intervention (Evans 1998; Jaggs 1986; Swain 1998; van Krieken 1991). The children's courts in most states during the same years introduced probation as an alternative to institutional care, but across the nation, child labor, primarily in street trades and the entertainment industries, faced increasing regulation. Typically, such legislation saw children of school age working in the streets after dark as being particularly at risk, prohibiting such employment for children under ten or fifteen, and sometimes for older girls as well, and introducing penalties for employers. It also allowed for the removal of girls from brothels, although such clauses were usually couched in terms of moral contamination rather than employment. In the early years of the twentieth century, a second wave of legislation sought to control the residual street traders, introducing licensing, and in some cases badges, for the small group of boys now permitted to sell newspapers in urban centers (Jaggs 1986; Maunders 1988).

Such legislation was largely reactive, seeking to control the minority of juveniles who remained in employment after the introduction of education and labor laws designed to restrict such activity. Compulsory education, introduced across the colonies from 1872, initially accommodated child employment, setting minimal attendance requirements, which allowed rural children to continue to help out with harvests and urban children to participate in family businesses or assist with child care during their parents' busy times. By the early years of the twentieth century, this flexibility had been removed, although provisions exempting children from the final years of compulsory education, if their wages were needed to support their families, remained in place (Hetherington 2002; Larson 1986; Wimshurst 1981). Labor legislation, passed in the period 1873–1897, complemented the Education Acts, prohibiting the employment of children in factories and workshops during school hours, unless they held such an exemption (Bowden and Penrose 2006; Davey 1956). Later legislation extended this control to other workplaces as well, prohibiting the employment of juveniles in mines and setting limits on the hours during which they could be employed in the retail industry (Davey 1956).

The introduction, in 1907, of a government-mandated basic wage, set at a level sufficient for a man to support a wife and three children, was believed to have removed the need for child labor, although, as women were guaranteed only 40 to 60 percent of the male wage, many female-headed families continued to live in poverty. Child welfare legislation passed in the first half of the twentieth century was focused largely on administrative change, and, while child labor clauses were retained, they were seldom used as a reason for bringing children under state control. Although most children went to work after completing their primary education at age fourteen, the conditions under which they were employed were controlled by union-influenced labor legislation designed to preserve adult male wage levels. For boys, juvenile employment was seen as an essential preparation for entering into their adult responsibilities (van Krieken 1991). For girls, it was an occupation to fill the time between education and marriage. Although education authorities attempted to draw the attention of child welfare activists to work required of children on family farms and girls spending long hours assisting their mothers with the arduous work of the household, their efforts did not meet with success (Scott and Swain 2002). This focus on street trading, to the exclusion of other forms of child labor, has led some scholars to argue that early-twentieth-century child welfare legislation was concerned more with restraining than protecting young people (Maunders 1988; van Krieken 1991).

"Protecting" Indigenous Children

Education and labor legislation had little impact on the lives of Aboriginal children. Beginning in Queensland in 1897, colonies with substantial surviving indigenous populations introduced legislation under which protectors were appointed to control the lives of Aboriginal people (Reekie and Wilson 1996). Such protectors used their guardianship powers to separate indigenous children from their parents and place them in domestic or rural employment after a short period in "training homes." The acts established minimal levels of pay and control over what had been a long-established practice, but under the guise of protection, the proportion of indigenous children sent to work increased. Children of mixed descent were particularly targeted, breaking bonds with family and community over several generations and perpetuating Aboriginal impoverishment (Haskins 2005; Hetherington 2002; Robinson 2002). The impact of these practices, which continued to be applied into the second half of the twentieth century, were examined by the *Bringing Them Home* inquiry (Human Rights and Equal Opportunity Commission 1997), in the aftermath of which successful campaigns have been undertaken to compel state governments to reimburse Aboriginal people for wages lost during their enforced employment (Kidd 2006).

Child Labor Regulation in the Twenty-first Century

As a result of the passage of state and federal acts outlawing racial discrimination, in the last quarter of the twentieth century, Aboriginal children became subject to the same controls as applied to nonindigenous children. The clauses regulating juvenile employment survive in most current child welfare legislation, but they are rarely cited as a reason for bringing children under supervision. Policy initiatives are now more focused on promoting than containing employment for young people. The prolongation of compulsory education and high levels of youth unemployment have led to an anxiety about the work readiness of children and the introduction of measures to increase participation in the workforce. While access to full-time employment continues to be linked to compulsory school-attendance regulations, large numbers of young people are engaged in part-time employment outside of school hours. Although legislation restricts the hours and locations in which such work can be undertaken, there is no protection for children working in family businesses outside school hours, and the protective clauses that govern industrial and commercial workplaces are increasingly being undermined by moves to deregulate the workforce. The skills-based award wages, which replaced youth wages in 1993, are now being superseded by individual workplace agreements negotiated between the juvenile worker and the employer. Unemployed young people in receipt of government benefits can now be compelled to undertake training programs or to "work for the dole" in order to prove work readiness. In an economy that prolongs childhood dependence in the interests of attaining higher skill levels, welfare legislation is once again preoccupied with the dangers of idleness among those who are not contained within such education and training systems.

References and Further Reading

Behlmer, George. *Child Abuse and Moral Reform in England, 1870–1908.* Stanford, CA: Stanford University Press, 1982.

Bowden, Bradley, and Beris Penrose. "The Origins of Child Labour in Australia, 1880–1907: A Health and Safety Perspective." *Journal of Occupational Health and Safety* 22:2 (2006): 127–35.

Davey, Constance. *Children and Their Lawmakers: A Social-Historical Survey of the Growth and Development from 1836 to 1950 of South Australian Laws Relating to Children.* Adelaide, Australia: Griffin Press, 1956.

Evans, Caroline. "'Poor Wand'rers': Tasmania's Street Children and Social Policy in the 1890s." *Tasmanian Historical Studies* 6:1 (1998): 60–74.

Haskins, Victoria. "'& So We *Are* "Slave Owners"!': Employers and the NSW Aborigines Protection Board Trust Funds." *Labour History* 88 (2005): 147–64.

Hetherington, Penelope. *Settlers, Servants and Slaves: Aboriginal Children in Nineteenth-Century Western Australia.* Nedlands: University of Western Australia Press, 2002.

Human Rights and Equal Opportunity Commission. *Bringing Them Home: Report of the National Inquiry into the Separation of Aboriginal and Torres Strait Islander Children from Their Families.* Sydney: Human Rights and Equal Opportunity Commission, 1997.

Jaggs, Donella. *Neglected and Criminal: Foundations of Child Welfare Legislation in Victoria.* Melbourne: Centre for Youth and Community Studies, Phillip Institute of Technology, 1986.

Kidd, Ros. *Trustees on Trial.* Canberra: Aboriginal Studies Press, 2006.

Larson, Ann. "Who Wants to Go to School? The Effects of Free and Compulsory State Education in Nineteenth-Century Victoria." *History of Education Review* 15:1 (1986): 1–18.

Maunders, David. "Legislating for Dependence: The Development of Juvenile Trading Legislation in Victoria 1887–1927." *Journal of Australian Studies* 22 (1988): 94–104.

Murray, Maree. "'The Child Is Not a Servant': Children, Work and the Boarding-Out Scheme in New South Wales, 1880–1920." *Labour History* 77 (1999): 190–206.

Ramsland, John. *Children of the Backlanes: Destitute and Neglected Children in Colonial New South Wales.* Kensington, Australia: University of New South Wales Press, 1986.

Reekie, Gail, and Paul Wilson. "Criminal Children: Childhood and the Law Since 1865." *Queensland Review* 3:2 (1996): 76–85.

Robinson, Shirleene. "The Unregulated Employment of Aboriginal Children in Queensland, 1842–1902." *Labour History* 82 (2002): 1–15.

Scott, Dorothy, and Shurlee Swain. *Confronting Cruelty: Historical Perspectives on Child Abuse.* Carlton, Australia: Melbourne University Press, 2002.

Swain, Shurlee. "The State and the Child." *Australian Journal of Legal History* 4:1 (1998): 64–77.

Van Krieken, Robert. *Children and the State: Social Control and the Formation of Australian Child Welfare.* Sydney: Allen and Unwin, 1991.

Wimshurst, Kerry. "Child Labour and School Attendance in South Australia 1890–1915." *Historical Studies* 19:76 (1981): 388–411.

Aboriginal Child Labor in Colonial Australia

Shirleene Robinson, Assistant Professor, Bond University, Gold Coast, Australia

Thousands of Aboriginal child workers, like adult Aboriginal workers, provided much essential labor in Australia's colonial past. Across the continent, female Aboriginal children, some as young as three years of age, were employed as domestic servants. Male Aboriginal children, mostly aged between ten and twelve years, labored predominantly in the burgeoning pastoral industry. A substantial number of Aboriginal children were also employed in the pearling and bêche-de-mer (sea cucumber) industries off the coasts of Queensland and Western Australia. There are also accounts of Aboriginal children working as guides and interpreters, on the gold fields, as errand boys, as laborers, in circuses, and as jockeys.

Although it is apparent that large numbers of Aboriginal children worked for Europeans in colonial Australia, it was not until the sweeping social changes of the 1960s that historians began to consider the experiences of Aboriginal workers. Until recently, however, very little attention has been paid to the employment of Aboriginal children. This void is attributable to the disregard that Australian historians have generally shown toward children and childhood. Since the turn of the millennium, though, this historiographical trend has started to change, with greater numbers of historians recognizing the importance of Aboriginal child labor in Australia's past. Following convention, Australian scholarship treats people under the age of eighteen as children (Read 1981).

Legal Context

Both European and Aboriginal children were employed in large numbers in early-nineteenth-century Australia. By the 1870s, though, the governments of most Australian colonies had started to pass regulations requiring European children to receive an education until they had reached fourteen years of age. While the employment of very young European children became increasingly obsolete during the second half of the nineteenth century, the use of young Aboriginal labor remained widespread.

Educating Aboriginal children was not a matter of concern for colonial governments, and the employment of Aboriginal children was not monitored until the twentieth century. In Queensland, for example, the government did not set a minimum age for labor of Aboriginal children until 1919. Aboriginal children were considered to be such desirable employees, and were employed in such large numbers, that the various colonial governments would have attracted criticism had they attempted to control this labor.

Types of Labor Performed

Domestic service was the single-largest field of employment for female Aboriginal children in colonial Australia. Instances of physical, emotional, and sexual abuse were very common in domestic service. Australia's pastoral industry also relied heavily on labor provided by Aboriginal children, especially boys. The marine pearling and bêche-de-mer industries of Queensland and Western Australia were also heavily reliant on indigenous workers, a significant proportion of which were young children. This type of labor was arguably the most dangerous that Aboriginal children performed. The industry had a very high casualty rate, and most Europeans were reluctant to perform this type of labor. Aboriginal children who were employed in these maritime industries were among the most severely mistreated of all indigenous laborers in any field of employment.

While the majority of Aboriginal children worked as domestic servants, pastoral workers, or pearling and bêche-de-mer workers, indigenous children also worked in other capacities. In one of the earliest uses, Europeans employed Aboriginal children as guides, assistants, and interpreters. Indigenous children also worked on the gold fields across the continent. There are references to Aboriginal children acting as errand boys, particularly during the earlier period of settlement. Many male Aboriginal children were made to perform menial agricultural and laboring tasks. There are even accounts of a number of Aboriginal children working in colonial circuses.

While many sources prove that Aboriginal child labor was widespread and socially accepted all across Australia, colonial governments kept no detailed records of this employment. As a result, it is impossible to provide precise estimates of the number of Aboriginal children who worked in colonial Australia. From the records that are available, it appears that Aboriginal children constituted about one-third of the total Aboriginal workforce. Certainly, in both Queensland and Western Australia, at least 1,000 Aboriginal children labored in each colony. The individual patterns of settlement and labor requirements of Tasmania, New South Wales, Victoria, South Australia, and the area that would later become the Northern Territory make it more difficult to gauge the numbers of indigenous children employed. As a whole, though, we can be sure that thousands of Aboriginal children made valuable contributions to the developing colonial economic system (Robinson 2002).

Aboriginal children were heavily sought-after employees for several reasons. First, they were available in regions where other workers were scarce. Second, these children represented the cheapest form of labor obtainable. Third, settlers argued that Aboriginal children could be "civilized" and the indigenous threat thereby disbanded through the employment of these children. Finally, Europeans considered Aboriginal children to be pliable workers (Robinson 2002).

Aboriginal labor—of both adults and children—was vital to the development of colonial Australia. While there is some debate over the degree of agency that adult Aboriginal workers experienced, there is no question that younger indigenous workers had very little autonomy. There is much evidence that these young workers did not freely choose to enter the European workforce. Many young Aboriginal workers were kidnapped, with statistics indicating that the great majority of Aboriginal children who worked for Europeans were abducted from their family groups. Later, during the twentieth century, missions and reserves served as labor reserves for Europeans wishing to obtain Aboriginal child workers. Many of these young laborers formed part of the "stolen generations" of Aboriginal children who were removed from their parents and suffered devastating emotional and physical problems as a result.

Conclusion

Working Aboriginal children occupied a weak position in colonial Australia. These children were not only vulnerable because of their membership in a dispossessed subgroup; their status as children meant they were even more prone to exploitation. Their work was detrimental to the emotional and physical health of these children in all fields of labor. It was not unusual for Aboriginal child workers to be injured while performing labor that was physically strenuous. Furthermore, most Aboriginal children were not paid for their labor, were not educated, and did not receive the basic essentials of life. Moreover, many of these children were physically, sexually, and emotionally abused by their employers. Many Aboriginal children suffered further severe psychological trauma after being removed from, or being denied contact with, their indigenous family groups. While there is some evidence that Aboriginal children tried to resist the domination of European employers, overall these children occupied a uniquely subjugated position because of their racial categorization, their youth, and, for some, their sex. When the totality of their position is considered, it was comparable to slavery.

References and Further Reading

Hetherington, Penelope. *Settlers, Servants and Slaves: Aboriginal and European Children in Nineteenth-Century Western Australia.* Nedlands, Western Australia: University of Western Australia Press, 2002.

Read, Peter. *The Stolen Generations: The Removal of Aboriginal Children in New South Wales 1883 to 1969.* Sydney: New South Wales Department of Aboriginal Affairs, 1981.

Robinson, Shirleene. "The Unregulated Employment of Aboriginal Children in Queensland, 1842–1902." *Labour History* 82 (May 2002): 1–16.

———. "'We Do Not Want One Who Is Too Old . . .' Aboriginal Child Domestic Servants in Queensland in the Late Nineteenth and Early Twentieth Centuries." *Aboriginal History* 27 (2003): 162–82.

———. *Something Like Slavery? Queensland's Aboriginal Child Workers.* Melbourne: Australian Scholarly Publishing, 2007.

New Zealand

Child Labor in New Zealand

Jeanine Graham, Senior Lecturer in History, University of Waikato

Child labor in Aotearoa, the Maori name for New Zealand, is interpreted here within a framework of colonization, economic diversification, and changing social attitudes toward children and childhood. Both historically and in the contemporary era, many developments within this Pacific country reflect or parallel trends elsewhere, in the United Kingdom and North America especially. Since the experiences of young people in New Zealand have not been researched extensively, this essay represents an impressionistic foray, focusing on contributions within family and community economies as well as youth participation in the paid workforce.

Traditional and Transitional

Following the establishment of foundation Polynesian migrant populations in Aotearoa/New Zealand (around 1200), *tamariki* (children) and *rangatahi* (youths) probably contributed their labor in ways similar to those of young Aboriginals on the Australian continent and Indian communities in North America, as well as their ancestral forebears in the Pacific Ocean islands. The hunting, fishing, and gardening patterns associated with subsistence living would have seen young people involved in the seasonal rounds of mutton birding, fish netting and drying, bird snaring and preservation, *kūmara* (sweet potato) growing, and forest-resource gathering. They would have done so alongside adults, who instilled rituals of appropriate *tikanga* (custom) and propitiation of the gods. Many tasks were gendered. Only girls were taught the skills of the flax processing and weaving that were essential for producing the kits, mats, cloaks, and cords so integral to the evolving material culture of this Polynesian people. As founding populations grew, intertribal competition for territory and resources intensified. Yet fighting generally remained small-scale and cyclical. Hunting, fishing, and food production and preservation continued to be the priority for *whānau* (family) and *hapū* (subtribal) groups, and all the able-bodied, male and female, young and old, would participate in communal activities. Since the songs and stories of each tribe were transmitted orally, the presence of young people alongside their elders while such tasks were performed was of cultural importance as well. Adult expectations of youthful work contributions were probably relatively light and relaxed.

European exploration of the Pacific and subsequent exploitation of the region's whale, seal, flax, and timber resources began a transition phase in New Zealand's history, one that lasted for some fifty years, from 1769 to 1839. During these decades, cultural encounters between Maori (a collective term for the indigenous people that came into common use during the nineteenth century) and Pākehā (generally denoting those of European ancestry) involved trade; observation; intermarriage; misunderstandings; cooperation; conflict; sexual liaisons and sexually transmitted diseases; the introduction of muskets, metal goods, wheat, pigs, poultry, and potatoes; and the advent of a new religion—Christianity—with its emphasis on the written word. *Tamariki* and *rangatahi* were in the vanguard of cultural change. Mixed-blood children were accepted within their mothers' communities; those who grew up within settlements where the non-Maori father remained present, as at shore-based whaling stations, might access the language, customs, and artifacts of two cultures. In tribal areas where Protestant or Catholic missionaries sought to proselytize and promote literacy, young people were a focus for "civilization" and conversion. Some lived, temporarily, within mission stations, being instructed in aspects of (English) household management, or learning basic skills of animal husbandry and agricultural production. Missionaries frequently—and ruefully—recorded the departures of these potential converts.

Increasingly, literacy and some knowledge of English gave tribes a competitive advantage, particularly in the development of trade and acquisition of muskets. During this transition era, *rangatahi* do not seem to have been exploited in terms of their labor, though there is some evidence that young girls were used sexually, particularly in the northern harbors that became notorious for visiting sailors' drunken and licentious behavior. More common, perhaps, was an increased effort from youths in gardening and flax gathering. The ease with which potatoes could be cultivated, stored, and sold (in comparison with the *kūmara,* which required much more delicate handling) resulted in larger plantings of potato crops. The emphasis expanded from subsistence and provision for traditional hospitality to one of coastal and trans-Tasman supply. Pākehā traders exchanged material goods and guns for ever-increasing quantities of flax, timber, pork, and potatoes. The health of whole communities suffered as *hapū* diverted their energies into meeting the new commercial opportunities. They suffered, too, as a consequence of the internecine "musket wars" that ravaged most tribes during the 1820s. Death rates were high; the vanquished could be killed or used as captive labor. It seems likely that any captured *rangatahi* would be set to work in the gardens.

Settlement and Dispossession

The dominant position of Maori during the first phase of cultural encounter was reversed rapidly during the next half century. In 1840, New Zealand became a Crown colony within the British Empire. The Treaty of Waitangi, signed by some 500 chiefs and the queen's representative, established British sovereignty while acknowledging indigenous ownership of land and granting Maori equal status as British subjects. Within two decades, the immigrant and indigenous populations were roughly equal (approximately 56,000 Maori and 59,000 Europeans in 1858). By the mid-1890s, disease and dislocation had reduced tribal populations to their nadir of approximately 42,000, while continued immigration, gold discoveries, conquest, and colonial expansion had brought the Pākehā population to some 620,000.

Throughout this turbulent period of immigrant settlement and indigenous dispossession, the labor of Pākehā children and young persons was primarily within nuclear and extended families. Older children helped with younger siblings and household chores, tending poultry, chopping wood and kindling, gardening, and running errands. Free elementary schooling was introduced throughout the colony in 1877; the compulsory-attendance provisions were enforced for both Maori and Pākehā pupils by the turn of the century. Tensions between educational and income-earning opportunities were long-standing for many parents and children alike. Some youngsters found training and employment as pupil teachers: Most students left as soon as they turned thirteen or earned their proficiency qualification. As small-scale manufacturing developed in the expanding urban areas, on the more populous South Island especially, legislation governing apprenticeships and factory working conditions aimed to prevent the exploitation of women and children, since British migrants had arrived with a desire never to replicate the squalor and working conditions of industrial Victorian Britain. A colony-wide recession throughout the 1880s caused significant economic distress, but allegations of sweated labor among factory and piece workers, investigated in 1890, found relatively little evidence of underage youth employment. Further legislation passed by the reformist Liberal government of the 1890s aimed to forestall such occurrences. Owing to the advent of refrigerated shipping in 1882, however, New Zealand's future economic prosperity was to be built on pastoralism. Children and youths would be closely involved, usually in family circumstances where the state was loath to intervene, despite the protective role that successive governments would uphold in the areas of child health, education, and welfare.

Rural and Urban Developments

Within both rural and urban colonial households throughout the nineteenth century, youthful labor was significant and sustained. A shortage of domestic servants imposed a greater burden of domestic work on older daughters, particularly when a mother died while the family was still young. In North Island rural areas, where there were good working relationships between local *iwi* (tribe) and Pākehā lessees or landowners, younger girls might accompany older Maori women who cooked, cleaned, or did washing at the station homestead. Maori sheep-shearing gangs frequently included women and children. Youthful assistance with drafting the sheep, gathering up the fleece, or cooking for the regular meal breaks may well have been influential in shaping a pattern of later adult laboring, especially when school attendance was affected by a shearing gang's mobility.

A strong work ethic became well established as part of the colonial culture. Most immigrants had traveled 12,000 miles with a desire to succeed materially. Hard work offered them a pathway to financial success and upward social mobility, for their children especially. State-sponsored education complemented that ambition—though not all parents viewed schooling as a better training for life than physical work. Landownership was the hallmark of success for most colonists: That this was being made possible by a legal land alienation system that was having disastrous economic and social consequences for the indigenous people was a situation to which most colonists were either oblivious or indifferent. All demographic indicators pointed to the demise of the Maori as a people; Europeanization seemed to be the only way forward for their youth. With some notable exceptions, elders and officials alike generally advocated a vocational curriculum that would equip young Maori for a future as farm laborers or domesticated wives.

The thousands of family farms made possible by cheap land, cheap loans, and an expanding and secure British export market for dairy, produce, and frozen meat could not have succeeded without child labor. Schoolteachers in Taranaki, a prime North Island dairying province, complained constantly of the tyranny of the milking shed—of pupils falling asleep at their school desks, exhausted by the early-morning rising to round up the herd and help with the hand milking and the after-school repetition of the same arduous routine. Some parents deplored the necessity of relying on their children's assistance; others viewed such labor as more important than any "book learning." Generally, it was the older siblings within a family whose education ceased as soon as they reached the official school-leaving age (raised to fourteen in 1901). By the 1920s, milking machines and gradual electrification of rural areas would start to transform conditions on the country's farms, but it was usually the youngest siblings or the second generation of farming families whose children reaped those benefits. Many farmers relied on household rather than waged labor as they increased herd sizes in response to mechanized milking.

Early-twentieth-century school reports also made regular reference to low student attendance at the height of the hop-picking and fruit-harvesting seasons. In the major South Island horticultural province of Nelson, for example, some primary school boards advocated adjusting school holidays to coincide with peak demands for labor. Families frequently made their own decisions, irrespective of school-attendance regulations and an administrative practice that linked a teacher's salary to the daily average number of pupils present. The income earned from harvesting was greater than any fine for absenteeism. Similar patterns were recorded for Maori in Northland and in Hawke's Bay Province, where employment in kauri-gum digging, bush felling, fencing, shearing, or railway or road construction provided cash income for *whānau* whose subsistence lifestyle had been substantially destroyed. The financial assistance that enabled many Pākehā families to become established on dairy farms was not available to Maori to develop land held in customary collective ownership. Share milking became one option, and some tribes (Ngati Porou, for instance) embarked on tribal farming schemes, but Maori children were generally not as involved as their Pākehā contemporaries in the expansion of dairying. Poverty, poor living conditions, and low academic expectations were more likely to impact their well-being.

War and depression marred the lives of many young New Zealanders in the first half of the twentieth century. The distant theater of conflict was no impediment to young men eager for an overseas adventure. During World War I, high rates of volunteering from rural communities contributed to labor shortages. Older boys left school earlier than intended; younger brothers or sons undertook manual work that was often at or beyond their physical capacity to perform. Not all who returned from active service were capable of resuming their former lives, and their children or younger siblings could find their own futures affected by that.

Compulsory schooling and legislation governing wages and conditions for some youthful employees had given young people protection against overt exploitation in the workplace. Open access to free secondary education for fourteen- to nineteen-year-olds was provided in 1936. No government, however, would risk intervention in the family, even though the excessive work demands made by some parents continued to be well recognized by education and welfare officials. Both before and during the Great Depression of the 1930s, youths endeavored to augment the family income: gathering grass seed, collecting ergot or salable fungus; selling the eggs of birds deemed pests by local grain farmers; and exchanging discarded glass bottles for cash. Boys sold newspapers, delivered groceries after school, or worked in the early mornings on suburban milk runs. In mining towns, carting household supplies of coal was another option. Some youngsters assisted parents with door-to-door selling. Others undertook a greater share of child care, gardening, and laundry work as one or both parents endeavored to supplement very limited incomes. Recycling of clothing was commonplace. Girls especially were skilled in unraveling knitted garments; unpicking collars, cuffs, and seams; and darning and mending. Such work was performed within the family and unpaid.

Neighbors, too, often found ready assistance from youths willing to mow lawns, dig gardens, or chop kindling and firewood for pocket money. During World War II, these tasks were also undertaken voluntarily by youth groups, such as Boy Scout troops, for households where the male breadwinner was serving overseas. In farming regions, older pupils regularly helped to compensate for labor shortages. Seasonal silage or hay making, for instance, tended to involve all who had the physical capacity to fork hay or stack bales.

The rapid urbanization of Maori, and a general trend of rural depopulation in the decades following World War II, contributed to a decline in farm-related skills among urban-based generations. In the initial postwar decades of prosperity, full employment, and compulsory schooling extended to age fifteen (since 1944, which normally meant two years at the secondary level), even youths who left school with no educational qualifications could generally find laboring or unskilled work. Apprenticeship schemes continued to exist in most trades, and cadetships within government departments. Specific programs were introduced to assist young Maori school leavers make the transition from rural to urban living and find meaningful employment. Youthful workers in the fifteen- to nineteen-year-old range were nevertheless a vulnerable group, and many who migrated from the Pacific Islands or from rural Maori communities did not come from a family tradition that valued further education. Adult wage rates protected those age twenty and over: not until 1983 was there legislation establishing youth minimum-wage rates for young people ages sixteen to nineteen in the paid workforce.

Recent and Contemporary

The economic downturn of the 1970s, and major government restructuring of the economy during the 1980s, contributed to a dramatic rise in unemployment and social distress among working-class households, especially those in which the principal income earners had been engaged in the manufacturing and construction industries. A rapid withdrawal of farm subsidies had serious consequences for the viability of many small towns and country communities. In both rural and urban areas, problems of poverty and long-term unemployment have impacted the educational and career-related opportunities of youngsters reared in such households, especially those affected by reduction in welfare benefit levels and introduction of market rentals for state housing during the 1990s. There has also been a statistically significant growth in single-parent and female-headed households and in those in which both parents are in paid (though not always full-time) employment. Although legislation prohibits children under the age of fourteen from being left home alone, working parents often maintain that they have little choice about doing so. In such households, the contribution that older children are making to the family economy is implicit and primarily domestic—folding laundry, sweeping or vacuuming floors, preparing meals, cleaning bathrooms. Full-time paid employment is not legal until the official school-leaving age of sixteen (since 1993), but for those aged fourteen and fifteen, informal child-care and babysitting arrangements with friends, relatives, or neighbors are not unusual among schoolgirls. Delivering newspapers, direct-marketing brochures, and real-estate leaflets in suburban mailboxes are other income-earning tasks undertaken by girls as well as boys.

The range of part-time employment opportunities expanded significantly in urban areas in the late twentieth century. Changes in employment law, the advent of seven-day-a-week shopping, and the proliferation of supermarket chains and large retail complexes all contributed to the intensification of a consumer culture (with children and youths a clearly targeted group). Food supermarkets, often in close proximity to local high schools, provide part-time employment. Students work after school hours and on weekends, packing groceries, stocking shelves, preparing foodstuffs in the delicatessen and bakery sections, and gathering shopping carts from the parking lots. The more experienced may become checkout operators and supervisors, particularly when such part-time employment continues as they progress from secondary to tertiary study. Similar patterns of youth employment can be seen with the rapid growth in fast-food outlets (such as the ubiquitous McDonald's), multipurpose megastores (including the Warehouse), and other self-service retail centers. This type of paid work is highly sought after by students and is often seen as beneficial in enhancing time-management and social skills and a sense of self-esteem. The income earned by these youthful workers is generally retained by them for discretionary spending—their contribution to a circular pattern strengthening the youth market potential in the local consumer culture. At NZ$9 (about US$4.75) per hour in 2007, the youth minimum rate for sixteen- to seventeen-year-olds is 80 percent of the adult minimum wage. A majority of young employees are likely to be from middle-class households since they are the ones with the clothing, confidence, and access to cars, all of which tend to be essential for successful workforce participation. The negative aspects of such widespread casualization of the youthful workforce are not often acknowledged. Another recent trend, reflecting the more diverse immigration policy adopted in the past two decades, has seen children of immigrant families working alongside their parents in small businesses, such as bakeries, dairies, and small fast-food outlets, a contemporary recurrence of early-twentieth-century trends in the dairy industry.

Conclusion

Children and youths have clearly contributed much to the development of New Zealand's economy. Their involvement has been predominantly within a *whānau,* or family, setting. The types of work they have performed reflect the country's economic transitions over the past two centuries, from indigenous subsistence living to the establishment of a colonial trading economy and the expansion of the farming section by the end of the nineteenth century to the growth of a highly urbanized consumer-oriented society by the end of the twentieth century.

Overt exploitation of youths within the paid workforce has been limited. Preventative measures included the early establishment of a state-funded free and compulsory elementary education system; the eventual extension to compulsory secondary education by the 1940s; and the setting of a minimum age for entry into paid employment that was higher than the official school-leaving age. The twentieth-century trend toward smaller family sizes also affected adult expectations of children's work, as did emerging notions of children's rights. Yet despite the growing secularization of New Zealand society, there is still a widespread belief in the moral as well as the economic value of hard work, and a desire to see children and youths developing as citizens who share that outlook.

References and Further Reading

Brookes, Barbara, Annabel Cooper, and Robin Law, eds. *Sites of Gender: Women, Men and Modernity in Southern Dunedin, 1890–1939.* Auckland, New Zealand: Auckland University Press, 2003.

Daley, Caroline. *Girls and Women, Men and Boys: Gender in Taradale 1886–1930.* Auckland, New Zealand: Auckland University Press, 1999.

Dalley, Bronwyn. *Child Welfare in Twentieth-Century New Zealand.* Auckland, New Zealand: Auckland University Press, 1998.

Goodyear, Rosemary. "Overworked Children? Child Labour in New Zealand, 1919–1939." *New Zealand Journal of History* 40:1 (2006): 75–90.

Graham, Jeanine. "Child Employment in New Zealand." *New Zealand Journal of History* 21:2 (1986): 62–78.

Ihimaera, Witi, ed. *Growing Up Maori.* Auckland, New Zealand: Tandem Press, 1998.

Ministry of Youth Affairs. *15 to 25: A Youth Statistical Profile.* Wellington, New Zealand: Ministry of Youth Affairs, 1994.

Toynbee, Claire. *Her Work and His: Family, Kin and Community in New Zealand 1900–1930.* Wellington, New Zealand: Victoria University Press, 1995.

Statistics New Zealand. http://www.stats.govt.nz.

Index

Note: Illustrations are indicated by italics; tables are indicated by *t*; figures are indicated by *f*. Bold italics represent a country map with summary and quantitative indicators.

Index of Applications

Business and Economics

General Interest

Life Sciences

Social Sciences

Applied Calculus

Sixth Edition

Stefan Waner
Hofstra University

Steven R. Costenoble
Hofstra University

BROOKS/COLE
CENGAGE Learning®

Australia • Brazil • Japan • Korea • Mexico • Singapore • Spain • United Kingdom • United States

BROOKS/COLE
CENGAGE Learning

Applied Calculus, Sixth Edition
Stefan Waner, Steven R. Costenoble

Publisher: Richard Stratton

Development Editor: Jay Campbell

Editorial Assistant: Alex Gontar

Media Editor: Andrew Coppola

Brand Manager: Gordon Lee

Marketing Coordinator: Lindsy Lettre

Marketing Communications Manager: Linda Yip

Content Project Manager: Alison Eigel Zade

Senior Art Director: Linda May

Print Buyer: Doug Bertke

Rights Acquisition Specialist: Shalice Shah-Caldwell

Production Service: MPS Limited

Text Designer: RHDG Design

Cover Designer: Chris Miller

Cover Image: William Dudziak (dudziak.com)

Compositor: MPS Limited

Library of Congress Control Number: 2012947818

Student Edition:
ISBN-13: 978-1-133-60768-7
ISBN-10: 1-133-60768-3

Brooks/Cole
20 Channel Center Street
Boston, MA 02210
USA

Printed in Canada
1 2 3 4 5 6 7 16 15 14 13 12

Brief Contents

Contents

CHAPTER 3 Introduction to the Derivative 193

CHAPTER 4 Techniques of Differentiation with Applications 289

CHAPTER 5 Further Applications of the Derivative 369

CHAPTER 9 Trigonometric Models 655

Preface

Applied Calculus, sixth edition, is intended for a one- or two-term course for students majoring in business, the social sciences, or the liberal arts. Like the earlier editions, the sixth edition of *Applied Calculus* is designed to address the challenge of generating enthusiasm and mathematical sophistication in an audience that is often underprepared and lacks motivation for traditional mathematics courses. We meet this challenge by focusing on real-life applications and topics of current interest that students can relate to, by presenting mathematical concepts intuitively and thoroughly, and by employing a writing style that is informal, engaging, and occasionally even humorous.

The sixth edition goes further than earlier editions in implementing support for a wide range of instructional paradigms: from traditional face-to-face courses to online distance learning courses, from settings incorporating little or no technology to courses taught in computerized classrooms, and from classes in which a single form of technology is used exclusively to those incorporating several technologies. We fully support three forms of technology in this text: TI-83/84 Plus graphing calculators, spreadsheets, and powerful online utilities we have created for the book. In particular, our comprehensive support for spreadsheet technology, both in the text and online, is highly relevant for students who are studying business and economics, where skill with spreadsheets may be vital to their future careers.

Our Approach to Pedagogy

Real-World Orientation We are confident that you will appreciate the diversity, breadth, and abundance of examples and exercises included in this edition. A large number of these are based on real, referenced data from business, economics, the life sciences, and the social sciences. Examples and exercises based on dated information have generally been replaced by more current versions; applications based on unique or historically interesting data have been kept.

Adapting real data for pedagogical use can be tricky; available data can be numerically complex, intimidating for students, or incomplete. We have modified and streamlined many of the real-world applications, rendering them as tractable as any "made-up" application. At the same time, we have been careful to strike a pedagogically sound balance between applications based on real data and more traditional "generic" applications. Thus, the density and selection of real data–based applications has been tailored to the pedagogical goals and appropriate difficulty level for each section.

Readability We would like students to read this book. We would like students to *enjoy* reading this book. Thus, we have written the book in a conversational and student-oriented style, and have made frequent use of question-and-answer dialogues to encourage the development of the student's mathematical curiosity and intuition. We hope that this text will give the student insight into how a mathematician develops and thinks about mathematical ideas and their applications.

Rigor We feel that mathematical rigor need not be antithetical to the kind of applied focus and conceptual approach that are earmarks of this book. We have worked hard to ensure that we are always mathematically honest without being unnecessarily formal. Sometimes we do this through the question-and-answer dialogs and sometimes through the "Before we go on..." discussions that follow examples, but always in manner designed to provoke the interest of the student.

Five Elements of Mathematical Pedagogy to Address Different Learning Styles The "Rule of Four" is a common theme in many texts. Implementing this approach, we discuss many of the central concepts **numerically, graphically,** and **algebraically** and clearly delineate these distinctions. The fourth element, **verbal communication** of mathematical concepts, is emphasized through our discussions on translating English sentences into mathematical statements and in our extensive Communication and Reasoning exercises at the end of each section. A fifth element, **interactivity,** is implemented through expanded use of question-and-answer dialogues but is seen most dramatically in the student Website. Using this resource, students can interact with the material in several ways: through interactive tutorials in the form of games, chapter summaries, and chapter review exercises, all in reference to concepts and examples covered in sections and with online utilities that automate a variety of tasks, from graphing to regression and matrix algebra.

Exercise Sets Our comprehensive collection of exercises provides a wealth of material that can be used to challenge students at almost every level of preparation and includes everything from straightforward drill exercises to interesting and rather challenging applications. The exercise sets have been carefully graded to move from straightforward basic exercises and exercises that are similar to examples in the text to more interesting and advanced ones, marked as "more advanced" for easy reference. There are also several much more difficult exercises, designated as "challenging." We have also included, in virtually every section of every chapter, interesting applications based on real data, Communication and Reasoning exercises that help students articulate mathematical concepts and recognize common errors, and exercises ideal for the use of technology.

Many of the scenarios used in application examples and exercises are revisited several times throughout the book. Thus, for instance, students will find themselves using a variety of techniques, from graphing through the use of derivatives and elasticity, to analyze the same application. Reusing scenarios and important functions provides unifying threads and shows students the complex texture of real-life problems.

New to This Edition

Content

- Chapter 1 (page 39): We now include, in Section 1.1, careful discussion of the common practice of representing functions as equations and vice versa; for instance, a cost equation like $C = 10x + 50$ can be thought of as defining a cost *function* $C(x) = 10x + 50$. Instead of rejecting this practice, we encourage the student to see this connection between functions and equations and to be able to switch from one interpretation to the other.

  Our discussion of functions and models in Section 1.2 now includes a careful discussion of the algebra of functions presented through the context of important applications rather than as an abstract concept. Thus, the student will see from the outset *why* we want to talk about sums, products, etc. of functions rather than simply *how* to manipulate them.

- Chapter 3 (page 193): Our discussion of limits now discusses extensively when, and why, substitution can be used to obtain a limit. We now also follow the usual convention of allowing only one-sided limits at endpoints of domains. This approach also applies to derivatives, where we now disallow derivatives at endpoints of domains, as is the normal convention.
- Chapter 4 (page 289): The closed-form formula for the derivative of $|x|$, introduced in Section 4.1, is now more fully integrated into the text, as is that for its antiderivative (in Chapter 6). (It is puzzling that it is not standard fare in other calculus books.)
- Chapter 6 (page 451): The sections on antiderivatives and substitution have been reorganized and streamlined and now include discussion of the closed-form antiderivative of $|x|$ and well as new exercises featuring absolute values.

  The definite integral is now introduced in the realistic context of the volume of oil released in an oil spill comparable in size to the *BP* 2011 Gulf oil spill.
- Chapter 8 (page 587): The discussion of level curves in Section 8.1 is now more extensive and includes added examples and exercises.
- **Case Studies:** A number of the Case Studies at the ends of the chapters have been extensively revised, using updated real data, and continue to reflect topics of current interest, such as spending on housing construction, modeling tax revenues, and controlling pollution.

Current Topics in the Applications

- We have added and updated numerous real data exercises and examples based on topics that are either of intense current interest or of general interest to contemporary students, including Facebook, XBoxes, iPhones, Androids, iPads, foreclosure rates, the housing crisis, subprime mortgages, the *BP* 2011 Gulf oil spill, and the U.S. stock market "flash crash" of May 6, 2010. (Also see the list, in the inside back cover, of the corporations we reference in the applications.)

Exercises

- We have expanded the chapter review exercise sets to be more representative of the material within the chapter. Note that all the applications in the chapter review exercises revolve around the fictitious online bookseller, *OHaganBooks.com,* and the various—often amusing—travails of *OHaganBooks.com* CEO John O'Hagan and his business associate Marjory Duffin.
- We have added many new conceptual Communication and Reasoning exercises, including many dealing with common student errors and misconceptions.

End-of-Chapter Technology Guides

- Our end-of-chapter detailed Technology Guides now discuss the use of spreadsheets in general rather than focusing exclusively on Microsoft® Excel, thus enabling readers to use any of the several alternatives now available, such as Google's online Google Sheets®, Open Office®, and Apple's Numbers®.

Continuing Features

Case Study **Checking up on Malthus**

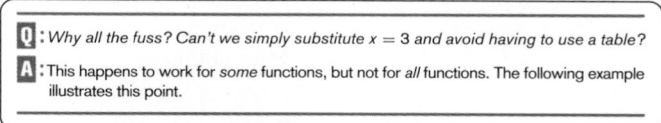

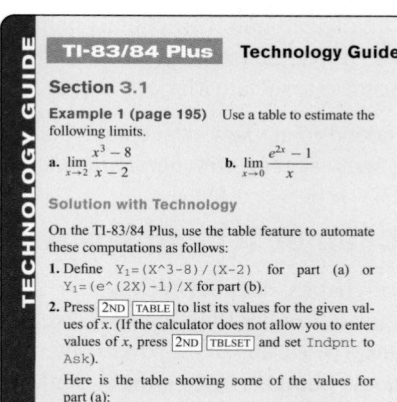

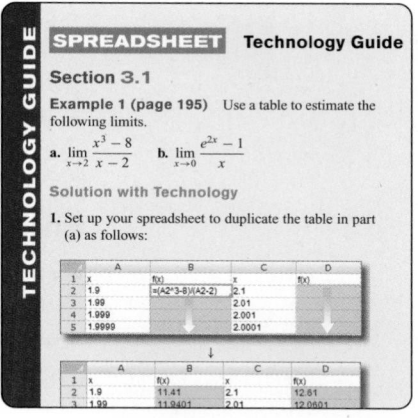

Robert Nickelsberg/Getty Images

In 1798 Thomas R. Malthus (1766–1834) published an influential pamphlet, later expanded into a book, titled *An Essay on the Principle of Population As It Affects the Future Improvement of Society.* One of his main contentions was that population grows geometrically (exponentially) while the supply of resources such as food grows only arithmetically (linearly). This led him to the pessimistic conclusion that population would always reach the limits of subsistence and precipitate famine, war, and ill health, unless population could be checked by other means. He advocated "moral restraint," which includes the pattern of late marriage common in Western Europe at the time and now common in most developed countries and which leads to a lower reproduction rate.

- **Case Studies** Each chapter ends with a section entitled "Case Study," an extended application that uses and illustrates the central ideas of the chapter, focusing on the development of mathematical models appropriate to the topics. These applications are ideal for assignment as projects, and to this end we have included groups of exercises at the end of each.
- **Before We Go On** Most examples are followed by supplementary discussions, which may include a check on the answer, a discussion of the feasibility and significance of a solution, or an in-depth look at what the solution means.
- **Quick Examples** Most definition boxes include quick, straightforward examples that a student can use to solidify each new concept.
- **Question-and-Answer Dialogue** We frequently use informal question-and-answer dialogues that anticipate the kinds of questions that may occur to the student and also guide the student through the development of new concepts.

Q: *Why all the fuss? Can't we simply substitute $x = 3$ and avoid having to use a table?*

A: This happens to work for *some* functions, but not for *all* functions. The following example illustrates this point.

- **Marginal Technology Notes** We give brief marginal technology notes to outline the use of graphing calculator, spreadsheet, and Website technology in appropriate examples. When necessary, the reader is referred to more detailed discussion in the end-of-chapter Technology Guides.
- **End-of-Chapter Technology Guides** We continue to include detailed TI-83/84 Plus and Spreadsheet Guides at the end of each chapter. These Guides are referenced liberally in marginal technology notes at appropriate points in the chapter, so instructors and students can easily use this material or not, as they prefer. Groups of exercises for which the use of technology is suggested or required appear throughout the exercise sets.

TECHNOLOGY GUIDE

TI-83/84 Plus Technology Guide

Section 3.1

Example 1 (page 195) Use a table to estimate the following limits.

a. $\lim_{x\to 2} \frac{x^3 - 8}{x - 2}$ **b.** $\lim_{x\to 0} \frac{e^{2x} - 1}{x}$

Solution with Technology

On the TI-83/84 Plus, use the table feature to automate these computations as follows:

1. Define `Y1=(X^3-8)/(X-2)` for part (a) or `Y1=(e^(2X)-1)/X` for part (b).
2. Press [2ND] [TABLE] to list its values for the given values of x. (If the calculator does not allow you to enter values of x, press [2ND] [TBLSET] and set `Indpnt` to `Ask`).

   Here is the table showing some of the values for part (a):

TECHNOLOGY GUIDE

SPREADSHEET Technology Guide

Section 3.1

Example 1 (page 195) Use a table to estimate the following limits.

a. $\lim_{x\to 2} \frac{x^3 - 8}{x - 2}$ **b.** $\lim_{x\to 0} \frac{e^{2x} - 1}{x}$

Solution with Technology

1. Set up your spreadsheet to duplicate the table in part (a) as follows:

	A	B	C	D
1	x	f(x)	x	f(x)
2	1.9	=(A2^3-8)/(A2-2)	2.1	
3	1.99		2.01	
4	1.999		2.001	
5	1.9999		2.0001	

↓

	A	B	C	D
1	x	f(x)	x	f(x)
2	1.9	11.41	2.1	12.61
3	1.99	11.9401	2.01	12.0601

- **Communication and Reasoning Exercises for Writing and Discussion** These are exercises designed to broaden the student's grasp of the mathematical concepts and develop modeling skills. They include exercises in which the student is asked to provide his or her own examples to illustrate a point or design an application with a given solution. They also include "fill in the blank" type exercises, exercises that invite discussion and debate, and exercises in which the student must identify common errors. These exercises often have no single correct answer.

Supplemental Material

For Instructors and Students

Enhanced WebAssign®

Content

Exclusively from Cengage Learning, Enhanced WebAssign® combines the exceptional mathematics content in Waner and Costenoble's text with the most powerful online homework solution, WebAssign. Enhanced WebAssign engages students with immediate feedback, rich tutorial content, videos, animations, and an interactive eBook, helping students to develop a deeper conceptual understanding of the subject matter. The interactive eBook contains helpful search, highlighting, and note-taking features.

Instructors can build online assignments by selecting from thousands of text-specific problems, supplemented if desired with problems from any Cengage Learning textbook. Flexible assignment options give instructors the ability to choose how feedback and tutorial content is released to students as well as the ability to release assignments conditionally based on students' prerequisite assignment scores. Increase student engagement, improve course outcomes, and experience the superior service offered through CourseCare. Visit us at http://webassign.net/cengage or www.cengage.com/ewa to learn more.

Service

Your adoption of Enhanced WebAssign® includes CourseCare, Cengage Learning's industry leading service and training program designed to ensure that you have everything that you need to make the most of your use of Enhanced WebAssign. CourseCare provides one-on-one service, from finding the right solutions for your course to training and support. A team of Cengage representatives, including Digital Solutions Managers and Coordinators as well as Service and Training Consultants, assists you every step of the way. For additional information about CourseCare, please visit www.cengage.com/coursecare.

Our Enhanced WebAssign training program provides a comprehensive curriculum of beginner, intermediate, and advanced sessions, designed to get you started and effectively integrate Enhanced WebAssign into your course. We offer a flexible online and recorded training program designed to accommodate your busy schedule. Whether you are using Enhanced WebAssign for the first time or an experienced user, there is a training option to meet your needs.

www.WanerMath.com

The authors' Website, accessible through www.WanerMath.com and linked within Enhanced WebAssign, has been evolving for more than a decade and has been receiving increasingly more recognition. Students, raised in an environment in which computers permeate both work and play, now use the Internet to engage with the material in an active way. The following features of the authors' Website are fully integrated with the text and can be used as a personalized study resource as well as a valuable teaching aid for instructors:

- *Interactive tutorials* on almost all topics, with guided exercises, which also can be used in classroom instruction or in distance learning courses
- *More challenging game versions of tutorials* with randomized questions that complement the traditional interactive tutorials and can be used as in-class quizzes
- *Detailed interactive chapter summaries* that review basic definitions and problem-solving techniques and can act as pre-test study tools
- *Downloadable Excel tutorials* keyed to examples given in the text
- *Online utilities for use in solving many of the technology-based application exercises.* The utilities, for instructor use in class and student use out of class, include a function grapher and evaluator that now also graphs derivatives and offers curve-fitting, regression tools, an interactive Riemann sum grapher with an improved numerical integrator, and a line entry calculator on the main page that does derivatives, expands polynomial expressions, does numerical integration and gives Taylor series.
- *Chapter true-false quizzes* with feedback for many incorrect answers
- *Supplemental topics* including interactive text and exercise sets for selected topics not found in the printed texts
- *Spanish versions* of chapter summaries, tutorials, game tutorials, and utilities

For Students

Student Solutions Manual *by Waner and Costenoble*
ISBN: 9781285085524
The student solutions manual provides worked-out solutions to the odd-numbered exercises in the text, plus problem-solving strategies and additional algebra steps and review for selected problems.

CENGAGE brain .com

To access this and other course materials and companion resources, please visit **www.cengagebrain.com**. At the CengageBrain.com home page, search for the ISBN of your title (from the back cover of your book) using the search box at the top of the page. This will take you to the product page where free companion resources can be found.

Microsoft Excel Computer Laboratory Manual *by Anne D. Henriksen*
This laboratory manual uses Microsoft Excel to solve real-world problems in a variety of scientific, technical, and business disciplines. It provides hands-on experience to demonstrate for students that calculus is a valuable tool for solving practical, real-world problems while helping students increase their knowledge of Microsoft Excel. The manual is a set of self-contained computer exercises that are meant to be used over the course of a 15-week semester in a separate, 75-minute computer laboratory period. The weekly labs parallel the material in the text. Available at www.cengagebrain.com.

For Instructors

Complete Solution Manual *by Waner and Costenoble*
ISBN: 9781285085531
The instructor's solutions manual provides worked-out solutions to all of the exercises in the text.

Solution Builder *by Waner and Costenoble*
ISBN: 9781285085548
This time-saving resource offers fully worked instructor solutions to all exercises in the text in customizable online format. Adopting instructors can sign up for access at www.cengage.com/solutionbuilder.

PowerLecture™ with ExamView® computerized testing *by Waner and Costenoble*
ISBN: 9781285085579
This CD-ROM provides the instructor with dynamic media tools for teaching, including Microsoft® PowerPoint® lecture slides, figures from the book, and the Test Bank. You can create, deliver, and customize tests (both print and online) in minutes with ExamView® computerized testing, which includes Test Bank items in electronic format. In addition, you can easily build solution sets for homework or exams by linking to Solution Builder's online solutions manual.

Instructor's Edition
ISBN: 9781133610571

www.WanerMath.com
The Instructor's Resource Page at www.WanerMath.com features an expanded collection of instructor resources, including an updated corrections page, an expanding set of author-created teaching videos for use in distance learning courses, and a utility that automatically updates homework exercise sets from the fifth edition to the sixth.

Acknowledgments

This project would not have been possible without the contributions and suggestions of numerous colleagues, students, and friends. We are particularly grateful to our colleagues at Hofstra and elsewhere who used and gave us useful feedback on previous editions. We are also grateful to everyone at Cengage for their encouragement and guidance throughout the project. Specifically, we would like to thank Richard Stratton and Jay Campbell for their unflagging enthusiasm and Alison Eigel Zade for whipping the book into shape.

We would also like to thank our accuracy checker, Jerrold Grossman, and the numerous reviewers who provided many helpful suggestions that have shaped the development of this book.

Christopher Brown, *California Lutheran University*
Nathan Carlson, *California Lutheran University*
Scott Fallstrom, *University of Oregon*
Latrice Laughlin, *University of Alaska Fairbanks*
Michael Price, *University of Oregon*
Christopher Quarles, *Everett Community College*
Leela Rakesh, *Central Michigan University*
Tom Rosenwinkel, *Concordia University Texas*
Larry Taylor, *North Dakota State University*

Stefan Waner
Steven R. Costenoble

0

Precalculus Review

DreamPictures/Taxi/Getty Images

Website
www.WanerMath.com

- At the Website you will find section-by-section interactive tutorials for further study and practice.

Introduction

In this chapter we review some topics from algebra that you need to know to get the most out of this book. This chapter can be used either as a refresher course or as a reference.

There is one crucial fact you must always keep in mind: The letters used in algebraic expressions stand for numbers. All the rules of algebra are just facts about the arithmetic of numbers. If you are not sure whether some algebraic manipulation you are about to do is legitimate, try it first with numbers. If it doesn't work with numbers, it doesn't work.

0.1 Real Numbers

The **real numbers** are the numbers that can be written in decimal notation, including those that require an infinite decimal expansion. The set of real numbers includes all integers, positive and negative; all fractions; and the irrational numbers, those with decimal expansions that never repeat. Examples of irrational numbers are

$$\sqrt{2} = 1.414213562373\ldots$$

and

$$\pi = 3.141592653589\ldots$$

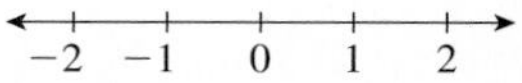

Figure 1

It is very useful to picture the real numbers as points on a line. As shown in Figure 1, larger numbers appear to the right, in the sense that if $a < b$ then the point corresponding to b is to the right of the one corresponding to a.

Intervals

Some subsets of the set of real numbers, called **intervals**, show up quite often and so we have a compact notation for them.

Interval Notation

Here is a list of types of intervals along with examples.

	Interval	*Description*	*Picture*	*Example*
Closed	$[a, b]$	Set of numbers x with $a \le x \le b$	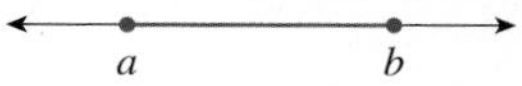 (includes end points)	$[0, 10]$
Open	(a, b)	Set of numbers x with $a < x < b$	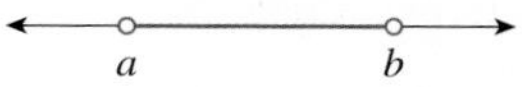 (excludes end points)	$(-1, 5)$
Half-Open	$(a, b]$	Set of numbers x with $a < x \le b$		$(-3, 1]$
	$[a, b)$	Set of numbers x with $a \le x < b$		$[0, 5)$

Infinite	$[a, +\infty)$	Set of numbers x with $a \le x$	a	$[10, +\infty)$
	$(a, +\infty)$	Set of numbers x with $a < x$	a	$(-3, +\infty)$
	$(-\infty, b]$	Set of numbers x with $x \le b$	b	$(-\infty, -3]$
	$(-\infty, b)$	Set of numbers x with $x < b$	b	$(-\infty, 10)$
	$(-\infty, +\infty)$	Set of all real numbers		$(-\infty, +\infty)$

Operations

There are five important operations on real numbers: addition, subtraction, multiplication, division, and exponentiation. "Exponentiation" means raising a real number to a power; for instance, $3^2 = 3 \cdot 3 = 9$; $2^3 = 2 \cdot 2 \cdot 2 = 8$.

A note on technology: Most graphing calculators and spreadsheets use an asterisk * for multiplication and a caret sign ^ for exponentiation. Thus, for instance, 3×5 is entered as `3*5`, $3x$ as `3*x`, and 3^2 as `3^2`.

When we write an expression involving two or more operations, like

$$2 \cdot 3 + 4$$

or

$$\frac{2 \cdot 3^2 - 5}{4 - (-1)}$$

we need to agree on the order in which to do the operations. Does $2 \cdot 3 + 4$ mean $(2 \cdot 3) + 4 = 10$ or $2 \cdot (3 + 4) = 14$? We all agree to use the following rules for the order in which we do the operations.

Standard Order of Operations

Parentheses and Fraction Bars First, calculate the values of all expressions inside parentheses or brackets, working from the innermost parentheses out, before using them in other operations. In a fraction, calculate the numerator and denominator separately before doing the division.

Quick Examples

1. $6(2 + [3 - 5] - 4) = 6(2 + (-2) - 4) = 6(-4) = -24$
2. $\dfrac{(4 - 2)}{3(-2 + 1)} = \dfrac{2}{3(-1)} = \dfrac{2}{-3} = -\dfrac{2}{3}$
3. $3/(2 + 4) = \dfrac{3}{2 + 4} = \dfrac{3}{6} = \dfrac{1}{2}$
4. $(x + 4x)/(y + 3y) = 5x/(4y)$

Exponents Next, perform exponentiation.

Quick Examples

1. $2 + 4^2 = 2 + 16 = 18$
2. $(2 + 4)^2 = 6^2 = 36$

Note the difference.

3. $2\left(\frac{3}{4-5}\right)^2 = 2\left(\frac{3}{-1}\right)^2 = 2(-3)^2 = 2 \times 9 = 18$
4. $2(1 + 1/10)^2 = 2(1.1)^2 = 2 \times 1.21 = 2.42$

Multiplication and Division Next, do all multiplications and divisions, from left to right.

Quick Examples

1. $2(3 - 5)/4 \cdot 2 = 2(-2)/4 \cdot 2$ — Parentheses first
   $= -4/4 \cdot 2$ — Left-most product
   $= -1 \cdot 2 = -2$ — Multiplications and divisions, left to right
2. $2(1 + 1/10)^2 \times 2/10 = 2(1.1)^2 \times 2/10$ — Parentheses first
   $= 2 \times 1.21 \times 2/10$ — Exponent
   $= 4.84/10 = 0.484$ — Multiplications and divisions, left to right
3. $4\frac{2(4-2)}{3(-2 \cdot 5)} = 4\frac{2(2)}{3(-10)} = 4\frac{4}{-30} = \frac{16}{-30} = -\frac{8}{15}$

Addition and Subtraction Last, do all additions and subtractions, from left to right.

Quick Examples

1. $2(3 - 5)^2 + 6 - 1 = 2(-2)^2 + 6 - 1 = 2(4) + 6 - 1$
   $= 8 + 6 - 1 = 13$
2. $\left(\frac{1}{2}\right)^2 - (-1)^2 + 4 = \frac{1}{4} - 1 + 4 = -\frac{3}{4} + 4 = \frac{13}{4}$
3. $3/2 + 4 = 1.5 + 4 = 5.5$
4. $3/(2 + 4) = 3/6 = 1/2 = 0.5$

Note the difference.

5. $4/2^2 + (4/2)^2 = 4/2^2 + 2^2 = 4/4 + 4 = 1 + 4 = 5$

T Entering Formulas

Any good calculator or spreadsheet will respect the standard order of operations. However, we must be careful with division and exponentiation and use parentheses as necessary. The following table gives some examples of simple mathematical expressions and their equivalents in the functional format used in most graphing calculators, spreadsheets, and computer programs.

Mathematical Expression	*Formula*	*Comments*
$\dfrac{2}{3-x}$	`2/(3-x)`	Note the use of parentheses instead of the fraction bar. If we omit the parentheses, we get the expression shown next.
$\dfrac{2}{3}-x$	`2/3-x`	The calculator follows the usual order of operations.
$\dfrac{2}{3\times 5}$	`2/(3*5)`	Putting the denominator in parentheses ensures that the multiplication is carried out first. The asterisk is usually used for multiplication in graphing calculators and computers.
$\dfrac{2}{x}\times 5$	`(2/x)*5`	Putting the fraction in parentheses ensures that it is calculated first. Some calculators will interpret `2/3*5` as $\dfrac{2}{3\times 5}$, but `2/3(5)` as $\dfrac{2}{3}\times 5$.
$\dfrac{2-3}{4+5}$	`(2-3)/(4+5)`	Note once again the use of parentheses in place of the fraction bar.
2^3	`2^3`	The caret ^ is commonly used to denote exponentiation.
2^{3-x}	`2^(3-x)`	Be careful to use parentheses to tell the calculator where the exponent ends. Enclose the *entire exponent* in parentheses.
2^3-x	`2^3-x`	Without parentheses, the calculator will follow the usual order of operations: exponentiation and then subtraction.
3×2^{-4}	`3*2^(-4)`	On some calculators, the negation key is separate from the minus key.
$2^{-4\times 3}\times 5$	`2^(-4*3)*5`	Note once again how parentheses enclose the entire exponent.
$100\left(1+\dfrac{0.05}{12}\right)^{60}$	`100*(1+0.05/12)^60`	This is a typical calculation for compound interest.
$PV\left(1+\dfrac{r}{m}\right)^{mt}$	`PV*(1+r/m)^(m*t)`	This is the compound interest formula. *PV* is understood to be a single number (present value) and not the product of *P* and *V* (or else we would have used `P*V`).
$\dfrac{2^{3-2}\times 5}{y-x}$	`2^(3-2)*5/(y-x)` or `(2^(3-2)*5)/(y -x)`	Notice again the use of parentheses to hold the denominator together. We could also have enclosed the numerator in parentheses, although this is optional. (Why?)
$\dfrac{2^y+1}{2-4^{3x}}$	`(2^y+1)/(2-4^(3*x))`	Here, it is necessary to enclose both the numerator and the denominator in parentheses.
$2^y+\dfrac{1}{2}-4^{3x}$	`2^y+1/2-4^(3*x)`	This is the effect of leaving out the parentheses around the numerator and denominator in the previous expression.

Accuracy and Rounding

When we use a calculator or computer, the results of our calculations are often given to far more decimal places than are useful. For example, suppose we are told that a square has an area of 2.0 square feet and we are asked how long its sides are. Each side is the square root of the area, which the calculator tells us is

$$\sqrt{2} \approx 1.414213562$$

However, the measurement of 2.0 square feet is probably accurate to only two digits, so our estimate of the lengths of the sides can be no more accurate than that. Therefore, we round the answer to two digits:

$$\text{Length of one side} \approx 1.4 \text{ feet}$$

The digits that follow 1.4 are meaningless. The following guide makes these ideas more precise.

Significant Digits, Decimal Places, and Rounding

The number of **significant digits** in a decimal representation of a number is the number of digits that are not leading zeros after the decimal point (as in .0005) or trailing zeros before the decimal point (as in 5,400,000). We say that a value is **accurate to *n* significant digits** if only the first n significant digits are meaningful.

When to Round

After doing a computation in which all the quantities are accurate to no more than n significant digits, round the final result to n significant digits.

Quick Examples

1. 0.00067 has two significant digits. — The 000 before 67 are leading zeros.
2. 0.000670 has three significant digits. — The 0 after 67 is significant.
3. 5,400,000 has two or more significant digits. — We can't say how many of the zeros are trailing.[1]
4. 5,400,001 has 7 significant digits. — The string of zeros is not trailing.
5. Rounding 63,918 to three significant digits gives 63,900.
6. Rounding 63,958 to three significant digits gives 64,000.
7. $\pi = 3.141592653...$ $\frac{22}{7} = 3.142857142...$ Therefore, $\frac{22}{7}$ is an approximation of π that is accurate to only three significant digits (3.14).
8. $4.02(1+0.02)^{1.4} \approx 4.13$ — We rounded to three significant digits.

[1]If we obtained 5,400,000 by rounding 5,401,011, then it has three significant digits because the zero after the 4 is significant. On the other hand, if we obtained it by rounding 5,411,234, then it has only two significant digits. The use of scientific notation avoids this ambiguity: 5.40×10^6 (or 5.40 E6 on a calculator or computer) is accurate to three digits and 5.4×10^6 is accurate to two.

One more point, though: If, in a long calculation, you round the intermediate results, your final answer may be even less accurate than you think. As a general rule,

When calculating, don't round intermediate results. Rather, use the most accurate results obtainable or have your calculator or computer store them for you.

When you are done with the calculation, *then* round your answer to the appropriate number of digits of accuracy.

0.1 EXERCISES

Calculate each expression in Exercises 1–24, giving the answer as a whole number or a fraction in lowest terms.

1. $2(4+(-1))(2\cdot -4)$ **2.** $3+([4-2]\cdot 9)$

3. `20/(3*4)-1` **4.** `2-(3*4)/10`

5. $\dfrac{3+([3+(-5)])}{3-2\times 2}$ **6.** $\dfrac{12-(1-4)}{2(5-1)\cdot 2-1}$

7. `(2-5*(-1))/1-2*(-1)`

8. `2-5*(-1)/(1-2*(-1))`

9. $2\cdot(-1)^2/2$ **10.** $2+4\cdot 3^2$

11. $2\cdot 4^2+1$ **12.** $1-3\cdot(-2)^2\times 2$

13. `3^2+2^2+1` **14.** `2^(2^2-2)`

15. $\dfrac{3-2(-3)^2}{-6(4-1)^2}$ **16.** $\dfrac{1-2(1-4)^2}{2(5-1)^2\cdot 2}$

17. `10*(1+1/10)^3` **18.** `121/(1+1/10)^2`

19. $3\left(\dfrac{-2\cdot 3^2}{-(4-1)^2}\right)$ **20.** $-\left(\dfrac{8(1-4)^2}{-9(5-1)^2}\right)$

21. $3\left(1-\left(-\frac{1}{2}\right)^2\right)^2+1$ **22.** $3\left(\frac{1}{9}-\left(\frac{2}{3}\right)^2\right)^2+1$

23. `(1/2)^2-1/2^2` **24.** `2/(1^2)-(2/1)^2`

Convert each expression in Exercises 25–50 into its technology formula equivalent as in the table in the text.

25. $3\times(2-5)$ **26.** $4+\dfrac{5}{9}$

27. $\dfrac{3}{2-5}$ **28.** $\dfrac{4-1}{3}$

29. $\dfrac{3-1}{8+6}$ **30.** $3+\dfrac{3}{2-9}$

31. $3-\dfrac{4+7}{8}$ **32.** $\dfrac{4\times 2}{\left(\frac{2}{3}\right)}$

33. $\dfrac{2}{3+x}-xy^2$ **34.** $3+\dfrac{3+x}{xy}$

35. $3.1x^3-4x^{-2}-\dfrac{60}{x^2-1}$ **36.** $2.1x^{-3}-x^{-1}+\dfrac{x^2-3}{2}$

37. $\dfrac{\left(\frac{2}{3}\right)}{5}$ **38.** $\dfrac{2}{\left(\frac{3}{5}\right)}$

39. $3^{4-5}\times 6$ **40.** $\dfrac{2}{3+5^{7-9}}$

41. $3\left(1+\dfrac{4}{100}\right)^{-3}$ **42.** $3\left(\dfrac{1+4}{100}\right)^{-3}$

43. $3^{2x-1}+4^x-1$ **44.** $2^{x^2}-(2^{2x})^2$

45. 2^{2x^2-x+1} **46.** $2^{2x^2-x}+1$

47. $\dfrac{4e^{-2x}}{2-3e^{-2x}}$ **48.** $\dfrac{e^{2x}+e^{-2x}}{e^{2x}-e^{-2x}}$

49. $3\left(1-\left(-\frac{1}{2}\right)^2\right)^2+1$ **50.** $3\left(\frac{1}{9}-\left(\frac{2}{3}\right)^2\right)^2+1$

0.2 Exponents and Radicals

In Section 1 we discussed exponentiation, or "raising to a power"; for example, $2^3=2\cdot 2\cdot 2$. In this section we discuss the algebra of exponentials more fully. First, we look at *integer* exponents: cases in which the powers are positive or negative whole numbers.

Integer Exponents

Positive Integer Exponents

If a is any real number and n is any positive integer, then by a^n we mean the quantity $a \cdot a \cdot \cdots \cdot a$ (n times); thus, $a^1 = a$, $a^2 = a \cdot a$, $a^5 = a \cdot a \cdot a \cdot a \cdot a$. In the expression a^n the number n is called the **exponent**, and the number a is called the **base**.

Quick Examples

$3^2 = 9$ $\quad$ $2^3 = 8$

$0^{34} = 0$ $\quad$ $(-1)^5 = -1$

$10^3 = 1{,}000$ $\quad$ $10^5 = 100{,}000$

Negative Integer Exponents

If a is any real number *other than zero* and n is any positive integer, then we define

$$a^{-n} = \frac{1}{a^n} = \frac{1}{a \cdot a \cdot \cdots \cdot a} \quad (n \text{ times})$$

Quick Examples

$2^{-3} = \frac{1}{2^3} = \frac{1}{8}$ $\quad$ $1^{-27} = \frac{1}{1^{27}} = 1$

$x^{-1} = \frac{1}{x^1} = \frac{1}{x}$ $\quad$ $(-3)^{-2} = \frac{1}{(-3)^2} = \frac{1}{9}$

$y^7y^{-2} = y^7\frac{1}{y^2} = y^5$ $\quad$ 0^{-2} is not defined

Zero Exponent

If a is any real number other than zero, then we define

$$a^0 = 1$$

Quick Examples

$3^0 = 1$ $\quad$ $1{,}000{,}000^0 = 1$

0^0 is not defined

When combining exponential expressions, we use the following identities.

Exponent Identity	Quick Examples
1. $a^m a^n = a^{m+n}$	$2^3 2^2 = 2^{3+2} = 2^5 = 32$ $x^3 x^{-4} = x^{3-4} = x^{-1} = \frac{1}{x}$ $\frac{x^3}{x^{-2}} = x^3 \frac{1}{x^{-2}} = x^3 x^2 = x^5$
2. $\frac{a^m}{a^n} = a^{m-n}$ if $a \neq 0$	$\frac{4^3}{4^2} = 4^{3-2} = 4^1 = 4$ $\frac{x^3}{x^{-2}} = x^{3-(-2)} = x^5$ $\frac{3^2}{3^4} = 3^{2-4} = 3^{-2} = \frac{1}{9}$
3. $(a^n)^m = a^{nm}$	$(3^2)^2 = 3^4 = 81$ $(2^x)^2 = 2^{2x}$
4. $(ab)^n = a^n b^n$	$(4 \cdot 2)^2 = 4^2 2^2 = 64$ $(-2y)^4 = (-2)^4 y^4 = 16y^4$
5. $\left(\frac{a}{b}\right)^n = \frac{a^n}{b^n}$ if $b \neq 0$	$\left(\frac{4}{3}\right)^2 = \frac{4^2}{3^2} = \frac{16}{9}$ $\left(\frac{x}{-y}\right)^3 = \frac{x^3}{(-y)^3} = -\frac{x^3}{y^3}$

Caution

- In the first two identities, the bases of the expressions must be the same. For example, the first gives $3^2 3^4 = 3^6$, but does *not* apply to $3^2 4^2$.
- People sometimes invent their own identities, such as $a^m + a^n = a^{m+n}$, which is wrong! (Try it with $a = m = n = 1$.) If you wind up with something like $2^3 + 2^4$, you are stuck with it; there are no identities around to simplify it further. (You can factor out 2^3, but whether or not that is a simplification depends on what you are going to do with the expression next.)

EXAMPLE 1 Combining the Identities

$$\begin{aligned} \frac{(x^2)^3}{x^3} &= \frac{x^6}{x^3} && \text{By (3)} \\ &= x^{6-3} && \text{By (2)} \\ &= x^3 \end{aligned}$$

$$\begin{aligned} \frac{(x^4 y)^3}{y} &= \frac{(x^4)^3 y^3}{y} && \text{By (4)} \\ &= \frac{x^{12} y^3}{y} && \text{By (3)} \\ &= x^{12} y^{3-1} && \text{By (2)} \\ &= x^{12} y^2 \end{aligned}$$

EXAMPLE 2 Eliminating Negative Exponents

Simplify the following and express the answer using no negative exponents.

a. $\dfrac{x^4y^{-3}}{x^5y^2}$ **b.** $\left(\dfrac{x^{-1}}{x^2y}\right)^5$

Solution

a. $\dfrac{x^4y^{-3}}{x^5y^2} = x^{4-5}y^{-3-2} = x^{-1}y^{-5} = \dfrac{1}{xy^5}$

b. $\left(\dfrac{x^{-1}}{x^2y}\right)^5 = \dfrac{(x^{-1})^5}{(x^2y)^5} = \dfrac{x^{-5}}{x^{10}y^5} = \dfrac{1}{x^{15}y^5}$

Radicals

If a is any non-negative real number, then its **square root** is the non-negative number whose square is a. For example, the square root of 16 is 4, because $4^2 = 16$. We write the square root of n as $\sqrt{n}$. (Roots are also referred to as **radicals**.) It is important to remember that $\sqrt{n}$ is never negative. Thus, for instance, $\sqrt{9}$ is 3, and not -3, even though $(-3)^2 = 9$. If we want to speak of the "negative square root" of 9, we write it as $-\sqrt{9} = -3$. If we want to write both square roots at once, we write $\pm\sqrt{9} = \pm 3$.

The **cube root** of a real number a is the number whose cube is a. The cube root of a is written as $\sqrt[3]{a}$ so that, for example, $\sqrt[3]{8} = 2$ (because $2^3 = 8$). Note that we can take the cube root of any number, positive, negative, or zero. For instance, the cube root of -8 is $\sqrt[3]{-8} = -2$ because $(-2)^3 = -8$. Unlike square roots, the cube root of a number may be negative. In fact, the cube root of a always has the same sign as a.

Higher roots are defined similarly. The **fourth root** of the *non-negative* number a is defined as the non-negative number whose fourth power is a, and written $\sqrt[4]{a}$. The **fifth root** of any number a is the number whose fifth power is a, and so on.

Note We cannot take an even-numbered root of a negative number, but we can take an odd-numbered root of any number. Even roots are always positive, whereas odd roots have the same sign as the number we start with. ■

EXAMPLE 3 *n*th Roots

$\sqrt{4} = 2$	Because $2^2 = 4$
$\sqrt{16} = 4$	Because $4^2 = 16$
$\sqrt{1} = 1$	Because $1^2 = 1$
If $x \geq 0$, then $\sqrt{x^2} = x$	Because $x^2 = x^2$
$\sqrt{2} \approx 1.414213562$	$\sqrt{2}$ is not a whole number.
$\sqrt{1+1} = \sqrt{2} \approx 1.414213562$	First add, then take the square root.[2]
$\sqrt{9+16} = \sqrt{25} = 5$	Contrast with $\sqrt{9} + \sqrt{16} = 3 + 4 = 7$.

[2]In general, $\sqrt{a+b}$ means the square root of the *quantity* $(a+b)$. The radical sign acts as a pair of parentheses or a fraction bar, telling us to evaluate what is inside before taking the root. (See the Caution on the next page.)

$\frac{1}{\sqrt{2}} = \frac{\sqrt{2}}{2}$ — Multiply top and bottom by $\sqrt{2}$.

$\sqrt[3]{27} = 3$ — Because $3^3 = 27$

$\sqrt[3]{-64} = -4$ — Because $(-4)^3 = -64$

$\sqrt[4]{16} = 2$ — Because $2^4 = 16$

$\sqrt[4]{-16}$ is not defined — Even-numbered root of a negative number

$\sqrt[5]{-1} = -1$, since $(-1)^5 = -1$ — Odd-numbered root of a negative number

$\sqrt[n]{-1} = -1$ if n is any odd number

Q: *In the example we saw that $\sqrt{x^2} = x$ if x is non-negative. What happens if x is negative?*

A: If x is negative, then x^2 is positive, and so $\sqrt{x^2}$ is still defined as the non-negative number whose square is x^2. This number must be $|x|$, the **absolute value of *x***, which is the non-negative number with the same size as x. For instance, $|-3| = 3$, while $|3| = 3$, and $|0| = 0$. It follows that

$$\sqrt{x^2} = |x|$$

for every real number x, positive or negative. For instance,

$$\sqrt{(-3)^2} = \sqrt{9} = 3 = |-3|$$

and $$\sqrt{3^2} = \sqrt{9} = 3 = |3|.$$

In general, we find that

$$\sqrt[n]{x^n} = x \text{ if } n \text{ is odd, and } \sqrt[n]{x^n} = |x| \text{ if } n \text{ is even.}$$

We use the following identities to evaluate radicals of products and quotients.

Radicals of Products and Quotients

If a and b are any real numbers (non-negative in the case of even-numbered roots), then

$\sqrt[n]{ab} = \sqrt[n]{a}\sqrt[n]{b}$ — Radical of a product = Product of radicals

$\sqrt[n]{\frac{a}{b}} = \frac{\sqrt[n]{a}}{\sqrt[n]{b}}$ if $b \neq 0$ — Radical of a quotient = Quotient of radicals

Notes

- The first rule is similar to the rule $(a \cdot b)^2 = a^2b^2$ for the square of a product, and the second rule is similar to the rule $\left(\frac{a}{b}\right)^2 = \frac{a^2}{b^2}$ for the square of a quotient.
- ***Caution*** There is no corresponding identity for addition:

  $\sqrt{a+b}$ is *not* equal to $\sqrt{a} + \sqrt{b}$

(Consider $a = b = 1$, for example.) Equating these expressions is a common error, so be careful! ■

Quick Examples

1. $\sqrt{9 \cdot 4} = \sqrt{9}\sqrt{4} = 3 \times 2 = 6$ — Alternatively, $\sqrt{9 \cdot 4} = \sqrt{36} = 6$
2. $\sqrt{\dfrac{9}{4}} = \dfrac{\sqrt{9}}{\sqrt{4}} = \dfrac{3}{2}$
3. $\dfrac{\sqrt{2}}{\sqrt{5}} = \dfrac{\sqrt{2}\sqrt{5}}{\sqrt{5}\sqrt{5}} = \dfrac{\sqrt{10}}{5}$
4. $\sqrt{4(3+13)} = \sqrt{4(16)} = \sqrt{4}\sqrt{16} = 2 \times 4 = 8$
5. $\sqrt[3]{-216} = \sqrt[3]{(-27)8} = \sqrt[3]{-27}\sqrt[3]{8} = (-3)2 = -6$
6. $\sqrt{x^3} = \sqrt{x^2 \cdot x} = \sqrt{x^2}\sqrt{x} = x\sqrt{x}$ if $x \geq 0$
7. $\sqrt{\dfrac{x^2+y^2}{z^2}} = \dfrac{\sqrt{x^2+y^2}}{\sqrt{z^2}} = \dfrac{\sqrt{x^2+y^2}}{|z|}$ — We can't simplify the numerator any further.

Rational Exponents

We already know what we mean by expressions such as x^4 and a^{-6}. The next step is to make sense of *rational* exponents: exponents of the form p/q with p and q integers as in $a^{1/2}$ and $3^{-2/3}$.

Q: *What should we mean by $a^{1/2}$?*

A: The overriding concern here is that all the exponent identities should remain true. In this case the identity to look at is the one that says that $(a^m)^n = a^{mn}$. This identity tells us that

$$(a^{1/2})^2 = a^1 = a.$$

That is, $a^{1/2}$, when squared, gives us a. But that must mean that $a^{1/2}$ is the *square root* of a, or

$$a^{1/2} = \sqrt{a}.$$

A similar argument tells us that, if q is any positive whole number, then

$$a^{1/q} = \sqrt[q]{a}, \text{ the } q\text{th root of } a.$$

Notice that if a is negative, this makes sense only for q odd. To avoid this problem, we usually stick to positive a.

Q: *If p and q are integers (q positive), what should we mean by $a^{p/q}$?*

A: By the exponent identities, $a^{p/q}$ should equal both $(a^p)^{1/q}$ and $(a^{1/q})^p$. The first is the qth root of a^p, and the second is the pth power of $a^{1/q}$, which gives us the following.

Conversion Between Rational Exponents and Radicals

If a is any non-negative number, then

$$a^{p/q} = \sqrt[q]{a^p} = \left(\sqrt[q]{a}\right)^p.$$

↑ Using exponents ↑ ↑ Using radicals

In particular,

$$a^{1/q} = \sqrt[q]{a}, \text{ the } q\text{th root of } a.$$

Notes

- If a is negative, all of this makes sense only if q is odd.
- All of the exponent identities continue to work when we allow rational exponents p/q. In other words, we are free to use all the exponent identities even though the exponents are not integers. ■

Quick Examples

1. $4^{3/2} = (\sqrt{4})^3 = 2^3 = 8$
2. $8^{2/3} = (\sqrt[3]{8})^2 = 2^2 = 4$
3. $9^{-3/2} = \dfrac{1}{9^{3/2}} = \dfrac{1}{(\sqrt{9})^3} = \dfrac{1}{3^3} = \dfrac{1}{27}$
4. $\dfrac{\sqrt{3}}{\sqrt[3]{3}} = \dfrac{3^{1/2}}{3^{1/3}} = 3^{1/2-1/3} = 3^{1/6} = \sqrt[6]{3}$
5. $2^2 2^{7/2} = 2^2 2^{3+1/2} = 2^2 2^3 2^{1/2} = 2^5 2^{1/2} = 2^5\sqrt{2}$

EXAMPLE 4 Simplifying Algebraic Expressions

Simplify the following.

a. $\dfrac{(x^3)^{5/3}}{x^3}$ **b.** $\sqrt[4]{a^6}$ **c.** $\dfrac{(xy)^{-3}y^{-3/2}}{x^{-2}\sqrt{y}}$

Solution

a. $\dfrac{(x^3)^{5/3}}{x^3} = \dfrac{x^5}{x^3} = x^2$

b. $\sqrt[4]{a^6} = a^{6/4} = a^{3/2} = a \cdot a^{1/2} = a\sqrt{a}$

c. $\dfrac{(xy)^{-3}y^{-3/2}}{x^{-2}\sqrt{y}} = \dfrac{x^{-3}y^{-3}y^{-3/2}}{x^{-2}y^{1/2}} = \dfrac{1}{x^{-2+3}y^{1/2+3+3/2}} = \dfrac{1}{xy^5}$

Converting Between Rational, Radical, and Exponent Form

In calculus we must often convert algebraic expressions involving powers of x, such as $\dfrac{3}{2x^2}$, into expressions in which x does not appear in the denominator, such as $\dfrac{3}{2}x^{-2}$. Also, we must often convert expressions with radicals, such as $\dfrac{1}{\sqrt{1+x^2}}$, into expressions with no radicals and all powers in the numerator, such as $(1+x^2)^{-1/2}$. In these cases, we are converting from **rational form** or **radical form** to **exponent form.**

Rational Form

An expression is in **rational form** if it is written with positive exponents only.

Quick Examples

1. $\frac{2}{3x^2}$ is in rational form.
2. $\frac{2x^{-1}}{3}$ is not in rational form because the exponent of x is negative.
3. $\frac{x}{6}+\frac{6}{x}$ is in rational form.

Radical Form

An expression is in **radical form** if it is written with integer powers and roots only.

Quick Examples

1. $\frac{2}{5\sqrt[3]{x}}+\frac{2}{x}$ is in radical form.
2. $\frac{2x^{-1/3}}{5}+2x^{-1}$ is not in radical form because $x^{-1/3}$ appears.
3. $\frac{1}{\sqrt{1+x^2}}$ is in radical form, but $(1+x^2)^{-1/2}$ is not.

Exponent Form

An expression is in **exponent form** if there are no radicals and all powers of unknowns occur in the numerator. We write such expressions as sums or differences of terms of the form

Constant × (Expression with x)^p As in $\frac{1}{3}x^{-3/2}$

Quick Examples

1. $\frac{2}{3}x^4-3x^{-1/3}$ is in exponent form.
2. $\frac{x}{6}+\frac{6}{x}$ is not in exponent form because the second expression has x in the denominator.
3. $\sqrt[3]{x}$ is not in exponent form because it has a radical.
4. $(1+x^2)^{-1/2}$ is in exponent form, but $\frac{1}{\sqrt{1+x^2}}$ is not.

EXAMPLE 5 Converting from One Form to Another

Convert the following to rational form:

a. $\frac{1}{2}x^{-2} + \frac{4}{3}x^{-5}$ **b.** $\frac{2}{\sqrt{x}} - \frac{2}{x^{-4}}$

Convert the following to radical form:

c. $\frac{1}{2}x^{-1/2} + \frac{4}{3}x^{-5/4}$ **d.** $\frac{(3+x)^{-1/3}}{5}$

Convert the following to exponent form:

e. $\frac{3}{4x^2} - \frac{x}{6} + \frac{6}{x} + \frac{4}{3\sqrt{x}}$ **f.** $\frac{2}{(x+1)^2} - \frac{3}{4\sqrt[5]{2x-1}}$

Solution For (a) and (b), we eliminate negative exponents as we did in Example 2:

a. $\frac{1}{2}x^{-2} + \frac{4}{3}x^{-5} = \frac{1}{2} \cdot \frac{1}{x^2} + \frac{4}{3} \cdot \frac{1}{x^5} = \frac{1}{2x^2} + \frac{4}{3x^5}$

b. $\frac{2}{\sqrt{x}} - \frac{2}{x^{-4}} = \frac{2}{\sqrt{x}} - 2x^4$

For (c) and (d), we rewrite all terms with fractional exponents as radicals:

c.
$$\frac{1}{2}x^{-1/2} + \frac{4}{3}x^{-5/4} = \frac{1}{2} \cdot \frac{1}{x^{1/2}} + \frac{4}{3} \cdot \frac{1}{x^{5/4}}$$
$$= \frac{1}{2} \cdot \frac{1}{\sqrt{x}} + \frac{4}{3} \cdot \frac{1}{\sqrt[4]{x^5}} = \frac{1}{2\sqrt{x}} + \frac{4}{3\sqrt[4]{x^5}}$$

d. $\frac{(3+x)^{-1/3}}{5} = \frac{1}{5(3+x)^{1/3}} = \frac{1}{5\sqrt[3]{3+x}}$

For (e) and (f), we eliminate any radicals and move all expressions involving x to the numerator:

e.
$$\frac{3}{4x^2} - \frac{x}{6} + \frac{6}{x} + \frac{4}{3\sqrt{x}} = \frac{3}{4}x^{-2} - \frac{1}{6}x + 6x^{-1} + \frac{4}{3x^{1/2}}$$
$$= \frac{3}{4}x^{-2} - \frac{1}{6}x + 6x^{-1} + \frac{4}{3}x^{-1/2}$$

f.
$$\frac{2}{(x+1)^2} - \frac{3}{4\sqrt[5]{2x-1}} = 2(x+1)^{-2} - \frac{3}{4(2x-1)^{1/5}}$$
$$= 2(x+1)^{-2} - \frac{3}{4}(2x-1)^{-1/5}$$

Solving Equations with Exponents

EXAMPLE 6 Solving Equations

Solve the following equations:

a. $x^3 + 8 = 0$ **b.** $x^2 - \frac{1}{2} = 0$ **c.** $x^{3/2} - 64 = 0$

Solution

a. Subtracting 8 from both sides gives $x^3 = -8$. Taking the cube root of both sides gives $x = -2$.

b. Adding $\frac{1}{2}$ to both sides gives $x^2 = \frac{1}{2}$. Thus, $x = \pm\sqrt{\frac{1}{2}} = \pm\frac{1}{\sqrt{2}}$.

c. Adding 64 to both sides gives $x^{3/2} = 64$. Taking the reciprocal (2/3) power of both sides gives

$$(x^{3/2})^{2/3} = 64^{2/3}$$
$$x^1 = \left(\sqrt[3]{64}\right)^2 = 4^2 = 16$$

so $x = 16$.

0.2 EXERCISES

Evaluate the expressions in Exercises 1–16.

1. 3^3 **2.** $(-2)^3$ **3.** $-(2 \cdot 3)^2$ **4.** $(4 \cdot 2)^2$

5. $\left(\frac{-2}{3}\right)^2$ **6.** $\left(\frac{3}{2}\right)^3$ **7.** $(-2)^{-3}$ **8.** -2^{-3}

9. $\left(\frac{1}{4}\right)^{-2}$ **10.** $\left(\frac{-2}{3}\right)^{-2}$ **11.** $2 \cdot 3^0$ **12.** $3 \cdot (-2)^0$

13. $2^3\,2^2$ **14.** $3^2 3$ **15.** $2^2 2^{-1} 2^4 2^{-4}$ **16.** $5^2 5^{-3} 5^2 5^{-2}$

Simplify each expression in Exercises 17–30, expressing your answer in rational form.

17. $x^3 x^2$ **18.** $x^4 x^{-1}$ **19.** $-x^2 x^{-3} y$ **20.** $-xy^{-1}x^{-1}$

21. $\frac{x^3}{x^4}$ **22.** $\frac{y^5}{y^3}$ **23.** $\frac{x^2y^2}{x^{-1}y}$ **24.** $\frac{x^{-1}y}{x^2y^2}$

25. $\frac{(xy^{-1}z^3)^2}{x^2yz^2}$ **26.** $\frac{x^2yz^2}{(xyz^{-1})^{-1}}$ **27.** $\left(\frac{xy^{-2}z}{x^{-1}z}\right)^3$

28. $\left(\frac{x^2y^{-1}z^0}{xyz}\right)^2$ **29.** $\left(\frac{x^{-1}y^{-2}z^2}{xy}\right)^{-2}$ **30.** $\left(\frac{xy^{-2}}{x^2y^{-1}z}\right)^{-3}$

Convert the expressions in Exercises 31–36 to rational form.

31. $3x^{-4}$ **32.** $\frac{1}{2}x^{-4}$ **33.** $\frac{3}{4}x^{-2/3}$

34. $\frac{4}{5}y^{-3/4}$ **35.** $1 - \frac{0.3}{x^{-2}} - \frac{6}{5}x^{-1}$ **36.** $\frac{1}{3x^{-4}} + \frac{0.1x^{-2}}{3}$

Evaluate the expressions in Exercises 37–56, rounding your answer to four significant digits where necessary.

37. $\sqrt{4}$ **38.** $\sqrt{5}$ **39.** $\sqrt{\frac{1}{4}}$

40. $\sqrt{\frac{1}{9}}$ **41.** $\sqrt{\frac{16}{9}}$ **42.** $\sqrt{\frac{9}{4}}$

43. $\frac{\sqrt{4}}{5}$ **44.** $\frac{6}{\sqrt{25}}$ **45.** $\sqrt{9} + \sqrt{16}$

46. $\sqrt{25} - \sqrt{16}$ **47.** $\sqrt{9 + 16}$ **48.** $\sqrt{25 - 16}$

49. $\sqrt[3]{8 - 27}$ **50.** $\sqrt[4]{81 - 16}$ **51.** $\sqrt[3]{27/8}$

52. $\sqrt[3]{8 \times 64}$ **53.** $\sqrt{(-2)^2}$ **54.** $\sqrt{(-1)^2}$

55. $\sqrt{\frac{1}{4}(1 + 15)}$ **56.** $\sqrt{\frac{1}{9}(3 + 33)}$

Simplify the expressions in Exercises 57–64, given that x, y, z, a, b, and c are positive real numbers.

57. $\sqrt{a^2b^2}$ **58.** $\sqrt{\frac{a^2}{b^2}}$ **59.** $\sqrt{(x + 9)^2}$

60. $(\sqrt{x + 9})^2$ **61.** $\sqrt[3]{x^3(a^3 + b^3)}$ **62.** $\sqrt[4]{\frac{x^4}{a^4b^4}}$

63. $\sqrt{\frac{4xy^3}{x^2y}}$ **64.** $\sqrt{\frac{4(x^2 + y^2)}{c^2}}$

Convert the expressions in Exercises 65–84 to exponent form.

65. $\sqrt{3}$ **66.** $\sqrt{8}$ **67.** $\sqrt{x^3}$

68. $\sqrt[3]{x^2}$ **69.** $\sqrt[3]{xy^2}$ **70.** $\sqrt{x^2y}$

71. $\frac{x^2}{\sqrt{x}}$ **72.** $\frac{x}{\sqrt{x}}$ **73.** $\frac{3}{5x^2}$

74. $\frac{2}{5x^{-3}}$ **75.** $\frac{3x^{-1.2}}{2} - \frac{1}{3x^{2.1}}$ **76.** $\frac{2}{3x^{-1.2}} - \frac{x^{2.1}}{3}$

77. $\frac{2x}{3} - \frac{x^{0.1}}{2} + \frac{4}{3x^{1.1}}$ **78.** $\frac{4x^2}{3} + \frac{x^{3/2}}{6} - \frac{2}{3x^2}$

79. $\frac{3\sqrt{x}}{4} - \frac{5}{3\sqrt{x}} + \frac{4}{3x\sqrt{x}}$ **80.** $\frac{3}{5\sqrt{x}} - \frac{5\sqrt{x}}{8} + \frac{7}{2\sqrt[3]{x}}$

81. $\frac{3\sqrt[5]{x^2}}{4} - \frac{7}{2\sqrt{x^3}}$ **82.** $\frac{1}{8x\sqrt{x}} - \frac{2}{3\sqrt[5]{x^3}}$

83. $\frac{1}{(x^2 + 1)^3} - \frac{3}{4\sqrt[3]{(x^2 + 1)}}$ **84.** $\frac{2}{3(x^2 + 1)^{-3}} - \frac{3\sqrt[3]{(x^2 + 1)^7}}{4}$

Convert the expressions in Exercises 85–96 to radical form.

85. $2^{2/3}$ **86.** $3^{4/5}$ **87.** $x^{4/3}$ **88.** $y^{7/4}$

89. $(x^{1/2}y^{1/3})^{1/5}$ **90.** $x^{-1/3}y^{3/2}$ **91.** $-\frac{3}{2}x^{-1/4}$ **92.** $\frac{4}{5}x^{3/2}$

93. $0.2x^{-2/3}+\frac{3}{7x^{-1/2}}$

94. $\frac{3.1}{x^{-4/3}}-\frac{11}{7}x^{-1/7}$

95. $\frac{3}{4(1-x)^{5/2}}$

96. $\frac{9}{4(1-x)^{-7/3}}$

Simplify the expressions in Exercises 97–106.

97. $4^{-1/2}4^{7/2}$

98. $2^{1/a}/2^{2/a}$

99. $3^{2/3}3^{-1/6}$

100. $2^{1/3}2^{-1}2^{2/3}2^{-1/3}$

101. $\frac{x^{3/2}}{x^{5/2}}$

102. $\frac{y^{5/4}}{y^{3/4}}$

103. $\frac{x^{1/2}y^2}{x^{-1/2}y}$

104. $\frac{x^{-1/2}y}{x^2y^{3/2}}$

105. $\left(\frac{x}{y}\right)^{1/3}\left(\frac{y}{x}\right)^{2/3}$

106. $\left(\frac{x}{y}\right)^{-1/3}\left(\frac{y}{x}\right)^{1/3}$

Solve each equation in Exercises 107–120 for x, rounding your answer to four significant digits where necessary.

107. $x^2-16=0$

108. $x^2-1=0$

109. $x^2-\frac{4}{9}=0$

110. $x^2-\frac{1}{10}=0$

111. $x^2-(1+2x)^2=0$

112. $x^2-(2-3x)^2=0$

113. $x^5+32=0$

114. $x^4-81=0$

115. $x^{1/2}-4=0$

116. $x^{1/3}-2=0$

117. $1-\frac{1}{x^2}=0$

118. $\frac{2}{x^3}-\frac{6}{x^4}=0$

119. $(x-4)^{-1/3}=2$

120. $(x-4)^{2/3}+1=5$

0.3 Multiplying and Factoring Algebraic Expressions

Multiplying Algebraic Expressions

Distributive Law

The **distributive law** for real numbers states that

$$a(b\pm c)=ab\pm ac$$
$$(a\pm b)c=ac\pm bc$$

for any real numbers a, b, and c.

Quick Examples

1. $2(x-3)$ is *not* equal to $2x-3$ but is equal to $2x-2(3)=2x-6$.
2. $x(x+1)=x^2+x$
3. $2x(3x-4)=6x^2-8x$
4. $(x-4)x^2=x^3-4x^2$
5. $(x+2)(x+3)=(x+2)x+(x+2)3$
$=(x^2+2x)+(3x+6)=x^2+5x+6$
6. $(x+2)(x-3)=(x+2)x-(x+2)3$
$=(x^2+2x)-(3x+6)=x^2-x-6$

There is a quicker way of expanding expressions like the last two, called the "FOIL" method (First, Outer, Inner, Last). Consider, for instance, the expression $(x+1)(x-2)$. The FOIL method says: Take the product of the first terms: $x\cdot x=x^2$, the product of the outer terms: $x\cdot(-2)=-2x$, the product of the inner terms: $1\cdot x=x$, and the product of the last terms: $1\cdot(-2)=-2$, and then add them all up, getting $x^2-2x+x-2=x^2-x-2$.

EXAMPLE 1 FOIL

a. $(x-2)(2x+5) = \underset{\text{First}}{2x^2} + \underset{\text{Outer}}{5x} - \underset{\text{Inner}}{4x} - \underset{\text{Last}}{10} = 2x^2 + x - 10$

b. $(x^2+1)(x-4) = x^3 - 4x^2 + x - 4$

c. $(a-b)(a+b) = a^2 + ab - ab - b^2 = a^2 - b^2$

d. $(a+b)^2 = (a+b)(a+b) = a^2 + ab + ab + b^2 = a^2 + 2ab + b^2$

e. $(a-b)^2 = (a-b)(a-b) = a^2 - ab - ab + b^2 = a^2 - 2ab + b^2$

The last three are particularly important and are worth memorizing.

Special Formulas

$(a-b)(a+b) = a^2 - b^2$ Difference of two squares

$(a+b)^2 = a^2 + 2ab + b^2$ Square of a sum

$(a-b)^2 = a^2 - 2ab + b^2$ Square of a difference

Quick Examples

1. $(2-x)(2+x) = 4 - x^2$

2. $(1+a)(1-a) = 1 - a^2$

3. $(x+3)^2 = x^2 + 6x + 9$

4. $(4-x)^2 = 16 - 8x + x^2$

Here are some longer examples that require the distributive law.

EXAMPLE 2 Multiplying Algebraic Expressions

a.
$$\begin{aligned}(x+1)(x^2+3x-4) &= (x+1)x^2 + (x+1)3x - (x+1)4\\ &= (x^3+x^2) + (3x^2+3x) - (4x+4)\\ &= x^3 + 4x^2 - x - 4\end{aligned}$$

b.
$$\begin{aligned}\left(x^2 - \frac{1}{x} + 1\right)(2x+5) &= \left(x^2 - \frac{1}{x} + 1\right)2x + \left(x^2 - \frac{1}{x} + 1\right)5\\ &= (2x^3 - 2 + 2x) + \left(5x^2 - \frac{5}{x} + 5\right)\\ &= 2x^3 + 5x^2 + 2x + 3 - \frac{5}{x}\end{aligned}$$

c.
$$\begin{aligned}(x-y)(x-y)(x-y) &= (x^2 - 2xy + y^2)(x-y)\\ &= (x^2 - 2xy + y^2)x - (x^2 - 2xy + y^2)y\\ &= (x^3 - 2x^2y + xy^2) - (x^2y - 2xy^2 + y^3)\\ &= x^3 - 3x^2y + 3xy^2 - y^3\end{aligned}$$

Factoring Algebraic Expressions

We can think of factoring as applying the distributive law in reverse—for example,

$$2x^2 + x = x(2x + 1),$$

which can be checked by using the distributive law. Factoring is an art that you will learn with experience and the help of a few useful techniques.

Factoring Using a Common Factor

To use this technique, locate a **common factor**—a term that occurs as a factor in each of the expressions being added or subtracted (for example, x is a common factor in $2x^2 + x$, because it is a factor of both $2x^2$ and x). Once you have located a common factor, "factor it out" by applying the distributive law.

Quick Examples

1. $2x^3 - x^2 + x$ has x as a common factor, so
$$2x^3 - x^2 + x = x(2x^2 - x + 1)$$

2. $2x^2 + 4x$ has $2x$ as a common factor, so
$$2x^2 + 4x = 2x(x + 2)$$

3. $2x^2y + xy^2 - x^2y^2$ has xy as a common factor, so
$$2x^2y + xy^2 - x^2y^2 = xy(2x + y - xy)$$

4. $(x^2 + 1)(x + 2) - (x^2 + 1)(x + 3)$ has $x^2 + 1$ as a common factor, so
$$\begin{aligned}(x^2 + 1)(x + 2) - (x^2 + 1)(x + 3) &= (x^2 + 1)[(x + 2) - (x + 3)] \\ &= (x^2 + 1)(x + 2 - x - 3) \\ &= (x^2 + 1)(-1) = -(x^2 + 1)\end{aligned}$$

5. $12x(x^2 - 1)^5(x^3 + 1)^6 + 18x^2(x^2 - 1)^6(x^3 + 1)^5$ has $6x(x^2 - 1)^5(x^3 + 1)^5$ as a common factor, so
$$\begin{aligned}&12x(x^2 - 1)^5(x^3 + 1)^6 + 18x^2(x^2 - 1)^6(x^3 + 1)^5 \\ &= 6x(x^2 - 1)^5(x^3 + 1)^5[2(x^3 + 1) + 3x(x^2 - 1)] \\ &= 6x(x^2 - 1)^5(x^3 + 1)^5(2x^3 + 2 + 3x^3 - 3x) \\ &= 6x(x^2 - 1)^5(x^3 + 1)^5(5x^3 - 3x + 2)\end{aligned}$$

We would also like to be able to reverse calculations such as $(x + 2)(2x - 5) = 2x^2 - x - 10$. That is, starting with the expression $2x^2 - x - 10$, we would like to **factor** it to get the expression $(x + 2)(2x - 5)$. An expression of the form $ax^2 + bx + c$, where a, b, and c are real numbers, is called a **quadratic** expression in x. Thus, given a quadratic expression $ax^2 + bx + c$, we would like to write it in the form $(dx + e)(fx + g)$ for some real numbers d, e, f, and g. There are some quadratics, such as $x^2 + x + 1$, that cannot be factored in this form at all. Here, we consider only quadratics that do factor, and in such a way that the numbers d, e, f, and g are integers (whole numbers; other cases are discussed in Section 5). The usual technique of factoring such quadratics is a "trial and error" approach.

Factoring Quadratics by Trial and Error

To factor the quadratic $ax^2 + bx + c$, factor ax^2 as $(a_1x)(a_2x)$ (with a_1 positive) and c as c_1c_2, and then check whether or not $ax^2 + bx + c = (a_1x \pm c_1)(a_2x \pm c_2)$. If not, try other factorizations of ax^2 and c.

Quick Examples

1. To factor $x^2 - 6x + 5$, first factor x^2 as $(x)(x)$, and 5 as (5)(1):

$(x + 5)(x + 1) = x^2 + 6x + 5.$ No good

$(x - 5)(x - 1) = x^2 - 6x + 5.$ Desired factorization

2. To factor $x^2 - 4x - 12$, first factor x^2 as $(x)(x)$, and -12 as $(1)(-12)$, $(2)(-6)$, or $(3)(-4)$. Trying them one by one gives

$(x + 1)(x - 12) = x^2 - 11x - 12.$ No good

$(x - 1)(x + 12) = x^2 + 11x - 12.$ No good

$(x + 2)(x - 6) = x^2 - 4x - 12.$ Desired factorization

3. To factor $4x^2 - 25$, we can follow the above procedure, or recognize $4x^2 - 25$ as the difference of two squares:

$$4x^2 - 25 = (2x)^2 - 5^2 = (2x - 5)(2x + 5).$$

Note: Not all quadratic expressions factor. In Section 5 we look at a test that tells us whether or not a given quadratic factors.

Here are examples requiring either a little more work or a little more thought.

EXAMPLE 3 Factoring Quadratics

Factor the following: **a.** $4x^2 - 5x - 6$ **b.** $x^4 - 5x^2 + 6$

Solution

a. Possible factorizations of $4x^2$ are $(2x)(2x)$ or $(x)(4x)$. Possible factorizations of -6 are $(1)(-6)$, $(2)(-3)$. We now systematically try out all the possibilities until we come up with the correct one.

$(2x)(2x)$ and $(1)(-6)$:	$(2x + 1)(2x - 6) = 4x^2 - 10x - 6$	No good
$(2x)(2x)$ and $(2)(-3)$:	$(2x + 2)(2x - 3) = 4x^2 - 2x - 6$	No good
$(x)(4x)$ and $(1)(-6)$:	$(x + 1)(4x - 6) = 4x^2 - 2x - 6$	No good
$(x)(4x)$ and $(2)(-3)$:	$(x + 2)(4x - 3) = 4x^2 + 5x - 6$	Almost!
Change signs:	$(x - 2)(4x + 3) = 4x^2 - 5x - 6$	Correct

b. The expression $x^4 - 5x^2 + 6$ is not a quadratic, you say? Correct. It's a quartic (a fourth degree expression). However, it looks rather like a quadratic. In fact, it is quadratic *in* x^2, meaning that it is

$$(x^2)^2 - 5(x^2) + 6 = y^2 - 5y + 6$$

where $y = x^2$. The quadratic $y^2 - 5y + 6$ factors as

$$y^2 - 5y + 6 = (y - 3)(y - 2)$$

so

$$x^4 - 5x^2 + 6 = (x^2 - 3)(x^2 - 2)$$

This is a sometimes useful technique.

Our last example is here to remind you why we should want to factor polynomials in the first place. We shall return to this in Section 5.

EXAMPLE 4 Solving a Quadratic Equation by Factoring

Solve the equation $3x^2 + 4x - 4 = 0$.

Solution We first factor the left-hand side to get

$$(3x - 2)(x + 2) = 0.$$

Thus, the product of the two quantities $(3x - 2)$ and $(x + 2)$ is zero. Now, if a product of two numbers is zero, one of the two must be zero. In other words, either $3x - 2 = 0$, giving $x = \frac{2}{3}$, or $x + 2 = 0$, giving $x = -2$. Thus, there are two solutions: $x = \frac{2}{3}$ and $x = -2$.

0.3 EXERCISES

Expand each expression in Exercises 1–22.

1. $x(4x + 6)$
2. $(4y - 2)y$
3. $(2x - y)y$
4. $x(3x + y)$
5. $(x + 1)(x - 3)$
6. $(y + 3)(y + 4)$
7. $(2y + 3)(y + 5)$
8. $(2x - 2)(3x - 4)$
9. $(2x - 3)^2$
10. $(3x + 1)^2$
11. $\left(x + \frac{1}{x}\right)^2$
12. $\left(y - \frac{1}{y}\right)^2$
13. $(2x - 3)(2x + 3)$
14. $(4 + 2x)(4 - 2x)$
15. $\left(y - \frac{1}{y}\right)\left(y + \frac{1}{y}\right)$
16. $(x - x^2)(x + x^2)$
17. $(x^2 + x - 1)(2x + 4)$
18. $(3x + 1)(2x^2 - x + 1)$
19. $(x^2 - 2x + 1)^2$
20. $(x + y - xy)^2$
21. $(y^3 + 2y^2 + y)(y^2 + 2y - 1)$
22. $(x^3 - 2x^2 + 4)(3x^2 - x + 2)$

In Exercises 23–30, factor each expression and simplify as much as possible.

23. $(x + 1)(x + 2) + (x + 1)(x + 3)$
24. $(x + 1)(x + 2)^2 + (x + 1)^2(x + 2)$
25. $(x^2 + 1)^5(x + 3)^4 + (x^2 + 1)^6(x + 3)^3$
26. $10x(x^2 + 1)^4(x^3 + 1)^5 + 15x^2(x^2 + 1)^5(x^3 + 1)^4$
27. $(x^3 + 1)\sqrt{x + 1} - (x^3 + 1)^2\sqrt{x + 1}$
28. $(x^2 + 1)\sqrt{x + 1} - \sqrt{(x + 1)^3}$
29. $\sqrt{(x + 1)^3} + \sqrt{(x + 1)^5}$
30. $(x^2 + 1)\sqrt[3]{(x + 1)^4} - \sqrt[3]{(x + 1)^7}$

*In Exercises 31–48, **(a)** factor the given expression; **(b)** set the expression equal to zero and solve for the unknown (x in the odd-numbered exercises and y in the even-numbered exercises).*

31. $2x + 3x^2$
32. $y^2 - 4y$
33. $6x^3 - 2x^2$
34. $3y^3 - 9y^2$
35. $x^2 - 8x + 7$
36. $y^2 + 6y + 8$
37. $x^2 + x - 12$
38. $y^2 + y - 6$
39. $2x^2 - 3x - 2$
40. $3y^2 - 8y - 3$
41. $6x^2 + 13x + 6$
42. $6y^2 + 17y + 12$
43. $12x^2 + x - 6$
44. $20y^2 + 7y - 3$
45. $x^2 + 4xy + 4y^2$
46. $4y^2 - 4xy + x^2$
47. $x^4 - 5x^2 + 4$
48. $y^4 + 2y^2 - 3$

0.4 Rational Expressions

Rational Expression

A **rational expression** is an algebraic expression of the form $\frac{P}{Q}$, where P and Q are simpler expressions (usually polynomials) and the denominator Q is not zero.

Quick Examples

1. $\frac{x^2 - 3x}{x}$ — $P = x^2 - 3x$, $Q = x$
2. $\frac{x + \frac{1}{x} + 1}{2x^2y + 1}$ — $P = x + \frac{1}{x} + 1$, $Q = 2x^2y + 1$
3. $3xy - x^2$ — $P = 3xy - x^2$, $Q = 1$

Algebra of Rational Expressions

We manipulate rational expressions in the same way that we manipulate fractions, using the following rules:

	Algebraic Rule	Quick Example
Product:	$\frac{P}{Q} \cdot \frac{R}{S} = \frac{PR}{QS}$	$\frac{x+1}{x} \cdot \frac{x-1}{2x+1} = \frac{(x+1)(x-1)}{x(2x+1)} = \frac{x^2-1}{2x^2+x}$
Sum:	$\frac{P}{Q} + \frac{R}{S} = \frac{PS + RQ}{QS}$	$\frac{2x-1}{3x+2} + \frac{1}{x} = \frac{(2x-1)x + 1(3x+2)}{x(3x+2)} = \frac{2x^2+2x+2}{3x^2+2x}$
Difference:	$\frac{P}{Q} - \frac{R}{S} = \frac{PS - RQ}{QS}$	$\frac{x}{3x+2} - \frac{x-4}{x} = \frac{x^2 - (x-4)(3x+2)}{x(3x+2)} = \frac{-2x^2+10x+8}{3x^2+2x}$
Reciprocal:	$\frac{1}{\left(\frac{P}{Q}\right)} = \frac{Q}{P}$	$\frac{1}{\left(\frac{2xy}{3x-1}\right)} = \frac{3x-1}{2xy}$
Quotient:	$\frac{\left(\frac{P}{Q}\right)}{\left(\frac{R}{S}\right)} = \frac{P}{Q} \cdot \frac{S}{R} = \frac{PS}{QR}$	$\frac{\left(\frac{x}{x-1}\right)}{\left(\frac{y-1}{y}\right)} = \frac{xy}{(x-1)(y-1)} = \frac{xy}{xy-x-y+1}$
Cancellation:	$\frac{P\cancel{R}}{Q\cancel{R}} = \frac{P}{Q}$	$\frac{(x-1)(xy+4)}{(x^2y-8)(x-1)} = \frac{xy+4}{x^2y-8}$

Caution Cancellation of summands is *invalid*. For instance,

$$\frac{\not{x} + (2xy^2 - y)}{\not{x} + 4y} = \frac{(2xy^2 - y)}{4y} \quad ✗ \textit{ WRONG!} \quad \text{Do } \textit{not} \text{ cancel a summand.}$$

$$\frac{\not{x}(2xy^2 - y)}{4\not{x}y} = \frac{(2xy^2 - y)}{4y} \quad ✔ \textit{ CORRECT} \quad \text{Do cancel a factor.}$$

Here are some examples that require several algebraic operations.

EXAMPLE 1 Simplifying Rational Expressions

a. $$\frac{\left(\frac{1}{x+y} - \frac{1}{x}\right)}{y} = \frac{\left(\frac{x-(x+y)}{x(x+y)}\right)}{y} = \frac{\left(\frac{-y}{x(x+y)}\right)}{y} = \frac{-y}{xy(x+y)} = -\frac{1}{x(x+y)}$$

b. $$\frac{(x+1)(x+2)^2 - (x+1)^2(x+2)}{(x+2)^4} = \frac{(x+1)(x+2)[(x+2)-(x+1)]}{(x+2)^4}$$

$$= \frac{(x+1)(x+2)(x+2-x-1)}{(x+2)^4} = \frac{(x+1)(x+2)}{(x+2)^4} = \frac{x+1}{(x+2)^3}$$

c. $$\frac{2x\sqrt{x+1} - \frac{x^2}{\sqrt{x+1}}}{x+1} = \frac{\left(\frac{2x(\sqrt{x+1})^2 - x^2}{\sqrt{x+1}}\right)}{x+1} = \frac{2x(x+1) - x^2}{(x+1)\sqrt{x+1}}$$

$$= \frac{2x^2 + 2x - x^2}{(x+1)\sqrt{x+1}} = \frac{x^2 + 2x}{\sqrt{(x+1)^3}} = \frac{x(x+2)}{\sqrt{(x+1)^3}}$$

0.4 EXERCISES

Rewrite each expression in Exercises 1–16 as a single rational expression, simplified as much as possible.

1. $\frac{x-4}{x+1} \cdot \frac{2x+1}{x-1}$

2. $\frac{2x-3}{x-2} \cdot \frac{x+3}{x+1}$

3. $\frac{x-4}{x+1} + \frac{2x+1}{x-1}$

4. $\frac{2x-3}{x-2} + \frac{x+3}{x+1}$

5. $\frac{x^2}{x+1} - \frac{x-1}{x+1}$

6. $\frac{x^2-1}{x-2} - \frac{1}{x-1}$

7. $\frac{1}{\left(\frac{x}{x-1}\right)} + x - 1$

8. $\frac{2}{\left(\frac{x-2}{x^2}\right)} - \frac{1}{x-2}$

9. $\frac{1}{x}\left[\frac{x-3}{xy} + \frac{1}{y}\right]$

10. $\frac{y^2}{x}\left[\frac{2x-3}{y} + \frac{x}{y}\right]$

11. $\frac{(x+1)^2(x+2)^3 - (x+1)^3(x+2)^2}{(x+2)^6}$

12. $\frac{6x(x^2+1)^2(x^3+2)^3 - 9x^2(x^2+1)^3(x^3+2)^2}{(x^3+2)^6}$

13. $\frac{(x^2-1)\sqrt{x^2+1} - \frac{x^4}{\sqrt{x^2+1}}}{x^2+1}$

14. $\frac{x\sqrt{x^3-1} - \frac{3x^4}{\sqrt{x^3-1}}}{x^3-1}$

15. $\frac{\frac{1}{(x+y)^2} - \frac{1}{x^2}}{y}$

16. $\frac{\frac{1}{(x+y)^3} - \frac{1}{x^3}}{y}$

0.5 Solving Polynomial Equations

Polynomial Equation

A **polynomial equation** in one unknown is an equation that can be written in the form

$$ax^n + bx^{n-1} + \cdots + rx + s = 0$$

where $a, b, \ldots, r$, and s are constants.

We call the largest exponent of x appearing in a nonzero term of a polynomial the **degree** of that polynomial.

Quick Examples

1. $3x + 1 = 0$ has degree 1 because the largest power of x that occurs is $x = x^1$. Degree 1 equations are called **linear** equations.
2. $x^2 - x - 1 = 0$ has degree 2 because the largest power of x that occurs is x^2. Degree 2 equations are also called **quadratic equations**, or just **quadratics**.
3. $x^3 = 2x^2 + 1$ is a degree 3 polynomial (or **cubic**) in disguise. It can be rewritten as $x^3 - 2x^2 - 1 = 0$, which is in the standard form for a degree 3 equation.
4. $x^4 - x = 0$ has degree 4. It is called a **quartic**.

Now comes the question: How do we solve these equations for x? This question was asked by mathematicians as early as 1600 BCE. Let's look at these equations one degree at a time.

Solution of Linear Equations

By definition, a linear equation can be written in the form

$$ax + b = 0. \qquad a \text{ and } b \text{ are fixed numbers with } a \neq 0.$$

Solving this is a nice mental exercise: Subtract b from both sides and then divide by a, getting $x = -b/a$. Don't bother memorizing this formula; just go ahead and solve linear equations as they arise. If you feel you need practice, see the exercises at the end of the section.

Solution of Quadratic Equations

By definition, a quadratic equation has the form

$$ax^2 + bx + c = 0. \qquad a, b, \text{ and } c \text{ are fixed numbers and } a \neq 0.^{3}$$

[3]What happens if $a = 0$?

The solutions of this equation are also called the **roots** of $ax^2 + bx + c$. We're assuming that you saw quadratic equations somewhere in high school but may be a little hazy about the details of their solution. There are two ways of solving these equations—one works sometimes, and the other works every time.

Solving Quadratic Equations by Factoring (works sometimes)

If we can factor[4] a quadratic equation $ax^2 + bx + c = 0$, we can solve the equation by setting each factor equal to zero.

Quick Examples

1. $x^2 + 7x + 10 = 0$
   $(x + 5)(x + 2) = 0$ — Factor the left-hand side.
   $x + 5 = 0$ or $x + 2 = 0$ — If a product is zero, one or both factors is zero.
   Solutions: $x = -5$ and $x = -2$
2. $2x^2 - 5x - 12 = 0$
   $(2x + 3)(x - 4) = 0$ — Factor the left-hand side.
   $2x + 3 = 0$ or $x - 4 = 0$
   Solutions: $x = -3/2$ and $x = 4$

Test for Factoring

The quadratic $ax^2 + bx + c$, with a, b, and c being integers (whole numbers), factors into an expression of the form $(rx + s)(tx + u)$ with r, s, t, and u integers precisely when the quantity $b^2 - 4ac$ is a perfect square. (That is, it is the square of an integer.) If this happens, we say that the quadratic **factors over the integers**.

Quick Examples

1. $x^2 + x + 1$ has $a = 1$, $b = 1$, and $c = 1$, so $b^2 - 4ac = -3$, which is not a perfect square. Therefore, this quadratic does not factor over the integers.
2. $2x^2 - 5x - 12$ has $a = 2$, $b = -5$, and $c = -12$, so $b^2 - 4ac = 121$. Because $121 = 11^2$, this quadratic does factor over the integers. (We factored it above.)

Solving Quadratic Equations with the Quadratic Formula (works every time)

The solutions of the general quadratic $ax^2 + bx + c = 0$ $(a \neq 0)$ are given by

$$x = \frac{-b \pm \sqrt{b^2 - 4ac}}{2a}.$$

[4]See the section on factoring for a review of how to factor quadratics.

We call the quantity $\Delta = b^2 - 4ac$ the **discriminant** of the quadratic (Δ is the Greek letter delta), and we have the following general rules:

- If Δ is positive, there are two distinct real solutions.
- If Δ is zero, there is only one real solution: $x = -\frac{b}{2a}$. (Why?)
- If Δ is negative, there are no real solutions.

Quick Examples

1. $2x^2 - 5x - 12 = 0$ has $a = 2$, $b = -5$, and $c = -12$.

$$x = \frac{-b \pm \sqrt{b^2 - 4ac}}{2a} = \frac{5 \pm \sqrt{25 + 96}}{4} = \frac{5 \pm \sqrt{121}}{4} = \frac{5 \pm 11}{4}$$

$$= \frac{16}{4} \text{ or } -\frac{6}{4} = 4 \text{ or } -3/2$$

Δ is positive in this example.

2. $4x^2 = 12x - 9$ can be rewritten as $4x^2 - 12x + 9 = 0$, which has $a = 4$, $b = -12$, and $c = 9$.

$$x = \frac{-b \pm \sqrt{b^2 - 4ac}}{2a} = \frac{12 \pm \sqrt{144 - 144}}{8} = \frac{12 \pm 0}{8} = \frac{12}{8} = \frac{3}{2}$$

Δ is zero in this example.

3. $x^2 + 2x - 1 = 0$ has $a = 1$, $b = 2$, and $c = -1$.

$$x = \frac{-b \pm \sqrt{b^2 - 4ac}}{2a} = \frac{-2 \pm \sqrt{8}}{2} = \frac{-2 \pm 2\sqrt{2}}{2} = -1 \pm \sqrt{2}$$

The two solutions are $x = -1 + \sqrt{2} = 0.414\ldots$ and $x = -1 - \sqrt{2} = -2.414\ldots$

Δ is positive in this example.

4. $x^2 + x + 1 = 0$ has $a = 1$, $b = 1$, and $c = 1$. Because $\Delta = -3$ is negative, there are no real solutions.

Δ is negative in this example.

Q: *This is all very useful, but where does the quadratic formula come from?*

A: To see where it comes from, we will solve a general quadratic equation using "brute force." Start with the general quadratic equation.

$$ax^2 + bx + c = 0.$$

First, divide out the nonzero number a to get

$$x^2 + \frac{bx}{a} + \frac{c}{a} = 0.$$

Now we **complete the square:** Add and subtract the quantity $\frac{b^2}{4a^2}$ to get

$$x^2 + \frac{bx}{a} + \frac{b^2}{4a^2} - \frac{b^2}{4a^2} + \frac{c}{a} = 0.$$

We do this to get the first three terms to factor as a perfect square:

$$\left(x + \frac{b}{2a}\right)^2 - \frac{b^2}{4a^2} + \frac{c}{a} = 0.$$

(Check this by multiplying out.) Adding $\frac{b^2}{4a^2} - \frac{c}{a}$ to both sides gives:

$$\left(x + \frac{b}{2a}\right)^2 = \frac{b^2}{4a^2} - \frac{c}{a} = \frac{b^2 - 4ac}{4a^2}.$$

Taking square roots gives

$$x + \frac{b}{2a} = \frac{\pm\sqrt{b^2 - 4ac}}{2a}.$$

Finally, adding $-\frac{b}{2a}$ to both sides yields the result:

$$x = -\frac{b}{2a} + \frac{\pm\sqrt{b^2 - 4ac}}{2a}$$

or

$$x = \frac{-b \pm \sqrt{b^2 - 4ac}}{2a}.$$

Solution of Cubic Equations

By definition, a cubic equation can be written in the form

$$ax^3 + bx^2 + cx + d = 0. \qquad a, b, c, \text{ and } d \text{ are fixed numbers and } a \neq 0.$$

Now we get into something of a bind. Although there is a perfectly respectable formula for the solutions, it is very complicated and involves the use of complex numbers rather heavily.[5] So we discuss instead a much simpler method that *sometimes* works nicely. Here is the method in a nutshell.

Solving Cubics by Finding One Factor

Start with a given cubic equation $ax^3 + bx^2 + cx + d = 0$.

Step 1 By trial and error, find one solution $x = s$. If a, b, c, and d are integers, the only possible *rational* solutions[6] are those of the form $s = \pm$(factor of d)/(factor of a).

Step 2 It will now be possible to factor the cubic as

$$ax^3 + bx^2 + cx + d = (x - s)(ax^2 + ex + f) = 0$$

To find $ax^2 + ex + f$, divide the cubic by $x - s$, using long division.[7]

Step 3 The factored equation says that either $x - s = 0$ or $ax^2 + ex + f = 0$. We already know that s is a solution, and now we see that the other solutions are the roots of the quadratic. Note that this quadratic may or may not have any real solutions, as usual.

[5] It was when this formula was discovered in the 16th century that complex numbers were first taken seriously. Although we would like to show you the formula, it is too large to fit in this footnote.

[6] There may be *irrational* solutions, however; for example, $x^3 - 2 = 0$ has the single solution $x = \sqrt[3]{2}$.

[7] Alternatively, use "synthetic division," a shortcut that would take us too far afield to describe.

Quick Example

To solve the cubic $x^3 - x^2 + x - 1 = 0$, we first find a single solution. Here, $a = 1$ and $d = -1$. Because the only factors of ± 1 are ± 1, the only possible rational solutions are $x = \pm 1$. By substitution, we see that $x = 1$ is a solution. Thus, $(x - 1)$ is a factor. Dividing by $(x - 1)$ yields the quotient $(x^2 + 1)$. Thus,

$$x^3 - x^2 + x - 1 = (x - 1)(x^2 + 1) = 0$$

so that either $x - 1 = 0$ or $x^2 + 1 = 0$.

Because the discriminant of the quadratic $x^2 + 1$ is negative, we don't get any real solutions from $x^2 + 1 = 0$, so the only real solution is $x = 1$.

Possible Outcomes When Solving a Cubic Equation

If you consider all the cases, there are three possible outcomes when solving a cubic equation:

1. One real solution (as in the Quick Example above)
2. Two real solutions (try, for example, $x^3 + x^2 - x - 1 = 0$)
3. Three real solutions (see the next example)

EXAMPLE 1 Solving a Cubic

Solve the cubic $2x^3 - 3x^2 - 17x + 30 = 0$.

Solution First we look for a single solution. Here, $a = 2$ and $d = 30$. The factors of a are ± 1 and ± 2, and the factors of d are $\pm 1, \pm 2, \pm 3, \pm 5, \pm 6, \pm 10, \pm 15$, and ± 30. This gives us a large number of possible ratios: $\pm 1, \pm 2, \pm 3, \pm 5, \pm 6, \pm 10, \pm 15, \pm 30, \pm 1/2, \pm 3/2, \pm 5/2, \pm 15/2$. Undaunted, we first try $x = 1$ and $x = -1$, getting nowhere. So we move on to $x = 2$, and we hit the jackpot, because substituting $x = 2$ gives $16 - 12 - 34 + 30 = 0$. Thus, $(x - 2)$ is a factor. Dividing yields the quotient $2x^2 + x - 15$. Here is the calculation:

$$\begin{array}{r|l} & 2x^2 + x - 15 \\ x - 2 & 2x^3 - 3x^2 - 17x + 30 \\ & \underline{2x^3 - 4x^2} \\ & \quad x^2 - 17x \\ & \quad \underline{x^2 - 2x} \\ & \qquad -15x + 30 \\ & \qquad \underline{-15x + 30} \\ & \qquad\qquad 0. \end{array}$$

Thus,

$$2x^3 - 3x^2 - 17x + 30 = (x - 2)(2x^2 + x - 15) = 0.$$

Setting the factors equal to zero gives either $x - 2 = 0$ or $2x^2 + x - 15 = 0$. We could solve the quadratic using the quadratic formula, but, luckily, we notice that it factors as

$$2x^2 + x - 15 = (x + 3)(2x - 5).$$

Thus, the solutions are $x = 2$, $x = -3$ and $x = 5/2$.

Solution of Higher-Order Polynomial Equations

Logically speaking, our next step should be a discussion of quartics, then quintics (fifth degree equations), and so on forever. Well, we've got to stop somewhere, and cubics may be as good a place as any. On the other hand, since we've gotten so far, we ought to at least tell you what is known about higher order polynomials.

Quartics Just as in the case of cubics, there is a formula to find the solutions of quartics.[8]

Quintics and Beyond All good things must come to an end, we're afraid. It turns out that there is no "quintic formula." In other words, there is no single algebraic formula or collection of algebraic formulas that gives the solutions to all quintics. This question was settled by the Norwegian mathematician Niels Henrik Abel in 1824 after almost 300 years of controversy about this question. (In fact, several notable mathematicians had previously claimed to have devised formulas for solving the quintic, but these were all shot down by other mathematicians—this being one of the favorite pastimes of practitioners of our art.) The same negative answer applies to polynomial equations of degree 6 and higher. It's not that these equations don't have solutions; it's just that they can't be found using algebraic formulas.[9] However, there are certain special classes of polynomial equations that can be solved with algebraic methods. The way of identifying such equations was discovered around 1829 by the French mathematician Évariste Galois.[10]

[8] See, for example, *First Course in the Theory of Equations* by L. E. Dickson (New York: Wiley, 1922), or *Modern Algebra* by B. L. van der Waerden (New York: Frederick Ungar, 1953).

[9] What we mean by an "algebraic formula" is a formula in the coefficients using the operations of addition, subtraction, multiplication, division, and the taking of radicals. Mathematicians call the use of such formulas in solving polynomial equations "solution by radicals." If you were a math major, you would eventually go on to study this under the heading of Galois theory.

[10] Both Abel (1802–1829) and Galois (1811–1832) died young. Abel died of tuberculosis at the age of 26, while Galois was killed in a duel at the age of 20.

0.5 EXERCISES

Solve the equations in Exercises 1–12 for x (mentally, if possible).

1. $x + 1 = 0$ **2.** $x - 3 = 1$ **3.** $-x + 5 = 0$

4. $2x + 4 = 1$ **5.** $4x - 5 = 8$ **6.** $\frac{3}{4}x + 1 = 0$

7. $7x + 55 = 98$ **8.** $3x + 1 = x$ **9.** $x + 1 = 2x + 2$

10. $x + 1 = 3x + 1$ **11.** $ax + b = c \quad (a \neq 0)$

12. $x - 1 = cx + d \quad (c \neq 1)$

By any method, determine all possible real solutions of each equation in Exercises 13–30. Check your answers by substitution.

13. $2x^2 + 7x - 4 = 0$

14. $x^2 + x + 1 = 0$

15. $x^2 - x + 1 = 0$

16. $2x^2 - 4x + 3 = 0$

17. $2x^2 - 5 = 0$

18. $3x^2 - 1 = 0$

19. $-x^2 - 2x - 1 = 0$

20. $2x^2 - x - 3 = 0$

21. $\frac{1}{2}x^2 - x - \frac{3}{2} = 0$

22. $-\frac{1}{2}x^2 - \frac{1}{2}x + 1 = 0$

23. $x^2 - x = 1$

24. $16x^2 = -24x - 9$

25. $x = 2 - \frac{1}{x}$

26. $x + 4 = \frac{1}{x - 2}$

27. $x^4 - 10x^2 + 9 = 0$

28. $x^4 - 2x^2 + 1 = 0$

29. $x^4 + x^2 - 1 = 0$

30. $x^3 + 2x^2 + x = 0$

Find all possible real solutions of each equation in Exercises 31–44.

31. $x^3 + 6x^2 + 11x + 6 = 0$

32. $x^3 - 6x^2 + 12x - 8 = 0$

33. $x^3 + 4x^2 + 4x + 3 = 0$

34. $y^3 + 64 = 0$

35. $x^3 - 1 = 0$

36. $x^3 - 27 = 0$

37. $y^3 + 3y^2 + 3y + 2 = 0$

38. $y^3 - 2y^2 - 2y - 3 = 0$

39. $x^3 - x^2 - 5x + 5 = 0$

40. $x^3 - x^2 - 3x + 3 = 0$

41. $2x^6 - x^4 - 2x^2 + 1 = 0$

42. $3x^6 - x^4 - 12x^2 + 4 = 0$

43. $(x^2 + 3x + 2)(x^2 - 5x + 6) = 0$

44. $(x^2 - 4x + 4)^2(x^2 + 6x + 5)^3 = 0$

0.6 Solving Miscellaneous Equations

Equations often arise in calculus that are not polynomial equations of low degree. Many of these complicated-looking equations can be solved easily if you remember the following, which we used in the previous section:

Solving an Equation of the Form $P \cdot Q = 0$

If a product is equal to 0, then at least one of the factors must be 0. That is, if $P \cdot Q = 0$, then either $P = 0$ or $Q = 0$.

Quick Examples

1. $x^5 - 4x^3 = 0$

$x^3(x^2 - 4) = 0$	Factor the left-hand side.
Either $x^3 = 0$ or $x^2 - 4 = 0$	Either $P = 0$ or $Q = 0$.
$x = 0, 2$ or -2.	Solve the individual equations.

2. $(x^2 - 1)(x + 2) + (x^2 - 1)(x + 4) = 0$

$(x^2 - 1)[(x + 2) + (x + 4)] = 0$	Factor the left-hand side.
$(x^2 - 1)(2x + 6) = 0$	
Either $x^2 - 1 = 0$ or $2x + 6 = 0$	Either $P = 0$ or $Q = 0$.
$x = -3, -1$, or 1.	Solve the individual equations.

EXAMPLE 1 Solving by Factoring

Solve $12x(x^2-4)^5(x^2+2)^6 + 12x(x^2-4)^6(x^2+2)^5 = 0$.

Solution

Again, we start by factoring the left-hand side:

$$\begin{aligned}
&12x(x^2-4)^5(x^2+2)^6 + 12x(x^2-4)^6(x^2+2)^5 \\
&\quad = 12x(x^2-4)^5(x^2+2)^5[(x^2+2)+(x^2-4)] \\
&\quad = 12x(x^2-4)^5(x^2+2)^5(2x^2-2) \\
&\quad = 24x(x^2-4)^5(x^2+2)^5(x^2-1).
\end{aligned}$$

Setting this equal to 0, we get:

$$24x(x^2-4)^5(x^2+2)^5(x^2-1) = 0,$$

which means that at least one of the factors of this product must be zero. Now it certainly cannot be the 24, but it could be the x: $x = 0$ is one solution. It could also be that

$$(x^2-4)^5 = 0$$

or

$$x^2 - 4 = 0,$$

which has solutions $x = \pm 2$. Could it be that $(x^2+2)^5 = 0$? If so, then $x^2 + 2 = 0$, but this is impossible because $x^2 + 2 \geq 2$, no matter what x is. Finally, it could be that $x^2 - 1 = 0$, which has solutions $x = \pm 1$. This gives us five solutions to the original equation:

$$x = -2, -1, 0, 1, \text{ or } 2.$$

EXAMPLE 2 Solving by Factoring

Solve $(x^2-1)(x^2-4) = 10$.

Solution Watch out! You may be tempted to say that $x^2 - 1 = 10$ or $x^2 - 4 = 10$, but this does not follow. If two numbers multiply to give you 10, what must they be? There are lots of possibilities: 2 and 5, 1 and 10, −500,000 and −0.00002 are just a few. The fact that the left-hand side is factored is nearly useless to us if we want to solve this equation. What we will have to do is multiply out, bring the 10 over to the left, and hope that we can factor what we get. Here goes:

$$\begin{aligned}
x^4 - 5x^2 + 4 &= 10 \\
x^4 - 5x^2 - 6 &= 0 \\
(x^2-6)(x^2+1) &= 0
\end{aligned}$$

(Here we used a sometimes useful trick that we mentioned in Section 3: We treated x^2 like x and x^4 like x^2, so factoring $x^4 - 5x^2 - 6$ is essentially the same as factoring $x^2 - 5x - 6$.) *Now* we are allowed to say that one of the factors must be 0: $x^2 - 6 = 0$ has solutions $x = \pm\sqrt{6} = \pm 2.449\ldots$ and $x^2 + 1 = 0$ has no real solutions. Therefore, we get exactly two solutions, $x = \pm\sqrt{6} = \pm 2.449\ldots$.

To solve equations involving rational expressions, the following rule is very useful.

Solving an Equation of the Form $P/Q = 0$

$$\text{If } \frac{P}{Q} = 0, \text{ then } P = 0.$$

How else could a fraction equal 0? If that is not convincing, multiply both sides by Q (which cannot be 0 if the quotient is defined).

Quick Example

$$\frac{(x+1)(x+2)^2 - (x+1)^2(x+2)}{(x+2)^4} = 0$$

$(x+1)(x+2)^2 - (x+1)^2(x+2) = 0$ — If $\frac{P}{Q} = 0$, then $P = 0$.

$(x+1)(x+2)[(x+2) - (x+1)] = 0$ — Factor.

$(x+1)(x+2)(1) = 0$

Either $x + 1 = 0$ or $x + 2 = 0$,

$x = -1$ or $x = -2$

$x = -1$ — $x = -2$ does not make sense in the original equation: it makes the denominator 0. So it is not a solution and $x = -1$ is the only solution.

EXAMPLE 3 Solving a Rational Equation

Solve $1 - \frac{1}{x^2} = 0$.

Solution Write 1 as $\frac{1}{1}$, so that we now have a difference of two rational expressions:

$$\frac{1}{1} - \frac{1}{x^2} = 0.$$

To combine these we can put both over a common denominator of x^2, which gives

$$\frac{x^2 - 1}{x^2} = 0.$$

Now we can set the numerator, $x^2 - 1$, equal to zero. Thus,

$$x^2 - 1 = 0$$

so

$$(x-1)(x+1) = 0,$$

giving $x = \pm 1$.

Before we go on... This equation could also have been solved by writing

$$1 = \frac{1}{x^2}$$

and then multiplying both sides by x^2. ■

EXAMPLE 4 Another Rational Equation

Solve $\frac{2x-1}{x} + \frac{3}{x-2} = 0$.

Solution We *could* first perform the addition on the left and then set the top equal to 0, but here is another approach. Subtracting the second expression from both sides gives

$$\frac{2x-1}{x} = \frac{-3}{x-2}$$

Cross-multiplying [multiplying both sides by both denominators—that is, by $x(x-2)$] now gives

$$(2x-1)(x-2) = -3x$$

so

$$2x^2 - 5x + 2 = -3x.$$

Adding $3x$ to both sides gives the quadratic equation

$$2x^2 - 2x + 1 = 0.$$

The discriminant is $(-2)^2 - 4 \cdot 2 \cdot 1 = -4 < 0$, so we conclude that there is no real solution.

Before we go on... Notice that when we said that $(2x-1)(x-2) = -3x$, we were *not* allowed to conclude that $2x - 1 = -3x$ or $x - 2 = -3x$. ■

EXAMPLE 5 A Rational Equation with Radicals

Solve $\frac{\left(2x\sqrt{x+1} - \frac{x^2}{\sqrt{x+1}}\right)}{x+1} = 0$.

Solution Setting the top equal to 0 gives

$$2x\sqrt{x+1} - \frac{x^2}{\sqrt{x+1}} = 0.$$

This still involves fractions. To get rid of the fractions, we could put everything over a common denominator ($\sqrt{x+1}$) and then set the top equal to 0, or we could multiply the whole equation by that common denominator in the first place to clear fractions. If we do the second, we get

$$2x(x+1) - x^2 = 0$$
$$2x^2 + 2x - x^2 = 0$$
$$x^2 + 2x = 0.$$

Factoring,

$$x(x+2) = 0$$

so either $x = 0$ or $x + 2 = 0$, giving us $x = 0$ or $x = -2$. Again, one of these is not really a solution. The problem is that $x = -2$ cannot be substituted into $\sqrt{x+1}$, because we would then have to take the square root of -1, and we are not allowing ourselves to do that. Therefore, $x = 0$ is the only solution.

0.6 EXERCISES

Solve the following equations:

1. $x^4 - 3x^3 = 0$

2. $x^6 - 9x^4 = 0$

3. $x^4 - 4x^2 = -4$

4. $x^4 - x^2 = 6$

5. $(x+1)(x+2) + (x+1)(x+3) = 0$

6. $(x+1)(x+2)^2 + (x+1)^2(x+2) = 0$

7. $(x^2+1)^5(x+3)^4 + (x^2+1)^6(x+3)^3 = 0$

8. $10x(x^2+1)^4(x^3+1)^5 - 10x^2(x^2+1)^5(x^3+1)^4 = 0$

9. $(x^3+1)\sqrt{x+1} - (x^3+1)^2\sqrt{x+1} = 0$

10. $(x^2+1)\sqrt{x+1} - \sqrt{(x+1)^3} = 0$

11. $\sqrt{(x+1)^3} + \sqrt{(x+1)^5} = 0$

12. $(x^2+1)\sqrt[3]{(x+1)^4} - \sqrt[3]{(x+1)^7} = 0$

13. $(x+1)^2(2x+3) - (x+1)(2x+3)^2 = 0$

14. $(x^2-1)^2(x+2)^3 - (x^2-1)^3(x+2)^2 = 0$

15. $\dfrac{(x+1)^2(x+2)^3 - (x+1)^3(x+2)^2}{(x+2)^6} = 0$

16. $\dfrac{6x(x^2+1)^2(x^2+2)^4 - 8x(x^2+1)^3(x^2+2)^3}{(x^2+2)^8} = 0$

17. $\dfrac{2(x^2-1)\sqrt{x^2+1} - \frac{x^4}{\sqrt{x^2+1}}}{x^2+1} = 0$

18. $\dfrac{4x\sqrt{x^3-1} - \frac{3x^4}{\sqrt{x^3-1}}}{x^3-1} = 0$

19. $x - \dfrac{1}{x} = 0$

20. $1 - \dfrac{4}{x^2} = 0$

21. $\dfrac{1}{x} - \dfrac{9}{x^3} = 0$

22. $\dfrac{1}{x^2} - \dfrac{1}{x+1} = 0$

23. $\dfrac{x-4}{x+1} - \dfrac{x}{x-1} = 0$

24. $\dfrac{2x-3}{x-1} - \dfrac{2x+3}{x+1} = 0$

25. $\dfrac{x+4}{x+1} + \dfrac{x+4}{3x} = 0$

26. $\dfrac{2x-3}{x} - \dfrac{2x-3}{x+1} = 0$

0.7 The Coordinate Plane

Q: *Just what is the xy-plane?*

A: The *xy*-plane is an infinite flat surface with two perpendicular lines, usually labeled the ***x*-axis** and ***y*-axis**. These axes are calibrated as shown in Figure 2. (Notice also how the plane is divided into four **quadrants**.)

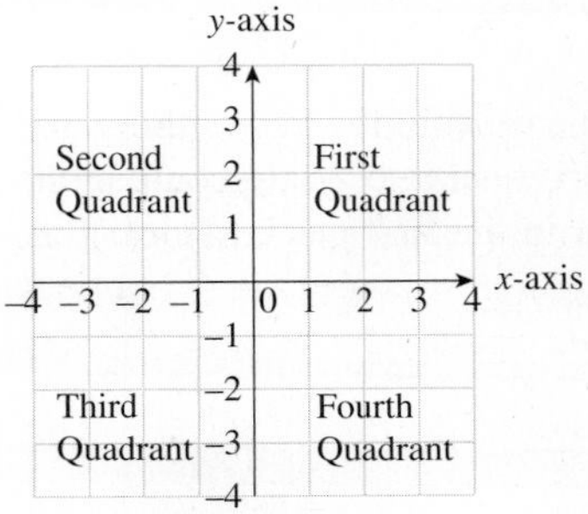

The *xy*-plane

Figure 2

Thus, the *xy*-plane is nothing more than a very large—in fact, infinitely large—flat surface. The purpose of the axes is to allow us to locate specific positions, or **points**, on the plane, with the use of **coordinates**. (If Captain Picard wants to have himself beamed to a specific location, he must supply its coordinates, or he's in trouble.)

Q: *So how do we use coordinates to locate points?*

A: The rule is simple. Each point in the plane has two coordinates, an ***x*-coordinate** and a ***y*-coordinate**. These can be determined in two ways:

1. The *x*-coordinate measures a point's distance to the right or left of the *y*-axis. It is positive if the point is to the right of the axis, negative if it is to the left of the axis, and 0 if it is on the axis. The *y*-coordinate measures a point's distance above or below the *x*-axis. It is positive if the point is above the axis, negative if it is below the axis, and 0 if it is on the axis. Briefly, the *x*-coordinate tells us the *horizontal* position (distance left or right), and the *y*-coordinate tells us the *vertical* position (height).

2. Given a point P, we get its x-coordinate by drawing a vertical line from P and seeing where it intersects the x-axis. Similarly, we get the y-coordinate by extending a horizontal line from P and seeing where it intersects the y-axis.

This way of assigning coordinates to points in the plane is often called the system of **Cartesian** coordinates, in honor of the mathematician and philosopher René Descartes (1596–1650), who was the first to use them extensively.

Here are a few examples to help you review coordinates.

EXAMPLE 1 Coordinates of Points

a. Find the coordinates of the indicated points. (See Figure 3. The grid lines are placed at intervals of one unit.)

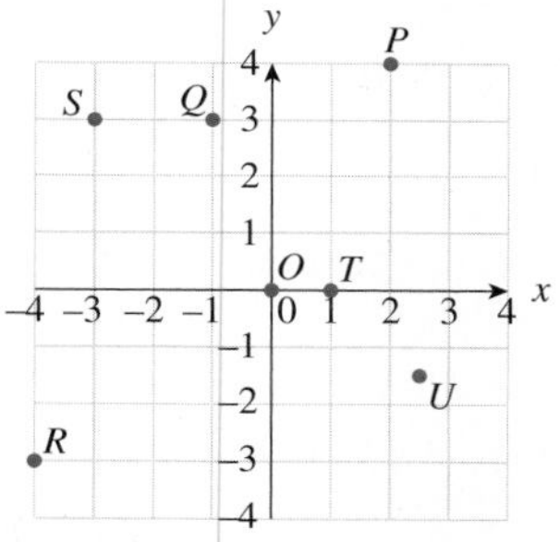

Figure 3

b. Locate the following points in the xy-plane.

$$A(2, 3),\ B(-4, 2),\ C(3, -2.5),\ D(0, -3),\ E(3.5, 0),\ F(-2.5, -1.5)$$

Solution

a. Taking them in alphabetical order, we start with the origin O. This point has height zero and is also zero units to the right of the y-axis, so its coordinates are (0, 0). Turning to P, dropping a vertical line gives $x = 2$ and extending a horizontal line gives $y = 4$. Thus, P has coordinates (2, 4). For practice, determine the coordinates of the remaining points, and check your work against the list that follows:

$$Q(-1, 3),\ R(-4, -3),\ S(-3, 3),\ T(1, 0),\ U(2.5, -1.5)$$

b. In order to locate the given points, we start at the origin (0, 0), and proceed as follows. (See Figure 4.)

To locate A, we move 2 units to the right and 3 up, as shown.

To locate B, we move −4 units to the right (that is, 4 to the *left*) and 2 up, as shown.

To locate C, we move 3 units right and 2.5 down.

We locate the remaining points in a similar way.

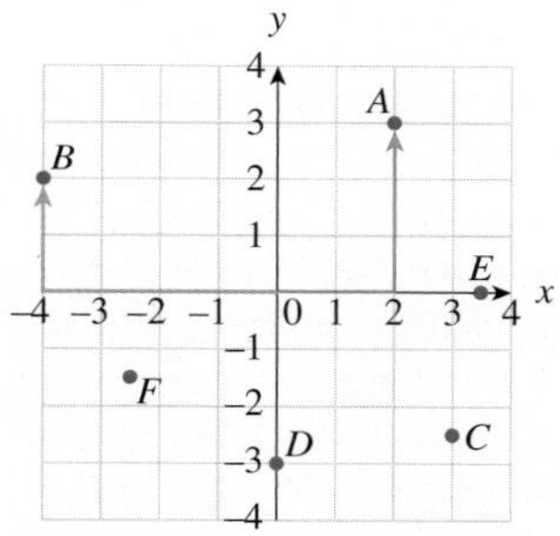

Figure 4

The Graph of an Equation

One of the more surprising developments of mathematics was the realization that equations, which are algebraic objects, can be represented by graphs, which are geometric objects. The kinds of equations that we have in mind are equations in x and y, such as

$$y = 4x - 1, \quad 2x^2 - y = 0, \quad y = 3x^2 + 1, \quad y = \sqrt{x - 1}.$$

The **graph** of an equation in the two variables x and y consists of all points (x, y) in the plane whose coordinates are solutions of the equation.

EXAMPLE 2 Graph of an Equation

Obtain the graph of the equation $y - x^2 = 0$.

Solution We can solve the equation for y to obtain $y = x^2$. Solutions can then be obtained by choosing values for x and then computing y by squaring the value of x, as shown in the following table:

x	-3	-2	-1	0	1	2	3
$y = x^2$	9	4	1	0	1	4	9

Plotting these points (x, y) gives the following picture (left side of Figure 5), suggesting the graph on the right in Figure 5.

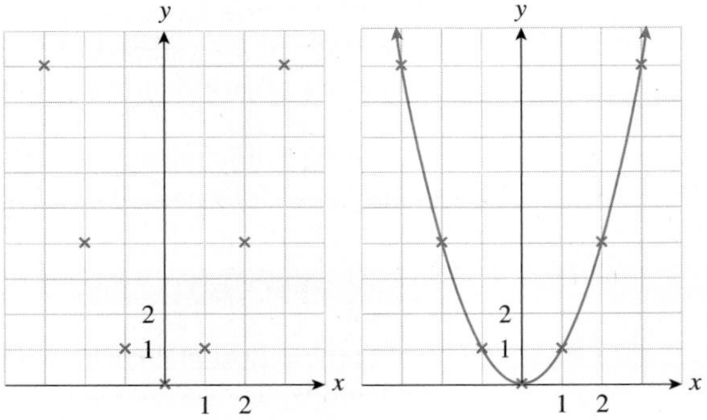

Figure 5

Distance

The distance between two points in the xy-plane can be expressed as a function of their coordinates, as follows:

Distance Formula

The distance between the points $P(x_1, y_1)$ and $Q(x_2, y_2)$ is

$$d = \sqrt{(x_2 - x_1)^2 + (y_2 - y_1)^2} = \sqrt{(\Delta x)^2 + (\Delta y)^2}.$$

Derivation

The distance d is shown in the figure below.

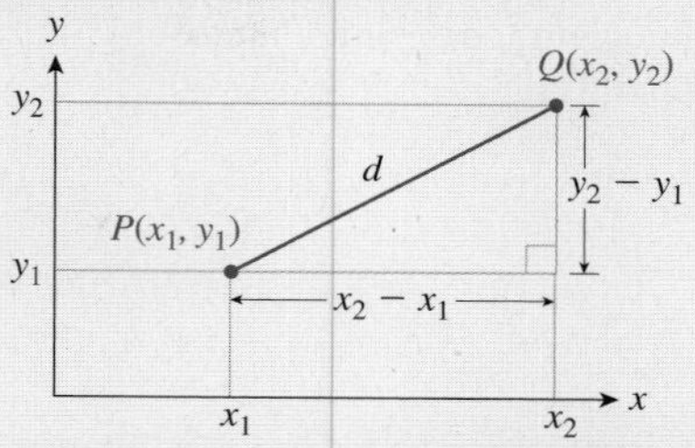

By the Pythagorean theorem applied to the right triangle shown, we get

$$d^2 = (x_2 - x_1)^2 + (y_2 - y_1)^2.$$

Taking square roots (d is a distance, so we take the positive square root), we get the distance formula. Notice that if we switch x_1 with x_2 or y_1 with y_2, we get the same result.

Quick Examples

1. The distance between the points $(3, -2)$ and $(-1, 1)$ is
$$d = \sqrt{(-1-3)^2 + (1+2)^2} = \sqrt{25} = 5.$$
2. The distance from (x, y) to the origin $(0, 0)$ is
$$d = \sqrt{(x-0)^2 + (y-0)^2} = \sqrt{x^2 + y^2}.$$ Distance to the origin

The set of all points (x, y) whose distance from the origin $(0, 0)$ is a fixed quantity r is a circle centered at the origin with radius r. From the second Quick Example, we get the following equation for the circle centered at the origin with radius r:

$$\sqrt{x^2 + y^2} = r.$$ Distance from the origin $= r$.

Squaring both sides gives the following equation:

Equation of the Circle of Radius *r* Centered at the Origin

$$x^2 + y^2 = r^2$$

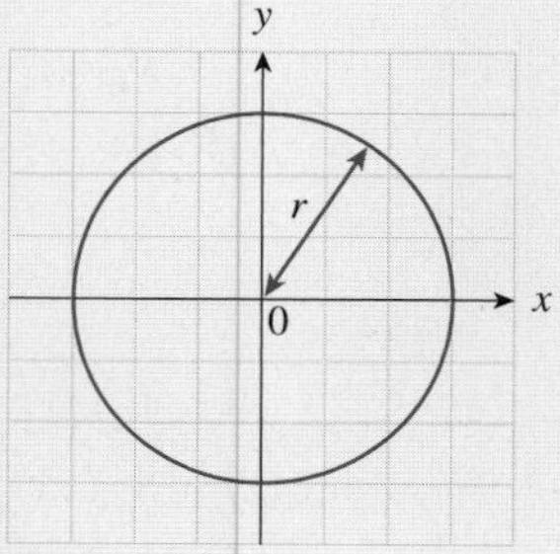

Quick Examples

1. The circle of radius 1 centered at the origin has equation $x^2 + y^2 = 1$.
2. The circle of radius 2 centered at the origin has equation $x^2 + y^2 = 4$.

0.7 EXERCISES

1. Referring to the following figure, determine the coordinates of the indicated points as accurately as you can.

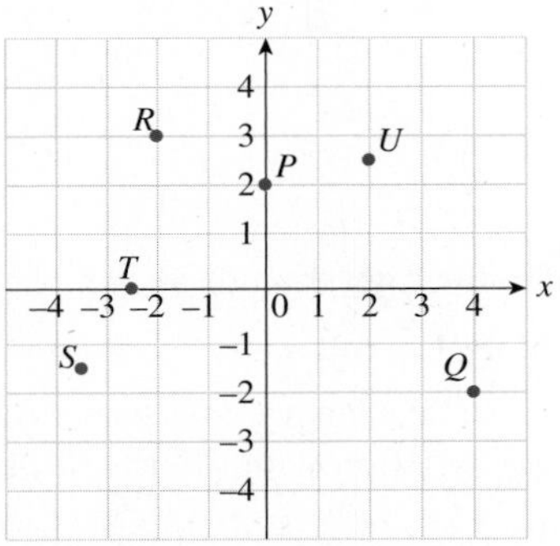

2. Referring to the following figure, determine the coordinates of the indicated points as accurately as you can.

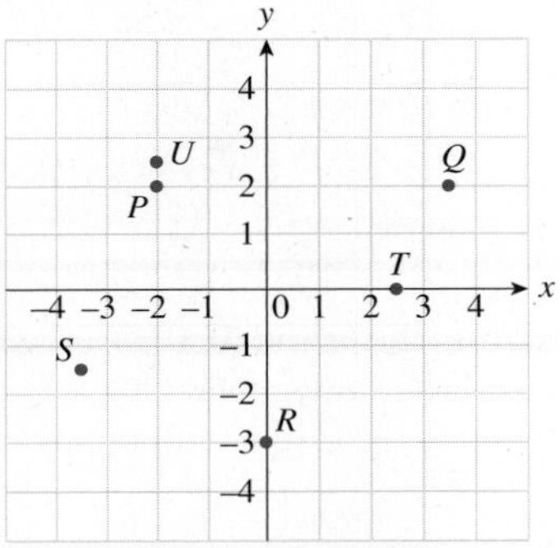

3. Graph the following points.

$P(4, 4)$, $Q(4, -4)$, $R(3, 0)$, $S(4, 0.5)$, $T(0.5, 2.5)$, $U(-2, 0)$, $V(-4, 4)$

4. Graph the following points.

$P(4, -2)$, $Q(2, -4)$, $R(1, -3)$, $S(-4, 2)$, $T(2, -1)$, $U(-2, 0)$, $V(-4, -4)$

Sketch the graphs of the equations in Exercises 5–12.

5. $x + y = 1$
6. $y - x = -1$
7. $2y - x^2 = 1$
8. $2y + \sqrt{x} = 1$
9. $xy = 4$
10. $x^2y = -1$
11. $xy = x^2 + 1$
12. $xy = 2x^3 + 1$

In Exercises 13–16, find the distance between the given pairs of points.

13. $(1, -1)$ and $(2, -2)$
14. $(1, 0)$ and $(6, 1)$
15. $(a, 0)$ and $(0, b)$
16. (a, a) and (b, b)
17. Find the value of k such that $(1, k)$ is equidistant from $(0, 0)$ and $(2, 1)$.
18. Find the value of k such that (k, k) is equidistant from $(-1, 0)$ and $(0, 2)$.
19. Describe the set of points (x, y) such that $x^2 + y^2 = 9$.
20. Describe the set of points (x, y) such that $x^2 + y^2 = 0$.

1

Functions and Applications

Case Study Modeling Spending on Internet Advertising

You are the new director of *Impact Advertising Inc.'s* Internet division, which has enjoyed a steady 0.25% of the Internet advertising market. You have drawn up an ambitious proposal to expand your division in light of your anticipation that Internet advertising will continue to skyrocket. The VP in charge of Financial Affairs feels that current projections (based on a linear model) do not warrant the level of expansion you propose. **How can you persuade the VP that those projections do not fit the data convincingly?**

Jeff Titcomb/Photographer's Choice / Getty Images

Website

www.WanerMath.com

At the Website you will find:

- Section-by-section tutorials, including game tutorials with randomized quizzes
- A detailed chapter summary
- A true/false quiz
- Additional review exercises
- Graphers, Excel tutorials, and other resources
- The following extra topic:

  New Functions from Old: Scaled and Shifted Functions

Introduction

To analyze recent trends in spending on Internet advertising and to make reasonable projections, we need a mathematical model of this spending. Where do we start? To apply mathematics to real-world situations like this, we need a good understanding of basic mathematical concepts. Perhaps the most fundamental of these concepts is that of a function: a relationship that shows how one quantity depends on another. Functions may be described numerically and, often, algebraically. They can also be described graphically—a viewpoint that is extremely useful.

The simplest functions—the ones with the simplest formulas and the simplest graphs—are linear functions. Because of their simplicity, they are also among the most useful functions and can often be used to model real-world situations, at least over short periods of time. In discussing linear functions, we will meet the concepts of slope and rate of change, which are the starting point of the mathematics of change.

algebra Review
For this chapter, you should be familiar with real numbers and intervals. To review this material, see **Chapter 0.**

In the last section of this chapter, we discuss *simple linear regression*: construction of linear functions that best fit given collections of data. Regression is used extensively in applied mathematics, statistics, and quantitative methods in business. The inclusion of regression utilities in computer spreadsheets like Excel® makes this powerful mathematical tool readily available for anyone to use.

1.1 Functions from the Numerical, Algebraic, and Graphical Viewpoints

The following table gives the approximate number of Facebook users at various times since its establishment early in 2004.[1]

Year t (Since start of 2004)	0	1	2	3	4	5	6
Facebook Members n (Millions)	0	1	5.5	12	58	150	450

Let's write $n(0)$ for the number of members (in millions) at time $t = 0$, $n(1)$ for the number at time $t = 1$, and so on (we read $n(0)$ as "n of 0"). Thus, $n(0) = 0$, $n(1) = 1$, $n(2) = 5.5, \ldots, n(6) = 450$. In general, we write $n(t)$ for the number of members (in millions) at time t. We call n a **function** of the variable t, meaning that for each value of t between 0 and 6, n gives us a single corresponding number $n(t)$ (the number of members at that time).

In general, we think of a function as a way of producing new objects from old ones. The functions we deal with in this text produce new numbers from old numbers. The numbers we have in mind are the *real* numbers, including not only positive and negative integers and fractions but also numbers like $\sqrt{2}$ or π. (See Chapter 0 for more on real numbers.) For this reason, the functions we use are called **real-valued functions of a real variable**. For example, the function n takes the year since the start of 2004 as input and returns the number of Facebook members as output (Figure 1).

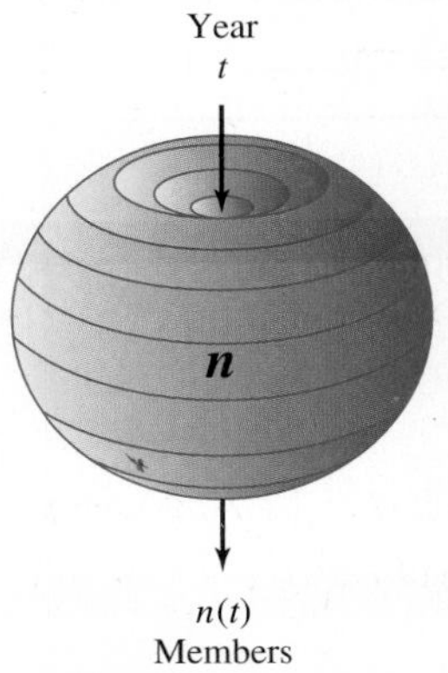

Figure 1

[1]Sources: www.facebook.com, www.insidefacebook.com.

The variable t is called the **independent variable**, while n is called the **dependent variable** as its value depends on t. A function may be specified in several different ways. Here, we have specified the function n **numerically** by giving the values of the function for a number of values of the independent variable, as in the preceding table.

Q: *For which values of t does it make sense to ask for n(t)? In other words, for which years t is the function n defined?*

A: Because $n(t)$ refers to the number of members from the start of 2004 to the start of 2010, $n(t)$ is defined when t is any number between 0 and 6, that is, when $0 \le t \le 6$. Using interval notation (see Chapter 0), we can say that $n(t)$ is defined when t is in the interval [0, 6].

The set of values of the independent variable for which a function is defined is called its **domain** and is a necessary part of the definition of the function. Notice that the preceding table gives the value of $n(t)$ at only some of the infinitely many possible values in the domain [0, 6]. The domain of a function is not always specified explicitly; if no domain is specified for the function f, we take the domain to be the largest set of numbers x for which $f(x)$ makes sense. This "largest possible domain" is sometimes called the **natural domain**.

The previous Facebook data can also be represented on a graph by plotting the given pairs of numbers $(t, n(t))$ in the xy-plane. (See Figure 2. We have connected successive points by line segments.) In general, the **graph** of a function f consists of all points $(x, f(x))$ in the plane with x in the domain of f.

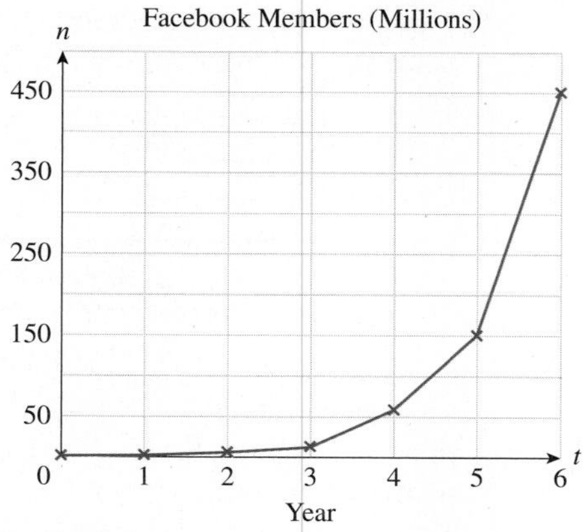

Figure 2

In Figure 2 we specified the function n **graphically** by using a graph to display its values. Suppose now that we had only the graph without the table of data. We could use the graph to find approximate values of n. For instance, to find $n(5)$ from the graph, we do the following:

1. Find the desired value of t at the bottom of the graph ($t = 5$ in this case).
2. Estimate the height (n-coordinate) of the corresponding point on the graph (around 150 in this case).

Thus, $n(5) \approx 150$ million members.*

* In a graphically defined function, we can never know the y-coordinates of points exactly; no matter how accurately a graph is drawn, we can obtain only *approximate* values of the coordinates of points. That is why we have been using the word *estimate* rather than *calculate* and why we say $n(5) \approx 150$ rather than $n(5) = 150$.

In some cases we may be able to use an algebraic formula to calculate the function, and we say that the function is specified **algebraically**. These are not the only ways in which a function can be specified; for instance, it could also be specified **verbally**, as in "Let $n(t)$ be the number of Facebook members, in millions, t years since the start of 2004."* Notice that any function can be represented graphically by plotting the points $(x, f(x))$ for a number of values of x in its domain.

* Specifying a function verbally in this way is useful for understanding what the function is doing, but it gives no numerical information.

Here is a summary of the terms we have just introduced.

Functions

A **real-valued function f of a real-valued variable x** assigns to each real number x in a specified set of numbers, called the **domain** of f, a unique real number $f(x)$, read "f of x." The variable x is called the **independent variable**, and f is called the **dependent variable**. A function is usually specified **numerically** using a table of values, **graphically** using a graph, or **algebraically** using a formula. The **graph of a function** consists of all points $(x, f(x))$ in the plane with x in the domain of f.

Quick Examples

1. **A function specified numerically:** Take $c(t)$ to be the world emission of carbon dioxide in year t since 2000, represented by the following table:[2]

t (Year Since 2000)	$c(t)$ (Billion Metric Tons of CO_2)
0	24
5	28
10	31
15	33
20	36
25	38
30	41

The domain of c is [0, 30], the independent variable is t, the number of years since 2000, and the dependent variable is c, the world production of carbon dioxide in a given year. Some values of c are:

$c(0) = 24$ — 24 billion metric tons of CO_2 were produced in 2000.

$c(10) = 31$ — 31 billion metric tons of CO_2 were produced in 2010.

$c(30) = 41$ — 41 billion metric tons of CO_2 were projected to be produced in 2030.

[2]Figures for 2015 and later are projections. Source: Energy Information Administration (EIA) (www.eia.doe.gov)

Graph of c: Plotting the pairs $(t, c(t))$ gives the following graph:

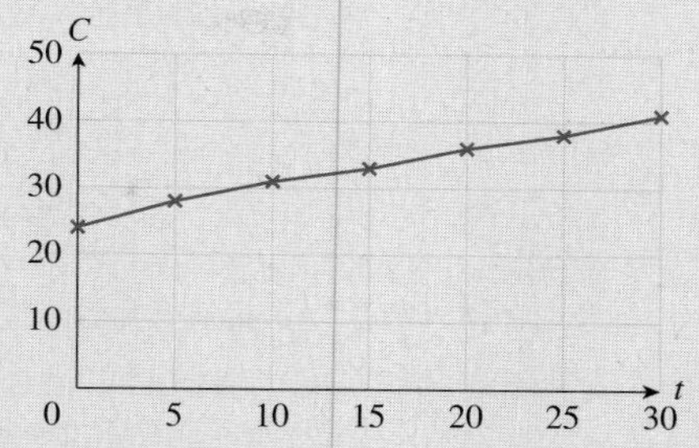

2. **A function specified graphically:** Take $m(t)$ to be the median U.S. home price in thousands of dollars, t years since 2000, as represented by the following graph:[3]

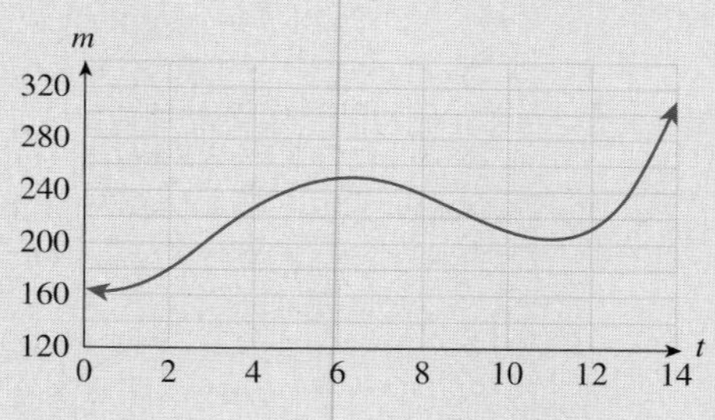

The domain of m is [0, 14], the independent variable is t, the number of years since 2000, and the dependent variable is m, the median U.S. home price in thousands of dollars. Some values of m are:

$m(2) \approx 180$ The median home price in 2002 was about $180,000.

$m(10) \approx 210.$ The median home price in 2010 was about $210,000.

3. **A function specified algebraically:** Let $f(x) = \frac{1}{x}$. The function f is specified algebraically. The independent variable is x and the dependent variable is f. The natural domain of f consists of all real numbers except zero because $f(x)$ makes sense for all values of x other than $x = 0$. Some specific values of f are

$$f(2) = \frac{1}{2} \qquad f(3) = \frac{1}{3} \qquad f(-1) = \frac{1}{-1} = -1$$

$f(0)$ is not defined because 0 is not in the domain of f.

[3]Source for data through end of 2010: www.zillow.com/local-info.

4. The graph of a function: Let $f(x) = x^2$, with domain the set of all real numbers. To draw the graph of f, first choose some convenient values of x in the domain and compute the corresponding y-coordinates $f(x)$:

x	-3	-2	-1	0	1	2	3
$f(x) = x^2$	9	4	1	0	1	4	9

Plotting these points $(x, f(x))$ gives the picture on the left, suggesting the graph on the right.*

* If you plot more points, you will find that they lie on a smooth curve as shown. That is why we did not use line segments to connect the points.

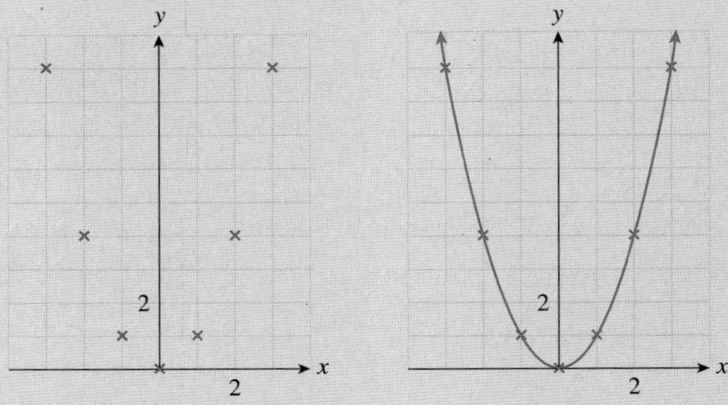

(This particular curve happens to be called a **parabola**, and its lowest point, at the origin, is called its **vertex**.)

EXAMPLE 1 iPod Sales

The total number of iPods sold by Apple up to the end of year x can be approximated by

$$f(x) = 4x^2 + 16x + 2 \text{ million iPods } (0 \le x \le 6),$$

where $x = 0$ represents 2003.[4]

a. What is the domain of f? Compute $f(0)$, $f(2)$, $f(4)$, and $f(6)$. What do these answers tell you about iPod sales? Is $f(-1)$ defined?

b. Compute $f(a)$, $f(-b)$, $f(a+h)$, and $f(a) + h$ assuming that the quantities a, $-b$, and $a + h$ are in the domain of f.

c. Sketch the graph of f. Does the shape of the curve suggest that iPod sales were accelerating or decelerating?

Solution

a. The domain of f is the set of numbers x with $0 \le x \le 6$—that is, the interval [0, 6]. If we substitute 0 for x in the formula for $f(x)$, we get

$$f(0) = 4(0)^2 + 16(0) + 2 = 2.$$

By the end of 2003 approximately 2 million iPods had been sold.

[4]Source for data: Apple quarterly earnings reports at www.apple.com/investor/.

Similarly,

$$f(2) = 4(2)^2 + 16(2) + 2 = 50$$ By the end of 2005 approximately 50 million iPods had been sold.

$$f(4) = 4(4)^2 + 16(4) + 2 = 130$$ By the end of 2007 approximately 130 million iPods had been sold.

$$f(6) = 4(6)^2 + 16(6) + 2 = 242.$$ By the end of 2009 approximately 242 million iPods had been sold.

As -1 is not in the domain of f, $f(-1)$ is not defined.

b. To find $f(a)$ we substitute a for x in the formula for $f(x)$ to get

$$f(a) = 4a^2 + 16a + 2.$$ Substitute a for x.

Similarly,

$$f(-b) = 4(-b)^2 + 16(-b) + 2$$ Substitute $-b$ for x.

$$= 4b^2 - 16b + 2$$ $(-b)^2 = b^2$

$$f(a+h) = 4(a+h)^2 + 16(a+h) + 2$$ Substitute $(a+h)$ for x.

$$= 4(a^2 + 2ah + h^2) + 16a + 16h + 2$$ Expand.

$$= 4a^2 + 8ah + 4h^2 + 16a + 16h + 2$$

$$f(a) + h = 4a^2 + 16a + 2 + h.$$ Add h to $f(a)$.

Note how we placed parentheses around the quantities at which we evaluated the function. If we tried to do without any of these parentheses we would likely get an error:

Correct expression: $f(a+h) = 4(a+h)^2 + 16(a+h) + 2.$ ✓

NOT $4a + h^2 + 16a + h + 2x$

Also notice the distinction between $f(a+h)$ and $f(a) + h$: To find $f(a+h)$, we replace x by the quantity $(a+h)$; to find $f(a) + h$ we add h to $f(a)$.

c. To draw the graph of f we plot points of the form $(x, f(x))$ for several values of x in the domain of f. Let us use the values we computed in part (a):

x	0	2	4	6
$f(x) = 4x^2 + 16x + 2$	2	50	130	242

Graphing these points gives the graph shown in Figure 3, suggesting the curve shown on the right.

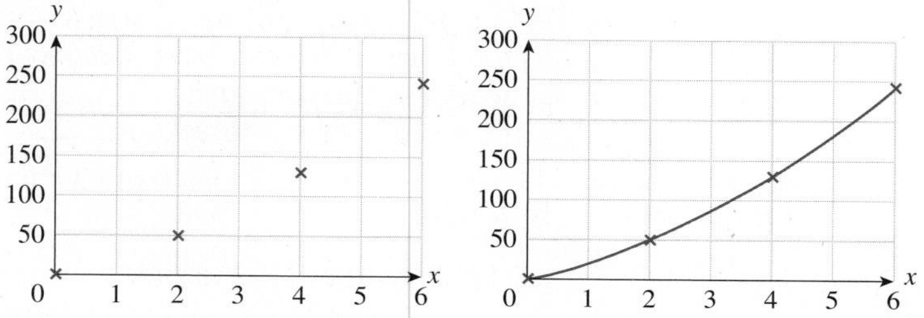

Figure 3

The graph becomes more steep as we move from left to right, suggesting that iPod sales were accelerating.

using Technology

See the Technology Guides at the end of the chapter for detailed instructions on how to obtain the table of values and graph in Example 1 using a TI-83/84 Plus or Excel. Here is an outline:

TI-83/84 Plus

Table of values:

`Y1=4X^2+16X+2`

[2ND] [TABLE].

Graph: [WINDOW];

Xmin = 0, Xmax = 6

[ZOOM] [0].

[More details on page 114.]

Spreadsheet

Table of values: Headings x and $f(x)$ in A1–B1; x-values 0, 2, 4, 6 in A2–A5.

`=4*A2^2+16*A2+2`

in B2; copy down through B5.

Graph: Highlight A1 through B5 and insert a Scatter chart. [More details on page 119.]

Website

www.WanerMath.com

Go to the Function Evaluator and Grapher under Online Utilities, and enter

`4x^2+16x+2`

for y_1. To obtain a table of values, enter the x-values 0, 1, 2, 3 in the Evaluator box, and press "Evaluate" at the top of the box. Graph: Set Xmin = 0, Xmax = 6, and press "Plot Graphs".

Before we go on... The following table compares the value of f in Example 1 with the actual sales figures:

x	0	2	4	6
$f(x) = 4x^2 + 16x + 2$	2	50	130	242
Actual iPod Sales (Millions)	2	32	141	240

The actual figures are only stated here for (some) integer values of x; for instance, $x = 4$ gives the total sales up to the end of 2007. But what were, for instance, the sales through June of 2008 ($x = 4.5$)? This is where our formula comes in handy: We can use the formula for f to **interpolate**—that is, to find sales at values of x other than those between values that are stated:

$$f(4.5) = 4(4.5)^2 + 16(4.5) + 2 = 155 \text{ million iPods.}$$

We can also use the formula to **extrapolate**—that is, to predict sales at values of x *outside* the domain—say, for $x = 6.5$ (that is, sales through June 2009):

$$f(6.5) = 4(6.5)^2 + 16(6.5) + 2 = 275 \text{ million iPods.}$$

As a general rule, extrapolation is far less reliable than interpolation: Predicting the future from current data is difficult, especially given the vagaries of the marketplace.

We call the algebraic function f an **algebraic model** of iPod sales because it uses an algebraic formula to model—or mathematically represent (approximately)—the annual sales. The particular kind of algebraic model we used is called a **quadratic model**. (See the end of this section for the names of some commonly used models.) ■

Functions and Equations

Instead of using the usual "function notation" to specify a function, as in, say,

$$f(x) = 4x^2 + 16x + 2, \qquad \text{Function notation}$$

we could have specified it by an equation by replacing $f(x)$ by y:

$$y = 4x^2 + 16x + 2 \qquad \text{Equation notation}$$

(the choice of the letter y is a convention, but any letter will do).

Technically, $y = 4x^2 + 16x + 2$ is an equation and not a function. However, an equation of this type, $y =$ *Expression in* x, can be thought of as "specifying y as a function of x." When we specify a function in this way, the variable x is the independent variable and y is the dependent variable.

We could also write the above function as $f = 4x^2 + 16x + 2$, in which case the dependent variable would be f.

Quick Example

If the cost to manufacture x items is given by the "cost function"* C specified by

$$C(x) = 40x + 2{,}000, \qquad \text{Cost function}$$

we could instead write

$$C = 40x + 2{,}000 \qquad \text{Cost equation}$$

and think of C, the cost, as a function of x.

* We will discuss cost functions more fully in the next section.

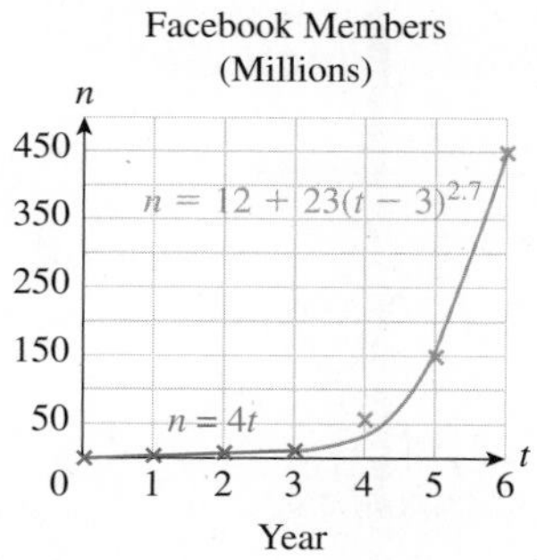

Facebook Members
(Millions)

Figure 4

Facebook Members
(Millions)

Figure 5

🖩 **using** Technology

See the Technology Guides at the end of the chapter for detailed instructions on how to obtain the table of values and graph in Example 2 using a TI-83/84 Plus or Excel. Here is an outline:

TI-83/84 Plus
Table of values:
$Y_1 = (X \leq 3) * (4X) + (X > 3) *$
$(12+23*\text{abs}(X-3)^{\wedge}2.7)$
2ND TABLE.
Graph: WINDOW; Xmin = 0,
Xmax = 6; ZOOM 0.
[More details on page 114.]

Spreadsheet
Table of values: Headings t and $n(t)$ in A1–B1; t-values 0, 1, . . . , 6 in A2–A8.
$=(\text{A2}<=3)*(4*\text{A2})+(\text{A2}>3)*$
$(12+23*\text{abs}(\text{A2}-3)^{\wedge}2.7)$
in B2; copy down through B8.
Graph: Highlight A1 through B8 and insert a Scatter chart.
[More details on page 120.]

Function notation and equation notation, sometimes using the same letter for the function name and the dependent variable, are often used interchangeably. It is important to be able to switch back and forth between function notation and equation notation, and we shall do so when it is convenient.

Look again at the graph of the number of Facebook users in Figure 2. From year 0 through year 3 the membership appears to increase more-or-less linearly (that is, the graph is almost a straight line), but then curves upward quite sharply from year 3 to year 6. This behavior can be modeled by using two different functions: one for the interval [0, 3] and another for the interval [3, 6] (see Figure 4).

A function specified by two or more different formulas like this is called a **piecewise-defined function**.

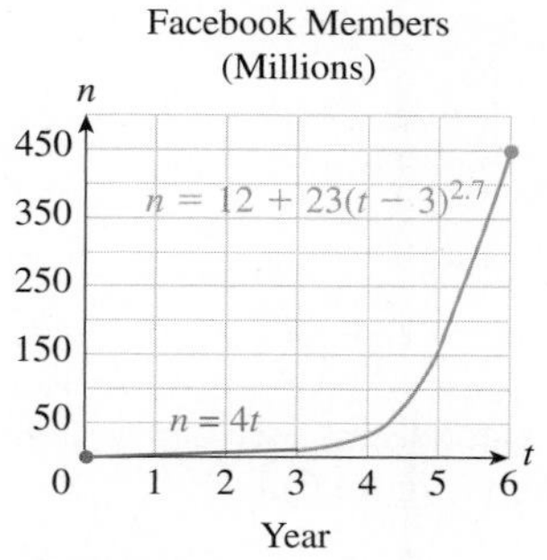

EXAMPLE 2 A Piecewise-Defined Function: Facebook Membership

The number $n(t)$ of Facebook members can be approximated by the following function of time t in years ($t = 0$ represents January 2004):

$$n(t) = \begin{cases} 4t & \text{if } 0 \leq t \leq 3 \\ 12 + 23(t-3)^{2.7} & \text{if } 3 < t \leq 6 \end{cases} \quad \text{million members.}$$

What was the approximate membership of Facebook in January 2005, January 2007, and June 2009? Sketch the graph of n by plotting several points.

Solution We evaluate the given function at the corresponding values of t:

Jan. 2005 ($t = 1$): $n(1) = 4(1) = 4$ Use the first formula because $0 \leq t \leq 3$.

Jan. 2007 ($t = 3$): $n(3) = 4(3) = 12$ Use the first formula because $0 \leq t \leq 3$.

June 2009 ($t = 5.5$): $n(5.5) = 12 + 23(5.5 - 3)^{2.7} \approx 285$. Use the second formula because $3 < t \leq 6$.

Thus, the number of Facebook members was approximately 4 million in January 2005, 12 million in January 2007, and 285 million in June 2009.

To sketch the graph of n we use a table of rounded values of $n(t)$ (some of which we have already calculated above), plot the points, and connect them to sketch the graph:

t	0	1	2	3	4	5	6
$n(t)$	0	4	8	12	35	161	459

First Formula Second Formula

The graph (Figure 5) has the following features:

1. The first formula (the line) is used for $0 \leq t \leq 3$.

2. The second formula (ascending curve) is used for $3 < t \leq 6$.

3. The domain is [0, 6], so the graph is cut off at $t = 0$ and $t = 6$.

4. The heavy solid dots at the ends indicate the endpoints of the domain.

Website
www.WanerMath.com
Go to the Function Evaluator and Grapher under Online Utilities, and enter

```
(x≤3)*(4x)+(x>3)*
  (12+23*abs(x-3)^2.7)
```

for y_1. To obtain a table of values, enter the x-values 0, 1, . . . , 6 in the Evaluator box, and press "Evaluate." at the top of the box. Graph: Set Xmin = 0, Xmax = 6, and press "Plot Graphs."

EXAMPLE 3 More Complicated Piecewise-Defined Functions

Let f be the function specified by

$$f(x) = \begin{cases} -1 & \text{if } -4 \le x < -1 \\ x & \text{if } -1 \le x \le 1 \\ x^2 - 1 & \text{if } 1 < x \le 2 \end{cases}.$$

a. What is the domain of f? Find $f(-2)$, $f(-1)$, $f(0)$, $f(1)$, and $f(2)$.

b. Sketch the graph of f.

Solution

a. The domain of f is $[-4, 2]$, because $f(x)$ is specified only when $-4 \le x \le 2$.

$f(-2) = -1$	We used the first formula because $-4 \le x < -1$.
$f(-1) = -1$	We used the second formula because $-1 \le x \le 1$.
$f(0) = 0$	We used the second formula because $-1 \le x \le 1$.
$f(1) = 1$	We used the second formula because $-1 \le x \le 1$.
$f(2) = 2^2 - 1 = 3$	We used the third formula because $1 < x \le 2$.

b. To sketch the graph by hand, we first sketch the three graphs $y = -1$, $y = x$, and $y = x^2 - 1$, and then use the appropriate portion of each (Figure 6).

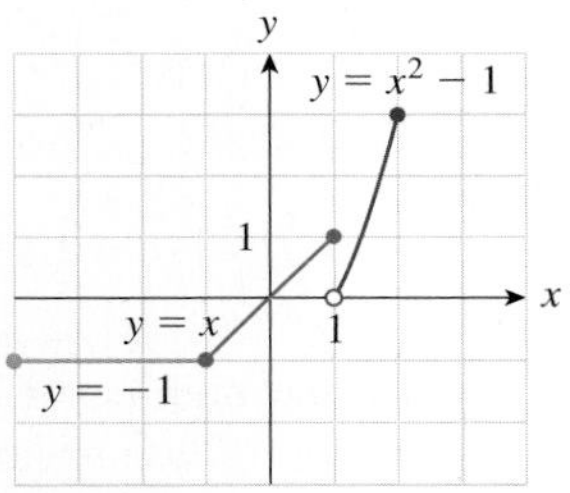

Figure 6

using Technology
For the function in Example 3, use the following technology formula (see the technology discussion for Example 2):

```
(X<-1)*(-1)
 +(-1≤X)*(X≤1)*X
 +(1<X)*(X^2-1)
```

Note that solid dots indicate points on the graph, whereas the open dots indicate points not on the graph. For example, when $x = 1$, the inequalities in the formula tell us that we are to use the middle formula (x) rather than the bottom one ($x^2 - 1$). Thus, $f(1) = 1$, not 0, so we place a solid dot at (1, 1) and an open dot at (1, 0).

Vertical Line Test

Every point in the graph of a function has the form $(x, f(x))$ for some x in the domain of f. Because f assigns a *single* value $f(x)$ to each value of x in the domain, it follows that, in the graph of f, there should be only one y corresponding to any such value of x—namely, $y = f(x)$. In other words, *the graph of a function cannot contain two or more points with the same x-coordinate—that is, two or more points on the same vertical line.* On the other hand, a vertical line at a value of x not in the domain will not contain any points in the graph. This gives us the following rule.

Vertical-Line Test

For a graph to be the graph of a function, every vertical line must intersect the graph in *at most* one point.

Quick Examples

As illustrated below, only graph B passes the vertical line test, so only graph B is the graph of a function.

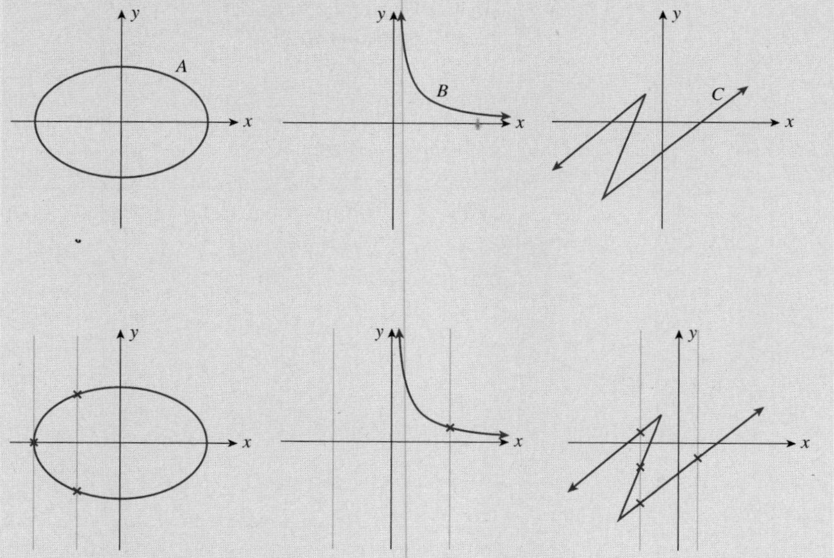

Table 1 lists some common types of functions that are often used to model real world situations.

Table 1 A Compendium of Functions and Their Graphs

Type of Function	***Examples***	
Linear $f(x) = mx + b$ m, b constant Graphs of linear functions are straight lines. The quantity m is the **slope** of the line; the quantity b is the ***y*-intercept** of the line. [See Section 1.3.]	$y = x$ 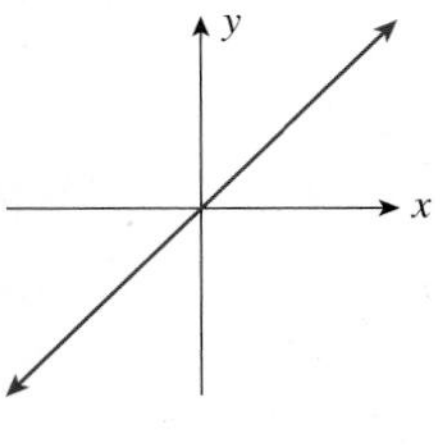	$y = -2x + 2$ 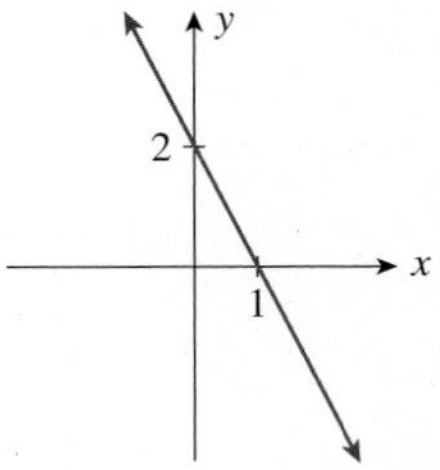
Technology formulas:	`x`	`-2*x+2`
Quadratic $f(x) = ax^2 + bx + c$ a, b, c constant $(a \neq 0)$ Graphs of quadratic functions are called **parabolas**.	$y = x^2$ 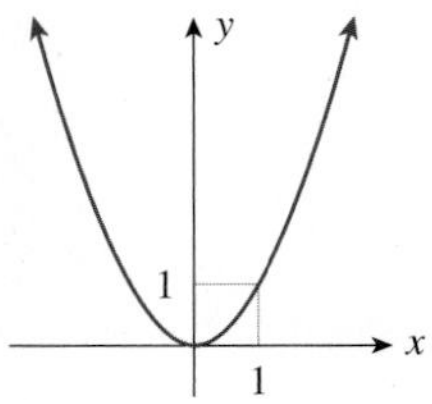	$y = -2x^2 + 2x + 4$ 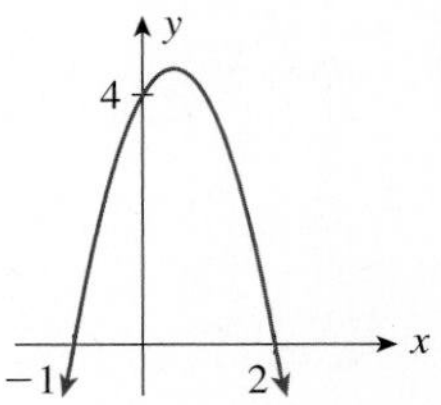
Technology formulas:	`x^2`	`-2*x^2+2*x+4`
Cubic $f(x) = ax^3 + bx^2 + cx + d$ a, b, c, d constant $(a \neq 0)$	$y = x^3$ 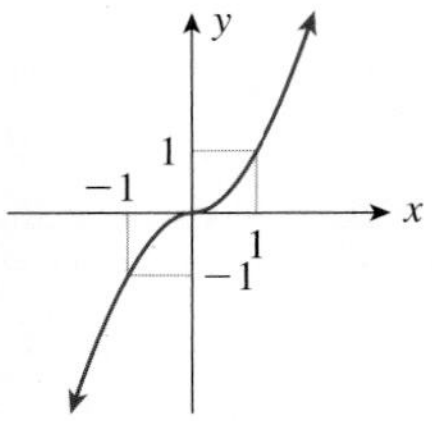	$y = -x^3 + 3x^2 + 1$ 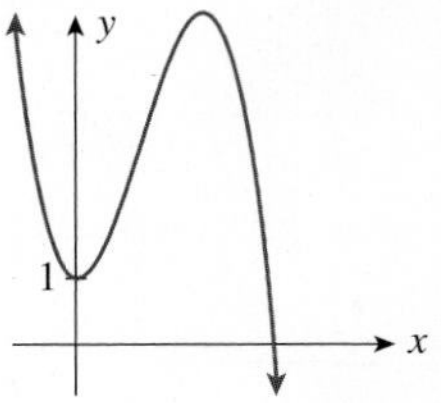
Technology formulas:	`x^3`	`-x^3+3*x^2+1`
Polynomial $f(x) = ax^n + bx^{n-1} + \ldots + rx + s$ $a, b, \ldots, r, s$ constant (includes all of the above functions)	All the above, and $f(x) = x^6 - 2x^5 - 2x^4 + 4x^2$ 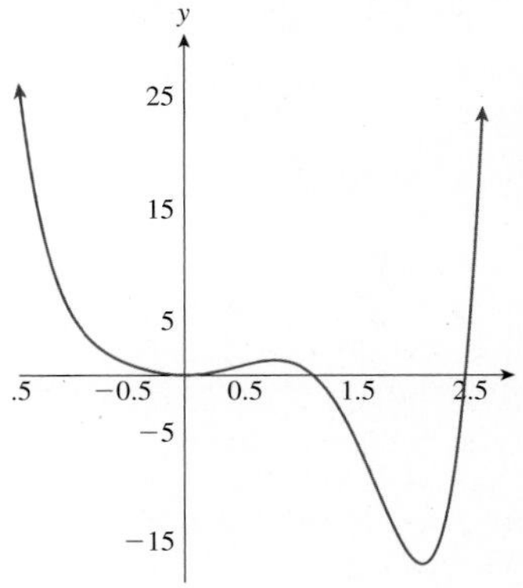	
Technology formula:	`x^6-2x^5-2x^4+4x^2`	

Table 1 (*Continued*)

Type of Function	*Examples*	
Exponential $f(x) = Ab^x$ A, b constant ($b > 0$ and $b \neq 1$) The y-coordinate is multiplied by b every time x increases by 1.	$y = 2^x$ 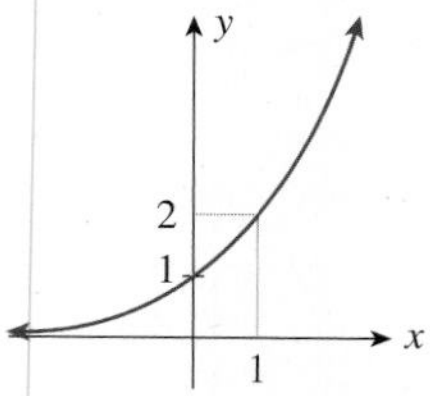 y is doubled every time x increases by 1.	$y = 4(0.5)^x$ 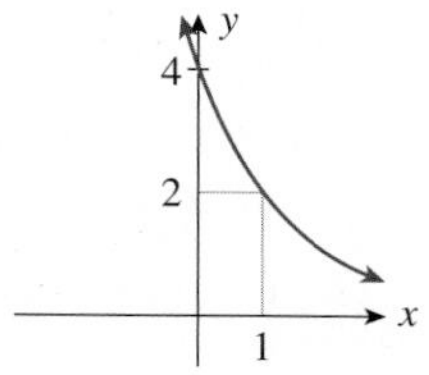 y is halved every time x increases by 1.
Technology formulas:	`2^x`	`4*0.5^x`
Rational $f(x) = \frac{P(x)}{Q(x)}$; $P(x)$ and $Q(x)$ polynomials The graph of $y = 1/x$ is a **hyperbola**. The domain excludes zero because $1/0$ is not defined.	$y = \frac{1}{x}$ 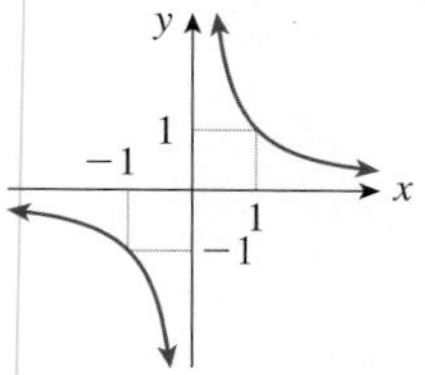	$y = \frac{x}{x-1}$ 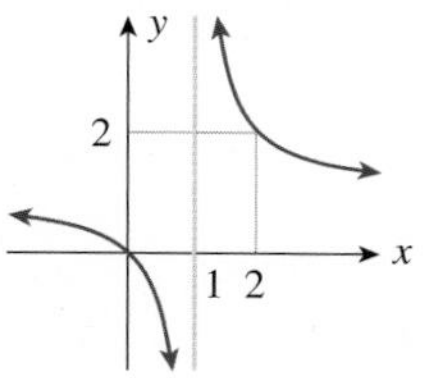
Technology formulas:	`1/x`	`x/(x-1)`
Absolute value For x positive or zero, the graph of $y = \lvert x \rvert$ is the same as that of $y = x$. For x negative or zero, it is the same as that of $y = -x$.	$y = \lvert x \rvert$ 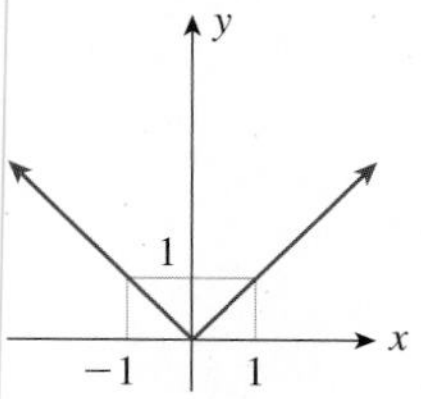	$y = \lvert 2x + 2 \rvert$ 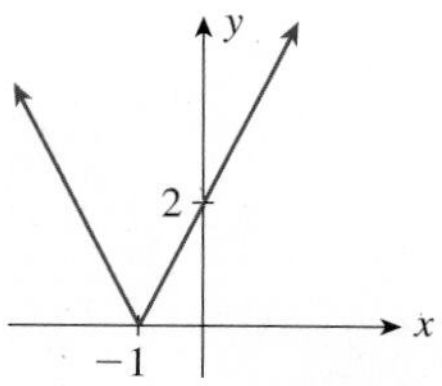
Technology formulas:	`abs(x)`	`abs(2*x+2)`
Square Root The domain of $y = \sqrt{x}$ must be restricted to the nonnegative numbers, because the square root of a negative number is not real. Its graph is the top half of a horizontally oriented parabola.	$y = \sqrt{x}$ 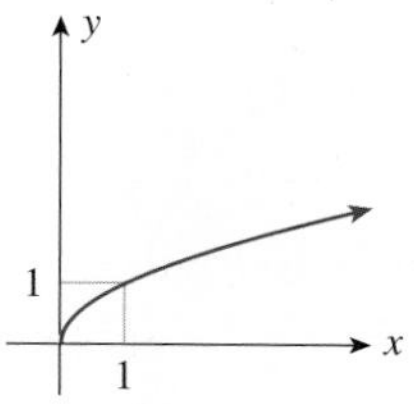	$y = \sqrt{4x - 2}$ 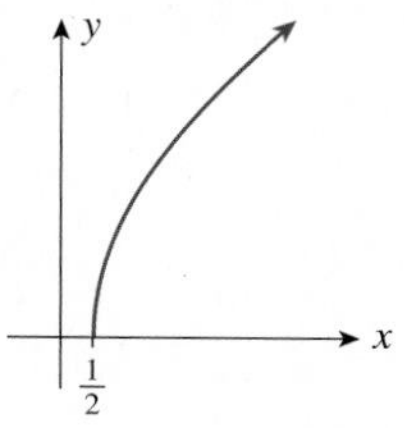
Technology formulas:	`x^0.5 or √(x)`	`(4*x-2)^0.5 or √(4*x-2)`

Go to the Website and follow the path

Online Text

→ New Functions from Old: Scaled and Shifted Functions

where you will find complete online interactive text, examples, and exercises on scaling and translating the graph of a function by changing the formula.

Functions and models other than linear ones are called **nonlinear**.

1.1 EXERCISES

▼ more advanced ◆ challenging

T indicates exercises that should be solved using technology

In Exercises 1–4, evaluate or estimate each expression based on the following table. HINT [See Quick Example 1 on page 42.]

x	-3	-2	-1	0	1	2	3
$f(x)$	1	2	4	2	1	0.5	0.25

1. **a.** $f(0)$ **b.** $f(2)$ **2.** **a.** $f(-1)$ **b.** $f(1)$

3. **a.** $f(2) - f(-2)$ **b.** $f(-1)f(-2)$ **c.** $-2f(-1)$

4. **a.** $f(1) - f(-1)$ **b.** $f(1)f(-2)$ **c.** $3f(-2)$

In Exercises 5–8, use the graph of the function f to find approximations of the given values. HINT [See Example 1.]

5.

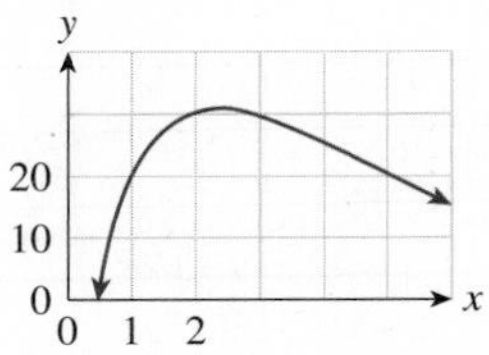

a. $f(1)$ **b.** $f(2)$
c. $f(3)$ **d.** $f(5)$
e. $f(3) - f(2)$

6.

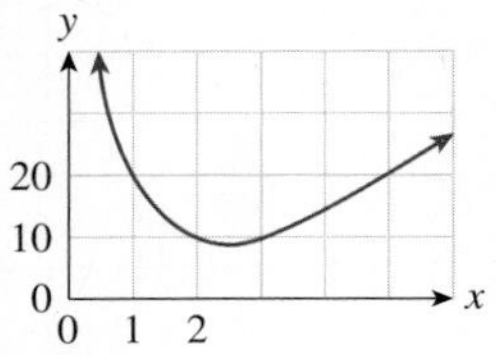

a. $f(1)$ **b.** $f(2)$
c. $f(3)$ **d.** $f(5)$
e. $f(3) - f(2)$

7.

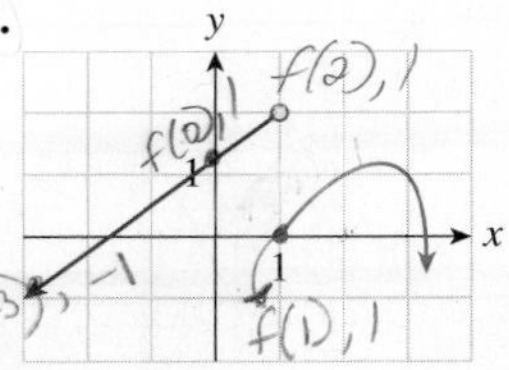

a. $f(-3)$ **b.** $f(0)$
c. $f(1)$ **d.** $f(2)$
e. $\dfrac{f(2) - f(1)}{2 - 1}$

8.

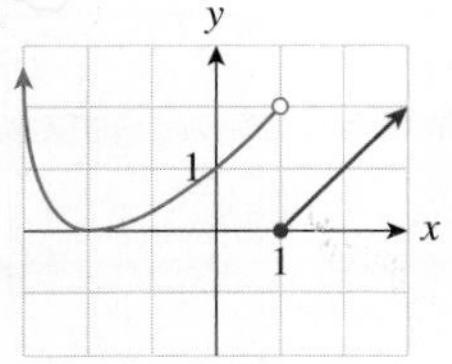

a. $f(-2)$ **b.** $f(0)$
c. $f(1)$ **d.** $f(3)$
e. $\dfrac{f(3) - f(1)}{3 - 1}$

In Exercises 9–12, say whether or not $f(x)$ is defined for the given values of x. If it is defined, give its value. HINT [See Quick Example 3 on page 43.]

9. $f(x) = x - \dfrac{1}{x^2}$, with domain $(0, +\infty)$
a. $x = 4$ **b.** $x = 0$ **c.** $x = -1$

10. $f(x) = \dfrac{2}{x} - x^2$, with domain $[2, +\infty)$
a. $x = 4$ **b.** $x = 0$ **c.** $x = 1$

11. $f(x) = \sqrt{x + 10}$, with domain $[-10, 0)$
a. $x = 0$ **b.** $x = 9$ **c.** $x = -10$

12. $f(x) = \sqrt{9 - x^2}$, with domain $(-3, 3)$
a. $x = 0$ **b.** $x = 3$ **c.** $x = -3$

13. Given $f(x) = 4x - 3$, find **a.** $f(-1)$ **b.** $f(0)$ **c.** $f(1)$ **d.** $f(y)$ **e.** $f(a + b)$ HINT [See Example 1.]

14. Given $f(x) = -3x + 4$, find
a. $f(-1)$ **b.** $f(0)$ **c.** $f(1)$ **d.** $f(y)$ **e.** $f(a + b)$

15. Given $f(x) = x^2 + 2x + 3$, find
a. $f(0)$ **b.** $f(1)$ **c.** $f(-1)$ **d.** $f(-3)$
e. $f(a)$ **f.** $f(x + h)$ HINT [See Example 1.]

16. Given $g(x) = 2x^2 - x + 1$, find
a. $g(0)$ **b.** $g(-1)$ **c.** $g(r)$ **d.** $g(x + h)$

17. Given $g(s) = s^2 + \dfrac{1}{s}$, find
a. $g(1)$ **b.** $g(-1)$ **c.** $g(4)$ **d.** $g(x)$ **e.** $g(s + h)$
f. $g(s + h) - g(s)$

18. Given $h(r) = \dfrac{1}{r + 4}$, find
a. $h(0)$ **b.** $h(-3)$ **c.** $h(-5)$ **d.** $h(x^2)$
e. $h(x^2 + 1)$ **f.** $h(x^2) + 1$

In Exercises 19–24, graph the given functions. Give the technology formula and use technology to check your graph. We suggest that you become familiar with these graphs in addition to those in Table 1. HINT [See Quick Example 4 on page 44.]

19. $f(x) = -x^3$ (domain $(-\infty, +\infty)$)

20. $f(x) = x^3$ (domain $[0, +\infty)$)

21. $f(x) = x^4$ (domain $(-\infty, +\infty)$)

22. $f(x) = \sqrt[3]{x}$ (domain $(-\infty, +\infty)$)

23. $f(x) = \dfrac{1}{x^2}$ $(x \neq 0)$ **24.** $f(x) = x + \dfrac{1}{x}$ $(x \neq 0)$

In Exercises 25 and 26, match the functions to the graphs. Using technology to draw the graphs is suggested, but not required.

25. T **a.** $f(x) = x$ $(-1 \le x \le 1)$
b. $f(x) = -x$ $(-1 \le x \le 1)$
c. $f(x) = \sqrt{x}$ $(0 < x < 4)$
d. $f(x) = x + \dfrac{1}{x} - 2$ $(0 < x < 4)$
e. $f(x) = |x|$ $(-1 \le x \le 1)$
f. $f(x) = x - 1$ $(-1 \le x \le 1)$

(I)

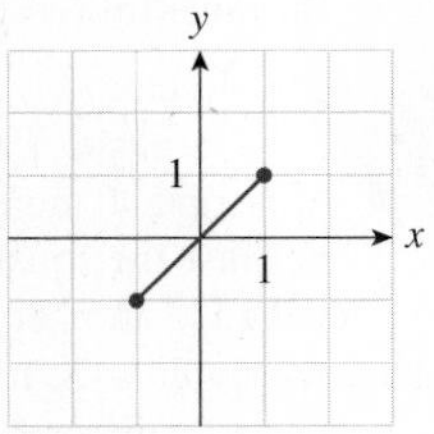

(II)

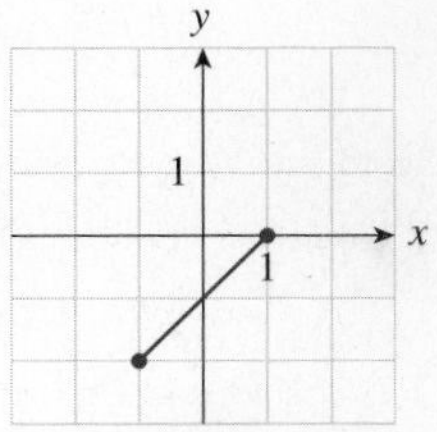

(III)

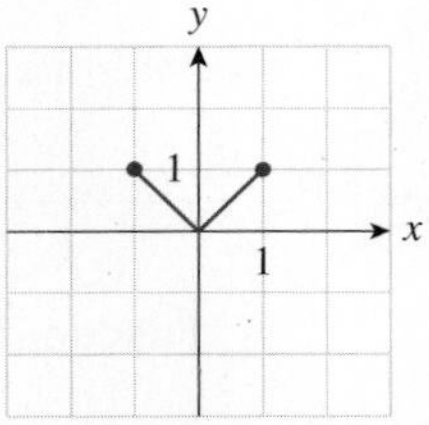

(IV)

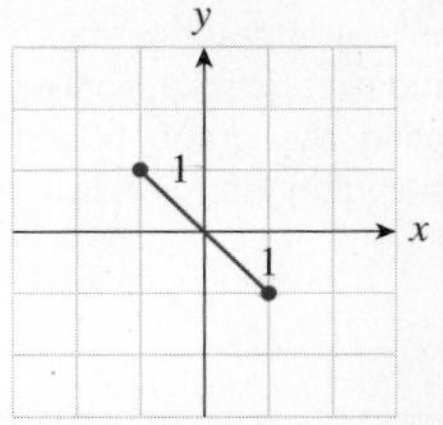

(V)

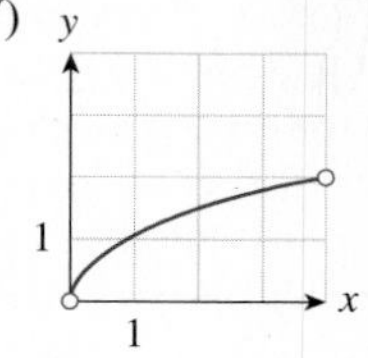

(VI)

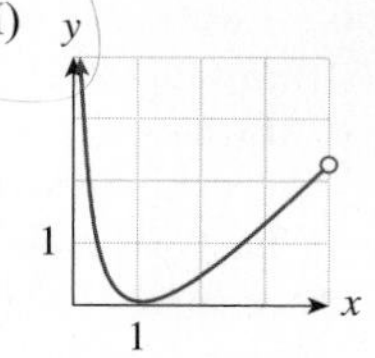

26. T **a.** $f(x) = -x + 4 \quad (0 < x \le 4)$
b. $f(x) = 2 - |x| \quad (-2 < x \le 2)$
c. $f(x) = \sqrt{x + 2} \quad (-2 < x \le 2)$
d. $f(x) = -x^2 + 2 \quad (-2 < x \le 2)$
e. $f(x) = \dfrac{1}{x} - 1 \quad (0 < x \le 4)$
f. $f(x) = x^2 - 1 \quad (-2 < x \le 2)$

(I)

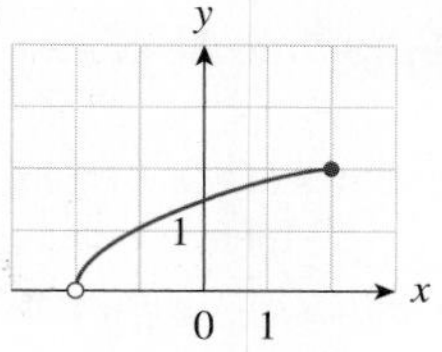

(II)

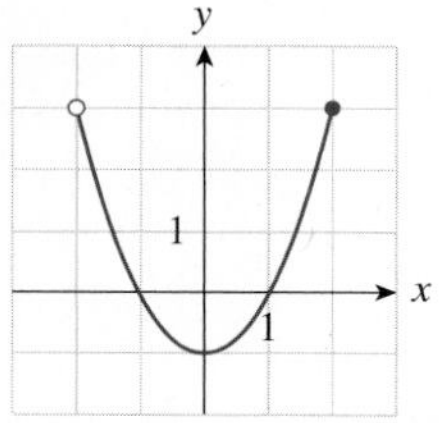

(III)

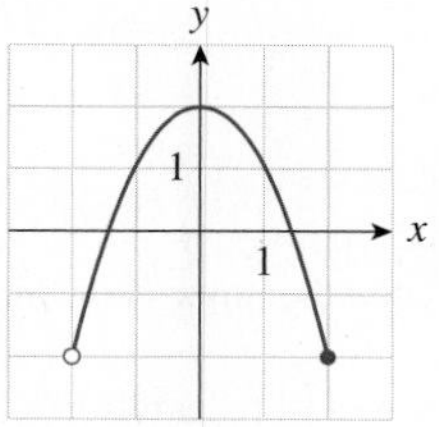

(IV)

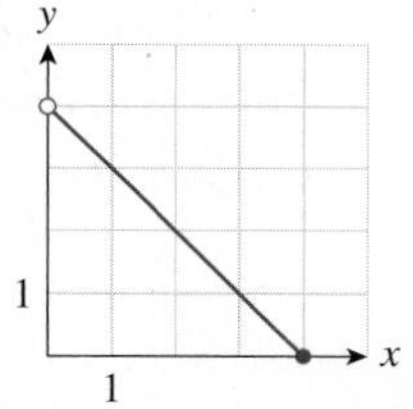

(V)

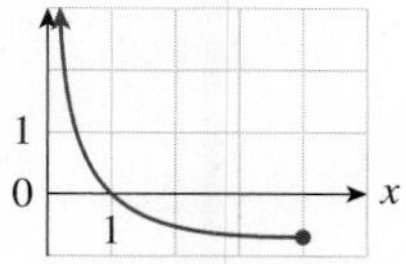

(VI)

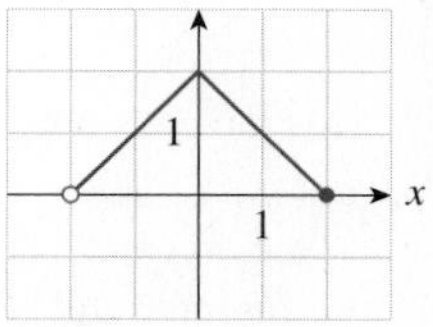

T *In Exercises 27–30, first give the technology formula for the given function and then use technology to evaluate the function for the given values of x (when defined there).*

27. T $f(x) = 0.1x^2 - 4x + 5;\ x = 0, 1, \ldots, 10$

28. T $g(x) = 0.4x^2 - 6x - 0.1;\ x = -5, -4, \ldots, 4, 5$

29. T $h(x) = \dfrac{x^2 - 1}{x^2 + 1};\ x = 0.5, 1.5, 2.5, \ldots, 10.5$ (Round all answers to four decimal places.)

30. T $r(x) = \dfrac{2x^2 + 1}{2x^2 - 1};\ x = -1, 0, 1, \ldots, 9$ (Round all answers to four decimal places.)

In Exercises 31–36, sketch the graph of the given function, evaluate the given expressions, and then use technology to duplicate the graphs. Give the technology formula. HINT [See Example 2.]

31. $f(x) = \begin{cases} x & \text{if } -4 \le x < 0 \\ 2 & \text{if } 0 \le x \le 4 \end{cases}$

a. $f(-1)$ **b.** $f(0)$ **c.** $f(1)$

32. $f(x) = \begin{cases} -1 & \text{if } -4 \le x \le 0 \\ x & \text{if } 0 < x \le 4 \end{cases}$

a. $f(-1)$ **b.** $f(0)$ **c.** $f(1)$

33. $f(x) = \begin{cases} x^2 & \text{if } -2 < x \le 0 \\ 1/x & \text{if } 0 < x \le 4 \end{cases}$

a. $f(-1)$ **b.** $f(0)$ **c.** $f(1)$

34. $f(x) = \begin{cases} -x^2 & \text{if } -2 < x \le 0 \\ \sqrt{x} & \text{if } 0 < x < 4 \end{cases}$

a. $f(-1)$ **b.** $f(0)$ **c.** $f(1)$

35. $f(x) = \begin{cases} x & \text{if } -1 < x \le 0 \\ x + 1 & \text{if } 0 < x \le 2 \\ x & \text{if } 2 < x \le 4 \end{cases}$

a. $f(0)$ **b.** $f(1)$ **c.** $f(2)$ **d.** $f(3)$ HINT [See Example 3.]

36. $f(x) = \begin{cases} -x & \text{if } -1 < x < 0 \\ x - 2 & \text{if } 0 \le x \le 2 \\ -x & \text{if } 2 < x \le 4 \end{cases}$

a. $f(0)$ **b.** $f(1)$ **c.** $f(2)$ **d.** $f(3)$

In Exercises 37–40, find and simplify ***(a)*** $f(x + h) - f(x)$ ***(b)*** $\dfrac{f(x + h) - f(x)}{h}$

37. ▼ $f(x) = x^2$

38. ▼ $f(x) = 3x - 1$

39. ▼ $f(x) = 2 - x^2$

40. ▼ $f(x) = x^2 + x$

APPLICATIONS

41. ***Petrochemical Sales: Mexico*** The following table shows annual petrochemical sales in Mexico by **Pemex**, Mexico's national oil company, for 2005–2010 ($t = 0$ represents 2005):[5]

Year *t* (Year since 2005)	0	1	2	3	4	5
Petrochemical Sales *s* (Billion metric tons)	3.7	3.8	4.0	4.1	4.0	4.1

a. Find $s(1)$, $s(4)$, and $s(5)$. Interpret your answers.
b. What is the domain of s?
c. Represent s graphically and use your graph to estimate $s(1.5)$. Interpret your answer. HINT [See Quick Example 1 on page 42.]

[5] 2010 figure is a projection based on data through May 2010. Source: www.pemex.com (July 2010).

42. ***Petrochemical Production: Mexico*** The following table shows annual petrochemical production in Mexico by **Pemex**, Mexico's national oil company, for 2005–2010 (t = 0 represents 2005):[6]

Year t (Year since 2005)	0	1	2	3	4	5
Petrochemical Production p (Billion metric tons)	10.8	11.0	11.8	12.0	12.0	13.3

a. Find $p(0)$, $p(2)$, and $p(4)$. Interpret your answers.
b. What is the domain of p?
c. Represent p graphically and use your graph to estimate $p(2.5)$. Interpret your answer. HINT [See Quick Example 1 on page 42]

Housing Starts *Exercises 43–46 refer to the following graph, which shows the number f(t) of housing starts in the U.S. each year from 2000 through 2010 (t = 0 represents 2000, and f(t) is the number of housing starts in year t in thousands of units).*[7]

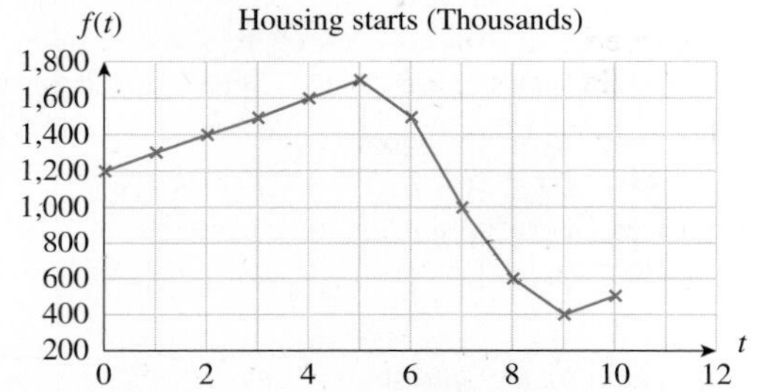

43. Estimate $f(4)$, $f(5)$, and $f(7.5)$. Interpret your answers.

44. Estimate $f(3)$, $f(6)$, and $f(8.5)$. Interpret your answers.

45. Which has the larger magnitude: $f(5) - f(0)$ or $f(8) - f(0)$? Interpret the answer.

46. Which has the larger magnitude: $f(5) - f(0)$ or $f(9) - f(7)$? Interpret the answer.

47. ***Airline Net Income*** The following graph shows the approximate annual after-tax net income $P(t)$, in millions of dollars, of **Continental Airlines** for 2005–2009 ($t = 0$ represents 2005):[8]

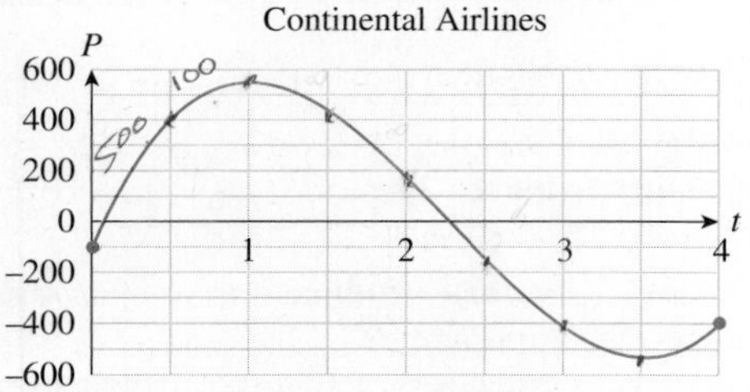

a. Estimate $P(0)$, $P(4)$, and $P(1.5)$ to the nearest 100. Interpret your answers.

b. At which of the following values of t is $P(t)$ *increasing* most rapidly: 0, 0.5, 1, 2.5, 3.5? Interpret the result.

c. At which of the following values of t is $P(t)$ *decreasing* most rapidly: 0, 0.5, 1, 2.5, 3.5? Interpret the result.

48. ***Airline Net Income*** The following graph shows the approximate annual after-tax net income $P(t)$, in millions of dollars, of **Delta Air Lines** for 2005–2009 ($t = 0$ represents 2005):[9]

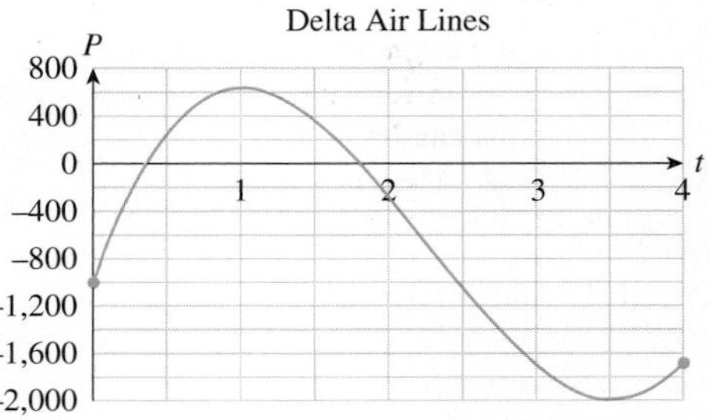

a. Estimate $P(0)$, $P(1)$, and $P(3.5)$ to the nearest 100. Interpret your answers.

b. At which of the following values of t is $P(t)$ *increasing* most rapidly: 0, 0.5, 1, 2.5, 3.5? Interpret the result.

c. At which of the following values of t is $P(t)$ *decreasing* most rapidly: 0, 0.5, 1, 2.5, 3.5? Interpret the result.

49. ***Trade with China*** The value of U.S. trade with China from 1994 through 2004 can be approximated by

$$C(t) = 3t^2 - 7t + 50 \text{ billion dollars}$$

(t is time in years since 1994).[10]

a. Find an appropriate domain of C. Is $t \geq 0$ an appropriate domain? Why or why not?

b. Compute $C(10)$. What does the answer say about trade with China?

50. ***Scientific Research*** The number of research articles in *Physical Review* that were written by researchers in the United States from 1983 through 2003 can be approximated by

$$A(t) = -0.01\,t^2 + 0.24t + 3.4 \text{ hundred articles}$$

(t is time in years since 1983).[11]

a. Find an appropriate domain of A. Is $t \leq 20$ an appropriate domain? Why or why not?

b. Compute $A(10)$. What does the answer say about the number of research articles?

51. T ***Acquisition of Language*** The percentage $p(t)$ of children who can speak in at least single words by the age of t months can be approximated by the equation[12]

$$p(t) = 100\left(1 - \frac{12{,}200}{t^{4.48}}\right) \quad (t \geq 8.5).$$

[6] *Ibid.*

[7] Sources for data: www.census.gov, www.forecast-chart.com

[8] "Net income" is an accounting term for profit (see Section 1.2). Model is the authors'. Source for data: Company reports.

[9] *Ibid.*

[10] Based on a regression by the authors. Source for data: U.S. Census Bureau/*New York Times*, September 23, 2004, p. C1.

[11] Based on a regression by the authors. Source for data: The American Physical Society/*New York Times*, May 3, 2003, p. A1.

[12] The model is the authors' and is based on data presented in the article *The Emergence of Intelligence* by William H. Calvin, *Scientific American*, October, 1994, pp. 101–107.

a. Give a technology formula for p.
b. Graph p for $8.5 \leq t \leq 20$ and $0 \leq p \leq 100$.
c. Create a table of values of p for $t = 9, 10, \ldots, 20$ (rounding answers to one decimal place).
d. What percentage of children can speak in at least single words by the age of 12 months?
e. By what age are 90% or more children speaking in at least single words?

52. T ***Acquisition of Language*** The percentage $p(t)$ of children who can speak in sentences of five or more words by the age of t months can be approximated by the equation[13]

$$p(t) = 100\left(1 - \frac{5.27 \times 10^{17}}{t^{12}}\right) \quad (t \geq 30).$$

a. Give a technology formula for p.
b. Graph p for $30 \leq t \leq 45$ and $0 \leq p \leq 100$.
c. Create a table of values of p for $t = 30, 31, \ldots, 40$ (rounding answers to one decimal place).
d. What percentage of children can speak in sentences of five or more words by the age of 36 months?
e. By what age are 75% or more children speaking in sentences of five or more words?

53. ▼ ***Processor Speeds*** The processor speed, in megahertz (MHz), of **Intel** processors during the period 1980–2010 could be approximated by the following function of time t in years since the start of 1980:[14]

$$v(t) = \begin{cases} 8(1.22)^t & \text{if } 0 \leq t < 16 \\ 400t - 6{,}200 & \text{if } 16 \leq t < 25 \\ 3{,}800 & \text{if } 25 \leq t \leq 30 \end{cases}$$

a. Evaluate $v(10)$, $v(16)$, and $v(28)$ and interpret the results.
b. Write down a technology formula for v.
c. T Use technology to sketch the graph of v and to generate a table of values for $v(t)$ with $t = 0, 2, \ldots, 30$. (Round values to two significant digits.)
d. When, to the nearest year, did processor speeds reach 3 gigahertz (1 gigahertz = 1,000 megahertz) according to the model?

54. ▼ ***Processor Speeds*** The processor speed, in megahertz (MHz), of **Intel** processors during the period 1970–2000 could be approximated by the following function of time t in years since the start of 1970:[15]

$$v(t) = \begin{cases} 0.12t^2 + 0.04t + 0.2 & \text{if } 0 \leq t < 12 \\ 1.1(1.22)^t & \text{if } 12 \leq t < 26 \\ 400t - 10{,}200 & \text{if } 26 \leq t \leq 30 \end{cases}$$

a. Evaluate $v(2)$, $v(12)$, and $v(28)$ and interpret the results.
b. Write down a technology formula for v.
c. T Use technology to sketch the graph of v and to generate a table of values for $v(t)$ with $t = 0, 2, \ldots, 30$. (Round values to two significant digits.)
d. When, to the nearest year, did processor speeds reach 500 megahertz?

55. ▼ ***Income Taxes*** The U.S. Federal income tax is a function of taxable income. Write $T(x)$ for the tax owed on a taxable income of x dollars. For tax year 2010, the function T for a single taxpayer was specified as follows:

If your taxable income was			
Over...	*But not over...*	*Your tax is*	*of the amount over...*
\$0	8,375	.... 10%	\$0
8,375	34,000	\$837.50 + 15%	\$8,375
34,000	82,400	4,663.25 + 25%	\$34,000
82,400	171,850	16,763.25 + 28%	\$82,400
171,850	373,650	41,809.25 + 33%	\$171,850
373,650	....	108,403.25 + 35%	\$373,650

a. Represent T as a piecewise-defined function of income x. HINT [Each row of the table defines a formula with a condition.]
b. Use your function to compute the tax owed by a single taxpayer on a taxable income of \$36,000.

56. ▼ ***Income Taxes*** Repeat Exercise 55 using the following information for tax year 2009.

If your taxable income was			
Over...	*But not over...*	*Your tax is*	*of the amount over...*
\$0	8,350	.... 10%	\$0
8,350	33,950	\$835.00 + 15%	\$8,350
33,950	82,250	4,675.00 + 25%	\$33,950
82,250	171,550	16,750.00 + 28%	\$82,250
171,550	372,950	41,754.00 + 33%	\$171,550
372,950	....	108,216.00 + 35%	\$372,950

COMMUNICATION AND REASONING EXERCISES

57. Complete the following sentence: If the market price m of gold varies with time t, then the independent variable is ___ and the dependent variable is ___.

58. Complete the following sentence: If weekly profit P is specified as a function of selling price s, then the independent variable is ___ and the dependent variable is ___.

59. Complete the following: The function notation for the equation $y = 4x^2 - 2$ is ____.

60. Complete the following: The equation notation for $C(t) = -0.34t^2 + 0.1t$ is ____.

[13] *Ibid.*

[14] Based on the fastest processors produced by Intel. Source for data: www.intel.com.

[15] *Ibid.*

61. True or false? Every graphically specified function can also be specified numerically. Explain.

62. True or false? Every algebraically specified function can also be specified graphically. Explain.

63. True or false? Every numerically specified function with domain [0, 10] can also be specified algebraically. Explain.

64. True or false? Every graphically specified function can also be specified algebraically. Explain.

65. ▼ True or false? Every function can be specified numerically. Explain.

66. ▼ Which supplies more information about a situation: a numerical model or an algebraic model?

67. ▼ Why is the following assertion false? "If $f(x) = x^2 - 1$, then $f(x + h) = x^2 + h - 1$."

68. ▼ Why is the following assertion false? "If $f(2) = 2$ and $f(4) = 4$, then $f(3) = 3$."

69. How do the graphs of two functions differ if they are specified by the same formula but have different domains?

70. How do the graphs of two functions f and g differ if $g(x) = f(x) + 10$? (Try an example.)

71. ▼ How do the graphs of two functions f and g differ if $g(x) = f(x - 5)$? (Try an example.)

72. ▼ How do the graphs of two functions f and g differ if $g(x) = f(-x)$? (Try an example.)

1.2 Functions and Models

The functions we used in Examples 1 and 2 in Section 1.1 are **mathematical models** of real-life situations, because they model, or represent, situations in mathematical terms.

Mathematical Modeling

To mathematically model a situation means to represent it in mathematical terms. The particular representation used is called a **mathematical model** of the situation. Mathematical models do not always represent a situation perfectly or completely. Some (like Example 1 of Section 1.1) represent a situation only approximately, whereas others represent only some aspects of the situation.

Quick Examples

1. The temperature is now 10°F and increasing by 20° per hour.
   Model: $T(t) = 10 + 20t$ (t = time in hours, T = temperature)
2. I invest $1,000 at 5% interest compounded quarterly. Find the value of the investment after t years.
   Model: $A(t) = 1{,}000\left(1 + \frac{0.05}{4}\right)^{4t}$ (This is the compound interest formula we will study in Example 6.)
3. I am fencing a rectangular area whose perimeter is 100 ft. Find the area as a function of the width x.
   Model: Take y to be the length, so the perimeter is
   $$100 = x + y + x + y = 2(x + y).$$
   This gives
   $$x + y = 50.$$
   Thus the length is $y = 50 - x$, and the area is
   $$A = xy = x(50 - x).$$

4. You work 8 hours a day Monday through Friday, 5 hours on Saturday, and have Sunday off. Model the number of hours you work as a function of the day of the week n, with $n = 1$ being Sunday.
Model: Take $f(n)$ to be the number of hours you work on the nth day of the week, so

$$f(n) = \begin{cases} 0 & \text{if } n = 1 \\ 8 & \text{if } 2 \le n \le 6 \\ 5 & \text{if } n = 7 \end{cases}.$$

Note that the domain of f is $\{1, 2, 3, 4, 5, 6, 7\}$—a discrete set rather than a continuous interval of the real line.

5. The function

$$f(x) = 4x^2 + 16x + 2 \text{ million iPods sold } (x = \text{years since 2003})$$

in Example 1 of Section 1.1 is a model of iPod sales.

6. The function

$$n(t) = \begin{cases} 4t & \text{if } 0 \le t \le 3 \\ 12 + 23(t - 3)^{2.7} & \text{if } 3 < t \le 6 \end{cases} \text{ million members}$$

(t = years since January 2004) in Example 2 of Section 1.1 is a model of Facebook membership.

Types of Models

Quick Examples 1–4 are **analytical models**, obtained by analyzing the situation being modeled, whereas Quick Examples 5 and 6 are **curve-fitting models**, obtained by finding mathematical formulas that approximate observed data. All the models except for Quick Example 4 are **continuous models**, defined by functions whose domains are intervals of the real line, whereas Quick Example 4 is a **discrete model** as its domain is a discrete set, as mentioned above. Discrete models are used extensively in probability and statistics.

Cost, Revenue, and Profit Models

EXAMPLE 1 Modeling Cost: Cost Function

As of August 2010, Yellow Cab Chicago's rates amounted to \$2.05 on entering the cab plus \$1.80 for each mile.[16]

a. Find the cost C of an x-mile trip.

b. Use your answer to calculate the cost of a 40-mile trip.

c. What is the cost of the second mile? What is the cost of the tenth mile?

d. Graph C as a function of x.

[16] According to their Web site at www.yellowcabchicago.com.

Solution

a. We are being asked to find how the cost C depends on the length x of the trip, or to find C as a function of x. Here is the cost in a few cases:

Cost of a 1-mile trip: $C = 1.80(1) + 2.05 = 3.85$ 1 mile at \$1.80 per mile plus \$2.05

Cost of a 2-mile trip: $C = 1.80(2) + 2.05 = 5.65$ 2 miles at \$1.80 per mile plus \$2.05

Cost of a 3-mile trip: $C = 1.80(3) + 2.05 = 7.45$ 3 miles at \$1.80 per mile plus \$2.05

Do you see the pattern? The cost of an x-mile trip is given by the linear function

$$C(x) = 1.80x + 2.05.$$

Notice that the cost function is a sum of two terms: The **variable cost** $1.80x$, which depends on x, and the **fixed cost** 2.05, which is independent of x:

$$\text{Cost} = \text{Variable Cost} + \text{Fixed Cost}.$$

The quantity 1.80 by itself is the incremental cost per mile; you might recognize it as the *slope* of the given linear function. In this context we call 1.80 the **marginal cost**. You might recognize the fixed cost 2.05 as the *C-intercept* of the given linear function.

b. We can use the formula for the cost function to calculate the cost of a 40-mile trip as

$$C(40) = 1.80(40) + 2.05 = \$74.05.$$

c. To calculate the cost of the second mile, we *could* proceed as follows:

Find the cost of a 1-mile trip: $C(1) = 1.80(1) + 2.05 = \$3.85$.

Find the cost of a 2-mile trip: $C(2) = 1.80(2) + 2.05 = \$5.65$.

Therefore, the cost of the second mile is $\$5.65 - \$3.85 = \$1.80$.

But notice that this is just the marginal cost. In fact, the marginal cost is the cost of each additional mile, so we could have done this more simply:

Cost of second mile = Cost of tenth mile = Marginal cost = \$1.80.

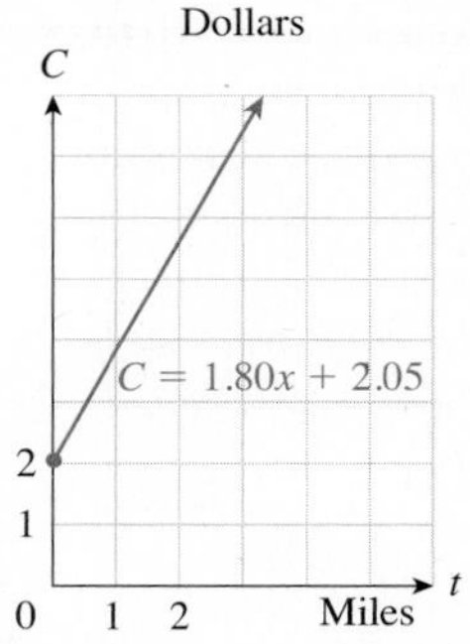

Figure 7

d. Figure 7 shows the graph of the cost function, which we can interpret as a *cost vs. miles* graph. The fixed cost is the starting height on the left, while the marginal cost is the slope of the line: It rises 1.80 units per unit of x. (See Section 1.3 for a discussion of properties of straight lines.)

➡ **Before we go on...** The cost function in Example 1 is an example of an *analytical model:* We derived the form of the cost function from a knowledge of the cost per mile and the fixed cost.

As we discussed in Section 1.1, we can specify the cost function in Example 1 using equation notation:

$$C = 1.80x + 2.05. \qquad \text{Equation notation}$$

Here, the independent variable is x, and the dependent variable is C. (This is the notation we have used in Figure 7. Remember that we will often switch between function and equation notation when it is convenient to do so.) ■

Here is a summary of some terms we used in Example 1, along with an introduction to some new terms:

Cost, Revenue, and Profit Functions

A **cost function** specifies the cost C as a function of the number of items x. Thus, $C(x)$ is the cost of x items, and has the form

$$\text{Cost} = \text{Variable cost} + \text{Fixed cost}$$

where the variable cost is a function of x and the fixed cost is a constant. A cost function of the form

$$C(x) = mx + b$$

is called a **linear cost function**; the variable cost is mx and the fixed cost is b. The slope m, the **marginal cost**, measures the incremental cost per item.

The **revenue**, or **net sales**, resulting from one or more business transactions is the total income received. If $R(x)$ is the revenue from selling x items at a price of m each, then R is the linear function $R(x) = mx$ and the selling price m can also be called the **marginal revenue**.

The **profit**, or **net income**, on the other hand, is what remains of the revenue when costs are subtracted. If the profit depends linearly on the number of items, the slope m is called the **marginal profit**. Profit, revenue, and cost are related by the following formula.

$$\text{Profit} = \text{Revenue} - \text{Cost}$$
$$P(x) = R(x) - C(x).^*$$

* We say that the profit function P is the **difference** between the revenue and cost functions, and express this fact as a formula about functions: $P = R - C$. (We will discuss this further when we talk about the algebra of functions at the end of this section.)

If the profit is negative, say $-\$500$, we refer to a **loss** (of \$500 in this case). To **break even** means to make neither a profit nor a loss. Thus, breakeven occurs when $P = 0$, or

$$R(x) = C(x). \qquad \text{Breakeven}$$

The **break-even point** is the number of items x at which breakeven occurs.

Quick Example

If the daily cost (including operating costs) of manufacturing x T-shirts is $C(x) = 8x + 100$, and the revenue obtained by selling x T-shirts is $R(x) = 10x$, then the daily profit resulting from the manufacture and sale of x T-shirts is

$$P(x) = R(x) - C(x) = 10x - (8x + 100) = 2x - 100.$$

Breakeven occurs when $P(x) = 0$, or $x = 50$.

EXAMPLE 2 Cost, Revenue, and Profit

The annual operating cost of *YSport* Fitness gym is estimated to be

$$C(x) = 100{,}000 + 160x - 0.2x^2 \text{ dollars} \qquad (0 \le x \le 400),$$

where x is the number of members. Annual revenue from membership averages \$800 per member. What is the variable cost? What is the fixed cost? What is the profit function? How many members must *YSport* have to make a profit? What will happen if it has fewer members? If it has more?

Solution The variable cost is the part of the cost function that depends on x:

$$\text{Variable cost} = 160x - 0.2x^2.$$

The fixed cost is the constant term:

$$\text{Fixed cost} = 100{,}000.$$

The annual revenue *YSport* obtains from a single member is \$800. So, if it has x members, it earns an annual revenue of

$$R(x) = 800x.$$

For the profit, we use the formula

$$\begin{aligned} P(x) &= R(x) - C(x) && \text{Formula for profit} \\ &= 800x - (100{,}000 + 160x - 0.2x^2) && \text{Substitute } R(x) \text{ and } C(x). \\ &= -100{,}000 + 640x + 0.2x^2. \end{aligned}$$

To make a profit, *YSport* needs to do better than break even, so let us find the break-even point: the value of x such that $P(x) = 0$. All we have to do is set $P(x) = 0$ and solve for x:

$$-100{,}000 + 640x + 0.2x^2 = 0.$$

Notice that we have a quadratic equation $ax^2 + bx + c = 0$ with $a = 0.2$, $b = 640$, and $c = -100{,}000$. Its solution is given by the quadratic formula:

using Technology

Excel has a feature called "Goal Seek," which can be used to find the point of intersection of the cost and revenue graphs numerically rather than graphically. See the downloadable Excel tutorial for this section at the Website.

$$\begin{aligned} x = \frac{-b \pm \sqrt{b^2 - 4ac}}{2a} &= \frac{-640 \pm \sqrt{640^2 + 4(0.2)(100{,}000)}}{2(0.2)} \\ &\approx \frac{-640 \pm 699.71}{2(0.2)} \\ &\approx 149.3 \text{ or } -3{,}349.3. \end{aligned}$$

We reject the negative solution (as the domain is $[0, 400]$) and conclude that $x \approx 149.3$ members. To make a profit, should *YSport* have 149 members or 150 members? To decide, take a look at Figure 8, which shows two graphs: On the left we see the graph of revenue and cost, and on the right we see the graph of the profit function.

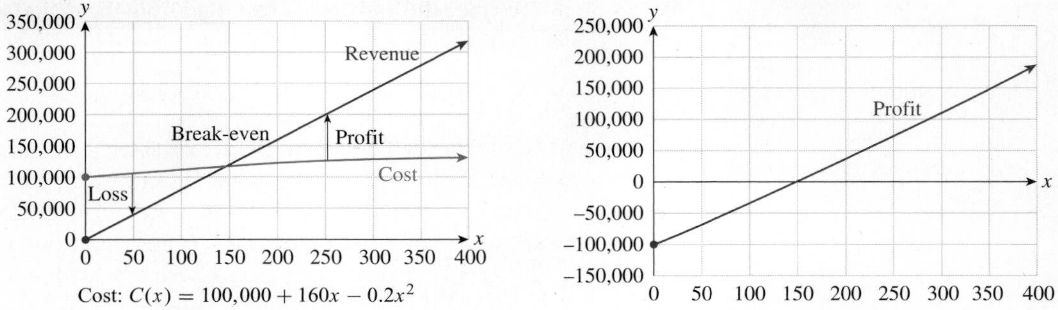

Cost: $C(x) = 100{,}000 + 160x - 0.2x^2$
Revenue: $R(x) = 800x$
Breakeven occurs at the point of intersection of the graphs of revenue and cost.

Profit: $P(x) = -100{,}000 + 640x + 0.2x^2$
Breakeven occurs when $P(x) = 0$

Figure 8

For values of x less than the break-even point of 149.3, $P(x)$ is negative, so the company will have a loss. For values of x greater than the break-even point, $P(x)$ is positive, so the company will make a profit. Thus, *YSport Fitness* needs at least 150 members to make a profit. (Note that we rounded 149.3 up to 150 in this case.)

Demand and Supply Models

The demand for a commodity usually goes down as its price goes up. It is traditional to use the letter q for the (quantity of) demand, as measured, for example, in sales. Consider the following example.

EXAMPLE 3 Demand: Private Schools

The demand for private schools in Michigan depends on the tuition cost and can be approximated by

$$q = 77.8p^{-0.11} \text{ thousand students} \qquad (200 \le p \le 2{,}200), \qquad \text{Demand curve}$$

where p is the net tuition cost in dollars.[17]

a. Use technology to plot the demand function.

b. What is the effect on demand if the tuition cost is increased from \$1,000 to \$1,500?

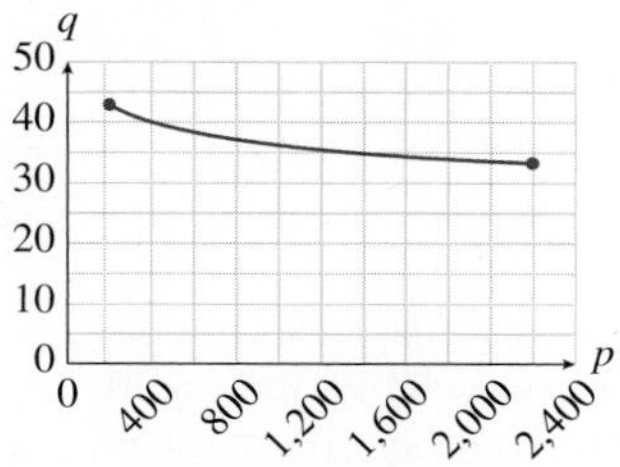

Technology Formula:
y = 77.8x^(-0.11)

Figure 9

Solution

a. The demand function is given by $q(p) = 77.8p^{-0.11}$. Its graph is known as a **demand curve** (Figure 9).

b. The demand at tuition costs of \$1,000 and \$1,500 is

$$q(1{,}000) = 77.8(1{,}000)^{-0.11} \approx 36.4 \text{ thousand students}$$
$$q(1{,}500) = 77.8(1{,}500)^{-0.11} \approx 34.8 \text{ thousand students.}$$

The change in demand is therefore

$$q(1{,}500) - q(1{,}000) \approx 34.8 - 36.4 = -1.6 \text{ thousand students.}$$

We have seen that a demand function gives the number of items consumers are willing to buy at a given price, and a higher price generally results in a lower demand. However, as the price rises, suppliers will be more inclined to produce these items (as opposed to spending their time and money on other products), so supply will generally rise. A **supply function** gives q, the number of items suppliers are willing to make available for sale*, as a function of p, the price per item.

* Although a bit confusing at first, it is traditional to use the same letter q for the quantity of supply and the quantity of demand, particularly when we want to compare them, as in the next example.

Demand, Supply, and Equilibrium Price

A **demand equation** or **demand function** expresses demand q (the number of items demanded) as a function of the unit price p (the price per item). A **supply equation** or **supply function** expresses supply q (the number of items a supplier is willing to make available) as a function of the unit price p (the price per item). It is usually the case that demand decreases and supply increases as the unit price increases.

[17]The tuition cost is net cost: tuition minus tax credit. The model is based on data in "The Universal Tuition Tax Credit: A Proposal to Advance Personal Choice in Education," Patrick L. Anderson, Richard McLellan, J.D., Joseph P. Overton, J.D., Gary Wolfram, Ph.D., Mackinac Center for Public Policy, www.mackinac.org/

Demand and supply are said to be in **equilibrium** when demand equals supply. The corresponding values of p and q are called the **equilibrium price** and **equilibrium demand**. To find the equilibrium price, determine the unit price p where the demand and supply curves cross (sometimes we can determine this value analytically by setting demand equal to supply and solving for p). To find the equilibrium demand, evaluate the demand (or supply) function at the equilibrium price.

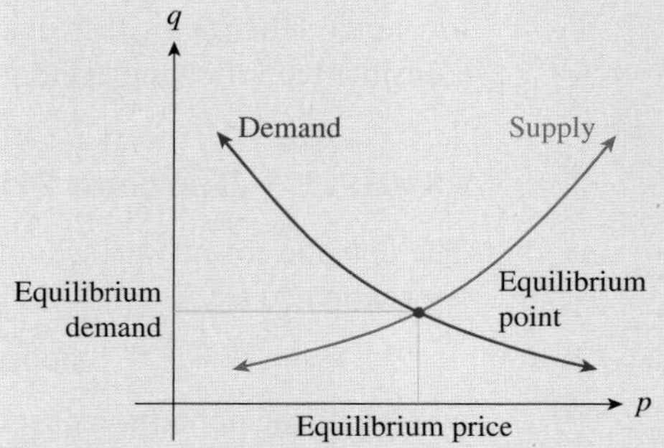

Quick Example

If the demand for your exclusive T-shirts is $q = -20p + 800$ shirts sold per day and the supply is $q = 10p - 100$ shirts per day, then the equilibrium point is obtained when demand = supply:

$$-20p + 800 = 10p - 100$$
$$30p = 900, \text{ giving } p = \$30.$$

The equilibrium price is therefore \$30 and the equilibrium demand is $q = -20(30) + 800 = 200$ shirts per day. What happens at prices other than the equilibrium price is discussed in Example 4.

Note In economics it is customary to plot the independent variable (price) on the vertical axis and the dependent variable (demand or supply) on the horizontal axis, but in this book we follow the usual mathematical convention for all graphs and plot the independent variable on the horizontal axis.

EXAMPLE 4 Demand, Supply, and Equilibrium Price

Continuing with Example 3, suppose that private school institutions are willing to create private schools to accommodate

$$q = 30.4 + 0.006p \text{ thousand students} \qquad (200 \le p \le 2{,}200) \qquad \text{Supply curve}$$

who pay a net tuition of p dollars.

a. Graph the demand curve of Example 3 and the supply curve given here on the same set of axes. Use your graph to estimate, to the nearest \$100, the tuition at which the demand equals the supply. Approximately how many students will be accommodated at that price, known as the **equilibrium price**?

b. What happens if the tuition is higher than the equilibrium price? What happens if it is lower?

c. Estimate the shortage or surplus of openings at private schools if tuition is set at \$1,200.

Solution

a. Figure 10 shows the graphs of demand $q = 77.8p^{-0.11}$ and supply $q = 30.4 + 0.006p$. (See the margin note for a brief description of how to plot them.)

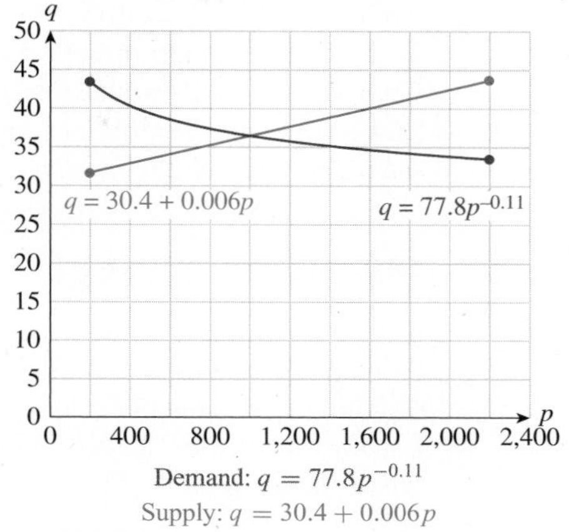

Figure 10

The lines cross close to $p = \$1{,}000$, so we conclude that demand = supply when $p \approx \$1{,}000$ (to the nearest \$100). This is the (approximate) equilibrium tuition price. At that price, we can estimate the demand or supply at around

Demand: $q = 77.8(1{,}000)^{-0.11} \approx 36.4$

Supply: $q = 30.4 + 0.006(1{,}000) = 36.4$ Demand = Supply at equilibrium

or 36,400 students.

b. Take a look at Figure 11, which shows what happens if schools charge more or less than the equilibrium price.

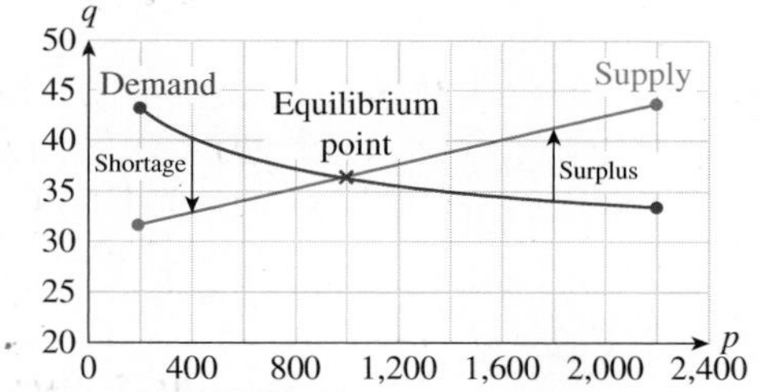

Figure 11

If tuition is, say, \$1,800, then the supply will be larger than demand and there will be a surplus of available openings at private schools. Similarly, if tuition is less—say \$400—then the supply will be less than the demand, and there will be a shortage of available openings.

c. The discussion in part (b) shows that if tuition is set at \$1,200 there will be a surplus of available openings. To estimate that number, we calculate the projected demand and supply when $p = \$1{,}200$:

Demand: $q = 77.8(1{,}200)^{-0.11} \approx 35.7$ thousand seats

Supply: $q = 30.4 + 0.006(1{,}200) = 37.6$ thousand seats

Surplus = Supply − Demand $\approx 37.6 - 35.7 = 1.9$ thousand seats.

So, there would be a surplus of around 1,900 available seats.

using Technology

See the Technology Guides at the end of the chapter for detailed instructions on how to obtain the table of values and graph in Example 4 using a TI-83/84 Plus or Excel. Here is an outline:

TI-83/84 Plus

Graphs:

```
Y1=77.8*X^(-0.11)
Y2=30.4+0.006*X
```

[2ND] [TABLE] Graph:

Xmin = 200, Xmax = 2200;

[ZOOM] [0] [More details on page 115.]

Spreadsheet

Headings p, Demand, Supply in A1–C1; p-values 200, 300, ..., 2200 in A2-A22.

`=77.8*A2^(-0.11)` in B2

`=30.4+0.006*A2` in C2

Copy down through C22.

Highlight A1–C22; insert Scatter chart. [More details on page 120.]

Website

www.WanerMath.com

Go to the Function Evaluator and Grapher under Online Utilities, and enter

`77.8*x^(-0.11)` for y_1 and `30.4+0.006*x` for y_2.

Graph: Set Xmin = 200, Xmax = 2200, and press "Plot Graphs".

Before we go on... We just saw in Example 4 that if tuition is less than the equilibrium price there will be a shortage. If schools were to raise their tuition toward the equilibrium, they would create and fill more openings and increase revenue, because it is the supply equation—and not the demand equation—that determines what one can sell below the equilibrium price. On the other hand, if they were to charge more than the equilibrium price, they will be left with a possibly costly surplus of unused openings (and will want to lower tuition to reduce the surplus). Prices tend to move toward the equilibrium, so supply tends to equal demand. When supply equals demand, we say that the market **clears**. ■

Modeling Change over Time

Things around us change with time. Thus, there are many quantities, such as your income or the temperature in Honolulu, that are natural to think of as functions of time. Example 1 on page 44 (on iPod sales) and Example 2 on page 47 (on Facebook membership) in Section 1.1 are models of change over time. Both of those models are curve-fitting models: We used algebraic functions to approximate observed data.

Note We usually use the independent variable t to denote time (in seconds, hours, days, years, etc.). If a quantity q changes with time, then we can regard q as a function of t. ■

In the next example we are asked to select from among several curve-fitting models for given data.

EXAMPLE 5 Model Selection: Sales

The following table shows annual sales, in billions of dollars, by Nike from 2005 through 2010:[18]

Year	2005	2006	2007	2008	2009	2010
Sales ($ billion)	13.5	15	16.5	18.5	19	19

Take t to be the number of years since 2005, and consider the following four models:

(1) $s(t) = 14 + 1.2t$ Linear model

(2) $s(t) = 13 + 2.2t - 0.2t^2$ Quadratic model

(3) $s(t) = 14(1.07^t)$ Exponential model

(4) $s(t) = \dfrac{19.5}{1 + 0.48(1.8^{-t})}$ Logistic model

a. Which models fit the data significantly better than the rest?

b. Of the models you selected in part (a), which gives the most reasonable prediction for 2013?

[18] Figures are rounded. Source: http://invest.nike.com.

Solution

a. The following table shows the original data together with the values, rounded to the nearest 0.5, for all four models:

t	0	1	2	3	4	5
Sales ($billion)	13.5	15	16.5	18.5	19	19
Linear: $s(t) = 14 + 1.2t$ Technology: `14+1.2*x`	14	15	16.5	17.5	19	20
Quadratic: $s(t) = 13 + 2.2t - 0.2t^2$ Technology: `13+2.2*x-0.2*x^2`	13	15	16.5	18	18.5	19
Exponential: $s(t) = 14(1.07^t)$ Technology: `14*1.07^x`	14	15	16	17	18.5	19.5
Logistic: $s(t) = \dfrac{19.5}{1 + 0.48(1.8^{-t})}$ Technology: `19.5/(1+0.48*1.8^(-x))`	13	15.5	17	18	18.5	19

Notice that all the models give values that seem reasonably close to the actual sales values. However, the quadratic and logistic curves seem to model their behavior more accurately than the others (see Figure 12).

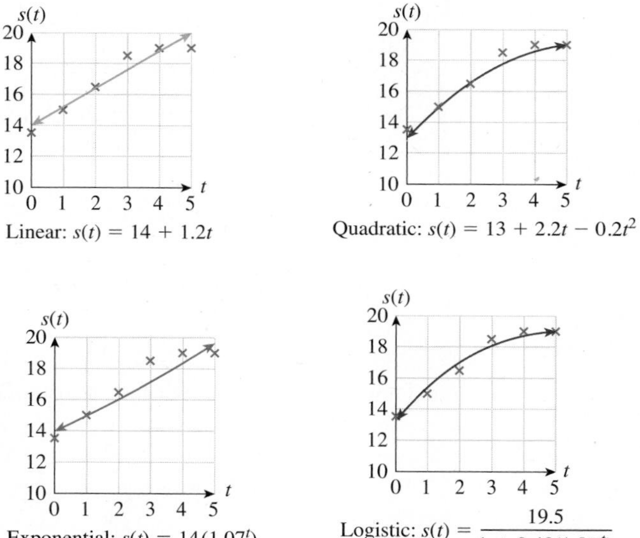

Linear: $s(t) = 14 + 1.2t$

Quadratic: $s(t) = 13 + 2.2t - 0.2t^2$

Exponential: $s(t) = 14(1.07^t)$

Logistic: $s(t) = \dfrac{19.5}{1 + 0.48(1.8^{-t})}$

Figure 12

We therefore conclude that the quadratic and logistic models fit the data significantly better than the others.

b. Although the quadratic and logistic models both appear to fit the data well, they do not both extrapolate to give reasonable predictions for 2013:

$$\text{Quadratic Model: } s(8) = 13 + 2.2(8) - 0.2(8)^2 = 17.8$$

$$\text{Logistic Model: } s(8) = \frac{19.5}{1 + 0.48(1.8^{-8})} \approx 19.4.$$

using Technology

See the Technology Guides at the end of the chapter for detailed instructions on how to obtain the table and graphs in Example 5 using a TI-83/84 Plus or Excel. Here is an outline:

TI-83/84 Plus
STAT EDIT; enter the values of t in L_1, and $r(t)$ in L_2.
Plotting the points: ZOOM 9
Adding a curve:
Turn on Plot1 in Y= screen. Then (for the second curve)
`Y1=13+2.2*X-0.2*X^2`
Press GRAPH [More details on page 115.]

Spreadsheet
Table of values: Headings t, Sales, $s(t)$ in A1–C1;
t-values in A2-A7; sales values in B2–B7. Formula in C2:
`=13+2.2*A2-0.2*A2^2`
(second model)
Copy down through C7
Graph: Highlight A1–C7; insert Scatter chart. [More details on page 121.]

Website
www.WanerMath.com
In the Function Evaluator and Grapher utility, enter the data and model(s) as shown below. Set xMin = 0, xMax = 5 and press "Plot Graphs".

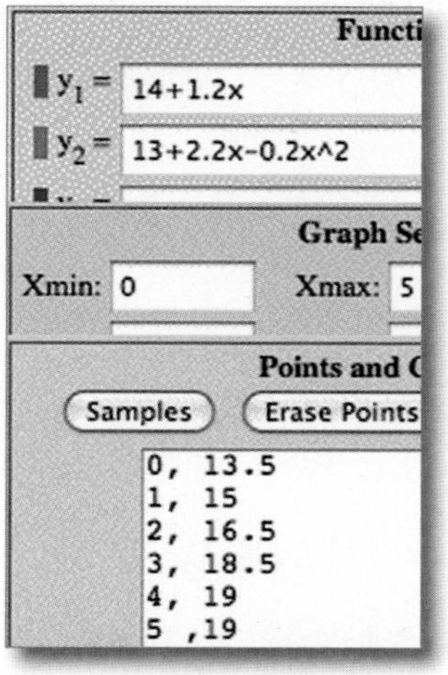

Notice that the quadratic model predicts a significant *decline* in sales whereas the logistic model predicts a more reasonable modest increase. This discrepancy can be seen quite dramatically in Figure 13.

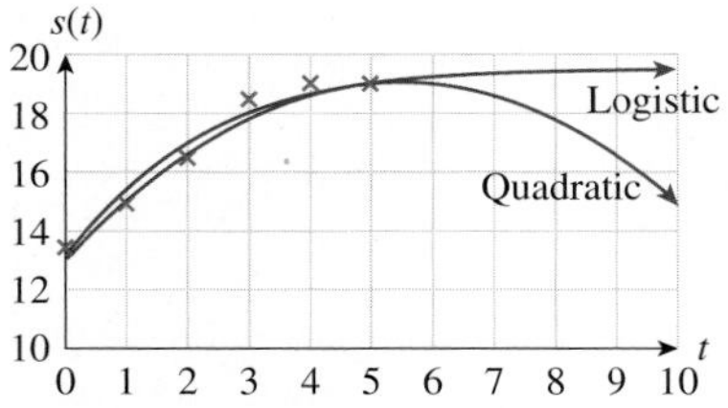

Figure 13

We now derive an analytical model of change over time based on the idea of **compound interest**. Suppose you invest \$500 (the **present value**) in an investment account with an annual yield of 15%, and the interest is reinvested at the end of every year (we say that the interest is **compounded** or **reinvested** once a year). Let t represent the number of years since you made the initial \$500 investment. Each year, the investment is worth 115% (or 1.15 times) of its value the previous year. The **future value** A of your investment changes over time t, so we think of A as a function of t. The following table illustrates how we can calculate the future value for several values of t:

t	0	1	2	3
Future Value $A(t)$	500	575	661.25	760.44
	A	$500(1.15)$	$500(1.15)^2$	$500(1.15)^3$
		$\times 1.15$	$\times 1.15$	$\times 1.15$

Thus, $A(t) = 500(1.15)^t$. A traditional way to write this formula is

$$A(t) = P(1 + r)^t,$$

where P is the present value ($P = 500$) and r is the annual interest rate ($r = 0.15$).

If, instead of compounding the interest once a year, we compound it every three months (four times a year), we would earn one quarter of the interest ($r/4$ of the current investment) every three months. Because this would happen $4t$ times in t years, the formula for the future value becomes

$$A(t) = P\left(1 + \frac{r}{4}\right)^{4t}.$$

Compound Interest

If an amount (**present value**) P is invested for t years at an annual rate of r, and if the interest is compounded (reinvested) m times per year, then the **future value** A is

$$A(t) = P\left(1 + \frac{r}{m}\right)^{mt}.$$

A special case is **interest compounded once a year**:

$$A(t) = P(1 + r)^t.$$

Quick Example

If \$2,000 is invested for two and a half years in a mutual fund with an annual yield of 12.6% and the earnings are reinvested each month, then $P = 2{,}000$, $r = 0.126$, $m = 12$, and $t = 2.5$, which gives

$$A(2.5) = 2{,}000\left(1 + \frac{0.126}{12}\right)^{12\times 2.5}$$ `2000*(1+0.126/12)^(12*2.5)`

$$= 2{,}000(1.0105)^{30} = \$2{,}736.02.$$

EXAMPLE 6 Compound Interest: Investments

Consider the scenario in the preceding Quick Example: You invest \$2,000 in a mutual fund with an annual yield of 12.6% and the interest is reinvested each month.

a. Find the associated exponential model.

b. T Use a table of values to estimate the year during which the value of your investment reaches \$5,000.

c. Use a graph to confirm your answer in part (b).

using Technology

TI-83/84 Plus
`Y1=2000(1+0.126/12)^(12X)`
[2ND] [TABLE]

Spreadsheet
Headings t and A in A1–B1; t-values 0–11 in A2–A13.
`=2000*(1+0.126/12)^(12*A2)`
in B2; copy down through B13.

Website
www.WanerMath.com
Go to the Function Evaluator and Grapher under Online Utilities, and enter
`2000(1+0.126/12)^(12x)`
for y_1. Scroll down to the Evaluator, enter the values 0–11 under x-values and press "Evaluate."

Solution

a. Apply the formula

$$A(t) = P\left(1 + \frac{r}{m}\right)^{mt}$$

with $P = 2{,}000$, $r = 0.126$, and $m = 12$. We get

$$A(t) = 2{,}000\left(1 + \frac{0.126}{12}\right)^{12t}$$

$$= 2{,}000(1.0105)^{12t}.$$ `2000*(1+0.126/12)^(12*t)`

This is the exponential model. (What would happen if we left out the last set of parentheses in the technology formula?)

b. We need to find the value of t for which $A(t) = \$5{,}000$, so we need to solve the equation

$$5{,}000 = 2{,}000(1.0105)^{12t}.$$

In Section 2.3 we will learn how to use logarithms to do this algebraically, but we can answer the question now using a graphing calculator, a spreadsheet, or the Function Evaluator and Grapher utility at the Website. Just enter the model and compute the balance at the end of several years. Here are examples of tables obtained using three forms of technology:

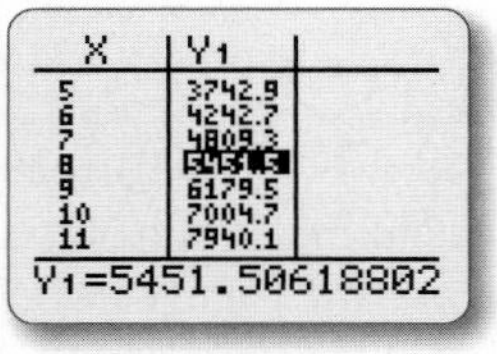

TI-83/84 Plus

	A	B
1	t	A
2	0	$ 2,000.00
3	1	$ 2,267.07
4	2	$ 2,569.81
5	3	$ 2,912.98
6	4	$ 3,301.97
7	5	$ 3,742.91
8	6	$ 4,242.72
9	7	$ 4,809.29
10	8	$ 5,451.51
11	9	$ 6,179.49

Excel

x-Values	y_1-Values
3	2912.98
4	3301.97
5	3742.91
6	4242.72
7	4809.29
8	5451.51

Website

Because the balance first exceeds $5,000 at $t = 8$ (the end of year 8), your investment has reached $5,000 during year 8.

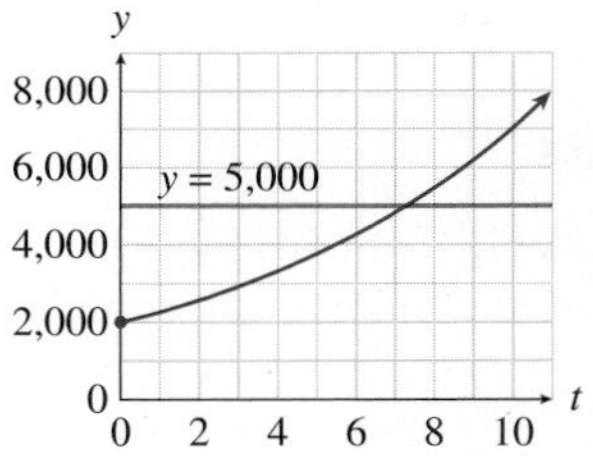

Technology formula:
`2000*1.0105^(12*x)`

Figure 14

c. Figure 14 shows the graph of $A(t) = 2{,}000(1.0105)^{12t}$ together with the horizontal line $y = 5{,}000$. The graphs cross between $t = 7$ and $t = 8$, confirming that year 8 is the first year during which the value of the investment reaches $5,000.

The compound interest examples we saw above are instances of **exponential growth:** a quantity whose magnitude is an increasing exponential function of time. The decay of unstable radioactive isotopes provides instances of **exponential decay:** a quantity whose magnitude is a *decreasing* exponential function of time. For example, carbon 14, an unstable isotope of carbon, decays exponentially to nitrogen. Because carbon 14 decay is extremely slow, it has important applications in the dating of fossils.

EXAMPLE 7 Exponential Decay: Carbon Dating

The amount of carbon 14 remaining in a sample that originally contained A grams is approximately

$$C(t) = A(0.999879)^t,$$

where t is time in years.

a. What percentage of the original amount remains after one year? After two years?

b. Graph the function C for a sample originally containing 50 g of carbon 14, and use your graph to estimate how long, to the nearest 1,000 years, it takes for half the original carbon 14 to decay.

c. A fossilized plant unearthed in an archaeological dig contains 0.50 g of carbon 14 and is known to be 50,000 years old. How much carbon 14 did the plant originally contain?

Solution

Notice that the given model is exponential as it has the form $f(t) = Ab^t$. (See page 51.)

a. At the start of the first year, $t = 0$, so there are

$$C(0) = A(0.999879)^0 = A \text{ grams.}$$

At the end of the first year, $t = 1$, so there are

$$C(1) = A(0.999879)^1 = 0.999879A \text{ grams;}$$

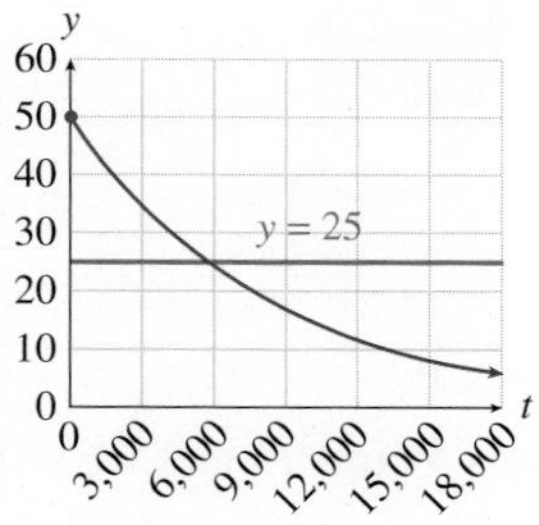

Technology formula:
`50*0.999879^x`

Figure 15

that is, 99.9879% of the original amount remains. After the second year, the amount remaining is

$$C(2) = A(0.999879)^2 \approx 0.999758A \text{ grams},$$

or about 99.9758% of the original sample.

b. For a sample originally containing 50 g of carbon 14, $A = 50$, so $C(t) = 50(0.999879)^t$. Its graph is shown in Figure 15. We have also plotted the line $y = 25$ on the same graph. The graphs intersect at the point where the original sample has decayed to 25 g: about $t = 6{,}000$ years.

c. We are given the following information: $C = 0.50$, $A =$ the unknown, and $t = 50{,}000$. Substituting gives

$$0.50 = A(0.999879)^{50{,}000}.$$

Solving for A gives

$$A = \frac{0.5}{0.999879^{50{,}000}} \approx 212 \text{ grams}.$$

Thus, the plant originally contained 212 g of carbon 14.

Before we go on...

The formula we used for A in Example 7(c) has the form

$$A(t) = \frac{C}{0.999879^t},$$

which gives the original amount of carbon 14 t years ago in terms of the amount C that is left now. A similar formula can be used in finance to find the present value, given the future value. ■

Algebra of Functions

If you look back at some of the functions considered in this section, you will notice that we frequently constructed them by combining simpler or previously constructed functions. For instance:

Quick Example 3 on page 56:	Area = Width × Length: $A(x) = x(50 - x)$
Example 1:	Cost = Variable Cost + Fixed Cost: $C(x) = 1.80x + 2.05$
Quick Example on page 59:	Profit = Revenue − Cost: $P(x) = 10x - (8x + 100)$.

Let us look a little more deeply at each of the above examples:

Area Example: $A(x) =$ Width × Length $= x(50 - x)$:
Think of the width and length as separate functions of x:

$$\text{Width: } W(x) = x; \qquad \text{Length: } L(x) = 50 - x$$

so that

$$A(x) = W(x)L(x). \qquad \text{Area = Width × Length}$$

We say that the area function A is the **product of the functions** W and L, and we write

$$A = WL. \qquad A \text{ is the product of the functions } W \text{ and } L.$$

To calculate $A(x)$, we multiply $W(x)$ by $L(x)$.

Cost Example: $C(x) =$ Variable Cost + Fixed Cost $= 1.80x + 2.05$:
Think of the variable and fixed costs as separate functions of x:

Variable Cost: $V(x) = 1.80x$; Fixed Cost: $F(x) = 2.05$*

* F is called a constant function as its value, 2.05, is the same for every value of x.

so that

$$C(x) = V(x) + F(x). \qquad \text{Cost = Variable Cost + Fixed Cost}$$

We say that the cost function C is the **sum of the functions V and F**, and we write

$$C = V + F. \qquad C \text{ is the sum of the functions } V \text{ and } F.$$

To calculate $C(x)$, we add $V(x)$ to $F(x)$.

Profit Example: $P(x) =$ Revenue − Cost $= 10x - (8x + 100)$:
Think of the revenue and cost as separate functions of x:

Revenue: $R(x) = 10x$; Cost: $C(x) = 8x + 100$

so that

$$P(x) = R(x) - C(x). \qquad \text{Profit = Revenue − Cost}$$

We say that the profit function P is the **difference between the functions R and C**, and we write

$$P = R - C. \qquad P \text{ is the difference of the functions } R \text{ and } C.$$

To calculate $P(x)$, we subtract $C(x)$ from $R(x)$.

Algebra of Functions

If f and g are real-valued functions of the real variable x, then we define their **sum s, difference d, product p,** and **quotient q** as follows:

$s = f + g$ is the function specified by $s(x) = f(x) + g(x)$.
$d = f - g$ is the function specified by $d(x) = f(x) - g(x)$.
$p = fg$ is the function specified by $p(x) = f(x)g(x)$.
$q = \dfrac{f}{g}$ is the function specified by $q(x) = \dfrac{f(x)}{g(x)}$.

Also, if f is as above and c is a constant (real number), then we define the associated **constant multiple m of f** by

$m = cf$ is the function specified by $m(x) = cf(x)$.

Note on Domains

In order for any of the expressions $f(x) + g(x)$, $f(x) - g(x)$, $f(x)g(x)$, or $f(x)/g(x)$ to make sense, x must be simultaneously in the domains of both f and g. Further, for the quotient, the denominator $g(x)$ cannot be zero. Thus, we specify the domains of these functions as follows:

Domain of $f + g$, $f - g$, and fg: All real numbers x simultaneously in the domains of f and g

Domain of f/g: All real numbers x simultaneously in the domains of f and g such that $g(x) \neq 0$

Domain of cf: Same as the domain of f

Quick Examples

1. If $f(x) = x^2 - 1$ and $g(x) = \sqrt{x}$ with domain $[0, +\infty)$, then the sum s of f and g has domain $[0, +\infty)$ and is specified by $s(x) = f(x) + g(x) = x^2 - 1 + \sqrt{x}$.
2. If $f(x) = x^2 - 1$ and $c = 3$, then the associated constant multiple m of f is specified by $m(x) = 3f(x) = 3(x^2 - 1)$.
3. If there are $N = 1{,}000t$ Mars shuttle passengers in year t who pay a total cost of $C = 40{,}000 + 800t$ million dollars, then the cost per passenger is given by the quotient of the two functions,

$$\text{Cost per passenger} = q(t) = \frac{C(t)}{N(t)}$$
$$= \frac{40{,}000 + 800t}{1{,}000t} \text{ million dollars per passenger.}$$

The largest possible domain of C/N is $(0, +\infty)$, as the quotient is not defined if $t = 0$.

1.2 EXERCISES

▼ more advanced ◆ challenging

T indicates exercises that should be solved using technology

Exercises 1–8 are based on the following functions:

$f(x) = x^2 + 1$ *with domain all real numbers*
$g(x) = x - 1$ *with domain all real numbers*
$h(x) = x + 4$ *with domain* $x \geq 10$
$u(x) = \sqrt{x + 10}$ *with domain* $[-10, 0)$
$v(x) = \sqrt{10 - x}$ *with domain* $[0, 10]$

In each exercise, **a.** *write a formula for the indicated function,* **b.** *give its domain, and* **c.** *specify its value at the given point a, if defined.*

1. $s = f + g; a = -3$

2. $d = g - f; a = -1$

3. $p = gu; a = -6$

4. $p = hv; a = 1$

5. $q = \dfrac{v}{g}; a = 1$

6. $q = \dfrac{g}{v}; a = 1$

7. $m = 5f; a = 1$

8. $m = 3u; a = -1$

APPLICATIONS

9. ***Resources*** You now have 200 music files on your hard drive, and this number is increasing by 10 music files each day. Find a mathematical model for this situation. HINT [See Quick Example 1 on page 56.]

10. ***Resources*** The amount of free space left on your hard drive is now 50 gigabytes (GB) and is decreasing by 5 GB/month. Find a mathematical model for this situation.

11. ***Soccer*** My rectangular soccer field site has a length equal to twice its width. Find its area in terms of its length x. HINT [See Quick Example 3 on page 56.]

12. ***Cabbage*** My rectangular cabbage patch has a total area of 100 sq. ft. Find its perimeter in terms of the width x.

13. ***Vegetables*** I want to fence in a square vegetable patch. The fencing for the east and west sides costs \$4 per foot, and the fencing for the north and south sides costs only \$2 per foot. Find the total cost of the fencing as a function of the length of a side x.

14. ***Orchids*** My square orchid garden abuts my house so that the house itself forms the northern boundary. The fencing for the southern boundary costs \$4 per foot, and the fencing for the east and west sides costs \$2 per foot. Find the total cost of the fencing as a function of the length of a side x.

15. ***Study*** You study math 4 hours a day Sunday through Thursday, and take the rest of the week off. Model the number of hours h you study math as a function of the day of the week n (with $n = 1$ being Sunday). HINT [See Quick Example 4 on page 57.]

16. ***Recreation*** You spend 5 hours per day on Saturdays and Sundays watching movies, but only two hours per day during the week. Model the number of hours h you watch movies as a function of the day of the week n (with $n = 1$ being Sunday).

17. ***Cost*** A piano manufacturer has a daily fixed cost of \$1,200 and a marginal cost of \$1,500 per piano. Find the cost $C(x)$ of manufacturing x pianos in one day. Use your function to answer the following questions:

a. On a given day, what is the cost of manufacturing 3 pianos?
b. What is the cost of manufacturing the 3rd piano that day?
c. What is the cost of manufacturing the 11th piano that day?
d. What is the variable cost? What is the fixed cost? What is the marginal cost?
e. Graph C as a function of x. HINT [See Example 1.]

18. ***Cost*** The cost of renting tuxes for the Choral Society's formal is \$20 down, plus \$88 per tux. Express the cost C as a function of x, the number of tuxedos rented. Use your function to answer the following questions.

a. What is the cost of renting 2 tuxes?
b. What is the cost of the 2nd tux?
c. What is the cost of the 4,098th tux?
d. What is the variable cost? What is the fixed cost? What is the marginal cost?
e. Graph C as a function of x.

19. ***Break-Even Analysis*** Your college newspaper, *The Collegiate Investigator*, has fixed production costs of \$70 per edition and marginal printing and distribution costs of 40¢ per copy. *The Collegiate Investigator* sells for 50¢ per copy.

a. Write down the associated cost, revenue, and profit functions. HINT [See Examples 1 and 2.]
b. What profit (or loss) results from the sale of 500 copies of *The Collegiate Investigator*?
c. How many copies should be sold in order to break even?

20. ***Break-Even Analysis*** The Audubon Society at Enormous State University (ESU) is planning its annual fund-raising "Eat-a-thon." The society will charge students 50¢ per serving of pasta. The only expenses the society will incur are the cost of the pasta, estimated at 15¢ per serving, and the \$350 cost of renting the facility for the evening.

a. Write down the associated cost, revenue, and profit functions.
b. How many servings of pasta must the Audubon Society sell in order to break even?
c. What profit (or loss) results from the sale of 1,500 servings of pasta?

21. ***Break-Even Analysis*** Gymnast Clothing manufactures expensive hockey jerseys for sale to college bookstores in runs of up to 200. Its cost (in dollars) for a run of x hockey jerseys is

$$C(x) = 2{,}000 + 10x + 0.2x^2 \quad (0 \le x \le 200).$$

Gymnast Clothing sells the jerseys at \$100 each. Find the revenue and profit functions. How many should Gymnast Clothing manufacture to make a profit? HINT [See Example 2.]

22. ***Break-Even Analysis*** Gymnast Clothing also manufactures expensive soccer cleats for sale to college bookstores in runs of up to 500. Its cost (in dollars) for a run of x pairs of cleats is

$$C(x) = 3{,}000 + 8x + 0.1x^2 \quad (0 \le x \le 500).$$

Gymnast Clothing sells the cleats at \$120 per pair. Find the revenue and profit functions. How many should Gymnast Clothing manufacture to make a profit?

23. ***Break-Even Analysis: School Construction Costs*** The cost, in millions of dollars, of building a two-story high school in New York State was estimated to be

$$C(x) = 1.7 + 0.12x - 0.0001x^2 \quad (20 \le x \le 400),$$

where x is the number of thousands of square feet.[19] Suppose that you are contemplating building a for-profit two-story high school and estimate that your total revenue will be \$0.1 million dollars per thousand square feet. What is the profit function? What size school should you build in order to break even?

24. ***Break-Even Analysis: School Construction Costs*** The cost, in millions of dollars, of building a three-story high school in New York State was estimated to be

$$C(x) = 1.7 + 0.14x - 0.0001x^2 \quad (20 \le x \le 400),$$

where x is the number of thousands of square feet.[20] Suppose that you are contemplating building a for-profit three-story high school and estimate that your total revenue will be \$0.2 million dollars per thousand square feet. What is the profit function? What size school should you build in order to break even?

25. ▼ ***Profit Analysis—Aviation*** The hourly operating cost of a Boeing 747-100, which seats up to 405 passengers, is estimated to be \$5,132.[21] If an airline charges each passenger a fare of \$100 per hour of flight, find the hourly profit P it earns operating a 747-100 as a function of the number of passengers x. (Be sure to specify the domain.) What is the least number of passengers it must carry in order to make a profit? HINT [The cost function is constant (Variable cost = 0).]

26. ▼ ***Profit Analysis—Aviation*** The hourly operating cost of a McDonnell Douglas DC 10-10, which seats up to 295 passengers, is estimated to be \$3,885.[22] If an airline charges each passenger a fare of \$100 per hour of flight, find the hourly profit P it earns operating a DC10-10 as a function of the number of passengers x. (Be sure to specify the domain.) What is the least number of passengers it must carry in order to make a profit? HINT [The cost function is constant (Variable cost = 0).]

27. ▼ ***Break-Even Analysis*** *(based on a question from a CPA exam)* The Oliver Company plans to market a new product. Based on its market studies, Oliver estimates that it can sell up to 5,500 units in 2005. The selling price will be \$2 per unit. Variable costs are estimated to be 40% of total revenue. Fixed costs are estimated to be \$6,000 for 2005. How many units should the company sell to break even?

---

[19] The model is the authors'. Source for data: *Project Labor Agreements and Public Construction Cost in New York State,* Paul Bachman and David Tuerck, Beacon Hill Institute at Suffolk University, April 2006, www.beaconhill.org.

[20] *Ibid.*

[21] In 1992. Source: Air Transportation Association of America.

[22] *Ibid.*

28. ▼ ***Break-Even Analysis*** *(based on a question from a CPA exam)* The Metropolitan Company sells its latest product at a unit price of \$5. Variable costs are estimated to be 30% of the total revenue, while fixed costs amount to \$7,000 per month. How many units should the company sell per month in order to break even, assuming that it can sell up to 5,000 units per month at the planned price?

29. ◆ ***Break-Even Analysis*** *(from a CPA exam)* Given the following notations, write a formula for the break-even sales level.

SP = Selling price per unit
FC = Total fixed cost
VC = Variable cost per unit

30. ◆ ***Break-Even Analysis*** *(based on a question from a CPA exam)* Given the following notation, give a formula for the total fixed cost.

SP = Selling price per unit
VC = Variable cost per unit
BE = Break even sales level in units

31. ◆ ***Break-Even Analysis—Organized Crime*** The organized crime boss and perfume king Butch (Stinky) Rose has daily overheads (bribes to corrupt officials, motel photographers, wages for hit men, explosives, and so on) amounting to \$20,000 per day. On the other hand, he has a substantial income from his counterfeit perfume racket: He buys imitation French perfume (Chanel № 22.5) at \$20 per gram, pays an additional \$30 per 100 grams for transportation, and sells it via his street thugs for \$600 per gram. Specify Stinky's profit function, $P(x)$, where x is the quantity (in grams) of perfume he buys and sells, and use your answer to calculate how much perfume should pass through his hands per day in order that he break even.

32. ◆ ***Break-Even Analysis—Disorganized Crime*** Butch (Stinky) Rose's counterfeit Chanel № 22.5 racket has run into difficulties; it seems that the *authentic* Chanel № 22.5 perfume is selling for less than his counterfeit perfume. However, he has managed to reduce his fixed costs to zero, and his overall costs are now \$400 per gram plus \$30 per gram transportation costs and commission. (The perfume's smell is easily detected by specially trained Chanel Hounds, and this necessitates elaborate packaging measures.) He therefore decides to sell it for \$420 per gram in order to undercut the competition. Specify Stinky's profit function, $P(x)$, where x is the quantity (in grams) of perfume he buys and sells, and use your answer to calculate how much perfume should pass through his hands per day in order that he break even. Interpret your answer.

33. ***Demand for Monorail Service, Las Vegas*** The demand for monorail service in Las Vegas can be approximated by

$$q(p) = 64p^{-0.76} \text{ thousand rides per day} \quad (3 \le p \le 5),$$

where p is the cost per ride in dollars.[23]

a. Graph the demand function.

b. What is the result on demand if the cost per ride is increased from \$3.00 to \$3.50? HINT [See Example 3.]

34. ***Demand for Monorail Service, Mars*** The demand for monorail service on the Utarek monorail, which links the three urbynes (or districts) of Utarek, Mars, can be approximated by

$$q(p) = 30p^{-0.49} \text{ million rides per day} \quad (3 \le p \le 5),$$

where p is the cost per ride in zonars ($\bar{\bar{Z}}$).[24]

a. Graph the demand function.

b. What is the result on demand if the cost per ride is decreased from $\bar{\bar{Z}}$5.00 to $\bar{\bar{Z}}$3.50?

35. ▼ ***Demand: Smart Phones*** The worldwide demand for smart phones may be modeled by

$$q(p) = 0.0009p^2 - 0.63p + 245 \text{ million units sold annually} \quad (50 \le p \le 150),$$

where p is the unit price in dollars.[25]

a. Graph the demand function.

b. Use the demand function to estimate, to the nearest million units, worldwide sales of smart phones if the price is \$60.

c. Extrapolate the demand function to estimate, to the nearest million units, worldwide sales of smart phones if the price is \$20.

d. Model the worldwide annual revenue from the sale of smart phones as a function of unit price, and use your model to estimate, to the nearest billion dollars, worldwide annual revenue when the price is set at \$60. HINT [Revenue = Price × Quantity = $p \cdot q(p)$]

36. ▼ ***Demand: Smart Phones*** (See Exercise 35.) Here is another model for worldwide demand for smart phones:

$$q(p) = 700p^{-0.284} \text{ million units sold annually} \quad (50 \le p \le 150),$$

where p is the unit price in dollars.[26]

a. Graph the demand function.

b. Use the demand function to estimate, to the nearest million units, worldwide sales of smart phones if the price is \$70.

c. Extrapolate the demand function to estimate, to the nearest million units, worldwide sales of smart phones if the price is \$180.

d. Model the worldwide annual revenue from the sale of smart phones as a function of unit price, and use your model to estimate, to the nearest billion dollars, worldwide annual revenue when the price is set at \$70. HINT [Revenue = Price × Quantity = $p \cdot q(p)$]

---

[23]Source: *New York Times,* February 10, 2007, p. A9.

[24]The zonar ($\bar{\bar{Z}}$) is the official currency in the city-state of Utarek, Mars (formerly www.Marsnext.com, a now extinct virtual society).

[25]The model is the authors' based on data available in 2010. Sources for Data: www.businessweek.com, http://techcrunch.com.

[26]*Ibid.*

37. ***Equilibrium Price*** The demand for your hand-made skateboards, in weekly sales, is $q = -3p + 700$ if the selling price is \$$p$. You are prepared to supply $q = 2p - 500$ per week at the price \$$p$. At what price should you sell your skateboards so that there is neither a shortage nor a surplus? HINT [See Quick Example on page 62.]

38. ***Equilibrium Price*** The demand for your factory-made skateboards, in weekly sales, is $q = -5p + 50$ if the selling price is \$$p$. If you are selling them at that price, you can obtain $q = 3p - 30$ per week from the factory. At what price should you sell your skateboards so that there is neither a shortage nor a surplus?

39. ***Equilibrium Price: Cell Phones*** Worldwide quarterly sales of Nokia® cell phones were approximately $q = -p + 156$ million phones when the wholesale price[27] was \$$p$.

a. If Nokia was prepared to supply $q = 4p - 394$ million phones per quarter at a wholesale price of \$$p$, what would have been the equilibrium price?

b. The actual wholesale price was \$105 in the fourth quarter of 2004. Estimate the projected shortage or surplus at that price. HINT [See Quick Example on page 62 and also Example 4.]

40. ***Equilibrium Price: Cell Phones*** Worldwide annual sales of all cell phones were approximately $-10p + 1{,}600$ million phones when the wholesale price[28] was \$$p$.

a. If manufacturers were prepared to supply $q = 14p - 800$ million phones per year at a wholesale price of \$$p$, what would have been the equilibrium price?

b. The actual wholesale price was projected to be \$80 in the fourth quarter of 2008. Estimate the projected shortage or surplus at that price.

41. T ***Equilibrium Price: Las Vegas Monorail Service*** The demand for monorail service in Las Vegas could be approximated by

$$q = 64p^{-0.76} \quad \text{thousand rides per day,}$$

where p was the fare the Las Vegas Monorail Company charges in dollars.[29] Assume the company was prepared to provide service for

$$q = 2.5p + 15.5 \quad \text{thousand rides per day}$$

at a fare of \$$p$.

a. Graph the demand and supply equations, and use your graph to estimate the equilibrium price (to the nearest 50¢).

b. Estimate, to the nearest 10 rides, the shortage or surplus of monorail service at the December 2005 fare of \$5 per ride.

[27]Source: Embedded.com/Company reports December, 2004.

[28]Wholesale price projections are the authors'. Source for sales prediction: I-Stat/NDR December, 2004.

[29]The model is the authors'. Source for data: *New York Times,* February 10, 2007, p. A9.

42. T ***Equilibrium Price: Mars Monorail Service*** The demand for monorail service in the three urbynes (or districts) of Utarek, Mars can be approximated by

$$q = 31p^{-0.49} \text{ million rides per day,}$$

where p is the fare the Utarek Monorail Cooperative charges in zonars (Z̿).[30] Assume the cooperative is prepared to provide service for

$$q = 2.5p + 17.5 \text{ million rides per day}$$

at a fare of Z̿p.

a. Graph the demand and supply equations, and use your graph to estimate the equilibrium price (to the nearest 0.50 zonars).

b. Estimate the shortage or surplus of monorail service at the December 2085 fare of Z̿1 per ride.

43. ▼ ***Toxic Waste Treatment*** The cost of treating waste by removing PCPs goes up rapidly as the quantity of PCPs removed goes up. Here is a possible model:

$$C(q) = 2{,}000 + 100q^2,$$

where q is the reduction in toxicity (in pounds of PCPs removed per day) and $C(q)$ is the daily cost (in dollars) of this reduction.

a. Find the cost of removing 10 pounds of PCPs per day.

b. Government subsidies for toxic waste cleanup amount to

$$S(q) = 500q,$$

where q is as above and $S(q)$ is the daily dollar subsidy. The *net cost* function is given by $N = C - S$. Give a formula for $N(q)$ and interpret your answer.

c. Find $N(20)$ and interpret your answer.

44. ▼ ***Dental Plans*** A company pays for its employees' dental coverage at an annual cost C given by

$$C(q) = 1{,}000 + 100\sqrt{q},$$

where q is the number of employees covered and $C(q)$ is the annual cost in dollars.

a. If the company has 100 employees, find its annual outlay for dental coverage.

b. Assume that the government subsidizes coverage by an annual dollar amount of

$$S(q) = 200q.$$

The *net cost* function is given by $N = C - S$. Give a formula for $N(q)$ and interpret your answer.

c. Find $N(100)$ and interpret your answer.

[30]The official currency of Utarek, Mars. (See the footnote to Exercise 34.)

45. ***Spending on Corrections in the 1990s*** The following table shows the annual spending by all states in the United States on corrections ($t = 0$ represents the year 1990):[31]

Year (t)	0	2	4	6	7
Spending ($ billion)	16	18	22	28	30

a. Which of the following functions best fits the given data? (Warning: None of them fits exactly, but one fits more closely than the others.) HINT [See Example 5.]

(A) $S(t) = -0.2t^2 + t + 16$
(B) $S(t) = 0.2t^2 + t + 16$
(C) $S(t) = t + 16$

b. Use your answer to part (a) to "predict" spending on corrections in 1998, assuming that the trend continued.

46. ***Spending on Corrections in the 1990s*** Repeat Exercise 45, this time choosing from the following functions:

(A) $S(t) = 16 + 2t$
(B) $S(t) = 16 + t + 0.5t^2$
(C) $S(t) = 16 + t - 0.5t^2$

47. ***Soccer Gear*** The East Coast College soccer team is planning to buy new gear for its road trip to California. The cost per shirt depends on the number of shirts the team orders as shown in the following table:

x **(Shirts ordered)**	5	25	40	100	125
***A*(*x*) (Cost/shirt, $)**	22.91	21.81	21.25	21.25	22.31

a. Which of the following functions best models the data?

(A) $A(x) = 0.005x + 20.75$
(B) $A(x) = 0.01x + 20 + \dfrac{25}{x}$
(C) $A(x) = 0.0005x^2 - 0.07x + 23.25$
(D) $A(x) = 25.5(1.08)^{(x-5)}$

b. Graph the model you chose in part (a) for $10 \le x \le 100$. Use your graph to estimate the lowest cost per shirt and the number of shirts the team should order to obtain the lowest price per shirt.

48. ***Hockey Gear*** The South Coast College hockey team wants to purchase wool hats for its road trip to Alaska. The cost per hat depends on the number of hats the team orders as shown in the following table:

x **(Hats ordered)**	5	25	40	100	125
***A*(*x*) (Cost/hat, $)**	25.50	23.50	24.63	30.25	32.70

a. Which of the following functions best models the data?

(A) $A(x) = 0.05x + 20.75$
(B) $A(x) = 0.1x + 20 + \dfrac{25}{x}$
(C) $A(x) = 0.0008x^2 - 0.07x + 23.25$
(D) $A(x) = 25.5(1.08)^{(x-5)}$

b. Graph the model you chose in part (a) with $5 \le x \le 30$. Use your graph to estimate the lowest cost per hat and the number of hats the team should order to obtain the lowest price per hat.

Cost: Hard Drive Storage *Exercises 49 and 50 are based on the following data showing how the approximate retail cost of a gigabyte of hard drive storage has fallen since 2000:*[32]

t **(Year since 2000)**	***c*(*t*) (Cost per Gigabyte ($))**
0	7.5
2	2.5
4	1.2
6	0.6
8	0.2
10	0.1
12	0.06

49. **a.** Graph each of the following models together with the data points above and use your graph to decide which two of the models best fit the data: HINT [See Example 5 and accompanying technology note.]

(A) $c(t) = 6.3(0.67)^t$
(B) $c(t) = 0.093t^2 - 1.6t + 6.7$
(C) $c(t) = 4.75 - 0.50t$
(D) $c(t) = \dfrac{12.8}{t^{1.7} + 1.7}$

b. Of the two models you chose in part (a), which predicts the lower price in 2020? What price does that model predict?

50. **a.** Graph each of the following models together with the data points above and use your graph to decide which three of the models best fit the given data:

(A) $c(t) = \dfrac{15}{1 + 2^t}$
(B) $c(t) = (7.32)0.59^t + 0.10$
(C) $c(t) = 0.00085(t - 9.6)^4$
(D) $c(t) = 7.5 - 0.82t$

b. One of the three best-fit models in part (a) gives an unreasonable prediction for the price in 2020. Which is it, what price does it predict, and why is the prediction unreasonable?

[31] Data are rounded. Source: National Association of State Budget Officers/*New York Times*, February 28, 1999, p. A1.

[32] 2012 price is estimated. Source for data: Historical Notes about the Cost of Hard Drive Storage Space http://ns1758.ca/winch/winchest.html.

51. ***Value of Euro*** The following table shows the approximate value V of one euro in U.S. dollars during three months in 2010. ($t = 1$ represents January, 2010.)[33]

t (Month)	1	5	6
V (Value in \$)	1.42	1.26	1.22

Which of the following kinds of models would best fit the given data? Explain your choice of model. (A, a, b, c, and m are constants.)

(A) Linear: $V(t) = mt + b$
(B) Quadratic: $V(t) = at^2 + bt + c$
(C) Exponential: $V(t) = Ab^t$

52. ***Value of Yen*** The following table shows the approximate value V of one yen in U.S. dollars during three months in 2010. ($t = 1$ represents January, 2010.)[34]

t (Month)	1	4	10
V (Value in \$)	0.0110	0.0107	0.0122

Which of the following kinds of models would best fit the given data? Explain your choice of model. (A, a, b, c, and m are constants.)

(A) Linear: $V(t) = mt + b$
(B) Quadratic: $V(t) = at^2 + bt + c$
(C) Exponential: $V(t) = Ab^t$

53. ***Petrochemical Sales: Mexico*** The following table shows annual petrochemial sales in Mexico by **Pemex**, Mexico's national oil company, for 2005–2010 ($t = 0$ represents 2005):[35]

Year t (Year since 2005)	0	2	3	4
Petrochemical Sales s (Billion metric tons)	3.7	4.0	4.1	4.0

Which of the following kinds of models would best fit the given data? Explain your choice of model. (A, a, b, and c are constants.)

(A) $s(t) = Ab^t$ $(b > 1)$
(B) $s(t) = Ab^t$ $(b < 1)$
(C) $s(t) = at^2 + bt + c$ $(a > 0)$
(D) $s(t) = at^2 + bt + c$ $(a < 0)$

54. ***Petrochemical Production: Mexico*** The following table shows annual petrochemical production in Mexico by **Pemex**, Mexico's national oil company, for 2005–2010 ($t = 0$ represents 2005):[36]

Year t (Year since 2005)	1	3	5
Petrochemical Production p (Billion metric tons)	11.0	12.0	13.3

Which of the following kinds of models would best fit the given data? Explain your choice of model. (A, a, b, c, and m are constants.)

(A) $s(t) = Ab^t$ $(b > 1)$
(B) $s(t) = Ab^t$ $(b < 1)$
(C) $s(t) = mt + b$ $(m > 0)$
(D) $s(t) = at^2 + bt + c$ $(a < 0)$

55. ***Investments*** In November 2010, **E*Trade Financial** was offering only 0.3% interest on its online savings accounts, with interest reinvested monthly.[37] Find the associated exponential model for the value of a \$5,000 deposit after t years. Assuming this rate of return continued for seven years, how much would a deposit of \$5,000 in November 2010 be worth in November 2017? (Answer to the nearest \$1.) HINT [See Quick Example on page 67.]

56. ***Investments*** In November 2010, **ING Direct** was offering 2.4% interest on its Orange Savings Account, with interest reinvested quarterly.[38] Find the associated exponential model for the value of a \$4,000 deposit after t years. Assuming this rate of return continued for eight years, how much would a deposit of \$4,000 in November 2010 be worth in November 2018? (Answer to the nearest \$1.)

57. T ***Investments*** Refer to Exercise 55. In November of which year will an investment of \$5,000 made in November of 2010 first exceed \$5,200? HINT [See Example 6.]

58. T ***Investments*** Refer to Exercise 56. In November of which year will an investment of \$4,000 made in November of 2010 first exceed \$5,200?

59. ***Carbon Dating*** A fossil originally contained 104 grams of carbon 14. Refer to the formula for $C(t)$ in Example 7 and estimate the amount of carbon 14 left in the sample after 10,000 years, 20,000 years, and 30,000 years. HINT [See Example 7.]

[33]Source: www.exchange-rates.org.

[34]*Ibid.*

[35]2010 figure is a projection based on data through May 2010. Source: www.pemex.com (July 2010)

[36]*Ibid.*

[37]Interest rate based on annual percentage yield. Source: https://us.etrade.com, November 2010.

[38]Interest rate based on annual percentage yield. Source: http://home.ingdirect.com, November 2010.

60. ***Carbon Dating*** A fossil contains 4.06 grams of carbon 14. Refer to the formula for $A(t)$ at the end of Example 7, and estimate the amount of carbon 14 in the sample 10,000 years, 20,000 years, and 30,000 years ago.

61. ***Carbon Dating*** A fossil contains 4.06 grams of carbon 14. It is estimated that the fossil originally contained 46 grams of carbon 14. By calculating the amount left after 5,000 years, 10,000 years, . . . , 35,000 years, estimate the age of the sample to the nearest 5,000 years. (Refer to the formula for $C(t)$ in Example 7.)

62. ***Carbon Dating*** A fossil contains 2.8 grams of carbon 14. It is estimated that the fossil originally contained 104 grams of carbon 14. By calculating the amount 5,000 years, 10,000 years, . . . , 35,000 years ago, estimate the age of the sample to the nearest 5,000 years. (Refer to the formula for $C(t)$ at the end of Example 7.)

63. ***Radium Decay*** The amount of radium 226 remaining in a sample that originally contained A grams is approximately

$$C(t) = A(0.999567)^t$$

where t is time in years.

a. Find, to the nearest whole number, the percentage of radium 226 left in an originally pure sample after 1,000 years, 2,000 years, and 3,000 years.
b. Use a graph to estimate, to the nearest 100 years, when one half of a sample of 100 grams will have decayed.

64. ***Iodine Decay*** The amount of iodine 131 remaining in a sample that originally contained A grams is approximately

$$C(t) = A(0.9175)^t$$

where t is time in days.

a. Find, to the nearest whole number, the percentage of iodine 131 left in an originally pure sample after 2 days, 4 days, and 6 days.
b. Use a graph to estimate, to the nearest day, when one half of a sample of 100 g will have decayed.

COMMUNICATION AND REASONING EXERCISES

65. If the population of the lunar station at Clavius has a population of $P = 200 + 30t$, where t is time in years since the station was established, then the population is increasing by ____ per year.

66. My bank balance can be modeled by $B(t) = 5{,}000 - 200t$ dollars, where t is time in days since I opened the account. The balance on my account is ________ by \$200 per day.

67. Classify the following model as analytical or curve fitting, and give a reason for your choice: The price of gold was \$700 on Monday, \$710 on Tuesday, and \$700 on Wednesday. Therefore, the price can be modeled by $p(t) = -10t^2 + 20t + 700$ where t is the day since Monday.

68. Classify the following model as analytical or curve fitting, and give a reason for your choice: The width of a small animated square on my computer screen is currently 10 mm and is growing by 2 mm per second. Therefore, its area can be modeled by $a(t) = (10 + 2t)^2$ square mm where t is time in seconds.

69. Fill in the missing information for the following *analytical model* (answers may vary): ____________. Therefore, the cost of downloading a movie can be modeled by $c(t) = 4 - 0.2t$, where t is time in months since January.

70. Repeat Exercise 69, but this time regard the given model as a *curve-fitting model*.

71. Fill in the blanks: In a linear cost function, the ______ cost is x times the ______ cost.

72. Complete the following sentence: In a linear cost function, the marginal cost is the ____________.

73. ▼ We said on page 61 that the demand for a commodity generally goes down as the price goes up. Assume that the demand for a certain commodity goes up as the price goes up. Is it still possible for there to be an equilibrium price? Explain with the aid of a demand and supply graph.

74. ▼ What would happen to the price of a certain commodity if the demand was always greater than the supply? Illustrate with a demand and supply graph.

75. You have a set of data points showing the sales of videos on your Web site versus time that are closely approximated by two different mathematical models. Give one criterion that would lead you to choose one over the other. (Answers may vary.)

76. Would it ever be reasonable to use a quadratic model $s(t) = at^2 + bt + c$ to predict long-term sales if a is negative? Explain.

77. If f and g are functions with $f(x) \geq g(x)$ for every x, what can you say about the values of the function $f - g$?

78. If f and g are functions with $f(x) > g(x) > 0$ for every x, what can you say about the values of the function $\frac{f}{g}$?

79. If f is measured in books, and g is measured in people, what are the units of measurement of the function $\frac{f}{g}$?

80. If f and g are linear functions, then what can you say about $f - g$?

1.3 Linear Functions and Models

Linear functions are among the simplest functions and are perhaps the most useful of all mathematical functions.

Linear Function

A **linear function** is one that can be written in the form

		Quick Example
$f(x) = mx + b$	Function form	$f(x) = 3x - 1$
or		
$y = mx + b$	Equation form	$y = 3x - 1$

where m and b are fixed numbers. (The names m and b are traditional.*)

* Actually, c is sometimes used instead of b. As for m, there has even been some research into the question of its origin, but no one knows exactly why the letter m is used.

Linear Functions from the Numerical and Graphical Point of View

The following table shows values of $y = 3x - 1$ ($m = 3, b = -1$) for some values of x:

x	−4	−3	−2	−1	0	1	2	3	4
y	−13	−10	−7	−4	−1	2	5	8	11

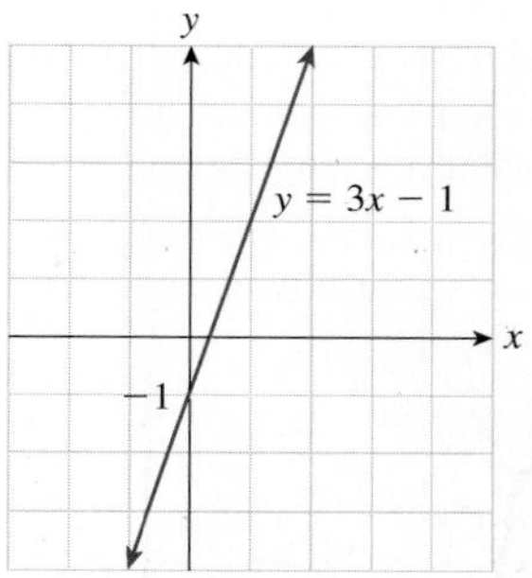

Figure 16

Its graph is shown in Figure 16.

Looking first at the table, notice that setting $x = 0$ gives $y = -1$, the value of b.

Numerically, b is the value of y when $x = 0$.

On the graph, the corresponding point $(0, -1)$ is the point where the graph crosses the y-axis, and we say that $b = -1$ is the **y-intercept** of the graph (Figure 17).

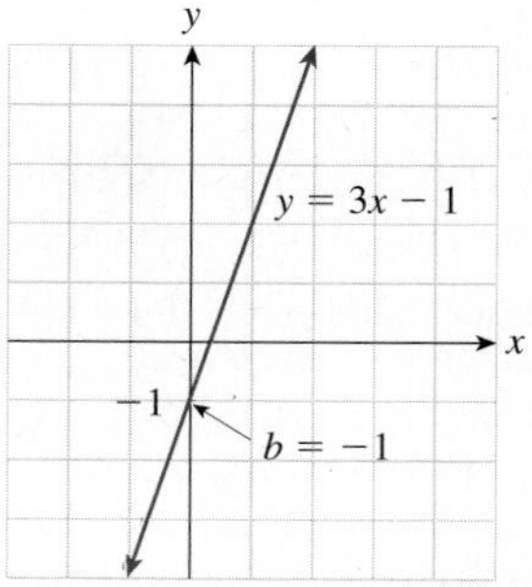

y-intercept $= b = -1$
Graphically, b is the y-intercept of the graph.

Figure 17

What about m? Looking once again at the table, notice that y increases by $m = 3$ units for every increase of 1 unit in x. This is caused by the term $3x$ in the formula: for every increase of 1 in x we get an increase of $3 \times 1 = 3$ in y.

Numerically, y increases by m units for every 1-unit increase of x.

Likewise, for every increase of 2 in x we get an increase of $3 \times 2 = 6$ in y. In general, if x increases by some amount, y will increase by three times that amount. We write:

$$\text{Change in } y = 3 \times \text{Change in } x.$$

The Change in a Quantity: Delta Notation

If a quantity q changes from q_1 to q_2, the **change in q** is just the difference:

$$\text{Change in } q = \text{Second value} - \text{First value}$$
$$= q_2 - q_1.$$

Mathematicians traditionally use Δ (delta, the Greek equivalent of the Roman letter D) to stand for change, and write the change in q as Δq.

$$\Delta q = \text{Change in } q = q_2 - q_1$$

Quick Examples

1. If x is changed from 1 to 3, we write

$$\Delta x = \text{Second value} - \text{First value} = 3 - 1 = 2.$$

2. Looking at our linear function, we see that, when x changes from 1 to 3, y changes from 2 to 8. So,

$$\Delta y = \text{Second value} - \text{First value} = 8 - 2 = 6.$$

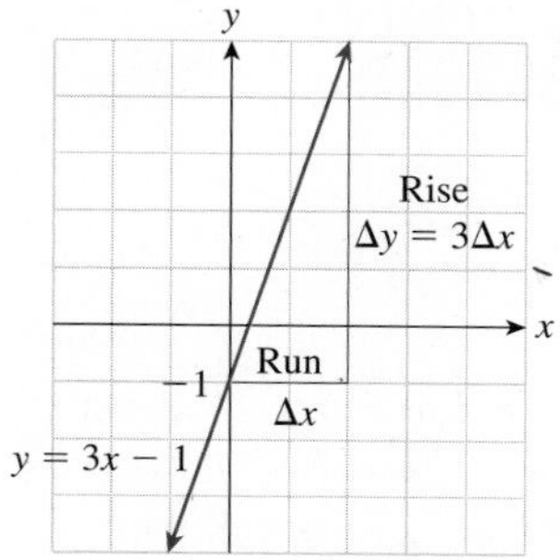

Using delta notation, we can now write, for our linear function,

$$\Delta y = 3\Delta x \qquad \text{Change in } y = 3 \times \text{Change in } x.$$

or

$$\frac{\Delta y}{\Delta x} = 3.$$

Because the value of y increases by exactly 3 units for every increase of 1 unit in x, the graph is a straight line rising by 3 units for every 1 unit we go to the right. We say that we have a **rise** of 3 units for each **run** of 1 unit. Because the value of y changes by $\Delta y = 3\Delta x$ units for every change of Δx units in x, in general we have a rise of $\Delta y = 3\Delta x$ units for each run of Δx units (Figure 18). Thus, we have a rise of 6 for a run of 2, a rise of 9 for a run of 3, and so on. So, $m = 3$ is a measure of the steepness of the line; we call m the **slope of the line**:

$$\text{Slope} = m = \frac{\Delta y}{\Delta x} = \frac{\text{Rise}}{\text{Run}}.$$

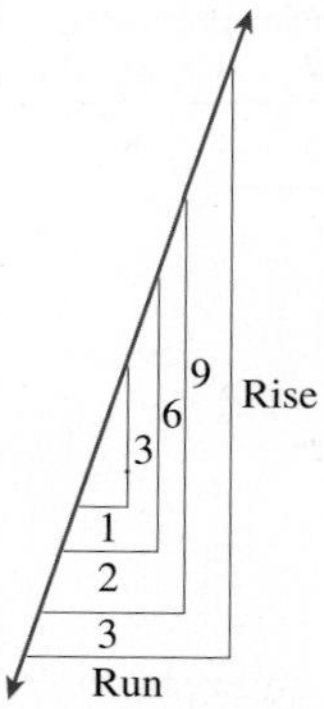

Slope $= m = 3$
Graphically, m is the slope of the graph.

Figure 18

In general (replace the number 3 by a general number m), we can say the following.

The Roles of m and b in the Linear Function $f(x) = mx + b$

Role of m

Numerically If $y = mx + b$, then y changes by m units for every 1-unit change in x. A change of Δx units in x results in a change of $\Delta y = m\Delta x$ units in y. Thus,

$$m = \frac{\Delta y}{\Delta x} = \frac{\text{Change in } y}{\text{Change in } x}.$$

Graphically m is the slope of the line $y = mx + b$:

$$m = \frac{\Delta y}{\Delta x} = \frac{\text{Rise}}{\text{Run}} = \text{Slope}.$$

For positive m, the graph rises m units for every 1-unit move to the right, and rises $\Delta y = m\Delta x$ units for every Δx units moved to the right. For negative m, the graph drops $|m|$ units for every 1-unit move to the right, and drops $|m|\Delta x$ units for every Δx units moved to the right.

Graph of $y = mx + b$

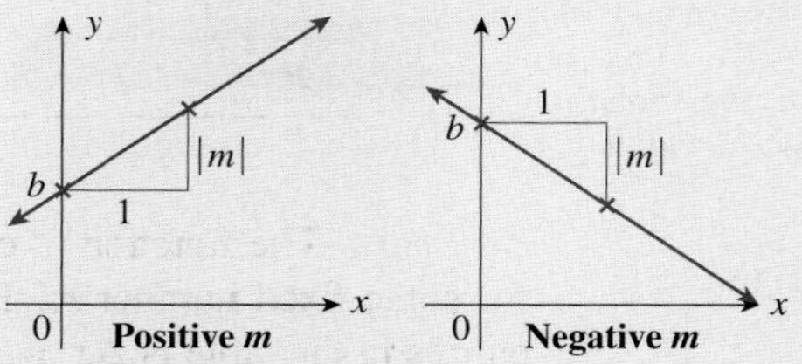

Role of *b*

Numerically When $x = 0$, $y = b$.

Graphically b is the y-intercept of the line $y = mx + b$.

Quick Examples

1. $f(x) = 2x + 1$ has slope $m = 2$ and y-intercept $b = 1$. To sketch the graph, we start at the y-intercept $b = 1$ on the y-axis, and then move 1 unit to the right and up $m = 2$ units to arrive at a second point on the graph. Now connect the two points to obtain the graph on the left.

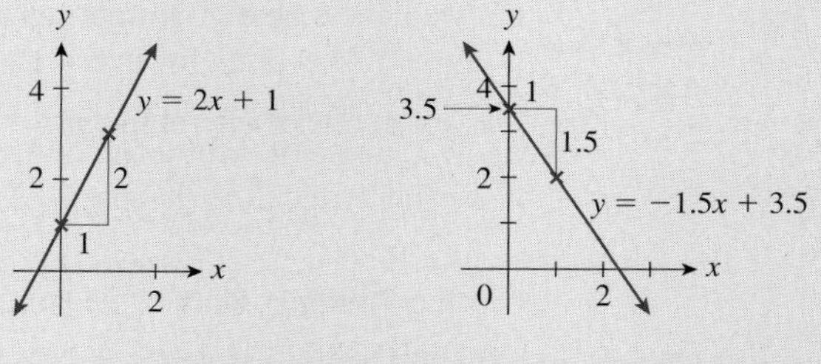

2. The line $y = -1.5x + 3.5$ has slope $m = -1.5$ and y-intercept $b = 3.5$. Because the slope is negative, the graph (above right) goes *down* 1.5 units for every 1 unit it moves to the right.

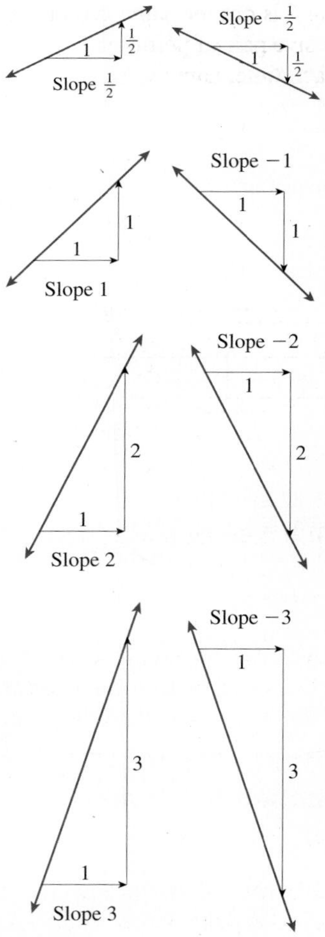

Figure 19

It helps to be able to picture what different slopes look like, as in Figure 19. Notice that the larger the absolute value of the slope, the steeper is the line.

using Technology

See the Technology Guides at the end of the chapter for detailed instructions on how to obtain a table with the successive quotients $m = \Delta y/\Delta x$ for the functions f and g in Example 1 using a TI-83/84 Plus or Excel. These tables show at a glance that f is not linear. Here is an outline:

TI-83/84 Plus

STAT EDIT; Enter values of x and $f(x)$ in lists L_1 and L_2.
Highlight the heading L_3 then enter the following formula (including the quotes)
"ΔList(L2)/ΔList(L1)"
[More details on page 116.]

Spreadsheet

Enter headings x, $f(x)$, Df/Dx in cells A1–C1, and the corresponding values from one of the tables in cells A2–B8. Enter
=(B3-B2)/(A3-A2)
in cell C2, and copy down through C8.
[More details on page 122.]

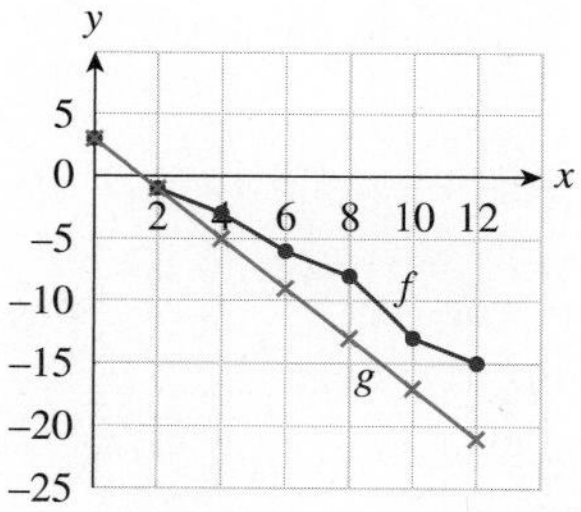

Figure 20

EXAMPLE 1 Recognizing Linear Data Numerically and Graphically

Which of the following two tables gives the values of a linear function? What is the formula for that function?

x	0	2	4	6	8	10	12
$f(x)$	3	−1	−3	−6	−8	−13	−15

x	0	2	4	6	8	10	12
$g(x)$	3	−1	−5	−9	−13	−17	−21

Solution The function f cannot be linear: If it were, we would have $\Delta f = m\Delta x$ for some fixed number m. However, although the change in x between successive entries in the table is $\Delta x = 2$ each time, the change in f is not the same each time. Thus, the ratio $\Delta f/\Delta x$ is not the same for every successive pair of points.

On the other hand, the ratio $\Delta g/\Delta x$ is the same each time, namely,

$$\frac{\Delta g}{\Delta x} = \frac{-4}{2} = -2$$

as we see in the following table:

Δx		$2-0=2$	$4-2=2$	$6-4=2$	$8-6=2$	$10-8=2$	$12-10=2$
x	0	2	4	6	8	10	12
$g(x)$	3	−1	−5	−9	−13	−17	−21
Δg		$-1-3 = -4$	$-5-(-1) = -4$	$-9-(-5) = -4$	$-13-(-9) = -4$	$-17-(-13) = -4$	$-21-(-17) = -4$

Thus, g is linear with slope $m = -2$. By the table, $g(0) = 3$, hence $b = 3$. Thus,

$$g(x) = -2x + 3.$$ Check that this formula gives the values in the table.

If you graph the points in the tables defining f and g above, it becomes easy to see that g is linear and f is not; the points of g lie on a straight line (with slope −2), whereas the points of f do not lie on a straight line (Figure 20).

Finding a Linear Equation from Data

If we happen to know the slope and y-intercept of a line, writing down its equation is straightforward. For example, if we know that the slope is 3 and the y-intercept is −1, then the equation is $y = 3x - 1$. Sadly, the information we are given is seldom so convenient. For instance, we may know the slope and a point other than the y-intercept, two points on the line, or other information. We therefore need to know how to use the information we are given to obtain the slope and the intercept.

Computing the Slope

We can always determine the slope of a line if we are given two (or more) points on the line, because any two points—say (x_1, y_1) and (x_2, y_2)—determine the line, and hence its slope. To compute the slope when given two points, recall the formula

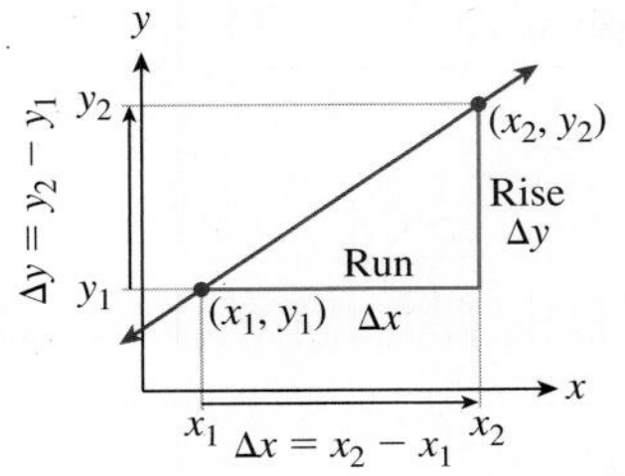

Figure 21

$$\text{Slope} = m = \frac{\text{Rise}}{\text{Run}} = \frac{\Delta y}{\Delta x}.$$

To find its slope, we need a run Δx and corresponding rise Δy. In Figure 21, we see that we can use $\Delta x = x_2 - x_1$, the change in the x-coordinate from the first point to the second, as our run, and $\Delta y = y_2 - y_1$, the change in the y-coordinate, as our rise. The resulting formula for computing the slope is given in the box.

Computing the Slope of a Line

We can compute the slope m of the line through the points (x_1, y_1) and (x_2, y_2) using

$$m = \frac{\Delta y}{\Delta x} = \frac{y_2 - y_1}{x_2 - x_1}.$$

Quick Examples

1. The slope of the line through $(x_1, y_1) = (1, 3)$ and $(x_2, y_2) = (5, 11)$ is

$$m = \frac{\Delta y}{\Delta x} = \frac{y_2 - y_1}{x_2 - x_1} = \frac{11 - 3}{5 - 1} = \frac{8}{4} = 2.$$

Notice that we can use the points in the reverse order: If we take $(x_1, y_1) = (5, 11)$ and $(x_2, y_2) = (1, 3)$, we obtain the same answer:

$$m = \frac{\Delta y}{\Delta x} = \frac{y_2 - y_1}{x_2 - x_1} = \frac{3 - 11}{1 - 5} = \frac{-8}{-4} = 2.$$

2. The slope of the line through $(x_1, y_1) = (1, 2)$ and $(x_2, y_2) = (2, 1)$ is

$$m = \frac{\Delta y}{\Delta x} = \frac{y_2 - y_1}{x_2 - x_1} = \frac{1 - 2}{2 - 1} = \frac{-1}{1} = -1.$$

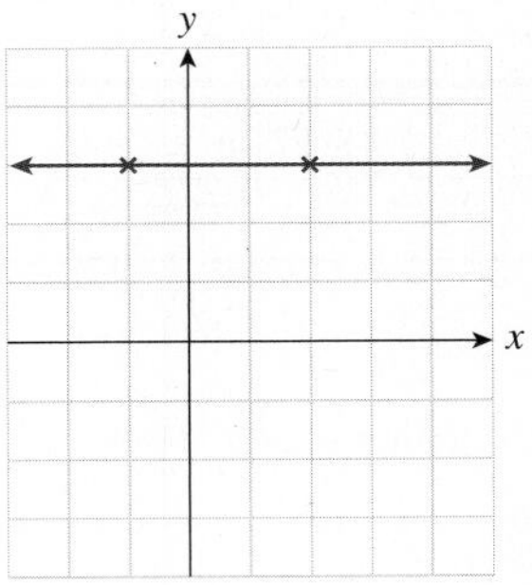

Figure 22

3. The slope of the line through $(2, 3)$ and $(-1, 3)$ is

$$m = \frac{\Delta y}{\Delta x} = \frac{y_2 - y_1}{x_2 - x_1} = \frac{3 - 3}{-1 - 2} = \frac{0}{-3} = 0.$$

A line of slope 0 has zero rise, so is a *horizontal* line, as shown in Figure 22.

4. The line through $(3, 2)$ and $(3, -1)$ has slope

$$m = \frac{\Delta y}{\Delta x} = \frac{y_2 - y_1}{x_2 - x_1} = \frac{-1 - 2}{3 - 3} = \frac{-3}{0},$$

which is undefined. The line passing through these points is *vertical*, as shown in Figure 23.

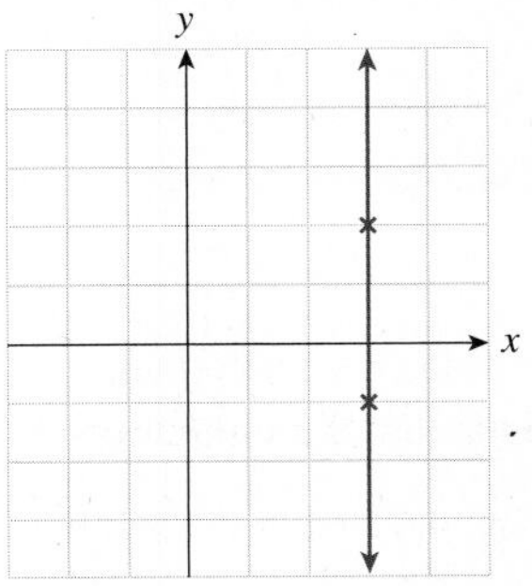

Vertical lines have undefined slope.

Figure 23

Computing the y-Intercept

Once we know the slope m of a line, and also the coordinates of a point (x_1, y_1), then we can calculate its y-intercept b as follows: The equation of the line must be

$$y = mx + b,$$

where b is as yet unknown. To determine b we use the fact that the line must pass through the point (x_1, y_1), so that (x_1, y_1) satisfies the equation $y = mx + b$. In other words,

$$y_1 = mx_1 + b.$$

Solving for b gives

$$b = y_1 - mx_1.$$

In summary:

Computing the y-Intercept of a Line

The y-intercept of the line passing through (x_1, y_1) with slope m is

$$b = y_1 - mx_1.$$

Quick Example

The line through (2, 3) with slope 4 has

$$b = y_1 - mx_1 = 3 - (4)(2) = -5.$$

Its equation is therefore

$$y = mx + b = 4x - 5.$$

EXAMPLE 2 Finding Linear Equations

Find equations for the following straight lines.

a. Through the points (1, 2) and (3, −1)

b. Through (2, −2) and parallel to the line $3x + 4y = 5$

c. Horizontal and through (−9, 5)

d. Vertical and through (−9, 5)

Solution

a. To write down the equation of the line, we need the slope m and the y-intercept b.

- ***Slope*** Because we are given two points on the line, we can use the slope formula:

$$m = \frac{y_2 - y_1}{x_2 - x_1} = \frac{-1 - 2}{3 - 1} = -\frac{3}{2}.$$

using Technology

See the Technology Guides at the end of the chapter for detailed instructions on how to obtain the slope and intercept in Example 2(a) using a TI-83/84 Plus or a spreadsheet. Here is an outline:

TI-83/84 Plus

STAT EDIT; Enter values of x and y in lists L_1 and L_2.
Slope: Home screen
`(L2(2)-L2(1))/(L1(2)-L1(1))→M`
Intercept: Home screen
`L2(1)-M*L1(1)`
[More details on page 117.]

Spreadsheet

Enter headings x, y, m, b, in cells A1–D1, and the values (x, y) in cells A2–B3. Enter
`=(B3-B2)/(A3-A2)`
in cell C2, and
`=B2-C2*A2`
in cell D2.
[More details on page 122.]

- ***Intercept*** We now have the slope of the line, $m = -3/2$, and also a point—we have two to choose from, so let us choose $(x_1, y_1) = (1, 2)$. We can now use the formula for the y-intercept:

$$b = y_1 - mx_1 = 2 - \left(-\frac{3}{2}\right)(1) = \frac{7}{2}.$$

Thus, the equation of the line is

$$y = -\frac{3}{2}x + \frac{7}{2}. \qquad y = mx + b$$

b. Proceeding as before,

- ***Slope*** We are not given two points on the line, but we are given a parallel line. We use the fact that *parallel lines have the same slope.* (Why?) We can find the slope of $3x + 4y = 5$ by solving for y and then looking at the coefficient of x:

$$y = -\frac{3}{4}x + \frac{5}{4} \qquad \text{To find the slope, solve for } y.$$

so the slope is $-3/4$.

- ***Intercept*** We now have the slope of the line, $m = -3/4$, and also a point $(x_1, y_1) = (2, -2)$. We can now use the formula for the y-intercept:

$$b = y_1 - mx_1 = -2 - \left(-\frac{3}{4}\right)(2) = -\frac{1}{2}.$$

Thus, the equation of the line is

$$y = -\frac{3}{4}x - \frac{1}{2}. \qquad y = mx + b$$

c. We are given a point: $(-9, 5)$. Furthermore, we are told that the line is horizontal, which tells us that the slope is $m = 0$. Therefore, all that remains is the calculation of the y-intercept:

$$b = y_1 - mx_1 = 5 - (0)(-9) = 5$$

so the equation of the line is

$$y = 5. \qquad y = mx + b$$

d. We are given a point: $(-9, 5)$. This time, we are told that the line is vertical, which means that the slope is undefined. Thus, we can't express the equation of the line in the form $y = mx + b$. (This formula makes sense only when the slope m of the line is defined.) What can we do? Well, here are some points on the desired line:

$$(-9, 1), (-9, 2), (-9, 3), \ldots$$

so $x = -9$ and $y = \textit{anything}$. If we simply say that $x = -9$, then these points are all solutions, so the equation is $x = -9$.

Applications: Linear Models

Using linear functions to describe or approximate relationships in the real world is called **linear modeling**.

Recall from Section 1.2 that a **cost function** specifies the cost C as a function of the number of items x.

EXAMPLE 3 Linear Cost Function from Data

The manager of the FrozenAir Refrigerator factory notices that on Monday it cost the company a total of \$25,000 to build 30 refrigerators and on Tuesday it cost \$30,000 to build 40 refrigerators. Find a linear cost function based on this information. What is the daily fixed cost, and what is the marginal cost?

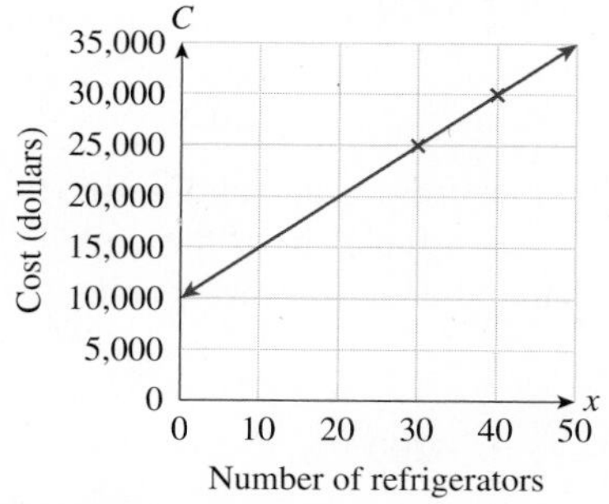

Figure 24

Solution We are seeking the cost C as a linear function of x, the number of refrigerators sold:

$$C = mx + b.$$

We are told that $C = 25{,}000$ when $x = 30$, and this amounts to being told that (30, 25,000) is a point on the graph of the cost function. Similarly, (40, 30,000) is another point on the line (Figure 24).

We can use the two points on the line to construct the linear cost equation:

- ***Slope*** $m = \dfrac{C_2 - C_1}{x_2 - x_1} = \dfrac{30{,}000 - 25{,}000}{40 - 30} = 500$ — C plays the role of y.
- ***Intercept*** $b = C_1 - mx_1 = 25{,}000 - (500)(30) = 10{,}000.$ — We used the point $(x_1, C_1) = (30, 25{,}000)$.

The linear cost function is therefore

$$C(x) = 500x + 10{,}000.$$

Because $m = 500$ and $b = 10{,}000$ the factory's fixed cost is \$10,000 each day, and its marginal cost is \$500 per refrigerator. (See page 59 in Section 1.2.) These are illustrated in Figure 25.

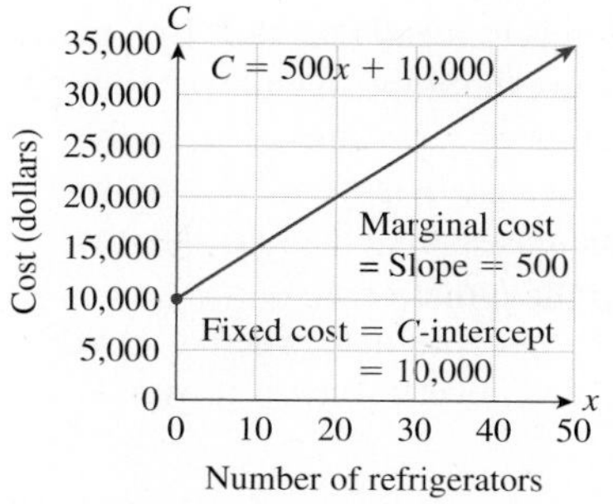

Figure 25

Before we go on... Recall that, in general, the slope m measures the number of units of change in y per 1-unit change in x, so it is measured in units of y per unit of x:

Units of Slope = Units of y per unit of x.

In Example 3, y is the cost C, measured in dollars, and x is the number of items, measured in refrigerators. Hence,

Units of Slope = Units of y per Unit of x = Dollars per refrigerator.

The y-intercept b, being a value of y, is measured in the same units as y. In Example 3, b is measured in dollars. ■

using Technology

To obtain the cost equation for Example 3 with technology, apply the Technology note for Example 2(a) to the given points (30, 25,000) and (40, 30,000) on the graph of the cost equation.

In Section 1.2 we saw that a **demand function** specifies the demand q as a function of the price p per item.

y-25 = 5(x-9)
y -25 = 5x -45
+45 +45
y+20 = 5x
5

EXAMPLE 4 Linear Demand Function from Data

You run a small supermarket and must determine how much to charge for Hot'n'Spicy brand baked beans. The following chart shows weekly sales figures (the demand) for Hot'n'Spicy at two different prices.

Price/Can	\$0.50	\$0.75
Demand (cans sold/week)	400	350

a. Model these data with a linear demand function. (See Example 4 in Section 1.2.)

b. How do we interpret the slope and q-intercept of the demand function?

Solution

a. Recall that a demand equation—or demand function—expresses demand q (in this case, the number of cans of beans sold per week) as a function of the unit price p (in this case, price per can). We model the demand using the two points we are given: (0.50, 400) and (0.75, 350).

$$\textit{Slope:} \quad m = \frac{q_2 - q_1}{p_2 - p_1} = \frac{350 - 400}{0.75 - 0.50} = \frac{-50}{0.25} = -200$$

$$\textit{Intercept:} \quad b = q_1 - mp_1 = 400 - (-200)(0.50) = 500$$

So, the demand equation is

$$q = -200p + 500. \qquad q = mp + b$$

using Technology

To obtain the demand equation for Example 4 with technology, apply the Technology note for Example 2(a) to the given points (0.50, 400) and (0.75, 350) on the graph of the demand equation.

b. The key to interpreting the slope in a demand equation is to recall (see the "Before we go on" note at the end of Example 3) that we measure the slope in *units of y per unit of x*. Here, $m = -200$, and the units of m are units of q per unit of p, or the number of cans sold per dollar change in the price. Because m is negative, we see that the number of cans sold decreases as the price increases. We conclude that the weekly sales will drop by 200 cans per \$1 increase in the price.

To interpret the q-intercept, recall that it gives the q-coordinate when $p = 0$. Hence it is the number of cans the supermarket can "sell" every week if it were to give them away.*

* Does this seem realistic? Demand is not always unlimited if items were given away. For instance, campus newspapers are sometimes given away, and yet piles of them are often left untaken. Also see the "Before we go on" discussion at the end of this example.

➡ Before we go on...

Q: *Just how reliable is the linear model used in Example 4?*

A: The *actual* demand graph could in principle be obtained by tabulating demand figures for a large number of different prices. If the resulting points were plotted on the *pq* plane, they would probably suggest a curve and not a straight line. However, if you looked at a small enough portion of any curve, you could closely *approximate* it by a straight line. In other words, *over a small range of values of p, a linear model is accurate*. Linear models of real-world situations are generally reliable only for small ranges of the variables. (This point will come up again in some of the exercises.)

■

The next example illustrates modeling change over time t with a linear function of t.

EXAMPLE 5 Modeling Change Over Time: Growth of Sales

The worldwide market for portable navigation devices was expected to grow from 50 million units in 2007 to around 530 million units in 2015.[39]

[39]Sales were expected to grow to more than 500 million in 2015 according to a January 2008 press release by Telematics Research Group. Source: www.telematicsresearch.com.

a. Use this information to model annual worldwide sales of portable navigation devices as a linear function of time t in years since 2007. What is the significance of the slope?

b. Use the model to predict when annual sales of mobile navigation devices will reach 440 million units.

Solution

a. Since we are interested in worldwide sales s of portable navigation devices as a function of time, we take time t to be the independent coordinate (playing the role of x) and the annual sales s, in million of units, to be the dependent coordinate (in the role of y). Notice that 2007 corresponds to $t = 0$ and 2015 corresponds to $t = 8$, so we are given the coordinates of two points on the graph of sales s as a function of time t: (0, 50) and (8, 530). We model the sales using these two points:

$$m = \frac{s_2 - s_1}{t_2 - t_1} = \frac{530 - 50}{8 - 0} = \frac{480}{8} = 60$$

$$b = s_1 - mt_1 = 50 - (60)(0) = 50$$

So, $s = 60t + 50$ million units. $\quad s = mt + b$

The slope m is measured in units of s per unit of t; that is, millions of devices per year, and is thus the *rate of change of annual sales*. To say that $m = 60$ is to say that annual sales are increasing at a rate of 60 million devices per year.

b. Our model of annual sales as a function of time is

$$s = 60t + 50 \text{ million units.}$$

Annual sales of mobile portable devices will reach 440 million when $s = 440$, or

$$440 = 60t + 50$$

Solving for t,

$$60t = 440 - 50 = 390$$

$$t = \frac{390}{60} = 6.5 \text{ years},$$

which is midway through 2013. Thus annual sales are expected to reach 440 million midway through 2013.

using Technology

To use technology to obtain s as a function of t in Example 5, apply the Technology note for Example 2(a) to the points (0, 50) and (8, 530) on its graph.

EXAMPLE 6 Velocity

You are driving down the Ohio Turnpike, watching the mileage markers to stay awake. Measuring time in hours after you see the 20-mile marker, you see the following markers each half hour:

Time (h)	0	0.5	1	1.5	2
Marker (mi)	20	47	74	101	128

Find your location s as a function of t, the number of hours you have been driving. (The number s is also called your **position** or **displacement**.)

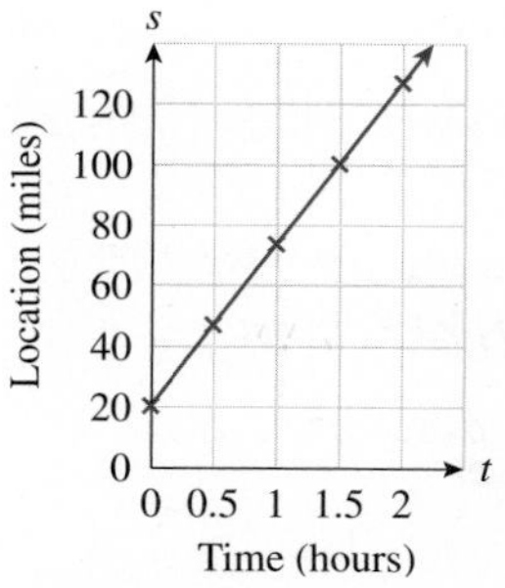

Figure 26

Solution

If we plot the location s versus the time t, the five markers listed give us the graph in Figure 26. These points appear to lie along a straight line. We can verify this by calculating how far you traveled in each half hour. In the first half hour, you traveled $47 - 20 = 27$ miles. In the second half hour you traveled $74 - 47 = 27$ miles also. In fact, you traveled exactly 27 miles each half hour. The points we plotted lie on a straight line that rises 27 units for every 0.5 unit we go to the right, for a slope of $27/0.5 = 54$.

To get the equation of that line, notice that we have the s-intercept, which is the starting marker of 20. Thus, the equation of s as a function of time t is

$$s(t) = 54t + 20.$$ We used s in place of y and t in place of x.

using Technology

To use technology to obtain s as a function of t in Example 6, apply the Technology note for Example 2(a) to the points (0, 20) and (1, 74) on its graph.

Notice the significance of the slope: For every hour you travel, you drive a distance of 54 miles. In other words, you are traveling at a constant velocity of 54 mph. We have uncovered a very important principle:

In the graph of displacement versus time, velocity is given by the slope.

Linear Change over Time

If a quantity q is a linear function of time t,

$$q = mt + b,$$

then the slope m measures the **rate of change** of q, and b is the quantity at time $t = 0$, the **initial quantity**. If q represents the position of a moving object, then the rate of change is also called the **velocity**.

Units of *m* and *b*

The units of measurement of m are units of q per unit of time; for instance, if q is income in dollars and t is time in years, then the rate of change m is measured in dollars per year.

The units of b are units of q; for instance, if q is income in dollars and t is time in years, then b is measured in dollars.

Quick Example

If the accumulated revenue from sales of your video game software is given by $R = 2{,}000t + 500$ dollars, where t is time in years from now, then you have earned \$500 in revenue so far, and the accumulated revenue is increasing at a rate of \$2,000 per year.

Examples 3–6 share the following common theme.

General Linear Models

If $y = mx + b$ is a linear model of changing quantities x and y, then the slope m is the rate at which y is increasing per unit increase in x, and the y-intercept b is the value of y that corresponds to $x = 0$.

Units of *m* and *b*

The slope m is measured in units of y per unit of x, and the intercept b is measured in units of y.

Quick Example

If the number n of spectators at a soccer game is related to the number g of goals your team has scored so far by the equation $n = 20g + 4$, then you can expect 4 spectators if no goals have been scored and 20 additional spectators per additional goal scored.

FAQs

What to Use as x and y, and How to Interpret a Linear Model

Q: *In a problem where I must find a linear relationship between two quantities, which quantity do I use as x and which do I use as y?*

A: The key is to decide which of the two quantities is the independent variable, and which is the dependent variable. Then use the independent variable as x and the dependent variable as y. In other words, *y depends on x.*

Here are examples of phrases that convey this information, usually of the form *Find y [dependent variable] in terms of x [independent variable]:*

- Find the cost in terms of the number of items. y = Cost, x = # Items
- How does color depend on wavelength? y = Color, x = Wavelength

If no information is conveyed about which variable is intended to be independent, then you can use whichever is convenient.

Q: *How do I interpret a general linear model $y = mx + b$?*

A: The key to interpreting a linear model is to remember the units we use to measure m and b:

The slope m is measured in units of y per unit of x; the intercept b is measured in units of y.

For instance, if $y = 4.3x + 8.1$ and you know that x is measured in feet and y in kilograms, then you can already say, "y is 8.1 kilograms when $x = 0$ feet, and increases at a rate of 4.3 kilograms per foot" without knowing anything more about the situation!

1.3 EXERCISES

▼ more advanced ◆ challenging

T indicates exercises that should be solved using technology

In Exercises 1–6, a table of values for a linear function is given. Fill in the missing value and calculate m in each case.

1.

x	−1	0	1
y	5	8	

2.

x	−1	0	1
y	−1	−3	

3.

x	2	3	5
y	−1	−2	

4.

x	2	4	5
y	−1	−2	

5.

x	-2	0	2
y	4		10

6.

x	0	3	6
y	-1		-5

In Exercises 7–10, first find f(0), if not supplied, and then find the equation of the given linear function.

7.

x	-2	0	2	4
$f(x)$	-1	-2	-3	-4

8.

x	-6	-3	0	3
$f(x)$	1	2	3	4

9.

x	-4	-3	-2	-1
$f(x)$	-1	-2	-3	-4

10.

x	1	2	3	4
$f(x)$	4	6	8	10

In each of Exercises 11–14, decide which of the two given functions is linear and find its equation. HINT [See Example 1.]

11.

x	0	1	2	3	4
$f(x)$	6	10	14	18	22
$g(x)$	8	10	12	16	22

12.

x	-10	0	10	20	30
$f(x)$	-1.5	0	1.5	2.5	3.5
$g(x)$	-9	-4	1	6	11

13.

x	0	3	6	10	15
$f(x)$	0	3	5	7	9
$g(x)$	-1	5	11	19	29

14.

x	0	3	5	6	9
$f(x)$	2	6	9	12	15
$g(x)$	-1	8	14	17	26

In Exercises 15–24, find the slope of the given line, if it is defined.

15. $y = -\frac{3}{2}x - 4$

16. $y = \frac{2x}{3} + 4$

17. $y = \frac{x+1}{6}$

18. $y = -\frac{2x-1}{3}$

19. $3x + 1 = 0$

20. $8x - 2y = 1$

21. $3y + 1 = 0$

22. $2x + 3 = 0$

23. $4x + 3y = 7$

24. $2y + 3 = 0$

In Exercises 25–38, graph the given equation. HINT [See Quick Examples on page 80.]

25. $y = 2x - 1$

26. $y = x - 3$

27. $y = -\frac{2}{3}x + 2$

28. $y = -\frac{1}{2}x + 3$

29. $y + \frac{1}{4}x = -4$

30. $y - \frac{1}{4}x = -2$

31. $7x - 2y = 7$

32. $2x - 3y = 1$

33. $3x = 8$

34. $2x = -7$

35. $6y = 9$

36. $3y = 4$

37. $2x = 3y$

38. $3x = -2y$

In Exercises 39–58, calculate the slope, if defined, of the straight line through the given pair of points. Try to do as many as you can without writing anything down except the answer. HINT [See Quick Examples on page 82.]

39. $(0, 0)$ and $(1, 2)$

40. $(0, 0)$ and $(-1, 2)$

41. $(-1, -2)$ and $(0, 0)$

42. $(2, 1)$ and $(0, 0)$

43. $(4, 3)$ and $(5, 1)$

44. $(4, 3)$ and $(4, 1)$

45. $(1, -1)$ and $(1, -2)$

46. $(-2, 2)$ and $(-1, -1)$

47. $(2, 3.5)$ and $(4, 6.5)$

48. $(10, -3.5)$ and $(0, -1.5)$

49. $(300, 20.2)$ and $(400, 11.2)$

50. $(1, -20.2)$ and $(2, 3.2)$

51. $(0, 1)$ and $\left(-\frac{1}{2}, \frac{3}{4}\right)$

52. $\left(\frac{1}{2}, 1\right)$ and $\left(-\frac{1}{2}, \frac{3}{4}\right)$

53. (a, b) and (c, d) $(a \neq c)$

54. (a, b) and (c, b) $(a \neq c)$

55. (a, b) and (a, d) $(b \neq d)$

56. (a, b) and $(-a, -b)$ $(a \neq 0)$

57. $(-a, b)$ and $(a, -b)$ $(a \neq 0)$

58. (a, b) and (b, a) $(a \neq b)$

59. In the following figure, estimate the slopes of all line segments.

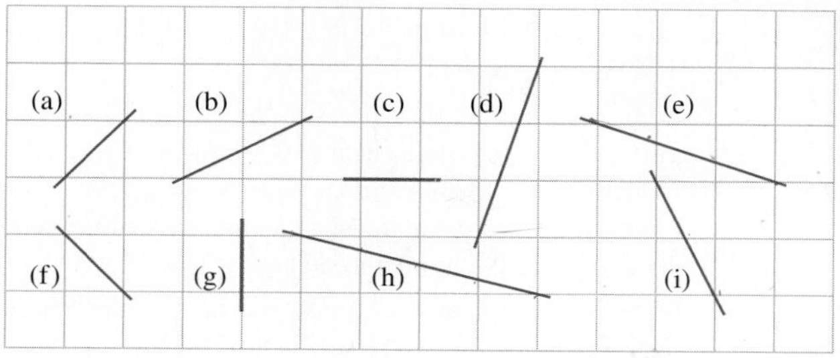

60. In the following figure, estimate the slopes of all line segments.

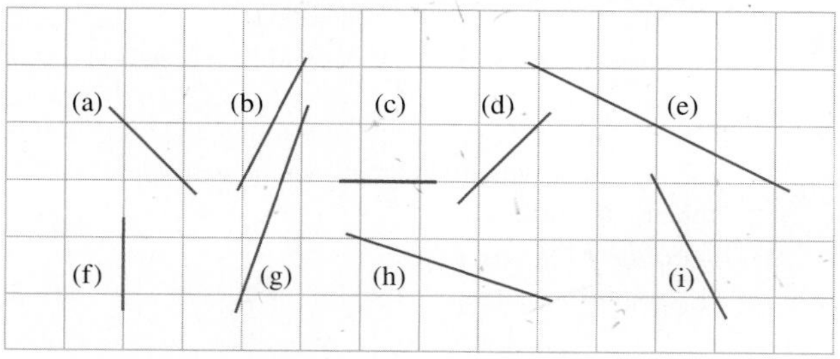

In Exercises 61–78, find a linear equation whose graph is the straight line with the given properties. HINT [See Example 2.]

61. Through (1, 3) with slope 3

62. Through (2, 1) with slope 2

63. Through $(1, -\frac{3}{4})$ with slope $\frac{1}{4}$

64. Through $(0, -\frac{1}{3})$ with slope $\frac{1}{3}$

65. Through (20, −3.5) and increasing at a rate of 10 units of y per unit of x

66. Through (3.5, −10) and increasing at a rate of 1 unit of y per 2 units of x

67. Through (2, −4) and (1, 1)

68. Through (1, −4) and (−1, −1)

69. Through (1, −0.75) and (0.5, 0.75)

70. Through (0.5, −0.75) and (1, −3.75)

71. Through (6, 6) and parallel to the line $x + y = 4$

72. Through (1/3, −1) and parallel to the line $3x - 4y = 8$

73. Through (0.5, 5) and parallel to the line $4x - 2y = 11$

74. Through (1/3, 0) and parallel to the line $6x - 2y = 11$

75. ▼ Through (0, 0) and (p, q) $(p \neq 0)$

76. ▼ Through (p, q) parallel to $y = rx + s$

77. ▼ Through (p, q) and (r, q) $(p \neq r)$

78. ▼ Through (p, q) and (r, s) $(p \neq r)$

APPLICATIONS

79. ***Cost*** The RideEm Bicycles factory can produce 100 bicycles in a day at a total cost of $10,500 and it can produce 120 bicycles in a day at a total cost of $11,000. What are the company's daily fixed costs, and what is the marginal cost per bicycle? HINT [See Example 3.]

80. ***Cost*** A soft-drink manufacturer can produce 1,000 cases of soda in a week at a total cost of $6,000, and 1,500 cases of soda at a total cost of $8,500. Find the manufacturer's weekly fixed costs and marginal cost per case of soda.

81. ***Cost: iPhones*** If it costs Apple $1,900 to manufacture 10 iPhone 4s per hour and $3,780 to manufacture 20 per hour at a particular plant,[40] obtain the corresponding linear cost function. What was the cost to manufacture each additional iPhone? Use the cost function to estimate the cost of manufacturing 40 iPhones in an hour.

82. ***Cost: Kinects*** If it costs Microsoft $1,230 to manufacture 8 Kinects per hour for the Xbox 360 and $2,430 to manufacture 16 per hour at a particular plant,[41] obtain the corresponding linear cost function. What was the cost to manufacture each additional Kinect? Use the cost function to estimate the cost of manufacturing 30 Kinects in an hour.

83. ***Demand*** Sales figures show that your company sold 1,960 pen sets each week when they were priced at $1/pen set and 1,800 pen sets each week when they were priced at $5/pen set. What is the linear demand function for your pen sets? HINT [See Example 4.]

84. ***Demand*** A large department store is prepared to buy 3,950 of your tie-dye shower curtains per month for $5 each, but only 3,700 shower curtains per month for $10 each. What is the linear demand function for your tie-dye shower curtains?

85. ***Demand for Cell Phones*** The following table shows worldwide sales of cell phones by Nokia and their average wholesale prices in the first quarters of 2009 and 2010:[42]

Quarter	*Q1 2009*	*Q1 2010*
Wholesale Price ($)	85	81
Sales (millions)	103	111

a. Use the data to obtain a linear demand function for (Nokia) cell phones, and use your demand equation to predict sales if Nokia lowered the price further to $75.

b. Fill in the blanks: For every ____ increase in price, sales of cell phones decrease by ____ units.

[40]Based on marginal cost data at www.isuppli.com.

[41]Based on marginal cost data provided by a "highly-positioned, trusted source." www.develop-online.net.

[42]Data are approximate. Source: www.nokia.com.

86. ***Demand for Smart Phones*** The following table shows worldwide sales of smart phones and their average wholesale prices in 2009 and 2010:[43]

Quarter	*Q1 2009*	*Q1 2010*
Wholesale Price ($)	162	152
Sales (millions)	174	213

a. Use the data to obtain a linear demand function for smart phones, and use your demand equation to predict sales to the nearest million phones if the price was set at $155.
b. Fill in the blanks: For every ____ increase in price, sales of smart phones decrease by ___ units.

87. ***Demand for Monorail Service, Las Vegas*** In 2005, the Las Vegas monorail charged $3 per ride and had an average ridership of about 28,000 per day. In December 2005 the Las Vegas Monorail Company raised the fare to $5 per ride, and average ridership in 2006 plunged to around 19,000 per day.[44]

a. Use the given information to find a linear demand equation.
b. Give the units of measurement and interpretation of the slope.
c. What would have been the effect on ridership of raising the fare to $6 per ride?

88. ***Demand for Monorail Service, Mars*** The Utarek monorail, which links the three urbynes (or districts) of Utarek, Mars, charged Z5 per ride[45] and sold about 14 million rides per day. When the Utarek City Council lowered the fare to Z3 per ride, the number of rides increased to 18 million per day.

a. Use the given information to find a linear demand equation.
b. Give the units of measurement and interpretation of the slope.
c. What would have been the effect on ridership of raising the fare to Z10 per ride?

89. ***Pasta Imports in the 90s*** During the period 1990–2001, U.S. imports of pasta increased from 290 million pounds in 1990 ($t = 0$) by an average of 40 million pounds/year.[46]

a. Use this information to express y, the annual U.S. imports of pasta (in millions of pounds), as a linear function of t, the number of years since 1990.
b. Use your model to estimate U.S. pasta imports in 2005, assuming the import trend continued.

[43] Data are approximate. Sources: www.techcrunch.com, www.businessweek.com.

[44] Source: *New York Times,* February 10, 2007, p. A9.

[45] The zonar (Z) is the official currency in the city-state of Utarek, Mars (formerly www.Marsnext.com, a now extinct virtual society).

[46] Data are rounded. Sources: Department of Commerce/*New York Times*, September 5, 1995, p. D4; International Trade Administration, March 31, 2002, www.ita.doc.gov/.

90. ***Mercury Imports in the 10s*** During the period 2210–2220, Martian imports of mercury (from the planet of that name) increased from 550 million kg in 2210 ($t = 0$) by an average of 60 million kg/year.

a. Use this information to express y, the annual Martian imports of mercury (in millions of kilograms), as a linear function of t, the number of years since 2210.
b. Use your model to estimate Martian mercury imports in 2230, assuming the import trend continued.

91. ***Net Income*** The net income of Amazon.com increased from $10 billion in 2006 to $25 billion in 2009.[47]

a. Use this information to find a linear model for Amazon's net income N (in billions of dollars) as a function of time t in years since 2000.
b. Give the units of measurement and interpretation of the slope.
c. Use the model from part (a) to estimate the 2008 net income. (The actual 2008 net income was approximately $19 billion.)

92. ***Operating Expenses*** The operating expenses of Amazon.com increased from $2.0 billion in 2006 to $4.4 billion in 2009.[48]

a. Use this information to find a linear model for Amazon's operating expenses E (in billions of dollars) as a function of time t in years since 2000.
b. Give the units of measurement and interpretation of the slope.
c. Use the model from part (a) to estimate the 2007 operating expenses. (The actual 2007 operating expenses were approximately $2.5 billion.)

93. ***Velocity*** The position of a model train, in feet along a railroad track, is given by

$$s(t) = 2.5t + 10$$

after t seconds.

a. How fast is the train moving?
b. Where is the train after 4 seconds?
c. When will it be 25 feet along the track?

94. ***Velocity*** The height of a falling sheet of paper, in feet from the ground, is given by

$$s(t) = -1.8t + 9$$

after t seconds.

a. What is the velocity of the sheet of paper?
b. How high is it after 4 seconds?
c. When will it reach the ground?

95. ▼ ***Fast Cars*** A police car was traveling down Ocean Parkway in a high-speed chase from Jones Beach. It was at Jones Beach at exactly 10 pm ($t = 10$) and was at Oak Beach, 13 miles from Jones Beach, at exactly 10:06 pm.

a. How fast was the police car traveling? HINT [See Example 6.]
b. How far was the police car from Jones Beach at time t?

[47] Recall that "net income" is another term for "profit." Source: www.wikinvest.com.

[48] *Ibid.*

96. ▼ ***Fast Cars*** The car that was being pursued by the police in Exercise 95 was at Jones Beach at exactly 9:54 pm ($t = 9.9$) and passed Oak Beach (13 miles from Jones Beach) at exactly 10:06 pm, where it was overtaken by the police.

a. How fast was the car traveling? HINT [See Example 6.]

b. How far was the car from Jones Beach at time t?

97. ***Textbook Sizes*** The second edition of *Applied Calculus* by Waner and Costenoble was 585 pages long. By the time we got to the fifth edition, the book had grown to 750 pages.

a. Use this information to obtain the page length L as a linear function of the edition number n.

b. What are the units of measurement of the slope? What does the slope tell you about the length of *Applied Calculus*?

c. At this rate, by which edition will the book have grown to over 1,500 pages?

98. ***Textbook Sizes*** The second edition of *Finite Mathematics* by Waner and Costenoble was 603 pages long. By the time we got to the fifth edition, the book had grown to 690 pages.

a. Use this information to obtain the page length L as a linear function of the edition number n.

b. What are the units of measurement of the slope? What does the slope tell you about the length of *Finite Mathematics*?

c. At this rate, by which edition will the book have grown to over 1,000 pages?

99. ***Fahrenheit and Celsius*** In the Fahrenheit temperature scale, water freezes at 32°F and boils at 212°F. In the Celsius scale, water freezes at 0°C and boils at 100°C. Further, the Fahrenheit temperature F and the Celsius temperature C are related by a linear equation. Find F in terms of C. Use your equation to find the Fahrenheit temperatures corresponding to 30°C, 22°C, −10°C, and −14°C, to the nearest degree.

100. ***Fahrenheit and Celsius*** Use the information about Celsius and Fahrenheit given in Exercise 99 to obtain a linear equation for C in terms of F, and use your equation to find the Celsius temperatures corresponding to 104°F, 77°F, 14°F, and −40°F, to the nearest degree.

Airline Net Income *Exercises 101 and 102 are based on the following table, which compares the net incomes, in millions of dollars, of* American Airlines, Continental Airlines, *and* Southwest Airlines:[49]

Year	2005	2006	2007	2008	2009	2010
American Airlines	−850	250	450	−2,100	−1,450	−300
Continental Airlines	−50	350	450	−600	−300	150
Southwest Airlines	550	500	650	200	100	300

101. **a.** Use the 2005 and 2009 data to obtain American's net income A as a linear function of Continental's net income C. (Use millions of dollars for all units.)

b. How far off is your model in estimating American's net income based on Continental's 2007 income?

c. What does the slope of the linear function from part (a) suggest about the net income of these two airlines?

102. **a.** Use the 2006 and 2010 data to obtain Continental's net income C as a linear function of Southwest's net income S. (Use millions of dollars for all units.)

b. How far off is your model in estimating Continental's net income based on Southwest's 2008 income?

c. What does the slope of the linear function from part (a) suggest about the net income of these two airlines?

103. ▼ ***Income*** The well-known romance novelist Celestine A. Lafleur (a.k.a. Bertha Snodgrass) has decided to sell the screen rights to her latest book, *Henrietta's Heaving Heart*, to Boxoffice Success Productions for \$50,000. In addition, the contract ensures Ms. Lafleur royalties of 5% of the net profits.[50] Express her income I as a function of the net profit N, and determine the net profit necessary to bring her an income of \$100,000. What is her marginal income (share of each dollar of net profit)?

104. ▼ ***Income*** Due to the enormous success of the movie *Henrietta's Heaving Heart* based on a novel by Celestine A. Lafleur (see Exercise 103), Boxoffice Success Productions decides to film the sequel, *Henrietta, Oh Henrietta.* At this point, Bertha Snodgrass (whose novels now top the best seller lists) feels she is in a position to demand \$100,000 for the screen rights and royalties of 8% of the net profits. Express her income I as a function of the net profit N and determine the net profit necessary to bring her an income of \$1,000,000. What is her marginal income (share of each dollar of net profit)?

105. ***Processor Speeds*** The processor speed, in megahertz (MHz), of Intel processors during the period 1996–2010 could be approximated by the following function of time t in years since the start of 1990:[51]

$$v(t) = \begin{cases} 400t - 2{,}200 & \text{if } 6 \le t < 15 \\ 3{,}800 & \text{if } 15 \le t \le 20. \end{cases}$$

How fast and in what direction was processor speed changing in 2000?

106. ***Processor Speeds*** The processor speed, in megahertz (MHz), of Intel processors during the period 1970–2000 could be approximated by the following function of time t in years since the start of 1970:[52]

$$v(t) = \begin{cases} 3t & \text{if } 0 \le t < 20 \\ 174t - 3{,}420 & \text{if } 20 \le t \le 30. \end{cases}$$

How fast and in what direction was processor speed changing in 1995?

[49] Data are rounded. 2010 net incomes projected based on first three quarters. Source: www.wikinvest.com.

[50] Percentages of net profit are commonly called "monkey points." Few movies ever make a net profit on paper, and anyone with any clout in the business gets a share of the *gross*, not the net.

[51] A rough model based on the fastest processors produced by Intel. Source: www.intel.com.

[52] *Ibid.*

Superbowl Advertising
Exercises 107 and 108 are based on the following graph and data from Wikipedia showing the increasing cost of a 30-second television ad during the Super Bowl.[53]

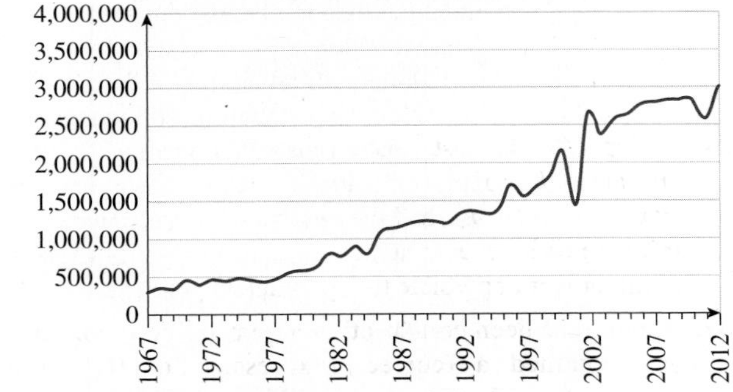

Year	1970	1980	1990	2000	2010
Cost (Thousands of $)	78	222	700	1,100	2,500

107. ▼ Take t to be the number of years since 1970 and y to be the cost, in thousands of dollars, of a Super Bowl ad.

a. Model the 1970 and 1990 data with a linear equation.
b. Model the 1990 and 2010 data with a linear equation.
c. Use the results of parts (a) and (b) to obtain a piecewise linear model of the cost of a Super Bowl ad during 1970–2010.
d. Use your model to estimate the cost in 2004. Is your answer in rough agreement with the graph? Explain any discrepancy.

108 ▼ Take t to be the number of years since 1980 and y to be the cost, in thousands of dollars, of a Super Bowl ad.

a. Model the 1980 and 2000 data with a linear equation.
b. Model the 2000 and 2010 data with a linear equation.
c. Use the results of parts (a) and (b) to obtain a piecewise linear model of the cost of a Super Bowl ad during 1980–2010.
d. Use your model to estimate the cost in 1992. Is your answer in rough agreement with the graph? Explain any discrepancy.

109. ▼ ***Employment in Mexico*** The number of workers employed in manufacturing jobs in Mexico was 3 million in 1995, rose to 4.1 million in 2000, and then dropped to 3.5 million in 2004.[54] Model this number N as a piecewise-linear function of the time t in years since 1995, and use your model to estimate the number of manufacturing jobs in Mexico in 2002. (Take the units of N to be millions.)

110. ▼ ***Mortgage Delinquencies*** The percentage of borrowers in the highest risk category who were delinquent on their payments decreased from 9.7% in 2001 to 4.3% in 2004 and then shot up to 10.3% in 2007.[55] Model this percentage P as a piecewise-linear function of the time t in years since 2001, and use your model to estimate the percentage of delinquent borrowers in 2006.

COMMUNICATION AND REASONING EXERCISES

111. How would you test a table of values of x and y to see if it comes from a linear function?

112. You have ascertained that a table of values of x and y corresponds to a linear function. How do you find an equation for that linear function?

113. To what linear function of x does the linear equation $ax + by = c$ $(b \neq 0)$ correspond? Why did we specify $b \neq 0$?

114. Complete the following. The slope of the line with equation $y = mx + b$ is the number of units that ____ increases per unit increase in ____.

115. Complete the following. If, in a straight line, y is increasing three times as fast as x, then its ____ is ____.

116. Suppose that y is decreasing at a rate of 4 units per 3-unit increase of x. What can we say about the slope of the linear relationship between x and y? What can we say about the intercept?

117. If y and x are related by the linear expression $y = mx + b$, how will y change as x changes if m is positive? negative? zero?

118. Your friend April tells you that $y = f(x)$ has the property that, whenever x is changed by Δx, the corresponding change in y is $\Delta y = -\Delta x$. What can you tell her about f?

119. T ▼ Consider the following worksheet:

	A	B	C	D
1	x	y	m	b
2	1	1	2 =(B3-B2)/(A3-A2)	=B2-C2*A2
3	3	3	-1 Slope	Intercept

What is the effect on the slope of increasing the y-coordinate of the second point (the point whose coordinates are in Row 3)? Explain.

120. T ▼ Referring to the worksheet in Exercise 119, what is the effect on the slope of increasing the x-coordinate of the second point (the point whose coordinates are in row 3)? Explain.

121. If y is measured in bootlags[56] and x is measured in zonars[57], and $y = mx + b$, then m is measured in _______ and b is measured in _______.

[53]Source: http//en.wikipedia.org/wiki/Super_Bowl_advertising.

[54]Source: *New York Times*, Februrary 18, 2007, p. WK4.

[55]The 2007 figure was projected from data through October 2006. Source: *New York Times*, Februrary 18, 2007, p. BU9.

[56]An ancient Martian unit of length; one bootlag is the mean distance from a Martian's foreleg to its rearleg.

[57]The official currency of Utarek, Mars. (See the footnote to Exercise 88.)

122. If the slope in a linear relationship is measured in miles per dollar, then the independent variable is measured in ______ and the dependent variable is measured in ______.

123. If a quantity is changing linearly with time, and it increases by 10 units in the first day, what can you say about its behavior in the third day?

124. The quantities Q and T are related by a linear equation of the form

$$Q = mT + b.$$

When $T = 0$, Q is positive, but decreases to a negative quantity when T is 10. What are the signs of m and b? Explain your answers.

125. ▼ The velocity of an object is given by $v = 0.1t + 20$ m/sec, where t is time in seconds. The object is

(A) moving with fixed speed **(B)** accelerating
(C) decelerating **(D)** impossible to say from the given information

126. ▼ The position of an object is given by $x = 0.2t - 4$, where t is time in seconds. The object is

(A) moving with fixed speed **(B)** accelerating
(C) decelerating **(D)** impossible to say from the given information

127. If f and g are linear functions with slope m and n respectively, then what can you say about $f + g$?

128. If f and g are linear functions, then is $\frac{f}{g}$ linear? Explain.

129. Give examples of nonlinear functions f and g whose product is linear.

130. Give examples of nonlinear functions f and g whose quotient is linear (on a suitable domain).

131. ▼ Suppose the cost function is $C(x) = mx + b$ (with m and b positive), the revenue function is $R(x) = kx$ $(k > m)$, and the number of items is increased from the break-even quantity. Does this result in a loss, a profit, or is it impossible to say? Explain your answer.

132. ▼ You have been constructing a demand equation, and you obtained a (correct) expression of the form $p = mq + b$, whereas you would have preferred one of the form $q = mp + b$. Should you simply switch p and q in the answer, should you start again from scratch, using p in the role of x and q in the role of y, or should you solve your demand equation for q? Give reasons for your decision.

1.4 Linear Regression

We have seen how to find a linear model given two data points: We find the equation of the line that passes through them. However, we often have more than two data points, and they will rarely all lie on a single straight line, but may often come close to doing so. The problem is to find the line coming *closest* to passing through all of the points.

Suppose, for example, that we are conducting research for a company interested in expanding into Mexico. Of interest to us would be current and projected growth in that country's economy. The following table shows past and projected per capita gross domestic product (GDP)[58] of Mexico for 2000–2014.[59]

Year t ($t = 0$ represents 2000)	0	2	4	6	8	10	12	14
Per Capita GDP y (\$1,000)	9	9	10	11	11	12	13	13

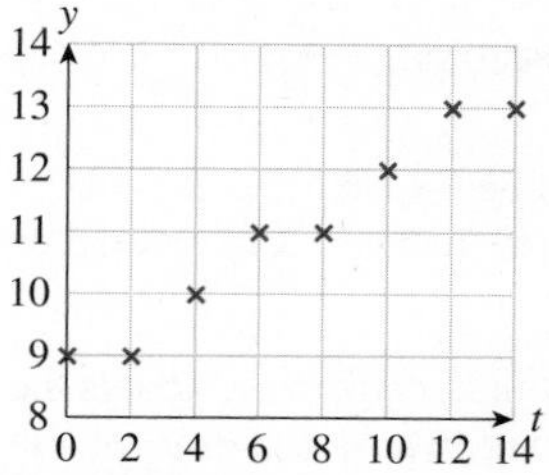

Figure 27(a)

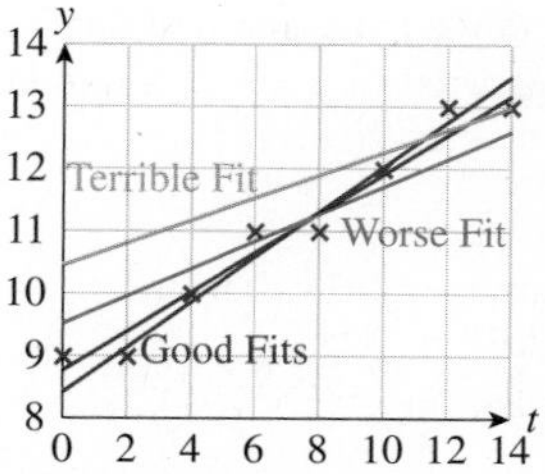

Figure 27(b)

A plot of these data suggests a roughly linear growth of the GDP (Figure 27(a)). These points suggest a roughly linear relationship between t and y, although they clearly do not all lie on a single straight line. Figure 27(b) shows the points together with several lines, some fitting better than others. Can we precisely measure which lines fit better than others? For instance, which of the two lines labeled as "good" fits in Figure 27(b) models the data more accurately? We begin by considering, for each value of t, the difference between the actual GDP (the **observed value**) and the GDP

[58]The GDP is a measure of the total market value of all goods and services produced within a country.

[59]Data are approximate and/or projected. Sources: CIA World Factbook/www.indexmundi.com, www.economist.com.

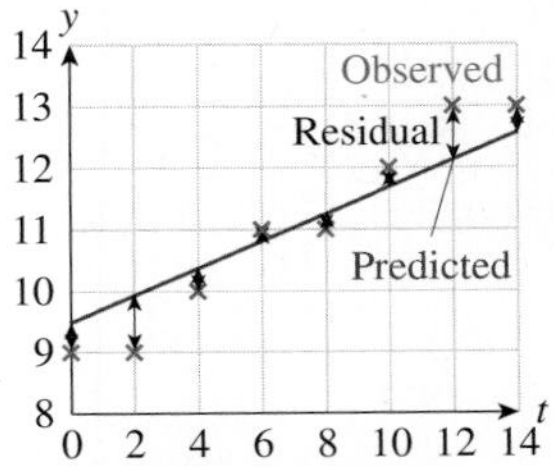

Residual = Observed Value – Predicted Value

Figure 28

predicted by a linear equation (the **predicted value**). The difference between the predicted value and the observed value is called the **residual**.

$$\text{Residual} = \text{Observed Value} - \text{Predicted Value}$$

On the graph, the residuals measure the vertical distances between the (observed) data points and the line (Figure 28) and they tell us how far the linear model is from predicting the actual GDP.

The more accurate our model, the smaller the residuals should be. We can combine all the residuals into a single measure of accuracy by adding their *squares.* (We square the residuals in part to make them all positive.*) The sum of the squares of the residuals is called the **sum-of-squares error, SSE**. Smaller values of SSE indicate more accurate models.

Here are some definitions and formulas for what we have been discussing.

* Why not add the absolute values of the residuals instead? Mathematically, using the squares rather than the absolute values results in a simpler and more elegant solution. Further, using the squares always results in a *single* best-fit line in cases where the *x*-coordinates are all different, whereas this is not the case if we use absolute values.

Observed and Predicted Values

Suppose we are given a collection of data points $(x_1, y_1), \ldots, (x_n, y_n)$. The n quantities $y_1, y_2, \ldots, y_n$ are called the **observed y-values**. If we model these data with a linear equation

$$\hat{y} = mx + b, \qquad \hat{y} \text{ stands for "estimated } y\text{" or "predicted } y\text{."}$$

then the y-values we get by substituting the given x-values into the equation are called the **predicted y-values**:

$$\hat{y}_1 = mx_1 + b \qquad \text{Substitute } x_1 \text{ for } x.$$

$$\hat{y}_2 = mx_2 + b \qquad \text{Substitute } x_2 \text{ for } x.$$

$$\ldots$$

$$\hat{y}_n = mx_n + b. \qquad \text{Substitute } x_n \text{ for } x.$$

Quick Example

Consider the three data points (0, 2), (2, 5), and (3, 6). The observed y-values are $y_1 = 2$, $y_2 = 5$, and $y_3 = 6$. If we model these data with the equation $\hat{y} = x + 2.5$, then the predicted values are:

$$\hat{y}_1 = x_1 + 2.5 = 0 + 2.5 = 2.5$$

$$\hat{y}_2 = x_2 + 2.5 = 2 + 2.5 = 4.5$$

$$\hat{y}_3 = x_3 + 2.5 = 3 + 2.5 = 5.5.$$

Residuals and Sum-of-Squares Error (SSE)

If we model a collection of data $(x_1, y_1), \ldots, (x_n, y_n)$ with a linear equation $\hat{y} = mx + b$, then the **residuals** are the n quantities (Observed Value – Predicted Value):

$$(y_1 - \hat{y}_1), (y_2 - \hat{y}_2), \ldots, (y_n - \hat{y}_n).$$

The **sum-of-squares error (SSE)** is the sum of the squares of the residuals:

$$\text{SSE} = (y_1 - \hat{y}_1)^2 + (y_2 - \hat{y}_2)^2 + \cdots + (y_n - \hat{y}_n)^2.$$

Quick Example

For the data and linear approximation given above, the residuals are:

$$y_1 - \hat{y}_1 = 2 - 2.5 = -0.5$$
$$y_2 - \hat{y}_2 = 5 - 4.5 = 0.5$$
$$y_3 - \hat{y}_3 = 6 - 5.5 = 0.5$$

and so $\text{SSE} = (-0.5)^2 + (0.5)^2 + (0.5)^2 = 0.75$.

EXAMPLE 1 Computing SSE

Using the data above on the GDP in Mexico, compute SSE for the linear models $y = 0.5t + 8$ and $y = 0.25t + 9$. Which model is the better fit?

Solution We begin by creating a table showing the values of t, the observed (given) values of y, and the values predicted by the first model.

Year t	Observed y	Predicted $\hat{y} = 0.5t + 8$
0	9	8
2	9	9
4	10	10
6	11	11
8	11	12
10	12	13
12	13	14
14	13	15

We now add two new columns for the residuals and their squares.

Year t	Observed y	Predicted $\hat{y} = 0.5t + 8$	Residual $y - \hat{y}$	Residual² $(y - \hat{y})^2$
0	9	8	$9 - 8 = 1$	$1^2 = 1$
2	9	9	$9 - 9 = 0$	$0^2 = 0$
4	10	10	$10 - 10 = 0$	$0^2 = 0$
6	11	11	$11 - 11 = 0$	$0^2 = 0$
8	11	12	$11 - 12 = -1$	$(-1)^2 = 1$
10	12	13	$12 - 13 = -1$	$(-1)^2 = 1$
12	13	14	$13 - 14 = -1$	$(-1)^2 = 1$
14	13	15	$13 - 15 = -2$	$(-2)^2 = 4$

using Technology

See the Technology Guides at the end of the chapter for detailed instructions on how to obtain the tables and graphs in Example 1 using a TI-83/84 Plus or a spreadsheet. Here is an outline:

TI-83/84 Plus

STAT EDIT

Values of t in L_1, and y in L_2.
Predicted y: Highlight L_3. Enter `0.5*L1+8`
Squares of residuals: Highlight L_4. Enter `(L2-L3)^2`
SSE: Home screen `sum(L4)`
Graph: `Y1=0.5X+8`
Y = screen: Turn on Plot 1 ZOOM (STAT) [More details on page 117.]

Spreadsheet

Headings t, y, y-hat, Residual^2, m, b, and SSE in A1–F1.
t-values in A2–A9, y-values in B2–B9; 0.25 for m and 9 for b in E2–F2
Predicted y: `=$E$2*A2+$F$2` in C2 and copy down to C9.
Squares of residuals: `=(B2-C2)^2` in D2 and copy down to D9.
SSE: `=SUM(D2:D9)` in G2
Graph: Highlight A1–C9. Insert a Scatter chart.
[More details on page 122.]

SSE, the sum of the squares of the residuals, is then the sum of the entries in the last column,

$$SSE = 8.$$

Repeating the process using the second model, $0.25t + 9$, yields the following table:

Year t	**Observed** y	**Predicted** $\hat{y} = 0.25t + 9$	**Residual** $y - \hat{y}$	**Residual** ^{2} $(y - \hat{y})^2$
0	9	9	$9 - 9 = 0$	$0^2 = 0$
2	9	9.5	$9 - 9.5 = -0.5$	$(-0.5)^2 = 0.25$
4	10	10	$10 - 10 = 0$	$0^2 = 0$
6	11	10.5	$11 - 10.5 = 0.5$	$0.5^2 = 0.25$
8	11	11	$11 - 11 = 0$	$0^2 = 0$
10	12	11.5	$12 - 11.5 = 0.5$	$0.5^2 = 0.25$
12	13	12	$13 - 12 = 1$	$1^2 = 1$
14	13	12.5	$13 - 12.5 = 0.5$	$0.5^2 = 0.25$

This time, $SSE = 2$ and so the second model is a better fit.

Figure 29 shows the data points and the two linear models in question.

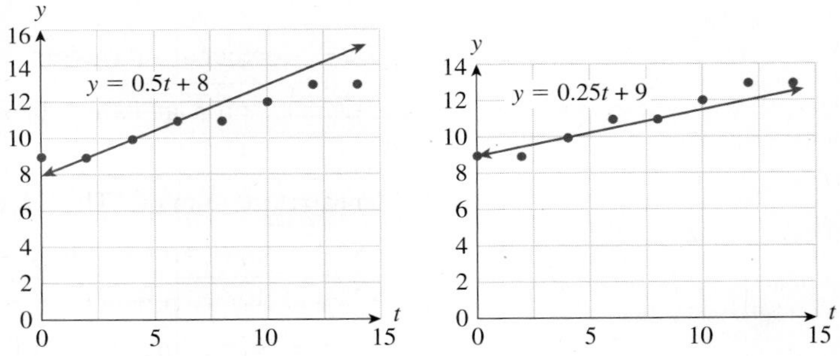

Figure 29

➡ Before we go on...

Q: *It seems clear from the figure that the second model in Example 1 gives a better fit. Why bother to compute SSE to tell me this?*

A: The difference between the two models we chose is so great that it is clear from the graphs which is the better fit. However, if we used a third model with $m = 0.25$ and $b = 9.1$, then its graph would be almost indistinguishable from that of the second, but a slightly better fit as measured by $SSE = 1.68$.

■

Among all possible lines, there ought to be one with the least possible value of SSE—that is, the greatest possible accuracy as a model. The line (and there is only one such line) that minimizes the sum of the squares of the residuals is called the **regression line**, the **least-squares line**, or the **best-fit line**.

To find the regression line, we need a way to find values of m and b that give the smallest possible value of SSE. As an example, let us take the second linear model in the example above. We said in the "Before we go on" discussion that increasing b from 9 to 9.1 had the desirable effect of decreasing SSE from 2 to 1.68. We could then increase m to 0.26, further reducing SSE to 1.328. Imagine this as a kind of game: Alternately alter the values of m and b by small amounts until SSE is as small as you can make it. This works, but is extremely tedious and time-consuming.

Fortunately, there is an algebraic way to find the regression line. Here is the calculation. To justify it rigorously requires calculus of several variables or linear algebra.

Regression Line

The **regression line (least squares line, best-fit line)** associated with the points $(x_1, y_1), (x_2, y_2), \ldots, (x_n, y_n)$ is the line that gives the minimum SSE. The regression line is

$$y = mx + b,$$

where m and b are computed as follows:

$$m = \frac{n\left(\sum xy\right) - \left(\sum x\right)\left(\sum y\right)}{n\left(\sum x^2\right) - \left(\sum x\right)^2}$$

$$b = \frac{\sum y - m\left(\sum x\right)}{n}$$

$n =$ number of data points.

The quantities m and b are called the **regression coefficients.**

Here, "$\sum$" means "the sum of." Thus, for example,

$$\sum x = \text{Sum of the } x\text{-values} = x_1 + x_2 + \cdots + x_n$$
$$\sum xy = \text{Sum of products} = x_1y_1 + x_2y_2 + \cdots + x_ny_n$$
$$\sum x^2 = \text{Sum of the squares of the } x\text{-values} = x_1^2 + x_2^2 + \cdots + x_n^2.$$

On the other hand,

$$\left(\sum x\right)^2 = \text{Square of } \sum x = \text{Square of the sum of the } x\text{-values.}$$

EXAMPLE 2 Per Capita Gross Domestic Product in Mexico

In Example 1 we considered the following data on the per capita gross domestic product (GDP) of Mexico:

Year x ($x = 0$ represents 2000)	0	2	4	6	8	10	12	14
Per Capita GDP y (\$1,000)	9	9	10	11	11	12	13	13

Find the best-fit linear model for these data and use the model to predict the per capita GDP in Mexico in 2016.

using Technology

See the Technology Guides at the end of the chapter for detailed instructions on how to obtain the regression line and graph in Example 2 using a TI-83/84 Plus or a spreadsheet. Here is an outline:

TI-83/84 Plus

STAT EDIT

Values of x in L_1, and y in L_2.

Regression equation: STAT CALC option #4: `LinReg(ax+b)`

Graph: Y= VARS 5 EQ 1, then ZOOM 9

[More details on page 118.]

Spreadsheet

x-values in A2–A9, y-values in B2–B9

Graph: Highlight A2–B9. Insert a Scatter Chart.

Regression line: Add a linear trendline. [More details on page 123.]

Website

www.WanerMath.com

The following two utilities will calculate and plot regression lines (link to either from Math Tools for Chapter 1):

Simple Regression

Function Evaluator and Grapher

Solution Let's organize our work in the form of a table, where the original data are entered in the first two columns and the bottom row contains the column sums.

	x	y	xy	x^2
	0	9	0	0
	2	9	18	4
	4	10	40	16
	6	11	66	36
	8	11	88	64
	10	12	120	100
	12	13	156	144
	14	13	182	196
$\sum$ (Sum)	56	88	670	560

Because there are $n = 8$ data points, we get

$$m = \frac{n(\sum xy) - (\sum x)(\sum y)}{n(\sum x^2) - (\sum x)^2} = \frac{8(670) - (56)(88)}{8(560) - (56)^2} \approx 0.321$$

and

$$b = \frac{\sum y - m(\sum x)}{n} \approx \frac{88 - (0.321)(56)}{8} \approx 8.75.$$

So, the regression line is

$$y = 0.321x + 8.75.$$

To predict the per capita GDP in Mexico in 2016 we substitute $x = 16$ and get $y \approx 14$, or \$14,000 per capita.

Figure 30 shows the data points and the regression line (which has SSE ≈ 0.643; a lot lower than in Example 1).

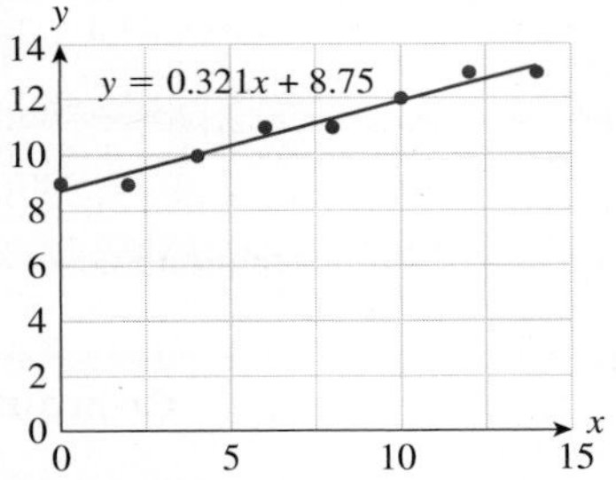

Figure 30

Coefficient of Correlation

If all the data points do not lie on one straight line, we would like to be able to measure how closely they can be approximated by a straight line. Recall that SSE measures the sum of the squares of the deviations from the regression line; therefore it constitutes a measurement of what is called "goodness of fit." (For instance, if SSE $= 0$, then all the points lie on a straight line.) However, SSE depends on the units we use to measure y, and also on the number of data points (the more data points we use, the larger SSE tends to be). Thus, while we can (and do) use SSE to compare the goodness of fit of two lines to the same data, we cannot use it to compare the goodness of fit of one line to one set of data with that of another to a different set of data.

To remove this dependency, statisticians have found a related quantity that can be used to compare the goodness of fit of lines to different sets of data. This quantity, called the **coefficient of correlation** or **correlation coefficient**, and usually denoted r, is between -1 and 1. The closer r is to -1 or 1, the better the fit. For an *exact* fit, we would have $r = -1$ (for a line with negative slope) or $r = 1$ (for a line with positive slope). For a bad fit, we would have r close to 0. Figure 31 shows several collections of data points with least-squares lines and the corresponding values of r.

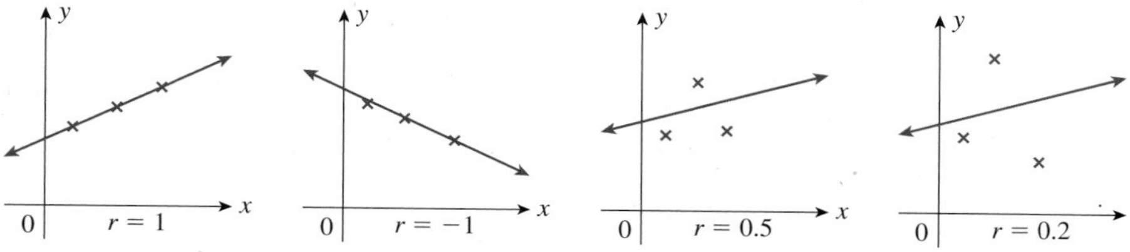

Figure 31

Correlation Coefficient

The coefficient of correlation of the n data points $(x_1, y_1), (x_2, y_2), \ldots, (x_n, y_n)$ is

$$r = \frac{n(\sum xy) - (\sum x)(\sum y)}{\sqrt{n(\sum x^2) - (\sum x)^2} \cdot \sqrt{n(\sum y^2) - (\sum y)^2}}.$$

It measures how closely the data points $(x_1, y_1), (x_2, y_2), \ldots, (x_n, y_n)$ fit the regression line. (The value r^2 is sometimes called the **coefficient of determination**.)

Interpretation

- If r is positive, the regression line has positive slope; if r is negative, the regression line has negative slope.
- If $r = 1$ or -1, then all the data points lie exactly on the regression line; if it is close to ± 1, then all the data points are close to the regression line.
- On the other hand, if r is not close to ± 1, then the data points are not close to the regression line, so the fit is not a good one. As a general rule of thumb, a value of $|r|$ less than around 0.8 indicates a poor fit of the data to the regression line.

using Technology

See the Technology Guides at the end of the chapter for detailed instructions on how to obtain the correlation coefficient in Example 3 using a TI-83/84 Plus or a spreadsheet. Here is an outline:

TI-83/84 Plus

[2ND] [CATALOG] `DiagnosticOn`

Then [STAT] CALC option #4: `LinReg(ax+b)` [More details on page 119.]

Spreadsheet

Add a trendline and select the option to "Display R-squared value on chart."

[More details and other alternatives on page 124.]

Website

www.WanerMath.com

The following two utilities will show regression lines and also r^2 (link to either from Math Tools for Chapter 1):

Simple Regression

Function Evaluator and Grapher

EXAMPLE 3 Computing the Coefficient of Correlation

Find the correlation coefficient for the data in Example 2. Is the regression line a good fit?

Solution The formula for r requires $\sum x, \sum x^2, \sum xy, \sum y$, and $\sum y^2$. We have all of these except for $\sum y^2$, which we find in a new column as shown.

	x	y	xy	x^2	y^2
	0	9	0	0	81
	2	9	18	4	81
	4	10	40	16	100
	6	11	66	36	121
	8	11	88	64	121
	10	12	120	100	144
	12	13	156	144	169
	14	13	182	196	169
$\sum$ (Sum)	56	88	670	560	986

Substituting these values into the formula, we get

$$r = \frac{n(\sum xy) - (\sum x)(\sum y)}{\sqrt{n(\sum x^2) - (\sum x)^2} \cdot \sqrt{n(\sum y^2) - (\sum y)^2}}$$

$$= \frac{8(670) - (56)(88)}{\sqrt{8(560) - 56^2} \cdot \sqrt{8(986) - 88^2}}$$

$$\approx 0.982.$$

As r is close to 1, the fit is a fairly good one; that is, the original points lie nearly along a straight line, as can be confirmed from the graph in Example 2.

1.4 EXERCISES

▼ more advanced ◆ challenging

T indicates exercises that should be solved using technology

In Exercises 1–4, compute the sum-of-squares error (SSE) by hand for the given set of data and linear model. HINT [See Example 1.]

1. (1, 1), (2, 2), (3, 4); $y = x - 1$

2. (0, 1), (1, 1), (2, 2); $y = x + 1$

3. (0, −1), (1, 3), (4, 6), (5, 0); $y = -x + 2$

4. (2, 4), (6, 8), (8, 12), (10, 0); $y = 2x - 8$

T *In Exercises 5–8, use technology to compute the sum-of-squares error (SSE) for the given set of data and linear models. Indicate which linear model gives the better fit.*

5. (1, 1), (2, 2), (3, 4); **a.** $y = 1.5x - 1$ **b.** $y = 2x - 1.5$

6. (0, 1), (1, 1), (2, 2); **a.** $y = 0.4x + 1.1$ **b.** $y = 0.5x + 0.9$

7. (0, −1), (1, 3), (4, 6), (5, 0); **a.** $y = 0.3x + 1.1$
b. $y = 0.4x + 0.9$

8. (2, 4), (6, 8), (8, 12), (10, 0); **a.** $y = -0.1x + 7$
b. $y = -0.2x + 6$

Find the regression line associated with each set of points in Exercises 9–12. Graph the data and the best-fit line. (Round all coefficients to 4 decimal places.) HINT [See Example 2.]

9. (1, 1), (2, 2), (3, 4)

10. (0, 1), (1, 1), (2, 2)

11. (0, −1), (1, 3), (3, 6), (4, 1)

12. (2, 4), (4, 8), (8, 12), (10, 0)

In the next two exercises, use correlation coefficients to determine which of the given sets of data is best fit by its associated regression line and which is fit worst. Is it a perfect fit for any of the data sets? HINT [See Example 3.]

13. a. {(1, 3), (2, 4), (5, 6)}
b. {(0, −1), (2, 1), (3, 4)}
c. {(4, −3), (5, 5), (0, 0)}

14. a. {(1, 3), (−2, 9), (2, 1)}
b. {(0, 1), (1, 0), (2, 1)}
c. {(0, 0), (5, −5), (2, −2.1)}

APPLICATIONS

15. ***Mobile Broadband Subscriptions*** The following table shows the number of mobile broadband subscribers worldwide (x is the number of years since 2000):[60]

Year x	2	6	10
Subscribers y (Millions)	0	70	900

Complete the following table and obtain the associated regression line. (Round coefficients to one decimal place.) HINT [See Example 3.]

	x	y	xy	x^2
	2	0		
	6	70		
	10	900		
Σ (Sum)				

Use your regression equation to project the number in 2012.

16. ***Investment in Gold*** Following are approximate values of the Amex Gold BUGS Index ($x = 0$ represents 2000):[61]

Year x	0	5	10
Index y	50	200	500

[60] Data are rounded (2010 figure is estimated). Source: International Telecommunication Union www.itu.int/ITU-D/ict/statistics/at_glance/KeyTelecom.html.

[61] BUGS stands for "basket of unhedged gold stocks." Figures are approximate. Source: www.google.com/finance.

Complete the following table and obtain the associated regression line. (Round coefficients to the nearest whole number.) HINT [See Example 3.]

	x	y	xy	x^2
	0	50		
	5	200		
	10	500		
Σ (Sum)				

Use your regression equation to project the index in 2011.

17. ***E-Commerce*** The following chart shows second quarter total retail e-commerce sales in the U.S. in 2000, 2005, and 2010 ($t = 0$ represents 2000):[62]

Year t	0	5	10
Sales (\$ billion) y	6	20	40

Find the regression line (round coefficients to one decimal place) and use it to estimate second quarter retail e-commerce sales in 2006. (The actual figure was approximately \$25 billion.)

18. ***Net Sales*** The following table show the reported net sales by Nokia in the third quarters of 2008, 2009, and 2010 ($t = 0$ represents the third quarter of 2008):[63]

Year t	0	1	2
Net Sales (€ billion) y	12	10	10

Find the regression line (round coefficients to one decimal place) and use it to "predict" Nokia's net income in the third quarter of 2011. (The actual figure was approximately €9.0 billion.)

19. ***Oil Recovery*** The Texas Bureau of Economic Geology published a study on the economic impact of using carbon dioxide enhanced oil recovery (EOR) technology to extract additional oil from fields that have reached the end of their conventional economic life. The following table gives the approximate number of jobs for the citizens of Texas that would be created at various levels of recovery.[64]

Percent Recovery (%)	20	40	80	100
Jobs Created (Millions)	3	6	9	15

Find the regression line and use it to estimate the number of jobs that would be created at a recovery level of 50%.

[62]Figures are rounded. Source: U.S. Census Bureau www.census.gov

[63]Data are approximate. Source: www.nokia.com.

[64]Source: "CO2–Enhanced Oil Recovery Resource Potential in Texas: Potential Positive Economic Impacts," Texas Bureau of Economic Geology, April 2004, www.rrc.state.tx.us/tepc/CO2-EOR_white_paper.pdf.

20. ***Oil Recovery*** (Refer to Exercise 19.) The following table gives the approximate economic value associated with various levels of oil recovery in Texas.[65]

Percent Recovery (%)	10	40	50	80
Economic Value (\$ billions)	200	900	1,000	2,000

Find the regression line and use it to estimate the economic value associated with a recovery level of 70%.

21. ***Profit: Amazon.com*** The following table shows Amazon.com's approximate net sales (revenue) and net income (profit) in the period 2006–2009:[66]

Net Sales (\$ billions)	10	15	20	25
Net Income (\$ millions)	200	500	600	900

a. Use this information to find a linear regression model for Amazon's net income I (in millions of dollars) as a function of net sales S (in billions of dollars).

b. Give the units of measurement and interpretation of the slope.

c. What, according to the model, would Amazon.com need to earn in net sales in order for its net income to be \$1 billion? (Round answer to the nearest \$ billion.)

d. Plot the data and regression line. Based on the graph, would you say that the linear model is reasonable? Why?

22. ***Operating Expenses: Amazon.com*** The following table shows Amazon.com's approximate net sales (revenue) and operating expenses in 2006–2009:[67]

Net Sales (\$ billions)	10	15	20	25
Operating Expenses (\$ billions)	2	2.5	3	4.5

a. Use this information to find a linear regression model for Amazon's operating expenses E (in billions of dollars) as a function of net sales S (in billions of dollars).

b. Give the units of measurement and interpretation of the slope.

c. What, according to the model, would Amazon.com need to earn in net sales in order for its operating expenses to be \$5 billion? (Round answer to the nearest \$ billion.)

d. Plot the data and regression line. Based on the graph, would you say that the linear model is reasonable? Why?

[65]*Ibid.*

[66]Figures are approximate. Source: www.wikinvest.com.

[67]*Ibid.*

23. **T** ***Textbook Sizes*** The following table shows the numbers of pages in previous editions of *Applied Calculus* by Waner and Costenoble:

Edition n	2	3	4	5
Number of Pages L	585	656	694	748

a. With the edition number as the independent variable, use technology to obtain a regression line and a plot of the points together with the regression line. (Round coefficients to two decimal places.)
b. Interpret the slope of the regression line.

24. **T** ***Textbook Sizes*** Repeat Exercise 23 using the following corresponding table for *Finite Mathematics* by Waner and Costenoble:

Edition n	2	3	4	5
Number of Pages L	603	608	676	692

25. **T** ***Soybean Production: Cerrados*** The following table shows soybean production, in millions of tons, in Brazil's *Cerrados* region, as a function of the cultivated area, in millions of acres.[68]

Area (millions of acres)	25	30	32	40	52
Production (millions of tons)	15	25	30	40	60

a. Use technology to obtain the regression line and to show a plot of the points together with the regression line. (Round coefficients to two decimal places.)
b. Interpret the slope of the regression line.

26. **T** ***Soybean Production: U.S.*** The following table shows soybean production, in millions of tons, in the U.S. as a function of the cultivated area, in millions of acres.[69]

Area (millions of acres)	30	42	69	59	74	74
Production (millions of tons)	20	33	55	57	83	88

a. Use technology to obtain the regression line and to show a plot of the points together with the regression line. (Round coefficients to two decimal places.)
b. Interpret the slope of the regression line.

27. **T** ***Airline Profits and the Price of Oil*** A common perception is that airline profits are strongly correlated with the price of oil. Following are annual net incomes of **Continental Airlines** together with the approximate price of oil in the period 2005–2010:[70]

Year	**2005**	**2006**	**2007**	**2008**	**2009**	**2010**
Price of Oil ($ per barrel)	56	63	67	92	54	71
Continental Net Income ($ million)	−70	370	430	−590	−280	150

a. Use technology to obtain a regression line showing Continental's net income as a function of the price of oil, and also the coefficient of correlation r.
b. What does the value of r suggest about the relationship of Continental's net income to the price of oil?
c. Support your answer to part (b) with a plot of the data and regression line.

28. **T** ***Airline Profits and the Price of Oil*** Repeat Exercise 27 using the following corresponding data for **American Airlines**:[71]

Year	**2005**	**2006**	**2007**	**2008**	**2009**	**2010**
Price of Oil ($ per barrel)	56	63	67	92	54	71
American Net Income ($ million)	−850	250	450	−2,100	−1,450	−700

T ***Doctorates in Mexico*** *Exercises 29–32 are based on the following table showing the annual number of PhD graduates in Mexico in various fields.*[72]

	Natural Sciences	**Engineering**	**Social Sciences**
1990	84	8	98
1995	107	55	161
2000	174	247	222
2005	515	371	584
2010	979	578	1,230

29. a. With x = the number of natural science doctorates and y = the number of engineering doctorates, use technology to obtain the regression equation and graph the associated points and regression line. (Round coefficients to three significant digits.)
b. What does the slope tell you about the relationship between the number of natural science doctorates and the number of engineering doctorates?
c. Use technology to obtain the coefficient of correlation r. Does the value of r suggest a strong correlation between x and y?
d. Judging from the graph, would you say that a linear relationship between x and y is appropriate? Why?

30. a. With x = the number of natural science doctorates and y = the number of social science doctorates, use technology to obtain the regression equation and graph the associated points and regression line. (Round coefficients to three significant digits.)

[68]Source: Brazil Agriculture Ministry/*New York Times*, December 12, 2004, p. N32.

[69]Data are approximate. Source for data: L. David Roper, June 2010, *Crop Production in the World & the United States*, www.roperld.com/science/cropsworld&us.htm.

[70]Figures are rounded and oil prices are inflation adjusted. Sources: www.wikinvest.com, www.inflationdata.com.

[71]*Ibid.*

[72]2010 data is estimated. Source: Instituto Nacional de Estadística y Geografía www.inegi.org.mx.

b. What does the slope tell you about the relationship between the number of natural science doctorates and the number of social science doctorates?

c. Use technology to obtain the coefficient of correlation r. Does the value of r suggest a strong correlation between x and y?

d. Judging from the graph, would you say that a linear relationship between x and y is appropriate? Why?

31. ▼ **a.** Use technology to obtain the regression equation and the coefficient of correlation r for the number of natural science doctorates as a function of time t in years since 1990, and graph the associated points and regression line. (Round coefficients to three significant digits.)

b. What does the slope tell you about the number of natural science doctorates?

c. Judging from the graph, would you say that the number of natural science doctorates is increasing at a faster and faster rate, a slower and slower rate, or neither? Why?

d. If r had been equal to 1, could you have drawn the same conclusion as in part (c)? Explain.

32. ▼ **a.** Use technology to obtain the regression equation and the coefficient of correlation r for the number of engineering doctorates as a function of time t in years since 1990, and graph the associated points and regression line. (Round coefficients to three significant digits.)

b. What does the slope tell you about the number of engineering doctorates?

c. Judging from the graph, would you say that the number of engineering doctorates is increasing at a faster and faster rate, a slower and slower rate, or neither? Why?

d. If r had been close to 0, could you have drawn the same conclusion as in part (c)? Explain.

33. ▮ ▼ *NY City Housing Costs: Downtown* The following table shows the average price of a two-bedroom apartment in downtown New York City from 1994 to 2004 ($t = 0$ represents 1994).[73]

Year t	0	2	4	6	8	10
Price p ($ million)	0.38	0.40	0.60	0.95	1.20	1.60

a. Use technology to obtain the linear regression line and correlation coefficient r, with all coefficients rounded to two decimal places, and plot the regression line and the given points.

b. Does the graph suggest that a non-linear relationship between t and p would be more appropriate than a linear one? Why?

c. Use technology to obtain the residuals. What can you say about the residuals in support of the claim in part (b)?

34. ▮ ▼ *Fiber Optic Connections* The following table shows the number of fiber optic cable connections to homes in the U.S. from 2000 to 2004 ($t = 0$ represents 2000):[74]

Year t	0	1	2	3	4
Connections c (Thousands)	0	10	25	65	150

a. Use technology to obtain the linear regression line and correlation coefficient r, with all coefficients rounded to two decimal places, and plot the regression line and the given points.

b. Does the graph suggest that a non-linear relationship between t and c would be more appropriate than a linear one? Why?

c. Use technology to obtain the residuals. What can you say about the residuals in support of the claim in part (b)?

COMMUNICATION AND REASONING EXERCISES

35. Why is the regression line associated with the two points (a, b) and (c, d) the same as the line that passes through both? (Assume that $a \neq c$.)

36. What is the smallest possible sum-of-squares error if the given points happen to lie on a straight line? Why?

37. If the points (x_1, y_1), (x_2, y_2), . . . , (x_n, y_n) lie on a straight line, what can you say about the regression line associated with these points?

38. If all but one of the points (x_1, y_1), (x_2, y_2), . . . , (x_n, y_n) lie on a straight line, must the regression line pass through all but one of these points?

39. ▼ Verify that the regression line for the points $(0, 0)$, $(-a, a)$, and (a, a) has slope 0. What is the value of r? (Assume that $a \neq 0$.)

40. ▼ Verify that the regression line for the points $(0, a)$, $(0, -a)$, and $(a, 0)$ has slope 0. What is the value of r? (Assume that $a \neq 0$.)

41. ▼ Must the regression line pass through at least one of the data points? Illustrate your answer with an example.

42. ▼ Why must care be taken when using mathematical models to extrapolate?

43. ▼ Your friend Imogen tells you that if r for a collection of data points is more than 0.9, then the most appropriate relationship between the variables is a linear one. Explain why she is wrong by referring to one of the exercises.

44. ▼ Your other friend Mervyn tells you that if r for a collection of data points has an absolute value less than 0.8, then the most appropriate relationship between the variables is a quadratic and not a linear one. Explain why *he* is wrong.

[73]Data are rounded and 2004 figure is an estimate. Source: Miller Samuel/*New York Times*, March 28, 2004, p. RE 11.

[74]Source: Render, Vanderslice & Associates/*New York Times*, October 11, 2004, p. C1.

CHAPTER 1 REVIEW

KEY CONCEPTS

Website www.WanerMath.com
Go to the Website at www.WanerMath.com to find a comprehensive and interactive Web-based summary of Chapter 1.

1.1 Functions from the Numerical, Algebraic, and Graphical Viewpoints

Real-valued function *f* of a real-valued variable *x*, domain *p. 42*
Independent and dependent variables *p. 42*
Graph of the function *f* *p. 42*
Numerically specified function *p. 42*
Graphically specified function *p. 42*
Algebraically defined function *p. 42*
Piecewise-defined function *p. 47*
Vertical line test *p. 49*
Common types of algebraic functions and their graphs *p. 50*

1.2 Functions and Models

Mathematical model *p. 56*
Analytical model *p. 57*
Curve-fitting model *p. 57*
Cost, revenue, and profit; marginal cost, revenue, and profit; break-even point *p. 59*
Demand, supply, and equilibrium price *pp. 61–62*
Selecting a model *p. 64*
Compound interest *p. 66*
Exponential growth and decay *p. 68*
Algebra of functions (sum, difference, product, quotient) *p. 70*

1.3 Linear Functions and Models

Linear function $f(x) = mx + b$ *p. 78*
Change in q: $\Delta q = q_2 - q_1$ *p. 79*
Slope of a line:

$$m = \frac{\Delta y}{\Delta x} = \frac{\text{Change in } y}{\text{Change in } x} \quad p.\ 79$$

Interpretations of m *p. 80*
Interpretation of b: y-intercept *p. 80*
Recognizing linear data *p. 81*
Computing the slope of a line *p. 82*
Slopes of horizontal and vertical lines *p. 82*
Computing the y-intercept *p. 83*
Linear modeling *p. 84*
Linear cost *p. 85*
Linear demand *p. 85*
Linear change over time; rate of change; velocity *p. 88*
General linear models *p. 88*

1.4 Linear Regression

Observed and predicted values *p. 96*
Residuals and sum-of-squares error (SSE) *p. 96*
Regression line (least-squares line, best-fit line) *p. 99*
Correlation coefficient; coefficient of determination *p. 101*

REVIEW EXERCISES

In Exercises 1–4, use the graph of the function f to find approximations of the given values.

1.

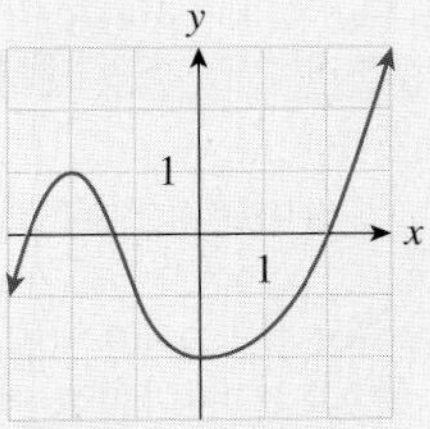

a. $f(-2)$ **b.** $f(0)$
c. $f(2)$ **d.** $f(2) - f(-2)$

2.

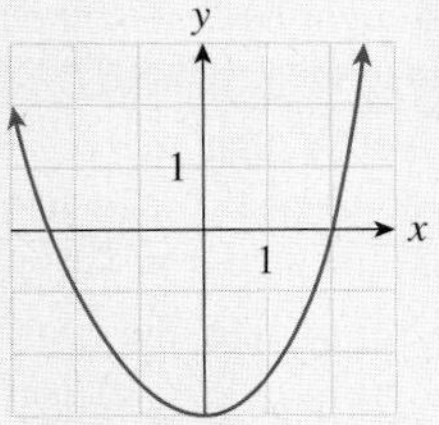

a. $f(-2)$ **b.** $f(0)$
c. $f(2)$ **d.** $f(2) - f(-2)$

3.

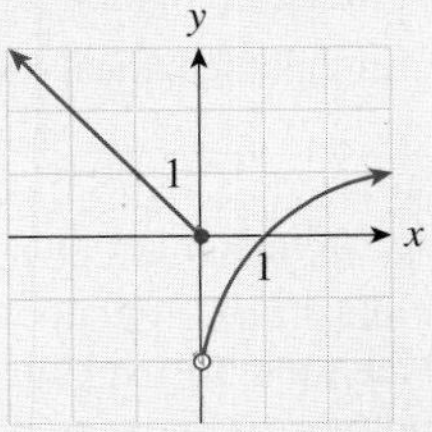

a. $f(-1)$ **b.** $f(0)$
c. $f(1)$ **d.** $f(1) - f(-1)$

4.

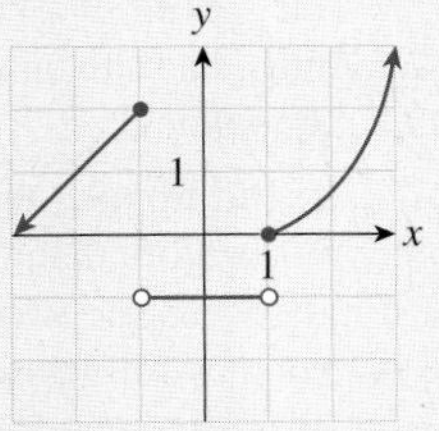

a. $f(-1)$ **b.** $f(0)$
c. $f(1)$ **d.** $f(1) - f(-1)$

In Exercises 5–8, graph the given function or equation.

5. $y = -2x + 5$ **6.** $2x - 3y = 12$

7. $y = \begin{cases} \frac{1}{2}x & \text{if } -1 \le x \le 1 \\ x - 1 & \text{if } 1 < x \le 3 \end{cases}$

8. $f(x) = 4x - x^2$ with domain $[0, 4]$

In Exercises 9–14, decide whether the specified values come from a linear, quadratic, exponential, or absolute value function.

9.

x	−2	0	1	2	4
$f(x)$	4	2	1	0	2

10.

x	−2	0	1	2	4
$g(x)$	−5	−3	−2	−1	1

11.

x	−2	0	1	2	4
$h(x)$	1.5	1	0.75	0.5	0

12.

x	−2	0	1	2	4
$k(x)$	0.25	1	2	4	16

13.

x	−2	0	1	2	4
$u(x)$	0	4	3	0	−12

14.

x	-2	0	1	2	4
$w(x)$	32	8	4	2	0.5

In Exercises 15–22, find the equation of the specified line.

15. Through (3, 2) with slope -3

16. Through $(-2, 4)$ with slope -1

17. Through $(1, -3)$ and (5, 2)

18. Through $(-1, 2)$ and (1, 0)

19. Through (1, 2) parallel to $x - 2y = 2$

20. Through $(-3, 1)$ parallel to $-2x - 4y = 5$

21. With slope 4 crossing $2x - 3y = 6$ at its x-intercept

22. With slope $1/2$ crossing $3x + y = 6$ at its x-intercept

In Exercises 23 and 24, determine which of the given lines better fits the given points.

23. $(-1, 1), (1, 2), (2, 0)$; $y = -x/2 + 1$ or $y = -x/4 + 1$

24. $(-2, -1), (-1, 1), (0, 1), (1, 2), (2, 4), (3, 3)$; $y = x + 1$ or $y = x/2 + 1$

In Exercises 25 and 26, find the line that best fits the given points and compute the correlation coefficient.

25. $(-1, 1), (1, 2), (2, 0)$

26. $(-2, -1), (-1, 1), (0, 1), (1, 2), (2, 4), (3, 3)$

APPLICATIONS: OHaganBooks.com

27. ***Web Site Traffic*** John Sean O'Hagan is CEO of the online bookstore OHaganBooks.com and notices that, since the establishment of the company Web site six years ago ($t = 0$), the number of visitors to the site has grown quite dramatically, as indicated by the following table:

Year t	0	1	2	3	4	5	6
Web site Traffic $V(t)$ (visits/day)	100	300	1,000	3,300	10,500	33,600	107,400

a. Graph the function V as a function of time t. Which of the following types of function seem to fit the curve best: linear, quadratic, or exponential?

b. Compute the ratios $\frac{V(1)}{V(0)}, \frac{V(2)}{V(1)}, \ldots,$ and $\frac{V(6)}{V(5)}$. What do you notice?

c. Use the result of part (b) to predict Web site traffic next year (to the nearest 100).

28. ***Publishing Costs*** Marjory Maureen Duffin is CEO of publisher Duffin House, a major supplier of paperback titles to OHaganBooks.com. She notices that publishing costs over the past five years have varied considerably as indicated by the following table, which shows the average cost to the company of publishing a paperback novel (t is time in years, and the current year is $t = 5$):

Year t	0	1	2	3	4	5
Cost $C(t)$	\$5.42	\$5.10	\$5.00	\$5.12	\$5.40	\$5.88

a. Graph the function C as a function of time t. Which of the following types of function seem to fit the curve best: linear, quadratic, or exponential?

b. Compute the differences $C(1) - C(0), C(2) - C(1), \ldots,$ and $C(5) - C(4)$, rounded to one decimal place. What do you notice?

c. Use the result of part (b) to predict the cost of producing a paperback novel next year.

29. ***Web Site Stability*** John O'Hagan is considering upgrading the Web server equipment at OHaganBooks.com because of frequent crashes. The tech services manager has been monitoring the frequency of crashes as a function of Web site traffic (measured in thousands of visits per day) and has obtained the following model:

$$c(x) = \begin{cases} 0.03x + 2 & \text{if } 0 \le x \le 50 \\ 0.05x + 1 & \text{if } x > 50 \end{cases}$$

where $c(x)$ is the average number of crashes in a day in which there are x thousand visitors.

a. On average, how many times will the Web site crash on a day when there are 10,000 visits? 50,000 visits? 100,000 visits?

b. What does the coefficient 0.03 tell you about the Web site's stability?

c. Last Friday, the Web site went down 8 times. Estimate the number of visits that day.

30. ***Book Sales*** As OHaganBooks.com has grown in popularity, the sales manager has been monitoring book sales as a function of the Web site traffic (measured in thousands of visits per day) and has obtained the following model:

$$s(x) = \begin{cases} 1.55x & \text{if } 0 \le x \le 100 \\ 1.75x - 20 & \text{if } 100 < x \le 250 \end{cases}$$

where $s(x)$ is the average number of books sold in a day in which there are x thousand visitors.

a. On average, how many books per day does the model predict OHaganBooks.com will sell when it has 60,000 visits in a day? 100,000 visits in a day? 160,000 visits in a day?

b. What does the coefficient 1.75 tell you about book sales?

c. According to the model, approximately how many visitors per day will be needed in order to sell an average of 300 books per day?

31. ***New Users*** The number of registered users at OHaganBooks.com has increased substantially over the past few months. The following table shows the number of new users registering each month for the past six months:

Month t	1	2	3	4	5	6
New Users (thousands)	12.5	37.5	62.5	72.0	74.5	75.0

a. Which of the following models best approximates the data?

(A) $n(t) = \dfrac{300}{4 + 100(5^{-t})}$ **(B)** $n(t) = 13.3t + 8.0$

(C) $n(t) = -2.3t^2 + 30.0t - 3.3$

(D) $n(t) = 7(3^{0.5t})$

b. What do each of the above models predict for the number of new users in the next few months: rising, falling, or leveling off?

32. *Purchases* OHaganBooks.com has been promoting a number of books published at Duffin House. The following table shows the number of books purchased each month from Duffin House for the past five months:

Month t	1	2	3	4	5
Purchases (books)	1,330	520	520	1,340	2,980

a. Which of the following models best approximates the data?

(A) $n(t) = \dfrac{3{,}000}{1 + 12(2^{-t})}$ **(B)** $n(t) = \dfrac{2{,}000}{4.2 - 0.7t}$

(C) $n(t) = 300(1.6^t)$

(D) $n(t) = 100(4.1t^2 - 20.4t + 29.5)$

b. What do each of the above models predict for the number of new users in the next few months: rising, falling, leveling off, or something else?

33. *Internet Advertising* Several months ago. John O'Hagan investigated the effect on the popularity of OHaganBooks.com of placing banner ads at well-known Internet portals. The following model was obtained from available data:

$v(c) = -0.000005c^2 + 0.085c + 1{,}750$ new visits per day

where c is the monthly expenditure on banner ads.

a. John O'Hagan is considering increasing expenditure on banner ads from the current level of \$5,000 to \$6,000 per month. What will be the resulting effect on Web site popularity?

b. According to the model, would the Web site popularity continue to grow at the same rate if he continued to raise expenditure on advertising \$1,000 each month? Explain.

c. Does this model give a reasonable prediction of traffic at expenditures larger than \$8,500 per month? Why?

34. *Production Costs* Over at Duffin House, Marjory Duffin is trying to decide on the size of the print runs for the best-selling new fantasy novel *Larry Plotter and the Simplex Method*. The following model shows a calculation of the total cost to produce a million copies of the novel, based on an analysis of setup and storage costs:

$$c(n) = 0.0008n^2 - 72n + 2{,}000{,}000 \text{ dollars}$$

where n is the print run size (the number of books printed in each run).

a. What would be the effect on cost if the run size was increased from 20,000 to 30,000?

b. Would increasing the run size in further steps of 10,000 result in the same changes in the total cost? Explain.

c. What approximate run size would you recommend that Marjoy Duffin use for a minimum cost?

35. *Internet Advertising* When OHaganBooks.com actually went ahead and increased Internet advertising from \$5,000 per month to \$6,000 per month (see Exercise 33) it was noticed that the number of new visits increased from an estimated 2,050 per day to 2,100 per day. Use this information to construct a linear model giving the average number v of new visits per day as a function of the monthly advertising expenditure c.

a. What is the model?

b. Based on the model, how many new visits per day could be anticipated if OHaganBooks.com budgets \$7,000 per month for Internet advertising?

c. The goal is to eventually increase the number of new visits to 2,500 per day. Based on the model, how much should be spent on Internet advertising in order to accomplish this?

36. *Production Costs* When Duffin House printed a million copies of *Larry Plotter and the Simplex Method* (see Exercise 34), it used print runs of 20,000, which cost the company \$880,000. For the sequel, *Larry Plotter and the Simplex Method, Phase 2* it used print runs of 40,000 which cost the company \$550,000. Use this information to construct a linear model giving the production cost c as a function of the run size n.

a. What is the model?

b. Based on the model, what would print runs of 25,000 have cost the company?

c. Marjory Duffin has decided to budget \$418,000 for production of the next book in the *Simplex Method* series. Based on the model, how large should the print runs be to accomplish this?

37. *Recreation* John O'Hagan has just returned from a sales convention at Puerto Vallarta, Mexico where, in order to win a bet he made with Marjory Duffin (Duffin House was also at the convention), he went bungee jumping at a nearby mountain retreat. The bungee cord he used had the property that a person weighing 70 kg would drop a total distance of 74.5 meters, while a 90 kg person would drop 93.5 meters. Express the distance d a jumper drops as a linear function of the jumper's weight w. John OHagan dropped 90 m. What was his approximate weight?

38. *Crickets* The mountain retreat near Puerto Vallarta was so quiet at night that all one could hear was the chirping of the snowy tree crickets. These crickets behave in a rather interesting way: The rate at which they chirp depends linearly on the temperature. Early in the evening, John O'Hagan counted 140 chirps/minute and noticed that the temperature was 80°F. Later in the evening the temperature dropped to 75°F, and the chirping slowed down to 120 chirps/minute. Express the temperature T as a function of the rate of chirping r. The temperature that night dropped to a low of 65°F. At approximately what rate were the crickets chirping at that point?

39. ***Break-Even Analysis*** OHaganBooks.com has recently decided to start selling music albums online through a service it calls *o'Tunes*.[75] Users pay a fee to download an entire music album. Composer royalties and copyright fees cost an average of \$5.50 per album, and the cost of operating and maintaining *o'Tunes* amounts to \$500 per week. The company is currently charging customers \$9.50 per album.

a. What are the associated (weekly) cost, revenue, and profit functions?

b. How many albums must be sold per week in order to make a profit?

c. If the charge is lowered to \$8.00 per album, how many albums must be sold per week in order to make a profit?

40. ***Break-Even Analysis*** OHaganBooks.com also generates revenue through its *o'Books* e-book service. Author royalties and copyright fees cost the company an average of \$4 per novel, and the monthly cost of operating and maintaining the service amounts to \$900 per month. The company is currently charging readers \$5.50 per novel.

a. What are the associated cost, revenue, and profit functions?

b. How many novels must be sold per month in order to break even?

c. If the charge is lowered to \$5.00 per novel, how many books must be sold in order to break even?

41. ***Demand and Profit*** In order to generate a profit from its new *o'Tunes* service, OHaganBooks.com needs to know how the demand for music albums depends on the price it charges. During the first week of the service, it was charging \$7 per album, and sold 500. Raising the price to \$9.50 had the effect of lowering demand to 300 albums per week.

a. Use the given data to construct a linear demand equation.

b. Use the demand equation you constructed in part (a) to estimate the demand if the price was raised to \$12 per album.

c. Using the information on cost given in Exercise 39, determine which of the three prices (\$7, \$9.50 and \$12) would result in the largest weekly profit, and the size of that profit.

42. ***Demand and Profit*** In order to generate a profit from its *o'Books* e-book service, OHaganBooks.com needs to know how the demand for novels depends on the price it charges. During the first month of the service, it was charging \$10 per novel, and sold 350. Lowering the price to \$5.50 per novel had the effect of increasing demand to 620 novels per month.

a. Use the given data to construct a linear demand equation.

b. Use the demand equation you constructed in part (a) to estimate the demand if the price was raised to \$15 per novel.

c. Using the information on cost given in Exercise 40, determine which of the three prices (\$5.50, \$10 and \$15) would result in the largest profit, and the size of that profit.

43. ***Demand*** OHaganBooks.com has tried selling music albums on *o'Tunes* at a variety of prices, with the following results:

Price	\$8.00	\$8.50	\$10	\$11.50
Demand (Weekly sales)	440	380	250	180

a. Use the given data to obtain a linear regression model of demand.

b. Use the demand model you constructed in part (a) to estimate the demand if the company charged \$10.50 per album. (Round the answer to the nearest album.)

44. ***Demand*** OHaganBooks.com has tried selling novels through *o'Books* at a variety of prices, with the following results:

Price	\$5.50	\$10	\$11.50	\$12
Demand (Monthly sales)	620	350	350	300

a. Use the given data to obtain a linear regression model of demand.

b. Use the demand model you constructed in part (a) to estimate the demand if the company charged \$8 per novel. (Round the answer to the nearest novel.)

[75] The (highly original) name was suggested to John O'Hagan by Marjory Duffin over cocktails one evening.

Case Study: Modeling Spending on Internet Advertising

Jeff Titcomb/Photographer's Choice / Getty Images

You are the new director of Impact Advertising Inc.'s Internet division, which has enjoyed a steady 0.25% of the Internet advertising market. You have drawn up an ambitious proposal to expand your division in light of your anticipation that Internet advertising will continue to skyrocket. However, upper management sees things differently and, based on the following email, does not seem likely to approve the budget for your proposal.

TO: JCheddar@impact.com (J. R. Cheddar)
CC: CVODoylePres@impact.com (C. V. O'Doyle, CEO)
FROM: SGLombardoVP@impact.com (S. G. Lombardo, VP Financial Affairs)
SUBJECT: Your Expansion Proposal
DATE: May 30, 2014

Hi John:

Your proposal reflects exactly the kind of ambitious planning and optimism we like to see in our new upper management personnel. Your presentation last week was most impressive, and obviously reflected a great deal of hard work and preparation.

I am in full agreement with you that Internet advertising is on the increase. Indeed, our Market Research department informs me that, based on a regression of the most recently available data, Internet advertising revenue in the United States will continue to grow at a rate of approximately $2.7 billion per year. This translates into approximately $6.75 million in increased revenues per year for Impact, given our 0.25% market share. This rate of expansion is exactly what our planned 2015 budget anticipates. Your proposal, on the other hand, would require a budget of approximately *twice* the 2015 budget allocation, even though your proposal provides no hard evidence to justify this degree of financial backing.

At this stage, therefore, I am sorry to say that I am inclined not to approve the funding for your project, although I would be happy to discuss this further with you. I plan to present my final decision on the 2015 budget at next week's divisional meeting.

Regards, Sylvia

Refusing to admit defeat, you contact the Market Research department and request the details of their projections on Internet advertising. They fax you the following information:[76]

Year	2007	2008	2009	2010	2011	2012	2013	2014
Internet Advertising Revenue ($ Billion)	21.2	23.4	22.7	25.8	28.5	32.6	36	40.5

Regression Model: $y = 2.744x + 19.233$ (x = time in years since 2007)

Correlation Coefficient: $r = 0.970$

Now you see where the VP got that $2.7 billion figure: The slope of the regression equation is close to 2.7, indicating a rate of increase of about $2.7 billion per year. Also, the correlation coefficient is very high—an indication that the linear model fits the data well. In view of this strong evidence, it seems difficult to argue that revenues will increase by significantly more than the projected $2.7 billion per year. To get a

[76]The 2011–2014 figures are projections by eMarketer. Source: www.eMarketer.com.

better picture of what's going on, you decide to graph the data together with the regression line in your spreadsheet. What you get is shown in Figure 32. You immediately notice that the data points seem to suggest a curve, and not a straight line. Then again, perhaps the suggestion of a curve is an illusion. Thus there are, you surmise, two possible interpretations of the data:

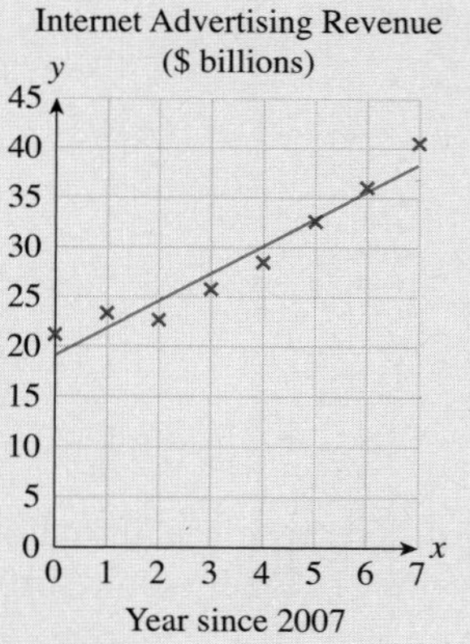

Figure 32

1. (Your first impression) As a function of time, Internet advertising revenue is nonlinear, and is in fact accelerating (the rate of change is increasing), so a linear model is inappropriate.
2. (Devil's advocate) Internet advertising revenue *is* a linear function of time; the fact that the points do not lie on the regression line is simply a consequence of random factors that do not reflect a long-term trend, such as world events, mergers and acquisitions, short-term fluctuations in economy or the stock market, etc.

You suspect that the VP will probably opt for the second interpretation and discount the graphical evidence of accelerating growth by claiming that it is an illusion: a "statistical fluctuation." That is, of course, a possibility, but you wonder how likely it really is.

For the sake of comparison, you decide to try a regression based on the simplest nonlinear model you can think of—a quadratic function.

$$y = ax^2 + bx + c$$

Your spreadsheet allows you to fit such a function with a click of the mouse. The result is the following.

$$y = 0.3208x^2 + 0.4982x + 21.479 \quad (x = \text{number of years since 2007})$$

$$r = 0.996$$

See Note.*

* Note that this r is *not* the linear correlation coefficient we defined on page 101; what this r measures is how closely the *quadratic* regression model fits the data.

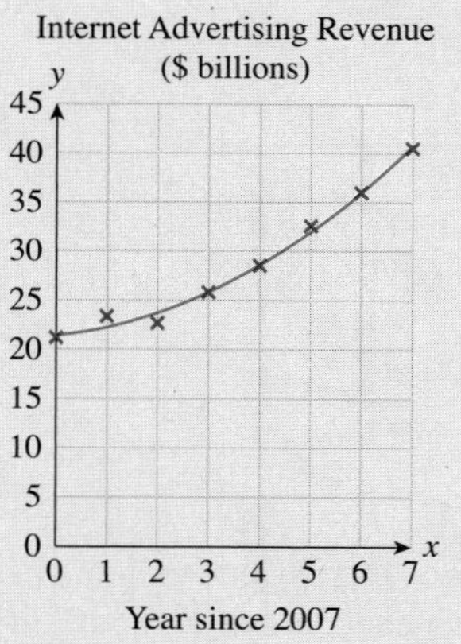

Figure 33

Figure 33 shows the graph of the regression function together with the original data.

Aha! The fit is visually far better, and the correlation coefficient is even higher! Further, the quadratic model predicts 2015 revenue as

$$y = 0.3208(8)^2 + 0.4982(8) + 21.479 \approx \$46.0 \text{ billion},$$

which is \$5.5 billion above the 2014 spending figure in the table above. Given Impact Advertising's 0.25% market share, this translates into an increase in revenues of \$13.75 million, which is about double the estimate predicted by the linear model!

You quickly draft an email to Lombardo, and are about to click "Send" when you decide, as a precaution, to check with a colleague who is knowledgeable in statistics. He tells you to be cautious: The value of r will always tend to increase if you pass from a linear model to a quadratic one because of the increase in "degrees of freedom."† A good way to test whether a quadratic model is more appropriate than a linear one is to compute a statistic called the "p-value" associated with the coefficient of x^2. A low value of p indicates a high degree of confidence that the coefficient of x^2 cannot be zero (see below). Notice that if the coefficient of x^2 *is* zero, then you have a linear model.

† The number of degrees of freedom in a regression model is 1 less than the number of coefficients. For a linear model, it is 1 (there are two coefficients: the slope m and the intercept b), and for a quadratic model it is 2. For a detailed discussion, consult a text on regression analysis.

You can, your colleague explains, obtain the p-value using your spreadsheet as follows (the method we describe here works on all the popular spreadsheets, including *Excel, Google Docs,* and *Open Office Calc*).

First, set up the data in columns, with an extra column for the values of x^2:

	A	B	C
1	y	x	x^2
2	21.2	0	0
3	23.4	1	1
4	22.7	2	4
5	25.8	3	9
6	28.5	4	16
7	32.6	5	25
8	36	6	36
9	40.5	7	49

Then, highlight a vacant 5 × 3 block (the block E1:G5 say), type the formula `=LINEST(A2:A9,B2:C9,,TRUE)`, and press Cntl+Shift+Enter (not just Enter!). You will see a table of statistics like the following:

	E	F	G
1	=LINEST(A2:A9,B2:C9,,TRUE)		
2			
3			
4			
5			

↓

Cntl+Shift+Enter

	E	F	G
1	0.32083333	0.49821429	21.4791667
2	0.05808804	0.42288732	0.63366572
3	0.99157395	0.75290706	#N/A
4	294.198816	5	#N/A
5	333.544405	2.83434524	#N/A

(Notice the coefficients of the quadratic model in the first row.) The *p*-value is then obtained by the formula `=TDIST(ABS(E1/E2),F4,2)`, which you can compute in any vacant cell. You should get $p \approx 0.00267$.

Q: *What does p actually measure?*

A: *Roughly speaking,* $1 - p \approx 0.997733$ gives the degree of confidence you can have (99.7733%) in asserting that the coefficient of x^2 is not zero. (Technically, p is the probability—allowing for random fluctuation in the data—that, if the coefficient of x^2 were in fact zero, the ratio E1/E2 could be as large as it is.)

In short, you can go ahead and send your email with almost 100% confidence!

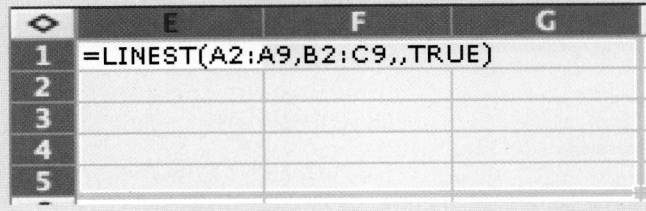

EXERCISES

Suppose you are given the following data for the spending on Internet advertising in a hypothetical country in which Impact Advertising also has a 0.25% share of the market.

Year	2010	2011	2012	2013	2014	2015	2016
Spending on Advertising ($ Billion)	0	0.3	1.5	2.6	3.4	4.3	5.0

1. Obtain a linear regression model and the correlation coefficient r. (Take t to be time in years since 2010.) According to the model, at what rate is spending on Internet Advertising increasing in this country? How does this translate to annual revenues for Impact Advertising?

2. Use a spreadsheet or other technology to graph the data together with the best-fit line. Does the graph suggest a quadratic model (parabola)?

3. Test your impression in the preceding exercise by using technology to fit a quadratic function and graphing the resulting curve together with the data. Does the graph suggest that the quadratic model is appropriate?

4. Perform a regression analysis using the quadratic model and find the associated p-value. What does it tell you about the appropriateness of a quadratic model?

TI-83/84 Plus Technology Guide

Section 1.1

Example 1(a) and (c) (page 44) The total number of iPods sold by Apple up to the end of year x can be approximated by $f(x) = 4x^2 + 16x + 2$ million iPods $(0 \le x \le 6)$, where $x = 0$ represents 2003. Compute $f(0)$, $f(2)$, $f(4)$, and $f(6)$, and obtain the graph of f.

Solution with Technology

You can use the Y= screen to enter an algebraically defined function.

1. Enter the function in the Y= screen, as

`Y1 = 4X^2+16X+2`

or `Y1 = 4X²+16X+2`

(See Chapter 0 for a discussion of technology formulas.)

2. To evaluate $f(0)$, for example, enter $Y_1(0)$ in the Home screen to evaluate the function Y_1 at 0. Alternatively, you can use the table feature: After entering the function under Y_1, press [2ND] [TBLSET], and set `Indpnt` to `Ask`. (You do this once and for all; it will permit you to specify values for x in the table screen.) Then, press [2ND] [TABLE], and you will be able to evaluate the function at several values of x. Below (top) is a table showing the values requested:

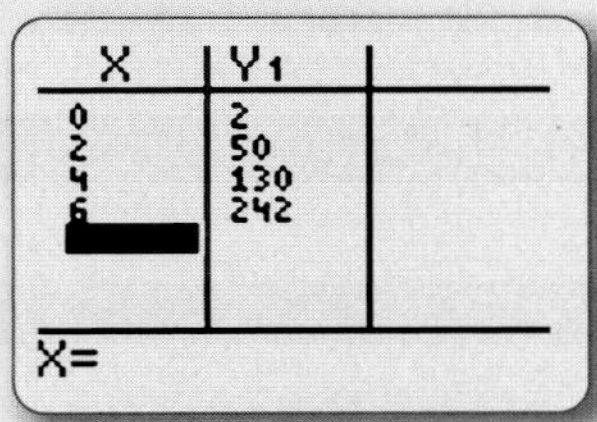

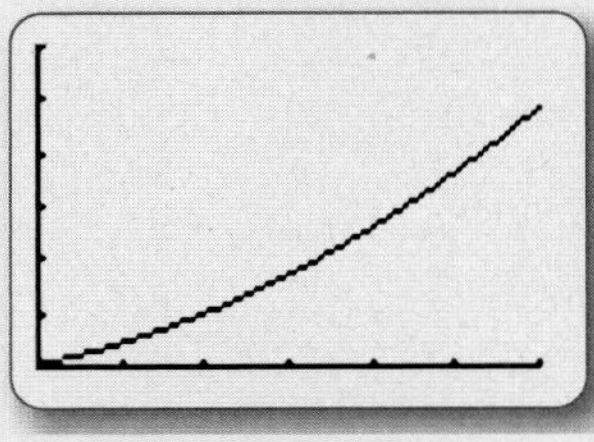

3. To obtain the graph above press [WINDOW], set Xmin = 0, Xmax = 6 (the range of x-values we are interested in), Ymin = 0, Ymax = 300 (we estimated Ymin and Ymax from the corresponding set of y-values in the table) and press [GRAPH] to obtain the curve. Alternatively, you can avoid having to estimate Ymin and Ymax by pressing ZoomFit ([ZOOM] [0]), which automatically sets Ymin and Ymax to the smallest and greatest values of y in the specified range for x.

Example 2 (page 47) The number $n(t)$ of Facebook members can be approximated by the following function of time t in years ($t = 0$ represents January 2004):

$$n(t) = \begin{cases} 4t & \text{if } 0 \le t \le 3 \\ 12 + 23(t-3)^{2.7} & \text{if } 3 < t \le 6 \end{cases} \text{ million members.}$$

Obtain a table showing the values $n(t)$ for $t = 0, \ldots, 6$ and also obtain the graph of n.

Solution with Technology

You can enter a piecewise-defined function using the logical inequality operators $<$, $>$, $\le$, and $\ge$, which are found by pressing [2ND] [TEST]:

1. Enter the function n in the Y= screen as:

`Y1=(X≤3)*(4X)+(X>3)*(12+23*abs(X-3)^2.7)`

When x is less than or equal to 3, the logical expression `(X≤3)` evaluates to 1 because it is true, and the expression `(X>3)` evaluates to 0 because it is false. The value of the function is therefore given by the expression `(4X)`. When x is greater than 3, the expression `(X≤3)` evaluates to 0 while the expression `(X>3)` evaluates to 1, so the value of the function is given by the expression `(12+23*abs(X-3)^2.7)`. (The reason we use the `abs` in the formula is to prevent an error in evaluating $(x - 3)^{2.7}$ when $x < 3$; even though we don't use that formula when $x < 3$, we are in fact evaluating it and multiplying it by zero.)

2. As in Example 1, use the Table feature to compute several values of the function at once by pressing [2ND] [TABLE].

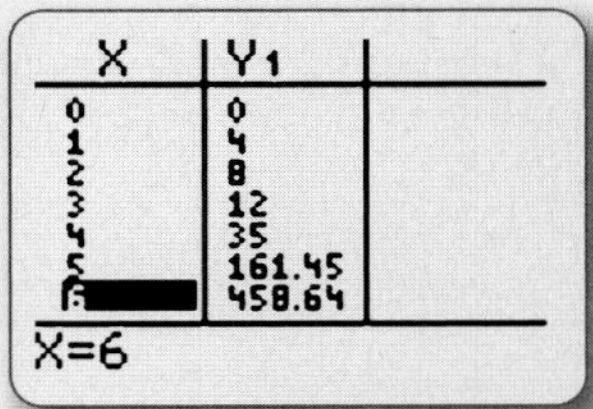

3. To obtain the graph, we proceed as in Example 1: Press [WINDOW], set Xmin = 0, Xmax = 6 (the range of x-values we are interested in), Ymin = 0, Ymax = 500 (see the y-values in the table) and press [GRAPH].

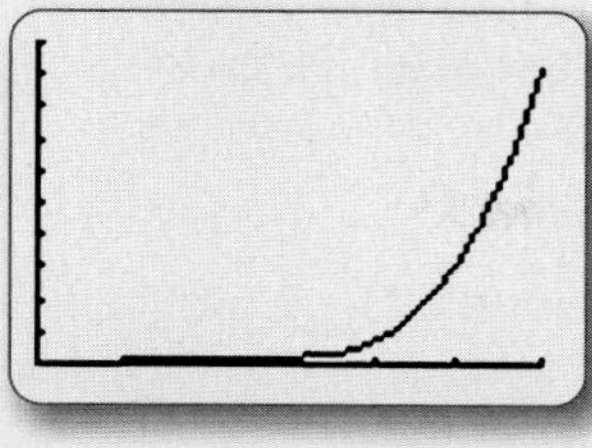

Section 1.2

Example 4(a) (page 62) The demand and supply curves for private schools in Michigan are $q = 77.8p^{-0.11}$ and $q = 30.4 + 0.006p$ thousand students, respectively $(200 \le p \le 2{,}200)$, where p is the net tuition cost in dollars. Graph the demand and supply curves on the same set of axes. Use your graph to estimate, to the nearest \$100, the tuition at which the demand equals the supply (equilibrium price). Approximately how many students will be accommodated at that price?

Solution with Technology

To obtain the graphs of demand and supply:

1. Enter `Y1=77.8*X^(-0.11)` and `Y2=30.4+0.006*X` in the "Y=" screen.
2. Press [WINDOW], enter Xmin = 200, Xmax = 2200, Ymin = 0, Ymax = 50 and press [GRAPH] for the graph shown below:

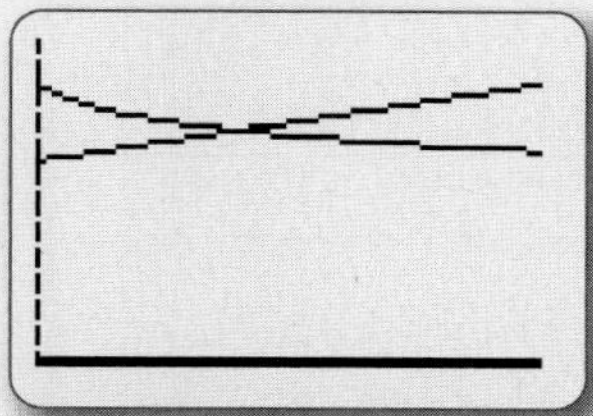

3. To estimate the equilibrium price, press [TRACE] and use the arrow keys to follow the curve to the approximate point of intersection (around X = 1008) as shown below.

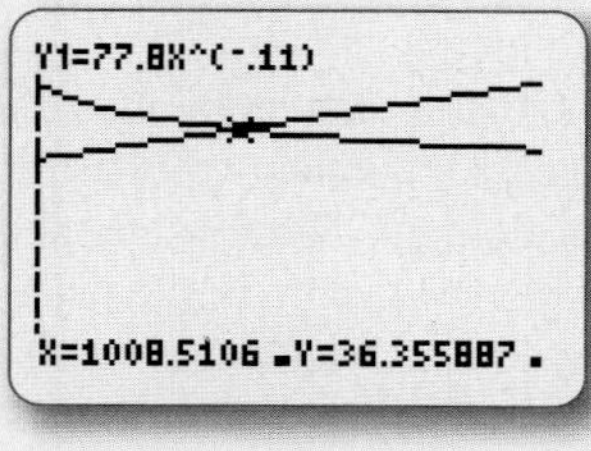

4. For a more accurate estimate, zoom in by pressing [ZOOM] and selecting Option 1 `ZBox`.
5. Move the curser to a point slightly above and to the left of the intersection, press [ENTER], and then move the curser to a point slightly below and to the right and press [ENTER] again to obtain a box.

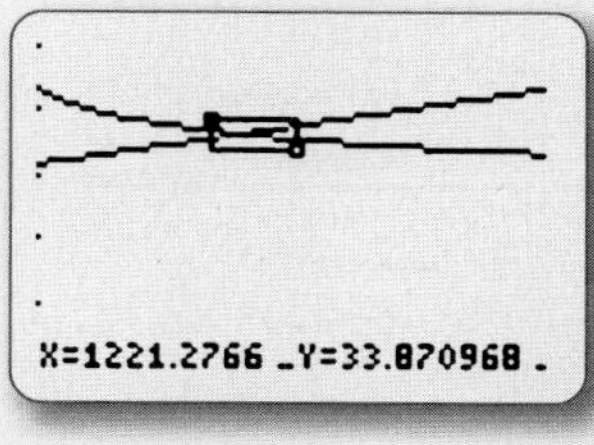

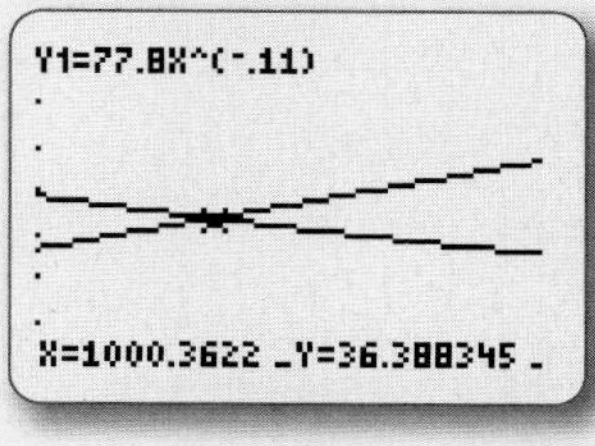

6. Now press [ENTER] again for a zoomed-in view of the intersection.
7. You can now use [TRACE] to obtain the intersection coordinates more accurately: X ≈ 1,000, representing a tuition cost of \$1,000. The associated demand is the Y-coordinate: around 36.4 thousand students.

Example 5(a) (page 64) The following table shows annual sales, in billions of dollars, by *Nike* from 2005 through 2010 ($t = 0$ represents 2005):

t	0	1	2	3	4	5
Sales (\$ billion)	13.5	15	16.5	18.5	19	19

Consider the following four models:

(1) $s(t) = 14 + 1.2t$ Linear model

(2) $s(t) = 13 + 2.2t - 0.2t^2$ Quadratic model

(3) $s(t) = 14(1.07^t)$ Exponential model

(4) $s(t) = \dfrac{19.5}{1 + 0.48(1.8^{-t})}$. Logistic model

a. Which models fit the data significantly better than the rest?

b. Of the models you selected in part (a), which gives the most reasonable prediction for 2013?

Solution with Technology

1. First enter the actual revenue data in the stat list editor (STAT EDIT) with the values of t in L_1, and the values of $s(t)$ in L_2.

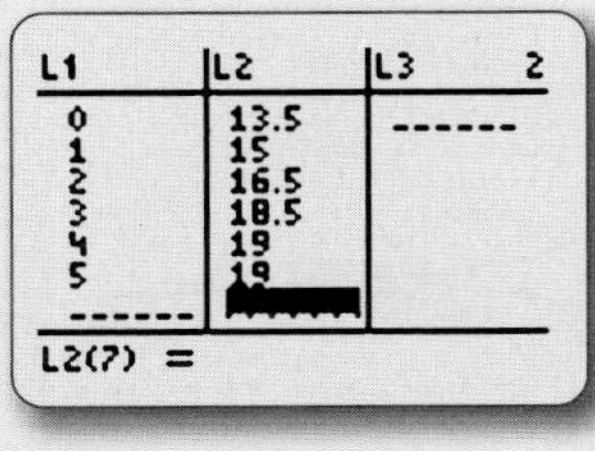

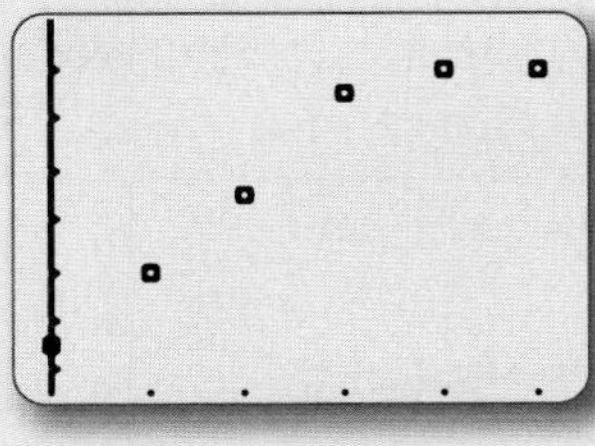

2. Now go to the `Y=` window and turn `Plot1` on by selecting it and pressing ENTER. (You can also turn it on in the 2ND STAT PLOT screen.) Then press ZoomStat (ZOOM 9) to obtain a plot of the points (above).
3. To see any of the four curves plotted along with the points, enter its formula in the Y= screen (for instance, Y_1=13+2.2x-0.2X^2 for the second model) and press GRAPH (figure on top below).

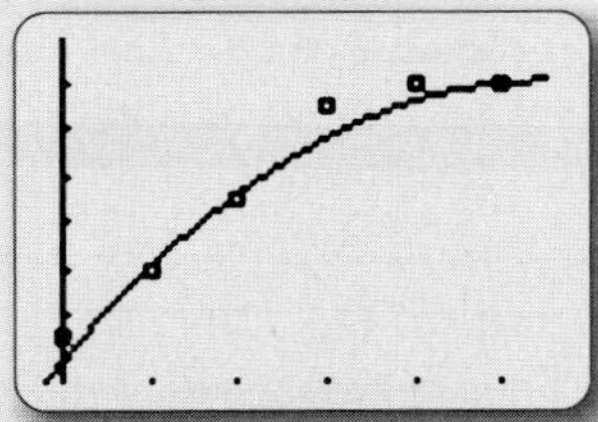

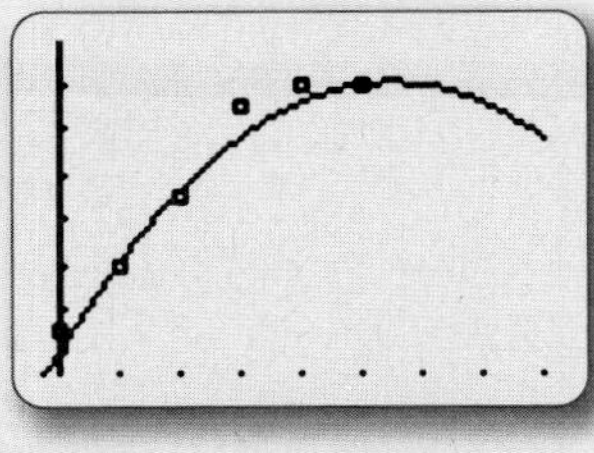

4. To see the extrapolation of the curve to 2013, just change Xmax to 8 (in the WINDOW screen) and press GRAPH again (lower figure above).
5. Now change Y_1 to see similar graphs for the remaining curves.
6. When you are done, turn `Plot1` off again so that the points you entered do not show up in other graphs.

Section 1.3

Example 1 (page 81) Which of the following two tables gives the values of a linear function? What is the formula for that function?

x	0	2	4	6	8	10	12
$f(x)$	3	−1	−3	−6	−8	−13	−15

x	0	2	4	6	8	10	12
$g(x)$	3	−1	−5	−9	−13	−17	−21

Solution with Technology

We can use the "List" feature in the TI-83/84 Plus to automatically compute the successive quotients $m = \Delta y/\Delta x$ for either f or g as follows:

1. Use the stat list editor (STAT EDIT) to enter the values of x and $f(x)$ in the first two columns, called L_1 and L_2, as shown in the screenshot below. (If there is already data in a column you want to use, you can clear it by highlighting the column heading (e.g., L_1) using the arrow key, and pressing CLEAR ENTER.)

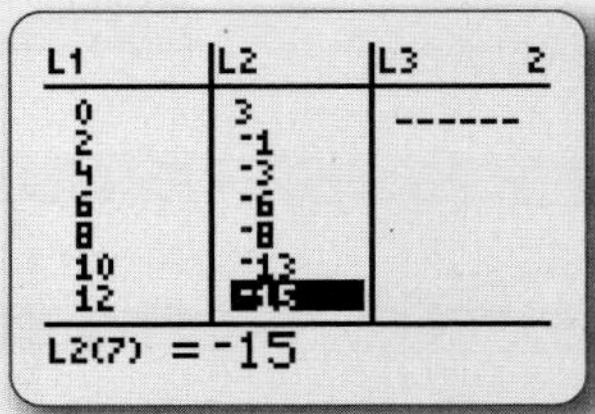

2. Highlight the heading L_3 by using the arrow keys, and enter the following formula (with the quotes, as explained below):

"ΔList(L$_2$)/ΔList(L$_1$)"   ΔList is found under 2ND LIST OPS. L_1 is 2ND 1

The "ΔList" function computes the differences between successive elements of a list, returning a list with one less element. The formula above then computes the quotients $\Delta y/\Delta x$ in the list L_3 as shown in the following screenshot. As you can see in the third column, $f(x)$ is not linear.

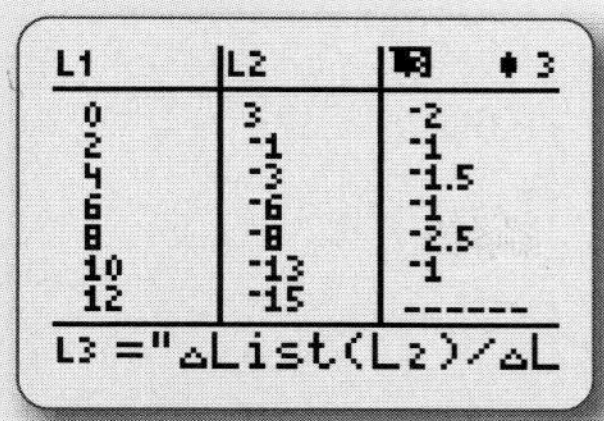

3. To redo the computation for $g(x)$, all you need to do is edit the values of L_2 in the stat list editor. By putting quotes around the formula we used for L_3, we told the calculator to remember the formula, so it automatically recalculates the values.

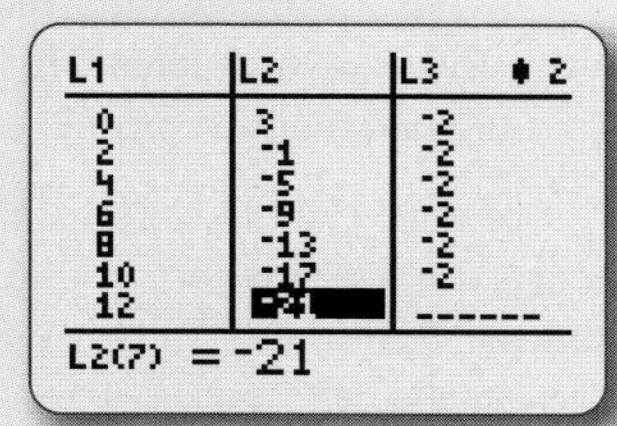

Example 2(a) (page 83) Find the equation of the line through the points (1, 2) and (3, −1).

Solution with Technology

1. Enter the coordinates of the given points in the stat list editor ([STAT] EDIT) with the values of x in L_1, and the values of y in L_2.

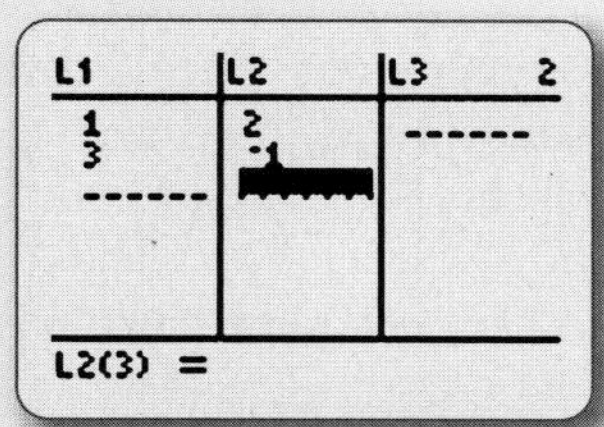

2. To compute the slope, enter the following formula in the Home screen:

```
(L2(2)-L2(1))/(L1(2)-L1(1))→M
```

L_1 and L_2 are under [2ND] [LIST] and the arrow is [STO]

3. Then, to compute the y-intercept, enter

```
L2(1)-M*L1(1)
```

Section 1.4

Example 1(a) (page 97) Using the data on the per capita GDP in Mexico given at the beginning of Section 1.4, compute SSE, the sum-of-squares error, for the linear models $y = 0.5t + 8$ and $y = 0.25t + 9$, and graph the data with the given models.

Solution with Technology

We can use the "List" feature in the TI-83/84 Plus to automate the computation of SSE.

1. Use the stat list editor ([STAT] EDIT) to enter the given data in the lists L_1 and L_2, as shown in the first screenshot below. (If there is already data in a column you want to use, you can clear it by highlighting the column heading (e.g., L_1) using the arrow key, and pressing [CLEAR] [ENTER].)

2. To compute the predicted values, highlight the heading L_3 using the arrow keys, and enter the following formula for the predicted values (figure on the top below):

```
0.5*L1+8
```

L_1 is [2ND] [1]

Pressing [ENTER] again will fill column 3 with the predicted values (below bottom). Note that only seven of the eight data points can be seen on the screen at one time.

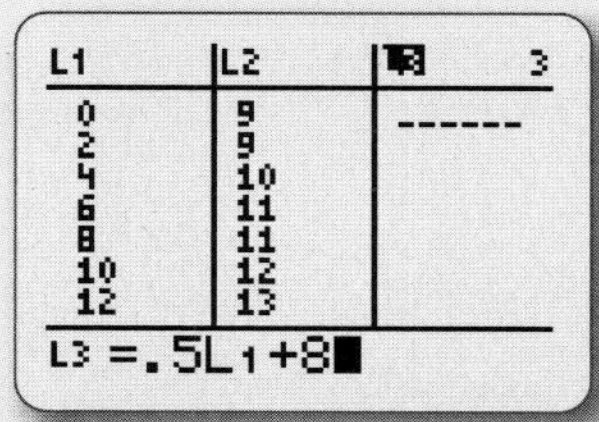

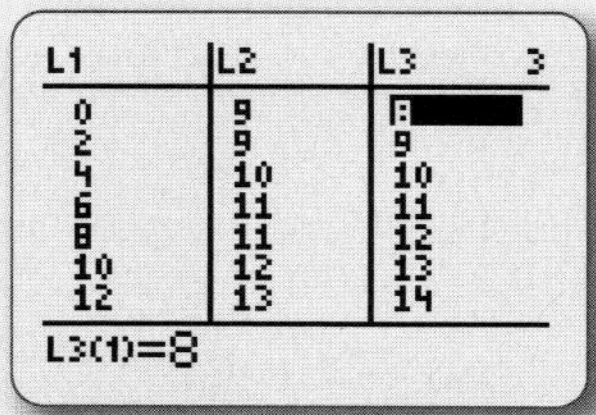

3. Highlight the heading L_4 and enter the following formula (including the quotes):

```
"(L2-L3)^2"
```

Squaring the residuals

TECHNOLOGY GUIDE

4. Pressing ENTER will fill L_4 with the squares of the residuals. (Putting quotes around the formula will allow us to easily check the second model, as we shall see.)

5. To compute SSE, the sum of the entries in L_4, go to the home screen and enter `sum(L4)` (see below; "sum" is under 2ND LIST MATH.)

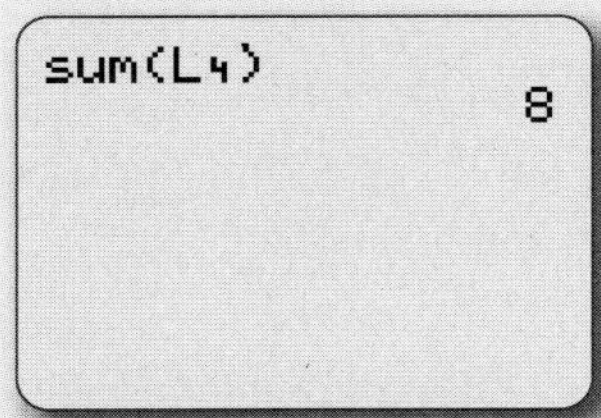

6. To check the second model, go back to the List screen, highlight the heading L_3, enter the formula for the second model, `0.25*L1+9`, and press ENTER. Because we put quotes around the formula for the residuals in L_4, the TI-83/84 Plus will remember the formula and automatically recalculate the values (below top). On the home screen we can again calculate `sum(L4)` to get SSE for the second model (below bottom).

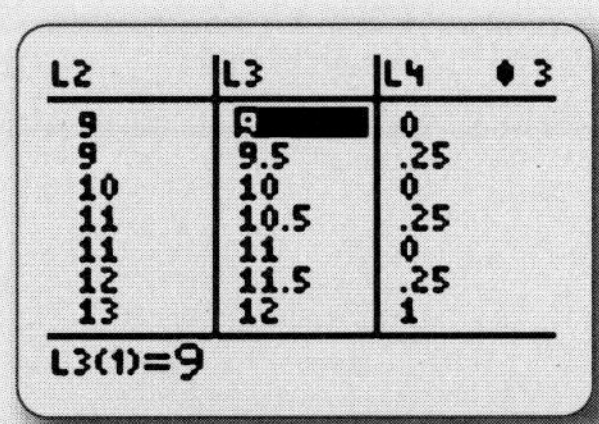

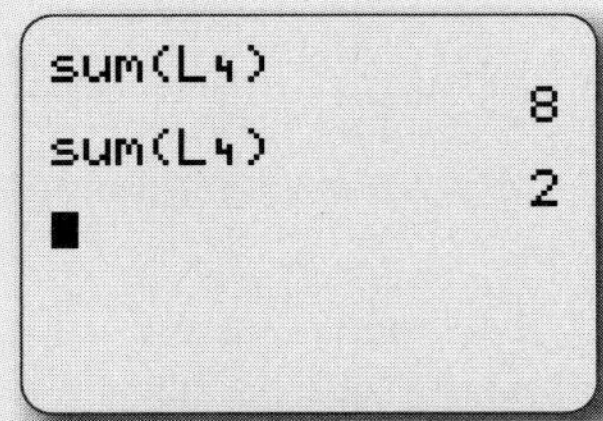

The second model gives a much smaller SSE, so is the better fit.

7. You can also use the TI-83/84 Plus to plot both the original data points and the two lines (see below). Turn `Plot1` on in the STAT PLOT window, obtained by pressing 2ND STAT PLOT. To show the lines, enter them in the "Y=" screen as usual. To obtain a convenient window showing all the points and the lines, press ZOOM and choose 9: `ZoomStat`.

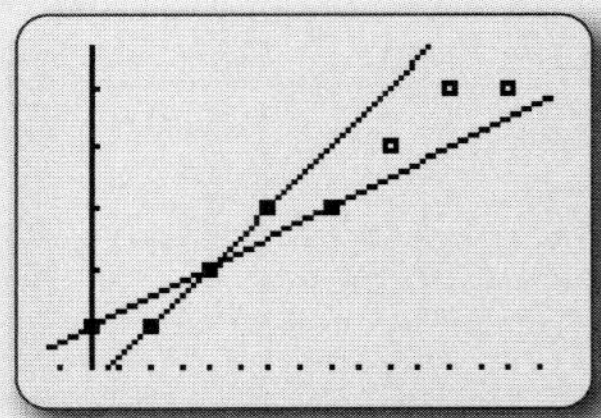

Example 2 (page 99) Use the data on the per capita GDP in Mexico to find the best-fit linear model.

Solution with Technology

1. Enter the data in the TI-83/84 Plus using the List feature, putting the x-coordinates in L_1 and the y-coordinates in L_2, just as in Example 1.

2. Press STAT, select CALC, and choose `#4: LinReg(ax+b)`. Pressing ENTER will cause the equation of the regression line to be displayed in the home screen:

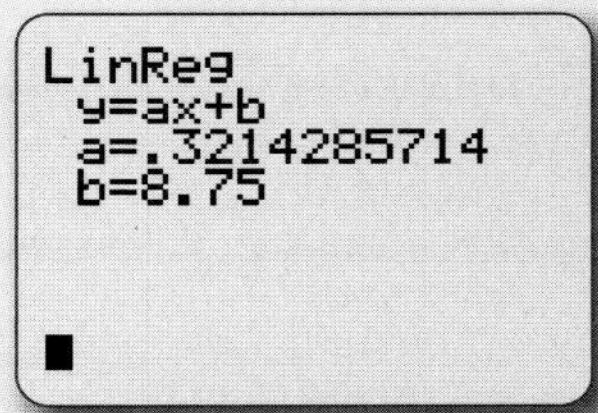

So, the regression line is $y \approx 0.321x + 8.75$.

3. To graph the regression line without having to enter it by hand in the "`Y=`" screen, press Y=, clear the contents of Y_1, press VARS, choose `#5: Statistics`, select `EQ`, and then choose `#1:RegEQ`. The regression equation will then be entered under Y_1.

4. To simultaneously show the data points, press 2ND STATPLOT and turn `Plot1` on as in Example 1. To obtain a convenient window showing all the points and the line (see below), press ZOOM and choose `#9: ZoomStat`.

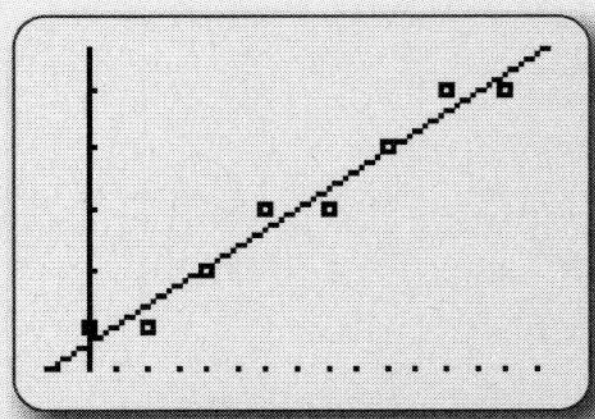

Example 3 (page 101) Find the correlation coefficient for the data in Example 2.

Solution with Technology

To find the correlation coefficient using a TI-83/84 Plus you need to tell the calculator to show you the coefficient at the same time that it shows you the regression line.

1. Press [2ND] [CATALOG] and select `DiagnosticOn` from the list. The command will be pasted to the home screen, and you should then press [ENTER] to execute the command.
2. Once you have done this, the `"LinReg(ax+b)"` command (see the discussion for Example 2) will show you not only a and b, but r and r^2 as well:

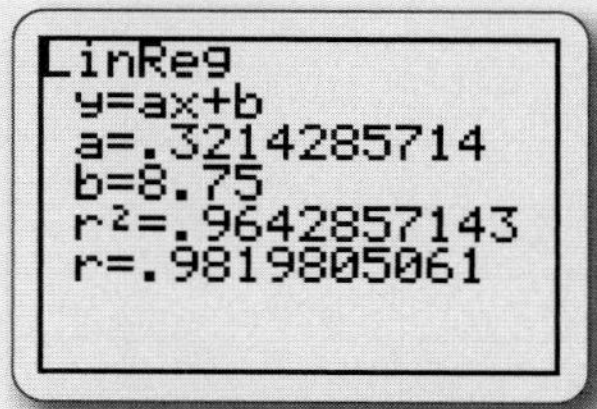

SPREADSHEET Technology Guide

Section 1.1

Example 1(a) and (c) (page 44) The total number of iPods sold by Apple up to the end of year x can be approximated by $f(x) = 4x^2 + 16x + 2$ million iPods $(0 \le x \le 6)$, where $x = 0$ represents 2003. Compute $f(0)$, $f(2)$, $f(4)$, and $f(6)$, and obtain the graph of f.

Solution with Technology

To create a table of values of f using a spreadsheet:

1. Set up two columns: one for the values of x and one for the values of $f(x)$. Then enter the sequence of values 0, 2, 4, 6 in the x column as shown.

◇	A	B
1	x	f(x)
2	0	
3	2	
4	4	
5	6	

2. Now we enter a formula for $f(x)$ in cell B2 (below). The technology formula is `4*x^2+16*x+2`. To use this formula in a spreadsheet, we modify it slightly:

`=4*A2^2+16*A2+2` Spreadsheet version of tech formula

Notice that we have preceded the Excel formula by an equals sign (=) and replaced each occurrence of x by the name of the cell holding the value of x (cell A2 in this case).

◇	A	B	C
1	x	f(x)	
2	0	=4*A2^2+16*A2+2	
3	2		
4	4		
5	6		

Note Instead of typing in the name of the cell "A2" each time, you can simply click on the cell A2, and "A2" will be automatically inserted. ■

3. Now highlight cell B2 and drag the **fill handle** (the little square at the lower right-hand corner of the selection) down until you reach Row 5 as shown below on the top, to obtain the result shown on the bottom.

◇	A	B	C
1	x	f(x)	
2	0	=4*A2^2+16*A2+2	
3	2		
4	4		
5	6		

◇	A	B
1	x	f(x)
2	0	2
3	2	50
4	4	130
5	6	242

4. To graph the data, highlight A1 through B5, and insert a "Scatter chart" (the exact method of doing this depends on the specific version of the spreadsheet program). When choosing the style of the chart,

choose a style that shows points connected by lines (if possible) to obtain a graph something like the following:

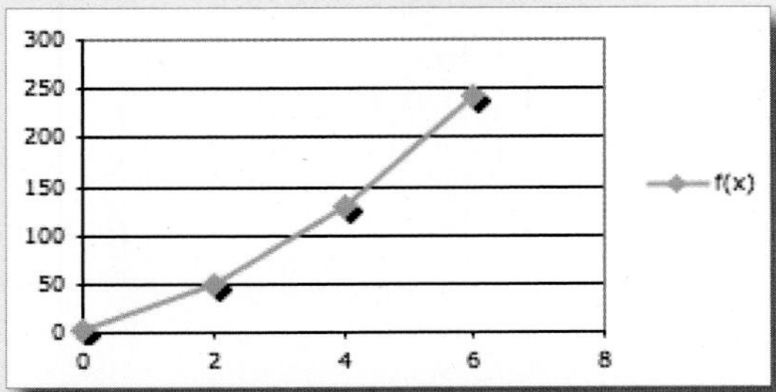

Example 2 (page 47) The number $n(t)$ of Facebook members can be approximated by the following function of time t in years ($t = 0$ represents January 2004):

$$n(t) = \begin{cases} 4t & \text{if } 0 \le t \le 3 \\ 12 + 23(t-3)^{2.7} & \text{if } 3 < t \le 6 \end{cases} \quad \text{million members.}$$

Obtain a table showing the values $n(t)$ for $t = 0, \ldots, 6$ and also obtain the graph of n.

Solution with Technology

We can generate a table of values of $n(t)$ for $t = 0, 1, \ldots, 6$ as follows:

1. Set up two columns; one for the values of t and one for the values of $n(t)$, and enter the values 0, 1, . . . , 6 in the t column as shown in the first screenshot below:
2. We must now enter the formula for n in cell B2. The following formula defines the function n in Excel:

```
=(x<=3)*(4*x)+(x>3)*(12+23*abs
 (x-3)^2.7)
```

When x is less than or equal to 3, the logical expression `(x≤3)` evaluates to 1 because it is true, and the expression `(x>3)` evaluates to 0 because it is false. The value of the function is therefore given by the expression `(4*x)`. When x is greater than 3, the expression `(x≤3)` evaluates to 0 while the expression `(x>3)` evaluates to 1, so the value of the function is given by the expression `(12+23*abs (x-3)^2.7)`. (The reason we use the `abs` in the formula is to prevent an error in evaluating $(x-3)^{2.7}$ when $x < 3$; even though we don't use that formula when $x < 3$, we are in fact evaluating it and multiplying it by zero.) We therefore enter the formula

```
=(A2<=3)*(4*A2)+(A2>3)*(12+23
 *ABS(A2-3)^2.7)
```

in cell B2 and then copy down to cell B8 (below top) to obtain the result shown on the bottom:

	A	B	C	D	E
1	t	n(t)			
2	0	=(A2<=3)*(4*A2)+(A2>3)*(12+23*ABS(A2-3)^2.7)			
3	1				
4	2				
5	3				
6	4				
7	5				
8	6				

	A	B
1	t	n(t)
2	0	0
3	1	4
4	2	8
5	3	12
6	4	35
7	5	161.454
8	6	458.638

3. To graph the data, highlight A1 through B8, and insert a "Scatter chart" as in Example 1 to obtain the result shown below:

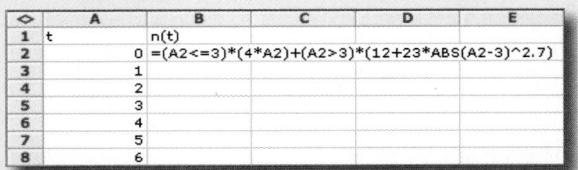

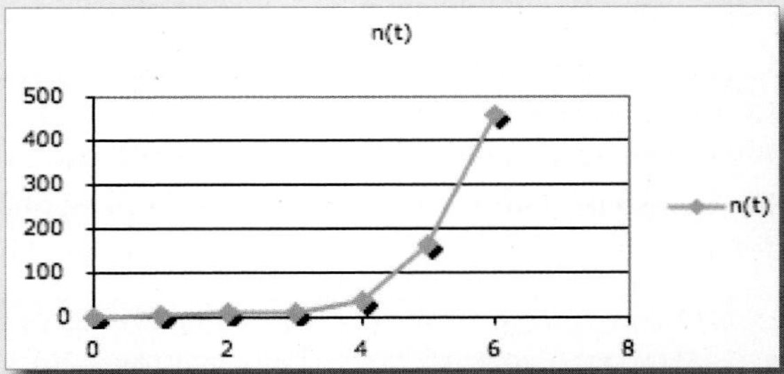

Section 1.2

Example 4(a) (page 62) The demand and supply curves for private schools in Michigan are $q = 77.8p^{-0.11}$ and $q = 30.4 + 0.006p$ thousand students, respectively ($200 \le p \le 2{,}200$), where p is the net tuition cost in dollars. Graph the demand and supply curves on the same set of axes. Use your graph to estimate, to the nearest \$100, the tuition at which the demand equals the supply (equilibrium price). Approximately how many students will be accommodated at that price?

Solution with Technology

To obtain the graphs of demand and supply:

1. Enter the headings p, Demand, and Supply in cells A1–C1 and the p-values 200, 300, . . . , 2,200 in A2–A22.

2. Next, enter the formulas for the demand and supply functions in cells B2 and C2.

Demand: `=77.8*A2^(-0.11)` in cell B2

Supply: `=30.4+0.006*A2` in cell C2

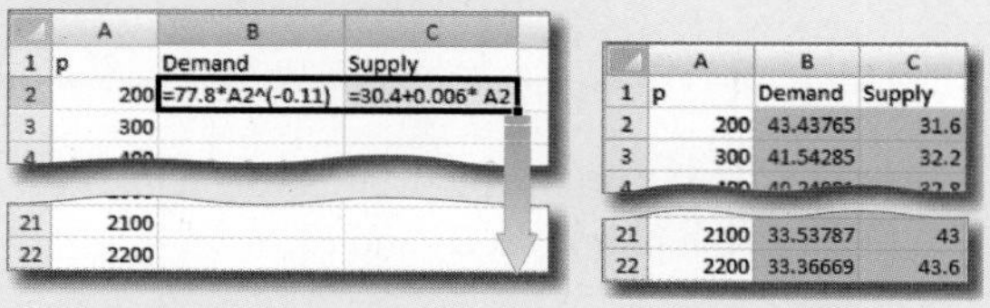

3. To graph the data, highlight A1 through C22, and insert a Scatter chart:

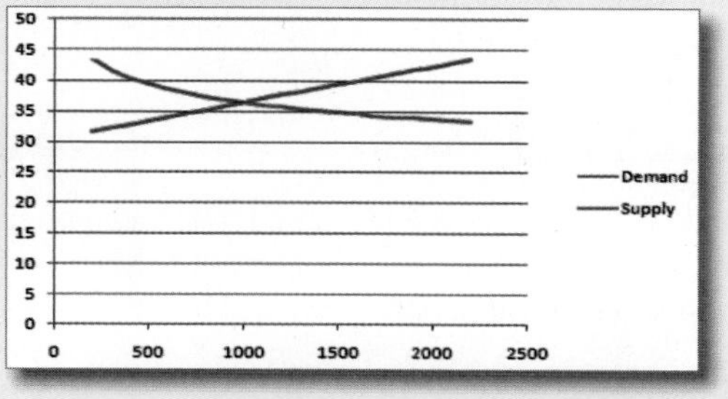

4. If you place the cursor as close as you can get to the intersection point (or just look at the table of values), you will see that the curves cross close to $p = \$1,000$ (to the nearest \$100).

5. To more accurately determine where the curves cross, you can narrow down the range of values shown on the x-axis by changing the p-values to 990, 991, . . . , 1010.

Example 5(a) (page 64) The following table shows annual sales, in billions of dollars, by *Nike* from 2005 through 2010 ($t = 0$ represents 2005):

t	0	1	2	3	4	5
Sales ($ billion)	13.5	15	16.5	18.5	19	19

Consider the following four models:

(1) $s(t) = 14t + 1.2t$ Linear model

(2) $s(t) = 13 + 2.2t - 0.2t^2$ Quadratic model

(3) $s(t) = 14(1.07^t)$ Exponential model

(4) $s(t) = \dfrac{19.5}{1 + 0.48(1.8^{-t})}$ Logistic model

a. Which models fit the data significantly better than the rest?

b. Of the models you selected in part (a), which gives the most reasonable prediction for 2013?

Solution with Technology

1. First create a scatter plot of the given data by tabulating the data as shown below, and selecting the Insert tab and choosing a "Scatter" chart:

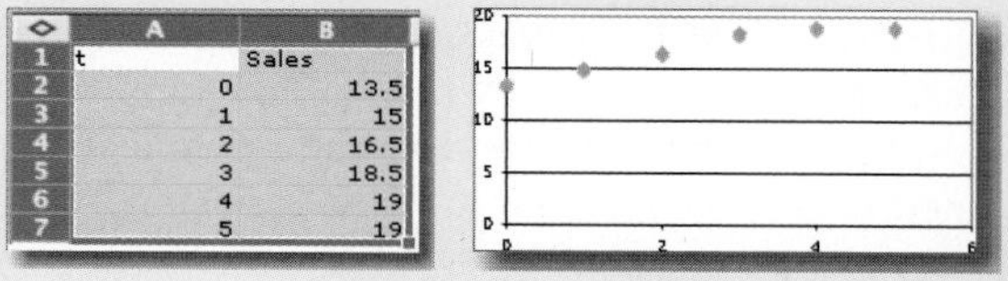

2. In column C use the formula for the model you are interested in seeing; for example, model (2): `=13+2.2*A2-0.2*A2^2`

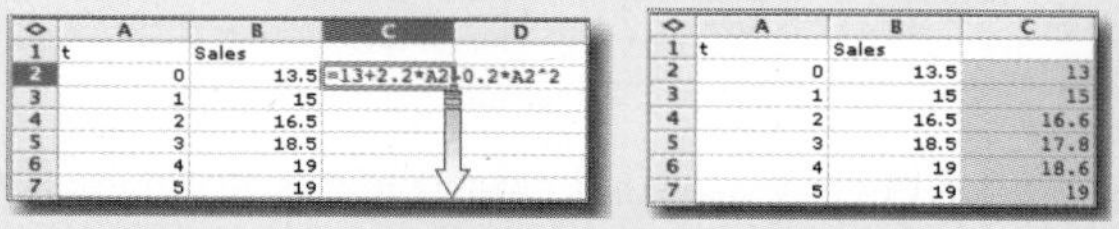

3. To adjust the graph to include the graph of the model you have added, you need to change the graph data from \$A\$2:\$B\$7 to \$A\$2:\$C\$7 so as to include column C. In Excel you can obtain this by right-clicking on the graph to select "Source Data". In OpenOffice, double-click on the graph and then right-click it to choose "Data Ranges". In Excel, you can also click once on the graph—the effect will be to outline the data you have graphed in columns A and B—and then use the fill handle at the bottom of Column B to extend the selection to Column C as shown:

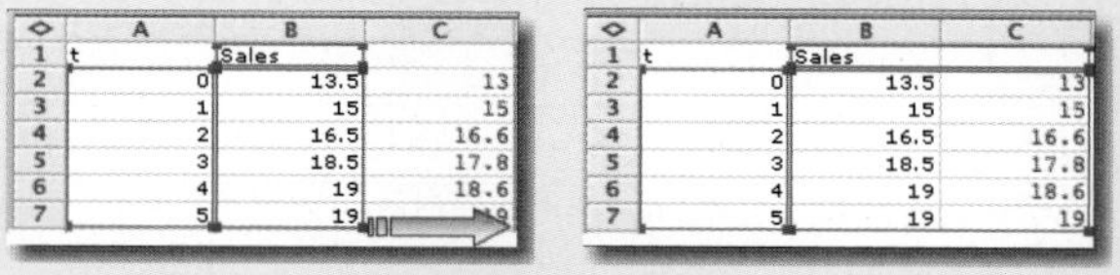

The graph will now include markers showing the values of both the actual sales and the model you inserted in Column C.

4. Right-click on any of the markers corresponding to column B in the graph (in OpenOffice you would first double-click on the graph), select "Format data series" to add lines connecting the points and remove the markers. The effect will be as shown below, with the model represented by a curve and the actual data points represented by dots:

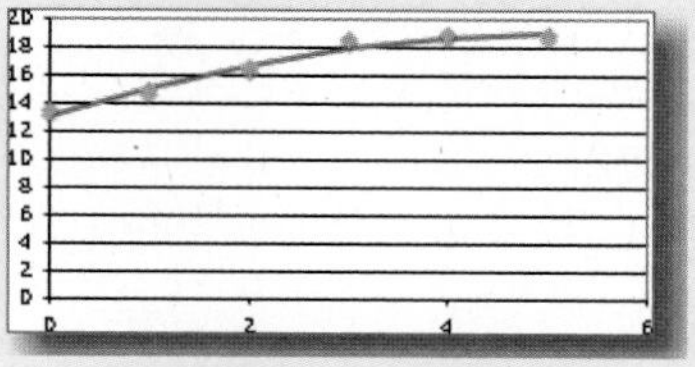

TECHNOLOGY GUIDE

5. To see the extrapolation of the curve to 2013, add the values 6, 7, 8 to Column A. The values of $s(t)$ may automatically be computed in Column C as you type, depending on the spreadsheet. If not, you will need to copy the formula in column C down to C10. (Do not touch Column B, as that contains the observed data up through $t = 5$ only.) Click on the graph, and use the fill handle at the base of Column C to include the new data in the graph:

	A	B	C
1	t	Sales	
2	0	13.5	13
3	1	15	15
4	2	16.5	16.6
5	3	18.5	17.8
6	4	19	18.6
7	5	19	19
8	6		19
9	7		18.6
10	8		17.8

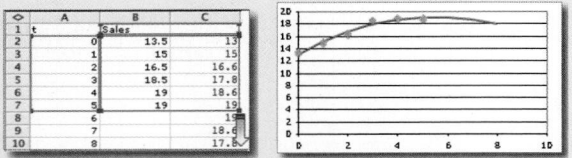

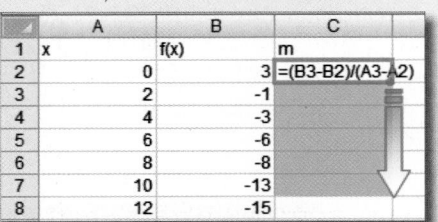

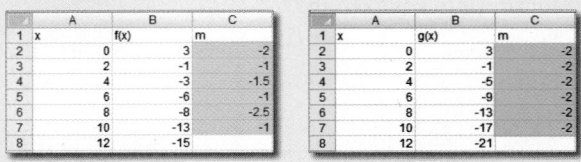

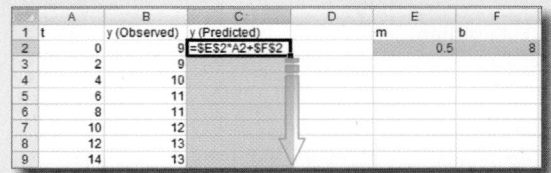

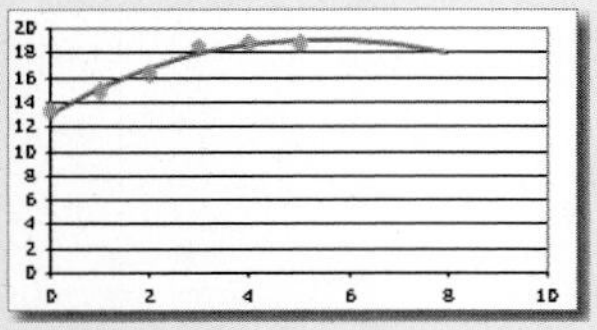

6. To see the plots for the remaining curves, change the formula in Column B (and don't forget to copy the new formula down to cell C10 when you do so).

Section 1.3

Example 1 (page 81) Which of the following two tables gives the values of a linear function? What is the formula for that function?

x	0	2	4	6	8	10	12
$f(x)$	3	−1	−3	−6	−8	−13	−15

x	0	2	4	6	8	10	12
$g(x)$	3	−1	−5	−9	−13	−17	−21

Solution with Technology

1. The following worksheet shows how you can compute the successive quotients $m = \Delta y/\Delta x$, and hence check whether a given set of data shows a linear relationship, in which case all the quotients will be the same. (The shading indicates that the formula is to be copied down only as far as cell C7. Why not cell C8?)

	A	B	C
1	x	f(x)	m
2	0	3	=(B3-B2)/(A3-A2)
3	2	-1	
4	4	-3	
5	6	-6	
6	8	-8	
7	10	-13	
8	12	-15	

2. Here are the results for both f and g.

	A	B	C
1	x	f(x)	m
2	0	3	-2
3	2	-1	-1
4	4	-3	-1.5
5	6	-6	-1
6	8	-8	-2.5
7	10	-13	-1
8	12	-15	

	A	B	C
1	x	g(x)	m
2	0	3	-2
3	2	-1	-2
4	4	-5	-2
5	6	-9	-2
6	8	-13	-2
7	10	-17	-2
8	12	-21	

Example 2(a) (page 83) Find the equation of the line through the points (1, 2) and (3, −1).

Solution with Technology

1. Enter the x- and y-coordinates in columns A and B, as shown below on the left.

	A	B
1	x	y
2	1	2
3	3	-1

	A	B	C	D
1	x	y	m	b
2	1	2	=(B3-B2)/(A3-A2)	=B2-C2*A2
3	3	-1	Slope	Intercept

2. Add the headings m and b in C1-D1, and then the formulas for the slope and intercept in C2-D2, as shown above on the right. The result will be as shown below:

	A	B	C	D
1	x	y	m	b
2	1	2	-1.5	3.5
3	3	-1	Slope	Intercept

Section 1.4

Example 1(a) (page 97) Using the data on the per capita GDP in Mexico given at the beginning of Section 1.4, compute SSE, the sum-of-squares error, for the linear models $y = 0.5t + 8$ and $y = 0.25t + 9$, and graph the data with the given models.

Solution with Technology

1. Begin by setting up your worksheet with the observed data in two columns, t and y, and the predicted data for the first model in the third.

	A	B	C	D	E	F
1	t	y (Observed)	y (Predicted)		m	b
2	0	9	=$E$2*A2+$F$2		0.5	8
3	2	9				
4	4	10				
5	6	11				
6	8	11				
7	10	12				
8	12	13				
9	14	13				

2. Notice that, instead of using the numerical equation for the first model in column C, we used absolute references to the cells containing the slope m and the intercept b. This way, we can switch from one linear model to the next by changing only m and b in cells E2 and F2. (We have deliberately left column D empty in anticipation of the next step.)

3. In column D we compute the squares of the residuals using the Excel formula `=(B2-C2)^2`.

	A	B	C	D	E	F
1	t	y (Observed)	y (Predicted)	Residual^2	m	b
2	0	9	8	=(B2-C2)^2	0.5	8
3	2	9	9			
4	4	10	10			
5	6	11	11			
6	8	11	12			
7	10	12	13			
8	12	13	14			
9	14	13	15			

4. We now compute SSE in cell F4 by summing the entries in column D:

	A	B	C	D	E	F
1	t	y (Observed)	y (Predicted)	Residual^2	m	b
2	0	9	8	1	0.5	8
3	2	9	9	0		
4	4	10	10	0	SSE:	=SUM(D2:D9)
5	6	11	11	0		
6	8	11	12	1		
7	10	12	13	1		
8	12	13	14	1		
9	14	13	15	4		

5. Here is the completed spreadsheet:

	A	B	C	D	E	F
1	t	y (Observed)	y (Predicted)	Residual^2	m	b
2	0	9	8	1	0.5	8
3	2	9	9	0		
4	4	10	10	0	SSE:	8
5	6	11	11	0		
6	8	11	12	1		
7	10	12	13	1		
8	12	13	14	1		
9	14	13	15	4		

6. Changing m to 0.25 and b to 9 gives the sum of squares error for the second model, SSE = 2.

	A	B	C	D	E	F
1	t	y (Observed)	y (Predicted)	Residual^2	m	b
2	0	9	9	0	0.25	9
3	2	9	9.5	0.25		
4	4	10	10	0	SSE:	2
5	6	11	10.5	0.25		
6	8	11	11	0		
7	10	12	11.5	0.25		
8	12	13	12	1		
9	14	13	12.5	0.25		

7. To plot both the original data points and each of the two lines, use a scatter plot to graph the data in columns A through C in each of the last two worksheets above.

$y = 0.5t + 8$

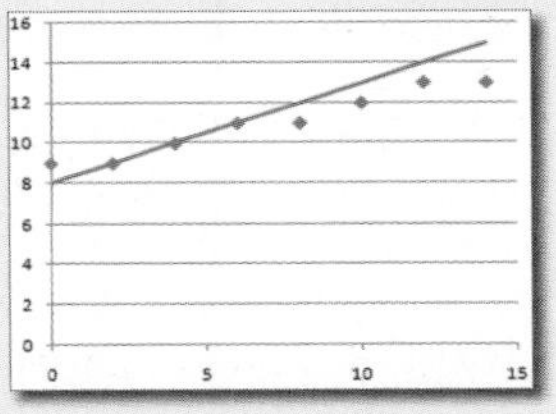

$y = 0.25t + 9$

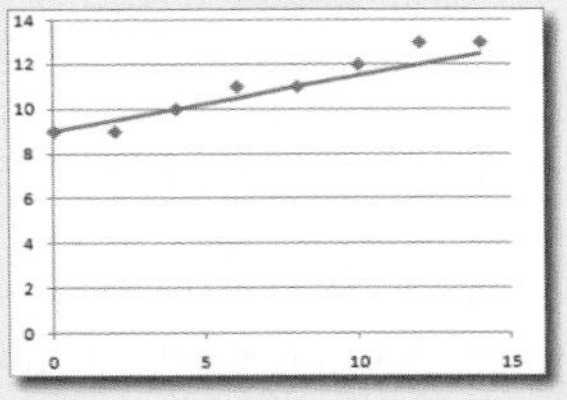

Example 2 (page 99) Use the data on the per capita GDP in Mexico to find the best-fit linear model.

Solution with Technology

Here are two spreadsheet shortcuts for linear regression; one graphical and one based on a spreadsheet formula:

Using a Trendline

1. Start with the original data and insert a scatter plot (below left and right).

	A	B
1	t	y
2	0	9
3	2	9
4	4	10
5	6	11
6	8	11
7	10	12
8	12	13
9	14	13

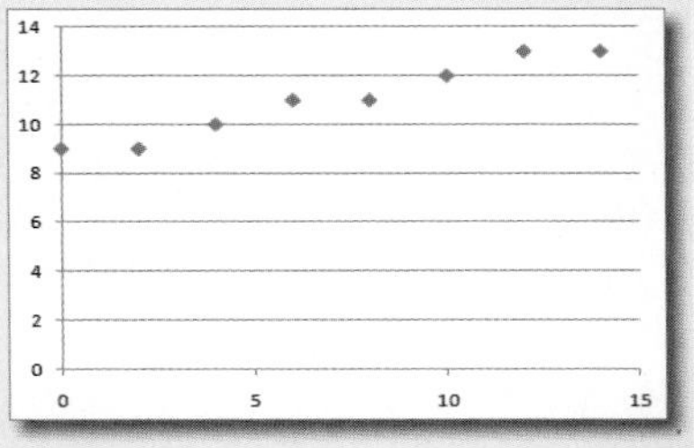

2. Insert a "linear trendline", choosing the option to display the equation on the chart. The method for doing so varies from spreadsheet to spreadsheet.[77] In Excel, you can right-click on one of the points in the graph and choose "Add Trendline" (in OpenOffice you would first double-click on the graph). Then, under "Trendline Options", select "Display Equation on chart". The procedure for OpenOffice is almost identical, but you first need to double-click on the graph. The result is shown below.

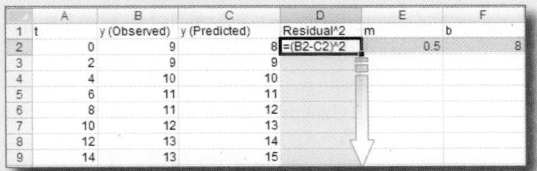

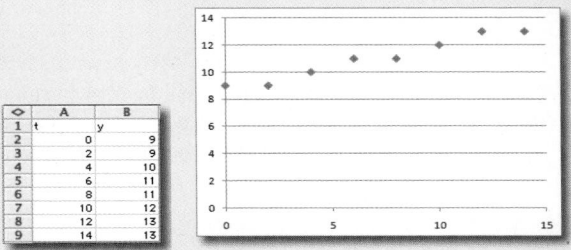

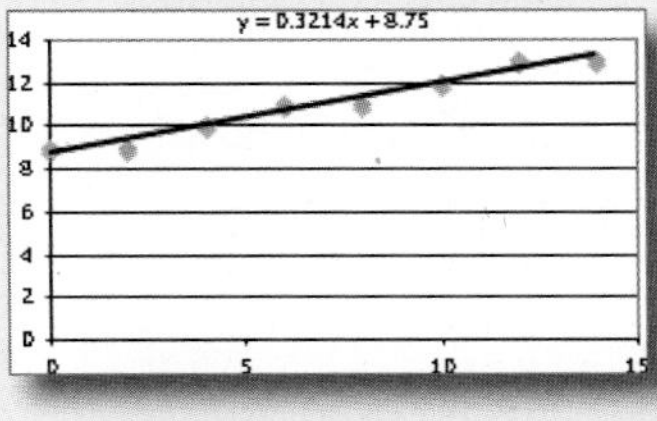

Using a Formula

1. Enter your data as above, and select a block of unused cells two wide and one tall; for example, C2:D2. Then enter the formula

```
=LINEST(B2:B9,A2:A9)
```

[77]At the time of this writing, Google Docs has no trendline feature for its spreadsheet, so you would need to use the formula method.

as shown on the left. Then press Control-Shift-Enter. The result should appear as on the right, with m and b appearing in cells C2 and D2 as shown:

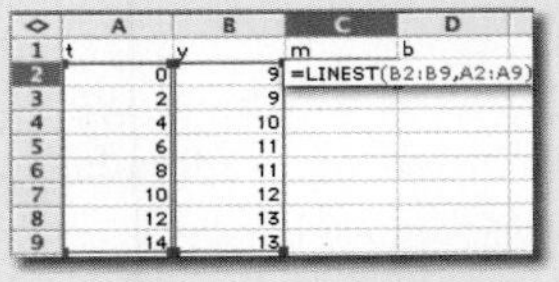

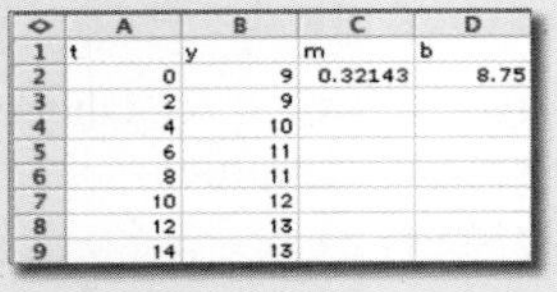

Example 3 (page 101) Find the correlation coefficient for the data in Example 2.

Solution with Technology

1. When you add a trendline to a chart you can select the option "Display R-squared value on chart" to show the value of r^2 on the chart (it is common to examine r^2, which takes on values between 0 and 1, instead of r).

2. Alternatively, the LINEST function we used above in 2 can be used to display quite a few statistics about a best-fit line, including r^2. Instead of selecting a block of cells two wide and one tall as we did in Example 2, we select one two wide and *five* tall. We now enter the requisite LINEST formula with two additional arguments set to "TRUE" as shown, and press Control-Shift-Enter:

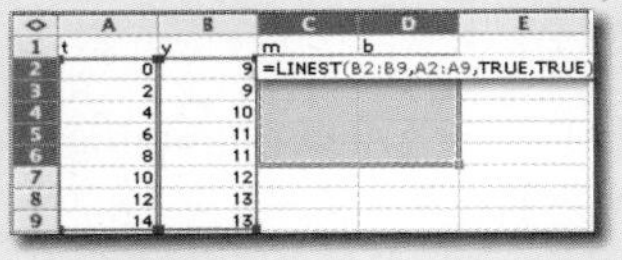

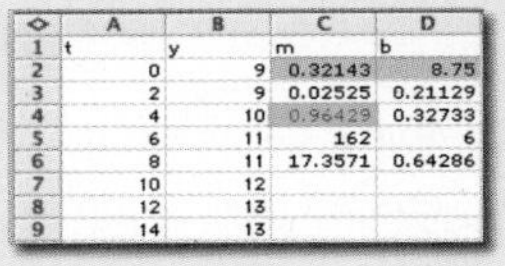

The values of m and b appear in cells C2 and D2 as before, and the value of r^2 in cell C4. (Among the other numbers shown is SSE in cell D6. For the meanings of the remaining numbers shown, do a Web search for "LINEST"; you will see numerous articles, including many that explain all the terms. A good course in statistics wouldn't hurt, either.)

2

Nonlinear Functions and Models

Website
www.WanerMath.com
At the Website you will find:

- Section-by-section tutorials, including game tutorials with randomized quizzes
- A detailed chapter summary
- A true/false quiz
- Additional review exercises
- Graphers, Excel tutorials, and other resources
- The following extra topics:
  - Inverse functions
  - Using and deriving algebraic properties of logarithms

Case Study Checking up on Malthus

In 1798 Thomas R. Malthus (1766–1834) published an influential pamphlet, later expanded into a book, titled *An Essay on the Principle of Population as It Affects the Future Improvement of Society*. One of his main contentions was that population grows geometrically (exponentially), while the supply of resources such as food grows only arithmetically (linearly). Some 200+ years later, you have been asked to check the validity of Malthus's contention. **How do you go about doing so?**

Robert Nickelsberg/Getty Images

Introduction

To see if Malthus was right, we need to see if the data fit the models (linear and exponential) that he suggested or if other models would be better. We saw in Chapter 1 how to fit a linear model. In this chapter we discuss how to construct models that use various *nonlinear* functions.

The nonlinear functions we consider in this chapter are the *quadratic* functions, the simplest nonlinear functions; the *exponential* functions, essential for discussing many kinds of growth and decay, including the growth (and decay) of money in finance and the initial growth of an epidemic; the *logarithmic* functions, needed to fully understand the exponential functions; and the *logistic* functions, used to model growth with an upper limit, such as the spread of an epidemic.

algebra Review
For this chapter, you should be familiar with the algebra reviewed in **Chapter 0, Section 2.**

2.1 Quadratic Functions and Models

In Chapter 1 we studied linear functions. Linear functions are useful, but in real-life applications, they are often accurate for only a limited range of values of the variables. The relationship between two quantities is often best modeled by a curved line rather than a straight line. The simplest function with a graph that is not a straight line is a *quadratic* function.

Quadratic Function

A **quadratic function** of the variable x is a function that can be written in the form

$$f(x) = ax^2 + bx + c \qquad \text{Function form}$$

or

$$y = ax^2 + bx + c \qquad \text{Equation form}$$

where a, b, and c are fixed numbers (with $a \neq 0$).

Quick Examples

1. $f(x) = 3x^2 - 2x + 1$ — $a = 3, b = -2, c = 1$
2. $g(x) = -x^2$ — $a = -1, b = 0, c = 0$
3. $R(p) = -5{,}600p^2 + 14{,}000p$ — $a = -5{,}600, b = 14{,}000, c = 0$

Every quadratic function $f(x) = ax^2 + bx + c$ $(a \neq 0)$ has a **parabola** as its graph. Following is a summary of some features of parabolas that we can use to sketch the graph of any quadratic function.*

* We shall not fully justify the formula for the vertex and the axis of symmetry until we have studied some calculus, although it is possible to do so with just algebra.

Features of a Parabola

The graph of $f(x) = ax^2 + bx + c\ (a \neq 0)$ is a **parabola**. If $a > 0$ the parabola opens upward (concave up) and if $a < 0$ it opens downward (concave down):

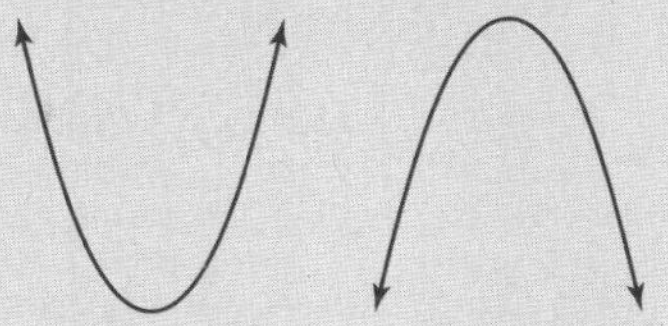

Vertex, Intercepts, and Symmetry

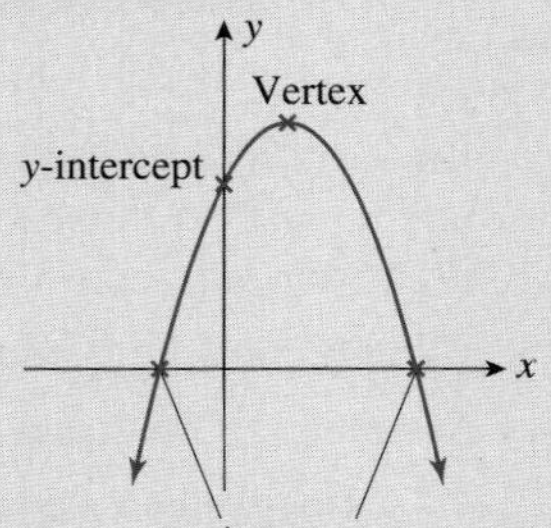

Vertex The vertex is the highest or lowest point of the parabola (see the figure above). Its x-coordinate is $-\dfrac{b}{2a}$. Its y-coordinate is $f\left(-\dfrac{b}{2a}\right)$.

***x*-Intercepts** (if any) These occur when $f(x) = 0$; that is, when

$$ax^2 + bx + c = 0.$$

Solve this equation for x by either factoring or using the quadratic formula. The x-intercepts are

$$x = \frac{-b \pm \sqrt{b^2 - 4ac}}{2a}.$$

If the **discriminant** $b^2 - 4ac$ is positive, there are two x-intercepts. If it is zero, there is a single x-intercept (at the vertex). If it is negative, there are no x-intercepts (so the parabola doesn't touch the x-axis at all).

***y*-Intercept** This occurs when $x = 0$, so

$$y = a(0)^2 + b(0) + c = c.$$

Symmetry The parabola is symmetric with respect to the vertical line through the vertex, which is the line $x = -\dfrac{b}{2a}$.

Note that the x-intercepts can also be written as

$$x = -\frac{b}{2a} \pm \frac{\sqrt{b^2 - 4ac}}{2a},$$

making it clear that they are located symmetrically on either side of the line $x = -b/(2a)$. This partially justifies the claim that the whole parabola is symmetric with respect to this line.

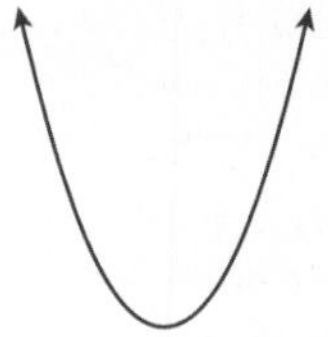

Figure 1

EXAMPLE 1 Sketching the Graph of a Quadratic Function

Sketch the graph of $f(x) = x^2 + 2x - 8$ by hand.

Solution Here, $a = 1$, $b = 2$, and $c = -8$. Because $a > 0$, the parabola is concave up (Figure 1).

Vertex: The x coordinate of the vertex is

$$x = -\frac{b}{2a} = -\frac{2}{2} = -1.$$

To get its y coordinate, we substitute the value of x back into $f(x)$ to get

$$y = f(-1) = (-1)^2 + 2(-1) - 8 = 1 - 2 - 8 = -9.$$

Thus, the coordinates of the vertex are $(-1, -9)$.

x-Intercepts: To calculate the x-intercepts (if any), we solve the equation

$$x^2 + 2x - 8 = 0.$$

Luckily, this equation factors as $(x + 4)(x - 2) = 0$. Thus, the solutions are $x = -4$ and $x = 2$, so these values are the x-intercepts. (We could also have used the quadratic formula here.)

y-Intercept: The y-intercept is given by $c = -8$.

Symmetry: The graph is symmetric around the vertical line $x = -1$.

Now we can sketch the curve as in Figure 2. (As we see in the figure, it is helpful to plot additional points by using the equation $y = x^2 + 2x - 8$, and to use symmetry to obtain others.)

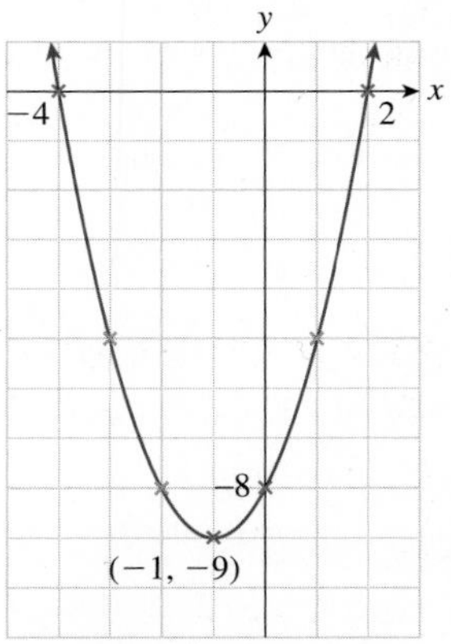

$y = x^2 + 2x - 8$

Figure 2

EXAMPLE 2 One x-Intercept and No x-Intercepts

Sketch the graph of each quadratic function, showing the location of the vertex and intercepts.

a. $f(x) = 4x^2 - 12x + 9$

b. $g(x) = -\frac{1}{2}x^2 + 4x - 12$

Solution

a. We have $a = 4$, $b = -12$, and $c = 9$. Because $a > 0$, this parabola is concave up.

Vertex: $x = -\frac{b}{2a} = \frac{12}{8} = \frac{3}{2}$ — *x coordinate of vertex*

$$y = f\left(\frac{3}{2}\right) = 4\left(\frac{3}{2}\right)^2 - 12\left(\frac{3}{2}\right) + 9 = 0$$ *y coordinate of vertex*

Thus, the vertex is at the point $(3/2, 0)$.

x-Intercepts:

$$4x^2 - 12x + 9 = 0$$
$$(2x - 3)^2 = 0$$

The only solution is $2x - 3 = 0$, or $x = 3/2$. Note that this coincides with the vertex, which lies on the x-axis.

y-Intercept: $c = 9$

Symmetry: The graph is symmetric around the vertical line $x = 3/2$.

The graph is the narrow parabola shown in Figure 3. (As we remarked in Example 1, plotting additional points and using symmetry helps us obtain an accurate sketch.)

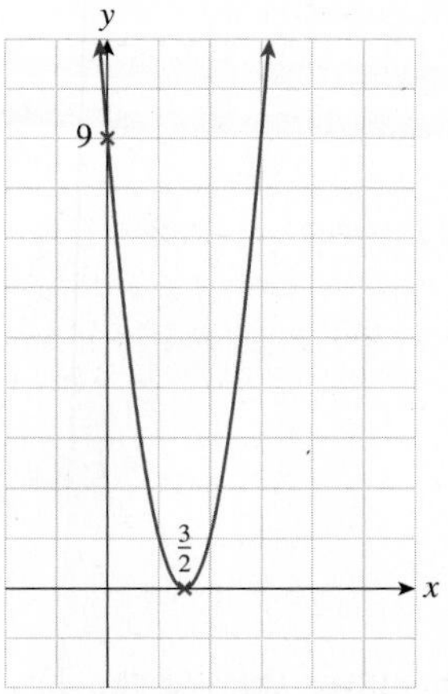

$y = 4x^2 - 12x + 9$

Figure 3

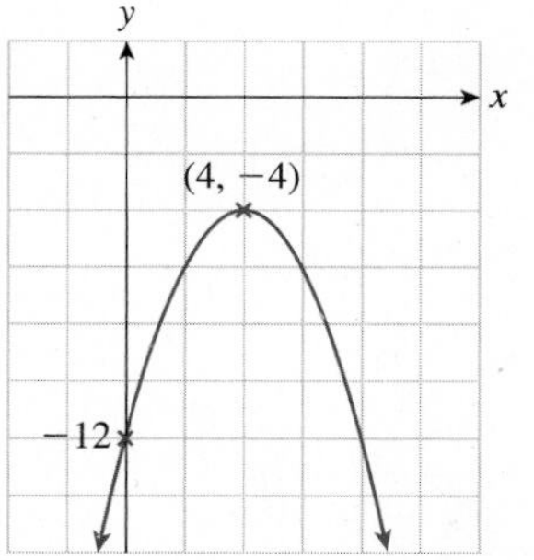

$y = -\frac{1}{2}x^2 + 4x - 12$

Figure 4

b. Here, $a = -1/2$, $b = 4$, and $c = -12$. Because $a < 0$, the parabola is concave down. The vertex has x coordinate $-b/(2a) = 4$, with corresponding y coordinate $f(4) = -\frac{1}{2}(4)^2 + 4(4) - 12 = -4$. Thus, the vertex is at (4, −4).

For the x-intercepts, we must solve $-\frac{1}{2}x^2 + 4x - 12 = 0$. If we try to use the quadratic formula, we discover that the discriminant is $b^2 - 4ac = 16 - 24 = -8$. Because the discriminant is negative, there are no solutions of the equation, so there are no x-intercepts.

The y-intercept is given by $c = -12$, and the graph is symmetric around the vertical line $x = 4$.

Because there are no x-intercepts, the graph lies entirely below the x-axis, as shown in Figure 4. (Again, you should plot additional points and use symmetry to ensure that your sketch is accurate.)

using Technology

To automate the computations in Example 2 using a graphing calculator or a spreadsheet, see the Technology Guides at the end of the chapter. Outline:

TI-83/84 Plus

```
Y1=AX^2+BX+C
4→A:-12→B:9→C
[WINDOW] Xmin=0, Xmax=3
[ZOOM] [0]
```

[More details on page 186.]

Spreadsheet

Enter x values in column A.
Compute the corresponding y values in column B.
Graph the data in columns A and B.
[More details on page 188.]

Website

www.WanerMath.com
In the Function Evaluator and Grapher, enter `4x^2-12x+9` for y_1. For a table of values, enter the various x-values in the Evaluator box, and press "Evaluate".

APPLICATIONS

Recall that the **revenue** resulting from one or more business transactions is the total payment received. Thus, if q units of some item are sold at p dollars per unit, the revenue resulting from the sale is

$$\text{revenue} = \text{price} \times \text{quantity}$$
$$R = pq.$$

EXAMPLE 3 Demand and Revenue

Alien Publications, Inc. predicts that the demand equation for the sale of its latest illustrated sci-fi novel *Episode 93: Yoda vs. Alien* is

$$q = -2{,}000p + 150{,}000$$

where q is the number of books it can sell each year at a price of $\$p$ per book. What price should Alien Publications, Inc., charge to obtain the maximum annual revenue?

Solution The total revenue depends on the price, as follows:

$$\begin{aligned} R &= pq && \text{Formula for revenue} \\ &= p(-2{,}000p + 150{,}000) && \text{Substitute for } q \text{ from demand equation.} \\ &= -2{,}000p^2 + 150{,}000p. && \text{Simplify.} \end{aligned}$$

We are after the price p that gives the maximum possible revenue. Notice that what we have is a quadratic function of the form $R(p) = ap^2 + bp + c$, where $a = -2{,}000$, $b = 150{,}000$, and $c = 0$. Because a is negative, the graph of the function is a parabola, concave down, so its vertex is its highest point (Figure 5). The p coordinate of the vertex is

$$p = -\frac{b}{2a} = -\frac{150{,}000}{-4{,}000} = 37.5.$$

This value of p gives the highest point on the graph and thus gives the largest value of $R(p)$. We may conclude that Alien Publications, Inc., should charge \$37.50 per book to maximize its annual revenue.

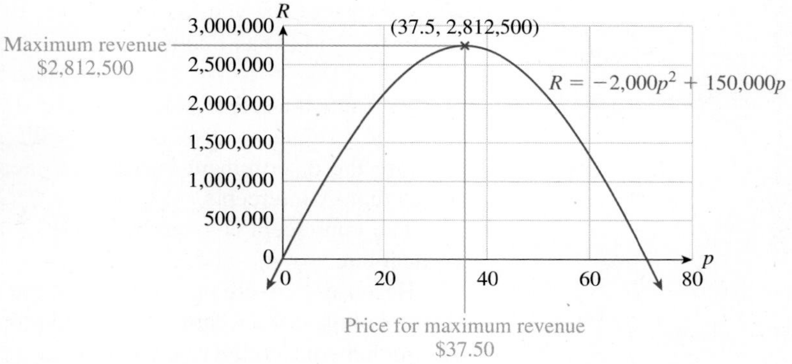

Figure 5

➡ **Before we go on...** You might ask what the maximum annual revenue is for the publisher in Example 3. Because $R(p)$ gives us the revenue at a price of $\$p$, the answer is $R(37.5) = -2,000(37.5)^2 + 150,000(37.5) = 2,812,500$. In other words, the company will earn total annual revenues from this book amounting to \$2,812,500. ■

EXAMPLE 4 Demand, Revenue, and Profit

As the operator of *YSport Fitness* gym, you calculate your demand equation to be

$$q = -0.06p + 84,$$

where q is the number of members in the club and p is the annual membership fee you charge.

a. Your annual operating costs are a fixed cost of \$20,000 per year plus a variable cost of \$20 per member. Find the annual revenue and profit as functions of the membership price p.

b. At what price should you set the annual membership fee to obtain the maximum revenue? What is the maximum possible revenue?

c. At what price should you set the annual membership fee to obtain the maximum profit? What is the maximum possible profit? What is the corresponding revenue?

Solution

a. The annual revenue is given by

$$R = pq \qquad \text{Formula for revenue}$$
$$= p(-0.06p + 84) \qquad \text{Substitute for } q \text{ from demand equation.}$$
$$= -0.06p^2 + 84p. \qquad \text{Simplify.}$$

The annual cost C is given by

$$C = 20,000 + 20q. \qquad \text{\$20,000 plus \$20 per member}$$

However, this is a function of q, and not p. To express C as a function of p we substitute for q using the demand equation $q = -0.06p + 84$:

$$C = 20,000 + 20(-0.06p + 84)$$
$$= 20,000 - 1.2p + 1,680$$
$$= -1.2p + 21,680.$$

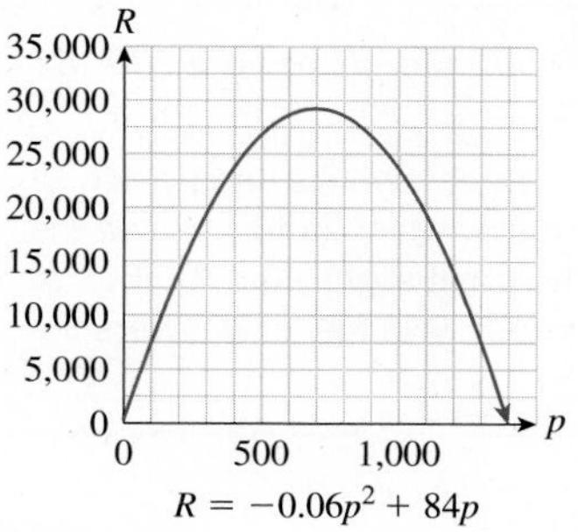

Figure 6

Thus, the profit function is:

$$P = R - C \quad \text{Formula for profit}$$

$$= -0.06p^2 + 84p - (-1.2p + 21{,}680) \quad \text{Substitute for revenue and cost.}$$

$$= -0.06p^2 + 85.2p - 21{,}680.$$

b. From part (a) the revenue function is given by

$$R = -0.06p^2 + 84p.$$

This is a quadratic function ($a = -0.06$, $b = 84$, $c = 0$) whose graph is a concave-down parabola (Figure 6). The maximum revenue corresponds to the highest point of the graph: the vertex, of which the p coordinate is

$$p = -\frac{b}{2a} = -\frac{84}{2(-0.06)} \approx \$700.$$

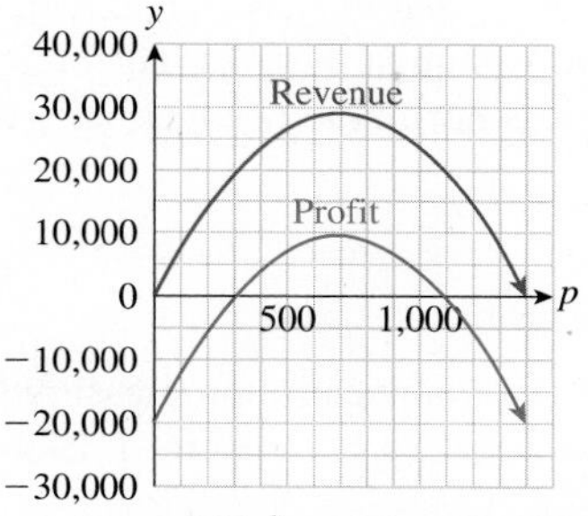

Figure 7

This is the membership fee you should charge for the maximum revenue. The corresponding maximum revenue is given by the y coordinate of the vertex in Figure 6:

$$R(700) = -0.06(700)^2 + 84(700) = \$29{,}400.$$

c. From part (a), the profit function is given by

$$P = -0.06p^2 + 85.2p - 21{,}680.$$

Like the revenue function, the profit function is quadratic ($a = -0.06$, $b = 85.2$, $c = -21{,}680$). Figure 7 shows both the revenue and profit functions. The maximum profit corresponds to the vertex, whose p coordinate is

$$p = -\frac{b}{2a} = -\frac{85.2}{2(-0.06)} \approx \$710.$$

This is the membership fee you should charge for the maximum profit. The corresponding maximum profit is given by the y coordinate of the vertex of the profit curve in Figure 7:

$$P(710) = -0.06(710)^2 + 85.2(710) - 21{,}680 = \$8{,}566.$$

The corresponding revenue is

$$R(710) = -0.06(710)^2 + 84(710) = \$29{,}394,$$

slightly less than the maximum possible revenue of \$29,400.

➡ **Before we go on...** The result of part (c) of Example 4 tells us that the vertex of the profit curve in Figure 7 is slightly to the right of the vertex in the revenue curve. However, the difference is tiny compared to the scale of the graphs, so the graphs appear to be parallel. ■

Q: *Charging \$710 membership brings in less revenue than charging \$700. So why charge \$710?*

A: A membership fee of \$700 does bring in slightly larger revenue than a fee of \$710, but it also brings in a slightly larger membership, which in turn raises the operating expense and has the effect of *lowering* the profit slightly (to \$8,560). In other words, the slightly higher fee, while bringing in less revenue, also lowers the cost, and the net result is a larger profit.

Fitting a Quadratic Function to Data: Quadratic Regression

In Section 1.4 we saw how to fit a regression line to a collection of data points. Here, we see how to use technology to obtain the **quadratic regression curve** associated with a set of points. The quadratic regression curve is the quadratic curve $y = ax^2 + bx + c$ that best fits the data points in the sense that the associated sum-of-squares error (SSE—see Section 1.4) is a minimum. Although there are algebraic methods for obtaining the quadratic regression curve, it is normal to use technology to do this.

EXAMPLE 5 Carbon Dioxide Concentration

The following table shows the annual mean carbon dioxide concentration measured at Mauna Loa Observatory in Hawaii, in parts per million, every 10 years from 1960 through 2010 ($t = 0$ represents 1960).[1]

Year t	0	10	20	30	40	50
PPM CO_2 C	317	326	339	354	369	390

a. Is a linear model appropriate for these data?

b. Find the quadratic model

$$C(t) = at^2 + bt + c$$

that best fits the data.

Solution

a. To see whether a linear model is appropriate, we plot the data points and the regression line using one of the methods of Example 2 in Section 1.4 (Figure 8).

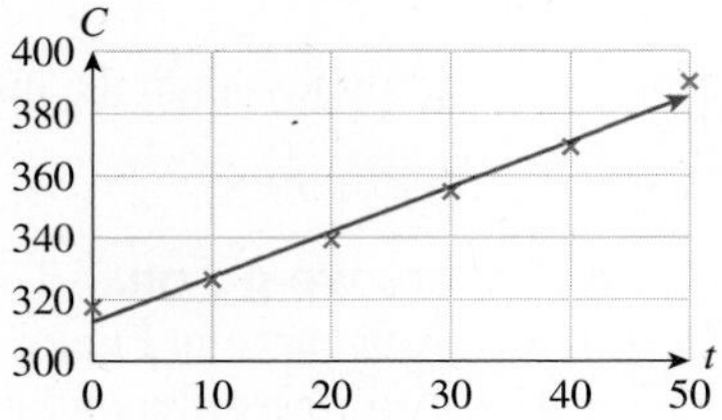

Figure 8

[1]Figures are approximate. Source: U.S. Department of Commerce/National Oceanic and Atmospheric Administration (NOAA) Earth System Research Laboratory, data downloaded from www.esrl.noaa.gov/gmd/ccgg/trends/ on March 13, 2011.

using Technology

For detailed instructions on how to find and graph the regression curve in Example 5 using a graphing calculator or a spreadsheet, see the Technology Guides at the end of the chapter. Outline:

TI-83/84 Plus

STAT EDIT values of t in L_1 and values of C in L_2
Regression curve: STAT CALC option 5 QuadReg ENTER
Graph: Y= VARS 5 EQ 1, then ZOOM 9
[More details on page 186.]

Spreadsheet

t- and C-values in Columns A and B.
Graph: Highlight data and insert a Scatter chart.
Regression curve: Right-click a datapoint and add polynomial order 2 trendline with option to show equation on chart.
[More details on page 189.]

Website

www.WanerMath.com
In the Simple Regression utility, enter the data in the x- and y-columns and press "y=ax^2+bx+c".

From the graph, we can see that the given data suggest a curve and not a straight line: The observed points are above the regression line at the ends but below in the middle. (We would expect the data points from a linear relation to fall randomly above and below the regression line.)

b. The quadratic model that best fits the data is the quadratic regression model. As with linear regression, there are algebraic formulas to compute a, b, and c, but they are rather involved. However, we exploit the fact that these formulas are built into graphing calculators, spreadsheets, and other technology and obtain the regression curve using technology (see Figure 9):

$$C(t) = 0.012t^2 + 0.85t + 320. \quad \text{Coefficients rounded to two significant digits}$$

Notice from the graphs that the quadratic regression model appears to give a better fit than the linear regression model. This impression is supported by the values of SSE: For the linear regression model, SSE $\approx$ 58, while for the quadratic regression model, SSE is much smaller, approximately 2.6, indicating a much better fit.

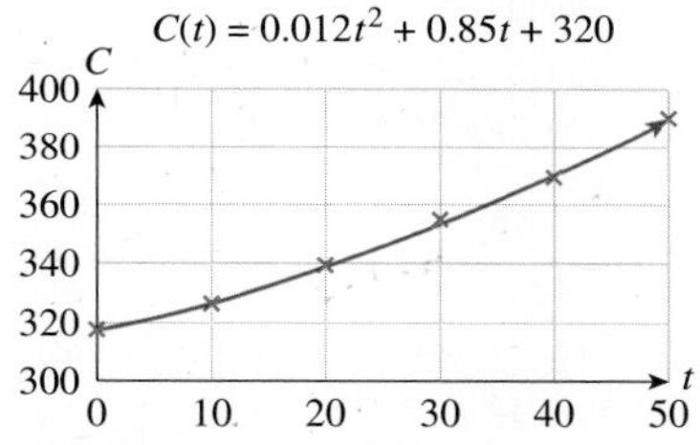

Figure 9

2.1 EXERCISES

▼ more advanced ◆ challenging

T indicates exercises that should be solved using technology

In Exercises 1–10, sketch the graphs of the quadratic functions, indicating the coordinates of the vertex, the y-intercept, and the x-intercepts (if any). HINT [See Example 1.]

1. $f(x) = x^2 + 3x + 2$ **2.** $f(x) = -x^2 - x$

3. $f(x) = -x^2 + 4x - 4$ **4.** $f(x) = x^2 + 2x + 1$

5. $f(x) = -x^2 - 40x + 500$ **6.** $f(x) = x^2 - 10x - 600$

7. $f(x) = x^2 + x - 1$ **8.** $f(x) = x^2 + \sqrt{2}x + 1$

9. $f(x) = x^2 + 1$ **10.** $f(x) = -x^2 + 5$

In Exercises 11–14, for each demand equation, express the total revenue R as a function of the price p per item, sketch the graph of the resulting function, and determine the price p that maximizes total revenue in each case. HINT [See Example 3.]

11. $q = -4p + 100$ **12.** $q = -3p + 300$

13. $q = -2p + 400$ **14.** $q = -5p + 1{,}200$

T *In Exercises 15–18, use technology to find the quadratic regression curve through the given points. (Round all coefficients to four decimal places.)* HINT [See Example 5.]

15. $\{(1, 2), (3, 5), (4, 3), (5, 1)\}$

16. $\{(-1, 2), (-3, 5), (-4, 3), (-5, 1)\}$

17. $\{(-1, 2), (-3, 5), (-4, 3)\}$

18. $\{(2, 5), (3, 5), (5, 3)\}$

APPLICATIONS

19. ***World Military Expenditure*** The following chart shows total military and arms trade expenditure from 1990 to 2008 ($t = 0$ represents 1990).[2]

[2] Approximate figures in constant 2005 dollars. The 2008 figure is an estimate, based on the increase in U.S. military expenditure.

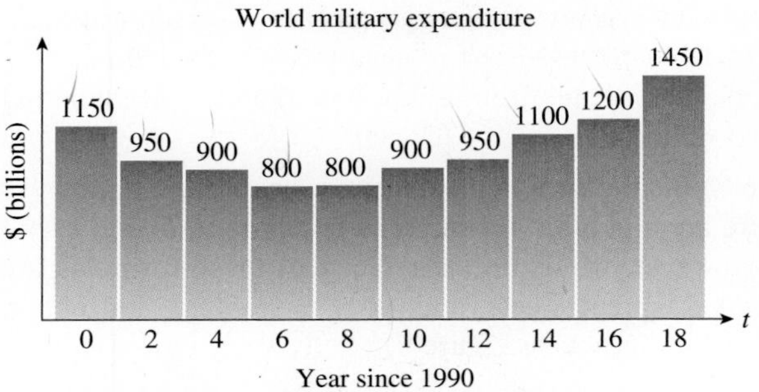

Source: www.globalissues.org/Geopolitics/ArmsTrade/Spending.asp

a. If you want to model the expenditure figures with a function of the form

$$f(t) = at^2 + bt + c,$$

would you expect the coefficient a to be positive or negative? Why? HINT [See "Features of a Parabola," page 127.]

b. Which of the following models best approximates the data given? (Try to answer this without actually computing values.)

(A) $f(t) = 5t^2 - 80t - 1{,}150$
(B) $f(t) = -5t^2 - 80t + 1{,}150$
(C) $f(t) = 5t^2 - 80t + 1{,}150$
(D) $f(t) = -5t^2 - 80t - 1{,}150$

c. What is the nearest year that would correspond to the vertex of the graph of the correct model from part (b)? What is the danger of extrapolating the data in either direction?

20. ***Education Expenditure*** The following chart shows the percentage of the U.S. Discretionary Budget allocated to education from 2003 to 2009 ($t = 3$ represents the start of 2003).

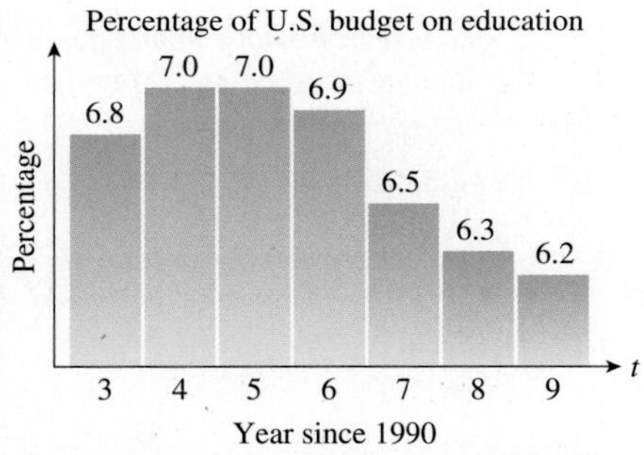

Source: www.globalissues.org/Geopolitics/ArmsTrade/Spending.asp

a. If you want to model the percentage figures with a function of the form

$$f(t) = at^2 + bt + c,$$

would you expect the coefficient a to be positive or negative? Why? HINT [See "Features of a Parabola," page 127.]

b. Which of the following models best approximates the data given? (Try to answer this without actually computing values)

(A) $f(t) = 0.04t^2 + 0.3t - 6$
(B) $f(t) = -0.04t^2 + 0.3t + 6$
(C) $f(t) = 0.04t^2 + 0.3t + 6$
(D) $f(t) = -0.04t^2 + 0.3t - 6$

c. What is the nearest year that would correspond to the vertex of the graph of the correct model from part (b)? What is the danger of extrapolating the data in either direction?

21. ***Oil Imports from Mexico*** Daily oil imports to the United States from Mexico can be approximated by

$$I(t) = -0.015t^2 + 0.1t + 1.4 \quad \text{million barrels/day} \quad (0 \le t \le 8)$$

where t is time in years since the start of 2000.[3] According to the model, in what year were oil imports to the United States greatest? How many barrels per day were imported that year? HINT [See Example 1.]

22. ***Oil Production in Mexico*** Daily oil production by Pemex, Mexico's national oil company, for 2001–2009 can be approximated by

$$P(t) = -0.022t^2 + 0.2t + 2.9 \quad \text{million barrels/day} \quad (1 \le t \le 9)$$

where t is time in years since the start of 2000.[4] According to the model, in what year was oil production by Pemex greatest? How many barrels per day were produced that year?

23. ***Net Income*** The annual net income of General Electric for the period 2005–2010 could be approximated by

$$P(t) = -2.0t^2 + 6.6t + 16 \text{ billion dollars } (0 \le t \le 5)$$

where t is time in years since 2005.[5] According to the model, in what year in this period was General Electric's net income highest? What was its net income that year? Would you trust this model to continue to be valid long past this period? Why?

24. ***Net Income*** The annual net income of General Electric for the period 2007–2012 could be approximated by

$$P(t) = 3.0t^2 - 24t + 59 \text{ billion dollars } (2 \le t \le 7)$$

where t is time in years since 2005.[6] According to the model, in what year in this period was General Electric's net income lowest? What was its net income that year? Would you trust this model to continue to be valid long past this period? Why?

[3]Source: Energy Information Administration/Pemex/www.eia.gov

[4]Figures are approximate, and 2008–2009 figures are projections by the Department of Energy. Source: Energy Information Administration: Pemex.

[5]Source for data: www.wikinvest.com/

[6]*Ibid.* 2011 net income is projected.

25. ***Revenue*** The market research department of the *Better Baby Buggy Co.* predicts that the demand equation for its buggies is given by $q = -0.5p + 140$, where q is the number of buggies it can sell in a month if the price is $\$p$ per buggy. At what price should it sell the buggies to get the largest revenue? What is the largest monthly revenue? HINT [See Example 3.]

26. ***Revenue*** The *Better Baby Buggy Co.* has just come out with a new model, the Turbo. The market research department predicts that the demand equation for Turbos is given by $q = -2p + 320$, where q is the number of buggies it can sell in a month if the price is $\$p$ per buggy. At what price should it sell the buggies to get the largest revenue? What is the largest monthly revenue?

27. ***Revenue*** *Pack-Em-In Real Estate* is building a new housing development. The more houses it builds, the less people will be willing to pay, due to the crowding and smaller lot sizes. In fact, if it builds 40 houses in this particular development, it can sell them for \$200,000 each, but if it builds 60 houses, it will only be able to get \$160,000 each. Obtain a linear demand equation and hence determine how many houses Pack-Em-In should build to get the largest revenue. What is the largest possible revenue? HINT [See Example 3.]

28. ***Revenue*** *Pack-Em-In* has another development in the works. If it builds 50 houses in this development, it will be able to sell them at \$190,000 each, but if it builds 70 houses, it will get only \$170,000 each. Obtain a linear demand equation and hence determine how many houses it should build to get the largest revenue. What is the largest possible revenue?

29. ▼ ***Revenue from Monorail Service, Las Vegas*** In 2005, the Las Vegas monorail charged \$3 per ride and had an average ridership of about 28,000 per day. In December 2005 the Las Vegas Monorail Company raised the fare to \$5 per ride, and average ridership in 2006 plunged to around 19,000 per day.[7]

a. Use the given information to find a linear demand equation.

b. Find the price the company should have charged to maximize revenue from ridership. What is the corresponding daily revenue?

c. The Las Vegas Monorail Company would have needed \$44.9 million in revenues from ridership to break even in 2006. Would it have been possible to break even in 2006 by charging a suitable price?

30. ▼ ***Revenue from Monorail Service, Mars*** The Utarek monorail, which links the three urbynes (or districts) of Utarek, Mars, charged Z5 per ride[8] and sold about 14 million rides per day. When the Utarek City Council lowered the fare to Z3 per ride, the number of rides increased to 18 million per day.

a. Use the given information to find a linear demand equation.

b. Find the price the City Council should have charged to maximize revenue from ridership. What is the corresponding daily revenue?

c. The City Council would have needed to raise Z48 billion in revenues from ridership each Martian year (670 days[9]) to finance the new Mars organism research lab. Would this have been possible by charging a suitable price?

31. ***Web Site Profit*** You operate a gaming Web site, www.mudbeast.net, where users must pay a small fee to log on. When you charged \$2 the demand was 280 log-ons per month. When you lowered the price to \$1.50, the demand increased to 560 log-ons per month.

a. Construct a linear demand function for your Web site and hence obtain the monthly revenue R as a function of the log-on fee x.

b. Your Internet provider charges you a monthly fee of \$30 to maintain your site. Express your monthly profit P as a function of the log-on fee x, and hence determine the log-on fee you should charge to obtain the largest possible monthly profit. What is the largest possible monthly profit? HINT [See Example 4.]

32. ***T-Shirt Profit*** Two fraternities, Sig Ep and Ep Sig, plan to raise money jointly to benefit homeless people on Long Island. They will sell *Yoda vs. Alien* T-shirts in the student center, but are not sure how much to charge. Sig Ep treasurer Augustus recalls that they once sold 400 shirts in a week at \$8 per shirt, but Ep Sig treasurer Julius has solid research indicating that it is possible to sell 600 per week at \$4 per shirt.

a. Based on this information, construct a linear demand equation for Yoda vs. Alien T-shirts, and hence obtain the weekly revenue R as a function of the unit price x.

b. The university administration charges the fraternities a weekly fee of \$500 for use of the Student Center. Write down the monthly profit P as a function of the unit price x, and hence determine how much the fraternities should charge to obtain the largest possible weekly profit. What is the largest possible weekly profit? HINT [See Example 4.]

33. ***Web Site Profit*** The latest demand equation for your gaming Web site, www.mudbeast.net, is given by

$$q = -400x + 1{,}200$$

where q is the number of users who log on per month and x is the log-on fee you charge. Your Internet provider bills you as follows:

Site maintenance fee:	\$20 per month
High-volume access fee:	50¢ per log-on

Find the monthly cost as a function of the log-on fee x. Hence, find the monthly profit as a function of x and determine the log-on fee you should charge to obtain the largest possible monthly profit. What is the largest possible monthly profit?

---

[7]Source: *New York Times*, Februrary 10, 2007, p. A9.

[8]The zonar (Z) is the official currency in the city-state of Utarek, Mars (formerly www.Marsnext.com, a now extinct virtual society).

[9]As measured in Mars days. The actual length of a Mars year is about 670.55 Mars days, so frequent leap years are designated by the Mars Planetary Authority to adjust.

34. ***T-Shirt Profit*** The latest demand equation for your *Yoda vs. Alien* T-shirts is given by

$$q = -40x + 600$$

where q is the number of shirts you can sell in one week if you charge $\$x$ per shirt. The Student Council charges you \$400 per week for use of their facilities, and the T-shirts cost you \$5 each. Find the weekly cost as a function of the unit price x. Hence, find the weekly profit as a function of x and determine the unit price you should charge to obtain the largest possible weekly profit. What is the largest possible weekly profit?

35. ▼ ***Nightclub Management*** You have just opened a new nightclub, *Russ' Techno Pitstop,* but are unsure of how high to set the cover charge (entrance fee). One week you charged \$10 per guest and averaged 300 guests per night. The next week you charged \$15 per guest and averaged 250 guests per night.

a. Find a linear demand equation showing the number of guests q per night as a function of the cover charge p.

b. Find the nightly revenue R as a function of the cover charge p.

c. The club will provide two free nonalcoholic drinks for each guest, costing the club \$3 per head. In addition, the nightly overheads (rent, salaries, dancers, DJ, etc.) amount to \$3,000. Find the cost C as a function of the cover charge p.

d. Now find the profit in terms of the cover charge p, and hence determine the entrance fee you should charge for a maximum profit.

36. ▼ ***Television Advertising*** As sales manager for *Montevideo Productions, Inc.,* you are planning to review the prices you charge clients for television advertisement development. You currently charge each client an hourly development fee of \$2,500. With this pricing structure, the demand, measured by the number of contracts Montevideo signs per month, is 15 contracts. This is down 5 contracts from the figure last year, when your company charged only \$2,000.

a. Construct a linear demand equation giving the number of contracts q as a function of the hourly fee p Montevideo charges for development.

b. On average, Montevideo bills for 50 hours of production time on each contract. Give a formula for the total revenue obtained by charging $\$p$ per hour.

c. The costs to Montevideo Productions are estimated as follows:

Fixed costs:	\$120,000 per month
Variable costs:	\$80,000 per contract

Express Montevideo Productions' monthly cost **(i)** as a function of the number q of contracts and **(ii)** as a function of the hourly production charge p.

d. Express Montevideo Productions' monthly profit as a function of the hourly development fee p and hence find the price it should charge to maximize the profit.

37. T ***World Military Expenditure*** The following table shows total military and arms trade expenditure in 1994, 1998, and 2006. (See Exercise 19; $t = 4$ represents 1994.)[10]

Year t	4	8	16
Military Expenditure (\$ billion)	900	800	1,200

Find a quadratic model for these data, and use your model to estimate world military expenditure in 2008. Compare your answer with the actual figure shown in Exercise 19. HINT [See Example 5.]

38. T ***Education Expenditure*** The following table shows the percentage of the U.S. Discretionary Budget allocated to education in 2003, 2005, and 2009. (See Exercise 20; $t = 3$ represents the start of 2003.)[11]

Year t	3	5	9
Percentage	6.8	7	6.2

Find a quadratic model for these data, and use your model to estimate the percentage of the U.S. Discretionary Budget allocated to education in 2008. Compare your answer with the actual figure shown in Exercise 20.

39. T ***iPod Sales*** The following table shows Apple iPod sales from the last quarter of 2009 through the last quarter of 2010.[12]

Quarter t	4	5	6	7	8
iPod Sales (millions)	21.0	10.9	9.4	9.1	19.5

a. Find a quadratic regression model for these data. (Round coefficients to two significant digits.) Graph the model together with the data.

b. What does the model predict for iPod sales in the first quarter of 2011 ($t = 9$), to the nearest million? Comment on the answer.

40. T ***iPod Sales*** The following table shows Apple iPod sales from the second quarter of 2009 through the second quarter of 2010.[13]

Quarter t	2	3	4	5	6
iPod Sales (millions)	10.2	10.2	21.0	10.9	9.4

[10] Approximate figures in constant 2005 dollars. The 2008 figure is an estimate, based on the increase in U.S. military expenditure. Source: www.globalissues.org/Geopolitics/ArmsTrade/Spending.asp.

[11] Source: www.globalissues.org/Geopolitics/ArmsTrade/Spending.asp.

[12] Source: Apple quarterly press releases (www.apple.com/investor/).

[13] *Ibid.*

a. Find a quadratic regression model for these data. (Round coefficients to two significant digits.) Graph the model together with the data.

b. What does the model predict for iPod sales in the third quarter of 2010 ($t = 7$), to the nearest million? Comment on the answer.

COMMUNICATION AND REASONING EXERCISES

41. What can you say about the graph of $f(x) = ax^2 + bx + c$ if $a = 0$?

42. What can you say about the graph of $f(x) = ax^2 + bx + c$ if $c = 0$?

43. **Multiple choice:** Following is the graph of $f(x) = ax^2 + bx + c$:

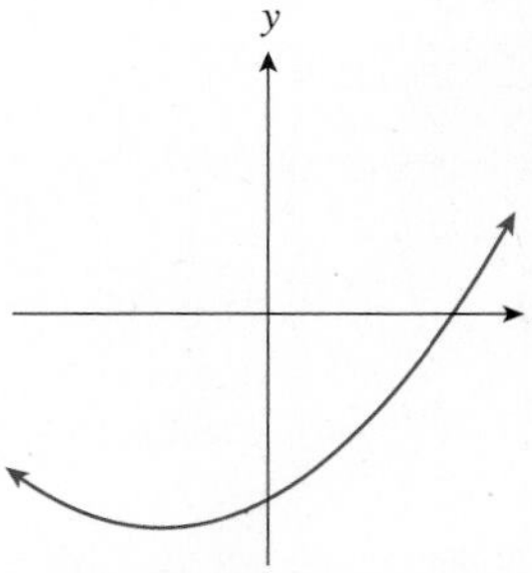

(A) a is positive and c is positive.
(B) a is negative and c is positive.
(C) a is positive and c is negative.
(D) a is negative and c is negative.

44. **Multiple choice:** Following is the graph of $f(x) = ax^2 + bx + c$:

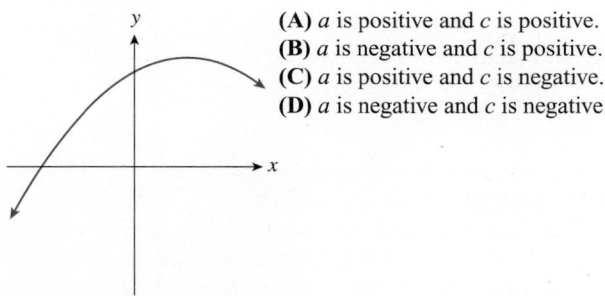

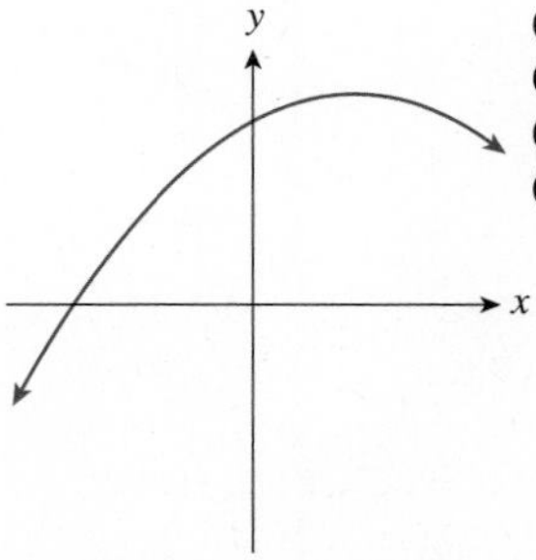

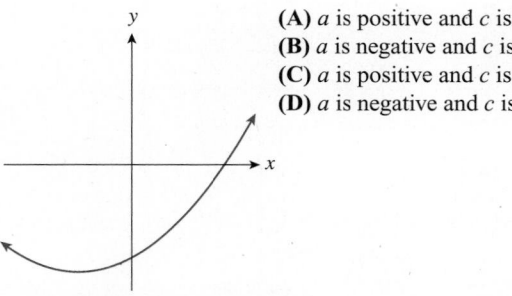

(A) a is positive and c is positive.
(B) a is negative and c is positive.
(C) a is positive and c is negative.
(D) a is negative and c is negative.

45. ▼ Refer to the graph of $f(x) = ax^2 + bx + c$ in Exercise 43. Is b positive or negative? Why?

46. ▼ Refer to the graph of $f(x) = ax^2 + bx + c$ in Exercise 44. Is b positive or negative? Why?

47. Suppose the graph of revenue as a function of unit price is a parabola that is concave down. What is the significance of the coordinates of the vertex, the x-intercepts, and the y-intercept?

48. Suppose the height of a stone thrown vertically upward is given by a quadratic function of time. What is the significance of the coordinates of the vertex, the (possible) x-intercepts, and the y-intercept?

49. How might you tell, roughly, whether a set of data should be modeled by a quadratic rather than by a linear equation?

50. A member of your study group tells you that, because the following set of data does not suggest a straight line, the data are best modeled by a quadratic.

x	0	2	4	6	8
y	1	2	1	0	1

Comment on her suggestion.

51. Is a quadratic model useful for long-term prediction of sales of an item? Why?

52. Of what use is a quadratic model, if not for long-term prediction?

53. ▼ Explain why, if demand is a linear function of unit price p (with negative slope), then there must be a *single value of* p that results in the maximum revenue.

54. ▼ Explain why, if the average cost of a commodity is given by $y = 0.1x^2 - 4x - 2$, where x is the number of units sold, there is a single choice of x that results in the lowest possible average cost.

55. ▼ If the revenue function for a particular commodity is $R(p) = -50p^2 + 60p$, what is the (linear) demand function? Give a reason for your answer.

56. ▼ If the revenue function for a particular commodity is $R(p) = -50p^2 + 60p + 50$, can the demand function be linear? What is the associated demand function?

2.2 Exponential Functions and Models

The quadratic functions we discussed in Section 2.1 can be used to model many nonlinear situations. However, exponential functions give better models in some applications, including population growth, radioactive decay, the growth or depreciation of financial investments, and many other phenomena. (We already saw some of these applications in Section 1.2.)

To work effectively with exponential functions, we need to know the laws of exponents. The following list, taken from the algebra review in Chapter 0, gives the laws of exponents we will be using.

The Laws of Exponents

If b and c are positive and x and y are any real numbers, then the following laws hold:

Law	Quick Examples	
1. $b^x b^y = b^{x+y}$	$2^3 2^2 = 2^5 = 32$	$2^{3-x} = 2^3 2^{-x}$
2. $\frac{b^x}{b^y} = b^{x-y}$	$\frac{4^3}{4^2} = 4^{3-2} = 4^1 = 4$	$3^{x-2} = \frac{3^x}{3^2} = \frac{3^x}{9}$
3. $\frac{1}{b^x} = b^{-x}$	$9^{-0.5} = \frac{1}{9^{0.5}} = \frac{1}{3}$	$2^{-x} = \frac{1}{2^x}$
4. $b^0 = 1$	$(3.3)^0 = 1$	$x^0 = 1$ if $x \neq 0$
5. $(b^x)^y = b^{xy}$	$(2^3)^2 = 2^6 = 64$	$\left(\frac{1}{2}\right)^x = (2^{-1})^x = 2^{-x}$
6. $(bc)^x = b^x c^x$	$(4 \cdot 2)^2 = 4^2 2^2 = 64$	$10^x = 5^x 2^x$
7. $\left(\frac{b}{c}\right)^x = \frac{b^x}{c^x}$	$\left(\frac{4}{3}\right)^2 = \frac{4^2}{3^2} = \frac{16}{9}$	$\left(\frac{1}{2}\right)^x = \frac{1^x}{2^x} = \frac{1}{2^x}$

Here are the functions we will study in this section.

Exponential Function

An **exponential function** has the form

$$f(x) = Ab^x, \qquad \text{Technology: } \texttt{A*b^x}$$

where A and b are constants with $A \neq 0$ and b positive and not equal to 1. We call b the **base** of the exponential function.

Quick Examples

1. $f(x) = 2^x$ — $A = 1, b = 2$; Technology: `2^x`

$f(1) = 2^1 = 2$ — `2^1`

$f(-3) = 2^{-3} = \frac{1}{8}$ — `2^(-3)`

$f(0) = 2^0 = 1$ — `2^0`

2. $g(x) = 20(3^x)$ — $A = 20, b = 3$; Technology: `20*3^x`

$g(2) = 20(3^2) = 20(9) = 180$ — `20*3^2`

$g(-1) = 20(3^{-1}) = 20\left(\frac{1}{3}\right) = 6\frac{2}{3}$ — `20*3^(-1)`

3. $h(x) = 2^{-x} = \left(\frac{1}{2}\right)^x$ — $A = 1, b = \frac{1}{2}$; Technology: `2^(-x)` or `(1/2)^x`

$h(1) = 2^{-1} = \frac{1}{2}$ — `2^(-1)` or `(1/2)^1`

$h(2) = 2^{-2} = \frac{1}{4}$ — `2^(-2)` or `(1/2)^2`

4. $k(x) = 3 \cdot 2^{-4x} = 3(2^{-4})^x$ — $A = 3, b = 2^{-4}$; Technology: `3*2^(-4*x)`

$k(-2) = 3 \cdot 2^{-4(-2)}$ — `3*2^(-4*(-2))`

$= 3 \cdot 2^8 = 3 \cdot 256 = 768$

Exponential Functions from the Numerical and Graphical Points of View

The following table shows values of $f(x) = 3(2^x)$ for some values of x ($A = 3$, $b = 2$):

x	−3	−2	−1	0	1	2	3
$f(x)$	$\frac{3}{8}$	$\frac{3}{4}$	$\frac{3}{2}$	3	6	12	24

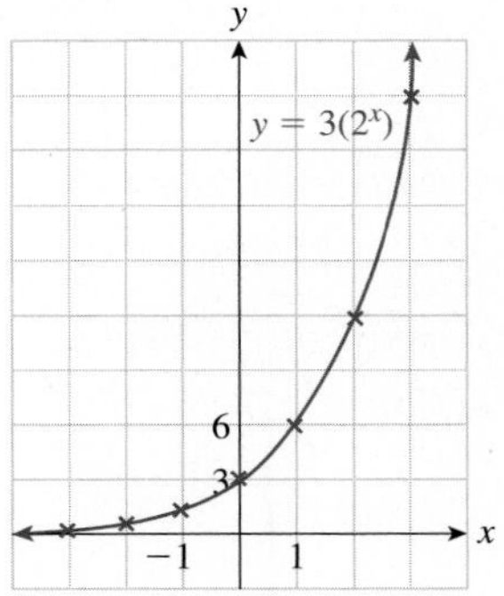

`3*2^x`

Figure 10

The graph of f is shown in Figure 10.

Notice that the y-intercept is $A = 3$ (obtained by setting $x = 0$). In general:

In the graph of $f(x) = Ab^x$, A is the y-intercept, or the value of y when $x = 0$.

What about b? Notice from the table that the value of y is multiplied by $b = 2$ for every increase of 1 in x. If we decrease x by 1, the y coordinate gets *divided* by $b = 2$.

The value of y is multiplied by b for every one-unit increase of x.

x	−3	−2	−1	0	1	2	3
$f(x)$	$\frac{3}{8}$	$\frac{3}{4}$	$\frac{3}{2}$	3	6	12	24

Multiply by 2.

On the graph, if we move one unit to the right from any point on the curve, the y coordinate doubles. Thus, the curve becomes dramatically steeper as the value of x increases. This phenomenon is called **exponential growth**. (See Section 1.2.)

Exponential Function Numerically and Graphically

For the exponential function $f(x) = Ab^x$:

Role of *A*

$f(0) = A$, so A is the y-intercept of the graph of f.

Role of *b*

If x increases by 1, $f(x)$ is multiplied by b.
If x increases by 2, $f(x)$ is multiplied by b^2.
⋮
If x increases by Δx, $f(x)$ is multiplied by $b^{\Delta x}$.

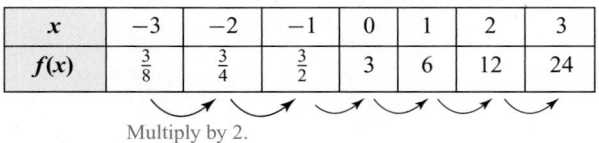

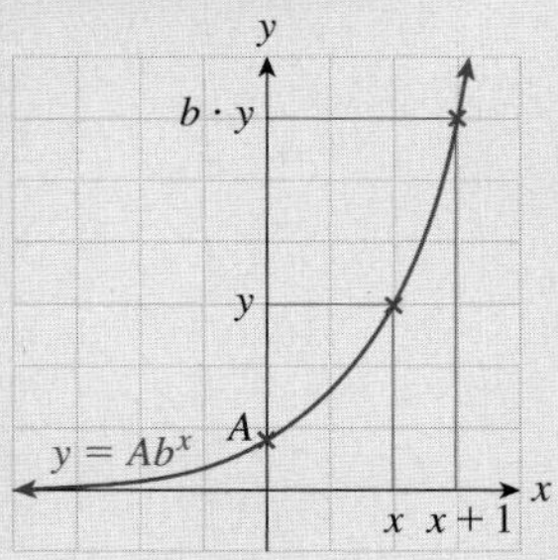

If x increases by 1, y is multiplied by b.

Quick Examples

1. $f_1(x) = 2^x,\ f_2(x) = \left(\frac{1}{2}\right)^x = 2^{-x}$

	A	B	C
1	x	2^x	2^(-x)
2	-3	1/8	8
3	-2	1/4	4
4	-1	1/2	2
5	0	1	1
6	1	2	1/2
7	2	4	1/4
8	3	8	1/8

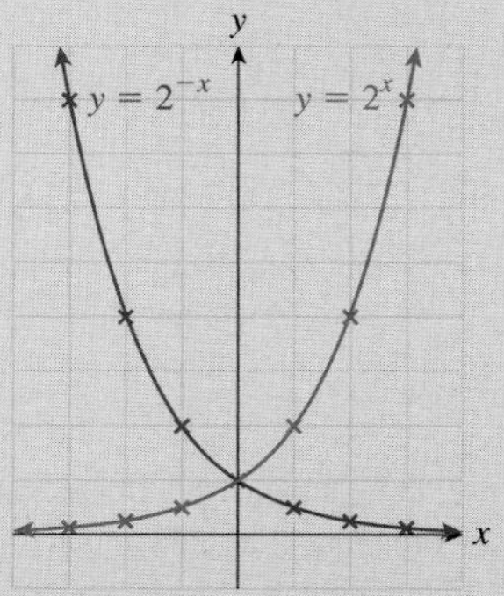

Technology: 2^x; 2^(-x)

When x increases by 1, $f_2(x)$ is multiplied by $\frac{1}{2}$. The function $f_1(x) = 2^x$ illustrates exponential growth, while $f_2(x) = \left(\frac{1}{2}\right)^x$ illustrates the opposite phenomenon: **exponential decay**.

2. $f_1(x) = 2^x,\ f_2(x) = 3^x,\ f_3(x) = 1^x$ (Can you see why f_3 is not an exponential function?)

	A	B	C	D
1	x	2^x	3^x	1^x
2	-3	1/8	1/27	1
3	-2	1/4	1/9	1
4	-1	1/2	1/3	1
5	0	1	1	1
6	1	2	3	1
7	2	4	9	1
8	3	8	27	1

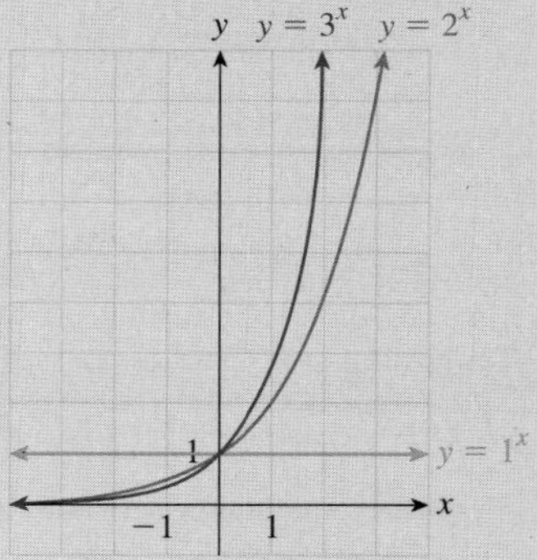

If x increases by 1, 3^x is multiplied by 3. Note also that all the graphs pass through (0, 1). (Why?)

EXAMPLE 1 Recognizing Exponential Data Numerically and Graphically

Some of the values of two functions, f and g, are given in the following table:

x	-2	-1	0	1	2
$f(x)$	-7	-3	1	5	9
$g(x)$	$\frac{2}{9}$	$\frac{2}{3}$	2	6	18

One of these functions is linear, and the other is exponential. Which is which?

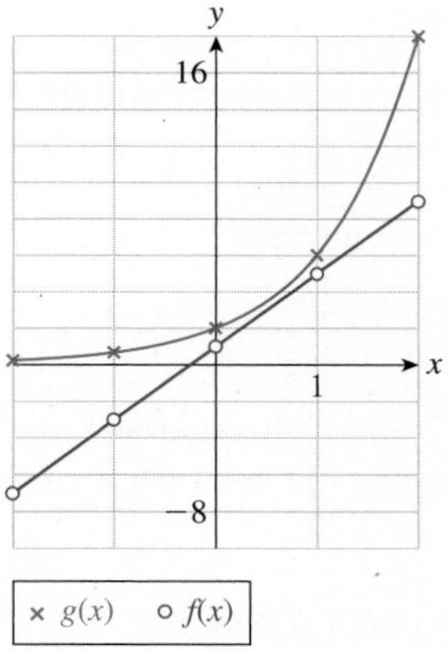

Figure 11

Solution Remember that a linear function increases (or decreases) by the same amount every time x increases by 1. The values of f behave this way: Every time x increases by 1, the value of $f(x)$ increases by 4. Therefore, f is a linear function with a *slope* of 4. Because $f(0) = 1$, we see that

$$f(x) = 4x + 1$$

is a linear formula that fits the data.

On the other hand, every time x increases by 1, the value of $g(x)$ is *multiplied* by 3. Because $g(0) = 2$, we find that

$$g(x) = 2(3^x)$$

is an exponential function fitting the data.

We can visualize the two functions f and g by plotting the data points (Figure 11). The data points for $f(x)$ clearly lie along a straight line, whereas the points for $g(x)$ lie along a curve. The y coordinate of each point for $g(x)$ is 3 times the y coordinate of the preceding point, demonstrating that the curve is an exponential one.

In Section 1.3, we discussed a method for calculating the equation of the line that passes through two given points. In the following example, we show a method for calculating the equation of the exponential curve through two given points.

EXAMPLE 2 Finding the Exponential Curve through Two Points

Find an equation of the exponential curve through (1, 6.3) and (4, 170.1).

Solution We want an equation of the form

$$y = Ab^x \quad (b > 0).$$

Substituting the coordinates of the given points, we get

$$6.3 = Ab^1 \qquad \text{Substitute (1, 6.3).}$$
$$170.1 = Ab^4. \qquad \text{Substitute (4, 170.1).}$$

If we now divide the second equation by the first, we get

$$\frac{170.1}{6.3} = \frac{Ab^4}{Ab} = b^3$$
$$b^3 = 27$$
$$b = 27^{1/3} \qquad \text{Take reciprocal power of both sides.}$$
$$b = 3.$$

Now that we have b, we can substitute its value into the first equation to obtain

$$6.3 = 3A \qquad \text{Substitute } b = 3 \text{ into the equation } 6.3 = Ab^1.$$
$$A = \frac{6.3}{3} = 2.1.$$

We have both constants, $A = 2.1$ and $b = 3$, so the model is

$$y = 2.1(3^x).$$

Example 6 will show how to use technology to fit an exponential function to two or more data points.

APPLICATIONS

Recall some terminology we mentioned earlier: A quantity y experiences **exponential growth** if $y = Ab^t$ with $b > 1$. (Here we use t for the independent variable, thinking of time.) It experiences **exponential decay** if $y = Ab^t$ with $0 < b < 1$. We already saw several examples of exponential growth and decay in Section 1.2.

EXAMPLE 3 Exponential Growth and Decay

a. Compound Interest (See Section 1.2 Example 6.) If \$2,000 is invested in a mutual fund with an annual yield of 12.6% and the earnings are reinvested each month, then the future value after t years is

$$A(t) = P\left(1 + \frac{r}{m}\right)^{mt} = 2{,}000\left(1 + \frac{0.126}{12}\right)^{12t} = 2{,}000(1.0105)^{12t},$$

which can be written as $2{,}000(1.0105^{12})^t$, so $A = 2{,}000$ and $b = 1.0105^{12}$. This is an example of exponential growth, because $b > 1$.

b. Carbon Decay (See Section 1.2 Example 7.) The amount of carbon 14 remaining in a sample that originally contained A grams is approximately

$$C(t) = A(0.999879)^t.$$

This is an instance of exponential decay, because $b < 1$.

➡ **Before we go on...** Refer again to part (a). In Example 6(b) of Section 1.2 we showed how to use technology to answer questions such as the following: "When, to the nearest year, will the value of your investment reach \$5,000?" ■

The next example shows an application to public health.

EXAMPLE 4 Exponential Growth: Epidemics

In the early stages of the AIDS epidemic during the 1980s, the number of cases in the United States was increasing by about 50% every 6 months. By the start of 1983, there were approximately 1,600 AIDS cases in the United States.[14]

a. Assuming an exponential growth model, find a function that predicts the number of people infected t years after the start of 1983.

b. Use the model to estimate the number of people infected by October 1, 1986, and also by the end of that year.

Solution

a. One way of finding the desired exponential function is to reason as follows: At time $t = 0$ (January 1, 1983), the number of people infected was 1,600, so $A = 1{,}600$. Every 6 months, the number of cases increased to 150% of the number 6 months earlier—that is, to 1.50 times that number. Each year, it therefore increased to $(1.50)^2 = 2.25$ times the number one year earlier. Hence, after t years, we need to multiply the original 1,600 by 2.25^t, so the model is

$$y = 1{,}600(2.25^t) \text{ cases.}$$

[14]Data based on regression of the 1982–1986 figures. Source for data: Centers for Disease Control and Prevention. HIV/AIDS Surveillance Report, 2000;12 (No. 2).

Alternatively, if we wish to use the method of Example 2, we need two data points. We are given one point: (0, 1,600). Because y increased by 50% every 6 months, 6 months later it reached $1{,}600 + 800 = 2{,}400$ ($t = 0.5$). This information gives a second point: (0.5, 2,400). We can now apply the method in Example 2 to find the model above.

b. October 1, 1986, corresponds to $t = 3.75$ (because October 1 is 9 months, or $9/12 = 0.75$ of a year after January 1). Substituting this value of t in the model gives

$$y = 1{,}600(2.25^{3.75}) \approx 33{,}481 \text{ cases}$$ `1600*2.25^3.75`

By the end of 1986, the model predicts that

$$y = 1{,}600(2.25^{4}) = 41{,}006 \text{ cases.}$$

(The actual number of cases was around 41,700.)

Before we go on... Increasing the number of cases by 50% every 6 months couldn't continue for very long and this is borne out by observations. If increasing by 50% every 6 months did continue, then by January 2003 ($t = 20$), the number of infected people would have been

$$1{,}600(2.25^{20}) \approx 17{,}700{,}000{,}000$$

a number that is more than 50 times the size of the U.S. population! Thus, although the exponential model is fairly reliable in the early stages of the epidemic, it is unreliable for predicting long-term trends. ■

Epidemiologists use more sophisticated models to measure the spread of epidemics, and these models predict a leveling-off phenomenon as the number of cases becomes a significant part of the total population. We discuss such a model, the **logistic function**, in Section 2.4.

The Number e and More Applications

In nature we find examples of growth that occurs *continuously*, as though "interest" is being added more often than every second or fraction of a second. To model this, we need to see what happens to the compound interest formula of Section 1.2 as we let m (the number of times interest is added per year) become extremely large. Something very interesting does happen: We end up with a more compact and elegant formula than we began with. To see why, let's look at a very simple situation.

	A	B
1	m	(1+1/m)^m
2	1	2
3	10	2.59374246
4	100	2.704813829
5	1000	2.716923932
6	10000	2.718145927
7	100000	2.718268237
8	1000000	2.718280469
9	10000000	2.718281694
10	100000000	2.718281786
11	1000000000	2.718282031

Suppose we invest \$1 in the bank for 1 year at 100% interest, compounded m times per year. If $m = 1$, then 100% interest is added every year, and so our money doubles at the end of the year. In general, the accumulated capital at the end of the year is

$$A = 1\left(1 + \frac{1}{m}\right)^m = \left(1 + \frac{1}{m}\right)^m.$$ `(1+1/m)^m`

Now, we are interested in what A becomes for large values of m. On the left is a spreadsheet showing the quantity $\left(1 + \frac{1}{m}\right)^m$ for larger and larger values of m.

Something interesting *does* seem to be happening! The numbers appear to be getting closer and closer to a specific value. In mathematical terminology, we say that the numbers **converge** to a fixed number, 2.71828..., called the **limiting value*** of the quantities $\left(1 + \frac{1}{m}\right)^m$. This number, called e, is one of the most important in mathematics. The number e is irrational, just as the more familiar number π is, so we cannot write down its exact numerical value. To 20 decimal places,

$$e = 2.71828182845904523536....$$

* See Chapter 3 for more on limits.

We now say that, if \$1 is invested for 1 year at 100% interest **compounded continuously**, the accumulated money at the end of that year will amount to $\$e = \$2.72$ (to the nearest cent). But what about the following more general question?

Q: *What about a more general scenario: If we invest an amount \$P for t years at an interest rate of r, compounded continuously, what will be the accumulated amount A at the end of that period?*

A: In the special case above (P, t, and r all equal 1), we took the compound interest formula and let m get larger and larger. We do the same more generally, after a little preliminary work with the algebra of exponentials.

$$A = P\left(1 + \frac{r}{m}\right)^{mt}$$

$$= P\left(1 + \frac{1}{(m/r)}\right)^{mt} \qquad \text{Substituting } \frac{r}{m} = \frac{1}{(m/r)}$$

$$= P\left(1 + \frac{1}{(m/r)}\right)^{(m/r)rt} \qquad \text{Substituting } m = \left(\frac{m}{r}\right)r$$

$$= P\left[\left(1 + \frac{1}{(m/r)}\right)^{(m/r)}\right]^{rt} \qquad \text{Using the rule } a^{bc} = (a^b)^c$$

For continuous compounding of interest, we let m, and hence m/r, get very large. This affects only the term in brackets, which converges to e, and we get the formula

$$A = Pe^{rt}.$$

Q: *How do I obtain powers of e or e itself on a TI-83/84 Plus or in a spreadsheet?*

A: On the TI-83/84 Plus, enter e^x as `e^(x)`, where `e^(` can be obtained by pressing [2ND] [LN]. To obtain the number e on the TI-83/84 Plus, enter `e^(1)`. Spreadsheets have a built-in function called `EXP`; `EXP(x)` gives the value of e^x. To obtain the number e in a spreadsheet, enter `=EXP(1)`.

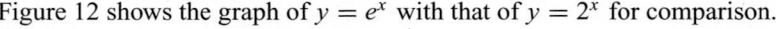

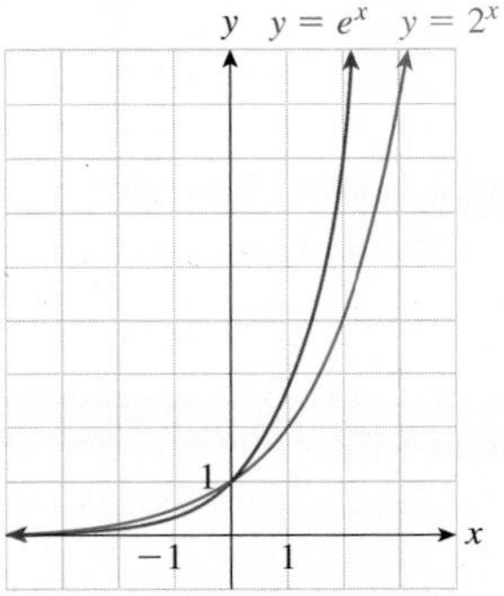

Technology formula: `e^(x)` or `EXP(x)`

Figure 12

Figure 12 shows the graph of $y = e^x$ with that of $y = 2^x$ for comparison.

The Number e and Continuous Compounding

The number e is the limiting value of the quantities $\left(1 + \frac{1}{m}\right)^m$ as m gets larger and larger, and has the value 2.71828182845904523536 ...

If \$P is invested at an annual interest rate r compounded continuously, the accumulated amount after t years is

$$A(t) = Pe^{rt}. \qquad \texttt{P*e^(r*t) or P*EXP(r*t)}$$

Quick Examples

1. If \$100 is invested in an account that bears 15% interest compounded continuously, at the end of 10 years the investment will be worth

$$A(10) = 100e^{(0.15)(10)} = \$448.17. \qquad \texttt{100*e^(0.15*10) or 100*EXP(0.15*10)}$$

2. If \$1 is invested in an account that bears 100% interest compounded continuously, at the end of x years the investment will be worth

$$A(x) = e^x \text{ dollars.}$$

EXAMPLE 5 Continuous Compounding

a. You invest \$10,000 at *Fastrack Savings & Loan,* which pays 6% compounded continuously. Express the balance in your account as a function of the number of years t and calculate the amount of money you will have after 5 years.

b. Your friend has just invested \$20,000 in *Constant Growth Funds,* whose stocks are continuously *declining* at a rate of 6% per year. How much will her investment be worth in 5 years?

c. T During which year will the value of your investment first exceed that of your friend?

Solution

a. We use the continuous growth formula with $P = 10{,}000$, $r = 0.06$, and t variable, getting

$$A(t) = Pe^{rt} = 10{,}000e^{0.06t}.$$

In 5 years,

$$\begin{aligned} A(5) &= 10{,}000e^{0.06(5)} \\ &= 10{,}000e^{0.3} \\ &\approx \$13{,}498.59. \end{aligned}$$

b. Because the investment is depreciating, we use a negative value for r and take $P = 20{,}000$, $r = -0.06$, and $t = 5$, getting

$$\begin{aligned} A(t) &= Pe^{rt} = 20{,}000e^{-0.06t} \\ A(5) &= 20{,}000e^{-0.06(5)} \\ &= 20{,}000e^{-0.3} \\ &\approx \$14{,}816.36. \end{aligned}$$

c. We can answer the question now using a graphing calculator, a spreadsheet, or the Function Evaluator and Grapher tool at the Website. Just enter the exponential models of parts (a) and (b) and create tables to compute the values at the end of several years:

TI-83/84 Plus

`Y1=10000e^(0.06X)`
`Y2=20000e^(-0.06X)`
[2ND] [TABLE]

X	Y1	Y2
1	10618	18835
2	11275	17738
3	11972	16705
4	12712	15733
5	13499	14816
6	14333	13954

X=

Spreadsheet

Headings *t*, Me, Friend in A1–C1; *t*-values 1, . . . , 6 in A2–A7.
`=10000*exp(0.06*A2)`
`=20000*exp(-0.06*A2)`
in B2 and C2 and copy down to C7.

	A	B	C
1	t	Me	Friend
2	1	10618.365	18835.291
3	2	11274.969	17738.409
4	3	11972.174	16705.404
5	4	12712.492	15732.557
6	5	13498.588	14816.364
7	6	14333.294	13953.527

Website www.WanerMath.com

`10000e^(0.06X)` under y_1
`20000e^(-0.06X)` under y_2 Enter 1, . . . , 6 as the x-Values in the Evaluator and press "Evaluate."

x-Values	y_1-Values	y_2-Values
1	10618	18835
2	11275	17738
3	11972	16705
4	12712	15733
5	13499	14816
6	14333	13954

From the table, we see that the value of your investment overtakes that of your friend after $t = 5$ (the end of year 5) and before $t = 6$ (the end of year 6). Thus your investment first exceeds that of your friend sometime during year 6.

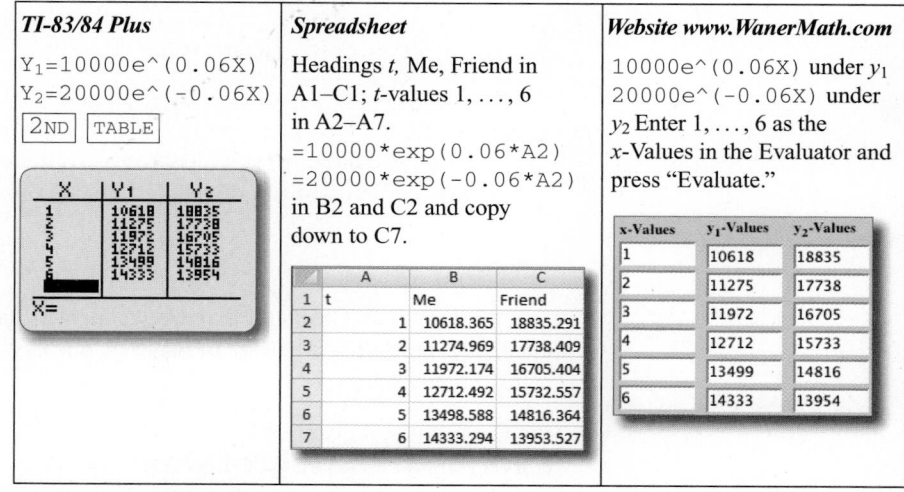

➡ Before we go on...

Q: *How does continuous compounding compare with monthly compounding?*

A: To repeat the calculation in part (a) of Example 5 using monthly compounding instead of continuous compounding, we use the compound interest formula with $P = 10{,}000$, $r = 0.06$, $m = 12$, and $t = 5$ and find

$$A(5) = 10{,}000(1 + 0.06/12)^{60} \approx \$13{,}488.50.$$

Thus, continuous compounding earns you approximately $10 more than monthly compounding on a 5-year, $10,000 investment. This is little to get excited about.

■

If we write the continuous compounding formula $A(t) = Pe^{rt}$ as $A(t) = P(e^r)^t$, we see that $A(t)$ is an exponential function of t, where the base is $b = e^r$, so we have really not introduced a new kind of function. In fact, exponential functions are often written in this way:

Exponential Functions: Alternative Form

We can write any exponential function in the following alternative form:

$$f(x) = Ae^{rx}$$

where A and r are constants. If r is positive, f models exponential growth; if r is negative, f models exponential decay.

Quick Examples

1. $f(x) = 100e^{0.15x}$ — Exponential growth $A = 100$, $r = 0.15$
2. $f(t) = Ae^{-0.000\,121\,01t}$ — Exponential decay of carbon 14; $r = -0.000\,121\,01$
3. $f(t) = 100e^{0.15t} = 100\left(e^{0.15}\right)^t$
   $= 100(1.1618)^t$ — Converting Ae^{rt} to the form Ab^t

We will see in Chapter 4 that the exponential function with base e exhibits some interesting properties when we measure its rate of change, and this is the real mathematical importance of e.

Exponential Regression

Starting with a set of data that suggests an exponential curve, we can use technology to compute the exponential regression curve in much the same way as we did for the quadratic regression curve in Example 5 of Section 2.1.

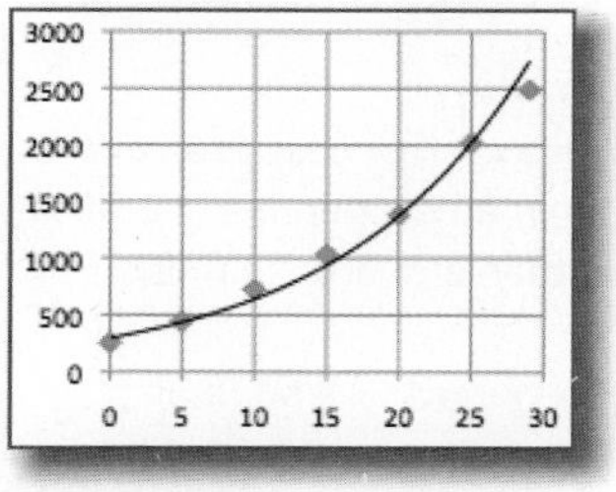

Figure 13

using Technology

See the Technology Guides at the end of the chapter for detailed instructions on how to obtain the regression curve and graph for Example 6 using a graphing calculator or spreadsheet. Outline:

TI-83/84 Plus

STAT EDIT values of t in L_1 and values of C in L_2
Regression curve: STAT CALC option #0 ExpReg ENTER
Graph: Y= VARS 5 EQ 1, then ZOOM 9
[More details on page 187.]

Spreadsheet

t- and C-values in Columns A and B, graph these data. Regression curve: Add exponential Trendline with option to show equation.
[More details on page 190.]

Website

www.WanerMath.com
In the Simple Regression utility, enter the data in the *x* and *y* columns and press "y=a(b^x)".

EXAMPLE 6 Exponential Regression: Health Expenditures

The following table shows annual expenditure on health in the U.S. from 1980 through 2009 ($t = 0$ represents 1980).[15]

Year t	0	5	10	15	20	25	29
Expenditure ($ billion)	256	444	724	1,030	1,380	2,020	2,490

a. Find the exponential regression model

$$C(t) = Ab^t$$

for the annual expenditure.

b. Use the regression model to estimate the expenditure in 2002 ($t = 22$; the actual expenditure was approximately $1,640 billion).

Solution

a. We use technology to obtain the exponential regression curve (See Figure 13):

$$C(t) \approx 296(1.08)^t.$$ Coefficients rounded

b. Using the model $C(t) \approx 296(1.08)^t$ we find that

$$C(22) \approx 296(1.08)^{22} \approx \$1,609 \text{ billion},$$

which is close to the actual number of about $1,640 billion.

Before we go on... We said in the preceding section that the regression curve gives the smallest value of the sum-of-squares error, SSE (the sum of the squares of the residuals). However, exponential regression as computed via technology generally minimizes the sum of the squares of the residuals of the *logarithms* (logarithms are discussed in the next section). Using logarithms allows one easily to convert an exponential function into a linear one and then use linear regression formulas. However, in Section 2.4, we will discuss a way of using Excel's Solver to minimize SSE directly, which allows us to find the best-fit exponential curve directly without the need for devices to simplify the mathematics. If we do this, we obtain a very different equation:

$$C(t) \approx 353(1.07)^t.$$

If you plot this function, you will notice that it seems to fit the data more closely than the regression curve. ■

FAQs

When to Use an Exponential Model for Data Points, and when to Use e in Your Model

Q: *Given a set of data points that appear to be curving upward, how can I tell whether to use a quadratic model or an exponential model?*

[15]Data are rounded. Source: U.S. Department of Health & Human Services/Centers for Medicare & Medicaid Services, National Health Expenditure Data, downloaded April 2011 from www.cms.gov.

A: Here are some things to look for:

- Do the data values appear to double at regular intervals? (For example, do the values approximately double every 5 units?) If so, then an exponential model is appropriate. If it takes longer and longer to double, then a quadratic model may be more appropriate.
- Do the values first decrease to a low point and then increase? If so, then a quadratic model is more appropriate.

It is also helpful to use technology to graph both the regression quadratic and exponential curves and to visually inspect the graphs to determine which gives the closest fit to the data.

Q: *We have two ways of writing exponential functions: $f(x) = Ab^x$ and $f(x) = Ae^{rx}$. How do we know which one to use?*

A: The two forms are equivalent, and it is always possible to convert from one form to the other.* So, use whichever form seems to be convenient for a particular situation. For instance, $f(t) = A(3^t)$ conveniently models exponential growth that is tripling every unit of time, whereas $f(t) = Ae^{0.06t}$ conveniently models an investment with continuous compounding at 6%.

* Quick Example 3 on page 146 shows how to convert Ae^{rx} to Ab^x. Conversion from Ab^x to Ae^{rx} involves logarithms: $r = \ln b$.

2.2 EXERCISES

▼ more advanced ◆ challenging

T indicates exercises that should be solved using technology

For each function in Exercises 1–12, compute the missing values in the following table and supply a valid technology formula for the given function: HINT [See Quick Examples on page 138.]

x	−3	−2	−1	0	1	2	3
$f(x)$							

1. $f(x) = 4^x$

2. $f(x) = 3^x$

3. $f(x) = 3^{-x}$

4. $f(x) = 4^{-x}$

5. $g(x) = 2(2^x)$

6. $g(x) = 2(3^x)$

7. $h(x) = -3(2^{-x})$

8. $h(x) = -2(3^{-x})$

9. $r(x) = 2^x - 1$

10. $r(x) = 2^{-x} + 1$

11. $s(x) = 2^{x-1}$

12. $s(x) = 2^{1-x}$

Using a chart of values, graph each of the functions in Exercises 13–18. (Use $-3 \le x \le 3$.)

13. $f(x) = 3^{-x}$

14. $f(x) = 4^{-x}$

15. $g(x) = 2(2^x)$

16. $g(x) = 2(3^x)$

17. $h(x) = -3(2^{-x})$

18. $h(x) = -2(3^{-x})$

In Exercises 19–24, the values of two functions, f and g, are given in a table. One, both, or neither of them may be exponential. Decide which, if any, are exponential, and give the exponential models for those that are. HINT [See Example 1.]

19.

x	−2	−1	0	1	2
$f(x)$	0.5	1.5	4.5	13.5	40.5
$g(x)$	8	4	2	1	$\frac{1}{2}$

20.

x	−2	−1	0	1	2
$f(x)$	$\frac{1}{2}$	1	2	4	8
$g(x)$	3	0	−1	0	3

21.

x	−2	−1	0	1	2
$f(x)$	22.5	7.5	2.5	7.5	22.5
$g(x)$	0.3	0.9	2.7	8.1	16.2

22.

x	−2	−1	0	1	2
$f(x)$	0.3	0.9	2.7	8.1	24.3
$g(x)$	3	1.5	0.75	0.375	0.1875

23.

x	−2	−1	0	1	2
$f(x)$	100	200	400	600	800
$g(x)$	100	20	4	0.8	0.16

24.

x	−2	−1	0	1	2
$f(x)$	0.8	0.2	0.1	0.05	0.025
$g(x)$	80	40	20	10	2

T *For each function in Exercises 25–30, supply a valid technology formula and then use technology to compute the missing values in the following table:* HINT [See Quick Examples on page 138.]

x	−3	−2	−1	0	1	2	3
$f(x)$							

25. $f(x) = e^{-2x}$

26. $g(x) = e^{x/5}$

27. $h(x) = 1.01(2.02^{-4x})$

28. $h(x) = 3.42(3^{-x/5})$

29. $r(x) = 50\left(1+\frac{1}{3.2}\right)^{2x}$

30. $r(x) = 0.043\left(4.5 - \frac{5}{1.2}\right)^{-x}$

In Exercises 31–38, supply a valid technology formula for the given function.

31. 2^{x-1}

32. 2^{-4x}

33. $\frac{2}{1-2^{-4x}}$

34. $\frac{2^{3-x}}{1-2^x}$

35. $\frac{(3+x)^{3x}}{x+1}$

36. $\frac{20.3^{3x}}{1+20.3^{2x}}$

37. $2e^{(1+x)/x}$

38. $\frac{2e^{2/x}}{x}$

T *On the same set of axes, use technology to graph the pairs of functions in Exercises 39–46 with $-3 \le x \le 3$. Identify which graph corresponds to which function.* HINT [See Quick Examples on page 139.]

39. $f_1(x) = 1.6^x$, $f_2(x) = 1.8^x$

40. $f_1(x) = 2.2^x$, $f_2(x) = 2.5^x$

41. $f_1(x) = 300(1.1^x)$, $f_2(x) = 300(1.1^{2x})$

42. $f_1(x) = 100(1.01^{2x})$, $f_2(x) = 100(1.01^{3x})$

43. $f_1(x) = 2.5^{1.02x}$, $f_2(x) = e^{1.02x}$

44. $f_1(x) = 2.5^{-1.02x}$, $f_2(x) = e^{-1.02x}$

45. $f_1(x) = 1{,}000(1.045^{-3x})$, $f_2(x) = 1{,}000(1.045^{3x})$

46. $f_1(x) = 1{,}202(1.034^{-3x})$, $f_2(x) = 1{,}202(1.034^{3x})$

For Exercises 47–54, model the data using an exponential function $f(x) = Ab^x$. HINT [See Example 1.]

47.

x	0	1	2
$f(x)$	500	250	125

48.

x	0	1	2
$f(x)$	500	1,000	2,000

49.

x	0	1	2
$f(x)$	10	30	90

50.

x	0	1	2
$f(x)$	90	30	10

51.

x	0	1	2
$f(x)$	500	225	101.25

52.

x	0	1	2
$f(x)$	5	3	1.8

53.

x	1	2
$f(x)$	−110	−121

54.

x	1	2
$f(x)$	−41	−42.025

Find equations for exponential functions that pass through the pairs of points given in Exercises 55–62. (Round all coefficients to 4 decimal places when necessary.) HINT [See Example 2.]

55. Through (2, 36) and (4, 324)

56. Through (2, −4) and (4, −16)

57. Through (−2, −25) and (1, −0.2)

58. Through (1, 1.2) and (3, 0.108)

59. Through (1, 3) and (3, 6)

60. Through (1, 2) and (4, 6)

61. Through (2, 3) and (6, 2)

62. Through (−1, 2) and (3, 1)

Obtain exponential functions in the form $f(t) = Ae^{rt}$ in Exercises 63–66. HINT [See Example 5.]

63. $f(t)$ is the value after t years of a \$5,000 investment earning 10% interest compounded continuously.

64. $f(t)$ is the value after t years of a \$2,000 investment earning 5.3% interest compounded continuously.

65. $f(t)$ is the value after t years of a \$1,000 investment depreciating continuously at an annual rate of 6.3%.

66. $f(t)$ is the value after t years of a \$10,000 investment depreciating continuously at an annual rate of 60%.

T *In Exercises 67–70, use technology to find the exponential regression function through the given points. (Round all coefficients to 4 decimal places.)* HINT [See Example 6.]

67. {(1, 2), (3, 5), (4, 9), (5, 20)}

68. {(−1, 2), (−3, 5), (−4, 9), (−5, 20)}

69. {(−1, 10), (−3, 5), (−4, 3)}

70. {(3, 3), (4, 5), (5, 10)}

APPLICATIONS

71. ***Aspirin*** Soon after taking an aspirin, a patient has absorbed 300 mg of the drug. After 2 hours, only 75 mg remain. Find an exponential model for the amount of aspirin in the bloodstream after t hours, and use your model to find the amount of aspirin in the bloodstream after 5 hours. HINT [See Example 2.]

72. ***Alcohol*** After a large number of drinks, a person has a blood alcohol level of 200 mg/dL (milligrams per deciliter). If the amount of alcohol in the blood decays exponentially, and after 2 hours, 112.5 mg/dL remain, find an exponential model for the person's blood alcohol level, and use your model to estimate the person's blood alcohol level after 4 hours. HINT [See Example 2.]

73. ***Freon Production*** The production of ozone-layer-damaging Freon 22 (chlorodifluoromethane) in developing countries rose from 200 tons in 2004 to a projected 590 tons in 2010.[16]

[16] Figures are approximate. Source: Lampert Kuijpers (Panel of the Montreal Protocol), National Bureau of Statistics in China, via CEIC Data/*New York Times*, February 23, 2007, p. C1.

a. Use this information to find both a linear model and an exponential model for the amount F of Freon 22 (in tons) as a function of time t in years since 2000. (Round all coefficients to three significant digits.) HINT [See Example 2.] Which of these models would you judge to be more appropriate to the data shown below?

t (year since 2000)	0	2	4	6	8	10
F (tons of Freon 22)	100	140	200	270	400	590

b. Use the better of the two models from part (a) to predict the 2008 figure and compare it with the projected figure above.

74. ***Revenue*** The annual revenue of Amazon.com rose from approximately \$10.7 billion in 2006 to \$34.2 billion in 2010.[17]

a. Use this information to find both a linear model and an exponential model for Amazon.com's annual revenue I (in billions of dollars) as a function of time t in years since 2000. (Round all coefficients to three significant digits.) HINT [See Example 2.] Which of these models would you judge to be more appropriate to the data shown below?

t (Year since 2000)	6	7	8	9	10
I (\$ billions)	10.7	14.8	19.2	24.5	34.2

b. Use the better of the two models from part (a) to predict the 2008 figure and compare it with the actual figure above.

75. ▼ ***U.S. Population*** The U.S. population was 180 million in 1960 and 309 million in 2010.[18]

a. Use these data to give an exponential growth model showing the U.S. population P as a function of time t in years since 1960. Round coefficients to 6 significant digits. HINT [See Example 2.]

b. By experimenting, determine the smallest number of significant digits to which you should round the coefficients in part (a) in order to obtain the correct 2010 population figure accurate to 3 significant digits.

c. Using the model in part (a), predict the population in 2020.

76. ▼ ***World Population*** World population was estimated at 2.56 billion people in 1950 and 6.91 billion people in 2011.[19]

a. Use these data to give an exponential growth model showing the world population P as a function of time t in years since 1950. Round coefficients to 6 significant digits. HINT [See Example 2.]

b. By experimenting, determine the smallest number of significant digits to which you should round the coefficients in part (a) in order to obtain the correct 2011 population figure to 3 significant digits.

c. Assuming the exponential growth model from part (a), estimate the world population in the year 1000. Comment on your answer.

77. ▼ ***Frogs*** Frogs have been breeding like flies at the Enormous State University (ESU) campus! Each year, the pledge class of the Epsilon Delta fraternity is instructed to tag all the frogs residing on the ESU campus. Two years ago they managed to tag all 50,000 of them (with little Epsilon Delta Fraternity tags). This year's pledge class discovered that last year's tags had all fallen off, and they wound up tagging a total of 75,000 frogs.

a. Find an exponential model for the frog population.

b. Assuming exponential population growth, and that all this year's tags have fallen off, how many tags should Epsilon Delta order for next year's pledge class?

78. ▼ ***Flies*** Flies in Suffolk County have been breeding like frogs! Three years ago the Health Commission caught 4,000 flies in a trap in 1 hour. This year it caught 7,000 flies in 1 hour.

a. Find an exponential model for the fly population.

b. Assuming exponential population growth, how many flies should the commission expect to catch next year?

79. ***Bacteria*** A bacteria culture starts with 1,000 bacteria and doubles in size every 3 hours. Find an exponential model for the size of the culture as a function of time t in hours and use the model to predict how many bacteria there will be after 2 days. HINT [See Example 4.]

80. ***Bacteria*** A bacteria culture starts with 1,000 bacteria. Two hours later there are 1,500 bacteria. Find an exponential model for the size of the culture as a function of time t in hours, and use the model to predict how many bacteria there will be after 2 days. HINT [See Example 4.]

81. ***SARS*** In the early stages of the deadly SARS (Severe Acute Respiratory Syndrome) epidemic in 2003, the number of cases was increasing by about 18% each day.[20] On March 17, 2003 (the first day for which statistics were reported by the World Health Organization), there were 167 cases. Find an exponential model that predicts the number of cases t days after March 17, 2003, and use it to estimate the number of cases on March 31, 2003. (The actual reported number of cases was 1,662.)

82. ***SARS*** A few weeks into the deadly SARS (Severe Acute Respiratory Syndrome) epidemic in 2003, the number of cases was increasing by about 4% each day.[21] On April 1,

[17] Source for data: www.wikinvest.com/

[18] Figures are rounded to 3 significant digits. Source: U.S. Census Bureau, www.census.gov.

[19] *Ibid.*

[20] Source: World Health Organization, www.who.int.

[21] *Ibid.*

2003 there were 1,804 cases. Find an exponential model that predicts the number of cases t days after April 1, 2003, and use it to estimate the number of cases on April 30, 2003. (The actual reported number of cases was 5,663.)

83. *Investments* In November 2010, E*TRADE Financial was offering only 0.3% interest on its online savings accounts, with interest reinvested monthly.[22] Find the associated exponential model for the value of a \$5,000 deposit after t years. Assuming this rate of return continued for seven years, how much would a deposit of \$5,000 in November 2010 be worth in November 2017? (Answer to the nearest \$1.) HINT [See Example 3; you saw this exercise before in Section 1.2.]

84. *Investments* In November 2010, ING Direct was offering 2.4% interest on its Orange Savings Account, with interest reinvested quarterly.[23] Find the associated exponential model for the value of a \$4,000 deposit after t years. Assuming this rate of return continued for 8 years, how much would a deposit of \$4,000 in November 2010 be worth in November 2018? (Answer to the nearest \$1.) HINT [See Example 3; you saw this exercise before in Section 1.2.]

85. T ***Investments*** Refer to Exercise 83. In November of which year will an investment of \$5,000 made in November of 2010 first exceed \$5,200? HINT [See Example 5; you saw this exercise before in Section 1.2.]

86. T ***Investments*** Refer to Exercise 84. In November of which year will an investment of \$4,000 made in November of 2010 first exceed \$5,200? HINT [See Example 5; you saw this exercise before in Section 1.2.]

87. *Investments* *Rock Solid Bank & Trust* is offering a CD (certificate of deposit) that pays 4% compounded continuously. How much interest would a \$1,000 deposit earn over 10 years? HINT [See Example 5.]

88. *Savings* *FlybynightSavings.com* is offering a savings account that pays 31% interest compounded continuously. How much interest would a deposit of \$2,000 earn over 10 years?

89. *Home Sales* Sales of existing homes in the U.S. rose continuously over the period 2008–2011 at the rate of 3.2% per year from 4.9 million in 2008.[24] Write down a formula that predicts sales of existing homes t years after 2008. Use your model to estimate, to the nearest 0.1 million, sales of existing homes in 2010 and 2012.

90. *Home Prices* The median selling price of an existing home in the U.S. declined continuously over the period 2008–2011 at the rate of 7.6% per year from approximately \$198 thousand in 2008.[25] Write down a formula that predicts the median selling price of an existing home t years after 2008. Use your model to estimate, to the nearest \$1,000, the median selling price of an existing home in 2011 and 2013.

91. *Global Warming* The most abundant greenhouse gas is carbon dioxide. According to figures from the Intergovernmental Panel on Climate Change (IPCC), the amount of carbon dioxide in the atmosphere (in parts of volume per million) can be approximated by

$$C(t) \approx 280e^{0.00119t} \text{ parts per million}$$

where t is time in years since 1750.[26]

a. Use the model to estimate the amount of carbon dioxide in the atmosphere in 1950, 2000, 2050, and 2100.

b. According to the model, when, to the nearest decade, will the level surpass 390 parts per million?

92. *Global Warming* Another greenhouse gas is methane. According to figures from the Intergovernmental Panel on Climate Change (IPCC), the amount of methane in the atmosphere (in parts of volume per billion) can be approximated by

$$C(t) \approx 715e^{0.00356t} \text{ parts per billion}$$

where t is time in years since 1750.[27]

a. Use the model to estimate the amount of methane in the atmosphere in 1950, 2000, 2050, and 2100. (Round your answers to the nearest 10 parts per billion.)

b. According to the model, when, to the nearest decade, will the level surpass 2,000 parts per billion?

93. T ***New York City Housing Costs: Downtown*** The following table shows the average price of a two-bedroom apartment in downtown New York City during the real estate boom from 1994 to 2004.[28]

t	0 (1994)	2	4	6	8	10 (2004)
Price (\$ million)	0.38	0.40	0.60	0.95	1.20	1.60

a. Use exponential regression to model the price $P(t)$ as a function of time t since 1994. Include a sketch of the points and the regression curve. (Round the coefficients to 3 decimal places.) HINT [See Example 6.]

b. Extrapolate your model to estimate the cost of a two-bedroom downtown apartment in 2005.

94. T ***New York City Housing Costs: Uptown*** The following table shows the average price of a two-bedroom apartment in uptown New York City during the real estate boom from 1994 to 2004.[29]

t	0 (1994)	2	4	6	8	10 (2004)
Price (\$ million)	0.18	0.18	0.19	0.2	0.35	0.4

[22] Interest rate based on annual percentage yield. Source: us.etrade.com, November 2010.

[23] Interest rate based on annual percentage yield. Source: home.ingdirect.com, November 2010.

[24] Source: National Association of Realtors, www.realtor.org.

[25] *Ibid.*

[26] Authors' exponential model based on the 1750 and 2005 figures. Source for data: IPCC Fourth Assessment Report: Climate Change 2007, www.ipcc.ch.

[27] *Ibid.*

[28] Data are rounded and 2004 figure is an estimate. Source: Miller Samuel/*New York Times*, March 28, 2004, p. RE 11.

[29] *Ibid.*

a. Use exponential regression to model the price $P(t)$ as a function of time t since 1994. Include a sketch of the points and the regression curve. (Round the coefficients to 3 decimal places.)

b. Extrapolate your model to estimate the cost of a two-bedroom uptown apartment in 2005.

95. T ***Facebook*** The following table gives the approximate numbers of Facebook members at various times early in its history.[30]

Year t (Since start of 2005)	0	0.5	1	1.5	2	2.5	3	3.5
Facebook Members n (millions)	1	2	5.5	7	12	30	58	80

a. Use exponential regression to model Facebook membership as a function of time in years since the start of 2005, and graph the data points and regression curve. (Round coefficients to 3 decimal places.)

b. Fill in the missing quantity: According to the model, Facebook membership each year was ____ times that of the year before.

c. Use your model to estimate Facebook membership in early 2009 to the nearest million.

96. T ***Freon Production*** The following table shows Freon 22 production in developing countries in various years since 2000.[31]

t (Year since 2000)	0	2	4	6	8	10
F (Tons of Freon 22)	100	140	200	270	400	590

a. Use exponential regression to model Freon production as a function of time in years since 2000, and graph the data points and regression curve. (Round coefficients to 3 decimal places.)

b. Fill in the missing quantity: According to the model, Freon production each year was ____ times that of the year before.

c. Use your model to estimate freon production in 2009 to the nearest ton.

COMMUNICATION AND REASONING EXERCISES

97. Which of the following three functions will be largest for large values of x?

(A) $f(x) = x^2$ **(B)** $r(x) = 2^x$ **(C)** $h(x) = x^{10}$

98. Which of the following three functions will be smallest for large values of x?

(A) $f(x) = x^{-2}$ **(B)** $r(x) = 2^{-x}$ **(C)** $h(x) = x^{-10}$

99. What limitations apply to using an exponential function to model growth in real-life situations? Illustrate your answer with an example.

100. Explain in words why 5% per year compounded continuously yields more interest than 5% per year compounded monthly.

101. ▼ The following commentary and graph appeared in politicalcalculations.blogspot.com on August 30, 2005:[32]

> One of the neater blogs I've recently encountered is The Real Returns, which offers a wealth of investing, market and economic data. Earlier this month, The Real Returns posted data related to the recent history of U.S. median house prices over the period from 1963 to 2004. The original source of the housing data is the U.S. Census Bureau.
>
> Well, that kind of data deserves some curve-fitting and a calculator to estimate what the future U.S. median house price might be, so Political Calculations has extracted the data from 1973 onward to create the following chart:

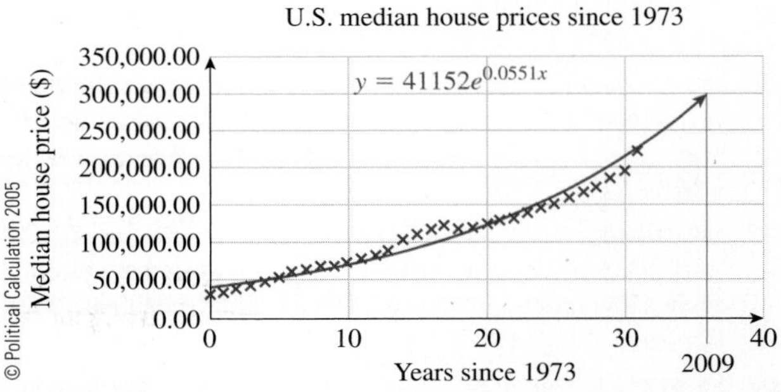

Comment on the article and graph. HINT [See Exercise 90.]

102. ▼ Refer to Exercise 101. Of what possible predictive use, then, is the kind of exponential model given by the blogger in the article referred to?

103. ▼ Describe two real-life situations in which a linear model would be more appropriate than an exponential model, and two situations in which an exponential model would be more appropriate than a linear model.

104. ▼ Describe a real-life situation in which a quadratic model would be more appropriate than an exponential model and one in which an exponential model would be more appropriate than a quadratic model.

105. How would you check whether data points of the form $(1, y_1)$, $(2, y_2)$, $(3, y_3)$ lie on an exponential curve?

[30] Sources: www.facebook.com, www.insidehighered.com. (Some data are interpolated.)

[31] Figures are approximate. Source: Lampert Kuijpers (Panel of the Montreal Protocol), National Bureau of Statistics in China, via CEIC Data/*New York Times*, February 23, 2007, p. C1.

[32] The graph was re-created by the authors using the blog author's data source.
Source for article: politicalcalculations.blogspot.com/2005/08/projecting-us-median-housing-prices.html.
Source for data: therealreturns.blogspot.com/2005_08_01_archive.html.

106. ▼ You are told that the points $(1, y_1)$, $(2, y_2)$, $(3, y_3)$ lie on an exponential curve. Express y_3 in terms of y_1 and y_2.

107. ▼ Your local banker tells you that the reason his bank doesn't compound interest continuously is that it would be too demanding of computer resources because the computer would need to spend a great deal of time keeping all accounts updated. Comment on his reasoning.

108. ▼ Your other local banker tells you that the reason *her* bank doesn't offer continuously compounded interest is that it is equivalent to offering a fractionally higher interest rate compounded daily. Comment on her reasoning.

2.3 Logarithmic Functions and Models

Logarithms were invented by John Napier (1550–1617) in the late sixteenth century as a means of aiding calculation. His invention made possible the prodigious hand calculations of astronomer Johannes Kepler (1571–1630), who was the first to describe accurately the orbits and the motions of the planets. Today, computers and calculators have done away with that use of logarithms, but many other uses remain. In particular, the logarithm is used to model real-world phenomena in numerous fields, including physics, finance, and economics.

From the equation

$$2^3 = 8$$

we can see that the power to which we need to raise 2 in order to get 8 is 3. We abbreviate the phrase "the power to which we need to raise 2 in order to get 8" as "$\log_2 8$." Thus, another way of writing the equation $2^3 = 8$ is

$$\log_2 8 = 3. \qquad \text{The power to which we need to raise 2 in order to get 8 is 3.}$$

This is read "the base 2 logarithm of 8 is 3" or "the log, base 2, of 8 is 3."

Here is the general definition.

Base *b* Logarithm

The **base *b* logarithm of *x***, $\log_b x$, is the power to which we need to raise b in order to get x. Symbolically,

$$\log_b x = y \qquad \text{means} \qquad b^y = x.$$

Logarithmic form — *Exponential form*

Quick Examples

1. The following table lists some exponential equations and their equivalent logarithmic forms:

Exponential Form	$10^3 = 1000$	$4^2 = 16$	$3^3 = 27$	$5^1 = 5$	$7^0 = 1$	$4^{-2} = \frac{1}{16}$	$25^{1/2} = 5$
Logarithmic Form	$\log_{10} 1000 = 3$	$\log_4 16 = 2$	$\log_3 27 = 3$	$\log_5 5 = 1$	$\log_7 1 = 0$	$\log_4 \frac{1}{16} = -2$	$\log_{25} 5 = \frac{1}{2}$

2. $\log_3 9$ = the power to which we need to raise 3 in order to get 9. Because $3^2 = 9$, this power is 2, so $\log_3 9 = 2$.

3. $\log_{10}10{,}000$ = the power to which we need to raise 10 in order to get 10,000. Because $10^4 = 10{,}000$, this power is 4, so $\log_{10}10{,}000 = 4$.

4. $\log_3\frac{1}{27}$ is the power to which we need to raise 3 in order to get $\frac{1}{27}$. Because $3^{-3} = \frac{1}{27}$ this power is –3, so $\log_3\frac{1}{27} = -3$.

5. $\log_b 1 = 0$ for every positive number b other than 1 because $b^0 = 1$.

Note The number $\log_b x$ is defined only if b and x are both positive and $b \neq 1$. Thus, it is impossible to compute, say, $\log_3(-9)$ (because there is no power of 3 that equals -9), or $\log_1(2)$ (because there is no power of 1 that equals 2). ■

Logarithms with base 10 and base e are frequently used, so they have special names and notations.

Common Logarithm, Natural Logarithm

The following are standard abbreviations.

		TI-83/84 Plus & Spreadsheet Formula
Base 10: $\log_{10} x = \log x$	*Common Logarithm*	`log(x)`
Base e: $\log_e x = \ln x$	*Natural Logarithm*	`ln(x)`

Quick Examples

Logarithmic Form	Exponential Form
1. $\log 10{,}000 = 4$	$10^4 = 10{,}000$
2. $\log 10 = 1$	$10^1 = 10$
3. $\log \dfrac{1}{10{,}000} = -4$	$10^{-4} = \dfrac{1}{10{,}000}$
4. $\ln e = 1$	$e^1 = e$
5. $\ln 1 = 0$	$e^0 = 1$
6. $\ln 2 = 0.69314718\ldots$	$e^{0.69314718\ldots} = 2$

Some technologies (such as calculators) do not permit direct calculation of logarithms other than common and natural logarithms. To compute logarithms with other bases with these technologies, we can use the following formula:

Change-of-Base Formula

$$\log_b a = \frac{\log a}{\log b} = \frac{\ln a}{\ln b}$$ Change-of-base formula*

Quick Examples

1. $\log_{11} 9 = \dfrac{\log 9}{\log 11} \approx 0.91631$ `log(9)/log(11)`

2. $\log_{11} 9 = \dfrac{\ln 9}{\ln 11} \approx 0.91631$ `ln(9)/ln(11)`

3. $\log_{3.2}\left(\dfrac{1.42}{3.4}\right) \approx -0.75065$ `log(1.42/3.4)/log(3.2)`

* Here is a quick explanation of why this formula works: To calculate $\log_b a$, we ask, "to what power must we raise b to get a?" To check the formula, we try using $\log a/\log b$ as the exponent.

$$b^{\frac{\log a}{\log b}} = (10^{\log b})^{\frac{\log a}{\log b}}$$
(because $b = 10^{\log b}$)
$$= 10^{\log a} = a$$

so this exponent works!

Using Technology to Compute Logarithms

To compute $\log_b x$ using technology, use the following formulas:

TI-83/84 Plus	`log(x)/log(b)`	Example: $\log_2(16)$ is `log(16)/log(2)`
Spreadsheet:	`=LOG(x,b)`	Example: $\log_2(16)$ is `=LOG(16,2)`

One important use of logarithms is to solve equations in which the unknown is in the exponent.

EXAMPLE 1 Solving Equations with Unknowns in the Exponent

Solve the following equations.

a. $5^{-x} = 125$ **b.** $3^{2x-1} = 6$ **c.** $100(1.005)^{3x} = 200$

Solution

a. Write the given equation $5^{-x} = 125$ in logarithmic form:

$$-x = \log_5 125$$

This gives $x = -\log_5 125 = -3$.

b. In logarithmic form, $3^{2x-1} = 6$ becomes

$$2x - 1 = \log_3 6$$
$$2x = 1 + \log_3 6$$

giving
$$x = \frac{1 + \log_3 6}{2} \approx \frac{1 + 1.6309}{2} \approx 1.3155.$$

c. We cannot write the given equation, $100(1.005)^{3x} = 200$, directly in logarithmic form. We must first divide both sides by 100:

$$1.005^{3x} = \frac{200}{100} = 2$$
$$3x = \log_{1.005} 2$$
$$x = \frac{\log_{1.005} 2}{3} \approx \frac{138.9757}{3} \approx 46.3252.$$

Now that we know what logarithms are, we can talk about functions based on logarithms:

Logarithmic Function

A **logarithmic function** has the form

$$f(x) = \log_b x + C \qquad \text{(b and C are constants with $b > 0$, $b \neq 1$)}$$

or, alternatively,

$$f(x) = A \ln x + C. \qquad \text{(A, C constants with $A \neq 0$)}$$

Quick Examples

1. $f(x) = \log x$
2. $g(x) = \ln x - 5$
3. $h(x) = \log_2 x + 1$
4. $k(x) = 3.2 \ln x + 7.2$

Q: *What is the difference between the two forms of the logarithmic function?*

A: None, really—they're equivalent: We can start with an equation in the first form and use the change-of-base formula to rewrite it:

$$f(x) = \log_b x + C$$

$$= \frac{\ln x}{\ln b} + C \qquad \text{Change-of-base formula}$$

$$= \left(\frac{1}{\ln b}\right) \ln x + C.$$

Our function now has the form $f(x) = A \ln x + C$, where $A = 1/\ln b$. We can go the other way as well, to rewrite $A \ln x + C$ in the form $\log_b x + C$.

EXAMPLE 2 Graphs of Logarithmic Functions

a. Sketch the graph of $f(x) = \log_2 x$ by hand.

b. Use technology to compare the graph in part (a) with the graphs of $\log_b x$ for $b = 1/4$, $1/2$, and 4.

Solution

a. To sketch the graph of $f(x) = \log_2 x$ by hand, we begin with a table of values. Because $\log_2 x$ is not defined when $x = 0$, we choose several values of x close to zero and also some larger values, all chosen so that their logarithms are easy to compute:

x	$\frac{1}{8}$	$\frac{1}{4}$	$\frac{1}{2}$	1	2	4	8
$f(x) = \log_2 x$	−3	−2	−1	0	1	2	3

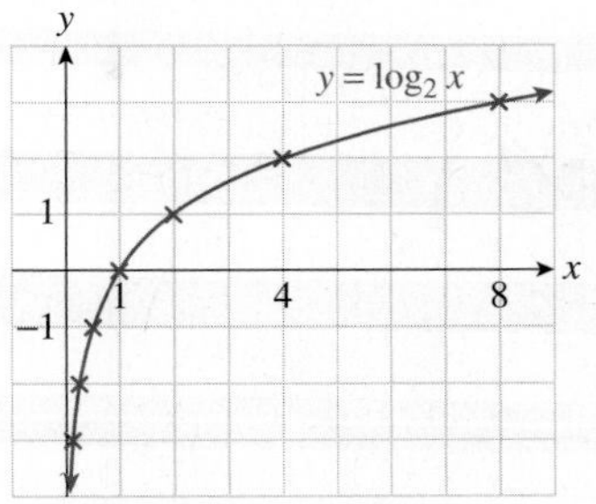

Figure 14

Graphing these points and joining them by a smooth curve gives us Figure 14.

b. We enter the logarithmic functions in graphing utilities as follows (note the use of the change-of-base formula in the TI-83/84 Plus version):

TI-83/84 Plus	Spreadsheet
`Y1=log(X)/log(0.25)`	`=LOG(x,0.25)`
`Y2=log(X)/log(0.5)`	`=LOG(x,0.5)`
`Y3=log(X)/log(2)`	`=LOG(x,2)`
`Y4=log(X)/log(4)`	`=LOG(x,4)`

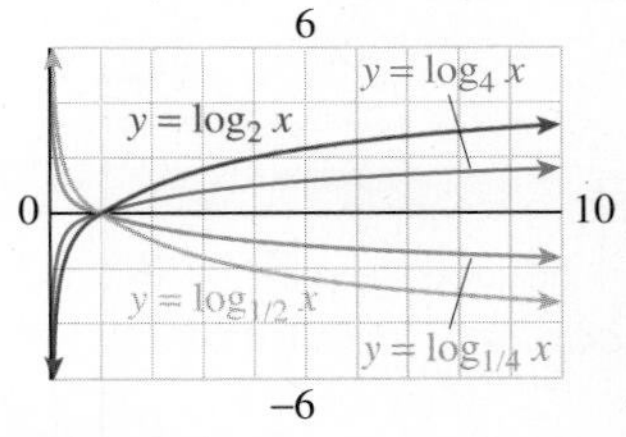

Figure 15

Figure 15 shows the resulting graphs.

➡ **Before we go on...** Notice that the graphs of the logarithmic functions in Example 2 all pass through the point (1, 0). (Why?) Notice further that the graphs of the logarithmic functions with bases less than 1 are upside-down versions of the others. Finally, how are these graphs related to the graphs of exponential functions? ■

Below are some important algebraic properties of logarithms we shall use throughout the rest of this section.

Website
www.WanerMath.com
Follow the path
Chapter 2
→ Using and Deriving Algebraic Properties of Logarithms
to find a list of logarithmic identities and a discussion on where they come from.
Follow the path
Chapter 2
→ Inverse Functions
for a general discussion of inverse functions, including further discussion of the relationship between logarithmic and exponential functions.

Logarithm Identities

The following identities hold for all positive bases $a \neq 1$ and $b \neq 1$, all positive numbers x and y, and every real number r. These identities follow from the laws of exponents.

Identity	Quick Examples
1. $\log_b(xy) = \log_b x + \log_b y$	$\log_2 16 = \log_2 8 + \log_2 2$
2. $\log_b\left(\frac{x}{y}\right) = \log_b x - \log_b y$	$\log_2\left(\frac{5}{3}\right) = \log_2 5 - \log_2 3$
3. $\log_b(x^r) = r \log_b x$	$\log_2(6^5) = 5 \log_2 6$
4. $\log_b b = 1; \log_b 1 = 0$	$\log_2 2 = 1; \ln e = 1; \log_{11} 1 = 0$
5. $\log_b\left(\frac{1}{x}\right) = -\log_b x$	$\log_2\left(\frac{1}{3}\right) = -\log_2 3$
6. $\log_b x = \frac{\log_a x}{\log_a b}$	$\log_2 5 = \frac{\log_{10} 5}{\log_{10} 2} = \frac{\log 5}{\log 2}$

Relationship with Exponential Functions

The following two identities demonstrate that the operations of taking the base b logarithm and raising b to a power are *inverse* to each other.

Identity	Quick Examples
1. $\log_b(b^x) = x$ *In words:* The power to which you raise b in order to get b^x is x. (!)	$\log_2(2^7) = 7$
2. $b^{\log_b x} = x$ *In words:* Raising b to the power to which it must be raised to get x yields x. (!)	$5^{\log_5 8} = 8$

APPLICATIONS

EXAMPLE 3 Investments: How Long?

Global bonds sold by Mexico are yielding an average of 2.51% per year.[33] At that interest rate, how long will it take a \$1,000 investment to be worth \$1,200 if the interest is compounded monthly?

[33] In 2011 (Bonds maturing 03/03/2015). Source: www.bloomberg.com.

Solution Substituting $A = 1{,}200$, $P = 1{,}000$, $r = 0.0251$, and $m = 12$ in the compound interest equation gives

$$A(t) = P\left(1 + \frac{r}{m}\right)^{mt}$$

$$1{,}200 = 1{,}000\left(1 + \frac{0.0251}{12}\right)^{12t}$$

$$\approx 1{,}000(1.002092)^{12t}$$

and we must solve for t. We first divide both sides by 1,000, getting an equation in exponential form:

$$1.2 = 1.002092^{12t}.$$

In logarithmic form, this becomes

$$12t = \log_{1.002092}(1.2).$$

We can now solve for t:

$$t = \frac{\log_{1.002092}(1.2)}{12} \approx 7.3 \text{ years.}$$ `log(1.2)/(log(1.002092)*12)`

Thus, it will take approximately 7.3 years for a \$1,000 investment to be worth \$1,200.

Before we go on... We can use the logarithm identities to solve the equation

$$1.2 = 1.002092^{12t}$$

that arose in Example 3 (and also more general equations with unknowns in the exponent) by taking the natural logarithm of both sides:

$$\ln 1.2 = \ln(1.002092^{12t})$$

$$= 12t \ln 1.002092.$$ By Identity 3

We can now solve this for t to get

$$t = \frac{\ln 1.2}{12 \ln 1.002092},$$

which, by the change-of-base formula, is equivalent to the answer we got in Example 3. ■

EXAMPLE 4 Half-Life

a. The weight of carbon 14 that remains in a sample that originally contained A grams is given by

$$C(t) = A(0.999879)^t$$

where t is time in years. Find the **half-life**, the time it takes half of the carbon 14 in a sample to decay.

b. Repeat part (a) using the following alternative form of the exponential model in part (a):

$$C(t) = Ae^{-0.000\,121\,01t}$$ See Quick Examples, page 146.

c. Another radioactive material has a half-life of 7,000 years. Find an exponential decay model in the form

$$R(t) = Ae^{-kt}$$

for the amount of undecayed material remaining. (The constant k is called the **decay constant**.)

d. How long will it take for 99.95% of the substance in a sample of the material in part (c) to decay?

Solution

a. We want to find the value of t for which $C(t) =$ the weight of undecayed carbon 14 left = half the original weight = $0.5A$. Substituting, we get

$$0.5A = A(0.999879)^t.$$

Dividing both sides by A gives

$$0.5 = 0.999879^t \qquad \text{Exponential form}$$

$$t = \log_{0.999879} 0.5 \approx 5{,}728 \text{ years.} \qquad \text{Logarithmic form}$$

b. This is similar to part (a): We want to solve the equation

$$0.5A = Ae^{-0.000\,121\,01t}$$

for t. Dividing both sides by A gives

$$0.5 = e^{-0.000\,121\,01t}.$$

Taking the natural logarithm of both sides gives

$$\ln(0.5) = \ln(e^{-0.000\,121\,01t}) = -0.000\,121\,01t \qquad \text{Identity 3: } \ln(e^a) = a\ln e = a$$

$$t = \frac{\ln(0.5)}{-0.000\,121\,01} \approx 5{,}728 \text{ years,}$$

as we obtained in part (a).

c. This time we are given the half-life, which we can use to find the exponential model $R(t) = Ae^{-kt}$. At time $t = 0$, the amount of radioactive material is

$$R(0) = Ae^0 = A.$$

Because half of the sample decays in 7,000 years, this sample will decay to $0.5A$ grams in 7,000 years ($t = 7{,}000$). Substituting this information gives

$$0.5A = Ae^{-k(7{,}000)}.$$

Canceling A and taking natural logarithms (again using Identity 3) gives

$$\ln(0.5) = -7{,}000k$$

so the decay constant k is

$$k = -\frac{\ln(0.5)}{7{,}000} \approx 0.000\,099\,021.$$

Therefore, the model is

$$R(t) = Ae^{-0.000\,099\,021t}.$$

d. If 99.95% of the substance in a sample has decayed, then the amount of undecayed material left is 0.05% of the original amount, or $0.0005A$. We have

$$\begin{aligned} 0.0005A &= Ae^{-0.000\,099\,021t} \\ 0.0005 &= e^{-0.000\,099\,021t} \\ \ln(0.0005) &= -0.000\,099\,021t \\ t &= \frac{\ln(0.0005)}{-0.000\,099\,021} \approx 76{,}760 \text{ years.} \end{aligned}$$

➡ Before we go on...

Q: *In parts (a) and (b) of Example 4 we were given two different forms of the model for carbon 14 decay. How do we convert an exponential function in one form to the other?*

A: We have already seen (See Quick Example 3 on page 146) how to convert from the form $f(t) = Ae^{rt}$ in part (b) to the form $f(t) = Ab^t$ in part (a). To go the other way, start with the model in part (a), and equate it to the desired form:

$$C(t) = A(0.999\,879)^t = Ae^{rt}.$$

To solve for r, cancel the As and take the natural logarithm of both sides:

$$t \ln(0.999\,879) = rt \ln e = rt$$

so $r = \ln(0.999\,879) \approx -0.000\,121\,007$,

giving

$$C(t) = Ae^{-0.000\,121\,01t}$$

as in part (b).

We can use the work we did in parts (b) and (c) of the above example to obtain a formula for the decay constant in an exponential decay model for any radioactive substance when we know its half-life. Write the half-life as t_h. Then the calculation in part (b) gives

$$k = -\frac{\ln(0.5)}{t_h} = \frac{\ln 2}{t_h}. \qquad -\ln(0.5) = -\ln\left(\frac{1}{2}\right) = \ln 2$$

Multiplying both sides by t_h gives us the relationship $t_h k = \ln 2$.

Exponential Decay Model and Half-Life

An **exponential decay function** has the form

$$Q(t) = Q_0 e^{-kt}. \qquad Q_0, k \text{ both positive}$$

Q_0 represents the value of Q at time $t = 0$, and k is the **decay constant.** The decay constant k and half-life t_h for Q are related by

$$t_h k = \ln 2.$$

Quick Examples

1. $Q(t) = Q_0e^{-0.000\,121\,01t}$ is the decay function for carbon 14 (see Example 4b).
2. If $t_h = 10$ years, then $10k = \ln 2$, so $k = \frac{\ln 2}{10} \approx 0.06931$ and the decay model is
$$Q(t) = Q_0e^{-0.06931t}.$$
3. If $k = 0.0123$, then $t_h(0.0123) = \ln 2$, so the half-life is
$$t_h = \frac{\ln 2}{0.0123} \approx 56.35 \text{ years.}$$

We can repeat the analysis above for exponential growth models:

Exponential Growth Model and Doubling Time

An **exponential growth function** has the form

$$Q(t) = Q_0e^{kt}. \qquad Q_0,\ k \text{ both positive}$$

Q_0 represents the value of Q at time $t = 0$, and k is the **growth constant**. The growth constant k and doubling time t_d for Q are related by

$$t_dk = \ln 2.$$

Quick Examples

1. $P(t) = 1{,}000e^{0.05t}$ — $1,000 invested at 5% annually with interest compounded continuously
2. If $t_d = 10$ years, then $10k = \ln 2$, so $k = \frac{\ln 2}{10} \approx 0.06931$ and the growth model is
$$Q(t) = Q_0e^{0.06931t}.$$
3. If $k = 0.0123$, then $t_d(0.0123) = \ln 2$, so the doubling time is
$$t_d = \frac{\ln 2}{0.0123} \approx 56.35 \text{ years.}$$

using Technology

To obtain the regression curve and graph for Example 5 using a graphing calculator or a spreadsheet, see the Technology Guides at the end of the chapter. Outline:

TI-83/84 Plus

[STAT] EDIT values of t in L_1 and values of S in L_2
Regression curve: [STAT] CALC option #9 LnReg [ENTER]
Graph: [Y=] [VARS] [5] EQ [1], then [ZOOM] [9]
[More details on page 187.]

Spreadsheet

t- and S-values in Columns A and B
Graph: Highlight data and insert a Scatter chart.
Regression curve: Right-click a datapoint and add logarithmic Trendline with option to show equation on chart.
[More details on page 190.]

Website

www.WanerMath.com
In the Function Evaluator and Grapher, enter the data as shown, press "Examples" until the logarithmic model `$1*ln(x)+$2` shows in the first box, and press "Fit Curve".

Logarithmic Regression

If we start with a set of data that suggests a logarithmic curve we can, by repeating the methods from previous sections, use technology to find the logarithmic regression curve $y = \log_b x + C$ approximating the data.

EXAMPLE 5 Research & Development

The following table shows the total spent on research and development by universities and colleges in the U.S., in billions of dollars, for the period 1998–2008 (t is the number of years since 1990).[34]

[34] 2008 data is preliminary. Source: National Science Foundation, Division of Science Resources Statistics. 2010. *National Patterns of R&D Resources: 2008 Data Update.* NSF 10-314. Arlington, VA. www.nsf.gov/statistics/nsf10314/.

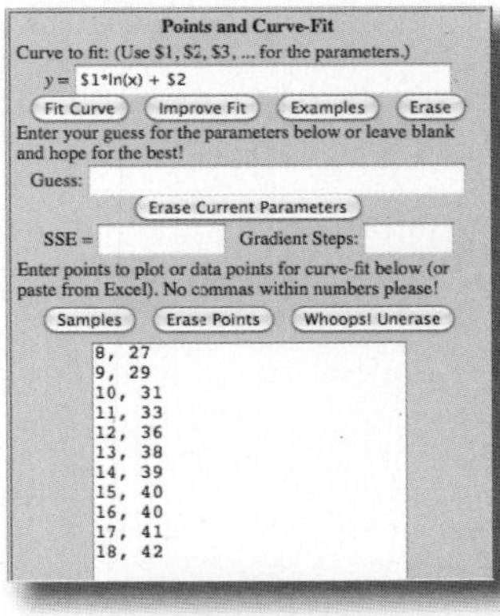

Year t	8	9	10	11	12	13	14	15	16	17	18
Spending ($ billions)	27	29	31	33	36	38	39	40	40	41	42

Find the best-fit logarithmic model of the form

$$S(t) = A \ln t + C$$

and use the model to project total spending on research by universities and colleges in 2012, assuming the trend continues.

Solution We use technology to get the following regression model:

$$S(t) = 19.3 \ln t - 12.8.$$ Coefficients rounded

Because 2012 is represented by $t = 22$, we have

$$S(22) = 19.3 \ln(22) - 12.8 \approx 47.$$ Why did we round the result to two significant digits?

So, research and development spending by universities and colleges is projected to be around $47 billion in 2012.

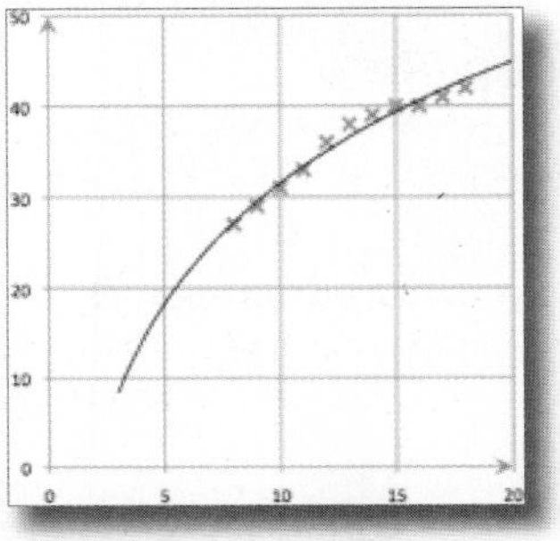

Figure 16

➡ **Before we go on...** The model in Example 5 seems to give reasonable estimates when we extrapolate forward, but extrapolating backward is quite another matter: The logarithm curve drops sharply to the left of the given range and becomes negative for small values of t (Figure 16). ■

2.3 EXERCISES

▼ more advanced ◆ challenging

T indicates exercises that should be solved using technology

In Exercises 1–4, complete the given tables. HINT [See Quick Examples on page 153.]

1.

Exponential Form	$10^4 = 10{,}000$	$4^2 = 16$	$3^3 = 27$	$5^1 = 5$	$7^0 = 1$	$4^{-2} = \frac{1}{16}$
Logarithmic Form						

2.

Exponential Form	$4^3 = 64$	$10^{-1} = 0.1$	$2^8 = 256$	$5^0 = 1$	$(0.5)^2 = 0.25$	$6^{-2} = \frac{1}{36}$
Logarithmic Form						

3.

Exponential Form						
Logarithmic Form	$\log_{0.5} 0.25 = 2$	$\log_5 1 = 0$	$\log_{10} 0.1 = -1$	$\log_4 64 = 3$	$\log_2 256 = 8$	$\log_2 \frac{1}{4} = -2$

4.

Exponential Form						
Logarithmic Form	$\log_5 5 = 1$	$\log_4 \frac{1}{16} = -2$	$\log_4 16 = 2$	$\log_{10} 10{,}000 = 4$	$\log_3 27 = 3$	$\log_7 1 = 0$

In Exercises 5–12, use logarithms to solve the given equation. (Round answers to 4 decimal places.) HINT [See Example 1.]

5. $3^x = 5$

6. $4^x = 3$

7. $5^{-2x} = 40$

8. $6^{3x+1} = 30$

9. $4.16e^x = 2$

10. $5.3(10^x) = 2$

11. $5(1.06^{2x+1}) = 11$

12. $4(1.5^{2x-1}) = 8$

In Exercises 13–18, graph the given function. HINT [See Example 2.]

13. $f(x) = \log_4 x$

14. $f(x) = \log_5 x$

15. $f(x) = \log_4(x - 1)$

16. $f(x) = \log_5(x + 1)$

17. $f(x) = \log_{1/4} x$

18. $f(x) = \log_{1/5} x$

In Exercises 19–22 find the associated exponential decay or growth model. HINT [See Quick Examples on page 161.]

19. $Q = 1{,}000$ when $t = 0$; half-life $= 1$

20. $Q = 2{,}000$ when $t = 0$; half-life $= 5$

21. $Q = 1{,}000$ when $t = 0$; doubling time $= 2$

22. $Q = 2{,}000$ when $t = 0$; doubling time $= 5$

In Exercises 23–26 find the associated half-life or doubling time. HINT [See Quick Examples on page 161.]

23. $Q = 1{,}000e^{0.5t}$

24. $Q = 1{,}000e^{-0.025t}$

25. $Q = Q_0e^{-4t}$

26. $Q = Q_0e^{t}$

In Exercises 27–32 convert the given exponential function to the form indicated. Round all coefficients to 4 significant digits. HINT [See Example 4 "Before we go on."]

27. $f(x) = 4e^{2x}$; $f(x) = Ab^x$

28. $f(x) = 2.1e^{-0.1x}$; $f(x) = Ab^x$

29. $f(t) = 2.1(1.001)^t$; $f(t) = Q_0e^{kt}$

30. $f(t) = 23.4(0.991)^t$; $f(t) = Q_0e^{-kt}$

31. $f(t) = 10(0.987)^t$; $f(t) = Q_0e^{-kt}$

32. $f(t) = 2.3(2.2)^t$; $f(t) = Q_0e^{kt}$

APPLICATIONS

33. ***Investments*** How long will it take a \$500 investment to be worth \$700 if it is continuously compounded at 10% per year? (Give the answer to two decimal places.) HINT [See Example 3.]

34. ***Investments*** How long will it take a \$500 investment to be worth \$700 if it is continuously compounded at 15% per year? (Give the answer to two decimal places.) HINT [See Example 3.]

35. ***Investments*** How long, to the nearest year, will it take an investment to triple if it is continuously compounded at 10% per year? HINT [See Example 3.]

36. ***Investments*** How long, to the nearest year, will it take me to become a millionaire if I invest \$1,000 at 10% interest compounded continuously? HINT [See Example 3.]

37. ***Investments*** I would like my investment to double in value every 3 years. At what rate of interest would I need to invest it, assuming the interest is compounded continuously? HINT [See Quick Examples page 161.]

38. ***Depreciation*** My investment in OHaganBooks.com stocks is losing half its value every 2 years. Find and interpret the associated decay rate. HINT [See Quick Examples page 161.]

39. ***Carbon Dating*** The amount of carbon 14 remaining in a sample that originally contained A grams is given by

$$C(t) = A(0.999879)^t$$

where t is time in years. If tests on a fossilized skull reveal that 99.95% of the carbon 14 has decayed, how old, to the nearest 1,000 years, is the skull? HINT [See Example 4.]

40. ***Carbon Dating*** Refer back to Exercise 39. How old, to the nearest 1,000 years, is a fossil in which only 30% of the carbon 14 has decayed? HINT [See Example 4.]

Long-Term Investments *Exercises 41–48 are based on the following table, which lists interest rates on long-term investments (based on 10-year government bonds) in several countries in 2011.*[35] HINT [See Example 3.]

Country	U.S.	Japan	Germany	Australia	Brazil
Yield	3.4%	1.2%	3.3%	5.5%	12.7%

41. Assuming that you invest \$10,000 in the U.S., how long (to the nearest year) must you wait before your investment is worth \$15,000 if the interest is compounded annually?

42. Assuming that you invest \$10,000 in Japan, how long (to the nearest year) must you wait before your investment is worth \$15,000 if the interest is compounded annually?

43. If you invest \$10,400 in Germany and the interest is compounded monthly, when, to the nearest month, will your investment be worth \$20,000?

44. If you invest \$10,400 in the U.S., and the interest is compounded monthly, when, to the nearest month, will your investment be worth \$20,000?

45. How long, to the nearest year, will it take an investment in Australia to double its value if the interest is compounded every 6 months?

46. How long, to the nearest year, will it take an investment in Brazil to double its value if the interest is compounded every 6 months?

47. If the interest on a long-term U.S. investment is compounded continuously, how long will it take the value of an investment to double? (Give the answer correct to 2 decimal places.)

[35] Approximate interest rates based on 10-year government bonds. Source: www.bloomberg.com.

48. If the interest on a long-term Australia investment is compounded continuously, how long will it take the value of an investment to double? (Give an answer correct to 2 decimal places.)

49. ***Half-Life*** The amount of radium 226 remaining in a sample that originally contained A grams is approximately

$$C(t) = A(0.999\,567)^t$$

where t is time in years. Find the half-life to the nearest 100 years. HINT [See Example 4a.]

50. ***Half-Life*** The amount of iodine 131 remaining in a sample that originally contained A grams is approximately

$$C(t) = A(0.9175)^t$$

where t is time in days. Find the half-life to 2 decimal places. HINT [See Example 4a.]

51. ***Automobiles*** The rate of auto thefts triples every 6 months.

a. Determine, to 2 decimal places, the base b for an exponential model $y = Ab^t$ of the rate of auto thefts as a function of time in months.

b. Find the doubling time to the nearest tenth of a month. HINT [(a) See Section 2.2 Example 2. (b) See Quick Examples page 161.]

52. ***Televisions*** The rate of television thefts is doubling every 4 months.

a. Determine, to 2 decimal places, the base b for an exponential model $y = Ab^t$ of the rate of television thefts as a function of time in months.

b. Find the tripling time to the nearest tenth of a month. HINT [(a) See Section 2.2 Example 2. (b) See Quick Examples page 161.]

53. ***Half-Life*** The half-life of cobalt 60 is 5 years.

a. Obtain an exponential decay model for cobalt 60 in the form $Q(t) = Q_0e^{-kt}$. (Round coefficients to 3 significant digits.)

b. Use your model to predict, to the nearest year, the time it takes one third of a sample of cobalt 60 to decay.

54. ***Half-Life*** The half-life of strontium 90 is 28 years.

a. Obtain an exponential decay model for strontium 90 in the form $Q(t) = Q_0e^{-kt}$. (Round coefficients to 3 significant digits.)

b. Use your model to predict, to the nearest year, the time it takes three fifths of a sample of strontium 90 to decay.

55. ***Radioactive Decay*** Uranium 235 is used as fuel for some nuclear reactors. It has a half-life of 710 million years. How long will it take 10 grams of uranium 235 to decay to 1 gram? (Round your answer to 3 significant digits.)

56. ***Radioactive Decay*** Plutonium 239 is used as fuel for some nuclear reactors, and also as the fissionable material in atomic bombs. It has a half-life of 24,400 years. How long would it take 10 grams of plutonium 239 to decay to 1 gram? (Round your answer to 3 significant digits.)

57. ▼ ***Aspirin*** Soon after taking an aspirin, a patient has absorbed 300 mg of the drug. If the amount of aspirin in the bloodstream decays exponentially, with half being removed every 2 hours, find, to the nearest 0.1 hour, the time it will take for the amount of aspirin in the bloodstream to decrease to 100 mg.

58. ▼ ***Alcohol*** After a large number of drinks, a person has a blood alcohol level of 200 mg/dL (milligrams per deciliter). If the amount of alcohol in the blood decays exponentially, with one fourth being removed every hour, find the time it will take for the person's blood alcohol level to decrease to 80 mg/dL. HINT [See Example 4.]

59. ▼ ***Radioactive Decay*** You are trying to determine the half-life of a new radioactive element you have isolated. You start with 1 gram, and 2 days later you determine that it has decayed down to 0.7 grams. What is its half-life? (Round your answer to 3 significant digits.) HINT [First find an exponential model, then see Example 4.]

60. ▼ ***Radioactive Decay*** You have just isolated a new radioactive element. If you can determine its half-life, you will win the Nobel Prize in physics. You purify a sample of 2 grams. One of your colleagues steals half of it, and 3 days later you find that 0.1 grams of the radioactive material is still left. What is the half-life? (Round your answer to 3 significant digits.) HINT [First find an exponential model, then see Example 4.]

61. T ***Population Aging*** The following table shows the percentage of U.S. residents over the age of 65 in 1950, 1960, . . . , 2010 (t is time in years since 1900):[36]

t **(Year since 1900)**	50	60	70	80	90	100	110
P **(% over 65)**	8.2	9.2	9.9	11.3	12.6	12.6	13

a. Find the logarithmic regression model of the form $P(t) = A \ln t + C$. (Round the coefficients to 4 significant digits). HINT [See Example 5.]

b. In 1940, 6.9% of the population was over 65. To how many significant digits does the model reflect this figure?

c. Which of the following is correct? The model, if extrapolated into the indefinite future, predicts that

(A) The percentage of U.S. residents over the age of 65 will increase without bound.

(B) The percentage of U.S. residents over the age of 65 will level off at around 14.2%.

(C) The percentage of U.S. residents over the age of 65 will eventually decrease.

62. T ***Population Aging*** The following table shows the percentage of U.S. residents over the age of 85 in 1950, 1960, . . . , 2010 (t is time in years since 1900):[37]

t **(Year since 1900)**	50	60	70	80	90	100	110
P **(% over 85)**	0.4	0.5	0.7	1	1.2	1.6	1.9

a. Find the logarithmic regression model of the form $P(t) = A \ln t + C$. (Round the coefficients to 4 significant digits). HINT [See Example 5.]

[36] Source: U.S. Census Bureau.

[37] *Ibid.*

b. In 2020, 2.1% of the population is projected to be over 85. To how many significant digits does the model reflect this figure?

c. Which of the following is correct? If you increase A by 0.1 and decrease C by 0.1 in the logarithmic model, then

(A) The new model predicts eventually lower percentages.
(B) The long-term prediction is essentially the same.
(C) The new model predicts eventually higher percentages.

63. T ***Research & Development: Industry*** The following table shows the total spent on research and development by industry in the United States, in billions of dollars, for the period 1998–2008 (t is the year since 1990).[38]

Year t	8	9	10	11	12	13	14	15	16	17	18
Spending ($ billions)	150	165	183	181	170	172	172	181	191	203	215

Find the logarithmic regression model of the form $S(t) = A \ln t + C$ with coefficients A and C rounded to 2 decimal places. Also obtain a graph showing the data points and the regression curve. In which direction is it more reasonable to extrapolate the model? Why?

64. T ***Research & Development: Federal*** The following table shows the total spent on research and development by the federal government in the United States, in billions of dollars, for the period 1998–2008 (t is the year since 1990).[39]

Year t	8	9	10	11	12	13	14	15	16	17	18
Spending ($ billions)	18	18	18	20	21	21	21	22	22	21	22

Find the logarithmic regression model of the form $S(t) = A \ln t + C$ with coefficients A and C rounded to 2 decimal places. Also obtain a graph showing the data points and the regression curve. In which direction is it more reasonable to extrapolate the model? Why?

65. ▼ ***Richter Scale*** The **Richter scale** is used to measure the intensity of earthquakes. The Richter scale rating of an earthquake is given by the formula

$$R = \frac{2}{3}(\log E - 11.8)$$

where E is the energy released by the earthquake (measured in ergs[40]).

a. The San Francisco earthquake of 1906 is estimated to have registered $R = 7.9$ on the Richter scale. How many ergs of energy were released?

b. The Japan earthquake of 2011 registered 9.0 on the Richter scale. Compare the two: The energy released in the 1906 earthquake was what percentage of the energy released in the 2011 quake?

c. Solve the equation given above for E in terms of R.

d. Use the result of part (c) to show that if two earthquakes registering R_1 and R_2 on the Richter scale release E_1 and E_2 ergs of energy, respectively, then

$$\frac{E_2}{E_1} = 10^{1.5(R_2 - R_1)}.$$

e. Fill in the blank: If one earthquake registers 2 points more on the Richter scale than another, then it releases ___ times the amount of energy.

66. ▼ ***Sound Intensity*** The loudness of a sound is measured in **decibels**. The decibel level of a sound is given by the formula

$$D = 10 \log \frac{I}{I_0},$$

where D is the decibel level (dB), I is its intensity in watts per square meter (W/m^2), and $I_0 = 10^{-12}$ W/m^2 is the intensity of a barely audible "threshold" sound. A sound intensity of 90 dB or greater causes damage to the average human ear.

a. Find the decibel levels of each of the following, rounding to the nearest decibel:

Whisper:	115×10^{-12} W/m^2
TV (average volume from 10 feet):	320×10^{-7} W/m^2
Loud music:	900×10^{-3} W/m^2
Jet aircraft (from 500 feet):	100 W/m^2

b. Which of the sounds above damages the average human ear?

c. Solve the given equation to express I in terms of D.

d. Use the answer to part (c) to show that if two sounds of intensity I_1 and I_2 register decibel levels of D_1 and D_2, respectively, then

$$\frac{I_2}{I_1} = 10^{0.1(D_2 - D_1)}.$$

e. Fill in the blank: If one sound registers one decibel more than another, then it is ___ times as intense.

67. ▼ ***Sound Intensity*** The decibel level of a TV set decreases with the distance from the set according to the formula

$$D = 10 \log\left(\frac{320 \times 10^7}{r^2}\right)$$

[38] Excludes Federal funding; 2008 data is preliminary. Source: National Science Foundation, Division of Science Resources Statistics. 2010. *National Patterns of R&D Resources: 2008 Data Update.* NSF 10-314. Arlington, VA. www.nsf.gov/statistics/nsf10314/.

[39] Excludes Federal funding to industry and nonprofit organizations; 2008 data is preliminary. Source: National Science Foundation, Division of Science Resources Statistics. 2010. *National Patterns of R&D Resources: 2008 Data Update.* NSF 10-314. Arlington, VA. www.nsf.gov/statistics/nsf10314/.

[40] An erg is a unit of energy. One erg is the amount of energy it takes to move a mass of one gram one centimeter in one second. The term "Richter scale" is used loosely to refer to several ways of measuring earthquake magnitudes, calibrated to agree where they overlap.

where D is the decibel level (dB) and r is the distance from the TV set in feet.

a. Find the decibel level (to the nearest decibel) at distances of 10, 20, and 50 feet.

b. Express D in the form $D = A + B \log r$ for suitable constants A and B. (Round A and D to 2 significant digits.)

c. How far must a listener be from a TV so that the decibel level drops to 0 dB? (Round the answer to two significant digits.)

68. ▼ *Acidity* The acidity of a solution is measured by its pH, which is given by the formula

$$pH = -\log(H^+)$$

where H^+ measures the concentration of hydrogen ions in moles per liter.[41] The pH of pure water is 7. A solution is referred to as *acidic* if its pH is below 7 and as *basic* if its pH is above 7.

a. Calculate the pH of each of the following substances.

Blood:	3.9×10^{-8} moles/liter
Milk:	4.0×10^{-7} moles/liter
Soap solution:	1.0×10^{-11} moles/liter
Black coffee:	1.2×10^{-7} moles/liter

b. How many moles of hydrogen ions are contained in a liter of acid rain that has a pH of 5.0?

c. Complete the following sentence: If the pH of a solution increases by 1.0, then the concentration of hydrogen ions _____.

COMMUNICATION AND REASONING EXERCISES

69. On the same set of axes, graph $y = \ln x$, $y = A \ln x$, and $y = A \ln x + C$ for various choices of *positive A* and *C*. What is the effect on the graph of $y = \ln x$ of multiplying by A? What is the effect of then adding C?

[41] A mole corresponds to about 6.0×10^{23} hydrogen ions. (This number is known as Avogadro's number.)

70. On the same set of axes, graph $y = -\ln x$, $y = A \ln x$, and $y = A \ln x + C$ for various choices of *negative A* and C. What is the effect on the graph of $y = \ln x$ of multiplying by A? What is the effect of then adding C?

71. Why is the logarithm of a negative number not defined?

72. Of what use are logarithms, now that they are no longer needed to perform complex calculations?

73. Your company's market share is undergoing steady growth. Explain why a logarithmic function is *not* appropriate for long-term future prediction of your market share.

74. Your company's market share is undergoing steady growth. Explain why a logarithmic function is *not* appropriate for long-term backward extrapolation of your market share.

75. If $y = 4^x$, then $x = $ _____.

76. If $y = \log_6 x$, then $x = $ _____.

77. Simplify: $2^{\log_2 8}$.

78. Simplify: $e^{\ln x}$.

79. Simplify: $\ln(e^x)$.

80. Simplify: $\ln \sqrt{a}$.

81. ▼ If a town's population is increasing exponentially with time, how is time increasing with population? Explain.

82. ▼ If a town's population is increasing logarithmically with time, how is time increasing with population? Explain.

83. ▼ If two quantities Q_1 and Q_2 are logarithmic functions of time t, show that their sum, $Q_1 + Q_2$, is also a logarithmic function of time t.

84. ⬜ ▼ In Exercise 83 we saw that the sum of two logarithmic functions is a logarithmic function. In Exercises 63 and 64 you modeled research and development expenditure by industry and government. Now do a logarithmic regression on the sum of the two sets of figures. Does the result coincide with the sum of the two individual regression models? What does your answer tell you about the sum of logarithmic regression models?

2.4 Logistic Functions and Models

Figure 17 shows wired broadband penetration in the United States as a function of time t in years ($t = 0$ represents 2000).[42]

The left-hand part of the curve in Figure 17, from $t = 2$ to, say, $t = 6$, looks roughly like exponential growth: P behaves (roughly) like an exponential function, with the y-coordinates growing by a factor of around 1.5 per year. Then, as the market starts to become saturated, the growth of P slows and its value approaches a "saturation" point that appears to be around 30%. **Logistic** functions have just this

[42] Broadband penetration is the number of broadband installations divided by the total population. Source for data: Organisation for Economic Co-operation and Development (OECD) Directorate for Science, Technology, and Industry, table of Historical Penetration Rates, June 2010, downloaded April 2011 from www.oecd.org/sti/ict/broadband.

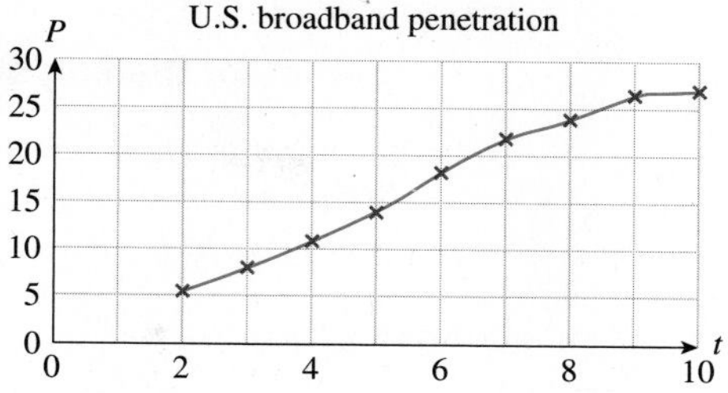

Figure 17

kind of behavior, growing exponentially at first and then leveling off. In addition to modeling the demand for a new technology or product, logistic functions are often used in epidemic and population modeling. In an epidemic, the number of infected people often grows exponentially at first and then slows when a significant proportion of the entire susceptible population is infected and the epidemic has "run its course." Similarly, populations may grow exponentially at first and then slow as they approach the capacity of the available resources.

Logistic Function

A **logistic function** has the form

$$f(x) = \frac{N}{1 + Ab^{-x}}$$

for nonzero constants N, A, and b (A and b positive and $b \neq 1$).

Quick Example

$N = 6, A = 2, b = 1.1$ gives $f(x) = \dfrac{6}{1 + 2(1.1^{-x})}$ `6/(1+2*1.1^-x)`

$f(0) = \dfrac{6}{1+2} = 2$ The y-intercept is $N/(1 + A)$.

$f(1{,}000) = \dfrac{6}{1 + 2(1.1^{-1{,}000})} \approx \dfrac{6}{1+0} = 6 = N$ When x is large, $f(x) \approx N$.

Graph of a Logistic Function

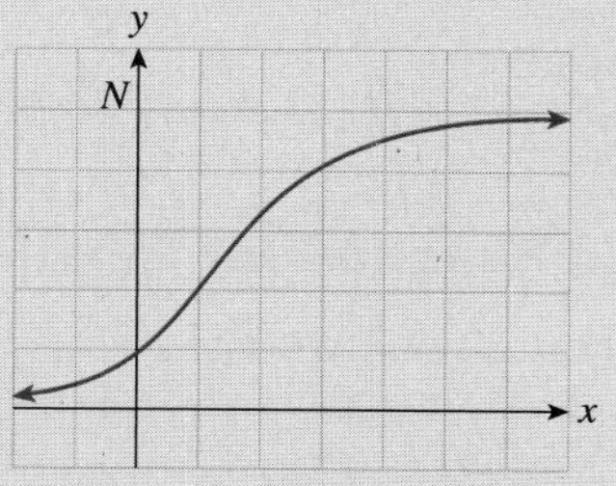

$b > 1$

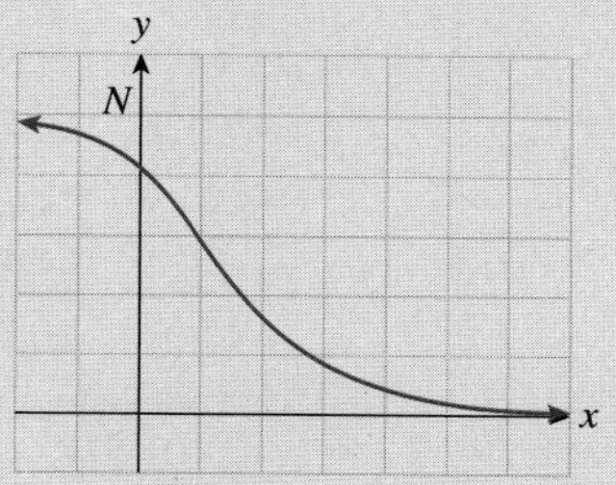

$0 < b < 1$

$$y = \frac{N}{1 + Ab^{-x}}$$

Properties of the Logistic Curve $y = \dfrac{N}{1 + Ab^{-x}}$

- The graph is an S-shaped curve sandwiched between the horizontal lines $y = 0$ and $y = N$. N is called the **limiting value** of the logistic curve.
- If $b > 1$ the graph rises; if $b < 1$, the graph falls.
- The y-intercept is $\dfrac{N}{1 + A}$.
- The curve is steepest when $t = \dfrac{\ln A}{\ln b}$. We will see why in Chapter 5.

Note If we write b^{-x} as e^{-kx} (so that $k = \ln b$), we get the following alternative form of the logistic function:

$$f(x) = \frac{N}{1 + Ae^{-kx}}.$$

■

Q: *How does the constant b affect the graph?*

A: To understand the role of b, we first rewrite the logistic function by multiplying top and bottom by b^x:

$$\begin{aligned} f(x) &= \frac{N}{1 + Ab^{-x}} \\ &= \frac{Nb^x}{(1 + Ab^{-x})b^x} \\ &= \frac{Nb^x}{b^x + A} \end{aligned}$$

Because $b^{-x}b^x = 1$

For values of x close to 0, the quantity b^x is close to 1, so the denominator is approximately $1 + A$, giving

$$f(x) \approx \frac{Nb^x}{1 + A} = \left(\frac{N}{1 + A}\right) b^x.$$

In other words, $f(x)$ is approximately exponential with base b for values of x close to 0. Put another way, if x represents time, then initially the logistic function behaves like an exponential function.

To summarize:

Logistic Function for Small *x* and the Role of *b*

For small values of x, we have

$$\frac{N}{1 + Ab^{-x}} \approx \left(\frac{N}{1 + A}\right) b^x.$$

Thus, for small x, the logistic function grows approximately exponentially with base b.

Quick Example

Let

$$f(x) = \frac{50}{1+24(3^{-x})}. \qquad N = 50,\ A = 24,\ b = 3$$

Then

$$f(x) \approx \left(\frac{50}{1+24}\right)(3^x) = 2(3^x)$$

for small values of x. The following figure compares their graphs:

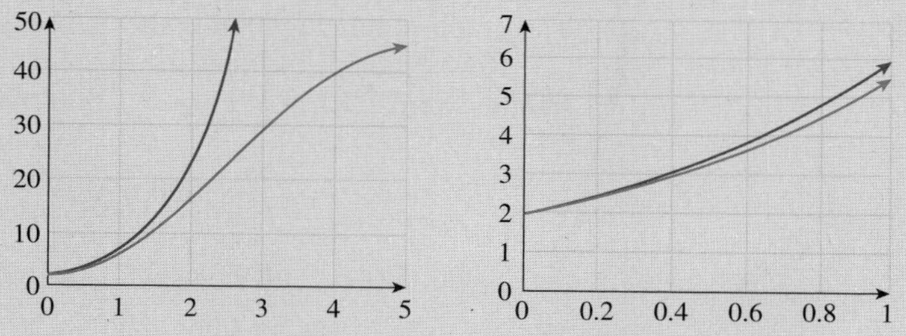

The upper curve is the exponential curve.

Modeling with the Logistic Function

EXAMPLE 1 Epidemics

A flu epidemic is spreading through the U.S. population. An estimated 150 million people are susceptible to this particular strain, and it is predicted that all susceptible people will eventually become infected. There are 10,000 people already infected, and the number is doubling every 2 weeks. Use a logistic function to model the number of people infected. Hence predict when, to the nearest week, 1 million people will be infected.

Solution Let t be time in weeks, and let $P(t)$ be the total number of people infected at time t. We want to express P as a logistic function of t, so that

$$P(t) = \frac{N}{1 + Ab^{-t}}.$$

We are told that, in the long run, 150 million people will be infected, so that

$$N = 150{,}000{,}000. \qquad \text{Limiting value of } P$$

At the current time ($t = 0$), 10,000 people are infected, so

$$10{,}000 = \frac{N}{1+A} = \frac{150{,}000{,}000}{1+A}. \qquad \text{Value of } P \text{ when } t = 0$$

Solving for A gives

$$\begin{aligned} 10{,}000(1 + A) &= 150{,}000{,}000 \\ 1 + A &= 15{,}000 \\ A &= 14{,}999. \end{aligned}$$

What about b? At the beginning of the epidemic (t near 0), P is growing approximately exponentially, doubling every 2 weeks. Using the technique of Section 2.2, we find that the exponential curve passing through the points (0, 10,000) and (2, 20,000) is

$$y = 10,000(\sqrt{2})^t$$

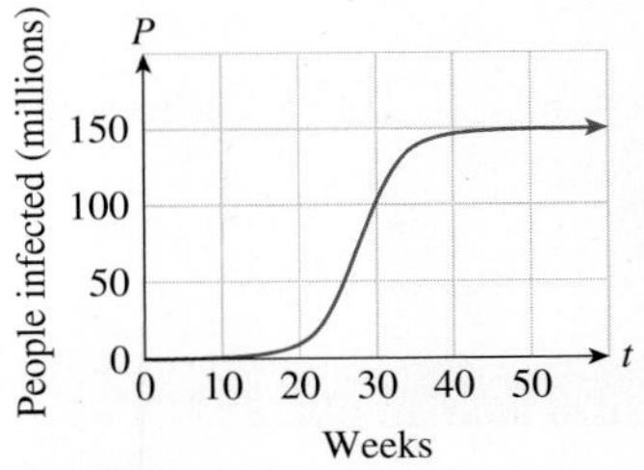

Figure 18

giving us $b = \sqrt{2}$. Now that we have the constants N, A, and b, we can write down the logistic model:

$$P(t) = \frac{150,000,000}{1 + 14,999(\sqrt{2})^{-t}}.$$

The graph of this function is shown in Figure 18.

Now we tackle the question of prediction: When will 1 million people be infected? In other words: When is $P(t) = 1,000,000$?

$$1,000,000 = \frac{150,000,000}{1 + 14,999(\sqrt{2})^{-t}}$$

$$1,000,000[1 + 14,999(\sqrt{2})^{-t}] = 150,000,000$$

$$1 + 14,999(\sqrt{2})^{-t} = 150$$

$$14,999(\sqrt{2})^{-t} = 149$$

$$(\sqrt{2})^{-t} = \frac{149}{14,999}$$

$$-t = \log_{\sqrt{2}}\left(\frac{149}{14,999}\right) \approx -13.31 \quad \text{Logarithmic form}$$

Thus, 1 million people will be infected by about the thirteenth week.

➡ **Before we go on...** We said earlier that the logistic curve is steepest when $t = \frac{\ln A}{\ln b}$. In Example 1, this occurs when $t = \frac{\ln 14,999}{\ln\sqrt{2}} \approx 28$ weeks into the epidemic. At that time, the number of cases is growing most rapidly (look at the apparent slope of the graph at the corresponding point). ■

Logistic Regression

Let's go back to the data on broadband penetration in the United States with which we began this section and try to determine the long-term percentage of broadband penetration. In order to be able to make predictions such as this, we require a model for the data, so we will need to do some form of regression.

EXAMPLE 2 Broadband Penetration

Here are the data graphed in Figure 17:

Year (t)	2	3	4	5	6	7	8	9	10
Penetration (%) (P)	5.5	7.9	10.9	14.2	18.2	21.9	23.9	26.5	27.1

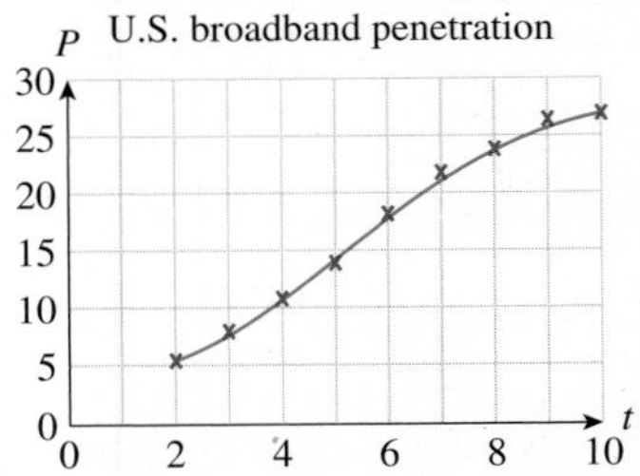

Figure 19

using Technology

See the Technology Guide at the end of the chapter for detailed instructions on how to obtain the regression curve and graph for Example 2 using a graphing calculator or spreadsheet. Outline:

TI-83/84 Plus

[STAT] EDIT values of t in L_1 and values of P in L_2

Regression curve: [STAT] CALC option #B Logistic [ENTER]

Graph: [Y=] [VARS] [5] EQ [1], then [ZOOM] [9] [More details on page 188.]

Spreadsheet

Use the Solver Add-in to obtain the best-fit logistic curve. [More details on page 190.]

Website

www.WanerMath.com

In the Function Evaluator and Grapher, enter the data as shown, press "Examples" until the logistic model `$1/(1+$2*$3^(-x))` shows in the first box, and press "Fit Curve".

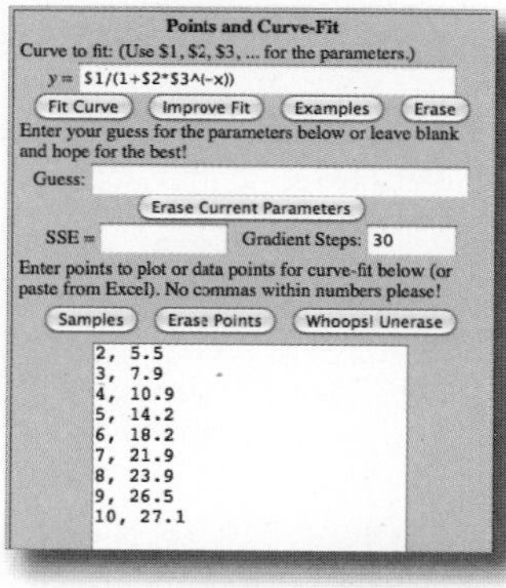

Find a logistic regression curve of the form

$$P(t) = \frac{N}{1 + Ab^{-t}}.$$

In the long term, what percentage of broadband penetration in the United States does the model predict?

Solution We can use technology to obtain the following regression model:

$$P(t) \approx \frac{29.842}{1 + 12.502(1.642)^{-t}}. \qquad \text{Coefficients rounded to 3 decimal places}$$

Its graph and the original data are shown in Figure 19. Because $N = 29.842$, this model predicts that, in the long term, the percentage of broadband penetration in the United States will be 29.842%, or about 30%.

Before we go on... Logistic regression programs generally estimate all three constants N, A, and b for a model $y = \dfrac{N}{1 + Ab^{-x}}$. However, there are times, as in Example 1, when we already know the limiting value N and require estimates of only A and b. In such cases, we can use technology like Excel Solver to find A and b for the best-fit curve with N fixed. Alternatively, we can use exponential regression to compute estimates of A and b as follows: First rewrite the logistic equation as

$$\frac{N}{y} = 1 + Ab^{-x},$$

so that

$$\frac{N}{y} - 1 = Ab^{-x} = A(b^{-1})^x.$$

This equation gives $N/y - 1$ as an exponential function of x. Thus, if we do exponential regression using the data points $(x, N/y - 1)$, we can obtain estimates for A and b^{-1} (and hence b). This is done in Exercises 35 and 36.

It is important to note that the resulting curve is not the best-fit curve (in the sense of minimizing SSE; see the "Before we go on" discussion on page 147 after Example 6 in Section 2.2) and will be thus be different from that obtained using the method in Example 2. ■

2.4 EXERCISES

▼ more advanced ◆ challenging

T indicates exercises that should be solved using technology

In Exercises 1–6, find N, A, and b, give a technology formula for the given function, and use technology to sketch its graph for the given range of values of x. HINT [See Quick Examples on page 167.]

1. $f(x) = \dfrac{7}{1 + 6(2^{-x})}$; $[0, 10]$

2. $g(x) = \dfrac{4}{1 + 0.333(4^{-x})}$; $[0, 2]$

3. $f(x) = \dfrac{10}{1 + 4(0.3^{-x})}$; $[-5, 5]$

4. $g(x) = \dfrac{100}{1 + 5(0.5^{-x})}$; $[-5, 5]$

5. $h(x) = \dfrac{2}{0.5 + 3.5(1.5^{-x})}$; $[0, 15]$
(First divide top and bottom by 0.5.)

6. $k(x) = \dfrac{17}{2 + 6.5(1.05^{-x})}$; $[0, 100]$

(First divide top and bottom by 2.)

In Exercises 7–10, find the logistic function f with the given properties. HINT [See Example 1.]

7. $f(0) = 10$, f has limiting value 200, and for small values of x, f is approximately exponential and doubles with every increase of 1 in x.

8. $f(0) = 1$, f has limiting value 10, and for small values of x, f is approximately exponential and grows by 50% with every increase of 1 in x.

9. f has limiting value 6 and passes through (0, 3) and (1, 4). HINT [First find *A*, then substitute.]

10. f has limiting value 4 and passes through (0, 1) and (1, 2). HINT [First find *A*, then substitute.]

In Exercises 11–16, choose the logistic function that best approximates the given curve.

11.

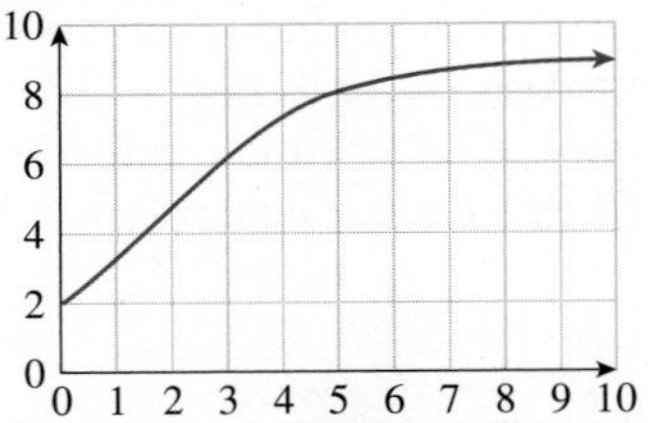

(A) $f(x) = \dfrac{6}{1 + 0.5(3^{-x})}$

(B) $f(x) = \dfrac{9}{1 + 3.5(2^{-x})}$

(C) $f(x) = \dfrac{9}{1 + 0.5(1.01)^{-x}}$

12.

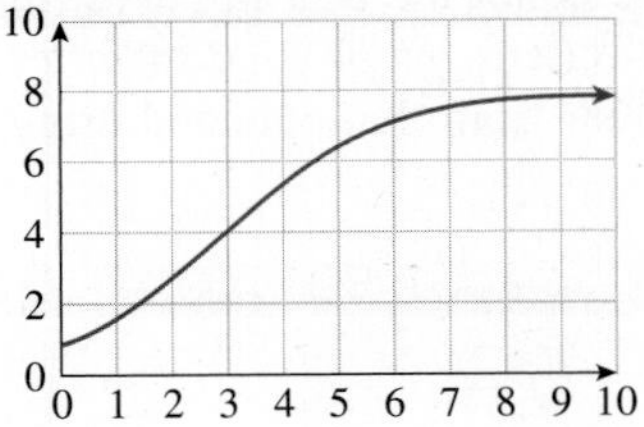

(A) $f(x) = \dfrac{8}{1 + 7(2)^{-x}}$ **(B)** $f(x) = \dfrac{8}{1 + 3(2)^{-x}}$

(C) $f(x) = \dfrac{6}{1 + 11(5)^{-x}}$

13.

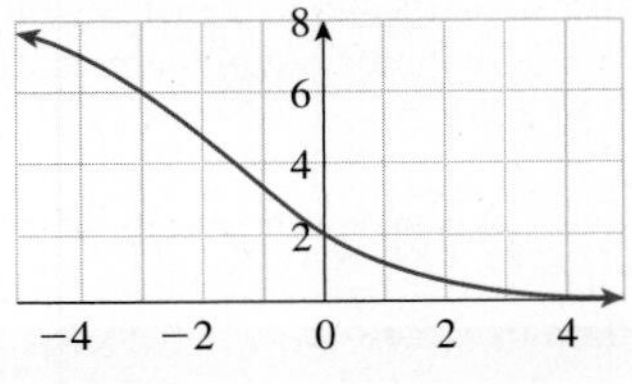

(A) $f(x) = \dfrac{8}{1 + 7(0.5)^{-x}}$ **(B)** $f(x) = \dfrac{8}{1 + 3(0.5)^{-x}}$

(C) $f(x) = \dfrac{8}{1 + 3(2)^{-x}}$

14.

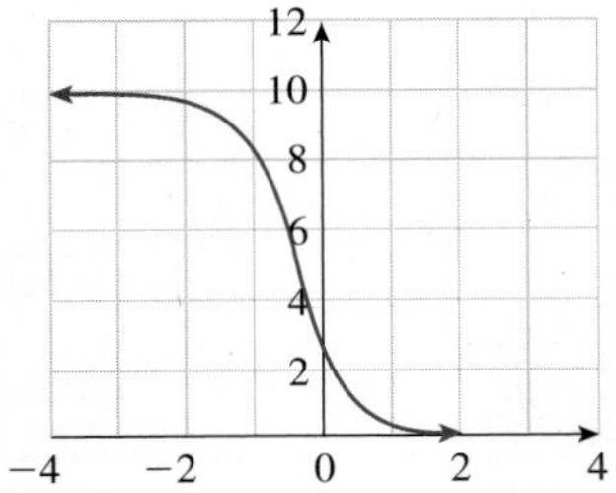

(A) $f(x) = \dfrac{10}{1 + 3(1.01)^{-x}}$ **(B)** $f(x) = \dfrac{8}{1 + 7(0.1)^{-x}}$

(C) $f(x) = \dfrac{10}{1 + 3(0.1)^{-x}}$

15.

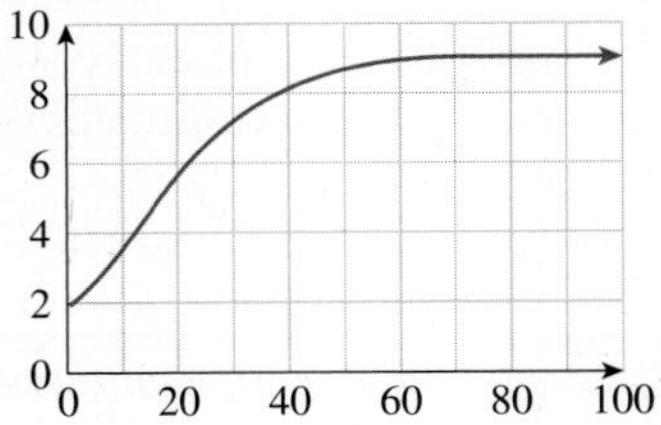

(A) $f(x) = \dfrac{18}{2 + 7(5)^{-x}}$ **(B)** $f(x) = \dfrac{18}{2 + 3(1.1)^{-x}}$

(C) $f(x) = \dfrac{18}{2 + 7(1.1)^{-x}}$

16.

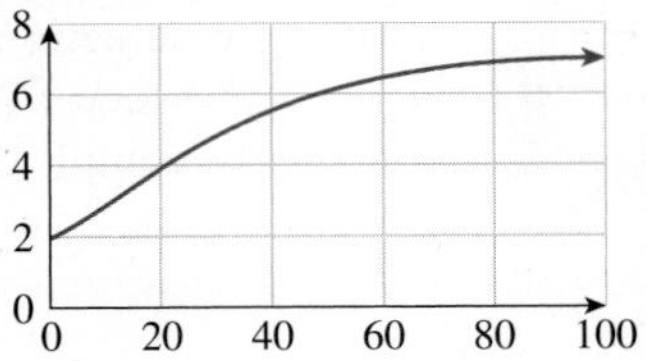

(A) $f(x) = \dfrac{14}{2 + 5(15)^{-x}}$ **(B)** $f(x) = \dfrac{14}{1 + 13(1.05)^{-x}}$

(C) $f(x) = \dfrac{14}{2 + 5(1.05)^{-x}}$

T *In Exercises 17–20, use technology to find a logistic regression curve* $y = \dfrac{N}{1 + Ab^{-x}}$ *approximating the given data. Draw a graph showing the data points and regression curve. (Round b to 3 significant digits and A and N to 2 significant digits.)* HINT [See Example 2.]

17.

x	0	20	40	60	80	100
y	2.1	3.6	5.0	6.1	6.8	6.9

18.

x	0	30	60	90	120	150
y	2.8	5.8	7.9	9.4	9.7	9.9

19.

x	0	20	40	60	80	100
y	30.1	11.6	3.8	1.2	0.4	0.1

20.

x	0	30	60	90	120	150
y	30.1	20	12	7.2	3.8	2.4

APPLICATIONS

21. ***Subprime Mortgages during the Housing Bubble*** The following graph shows the approximate percentage of mortgages issued in the United States during the real-estate run-up in 2000–2008 that were subprime (normally classified as risky) as well as the logistic regression curve:[43]

Subprime mortgages

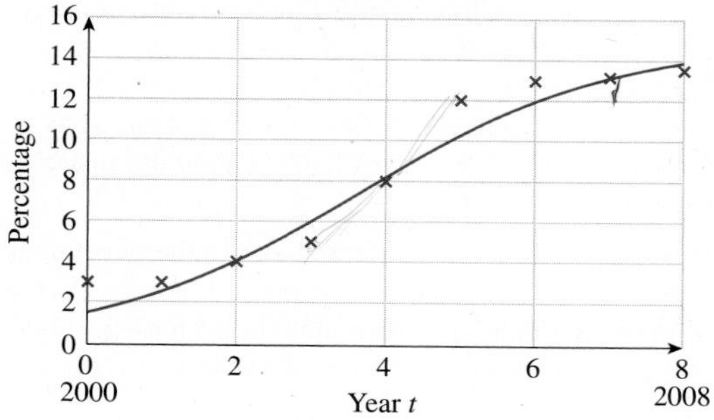

a. Which of the following logistic functions best approximates the curve? (t is the number of years since the start of 2000.) Try to determine the correct model without actually computing data points. HINT [See Properties of the Logistic Curve on page 168.]

(A) $A(t) = \dfrac{15.0}{1 + 8.6(1.8)^{-t}}$

(B) $A(t) = \dfrac{2.0}{1 + 6.8(0.8)^{-t}}$

(C) $A(t) = \dfrac{2.0}{1 + 6.8(1.8)^{-t}}$

(D) $A(t) = \dfrac{15.0}{1 + 8.6(0.8)^{-t}}$

b. According to the model you selected, during which year was the percentage growing fastest? HINT [See the "Before we go on" discussion after Example 1.]

22. ***Subprime Mortgage Debt during the Housing Bubble*** The following graph shows the approximate value of subprime (normally classified as risky) mortgage debt outstanding in the United States during the real-estate run-up in 2000–2008 as well as the logistic regression curve:[44]

Subprime debt outstanding

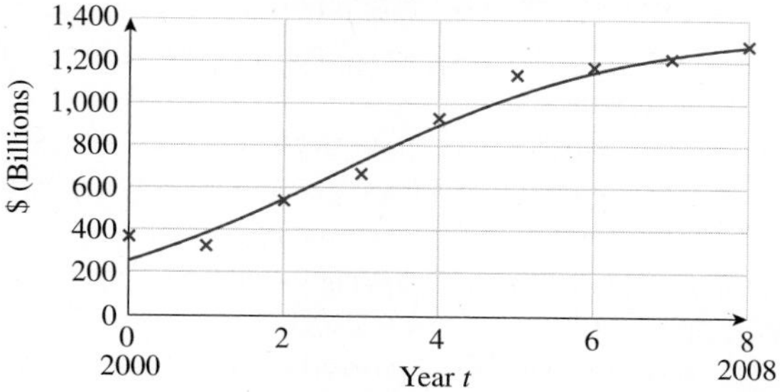

a. Which of the following logistic functions best approximates the curve? (t is the number of years since the start of 2000.) Try to determine the correct model without actually computing data points. HINT [See Properties of the Logistic Curve on page 168.]

(A) $A(t) = \dfrac{1{,}850}{1 + 5.36(1.8)^{-t}}$

(B) $A(t) = \dfrac{1{,}350}{1 + 4.2(1.7)^{-t}}$

(C) $A(t) = \dfrac{1{,}020}{1 + 5.3(1.8)^{-t}}$

(D) $A(t) = \dfrac{1{,}300}{1 + 4.2(0.9)^{-t}}$

b. According to the model you selected, during which year was outstanding debt growing fastest? HINT [See the "Before we go on" discussion after Example 1.]

23. ***Scientific Research*** The following graph shows the number of research articles in the prominent journal *Physical Review* that were written by researchers in Europe during 1983–2003 ($t = 0$ represents 1983).[45]

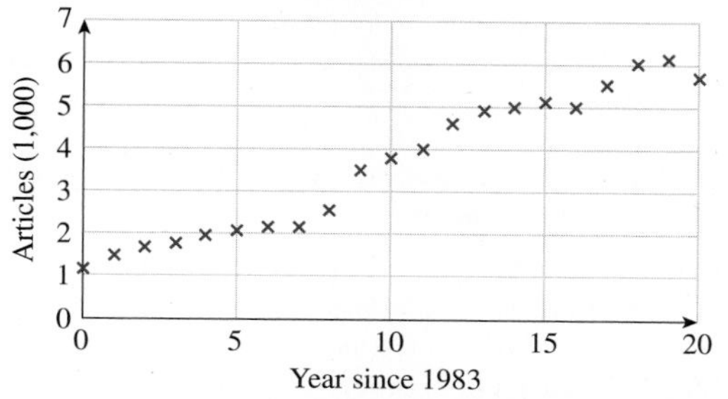

a. Which of the following logistic functions best models the data? (t is the number of years since 1983.) Try to determine the correct model without actually computing data points.

[43] 2008 figure is an estimate. Sources: Mortgage Bankers Association, UBS.

[44] 2008–2009 figures are estimates. Source: www.data360.org/dataset.aspx?Data_Set_Id=9549.

[45] Source: The American Physical Society/*New York Times* May 3, 2003, p. A1.

(A) $A(t) = \dfrac{7.0}{1 + 5.4(1.2)^{-t}}$

(B) $A(t) = \dfrac{4.0}{1 + 3.4(1.2)^{-t}}$

(C) $A(t) = \dfrac{4.0}{1 + 3.4(0.8)^{-t}}$

(D) $A(t) = \dfrac{7.0}{1 + 5.4(6.2)^{-t}}$

b. According to the model you selected, at what percentage was the number of articles growing around 1985?

24. ***Scientific Research*** The following graph shows the percentage, above 25%, of research articles in the prominent journal *Physical Review* that were written by researchers in the United States during 1983–2003 ($t = 0$ represents 1983).[46]

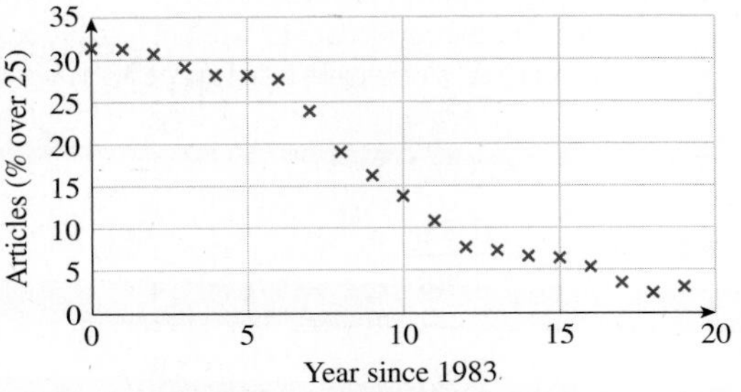

a. Which of the following logistic functions best models the data? (t is the number of years since 1983 and P is the actual percentage.) Try to determine the correct model without actually computing data points.

(A) $P(t) = \dfrac{36}{1 + 0.06(0.02)^{-t}}$

(B) $P(t) = \dfrac{12}{1 + 0.06(1.7)^{-t}}$

(C) $P(t) = \dfrac{12}{1 + 0.06(0.7)^{-t}}$

(D) $P(t) = \dfrac{36}{1 + 0.06(0.7)^{-t}}$

b. According to the model you selected, how fast was the value of P declining around 1985?

25. ***Internet Use*** The following graph shows the percentage of U.S. households using the Internet at home in 2010 as a function of household income (the data points) and a logistic model of these data (the curve).[47]

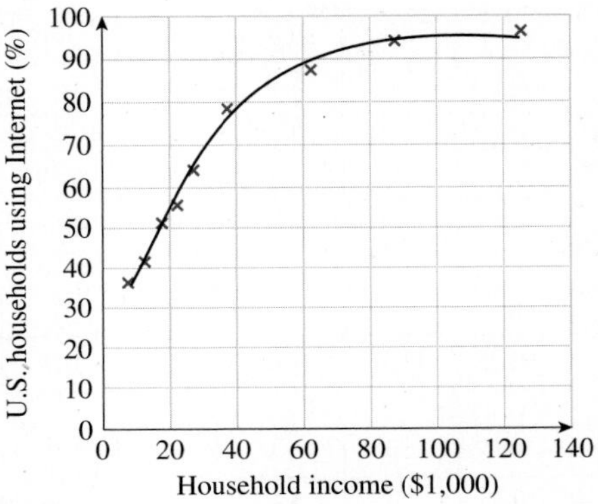

The logistic model is

$$P(x) = \frac{95.0}{1 + 2.78(1.064)^{-x}} \text{ percent}$$

where x is the household income in thousands of dollars.

a. According to the model, what percentage of extremely wealthy households used the Internet?

b. For low incomes, the logistic model is approximately exponential. Which exponential model best approximates $P(x)$ for small x?

c. According to the model, 50% of households of what income used the Internet in 2010? (Round the answer to the nearest $1,000.)

26. ***Internet Use*** The following graph shows the percentage of U.S. residents who used the Internet at home in 2010 as a function of income (the data points) and a logistic model of these data (the curve).[48]

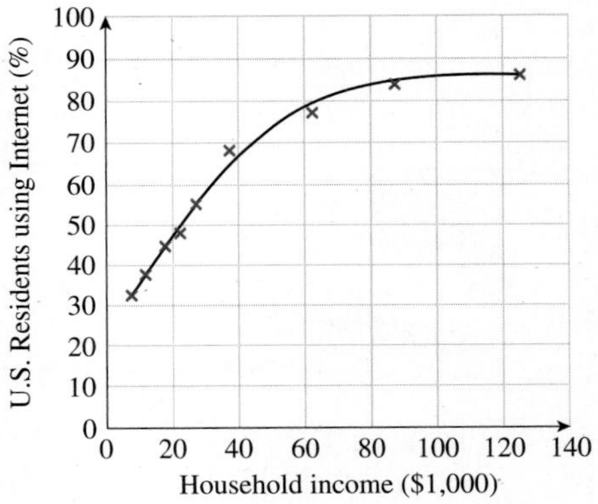

The logistic model is given by

$$P(x) = \frac{86.2}{1 + 2.49(1.054)^{-x}} \text{ percent}$$

where x is the household income in thousands of dollars.

---

[46] Source: The American Physical Society/*New York Times* May 3, 2003, p. A1.

[47] Income levels are midpoints of income brackets. Source: *Current Population Survey (CPS) Internet Use 2010,* National Telecommunications and Information Administration, www.ntia.doc.gov, January 2011.

[48] *Ibid.*

a. According to the model, what percentage of extremely wealthy people used the Internet at home?

b. For low incomes, the logistic model is approximately exponential. Which exponential model best approximates $P(x)$ for small x?

c. According to the model, 50% of individuals with what household income used the Internet at home in 2010? (Round the answer to the nearest $1,000.)

27. ***Epidemics*** There are currently 1,000 cases of Venusian flu in a total susceptible population of 10,000 and the number of cases is increasing by 25% each day. Find a logistic model for the number of cases of Venusian flu and use your model to predict the number of flu cases a week from now. HINT [See Example 1.]

28. ***Epidemics*** Last year's epidemic of Martian flu began with a single case in a total susceptible population of 10,000. The number of cases was increasing initially by 40% per day. Find a logistic model for the number of cases of Martian flu and use your model to predict the number of flu cases 3 weeks into the epidemic. HINT [See Example 1.]

29. ***Sales*** You have sold 100 "I ♥ Calculus" T-shirts and sales appear to be doubling every 5 days. You estimate the total market for "I ♥ Calculus" T-shirts to be 3,000. Give a logistic model for your sales and use it to predict, to the nearest day, when you will have sold 700 T-shirts.

30. ***Sales*** In Russia the average consumer drank two servings of Coca-Cola® in 1993. This amount appeared to be increasing exponentially with a doubling time of 2 years.[49] Given a long-range market saturation estimate of 100 servings per year, find a logistic model for the consumption of Coca-Cola in Russia and use your model to predict when, to the nearest year, the average consumption reached 50 servings per year.

31. T ***Scientific Research*** The following chart shows some the data shown in the graph in Exercise 23 ($t = 0$ represents 1983).[50]

Year t	0	5	10	15	20
Research Articles A (1,000)	1.2	2.1	3.8	5.1	5.7

a. What is the logistic regression model for the data? (Round all coefficients to 2 significant digits.) At what value does the model predict that the number of research articles will level off? HINT [See Example 2.]

b. According to the model, how many *Physical Review* articles were published by U.S. researchers in 2000 ($t = 17$)? (The actual number was about 5,500 articles.)

32. T ***Scientific Research*** The following chart shows some the data shown in the graph in Exercise 24 ($t = 0$ represents 1983).[51]

Year t	0	5	10	15	20
Percentage P (over 25)	36	28	16	7	3

a. What is the logistic regression model for the data? (Round all coefficients to 2 significant digits.) HINT [See Example 2.]

b. According to the model, what percentage of *Physical Review* articles were published by researchers in the United States in 2000 ($t = 17$)? (The actual figure was about 30.1%.)

33. T ***College Basketball: Men*** The following table shows the number of NCAA men's college basketball teams in the U.S. for various years since 1990.[52]

t (Year since 1990)	0	5	10	11	12	13	14
Teams	767	868	932	937	936	967	981
t (Year since 1990)	15	16	17	18	19	20	
Teams	983	984	982	1,017	1,017	1,011	

a. What is the logistic regression model for the data? (Round all coefficients to 3 significant digits.) At what value does the model predict that the number of basketball teams will level off?

b. According to the model, for what value of t is the regression curve steepest? Interpret the answer.

c. Interpret the coefficient b in the context of the number of men's basketball teams.

34. T ***College Basketball: Women*** The following table shows the number of NCAA women's college basketball teams in the U.S. for various years since 1990.[53]

t (Year since 1990)	0	5	10	11	12	13	14
Teams	782	864	956	958	975	1,009	1,008
t (Year since 1990)	15	16	17	18	19	20	
Teams	1,036	1,018	1,003	1,013	1,032	1,036	

a. What is the logistic regression model for the data? (Round all coefficients to 3 significant digits.) At what value does the model predict that the number of basketball teams will level off?

[49] The doubling time is based on retail sales of Coca-Cola products in Russia. Sales in 1993 were double those in 1991, and were expected to double again by 1995. Source: *New York Times*, September 26, 1994, p. D2.

[50] Source: The American Physical Society/*New York Times* May 3, 2003, p. A1.

[51] *Ibid.*

[52] 2010 figure is an estimate. Source: www.census.gov.

[53] *Ibid.*

b. According to the model, for what value of t is the regression curve steepest? Interpret the answer.

c. Interpret the coefficient b in the context of the number of women's basketball teams.

T *Exercises 35 and 36 are based on the discussion following Example 2. If the limiting value N is known, then*

$$\frac{N}{y} - 1 = A(b^{-1})^x$$

and so $N/y - 1$ is an exponential function of x. In Exercises 35 and 36, use the given value of N and the data points $(x, N/y - 1)$ to obtain A and b, and hence a logistic model.

35. T ◆ ***Population: Puerto Rico*** The following table and graph show the population of Puerto Rico in thousands from 1950 to 2025.[54]

t (year since 1950)	0	10	20	30	40	50
Population (thousands)	2,220	2,360	2,720	3,210	3,540	3,820
t (year since 1950)	55	60	65	70	75	
Population (thousands)	3,910	3,990	4,050	4,080	4,100	

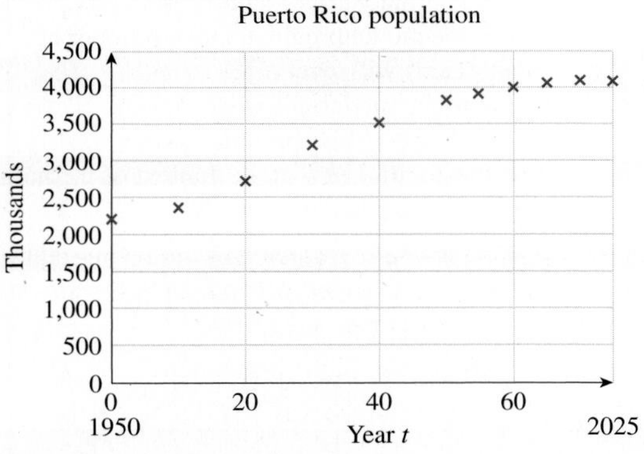

Take t to be the number of years since 1950, and find a logistic model based on the assumption that, eventually, the population of Puerto Rico will grow to 4.5 million. (Round coefficients to 4 decimal places.) In what year does your model predict the population of Puerto Rico will first reach 4.0 million?

36. T ◆ ***Population: Virgin Islands*** The following table and graph show the population of the Virgin Islands in thousands from 1950 to 2025.[55]

t (year since 1950)	0	10	20	30	40	50
Population (thousands)	27	33	63	98	104	106
t (year since 1950)	55	60	65	70	75	
Population (thousands)	108	108	107	107	108	

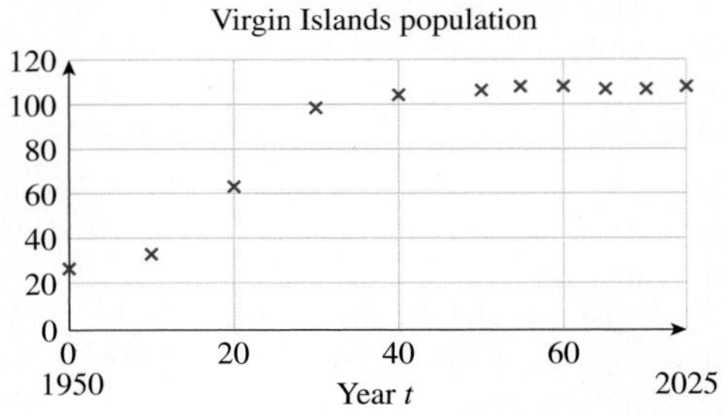

Take t to be the number of years since 1950, and find a logistic model based on the assumption that, eventually, the population of the Virgin Islands will grow to 110,000. (Round coefficients to 4 decimal places.) In what year does your model predict the population of the Virgin Islands first reached 80,000?

COMMUNICATION AND REASONING EXERCISES

37. Logistic functions are commonly used to model the spread of epidemics. Given this fact, explain why a logistic function is also useful to model the spread of a new technology.

38. Why is a logistic function more appropriate than an exponential function for modeling the spread of an epidemic?

39. Give one practical use for logistic regression.

40. Refer to an exercise or example in this section to find a scenario in which a logistic model may not be a good predictor of long-term behavior.

41. What happens to the function $P(t) = \dfrac{N}{1 + Ab^{-t}}$ if we replace b^{-t} by b^t when $b > 1$? When $b < 1$?

42. ▼ What happens to the function $P(t) = \dfrac{N}{1 + Ab^{-t}}$ if $A = 0$? If $A < 0$?

43. ▼ We said that the logistic curve $y = \dfrac{N}{1 + Ab^{-t}}$ is steepest when $t = \dfrac{\ln A}{\ln b}$. Show that the corresponding value of y is $N/2$. HINT [Use the fact that $\dfrac{\ln A}{\ln b} = \log_b A$.]

44. ▼ We said that the logistic curve $y = \dfrac{N}{1 + Ab^{-t}}$ is steepest when $t = \dfrac{\ln A}{\ln b}$. For which values of A and b is this value of t positive, zero, and negative?

[54] Figures from 2010 on are U.S. census projections. Source: The 2008 Statistical Abstract, www.census.gov.

[55] *Ibid.*

CHAPTER 2 REVIEW

KEY CONCEPTS

WW Website www.WanerMath.com
Go to the Website at www.WanerMath .com to find a comprehensive and interactive Web-based summary of Chapter 2.

2.1 Quadratic Functions and Models

A **quadratic function** has the form $f(x) = ax^2 + bx + c$. *p. 126*

The graph of $f(x) = ax^2 + bx + c$ $(a \neq 0)$ is a **parabola.** *p. 127*

The x-coordinate of the **vertex** is $-\frac{b}{2a}$. The y-coordinate is $f\left(-\frac{b}{2a}\right)$. *p. 127*

***x*-intercepts** (if any) occur at
$$x = \frac{-b \pm \sqrt{b^2 - 4ac}}{2a}.\quad p.\ 127$$

The ***y*-intercept** occurs at $y = c$. *p. 127*

The parabola is **symmetric** with respect to the vertical line through the vertex. *p. 127*

Sketching the graph of a quadratic function *p. 128*

Application to maximizing revenue *p. 130*

Application to maximizing profit *p. 130*

Finding the quadratic regression curve *p. 132*

2.2 Exponential Functions and Models

An **exponential function** has the form $f(x) = Ab^x$. *p. 138*

Roles of the constants A and b in an exponential function $f(x) = Ab^x$ *p. 139*

Recognizing exponential data *p. 140*

Finding the exponential curve through two points *p. 141*

Application to compound interest *p. 142*

Application to exponential decay (carbon dating) *p. 142*

Application to exponential growth (epidemics) *p. 142*

The number e and continuous compounding *p. 144*

Alternative form of an exponential function: $f(x) = Ae^{rx}$ *p. 146*

Finding the exponential regression curve *p. 146*

2.3 Logarithmic Functions and Models

The **base *b* logarithm of *x***: $y = \log_b x$ means $b^y = x$ *p. 153*

Common logarithm, $\log x = \log_{10} x$, and **natural logarithm**, $\ln x = \log_e x$ *p. 154*

Change-of-base formula *p. 154*

Solving equations with unknowns in the exponent *p. 155*

A **logarithmic function** has the form $f(x) = \log_b x + C$ or $f(x) = A \ln x + C$. *p. 155*

Graphs of logarithmic functions *p. 156*

Logarithm identities *p. 157*

Application to investments (How long?) *p. 157*

Application to half-life *p. 158*

Exponential decay models and half-life *p. 160*

Exponential growth models and doubling time *p. 161*

Finding the logarithmic regression curve *p. 161*

2.4 Logistic Functions and Models

A **logistic function** has the form
$$f(x) = \frac{N}{1 + Ab^{-x}}.\quad p.\ 167$$

Properties of the logistic curve, point where curve is steepest *p. 168*

Logistic function for small x, the role of b *p. 168*

Application to epidemics *p. 169*

Finding the logistic regression curve *p. 170*

REVIEW EXERCISES

Sketch the graph of the quadratic functions in Exercises 1 and 2, indicating the coordinates of the vertex, the y-intercept, and the x-intercepts (if any).

1. $f(x) = x^2 + 2x - 3$

2. $f(x) = -x^2 - x - 1$

In Exercises 3 and 4, the values of two functions, f and g, are given in a table. One, both, or neither of them may be exponential. Decide which, if any, are exponential, and give the exponential models for those that are.

3.

x	-2	-1	0	1	2
$f(x)$	20	10	5	2.5	1.25
$g(x)$	8	4	2	1	0

4.

x	-2	-1	0	1	2
$f(x)$	8	6	4	2	1
$g(x)$	$\frac{3}{4}$	$\frac{3}{2}$	3	6	12

In Exercises 5 and 6, graph the given pairs of functions on the same set of axes with $-3 \le x \le 3$.

5. $f(x) = \frac{1}{2}(3^x)$; $g(x) = \frac{1}{2}(3^{-x})$

6. $f(x) = 2(4^x)$; $g(x) = 2(4^{-x})$

T *On the same set of axes, use technology to graph the pairs of functions in Exercises 7 and 8 for the given range of x. Identify which graph corresponds to which function.*

7. $f(x) = e^x$; $g(x) = e^{0.8x}$; $-3 \le x \le 3$

8. $f(x) = 2(1.01)^x$; $g(x) = 2(0.99)^x$; $-100 \le x \le 100$

In Exercises 9–14, compute the indicated quantity.

9. A \$3,000 investment earns 3% interest, compounded monthly. Find its value after 5 years.

10. A \$10,000 investment earns 2.5% interest, compounded quarterly. Find its value after 10 years.

11. An investment earns 3% interest, compounded monthly, and is worth \$5,000 after 10 years. Find its initial value.

12. An investment earns 2.5% interest, compounded quarterly, and is worth \$10,000 after 10 years. Find its initial value.

13. A \$3,000 investment earns 3% interest, compounded continuously. Find its value after 5 years.

14. A \$10,000 investment earns 2.5% interest, compounded continuously. Find its value after 10 years.

In Exercises 15–18, find a formula of the form $f(x) = Ab^x$ *using the given information.*

15. $f(0) = 4.5$; the value of f triples for every half-unit increase in x.

16. $f(0) = 5$; the value of f decreases by 75% for every 1-unit increase in x.

17. $f(1) = 2$, $f(3) = 18$.

18. $f(1) = 10$, $f(3) = 5$.

In Exercises 19–22, use logarithms to solve the given equation for x.

19. $3^{-2x} = 4$ **20.** $2^{2x^2-1} = 2$

21. $300(10^{3x}) = 315$ **22.** $P(1+i)^{mx} = A$

On the same set of axes, graph the pairs of functions in Exercises 23 and 24.

23. $f(x) = \log_3 x$; $g(x) = \log_{(1/3)} x$

24. $f(x) = \log x$; $g(x) = \log_{(1/10)} x$

In Exercises 25–28, use the given information to find an exponential model of the form $Q = Q_0e^{-kt}$ *or* $Q = Q_0e^{kt}$, *as appropriate. Round all coefficients to 3 significant digits when rounding is necessary.*

25. Q is the amount of radioactive substance with a half-life of 100 years in a sample originally containing 5 g (t is time in years).

26. Q is the number of cats on an island whose cat population was originally 10,000 but is being cut in half every 5 years (t is time in years).

27. Q is the diameter (in cm) of a circular patch of mold on your roommate's damp towel you have been monitoring with morbid fascination. You measured the patch at 2.5 cm across 4 days ago, and have observed that it is doubling in diameter every 2 days (t is time in days).

28. Q is the population of cats on another island whose cat population was originally 10,000 but is doubling every 15 months (t is time in months).

In Exercises 29–32, find the time required, to the nearest 0.1 year, for the investment to reach the desired goal.

29. \$2,000 invested at 4%, compounded monthly; goal: \$3,000

30. \$2,000 invested at 6.75%, compounded daily; goal: \$3,000

31. \$2,000 invested at 3.75%, compounded continuously; goal: \$3,000

32. \$1,000 invested at 100%, compounded quarterly; goal: \$1,200

In Exercises 33–36, find equations for the logistic functions of x with the stated properties.

33. Through (0, 100), initially increasing by 50% per unit of x, and limiting value 900.

34. Initially exponential of the form $y = 5(1.1)^x$ with limiting value 25.

35. Passing through (0, 5) and decreasing from a limiting value of 20 to 0 at a rate of 20% per unit of x when x is near 0.

36. Initially exponential of the form $y = 2(0.8)^x$ with a value close to 10 when $x = -60$.

APPLICATIONS: OHaganBooks.com

37. ***Web Site Traffic*** The daily traffic ("hits per day") at OHaganBooks.com apparently depends on the monthly expenditure on Internet advertising. The following model is based on information collected over the past few months:

$$h = -0.000005c^2 + 0.085c + 1{,}750.$$

Here, h is the average number of hits per day at OHaganBooks.com, and c is the monthly advertising expenditure.

a. According to the model, what monthly advertising expenditure will result in the largest volume of traffic at OHaganBooks.com? What is that volume?

b. In addition to predicting a maximum volume of traffic, the model predicts that the traffic will eventually drop to zero if the advertising expenditure is increased too far. What expenditure (to the nearest dollar) results in no Web site traffic?

c. What feature of the formula for this quadratic model indicates that it will predict an eventual decline in traffic as advertising expenditure increases?

38. ***Broadband Access*** Pablo Pelogrande, a new summer intern at OHaganBooks.com in 2013, was asked by John O'Hagan to research the extent of broadband access in the United States. Pelogrande found some very old data online on broadband access from the start of 2001 to the end of 2003 and used it to construct the following quadratic model of the growth rate of broadband access:

$n(t) = 2t^2 - 6t + 12$ million new American adults with broadband per year

(t is time in years; $t = 0$ represents the start 2000).[56]

a. What is the appropriate domain of n?

b. According to the model, when was the growth rate at a minimum?

c. Does the model predict a zero growth rate at any particular time? If so, when?

d. What feature of the formula for this quadratic model indicates that the growth rate eventually increases?

e. Does the fact that $n(t)$ decreases for $t \le 1.5$ suggest that the number of broadband users actually declined before June 2001? Explain.

[56]Based on data for 2001–2003. Source for data: Pew Internet and American Life Project data memos dated May 18, 2003 and April 19, 2004, downloaded from www.pewinternet.org.

f. Pelogande extrapolated the model in order to estimate the growth rate at the beginning of 2013 and 2014. What did he find? Comment on the answer.

39. ***Revenue and Profit*** Some time ago, a consultant formulated the following linear model of demand for online novels:

$$q = -60p + 950$$

where q is the monthly demand for OHaganBooks.com's online novels at a price of p dollars per novel.

a. Use this model to express the monthly revenue as a function of the unit price p, and hence determine the price you should charge for a maximum monthly revenue.

b. Author royalties and copyright fees cost the company an average of $4 per novel, and the monthly cost of operating and maintaining the online publishing service amounts to $900 per month. Express the monthly profit P as a function of the unit price p, and hence determine the unit price you should charge for a maximum monthly profit. What is the resulting profit (or loss)?

40. ***Revenue and Profit*** Billy-Sean O'Hagan is John O'Hagan's son and a freshman in college. He notices that the demand for the college newspaper was 2,000 copies each week when the paper was given away free of charge, but dropped to 1,000 each week when the college started charging 10¢/copy.

a. Write down the associated linear demand function.

b. Use your demand function to express the revenue as a function of the unit price p, and hence determine the price the college should charge for a maximum revenue. At that price, what is the revenue from sales of one edition of the newspaper?

c. It costs the college 4¢ to produce each copy of the paper, plus an additional fixed cost of $200. Express the profit P as a function of the unit price p, and hence determine the unit price the college should charge for a maximum monthly profit (or minimum loss). What is the resulting profit (or loss)?

41. ***Lobsters*** Marjory Duffin, CEO of Duffin House, is particularly fond of having steamed lobster at working lunches with executives from OHaganBooks.com and is therefore alarmed by the fact that the yearly lobster harvest from New York's Long Island Sound has been decreasing dramatically since 1997. Indeed, the size of the annual harvest can be approximated by

$$n(t) = 9.1(0.81^t) \text{ million pounds}$$

where t is time in years since 1997.[57]

a. The model tells us that the harvest was ____ million pounds in 1997 and decreasing by ___% each year.

b. What does the model predict for the 2013 harvest?

42. ***Stock Prices*** In the period immediately following its initial public offering (IPO), OHaganBooks.com's stock was doubling in value every 3 hours. If you bought $10,000 worth of the stock when it was first offered, how much was your stock worth after 8 hours?

[57]Authors' regression model. Source for data: Long Island Sound Study, data downloaded May 2011 from longislandsoundstudy.net/2010/07/lobster-landings/.

43. ***Lobsters*** (See Exercise 41.) Marjory Duffin has just left John O'Hagan, CEO of OHaganBooks.com, a frantic phone message to the effect that this year's lobster harvest from New York's Long Island Sound is predicted to dip below 200,000 pounds, making that planned lobster working lunch more urgent than ever. What year is it?

44. ***Stock Prices*** We saw in Exercise 42 that OHaganBooks.com's stock was doubling in value every 3 hours, following its IPO. If you bought $10,000 worth of the stock when it was first offered, how long from the initial offering did it take your investment to reach $50,000?

45. ***Lobsters*** We saw in Exercise 41 that the Long Island Sound lobster harvest was given by $n(t) = 9.1(0.81^t)$ million pounds t years after 1997. However, in 2010, thanks to the efforts of Duffin House, Inc. it turned around and started increasing by 24% each year.[58] What, to the nearest 10,000 pounds, was the actual size of the harvest in 2013?

46. ***Stock Prices*** We saw in Exercise 42 that OHaganBooks.com's stock was doubling in value every 3 hours, following its IPO. After 10 hours of trading, the stock turns around and starts losing one third of its value every 4 hours. How long (from the initial offering) will it be before your stock is once again worth $10,000?

47. T ***Lobsters*** The following chart shows some of the data that went into the model in Exercise 41:

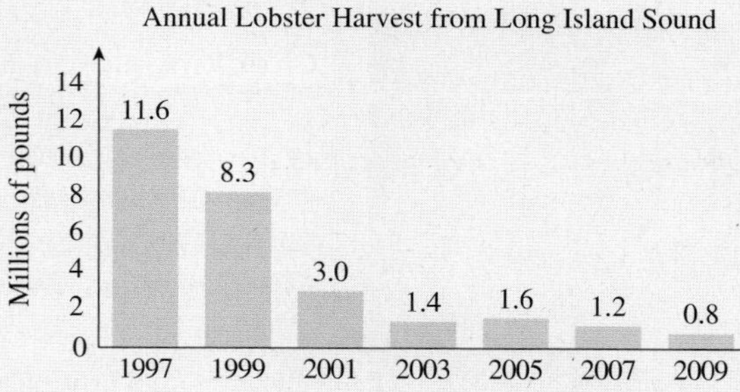

Use these data to obtain an exponential regression curve of the form $n(t) = Ab^t$, with $t = 0$ corresponding to 1997 and coefficients rounded to 2 significant digits.

48. T ***Stock Prices*** The actual stock price of OHaganBooks.com in the hours following its IPO is shown in the following chart:

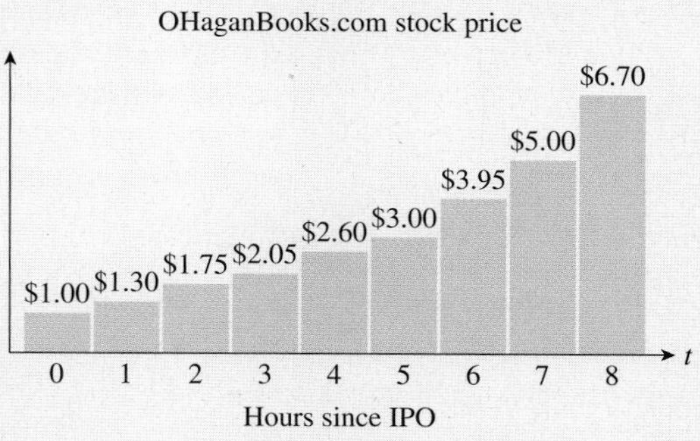

[58]This claim, like Duffin House, is fiction.

Use the data to obtain an exponential regression curve of the form $P(t) = Ab^t$, with $t = 0$ the time in hours since the IPO and coefficients rounded to 3 significant digits. At the end of which hour will the stock price first be above $10?

49. ***Hardware Life*** *(Based on a question from the GRE economics exam)* To estimate the rate at which new computer hard drives will have to be retired, OHaganBooks.com uses the "survivor curve":

$$L_x = L_0 e^{-x/t}$$

where

L_x = number of surviving hard drives at age x
L_0 = number of hard drives initially
t = average life in years.

All of the following are implied by the curve *except:*

(A) Some of the equipment is retired during the first year of service.
(B) Some equipment survives three average lives.
(C) More than half the equipment survives the average life.
(D) Increasing the average life of equipment by using more durable materials would increase the number surviving at every age.
(E) The number of survivors never reaches zero.

50. ***Sales*** OHaganBooks.com modeled its weekly sales over a period of time with the function

$$s(t) = 6{,}050 + \frac{4{,}470}{1 + 14(1.73^{-t})}$$

as shown in the following graph (t is measured in weeks):

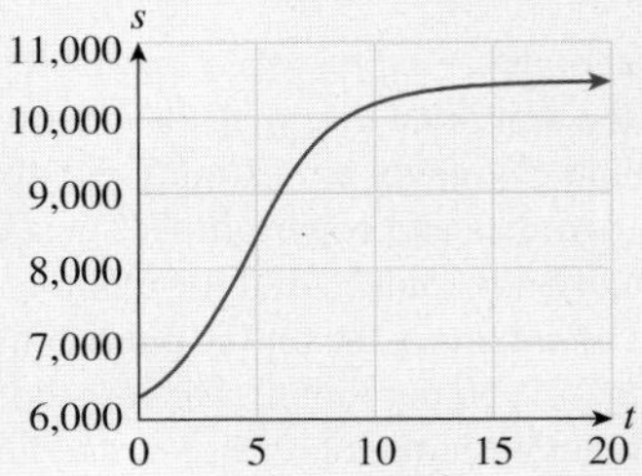

a. As time goes on, it appears that weekly sales are leveling off. At what value are they leveling off?
b. When did weekly sales rise above 10,000?
c. When, to the nearest week, were sales rising most rapidly?

Case Study

Checking up on Malthus

Robert Nickelsberg/Getty Images

In 1798 Thomas R. Malthus (1766–1834) published an influential pamphlet, later expanded into a book, titled *An Essay on the Principle of Population As It Affects the Future Improvement of Society.* One of his main contentions was that population grows geometrically (exponentially) while the supply of resources such as food grows only arithmetically (linearly). This led him to the pessimistic conclusion that population would always reach the limits of subsistence and precipitate famine, war, and ill health, unless population could be checked by other means. He advocated "moral restraint," which includes the pattern of late marriage common in Western Europe at the time and now common in most developed countries and which leads to a lower reproduction rate.

Two hundred years later, you have been asked to check the validity of Malthus's contention. That population grows geometrically, at least over short periods of time, is commonly assumed. That resources grow linearly is more questionable. You decide to check the actual production of a common crop, wheat, in the United States. Agricultural statistics like these are available from the U.S. government on the Internet, through the U.S. Department of Agriculture's National Agricultural Statistics Service (NASS). As of 2011, this service was available at www.nass.usda.gov. Looking through this site, you locate data on the annual production of all wheat in the United States from 1900 through 2010.

Website
www.WanerMath.com
To download an Excel sheet with the data used in the case study, go to Everything for Calculus, scroll down to the case study for Chapter 2, and click on "Wheat Production Data (Excel)".

Year	1900	1901	. . .	2009	2010
Thousands of Bushels	599,315	762,546	. . .	2,218,061	2,208,391

Graphing these data (using Excel, for example), you obtain the graph in Figure 20.

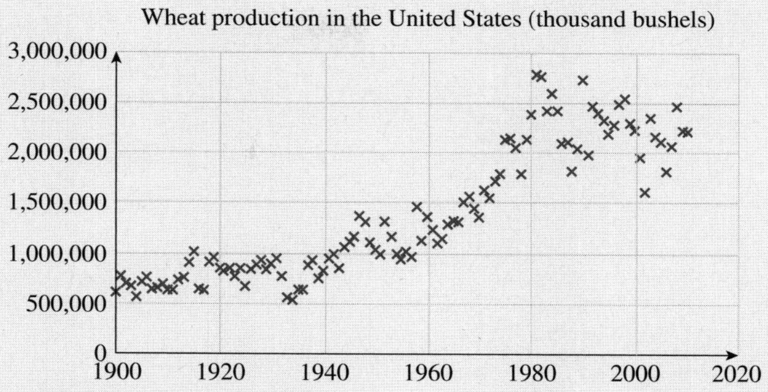

Figure 20

This does not look very linear, particularly in the last half of the twentieth century, but you continue checking the mathematics. Using Excel's built-in linear regression capabilities, you find that the line that best fits these data, shown in Figure 21, has $r^2 = 0.8039$. (Recall the discussion of the correlation coefficient r in Section 1.4. A similar statistic is available for other types of regression as well.)

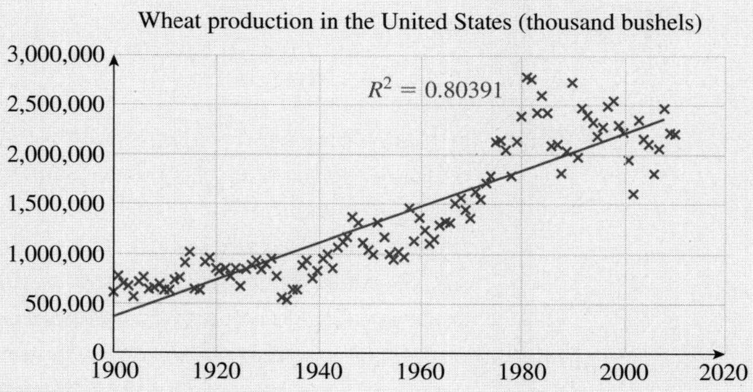

Figure 21

* Recall that the residuals are defined as $y_{\text{Observed}} - y_{\text{Predicted}}$ (see Section 1.4) and are the vertical distances between the observed data points and the regression line.

Although that is a fairly high correlation, you notice that the residuals* are not distributed randomly: The actual wheat production starts out higher than the line, dips below the line from about 1920 to about 1970, then rises above the line, and finally appears to dip below the line around 2002. This behavior seems to suggest a logistic curve or perhaps a cubic curve. On the other hand, it is also possible that the apparent dip at the end of the data is not statistically significant—it could be nothing more than a transitory fluctuation in the wheat production industry—so perhaps we should also consider models that do not bend downward, like exponential and quadratic models.

Following is a comparison of the four proposed models (with coefficients rounded to 3 significant digits). For the independent variable, we used t = time in years since 1900. SSE is the sum-of-squares error.

Quadratic

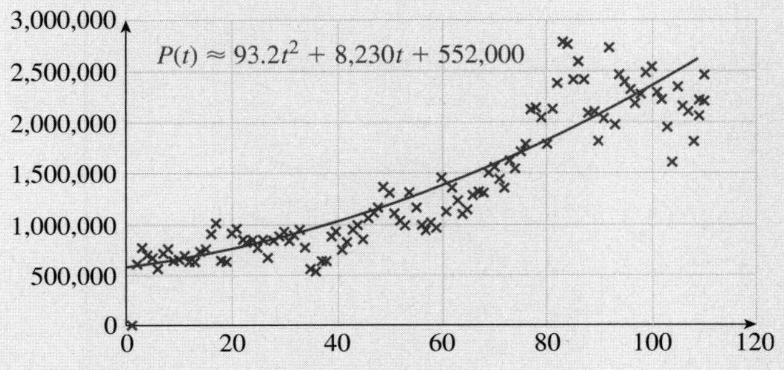

SSE $\approx 8.68 \times 10^{12}$

Cubic

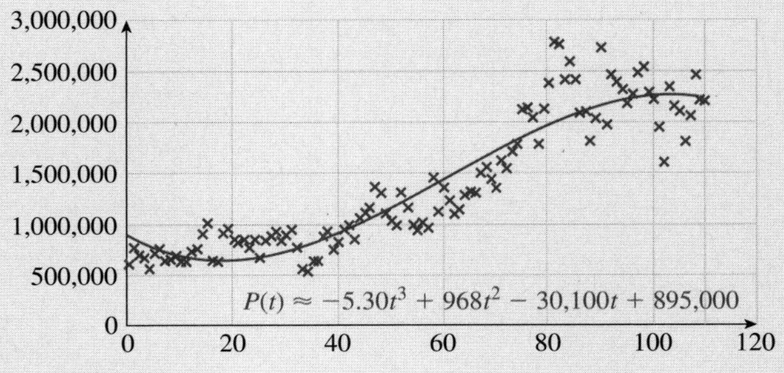

SSE $\approx 6.60 \times 10^{12}$

Exponential

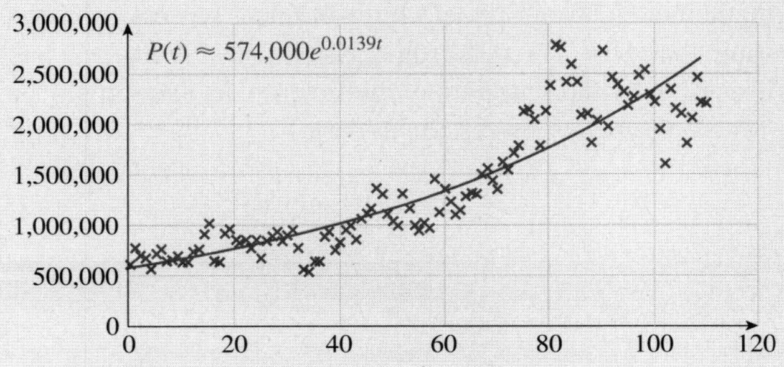

SSE $\approx 9.34 \times 10^{12}$

Logistic

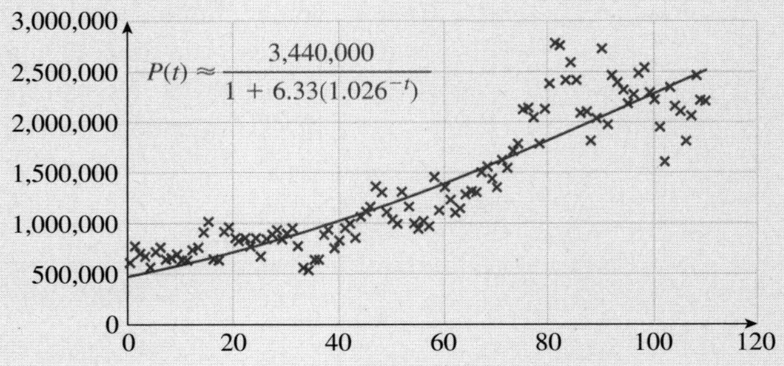

SSE $\approx 8.26 \times 10^{12}$

The model that appears to best fit the data seems to be the cubic model; both visually and by virtúe of SSE. Notice also that the cubic model predicts a *decrease* in the production of wheat in the near term (see Figure 22).

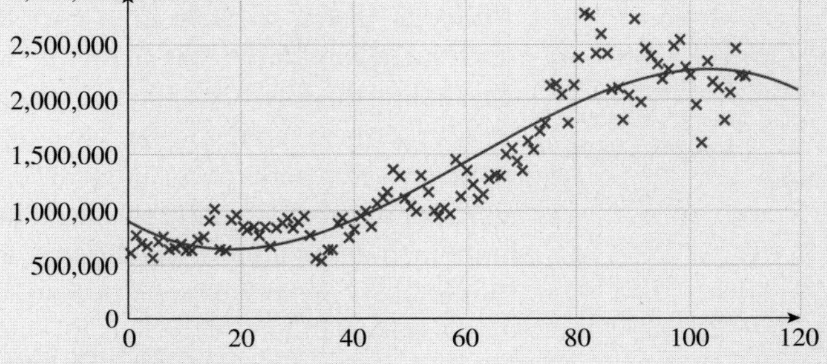

Figure 22

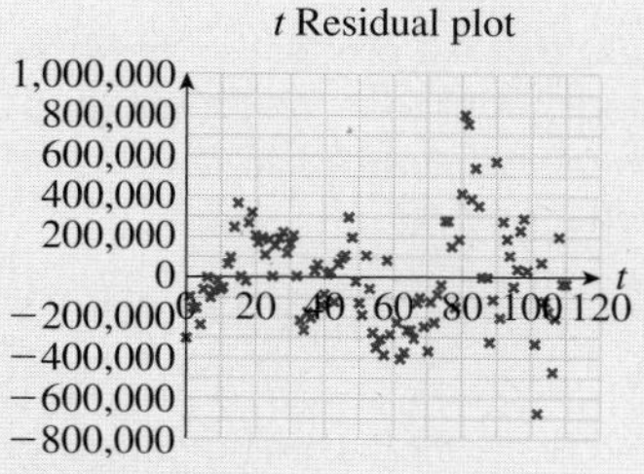

Figure 23

So you prepare a report that documents your findings and concludes that things are even worse than Malthus predicted, at least as far as wheat production in the United States is concerned: The supply is deceasing while the population is still increasing more-or-less exponentially. (See Exercise 75 in Section 2.2.)

You are about to hit "Send," which will dispatch copies of your report to a significant number of people on whom the success of your career depends, when you notice something strange about the pattern of data in Figure 22: The observed data points appear to hug the regression curve quite closely for small values of t, but appear to become more and more scattered as the value of t increases. In the language of residuals, the residuals are small for small values of t but then tend to get larger with increasing t. Figure 23 shows a plot of the residuals that shows this trend even more clearly.

This reminds you vaguely of something that came up in your college business statistics course, so you consult the textbook from that class that (fortunately) you still own and discover that a pattern of residuals with increasing magnitude suggests that, instead of modeling y versus t directly, you instead model $\ln y$ versus t. (The residuals for large values of t will then be scaled down by the logarithm.)

Figure 24 shows the resulting plot together with the regression line (what we call the "linear transformed model").

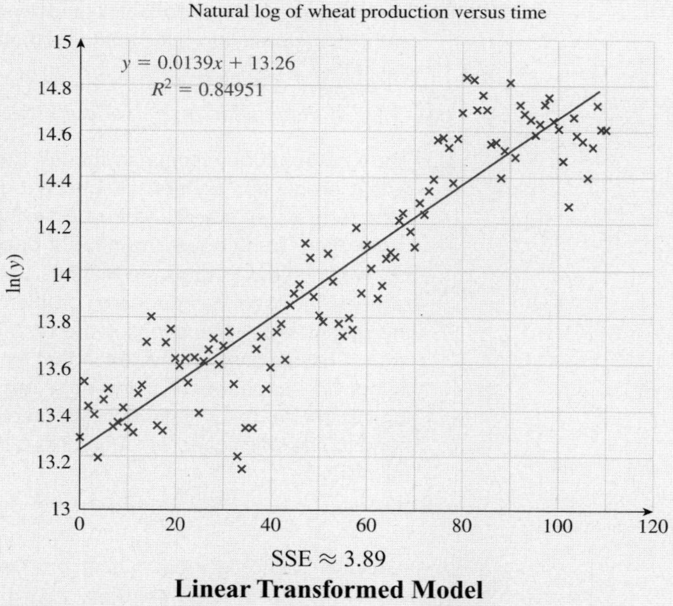

Figure 24

Notice that this time, the regression patterns no longer suggest an obvious curve. Further, they no longer appear to grow with increasing t. Although SSE is dramatically lower than the values for the earlier models, the contrast is a false one; the units of y are now different, and comparing SSE with that of the earlier models is like comparing apples and oranges. While SSE depends on the units of measurement used, the coefficient of determination r^2 discussed in Section 1.4 is independent of the units used. A similar statistic is available for other types of regression as well, as well as something called "adjusted r^2."

The value of r^2 for the transformed model is approximately 0.850, while r^2 for the cubic model* is about 0.861, which is fairly close.

* The "adjusted r^2" from statistics that corrects for model size.

Q: *If the cubic model and the linear transformed model have similar values of r^2, how do I decide which is more appropriate?*

A: The cubic model, if extrapolated, predicts unrealistically that the production of wheat will plunge in the near future, but the linear transformed model sees the recent drop-off as just one of several market fluctuations that show up in the residuals. You should therefore favor the more reasonable linear transformed model.

Q: *The linear transformed model gives us ln y versus t. What does it say about y versus t?*

A: Accurately write down the equation of the transformed linear model, being careful to replace y by $\ln y$:

$$\ln y = 0.0139t + 13.26.$$

Rewriting this in exponential form gives

$$\begin{aligned} y &= e^{0.0139t+13.26} \\ &= e^{13.26}e^{0.0139t} \\ &\approx 574{,}000e^{0.0139t}, \end{aligned}$$ Coefficients rounded to 3 digits

which is exactly the exponential model we found earlier! (In fact, using the natural logarithm transformation is the standard method of computing the regression exponential curve.)

Q: *What of the logistic model; should that not be the most realistic?*

A: The logistic model seems as though it *ought* to be the most appropriate, because wheat production cannot reasonably be expected to continue increasing exponentially forever; eventually resource limitations must lead to a leveling off of wheat production. Such a leveling off, if it occurred before the population started to level off, would seem to vindicate Malthus's pessimistic predictions. However, the logistic regression model has the same problem as the cubic model: It is trying to interpret the recent large fluctuations in the data as evidence of leveling off, but we really do not yet have significant evidence that that is occurring. Wheat production—even if it is logistic—appears still in the early (exponential) stage of growth. In general, for a logistic model to be reliable in its prediction of the leveling-off value N, we would need to see significant evidence of leveling off in the data. (See, however, Exercise 2 following.)

You now conclude that wheat production for the past 100 years is better described as increasing exponentially than linearly, contradicting Malthus, and moreover that it shows no sign of leveling off as yet.

EXERCISES

1. Use the wheat production data starting at 1950 to construct the exponential regression model in two ways: directly, and using a linear transformed model as above. (Round coefficients to 3 digits.) Compare the growth constant k of your model with that of the exponential model based on the data from 1900 on. How would you interpret the difference?
2. Compute the least-squares logistic model for the data in the preceding exercise. (Round coefficients to 3 significant digits.) At what level does it predict that wheat production will level off? (Note on using Excel Solver for logistic regression: Before running Solver, press Options in the Solver window and turn "Automatic Scaling" on. This adjusts the algorithm for the fact that the constants A, N, and b have vastly different orders of magnitude.) Give

two graphs: one showing the data with the exponential regression model, and the other showing the data with the logistic regression model. Which model gives a better fit visually? Justify your observation by computing SSE directly for both models. Comment on your answer in terms of Malthus's assertions.

3. Find the production figures for another common crop grown in the United States. Compare the linear, quadratic, cubic, exponential, and logistic models. What can you conclude?

4. Below are the census figures for the population of the U.S. (in thousands) from 1820 to 2010.[59] Compare the linear, quadratic, and exponential models. What can you conclude?

Year	1820	1830	1840	1850	1860	1870	1880	1890	1900	1910
Population (1000s)	9,638	12,861	17,063	23,192	31,443	38,558	50,189	62,980	76,212	92,228
Year	1920	1930	1940	1950	1960	1970	1980	1990	2000	2010
Population (1000s)	106,022	123,203	132,165	151,326	179,323	203,302	226,542	248,710	281,422	308,746

[59] Source: Bureau of the Census, U.S. Department of Commerce.

TI-83/84 Plus Technology Guide

Section 2.1

Example 2 (page 128) Sketch the graph of each quadratic function, showing the location of the vertex and intercepts.

a. $f(x) = 4x^2 - 12x + 9$ **b.** $g(x) = -\frac{1}{2}x^2 + 4x - 12$

Solution with Technology

We will do part (a).

1. Start by storing the coefficients a, b, c using

 $4 \rightarrow A: -12 \rightarrow B: 9 \rightarrow C$
 $\boxed{\text{STO>}}$ gives the arrow $\boxed{\text{ALPHA}}\boxed{.}$ gives the colon

2. Save your quadratic as Y_1 using the $Y =$ screen:

 $Y_1 = AX\text{^}2 + BX + C$

3. To obtain the x-coordinate of the vertex, enter its formula as shown below on the left.

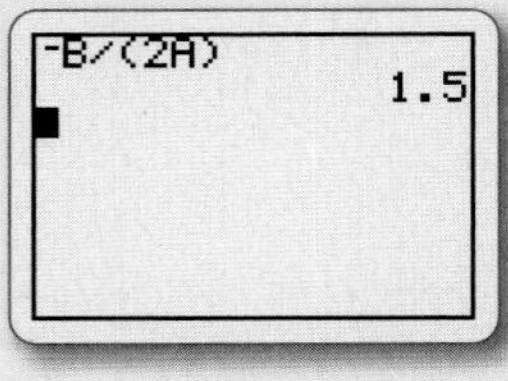

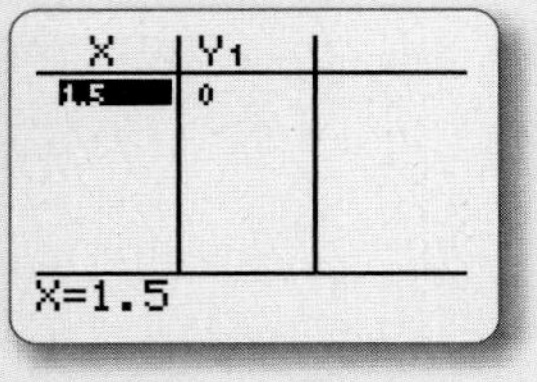

4. The y-coordinate of the vertex can be obtained from the Table screen by entering $x = 1.5$ as shown above on the right. (If you can't enter values of x, press $\boxed{\text{2ND}}$ $\boxed{\text{TBLSET}}$, and set Indpnt to Ask.) From the table, we see that the vertex is at the point (1.5, 0).

5. To obtain the x-intercepts, enter the quadratic formula on the home screen as shown:

    ```
    (-B+√(B²-4AC))/(
    2A)
                1.5
    (-B-√(B²-4AC))/(
    2A)
                1.5
    ```

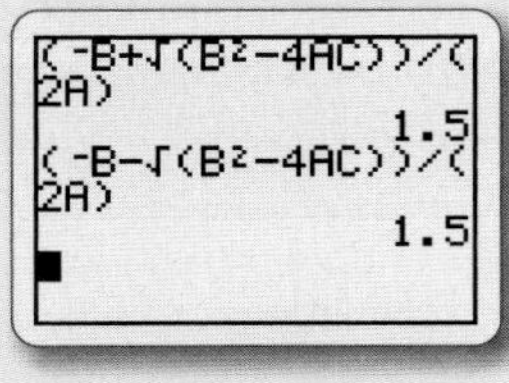

 Because both intercepts agree, we conclude that the graph intersects the x-axis on a single point (at the vertex).

6. To graph the function, we need to select good values for Xmin and Xmax. In general, we would like our graph to show the vertex as well as all the intercepts. To see the vertex, make sure that its x coordinate (1.5) is between Xmin and Xmax. To see the x-intercepts, make sure that they are also between Xmin and

Xmax. To see the y-intercept, make sure that $x = 0$ is between Xmin and Xmax. Thus, to see everything, choose Xmin and Xmax so that the interval [xMin, xMax] contains the x coordinate of the vertex, the x-intercepts, and 0. For this example, we can choose an interval like $[-1, 3]$.

7. Once xMin and xMax are chosen, you can obtain convenient values of yMin and yMax by pressing $\boxed{\text{ZOOM}}$ and selecting the option ZoomFit. (Make sure that your quadratic equation is entered in the $Y =$ screen before doing this!)

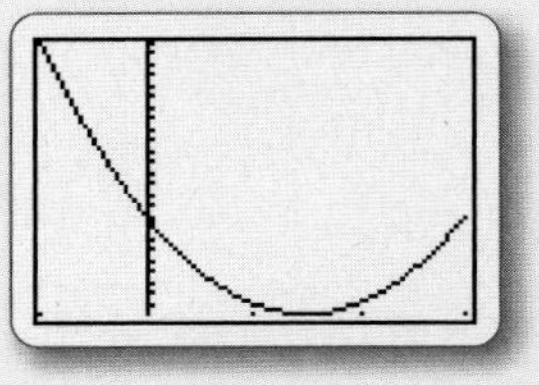

Example 5 (page 132) The following table shows the annual mean carbon dioxide concentration measured at Mauna Loa Observatory in Hawaii, in parts per million, every 10 years from 1960 through 2010 ($t = 0$ represents 1960).

Year t	0	10	20	30	40	50
PPM CO_2 C	317	326	339	354	369	390

Find the quadratic model

$$C(t) = at^2 + bt + c$$

that best fits the data.

Solution with Technology

1. Using $\boxed{\text{STAT}}$ EDIT enter the data with the x-coordinates (values of t) in L_1 and the y-coordinates (values of C) in L_2, just as in Section 1.4:

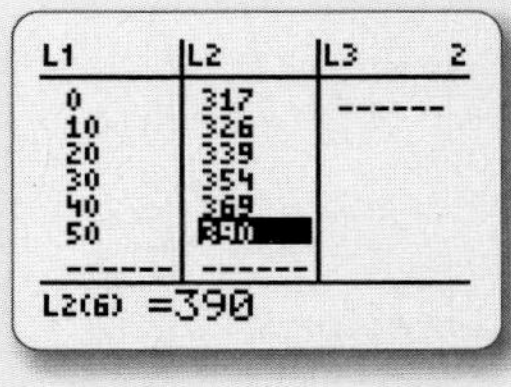

2. Press STAT, select CALC, and choose option #5 QuadReg. Pressing ENTER gives the quadratic regression curve in the home screen:

$$y \approx 0.01214x^2 + 0.8471x + 316.9. \quad \text{Coefficients rounded to 4 decimal places}$$

3. Now go to the Y= window and turn Plot1 on by selecting it and pressing ENTER. (You can also turn it on in the 2ND STAT PLOT screen.)
4. Next, enter the regression equation in the Y= screen by pressing Y=, clearing out whatever function is there, and pressing VARS 5 and selecting EQ option #1: RegEq as shown below left.

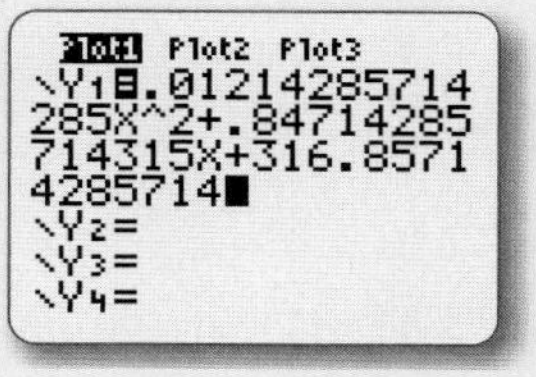

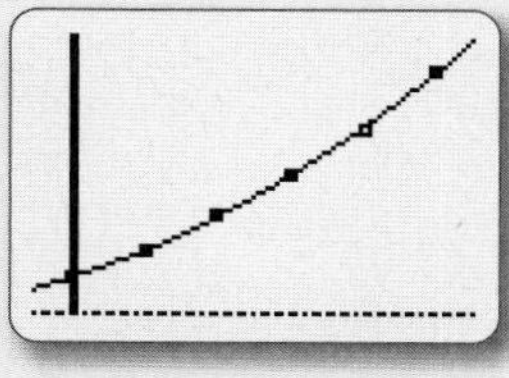

5. To obtain a convenient window showing all the points and the lines, press ZOOM and choose option #9: ZoomStat as shown above on the right.

Note When you are done viewing the graph, it is a good idea to turn Plot1 off again to avoid errors in graphing or data points showing up in your other graphs. ■

Section 2.2

Example 6(a) (page 147) The following table shows annual expenditure on health in the U.S. from 1980 through 2009 ($t = 0$ represents 1980).

Year t	0	5	10	15	20	25	29
Expenditure ($ billion)	256	444	724	1,030	1,380	2,020	2,490

Find the exponential regression model

$$C(t) = Ab^t$$

for the annual expenditure.

Solution with Technology

This is very similar to Example 5 in Section 2.1 (see the Technology Guide for Section 2.1):

1. Use STAT EDIT to enter the table of values.

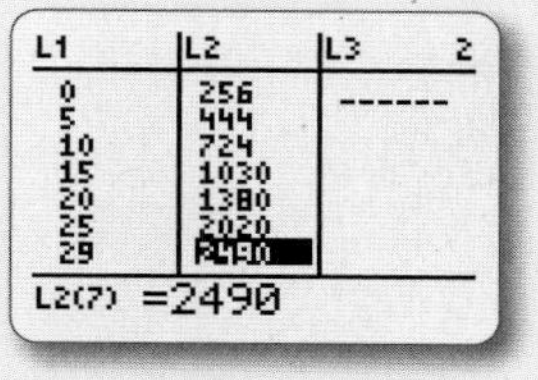

2. Press STAT, select CALC, and choose option #0 ExpReg. Pressing ENTER gives the exponential regression curve in the home screen:

$$C(t) \approx 296.25(1.0798)^t. \quad \text{Coefficients rounded}$$

3. To graph the points and regression line in the same window, turn Plot1 on (see the Technology Guide for Example 5 in Section 2.1) and enter the regression equation in the Y= screen by pressing Y=, clearing out whatever function is there, and pressing VARS 5 and selecting EQ option #1: RegEq. Then press ZOOM and choose option #9: ZoomStat to see the graph.

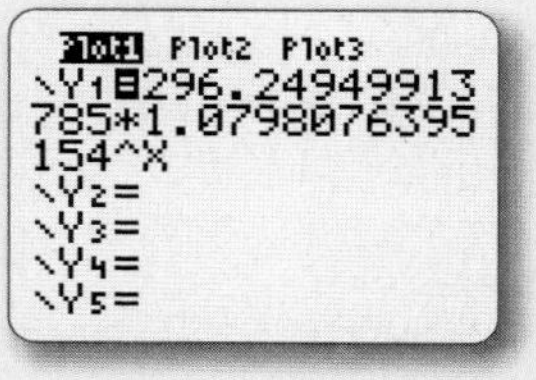

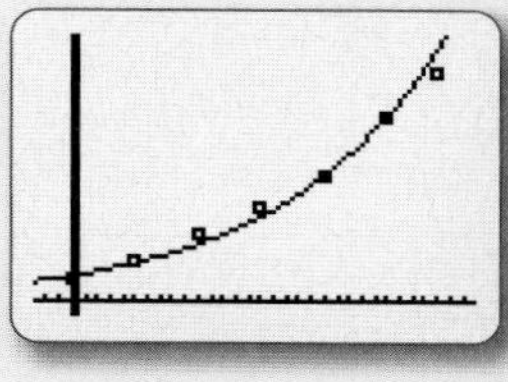

Note When you are done viewing the graph, it is a good idea to turn Plot1 off again to avoid errors in graphing or data points showing up in your other graphs. ■

Section 2.3

Example 5 (page 161) The following table shows the total spent on research and development by universities and colleges in the U.S., in billions of dollars, for the period 1998–2008 (t is the year since 1990).

Year t	8	9	10	11	12	13
Spending ($ billions)	27	29	31	33	36	38
Year t	14	15	16	17	18	
Spending ($ billions)	39	40	40	41	42	

Find the best-fit logarithmic model of the form

$$S(t) = A \ln t + C$$

and use the model to project total spending on research by universities and colleges in 2012, assuming the trend continues.

Solution with Technology

This is very similar to Example 5 in Section 2.1 (see the Technology Guide for Section 2.1):

1. Use `STAT` EDIT to enter the table of values.
2. Press `STAT`, select CALC, and choose option #9 LnReg. Pressing `ENTER` gives the logarithmic regression curve in the home screen:

$$S(t) \approx 19.25 \ln t - 12.78. \qquad \text{Coefficients rounded}$$

3. To graph the points and regression line in the same window, turn Plot1 on (see the Technology Guide for Example 5 in Section 2.1) and enter the regression equation in the Y= screen by pressing `Y=`, clearing out whatever function is there, and pressing `VARS` `5` and selecting EQ option #1: RegEq. Then press `ZOOM` and choose option #9: ZoomStat to see the graph.

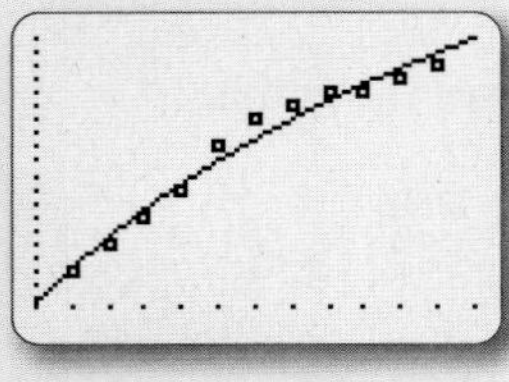

Section 2.4

Example 2 (page 170) The following table shows wired broadband penetration in the United States as a function of time t in years ($t = 0$ represents 2000).

Year (t)	2	3	4	5	6	7	8	9	10
Penetration (%) (P)	5.5	7.9	10.9	14.2	18.2	21.9	23.9	26.5	27.1

Find a logistic regression curve of the form

$$P(t) = \frac{N}{1 + Ab^{-t}}.$$

Solution with Technology

This is very similar to Example 5 in Section 2.1 (see the Technology Guide for Section 2.1):

1. Use `STAT` EDIT to enter the table of values.
2. Press `STAT`, select CALC, and choose option #B Logistic. Pressing `ENTER` gives the logistic regression curve in the home screen:

$$P(t) \approx \frac{29.842}{1 + 12.502e^{-0.49592t}}. \qquad \text{Coefficients rounded}$$

This is not exactly the form we are seeking, but we can convert it to that form by writing

$$e^{-0.49592t} = (e^{0.49592})^{-t} \approx 1.642^{-t}$$

so

$$P(t) \approx \frac{29.842}{1 + 12.502(1.642)^{-t}}.$$

3. To graph the points and regression line in the same window, turn Plot1 on (see the Technology Guide for Example 5 in Section 2.1) and enter the regression equation in the Y= screen by pressing `Y=`, clearing out whatever function is there, and pressing `VARS` `5` and selecting EQ option #1: RegEq. Then press `ZOOM` and choose option #9: ZoomStat to see the graph.

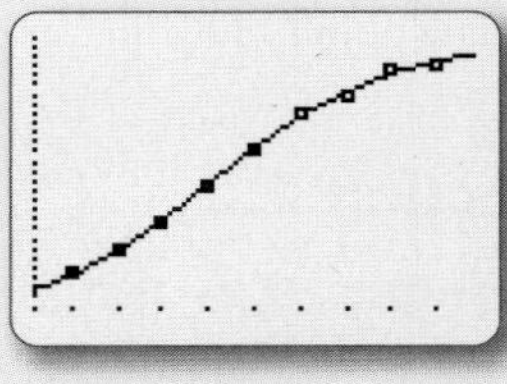

SPREADSHEET Technology Guide

Section 2.1

Example 2 (page 128) Sketch the graph of each quadratic function, showing the location of the vertex and intercepts.

a. $f(x) = 4x^2 - 12x + 9$

b. $g(x) = -\frac{1}{2}x^2 + 4x - 12$

Solution with Technology

We can set up a worksheet so that all we have to enter are the coefficients a, b, and c, and a range of x-values for the graph. Here is a possible layout that will plot 101 points using the coefficients for part (a).

1. First, we compute the x coordinates:

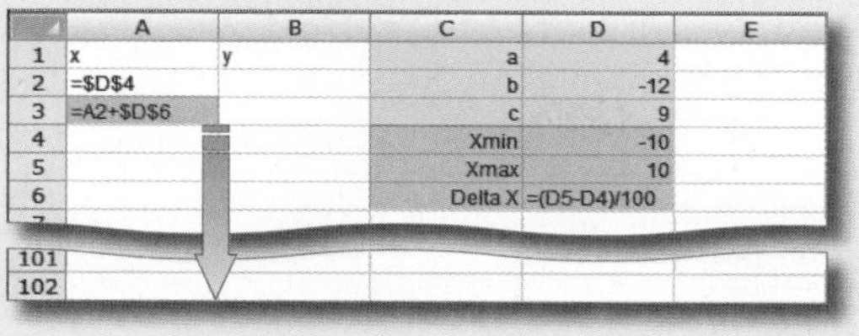

2. To add the y coordinates, we use the technology formula

```
a*x^2+b*x+c
```

replacing a, b, and c with (absolute) references to the cells containing their values.

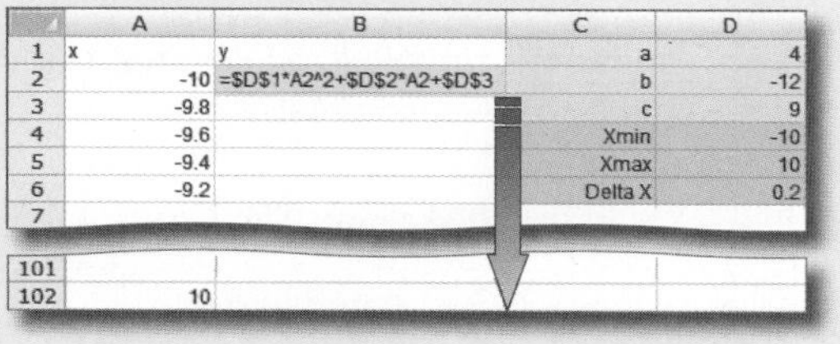

3. Graphing the data in columns A and B gives the graph shown here:

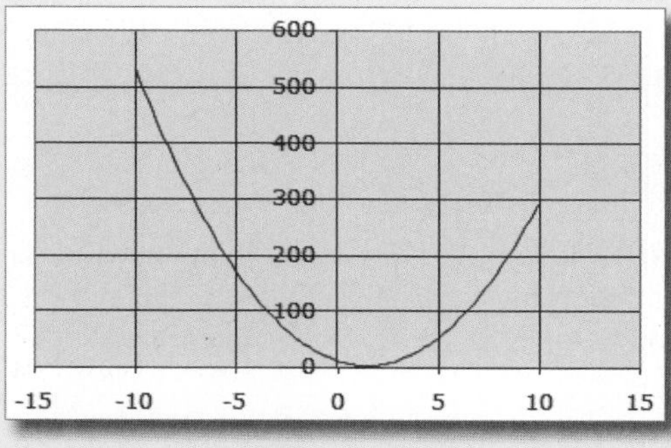

$$y = 4x^2 - 12x + 9$$

4. We can go further and compute the exact coordinates of the vertex and intercepts:

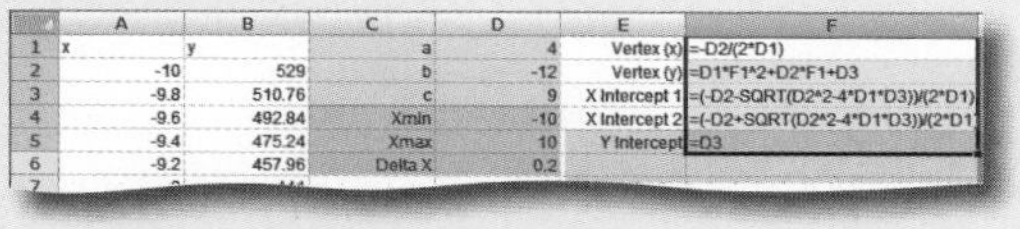

The completed sheet should look like this:

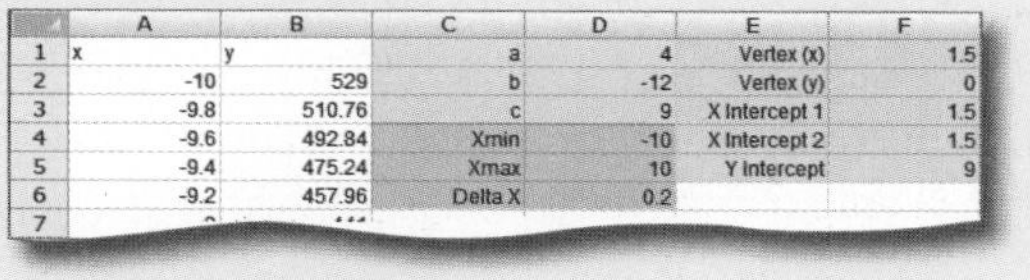

We can now save this sheet as a template to handle all quadratic functions. For instance, to do part (b), we just change the values of a, b, and c in column D to $a = -1/2$, $b = 4$, and $c = -12$.

Example 5 (page 132) The following table shows the annual mean carbon dioxide concentration measured at Mauna Loa Observatory in Hawaii, in parts per million, every 10 years from 1960 through 2010 ($t = 0$ represents 1960).

Year t	0	10	20	30	40	50
PPM CO_2 C	317	326	339	354	369	390

Find the quadratic model

$$C(t) = at^2 + bt + c$$

that best fits the data.

Solution with Technology

As in Section 1.4, Example 2, we start with a scatter plot of the original data, and add a trendline:

1. Start with the original data and a "Scatter plot" (see Section 1.2 Example 5).

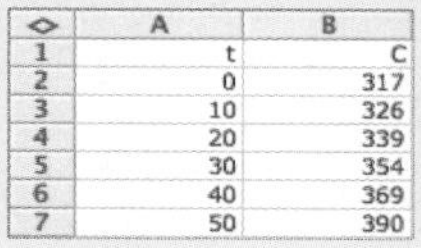

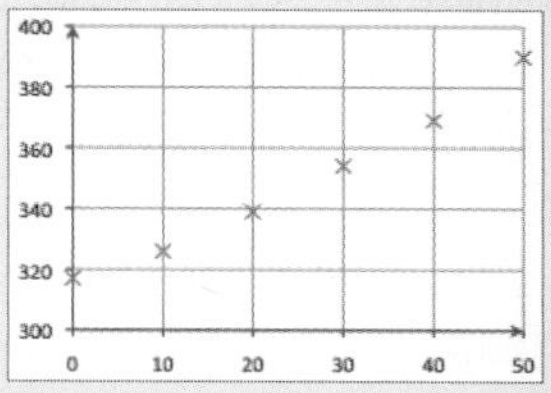

2. Add a quadratic trend line. (As of the time of this writing, among the common spreadsheets only Excel has the ability to add a polynomial trendline.) Right-click on any data point in the chart and select "Add Trendline," then select a "Polynomial" type of order 2 and check the option to "Display Equation on chart."

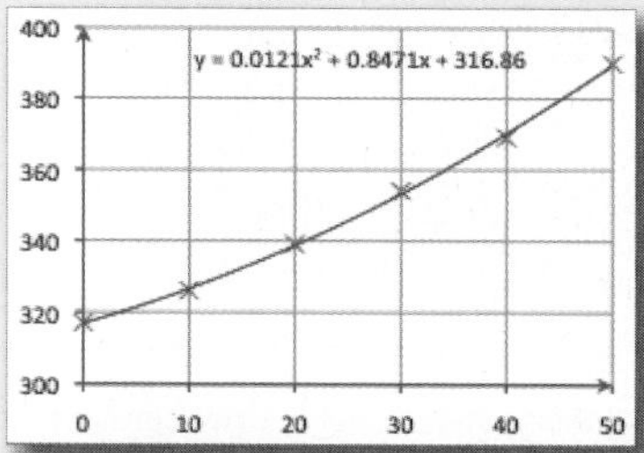

Section 2.2

Example 6(a) (page 147) The following table shows annual expenditure on health in the U.S. from 1980 through 2009 ($t = 0$ represents 1980).

Year t	0	5	10	15	20	25	29
Expenditure ($ billion)	256	444	724	1,030	1,380	2,020	2,490

Find the exponential regression model

$$C(t) = Ab^t$$

for the annual expenditure.

Solution with Technology

This is very similar to Example 5 in Section 2.1 (see the Technology Guide for Section 2.1):

1. Start with a "Scatter plot" of the observed data.
2. Add an exponential trendline:[60] The details vary from spreadsheet to spreadsheet—in OpenOffice, first double-click on the graph. Right-click on any data point in the chart and select "Add Trendline," then select an "Exponential" type and check the option to "Display Equation on chart."

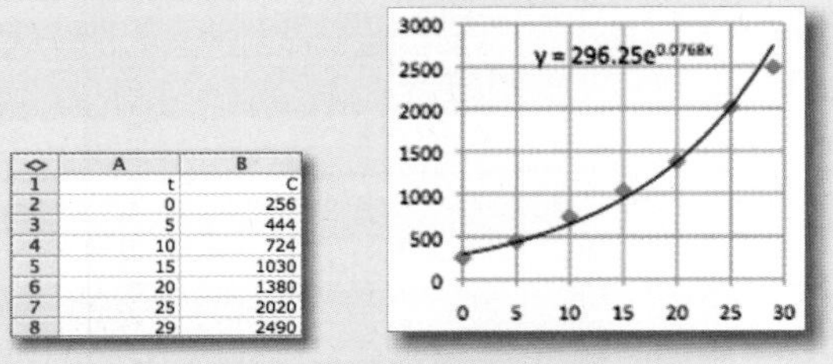

Notice that the regression curve is given in the form Ae^{kt} rather than Ab^t. To transform it, write

$$296.25e^{0.0768t} = 296.25(e^{0.0768})^t$$
$$\approx 296.25(1.0798)^t. \qquad e^{0.0768} \approx 1.0798$$

Section 2.3

Example 5 (page 161) The following table shows the total spent on research and development by universities and colleges in the U.S., in billions of dollars, for the period 1998–2008 (t is the year since 1990).

Year t	8	9	10	11	12	13
Spending ($ billions)	27	29	31	33	36	38
Year t	14	15	16	17	18	
Spending ($ billions)	39	40	40	41	42	

Find the best-fit logarithmic model of the form

$$S(t) = A \ln t + C$$

and use the model to project total spending on research by universities and colleges in 2012, assuming the trend continues.

Solution with Technology

This is very similar to Example 5 in Section 2.1 (see the Technology Guide for Section 2.1): We start, as usual, with a "Scatter plot" of the observed data and add a Logarithmic trendline. Here is the result:

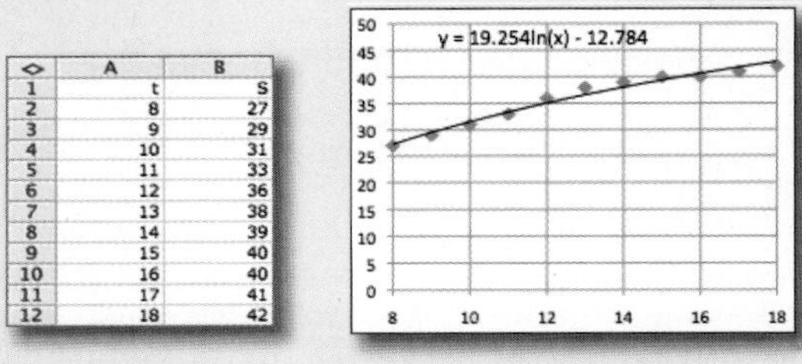

Section 2.4

Example 2 (page 170) The following table shows wired broadband penetration in the United States as a function of time t in years ($t = 0$ represents 2000).

Year (t)	2	3	4	5	6	7	8	9	10
Penetration (%) (P)	5.5	7.9	10.9	14.2	18.2	21.9	23.9	26.5	27.1

Find a logistic regression curve of the form

$$P(t) = \frac{N}{1 + Ab^{-t}}.$$

Solution with Technology

At the time of this writing, available spreadsheets did not have a built-in logistic regression calculation, so we use an alternative method that works for any type of regression curve. The Solver included with Windows versions of Excel and some Mac versions can find logistic regression curves while the Solver included with some other spreadsheets is not yet capable of this, so the instructions here are specific to Excel.

[60] At the time of this writing, Google Docs has no trendline feature for its spreadsheet.

1. First use rough estimates for N, A, and b, and compute the sum-of-squares error (SSE; see Section 1.4) directly:

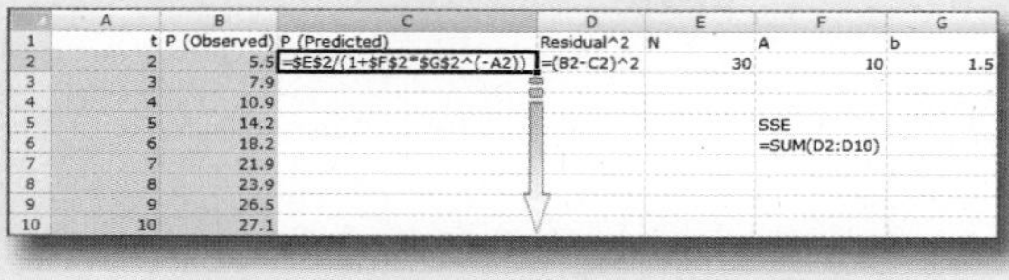

	A	B	C	D	E	F	G
1	t	P (Observed)	P (Predicted)	Residual^2	N	A	b
2	2	5.5	=$E$2/(1+$F$2*$G$2^(-A2))	=(B2-C2)^2	30	10	1.5
3	3	7.9					
4	4	10.9					
5	5	14.2				SSE	
6	6	18.2				=SUM(D2:D10)	
7	7	21.9					
8	8	23.9					
9	9	26.5					
10	10	27.1					

Cells E2:G2 contain our initial rough estimates of N, A, and b. For N, we used 30 (notice that the y-coordinates do appear to level off around 30). For A, we used the fact that the y-intercept is $N/(1+A)$ and the y-intercept appears to be approximately 3. In other words,

$$3 = \frac{30}{1+A}.$$

Because a very rough estimate is all we are after, using $A = 10$ will do just fine. For b, we chose 1.5 as the values of P appear to be increasing by around 50% per year initially (again, this is rough).

2. Cell C2 contains the formula for $P(t)$, and the square of the resulting residual is computed in D2.

3. Cell F6 will contain SSE. The completed spreadsheet should look like this:

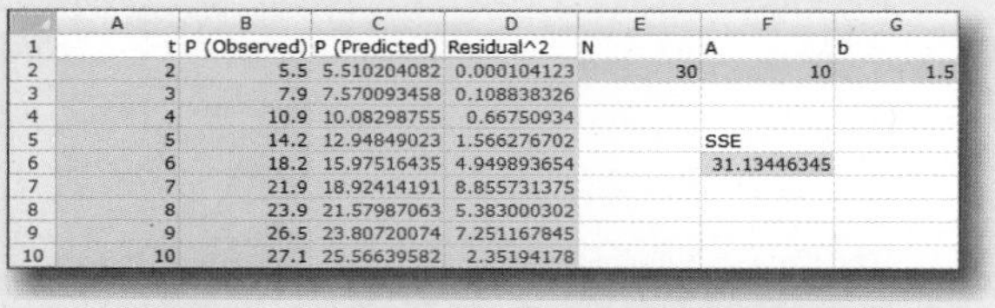

	A	B	C	D	E	F	G
1	t	P (Observed)	P (Predicted)	Residual^2	N	A	b
2	2	5.5	5.510204082	0.000104123	30	10	1.5
3	3	7.9	7.570093458	0.108838326			
4	4	10.9	10.08298755	0.66750934			
5	5	14.2	12.94849023	1.566276702		SSE	
6	6	18.2	15.97516435	4.949893654		31.13446345	
7	7	21.9	18.92414191	8.855731375			
8	8	23.9	21.57987063	5.383000302			
9	9	26.5	23.80720074	7.251167845			
10	10	27.1	25.56639582	2.35194178			

The best-fit curve will result from values of N, A, and b that give a minimum value for SSE. We shall use Excel's "Solver," found in the "Analysis" group on the "Data" tab. (If "Solver" does not appear in the Analysis group, you will have to install the Solver Add-in using the Excel Options dialogue.) The Solver dialogue box with the necessary fields completed to solve the problem looks like this:

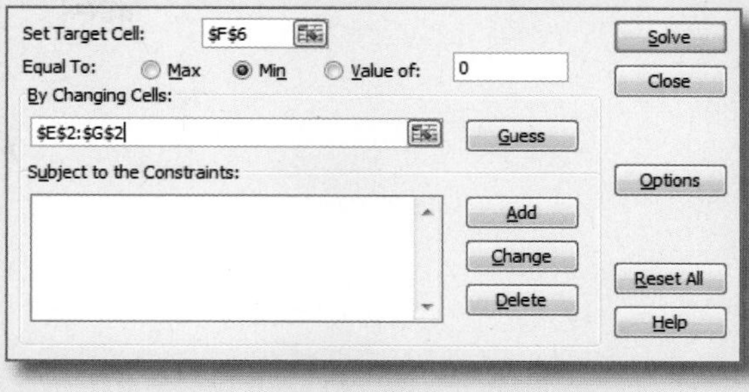

- The Target Cell refers to the cell that contains SSE.
- "Min" is selected because we are minimizing SSE.
- "Changing Cells" are obtained by selecting the cells that contain the current values of N, A, and b.

4. When you have filled in the values for the three items above, press "Solve" and tell Solver to Keep Solver Solution when done. You will find $N \approx 29.842$, $A \approx 12.501$, and $b \approx 1.642$ so that

$$P(t) \approx \frac{29.842}{1 + 12.501(1.642)^{-t}}.$$

If you use a scatter plot to graph the data in columns A, B and C, you will obtain the following graph:

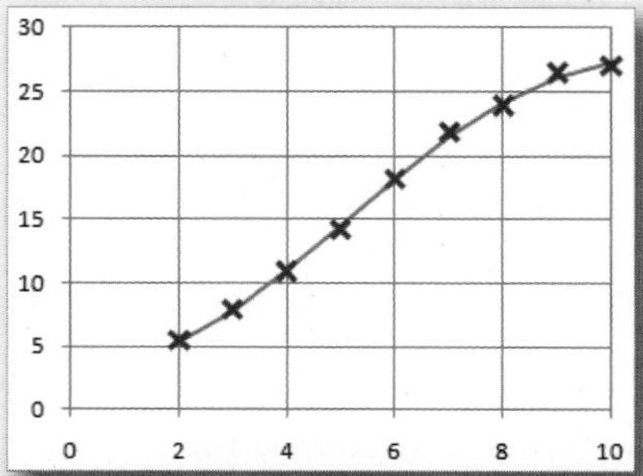

3

Introduction to the Derivative

Website
www.WanerMath.com
At the Website you will find:

- Section-by-section tutorials, including game tutorials with randomized quizzes
- A detailed chapter summary
- A true/false quiz
- Additional review exercises
- Graphers, Excel tutorials, and other resources
- The following extra topics:

  Sketching the graph of the derivative

  Continuity and differentiability

Case Study Reducing Sulfur Emissions

The Environmental Protection Agency (EPA) wants to formulate a policy that will encourage utilities to reduce sulfur emissions. Its goal is to reduce annual emissions of sulfur dioxide by a total of 10 million tons from the current level of 25 million tons by imposing a fixed charge for every ton of sulfur released into the environment per year. The EPA has some data showing the marginal cost to utilities of reducing sulfur emissions. As a consultant to the EPA, you must determine the amount to be charged per ton of sulfur emissions in light of these data.

Norbert Schaefer/CORBIS

Introduction

In the world around us, everything is changing. The mathematics of change is largely about the rate of change: how fast and in which direction the change is occurring. Is the Dow Jones average going up, and if so, how fast? If I raise my prices, how many customers will I lose? If I launch this missile, how fast will it be traveling after two seconds, how high will it go, and where will it come down?

We have already discussed the concept of rate of change for linear functions (straight lines), where the slope measures the rate of change. But this works only because a straight line maintains a constant rate of change along its whole length. Other functions rise faster here than there—or rise in one place and fall in another—so that the rate of change varies along the graph. The first achievement of calculus is to provide a systematic and straightforward way of calculating (hence the name) these rates of change. To describe a changing world, we need a language of change, and that is what calculus is.

The history of calculus is an interesting story of personalities, intellectual movements, and controversy. Credit for its invention is given to two mathematicians: Isaac Newton (1642–1727) and Gottfried Leibniz (1646–1716). Newton, an English mathematician and scientist, developed calculus first, probably in the 1660s. We say "probably" because, for various reasons, he did not publish his ideas until much later. This allowed Leibniz, a German mathematician and philosopher, to publish his own version of calculus first, in 1684. Fifteen years later, stirred up by nationalist fervor in England and on the continent, controversy erupted over who should get the credit for the invention of calculus. The debate got so heated that the Royal Society (of which Newton and Leibniz were both members) set up a commission to investigate the question. The commission decided in favor of Newton, who happened to be president of the society at the time. The consensus today is that both mathematicians deserve credit because they came to the same conclusions working independently. This is not really surprising: Both built on well-known work of other people, and it was almost inevitable that someone would put it all together at about that time.

algebra Review
For this chapter, you should be familiar with the algebra reviewed in **Chapter 0, Section 2.**

3.1 Limits: Numerical and Graphical Viewpoints

Rates of change are calculated by derivatives, but an important part of the definition of the derivative is something called a **limit**. Arguably, much of mathematics since the eighteenth century has revolved around understanding, refining, and exploiting the idea of the limit. The basic idea is easy, but getting the technicalities right is not.

Evaluating Limits Numerically

Start with a very simple example: Look at the function $f(x) = 2 + x$ and ask: What happens to $f(x)$ as x approaches 3? The following table shows the value of $f(x)$ for values of x close to and on either side of 3:

	x approaching 3 from the left →					← *x* approaching 3 from the right			
x	2.9	2.99	2.999	2.9999	3	3.0001	3.001	3.01	3.1
$f(x) = 2 + x$	4.9	4.99	4.999	4.9999		5.0001	5.001	5.01	5.1

We have left the entry under 3 blank to emphasize that when calculating the limit of $f(x)$ as x *approaches* 3, we are not interested in its value when x *equals* 3.

Notice from the table that the closer x gets to 3 from either side, the closer $f(x)$ gets to 5. We write this as

$$\lim_{x \to 3} f(x) = 5. \qquad \text{The limit of } f(x) \text{, as } x \text{ approaches 3, equals 5.}$$

Q: *Why all the fuss? Can't we simply substitute $x = 3$ and avoid having to use a table?*

A: This happens to work for *some* functions, but not for *all* functions. The following example illustrates this point.

EXAMPLE 1 Estimating a Limit Numerically

Use a table to estimate the following limits:

a. $\lim_{x \to 2} \dfrac{x^3 - 8}{x - 2}$ **b.** $\lim_{x \to 0} \dfrac{e^{2x} - 1}{x}$

Solution

a. We cannot simply substitute $x = 2$, because the function $f(x) = \dfrac{x^3 - 8}{x - 2}$ is not defined at $x = 2$. (Why?)* Instead, we use a table of values as we did above, with x approaching 2 from both sides.

x approaching 2 from the left → ← x approaching 2 from the right

x	1.9	1.99	1.999	1.9999	2	2.0001	2.001	2.01	2.1
$f(x) = \dfrac{x^3 - 8}{x - 2}$	11.41	11.9401	11.9940	11.9994		12.0006	12.0060	12.0601	12.61

We notice that as x approaches 2 from either side, $f(x)$ appears to be approaching 12. This suggests that the limit is 12, and we write

$$\lim_{x \to 2} \frac{x^3 - 8}{x - 2} = 12.$$

b. The function $g(x) = \dfrac{e^{2x} - 1}{x}$ is not defined at $x = 0$ (nor can it even be simplified to one which *is* defined at $x = 0$). In the following table, we allow x to approach 0 from both sides:

x approaching 0 from the left → ← x approaching 0 from the right

x	−0.1	−0.01	−0.001	−0.0001	0	0.0001	0.001	0.01	0.1
$g(x) = \dfrac{e^{2x} - 1}{x}$	1.8127	1.9801	1.9980	1.9998		2.0002	2.0020	2.0201	2.2140

The table suggests that $\lim_{x \to 0} \dfrac{e^{2x} - 1}{x} = 2$.

* However, if you factor $x^3 - 8$, you will find that $f(x)$ can be simplified to a function that *is* defined at $x = 2$. This point will be discussed (and this example redone) in Section 3.3. The function in part (b) cannot be simplified by factoring.

using Technology

To automate the computations in Example 1 using a graphing calculator or a spreadsheet, see the Technology Guides at the end of the chapter. Outline for part (a):

TI-83/84 Plus

Home screen: `Y1=(X^3-8)/(X-2)`

`2ND` `TBLSET` `Indpnt` set to `Ask`

`2ND` `TABLE` Enter some values of x from the example: 1.9, 1.99, 1.999 . . .

[More details on page 284.]

Spreadsheet
Headings x, $f(x)$ in A1–B1 and again in C1–D1.
In A2–A5 enter 1.9, 1.99, 1.999, 1.9999.
In C1–C5 enter 2.1, 2.01, 2.001, 2.0001. Enter
`=(A2^3-8)/(A2-2)`
in B2 and copy down to B5.
Copy and paste the same formula in D2–D5.
[More details on page 286.]

Website
www.WanerMath.com
In the Function Evaluator and Grapher, enter `(x^3-8)/(x-2)` for y_1. For a table of values, enter the various x-values in the Evaluator box, and press "Evaluate".

Before we go on... Although the table *suggests* that the limit in Example 1 part (b) is 2, it by no means establishes that fact conclusively. It is *conceivable* (though not in fact the case here) that putting $x = 0.000000087$ could result in, say, $g(x) = 426$. Using a table can only *suggest* a value for the limit. In the next two sections we shall discuss algebraic techniques to allow us to actually *calculate* limits. ■

Before we continue, let us make a more formal definition.

Definition of a Limit

If $f(x)$ approaches the number L as x approaches (but is not equal to) a from both sides, then we say that $f(x)$ **approaches L as $x \to a$** ("x approaches a") or that the **limit** of $f(x)$ as $x \to a$ is L. More precisely, *we can make $f(x)$ be as close to L as we like by choosing any x sufficiently close to (but not equal to) a on either side*. We write

$$\lim_{x \to a} f(x) = L$$

or

$$f(x) \to L \text{ as } x \to a.$$

If $f(x)$ *fails* to approach *a single fixed number* as x approaches a from both sides, then we say that $f(x)$ **has no limit** as $x \to a$, or

$$\lim_{x \to a} f(x) \textbf{ does not exist.}$$

Quick Examples

1. $\lim_{x \to 3}(2 + x) = 5$ — See discussion before Example 1.
2. $\lim_{x \to -2}(3x) = -6$ — As x approaches -2, $3x$ approaches -6.
3. $\lim_{x \to 0}(x^2 - 2x + 1)$ exists. — In fact, the limit is 1.
4. $\lim_{x \to 5} \frac{1}{x} = \frac{1}{5}$ — As x approaches 5, $\frac{1}{x}$ approaches $\frac{1}{5}$.
5. $\lim_{x \to 2} \frac{x^3 - 8}{x - 2} = 12$ — See Example 1. (We cannot just put $x = 2$ here.)

(For examples where the limit does not exist, see Example 2.)

Notes

1. It is important that $f(x)$ approach the same number as x approaches a from *both sides*. For instance, if $f(x)$ approaches 5 for $x = 1.9, 1.99, 1.999, \ldots$, but approaches 4 for $x = 2.1, 2.01, 2.001, \ldots$, then the limit as $x \to 2$ does not exist. (See Example 2 for such a situation.)
2. It may happen that $f(x)$ does not approach any fixed number at all as $x \to a$ from either side. In this case, we also say that the limit does not exist.
3. If a happens to be an endpoint of the domain of f, then the function is only defined on one side of a, and so the limit as $x \to a$ does not exist. For example, the natural domain of $f(x) = \sqrt{x}$ is $[0, +\infty)$, so the limit of $f(x)$ as $x \to 0$ does not exist. The appropriate kind of limit to consider in such a case is a **one-sided limit** (see Example 2). ■

The next example gives instances in which a stated limit does not exist.

EXAMPLE 2 Limits Do Not Always Exist

Do the following limits exist?

a. $\lim_{x \to 0} \frac{1}{x^2}$ **b.** $\lim_{x \to 0} \frac{|x|}{x}$ **c.** $\lim_{x \to 2} \frac{1}{x-2}$ **d.** $\lim_{x \to 1} \sqrt{x-1}$

Solution

a. Here is a table of values for $f(x) = \frac{1}{x^2}$, with x approaching 0 from both sides.

x approaching 0 from the left → ← x approaching 0 from the right

x	−0.1	−0.01	−0.001	−0.0001	0	0.0001	0.001	0.01	0.1
$f(x) = \frac{1}{x^2}$	100	10,000	1,000,000	100,000,000		100,000,000	1,000,000	10,000	100

The table shows that as x gets closer to zero on either side, $f(x)$ gets larger and larger **without bound**—that is, if you name any number, no matter how large, $f(x)$ will be even larger than that if x is sufficiently close to 0. Because $f(x)$ is not approaching any real number, we conclude that $\lim_{x \to 0} \frac{1}{x^2}$ does not exist. Because $f(x)$ is becoming arbitrarily large, we also say that $\lim_{x \to 0} \frac{1}{x^2}$ **diverges to** $+\infty$, or just

$$\lim_{x \to 0} \frac{1}{x^2} = +\infty.$$

Note This is not meant to imply that the limit exists; the symbol $+\infty$ does not represent any real number. We write $\lim_{x \to a} f(x) = +\infty$ to indicate two things: (1) The limit does not exist and (2) the function gets large without bound as x approaches a. ■

b. Here is a table of values for $f(x) = \frac{|x|}{x}$, with x approaching 0 from both sides.

x approaching 0 from the left → ← x approaching 0 from the right

x	−0.1	−0.01	−0.001	−0.0001	0	0.0001	0.001	0.01	0.1
$f(x) = \frac{\lvert x \rvert}{x}$	−1	−1	−1	−1		1	1	1	1

The table shows that $f(x)$ does not approach the same limit as x approaches 0 from both sides. There appear to be two *different* limits: the limit as we approach 0 from the left and the limit as we approach from the right. We write

$$\lim_{x \to 0^-} f(x) = -1$$

read as "the limit as x approaches 0 from the left (or from below) is −1" and

$$\lim_{x \to 0^+} f(x) = 1$$

read as "the limit as x approaches 0 from the right (or from above) is 1." These are called the **one-sided limits** of $f(x)$. In order for f to have a **two-sided limit**, the two one-sided limits must be equal. Because they are not, we conclude that $\lim_{x \to 0} f(x)$ does not exist.

c. Near $x = 2$, we have the following table of values for $f(x) = \dfrac{1}{x-2}$:

	x approaching 2 from the left →					← x approaching 2 from the right			
x	1.9	1.99	1.999	1.9999	2	2.0001	2.001	2.01	2.1
$f(x) = \dfrac{1}{x-2}$	−10	−100	−1,000	−10,000		10,000	1,000	100	10

Because $f(x)$ is approaching no (single) real number as $x \to 2$, we see that $\lim_{x\to 2} \dfrac{1}{x-2}$ does not exist. Notice also that $\dfrac{1}{x-2}$ diverges to $+\infty$ as $x \to 2$ from the positive side (right half of the table) and to $-\infty$ as $x \to 2$ from the left (left half of the table). In other words,

$$\lim_{x\to 2^-} \frac{1}{x-2} = -\infty$$

$$\lim_{x\to 2^+} \frac{1}{x-2} = +\infty$$

$$\lim_{x\to 2} \frac{1}{x-2} \text{ does not exist.}$$

d. The natural domain of $f(x) = \sqrt{x-1}$ is $[1, +\infty)$, as $f(x)$ is defined only when $x \geq 1$. Thus we cannot evaluate $f(x)$ if x is to the left of 1. This means that

$$\lim_{x\to 1^-} \sqrt{x-1} \text{ does not exist,}$$

and our table looks like this:

		← x approaching 1 from the right				
x	1	1.00001	1.0001	1.001	1.01	1.1
$f(x) = \sqrt{x-1}$		0.0032	0.0100	0.0316	0.1000	0.3162

The values suggest that

$$\lim_{x\to 1^+} \sqrt{x-1} = 0.$$

In fact, we can obtain this limit by substituting $x = 1$ in the formula for $f(x)$ (see the comments after the example).

Q: *In Example 2(d) (and also in some of the Quick Examples before that) we could find a limit of an algebraically specified function by simply substituting the value of x in the formula for f(x). Does this always work?*

A: Short answer: Yes, when it makes sense. If the function is specified by a *single* algebraic formula and if $x = a$ is in the domain of f, then the limit can be obtained by substituting. We will say more about this when we discuss the algebraic approach to limits in Section 3.3. Remember, however, that, by definition, the limit of a function as $x \to a$ has nothing to do with its value at $x = a$, but rather its values for x *close to* a.

Q: *If f(x) is undefined when x = a, then the limit does not exist, right?*

A: Wrong. If $f(a)$ is not defined, then the limit may or may not exist. Example 1 shows instances where the limit *does* exist, and Example 2 shows instances where it does not. Again, the limit of a function as $x \to a$ has nothing to do with its value at $x = a$, but rather its values for x *close to a*.

In another useful kind of limit, we let x approach either $+\infty$ or $-\infty$, by which we mean that we let x get arbitrarily large or let x become an arbitrarily large negative number. The next example illustrates this.

EXAMPLE 3 Limits at Infinity

Use a table to estimate: **a.** $\lim_{x\to+\infty} \dfrac{2x^2-4x}{x^2-1}$ and **b.** $\lim_{x\to-\infty} \dfrac{2x^2-4x}{x^2-1}$.

Solution

a. By saying that x is "approaching $+\infty$," we mean that x is getting larger and larger without bound, so we make the following table:

x approaching $+\infty$ →

x	10	100	1,000	10,000	100,000
$f(x) = \dfrac{2x^2-4x}{x^2-1}$	1.6162	1.9602	1.9960	1.9996	2.0000

(Note that we are only approaching $+\infty$ from the left because we can hardly approach it from the right!) What seems to be happening is that $f(x)$ is approaching 2. Thus we write

$$\lim_{x\to+\infty} f(x) = 2.$$

b. Here, x is approaching $-\infty$, so we make a similar table, this time with x assuming negative values of greater and greater magnitude (read this table from right to left):

← x approaching $-\infty$

x	−100,000	−10,000	−1,000	−100	−10
$f(x) = \dfrac{2x^2-4x}{x^2-1}$	2.0000	2.0004	2.0040	2.0402	2.4242

Once again, $f(x)$ is approaching 2. Thus, $\lim_{x\to-\infty} f(x) = 2$.

Cars don't "crash" limit doesn't exist

Estimating Limits Graphically

We can often estimate a limit from a graph, as the next example shows.

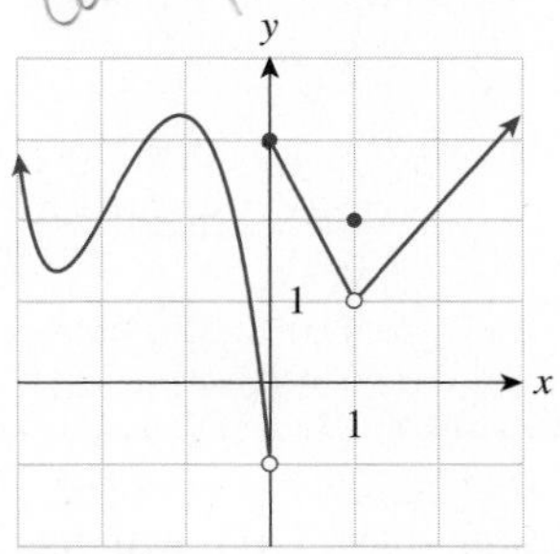

Figure 1

EXAMPLE 4 Estimating Limits Graphically

The graph of a function f is shown in Figure 1. (Recall that the solid dots indicate points on the graph, and the hollow dots indicate points not on the graph.) From the graph, analyze the following limits.

a. $\lim_{x\to-2} f(x)$ **b.** $\lim_{x\to0} f(x)$ **c.** $\lim_{x\to1} f(x)$ **d.** $\lim_{x\to+\infty} f(x)$

Solution Since we are given only a graph of f, we must analyze these limits graphically.

a. Imagine that Figure 1 was drawn on a graphing calculator equipped with a trace feature that allows us to move a cursor along the graph and see the coordinates as we go. To simulate this, place a pencil point on the graph to the left of $x = -2$, and move it along the curve so that the x-coordinate approaches -2. (See Figure 2.) We evaluate the limit numerically by noting the behavior of the y-coordinates.*

However, we can see directly from the graph that the y-coordinate approaches 2. Similarly, if we place our pencil point to the right of $x = -2$ and move it to the left, the y coordinate will approach 2 from that side as well (Figure 3). Therefore, as x approaches -2 from either side, $f(x)$ approaches 2, so

$$\lim_{x \to -2} f(x) = 2.$$

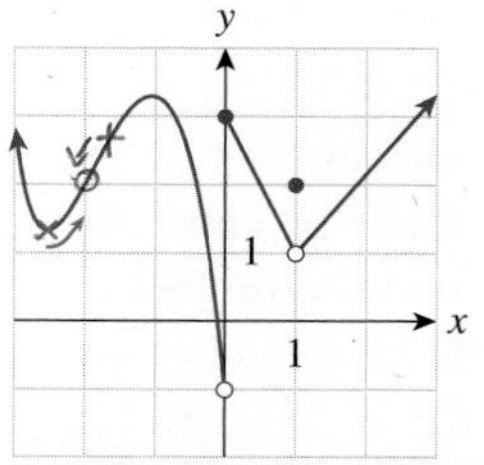

Figure 2

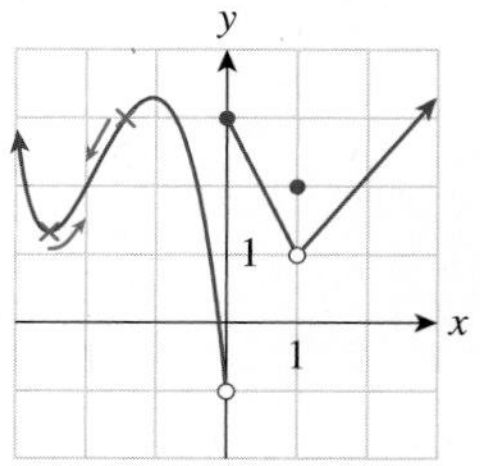

Figure 3

b. This time we move our pencil point toward $x = 0$. Referring to Figure 4, if we start from the left of $x = 0$ and approach 0 (by moving right), the y-coordinate approaches -1. However, if we start from the right of $x = 0$ and approach 0 (by moving left), the y-coordinate approaches 3. Thus (see Example 2),

$$\lim_{x \to 0^-} f(x) = -1$$

and

$$\lim_{x \to 0^+} f(x) = 3.$$

Because these limits are not equal, we conclude that

$$\lim_{x \to 0} f(x) \text{ does not exist.}$$

In this case there is a "break" in the graph at $x = 0$, and we say that the function is **discontinuous** at $x = 0$ (see Section 3.2).

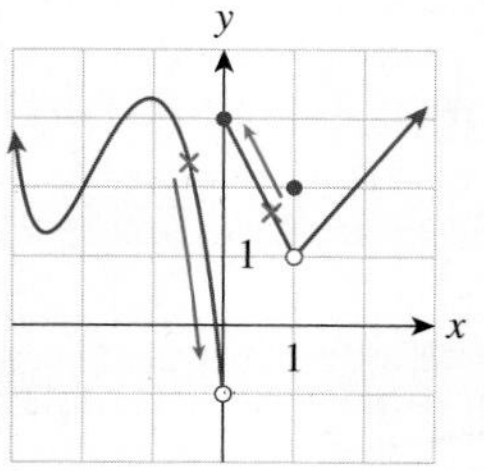

Figure 4

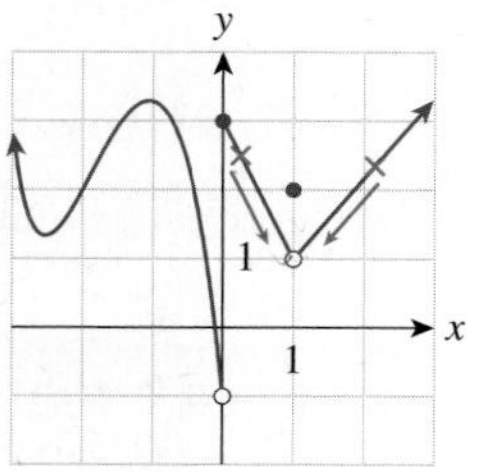

Figure 5

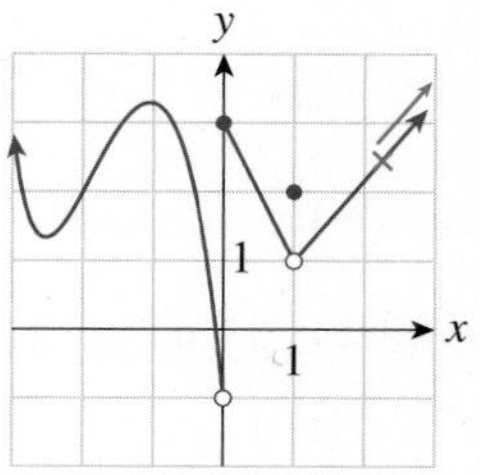

Figure 6

c. Once more we think about a pencil point moving along the graph with the x-coordinate this time approaching $x = 1$ from the left and from the right (Figure 5).

* For a visual animation of this process, look at the online tutorial for this section at the Website.

As the x-coordinate of the point approaches 1 from either side, the y-coordinate approaches 1 also. Therefore,

$$\lim_{x \to 1} f(x) = 1.$$

d. For this limit, x is supposed to approach infinity. We think about a pencil point moving along the graph further and further to the right as shown in Figure 6.

As the x-coordinate gets larger, the y-coordinate also gets larger and larger without bound. Thus, $f(x)$ diverges to $+\infty$:

$$\lim_{x \to +\infty} f(x) = +\infty.$$

Similarly,

$$\lim_{x \to -\infty} f(x) = +\infty.$$

Before we go on... In Example 4(c) $\lim_{x \to 1} f(x) = 1$ but $f(1) = 2$ (why?). Thus, $\lim_{x \to 1} f(x) \neq f(1)$. In other words, the limit of $f(x)$ as x *approaches* 1 is not the same as the value of f *at* $x = 1$. Always keep in mind that when we evaluate a limit as $x \to a$, *we do not care about the value of the function at* $x = a$. We only care about the value of $f(x)$ as x *approaches* a. In other words, $f(a)$ may or may not equal $\lim_{x \to a} f(x)$. ■

Here is a summary of the graphical method we used in Example 4, together with some additional information:

Evaluating Limits Graphically

To decide whether $\lim_{x \to a} f(x)$ exists and to find its value if it does:

1. Draw the graph of $f(x)$ by hand or with graphing technology.
2. Position your pencil point (or the Trace cursor) on a point of the graph to the right of $x = a$.
3. Move the point *along the graph* toward $x = a$ from the right and read the y-coordinate as you go. The value the y-coordinate approaches (if any) is the limit $\lim_{x \to a^+} f(x)$.
4. Repeat Steps 2 and 3, this time starting from a point on the graph to the left of $x = a$, and approaching $x = a$ along the graph from the left. The value the y-coordinate approaches (if any) is $\lim_{x \to a^-} f(x)$.
5. If the left and right limits both exist and have the same value L, then $\lim_{x \to a} f(x) = L$. Otherwise, the limit does not exist. The value $f(a)$ has no relevance whatsoever.
6. To evaluate $\lim_{x \to +\infty} f(x)$, move the pencil point toward the far right of the graph and estimate the value the y-coordinate approaches (if any). For $\lim_{x \to -\infty} f(x)$, move the pencil point toward the far left.
7. If $x = a$ happens to be an endpoint of the domain of f, then only a one-sided limit is possible at $x = a$. For instance, if the domain is $(-\infty, 4]$, then $\lim_{x \to 4^-} f(x)$ may exist, but neither $\lim_{x \to 4^+} f(x)$ nor $\lim_{x \to 4} f(x)$ exists.

In the next example we use both the numerical and graphical approaches.

EXAMPLE 5 Infinite Limit

Does $\lim_{x \to 0^+} \frac{1}{x}$ exist?

Solution

Numerical Method Because we are asked for only the right-hand limit, we need only list values of x approaching 0 from the right.

← x approaching 0 from the right

x	0	0.0001	0.001	0.01	0.1
$f(x) = \frac{1}{x}$		10,000	1,000	100	10

What seems to be happening as x approaches 0 from the right is that $f(x)$ is increasing without bound, as in Example 4(d). That is, if you name any number, no matter how large, $f(x)$ will be even larger than that if x is sufficiently close to zero. Thus, the limit diverges to $+\infty$, so

$$\lim_{x \to 0^+} \frac{1}{x} = +\infty$$

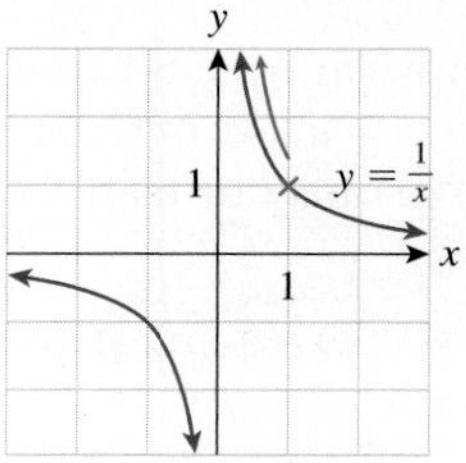

Figure 7

Graphical Method Recall that the graph of $f(x) = \frac{1}{x}$ is the standard hyperbola shown in Figure 7. The figure also shows the pencil point moving so that its x-coordinate approaches 0 from the right. Because the point moves along the graph, it is forced to go higher and higher. In other words, its y-coordinate becomes larger and larger, approaching $+\infty$. Thus, we conclude that

$$\lim_{x \to 0^+} \frac{1}{x} = +\infty.$$

Before we go on... In Example 5 you should check that

$$\lim_{x \to 0^-} \frac{1}{x} = -\infty.$$

$\frac{1}{x}$ diverges to $-\infty$ as $x \to 0^-$.

Also, check that

$$\lim_{x \to +\infty} \frac{1}{x} = \lim_{x \to -\infty} \frac{1}{x} = 0. \blacksquare$$

APPLICATION

EXAMPLE 6 Broadband Penetration

Wired broadband penetration in the United States can be modeled by

$$P(t) = \frac{29.842}{1 + 12.502(1.642)^{-t}} \quad (t \geq 0),$$

where t is time in years since 2000.[1]

[1]See Example 2 in Section 2.4. Broadband penetration is the number of broadband installations divided by the total population. Source for data: Organization for Economic Cooperation and Development (OECD) Directorate for Science, Technology, and Industry, table of Historical Penetration Rates, June 2010, downloaded April 2011 from www.oecd.org/sti /ict/broadband.

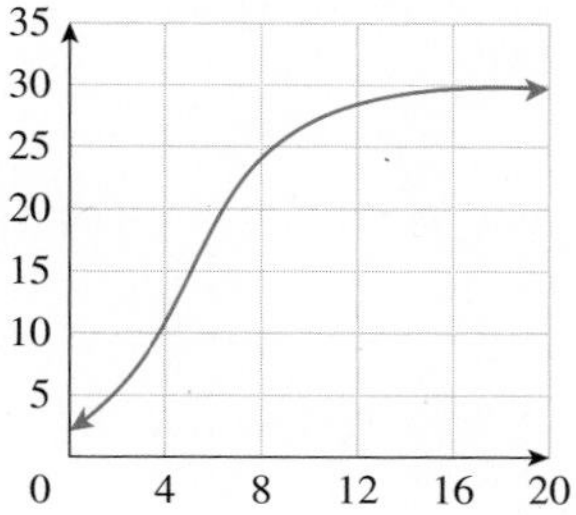

Figure 8

a. Estimate $\lim_{t \to +\infty} P(t)$ and interpret the answer.

b. Estimate $\lim_{t \to 0^+} P(t)$ and interpret the answer.

Solution

a. Figure 8 shows a plot of $P(t)$ for $0 \le t \le 20$. Using either the numerical or the graphical approach, we find

$$\lim_{t \to +\infty} P(t) = \lim_{t \to +\infty} \frac{29.842}{1 + 12.502(1.642)^{-t}} \approx 30.$$

(The actual limit is 29.842. Why?) Thus, in the long term (as t gets larger and larger), broadband penetration in the United States is expected to approach 30%; that is, the number of installations is expected to approach 30% of the total population.

b. The limit here is

$$\lim_{t \to 0^+} P(t) = \lim_{t \to 0^+} \frac{29.842}{1 + 12.502(1.642)^{-t}} \approx 2.21.$$

(Notice that in this case, we can simply put $t = 0$ to evaluate this limit.) Thus, the closer t gets to 0 (representing 2000) from the right, the closer $P(t)$ gets to 2.21%, meaning that, in 2000, broadband penetration was about 2.2% of the population.

FAQs

Determining when a Limit Does or Does Not Exist

Q: *If I substitute $x = a$ in the formula for a function and find that the function is defined there, it means that $\lim_{x \to a} f(x)$ exists and equals $f(a)$, right?*

A: Correct, provided the function is specified by *a single algebraic formula* and is not, say, piecewise-defined. We shall say more about this in the next two sections.

Q: *If I substitute $x = a$ in the formula for a function and find that the function is* not *defined there, it means that $\lim_{x \to a} f(x)$ does not exist, right?*

A: Wrong. The limit may still exist, as in Example 1, or may not exist, as in Example 2. In general, whether or not $\lim_{x \to a} f(x)$ exists has nothing to do with $f(a)$, but rather the values of f when x is *very close to, but not equal to a*.

Q: *Is there a quick and easy way of telling from a graph whether $\lim_{x \to a} f(x)$ exists?*

A: Yes. If you cover up the portion of the graph corresponding to $x = a$ and it appears as though the visible part of the graph could be made into a continuous curve by filling in a suitable point at $x = a$, then the limit exists. (The "suitable point" need not be $(a, f(a))$.) Otherwise, it does not. Try this method with the curves in Example 4.

3.1 EXERCISES

▼ more advanced ◆ challenging

T indicates exercises that should be solved using technology

Estimate the limits in Exercises 1–20 numerically. HINT [See Examples 1–3.]

1. $\lim_{x\to 0} \frac{x^2}{x+1}$

2. $\lim_{x\to 0} \frac{x-3}{x-1}$

3. $\lim_{x\to 2} \frac{x^2-4}{x-2}$

4. $\lim_{x\to 2} \frac{x^2-1}{x-2}$

5. $\lim_{x\to -1} \frac{x^2+1}{x+1}$

6. $\lim_{x\to -1} \frac{x^2+2x+1}{x+1}$

7. $\lim_{x\to +\infty} \frac{3x^2+10x-1}{2x^2-5x}$

8. $\lim_{x\to +\infty} \frac{6x^2+5x+100}{3x^2-9}$

9. $\lim_{x\to -\infty} \frac{x^5-1{,}000x^4}{2x^5+10{,}000}$

10. $\lim_{x\to -\infty} \frac{x^6+3{,}000x^3+1{,}000{,}000}{2x^6+1{,}000x^3}$

11. $\lim_{x\to +\infty} \frac{10x^2+300x+1}{5x+2}$

12. $\lim_{x\to +\infty} \frac{2x^4+20x^3}{1{,}000x^6+6}$

13. $\lim_{x\to +\infty} \frac{10x^2+300x+1}{5x^3+2}$

14. $\lim_{x\to +\infty} \frac{2x^4+20x^3}{1{,}000x^3+6}$

15. $\lim_{x\to 2} e^{x-2}$

16. $\lim_{x\to +\infty} e^{-x}$

17. $\lim_{x\to +\infty} xe^{-x}$

18. $\lim_{x\to -\infty} xe^{x}$

19. $\lim_{x\to -\infty} (x^{10}+2x^5+1)e^{x}$

20. $\lim_{x\to +\infty} (x^{50}+x^{30}+1)e^{-x}$

In each of Exercises 21–34, the graph of f is given. Use the graph to compute the quantities asked for. HINT [See Examples 4–5.]

21. a. $\lim_{x\to 1} f(x)$ **b.** $\lim_{x\to -1} f(x)$

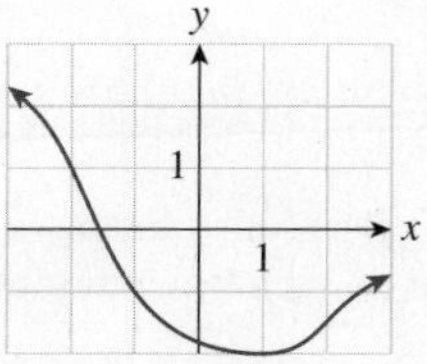

22. a. $\lim_{x\to -1} f(x)$ **b.** $\lim_{x\to 1} f(x)$

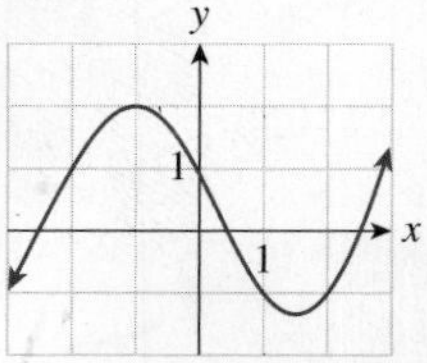

23. a. $\lim_{x\to 0} f(x)$ **b.** $\lim_{x\to 2} f(x)$ **c.** $\lim_{x\to -\infty} f(x)$ **d.** $\lim_{x\to +\infty} f(x)$

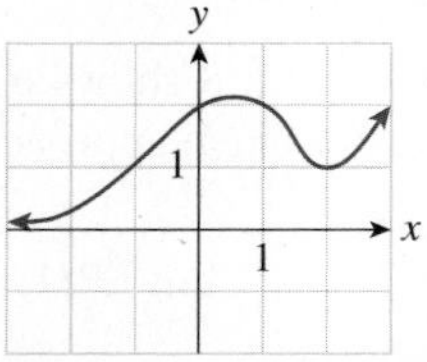

24. a. $\lim_{x\to -1} f(x)$ **b.** $\lim_{x\to 1} f(x)$ **c.** $\lim_{x\to +\infty} f(x)$ **d.** $\lim_{x\to -\infty} f(x)$

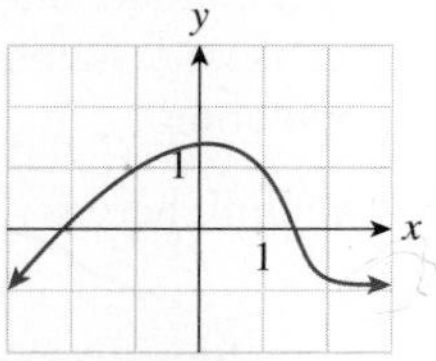

25. a. $\lim_{x\to 2} f(x)$ **b.** $\lim_{x\to 0^+} f(x)$ **c.** $\lim_{x\to 0^-} f(x)$

d. $\lim_{x\to 0} f(x)$ **e.** $f(0)$ **f.** $\lim_{x\to -\infty} f(x)$

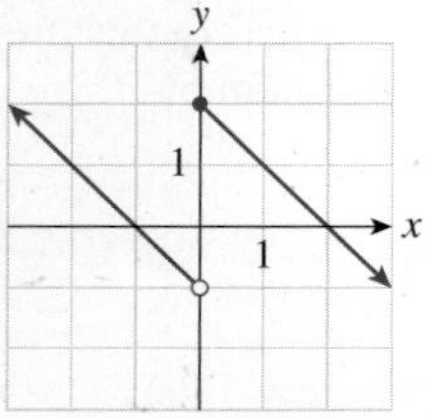

26. a. $\lim_{x\to 3} f(x)$ **b.** $\lim_{x\to 1^+} f(x)$ **c.** $\lim_{x\to 1^-} f(x)$

d. $\lim_{x\to 1} f(x)$ **e.** $f(1)$ **f.** $\lim_{x\to +\infty} f(x)$

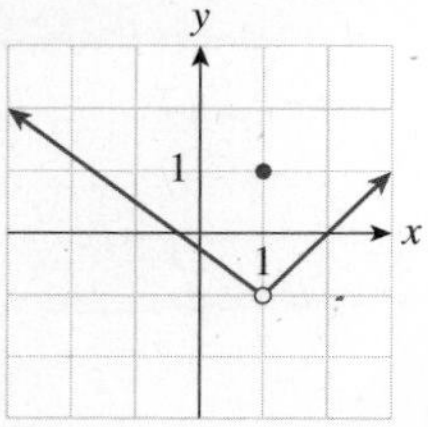

27. a. $\lim_{x\to -2} f(x)$ **b.** $\lim_{x\to -1^+} f(x)$ **c.** $\lim_{x\to -1^-} f(x)$

d. $\lim_{x\to -1} f(x)$ **e.** $f(-1)$ **f.** $\lim_{x\to +\infty} f(x)$

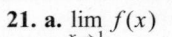

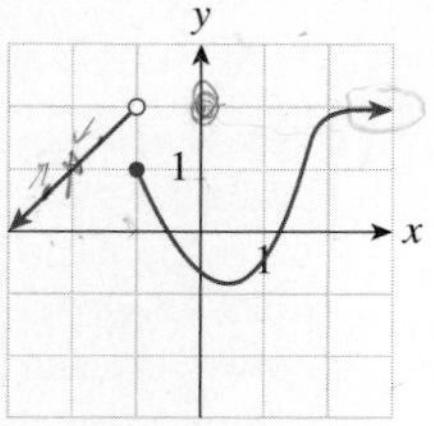

28. **a.** $\lim_{x\to -1} f(x)$ **b.** $\lim_{x\to 0^+} f(x)$ **c.** $\lim_{x\to 0^-} f(x)$
d. $\lim_{x\to 0} f(x)$ **e.** $f(0)$ **f.** $\lim_{x\to -\infty} f(x)$

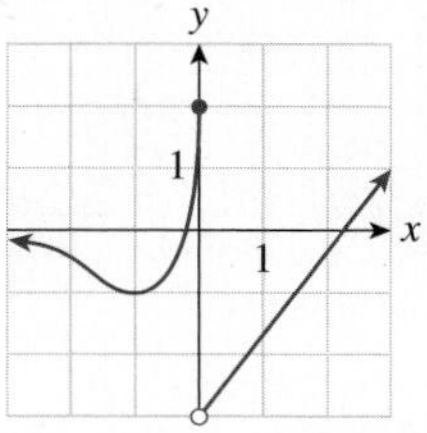

29. **a.** $\lim_{x\to -1^+} f(x)$ **b.** $\lim_{x\to -1^-} f(x)$ **c.** $\lim_{x\to -1} f(x)$ **d.** $f(-1)$

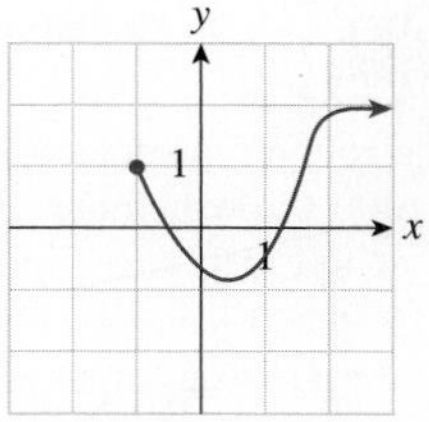

30. **a.** $\lim_{x\to 0^+} f(x)$ **b.** $\lim_{x\to 0^-} f(x)$ **c.** $\lim_{x\to 0} f(x)$ **d.** $f(0)$

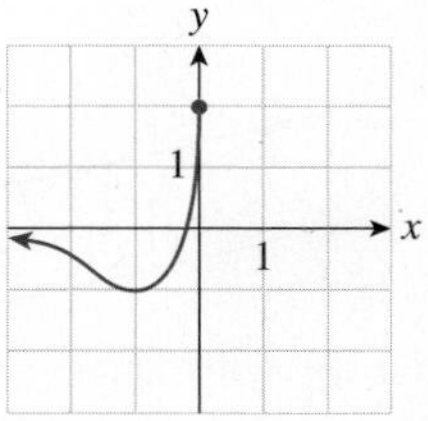

31. **a.** $\lim_{x\to -1} f(x)$ **b.** $\lim_{x\to 0^+} f(x)$ **c.** $\lim_{x\to 0^-} f(x)$
d. $\lim_{x\to 0} f(x)$ **e.** $f(0)$ **f.** $\lim_{x\to +\infty} f(x)$

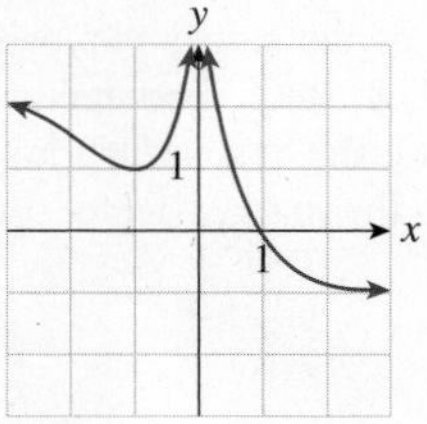

32. **a.** $\lim_{x\to 1} f(x)$ **b.** $\lim_{x\to 0^+} f(x)$ **c.** $\lim_{x\to 0^-} f(x)$
d. $\lim_{x\to 0} f(x)$ **e.** $f(0)$ **f.** $\lim_{x\to -\infty} f(x)$

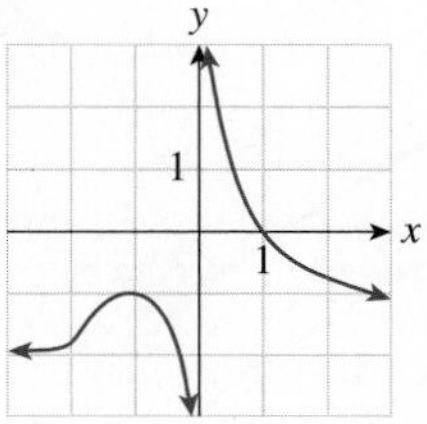

33. **a.** $\lim_{x\to -1} f(x)$ **b.** $\lim_{x\to 0^+} f(x)$ **c.** $\lim_{x\to 0^-} f(x)$
d. $\lim_{x\to 0} f(x)$ **e.** $f(0)$ **f.** $f(-1)$

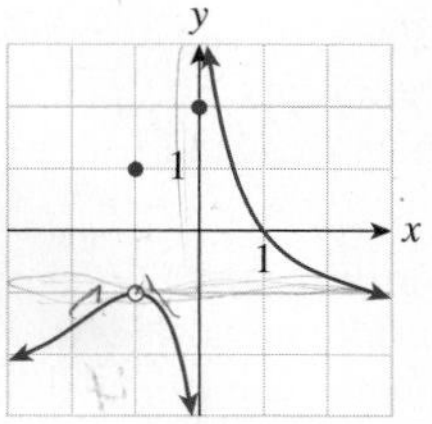

34. **a.** $\lim_{x\to 0^-} f(x)$ **b.** $\lim_{x\to 1^+} f(x)$ **c.** $\lim_{x\to 0} f(x)$
d. $\lim_{x\to 1} f(x)$ **e.** $f(0)$ **f.** $f(1)$

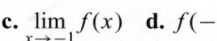

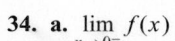

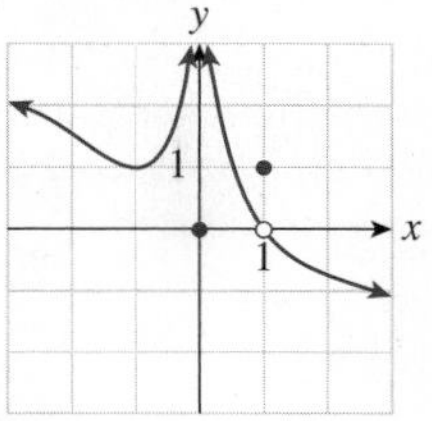

APPLICATIONS

35. ***Economic Growth*** The value of sold goods in Mexico can be approximated by

$$v(t) = 210 - 62e^{-0.05t} \text{ trillion pesos per month} \quad (t \geq 0),$$

where t is time in months since January 2005.[2] Numerically estimate $\lim_{t\to +\infty} v(t)$ and interpret the answer. HINT [See Example 6.]

36. ***Economic Growth*** The number of housing starts for single family homes in the U.S. can be approximated by

$$n(t) = 400 + 1{,}420e^{-0.48t} \text{ thousand housing starts per year} \quad (t \geq 0),$$

where t is time in years since January 2005.[3] Numerically estimate $\lim_{t\to +\infty} n(t)$ and interpret the answer.

37. ***Revenue*** The annual revenue of Amazon.com for the period 2006–2010 could be approximated by

$$P(t) = 870t^2 + 2{,}200t + 11{,}000 \text{ million dollars } (0 \leq t \leq 4),$$

where t is time in years since 2006.[4] If one extrapolates the function and numerically estimates $\lim_{t\to +\infty} P(t)$, what does the answer suggest about Amazon's revenue?

[2]Source: Instituto Nacional de Estadística y Geografía (INEGI), www.inegi.org.mx.

[3]Source for data: www.census.gov.

[4]Source for data: www.wikinvest.com.

38. ***Net Income*** The annual net income of General Electric for the period 2005–2010 could be approximated by

$$P(t) = -2.0t^2 + 6.6t + 16 \text{ billion dollars} \quad (0 \le t \le 5),$$

where t is time in years since 2005.[5] If one extrapolates the function and numerically estimates $\lim_{t\to+\infty} P(t)$, what does the answer suggest about General Electric's net income?

39. ***Scientific Research*** The number of research articles per year, in thousands, in the prominent journal *Physical Review* written by researchers in Europe can be modeled by

$$A(t) = \frac{7.0}{1 + 5.4(1.2)^{-t}},$$

where t is time in years ($t = 0$ represents 1983).[6] Numerically estimate $\lim_{t\to+\infty} A(t)$ and interpret the answer.

40. ***Scientific Research*** The percentage of research articles in the prominent journal *Physical Review* written by researchers in the United States can be modeled by

$$A(t) = 25 + \frac{36}{1 + 0.6(0.7)^{-t}},$$

where t is time in years ($t = 0$ represents 1983).[7] Numerically estimate $\lim_{t\to+\infty} A(t)$ and interpret the answer.

41. ***SAT Scores by Income*** The following bar graph shows U.S. math SAT scores as a function of household income:[8]

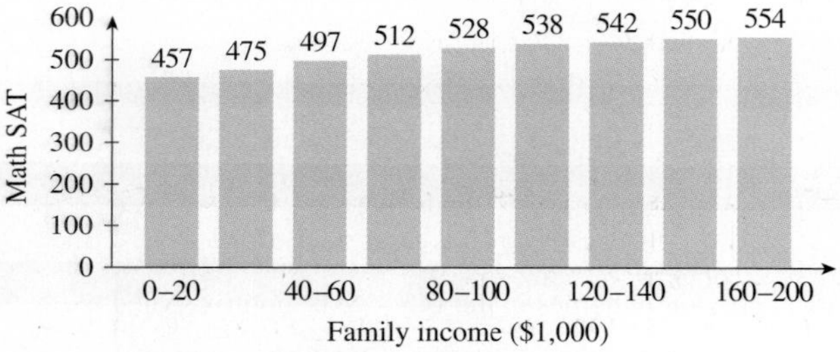

These data can be modeled by

$$S(x) = 573 - 133(0.987)^x,$$

where $S(x)$ is the average math SAT score of students whose household income is x thousand dollars per year. Numerically estimate $\lim_{x\to+\infty} S(x)$ and interpret the answer.

42. ***SAT Scores by Income*** The following bar graph shows U.S. critical reading SAT scores as a function of household income:[9]

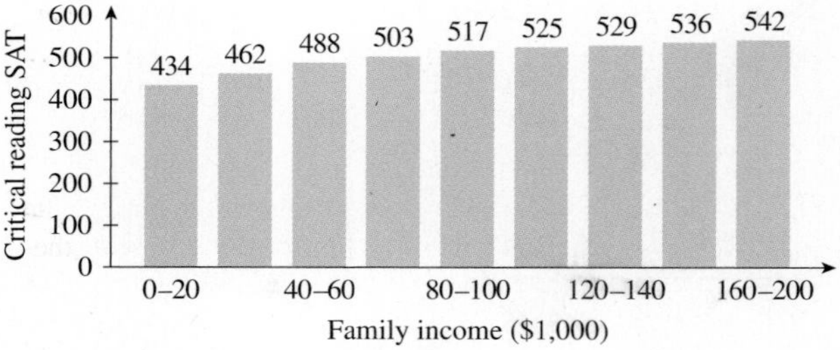

These data can be modeled by

$$S(x) = 550 - 136(0.985)^x,$$

where $S(x)$ is the average critical reading SAT score of students whose household income is x thousand dollars per year. Numerically estimate $\lim_{x\to+\infty} S(x)$ and interpret the answer.

43. ***Flash Crash*** The graph shows a rough representation of what happened to the Russel 1000 Growth Index Fund (IWF) stock price on the day of the U.S. stock market crash at 2:45 pm on May 6, 2010 (the "Flash Crash"; t is the time of the day in hours, and $r(t)$ is the price of the stock in dollars).[10]

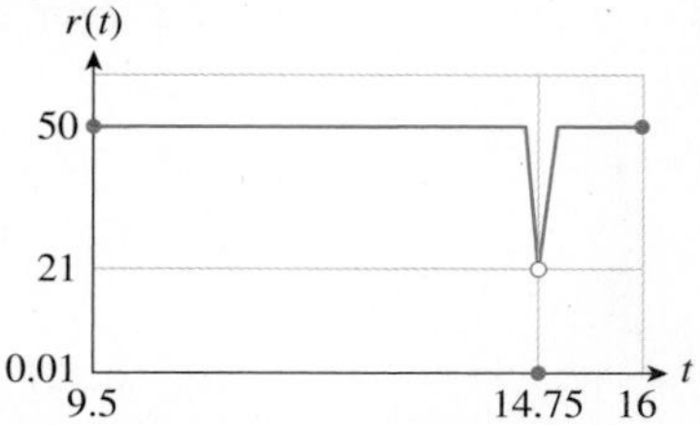

a. Compute the following (if a limit does not exist, say why):

$$\lim_{t\to14.75^-} r(t), \quad \lim_{t\to14.75^+} r(t), \quad \lim_{t\to14.75} r(t), \quad r(14.75).$$

b. What do the answers to part (a) tell you about the IWF stock price?

44. ***Flash Crash*** The graph shows a rough representation of the (aggregate) market depth[11] of the stocks comprising the S&P 500 on the day of the U.S. stock market crash at 2:45 pm on May 6, 2010 (the "Flash Crash"; t is the time of the day in hours, and $m(t)$ is the market depth in millions of shares).

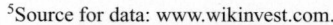

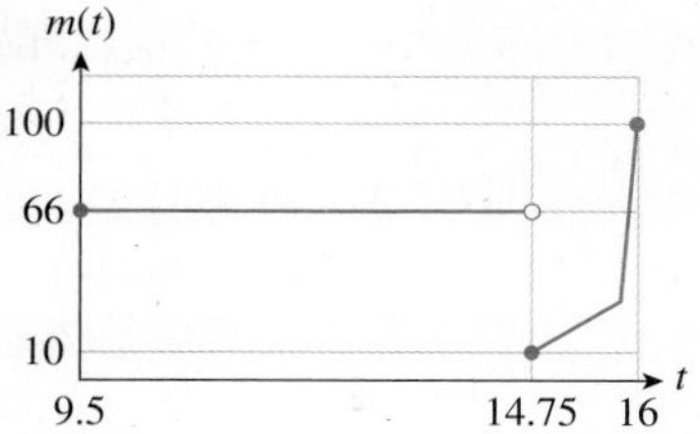

[5]Source for data: www.wikinvest.com.

[6]Based on data from 1983 to 2003. Source: The American Physical Society/*New York Times*, May 3, 2003, p. A1.

[7]*Ibid.*

[8]2009 data. Source: College Board/*New York Times* http://economix.blogs.nytimes.com.

[9]*Ibid.*

[10]The actual graph can be seen at http://seekingalpha.com.

[11]The market depth of a stock is a measure of its ability to withstand relatively large market orders, and is measured in orders to buy or sell the given stock. Source for data on graph: *Findings Regarding the Market Events of May 6, 2010,* U.S. Commodity Futures Trading Commission, U.S. Securities & Exchange Commission.

a. Compute the following (if a limit does not exist, say why):
$\lim_{t\to 14.75^-} m(t)$, $\lim_{t\to 14.75^+} m(t)$, $\lim_{t\to 14.75} m(t)$, $m(14.75)$.

b. What do the answers to part (a) tell you about the market depth?

45. ***Home Prices*** The following graph shows the values of the home price index[12] for 2000–2010 together with a mathematical model I extrapolating the data.

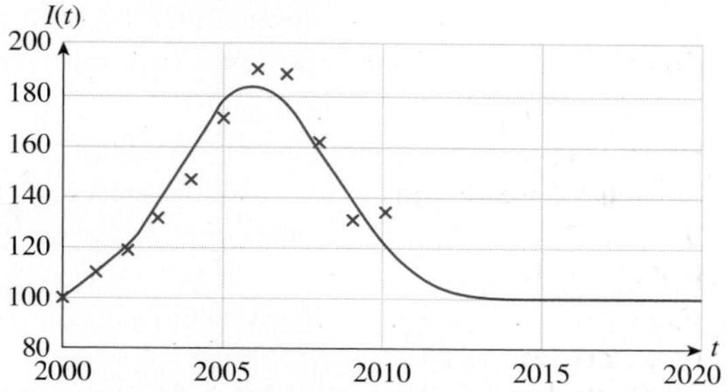

Estimate and interpret $\lim_{t\to+\infty} I(t)$.

46. ***Home Prices: Optimist Projection*** The following graph shows the values of the home price index[13] for 2000–2010 together with another mathematical model I extrapolating the data.

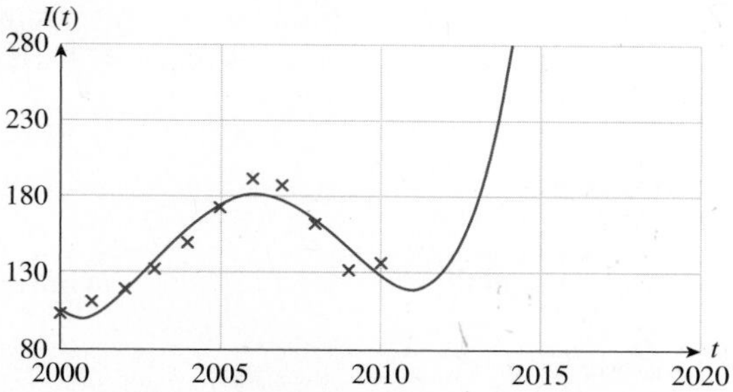

Estimate and interpret $\lim_{t\to+\infty} I(t)$.

47. ***Electric Rates*** The cost of electricity in Portland, Oregon, for residential customers increased suddenly on October 1, 2001, from around \$0.06 to around \$0.08 per kilowatt hour.[14] Let $C(t)$ be this cost at time t, and take $t = 1$ to represent October 1, 2001. What does the given information tell you about $\lim_{t\to 1} C(t)$?

48. ***Airline Stocks*** Prior to the September 11, 2001 attacks, United Airlines stock was trading at around \$35 per share. Immediately following the attacks, the share price dropped by \$15.[15] Let $U(t)$ be this cost at time t, and take $t = 11$ to represent September 11, 2001. What does the given information tell you about $\lim_{t\to 11} U(t)$?

Foreign Trade *Annual U.S. imports from China in the years 1996 through 2003 can be approximated by*

$$I(t) = t^2 + 3.5t + 50 \qquad (1 \le t \le 9)$$

billion dollars, where t represents time in years since 1995. Annual U.S. exports to China in the same years can be approximated by

$$E(t) = 0.4t^2 - 1.6t + 14$$

billion dollars.[16] *Exercises 49 and 50 are based on these models.*

49. ▼ Assuming the trends shown in the above models continued indefinitely, numerically estimate

$$\lim_{t\to+\infty} I(t) \text{ and } \lim_{t\to+\infty} \frac{I(t)}{E(t)},$$

interpret your answers, and comment on the results.

50. ▼ Repeat Exercise 49, this time calculating

$$\lim_{t\to+\infty} E(t) \text{ and } \lim_{t\to+\infty} \frac{E(t)}{I(t)}.$$

COMMUNICATION AND REASONING EXERCISES

51. Describe the method of evaluating limits numerically. Give at least one disadvantage of this method.

52. Describe the method of evaluating limits graphically. Give at least one disadvantage of this method.

53. Your friend Dion, a business student, claims that the study of limits that do not exist is completely unrealistic and has nothing to do with the world of business. Give two examples from the world of business that might convince him that he is wrong.

54. Your other friend Fiona claims that the study of limits is a complete farce; all you ever need to do to find the limit as x approaches a is substitute $x = a$. Give two examples that show she is wrong.

55. ▼ What is wrong with the following statement? "Because $f(a)$ is not defined, $\lim_{x\to a} f(x)$ does not exist." Illustrate your claim with an example.

56. ▼ What is wrong with the following statement? "Because $f(a)$ is defined, $\lim_{x\to a} f(x)$ exists." Illustrate your claim with an example.

57. ◆ Give an example of a function f with $\lim_{x\to 1} f(x) = f(2)$.

58. ◆ If $S(t)$ represents the size of the universe in billions of light years at time t years since the big bang and $\lim_{t\to+\infty} S(t) = 130{,}000$, is it possible that the universe will continue to expand forever?

59. ◆ Investigate $\lim_{x\to+\infty} x^n e^{-x}$ for some large values of n. What do you find? What do you think is the value of $\lim_{x\to+\infty} p(x)e^{-x}$ if $p(x)$ is any polynomial?

60. ◆ Investigate $\lim_{x\to-\infty} x^n e^{x}$ for some large values of n. What do you find? What do you think is the value of $\lim_{x\to-\infty} p(x)e^{x}$ if $p(x)$ is any polynomial?

[12] The index is the Standard & Poor/Case-Shiller Home Price Index. Source for data: www.standardandpoors.com.

[13] *Ibid.*

[14] Source: Portland General Electric/*New York Times*, February 2, 2002, p. C1.

[15] Stock prices are approximate.

[16] Based on quadratic regression using data from the U.S. Census Bureau Foreign Trade Division Web site www.census.gov/foreign-trade/sitc1/ as of December 2004.

3.2 Limits and Continuity

In the last section we saw examples of graphs that had various kinds of "breaks" or "jumps." For instance, in Example 4 we looked at the graph in Figure 9. This graph appears to have breaks, or **discontinuities**, at $x = 0$ and at $x = 1$. At $x = 0$ we saw that $\lim_{x\to 0} f(x)$ does not exist because the left- and right-hand limits are not the same. Thus, the discontinuity at $x = 0$ seems to be due to the fact that the limit does not exist there. On the other hand, at $x = 1$, $\lim_{x\to 1} f(x)$ *does* exist (it is equal to 1), but is not equal to $f(1) = 2$.

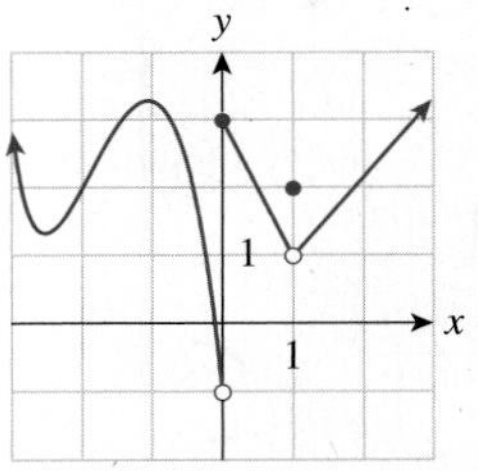

Figure 9

Thus, we have identified two kinds of discontinuity:

1. Points where the limit of the function does not exist.

$x = 0$ in Figure 9 because $\lim_{x\to 0} f(x)$ does not exist.

2. Points where the limit exists but does not equal the value of the function.

$x = 1$ in Figure 9 because $\lim_{x\to 1} f(x) = 1 \neq f(1)$

On the other hand, there is no discontinuity at, say, $x = -2$, where we find that $\lim_{x\to -2} f(x)$ exists and equals 2 and $f(-2)$ is also equal to 2. In other words,

$$\lim_{x\to -2} f(x) = 2 = f(-2).$$

The point $x = -2$ is an example of a point where f is **continuous**. (Notice that you can draw the portion of the graph near $x = -2$ without lifting your pencil from the paper.) Similarly, f is continuous at *every* point other than $x = 0$ and $x = 1$. Here is the mathematical definition.

Continuous Function

Let f be a function and let a be a number in the domain of f. Then f is **continuous at a** if

a. $\lim_{x\to a} f(x)$ exists, and

b. $\lim_{x\to a} f(x) = f(a)$.

If the number a is an endpoint of the domain, we will understand that the limit is the left or right limit, as appropriate.

The function f is said to be **continuous on its domain** if it is continuous at each point in its domain.

If f is not continuous at a particular a in its domain, we say that f is **discontinuous** at a or that f has a **discontinuity** at a. Thus, a discontinuity can occur at $x = a$ if either

a. $\lim_{x\to a} f(x)$ does not exist, or

b. $\lim_{x\to a} f(x)$ exists but is not equal to $f(a)$.

Quick Examples

1. The function shown in Figure 9 is continuous at $x = -1$ and $x = 2$. It is discontinuous at $x = 0$ and $x = 1$, and so is not continuous on its domain.
2. The function $f(x) = x^2$ is continuous on its domain. (Think of its graph, which contains no breaks.)

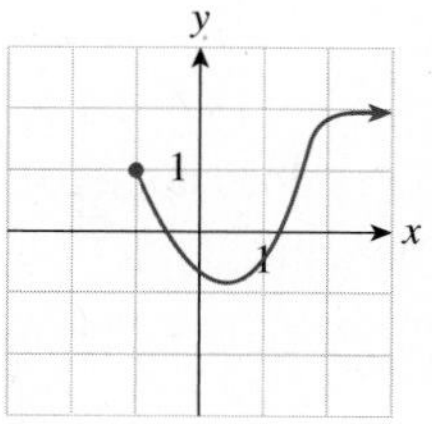

Figure 10

3. The function shown in Figure 10 is continuous on its domain. In particular, it is continuous at the left endpoint $x = -1$ of its domain, because $\lim_{x \to -1^+} f(x) = 1 = f(-1)$ (recall that we use only a one-sided limit at an endpoint of the domain).
4. The function *f* whose graph is shown on the left in the following figure is continuous on its domain. (Although the graph breaks at $x = 2$, that is not a point of its domain.) The function *g* whose graph is shown on the right is not continuous on its domain because it has a discontinuity at $x = 2$. (Here, $x = 2$ is a point of the domain of *g*.)

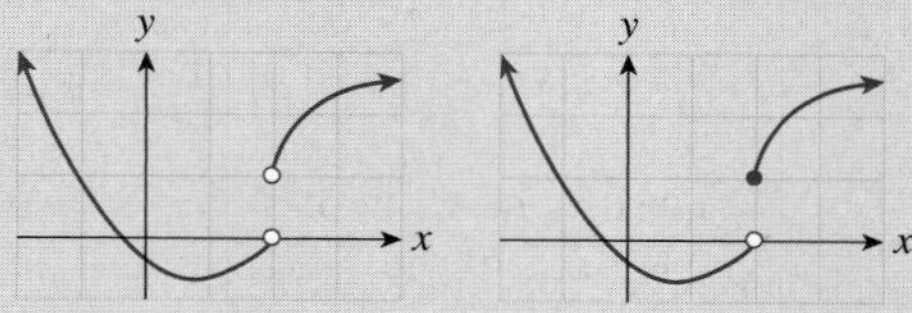

$y = f(x)$: Continuous on its domain　　$y = g(x)$: Not continuous on its domain

Note Continuity and discontinuity of a function are defined only for points in a function's domain; a function cannot be continuous at a point not in its domain, and it cannot be discontinuous there either. So, if a is not in the domain of *f*—that is, if $f(a)$ is not defined—then it is meaningless to talk about whether *f* is continuous or discontinuous at a. ■

EXAMPLE 1 Continuous and Discontinuous Functions

Which of the following functions are continuous on their domains?

a. $h(x) = \begin{cases} x + 3 & \text{if } x \le 1 \\ 5 - x & \text{if } x > 1 \end{cases}$　　**b.** $k(x) = \begin{cases} x + 3 & \text{if } x \le 1 \\ 1 - x & \text{if } x > 1 \end{cases}$

c. $f(x) = \dfrac{1}{x}$　　**d.** $g(x) = \begin{cases} \dfrac{1}{x} & \text{if } x \ne 0 \\ 0 & \text{if } x = 0 \end{cases}$

Solution

a and **b.** The graphs of *h* and *k* are shown in Figure 11.

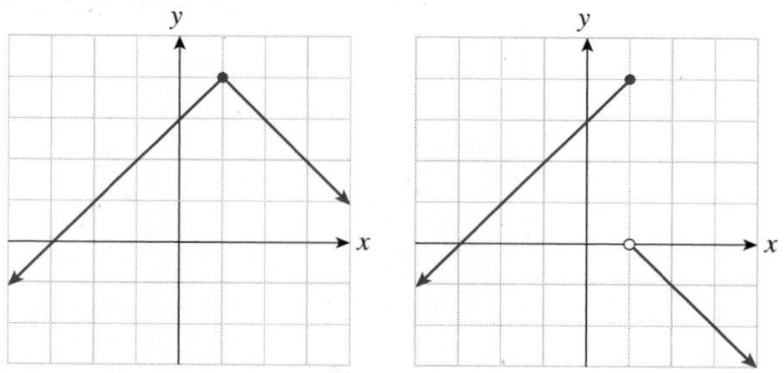

$y = h(x)$　　$y = k(x)$

Figure 11

Even though the graph of h is made up of two different line segments, it is continuous at every point of its domain, including $x = 1$ because

$$\lim_{x \to 1} h(x) = 4 = h(1).$$

On the other hand, $x = 1$ is also in the domain of k, but $\lim_{x \to 1} k(x)$ does not exist. Thus, k is discontinuous at $x = 1$ and thus not continuous on its domain.

c and **d.** The graphs of f and g are shown in Figure 12.

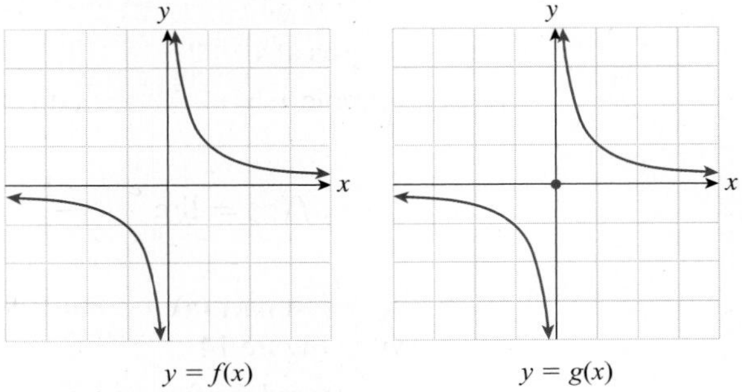

Figure 12

using Technology

We can use technology to draw (approximate) graphs of the functions in Example 1(a), (b), and (c). Here are the technology formulas that will work for the TI-83/84 Plus, spreadsheets, and Website function evaluator and grapher. (In the TI-83/84 Plus, replace `<=` by ≤. In spreadsheets, replace `x` by a cell reference and insert an equals sign in front of the formula.)

a. `(x+3)*(x<=1)+(5-x)*(x>1)`

b. `(x+3)*(x<=1)+(1-x)*(x>1)`

c. `(1/x)`

Observe in each case how technology handles the breaks in the curves.

The domain of f consists of all real numbers except 0 and f is continuous at all such numbers. (Notice that 0 is not in the domain of f, so the question of continuity at 0 does not arise.) Thus, f is continuous on its domain.

The function g, on the other hand, has its domain expanded to include 0, so we now need to check whether g is continuous at 0. From the graph, it is easy to see that g is discontinuous there because $\lim_{x \to 0} g(x)$ does not exist. Thus, g is not continuous on its domain because it is discontinuous at 0.

Before we go on...

Q: *Wait a minute! How can a function like $f(x) = 1/x$ be continuous when its graph has a break in it?*

A: We are not claiming that f is continuous *at every real number.* What we are saying is that f is continuous *on its domain;* the break in the graph occurs at a point not in the domain of f. In other words, f is continuous on the set of all nonzero real numbers; it is not continuous on the set of *all* real numbers because it is not even defined on that set.

EXAMPLE 2 Continuous Except at a Point

In each case, say what, if any, value of $f(a)$ would make f continuous at a.

a. $f(x) = \dfrac{x^3 - 8}{x - 2}$; $a = 2$ **b.** $f(x) = \dfrac{e^{2x} - 1}{x}$; $a = 0$ **c.** $f(x) = \dfrac{|x|}{x}$; $a = 0$

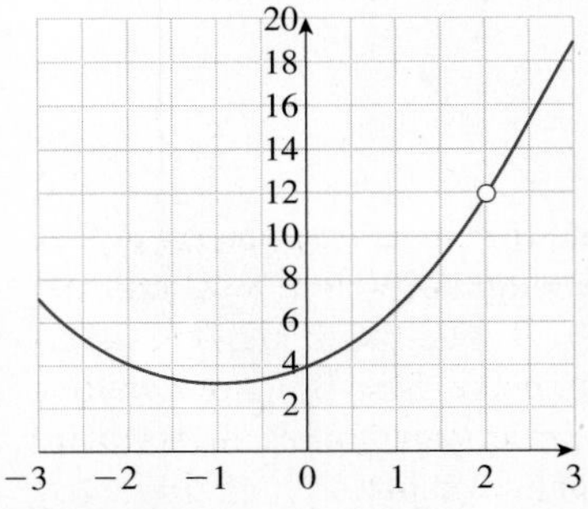

Figure 13

Solution

a. In Figure 13 we see the graph of $f(x) = \dfrac{x^3 - 8}{x - 2}$. The point corresponding to $x = 2$ is missing because f is not (yet) defined there. (Your graphing utility will probably miss this subtlety and render a continuous curve. See the technology note in the margin.) To turn f into a function that is continuous at $x = 2$, we need to "fill in the gap" so as to obtain a continuous curve. Since the graph suggests that the missing point is (2, 12), let us define $f(2) = 12$.

Does f now become continuous if we take $f(2) = 12$? From the graph, or Example 1(a) of Section 3.1,

$$\lim_{x\to 2} f(x) = \lim_{x\to 2} \frac{x^3 - 8}{x - 2} = 12,$$

which is now equal to $f(2)$. Thus, $\lim_{x\to 2} f(x) = f(2)$, showing that f is now continuous at $x = 2$.

b. In Example 1(b) of the preceding section, we saw that

$$\lim_{x\to 0} f(x) = \lim_{x\to 0} \frac{e^{2x} - 1}{x} = 2,$$

and so, as in part (a), we must define $f(0) = 2$. This is confirmed by the graph, shown in Figure 14.

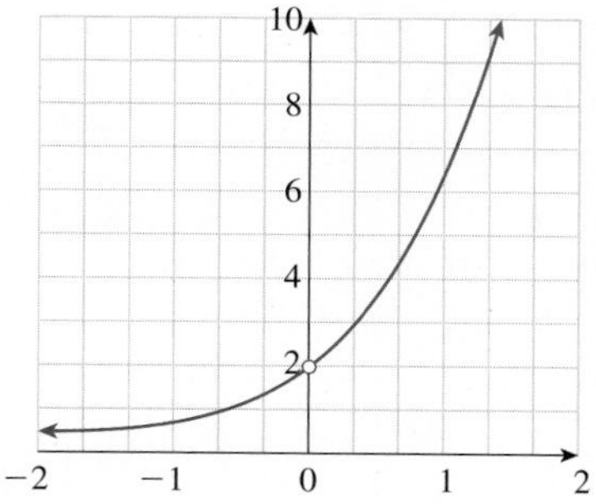

Figure 14

c. We considered the function $f(x) = |x|/x$ in Example 2 in Section 3.1. Its graph is shown in Figure 15.

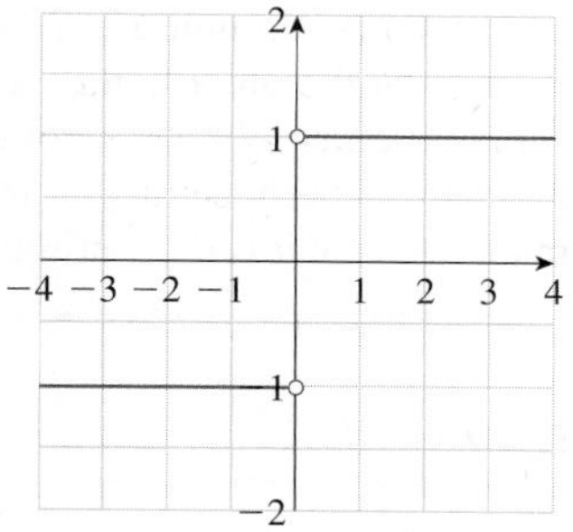

Figure 15

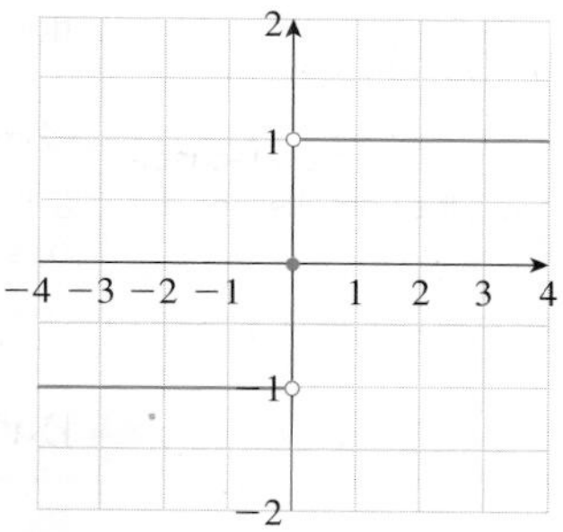

Figure 16

Now we encounter a problem: No matter how we try to fill in the gap at $x = 0$, the result will be a discontinuous function. For example, setting $f(0) = 0$ will result in the discontinuous function shown in Figure 16. We conclude that it is impossible to assign any value to $f(0)$ to turn f into a function that is continuous at $x = 0$.

We can also see this result algebraically: In Example 2 of Section 3.1, we saw that $\lim_{x\to 0} \frac{|x|}{x}$ does not exist. Thus, the resulting function will fail to be continuous at 0, no matter how we define $f(0)$.

using Technology

It is instructive to see how technology handles the functions in Example 2. Here are the technology formulas that will work for the TI-83/84 Plus, spreadsheets, and Website function evaluator and grapher. (In spreadsheets, replace `x` by a cell reference and insert an equal sign in front of the formula.)

a. `(x^3-8)/(x-2)`

b. `(e^(2x)-1)/x`

Spreadsheet:
`=(exp(2*A2)-1)/A2`

c. `abs(x)/x`

In each case, compare the graph rendered by technology with the corresponding figure in Example 2.

A function not defined at an isolated point is said to have a **singularity** at that point. The function in part (a) of Example 2 has a singularity at $x = 2$, and the functions in parts (b) and (c) have singularities at $x = 0$. The functions in parts (a) and (b) have **removable singularities** because we can make these functions continuous at $x = a$ by properly defining $f(a)$. The function in part (c) has an **essential singularity** because we cannot make f continuous at $x = a$ just by defining $f(a)$ properly.

3.2 EXERCISES

▼ more advanced ◆ challenging

T indicates exercises that should be solved using technology

In Exercises 1–14, the graph of a function f is given. Determine whether f is continuous on its domain. If it is not continuous on its domain, say why. HINT [See Quick Examples page 208.]

1.

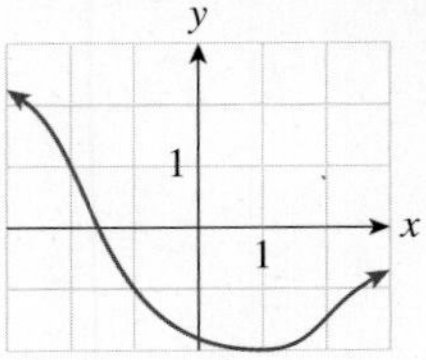

2.

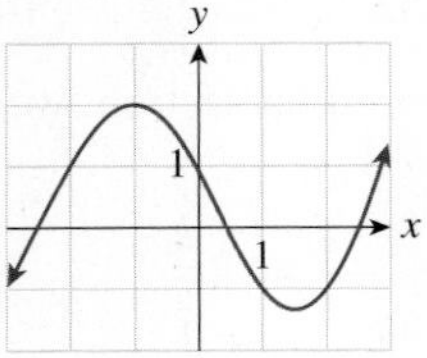

3.

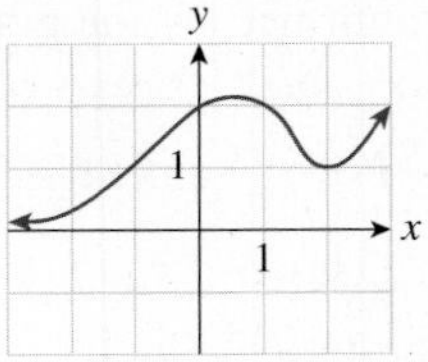

4.

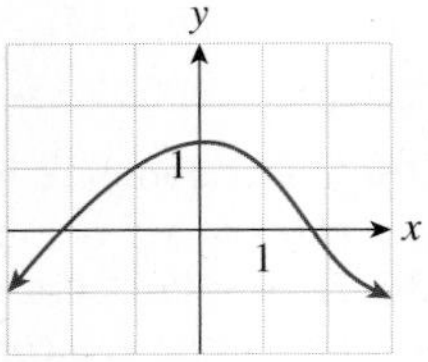

5.

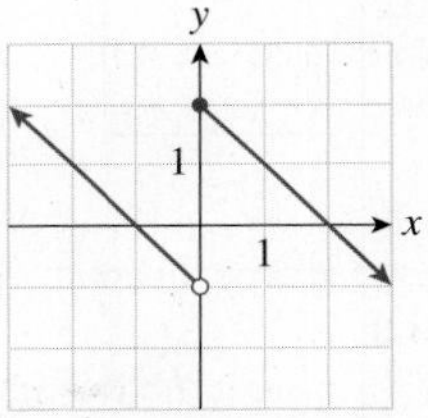

6.

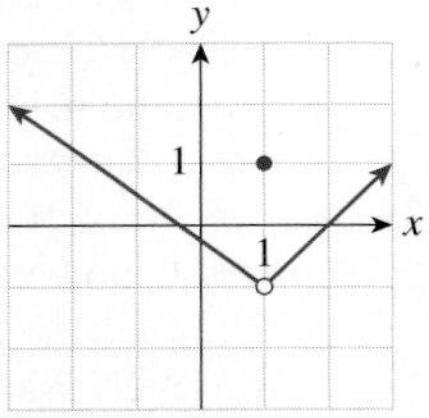

7.

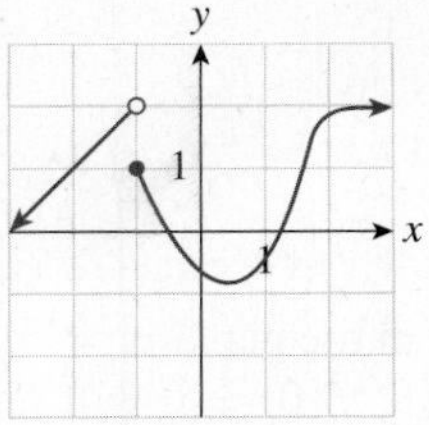

8.

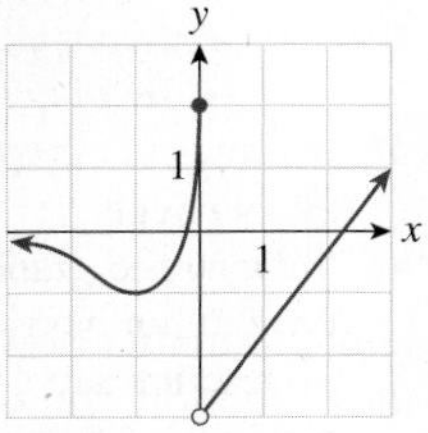

9.

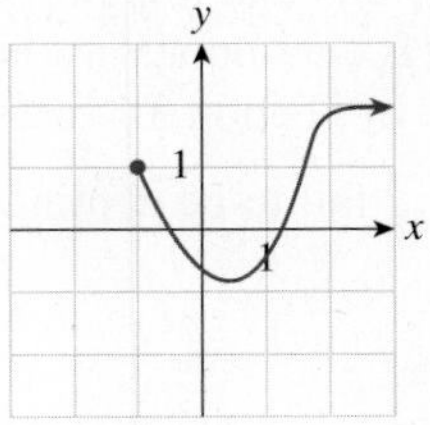

10.

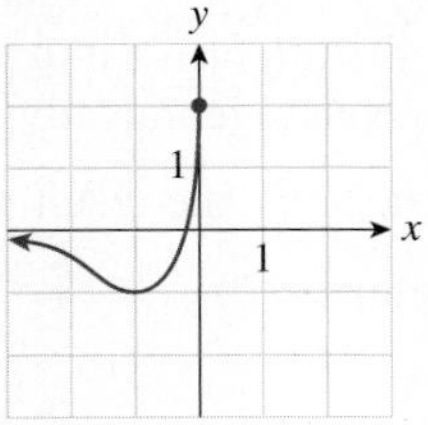

11.

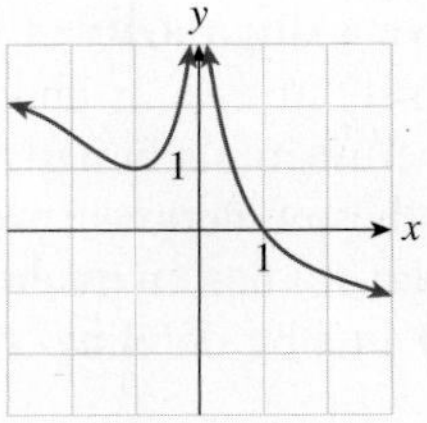

12.

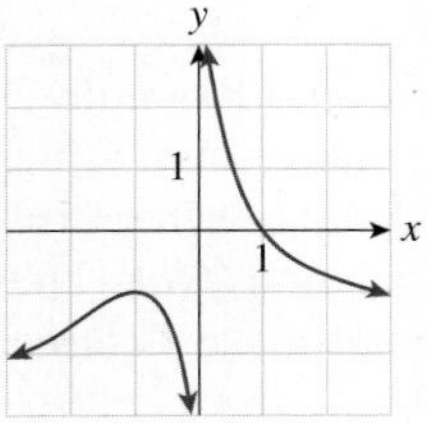

13.

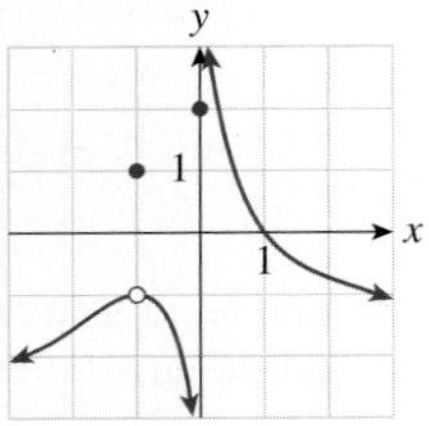

14.

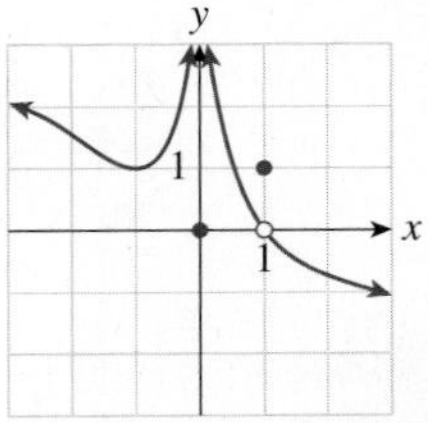

In Exercises 15 and 16, identify which (if any) of the given graphs represent functions continuous on their domains. HINT [See Quick Examples page 208.]

15. (A)

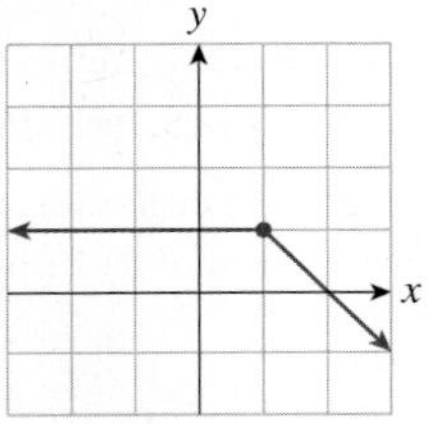

(B)

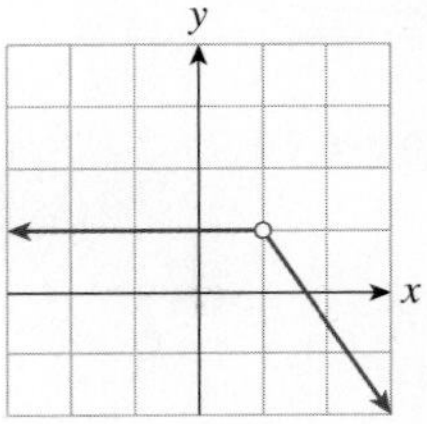

(C)

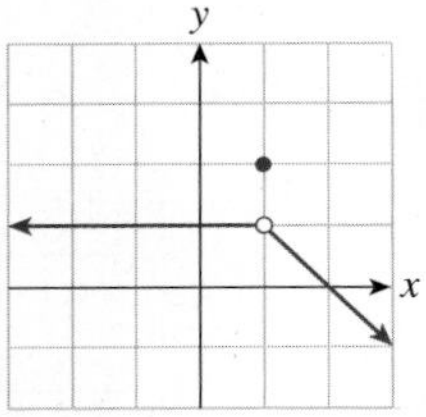

(D)

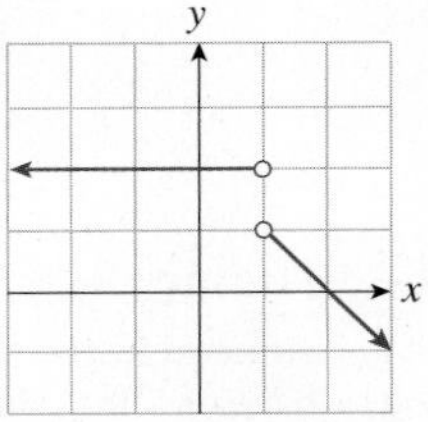

(E)

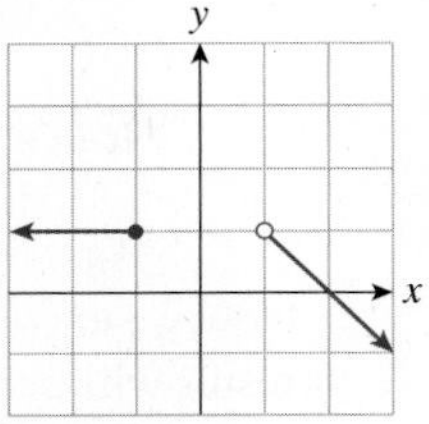

(F)

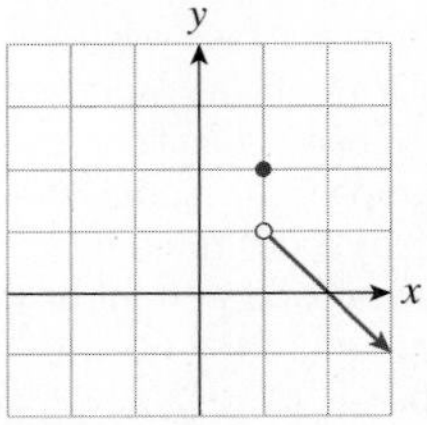

16. (A)

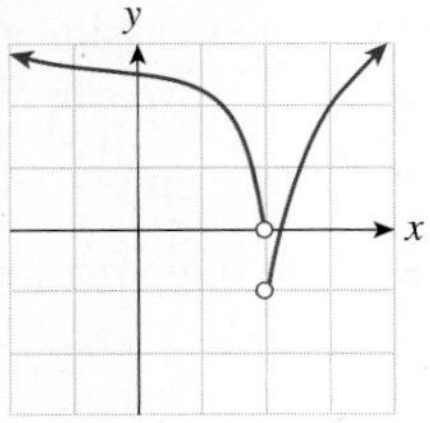

(B)

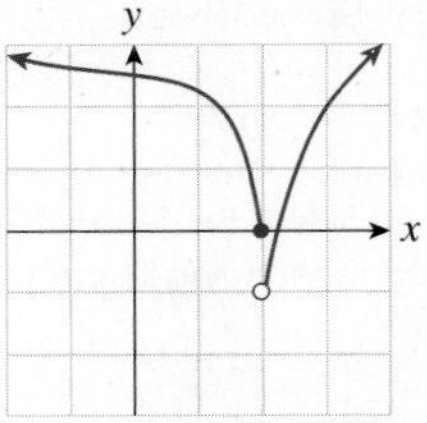

(C)

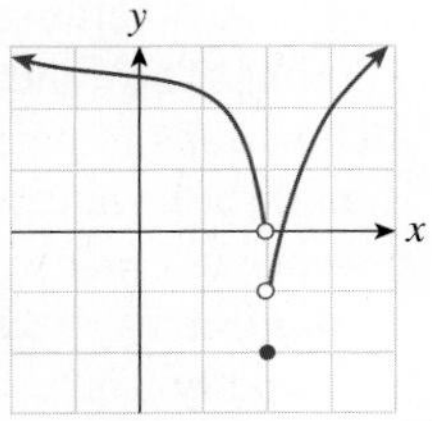

(D)

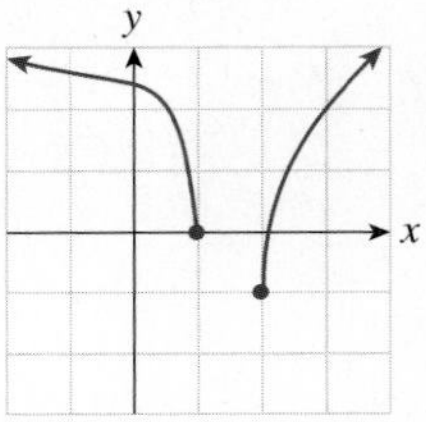

(E)

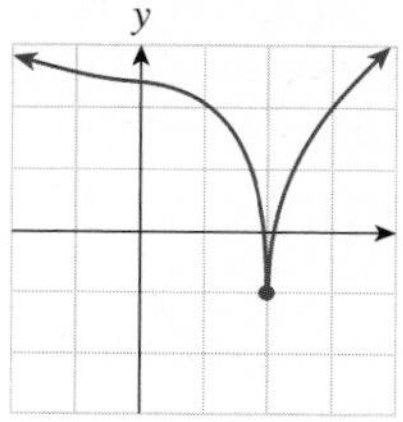

(F)

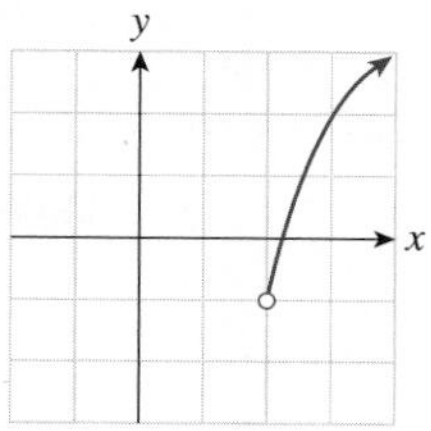

In Exercises 17–24, use a graph of f or some other method to determine what, if any, value to assign to f(a) to make f continuous at x = a. HINT [See Example 2.]

17. $f(x) = \dfrac{x^2 - 2x + 1}{x - 1}$; $a = 1$

18. $f(x) = \dfrac{x^2 + 3x + 2}{x + 1}$; $a = -1$

19. $f(x) = \dfrac{x}{3x^2 - x}$; $a = 0$

20. $f(x) = \dfrac{x^2 - 3x}{x + 4}$; $a = -4$

21. $f(x) = \dfrac{3}{3x^2 - x}$; $a = 0$

22. $f(x) = \dfrac{x - 1}{x^3 - 1}$; $a = 1$

23. $f(x) = \dfrac{1 - e^x}{x}$; $a = 0$

24. $f(x) = \dfrac{1 + e^x}{1 - e^x}$; $a = 0$

In Exercises 25–34, use a graph to determine whether the given function is continuous on its domain. If it is not continuous on its domain, list the points of discontinuity. HINT [See Example 1.]

25. $f(x) = |x|$

26. $f(x) = \dfrac{|x|}{x}$

27. $g(x) = \dfrac{1}{x^2 - 1}$

28. $g(x) = \dfrac{x - 1}{x + 2}$

29. $f(x) = \begin{cases} x + 2 & \text{if } x < 0 \\ 2x - 1 & \text{if } x \geq 0 \end{cases}$

30. $f(x) = \begin{cases} 1 - x & \text{if } x \leq 1 \\ x - 1 & \text{if } x > 1 \end{cases}$

31. $h(x) = \begin{cases} \dfrac{|x|}{x} & \text{if } x \neq 0 \\ 0 & \text{if } x = 0 \end{cases}$

32. $h(x) = \begin{cases} \dfrac{1}{x^2} & \text{if } x \neq 0 \\ 2 & \text{if } x = 0 \end{cases}$

33. $g(x) = \begin{cases} x + 2 & \text{if } x < 0 \\ 2x + 2 & \text{if } x \geq 0 \end{cases}$

34. $g(x) = \begin{cases} 1 - x & \text{if } x \leq 1 \\ x + 1 & \text{if } x > 1 \end{cases}$

COMMUNICATION AND REASONING EXERCISES

35. If a function is continuous on its domain, is it continuous at every real number? Explain.

36. True or false? The graph of a function that is continuous on its domain is a continuous curve with no breaks in it. Explain your answer.

37. True or false? The graph of a function that is continuous at every real number is a continuous curve with no breaks in it. Explain your answer.

38. True or false? If the graph of a function is a continuous curve with no breaks in it, then the function is continuous on its domain. Explain your answer.

39. ▼ Give a formula for a function that is continuous on its domain but whose graph consists of three distinct curves.

40. ▼ Give a formula for a function that is not continuous at $x = -1$ but is not discontinuous there either.

41. ▼ Draw the graph of a function that is discontinuous at every integer.

42. ▼ Draw the graph of a function that is continuous on its domain but whose graph has a break at every integer.

43. ▼ Describe a real-life scenario in the stock market that can be modeled by a discontinuous function.

44. ▼ Describe a real-life scenario in your room that can be modeled by a discontinuous function.

3.3 Limits and Continuity: Algebraic Viewpoint

Although numerical and graphical estimation of limits is effective, the estimates these methods yield may not be perfectly accurate. The algebraic method, when it can be used, will always yield an exact answer. Moreover, algebraic analysis of a function often enables us to take a function apart and see "what makes it tick."

Let's start with the function $f(x) = 2 + x$ and ask: What happens to $f(x)$ as x approaches 3? To answer this algebraically, notice that as x gets closer and closer to 3, the quantity $2 + x$ must get closer and closer to $2 + 3 = 5$. Hence,

$$\lim_{x \to 3} f(x) = \lim_{x \to 3}(2 + x) = 2 + 3 = 5$$

Q: *Is that all there is to the algebraic method? Just substitute $x = a$?*

A: Under certain circumstances: Notice that by substituting $x = 3$ we *evaluated the function at $x = 3$*. In other words, we relied on the fact that

$$\lim_{x \to 3} f(x) = f(3).$$

In Section 3.2 we said that a function satisfying this equation is *continuous* at $x = 3$.

Thus,

If we know that the function f is continuous at a point a, we can compute $\lim_{x \to a} f(x)$ by simply substituting $x = a$ into $f(x)$.

To use this fact, we need to know how to recognize continuous functions when we see them. Geometrically, they are easy to spot: A function is continuous at $x = a$ if its graph has no break at $x = a$. Algebraically, a large class of functions are known to be continuous on their domains—those, roughly speaking, that are *specified by a single formula*.

We can be more precise: A **closed-form function** is any function that can be obtained by combining constants, powers of x, exponential functions, radicals, logarithms, absolute values, trigonometric functions (and some other functions we do not encounter in this text) into a *single* mathematical formula by means of the usual arithmetic operations and composition of functions. (They can be as complicated as we like.)

Closed-Form Functions

A function is **written in closed form** if it is specified by combining constants, powers of x, exponential functions, radicals, logarithms, absolute values, trigonometric functions (and some other functions we do not encounter in this text) into a *single* mathematical formula by means of the usual arithmetic operations and composition of functions. A **closed-form function** is any function that can be written in closed form.

Quick Examples

1. $3x^2 - |x| + 1$, $\dfrac{\sqrt{x^2 - 1}}{6x - 1}$, $e^{-\frac{4x^2-1}{x}}$, and $\sqrt{\log_3(x^2 - 1)}$ are written in closed form, so they are all closed-form functions.

2. $f(x) = \begin{cases} -1 & \text{if } x \le -1 \\ x^2 + x & \text{if } -1 < x \le 1 \\ 2 - x & \text{if } 1 < x \le 2 \end{cases}$ is not written in closed-form because $f(x)$ is not expressed by a *single* mathematical formula.*

* It is possible to rewrite some piecewise-defined functions in closed form (using a single formula), but not this particular function, so $f(x)$ is not a closed-form function.

What is so special about closed-form functions is the following theorem.

Theorem 3.1 Continuity of Closed-Form Functions

Every closed-form function is continuous on its domain. Thus, if f is a closed-form function and $f(a)$ is defined, then $\lim_{x \to a} f(x)$ exists, and equals $f(a)$. (When a is an endpoint of the domain of f, we understand the limit to be the appropriate one-sided limit.)

Quick Example

$f(x) = 1/x$ is a closed-form function, and its natural domain consists of all real numbers except 0. Thus, f is continuous at every nonzero real number. That is,

$$\lim_{x \to a} \frac{1}{x} = \frac{1}{a}$$

provided $a \neq 0$.

Mathematics majors spend a great deal of time studying the proof of this theorem. We ask you to accept it without proof.

EXAMPLE 1 Limit of a Closed-Form Function

Evaluate the following limits algebraically:

a. $\lim_{x \to 1} \dfrac{x^3 - 8}{x - 2}$ **b.** $\lim_{x \to 2} \dfrac{x^3 - 8}{x - 2}$.

Solution

a. First, notice that $(x^3 - 8)/(x - 2)$ is a closed-form function because it is specified by a single algebraic formula. Also, $x = 1$ is in the domain of this function. Therefore the theorem applies, and

$$\lim_{x \to 1} \frac{x^3 - 8}{x - 2} = \frac{1^3 - 8}{1 - 2} = 7.$$

b. Although $(x^3 - 8)/(x - 2)$ is a closed-form function, $x = 2$ is not in its domain. Thus, the theorem does not apply and we cannot obtain the limit by substitution. However—and this is the key to finding such limits—*some preliminary algebraic simplification will allow us to obtain a closed-form function with $x = 2$ in its domain.* To do this, notice first that the numerator can be factored as

$$x^3 - 8 = (x - 2)(x^2 + 2x + 4).$$

Thus,

$$\frac{x^3 - 8}{x - 2} = \frac{(x - 2)(x^2 + 2x + 4)}{x - 2} = x^2 + 2x + 4.$$

Once we have canceled the offending $(x - 2)$ in the denominator, we are left with a closed-form function *with 2 in its domain*. Thus,

$$\lim_{x\to 2} \frac{x^3 - 8}{x - 2} = \lim_{x\to 2}(x^2 + 2x + 4)$$

$$= 2^2 + 2(2) + 4 = 12. \quad \text{Substitute } x = 2.$$

This confirms the answer we found numerically in Example 1 in Section 3.1.

➡ **Before we go on...** Notice that in Example 1(b) before simplification, the substitution $x = 2$ yields

$$\frac{x^3 - 8}{x - 2} = \frac{8 - 8}{2 - 2} = \frac{0}{0}.$$

Worse than the fact that 0/0 is undefined, it also conveys absolutely no information as to what the limit might be. (The limit turned out to be 12!) We therefore call the expression 0/0 an **indeterminate form**. Once simplified, the function became $x^2 + 2x + 4$, which, upon the substitution $x = 2$, yielded 12—no longer an indeterminate form. In general, we have the following rule of thumb:

If the substitution $x = a$ yields the indeterminate form 0/0, try simplifying by the method in Example 1.

We will say more about indeterminate forms in Example 2. ■

Q: *There is something suspicious about Example 1(b). If 2 was not in the domain before simplifying but was in the domain after simplifying, we must have changed the function, right?*

A: Correct. In fact, when we said that

$$\frac{x^3 - 8}{x - 2} = x^2 + 2x + 4$$

Domain excludes 2 Domain includes 2

we were lying a little bit. What we really meant is that these two expressions are equal *where both are defined.* The functions $(x^3 - 8)/(x - 2)$ and $x^2 + 2x + 4$ are different functions. The difference is that $x = 2$ is not in the domain of $(x^3 - 8)/(x - 2)$ and is in the domain of $x^2 + 2x + 4$. Since $\lim_{x\to 2} f(x)$ explicitly *ignores* any value that f may have at 2, this does not affect the limit. From the point of view of the limit at 2, these functions *are* equal. In general we have the following rule.

Functions with Equal Limits

If $f(x) = g(x)$ for all x except possibly $x = a$, then

$$\lim_{x\to a} f(x) = \lim_{x\to a} g(x).$$

Quick Example

$$\frac{x^2 - 1}{x - 1} = x + 1 \text{ for all } x \text{ except } x = 1.$$

Write $\frac{x^2 - 1}{x - 1}$ as $\frac{(x + 1)(x - 1)}{x - 1}$ and cancel the $(x - 1)$.

Therefore,

$$\lim_{x\to 1} \frac{x^2 - 1}{x - 1} = \lim_{x\to 1} (x + 1) = 1 + 1 = 2.$$

Q: *How do we find $\lim_{x \to a} f(x)$ when $x = a$ is not in the domain of the function f and we cannot simplify the given function to make a a point of the domain?*

A: In such a case, it might be necessary to analyze the function by some other method, such as numerically or graphically. However, if we do not obtain the indeterminate form 0/0 upon substitution, we can often say what the limit is, as the following example shows.

EXAMPLE 2 Limit of a Closed-Form Function at a Point Not in Its Domain: The Determinate Form $k/0$

Evaluate the following limits, if they exist:

a. $\lim_{x \to 1^+} \dfrac{x^2 - 4x + 1}{x - 1}$ **b.** $\lim_{x \to 1} \dfrac{x^2 - 4x + 1}{x - 1}$ **c.** $\lim_{x \to 1} \dfrac{x^2 - 4x + 1}{x^2 - 2x + 1}$

Solution

a. Although the function $f(x) = \dfrac{x^2 - 4x + 1}{x - 1}$ is a closed-form function, $x = 1$ is not in its domain. Notice that substituting $x = 1$ gives

$$\frac{x^2 - 4x + 1}{x - 1} = \frac{1^2 - 4 + 1}{1 - 1} = \frac{-2}{0}$$

The **determinate** form $\frac{k}{0}$

which, although not defined, conveys important information to us: As x gets closer and closer to 1, the numerator approaches -2 and the denominator gets closer and closer to 0. Now, if we divide a number close to -2 by a number close to zero, we get a number of large absolute value; for instance,

$$\frac{-2.1}{0.0001} = -21{,}000 \quad \text{and} \quad \frac{-2.1}{-0.0001} = 21{,}000$$

$$\frac{-2.01}{0.00001} = -201{,}000 \quad \text{and} \quad \frac{-2.01}{-0.00001} = 201{,}000.$$

(Compare Example 5 in Section 3.1.) In our limit for part (a), x is approaching 1 from the right, so the denominator $x - 1$ is positive (as x is to the right of 1). Thus we have the scenario illustrated previously on the left, and we can conclude that

$$\lim_{x \to 1^+} \frac{x^2 - 4x + 1}{x - 1} = -\infty.$$

Think of this as $\frac{-2}{0^+} = -\infty$.

b. This time, x could be approaching 1 from either side. We already have, from part (a)

$$\lim_{x \to 1^+} \frac{x^2 - 4x + 1}{x - 1} = -\infty.$$

The same reasoning we used in part (a) gives

$$\lim_{x \to 1^-} \frac{x^2 - 4x + 1}{x - 1} = +\infty$$

Think of this as $\frac{-2}{0^-} = +\infty$.

because now the denominator is negative and still approaching zero while the numerator still approaches -2 and therefore is also negative. (See the numerical calculations above on the right.) Because the left and right limits do not agree, we conclude that

$$\lim_{x \to 1} \frac{x^2 - 4x + 1}{x - 1} \text{ does not exist.}$$

c. First notice that the denominator factors:

$$\lim_{x\to 1}\frac{x^2-4x+1}{x^2-2x+1}=\lim_{x\to 1}\frac{x^2-4x+1}{(x-1)^2}.$$

As x approaches 1, the numerator approaches -2 as before, and the denominator approaches 0. However, this time, the denominator $(x-1)^2$, being a square, is ≥ 0, regardless of from which side x is approaching 1. Thus, the entire function is negative as x approaches 1, and

$$\lim_{x\to 1}\frac{x^2-4x+1}{(x-1)^2}=-\infty. \qquad \frac{-2}{0^+}=-\infty$$

Before we go on... In general, the determinate forms $\frac{k}{0^+}$ and $\frac{k}{0^-}$ will always yield $\pm\infty$, with the sign depending on the sign of the overall expression as $x \to a$. (When we write the form $\frac{k}{0}$ we always mean $k \neq 0$.) This and other determinate forms are discussed further after Example 4.

Figure 17 shows the graphs of $\frac{x^2-4x+1}{x-1}$ and $\frac{x^2-4x+1}{(x-1)^2}$ from Example 2. You should check that results we obtained above agree with a geometric analysis of these graphs near $x = 1$.

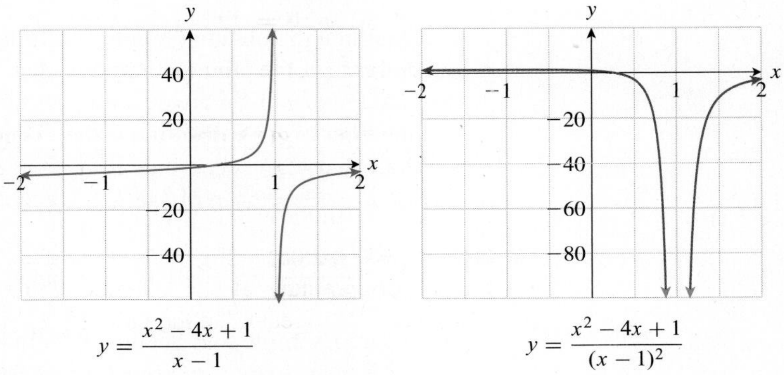

Figure 17

■

We can also use algebraic techniques to analyze functions that are not given in closed form.

EXAMPLE 3 Functions Not Written in Closed Form

For which values of x are the following piecewise defined functions continuous?

a. $f(x)=\begin{cases}x^2+2 & \text{if } x<1\\ 2x-1 & \text{if } x\geq 1\end{cases}$ **b.** $g(x)=\begin{cases}x^2-x+1 & \text{if } x\leq 0\\ 1-x & \text{if } 0<x\leq 1\\ x-3 & \text{if } x>1\end{cases}$

Solution

a. The function $f(x)$ is given in closed form over the intervals $(-\infty, 1)$ and $[1, +\infty)$. At $x = 1$, $f(x)$ suddenly switches from one closed-form formula to another, so

$x = 1$ is the only place where there is a potential problem with continuity. To investigate the continuity of $f(x)$ at $x = 1$, let's calculate the limit there:

$$\lim_{x\to 1^-} f(x) = \lim_{x\to 1^-} (x^2 + 2) \qquad f(x) = x^2 + 2 \text{ for } x < 1.$$
$$= (1)^2 + 2 = 3 \qquad x^2 + 2 \text{ is closed-form.}$$
$$\lim_{x\to 1^+} f(x) = \lim_{x\to 1^+} (2x - 1) \qquad f(x) = 2x - 1 \text{ for } x > 1.$$
$$= 2(1) - 1 = 1. \qquad 2x - 1 \text{ is closed-form.}$$

Because the left and right limits are different, $\lim_{x\to 1} f(x)$ does not exist, and so $f(x)$ is discontinuous at $x = 1$.

b. The only potential points of discontinuity for $g(x)$ occur at $x = 0$ and $x = 1$:

$$\lim_{x\to 0^-} g(x) = \lim_{x\to 0^-} (x^2 - x + 1) = 1$$
$$\lim_{x\to 0^+} g(x) = \lim_{x\to 0^+} (1 - x) = 1.$$

Thus, $\lim_{x\to 0} g(x) = 1$. Further, $g(0) = 0^2 - 0 + 1 = 1$ from the formula, and so

$$\lim_{x\to 0} g(x) = g(0),$$

which shows that $g(x)$ is continuous at $x = 0$. At $x = 1$ we have

$$\lim_{x\to 1^-} g(x) = \lim_{x\to 1^-} (1 - x) = 0$$
$$\lim_{x\to 1^+} g(x) = \lim_{x\to 1^+} (x - 3) = -2$$

so that $\lim_{x\to 1} g(x)$ does not exist. Thus, $g(x)$ is discontinuous at $x = 1$. We conclude that $g(x)$ is continuous at every real number x except $x = 1$.

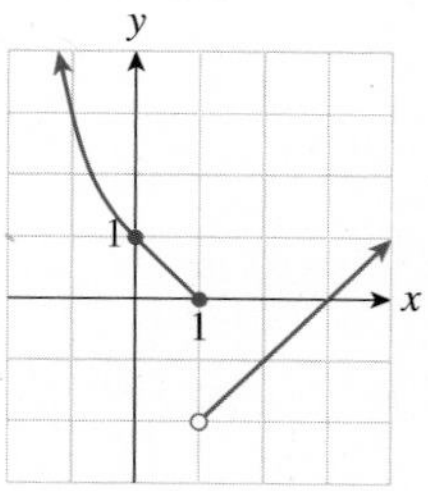

$y = g(x)$

Figure 18

➡ **Before we go on...** Figure 18 shows the graph of g from Example 3(b). Notice how the discontinuity at $x = 1$ shows up as a break in the graph, whereas at $x = 0$ the two pieces "fit together" at the point (0, 1). ■

Limits at Infinity

Let's look once again at some limits similar to those in Examples 3 and 6 in Section 3.1.

EXAMPLE 4 Limits at Infinity

Compute the following limits, if they exist:

a. $\displaystyle\lim_{x\to+\infty} \frac{2x^2 - 4x}{x^2 - 1}$ **b.** $\displaystyle\lim_{x\to-\infty} \frac{2x^2 - 4x}{x^2 - 1}$

c. $\displaystyle\lim_{x\to+\infty} \frac{-x^3 - 4x}{2x^2 - 1}$ **d.** $\displaystyle\lim_{x\to+\infty} \frac{2x^2 - 4x}{5x^3 - 3x + 5}$

e. $\displaystyle\lim_{t\to+\infty} (e^{0.1t} - 20)$ **f.** $\displaystyle\lim_{t\to+\infty} \frac{80}{1 + 2.2(3.68)^{-t}}$

Solution **a** and **b.** While calculating the values for the tables used in Example 3 in Section 3.1, you might have noticed that the highest power of x in both the numerator and denominator dominated the calculations. For instance, when $x = 100{,}000$, the term $2x^2$ in the numerator has the value of 20,000,000,000, whereas the term $4x$ has the comparatively insignificant value of 400,000. Similarly, the term x^2 in the denominator overwhelms the term -1. In other words, for large values of x (or negative values with large magnitude),

$$\frac{2x^2 - 4x}{x^2 - 1} \approx \frac{2x^2}{x^2} = 2.$$ Use only the highest powers top and bottom.

Therefore,

$$\lim_{x\to\pm\infty} \frac{2x^2 - 4x}{x^2 - 1} = \lim_{x\to\pm\infty} \frac{2x^2}{x^2} = \lim_{x\to\pm\infty} 2 = 2.$$

The procedure of using only the highest powers of x to compute the limit is stated formally and justified after this example.

c. Applying the previous technique of looking only at highest powers gives

$$\lim_{x\to+\infty} \frac{-x^3 - 4x}{2x^2 - 1} = \lim_{x\to+\infty} \frac{-x^3}{2x^2}$$ Use only the highest powers top and bottom.

$$= \lim_{x\to+\infty} \frac{-x}{2}.$$ Simplify.

As x gets large, $-x/2$ gets large in magnitude but negative, so the limit is

$$\lim_{x\to+\infty} \frac{-x}{2} = -\infty.$$ $\frac{-\infty}{2} = -\infty$ (See below.)

d. $$\lim_{x\to+\infty} \frac{2x^2 - 4x}{5x^3 - 3x + 5} = \lim_{x\to+\infty} \frac{2x^2}{5x^3}$$ Use only the highest powers top and bottom.

$$= \lim_{x\to+\infty} \frac{2}{5x}.$$

As x gets large, $2/(5x)$ gets close to zero, so the limit is

$$\lim_{x\to+\infty} \frac{2}{5x} = 0.$$ $\frac{2}{\infty} = 0$ (See below.)

e. Here we do not have a ratio of polynomials. However, we know that, as t becomes large and positive, so does $e^{0.1t}$, and hence also $e^{0.1t} - 20$. Thus,

$$\lim_{t\to+\infty} (e^{0.1t} - 20) = +\infty$$ $e^{+\infty} = +\infty$ (See below.)

f. As $t \to +\infty$, the term $(3.68)^{-t} = \frac{1}{3.68^t}$ in the denominator, being 1 divided by a very large number, approaches zero. Hence the denominator $1 + 2.2(3.68)^{-t}$ approaches $1 + 2.2(0) = 1$ as $t \to +\infty$. Thus,

$$\lim_{t\to+\infty} \frac{80}{1 + 2.2(3.68)^{-t}} = \frac{80}{1 + 2.2(0)} = 80$$ $(3.68)^{-\infty} = 0$ (See below.)

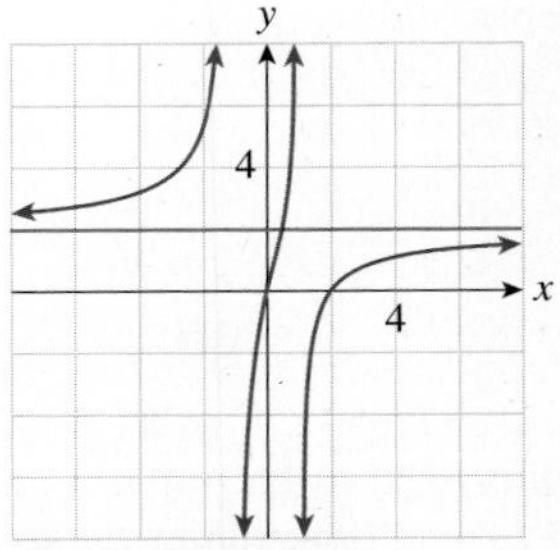

Figure 19

Before we go on... Let's now look at the graph of the function $\frac{2x^2 - 4x}{x^2 - 1}$ in parts (a)and (b) of Example 4. We say that the graph of f has a **horizontal asymptote** at $y = 2$ because of the limits we have just calculated. This means that the graph approaches the horizontal line $y = 2$ far to the right or left (in this case, to both the right and left). Figure 19 shows the graph of f together with the line $y = 2$.

The graph reveals some additional interesting information: as $x \to 1^+$, $f(x) \to -\infty$, and as $x \to 1^-$, $f(x) \to +\infty$. Thus,

$$\lim_{x\to 1} f(x) \text{ does not exist.}$$

See if you can determine what happens as $x \to -1$.

If you graph the functions in parts (d) and (f) of Example 4, you will again see a horizontal asymptote. Do the limits in parts (c) and (e) show horizontal asymptotes? ■

It is worthwhile looking again at what we did in each of the limits in Example 4:

a and **b.** We saw that $\dfrac{2x^2 - 4x}{x^2 - 1} \approx \dfrac{2x^2}{x^2}$, and then we canceled the x^2. Notice that, before we cancel, letting x approach $\pm\infty$ in the numerator and denominator yields the ratio $\dfrac{\infty}{\infty}$, which, like $\dfrac{0}{0}$, is another *indeterminate form*, and indicates to us that further work is needed—in this case cancellation—before we can write down the limit.

c. We obtained $\dfrac{-x^3 - 4x}{2x^2 - 1} \approx \dfrac{-x^3}{2x^2}$, which results in another indeterminate form, $\dfrac{-\infty}{\infty}$, as $x \to +\infty$. Cancellation of the x^2 gave us $\dfrac{-x}{2}$, resulting in the *determinate* form $\dfrac{-\infty}{2} = -\infty$ (a very large number divided by 2 is again a very large number).

d. Here, $\dfrac{2x^2 - 4x}{5x^3 - 3x + 5} \approx \dfrac{2x^2}{5x^3} = \dfrac{2}{5x}$, and the cancellation step turns the indeterminate form $\dfrac{\infty}{\infty}$ into the determinate form $\dfrac{2}{\infty} = 0$ (dividing 2 by a very large number yields a very small number).

e. We reasoned that e raised to a large positive number is large and positive. Putting $t = +\infty$ gives us the determinate form $e^{+\infty} = +\infty$.

f. Here we reasoned that 3.68 raised to a large *negative* number is close to zero. Putting $t = -\infty$ gives us the determinate form $3.68^{-\infty} = 1/3.68^{+\infty} = 1/\infty = 0$ (see (d)).

In parts (a)–(d) of Example 4, $f(x)$ was a **rational function**: a quotient of polynomial functions. We calculated the limit of $f(x)$ at $\pm\infty$ by ignoring all powers of x in both the numerator and denominator except for the largest. Following is a theorem that justifies this procedure.

Theorem 3.2 Evaluating the Limit of a Rational Function at $\pm\infty$

If $f(x)$ has the form

$$f(x) = \frac{c_n x^n + c_{n-1}x^{n-1} + \cdots + c_1 x + c_0}{d_m x^m + d_{m-1}x^{m-1} + \cdots + d_1 x + d_0}$$

with the c_i and d_i constants ($c_n \neq 0$ and $d_m \neq 0$), then we can calculate the limit of $f(x)$ as $x \to \pm\infty$ by ignoring all powers of x except the highest in both the numerator and denominator. Thus,

$$\lim_{x\to\pm\infty} f(x) = \lim_{x\to\pm\infty} \frac{c_n x^n}{d_m x^m}.$$

Quick Examples

(See Example 4.)

1. $\lim_{x \to +\infty} \frac{2x^2 - 4x}{x^2 - 1} = \lim_{x \to +\infty} \frac{2x^2}{x^2} = \lim_{x \to +\infty} 2 = 2$

2. $\lim_{x \to +\infty} \frac{-x^3 - 4x}{2x^2 - 1} = \lim_{x \to +\infty} \frac{-x^3}{2x^2} = \lim_{x \to +\infty} \frac{-x}{2} = -\infty$

3. $\lim_{x \to +\infty} \frac{2x^2 - 4x}{5x^3 - 3x + 5} = \lim_{x \to +\infty} \frac{2x^2}{5x^3} = \lim_{x \to +\infty} \frac{2}{5x} = 0$

Proof Our function $f(x)$ is a polynomial of degree n divided by a polynomial of degree m. If n happens to be larger than m, then dividing the top and bottom by the largest power x^n of x gives

$$f(x) = \frac{c_n x^n + c_{n-1}x^{n-1} + \cdots + c_1 x + c_0}{d_m x^m + d_{m-1}x^{m-1} + \cdots + d_1 x + d_0}$$

$$= \frac{c_n x^n/x^n + c_{n-1}x^{n-1}/x^n + \cdots + c_1 x/x^n + c_0/x^n}{d_m x^m/x^n + d_{m-1}x^{m-1}/x^n + \cdots + d_1 x/x^n + d_0/x^n}.$$

Canceling powers of x in each term and remembering that $n > m$ leaves us with

$$f(x) = \frac{c_n + c_{n-1}/x + \cdots + c_1/x^{n-1} + c_0/x^n}{d_m/x^{n-m} + d_{m-1}/x^{n-m+1} + \cdots + d_1/x^{n-1} + d_0/x^n}.$$

As $x \to \pm\infty$, all the terms shown in red approach 0, so we can ignore them in taking the limit. (The first term in the denominator happens to approach 0 as well, but we retain it for convenience.) Thus,

$$\lim_{x \to \pm\infty} f(x) = \lim_{x \to \pm\infty} \frac{c_n}{d_m/x^{n-m}} = \lim_{x \to \pm\infty} \frac{c_n x^n}{d_m x^m},$$

as required. The cases when n is smaller than m and $m = n$ are proved similarly by dividing top and bottom by the largest power of x in each case.

Some Determinate and Indeterminate Forms

The following table brings these ideas together with our observations in Example 2.

Some Determinate and Indeterminate Forms

$\frac{0}{0}$ and $\pm\frac{\infty}{\infty}$ are **indeterminate**; evaluating limits in which these arise requires simplification or further analysis.[†]

The following are **determinate** forms for any nonzero number k:

$\frac{k}{0^{\pm}} = \pm\infty$	$\frac{k}{\text{Small}} = \text{Big}^*$ (See Example 2.)
$k(\pm\infty) = \pm\infty$	$k \times \text{Big} = \text{Big}^*$
$k \pm \infty = \pm\infty$	$k \pm \text{Big} = \pm\text{Big}$

† Some other indeterminate forms are: $\pm\infty \cdot 0$, $\infty - \infty$, and 1^{∞}. (These are not discussed in this text, but see the Communication and Reasoning exercises for this section.)

$\pm\frac{\infty}{k} = \pm\infty$	$\frac{\text{Big}}{k} = \text{Big}^*$
$\pm\frac{k}{\infty} = 0$	$\frac{k}{\text{Big}} = \text{Small}$

and, if $k > 1$, then

$k^{+\infty} = +\infty$	$k^{\text{Big positive}} = \text{Big}$
$k^{-\infty} = 0.$	$k^{\text{Big negative}} = \text{Small}$

*The sign gets switched in these forms if k is negative.

Quick Examples

1. $\lim_{x\to 0} \frac{60}{2x^2} = +\infty$	$\frac{k}{0^+} = +\infty$
2. $\lim_{x\to -1^-} \frac{2x-6}{x+1} = +\infty$	$\frac{-8}{0^-} = +\infty$
3. $\lim_{x\to -\infty} 3x - 5 = -\infty$	$3(-\infty) - 5 = -\infty - 5 = -\infty$
4. $\lim_{x\to +\infty} \frac{2x}{60} = +\infty$	$\frac{2(\infty)}{60} = \infty$
5. $\lim_{x\to -\infty} \frac{60}{2x} = 0$	$\frac{60}{2(-\infty)} = 0$
6. $\lim_{x\to +\infty} \frac{60x}{2x} = 30$	$\frac{\infty}{\infty}$ is indeterminate but we can cancel.
7. $\lim_{x\to -\infty} \frac{60}{e^x - 1} = \frac{60}{0-1} = -60$	$e^{-\infty} = 0$

FAQs

Strategy for Evaluating Limits Algebraically

Q: *Is there a systematic way to evaluate a limit* $\lim_{x\to a} f(x)$ *algebraically?*

A: The following approach is often successful:

Case 1: a Is a Finite Number (Not $\pm\infty$)

1. Decide whether f is a closed-form function. If it is not, then find the left and right limits at the values of x where the function changes from one formula to another.
2. If f is a closed-form function, try substituting $x = a$ in the formula for $f(x)$. Then one of the following three things may happen:

   $f(a)$ is defined. Then $\lim_{x\to a} f(x) = f(a)$.

   $f(a)$ is not defined and has the indeterminate form 0/0. Try to simplify the expression for f to cancel one of the terms that gives 0.

   $f(a)$ is not defined and has one of the determinate forms listed above in the above table. Use the table to determine the limit as in the Quick Examples.

Case 2: $a = \pm\infty$

Remember that we can use the determinate forms $k^{+\infty} = \infty$ and $k^{-\infty} = 0$ if $k > 1$. Further, if the given function is a polynomial or ratio of polynomials, use the technique of Example 4: Focus only on the highest powers of x and then simplify to obtain either a number L, in which case the limit exists and equals L, or one of the determinate forms $\pm\infty/k = \pm\infty$ or $\pm k/\infty = 0$.

There is another technique for evaluating certain difficult limits, called *l'Hospital's rule,* but this uses derivatives, so we'll have to wait to discuss it until Section 4.1.

3.3 EXERCISES

▼ more advanced ◆ challenging
T indicates exercises that should be solved using technology

In Exercises 1–4, complete the given sentence.

1. The closed-form function $f(x) = \dfrac{1}{x-1}$ is continuous for all x except ______. HINT [See Quick Example on page 215.]
2. The closed-form function $f(x) = \dfrac{1}{x^2-1}$ is continuous for all x except ______. HINT [See Quick Example on page 215.]
3. The closed-form function $f(x) = \sqrt{x+1}$ has $x = 3$ in its domain. Therefore, $\lim_{x\to 3}\sqrt{x+1} =$ ___. HINT [See Example 1.]
4. The closed-form function $f(x) = \sqrt{x-1}$ has $x = 10$ in its domain. Therefore, $\lim_{x\to 10}\sqrt{x-1} =$ ___. HINT [See Example 1.]

In Exercises 5–20, determine whether the given limit leads to a determinate or indeterminate form. Evaluate the limit if it exists, or say why if not. HINT [See Example 2 and Quick Examples on page 223.]

5. $\displaystyle\lim_{x\to 0}\frac{60}{x^4}$
6. $\displaystyle\lim_{x\to 0}\frac{2x^2}{x^2}$
7. $\displaystyle\lim_{x\to 0}\frac{x^3-1}{x^3}$
8. $\displaystyle\lim_{x\to 0}\frac{-2}{x^2}$
9. $\displaystyle\lim_{x\to -\infty}(-x^2+5)$
10. $\displaystyle\lim_{x\to 0}\frac{2x^2+4}{x}$
11. $\displaystyle\lim_{x\to +\infty}4^{-x}$
12. $\displaystyle\lim_{x\to +\infty}\frac{60+e^{-x}}{2-e^{-x}}$
13. $\displaystyle\lim_{x\to 0}\frac{-x^3}{3x^3}$
14. $\displaystyle\lim_{x\to -\infty}3x^2+6$
15. $\displaystyle\lim_{x\to -\infty}\frac{-x^3}{3x^6}$
16. $\displaystyle\lim_{x\to +\infty}\frac{-x^6}{3x^3}$
17. $\displaystyle\lim_{x\to -\infty}\frac{4}{-x+2}$
18. $\displaystyle\lim_{x\to -\infty}e^x$
19. $\displaystyle\lim_{x\to -\infty}\frac{60}{e^x-1}$
20. $\displaystyle\lim_{x\to -\infty}\frac{2}{2x^2+3}$

Calculate the limits in Exercises 21–74 algebraically. If a limit does not exist, say why.

21. $\displaystyle\lim_{x\to 0}(x+1)$ HINT [See Example 1(a).]
22. $\displaystyle\lim_{x\to 0}(2x-4)$ HINT [See Example 1(a).]
23. $\displaystyle\lim_{x\to 2}\frac{2+x}{x}$
24. $\displaystyle\lim_{x\to -1}\frac{4x^2+1}{x}$
25. $\displaystyle\lim_{x\to -1}\frac{x+1}{x}$
26. $\displaystyle\lim_{x\to 4}(x+\sqrt{x})$
27. $\displaystyle\lim_{x\to 8}(x-\sqrt[3]{x})$
28. $\displaystyle\lim_{x\to 1}\frac{x-2}{x+1}$
29. $\displaystyle\lim_{h\to 1}(h^2+2h+1)$
30. $\displaystyle\lim_{h\to 0}(h^3-4)$
31. $\displaystyle\lim_{h\to 3}2$
32. $\displaystyle\lim_{h\to 0}-5$
33. $\displaystyle\lim_{h\to 0}\frac{h^2}{h+h^2}$ HINT [See Example 1(b).]
34. $\displaystyle\lim_{h\to 0}\frac{h^2+h}{h^2+2h}$ HINT [See Example 1(b).]
35. $\displaystyle\lim_{x\to 1}\frac{x^2-2x+1}{x^2-x}$
36. $\displaystyle\lim_{x\to -1}\frac{x^2+3x+2}{x^2+x}$
37. $\displaystyle\lim_{x\to 2}\frac{x^3-8}{x-2}$
38. $\displaystyle\lim_{x\to -2}\frac{x^3+8}{x^2+3x+2}$
39. $\displaystyle\lim_{x\to 0^+}\frac{1}{x^2}$ HINT [See Example 2.]
40. $\displaystyle\lim_{x\to 0^+}\frac{1}{x^2-x}$ HINT [See Example 2.]
41. $\displaystyle\lim_{x\to -1}\frac{x^2+1}{x+1}$
42. $\displaystyle\lim_{x\to -1^-}\frac{x^2+1}{x+1}$
43. $\displaystyle\lim_{x\to -2^+}\frac{x^2+8}{x^2+3x+2}$
44. $\displaystyle\lim_{x\to -1}\frac{x^2+3x}{x^2+x}$

45. $\lim_{x\to -2} \frac{x^2+8}{x^2+3x+2}$

46. $\lim_{x\to -1} \frac{x^2+3x}{x^2+2x+1}$

47. $\lim_{x\to 2} \frac{x^2+8}{x^2-4x+4}$

48. $\lim_{x\to -1} \frac{x^2+3x}{x^2+3x+2}$

49. ▼ $\lim_{x\to 2^+} \frac{x-2}{\sqrt{x-2}}$

50. ▼ $\lim_{x\to 3^-} \frac{\sqrt{3-x}}{3-x}$

51. ▼ $\lim_{x\to 9} \frac{\sqrt{x}-3}{x-9}$

52. ▼ $\lim_{x\to 4} \frac{x-4}{\sqrt{x}-2}$

53. $\lim_{x\to +\infty} \frac{3x^2+10x-1}{2x^2-5x}$ HINT [See Example 4.]

54. $\lim_{x\to +\infty} \frac{6x^2+5x+100}{3x^2-9}$ HINT [See Example 4.]

55. $\lim_{x\to +\infty} \frac{x^5-1{,}000x^4}{2x^5+10{,}000}$

56. $\lim_{x\to +\infty} \frac{x^6+3{,}000x^3+1{,}000{,}000}{2x^6+1{,}000x^3}$

57. $\lim_{x\to +\infty} \frac{10x^2+300x+1}{5x+2}$

58. $\lim_{x\to +\infty} \frac{2x^4+20x^3}{1{,}000x^3+6}$

59. $\lim_{x\to -\infty} \frac{3x^2+10x-1}{2x^2-5x}$

60. $\lim_{x\to -\infty} \frac{6x^2+5x+100}{3x^2-9}$

61. $\lim_{x\to -\infty} \frac{x^5-1{,}000x^4}{2x^5+10{,}000}$

62. $\lim_{x\to -\infty} \frac{x^6+3000x^3+1{,}000{,}000}{2x^6+1{,}000x^3}$

63. $\lim_{x\to -\infty} \frac{10x^2+300x+1}{5x+2}$

64. $\lim_{x\to -\infty} \frac{2x^4+20x^3}{1{,}000x^3+6}$

65. $\lim_{x\to -\infty} \frac{10x^2+300x+1}{5x^3+2}$

66. $\lim_{x\to -\infty} \frac{2x^4+20x^3}{1{,}000x^6+6}$

67. $\lim_{x\to +\infty} (4e^{-3x}+12)$

68. $\lim_{x\to +\infty} \frac{2}{5-5.3e^{-3x}}$

69. $\lim_{t\to +\infty} \frac{2}{5-5.3(3^{3t})}$

70. $\lim_{t\to +\infty} (4.1-2e^{3t})$

71. $\lim_{t\to +\infty} \frac{2^{3t}}{1+5.3e^{-t}}$

72. $\lim_{x\to -\infty} \frac{4.2}{2-3^{2x}}$

73. $\lim_{x\to -\infty} \frac{-3^{2x}}{2+e^x}$

74. $\lim_{x\to +\infty} \frac{2^{-3x}}{1+5.3e^{-x}}$

In each of Exercises 75–82, find all points of discontinuity of the given function. HINT [See Example 3.]

75. $f(x) = \begin{cases} x+2 & \text{if } x<0 \\ 2x-1 & \text{if } x\ge 0 \end{cases}$

76. $g(x) = \begin{cases} 1-x & \text{if } x\le 1 \\ x-1 & \text{if } x>1 \end{cases}$

77. $g(x) = \begin{cases} x+2 & \text{if } x<0 \\ 2x+2 & \text{if } 0\le x<2 \\ x^2+2 & \text{if } x\ge 2 \end{cases}$

78. $f(x) = \begin{cases} 1-x & \text{if } x\le 1 \\ x+2 & \text{if } 1<x<3 \\ x^2-4 & \text{if } x\ge 3 \end{cases}$

79. ▼ $h(x) = \begin{cases} x+2 & \text{if } x<0 \\ 0 & \text{if } x=0 \\ 2x+2 & \text{if } x>0 \end{cases}$

80. ▼ $h(x) = \begin{cases} 1-x & \text{if } x<1 \\ 1 & \text{if } x=1 \\ x+2 & \text{if } x>1 \end{cases}$

81. ▼ $f(x) = \begin{cases} 1/x & \text{if } x<0 \\ x & \text{if } 0\le x\le 2 \\ 2^{x-1} & \text{if } x>2 \end{cases}$

82. ▼ $f(x) = \begin{cases} x^3+2 & \text{if } x\le -1 \\ x^2 & \text{if } -1<x<0 \\ x & \text{if } x\ge 0 \end{cases}$

APPLICATIONS

83. ***Processor Speeds*** The processor speeds, in megahertz (MHz), of Intel processors during the period 1996–2010 can be approximated by the following function of time t in years since the start of 1990:[17]

$$v(t) = \begin{cases} 400t-2{,}200 & \text{if } 6\le t<15 \\ 3{,}800 & \text{if } 15\le t\le 20. \end{cases}$$

a. Compute $\lim_{t\to 15^-} v(t)$ and $\lim_{t\to 15^+} v(t)$ and interpret each answer. HINT [See Example 3.]

b. Is the function v continuous at $t=15$? According to the model, was there any abrupt change in processor speeds during the period 1996–2010?

84. ***Processor Speeds*** The processor speeds, in megahertz (MHz), of Intel processors during the period 1970–2000 can be approximated by the following function of time t in years since the start of 1970:[18]

$$v(t) = \begin{cases} 3t & \text{if } 0\le t<20 \\ 174t-3{,}420 & \text{if } 20\le t\le 30. \end{cases}$$

[17] A rough model based on the fastest processors produced by Intel. Source for data: www.intel.com.

[18] *Ibid.*

a. Compute $\lim_{t\to 20^-} v(t)$ and $\lim_{t\to 20^+} v(t)$ and interpret each answer.

b. Is the function v continuous at $t = 20$? According to the model, was there any abrupt change in processor speeds during the period 1970–2000?

85. ***Movie Advertising*** Movie expenditures, in billions of dollars, on advertising in newspapers from 1995 to 2004 can be approximated by

$$f(t) = \begin{cases} 0.04t + 0.33 & \text{if } t \le 4 \\ -0.01t + 1.2 & \text{if } t > 4 \end{cases}$$

where t is time in years since 1995.[19]

a. Compute $\lim_{t\to 4^-} f(t)$ and $\lim_{t\to 4^+} f(t)$, and interpret each answer. HINT [See Example 3.]

b. Is the function f continuous at $t = 4$? What does the answer tell you about movie advertising expenditures?

86. ***Movie Advertising*** The percentage of movie advertising as a share of newspapers' total advertising revenue from 1995 to 2004 can be approximated by

$$p(t) = \begin{cases} -0.07t + 6.0 & \text{if } t \le 4 \\ 0.3t + 17.0 & \text{if } t > 4 \end{cases}$$

where t is time in years since 1995.[20]

a. Compute $\lim_{t\to 4^-} p(t)$ and $\lim_{t\to 4^+} p(t)$, and interpret each answer. HINT [See Example 3.]

b. Is the function p continuous at $t = 4$? What does the answer tell you about newspaper revenues?

87. ***Law Enforcement in the 1980s and 1990s*** The cost of fighting crime in the United States increased significantly during the period 1982–1999. Total spending on police and courts can be approximated, respectively, by[21]

$$P(t) = 1.745t + 29.84 \text{ billion dollars} \qquad (2 \le t \le 19)$$
$$C(t) = 1.097t + 10.65 \text{ billion dollars} \qquad (2 \le t \le 19),$$

where t is time in years since 1980. Compute $\lim_{t\to +\infty} \frac{P(t)}{C(t)}$ to two decimal places and interpret the result. HINT [See Example 4.]

88. ***Law Enforcement in the 1980s and 1990s*** Refer to Exercise 87. Total spending on police, courts, and prisons in the period 1982–1999 could be approximated, respectively, by[22]

$$P(t) = 1.745t + 29.84 \text{ billion dollars} \qquad (2 \le t \le 19)$$
$$C(t) = 1.097t + 10.65 \text{ billion dollars} \qquad (2 \le t \le 19)$$
$$J(t) = 1.919t + 12.36 \text{ billion dollars} \qquad (2 \le t \le 19),$$

where t is time in years since 1980. Compute $\lim_{t\to +\infty} \frac{P(t)}{P(t) + C(t) + J(t)}$ to two decimal places and interpret the result. HINT [See Example 4.]

89. ***SAT Scores by Income*** The following bar graph shows U.S. math SAT scores as a function of household income:[23]

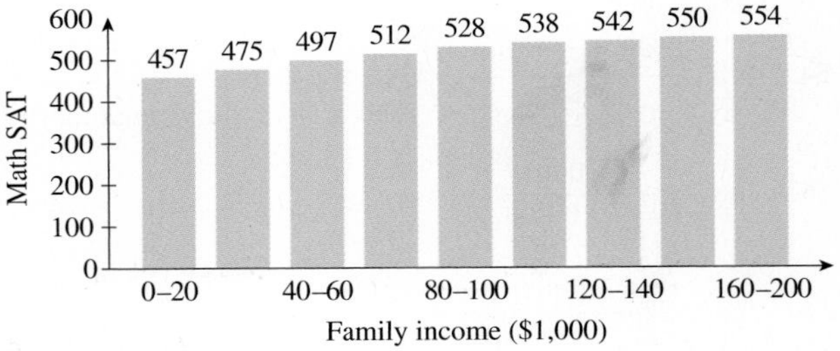

These data can be modeled by

$$S(x) = 573 - 33e^{-0.0131x},$$

where $S(x)$ is the average math SAT score of students whose household income is x thousand dollars per year. Calculate $\lim_{x\to +\infty} S(x)$ and interpret the answer.

90. ***SAT Scores by Income*** The following bar graph shows U.S. critical reading SAT scores as a function of household income:[24]

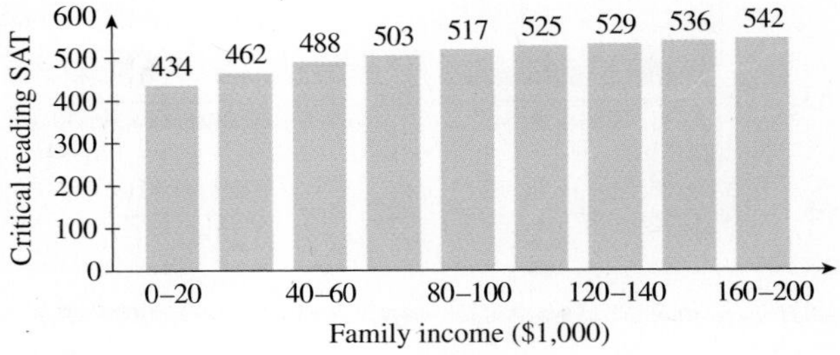

These data can be modeled by

$$S(x) = 550 - 136e^{-0.0151x},$$

where $S(x)$ is the average critical reading SAT score of students whose household income is x thousand dollars per year. Calculate $\lim_{x\to +\infty} S(x)$ and interpret the answer.

[19] Model by the authors. Source for data: Newspaper Association of America Business Analysis and Research/*New York Times*, May 16, 2005.

[20] *Ibid.*

[21] Spending is adjusted for inflation and shown in 1999 dollars. Models are based on a linear regression. Source for data: Bureau of Justice Statistics/*New York Times*, February 11, 2002, p. A14.

[22] *Ibid.*

[23] 2009 data. Source: College Board/*New York Times* http://economix.blogs.nytimes.com.

[24] *Ibid.*

Foreign Trade *Annual U.S. imports from China in the years 1996 through 2003 could be approximated by*

$$I(t) = t^2 + 3.5t + 50 \quad (1 \le t \le 9)$$

billion dollars, where t represents time in years since 1995. Annual U.S. exports to China in the same years could be approximated by

$$E(t) = 0.4t^2 - 1.6t + 14 \quad (0 \le t \le 10)$$

billion dollars.[25] *Exercises 91 and 92 are based on these models.*

91. Assuming that the trends shown in the above models continue indefinitely, calculate the limits

$$\lim_{t\to+\infty} I(t) \text{ and } \lim_{t\to+\infty} \frac{I(t)}{E(t)}$$

algebraically, interpret your answers, and comment on the results. HINT [See Example 4.]

92. Repeat Exercise 91, this time calculating

$$\lim_{t\to+\infty} E(t) \text{ and } \lim_{t\to+\infty} \frac{E(t)}{I(t)}$$ HINT [See Example 4.]

93. ***Acquisition of Language*** The percentage $p(t)$ of children who can speak in at least single words by the age of t months can be approximated by the equation[26]

$$p(t) = 100\left(\frac{1 - 12{,}200}{t^{4.48}}\right) \quad (t \ge 8.5).$$

Calculate $\lim_{t\to+\infty} p(t)$ and interpret the result. HINT [See Example 4.]

94. ***Acquisition of Language*** The percentage $q(t)$ of children who can speak in sentences of five or more words by the age of t months can be approximated by the equation[27]

$$q(t) = 100\left(1 - \frac{5.27 \times 10^{17}}{t^{12}}\right) \quad (t \ge 30).$$

If p is the function referred to in the preceding exercise, calculate $\lim_{t\to+\infty}[p(t) - q(t)]$ and interpret the result. HINT [See Example 4.]

COMMUNICATION AND REASONING EXERCISES

95. Describe the algebraic method of evaluating limits as discussed in this section and give at least one disadvantage of this method.

96. What is a closed-form function? What can we say about such functions?

97. Why was the following marked wrong? What is the correct answer?

$$\lim_{x\to 3} \frac{x^3 - 27}{x - 3} = \frac{0}{0} \text{ undefined} \qquad \text{✗ WRONG!}$$

98. Why was the following marked wrong? What is the correct answer?

$$\lim_{x\to 1^-} \frac{x - 1}{x^2 - 2x + 1} = \frac{0}{0} = 0 \qquad \text{✗ WRONG!}$$

99. ▼ Your friend Karin tells you that $f(x) = 1/(x-2)^2$ cannot be a closed-form function because it is not continuous at $x = 2$. Comment on her assertion.

100. ▼ Give an example of a function f specified by means of algebraic formulas such that the domain of f consists of all real numbers and f is not continuous at $x = 2$. Is f a closed-form function?

101. Give examples of two limits that lead to two different indeterminate forms, but where both limits exist.

102. Give examples of two limits: one that leads to a determinate form and another that leads to an indeterminate form, but where neither limit exists.

103. ▼ (Compare Exercise 59 in Section 3.1.) Which indeterminate form results from $\lim_{x\to+\infty} \frac{p(x)}{e^x}$ if $p(x)$ is a polynomial? Numerically or graphically estimate these limits for various polynomials $p(x)$. What does this suggest about limits that result in $\frac{p(\infty)}{e^\infty}$?

104. ▼ (Compare Exercise 60 in Section 3.1.) Which indeterminate form results from $\lim_{x\to-\infty} p(x)e^x$ if $p(x)$ is a polynomial? What does this suggest about the limits that result in $p(\infty)e^{-\infty}$?

105. ▼ What is wrong with the following statement? If $f(x)$ is specified algebraically and $f(a)$ is defined, then $\lim_{x\to a} f(x)$ exists and equals $f(a)$. How can it be corrected?

106. ▼ What is wrong with the following statement? If $f(x)$ is specified algebraically and $f(a)$ is not defined, then $\lim_{x\to a} f(x)$ does not exist.

107. ▼ Give the formula for a function that is continuous everywhere except at two points.

108. ▼ Give the formula for a function that is continuous everywhere except at three points.

109. ◆ ***The Indeterminate Form*** $\infty - \infty$ An indeterminate form not mentioned in Section 3.3 is $\infty - \infty$. Give examples of three limits that lead to this indeterminate form, and where the first limit exists and equals 5, where the second limit diverges to $+\infty$, and where the third exists and equals –5.

110. ◆ ***The Indeterminate Form*** 1^∞ An indeterminate form not mentioned in Section 3.3 is 1^∞. Give examples of three limits that lead to this indeterminate form, and where the first limit exists and equals 1, where the second limit exists and equals e, and where the third diverges to $+\infty$. HINT [For the third, consider modifying the second.]

---

[25] Based on quadratic regression using data from the U.S. Census Bureau Foreign Trade Division Web site www.census.gov/foreign-trade/sitc1/ as of December 2004.

[26] The model is the authors' and is based on data presented in the article *The Emergence of Intelligence* by William H. Calvin, *Scientific American,* October, 1994, pp. 101–107.

[27] *Ibid.*

3.4 Average Rate of Change

Calculus is the mathematics of change, inspired largely by observation of continuously changing quantities around us in the real world. As an example, the Consumer Price Index (CPI) C increased from 211 points in January 2009 to 220 points in January 2011.[28] As we saw in Chapter 1, the **change** in this index can be measured as the difference:

$$\Delta C = \text{Second value} - \text{First value} = 220 - 211 = 9 \text{ points.}$$

(The fact that the CPI increased is reflected in the positive sign of the change.) The kind of question we will concentrate on is *how fast* the CPI was changing. Because C increased by 9 points in 2 years, we say it averaged a $9/2 = 4.5$ point rise each year. (It actually rose 5 points the first year and 4 the second, giving an average rise of 4.5 points each year.)

Alternatively, we might want to measure this rate in points per month rather than points per year. Because C increased by 9 points in 24 months, it increased at an average rate of $9/24 = 0.375$ points per month.

In both cases, we obtained the average rate of change by dividing the change by the corresponding length of time:

$$\text{Average rate of change} = \frac{\text{Change in } C}{\text{Change in time}} = \frac{9}{2} = 4.50 \text{ points per year}$$

$$\text{Average rate of change} = \frac{\text{Change in } C}{\text{Change in time}} = \frac{9}{24} = 0.375 \text{ points per month.}$$

Average Rate of Change of a Function Numerically and Graphically

EXAMPLE 1 Standard and Poor's 500

The following table lists the approximate value of Standard and Poor's 500 stock market index (S&P) during the period 2005–2011[29] ($t = 5$ represents 2005):

***t* (year)**	5	6	7	8	9	10	11
***S*(*t*) (points)**	1,200	1,300	1,400	1,400	900	1,150	1,300

a. What was the average rate of change in the S&P over the 2-year period 2005–2007 (the period $5 \le t \le 7$ or $[5, 7]$ in interval notation); over the 4-year period 2005–2009 (the period $5 \le t \le 9$ or $[5, 9]$); and over the period $[6, 11]$?

b. Graph the values shown in the table. How are the rates of change reflected in the graph?

[28]Figures are approximate. Source: Bureau of Labor Statistics www.bls.gov.

[29]The values are approximate values at the start of the given year. Source: http://finance.google.com.

Solution

a. During the 2-year period [5, 7], the S&P changed as follows:

Start of the period ($t = 5$):	$S(5) = 1{,}200$
End of the period ($t = 7$):	$S(7) = 1{,}400$
Change during the period [5, 7]:	$S(7) - S(5) = 200$

Thus, the S&P increased by 200 points in 2 years, giving an average rate of change of $200/2 = 100$ points per year. We can write the calculation this way:

$$\text{Average rate of change of } S = \frac{\text{Change in } S}{\text{Change in } t} = \frac{\Delta S}{\Delta t} = \frac{S(7) - S(5)}{7 - 5} = \frac{1{,}400 - 1{,}200}{7 - 5} = \frac{200}{2} = 100 \text{ points per year.}$$

Interpreting the result: During the period [5, 7] (that is, 2005–2007), the S&P increased at an average rate of 100 points per year.

Similarly, the average rate of change during the period [5, 9] was

$$\text{Average rate of change of } S = \frac{\Delta S}{\Delta t} = \frac{S(9) - S(5)}{9 - 5} = \frac{900 - 1{,}200}{9 - 5} = \frac{-300}{4} = -75 \text{ points per year.}$$

Interpreting the result: During the period [5, 9] (that is, 2005–2009), the S&P *decreased* at an average rate of 75 points per year.

Finally, during the period [6, 11], the average change was

$$\text{Average rate of change of } S = \frac{\Delta S}{\Delta t} = \frac{S(11) - S(6)}{11 - 6} = \frac{1{,}300 - 1{,}300}{11 - 6} = \frac{0}{5} = 0 \text{ points per year.}$$

Interpreting the result: During the period [6, 11] the average rate of change of the S&P was zero points per year (even though its value did fluctuate during that period).

b. In Chapter 1, we saw that the rate of change of a quantity that changes linearly with time is measured by the slope of its graph. However, the S&P index does not change linearly with time. Figure 20 shows the data plotted two different ways: (a) as a bar chart and (b) as a piecewise linear graph. Bar charts are more commonly used in the media, but Figure 20(b) on the right illustrates the changing index more clearly.

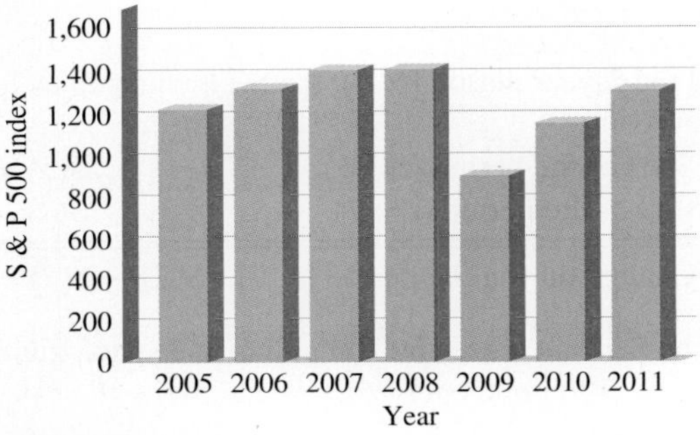

Figure 20(a)

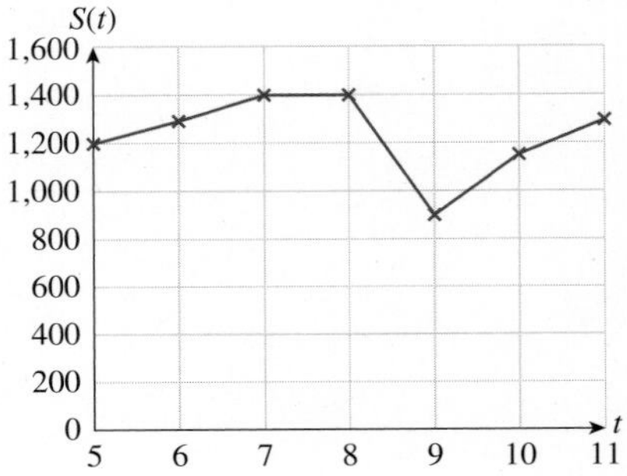

Figure 20(b)

We saw in part (a) that the average rate of change of S over the interval [5, 9] is the ratio

$$\text{Average rate of change of } S = \frac{\Delta S}{\Delta t} = \frac{S(9) - S(5)}{9 - 5} = -75 \text{ points per year.}$$

Notice that this rate of change is also the slope of the line through P and Q shown in Figure 21, and we can estimate this slope directly from the graph as shown.

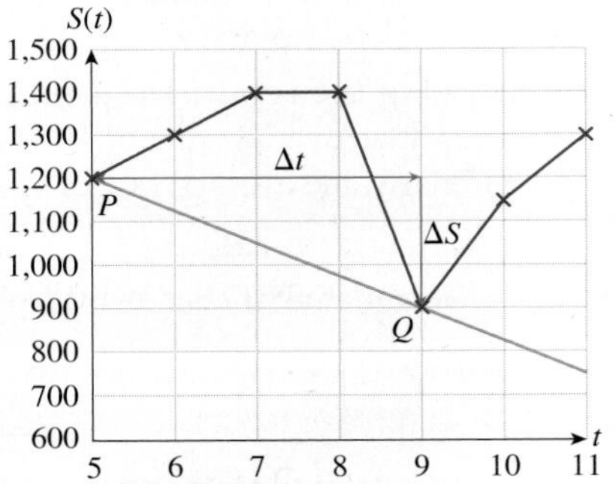

$$\text{Slope } PQ = \frac{\Delta S}{\Delta t} = \frac{900 - 1{,}200}{9 - 5} = -75$$

Figure 21

Average Rate of Change as Slope: The average rate of change of the S&P over the interval [5, 9] is the slope of the line passing through the points on the graph where $t = 5$ and $t = 9$.

Similarly, the average rates of change of the S&P over the intervals [5, 7] and [6, 11] are the slopes of the lines through pairs of corresponding points.

Here is the formal definition of the average rate of change of a function over an interval.

Change and Average Rate of Change of *f* over [*a*, *b*]: Difference Quotient

The **change** in $f(x)$ over the interval $[a, b]$ is

$$\begin{aligned}\text{Change in } f &= \Delta f \\ &= \text{Second value} - \text{First value} \\ &= f(b) - f(a).\end{aligned}$$

The **average rate of change** of $f(x)$ over the interval $[a, b]$ is

$$\text{Average rate of change of } f = \frac{\text{Change in } f}{\text{Change in } x}$$
$$= \frac{\Delta f}{\Delta x} = \frac{f(b) - f(a)}{b - a}$$
$$= \text{Slope of line through points } P \text{ and } Q \text{ (see figure).}$$

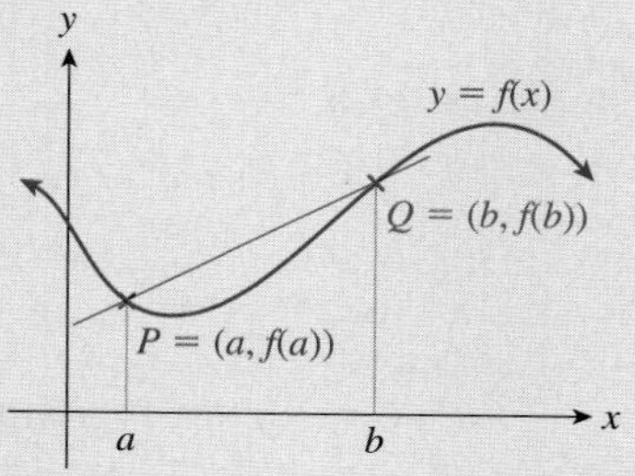

Average rate of change = Slope of PQ

We also call this average rate of change the **difference quotient** of f over the interval $[a, b]$. (It is the *quotient* of the *differences* $f(b) - f(a)$ and $b - a$.) A line through two points of a graph like P and Q is called a **secant line** of the graph.

Units

The units of the change Δf in f are the units of $f(x)$.
The units of the average rate of change of f are units of $f(x)$ per unit of x.*

* The average rate of change is a slope, and so it is measured in the same units as the slope: units of y (or $f(x)$) per unit of x.

Quick Example

If $f(3) = -1$ billion dollars, $f(5) = 0.5$ billion dollars, and x is measured in years, then the change and average rate of change of f over the interval $[3, 5]$ are given by

$$\text{Change in } f = f(5) - f(3) = 0.5 - (-1) = 1.5 \text{ billion dollars}$$
$$\text{Average rate of change} = \frac{f(5) - f(3)}{5 - 3} = \frac{0.5 - (-1)}{2}$$
$$= 0.75 \text{ billion dollars/year.}$$

Alternative Formula: Average Rate of Change of *f* over [*a*, *a* + *h*]

(Replace b in the formula for the average rate of change by $a + h$.) The average rate of change of f over the interval $[a, a + h]$ is

$$\text{Average rate of change of } f = \frac{f(a + h) - f(a)}{h}. \qquad \text{Replace } b \text{ by } a + h.$$

In Example 1 we saw that the average rate of change of a quantity can be estimated directly from a graph. Here is an example that further illustrates the graphical approach.

EXAMPLE 2 Freon 22 Production

Figure 22 shows the number of tons $f(t)$ of ozone-layer-damaging Freon 22 (chlorodifluoromethane) produced annually in developing countries for the period 2000–2010 (t is time in years, and $t = 0$ represents 2000).[30]

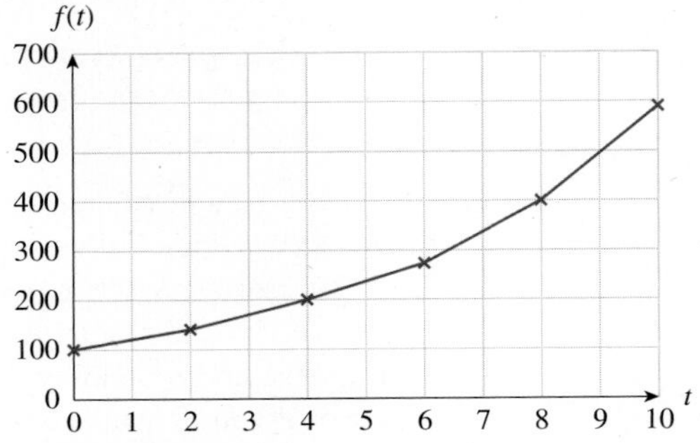

Figure 22

a. Use the graph to estimate the average rate of change of $f(t)$ with respect to t over the interval [4, 8] and interpret the result.

b. Over which 2-year period(s) was the average rate of change of Freon 22 production the greatest?

c. Multiple choice: For the period of time under consideration, Freon 22 production was

(A) increasing at a faster and faster rate.
(B) increasing at a slower and slower rate.
(C) decreasing at a faster and faster rate.
(D) decreasing at a slower and slower rate.

Solution

a. The average rate of change of f over the interval [4, 8] is given by the slope of the line through the points P and Q shown in Figure 23.

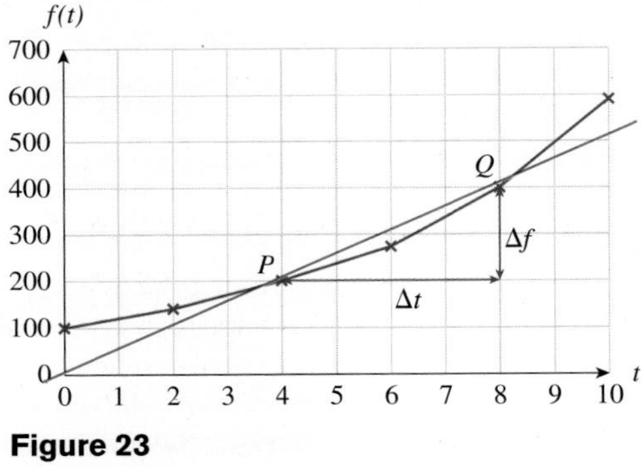

Figure 23

From the figure,

$$\text{Average rate of change of } f = \frac{\Delta f}{\Delta t} = \text{slope } PQ \approx \frac{400 - 200}{8 - 4} = \frac{200}{4} = 50.$$

Thus, the rate of change of f over the interval [4, 8] is approximately 50.

[30]Figures from 2007 on were projected. Source: *New York Times*, February 23, 2007, p. C1.

Q: *How do we interpret the result?*

A: A clue is given by the units of the average rate of change: units of f per unit of t. The units of f are tons of Freon 22 and the units of t are years. Thus, the average rate of change of f is measured in tons of Freon 22 per year, and we can now interpret the result as follows:

Interpreting the average rate of change: Annual production of Freon 22 was increasing at an average rate of 50 tons of Freon 22 per year from 2004 to 2008.

b. The rates of change of Freon 22 production over successive 2-year periods are given by the slopes of the individual line segments that make up the graph in Figure 22. Thus, the greatest average rate of change in a single 2-year period corresponds to the segment(s) with the largest slope. If you look at the figure, you will notice that the segment corresponding to [8, 10] is the steepest. Thus, the average rate of change of Freon 22 production was largest over the 2-year period from 2008 to 2010.

c. Looking again at the figure, notice that the graph rises as we go from left to right; that is, the value of the function (Freon 22 production) is increasing with increasing t. At the same time, the fact that the curve bends up (is concave up) with increasing t tells us that the successive slopes get steeper, and so the average rates of change increase as well (Choice (A)).

Before we go on... Notice in Example 2 that we do not get exact answers from a graph; the best we can do is *estimate* the rates of change: Was the exact answer to part (a) closer to 49 or 51? Two people can reasonably disagree about results read from a graph, and you should bear this in mind when you check the answers to the exercises. ■

Perhaps the most sophisticated way to compute the average rate of change of a quantity is through the use of a mathematical formula or model for the quantity in question.

Average Rate of Change of a Function Using Algebraic Data

EXAMPLE 3 Average Rate of Change from a Formula

You are a commodities trader and you monitor the price of gold on the spot market very closely during an active morning. Suppose you find that the price of an ounce of gold can be approximated by the function

$$G(t) = 5t^2 - 85t + 1{,}762 \qquad (7.5 \le t \le 10.5),$$

where t is time in hours. (See Figure 24. $t = 8$ represents 8:00 am.)

Looking at the graph on the right, we can see that the price of gold was falling at the beginning of the time period, but by $t = 8.5$ the fall had slowed to a stop, whereupon the market turned around and the price began to rise more and more rapidly toward the end of the period. What was the average rate of change of the price of gold over the $1\frac{1}{2}$-hour period starting at 8:00 am (the interval [8, 9.5] on the t-axis)?

using Technology

See the Technology Guides at the end of the chapter for detailed instructions on how to calculate the average rate of change of the function in Example 3 using a TI-83/84 Plus or a spreadsheet. Here is an outline:

TI-83/84 Plus

`Y1=5X^2-85X+1762`

Home screen: `(Y1(9.5)-Y1(8))/(9.5-8)`

[More details on page 284.]

Spreadsheet

Headings t, $G(t)$, Rate of Change in A1–C1

t-values 8, 9.5 in A2–A3

`=5*A2^2-85*A2+1762` in B2, copied down to B3

`=(B3-B2)/(A3-A2)` in C2.

[More details on page 286.]

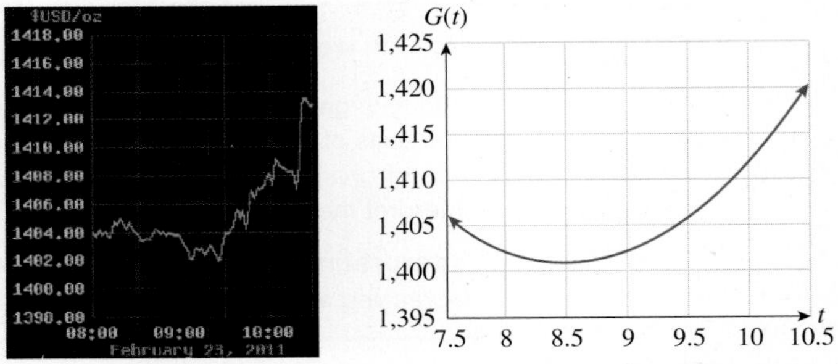

Source: www.kitco.com

$G(t) = 5t^2 - 85t + 1,762$

Figure 24

Solution We have

$$\text{Average rate of change of } G \text{ over } [8, 9.5] = \frac{\Delta G}{\Delta t} = \frac{G(9.5) - G(8)}{9.5 - 8}.$$

From the formula for $G(t)$, we find

$$G(9.5) = 5(9.5)^2 - 85(9.5) + 1,762 = 1,405.75$$
$$G(8) = 5(8)^2 - 85(8) + 1,762 = 1,402.$$

Thus, the average rate of change of G is given by

$$\frac{G(9.5) - G(8)}{9.5 - 8} = \frac{1,405.75 - 1,402}{1.5} = \frac{3.75}{1.5} = \$2.50 \text{ per hour.}$$

In other words, the price of gold increased at an average rate of \$2.50 per hour over the $1\frac{1}{2}$-hour period.

EXAMPLE 4 Rates of Change over Shorter Intervals

Continuing with Example 3, use technology to compute the average rate of change of

$$G(t) = 5t^2 - 85t + 1,762 \qquad (7.5 \le t \le 10.5)$$

over the intervals $[8, 8 + h]$, where $h = 1, 0.1, 0.01, 0.001$, and 0.0001. What do the answers tell you about the price of gold?

Solution

We use the "alternative" formula

$$\text{Average rate of change of } G \text{ over } [a, a + h] = \frac{G(a + h) - G(a)}{h}$$

so

$$\text{Average rate of change of } G \text{ over } [8, 8 + h] = \frac{G(8 + h) - G(8)}{h}.$$

using Technology

Example 4 is the kind of example where the use of technology can make a huge difference. See the Technology Guides at the end of the chapter to find out how to do the above computations almost effortlessly using a TI-83/84 Plus or a spreadsheet. Here is an outline:

TI-83/84 Plus

```
Y1=5X^2-85X+1762
```

Home screen:

```
(Y1(8+1)-Y1(8))/1
(Y1(8+0.1)-Y1(8))/0.1
(Y1(8+0.01)-Y1(8))/0.01
```

etc.

[More details on page 284.]

Spreadsheet

Headings *a*, *h*, *t*, *G*(*t*), Rate of Change in A1–E1

`8` in A2, `1` in B2,

`=A2` in C2, `=A2+B2` in C3

`=5*C2^2-85*C2+1762` in D2; copy down to D3

`=(D3-D2)/(C3-C2)` in E2

[More details on page 286.]

Let us calculate this average rate of change for some of the values of h listed:

$h = 1$: $\quad G(8+h) = G(8+1) = G(9) = 5(9)^2 - 85(9) + 1{,}762 = 1{,}402$

$$G(8) = 5(8)^2 - 85(8) + 1{,}762 = 1{,}402$$

$$\text{Average rate of change of } G = \frac{G(9) - G(8)}{1} = \frac{1{,}402 - 1{,}402}{1} = 0$$

$h = 0.1$: $\quad G(8+h) = G(8+0.1) = G(8.1) = 5(8.1)^2 - 85(8.1) + 1{,}762$

$$= 1{,}401.55$$

$$G(8) = 5(8)^2 - 85(8) + 1{,}762 = 1{,}402$$

$$\text{Average rate of change of } G = \frac{G(8.1) - G(8)}{0.1} = \frac{1{,}401.55 - 1{,}402}{0.1} = \frac{-0.45}{0.1}$$

$$= -4.5$$

$h = 0.01$: $\quad G(8+h) = G(8+0.01) = G(8.01) = 5(8.01)^2 - 85(8.01) + 1{,}762$

$$= 1{,}401.9505$$

$$G(8) = 5(8)^2 - 85(8) + 1{,}762 = 1{,}402$$

$$\text{Average rate of change of } G = \frac{G(8.01) - G(8)}{0.01} = \frac{1{,}401.9505 - 1{,}402}{0.01} = \frac{-0.0495}{0.01}$$

$$= -4.95$$

Continuing in this way, we get the values in the following table:

h	1	0.1	0.01	0.001	0.0001
Ave. Rate of Change $\dfrac{G(8+h) - G(8)}{h}$	0	−4.5	−4.95	−4.995	−4.9995

Each value is an average rate of change of G. For example, the value corresponding to $h = 0.01$ is -4.95, which tells us:

> *Over the interval* [8, 8.01] *the price of gold was decreasing at an average rate of* \$4.95 *per hour.*

In other words, during the first one hundredth of an hour (or 36 seconds) starting at $t = 8{:}00$ am, the price of gold was decreasing at an average rate of \$4.95 per hour. Put another way, in those 36 seconds, the price of gold decreased at a rate that, if continued, would have produced a decrease of \$4.95 in the price of gold during the next hour. We will return to this example at the beginning of Section 3.5.

FAQs

Recognizing When and How to Compute the Average Rate of Change and How to Interpret the Answer

Q: *How do I know, by looking at the wording of a problem, that it is asking for an average rate of change?*

A: If a problem does not ask for an average rate of change directly, it might do so indirectly, as in "On average, how fast is quantity q increasing?"

Q: *If I know that a problem calls for computing an average rate of change, how should I compute it? By hand or using technology?*

A: All the computations can be done by hand, but when hand calculations are not called for, using technology might save time.

Q: *Lots of problems ask us to "interpret" the answer. How do I do that for questions involving average rates of change?*

A: The *units* of the average rate of change are often the key to interpreting the results:

The units of the average rate of change of f(x) are units of f(x) per unit of x.

Thus, for instance, if $f(x)$ is the cost, in dollars, of a trip of x miles in length, and the average rate of change of f is calculated to be 10, then the units of the average rate of change are dollars per mile, and so we can interpret the answer by saying that the cost of a trip rises an average of $10 for each additional mile.

3.4 EXERCISES

▼ more advanced ◆ challenging

T indicates exercises that should be solved using technology

In Exercises 1–18, calculate the average rate of change of the given function over the given interval. Where appropriate, specify the units of measurement. HINT [See Example 1.]

1.

x	0	1	2	3
$f(x)$	3	5	2	−1

Interval: [1, 3]

2.

x	0	1	2	3
$f(x)$	−1	3	2	1

Interval: [0, 2]

3.

x	−3	−2	−1	0
$f(x)$	−2.1	0	−1.5	0

Interval: [−3, −1]

4.

x	−2	−1	0	1
$f(x)$	−1.5	−0.5	4	6.5

Interval: [−1, 1]

5.

t (months)	2	4	6
$R(t)$ ($ millions)	20.2	24.3	20.1

Interval: [2, 6]

6.

x (kilos)	1	2	3
$C(x)$ (£)	2.20	3.30	4.00

Interval: [1, 3]

7.

p ($)	5.00	5.50	6.00
$q(p)$ (items)	400	300	150

Interval: [5, 5.5]

8.

t (hours)	0	0.1	0.2
$D(t)$ (miles)	0	3	6

Interval: [0.1, 0.2]

9. Apple Computer Stock Price ($)

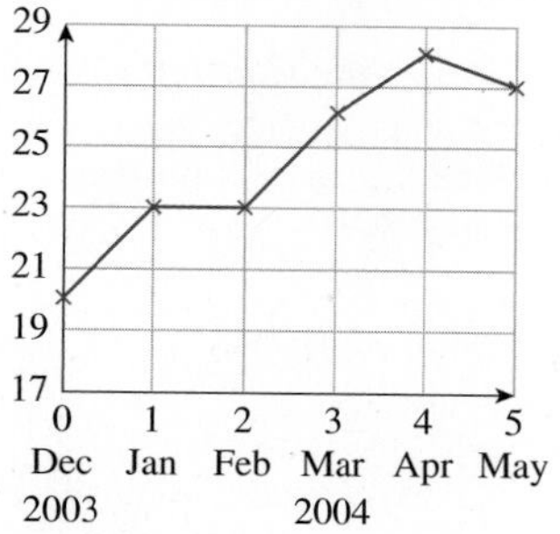

Interval: [2, 5]
HINT [See Example 2.]

10. Cisco Systems Stock Price ($)

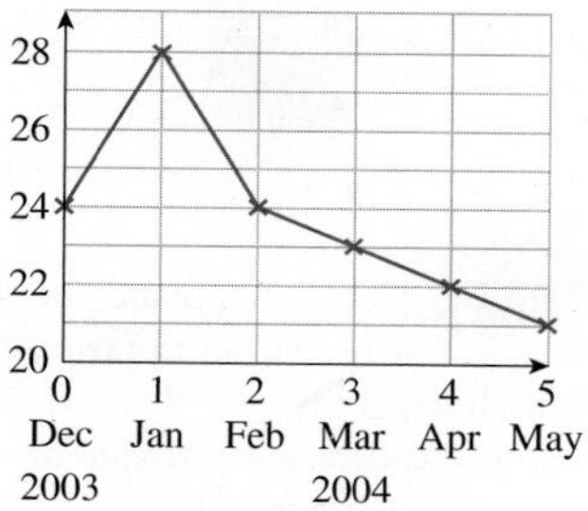

Interval: [1, 5]
HINT [See Example 2.]

11. Unemployment (%)

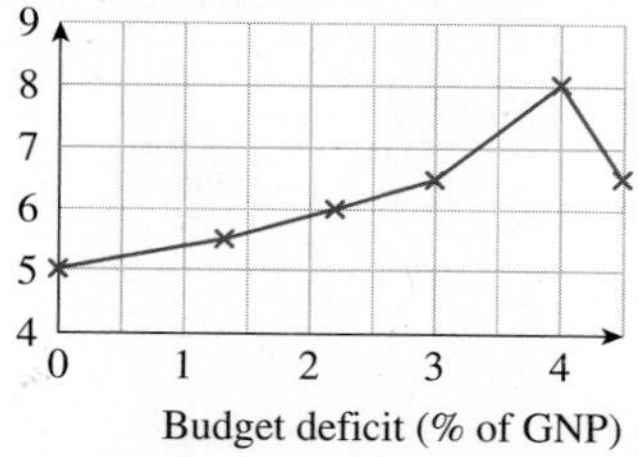

Interval: [0, 4]

12. Inflation (%)

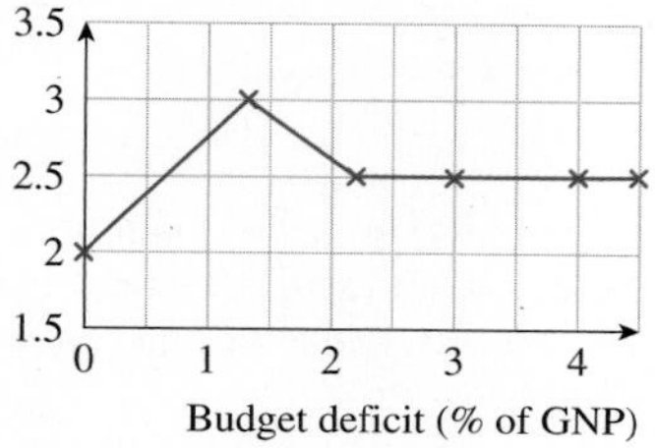

Interval: [0, 4]

13. $f(x) = x^2 - 3$; [1, 3] HINT [See Example 3.]

14. $f(x) = 2x^2 + 4$; [−1, 2] HINT [See Example 3.]

15. $f(x) = 2x + 4$; [−2, 0]

16. $f(x) = \frac{1}{x}$; [1, 4]

17. $f(x) = \frac{x^2}{2} + \frac{1}{x}$; [2, 3] 18. $f(x) = 3x^2 - \frac{x}{2}$; [3, 4]

In Exercises 19–24, calculate the average rate of change of the given function f over the intervals [a, a + h] where h = 1, 0.1, 0.01, 0.001, and 0.0001. (Technology is recommended for the cases h = 0.01, 0.001, and 0.0001.) HINT [See Example 4.]

19. $f(x) = 2x^2; a = 0$

20. $f(x) = \frac{x^2}{2}; a = 1$

21. $f(x) = \frac{1}{x}; a = 2$

22. $f(x) = \frac{2}{x}; a = 1$

23. $f(x) = x^2 + 2x; a = 3$

24. $f(x) = 3x^2 - 2x; a = 0$

APPLICATIONS

25. ***World Military Expenditure*** The following table shows total military and arms trade expenditure in 2000, 2005, and 2010 ($t = 0$ represents 2000):[31]

Year *t*	0	5	10
Military Expenditure *C*(*t*) ($ billion)	1,100	1,300	1,600

Compute and interpret the average rate of change of $C(t)$ **(a)** over the period 2005–2010 (that is, [5, 10]), and **(b)** over the period [0, 10]. Be sure to state the units of measurement. HINT [See Example 1.]

26. ***Education Expenditure*** The following table shows the percentage of the U.S. Discretionary Budget allocated to education in 2003, 2005, and 2009 ($t = 0$ represents 2000):[32]

Year *t*	3	5	9
Percentage *P*(*t*)	6.8	7	6.2

Compute and interpret the average rate of change of $P(t)$ **(a)** over the period 2003–2009 (that is, [3, 9]), and **(b)** over the period [5, 9]. Be sure to state the units of measurement. HINT [See Example 1.]

27. ***Oil Production in Mexico*** The following table shows approximate daily oil production by Pemex, Mexico's national oil company, for 2001–2009 ($t = 1$ represents the start of 2001):[33]

***t* (year since 2000)**	1	2	3	4	5	6	7	8	9
***P*(*t*) (million barrels)**	3.1	3.3	3.4	3.4	3.4	3.3	3.2	3.1	3.0

[31] Source: www.globalissues.org/Geopolitics/ArmsTrade/Spending.asp.

[32] *Ibid.*

[33] Figures are approximate, and 2008–2009 figures are projections by the Department of Energy. Source: Energy Information Administration/Pemex (www.eia.doe.gov).

a. Compute the average rate of change of $P(t)$ over the period 2002–2007. Interpret the result. HINT [See Example 1.]

b. Which of the following is true? From 2001 to 2008, the one-year average rate of change of oil production by Pemex

(A) increased in value.
(B) decreased in value.
(C) never increased in value.
(D) never decreased in value.
HINT [See Example 2.]

28. ***Oil Imports from Mexico*** The following table shows U.S. daily oil imports from Mexico, for 2001–2009 ($t = 1$ represents the start of 2001):[34]

***t* (year since 2000)**	1	2	3	4	5	6	7	8	9
***I*(*t*) (million barrels)**	1.4	1.35	1.5	1.55	1.6	1.5	1.5	1.5	1.2

a. Use the data in the table to compute the average rate of change of $I(t)$ over the period 2001–2006. Interpret the result.

b. Which of the following is true? From 2002 to 2006, the one-year average rate of change of oil imports from Mexico

(A) increased in value.
(B) decreased in value.
(C) never increased in value.
(D) never decreased in value.

29. ***Subprime Mortgages during the Housing Crisis*** The following graph shows the approximate percentage $P(t)$ of mortgages issued in the U.S. that were subprime (normally classified as risky):[35]

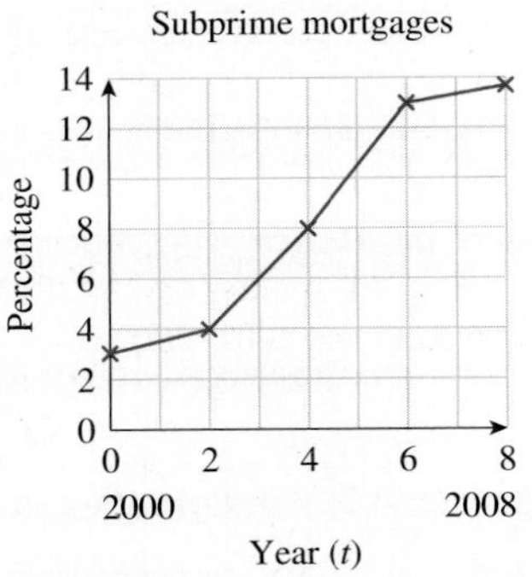

a. Use the graph to estimate, to one decimal place, the average rate of change of $P(t)$ with respect to t over the interval [0, 6] and interpret the result.

b. Over which 2-year period(s) was the average rate of change of $P(t)$ the greatest? HINT [See Example 2.]

30. ***Subprime Mortgage Debt during the Housing Crisis*** The following graph shows the approximate value $V(t)$ of subprime (normally classified as risky) mortgage debt outstanding in the United States:[36]

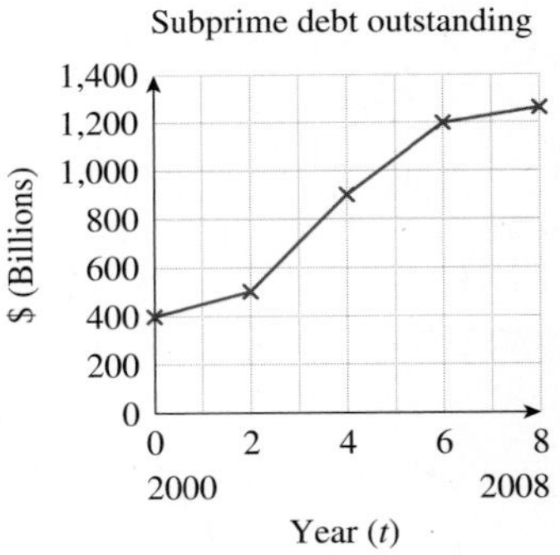

a. Use the graph to estimate, to one decimal place, the average rate of change of $V(t)$ with respect to t over the interval [2, 6] and interpret the result.

b. Over which 2-year period(s) was the average rate of change of $V(t)$ the least? HINT [See Example 2.]

31. ***Immigration to Ireland*** The following graph shows the approximate number (in thousands) of people who immigrated to Ireland during the period 2006–2010 (t is time in years since 2000):[37]

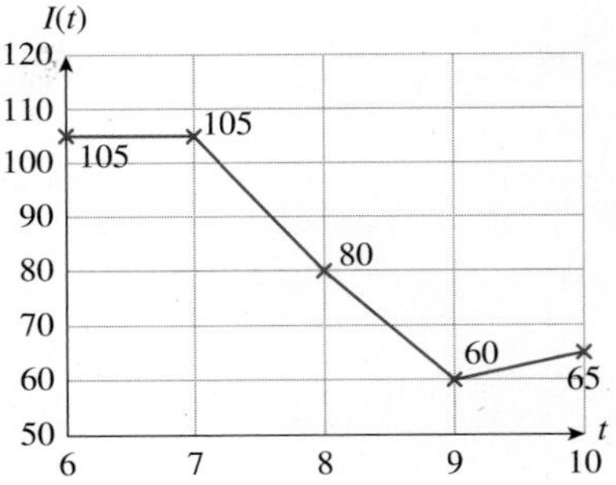

During which 2-year interval(s) was the magnitude of the average rate of change of $I(t)$ **(a)** greatest **(b)** least? Interpret your answers by referring to the rates of change.

32. ***Emigration from Ireland*** The following graph shows the approximate number (in thousands) of people who emigrated from Ireland during the period 2006–2010.[38]

---

[34] Figures are approximate, and 2008–2009 figures are projections by the Department of Energy. Source: Energy Information Administration/Pemex (www.eia.doe.gov).

[35] Sources: Mortgage Bankers Association, UBS.

[36] Source: Data 360 www.data360.org.

[37] Sources: Ireland Central Statistic Office/Data 360 www.data360.org.

[38] *Ibid.*

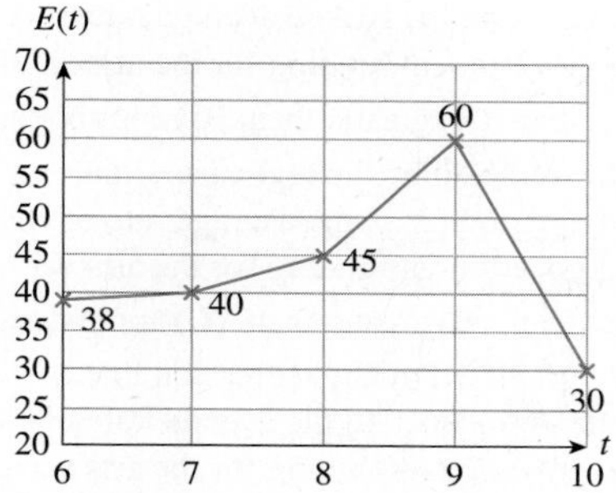

During which 2-year interval(s) was the magnitude of the average rate of change of $E(t)$ (**a**) greatest (**b**) least? Interpret your answers by referring to the rates of change.

33. ▼ ***Physics Research in the U.S.*** The following table shows the number of research articles in the journal *Physical Review* authored by U.S researchers during the period 1993–2003 ($t = 3$ represents 1993):[39]

***t* (year since 1990)**	3	5	7	9	11	13
***N(t)* (articles, thousands)**	5.1	4.6	4.3	4.3	4.5	4.2

a. Find the interval(s) over which the average rate of change of N was the most negative. What was that rate of change? Interpret your answer.

b. The **percentage change of *N* over the interval [*a*, *b*]** is defined to be

$$\text{Percentage change of } N = \frac{\text{Change in } N}{\text{First value}} = \frac{N(b) - N(a)}{N(a)}.$$

Compute the percentage change of N over the interval [3, 13] and also the average rate of change. Interpret the answers.

34. ▼ ***Physics Research in Europe*** The following table shows the number of research articles in the journal *Physical Review* authored by researchers in Europe during the period 1993–2003 ($t = 3$ represents 1993):[40]

***t* (year since 1990)**	3	5	7	9	11	13
***N(t)* (articles, thousands)**	3.8	4.6	5.0	5.0	6.0	5.7

a. Find the interval(s) over which the average rate of change of N was the most positive. What was that rate of change? Interpret your answer.

b. The **percentage change of *N* over the interval [*a*, *b*]** is defined to be

$$\text{Percentage change of } N = \frac{\text{Change in } N}{\text{First value}} = \frac{N(b) - N(a)}{N(a)}.$$

Compute the percentage change of N over the interval [7, 13] and also the average rate of change. Interpret the answers.

35. ***College Basketball: Men*** The following chart shows the number of NCAA men's college basketball teams in the United States during the period 2000–2010:[41]

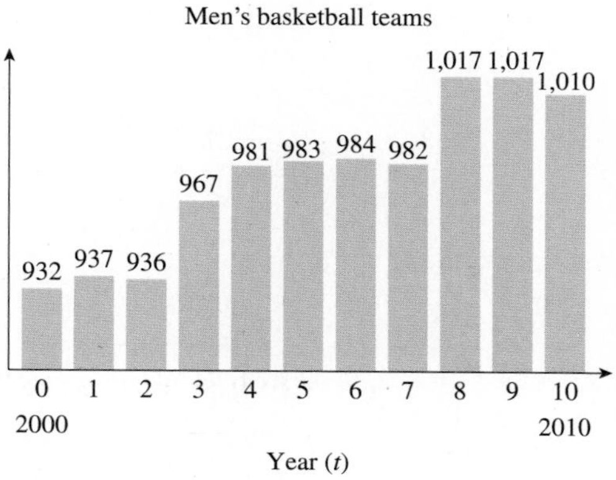

a. On average, how fast was the number of men's college basketball teams growing over the 4-year period beginning in 2002?

b. By inspecting the chart, determine whether the 3-year average rates of change increased or decreased beginning in 2005. HINT [See Example 2.]

36. ***College Basketball: Women*** The following chart shows the number of NCAA women's college basketball teams in the United States during the period 2000–2010:[42]

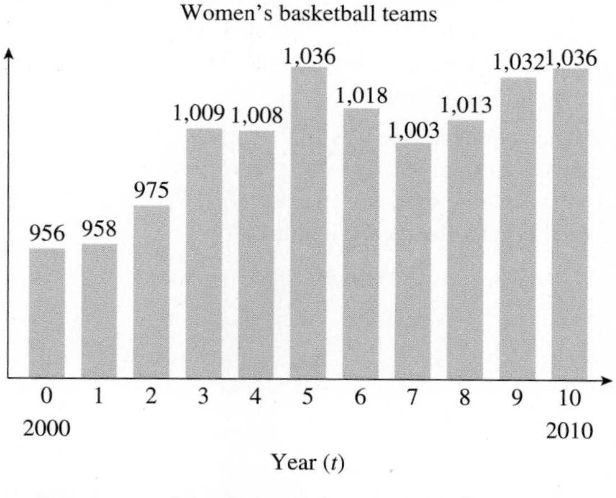

a. On average, how fast was the number of women's college basketball teams growing over the 4-year period beginning in 2004?

b. By inspecting the graph, find the 3-year period over which the average rate of change was largest.

[39] Source: The Americal Physical Society/*New York Times*, May 3, 2003, p. A1.

[40] *Ibid.*

[41] 2010 figure is an estimate. Source: www.census.gov.

[42] *Ibid.*

37. ***Funding for the Arts*** State governments in the United States spend a total of between \$1 and \$2 per person on the arts and culture each year. The following chart shows the data for 2002–2010, together with the regression line:[43]

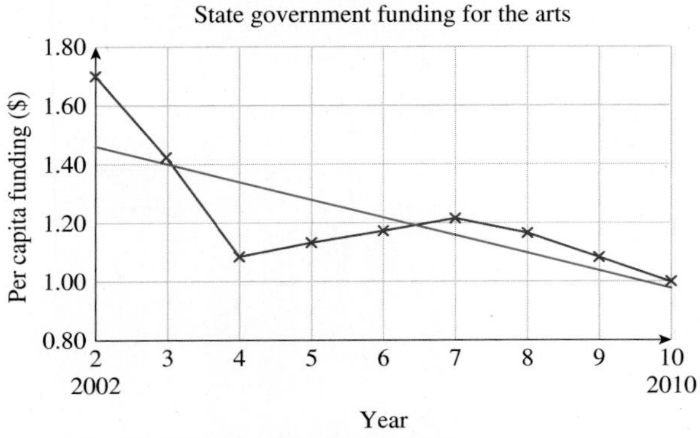

a. Over the period [2, 6] the average rate of change of state government funding for the arts was

(A) less than **(B)** greater than **(C)** approximately equal to

the rate predicted by the regression line.

b. Over the period [3, 10] the average rate of change of state government funding for the arts was

(A) less than **(B)** greater than **(C)** approximately equal to

the rate predicted by the regression line.

c. Over the period [4, 8] the average rate of change of state government funding for the arts was

(A) less than **(B)** greater than **(C)** approximately equal to

the rate predicted by the regression line.

d. Estimate, to two significant digits, the average rate of change of per capita state government funding for the arts over the period [2, 10]. (Be careful to state the units of measurement.) How does it compare to the slope of the regression line?

38. ***Funding for the Arts*** The U.S. federal government spends a total of between \$6 and \$7 per person on the arts and culture each year. The following chart shows the data for 2002–2010, together with the regression line:[44]

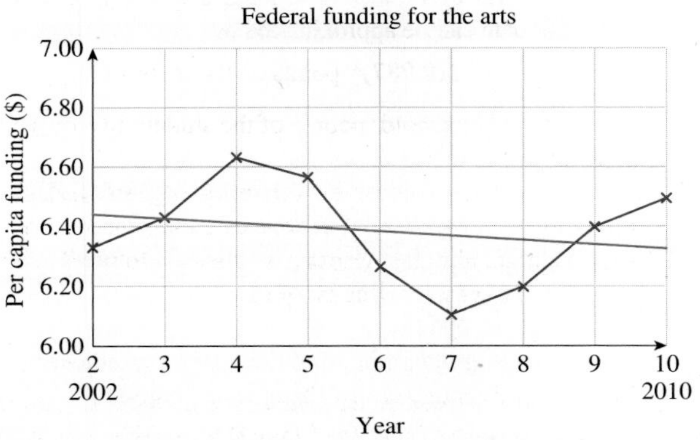

a. Over the period [4, 10] the average rate of change of federal government funding for the arts was

(A) less than **(B)** greater than **(C)** approximately equal to

the rate predicted by the regression line.

b. Over the period [2, 7] the average rate of change of federal government funding for the arts was

(A) less than **(B)** greater than **(C)** approximately equal to

the rate predicted by the regression line.

c. Over the period [3, 10] the average rate of change of federal government funding for the arts was

(A) less than **(B)** greater than **(C)** approximately equal to

the rate predicted by the regression line.

d. Estimate, to one significant digit, the average rate of change of per capita federal government funding for the arts over the period [2, 10]. (Be careful to state the units of measurement.) How does it compare to the slope of the regression line?

39. ▼ ***Market Volatility during the Dot-com Boom*** A volatility index generally measures the extent to which a market undergoes sudden changes in value. The volatility of the S&P 500 (as measured by one such index) was decreasing at an average rate of 0.2 points per year during 1991–1995, and was increasing at an average rate of about 0.3 points per year during 1995–1999. In 1995, the volatility of the S&P was 1.1.[45] Use this information to give a rough sketch of the volatility of the S&P 500 as a function of time, showing its values in 1991 and 1999.

40. ▼ ***Market Volatility during the Dot-com Boom*** The volatility (see the preceding exercise) of the NASDAQ had an average rate of change of 0 points per year during 1992–1995, and increased at an average rate of 0.2 points per year during 1995–1998. In 1995, the volatility of the NASDAQ was 1.1.[46] Use this information to give a rough sketch of the volatility of the NASDAQ as a function of time.

41. ***Market Index*** Joe Downs runs a small investment company from his basement. Every week he publishes a report on the success of his investments, including the progress of the "Joe Downs Index." At the end of one particularly memorable week, he reported that the index for that week had the value $I(t) = 1{,}000 + 1{,}500t - 800t^2 + 100t^3$ points, where t represents the number of business days into the week; t ranges from 0 at the beginning of the week to 5 at the end of the week. The graph of I is shown below.

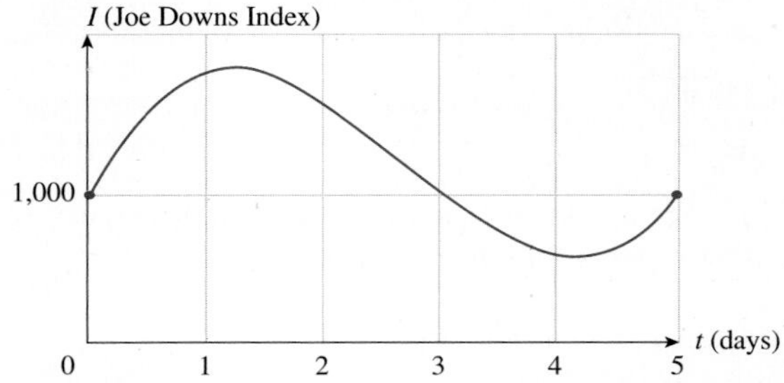

[43] Figures are in constant 2008 dollars, and the 2010 figure is the authors' estimate. Source: *Americans for the Arts* www.artsusa.org.

[44] *Ibid.*

[45] Source for data: Sanford C. Bernstein Company/*New York Times*, March 24, 2000, p. C1.

[46] *Ibid.*

On average, how fast, and in what direction, was the index changing over the first two business days (the interval [0, 2])? HINT [See Example 3.]

42. ***Market Index*** Refer to the Joe Downs Index in the preceding exercise. On average, how fast, and in which direction, was the index changing over the last three business days (the interval [2, 5])? HINT [See Example 3.]

43. ***Crude Oil Prices*** The price per barrel of crude oil in constant 2008 dollars can be approximated by

$$P(t) = 0.45t^2 - 12t + 105 \text{ dollars} \quad (0 \le t \le 28),$$

where t is time in years since the start of 1980.[47]

a. What, in constant 2008 dollars, was the average rate of change of the price of oil from the start of 1981 ($t = 1$) to the start of 2006 ($t = 26$)? HINT [See Example 3.]

b. Your answer to part (a) is quite small. Can you conclude that the price of oil hardly changed at all over the 25-year period 1981 to 2006? Explain.

44. ***Median Home Price*** The median home price in the U.S. over the period 2003–2011 can be approximated by

$$P(t) = -5t^2 + 75t - 30 \text{ thousand dollars} \quad (3 \le t \le 11),$$

where t is time in years since the start of 2000.[48]

a. What was the average rate of change of the median home price from the start of 2007 to the start of 2009? HINT [See Example 3.]

b. What, if anything, does your answer to part (a) say about the median home price in 2008? Explain.

45. ***SARS*** In the early stages of the deadly SARS (Severe Acute Respiratory Syndrome) epidemic in 2003, the number of reported cases could be approximated by

$$A(t) = 167(1.18)^t \quad (0 \le t \le 20)$$

t days after March 17, 2003 (the first day for which statistics were reported by the World Health Organization).

a. What was the average rate of change of $A(t)$ from March 17 to March 23? Interpret the result.

b. Which of the following is true? For the first 20 days of the epidemic, the number of reported cases
(A) increased at a faster and faster rate
(B) increased at a slower and slower rate
(C) decreased at a faster and faster rate
(D) decreased at a slower and slower rate HINT [See Example 2.]

46. ***SARS*** A few weeks into the deadly SARS (Severe Acute Respiratory Syndrome) epidemic in 2003, the number of reported cases could be approximated by

$$A(t) = 1{,}804(1.04)^t \quad (0 \le t \le 30)$$

t days after April 1, 2003.

a. What was the average rate of change of $A(t)$ from April 19 ($t = 18$) to April 29? Interpret the result.

b. Which of the following is true? During the 30-day period beginning April 1, the number of reported cases
(A) increased at a faster and faster rate
(B) increased at a slower and slower rate
(C) decreased at a faster and faster rate
(D) decreased at a slower and slower rate
HINT [See Example 2.]

47. ▼ ***Ecology*** Increasing numbers of manatees ("sea sirens") have been killed by boats off the Florida coast. The following graph shows the relationship between the number of boats registered in Florida and the number of manatees killed each year:

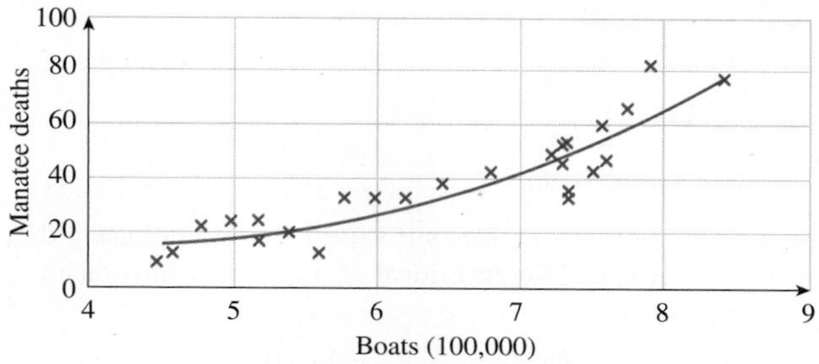

The regression curve shown is given by

$$f(x) = 3.55x^2 - 30.2x + 81 \text{ manatees} \quad (4.5 < x < 8.5),$$

where x is the number of boats (in hundreds of thousands) registered in Florida in a particular year, and $f(x)$ is the number of manatees killed by boats in Florida that year.[49]

a. Compute the average rate of change of f over the intervals [5, 6] and [7, 8].

b. What does the answer to part (a) tell you about the manatee deaths per boat?

48. ▼ ***Ecology*** Refer to Exercise 47.

a. Compute the average rate of change of f over the intervals [5, 7] and [6, 8].

b. Had we used a linear model instead of a quadratic one, how would the two answers in part (a) be related to each other?

49. T ▼ ***SAT Scores by Income*** The math SAT score of a high school graduate can be approximated by

$$S(x) = 573 - 133(0.987)^x \text{ points on the math SAT test,}$$

where x is the household income of the student in thousands of dollars per year.[50]

a. Use technology to complete the following table, which shows the average rate of change of S over successive intervals of length 40. (Round all answers to two decimal places.) HINT [See Example 4.]

[47] Source for data: www.inflationdata.com.

[48] Source for data: www.zillow.com.

[49] Regression model is based on data from 1976 to 2000. Sources for data: Florida Department of Highway Safety & Motor Vehicles, Florida Marine Institute/*New York Times*, February 12, 2002, p. F4.

[50] The model is the authors'. Source for data: College Board/*New York Times* http://economix.blogs.nytimes.com.

Interval	[0, 40]	[40, 80]	[80, 120]	[120, 160]	[160, 200]
Average Rate of change of S					

b. Interpret your answer for the interval [40, 80], being sure to indicate the direction of change and the units of measurement.

c. Multiple choice: As her household income rises, a student's SAT score

(A) increases.
(B) decreases.
(C) increases, then decreases.
(D) decreases, then increases.

d. Multiple choice: As the household income increases, the effect on a student's SAT score is

(A) more pronounced.
(B) less pronounced.

50. *SAT Scores by Income* Repeat Exercise 49 using the following model for the critical reading SAT score of a high school graduate:

$S(x) = 550 - 136(0.985)^x$ points on the critical reading SAT test,

where x is the household income of the student in thousands of dollars per year.[51]

COMMUNICATION AND REASONING EXERCISES

51. Describe three ways we have used to determine the average rate of change of f over an interval $[a, b]$. Which of the three ways is *least* precise? Explain.

52. If f is a linear function of x with slope m, what is its average rate of change over any interval $[a, b]$?

53. Is the average rate of change of a function over $[a, b]$ affected by the values of the function between a and b? Explain.

54. If the average rate of change of a function over $[a, b]$ is zero, this means that the function has not changed over $[a, b]$, right?

55. Sketch the graph of a function whose average rate of change over [0, 3] is negative but whose average rate of change over [1, 3] is positive.

56. Sketch the graph of a function whose average rate of change over [0, 2] is positive but whose average rate of change over [0, 1] is negative.

57. If the rate of change of quantity A is 2 units of quantity A per unit of quantity B, and the rate of change of quantity B is 3 units of quantity B per unit of quantity C, what is the rate of change of quantity A with respect to quantity C?

58. If the rate of change of quantity A is 2 units of quantity A per unit of quantity B, what is the rate of change of quantity B with respect to quantity A?

59. A certain function f has the property that its average rate of change over the interval $[1, 1+h]$ (for positive h) increases as h decreases. Which of the following graphs could be the graph of f?

(A)

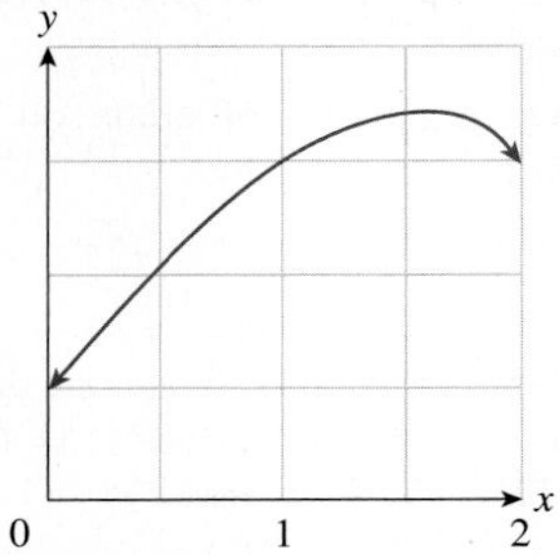

(B)

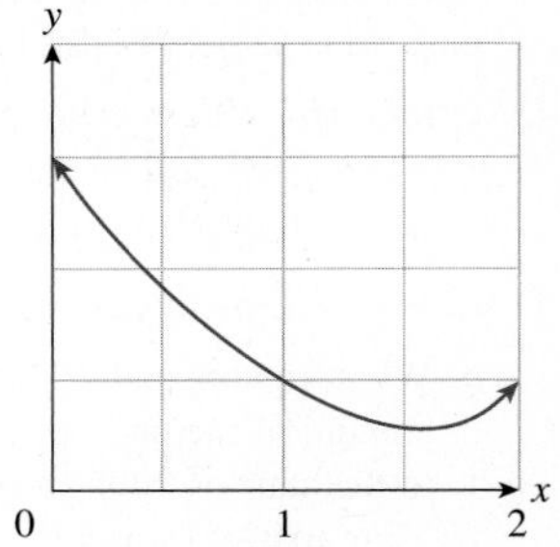

(C)

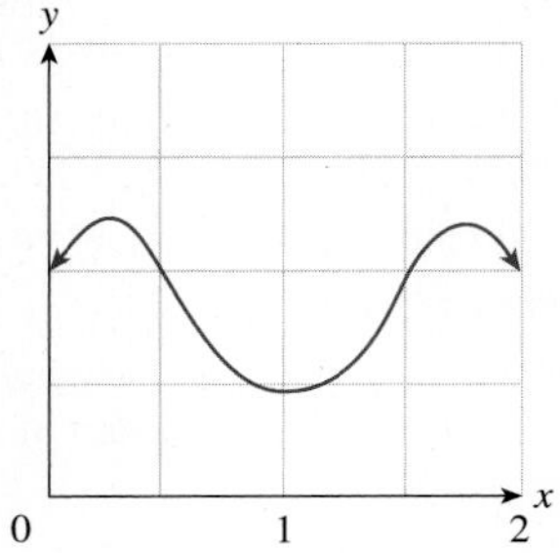

60. A certain function f has the property that its average rate of change over the interval $[1, 1 + h]$ (for positive h) decreases as h decreases. Which of the following graphs could be the graph of f?

(A)

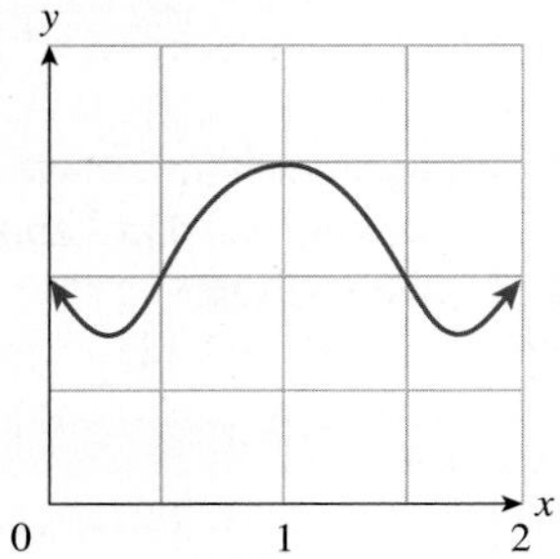

(B)

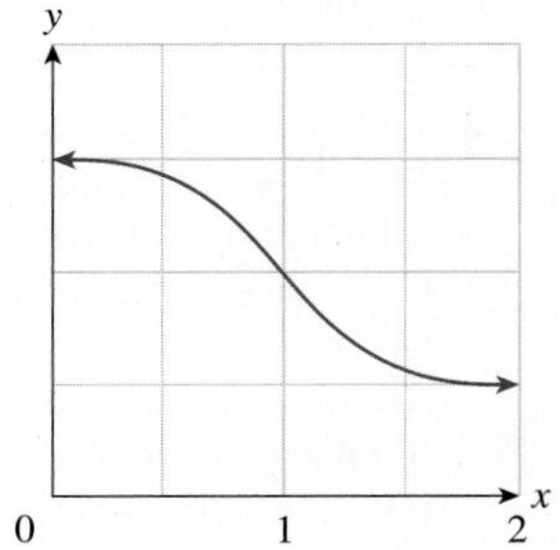

(C)

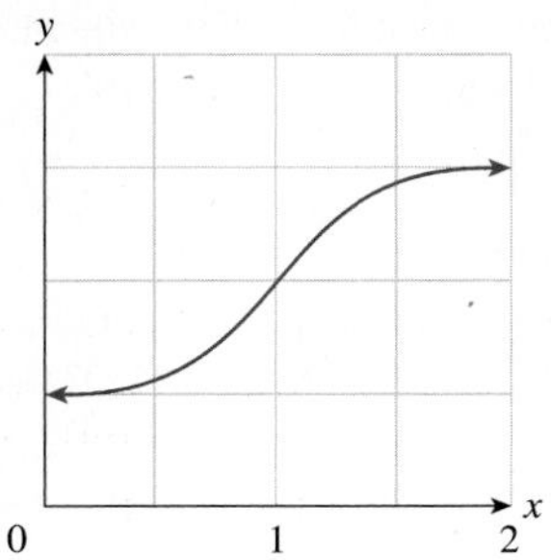

[51] The model is the authors'. Source for data: College Board/*New York Times* http://economix.blogs.nytimes.com.

61. ▼ Is it possible for a company's revenue to have a negative 3-year average rate of growth, but a positive average rate of growth in 2 of the 3 years? (If not, explain; if so, illustrate with an example.)

62. ▼ Is it possible for a company's revenue to have a larger 2-year average rate of change than either of the 1-year average rates of change? (If not, explain why with the aid of a graph; if so, illustrate with an example.)

63. ◆ The average rate of change of f over [1, 3] is
(A) always equal to **(B)** never equal to
(C) sometimes equal to
the average of its average rates of change over [1, 2] and [2, 3].

64. ◆ The average rate of change of f over [1, 4] is
(A) always equal to **(B)** never equal to
(C) sometimes equal to
the average of its average rates of change over [1, 2], [2, 3], and [3, 4].

3.5 Derivatives: Numerical and Graphical Viewpoints

In Example 4 of Section 3.4, we looked at the average rate of change of the function $G(t) = 5t^2 - 85t + 1{,}762$ approximating the price of gold on the spot market over smaller and smaller intervals of time. We obtained the following table showing the average rates of change of G over the intervals $[8, 8 + h]$ for successively smaller values of h:

h getting smaller; interval $[8, 8 + h]$ getting smaller →

h	1	0.1	0.01	0.001	0.0001
Ave. Rate of Change over $[8, 8 + h]$	0	−4.5	−4.95	−4.995	−4.9995

Rate of change approaching −$5 per hour →

The average rates of change of the price of gold over smaller and smaller periods of time, starting at the instant $t = 8$ (8:00 am), appear to be getting closer and closer to −$5 per hour. As we look at these shrinking periods of time, we are getting closer to looking at what happens at the *instant* $t = 8$. So it seems reasonable to say that the average rates of change are approaching the **instantaneous rate of change** at $t = 8$, which the table suggests is −$5 per hour. This is how fast the price of gold was changing *exactly* at 8:00 am.

At $t = 8$, *the instantaneous rate of change of* $G(t)$ *is* −5.

We express this fact mathematically by writing $G'(8) = -5$ (which we read as "G prime of 8 equals −5"). Thus

$G'(8) = -5$ *means that, at* $t = 8$, *the instantaneous rate of change of* $G(t)$ *is* −5.

The process of letting h get smaller and smaller is called taking the **limit** as h approaches 0 (as you recognize if you've done the sections on limits). As in the sections on limits, we write $h \to 0$ as shorthand for "h approaches 0." Thus, taking the limit of the average rates of change as $h \to 0$ gives us the instantaneous rate of change.

Q: *All these intervals [8, 8 + h] are intervals to the right of 8. What about small intervals to the left of 8, such as [7.9, 8]?*

A: We can compute the average rate of change of our function for such intervals by choosing h to be negative ($h = -0.1, -0.01$, etc.) and using the same difference quotient formula we used for positive h:

$$\text{Average rate of change of } G \text{ over } [8+h, 8] = \frac{G(8) - G(8+h)}{8 - (8+h)}$$

Here are the results we get using negative h:

h getting closer to 0; interval $[8 + h, 8]$ getting smaller →

h	−1	−0.1	−0.01	−0.001	−0.0001
Ave. Rate of Change over [8 + *h*, 8]	−10	−5.5	−5.05	−5.005	−5.0005

Rate of change approaching −$5 per hour →

Notice that the average rates of change are again getting closer and closer to −5 as h approaches 0, suggesting once again that the instantaneous rate of change is −$5 per hour.

Instantaneous Rate of Change of *f*(*x*) at *x* = *a*: Derivative

The **instantaneous rate of change** of $f(x)$ at $x = a$ is defined as

$$f'(a) = \lim_{h \to 0} \frac{f(a+h) - f(a)}{h}.$$

f prime of a equals the limit, as h approaches 0, of the ratio $\frac{f(a+h) - f(a)}{h}$.

The quantity $f'(a)$ is also called the **derivative of *f*(*x*) at *x* = *a*.** Finding the derivative of f is called **differentiating *f*.**

Units

The units of $f'(a)$ are the same as the units of the average rate of change: units of f per unit of x.

Quick Examples

1. If $f(x) = 5x^2 - 85x + 1{,}762$, then the two tables above suggest that

$$f'(8) = \lim_{h \to 0} \frac{f(8+h) - f(8)}{h} = -5.$$

2. If $f(t)$ is the number of insects in your dorm room at time t hours, and you know that $f(3) = 5$ and $f'(3) = 8$, this means that, at time $t = 3$ hours, there are 5 insects in your room, and this number is growing at an instantaneous rate of 8 insects per hour.

IMPORTANT NOTES

1. Sections 3.1–3.3 discuss limits in some detail. If you have not (yet) covered those sections, you can trust to your intuition.
2. The formula for the derivative tells us that the instantaneous rate of change is the limit of the average rates of change $[f(a+h)-f(a)]/h$ over smaller and smaller intervals. Thus, the value of $f'(a)$ can be approximated by computing the average rate of change for smaller and smaller values of h, both positive and negative.
3. If a happens to be an endpoint of the domain of f, then $f'(a)$ does not exist, as then $[f(a+h)-f(a)]/h$ only has a one-sided limit as $h \to 0$, and so

   $\lim_{h\to 0} \frac{f(a+h)-f(a)}{h}$ does not exist.*

* One could define the derivative at an endpoint by instead using the associated one-sided limit; for instance, if a is a left endpoint of the domain of f, then one could define

$$f'(a) = \lim_{h\to 0^+} \frac{f(a+h)-f(a)}{h}$$

as we did in previous editions of this book. However, in this edition we have decided to follow the usual convention and say that the derivative at an endpoint does not exist.

4. In this section we will only *approximate* derivatives. In Section 3.6 we will begin to see how we find the *exact* values of derivatives.
5. $f'(a)$ is a number we can calculate, or at least approximate, for various values of a, as we have done in the earlier example. Since $f'(a)$ depends on the value of a, we can think of f' as *a function of a*. (We return to this idea at the end of this section.) An old name for f' is "the function *derived from f*," which has been shortened to the *derivative* of f.
6. It is because f' is a function that we sometimes refer to $f'(a)$ as "the derivative of *f evaluated at a*," or the "derivative of $f(x)$ evaluated at $x = a$."

It may happen that the average rates of change $[f(a+h)-f(a)]/h$ do not approach any fixed number at all as h approaches zero, or that they approach one number on the intervals using positive h, and another on those using negative h. If this happens, $\lim_{h\to 0}[f(a+h)-f(a)]/h$ does not exist, and we say that f is **not differentiable** at $x = a$, or $\boldsymbol{f'(a)}$ **does not exist**. When the limit *does* exist, we say that f is **differentiable** at the point $x = a$, or $\boldsymbol{f'(a)}$ **exists**. It is comforting to know that all polynomials and exponential functions are differentiable at *every* point. On the other hand, certain functions are not differentiable. Examples are $f(x) = |x|$ and $f(x) = x^{1/3}$, neither of which is differentiable at $x = 0$. (See Section 4.1.)

EXAMPLE 1 Instantaneous Rate of Change: Numerically and Graphically

The air temperature one spring morning, t hours after 7:00 am, was given by the function $f(t) = 50 + 0.1t^4$ degrees Fahrenheit $(0 \le t \le 4)$.

a. How fast was the temperature rising at 9:00 am?

b. How is the instantaneous rate of change of temperature at 9:00 am reflected in the graph of temperature vs. time?

Solution

a. We are being asked to find the instantaneous rate of change of the temperature at $t = 2$, so we need to find $f'(2)$. To do this we examine the average rates of change

$$\frac{f(2+h)-f(2)}{h} \qquad \text{Average rate of change = difference quotient}$$

for values of h approaching 0. Calculating the average rate of change over $[2, 2 + h]$ for $h = 1$, 0.1, 0.01, 0.001, and 0.0001 we get the following values (rounded to four decimal places):*

* We can quickly compute these values using technology as in Example 4 in Section 3.4. (See the Technology Guides at the end of the chapter.)

h	1	0.1	0.01	0.001	0.0001
Average Rate of Change Over [2, 2 + h]	6.5	3.4481	3.2241	3.2024	3.2002

Here are the values we get using negative values of h:

h	−1	−0.1	−0.01	−0.001	−0.0001
Average Rate of Change Over [2 + h, 2]	1.5	2.9679	3.1761	3.1976	3.1998

The average rates of change are clearly approaching the number 3.2, so we can say that $f'(2) = 3.2$. Thus, at 9:00 in the morning, the temperature was rising at the rate of 3.2 degrees per hour.

b. We saw in Section 3.4 that the average rate of change of f over an interval is the slope of the secant line through the corresponding points on the graph of f. Figure 25 illustrates this for the intervals $[2, 2 + h]$ with $h = 1$, 0.5, and 0.1.

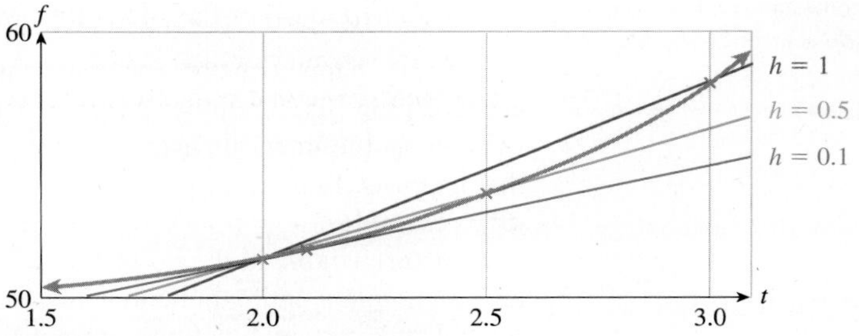

Figure 25

All three secant lines pass though the point $(2, f(2)) = (2, 51.6)$ on the graph of f. Each of them passes through a second point on the curve (the second point is different for each secant line) and this second point gets closer and closer to (2, 51.6) as h gets closer to 0. What seems to be happening is that the secant lines are getting closer and closer to a line that just touches the curve at (2, 51.6): the **tangent line** at (2, 51.6), shown in Figure 26.

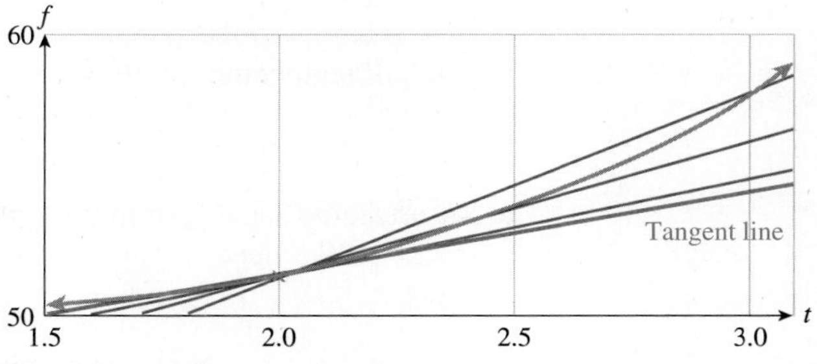

Figure 26

Q: *What is the slope of this tangent line?*

A: Because the slopes of the secant lines are getting closer and closer to 3.2, and because the secant lines are approaching the tangent line, the tangent line must have slope 3.2. In other words,

At the point on the graph where $x = 2$, the slope of the tangent line is $f'(2)$.

Q: *What is the difference between $f(2)$ and $f'(2)$?*

A: An important question. Briefly, $f(2)$ is the *value of f* when $t = 2$, while $f'(2)$ is the *rate at which f is changing* when $t = 2$. Here,

$$f(2) = 50 + 0.1(2)^4 = 51.6 \text{ degrees.}$$

Thus, at 9:00 am ($t = 2$), the temperature was 51.6 degrees. On the other hand,

$$f'(2) = 3.2 \text{ degrees per hour.}$$

Units of slope are units of f per unit of t.

This means that, at 9:00 am ($t = 2$), the temperature was increasing at a rate of 3.2 degrees per hour.

Because we have been talking about tangent lines, we should say more about what they *are*. A tangent line to a *circle* is a line that touches the circle in just one point. A tangent line gives the circle "a glancing blow," as shown in Figure 27.

For a smooth curve other than a circle, a tangent line may touch the curve at more than one point, or pass through it (Figure 28).

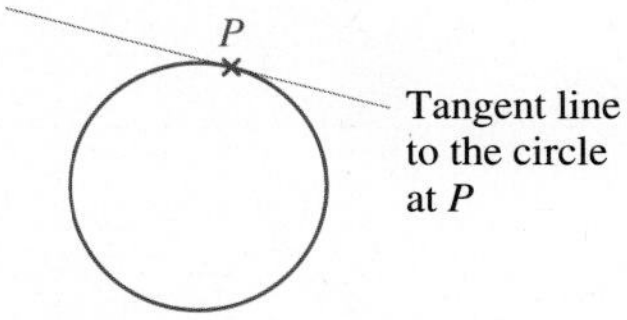

Figure 27

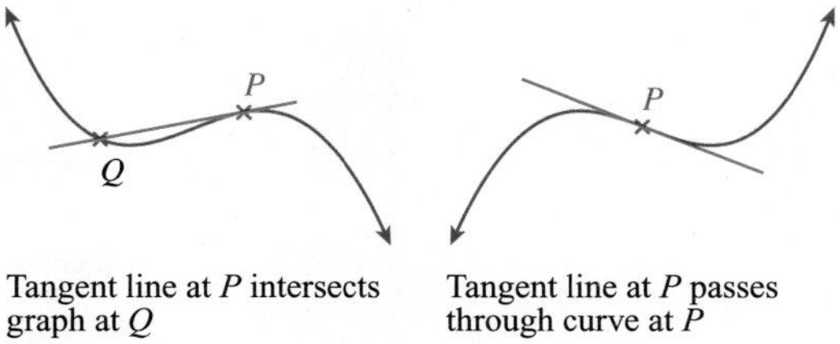

Figure 28

However, all tangent lines have the following interesting property in common: If we focus on a small portion of the curve very close to the point P—in other words, if we "zoom in" to the graph near the point P—the curve will appear almost straight, and almost indistinguishable from the tangent line (Figure 29).

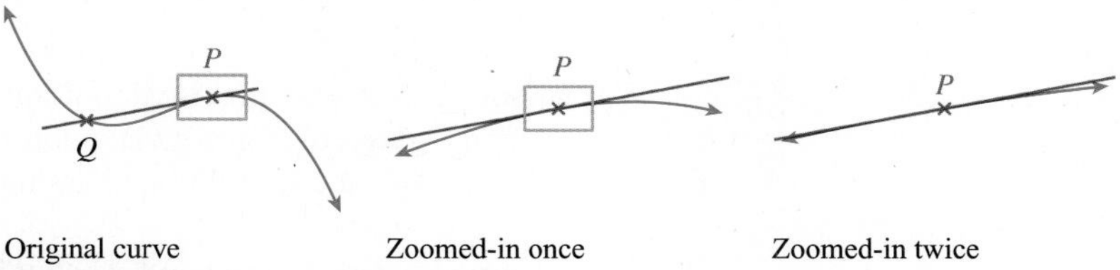

Figure 29

You can check this property by zooming in on the curve shown in Figures 25 and 26 in the previous example near the point where $x = 2$.

Secant and Tangent Lines

The *slope of the secant line* through the points on the graph of f where $x = a$ and $x = a + h$ is given by the average rate of change, or difference quotient,

$$m_{\text{sec}} = \text{slope of secant} = \text{average rate of change} = \frac{f(a+h) - f(a)}{h}.$$

The *slope of the tangent line* through the point on the graph of f where $x = a$ is given by the instantaneous rate of change, or derivative

$$m_{\text{tan}} = \text{slope of tangent} = \text{instantaneous rate of change} = \text{derivative}$$
$$= f'(a) = \lim_{h \to 0} \frac{f(a+h) - f(a)}{h},$$

assuming the limit exists.

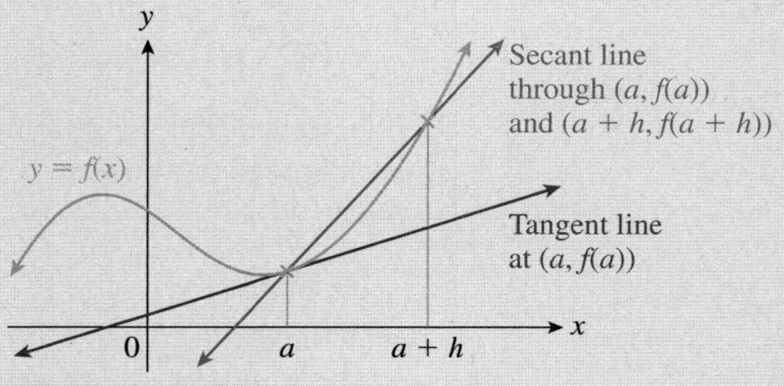

Quick Example

In the following graph, the tangent line at the point where $x = 2$ has slope 3. Therefore, the derivative at $x = 2$ is 3. That is, $f'(2) = 3$.

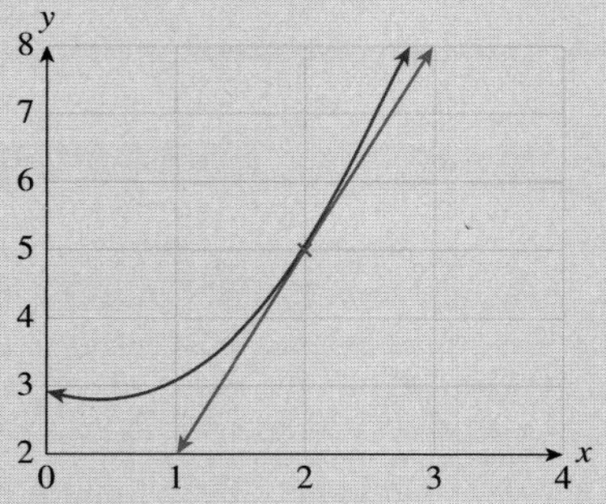

Note It might happen that the tangent line is vertical at some point or does not exist at all. These are the cases in which f is not differentiable at the given point. (See Section 3.6.) ■

We can now give a more precise definition of what we mean by the tangent line to a point P on the graph of f at a given point: The **tangent line** to the graph of f at the point $P(a, f(a))$ is the straight line passing through P with slope $f'(a)$.

Quick Approximation of the Derivative

Q: *Do we always need to make tables of difference quotients as above in order to calculate an approximate value for the derivative? That seems like a large amount of work just to get an approximation.*

A: We can usually *approximate* the value of the derivative by using a single, small value of h. In the example above, the value $h = 0.0001$ would have given a pretty good approximation. The problems with using a fixed value of h are that (1) we do not get an *exact* answer, only an *approximation* of the derivative, and (2) how good an approximation it is depends on the function we're differentiating.* However, with most of the functions we'll be considering, setting $h = 0.0001$ does give us a good approximation.

* In fact, no matter how small the value we decide to use for h, it is possible to craft a function f for which the difference quotient at a is not even close to $f'(a)$.

Calculating a Quick Approximation of the Derivative

We can calculate an approximate value of $f'(a)$ by using the formula

$$f'(a) \approx \frac{f(a+h) - f(a)}{h} \qquad \text{Rate of change over } [a,\ a+h]$$

with a small value of h. The value $h = 0.0001$ works for most examples we encounter (students of numerical methods study the question of exactly how accurate this approximation is).

Alternative Formula: The Balanced Difference Quotient

The following alternative formula, which measures the rate of change of f over the interval $[a - h, a + h]$, often gives a more accurate result, and is the one used in many calculators:

$$f'(a) \approx \frac{f(a+h) - f(a-h)}{2h}. \qquad \text{Rate of change over } [a-h,\ a+h]$$

Note For the quick approximations to be valid, the function f must be differentiable; that is, $f'(a)$ must exist. ■

EXAMPLE 2 Quick Approximation of the Derivative

a. Calculate an approximate value of $f'(1.5)$ if $f(x) = x^2 - 4x$.

b. Find the equation of the tangent line at the point on the graph where $x = 1.5$.

Solution

a. We shall compute both the ordinary difference quotient and the balanced difference quotient.

Ordinary Difference Quotient: Using $h = 0.0001$, the ordinary difference quotient is:

$$f'(1.5) \approx \frac{f(1.5 + 0.0001) - f(1.5)}{0.0001} \qquad \text{Ordinary difference quotient}$$

$$= \frac{f(1.5001) - f(1.5)}{0.0001}$$

$$= \frac{(1.5001^2 - 4 \times 1.5001) - (1.5^2 - 4 \times 1.5)}{0.0001} = -0.9999.$$

This answer is accurate to 0.0001; in fact, $f'(1.5) = -1$.

Graphically, we can picture this approximation as follows: Zoom in on the curve using the window $1.5 \le x \le 1.5001$ and measure the slope of the secant line joining both ends of the curve segment. Figure 30 shows close-up views of the curve and tangent line near the point P in which we are interested, the third view being the zoomed-in view used for this approximation.

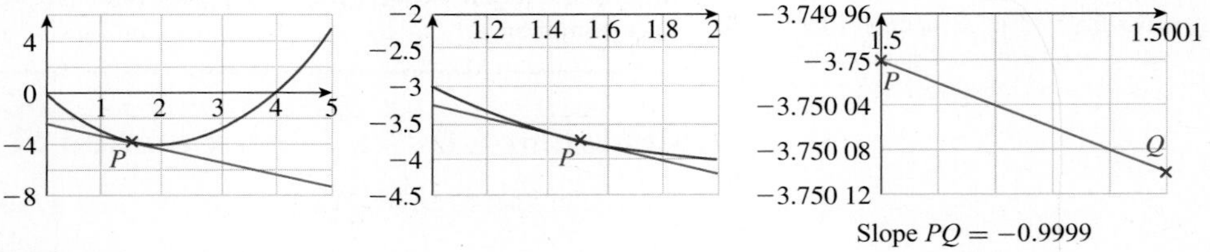

Figure 30

Notice that in the third window the tangent line and curve are indistinguishable. Also, the point P in which we are interested is on the left edge of the window.

Balanced Difference Quotient: For the balanced difference quotient, we get

$$f'(1.5) \approx \frac{f(1.5+0.0001)-f(1.5-0.0001)}{2(0.0001)} \qquad \text{Balanced difference quotient}$$

$$= \frac{f(1.5001)-f(1.4999)}{0.0002}$$

$$= \frac{(1.5001^2 - 4\times 1.5001)-(1.4999^2 - 4\times 1.4999)}{0.0002} = -1.$$

This balanced difference quotient gives the exact answer in this case!* Graphically, it is as though we have zoomed in using a window that puts the point P in the *center* of the screen (Figure 31) rather than at the left edge.

* The balanced difference quotient always gives the exact derivative for a quadratic function.

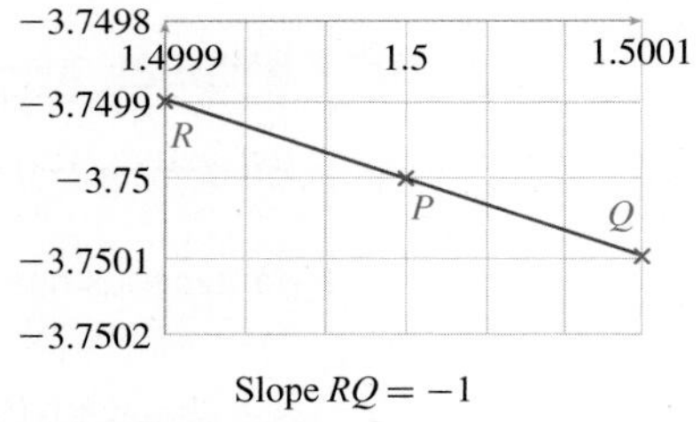

Figure 31

b. We find the equation of the tangent line from a point on the line and its slope, as we did in Chapter 1:

- ***Point*** $(1.5, f(1.5)) = (1.5, -3.75)$.
- ***Slope*** $m = f'(1.5) = -1$. Slope of the tangent line = derivative.

The equation is

$$y = mx + b,$$

where $m = -1$ and $b = y_1 - mx_1 = -3.75 - (-1)(1.5) = -2.25$. Thus, the equation of the tangent line is

$$y = -x - 2.25.$$

using Technology

See the Technology Guides at the end of the chapter to find out how to calculate the quick approximations to the derivative in Example 2 using a TI-83/84 Plus or a spreadsheet. Here is an outline:

TI-83/84 Plus

`Y₁=X^2-4*X`

Home screen:

`(Y₁(1.5001)-Y₁(1.5))/0.0001`

`(Y₁(1.5001)-Y₁(1.4999))/0.0002`

[More details on page 285.]

Spreadsheet

Headings *a*, *h*, *x*, *f*(*x*), Diff Quotient, Balanced Diff Quotient in A1–F1

`1.5` in A2, `0.0001` in B2,

`=A2-B2` in C2, `=A2` in C3, `=A2+B2` in C4

`=C2^2-4*C2` in D2; copy down to D4

`=(D3-D2)/(C3-C2)` in E2

`=(D4-D2)/(C4-C2)` in E3

[More details on page 287.]

Q: *Why can't we simply put $h = 0.000\,000\,000\,000\,000\,000\,01$ for an incredibly accurate approximation to the instantaneous rate of change and be done with it?*

A: This approach would certainly work if you were patient enough to do the (thankless) calculation by hand! However, doing it with the help of technology—even an ordinary calculator—will cause problems: The issue is that calculators and spreadsheets represent numbers with a maximum number of significant digits (15 in the case of Excel). As the value of h gets smaller, the value of $f(a+h)$ gets closer and closer to the value of $f(a)$. For example, if $f(x) = 50 + 0.1x^4$, Excel might compute

$$\begin{aligned} &f(2 + 0.000\,000\,000\,000\,1) - f(2) \\ &= 51.600\,000\,000\,000\,3 - 51.6 \qquad \text{Rounded to 15 digits} \\ &= 0.000\,000\,000\,000\,3 \end{aligned}$$

and the corresponding difference quotient would be 3, not 3.2 as it should be. If h gets even smaller, Excel will not be able to distinguish between $f(a+h)$ and $f(a)$ at all, in which case it will compute 0 for the rate of change. This loss in accuracy when subtracting two very close numbers is called **subtractive error**.

Thus, there is a trade-off in lowering the value of h: Smaller values of h yield *mathematically* more accurate approximations of the derivative, but if h gets too small, subtractive error becomes a problem and decreases the accuracy of computations that use technology.

Leibniz *d* Notation

We introduced the notation $f'(x)$ for the derivative of f at x, but there is another interesting notation. We have written the average rate of change as

$$\text{Average rate of change} = \frac{\Delta f}{\Delta x}. \qquad \frac{\text{Change in } f}{\text{Change in } x}$$

As we use smaller and smaller values for Δx, we approach the instantaneous rate of change, or derivative, for which we also have the notation df/dx, due to Leibniz:

$$\text{Instantaneous rate of change} = \lim_{\Delta x \to 0} \frac{\Delta f}{\Delta x} = \frac{df}{dx}.$$

That is, df/dx is just another notation for $f'(x)$. Do not think of df/dx as an actual quotient of two numbers: Remember that we only use an actual quotient $\Delta f/\Delta x$ to *approximate* the value of df/dx.

In Example 3, we apply the quick approximation method of estimating the derivative.

EXAMPLE 3 Velocity

My friend Eric, an enthusiastic baseball player, claims he can "probably" throw a ball upward at a speed of 100 feet per second (ft/s).* Our physicist friends tell us that its height s (in feet) t seconds later would be $s = 100t - 16t^2$. Find its average velocity over the interval [2, 3] and its instantaneous velocity exactly 2 seconds after Eric throws it.

* Eric's claim is difficult to believe; 100 ft/s corresponds to around 68 mph, and professional pitchers can throw *forward* at about 100 mph.

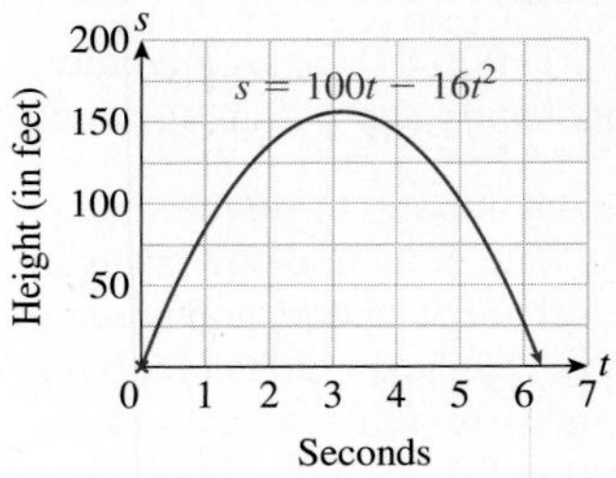

Figure 32

Solution The graph of the ball's height as a function of time is shown in Figure 32. Asking for the velocity is really asking for the rate of change of height with respect to time. (Why?) Consider average velocity first. To compute the **average velocity** of the ball from time 2 to time 3, we first compute the change in height:

$$\Delta s = s(3) - s(2) = 156 - 136 = 20 \text{ ft}.$$

Since it rises 20 feet in $\Delta t = 1$ second, we use the defining formula *speed = distance/time* to get the average velocity:

$$\text{Average velocity} = \frac{\Delta s}{\Delta t} = \frac{20}{1} = 20 \text{ ft/sec.}$$

from time $t = 2$ to $t = 3$. This is just the difference quotient, so

The average velocity is the average rate of change of height.

To get the **instantaneous velocity** at $t = 2$, we find the instantaneous rate of change of height. In other words, we need to calculate the derivative ds/dt at $t = 2$. Using the balanced quick approximation described earlier, we get

$$\begin{aligned}\frac{ds}{dt} &\approx \frac{s(2+0.0001) - s(2-0.0001)}{2(0.0001)} \\ &= \frac{s(2.0001) - s(1.9999)}{0.0002} \\ &= \frac{100(2.0001) - 16(2.0001)^2 - (100(1.9999) - 16(1.9999)^2)}{0.0002} \\ &= 36 \text{ ft/sec.}\end{aligned}$$

In fact, this happens to be the exact answer; the instantaneous velocity at $t = 2$ is exactly 36 ft/sec. (Try an even smaller value of h to persuade yourself.)

➡ **Before we go on...** If we repeat the calculation in Example 3 at time $t = 5$, we get

$$\frac{ds}{dt} = -60 \text{ ft/sec.}$$

The negative sign tells us that the ball is *falling* at a rate of 60 feet per second at time $t = 5$. (How does the fact that it is falling at $t = 5$ show up on the graph?) ■

The preceding example gives another interpretation of the derivative.

Average and Instantaneous Velocity

For an object moving in a straight line with position $s(t)$ at time t, the **average velocity** from time t to time $t + h$ is the average rate of change of position with respect to time:

$$v_{ave} = \frac{s(t+h) - s(t)}{h} = \frac{\Delta s}{\Delta t}.$$

Average velocity = Average rate of change of position

The **instantaneous velocity** at time t is

$$v = \lim_{h \to 0} \frac{s(t+h) - s(t)}{h} = \frac{ds}{dt}.$$

Instantaneous velocity = Instantaneous rate of change of position

In other words, *instantaneous velocity is the derivative of position with respect to time.*

Here is one last comment on Leibniz notation. In Example 3, we could have written the velocity either as s' or as ds/dt, as we chose to do. To write the answer to the question, that the velocity at $t = 2$ sec was 36 ft/sec, we can write either

$$s'(2) = 36$$

or

$$\left.\frac{ds}{dt}\right|_{t=2} = 36.$$

The notation "$|_{t=2}$" is read "evaluated at $t = 2$." Similarly, if $y = f(x)$, we can write the instantaneous rate of change of f at $x = 5$ in either functional notation as

$$f'(5) \qquad \text{The derivative of } f \text{, evaluated at } x = 5$$

or in Leibniz notation as

$$\left.\frac{dy}{dx}\right|_{x=5}. \qquad \text{The derivative of } y \text{, evaluated at } x = 5$$

The latter notation is obviously more cumbersome than the functional notation $f'(5)$, but the notation dy/dx has compensating advantages. You should practice using both notations.

The Derivative Function

The derivative $f'(x)$ is a number we can calculate, or at least approximate, for various values of x. Because $f'(x)$ depends on the value of x, we may think of f' as a function of x. This function is the **derivative function**.

Derivative Function

If f is a function, its **derivative function** f' is the function whose value $f'(x)$ is the derivative of f at x. Its domain is the set of all x at which f is differentiable. Equivalently, f' associates to each x the slope of the tangent to the graph of the function f at x, or the rate of change of f at x. The formula for the derivative function is

$$f'(x) = \lim_{h \to 0} \frac{f(x+h) - f(x)}{h}. \qquad \text{Derivative function}$$

Quick Examples

1. Let $f(x) = 3x - 1$. The graph of f is a straight line that has slope 3 everywhere. In other words, $f'(x) = 3$ for every choice of x; that is, f' is a constant function.

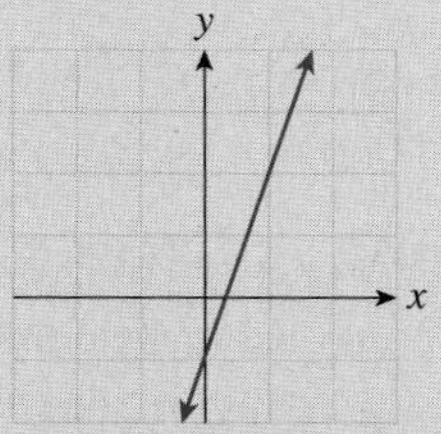

Original Function f
$f(x) = 3x - 1$

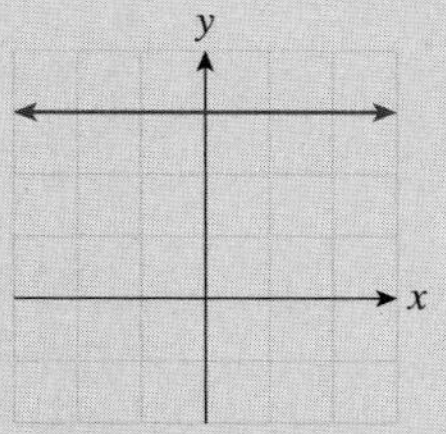

Derivative Function f'
$f'(x) = 3$

* This method is discussed in detail on the Website at Online Text → Sketching the Graph of the Derivative.

2. Given the graph of a function f, we can get a rough sketch of the graph of f' by estimating the slope of the tangent to the graph of f at several points, as illustrated below.*

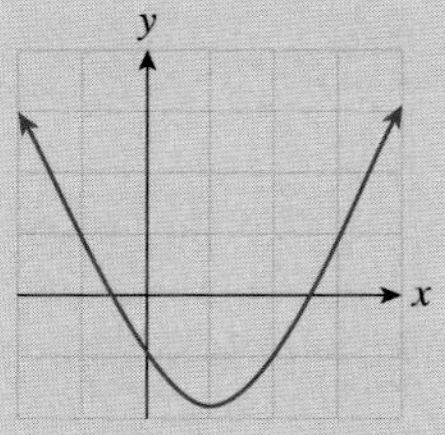

Original Function f
$y = f(x)$

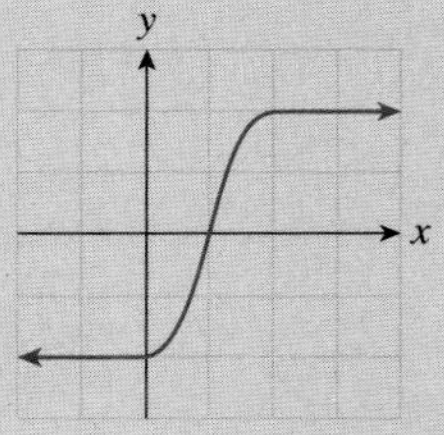

Derivative Function f'
$y = f'(x)$

For x between -2 and 0, the graph of f is linear with slope -2. As x increases from 0 to 2, the slope increases from -2 to 2. For x larger than 2, the graph of f is linear with slope 2. (Notice that, when $x = 1$, the graph of f has a horizontal tangent, so $f'(1) = 0$.)

3. Look again at the graph on the left in Quick Example 2. When $x < 1$ the derivative $f'(x)$ is negative, so the graph has negative slope and f is **decreasing**; its values are going down as x increases. When $x > 1$ the derivative $f'(x)$ is positive, so the graph has positive slope and f is **increasing**; its values are going up as x increases.

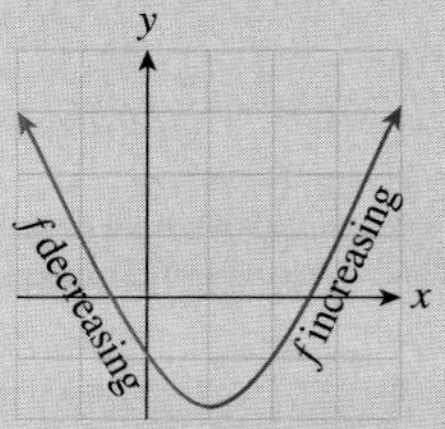

f decreasing for $x < 1$
f increasing for $x > 1$

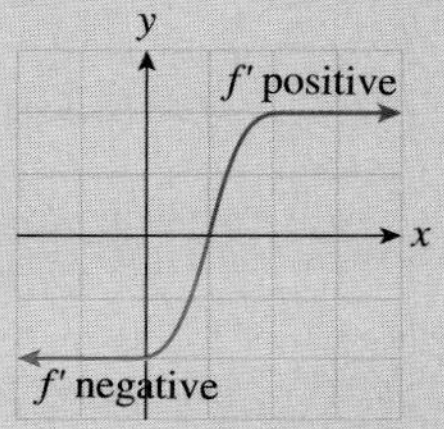

f' negative for $x < 1$
f' positive for $x > 1$

The following example shows how we can use technology to graph the (approximate) derivative of a function, where it exists.

EXAMPLE 4 T Graphing the Derivative with Technology

Use technology to graph the derivative of $f(x) = -2x^2 + 6x + 5$ for values of x starting at -5.

Solution The TI-83/84 Plus has a built-in function that approximates the derivative, and we can use it to graph the derivative of a function. In a spreadsheet, we need to create the approximation using one of the quick approximation formulas and we can then graph a table of its values. See the technology note in the margin on the next page to find out how to graph the derivative (Figure 33) using the Website graphing utility, the TI-83/84 Plus, and a spreadsheet.

using Technology

See the Technology Guides at the end of the chapter to find out how to obtain a table of values of and graph the derivative in Example 4 using a TI-83/84 Plus or a spreadsheet. Here is an outline:

TI-83/84 Plus

```
Y1=-2X^2+6X+5
Y2=nDeriv(Y1,X,X)
```

[More details on page 285.]

Spreadsheet

Value of *h* in E2

Values of *x* from A2 down increasing by *h*

`-2*A2^2+6*A2+5` from B2 down

`=(B3-B2)/$E$2` from C2 down

Insert scatter chart using columns A and C [More details on page 287.]

Website

www.WanerMath.com

Web grapher:

Online Utilities→ Function Evaluator and Grapher

Enter `deriv(-2*x^2+6*x+5)` for y_1. Alternatively, enter `-2*x^2+6*x+5` for y_1 and `deriv(y1)` for y_2.

Excel grapher:

Student Home→ Online Utilities→ Excel First and Second Derivative Graphing Utility

Function: `-2*x^2+6*x+5`

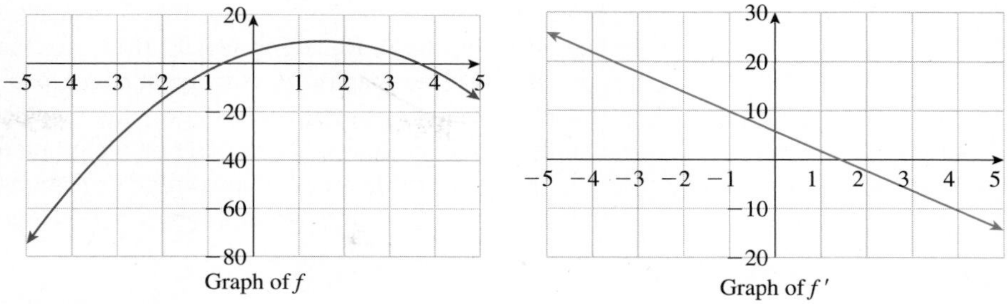

Figure 33

We said that f' records the slope of (the tangent line to) the function f at each point. Notice that the graph of f' confirms that the slope of the graph of f is decreasing as x increases from -5 to 5. Note also that the graph of f reaches a high point at $x = 1.5$ (the vertex of the parabola). At that point, the slope of the tangent is zero; that is, $f'(1.5) = 0$, as we see in the graph of f'.

EXAMPLE 5 An Application: Broadband Penetration

Wired broadband penetration in the United States can be modeled by

$$P(t) = \frac{29.842}{1 + 12.502(1.642)^{-t}} \qquad (0 \le t \le 12),$$

where t is time in years since 2000.[52] Graph both P and its derivative, and determine when broadband penetration was growing most rapidly.

Solution Using one of the methods in Example 4, we obtain the graphs shown in Figure 34.

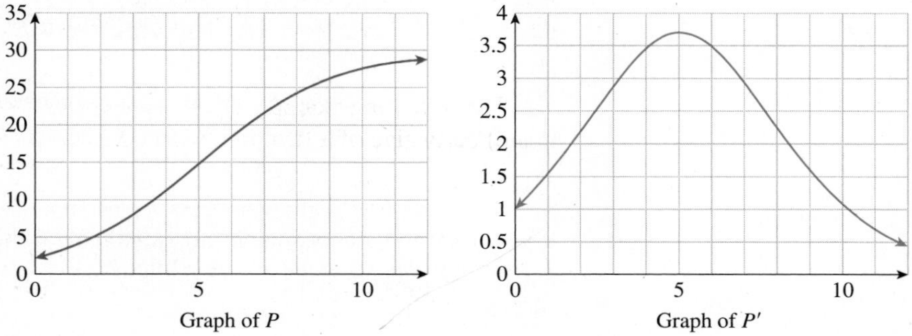

Figure 34

[52]Broadband penetration is the number of broadband installations divided by the total population. Source for data: Organisation for Economic Co-operation and Development (OECD) Directorate for Science, Technology, and Industry, table of Historical Penetration Rates, June 2010, downloaded April 2011 from www.oecd.org/sti/ict/broadband.

From the graph on the right, we see that P' reaches a peak somewhere near $t = 5$ (the beginning of 2005). Recalling that P' measures the *slope* of the graph of P, we can conclude that the graph of P is steepest near $t = 5$, indicating that, according to the model, broadband penetration was growing most rapidly at the start of 2005. Notice that this is not so easy to see directly on the graph of P.

To determine the point of maximum growth more accurately, we can zoom in on the graph of P' using the range $4.5 \leq t \leq 5.5$ (Figure 35).

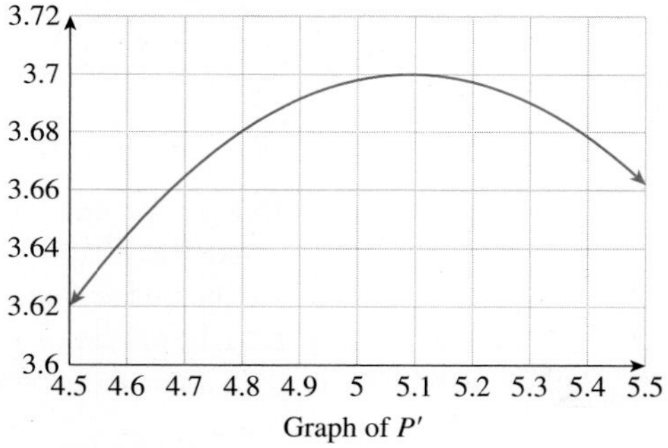

Figure 35

We can now see that P' reaches its highest point around $t = 5.1$, so we conclude that broadband penetration was growing most rapidly in early 2005.

➡ **Before we go on...** Besides helping us to determine the point of maximum growth, the graph of P' in Example 5 gives us a great deal of additional information. As just one example, in Figure 35 we can see that the maximum value of P' is about 3.7, indicating that broadband penetration grew at a fastest rate of about 3.7 percentage points per year. ■

FAQs

Recognizing When and How to Compute the Instantaneous Rate of Change

Q: *How do I know, by looking at the wording of a problem, that it is asking for an instantaneous rate of change?*

A: If a problem does not ask for an instantaneous rate of change directly, it might do so indirectly, as in "How fast is quantity q increasing?" or "Find the rate of increase of q."

Q: *If I know that a problem calls for estimating an instantaneous rate of change, how should I estimate it: with a table showing smaller and smaller values of h, or by using a quick approximation?*

A: For most practical purposes, a quick approximation is accurate enough. Use a table showing smaller and smaller values of h when you would like to check the accuracy.

Q: *Which should I use in computing a quick approximation: the balanced difference quotient or the ordinary difference quotient?*

A: In general, the balanced difference quotient gives a more accurate answer.

WW Website
www.WanerMath.com
At the Website you can find the following optional interactive online sections:
- **Continuity and Differentiability**
- **Sketching the Graph of the Derivative**

You can find these sections by following
Everything for Calculus → Chapter 3 (Online Sections)

3.5 EXERCISES

▼ more advanced ◆ challenging

T indicates exercises that should be solved using technology

In Exercises 1–4, estimate the derivative from the table of average rates of change. HINT [See discussion at the beginning of the section.]

1.

h	1	0.1	0.01	0.001	0.0001
Average Rate of Change of f Over [5, 5 + h]	12	6.4	6.04	6.004	6.0004
h	−1	−0.1	−0.01	−0.001	−0.0001
Average Rate of Change of f Over [5 + h, 5]	3	5.6	5.96	5.996	5.9996

Estimate $f'(5)$.

2.

h	1	0.1	0.01	0.001	0.0001
Average Rate of Change of g Over [7, 7 + h]	4	4.8	4.98	4.998	4.9998
h	−1	−0.1	−0.01	−0.001	−0.0001
Average Rate of Change of g Over [7 + h, 7]	5	5.3	5.03	5.003	5.0003

Estimate $g'(7)$.

3.

h	1	0.1	0.01	0.001	0.0001
Average Rate of Change of r Over [−6, −6 + h]	−5.4	−5.498	−5.4998	−5.499982	−5.49999822
h	−1	−0.1	−0.01	−0.001	−0.0001
Average Rate of Change of r Over [−6 + h, −6]	−7.52	−6.13	−5.5014	−5.5000144	−5.500001444

Estimate $r'(-6)$.

4.

h	1	0.1	0.01	0.001	0.0001
Average Rate of Change of s Over [0, h]	−2.52	−1.13	−0.6014	−0.6000144	−0.600001444
h	−1	−0.1	−0.01	−0.001	−0.0001
Average Rate of Change of s Over [h, 0]	−0.4	−0.598	−0.5998	−0.599982	−0.59999822

Estimate $s'(0)$.

Consider the functions in Exercises 5–8 as representing the value of an ounce of palladium in U.S. dollars as a function of the time t in days.[53] *Find the average rates of change of $R(t)$ over the time intervals $[t, t + h]$, where t is as indicated and $h = 1, 0.1,$ and 0.01 days. Hence, estimate the instantaneous rate of change of R at time t, specifying the units of measurement. (Use smaller values of h to check your estimates.)* HINT [See Example 1.]

5. $R(t) = 60 + 50t - t^2; t = 5$

6. $R(t) = 60t - 2t^2; t = 3$

7. $R(t) = 270 + 20t^3; t = 1$

8. $R(t) = 200 + 50t - t^3; t = 2$

Each of the functions in Exercises 9–12 gives the cost to manufacture x items. Find the average cost per unit of manufacturing h more items (i.e., the average rate of change of the total cost) at a production level of x, where x is as indicated and $h = 10$ and 1. Hence, estimate the instantaneous rate of change of the total cost at the given production level x, specifying the units of measurement. (Use smaller values of h to check your estimates.) HINT [See Example 1.]

9. $C(x) = 10{,}000 + 5x - \dfrac{x^2}{10{,}000}; x = 1{,}000$

10. $C(x) = 20{,}000 + 7x - \dfrac{x^2}{20{,}000}; x = 10{,}000$

11. $C(x) = 15{,}000 + 100x + \dfrac{1{,}000}{x}; \ x = 100$

12. $C(x) = 20{,}000 + 50x + \dfrac{10{,}000}{x}; x = 100$

In Exercises 13–16, the graph of a function is shown together with the tangent line at a point P. Estimate the derivative of f at the corresponding x value. HINT [See Quick Example page 248.]

13.

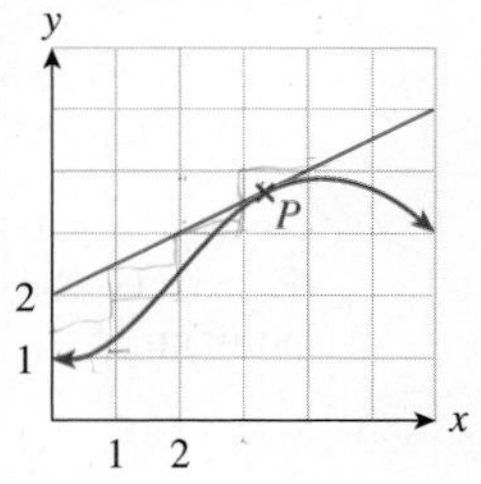

14.

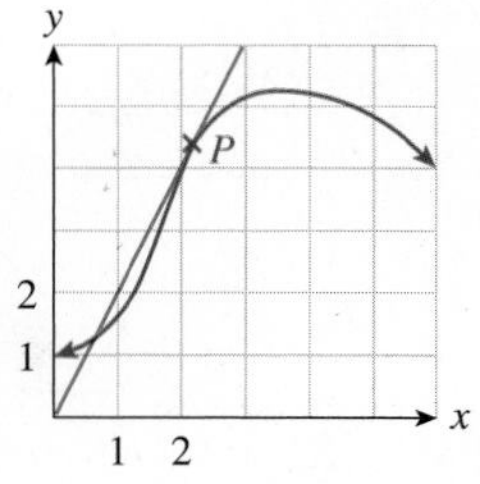

15.

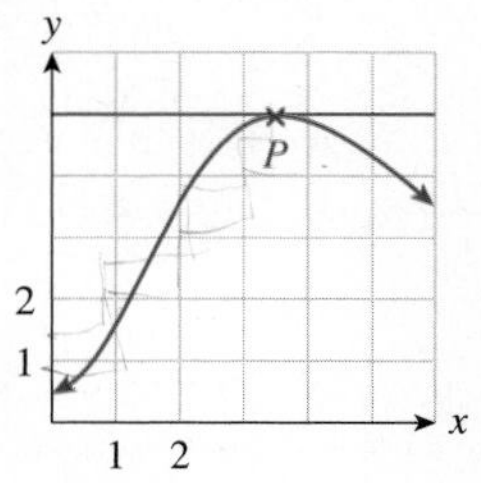

16.

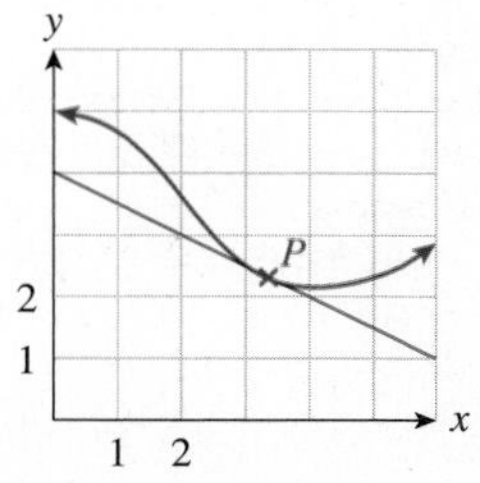

[53] Palladium was trading at around $290 in August 2008.

*In each of the graphs given in Exercises 17–22, say at which labeled point the slope of the tangent is **(a)** greatest and **(b)** least (in the sense that -7 is less than 1).* HINT [See Quick Example page 248.]

17.

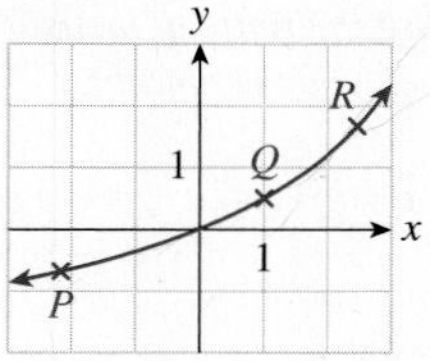

18.

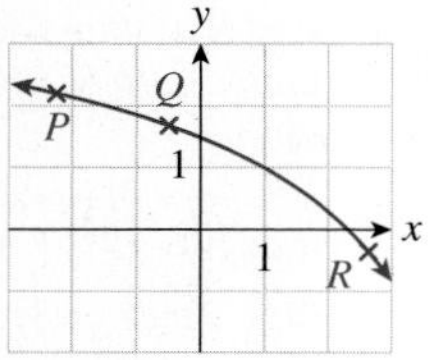

19.

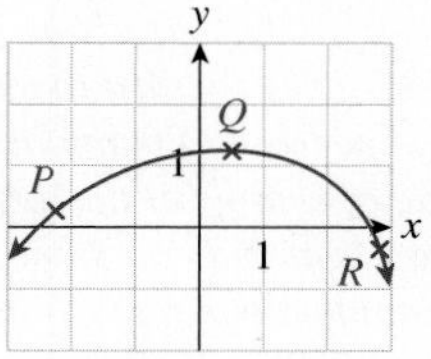

20.

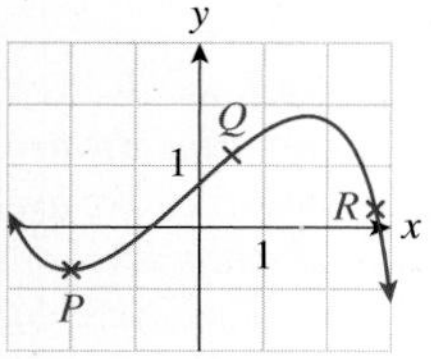

21.

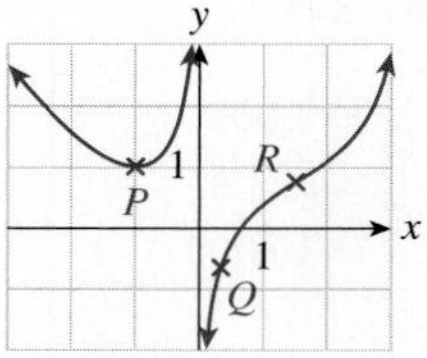

22.

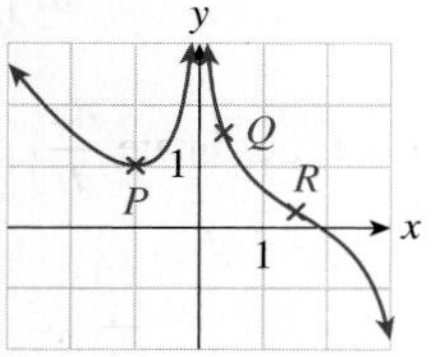

In each of Exercises 23–26, three slopes are given. For each slope, determine at which of the labeled points on the graph the tangent line has that slope.

23. **a.** 0 **b.** 4 **c.** -1

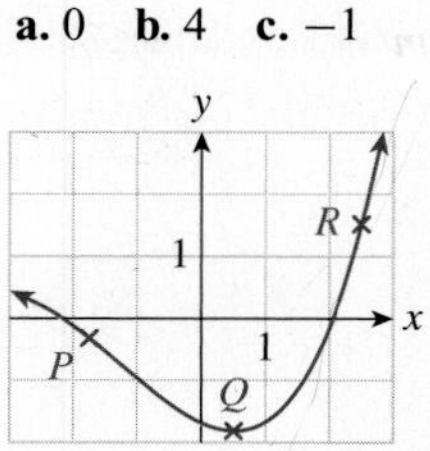

24. **a.** 0 **b.** 1 **c.** -1

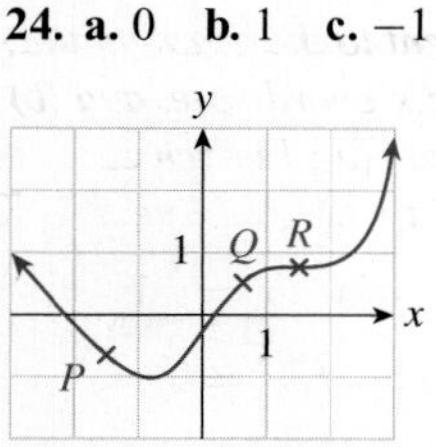

25. **a.** 0 **b.** 3 **c.** -3

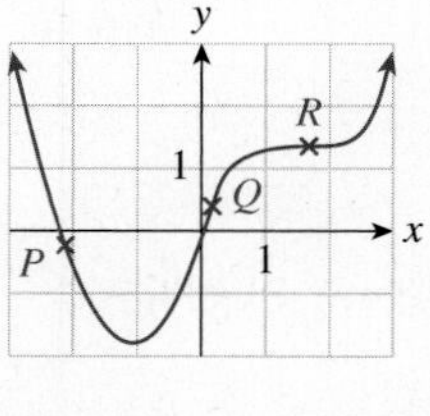

26. **a.** 0 **b.** 3 **c.** 1

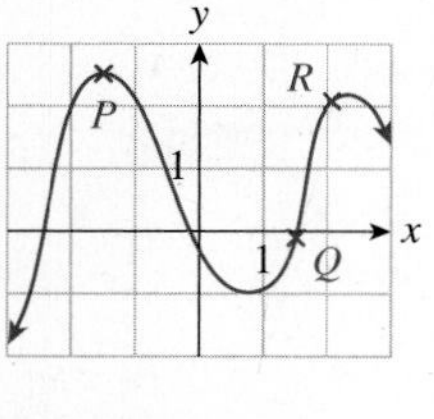

*In each of Exercises 27–30, find the approximate coordinates of all points (if any) where the slope of the tangent is: **(a)** 0, **(b)** 1, **(c)** -1.* HINT [See Quick Example page 248.]

27.

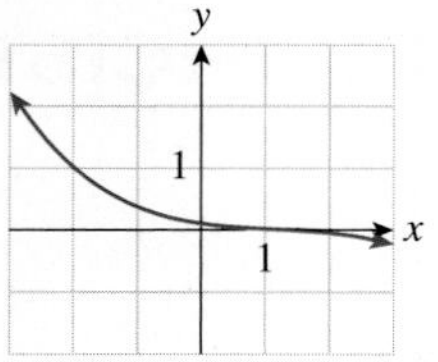

28.

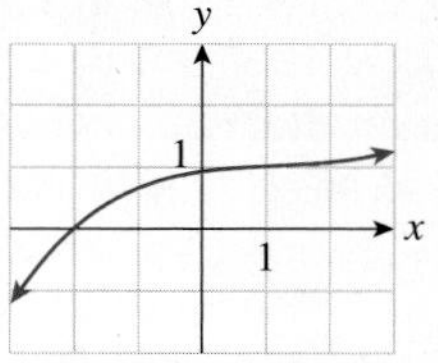

29.

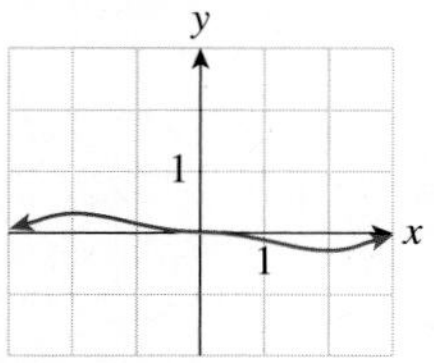

30.

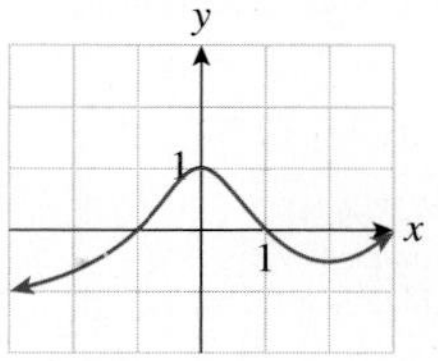

31. Complete the following: The tangent to the graph of the function f at the point where $x = a$ is the line passing through the point ____ with slope ____ .

32. Complete the following: The difference quotient for f at the point where $x = a$ gives the slope of the ____ line that passes through _____ .

33. Which is correct? The derivative function assigns to each value x

(A) the average rate of change of f at x.
(B) the slope of the tangent to the graph of f at $(x, f(x))$.
(C) the rate at which f is changing over the interval $[x, x+h]$ for $h = 0.0001$.
(D) the balanced difference quotient $[f(x+h) - f(x-h)]/(2h)$ for $h \approx 0.0001$.

34. Which is correct? The derivative function $f'(x)$ tells us
(A) the slope of the tangent line at each of the points $(x, f(x))$.
(B) the approximate slope of the tangent line at each of the points $(x, f(x))$.
(C) the slope of the secant line through $(x, f(x))$ and $(x+h, f(x+h))$ for $h = 0.0001$.
(D) the slope of a certain secant line through each of the points $(x, f(x))$.

35. ▼ Let f have the graph shown.

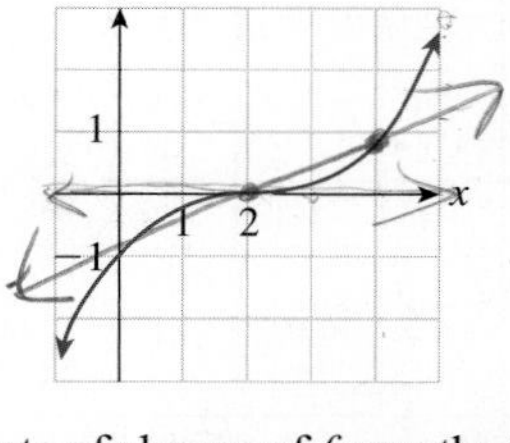

a. The average rate of change of f over the interval $[2, 4]$ is
(A) greater than $f'(2)$. **(B)** less than $f'(2)$.
(C) approximately equal to $f'(2)$.

b. The average rate of change of f over the interval $[-1, 1]$ is
(A) greater than $f'(0)$. **(B)** less than $f'(0)$.
(C) approximately equal to $f'(0)$.

c. Over the interval [0, 2], the instantaneous rate of change of *f* is
(A) increasing. **(B)** decreasing. **(C)** neither.

d. Over the interval [0, 4], the instantaneous rate of change of *f* is
(A) increasing, then decreasing.
(B) decreasing, then increasing.
(C) always increasing.
(D) always decreasing.

e. When $x = 4$, $f(x)$ is
(A) approximately 0, and increasing at a rate of about 0.7 units per unit of *x*.
(B) approximately 0, and decreasing at a rate of about 0.7 units per unit of *x*.
(C) approximately 0.7, and increasing at a rate of about 1 unit per unit of *x*.
(D) approximately 0.7, and increasing at a rate of about 3 units per unit of *x*.

36. ▼ A function *f* has the following graph.

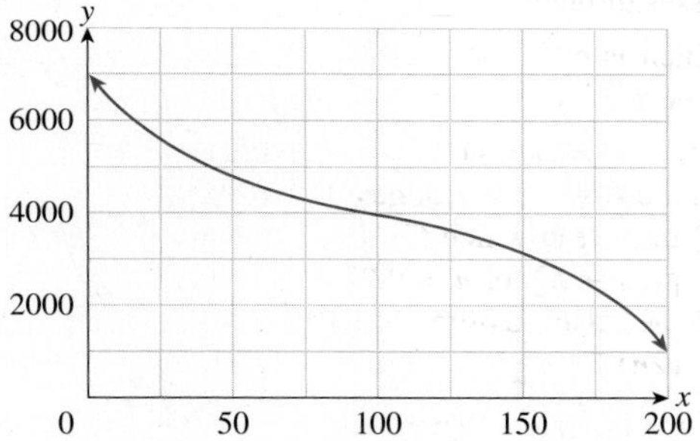

a. The average rate of change of *f* over [0, 200] is
(A) greater than
(B) less than
(C) approximately equal to
the instantaneous rate of change at $x = 100$.

b. The average rate of change of *f* over [0, 200] is
(A) greater than
(B) less than
(C) approximately equal to
the instantaneous rate of change at $x = 150$.

c. Over the interval [0, 50] the instantaneous rate of change of *f* is
(A) increasing, then decreasing.
(B) decreasing, then increasing.
(C) always increasing.
(D) always decreasing.

d. On the interval [0, 200], the instantaneous rate of change of *f* is
(A) always positive. **(B)** always negative.
(C) negative, positive, and then negative.

e. $f'(100)$ is
(A) greater than $f'(25)$. **(B)** less than $f'(25)$.
(C) approximately equal to $f'(25)$.

In Exercises 37–40, use a quick approximation to estimate the derivative of the given function at the indicated point. HINT [See Example 2(a).]

37. $f(x) = 1 - 2x;\ x = 2$

38. $f(x) = \frac{x}{3} - 1;\ x = -3$

39. $f(x) = \frac{x^2}{4} - \frac{x^3}{3};\ x = -1$

40. $f(x) = \frac{x^2}{2} + \frac{x}{4};\ x = 2$

In Exercises 41–48, estimate the indicated derivative by any method. HINT [See Example 2.]

41. $g(t) = \frac{1}{t^5}$; estimate $g'(1)$

42. $s(t) = \frac{1}{t^3}$; estimate $s'(-2)$

43. $y = 4x^2$; estimate $\left.\frac{dy}{dx}\right|_{x=2}$

44. $y = 1 - x^2$; estimate $\left.\frac{dy}{dx}\right|_{x=-1}$

45. $s = 4t + t^2$; estimate $\left.\frac{ds}{dt}\right|_{t=-2}$

46. $s = t - t^2$; estimate $\left.\frac{ds}{dt}\right|_{t=2}$

47. $R = \frac{1}{p}$; estimate $\left.\frac{dR}{dp}\right|_{p=20}$

48. $R = \sqrt{p}$; estimate $\left.\frac{dR}{dp}\right|_{p=400}$

*In Exercises 49–54, **(a)** use any method to estimate the slope of the tangent to the graph of the given function at the point with the given x-coordinate, and **(b)** find an equation of the tangent line in part (a). In each case, sketch the curve together with the appropriate tangent line.* HINT [See Example 2(b).]

49. $f(x) = x^3;\ x = -1$

50. $f(x) = x^2;\ x = 0$

51. $f(x) = x + \frac{1}{x};\ x = 2$

52. $f(x) = \frac{1}{x^2};\ x = 1$

53. $f(x) = \sqrt{x};\ x = 4$

54. $f(x) = 2x + 4;\ x = -1$

In each of Exercises 55–58, estimate the given quantity.

55. $f(x) = e^x$; estimate $f'(0)$

56. $f(x) = 2e^x$; estimate $f'(1)$

57. $f(x) = \ln x$; estimate $f'(1)$

58. $f(x) = \ln x$; estimate $f'(2)$

In Exercises 59–64, match the graph of f to the graph of f' (the graphs of f' are shown after Exercise 64).

59. ▼

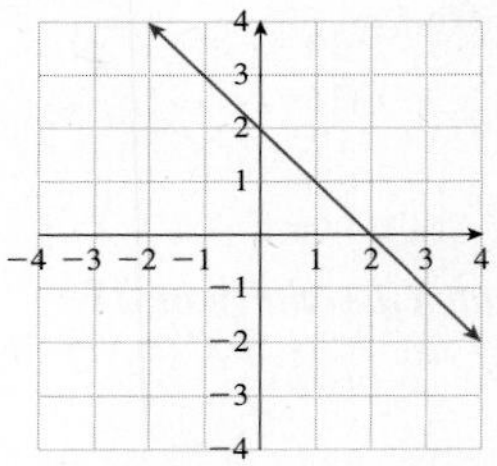

60. ▼

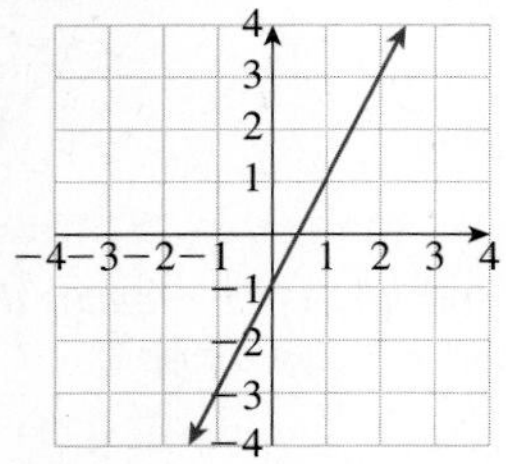

61. ▼

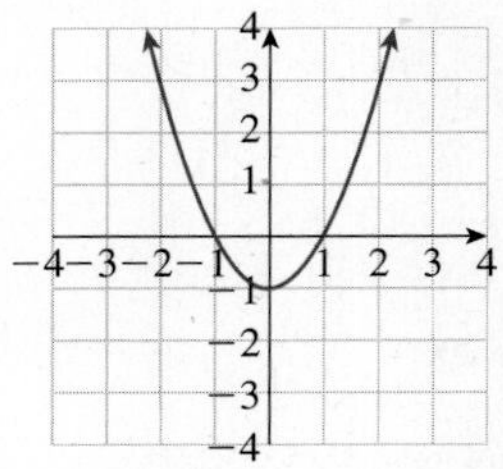

62. ▼

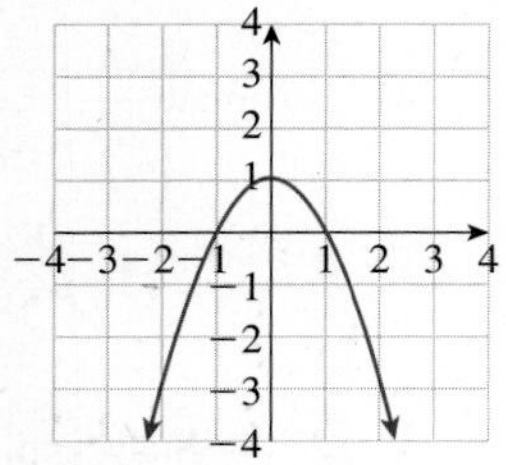

63. ▼

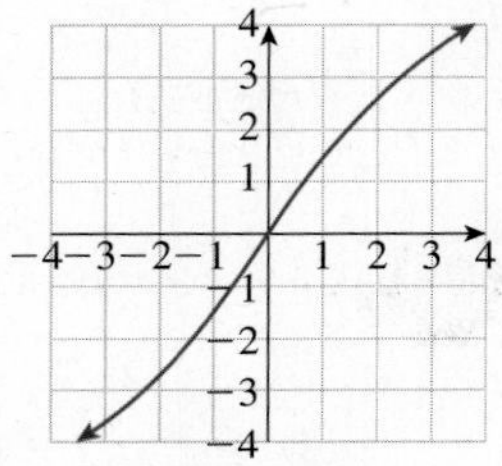

64. ▼

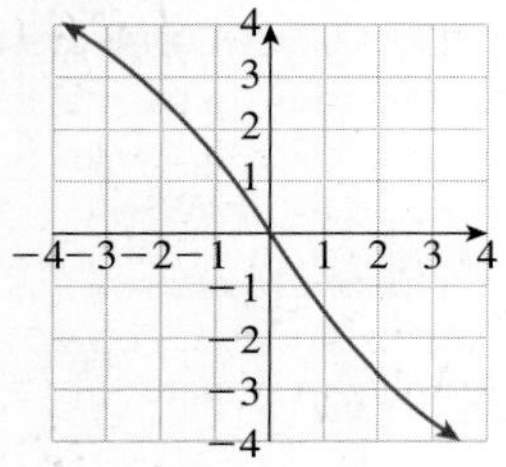

Graphs of derivatives for Exercises 59–64:

(A)

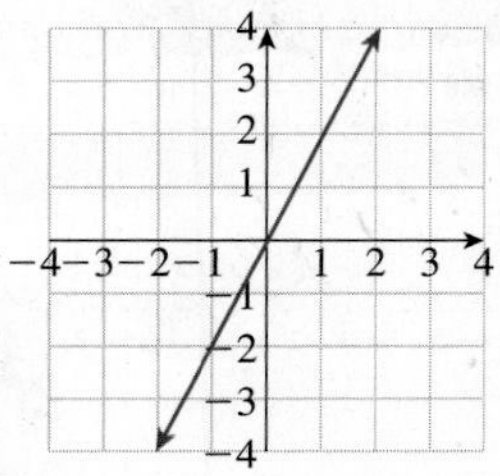

(B)

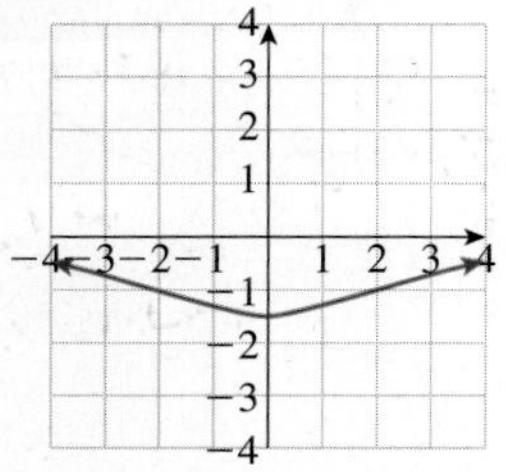

(C)

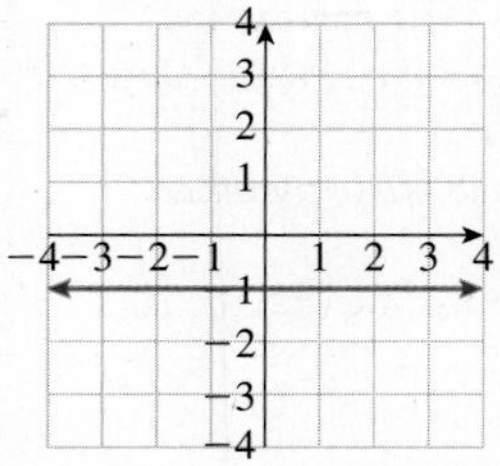

(D)

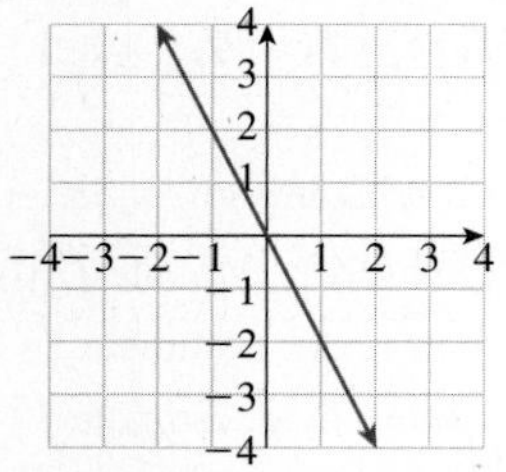

(E)

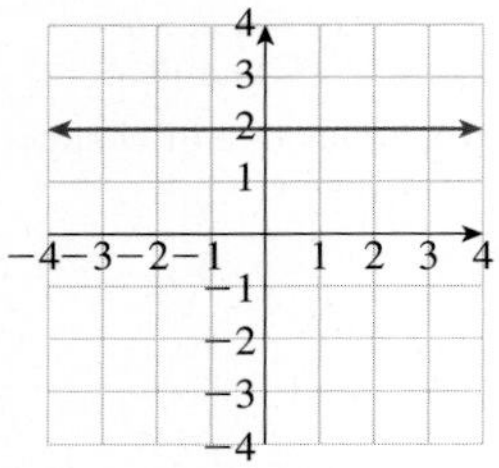

(F)

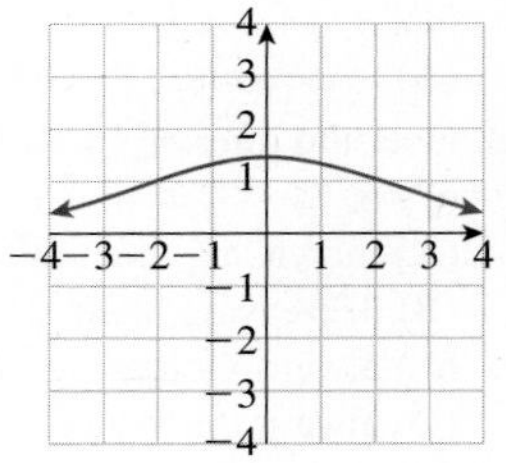

In Exercises 65–68, the graph of a function is given. For which x in the range shown is the function increasing? For which x is the function decreasing? HINT [See Quick Example 3 page 254.]

65.

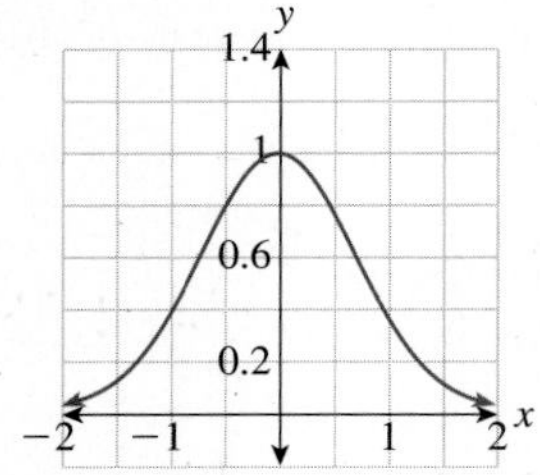

66.

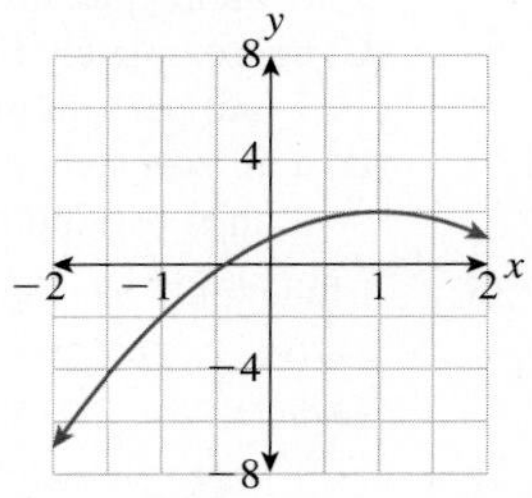

67.

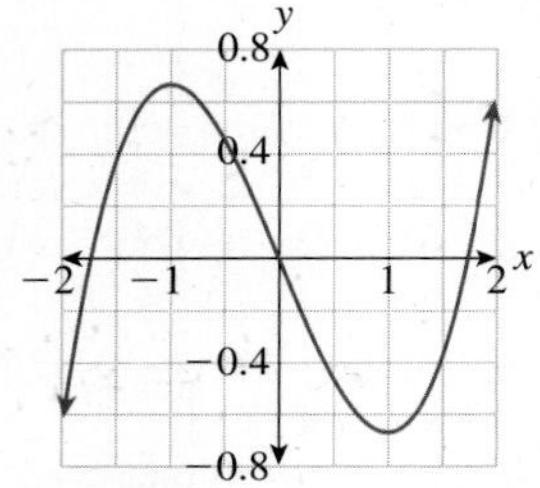

68.

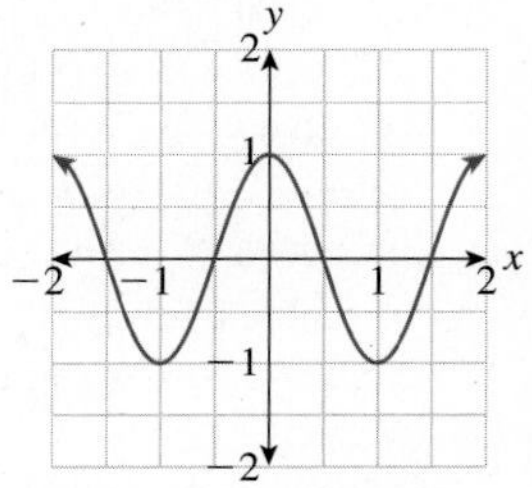

In Exercises 69–72, the graph of the derivative of a function is given. For which x is the (original) function increasing? For which x is the (original) function decreasing? HINT [See Quick Example 3 page 254.]

69.

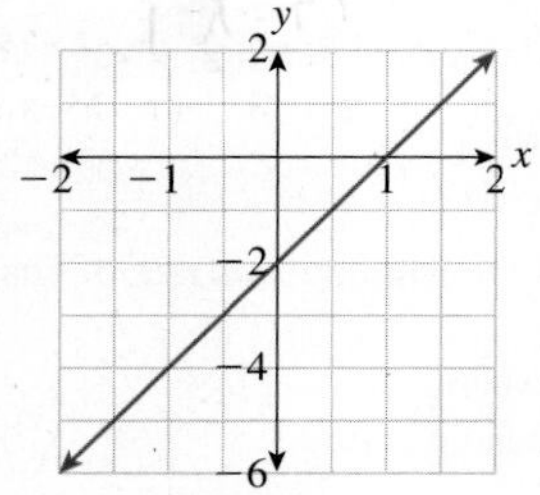

70.

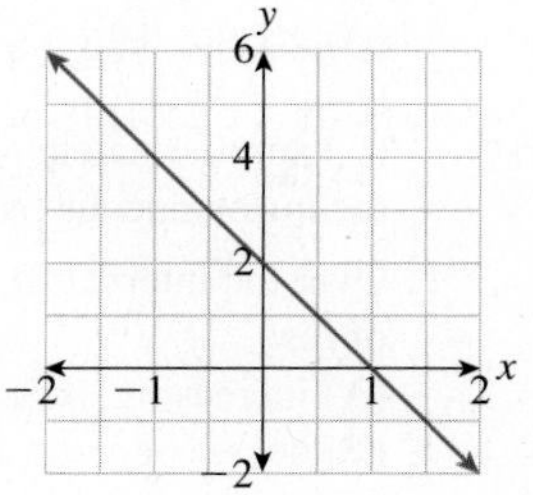

71.

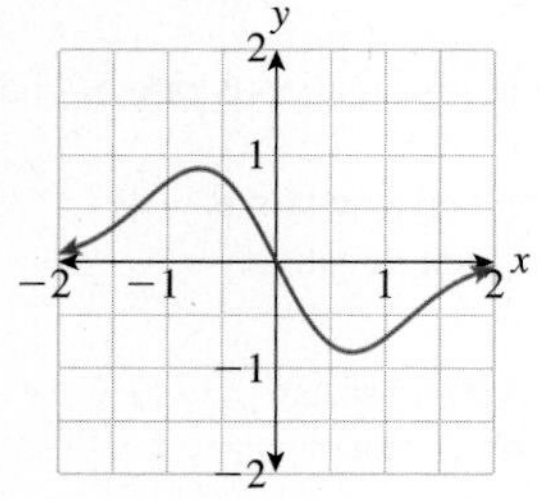

72.

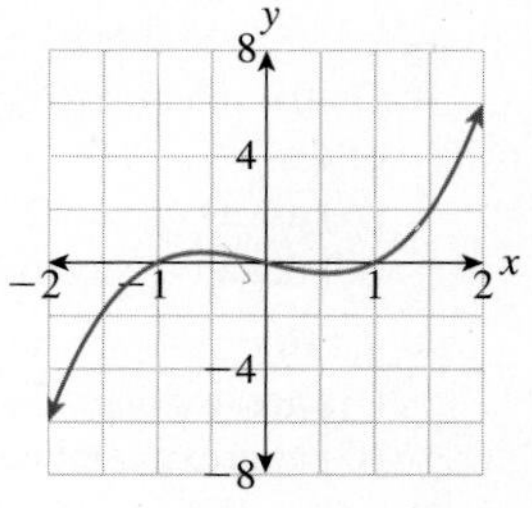

T *In Exercises 73 and 74, use technology to graph the derivative of the given function for the given range of values of x. Then use your graph to estimate all values of x (if any) where the tangent line to the graph of the given function is horizontal. Round answers to one decimal place.* HINT [See Example 4.]

73. $f(x) = x^4 + 2x^3 - 1; \quad -2 \le x \le 1$

74. $f(x) = -x^3 - 3x^2 - 1; \quad -3 \le x \le 1$

T *In Exercises 75 and 76, use the method of Example 4 to list approximate values of f′(x) for x in the given range. Graph f(x) together with f′(x) for x in the given range.*

75. $f(x) = \dfrac{x+2}{x-3}; \quad 4 \le x \le 5$

76. $f(x) = \dfrac{10x}{x-2}; \quad 2.5 \le x \le 3$

APPLICATIONS

77. ***Demand*** Suppose the demand for a new brand of sneakers is given by

$$q = \frac{5{,}000{,}000}{p}$$

where p is the price per pair of sneakers, in dollars, and q is the number of pairs of sneakers that can be sold at price p. Find $q(100)$ and estimate $q'(100)$. Interpret your answers. HINT [See Example 1.]

78. ***Demand*** Suppose the demand for an old brand of TV is given by

$$q = \frac{100{,}000}{p+10}$$

where p is the price per TV set, in dollars, and q is the number of TV sets that can be sold at price p. Find $q(190)$ and estimate $q'(190)$. Interpret your answers. HINT [See Example 1.]

79. ***Oil Imports from Mexico*** The following graph shows approximate daily oil imports to the U.S. from Mexico.[54] Also shown is the tangent line at the point corresponding to year 2005.

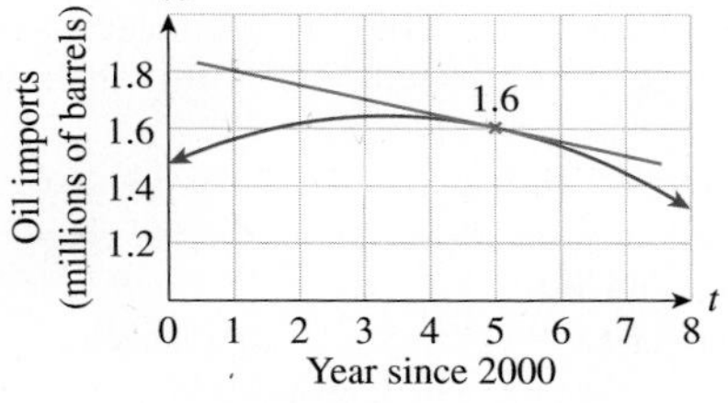

a. Estimate the slope of the tangent line shown on the graph. What does the graph tell you about oil imports from Mexico in 2005? HINT [Identify two points on the tangent line. Then see Quick Example page 248.]

b. According to the graph, is the rate of change of oil imports from Mexico increasing, decreasing, or increasing then decreasing? Why?

80. ***Oil Production in Mexico*** The following graph shows approximate daily oil production by Pemex, Mexico's national oil company.[55] Also shown is the tangent line at the point corresponding to year 2003.

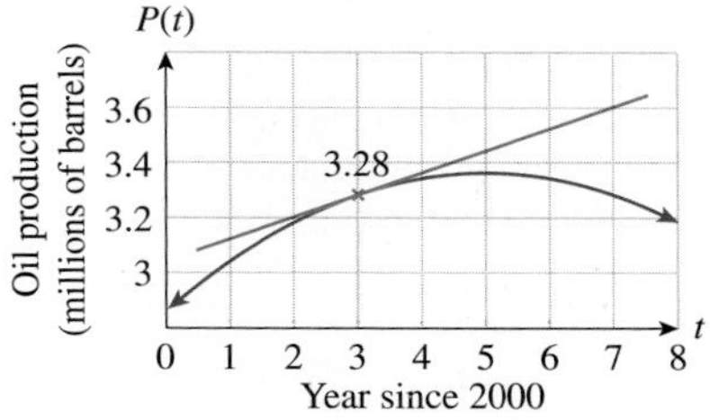

a. Estimate the slope of the tangent line shown on the graph. What does the graph tell you about oil production by Pemex in 2003? HINT [Identify two points on the tangent line. Then see Quick Example page 248.]

b. According to the graph, is the rate of change of oil production by Pemex increasing or decreasing over the range [0, 4]? Why?

81. ▼ ***Prison Population*** The following curve is a model of the total U.S. prison population as a function of time in years ($t = 0$ represents 2000).[56]

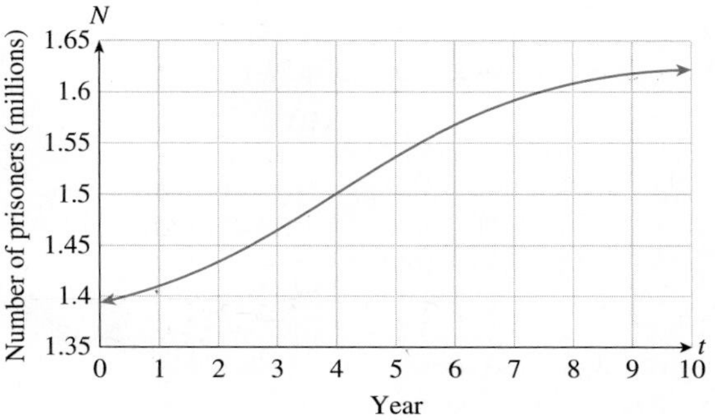

a. Which is correct? Over the period [5, 10] the instantaneous rate of change of N is

(A) increasing. **(B)** decreasing.

b. Which is correct? The instantaneous rate of change of prison population at $t = 4$ was

(A) less than **(B)** greater than

(C) approximately equal to

the average rate of change over the interval [0, 10].

[54] Figures are approximate, and 2008–2009 figures are projections by the Department of Energy. Source: Energy Information Administration/Pemex (www.eia.doe.gov).

[55] *Ibid.*

[56] Source: Bureau of Justice Statistics http://bjs.ojp.usdoj.gov.

c. Which is correct? Over the period [0, 10] the instantaneous rate of change of N is
(A) increasing, then decreasing.
(B) decreasing, then increasing.
(C) always increasing.
(D) always decreasing.

d. According to the model, the U.S. prison population was increasing fastest around what year?

e. Roughly estimate the instantaneous rate of change of N at $t = 4$ by using a balanced difference quotient with $h = 1.5$. Interpret the result.

82. ▼ ***Demand for Freon 12*** The demand for chlorofluorocarbon-12 (CFC-12)—the ozone-depleting refrigerant commonly known as Freon 12[57]—has been declining significantly in response to regulation and concern about the ozone layer. The graph below represents a model for the projected demand for CFC-12 as a function of time in years ($t = 0$ represents 1990).[58]

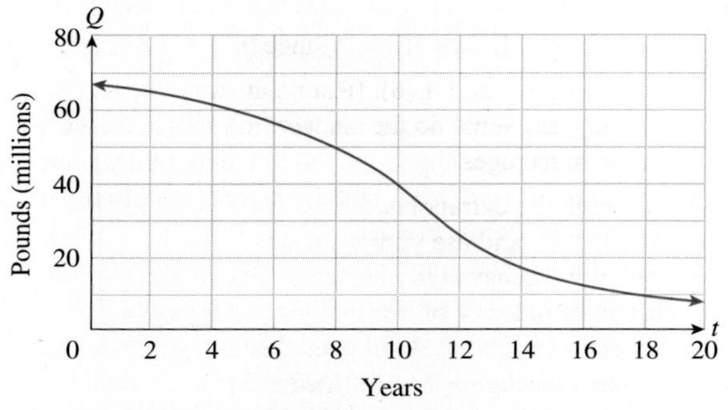

a. Which is correct? Over the period [12, 20] the instantaneous rate of change of Q is
(A) increasing. **(B)** decreasing.

b. Which is correct? The instantaneous rate of change of demand for Freon 12 at $t = 10$ was
(A) less than **(B)** greater than
(C) approximately equal to
the average rate of change over the interval [0, 20].

c. Which is correct? Over the period [0, 20] the instantaneous rate of change of Q is
(A) increasing, then decreasing.
(B) decreasing, then increasing.
(C) always increasing.
(D) always decreasing.

d. According to the model, the demand for Freon 12 was decreasing most rapidly around what year?

e. Roughly estimate the instantaneous rate of change of Q at $t = 13$ by using a balanced difference quotient with $h = 5$. Interpret the result.

[57]The name given to it by DuPont. Freon 12 (dichlorodifluoromethane) is distinct from Freon 22 (chlorodifluoromethane, also registered by DuPont; see p. 232).

[58]Source for data: The Automobile Consulting Group (*New York Times*, December 26, 1993, p. F23). The exact figures were not given, and the chart is a reasonable facsimile of the chart that appeared in *New York Times*.

83. ***Velocity*** If a stone is dropped from a height of 400 feet, its height after t seconds is given by $s = 400 - 16t^2$.

a. Find its average velocity over the period [2, 4].

b. Estimate its instantaneous velocity at time $t = 4$. HINT [See Example 3.]

84. ***Velocity*** If a stone is thrown down at 120 ft/s from a height of 1,000 feet, its height after t seconds is given by $s = 1{,}000 - 120t - 16t^2$.

a. Find its average velocity over the period [1, 3].

b. Estimate its instantaneous velocity at time $t = 3$. HINT [See Example 3.]

85. ***Crude Oil Prices*** The price per barrel of crude oil in constant 2008 dollars can be approximated by

$$P(t) = 0.45t^2 - 12t + 105 \text{ dollars} \quad (0 \le t \le 28),$$

where t is time in years since the start of 1980.[59]

a. Compute the average rate of change of $P(t)$ over the interval [0, 28], and interpret your answer. HINT [See Section 3.4 Example 3.]

b. Estimate the instantaneous rate of change of $P(t)$ at $t = 0$, and interpret your answer. HINT [See Example 2(a).]

c. The answers to part (a) and part (b) have opposite signs. What does this indicate about the price of oil?

86. ***Median Home Prices*** The median home price in the U.S. over the period 2003–2011 can be approximated by

$$P(t) = -5t^2 + 75t - 30 \text{ thousand dollars} \quad (3 \le t \le 11),$$

where t is time in years since the start of 2000.[60]

a. Compute the average rate of change of $P(t)$ over the interval [5, 9], and interpret your answer. HINT [See Section 3.4 Example 3.]

b. Estimate the instantaneous rate of change of $P(t)$ at $t = 5$, and interpret your answer. HINT [See Example 2(a).]

c. The answer to part (b) has larger absolute value than the answer to part (a). What does this indicate about the median home price?

87. ***SARS*** In the early stages of the deadly SARS (Severe Acute Respiratory Syndrome) epidemic in 2003, the number of reported cases could be approximated by

$$A(t) = 167(1.18)^t \quad (0 \le t \le 20)$$

t days after March 17, 2003 (the first day in which statistics were reported by the World Health Organization).

a. What, approximately, was the instantaneous rate of change of $A(t)$ on March 27 ($t = 10$)? Interpret the result.

b. Which of the following is true? For the first 20 days of the epidemic, the instantaneous rate of change of the number of cases
(A) increased. **(B)** decreased.
(C) increased and then decreased.
(D) decreased and then increased.

[59]Source for data: www.inflationdata.com.
[60]Source for data: www.zillow.com.

88. ***SARS*** A few weeks into the deadly SARS (Severe Acute Respiratory Syndrome) epidemic in 2003, the number of reported cases could be approximated by

$$A(t) = 1{,}804(1.04)^t \quad (0 \le t \le 30)$$

t days after April 1, 2003.

a. What, approximately, was the instantaneous rate of change of $A(t)$ on April 21 ($t = 20$)? Interpret the result.

b. Which of the following is true? During April, the instantaneous rate of change of the number of cases
(A) increased. **(B)** decreased.
(C) increased and then decreased.
(D) decreased and then increased.

89. ***Sales*** Weekly sales of a new brand of sneakers are given by

$$S(t) = 200 - 150e^{-t/10}$$

pairs sold per week, where t is the number of weeks since the introduction of the brand. Estimate $S(5)$ and $\left.\frac{dS}{dt}\right|_{t=5}$ and interpret your answers.

90. ***Sales*** Weekly sales of an old brand of TV are given by

$$S(t) = 100e^{-t/5}$$

sets per week, where t is the number of weeks after the introduction of a competing brand. Estimate $S(5)$ and $\left.\frac{dS}{dt}\right|_{t=5}$ and interpret your answers.

91. ***Early Internet Services*** On January 1, 1996, America Online was the biggest online service provider, with 4.5 million subscribers, and was adding new subscribers at a rate of 60,000 per week.[61] If $A(t)$ is the number of America Online subscribers t weeks after January 1, 1996, what do the given data tell you about values of the function A and its derivative? HINT [See Quick Example 2 on page 244.]

92. ***Early Internet Services*** On January 1, 1996, Prodigy was the third-biggest online service provider, with 1.6 million subscribers, but was losing subscribers.[62] If $P(t)$ is the number of Prodigy subscribers t weeks after January 1, 1996, what do the given data tell you about values of the function P and its derivative? HINT [See Quick Example 2 on page 244.]

93. ▼ ***Learning to Speak*** Let $p(t)$ represent the percentage of children who are able to speak at the age of t months.

a. It is found that $p(10) = 60$ and $\left.\frac{dp}{dt}\right|_{t=10} = 18.2$. What does this mean?[63] HINT [See Quick Example 2 on page 244.]

b. As t increases, what happens to p and $\frac{dp}{dt}$?

94. ▼ ***Learning to Read*** Let $p(t)$ represent the percentage of children in your class who learned to read at the age of t years.

a. Assuming that everyone in your class could read by the age of 7, what does this tell you about $p(7)$ and $\left.\frac{dp}{dt}\right|_{t=7}$? HINT [See Quick Example 2 on page 244.]

b. Assuming that 25.0% of the people in your class could read by the age of 5, and that 25.3% of them could read by the age of 5 years and one month, estimate $\left.\frac{dp}{dt}\right|_{t=5}$. Remember to give its units.

95. ***Subprime Mortgages during the Housing Crisis*** (Compare Exercise 29 of Section 3.4.) The percentage of mortgages issued in the United States during the period 2000–2009 that were subprime (normally classified as risky) can be approximated by

$$A(t) = \frac{15}{1 + 8.6(1.8)^{-t}} \quad (0 \le t \le 9),$$

where t is the number of years since the start of 2000.[64]

a. Estimate $A(6)$ and $A'(6)$. (Round answers to two significant digits.) What do the answers tell you about subprime mortgages?

b. T Graph the extrapolated function and its derivative for $0 \le t \le 16$ and use your graphs to describe how the derivative behaves as t becomes large. (Express this behavior in terms of limits if you have studied the sections on limits.) What does this tell you about subprime mortgages? HINT [See Example 5.]

96. ***Subprime Mortgage Debt during the Housing Crisis*** (Compare Exercise 30 of Section 3.4.) The value of subprime (normally classified as risky) mortgage debt outstanding in the U.S. during the period 2000–2009 can be approximated by

$$A(t) = \frac{1{,}350}{1 + 4.2(1.7)^{-t}} \text{ billion dollars} \quad (0 \le t \le 9),$$

where t is the number of years since the start of 2000.[65]

a. Estimate $A(7)$ and $A'(7)$. (Round answers to three significant digits.) What do the answers tell you about subprime mortgages?

b. T Graph the function and its derivative and use your graphs to estimate when, to the nearest year, $A'(t)$ is greatest. What does this tell you about subprime mortgages? HINT [See Example 5.]

97. T ▼ ***Embryo Development*** The oxygen consumption of a turkey embryo increases from the time the egg is laid through the time the turkey chick hatches. In a brush turkey, the oxygen consumption (in milliliters per hour) can be approximated by

$$c(t) = -0.0012t^3 + 0.12t^2 - 1.83t + 3.97 \quad (20 \le t \le 50),$$

---

[61] Source: Information and Interactive Services Report/*New York Times*, January 2, 1996, p. C14.

[62] *Ibid.*

[63] Based on data presented in the article *The Emergence of Intelligence* by William H. Calvin, *Scientific American*, October, 1994, pp. 101–107.

[64] Sources: Mortgage Bankers Association, UBS.

[65] Source: Data 360 www.data360.org.

where t is the time (in days) since the egg was laid.[66] (An egg will typically hatch at around $t = 50$.) Use technology to graph $c'(t)$ and use your graph to answer the following questions. HINT [See Example 5.]

a. Over the interval [20, 32] the derivative c' is
   (A) increasing, then decreasing.
   (B) decreasing, then increasing.
   (C) decreasing. **(D)** increasing.

b. When, to the nearest day, is the oxygen consumption increasing at the fastest rate?

c. When, to the nearest day, is the oxygen consumption increasing at the slowest rate?

98. T ▼ ***Embryo Development*** The oxygen consumption of a bird embryo increases from the time the egg is laid through the time the chick hatches. In a typical galliform bird, the oxygen consumption (in milliliters per hour) can be approximated by

$$c(t) = -0.0027t^3 + 0.14t^2 - 0.89t + 0.15 \quad (8 \le t \le 30),$$

where t is the time (in days) since the egg was laid.[67] (An egg will typically hatch at around $t = 28$.) Use technology to graph $c'(t)$ and use your graph to answer the following questions. HINT [See Example 5.]

a. Over the interval [8, 30] the derivative c' is
   (A) increasing, then decreasing.
   (B) decreasing, then increasing.
   (C) decreasing. **(D)** increasing.

b. When, to the nearest day, is the oxygen consumption increasing the fastest?

c. When, to the nearest day, is the oxygen consumption increasing at the slowest rate?

The next two exercises are applications of Einstein's Special Theory of Relativity and relate to objects that are moving extremely fast. In science fiction terminology, a speed of warp 1 *is the speed of light—about* 3×10^8 *meters per second. (Thus, for instance, a speed of warp* 0.8 *corresponds to 80% of the speed of light—about* 2.4×10^8 *meters per second.)*

99. ◆ ***Lorentz Contraction*** According to Einstein's Special Theory of Relativity, a moving object appears to get shorter to a stationary observer as its speed approaches the speed of light. If a spaceship that has a length of 100 meters at rest travels at a speed of warp p, its length in meters, as measured by a stationary observer, is given by

$$L(p) = 100\sqrt{1 - p^2}$$

with domain [0, 1). Estimate $L(0.95)$ and $L'(0.95)$. What do these figures tell you?

100. ◆ ***Time Dilation*** Another prediction of Einstein's Special Theory of Relativity is that, to a stationary observer, clocks (as well as all biological processes) in a moving object appear to go more and more slowly as the speed of the object approaches that of light. If a spaceship travels at a speed of warp p, the time it takes for an onboard clock to register one second, as measured by a stationary observer, will be given by

$$T(p) = \frac{1}{\sqrt{1 - p^2}} \text{ seconds}$$

with domain [0, 1). Estimate $T(0.95)$ and $T'(0.95)$. What do these figures tell you?

COMMUNICATION AND REASONING EXERCISES

101. Explain why we cannot put $h = 0$ in the approximation

$$f'(x) \approx \frac{f(x+h) - f(x)}{h}$$

for the derivative of f.

102. The balanced difference quotient

$$f'(a) \approx \frac{f(a + 0.0001) - f(a - 0.0001)}{0.0002}$$

is the average rate of change of f on what interval?

103. Let $H(t)$ represent the number of Handbook members in millions t years after its inception in 2020. It is found that $H(10) = 50$ and $H'(10) = -6$. This means that, in 2030 (Multiple Choice):

(A) There were 6 million members and this number was decreasing at a rate of 50 million per year.
(B) There were –6 million members and this number was increasing at a rate of 50 million per year.
(C) Membership had dropped by 6 million since the previous year, but was now increasing at a rate of 50 million per year.
(D) There were 50 million members and this number was decreasing at a rate of 6 million per year.
(E) There were 50 million members and membership had dropped by 6 million since the previous year.

104. Let $F(t)$ represent the net earnings of Footbook Inc. in millions of dollars t years after its inception in 3020. It is found that $F(100) = -10$ and $F'(100) = 60$. This means that, in 3120 (Multiple Choice):

(A) Footbook lost $10 million but its net earnings were increasing at a rate of $60 million per year.
(B) Footbook earned $60 million but its earnings were decreasing at a rate of $10 million per year.
(C) Footbook's net earnings had increased by $60 million since the year before, but it still lost $10 million.

[66] The model approximates graphical data published in the article *The Brush Turkey* by Roger S. Seymour, *Scientific American*, December, 1991, pp. 108–114.

[67] *Ibid.*

(D) Footbook earned $10 million but its net earnings were decreasing at a rate of $60 million per year.

(E) Footbook's net earnings had decreased by $10 million since the year before, but it still earned $60 million.

105. It is now eight months since the Garden City lacrosse team won the national championship, and sales of team paraphernalia, while still increasing, have been leveling off. What does this tell you about the derivative of the sales curve?

106. Having been soundly defeated in the national lacrosse championships, Brakpan High has been faced with decreasing sales of its team paraphernalia. However, sales, while still decreasing, appear to be bottoming out. What does this tell you about the derivative of the sales curve?

107. ▼ Company A's profits are given by $P(0) = \$1$ million and $P'(0) = -\$1$ million/month. Company B's profits are given by $P(0) = -\$1$ million and $P'(0) = \$1$ million/month. In which company would you rather invest? Why?

108. ▼ Company C's profits are given by $P(0) = \$1$ million and $P'(0) = \$0.5$ million/month. Company D's profits are given by $P(0) = \$0.5$ million and $P'(0) = \$1$ million/month. In which company would you rather invest? Why?

109. ▼ During the one-month period starting last January 1, your company's profits increased at an average rate of change of $4 million per month. On January 1, profits were increasing at an instantaneous rate of $5 million per month. Which of the following graphs could represent your company's profits? Why?

(A)

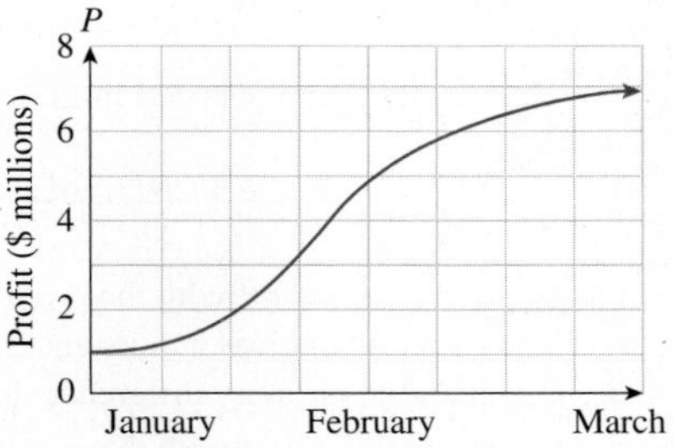

(B)

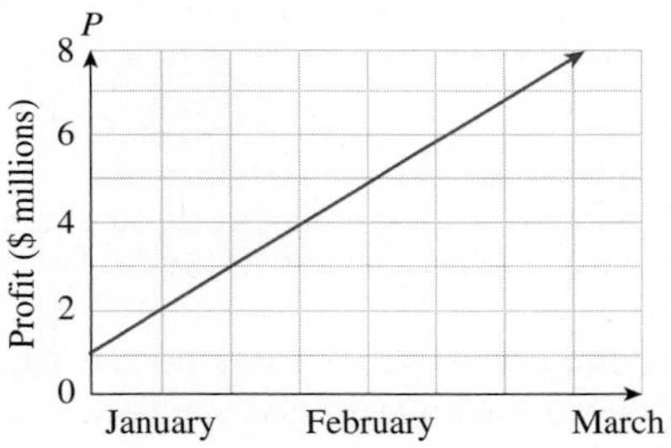

(C)

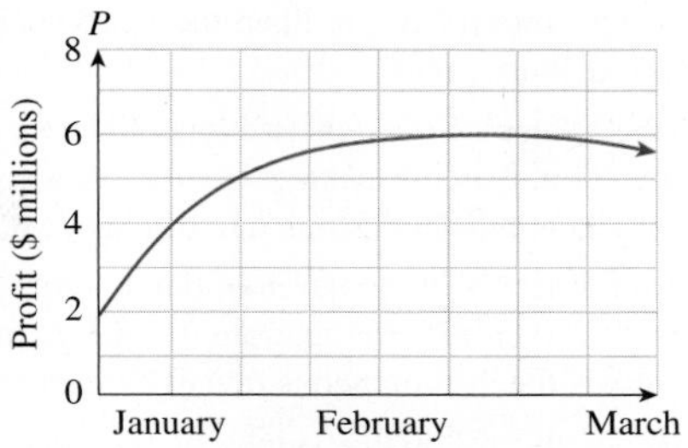

110. ▼ During the one-month period starting last January 1, your company's sales increased at an average rate of change of $3,000 per month. On January 1, sales were changing at an instantaneous rate of –$1,000 per month. Which of the following graphs could represent your company's sales? Why?

(A)

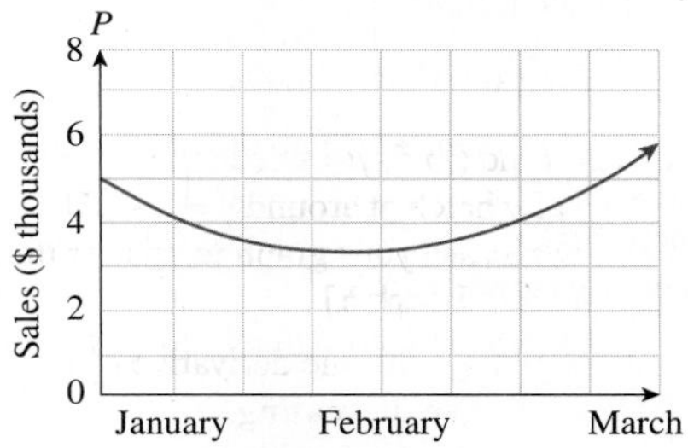

(B)

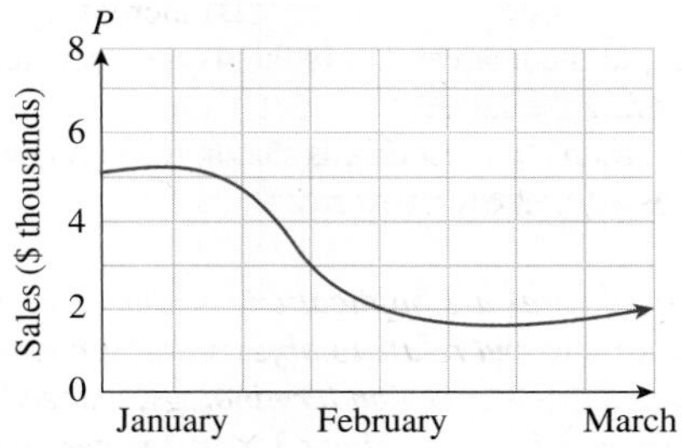

(C)

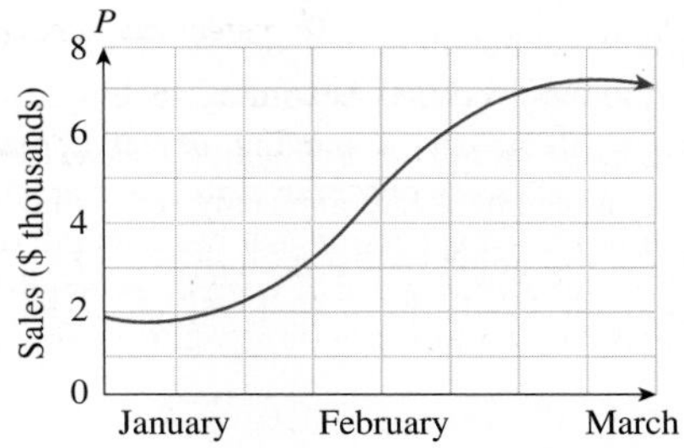

111. ▼ If the derivative of *f* is zero at a point, what do you know about the graph of *f* near that point?

112. ▼ Sketch the graph of a function whose derivative never exceeds 1.

113. ▼ Sketch the graph of a function whose derivative exceeds 1 at every point.

114. ▼ Sketch the graph of a function whose derivative is exactly 1 at every point.

115. ▼ Use the difference quotient to explain the fact that if *f* is a linear function, then the average rate of change over any interval equals the instantaneous rate of change at any point.

116. ▼ Give a numerical explanation of the fact that if *f* is a linear function, then the average rate of change over any interval equals the instantaneous rate of change at any point.

117. ◆ Consider the following values of the function f from Exercise 1.

h	0.1	0.01	0.001	0.0001
Average Rate of Change of f over $[5, 5+h]$	6.4	6.04	6.004	6.0004
h	−0.1	−0.01	−0.001	−0.0001
Average Rate of Change of f over $[5+h, 5]$	5.6	5.96	5.996	5.9996

Does the table suggests that the instantaneous rate of change of *f* is

(A) increasing **(B)** decreasing

as x increases toward 5?

118. ◆ Consider the following values of the function g from Exercise 2.

h	0.1	0.01	0.001	0.0001
Average Rate of Change of g over $[7, 7+h]$	4.8	4.98	4.998	4.9998
h	−0.1	−0.01	−0.001	−0.0001
Average Rate of Change of g over $[7+h, 7]$	5.3	5.03	5.003	5.0003

Does the table suggest that the instantaneous rate of change of g is

(A) increasing **(B)** decreasing

as x increases toward 7?

119. ▼ Sketch the graph of a function whose derivative is never zero but decreases as x increases.

120. ▼ Sketch the graph of a function whose derivative is never negative but is zero at exactly two points.

121. ◆ Here is the graph of the derivative f' of a function f. Give a rough sketch of the graph of f, given that $f(0) = 0$.

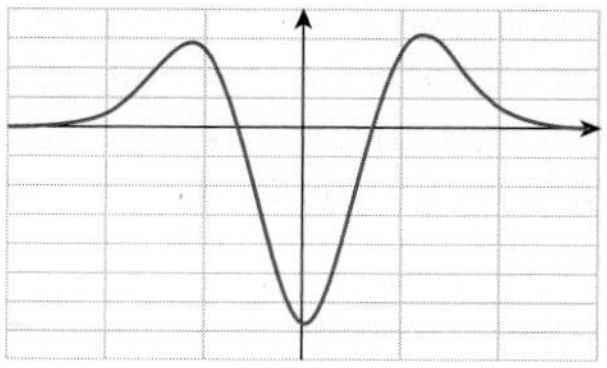

122. ◆ Here is the graph of the derivative f' of a function f. Give a rough sketch of the graph of f, given that $f(0) = 0$.

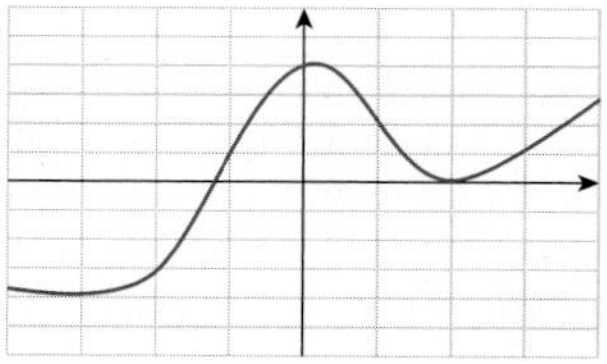

123. ◆ Professor Talker of the physics department drove a 60-mile stretch of road in exactly one hour. The speed limit along that stretch was 55 miles per hour. Which of the following must be correct?

(A) He exceeded the speed limit at no point of the journey.

(B) He exceeded the speed limit at some point of the journey.

(C) He exceeded the speed limit throughout the journey.

(D) He traveled slower than the speed limit at some point of the journey.

124. ◆ Professor Silent, another physics professor, drove a 50-mile stretch of road in exactly one hour. The speed limit along that stretch was 55 miles per hour. Which of the following must be correct?

(A) She exceeded the speed limit at no point of the journey.

(B) She exceeded the speed limit at some point of the journey.

(C) She traveled slower than the speed limit throughout the journey.

(D) She traveled slower than the speed limit at some point of the journey.

125. ◆ Draw the graph of a function f with the property that the balanced difference quotient gives a more accurate approximation of $f'(1)$ than the ordinary difference quotient.

126. ◆ Draw the graph of a function f with the property that the balanced difference quotient gives a less accurate approximation of $f'(1)$ than the ordinary difference quotient.

3.6 Derivatives: Algebraic Viewpoint

In Section 3.5 we saw how to estimate the derivative of a function using numerical and graphical approaches. In this section we use an algebraic approach that will give us the *exact value* of the derivative, rather than just an approximation, when the function is specified algebraically.

This algebraic approach is quite straightforward: Instead of subtracting numbers to estimate the average rate of change over smaller and smaller intervals, we subtract algebraic expressions. Our starting point is the definition of the derivative in terms of the difference quotient:

$$f'(a) = \lim_{h \to 0} \frac{f(a+h) - f(a)}{h}.$$

EXAMPLE 1 Calculating the Derivative at a Point Algebraically

Let $f(x) = x^2$. Use the definition of the derivative to compute $f'(3)$ algebraically.

Solution Substituting $a = 3$ into the definition of the derivative, we get:

$$f'(3) = \lim_{h \to 0} \frac{f(3+h) - f(3)}{h}$$ Formula for the derivative

$$= \lim_{h \to 0} \frac{\overbrace{(3+h)^2}^{f(3+h)} - \overbrace{3^2}^{f(3)}}{h}$$ Substitute for $f(3)$ and $f(3+h)$.

$$= \lim_{h \to 0} \frac{(9 + 6h + h^2) - 9}{h}$$ Expand $(3+h)^2$.

$$= \lim_{h \to 0} \frac{6h + h^2}{h}$$ Cancel the 9.

$$= \lim_{h \to 0} \frac{h(6+h)}{h}$$ Factor out h.

$$= \lim_{h \to 0} (6+h).$$ Cancel the h.

Now we let h approach 0. As h gets closer and closer to 0, the sum $6 + h$ clearly gets closer and closer to $6 + 0 = 6$. Thus,

$$f'(3) = \lim_{h \to 0} (6+h) = 6.$$ As $h \to 0$, $(6+h) \to 6$

(Calculations of limits like this are discussed and justified more fully in Sections 3.2 and 3.3.)

➡ **Before we go on...** We did the following calculation in Example 1: If $f(x) = x^2$, then $f'(3) = 6$. In other words, the tangent to the graph of $y = x^2$ at the point (3, 9) has slope 6 (Figure 36). ■

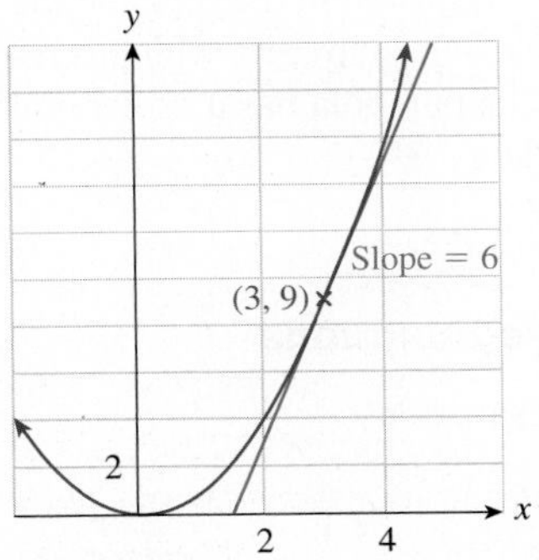

Figure 36

There is nothing very special about $a = 3$ in Example 1. Let's try to compute $f'(x)$ for general x.

EXAMPLE 2 Calculating the Derivative Function Algebraically

Let $f(x) = x^2$.

a. Use the definition of the derivative to compute $f'(x)$ algebraically.
b. Use the answer to evaluate $f'(3)$.

Solution

a. Once again, our starting point is the definition of the derivative in terms of the difference quotient:

$$f'(x) = \lim_{h\to 0} \frac{f(x+h) - f(x)}{h} \qquad \text{Formula for the derivative}$$

$$= \lim_{h\to 0} \frac{\overbrace{(x+h)^2}^{f(x+h)} - \overbrace{x^2}^{f(x)}}{h} \qquad \text{Substitute for } f(x) \text{ and } f(x+h).$$

$$= \lim_{h\to 0} \frac{(x^2 + 2xh + h^2) - x^2}{h} \qquad \text{Expand } (x+h)^2.$$

$$= \lim_{h\to 0} \frac{2xh + h^2}{h} \qquad \text{Cancel the } x^2.$$

$$= \lim_{h\to 0} \frac{h(2x+h)}{h} \qquad \text{Factor out } h.$$

$$= \lim_{h\to 0} (2x+h). \qquad \text{Cancel the } h.$$

Now we let h approach 0. As h gets closer and closer to 0, the sum $2x + h$ clearly gets closer and closer to $2x + 0 = 2x$. Thus,

$$f'(x) = \lim_{h\to 0} (2x+h) = 2x.$$

This is the derivative function.

b. Now that we have a *formula* for the derivative of *f*, we can obtain $f'(a)$ for any value of a we choose by simply evaluating f' there. For instance,

$$f'(3) = 2(3) = 6$$

as we saw in Example 1.

Before we go on... The graphs of $f(x) = x^2$ and $f'(x) = 2x$ from Example 2 are familiar. Their graphs are shown in Figure 37.

When $x < 0$, the parabola slopes downward, which is reflected in the fact that the derivative $2x$ is negative there. When $x > 0$, the parabola slopes upward, which is reflected in the fact that the derivative is positive there. The parabola has a horizontal tangent line at $x = 0$, reflected in the fact that $2x = 0$ there. ■

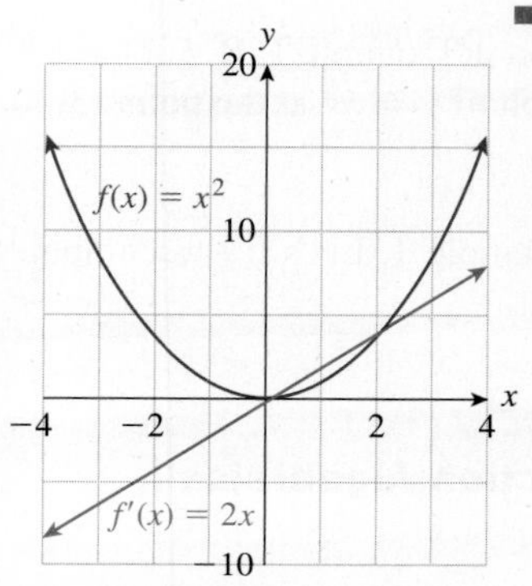

Figure 37

EXAMPLE 3 More Computations of Derivative Functions

Compute the derivative $f'(x)$ for each of the following functions:

a. $f(x) = x^3$ **b.** $f(x) = 2x^2 - x$ **c.** $f(x) = \frac{1}{x}$

Solution

a. $f'(x) = \lim_{h\to 0} \frac{f(x+h) - f(x)}{h}$ — Derivative formula

$= \lim_{h\to 0} \frac{\overbrace{(x+h)^3}^{f(x+h)} - \overbrace{x^3}^{f(x)}}{h}$ — Substitute for $f(x)$ and $f(x+h)$.

$= \lim_{h\to 0} \frac{(x^3 + 3x^2h + 3xh^2 + h^3) - x^3}{h}$ — Expand $(x+h)^3$.

$= \lim_{h\to 0} \frac{3x^2h + 3xh^2 + h^3}{h}$ — Cancel the x^3.

$= \lim_{h\to 0} \frac{h(3x^2 + 3xh + h^2)}{h}$ — Factor out h.

$= \lim_{h\to 0} (3x^2 + 3xh + h^2)$ — Cancel the h.

$= 3x^2.$ — Let h approach 0.

b. $f'(x) = \lim_{h\to 0} \frac{f(x+h) - f(x)}{h}$ — Derivative formula

$= \lim_{h\to 0} \frac{\overbrace{(2(x+h)^2 - (x+h))}^{f(x+h)} - \overbrace{(2x^2 - x)}^{f(x)}}{h}$ — Substitute for $f(x)$ and $f(x+h)$.

$= \lim_{h\to 0} \frac{(2x^2 + 4xh + 2h^2 - x - h) - (2x^2 - x)}{h}$ — Expand.

$= \lim_{h\to 0} \frac{4xh + 2h^2 - h}{h}$ — Cancel the $2x^2$ and x.

$= \lim_{h\to 0} \frac{h(4x + 2h - 1)}{h}$ — Factor out h.

$= \lim_{h\to 0} (4x + 2h - 1)$ — Cancel the h.

$= 4x - 1.$ — Let h approach 0.

c. $f'(x) = \lim_{h\to 0} \frac{f(x+h) - f(x)}{h}$ — Derivative formula

$= \lim_{h\to 0} \frac{\left[\overbrace{\frac{1}{x+h}}^{f(x+h)} - \overbrace{\frac{1}{x}}^{f(x)}\right]}{h}$ — Substitute for $f(x)$ and $f(x+h)$.

$= \lim_{h\to 0} \frac{\left[\frac{x - (x+h)}{(x+h)x}\right]}{h}$ — Subtract the fractions.

$= \lim_{h\to 0} \frac{1}{h}\left[\frac{x - (x+h)}{(x+h)x}\right]$ — Dividing by h = Multiplying by $1/h$.

$$= \lim_{h\to 0}\left[\frac{-h}{h(x+h)x}\right] \qquad \text{Simplify.}$$

$$= \lim_{h\to 0}\left[\frac{-1}{(x+h)x}\right] \qquad \text{Cancel the } h.$$

$$= \frac{-1}{x^2} \qquad \text{Let } h \text{ approach 0.}$$

In Example 4, we redo Example 3 of Section 3.5, this time getting an exact, rather than approximate, answer.

EXAMPLE 4 Velocity

My friend Eric, an enthusiastic baseball player, claims he can "probably" throw a ball upward at a speed of 100 feet per second (ft/sec). Our physicist friends tell us that its height s (in feet) t seconds later would be $s(t) = 100t - 16t^2$. Find the ball's instantaneous velocity function and its velocity exactly 2 seconds after Eric throws it.

Solution The instantaneous velocity function is the derivative ds/dt, which we calculate as follows:

$$\frac{ds}{dt} = \lim_{h\to 0}\frac{s(t+h)-s(t)}{h}.$$

Let us compute $s(t+h)$ and $s(t)$ separately:

$$\begin{aligned} s(t) &= 100t - 16t^2 \\ s(t+h) &= 100(t+h) - 16(t+h)^2 \\ &= 100t + 100h - 16(t^2 + 2th + h^2) \\ &= 100t + 100h - 16t^2 - 32th - 16h^2. \end{aligned}$$

Therefore,

$$\begin{aligned} \frac{ds}{dt} &= \lim_{h\to 0}\frac{s(t+h)-s(t)}{h} \\ &= \lim_{h\to 0}\frac{100t + 100h - 16t^2 - 32th - 16h^2 - (100t - 16t^2)}{h} \\ &= \lim_{h\to 0}\frac{100h - 32th - 16h^2}{h} \\ &= \lim_{h\to 0}\frac{h(100 - 32t - 16h)}{h} \\ &= \lim_{h\to 0}(100 - 32t - 16h) \\ &= 100 - 32t \text{ ft/sec.} \end{aligned}$$

Thus, the velocity exactly 2 seconds after Eric throws it is

$$\left.\frac{ds}{dt}\right|_{t=2} = 100 - 32(2) = 36 \text{ ft/sec.}$$

This verifies the accuracy of the approximation we made in Section 3.5.

➡ **Before we go on...** From the derivative function in Example 4, we can now describe the behavior of the velocity of the ball: Immediately on release ($t = 0$) the ball is traveling at 100 feet per second upward. The ball then slows down; precisely, it loses 32 feet per second of speed every second. When, exactly, does the velocity become zero and what happens after that? ■

Q: *Do we always have to calculate the limit of the difference quotient to find a formula for the derivative function?*

A: As it turns out, no. In Section 4.1 we will start to look at shortcuts for finding derivatives that allow us to bypass the definition of the derivative in many cases.

A Function Not Differentiable at a Point

Recall from Section 3.5 that a function is **differentiable** at a point a if $f'(a)$ exists; that is, if the difference quotient $[f(a+h) - f(a)]/h$ approaches a fixed value as h approaches 0. In Section 3.5, we mentioned that the function $f(x) = |x|$ is not differentiable at $x = 0$. In Example 5, we find out why.

EXAMPLE 5 A Function Not Differentiable at 0

Numerically, graphically, and algebraically investigate the differentiability of the function $f(x) = |x|$ at the points **(a)** $x = 1$ and **(b)** $x = 0$.

Solution

a. We compute

$$f'(1) = \lim_{h\to 0} \frac{f(1+h) - f(1)}{h}$$
$$= \lim_{h\to 0} \frac{|1+h| - 1}{h}.$$

Numerically, we can make tables of the values of the average rate of change $(|1+h| - 1)/h$ for h positive or negative and approaching 0:

h	1	0.1	0.01	0.001	0.0001
Average Rate of Change Over [1, 1 + *h*]	1	1	1	1	1

h	−1	−0.1	−0.01	−0.001	−0.0001
Average Rate of Change Over [1 + *h*, 1]	1	1	1	1	1

From these tables it appears that $f'(1)$ is equal to 1. We can verify that algebraically: For h that is sufficiently small, $1 + h$ is positive (even if h is negative) and so

$$f'(1) = \lim_{h\to 0} \frac{1+h-1}{h}$$
$$= \lim_{h\to 0} \frac{h}{h} \qquad \text{Cancel the 1s.}$$
$$= \lim_{h\to 0} 1 \qquad \text{Cancel the } h.$$
$$= 1.$$

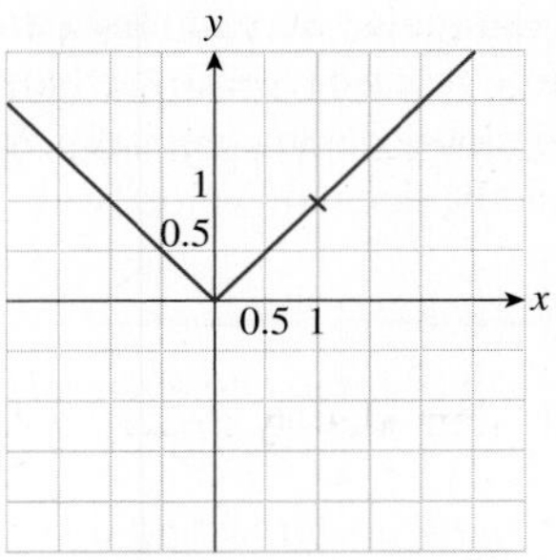

Figure 38

Graphically, we are seeing the fact that the tangent line at the point (1, 1) has slope 1 because the graph is a straight line with slope 1 near that point (Figure 38).

b. $$f'(0) = \lim_{h \to 0} \frac{f(0+h) - f(0)}{h} = \lim_{h \to 0} \frac{|0+h| - 0}{h} = \lim_{h \to 0} \frac{|h|}{h}$$

If we make tables of values in this case we get the following:

h	1	0.1	0.01	0.001	0.0001
Average Rate of Change over [0, 0 + *h*]	1	1	1	1	1

h	−1	−0.1	−0.01	−0.001	−0.0001
Average Rate of Change over [0 + *h*, 0]	−1	−1	−1	−1	−1

For the limit and hence the derivative $f'(0)$ to exist, the average rates of change should approach the same number for both positive and negative h. Because they do not, f is not differentiable at $x = 0$. We can verify this conclusion algebraically: If h is positive, then $|h| = h$, and so the ratio $|h|/h$ is 1, regardless of how small h is. Thus, according to the values of the difference quotients with $h > 0$, the limit should be 1. On the other hand if h is negative, then $|h| = -h$ (positive) and so $|h|/h = -1$, meaning that the limit should be -1. Because the limit cannot be both -1 and 1 (it must be a single number for the derivative to exist), we conclude that $f'(0)$ does not exist.

To see what is happening graphically, take a look at Figure 39, which shows zoomed-in views of the graph of f near $x = 0$.

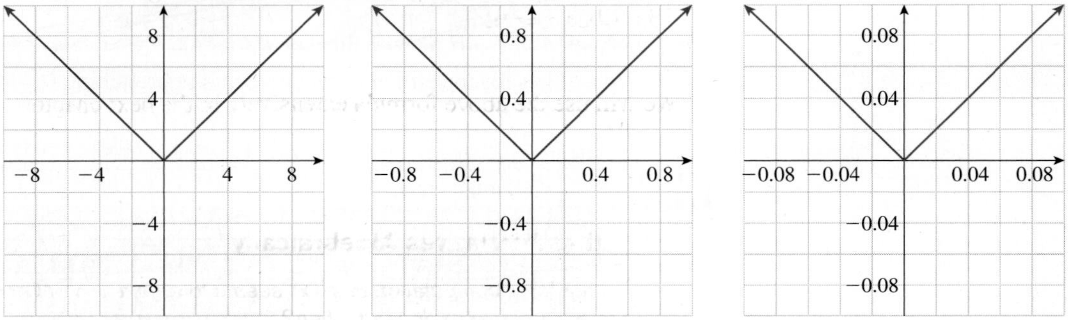

Figure 39

No matter what scale we use to view the graph, it has a sharp corner at $x = 0$ and hence has no tangent line there. Since there is no tangent line at $x = 0$, the function is not differentiable there.

➡ **Before we go on...** Notice that $|x| = \begin{cases} -x & \text{if } x < 0 \\ x & \text{if } x \geq 0 \end{cases}$ is an example of a piecewise-linear function whose graph comes to a point at $x = 0$. In general, if $f(x)$ is any piecewise linear function whose graph comes to a point at $x = a$, it will be nondifferentiable at $x = a$ for the same reason that $|x|$ fails to be differentiable at $x = 0$.

If we repeat the computation in Example 5(a) using any nonzero value for a in place of 1, we see that f is differentiable there as well. If a is positive, we find that $f'(a) = 1$ and, if a is negative, $f'(a) = -1$. In other words, the derivative function is

$$f'(x) = \begin{cases} -1 & \text{if } x < 0 \\ 1 & \text{if } x > 0 \end{cases}.$$

Immediately to the left of $x = 0$, we see that $f'(x) = -1$, immediately to the right, $f'(x) = 1$; and when $x = 0$, $f'(x)$ is not defined. ■

Q: *So does that mean there is no single formula for the derivative of $|x|$?*

A: Actually, there is a convenient formula. Consider the ratio $\frac{|x|}{x}$. If x is positive, then $|x| = x$, so $\frac{|x|}{x} = \frac{x}{x} = 1$. On the other hand, if x is negative, then $|x| = -x$, so $\frac{|x|}{x} = \frac{-x}{x} = -1$. In other words,

$$\frac{|x|}{x} = \begin{cases} -1 & \text{if } x < 0 \\ 1 & \text{if } x > 0 \end{cases},$$

which is exactly the formula we obtained for $f'(x)$. We have therefore obtained a convenient closed-form formula for the derivative of $|x|$!

Derivative of |x|

If $f(x) = |x|$, then $f'(x) = \frac{|x|}{x}$.

Note that $|x|/x$ is not defined if $x = 0$, reflecting the fact that $f'(x)$ does not exist when $x = 0$.

We will use the above formula extensively in the next chapter.

FAQ

Computing Derivatives Algebraically

Q: *The algebraic computation of $f'(x)$ seems to require a number of steps. How do I remember what to do, and when?*

A: If you examine the computations in the examples above, you will find the following pattern:

1. Write out the formula for $f'(x)$, as the limit of the difference quotient, then substitute $f(x+h)$ and $f(x)$.
2. Expand and simplify the *numerator* of the expression, but not the denominator.
3. After simplifying the numerator, factor out an h to cancel with the h in the denominator. If h does not factor out of the numerator, you might have made an error. (A frequent error is a wrong sign.)
4. After canceling the h, you should be able to see what the limit is by letting $h \to 0$.

3.6 EXERCISES

▼ more advanced ◆ challenging

T indicates exercises that should be solved using technology

In Exercises 1–14, compute $f'(a)$ algebraically for the given value of a. HINT [See Example 1.]

1. $f(x) = x^2 + 1; a = 2$

2. $f(x) = x^2 - 3; a = 1$

3. $f(x) = 3x - 4; a = -1$

4. $f(x) = -2x + 4; a = -1$

5. $f(x) = 3x^2 + x; a = 1$

6. $f(x) = 2x^2 + x; a = -2$

7. $f(x) = 2x - x^2; a = -1$

8. $f(x) = -x - x^2; a = 0$

9. $f(x) = x^3 + 2x; a = 2$

10. $f(x) = x - 2x^3; a = 1$

11. $f(x) = \frac{-1}{x}; a = 1$ HINT [See Example 3.]

12. $f(x) = \frac{2}{x}; a = 5$ HINT [See Example 3.]

13. ▼ $f(x) = mx + b; a = 43$

14. ▼ $f(x) = \frac{x}{k} - b\ (k \neq 0); a = 12$

In Exercises 15–28, compute the derivative function $f'(x)$ algebraically. (Notice that the functions are the same as those in Exercises 1–14.) HINT [See Examples 2 and 3.]

15. $f(x) = x^2 + 1$
16. $f(x) = x^2 - 3$
17. $f(x) = 3x - 4$
18. $f(x) = -2x + 4$
19. $f(x) = 3x^2 + x$
20. $f(x) = 2x^2 + x$
21. $f(x) = 2x - x^2$
22. $f(x) = -x - x^2$
23. $f(x) = x^3 + 2x$
24. $f(x) = x - 2x^3$
25. ▼ $f(x) = \frac{-1}{x}$
26. ▼ $f(x) = \frac{2}{x}$
27. ▼ $f(x) = mx + b$
28. ▼ $f(x) = \frac{x}{k} - b\ (k \neq 0)$

In Exercises 29–38, compute the indicated derivative.

29. $R(t) = -0.3t^2; R'(2)$

30. $S(t) = 1.4t^2; S'(-1)$

31. $U(t) = 5.1t^2 + 5.1; U'(3)$

32. $U(t) = -1.3t^2 + 1.1; U'(4)$

33. $U(t) = -1.3t^2 - 4.5t; U'(1)$

34. $U(t) = 5.1t^2 - 1.1t; U'(1)$

35. $L(r) = 4.25r - 5.01; L'(1.2)$

36. $L(r) = -1.02r + 5.7; L'(3.1)$

37. ▼ $q(p) = \frac{2.4}{p} + 3.1; q'(2)$

38. ▼ $q(p) = \frac{1}{0.5p} - 3.1; q'(2)$

In Exercises 39–44, find the equation of the tangent to the graph at the indicated point. HINT [Compute the derivative algebraically; then see Example 2(b) in Section 3.5.]

39. ▼ $f(x) = x^2 - 3; a = 2$
40. ▼ $f(x) = x^2 + 1; a = 2$
41. ▼ $f(x) = -2x - 4; a = 3$
42. ▼ $f(x) = 3x + 1; a = 1$
43. ▼ $f(x) = x^2 - x; a = -1$
44. ▼ $f(x) = x^2 + x; a = -1$

APPLICATIONS

45. ***Velocity*** If a stone is dropped from a height of 400 feet, its height after t seconds is given by $s = 400 - 16t^2$. Find its instantaneous velocity function and its velocity at time $t = 4$. HINT [See Example 4.]

46. ***Velocity*** If a stone is thrown down at 120 feet per second from a height of 1,000 feet, its height after t seconds is given by $s = 1{,}000 - 120t - 16t^2$. Find its instantaneous velocity function and its velocity at time $t = 3$. HINT [See Example 4.]

47. ***Oil Imports from Mexico*** Daily oil imports to the United States from Mexico can be approximated by

$$I(t) = -0.015t^2 + 0.1t + 1.4 \text{ million barrels} \quad (0 \leq t \leq 8),$$

where t is time in years since the start of 2000.[68] Find the derivative function $\frac{dI}{dt}$. At what rate were oil imports changing at the start of 2007 ($t = 7$)? HINT [See Example 4.]

48. ***Oil Production in Mexico*** Daily oil production by Pemex, Mexico's national oil company, can be approximated by

$$P(t) = -0.022t^2 + 0.2t + 2.9 \text{ million barrels} \quad (1 \leq t \leq 9),$$

where t is time in years since the start of 2000.[69] Find the derivative function $\frac{dP}{dt}$. At what rate was oil production changing at the start of 2004 ($t = 4$)? HINT [See Example 4.]

49. ***Bottled Water Sales*** The following chart shows the amount of bottled water sold in the United States for the period 2000–2010:[70]

---

[68] Source for data: Energy Information Administration/Pemex (www.eia.doe.gov).

[69] *Ibid.*

[70] The 2010 figure is an estimate. Source: Beverage Marketing Corporation/www.bottledwater.org.

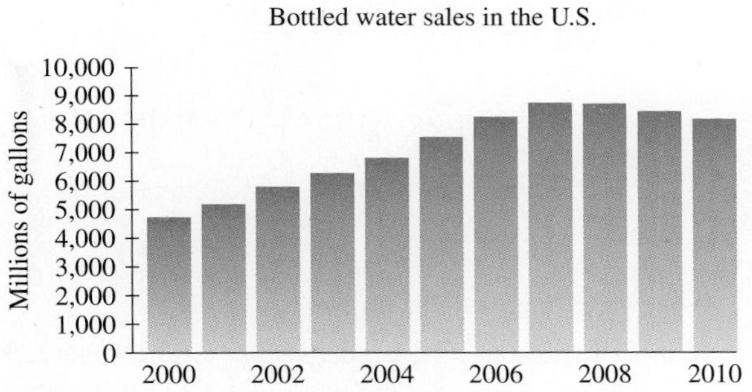

The function

$$R(t) = -45t^2 + 900t + 4{,}200 \text{ million gallons} \quad (0 \le t \le 10)$$

gives a good approximation, where t is time in years since 2000. Find the derivative function $R'(t)$. According to the model, how fast were annual sales of bottled water changing in 2005?

50. ***Bottled Water Sales*** The following chart shows annual per capita sales of bottled water in the United States for the period 2000–2010:[71]

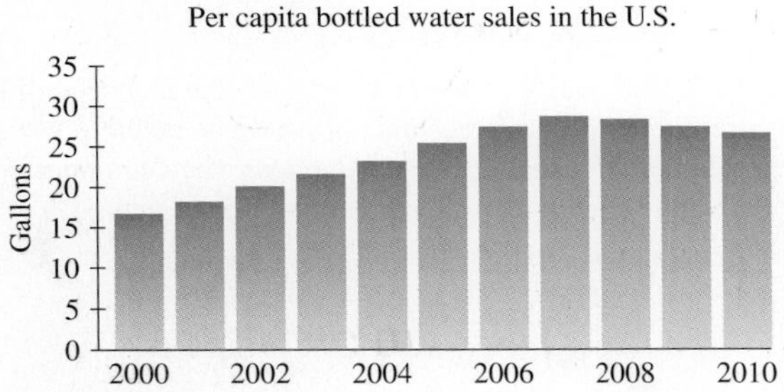

The function

$$R(t) = -0.18t^2 + 3t + 15 \text{ gallons} \qquad (0 \le t \le 10)$$

gives a good approximation, where t is time in years since 2000. Find the derivative function $R'(t)$. According to the model, how fast were per capita sales of bottled water changing in 2009?

51. ▼ ***Ecology*** Increasing numbers of manatees ("sea sirens") have been killed by boats off the Florida coast. The following graph shows the relationship between the number of boats registered in Florida and the number of manatees killed each year.

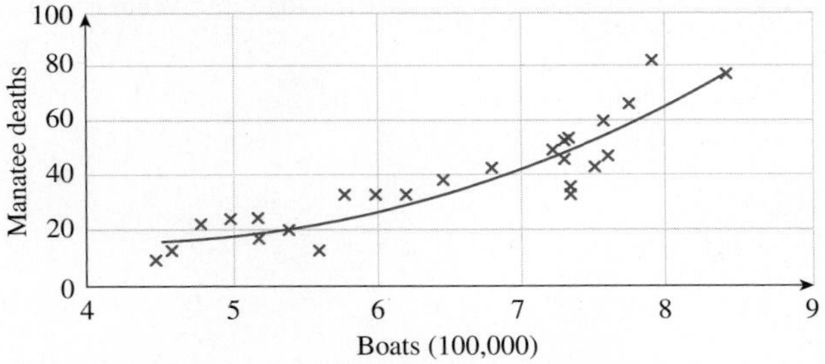

The regression curve shown is given by

$$f(x) = 3.55x^2 - 30.2x + 81 \text{ manatee deaths} \quad (4.5 \le x \le 8.5),$$

where x is the number of boats (hundreds of thousands) registered in Florida in a particular year and $f(x)$ is the number of manatees killed by boats in Florida that year.[72] Compute and interpret $f'(8)$.

52. ▼ ***SAT Scores by Income*** The following graph shows U.S. math SAT scores as a function of parents' income level.[73]

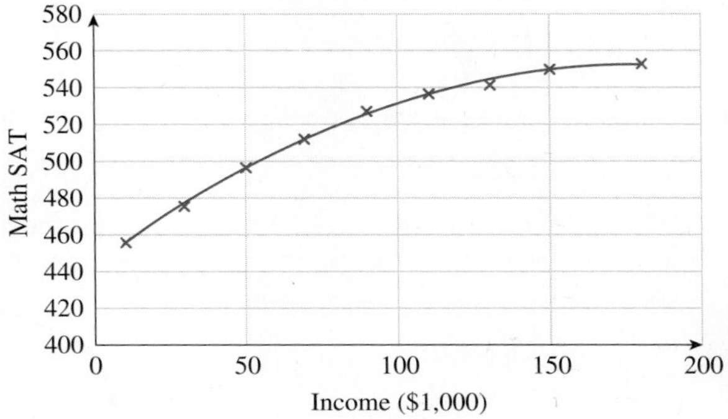

The regression curve shown is given by

$$f(x) = -0.0034x^2 + 1.2x + 444 \qquad (10 \le x \le 180),$$

where $f(x)$ is the average math SAT score of a student whose parents earn x thousand dollars per year. Compute and interpret $f'(30)$.

53. ▼ ***Television Advertising*** The cost, in thousands of dollars, of a 30-second television ad during the Super Bowl in the years 1970 to 2010 can be approximated by the following piecewise linear function ($t = 0$ represents 1970):[74]

$$C(t) = \begin{cases} 31.1t + 78 & \text{if } 0 \le t < 20 \\ 90t - 1{,}100 & \text{if } 20 \le t \le 40 \end{cases}.$$

a. Is C a continuous function of t? Why? HINT [See Example 4 of Section 3.3.]

b. Is C a differentiable function of t? Compute $\lim_{t\to 20^-} C'(t)$ and $\lim_{t\to 20^+} C'(t)$ and interpret the results. HINT [See *Before we go on...* after Example 5.]

54. ▼ ***Television Advertising*** (Compare Exercise 53.) The cost, in thousands of dollars, of a 30-second television ad during the Super Bowl in the years 1980 to 2010 can be approximated by the following piecewise linear function ($t = 0$ represents 1980):[75]

$$C(t) = \begin{cases} 43.9t + 222 & \text{if } 0 \le t \le 20 \\ 140t - 1{,}700 & \text{if } 20 < t \le 30 \end{cases}.$$

[71] The 2010 figure is an estimate. Source: Beverage Marketing Corporation/www.bottledwater.org.

[72] Regression model is based on data from 1976 to 2000. Sources for data: Florida Department of Highway Safety & Motor Vehicles, Florida Marine Institute/*New York Times*, February 12, 2002, p. F4.

[73] Regression model is based on 2009 data. Source: College Board/*New York Times* http://economix.blogs.nytimes.com.

[74] Source: http://en.wikipedia.org/wiki/Super_Bowl_advertising.

[75] *Ibid.*

a. Is C a continuous function of t? Why? HINT [See Example 4 of Section 3.3.]

b. Is C a differentiable function of t? Compute $\lim_{t\to 20^-} C'(t)$ and $\lim_{t\to 20^+} C'(t)$ and interpret the results. HINT [See *Before we go on...* after Example 5.]

COMMUNICATION AND REASONING EXERCISES

55. Of the three methods (numerical, graphical, algebraic) we can use to estimate the derivative of a function at a given value of x, which is always the most accurate? Explain.

56. Explain why we cannot put $h = 0$ in the formula

$$f'(a) = \lim_{h\to 0} \frac{f(a+h) - f(a)}{h}$$

for the derivative of f.

57. You just got your derivatives test back and you can't understand why that teacher of yours deducted so many points for what you thought was your best work:

$$\begin{aligned} &\lim_{h\to 0} \frac{f(x+h) - f(x)}{h} \\ &= \lim_{h\to 0} \frac{f(x) + h - f(x)}{h} \\ &= \lim_{h\to 0} \frac{h}{h} && \text{Canceled the } f(x) \\ &= 1. && \text{✗ WRONG } -10 \end{aligned}$$

What was wrong with your answer?

58. Your friend just got his derivatives test back and can't understand why that teacher of his deducted so many points for the following:

$$\begin{aligned} &\lim_{h\to 0} \frac{f(x+h) - f(x)}{h} \\ &= \lim_{h\to 0} \frac{f(x) + f(h) - f(x)}{h} \\ &= \lim_{h\to 0} \frac{f(h)}{h} && \text{Canceled the } f(x) \\ &= \lim_{h\to 0} \frac{f(\not h)}{\not h} && \text{Now cancel the } h. \\ &= f. && \text{✗ WRONG } -50 \end{aligned}$$

What was wrong with his answer?

59. Your other friend just got her derivatives test back and can't understand why that teacher of hers took off so many points for the following:

$$\begin{aligned} &\lim_{h\to 0} \frac{f(x+h) - f(x)}{h} \\ &= \lim_{h\to 0} \frac{f(x+\not h) - f(x)}{\not h} && \text{Now cancel the } h. \\ &= \lim_{h\to 0} f(x) - f(x) && \text{Cancel the } f(x) \\ &= 0. && \text{✗ WRONG } -15 \end{aligned}$$

What was wrong with her answer?

60. Your third friend just got her derivatives test back and can't understand why that teacher of hers took off so many points for the following:

$$\begin{aligned} &\lim_{h\to 0} \frac{f(x+h) - f(x)}{h} \\ &= \lim_{h\to 0} \frac{f(x) + h - f(x)}{h} \\ &= \lim_{h\to 0} \frac{f(x) + \not h - f(x)}{\not h} && \text{Now cancel the } h. \\ &= \lim_{h\to 0} f(x) - f(x) && \text{Cancel the } f(x) \\ &= 0. && \text{✗ WRONG } -25 \end{aligned}$$

What was wrong with her answer?

61. Your friend Muffy claims that, because the balanced difference quotient is more accurate, it would be better to use that instead of the usual difference quotient when computing the derivative algebraically. Comment on this advice.

62. Use the balanced difference quotient formula,

$$f'(a) = \lim_{h\to 0} \frac{f(a+h) - f(a-h)}{2h},$$

to compute $f'(3)$ when $f(x) = x^2$. What do you find?

63. ▼ A certain function f has the property that $f'(a)$ does not exist. How is that reflected in the attempt to compute $f'(a)$ algebraically?

64. ▼ One cannot put $h = 0$ in the formula

$$f'(a) = \lim_{h\to 0} \frac{f(a+h) - f(a)}{h}$$

for the derivative of f. (See Exercise 56.) However, in the last step of each of the computations in the text, we are effectively setting $h = 0$ when taking the limit. What is going on here?

CHAPTER 3 REVIEW

KEY CONCEPTS

Website www.WanerMath.com
Go to the Website at www.WanerMath.com to find a comprehensive and interactive Web-based summary of Chapter 3.

3.1 Limits: Numerical and Graphical Viewpoints

$\lim_{x\to a} f(x) = L$ means that $f(x)$ approaches L as x approaches a *p. 196*
What it means for a limit to exist *p. 197*
Limits at infinity *p. 199*
Estimating limits graphically *p. 199*
Interpreting limits in real-world situations *p. 202*

3.2 Limits and Continuity

f is continuous at a if $\lim_{x\to a} f(x)$ exists and $\lim_{x\to a} f(x) = f(a)$ *p. 208*
Discontinuous, continuous on domain *p. 208*
Determining whether a given function is continuous *p. 209*

3.3 Limits and Continuity: Algebraic Viewpoint

Closed-form function *p. 214*
Limits of closed form functions *p. 215*
Simplifying to obtain limits *p. 215*
The indeterminate form 0/0 *p. 216*
The determinate form $k/0$ *p. 217*
Limits of piecewise-defined functions *p. 218*
Limits at infinity *p. 219*
Determinate and indeterminate forms *p. 222*

3.4 Average Rate of Change

Average rate of change of $f(x)$ over $[a, b]$: $\dfrac{\Delta f}{\Delta x} = \dfrac{f(b) - f(a)}{b - a}$ *p. 230*
Average rate of change as slope of the secant line *p. 231*
Computing the average rate of change from a graph *p. 232*
Computing the average rate of change from a formula *p. 233*
Computing the average rate of change over short intervals $[a, a + h]$ *p. 234*

3.5 Derivatives: Numerical and Graphical Viewpoints

Instantaneous rate of change of $f(x)$ (derivative of f at a);
$f'(a) = \lim_{h\to 0} \dfrac{f(a+h) - f(a)}{h}$ *p. 244*
The derivative as slope of the tangent line *p. 248*
Quick approximation of the derivative *p. 249*
$\dfrac{d}{dx}$ Notation *p. 251*
The derivative as velocity *p. 251*
Average and instantaneous velocity *p. 252*
The derivative function *p. 253*
Graphing the derivative function with technology *p. 254*

3.6 Derivatives: Algebraic Viewpoint

Derivative at the point $x = a$:
$f'(a) = \lim_{h\to 0} \dfrac{f(a+h) - f(a)}{h}$ *p. 267*
Derivative function:
$f'(x) = \lim_{h\to 0} \dfrac{f(x+h) - f(x)}{h}$ *p. 268*
Examples of the computation of $f'(x)$ *p. 269*
$f(x) = |x|$ is not differentiable at $x = 0$ *p. 271*

REVIEW EXERCISES

T indicates exercises that must be solved using technology

Numerically *estimate whether the limits in Exercises 1–4 exist. If a limit does exist, give its approximate value.*

1. $\lim_{x\to 3} \dfrac{x^2 - x - 6}{x - 3}$ **2.** $\lim_{x\to 3} \dfrac{x^2 - 2x - 6}{x - 3}$

3. $\lim_{x\to -1} \dfrac{|x + 1|}{x^2 - x - 2}$ **4.** $\lim_{x\to -1} \dfrac{|x + 1|}{x^2 + x - 2}$

In Exercises 5 and 6, the graph of a function f is shown. Graphically determine whether the given limits exist. If a limit does exist, give its approximate value.

5.

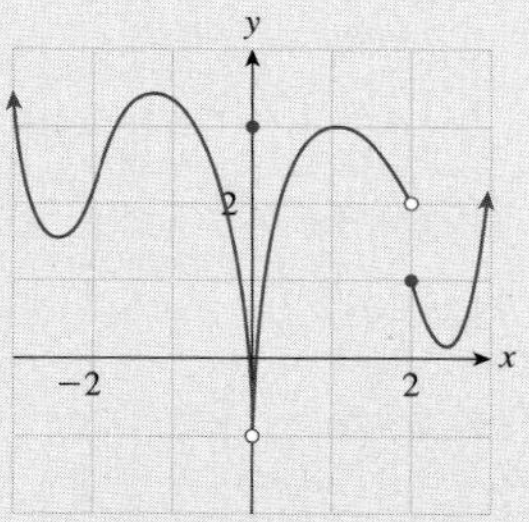

a. $\lim_{x\to 0} f(x)$ **b.** $\lim_{x\to 1} f(x)$
c. $\lim_{x\to 2} f(x)$

6.

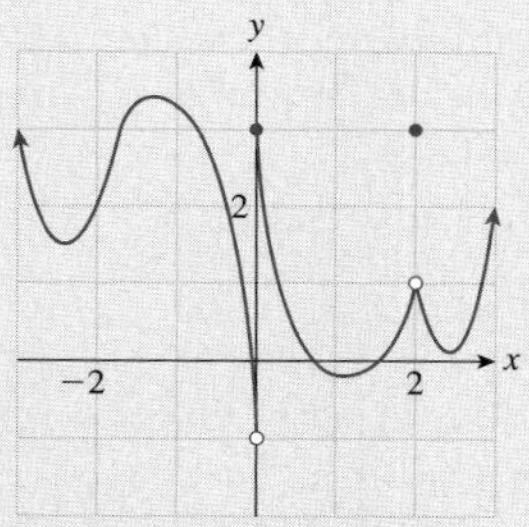

a. $\lim_{x\to 0} f(x)$ **b.** $\lim_{x\to -2} f(x)$
c. $\lim_{x\to 2} f(x)$

Calculate the limits in Exercises 7–30 algebraically. If a limit does not exist, say why.

7. $\lim_{x\to -2} \dfrac{x^2}{x - 3}$ **8.** $\lim_{x\to 3} \dfrac{x^2 - 9}{2x - 6}$

9. $\lim_{x\to -2} \dfrac{x^2 - 4}{x^3 + 2x^2}$ **10.** $\lim_{x\to -1} \dfrac{x^2 - 9}{2x - 6}$

11. $\lim_{x\to 0} \dfrac{x}{2x^2 - x}$ **12.** $\lim_{x\to 1} \dfrac{x^2 - 9}{x - 1}$

13. $\lim_{x\to -1} \dfrac{x^2 + 3x}{x^2 - x - 2}$ **14.** $\lim_{x\to -1^+} \dfrac{x^2 + 1}{x^2 + 3x + 2}$

15. $\lim_{x\to 8} \dfrac{x^2 - 6x - 16}{x^2 - 9x + 8}$ **16.** $\lim_{x\to 4} \dfrac{x^2 + 3x}{x^2 - 8x + 16}$

17. $\lim_{x\to 4} \dfrac{x^2 + 8}{x^2 - 2x - 8}$ **18.** $\lim_{x\to 6} \dfrac{x^2 - 5x - 6}{x^2 - 36}$

19. $\lim_{x\to 1/2} \dfrac{x^2 + 8}{4x^2 - 4x + 1}$ **20.** $\lim_{x\to 1/2} \dfrac{x^2 + 3x}{2x^2 + 3x - 1}$

21. $\lim_{x\to +\infty} \dfrac{10x^2 + 300x + 1}{5x^3 + 2}$ **22.** $\lim_{x\to +\infty} \dfrac{2x^4 + 20x^3}{1{,}000x^6 + 6}$

23. $\lim_{x\to -\infty} \dfrac{x^2 - x - 6}{x - 3}$ **24.** $\lim_{x\to +\infty} \dfrac{x^2 - x - 6}{4x^2 - 3}$

25. $\lim_{t\to+\infty} \frac{-5}{5+5.3(3^{2t})}$

26. $\lim_{t\to+\infty} \left(3+\frac{2}{e^{4t}}\right)$

27. $\lim_{x\to+\infty} \frac{2}{5+4e^{-3x}}$

28. $\lim_{x\to+\infty} (4e^{3x}+12)$

29. $\lim_{t\to+\infty} \frac{1+2^{-3t}}{1+5.3e^{-t}}$

30. $\lim_{x\to-\infty} \frac{8+0.5^x}{2-3^{2x}}$

In Exercises 31–34, find the average rate of change of the given function over the interval $[a, a+h]$ *for* $h = 1, 0.01,$ *and* 0.001. *(Round answers to four decimal places.) Then estimate the slope of the tangent line to the graph of the function at a.*

31. $f(x) = \frac{1}{x+1}$; $a = 0$

32. $f(x) = x^x$; $a = 2$

33. $f(x) = e^{2x}$; $a = 0$

34. $f(x) = \ln(2x)$; $a = 1$

In Exercises 35–38, you are given the graph of a function with four points marked. Determine at which (if any) of these points the derivative of the function is: ***(a)*** -1, ***(b)*** 0, ***(c)*** 1, *and* ***(d)*** 2.

35.

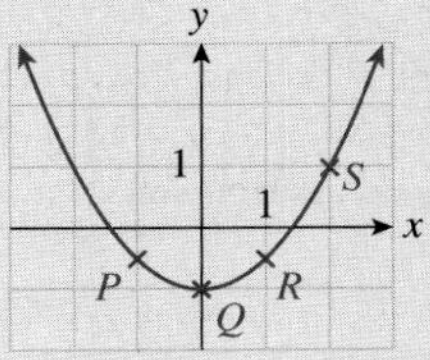

36.

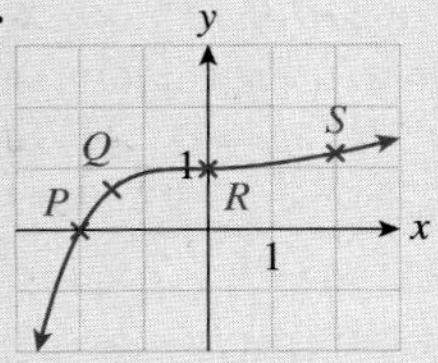

37.

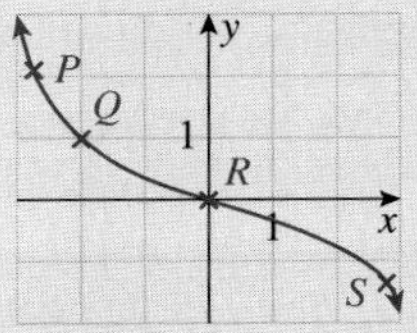

38.

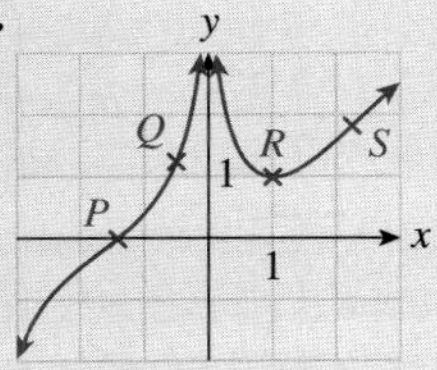

39. Let f have the graph shown.

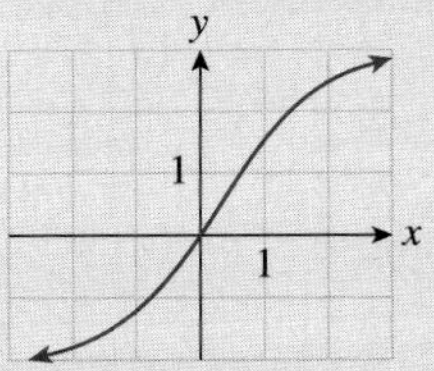

Select the correct answer.

a. The average rate of change of f over the interval [0, 2] is
(A) greater than $f'(0)$. **(B)** less than $f'(0)$.
(C) approximately equal to $f'(0)$.

b. The average rate of change of f over the interval [−1, 1] is
(A) greater than $f'(0)$. **(B)** less than $f'(0)$.
(C) approximately equal to $f'(0)$.

c. Over the interval [0, 2], the instantaneous rate of change of f is
(A) increasing. **(B)** decreasing.
(C) neither increasing nor decreasing.

d. Over the interval [−2, 2], the instantaneous rate of change of f is
(A) increasing, then decreasing.
(B) decreasing, then increasing.
(C) approximately constant.

e. When $x = 2$, $f(x)$ is
(A) approximately 1 and increasing at a rate of about 2.5 units per unit of x.
(B) approximately 1.2 and increasing at a rate of about 1 unit per unit of x.
(C) approximately 2.5 and increasing at a rate of about 0.5 units per unit of x.
(D) approximately 2.5 and increasing at a rate of about 2.5 units per unit of x.

40. Let f have the graph shown.

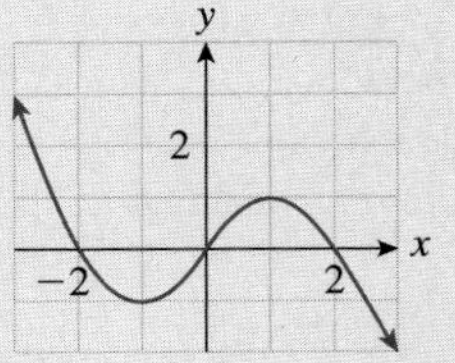

Select the correct answer.

a. The average rate of change of f over the interval [0, 1] is
(A) greater than $f'(0)$. **(B)** less than $f'(0)$.
(C) approximately equal to $f'(0)$.

b. The average rate of change of f over the interval [0, 2] is
(A) greater than $f'(1)$. **(B)** less than $f'(1)$.
(C) approximately equal to $f'(1)$.

c. Over the interval [−2, 0], the instantaneous rate of change of f is
(A) increasing. **(B)** decreasing.
(C) neither increasing nor decreasing.

d. Over the interval [−2, 2], the instantaneous rate of change of f is
(A) increasing, then decreasing.
(B) decreasing, then increasing.
(C) approximately constant.

e. When $x = 0$, $f(x)$ is
(A) approximately 0 and increasing at a rate of about 1.5 units per unit of x.
(B) approximately 0 and decreasing at a rate of about 1.5 units per unit of x.
(C) approximately 1.5 and neither increasing nor decreasing.
(D) approximately 0 and neither increasing nor decreasing.

In Exercises 41–44, use the definition of the derivative to calculate the derivative of each of the given functions algebraically.

41. $f(x) = x^2 + x$

42. $f(x) = 3x^2 - x + 1$

43. $f(x) = 1 - \frac{2}{x}$

44. $f(x) = \frac{1}{x} + 1$

T *In Exercises 45–48, use technology to graph the derivative of the given function. In each case, choose a range of x-values and y-values that shows the interesting features of the graph.*

45. $f(x) = 10x^5 + \frac{1}{2}x^4 - x + 2$

46. $f(x) = \frac{10}{x^5} + \frac{1}{2x^4} - \frac{1}{x} + 2$

47. $f(x) = 3x^3 + 3\sqrt[3]{x}$

48. $f(x) = \frac{2}{x^{2.1}} - \frac{x^{0.1}}{2}$

APPLICATIONS: OHaganBooks.com

49. ***Stock Investments*** OHaganBooks.com CEO John O'Hagan has terrible luck with stocks. The following graph shows the value of Fly-By-Night Airlines stock that he bought acting on a "hot tip" from Marjory Duffin (CEO of Duffin House publishers and a close business associate):

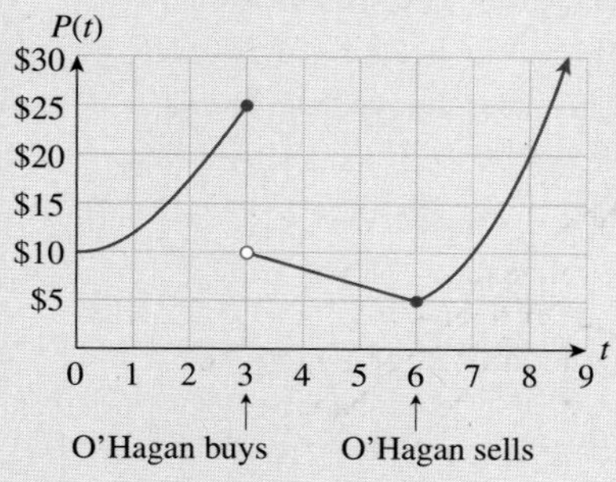

a. Compute $P(3)$, $\lim_{t\to 3^-} P(t)$ and $\lim_{t\to 3^+} P(t)$. Does $\lim_{t\to 3} P(t)$ exist? Interpret your answers in terms of Fly-By-Night stock.

b. Is P continuous at $t = 6$? Is P differentiable at $t = 6$? Interpret your answers in terms of Fly-By-Night stock.

50. ***Stock Investments*** John O'Hagan's golf partner Juan Robles seems to have had better luck with his investment in Gapple Gomputer Inc. stocks as shown in the following graph:

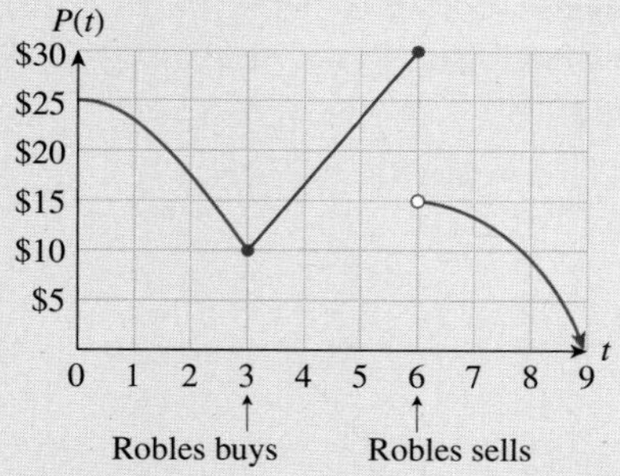

a. Compute $P(6)$, $\lim_{t\to 6^-} P(t)$ and $\lim_{t\to 6^+} P(t)$. Does $\lim_{t\to 6} P(t)$ exist? Interpret your answers in terms of Gapple stock.

b. Is P continuous at $t = 3$? Is P differentiable at $t = 3$? Interpret your answers in terms of Gapple stock.

51. ***Real Estate*** Marjory Duffin has persuaded John O'Hagan to consider investing a portion of OHaganBooks.com profits in real estate, now that the real estate market seems to have bottomed out. A real estate broker friend of hers emailed her the following (somewhat optimistic) graph from brokersadvocacy.com:[76]

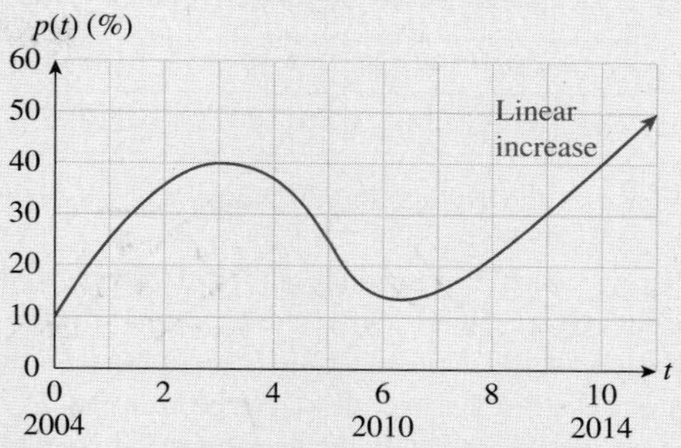

Here, $p(t)$ is the home price percentage over the 2003 level.

a. Assuming the trend shown in the graph were to continue indefinitely, estimate $\lim_{t\to 3} p(t)$ and $\lim_{t\to +\infty} p(t)$ and interpret the results.

b. Estimate $\lim_{t\to +\infty} p'(t)$ and interpret the result.

52. ***Advertising Costs*** OHaganBooks.com has (on further advice from Marjory Duffin) mounted an aggressive online marketing strategy. The following graph shows the weekly cost of this campaign for the six-week period since the start of July (t is time in weeks):

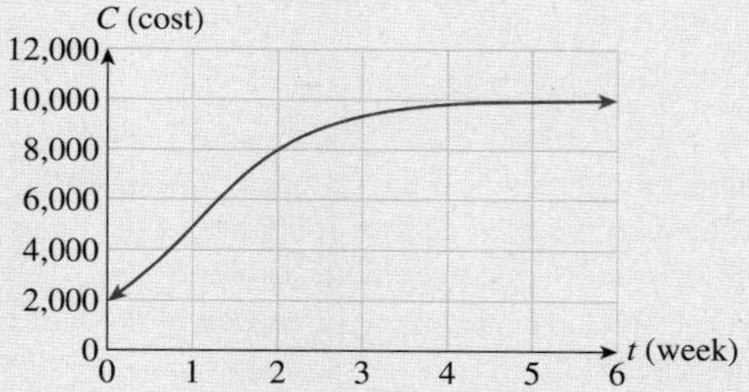

a. Assuming the trend shown in the graph were to continue indefinitely, estimate $\lim_{t\to 2} C(t)$ and $\lim_{t\to +\infty} C(t)$ and interpret the results.

b. Estimate $\lim_{t\to +\infty} C'(t)$ and interpret the result.

53. ***Sales*** Since the start of July, OHaganBooks.com has seen its weekly sales increase, as shown in the following table:

Week	1	2	3	4	5	6
Sales (books)	6,500	7,000	7,200	7,800	8,500	9,000

a. What was the average rate of increase of weekly sales over this entire period?

b. During which 1-week interval(s) did the rate of increase of sales exceed the average rate?

c. During which 2-week interval(s) did the weekly sales rise at the highest average rate, and what was that average rate?

[76] Authors' note: As of August 2012, brokersadvocacy.com is unregistered.

54. ***Rising Sea Level*** Marjory Duffin recently purchased a beachfront condominium in New York and is now in a panic, having just seen some disturbing figures about rising sea levels (sea levels as measured in New York relative to the 1900 level).[77]

Year since 1900	0	25	50	75	100	125
Sea Level (mm)	0	60	140	240	310	390

a. What was the average rate of increase of the sea level over this entire period?
b. During which 25-year interval(s) did the rate of increase of the sea level exceed the average rate?
c. Marjory Duffin's condominium is about 2 meters above sea level. Using the average rate of change from part (a), estimate how long she has before the sea rises to her condominium.

55. ***Real Estate*** The following graph (see Exercise 51) shows the home price index chart emailed to Marjory Duffin by a real estate broker:

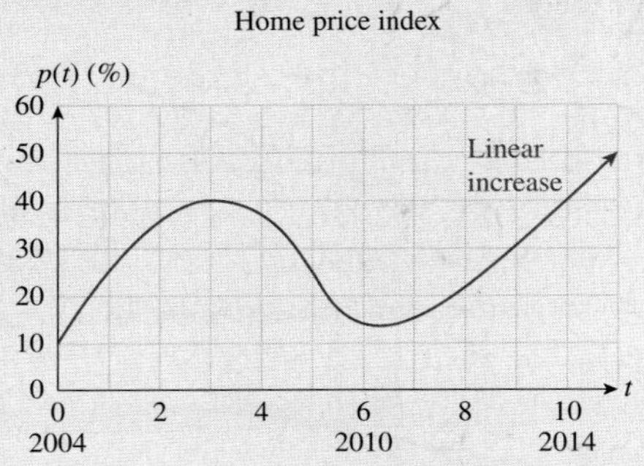

Use the graph to answer the following questions:
a. What was the average rate of change of the index over the 10-year period beginning 2004?
b. What was the average rate of change of the index over the period [3, 10]?
c. Which of the following is correct? Over the period [4, 6],
(A) The rate of change of the index increased.
(B) The rate of change of the index increased and then decreased.
(C) The rate of change of the index decreased.
(D) The rate of change of the index decreased and then increased.

56. ***Advertising Costs*** The following graph (see Exercise 52) shows the weekly cost of OHaganBooks.com's online ad campaign for the 6-week period since the start of July (t is time in weeks).

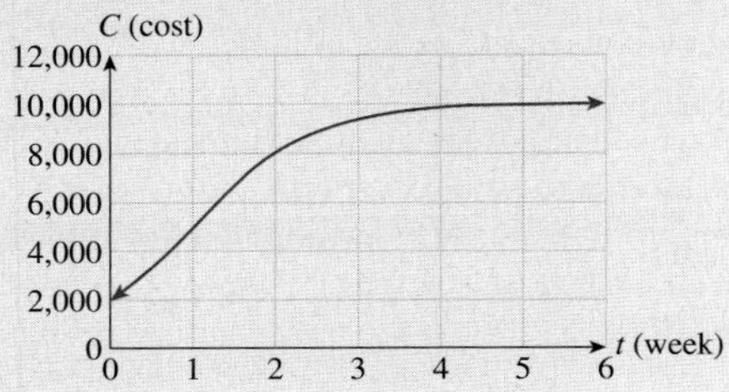

Use the graph to answer the following questions:
a. What was the average rate of change of cost over the entire six-week period?
b. What was the average rate of change of cost over the period [2, 6]?
c. Which of the following is correct? Over the period [2, 6],
(A) The rate of change of cost increased and the cost increased.
(B) The rate of change of cost decreased and the cost increased.
(C) The rate of change of cost increased and the cost decreased.
(D) The rate of change of cost decreased and the cost decreased.

57. ***Sales*** OHaganBooks.com fits the curve

$$w(t) = 36t^2 + 250t + 6{,}240 \quad (0 \le t \le 6)$$

to its weekly sales figures from Exercise 53, as shown in the following graph:

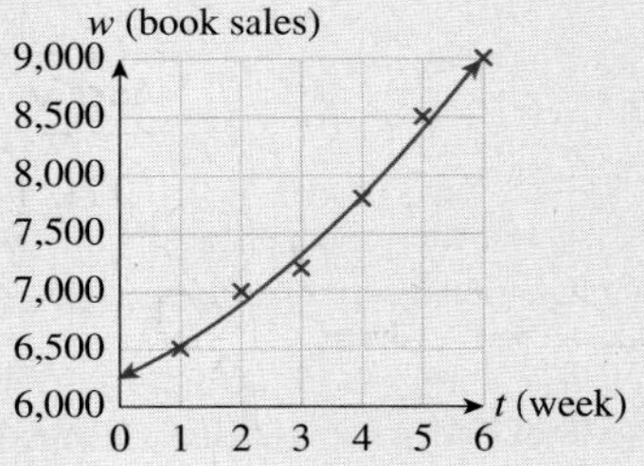

a. Compute the derivative function $w'(t)$.
b. According to the model, what was the rate of increase of sales at the beginning of the second week ($t = 1$)?
c. If we extrapolate the model, what would be the rate of increase of weekly sales at the beginning of the 8th week ($t = 7$)?

58. ***Sea Levels*** Marjory Duffin fit the curve

$$s(t) = 0.002t^2 + 3t - 6.4 \quad (0 \le t \le 125)$$

to her sea level figures from Exercise 54, as shown in the following graph:

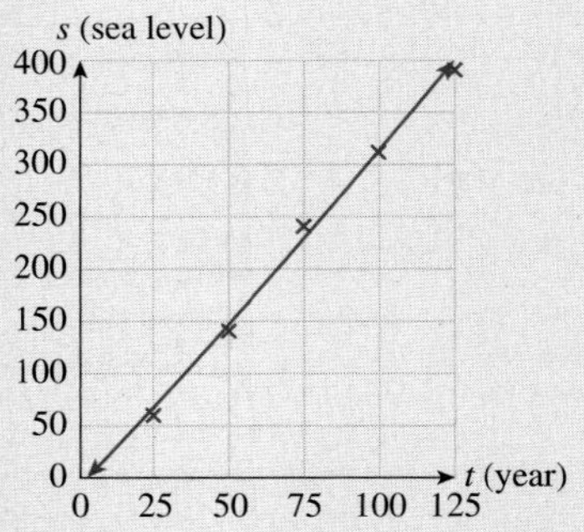

a. Compute the derivative function $s'(t)$.
b. According to the model, what was the rate of increase of the sea level in 2000 ($t = 100$)?
c. If we extrapolate the model, what would be the rate of increase of the sea level in 2100 ($t = 200$)?

[77] The 2025 level is a projection. Source: New England Integrated Science & Assessment (www.neisa.unh.edu/Climate/index.html).

Case Study

Reducing Sulfur Emissions

The Environmental Protection Agency (EPA) wishes to formulate a policy that will encourage utilities to reduce sulfur emissions. Its goal is to reduce annual emissions of sulfur dioxide by a total of 10 million tons from the current level of 25 million tons by imposing a fixed charge for every ton of sulfur released into the environment per year. As a consultant to the EPA, you must determine the amount to be charged per ton of sulfur emissions.

You would like first to know the cost to the utility industry of reducing sulfur emissions. In other words, you would like to have a cost function of the form

$$C(q) = \text{Cost of removing } q \text{ tons of sulfur dioxide.}$$

Unfortunately, you do not have such a function handy. You do, however, have the following data, which show the *marginal* cost (that is, the *rate of change* of cost) to the utility industry of reducing sulfur emissions at several levels of reduction.[78]

Reduction (tons) q	8,000,000	10,000,000	12,000,000
Marginal Cost ($ per ton) $C'(q)$	270	360	779

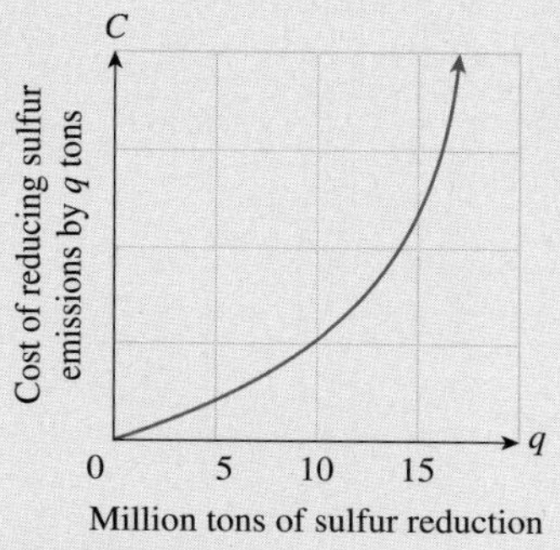

Figure 40

The table tells you that $C'(8{,}000{,}000) = \$270$ per ton, $C'(10{,}000{,}000) = \$360$ per ton, and $C'(12{,}000{,}000) = \$779$ per ton. Recalling that $C'(q)$ is the slope of the tangent to the graph of the cost function, you can see from the table that this slope is positive and increasing as q increases, so the graph of the cost function has the general shape shown in Figure 40.

Notice that the slope (additional cost) is increasing as you move to the right, so the utility industry has no cost incentive to reduce emissions further, as it costs the industry significantly more per ton for each additional ton of sulfur it removes. What you would like—if the goal of reducing total emissions by 10 million tons is to be reached—is that, somehow, the imposition of a fixed charge for every ton of sulfur dioxide released will *alter* the form of the cost curve so that it has the general shape shown in Figure 41. In this ideal curve, the cost D to utilities is lowest at a reduction level of 10 million tons, so if the utilities act to minimize cost, they can be expected to reduce emissions by 10 million tons, which is exactly the EPA goal! From the graph, you can see that the tangent line to the curve at the point where $q = 10$ million tons is horizontal, and thus has zero slope: $D'(10{,}000{,}000) = \$0$ per ton. Further, the slope $D'(q)$ is negative for values of q to the left of 10 million tons and positive for values to the right.

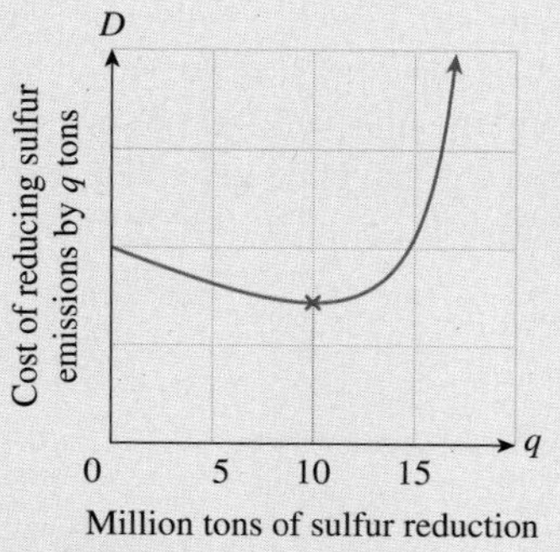

Figure 41

So, how much should the EPA charge per ton of sulfur released into the environment? Suppose the EPA charges $\$k$ per ton, so that

$$\text{Emission charge to utilities} = k \times \text{Sulfur emissions.}$$

It is your job to calculate k. Because you are working with q as the independent variable, you decide that it would be best to formulate the emission charge as a function of q. However, q represents the amount by which sulfur emissions have been reduced from the original 25 million tons; that is, the amount by which sulfur emissions are *lower than* the original 25 million tons:

$$q = 25{,}000{,}000 - \text{Sulfur emissions.}$$

[78] These figures were produced in a computerized study of reducing sulfur emissions from the 1980 level by the given amounts. Source: Congress of the United States, Congressional Budget Office, *Curbing Acid Rain: Cost, Budget and Coal Market Effects* (Washington, DC: Government Printing Office, 1986): xx, xxii, 23, 80.

Thus, the total annual emission charge to the utilities is

$$k \times \text{Sulfur emissions} = k(25{,}000{,}000 - q) = 25{,}000{,}000k - kq.$$

This results in a total cost to the utilities of

$$\begin{aligned} \text{Total cost} &= \text{Cost of reducing emissions} + \text{Emission charge} \\ D(q) &= C(q) + 25{,}000{,}000k - kq. \end{aligned}$$

You now recall from calculus that the derivative of a sum of two functions is the sum of their derivatives (you will see why in Section 4.1*), so the derivative of D is given by

* This statement makes intuitive sense: For instance, if C is changing at a rate of 3 units per second and D is changing at a rate of 2 units per second, then their sum is changing at a rate of $3 + 2 = 5$ units per second.

$$D'(q) = \text{Derivative of } C + \text{Derivative of } (25{,}000{,}000k - kq).$$

The function $y = 25{,}000{,}000k - kq$ is a linear function of q with slope $-k$ and intercept $25{,}000{,}000k$. Thus its derivative is just its slope: $-k$. Therefore:

$$D'(q) = C'(q) - k.$$

Remember that you want

$$D'(10{,}000{,}000) = 0.$$

Thus,

$$C'(10{,}000{,}000) - k = 0.$$

Referring to the table, you see that

$$360 - k = 0$$

or

$$k = \$360 \text{ per ton.}$$

In other words, all you need to do is set the emission charge at $k = \$360$ per ton of sulfur emitted. Further, to ensure that the resulting curve will have the general shape shown in Figure 40, you would like to have $D'(q)$ negative for $q < 10{,}000{,}000$ and positive for $q > 10{,}000{,}000$. To check this, write

$$\begin{aligned} D'(q) &= C'(q) - k \\ &= C'(q) - 360 \end{aligned}$$

and refer to the table to obtain

$$D'(8{,}000{,}000) = 270 - 360 = -90 < 0 \checkmark$$

and

$$D'(12{,}000{,}000) = 779 - 360 = 419 > 0 \checkmark$$

Thus, based on the given data, the resulting curve will have the shape you require. You therefore inform the EPA that an annual emissions charge of \$360 per ton of sulfur released into the environment will create the desired incentive: to reduce sulfur emissions by 10 million tons per year.

One week later, you are informed that this charge would be unrealistic because the utilities cannot possibly afford such a cost. You are asked whether there is an alternative plan that accomplishes the 10-million-ton reduction goal and yet is cheaper to the utilities by \$5 billion per year. You then look at your expression for the emission charge

$$25{,}000{,}000k - kq$$

and notice that, if you decrease this amount by \$5 billion, the derivative will not change at all because it will still have the same slope (only the intercept is affected). Thus, you propose the following revised formula for the emission charge:

$$\begin{aligned}&25{,}000{,}000k - kq - 5{,}000{,}000{,}000\\ &= 25{,}000{,}000(360) - 360q - 5{,}000{,}000{,}000\\ &= 4{,}000{,}000{,}000 - 360q.\end{aligned}$$

At the expected reduction level of 10 million tons, the total amount paid by the utilities will then be

$$4{,}000{,}000{,}000 - 360(10{,}000{,}000) = \$400{,}000{,}000.$$

Thus, your revised proposal is the following: Impose an annual emissions charge of \$360 per ton of sulfur released into the environment and hand back \$5 billion in the form of subsidies. The effect of this policy will be to cause the utilities industry to reduce sulfur emissions by 10 million tons per year and will result in \$400 million in annual revenues to the government.

Notice that this policy also provides an incentive for the utilities to search for cheaper ways to reduce emissions. For instance, if they lowered costs to the point where they could achieve a reduction level of 12 million tons, they would have a total emission charge of

$$4{,}000{,}000{,}000 - 360(12{,}000{,}000) = -\$320{,}000{,}000.$$

The fact that this is negative means that the government would be paying the utilities industry \$320 million more in annual subsidies than the industry is paying in per ton emission charges.

EXERCISES

1. Excluding subsidies, what should the annual emission charge be if the goal is to reduce sulfur emissions by 8 million tons?
2. Excluding subsidies, what should the annual emission charge be if the goal is to reduce sulfur emissions by 12 million tons?
3. What is the *marginal emission charge* (derivative of emission charge) in your revised proposal (as stated before the exercise set)? What is the relationship between the marginal cost of reducing sulfur emissions before emissions charges are implemented and the marginal emission charge, at the optimal reduction under your revised proposal?
4. We said that the revised policy provided an incentive for utilities to find cheaper ways to reduce emissions. How would $C(q)$ have to change to make 12 million tons the optimum reduction?
5. What change in $C(q)$ would make 8 million tons the optimum reduction?
6. If the scenario in Exercise 5 took place, what would the EPA have to do in order to make 10 million tons the optimal reduction once again?
7. Due to intense lobbying by the utility industry, you are asked to revise the proposed policy so that the utility industry will pay no charge if sulfur emissions are reduced by the desired 10 million tons. How can you accomplish this?
8. Suppose that instead of imposing a fixed charge per ton of emission, you decide to use a sliding scale, so that the total charge to the industry for annual emissions of x tons will be $\$kx^2$ for some k. What must k be to again make 10 million tons the optimum reduction? HINT [The derivative of kx^2 is $2kx$.]

TI-83/84 Plus Technology Guide

Section 3.1

Example 1 (page 195) Use a table to estimate the following limits.

a. $\lim_{x\to 2} \frac{x^3 - 8}{x - 2}$ **b.** $\lim_{x\to 0} \frac{e^{2x} - 1}{x}$

Solution with Technology

On the TI-83/84 Plus, use the table feature to automate these computations as follows:

1. Define `Y1=(X^3-8)/(X-2)` for part (a) or `Y1=(e^(2X)-1)/X` for part (b).
2. Press [2ND] [TABLE] to list its values for the given values of x. (If the calculator does not allow you to enter values of x, press [2ND] [TBLSET] and set `Indpnt` to `Ask`).

   Here is the table showing some of the values for part (a):

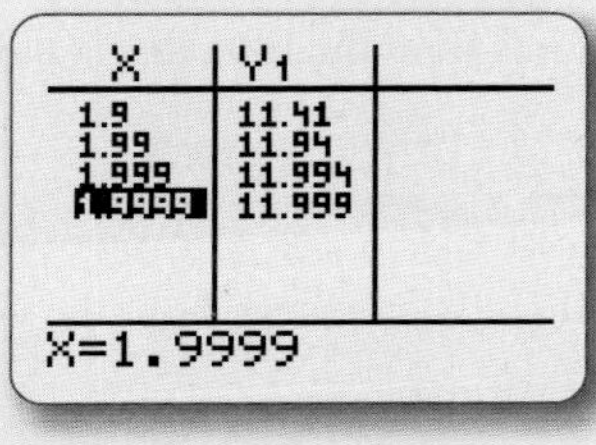

3. For part (b) use `Y1=(e^(2X)-1)/X` and use values of x approaching 0 from either side.

Section 3.4

Example 3 (page 233) The price of an ounce of gold can be approximated by the function

$$G(t) = 5t^2 - 85t + 1{,}762 \quad (7.5 \le t \le 10.5)$$

where t is time in hours. ($t = 8$ represents 8:00 am.) What was the average rate of change of the price of gold over the $1\frac{1}{2}$-hour period starting at 8:00 am (the interval [8, 9.5] on the t-axis)?

Solution with Technology

On the TI-83/84 Plus:

1. Enter the function G as `Y1` (using X for t):

   `Y1=5X^2-85X+1762`

2. Now find the average rate of change over [8, 9.5] by evaluating the following on the home screen:

   `(Y1(9.5)-Y1(8))/(9.5-8)`

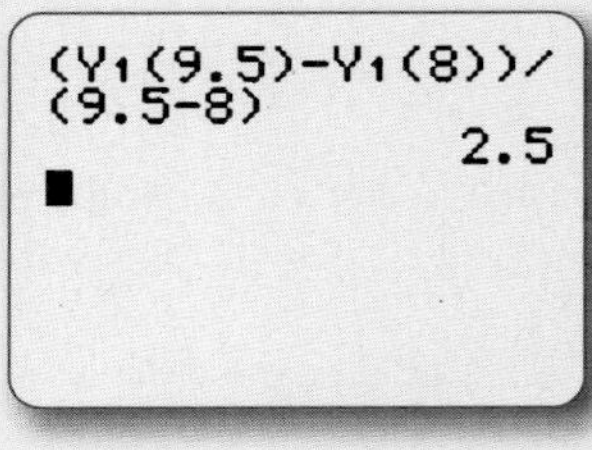

As shown on the screen, the average rate is of change is 2.5.

Example 4 (page 234) Continuing with Example 3, use technology to compute the average rate of change of

$$G(t) = 5t^2 - 85t + 1{,}762 \qquad (7.5 \le t \le 10.5)$$

over the intervals $[8, 8 + h]$, where $h = 1$, 0.1, 0.01, 0.001, and 0.0001.

Solution with Technology

1. As in Example 4, enter the function G as `Y1` (using X for t):

   `Y1=5X^2-85X+1762`

2. Now find the average rate of change for $h = 1$ by evaluating, on the home screen,

   `(Y1(8+1)-Y1(8))/1`,

   which gives 0.

3. To evaluate for $h = 0.1$, recall the expression using [2ND] [ENTER] and then change the 1, both places it occurs, to 0.1, getting

   `(Y1(8+0.1)-Y1(8))/0.1`,

   which gives −4.95.

4. Continuing, we can evaluate the average rate of change for all the desired values of h:

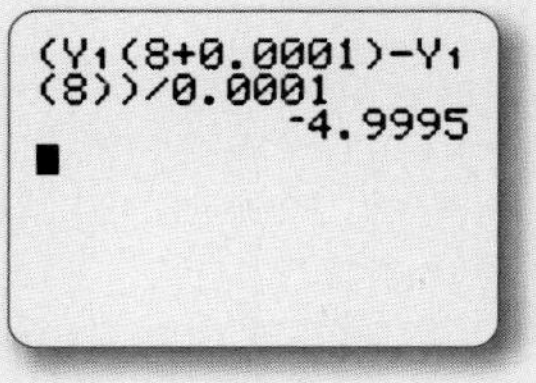

Section 3.5

Example 2 (page 249) Calculate an approximate value of $f'(1.5)$ if $f(x) = x^2 - 4x$, and then find the equation of the tangent line at the point on the graph where $x = 1.5$.

Solution with Technology

1. In the TI-83/84 Plus, enter the function f as Y_1

$$Y_1\text{=X^2-4*X}$$

2. Go to the home screen to compute the approximations:

`(Y₁(1.5001)-Y₁(1.5))/0.0001`

Usual difference quotient

`(Y₁(1.5001)-Y₁(1.4999))/0.0002`

Balanced difference quotient

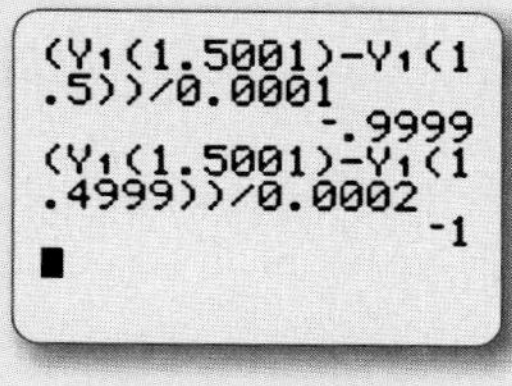

From the display on the right, we find that the difference quotient quick approximation is -0.9999 and the balanced difference quotient quick approximation is -1, which is in fact the exact value of $f'(1.5)$. See the discussion in the text for the calculation of the equation of the tangent line.

Example 4 (page 254) Use technology to graph the derivative of $f(x) = -2x^2 + 6x + 5$ for values of x in starting at -5.

Solution with Technology

On the TI-83/84 Plus, the easiest way to obtain quick approximations of the derivative of a given function is to use the built-in `nDeriv` function, which calculates balanced difference quotients.

1. On the `Y=` screen, first enter the function:

`Y₁=-2X^2+6X+5`

2. Then set

`Y₂=nDeriv(Y₁,X,X)` For `nDeriv` press [MATH] [8]

which is the TI-83/84 Plus's approximation of $f'(x)$ (see figure on the left below). Alternatively, we can enter the balanced difference quotient directly:

`Y₂=(Y₁(X+0.001)-Y₁(X-0.001))/0.002`

(The TI-83/84 Plus uses $h = 0.001$ by default in the balanced difference quotient when calculating `nDeriv`, but this can be changed by giving a value of h as a fourth argument, like `nDeriv(Y₁,X,X,0.0001)`.) To see a table of approximate values of the derivative, we press [2ND] [TABLE] and choose a collection of values for x (shown on the right below):

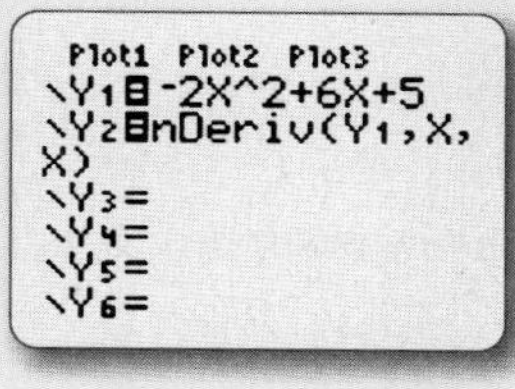

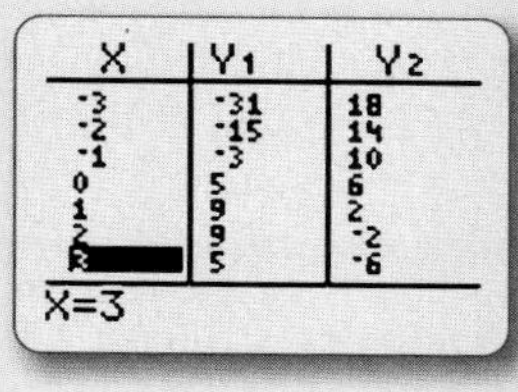

Here, Y_1 shows the value of f and Y_2 shows the values of f'.

To graph the function or its derivative, we can graph Y_1 or Y_2 in a window showing the given domain $[-5, 5]$:

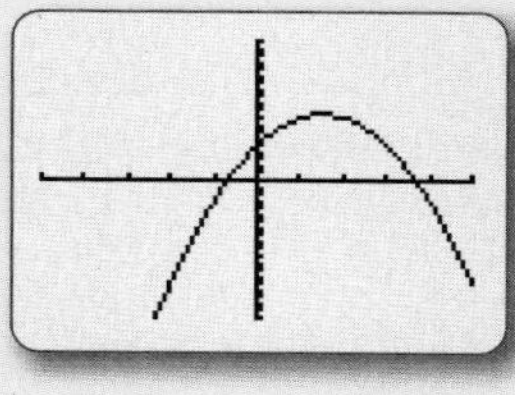

Graph of f

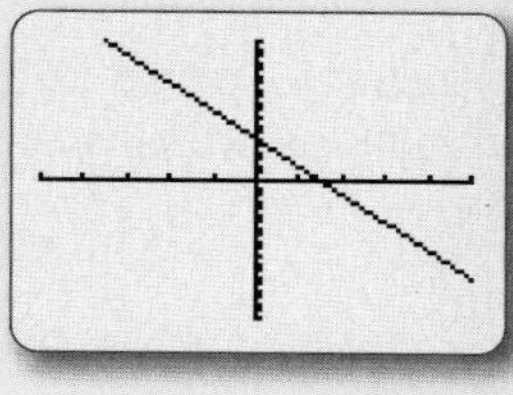

Graph of f'

TECHNOLOGY GUIDE

SPREADSHEET Technology Guide

Section 3.1

Example 1 (page 195) Use a table to estimate the following limits.

a. $\lim_{x \to 2} \frac{x^3 - 8}{x - 2}$ **b.** $\lim_{x \to 0} \frac{e^{2x} - 1}{x}$

Solution with Technology

1. Set up your spreadsheet to duplicate the table in part (a) as follows:

	A	B	C	D
1	x	f(x)	x	f(x)
2	1.9	=(A2^3-8)/(A2-2)	2.1	
3	1.99		2.01	
4	1.999		2.001	
5	1.9999		2.0001	

↓

	A	B	C	D
1	x	f(x)	x	f(x)
2	1.9	11.41	2.1	12.61
3	1.99	11.9401	2.01	12.0601
4	1.999	11.994001	2.001	12.006001
5	1.9999	11.99940001	2.0001	12.00060001

(The formula in cell B2 is copied to columns B and D as indicated by the shading.) The values of $f(x)$ will be calculated in columns B and D.

2. For part (b), use the formula `=(EXP(2*A2)-1)/A2` in cell B2 and, in columns A and C, use values of x approaching 0 from either side.

Section 3.4

Example 3 (page 233) The price of an ounce of gold can be approximated by the function

$$G(t) = 5t^2 + 85t + 1,762 \quad (7.5 \le t \le 10.5)$$

where t is time in hours. ($t = 8$ represents 8:00 am.) What was the average rate of change of the price of gold over the $1\frac{1}{2}$-hour period starting at 8:00 am (the interval [8, 9.5] on the t-axis)?

Solution with Technology

To use a spreadsheet to compute the average rate of change of G:

1. Start with two columns, one for values of t and one for values of $G(t)$, which you enter using the formula for G:

`=5*A2^2-85*A2+1762`

	A	B
1	t	G(t)
2	8	=5*A2^2-85*A2+1762
3	9.5	

2. Next, calculate the average rate of change as shown here:

	A	B	C	D
1	t	G(t)		
2	8	1402	Rate of change over [8, 9.5]:	
3	9.5	1405.75	=(B3-B2)/(A3-A2)	

↓

	A	B	C	D
1	t	G(t)		
2	8	1402	Rate of change over [8, 9.5]:	
3	9.5	1405.75	2.5	

In Example 4, we describe another, more versatile Excel template for computing rates of change.

Example 4 (page 234) Continuing with Example 3, use technology to compute the average rate of change of

$$G(t) = 5t^2 + 85t + 1,762 \qquad (7.5 \le t \le 10.5)$$

over the intervals $[8, 8 + h]$, where $h = 1$, 0.1, 0.01, 0.001, and 0.0001.

Solution with Technology

The template we can use to compute the rates of change is an extension of what we used in Example 3:

	A	B	C	D	E
1	a	h	t	G(t)	Rate of Change
2	8	0.001	=A2	=5*C2^2-85*C2+1762	=(D3-D2)/(C3-C2)
3			=A2+B2		

↓

	A	B	C	D	E
1	a	h	t	G(t)	Rate of Change
2	8	0.001	8	1402	-4.995
3			8.001	1401.99501	

1. Column C contains the values $t = a$ and $t = a + h$ we are using for the independent variable.

2. The formula in cell E2 is the average-rate-of-change formula $\Delta G/\Delta t$. Entering the different values $h = 1$, 0.1, 0.01, 0.001, and 0.0001 in cell B2 gives the results shown in Example 4.

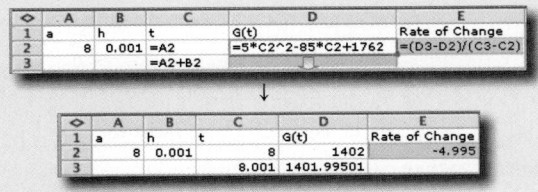

Section 3.5

Example 2 (page 249) Calculate an approximate value of $f'(1.5)$ if $f(x) = x^2 - 4x$, and then find the equation of the tangent line at the point on the graph where $x = 1.5$.

Solution with Technology

You can compute both the difference quotient and the balanced difference quotient approximations in a spreadsheet using the following extension of the worksheet in Example 4 in Section 3.4:

	A	B	C	D	E	F
1	a	h	x	f(x)	Diff Quotients	Balanced Diff Quotient
2	1.5	0.0001	=A2-B2	=C2^2-4*C2	=(D3-D2)/(C3-C2)	=(D4-D2)/(C4-C2)
3			=A2			
4			=A2+B2			

Notice that we get two difference quotients in column E. The first uses $h = -0.0001$ while the second uses $h = 0.0001$ and is the one we use for our quick approximation. The balanced quotient is their average (column F). The results are as follows.

	A	B	C	D	E	F
1	a	h	x	f(x)	Diff Quotients	Balanced Diff Quotient
2	1.5	0.0001	1.4999	-3.7499	-1.0001	-1
3			1.5	-3.75	-0.9999	
4			1.5001	-3.7501		

From the results shown above, we find that the difference quotient quick approximation is -0.9999 and that the balanced difference quotient quick approximation is -1, which is in fact the exact value of $f'(1.5)$. See the discussion in the text for the calculation of the equation of the tangent line.

Example 4 (page 254) Use technology to graph the derivative of $f(x) = -2x^2 + 6x + 5$ for values of x starting at -5.

Solution with Technology

1. Start with a table of values for the function f:

	A	B	C	D	E
1	x	f(x)		Xmin	-5
2	=$E$1	=-2*A2^2+6*A2+5		h	0.1
3	=A2+$E$2				
4					
5					
101					
102					

2. Next, compute approximate derivatives in Column C:

	A	B	C	D	E
1	x	f(x)	f'(x)	Xmin	-5
2	-5	-75	=(B3-B2)/$E$2	h	0.1
3	-4.9	-72.42			
4	-4.8	-69.88			
5	-4.7	-67.38			
101	4.9	-13.62			
102	5	-15			

	A	B	C	D	E
1	x	f(x)	f'(x)	Xmin	-5
2	-5	-75	25.8	h	0.1
3	-4.9	-72.42	25.4		
4	-4.8	-69.88	25		
5	-4.7	-67.38	24.6		
101	4.9	-13.62	-13.8		
102	5	-15			

You cannot paste the difference quotient formula into cell C102. (Why?) Notice that this worksheet uses the ordinary difference quotients, $[f(x+h) - f(x)]/h$. If you prefer, you can use balanced difference quotients $[f(x+h) - f(x-h)]/(2h)$, in which case cells C2 and C102 would both have to be left blank.

We now graph the function and the derivative on different graphs as follows:

1. First, graph the function f in the usual way, using Columns A and B.
2. Make a copy of this graph and click on it once. Columns A and B should be outlined, indicating that these are the columns used in the graph.
3. By dragging from the center of the bottom edge of the box, move the Column B box over to Column C as shown:

	A	B	C
96	4.4	-7.32	-11.8
97	4.5	-8.5	-12.2
98	4.6	-9.72	-12.6
99	4.7	-10.98	-13
100	4.8	-12.28	-13.4
101	4.9	-13.62	-13.8
102	5	-15	

↓

	A	B	C
96	4.4	-7.32	-11.8
97	4.5	-8.5	-12.2
98	4.6	-9.72	-12.6
99	4.7	-10.98	-13
100	4.8	-12.28	-13.4
101	4.9	-13.62	-13.8
102	5	-15	

TECHNOLOGY GUIDE

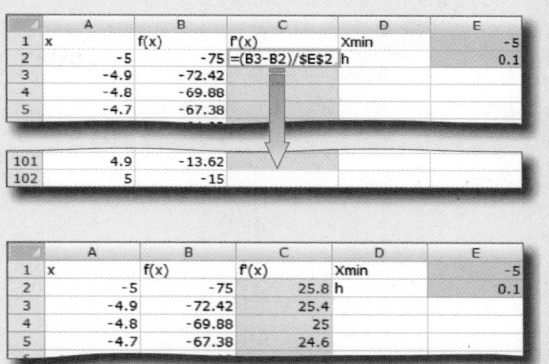

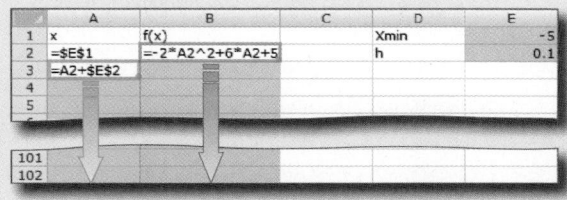

The graph will then show the derivative (Columns A and C):

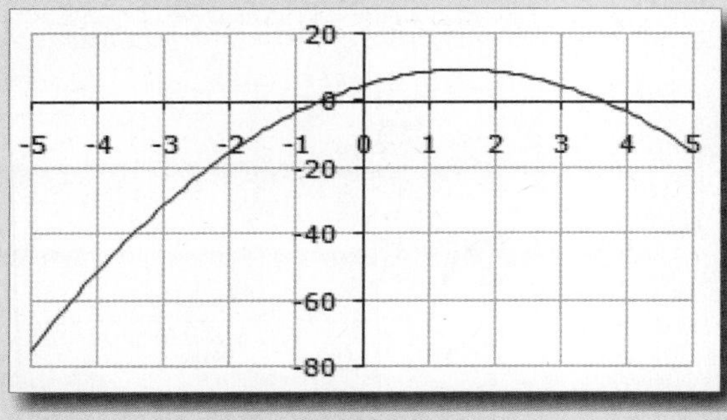

Graph of f

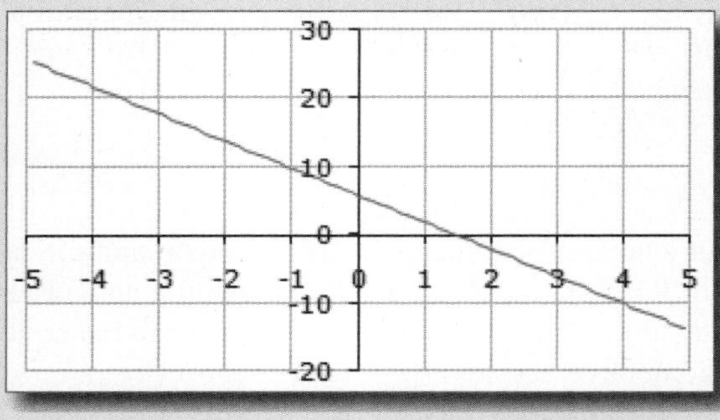

Graph of f'

4

Techniques of Differentiation with Applications

Website
www.WanerMath.com
At the Website you will find:

- Section-by-section tutorials, including game tutorials with randomized quizzes
- A detailed chapter summary
- A true/false quiz
- Additional review exercises
- Graphers, Excel tutorials, and other resources
- The following extra topic:
  Linear Approximation and Error Estimation

Case Study Projecting Market Growth

You are on the board of directors at Fullcourt Academic Press. The sales director of the high school division has just burst into your office with a proposal for an expansion strategy based on the assumption that the number of graduates from private high schools in the U.S. will grow at a rate of at least 4,000 per year through the year 2015. Because the figures actually appear to be leveling off, you are suspicious about this estimate. You would like to devise a model that predicts this trend before tomorrow's scheduled board meeting. **How do you go about doing this?**

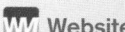

Yuri Arcurs/Shutterstock

Introduction

In Chapter 3 we studied the concept of the derivative of a function, and we saw some of the applications for which derivatives are useful. However, computing the derivative of a function algebraically seemed to be a time-consuming process, forcing us to restrict attention to fairly simply functions.

In this chapter we develop shortcut techniques that will allow us to write down the derivative of a function directly without having to calculate any limit. These techniques will also enable us to differentiate any closed-form function—that is, any function, no matter how complicated, that can be specified by a formula involving powers, radicals, absolute values, exponents, and logarithms. (In Chapter 9 we will discuss how to add trigonometric functions to this list.) We also show how to find the derivatives of functions that are only specified *implicitly*—that is, functions for which we are not given an explicit formula for y in terms of x but only an equation relating x and y.

algebra Review

For this chapter, you should be familiar with the algebra reviewed in **Chapter 0, Sections 3 and 4.**

4.1 Derivatives of Powers, Sums, and Constant Multiples

Up to this point we have approximated derivatives using difference quotients, and we have done exact calculations using the definition of the derivative as the limit of a difference quotient. In general, we would prefer to have an exact calculation, and it is also very useful to have a formula for the derivative function when we can find one. However, the calculation of a derivative as a limit is often tedious, so it would be nice to have a quicker method. We discuss the first of the shortcut rules in this section. By the end of this chapter, we will be able to find fairly quickly the derivative of almost any function we can write.

Shortcut Formula: The Power Rule

If you look at Examples 2 and 3 in Section 3.6, you may notice a pattern:

$$f(x) = x^2 \quad \Rightarrow \quad f'(x) = 2x$$
$$f(x) = x^3 \quad \Rightarrow \quad f'(x) = 3x^2.$$

This pattern generalizes to any power of x:

Theorem 4.1 The Power Rule

If n is any constant and $f(x) = x^n$, then

$$f'(x) = nx^{n-1}.$$

Quick Examples

1. If $f(x) = x^2$, then $f'(x) = 2x^1 = 2x$.
2. If $f(x) = x^3$, then $f'(x) = 3x^2$.
3. If $f(x) = x$, rewrite as $f(x) = x^1$, so $f'(x) = 1x^0 = 1$.
4. If $f(x) = 1$, rewrite as $f(x) = x^0$, so $f'(x) = 0x^{-1} = 0$.

Website
www.WanerMath.com
At the Website you can find a proof of the power rule by following:
Everything for Calculus
→ Chapter 4
→ Proof of the Power Rule

The proof of the power rule involves first studying the case when n is a positive integer, and then studying the cases of other types of exponents (negative integer, rational number, irrational number). You can find a proof at the Website.

EXAMPLE 1 Using the Power Rule for Negative and Fractional Exponents

Calculate the derivatives of the following:

a. $f(x) = \dfrac{1}{x}$ **b.** $f(x) = \dfrac{1}{x^2}$ **c.** $f(x) = \sqrt{x}$

Solution

a. Rewrite* as $f(x) = x^{-1}$. Then $f'(x) = (-1)x^{-2} = -\dfrac{1}{x^2}$.

b. Rewrite as $f(x) = x^{-2}$. Then $f'(x) = (-2)x^{-3} = -\dfrac{2}{x^3}$.

c. Rewrite as $f(x) = x^{0.5}$. Then $f'(x) = 0.5x^{-0.5} = \dfrac{0.5}{x^{0.5}}$. Alternatively, rewrite $f(x)$ as $x^{1/2}$, so that $f'(x) = \dfrac{1}{2}x^{-1/2} = \dfrac{1}{2x^{1/2}} = \dfrac{1}{2\sqrt{x}}$.

* See Section 0.2 in the Precalculus Review to brush up on negative and fractional exponents. Pay particular attention to rational, radical, and exponent forms.

By rewriting the given functions in Example 1 before taking derivatives, we converted them from **rational** or **radical form** (as in, say, $\dfrac{1}{x^2}$ and $\sqrt{x}$) to **exponent form** (as in x^{-2} and $x^{0.5}$; see the Precalculus Review, Section 0.2) to enable us to use the power rule. (See the Caution below.)

Caution

We cannot apply the power rule to terms in the denominators or under square roots. For example:

1. The derivative of $\dfrac{1}{x^2}$ is **NOT** $\dfrac{1}{2x}$; it is $-\dfrac{2}{x^3}$. See Example 1(b).
2. The derivative of $\sqrt{x^3}$ is **NOT** $\sqrt{3x^2}$; it is $1.5x^{0.5}$. Rewrite $\sqrt{x^3}$ as $x^{3/2}$ or $x^{1.5}$ and apply the power rule.

Some of the derivatives in Example 1 are very useful to remember, so we summarize them in Table 1. We suggest that you add to this table as you learn more derivatives. It is *extremely* helpful to remember the derivatives of common functions such as $1/x$ and $\sqrt{x}$, even though they can be obtained by using the power rule as in the above example.

Table 1 Table of Derivative Formulas

$f(x)$	$f'(x)$
1	0
x	1
x^2	$2x$
x^3	$3x^2$
x^n	nx^{n-1}
$\dfrac{1}{x}$	$-\dfrac{1}{x^2}$
$\dfrac{1}{x^2}$	$-\dfrac{2}{x^3}$
$\sqrt{x}$	$\dfrac{1}{2\sqrt{x}}$

Another Notation: Differential Notation

Here is a useful notation based on the "d-notation" we discussed in Section 3.5. **Differential notation** is based on an abbreviation for the phrase "the derivative with respect to x." For example, we learned that if $f(x) = x^3$, then $f'(x) = 3x^2$. When we say "$f'(x) = 3x^2$," we mean the following:

The derivative of x^3 with respect to x equals $3x^2$.

You may wonder why we sneaked in the words "with respect to x." All this means is that the variable of the function is x, and not any other variable.* Because we use the phrase "the derivative with respect to x" often, we use the following abbreviation.

* This may seem odd in the case of $f(x) = x^3$ because there are no other variables to worry about. But in expressions like st^3 that involve variables other than x, it is necessary to specify just what the variable of the function is. This is the same reason that we write "$f(x) = x^3$" rather than just "$f = x^3$."

Differential Notation; Differentiation

$\frac{d}{dx}$ means "the derivative with respect to x."

Thus, $\frac{d}{dx}[f(x)]$ is the same thing as $f'(x)$, the derivative of $f(x)$ with respect to x. If y is a function of x, then the derivative of y with respect to x is

$$\frac{d}{dx}(y) \quad \text{or, more compactly,} \quad \frac{dy}{dx}.$$

To **differentiate** a function $f(x)$ with respect to x means to take its derivative with respect to x.

Quick Examples

In Words	Formula
1. The derivative with respect to x of x^3 is $3x^2$.	$\frac{d}{dx}(x^3) = 3x^2$
2. The derivative with respect to t of $\frac{1}{t}$ is $-\frac{1}{t^2}$.	$\frac{d}{dt}\left(\frac{1}{t}\right) = -\frac{1}{t^2}$
3. If $y = x^4$, then $\frac{dy}{dx} = 4x^3$.	
4. If $u = \frac{1}{t^2}$, then $\frac{du}{dt} = -\frac{2}{t^3}$.	

Notes

1. $\frac{dy}{dx}$ is Leibniz's notation for the derivative we discussed in Section 3.5. (See the discussion before Example 3 there.)

2. Leibniz notation illustrates units nicely: Units of $\frac{dy}{dx}$ are units of y per unit of x.

3. We can (and often do!) use different kind of brackets or parentheses in Liebniz notation; for instance, $\frac{d}{dx}[x^3]$, $\frac{d}{dx}(x^3)$, and $\frac{d}{dx}\{x^3\}$ all mean the same thing (and equal $3x^2$). ■

The Rules for Sums and Constant Multiples

We can now find the derivatives of more complicated functions, such as polynomials, using the following rules. If f and g are functions and if c is a constant, we saw in Section 1.2 how to obtain the **sum**, $\boldsymbol{f + g}$, **difference**, $\boldsymbol{f - g}$, and **constant multiple**, $\boldsymbol{cf}$.

Theorem 4.2 Derivatives of Sums, Differences, and Constant Multiples

If f and g are any two differentiable functions, and if c is any constant, then the sum, $f+g$, the difference, $f-g$, and the constant multiple, cf, are differentiable, and

$$[f \pm g]'(x) = f'(x) \pm g'(x) \qquad \text{Sum Rule}$$

$$[cf]'(x) = cf'(x). \qquad \text{Constant Multiple Rule}$$

In Words:

- The derivative of a sum is the sum of the derivatives, and the derivative of a difference is the difference of the derivatives.
- The derivative of c times a function is c times the derivative of the function.

Differential Notation:

$$\frac{d}{dx}[f(x) \pm g(x)] = \frac{d}{dx}f(x) \pm \frac{d}{dx}g(x)$$

$$\frac{d}{dx}[cf(x)] = c\frac{d}{dx}f(x)$$

Quick Examples

1. $\frac{d}{dx}(x^2 - x^4) = \frac{d}{dx}(x^2) - \frac{d}{dx}(x^4) = 2x - 4x^3$
2. $\frac{d}{dx}(7x^3) = 7\frac{d}{dx}(x^3) = 7(3x^2) = 21x^2$

   In other words, we multiply the coefficient (7) by the exponent (3), and then decrease the exponent by 1.
3. $\frac{d}{dx}(12x) = 12\frac{d}{dx}(x) = 12(1) = 12$

   In other words, the derivative of a constant times x is that constant.
4. $\frac{d}{dx}(-x^{0.5}) = \frac{d}{dx}[(-1)x^{0.5}] = (-1)\frac{d}{dx}(x^{0.5}) = (-1)(0.5)x^{-0.5}$
   $= -0.5x^{-0.5}$
5. $\frac{d}{dx}(12) = \frac{d}{dx}[12(1)] = 12\frac{d}{dx}(1) = 12(0) = 0.$

   In other words, the derivative of a constant is zero.
6. If my company earns twice as much (annual) revenue as yours and the derivative of your revenue function is the curve on the left, then the derivative of my revenue function is the curve on the right.

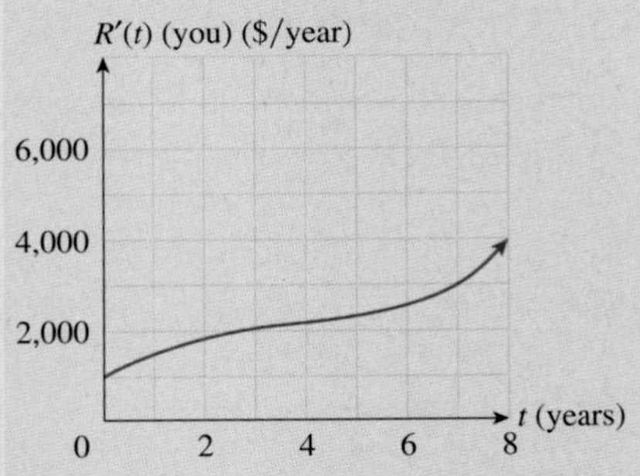

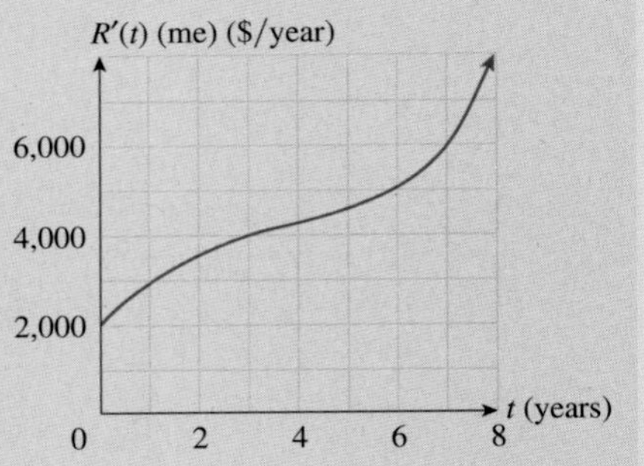

7. Suppose that a company's revenue R and cost C are changing with time. Then so is the profit, $P(t) = R(t) - C(t)$, and the rate of change of the profit is

$$P'(t) = R'(t) - C'(t).$$

In words: *The derivative of the profit is the derivative of revenue minus the derivative of cost.*

Proof of the Sum Rule

By the definition of the derivative of a function,

$$\begin{aligned}
\frac{d}{dx}[f(x) + g(x)] &= \lim_{h\to 0} \frac{[f(x+h) + g(x+h)] - [f(x) + g(x)]}{h} \\
&= \lim_{h\to 0} \frac{[f(x+h) - f(x)] + [g(x+h) - g(x)]}{h} \\
&= \lim_{h\to 0} \left[\frac{f(x+h) - f(x)}{h} + \frac{g(x+h) - g(x)}{h}\right] \\
&= \lim_{h\to 0} \frac{f(x+h) - f(x)}{h} + \lim_{h\to 0} \frac{g(x+h) - g(x)}{h} \\
&= \frac{d}{dx}[f(x)] + \frac{d}{dx}[g(x)].
\end{aligned}$$

The next-to-last step uses a property of limits: The limit of a sum is the sum of the limits. Think about why this should be true. The last step uses the definition of the derivative again (and the fact that the functions are differentiable).

The proof of the rule for constant multiples is similar.

EXAMPLE 2 Combining the Sum and Constant Multiple Rules, and Dealing with *x* in the Denominator

Find the derivatives of the following:

a. $f(x) = 3x^2 + 2x - 4$

b. $f(x) = \dfrac{2x}{3} - \dfrac{6}{x} + \dfrac{2}{3x^{0.2}} - \dfrac{x^4}{2}$

c. $f(x) = \dfrac{|x|}{4} + \dfrac{1}{2\sqrt{x}}$

Solution

a. $$\frac{d}{dx}(3x^2+2x-4) = \frac{d}{dx}(3x^2) + \frac{d}{dx}(2x-4)$$ Rule for sums

$$= \frac{d}{dx}(3x^2) + \frac{d}{dx}(2x) - \frac{d}{dx}(4)$$ Rule for differences

$$= 3(2x) + 2(1) - 0$$ See Quick Example 2.

$$= 6x + 2$$

b. Notice that f has x and powers of x in the denominator. We deal with these terms the same way we did in Example 1, by rewriting them in exponent form (that is, in the form constant × power of x; see Section 0.2 in the Precalculus Review):

$$f(x) = \frac{2x}{3} - \frac{6}{x} + \frac{2}{3x^{0.2}} - \frac{x^4}{2}$$ Rational form

$$= \frac{2}{3}x - 6x^{-1} + \frac{2}{3}x^{-0.2} - \frac{1}{2}x^4.$$ Exponent form

We are now ready to take the derivative:

$$f'(x) = \frac{2}{3}(1) - 6(-1)x^{-2} + \frac{2}{3}(-0.2)x^{-1.2} - \frac{1}{2}(4x^3)$$

$$= \frac{2}{3} + 6x^{-2} - \frac{0.4}{3}x^{-1.2} - 2x^3$$ Exponent form

$$= \frac{2}{3} + \frac{6}{x^2} - \frac{0.4}{3x^{1.2}} - 2x^3.$$ Rational form

c. Rewrite $f(x)$ using exponent form as follows:

$$f(x) = \frac{|x|}{4} + \frac{1}{2\sqrt{x}}$$ Rational form

$$= \frac{1}{4}|x| + \frac{1}{2}x^{-1/2}.$$ Exponent form

Now recall from the end of Section 3.6 that the derivative of $|x|$ is $\frac{|x|}{x}$. Thus,

$$f'(x) = \frac{1}{4}\frac{|x|}{x} + \frac{1}{2}\left(\frac{-1}{2}x^{-3/2}\right)$$

$$= \frac{|x|}{4x} - \frac{1}{4}x^{-3/2}$$ Simplify

$$= \frac{|x|}{4x} - \frac{1}{4x^{3/2}}.$$ Rational form

Notice that in Example 2(a) we had three terms in the expression for $f(x)$, not just two. By applying the rule for sums and differences twice, we saw that the derivative of a sum or difference of three terms is the sum or difference of the derivatives of the terms. (One of those terms had zero derivative, so the final answer had only two terms.) In fact, the derivative of a sum or difference of any number of terms is the sum or difference of the derivatives of the terms. Put another way, to take the derivative of a sum or difference of any number of terms, we take derivatives term by term.

Note Nothing forces us to use only x as the independent variable when taking derivatives (although it is traditional to give x preference). For instance, part (a) in Example 2 can be rewritten as

$$\frac{d}{dt}(3t^2 + 2t - 4) = 6t + 2. \qquad \frac{d}{dt} \text{ means "derivative with respect to } t\text{."}$$

or

$$\frac{d}{du}(3u^2 + 2u - 4) = 6u + 2. \qquad \frac{d}{du} \text{ means "derivative with respect to } u\text{."}$$

■

In the previous examples, we saw instances of the following important facts. (Think about these graphically to see why they must be true.)

The Derivative of a Constant Times x and the Derivative of a Constant

If c is any constant, then:

Rule	Quick Examples	
$\frac{d}{dx}(cx) = c$	$\frac{d}{dx}(6x) = 6$	$\frac{d}{dx}(-x) = -1$
$\frac{d}{dx}(c) = 0$	$\frac{d}{dx}(5) = 0$	$\frac{d}{dx}(\pi) = 0$

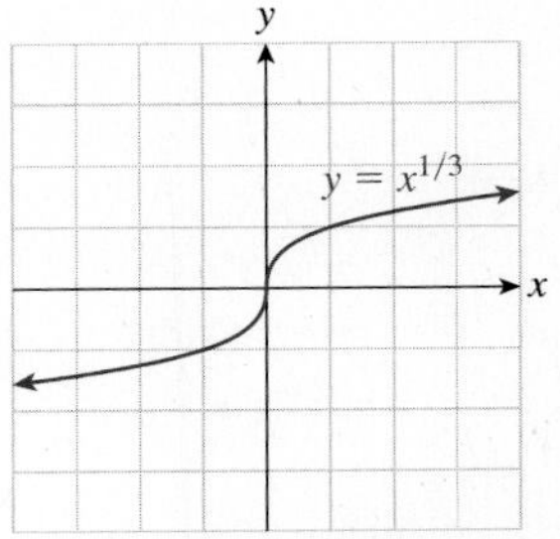

$f(x) = x^{1/3}$

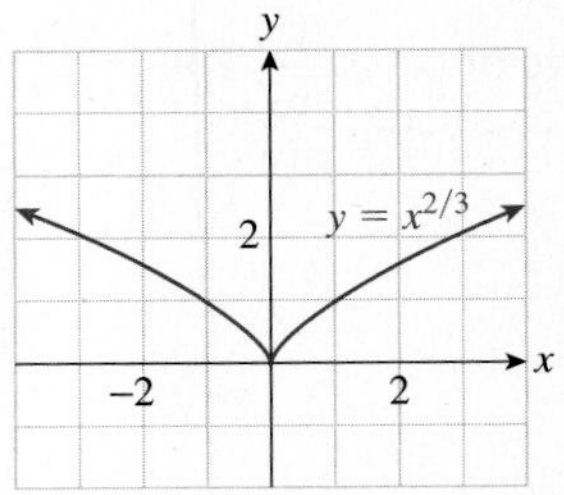

$g(x) = x^{2/3}$

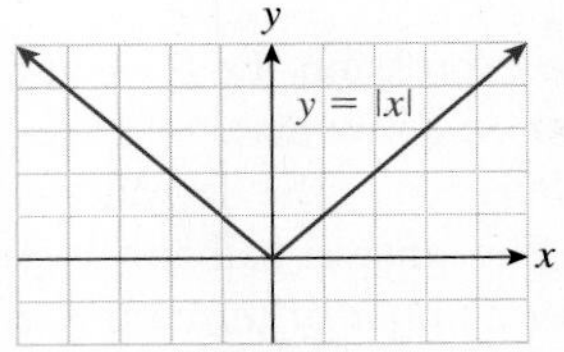

$h(x) = |x|$

Figure 1

In Section 3.5 we pointed out that the derivative of a function cannot exist at an endpoint of its domain, as the defining limit does not exist there (see the "Important Notes" after the definition of instantaneous rate of change). Thus, for instance, $f(x) = \sqrt{x}$ and $g(x) = x^{1/4}$ are not differentiable at the endpoint $x = 0$ of their domains. In Example 5 of Section 3.6 we saw that $h(x) = |x|$ also fails to be differentiable at $x = 0$, even though $x = 0$ is not an endpoint of its domain (the domain of h is the set of all real numbers). In the next example we see how to spot the non-differentiability at a point of this and other functions simply by looking at the formulas for their derivatives.

EXAMPLE 3 Functions Not Differentiable at a Point

Find the natural domains of the derivatives of $f(x) = x^{1/3}$, $g(x) = x^{2/3}$, and $h(x) = |x|$.

Solution Let's look at the derivatives of the three functions given:

$$f(x) = x^{1/3}, \text{ so } f'(x) = \frac{1}{3}x^{-2/3} = \frac{1}{3x^{2/3}}.$$

$$g(x) = x^{2/3}, \text{ so } g'(x) = \frac{2}{3}x^{-1/3} = \frac{2}{3x^{1/3}}.$$

$$h(x) = |x|, \text{ so } h'(x) = \frac{|x|}{x}.$$

The derivatives of all three functions are defined only for nonzero values of x, and their natural domains consist of all real numbers except 0. Thus, the derivatives f', g', and h' do not exist at $x = 0$. In other words, these functions are not differentiable at $x = 0$. If we look at Figure 1 we notice why these functions fail to be differentiable at $x = 0$: The graph of f has a vertical tangent line at 0. Because a vertical line

using Technology

If you try to graph the function $f(x) = x^{2/3}$ using the format

```
X^(2/3)
```

you may get only the right-hand portion of the graph of g in Figure 1 because graphing utilities are (often) not programmed to raise negative numbers to fractional exponents. (However, many will handle `X^(1/3)` correctly, as a special case they recognize.) To avoid this difficulty, you can take advantage of the identity

$$x^{2/3} = (x^2)^{1/3}$$

so that it is always a nonnegative number that is being raised to a fractional exponent. Thus, use the format

```
(X^2)^(1/3)
```

to obtain both portions of the graph.

has undefined slope, the derivative is undefined at that point. The graphs of g and h come to a sharp point at 0, where it is not meaningful to speak about the slope of the tangent line; therefore, the derivatives of g and h are not defined there. (In the case of g, where the sharp point is called a *cusp,* a vertical tangent line would seem appropriate, but as in the case of f, its slope is undefined.)

You can also detect this nondifferentiability by computing some difference quotients numerically, as we did for h in Section 3.6.

APPLICATION

EXAMPLE 4 Gold Price

You are a commodities trader and you monitor the price of gold on the spot market very closely during an active morning. Suppose you find that the price of an ounce of gold can be approximated by the function

$$G(t) = 5t^2 - 85t + 1{,}762 \quad (7.5 \le t \le 10.5),$$

where t is time in hours. (See Figure 2. $t = 8$ represents 8:00 am.)

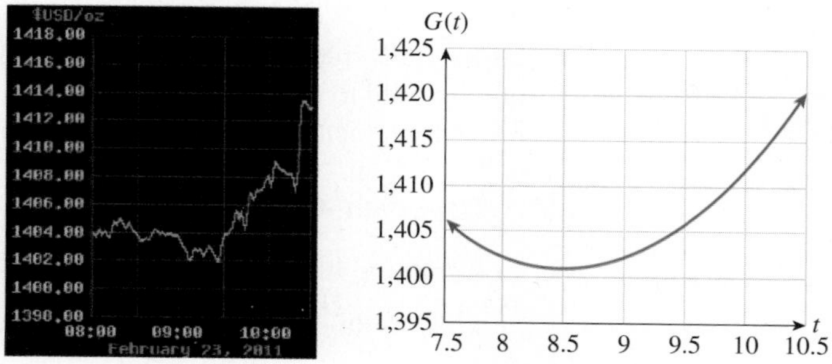

Source: www.kitco.com

$G(t) = 5t^2 - 85t + 1{,}762$

Figure 2

a. According to the model, how fast was the price of gold changing at 8:00 am?

b. According to the model, the price of gold

(A) increased at a faster and faster rate
(B) increased at a slower and slower rate
(C) decreased at a faster and faster rate
(D) decreased at a slower and slower rate

between 7:30 and 8:30 am.

Solution

a. Differentiating the given function with respect to t gives

$$G'(t) = 10t - 85.$$

Because 8:00 am corresponds to $t = 8$, we obtain

$$G'(8) = 10(8) - 85 = -5.$$

The units of the derivative are dollars per hour, so we conclude that, at 8:00 am, the price of gold was dropping at a rate of \$5 per hour.

b. From the graph, we can see that, between 7:30 and 8:30 am (the interval [7.5, 8.5]), the price of gold was decreasing. Also from the graph, we see that the slope of the tangent becomes less and less negative as t increases, so the price of gold is decreasing at a slower and slower rate (choice (D)).

We can also see this algebraically from the derivative, $G'(t) = 10t - 85$: For values of t less than 8.5, $G'(t)$ is negative; that is, the rate of change of G is negative, so the price of gold is decreasing. Further, as t increases, $G'(t)$ becomes less and less negative, so the price of gold is decreasing at a slower and slower rate, confirming that choice (D) is the correct one.

An Application to Limits: L'Hospital's Rule

The limits that caused us some trouble in Sections 3.1–3.3 are those of the form $\lim_{x\to a} f(x)$ in which substituting $x = a$ gave us an indeterminate form, such as

$$\lim_{x\to 2} \frac{x^3 - 8}{x - 2} \qquad \text{Substituting } x = 2 \text{ yields } \tfrac{0}{0}.$$

$$\lim_{x\to +\infty} \frac{2x - 4}{x - 1}. \qquad \text{Substituting } x = +\infty \text{ yields } \tfrac{\infty}{\infty}.$$

L'Hospital's rule* gives us an alternate way of computing limits such as these without the need to do any preliminary simplification. It also allows us to compute some limits for which algebraic simplification does not work.

* Guillaume François Antoine, Marquis de l'Hospital (1661–1704) wrote the first textbook on calculus, *Analyse des infiniment petits pour l'intelligence des lignes courbes,* in 1692. The rule now known as l'Hospital's rule appeared first in this book.

Theorem 4.3 L'Hospital's Rule

If f and g are two differentiable functions such that substituting $x = a$ in the expression $\dfrac{f(x)}{g(x)}$ gives the indeterminate form $\dfrac{0}{0}$ or $\dfrac{\infty}{\infty}$, then

$$\lim_{x\to a} \frac{f(x)}{g(x)} = \lim_{x\to a} \frac{f'(x)}{g'(x)}.$$

That is, we can replace $f(x)$ and $g(x)$ with their *derivatives* and try again to take the limit.

Quick Examples

1. Substituting $x = 2$ in $\dfrac{x^3 - 8}{x - 2}$ yields $\dfrac{0}{0}$. Therefore, l'Hospital's rule applies and

$$\lim_{x\to 2} \frac{x^3 - 8}{x - 2} = \lim_{x\to 2} \frac{3x^2}{1} = \frac{3(2)^2}{1} = 12.$$

2. Substituting $x = +\infty$ in $\dfrac{2x - 4}{x - 1}$ yields $\dfrac{\infty}{\infty}$. Therefore, l'Hospital's rule applies and

$$\lim_{x\to +\infty} \frac{2x - 4}{x - 1} = \lim_{x\to +\infty} \frac{2}{1} = 2.$$

The proof of l'Hospital's rule is beyond the scope of this text.†

† A proof of l'Hospital's rule can be found in most advanced calculus textbooks.

EXAMPLE 5 Applying L'Hospital's Rule

Check whether l'Hospital's rule applies to each of the following limits. If it does, use it to evaluate the limit. Otherwise, use some other method to evaluate the limit.

a. $\lim_{x\to 1} \dfrac{x^2 - 2x + 1}{4x^3 - 3x^2 - 6x + 5}$ **b.** $\lim_{x\to +\infty} \dfrac{2x^2 - 4x}{5x^3 - 3x + 5}$

c. $\lim_{x\to 1} \dfrac{x - 1}{x^3 - 3x^2 + 3x - 1}$ **d.** $\lim_{x\to 1} \dfrac{x}{x^3 - 3x^2 + 3x - 1}$

Solution

a. Setting $x = 1$ yields

$$\frac{1 - 2 + 1}{4 - 3 - 6 + 5} = \frac{0}{0}.$$

Therefore, l'Hospital's rule applies and

$$\lim_{x\to 1} \frac{x^2 - 2x + 1}{4x^3 - 3x^2 - 6x + 5} = \lim_{x\to 1} \frac{2x - 2}{12x^2 - 6x - 6}.$$

We are left with a closed-form function. However, we cannot substitute $x = 1$ to find the limit because the function $(2x - 2)/(12x^2 - 6x - 6)$ is still not defined at $x = 1$. In fact, if we set $x = 1$, we again get $0/0$. Thus, l'Hospital's rule applies again, and

$$\lim_{x\to 1} \frac{2x - 2}{12x^2 - 6x - 6} = \lim_{x\to 1} \frac{2}{24x - 6}.$$

Once again we have a closed-form function, but this time it is defined when $x = 1$, giving

$$\frac{2}{24 - 6} = \frac{1}{9}.$$

Thus,

$$\lim_{x\to 1} \frac{x^2 - 2x + 1}{4x^3 - 3x^2 - 6x + 5} = \frac{1}{9}.$$

b. Setting $x = +\infty$ yields $\dfrac{\infty}{\infty}$, so

$$\lim_{x\to +\infty} \frac{2x^2 - 4x}{5x^3 - 3x + 5} = \lim_{x\to +\infty} \frac{4x - 4}{15x^2 - 3}.$$

Setting $x = +\infty$ again yields $\dfrac{\infty}{\infty}$, so we can apply the rule again to obtain

$$\lim_{x\to +\infty} \frac{4x - 4}{15x^2 - 3} = \lim_{x\to +\infty} \frac{4}{30x}.$$

Note that we cannot apply l'Hospital's rule a third time because setting $x = +\infty$ yields the *determinate* form $4/\infty = 0$ (see the discussion at the end of Section 3.3). Thus, the limit is 0.

c. Setting $x = 1$ yields $0/0$ so, by l'Hospital's rule,

$$\lim_{x\to 1} \frac{x - 1}{x^3 - 3x^2 + 3x - 1} = \lim_{x\to 1} \frac{1}{3x^2 - 6x + 3}.$$

We are left with a closed-form function that is still not defined at $x = 1$. Further, l'Hospital's rule no longer applies because putting $x = 1$ yields the determinate form 1/0. To investigate this limit, we refer to the discussion at the end of Section 3.3 and find

$$\lim_{x\to 1} \frac{1}{3x^2 - 6x + 3} = \lim_{x\to 1} \frac{1}{3(x-1)^2} = +\infty. \qquad \frac{1}{0^+} = +\infty$$

d. Setting $x = 1$ in the expression yields the determinate form 1/0, so l'Hospital's rule does not apply here. Using the methods of Section 3.3 again, we find that the limit does not exist.

FAQs

Using the Rules and Recognizing when a Function Is Not Differentiable

Q: I would *like* to say that the derivative of $5x^2 - 8x + 4$ is just $10x - 8$ without having to go through all that stuff about derivatives of sums and constant multiples. Can I simply forget about all the rules and write down the answer?

A: We developed the rules for sums and constant multiples precisely for that reason: so that we could simply write down a derivative without having to think about it too hard. So, you are perfectly justified in simply writing down the derivative without going through the rules, but bear in mind that what you are really doing is applying the power rule, the rule for sums, and the rule for multiples over and over.

Q: Is there a way of telling from its formula whether a function f is not differentiable at a point?

A: Here are some indicators to look for in the formula for f:

- The absolute value of some expression; f may not be differentiable at points where that expression is zero.

  Example: $f(x) = 3x^2 - |x - 4|$ is not differentiable at $x = 4$.

- A fractional power smaller than 1 of some expression; f may not be differentiable at points where that expression is zero.

  Example: $f(x) = (x^2 - 16)^{2/3}$ is not differentiable at $x = \pm 4$.

4.1 EXERCISES

▼ more advanced ◆ challenging

T indicates exercises that should be solved using technology

*In Exercises 1–10, use the shortcut rules to **mentally** calculate the derivative of the given function.* HINT [See Examples 1 and 2.]

1. $f(x) = x^5$ **2.** $f(x) = x^4$

3. $f(x) = 2x^{-2}$ **4.** $f(x) = 3x^{-1}$

5. $f(x) = -x^{0.25}$ **6.** $f(x) = -x^{-0.5}$

7. $f(x) = 2x^4 + 3x^3 - 1$ **8.** $f(x) = -x^3 - 3x^2 - 1$

9. $f(x) = -x + \frac{1}{x} + 1$ **10.** $f(x) = \frac{1}{x} + \frac{1}{x^2}$

In Exercises 11–16, obtain the derivative dy/dx and state the rules that you use. HINT [See Example 2.]

11. $y = 10$ **12.** $y = x^3$

13. $y = x^2 + x$ **14.** $y = x - 5$

15. $y = 4x^3 + 2x - 1$ **16.** $y = 4x^{-1} - 2x - 10$

In Exercises 17–40, find the derivative of each function. HINT [See Examples 1 and 2.]

17. $f(x) = x^2 - 3x + 5$ **18.** $f(x) = 3x^3 - 2x^2 + x$

19. $f(x) = x + x^{0.5}$ **20.** $f(x) = x^{0.5} + 2x^{-0.5}$

21. $g(x) = x^{-2} - 3x^{-1} - 2$

22. $g(x) = 2x^{-1} + 4x^{-2}$

23. $g(x) = \frac{1}{x} - \frac{1}{x^2}$

24. $g(x) = \frac{1}{x^2} + \frac{1}{x^3}$

25. $h(x) = \frac{2}{x^{0.4}}$

26. $h(x) = -\frac{1}{2x^{0.2}}$

27. $h(x) = \frac{1}{x^2} + \frac{2}{x^3}$

28. $h(x) = \frac{2}{x} - \frac{2}{x^3} + \frac{1}{x^4}$

29. $r(x) = \frac{2}{3x} - \frac{1}{2x^{0.1}}$

30. $r(x) = \frac{4}{3x^2} + \frac{1}{x^{3.2}}$

31. $r(x) = \frac{2x}{3} - \frac{x^{0.1}}{2} + \frac{4}{3x^{1.1}} - 2$

32. $r(x) = \frac{4x^2}{3} + \frac{x^{3.2}}{6} - \frac{2}{3x^2} + 4$

33. $t(x) = |x| + \frac{1}{x}$

34. $t(x) = 3|x| - \sqrt{x}$

35. $s(x) = \sqrt{x} + \frac{1}{\sqrt{x}}$

36. $s(x) = x + \frac{7}{\sqrt{x}}$

HINT [For Exercises 37–38, first expand the given function.]

37. ▼ $s(x) = x\left(x^2 - \frac{1}{x}\right)$

38. ▼ $s(x) = x^{-1}\left(x - \frac{2}{x}\right)$

HINT [For Exercises 39–40, first rewrite the given function.]

39. ▼ $t(x) = \frac{x^2 - 2x^3}{x}$

40. ▼ $t(x) = \frac{2x + x^2}{x}$

In Exercises 41–46, evaluate the given expression.

41. $\frac{d}{dx}(2x^{1.3} - x^{-1.2})$

42. $\frac{d}{dx}(2x^{4.3} + x^{0.6})$

43. ▼ $\frac{d}{dx}[1.2(x - |x|)]$

44. ▼ $\frac{d}{dx}[4(x^2 + 3|x|)]$

45. ▼ $\frac{d}{dt}(at^3 - 4at)$; (a constant)

46. ▼ $\frac{d}{dt}(at^2 + bt + c)$; ($a$, b, c constant)

In Exercises 47–52, find the indicated derivative.

47. $y = \frac{x^{10.3}}{2} + 99x^{-1}$; $\frac{dy}{dx}$

48. $y = \frac{x^{1.2}}{3} - \frac{x^{0.9}}{2}$; $\frac{dy}{dx}$

49. $s = 2.3 + \frac{2.1}{t^{1.1}} - \frac{t^{0.6}}{2}$; $\frac{ds}{dt}$

50. $s = \frac{2}{t^{1.1}} + t^{-1.2}$; $\frac{ds}{dt}$

51. ▼ $V = \frac{4}{3}\pi r^3$; $\frac{dV}{dr}$

52. ▼ $A = 4\pi r^2$; $\frac{dA}{dr}$

In Exercises 53–58, find the slope of the tangent to the graph of the given function at the indicated point. HINT [Recall that the slope of the tangent to the graph of f at $x = a$ is $f'(a)$.]

53. $f(x) = x^3$; $(-1, -1)$

54. $g(x) = x^4$; $(-2, 16)$

55. $f(x) = 1 - 2x$; $(2, -3)$

56. $f(x) = \frac{x}{3} - 1$; $(-3, -2)$

57. $g(t) = \frac{1}{t^5}$; $(1, 1)$

58. $s(t) = \frac{1}{t^3}$; $\left(-2, -\frac{1}{8}\right)$

In Exercises 59–64, find the equation of the tangent line to the graph of the given function at the point with the indicated x-coordinate. In each case, sketch the curve together with the appropriate tangent line.

59. ▼ $f(x) = x^3$; $x = -1$

60. ▼ $f(x) = x^2$; $x = 0$

61. ▼ $f(x) = x + \frac{1}{x}$; $x = 2$

62. ▼ $f(x) = \frac{1}{x^2}$; $x = 1$

63. ▼ $f(x) = \sqrt{x}$; $x = 4$

64. ▼ $f(x) = 2x + 4$; $x = -1$

In Exercises 65–70, find all values of x (if any) where the tangent line to the graph of the given equation is horizontal. HINT [The tangent line is horizontal when its slope is zero.]

65. ▼ $y = 2x^2 + 3x - 1$

66. ▼ $y = -3x^2 - x$

67. ▼ $y = 2x + 8$

68. ▼ $y = -x + 1$

69. ▼ $y = x + \frac{1}{x}$

70. ▼ $y = x - \sqrt{x}$

71. ◆ Write out the proof that $\frac{d}{dx}(x^4) = 4x^3$.

72. ◆ Write out the proof that $\frac{d}{dx}(x^5) = 5x^4$.

In Exercises 73–76, determine whether f is differentiable at the given point. If f′(a) exists, give its value. HINT [See Example 3.]

73. $f(x) = x - x^{1/3}$ **a.** $a = 1$ **b.** $a = 0$

74. $f(x) = 2x + x^{4/3}$ **a.** $a = 8$ **b.** $a = 0$

75. $f(x) = x^{5/4} - 1$ **a.** $a = 16$ **b.** $a = 0$

76. $f(x) = x^{1/5} + 5$ **a.** $a = 1$ **b.** $a = 0$

In Exercises 77–88 say whether l'Hospital's rule applies. If is does, use it to evaluate the given limit. If not, use some other method.

77. $\lim_{x \to 1} \frac{x^2 - 2x + 1}{x^2 - x}$

78. $\lim_{x \to -1} \frac{x^2 + 3x + 2}{x^2 + x}$

79. $\lim_{x \to 2} \frac{x^3 - 8}{x - 2}$

80. $\lim_{x \to 0} \frac{x^3 + 8}{x^2 + 3x + 2}$

81. $\lim_{x \to 1} \frac{x^2 + 3x + 2}{x^2 + x}$

82. $\lim_{x \to -2} \frac{x^3 + 8}{x^2 + 3x + 2}$

83. $\lim_{x \to -\infty} \frac{3x^2 + 10x - 1}{2x^2 - 5x}$

84. $\lim_{x \to -\infty} \frac{6x^2 + 5x + 100}{3x^2 - 9}$

85. $\lim_{x \to -\infty} \frac{10x^2 + 300x + 1}{5x + 2}$

86. $\lim_{x \to -\infty} \frac{2x^4 + 20x^3}{1{,}000x^3 + 6}$

87. $\lim_{x \to -\infty} \frac{x^3 - 100}{2x^2 + 500}$

88. $\lim_{x \to -\infty} \frac{x^2 + 30x}{2x^6 + 10x}$

APPLICATIONS

89. ***Crude Oil Prices*** The price per barrel of crude oil in constant 2008 dollars can be approximated by

$$P(t) = 0.45t^2 - 12t + 105 \text{ dollars} \quad (0 \le t \le 28),$$

where t is time in years since the start of 1980.[1] Find $P'(t)$ and $P'(20)$. What does the answer tell you about the price of crude oil? HINT [See Example 2.]

90. ***Median Home Prices*** The median home price in the United States over the period 2003–2011 can be approximated by

$$P(t) = -5t^2 + 75t - 30 \text{ thousand dollars} \quad (3 \le t \le 11),$$

where t is time in years since the start of 2000.[2] Find $P'(t)$ and $P'(6)$. What does the answer tell you about home prices? HINT [See Example 2.]

91. ***Food versus Education*** The following equation shows the approximate relationship between the percentage y of total personal consumption spent on food and the corresponding percentage x spent on education.[3]

$$y = \frac{35}{x^{0.35}} \text{ percentage points} \quad (6.5 \le x \le 17.5).$$

According to the model, spending on food is decreasing at a rate of _____ percentage points per one percentage point increase in spending on education when 10% of total consumption is spent on education. (Answer should be rounded to two significant digits.) HINT [See Example 2(b).]

92. ***Food versus Recreation*** The following equation shows the approximate relationship between the percentage y of total personal consumption spent on food and the corresponding percentage x spent on recreation.[4]

$$y = \frac{33}{x^{0.63}} \text{ percentage points} \quad (6.5 \le x \le 17.5).$$

According to the model, spending on food is decreasing at a rate of _____ percentage points per one percentage point increase in spending on recreation when 3% of total consumption is spent on recreation. (Answer should be rounded to two significant digits.) HINT [See Example 2(b).]

93. ***Velocity*** If a stone is dropped from a height of 400 feet, its height s after t seconds is given by $s(t) = 400 - 16t^2$, with s in feet.

a. Compute $s'(t)$ and hence find its velocity at times $t = 0, 1, 2, 3$, and 4 seconds.

b. When does it reach the ground, and how fast is it traveling when it hits the ground? HINT [It reaches the ground when $s(t) = 0$.]

94. ***Velocity*** If a stone is thrown down at 120 ft/s from a height of 1,000 feet, its height s after t seconds is given by $s(t) = 1{,}000 - 120t - 16t^2$, with s in feet.

a. Compute $s'(t)$ and hence find its velocity at times $t = 0$, 1, 2, 3, and 4 seconds.

b. When does it reach the ground, and how fast is it traveling when it hits the ground? HINT [It reaches the ground when $s(t) = 0$.]

95. ***GE Net Income 2005–2009*** The annual net income of General Electric for the period 2005–2009 could be approximated by[5]

$$P(t) = -2.0t^2 + 6.6t + 16 \text{ billion dollars} \quad (0 \le t \le 4),$$

where t is time in years since 2005.

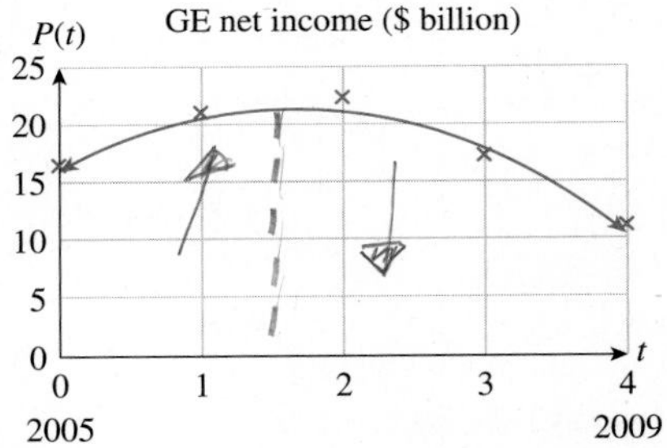

a. Compute $P'(t)$. How fast was GE's annual net income changing in 2008? (Be careful to give correct units of measurement.)

b. According to the model, GE's annual net income

(A) increased at a faster and faster rate
(B) increased at a slower and slower rate
(C) decreased at a faster and faster rate
(D) decreased at a slower and slower rate

during the first year and a half shown (the interval [0, 1.5]). Justify your answer in two ways: geometrically, reasoning entirely from the graph; and algebraically, reasoning from the derivative of P. HINT [See Example 4.]

96. ***GE Net Income 2007–2011*** The annual net income of General Electric for the period 2007–2011 could be approximated by[6]

$$P(t) = 3t^2 - 24t + 59 \text{ billion dollars} \quad (2 \le t \le 6),$$

where t is time in years since 2005.

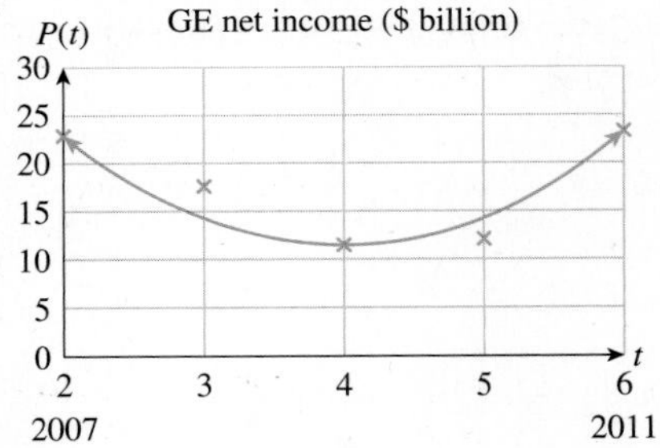

[1] Source for data: www.inflationdata.com.

[2] Source for data: www.zillow.com.

[3] Model based on historical and projected data from 1908–2010. Sources: Historical data, Bureau of Economic Analysis; projected data, Bureau of Labor Statistics/*New York Times*, December 1, 2003, p. C2.

[4] *Ibid.*

[5] Source for data: www.wikinvest.com.

[6] 2011 value estimated. Source: *Ibid.*

a. Compute $P'(t)$. How fast was GE's annual net income changing in 2010? (Be careful to give correct units of measurement.)

b. According to the model, GE's annual net income

(A) increased at a faster and faster rate
(B) increased at a slower and slower rate
(C) decreased at a faster and faster rate
(D) decreased at a slower and slower rate

during the first two years shown (the interval [2, 4]). Justify your answer in two ways: geometrically, reasoning entirely from the graph; and algebraically, reasoning from the derivative of P. HINT [See Example 4.]

97. ***Ecology*** Increasing numbers of manatees ("sea sirens") have been killed by boats off the Florida coast. The following graph shows the relationship between the number of boats registered in Florida and the number of manatees killed each year.

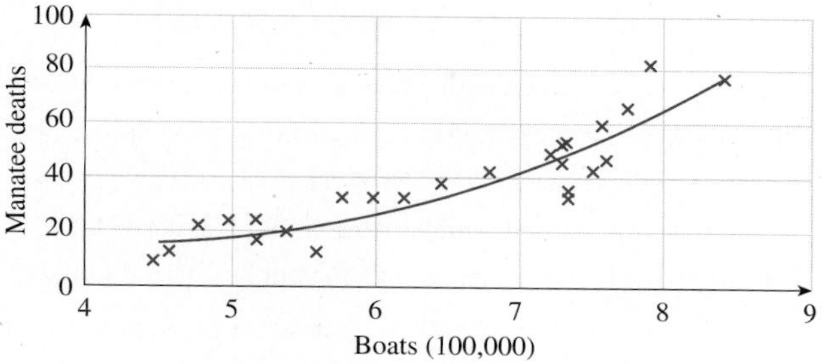

The regression curve shown is given by

$$f(x) = 3.55x^2 - 30.2x + 81 \quad (4.5 \le x \le 8.5),$$

where x is the number of boats (hundreds of thousands) registered in Florida in a particular year and $f(x)$ is the number of manatees killed by boats in Florida that year.[7]

a. Find $f'(x)$, and use your formula to compute $f'(8)$, stating its units of measurement. What does the answer say about manatee deaths?

b. Is $f'(x)$ increasing or decreasing with increasing x? Interpret the answer. HINT [See Example 4.]

98. ***SAT Scores by Income*** The following graph shows U.S. math SAT scores as a function of parents' income level.[8]

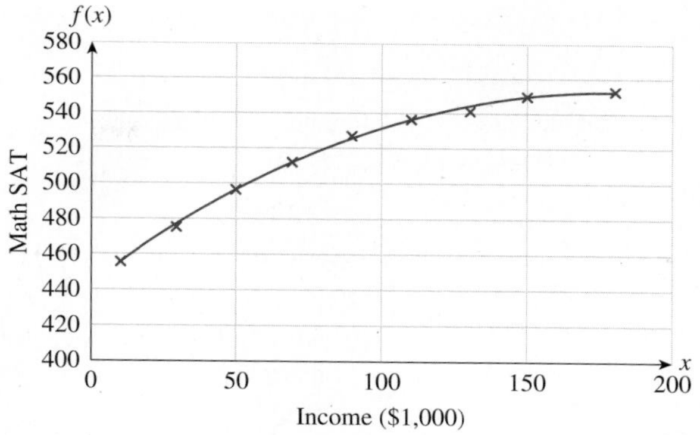

The regression curve shown is given by

$$f(x) = -0.0034x^2 + 1.2x + 444 \quad (10 \le x \le 180),$$

where $f(x)$ is the average math SAT score of a student whose parents earn x thousand dollars per year.

a. Find $f'(x)$, and use your formula to compute $f'(100)$, stating its units of measurement. What does the answer say about math SAT scores?

b. Does $f'(x)$ increase or decrease with increasing x? What does your answer say about math SAT scores? HINT [See Example 4.]

99. ▼ ***Market Share: Smart Phones*** The following graph shows the approximate market shares, in percentage points, of **Apple's** *iPhone* and **Google's** *Android*-based smart phones from January 2009 to May 2010 (t is time in months, and $t = 0$ represents January, 2009):[9]

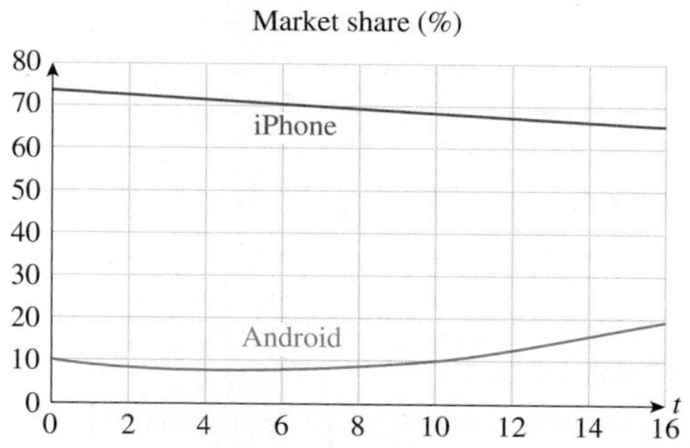

Let $I(t)$ be the iPhone market share at time t, and let $A(t)$ be the Android market share at time t.

a. What does the function $I - A$ measure? What does its derivative $(I - A)'$ measure?

b. The graph suggests that, on the interval [6, 16], $I - A$ is

(A) increasing.
(B) decreasing.
(C) increasing, then decreasing.
(D) decreasing, then increasing.

[7] Regression model is based on data from 1976 to 2000. Sources for data: Florida Department of Highway Safety & Motor Vehicles, Florida Marine Institute/*New York Times*, February 12, 2002, p. F4.

[8] Regression model is based on 2009 data. Source: College Board/*New York Times* http://economix.blogs.nytimes.com.

[9] Source for data: Quantcast www.quantcast.com.

c. The two market shares are approximated by
iPhone: $I(t) = -0.5t + 73$
Android: $A(t) = 0.1t^2 - t + 10$.
Compute $(I - A)'$, stating its units of measurement. On the interval [0, 16], $(I - A)'$ is
(A) positive.
(B) negative.
(C) positive, then negative.
(D) negative, then positive.
How is this behavior reflected in the graph, and what does it mean about the market shares of iPhone and Android?

d. Compute $(I - A)'(4)$. Interpret your answer.

100. ▼ ***Market Share: Smart Phones*** The following graph shows the approximate market shares, in percentage points, of **Research In Motion's** *BlackBerry* smartphones and **Google's** *Android*-based smartphones from July 2009 to May 2010 (t is time in months, and $t = 0$ represents January 2009):[10]

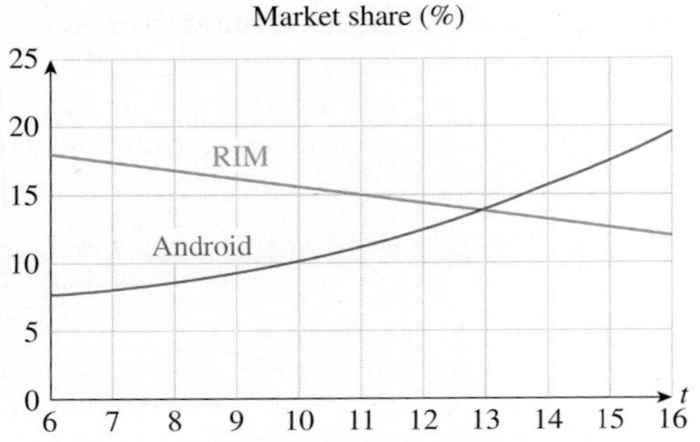

Let $B(t)$ be the BlackBerry market share at time t, and let $A(t)$ be the Android market share at time t.

a. What does the function $B - A$ measure? What does its derivative $(B - A)'$ measure?

b. The graph suggests that, on the interval [6, 16], $B - A$ is
(A) increasing.
(B) decreasing.
(C) increasing, then decreasing.
(D) decreasing, then increasing.

c. The two market shares are approximated by
BlackBerry: $B(t) = -0.6t + 21.6$
Android: $A(t) = 0.1t^2 - t + 10$.
Compute $(B - A)'$, stating its units of measurement. On the interval [6, 16], $(B - A)'$ is
(A) positive.
(B) negative.
(C) positive, then negative.
(D) negative, then positive.
How is this reflected in the graph, and what does it mean about the market shares of BlackBerry and Android?

d. Compute $(B - A)'(10)$. Interpret your answer.

[10]Source for data: Quantcast www.quantcast.com.

COMMUNICATION AND REASONING EXERCISES

101. What instructions would you give to a fellow student who wanted to accurately graph the tangent line to the curve $y = 3x^2$ at the point $(-1, 3)$?

102. What instructions would you give to a fellow student who wanted to accurately graph a line at right angles to the curve $y = 4/x$ at the point where $x = 0.5$?

103. Consider $f(x) = x^2$ and $g(x) = 2x^2$. How do the slopes of the tangent lines of f and g at the same x compare?

104. Consider $f(x) = x^3$ and $g(x) = x^3 + 3$. How do the slopes of the tangent lines of f and g compare?

105. Suppose $g(x) = -f(x)$. How do the derivatives of f and g compare?

106. Suppose $g(x) = f(x) - 50$. How do the derivatives of f and g compare?

107. Following is an excerpt from your best friend's graded homework:

$$3x^4 + 11x^5 = 12x^3 + 55x^4. \quad \text{✗ } \textit{WRONG} \quad -8$$

Why was it marked wrong? How would you correct it?

108. Following is an excerpt from your own graded homework:

$$x^n = nx^{n-1}. \quad \text{✗ } \textit{WRONG} \quad -10$$

Why was it marked wrong? How would you correct it?

109. Following is another excerpt from your best friend's graded homework:

$$y = \frac{1}{2x} = 2x^{-1}, \text{ so } \frac{dy}{dx} = -2x^{-2}. \quad \text{✗ } \textit{WRONG} \quad -5$$

Why was it marked wrong? How would you correct it?

110. Following is an excerpt from your second best friend's graded homework:

$$f(x) = \frac{3}{4x^2};\ f'(x) = \frac{3}{8x}. \quad \text{✗ } \textit{WRONG} \quad -10$$

Why was it marked wrong? How would you correct it?

111. Following is an excerpt from your worst enemy's graded homework:

$$f(x) = 4x^2;\ f'(x) = (0)(2x) = 0. \quad \text{✗ } \textit{WRONG} \quad -6$$

Why was it marked wrong? How would you correct it?

112. Following is an excerpt from your second worst enemy's graded homework:

$$f(x) = \frac{3}{4x};\ f'(x) = \frac{0}{4} = 0. \quad \text{✗ } \textit{WRONG} \quad -10$$

Why was it marked wrong? How would you correct it?

113. One of the questions in your last calculus test was "**Question 1(a)** Give the definition of the derivative of a function f." Following is your answer and the grade you received:

$$nx^{n-1}. \quad \text{✗ } \textit{WRONG} \quad -10$$

Why was it marked wrong? What is the correct answer?

114. ▼ How would you respond to an acquaintance who says, "I finally understand what the derivative is: It is nx^{n-1}! Why weren't we taught that in the first place instead of the difficult way using limits?"

115. ▼ Sketch the graph of a function whose derivative is undefined at exactly two points but that has a tangent line at all but one point.

116. ▼ Sketch the graph of a function that has a tangent line at each of its points, but whose derivative is undefined at exactly two points.

4.2 A First Application: Marginal Analysis

In Chapter 1, we considered linear *cost functions* of the form $C(x) = mx + b$, where C is the total cost, x is the number of items, and m and b are constants. The slope m is the *marginal cost.* It measures the *cost of one more item.* Notice that the derivative of $C(x) = mx + b$ is $C'(x) = m$. In other words, for a linear cost function, *the marginal cost is the derivative of the cost function.*

In general, we make the following definition.

Marginal Cost

Recall from Section 1.2 that a **cost function** C specifies the total cost as a function of the number of items x, so that $C(x)$ is the total cost of x items. The **marginal cost function** is the derivative C' of the cost function C. Thus, $C'(x)$ measures the rate of change of cost with respect to x.

Units

The units of marginal cost are units of cost (dollars, say) per item.

Interpretation

*We interpret $C'(x)$ as the approximate cost of one more item.**

* See Example 1.

Quick Example

If $C(x) = 400x + 1{,}000$ dollars, then the marginal cost function is $C'(x) = \$400$ per item (a constant).

EXAMPLE 1 Marginal Cost

Suppose that the cost in dollars to manufacture portable music players is given by

$$C(x) = 150{,}000 + 20x - 0.0001x^2$$

where x is the number of music players manufactured.† Find the marginal cost function C' and use it to estimate the cost of manufacturing the 50,001st music player.

† The term $0.0001x^2$ may reflect a cost saving for high levels of production, such as a bulk discount in the cost of electronic components.

Solution Since

$$C(x) = 150{,}000 + 20x - 0.0001x^2$$

the marginal cost function is

$$C'(x) = 20 - 0.0002x.$$

The units of $C'(x)$ are units of C (dollars) per unit of x (music players). Thus, $C'(x)$ is measured in dollars per music player.

The cost of the 50,001st music player is the amount by which the total cost would rise if we increased production from 50,000 music players to 50,001. Thus, we need to know the rate at which the total cost rises as we increase production. This rate of change is measured by the derivative, or marginal cost, which we just computed. At $x = 50{,}000$, we get

$$C'(50{,}000) = 20 - 0.0002(50{,}000) = \$10 \text{ per music player.}$$

In other words, we estimate that the 50,001st music player will cost approximately $10.

➡ Before we go on... In Example 1, the marginal cost is really only an *approximation* to the cost of the 50,001st music player:

$$\begin{aligned} C'(50{,}000) &\approx \frac{C(50{,}001) - C(50{,}000)}{1} && \text{Set } h = 1 \text{ in the definition of the derivative.} \\ &= C(50{,}001) - C(50{,}000) \\ &= \text{cost of the 50,001st music player} \end{aligned}$$

The exact cost of the 50,001st music player is

$$\begin{aligned} C(50{,}001) - C(50{,}000) &= [150{,}000 + 20(50{,}001) - 0.0001(50{,}001)^2] \\ &\quad - [150{,}000 + 20(50{,}000) - 0.0001(50{,}000)^2] \\ &= \$9.9999 \end{aligned}$$

So, the marginal cost is a good approximation to the actual cost.

Graphically, we are using the tangent line to approximate the cost function near a production level of 50,000. Figure 3 shows the graph of the cost function together with the tangent line at $x = 50{,}000$. Notice that the tangent line is essentially indistinguishable from the graph of the function for some distance on either side of 50,000.

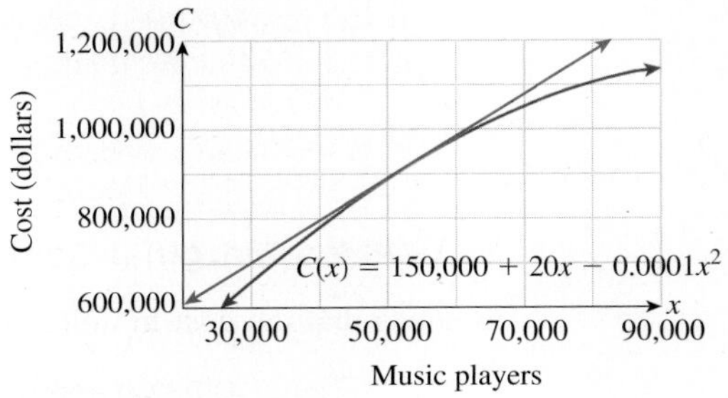

Figure 3 ■

Notes

1. In general, the difference quotient $[C(x + h) - C(x)]/h$ gives the **average cost per item** to produce h more items at a current production level of x items. (Why?)
2. Notice that $C'(x)$ is much easier to calculate than $[C(x + h) - C(x)]/h$. (Try it.) ■

We can extend the idea of marginal cost to include other functions we discussed in Section 1.2, like revenue and profit:

Marginal Revenue and Profit

Recall that a **revenue** or **profit function** specifies the total revenue R or profit P as a function of the number of items x. The derivatives, R' and P', of these functions are called the **marginal revenue** and **marginal profit** functions. They measure the rate of change of revenue and profit with respect to the number of items.

Units

The units of marginal revenue and profit are the same as those of marginal cost: dollars (or euros, pesos, etc.) per item.

Interpretation

We interpret $R'(x)$ and $P'(x)$ as the approximate revenue and profit from the sale of one more item.

EXAMPLE 2 Marginal Revenue and Profit

You operate an *iPod* refurbishing service (a typical refurbished iPod might have a custom color case with blinking lights and a personalized logo). The cost to refurbish x iPods in a month is calculated to be

$$C(x) = 0.25x^2 + 40x + 1{,}000 \text{ dollars.}$$

You charge customers \$80 per iPod for the work.

a. Calculate the marginal revenue and profit functions. Interpret the results.

b. Compute the revenue and profit, and also the marginal revenue and profit, if you have refurbished 20 units this month. Interpret the results.

c. For which value of x is the marginal profit zero? Interpret your answer.

Solution

a. We first calculate the revenue and profit functions:

$$R(x) = 80x \qquad \text{Revenue} = \text{Price} \times \text{Quantity}$$

$$P(x) = R(x) - C(x) \qquad \text{Profit} = \text{Revenue} - \text{Cost}$$

$$= 80x - (0.25x^2 + 40x + 1{,}000)$$

$$P(x) = -0.25x^2 + 40x - 1{,}000.$$

The marginal revenue and profit functions are then the derivatives:

$$\text{Marginal revenue} = R'(x) = 80$$

$$\text{Marginal profit} = P'(x) = -0.5x + 40.$$

Interpretation: $R'(x)$ gives the approximate revenue from the refurbishing of one more item, and $P'(x)$ gives the approximate profit from the refurbishing of one more item. Thus, if x iPods have been refurbished in a month, you will earn a revenue of \$80 and make a profit of approximately $\$(-0.5x + 40)$ if you refurbish one more that month.

Notice that the marginal revenue is a constant, so you earn the same revenue (\$80) for each iPod you refurbish. However, the marginal profit, $\$(-0.5x + 40)$, decreases as x increases, so your additional profit is about 50¢ less for each additional iPod you refurbish.

b. From part (a), the revenue, profit, marginal revenue, and marginal profit functions are

$$R(x) = 80x$$
$$P(x) = -0.25x^2 + 40x - 1{,}000$$
$$R'(x) = 80$$
$$P'(x) = -0.5x + 40$$

Because you have refurbished $x = 20$ iPods this month, $x = 20$, so

$$R(20) = 80(20) = \$1{,}600$$ Total revenue from 20 iPods

$$P(20) = -0.25(20)^2 + 40(20) - 1{,}000 = -\$300$$ Total profit from 20 iPods

$$R'(20) = \$80 \text{ per unit}$$ Approximate revenue from the 21st iPod

$$P'(20) = -0.5(20) + 40 = \$30 \text{ per unit}$$ Approximate profit from the 21st iPod

Interpretation: If you refurbish 20 iPods in a month, you will earn a total revenue of \$160 and a profit of –\$300 (indicating a loss of \$300). Refurbishing one more iPod that month will earn you an additional revenue of \$80 and an additional profit of about \$30.

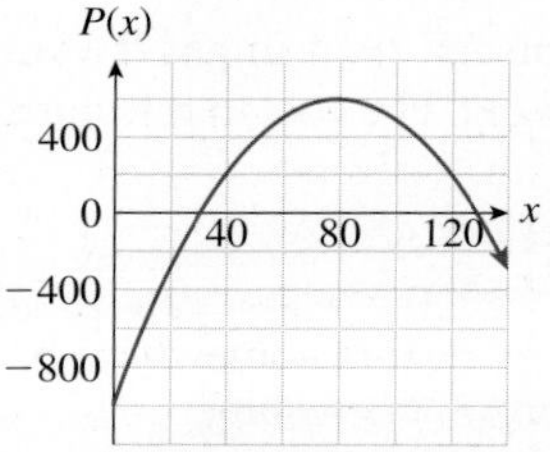

$P(x) = -0.25x^2 + 40x - 1{,}000$

Figure 4

c. The marginal profit is zero when $P'(x) = 0$:

$$-0.5x + 40 = 0$$
$$x = \frac{40}{0.5} = 80 \text{ iPods}$$

Thus, if you refurbish 80 iPods in a month, refurbishing one more will get you (approximately) zero additional profit. To understand this further, let us take a look at the graph of the profit function, shown in Figure 4. Notice that the graph is a parabola (the profit function is quadratic) with vertex at the point $x = 80$, where $P'(x) = 0$, so the profit is a maximum at this value of x.

➡ **Before we go on...** In general, setting $P'(x) = 0$ and solving for x will always give the exact values of x for which the profit peaks as in Figure 4, assuming there is such a value. We recommend that you graph the profit function to check whether the profit is indeed a maximum at such a point. ■

EXAMPLE 3 Marginal Product

A consultant determines that *Precision Manufacturers'* annual profit (in dollars) is given by

$$P(n) = -200{,}000 + 400{,}000n - 4{,}600n^2 - 10n^3 \qquad (10 \le n \le 50),$$

where n is the number of assembly-line workers it employs.

a. Compute $P'(n)$. $P'(n)$ is called the **marginal product** at the employment level of n assembly-line workers. What are its units?

b. Calculate $P(20)$ and $P'(20)$, and interpret the results.

c. Precision Manufacturers currently employs 20 assembly-line workers and is considering laying off some of them. What advice would you give the company's management?

Solution

a. Taking the derivative gives

$$P'(n) = 400{,}000 - 9{,}200n - 30n^2.$$

The units of $P'(n)$ are profit (in dollars) per worker.

b. Substituting into the formula for $P(n)$, we get

$$P(20) = -200{,}000 + 400{,}000(20) - 4{,}600(20)^2 - 10(20)^3 = \$5{,}880{,}000.$$

Thus, Precision Manufacturers will make an annual profit of \$5,880,000 if it employs 20 assembly-line workers. On the other hand,

$$P'(20) = 400{,}000 - 9{,}200(20) - 30(20)^2 = \$204{,}000/\text{worker}.$$

Thus, at an employment level of 20 assembly-line workers, annual profit is increasing at a rate of \$204,000 per additional worker. In other words, if the company were to employ one more assembly-line worker, its annual profit would increase by approximately \$204,000.

c. Because the marginal product is positive, profits will increase if the company increases the number of workers and will decrease if it decreases the number of workers, so your advice would be to hire additional assembly-line workers. Downsizing the assembly-line workforce would reduce its annual profits.

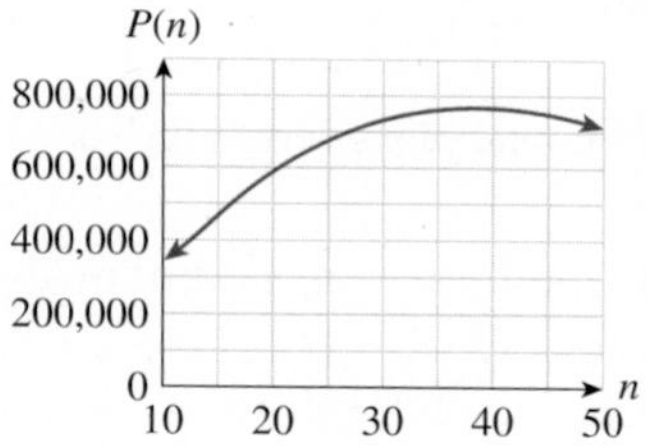

Figure 5

Before we go on... In Example 3, it would be interesting for Precision Manufacturers to ascertain how many additional assembly-line workers it should hire to obtain the *maximum* annual profit. Taking our cue from Example 2, we suspect that such a value of n would correspond to a point where $P'(n) = 0$. Figure 5 shows the graph of P, and on it we see that the highest point of the graph is indeed a point where the tangent line is horizontal; that is, $P'(n) = 0$, and occurs somewhere between $n = 35$ and 40. To compute this value of n more accurately, set $P'(n) = 0$ and solve for n:

$$P'(n) = 400{,}000 - 9{,}200n - 30n^2 = 0 \quad \text{or} \quad 40{,}000 - 920n - 3n^2 = 0.$$

We can now obtain n using the quadratic formula:

$$n = \frac{-b \pm \sqrt{b^2 - 4ac}}{2a} = \frac{920 \pm \sqrt{920^2 - 4(-3)(40{,}000)}}{2(-3)}$$

$$= \frac{920 \pm \sqrt{1{,}326{,}400}}{-6} \approx -345.3 \text{ or } 38.6.$$

The only meaningful solution is the positive one, $n \approx 38.6$ workers, and we conclude that the company should employ between 38 and 39 assembly-line workers for a maximum profit. To see which gives the larger profit, 38 or 39, we check:

$$P(38) = \$7{,}808{,}880$$

while

$$P(39) = \$7{,}810{,}210.$$

This tells us that the company should employ 39 assembly-line workers for a maximum profit. Thus, instead of laying off any of its 20 assembly-line workers, the company should hire 19 additional assembly-line workers for a total of 39. ■

Average Cost

EXAMPLE 4 Average Cost

Suppose the cost in dollars to manufacture portable music players is given by

$$C(x) = 150{,}000 + 20x - 0.0001x^2$$

where x is the number of music players manufactured. (This is the cost equation we saw in Example 1.)

a. Find the average cost per music player if 50,000 music players are manufactured.

b. Find a formula for the average cost per music player if x music players are manufactured. This function of x is called the **average cost function, $\bar{C}(x)$.**

Solution

a. The total cost of manufacturing 50,000 music players is given by

$$\begin{aligned} C(50{,}000) &= 150{,}000 + 20(50{,}000) - 0.0001(50{,}000)^2 \\ &= \$900{,}000. \end{aligned}$$

Because 50,000 music players cost a total of \$900,000 to manufacture, the average cost of manufacturing one music player is this total cost divided by 50,000:

$$\bar{C}(50{,}000) = \frac{900{,}000}{50{,}000} = \$18.00 \text{ per music player.}$$

Thus, if 50,000 music players are manufactured, each music player costs the manufacturer an average of \$18.00 to manufacture.

b. If we replace 50,000 by x, we get the general formula for the average cost of manufacturing x music players:

$$\begin{aligned} \bar{C}(x) &= \frac{C(x)}{x} \\ &= \frac{1}{x}(150{,}000 + 20x - 0.0001x^2) \\ &= \frac{150{,}000}{x} + 20 - 0.0001x. \end{aligned}$$ Average cost function

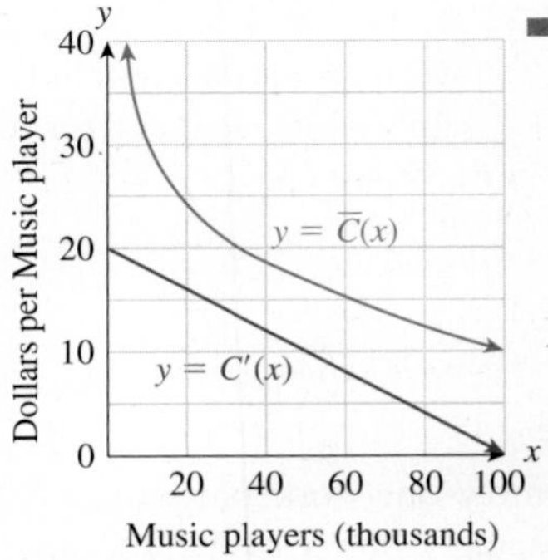

Figure 6

➡ **Before we go on...** Average cost and marginal cost convey different but related information. The average cost $\bar{C}(50{,}000) = \$18$ that we calculated in Example 4 is the cost per item of manufacturing the first 50,000 music players, whereas the marginal cost $C'(50{,}000) = \$10$ that we calculated in Example 1 gives the (approximate) cost of manufacturing the *next* music player. Thus, according to our calculations, the first 50,000 music players cost an average of \$18 to manufacture, but it costs only about \$10 to manufacture the next one. Note that the marginal cost at a production level of 50,000 music players is lower than the average cost. This means that the average cost to manufacture CDs is going down with increasing volume. (Think about why.)

Figure 6 shows the graphs of average and marginal cost. Notice how the decreasing marginal cost seems to pull the average cost down with it. ■

To summarize:

Average Cost

Given a cost function C, the **average cost** of the first x items is given by

$$\bar{C}(x) = \frac{C(x)}{x}.$$

The average cost is distinct from the **marginal cost** $C'(x)$, which tells us the approximate cost of the *next* item.

Quick Example

For the cost function $C(x) = 20x + 100$ dollars

Marginal Cost $= C'(x) = \$20$ per additional item.

Average Cost $= \bar{C}(x) = \dfrac{C(x)}{x} = \dfrac{20x + 100}{x} = \$(20 + 100/x)$ per item.

4.2 EXERCISES

▼ more advanced ◆ challenging

T indicates exercises that should be solved using technology

In Exercises 1–4, for each cost function, find the marginal cost at the given production level x, and state the units of measurement. (All costs are in dollars.) HINT [See Example 1.]

1. $C(x) = 10{,}000 + 5x - 0.0001x^2$; $x = 1{,}000$
2. $C(x) = 20{,}000 + 7x - 0.00005x^2$; $x = 10{,}000$
3. $C(x) = 15{,}000 + 100x + \dfrac{1{,}000}{x}$; $x = 100$
4. $C(x) = 20{,}000 + 50x + \dfrac{10{,}000}{x}$; $x = 100$

In Exercises 5 and 6, find the marginal cost, marginal revenue, and marginal profit functions, and find all values of x for which the marginal profit is zero. Interpret your answer. HINT [See Example 2.]

5. $C(x) = 4x$; $R(x) = 8x - 0.001x^2$
6. $C(x) = 5x^2$; $R(x) = x^3 + 7x + 10$
7. ▼ A certain cost function has the following graph:

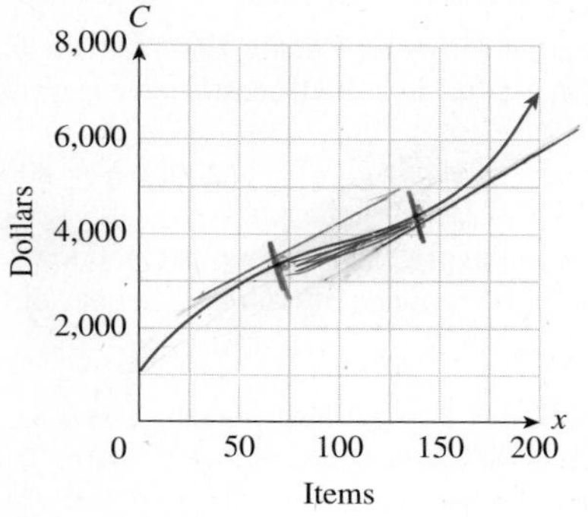

a. The associated marginal cost is
   (A) increasing, then decreasing.
   (B) decreasing, then increasing.
   (C) always increasing.
   (D) always decreasing.

b. The marginal cost is least at approximately
   (A) $x = 0$. (B) $x = 50$. (C) $x = 100$. (D) $x = 150$.

c. The cost of 50 items is
   (A) approximately \$20, and increasing at a rate of about \$3,000 per item.
   (B) approximately \$0.50, and increasing at a rate of about \$3,000 per item.
   (C) approximately \$3,000, and increasing at a rate of about \$20 per item.
   (D) approximately \$3,000, and increasing at a rate of about \$0.50 per item.

8. ▼ A certain cost function has the following graph:

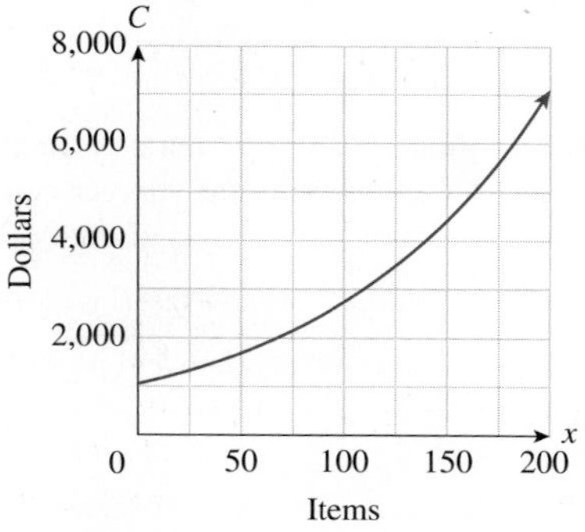

a. The associated marginal cost is

(A) increasing, then decreasing.
(B) decreasing, then increasing.
(C) always increasing.
(D) always decreasing.

b. When $x = 100$, the marginal cost is

(A) greater than the average cost.
(B) less than the average cost.
(C) approximately equal to the average cost.

c. The cost of 150 items is

(A) approximately \$4,400, and increasing at a rate of about \$40 per item.
(B) approximately \$40, and increasing at a rate of about \$4,400 per item.
(C) approximately \$4,400, and increasing at a rate of about \$1 per item.
(D) approximately \$1, and increasing at a rate of about \$4,400 per item.

APPLICATIONS

9. ***Advertising Costs*** The cost, in thousands of dollars, of airing x television commercials during a Super Bowl game is given by[11]

$$C(x) = 150 + 2{,}500x - 0.02x^2.$$

a. Find the marginal cost function and use it to estimate how fast the cost is increasing when $x = 4$. Compare this with the exact cost of airing the fifth commercial. HINT [See Example 1.]

b. Find the average cost function $\bar{C}$, and evaluate $\bar{C}(4)$. What does the answer tell you? HINT [See Example 4.]

10. ***Marginal Cost and Average Cost*** The cost of producing x teddy bears per day at the *Cuddly Companion Co.* is calculated by the company's marketing staff to be given by the formula

$$C(x) = 100 + 40x - 0.001x^2.$$

a. Find the marginal cost function and use it to estimate how fast the cost is going up at a production level of 100 teddy bears. Compare this with the exact cost of producing the 101st teddy bear. HINT [See Example 1.]

b. Find the average cost function $\bar{C}$, and evaluate $\bar{C}(100)$. What does the answer tell you? HINT [See Example 4.]

11. ***Marginal Revenue and Profit*** Your college newspaper, *The Collegiate Investigator*, sells for 90¢ per copy. The cost of producing x copies of an edition is given by

$$C(x) = 70 + 0.10x + 0.001x^2 \text{ dollars.}$$

a. Calculate the marginal revenue and profit functions. HINT [See Example 2.]

b. Compute the revenue and profit, and also the marginal revenue and profit, if you have produced and sold 500 copies of the latest edition. Interpret the results.

c. For which value of x is the marginal profit zero? Interpret your answer.

12. ***Marginal Revenue and Profit*** The Audubon Society at Enormous State University (ESU) is planning its annual fund-raising "Eatathon." The society will charge students \$1.10 per serving of pasta. The society estimates that the total cost of producing x servings of pasta at the event will be

$$C(x) = 350 + 0.10x + 0.002x^2 \text{ dollars.}$$

a. Calculate the marginal revenue and profit functions. HINT [See Example 2.]

b. Compute the revenue and profit, and also the marginal revenue and profit, if you have produced and sold 200 servings of pasta. Interpret the results.

c. For which value of x is the marginal profit zero? Interpret your answer.

13. ***Marginal Profit*** Suppose $P(x)$ represents the profit in dollars on the sale of x DVDs. If $P(1{,}000) = 3{,}000$ and $P'(1{,}000) = -3$, what do these values tell you about the profit?

14. ***Marginal Loss*** An automobile retailer calculates that its loss in dollars on the sale of *Type M* cars is given by $L(50) = 5{,}000$ and $L'(50) = -200$, where $L(x)$ represents the loss on the sale of x Type M cars. What do these values tell you about losses?

15. ***Marginal Profit*** Your monthly profit (in dollars) from selling magazines is given by

$$P = 5x + \sqrt{x}$$

where x is the number of magazines you sell in a month. If you are currently selling 50 magazines per month, find your profit and your marginal profit. Interpret your answers.

16. ***Marginal Profit*** Your monthly profit (in dollars) from your newspaper route is given by

$$P = 2n - \sqrt{n}$$

where n is the number of subscribers on your route. If you currently have 100 subscribers, find your profit and your marginal profit. Interpret your answers.

17. ▼ ***Marginal Revenue: Pricing Tuna*** Assume that the demand equation for tuna in a small coastal town is given by

$$p = \frac{20{,}000}{q^{1.5}} \quad (200 \le q \le 800),$$

where p is the price (in dollars) per pound of tuna, and q is the number of pounds of tuna that can be sold at the price p in one month.[12]

---

[11] The cost of a 30-second ad during the 2010 Super Bowl game was about \$2.5 million. This explains the coefficient of x in the cost function. Source: http://en.wikipedia.org/wiki/Super_Bowl_advertising.

[12] Notice that here we have specified p as a function of q, and not the other way around as we did in Section 1.2. Economists frequently specify demand curves this way.

a. Calculate the price that the town's fishery should charge for tuna in order to produce a demand of 400 pounds of tuna per month.

b. Calculate the monthly revenue R as a function of the number of pounds of tuna q.

c. Calculate the revenue and marginal revenue (derivative of the revenue with respect to q) at a demand level of 400 pounds per month, and interpret the results.

d. If the town fishery's monthly tuna catch amounted to 400 pounds of tuna, and the price is at the level in part (a), would you recommend that the fishery raise or lower the price of tuna in order to increase its revenue?

18. ▼ ***Marginal Revenue: Pricing Tuna*** Repeat Exercise 17, assuming a demand equation of

$$p = \frac{60}{q^{0.5}} \qquad (200 \le q \le 800).$$

19. ***Marginal Product*** A car wash firm calculates that its daily profit (in dollars) depends on the number n of workers it employs according to the formula

$$P = 400n - 0.5n^2.$$

Calculate the marginal product at an employment level of 50 workers, and interpret the result. HINT [See Example 3.]

20. ***Marginal Product*** Repeat the preceding exercise using the formula

$$P = -100n + 25n^2 - 0.005n^4.$$

HINT [See Example 3.]

21. ***Average and Marginal Cost*** The daily cost to manufacture generic trinkets for gullible tourists is given by the cost function

$$C(x) = -0.001x^2 + 0.3x + 500 \text{ dollars}$$

where x is the number of trinkets.

a. As x increases, the marginal cost
(A) increases. **(B)** decreases. **(C)** increases, then decreases. **(D)** decreases, then increases.

b. As x increases, the average cost
(A) increases. **(B)** decreases. **(C)** increases, then decreases. **(D)** decreases, then increases.

c. The marginal cost is
(A) greater than **(B)** equal to **(C)** less than
the average cost when $x = 100$. HINT [See Example 4.]

22. ***Average and Marginal Cost*** Repeat Exercise 21, using the following cost function for imitation oil paintings (x is the number of "oil paintings" manufactured):

$$C(x) = 0.1x^2 - 3.5x + 500 \text{ dollars.}$$

HINT [See Example 4.]

23. ***Advertising Cost*** Your company is planning to air a number of television commercials during the **ABC Television Network's** presentation of the Academy Awards. ABC is charging your company \$1.6 million per 30-second spot.[13] Additional fixed costs (development and personnel costs) amount to \$500,000, and the network has agreed to provide a discount of $\$10{,}000\sqrt{x}$ for x television spots.

a. Write down the cost function C, marginal cost function C', and average cost function $\bar{C}$.

b. Compute $C'(3)$ and $\bar{C}(3)$. (Round all answers to three significant digits.) Use these two answers to say whether the average cost is increasing or decreasing as x increases.

24. ***Housing Costs*** The cost C of building a house is related to the number k of carpenters used and the number x of electricians used by the formula[14]

$$C = 15{,}000 + 50k^2 + 60x^2.$$

a. Assuming that 10 carpenters are currently being used, find the cost function C, marginal cost function C', and average cost function $\bar{C}$, all as functions of x.

b. Use the functions you obtained in part (a) to compute $C'(15)$ and $\bar{C}(15)$. Use these two answers to say whether the average cost is increasing or decreasing as the number of electricians increases.

25. ▼ ***Emission Control*** The cost of controlling emissions at a firm rises rapidly as the amount of emissions reduced increases. Here is a possible model:

$$C(q) = 4{,}000 + 100q^2$$

where q is the reduction in emissions (in pounds of pollutant per day) and C is the daily cost (in dollars) of this reduction.

a. If a firm is currently reducing its emissions by 10 pounds each day, what is the marginal cost of reducing emissions further?

b. Government clean-air subsidies to the firm are based on the formula

$$S(q) = 500q$$

where q is again the reduction in emissions (in pounds per day) and S is the subsidy (in dollars). At what reduction level does the marginal cost surpass the marginal subsidy?

c. Calculate the net cost function, $N(q) = C(q) - S(q)$, given the cost function and subsidy above, and find the value of q that gives the lowest net cost. What is this lowest net cost? Compare your answer to that for part (b) and comment on what you find.

26. ▼ ***Taxation Schemes*** In order to raise revenues during the recent recession, the governor of your state proposed the following taxation formula:

$$T(i) = 0.001i^{0.5},$$

[13] ABC charged an average of \$1.6 million for a 30-second spot during the 2005 Academy Awards presentation. Source: CNN/Reuters, www.cnn.com, February 9, 2005.

[14] Based on an exercise in *Introduction to Mathematical Economics* by A. L. Ostrosky, Jr., and J. V. Koch (Waveland Press, Prospect Heights, Illinois, 1979).

where i represents total annual income earned by an individual in dollars and $T(i)$ is the income tax rate as a percentage of total annual income. (Thus, for example, an income of \$50,000 per year would be taxed at about 22%, while an income of double that amount would be taxed at about 32%.)[15]

a. Calculate the after-tax (net) income $N(i)$ an individual can expect to earn as a function of income i.

b. Calculate an individual's marginal after-tax income at income levels of \$100,000 and \$500,000.

c. At what income does an individual's marginal after-tax income become negative? What is the after-tax income at that level, and what happens at higher income levels?

d. What do you suspect is the most anyone can earn after taxes? (See NOTE at the bottom of this page.)

27. ▼ ***Fuel Economy*** Your Porsche's gas mileage (in miles per gallon) is given as a function $M(x)$ of speed x in miles per hour. It is found that

$$M'(x) = \frac{3{,}600x^{-2} - 1}{(3{,}600x^{-1} + x)^2}.$$

Estimate $M'(10)$, $M'(60)$, and $M'(70)$. What do the answers tell you about your car?

28. ▼ ***Marginal Revenue*** The estimated marginal revenue for sales of ESU soccer team T-shirts is given by

$$R'(p) = \frac{(8 - 2p)e^{-p^2+8p}}{10{,}000{,}000}$$

where p is the price (in dollars) that the soccer players charge for each shirt. Estimate $R'(3)$, $R'(4)$, and $R'(5)$. What do the answers tell you?

29. ◆ ***Marginal Cost*** *(from the GRE Economics Test)* In a multiplant firm in which the different plants have different and continuous cost schedules, if costs of production for a given output level are to be minimized, which of the following is essential?

(A) Marginal costs must equal marginal revenue.
(B) Average variable costs must be the same in all plants.
(C) Marginal costs must be the same in all plants.
(D) Total costs must be the same in all plants.
(E) Output per worker per hour must be the same in all plants.

30. ◆ ***Study Time*** *(from the GRE economics test)* A student has a fixed number of hours to devote to study and is certain of the relationship between hours of study and the final grade for each course. Grades are given on a numerical scale (0 to 100), and each course is counted equally in computing the grade average. In order to maximize his or her grade average, the student should allocate these hours to different courses so that

(A) the grade in each course is the same.
(B) the marginal product of an hour's study (in terms of final grade) in each course is zero.
(C) the marginal product of an hour's study (in terms of final grade) in each course is equal, although not necessarily equal to zero.
(D) the average product of an hour's study (in terms of final grade) in each course is equal.
(E) the number of hours spent in study for each course is equal.

31. ◆ ***Marginal Product*** *(from the GRE Economics Test)* Assume that the marginal product of an additional senior professor is 50% higher than the marginal product of an additional junior professor and that junior professors are paid one half the amount that senior professors receive. With a fixed overall budget, a university that wishes to maximize its quantity of output from professors should do which of the following?

(A) Hire equal numbers of senior professors and junior professors.
(B) Hire more senior professors and junior professors.
(C) Hire more senior professors and discharge junior professors.
(D) Discharge senior professors and hire more junior professors.
(E) Discharge all senior professors and half of the junior professors.

32. ◆ ***Marginal Product (based on a question from the GRE Economics Test)*** Assume that the marginal product of an additional senior professor is twice the marginal product of an additional junior professor and that junior professors are paid two thirds the amount that senior professors receive. With a fixed overall budget, a university that wishes to maximize its quantity of output from professors should do which of the following?

(A) Hire equal numbers of senior professors and junior professors.
(B) Hire more senior professors and junior professors.
(C) Hire more senior professors and discharge junior professors.
(D) Discharge senior professors and hire more junior professors.
(E) Discharge all senior professors and half of the junior professors.

COMMUNICATION AND REASONING EXERCISES

33. The marginal cost of producing the 1,001st item is

(A) equal to
(B) approximately equal to
(C) always slightly greater than
(D) always slightly less than

the actual cost of producing the 1,001st item.

34. For the cost function $C(x) = mx + b$, the marginal cost of producing the 1,001st item is,

(A) equal to
(B) approximately equal to
(C) always slightly greater than
(D) always slightly less than

the actual cost of producing the 1,001st item.

[15] This model has the following interesting feature: An income of \$1 million per year would be taxed at 100%, leaving the individual penniless!

35. What is a cost function? Carefully explain the difference between *average cost* and *marginal cost* in terms of **(a)** their mathematical definition, **(b)** graphs, and **(c)** interpretation.

36. The cost function for your grand piano manufacturing plant has the property that $\bar{C}(1{,}000) = \$3{,}000$ per unit and $C'(1{,}000) = \$2{,}500$ per unit. Will the average cost increase or decrease if your company manufactures a slightly larger number of pianos? Explain your reasoning.

37. Give an example of a cost function for which the marginal cost function is the same as the average cost function.

38. Give an example of a cost function for which the marginal cost function is always less than the average cost function.

39. If the average cost to manufacture one grand piano increases as the production level increases, which is greater, the marginal cost or the average cost?

40. If your analysis of a manufacturing company yielded positive marginal profit but negative profit at the company's current production levels, what would you advise the company to do?

41. ▼ If the marginal cost is decreasing, is the average cost necessarily decreasing? Explain.

42. ▼ If the average cost is decreasing, is the marginal cost necessarily decreasing? Explain.

43. ◆ If a company's marginal average cost is zero at the current production level, positive for a slightly higher production level, and negative for a slightly lower production level, what should you advise the company to do?

44. ◆ The **acceleration** of cost is defined as the derivative of the marginal cost function: that is, the derivative of the derivative—or *second derivative*—of the cost function. What are the units of acceleration of cost, and how does one interpret this measure?

4.3 The Product and Quotient Rules

We know how to find the derivatives of functions that are sums of powers, such as polynomials. In general, if a function is a sum or difference of functions whose derivatives we know, then we know how to find its derivative. But what about *products and quotients* of functions whose derivatives we know? For instance, how do we calculate the derivative of something like $x^2/(x+1)$? The derivative of $x^2/(x+1)$ is not, as one might suspect, $2x/1 = 2x$. That calculation is based on an assumption that the derivative of a quotient is the quotient of the derivatives. But it is easy to see that this assumption is false: For instance, the derivative of $1/x$ is not $0/1 = 0$, but $-1/x^2$. Similarly, the derivative of a product is not the product of the derivatives: For instance, the derivative of $x = 1 \cdot x$ is not $0 \cdot 1 = 0$, but 1.

To identify the correct method of computing the derivatives of products and quotients, let's look at a simple example. We know that the daily revenue resulting from the sale of q items per day at a price of p dollars per item is given by the product, $R = pq$ dollars. Suppose you are currently selling wall posters on campus. At this time your daily sales are 50 posters, and sales are increasing at a rate of 4 per day. Furthermore, you are currently charging \$10 per poster, and you are also raising the price at a rate of \$2 per day. Let's use this information to estimate how fast your daily revenue is increasing. In other words, let us estimate the rate of change, dR/dt, of the revenue R.

There are two contributions to the rate of change of daily revenue: the increase in daily sales and the increase in the unit price. We have

$$\frac{dR}{dt} \text{ due to increasing price: } \quad \$2 \text{ per day} \times 50 \text{ posters} = \$100 \text{ per day}$$

$$\frac{dR}{dt} \text{ due to increasing sales: } \quad \$10 \text{ per poster} \times 4 \text{ posters per day} = \$40 \text{ per day.}$$

Thus, we estimate the daily revenue to be increasing at a rate of \$100 + \$40 = \$140 per day. Let us translate what we have said into symbols:

$$\frac{dR}{dt} \text{ due to increasing price: } \quad \frac{dp}{dt} \times q$$

$$\frac{dR}{dt} \text{ due to increasing sales: } \quad p \times \frac{dq}{dt}.$$

Thus, the rate of change of revenue is given by

$$\frac{dR}{dt} = \frac{dp}{dt}q + p\frac{dq}{dt}.$$

Because $R = pq$, we have discovered the following rule for differentiating a product:

$$\frac{d}{dt}(pq) = \frac{dp}{dt}q + p\frac{dq}{dt}.$$

The derivative of a product is the derivative of the first times the second, plus the first times the derivative of the second.

This rule and a similar rule for differentiating quotients are given next, and also a discussion of how these results are proved rigorously.

Product Rule

If f and g are differentiable functions of x, then so is their product fg, and

$$\frac{d}{dx}[f(x)g(x)] = f'(x)g(x) + f(x)g'(x).$$

Product Rule in Words

The derivative of a product is the derivative of the first times the second, plus the first times the derivative of the second.

Quick Example

Let $f(x) = x^2$ and $g(x) = 3x - 1$. Because f and g are both differentiable functions of x, so is their product fg, and its derivative is

$$\frac{d}{dx}[x^2(3x-1)] = \underset{\uparrow\ \text{Derivative of first}}{2x} \cdot \underset{\uparrow\ \text{Second}}{(3x-1)} + \underset{\uparrow\ \text{First}}{x^2} \cdot \underset{\uparrow\ \text{Derivative of second}}{(3)}.$$

Quotient Rule

If f and g are differentiable functions of x, then so is their quotient f/g, and

$$\frac{d}{dx}\left(\frac{f(x)}{g(x)}\right) = \frac{f'(x)g(x) - f(x)g'(x)}{[g(x)]^2}.$$

provided $g(x) \neq 0$.*

Quotient Rule in Words

The derivative of a quotient is the derivative of the top times the bottom, minus the top times the derivative of the bottom, all over the bottom squared.

* If $g(x)$ is zero, then the quotient $f(x)/g(x)$ is not defined in the first place.

Quick Example

Let $f(x) = x^3$ and $g(x) = x^2 - 1$. Because f and g are both differentiable functions of x, so is their quotient f/g, and its derivative is

$$\frac{d}{dx}\left(\frac{x^3}{x^2-1}\right) = \frac{\overset{\text{Derivative of top}}{\downarrow}\; 3x^2 \overset{\text{Bottom}}{\downarrow}(x^2-1) - \overset{\text{Top}}{\downarrow} x^3 \cdot \overset{\text{Derivative of bottom}}{\downarrow} 2x}{\underset{\text{Bottom squared}}{(x^2-1)^2}},$$

provided $x \neq 1$ or -1.

Notes

1. Don't try to remember the rules by the symbols we have used, but remember them in words. (The slogans are easy to remember, even if the terms are not precise.)
2. One more time: *The derivative of a product is* NOT *the product of the derivatives, and the derivative of a quotient is* NOT *the quotient of the derivatives.* To find the derivative of a product, you must use the product rule, and to find the derivative of a quotient, you must use the quotient rule.* ■

* Leibniz made this mistake at first, too, so you would be in good company if you forgot to use the product or quotient rule.

Q: *Wait a minute! The expression $2x^3$ is a product, and we already know that its derivative is $6x^2$. Where did we use the product rule?*

A: To differentiate functions such as $2x^3$, we have used the rule from Section 4.1:

The derivative of c times a function is c times the derivative of the function.

However, the product rule gives us the same result:

$\frac{d}{dx}(2x^3) = \underset{\text{Derivative of first}}{(0)}\underset{\text{Second}}{(x^3)} + \underset{\text{First}}{(2)}\underset{\text{Derivative of second}}{(3x^2)} = 6x^2$	Product rule
$\frac{d}{dx}(2x^3) = (2)(3x^2) = 6x^2$	Derivative of a constant times a function

We do not recommend that you use the product rule to differentiate functions such as $2x^3$; continue to use the simpler rule when one of the factors is a constant.

Derivation of the Product Rule

Before we look at more examples of using the product and quotient rules, let's see why the product rule is true. To calculate the derivative of the product $f(x)g(x)$ of two differentiable functions, we go back to the definition of the derivative:

$$\frac{d}{dx}[f(x)g(x)] = \lim_{h\to 0} \frac{f(x+h)g(x+h) - f(x)g(x)}{h}.$$

We now rewrite this expression so that we can evaluate the limit: Notice that the numerator reflects a simultaneous change in f [from $f(x)$ to $f(x+h)$] and g [from

$g(x)$ to $g(x+h)$]. To separate the two effects, we add and subtract a quantity in the numerator that reflects a change in only one of the functions:

$$\frac{d}{dx}[f(x)g(x)] = \lim_{h\to 0}\frac{f(x+h)g(x+h) - f(x)g(x)}{h}$$

$$= \lim_{h\to 0}\frac{f(x+h)g(x+h) - f(x)g(x+h) + f(x)g(x+h) - f(x)g(x)}{h}$$ We subtracted and added the quantity* $f(x)g(x+h)$.

$$= \lim_{h\to 0}\frac{[f(x+h) - f(x)]\,g(x+h) + f(x)[g(x+h) - g(x)]}{h}$$ Common factors

$$= \lim_{h\to 0}\left(\frac{f(x+h)-f(x)}{h}\right)g(x+h) + \lim_{h\to 0} f(x)\left(\frac{g(x+h)-g(x)}{h}\right)$$ Limit of sum

$$= \lim_{h\to 0}\left(\frac{f(x+h)-f(x)}{h}\right)\lim_{h\to 0} g(x+h) + \lim_{h\to 0} f(x)\lim_{h\to 0}\left(\frac{g(x+h)-g(x)}{h}\right)$$ Limit of product

Now we already know the following four limits:

$$\lim_{h\to 0}\frac{f(x+h)-f(x)}{h} = f'(x)$$ Definition of derivative of f; f is differentiable.

$$\lim_{h\to 0}\frac{g(x+h)-g(x)}{h} = g'(x)$$ Definition of derivative of g; g is differentiable.

$$\lim_{h\to 0} g(x+h) = g(x)$$ If g is differentiable, it must be continuous.†

$$\lim_{h\to 0} f(x) = f(x)$$ Limit of a constant

Putting these limits into the one we're calculating, we get

$$\frac{d}{dx}[f(x)g(x)] = f'(x)g(x) + f(x)g'(x)$$

which is the product rule.

* Adding an appropriate form of zero is an age-old mathematical ploy.

† For a proof of the fact that, if g is differentiable, it must be continuous, go to the Website and follow the path

Everything for Calculus
→ Chapter 4
→ Continuity and Differentiability

EXAMPLE 1 Using the Product Rule

Compute the following derivatives.

a. $\frac{d}{dx}[(x^{3.2}+1)(1-x)]$ Simplify the answer.

b. $\frac{d}{dx}[(x+1)(x^2+1)(x^3+1)]$ Do not expand the answer.

c. $\frac{d}{dx}\left[\frac{x|x|}{2}\right]$

Website
www.WanerMath.com
The quotient rule can be proved in a very similar way. Go to the Website and follow the path

Everything for Calculus
→ Chapter 4
→ Proof of Quotient Rule

Solution

a. We can do the calculation in two ways.

Using the Product Rule:

(Derivative of first ↓ $(3.2x^{2.2})$; Second ↓ $(1-x)$; First ↓ $(x^{3.2}+1)$; Derivative of second ↓ (-1))

$$\frac{d}{dx}[(x^{3.2}+1)(1-x)] = (3.2x^{2.2})(1-x) + (x^{3.2}+1)(-1)$$

$$= 3.2x^{2.2} - 3.2x^{3.2} - x^{3.2} - 1$$ Expand the answer.

$$= -4.2x^{3.2} + 3.2x^{2.2} - 1$$

Not Using the Product Rule: First, expand the given expression.

$$(x^{3.2}+1)(1-x) = -x^{4.2}+x^{3.2}-x+1$$

Thus,

$$\frac{d}{dx}[(x^{3.2}+1)(1-x)] = \frac{d}{dx}(-x^{4.2}+x^{3.2}-x+1)$$
$$= -4.2x^{3.2}+3.2x^{2.2}-1$$

In this example the product rule saves us little or no work, but in later sections we shall see examples that can be done in no other way. Learn how to use the product rule now!

b. Here we have a product of *three* functions, not just two. We can find the derivative by using the product rule twice:

$$\frac{d}{dx}[(x+1)(x^2+1)(x^3+1)]$$
$$= \frac{d}{dx}(x+1)\cdot[(x^2+1)(x^3+1)] + (x+1)\cdot\frac{d}{dx}[(x^2+1)(x^3+1)]$$
$$= (1)(x^2+1)(x^3+1) + (x+1)[(2x)(x^3+1)+(x^2+1)(3x^2)]$$
$$= (1)(x^2+1)(x^3+1) + (x+1)(2x)(x^3+1) + (x+1)(x^2+1)(3x^2)$$

We can see here a more general product rule:

$$(fgh)' = f'gh + fg'h + fgh'$$

Notice that every factor has a chance to contribute to the rate of change of the product. There are similar formulas for products of four or more functions.

c. First write $\frac{x|x|}{2}$ as $\frac{1}{2}x|x|$.

$$\frac{d}{dx}\left[\frac{1}{2}x|x|\right] = \frac{1}{2}\frac{d}{dx}[x|x|] \qquad \text{Constant multiple rule}$$
$$= \frac{1}{2}\left((1)\cdot|x| + x\cdot\frac{|x|}{x}\right) \qquad \text{Recall that } \frac{d}{dx}|x| = \frac{|x|}{x}.$$
$$= \frac{1}{2}(|x|+|x|) \qquad \text{Cancel the } x.$$
$$= \frac{1}{2}(2|x|) = |x| \qquad \text{See the note.*}$$

* Notice that we have found a function whose derivative is $|x|$; namely $x|x|/2$. Notice also that the derivation we gave assumes that $x \neq 0$ because we divided by x in the third step. However, one can verify, using the definition of the derivative as a limit, that $x|x|/2$ is differentiable at $x = 0$ as well, and that its derivative at $x = 0$ is 0, implying that the formula $\frac{d}{dx}(x|x|/2) = |x|$ is valid for all values of x, including 0.

EXAMPLE 2 Using the Quotient Rule

Compute the derivatives **a.** $\frac{d}{dx}\left[\frac{1-3.2x^{-0.1}}{x+1}\right]$ **b.** $\frac{d}{dx}\left[\frac{(x+1)(x+2)}{x-1}\right]$

Solution

Derivative of top ↓ Bottom ↓ Top ↓ Derivative of bottom ↓

a. $$\frac{d}{dx}\left[\frac{1-3.2x^{-0.1}}{x+1}\right] = \frac{(0.32x^{-1.1})(x+1) - (1-3.2x^{-0.1})(1)}{(x+1)^2}$$

↑ Bottom squared

$$= \frac{0.32x^{-0.1} + 0.32x^{-1.1} - 1 + 3.2x^{-0.1}}{(x+1)^2} \qquad \text{Expand the numerator.}$$

$$= \frac{3.52x^{-0.1} + 0.32x^{-1.1} - 1}{(x+1)^2}$$

b. Here we have both a product and a quotient. Which rule do we use, the product or the quotient rule? Here is a way to decide. Think about how we would calculate, step by step, the value of $(x+1)(x+2)/(x-1)$ for a specific value of x—say $x = 11$. Here is how we would probably do it:

1. Calculate $(x+1)(x+2) = (11+1)(11+2) = 156$.

2. Calculate $x - 1 = 11 - 1 = 10$.

3. Divide 156 by 10 to get 15.6.

Now ask: *What was the last operation we performed?* The last operation we performed was division, so we can regard the whole expression as a *quotient*—that is, as $(x+1)(x+2)$ *divided by* $(x-1)$. Therefore, we should use the quotient rule.

The first thing the quotient rule tells us to do is to take the derivative of the numerator. Now, the numerator is a product, so we must use the product rule to take its derivative. Here is the calculation:

$$\frac{d}{dx}\left[\frac{(x+1)(x+2)}{x-1}\right] = \frac{\overbrace{[(1)(x+2)+(x+1)(1)]}^{\text{Derivative of top}}\overbrace{(x-1)}^{\text{Bottom}} - \overbrace{[(x+1)(x+2)]}^{\text{Top}}\overbrace{(1)}^{\text{Derivative of bottom}}}{\underbrace{(x-1)^2}_{\text{Bottom squared}}}$$

$$= \frac{(2x+3)(x-1) - (x+1)(x+2)}{(x-1)^2}$$

$$= \frac{x^2 - 2x - 5}{(x-1)^2}$$

What is important is to determine the *order of operations* and, in particular, to determine the last operation to be performed. Pretending to do an actual calculation reminds us of the order of operations; we call this technique the **calculation thought experiment**.

➡ **Before we go on...** We used the quotient rule in Example 2 because the function was a quotient; we used the product rule to calculate the derivative of the numerator because the numerator was a product. Get used to this: Differentiation rules usually must be used in combination.

Here is another way we could have done this problem: Our calculation thought experiment could have taken the following form.

1. Calculate $(x+1)/(x-1) = (11+1)/(11-1) = 1.2$.

2. Calculate $x + 2 = 11 + 2 = 13$.

3. Multiply 1.2 by 13 to get 15.6.

We would have then regarded the expression as a *product*—the product of the factors $(x+1)/(x-1)$ and $(x+2)$—and used the product rule instead. We can't escape the quotient rule, however: We need to use it to take the derivative of the first factor, $(x+1)/(x-1)$. Try this approach for practice and check that you get the same answer. ■

Calculation Thought Experiment

The **calculation thought experiment** is a technique to determine whether to treat an algebraic expression as a product, quotient, sum, or difference. Given an expression, consider the steps you would use in computing its value. If the last operation is multiplication, treat the expression as a product; if the last operation is division, treat the expression as a quotient; and so on.

Quick Examples

1. $(3x^2-4)(2x+1)$ can be computed by first calculating the expressions in parentheses and then multiplying. Because the last step is multiplication, we can treat the expression as a product.
2. $\dfrac{2x-1}{x}$ can be computed by first calculating the numerator and denominator and then dividing one by the other. Because the last step is division, we can treat the expression as a quotient.
3. $x^2+(4x-1)(x+2)$ can be computed by first calculating x^2, then calculating the product $(4x-1)(x+2)$, and finally adding the two answers. Thus, we can treat the expression as a sum.
4. $(3x^2-1)^5$ can be computed by first calculating the expression in parentheses and then raising the answer to the fifth power. Thus, we can treat the expression as a power. (We shall see how to differentiate powers of expressions in Section 4.4.)
5. The expression $(x+1)(x+2)/(x-1)$ can be treated as either a quotient or a product: We can write it as a quotient: $\dfrac{(x+1)(x+2)}{x-1}$ or as a product: $(x+1)\left(\dfrac{x+2}{x-1}\right)$. (See Example 2(b).)

EXAMPLE 3 Using the Calculation Thought Experiment

Find $\dfrac{d}{dx}\left[6x^2+5\left(\dfrac{x}{x-1}\right)\right]$.

Solution The calculation thought experiment tells us that the expression we are asked to differentiate can be treated as a *sum*. Because the derivative of a sum is the sum of the derivatives, we get

$$\frac{d}{dx}\left[6x^2+5\left(\frac{x}{x-1}\right)\right]=\frac{d}{dx}(6x^2)+\frac{d}{dx}\left[5\left(\frac{x}{x-1}\right)\right].$$

In other words, we must take the derivatives of $6x^2$ and $5\left(\frac{x}{x-1}\right)$ separately and then add the answers. The derivative of $6x^2$ is $12x$. There are two ways of taking the derivative of $5\left(\frac{x}{x-1}\right)$: We could either first multiply the expression $\left(\frac{x}{x-1}\right)$ by 5 to get $\left(\frac{5x}{x-1}\right)$ and then take its derivative using the quotient rule, or we could pull the 5 out, as we do next.

$$\frac{d}{dx}\left[6x^2 + 5\left(\frac{x}{x-1}\right)\right] = \frac{d}{dx}(6x^2) + \frac{d}{dx}\left[5\left(\frac{x}{x-1}\right)\right] \qquad \text{Derivative of sum}$$

$$= 12x + 5\frac{d}{dx}\left(\frac{x}{x-1}\right) \qquad \text{Constant} \times \text{Function}$$

$$= 12x + 5\left(\frac{(1)(x-1)-(x)(1)}{(x-1)^2}\right) \qquad \text{Quotient rule}$$

$$= 12x + 5\left(\frac{-1}{(x-1)^2}\right)$$

$$= 12x - \frac{5}{(x-1)^2}$$

APPLICATIONS

In the next example, we return to a scenario similar to the one discussed at the start of this section.

EXAMPLE 4 Applying the Product and Quotient Rules: Revenue and Average Cost

Sales of your newly launched miniature wall posters for college dorms, *iMiniPosters,* are really taking off. (Those old-fashioned large wall posters no longer fit in today's "downsized" college dorm rooms.) Monthly sales to students at the start of this year were 1,500 iMiniPosters, and since that time, sales have been increasing by 300 posters each month, even though the price you charge has also been going up.

a. The price you charge for iMiniPosters is given by

$$p(t) = 10 + 0.05t^2 \text{ dollars per poster,}$$

where t is time in months since the start of January of this year. Find a formula for the monthly revenue, and then compute its rate of change at the beginning of March.

b. The number of students who purchase iMiniPosters in a month is given by

$$n(t) = 800 + 0.2t,$$

where t is as in part (a). Find a formula for the average number of posters each student buys, and hence estimate the rate at which this number was growing at the beginning of March.

Solution

a. To compute monthly revenue as a function of time t, we use

$$R(t) = p(t)q(t). \qquad \text{Revenue} = \text{Price} \times \text{Quantity}$$

We already have a formula for $p(t)$. The function $q(t)$ measures sales, which were 1,500 posters/month at time $t = 0$, and were rising by 300 per month:

$$q(t) = 1{,}500 + 300t.$$

Therefore, the formula for revenue is

$$R(t) = p(t)q(t)$$
$$R(t) = (10 + 0.05t^2)(1{,}500 + 300t).$$

Rather than expand this expression, we shall leave it as a product so that we can use the product rule in computing its rate of change:

$$\begin{aligned} R'(t) &= p'(t)q(t) + p(t)q'(t) \\ &= [0.10t][1{,}500 + 300t] + [10 + 0.05t^2][300]. \end{aligned}$$

Because the beginning of March corresponds to $t = 2$, we have

$$\begin{aligned} R'(2) &= [0.10(2)][1{,}500 + 300(2)] + [10 + 0.05(2)^2][300] \\ &= (0.2)(2{,}100) + (10.2)(300) = \$3{,}480 \text{ per month.} \end{aligned}$$

Therefore, your monthly revenue was increasing at a rate of \$3,480 per month at the beginning of March.

b. The average number of posters sold to each student is

$$k(t) = \frac{\text{Number of posters}}{\text{Number of students}} = \frac{q(t)}{n(t)} = \frac{1{,}500 + 300t}{800 + 0.2t}.$$

The rate of change of $k(t)$ is computed with the quotient rule:

$$\begin{aligned} k'(t) &= \frac{q'(t)n(t) - q(t)n'(t)}{n(t)^2} \\ &= \frac{(300)(800 + 0.2t) - (1{,}500 + 300t)(0.2)}{(800 + 0.2t)^2} \end{aligned}$$

so that

$$\begin{aligned} k'(2) &= \frac{(300)[800 + 0.2(2)] - [1{,}500 + 300(2)](0.2)}{[800 + 0.2(2)]^2} \\ &= \frac{(300)(800.4) - (2{,}100)(0.2)}{800.4^2} \approx 0.37 \text{ posters/student per month.} \end{aligned}$$

Therefore, the average number of posters sold to each student was increasing at a rate of about 0.37 posters/student per month.

4.3 EXERCISES

▼ more advanced ◆ challenging

T indicates exercises that should be solved using technology

In Exercises 1–12:

a. *Calculate the derivative of the given function without using either the product or quotient rule.*

b. *Use the product or quotient rule to find the derivative. Check that you obtain the same answer.* HINT [See Quick Examples on pages 316–317.]

1. $f(x) = 3x$ **2.** $f(x) = 2x^2$

3. $g(x) = x \cdot x^2$ **4.** $g(x) = x \cdot x$

5. $h(x) = x(x + 3)$ **6.** $h(x) = x(1 + 2x)$

7. $r(x) = 100x^{2.1}$ **8.** $r(x) = 0.2x^{-1}$ **9.** $s(x) = \dfrac{2}{x}$

10. $t(x) = \dfrac{x}{3}$ **11.** $u(x) = \dfrac{x^2}{3}$ **12.** $s(x) = \dfrac{3}{x^2}$

Calculate $\frac{dy}{dx}$ *in Exercises 13–28. Simplify your answer.* HINT [See Examples 1 and 2.]

13. $y = 3x(4x^2 - 1)$
14. $y = 3x^2(2x + 1)$
15. $y = x^3(1 - x^2)$
16. $y = x^5(1 - x)$
17. $y = (2x + 3)^2$
18. $y = (4x - 1)^2$
19. $y = \frac{4x}{5x - 2}$
20. $y = \frac{3x}{-3x + 2}$
21. $y = \frac{2x + 4}{3x - 1}$
22. $y = \frac{3x - 9}{2x + 4}$
23. $y = \frac{|x|}{x}$
24. $y = \frac{x}{|x|}$
25. $y = \frac{|x|}{x^2}$
26. $y = \frac{x^2}{|x|}$
27. $y = x\sqrt{x}$
28. $y = x^2\sqrt{x}$

Calculate $\frac{dy}{dx}$ *in Exercises 29–56. You need not expand your answers.* HINT [See Examples 1 and 2.]

29. $y = (x + 1)(x^2 - 1)$
30. $y = (4x^2 + x)(x - x^2)$
31. $y = (2x^{0.5} + 4x - 5)(x - x^{-1})$
32. $y = (x^{0.7} - 4x - 5)(x^{-1} + x^{-2})$
33. $y = (2x^2 - 4x + 1)^2$
34. $y = (2x^{0.5} - x^2)^2$
35. $y = \left(\frac{x}{3.2} + \frac{3.2}{x}\right)(x^2 + 1)$
36. $y = \left(\frac{x^{2.1}}{7} + \frac{2}{x^{2.1}}\right)(7x - 1)$
37. $y = x^2(2x + 3)(7x + 2)$ HINT [See Example 1(b).]
38. $y = x(x^2 - 3)(2x^2 + 1)$ HINT [See Example 1(b).]
39. $y = (5.3x - 1)(1 - x^{2.1})(x^{-2.3} - 3.4)$
40. $y = (1.1x + 4)(x^{2.1} - x)(3.4 - x^{-2.1})$
41. ▼ $y = (\sqrt{x} + 1)\left(\sqrt{x} + \frac{1}{x^2}\right)$
42. ▼ $y = (4x^2 - \sqrt{x})\left(\sqrt{x} - \frac{2}{x^2}\right)$
43. $y = \frac{2x^2 + 4x + 1}{3x - 1}$
44. $y = \frac{3x^2 - 9x + 11}{2x + 4}$
45. $y = \frac{x^2 - 4x + 1}{x^2 + x + 1}$
46. $y = \frac{x^2 + 9x - 1}{x^2 + 2x - 1}$
47. $y = \frac{x^{0.23} - 5.7x}{1 - x^{-2.9}}$
48. $y = \frac{8.43x^{-0.1} - 0.5x^{-1}}{3.2 + x^{2.9}}$
49. ▼ $y = \frac{\sqrt{x} + 1}{\sqrt{x} - 1}$
50. ▼ $y = \frac{\sqrt{x} - 1}{\sqrt{x} + 1}$
51. ▼ $y = \frac{\left(\frac{1}{x} + \frac{1}{x^2}\right)}{x + x^2}$
52. ▼ $y = \frac{\left(1 - \frac{1}{x^2}\right)}{x^2 - 1}$
53. $y = \frac{(x + 3)(x + 1)}{3x - 1}$ HINT [See Example 2(b).]
54. $y = \frac{x}{(x - 5)(x - 4)}$ HINT [See Example 2(b).]
55. $y = \frac{(x + 3)(x + 1)(x + 2)}{3x - 1}$
56. $y = \frac{3x - 1}{(x - 5)(x - 4)(x - 1)}$

In Exercises 57–62, compute the indicated derivatives.

57. $\frac{d}{dx}[(x^2 + x)(x^2 - x)]$
58. $\frac{d}{dx}[(x^2 + x^3)(x + 1)]$
59. $\frac{d}{dx}[(x^3 + 2x)(x^2 - x)]\Big|_{x=2}$
60. $\frac{d}{dx}[(x^2 + x)(x^2 - x)]\Big|_{x=1}$
61. $\frac{d}{dt}[(t^2 - t^{0.5})(t^{0.5} + t^{-0.5})]\Big|_{t=1}$
62. $\frac{d}{dt}[(t^2 + t^{0.5})(t^{0.5} - t^{-0.5})]\Big|_{t=1}$

In Exercises 63–70, use the calculation thought experiment to say whether the expression is written as a sum, difference, scalar multiple, product, or quotient. Then use the appropriate rules to find its derivative. HINT [See Quick Examples on page 321 and Example 3.]

63. $y = x^4 - (x^2 + 120)(4x - 1)$
64. $y = x^4 - \frac{x^2 + 120}{4x - 1}$
65. $y = x + 1 + 2\left(\frac{x}{x + 1}\right)$
66. $y = (x + 2) - 4(x^2 - x)\left(x + \frac{1}{x}\right)$
(Do not simplify the answer.)
67. $y = (x + 2)\left(\frac{x}{x + 1}\right)$ (Do not simplify the answer.)
68. $y = \frac{(x + 2)x}{x + 1}$ (Do not simplify the answer.)
69. $y = (x + 1)(x - 2) - 2\left(\frac{x}{x + 1}\right)$
70. $y = \frac{x + 2}{x + 1} + (x + 1)(x - 2)$

In Exercises 71–76, find the equation of the line tangent to the graph of the given function at the point with the indicated x-coordinate.

71. $f(x) = (x^2 + 1)(x^3 + x)$; $x = 1$
72. $f(x) = (x^{0.5} + 1)(x^2 + x)$; $x = 1$

73. $f(x) = \frac{x+1}{x+2}; x = 0$

74. $f(x) = \frac{\sqrt{x}+1}{\sqrt{x}+2}; x = 4$

75. $f(x) = \frac{x^2+1}{x}; x = -1$

76. $f(x) = \frac{x}{x^2+1}; x = 1$

APPLICATIONS

77. ***Revenue*** The monthly sales of *Sunny Electronics'* new sound system are given by $q(t) = 2{,}000t - 100t^2$ units per month, t months after its introduction. The price Sunny charges is $p(t) = 1{,}000 - t^2$ dollars per sound system, t months after introduction. Find the rate of change of monthly sales, the rate of change of the price, and the rate of change of monthly revenue 5 months after the introduction of the sound system. Interpret your answers. HINT [See Example 4(a).]

78. ***Revenue*** The monthly sales of *Sunny Electronics'* new *iSun* walkman is given by $q(t) = 2{,}000t - 100t^2$ units per month, t months after its introduction. The price Sunny charges is $p(t) = 100 - t^2$ dollars per iSun, t months after introduction. Find the rate of change of monthly sales, the rate of change of the price, and the rate of change of monthly revenue 6 months after the introduction of the iSun. Interpret your answers. HINT [See Example 4(a).]

79. ***Saudi Oil Revenues*** The price of crude oil during the period 2000–2010 can be approximated by

$$P(t) = 6t + 18 \text{ dollars per barrel} \quad (0 \le t \le 10)$$

in year t, where $t = 0$ represents 2000. Saudi Arabia's crude oil production over the same period can be approximated by[16]

$$Q(t) = -0.036t^2 + 0.62t + 8 \text{ million barrels per day.} \quad (0 \le t \le 10).$$

Use these models to estimate Saudi Arabia's daily oil revenue and also its rate of change in 2008. (Round your answers to the nearest $1 million.)

80. ***Russian Oil Revenues*** The price of crude oil during the period 2000–2010 can be approximated by

$$P(t) = 6t + 18 \text{ dollars per barrels} \quad (0 \le t \le 10)$$

in year t, where $t = 0$ represents 2000. Russia's crude oil production over the same period can be approximated by[17]

$$Q(t) = -0.08t^2 + 1.2t + 5.5 \text{ million barrels per day} \quad (0 \le t \le 10).$$

Use these models to estimate Russia's daily oil revenue and also its rate of change in 2005. (Round your answers to the nearest $1 million.)

81. ***Revenue*** Dorothy Wagner is currently selling 20 "I ♥ Calculus" T-shirts per day, but sales are dropping at a rate of 3 per day. She is currently charging $7 per T-shirt, but to compensate for dwindling sales, she is increasing the unit price by $1 per day. How fast, and in what direction, is her daily revenue currently changing?

82. ***Pricing Policy*** Let us turn Exercise 81 around a little: Dorothy Wagner is currently selling 20 "I ♥ Calculus" T-shirts per day, but sales are dropping at a rate of 3 per day. She is currently charging $7 per T-shirt, and she wishes to increase her daily revenue by $10 per day. At what rate should she increase the unit price to accomplish this (assuming that the price increase does not affect sales)?

83. ***Bus Travel*** *Thoroughbred Bus Company* finds that its monthly costs for one particular year were given by $C(t) = 10{,}000 + t^2$ dollars after t months. After t months the company had $P(t) = 1{,}000 + t^2$ passengers per month. How fast is its cost per passenger changing after 6 months? HINT [See Example 4(b).]

84. ***Bus Travel*** *Thoroughbred Bus Company* finds that its monthly costs for one particular year were given by $C(t) = 100 + t^2$ dollars after t months. After t months, the company had $P(t) = 1{,}000 + t^2$ passengers per month. How fast is its cost per passenger changing after 6 months? HINT [See Example 4(b).]

85. ***Fuel Economy*** Your muscle car's gas mileage (in miles per gallon) is given as a function $M(x)$ of speed x in mph, where

$$M(x) = \frac{3{,}000}{x + 3{,}600x^{-1}}.$$

Calculate $M'(x)$, and then $M'(10)$, $M'(60)$, and $M'(70)$. What do the answers tell you about your car?

86. ***Fuel Economy*** Your used Chevy's gas mileage (in miles per gallon) is given as a function $M(x)$ of speed x in mph, where

$$M(x) = \frac{4{,}000}{x + 3{,}025x^{-1}}.$$

Calculate $M'(x)$ and hence determine *the sign* of each of the following: $M'(40)$, $M'(55)$, and $M'(60)$. Interpret your results.

87. ▼ ***Oil Imports from Mexico*** Daily oil production in Mexico and daily U.S. oil imports from Mexico during 2005–2009 could be approximated by

$$P(t) = 3.9 - 0.10t \text{ million barrels} \quad (5 \le t \le 9)$$
$$I(t) = 2.1 - 0.11t \text{ million barrels} \quad (5 \le t \le 9),$$

where t is time in years since the start of 2000.[18]

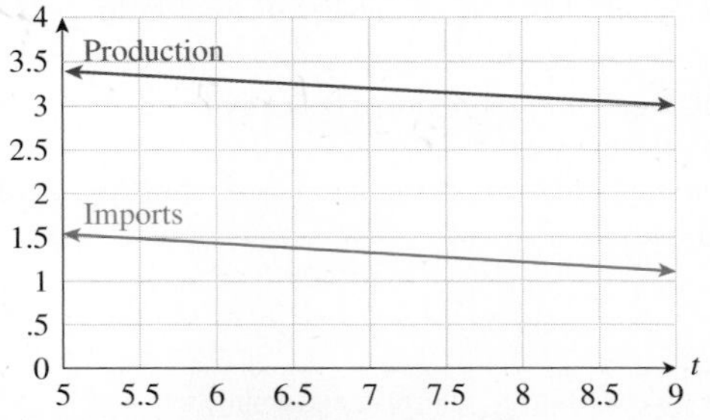

a. What are represented by the functions $P(t) - I(t)$ and $I(t)/P(t)$?

[16]Sources for data: Oil price: InflationData.com www.inflationdata.com, Production: Energy Bulletin www.energybulletin.net.

[17]*Ibid.*

[18]Source for data: Energy Information Administration (www.eia.doe.gov)/Pemex.

b. Compute $\frac{d}{dt}\left[\frac{I(t)}{P(t)}\right]\bigg|_{t=8}$ to two significant digits. What does the answer tell you about oil imports from Mexico?

88. ▼ ***Oil Imports from Mexico*** Daily oil production in Mexico and daily U.S. oil imports from Mexico during 2000–2004 could be approximated by

$$P(t) = 3.0 + 0.13t \text{ million barrels} \quad (0 \le t \le 4)$$

$$I(t) = 1.4 + 0.06t \text{ million barrels} \quad (0 \le t \le 4),$$

where t is time in years since the start of 2000.[19]

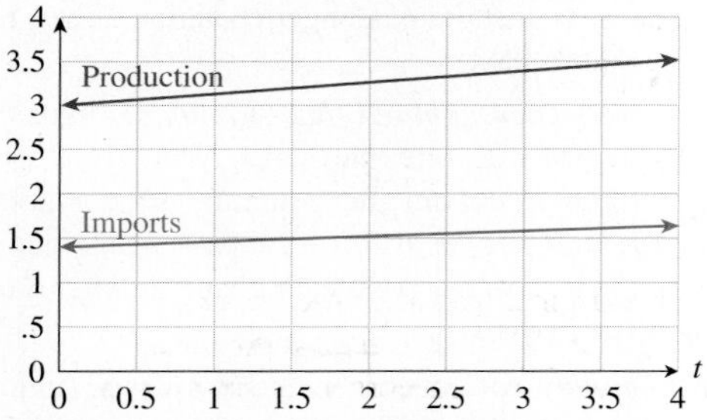

a. What are represented by the functions $P(t) - I(t)$ and $I(t)/P(t)$?

b. Compute $\frac{d}{dt}\left[\frac{I(t)}{P(t)}\right]\bigg|_{t=3}$ to two significant digits. What does the answer tell you about oil imports from Mexico?

89. ▼ ***Military Spending*** The annual cost per active-duty armed service member in the United States increased from \$80,000 in 1995 to a projected \$120,000 in 2007. In 1995, there were 1.5 million armed service personnel, and this number was projected to decrease to 1.4 million in 2003.[20] Use linear models for annual cost and personnel to estimate, to the nearest \$10 million, the rate of change of total military personnel costs in 2002.

90. ▼ ***Military Spending in the 1990s*** The annual cost per active-duty armed service member in the United States increased from \$80,000 in 1995 to \$90,000 in 2000. In 1990, there were 2 million armed service personnel and this number decreased to 1.5 million in 2000.[21] Use linear models for annual cost and personnel to estimate, to the nearest \$10 million, the rate of change of total military personnel costs in 1995.

91. ▼ ***Biology—Reproduction*** The Verhulst model for population growth specifies the reproductive rate of an organism as a function of the total population according to the following formula:

$$R(p) = \frac{r}{1 + kp}$$

where p is the total population in thousands of organisms, r and k are constants that depend on the particular circumstances and the organism being studied, and $R(p)$ is the reproduction rate in thousands of organisms per hour.[22] If $k = 0.125$ and $r = 45$, find $R'(p)$ and then $R'(4)$. Interpret the result.

92. ▼ ***Biology—Reproduction*** Another model, the predator satiation model for population growth, specifies that the reproductive rate of an organism as a function of the total population varies according to the following formula:

$$R(p) = \frac{rp}{1 + kp}$$

where p is the total population in thousands of organisms, r and k are constants that depend on the particular circumstances and the organism being studied, and $R(p)$ is the reproduction rate in new organisms per hour.[23] Given that $k = 0.2$ and $r = 0.08$, find $R'(p)$ and $R'(2)$. Interpret the result.

93. ▼ ***Embryo Development*** Bird embryos consume oxygen from the time the egg is laid through the time the chick hatches. For a typical galliform bird egg, the oxygen consumption (in milliliters) t days after the egg was laid can be approximated by[24]

$$C(t) = -0.016t^4 + 1.1t^3 - 11t^2 + 3.6t \quad (15 \le t \le 30).$$

(An egg will usually hatch at around $t = 28$.) Suppose that at time $t = 0$ you have a collection of 30 newly laid eggs and that the number of eggs decreases linearly to zero at time $t = 30$ days. How fast is the total oxygen consumption of your collection of embryos changing after 25 days? (Round your answers to two significant digits.) Comment on the result. HINT [Total oxygen consumption = Oxygen consumption per egg × Number of eggs.]

94. ▼ ***Embryo Development*** Turkey embryos consume oxygen from the time the egg is laid through the time the chick hatches. For a brush turkey, the oxygen consumption (in milliliters) t days after the egg was laid can be approximated by[25]

$$C(t) = -0.0071t^4 + 0.95t^3 - 22t^2 + 95t \quad (25 \le t \le 50).$$

(An egg will typically hatch at around $t = 50$.) Suppose that at time $t = 0$ you have a collection of 100 newly laid eggs and that the number of eggs decreases linearly to zero at time $t = 50$ days. How fast is the total oxygen consumption of your collection of embryos changing after 40 days? (Round your answer to two significant digits.) Interpret the result. HINT [Total oxygen consumption = Oxygen consumption per egg × Number of eggs.]

---

[19] Source for data: Energy Information Administration (www.eia.doe.gov)/Pemex.

[20] Annual costs are adjusted for inflation. Sources: Department of Defense, Stephen Daggett, military analyst, Congressional Research Service/*New York Times*, April 19, 2002, p. A21.

[21] *Ibid.*

[22] Source: *Mathematics in Medicine and the Life Sciences* by F. C. Hoppensteadt and C. S. Peskin (Springer-Verlag, New York, 1992) pp. 20–22.

[23] *Ibid.*

[24] The model is derived from graphical data published in the article "The Brush Turkey" by Roger S. Seymour, *Scientific American*, December, 1991, pp. 108–114.

[25] *Ibid.*

COMMUNICATION AND REASONING EXERCISES

95. If f and g are functions of time, and at time $t = 3$, f equals 5 and is rising at a rate of 2 units per second, and g equals 4 and is rising at a rate of 5 units per second, then the product fg equals ____ and is rising at a rate of ____ units per second.

96. If f and g are functions of time, and at time $t = 2$, f equals 3 and is rising at a rate of 4 units per second, and g equals 5 and is rising at a rate of 6 units per second, then fg equals ____ and is rising at a rate of ____ units per second.

97. If f and g are functions of time, and at time $t = 3$, f equals 5 and is rising at a rate of 2 units per second, and g equals 4 and is rising at a rate of 5 units per second, then f/g equals ____ and is changing at a rate of ____ units per second.

98. If f and g are functions of time, and at time $t = 2$, f equals 3 and is rising at a rate of 4 units per second, and g equals 5 and is rising at a rate of 6 units per second, then f/g equals ____ and is changing at a rate of ____ units per second.

99. You have come across the following in a newspaper article: "Revenues of HAL Home Heating Oil Inc. are rising by \$4.2 million per year. This is due to an annual increase of 70¢ per gallon in the price HAL charges for heating oil and an increase in sales of 6 million gallons of oil per year." Comment on this analysis.

100. Your friend says that because average cost is obtained by dividing the cost function by the number of units x, it follows that the derivative of average cost is the same as marginal cost because the derivative of x is 1. Comment on this analysis.

101. ▼ Find a demand function $q(p)$ such that, at a price per item of $p = \$100$, revenue will rise if the price per item is increased.

102. ▼ What must be true about a demand function $q(p)$ so that, at a price per item of $p = \$100$, revenue will decrease if the price per item is increased?

103. ▼ You and I are both selling a steady 20 T-shirts per day. The price I am getting for my T-shirts is increasing twice as fast as yours, but your T-shirts are currently selling for twice the price of mine. Whose revenue is increasing faster: yours, mine, or neither? Explain.

104. ▼ You and I are both selling T-shirts for a steady \$20 per shirt. Sales of my T-shirts are increasing at twice the rate of yours, but you are currently selling twice as many as I am. Whose revenue is increasing faster: yours, mine, or neither? Explain.

105. ◆***Marginal Product*** *(from the GRE Economics Test)* Which of the following statements about average product and marginal product is correct?

(A) If average product is decreasing, marginal product must be less than average product.
(B) If average product is increasing, marginal product must be increasing.
(C) If marginal product is decreasing, average product must be less than marginal product.
(D) If marginal product is increasing, average product must be decreasing.
(E) If marginal product is constant over some range, average product must be constant over that range.

106. ◆***Marginal Cost*** *(based on a question from the GRE Economics Test)* Which of the following statements about average cost and marginal cost is correct?

(A) If average cost is increasing, marginal cost must be increasing.
(B) If average cost is increasing, marginal cost must be decreasing.
(C) If average cost is increasing, marginal cost must be more than average cost.
(D) If marginal cost is increasing, average cost must be increasing.
(E) If marginal cost is increasing, average cost must be larger than marginal cost.

4.4 The Chain Rule

We can now find the derivatives of expressions involving powers of x combined using addition, subtraction, multiplication, and division, but we still cannot take the derivative of an expression like $(3x + 1)^{0.5}$. For this we need one more rule. The function $h(x) = (3x + 1)^{0.5}$ is not a sum, difference, product, or quotient. To find out what it is, we can use the calculation thought experiment and think about the last operation we would perform in calculating $h(x)$.

1. Calculate $3x + 1$.

2. Take the 0.5 power (square root) of the answer.

The last operation is "take the 0.5 power." We do not yet have a rule for finding the derivative of the 0.5 power of a quantity other than x.

There is a way to build $h(x) = (3x + 1)^{0.5}$ out of two simpler functions: $u(x) = 3x + 1$ (the function that corresponds to the first step in the calculation above) and $f(x) = x^{0.5}$ (the function that corresponds to the second step):

$$\begin{aligned} h(x) &= (3x + 1)^{0.5} \\ &= [u(x)]^{0.5} && u(x) = 3x + 1 \\ &= f(u(x)). && f(x) = x^{0.5} \end{aligned}$$

We say that h is the **composite** of f and u. We read $f(u(x))$ as "f of u of x."

To compute $h(1)$, say, we first compute $3 \cdot 1 + 1 = 4$ and then take the square root of 4, giving $h(1) = 2$. To compute $f(u(1))$ we follow exactly the same steps: First compute $u(1) = 4$ and then $f(u(1)) = f(4) = 2$. We always compute $f(u(x))$ from the inside out: Given x, first compute $u(x)$ and then $f(u(x))$.

Now, f and u are functions *whose derivatives we know.* The *chain rule* allows us to use our knowledge of the derivatives of f and u to find the derivative of $f(u(x))$. For the purposes of stating the rule, let us avoid some of the nested parentheses by abbreviating $u(x)$ as u. Thus, we write $f(u)$ instead of $f(u(x))$ and remember that u is a function of x.

Chain Rule

If f is a differentiable function of u and u is a differentiable function of x, then the composite $f(u)$ is a differentiable function of x, and

$$\frac{d}{dx}[f(u)] = f'(u)\frac{du}{dx}. \qquad \text{Chain rule}$$

In words *The derivative of f(quantity) is the derivative of f, evaluated at that quantity, times the derivative of the quantity.*

Quick Examples

In the Quick Examples that follow, u, "the quantity," is some (unspecified) differentiable function of x.

1. Take $f(u) = u^2$. Then

$$\frac{d}{dx}(u^2) = 2u\frac{du}{dx}. \qquad \text{Because } f'(u) = 2u$$

The derivative of a quantity squared is two times the quantity, times the derivative of the quantity.

2. Take $f(u) = u^{0.5}$. Then

$$\frac{d}{dx}(u^{0.5}) = 0.5u^{-0.5}\frac{du}{dx}. \qquad \text{Because } f'(u) = 0.5u^{-0.5}$$

The derivative of a quantity raised to the 0.5 is 0.5 times the quantity raised to the −0.5, times the derivative of the quantity.

As the quick examples illustrate, for every power of a function u whose derivative we know, we now get a "generalized" differentiation rule. The following table gives more examples.

Original Rule	*Generalized Rule*	*In Words*
$\frac{d}{dx}(x^2) = 2x$	$\frac{d}{dx}(u^2) = 2u\frac{du}{dx}$	*The derivative of a quantity squared is twice the quantity, times the derivative of the quantity.*
$\frac{d}{dx}(x^3) = 3x^2$	$\frac{d}{dx}(u^3) = 3u^2\frac{du}{dx}$	*The derivative of a quantity cubed is 3 times the quantity squared, times the derivative of the quantity.*
$\frac{d}{dx}\left(\frac{1}{x}\right) = -\frac{1}{x^2}$	$\frac{d}{dx}\left(\frac{1}{u}\right) = -\frac{1}{u^2}\frac{du}{dx}$	*The derivative of 1 over a quantity is negative 1 over the quantity squared, times the derivative of the quantity.*
Power Rule	***Generalized Power Rule***	***In Words***
$\frac{d}{dx}(x^n) = nx^{n-1}$	$\frac{d}{dx}(u^n) = nu^{n-1}\frac{du}{dx}$	*The derivative of a quantity raised to the n is n times the quantity raised to the n − 1, times the derivative of the quantity.*
$\frac{d}{dx}\lvert x\rvert = \frac{\lvert x\rvert}{x}$	$\frac{d}{dx}\lvert u\rvert = \frac{\lvert u\rvert}{u}\frac{du}{dx}$	*The derivative of the absolute value of a quantity is the absolute value of the quantity divided by the quantity, times the derivative of the quantity.*

To motivate the chain rule, let us see why it is true in the special case when $f(u) = u^3$, where the chain rule tells us that

$$\frac{d}{dx}(u^3) = 3u^2\frac{du}{dx}. \qquad \text{Generalized power rule with } n = 3$$

But we could have done this using the product rule instead:

$$\frac{d}{dx}(u^3) = \frac{d}{dx}(u \cdot u \cdot u) = \frac{du}{dx}u \cdot u + u\frac{du}{dx}u + u \cdot u\frac{du}{dx} = 3u^2\frac{du}{dx},$$

which gives us the same result. A similar argument works for $f(u) = u^n$, where $n = 2, 3, 4, \ldots$. We can then use the quotient rule and the chain rule for positive powers to verify the generalized power rule for *negative* powers as well. For the case of a general differentiable function *f*, the proof of the chain rule is beyond the scope of this book, but you can find one on the Website by following the path

Website → Everything for Calculus → Chapter 4 → Proof of Chain Rule.

EXAMPLE 1 Using the Chain Rule

Compute the following derivatives.

a. $\frac{d}{dx}[(2x^2 + x)^3]$ **b.** $\frac{d}{dx}[(x^3 + x)^{100}]$ **c.** $\frac{d}{dx}\sqrt{3x + 1}$ **d.** $\frac{d}{dx}|4x^2 - x|$

Solution

a. Using the calculation thought experiment, we see that the last operation we would perform in calculating $(2x^2 + x)^3$ is that of *cubing.* Thus we think of $(2x^2 + x)^3$ as *a quantity cubed.* There are two similar methods we can use to calculate its derivative.

Method 1: Using the formula We think of $(2x^2+x)^3$ as u^3, where $u = 2x^2+x$. By the formula,

$$\frac{d}{dx}(u^3) = 3u^2\frac{du}{dx}. \qquad \text{Generalized power rule}$$

Now substitute for u:

$$\begin{aligned}\frac{d}{dx}[(2x^2+x)^3] &= 3(2x^2+x)^2\frac{d}{dx}(2x^2+x)\\ &= 3(2x^2+x)^2(4x+1)\end{aligned}$$

Method 2: Using the verbal form If we prefer to use the verbal form, we get:

The derivative of $(2x^2+x)$ *cubed is three times* $(2x^2+x)$ *squared, times the derivative of* $(2x^2+x)$.

In symbols,

$$\frac{d}{dx}[(2x^2+x)^3] = 3(2x^2+x)^2(4x+1),$$

as we obtained above.

b. First, the calculation thought experiment: If we were computing $(x^3+x)^{100}$, the last operation we would perform is *raising a quantity to the power* 100. Thus we are dealing with *a quantity raised to the power* 100, and so we must again use the generalized power rule. According to the verbal form of the generalized power rule, the derivative of a quantity raised to the power 100 is 100 times that quantity to the power 99, times the derivative of that quantity. In symbols,

$$\frac{d}{dx}[(x^3+x)^{100}] = 100(x^3+x)^{99}(3x^2+1).$$

c. We first rewrite the expression $\sqrt{3x+1}$ as $(3x+1)^{0.5}$ and then use the generalized power rule as in parts (a) and (b):

The derivative of a quantity raised to the 0.5 *is* 0.5 *times the quantity raised to the* −0.5, *times the derivative of the quantity.*

Thus,

$$\frac{d}{dx}[(3x+1)^{0.5}] = 0.5(3x+1)^{-0.5}\cdot 3 = 1.5(3x+1)^{-0.5}.$$

d. The calculation thought experiment tells us that $|4x^2-x|$ is the absolute value of a quantity, so we use the generalized rule for absolute values (above):

$$\frac{d}{dx}|u| = \frac{|u|}{u}\frac{du}{dx}, \text{ or, in words,}$$

The derivative of the absolute value of a quantity is the absolute value of the quantity divided by the quantity, times the derivative of the quantity.

Thus,

$$\frac{d}{dx}|4x^2-x| = \frac{|4x^2-x|}{4x^2-x}\cdot(8x-1). \qquad \frac{d}{dx}|u| = \frac{|u|}{u}\frac{du}{dx}$$

➡ **Before we go on...** The following are examples of common errors in solving Example 1(b):

$$\text{“}\frac{d}{dx}[(x^3+x)^{100}] = 100(3x^2+1)^{99}\text{”} \qquad ✗ \textit{ WRONG!}$$

$$\text{“}\frac{d}{dx}[(x^3+x)^{100}] = 100(x^3+x)^{99}.\text{”} \qquad ✗ \textit{ WRONG!}$$

Remember that the generalized power rule says that the derivative of a quantity to the power 100 is 100 times *that same quantity* raised to the power 99, *times the derivative of that quantity.* ■

Q: *It seems that there are now two formulas for the derivative of an nth power:*

1. $\frac{d}{dx}[x^n] = nx^{n-1}$
2. $\frac{d}{dx}[u^n] = nu^{n-1}\frac{du}{dx}.$

Which one do I use?

A: Formula 1 is actually a special case of Formula 2: Formula 1 is the original power rule, which applies only to a power of x. For instance, it applies to x^{10}, but it does not apply to $(2x+1)^{10}$ because the quantity that is being raised to a power is not x. Formula 2 applies to a power of any *function of x*, such as $(2x+1)^{10}$. It can even be used in place of the original power rule. For example, if we take $u = x$ in Formula 2, we obtain

$$\frac{d}{dx}[x^n] = nx^{n-1}\frac{dx}{dx}$$

$$= nx^{n-1}. \quad \text{The derivative of } x \text{ with respect to } x \text{ is 1.}$$

Thus, the generalized power rule really *is* a generalization of the original power rule, as its name suggests.

EXAMPLE 2 More Examples Using the Chain Rule

Find: **a.** $\frac{d}{dx}[(2x^5 + x^2 - 20)^{-2/3}]$ **b.** $\frac{d}{dx}\left[\frac{1}{\sqrt{x+2}}\right]$ **c.** $\frac{d}{dx}\left[\frac{1}{x^2+x}\right]$

Solution Each of the given functions is, or can be rewritten as, a power of a function whose derivative we know. Thus, we can use the method of Example 1.

a. $\frac{d}{dx}[(2x^5 + x^2 - 20)^{-2/3}] = -\frac{2}{3}(2x^5 + x^2 - 20)^{-5/3}(10x^4 + 2x)$

b. $\frac{d}{dx}\left[\frac{1}{\sqrt{x+2}}\right] = \frac{d}{dx}(x+2)^{-1/2} = -\frac{1}{2}(x+2)^{-3/2} \cdot 1 = -\frac{1}{2(x+2)^{3/2}}$

c. $\frac{d}{dx}\left[\frac{1}{x^2+x}\right] = \frac{d}{dx}(x^2+x)^{-1} = -(x^2+x)^{-2}(2x+1) = -\frac{2x+1}{(x^2+x)^2}$

➡ **Before we go on...** In Example 2(c), we could have used the quotient rule instead of the generalized power rule. We can think of the quantity $1/(x^2+x)$ in two different ways using the calculation thought experiment:

1. As 1 divided by something—in other words, as a quotient

2. As something raised to the -1 power

Of course, we get the same derivative using either approach. ■

We now look at some more complicated examples.

EXAMPLE 3 Harder Examples Using the Chain Rule

Find $\frac{dy}{dx}$ in each case. **a.** $y = [(x+1)^{-2.5} + 3x]^{-3}$ **b.** $y = (x+10)^3\sqrt{1-x^2}$

Solution

a. The calculation thought experiment tells us that the last operation we would perform in calculating y is raising the quantity $[(x+1)^{-2.5} + 3x]$ to the power -3. Thus, we use the generalized power rule.

$$\frac{dy}{dx} = -3[(x+1)^{-2.5} + 3x]^{-4}\frac{d}{dx}[(x+1)^{-2.5} + 3x]$$

We are not yet done; we must still find the derivative of $(x+1)^{-2.5} + 3x$. Finding the derivative of a complicated function in several steps helps to keep the problem manageable. Continuing, we have

$$\frac{dy}{dx} = -3[(x+1)^{-2.5} + 3x]^{-4}\frac{d}{dx}[(x+1)^{-2.5} + 3x]$$

$$= -3[(x+1)^{-2.5} + 3x]^{-4}\left(\frac{d}{dx}[(x+1)^{-2.5}] + \frac{d}{dx}(3x)\right). \quad \text{Derivative of a sum}$$

Now we have two derivatives left to calculate. The second of these we know to be 3, and the first is the derivative of a quantity raised to the -2.5 power. Thus

$$\frac{dy}{dx} = -3[(x+1)^{-2.5} + 3x]^{-4}[-2.5(x+1)^{-3.5}\cdot 1 + 3].$$

b. The expression $(x+10)^3\sqrt{1-x^2}$ is a product, so we use the product rule:

$$\frac{d}{dx}[(x+10)^3\sqrt{1-x^2}] = \left(\frac{d}{dx}[(x+10)^3]\right)\sqrt{1-x^2} + (x+10)^3\left(\frac{d}{dx}\sqrt{1-x^2}\right)$$

$$= 3(x+10)^2\sqrt{1-x^2} + (x+10)^3\frac{1}{2\sqrt{1-x^2}}(-2x)$$

$$= 3(x+10)^2\sqrt{1-x^2} - \frac{x(x+10)^3}{\sqrt{1-x^2}}.$$

APPLICATIONS

The next example is a new way of looking at Example 3 from Section 4.2.

EXAMPLE 4 Marginal Product

A consultant determines that *Precision Manufacturers'* annual profit (in dollars) is given by

$$P = -200{,}000 + 4{,}000q - 0.46q^2 - 0.00001q^3,$$

where q is the number of surgical lasers it sells each year. The consultant also informs Precision that the number of surgical lasers it can manufacture each year depends on the number n of assembly-line workers it employs according to the equation

$$q = 100n. \quad \text{Each worker contributes 100 lasers per year.}$$

Use the chain rule to find the marginal product $\frac{dP}{dn}$.

Solution We could calculate the marginal product by substituting the expression for q in the expression for P to obtain P as a function of n (as given in Example 3 from Section 4.2) and then finding dP/dn. Alternatively—and this will simplify the calculation—we can use the chain rule. To see how the chain rule applies, notice that P is a function of q, where q in turn is given as a function of n. By the chain rule,

$$\frac{dP}{dn} = P'(q)\frac{dq}{dn} \qquad \text{Chain rule}$$

$$= \frac{dP}{dq}\frac{dq}{dn}. \qquad \text{Notice how the "quantities" } dq \text{ appear to cancel.}$$

Now we compute

$$\frac{dP}{dq} = 4{,}000 - 0.92q - 0.00003q^2$$

and $$\frac{dq}{dn} = 100.$$

Substituting into the equation for $\frac{dP}{dn}$ gives

$$\frac{dP}{dn} = (4{,}000 - 0.92q - 0.00003q^2)(100)$$

$$= 400{,}000 - 92q - 0.003q^2.$$

Notice that the answer has q as a variable. We can express dP/dn as a function of n by substituting $100n$ for q:

$$\frac{dP}{dn} = 400{,}000 - 92(100n) - 0.003(100n)^2$$

$$= 400{,}000 - 9{,}200n - 30n^2.$$

The equation

$$\frac{dP}{dn} = \frac{dP}{dq}\frac{dq}{dn}$$

in the example above is an appealing way of writing the chain rule because it suggests that the "quantities" dq cancel. In general, we can write the chain rule as follows.

Chain Rule in Differential Notation

If y is a differentiable function of u, and u is a differentiable function of x, then

$$\frac{dy}{dx} = \frac{dy}{du}\frac{du}{dx}. \qquad \text{The terms } du \text{ cancel.}$$

Notice how the units of measurement also cancel:

$$\frac{\text{Units of } y}{\text{Units of } x} = \frac{\text{Units of } y}{\cancel{\text{Units of } u}}\frac{\cancel{\text{Units of } u}}{\text{Units of } x}.$$

Quick Examples

1. If $y = u^3$, where $u = 4x + 1$, then

$$\frac{dy}{dx} = \frac{dy}{du}\frac{du}{dx} = 3u^2 \cdot 4 = 12u^2 = 12(4x+1)^2.$$

2. If $q = 43p^2$, where p (and hence q also) is a differentiable function of t, then

$$\frac{dq}{dt} = \frac{dq}{dp}\frac{dp}{dt}$$

$$= 86p\frac{dp}{dt}.$$ p is not specified, so we leave dp/dt as is.

EXAMPLE 5 Marginal Revenue

Suppose a company's weekly revenue R is given as a function of the unit price p, and p in turn is given as a function of weekly sales q (by means of a demand equation). If

$$\left.\frac{dR}{dp}\right|_{q=1,000} = \$40 \text{ per } \$1 \text{ increase in price}$$

and

$$\left.\frac{dp}{dq}\right|_{q=1,000} = -\$20 \text{ per additional item sold per week}$$

find the marginal revenue when sales are 1,000 items per week.

Solution The marginal revenue is $\frac{dR}{dq}$. By the chain rule, we have

$$\frac{dR}{dq} = \frac{dR}{dp}\frac{dp}{dq}.$$ Units: Revenue per item
= Revenue per \$1 price increase × price increase per additional item.

Because we are interested in the marginal revenue at a demand level of 1,000 items per week, we have

$$\left.\frac{dR}{dq}\right|_{q=1,000} = (40)(-20) = -\$800 \text{ per additional item sold.}$$

Thus, if the price is lowered to increase the demand from 1,000 to 1,001 items per week, the weekly revenue will drop by approximately \$800.

Look again at the way the terms "du" appeared to cancel in the differential formula $\frac{dy}{dx} = \frac{dy}{du}\frac{du}{dx}$. In fact, the chain rule tells us more:

* The notion of "thinking of x as a function of y" will be made more precise in Section 4.6.

Manipulating Derivatives in Differential Notation

1. Suppose y is a function of x. Then, thinking of x as a function of y (as, for instance, when we can solve for x)* we have

$$\frac{dx}{dy} = \frac{1}{\left(\frac{dy}{dx}\right)}, \text{ provided } \frac{dy}{dx} \neq 0.$$ Notice again how $\frac{dy}{dx}$ behaves like a fraction.

Quick Example

In the demand equation $q = -0.2p - 8$, we have $\frac{dq}{dp} = -0.2$. Therefore,

$$\frac{dp}{dq} = \frac{1}{\left(\frac{dq}{dp}\right)} = \frac{1}{-0.2} = -5.$$

2. Suppose x and y are functions of t. Then, thinking of y as a function of x (as, for instance, when we can solve for t as a function of x, and hence obtain y as a function of x), we have

$$\frac{dy}{dx} = \frac{dy/dt}{dx/dt}.$$ The terms dt appear to cancel.

Quick Example

If $x = 3 - 0.2t$ and $y = 6 + 6t$, then

$$\frac{dy}{dx} = \frac{dy/dt}{dx/dt} = \frac{6}{-0.2} = -30.$$

To see why the above formulas work, notice that the second formula,

$$\frac{dy}{dx} = \frac{\left(\frac{dy}{dt}\right)}{\left(\frac{dx}{dt}\right)}$$

can be written as

$$\frac{dy}{dx}\frac{dx}{dt} = \frac{dy}{dt},$$ Multiply both sides by $\frac{dx}{dt}$.

which is just the differential form of the chain rule. For the first formula, use the second formula with y playing the role of t:

$$\frac{dy}{dx} = \frac{dy/dy}{dx/dy}$$

$$= \frac{1}{dx/dy}.$$ $\frac{dy}{dy} = \frac{d}{dy}[y] = 1$

FAQs

Using the Chain Rule

Q: *How do I decide whether or not to use the chain rule when taking a derivative?*

A: Use the calculation thought experiment (Section 4.3): Given an expression, consider the steps you would use in computing its value.

- If the last step is *raising a quantity to a power,* as in $\left(\frac{x^2-1}{x+4}\right)^4$, then the first step to use is the chain rule (in the form of the generalized power rule):

$$\frac{d}{dx}\left(\frac{x^2-1}{x+4}\right)^4 = 4\left(\frac{x^2-1}{x+4}\right)^3 \frac{d}{dx}\left(\frac{x^2-1}{x+4}\right).$$

Then use the appropriate rules to finish the computation. You may need to again use the calculation thought experiment to decide on the next step (here the quotient rule):

$$= 4\left(\frac{x^2-1}{x+4}\right)^3 \frac{(2x)(x+4)-(x^2-1)(1)}{(x+4)^2}.$$

- If the last step is *division,* as in $\frac{(x^2-1)}{(3x+4)^4}$, then the first step to use is the quotient rule:

$$\frac{d}{dx}\frac{(x^2-1)}{(3x+4)^4} = \frac{(2x)(3x+4)^4-(x^2-1)\frac{d}{dx}(3x+4)^4}{(3x+4)^8}.$$

Then use the appropriate rules to finish the computation (here the chain rule):

$$= \frac{(2x)(3x+4)^4-(x^2-1)[4(3x+4)^3(3)]}{(3x+4)^8}.$$

- If the last step is *multiplication, addition, subtraction, or multiplication by a constant,* then the first rule to use is the product rule, or the rule for sums, differences, or constant multiples as appropriate.

Q: *Every time I compute a derivative, I leave something out. How do I make sure I am really done when taking the derivative of a complicated-looking expression?*

A: Until you are an expert at taking derivatives, the key is to use one rule at a time and write out each step, rather than trying to compute the derivative in a single step. To illustrate this, try computing the derivative of $(x+10)^3\sqrt{1-x^2}$ in Example 3(b) in two ways: First try to compute it in a single step, and then compute it by writing out each step as shown in the example. How do your results compare? For more practice, try Exercises 87 and 88 following.

4.4 EXERCISES

▼ more advanced ◆ challenging

T indicates exercises that should be solved using technology

Calculate the derivatives of the functions in Exercises 1–50. HINT [See Example 1.]

1. $f(x) = (2x+1)^2$

2. $f(x) = (3x-1)^2$

3. $f(x) = (x-1)^{-1}$

4. $f(x) = (2x-1)^{-2}$

5. $f(x) = (2-x)^{-2}$

6. $f(x) = (1-x)^{-1}$

7. $f(x) = (2x+1)^{0.5}$

8. $f(x) = (-x+2)^{1.5}$

9. $f(x) = \dfrac{1}{3x-1}$

10. $f(x) = \dfrac{1}{(x+1)^2}$

11. $f(x) = (x^2+2x)^4$

12. $f(x) = (x^3-x)^3$

13. $f(x) = (2x^2-2)^{-1}$

14. $f(x) = (2x^3+x)^{-2}$

15. $g(x) = (x^2-3x-1)^{-5}$

16. $g(x) = (2x^2+x+1)^{-3}$

17. $h(x) = \dfrac{1}{(x^2+1)^3}$ HINT [See Example 2.]

18. $h(x) = \dfrac{1}{(x^2+x+1)^2}$ HINT [See Example 2.]

19. $r(x) = (0.1x^2-4.2x+9.5)^{1.5}$

20. $r(x) = (0.1x-4.2x^{-1})^{0.5}$

21. $r(s) = (s^2-s^{0.5})^4$

22. $r(s) = (2s+s^{0.5})^{-1}$

23. $f(x) = \sqrt{1-x^2}$

24. $f(x) = \sqrt{x+x^2}$

25. $f(x) = |3x-6|$ HINT [See Example 1(d).]

26. $f(x) = |-5x+1|$ HINT [See Example 1(d).]

27. $f(x) = |-x^3+5x|$

28. $f(x) = |x-x^4|$

29. $h(x) = 2[(x+1)(x^2-1)]^{-1/2}$ HINT [See Example 3.]

30. $h(x) = 3[(2x-1)(x-1)]^{-1/3}$ HINT [See Example 3.]

31. $h(x) = (3.1x-2)^2 - \dfrac{1}{(3.1x-2)^2}$

32. $h(x) = \left[3.1x^2 - 2 - \dfrac{1}{3.1x-2}\right]^2$

33. $f(x) = [(6.4x-1)^2 + (5.4x-2)^3]^2$

34. $f(x) = (6.4x-3)^{-2} + (4.3x-1)^{-2}$

35. $f(x) = (x^2-3x)^{-2}(1-x^2)^{0.5}$

36. $f(x) = (3x^2+x)(1-x^2)^{0.5}$

37. $s(x) = \left(\dfrac{2x+4}{3x-1}\right)^2$

38. $s(x) = \left(\dfrac{3x-9}{2x+4}\right)^3$

39. $g(z) = \left(\dfrac{z}{1+z^2}\right)^3$

40. $g(z) = \left(\dfrac{z^2}{1+z}\right)^2$

41. $f(x) = [(1+2x)^4 - (1-x)^2]^3$

42. $f(x) = [(3x-1)^2 + (1-x)^5]^2$

43. $f(x) = (3x-1)|3x-1|$

44. $f(x) = |(x-3)^{1/3}|$

45. $f(x) = |x-(2x-3)^{1/2}|$

46. $f(x) = (3-|3x-1|)^{-2}$

47. ▼ $r(x) = (\sqrt{2x+1} - x^2)^{-1}$

48. ▼ $r(x) = (\sqrt{x+1} + \sqrt{x})^3$

49. ▼ $f(x) = (1+(1+(1+2x)^3)^3)^3$

50. ▼ $f(x) = 2x + (2x + (2x+1)^3)^3$

Find the indicated derivatives in Exercises 51–58. In each case, the independent variable is a (unspecified) differentiable function of t. HINT [See Quick Example 2 on page 334.]

51. $y = x^{100} + 99x^{-1}$. Find $\dfrac{dy}{dt}$.

52. $y = x^{0.5}(1+x)$. Find $\dfrac{dy}{dt}$.

53. $s = \dfrac{1}{r^3} + r^{0.5}$. Find $\dfrac{ds}{dt}$.

54. $s = r + r^{-1}$. Find $\dfrac{ds}{dt}$.

55. $V = \dfrac{4}{3}\pi r^3$. Find $\dfrac{dV}{dt}$.

56. $A = 4\pi r^2$. Find $\dfrac{dA}{dt}$.

57. ▼ $y = x^3 + \dfrac{1}{x}$, $x = 2$ when $t = 1$, $\left.\dfrac{dx}{dt}\right|_{t=1} = -1$

Find $\left.\dfrac{dy}{dt}\right|_{t=1}$.

58. ▼ $y = \sqrt{x} + \dfrac{1}{\sqrt{x}}$, $x = 9$ when $t = 1$, $\left.\dfrac{dx}{dt}\right|_{t=1} = -1$

Find $\left.\dfrac{dy}{dt}\right|_{t=1}$.

In Exercises 59–64, compute the indicated derivative using the chain rule. HINT [See Quick Examples on page 335.]

59. $y = 3x - 2$; $\dfrac{dx}{dy}$

60. $y = 8x + 4$; $\dfrac{dx}{dy}$

61. $x = 2 + 3t$, $y = -5t$; $\dfrac{dy}{dx}$

62. $x = 1 - t/2$, $y = 4t - 1$; $\dfrac{dy}{dx}$

63. $y = 3x^2 - 2x$; $\left.\dfrac{dx}{dy}\right|_{x=1}$

64. $y = 3x - \dfrac{2}{x}$; $\left.\dfrac{dx}{dy}\right|_{x=2}$

APPLICATIONS

65. ***Marginal Product*** *Paramount Electronics* has an annual profit given by

$$P = -100{,}000 + 5{,}000q - 0.25q^2 \text{ dollars,}$$

where q is the number of laptop computers it sells each year. The number of laptop computers it can make and sell each year depends on the number n of electrical engineers Paramount employs, according to the equation

$$q = 30n + 0.01n^2.$$

Use the chain rule to find $\left.\frac{dP}{dn}\right|_{n=10}$ and interpret the result.

HINT [See Example 3.]

66. *Marginal Product* Refer back to Exercise 65. The average profit $\bar{P}$ per computer is given by dividing the total profit P by q:

$$\bar{P} = -\frac{100{,}000}{q} + 5{,}000 - 0.25q \text{ dollars.}$$

Determine the **marginal average product**, $d\bar{P}/dn$ at an employee level of 10 engineers. Interpret the result.
HINT [See Example 3.]

67. *Food versus Education* The percentage y (of total personal consumption) an individual spends on food is approximately

$$y = 35x^{-0.25} \text{ percentage points} \quad (6.5 \le x \le 17.5),$$

where x is the percentage the individual spends on education.[26] An individual finds that she is spending

$$x = 7 + 0.2t$$

percent of her personal consumption on education, where t is time in months since January 1. Use direct substitution to express the percentage y as a function of time t (do not simplify the expression) and then use the chain rule to estimate how fast the percentage she spends on food is changing on November 1. Be sure to specify the units.

68. *Food versus Recreation* The percentage y (of total personal consumption) an individual spends on food is approximately

$$y = 33x^{-0.63} \text{ percentage points} \quad (2.5 \le x \le 4.5),$$

where x is the percentage the individual spends on recreation.[27] A college student finds that he is spending

$$x = 3.5 + 0.1t$$

percent of his personal consumption on recreation, where t is time in months since January 1. Use direct substitution to express the percentage y as a function of time t (do not simplify the expression) and then use the chain rule to estimate how fast the percentage he spends on food is changing on November 1. Be sure to specify the units.

69. *Marginal Revenue* The weekly revenue from the sale of rubies at *Royal Ruby Retailers* (RRR) is increasing at a rate of \$40 per \$1 increase in price, and the price is decreasing at a rate of \$0.75 per additional ruby sold. What is the marginal revenue? (Be sure to state the units of measurement.) Interpret the result. HINT [See Example 5.]

[26]Model based on historical and projected data from 1908–2010. Sources: Historical data, Bureau of Economic Analysis; projected data, Bureau of Labor Statistics/*New York Times*, December 1, 2003, p. C2.

[27]*Ibid.*

70. *Marginal Revenue* The weekly revenue from the sale of emeralds at *Eduardo's Emerald Emporium* (EEE) is decreasing at a rate of €500 per €1 increase in price, and the price is decreasing at a rate of €0.45 per additional emerald sold. What is the marginal revenue? (Be sure to state the units of measurement.) Interpret the result. HINT [See Example 5.]

71. *Crime Statistics* The murder rate in large cities (over 1 million residents) can be related to that in smaller cities (500,000–1,000,000 residents) by the following linear model:[28]

$$y = 1.5x - 1.9 \quad (15 \le x \le 25),$$

where y is the murder rate (in murders per 100,000 residents each year) in large cities and x is the murder rate in smaller cities. During the period 1991–1998, the murder rate in small cities was decreasing at an average rate of 2 murders per 100,000 residents each year. Use the chain rule to estimate how fast the murder rate was changing in larger cities during that period. (Show how you used the chain rule in your answer.)

72. *Crime Statistics* Following is a quadratic model relating the murder rates described in the preceding exercise:

$$y = 0.1x^2 - 3x + 39 \quad (15 \le x \le 25).$$

In 1996, the murder rate in smaller cities was approximately 22 murders per 100,000 residents each year and was decreasing at a rate of approximately 2.5 murders per 100,000 residents each year. Use the chain rule to estimate how fast the murder rate was changing for large cities. (Show how you used the chain rule in your answer.)

73. *Existing Home Sales* The following graph shows the approximate value of home prices and existing home sales in 2006–2010 as a percentage change from 2003, together with quadratic approximations.[29]

Home prices and sales of existing homes

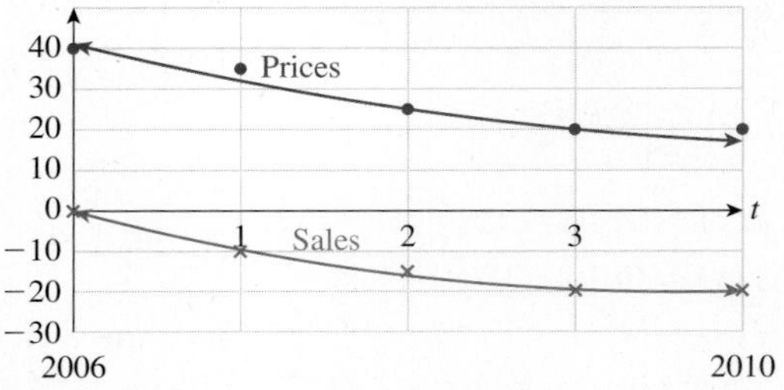

The quadratic approximations are given by

$$\text{Home Prices: } P(t) = t^2 - 10t + 41 \quad (0 \le t \le 4)$$
$$\text{Existing Home Sales: } S(t) = 1.5t^2 - 11t \quad (0 \le t \le 4),$$

[28]The model is a linear regression model. Source for data: Federal Bureau of Investigation, Supplementary Homicide Reports/*New York Times*, May 29, 2000, p. A12.

[29]Sources: Standard & Poors/Bloomberg Financial Markets/*New York Times*, September 29, 2007, p. C3. Projection is the authors'.

where t is time in years since the start of 2006. Use the chain rule to estimate $\left.\frac{dS}{dP}\right|_{t=2}$. What does the answer tell you about home sales and prices? HINT [See the second Quick Example on page 335.]

74. ***Existing Home Sales Leading to the Financial Crisis*** The following graph shows the approximate value of home prices and existing home sales in 2004–2007 (the 3 years prior to the 2008 economic crisis) as a percentage change from 2003, together with quadratic approximations.[30]

Home prices and sales of existing homes

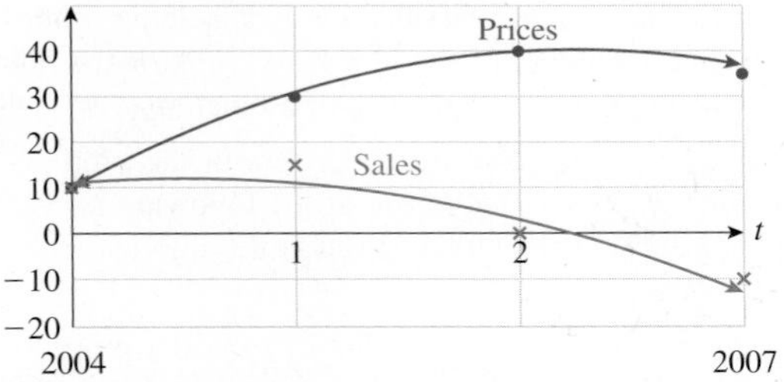

The quadratic approximations are given by

$$\text{Home Prices:} \quad P(t) = -6t^2 + 27t + 10 \quad (0 \le t \le 3)$$
$$\text{Existing Home Sales:} \quad S(t) = -4t^2 + 4t + 11 \quad (0 \le t \le 3),$$

where t is time in years since the start of 2004. Use the chain rule to estimate $\left.\frac{dS}{dP}\right|_{t=2}$. What does the answer tell you about home sales and prices? HINT [See the second Quick Example on page 335.]

75. ▼ ***Pollution*** An offshore oil well is leaking oil and creating a circular oil slick. If the radius of the slick is growing at a rate of 2 miles/hour, find the rate at which the area is increasing when the radius is 3 miles. (The area of a disc of radius r is $A = \pi r^2$.) HINT [See Quick Example 2 on page 334.]

76. ▼ ***Mold*** A mold culture in a dorm refrigerator is circular and growing. The radius is growing at a rate of 0.3 cm/day. How fast is the area growing when the culture is 4 centimeters in radius? (The area of a disc of radius r is $A = \pi r^2$.) HINT [See Quick Example 2 on page 334.]

77. ▼ ***Budget Overruns*** The Pentagon is planning to build a new, spherical satellite. As is typical in these cases, the specifications keep changing, so that the size of the satellite keeps growing. In fact, the radius of the planned satellite is growing 0.5 feet per week. Its cost will be $1,000 per cubic foot. At the point when the plans call for a satellite 10 feet in radius, how fast is the cost growing? (The volume of a solid sphere of radius r is $V = \frac{4}{3}\pi r^3$.)

78. ▼ ***Soap Bubbles*** The soap bubble I am blowing has a radius that is growing at a rate of 4 cm/sec. How fast is the surface area growing when the radius is 10 cm? (The surface area of a sphere of radius r is $S = 4\pi r^2$.)

79. T ▼ ***Revenue Growth*** The demand for the Cyberpunk II arcade video game is modeled by the logistic curve

$$q(t) = \frac{10{,}000}{1 + 0.5e^{-0.4t}}$$

where $q(t)$ is the total number of units sold t months after its introduction.

a. Use technology to estimate $q'(4)$.

b. Assume that the manufacturers of Cyberpunk II sell each unit for $800. What is the company's marginal revenue dR/dq?

c. Use the chain rule to estimate the rate at which revenue is growing 4 months after the introduction of the video game.

80. T ▼ ***Information Highway*** The amount of information transmitted each month in the early years of the Internet (1988 to 1994) can be modeled by the equation

$$q(t) = \frac{2e^{0.69t}}{3 + 1.5e^{-0.4t}} \qquad (0 \le t \le 6),$$

where q is the amount of information transmitted each month in billions of data packets and t is the number of years since the start of 1988.[31]

a. Use technology to estimate $q'(2)$.

b. Assume that it costs $5 to transmit a million packets of data. What is the marginal cost $C'(q)$?

c. How fast was the cost increasing at the start of 1990?

Money Stock *Exercises 81–84 are based on the following demand function for money (taken from a question on the GRE Economics Test):*

$$M_d = 2 \times y^{0.6} \times r^{-0.3} \times p,$$

where

M_d = *demand for nominal money balances (money stock)*
y = *real income*
r = *an index of interest rates*
p = *an index of prices*

These exercises also use the idea of ***percentage rate of growth****:*

$$\text{Percentage Rate of Growth of } M = \frac{\text{Rate of Growth of } M}{M} = \frac{dM/dt}{M}.$$

81. ◆ (from the GRE Economics Test) If the interest rate and price level are to remain constant while real income grows at 5 percent per year, the money stock must grow at what percent per year?

82. ◆ (from the GRE Economics Test) If real income and price level are to remain constant while the interest rate grows at 5 percent per year, the money stock must change by what percent per year?

[30]Sources: Standard & Poors /Bloomberg Financial Markets/*New York Times*, September 29, 2007, p. C3. Projection is the authors'.

[31]This is the authors' model, based on figures published in *New York Times*, Nov. 3, 1993.

83. ◆ (from the GRE Economics Test) If the interest rate is to remain constant while real income grows at 5 percent per year and the price level rises at 5 percent per year, the money stock must grow at what percent per year?

84. ◆ (from the GRE Economics Test) If real income grows by 5 percent per year, the interest rate grows by 2 percent per year, and the price level drops by 3 percent per year, the money stock must change by what percent per year?

COMMUNICATION AND REASONING EXERCISES

85. Complete the following: The derivative of 1 over a glob is −1 over . . . .

86. Complete the following: The derivative of the square root of a glob is 1 over . . . .

87. Say why the following was marked wrong and give the correct answer.

$$\frac{d}{dx}[(3x^3 - x)^3] = 3(9x^2 - 1)^2 \quad ✗ \text{ WRONG!}$$

88. Say why the following was marked wrong and give the correct answer.

$$\frac{d}{dx}\left[\left(\frac{3x^2-1}{2x-2}\right)^3\right] = 3\left(\frac{3x^2-1}{2x-2}\right)^2\left(\frac{6x}{2}\right) \quad ✗ \text{ WRONG!}$$

89. Name two major errors in the following graded test question and give the correct answer.

$$\frac{d}{dx}\left[\left(\frac{3x^2-1}{2x-2}\right)^3\right] = 3\left(\frac{6x}{2}\right)^2 \quad ✗ \text{ WRONG! SEE ME!}$$

90. Name two major errors in the following graded test question and give the correct answer.

$$\frac{d}{dx}[(3x^3 - x)(2x + 1)]^4 = 4[(9x^2 - 1)(2)]^3 \quad ✗ \text{ WRONG! SEE ME!}$$

91. ▼ Formulate a simple procedure for deciding whether to apply first the chain rule, the product rule, or the quotient rule when finding the derivative of a function.

92. ▼ Give an example of a function f with the property that calculating $f'(x)$ requires use of the following rules in the given order: (1) the chain rule, (2) the quotient rule, and (3) the chain rule.

93. ◆ Give an example of a function f with the property that calculating $f'(x)$ requires use of the chain rule five times in succession.

94. ◆ What can you say about the composite of two linear functions and what can you say about its derivative?

4.5 Derivatives of Logarithmic and Exponential Functions

At this point, we know how to take the derivative of any algebraic expression in x (involving powers, radicals, and so on). We now turn to the derivatives of logarithmic and exponential functions.

Derivative of the Natural Logarithm

$$\frac{d}{dx}[\ln x] = \frac{1}{x}$$

Recall that $\ln x = \log_e x$.

Quick Examples

1. $\frac{d}{dx}[3 \ln x] = 3 \cdot \frac{1}{x} = \frac{3}{x}$ — Derivative of a constant times a function

2. $\frac{d}{dx}[x \ln x] = 1 \cdot \ln x + x \cdot \frac{1}{x} = \ln x + 1.$ — Product rule, because $x \ln x$ is a product

The above simple formula works only for the natural logarithm (the logarithm with base e). For logarithms with bases other than e, we have the following:

Derivative of the Logarithm with Base b

$$\frac{d}{dx}[\log_b x] = \frac{1}{x \ln b}$$ Notice that, if $b = e$, we get the same formula as previously.

Quick Examples

1. $\frac{d}{dx}[\log_3 x] = \frac{1}{x \ln 3} \approx \frac{1}{1.0986x}$

2. $\frac{d}{dx}[\log_2(x^4)] = \frac{d}{dx}(4 \log_2 x)$ We used the logarithm identity $\log_b(x^r) = r \log_b x$.

$$= 4 \cdot \frac{1}{x \ln 2} \approx \frac{4}{0.6931x}$$

Derivation of the formulas $\frac{d}{dx}[\ln x] = \frac{1}{x}$ and $\frac{d}{dx}[\log_b x] = \frac{1}{x \ln b}$

To compute $\frac{d}{dx}[\ln x]$, we need to use the definition of the derivative. We also use properties of the logarithm to help evaluate the limit.

$$\frac{d}{dx}[\ln x] = \lim_{h\to 0} \frac{\ln(x+h) - \ln x}{h}$$ Definition of the derivative

$$= \lim_{h\to 0} \frac{1}{h}[\ln(x+h) - \ln x]$$ Algebra

$$= \lim_{h\to 0} \frac{1}{h} \ln\left(\frac{x+h}{x}\right)$$ Properties of the logarithm

$$= \lim_{h\to 0} \frac{1}{h} \ln\left(1 + \frac{h}{x}\right)$$ Algebra

$$= \lim_{h\to 0} \ln\left(1 + \frac{h}{x}\right)^{1/h}$$ Properties of the logarithm

which we rewrite as

$$\lim_{h\to 0} \ln\left[\left(1 + \frac{1}{(x/h)}\right)^{x/h}\right]^{1/x}.$$

As $h \to 0^+$, the quantity x/h gets large and positive, and so the quantity in brackets approaches e (see the definition of e in Section 2.2), which leaves us with

$$\ln[e]^{1/x} = \frac{1}{x} \ln e = \frac{1}{x}$$

which is the derivative we are after.* What about the limit as $h \to 0^-$? We will glide over that case and leave it for the interested reader to pursue.†

The rule for the derivative of $\log_b x$ follows from the fact that $\log_b x = \ln x / \ln b$.

If we were to take the derivative of the natural logarithm of a *quantity* (a function of x), rather than just x, we would need to use the chain rule:

* We actually used the fact that the logarithm function is continuous when we took the limit.

† Here is an outline of the argument for negative h. Because x must be positive for $\ln x$ to be defined, we find that $x/h \to -\infty$ as $h \to 0^-$, and so we must consider the quantity $(1 + 1/m)^m$ for large *negative* m. It turns out the limit is still e (check it numerically!) and so the computation above still works.

Derivatives of Logarithms of Functions

Original Rule	*Generalized Rule*	*In Words*
$\frac{d}{dx}[\ln x] = \frac{1}{x}$	$\frac{d}{dx}[\ln u] = \frac{1}{u}\frac{du}{dx}$	*The derivative of the natural logarithm of a quantity is* 1 *over that quantity, times the derivative of that quantity.*
$\frac{d}{dx}[\log_b x] = \frac{1}{x \ln b}$	$\frac{d}{dx}[\log_b u] = \frac{1}{u \ln b}\frac{du}{dx}$	*The derivative of the log to base b of a quantity is* 1 *over the product of* ln *b and that quantity, times the derivative of that quantity.*

Quick Examples

1. $\frac{d}{dx}\ln[x^2+1] = \frac{1}{x^2+1}\frac{d}{dx}(x^2+1)$ $\quad u = x^2 + 1$ (See the margin note.§)

$$= \frac{1}{x^2+1}(2x) = \frac{2x}{x^2+1}$$

2. $\frac{d}{dx}\log_2[x^3+x] = \frac{1}{(x^3+x)\ln 2}\frac{d}{dx}(x^3+x)$ $\quad u = x^3 + x$

$$= \frac{1}{(x^3+x)\ln 2}(3x^2+1) = \frac{3x^2+1}{(x^3+x)\ln 2}$$

§ If we were to evaluate $\ln(x^2+1)$, the last operation we would perform would be to take the natural logarithm of a quantity. Thus, the calculation thought experiment tells us that we are dealing with ln *of a quantity*, and so we need the generalized logarithm rule as stated above.

EXAMPLE 1 Derivative of Logarithmic Function

Compute the following derivatives:

a. $\frac{d}{dx}[\ln\sqrt{x+1}]$ **b.** $\frac{d}{dx}[\ln[(1+x)(2-x)]]$ **c.** $\frac{d}{dx}[\ln|x|]$

Solution

a. The calculation thought experiment tells us that we have the natural logarithm of a quantity, so

$$\frac{d}{dx}[\ln\sqrt{x+1}] = \frac{1}{\sqrt{x+1}}\frac{d}{dx}\sqrt{x+1} \qquad \frac{d}{dx}\ln u = \frac{1}{u}\frac{du}{dx}$$

$$= \frac{1}{\sqrt{x+1}} \cdot \frac{1}{2\sqrt{x+1}} \qquad \frac{d}{dx}\sqrt{u} = \frac{1}{2\sqrt{u}}\frac{du}{dx}$$

$$= \frac{1}{2(x+1)}.$$

Q: *What happened to the square root?*

A: As with many problems involving logarithms, we could have done this one differently and much more easily if we had simplified the expression ln $\sqrt{x+1}$ using the properties of logarithms *before* differentiating. Doing this, we get the following:

Part (a) redone by simplifying first:

$$\ln\sqrt{x+1} = \ln(x+1)^{1/2} = \frac{1}{2}\ln(x+1). \qquad \text{Simplify the logarithm first.}$$

Thus,

$$\frac{d}{dx}[\ln\sqrt{x+1}] = \frac{d}{dx}\left[\frac{1}{2}\ln(x+1)\right]$$

$$= \frac{1}{2}\left[\frac{1}{x+1}\right]\cdot 1 = \frac{1}{2(x+1)}.$$

A *lot* easier!

b. This time, we simplify the expression $\ln[(1+x)(2-x)]$ before taking the derivative:

$$\ln[(1+x)(2-x)] = \ln(1+x) + \ln(2-x). \qquad \text{Simplify the logarithm first.}$$

Thus,

$$\frac{d}{dx}[\ln[(1+x)(2-x)]] = \frac{d}{dx}[\ln[(1+x)]] + \frac{d}{dx}[\ln[(2-x)]]$$

$$= \frac{1}{1+x} - \frac{1}{2-x}. \qquad \frac{d}{dx}\ln u = \frac{1}{u}\frac{du}{dx}$$

For practice, try doing this calculation without simplifying first. What other differentiation rule do you need to use?

c. Before we start, we note that $\ln x$ is defined only for positive values of x, so its domain is the set of positive real numbers. The domain of $\ln|x|$, on the other hand, is the set of *all* nonzero real numbers. For example, $\ln|-2| = \ln 2 \approx 0.6931$. For this reason, $\ln|x|$ often turns out to be more useful than the ordinary logarithm function.

$$\frac{d}{dx}[\ln|x|] = \frac{1}{|x|}\frac{d}{dx}|x| \qquad \frac{d}{dx}\ln u = \frac{1}{u}\frac{du}{dx}$$

$$= \frac{1}{|x|}\frac{|x|}{x} \qquad \text{Recall that } \frac{d}{dx}|x| = \frac{|x|}{x}.$$

$$= \frac{1}{x}$$

➡ **Before we go on...** Figure 7(a) shows the graphs of $y = \ln |x|$ and $y = 1/x$. Figure 7(b) shows the graphs of $y = \ln |x|$ and $y = 1/|x|$. You should be able to see from these graphs why the derivative of $\ln |x|$ is $1/x$ and not $1/|x|$.

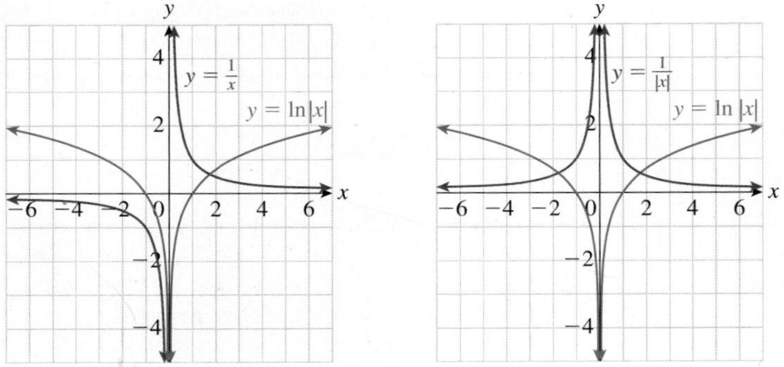

Figure 7(a) **Figure 7(b)** ■

This last example, in conjunction with the chain rule, gives us the following formulas.

Derivative of Logarithms of Absolute Values

Original Rule	*Generalized Rule*	*In Words*
$\frac{d}{dx}[\ln \lvert x \rvert] = \frac{1}{x}$	$\frac{d}{dx}[\ln \lvert u \rvert] = \frac{1}{u}\frac{du}{dx}$	*The derivative of the natural logarithm of the absolute value of a quantity is 1 over that quantity, times the derivative of that quantity.*
$\frac{d}{dx}[\log_b \lvert x \rvert] = \frac{1}{x \ln b}$	$\frac{d}{dx}[\log_b \lvert u \rvert] = \frac{1}{u \ln b}\frac{du}{dx}$	*The derivative of the log to base b of the absolute value of a quantity is 1 over the product of ln b and that quantity, times the derivative of that quantity.*

Note: Compare the above formulas with those on page 342. They tell us that we can simply ignore the absolute values in $\ln |u|$ or $\log_b |u|$ when taking the derivative.

Quick Examples

1. $\frac{d}{dx}[\ln |x^2 - 1|] = \frac{1}{x^2 - 1}\frac{d}{dx}(x^2 - 1)$ $\quad u = x^2 - 1$

$$= \frac{1}{x^2 - 1}(2x) = \frac{2x}{x^2 - 1}$$

2. $\frac{d}{dx}[\log_2|x^3+x|] = \frac{1}{(x^3+x)\ln 2}\frac{d}{dx}(x^3+x)$ $u = x^3 + x$

$= \frac{1}{(x^3+x)\ln 2}(3x^2+1) = \frac{3x^2+1}{(x^3+x)\ln 2}$

We now turn to the derivatives of *exponential* functions—that is, functions of the form $f(x) = b^x$. We begin by showing how *not* to differentiate them.

Caution The derivative of b^x is *not* xb^{x-1}. The power rule applies only to *constant* exponents. In this case the exponent is decidedly *not* constant, and so the power rule does not apply.

The following shows the correct way of differentiating b^x, beginning with a special case.

Derivative of e^x

$$\frac{d}{dx}[e^x] = e^x$$

Quick Examples

1. $\frac{d}{dx}[3e^x] = 3\frac{d}{dx}[e^x] = 3e^x$ Constant multiple rule

2. $\frac{d}{dx}\left[\frac{e^x}{x}\right] = \frac{e^x x - e^x(1)}{x^2}$ Quotient rule

$= \frac{e^x(x-1)}{x^2}$

Thus, e^x has the amazing property that its derivative is itself!* For bases other than e, we have the following generalization:

* There is another—very simple—function that is its own derivative. What is it?

Derivative of b^x

If b is any positive number, then

$$\frac{d}{dx}[b^x] = b^x \ln b.$$

Note that if $b = e$, we obtain the previous formula.

Quick Example

$$\frac{d}{dx}[3^x] = 3^x \ln 3$$

Derivation of the Formula $\frac{d}{dx}[e^x] = e^x$

To find the derivative of e^x, we use a shortcut.* Write $g(x) = e^x$. Then

$$\ln g(x) = x.$$

Take the derivative of both sides of this equation to get

$$\frac{g'(x)}{g(x)} = 1$$

or

$$g'(x) = g(x) = e^x.$$

In other words, the exponential function with base e is its own derivative. The rule for exponential functions with other bases follows from the equality $b^x = e^{x\ln b}$ (why?) and the chain rule. (Try it.)

If we were to take the derivative of e raised to a *quantity*, not just x, we would need to use the chain rule, as follows.

* This shortcut is an example of a technique called *logarithmic differentiation*, which is occasionally useful. We will see it again in the next section.

Derivatives of Exponentials of Functions

Original Rule	*Generalized Rule*	*In Words*
$\frac{d}{dx}[e^x] = e^x$	$\frac{d}{dx}[e^u] = e^u\frac{du}{dx}$	*The derivative of e raised to a quantity is e raised to that quantity, times the derivative of that quantity.*
$\frac{d}{dx}[b^x] = b^x \ln b$	$\frac{d}{dx}[b^u] = b^u \ln b\frac{du}{dx}$	*The derivative of b raised to a quantity is b raised to that quantity, times* ln *b, times the derivative of that quantity.*

Quick Examples

1. $\frac{d}{dx}\left[e^{x^2+1}\right] = e^{x^2+1}\frac{d}{dx}[x^2+1]$ $\quad u = x^2+1$ (See margin note.†)

$$= e^{x^2+1}(2x) = 2x\, e^{x^2+1}$$

2. $\frac{d}{dx}[2^{3x}] = 2^{3x}\ln 2\frac{d}{dx}[3x]$ $\quad u = 3x$

$$= 2^{3x}(\ln 2)(3) = (3\ln 2)2^{3x}$$

3. $\frac{d}{dt}[30e^{1.02t}] = 30e^{1.02t}(1.02) = 30.6e^{1.02t}$ $\quad u = 1.02t$

4. If \$1,000 is invested in an account earning 5% per year compounded continuously, then the rate of change of the account balance after t years is

$$\frac{d}{dt}[1{,}000e^{0.05t}] = 1{,}000(0.05)e^{0.05t} = 50e^{0.05t} \text{ dollars/year.}$$

† The calculation thought experiment tells us that we have e raised to a quantity.

APPLICATIONS

EXAMPLE 2 Epidemics

In the early stages of the AIDS epidemic during the 1980s, the number of cases in the United States was increasing by about 50% every 6 months. By the start of 1983, there were approximately 1,600 AIDS cases in the United States.[32] Had this trend continued, how many new cases per year would have been occurring by the start of 1993?

Solution To find the answer, we must first model this exponential growth using the methods of Chapter 2. Referring to Example 4 in Section 2.2, we find that t years after the start of 1983 the number of cases is

$$A = 1{,}600(2.25^t).$$

We are asking for the number of new cases each year. In other words, we want the rate of change, dA/dt:

$$\frac{dA}{dt} = 1{,}600(2.25)^t \ln 2.25 \text{ cases per year.}$$

At the start of 1993, $t = 10$, so the number of new cases per year is

$$\left.\frac{dA}{dt}\right|_{t=10} = 1{,}600(2.25)^{10} \ln 2.25 \approx 4{,}300{,}000 \text{ cases per year.}$$

➡ **Before we go on...** In Example 2, the figure for the number of new cases per year is so large because we assumed that exponential growth—the 50% increase every 6 months—would continue. A more realistic model for the spread of a disease is the logistic model. (See Section 2.4, as well as the next example.) ■

EXAMPLE 3 Sales Growth

The sales of the *Cyberpunk II* video game can be modeled by the logistic curve

$$q(t) = \frac{10{,}000}{1 + 0.5e^{-0.4t}}$$

where $q(t)$ is the total number of units sold t months after its introduction. How fast is the game selling 2 years after its introduction?

Solution We are asked for $q'(24)$. We can find the derivative of $q(t)$ using the quotient rule, or we can first write

$$q(t) = 10{,}000(1 + 0.5e^{-0.4t})^{-1}$$

and then use the generalized power rule:

$$q'(t) = -10{,}000(1 + 0.5e^{-0.4t})^{-2}(0.5e^{-0.4t})(-0.4)$$

$$= \frac{2{,}000e^{-0.4t}}{(1 + 0.5e^{-0.4t})^2}.$$

[32]Data based on regression of 1982–1986 figures. Source for data: Centers for Disease Control and Prevention. HIV/AIDS Surveillance Report, 2000;12 (No. 2).

Thus,

$$q'(24) = \frac{2{,}000e^{-0.4(24)}}{(1+0.5e^{-0.4(24)})^2} \approx 0.135 \text{ units per month.}$$

So, after 2 years, sales are quite slow.

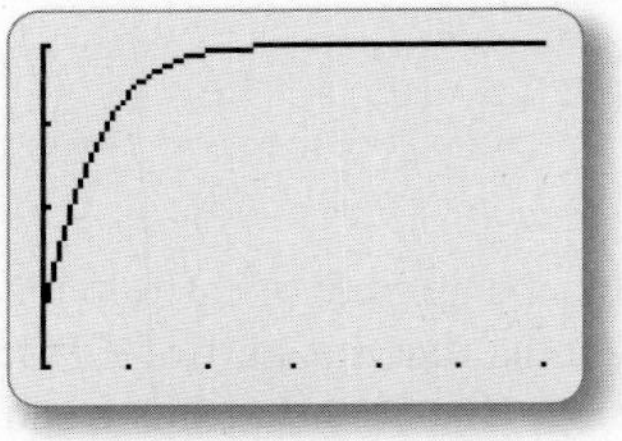

Figure 8

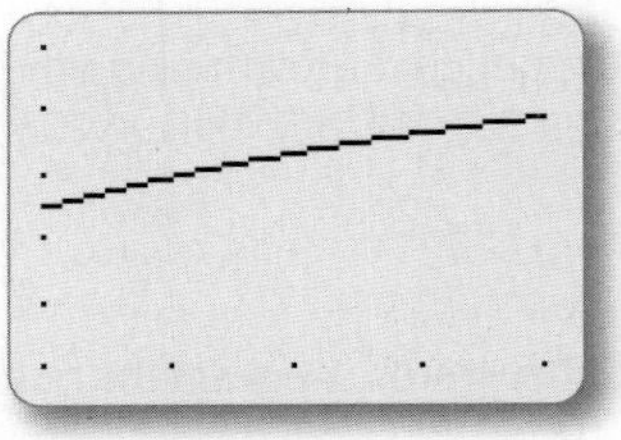

Figure 9

Before we go on... We can check the answer in Example 3 graphically. If we plot the total sales curve for $0 \le t \le 30$ and $6{,}000 \le q \le 10{,}000$, on a TI-83/84 Plus, for example, we get the graph shown in Figure 8. Notice that total sales level off at about 10,000 units.* We computed $q'(24)$, which is the slope of the curve at the point with t-coordinate 24. If we zoom in to the portion of the curve near $t = 24$, we obtain the graph shown in Figure 9, with $23 \le t \le 25$ and $9{,}999 \le q \le 10{,}000$. The curve is almost linear in this range. If we use the two endpoints of this segment of the curve, (23, 9,999.4948) and (25, 9,999.7730), we can approximate the derivative as

$$\frac{9{,}999.7730 - 9{,}999.4948}{25 - 23} = 0.1391$$

which is accurate to two decimal places. ■

* We can also say this using limits: $\lim_{t\to+\infty} q(t) = 10{,}000$.

4.5 EXERCISES

▼ more advanced ◆ challenging

T indicates exercises that should be solved using technology

Find the derivatives of the functions in Exercises 1–76.
HINT [See Quick Examples on page 342.]

1. $f(x) = \ln(x-1)$
2. $f(x) = \ln(x+3)$
3. $f(x) = \log_2 x$
4. $f(x) = \log_3 x$
5. $g(x) = \ln|x^2+3|$
6. $g(x) = \ln|2x-4|$
7. $h(x) = e^{x+3}$ HINT [See Quick Examples on page 346.]
8. $h(x) = e^{x^2}$ HINT [See Quick Examples on page 346.]
9. $f(x) = e^{-x}$
10. $f(x) = e^{1-x}$
11. $g(x) = 4^x$
12. $g(x) = 5^x$
13. $h(x) = 2^{x^2-1}$
14. $h(x) = 3^{x^2-x}$
15. $f(x) = x\ln x$
16. $f(x) = 3\ln x$
17. $f(x) = (x^2+1)\ln x$
18. $f(x) = (4x^2-x)\ln x$
19. $f(x) = (x^2+1)^5\ln x$
20. $f(x) = (x+1)^{0.5}\ln x$
21. $g(x) = \ln|3x-1|$
22. $g(x) = \ln|5-9x|$
23. $g(x) = \ln|2x^2+1|$
24. $g(x) = \ln|x^2-x|$
25. $g(x) = \ln(x^2-2.1x^{0.3})$
26. $g(x) = \ln(x-3.1x^{-1})$
27. $h(x) = \ln[(-2x+1)(x+1)]$ HINT [See Example 1b.]
28. $h(x) = \ln[(3x+1)(-x+1)]$ HINT [See Example 1b.]
29. $h(x) = \ln\left(\frac{3x+1}{4x-2}\right)$
30. $h(x) = \ln\left(\frac{9x}{4x-2}\right)$
31. $r(x) = \ln\left|\frac{(x+1)(x-3)}{-2x-9}\right|$
32. $r(x) = \ln\left|\frac{-x+1}{(3x-4)(x-9)}\right|$
33. $s(x) = \ln(4x-2)^{1.3}$ HINT [See Example 1a.]
34. $s(x) = \ln(x-8)^{-2}$ HINT [See Example 1a.]
35. $s(x) = \ln\left|\frac{(x+1)^2}{(3x-4)^3(x-9)}\right|$
36. $s(x) = \ln\left|\frac{(x+1)^2(x-3)^4}{2x+9}\right|$
37. $h(x) = \log_2(x+1)$
38. $h(x) = \log_3(x^2+x)$
39. $r(t) = \log_3(t+1/t)$
40. $r(t) = \log_3\left(t+\sqrt{t}\right)$
41. $f(x) = (\ln|x|)^2$
42. $f(x) = \frac{1}{\ln|x|}$
43. $r(x) = \ln(x^2) - [\ln(x-1)]^2$
44. $r(x) = (\ln(x^2))^2$
45. $f(x) = xe^x$
46. $f(x) = 2e^x - x^2e^x$
47. $r(x) = \ln(x+1) + 3x^3e^x$
48. $r(x) = \ln|x+e^x|$
49. $f(x) = e^x\ln|x|$
50. $f(x) = e^x\log_2|x|$
51. $f(x) = e^{2x+1}$
52. $f(x) = e^{4x-5}$
53. $h(x) = e^{x^2-x+1}$
54. $h(x) = e^{2x^2-x+1/x}$
55. $s(x) = x^2e^{2x-1}$
56. $s(x) = \frac{e^{4x-1}}{x^3-1}$
57. $r(x) = (e^{2x-1})^2$
58. $r(x) = (e^{2x^2})^3$
59. $t(x) = 3^{2x-4}$
60. $t(x) = 4^{-x+5}$
61. $v(x) = 3^{2x+1} + e^{3x+1}$
62. $v(x) = e^{2x}4^{2x}$

63. $u(x) = \dfrac{3^{x^2}}{x^2+1}$

64. $u(x) = (x^2+1)4^{x^2-1}$

65. $g(x) = \dfrac{e^x + e^{-x}}{e^x - e^{-x}}$

66. $g(x) = \dfrac{1}{e^x + e^{-x}}$

67. ▼ $g(x) = e^{3x-1}e^{x-2}e^x$

68. ▼ $g(x) = e^{-x+3}e^{2x-1}e^{-x+11}$

69. ▼ $f(x) = \dfrac{1}{x \ln x}$

70. ▼ $f(x) = \dfrac{e^{-x}}{xe^x}$

71. ▼ $f(x) = [\ln(e^x)]^2 - \ln[(e^x)^2]$

72. ▼ $f(x) = e^{\ln x} - e^{2\ln(x^2)}$

73. ▼ $f(x) = \ln|\ln x|$

74. ▼ $f(x) = \ln|\ln|\ln x||$

75. ▼ $s(x) = \ln\sqrt{\ln x}$

76. ▼ $s(x) = \sqrt{\ln(\ln x)}$

Find the equations of the straight lines described in Exercises 77–82. Use graphing technology to check your answers by plotting the given curve together with the tangent line.

77. Tangent to $y = e^x \log_2 x$ at the point $(1, 0)$

78. Tangent to $y = e^x + e^{-x}$ at the point $(0, 2)$

79. Tangent to $y = \ln\sqrt{2x+1}$ at the point where $x = 0$

80. Tangent to $y = \ln\sqrt{2x^2+1}$ at the point where $x = 1$

81. At right angles to $y = e^{x^2}$ at the point where $x = 1$

82. At right angles to $y = \log_2(3x+1)$ at the point where $x = 1$

APPLICATIONS

83. ***Research and Development: Industry*** The total spent on research and development by industry in the United States during 1995–2007 can be approximated by

$$S(t) = 57.5 \ln t + 31 \text{ billion dollars} \quad (5 \le t \le 17),$$

where t is the year since 1990.[33] What was the total spent in 2000 ($t = 10$) and how fast was it increasing? HINT [See Quick Examples on page 340.]

84. ***Research and Development: Federal*** The total spent on research and development by the federal government in the United States during 1995–2007 can be approximated by

$$S(t) = 7.4 \ln t + 3 \text{ billion dollars} \quad (5 \le t \le 17),$$

where t is the year since 1990.[34] What was the total spent in 2005 ($t = 15$) and how fast was it increasing? HINT [See Quick Examples on page 340.]

85. ***Research and Development: Industry*** The function $S(t)$ in Exercise 83 can also be written (approximately) as

$$S(t) = 57.5 \ln(1.71t + 17.1) \text{ billion dollars} \quad (-5 \le t \le 7),$$

where this time t is the year since 2000. Use this alternative formula to estimate the amount spent in 2000 and its rate of change, and check your answers by comparing them with those in Exercise 83.

86. ***Research and Development: Federal*** The function $S(t)$ in Exercise 84 can also be written (approximately) as

$$S(t) = 7.4 \ln(1.5t + 15) \text{ billion dollars} \quad (-5 \le t \le 7),$$

where this time t is the year since 2000. Use this alternative formula to estimate the amount spent in 2005 and its rate of change, and check your answers by comparing them with those in Exercise 84.

87. ▼ ***Carbon Dating*** The age in years of a specimen that originally contained 10g of carbon 14 is given by

$$y = \log_{0.999879}(0.1x),$$

where x is the amount of carbon 14 it currently contains. Compute $\left.\dfrac{dy}{dx}\right|_{x=5}$ and interpret your answer. HINT [For the calculation, see Quick Examples on page 342.]

88. ▼ ***Iodine Dating*** The age in years of a specimen that originally contained 10g of iodine 131 is given by

$$y = \log_{0.999567}(0.1x),$$

where x is the amount of iodine 131 it currently contains. Compute $\left.\dfrac{dy}{dx}\right|_{x=8}$ and interpret your answer. HINT [For the calculation, see Quick Examples on page 342.]

89. ***New York City Housing Costs: Downtown*** The average price of a two-bedroom apartment in downtown New York City during the real estate boom from 1994 to 2004 can be approximated by

$$p(t) = 0.33e^{0.16t} \text{ million dollars} \quad (0 \le t \le 10),$$

where t is time in years ($t = 0$ represents 1994).[35] What was the average price of a two-bedroom apartment in downtown New York City in 2003, and how fast was it increasing? (Round your answers to two significant digits.) HINT [See Quick Example 3 on page 346.]

90. ***New York City Housing Costs: Uptown*** The average price of a two-bedroom apartment in uptown New York City during the real estate boom from 1994 to 2004 can be approximated by

$$p(t) = 0.14e^{0.10t} \text{ million dollars} \quad (0 \le t \le 10),$$

where t is time in years ($t = 0$ represents 1994).[36] What was the average price of a two-bedroom apartment in uptown

[33] Spending is in constant 2000 dollars. Source for data through 2006: National Science Foundation, Division of Science Resources Statistics, National Patterns of R&D Resources (www.nsf.gov/statistics) August 2008.

[34] Federal funding excluding grants to industry and nonprofit organizations. Spending is in constant 2000 dollars. Source for data through 2006: National Science Foundation, Division of Science Resources Statistics, National Patterns of R&D Resources (www.nsf.gov/statistics) August 2008.

[35] Model is based on a exponential regression. Source for data: Miller Samuel/*New York Times*, March 28, 2004, p. RE 11.

[36] *Ibid.*

New York City in 2002, and how fast was it increasing? (Round your answers to two significant digits.) HINT [See Quick Example 3 on page 346.]

91. ***Big Brother*** The following chart shows the total number of wiretaps authorized each year by U.S. state and federal courts from 1990 to 2009 ($t = 0$ represents 1990):[37]

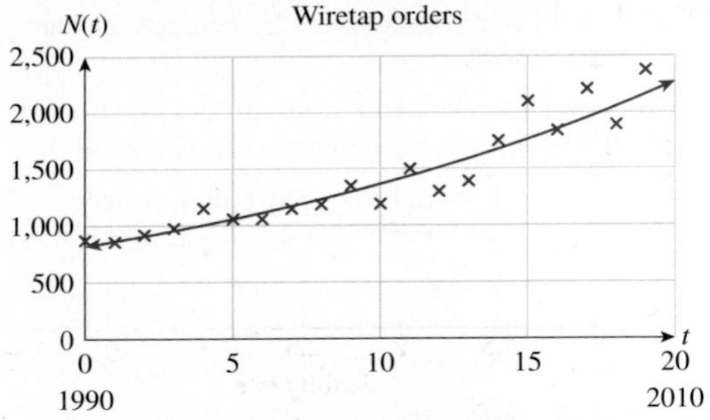

These data can be approximated with the model

$$N(t) = 820e^{0.051t} \quad (0 \le t \le 19).$$

a. Find $N(15)$ and $N'(15)$. Be sure to state the units of measurement. To how many significant digits should we round the answers? Why?

b. The number of people whose communications are intercepted averages around 100 per wiretap order. What does the answer to part (a) tell you about the number of people whose communications were intercepted?[38]

c. According to the model, the number of wiretaps orders each year (choose one)

(A) increased at a linear rate
(B) decreased at a quadratic rate
(C) increased at an exponential rate
(D) increased at a logarithmic rate

over the period shown.

92. ***Big Brother*** The following chart shows the total number of wiretaps authorized each year by U.S. state courts from 1990 to 2009 ($t = 0$ represents 1990):[39]

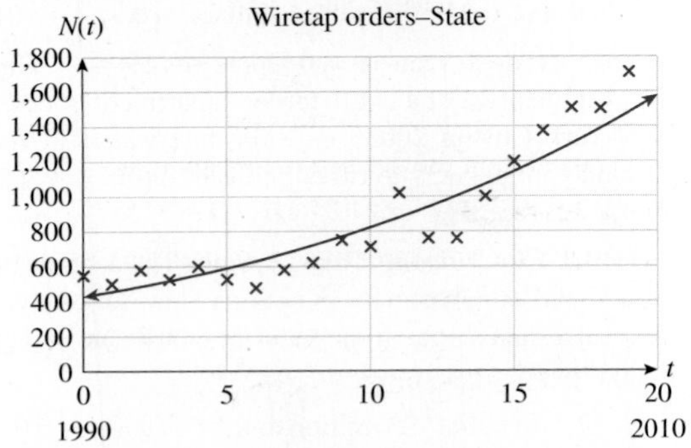

These data can be approximated with the model

$$N(t) = 430e^{0.065t} \quad (0 \le t \le 19).$$

a. Find $N(10)$ and $N'(10)$. Be sure to state the units of measurement. To how many significant digits should we round the answers? Why?

b. The number of people whose communications are intercepted averages around 100 per wiretap order. What does the answer to part (a) tell you about the number of people whose communications were intercepted?[40]

c. According to the model, the number of wiretaps orders each year (choose one)

(A) increased at a linear rate
(B) decreased at a quadratic rate
(C) increased at an exponential rate
(D) increased at a logarithmic rate

over the period shown.

93. ***Investments*** If \$10,000 is invested in a savings account offering 4% per year, compounded continuously, how fast is the balance growing after 3 years?

94. ***Investments*** If \$20,000 is invested in a savings account offering 3.5% per year, compounded continuously, how fast is the balance growing after 3 years?

95. ***Investments*** If \$10,000 is invested in a savings account offering 4% per year, compounded semiannually, how fast is the balance growing after 3 years?

96. ***Investments*** If \$20,000 is invested in a savings account offering 3.5% per year, compounded semiannually, how fast is the balance growing after 3 years?

97. ***SARS*** In the early stages of the deadly SARS (Severe Acute Respiratory Syndrome) epidemic in 2003, the number of cases was increasing by about 18% each day.[41] On March 17, 2003 (the first day for which statistics were reported by the World Health Organization) there were 167 cases. Find an exponential model that predicts the number of people infected t days after March 17, 2003, and use it to estimate how fast the epidemic was spreading on March 31, 2003. (Round your answer to the nearest whole number of new cases per day.) HINT [See Example 2.]

98. ***SARS*** A few weeks into the deadly SARS (Severe Acute Respiratory Syndrome) epidemic in 2003, the number of cases was increasing by about 4% each day.[42] On April 1, 2003 there were 1,804 cases. Find an exponential model that predicts the number $A(t)$ of people infected t days after April 1, 2003, and use it to estimate how fast the epidemic was spreading on April 30, 2003. (Round your answer to the nearest whole number of new cases per day.) HINT [See Example 2.]

[37] Source for data: Wiretap Reports, Administrative Office of the United States Courts www.uscourts.gov/Statistics/WiretapReports.

[38] Assume there is no significant overlap between the people whose communications are intercepted in different wiretap orders.

[39] See Footnote 37.

[40] See Footnote 38.

[41] World Health Organization (www.who.int).

[42] *Ibid.*

99. ▼ ***SAT Scores by Income*** The following bar graph shows U.S. math SAT scores as a function of household income:[43]

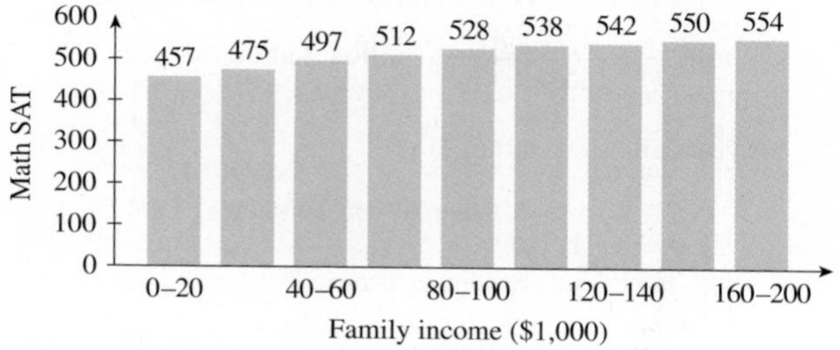

a. Which of the following best models the data (C is a constant)?

(A) $S(x) = C - 133e^{-0.0131x}$

(B) $S(x) = C + 133e^{-0.0131x}$

(C) $S(x) = C + 133e^{0.0131x}$

(D) $S(x) = C - 133e^{0.0131x}$

($S(x)$ is the average math SAT score of students whose household income is x thousand dollars per year.)

b. Use $S'(x)$ to predict how a student's math SAT score is affected by a $1,000 increase in parents' income for a student whose parents earn $45,000.

c. Does $S'(x)$ increase or decrease as x increases? Interpret your answer.

100. ***SAT Scores by Income*** The following bar graph shows U.S. critical reading SAT scores as a function of household income:[44]

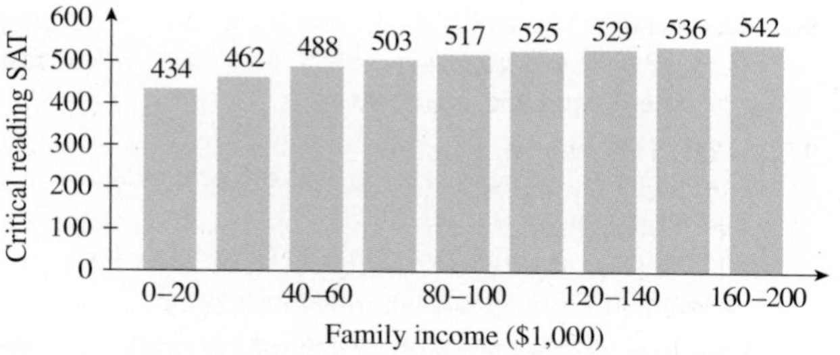

a. Which of the following best models the data (C is a constant)?

(A) $S(x) = C + \dfrac{1}{136e^{0.015x}}$

(B) $S(x) = C - 136e^{0.015x}$

(C) $S(x) = C - \dfrac{136}{e^{0.015x}}$

(D) $S(x) = C - \dfrac{e^{0.015x}}{136}$

($S(x)$ is the average critical reading SAT score of students whose household income is x thousand dollars per year.)

b. Use $S'(x)$ to predict how a student's critical reading SAT score is affected by a $1,000 increase in parents' income for a student whose parents earn $45,000.

c. Does $S'(x)$ increase or decrease as x increases? Interpret your answer.

101. ▼ ***Demographics: Average Age and Fertility*** The following graph shows a plot of average age of a population versus fertility rate (the average number of children each woman has in her lifetime) in the United States and Europe over the period 1950–2005.[45]

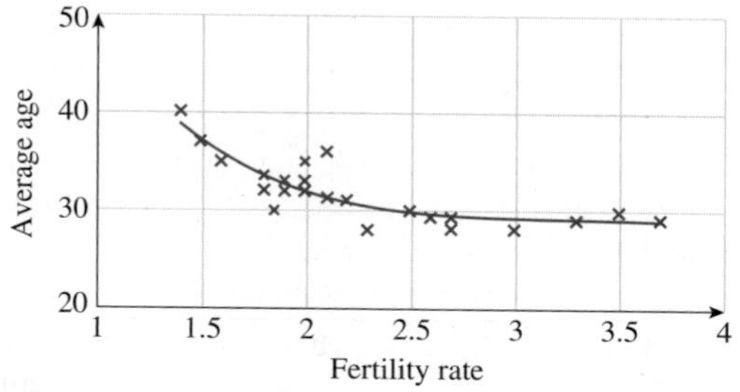

The equation of the accompanying curve is

$$a = 28.5 + 120(0.172)^x \quad (1.4 \le x \le 3.7),$$

where a is the average age (in years) of the population and x is the fertility rate.

a. Compute $a'(2)$. What does the answer tell you about average age and fertility rates?

b. Use the answer to part (a) to estimate how much the fertility rate would need to increase from a level of 2 children per woman to lower the average age of a population by about 1 year.

102. ▼ ***Demographics: Average Age and Fertility*** The following graph shows a plot of average age of a population versus fertility rate (the average number of children each woman has in her lifetime) in Europe over the period 1950–2005.[46]

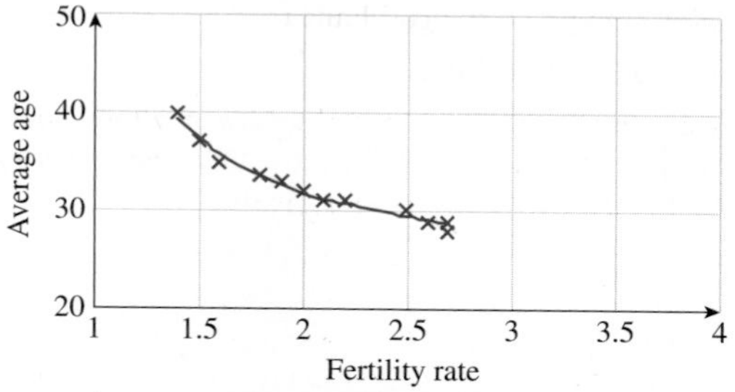

The equation of the accompanying curve is

$$g = 27.6 + 128(0.181)^x \quad (1.4 \le x \le 3.7),$$

where g is the average age (in years) of the population and x is the fertility rate.

a. Compute $g'(2.5)$. What does the answer tell you about average age and fertility rates?

[43] 2009 data. Source: College Board/*New York Times* http://economix.blogs.nytimes.com.

[44] *Ibid.*

[45] The separate data for Europe and the United States are collected in the same graph. 2005 figures are estimates. Source: United Nations World Population Division/*New York Times*, June 29, 2003, p. 3.

[46] All European countries including the Russian Federation. 2005 figures are estimates. Source: United Nations World Population Division/*New York Times*, June 29, 2003, p. 3.

b. Referring to the model that combines the data for Europe and the United States in Exercise 101, which population's average age is affected more by a changing fertility rate at the level of 2.5 children per woman?

103. ***Epidemics*** A flu epidemic described in Example 1 in Section 2.4 approximately followed the curve

$$P = \frac{150}{1 + 15{,}000e^{-0.35t}} \text{ million people,}$$

where P is the number of people infected and t is the number of weeks after the start of the epidemic. How fast is the epidemic growing (that is, how many new cases are there each week) after 20 weeks? After 30 weeks? After 40 weeks? (Round your answers to two significant digits.) HINT [See Example 3.]

104. ***Epidemics*** Another epidemic follows the curve

$$P = \frac{200}{1 + 20{,}000e^{-0.549t}} \text{ million people,}$$

where t is in years. How fast is the epidemic growing after 10 years? After 20 years? After 30 years? (Round your answers to two significant digits.) HINT [See Example 3.]

105. ***Subprime Mortgages during the Housing Bubble*** During the real estate run-up in 2000–2008, the percentage of mortgages issued in the U.S. that were subprime (normally classified as risky) could be approximated by

$$A(t) = \frac{15.0}{1 + 8.6e^{-0.59t}} \text{ percent} \quad (0 \le t \le 8)$$

t years after the start of 2000.[47]

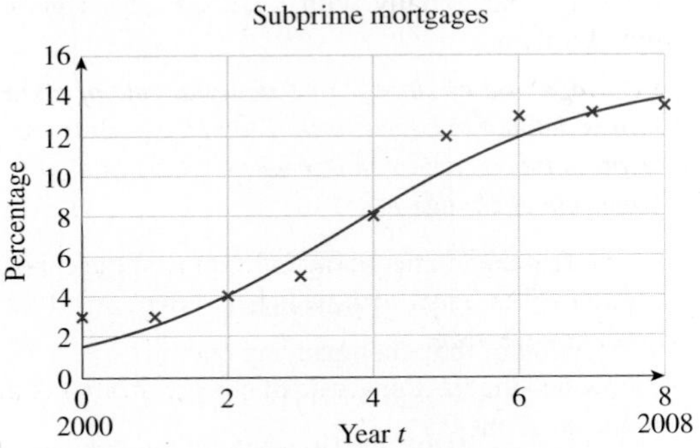

How fast, to the nearest 0.1%, was the percentage increasing at the start of 2003? How would you check that the answer is approximately correct by looking at the graph? HINT [See Example 3.]

106. ***Subprime Mortgage Debt during the Housing Bubble*** During the real estate run-up in 2000–2008, the value of subprime (normally classified as risky) mortgage debt outstanding in the U.S. was approximately

$$A(t) = \frac{1{,}350}{1 + 4.2e^{-0.53t}} \text{ billion dollars} \quad (0 \le t \le 8)$$

t years after the start of 2000.[48]

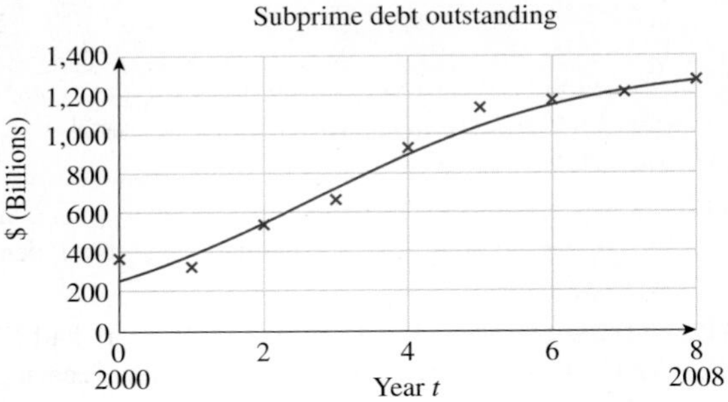

How fast, to the nearest $1 billion, was subprime mortgage debt increasing at the start of 2005? How would you check that the answer is approximately correct by looking at the graph? HINT [See Example 3.]

107. ***Subprime Mortgages during the Housing Bubble*** (Compare Exercise 105.) During the real estate run-up in 2000–2008, the percentage of mortgages issued in the U.S. that were subprime (normally classified as risky) could be approximated by

$$A(t) = \frac{15.0}{1 + 8.6(1.8)^{-t}} \text{ percent} \quad (0 \le t \le 8)$$

t years after the start of 2000.[49]

a. How fast, to the nearest 0.1%, was the percentage increasing at the start of 2003?

b. Compute $\lim_{t\to+\infty} A(t)$ and $\lim_{t\to+\infty} A'(t)$. What do the answers tell you about subprime mortgages?

108. ***Subprime Mortgage Debt during the Housing Bubble*** (Compare Exercise 106.) During the real estate run-up in 2000–2008, the value of subprime (normally classified as risky) mortgage debt outstanding in the U.S. could be approximated by

$$A(t) = \frac{1{,}350}{1 + 4.2(1.7)^{-t}} \text{ billion dollars} \quad (0 \le t \le 8)$$

t years after the start of 2000.[50]

a. How fast, to the nearest $1 billion, was subprime mortgage debt increasing at the start of 2005?

b. Compute $\lim_{t\to+\infty} A(t)$ and $\lim_{t\to+\infty} A'(t)$. What do the answers tell you about subprime mortgages?

[47] 2009 figure is an estimate. Sources: Mortgage Bankers Association, UBS.

[48] 2008–2009 figures are estimates. Source: www.data360.org/dataset.aspx? Data_Set_Id=9549.

[49] *Ibid.*

[50] *Ibid.*

109. ▼ ***Population Growth*** The population of Lower Anchovia was 4,000,000 at the start of 2010 and was doubling every 10 years. How fast was it growing per year at the start of 2010? (Round your answer to three significant digits.) HINT [Use the method of Example 2 in Section 2.2 to obtain an exponential model for the population.]

110. ▼ ***Population Growth*** The population of Upper Anchovia was 3,000,000 at the start of 2011 and doubling every 7 years. How fast was it growing per year at the start of 2011? (Round your answer to three significant digits.) HINT [Use the method of Example 2 in Section 2.2 to obtain an exponential model for the population.]

111. ▼ ***Radioactive Decay*** Plutonium 239 has a half-life of 24,400 years. How fast is a lump of 10 grams decaying after 100 years?

112. ▼ ***Radioactive Decay*** Carbon 14 has a half-life of 5,730 years. How fast is a lump of 20 grams decaying after 100 years?

113. ◆ ***Cellphone Revenues*** The number of cellphone subscribers in China for the period 2000–2005 was projected to follow the equation[51]

$$N(t) = 39t + 68 \text{ million subscribers}$$

in year t ($t = 0$ represents 2000). The average annual revenue per cellphone user was \$350 in 2000. Assuming that, due to competition, the revenue per cellphone user decreases continuously at an annual rate of 10%, give a formula for the annual revenue in year t. Hence, project the annual revenue and its rate of change in 2002. Round all answers to the nearest billion dollars or billion dollars per year.

114. ◆ ***Cellphone Revenues*** The annual revenue for cellphone use in China for the period 2000–2005 was projected to follow the equation[52]

$$R(t) = 14t + 24 \text{ billion dollars}$$

in year t ($t = 0$ represents 2000). At the same time, there were approximately 68 million subscribers in 2000. Assuming that the number of subscribers increases continuously at an annual rate of 10%, give a formula for the annual revenue per subscriber in year t. Hence, project to the nearest dollar the annual revenue per subscriber and its rate of change in 2002. (Be careful with units!)

[51]Based on a regression of projected figures (coefficients are rounded). Source: Intrinsic Technology/*New York Times*, Nov. 24, 2000, p. C1.

[52]Not allowing for discounting due to increased competition. Source: Ibid.

COMMUNICATION AND REASONING EXERCISES

115. Complete the following: The derivative of e raised to a glob is . . . .

116. Complete the following: The derivative of the natural logarithm of a glob is . . . .

117. Complete the following: The derivative of 2 raised to a glob is . . . .

118. Complete the following: The derivative of the base 2 logarithm of a glob is . . . .

119. What is wrong with the following?

$$\frac{d}{dx}\ln|3x+1| = \frac{3}{|3x+1|} \quad ✗ \textit{ WRONG!}$$

120. What is wrong with the following?

$$\frac{d}{dx}2^{2x} = (2)2^{2x} \quad ✗ \textit{ WRONG!}$$

121. What is wrong with the following?

$$\frac{d}{dx}3^{2x} = (2x)3^{2x-1} \quad ✗ \textit{ WRONG!}$$

122. What is wrong with the following?

$$\frac{d}{dx}\ln(3x^2-1) = \frac{1}{6x} \quad ✗ \textit{ WRONG!}$$

123. ▼ The number N of music downloads on campus is growing exponentially with time. Can $N'(t)$ grow linearly with time? Explain.

124. ▼ The number N of graphing calculators sold on campus is decaying exponentially with time. Can $N'(t)$ grow with time? Explain.

*The **percentage rate of change** or **fractional rate of change** of a function is defined to be the ratio $f'(x)/f(x)$. (It is customary to express this as a percentage when speaking about percentage rate of change.)*

125. ◆ Show that the fractional rate of change of the exponential function e^{kx} is equal to k, which is often called its **fractional growth rate**.

126. ◆ Show that the fractional rate of change of $f(x)$ is the rate of change of $\ln(f(x))$.

127. ◆ Let $A(t)$ represent a quantity growing exponentially. Show that the percentage rate of change, $A'(t)/A(t)$, is constant.

128. ◆ Let $A(t)$ be the amount of money in an account that pays interest that is compounded some number of times per year. Show that the percentage rate of growth, $A'(t)/A(t)$, is constant. What might this constant represent?

4.6 Implicit Differentiation

Consider the equation $y^5 + y + x = 0$, whose graph is shown in Figure 10.

How did we obtain this graph? We did not solve for y as a function of x; that is impossible. In fact, we solved for x in terms of y to find points to plot. Nonetheless, the graph in Figure 10 is the graph of a function because it passes the vertical line test: Every vertical line crosses the graph no more than once, so for each value of x there is no more than one corresponding value of y. Because we cannot solve for y explicitly in terms of x, we say that the equation $y^5 + y + x = 0$ determines y as an **implicit function** of x.

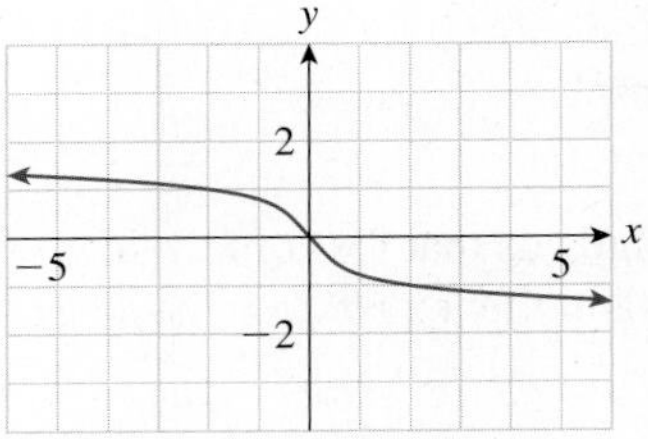

Figure 10

Now, suppose we want to find the slope of the tangent line to this curve at, say, the point $(2, -1)$ (which, you should check, is a point on the curve). In the following example we find, surprisingly, that it is possible to obtain a formula for dy/dx without having to first solve the equation for y.

EXAMPLE 1 Implicit Differentiation

Find $\dfrac{dy}{dx}$, given that $y^5 + y + x = 0$.

Solution We use the chain rule and a little cleverness. Think of y as a function of x and take the derivative with respect to x of both sides of the equation:

$$y^5 + y + x = 0 \qquad \text{Original equation}$$

$$\frac{d}{dx}[y^5 + y + x] = \frac{d}{dx}[0] \qquad \text{Derivative with respect to } x \text{ of both sides}$$

$$\frac{d}{dx}[y^5] + \frac{d}{dx}[y] + \frac{d}{dx}[x] = 0. \qquad \text{Derivative rules}$$

Now we must be careful. The derivative *with respect to* x of y^5 is *not* $5y^4$. Rather, because y is a function of x, we must use the chain rule, which tells us that

$$\frac{d}{dx}[y^5] = 5y^4\frac{dy}{dx}.$$

Thus, we get

$$5y^4\frac{dy}{dx} + \frac{dy}{dx} + 1 = 0.$$

We want to find dy/dx, so we *solve for it*:

$$(5y^4 + 1)\frac{dy}{dx} = -1 \qquad \text{Isolate } dy/dx \text{ on one side.}$$

$$\frac{dy}{dx} = -\frac{1}{5y^4 + 1}. \qquad \text{Divide both sides by } 5y^4 + 1.$$

➡ **Before we go on...** Note that we should not expect to obtain dy/dx as an explicit function of x if y was not an explicit function of x to begin with. For example, the formula we found for dy/dx in Example 1 is not a function of x because there is a y in

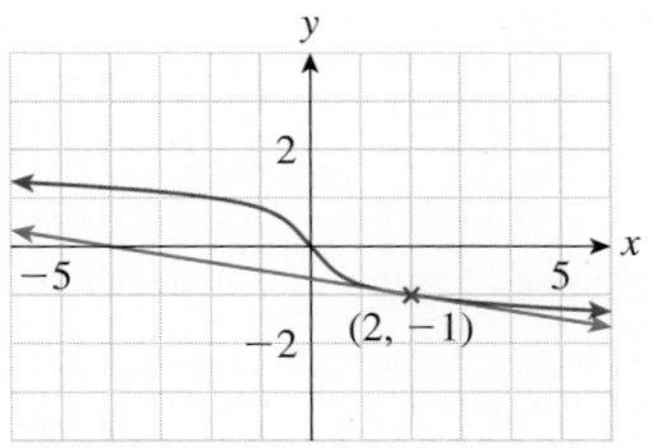

Figure 11

it. However, the result is still useful because we can evaluate the derivative at any point on the graph. For instance, at the point (2, −1) on the graph, we get

$$\frac{dy}{dx} = -\frac{1}{5y^4+1} = -\frac{1}{5(-1)^4+1} = -\frac{1}{6}.$$

Thus, the slope of the tangent line to the curve $y^5 + y + x = 0$ at the point (2, −1) is −1/6. Figure 11 shows the graph and this tangent line. ■

This procedure we just used—differentiating an equation to find dy/dx without first solving the equation for y—is called **implicit differentiation**.

In Example 1 we were given an equation in x and y that determined y as an (implicit) function of x, even though we could not solve for y. But an equation in x and y need not always determine y as a function of x. Consider, for example, the equation

$$2x^2 + y^2 = 2.$$

Solving for y yields $y = \pm\sqrt{2-2x^2}$. The ± sign reminds us that for some values of x there are two corresponding values for y. We can graph this equation by superimposing the graphs of

$$y = \sqrt{2-2x^2} \qquad \text{and} \qquad y = -\sqrt{2-2x^2}.$$

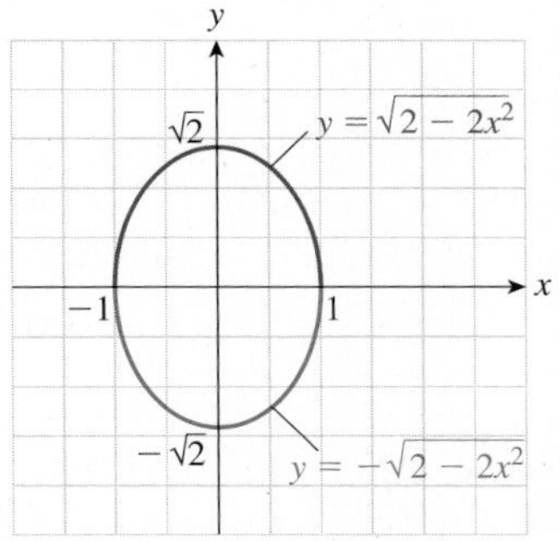

Figure 12

The graph, an *ellipse*, is shown in Figure 12.

The graph of $y = \sqrt{2-2x^2}$ constitutes the top half of the ellipse, and the graph of $y = -\sqrt{2-2x^2}$ constitutes the bottom half.

EXAMPLE 2 Slope of Tangent Line

Refer to Figure 12. Find the slope of the tangent line to the ellipse $2x^2 + y^2 = 2$ at the point $(1/\sqrt{2}, 1)$.

Solution Because $(1/\sqrt{2}, 1)$ is on the top half of the ellipse in Figure 12, we *could* differentiate the function $y = \sqrt{2-2x^2}$ to obtain the result, but it is actually easier to apply implicit differentiation to the original equation.

$$2x^2 + y^2 = 2 \qquad \text{Original equation}$$

$$\frac{d}{dx}[2x^2 + y^2] = \frac{d}{dx}[2] \qquad \text{Derivative with respect to } x \text{ of both sides}$$

$$4x + 2y\frac{dy}{dx} = 0$$

$$2y\frac{dy}{dx} = -4x \qquad \text{Solve for } dy/dx.$$

$$\frac{dy}{dx} = -\frac{4x}{2y} = -\frac{2x}{y}$$

To find the slope at $(1/\sqrt{2}, 1)$ we now substitute for x and y:

$$\left.\frac{dy}{dx}\right|_{(1/\sqrt{2},1)} = -\frac{2/\sqrt{2}}{1} = -\sqrt{2}.$$

Thus, the slope of the tangent to the ellipse at the point $(1/\sqrt{2}, 1)$ is $-\sqrt{2} \approx -1.414$.

EXAMPLE 3 Tangent Line for an Implicit Function

Find the equation of the tangent line to the curve $\ln y = xy$ at the point where $y = 1$.

Solution First, we use implicit differentiation to find dy/dx:

$$\frac{d}{dx}[\ln y] = \frac{d}{dx}[xy] \qquad \text{Take } d/dx \text{ of both sides.}$$

$$\frac{1}{y}\frac{dy}{dx} = (1)y + x\frac{dy}{dx}. \qquad \text{Chain rule on left, product rule on right}$$

To solve for dy/dx, we bring all the terms containing dy/dx to the left-hand side and all terms not containing it to the right-hand side:

$$\frac{1}{y}\frac{dy}{dx} - x\frac{dy}{dx} = y \qquad \text{Bring the terms with } dy/dx \text{ to the left.}$$

$$\frac{dy}{dx}\left(\frac{1}{y} - x\right) = y \qquad \text{Factor out } dy/dx.$$

$$\frac{dy}{dx}\left(\frac{1 - xy}{y}\right) = y$$

$$\frac{dy}{dx} = y\left(\frac{y}{1 - xy}\right) = \frac{y^2}{1 - xy}. \qquad \text{Solve for } dy/dx.$$

The derivative gives the slope of the tangent line, so we want to evaluate the derivative at the point where $y = 1$. However, the formula for dy/dx requires values for both x and y. We get the value of x by substituting $y = 1$ in the original equation:

$$\ln y = xy$$

$$\ln 1 = x \cdot 1$$

But $\ln 1 = 0$, and so $x = 0$ for this point. Thus,

$$\left.\frac{dy}{dx}\right|_{(0,1)} = \frac{1^2}{1 - (0)(1)} = 1.$$

Therefore, the tangent line is the line through $(x, y) = (0, 1)$ with slope 1, which is

$$y = x + 1.$$

➡ **Before we go on...** Example 3 presents an instance of an implicit function in which it is simply not possible to solve for y. Try it. ■

Sometimes, it is easiest to differentiate a complicated function of x by first taking the logarithm and then using implicit differentiation—a technique called **logarithmic differentiation**.

EXAMPLE 4 Logarithmic Differentiation

Find $\frac{d}{dx}\left[\frac{(x+1)^{10}(x^2+1)^{11}}{(x^3+1)^{12}}\right]$ without using the product or quotient rules.

Solution Write

$$y = \frac{(x+1)^{10}(x^2+1)^{11}}{(x^3+1)^{12}}$$

and then take the natural logarithm of both sides:

$$\ln y = \ln\left[\frac{(x+1)^{10}(x^2+1)^{11}}{(x^3+1)^{12}}\right].$$

We can use properties of the logarithm to simplify the right-hand side:

$$\begin{aligned}\ln y &= \ln(x+1)^{10} + \ln(x^2+1)^{11} - \ln(x^3+1)^{12} \\ &= 10\ln(x+1) + 11\ln(x^2+1) - 12\ln(x^3+1).\end{aligned}$$

Now we can find $\frac{dy}{dx}$ using implicit differentiation:

$$\frac{1}{y}\frac{dy}{dx} = \frac{10}{x+1} + \frac{22x}{x^2+1} - \frac{36x^2}{x^3+1}$$ Take d/dx of both sides.

$$\frac{dy}{dx} = y\left(\frac{10}{x+1} + \frac{22x}{x^2+1} - \frac{36x^2}{x^3+1}\right)$$ Solve for dy/dx.

$$= \frac{(x+1)^{10}(x^2+1)^{11}}{(x^3+1)^{12}}\left(\frac{10}{x+1} + \frac{22x}{x^2+1} - \frac{36x^2}{x^3+1}\right).$$ Substitute for y.

➡ **Before we go on...** Redo Example 4 using the product and quotient rules (and the chain rule) instead of logarithmic differentiation and compare the answers. Compare also the amount of work involved in both methods. ■

APPLICATION

Productivity usually depends on both labor and capital. Suppose, for example, you are managing a surfboard manufacturing company. You can measure its productivity by counting the number of surfboards the company makes each year. As a measure of labor, you can use the number of employees, and as a measure of capital you can use its operating budget. The so-called *Cobb-Douglas* model uses a function of the form:

$$P = Kx^a y^{1-a},$$ Cobb-Douglas model for productivity

where P stands for the number of surfboards made each year, x is the number of employees, and y is the operating budget. The numbers K and a are constants that depend on the particular situation studied, with a between 0 and 1.

EXAMPLE 5 Cobb-Douglas Production Function

The surfboard company you own has the Cobb-Douglas production function

$$P = x^{0.3}y^{0.7}$$

where P is the number of surfboards it produces per year, x is the number of employees, and y is the daily operating budget (in dollars). Assume that the production level P is constant.

a. Find $\frac{dy}{dx}$.

b. Evaluate this derivative at $x = 30$ and $y = 10{,}000$, and interpret the answer.

Solution

a. We are given the equation $P = x^{0.3}y^{0.7}$, in which P is constant. We find $\frac{dy}{dx}$ by implicit differentiation.

$$0 = \frac{d}{dx}[x^{0.3}y^{0.7}]$$ d/dx of both sides

$$0 = 0.3x^{-0.7}y^{0.7} + x^{0.3}(0.7)y^{-0.3}\frac{dy}{dx}$$ Product and chain rules

$$-0.7x^{0.3}y^{-0.3}\frac{dy}{dx} = 0.3x^{-0.7}y^{0.7}$$ Bring term with dy/dx to left.

$$\frac{dy}{dx} = -\frac{0.3x^{-0.7}y^{0.7}}{0.7x^{0.3}y^{-0.3}}$$ Solve for dy/dx.

$$= -\frac{3y}{7x}.$$ Simplify.

b. Evaluating this derivative at $x = 30$ and $y = 10,000$ gives

$$\left.\frac{dy}{dx}\right|_{x=30,\ y=10,000} = -\frac{3(10,000)}{7(30)} \approx -143.$$

To interpret this result, first look at the units of the derivative: We recall that the units of dy/dx are units of y per unit of x. Because y is the daily budget, its units are dollars; because x is the number of employees, its units are employees. Thus,

$$\left.\frac{dy}{dx}\right|_{x=30,\ y=10,000} \approx -\$143 \text{ per employee.}$$

Next, recall that dy/dx measures the rate of change of y as x changes. Because the answer is negative, the daily budget to maintain production at the fixed level is decreasing by approximately \$143 per additional employee at an employment level of 30 employees and a daily operating budget of \$10,000. In other words, increasing the workforce by one worker will result in a savings of approximately \$143 per day. Roughly speaking, *a new employee is worth \$143 per day* at the current levels of employment and production.

4.6 EXERCISES

▼ more advanced ◆ challenging

T indicates exercises that should be solved using technology

In Exercises 1–10, find dy/dx, using implicit differentiation. In each case, compare your answer with the result obtained by first solving for y as a function of x and then taking the derivative. HINT [See Example 1.]

1. $2x + 3y = 7$

2. $4x - 5y = 9$

3. $x^2 - 2y = 6$

4. $3y + x^2 = 5$

5. $2x + 3y = xy$

6. $x - y = xy$

7. $e^x y = 1$

8. $e^x y - y = 2$

9. $y \ln x + y = 2$

10. $\frac{\ln x}{y} = 2 - x$

In Exercises 11–30, find the indicated derivative using implicit differentiation. HINT [See Example 1.]

11. $x^2 + y^2 = 5;\ \frac{dy}{dx}$

12. $2x^2 - y^2 = 4;\ \frac{dy}{dx}$

13. $x^2y - y^2 = 4;\ \frac{dy}{dx}$

14. $xy^2 - y = x;\ \frac{dy}{dx}$

15. $3xy - \frac{y}{3} = \frac{2}{x};\ \frac{dy}{dx}$

16. $\frac{xy}{2} - y^2 = 3;\ \frac{dy}{dx}$

17. $x^2 - 3y^2 = 8;\ \frac{dx}{dy}$

18. $(xy)^2 + y^2 = 8;\ \frac{dx}{dy}$

19. $p^2 - pq = 5p^2q^2;\ \frac{dp}{dq}$

20. $q^2 - pq = 5p^2q^2;\ \frac{dp}{dq}$

21. $xe^y - ye^x = 1;\ \frac{dy}{dx}$

22. $x^2e^y - y^2 = e^x;\ \frac{dy}{dx}$

23. ▼ $e^{st} = s^2;\ \frac{ds}{dt}$

24. ▼ $e^{s^2t} - st = 1;\ \frac{ds}{dt}$

25. ▼ $\frac{e^x}{y^2} = 1 + e^y;\ \frac{dy}{dx}$

26. ▼ $\frac{x}{e^y} + xy = 9y;\ \frac{dy}{dx}$

27. ▼ $\ln(y^2 - y) + x = y;\ \frac{dy}{dx}$

28. ▼ $\ln(xy) - x\ln y = y;\ \frac{dy}{dx}$

29. ▼ $\ln(xy + y^2) = e^y;\ \frac{dy}{dx}$

30. ▼ $\ln(1 + e^{xy}) = y;\ \frac{dy}{dx}$

In Exercises 31–42, use implicit differentiation to find **(a)** *the slope of the tangent line, and* **(b)** *the equation of the tangent line at the indicated point on the graph. (Round answers to four decimal places as needed.) If only the x-coordinate is given, you must also find the y-coordinate.* HINT [See Examples 2, 3.]

31. $4x^2 + 2y^2 = 12, (1, -2)$

32. $3x^2 - y^2 = 11, (-2, 1)$

33. $2x^2 - y^2 = xy, (-1, 2)$

34. $2x^2 + xy = 3y^2, (-1, -1)$

35. $x^2y - y^2 + x = 1, (1, 0)$

36. $(xy)^2 + xy - x = 8, (-8, 0)$

37. $xy - 2000 = y, x = 2$

38. $x^2 - 10xy = 200, x = 10$

39. ▼ $\ln(x + y) - x = 3x^2, x = 0$

40. ▼ $\ln(x - y) + 1 = 3x^2, x = 0$

41. ▼ $e^{xy} - x = 4x, x = 3$

42. ▼ $e^{-xy} + 2x = 1, x = -1$

In Exercises 43–52, use logarithmic differentiation to find dy/dx. Do not simplify the result. HINT [See Example 4.]

43. $y = \frac{2x + 1}{4x - 2}$

44. $y = (3x + 2)(8x - 5)$

45. $y = \frac{(3x + 1)^2}{4x(2x - 1)^3}$

46. $y = \frac{x^2(3x + 1)^2}{(2x - 1)^3}$

47. $y = (8x - 1)^{1/3}(x - 1)$

48. $y = \frac{(3x + 2)^{2/3}}{3x - 1}$

49. $y = (x^3 + x)\sqrt{x^3 + 2}$

50. $y = \sqrt{\frac{x - 1}{x^2 + 2}}$

51. ▼ $y = x^x$

52. ▼ $y = x^{-x}$

APPLICATIONS

53. ***Productivity*** The number of CDs per hour that *Snappy Hardware* can manufacture at its plant is given by

$$P = x^{0.6}y^{0.4},$$

where x is the number of workers at the plant and y is the monthly budget (in dollars). Assume P is constant, and compute $\frac{dy}{dx}$ when $x = 100$ and $y = 200{,}000$. Interpret the result. HINT [See Example 5.]

54. ***Productivity*** The number of cellphone accessory kits (neon lights, matching covers, and earpods) per day that *USA Cellular Makeover Inc,* can manufacture at its plant in Cambodia is given by

$$P = x^{0.5}y^{0.5},$$

where x is the number of workers at the plant and y is the monthly budget (in dollars). Assume P is constant, and compute $\frac{dy}{dx}$ when $x = 200$ and $y = 100{,}000$. Interpret the result. HINT [See Example 5.]

55. ***Demand*** The demand equation for soccer tournament T-shirts is

$$xy - 2{,}000 = y,$$

where y is the number of T-shirts the Enormous State University soccer team can sell at a price of $\$x$ per shirt. Find $\left.\frac{dy}{dx}\right|_{x=5}$, and interpret the result.

56. ***Cost Equations*** The cost y (in cents) of producing x gallons of *Ectoplasm* hair gel is given by the cost equation

$$y^2 - 10xy = 200.$$

Evaluate $\frac{dy}{dx}$ at $x = 1$ and interpret the result.

57. ***Housing Costs***[53] The cost C (in dollars) of building a house is related to the number k of carpenters used and the number e of electricians used by the formula

$$C = 15{,}000 + 50k^2 + 60e^2.$$

If the cost of the house is fixed at \$200,000, find $\left.\frac{dk}{de}\right|_{e=15}$ and interpret your result.

58. ***Employment*** An employment research company estimates that the value of a recent MBA graduate to an accounting company is

$$V = 3e^2 + 5g^3,$$

where V is the value of the graduate, e is the number of years of prior business experience, and g is the graduate school grade-point average. If V is fixed at 200, find $\frac{de}{dg}$ when $g = 3.0$ and interpret the result.

59. ▼ ***Grades***[54] A productivity formula for a student's performance on a difficult English examination is

$$g = 4tx - 0.2t^2 - 10x^2 \quad (t < 30),$$

where g is the score the student can expect to obtain, t is the number of hours of study for the examination, and x is the student's grade-point average.

a. For how long should a student with a 3.0 grade-point average study in order to score 80 on the examination?

b. Find $\frac{dt}{dx}$ for a student who earns a score of 80, evaluate it when $x = 3.0$, and interpret the result.

60. ▼ ***Grades*** Repeat the preceding exercise using the following productivity formula for a basket-weaving examination:

$$g = 10tx - 0.2t^2 - 10x^2 \quad (t < 10).$$

Comment on the result.

---

[53]Based on an exercise in *Introduction to Mathematical Economics* by A. L. Ostrosky Jr., and J. V. Koch (Waveland Press, Springfield, Illinois, 1979).

[54]*Ibid.*

Exercises 61 and 62 are based on the following demand function for money (taken from a question on the GRE Economics Test):

$$M_d = (2) \times (y)^{0.6} \times (r)^{-0.3} \times (p)$$

where

M_d = *demand for nominal money balances (money stock)*

y = *real income*

r = *an index of interest rates*

p = *an index of prices.*

61. ◆ ***Money Stock*** If real income grows while the money stock and the price level remain constant, the interest rate must change at what rate? (First find dr/dy, then dr/dt; your answers will be expressed in terms of r, y, and $\frac{dy}{dt}$.)

62. ◆ ***Money Stock*** If real income grows while the money stock and the interest rate remain constant, the price level must change at what rate?

COMMUNICATION AND REASONING EXERCISES

63. Fill in the missing terms: The equation $x = y^3 + y - 3$ specifies ___ as a function of ___, and ___ as an implicit function of ___.

64. Fill in the missing terms: When $x \neq 0$ in the equation $xy = x^3 + 4$, it is possible to specify ___ as a function of ___. However, ___ is only an implicit function of ___.

65. ▼ Use logarithmic differentiation to give another proof of the product rule.

66. ▼ Use logarithmic differentiation to give a proof of the quotient rule.

67. ▼ If y is given explicitly as a function of x by an equation $y = f(x)$, compare finding dy/dx by implicit differentiation to finding it explicitly in the usual way.

68. ▼ Explain why one should not expect dy/dx to be a function of x if y is not a function of x.

69. ◆ If y is a function of x and $dy/dx \neq 0$ at some point, regard x as an implicit function of y and use implicit differentiation to obtain the equation

$$\frac{dx}{dy} = \frac{1}{dy/dx}.$$

70. ◆ If you are given an equation in x and y such that dy/dx is a function of x only, what can you say about the graph of the equation?

CHAPTER 4 REVIEW

KEY CONCEPTS

WM Website www.WanerMath.com

Go to the Website at www.WanerMath.com to find a comprehensive and interactive Web-based summary of Chapter 4.

4.1 Derivatives of Powers, Sums, and Constant Multiples

Power Rule: If n is any constant and $f(x) = x^n$, then $f'(x) = nx^{n-1}$. *p. 290*

Using the power rule for negative and fractional exponents *p. 291*

Sums, differences, and constant multiples *p. 293*

Combining the rules *p. 294*

$\frac{d}{dx}(cx) = c$, $\frac{d}{dx}(c) = 0$ *p. 296*

$f(x) = x^{1/3}$, $g(x) = x^{2/3}$, and $h(x) = |x|$ are not differentiable at $x = 0$. *p. 296*

L'Hospital's rule *p. 298*

4.2 A First Application: Marginal Analysis

Marginal cost function $C'(x)$ *p. 305*

Marginal revenue and profit functions $R'(x)$ and $P'(x)$ *p. 307*

What it means when the marginal profit is zero *p. 308*

Marginal product *p. 308*

Average cost of the first x items: $\bar{C}(x) = \frac{C(x)}{x}$ *p. 311*

4.3 The Product and Quotient Rules

Product rule: $\frac{d}{dx}[f(x)g(x)] = f'(x)g(x) + f(x)g'(x)$ *p. 316*

Quotient rule: $\frac{d}{dx}\left[\frac{f(x)}{g(x)}\right] = \frac{f'(x)g(x) - f(x)g'(x)}{[g(x)]^2}$ *p. 316*

Using the product rule *p. 318*

Using the quotient rule *p. 319*

Calculation thought experiment *p. 321*

Application to revenue and average cost *p. 322*

4.4 The Chain Rule

Chain rule: $\frac{d}{dx}[f(u)] = f'(u)\frac{du}{dx}$ *p. 328*

Generalized power rule:

$\frac{d}{dx}[u^n] = nu^{n-1}\frac{du}{dx}$ *p. 329*

Using the chain rule *p. 329*

Application to marginal product *p. 332*

Chain rule in differential notation:

$\frac{dy}{dx} = \frac{dy}{du}\frac{du}{dx}$ *p. 333*

Manipulating derivatives in differential notation *p. 335*

4.5 Derivatives of Logarithmic and Exponential Functions

Derivative of the natural logarithm:

$\frac{d}{dx}[\ln x] = \frac{1}{x}$ *p. 340*

Derivative of logarithm with base b:

$\frac{d}{dx}[\log_b x] = \frac{1}{x \ln b}$ *p. 341*

Derivatives of logarithms of functions:

$\frac{d}{dx}[\ln u] = \frac{1}{u}\frac{du}{dx}$

$\frac{d}{dx}[\log_b u] = \frac{1}{u \ln b}\frac{du}{dx}$ *p. 342*

Derivatives of logarithms of absolute values:

$\frac{d}{dx}[\ln|x|] = \frac{1}{x}$ $\quad \frac{d}{dx}[\ln|u|] = \frac{1}{u}\frac{du}{dx}$

$\frac{d}{dx}[\log_b|x|] = \frac{1}{x \ln b}$

$\frac{d}{dx}[\log_b|u|] = \frac{1}{u \ln b}\frac{du}{dx}$ *p. 344*

Derivative of e^x: $\frac{d}{dx}[e^x] = e^x$ *p. 345*

Derivative of b^x: $\frac{d}{dx}[b^x] = b^x \ln b$ *p. 345*

Derivatives of exponential functions *p. 346*

Application to epidemics *p. 347*

Application to sales growth (logistic function) *p. 347*

4.6 Implicit Differentiation

Implicit function of x *p. 354*

Implicit differentiation *p. 354*

Using implicit differentiation *p. 355*

Finding a tangent line *p. 355*

Logarithmic differentiation *p. 356*

REVIEW EXERCISES

In Exercises 1–26, find the derivative of the given function.

1. $f(x) = 10x^5 + \frac{1}{2}x^4 - x + 2$

2. $f(x) = \frac{10}{x^5} + \frac{1}{2x^4} - \frac{1}{x} + 2$

3. $f(x) = 3x^3 + 3\sqrt[3]{x}$

4. $f(x) = \frac{2}{x^{2.1}} - \frac{x^{0.1}}{2}$

5. $f(x) = x + \frac{1}{x^2}$

6. $f(x) = 2x - \frac{1}{x}$

7. $f(x) = \frac{4}{3x} - \frac{2}{x^{0.1}} + \frac{x^{1.1}}{3.2} - 4$

8. $f(x) = \frac{4}{x} + \frac{x}{4} - |x|$

9. $f(x) = e^x(x^2 - 1)$

10. $f(x) = \frac{x^2 + 1}{x^2 - 1}$

11. $f(x) = \frac{|x| + 1}{3x^2 + 1}$

12. $f(x) = (|x| + x)(2 - 3x^2)$

13. $f(x) = (4x - 1)^{-1}$

14. $f(x) = (x + 7)^{-2}$

15. $f(x) = (x^2 - 1)^{10}$

16. $f(x) = \frac{1}{(x^2 - 1)^{10}}$

17. $f(x) = [2 + (x + 1)^{-0.1}]^{4.3}$

18. $f(x) = [(x + 1)^{0.1} - 4x]^{-5.1}$

19. $f(x) = e^x(x^2 + 1)^{10}$

20. $f(x) = \left[\dfrac{x-1}{3x+1}\right]^3$ **21.** $f(x) = \dfrac{3^x}{x-1}$

22. $f(x) = 4^{-x}(x+1)$ **23.** $f(x) = e^{x^2-1}$

24. $f(x) = (x^2+1)e^{x^2-1}$ **25.** $f(x) = \ln(x^2-1)$

26. $f(x) = \dfrac{\ln(x^2-1)}{x^2-1}$

In Exercises 27–34, find all values of x (if any) where the tangent line to the graph of the given equation is horizontal.

27. $y = -3x^2 + 7x - 1$ **28.** $y = 5x^2 - 2x + 1$

29. $y = \dfrac{x}{2} + \dfrac{2}{x}$ **30.** $y = \dfrac{x^2}{2} - \dfrac{8}{x^2}$

31. $y = x - e^{2x-1}$ **32.** $y = e^{x^2}$

33. $y = \dfrac{x}{x+1}$ **34.** $y = \sqrt{x}(x-1)$

In Exercises 35–40, find dy/dx for the given equation.

35. $x^2 - y^2 = x$ **36.** $2xy + y^2 = y$

37. $e^{xy} + xy = 2$ **38.** $\ln\left(\dfrac{y}{x}\right) = y$

39. $y = \dfrac{(2x-1)^4(3x+4)}{(x+1)(3x-1)^3}$ **40.** $y = x^{x-1}3^x$

In Exercises 41–46, find the equation of the tangent line to the graph of the given equation at the specified point.

41. $y = (x^2 - 3x)^{-2}$; $x = 1$ **42.** $y = (2x^2 - 3)^{-3}$; $x = -1$

43. $y = x^2e^{-x}$; $x = -1$ **44.** $y = \dfrac{x}{1+e^x}$; $x = 0$

45. $xy - y^2 = x^2 - 3$; $(-1, 1)$

46. $\ln(xy) + y^2 = 1$; $(-1, -1)$

APPLICATIONS: OHaganBooks.com

47. ***Sales*** OHaganBooks.com fits the cubic curve

$$w(t) = -3.7t^3 + 74.6t^2 + 135.5t + 6{,}300$$

to its weekly sales figures (see Chapter 3 Review Exercise 57; t is time in weeks), as shown in the following graph:

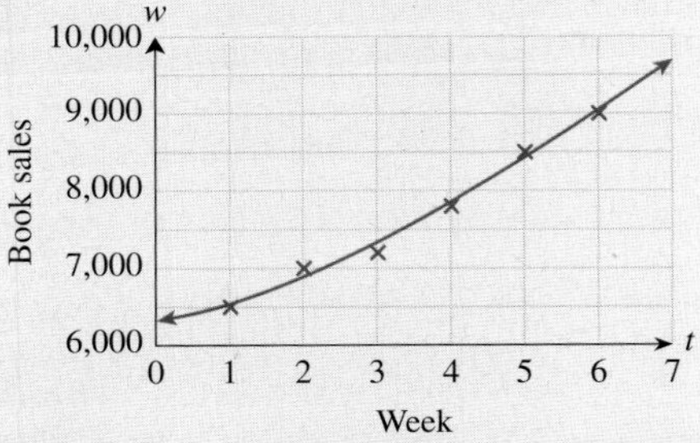

a. According to the cubic model, what was the rate of increase of sales at the beginning of the second week ($t = 1$)? (Round your answer to the nearest unit.)

b. If we extrapolate the model, what would be the rate of increase of weekly sales at the beginning of the eighth week ($t = 7$)?

c. Graph the function w for $0 \le t \le 20$. Would it be realistic to use the function to predict sales through week 20? Why?

d. By examining the graph, say why the choice of a quadratic model would result in radically different long-term predictions of sales.

48. ***Rising Sea Level*** Marjory Duffin is still toying with various models to fit to the New York sea level figures she had seen after purchasing a beachfront condominium in New York (see Chapter 3 Review Exercise 58). Following is a cubic curve she obtained using regression:

$$L(t) = -0.0001t^3 + 0.02t^2 + 2.2t \text{ mm}$$

(t is time in years since 1900). The curve and data are shown in the following graph:

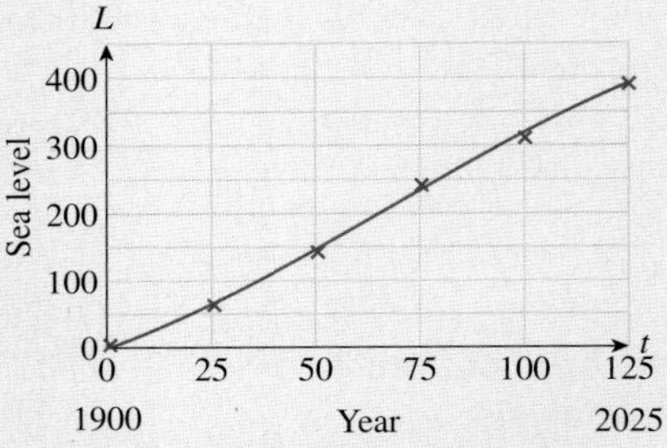

Sea Level Change since 1900

a. According to the cubic model, what was the rate at which the sea level was rising in 2000 ($t = 100$)? (Round your answer to two significant digits.)

b. If we extrapolate the model, what would be the rate at which the sea level is rising in 2025 ($t = 125$)?

c. Graph the function L for $0 \le t \le 200$. Why is it not realistic to use the function to predict the sea level through 2100?

d. James Stewart, a summer intern at Duffin House Publishers, differs. As he puts it, "The cubic curve came from doing regression on the actual data, and thus reflects the actual trend of the data. We can't argue against reality!" Comment on this assertion.

49. ***Cost*** As OHaganBooks.com's sales increase, so do its costs. If we take into account volume discounts from suppliers and shippers, the weekly cost of selling x books is

$$C(x) = -0.00002x^2 + 3.2x + 5{,}400 \text{ dollars.}$$

a. What is the marginal cost at a sales level of 8,000 books per week?

b. What is the average cost per book at a sales level of 8,000 books per week?

c. What is the marginal average cost ($d\bar{C}/dx$) at a sales level of 8,000 books per week?

d. Interpret the results of parts (a)–(c).

50. ***Cost*** OHaganBooks.com has been experiencing a run of bad luck with its summer college intern program in association with PCU (Party Central University), begun as a result of a suggestion by Marjory Duffin over dinner one evening. The frequent errors in filling orders, charges from movie download sites and dating sites, and beverages spilled on computer equipment have resulted in an estimated weekly cost to the company of

$$C(x) = 25x^2 - 5.2x + 4{,}000 \text{ dollars},$$

where x is the number of college interns employed.

a. What is the marginal cost at a level of 10 interns?
b. What is the average cost per intern at a level of 10 interns?
c. What is the marginal average cost at a level of 10 interns?
d. Interpret the results of parts (a)–(c).

51. ***Revenue*** At the moment, OHaganBooks.com is selling 1,000 books per week and its sales are rising at a rate of 200 books per week. Also, it is now selling all its books for \$20 each, but its price is dropping at a rate of \$1 per week.

a. At what rate is OHaganBooks.com's weekly revenue rising or falling?
b. John O'Hagan would like to see the company's weekly revenue increase at a rate of \$5,000 per week. At what rate would sales have to have been increasing to accomplish that goal, assuming all the other information is as given above?

52. ***Revenue*** Due to ongoing problems with its large college intern program in association with PCU (see Exercise 50), OHaganBooks.com has arranged to transfer its interns to its competitor JungleBooks.com (whose headquarters happens to be across the road) for a small fee. At the moment, it is transferring 5 students per week, and this number is rising at a rate of 4 students per week. Also, it is now charging JungleBooks \$400 per intern, but this amount is decreasing at a rate of \$20 per week.

a. At what rate is OHaganBooks.com's weekly revenue from this transaction rising or falling?
b. Flush with success of the transfer program, John O'Hagan would like to see the company's resulting revenue increase at a rate of \$3,900 per week. At what rate would the transfer of interns have to increase to accomplish that goal, assuming all the other information is as given above?

53. ***Percentage Rate of Change of Revenue*** The percentage rate of change of a quantity Q is Q'/Q. Why is the percentage rate of change of revenue always equal to the sum of the percentage rates of change of unit price and weekly sales?

54. ***P/E Ratios*** At the beginning of last week, OHaganBooks.com stock was selling for \$100 per share, rising at a rate of \$50 per year. Its earnings amounted to \$1 per share, rising at a rate of \$0.10 per year. At what rate was its price-to-earnings (P/E) ratio, the ratio of its stock price to its earnings per share, rising or falling?

55. ***P/E Ratios*** Refer to Exercise 54. Jay Campbell, who recently invested in OHaganBooks.com stock, would have liked to see the P/E ratio increase at a rate of 100 points per year. How fast would the stock have to have been rising, assuming all the other information is as given in Exercise 54?

56. ***Percentage Rate of Change of P/E Ratios*** Refer to Exercise 54. The percentage rate of change of a quantity Q is Q'/Q. Why is the percentage rate of change of P/E always equal to the percentage rate of change of unit price minus the percentage rate of change of earnings?

57. ***Sales*** OHaganBooks.com decided that the cubic curve in Exercise 47 was not suitable for extrapolation, so instead it tried

$$s(t) = 6{,}000 + \frac{4{,}500}{1 + e^{-0.55(t-4.8)}}$$

as shown in the following graph:

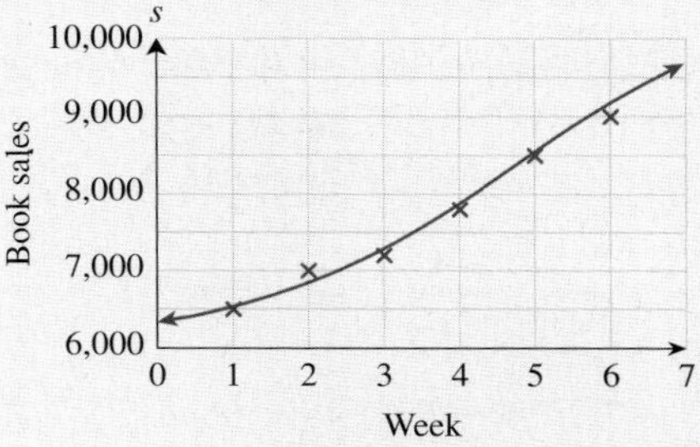

a. Compute $s'(t)$ and use the answer to estimate the rate of increase of weekly sales at the beginning of the seventh week ($t = 6$). (Round your answer to the nearest unit.)
b. Compute $\lim_{t\to+\infty} s'(t)$ and interpret the answer.

58. ***Rising Sea Level*** Upon some reflection, Marjory Duffin decided that the curve in Exercise 48 was not suitable for extrapolation, so instead she tried

$$L(t) = \frac{418}{1 + 17.2e^{-0.041t}} \qquad (0 \le t \le 125)$$

(t is time in years since 1900) as shown in the following graph:

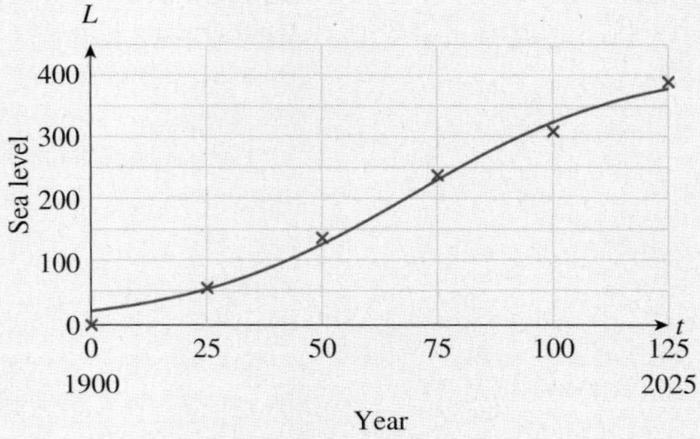

a. Compute $L'(t)$ and use the answer to estimate the rate at which the sea level was rising in 2000 ($t = 100$). (Round your answer to two decimal places.)
b. Compute $\lim_{t\to+\infty} L'(t)$ and interpret the answer.

59. ***Web Site Activity*** The number of "hits" on OHaganBooks.com's Web site was 1,000 per day at the beginning of the year, and was growing at a rate of 5% per week. If this growth rate continued for the whole year (52 weeks), find the rate of increase (in hits per day per week) at the end of the year.

60. ***Web Site Activity*** The number of "hits" on ShadyDownload.net during the summer intern program at OHaganBooks.com was 100 per day at the beginning of the intern program, and was growing at a rate of 15% per day. If this growth rate continued for the duration of the whole summer intern program (85 days), find the rate of increase (in hits per day per day) at the end of the program.

61. ***Demand and Revenue*** The price p that OHaganBooks.com charges for its latest leather-bound gift edition of *The Complete Larry Potter* is related to the demand q in weekly sales by the equation

$$250pq + q^2 = 13{,}500{,}000.$$

Suppose the price is set at \$50, which would make the demand 1,000 copies per week.

a. Using implicit differentiation, compute the rate of change of demand with respect to price, and interpret the result. (Round the answer to two decimal places.)

b. Use the result of part (a) to compute the rate of change of revenue with respect to price. Should the price be raised or lowered to increase revenue?

62. ***Demand and Revenue*** The price p that OHaganBooks.com charges for its latest leather-bound gift edition of *Lord of the Fields* is related to the demand q in weekly sales by the equation

$$100pq + q^2 = 5{,}000{,}000.$$

Suppose the price is set at \$40, which would make the demand 1,000 copies per week.

a. Using implicit differentiation, compute the rate of change of demand with respect to price, and interpret the result. (Round the answer to two decimal places.)

b. Use the result of part (a) to compute the rate of change of revenue with respect to price. Should the price be raised or lowered to increase revenue?

Case Study

Yuri Arcurs/Shutterstock

Projecting Market Growth

You are on the board of directors at *Fullcourt Academic Press,* a major textbook supplier to private schools, and various expansion strategies will be discussed at tomorrow's board meeting. TJM, the sales director of the high school division, has just burst into your office with his last-minute proposal based on data showing the number of private high school graduates in the U.S. each year over the past 18 years:[55]

Year	1995	1996	1997	1998	1999	2000	2001	2002	2003
Graduates (thousands)	245	254	265	273	279	279	285	296	301
Year	2004	2005	2006	2007	2008	2009	2010	2011	2012
Graduates (thousands)	307	307	307	314	314	315	315	316	316

He is asserts that, despite the unspectacular numbers in the past few years, the long-term trend appears to support a basic premise of his proposal for an expansion strategy: that the number of high school seniors in private schools in the U.S. will be growing at a rate of about 4,000 per year through 2015. He points out that the rate of increase predicted by the regression line is approximately 4,080 students per year, supporting his premise.

In order to decide whether to support TJM's proposal at tomorrow's board meeting, you would like to first determine whether the linear regression prediction of around 4,000 students per year is reasonable, especially in view of the more recent figures. You open your spreadsheet and graph the data with the regression line (Figure 13). The data suggest that the number of graduates began to "level off" (in the language of calculus, the *derivative appears to be decreasing*) toward the end of the

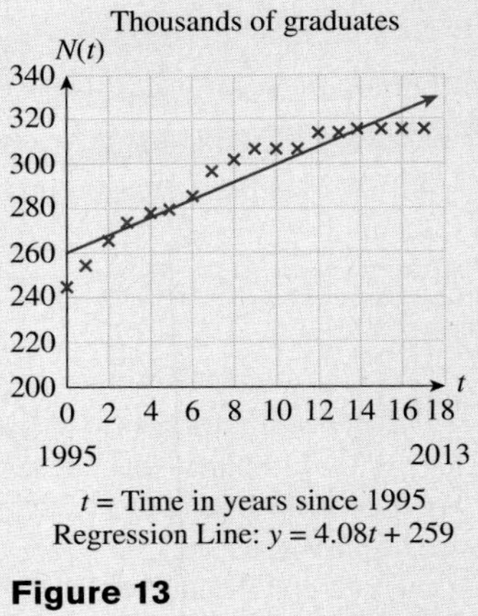

t = Time in years since 1995
Regression Line: $y = 4.08t + 259$

Figure 13

[55]Data through 2011 are National Center for Educational Statistics actual and projected data as of April 2010. Source: National Center for Educational Statistics http://nces.ed.gov/.

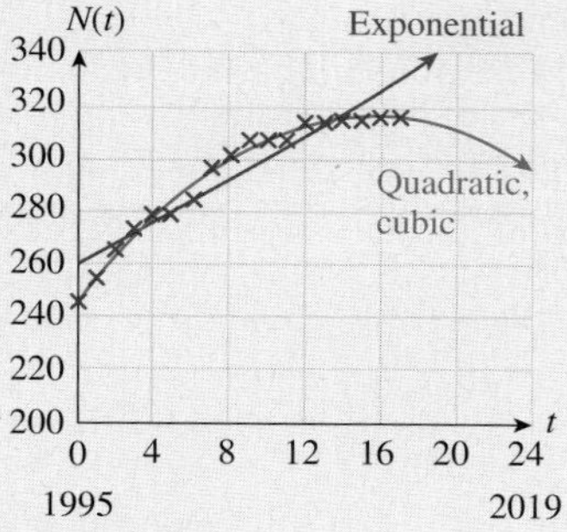

Figure 14

period. Moreover, you recall reading somewhere that the numbers of students in the lower grades have also begun to level off, so it is safe to predict that the slowing of growth in the senior class will continue over the next few years, contrary to what TJM has claimed. In order to make a meaningful prediction, you would really need some precise data about numbers in the lower grades, but the meeting is tomorrow and you would like a quick and easy way of extrapolating the data by "extending the curve to the right."

It would certainly be helpful if you had a mathematical model of the data in Figure 13 that you could use to project the current trend. But what kind of model should you use? The linear model is no good because it does not show any change in the derivative (the derivative of a linear function is constant). In addition, best-fit polynomial and exponential functions do not accurately reflect the leveling off, as you realize after trying to fit a few of them (Figure 14).

You then recall that a logistic curve can model the leveling-off property you desire, and so you try a model of the form

$$N(t) = \frac{M}{1 + Ab^{-t}}.$$

Figure 15 shows the best-fit logistic curve, which has a sum-of-squares error (SSE) of around 109. (See Section 1.4 or any of the regression examples in Chapter 2 for a discussion of SSE.)

$$N(t) = \frac{323.9}{1 + 0.3234(1.186)^{-t}} \qquad \text{SSE} \approx 109$$

Its graph shows the leveling off and also gives more reasonable long-term predictions.

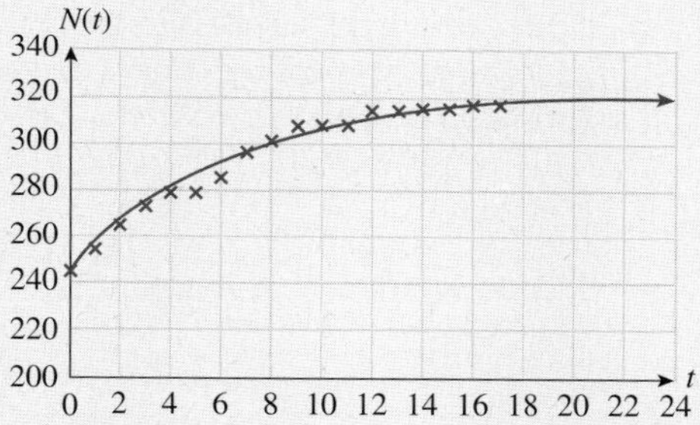

Figure 15

The rate of increase of high school students—pertinent to TJM's report—is given by the derivative, $N'(t)$:

$$N(t) = \frac{M}{1 + Ab^{-t}}$$

$$N'(t) = -\frac{M}{(1 + Ab^{-t})^2}\frac{d}{dt}[1 + Ab^{-t}]$$

$$= \frac{MAb^{-t}\ln b}{(1 + Ab^{-t})^2}.$$

The rate of increase in the number of high school students in 2015 ($t = 20$) is given by

$$N'(20) = \frac{(323.9)(0.3234)(1.186)^{-20}\ln 1.186}{(1 + 0.3234(1.186)^{-20})^2}$$

$$\approx 0.577 \text{ thousand students per year,}$$

using Technology

You can obtain the best-fit logistic curve using technology.

TI-83/84 Plus

[STAT] EDIT

Enter 0–17 in L_1 and the values of $N(t)$ in L_2.

[STAT] CALC and select Option #B `Logistic`

To plot the regression curve with the data: Graph: [Y=] [VARS] [5] EQ [1], then [ZOOM] [9]

[See the TI-83/84 Plus Technology Guide for Section 1.4 for more details on plotting the data and curve.]

Website

www.WanerMath.com

In the Function Ealuator and Grapher, enter the data as shown, press "Examples" until the logistic model `$1/(1+$2*$3^(-x))` shows in the first box, and press "Fit Curve". (You might need to press "Fit Curve" several times before it manages to find the curve. It also helps to read the instructions (link near the top of the Web page under the heading).)

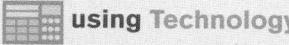

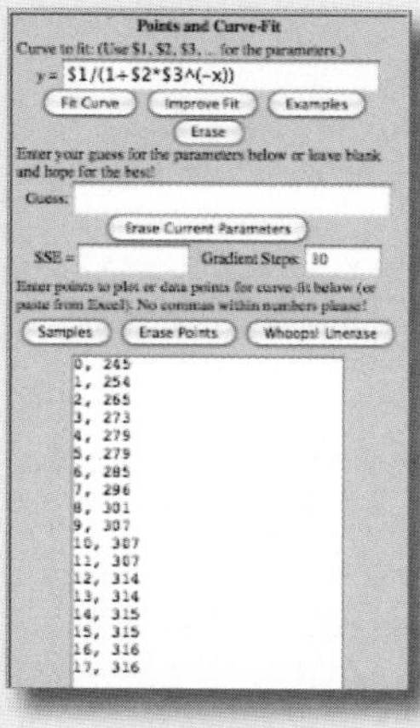

or about 580 students per year—far less than the optimistic estimate of 4,000 in the proposal! Thus, TJM's prediction is suspect and further research will have to be done before the board can even consider the proposal.

To reassure yourself, you decide to look for another kind of S-shaped model as a backup. After flipping through a calculus book, you stumble across a function that is slightly more general than the one you have:

$$N(t) = \frac{M}{1 + Ab^{-t}} + C. \qquad \text{Shifted Logistic Curve}^*$$

* To find a detailed discussion of scaled and shifted functions, visit the Website and follow

Chapter 1
→ New Functions from Old: Scaled and Shifted Functions.

The added term C has the effect of shifting the graph up C units. Turning once again to your calculus book (see the discussion of logistic regression in Section 2.4), you see that a best-fit curve is one that minimizes the sum-of-squares error, and you find the best-fit curve by again using the utility on the Website (this time, with the model `$1/(1+$2*$3^(-x))+$4` and initial guess 323.9, 0.3234, 1.186, 0; that is, keeping the current values and setting $c = 0$). You obtain the model

$$N(t) = \frac{135.5}{1 + 1.192(1.268)^{-t}} + 184.6. \qquad \text{SSE} \approx 100$$

The value of SSE has decreased only slightly, and, as seen in Figure 16, the shifted logistic curve seems almost identical to the unshifted curve, but does seem to level off slightly faster (compare the portions of the two curves on the extreme right).

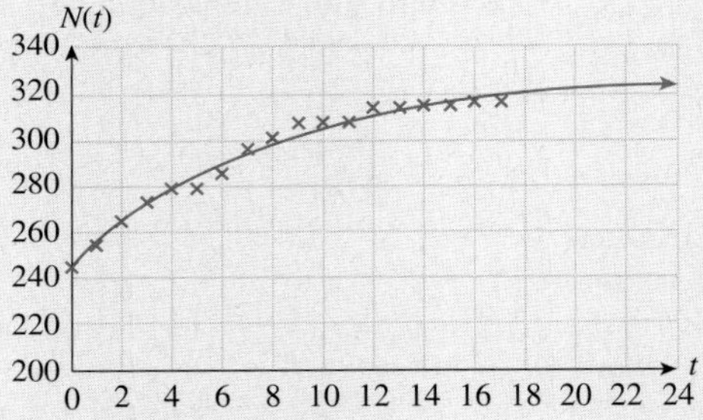

Figure 16

You decide to use the shifted model to obtain another estimate of the projected rate of change in 2015. As the two models differ by a constant, their derivatives are given by the same formula, so you compute

$$N'(20) = \frac{(135.5)(1.192)(1.268)^{-20} \ln 1.268}{(1 + 1.192(1.268)^{-20})^2}$$

$$\approx 0.325 \text{ thousand students per year,}$$

or about 325 students per year, even less than the prediction of the logistic model.

Q: *Why do the two models give very different predictions of the rate of change in 2015?*

A: The long-term prediction in any logistic model is highly sensitive to small changes in the data and/or the model. This is one reason why using regression curve-fitting models to make long-term projections can be a risky undertaking.

Q: *Then what is the point of using any model to project in the first place?*

A: Projections are always tricky as we cannot foresee the future. But a *good* model is not merely one that seems to fit the data well, but rather a model whose structure is based on the situation being modeled. For instance, a *good* model of student graduation rates should take into account such factors as the birth rate, current school populations at all levels, and the relative popularity of private schools as opposed to public schools. It is by using models of this kind that the National Center for Educational Statistics is able to make the projections shown in the data above.

EXERCISES

1. In 1994 there were 246,000 private high school graduates. What do the two logistic models (unshifted and shifted) "predict" for 1994? (Round answer to the nearest 1,000.) Which gives the better prediction?

2. What is the long-term prediction of each of the two models? (Round answer to the nearest 1,000.)

3. Find $\lim_{t\to+\infty} N'(t)$ for both models, and interpret the results.

4. T You receive a last-minute memo from TJM to the effect that, sorry, the 2011 and 2012 figures are not accurate. Use technology to re-estimate M, A, b, and C for the shifted logistic model in the absence of this data and obtain new estimates for the 2011 and 2012 data. What does the new model predict the rate of change in the number of high school seniors will be in 2015?

5. T ***Another Model*** Using the original data, find the best-fit shifted logistic curve of the form

$$N(t) = c + b\frac{a(t-m)}{1+a|t-m|}. \qquad (a, b, c, m \text{ constant})$$

Its graph is shown below:

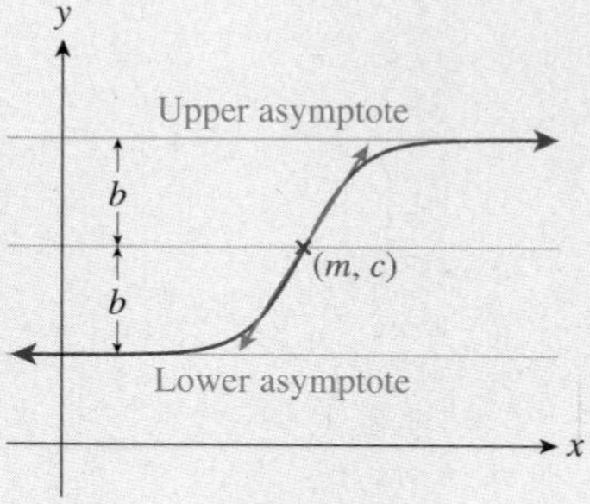

$$a = \frac{\text{Slope of tangent}}{b}$$

(Use the model `$1+$2*$3*(x-$4)/(1+$3*abs(x-$4))` and start with the following values: $a = 0.05$, $b = 160$, $c = 250$, $m = 5$; that is, input `250, 160, 0.05, 5` in the "Guess" field.) Graph the data together with the model. What is SSE? Is the model as accurate a fit as the model used in the text? What does this model predict will be the growth rate of the number of high school graduates in 2015? Comment on the answer. (Round the coefficients in the model and all answers to four decimal places.)

6. T ***Demand for Freon*** The demand for chlorofluorocarbon-12 (CFC-12)—the ozone-depleting refrigerant commonly known as Freon 12 (the name given to it by Du Pont)—has

been declining significantly in response to regulation and concern about the ozone layer. The chart below shows the projected demand for CFC-12 for the period 1994–2005.[56]

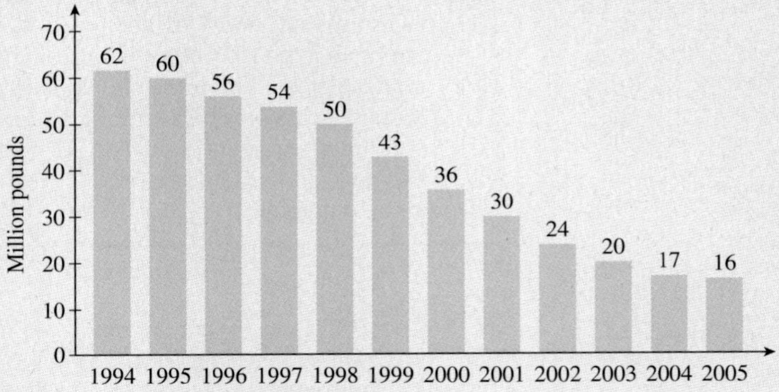

a. Use technology to obtain the best-fit equation of the form

$$N(t) = c + b\frac{a(t-m)}{1+a|t-m|}, \qquad (a, b, c, m \text{ constant})$$

where t is the number of years since 1990. Use your function to estimate the total demand for CFC-12 from the start of the year 2000 to the start of 2010. [Start with the following values: $a = 1$, $b = -25$, $c = 35$, and $m = 10$, and round your answers to four decimal places.]

b. According to your model, how fast is the demand for Freon declining in 2000?

[56]Source: The Automobile Consulting Group (*New York Times,* December 26, 1993, p. F23). The exact figures were not given, and the chart is a reasonable facsimile of the chart that appeared in *New York Times.*

5

Further Applications of the Derivative

Website
www.WanerMath.com
At the Website you will find:

- Section-by-section tutorials, including game tutorials with randomized quizzes
- A detailed chapter summary
- A true/false quiz
- Additional review exercises
- Graphers, Excel tutorials, and other resources
- The following extra topic:

  Linear Approximation and Error Estimation

Case Study Production Lot Size Management

Your publishing company is planning the production of its latest best seller, which it predicts will sell 100,000 copies each month over the coming year. The book will be printed in several batches of the same number, evenly spaced throughout the year. Each print run has a setup cost of $5,000, a single book costs $1 to produce, and monthly storage costs for books awaiting shipment average 1¢ per book. **To meet the anticipated demand at minimum total cost to your company, how many printing runs should you plan?**

SERDAR/Alamy

Introduction

In this chapter we begin to see the power of calculus as an optimization tool. In Chapter 2 we saw how to price an item in order to get the largest revenue when the demand function is linear. Using calculus, we can handle nonlinear functions, which are much more general. In Section 5.1 we show how calculus can be used to solve the problem of finding the values of a variable that lead to a maximum or minimum value of a given function. In Section 5.2 we show how this helps us in various real-world applications.

Another theme in this chapter is that calculus can help us to draw and understand the graph of a function. By the time you have completed the material in Section 5.1, you will be able to locate and sketch some of the important features of a graph, such as where it rises and where it falls. In Section 5.3 we look at the *second derivative,* the derivative of the derivative function, and what it tells us about how the graph *curves*. We also see how the second derivative is used to model the notion of *acceleration*. In Section 5.4 we put a number of ideas together that help to explain what you see in a graph (drawn, for example, using graphing technology) and to locate its most important points.

We also include sections on related rates and elasticity of demand. The first of these (Section 5.5) examines further the concept of the derivative as a rate of change. The second (Section 5.6) returns to the problem of optimizing revenue based on the demand equation, looking at it in a new way that leads to an important idea in economics—elasticity.

algebra Review
For this chapter, you should be familiar with the algebra reviewed in **Chapter 0, sections 5 and 6**.

5.1 Maxima and Minima

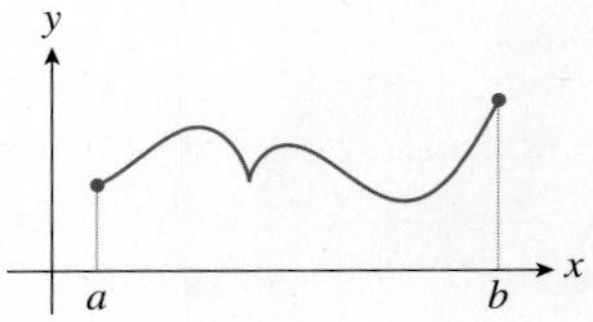

Figure 1

Figure 1 shows the graph of a function f whose domain is the closed interval $[a, b]$. A mathematician sees lots of interesting things going on here. There are hills and valleys, and even a small chasm (called a *cusp*) near the center. For many purposes, the important features of this curve are the highs and lows. Suppose, for example, you know that the price of the stock of a certain company will follow this graph during the course of a week. Although you would certainly make a handsome profit if you bought at time a and sold at time b, your best strategy would be to follow the old adage to "buy low and sell high," buying at all the lows and selling at all the highs.

Figure 2 shows the graph once again with the highs and lows marked. Mathematicians have names for these points: the highs (at the x-values p, r, and b) are referred to as **relative maxima**, and the lows (at the x-values a, q, and s) are referred to as **relative minima**. Collectively, these highs and lows are referred to as **relative extrema**. (A point of language: The singular forms of the plurals *minima, maxima,* and *extrema* are *minimum, maximum,* and *extremum.*)

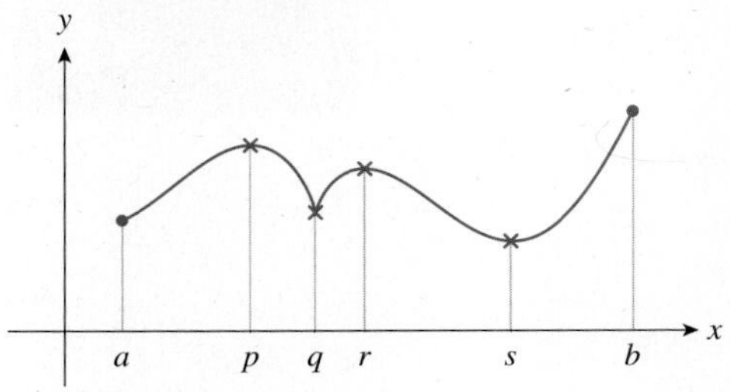

Figure 2

Why do we refer to these points as relative extrema? Take a look at the point corresponding to $x = r$. It is the highest point of the graph *compared to other points nearby*. If you were an extremely nearsighted mountaineer standing at the point

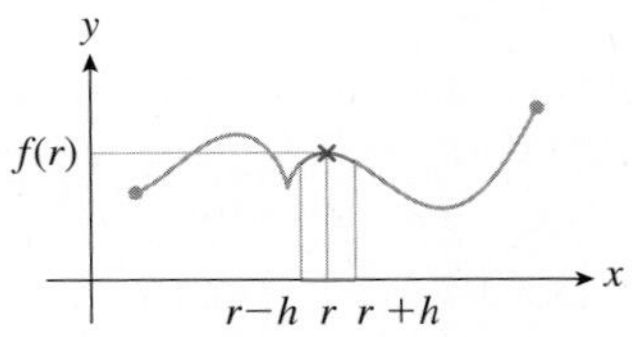

Figure 3

where $x = r$, you would *think* that you were at the highest point of the graph, not being able to see the distant peaks at $x = p$ and $x = b$.

Let's translate into mathematical terms. We are talking about the heights of various points on the curve. The height of the curve at $x = r$ is $f(r)$, so we are saying that $f(r)$ is greater than or equal to $f(x)$ for every x near r. In other words, *$f(r)$ is the greatest value that $f(x)$ has for all choices of x between $r - h$ and $r + h$* for some (possibly small) h. (See Figure 3.)

We can phrase the formal definition as follows.

Relative Extrema

f has a **relative maximum** at $x = r$ if there is some interval $(r - h, r + h)$ (even a very small one) for which $f(r) \geq f(x)$ for all x in $(r - h, r + h)$ for which $f(x)$ is defined.

f has a **relative minimum** at $x = r$ if there is some interval $(r - h, r + h)$ (even a very small one) for which $f(r) \leq f(x)$ for all x in $(r - h, r + h)$ for which $f(x)$ is defined.

Quick Examples

In Figure 2, f has the following relative extrema:

1. Relative maxima at p and r.
2. A relative maximum at b. (See Figure 4.) Note that $f(x)$ is not defined for $x > b$. However, $f(b) \geq f(x)$ for every x in the interval $(b - h, b + h)$ *for which $f(x)$ is defined*—that is, for every x in $(b - h, b]$.*
3. Relative minima at a, q, and s.

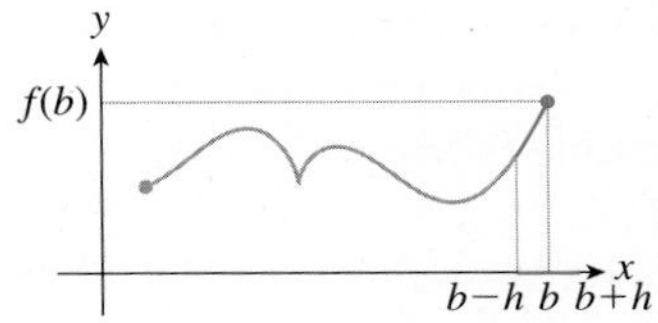

Figure 4

* Our definition of relative extremum allows f to have a relative extremum at an endpoint of its domain; the definitions used in some books do not. In view of examples like the stock market investing strategy mentioned above, we find it more useful to allow endpoints as relative extrema.

Looking carefully at Figure 2, we can see that the lowest point on the whole graph is where $x = s$ and the highest point is where $x = b$. This means that $f(s)$ is the least value of f on the whole domain of f (the interval $[a, b]$) and $f(b)$ is the greatest value. We call these the *absolute* minimum and maximum.

Absolute Extrema

f has an **absolute maximum** at $x = r$ if $f(r) \geq f(x)$ for every x in the domain of f.

f has an **absolute minimum** at $x = r$ if $f(r) \leq f(x)$ for every x in the domain of f.

Quick Examples

1. In Figure 2, f has an absolute maximum at b and an absolute minimum at s.
2. If $f(x) = x^2$, then $f(x) \geq f(0)$ for every real number x. Therefore, $f(x) = x^2$ has an absolute minimum at $x = 0$. (See Figure 5.)
3. Generalizing (2), every quadratic function $f(x) = ax^2 + bx + c$ has an absolute extremum at its vertex $x = -b/(2a)$; an absolute minimum if $a > 0$, and an absolute maximum if $a < 0$.

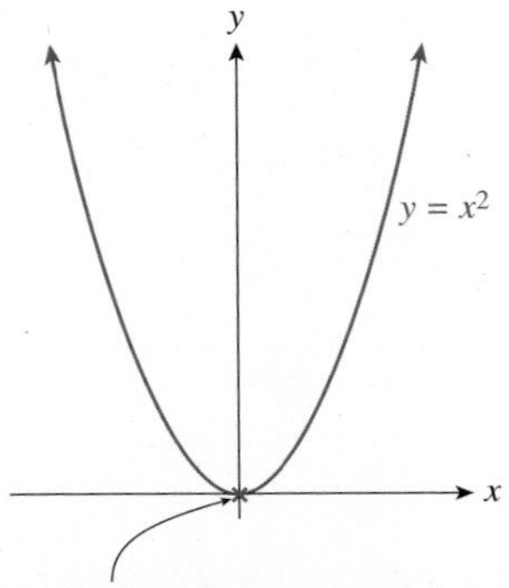

Absolute minimum at $x = 0$

Figure 5

Note If f has an absolute extremum at $x = r$, then it automatically satisfies the requirement for a *relative* extremum there as well; take $h = 1$ (or any other value) in the definition of relative extremum. Thus, absolute extrema are special types of relative extrema. ■

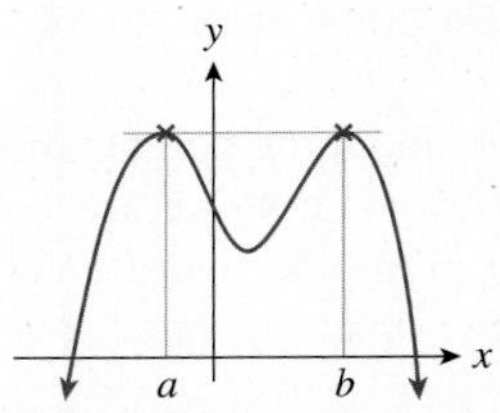

Absolute maxima at $x = a$ and $x = b$

Figure 6

Some graphs have no absolute extrema at all (think of the graph of $y = x$), while others might have an absolute minimum but no absolute maximum (like $y = x^2$), or vice versa. When *f* does have an absolute maximum, there is only one absolute maximum *value* of *f*, but this value may occur at different values of *x*, and similarly for absolute minima. (See Figure 6.)

Q: *At how many different values of x can f take on its absolute maximum value?*

A: An extreme case is that of a constant function; because we use $\geq$ in the definition of absolute maximum, a constant function has an absolute maximum (and minimum) at every point in its domain.

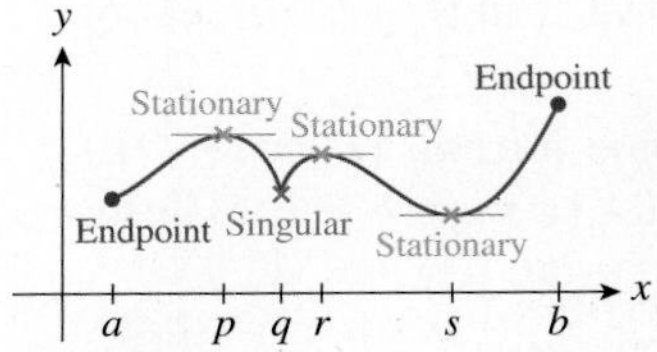

Figure 7

Now, how do we go about locating extrema? In many cases we can get a good idea by using graphing technology to zoom in on a maximum or minimum and approximate its coordinates. However, calculus gives us a way to find the exact locations of the extrema and at the same time to understand why the graph of a function behaves the way it does. In fact, it is often best to combine the powers of graphing technology with those of calculus, as we shall see.

In Figure 7 we see the graph from Figure 1 once more, but we have labeled each extreme point as one of three types. Notice that two extrema occur at endpoints and the others at **interior points;** that is, points other than endpoints. Let us look first at the extrema occurring at interior points: At the points labeled "Stationary," the tangent lines to the graph are horizontal, and so have slope 0, so f' (which gives the slope) is 0. Any time $f'(x) = 0$, we say that *f* has a **stationary point** at *x* because the rate of change of *f* is zero there. We call an extremum that occurs at a stationary point a **stationary extremum.** In general, to find the exact location of each stationary point, we need to solve the equation $f'(x) = 0$. Note that stationary points are always interior points, as f' is not defined at endpoints of the domain.

There is a relative minimum in Figure 7 at $x = q$, but there is no horizontal tangent there. In fact, there is no tangent line at all; $f'(q)$ is not defined. (Recall a similar situation with the graph of $f(x) = |x|$ at $x = 0$.) When $f'(x)$ does not exist for some interior point *x* in the domain of *f*, we say that *f* has a **singular point** at *x*. We shall call an extremum that occurs at a singular point a **singular extremum.** The points that are either stationary or singular we call collectively the **critical points** of *f*.

The remaining two extrema are at the **endpoints** of the domain (remember that we do allow relative extrema at endpoints). As we see in the figure, they are (almost) always either relative maxima or relative minima.

We bring all the above information together in Figure 8:

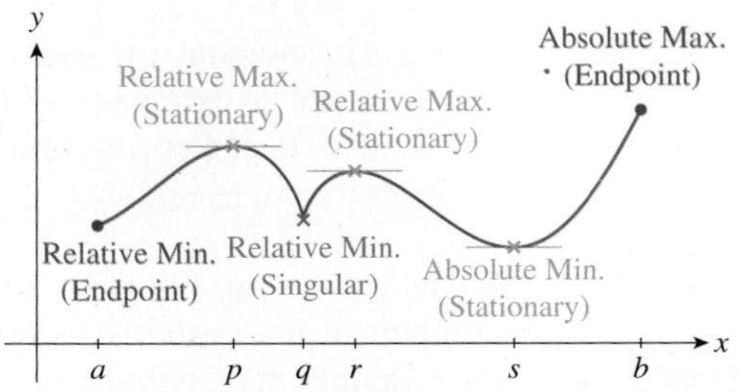

Figure 8

Q: *Are there any other types of relative extrema?*

A: No; relative extrema of a function always occur at critical points or endpoints. (A rigorous proof is beyond the scope of this book.)*

* Here is an outline of the argument. Suppose f has a maximum, say, at $x = a$, at some interior point of its domain. Then either f is differentiable there, or it is not. If it is not, then we have a singular point. If f is differentiable at $x = a$, then consider the slope of the secant line through the points where $x = a$ and $x = a + h$ for small positive h. Because f has a maximum at $x = a$, it is falling (or level) to the right of $x = a$, and so the slope of this secant line must be ≤ 0. Thus, we must have $f'(a) \leq 0$ in the limit as $h \to 0$. On the other hand, if h is small and *negative,* then the corresponding secant line must have slope ≥ 0 because f is also falling (or level) as we move left from $x = a$, and so $f'(a) \geq 0$. Because $f'(a)$ is both ≥ 0 and ≤ 0, it must be zero, and so we have a stationary point at $x = a$.

Locating Candidates for Extrema

If f is a real-valued function, then its extrema occur among the following types of points:

1. **Stationary Points:** f has a stationary point at x if x is in the interior of the domain and $f'(x) = 0$. To locate stationary points, set $f'(x) = 0$ and solve for x.
2. **Singular Points:** f has a singular point at x if x is in the interior of the domain and $f'(x)$ is not defined. To locate singular points, find values of x where $f'(x)$ is *not* defined, but $f(x)$ *is* defined.
3. **Endpoints:** These are the endpoints, if any, of the domain. Recall that closed intervals contain endpoints, but open intervals do not. If the domain of f is an open interval or the whole real line, then there are no endpoints.

Once we have a candidate for an extremum of f, we find the corresponding point (x, y) on the graph of f using $y = f(x)$.

Quick Examples

1. **Stationary Points:** Let $f(x) = x^3 - 12x$. Then to locate the stationary points, set $f'(x) = 0$ and solve for x. This gives $3x^2 - 12 = 0$, so f has stationary points at $x = \pm 2$. The corresponding points on the graph are $(-2, f(-2)) = (-2, 16)$ and $(2, f(2)) = (2, -16)$.
2. **Singular Points:** Let $f(x) = 3(x - 1)^{1/3}$. Then $f'(x) = (x - 1)^{-2/3} = 1/(x - 1)^{2/3}$. $f'(1)$ is not defined, although $f(1)$ *is* defined. Thus, the (only) singular point occurs at $x = 1$. The corresponding point on the graph is $(1, f(1)) = (1, 0)$.
3. **Endpoints:** Let $f(x) = 1/x$, with domain $(-\infty, 0) \cup [1, +\infty)$. Then the only endpoint in the domain of f occurs at $x = 1$. The corresponding point on the graph is $(1, 1)$. The natural domain of $1/x$, on the other hand, has no endpoints.

Remember, though, that the three types of points we identify above are only *candidates* for extrema. It is quite possible, as we shall see, to have a stationary point or a singular point that is neither a maximum nor a minimum. (It is also possible for an endpoint to be neither a maximum nor a minimum, but only in functions whose graphs are rather bizarre—see Exercise 65.)

Now let's look at some examples of finding maxima and minima. In all of these examples, we will use the following procedure: First, we find the derivative, which we examine to find the stationary points and singular points. Next, we make a table listing the x-coordinates of the critical points and endpoints, together with their y-coordinates. We use this table to make a rough sketch of the graph. From the table and rough sketch, we usually have enough data to be able to say where the extreme points are and what kind they are.

EXAMPLE 1 Maxima and Minima

Find the relative and absolute maxima and minima of

$$f(x) = x^2 - 2x$$

on the interval [0, 4].

Solution We first calculate $f'(x) = 2x - 2$. We use this derivative to locate the critical points (stationary and singular points).

Stationary Points To locate the stationary points, we solve the equation $f'(x) = 0$, or

$$2x - 2 = 0,$$

getting $x = 1$. The domain of the function is [0, 4], so $x = 1$ is in the interior of the domain. Thus, the only candidate for a stationary relative extremum occurs when $x = 1$.

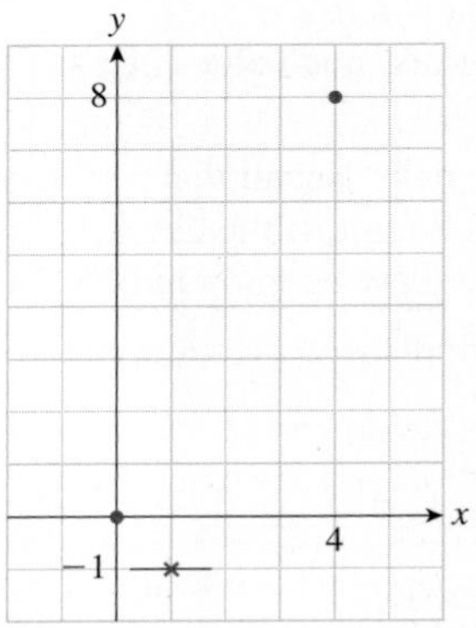

Figure 9

Singular Points We look for interior points where the derivative is not defined. However, the derivative is $2x - 2$, which is defined for every x. Thus, there are no singular points and hence no candidates for singular relative extrema.

Endpoints The domain is [0, 4], so the endpoints occur when $x = 0$ and $x = 4$.

We record these values of x in a table, together with the corresponding y-coordinates (values of f):

x	0	1	4
$f(x) = x^2 - 2x$	0	−1	8

This gives us three points on the graph, (0, 0), (1, −1), and (4, 8), which we plot in Figure 9. We remind ourselves that the point (1, −1) is a stationary point of the graph by drawing in a part of the horizontal tangent line. Connecting these points must give us a graph something like that in Figure 10.

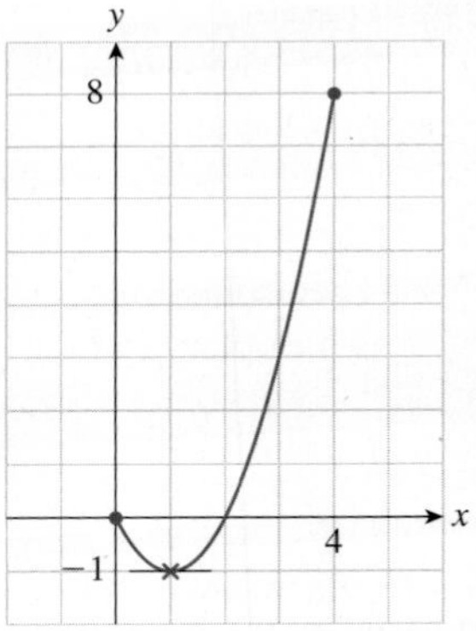

Figure 10

From Figure 10 we can see that f has the following extrema:

x	$y = x^2 - 2x$	*Classification*
0	0	Relative maximum (endpoint)
1	−1	Absolute minimum (stationary point)
4	8	Absolute maximum (endpoint)

➡ **Before we go on...** A little terminology: If the point (a, b) on the graph of f represents a maximum (or minimum) of f, we will sometimes say that ***f* has a maximum (or minimum) value of *b* at $x = a$**, or simply that ***f* has a maximum (or minimum) at (*a*, *b*).** Thus, in the above example, we could have said the following:

- "f has a relative maximum value of 0 at $x = 0$," or "f has a relative maximum at (0, 0)."
- "f has an absolute minimum value of −1 at $x = 1$," or "f has an absolute minimum at (1, −1)."
- "f has an absolute maximum value of 8 at $x = 4$," or "f has an absolute maximum at (4, 8)."

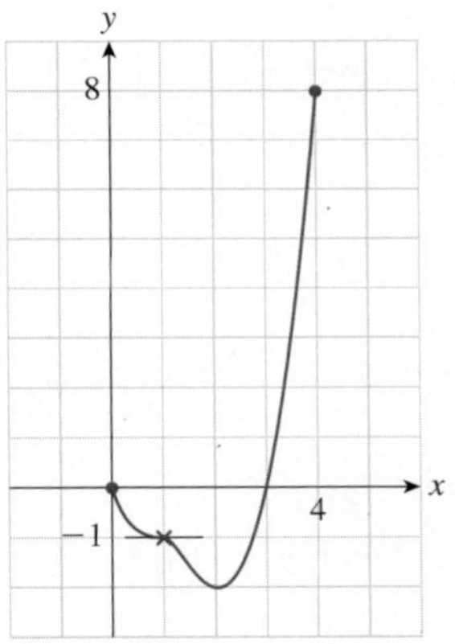

Figure 11

Q: *How can we be sure that the graph in Example 1 doesn't look like Figure 11?*

A: If it did, there would be another critical point somewhere between $x = 1$ and $x = 4$. But we already know that there aren't any other critical points. The table we made listed all of the possible extrema; there can be no more.

First Derivative Test

The **first derivative test*** gives another, very systematic, way of checking whether a critical point is a maximum or minimum. To motivate the first derivative test, consider again the critical point $x = 1$ in Example 1. If we look at some values of $f'(x)$ to the left and right of the critical point, we obtain the information shown in the following table:

* Why "first" derivative test? To distinguish it from a test based on the **second derivative** of a function, which we shall discuss in Section 5.3.

	Point to the Left	Critical Point	Point to the Right
x	0.5	1	2
$f'(x) = 2x - 2$	-1	0	2
Direction of Graph	↘	→	↗

At $x = 0.5$ (to the left of the critical point) we see that $f'(0.5) = -1 < 0$, so the graph has negative slope and f is decreasing. We note this with the downward pointing arrow. At $x = 2$ (to the right of the critical point), we find $f'(2) = 2 > 0$, so the graph has positive slope and f is increasing. In fact, because $f'(x) = 0$ only at $x = 1$, we know that $f'(x) < 0$ for all x in $(0, 1)$, and we can say that f is decreasing on the interval $(0, 1)$. Similarly, f is increasing on $(1, 4)$.

So, starting at $x = 0$, the graph of f goes down until we reach $x = 1$ and then it goes back up, telling us that $x = 1$ must be a minimum. Notice how the minimum is suggested by the arrows to the left and right.

First Derivative Test for Extrema

Suppose that c is a critical point of the continuous function f, and that its derivative is defined for x close to, and on both sides of, $x = c$. Then, determine the sign of the derivative to the left and right of $x = c$.

1. If $f'(x)$ is positive to the left of $x = c$ and negative to the right, then f has a maximum at $x = c$.
2. If $f'(x)$ is negative to the left of $x = c$ and positive to the right, then f has a minimum at $x = c$.
3. If $f'(x)$ has the same sign on both sides of $x = c$, then f has neither a maximum nor a minimum at $x = c$.

Quick Examples

1. In Example 1 above, we saw that $f(x) = x^2 - 2x$ has a critical point at $x = 1$ with $f'(x)$ negative to the left of $x = 1$ and positive to the right (see the table). Therefore, f has a minimum at $x = 1$.

2. Here is a graph showing a function f with a singular point at $x = 1$:

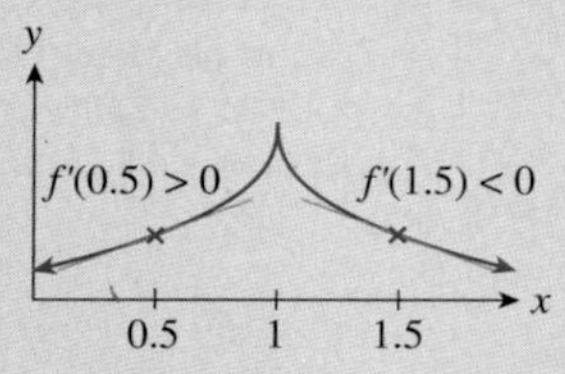

The graph gives us the information shown in the table:

	Point to the Left	Critical Point	Point to the Right
x	0.5	1	1.5
$f'(x)$	+	Undefined	−
Direction of Graph	↗		↘

Since $f'(x)$ is positive to the left of $x = 1$ and negative to the right, we see that f has a maximum at $x = 1$. (Notice again how this is suggested by the direction of the arrows.)

EXAMPLE 2 Unbounded Interval

Find all extrema of $f(x) = 3x^4 - 4x^3$ on $[-1, \infty)$.

Solution We first calculate $f'(x) = 12x^3 - 12x^2$.

Stationary points We solve the equation $f'(x) = 0$, which is

$$12x^3 - 12x^2 = 0 \text{ or}$$
$$12x^2(x - 1) = 0.$$

There are two solutions, $x = 0$ and $x = 1$, and both are in the domain. These are our candidates for the x-coordinates of stationary extrema.

Singular points There are no points where $f'(x)$ is not defined, so there are no singular points.

Endpoints The domain is $[-1, \infty)$, so there is one endpoint, at $x = -1$.

We record these points in a table with the corresponding y-coordinates:

x	−1	0	1
$f(x) = 3x^4 - 4x^3$	7	0	−1

We will illustrate three methods we can use to determine which are minima, which are maxima, and which are neither:

1. Plot these points and sketch the graph by hand.

2. Use the first derivative test.

3. Use technology to help us.

Use the method you find most convenient.

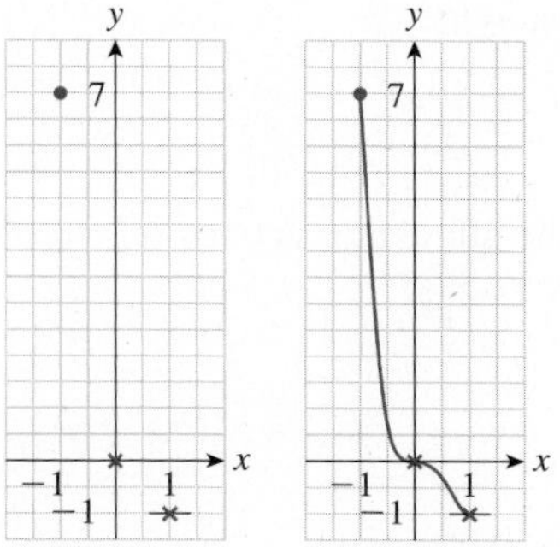

(a) (b)

Figure 12

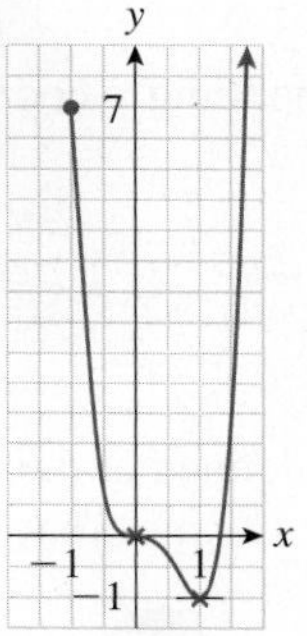

Figure 13

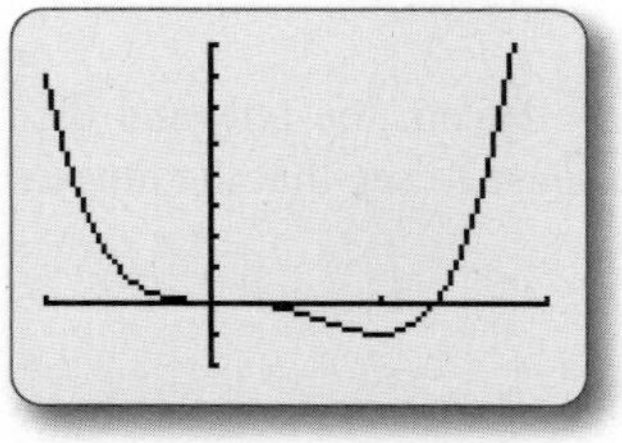

Figure 14

Using a Hand Plot: If we plot these points by hand, we obtain Figure 12(a), which suggests Figure 12(b).

We can't be sure what happens to the right of $x = 1$. Does the curve go up, or does it go down? To find out, let's plot a "test point" to the right of $x = 1$. Choosing $x = 2$, we obtain $y = 3(2)^4 - 4(2)^3 = 16$, so (2, 16) is another point on the graph. Thus, it must turn upward to the right of $x = 1$, as shown in Figure 13.

From the graph, we find that f has the following extrema:

A relative (endpoint) maximum at $(-1, 7)$

An absolute (stationary) minimum at $(1, -1)$

Using the First Derivative Test: List the critical and endpoints in a table, and add additional points as necessary so that each critical point has a noncritical point on either side. Then compute the derivative at each of these points, and draw an arrow to indicate the direction of the graph.

	Endpoint		**Critical Point**		**Critical Point**	
x	−1	−0.5	0	0.5	1	2
$f'(x) = 12x^3 - 12x^2$	−24	−1.5	0	−1.5	0	48
Direction of Graph		↘	→	↘	→	↗

Notice that the arrows now suggest the shape of the curve in Figure 13. The first derivative test tells us that the function has a relative maximum at $x = -1$, neither a maximum nor a minimum at $x = 0$, and a relative minimum at $x = 1$. Deciding which of these extrema are absolute and which are relative requires us to compute y-coordinates and plot the corresponding points on the graph by hand, as we did in the first method.

using Technology

If we use technology to show the graph, we should choose the viewing window so that it contains the three interesting points we found: $x = -1$, $x = 0$, and $x = 1$. Again, we can't be sure yet what happens to the right of $x = 1$; does the graph go up or down from that point? If we set the viewing window to an interval of $[-1, 2]$ for x and $[-2, 8]$ for y, we will leave enough room to the right of $x = 1$ and below $y = -1$ to see what the graph will do. The result will be something like Figure 14.

Now we can tell what happens to the right of $x = 1$: the function increases. We know that it cannot later decrease again because if it did, there would have to be another critical point where it turns around, and we found that there are no other critical points. ■

➡ **Before we go on...** Notice that the stationary point at $x = 0$ in Example 2 is neither a relative maximum nor a relative minimum. It is simply a place where the graph of f flattens out for a moment before it continues to fall. Notice also that f has no absolute maximum because $f(x)$ increases without bound as x gets large. ■

EXAMPLE 3 Singular Point

Find all extrema of $f(t) = t^{2/3}$ on $[-1, 1]$.

Solution First, $f'(t) = \frac{2}{3}t^{-1/3}$.

Stationary points We need to solve

$$\frac{2}{3}t^{-1/3} = 0.$$

We can rewrite this equation without the negative exponent:

$$\frac{2}{3t^{1/3}} = 0.$$

Now, the only way that a fraction can equal 0 is if the numerator is 0, so this fraction can never equal 0. Thus, there are no stationary points.

Singular Points The derivative

$$f'(t) = \frac{2}{3t^{1/3}}$$

is not defined for $t = 0$. However, 0 is in the interior of the domain of f (although f' is not defined at $t = 0$, f itself is). Thus, f has a singular point at $t = 0$.

Endpoints There are two endpoints, -1 and 1.

We now put these three points in a table with the corresponding y-coordinates:

t	-1	0	1
$f(t)$	1	0	1

Using a Hand Plot: The derivative, $f'(t) = 2/(3t^{1/3})$, is not defined at the singular point $t = 0$. To help us sketch the graph, let's use limits to investigate what happens to the derivative as we approach 0 from either side:

$$\lim_{t \to 0^-} f'(t) = \lim_{t \to 0^-} \frac{2}{3t^{1/3}} = -\infty$$

$$\lim_{t \to 0^+} f'(t) = \lim_{t \to 0^+} \frac{2}{3t^{1/3}} = +\infty.$$

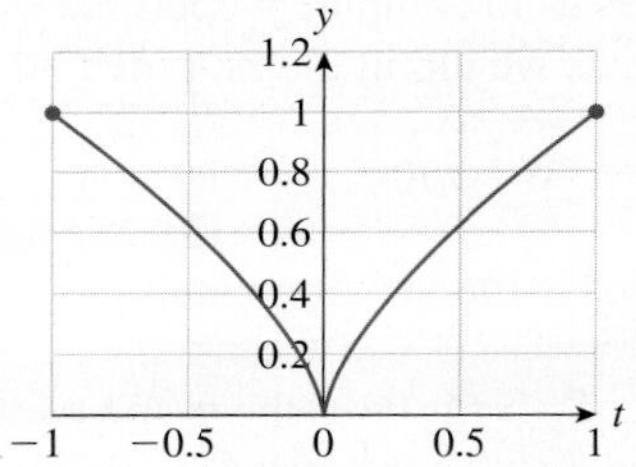

Figure 15

Thus, the graph decreases very steeply, approaching $t = 0$ from the left, and then rises very steeply as it leaves to the right. It would make sense to say that the tangent line at $x = 0$ is vertical, as seen in Figure 15.

From this graph, we find the following extrema for f:

An absolute (endpoint) maximum at $(-1, 1)$

An absolute (singular) minimum at $(0, 0)$

An absolute (endpoint) maximum at $(1, 1)$.

Notice that the absolute maximum value of f is achieved at two values of t: $t = -1$ and $t = 1$.

First Derivative Test: Here is the corresponding table for the first derivative test.

t	-0.5	0	0.5
$f'(t) = \frac{2}{3t^{1/3}}$	$-\frac{2}{3(0.5)^{1/3}}$	Undefined	$\frac{2}{3(0.5)^{1/3}}$
Direction of Graph	↘	↕	↗

(We drew a vertical arrow at $t = 0$ to indicate a vertical tangent.) Again, notice how the arrows suggest the shape of the curve in Figure 15, and the first derivative test confirms that we have a minimum at $x = 0$.

using Technology

Because there is only one critical point, at $t = 0$, it is clear from this table that f must decrease from $t = -1$ to $t = 0$ and then increase from $t = 0$ to $t = 1$. To graph f using technology, choose a viewing window with an interval of $[-1, 1]$ for t and $[0, 1]$ for y. The result will be something like Figure 15.* ■

* Many graphing calculators will give you only the right-hand half of the graph shown in Figure 15 because fractional powers of negative numbers are not, in general, real numbers. To obtain the whole curve, enter the formula as `Y=(x^2)^(1/3)`, a fractional power of the non-negative function x^2.

In Examples 1 and 3, we could have found the absolute maxima and minima without doing any graphing. In Example 1, after finding the critical points and endpoints, we created the following table:

x	0	1	4
$f(x)$	0	-1	8

From this table we can see that f must decrease from its value of 0 at $x = 0$ to -1 at $x = 1$, and then increase to 8 at $x = 4$. The value of 8 must be the largest value it takes on, and the value of -1 must be the smallest, on the interval $[0, 4]$. Similarly, in Example 3 we created the following table:

t	-1	0	1
$f(t)$	1	0	1

From this table we can see that the largest value of f on the interval $[-1, 1]$ is 1 and the smallest value is 0. We are taking advantage of the following fact, the proof of which uses some deep and beautiful mathematics (alas, beyond the scope of this book):

Extreme Value Theorem

If f is *continuous* on a *closed interval* $[a, b]$, then it will have an absolute maximum and an absolute minimum value on that interval. Each absolute extremum must occur at either an endpoint or a critical point. Therefore, the absolute maximum is the largest value in a table of the values of f at the endpoints and critical points, and the absolute minimum is the smallest value.

Quick Example

The function $f(x) = 3x - x^3$ on the interval $[0, 2]$ has one critical point at $x = 1$. The values of f at the critical point and the endpoints of the interval are given in the following table:

	Endpoint	**Critical point**	**Endpoint**
x	0	1	2
$f(x)$	0	2	-2

From this table we can say that the absolute maximum value of f on $[0, 2]$ is 2, which occurs at $x = 1$, and the absolute minimum value of f is -2, which occurs at $x = 2$.

As we can see in Example 2 and the following examples, if the domain is not a closed interval, then f may not have an absolute maximum and minimum, and a table of values as above is of little help in determining whether it does.

EXAMPLE 4 Domain Not a Closed Interval

Find all extrema of $f(x) = x + \dfrac{1}{x}$.

Solution Because no domain is specified, we take the domain to be as large as possible. The function is not defined at $x = 0$ but is at all other points, so we take its domain to be $(-\infty, 0) \cup (0, +\infty)$. We calculate

$$f'(x) = 1 - \frac{1}{x^2}.$$

Stationary Points Setting $f'(x) = 0$, we solve

$$1 - \frac{1}{x^2} = 0$$

to find $x = \pm 1$. Calculating the corresponding values of f, we get the two stationary points $(1, 2)$ and $(-1, -2)$.

Singular Points The only value of x for which $f'(x)$ is not defined is $x = 0$, but then f is not defined there either, so there are no singular points in the domain.

Endpoints The domain, $(-\infty, 0) \cup (0, +\infty)$, has no endpoints.

From this scant information, it is hard to tell what f does. If we are sketching the graph by hand, or using the first derivative test, we will need to plot additional "test points" to the left and right of the stationary points $x = \pm 1$.

using Technology

For the technology approach, let's choose a viewing window with an interval of $[-3, 3]$ for x and $[-4, 4]$ for y, which should leave plenty of room to see how f behaves near the stationary points. The result is something like Figure 16.

From this graph we can see that f has:

A relative (stationary) maximum at $(-1, -2)$

A relative (stationary) minimum at $(1, 2)$

Curiously, the relative maximum is lower than the relative minimum! Notice also that, because of the break in the graph at $x = 0$, the graph did not need to rise to get from $(-1, -2)$ to $(1, 2)$. ■

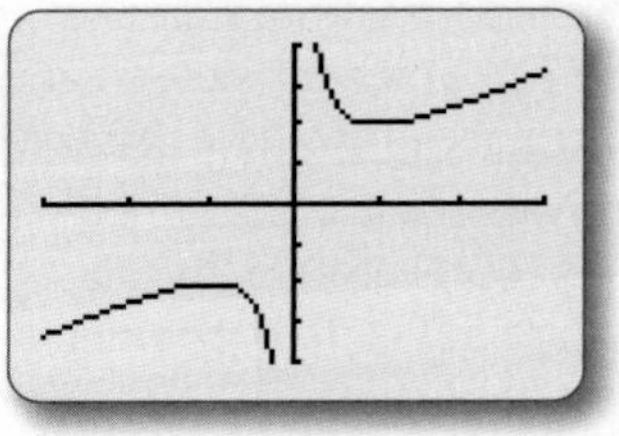

Figure 16

So far we have been solving the equation $f'(x) = 0$ to obtain our candidates for stationary extrema. However, it is often not easy—or even possible—to solve equations analytically. In the next example, we show a way around this problem by using graphing technology.

EXAMPLE 5 Finding Approximate Extrema Using Technology

Graph the function $f(x) = (x - 1)^{2/3} - \dfrac{x^2}{2}$ with domain $[-2, +\infty)$. Also graph its derivative and hence locate and classify all extrema of f, with coordinates accurate to two decimal places.

Solution In Example 4 of Section 3.5, we saw how to draw the graphs of f and f' using technology. Note that the technology formula to use for the graph of f is

```
((x-1)^2)^(1/3)-0.5*x^2
```

instead of

```
(x-1)^(2/3)-0.5*x^2
```

(Why?)

Figure 17 shows the resulting graphs of f and f'.

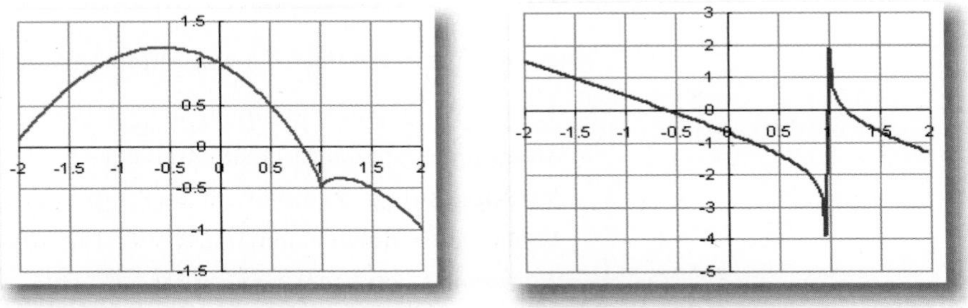

Graph of f Graph of f'

Figure 17 **(a)** **(b)**

If we extend Xmax beyond $x = 2$, we find that the graph continues downward, apparently without any further interesting behavior.

Stationary Points The graph of f shows two stationary points, both maxima, at around $x = -0.6$ and $x = 1.2$. Notice that the graph of f' is zero at these points. Moreover, it is easier to locate these values accurately on the graph of f' because it is easier to pinpoint where a graph crosses the x-axis than to locate a stationary point. Zooming in to the stationary point at $x \approx -0.6$ results in Figure 18.

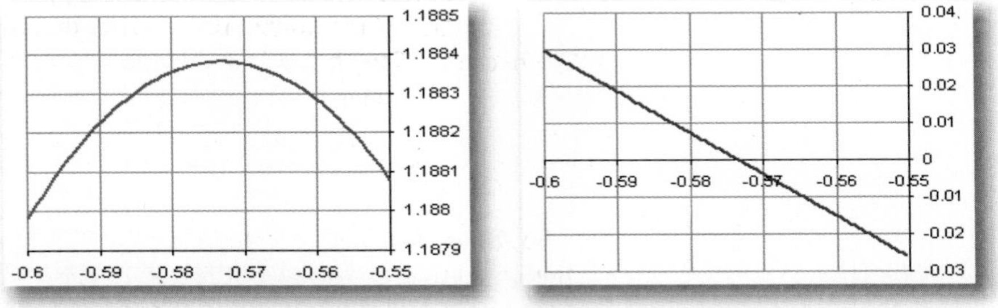

Graph of f Graph of f'

Figure 18 **(a)** **(b)**

From the graph of f, we can see that the stationary point is somewhere between -0.58 and -0.57. The graph of f' shows more clearly that the zero of f', hence the stationary point of f lies somewhat closer to -0.57 than to -0.58. Thus, the stationary point occurs at $x \approx -0.57$, rounded to two decimal places.

In a similar way, we find the second stationary point at $x \approx 1.18$.

Singular Points Going back to Figure 17, we notice what appears to be a cusp (singular point) at the relative minimum around $x = 1$, and this is confirmed by a glance at the graph of f', which seems to take a sudden jump at that value. Zooming in closer suggests that the singular point occurs at exactly $x = 1$. In fact, we can calculate

$$f'(x) = \frac{2}{3(x-1)^{1/3}} - x.$$

From this formula we see clearly that $f'(x)$ is defined everywhere except at $x = 1$.

Endpoints The only endpoint in the domain is $x = -2$, which gives a relative minimum.

Thus, we have found the following approximate extrema for f:

A relative (endpoint) minimum at $(-2, 0.08)$

An absolute (stationary) maximum at $(-0.57, 1.19)$

A relative (singular) minimum at $(1, -0.5)$

A relative (stationary) maximum at $(1.18, -0.38)$.

5.1 EXERCISES

▼ more advanced ◆ challenging

T indicates exercises that should be solved using technology

In Exercises 1–12, locate and classify all extrema in each graph. (By classifying the extrema, we mean listing whether each extremum is a relative or absolute maximum or minimum.) Also, locate any stationary points or singular points that are not relative extrema. HINT [See Figure 8.]

1.

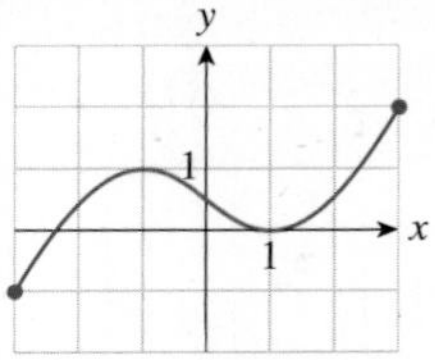

2.

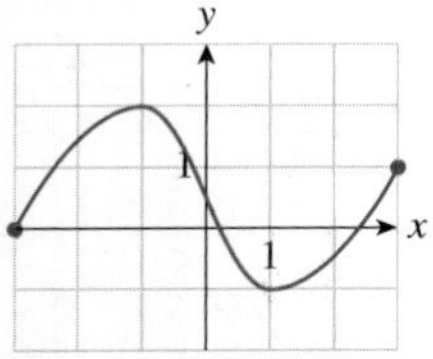

3.

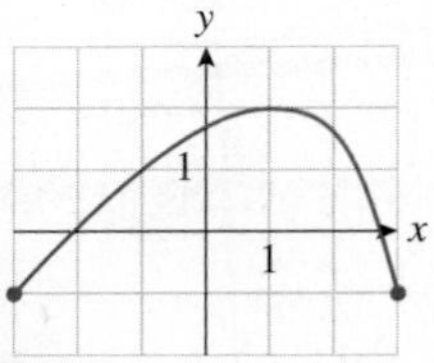

4.

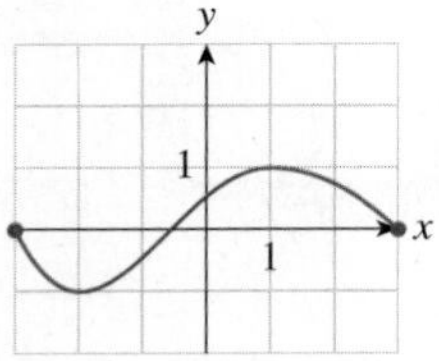

5.

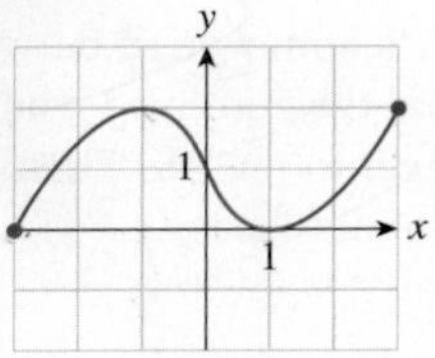

6.

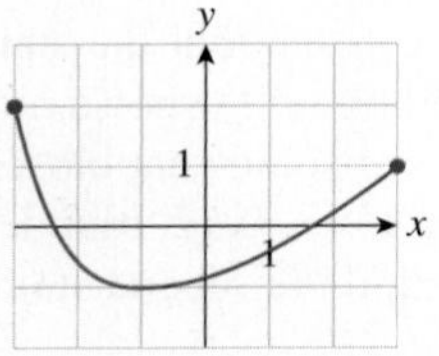

7.

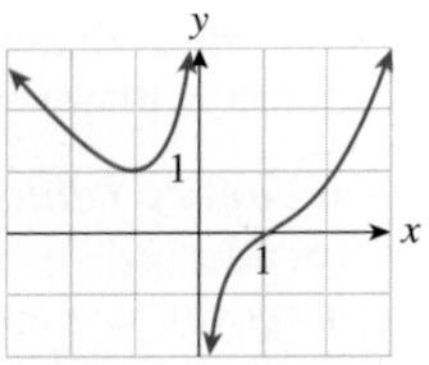

8.

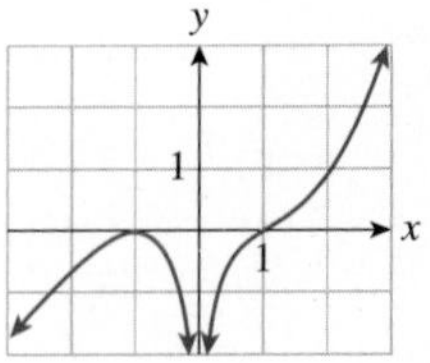

9.

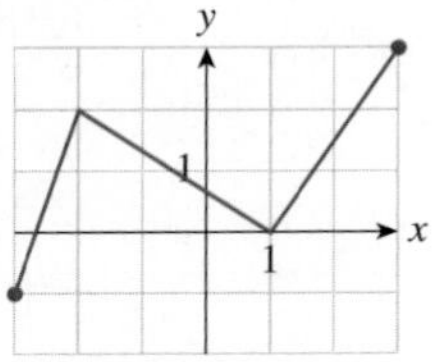

10.

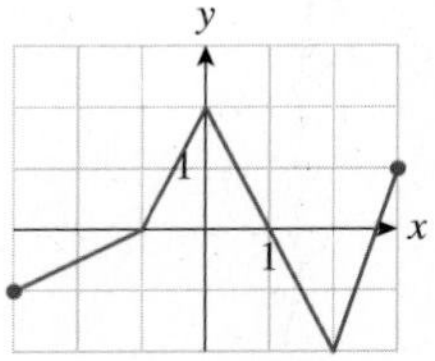

11.

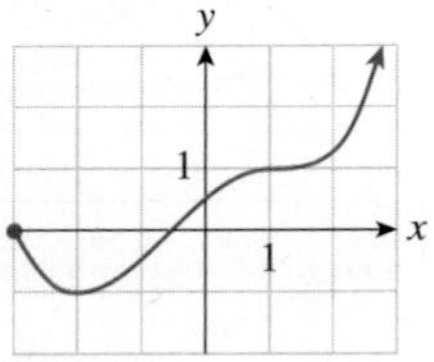

12.

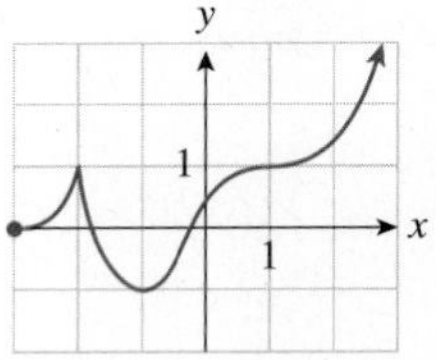

Find the exact location of all the relative and absolute extrema of each function in Exercises 13–44. HINT [See Example 1.]

13. $f(x) = x^2 - 4x + 1$ with domain $[0, 3]$

14. $f(x) = 2x^2 - 2x + 3$ with domain $[0, 3]$

15. $g(x) = x^3 - 12x$ with domain $[-4, 4]$

16. $g(x) = 2x^3 - 6x + 3$ with domain $[-2, 2]$

17. $f(t) = t^3 + t$ with domain $[-2, 2]$

18. $f(t) = -2t^3 - 3t$ with domain $[-1, 1]$

19. $h(t) = 2t^3 + 3t^2$ with domain $[-2, +\infty)$ HINT [See Example 2.]

20. $h(t) = t^3 - 3t^2$ with domain $[-1, +\infty)$ HINT [See Example 2.]

21. $f(x) = x^4 - 4x^3$ with domain $[-1, +\infty)$

22. $f(x) = 3x^4 - 2x^3$ with domain $[-1, +\infty)$

23. $g(t) = \frac{1}{4}t^4 - \frac{2}{3}t^3 + \frac{1}{2}t^2$ with domain $(-\infty, +\infty)$

24. $g(t) = 3t^4 - 16t^3 + 24t^2 + 1$ with domain $(-\infty, +\infty)$

25. $h(x) = (x - 1)^{2/3}$ with domain $[0, 2]$ HINT [See Example 3.]

26. $h(x) = (x + 1)^{2/5}$ with domain $[-2, 0]$ HINT [See Example 3.]

27. $k(x) = \frac{2x}{3} + (x + 1)^{2/3}$ with domain $(-\infty, 0]$

28. $k(x) = \frac{2x}{5} - (x - 1)^{2/5}$ with domain $[0, +\infty)$

29. ▼ $f(t) = \frac{t^2 + 1}{t^2 - 1}; -2 \le t \le 2, t \ne \pm 1$

30. ▼ $f(t) = \frac{t^2 - 1}{t^2 + 1}$ with domain $[-2, 2]$

31. ▼ $f(x) = \sqrt{x}(x - 1); x \ge 0$

32. ▼ $f(x) = \sqrt{x}(x + 1); x \ge 0$

33. ▼ $g(x) = x^2 - 4\sqrt{x}$

34. ▼ $g(x) = \frac{1}{x} - \frac{1}{x^2}$

35. ▼ $g(x) = \frac{x^3}{x^2 + 3}$

36. ▼ $g(x) = \frac{x^3}{x^2 - 3}$

37. ▼ $f(x) = x - \ln x$ with domain $(0, +\infty)$

38. ▼ $f(x) = x - \ln x^2$ with domain $(0, +\infty)$

39. ▼ $g(t) = e^t - t$ with domain $[-1, 1]$

40. ▼ $g(t) = e^{-t^2}$ with domain $(-\infty, +\infty)$

41. ▼ $f(x) = \frac{2x^2 - 24}{x + 4}$

42. ▼ $f(x) = \frac{x - 4}{x^2 + 20}$

43. ▼ $f(x) = xe^{1-x^2}$

44. ▼ $f(x) = x \ln x$ with domain $(0, +\infty)$

In Exercises 45–48, use graphing technology and the method in Example 5 to find the x-coordinates of the critical points, accurate to two decimal places. Find all relative and absolute maxima and minima. HINT [See Example 5.]

45. T $y = x^2 + \frac{1}{x - 2}$ with domain $(-3, 2) \cup (2, 6)$

46. T $y = x^2 - 10(x - 1)^{2/3}$ with domain $(-4, 4)$

47. T $f(x) = (x - 5)^2(x + 4)(x - 2)$ with domain $[-5, 6]$

48. T $f(x) = (x + 3)^2(x - 2)^2$ with domain $[-5, 5]$

In Exercises 49–56, the graph of the derivative of a function f is shown. Determine the x-coordinates of all stationary and singular points of f, and classify each as a relative maximum, relative minimum, or neither. (Assume that f(x) is defined and continuous everywhere in [−3, 3].) HINT [See Example 5.]

49. ▼

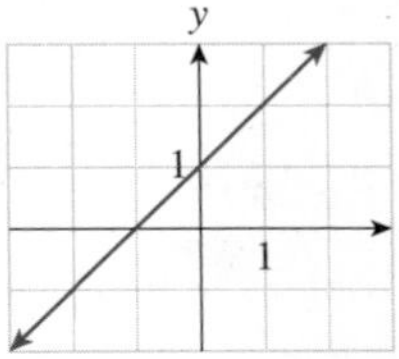

50. ▼

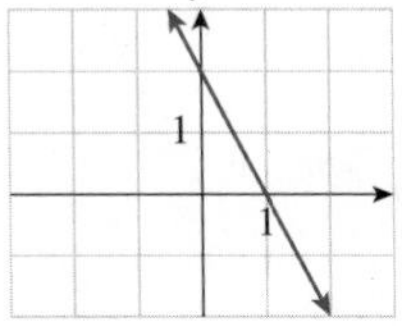

51. ▼

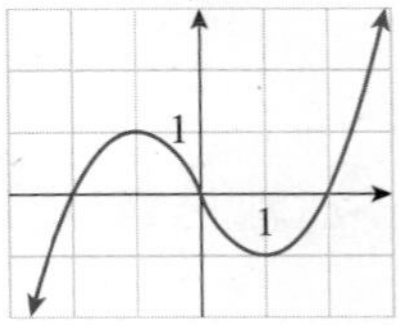

52. ▼

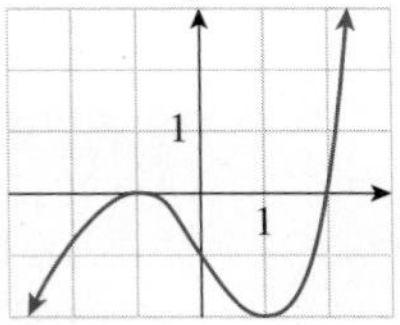

53. ▼

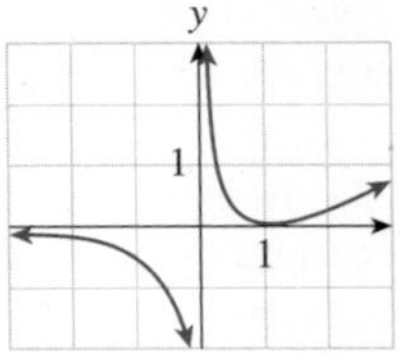

54. ▼

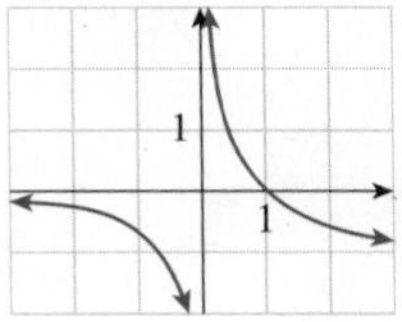

55. ▼

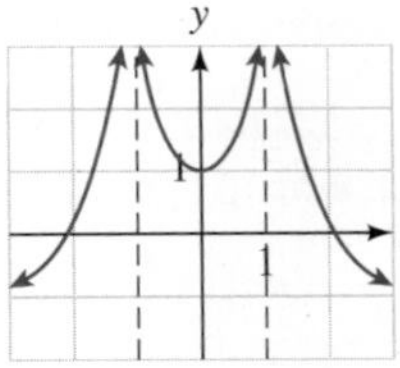

56. ▼

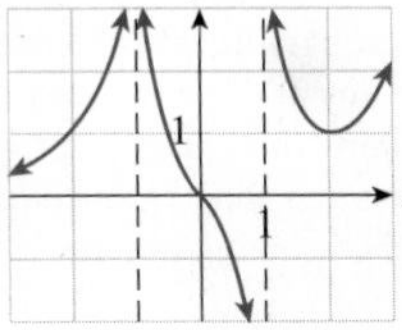

COMMUNICATION AND REASONING EXERCISES

57. Draw the graph of a function f with domain the set of all real numbers, such that f is not linear and has no relative extrema.

58. Draw the graph of a function g with domain the set of all real numbers, such that g has a relative maximum and minimum but no absolute extrema.

59. Draw the graph of a function that has stationary and singular points but no relative extrema.

60. Draw the graph of a function that has relative, not absolute, maxima and minima, but has no stationary or singular points.

61. If a stationary point is not a relative maximum, then must it be a relative minimum? Explain your answer.

62. If one endpoint is a relative maximum, must the other be a relative minimum? Explain your answer.

63. ▼ We said that if f is continuous on a closed interval $[a, b]$, then it will have an absolute maximum and an absolute minimum. Draw the graph of a function with domain $[0, 1]$ having an absolute maximum but no absolute minimum.

64. ▼ Refer to Exercise 63. Draw the graph of a function with domain $[0, 1]$ having no absolute extrema.

65. T ▼ Must endpoints always be extrema? Consider the following function (based on the trigonometric sine function—see Chapter 9 for a discussion of its properties):

$$f(x) = \begin{cases} x \sin\left(\frac{1}{x}\right) & \text{if } x > 0 \\ 0 & \text{if } x = 0 \end{cases}.$$

Technology formula: `x*sin(1/x)`

Graph this function using the technology formula above for $0 \le x \le h$, choosing smaller and smaller values of h, and decide whether f has a either a relative maximum or relative minimum at the endpoint $x = 0$. Explain your answer. (Note: Very few graphers can draw this curve accurately; the grapher on the Website does a good job (you can increase the number of points to plot for more beautiful results), the grapher that comes with Mac computers is probably among the best, while the TI-83/84 Plus is probably among the worst.)

66. T ▼ Refer to the preceding exercise, and consider the function

$$f(x) = \begin{cases} x^2 \sin\left(\frac{1}{x}\right) & \text{if } x \neq 0 \\ 0 & \text{if } x = 0 \end{cases}.$$

Technology formula: `x^2*sin(1/x)`

Graph this function using the technology formula above for $-h \le x \le h$, choosing smaller and smaller values of h, and decide **(a)** whether $x = 0$ is a stationary point, and **(b)** whether f has either a relative maximum or a relative minimum at $x = 0$. Explain your answers. HINT [For part (a), use technology to estimate the derivative at $x = 0$.]

5.2 Applications of Maxima and Minima

In many applications we would like to find the largest or smallest possible value of some quantity—for instance, the greatest possible profit or the lowest cost. We call this the *optimal* (best) value. In this section we consider several such examples and use calculus to find the optimal value in each.

In all applications the first step is to translate a written description into a mathematical problem. In the problems we look at in this section, there are *unknowns* that we are asked to find, there is an expression involving those unknowns that must be made as large or as small as possible—the **objective function**—and there may be **constraints**—equations or inequalities relating the variables.*

* If you have studied linear programming, you will notice a similarity here, but unlike the situation in linear programming, neither the objective function nor the constraints need be linear.

EXAMPLE 1 Minimizing Average Cost

Gymnast Clothing manufactures expensive hockey jerseys for sale to college bookstores in runs of up to 500. Its cost (in dollars) for a run of x hockey jerseys is

$$C(x) = 2{,}000 + 10x + 0.2x^2.$$

How many jerseys should Gymnast produce per run in order to minimize average cost?†

† Why don't we seek to minimize total cost? The answer would be uninteresting; to minimize total cost, we would make *no* jerseys at all. Minimizing the average cost is a more practical objective.

Solution Here is the procedure we will follow to solve problems like this.

1. ***Identify the unknown(s).*** There is one unknown: x, the number of hockey jerseys Gymnast should produce per run. (We know this because the question is, How many jerseys . . . ?)
2. ***Identify the objective function.*** The objective function is the quantity that must be made as small (in this case) as possible. In this example it is the average cost, which is given by

$$\bar{C}(x) = \frac{C(x)}{x} = \frac{2{,}000 + 10x + 0.2x^2}{x}$$
$$= \frac{2{,}000}{x} + 10 + 0.2x \text{ dollars/jersey.}$$

3. ***Identify the constraints (if any).*** At most 500 jerseys can be manufactured in a run. Also, $\bar{C}(0)$ is not defined. Thus, x is constrained by

$$0 < x \leq 500.$$

Put another way, the domain of the objective function $\bar{C}(x)$ is (0, 500].

4. ***State and solve the resulting optimization problem.*** Our optimization problem is:

$$\text{Minimize } \bar{C}(x) = \frac{2{,}000}{x} + 10 + 0.2x \qquad \text{Objective function}$$

$$\text{subject to } 0 < x \leq 500. \qquad \text{Constraint}$$

We now solve this problem as in Section 5.1. We first calculate

$$\bar{C}'(x) = -\frac{2{,}000}{x^2} + 0.2.$$

We solve $\bar{C}'(x) = 0$ to find $x = \pm 100$. We reject $x = -100$ because -100 is not in the domain of $\bar{C}$ (and makes no sense), so we have one stationary point, at $x = 100$. There, the average cost is $\bar{C}(100) = \$50$ per jersey.

The only point at which the formula for $\bar{C}'$ is not defined is $x = 0$, but that is not in the domain of $\bar{C}$, so we have no singular points. We have one endpoint in the domain, at $x = 500$. There, the average cost is $\bar{C}(500) = \$114$.

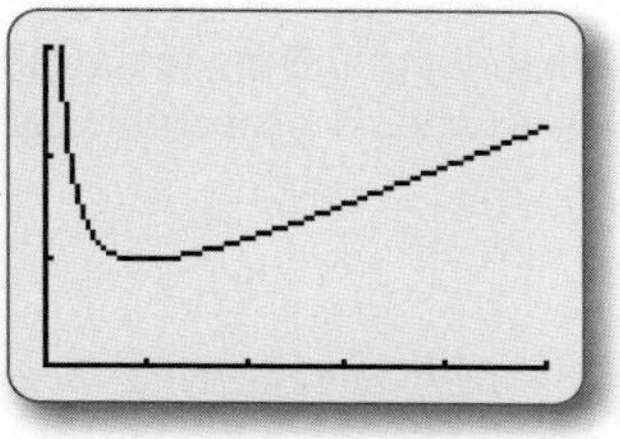
Figure 19

using Technology

Let's plot $\bar{C}$ in a viewing window with the intervals [0, 500] for x and [0, 150] for y, which will show the whole domain and the two interesting points we've found so far. The result is Figure 19.

From the graph of $\bar{C}$, we can see that the stationary point at $x = 100$ gives the absolute minimum. We can therefore say that Gymnast Clothing should produce 100 jerseys per run, for a lowest possible average cost of \$50 per jersey. ■

EXAMPLE 2 Maximizing Area

Slim wants to build a rectangular enclosure for his pet rabbit, Killer, against the side of his house, as shown in Figure 20. He has bought 100 feet of fencing. What are the dimensions of the largest area that he can enclose?

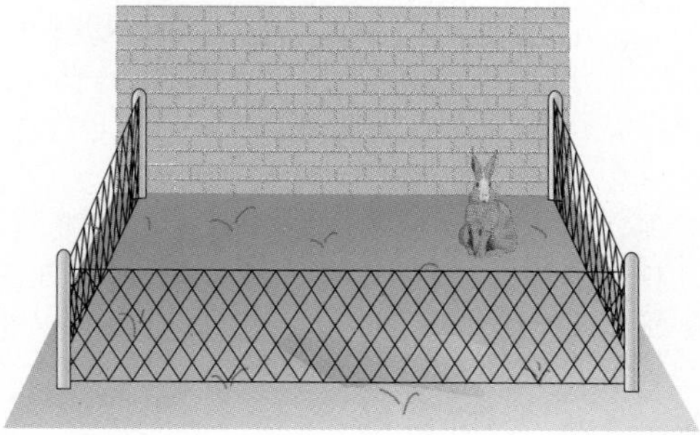
Figure 20

Solution

1. ***Identify the unknown(s).*** To identify the unknown(s), we look at the question: What are the *dimensions* of the largest area he can enclose? Thus, the unknowns are the dimensions of the fence. We call these x and y, as shown in Figure 21.

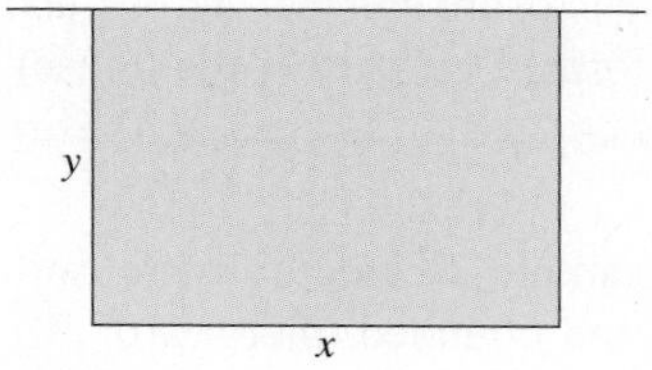

Figure 21

2. ***Identify the objective function.*** We look for what it is that we are trying to maximize (or minimize). The phrase "largest area" tells us that our object is to *maximize the area*, which is the product of length and width, so our objective function is

$$A = xy, \text{ where } A \text{ is the area of the enclosure.}$$

3. ***Identify the constraints (if any).*** What stops Slim from making the area as large as he wants? He has only 100 feet of fencing to work with. Looking again at Figure 21, we see that the sum of the lengths of the three sides must equal 100, so

$$x + 2y = 100.$$

One more point: Because x and y represent the lengths of the sides of the enclosure, neither can be a negative number.

4. ***State and solve the resulting optimization problem.*** Our mathematical problem is:

Maximize $A = xy$ — Objective function

subject to $x + 2y = 100$, $x \geq 0$, and $y \geq 0$. — Constraints

We know how to find maxima and minima of a function of one variable, but A appears to depend on two variables. We can remedy this by using a constraint to express one variable in terms of the other. Let's take the constraint $x + 2y = 100$ and solve for x in terms of y:

$$x = 100 - 2y.$$

Substituting into the objective function gives

$$A = xy = (100 - 2y)y = 100y - 2y^2$$

and we have eliminated x from the objective function. What about the inequalities? One says that $x \geq 0$, but we want to eliminate x from this as well. We substitute for x again, getting

$$100 - 2y \geq 0.$$

Solving this inequality for y gives $y \leq 50$. The second inequality says that $y \geq 0$. Now, we can restate our problem with x eliminated:

Maximize $A(y) = 100y - 2y^2$ subject to $0 \leq y \leq 50$.

We now proceed with our usual method of solving such problems. We calculate $A'(y) = 100 - 4y$. Solving $100 - 4y = 0$, we get one stationary point at $y = 25$. There, $A(25) = 1{,}250$. There are no points at which $A'(y)$ is not defined, so there are no singular points. We have two endpoints, at $y = 0$ and $y = 50$. The corresponding areas are $A(0) = 0$ and $A(50) = 0$. We record the three points we found in a table:

y	0	25	50
$A(y)$	0	1,250	0

It's clear now how A must behave: It increases from 0 at $y = 0$ to 1,250 at $y = 25$ and then decreases back to 0 at $y = 50$. Thus, the largest possible value of A is 1,250 square feet, which occurs when $y = 25$. To completely answer the question that was asked, we need to know the corresponding value of x. We have $x = 100 - 2y$, so $x = 50$ when $y = 25$. Thus, Slim should build his enclosure 50 feet across and 25 feet deep (with the "missing" 50-foot side being formed by part of the house).

➡ **Before we go on...** Notice that the problem in Example 2 came down to finding the absolute maximum value of A on the closed and bounded interval [0, 50]. As noted in the preceding section, the table of values of A at its critical points and the endpoints of the interval gives us enough information to find the absolute maximum. ■

Let's stop for a moment and summarize the steps we've taken in these two examples.

Solving an Optimization Problem

1. **Identify the unknown(s), possibly with the aid of a diagram.** These are usually the quantities asked for in the problem.
2. **Identify the objective function.** This is the quantity you are asked to maximize or minimize. You should name it explicitly, as in "Let S = surface area."
3. **Identify the constraint(s).** These can be equations relating variables or inequalities expressing limitations on the values of variables.
4. **State the optimization problem.** This will have the form "Maximize [minimize] the objective function subject to the constraint(s)."
5. **Eliminate extra variables.** If the objective function depends on several variables, solve the constraint equations to express all variables in terms of one particular variable. Substitute these expressions into the objective function to rewrite it as a function of a single variable. In short, if there is only one constraint equation:

   Solve the constraint for one of the unknowns and substitute into the objective.

   Also substitute the expressions into any inequality constraints to help determine the domain of the objective function.
6. **Find the absolute maximum (or minimum) of the objective function.** Use the techniques of the preceding section.

Now for some further examples.

EXAMPLE 3 Maximizing Revenue

Cozy Carriage Company builds baby strollers. Using market research, the company estimates that if it sets the price of a stroller at p dollars, then it can sell $q = 300{,}000 - 10p^2$ strollers per year.* What price will bring in the greatest annual revenue?

* This equation is, of course, the demand equation for the baby strollers. However, coming up with a suitable demand equation in real life is hard, to say the least. In this regard, the very entertaining and also insightful article, *Camels and Rubber Duckies* by Joel Spolsky at www.joelonsoftware.com/articles/CamelsandRubberDuckies.html is a must-read.

Solution The question we are asked identifies our main unknown, the price p. However, there is another quantity that we do not know, q, the number of strollers the company will sell per year. The question also identifies the objective function, revenue, which is

$$R = pq.$$

Including the equality constraint given to us, that $q = 300{,}000 - 10p^2$, and the "reality" inequality constraints $p \geq 0$ and $q \geq 0$, we can write our problem as

$$\text{Maximize } R = pq \text{ subject to } q = 300{,}000 - 10p^2,\ p \geq 0, \text{ and } q \geq 0.$$

We are given q in terms of p, so let's substitute to eliminate q:

$$R = pq = p(300{,}000 - 10p^2) = 300{,}000p - 10p^3.$$

Substituting in the inequality $q \geq 0$, we get

$$300{,}000 - 10p^2 \geq 0.$$

Thus, $p^2 \leq 30{,}000$, which gives $-100\sqrt{3} \leq p \leq 100\sqrt{3}$. When we combine this with $p \geq 0$, we get the following restatement of our problem:

$$\text{Maximize } R(p) = 300{,}000p - 10p^3 \text{ such that } 0 \leq p \leq 100\sqrt{3}.$$

We solve this problem in much the same way we did the preceding one. We calculate $R'(p) = 300{,}000 - 30p^2$. Setting $300{,}000 - 30p^2 = 0$, we find one stationary point at $p = 100$. There are no singular points and we have the endpoints $p = 0$ and $p = 100\sqrt{3}$. Putting these points in a table and computing the corresponding values of R, we get the following:

p	0	100	$100\sqrt{3}$
$R(p)$	0	20,000,000	0

Thus, Cozy Carriage should price its strollers at \$100 each, which will bring in the largest possible revenue of \$20,000,000.

Figure 22

EXAMPLE 4 Optimizing Resources

The Metal Can Company has an order to make cylindrical cans with a volume of 250 cubic centimeters. What should be the dimensions of the cans in order to use the least amount of metal in their production?

Solution We are asked to find the dimensions of the cans. It is traditional to take as the dimensions of a cylinder the height h and the radius of the base r, as in Figure 22.

We are also asked to minimize the amount of metal used in the can, which is the area of the surface of the cylinder. We can look up the formula or figure it out ourselves: Imagine removing the circular top and bottom and then cutting vertically and flattening out the hollow cylinder to get a rectangle, as shown in Figure 23.

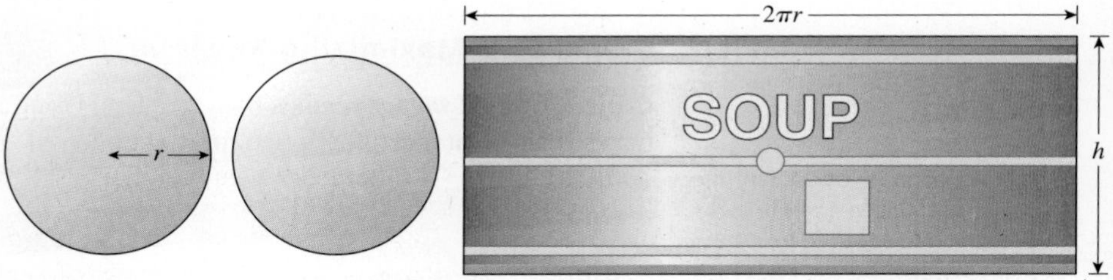

Figure 23

Our objective function is the (total) surface area S of the can. The area of each disc is πr^2, while the area of the rectangular piece is $2\pi rh$. Thus, our objective function is

$$S = 2\pi r^2 + 2\pi rh.$$

As usual, there is a constraint: The volume must be exactly 250 cubic centimeters. The formula for the volume of a cylinder is $V = \pi r^2 h$, so

$$\pi r^2 h = 250.$$

It is easiest to solve this constraint for h in terms of r:

$$h = \frac{250}{\pi r^2}.$$

Substituting in the objective function, we get

$$S = 2\pi r^2 + 2\pi r\frac{250}{\pi r^2} = 2\pi r^2 + \frac{500}{r}.$$

Now r cannot be negative or 0, but it can become very large (a very wide but very short can could have the right volume). We therefore take the domain of $S(r)$ to be $(0, +\infty)$, so our mathematical problem is as follows:

$$\text{Minimize } S(r) = 2\pi r^2 + \frac{500}{r} \text{ subject to } r > 0.$$

Now we calculate

$$S'(r) = 4\pi r - \frac{500}{r^2}.$$

To find stationary points, we set this equal to 0 and solve:

$$\begin{aligned} 4\pi r - \frac{500}{r^2} &= 0 \\ 4\pi r &= \frac{500}{r^2} \\ 4\pi r^3 &= 500 \\ r^3 &= \frac{125}{\pi}. \end{aligned}$$

So

$$r = \sqrt[3]{\frac{125}{\pi}} = \frac{5}{\sqrt[3]{\pi}} \approx 3.41.$$

The corresponding surface area is approximately $S(3.41) \approx 220$. There are no singular points or endpoints in the domain.

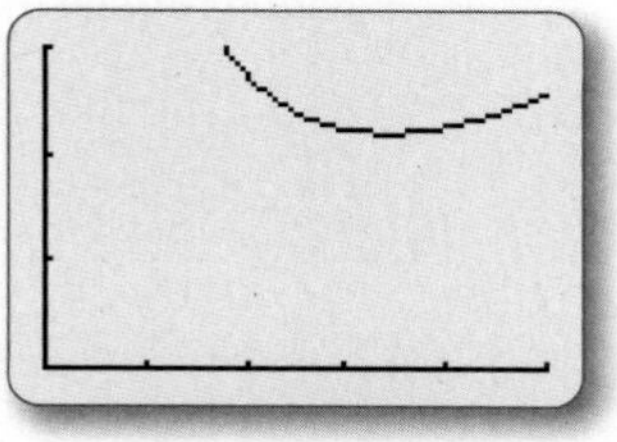

Figure 24

using Technology

To see how S behaves near the one stationary point, let's graph it in a viewing window with interval [0, 5] for r and [0, 300] for S. The result is Figure 24.

From the graph we can clearly see that the smallest surface area occurs at the stationary point at $r \approx 3.41$. The height of the can will be

$$h = \frac{250}{\pi r^2} \approx 6.83.$$

Thus, the can that uses the least amount of metal has a height of approximately 6.83 centimeters and a radius of approximately 3.41 centimeters. Such a can will use approximately 220 square centimeters of metal.

Before we go on... We obtained the value of r in Example 4 by solving the equation

$$4\pi r = \frac{500}{r^2}.$$

This time, let us do things differently: Divide both sides by 4π to obtain

$$r = \frac{500}{4\pi r^2} = \frac{125}{\pi r^2}$$

and compare what we got with the expression for h:

$$h = \frac{250}{\pi r^2},$$

which we see is exactly twice the expression for r. Put another way, the height is exactly equal to the diameter so that the can looks square when viewed from the side. Have you ever seen cans with that shape? Why do you think most cans do not have this shape? ■

EXAMPLE 5 Allocation of Labor

The Gym Sock Company manufactures cotton athletic socks. Production is partially automated through the use of robots. Daily operating costs amount to \$50 per laborer and \$30 per robot. The number of pairs of socks the company can manufacture in a day is given by a Cobb-Douglas* production formula

* Cobb-Douglas production formulas were discussed in Section 4.6.

$$q = 50n^{0.6}r^{0.4},$$

where q is the number of pairs of socks that can be manufactured by n laborers and r robots. Assuming that the company wishes to produce 1,000 pairs of socks per day at a minimum cost, how many laborers and how many robots should it use?

Solution The unknowns are the number of laborers n and the number of robots r. The objective is to minimize the daily cost:

$$C = 50n + 30r.$$

The constraints are given by the daily quota

$$1{,}000 = 50n^{0.6}r^{0.4}$$

and the fact that n and r are nonnegative. We solve the constraint equation for one of the variables; let's solve for n:

$$n^{0.6} = \frac{1{,}000}{50r^{0.4}} = \frac{20}{r^{0.4}}.$$

Taking the $1/0.6$ power of both sides gives

$$n = \left(\frac{20}{r^{0.4}}\right)^{1/0.6} = \frac{20^{1/0.6}}{r^{0.4/0.6}} = \frac{20^{5/3}}{r^{2/3}} \approx \frac{147.36}{r^{2/3}}.$$

Substituting in the objective equation gives us the cost as a function of r:

$$C(r) \approx 50\left(\frac{147.36}{r^{2/3}}\right) + 30r$$
$$= 7{,}368r^{-2/3} + 30r.$$

The only remaining constraint on r is that $r > 0$. To find the minimum value of $C(r)$, we first take the derivative:

$$C'(r) \approx -4{,}912r^{-5/3} + 30.$$

Setting this equal to zero, we solve for r:

$$r^{-5/3} \approx 0.006107$$
$$r \approx (0.006107)^{-3/5} \approx 21.3.$$

The corresponding cost is $C(21.3) \approx \$1{,}600$. There are no singular points or endpoints in the domain of C.

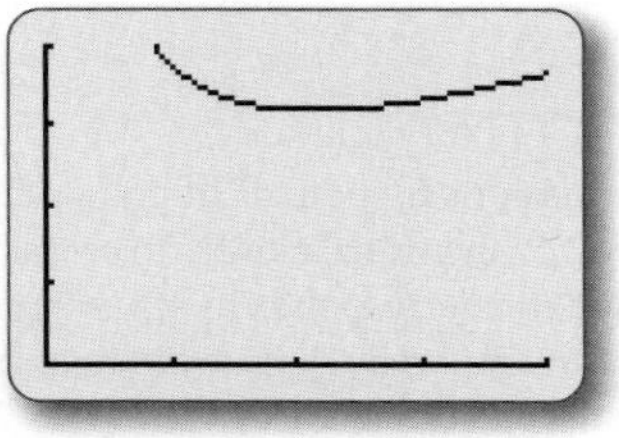

Figure 25

using Technology

To see how C behaves near its stationary point, let's draw its graph in a viewing window with an interval of [0, 40] for r and [0, 2,000] for C. The result is Figure 25.

From the graph we can see that C does have its minimum at the stationary point. The corresponding value of n is

$$n \approx \frac{147.36}{r^{2/3}} \approx 19.2.$$

At this point, our solution appears to be this: Use (approximately) 19.2 laborers and (approximately) 21.3 robots to meet the manufacturing quota at a minimum cost. However, we are not interested in fractions of robots or people, so we need to find integer solutions for n and r. If we round these numbers, we get the solution $(n, r) = (19, 21)$. However, a quick calculation shows that

$$q = 50(19)^{0.6}(21)^{0.4} \approx 989 \text{ pairs of socks,}$$

which fails to meet the quota of 1,000. Thus, we need to round at least one of the quantities n and r *upward* in order to meet the quota. The three possibilities, with corresponding values of q and C, are as follows:

$$(n, r) = (20, 21), \text{ with } q \approx 1{,}020 \text{ and } C = \$1{,}630$$
$$(n, r) = (19, 22), \text{ with } q \approx 1{,}007 \text{ and } C = \$1{,}610$$
$$(n, r) = (20, 22), \text{ with } q \approx 1{,}039 \text{ and } C = \$1{,}660.$$

Of these, the solution that meets the quota at a minimum cost is $(n, r) = (19, 22)$. Thus, the Gym Sock Co. should use 19 laborers and 22 robots, at a cost of $50 \times 19 + 30 \times 22 = \$1{,}610$, to manufacture $50 \times 19^{0.6} \times 22^{0.4} \approx 1{,}007$ pairs of socks.

FAQs

Constraints and Objectives

Q: *How do I know whether or not there are constraints in an applied optimization problem?*

A: There are usually at least *inequality* constraints; the variables usually represent real quantities, such as length or number of items, and so cannot be negative, leading to constraints like $x \geq 0$ (or $0 \leq x \leq 100$ in the event that there is an upper limit). *Equation* constraints usually arise when there is more than one unknown in the objective, and dictate how one unknown is related to others; as in, say "the length is twice the width," or "the demand is 8 divided by the price" (a demand equation).

Q: *How do I know what to use as the objective, and what to use as the constraint(s)?*

A: To identify the objective, look for a phrase such as "find the maximum (or minimum) value of." The amount you are trying to maximize or minimize is the objective. For example,

- . . . *at the least cost*. . . The objective function is the equation for cost, $C = \ldots.$
- . . . *the greatest area*. . . The objective function is the equation for area, $A = \ldots.$

To determine the constraint *inequalities*, ask yourself what limitations are placed on the unknown variables as above—are they nonnegative? are there upper limits? To identify the constraint *equations*, look for sentences that dictate restrictions in the form of relationships between the variables, as in the answer to the first question above.

5.2 EXERCISES

▼ more advanced ◆ challenging

T indicates exercises that should be solved using technology

Solve the optimization problems in Exercises 1–8. HINT [See Example 2.]

1. Maximize $P = xy$ subject to $x + y = 10$.
2. Maximize $P = xy$ subject to $x + 2y = 40$.
3. Minimize $S = x + y$ subject to $xy = 9$ and both x and $y > 0$.
4. Minimize $S = x + 2y$ subject to $xy = 2$ and both x and $y > 0$.
5. Minimize $F = x^2 + y^2$ subject to $x + 2y = 10$.
6. Minimize $F = x^2 + y^2$ subject to $xy^2 = 16$.
7. Maximize $P = xyz$ subject to $x + y = 30$, $y + z = 30$, and $x, y, z \geq 0$.
8. Maximize $P = xyz$ subject to $x + z = 12$, $y + z = 12$, and $x, y, z \geq 0$.
9. For a rectangle with perimeter 20 to have the largest area, what dimensions should it have?
10. For a rectangle with area 100 to have the smallest perimeter, what dimensions should it have?

APPLICATIONS

11. ***Average Cost: iPods*** Assume that it costs Apple approximately

$$C(x) = 22{,}500 + 100x + 0.01x^2$$

dollars to manufacture x 32GB iPods in a day.[1] How many iPods should be manufactured in order to minimize average cost? What is the resulting average cost of an iPod? (Give your answer to the nearest dollar.) HINT [See Example 1.]

12. ***Average Cost: Xboxes*** Assume that it costs Microsoft approximately

$$C(x) = 14{,}400 + 550x + 0.01x^2$$

dollars to manufacture x Xbox 360s in a day.[2] How many Xboxes should be manufactured in order to minimize average cost? What is the resulting average cost of an Xbox? (Give your answer to the nearest dollar.) HINT [See Example 1.]

13. ***Pollution Control*** The cost of controlling emissions at a firm rises rapidly as the amount of emissions reduced increases. Here is a possible model:

$$C(q) = 4{,}000 + 100q^2$$

where q is the reduction in emissions (in pounds of pollutant per day) and C is the daily cost to the firm (in dollars) of this reduction. What level of reduction corresponds to the lowest average cost per pound of pollutant, and what would be the resulting average cost to the nearest dollar?

14. ***Pollution Control*** Repeat the preceding exercise using the following cost function:

$$C(q) = 2{,}000 + 200q^2.$$

15. ***Pollution Control*** (Compare Exercise 13.) The cost of controlling emissions at a firm is given by

$$C(q) = 4{,}000 + 100q^2,$$

where q is the reduction in emissions (in pounds of pollutant per day) and C is the daily cost to the firm (in dollars) of this reduction. Government clean-air subsidies amount to \$500 per pound of pollutant removed. How many pounds of pollutant should the firm remove each day in order to minimize *net* cost (cost minus subsidy)?

16. ***Pollution Control*** (Compare Exercise 14.) Repeat the preceding exercise, using the following cost function:

$$C(q) = 2{,}000 + 200q^2$$

with government subsidies amounting to \$100 per pound of pollutant removed per day.

17. ***Fences*** I would like to create a rectangular vegetable patch. The fencing for the east and west sides costs \$4 per foot, and the fencing for the north and south sides costs only \$2 per foot. I have a budget of \$80 for the project. What are the dimensions of the vegetable patch with the largest area I can enclose? HINT [See Example 2.]

18. ***Fences*** I would like to create a rectangular orchid garden that abuts my house so that the house itself forms the northern boundary. The fencing for the southern boundary costs \$4 per foot, and the fencing for the east and west sides costs \$2 per foot. If I have a budget of \$80 for the project, what are the dimensions of the garden with the largest area I can enclose? HINT [See Example 2.]

19. ***Fences*** You are building a right-angled triangular flower garden along a stream as shown in the figure. (The borders can be in any directions as long as they are at right angles as shown.)

[1] Not the actual cost equation; the authors do not know Apple's actual cost equation. The marginal cost in the model given is in rough agreement with the actual marginal cost for reasonable values of x for one of the 2007 models. Source for cost data: *Manufacturing & Technology News*, July 31, 2007 Volume 14, No. 14 (www.manufacturingnews.com).

[2] Not the actual cost equation; the authors do not know Microsoft's actual cost equation. The marginal cost in the model given is in rough agreement with the actual marginal cost for reasonable values of x. Source for estimate of marginal cost: iSuppli (www.isuppli.com).

The fencing of the left border costs \$5 per foot, while the fencing of the lower border costs \$1 per foot. (No fencing is required along the river.) You want to spend \$100 and enclose as much area as possible. What are the dimensions of your garden, and what area does it enclose? HINT [The area of a right-triangle is given by $A = xy/2$.]

20. ***Fences*** Repeat Exercise 19, this time assuming that the fencing of the left border costs \$8 per foot, while the fencing of the lower border costs \$2 per foot, and that you can spend \$400.

21. ▼ ***Fences*** (Compare Exercise 17.) For tax reasons, I need to create a rectangular vegetable patch with an area of exactly 242 sq. ft. The fencing for the east and west sides costs \$4 per foot, and the fencing for the north and south sides costs only \$2 per foot. What are the dimensions of the vegetable patch with the least expensive fence? HINT [Compare Exercise 3.]

22. ▼ ***Fences*** (Compare Exercise 18.) For reasons too complicated to explain, I need to create a rectangular orchid garden with an area of exactly 324 sq. ft. abutting my house so that the house itself forms the northern boundary. The fencing for the southern boundary costs \$4 per foot, and the fencing for the east and west sides costs \$2 per foot. What are the dimensions of the orchid garden with the least expensive fence? HINT [Compare Exercise 4.]

23. ***Revenue*** *Hercules Films* is deciding on the price of the video release of its film *Son of Frankenstein.* Its marketing people estimate that at a price of p dollars, it can sell a total of $q = 200{,}000 - 10{,}000p$ copies. What price will bring in the greatest revenue? HINT [See Example 3.]

24. ***Profit*** *Hercules Films* is also deciding on the price of the video release of its film *Bride of the Son of Frankenstein.* Again, marketing estimates that at a price of p dollars, it can sell $q = 200{,}000 - 10{,}000p$ copies, but each copy costs \$4 to make. What price will give the greatest *profit*?

25. ***Revenue: Cellphones*** Worldwide quarterly sales of Nokia cellphones were approximately $q = -p + 156$ million phones when the wholesale price was \$$p$. At what wholesale price should Nokia have sold its phones to maximize its quarterly revenue? What would have been the resulting revenue?[3]

26. ***Revenue: Cellphones*** Worldwide annual sales of all cellphones were approximately $-10p + 1{,}600$ million phones when the wholesale price was \$$p$. At what wholesale price should cellphones have been sold to maximize annual revenue? What would have been the resulting revenue?[4]

27. ***Revenue: Monorail Service*** The demand, in rides per day, for monorail service in Las Vegas in 2005 can be approximated by $q = -4{,}500p + 41{,}500$ when the fare was \$$p$. What price should have been charged to maximize total revenue?[5]

28. ***Revenue: Mars Monorail*** The demand, in rides per day, for monorail service in the three urbynes (or districts) of Utarek, Mars, can be approximated by $q = -2p + 24$ million riders when the fare is Ƶp. What price should be charged to maximize total revenue?[6]

29. ***Revenue*** Assume that the demand for tuna in a small coastal town is given by

$$p = \frac{500{,}000}{q^{1.5}},$$

where q is the number of pounds of tuna that can be sold in a month at p dollars per pound. Assume that the town's fishery wishes to sell at least 5,000 pounds of tuna per month.

a. How much should the town's fishery charge for tuna in order to maximize monthly revenue? HINT [See Example 3, and don't neglect endpoints.]

b. How much tuna will it sell per month at that price?

c. What will be its resulting revenue?

30. ***Revenue*** In the 1930s the economist Henry Schultz devised the following demand function for corn:

$$p = \frac{6{,}570{,}000}{q^{1.3}},$$

where q is the number of bushels of corn that could be sold at p dollars per bushel in one year.[7] Assume that at least 10,000 bushels of corn per year must be sold.

a. How much should farmers charge per bushel of corn to maximize annual revenue? HINT [See Example 3, and don't neglect endpoints.]

b. How much corn can farmers sell per year at that price?

c. What will be the farmers' resulting revenue?

31. ***Revenue*** During the 1950s the wholesale price for chicken in the United States fell from 25¢ per pound to 14¢ per pound, while per capita chicken consumption rose from 22 pounds per year to 27.5 pounds per year.[8] Assuming that the demand for chicken depended linearly on the price, what wholesale price for chicken would have maximized revenues for poultry farmers, and what would that revenue have amounted to?

32. ***Revenue*** Your underground used-book business is booming. Your policy is to sell all used versions of *Calculus and You* at the same price (regardless of condition). When you set the price at \$10, sales amounted to 120 volumes during the first week of classes. The following semester, you set the price at \$30 and sales dropped to zero. Assuming that the demand for

---

[3] Demand equation based on second- and fourth-quarter sales. Source: Embedded.com/Company reports December, 2004.

[4] Demand equation based on estimated 2004 sales and projected 2008 sales. Source: I-Stat/NDR, December 2004.

[5] Source for ridership data: *New York Times*, February 10, 2007, p. A9.

[6] The zonar (Ƶ) is the official currency in the city-state of Utarek, Mars (formerly www.Marsnext.com, a now extinct virtual society).

[7] Based on data for the period 1915–1929. Source: Henry Schultz (1938), *The Theory and Measurement of Demand,* University of Chicago Press, Chicago.

[8] Data are provided for the years 1951–1958. Source: U.S. Department of Agriculture, *Agricultural Statistics.*

books depends linearly on the price, what price gives you the maximum revenue, and what does that revenue amount to?

33. ***Profit: Cellphones*** (Compare Exercise 25.) Worldwide quarterly sales of Nokia cellphones were approximately $q = -p + 156$ million phones when the wholesale price was \$$p$. Assuming that it cost Nokia \$40 to manufacture each cellphone, at what wholesale price should Nokia have sold its phones to maximize its quarterly profit? What would have been the resulting profit?[9] (The actual wholesale price was \$105 in the fourth quarter of 2004.) HINT [See Example 3, and recall that Profit = Revenue − Cost.]

34. ***Profit: Cellphones*** (Compare Exercise 26.) Worldwide annual sales of all cellphones were approximately $-10p + 1{,}600$ million phones when the wholesale price was \$$p$. Assuming that it costs \$30 to manufacture each cellphone, at what wholesale price should cellphones have been sold to maximize annual profit? What would have been the resulting profit?[10] HINT [See Example 3, and recall that Profit = Revenue − Cost.]

35. ▼ ***Profit*** The demand equation for your company's virtual reality video headsets is

$$p = \frac{1{,}000}{q^{0.3}},$$

where q is the total number of headsets that your company can sell in a week at a price of p dollars. The total manufacturing and shipping cost amounts to \$100 per headset.

a. What is the greatest profit your company can make in a week, and how many headsets will your company sell at this level of profit? (Give answers to the nearest whole number.)

b. How much, to the nearest \$1, should your company charge per headset for the maximum profit?

36. ▼ ***Profit*** Due to sales by a competing company, your company's sales of virtual reality video headsets have dropped, and your financial consultant revises the demand equation to

$$p = \frac{800}{q^{0.35}},$$

where q is the total number of headsets that your company can sell in a week at a price of p dollars. The total manufacturing and shipping cost still amounts to \$100 per headset.

a. What is the greatest profit your company can make in a week, and how many headsets will your company sell at this level of profit? (Give answers to the nearest whole number.)

b. How much, to the nearest \$1, should your company charge per headset for the maximum profit?

37. ***Paint Cans*** A company manufactures cylindrical paint cans with open tops with a volume of 27,000 cubic centimeters. What should be the dimensions of the cans in order to use the least amount of metal in their production? HINT [See Example 4.]

38. ***Metal Drums*** A company manufactures cylindrical metal drums with open tops with a volume of 1 cubic meter. What should be the dimensions of the drum in order to use the least amount of metal in their production? HINT [See Example 4.]

39. ***Tin Cans*** A company manufactures cylindrical tin cans with closed tops with a volume of 250 cubic centimeters. The metal used to manufacture the cans costs \$0.01 per square cm for the sides and \$0.02 per square cm for the (thicker) top and bottom. What should be the dimensions of the cans in order to minimize the cost of metal in their production? What is the ratio height/radius? HINT [See Example 4.]

40. ***Metal Drums*** A company manufactures cylindrical metal drums with open tops with a volume of 2 cubic meters. The metal used to manufacture the cans costs \$2 per square meter for the sides and \$3 per square meter for the (thicker) bottom. What should be the dimensions of the drums in order to minimize the cost of metal in their production? What is the ratio height/radius? HINT [See Example 4.]

41. ▼ ***Box Design*** *Chocolate Box Company* is going to make open-topped boxes out of 6 × 16-inch rectangles of cardboard by cutting squares out of the corners and folding up the sides. What is the largest volume box it can make this way?

42. ▼ ***Box Design*** *Vanilla Box Company* is going to make open-topped boxes out of 12 × 12-inch rectangles of cardboard by cutting squares out of the corners and folding up the sides. What is the largest volume box it can make this way?

43. ▼ ***Box Design*** A packaging company is going to make closed boxes, with square bases, that hold 125 cubic centimeters. What are the dimensions of the box that can be built with the least material?

44. ▼ ***Box Design*** A packaging company is going to make open-topped boxes, with square bases, that hold 108 cubic centimeters. What are the dimensions of the box that can be built with the least material?

45. ▼ ***Luggage Dimensions*** American Airlines requires that the total outside dimensions (length + width + height) of a checked bag not exceed 62 inches.[11] Suppose you want to check a bag whose height equals its width. What is the largest volume bag of this shape that you can check on an American flight?

46. ▼ ***Carry-on Dimensions*** American Airlines requires that the total outside dimensions (length + width + height) of a carry-on bag not exceed 45 inches.[12] Suppose you want to carry on a bag whose length is twice its height. What is the largest volume bag of this shape that you can carry on an American flight?

47. ▼ ***Luggage Dimensions*** *Fly-by-Night Airlines* has a peculiar rule about luggage: The length and width of a bag must add up to at most 45 inches, and the width and height must also add up to at most 45 inches. What are the dimensions of the bag with the largest volume that Fly-by-Night will accept?

---

[9] See Exercise 25.

[10] See Exercise 26.

[11] According to information on its Web site (www.aa.com/).

[12] *Ibid.*

48. ▼ ***Luggage Dimensions*** *Fair Weather Airlines* has a similar rule. It will accept only bags for which the sum of the length and width is at most 36 inches, while the sum of length, height, and twice the width is at most 72 inches. What are the dimensions of the bag with the largest volume that Fair Weather will accept?

49. ▼ ***Package Dimensions*** The U.S. Postal Service (USPS) will accept packages only if the length plus girth is no more than 108 inches.[13] (See the figure.)

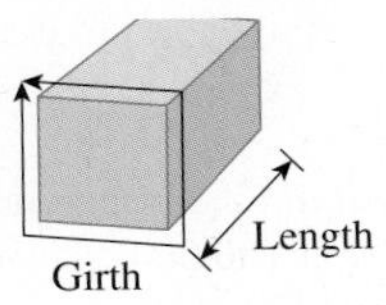

Assuming that the front face of the package (as shown in the figure) is square, what is the largest volume package that the USPS will accept?

50. ▼ ***Package Dimensions*** United Parcel Service (UPS) will accept only packages with a length of no more than 108 inches and length plus girth of no more than 165 inches.[14] (See figure for the preceding exercise.) Assuming that the front face of the package (as shown in the figure) is square, what is the largest volume package that UPS will accept?

51. ▼ ***Cellphone Revenues*** The number of cellphone subscribers in China in the years 2000–2005 was projected to follow the equation $N(t) = 39t + 68$ million subscribers in year t ($t = 0$ represents January 2000). The average annual revenue per cellphone user was \$350 in 2000.[15] If we assume that due to competition the revenue per cellphone user decreases continuously at an annual rate of 30%, we can model the annual revenue as

$$R(t) = 350(39t + 68)e^{-0.3t} \text{ million dollars.}$$

Determine **a.** when to the nearest 0.1 year the revenue was projected to peak and **b.** the revenue, to the nearest \$1 million, at that time.

52. ▼ ***Cellphone Revenues*** (Refer to Exercise 51.) If we assume instead that the revenue per cellphone user decreases continuously at an annual rate of 20%, we obtain the revenue model

$$R(t) = 350(39t + 68)e^{-0.2t} \text{ million dollars.}$$

Determine **a.** when to the nearest 0.1 year the revenue was projected to peak and **b.** the revenue, to the nearest \$1 million, at that time.

53. ▼ ***Research and Development*** Spending on research and development by drug companies in the United States t years after 1970 can be modeled by

$$S(t) = 2.5e^{0.08t} \text{ billion dollars} \quad (0 \le t \le 31).$$

The number of new drugs approved by the Federal Drug Administration (FDA) over the same period can be modeled by

$$D(t) = 10 + t \text{ drugs per year}^{16} \quad (0 \le t \le 31).$$

When was the function $D(t)/S(t)$ at a maximum? What is the maximum value of $D(t)/S(t)$? What does the answer tell you about the cost of developing new drugs?

54. ▼ ***Research and Development*** (Refer to Exercise 53.) If the number of new drugs approved by the FDA had been $10 + 2t$ new drugs each year, when would the function $D(t)/S(t)$ have reached a maximum? What does the answer tell you about the cost of developing new drugs?

55. ▼ ***Asset Appreciation*** As the financial consultant to a classic auto dealership, you estimate that the total value (in dollars) of its collection of 1959 Chevrolets and Fords is given by the formula

$$v = 300{,}000 + 1{,}000t^2 \quad (t \ge 5),$$

where t is the number of years from now. You anticipate a continuous inflation rate of 5% per year, so that the discounted (present) value of an item that will be worth \$$v$ in t years' time is

$$p = ve^{-0.05t}.$$

When would you advise the dealership to sell the vehicles to maximize their discounted value?

56. ▼ ***Plantation Management*** The value of a fir tree in your plantation increases with the age of the tree according to the formula

$$v = \frac{20t}{1 + 0.05t},$$

where t is the age of the tree in years. Given a continuous inflation rate of 5% per year, the discounted (present) value of a newly planted seedling is

$$p = ve^{-0.05t}.$$

At what age (to the nearest year) should you harvest your trees in order to ensure the greatest possible discounted value?

57. ▼ ***Marketing Strategy*** *FeatureRich Software Company* has a dilemma. Its new program, Doors-X 10.27, is almost ready to go on the market. However, the longer the company works on it, the better it can make the program and the more it can charge for it. The company's marketing analysts estimate that if it delays t days, it can set the price at $100 + 2t$ dollars. On the other hand, the longer it delays, the more market share it will lose to its main competitor (see the next exercise) so that if it delays t days it will be able to sell $400{,}000 - 2{,}500t$ copies of

[13]The requirement for packages sent other than Parcel Post, as of August 2011 (www.usps.com/).

[14]The requirement as of August, 2011 (www.ups.com/).

[15]Based on a regression of projected figures (coefficients are rounded). Source: Intrinsic Technology/*New York Times*, Nov. 24, 2000, p. C1.

[16]The exponential model for R&D is based on the 1970 and 2001 spending in constant 2001 dollars, while the linear model for new drugs approved is based on the 6-year moving average from data from 1970 to 2000. Source for data: Pharmaceutical Research and Manufacturers of America, FDA/*New York Times*, April 19, 2002, p. C1.

the program. How many days should FeatureRich delay the release in order to get the greatest revenue?

58. ▼ ***Marketing Strategy*** *FeatureRich Software's* main competitor (see previous exercise) is Moon Systems, and Moon is in a similar predicament. Its product, Walls-Y 11.4, could be sold now for \$200, but for each day Moon delays, it could increase the price by \$4. On the other hand, it could sell 300,000 copies now, but each day it waits will cut sales by 1,500. How many days should Moon delay the release in order to get the greatest revenue?

59. ▼ ***Average Profit*** The *FeatureRich Software Company* sells its graphing program, Dogwood, with a volume discount. If a customer buys x copies, then he or she pays[17] $\$500\sqrt{x}$. It cost the company \$10,000 to develop the program and \$2 to manufacture each copy. If a single customer were to buy all the copies of Dogwood, how many copies would the customer have to buy for FeatureRich Software's average profit per copy to be maximized? How are average profit and marginal profit related at this number of copies?

60. ▼ ***Average Profit*** Repeat the preceding exercise with the charge to the customer $\$600\sqrt{x}$ and the cost to develop the program \$9,000.

61. ***Resource Allocation*** Your company manufactures automobile alternators, and production is partially automated through the use of robots. Daily operating costs amount to \$100 per laborer and \$16 per robot. In order to meet production deadlines, the company calculates that the numbers of laborers and robots must satisfy the constraint

$$xy = 10{,}000,$$

where x is the number of laborers and y is the number of robots. Assuming that the company wishes to meet production deadlines at a minimum cost, how many laborers and how many robots should it use? HINT [See Example 5.]

62. ***Resource Allocation*** Your company is the largest sock manufacturer in the Solar System, and production is automated through the use of androids and robots. Daily operating costs amount to ₩200 per android and ₩8 per robot.[18] In order to meet production deadlines, the company calculates that the numbers of androids and robots must satisfy the constraint

$$xy = 1{,}000{,}000,$$

where x is the number of androids and y is the number of robots. Assuming that the company wishes to meet production deadlines at a minimum cost, how many androids and how many robots should it use? HINT [See Example 5.]

63. ▼ ***Resource Allocation*** Your automobile assembly plant has a Cobb-Douglas production function given by

$$q = x^{0.4}y^{0.6},$$

where q is the number of automobiles it produces per year, x is the number of employees, and y is the daily operating budget (in dollars). Annual operating costs amount to an average of \$20,000 per employee plus the operating budget of $\$365y$. Assume that you wish to produce 1,000 automobiles per year at a minimum cost. How many employees should you hire? HINT [See Example 5.]

64. ▼ ***Resource Allocation*** Repeat the preceding exercise using the production formula

$$q = x^{0.5}y^{0.5}.$$

HINT [See Example 5.]

65. ▼ ***Incarceration Rate*** The incarceration rate (the number of persons in prison per 100,000 residents) in the United States can be approximated by

$$N(t) = 0.04t^3 - 2t^2 + 40t + 460 \quad (0 \le t \le 18)$$

(t is the year since 1990).[19] When, to the nearest year, was the incarceration rate increasing most rapidly? When was it increasing least rapidly? HINT [You are being asked to find the extreme values of the rate of change of the incarceration rate.]

66. ▼ ***Prison Population*** The prison population in the United States can be approximated by

$$N(t) = 0.02t^3 - 2t^2 + 100t + 1{,}100 \text{ thousand people} \quad (0 \le t \le 18)$$

(t is the year since 1990).[20] When, to the nearest year, was the prison population increasing most rapidly? When was it increasing least rapidly? HINT [You are being asked to find the extreme values of the rate of change of the prison population.]

67. ▼ ***Embryo Development*** The oxygen consumption of a bird embryo increases from the time the egg is laid through the time the chick hatches. In a typical galliform bird, the oxygen consumption can be approximated by

$$c(t) = -0.065t^3 + 3.4t^2 - 22t + 3.6 \text{ milliliters per day} \quad (8 \le t \le 30),$$

where t is the time (in days) since the egg was laid.[21] (An egg will typically hatch at around $t = 28$.) When, to the nearest day, is $c'(t)$ a maximum? What does the answer tell you?

68. ▼ ***Embryo Development*** The oxygen consumption of a turkey embryo increases from the time the egg is laid through the time the chick hatches. In a brush turkey, the oxygen consumption can be approximated by

$$c(t) = -0.028t^3 + 2.9t^2 - 44t + 95 \text{ milliliters per day} \quad (20 \le t \le 50),$$

[17] This is similar to the way site licenses have been structured for the program Maple®.

[18] ₩are Neptunian Standard Solar Units of currency.

[19] Source for data: Sourcebook of Criminal Justice Statistics Online (www.albany.edu/sourcebook).

[20] *Ibid.*

[21] The model approximates graphical data published in the article "The Brush Turkey" by Roger S. Seymour, *Scientific American,* December, 1991, pp. 108–114.

where t is the time (in days) since the egg was laid.[22] (An egg will typically hatch at around $t = 50$.) When, to the nearest day, is $c'(t)$ a maximum? What does the answer tell you?

69. **T** ▼ ***Subprime Mortgages during the Housing Bubble*** During the real estate run-up in 2000–2008, the percentage of mortgages issued in the United States that were subprime (normally classified as risky) could be approximated by

$$A(t) = \frac{15.0}{1 + 8.6(1.8)^{-t}} \text{ percent} \quad (0 \le t \le 8)$$

t years after the start of 2000.[23] Graph the *derivative* of $A(t)$ and determine the year during which this derivative had an absolute maximum and also its value at that point. What does the answer tell you?

70. **T** ▼ ***Subprime Mortgage Debt during the Housing Bubble*** During the real estate run-up in 2000–2008, the value of subprime (normally classified as risky) mortgage debt outstanding in the United States was approximately

$$A(t) = \frac{1{,}350}{1 + 4.2(1.7)^{-t}} \text{ billion dollars} \quad (0 \le t \le 8)$$

t years after the start of 2000.[24] Graph the *derivative* of $A(t)$ and determine the year during which this derivative had an absolute maximum and also its value at that point. What does the answer tell you?

71. **T** ▼ ***Asset Appreciation*** You manage a small antique company that owns a collection of Louis XVI jewelry boxes. Their value v is increasing according to the formula

$$v = \frac{10{,}000}{1 + 500e^{-0.5t}},$$

where t is the number of years from now. You anticipate an inflation rate of 5% per year, so that the present value of an item that will be worth \$$v$ in t years' time is given by

$$p = v \cdot (1.05)^{-t}.$$

When (to the nearest year) should you sell the jewelry boxes to maximize their present value? How much (to the nearest constant dollar) will they be worth at that time?

72. **T** ▼ ***Harvesting Forests*** The following equation models the approximate volume in cubic feet of a typical Douglas fir tree of age t years.[25]

$$V = \frac{22{,}514}{1 + 22{,}514t^{-2.55}}$$

The lumber will be sold at \$10 per cubic foot, and you do not expect the price of lumber to appreciate in the foreseeable future. On the other hand, you anticipate a general inflation rate of 5% per year, so that the present value of an item that will be worth \$$v$ in t years' time is given by

$$p = v \cdot (1.05)^{-t}.$$

At what age (to the nearest year) should you harvest a Douglas fir tree in order to maximize its present value? How much (to the nearest constant dollar) will a Douglas fir tree be worth at that time?

73. ◆ ***Agriculture*** The fruit yield per tree in an orchard containing 50 trees is 100 pounds per tree each year. Due to crowding, the yield decreases by 1 pound per season for every additional tree planted. How many additional trees should be planted for a maximum total annual yield?

74. ◆ ***Agriculture*** Two years ago your orange orchard contained 50 trees and the yield per tree was 75 bags of oranges. Last year you removed 10 of the trees and noticed that the yield per tree increased to 80 bags. Assuming that the yield per tree depends linearly on the number of trees in the orchard, what should you do this year to maximize your total yield?

75. ◆ ***Revenue*** (based on a question on the GRE Economics Test[26]) If total revenue (*TR*) is specified by $TR = a + bQ - cQ^2$, where Q is quantity of output and a, b, and c are positive parameters, then *TR* is maximized for this firm when it produces Q equal to:

(A) $b/2ac$. **(B)** $b/4c$. **(C)** $(a + b)/c$. **(D)** $b/2c$. **(E)** $c/2b$.

76. ◆ ***Revenue*** (based on a question on the GRE Economics Test) If total demand (Q) is specified by $Q = -aP + b$, where P is unit price and a and b are positive parameters, then total revenue is maximized for this firm when it charges P equal to:

(A) $b/2a$. **(B)** $b/4a$. **(C)** a/b. **(D)** $a/2b$. **(E)** $-b/2a$.

COMMUNICATION AND REASONING EXERCISES

77. You are interested in knowing the height of the tallest condominium complex that meets the city zoning requirements that the height H should not exceed eight times the distance D from the road and that it must provide parking for at least 50 cars. The objective function of the associated optimization problem is then:

(A) H. **(B)** $H - 8D$. **(C)** D. **(D)** $D - 8H$.

One of the constraints is:

(A) $8H = D$. **(B)** $8D = H$.
(C) $H'(D) = 0$. **(D)** $D'(H) = 0$.

78. You are interested in building a condominium complex with a height H of at least 8 times the distance D from the road and parking area of at least 1,000 sq. ft. at the cheapest cost C. The objective function of the associated optimization problem is then:

(A) H. **(B)** D. **(C)** C. **(D)** $H + D - C$.

---

[22] The model approximates graphical data published in the article "The Brush Turkey" by Roger S. Seymour, *Scientific American*, December, 1991, pp. 108–114.

[23] Sources: Mortgage Bankers Association, UBS.

[24] Source: www.data360.org/dataset.aspx?Data_Set_Id=9549.

[25] The model is the authors' and is based on data in *Environmental and Natural Resource Economics* by Tom Tietenberg, third edition (New York: HarperCollins, 1992), p. 282.

[26] Source: GRE Economics Test, by G. Gallagher, G. E. Pollock, W. J. Simeone, G. Yohe (Piscataway, NJ: Research and Education Association, 1989).

One of the constraints is:

(A) $H - 8D = 0$. **(B)** $H + D - C = 0$.
(C) $C'(D) = 0$. **(D)** $8H = D$.

79. Explain why the following problem is uninteresting: A packaging company wishes to make cardboard boxes with open tops by cutting square pieces from the corners of a square sheet of cardboard and folding up the sides. What is the box with the least surface area it can make this way?

80. Explain why finding the production level that minimizes a cost function is frequently uninteresting. What would a more interesting objective be?

81. Your friend Margo claims that all you have to do to find the absolute maxima and minima in applications is set the derivative equal to zero and solve. "All that other stuff about endpoints and so on is a waste of time just to make life hard for us," according to Margo. Explain why she is wrong, and find at least one exercise in this exercise set to illustrate your point.

82. You are having a hard time persuading your friend Marco that maximizing revenue is not the same as maximizing profit. "How on earth can you expect to obtain the largest profit if you are not taking in the largest revenue?" Explain why he is wrong, and find at least one exercise in this exercise set to illustrate your point.

83. ▼ If demand q decreases as price p increases, what does the minimum value of dq/dp measure?

84. ▼ Explain how you would solve an optimization problem of the following form. Maximize $P = f(x, y, z)$ subject to $z = g(x, y)$ and $y = h(x)$.

5.3 Higher Order Derivatives: Acceleration and Concavity

The **second derivative** is simply the derivative of the derivative function. To explain why we would be interested in such a thing, we start by discussing one of its interpretations.

Acceleration

Recall that if $s(t)$ represents the position of a car at time t, then its velocity is given by the derivative: $v(t) = s'(t)$. But one rarely drives a car at a constant speed; the velocity itself may be changing. The rate at which the velocity is changing is the **acceleration**. Because the derivative measures the rate of change, acceleration is the derivative of velocity: $a(t) = v'(t)$. Because v is the derivative of s, we can express the acceleration in terms of s:

$$a(t) = v'(t) = (s')'(t) = s''(t).$$

That is, a is the derivative of the derivative of s; in other words, the second derivative of s, which we write as s''. (In this context you will often hear the derivative s' referred to as the **first derivative**.)

Second Derivative, Acceleration

If a function f has a derivative that is in turn differentiable, then its **second derivative** is the derivative of the derivative of f, written as f''. If $f''(a)$ exists, we say that f is **twice differentiable at** $x = a$.

Quick Examples

1. If $f(x) = x^3 - x$, then $f'(x) = 3x^2 - 1$, so $f''(x) = 6x$ and $f''(-2) = -12$.
2. If $f(x) = 3x + 1$, then $f'(x) = 3$, so $f''(x) = 0$.
3. If $f(x) = e^x$, then $f'(x) = e^x$, so $f''(x) = e^x$ as well.

The **acceleration** of a moving object is the derivative of its velocity—that is, the second derivative of the position function.

Quick Example

If t is time in hours and the position of a car at time t is $s(t) = t^3 + 2t^2$ miles, then the car's velocity is $v(t) = s'(t) = 3t^2 + 4t$ miles per hour and its acceleration is $a(t) = s''(t) = v'(t) = 6t + 4$ miles per hour per hour.

Differential Notation for the Second Derivative

We have written the second derivative of $f(x)$ as $f''(x)$. We could also use differential notation:

$$f''(x) = \frac{d^2 f}{dx^2}.$$

This notation comes from writing the second derivative as the derivative of the derivative in differential notation:

$$f''(x) = \frac{d}{dx}\left[\frac{df}{dx}\right] = \frac{d^2 f}{dx^2}.$$

Similarly, if $y = f(x)$, we write $f''(x)$ as $\frac{d}{dx}\left[\frac{dy}{dx}\right] = \frac{d^2 y}{dx^2}$. For example, if $y = x^3$, then $\frac{d^2 y}{dx^2} = 6x$.

An important example of acceleration is the acceleration due to gravity.

EXAMPLE 1 Acceleration Due to Gravity

According to the laws of physics, the height of an object near the surface of the earth falling in a vacuum from an initial rest position 100 feet above the ground under the influence of gravity is approximately

$$s(t) = 100 - 16t^2 \text{ feet}$$

in t seconds. Find its acceleration.

Solution The velocity of the object is

$$v(t) = s'(t) = -32t \text{ ft/sec.}$$

Differential notation: $v = \frac{ds}{dt} = -32t$ ft/sec

The reason for the negative sign is that the height of the object is decreasing with time, so its velocity is negative. Hence, the acceleration is

$$a(t) = s''(t) = -32 \text{ ft/sec}^2.$$

Differential notation: $a = \frac{d^2 s}{dt^2} = -32$ ft/sec^2

(We write ft/sec^2 as an abbreviation for feet/second/second—that is, feet per second per second. It is often read "feet per second squared.") Thus, the *downward* velocity is increasing by 32 ft/sec every second. We say that 32 ft/sec^2 is the **acceleration due to gravity**. In the absence of air resistance, all falling bodies near the surface of the earth, no matter what their weight, will fall with this acceleration.*

➡ **Before we go on...** In very careful experiments using balls rolling down inclined planes, Galileo made one of his most important discoveries—that the acceleration due to gravity is constant and does not depend on the weight or composition of the object falling.† A famous, though probably apocryphal, story has him dropping cannonballs of different weights off the Leaning Tower of Pisa to prove his point.§ ■

* On other planets the acceleration due to gravity is different. For example, on Jupiter, it is about three times as large as on Earth.

† An interesting aside: Galileo's experiments depended on getting extremely accurate timings. Because the timepieces of his day were very inaccurate, he used the most accurate time measurement he could: He sang and used the beat as his stopwatch.

§ Here is a true story: The point was made again during the Apollo 15 mission to the moon (July 1971) when astronaut David R. Scott dropped a feather and a hammer from the same height. The moon has no atmosphere, so the two hit the surface of the moon simultaneously.

EXAMPLE 2 Acceleration of Sales

For the first 15 months after the introduction of a new video game, the total sales can be modeled by the curve

$$S(t) = 20e^{0.4t} \text{ units sold,}$$

where t is the time in months since the game was introduced. After about 25 months total sales follow more closely the curve

$$S(t) = 100{,}000 - 20e^{17-0.4t}.$$

How fast are total sales accelerating after 10 months? How fast are they accelerating after 30 months? What do these numbers mean?

Solution By acceleration we mean the rate of change of the rate of change, which is the second derivative. During the first 15 months, the first derivative of sales is

$$\frac{dS}{dt} = 8e^{0.4t}$$

and so the second derivative is

$$\frac{d^2S}{dt^2} = 3.2e^{0.4t}.$$

Thus, after 10 months the acceleration of sales is

$$\left.\frac{d^2S}{dt^2}\right|_{t=10} = 3.2e^4 \approx 175 \text{ units/month/month, or units/month}^2.$$

We can also compute total sales

$$S(10) = 20e^4 \approx 1{,}092 \text{ units}$$

and the rate of change of sales

$$\left.\frac{dS}{dt}\right|_{t=10} = 8e^4 \approx 437 \text{ units/month.}$$

What do these numbers mean? By the end of the tenth month, a total of 1,092 video games have been sold. At that time the game is selling at the rate of 437 units per month. This rate of sales is increasing by 175 units per month per month. More games will be sold each month than the month before.

Analysis of the sales after 30 months is done similarly, using the formula

$$S(t) = 100{,}000 - 20e^{17-0.4t}.$$

The derivative is

$$\frac{dS}{dt} = 8e^{17-0.4t}$$

and the second derivative is

$$\frac{d^2S}{dt^2} = -3.2e^{17-0.4t}.$$

After 30 months,

$$S(30) = 100{,}000 - 20e^{17-12} \approx 97{,}032 \text{ units}$$

$$\left.\frac{dS}{dt}\right|_{t=30} = 8e^{17-12} \approx 1{,}187 \text{ units/month}$$

$$\left.\frac{d^2S}{dt^2}\right|_{t=30} = -3.2e^{17-12} \approx -475 \text{ units/month}^2.$$

By the end of the thirtieth month, 97,032 video games have been sold, the game is selling at a rate of 1,187 units per month, and the rate of sales is *decreasing* by 475 units per month. Fewer games are sold each month than the month before.

Geometric Interpretation of Second Derivative: Concavity

The first derivative of f tells us where the graph of f is rising [where $f'(x) > 0$] and where it is falling [where $f'(x) < 0$]. The second derivative tells in what direction the graph of f *curves* or *bends*. Consider the graphs in Figures 26 and 27.

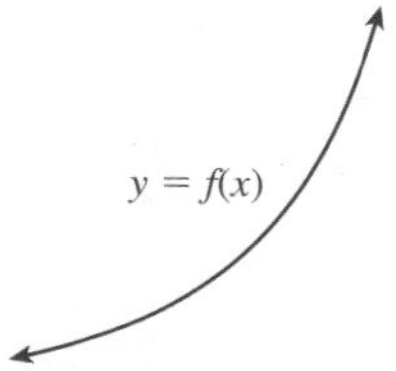

Figure 26

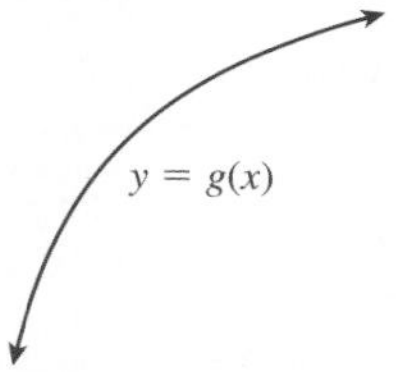

Figure 27

Think of a car driving from left to right along each of the roads shown in the two figures. A car driving along the graph of f in Figure 26 will turn to the left (upward); a car driving along the graph of g in Figure 27 will turn to the right (downward). We say that the graph of f is **concave up** and the graph of g is **concave down**. Now think about the derivatives of f and g. The derivative $f'(x)$ starts small but *increases* as the graph gets steeper. Because $f'(x)$ is increasing, its derivative $f''(x)$ must be positive. On the other hand, $g'(x)$ *decreases* as we go to the right. Because $g'(x)$ is decreasing, its derivative $g''(x)$ must be negative. Summarizing, we have the following.

Concavity and the Second Derivative

A curve is **concave up** if its slope is increasing, in which case the second derivative is positive. A curve is **concave down** if its slope is decreasing, in which case the second derivative is negative. A point in the domain of f where the graph of f changes concavity, from concave up to concave down or vice versa, is called a **point of inflection**. At a point of inflection, the second derivative is either zero or undefined.

Locating Points of Inflection

To locate possible points of inflection, list points where $f''(x) = 0$ and also interior points where $f''(x)$ is not defined.

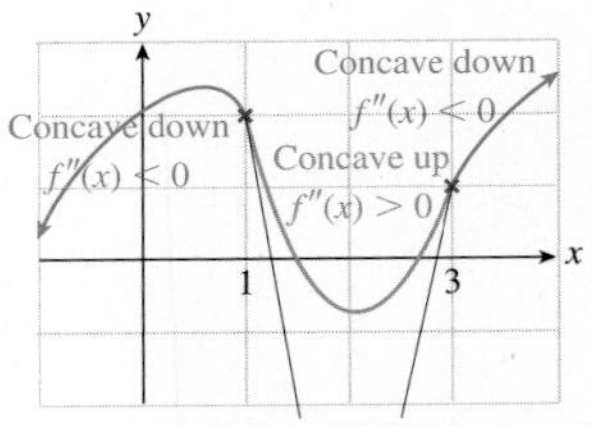

Figure 28

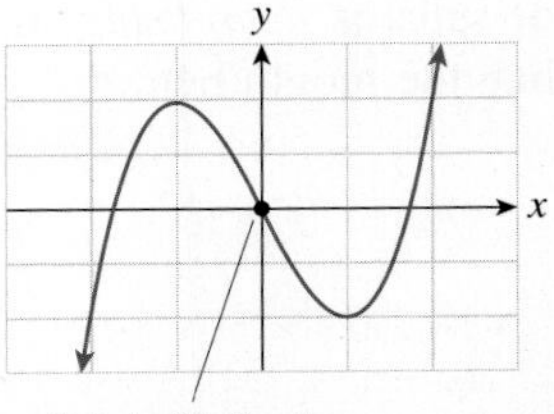

Figure 29

Quick Examples

1. The graph of the function f shown in Figure 28 is concave up when $1 < x < 3$, so $f''(x) > 0$ for $1 < x < 3$. It is concave down when $x < 1$ and $x > 3$, so $f''(x) < 0$ when $x < 1$ and $x > 3$. It has points of inflection at $x = 1$ and $x = 3$.
2. Consider $f(x) = x^3 - 3x$, whose graph is shown in Figure 29. $f''(x) = 6x$ is negative when $x < 0$ and positive when $x > 0$. The graph of f is concave down when $x < 0$ and concave up when $x > 0$. f has a point of inflection at $x = 0$, where the second derivative is 0.

The following example shows one of the reasons it's useful to look at concavity.

EXAMPLE 3 Inflation

Figure 30 shows the value of the U.S. Consumer Price Index (CPI) from January 2010 through April 2011.[27]

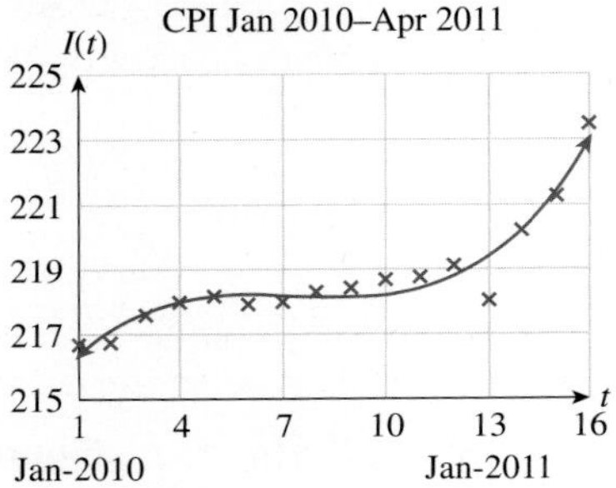

Figure 30

The approximating curve shown on the figure is given by

$$I(t) = 0.0081t^3 - 0.18t^2 + 1.3t + 215 \qquad (1 \le t \le 16),$$

where t is time in months ($t = 1$ represents January 2010). When the CPI is increasing, the U.S. economy is **experiencing inflation**. In terms of the model, this means that the derivative is positive: $I'(t) > 0$. Notice that $I'(t) > 0$ for most of the period shown (the graph is sloping upward), so the U.S. economy experienced inflation for most of $1 \le t \le 16$. We could measure **inflation** by the first derivative $I'(t)$ of the CPI, but we traditionally measure it as a ratio:

$$\text{Inflation rate} = \frac{I'(t)}{I(t)}, \qquad \text{Relative rate of change of the CPI}$$

expressed as a percentage per unit time (per month in this case).

a. Use the model to estimate the inflation rate in March 2010.

b. Was inflation slowing or speeding up in March 2010?

c. When was inflation slowing? When was inflation speeding up? When was inflation slowest?

[27]The CPI is compiled by the Bureau of Labor Statistics and is based upon a 1982 value of 100. For instance, a CPI of 200 means the CPI has doubled since 1982. Source: InflationData.com (www.inflationdata.com).

Solution

a. We need to compute $I'(t)$:

$$I'(t) = 0.0243t^2 - 0.36t + 1.3.$$

Thus, the inflation rate in March 2010 was given by

$$\text{Inflation rate} = \frac{I'(3)}{I(3)} = \frac{0.0243(3)^2 - 0.36(3) + 1.3}{0.0081(3)^3 - 0.18(3)^2 + 1.3(3) + 215}$$

$$= \frac{0.4387}{217.4987} \approx 0.0020,$$

or 0.20% per month.*

* The 0.20% monthly inflation rate corresponds to a $12 \times 0.20 =$ 2.40% annual inflation rate. This result could be obtained directly by changing the units of the *t*-axis from months to years and then redoing the calculation.

b. We say that inflation is "slowing" when the CPI is decelerating ($I''(t) < 0$; the index rises at a slower rate or falls at a faster rate†). Similarly, inflation is "speeding up" when the CPI is accelerating ($I''(t) > 0$; the index rises at a faster rate or falls at a slower rate). From the formula for $I'(t)$, the second derivative is

$$I''(t) = 0.0486t - 0.36$$
$$I''(3) = 0.0486(3) - 0.36 = -0.2142.$$

† When the CPI is falling, the inflation rate is negative and we experience *deflation*.

Because this quantity is negative, we conclude that inflation was slowing down in March 2010.

c. When inflation is slowing, $I''(t)$ is negative, so the graph of the CPI is concave down. When inflation is speeding up, it is concave up. At the point at which it switches, there is a point of inflection (Figure 31).

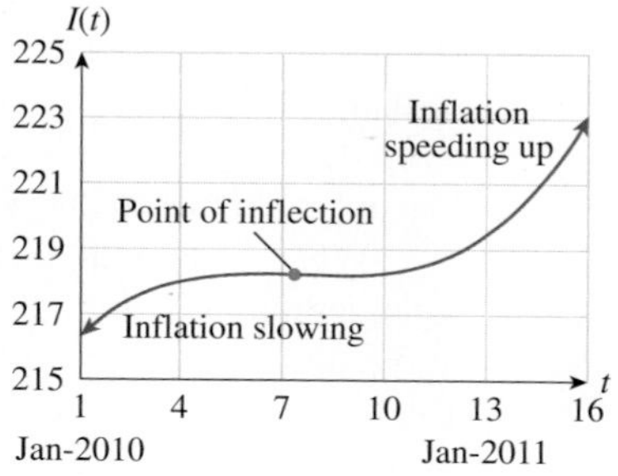

Figure 31

The point of inflection occurs when $I''(t) = 0$; that is,

$$0.0486t - 0.36 = 0$$

$$t = \frac{0.36}{0.0486} \approx 7.4.$$

Thus, inflation was slowing when $t < 7.4$ (that is, until around the middle of July), and speeding up when $t > 7.4$ (after that time). Inflation was slowest at the point when it stopped slowing down and began to speed up, $t \approx 7.4$ (in fact there was slight deflation at that particular point as $I'(7.4)$ is negative); notice that the graph has the least slope at that point.

EXAMPLE 4 The Point of Diminishing Returns

After the introduction of a new video game, the total worldwide sales are modeled by the curve

$$S(t) = \frac{1}{1 + 50e^{-0.2t}} \text{ million units sold,}$$

where t is the time in months since the game was introduced (compare Example 2). The graphs of $S(t)$, $S'(t)$, and $S''(t)$ are shown in Figure 32. Where is the graph of S concave up, and where is it concave down? Where are any points of inflection? What does this all mean?

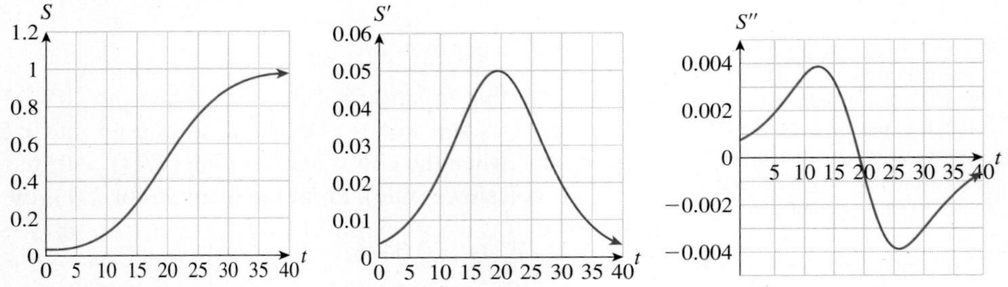

(a) Graph of S (b) Graph of S' (c) Graph of S''

Figure 32

using Technology

You can use a TI-83/84 Plus, a downloadable Excel sheet at the Website, or the Function Evaluator and Grapher at the Website to graph the second derivative of the function in Example 4:

TI-83/84 Plus

```
Y1=1/(1+50*e^(-0.2X))
Y2=nDeriv(Y1,X,X)
Y3=nDeriv(Y2,X,X)
```

Website

www.WanerMath.com

In the Function Evaluator and Grapher, enter the functions as shown.

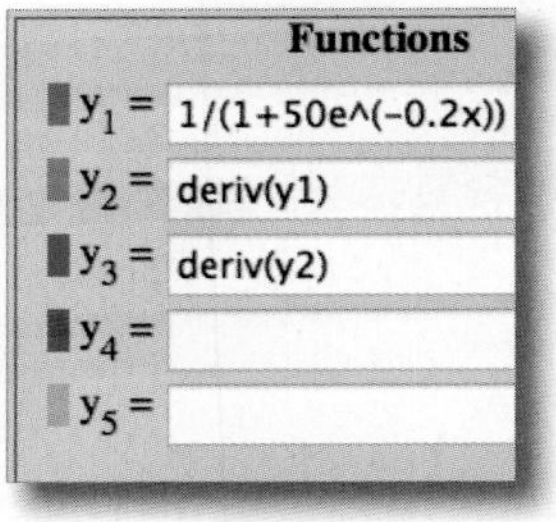

(Use Ymin = 0, yMax = 0.1 for a nice view of S' and Ymin = −0.01 and yMax = 0.01 for S''.)

For an Excel utility, try:

On Line Utilities
↓
Excel First and Second Derivative Graphing Utility

(This utility needs macros, so ensure they are enabled.)

Solution Look at the graph of S. We see that the graph of S is concave up in the early months and then becomes concave down later. The point of inflection, where the concavity changes, is somewhere between 15 and 25 months.

Now look at the graph of S''. This graph crosses the t-axis very close to $t = 20$, is positive before that point, and negative after that point. Because positive values of S'' indicate S is concave up and negative values concave down, we conclude that the graph of S is concave up for about the first 20 months; that is, for $0 < t < 20$ and concave down for $20 < t < 40$. The concavity switches at the point of inflection, which occurs at about $t = 20$ (when $S''(t) = 0$; a more accurate answer is $t \approx 19.56$).

What does this all mean? Look at the graph of S', which shows sales per unit time, or monthly sales. From this graph we see that monthly sales are increasing for $t < 20$: more units are being sold each month than the month before. Monthly sales reach a peak of 0.05 million = 50,000 games per month at the point of inflection $t = 20$ and then begin to drop off. Thus, the point of inflection occurs at the time when monthly sales stop increasing and start to fall off; that is, the time when monthly sales peak. The point of inflection is sometimes called the **point of diminishing returns**. Although the total sales figure continues to rise (see the graph of S: game units continue to be sold), the *rate* at which units are sold starts to drop. (See Figure 33.)

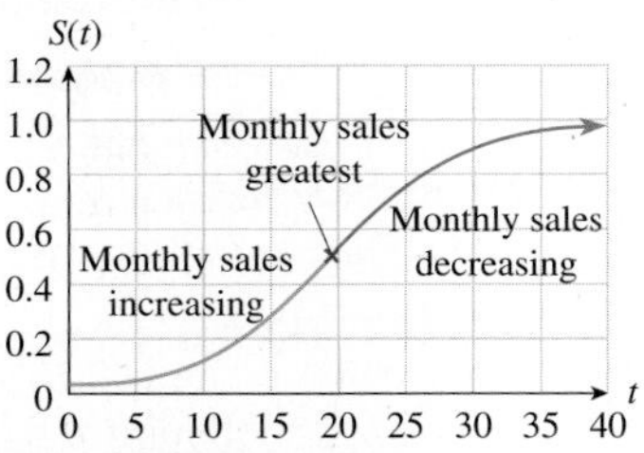

Figure 33

The Second Derivative Test for Relative Extrema

The second derivative often gives us a way of knowing whether or not a stationary point is a relative extremum. Figure 34 shows a graph with two stationary points: a relative maximum at $x = a$ and a relative minimum at $x = b$.

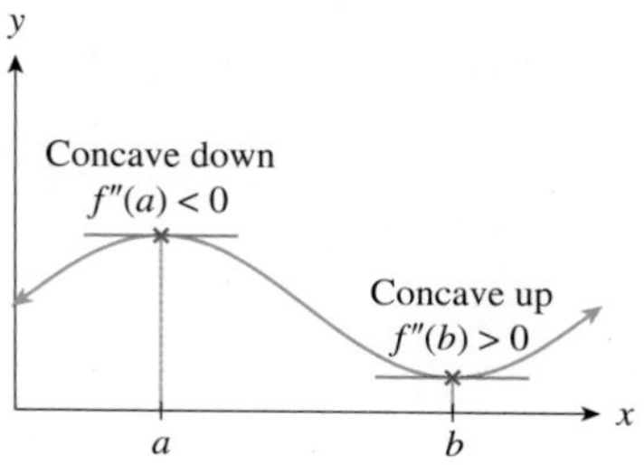

Figure 34

Notice that the curve is *concave down* at the relative maximum ($x = a$), so that $f''(a) < 0$, and *concave up* at the relative minimum ($x = b$), so that $f''(b) > 0$. This suggests the following (compare the First Derivative Test in Section 5.1).

Second Derivative Test for Relative Extrema

Suppose that the function f has a stationary point at $x = c$, and that $f''(c)$ exists. Determine the sign of $f''(c)$.

1. If $f''(c) > 0$, then f has a relative minimum at $x = c$.

2. If $f''(c) < 0$, then f has a relative maximum at $x = c$.

If $f''(c) = 0$, then the test is inconclusive and you need to use one of the methods of Section 5.1 (such as the first derivative test) to determine whether or not f has a relative extremum at $x = c$.

Quick Examples

1. $f(x) = x^2 - 2x$ has $f'(x) = 2x - 2$ and hence a stationary point at $x = 1$. $f''(x) = 2$, and so $f''(1) = 2$, which is positive, so f has a relative minimum at $x = 1$.
2. Let $f(x) = x^3 - 3x^2 - 9x$. Then

   $f'(x) = 3x^2 - 6x - 9 = 3(x + 1)(x - 3)$

   Stationary points at $x = -1$, $x = 3$

   $f''(x) = 6x - 6$

   $f''(-1) = -12$, so there is a relative maximum at $x = -1$

   $f''(3) = 12$, so there is a relative minimum at $x = 3$.
3. $f(x) = x^4$ has $f'(x) = 4x^3$ and hence a stationary point at $x = 0$. $f''(x) = 12x^2$ and so $f''(0) = 0$, telling us that the second derivative test is inconclusive. However, we can see from the graph of f or the first derivative test that f has a minimum at $x = 0$.

Higher Order Derivatives

There is no reason to stop at the second derivative; we could once again take the *derivative* of the second derivative to obtain the **third derivative**, f''', and we could take the derivative once again to obtain the **fourth derivative**, written $f^{(4)}$, and then continue to obtain $f^{(5)}$, $f^{(6)}$, and so on (assuming we get a differentiable function at each stage).

Higher Order Derivatives

We define

$$f'''(x) = \frac{d}{dx}[f''(x)]$$

$$f^{(4)}(x) = \frac{d}{dx}[f'''(x)]$$

$$f^{(5)}(x) = \frac{d}{dx}[f^{(4)}(x)],$$

and so on, assuming all these derivatives exist.

Different Notations

$$f'(x), f''(x), f'''(x), f^{(4)}(x), \ldots, f^{(n)}(x), \ldots$$

$$\frac{df}{dx}, \frac{d^2f}{dx^2}, \frac{d^3f}{dx^3}, \frac{d^4f}{dx^4}, \ldots, \frac{d^nf}{dx^n}, \ldots$$

$$\frac{dy}{dx}, \frac{d^2y}{dx^2}, \frac{d^3y}{dx^3}, \frac{d^4y}{dx^4}, \ldots, \frac{d^ny}{dx^n}, \ldots \qquad \text{When } y = f(x)$$

$$y, y', y'', y''', y^{(4)}, \ldots, y^{(n)}, \ldots \qquad \text{When } y = f(x)$$

Quick Examples

1. If $f(x) = x^3 - x$, then $f'(x) = 3x^2 - 1$, $f''(x) = 6x$, $f'''(x) = 6$, $f^{(4)}(x) = f^{(5)}(x) = \cdots = 0$.
2. If $f(x) = e^x$, then $f'(x) = e^x$, $f''(x) = e^x$, $f'''(x) = e^x$, $f^{(4)}(x) = f^{(5)}(x) = \cdots = e^x$.

Q: *We know that the second derivative can be interpreted as acceleration. How do we interpret the third derivative; and the fourth, fifth, and so on?*

A: Think of a car traveling down the road (with position $s(t)$ at time t) in such a way that its acceleration $\frac{d^2s}{dt^2}$ is changing with time (for instance, the driver may be slowly increasing pressure on the accelerator, causing the car to accelerate at a greater and greater rate). Then $\frac{d^3s}{dt^3}$ is the rate of change of acceleration. $\frac{d^4s}{dt^4}$ would then be the *acceleration* of the acceleration, and so on.

Q: *How are these higher order derivatives reflected in the graph of a function f?*

A: Because the concavity is measured by f'', its derivative f''' tells us the rate of change of concavity. Similarly, $f^{(4)}$ would tell us the *acceleration* of concavity, and so on. These properties are very subtle and hard to discern by simply looking at the curve; the higher the order, the more subtle the property. There is a remarkable theorem by Taylor* that tells us that, for a large class of functions (including polynomial, exponential, logarithmic, and trigonometric functions) the values of all orders of derivative $f(a)$, $f'(a)$, $f''(a)$, $f'''(a)$, and so on at the single point $x = a$ are enough to describe the entire graph (even at points very far from $x = a$)! In other words, the smallest piece of a graph near any point a contains sufficient information to "clone" the entire graph!

* Brook Taylor (1685–1731) was an English mathematician.

FAQs

Interpreting Points of Inflection and Using the Second Derivative Test

Q: *It says in Example 4 that monthly sales reach a maximum at the point of inflection (second derivative is zero), but the second derivative test says that, for a maximum, the second derivative must be negative. What is going on here?*

A: What is a maximum in Example 4 is the *rate of change of* sales: which is measured in sales per unit time (monthly sales in the example). In other words, it is the *derivative* of the total sales function that is a maximum, so we located the maximum by setting its derivative (which is the *second* derivative of total sales) equal to zero. In general: To find relative (stationary) extrema of the *original* function, set $f'(x)$ equal to zero and solve for x as usual. The second derivative test can then be used to test the stationary point obtained. To find relative (stationary) extrema of the *rate of change of f*, set $f''(x) = 0$ and solve for x.

Q: *I used the second derivative test and it was inconclusive. That means that there is neither a relative maximum nor a relative minimum at $x = a$, right?*

A: Wrong. If (as is often the case) the second derivative is zero at a stationary point, all it means is that the second derivative test itself cannot determine whether the given point is a relative maximum, minimum, or neither. For instance, $f(x) = x^4$ has a stationary minimum at $x = 0$, but the second derivative test is inconclusive. In such cases, one should use another test (such as the first derivative test) to decide if the point is a relative maximum, minimum, or neither.

5.3 EXERCISES

▼ more advanced ◆ challenging

T indicates exercises that should be solved using technology

In Exercises 1–10, calculate $\frac{d^2y}{dx^2}$. HINT [See Quick Examples on page 398.]

1. $y = 3x^2 - 6$
2. $y = -x^2 + x$
3. $y = \frac{2}{x}$
4. $y = -\frac{2}{x^2}$
5. $y = 4x^{0.4} - x$
6. $y = 0.2x^{-0.1}$
7. $y = e^{-(x-1)} - x$
8. $y = e^{-x} + e^x$
9. $y = \frac{1}{x} - \ln x$
10. $y = x^{-2} + \ln x$

In Exercises 11–16, the position s of a point (in feet) is given as a function of time t (in seconds). Find (a) its acceleration as a function of t and (b) its acceleration at the specified time. HINT [See Example 1.]

11. $s = 12 + 3t - 16t^2$; $t = 2$

12. $s = -12 + t - 16t^2$; $t = 2$

13. $s = \frac{1}{t} + \frac{1}{t^2}$; $t = 1$ **14.** $s = \frac{1}{t} - \frac{1}{t^2}$; $t = 2$

15. $s = \sqrt{t} + t^2$; $t = 4$ **16.** $s = 2\sqrt{t} + t^3$; $t = 1$

In Exercises 17–24, the graph of a function is given. Find the approximate coordinates of all points of inflection of each function (if any). HINT [See Quick Examples on page 402.]

17.
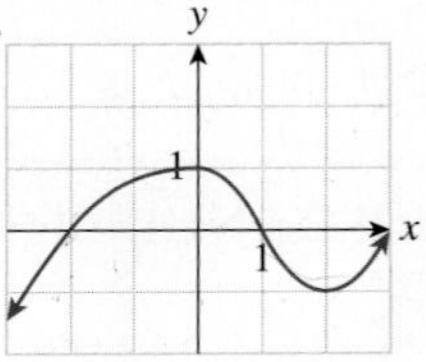

18.
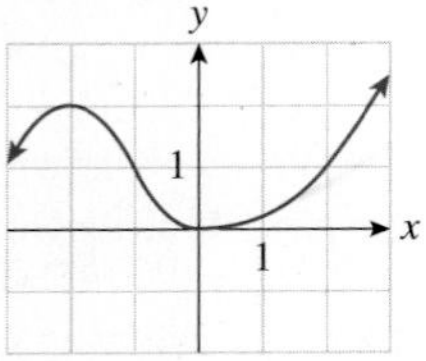

19.
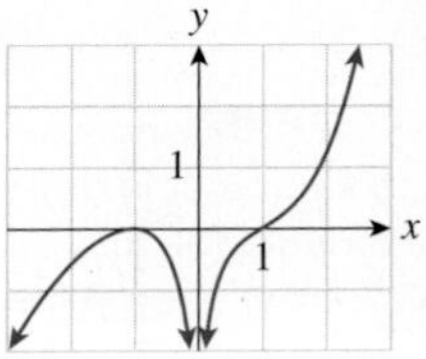

20.
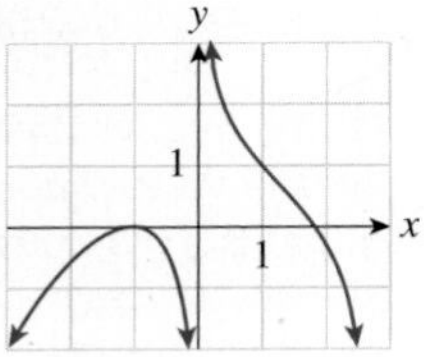

21.
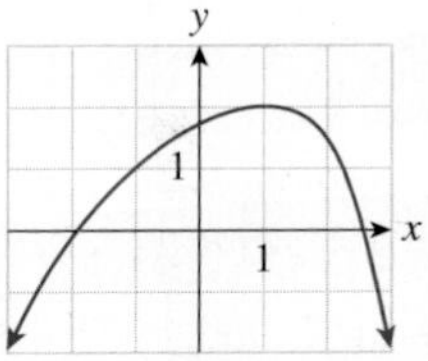

22.
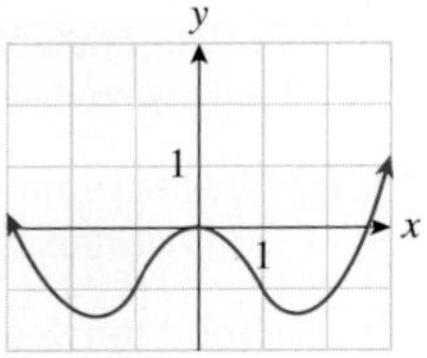

23.
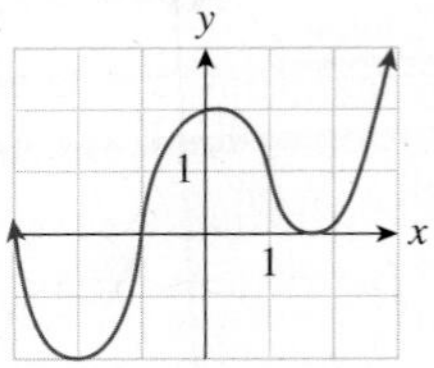

24.
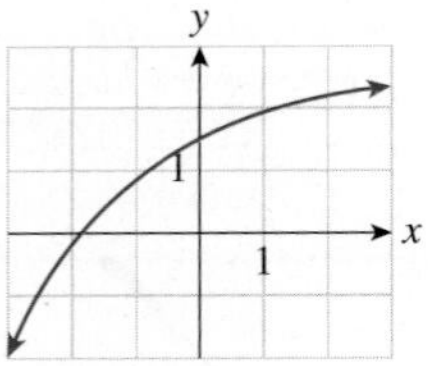

In Exercises 25–28, the graph of the derivative, $f'(x)$, *is given. Determine the x-coordinates of all points of inflection of f(x), if any. (Assume that f(x) is defined and continuous everywhere in* $[-3, 3]$.) HINT [See the **Before we go on** discussion in Example 4.]

25.
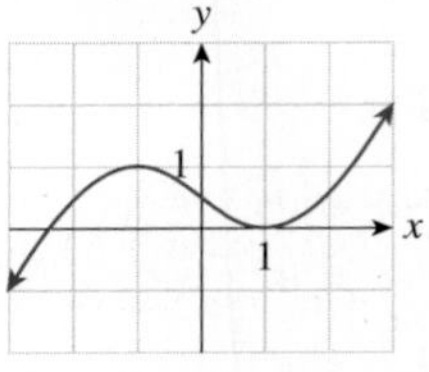

26.
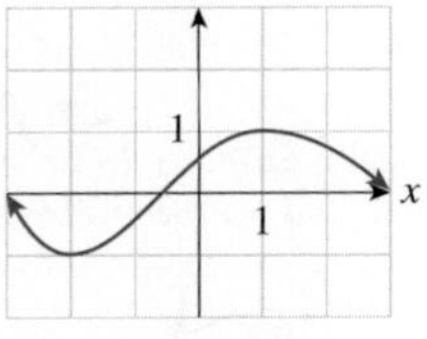

27.
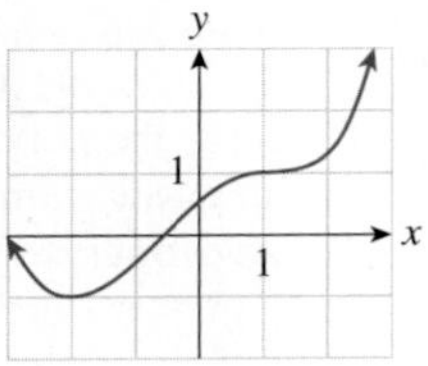

28.
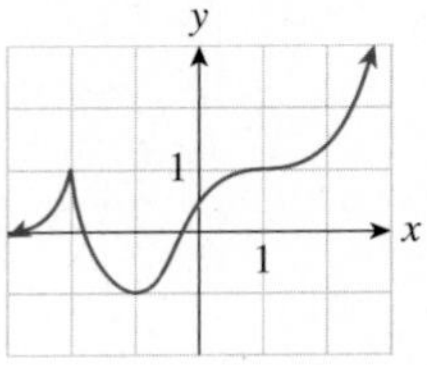

In Exercises 29–32, the graph of the second derivative, $f''(x)$, *is given. Determine the x-coordinates of all points of inflection of f(x), if any. (Assume that f(x) is defined and continuous everywhere in* $[-3, 3]$.) HINT [Remember that a point of inflection of f corresponds to a point at which f'' changes sign, from positive to negative or vice versa. This could be a point where its graph crosses the x-axis, or a point where its graph is broken: positive on one side of the break and negative on the other.]

29.
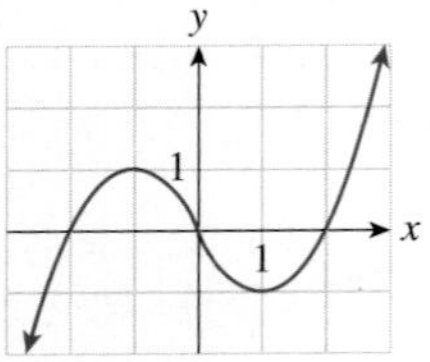

30.
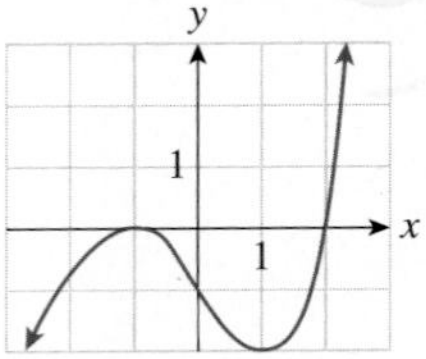

31.
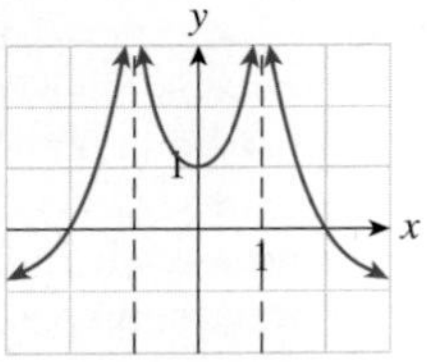

32.
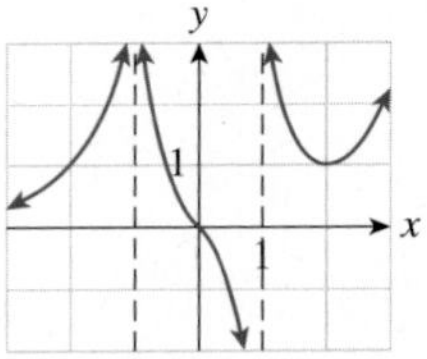

In Exercises 33–44, find the x-coordinates of all critical points of the given function. Determine whether each critical point is a relative maximum, minimum, or neither by first applying the second derivative test, and, if the test fails, by some other method. HINT [See Quick Examples on page 405.]

33. $f(x) = x^2 - 4x + 1$ **34.** $f(x) = 2x^2 - 2x + 3$

35. $g(x) = x^3 - 12x$ **36.** $g(x) = 2x^3 - 6x + 3$

37. $f(t) = t^3 - t$ **38.** $f(t) = -2t^3 + 3t$

39. $f(x) = x^4 - 4x^3$ **40.** $f(x) = 3x^4 - 2x^3$

41. $f(x) = e^{-x^2}$ **42.** $f(x) = e^{2-x^2}$

43. $f(x) = xe^{1-x^2}$ **44.** $f(x) = xe^{-x^2}$

In Exercises 45–54, calculate the derivatives of all orders: $f'(x), f''(x), f'''(x), f^{(4)}(x), \ldots, f^{(n)}(x), \ldots$ HINT [See Quick Examples on page 406.]

45. $f(x) = 4x^2 - x + 1$ **46.** $f(x) = -3x^3 + 4x$

47. $f(x) = -x^4 + 3x^2$ **48.** $f(x) = x^4 + x^3$

49. $f(x) = (2x + 1)^4$ **50.** $f(x) = (-2x + 1)^3$

51. $f(x) = e^{-x}$ **52.** $f(x) = e^{2x}$

53. $f(x) = e^{3x-1}$ **54.** $f(x) = 2e^{-x+3}$

APPLICATIONS

55. ***Acceleration on Mars*** If a stone is dropped from a height of 40 meters above the Martian surface, its height in meters after t seconds is given by $s = 40 - 1.9t^2$. What is its acceleration? HINT [See Example 1.]

56. ***Acceleration on the Moon*** If a stone is thrown up at 10 m per second from a height of 100 meters above the surface of the Moon, its height in meters after t seconds is given by $s = 100 + 10t - 0.8t^2$. What is its acceleration? HINT [See Example 1.]

57. ***Motion in a Straight Line*** The position of a particle moving in a straight line is given by $s = t^3 - t^2$ ft after t seconds. Find an expression for its acceleration after a time t. Is its velocity increasing or decreasing when $t = 1$?

58. ***Motion in a Straight Line*** The position of a particle moving in a straight line is given by $s = 3e^t - 8t^2$ ft after t seconds. Find an expression for its acceleration after a time t. Is its velocity increasing or decreasing when $t = 1$?

59. ***Bottled Water Sales*** Annual sales of bottled water in the United States in the period 2000–2010 could be approximated by

$$R(t) = -45t^2 + 900t + 4{,}200 \text{ million gallons} \quad (0 \le t \le 10),$$

where t is time in years since 2000.[28] According to the model, were annual sales of bottled water accelerating or decelerating in 2009? How fast? HINT [See Example 2.]

60. ***Bottled Water Sales*** Annual U.S. per capita sales of bottled water in the period 2000–2010 could be approximated by

$$Q(t) = -0.18t^2 + 3t + 15 \text{ gallons} \quad (0 \le t \le 10),$$

where t is time in years since 2000.[29] According to the model, were annual U.S. per capita sales of bottled water accelerating or decelerating in 2009? How fast?

61. ***Embryo Development*** The daily oxygen consumption of a bird embryo increases from the time the egg is laid through the time the chick hatches. In a typical galliform bird, the oxygen consumption can be approximated by

$$c(t) = -0.065t^3 + 3.4t^2 - 22t + 3.6 \text{ ml} \quad (8 \le t \le 30),$$

where t is the time (in days) since the egg was laid.[30] (An egg will typically hatch at around $t = 28$.) Use the model to estimate the following (give the units of measurement for each answer and round all answers to two significant digits):

a. The daily oxygen consumption 20 days after the egg was laid

b. The rate at which the oxygen consumption is changing 20 days after the egg was laid

c. The rate at which the oxygen consumption is accelerating 20 days after the egg was laid

62. ***Embryo Development*** The daily oxygen consumption of a turkey embryo increases from the time the egg is laid through the time the chick hatches. In a brush turkey, the oxygen consumption can be approximated by

$$c(t) = -0.028t^3 + 2.9t^2 - 44t + 95 \text{ ml} \quad (20 \le t \le 50),$$

where t is the time (in days) since the egg was laid.[31] (An egg will typically hatch at around $t = 50$.) Use the model to estimate the following (give the units of measurement for each answer and round all answers to two significant digits):

a. The daily oxygen consumption 40 days after the egg was laid

b. The rate at which the oxygen consumption is changing 40 days after the egg was laid

c. The rate at which the oxygen consumption is accelerating 40 days after the egg was laid

63. ***Inflation*** The following graph shows the approximate value of the United States Consumer Price Index (CPI) from December 2006 through July 2007.[32]

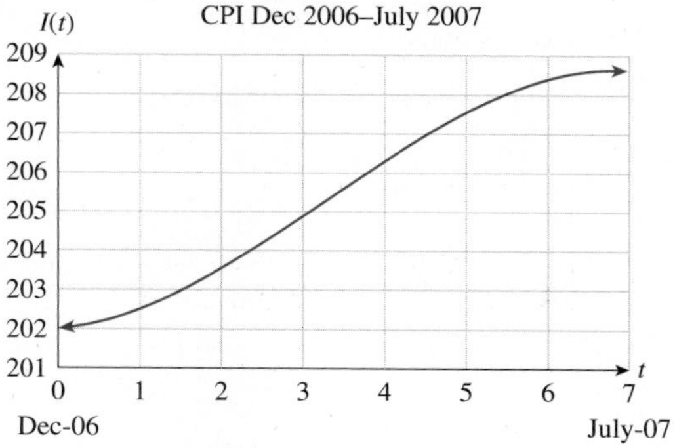

The approximating curve shown on the figure is given by

$$I(t) = -0.04t^3 + 0.4t^2 + 0.1t + 202 \quad (0 \le t \le 7),$$

where t is time in months ($t = 0$ represents December 2006).

a. Use the model to estimate the monthly inflation rate in February 2007 ($t = 2$). [Recall that the inflation *rate* is $I'(t)/I(t)$.]

b. Was inflation slowing or speeding up in February 2007?

c. When was inflation speeding up? When was inflation slowing? HINT [See Example 3.]

64. ***Inflation*** The following graph shows the approximate value of the U.S. Consumer Price Index (CPI) from September 2004 through November 2005.[33]

[28]Source for data: Beverage Marketing Corporation (www.bottledwater.org).

[29]*Ibid.*

[30]The model approximates graphical data published in the article "The Brush Turkey" by Roger S. Seymour, *Scientific American,* December, 1991, pp. 108–114.

[31]*Ibid.*

[32]The CPI is compiled by the Bureau of Labor Statistics and is based upon a 1982 value of 100. For instance, a CPI of 200 means the CPI has doubled since 1982. Source: InflationData.com (www.inflationdata.com).

[33]*Ibid.*

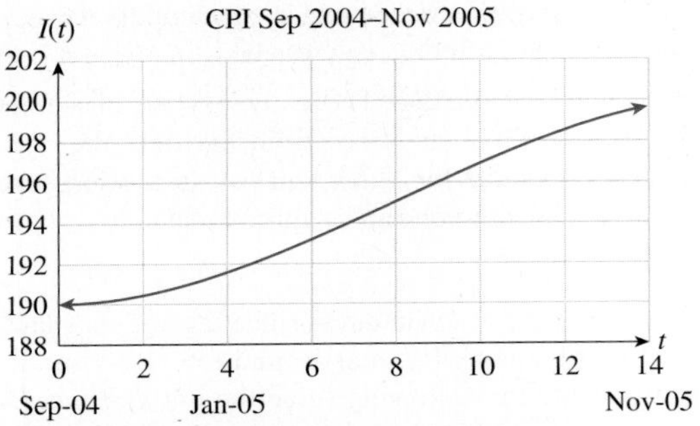

The approximating curve shown on the figure is given by

$$I(t) = -0.005t^3 + 0.12t^2 - 0.01t + 190 \quad (0 \le t \le 14),$$

where t is time in months ($t = 0$ represents September 2004).

a. Use the model to estimate the monthly inflation rate in July 2005 ($t = 10$). [Recall that the inflation *rate* is $I'(t)/I(t)$.]

b. Was inflation slowing or speeding up in July 2005?

c. When was inflation speeding up? When was inflation slowing? HINT [See Example 3.]

65. ***Inflation*** The following graph shows the approximate value of the U.S. Consumer Price Index (CPI) from July 2005 through March 2006.[34]

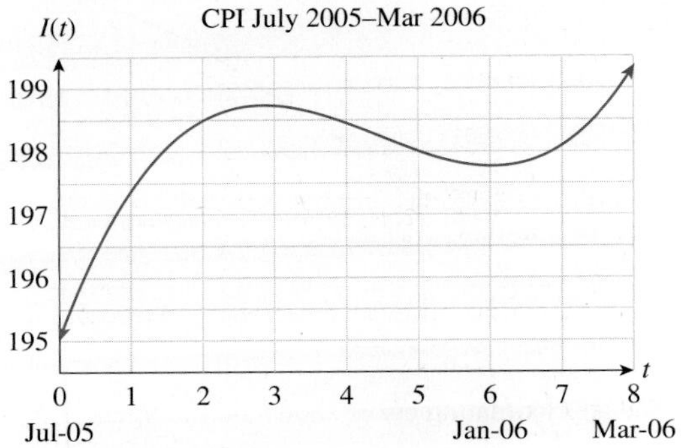

The approximating curve shown on the figure is given by

$$I(t) = 0.06t^3 - 0.8t^2 + 3.1t + 195 \quad (0 \le t \le 8),$$

where t is time in months ($t = 0$ represents July 2005).

a. Use the model to estimate the monthly inflation rates in December 2005 and February 2006 ($t = 5$ and $t = 7$).

b. Was inflation slowing or speeding up in February 2006?

c. When was inflation speeding up? When was inflation slowing?

66. ***Inflation*** The following graph shows the approximate value of the U.S. Consumer Price Index (CPI) from March 2006 through May 2007.[35]

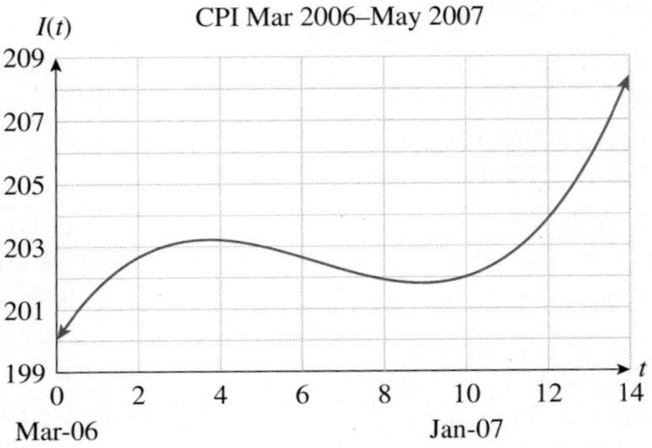

The approximating curve shown on the figure is given by

$$I(t) = 0.02t^3 - 0.38t^2 + 2t + 200 \quad (0 \le t \le 14),$$

where t is time in months ($t = 0$ represents March, 2006).

a. Use the model to estimate the monthly inflation rates in September 2006 and January 2007 ($t = 6$ and $t = 10$).

b. Was inflation slowing or speeding up in January 2007?

c. When was inflation speeding up? When was inflation slowing?

67. ***Scientific Research*** The percentage of research articles in the prominent journal *Physical Review* that were written by researchers in the United States during the years 1983–2003 can be modeled by

$$P(t) = 25 + \frac{36}{1 + 0.06(0.7)^{-t}},$$

where t is time in years since 1983.[36] The graphs of P, P', and P'' are shown here:

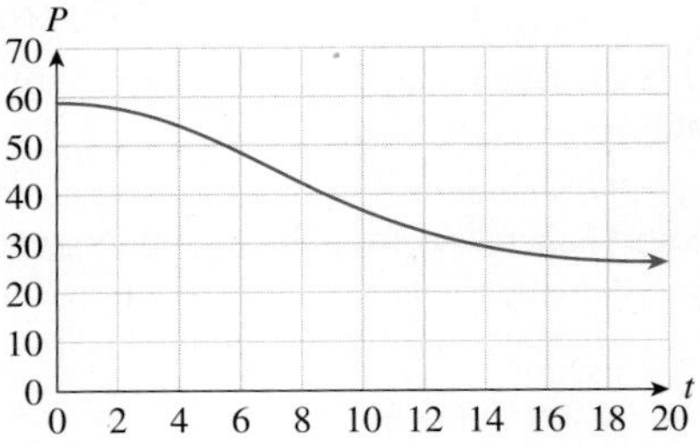

Graph of P

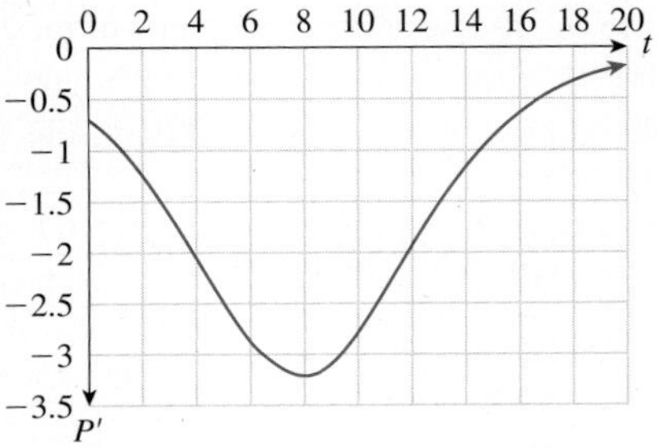

Graph of P'

[34] The CPI is compiled by the Bureau of Labor Statistics and is based upon a 1982 value of 100. For instance, a CPI of 200 means the CPI has doubled since 1982. Source: InflationData.com (www.inflationdata.com).

[35] *Ibid.*

[36] Source: The American Physical Society/*New York Times*, May 3, 2003, p. A1.

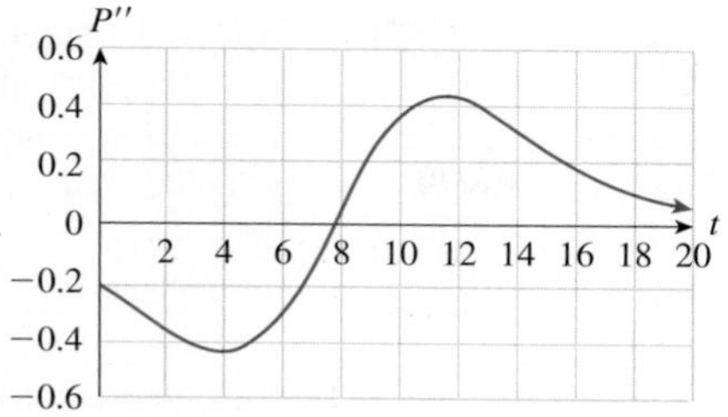

Graph of P''

Determine, to the nearest whole number, the values of t for which the graph of P is concave up and where it is concave down, and locate any points of inflection. What does the point of inflection tell you about science articles? HINT [See Example 4.]

68. ***Scientific Research*** The number of research articles in the prominent journal *Physical Review* that were written by researchers in Europe during the years 1983–2003 can be modeled by

$$P(t) = \frac{7.0}{1 + 5.4(1.2)^{-t}},$$

where t is time in years since 1983.[37] The graphs of P, P', and P'' are shown here:

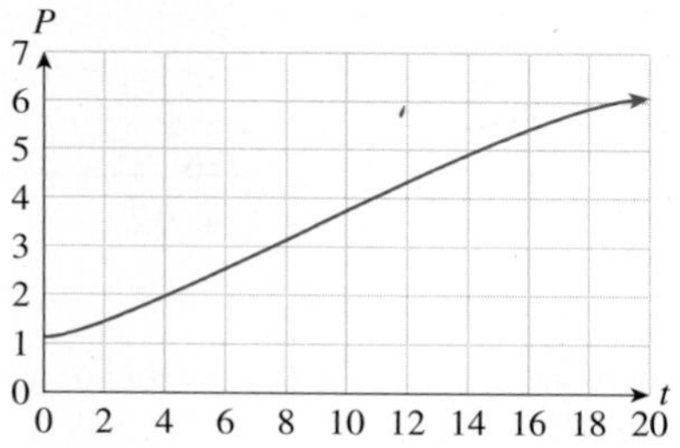

Graph of P

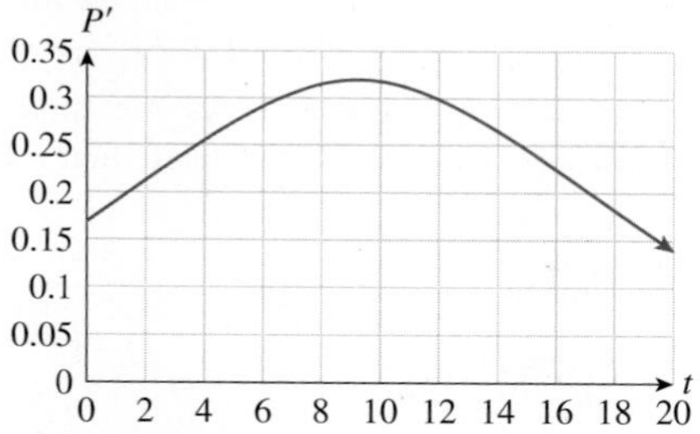

Graph of P'

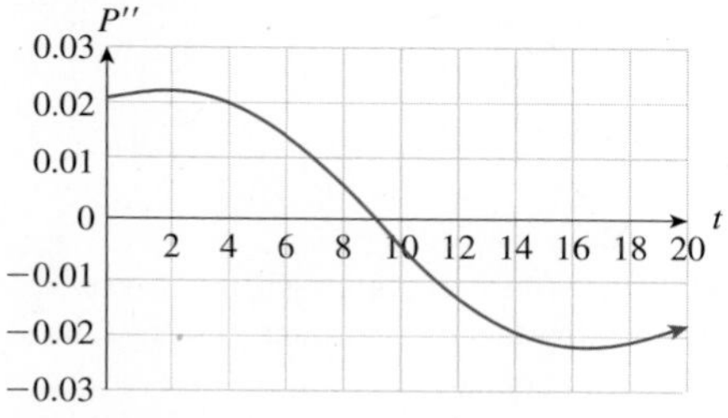

Graph of P''

Determine, to the nearest whole number, the values of t for which the graph of P is concave up and where it is concave down, and locate any points of inflection. What does the point of inflection tell you about science articles?

69. ***Embryo Development*** Here are sketches of the graphs of c, c', and c'' from Exercise 61:

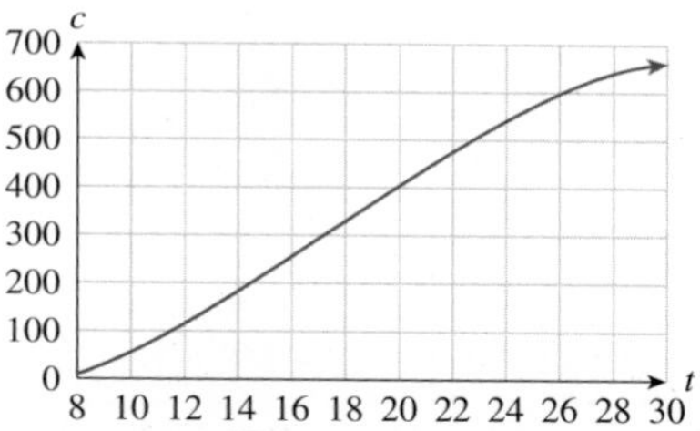

Graph of c

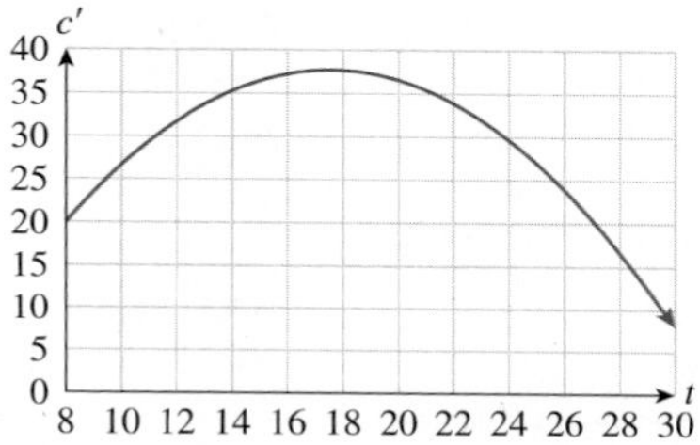

Graph of c'

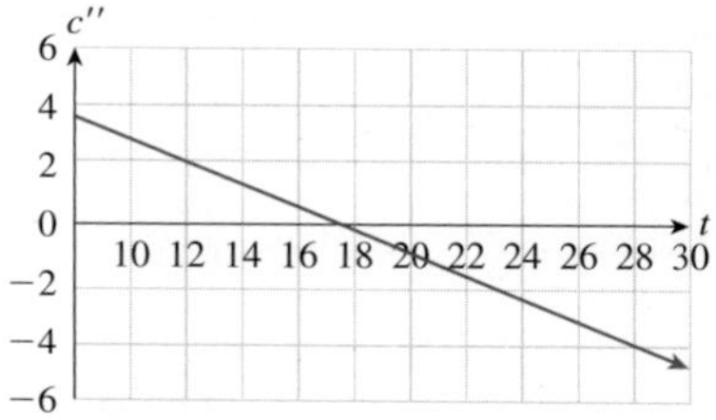

Graph of c''

Multiple choice:

a. The graph of c' **(A)** has a point of inflection. **(B)** has no points of inflection.

b. At around 18 days after the egg is laid, daily oxygen consumption is: **(A)** at a maximum. **(B)** increasing at a maximum rate. **(C)** just beginning to decrease.

c. For $t > 18$ days, the oxygen consumption is **(A)** increasing at a decreasing rate. **(B)** decreasing at an increasing rate. **(C)** increasing at an increasing rate.

70. ***Embryo Development*** Here are sketches of the graphs of c, c', and c'' from Exercise 62:

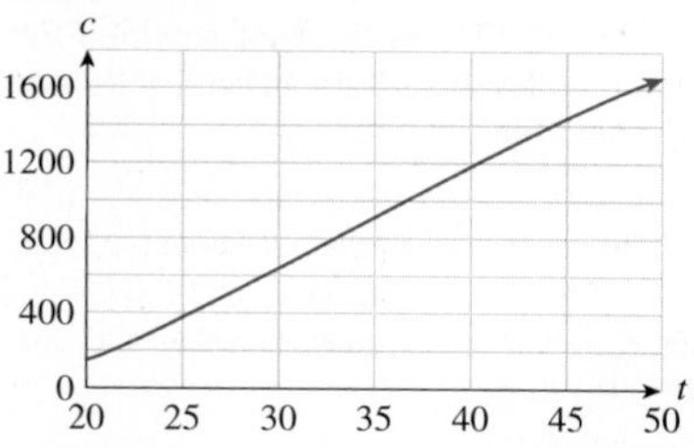

Graph of c

[37] Source: The American Physical Society/*New York Times*, May 3, 2003, p. A1.

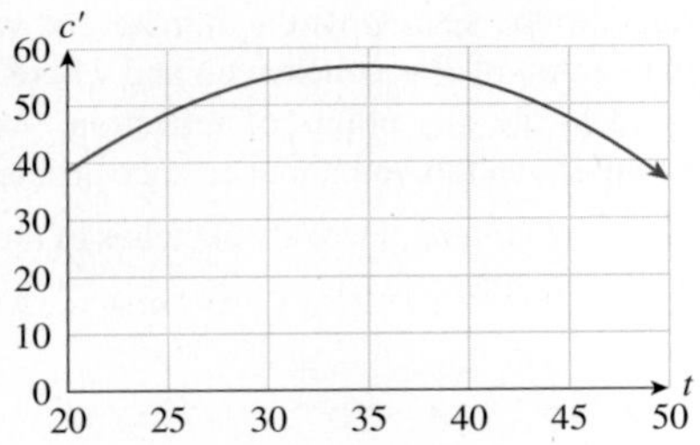

Graph of c'

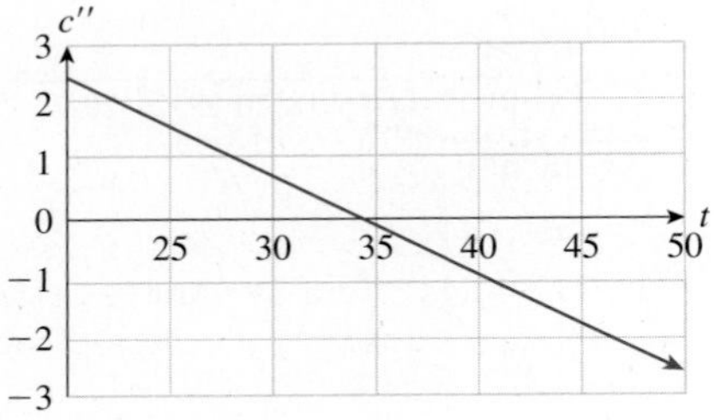

Graph of c''

Multiple choice:

a. The graph of c: **(A)** has points of inflection. **(B)** has no points of inflection. **(C)** may or may not have a point of inflection, but the graphs do not provide enough information.

b. At around 35 days after the egg is laid, the rate of change of daily oxygen consumption is: **(A)** at a maximum. **(B)** increasing at a maximum rate. **(C)** just becoming negative.

c. For $t < 35$ days, the oxygen consumption is: **(A)** increasing at an increasing rate. **(B)** increasing at a decreasing rate. **(C)** decreasing at an increasing rate.

71. T ***Subprime Mortgages during the Housing Bubble*** During the real estate run-up in 2000–2008, the percentage of mortgages issued in the United States that were subprime (normally classified as risky) could be approximated by

$$A(t) = \frac{15.0}{1 + 8.6(1.8)^{-t}} \text{ percent} \quad (0 \le t \le 8)$$

t years after the start of 2000.[38] Graph the function as well as its first and second derivatives. Determine, to the nearest whole number, the values of t for which the graph of A is concave up and concave down, and the t-coordinate of any points of inflection. What does the point of inflection tell you about subprime mortgages? HINT [To graph the second derivative, see the note in the margin after Example 4.]

72. T ***Subprime Mortgage Debt during the Housing Bubble*** During the real estate run-up in 2000–2008, the value of subprime (normally classified as risky) mortgage debt outstanding in the United States was approximately

$$A(t) = \frac{1{,}350}{1 + 4.2(1.7)^{-t}} \text{ billion dollars} \quad (0 \le t \le 8)$$

t years after the start of 2000.[39] Graph the function as well as its first and second derivatives. Determine, to the nearest whole number, the values of t for which the graph of A is concave up and concave down, and the t-coordinate of any points of inflection. What does the point of inflection tell you about subprime mortgages? HINT [To graph the second derivative, see the note in the margin after Example 4.]

73. ***Epidemics*** The following graph shows the total number n of people (in millions) infected in an epidemic as a function of time t (in years):

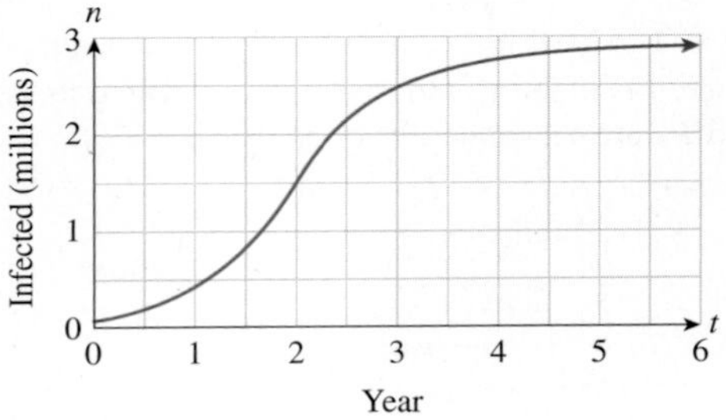

a. When to the nearest year was the rate of new infection largest?

b. When could the Centers for Disease Control and Prevention announce that the rate of new infection was beginning to drop? HINT [See Example 4.]

74. ***Sales*** The following graph shows the total number of *Pomegranate Q4* computers sold since their release (t is in years):

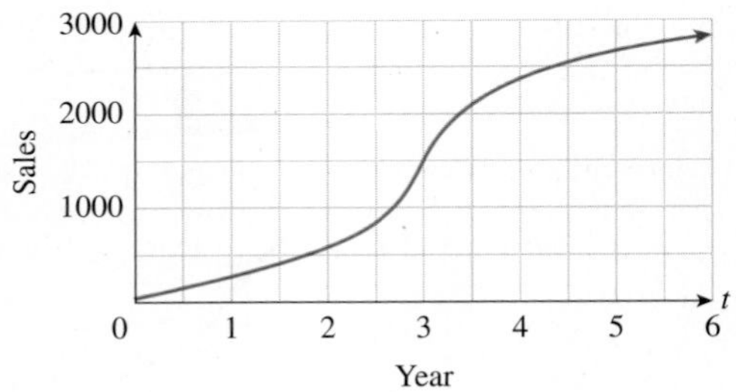

a. When were the computers selling fastest?

b. Explain why this graph might look as it does. HINT [See Example 4.]

[38] Sources: Mortgage Bankers Association, UBS.

[39] 2008 figure is an estimate.
Source: www.data360.org/dataset.aspx?Data_Set_Id=9549.

75. ***Industrial Output*** The following graph shows the yearly industrial output (measured in billions of zonars) of the city-state of Utarek, Mars over a seven-year period:

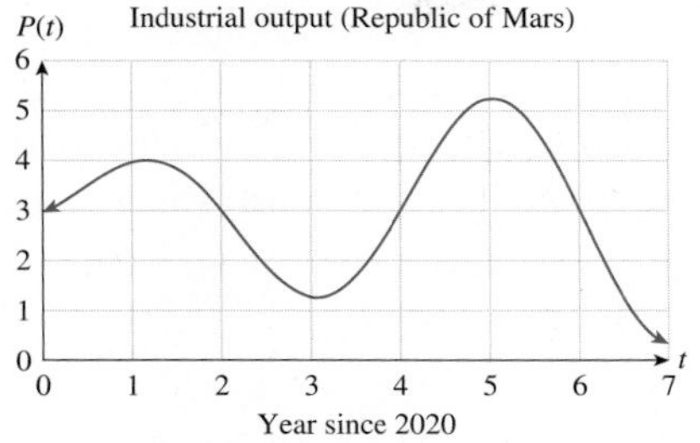

a. When to the nearest year did the rate of change of yearly industrial output reach a maximum?
b. When to the nearest year did the rate of change of yearly industrial output reach a minimum?
c. When to the nearest year does the graph first change from concave down to concave up? The result tells you that:
   (A) In that year the rate of change of industrial output reached a minimum compared with nearby years.
   (B) In that year the rate of change of industrial output reached a maximum compared with nearby years.

76. ***Profits*** The following graph shows the yearly profits of Gigantic Conglomerate, Inc. (GCI) from 2020 to 2035:

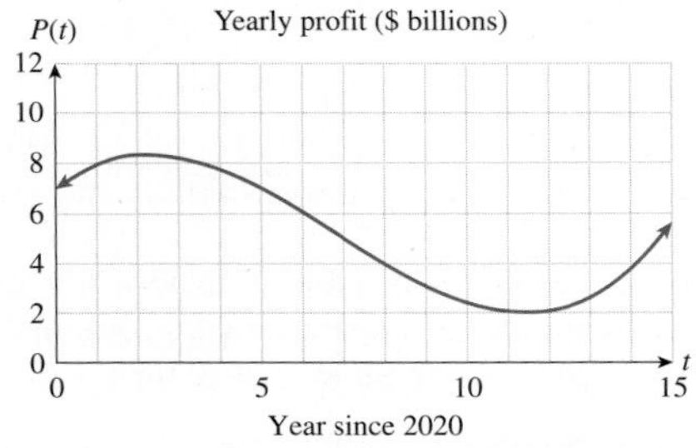

a. Approximately when were the profits rising most rapidly?
b. Approximately when were the profits falling most rapidly?
c. Approximately when could GCI's board of directors legitimately tell stockholders that they had "turned the company around"?

77. ▼ ***Education and Crime*** The following graph compares the total U.S. prison population and the average combined SAT score in the United States during the 1970s and 1980s:

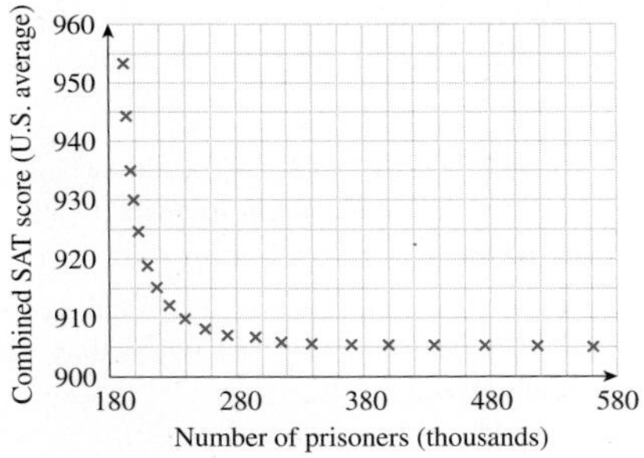

These data can be accurately modeled by

$$S(n) = 904 + \frac{1{,}326}{(n - 180)^{1.325}} \quad (192 \le n \le 563).$$

Here, $S(n)$ is the combined U.S. average SAT score at a time when the total U.S. prison population was n thousand.[40]

a. Are there any points of inflection on the graph of S?
b. What does the concavity of the graph of S tell you about prison populations and SAT scores?

78. ▼ ***Education and Crime*** Refer back to the model in the preceding exercise.

a. Are there any points of inflection on the graph of S'?
b. What does the concavity of the graph of S' tell you about prison populations and SAT scores?

79. ▼ ***Patents*** In 1965, the economist F. M. Scherer modeled the number, n, of patents produced by a firm as a function of the size, s, of the firm (measured in annual sales in millions of dollars). He came up with the following equation based on a study of 448 large firms:[41]

$$n = -3.79 + 144.42s - 23.86s^2 + 1.457s^3.$$

a. Find $\left.\dfrac{d^2n}{ds^2}\right|_{s=3}$. Is the rate at which patents are produced as the size of a firm goes up increasing or decreasing with size when $s = 3$? Comment on Scherer's words, "... we find diminishing returns dominating."
b. Find $\left.\dfrac{d^2n}{ds^2}\right|_{s=7}$ and interpret the answer.
c. Find the s-coordinate of any points of inflection and interpret the result.

80. ▼ ***Returns on Investments*** A company finds that the number of new products it develops per year depends on the size of its annual R&D budget, x (in thousands of dollars), according to the formula

$$n(x) = -1 + 8x + 2x^2 - 0.4x^3.$$

a. Find $n''(1)$ and $n''(3)$, and interpret the results.
b. Find the size of the budget that gives the largest rate of return as measured in new products per dollar (again, called the point of diminishing returns).

81. T ▼ ***Oil Imports from Mexico*** Daily oil production in Mexico and daily U.S. oil imports from Mexico during 2005–2009 can be approximated by

$$P(t) = 3.9 - 0.10t \text{ million barrels} \quad (5 \le t \le 9)$$
$$I(t) = 2.1 - 0.11t \text{ million barrels} \quad (5 \le t \le 9),$$

[40] Based on data for the years 1967–1989. Sources: *Sourcebook of Criminal Justice Statistics*, 1990, p. 604/Educational Testing Service.

[41] Source: F. M. Scherer, "Firm Size, Market Structure, Opportunity, and the Output of Patented Inventions," *American Economic Review* 55 (December 1965): pp. 1097–1125.

where t is time in years since the start of 2000.[42]

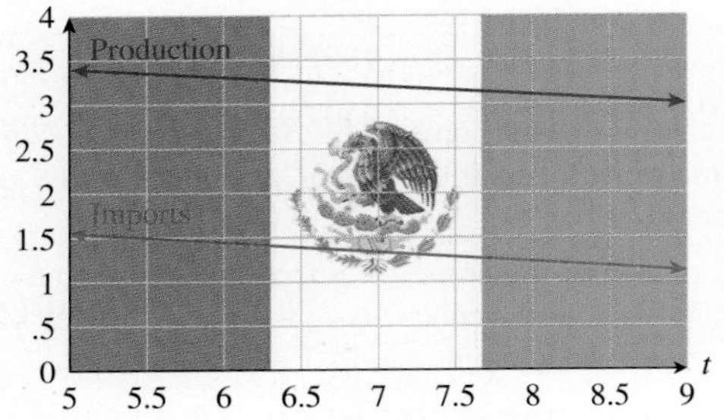

Graph the function $I(t)/P(t)$ and its derivative. Is the graph of $I(t)/P(t)$ concave up or concave down? The concavity of $I(t)/P(t)$ tells you that

(A) the percentage of oil produced in Mexico that was exported to the United States was decreasing.
(B) the percentage of oil produced in Mexico that was not exported to the United States was increasing.
(C) the percentage of oil produced in Mexico that was exported to the United States was decreasing at a slower rate.
(D) the percentage of oil produced in Mexico that was exported to the United States was decreasing at a faster rate.

82. T ▼ ***Oil Imports from Mexico*** Repeat Exercise 81 using instead the models for 2000–2004 shown below:

$$P(t) = 3.0 + 0.13t \text{ million barrels} \quad (0 \le t \le 4)$$
$$I(t) = 1.4 + 0.06t \text{ million barrels} \quad (0 \le t \le 4)$$

(t is time in years since the start of 2000).[43]

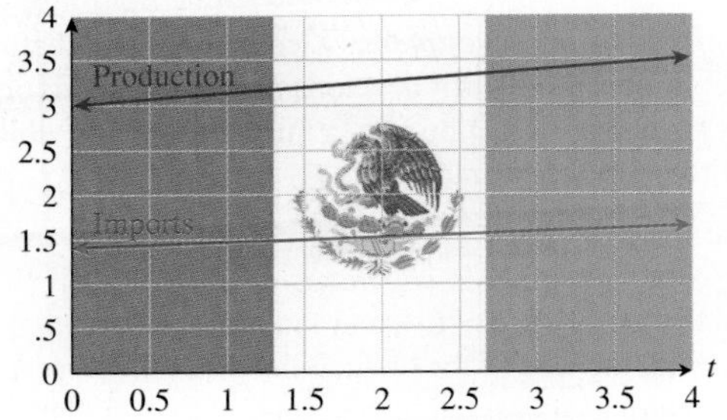

83. ◆ ***Logistic Models*** Let

$$f(x) = \frac{N}{1 + Ab^{-x}}$$

for constants N, A, and b (A and b positive and $b \neq 1$). Show that f has a single point of inflection at $x = \ln A/\ln b$.

[42] Source for data: Energy Information Administration/Pemex (www.eia.doe.gov).

[43] *Ibid.*

84. ◆ ***Logistic Models*** Let

$$f(x) = \frac{N}{1 + Ae^{-kx}}$$

for constants N, A, and k (A and k positive). Show that f has a single point of inflection at $x = \ln A/k$.

85. T ***Population: Puerto Rico*** The population of Puerto Rico in 1950–2025 can be approximated by

$$P(t) = \frac{4{,}500}{1 + 1.1466\,(1.0357)^{-t}} \text{ thousand people} \quad (0 \le t \le 75)$$

(t is the year since 1950).[44] Use the result of Exercise 83 to find the location of the point of inflection in the graph of P. What does the result tell you about the population of Puerto Rico?

86. T ***Population: Virgin Islands*** The population of the Virgin Islands in 1950–2025 can be approximated by

$$P(t) = \frac{110}{1 + 2.3596\,(1.0767)^{-t}} \text{ thousand people} \quad (0 \le t \le 75)$$

(t is the year since 1950).[45] Use the result of Exercise 83 to find the location of the point of inflection in the graph of P. What does the result tell you about the population of the Virgin Islands?

87. T ▼ ***Asset Appreciation*** You manage a small antique store that owns a collection of Louis XVI jewelry boxes. Their value v is increasing according to the formula

$$v = \frac{10{,}000}{1 + 500e^{-0.5t}},$$

where t is the number of years from now. You anticipate an inflation rate of 5% per year, so that the present value of an item that will be worth \$$v$ in t years' time is given by

$$p = v \cdot (1.05)^{-t}.$$

What is the greatest rate of increase of the value of your antiques, and when is this rate attained?

88. T ▼ ***Harvesting Forests*** The following equation models the approximate volume in cubic feet of a typical Douglas fir tree of age t years[46]:

$$V = \frac{22{,}514}{1 + 22{,}514t^{-2.55}}.$$

The lumber will be sold at \$10 per cubic foot, and you do not expect the price of lumber to appreciate in the foreseeable

[44] Figures from 2010 on are U.S. census projections. Source for data: The 2008 Statistical Abstract (www.census.gov/).

[45] *Ibid.*

[46] The model is the authors', and is based on data in *Environmental and Natural Resource Economics* by Tom Tietenberg, third edition (New York: HarperCollins, 1992), p. 282.

future. On the other hand, you anticipate a general inflation rate of 5% per year, so that the present value of an item that will be worth v in t years time is given by

$$p = v \cdot (1.05)^{-t}.$$

What is the largest rate of increase of the value of a fir tree, and when is this rate attained?

89. ⊡ ▽ *Asset Appreciation* As the financial consultant to a classic auto dealership, you estimate that the total value of its collection of 1959 Chevrolets and Fords is given by the formula

$$v = 300,000 + 1,000t^2,$$

where t is the number of years from now. You anticipate a continuous inflation rate of 5% per year, so that the discounted (present) value of an item that will be worth v in t years' time is given by

$$p = ve^{-0.05t}.$$

When is the value of the collection of classic cars increasing most rapidly? When is it decreasing most rapidly?

90. ⊡ ▽ *Plantation Management* The value of a fir tree in your plantation increases with the age of the tree according to the formula

$$v = \frac{20t}{1 + 0.05t},$$

where t is the age of the tree in years. Given a continuous inflation rate of 5% per year, the discounted (present) value of a newly planted seedling is

$$p = ve^{-0.05t}.$$

When is the discounted value of a tree increasing most rapidly? Decreasing most rapidly?

COMMUNICATION AND REASONING EXERCISES

91. Complete the following: If the graph of a function is concave up on its entire domain, then its second derivative is _____ on the domain.

92. Complete the following: If the graph of a function is concave up on its entire domain, then its first derivative is _____ on the domain.

93. Daily sales of *Kent's Tents* reached a maximum in January 2002 and declined to a minimum in January 2003 before starting to climb again. The graph of daily sales shows a point of inflection at June 2002. What is the significance of the point of inflection?

94. The graph of daily sales of *Luddington's Wellington* boots is concave down, although sales continue to increase. What properties of the graph of daily sales versus time are reflected in the following behaviors?

a. a point of inflection next year
b. a horizontal asymptote

95. ▽ Company A's profits satisfy $P(0) = \$1$ million, $P'(0) = \$1$ million per year, and $P''(0) = -\$1$ million per year per year. Company B's profits satisfy $P(0) = \$1$ million, $P'(0) = -\$1$ million per year, and $P''(0) = \$1$ million per year per year. There are no points of inflection in either company's profit curve. Sketch two pairs of profit curves: one in which Company A ultimately outperforms Company B and another in which Company B ultimately outperforms Company A.

96. ▽ Company C's profits satisfy $P(0) = \$1$ million, $P'(0) = \$1$ million per year, and $P''(0) = -\$1$ million per year per year. Company D's profits satisfy $P(0) = \$0$ million, $P'(0) = \$0$ million per year, and $P''(0) = \$1$ million per year per year. There are no points of inflection in either company's profit curve. Sketch two pairs of profit curves: one in which Company C ultimately outperforms Company D and another in which Company D ultimately outperforms Company C.

97. ▽ Explain geometrically why the derivative of a function has a relative extremum at a point of inflection, if it is defined there. Which points of inflection give rise to relative maxima in the derivative?

98. ▽ If we regard position, s, as a function of time, t, what is the significance of the *third* derivative, $s'''(t)$? Describe an everyday scenario in which this arises.

5.4 Analyzing Graphs

Mathematical curves are beautiful—their subtle form can be imitated by only the best of artists—and calculus gives us the tools we need to probe their secrets. While it is easy to use graphing technology to draw a graph, we must use calculus to understand what we are seeing. Following is a list of some of the most interesting features of the graph of a function.

Features of a Graph

1. ***The x- and y-intercepts:*** If $y = f(x)$, find the x-intercept(s) by setting $y = 0$ and solving for x; find the y-intercept by setting $x = 0$ and solving for y:

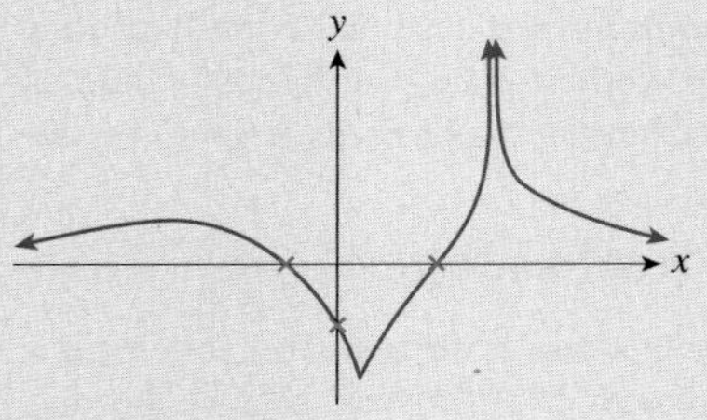

2. ***Extrema:*** Use the techniques of Section 5.1 to locate the maxima and minima:

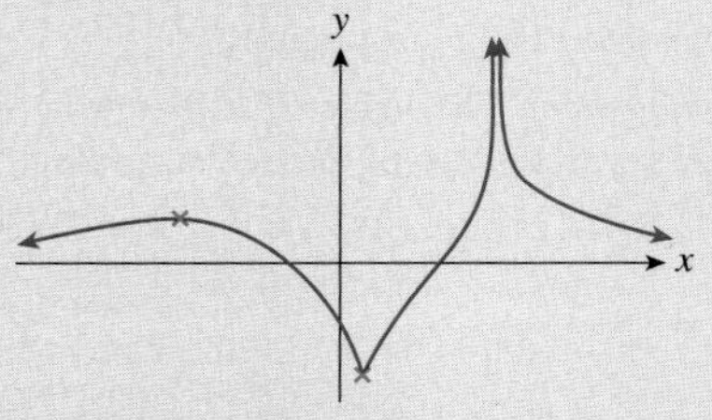

3. ***Points of inflection:*** Use the techniques of Section 5.2 to locate the points of inflection:

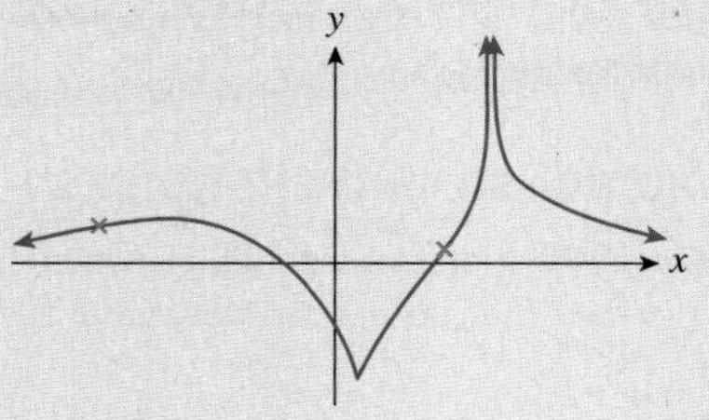

4. ***Behavior near points where the function is not defined:*** If $f(x)$ is not defined at $x = a$, consider $\lim_{x \to a^-} f(x)$ and $\lim_{x \to a^+} f(x)$ to see how the graph of f behaves as x approaches a:

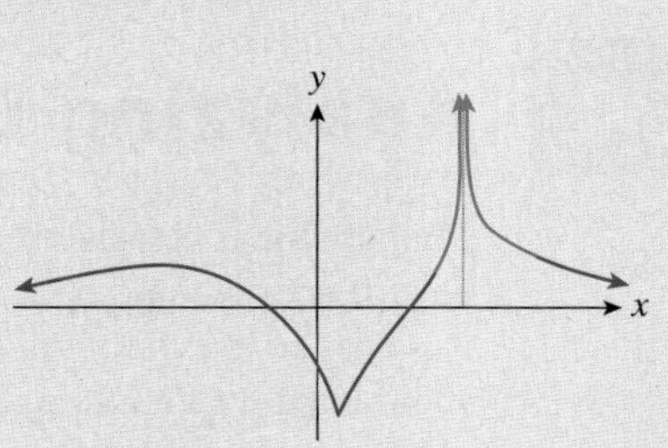

5. ***Behavior at infinity:*** Consider $\lim_{x\to-\infty} f(x)$ and $\lim_{x\to+\infty} f(x)$ if appropriate, to see how the graph of f behaves far to the left and right:

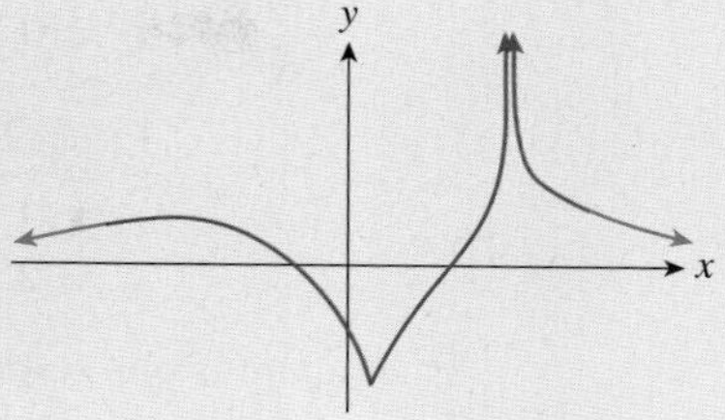

Note It is sometimes difficult or impossible to solve all of the equations that come up in Steps 1, 2, and 3 of the previous analysis. As a consequence, we might not be able to say exactly where the x-intercept, extrema, or points of inflection are. When this happens, we will use graphing technology to assist us in determining accurate numerical approximations. ■

EXAMPLE 1 Analyzing a Graph

Analyze the graph of $f(x) = \dfrac{1}{x} - \dfrac{1}{x^2}$.

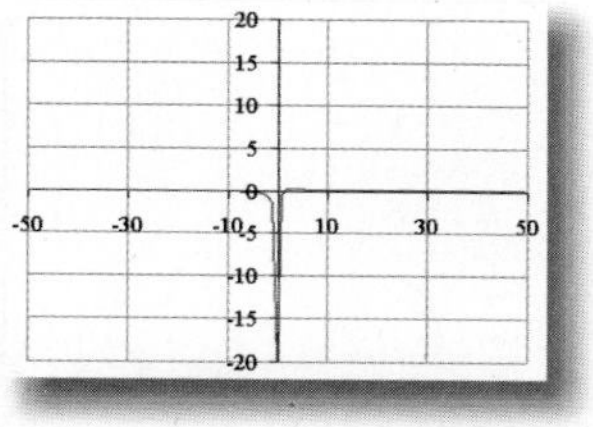

$-50 \le x \le 50, -20 \le y \le 20$

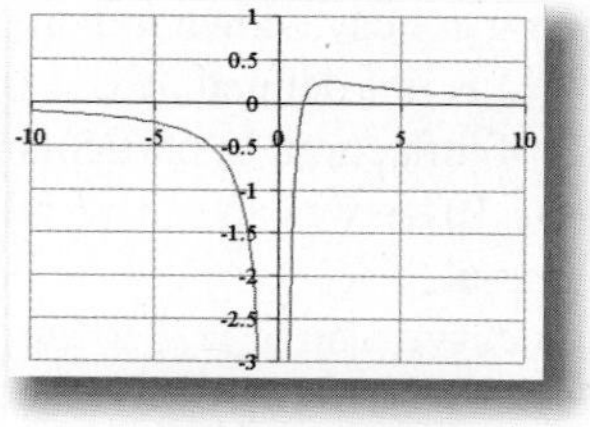

$-10 \le x \le 10, -3 \le y \le 1$

Figure 35

Solution The graph, as drawn using graphing technology, is shown in Figure 35, using two different viewing windows. (Note that $x = 0$ is not in the domain of f.) The second window in Figure 35 seems to show the features of the graph better than the first. Does the second viewing window include *all* the interesting features of the graph? Or are there perhaps some interesting features to the right of $x = 10$ or to the left of $x = -10$? Also, where exactly do features like maxima, minima, and points of inflection occur? In our five-step process of analyzing the interesting features of the graph, we will be able to sketch the curve by hand, and also answer these questions.

1. ***The x- and y-intercepts:*** We consider $y = \dfrac{1}{x} - \dfrac{1}{x^2}$. To find the x-intercept(s), we set $y = 0$ and solve for x:

$$0 = \frac{1}{x} - \frac{1}{x^2}$$
$$\frac{1}{x} = \frac{1}{x^2}.$$

Multiplying both sides by x^2 (we know that x cannot be zero, so we are not multiplying both sides by 0) gives

$$x = 1.$$

Thus, there is one x-intercept (which we can see in Figure 35) at $x = 1$.

For the y-intercept, we would substitute $x = 0$ and solve for y. However, we cannot substitute $x = 0$; because $f(0)$ is not defined, the graph does not meet the y-axis.

We add features to our freehand sketch as we go. Figure 36 shows what we have so far.

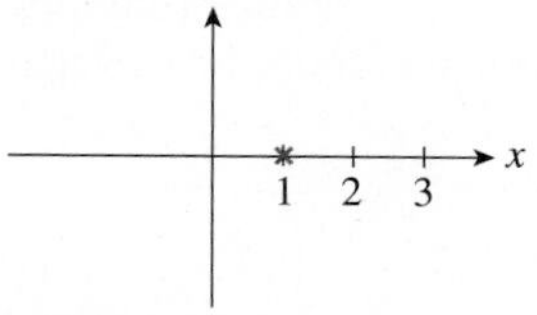

Figure 36

2. ***Relative extrema:*** We calculate $f'(x) = -\frac{1}{x^2} + \frac{2}{x^3}$. To find any stationary points, we set the derivative equal to 0 and solve for x:

$$-\frac{1}{x^2} + \frac{2}{x^3} = 0$$
$$\frac{1}{x^2} = \frac{2}{x^3}$$
$$x = 2.$$

Thus, there is one stationary point, at $x = 2$. We can use a test point to the right to determine that this stationary point is a relative maximum:

x	1 (Intercept)	2	3 (Test point)
$y = \frac{1}{x} - \frac{1}{x^2}$	0	$\frac{1}{4}$	$\frac{2}{9}$

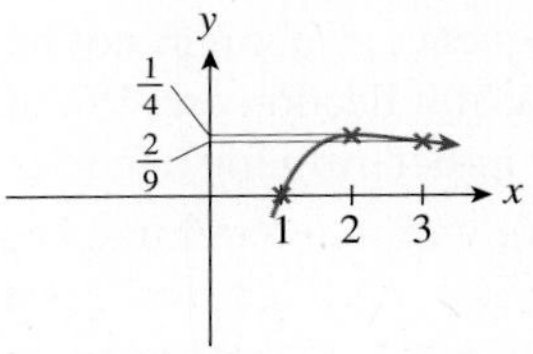

Figure 37

The only possible singular point is at $x = 0$ because $f'(0)$ is not defined. However, $f(0)$ is not defined either, so there are no singular points. Figure 37 shows our graph so far.

3. ***Points of inflection:*** We calculate $f''(x) = \frac{2}{x^3} - \frac{6}{x^4}$. To find points of inflection, we set the second derivative equal to 0 and solve for x:

$$\frac{2}{x^3} - \frac{6}{x^4} = 0$$
$$\frac{2}{x^3} = \frac{6}{x^4}$$
$$2x = 6$$
$$x = 3.$$

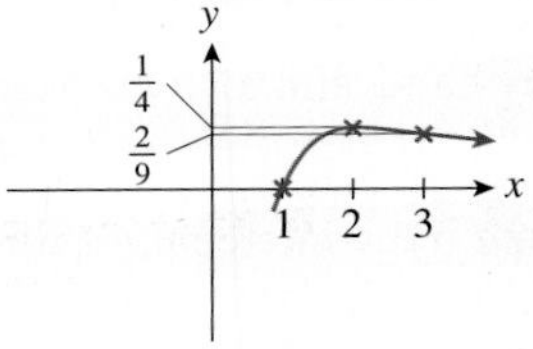

Figure 38

Figure 35 confirms that the graph of f changes from being concave down to being concave up at $x = 3$, so this is a point of inflection. $f''(x)$ is not defined at $x = 0$, but that is not in the domain, so there are no other points of inflection. In particular, the graph must be concave down in the whole region $(-\infty, 0)$, as we can see by calculating the second derivative at any one point in that interval: $f''(-1) = -8 < 0$.

Figure 38 shows our graph so far (we extended the curve near $x = 3$ to suggest a point of inflection at $x = 3$).

4. ***Behavior near points where f is not defined:*** The only point where $f(x)$ is not defined is $x = 0$. From the graph, $f(x)$ appears to go to $-\infty$ as x approaches 0 from either side. To calculate these limits, we rewrite $f(x)$:

$$f(x) = \frac{1}{x} - \frac{1}{x^2} = \frac{x-1}{x^2}.$$

Now, if x is close to 0 (on either side), the numerator $x - 1$ is close to -1 and the denominator is a very small but positive number. The quotient is therefore a negative number of very large magnitude. Therefore,

$$\lim_{x\to 0^-} f(x) = -\infty$$

and

$$\lim_{x\to 0^+} f(x) = -\infty.$$

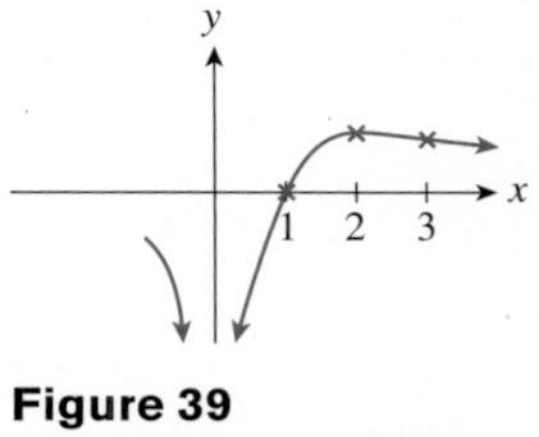

Figure 39

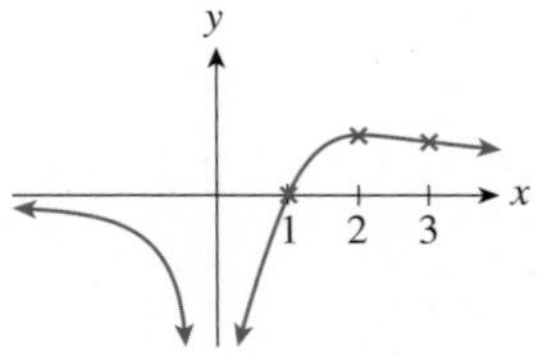

Figure 40

From these limits, we see the following:

(1) Immediately to the *left* of $x = 0$, the graph plunges down toward $-\infty$.

(2) Immediately to the *right* of $x = 0$, the graph also plunges down toward $-\infty$.

Figure 39 shows our graph with these features added. We say that f has a **vertical asymptote** at $x = 0$, meaning that the points on the graph of f get closer and closer to points on a vertical line (the y-axis in this case) further and further from the origin.

5. ***Behavior at infinity:*** Both $1/x$ and $1/x^2$ go to 0 as x goes to $-\infty$ or $+\infty$; that is,

$$\lim_{x \to -\infty} f(x) = 0$$

and

$$\lim_{x \to +\infty} f(x) = 0.$$

Thus, on the extreme left and right of our picture, the height of the curve levels off toward zero. Figure 40 shows the completed freehand sketch of the graph.

We say that f has a **horizontal asymptote** at $y = 0$. (Notice another thing: We haven't plotted a single point to the left of the y-axis, and yet we have a pretty good idea of what the curve looks like there! Compare the technology-drawn curve in Figure 35.)

In summary, there is one x-intercept at $x = 1$; there is one relative maximum (which, we can now see, is also an absolute maximum) at $x = 2$; there is one point of inflection at $x = 3$, where the graph changes from being concave down to concave up. There is a vertical asymptote at $x = 0$, on both sides of which the graph goes down toward $-\infty$, and a horizontal asymptote at $y = 0$.

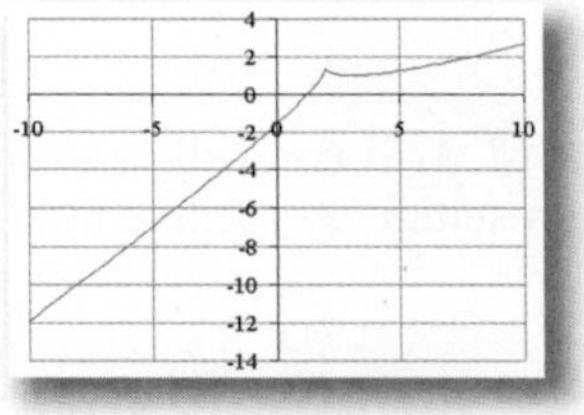

Technology:
`2*x/3-((x-2)^2)^(1/3)`

Figure 41

EXAMPLE 2 Analyzing a Graph

Analyze the graph of $f(x) = \dfrac{2x}{3} - (x-2)^{2/3}$.

Solution Figure 41 shows a technology-generated version of the graph. Note that in the technology formulation $(x-2)^{2/3}$ is written as $[(x-2)^2]^{1/3}$ to avoid problems with some graphing calculators and Excel.

Let us now re-create this graph by hand, and in the process identify the features we see in Figure 41.

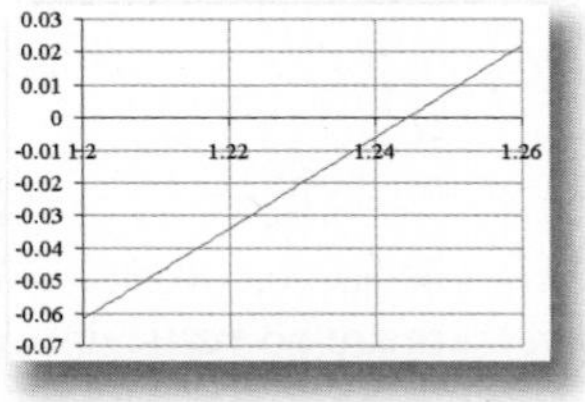

Figure 42

1. ***The x- and y-intercepts:*** We consider $y = \dfrac{2x}{3} - (x-2)^{2/3}$. For the y-intercept, we set $x = 0$ and solve for y:

$$y = \frac{2(0)}{3} - (0-2)^{2/3} = -2^{2/3} \approx -1.59.$$

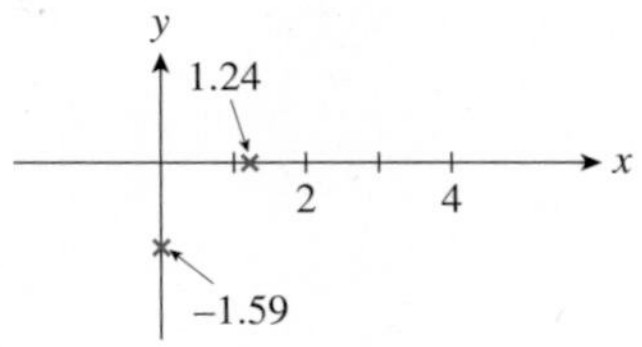

Figure 43

To find the x-intercept(s), we set $y = 0$ and solve for x. However, if we attempt this, we will find ourselves with a cubic equation that is hard to solve. (Try it!) Following the advice in the note on page 417, we use graphing technology to locate the x-intercept we see in Figure 41 by zooming in (Figure 42). From Figure 42, we find $x \approx 1.24$. We shall see in the discussion to follow that there can be no other x-intercepts.

Figure 43 shows our freehand sketch so far.

2. *Relative extrema:* We calculate

$$f'(x) = \frac{2}{3} - \frac{2}{3}(x-2)^{-1/3}$$
$$= \frac{2}{3} - \frac{2}{3(x-2)^{1/3}}.$$

To find any stationary points, we set the derivative equal to 0 and solve for x:

$$\frac{2}{3} - \frac{2}{3(x-2)^{1/3}} = 0$$
$$(x-2)^{1/3} = 1$$
$$x - 2 = 1^3 = 1$$
$$x = 3.$$

To check for singular points, look for points where $f(x)$ is defined and $f'(x)$ is not defined. The only such point is $x = 2$: $f'(x)$ is not defined at $x = 2$, whereas $f(x)$ is defined there, so we have a singular point at $x = 2$.

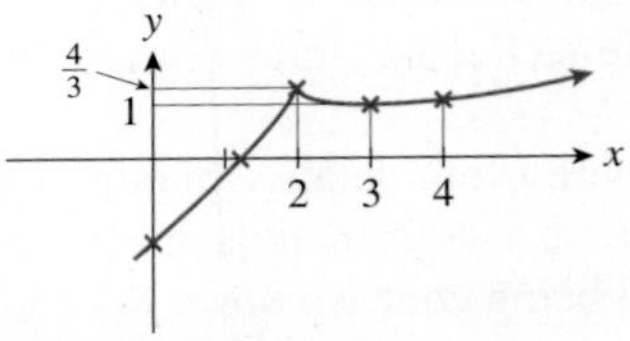

Figure 44

x	2 (Singular point)	3 (Stationary point)	4 (Test point)
$y = \frac{2x}{3} - (x-2)^{2/3}$	$\frac{4}{3}$	1	1.079

Figure 44 shows our graph so far.

We see that there is a singular relative maximum at (2, 4/3) (we will confirm that the graph eventually gets higher on the right) and a stationary relative minimum at $x = 3$.

3. *Points of inflection:* We calculate

$$f''(x) = \frac{2}{9(x-2)^{4/3}}.$$

To find points of inflection, we set the second derivative equal to 0 and solve for x. But the equation

$$0 = \frac{2}{9(x-2)^{4/3}}$$

has no solution for x, so there are no points of inflection on the graph.

4. *Behavior near points where f is not defined:* Because $f(x)$ is defined everywhere, there are no such points to consider. In particular, there are no vertical asymptotes.

5. *Behavior at infinity:* We estimate the following limits numerically:

$$\lim_{x\to-\infty}\left[\frac{2x}{3} - (x-2)^{2/3}\right] = -\infty$$

and

$$\lim_{x\to+\infty}\left[\frac{2x}{3} - (x-2)^{2/3}\right] = +\infty.$$

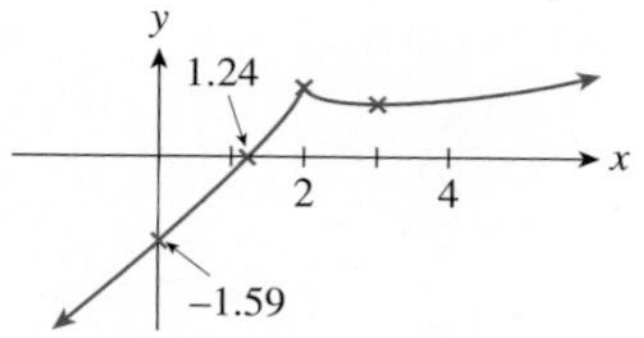

Figure 45

Thus, on the extreme left the curve goes down toward $-\infty$, and on the extreme right the curve rises toward $+\infty$. In particular, there are no horizontal asymptotes. (There can also be no other x-intercepts.)

Figure 45 shows the completed graph.

5.4 EXERCISES

▼ more advanced ◆ challenging

T indicates exercises that should be solved using technology

In Exercises 1–26, sketch the graph of the given function, indicating (a) x- and y-intercepts, (b) extrema, (c) points of inflection, (d) behavior near points where the function is not defined, and (e) behavior at infinity. Where indicated, technology should be used to approximate the intercepts, coordinates of extrema, and/or points of inflection to one decimal place. Check your sketch using technology. HINT [See Example 1.]

1. $f(x) = x^2 + 2x + 1$
2. $f(x) = -x^2 - 2x - 1$
3. $g(x) = x^3 - 12x$, domain $[-4, 4]$
4. $g(x) = 2x^3 - 6x$, domain $[-4, 4]$
5. $h(x) = 2x^3 - 3x^2 - 36x$ [Use technology for x-intercepts.]
6. $h(x) = -2x^3 - 3x^2 + 36x$ [Use technology for x-intercepts.]
7. $f(x) = 2x^3 + 3x^2 - 12x + 1$ [Use technology for x-intercepts.]
8. $f(x) = 4x^3 + 3x^2 + 2$ [Use technology for x-intercepts.]
9. $k(x) = -3x^4 + 4x^3 + 36x^2 + 10$ [Use technology for x-intercepts.]
10. $k(x) = 3x^4 + 4x^3 - 36x^2 - 10$ [Use technology for x-intercepts.]
11. $g(t) = \frac{1}{4}t^4 - \frac{2}{3}t^3 + \frac{1}{2}t^2$
12. $g(t) = 3t^4 - 16t^3 + 24t^2 + 1$
13. $f(x) = x + \frac{1}{x}$
14. $f(x) = x^2 + \frac{1}{x^2}$
15. $g(x) = x^3/(x^2 + 3)$
16. $g(x) = x^3/(x^2 - 3)$
17. $f(t) = \frac{t^2 + 1}{t^2 - 1}$, domain $[-2, 2]$, $t \neq \pm 1$
18. $f(t) = \frac{t^2 - 1}{t^2 + 1}$, domain $[-2, 2]$
19. $k(x) = \frac{2x}{3} + (x + 1)^{2/3}$ [Use technology for x-intercepts. HINT [See Example 2.]
20. $k(x) = \frac{2x}{5} - (x - 1)^{2/5}$ [Use technology for x-intercepts. HINT [See Example 2.]
21. $f(x) = x - \ln x$, domain $(0, +\infty)$
22. $f(x) = x - \ln x^2$, domain $(0, +\infty)$
23. $f(x) = x^2 + \ln x^2$ [Use technology for x-intercepts.]
24. $f(x) = 2x^2 + \ln x$ [Use technology for x-intercepts.]
25. $g(t) = e^t - t$, domain $[-1, 1]$
26. $g(t) = e^{-t^2}$

T *In Exercises 27–30, use technology to sketch the graph of the given function, labeling all relative and absolute extrema and points of inflection, and vertical and horizontal asymptotes. The coordinates of the extrema and points of inflection should be accurate to two decimal places.* HINT [To locate extrema accurately, plot the first derivative; to locate points of inflection accurately, plot the second derivative.]

27. ▼ $f(x) = x^4 - 2x^3 + x^2 - 2x + 1$
28. ▼ $f(x) = x^4 + x^3 + x^2 + x + 1$
29. ▼ $f(x) = e^x - x^3$
30. ▼ $f(x) = e^x - \frac{x^4}{4}$

APPLICATIONS

31. ***Home Prices*** The following graph approximates historical and projected median home prices in the United States for the period 2000–2020:[47]

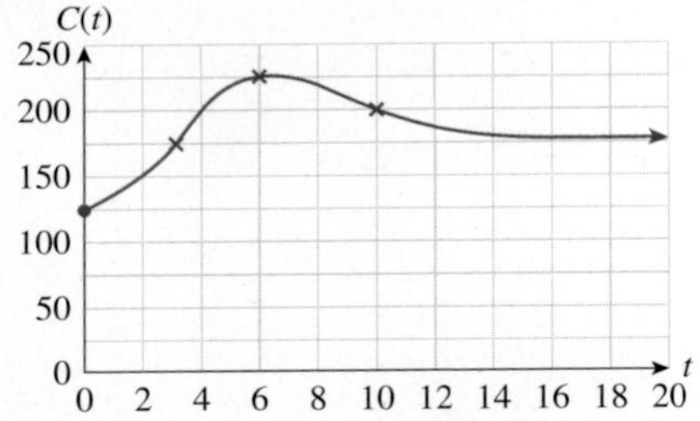

Here, t is time in years since the start of 2000 and $C(t)$ is the median home price in thousands of dollars. The locations of extrema and points of inflection are indicated on the graph. Analyze the graph's important features and interpret each feature in terms of the median home price.

32. ***Housing Starts*** The following graph approximates historical and projected numbers of housing starts of single-family homes each year in the United States for the period 2000–2020:[48]

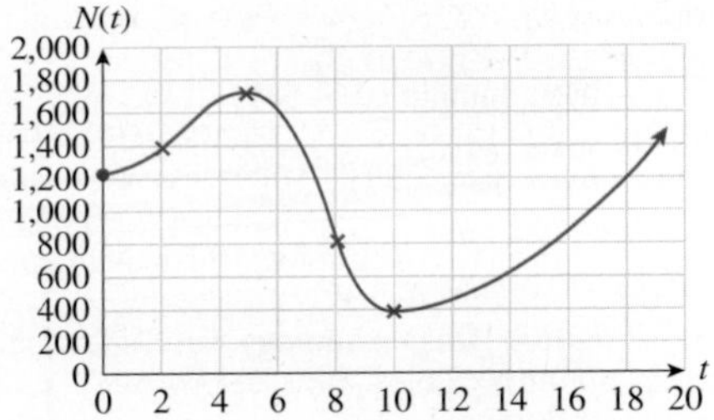

Here, t is time in years since 2000 and $N(t)$ is the number, in thousands, of housing starts per year. The locations of extrema and points of inflection are indicated on the graph. Analyze the graph's important features and interpret each feature in terms of the number of housing starts.

33. ***Consumer Price Index*** The following graph shows the approximate value of the U.S. Consumer Price Index (CPI) from July 2005 through March 2006.[49]

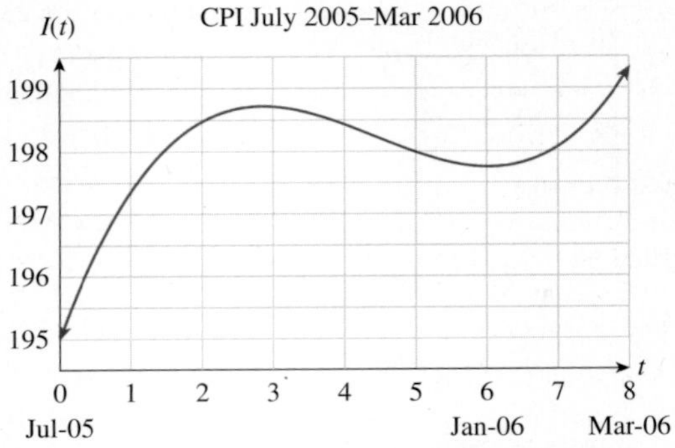

The approximating curve shown on the figure is given by

$$I(t) = 0.06t^3 - 0.8t^2 + 3.1t + 195 \quad (0 \le t \le 8),$$

where t is time in months ($t = 0$ represents July 2005).

a. Locate the intercepts, extrema, and points of inflection of the curve and interpret each feature in terms of the CPI. (Approximate all coordinates to one decimal place.) HINT [See Example 1.]

b. Recall from Section 5.2 that the inflation rate is defined to be $\dfrac{I'(t)}{I(t)}$. What do the stationary extrema of the curve shown above tell you about the inflation rate?

34. ***Consumer Price Index*** The following graph shows the approximate value of the U.S. Consumer Price Index (CPI) from March 2006 through May 2007.[50]

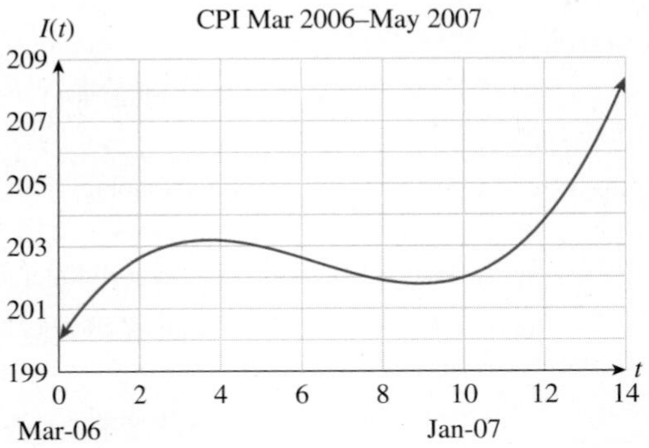

The approximating curve shown on the figure is given by

$$I(t) = 0.02t^3 - 0.38t^2 + 2t + 200 \quad (0 \le t \le 14),$$

where t is time in months ($t = 0$ represents March, 2006).

a. Locate the intercepts, extrema, and points of inflection of the curve and interpret each feature in terms of the CPI. (Approximate all coordinates to one decimal place.) HINT [See Example 1.]

[47] Values from 2012 on are authors' projections. Source for data through 2011: Zillow (www.zillow.com).

[48] Values from 2011 on are authors' projections. Source for data through 2010: U.S. Census Bureau (www.census.gov).

[49] The CPI is compiled by the Bureau of Labor Statistics and is based upon a 1982 value of 100. For instance, a CPI of 200 means the CPI has doubled since 1982. Source: InflationData.com. (www.inflationdata.com).

[50] *Ibid.*

b. Recall from Section 5.2 that the inflation rate is defined to be $\frac{I'(t)}{I(t)}$. What do the stationary extrema of the curve shown above tell you about the inflation rate?

35. ***Motion in a Straight Line*** The distance of a UFO from an observer is given by $s = 2t^3 - 3t^2 + 100$ feet after t seconds ($t \geq 0$). Obtain the extrema, points of inflection, and behavior at infinity. Sketch the curve and interpret these features in terms of the movement of the UFO.

36. ***Motion in a Straight Line*** The distance of the Mars orbiter from your location in Utarek, Mars is given by $s = 2(t-1)^3 - 3(t-1)^2 + 100$ km after t seconds ($t \geq 0$). Obtain the extrema, points of inflection, and behavior at infinity. Sketch the curve and interpret these features in terms of the movement of the Mars orbiter.

37. ***Average Cost: iPods*** Assume that it costs Apple approximately

$$C(x) = 22{,}500 + 100x + 0.01x^2$$

dollars to manufacture x 32 GB iPods in a day.[51] Obtain the average cost function, sketch its graph, and analyze the graph's important features. Interpret each feature in terms of iPods. HINT [Recall that the average cost function is $\bar{C}(x) = C(x)/x$.]

38. ***Average Cost: Xboxes*** Assume that it costs Microsoft approximately

$$C(x) = 14{,}400 + 550x + 0.01x^2$$

dollars to manufacture x Xbox 360s in a day.[52] Obtain the average cost function, sketch its graph, and analyze the graph's important features. Interpret each feature in terms of Xboxes. HINT [Recall that the average cost function is $\bar{C}(x) = C(x)/x$.]

39. T ▼ ***Subprime Mortgages during the Housing Bubble*** During the real estate run-up in 2000–2008, the percentage of mortgages issued in the United States that were subprime (normally classified as risky) could be approximated by

$$A(t) = \frac{15.0}{1 + 8.6(1.8)^{-t}} \text{ percent} \qquad (0 \leq t \leq 8)$$

t years after the start of 2000.[53] Graph the *derivative* $A'(t)$ of $A(t)$ using an extended domain of $0 \leq t \leq 15$. Determine the approximate coordinates of the maximum and determine the behavior of $A'(t)$ at infinity. What do the answers tell you?

40. T ▼ ***Subprime Mortgage Debt during the Housing Bubble*** During the real estate run-up in 2000–2008, the value of subprime (normally classified as risky) mortgage debt outstanding in the United States was approximately

$$A(t) = \frac{1{,}350}{1 + 4.2(1.7)^{-t}} \text{ billion dollars} \qquad (0 \leq t \leq 8)$$

t years after the start of 2000.[54] Graph the *derivative* $A'(t)$ of $A(t)$ using an extended domain of $0 \leq t \leq 15$. Determine the approximate coordinates of the maximum and determine the behavior of $A'(t)$ at infinity. What do the answers tell you?

COMMUNICATION AND REASONING EXERCISES

41. A function is *bounded* if its entire graph lies between two horizontal lines. Can a bounded function have vertical asymptotes? Can a bounded function have horizontal asymptotes? Explain.

42. A function is *bounded above* if its entire graph lies below some horizontal line. Can a bounded above function have vertical asymptotes? Can a bounded above function have horizontal asymptotes? Explain.

43. If the graph of a function has a vertical asymptote at $x = a$ in such a way that y increases to $+\infty$ as $x \to a$, what can you say about the graph of its derivative? Explain.

44. If the graph of a function has a horizontal asymptote at $y = a$ in such a way that y decreases to a as $x \to +\infty$, what can you say about the graph of its derivative? Explain.

45. Your friend tells you that he has found a continuous function defined on $(-\infty, +\infty)$ with exactly two critical points, each of which is a relative maximum. Can he be right?

46. Your other friend tells you that she has found a continuous function with two critical points, one a relative minimum and one a relative maximum, and no point of inflection between them. Can she be right?

47. ▼ By thinking about extrema, show that, if $f(x)$ is a polynomial, then between every pair of zeros (x-intercepts) of $f(x)$ there is a zero of $f'(x)$.

48. ▼ If $f(x)$ is a polynomial of degree 2 or higher, show that between every pair of relative extrema of $f(x)$ there is a point of inflection of $f(x)$.

---

[51] Not the actual cost equation; the authors do not know Apple's actual cost equation. The marginal cost in the model given is in rough agreement with the actual marginal cost for reasonable values of x for one of the 2007 models. Source for cost data: *Manufacturing & Technology News,* July 31, 2007 Volume 14, No. 14 (www.manufacturingnews.com).

[52] Not the actual cost equation; the authors do not know Microsoft's actual cost equation. The marginal cost in the model given is in rough agreement with the actual marginal cost for reasonable values of x. Source for estimate of marginal cost: iSuppli: (www.isuppli.com/news/xbox/).

[53] 2009 figure is an estimate. Sources: Mortgage Bankers Association, UBS.

[54] 2008–2009 figure are estimates. Source: www.data360.org/dataset.aspx?Data_Set_Id=9549.

5.5 Related Rates

We start by recalling some basic facts about the rate of change of a quantity:

Rate of Change of Q

If Q is a quantity changing over time t, then the derivative dQ/dt is the rate at which Q changes over time.

Quick Examples

1. If A is the area of an expanding circle, then dA/dt is the rate at which the area is increasing.
2. *Words:* The radius r of a sphere is currently 3 cm and increasing at a rate of 2 cm/sec.

   Symbols: $r = 3$ cm and $dr/dt = 2$ cm/sec.

In this section we are concerned with what are called **related rates** problems. In such a problem we have two (sometimes more) related quantities, we know the rate at which one is changing, and we wish to find the rate at which another is changing. A typical example is the following.

EXAMPLE 1 The Expanding Circle

The radius of a circle is increasing at a rate of 10 cm/sec. How fast is the area increasing at the instant when the radius has reached 5 cm?

Solution We have two related quantities: the radius of the circle, r, and its area, A. The first sentence of the problem tells us that r is increasing at a certain rate. When we see a sentence referring to speed or change, it is very helpful to rephrase the sentence using the phrase "the rate of change of." Here, we can say

The rate of change of r is 10 cm/sec.

Because the rate of change is the derivative, we can rewrite this sentence as the equation

$$\frac{dr}{dt} = 10.$$

Similarly, the second sentence of the problem asks how A is changing. We can rewrite that question:

What is the rate of change of A when the radius is 5 cm?

Using mathematical notation, the question is:

$$\text{What is } \frac{dA}{dt} \text{ when } r = 5?$$

Thus, knowing one rate of change, dr/dt, we wish to find a related rate of change, dA/dt. To find exactly how these derivatives are related, we need the equation relating the variables, which is

$$A = \pi r^2.$$

To find the relationship between the derivatives, we take the derivative of both sides of this equation *with respect to t*. On the left we get dA/dt. On the right we need to remember that r is a function of t and use the chain rule. We get

$$\frac{dA}{dt} = 2\pi r \frac{dr}{dt}.$$

Now we substitute the given values $r = 5$ and $dr/dt = 10$. This gives

$$\left.\frac{dA}{dt}\right|_{r=5} = 2\pi(5)(10) = 100\pi \approx 314 \text{ cm}^2/\text{sec}.$$

Thus, the area is increasing at the rate of 314 cm^2/sec when the radius is 5 cm.

We can organize our work as follows:

Solving a Related Rates Problem

A. The Problem

1. List the related, changing quantities.
2. Restate the problem in terms of rates of change. Rewrite the problem using mathematical notation for the changing quantities and their derivatives.

B. The Relationship

1. Draw a diagram, if appropriate, showing the changing quantities.
2. Find an equation or equations relating the changing quantities.
3. Take the derivative with respect to time of the equation(s) relating the quantities to get the **derived equation(s)**, which relate the rates of change of the quantities.

C. The Solution

1. Substitute into the derived equation(s) the given values of the quantities and their derivatives.
2. Solve for the derivative required.

We can illustrate the procedure with the "ladder problem" found in almost every calculus textbook.

EXAMPLE 2 The Falling Ladder

Jane is at the top of a 5-foot ladder when it starts to slide down the wall at a rate of 3 feet per minute. Jack is standing on the ground behind her. How fast is the base of the ladder moving when it hits him if Jane is 4 feet from the ground at that instant?

Solution The first sentence talks about (the top of) the ladder sliding down the wall. Thus, one of the changing quantities is the height of the top of the ladder. The question asked refers to the motion of the base of the ladder, so another changing quantity is the distance of the base of the ladder from the wall. Let's record these variables and follow the outline above to obtain the solution.

A. The Problem

1. The changing quantities are

$h =$ height of the top of the ladder
$b =$ distance of the base of the ladder from the wall

2. We rephrase the problem in words, using the phrase "rate of change":

The rate of change of the height of the top of the ladder is -3 *feet per minute. What is the rate of change of the distance of the base from the wall when the top of the ladder is* 4 *feet from the ground?*

We can now rewrite the problem mathematically:

$$\frac{dh}{dt} = -3. \text{ Find } \frac{db}{dt} \text{ when } h = 4.$$

Figure 46

B. The Relationship

1. Figure 46 shows the ladder and the variables h and b. Notice that we put in the figure the fixed length, 5, of the ladder, but any changing quantities, like h and b, we leave as variables. We shall not use any specific values for h or b until the very end.

2. From the figure, we can see that h and b are related by the Pythagorean theorem:

$$h^2 + b^2 = 25.$$

3. Taking the derivative with respect to time of the equation above gives us the derived equation:

$$2h\frac{dh}{dt} + 2b\frac{db}{dt} = 0.$$

C. The Solution

1. We substitute the known values $dh/dt = -3$ and $h = 4$ into the derived equation:

$$2(4)(-3) + 2b\frac{db}{dt} = 0.$$

We would like to solve for db/dt, but first we need the value of b, which we can determine from the equation $h^2 + b^2 = 25$, using the value $h = 4$:

$$\begin{aligned} 16 + b^2 &= 25 \\ b^2 &= 9 \\ b &= 3. \end{aligned}$$

Substituting into the derived equation, we get

$$-24 + 2(3)\frac{db}{dt} = 0.$$

2. Solving for db/dt gives

$$\frac{db}{dt} = \frac{24}{6} = 4.$$

Thus, the base of the ladder is sliding away from the wall at 4 ft/min when it hits Jack.

EXAMPLE 3 Average Cost

The cost to manufacture x cellphones in a day is

$$C(x) = 10{,}000 + 20x + \frac{x^2}{10{,}000} \text{ dollars.}$$

The daily production level is currently $x = 5{,}000$ cellphones and is increasing at a rate of 100 units per day. How fast is the average cost changing?

Solution

A. The Problem

1. The changing quantities are the production level x and the average cost, $\bar{C}$.

2. We rephrase the problem as follows:

The daily production level is $x = 5{,}000$ *units and the rate of change of* x *is* 100 *units/day. What is the rate of change of the average cost,* $\bar{C}$*?*

In mathematical notation,

$$x = 5{,}000 \text{ and } \frac{dx}{dt} = 100. \text{ Find } \frac{d\bar{C}}{dt}.$$

B. The Relationship

1. In this example the changing quantities cannot easily be depicted geometrically.

2. We are given a formula for the *total* cost. We get the *average* cost by dividing the total cost by x:

$$\bar{C} = \frac{C}{x}.$$

So,

$$\bar{C} = \frac{10{,}000}{x} + 20 + \frac{x}{10{,}000}.$$

3. Taking derivatives with respect to t of both sides, we get the derived equation:

$$\frac{d\bar{C}}{dt} = \left(-\frac{10{,}000}{x^2} + \frac{1}{10{,}000}\right)\frac{dx}{dt}.$$

C. The Solution

Substituting the values from part A into the derived equation, we get

$$\frac{d\bar{C}}{dt} = \left(-\frac{10{,}000}{5{,}000^2} + \frac{1}{10{,}000}\right)100$$

$$= -0.03 \text{ dollars/day.}$$

Thus, the average cost is decreasing by 3¢ per day.

The scenario in the following example is similar to Example 5 in Section 5.2.

EXAMPLE 4 Allocation of Labor

The Gym Sock Company manufactures cotton athletic socks. Production is partially automated through the use of robots. The number of pairs of socks the company can manufacture in a day is given by a Cobb-Douglas production formula:

$$q = 50n^{0.6}r^{0.4},$$

where q is the number of pairs of socks that can be manufactured by n laborers and r robots. The company currently produces 1,000 pairs of socks each day and employs 20 laborers. It is bringing one new robot on line every month. At what rate are laborers being laid off, assuming that the number of socks produced remains constant?

Solution

A. The Problem

1. The changing quantities are the number of laborers n and the number of robots r.

2. $\frac{dr}{dt} = 1$. Find $\frac{dn}{dt}$ when $n = 20$.

B. The Relationship

1. No diagram is appropriate here.

2. The equation relating the changing quantities:

$$1{,}000 = 50n^{0.6}r^{0.4} \quad \text{Productivity is constant at 1,000 pairs of socks each day.}$$

or

$$20 = n^{0.6}r^{0.4}.$$

3. The derived equation is

$$0 = 0.6n^{-0.4}\left(\frac{dn}{dt}\right)r^{0.4} + 0.4n^{0.6}r^{-0.6}\left(\frac{dr}{dt}\right)$$

$$= 0.6\left(\frac{r}{n}\right)^{0.4}\left(\frac{dn}{dt}\right) + 0.4\left(\frac{n}{r}\right)^{0.6}\left(\frac{dr}{dt}\right).$$

We solve this equation for dn/dt because we shall want to find dn/dt below and because the equation becomes simpler when we do this:

$$0.6\left(\frac{r}{n}\right)^{0.4}\left(\frac{dn}{dt}\right) = -0.4\left(\frac{n}{r}\right)^{0.6}\left(\frac{dr}{dt}\right)$$

$$\frac{dn}{dt} = -\frac{0.4}{0.6}\left(\frac{n}{r}\right)^{0.6}\left(\frac{n}{r}\right)^{0.4}\left(\frac{dr}{dt}\right)$$

$$= -\frac{2}{3}\left(\frac{n}{r}\right)\left(\frac{dr}{dt}\right).$$

C. The Solution

Substituting the numbers in A into the last equation in B, we get

$$\frac{dn}{dt} = -\frac{2}{3}\left(\frac{20}{r}\right)(1).$$

We need to compute r by substituting the known value of n in the original formula:

$$20 = n^{0.6}r^{0.4}$$
$$20 = 20^{0.6}r^{0.4}$$
$$r^{0.4} = \frac{20}{20^{0.6}} = 20^{0.4}$$
$$r = 20.$$

Thus,

$$\frac{dn}{dt} = -\frac{2}{3}\left(\frac{20}{20}\right)(1) = -\frac{2}{3} \text{ laborers per month.}$$

The company is laying off laborers at a rate of $2/3$ per month, or two every three months.

We can interpret this result as saying that, at the current level of production and number of laborers, one robot is as productive as $2/3$ of a laborer, or 3 robots are as productive as 2 laborers.

5.5 EXERCISES

▼ more advanced ◆ challenging

T indicates exercises that should be solved using technology

Rewrite the statements and questions in Exercises 1–8 in mathematical notation. HINT [See Quick Examples on page 424.]

1. The population P is currently 10,000 and growing at a rate of 1,000 per year.
2. There are presently 400 cases of Bangkok flu, and the number is growing by 30 new cases every month.
3. The annual revenue of your tie-dye T-shirt operation is currently \$7,000 but is decreasing by \$700 each year. How fast are annual sales changing?
4. A ladder is sliding down a wall so that the distance between the top of the ladder and the floor is decreasing at a rate of 3 feet per second. How fast is the base of the ladder receding from the wall?
5. The price of shoes is rising \$5 per year. How fast is the demand changing?
6. Stock prices are rising \$1,000 per year. How fast is the value of your portfolio increasing?
7. The average global temperature is 60°F and rising by 0.1°F per decade. How fast are annual sales of Bermuda shorts increasing?
8. The country's population is now 260,000,000 and is increasing by 1,000,000 people per year. How fast is the annual demand for diapers increasing?

APPLICATIONS

9. ***Sun Spots*** The area of a circular sun spot is growing at a rate of 1,200 km^2/sec.
   a. How fast is the radius growing at the instant when it equals 10,000 km? HINT [See Example 1.]
   b. How fast is the radius growing at the instant when the sun spot has an area of 640,000 km^2? HINT [Use the area formula to determine the radius at that instant.]
10. ***Puddles*** The radius of a circular puddle is growing at a rate of 5 cm/sec.
    a. How fast is its area growing at the instant when the radius is 10 cm? HINT [See Example 1.]
    b. How fast is the area growing at the instant when it equals 36 cm^2? HINT [Use the area formula to determine the radius at that instant.]
11. ***Balloons*** A spherical party balloon is being inflated with helium pumped in at a rate of 3 cubic feet per minute. How fast is the radius growing at the instant when the radius has reached 1 foot? (The volume of a sphere of radius r is $V = \frac{4}{3}\pi r^3$.) HINT [See Example 1.]
12. ***More Balloons*** A rather flimsy spherical balloon is designed to pop at the instant its radius has reached 10 centimeters. Assuming the balloon is filled with helium at a rate of 10 cubic centimeters per second, calculate how fast the radius is growing at the instant it pops. (The volume of a sphere of radius r is $V = \frac{4}{3}\pi r^3$.) HINT [See Example 1.]

13. ***Sliding Ladders*** The base of a 50-foot ladder is being pulled away from a wall at a rate of 10 feet per second. How fast is the top of the ladder sliding down the wall at the instant when the base of the ladder is 30 feet from the wall? HINT [See Example 2.]

14. ***Sliding Ladders*** The top of a 5-foot ladder is sliding down a wall at a rate of 10 feet per second. How fast is the base of the ladder sliding away from the wall at the instant when the top of the ladder is 3 feet from the ground? HINT [See Example 2.]

15. ***Average Cost*** The average cost function for the weekly manufacture of portable CD players is given by

$$\bar{C}(x) = 150{,}000x^{-1} + 20 + 0.0001x \text{ dollars per player,}$$

where x is the number of CD players manufactured that week. Weekly production is currently 3,000 players and is increasing at a rate of 100 players per week. What is happening to the average cost? HINT [See Example 3.]

16. ***Average Cost*** Repeat the preceding exercise, using the revised average cost function

$$\bar{C}(x) = 150{,}000x^{-1} + 20 + 0.01x \text{ dollars per player.}$$

HINT [See Example 3.]

17. ***Demand*** Demand for your tie-dyed T-shirts is given by the formula

$$q = 500 - 100p^{0.5},$$

where q is the number of T-shirts you can sell each month at a price of p dollars. If you currently sell T-shirts for \$15 each and you raise your price by \$2 per month, how fast will the demand drop? (Round your answer to the nearest whole number.)

18. ***Supply*** The number of portable CD players you are prepared to supply to a retail outlet every week is given by the formula

$$q = 0.1p^2 + 3p,$$

where p is the price it offers you. The retail outlet is currently offering you \$40 per CD player. If the price it offers decreases at a rate of \$2 per week, how will this affect the number you supply?

19. ***Revenue*** You can now sell 50 cups of lemonade per week at 30¢ per cup, but demand is dropping at a rate of 5 cups per week each week. Assuming that raising the price does not affect demand, how fast do you have to raise your price if you want to keep your weekly revenue constant? HINT [Revenue = Price × Quantity.]

20. ***Revenue*** You can now sell 40 cars per month at \$20,000 per car, and demand is increasing at a rate of 3 cars per month each month. What is the fastest you could drop your price before your monthly revenue starts to drop? HINT [Revenue = Price × Quantity.]

21. ▼ ***Oil Revenues*** Daily oil production by **Pemex**, Mexico's national oil company, can be approximated by

$$q(t) = -0.022t^2 + 0.2t + 2.9 \text{ million barrels} \quad (1 \le t \le 9),$$

where t is time in years since the start of 2000.[55]

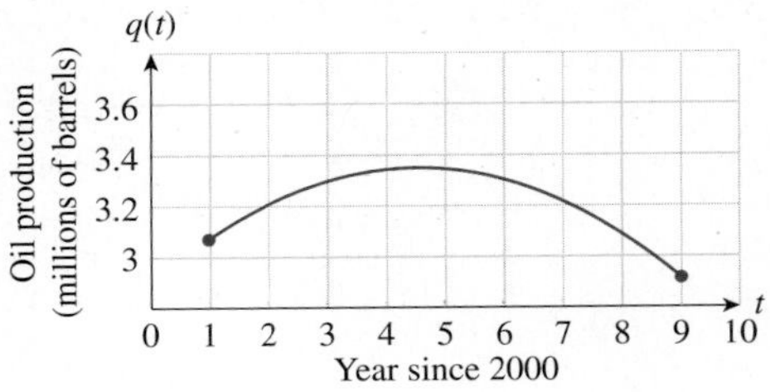

At the start of 2008 the price of oil was \$90 per barrel and increasing at a rate of \$80 per year.[56] How fast was Pemex's oil (daily) revenue changing at that time?

22. ▼ ***Oil Expenditures*** Daily oil imports to the United States from Mexico can be approximated by

$$q(t) = -0.015t^2 + 0.1t + 1.4 \text{ million barrels} \quad (0 \le t \le 8),$$

where t is time in years since the start of 2000.[57]

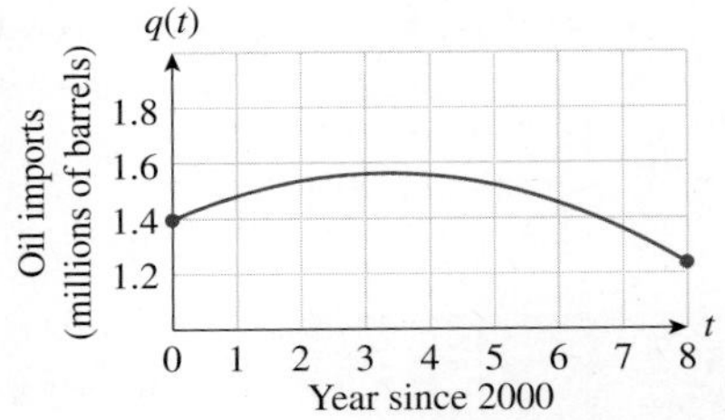

At the start of 2004 the price of oil was \$30 per barrel and increasing at a rate of \$40 per year.[58] How fast was (daily) oil expenditure for imports from Mexico changing at that time?

23. ***Resource Allocation*** Your company manufactures automobile alternators, and production is partially automated through the use of robots. In order to meet production deadlines, your company calculates that the numbers of laborers and robots must satisfy the constraint

$$xy = 10{,}000,$$

where x is the number of laborers and y is the number of robots. Your company currently uses 400 robots and is increasing robot deployment at a rate of 16 per month. How fast is it laying off laborers? HINT [See Example 4.]

24. ***Resource Allocation*** Your company is the largest sock manufacturer in the Solar System, and production is automated through the use of androids and robots. In order to meet production deadlines, your company calculates that the numbers of androids and robots must satisfy the constraint

$$xy = 1{,}000{,}000,$$

[55] Source for data: Energy Information Administration/Pemex (www.eia.doe.gov).

[56] Based on NYMEX crude oil futures; average rate of change during January–June, 2008.

[57] Source for data: Energy Information Administration/Pemex (www.eia.doe.gov).

[58] Based on NYMEX crude oil futures; average rate of change during 2004–2005.

where x is the number of androids and y is the number of robots. Your company currently uses 5000 androids and is increasing android deployment at a rate of 200 per month. How fast is it scrapping robots? HINT [See Example 4.]

25. ***Production*** The automobile assembly plant you manage has a Cobb-Douglas production function given by

$$P = 10x^{0.3}y^{0.7},$$

where P is the number of automobiles it produces per year, x is the number of employees, and y is the daily operating budget (in dollars). You maintain a production level of 1,000 automobiles per year. If you currently employ 150 workers and are hiring new workers at a rate of 10 per year, how fast is your daily operating budget changing? HINT [See Example 4.]

26. ***Production*** Refer back to the Cobb-Douglas production formula in the preceding exercise. Assume that you maintain a constant workforce of 200 workers and wish to increase production in order to meet a demand that is increasing by 100 automobiles per year. The current demand is 1000 automobiles per year. How fast should your daily operating budget be increasing? HINT [See Example 4.]

27. ***Demand*** Assume that the demand equation for tuna in a small coastal town is

$$pq^{1.5} = 50{,}000,$$

where q is the number of pounds of tuna that can be sold in one month at the price of p dollars per pound. The town's fishery finds that the demand for tuna is currently 900 pounds per month and is increasing at a rate of 100 pounds per month each month. How fast is the price changing?

28. ***Demand*** The demand equation for rubies at *Royal Ruby Retailers* is

$$q + \frac{4}{3}p = 80,$$

where q is the number of rubies RRR can sell per week at p dollars per ruby. RRR finds that the demand for its rubies is currently 20 rubies per week and is dropping at a rate of one ruby per week. How fast is the price changing?

29. ▼ ***Ships Sailing Apart*** The H.M.S. *Dreadnaught* is 40 miles south of Montauk and steaming due south at 20 miles/hour, while the U.S.S. *Mona Lisa* is 50 miles east of Montauk and steaming due east at an even 30 miles/hour. How fast is their distance apart increasing?

30. ▼ ***Near Miss*** My aunt and I were approaching the same intersection, she from the south and I from the west. She was traveling at a steady speed of 10 miles/hour, while I was approaching the intersection at 60 miles/hour. At a certain instant in time, I was one tenth of a mile from the intersection, while she was one twentieth of a mile from it. How fast were we approaching each other at that instant?

31. ▼ ***Baseball*** A baseball diamond is a square with side 90 ft.

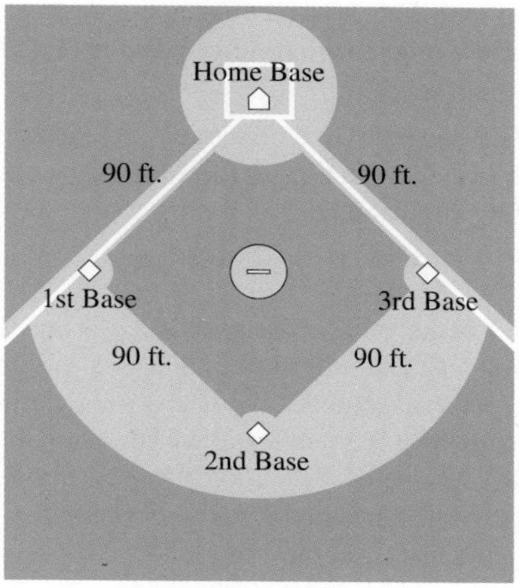

A batter at home base hits the ball and runs toward first base with a speed of 24 ft/sec. At what rate is his distance from third base increasing when he is halfway to first base?

32. ▼ ***Baseball*** Refer to Exercise 31. Another player is running from third base to home at 30 ft/sec. How fast is her distance from second base increasing when she is 60 feet from third base?

33. ▼ ***Movement along a Graph*** A point on the graph of $y = 1/x$ is moving along the curve in such a way that its x-coordinate is increasing at a rate of 4 units per second. What is happening to the y-coordinate at the instant the y-coordinate is equal to 2?

34. ▼ ***Motion around a Circle*** A point is moving along the circle $x^2 + (y - 1)^2 = 8$ in such a way that its x-coordinate is decreasing at a rate of 1 unit per second. What is happening to the y-coordinate at the instant when the point has reached $(-2, 3)$?

35. ▼ ***Education*** In 1991, the expected income of an individual depended on his or her educational level according to the following formula:

$$I(n) = 2.929n^3 - 115.9n^2 + 1{,}530n - 6{,}760 \text{ thousand dollars } (12 \le n \le 15).$$

Here, n is the number of school years completed and $I(n)$ is the individual's expected income in thousands of dollars.[59] It is 1991, and you have completed 13 years of school and are currently a part-time student. Your schedule is such that you will complete the equivalent of one year of college every three years. Assuming that your salary is linked to the above model, how fast is your income going up? (Round your answer to the nearest $1.)

[59]The model is a based on Table 358, U.S. Department of Education, *Digest of Education Statistics, 1991*, Washington, DC: Government Printing Office, 1991.

36. ▼ ***Education*** Refer back to the model in the preceding exercise. Assume that you have completed 14 years of school and that your income is increasing by \$5,000 per year. How much schooling per year is this rate of increase equivalent to?

37. ▼ ***Employment*** An employment research company estimates that the value of a recent MBA graduate to an accounting company is

$$V = 3e^2 + 5g^3,$$

where V is the value of the graduate, e is the number of years of prior business experience, and g is the graduate school grade-point average. A company that currently employs graduates with a 3.0 average wishes to maintain a constant employee value of $V = 200$, but finds that the grade-point average of its new employees is dropping at a rate of 0.2 per year. How fast must the experience of its new employees be growing in order to compensate for the decline in grade point average?

38. ▼ ***Grades***[60] A production formula for a student's performance on a difficult English examination is given by

$$g = 4hx - 0.2h^2 - 10x^2,$$

where g is the grade the student can expect to obtain, h is the number of hours of study for the examination, and x is the student's grade point average. The instructor finds that students' grade point averages have remained constant at 3.0 over the years, and that students currently spend an average of 15 hours studying for the examination. However, scores on the examination are dropping at a rate of 10 points per year. At what rate is the average study time decreasing?

39. ▼ ***Cones*** A right circular conical vessel is being filled with green industrial waste at a rate of 100 cubic meters per second. How fast is the level rising after 200π cubic meters have been poured in? The cone has a height of 50 m and a radius of 30 m at its brim. (The volume of a cone of height h and cross-sectional radius r at its brim is given by $V = \frac{1}{3}\pi r^2 h$.)

40. ▼ ***More Cones*** A circular conical vessel is being filled with ink at a rate of 10 cm^3/sec. How fast is the level rising after 20 cm^3 have been poured in? The cone has height 50 cm and radius 20 cm at its brim. (The volume of a cone of height h and cross-sectional radius r at its brim is given by $V = \frac{1}{3}\pi r^2 h$.)

41. ▼ ***Cylinders*** The volume of paint in a right cylindrical can is given by $V = 4t^2 - t$ where t is time in seconds and V is the volume in cm^3. How fast is the level rising when the height is 2 cm? The can has a height of 4 cm and a radius of 2 cm. HINT [To get h as a function of t, first solve the volume $V = \pi r^2 h$ for h.]

42. ▼ ***Cylinders*** A cylindrical bucket is being filled with paint at a rate of 6 cm^3 per minute. How fast is the level rising when the bucket starts to overflow? The bucket has a radius of 30 cm and a height of 60 cm.

[60] Based on an Exercise in *Introduction to Mathematical Economics* by A.L. Ostrosky Jr. and J.V. Koch (Waveland Press, Illinois, 1979).

43. ▼ ***Computers vs. Income*** The demand for personal computers in the home goes up with household income. For a given community, we can approximate the average number of computers in a home as

$$q = 0.3454 \ln x - 3.047 \quad (10{,}000 \le x \le 125{,}000),$$

where x is mean household income.[61] Your community has a mean income of \$30,000, increasing at a rate of \$2,000 per year. How many computers per household are there, and how fast is the number of computers in a home increasing? (Round your answer to four decimal places.)

44. ▼ ***Computers vs. Income*** Refer back to the model in the preceding exercise. The average number of computers per household in your town is 0.5 and is increasing at a rate of 0.02 computers per household per year. What is the average household income in your town, and how fast is it increasing? (Round your answers to the nearest \$10).

Education and Crime *The following graph compares the total U.S. prison population and the average combined SAT score in the United States during the 1970s and 1980s:*

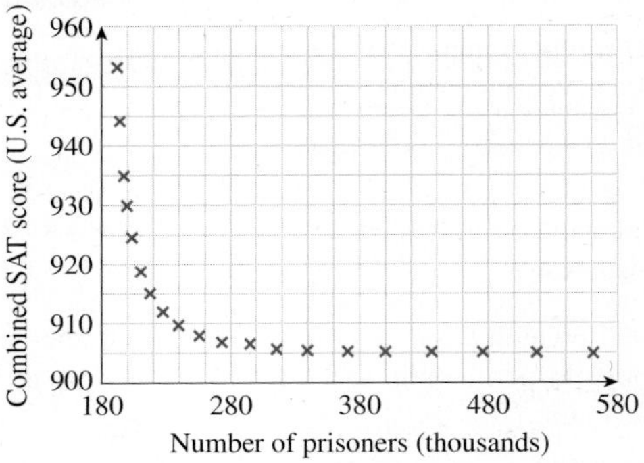

Exercises 45 and 46 are based on the following model for these data:

$$S(n) = 904 + \frac{1{,}326}{(n - 180)^{1.325}} \quad (192 \le n \le 563).$$

Here, S(n) is the combined average SAT score at a time when the total prison population is n thousand.[62]

45. ▼ In 1985, the U.S. prison population was 475,000 and increasing at a rate of 35,000 per year. What was the average SAT score, and how fast, and in what direction, was it changing? (Round your answers to two decimal places.)

[61] The model is a regression model. Source for data: Income distribution: Computer data: Forrester Research/*New York Times*, August 8, 1999, p. BU4.

[62] Based on data for the years 1967–1989. Sources: Sourcebook of Criminal Justice Statistics, 1990, p. 604/Educational Testing Service.

46. ▼ In 1970, the U.S. combined SAT average was 940 and dropping by 10 points per year. What was the U.S. prison population, and how fast, and in what direction, was it changing? (Round your answers to the nearest 100.)

Divorce Rates *A study found that the divorce rate d (given as a percentage) appears to depend on the ratio r of available men to available women.*[63] *This function can be approximated by*

$$d(r) = \begin{cases} -40r + 74 & \text{if } r \le 1.3 \\ \dfrac{130r}{3} - \dfrac{103}{3} & \text{if } r > 1.3 \end{cases}.$$

Exercises 47 and 48 are based on this model.

47. ◆ There are currently 1.1 available men per available woman in Littleville, and this ratio is increasing by 0.05 per year. What is happening to the divorce rate?

48. ◆ There are currently 1.5 available men per available woman in Largeville, and this ratio is decreasing by 0.03 per year. What is happening to the divorce rate?

COMMUNICATION AND REASONING EXERCISES

49. Why is this section titled "related rates"?

50. If you know how fast one quantity is changing and need to compute how fast a second quantity is changing, what kind of information do you need?

51. In a related rates problem, there is no limit to the number of changing quantities we can consider. Illustrate this by creating a related rates problem with four changing quantities.

[63]The cited study, by Scott J. South and associates, appeared in the *American Sociological Review* (February, 1995). Figures are rounded. Source: *New York Times*, February 19, 1995, p. 40.

52. If three quantities are related by a single equation, how would you go about computing how fast one of them is changing based on a knowledge of the other two?

53. ▼ The demand and unit price for your store's checkered T-shirts are changing with time. Show that the percentage rate of change of revenue equals the sum of the percentage rates of change of price and demand. (The percentage rate of change of a quantity Q is $Q'(t)/Q(t)$.)

54. ▼ The number N of employees and the total floor space S of your company are both changing with time. Show that the percentage rate of change of square footage per employee equals the percentage rate of change of S minus the percentage rate of change of N. (The percentage rate of change of a quantity Q is $Q'(t)/Q(t)$.)

55. ▼ In solving a related rates problem, a key step is solving the derived equation for the unknown rate of change (once we have substituted the other values into the equation). Call the unknown rate of change X. The derived equation is what kind of equation in X?

56. ▼ On a recent exam, you were given a related rates problem based on an algebraic equation relating two variables x and y. Your friend told you that the correct relationship between dx/dt and dy/dt was given by

$$\left(\frac{dx}{dt}\right) = \left(\frac{dy}{dt}\right)^2.$$

Could he be correct?

57. ▼ Transform the following into a mathematical statement about derivatives: If my grades are improving at twice the speed of yours, then your grades are improving at half the speed of mine.

58. ▼ If two quantities x and y are related by a linear equation, how are their rates of change related?

5.6 Elasticity

You manufacture an extremely popular brand of sneakers and want to know what will happen if you increase the selling price. Common sense tells you that demand will drop as you raise the price. But will the drop in demand be enough to cause your revenue to fall? Or will it be small enough that your revenue will rise because of the higher selling price? For example, if you raise the price by 1%, you might suffer only a 0.5% loss in sales. In this case, the loss in sales will be more than offset by the increase in price and your revenue will rise. In such a case, we say that the demand is **inelastic**, because it is not very sensitive to the increase in price. On the other hand, if your 1% price increase results in a 2% drop in demand, then raising the price will cause a drop in revenues. We then say that the demand is **elastic** because it reacts strongly to a price change.

* Coming up with a good demand equation is not always easy. We saw in Chapter 1 that it is possible to find a linear demand equation if we know the sales figures at two different prices. However, such an equation is only a first approximation. To come up with a more accurate demand equation, we might need to gather data corresponding to sales at several different prices and use curve-fitting techniques like regression. Another approach would be an analytic one, based on mathematical modeling techniques that an economist might use.

That said, we refer you again to *Camels and Rubber Duckies* by Joel Spolsky at www.joelonsoftware.com/articles/CamelsandRubberDuckies.html just in case you think there is nothing more to demand curves.

We can use calculus to measure the response of demand to price changes if we have a demand equation for the item we are selling.* We need to know the *percentage drop in demand per percentage increase in price.* This ratio is called the **elasticity of demand**, or **price elasticity of demand**, and is usually denoted by E. Let's derive a formula for E in terms of the demand equation.

Assume that we have a demand equation

$$q = f(p),$$

where q stands for the number of items we would sell (per week, per month, or what have you) if we set the price per item at p. Now suppose we increase the price p by a very small amount, Δp. Then our percentage increase in price is $(\Delta p/p) \times 100\%$. This increase in p will presumably result in a decrease in the demand q. Let's denote this corresponding decrease in q by $-\Delta q$ (we use the minus sign because, by convention, Δq stands for the *increase* in demand). Thus, the percentage decrease in demand is $(-\Delta q/q) \times 100\%$.

Now E is the ratio

$$E = \frac{\text{Percentage decrease in demand}}{\text{Percentage increase in price}}$$

so

$$E = \frac{-\dfrac{\Delta q}{q} \times 100\%}{\dfrac{\Delta p}{p} \times 100\%}.$$

Canceling the 100%s and reorganizing, we get

$$E = -\frac{\Delta q}{\Delta p} \cdot \frac{p}{q}.$$

Q: *What small change in price will we use for Δp?*

A: It should probably be pretty small. If, say, we increased the price of sneakers to $1 million per pair, the sales would likely drop to zero. But knowing this tells us nothing about how the market would respond to a modest increase in price. In fact, we'll do the usual thing we do in calculus and let Δp approach 0.

In the expression for E, if we let Δp go to 0, then the ratio $\Delta q/\Delta p$ goes to the derivative dq/dp. This gives us our final and most useful definition of the elasticity.

Price Elasticity of Demand

The **price elasticity of demand *E*** is the percentage rate of decrease of demand per percentage increase in price. E is given by the formula

$$E = -\frac{dq}{dp} \cdot \frac{p}{q}.$$

We say that the demand is **elastic** if $E > 1$, is **inelastic** if $E < 1$, and has **unit elasticity** if $E = 1$.

Quick Example

Suppose that the demand equation is $q = 20{,}000 - 2p$, where p is the price in dollars. Then

$$E = -(-2)\frac{p}{20{,}000 - 2p} = \frac{p}{10{,}000 - p}.$$

If $p = \$2{,}000$, then $E = 1/4$, and demand is inelastic at this price.
If $p = \$8{,}000$, then $E = 4$, and demand is elastic at this price.
If $p = \$5{,}000$, then $E = 1$, and the demand has unit elasticity at this price.

We are generally interested in the price that maximizes revenue and, in ordinary cases, the price that maximizes revenue must give unit elasticity. One way of seeing this is as follows:* If the demand is inelastic (which ordinarily occurs at a low unit price), then raising the price by a small percentage—1% say—results in a smaller percentage drop in demand. For example, in the Quick Example above, if $p = \$2{,}000$, then the demand would drop by only $\frac{1}{4}\%$ for every 1% increase in price. To see the effect on revenue, we use the fact† that, for small changes in price,

$$\begin{aligned}\text{Percentage change in revenue} &\approx \text{Percentage change in price} \\ &\quad + \text{Percentage change in demand} \\ &= 1 + \left(-\frac{1}{4}\right) = \frac{3}{4}\%.\end{aligned}$$

Thus, the revenue will increase by about 3/4%. Put another way:

If the demand is inelastic, raising the price increases revenue.

On the other hand, if the price is elastic (which ordinarily occurs at a high unit price), then increasing the price slightly will lower the revenue, so:

If the demand is elastic, lowering the price increases revenue.

The price that results in the largest revenue must therefore be at unit elasticity.

* For another—more rigorous—argument, see Exercise 29.

† See, for example, Exercise 53 in Section 5.5.

EXAMPLE 1 Price Elasticity of Demand: Dolls

Suppose that the demand equation for *Bobby Dolls* is given by $q = 216 - p^2$, where p is the price per doll in dollars and q is the number of dolls sold per week.

a. Compute the price elasticity of demand when $p = \$5$ and $p = \$10$, and interpret the results.

b. Find the range of prices for which the demand is elastic and the range for which the demand is inelastic.

c. Find the price at which the weekly revenue is maximized. What is the maximum weekly revenue?

Solution

a. The price elasticity of demand is

$$E = -\frac{dq}{dp} \cdot \frac{p}{q}.$$

Taking the derivative and substituting for q gives

$$E = 2p \cdot \frac{p}{216 - p^2} = \frac{2p^2}{216 - p^2}.$$

When $p = \$5$,

$$E = \frac{2(5)^2}{216 - 5^2} = \frac{50}{191} \approx 0.26.$$

Thus, when the price is set at \$5, the demand is dropping at a rate of 0.26% per 1% increase in the price. Because $E < 1$, the demand is inelastic at this price, so raising the price will increase revenue.

When $p = \$10$,

$$E = \frac{2(10)^2}{216 - 10^2} = \frac{200}{116} \approx 1.72.$$

Thus, when the price is set at \$10, the demand is dropping at a rate of 1.72% per 1% increase in the price. Because $E > 1$, demand is elastic at this price, so raising the price will decrease revenue; lowering the price will increase revenue.

b. and **c.** We answer part (c) first. Setting $E = 1$, we get

$$\frac{2p^2}{216 - p^2} = 1$$

$$p^2 = 72.$$

Thus, we conclude that the maximum revenue occurs when $p = \sqrt{72} \approx \$8.49$. We can now answer part (b): The demand is elastic when $p > \$8.49$ (the price is too high), and the demand is inelastic when $p < \$8.49$ (the price is too low). Finally, we calculate the maximum weekly revenue, which equals the revenue corresponding to the price of \$8.49:

$$R = qp = (216 - p^2)p = (216 - 72)\sqrt{72} = 144\sqrt{72} \approx \$1{,}222.$$

using Technology

See the Technology Guides at the end of the chapter to find out how to automate computations like those in part (a) of Example 1 using a graphing calculator or Excel. Here is an outline:

TI-83/84 Plus

```
Y1=216-X^2
Y2=-nDeriv(Y1,X,X)*X/Y1
```

[2ND] [TABLE] Enter $x = 5$

[More details on page 449.]

Spreadsheet

Enter values of p: 4.9, 4.91, . . . , 5.0, 5.01, . . . , 5.1 in A5–A25.

In B5 enter `216-A5^2` and copy down to B25.

In C5 enter `=(A6-A5)/A5` and paste the formula in C5–D24.

In E5 enter =–D5/C5 and copy down to E24. This column contains the values of E for the values of p in column A.

[More details on page 449.]

The concept of elasticity can be applied in other situations. In the following example we consider *income* elasticity of demand—the percentage increase in demand for a particular item per percentage increase in personal income.

EXAMPLE 2 Income Elasticity of Demand: Porsches

You are the sales director at *Suburban Porsche* and have noticed that demand for Porsches depends on income according to

$$q = 0.005e^{-0.05x^2+x} \qquad (1 \le x \le 10).$$

Here, x is the income of a potential customer in hundreds of thousands of dollars and q is the probability that the person will actually purchase a Porsche.* The **income elasticity of demand** is

$$E = \frac{dq}{dx}\frac{x}{q}.$$

Compute and interpret E for $x = 2$ and 9.

* In other words, q is the fraction of visitors to your showroom having income x who actually purchase a Porsche.

Solution

Q: *Why is there no negative sign in the formula?*

A: Because we anticipate that the demand will increase as income increases, the ratio

$$\frac{\text{Percentage increase in demand}}{\text{Percentage increase in income}}$$

will be positive, so there is no need to introduce a negative sign.

Turning to the calculation, since $q = 0.005e^{-0.05x^2+x}$,

$$\frac{dq}{dx} = 0.005e^{-0.05x^2+x}(-0.1x+1)$$

and so

$$\begin{aligned} E &= \frac{dq}{dx}\frac{x}{q} \\ &= 0.005e^{-0.05x^2+x}(-0.1x+1)\frac{x}{0.005e^{-0.05x^2+x}} \\ &= x(-0.1x+1). \end{aligned}$$

When $x = 2$, $E = 2[-0.1(2)+1)] = 1.6$. Thus, at an income level of \$200,000, the probability that a customer will purchase a Porsche increases at a rate of 1.6% per 1% increase in income.

When $x = 9$, $E = 9[-0.1(9)+1)] = 0.9$. Thus, at an income level of \$900,000, the probability that a customer will purchase a Porsche increases at a rate of 0.9% per 1% increase in income.

5.6 EXERCISES

▼ more advanced ◆ challenging

T indicates exercises that should be solved using technology

APPLICATIONS

1. ***Demand for Oranges*** The weekly sales of *Honolulu Red Oranges* is given by $q = 1{,}000 - 20p$. Calculate the price elasticity of demand when the price is \$30 per orange (yes, \$30 per orange[64]). Interpret your answer. Also, calculate the price that gives a maximum weekly revenue, and find this maximum revenue. HINT [See Example 1.]

2. ***Demand for Oranges*** Repeat the preceding exercise for weekly sales of $1{,}000 - 10p$. HINT [See Example 1.]

3. ***Tissues*** The consumer demand equation for tissues is given by $q = (100 - p)^2$, where p is the price per case of tissues and q is the demand in weekly sales.

   a. Determine the price elasticity of demand E when the price is set at \$30, and interpret your answer.

   b. At what price should tissues be sold in order to maximize the revenue?

   c. Approximately how many cases of tissues would be demanded at that price?

4. ***Bodybuilding*** The consumer demand curve for *Professor Stefan Schwarzenegger* dumbbells is given by $q = (100 - 2p)^2$, where p is the price per dumbbell, and q is the demand in weekly sales. Find the price Professor Schwarzenegger should charge for his dumbbells in order to maximize revenue.

5. ***T-Shirts*** The Physics Club sells $E = mc^2$ T-shirts at the local flea market. Unfortunately, the club's previous administration has been losing money for years, so you decide to do an analysis of the sales. A quadratic regression based on old sales data reveals the following demand equation for the T-shirts:

$$q = -2p^2 + 33p \quad (9 \le p \le 15).$$

   Here, p is the price the club charges per T-shirt, and q is the number it can sell each day at the flea market.

   a. Obtain a formula for the price elasticity of demand for $E = mc^2$ T-shirts.

[64] They are very hard to find, and their possession confers considerable social status.

b. Compute the elasticity of demand if the price is set at \$10 per shirt. *Interpret the result.*

c. How much should the Physics Club charge for the T-shirts in order to obtain the maximum daily revenue? What will this revenue be?

6. ***Comics*** The demand curve for original *Iguanawoman* comics is given by

$$q = \frac{(400 - p)^2}{100} \quad (0 \leq p \leq 400),$$

where q is the number of copies the publisher can sell per week if it sets the price at \$$p$.

a. Find the price elasticity of demand when the price is set at \$40 per copy.

b. Find the price at which the publisher should sell the books in order to maximize weekly revenue.

c. What, to the nearest \$1, is the maximum weekly revenue the publisher can realize from sales of *Iguanawoman* comics?

7. ***College Tuition*** A study of about 1,800 U.S. colleges and universities resulted in the demand equation $q = 9{,}900 - 2.2p$, where q is the enrollment at a college or university, and p is the average annual tuition (plus fees) it charges.[65]

a. The study also found that the average tuition charged by universities and colleges was \$2,900. What is the corresponding price elasticity of demand? Is the price elastic or inelastic? Should colleges charge more or less on average to maximize revenue?

b. Based on the study, what would you advise a college to charge its students in order to maximize total revenue, and what would the revenue be?

8. ***Demand for Fried Chicken*** A fried chicken franchise finds that the demand equation for its new roast chicken product, "Roasted Rooster," is given by

$$p = \frac{40}{q^{1.5}},$$

where p is the price (in dollars) per quarter-chicken serving and q is the number of quarter-chicken servings that can be sold per hour at this price. Express q as a function of p and find the price elasticity of demand when the price is set at \$4 per serving. Interpret the result.

9. ***Paint-By-Number*** The estimated monthly sales of *Mona Lisa* paint-by-number sets is given by the formula $q = 100e^{-3p^2+p}$, where q is the demand in monthly sales and p is the retail price in hundreds of yen.

a. Determine the price elasticity of demand E when the retail price is set at ¥300 and interpret your answer.

b. At what price will revenue be a maximum?

c. Approximately how many paint-by-number sets will be sold per month at the price in part (b)?

[65]Based on a study by A.L. Ostrosky Jr. and J.V. Koch, as cited in their book *Introduction to Mathematical Economics* (Waveland Press, Illinois, 1979) p. 133.

10. ***Paint-By-Number*** Repeat the preceding exercise using the demand equation $q = 100e^{p-3p^2/2}$.

11. ▼ ***Linear Demand Functions*** A general linear demand function has the form $q = mp + b$ (m and b constants, $m \neq 0$).

a. Obtain a formula for the price elasticity of demand at a unit price of p.

b. Obtain a formula for the price that maximizes revenue.

12. ▼ ***Exponential Demand Functions*** A general exponential demand function has the form $q = Ae^{-bp}$ (A and b nonzero constants).

a. Obtain a formula for the price elasticity of demand at a unit price of p.

b. Obtain a formula for the price that maximizes revenue.

13. ▼ ***Hyperbolic Demand Functions*** A general hyperbolic demand function has the form $q = \dfrac{k}{p^r}$ (r and k nonzero constants).

a. Obtain a formula for the price elasticity of demand at unit price p.

b. How does E vary with p?

c. What does the answer to part (b) say about the model?

14. ▼ ***Quadratic Demand Functions*** A general quadratic demand function has the form $q = ap^2 + bp + c$ (a, b, and c constants with $a \neq 0$).

a. Obtain a formula for the price elasticity of demand at a unit price p.

b. Obtain a formula for the price or prices that could maximize revenue.

15. ▼ ***Modeling Linear Demand*** You have been hired as a marketing consultant to *Johannesburg Burger Supply, Inc.*, and you wish to come up with a unit price for its hamburgers in order to maximize its weekly revenue. To make life as simple as possible, you assume that the demand equation for Johannesburg hamburgers has the linear form $q = mp + b$, where p is the price per hamburger, q is the demand in weekly sales, and m and b are certain constants you must determine.

a. Your market studies reveal the following sales figures: When the price is set at \$2.00 per hamburger, the sales amount to 3,000 per week, but when the price is set at \$4.00 per hamburger, the sales drop to zero. Use these data to calculate the demand equation.

b. Now estimate the unit price that maximizes weekly revenue and predict what the weekly revenue will be at that price.

16. ▼ ***Modeling Linear Demand*** You have been hired as a marketing consultant to *Big Book Publishing, Inc.*, and you have been approached to determine the best selling price for the hit calculus text by Whiner and Istanbul entitled *Fun with Derivatives*. You decide to make life easy and assume that the demand equation for *Fun with Derivatives* has the linear form $q = mp + b$, where p is the price per book, q is the demand in annual sales, and m and b are certain constants you must determine.

a. Your market studies reveal the following sales figures: When the price is set at \$50.00 per book, the sales amount to 10,000 per year; when the price is set at \$80.00 per book, the sales drop to 1000 per year. Use these data to calculate the demand equation.

b. Now estimate the unit price that maximizes annual revenue and predict what Big Book Publishing, Inc.'s annual revenue will be at that price.

17. ***Income Elasticity of Demand: Live Drama*** The likelihood that a child will attend a live theatrical performance can be modeled by

$$q = 0.01(-0.0078x^2 + 1.5x + 4.1) \qquad (15 \le x \le 100).$$

Here, q is the fraction of children with annual household income x thousand dollars who will attend a live dramatic performance at a theater during the year.[66] Compute the income elasticity of demand at an income level of \$20,000 and interpret the result. (Round your answer to two significant digits.) HINT [See Example 2.]

18. ***Income Elasticity of Demand: Live Concerts*** The likelihood that a child will attend a live musical performance can be modeled by

$$q = 0.01(0.0006x^2 + 0.38x + 35) \quad (15 \le x \le 100).$$

Here, q is the fraction of children with annual household income x who will attend a live musical performance during the year.[67] Compute the income elasticity of demand at an income level of \$30,000 and interpret the result. (Round your answer to two significant digits.) HINT [See Example 2.]

19. ***Income Elasticity of Demand: Broadband in 2010*** The following graph shows the percentage q of people in households with annual income x thousand dollars using broadband Internet access in 2010, together with the exponential curve $q = -74e^{-0.021x} + 92$.[68]

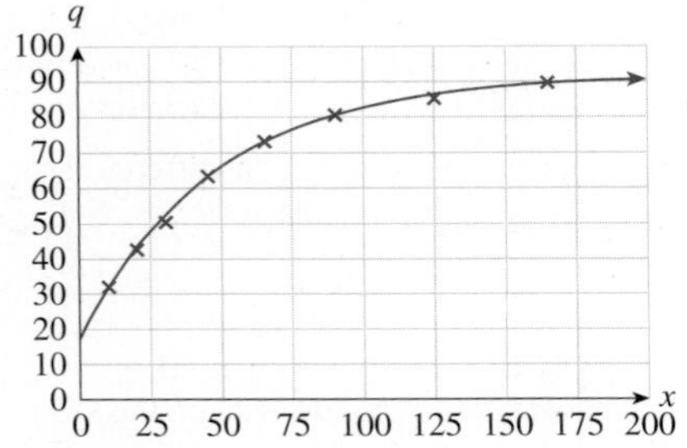

a. Find an equation for the income elasticity of demand for broadband usage, and use it to compute the elasticity for a household with annual income \$100,000 to two decimal places. Interpret the result.

b. What does the model predict as the elasticity of demand for households with very large incomes?

20. ***Income Elasticity of Demand: Broadband in 2007*** The following graph shows the percentage q of people in households with annual income x thousand dollars using broadband Internet access in 2007, together with the exponential curve $q = -86e^{-0.013x} + 92$.[69]

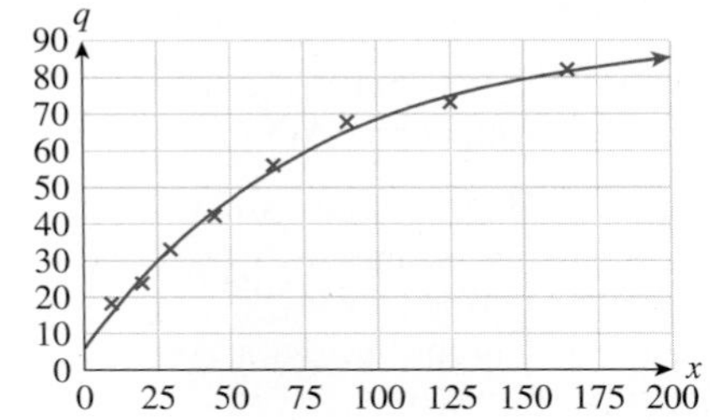

a. Find an equation for the income elasticity of demand for broadband usage, and use it to compute the elasticity for a household with annual income \$60,000 to two decimal places. Interpret the result.

b. What does the model predict as the elasticity of demand for households with very large incomes?

21. ***Income Elasticity of Demand: Computer Usage in the 1990s*** The following graph shows the probability q that a household in the 1990s with annual income x dollars had a computer, together with the logarithmic curve $q = 0.3454 \ln x - 3.047$.[70]

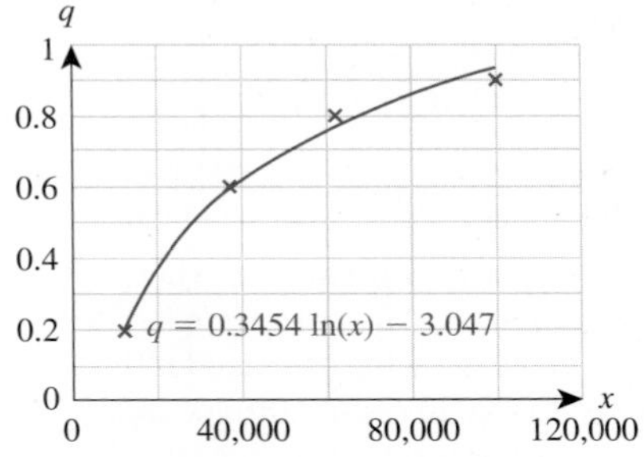

a. Compute the income elasticity of demand for computers, to two decimal places, for a household income of \$60,000 and interpret the result.

b. As household income increases, how is income elasticity of demand affected?

c. How reliable is the given model of demand for incomes well above \$120,000? Explain.

d. What can you say about E for incomes much larger than those shown?

---

[66] Based on a quadratic regression of data from a 2001 survey. Source for data: New York Foundation of the Arts (www.nyfa.org/culturalblueprint).

[67] *Ibid.*

[68] Source for data: *Digital Nation: Expanding Internet Usage,* National Telecommunications and Information Administration (U.S. Department of Commerce) (http://search.ntia.doc.gov).

[69] *Ibid.*

[70] Source for data: Income distribution computer data: Forrester Research/*New York Times*, August 8, 1999, p. BU4.

22. ***Income Elasticity of Demand: Internet Usage in the 1990s*** The following graph shows the probability q that a person in the 1990s with household annual income x dollars used the Internet, together with the logarithmic curve $q = 0.2802 \ln x - 2.505$.[71]

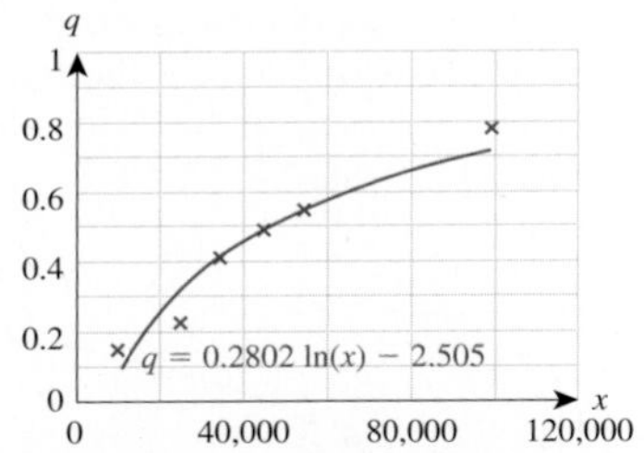

a. Compute the income elasticity of demand for Internet usage, to two decimal places, for a household income of $60,000 and interpret the result.
b. As household income increases, how is income elasticity of demand affected?
c. The logarithmic model shown above is not appropriate for incomes well above $100,000. Suggest a model that might be more appropriate.
d. In the model you propose, how would E behave for very large incomes?

23. ▼ ***Income Elasticity of Demand*** *(based on a question on the GRE Economics Test)* If $Q = aP^\alpha Y^\beta$ is the individual's demand function for a commodity, where P is the (fixed) price of the commodity, Y is the individual's income, and a, α, and β are parameters, explain why β can be interpreted as the income elasticity of demand.

24. ▼ ***College Tuition*** *(from the GRE Economics Test)* A time-series study of the demand for higher education, using tuition charges as a price variable, yields the following result:

$$\frac{dq}{dp} \cdot \frac{p}{q} = -0.4,$$

where p is tuition and q is the quantity of higher education. Which of the following is suggested by the result?

(A) As tuition rises, students want to buy a greater quantity of education.
(B) As a determinant of the demand for higher education, income is more important than price.
(C) If colleges lowered tuition slightly, their total tuition receipts would increase.
(D) If colleges raised tuition slightly, their total tuition receipts would increase.
(E) Colleges cannot increase enrollments by offering larger scholarships.

25. ▼ ***Modeling Exponential Demand*** As the new owner of a supermarket, you have inherited a large inventory of unsold imported Limburger cheese, and you would like to set the price so that your revenue from selling it is as large as possible. Previous sales figures of the cheese are shown in the following table:

Price per Pound, p	\$3.00	\$4.00	\$5.00
Monthly Sales in Pounds, q	407	287	223

a. Use the sales figures for the prices \$3 and \$5 per pound to construct a demand function of the form $q = Ae^{-bp}$, where A and b are constants you must determine. (Round A and b to two significant digits.)
b. Use your demand function to find the price elasticity of demand at each of the prices listed.
c. At what price should you sell the cheese in order to maximize monthly revenue?
d. If your total inventory of cheese amounts to only 200 pounds, and it will spoil one month from now, how should you price it in order to receive the greatest revenue? Is this the same answer you got in part (c)? If not, give a brief explanation.

26. ▼ ***Modeling Exponential Demand*** Repeat the preceding exercise, but this time use the sales figures for \$4 and \$5 per pound to construct the demand function.

COMMUNICATION AND REASONING EXERCISES

27. Complete the following: When demand is inelastic, revenue will decrease if____ .

28. Complete the following: When demand has unit elasticity, revenue will decrease if____ .

29. ▼ Given that the demand q is a differentiable function of the unit price p, show that the revenue $R = pq$ has a stationary point when

$$q + p\frac{dq}{dp} = 0.$$

Deduce that the stationary points of R are the same as the points of unit price elasticity of demand. (Ordinarily, there is only one such stationary point, corresponding to the absolute maximum of R.) HINT [Differentiate R with respect to p.]

30. ▼ Given that the demand q is a differentiable function of income x, show that the quantity $R = q/x$ has a stationary point when

$$q - x\frac{dq}{dx} = 0.$$

Deduce that stationary points of R are the same as the points of unit income elasticity of demand. HINT [Differentiate R with respect to x.]

31. ◆ Your calculus study group is discussing price elasticity of demand, and a member of the group asks the following question: "Since elasticity of demand measures the response of demand to change in unit price, what is the difference between elasticity of demand and the quantity $-dq/dp$?" How would you respond?

32. ◆ Another member of your study group claims that unit price elasticity of demand need not always correspond to maximum revenue. Is he correct? Explain your answer.

[71]Sources: Luxembourg Income Study/*New York Times*, August 14, 1995, p. A9, Commerce Department, Deloitte & Touche Survey/*New York Times*, November 24, 1999, p. C1.

CHAPTER 5 REVIEW

KEY CONCEPTS

WW Website www.WanerMath.com

Go to the Website at www.WanerMath.com to find a comprehensive and interactive Web-based summary of Chapter 5.

5.1 Maxima and Minima

Relative maximum, relative minimum *p. 371*

Absolute maximum, absolute minimum *p. 371*

Stationary points, singular points, endpoints *p. 373*

Finding and classifying maxima and minima *p. 374*

First derivative test for relative extrema *p. 375*

Extreme value theorem *p. 379*

Using technology to locate approximate extrema *p. 380*

5.2 Applications of Maxima and Minima

Minimizing average cost *p. 384*

Maximizing area *p. 385*

Steps in solving optimization problems *p. 387*

Maximizing revenue *p. 387*

Optimizing resources *p. 388*

Allocation of labor *p. 390*

5.3 Higher Order Derivatives: Acceleration and Concavity

The second derivative of a function f is the derivative of the derivative of f, written as f'' *p. 398*

The acceleration of a moving object is the second derivative of the position function *p. 398*

Acceleration due to gravity *p. 399*

Acceleration of sales *p. 400*

Concave up, concave down, point of inflection *p. 401*

Locating points of inflection *p. 401*

Application to inflation *p. 402*

Second derivative test for relative extrema *p. 405*

Higher order derivatives *p. 406*

5.4 Analyzing Graphs

Features of a graph: x- and y-intercepts, relative extrema, points of inflection; behavior near points where the function is not defined, behavior at infinity *pp. 416–417*

Analyzing a graph *p. 417*

5.5 Related Rates

If Q is a quantity changing over time t, then the derivative dQ/dt is the rate at which Q changes over time *p. 424*

The expanding circle *p. 424*

Steps in solving related rates problems *p. 425*

The falling ladder *p. 425*

Average cost *p. 427*

Allocation of labor *p. 428*

5.6 Elasticity

Price elasticity of demand $E = -\frac{dq}{dp} \cdot \frac{p}{q}$; demand is elastic if $E > 1$, inelastic if $E < 1$, has unit elasticity if $E = 1$ *p. 434*

Computing and interpreting elasticity, and maximizing revenue *p. 435*

Using technology to compute elasticity *p. 436*

Income elasticity of demand *p. 436*

REVIEW EXERCISES

In Exercises 1–8, find all the relative and absolute extrema of the given functions on the given domain (if supplied) or on the largest possible domain (if no domain is supplied).

1. $f(x) = 2x^3 - 6x + 1$ on $[-2, +\infty)$

2. $f(x) = x^3 - x^2 - x - 1$ on $(-\infty, \infty)$

3. $g(x) = x^4 - 4x$ on $[-1, 1]$

4. $f(x) = \dfrac{x+1}{(x-1)^2}$ for $-2 \le x \le 2, x \ne 1$

5. $g(x) = (x-1)^{2/3}$ **6.** $g(x) = x^2 + \ln x$ on $(0, +\infty)$

7. $h(x) = \dfrac{1}{x} + \dfrac{1}{x^2}$ **8.** $h(x) = e^{x^2} + 1$

In Exercises 9–12, the graph of the function f or its derivative is given. Find the approximate x-coordinates of all relative extrema and points of inflection of the original function f (if any).

9. Graph of f:

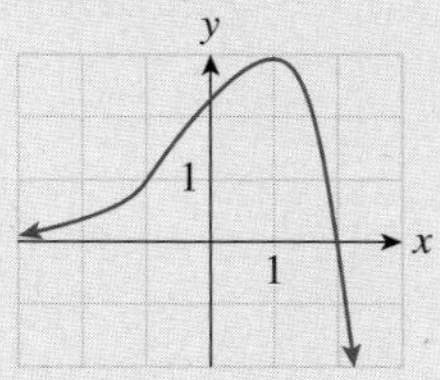

10. Graph of f:

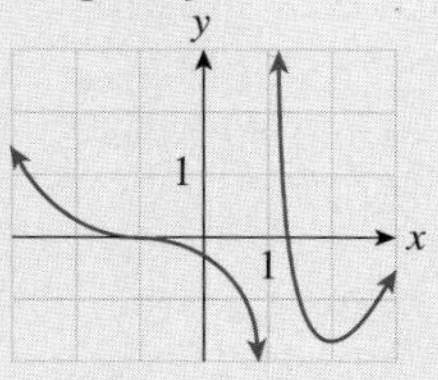

11. Graph of f':

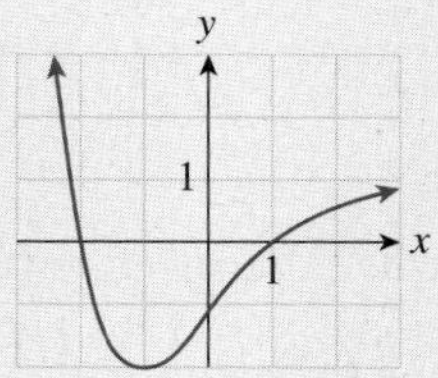

12. Graph of f':

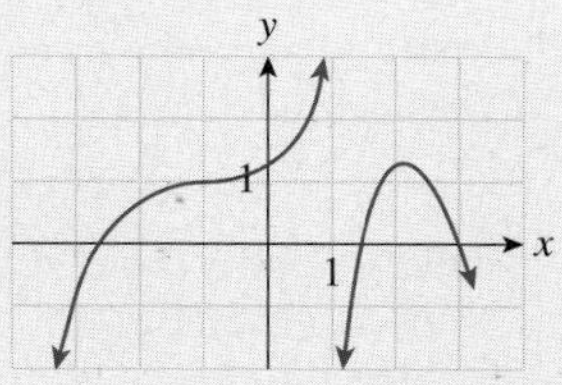

In Exercises 13 and 14, the graph of the second derivative of a function f is given. Find the approximate x-coordinates of all points of inflection of the original function f (if any).

13. Graph of f''

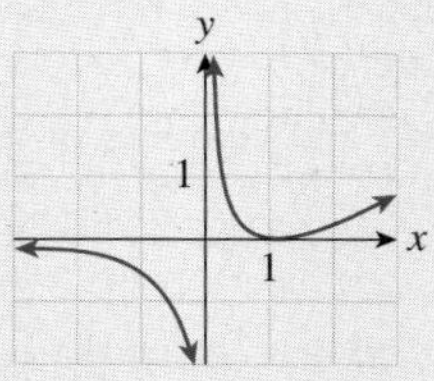

14. Graph of f''

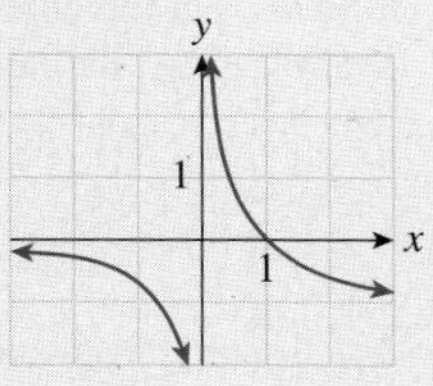

*In Exercises 15 and 16, the position s of a point (in meters) is given as a function of time t (in seconds). Find **(a)** its acceleration as a function of t and **(b)** its acceleration at the specified time.*

15. $s = \frac{2}{3t^2} - \frac{1}{t}; t = 1$

16. $s = \frac{4}{t^2} - \frac{3t}{4}; t = 2$

In Exercises 17–22, sketch the graph of the given function, indicating all relative and absolute extrema and points of inflection. Find the coordinates of these points exactly, where possible. Also indicate any horizontal and vertical asymptotes.

17. $f(x) = x^3 - 12x$ on $[-2, +\infty)$

18. $g(x) = x^4 - 4x$ on $[-1, 1]$

19. $f(x) = \frac{x^2 - 3}{x^3}$

20. $f(x) = (x - 1)^{2/3} + \frac{2x}{3}$

21. $g(x) = (x - 3)\sqrt{x}$

22. $g(x) = (x + 3)\sqrt{x}$

APPLICATIONS: OHaganBooks.com

23. ***Revenue*** Demand for the latest best-seller at OHaganBooks.com, *A River Burns through It*, is given by

$$q = -p^2 + 33p + 9 \qquad (18 \le p \le 28)$$

copies sold per week when the price is p dollars. What price should the company charge to obtain the largest revenue?

24. ***Revenue*** Demand for *The Secret Loves of John O*, a romance novel by Margó Dufón that flopped after two weeks on the market, is given by

$$q = -2p^2 + 5p + 6 \qquad (0 \le p \le 3.3)$$

copies sold per week when the price is p dollars. What price should OHaganBooks charge to obtain the largest revenue?

25. ***Profit*** Taking into account storage and shipping, it costs OHaganBooks.com

$$C = 9q + 100$$

dollars to sell q copies of *A River Burns through It* in a week (see Exercise 23).

a. If demand is as in Exercise 23, express the weekly profit earned by OHaganBooks.com from the sale of *A River Burns through It* as a function of unit price p.

b. What price should the company charge to get the largest weekly profit? What is the maximum possible weekly profit?

c. Compare your answer in part (b) with the price the company should charge to obtain the largest revenue (Exercise 23). Explain any difference.

26. ***Profit*** Taking into account storage and shipping, it costs OHaganBooks.com

$$C = 3q$$

dollars to sell q copies of Margó Dufón's *The Secret Loves of John O* in a week (see Exercise 24).

a. If demand is as in Exercise 24, express the weekly profit earned by OHaganBooks.com from the sale of *The Secret Loves of John O* as a function of unit price p.

b. What price should the company charge to get the largest weekly profit? What is the maximum possible weekly profit?

c. Compare your answer in part (b) with the price the company should charge to obtain the largest revenue (Exercise 24). Explain any difference.

27. ***Box Design*** The sales department at OHaganBooks.com, which has decided to send chocolate lobsters to each of its customers, is trying to design a shipping box with a square base. It has a roll of cardboard 36 inches wide from which to make the boxes. Each box will be obtained by cutting out corners from a rectangle of cardboard as shown in the following diagram:

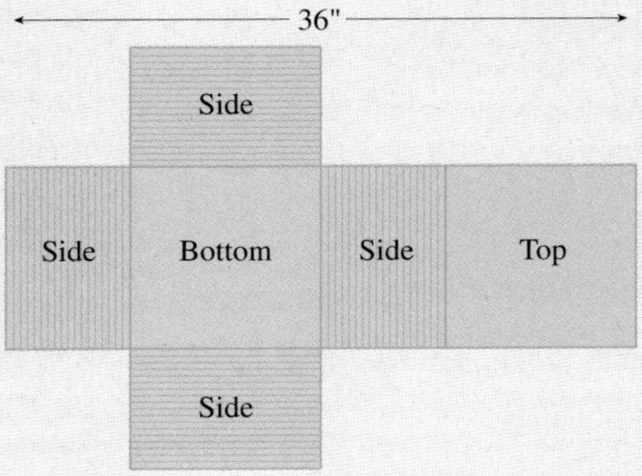

(Notice that the top and bottom of each box will be square, but the sides will not necessarily be square.) What are the dimensions of the boxes with the largest volume that can be made in this way? What is the maximum volume?

28. ***Box Redesign*** The sales department at OHaganBooks.com was not pleased with the result of the box design in the preceding exercise; the resulting box was too large for the chocolate lobsters, so, following a suggestion by a math major student intern, the department decided to redesign the boxes to meet the following specifications: As in Exercise 27, each box would be obtained by cutting out corners from a rectangle of cardboard as shown in the following diagram:

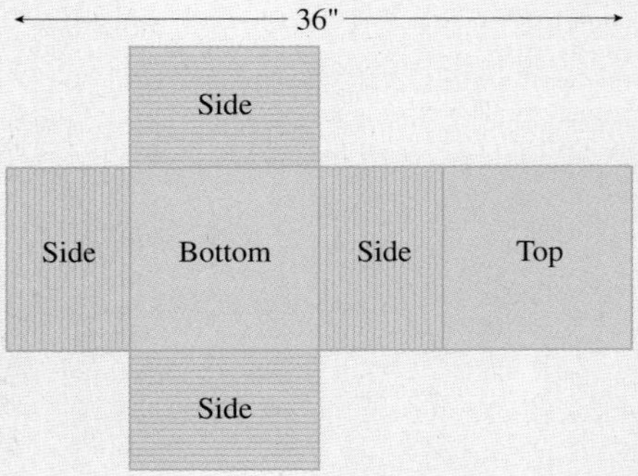

(Notice that the top and bottom of each box would be square, but not necessarily the sides.) The dimensions would be such that the total surface area of the sides plus the bottom of the box would be as large as possible. What are the dimensions of the boxes with the largest area that can be made in this way? How does this box compare with that obtained in Exercise 27?

29. ***Elasticity of Demand*** (Compare Exercise 23.) Demand for the latest best-seller at OHaganBooks.com, *A River Burns through It*, is given by

$$q = -p^2 + 33p + 9 \qquad (18 \le p \le 28)$$

copies sold per week when the price is p dollars.

a. Find the price elasticity of demand as a function of p.
b. Find the elasticity of demand for this book at a price of \$20 and at a price of \$25. (Round your answers to two decimal places.) Interpret the answers.
c. What price should the company charge to obtain the largest revenue?

30. ***Elasticity of Demand*** (Compare Exercise 24.) Demand for *The Secret Loves of John O*, a romance novel by Margó Dufón that flopped after two weeks on the market, is given by

$$q = -2p^2 + 5p + 6 \qquad (0 \le p \le 3.3)$$

copies sold per week when the price is p dollars.

a. Find the price elasticity of demand as a function of p.
b. Find the elasticity of demand for this book at a price of \$2 and at a price of \$3. (Round your answers to two decimal places.) Interpret the answers.
c. What price should the company charge to obtain the largest revenue?

31. ***Elasticity of Demand*** Last year OHaganBooks.com experimented with an online subscriber service, Red On Line (ROL), for its electronic book service. The consumer demand for ROL was modeled by the equation

$$q = 1{,}000e^{-p^2+p},$$

where p was the monthly access charge and q is the number of subscribers.

a. Obtain a formula for the price elasticity of demand, E, for ROL services.
b. Compute the elasticity of demand if the monthly access charge is set at \$2 per month. Interpret the result.
c. How much should the company have charged in order to obtain the maximum monthly revenue? What would this revenue have been?

32. ***Elasticity of Demand*** JungleBooks.com (one of OHaganBooks' main competitors) responded with its own online subscriber service, Better On Line (BOL), for its electronic book service. The consumer demand for BOL was modeled by the equation

$$q = 2{,}000e^{-3p^2+2p},$$

where p was the monthly access charge and q is the number of subscribers.

a. Obtain a formula for the price elasticity of demand, E, for BOL services.
b. Compute the elasticity of demand if the monthly access charge is set at \$2 per month. Interpret the result.
c. How much should the company have charged in order to obtain the maximum monthly revenue? What would this revenue have been?

33. ***Sales*** OHaganBooks.com modeled its weekly sales over a period of time with the function

$$s(t) = 6{,}053 + \frac{4{,}474}{1 + e^{-0.55(t-4.8)}},$$

where t is the time in weeks. Following are the graphs of s, s', and s'':

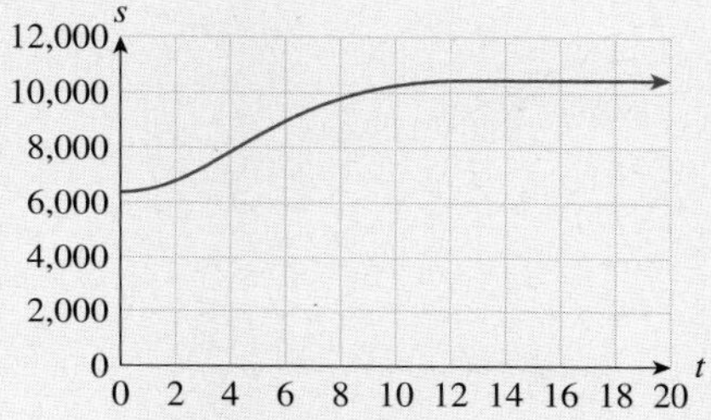

Graph of s

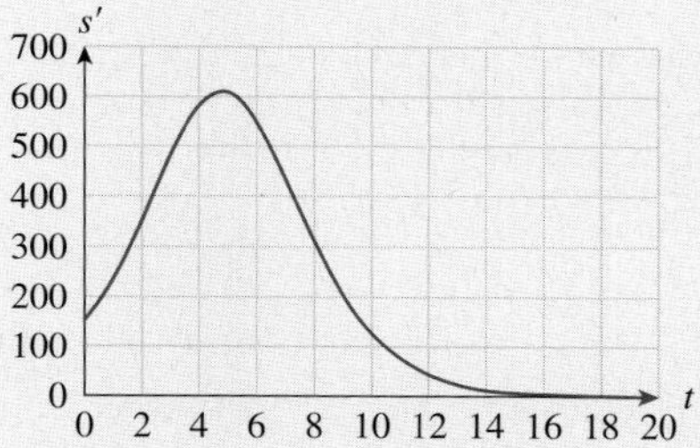

Graph of s'

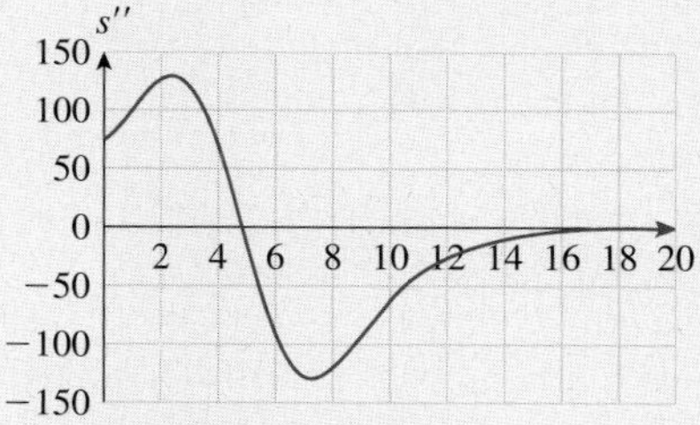

Graph of s''

a. Estimate when, to the nearest week, the weekly sales were growing fastest.
b. To what features on the graphs of s, s', and s'' does your answer to part (a) correspond?
c. The graph of s has a horizontal asymptote. What is the approximate value (s-coordinate) of this asymptote, and what is its significance in terms of weekly sales at OHaganBooks.com?

d. The graph of s' has a horizontal asymptote. What is the value (s'-coordinate) of this asymptote, and what is its significance in terms of weekly sales at OHaganBooks.com?

34. ***Sales*** The quarterly sales of OHagan *oPods* (OHaganBooks' answer to the *iPod*; a portable audio book unit with an incidental music feature) from the fourth quarter of 2009 can be roughly approximated by the function

$$N(t) = \frac{1{,}100}{1 + 9(1.8)^{-t}} \, oPods \ (t \geq 0),$$

where t is time in quarters since the fourth quarter of 2009. Following are the graphs of N, N', and N'':

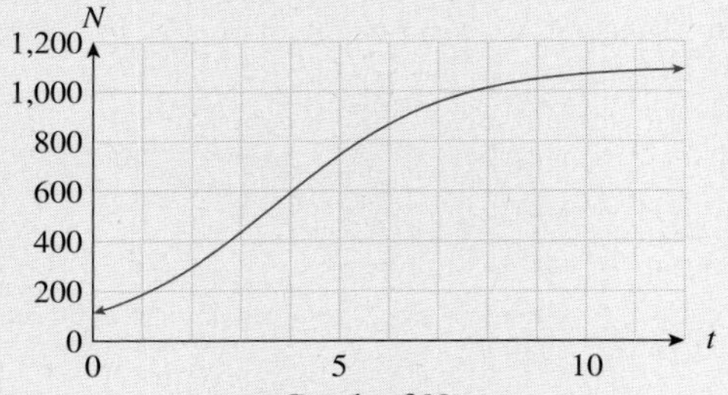

Graph of N

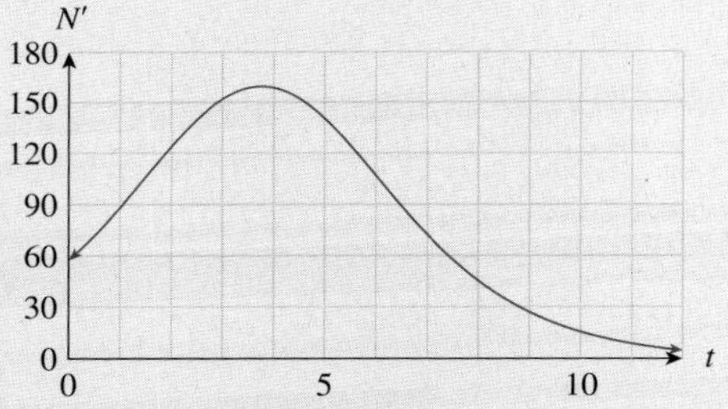

Graph of N'

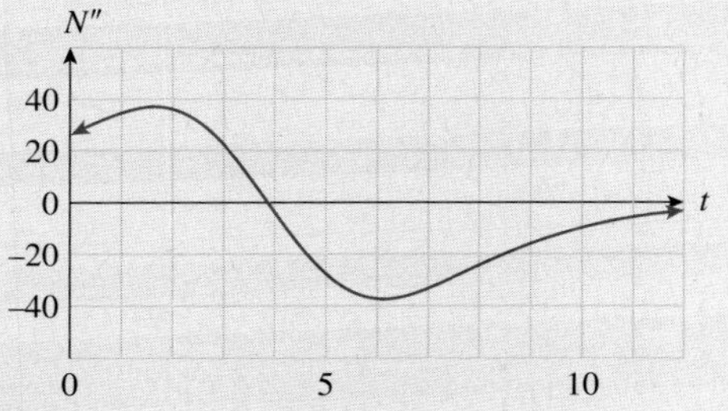

Graph of N''

a. Estimate when, to the nearest quarter, the quarterly sales were growing fastest.

b. To what features on the graphs of N, N', and N'' does your answer to part (a) correspond?

c. The graph of N has a horizontal asymptote. What is the approximate value (N-coordinate) of this asymptote, and what is its significance in terms of quarterly sales of *oPods*?

d. The graph of N' has a horizontal asymptote. What is the value (N'-coordinate) of this asymptote, and what is its significance in terms of quarterly sales of *oPods*?

35. ***Chance Encounter*** Marjory Duffin is walking north towards the corner entrance of OHaganBooks.com company headquarters at 5 ft/sec, while John O'Hagan is walking west toward the same entrance, also at 5 ft/sec. How fast is their distance apart decreasing when

a. each of them is 2 ft from the corner?

b. each of them is 1 ft from the corner?

c. each of them is h ft from the corner?

d. they collide on the corner?

36. ***Company Logos*** OHaganBooks.com's Web site has an animated graphic with its name in a rectangle whose height and width change; on either side of the rectangle are semicircles, as in the figure, whose diameters are the same as the height of the rectangle.

For reasons too complicated to explain, the designer wanted the combined area of the rectangle and semicircles to remain constant. At one point during the animation, the width of the rectangle is 1 inch, growing at a rate of 0.5 inches per second, while the height is 3 inches. How fast is the height changing?

Case Study

SERDAR/Alamy

Production Lot Size Management

Your publishing company, *Knockem Dead Paperbacks, Inc.,* is about to release its next best-seller, *Henrietta's Heaving Heart* by Celestine A. Lafleur. The company expects to sell 100,000 books each month in the next year. You have been given the job of scheduling print runs to meet the anticipated demand and minimize total costs to the company. Each print run has a setup cost of \$5,000, each book costs \$1 to produce, and monthly storage costs for books awaiting shipment average 1¢ per book. What will you do?

If you decide to print all 1,200,000 books (the total demand for the year, 100,000 books per month for 12 months) in a single run at the start of the year and sales run as predicted, then the number of books in stock would begin at 1,200,000 and decrease to zero by the end of the year, as shown in Figure 47.

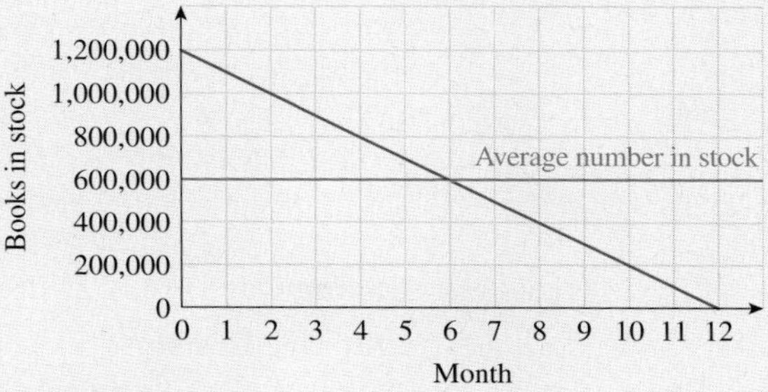

Figure 47

On average, you would be storing 600,000 books for 12 months at 1¢ per book, giving a total storage cost of $600{,}000 \times 12 \times .01 = \$72{,}000$. The setup cost for the single print run would be \$5,000. When you add to these the total cost of producing 1,200,000 books at \$1 per book, your total cost would be \$1,277,000.

If, on the other hand, you decide to cut down on storage costs by printing the book in two runs of 600,000 each, you would get the picture shown in Figure 48.

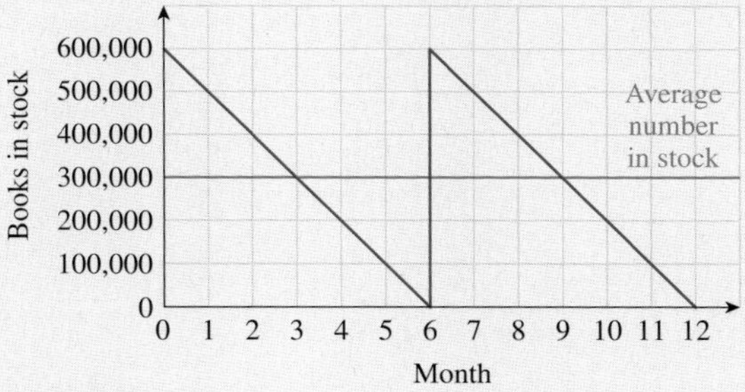

Figure 48

Now, the storage cost would be cut in half because on average there would be only 300,000 books in stock. Thus, the total storage cost would be \$36,000, and the setup cost would double to \$10,000 (because there would now be two runs). The production costs would be the same: 1,200,000 books @ \$1 per book. The total cost would therefore be reduced to \$1,246,000, a savings of \$31,000 compared to your first scenario.

"Aha!" you say to yourself, after doing these calculations. "Why not drastically cut costs by setting up a run every month?" You calculate that the setup costs alone would be 12 × \$5,000 = \$60,000, which is already more than the setup plus storage costs for two runs, so a run every month will cost too much. Perhaps, then, you should investigate three runs, four runs, and so on, until you find the lowest cost. This strikes you as too laborious a process, especially considering that you will have to do it all over again when planning for Lafleur's sequel, *Lorenzo's Lost Love,* due to be released next year. Realizing that this is an optimization problem, you decide to use some calculus to help you come up with a *formula* that you can use for all future plans. So you get to work.

Instead of working with the number 1,200,000, you use the letter N so that you can be as flexible as possible. (What if *Lorenzo's Lost Love* sells more copies?) Thus, you have a total of N books to be produced for the year. You now calculate the total cost of using x print runs per year. Because you are to produce a total of N books in x print runs, you will have to produce N/x books in each print run. N/x is called the **lot size**. As you can see from the diagrams above, the average number of books in storage will be half that amount, $N/(2x)$.

Now you can calculate the total cost for a year. Write P for the setup cost of a single print run ($P =$ \$5,000 in your case) and c for the *annual* cost of storing a book (to convert all of the time measurements to years; $c =$ \$0.12 here). Finally, write b for the cost of producing a single book ($b =$ \$1 here). The costs break down as follows.

Setup Costs: x print runs @ P dollars per run:	Px
Storage Costs: $N/(2x)$ books stored @ c dollars per year:	$cN/(2x)$
Production Costs: N books @ b dollars per book:	Nb
Total Cost:	$Px + \dfrac{cN}{2x} + Nb$

Remember that P, N, c, and b are all constants and x is the only variable. Thus, your cost function is

$$C(x) = Px + \frac{cN}{2x} + Nb$$

and you need to find the value of x that will minimize $C(x)$. But that's easy! All you need to do is find the relative extrema and select the absolute minimum (if any).

The domain of $C(x)$ is $(0, +\infty)$ because there is an x in the denominator and x can't be negative. To locate the extrema, you start by locating the critical points:

$$C'(x) = P - \frac{cN}{2x^2}.$$

The only singular point would be at $x = 0$, but 0 is not in the domain. To find stationary points, you set $C'(x) = 0$ and solve for x:

$$P - \frac{cN}{2x^2} = 0$$

$$2x^2 = \frac{cN}{P}$$

so

$$x = \sqrt{\frac{cN}{2P}}.$$

There is only one stationary point, and there are no singular points or endpoints. To graph the function you will need to put in numbers for the various constants. Substituting $N = 1{,}200{,}000$, $P = 5{,}000$, $c = 0.12$, and $b = 1$, you get

$$C(x) = 5{,}000x + \frac{72{,}000}{x} + 1{,}200{,}000$$

with the stationary point at

$$x = \sqrt{\frac{(0.12)(1{,}200{,}000)}{2(5000)}} \approx 3.79.$$

The total cost at the stationary point is

$$C(3.79) \approx 1{,}237{,}900.$$

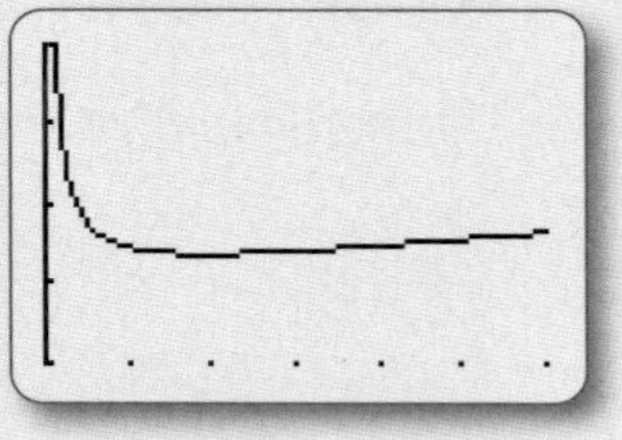

Figure 49

You now graph $C(x)$ in a window that includes the stationary point, say, $0 \le x \le 12$ and $1{,}100{,}000 \le C \le 1{,}500{,}000$, getting Figure 49.

From the graph, you can see that the stationary point is an absolute minimum. In the graph it appears that the graph is always concave up, which also tells you that your stationary point is a minimum. You can check the concavity by computing the second derivative:

$$C''(x) = \frac{cN}{x^3} > 0.$$

The second derivative is always positive because c, N, and x are all positive numbers, so indeed the graph is always concave up. Now you also know that it works regardless of the particular values of the constants.

So now you are practically done! You know that the absolute minimum cost occurs when you have $x \approx 3.79$ print runs per year. Don't be disappointed that the answer is not a whole number; whole number solutions are rarely found in real scenarios. What the answer (and the graph) do indicate is that either three or four print runs per year will cost the least money. If you take $x = 3$, you get a total cost of

$$C(3) = \$1{,}239{,}000.$$

If you take $x = 4$, you get a total cost of

$$C(4) = \$1{,}238{,}000.$$

So, four print runs per year will allow you to minimize your total costs.

EXERCISES

1. *Lorenzo's Lost Love* will sell 2,000,000 copies in a year. The remaining costs are the same. How many print runs should you use now?
2. In general, what happens to the number of runs that minimizes cost if both the setup cost and the total number of books are doubled?
3. In general, what happens to the number of runs that minimizes cost if the setup cost increases by a factor of 4?
4. Assuming that the total number of copies and storage costs are as originally stated, find the setup cost that would result in a single print run.
5. Assuming that the total number of copies and setup cost are as originally stated, find the storage cost that would result in a print run each month.

6. In Figure 48 we assumed that all the books in each run were manufactured in a very short time; otherwise the figure might have looked more like the following graph, which shows the inventory, assuming a slower rate of production.

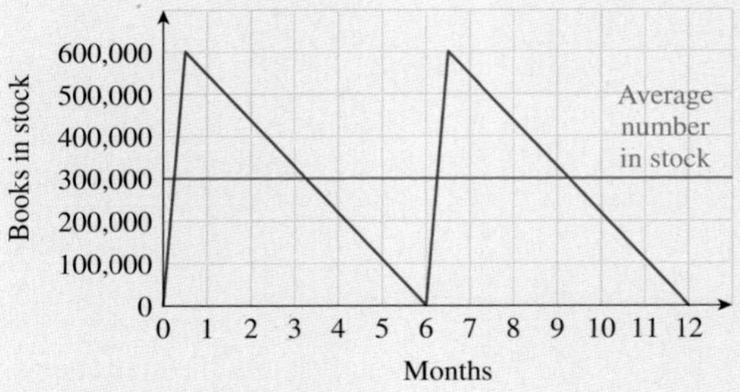

How would this affect the answer?

7. Referring to the general situation discussed in the text, find the cost as a function of the total number of books produced, assuming that the number of runs is chosen to minimize total cost. Also find the average cost per book.
8. Let $\bar{C}$ be the average cost function found in the preceding exercise. Calculate $\lim_{N\to+\infty} \bar{C}(N)$ and interpret the result.

TI-83/84 Plus Technology Guide

Section 5.6

Example 1(a) (page 435) Suppose that the demand equation for *Bobby Dolls* is given by $q = 216 - p^2$, where p is the price per doll in dollars and q is the number of dolls sold per week. Compute the price elasticity of demand when $p = \$5$ and $p = \$10$, and interpret the results.

Solution with Technology

The TI-83/84 Plus function `nDeriv` can be used to compute approximations of the elasticity E at various prices.

1. Set

```
Y1= 216-X^2                        Demand equation
Y2= -nDeriv(Y1,X,X)* X/Y1          Formula for E
```

2. Use the table feature to list the values of elasticity for a range of prices. For part (a) we chose values of `X` close to 5:

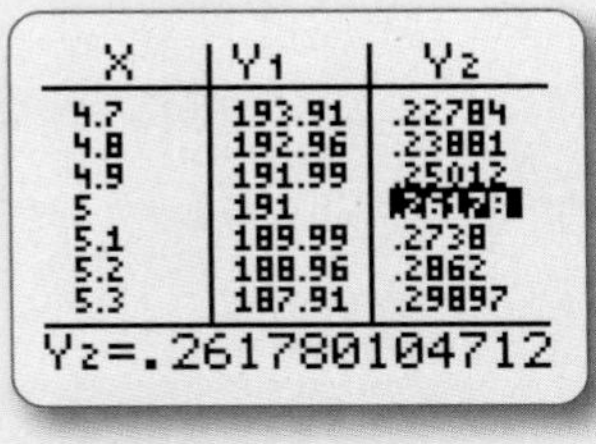

SPREADSHEET Technology Guide

Section 5.6

Example 1(a) (page 435) Suppose that the demand equation for *Bobby Dolls* is given by $q = 216 - p^2$, where p is the price per doll in dollars and q is the number of dolls sold per week. Compute the price elasticity of demand when $p = \$5$ and $p = \$10$, and interpret the results.

Solution with Technology

To approximate E in a spreadsheet, we can use the following approximation of E.

$$E \approx \frac{\text{Percentage decrease in demand}}{\text{Percentage increase in price}} \approx -\frac{\left(\dfrac{\Delta q}{q}\right)}{\left(\dfrac{\Delta p}{p}\right)}$$

The smaller Δp is, the better the approximation. Let's use $\Delta p = 1¢$, or 0.01 (which is small compared with the typical prices we consider—around \$5 to \$10).

1. We start by setting up our worksheet to list a range of prices, in increments of Δp, on either side of a price in which we are interested, such as $p_0 = \$5$:

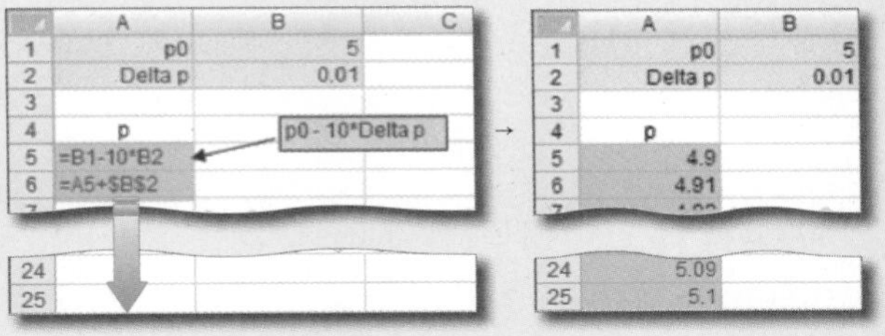

We start in cell A5 with the formula for $p_0 - 10\Delta p$ and then successively add Δp going down column A. You will find that the value $p_0 = 5$ appears midway down the list.

2. Next, we compute the corresponding values for the demand q in column B.

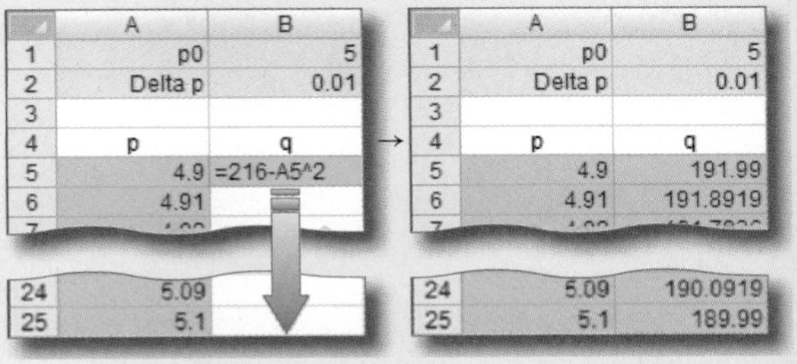

3. We add two new columns for the percentage changes in p and q. The formula shown in cell C5 is copied down columns C and D, to Row 24. (Why not row 25?)

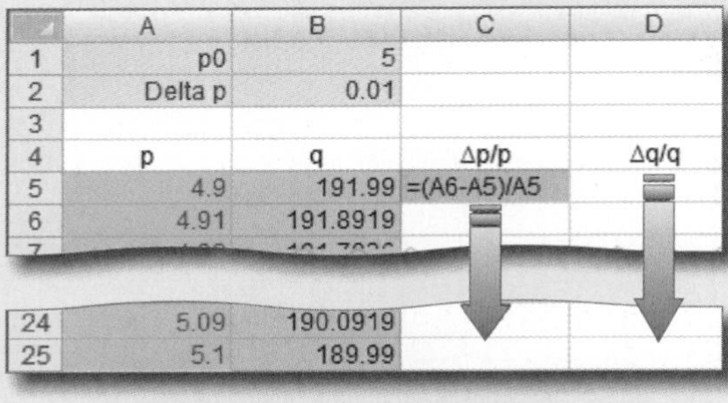

	A	B	C	D
1	p0	5		
2	Delta p	0.01		
3				
4	p	q	Δp/p	Δq/q
5	4.9	191.99	=(A6-A5)/A5	
6	4.91	191.8919		
24	5.09	190.0919		
25	5.1	189.99		

4. The elasticity can now be computed in column E as shown:

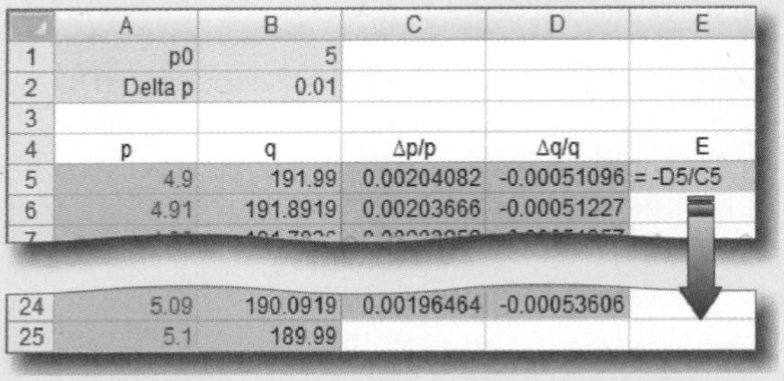

	A	B	C	D	E
1	p0	5			
2	Delta p	0.01			
3					
4	p	q	Δp/p	Δq/q	E
5	4.9	191.99	0.00204082	-0.00051096	= -D5/C5
6	4.91	191.8919	0.00203666	-0.00051227	
24	5.09	190.0919	0.00196464	-0.00053606	
25	5.1	189.99			

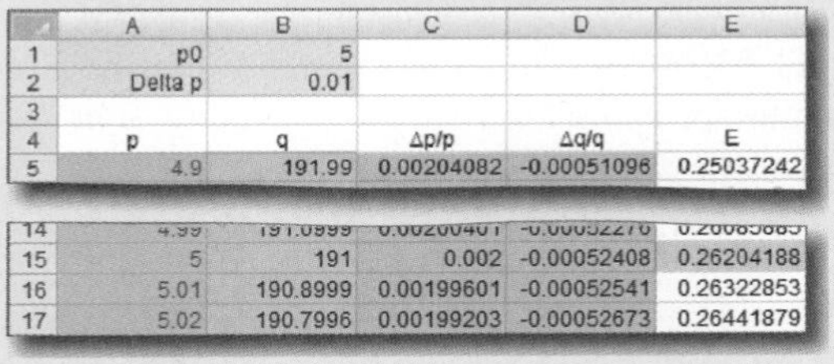

	A	B	C	D	E
1	p0	5			
2	Delta p	0.01			
3					
4	p	q	Δp/p	Δq/q	E
5	4.9	191.99	0.00204082	-0.00051096	0.25037242
14	4.99	191.0999	0.00200401	-0.00052276	[illegible]
15	5	191	0.002	-0.00052408	0.26204188
16	5.01	190.8999	0.00199601	-0.00052541	0.26322853
17	5.02	190.7996	0.00199203	-0.00052673	0.26441879

6

The Integral

Case Study Spending on Housing Construction

It is March 2007, and *Time* magazine, in its latest edition, is asking "Will the Housing Bubble Burst in 2007?" You are a summer intern at *Ronald Ramp Real Estate Development, Inc.,* which is considering a major luxury condominium development in Tampa, Florida, nicknamed the "Ramp Towers Tampa." You have been asked to find formulas for monthly spending on housing construction in the United States and for the average spent per month starting one year ago. You have data about percentage spending changes. **How will you model the trend and estimate the total?**

Bill Varie/Flirt/Corbis

Website

www.WanerMath.com

At the Website you will find:

- Section-by-section tutorials, including game tutorials with randomized quizzes
- A detailed chapter summary
- A true/false quiz
- Additional review exercises
- A numerical integration utility with Riemann sum grapher
- Graphing calculator programs for numerical integration
- Graphers, Excel tutorials, and other resources
- The following extra topic:

  Numerical Integration

Introduction

Roughly speaking, calculus is divided into two parts: **differential calculus** (the calculus of derivatives) and **integral calculus**, which is the subject of this chapter and the next. Integral calculus is concerned with problems that are in some sense the reverse of the problems seen in differential calculus. For example, where differential calculus shows how to compute the rate of change of a quantity, integral calculus shows how to find the quantity if we know its rate of change. This idea is made precise in the **Fundamental Theorem of Calculus**. Integral calculus and the Fundamental Theorem of Calculus allow us to solve many problems in economics, physics, and geometry, including one of the oldest problems in mathematics—computing areas of regions with curved boundaries.

6.1 The Indefinite Integral

Suppose that we knew the marginal cost to manufacture an item and we wanted to reconstruct the cost function. We would have to *reverse* the process of differentiation, to go from the derivative (the marginal cost function) back to the original function (the total cost). We'll first discuss how to do that and then look at some applications.

Here is an example: If the derivative of $F(x)$ is $4x^3$, what was $F(x)$? We recognize $4x^3$ as the derivative of x^4. So, we might have $F(x) = x^4$. However, $F(x) = x^4 + 7$ works just as well. In fact, $F(x) = x^4 + C$ works for any number C. Thus, there are *infinitely many* possible answers to this question.

In fact, we will see shortly that the formula $F(x) = x^4 + C$ covers *all* possible answers to the question. Let's give a name to what we are doing.

Antiderivative

An **antiderivative** of a function f is a function F such that $F' = f$.

Quick Examples

1. An antiderivative of $4x^3$ is x^4. Because the derivative of x^4 is $4x^3$
2. Another antiderivative of $4x^3$ is $x^4 + 7$. Because the derivative of $x^4 + 7$ is $4x^3$
3. An antiderivative of $2x$ is $x^2 + 12$. Because the derivative of $x^2 + 12$ is $2x$

Thus,

If the derivative of $A(x)$ is $B(x)$, then an antiderivative of $B(x)$ is $A(x)$.

We call the set of *all* antiderivatives of a function the **indefinite integral** of the function.

Indefinite Integral

$$\int f(x)\,dx$$

is read "the **indefinite integral** of $f(x)$ with respect to x" and stands for the set of all antiderivatives of f. Thus, $\int f(x)\,dx$ is a *collection of functions*; it is not a single function or a number. The function f that is being **integrated** is called the **integrand**, and the variable x is called the **variable of integration**.

Quick Examples

1. $\int 4x^3\,dx = x^4 + C$ — Every possible antiderivative of $4x^3$ has the form $x^4 + C$.
2. $\int 2x\,dx = x^2 + C$ — Every possible antiderivative of $2x$ has the form $x^2 + C$.

The **constant of integration** C reminds us that we can add any constant and get a different antiderivative.

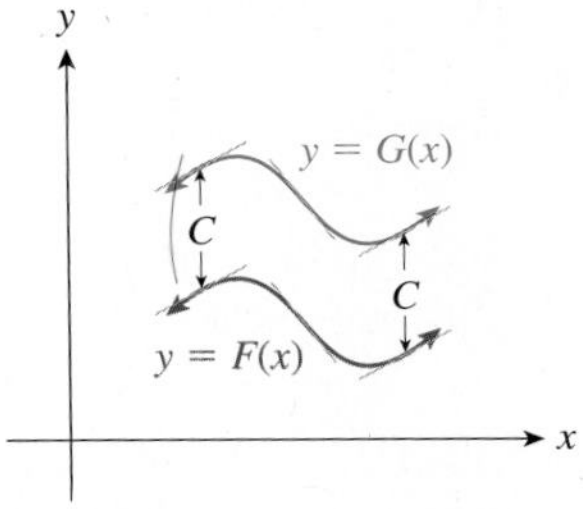

Figure 1

Q: *If $F(x)$ is one antiderivative of $f(x)$, why must all other antiderivatives have the form $F(x) + C$?*

A: Suppose $F(x)$ and $G(x)$ are both antiderivatives of $f(x)$, so that $F'(x) = G'(x)$. Consider what this means by looking at Figure 1. If $F'(x) = G'(x)$ for all x, then F and G have the *same slope* at each value of x. This means that their graphs must be *parallel* and hence remain exactly the same vertical distance apart. But that is the same as saying that the functions differ by a constant—that is, that $G(x) = F(x) + C$ for some constant C.*

* This argument can be turned into a more rigorous proof—that is, a proof that does not rely on geometric concepts such as "parallel graphs." We should also say that the result (and our geometric argument as well!) requires that the domain of F and G be a single (possibly infinite) open interval.

EXAMPLE 1 Indefinite Integral

Check that

a. $\int x\,dx = \frac{x^2}{2} + C$ **b.** $\int x^2\,dx = \frac{x^3}{3} + C$ **c.** $\int x^{-1}\,dx = \ln|x| + C$

Solution We check each equation by taking the derivative of its right-hand side and checking whether it equals the integrand on the left:

a. $\frac{d}{dx}\left(\frac{x^2}{2} + C\right) = \frac{2x}{2} + 0 = x$ ✔

b. $\frac{d}{dx}\left(\frac{x^3}{3} + C\right) = \frac{3x^2}{3} + 0 = x^2$ ✔

c. $\frac{d}{dx}(\ln|x| + C) = \frac{1}{x} + 0 = x^{-1}$. ✔

Because the derivative of the right-hand side is the integrand in each case, we can conclude that the given statements are all valid.†

† We are glossing over a subtlety in part (c): The constant of integration C can be different for $x < 0$ and $x > 0$ because the graph breaks at $x = 0$. (See the comment at the end of the last marginal note.) In general, our understanding will be that the constant of integration may be different on disconnected intervals of the domain.

➡ **Before we go on...** Example 1 gives us a very useful technique to check our answer every time we calculate an integral:

Take the derivative of the answer and check that it equals the integrand. ■

Now, we would like to make the process of finding indefinite integrals (antiderivatives) more mechanical. For example, it would be nice to have a power rule for indefinite integrals similar to the one we already have for derivatives. Example 1 already suggests such a rule for us:

Power Rule for the Indefinite Integral

$$\int x^n\,dx = \frac{x^{n+1}}{n+1} + C$$ This holds only if $n \neq -1$.*

$$\int x^{-1}\,dx = \ln|x| + C$$ For the special case $n = -1$

Equivalent Form of Second Formula: $\int \frac{1}{x}\,dx = \ln|x| + C$ Because $x^{-1} = \frac{1}{x}$

In Words For n other than -1, to find the integral of x^n, add 1 to the exponent, and then divide by the new exponent. When $n = -1$, the answer is the natural logarithm of the absolute value of x.

* Note that the right-hand side of the formula makes no sense if $n = -1$ because it has $n + 1$ in the denominator.

Quick Examples

1. $\int x^{55}\,dx = \frac{x^{56}}{56} + C$

2. $\int \frac{1}{x^{55}}\,dx = \int x^{-55}\,dx$ Exponent form

$= \frac{x^{-54}}{-54} + C$ When we add 1 to -55, we get -54, *not* -56.

$= -\frac{1}{54x^{54}} + C$

3. $\int 1\,dx = x + C$ Because $1 = x^0$. This is an important special case.

4. $\int \sqrt{x}\,dx = \int x^{1/2}dx$ Exponent form

$= \frac{x^{3/2}}{3/2} + C$

$= \frac{2x^{3/2}}{3} + C$

Notes

1. The integral $\int 1\,dx$ is commonly written as $\int dx$. Similarly, the integral $\int \frac{1}{x^{55}}\,dx$ may be written as $\int \frac{dx}{x^{55}}$.

2. We can easily check the power rule formula by taking the derivative of the right-hand side:

$$\frac{d}{dx}\left(\frac{x^{n+1}}{n+1} + C\right) = \frac{(n+1)x^n}{n+1} = x^n \quad ✔$$

3. Because the derivative of $\ln x$ is also $1/x$, you might be tempted to write $\int x^{-1}dx = \ln x + C$. But $\ln x$, being defined only for positive x, does not have the same domain as $1/x$, whereas $\ln |x|$ does. So, we must use $\ln |x| + C$ instead. ■

Following are more indefinite integrals that come from formulas for differentiation we have encountered before:

Indefinite Integral of e^x, b^x, and $|x|$

$$\int e^x\,dx = e^x + C \qquad \text{Because } \frac{d}{dx}(e^x) = e^x$$

If b is any positive number other than 1, then

$$\int b^x\,dx = \frac{b^x}{\ln b} + C \qquad \text{Because } \frac{d}{dx}\left(\frac{b^x}{\ln b}\right) = \frac{b^x \ln b}{\ln b} = b^x$$

$$\int |x|\,dx = \frac{x|x|}{2} + C. \qquad \text{Because } \frac{d}{dx}\left(\frac{x|x|}{2}\right) = |x| \text{ (Check this yourself!)}$$

Quick Example

$$\int 2^x\,dx = \frac{2^x}{\ln 2} + C$$

For more complicated functions, like $2x^3 + 6x^5 - 1$, we need the following rules for integrating sums, differences, and constant multiples.

Sums, Differences, and Constant Multiples

Sum and Difference Rules

$$\int [f(x) \pm g(x)]\,dx = \int f(x)\,dx \pm \int g(x)\,dx$$

In Words: The integral of a sum is the sum of the integrals, and the integral of a difference is the difference of the integrals.

Constant Multiple Rule

$$\int kf(x)\,dx = k\int f(x)\,dx \quad (k \text{ constant})$$

In Words: The integral of a constant times a function is the constant times the integral of the function. (In other words, the constant "goes along for the ride.")

Quick Examples

Sum Rule: $\int (x^3 + 1)\,dx = \int x^3\,dx + \int 1\,dx = \frac{x^4}{4} + x + C$ — $f(x) = x^3;\ g(x) = 1$

Constant Multiple Rule: $\int 5x^3\,dx = 5\int x^3\,dx = 5\frac{x^4}{4} + C$ — $k = 5;\ f(x) = x^3$

Constant Multiple Rule: $\int 4\,dx = 4\int 1\,dx = 4x + C$ — $k = 4;\ f(x) = 1$

Constant Multiple Rule: $\int 4e^x\,dx = 4\int e^x\,dx = 4e^x + C$ — $k = 4;\ f(x) = e^x$

Proof of the Sum Rule

We saw above that if two functions have the same derivative, they differ by a (possibly zero) constant. Look at the rule for sums:

$$\int [f(x) + g(x)]\,dx = \int f(x)\,dx + \int g(x)\,dx$$

If we take the derivative of the left-hand side with respect to x, we get the integrand, $f(x) + g(x)$. If we take the derivative of the right-hand side, we get

$$\frac{d}{dx}\left[\int f(x)\,dx + \int g(x)\,dx\right] = \frac{d}{dx}\left[\int f(x)\,dx\right] + \frac{d}{dx}\left[\int g(x)\,dx\right]$$

Derivative of a sum = Sum of derivatives.

$$= f(x) + g(x)$$

Because the left- and right-hand sides have the same derivative, they differ by a constant. But, because both expressions are indefinite integrals, adding a constant does not affect their value, so they are the same as indefinite integrals.

Notice that a key step in the proof was the fact that the derivative of a sum is the sum of the derivatives.

A similar proof works for the difference and constant multiple rules.

EXAMPLE 2 Using the Sum and Difference Rules

Find the integrals.

a. $\int (x^3 + x^5 - 1)\,dx$ **b.** $\int \left(x^{2.1} + \frac{1}{x^{1.1}} + \frac{1}{x} + e^x\right)dx$ **c.** $\int (e^x + 3^x - |x|)\,dx$

Solution

a. $\int (x^3 + x^5 - 1)\,dx = \int x^3\,dx + \int x^5\,dx - \int 1\,dx$ — Sum/difference rule

$= \frac{x^4}{4} + \frac{x^6}{6} - x + C$ — Power rule

b. $\int \left(x^{2.1} + \frac{1}{x^{1.1}} + \frac{1}{x} + e^x \right) dx$

$$= \int (x^{2.1} + x^{-1.1} + x^{-1} + e^x)\, dx \qquad \text{Exponent form}$$

$$= \int x^{2.1}\, dx + \int x^{-1.1}\, dx + \int x^{-1}\, dx + \int e^x\, dx \qquad \text{Sum rule}$$

$$= \frac{x^{3.1}}{3.1} + \frac{x^{-0.1}}{-0.1} + \ln|x| + e^x + C \qquad \text{Power rule and exponential rule}$$

$$= \frac{x^{3.1}}{3.1} - \frac{10}{x^{0.1}} + \ln|x| + e^x + C$$

c. $\int (e^x + 3^x - |x|)\, dx = \int e^x\, dx + \int 3^x\, dx - \int |x|\, dx$ Sum/difference rule

$$= e^x + \frac{3^x}{\ln 3} - \frac{x|x|}{2} + C$$ Rules for powers, exponentials, and absolute value

➡ **Before we go on...** You should check each of the answers in Example 2 by differentiating.

Q: *Why is there only a single arbitrary constant C in each of the answers?*

A: We could have written the answer to part (a) as

$$\frac{x^4}{4} + D + \frac{x^6}{6} + E - x + F$$

where D, E, and F are all arbitrary constants. Now suppose, for example, we set $D = 1$, $E = -2$, and $F = 6$. Then the particular antiderivative we get is $x^4/4 + x^6/6 - x + 5$, which has the form $x^4/4 + x^6/6 - x + C$. Thus, we could have chosen the single constant C to be 5 and obtained the same answer. In other words, the answer $x^4/4 + x^6/6 - x + C$ is just as general as the answer $x^4/4 + D + x^6/6 + E - x + F$, but simpler.

■

In practice we do not explicitly write the integral of a sum as a sum of integrals but just "integrate term by term," much as we learned to differentiate term by term.

EXAMPLE 3 Combining the Rules

Find the integrals.

a. $\int (10x^4 + 2x^2 - 3e^x)\, dx$ **b.** $\int \left(\frac{2}{x^{0.1}} + \frac{x^{0.1}}{2} - \frac{3}{4x} \right) dx$

c. $\int (3e^x - 2(1.2^x) + 5|x|)\, dx$

Solution

a. We need to integrate separately each of the terms $10x^4$, $2x^2$, and $3e^x$. To integrate $10x^4$ we use the rules for constant multiples and powers:

$$\int 10x^4\,dx = 10\int x^4\,dx = 10\frac{x^5}{5} + C = 2x^5 + C.$$

The other two terms are similar. We get

$$\int (10x^4 + 2x^2 - 3e^x)\,dx = 10\frac{x^5}{5} + 2\frac{x^3}{3} - 3e^x + C = 2x^5 + \frac{2}{3}x^3 - 3e^x + C.$$

b. We first convert to exponent form and then integrate term by term:

$$\int \left(\frac{2}{x^{0.1}} + \frac{x^{0.1}}{2} - \frac{3}{4x}\right)dx = \int \left(2x^{-0.1} + \frac{1}{2}x^{0.1} - \frac{3}{4}x^{-1}\right)dx$$ Exponent form

$$= 2\frac{x^{0.9}}{0.9} + \frac{1}{2}\frac{x^{1.1}}{1.1} - \frac{3}{4}\ln|x| + C$$ Integrate term by term.

$$= \frac{20x^{0.9}}{9} + \frac{x^{1.1}}{2.2} - \frac{3}{4}\ln|x| + C.$$ Back to rational form

c. $$\int (3e^x - 2(1.2^x) + 5|x|)\,dx = 3e^x - 2\frac{1.2^x}{\ln 1.2} + 5\frac{x|x|}{2} + C$$

EXAMPLE 4 Different Variable Name

Find $\int \left(\frac{1}{u} + \frac{1}{u^2}\right)du.$

Solution This integral may look a little strange because we are using the letter u instead of x, but there is really nothing special about x. Using u as the variable of integration, we get

$$\int \left(\frac{1}{u} + \frac{1}{u^2}\right)du = \int (u^{-1} + u^{-2})\,du$$ Exponent form.

$$= \ln|u| + \frac{u^{-1}}{-1} + C$$ Integrate term by term.

$$= \ln|u| - \frac{1}{u} + C.$$ Simplify the result.

➡ **Before we go on...** When we compute an indefinite integral, we want the independent variable in the answer to be the same as the variable of integration. Thus, if the integral in Example 4 had been written in terms of x rather than u, we would have written

$$\int \left(\frac{1}{x} + \frac{1}{x^2}\right)dx = \ln|x| - \frac{1}{x} + C.$$

■

APPLICATIONS

EXAMPLE 5 Finding Cost from Marginal Cost

The marginal cost to produce baseball caps at a production level of x caps is $4 - 0.001x$ dollars per cap, and the cost of producing 100 caps is \$500. Find the cost function.

Solution We are asked to find the cost function $C(x)$, given that the *marginal* cost function is $4 - 0.001x$. Recalling that the marginal cost function is the derivative of the cost function, we can write

$$C'(x) = 4 - 0.001x$$

and must find $C(x)$. Now $C(x)$ must be an antiderivative of $C'(x)$, so

$$\begin{aligned} C(x) &= \int (4 - 0.001x)\,dx \\ &= 4x - 0.001\frac{x^2}{2} + K \qquad \text{K is the constant of integration.*} \\ &= 4x - 0.0005x^2 + K. \end{aligned}$$

* We used K and not C for the constant of integration because we are using C for cost.

Now, unless we have a value for K, we don't really know what the cost function is. However, there is another piece of information we have ignored: The cost of producing 100 baseball caps is \$500. In symbols

$$C(100) = 500.$$

Substituting in our formula for $C(x)$, we have

$$\begin{aligned} C(100) &= 4(100) - 0.0005(100)^2 + K \\ 500 &= 395 + K \\ K &= 105. \end{aligned}$$

Now that we know what K is, we can write down the cost function:

$$C(x) = 4x - 0.0005x^2 + 105.$$

➡ **Before we go on...** Let us consider the significance of the constant term 105 in Example 5. If we substitute $x = 0$ into the cost function, we get

$$C(0) = 4(0) - 0.0005(0)^2 + 105 = 105.$$

Thus, \$105 is the cost of producing zero items; in other words, it is the **fixed cost.** ■

EXAMPLE 6 Total Sales from Annual Sales

By the start of 2008, Apple had sold a total of about 3.5 million iPhones. From the start of 2008 through the end of 2010, sales of iPhones were approximately

$$s(t) = 4.5t^2 + 5.8t + 6.5 \text{ million iPhones per year} \qquad (0 \le t \le 3),$$

where t is time in years since the start of 2008.[1]

[1] Source for data: Apple quarterly press releases (www.apple.com/investor/).

a. Find an expression for the total sales of iPhones up to time t.

b. Use the answer to part (a) to estimate the total sales of iPhones by the end of 2010. (The actual figure was 89.7 million.)

Solution

a. Let $S(t)$ be the total sales of iPhones, in millions, up to time t, where t is measured in years since the start of 2008, so we know that $S(0) = 3.5$. We are also given an expression for the number of iPhones sold per year. This function is the *derivative* of $S(t)$:

$$S'(t) = 4.5t^2 + 5.8t + 6.5.$$

Thus, the desired total sales function must be an antiderivative of $S'(t)$:

$$\begin{aligned} S(t) &= \int (4.5t^2 + 5.8t + 6.5)\, dt \\ &= \frac{4.5t^3}{3} + 5.8\frac{t^2}{2} + 6.5t + C \\ &= 1.5t^3 + 2.9t^2 + 6.5t + C. \end{aligned}$$

To calculate the value of the constant C, we can, as in the preceding example, use the known value of S: $S(0) = 3.5$.

$$S(0) = 1.5(0)^3 + 2.9(0)^2 + 6.5(0) + C = 3.5,$$

so

$$C = 3.5.$$

We can now write down the total sales function:

$$S(t) = 1.5t^3 + 2.9t^2 + 6.5t + 3.5 \text{ million iPhones.}$$

b. Because the end of 2010 (or the start of 2011) corresponds to $t = 3$, we calculate total sales as

$$S(3) = 1.5(3)^3 + 2.9(3)^2 + 6.5(3) + 3.5 = 89.6 \text{ million iPhones.}$$

Motion in a Straight Line

An important application of the indefinite integral is to the study of motion. The application of calculus to problems about motion is an example of the intertwining of mathematics and physics. We begin by bringing together some facts, scattered through the last several chapters, that have to do with an object moving in a straight line, and then restating them in terms of antiderivatives.

Position, Velocity, and Acceleration: Derivative Form

If $s = s(t)$ is the **position** of an object at time t, then its **velocity** is given by the derivative

$$v = \frac{ds}{dt}.$$

In Words: Velocity is the derivative of position.

The **acceleration** of an object is given by the derivative

$$a = \frac{dv}{dt}.$$

In Words: Acceleration is the derivative of velocity.

Position, Velocity, and Acceleration: Integral Form

$$s(t) = \int v(t)\,dt \qquad \text{Because } v = \frac{ds}{dt}$$

$$v(t) = \int a(t)\,dt \qquad \text{Because } a = \frac{dv}{dt}$$

Quick Examples

1. If the velocity of a particle moving in a straight line is given by $v(t) = 4t + 1$, then its position after t seconds is given by $s(t) = \int v(t)\,dt = \int (4t+1)\,dt = 2t^2 + t + C$.
2. If sales are accelerating at 2 golf balls/day^2, then the rate of change of sales ("velocity of sales") is $v(t) = \int a(t)\,dt = \int 2\,dt = 2t + C$ golf balls/day.
3. If the rate of change of sales is $v(t) = 2t + 5$ golf balls per day, then the total sales are $s(t) = \int v(t)\,dt = \int (2t+5)\,dt = t^2 + 5t + C$ golf balls sold through time t.

EXAMPLE 7 Motion in a Straight Line

a. The velocity of a particle moving along a straight line is given by $v(t) = 4t + 1$ m/sec. Given that the particle is at position $s = 2$ meters at time $t = 1$, find an expression for s in terms of t.

b. For a freely falling body experiencing no air resistance and zero initial velocity, find an expression for the velocity v in terms of t. [Note: On Earth, a freely falling body experiencing no air resistance accelerates downward at approximately 9.8 meters per second per second, or 9.8 m/sec^2 (or 32 ft/sec^2).]

Solution

a. As we saw in the Quick Example above, the position of the particle after t seconds is given by

$$\begin{aligned} s(t) &= \int v(t)\,dt \\ &= \int (4t+1)\,dt = 2t^2 + t + C. \end{aligned}$$

But what is the value of C? Now, we are told that the particle is at position $s = 2$ at time $t = 1$. In other words, $s(1) = 2$. Substituting this into the expression for $s(t)$ gives

$$2 = 2(1)^2 + 1 + C$$

so

$$C = -1.$$

Hence the position after t seconds is given by

$$s(t) = 2t^2 + t - 1 \text{ meters.}$$

b. Let's measure heights above the ground as positive, so that a rising object has positive velocity and the acceleration due to gravity is negative. (It causes the upward velocity to decrease in value.) Thus, the acceleration of the object is given by

$$a(t) = -9.8 \text{ m/sec}^2.$$

We wish to know the velocity, which is an antiderivative of acceleration, so we compute

$$v(t) = \int a(t)\, dt = \int (-9.8)\, dt = -9.8t + C.$$

To find the value of C, we use the given information that at time $t = 0$ the velocity is 0: $v(0) = 0$. Substituting this into the expression for $v(t)$ gives

$$0 = -9.8(0) + C$$

so

$$C = 0.$$

Hence, the velocity after t seconds is given by

$$v(t) = -9.8t \text{ m/sec.}$$

EXAMPLE 8 Vertical Motion under Gravity

You are standing on the edge of a cliff and toss a stone upward at a speed of $v_0 = 30$ feet per second (v_0 is called the *initial velocity*).

a. Find the stone's velocity as a function of time. How fast and in what direction is it going after 5 seconds? (Neglect the effects of air resistance.)

b. Find the position of the stone as a function of time. Where will it be after 5 seconds?

c. When and where will the stone reach its zenith, its highest point?

Solution

a. This is similar to Example 7(b): Measuring height above the ground as positive, the acceleration of the stone is given by $a(t) = -32$ ft/s^2, and so

$$v(t) = \int (-32)\, dt = -32t + C.$$

To obtain C, we use the fact that you tossed the stone upward at 30 ft/s; that is, when $t = 0$, $v = 30$, or $v(0) = 30$. Thus,

$$30 = v(0) = -32(0) + C.$$

So, $C = 30$ and the formula for velocity is

$$v(t) = -32t + 30 \text{ ft/sec.} \qquad v(t) = -32t + v_0$$

In particular, after 5 seconds the velocity will be

$$v(5) = -32(5) + 30 = -130 \text{ ft/sec.}$$

After 5 seconds the stone is *falling* with a speed of 130 ft/sec.

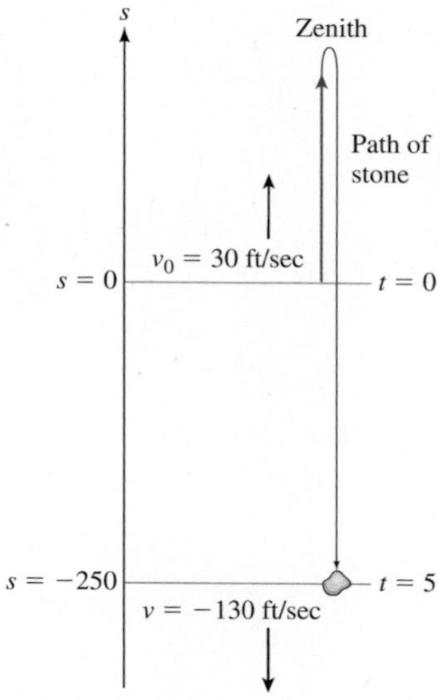

Figure 2

b. We wish to know the position, but position is an antiderivative of velocity. Thus,

$$s(t) = \int v(t)\, dt = \int (-32t + 30)\, dt = -16t^2 + 30t + C.$$

Now to find C, we need to know the initial position $s(0)$. We are not told this, so let's measure heights so that the initial position is zero. Then

$$0 = s(0) = C$$

and

$$s(t) = -16t^2 + 30t \text{ ft.}$$

$s(t) = -16t^2 + v_0t + s_0$
$s_0 =$ initial position

In particular, after 5 seconds the stone has a height of

$$s(5) = -16(5)^2 + 30(5) = -250 \text{ ft.}$$

In other words, the stone is now 250 ft *below* where it was when you first threw it, as shown in Figure 2.

c. The stone reaches its zenith when its height $s(t)$ is at its maximum value, which occurs when $v(t) = s'(t)$ is zero. So we solve

$$v(t) = -32t + 30 = 0$$

getting $t = 30/32 = 15/16 = 0.9375$ sec. This is the time when the stone reaches its zenith. The height of the stone at that time is

$$s(15/16) = -16(15/16)^2 + 30(15/16) = 14.0625 \text{ ft.}$$

➡ **Before we go on...** Here again are the formulas we obtained in Example 8, together with their metric equivalents:

Vertical Motion under Gravity: Velocity and Position

If we ignore air resistance, the vertical velocity and position of an object moving under gravity are given by

British Units	Metric Units
Velocity: $v(t) = -32t + v_0$ ft/sec	$v(t) = -9.8t + v_0$ m/sec
Position: $s(t) = -16t^2 + v_0t + s_0$ ft	$s(t) = -4.9t^2 + v_0t + s_0$ m

$v_0 =$ initial velocity $=$ velocity at time 0
$s_0 =$ initial position $=$ position at time 0

Quick Example

If a ball is thrown down at 2 ft/sec from a height of 200 ft, then its velocity and position after t seconds are $v(t) = -32t - 2$ ft/sec and $s(t) = -16t^2 - 2t + 200$ ft. ■

6.1 EXERCISES

▼ more advanced ◆ challenging

T indicates exercises that should be solved using technology

Evaluate the integrals in Exercises 1–42.
HINT [for 1–6: See Quick Examples on page 453.]

1. $\int x^5\,dx$
2. $\int x^7\,dx$
3. $\int 6\,dx$
4. $\int (-5)\,dx$
5. $\int x\,dx$
6. $\int (-x)\,dx$

HINT [for 7–18: See Example 2.]

7. $\int (x^2 - x)\,dx$
8. $\int (x + x^3)\,dx$
9. $\int (1 + x)\,dx$
10. $\int (4 - x)\,dx$
11. $\int x^{-5}\,dx$
12. $\int x^{-7}\,dx$
13. $\int (x^{2.3} + x^{-1.3})\,dx$
14. $\int (x^{-0.2} - x^{0.2})\,dx$
15. $\int (u^2 - u^{-1})\,du$ HINT [See Example 4.]
16. $\int (v^{-2} + 2v^{-1})\,dv$ HINT [See Example 4.]
17. $\int \sqrt[4]{x}\,dx$
18. $\int \sqrt[3]{x}\,dx$

HINT [for 19–42: See Example 3.]

19. $\int (3x^4 - 2x^{-2} + x^{-5} + 4)\,dx$
20. $\int (4x^7 - x^{-3} + 1)\,dx$
21. $\int \left(\frac{2}{u} + \frac{u}{4}\right) du$
22. $\int \left(\frac{2}{u^2} + \frac{u^2}{4}\right) du$
23. $\int \left(\frac{1}{x} + \frac{2}{x^2} - \frac{1}{x^3}\right) dx$
24. $\int \left(\frac{3}{x} - \frac{1}{x^5} + \frac{1}{x^7}\right) dx$
25. $\int (3x^{0.1} - x^{4.3} - 4.1)\,dx$
26. $\int \left(\frac{x^{2.1}}{2} - 2.3\right) dx$
27. $\int \left(\frac{3}{x^{0.1}} - \frac{4}{x^{1.1}}\right) dx$
28. $\int \left(\frac{1}{x^{1.1}} - \frac{1}{x}\right) dx$
29. $\int \left(5.1t - \frac{1.2}{t} + \frac{3}{t^{1.2}}\right) dt$
30. $\int \left(3.2 + \frac{1}{t^{0.9}} + \frac{t^{1.2}}{3}\right) dt$
31. $\int (2e^x + 5|x| + 1/4)\,dx$
32. $\int (-4e^x + |x|/3 - 1/8)\,dx$
33. $\int \left(\frac{6.1}{x^{0.5}} + \frac{x^{0.5}}{6} - e^x\right) dx$
34. $\int \left(\frac{4.2}{x^{0.4}} + \frac{x^{0.4}}{3} - 2e^x\right) dx$
35. $\int (2^x - 3^x)\,dx$
36. $\int (1.1^x + 2^x)\,dx$
37. $\int \left(100(1.1^x) - \frac{2|x|}{3}\right) dx$
38. $\int \left(1{,}000(0.9^x) + \frac{4|x|}{5}\right) dx$
39. ▼ $\int x^{-2}\left(x^4 - \frac{3}{2x^4}\right) dx$
40. ▼ $\int 3x^4\left(\frac{2}{x^4} + \frac{3}{5x^6}\right) dx$
41. ▼ $\int \frac{x+2}{x^3}\,dx$
42. ▼ $\int \frac{x^2-2}{x}\,dx$
43. Find $f(x)$ if $f(0) = 1$ and the tangent line at $(x, f(x))$ has slope x. HINT [See Example 5.]
44. Find $f(x)$ if $f(1) = 1$ and the tangent line at $(x, f(x))$ has slope $\frac{1}{x}$. HINT [See Example 5.]
45. Find $f(x)$ if $f(0) = 0$ and the tangent line at $(x, f(x))$ has slope $e^x - 1$.
46. Find $f(x)$ if $f(1) = -1$ and the tangent line at $(x, f(x))$ has slope $2e^x + 1$.

APPLICATIONS

47. ***Marginal Cost*** The marginal cost of producing the xth box of light bulbs is $5 - \frac{x}{10{,}000}$ and the fixed cost is \$20,000. Find the cost function $C(x)$. HINT [See Example 5.]
48. ***Marginal Cost*** The marginal cost of producing the xth box of DVDs is $10 + \frac{x^2}{100{,}000}$ and the fixed cost is \$100,000. Find the cost function $C(x)$. HINT [See Example 5.]
49. ***Marginal Cost*** The marginal cost of producing the xth roll of film is $5 + 2x + \frac{1}{x}$. The total cost to produce one roll is \$1,000. Find the cost function $C(x)$. HINT [See Example 5.]
50. ***Marginal Cost*** The marginal cost of producing the xth box of CDs is $10 + x + \frac{1}{x^2}$. The total cost to produce 100 boxes is \$10,000. Find the cost function $C(x)$. HINT [See Example 5.]
51. ***Facebook Membership*** At the start of 2005, Facebook had 1 million members. Since that time, new members joined at a rate of roughly

$$m(t) = 3.2t^3 - 12t + 10 \text{ million members per year} \quad (0 \le t \le 5),$$

where t is time in years since the start of 2005.[2]

a. Find an expression for total Facebook membership $M(t)$ at time t. HINT [See Example 6.]

b. Use the answer to part (a) to estimate Facebook membership midway through 2008. (Round your answer to the nearest 1 million members. The actual figure was 80 million.)

52. ***Uploads to YouTube*** Since YouTube first became available to the public in mid-2005, the rate at which video has been uploaded to the site can be approximated by

$$v(t) = 525{,}600(0.42t^2 + 2.7t - 1) \text{ hours of video per year} \quad (0.5 \le t \le 7),$$

where t is time in years since the start of 2005.[3]

a. Find an expression for the total number of hours $V(t)$ of video at time t (starting from zero hours of video at $t = 0.5$). HINT [See Example 6.]

b. Use the answer to part (a) to estimate the total number of hours of video uploaded by the start of 2012. (Round your answer to the nearest million hours of video.)

53. ***Median Household Income*** From 2000 to 2007, median household income in the United States rose by an average of approximately \$1,200 per year.[4] Given that the median household income in 2000 was approximately \$42,000, use an indefinite integral to find a formula for the median household income I as a function of the year t ($t = 0$ represents 2000), and use your formula to estimate the median household income in 2005. (You can do this exercise without integration using the methods of Section 1.3, but here you should use an indefinite integral.)

54. ***Mean Household Income*** From 2000 to 2007, the mean household income in the United States rose by an average of approximately \$1,500 per year.[5] Given that the mean household income in 2000 was approximately \$57,000, use an indefinite integral to find a formula for the mean household income I as a function of the year t ($t = 0$ represents 2000), and use your formula to estimate the mean household income in 2006. (You can do this exercise without integration using the methods of Section 1.3, but here you should use an indefinite integral.)

55. ***Bottled Water Sales*** The rate of U.S. sales of bottled water for the period 2000–2010 can be approximated by

$$s(t) = -45t^2 + 900t + 4{,}200 \text{ million gallons per year} \quad (0 \le t \le 10),$$

where t is time in years since the start of 2000.[6] Use an indefinite integral to approximate the total sales $S(t)$ of bottled water since the start of 2000. Approximately how much bottled water was sold from the start of 2000 to the start of 2008? HINT [At the start of 2000, sales since that time are zero.]

56. ***Bottled Water Sales*** The rate of U.S. per capita sales of bottled water for the period 2000–2010 can be approximated by

$$s(t) = -0.18t^2 + 3t + 15 \text{ gallons per year} \quad (0 \le t \le 10),$$

where t is time in years since the start of 2000.[7] Use an indefinite integral to approximate the total per capita sales $S(t)$ of bottled water since the start of 2000. Approximately how much bottled water was sold, per capita, from the start of 2000 to the end of 2009? HINT [At the start of 2000, sales since that time are zero.]

57. ▼ ***Health-Care Spending in the 1990s*** Write $H(t)$ for the amount spent in the United States on health care in year t, where t is measured in years since 1990. The rate of increase of $H(t)$ was approximately \$65 billion per year in 1990 and rose to \$100 billion per year in 2000.[8]

a. Find a linear model for the rate of change $H'(t)$.

b. Given that \$700 billion was spent on health care in the United States in 1990, find the function $H(t)$.

58. ▼ ***Health-Care Spending in the 2000s*** Write $H(t)$ for the amount spent in the United States on health care in year t, where t is measured in years since 2000. The rate of increase of $H(t)$ was projected to rise from \$100 billion per year in 2000 to approximately \$190 billion per year in 2010.[9]

a. Find a linear model for the rate of change $H'(t)$.

b. Given that \$1,300 billion was spent on health care in the United States in 2000, find the function $H(t)$.

59. ▼ ***Subprime Mortgage during the Housing Bubble*** At the start of 2007, the percentage of U.S. mortgages that were subprime was about 13%, was increasing at a rate of 1 percentage point per year, but was decelerating at 0.4 percentage points per year per year.[10]

a. Find an expression for the rate of change (velocity) of this percentage at time t in years since the start of 2007.

b. Use the result of part (a) to find an expression for the percentage of mortgages that were subprime at time t, and use it to estimate the rate at the start of 2008. HINT [See Quick Examples 2 and 3 on page 461.]

---

[2] Sources for data: www.facebook.com, www.insidefacebook.com.

[3] Source for data: www.YouTube.com.

[4] In current dollars, unadjusted for inflation. Source for data: U.S. Census Bureau (www.census.gov).

[5] *Ibid.*

[6] Source for data: Beverage Marketing Corporation (www.bottledwater.org).

[7] *Ibid.*

[8] Source: Centers for Medicare and Medicaid Services, "National Health Expenditures," 2002 version, released January 2004 (www.cms.hhs.gov/statistics/nhe/).

[9] Source: Centers for Medicare and Medicaid Services, "National Health Expenditures 1965–2013, History and Projections" (www.cms.hhs.gov/statistics/nhe/).

[10] Sources: Mortgage Bankers Association, UBS.

60. ▼ ***Subprime Mortgage Debt during the Housing Bubble*** At the start of 2008, the value of subprime mortgage debt outstanding in the U.S. was about \$1,300 billion, was increasing at a rate of 40 billion dollars per year, but was decelerating at 20 billion dollars per year per year.[11]

a. Find an expression for the rate of change (velocity) of the value of subprime mortgage debt at time t in years since the start of 2008.

b. Use the result of part (a) to find an expression for the value of subprime mortgage debt at time t, and use it to estimate the value at the start of 2009. HINT [See Quick Examples 2 and 3 on page 461.]

61. ***Motion in a Straight Line*** The velocity of a particle moving in a straight line is given by $v = t^2 + 1$.

a. Find an expression for the position s after a time t.

b. Given that $s = 1$ at time $t = 0$, find the constant of integration C, and hence find an expression for s in terms of t without any unknown constants. HINT [See Example 7.]

62. ***Motion in a Straight Line*** The velocity of a particle moving in a straight line is given by $v = 3e^t + t$.

a. Find an expression for the position s after a time t.

b. Given that $s = 3$ at time $t = 0$, find the constant of integration C, and hence find an expression for s in terms of t without any unknown constants. HINT [See Example 7.]

63. ***Vertical Motion under Gravity*** If a stone is dropped from a rest position above the ground, how fast (in feet per second) and in what direction will it be traveling after 10 seconds? (Neglect the effects of air resistance.) HINT [See Example 8.]

64. ***Vertical Motion under Gravity*** If a stone is thrown upward at 10 feet per second, how fast (in feet per second) and in what direction will it be traveling after 10 seconds? (Neglect the effects of air resistance.) HINT [See Example 8.]

65. ***Vertical Motion under Gravity*** Your name is Galileo Galilei and you toss a weight upward at 16 feet per second from the top of the Leaning Tower of Pisa (height 185 ft).

a. Neglecting air resistance, find the weight's velocity as a function of time t in seconds.

b. Find the height of the weight above the ground as a function of time. Where and when will it reach its zenith? HINT [See Example 8 and the formulas that follow.]

66. ***Vertical Motion under Gravity*** Your name is Spaghettini Bologna (an assistant of Galileo Galilei) and, to impress your boss, you toss a weight upward at 24 feet per second from the top of the Leaning Tower of Pisa (height 185 ft).

a. Neglecting air resistance, find the weight's velocity as a function of time t in seconds.

b. Find the height of the weight above the ground as a function of time. Where and when will it reach its zenith? HINT [See Example 8 and the formulas that follow.]

67. ▼ ***Tail Winds*** The ground speed of an airliner is obtained by adding its air speed and the tail-wind speed. On your recent trip from Mexico to the United States your plane was traveling at an air speed of 500 miles per hour and experienced tail winds of $25 + 50t$ miles per hour, where t is the time in hours since takeoff.

a. Obtain an expression for the distance traveled in terms of the time since takeoff. HINT [Ground speed = Air speed + Tail-wind speed.]

b. Use the result of part (a) to estimate the time of your 1,800-mile trip.

c. The equation solved in part (b) leads mathematically to two solutions. Explain the meaning of the solution you rejected.

68. ▼ ***Head Winds*** The ground speed of an airliner is obtained by subtracting its head-wind speed from its air speed. On your recent trip to Mexico from the United States your plane was traveling at an air speed of 500 miles per hour and experienced head winds of $25 + 50t$ miles per hour, where t is the time in hours since takeoff. HINT [Ground speed = Air speed − Head-wind speed.]

a. Obtain an expression for the distance traveled in terms of the time since takeoff.

b. Use the result of part (a) to estimate the time of your 1,500-mile trip.

c. The equation solved in part (b) leads mathematically to two solutions. Explain the meaning of the solution you rejected.

69. ▼ ***Vertical Motion*** Show that if a projectile is thrown upward with a velocity of v_0 ft/sec, then (neglecting air resistance) it will reach its highest point after $v_0/32$ seconds. HINT [See the formulas after Example 8.]

70. ▼ ***Vertical Motion*** Use the result of the preceding exercise to show that if a projectile is thrown upward with a velocity of v_0 ft/sec, its highest point will be $v_0^2/64$ feet above the starting point (if we neglect the effects of air resistance).

Exercises 71–76 use the results in the preceding two exercises.

71. ▼ I threw a ball up in the air to a height of 20 feet. How fast was the ball traveling when it left my hand?

72. ▼ I threw a ball up in the air to a height of 40 feet. How fast was the ball traveling when it left my hand?

73. ▼ A piece of chalk is tossed vertically upward by Prof. Schwarzenegger and hits the ceiling 100 feet above with a *BANG.*

a. What is the minimum speed the piece of chalk must have been traveling to enable it to hit the ceiling?

b. Assuming that Prof. Schwarzenegger in fact tossed the piece of chalk up at 100 ft/sec, how fast was it moving when it struck the ceiling?

c. Assuming that Prof. Schwarzenegger tossed the chalk up at 100 ft/sec, and that it recoils from the ceiling with the same speed it had at the instant it hit, how long will it take the chalk to make the return journey and hit the ground?

[11] Source: www.data360.org/dataset.aspx?Data_Set_Id=9549.

74. ▼ A projectile is fired vertically upward from ground level at 16,000 feet per second.

a. How high does the projectile go?
b. How long does it take to reach its zenith (highest point)?
c. How fast is it traveling when it hits the ground?

75. ▼ ***Strength*** Prof. Strong can throw a 10-pound dumbbell twice as high as Prof. Weak can. How much faster can Prof. Strong throw it?

76. ▼ ***Weakness*** Prof. Weak can throw a book three times as high as Prof. Strong can. How much faster can Prof. Weak throw it?

COMMUNICATION AND REASONING EXERCISES

77. Why is this section called "The *Indefinite* Integral?"

78. If the derivative of Julius is Augustus, then Augustus is __________ of Julius.

79. Linear functions are antiderivatives of what kind of function? Explain.

80. Constant functions are antiderivatives of what kind of function? Explain.

81. If we know the *derivative* of a function, do we know the function? Explain. If not, what further information will suffice?

82. If we know an *antiderivative* of a function, do we know the function? Explain. If not, what further information will suffice?

83. If $F(x)$ and $G(x)$ are both antiderivatives of $f(x)$, how are $F(x)$ and $G(x)$ related?

84. Your friend Marco claims that once you have one antiderivative of $f(x)$, you have all of them. Explain what he means.

85. Complete the following: The total cost function is a(n) ______ of the ______ cost function.

86. Complete the following: The distance covered is an antiderivative of the ______ function, and the velocity is an antiderivative of the ______ function.

87. If x represents the number of items manufactured and $f(x)$ represents dollars per item, what does $\int f(x)\,dx$ represent? In general, how are the units of $f(x)$ and the units of $\int f(x)\,dx$ related?

88. If t represents time in seconds since liftoff and $g(t)$ represents the volume of rocket fuel burned per second, what does $\int g(t)\,dt$ represent?

89. Why was the following marked wrong? What is the correct answer?

$$\int (3x+1)\,dx = \frac{3x^2}{2} + 0 + C = \frac{3x^2}{2} + C \quad \text{✗ WRONG!}$$

90. Why was the following marked wrong? What is the correct answer?

$$\int (3x^2 - 11x)\,dx = x^3 - 11 + C \quad \text{✗ WRONG!}$$

91. Why was the following marked wrong? What is the correct answer?

$$\int (12x^5 - 4x)\,dx = \int 2x^6 - 2x^2 + C \quad \text{✗ WRONG!}$$

92. Why was the following marked wrong? What is the correct answer?

$$\int 5\,dt = 5x + C \quad \text{✗ WRONG!}$$

93. Why was the following marked wrong? What is the correct answer?

$$\int 4(e^x - 2x)\,dx = (4x)(e^x - x^2) + C \quad \text{✗ WRONG!}$$

94. Why was the following marked wrong? What is the correct answer?

$$\int (2^x - 1)\,dx = \frac{2^{x+1}}{x+1} - x + C \quad \text{✗ WRONG!}$$

95. Why was the following marked wrong? How should it be corrected?

$$\frac{1}{x} = \ln|x| + C \quad \text{✗ WRONG!}$$

96. Why was the following marked wrong? What is the correct answer?

$$\int \frac{1}{x^3}\,dx = \ln|x^3| + C \quad \text{✗ WRONG!}$$

97. ▼ Give an argument for the rule that the integral of a sum is the sum of the integrals.

98. ▼ Give an argument for the rule that the integral of a constant multiple is the constant multiple of the integrals.

99. ▼ Give an example to show that the integral of a product is not the product of the integrals.

100. ▼ Give an example to show that the integral of a quotient is not the quotient of the integrals.

101. ▼ Complete the following: If you take the ______ of the ______ of $f(x)$, you obtain $f(x)$ back. On the other hand, if you take the ______ of the ______ of $f(x)$, you obtain $f(x) + C$.

102. ▼ If a Martian told you that the *Institute of Alien Mathematics*, after a long and difficult search, has announced the discovery of a new antiderivative of $x - 1$ called $M(x)$ [the formula for $M(x)$ is classified information and cannot be revealed here], how would you respond?

6.2 Substitution

The chain rule for derivatives gives us an extremely useful technique for finding antiderivatives. This technique is called **change of variables** or **substitution**.

Recall that to differentiate a function like $(x^2+1)^6$, we first think of the function as $g(u)$, where $u = x^2 + 1$ and $g(u) = u^6$. We then compute the derivative, using the chain rule, as

$$\frac{d}{dx} g(u) = g'(u)\frac{du}{dx}.$$

Any rule for derivatives can be turned into a technique for finding antiderivatives by writing it in integral form. The integral form of the above formula is

$$\int g'(u)\frac{du}{dx}\,dx = g(u) + C.$$

But, if we write $g(u) + C = \int g'(u)\,du$, we get the following interesting equation:

$$\int g'(u)\frac{du}{dx}\,dx = \int g'(u)\,du.$$

This equation is the one usually called the *change of variables formula.* We can turn it into a more useful integration technique as follows. Let $f = g'(u)(du/dx)$. We can rewrite the above change of variables formula using f:

$$\int f\,dx = \int \left(\frac{f}{du/dx}\right) du.$$

In essence, we are making the formal substitution

$$dx = \frac{1}{du/dx}\,du.$$

Here's the technique:

Substitution Rule

If u is a function of x, then we can use the following formula to evaluate an integral:

$$\int f\,dx = \int \left(\frac{f}{du/dx}\right) du.$$

Rather than use the formula directly, we use the following step-by-step procedure:

1. Write u as a function of x.
2. Take the derivative du/dx and solve for the quantity dx in terms of du.
3. Use the expression you obtain in step 2 to substitute for dx in the given integral and substitute u for its defining expression.

Now let's see how this procedure works in practice.

EXAMPLE 1 Substitution

Find $\int 4x(x^2+1)^6\,dx$.

Solution To use substitution we need to choose an expression to be u. There is no hard and fast rule, but here is one hint that often works:

Take u to be an expression that is being raised to a power.

In this case, let's set $u = x^2 + 1$. Continuing the procedure above, we place the calculations for Step 2 in a box.

$u = x^2 + 1$	Write u as a function of x.
$\dfrac{du}{dx} = 2x$	Take the derivative of u with respect to x.
$dx = \dfrac{1}{2x}\,du$	Solve for dx: $dx = \dfrac{1}{du/dx}\,du$.

Now we *substitute u for its defining expression and substitute for dx* in the original integral:

$$\int 4x(x^2+1)^6\,dx = \int 4xu^6\frac{1}{2x}\,du \qquad \text{Substitute* for } u \text{ and } dx.$$

$$= \int 2u^6\,du. \qquad \text{Cancel the } x\text{s and simplify.}$$

* This step is equivalent to using the formula stated in the Substitution Rule box. If it should bother you that the integral contains both x and u, note that x is now a function of u.

We have boiled the given integral down to the much simpler integral $\int 2u^6\,du$, and we can now write down the solution:

$$2\frac{u^7}{7} + C = \frac{2(x^2+1)^7}{7} + C. \qquad \text{Substitute } (x^2+1) \text{ for } u \text{ in the answer.}$$

➡ **Before we go on...** There are two points to notice in Example 1. First, before we can actually integrate with respect to u, *we must eliminate all x's from the integrand.* If we cannot, we may have chosen the wrong expression for u. Second, after integrating, we must substitute back to obtain an expression involving x.

It is easy to check our answer. We differentiate:

$$\frac{d}{dx}\left[\frac{2(x^2+1)^7}{7}\right] = \frac{2(7)(x^2+1)^6(2x)}{7} = 4x(x^2+1)^6. \quad ✔$$

Notice how we used the chain rule to check the result obtained by substitution. ■

When we use substitution, the first step is always to decide what to take as u. Again, there are no set rules, but we see some common cases in the examples.

EXAMPLE 2 More Substitution

Evaluate the following:

a. $\int x^2(x^3+1)^2\,dx$ **b.** $\int 3xe^{x^2}\,dx$ **c.** $\int \frac{1}{2x+5}\,dx$ **d.** $\int \left(\frac{1}{2x+5}+4x^2+1\right)dx$

Solution

a. As we said in Example 1, it often works to take u to be an expression that is being raised to a power. We usually also want to see the derivative of u as a factor in the integrand so that we can cancel terms involving x. In this case, x^3+1 is being raised to a power, so let's set $u = x^3+1$. Its derivative is $3x^2$; in the integrand we see x^2, which is missing the factor 3, but missing or incorrect constant factors are not a problem.

$u = x^3+1$	Write u as a function of x.
$\frac{du}{dx} = 3x^2$	Take the derivative of u with respect to x.
$dx = \frac{1}{3x^2}\,du$	Solve for dx: $dx = \frac{1}{du/dx}\,du$.

$$\int x^2(x^3+1)^2\,dx = \int x^2u^2\frac{1}{3x^2}du \qquad \text{Substitute for } u \text{ and } dx.$$

$$= \int \frac{1}{3}u^2\,du \qquad \text{Cancel the terms with } x.$$

$$= \frac{1}{9}u^3 + C \qquad \text{Take the antiderivative.}$$

$$= \frac{1}{9}(x^3+1)^3 + C \qquad \text{Substitute for } u \text{ in the answer.}$$

b. When we have an exponential with an expression in the exponent, it often works to substitute u for that expression. In this case, let's set $u = x^2$. (Notice again that we see a constant multiple of its derivative $2x$ as a factor in the integrand—a good sign.)

$$u = x^2$$
$$\frac{du}{dx} = 2x$$
$$dx = \frac{1}{2x}\,du$$

Substituting into the integral, we have

$$\int 3xe^{x^2}dx = \int 3xe^u\frac{1}{2x}\,du = \int \frac{3}{2}e^u du$$
$$= \frac{3}{2}e^u + C = \frac{3}{2}e^{x^2} + C.$$

c. We begin by rewriting the integrand as a power:

$$\int \frac{1}{2x+5}\,dx = \int (2x+5)^{-1}\,dx.$$

Now we take our earlier advice and set u equal to the expression that is being raised to a power:

$$u = 2x + 5$$
$$\frac{du}{dx} = 2$$
$$dx = \frac{1}{2}\,du$$

Substituting into the integral, we have

$$\int \frac{1}{2x+5}\,dx = \int \frac{1}{2}u^{-1}\,du = \frac{1}{2}\ln|u| + C$$
$$= \frac{1}{2}\ln|2x+5| + C.$$

d. Here, the substitution $u = 2x + 5$ works for the first part of the integrand, $1/(2x+5)$, but not for the rest of it, so we break up the integral:

$$\int \left(\frac{1}{2x+5} + 4x^2 + 1\right) dx = \int \frac{1}{2x+5}\,dx + \int (4x^2+1)\,dx.$$

For the first integral we can use the substitution $u = 2x + 5$ [which we did in part (a)], and for the second, no substitution is necessary:

$$\int \frac{1}{2x+5}\,dx + \int (4x^2+1)\,dx = \frac{1}{2}\ln|2x+5| + \frac{4x^3}{3} + x + C.$$

EXAMPLE 3 Choosing *u*

Evaluate $\int (x+3)\sqrt{x^2+6x}\,dx$.

Solution There are two parenthetical expressions. Notice, however, that the derivative of the expression $(x^2 + 6x)$ is $2x + 6$, which is twice the term $(x + 3)$ in front of the radical. Recall that we would like the derivative of u to appear as a factor. Thus, let's take $u = x^2 + 6x$.

$$u = x^2 + 6x$$
$$\frac{du}{dx} = 2x + 6 = 2(x+3)$$
$$dx = \frac{1}{2(x+3)}\,du$$

Substituting into the integral, we have

$$\int (x+3)\sqrt{x^2+6x}\,dx$$
$$= \int (x+3)\sqrt{u}\left(\frac{1}{2(x+3)}\right) du$$
$$= \int \frac{1}{2}\sqrt{u}\,du = \frac{1}{2}\int u^{1/2}du$$
$$= \frac{1}{2}\frac{2}{3}u^{3/2} + C = \frac{1}{3}(x^2+6x)^{3/2} + C.$$

Some cases require a little more work.

EXAMPLE 4 When the *x* Terms Do Not Cancel

Evaluate $\int \frac{2x}{(x-5)^2}\,dx$.

Solution We first rewrite

$$\int \frac{2x}{(x-5)^2}\,dx = \int 2x(x-5)^{-2}\,dx.$$

This suggests that we should set $u = x - 5$.

$$u = x - 5$$
$$\frac{du}{dx} = 1$$
$$dx = du$$

Substituting, we have

$$\int \frac{2x}{(x-5)^2}\,dx = \int 2xu^{-2}\,du.$$

Now, there is nothing in the integrand to cancel the x that appears. If, as here, there is still an x in the integrand after substituting, we go back to the expression for u, solve for x, and substitute the expression we obtain for x in the integrand. So, we take $u = x - 5$ and solve for $x = u + 5$. Substituting, we get

$$\begin{aligned}\int 2xu^{-2}\,du &= \int 2(u+5)u^{-2}\,du \\ &= 2\int (u^{-1} + 5u^{-2})\,du \\ &= 2\ln|u| - \frac{10}{u} + C \\ &= 2\ln|x-5| - \frac{10}{x-5} + C.\end{aligned}$$

EXAMPLE 5 Application: Bottled Water for Pets

Annual sales of bottled spring water for pets can be modeled by the logistic function

$$s(t) = \frac{3{,}000e^{0.5t}}{3 + e^{0.5t}} \text{ million gallons per year} \qquad (0 \le t \le 12),$$

where t is time in years since the start of 2000.[12]

a. Find an expression for the total amount of bottled spring water for pets sold since the start of 2000.

b. How much bottled spring water for pets was sold from the start of 2005 to the start of 2008?

Solution

a. If we write the total amount of pet spring water sold since the start of 2000 as $S(t)$, then the information we are given says that

$$S'(t) = s(t) = \frac{3{,}000e^{0.5t}}{3 + e^{0.5t}}.$$

[12]Based on data through 2008 and the recovery in 2010 of the general bottled water market to pre-recession levels. Sources: "*Liquid Assets: America's Expensive Love Affair with Bottled Water*" Daniel Gross, April 26, 2011 (finance.yahoo.com), Beverage Marketing Corporation (www.beveragemarketing.com).

Thus,

$$S(t) = \int \frac{3{,}000e^{0.5t}}{3 + e^{0.5t}}\,dt$$

is the function we are after. To integrate the expression, take u to be the denominator of the integrand:

$$u = 3 + e^{0.5t}$$
$$\frac{du}{dt} = 0.5e^{0.5t}$$
$$dt = \frac{1}{0.5e^{0.5t}}\,du$$

$$\begin{aligned} S(t) &= \int \frac{3{,}000e^{0.5t}}{3 + e^{0.5t}}\,dt \\ &= \int \frac{3{,}000e^{0.5t}}{u} \cdot \frac{1}{0.5e^{0.5t}}\,du \\ &= \frac{3{,}000}{0.5}\int \frac{1}{u}\,du \\ &= 6{,}000 \ln|u| + C = 6{,}000 \ln(3 + e^{0.5t}) + C. \end{aligned}$$

(Why could we drop the absolute value in the last step?)

Now what is C? Because $S(t)$ represents the total amount of bottled spring water for pets sold *since time* $t = 0$, we have $S(0) = 0$ (because that is when we started counting). Thus,

$$\begin{aligned} 0 &= 6{,}000 \ln\left(3 + e^{0.5(0)}\right) + C \\ &= 6{,}000 \ln 4 + C \\ C &= -6{,}000 \ln 4 \approx -8{,}318. \end{aligned}$$

Therefore, the total sales from the start of 2000 is approximately

$$S(t) = 6{,}000 \ln(3 + e^{0.5t}) - 8{,}318 \text{ million gallons.}$$

b. The period from the start of 2005 to the start of 2008 is represented by the interval [5, 8]. From part (a):

Sales through the start of 2005 $= S(5)$
$= 6{,}000 \ln\left(3 + e^{0.5(5)}\right) - 8{,}318 \approx 8{,}003$ million gallons.

Sales through the start of 2008 $= S(8)$
$= 6{,}000 \ln\left(3 + e^{0.5(8)}\right) - 8{,}318 \approx 16{,}003$ million gallons.

Therefore, sales over the period were about $16{,}003 - 8{,}003 = 8{,}000$ million gallons.

Before we go on... You might wonder why we are writing a logistic function in the form we used in Example 5 rather than in one of the "standard" forms $\dfrac{N}{1 + Ab^{-t}}$ or $\dfrac{N}{1 + Ae^{-kt}}$. Our only reason for doing this is to make the substitution work. To convert from the second "standard" form to the form we used in the example, multiply top and bottom by e^{kt}. (See Exercises 81 and 82 in Section 6.4 for further discussion.) ■

Shortcuts

The following rule allows us to simply write down the antiderivative in cases where we would otherwise need the substitution $u = ax + b$, as in Example 2 (a and b are constants with $a \neq 0$):

Shortcut Rule: Integrals of Expressions Involving $(ax + b)$

If $\int f(x)\,dx = F(x) + C$ and a and b are constants, with $a \neq 0$, then*

$$\int f(ax + b)\,dx = \frac{1}{a}F(ax + b) + C.$$

Quick Example

(Also see the examples in the table below.)

Because $\int x^4\,dx = \frac{x^5}{5} + C$, it follows that

$$\int (3x - 1)^4\,dx = \frac{1}{3}\frac{(3x-1)^5}{5} + C = \frac{(3x-1)^5}{15} + C.$$

* The shortcut rule can be justified by making the substitution $u = ax + b$ in the general case as stated.

Below are some instances of the shortcut rule with additional examples (their individual derivations using the substitution $u = ax + b$ will appear in the exercises):

Shortcut Rule	*Example*
$\int (ax+b)^n\,dx = \frac{1}{a}\frac{(ax+b)^{n+1}}{n+1} + C$ (if $n \neq -1$)	$\int (3x-1)^2\,dx = \frac{(3x-1)^3}{3(3)} + C = \frac{(3x-1)^3}{9} + C$
$\int (ax+b)^{-1}\,dx = \frac{1}{a}\ln\lvert ax+b\rvert + C$	$\int (3-2x)^{-1}\,dx = \frac{1}{(-2)}\ln\lvert 3-2x\rvert + C = -\frac{1}{2}\ln\lvert 3-2x\rvert + C$
$\int e^{ax+b}\,dx = \frac{1}{a}e^{ax+b} + C$	$\int e^{-x+4}\,dx = \frac{1}{(-1)}e^{-x+4} + C = -e^{-x+4} + C$
$\int c^{ax+b}\,dx = \frac{1}{a\ln c}c^{ax+b} + C$	$\int 2^{-3x+4}\,dx = \frac{1}{(-3\ln 2)}2^{-3x+4} + C = -\frac{1}{3\ln 2}2^{-3x+4} + C$
$\int \lvert ax+b\rvert\,dx = \frac{1}{2a}(ax+b)\lvert ax+b\rvert + C$	$\int \lvert 2x-1\rvert\,dx = \frac{1}{4}(2x-1)\lvert 2x-1\rvert + C$

The following more general version of the shortcut rule was suggested by a student.† We have marked it as optional so that you could skip it on a first reading, but we strongly suggest you come back to it afterward, as the rule will allow you to

† Mike Fuschetto, who was a Hofstra business calculus student in Spring 2010.

easily write down the answers in most of the exercises, as well as in almost all the examples of this section.

(Optional) Mike's Shortcut Rule: Integrals of More General Expressions

If $\int f(x)\,dx = F(x) + C$ and g and u are any differentiable functions of x, then

$$\int g \cdot f(u)\,dx = \frac{g}{u'} \cdot F(u) + C \text{ provided that } \frac{g}{u'} \text{ is constant.}$$

Quick Example

(Also see the examples in the table below.)

$$\int x^4\,dx = \frac{x^5}{5} + C, \quad \text{so}$$

$$\int 5x^2(x^3 - 1)^4\,dx = \frac{5x^2}{3x^2} \cdot \frac{(x^3-1)^5}{5} + C$$

$$= \frac{5}{3} \cdot \frac{(x^3-1)^5}{5} + C = \frac{(x^3-1)^5}{3} + C.$$

Caution

If g/u' is not constant, then Mike's rule does not apply; for instance, the following calculation is *wrong*:

$$\int x(2x-1)^2 dx = \frac{x}{2} \cdot \frac{(2x-1)^3}{3} + C \quad ✗ \textit{ WRONG! because } \frac{x}{2} \text{ is not constant.}$$

Here are some instances of Mike's rule with additional examples.

Shortcut Rule	***Example***
$\int g \cdot u^n\,dx = \frac{g}{u'}\frac{u^{n+1}}{n+1} + C$ (if $n \neq -1$)	$\int 3x(x^2-1)^3\,dx = \frac{3x}{2x}\frac{(x^2-1)^4}{4} + C = \frac{3(x^2-1)^4}{8} + C$
$\int g \cdot u^{-1}\,dx = \frac{g}{u'}\ln\|u\| + C$	$\int e^x(3-2e^x)^{-1}\,dx = \frac{e^x}{-2e^x}\ln\|3-2e^x\| + C = -\frac{1}{2}\ln\|3-2e^x\| + C$
$\int g \cdot e^u dx = \frac{g}{u'}e^u + C$	$\int x^2 e^{-x^3+4}\,dx = \frac{x^2}{-3x^2}e^{-x^3+4} + C = -\frac{1}{3}e^{-x^3+4} + C$
$\int g \cdot c^u dx = \frac{g}{u'\ln c}c^u + C$	$\int x^3 2^{x^4-1}\,dx = \frac{x^3}{4x^3\ln 2}2^{x^4-1} + C = -\frac{1}{4\ln 2}2^{x^4-1} + C$
$\int g \cdot \|u\|\,dx = \frac{g}{2u'}u\|u\| + C$	$\int x\|x^2-1\|\,dx = \frac{x}{4x}(x^2-1)\|x^2-1\| + C = \frac{1}{4}(x^2-1)\|x^2-1\| + C$

FAQs

When to Use Substitution and What to Use for *u*

Q: *If I am asked to calculate an antiderivative, how do I know when to use a substitution and when not to use one?*

A: Do *not* use substitution when integrating sums, differences, and/or constant multiples of powers of x and exponential functions, such as $2x^3 - \frac{4}{x^2} + \frac{1}{2x} + 3^x + \frac{2^x}{3}$.

To recognize when you should try a substitution, pretend that you are *differentiating* the given expression instead of integrating it. If differentiating the expression would require use of the chain rule, then integrating that expression may well require a substitution, as in, say, $x(3x^2 - 4)^3$ or $(x+1)e^{x^2+2x-1}$. (In the first we have a *quantity* cubed, and in the second we have e raised to a *quantity*.)

Q: *If an integral seems to call for a substitution, what should I use for u?*

A: There are no set rules for deciding what to use for u, but the preceding examples show some common patterns:

- If you see a linear expression raised to a power, try setting u equal to that linear expression. For example, in $(3x - 2)^{-3}$, set $u = 3x - 2$. (Alternatively, try using the shortcuts above.)
- If you see a constant raised to a linear expression, try setting u equal to that linear expression. For example, in $3^{(2x+1)}$, set $u = 2x + 1$. (Alternatively, try a shortcut.)
- If you see an expression raised to a power multiplied by the derivative of that expression (or a constant multiple of the derivative), try setting u equal to that expression. For example, in $x^2(3x^3 - 4)^{-1}$, set $u = 3x^3 - 4$.
- If you see a constant raised to an expression, multiplied by the derivative of that expression (or a constant multiple of its derivative), try setting u equal to that expression. For example, in $5(x+1)e^{x^2+2x-1}$, set $u = x^2 + 2x - 1$.
- If you see an expression in the denominator and its derivative (or a constant multiple of its derivative) in the numerator, try setting u equal to that expression. For example, in $\frac{2^{3x}}{3 - 2^{3x}}$, set $u = 3 - 2^{3x}$.

Persistence often pays off: If a certain substitution does not work, try another approach or a different substitution.

6.2 EXERCISES

▼ more advanced ◆ challenging

T indicates exercises that should be solved using technology

In Exercises 1–10, evaluate the given integral using the substitution (or method) indicated.

1. $\int (3x - 5)^3\,dx$; $u = 3x - 5$

2. $\int (2x + 5)^{-2}\,dx$; $u = 2x + 5$

3. $\int (3x - 5)^3\,dx$; shortcut page 474

4. $\int (2x + 5)^{-2}\,dx$; shortcut page 474

5. $\int e^{-x}\,dx$; $u = -x$

6. $\int e^{x/2}\,dx$; $u = x/2$

7. $\int e^{-x}\,dx$; shortcut page 474

8. $\int e^{x/2}\,dx$; shortcut page 474

9. $\int (x+1)e^{(x+1)^2}\,dx$; $u = (x+1)^2$

10. $\int (x-1)^2 e^{(x-1)^3}\,dx$; $u = (x-1)^3$

In Exercises 11–52, decide on what substitution to use, and then evaluate the given integral using a substitution. HINT [See the FAQ at the end of the section for advice on deciding on *u*, and the examples for the mechanics of doing the substitution.]

11. $\int (3x+1)^5\,dx$

12. $\int (-x-1)^7\,dx$

13. $\int 7.2\sqrt{3x-4}\,dx$

14. $\int 4.4e^{(-3x+4)}\,dx$

15. $\int 1.2e^{(0.6x+2)}\,dx$

16. $\int 8.1\sqrt{-3x+4}\,dx$

17. $\int x(3x^2+3)^3\,dx$

18. $\int x(-x^2-1)^3\,dx$

19. $\int 2x\sqrt{3x^2-1}\,dx$

20. $\int 3x\sqrt{-x^2+1}\,dx$

21. $\int \frac{x}{(x^2+1)^{1.3}}\,dx$

22. $\int \frac{x^2}{(1+x^3)^{1.4}}\,dx$

23. $\int x|4x^2-1|\,dx$

24. $\int x^2|4x^3+1|\,dx$

25. $\int (1+9.3e^{3.1x-2})\,dx$

26. $\int (3.2-4e^{1.2x-3})\,dx$

27. $\int xe^{-x^2+1}\,dx$

28. $\int xe^{2x^2-1}\,dx$

29. $\int (x+1)e^{-(x^2+2x)}\,dx$ HINT [See Example 2(b).]

30. $\int (2x-1)e^{2x^2-2x}\,dx$ HINT [See Example 2(b).]

31. $\int \frac{-2x-1}{(x^2+x+1)^3}\,dx$

32. $\int \frac{x^3-x^2}{3x^4-4x^3}\,dx$

33. $\int \frac{x^2+x^5}{\sqrt{2x^3+x^6-5}}\,dx$ HINT [See Example 3.]

34. $\int \frac{2(x^3-x^4)}{(5x^4-4x^5)^5}\,dx$ HINT [See Example 3.]

35. $\int x(x-2)^5\,dx$
HINT [See Example 4.]

36. $\int x(x-2)^{1/3}\,dx$
HINT [See Example 4.]

37. $\int 2x\sqrt{x+1}\,dx$

38. $\int \frac{x}{\sqrt{x+1}}\,dx$

39. $\int \frac{e^{-0.05x}}{1-e^{-0.05x}}\,dx$ HINT [See Example 5.]

40. $\int \frac{3e^{1.2x}}{2+e^{1.2x}}\,dx$ HINT [See Example 5.]

41. ▼ $\int \frac{3e^{-1/x}}{x^2}\,dx$

42. ▼ $\int \frac{2e^{2/x}}{x^2}\,dx$

43. ▼ $\int \frac{(4+1/x^2)^3}{x^3}\,dx$

44. ▼ $\int \frac{1}{x^2(2-1/x)}\,dx$

45. ▼ $\int \frac{e^x+e^{-x}}{2}\,dx$ HINT [See Example 2(d).]

46. ▼ $\int (e^{x/2}+e^{-x/2})\,dx$ HINT [See Example 2(d).]

47. ▼ $\int \frac{e^x-e^{-x}}{e^x+e^{-x}}\,dx$

48. ▼ $\int \frac{e^{x/2}+e^{-x/2}}{e^{x/2}-e^{-x/2}}\,dx$

49. ▼ $\int e^{3x-1}|1-e^{3x-1}|dx$

50. ▼ $\int |e^{-x-1}-1|(e^{-x-1})\,dx$

51. ▼ $\int \left((2x-1)e^{2x^2-2x}+xe^{x^2}\right)dx$

52. ▼ $\int \left(xe^{-x^2+1}+e^{2x}\right)dx$

In Exercises 53–56, derive the given equation, where a and b are constants with $a \neq 0$.

53. $\int (ax+b)^n\,dx = \frac{(ax+b)^{n+1}}{a(n+1)} + C \quad (\text{if } n \neq -1)$

54. $\int (ax+b)^{-1}\,dx = \frac{1}{a}\ln|ax+b| + C$

55. $\int |ax+b|\,dx = \frac{1}{2a}(ax+b)|ax+b| + C$

56. $\int e^{ax+b}\,dx = \frac{1}{a}e^{ax+b} + C$

In Exercises 57–72, use the shortcut formulas (see page 474 and Exercises 53–56) to calculate the given integral.

57. $\int e^{-x}\,dx$

58. $\int e^{x-1}\,dx$

59. $\int e^{2x-1}\,dx$

60. $\int e^{-3x}\,dx$

61. $\int (2x+4)^2\,dx$

62. $\int (3x-2)^4\,dx$

63. $\int \frac{1}{5x-1}\,dx$

64. $\int (x-1)^{-1}\,dx$

65. $\int (1.5x)^3\,dx$

66. $\int e^{2.1x}\,dx$

67. $\int 1.5^{3x}\,dx$

68. $\int 4^{-2x}\,dx$

69. $\int |2x+4|\,dx$

70. $\int |3x-2|\,dx$

71. $\int (2^{3x+4}+2^{-3x+4})\,dx$

72. $\int (1.1^{-x+4}+1.1^{x+4})\,dx$

73. Find $f(x)$ if $f(0)=0$ and the tangent line at $(x, f(x))$ has slope $x(x^2+1)^3$.

74. Find $f(x)$ if $f(1)=0$ and the tangent line at $(x, f(x))$ has slope $\frac{x}{x^2+1}$.

75. Find $f(x)$ if $f(1)=1/2$ and the tangent line at $(x, f(x))$ has slope xe^{x^2-1}.

76. Find $f(x)$ if $f(2)=1$ and the tangent line at x has slope $(x-1)e^{x^2-2x}$.

In Exercises 77–84, use Mike's shortcut method (see p. 475 and the examples that follow) to calculate the given integral.

77. $\int x(5x^2-3)^6\,dx$

78. $\int \frac{x}{(5x^2-3)^6}\,dx$

79. $\int \frac{e^x}{\sqrt{3e^x-1}}\,dx$

80. $\int e^x\sqrt{1+2e^x}\,dx$

81. $\int x^3 e^{(x^4-8)}\,dx$

82. $\int \frac{x^3}{e^{(x^4-8)}}\,dx$

83. $\int \frac{e^{3x}}{1+2e^{3x}}\,dx$

84. $\int \frac{e^{-2x}}{e^{-2x}-3}\,dx$

APPLICATIONS

85. ***Economic Growth*** The value of sold goods in Mexico can be approximated by

$$v(t) = 210 - 62e^{-0.05t} \text{ trillion pesos per month} \quad (t \geq 0),$$

where t is time in months since January 2005.[13] Find an expression for the total value $V(t)$ of sold goods in Mexico from January 2005 to time t. HINT [Use the shortcut on page 474.]

86. ***Economic Contraction*** The number of housing starts in the United States can be approximated by

$$n(t) = 1.1 + 1.2e^{-0.08t} \text{ million homes per year } (t \geq 0),$$

where t is time in years from the start of 2006.[14] Find an expression for the total number $N(t)$ of housing starts in the United States from January 2006 to time t. HINT [Use the shortcut on page 474.]

87. ***Revenue*** The annual revenue of Amazon.com over the period 2006–2010 can be approximated by

$$a(t) = 2e^{0.25t} \text{ billion dollars per year} \quad (6 \leq t \leq 10),$$

where t is time in years since the start of 2000.[15] Find an expression for the total revenue $A(t)$ earned since the start of 2006, and hence estimate the total revenue earned from the start of 2006 to the start of 2010. (Round your answer to the nearest \$ billion.)

88. ***Lobster Harvests*** The size of the annual lobster harvest from Long Island Sound over the period 1997–2010 can be approximated by

$$h(t) = 9.1e^{-0.21t} \text{ million pounds of lobster per year} \quad (0 \leq t \leq 13),$$

where t is time in years since mid-1997.[16] Find an expression for the total lobster harvest $H(t)$ since mid-1997, and hence estimate the total lobster harvest from mid-1997 to mid-2010. (Round your answer to the nearest million pounds.)

89. ***Cost*** The marginal cost of producing the xth roll of film is given by $5 + 1/(x+1)^2$. The total cost to produce one roll is \$1,000. Find the total cost function $C(x)$.

90. ***Cost*** The marginal cost of producing the xth box of CDs is given by $10 - x/(x^2+1)^2$. The total cost to produce 2 boxes is \$1,000. Find the total cost function $C(x)$.

91. ***Scientific Research*** The number of research articles in the prominent journal *Physical Review* written by researchers in Europe can be approximated by

$$E(t) = \frac{7e^{0.2t}}{5+e^{0.2t}} \text{ thousand articles per year} \quad (t \geq 0),$$

where t is time in years ($t = 0$ represents 1983).[17]

a. Find an (approximate) expression for the total number of articles written by researchers in Europe since 1983 ($t = 0$). HINT [See Example 5.]

b. Roughly how many articles were written by researchers in Europe from 1983 to 2003? (Round your answer to the nearest 1,000 articles.)

---

[13]Source: Instituto Nacional de Estadística y Geografía (INEGI) (www.inegi.gob.mx).

[14]Source for data: *New York Times*, February 17, 2007, p. C3.

[15]Source for data: www.wikinvest.com.

[16]Authors' regression model. Source for data: Long Island Sound Study, data downloaded May 2011 from longislandsoundstudy.net/2010/07/lobster-landings.

[17]Based on data from 1983 to 2003. Source: The American Physical Society/*New York Times*, May 3, 2003, p. A1.

92. ***Scientific Research*** The number of research articles in the prominent journal *Physical Review* written by researchers in the United States can be approximated by

$$U(t) = \frac{4.6e^{0.6t}}{0.4 + e^{0.6t}} \text{ thousand articles per year} \quad (t \geq 0),$$

where t is time in years ($t = 0$ represents 1983).[18]

a. Find an (approximate) expression for the total number of articles written by researchers in the United States since 1983 ($t = 0$). HINT [See Example 5.]

b. Roughly how many articles were written by researchers in the United States from 1983 to 2003?

93. ***Sales*** The rate of sales of your company's *Jackson Pollock Advanced Paint-by-Number* sets can be modeled by

$$s(t) = \frac{900e^{0.25t}}{3 + e^{0.25t}} \text{ sets per month}$$

t months after their introduction. Find an expression for the total number of paint-by-number sets $S(t)$ sold t months after their introduction, and use it to estimate the total sold in the first 12 months. HINT [See Example 5.]

94. ***Sales*** The rate of sales of your company's *Jackson Pollock Beginners Paint-by-Number* sets can be modeled by

$$s(t) = \frac{1{,}800e^{0.75t}}{10 + e^{0.75t}} \text{ sets per month}$$

t months after their introduction. Find an expression for the total number of paint-by-number sets $S(t)$ sold t months after their introduction, and use it to estimate the total sold in the first 12 months. HINT [See Example 5.]

95. ***Motion in a Straight Line*** The velocity of a particle moving in a straight line is given by $v = t(t^2 + 1)^4 + t$.

a. Find an expression for the position s after a time t. HINT [See Example 2(d).]

b. Given that $s = 1$ at time $t = 0$, find the constant of integration C and hence an expression for s in terms of t without any unknown constants.

96. ***Motion in a Straight Line*** The velocity of a particle moving in a straight line is given by $v = 3te^{t^2} + t$.

a. Find an expression for the position s after a time t. HINT [See Example 2(d).]

b. Given that $s = 3$ at time $t = 0$, find the constant of integration C and hence an expression for s in terms of t without any unknown constants.

97. ***Bottled Water Sales*** The rate of U.S. sales of bottled water for the period 2000–2010 could be approximated by

$$s(t) = -45(t - 2{,}000)^2 + 900(t - 2{,}000) + 4{,}200 \text{ million gallons per year} \quad (2{,}000 \leq t \leq 2{,}010),$$

where t is the year.[19] Use an indefinite integral to approximate the total sales $S(t)$ of bottled water since 2003 ($t = 2003$). Approximately how much bottled water was sold from $t = 2003$ to $t = 2008$?

98. ***Bottled Water Sales*** The rate of U.S. per capita sales of bottled water for the period 2000–2010 could be approximated by

$$s(t) = -0.18(t - 2{,}000)^2 + 3(t - 2{,}000) + 15 \text{ gallons per year} \quad (2{,}000 \leq t \leq 2{,}010),$$

where t is the year.[20] Use an indefinite integral to approximate the total per capita sales $S(t)$ of bottled water since the start of 2006. Approximately how much bottled water was sold, per capita, from $t = 2006$ to $t = 2008$?

COMMUNICATION AND REASONING EXERCISES

99. Are there any circumstances in which you should use the substitution $u = x$? Illustrate your answer by giving an example that shows the effect of this substitution.

100. You are asked to calculate $\int \frac{u}{u^2 + 1}\, du$. What is wrong with the substitution $u = u^2 + 1$?

101. If the x's do not cancel in a substitution, that means you chose the wrong expression for u, right?

102. At what stage of a calculation using a u substitution should you substitute back for u in terms of x: before or after taking the antiderivative?

103. Consider $\int \left(\frac{x}{x^2 - 1} + \frac{3x}{x^2 + 1}\right) dx$. To compute it, you should use which of the following?

(A) $u = x^2 - 1$ **(B)** $u = x^2 + 1$ **(C)** Neither **(D)** Both

Explain your answer.

104. If the substitution $u = x^2 - 1$ works in $\int \frac{x}{x^2 - 1}\, dx$, why does it not work nearly so easily in $\int \frac{x^2 - 1}{x}\, dx$? How would you do the second integral most simply?

105. Why was the following calculation marked wrong? What is the correct answer?

$$u = x^2 - 1$$
$$\frac{du}{dx} = 2x$$
$$dx = \frac{1}{2x}\, du$$

$$\int 3x(x^2 - 1) = \int 3xu = 3x\frac{u^2}{2} + C = 3x\frac{(x^2 - 1)^2}{2} + C$$

✗ *WRONG!*

[18]Based on data from 1983 to 2003. Source: The American Physical Society/*New York Times*, May 3, 2003, p. A1.

[19]Source for data: Beverage Marketing Corporation (www.bottledwater.org).

[20]*Ibid.*

106. Why was the following calculation marked wrong? What is the correct answer?

$u = x^3 - 1$	$\int x^2(x^3-1)^2 dx = \int x^2 u^2 \frac{1}{3x^2} du$
$\frac{du}{dx} = 3x^2$	$= \frac{1}{3}u^2 + C = \frac{1}{3}(x^3-1)^2 + C$
$dx = \frac{1}{3x^2}du$	✗ *WRONG!*

107. Why was the following calculation marked wrong? What is the correct answer?

$u = x^3 - 1$	$\int x^2(x^3-1)\,dx = \int x^2 u \frac{1}{3x^2} du$
$\frac{du}{dx} = 3x^2$	$= \int \frac{1}{3}u\,du = \int \frac{1}{3}(x^3-1)\,dx$
$dx = \frac{1}{3x^2}du$	$= \frac{1}{3}\left(\frac{x^4}{4} - x\right) + C$ ✗ *WRONG!*

108. Why was the following calculation marked wrong? What is the correct answer?

$u = x^2 - 1$	$\int \frac{x}{x^2-1}dx = \int \frac{x}{u}du$
$\frac{du}{dx} = 2x$	$= x\int \frac{1}{u}du = x \ln\|u\| + C$
$dx = \frac{1}{2x}du$	$= x\ln\|x^2-1\| + C$ ✗ *WRONG!*

109. ▼ Show that *none* of the following substitutions work for $\int e^{-x^2}dx$: $u = -x$, $u = x^2$, $u = -x^2$. (The antiderivative of e^{-x^2} involves the *error function* erf(x).)

110. ▼ Show that *none* of the following substitutions work for $\int \sqrt{1-x^2}\,dx$: $u = 1 - x^2$, $u = x^2$, and $u = -x^2$. (The antiderivative of $\sqrt{1-x^2}$ involves inverse trigonometric functions, discussion of which is beyond the scope of this book.)

6.3 The Definite Integral: Numerical and Graphical Viewpoints

In Sections 6.1 and 6.2, we discussed the indefinite integral. There is an older, related concept called the **definite integral**. Let's introduce this new idea with an example. (We'll drop hints now and then about how the two types of integral are related. In Section 6.4 we discuss the exact relationship, which is one of the most important results in calculus.)

In Section 6.1, we used antiderivatives to answer questions of the form "Given the marginal cost, compute the total cost." (See Example 5 in Section 6.1.) In this section we approach such questions more directly, and we will forget about antiderivatives for now.

EXAMPLE 1 Oil Spill

Your deep ocean oil rig has suffered a catastrophic failure, and oil is leaking from the ocean floor wellhead at a rate of

$$v(t) = 0.08t^2 - 4t + 60 \text{ thousand barrels per day } (0 \le t \le 20),$$

where t is time in days since the failure.[21] Use a numerical calculation to estimate the total volume of oil released during the first 20 days.

[21]The model is consistent with the order of magnitude of the BP Deepwater Horizon oil spill of April 20–June 15, 2010, when the rate of flow of oil was estimated by the Federal Emergency Management Agency's Flow Rate Technical Group to be between 35,000 and 60,000 barrels per day (one barrel of oil is equivalent to about 0.16 cubic meters). Source: www.doi.gov/deepwaterhorizon.

Solution The graph of $v(t)$ is shown in Figure 3.

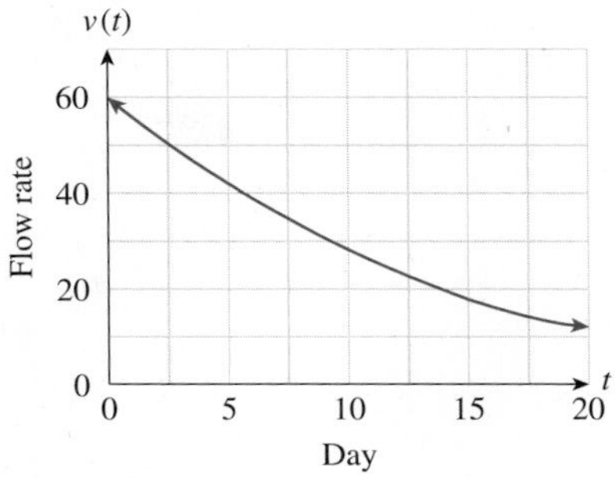

Figure 3

Let's start with a very crude estimate of the total volume of oil released, using the graph as a guide. The rate of change of this total volume at the beginning of the time period is $v(0) = 60$ thousand barrels per day. If this rate were to remain constant for the entire 20-day period, the total volume of oil released would be

$$\text{Total volume} = \text{Volume per day} \times \text{Number of days} = 60 \times 20$$
$$= 1{,}200 \text{ thousand barrels.}$$

Figure 4 shows how we can represent this calculation on the graph of $v(t)$.

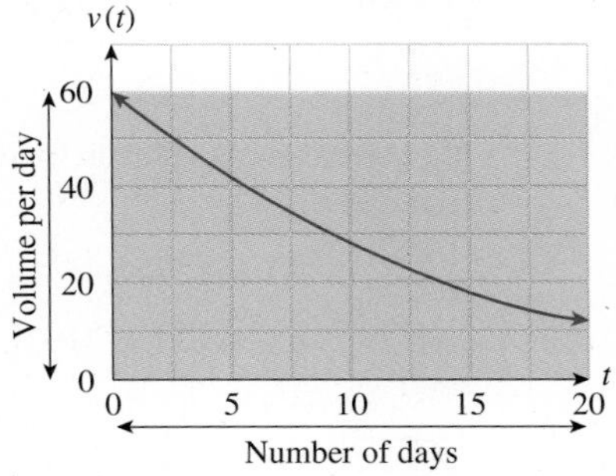

Figure 4

The volume per day based on $v(0) = 60$ is represented by the y-coordinate of the graph at its left edge, while the number of days is represented by the width of the interval [0, 20] on the x-axis. Therefore, computing the area of the shaded rectangle in the figure gives the same calculation:

$$\text{Area of rectangle} = \text{Volume per day} \times \text{Number of days}$$
$$= 60 \times 20 = 1{,}200 = \text{Total volume.}$$

But, as we see in the graph, the flow rate does not remain constant, but goes down quite significantly over the course of the 20-day interval. We can obtain a somewhat more accurate estimate of the total volume by re-estimating the volume using 10-day periods—that is, by dividing the interval [0, 20] into two equal intervals, or subdivisions. We estimate the volume over each 10-day period using the flow rate at the beginning of that period.

$$\text{Volume in first period} = \text{Volume per day} \times \text{Number of days}$$
$$= v(0) \times 10 = 60 \times 10 = 600 \text{ thousand barrels}$$

$$\text{Volume in second period} = \text{Volume per day} \times \text{Number of days}$$
$$= v(10) \times 10 = 28 \times 10 = 280 \text{ thousand barrels}$$

Adding these volumes gives us the more accurate estimate

$$v(0) \times 10 + v(10) \times 10 = 880 \text{ thousand barrels.}$$ Calculation using 2 subdivisions

In Figure 5 we see that we are computing the combined area of two rectangles, each of whose heights is determined by the height of the graph at its left edge:

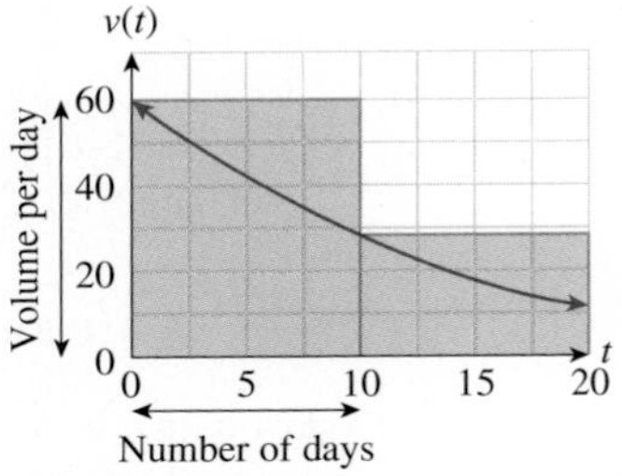

The areas of the rectangles are estimates of the volumes for successive 10-day periods.

Figure 5

$$\text{Area of first rectangle} = \text{Volume per day} \times \text{Number of days}$$
$$= v(0) \times 10 = 60 \times 10 = 600 = \text{Volume for first 10 days}$$
$$\text{Area of second rectangle} = \text{Volume per day} \times \text{Number of days} = v(10) \times 10$$
$$= 28 \times 10 = 280 = \text{Volume for second 10 days.}$$

We can get an even better estimate of the volume by using four divisions of [0, 20] instead of two:

$$v(0) \times 5 + v(5) \times 5 + v(10) \times 5 + v(15) \times 5$$ Calculation using 4 subdivisions
$$= 300 + 210 + 140 + 90 = 740 \text{ thousand barrels.}$$

As we see in Figure 6, we have now computed the combined area of *four* rectangles, each of whose heights is again determined by the height of the graph at its left edge.

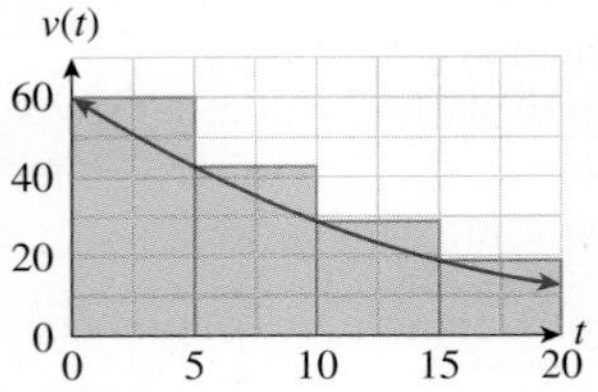

Estimated Volume Using 4 Subdivisions
The areas of the rectangles are estimates of the volumes for successive 5-day periods.

Figure 6

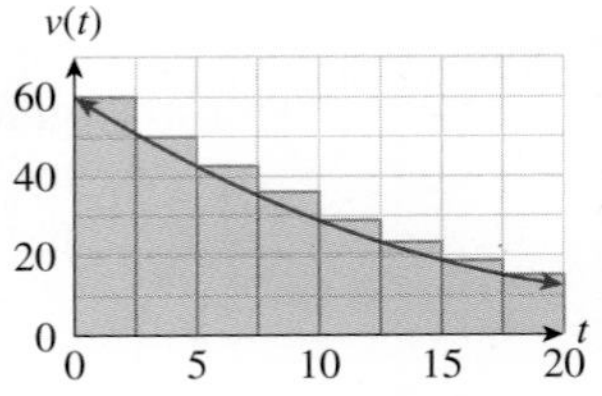

Estimated Volume Using 8 Subdivisions
The areas of the rectangles are estimates of the volumes for successive 2.5-day periods.

Figure 7

Notice how the volume seems to be decreasing as we use more subdivisions. More importantly, total volume seems to be getting closer to the area under the graph. Figure 7 illustrates the calculation for 8 equal subdivisions. The approximate total volume using 8 subdivisions is the total area of the shaded region in Figure 7:

$$v(0) \times 2.5 + v(2.5) \times 2.5 + v(5) \times 2.5 + \cdots + v(17.5) \times 2.5$$
$$= 675 \text{ thousand barrels.}$$ Calculation using 8 subdivisions

Looking at Figure 7, we still get the impression that we are overestimating the volume. If we want to be *really* accurate in our estimation of the volume, we should really be calculating the volume *continuously* every few hours or, better yet, minute by minute, as illustrated in Figure 8.

using Technology

Website
www.WanerMath.com
At the Website, select the Online Utilities tab, and choose the Numerical Integration Utility and Grapher. There, enter the formula

```
0.08x^2-4x+60
```

for $f(x)$, enter 0 and 20 for the lower and upper limits, and press "Left Sum" to compute and see a Riemann sum. You can then adjust the number of subdivisions to see the effect on the graph and on the calculation, and thus replicate the information in Figure 8.

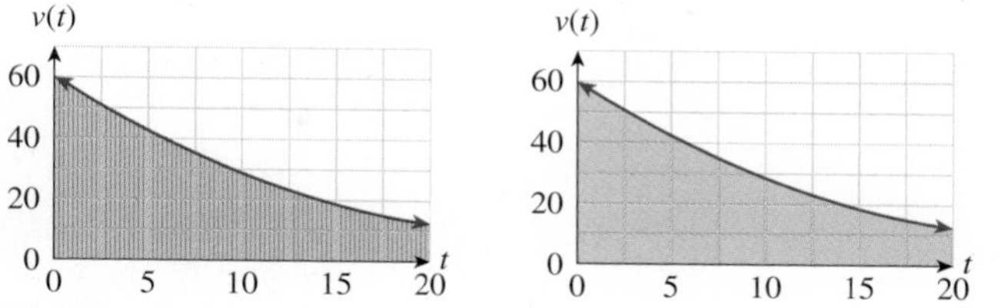

Every Six Hours (80 subdivisions)
Volume ≈ 619.35 thousand barrels

Every Minute (28,800 subdivisions)
Volume ≈ 613.35 thousand barrels

Figure 8

Figure 8 strongly suggests that the more accurately we estimate the total volume, the closer the answer gets to the exact area under the portion of the graph of $v(t)$ with $0 \le t \le 20$, and leads us to the conclusion that the *exact* total volume is the exact area under the rate of change of volume curve for $0 \le t \le 20$. In other words, we have made the following remarkable discovery:

Total volume is the area under the rate of change of volume curve!

Before we go on... The 80-subdivision calculation in Example 1 is tedious to do by hand, and no one in his or her right mind would even *attempt* to do the minute-by-minute calculation by hand! Below we discuss ways of doing these calculations with the aid of technology. ■

The type of calculation done in Example 1 is useful in many applications. Let's look at the general case and give the result a name.

In general, we have a function f (such as the function v in the example), and we consider an interval $[a, b]$ of possible values of the independent variable x. We subdivide the interval $[a, b]$ into some number of segments of equal length. Write n for the number of segments, or **subdivisions**.

Next, we label the endpoints of these subdivisions x_0 for a, x_1 for the end of the first subdivision, x_2 for the end of the second subdivision, and so on until we get to x_n, the end of the nth subdivision, so that $x_n = b$. Thus,

$$a = x_0 < x_1 < \cdots < x_n = b.$$

The first subdivision is the interval $[x_0, x_1]$, the second subdivision is $[x_1, x_2]$, and so on until we get to the last subdivision, which is $[x_{n-1}, x_n]$. We are dividing the interval $[a, b]$ into n subdivisions of equal length, so each segment has length $(b - a)/n$. We write Δx for $(b - a)/n$ (Figure 9).

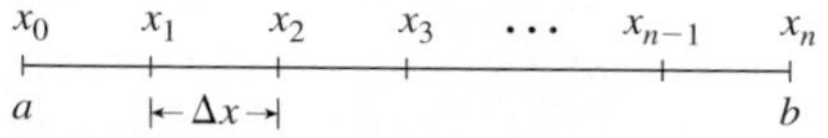

Figure 9

Having established this notation, we can write the calculation that we want to do as follows: For each subdivision $[x_{k-1}, x_k]$, compute $f(x_{k-1})$, the value of the function

f at the left endpoint. Multiply this value by the length of the interval, which is Δx. Then add together all n of these products to get the number

$$f(x_0)\Delta x + f(x_1)\Delta x + \cdots + f(x_{n-1})\Delta x.$$

* After Georg Friedrich Bernhard Riemann (1826–1866).

This sum is called a **(left) Riemann* sum** for f. In Example 1 we computed several different Riemann sums. Here is the computation for $n = 4$ we used in the oil spill example (see Figure 10):

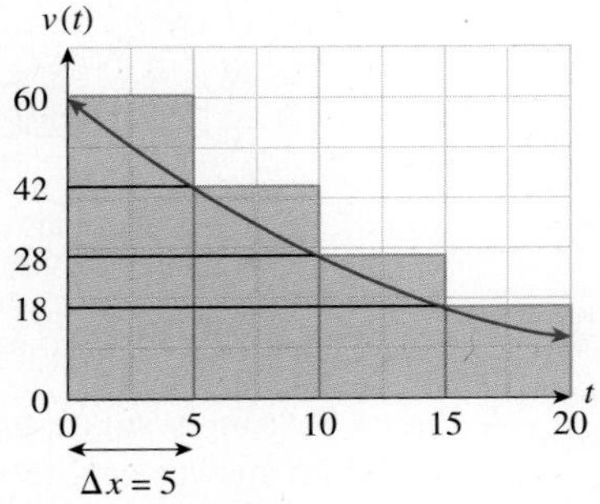

Figure 10

$$\begin{aligned}\text{Left Riemann sum} &= f(x_0)\Delta x + f(x_1)\Delta x + \cdots + f(x_{n-1})\Delta x \\ &= f(0)(5) + f(5)(5) + f(10)(5) + f(15)(5) \\ &= 60(5) + 42(5) + 28(5) + 18(5) = 740.\end{aligned}$$

Because sums are often used in mathematics, mathematicians have developed a shorthand notation for them. We write

$$f(x_0)\Delta x + f(x_1)\Delta x + \cdots + f(x_{n-1})\Delta x \text{ as } \sum_{k=0}^{n-1} f(x_k)\Delta x.$$

The symbol $\sum$ is the Greek letter sigma and stands for **summation**. The letter k here is called the index of summation, and we can think of it as counting off the segments. We read the notation as "the sum from $k = 0$ to $n - 1$ of the quantities $f(x_k)\Delta x$." Think of it as a set of instructions:

Set $k = 0$, and calculate $f(x_0)\Delta x$. — $f(0)(5)$ in the above calculation

Set $k = 1$, and calculate $f(x_1)\Delta x$. — $f(5)(5)$ in the above calculation

...

Set $k = n - 1$, and calculate $f(x_{n-1})\Delta x$. — $f(15)(5)$ in the above calculation

Then sum all the quantities so calculated.

Riemann Sum

If f is a continuous function, the **left Riemann sum** with n equal subdivisions for f over the interval $[a, b]$ is defined to be

$$\begin{aligned}\text{Left Riemann sum} &= \sum_{k=0}^{n-1} f(x_k)\Delta x \\ &= f(x_0)\Delta x + f(x_1)\Delta x + \cdots + f(x_{n-1})\Delta x \\ &= [f(x_0) + f(x_1) + \cdots + f(x_{n-1})]\Delta x,\end{aligned}$$

where $a = x_0 < x_1 < \cdots < x_n = b$ are the endpoints of the subdivisions, and $\Delta x = (b - a)/n$.

Interpretation of the Riemann Sum

If f is the rate of change of a quantity F (that is, $f = F'$), then the Riemann sum of f approximates the total change of F from $x = a$ to $x = b$. The approximation improves as the number of subdivisions increases toward infinity.

Quick Examples

1. If $f(t)$ is the rate of change in the number of bats in a belfry and $[a, b] = [2, 3]$, then the Riemann sum approximates the total change in the number of bats in the belfry from time $t = 2$ to time $t = 3$.
2. If $c(x)$ is the marginal cost of producing the xth item and $[a, b] = [10, 20]$, then the Riemann sum approximates the cost of producing items 11 through 20.

Visualizing a Left Riemann Sum (Non-negative Function)

Graphically, we can represent a left Riemann sum of a non-negative function as an approximation of the area under a curve:

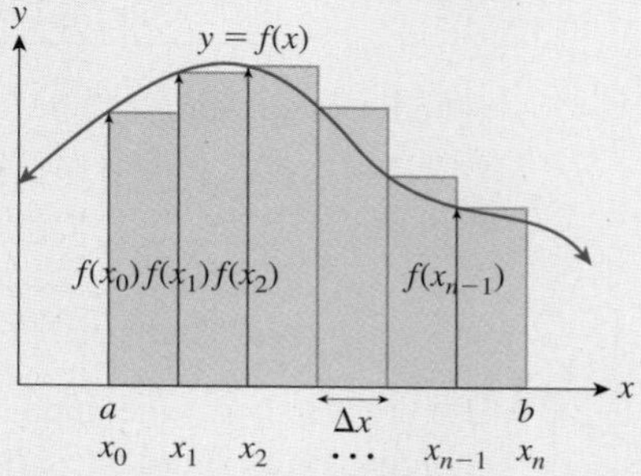

Riemann sum = Shaded area = Area of first rectangle + Area of second rectangle + · · · + Area of nth rectangle $= f(x_0)\Delta x + f(x_1)\Delta x + f(x_2)\Delta x + \cdots + f(x_{n-1})\Delta x$.

Quick Example

In Example 1 we computed several Riemann sums, including these:

$n = 1$: Riemann sum $= v(0)\Delta t = 60 \times 20 = 1{,}200$

$n = 2$: Riemann sum $= [v(t_0) + v(t_1)]\Delta t$
$= [v(0) + v(10)](10) = 880$

$n = 4$: Riemann sum $= [v(t_0) + v(t_1) + v(t_2) + v(t_3)]\Delta t$
$= [v(0) + v(5) + v(10) + v(15)](5) = 740$

$n = 8$: Riemann sum $= [v(t_0) + v(t_1) + \cdots + v(t_7)]\Delta t$
$= [v(0) + v(2.5) + \cdots + v(17.5)](2.5) = 675$

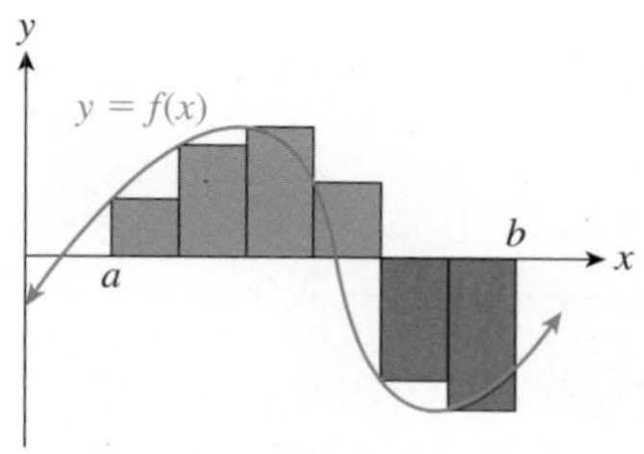

Riemann sum = Area above x-axis − Area below x-axis

Figure 11

Note To visualize the Riemann sum of a function that is negative, look again at the formula $f(x_0)\Delta x + f(x_1)\Delta x + f(x_2)\Delta x + \cdots + f(x_{n-1})\Delta x$ for the Riemann sum. Each term $f(x_k)\Delta x_k$ represents the area of one rectangle in the figure above. So, the areas of the rectangles with negative values of $f(x_k)$ are automatically counted as negative. They appear as red rectangles in Figure 11. ■

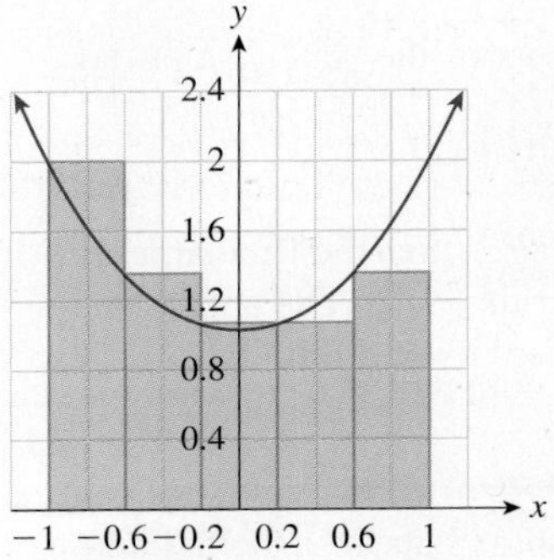

Figure 12

EXAMPLE 2 Computing a Riemann Sum from a Formula

Compute the left Riemann sum for $f(x) = x^2 + 1$ over the interval $[-1, 1]$, using $n = 5$ subdivisions.

Solution Because the interval is $[a, b] = [-1, 1]$ and $n = 5$, we have

$$\Delta x = \frac{b-a}{n} = \frac{1-(-1)}{5} = 0.4. \quad \text{Width of subdivisions}$$

Thus, the subdivisions of $[-1, 1]$ are determined by

$$-1 < -0.6 < -0.2 < 0.2 < 0.6 < 1. \quad \text{Start with } -1 \text{ and keep adding } \Delta x = 0.4.$$

Figure 12 shows the graph with a representation of the Riemann sum.

The Riemann sum we want is

$$[f(x_0) + f(x_1) + \cdots + f(x_4)]\Delta x$$
$$= [f(-1) + f(-0.6) + f(-0.2) + f(0.2) + f(0.6)]0.4.$$

We can conveniently organize this calculation in a table as follows:

x	−1	−0.6	−0.2	0.2	0.6	**Total**
$f(x) = x^2 + 1$	2	1.36	1.04	1.04	1.36	6.8

The Riemann sum is therefore

$$6.8\Delta x = 6.8 \times 0.4 = 2.72.$$

EXAMPLE 3 Computing a Riemann Sum from a Graph

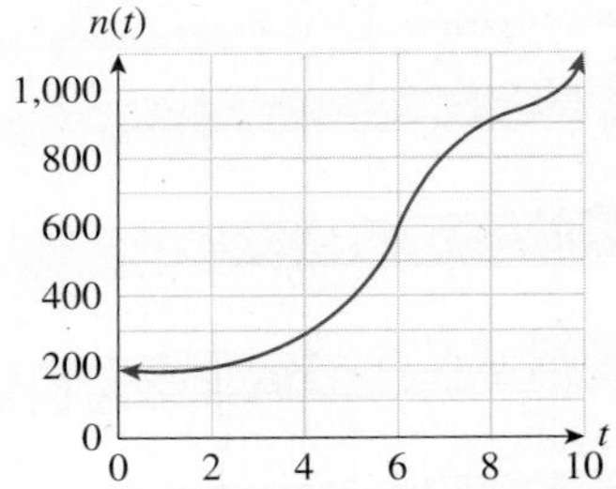

Figure 13

Figure 13 shows the approximate annual production $n(t)$ of engineering and technology Ph.D. graduates in Mexico during the period 2000–2010.[22] Use a left Riemann sum with four subdivisions to estimate the total number of Ph.D. graduates from 2002 to 2010.

Solution Let us represent the total number of (engineering and technology) Ph.D. graduates up to time t (measured in years since 2000) by $N(t)$. The total number of Ph.D. graduates from 2002 to 2010 is then the total change in $N(t)$ over the interval [2, 10]. In view of the above discussion, we can approximate the total change in $N(t)$ using a Riemann sum of its rate of change $n(t)$. Because $n = 4$ subdivisions are specified, the width of each subdivision is

$$\Delta t = \frac{b-a}{n} = \frac{10-2}{4} = 2.$$

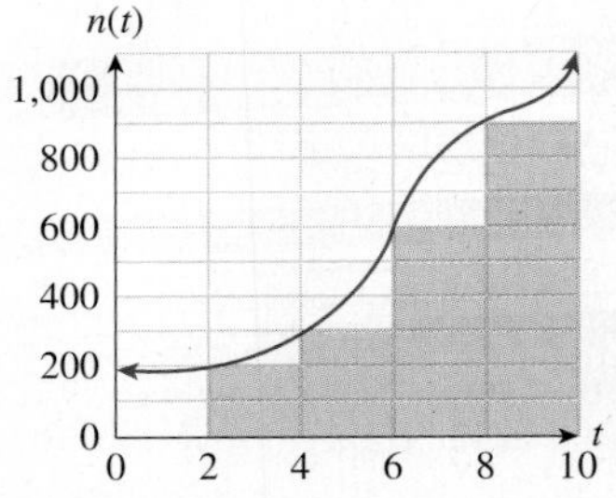

Figure 14

We can therefore represent the left Riemann sum by the shaded area shown in Figure 14.

From the graph,

$$\text{Left sum} = n(2)\Delta t + n(4)\Delta t + n(6)\Delta t + n(8)\Delta t$$
$$= (200)(2) + (300)(2) + (600)(2) + (900)(2) = 4{,}000.$$

So, we estimate that there was a total of about 4,000 engineering and technology Ph.D. graduates during the given period.

[22]Source for data: Instituto Nacional de Estadística y Geografía (www.inegi.org.mx).

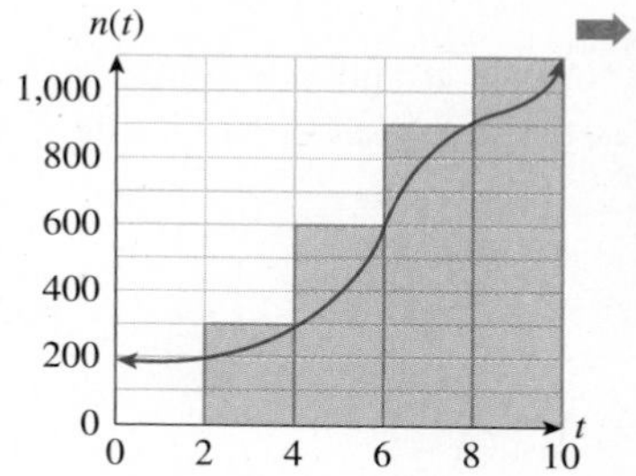

Right riemann sum = (300)(2) + (600)(2) + (900)(2) + (1,100)(2) = 5,800

Height of each ractangle is determined by height of graph at right edge.

Figure 15

➡ **Before we go on...** A glance at Figure 14 tells us that we have significantly underestimated the actual number of graduates, as the actual area under the curve is considerably larger. Figure 15 shows a **right Riemann sum** and gives us a much larger estimate. For continuous functions, the difference between these two types of Riemann sums approaches zero as the number of subdivisions approaches infinity (see below) so we will focus primarily on only one type: left Riemann sums. ■

As in Example 1, we're most interested in what happens to the Riemann sum when we let n get very large. When f is continuous,* its Riemann sums will always approach a limit as n goes to infinity. (This is not meant to be obvious. Proofs may be found in advanced calculus texts.) We give the limit a name.

* This applies to some other functions as well, including "piecewise continuous" functions discussed in the next section.

The Definite Integral

If f is a continuous function, the **definite integral of f from a to b** is defined to be the limit of the Riemann sums as the number of subdivisions approaches infinity:

$$\int_a^b f(x)\,dx = \lim_{n\to\infty} \sum_{k=0}^{n-1} f(x_k)\,\Delta x.$$

In Words: The integral, from a to b, of $f(x)\,dx$ equals the limit, as $n \to \infty$, of the Riemann Sum with a partition of n subdivisions.

The function f is called the **integrand**, the numbers a and b are the **limits of integration**, and the variable x is the **variable of integration**. A Riemann sum with a large number of subdivisions may be used to approximate the definite integral.

Interpretation of the Definite Integral

If f is the rate of change of a quantity F (that is, $f = F'$), then $\int_a^b f(x)\,dx$ is the (exact) total change of F from $x = a$ to $x = b$.

Quick Examples

1. If $f(t)$ is the rate of change in the number of bats in a belfry and $[a, b] = [2, 3]$, then $\int_2^3 f(t)\,dt$ is the total change in the number of bats in the belfry from time $t = 2$ to time $t = 3$.
2. If, at time t hours, you are selling wall posters at a rate of $s(t)$ posters per hour, then

$$\text{Total number of posters sold from hour 3 to hour 5} = \int_3^5 s(t)\,dt.$$

Visualizing the Definite Integral

Non-negative Functions: If $f(x) \geq 0$ for all x in $[a, b]$, then $\int_a^b f(x)\,dx$ is the area under the graph of f over the interval $[a, b]$, as shaded in the figure.

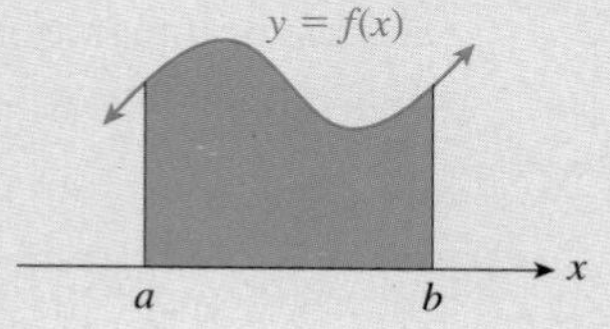

General Functions: $\int_a^b f(x)\,dx$ is the area between $x = a$ and $x = b$ that is above the x-axis and below the graph of f, minus the area that is below the x-axis and above the graph of f:

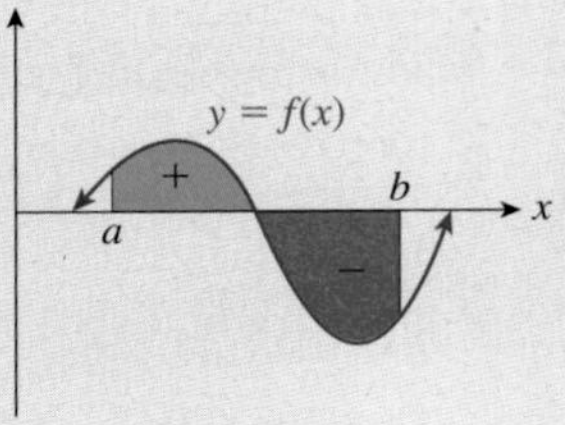

$$\int_a^b f(x)\,dx = \text{Area above } x\text{-axis} - \text{Area below } x\text{-axis}$$

Quick Examples

1.

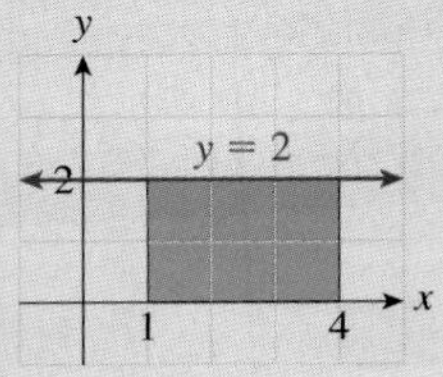

$$\int_1^4 2\,dx = \text{Area of rectangle} = 6$$

2.

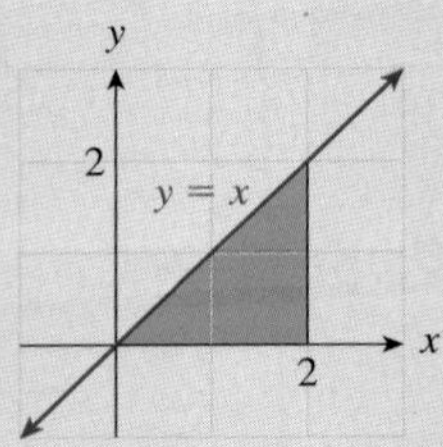

$$\int_0^2 x\,dx = \text{Area of triangle} = \frac{1}{2}\text{base} \times \text{height} = 2$$

3.

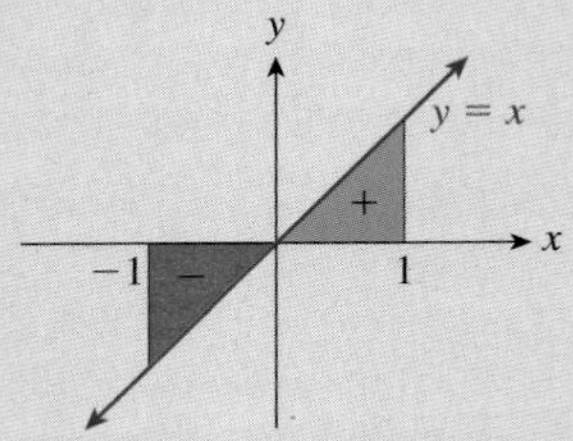

$$\int_{-1}^1 x\,dx = 0$$ The areas above and below the x-axis are equal.

Notes

1. Remember that $\int_a^b f(x)\,dx$ stands for a number that depends on f, a, and b. The variable of integration x that appears is called a **dummy variable** because it has no effect on the answer. In other words,

$$\int_a^b f(x)\,dx = \int_a^b f(t)\,dt.$$ x or t is just a name we give the variable.

2. The notation for the definite integral (due to Leibniz) comes from the notation for the Riemann sum. The integral sign $\int$ is an elongated S, the Roman equivalent of the Greek $\sum$. The d in dx is the lowercase Roman equivalent of the Greek Δ.
3. The definition above is adequate for continuous functions, but more complicated definitions are needed to handle other functions. For example, we broke the interval $[a, b]$ into n subdivisions of equal length, but other definitions allow a **partition** of the interval into subdivisions of possibly unequal lengths. We have evaluated f at the left endpoint of each subdivision, but we could equally well have used the right endpoint or any other point in the subdivision. All of these variations lead to the same answer when f is continuous.
4. The similarity between the notations for the definite integral and the indefinite integral is no mistake. We will discuss the exact connection in the next section. ■

Computing Definite Integrals

In some cases, we can compute the definite integral directly from the graph (see the quick examples above and the next example below). In general, the only method of computing definite integrals we have discussed so far is numerical estimation: Compute the Riemann sums for larger and larger values of n and then estimate the number it seems to be approaching as we did in Example 1. (In the next section we will discuss an algebraic method for computing them.)

EXAMPLE 4 Estimating a Definite Integral from a Graph

Figure 16 shows the graph of the (approximate) rate $f'(t)$, at which the United States consumed gasoline from 2000 through 2008. (t is time in years since 2000.)[23]

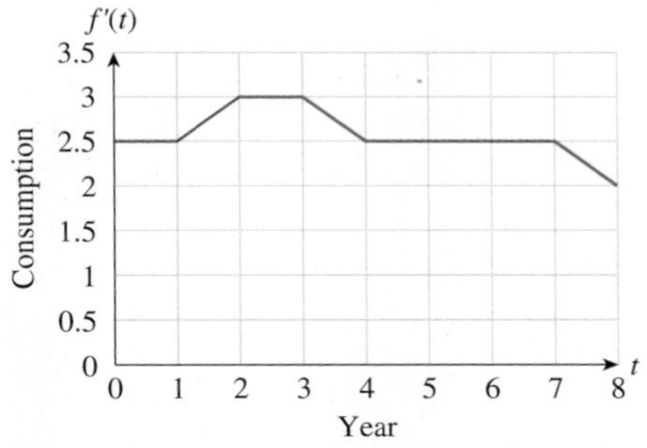

$f'(t)$ = Gasoline consumption (100 million gals per year)

Figure 16

Use the graph to estimate the total U.S. consumption of gasoline over the period shown.

Solution The derivative $f'(t)$ represents the rate of change of the total U.S. consumption of gasoline, and so the total U.S. consumption of gasoline over the given period [0, 8] is given by the definite integral:

$$\text{Total U.S. consumption of gasoline} = \text{Total change in } f(t) = \int_0^8 f'(t)\,dt$$

and is given by the area under the graph (Figure 17).

---

[23] Source: Energy Information Administration (Department of Energy). (www.eia.doe.gov).

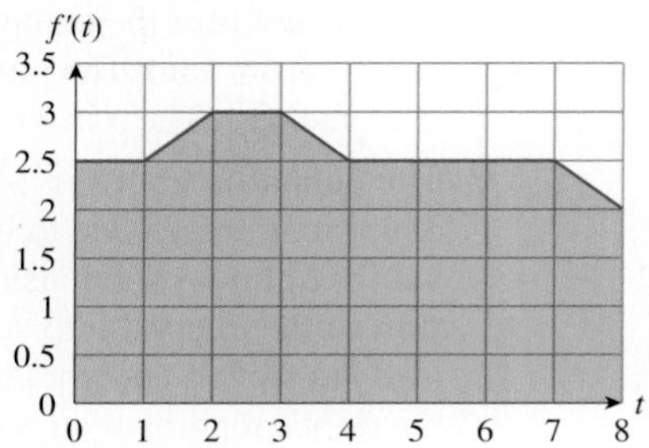

Figure 17

One way to determine the area is to count the number of filled rectangles as defined by the grid. Each rectangle has an area of $1 \times 0.5 = 0.5$ units (and the half-rectangles determined by diagonal portions of the graph have half that area). Counting rectangles, we find a total of 41.5 complete rectangles, so

$$\text{Total area} = 20.75.$$

Because $f'(t)$ is in 100 million gallons per year, we conclude that the total U.S. consumption of gasoline over the given period was about 2,075 million gallons, or 2.075 billion gallons.

While counting rectangles might seem easy, it becomes awkward in cases involving large numbers of rectangles or partial rectangles whose area is not easy to determine. In a case like this, in which the graph consists of straight lines, rather than counting rectangles, we can get the area by averaging the left and right Riemann sums whose subdivisions are determined by the grid:

$$\text{Left sum} = (2.5 + 2.5 + 3 + 3 + 2.5 + 2.5 + 2.5 + 2.5)(1) = 21$$

$$\text{Right sum} = (2.5 + 3 + 3 + 2.5 + 2.5 + 2.5 + 2.5 + 2)(1) = 20.5$$

$$\text{Average} = \frac{21 + 20.5}{2} = 20.75.$$

To see why this works, look at the single interval [1, 2]. The left sum contributes $2.5 \times 1 = 2.5$ and the right sum contributes $3 \times 1 = 3$. The exact area is their average, 2.75 (Figure 18).

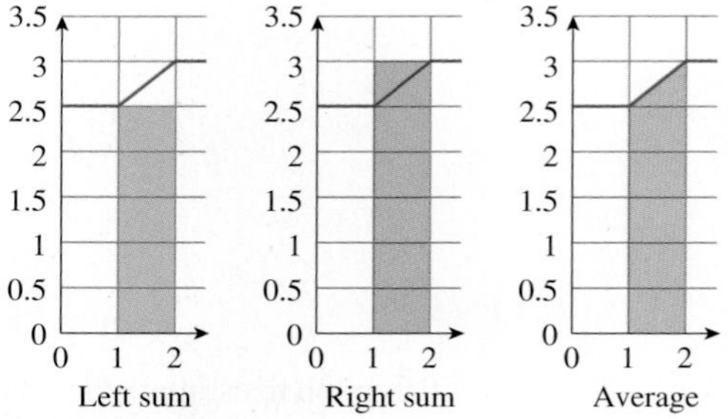

Figure 18

The average of the left and right Riemann sums is frequently a better estimate of the definite integral than either is alone.

➡ **Before we go on...** It is important to check that the units we are using in Example 4 match up correctly: t is given in *years* and $f'(t)$ is given in 100 million gallons per *year*. The integral is then given in

$$\text{Years} \times \frac{\text{100 million gallons}}{\text{Year}} = \text{100 million gallons.}$$

If we had specified $f'(t)$ in, say, 100 million gallons per *day* but t in years, then we would have needed to convert either t or $f'(t)$ so that the units of time match. ■

The next example illustrates the use of technology in estimating definite integrals using Riemann sums.

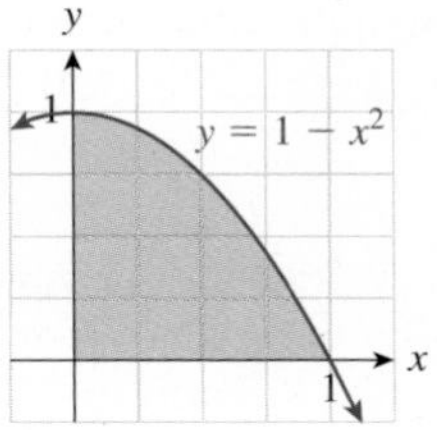

Figure 19

using Technology
See the Technology Guides at the end of the chapter to find out how to compute these sums on a TI-83/84 Plus and a spreadsheet.

Website
www.WanerMath.com
At the Website, select the Online Utilities tab, and choose the Numerical Integration Utility and Grapher. This utility computes left and right Riemann sums, as well as a good numerical approximation of the integral. There is also a downloadable Excel spreadsheet that computes and graphs Riemann sums (Riemann Sum Grapher).

EXAMPLE 5 T Using Technology to Approximate the Definite Integral

Use technology to estimate the area under the graph of $f(x) = 1 - x^2$ over the interval [0, 1] using $n = 100$, $n = 200$, and $n = 500$ subdivisions.

Solution We need to estimate the area under the parabola shown in Figure 19.

From the discussion above,

$$\text{Area} = \int_0^1 (1 - x^2)\,dx.$$

The Riemann sum with $n = 100$ has $\Delta x = (b - a)/n = (1 - 0)/100 = 0.01$ and is given by

$$\sum_{k=0}^{99} f(x_k)\Delta x = [f(0) + f(0.01) + \cdots + f(0.99)](0.01).$$

Similarly, the Riemann sum with $n = 200$ has $\Delta x = (b - a)/n = (1 - 0)/200 = 0.005$ and is given by

$$\sum_{k=0}^{199} f(x_k)\Delta x = [f(0) + f(0.005) + \cdots + f(0.995)](0.005).$$

For $n = 500$, $x = (b - a)/n = (1 - 0)/500 = 0.002$ and the Riemann sum is

$$\sum_{k=0}^{499} f(x_k)\Delta x = [f(0) + f(0.002) + \cdots + f(0.998)](0.002).$$

Using technology to evaluate these Riemann sums, we find:

$$n = 100\text{: } \sum_{k=0}^{99} f(x_k)\Delta x = 0.67165$$

$$n = 200\text{: } \sum_{k=0}^{199} f(x_k)\Delta x = 0.6691625$$

$$n = 500\text{: } \sum_{k=0}^{499} f(x_k)\Delta x = 0.667666$$

so we estimate that the area under the curve is about 0.667. (The exact answer is $2/3$, as we will be able to verify using the techniques in the next section.)

EXAMPLE 6 Motion

A fast car has velocity $v(t) = 6t^2 + 10t$ ft/sec after t seconds (as measured by a radar gun). Use several values of n to find the distance covered by the car from time $t = 3$ seconds to time $t = 4$ seconds.

Solution Because the velocity $v(t)$ is rate of change of position, the total change in position over the interval [3, 4] is

$$\text{Distance covered} = \text{Total change in position} = \int_3^4 v(t)\,dt = \int_3^4 (6t^2 + 10t)\,dt.$$

As in Examples 1 and 5, we can subdivide the one-second interval [3, 4] into smaller and smaller pieces to get more and more accurate approximations of the integral. By computing Riemann sums for various values of n, we get the following results.

$$n = 10: \sum_{k=0}^{9} v(t_k)\Delta t = 106.41 \qquad n = 100: \sum_{k=0}^{99} v(t_k)\Delta t \approx 108.740$$

$$n = 1{,}000: \sum_{k=0}^{999} v(t_k)\Delta t \approx 108.974 \qquad n = 10{,}000: \sum_{k=0}^{9999} v(t_k)\Delta t \approx 108.997$$

WW Website
www.WanerMath.com
At the Website you will find the following optional online interactive section: Internet Topic: Numerical Integration.

These calculations suggest that the total distance covered by the car, the value of the definite integral, is approximately 109 feet.

➡ **Before we go on...** Do Example 6 using antiderivatives instead of Riemann sums, as in Section 6.1. Do you notice a relationship between antiderivatives and definite integrals? This will be explored in the next section. ■

6.3 EXERCISES

▼ more advanced ◆ challenging

T indicates exercises that should be solved using technology

Calculate the left Riemann sums for the given functions over the given intervals in Exercises 1–10, using the given values of n. (When rounding, round answers to four decimal places.) HINT [See Example 2.]

1. $f(x) = 4x - 1$ over [0, 2], $n = 4$
2. $f(x) = 1 - 3x$ over [−1, 1], $n = 4$
3. $f(x) = x^2$ over [−2, 2], $n = 4$
4. $f(x) = x^2$ over [1, 5], $n = 4$
5. $f(x) = \dfrac{1}{1+x}$ over [0, 1], $n = 5$
6. $f(x) = \dfrac{x}{1+x^2}$ over [0, 1], $n = 5$
7. $f(x) = e^{-x}$ over [0, 10], $n = 5$
8. $f(x) = e^{-x}$ over [−5, 5], $n = 5$
9. $f(x) = e^{-x^2}$ over [0, 10], $n = 4$
10. $f(x) = e^{-x^2}$ over [0, 100], $n = 4$

In Exercises 11–18, use the given graph to estimate the left Riemann sum for the given interval with the stated number of subdivisions. HINT [See Example 3.]

11. [0, 5], $n = 5$

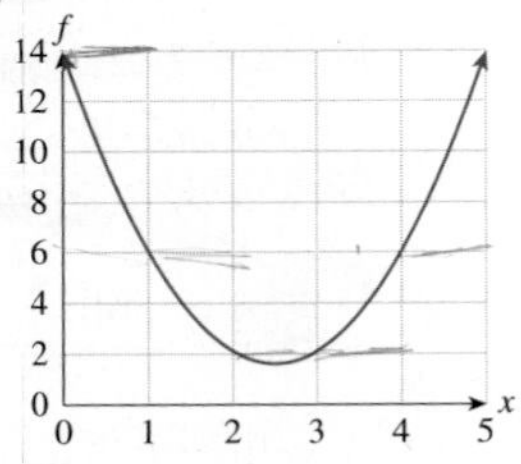

12. [0, 8], $n = 4$

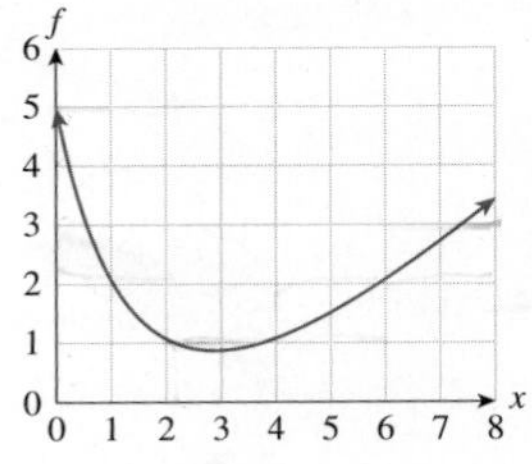

13. [1, 9], $n = 4$

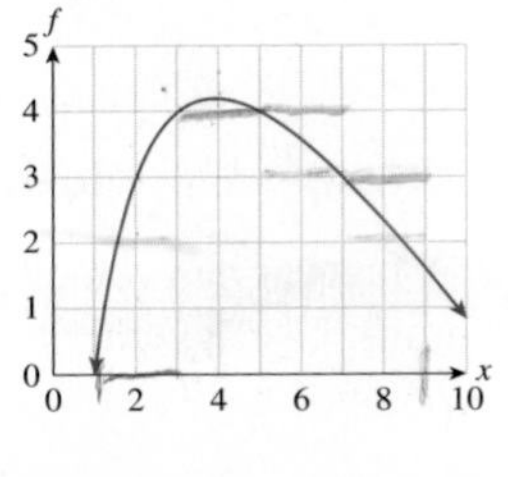

14. [0.5, 2.5], $n = 4$

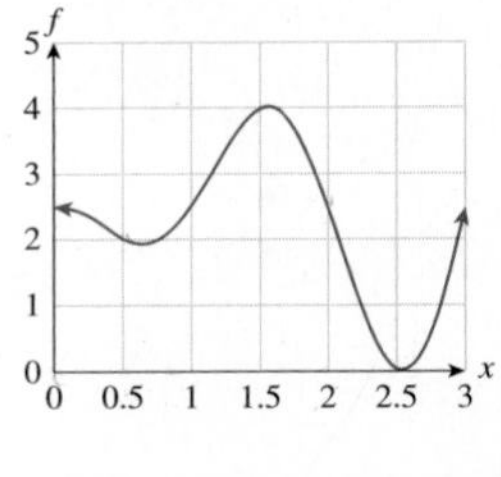

15. $[1, 3.5]$, $n = 5$

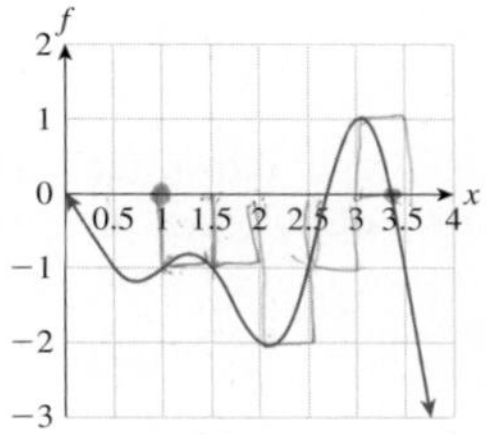

16. $[0.5, 3.5]$, $n = 3$

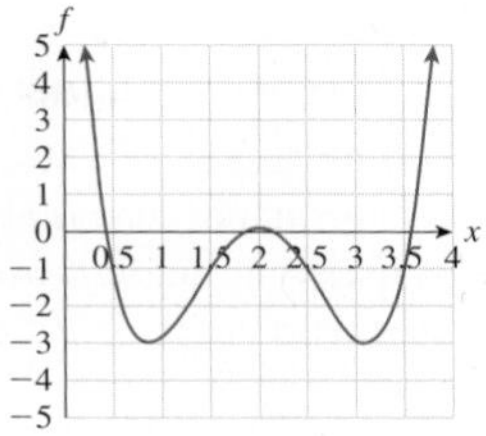

17. $[0, 3]$; $n = 3$

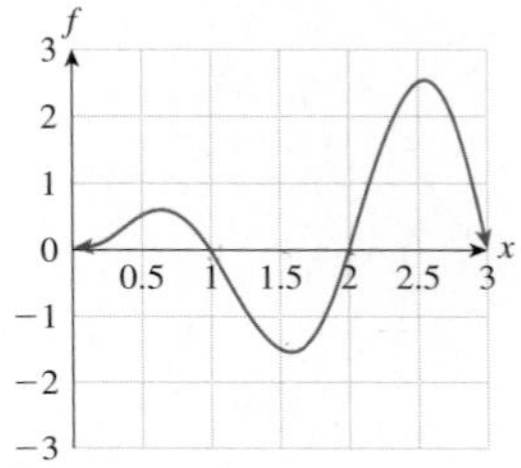

18. $[0.5, 3]$; $n = 5$

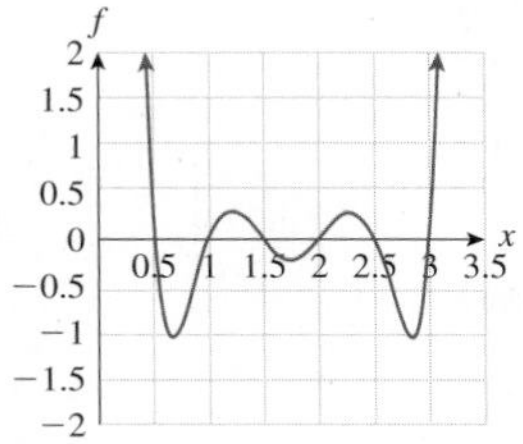

Use geometry (not Riemann sums) to compute the integrals in Exercises 19–28. HINT [See Quick Examples page 488.]

19. $\int_0^1 1\,dx$

20. $\int_0^2 5\,dx$

21. $\int_0^1 x\,dx$

22. $\int_1^2 x\,dx$

23. $\int_0^1 \frac{x}{2}\,dx$

24. $\int_1^2 \frac{x}{2}\,dx$

25. $\int_2^4 (x-2)\,dx$

26. $\int_3^6 (x-3)\,dx$

27. $\int_{-1}^1 x^3\,dx$

28. $\int_{-2}^2 \frac{x}{2}\,dx$

In Exercises 29–34, the graph of the derivative $f'(t)$ of $f(t)$ is shown. Compute the total change of $f(t)$ over the given interval. HINT [See Example 4.]

29. $[1, 5]$

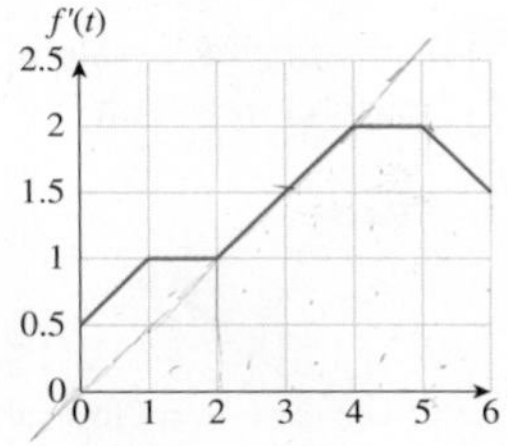

30. $[2, 6]$

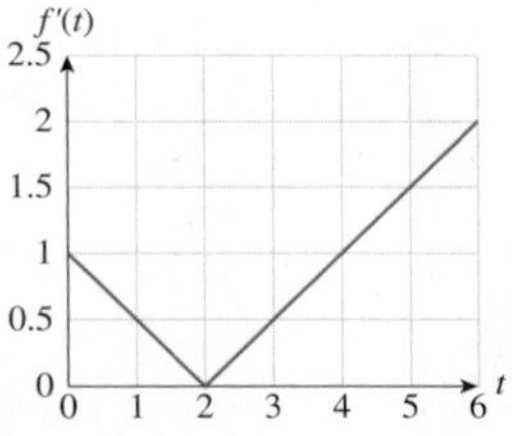

31. $[2, 6]$

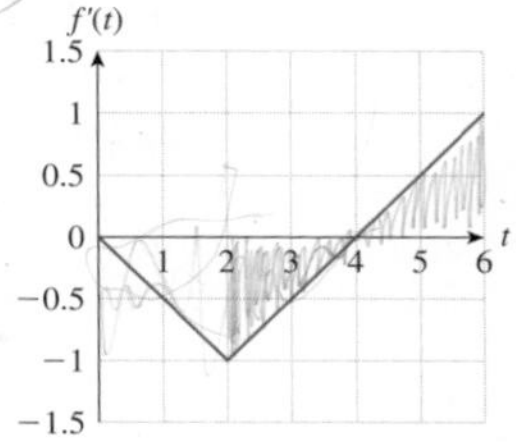

32. $[0, 5]$

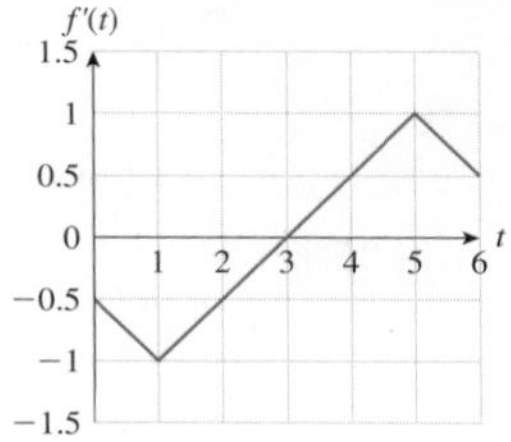

33. $[-1, 2]$

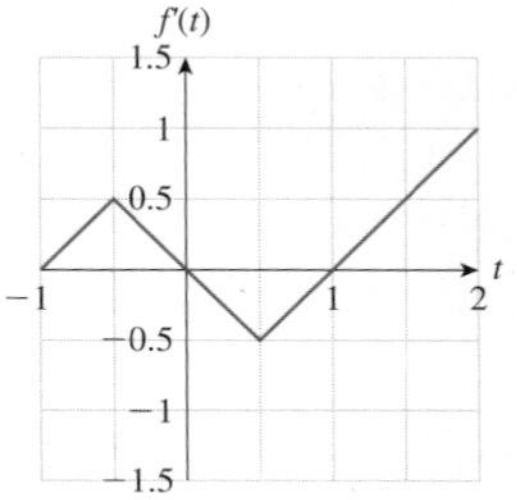

34. $[-1, 2]$

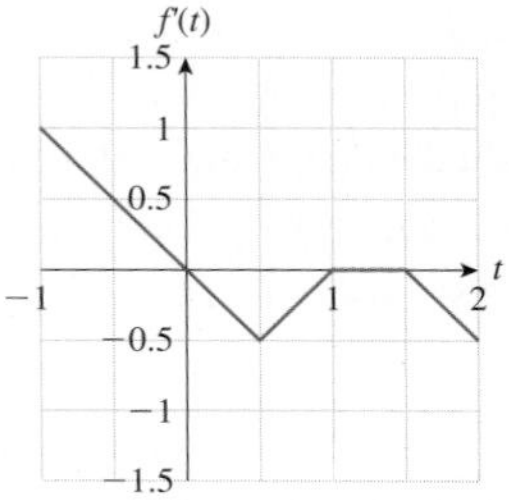

T *In Exercises 35–38, use technology to approximate the given integrals with Riemann sums, using **(a)** $n = 10$, **(b)** $n = 100$, and **(c)** $n = 1{,}000$. Round all answers to four decimal places.* HINT [See Example 5.]

35. $\int_0^1 4\sqrt{1-x^2}\,dx$

36. $\int_0^1 \frac{4}{1+x^2}\,dx$

37. $\int_2^3 \frac{2x^{1.2}}{1+3.5x^{4.7}}\,dx$

38. $\int_3^4 3xe^{1.3x}\,dx$

APPLICATIONS

39. *Pumps* A pump is delivering water into a tank at a rate of

$$r(t) = 3t^2 + 5 \text{ liters/minute,}$$

where t is time in minutes since the pump is turned on. Use a Riemann sum with $n = 5$ subdivisions to estimate the total volume of water pumped in during the first two minutes. HINT [See Examples 1 and 2. This exercise is also discussed in the tutorial on the Website.]

40. *Pumps* A pump is delivering water into a tank at a rate of

$$r(t) = 6t^2 + 40 \text{ liters/minute,}$$

where t is time in minutes since the pump is turned on. Use a Riemann sum with $n = 6$ subdivisions to estimate the total volume of water pumped in during the first three minutes. HINT [See Examples 1 and 2. A similar exercise is also discussed in the tutorial on the Website.]

41. ***Cost*** The marginal cost function for the manufacture of portable MP3 players is given by

$$C'(x) = 20 - \frac{x}{200},$$

where x is the number of MP3 players manufactured. Use a Riemann sum with $n = 5$ to estimate the cost of producing the first 5 MP3 players. HINT [See Examples 1 and 2 and Quick Example 2 on page 485.]

42. ***Cost*** Repeat the preceding exercise using the marginal cost function

$$C'(x) = 25 - \frac{x}{50}.$$

HINT [See Examples 1 and 2 and Quick Example 2 on page 485.]

43. ***Bottled Water Sales*** The rate of U.S. sales of bottled water for the period 2000–2010 could be approximated by

$$s(t) = -45t^2 + 900t + 4{,}200 \text{ million gallons per year} \quad (0 \le t \le 10),$$

where t is time in years since the start of 2000.[24] Use a Riemann sum with $n = 5$ to estimate the total U.S. sales of bottled water from the start of 2005 to the start of 2010. (Round your answer to the nearest billion gallons.) HINT [See Example 2.]

44. ***Bottled Water Sales*** The rate of U.S. per capita sales of bottled water for the period 2000–2010 could be approximated by

$$s(t) = -0.18t^2 + 3t + 15 \text{ gallons per year} \quad (0 \le t \le 10),$$

where t is time in years since the start of 2000.[25] Use a Riemann sum with $n = 5$ to estimate the total U.S. per capita sales of bottled water from the start of 2003 to the start of 2008. (Round your answer to the nearest gallon.) HINT [See Example 2.]

45. ***Online Vehicle Sales*** The following graph shows the rate of change $v(t)$ of the value of vehicle transactions on eBay, in billions of dollars per quarter from the first quarter of 2008 through the first quarter of 2011 (t is time in quarters; $t = 1$ represents the first quarter of 2008).[26]

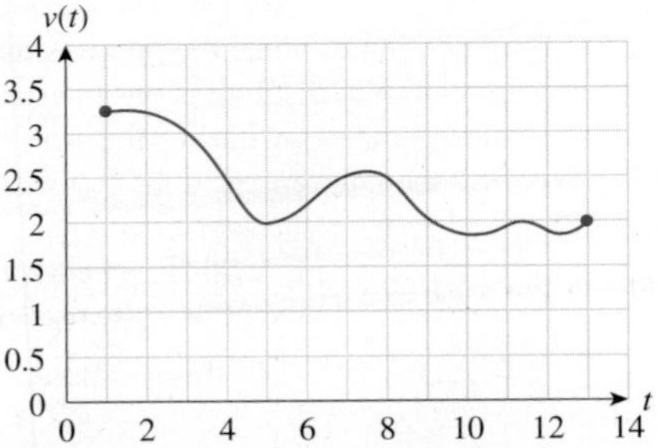

Use a left Riemann sum with four subdivisions to estimate the total value of vehicle transactions on eBay from the third quarter of 2008 to the third quarter of 2010 (the interval [3, 11]). HINT [See Example 3.]

46. ***Online Auctions*** The following graph shows the rate of change $n(t)$ of the number of active eBay users, in millions of users per quarter, from the first quarter of 2008 through the first quarter of 2011 (t is time in quarters; $t = 1$ represents the first quarter of 2008).[27]

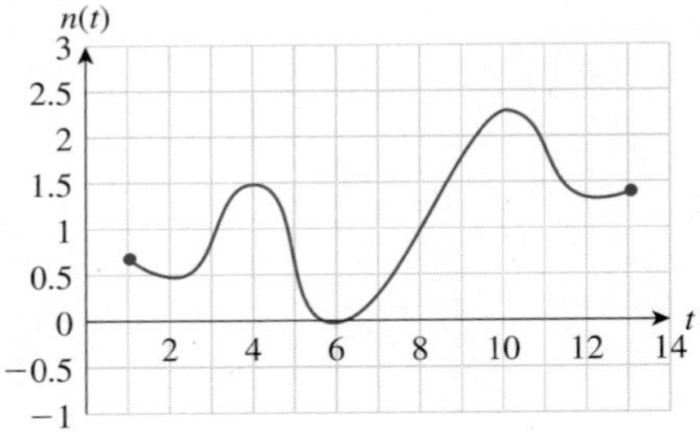

Use a left Riemann sum with four subdivisions to estimate the total change in the number of active users from the second quarter of 2008 to the second quarter of 2010 (the interval [2, 10]). HINT [See Example 3.]

47. ***Scientific Research*** The rate of change $r(t)$ of the total number of research articles in the prominent journal *Physical Review* written by researchers in Europe is shown in the following graph:

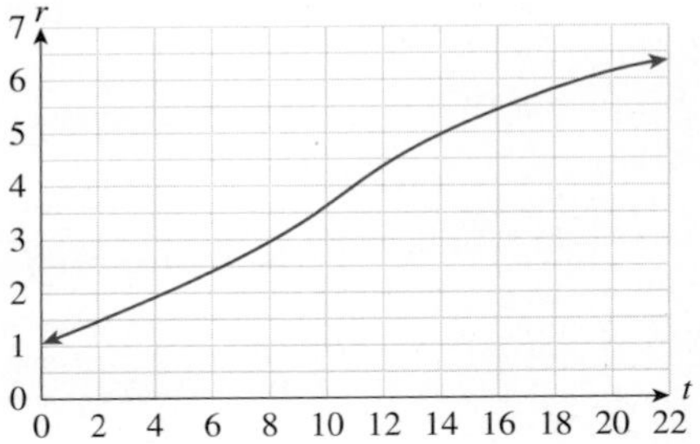

Here, t is time in years ($t = 0$ represents the start of 1983).[28]

a. Use both left and right Riemann sums with eight subdivisions to estimate the total number of articles in *Physical Review* written by researchers in Europe during the 16-year period beginning at the start of 1983. (Estimate each value of $r(t)$ to the nearest 0.5.) HINT [See Example 3.]

b. Use the answers from part (a) to obtain an estimate of $\int_0^{16} r(t)\,dt$. HINT [See Example 4.] Interpret the result.

[24]Source for data: Beverage Marketing Corporation (www.bottledwater.org).

[25]*Ibid.*

[26]Source for data: eBay company reports (http://investor.ebay.com).

[27]*Ibid.*

[28]Based on data from 1983 to 2003. Source: The American Physical Society/*New York Times*, May 3, 2003, p. A1.

48. ***Scientific Research*** The rate of change $r(t)$ of the total number of research articles in the prominent journal *Physical Review* written by researchers in the United States is shown in the following graph:

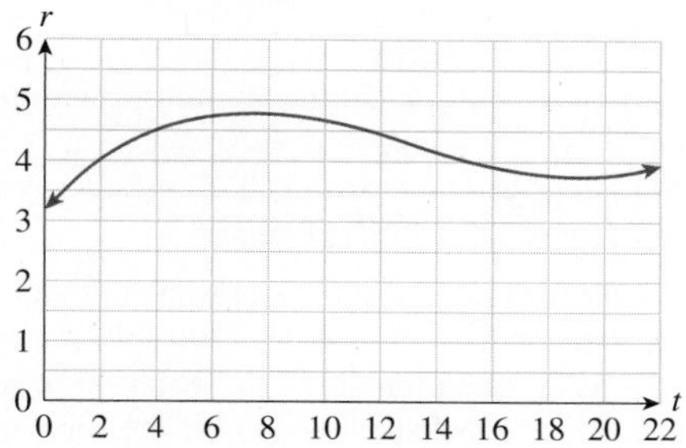

Here, t is time in years ($t = 0$ represents the start of 1983).[29]

a. Use both left and right Riemann sums with six subdivisions to estimate the total number of articles in *Physical Review* written by researchers in the United States during the 12-year period beginning at the start of 1993. (Estimate each value of $r(t)$ to the nearest 0.25.) HINT [See Example 3.]

b. Use the answers from part (a) to obtain an estimate of $\int_{10}^{22} r(t)\,dt$. HINT [See Example 4.] Interpret the result.

49. ***Graduate Degrees: Women*** The following graph shows the approximate number $f'(t)$ of doctoral degrees per year awarded to women in the United States during 2005–2014 ($t = 0$ represents 2005 and each unit of the y-axis represents 10,000 degrees).[30]

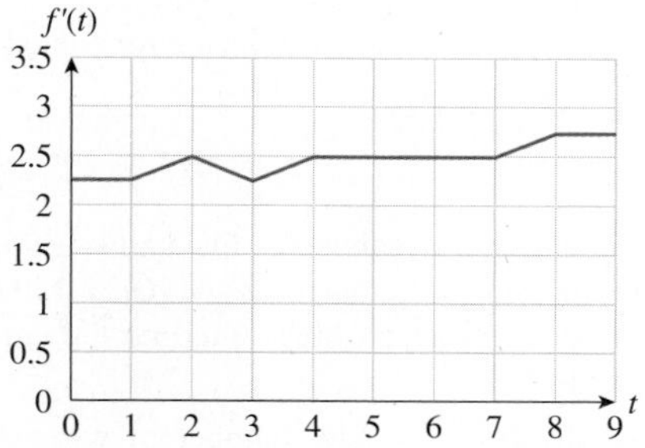

Use the graph to estimate the total number of doctoral degrees awarded to women from 2005 to 2010. HINT [See Example 4.]

50. ***Graduate Degrees: Men*** The following graph shows the approximate number $m'(t)$ of doctoral degrees per year awarded to men in the United States during 2005–2014 ($t = 0$ represents 2005 and each unit of the y-axis represents 10,000 degrees).[31]

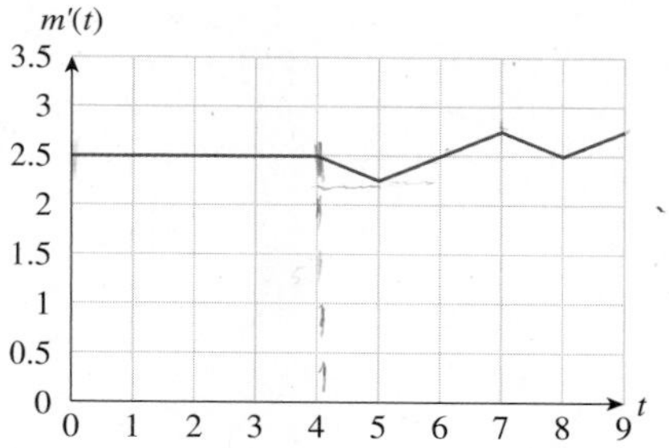

Use the graph to estimate the total number of doctoral degrees awarded to men from 2009 to 2014. HINT [See Example 4.]

51. ***Visiting Students in the Early 2000s*** The aftermath of the September 11 attacks saw a decrease in the number of students visiting the United States. The following graph shows the approximate rate of change $c'(t)$ in the number of students from China who had taken the GRE exam required for admission to U.S. universities (t is time in years since 2000):[32]

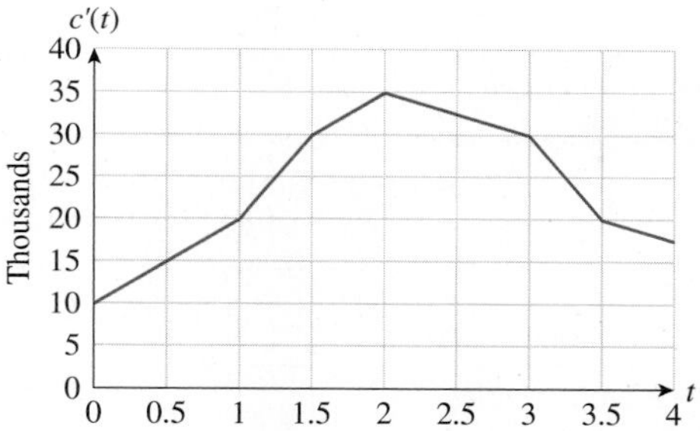

Use the graph to estimate, to the nearest 1,000, the total number of students from China who took the GRE exams during the period 2002–2004.

52. ***Visiting Students in the Early 2000s*** Repeat Exercise 51, using the following graph for students from India:[33]

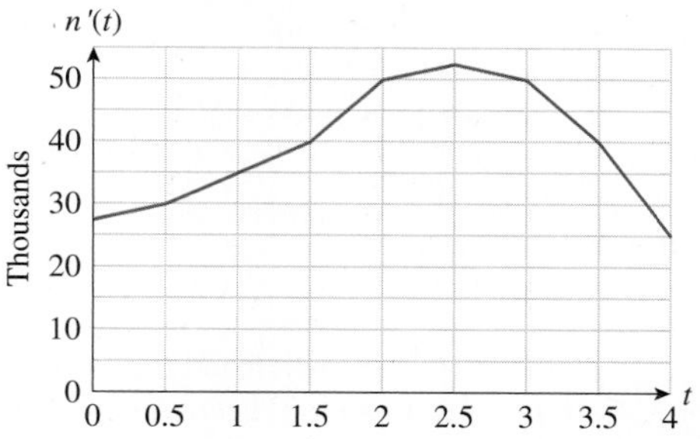

[29]Based on data from 1983 to 2003. Source: The American Physical Society/*New York Times*, May 3, 2003, p. A1.

[30]Source for data and projections: National Center for Education Statistics (www.nces.ed.gov).

[31]*Ibid.*

[32]Source: Educational Testing Services/Shanghai and Jiao Tong University/*New York Times*, December 21, 2004, p. A25.

[33]*Ibid.*

Net Income: Exercises 53 and 54 are based on the following graph, which shows **General Electric**'s *approximate net income in billions of dollars each year from 2005 to 2011.*[34]

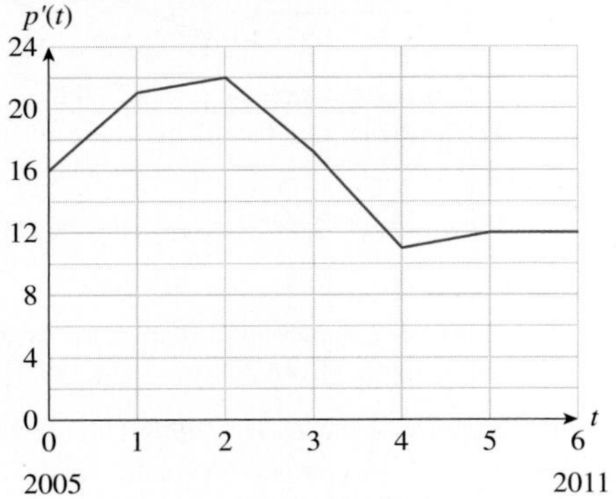

53. Compute the left and right Riemann sum estimates of $\int_0^4 p'(t)\,dt$ using $\Delta t = 1$. Which of these two sums gives the actual total net income earned by **GE** during the years 2005 through 2008? Explain.

54. Compute the left and right Riemann sum estimates of $\int_2^6 p'(t)\,dt$ using $\Delta t = 1$. Which of these two sums gives the actual total net income earned by **GE** during the years 2008 through 2011? Explain.

55. ***Petrochemical Sales: Mexico*** The following table shows annual petrochemical sales in Mexico by **Pemex**, Mexico's national oil company, for 2005–2010 ($t = 0$ represents 2005).[35]

Year t (Year since 2005)	0	1	2	3	4	5
Petrochemical Sales s (Billion metric tons)	3.7	3.8	4.0	4.1	4.0	4.1

a. Use the table to compute the left and right Riemann sums for $s(t)$ over the interval [0, 4] using 4 subdivisions.

b. What does the *right* Riemann sum in part (a) tell you about petrochemical sales by Pemex?

56. ***Petrochemical Production: Mexico*** The following table shows annual petrochemical production in Mexico by **Pemex**, Mexico's national oil company, for 2005–2010 ($t = 0$ represents 2005):[36]

Year t (Year since 2005)	0	1	2	3	4	5
Petrochemical Production p (Billion metric tons)	10.8	11.0	11.8	12.0	12.0	13.3

a. Use the table to compute the left and right Riemann sums for $p(t)$ over the interval [1, 5] using 4 subdivisions.

b. What does the *left* Riemann sum in part (a) tell you about production of petrochemicals by Pemex?

57. ***Motion under Gravity*** The velocity of a stone moving under gravity t seconds after being thrown up at 30 ft/s is given by $v(t) = -32t + 30$ ft/sec. Use a Riemann sum with 5 subdivisions to estimate $\int_0^4 v(t)\,dt$. What does the answer represent? HINT [See Example 6.]

58. ***Motion under Gravity*** The velocity of a stone moving under gravity t seconds after being thrown up at 4 m/s is given by $v(t) = -9.8t + 4$ m/sec. Use a Riemann sum with 5 subdivisions to estimate $\int_0^1 v(t)\,dt$. What does the answer represent? HINT [See Example 6.]

59. T ***Motion*** A model rocket has upward velocity $v(t) = 40t^2$ ft/sec, t seconds after launch. Use a Riemann sum with $n = 10$ to estimate how high the rocket is 2 seconds after launch. (Use technology to compute the Riemann sum.)

60. T ***Motion*** A race car has a velocity of $v(t) = 600(1 - e^{-0.5t})$ ft/sec, t seconds after starting. Use a Riemann sum with $n = 10$ to estimate how far the car has traveled in the first 4 seconds. (Round your answer to the nearest whole number.) (Use technology to compute the Riemann sum.)

61. T ***Facebook Membership*** Since the start of 2005, new members joined **Facebook** at a rate of roughly

$$m(t) = 3.2t^3 - 12t + 10 \text{ million members per year} \quad (0 \le t \le 5),$$

where t is time in years since the start of 2005.[37] Estimate $\int_0^5 m(t)\,dt$ using a Riemann sum with $n = 150$. (Round your answer to the nearest whole number.) Interpret the answer. HINT [See Example 5.]

62. T ***Uploads to YouTube*** Since **YouTube** first became available to the public in mid-2005, the rate at which video has been uploaded to the site can be approximated by

$$v(t) = 525{,}600(0.42t^2 + 2.7t - 1) \text{ hours of video per year} \quad (0.5 \le t \le 7),$$

where t is time in years since the start of 2005.[38] Estimate $\int_1^7 v(t)\,dt$ using a Riemann sum with $n = 150$. (Round your answer to the nearest 1,000.) Interpret the answer. HINT [See Example 5.]

63. T ***Big Brother*** The total number of wiretaps authorized each year by U.S. state and federal courts from 1990 to 2010 can be approximated by

$$w(t) = 820e^{0.051t} \quad (0 \le t \le 20)$$

(t is time in years since the start of 1990).[39] Estimate $\int_0^{15} w(t)\,dt$ using a (left) Riemann sum with $n = 100$. (Round your answer to the nearest 10.) Interpret the answer. HINT [See Example 5.]

[34] Source: Company reports (www.ge.com/investors).

[35] 2010 figure is a projection based on data through May 2010. Source: www.pemex.com (July 2010).

[36] *Ibid.*

[37] Sources for data: www.facebook.com, www.insidefacebook.com.

[38] Source for data: www.YouTube.com.

[39] Source for data: Wiretap Reports, Administrative Office of the United States Courts (www.uscourts.gov/Statistics/WiretapReports.aspx).

64. T ***Big Brother*** The number of wiretaps authorized each year by U.S. state courts from 1990 to 2010 can be approximated by

$$w(t) = 430e^{0.065t} \quad (0 \le t \le 20)$$

(t is time in years since the start of 1990).[40] Estimate $\int_{10}^{15} w(t)\,dt$ using a (left) Riemann sum with $n = 100$. (Round your answer to the nearest 10.) Interpret the answer. HINT [See Example 5.]

65. ▼ ***Surveying*** My uncle intends to build a kidney-shaped swimming pool in his small yard, and the town zoning board will approve the project only if the total area of the pool does not exceed 500 square feet. The accompanying figure shows a diagram of the planned swimming pool, with measurements of its width at the indicated points. Will my uncle's plans be approved? Use a (left) Riemann sum to approximate the area.

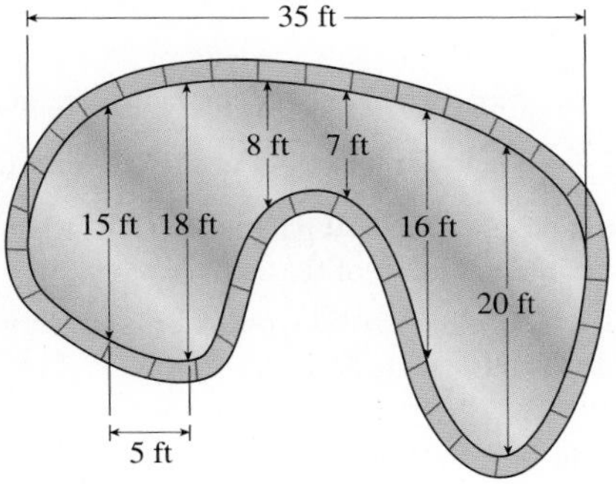

66. ▼ ***Pollution*** An aerial photograph of an ocean oil spill shows the pattern in the accompanying diagram. Assuming that the oil slick has a uniform depth of 0.01 m, how many cubic meters of oil would you estimate to be in the spill? (Volume = Area × Thickness. Use a (left) Riemann sum to approximate the area.)

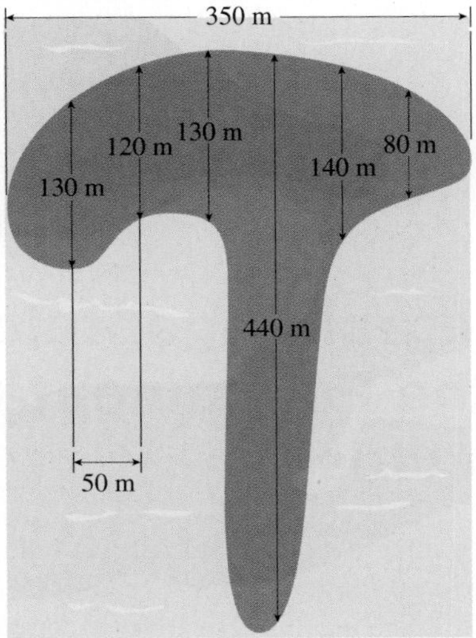

67. T ▼ ***Oil Consumption: United States*** During the period 1980–2008 the United States was consuming oil at a rate of about

$$q(t) = 76t + 5{,}540 \text{ million barrels per year} \quad (0 \le t \le 28),$$

where t is time in years since the start of 1980.[41] During the same period, the price per barrel of crude oil in constant 2008 dollars was about

$$p(t) = 0.45t^2 - 12t + 105 \text{ dollars}^{42} \quad (0 \le t \le 28).$$

a. Graph the function $r(t) = p(t)q(t)$ for $0 \le t \le 28$, indicating the area that represents $\int_{10}^{20} r(t)\,dt$. What does this area signify?

b. Estimate the area in part (a) using a Riemann sum with $n = 200$. (Round the answer to 3 significant digits.) Interpret the answer.

68. T ▼ ***Oil Consumption: China*** Repeat Exercise 67 using instead the rate of consumption of oil in China:

$$q(t) = 82t + 221 \text{ million barrels per year}^{43} \quad (0 \le t \le 28).$$

The Normal Curve *The normal distribution curve, which models the distributions of data in a wide range of applications, is given by the function*

$$p(x) = \frac{1}{\sqrt{2\pi}\,\sigma} e^{-(x-\mu)^2/2\sigma^2},$$

where $\pi = 3.14159265\ldots$ *and* σ *and* μ *are constants called the* ***standard deviation*** *and the* ***mean****, respectively. The graph of the normal distribution (when* $\sigma = 1$ *and* $\mu = 2$*) is shown in the figure. Exercises 69 and 70 illustrate its use.*

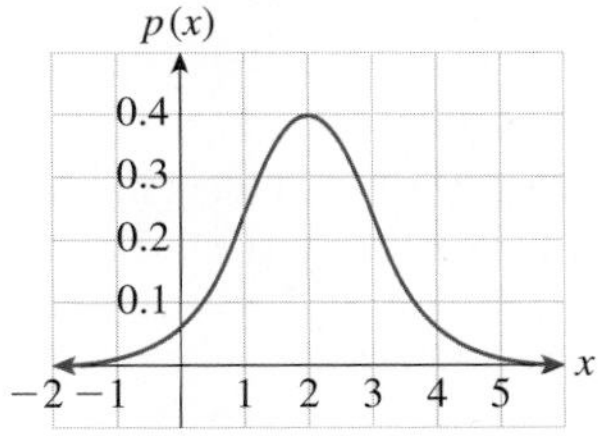

69. T ▼ ***Test Scores*** Enormous State University's Calculus I test scores are modeled by a normal distribution with $\mu = 72.6$ and $\sigma = 5.2$. The percentage of students who obtained scores between a and b on the test is given by

$$\int_a^b p(x)\,dx.$$

a. Use a Riemann sum with $n = 40$ to estimate the percentage of students who obtained between 60 and 100 on the test.

b. What percentage of students scored less than 30?

[40] Source for data: Wiretap Reports, Administrative Office of the United States Courts (www.uscourts.gov/Statistics/WiretapReports.aspx).

[41] Source for data: BP Statistical Review of World Energy (www.bp.com/statisticalreview).

[42] Source for data: www.inflationdata.com.

[43] Source for data: BP Statistical Review of World Energy (www.bp.com/statisticalreview).

70. T ▼ ***Consumer Satisfaction*** In a survey, consumers were asked to rate a new toothpaste on a scale of 1–10. The resulting data are modeled by a normal distribution with $\mu = 4.5$ and $\sigma = 1.0$. The percentage of consumers who rated the toothpaste with a score between a and b on the test is given by

$$\int_a^b p(x)\,dx.$$

a. Use a Riemann sum with $n = 10$ to estimate the percentage of customers who rated the toothpaste 5 or above. (Use the range 4.5 to 10.5.)

b. What percentage of customers rated the toothpaste 0 or 1? (Use the range −0.5 to 1.5.)

COMMUNICATION AND REASONING EXERCISES

71. If $f(x) = 6$, then the left Riemann sum _______ (increases/decreases/stays the same) as n increases.

72. If $f(x) = -1$, then the left Riemann sum _______ (increases/decreases/stays the same) as n increases.

73. If f is an increasing function of x, then the left Riemann sum _______ (increases/decreases/stays the same) as n increases.

74. If f is a decreasing function of x, then the left Riemann sum _______ (increases/decreases/stays the same) as n increases.

75. If $\int_a^b f(x)\,dx = 0$, what can you say about the graph of f?

76. Sketch the graphs of two (different) functions f and g such that $\int_a^b f(x)\,dx = \int_a^b g(x)\,dx$.

77. ▼ The definite integral counts the area under the x-axis as negative. Give an example that shows how this can be useful in applications.

78. ▼ Sketch the graph of a nonconstant function whose Riemann sum with $n = 1$ gives the exact value of the definite integral.

79. ▼ Sketch the graph of a nonconstant function whose Riemann sums with $n = 1$, 5, and 10 are all zero.

80. ▼ Besides left and right Riemann sums, another approximation of the integral is the **midpoint** approximation, in which we compute the sum

$$\sum_{k=1}^{n} f(\bar{x}_k)\,\Delta x$$

where $\bar{x}_k = (x_{k-1} + x_k)/2$ is the point midway between the left and right endpoints of the interval $[x_{k-1}, x_k]$. Why is it true that the midpoint approximation is exact if f is linear? (Draw a picture.)

81. ▼ Your cellphone company charges you $c(t) = \dfrac{20}{t + 100}$ dollars for the tth minute. You make a 60-minute phone call. What kind of (left) Riemann sum represents the total cost of the call? Explain.

82. ▼ Your friend's cellphone company charges her $c(t) = \dfrac{20}{t + 100}$ dollars for the $(t + 1)$st minute. Your friend makes a 60-minute phone call. What kind of (left) Riemann sum represents the total cost of the call? Explain.

83. ▼ Give a formula for the **right Riemann Sum** with n equal subdivisions $a = x_0 < x_1 < \cdots < x_n = b$ for f over the interval $[a, b]$.

84. ▼ Refer to Exercise 83. If f is continuous, what happens to the difference between the left and right Riemann sums as $n \to \infty$? Explain.

85. ▼ Sketch the graph of a nonzero function whose left Riemann sum with n subdivisions is zero for every *even* number n.

86. ▼ When approximating a definite integral by computing Riemann sums, how might you judge whether you have chosen n large enough to get your answer accurate to, say, three decimal places?

6.4 The Definite Integral: Algebraic Viewpoint and the Fundamental Theorem of Calculus

In Section 6.3 we saw that the definite integral of the marginal cost function gives the total cost. However, in Section 6.1 we used antiderivatives to recover the cost function from the marginal cost function, so we *could* use antiderivatives to compute total cost. The following example, based on Example 5 in Section 6.1, compares these two approaches.

EXAMPLE 1 Finding Cost from Marginal Cost

The marginal cost of producing baseball caps at a production level of x caps is $4 - 0.001x$ dollars per cap. Find the total change of cost if production is increased from 100 to 200 caps.

Solution

Method 1: Using an Antiderivative (based on Example 5 in Section 6.1): Let $C(x)$ be the cost function. Because the marginal cost function is the derivative of the cost function, we have $C'(x) = 4 - 0.001x$ and so

$$C(x) = \int (4 - 0.001x)\, dx$$

$$= 4x - 0.001\frac{x^2}{2} + K \qquad K \text{ is the constant of integration.}$$

$$= 4x - 0.0005x^2 + K.$$

Although we do not know what to use for the value of the constant K, we can say:

$$\text{Cost at production level of 100 caps} = C(100) = 4(100) - 0.0005(100)^2 + K = \$395 + K$$

$$\text{Cost at production level of 200 caps} = C(200) = 4(200) - 0.0005(200)^2 + K = \$780 + K.$$

Therefore,

$$\text{Total change in cost} = C(200) - C(100) = (\$780 + K) - (\$395 + K) = \$385.$$

Notice how the constant of integration simply canceled out! So, we could choose any value for K that we wanted (such as $K = 0$) and still come out with the correct total change. Put another way, we could use *any antiderivative* of $C'(x)$, such as

$$F(x) = 4x - 0.0005x^2 \qquad F(x) \text{ is } any \text{ antiderivative of } C'(x) \text{ whereas } C(x) \text{ is the actual cost function.}$$

or

$$F(x) = 4x - 0.0005x^2 + 4,$$

compute $F(200) - F(100)$, and obtain the total change, \$385.

Summarizing this method: To compute the total change of $C(x)$ over the interval [100, 200], use any antiderivative $F(x)$ of $C'(x)$, and compute $F(200) - F(100)$.

Method 2: Using a Definite Integral (based on the interpretation of the definite integral as total change discussed in Section 6.3): Because the marginal cost $C'(x)$ is the rate of change of the total cost function $C(x)$, the total change in $C(x)$ over the interval [100, 200] is given by

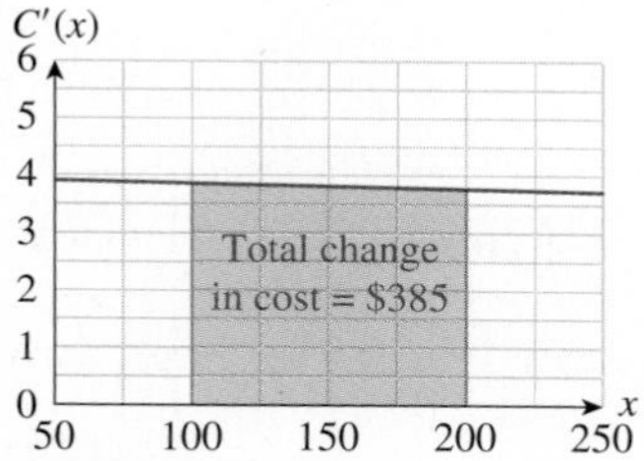

Figure 20

$$\text{Total change in cost} = \text{Area under the marginal cost function curve}$$

$$= \int_{100}^{200} C'(x)\, dx$$

$$= \int_{100}^{200} (4 - 0.001x)\, dx \qquad \text{See Figure 20.}$$

$$= \$385. \qquad \text{Using geometry or Riemann sums}$$

Putting these two methods together gives us the following surprising result:

$$\int_{100}^{200} C'(x)\,dx = F(200) - F(100),$$

where $F(x)$ is any antiderivative of $C'(x)$.

Now, there is nothing special in Example 1 about the specific function $C'(x)$ or the choice of endpoints of integration. So if we replace $C'(x)$ by a general continuous function $f(x)$, we can write

$$\int_a^b f(x)\,dx = F(b) - F(a),$$

where $F(x)$ is any antiderivative of $f(x)$. This result is known as the **Fundamental Theorem of Calculus**.

The Fundamental Theorem of Calculus (FTC)

Let f be a continuous function defined on the interval $[a, b]$ and let F be *any* antiderivative of f defined on $[a, b]$. Then

$$\int_a^b f(x)\,dx = F(b) - F(a).$$

Moreover, an antiderivative of f is guaranteed to exist.

In Words: Every continuous function has an antiderivative. To compute the definite integral of $f(x)$ over $[a, b]$, first find an antiderivative $F(x)$, then evaluate it at $x = b$, evaluate it at $x = a$, and subtract the two answers.

Quick Example

Because $F(x) = x^2$ is an antiderivative of $f(x) = 2x$,

$$\int_0^1 2x\,dx = F(1) - F(0) = 1^2 - 0^2 = 1.$$

Note The Fundamental Theorem of Calculus actually applies to some other functions besides the continuous ones. The function f is **piecewise continuous** on $[a, b]$ if it is defined and continuous at all but finitely many points in the interval, and at each point where the function is not defined or is discontinuous, the left and right limits of f exist and are finite. (See Figure 21.)

$$f(x) = \frac{|x|}{x} \qquad f(x) = \begin{cases} 1 + \dfrac{x^2}{8} & \text{if } x < 1 \\ 3 - \dfrac{x^2}{8} & \text{if } x > 1 \end{cases} \qquad f(x) = \frac{1}{2}\left[\frac{|x-1|}{x-1} + \frac{|x-2|}{x-2}\right]$$

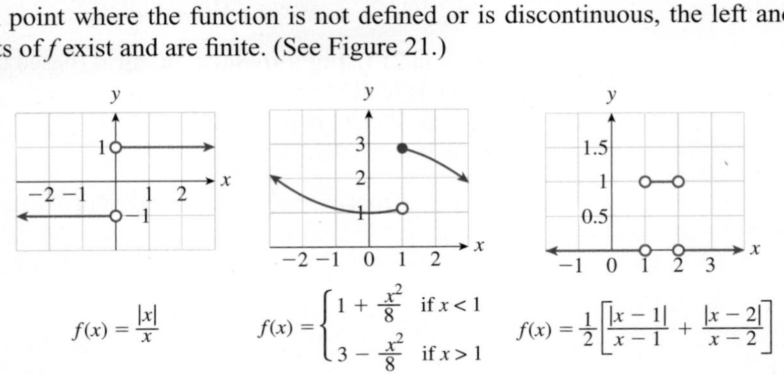

Figure 21

The FTC also applies to any piecewise continuous function f, as long as we specify that the antiderivative F that we choose be continuous. To be precise, to say that F is an antiderivative of f means here that $F'(x) = f(x)$ except at the points at which f is discontinuous or not defined, where $F'(x)$ may not exist. For example, if f is the step function $f(x) = |x|/x$, shown on the left in Figure 21, then we can use $F(x) = |x|$. (Note that F is continuous, and $F'(x) = |x|/x$ except when $x = 0$.) ■

EXAMPLE 2 Using the FTC to Calculate a Definite Integral

Calculate $\int_0^1 (1 - x^2)\,dx$.

Solution To use the FTC, we need to find an antiderivative of $1 - x^2$. But we know that

$$\int (1 - x^2)\,dx = x - \frac{x^3}{3} + C.$$

We need only one antiderivative, so let's take $F(x) = x - x^3/3$. The FTC tells us that

$$\int_0^1 (1 - x^2)\,dx = F(1) - F(0) = \left(1 - \frac{1}{3}\right) - (0) = \frac{2}{3}$$

which is the value we estimated in Section 6.3.

Before we go on... A useful piece of notation is often used here. We write*

$$[F(x)]_a^b = F(b) - F(a).$$

Thus, we can rewrite the computation in Example 2 more simply as follows:

$$\int_0^1 (1 - x^2)\,dx = \left[x - \frac{x^3}{3}\right]_0^1$$

Substitute $x = 1$. Substitute $x = 0$.

$$= \left(1 - \frac{1}{3}\right) - \left(0 - \frac{0}{3}\right)$$

$$= \left(1 - \frac{1}{3}\right) - (0) = \frac{2}{3}.$$ ■

* There seem to be several notations in use, actually. Another common notation is $F(x)\Big|_a^b$.

EXAMPLE 3 More Use of the FTC

Compute the following definite integrals.

a. $\int_0^1 (2x^3 + 10x + 1)\,dx$ **b.** $\int_1^5 \left(\frac{1}{x^2} + \frac{1}{x}\right) dx$

Solution

a. $$\int_0^1 (2x^3 + 10x + 1)\,dx = \left[\frac{1}{2}x^4 + 5x^2 + x\right]_0^1$$

Substitute $x = 1$. Substitute $x = 0$.

$$= \left(\frac{1}{2} + 5 + 1\right) - \left(\frac{1}{2}(0) + 5(0) + 0\right)$$

$$= \left(\frac{1}{2} + 5 + 1\right) - (0) = \frac{13}{2}$$

b. $\int_1^5 \left(\frac{1}{x^2}+\frac{1}{x}\right) dx = \int_1^5 (x^{-2}+x^{-1})\, dx$

$= \left[-x^{-1} + \ln|x|\right]_1^5$

Substitute $x = 5$. Substitute $x = 1$.

$= \left(-\frac{1}{5} + \ln 5\right) - (-1 + \ln 1)$

$= \frac{4}{5} + \ln 5$

When calculating a definite integral, we may have to use substitution to find the necessary antiderivative. We could substitute, evaluate the indefinite integral with respect to u, express the answer in terms of x, and then evaluate at the limits of integration. However, there is a shortcut, as we shall see in the next example.

EXAMPLE 4 Using the FTC with Substitution

Evaluate $\int_1^2 (2x-1)e^{2x^2-2x}\, dx$.

Solution The shortcut we promised is to put *everything* in terms of u, including the limits of integration.

$u = 2x^2 - 2x$

$\frac{du}{dx} = 4x - 2$

$dx = \frac{1}{4x-2}\, du$

When $x = 1$, $u = 0$. Substitute $x = 1$ in the formula for u.

When $x = 2$, $u = 4$. Substitute $x = 2$ in the formula for u.

We get the value $u = 0$, for example, by substituting $x = 1$ in the equation $u = 2x^2 - 2x$. We can now rewrite the integral.

$$\int_1^2 (2x-1)e^{2x^2-2x}\, dx = \int_0^4 (2x-1)e^u \frac{1}{4x-2}\, du$$

$$= \int_0^4 \frac{1}{2} e^u\, du$$

$$= \left[\frac{1}{2}e^u\right]_0^4 = \frac{1}{2}e^4 - \frac{1}{2}$$

Before we go on... The alternative, longer calculation in Example 4 is first to calculate the indefinite integral:

$$\int (2x-1)e^{2x^2-2x}\, dx = \int \frac{1}{2}e^u\, du$$

$$= \frac{1}{2}e^u + C = \frac{1}{2}e^{2x^2-2x} + C.$$

Then we can say that

$$\int_1^2 (2x-1)e^{2x^2-2x}\,dx = \left[\frac{1}{2}e^{2x^2-2x}\right]_1^2 = \frac{1}{2}e^4 - \frac{1}{2}.$$ ■

APPLICATIONS

EXAMPLE 5 Oil Spill

In Section 6.3 we considered the following example: Your deep ocean oil rig has suffered a catastrophic failure, and oil is leaking from the ocean floor wellhead at a rate of

$$v(t) = 0.08t^2 - 4t + 60 \text{ thousand barrels per day } (0 \le t \le 20),$$

where t is time in days since the failure. Compute the total volume of oil released during the first 20 days.

using Technology

TI-83/84 Plus
Home Screen:
`fnInt(0.08x^2-4x+60,x,0,20)`
(`fnInt` is MATH → 9)

Website
www.WanerMath.com
At the Website, select the Online Utilities tab, and choose the Numerical Integration Utility and Grapher. There, enter the formula

`0.08x^2-4x+60`

for $f(x)$, enter 0 and 20 for the lower and upper limits, and press "Integral".

Solution We calculate

$$\text{Total volume} = \int_0^{20}(0.08t^2 - 4t + 60)\,dt = \left[0.08\frac{t^3}{3} - 2t^2 + 60t\right]_0^{20}$$

$$= \left[0.08\frac{20^3}{3} - 2(20)^2 + 60(20)\right] - [0.08(0) - 2(0) + 60(0)]$$

$$= \frac{640}{3} - 800 + 1{,}200 \approx 613.3 \text{ thousand barrels.}$$

EXAMPLE 6 Computing Area

Find the total area of the region enclosed by the graph of $y = xe^{x^2}$, the x-axis, and the vertical lines $x = -1$ and $x = 1$.

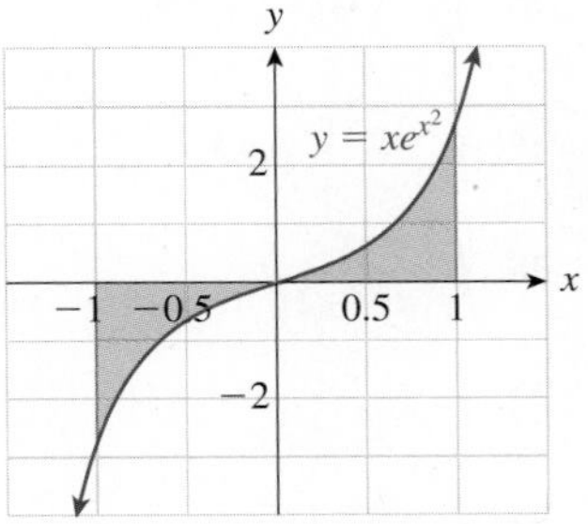

$\int_{-1}^{1} xe^{x^2}\,dx$

Figure 22

Solution The region whose area we want is shown in Figure 22. Notice the symmetry of the graph. Also, half the region we are interested in is above the x-axis, while the other half is below. If we calculated the integral $\int_{-1}^{1} xe^{x^2}\,dx$, the result would be

$$\text{Area above } x\text{-axis} - \text{Area below } x\text{-axis} = 0,$$

which does not give us the total area. To prevent the area below the x-axis from being combined with the area above the axis, we do the calculation in two parts, as illustrated in Figure 23.

(In Figure 23 we broke the integral at $x = 0$ because that is where the graph crosses the x-axis.) These integrals can be calculated using the substitution $u = x^2$:

$$\int_{-1}^{0} xe^{x^2}\,dx = \frac{1}{2}\left[e^{x^2}\right]_{-1}^{0} = \frac{1}{2}(1-e) \approx -0.85914$$ Why is it negative?

$$\int_{0}^{1} xe^{x^2}\,dx = \frac{1}{2}\left[e^{x^2}\right]_{0}^{1} = \frac{1}{2}(e-1) \approx 0.85914$$

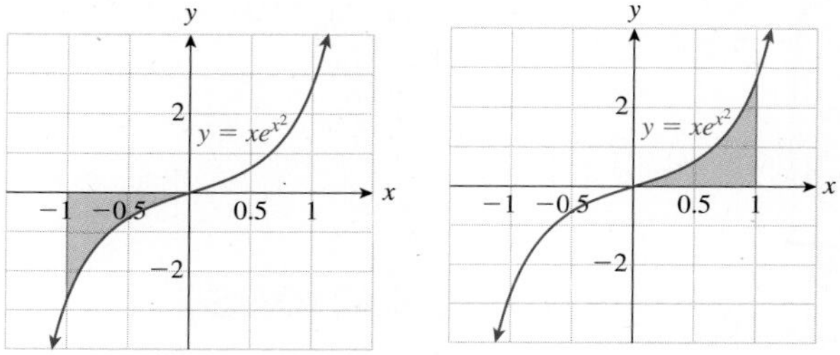

$\int_{-1}^{0} xe^{x^2}\,dx$ $\int_{0}^{1} xe^{x^2}\,dx$

Figure 23

To obtain the total area, we should add the *absolute* values of these answers because we don't wish to count any area as negative. Thus,

$$\text{Total area} \approx 0.85914 + 0.85914 = 1.71828.$$

6.4 EXERCISES

▼ more advanced ◆ challenging

T indicates exercises that should be solved using technology

Evaluate the integrals in Exercises 1–44. HINT [See Example 2.]

1. $\int_{-1}^{1} (x^2 + 2)\,dx$
2. $\int_{-2}^{1} (x - 2)\,dx$
3. $\int_{0}^{1} (12x^5 + 5x^4 - 6x^2 + 4)\,dx$
4. $\int_{0}^{1} (4x^3 - 3x^2 + 4x - 1)\,dx$
5. $\int_{-2}^{2} (x^3 - 2x)\,dx$
6. $\int_{-1}^{1} (2x^3 + x)\,dx$
7. $\int_{1}^{3} \left(\frac{2}{x^2} + 3x\right) dx$
8. $\int_{2}^{3} \left(x + \frac{1}{x}\right) dx$
9. $\int_{0}^{1} (2.1x - 4.3x^{1.2})\,dx$
10. $\int_{-1}^{0} (4.3x^2 - 1)\,dx$
11. $\int_{0}^{1} 2e^x\,dx$
12. $\int_{-1}^{0} 3e^x\,dx$
13. $\int_{0}^{1} \sqrt{x}\,dx$
14. $\int_{-1}^{1} \sqrt[3]{x}\,dx$
15. $\int_{0}^{1} 2^x\,dx$
16. $\int_{0}^{1} 3^x\,dx$

HINT [In Exercises 17–44 use a shortcut or see Example 4.]

17. $\int_{0}^{1} 18(3x + 1)^5\,dx$
18. $\int_{0}^{1} 8(-x + 1)^7\,dx$
19. $\int_{-1}^{1} e^{2x-1}\,dx$
20. $\int_{0}^{2} e^{-x+1}\,dx$
21. $\int_{0}^{2} 2^{-x+1}\,dx$
22. $\int_{-1}^{1} 3^{2x-1}\,dx$
23. $\int_{0}^{4} |-3x + 4|\,dx$
24. $\int_{-4}^{4} |-x - 2|\,dx$
25. $\int_{0}^{1} 5x(8x^2 + 1)^{-1/2}\,dx$
26. $\int_{0}^{\sqrt{2}} x\sqrt{2x^2 + 1}\,dx$
27. $\int_{-\sqrt{2}}^{\sqrt{2}} 3x\sqrt{2x^2 + 1}\,dx$
28. $\int_{-2}^{2} xe^{-x^2+1}\,dx$
29. $\int_{0}^{1} 5xe^{x^2+2}\,dx$
30. $\int_{0}^{2} \frac{3x}{x^2 + 2}\,dx$
31. $\int_{2}^{3} \frac{x^2}{x^3 - 1}\,dx$
32. $\int_{2}^{3} \frac{x}{2x^2 - 5}\,dx$
33. $\int_{0}^{1} x(1.1)^{-x^2}\,dx$
34. $\int_{0}^{1} x^2(2.1)^{x^3}\,dx$
35. $\int_{1}^{2} \frac{e^{1/x}}{x^2}\,dx$
36. $\int_{1}^{2} \frac{\sqrt{\ln x}}{x}\,dx$
37. $\int_{0}^{2} \frac{e^{-2x}}{1 + 3e^{-2x}}\,dx$ (Round the answer to four decimal places.)
38. $\int_{0}^{1} \frac{e^{2x}}{1 - 3e^{2x}}\,dx$ (Round the answer to four decimal places.)

39. ▼ $\int_0^2 \frac{x}{x+1}\,dx$

40. ▼ $\int_{-1}^1 \frac{2x}{x+2}\,dx$

41. ▼ $\int_1^2 x(x-2)^5\,dx$

42. ▼ $\int_1^2 x(x-2)^{1/3}\,dx$

43. ▼ $\int_0^1 x\sqrt{2x+1}\,dx$

44. ▼ $\int_{-1}^0 2x\sqrt{x+1}\,dx$

Calculate the total area of the regions described in Exercises 45–54. Do not count area beneath the x-axis as negative. HINT [See Example 6.]

45. Bounded by the line $y = x$, the x-axis, and the lines $x = 0$ and $x = 1$

46. Bounded by the line $y = 2x$, the x-axis, and the lines $x = 1$ and $x = 2$

47. Bounded by the curve $y = \sqrt{x}$, the x-axis, and the lines $x = 0$ and $x = 4$

48. Bounded by the curve $y = 2\sqrt{x}$, the x-axis, and the lines $x = 0$ and $x = 16$

49. Bounded by the graph of $y = |2x - 3|$, the x-axis, and the lines $x = 0$ and $x = 3$

50. Bounded by the graph of $y = |3x - 2|$, the x-axis, and the lines $x = 0$ and $x = 3$

51. ▼ Bounded by the curve $y = x^2 - 1$, the x-axis, and the lines $x = 0$ and $x = 4$

52. ▼ Bounded by the curve $y = 1 - x^2$, the x-axis, and the lines $x = -1$ and $x = 2$

53. ▼ Bounded by the x-axis, the curve $y = xe^{x^2}$, and the lines $x = 0$ and $x = (\ln 2)^{1/2}$

54. ▼ Bounded by the x-axis, the curve $y = xe^{x^2-1}$, and the lines $x = 0$ and $x = 1$

APPLICATIONS

55. ***Cost*** The marginal cost of producing the xth box of light bulbs is $5 + x^2/1{,}000$ dollars. Determine how much is added to the total cost by a change in production from $x = 10$ to $x = 100$ boxes. HINT [See Example 5.]

56. ***Revenue*** The marginal revenue of the xth box of flash cards sold is $100e^{-0.001x}$ dollars. Find the revenue generated by selling items 101 through 1,000. HINT [See Example 5.]

57. ***Motion*** A car traveling down a road has a velocity of $v(t) = 60 - e^{-t/10}$ mph at time t hours. Find the distance it has traveled from time $t = 1$ hour to time $t = 6$ hours. (Round your answer to the nearest mile.)

58. ***Motion*** A ball thrown in the air has a velocity of $v(t) = 100 - 32t$ ft/sec at time t seconds. Find the total displacement of the ball between times $t = 1$ second and $t = 7$ seconds, and interpret your answer.

59. ***Motion*** A car slows to a stop at a stop sign, then starts up again, in such a way that its speed at time t seconds after it starts to slow is $v(t) = |-10t + 40|$ ft/sec. How far does the car travel from time $t = 0$ to time $t = 10$ sec?

60. ***Motion*** A truck slows, doesn't quite stop at a stop sign, and then speeds up again in such a way that its speed at time t seconds is $v(t) = 10 + |-5t + 30|$ ft/sec. How far does the truck travel from time $t = 0$ to time $t = 10$?

61. ***Bottled Water Sales*** (Compare Exercise 55 in Section 6.1.) The rate of U.S. sales of bottled water for the period 2000–2010 could be approximated by

$$s(t) = -45t^2 + 900t + 4{,}200 \text{ million gallons per year} \quad (0 \le t \le 10),$$

where t is time in years since the start of 2000.[44] Use a definite integral to estimate the total sales $S(t)$ of bottled water from the start of 2000 to the start of 2008.

62. ***Bottled Water Sales*** (Compare Exercise 56 in Section 6.1.) The rate of U.S. per capita sales of bottled water for the period 2000–2010 could be approximated by

$$s(t) = -0.18t^2 + 3t + 15 \text{ gallons per year} \quad (0 \le t \le 10),$$

where t is time in years since the start of 2000.[45] Use a definite integral to estimate the total U.S. per capita sales of bottled water from the start of 2000 to the end of 2009.

63. ***Facebook Membership*** At the start of 2005, Facebook had 1 million members. Since that time, new members joined at a rate of roughly

$$m(t) = 3.2t^3 - 12t + 10 \text{ million members per year} \quad (0 \le t \le 5),$$

where t is time in years since the start of 2005.[46] Use a definite integral to estimate the total number of new Facebook members from the start of 2007 to the start of 2010.

64. ***Uploads to YouTube*** Since YouTube first became available to the public in mid-2005, the rate at which video has been uploaded to the site can be approximated by

$$v(t) = 525{,}600(0.42t^2 + 2.7t - 1) \text{ hours of video per year} \quad (0.5 \le t \le 7),$$

where t is time in years since the start of 2005.[47] Use a definite integral to estimate the total number of hours of video uploaded from the start of 2006 to the start of 2012. (Round your answer to the nearest million hours of video.)

65. ***Big Brother*** (Compare Exercise 69 in Section 6.3.) The total number of wiretaps authorized each year by U.S. state and federal courts from 1990 to 2010 can be approximated by

$$w(t) = 820e^{0.051t} \quad (0 \le t \le 20)$$

(t is time in years since the start of 1990).[48] Compute $\int_0^{15} w(t)\,dt$. (Round your answer to the nearest 10.) Interpret the answer.

---

[44] Source for data: Beverage Marketing Corporation (www.bottledwater.org).

[45] *Ibid.*

[46] Sources for data: www.facebook.com, www.insidefacebook.com.

[47] Source for data: www.YouTube.com.

[48] Source for data: 2007 Wiretap Report, Administrative Office of the United States Courts (www.uscourts.gov/wiretap07/2007WTText.pdf).

66. ***Big Brother*** (Compare Exercise 64 in Section 6.3.) The number of wiretaps authorized each year by U.S. state courts from 1990 to 2010 can be approximated by

$$w(t) = 430e^{0.065t} \quad (0 \le t \le 20)$$

(t is time in years since the start of 1990).[49] Compute $\int_{10}^{15} w(t)\,dt$. (Round your answer to the nearest 10.) Interpret the answer.

67. ***Economic Growth*** (Compare Exercise 85 in Section 6.2.) The value of sold goods in Mexico can be approximated by

$$v(x) = 210 - 62e^{-0.05x} \text{ trillion pesos per month } (x \ge 0),$$

where x is time in months since January 2005.[50] Find an expression for the total value $V(t)$ of sold goods in Mexico from January 2005 to time t.

68. ***Economic Contraction*** (Compare Exercise 86 in Section 6.2.) Housing starts in the United States can be approximated by

$$n(x) = 1.1 + 1.2e^{-0.08x} \text{ million homes per year } (x \ge 0),$$

where x is time in years since January 2006.[51] Find an expression for the total number $N(t)$ of housing starts in the United States from January 2006 to time t.

69. ***Fuel Consumption*** The way Professor Waner drives, he burns gas at the rate of $1 - e^{-t}$ gallons each hour, t hours after a fill-up. Find the number of gallons of gas he burns in the first 10 hours after a fill-up.

70. ***Fuel Consumption*** The way Professor Costenoble drives, he burns gas at the rate of $1/(t + 1)$ gallons each hour, t hours after a fill-up. Find the number of gallons of gas he burns in the first 10 hours after a fill-up.

71. ▼ ***Sales*** Weekly sales of your *Lord of the Rings* T-shirts have been falling by 5% per week. Assuming you are now selling 50 T-shirts per week, how many shirts will you sell during the coming year? (Round your answer to the nearest shirt.)

72. ▼ ***Sales*** Annual sales of fountain pens in Littleville are 4,000 per year and are increasing by 10% per year. How many fountain pens will be sold over the next five years?

73. T ***Embryo Development*** The oxygen consumption of a bird embryo increases from the time the egg is laid through the time the chick hatches. In a typical galliform bird, the oxygen consumption can be approximated by

$$c(t) = -0.065t^3 + 3.4t^2 - 22t + 3.6 \text{ milliliters per day } (8 \le t \le 30),$$

where t is the time (in days) since the egg was laid.[52] (An egg will typically hatch at around $t = 28$.) Use technology to estimate the total amount of oxygen consumed during the ninth and tenth days ($t = 8$ to $t = 10$). Round your answer to the nearest milliliter. HINT [See the technology note in the margin on page 503.]

74. T ***Embryo Development*** The oxygen consumption of a turkey embryo increases from the time the egg is laid through the time the chick hatches. In a brush turkey, the oxygen consumption can be approximated by

$$c(t) = -0.028t^3 + 2.9t^2 - 44t + 95 \text{ milliliters per day } (20 \le t \le 50),$$

where t is the time (in days) since the egg was laid.[53] (An egg will typically hatch at around $t = 50$.) Use technology to estimate the total amount of oxygen consumed during the 21st and 22nd days ($t = 20$ to $t = 22$). Round your answer to the nearest 10 milliliters. HINT [See the technology note in the margin on page 503.]

75. T ***Online Vehicle Sales*** The rate of change $v(t)$ of the value of vehicle transactions on **eBay** could be approximated by

$$v(t) = -0.002t^3 + 0.06t^2 - 0.55t + 3.9 \text{ billion dollars per quarter } (1 \le t \le 13)$$

(t is time in quarters; $t = 1$ represents the first quarter of 2008).[54] Use technology to estimate $\int_1^9 v(t)\,dt$. Interpret your answer.

76. T ***Online Auctions*** The rate of change $n(t)$ of the number of active **eBay** users could be approximated by

$$n(t) = -0.002t^4 + 0.06t^3 - 0.55t^2 + 1.9t - 1 \text{ million users per quarter } (1 \le t \le 13)$$

(t is time in quarters; $t = 1$ represents the first quarter of 2008).[55] Use technology to compute $\int_5^{13} n(t)\,dt$ correct to the nearest whole number. Interpret your answer.

77. ▼ ***Cost*** Use the Fundamental Theorem of Calculus to show that if $m(x)$ is the marginal cost at a production level of x items, then the cost function $C(x)$ is given by

$$C(x) = C(0) + \int_0^x m(t)\,dt.$$

What do we call $C(0)$?

78. ▼ ***Cost*** The total cost of producing x items is given by

$$C(x) = 246.76 + \int_0^x 5t\,dt.$$

Find the fixed cost and the marginal cost of producing the 10th item.

---

[49] Source for data: Wiretap Reports, Administrative Office of the United States Courts (www.uscourts.gov/Statistics/WiretapReports.aspx).

[50] Source: Instituto Nacional de Estadística y Geografía (INEGI) (www.inegi.org.mx).

[51] Source for data: *New York Times*, February 17, 2007, p. C3.

[52] The model approximates graphical data published in the article "The Brush Turkey" by Roger S. Seymour, *Scientific American*, December 1991, pp. 108–114.

[53] *Ibid.*

[54] Source for data: eBay company reports (http://investor.ebay.com).

[55] *Ibid.*

79. ***Scientific Research*** (Compare Exercise 91 in Section 6.2.) The number of research articles in the prominent journal *Physical Review* written by researchers in Europe can be approximated by

$$E(t) = \frac{7e^{0.2t}}{5 + e^{0.2t}} \text{ thousand articles per year} \quad (t \ge 0),$$

where t is time in years ($t = 0$ represents 1983).[56] Use a definite integral to estimate the number of articles written by researchers in Europe from 1983 to 2003. (Round your answer to the nearest 1,000 articles.) HINT [See Example 5 in Section 6.2.]

80. ***Scientific Research*** (Compare Exercise 92 in Section 6.2.) The number of research articles in the prominent journal *Physical Review* written by researchers in the United States can be approximated by

$$U(t) = \frac{4.6e^{0.6t}}{0.4 + e^{0.6t}} \text{ thousand articles per year} \quad (t \ge 0),$$

where t is time in years ($t = 0$ represents 1983).[57] Use a definite integral to estimate the total number of articles written by researchers in the United States from 1983 to 2003. (Round your answer to the nearest 1,000 articles.) HINT [See Example 5 in Section 6.2.]

81. ▼ ***The Logistic Function and High School Graduates***

a. Show that the logistic function $f(x) = \dfrac{N}{1 + Ab^{-x}}$ can be written in the form

$$f(x) = \frac{Nb^x}{A + b^x}.$$

HINT [See the note after Example 5 in Section 6.2.]

b. Use the result of part (a) and a suitable substitution to show that

$$\int \frac{N}{1 + Ab^{-x}}\,dx = \frac{N \ln(A + b^x)}{\ln b} + C.$$

c. The rate of graduation of private high school students in the United States for the period 1994–2008 was approximately

$$r(t) = 220 + \frac{110}{1 + 3.8(1.27)^{-t}} \text{ thousand students per year} \quad (0 \le t \le 14)$$

t years since 1994.[58] Use the result of part (b) to estimate the total number of private high school graduates over the period 2000–2008.

82. ▼ ***The Logistic Function and Grant Spending***

a. Show that the logistic function $f(x) = \dfrac{N}{1 + Ae^{-kx}}$ can be written in the form

$$f(x) = \frac{Ne^{kx}}{A + e^{kx}}.$$

HINT [See the note after Example 5 in Section 6.2.]

b. Use the result of part (a) and a suitable substitution to show that

$$\int \frac{N}{1 + Ae^{-kx}}\,dx = \frac{N \ln(A + e^{kx})}{k} + C.$$

c. The rate of spending on grants by U.S. foundations in the period 1993–2003 was approximately

$$s(t) = 11 + \frac{20}{1 + 1{,}800e^{-0.9t}} \text{ billion dollars per year} \quad (3 \le t \le 13),$$

where t is the number of years since 1990.[59] Use the result of part (b) to estimate, to the nearest \$10 billion, the total spending on grants from 1998 to 2003.

83. ◆ ***Kinetic Energy*** The work done in accelerating an object from velocity v_0 to velocity v_1 is given by

$$W = \int_{v_0}^{v_1} v\frac{dp}{dv}\,dv,$$

where p is its momentum, given by $p = mv$ (m = mass). Assuming that m is a constant, show that

$$W = \frac{1}{2}mv_1^2 - \frac{1}{2}mv_0^2.$$

The quantity $\frac{1}{2}mv^2$ is referred to as the **kinetic energy** of the object, so the work required to accelerate an object is given by its change in kinetic energy.

84. ◆ ***Einstein's Energy Equation*** According to the special theory of relativity, the apparent mass of an object depends on its velocity according to the formula

$$m = \frac{m_0}{\left(1 - \dfrac{v^2}{c^2}\right)^{1/2}},$$

where v is its velocity, m_0 is the "rest mass" of the object (that is, its mass when $v = 0$), and c is the velocity of light: approximately 3×10^8 meters per second.

a. Show that, if $p = mv$ is the momentum,

$$\frac{dp}{dv} = \frac{m_0}{\left(1 - \dfrac{v^2}{c^2}\right)^{3/2}}.$$

b. Use the integral formula for W in the preceding exercise, together with the result in part (a) to show that the work required to accelerate an object from a velocity of v_0 to v_1 is given by

$$W = \frac{m_0c^2}{\sqrt{1 - \dfrac{v_1^2}{c^2}}} - \frac{m_0c^2}{\sqrt{1 - \dfrac{v_0^2}{c^2}}}.$$

---

[56] Based on data from 1983 to 2003. Source: The American Physical Society/*New York Times*, May 3, 2003, p. A1.

[57] *Ibid.*

[58] Based on a logistic regression. Source for data: National Center for Educational Statistics (www.nces.ed.gov).

[59] Based on a logistic regression. Source for data: The Foundation Center, *Foundation Growth and Giving Estimates*, 2004, downloaded from the Center's Web site (www.fdncenter.org).

We call the quantity $\dfrac{m_0c^2}{\sqrt{1-\frac{v^2}{c^2}}}$ the **total relativistic energy** of an object moving at velocity v. Thus, the work to accelerate an object from one velocity to another is given by the change in its total relativistic energy.

c. Deduce (as Albert Einstein did) that the total relativistic energy E of a body at rest with rest mass m is given by the famous equation

$$E = mc^2.$$

COMMUNICATION AND REASONING EXERCISES

85. Explain how the indefinite integral and the definite integral are related.

86. What is "definite" about the definite integral?

87. The total change of a quantity from time a to time b can be obtained from its rate of change by doing what?

88. Complete the following: The total sales from time a to time b are obtained from the marginal sales by taking its _____ _____ from _____ to _____ .

89. What does the Fundamental Theorem of Calculus permit one to do?

90. If Felice and Philipe have different antiderivatives of f and each uses his or her own antiderivative to compute $\int_a^b f(x)\,dx$, they might get different answers, right?

91. ▼ Give an example of a nonzero velocity function that will produce a displacement of 0 from time $t = 0$ to time $t = 10$.

92. ▼ Give an example of a nonzero function whose definite integral over the interval [4, 6] is zero.

93. ▼ Give an example of a decreasing function $f(x)$ with the property that $\int_a^b f(x)\,dx$ is positive for every choice of a and $b > a$.

94. ▼ Explain why, in computing the total change of a quantity from its rate of change, it is useful to have the definite integral subtract area below the x-axis.

95. ◆ If $f(x)$ is a continuous function defined for $x \geq a$, define a new function $F(x)$ by the formula

$$F(x) = \int_a^x f(t)\,dt.$$

Use the Fundamental Theorem of Calculus to deduce that $F'(x) = f(x)$. What, if anything, is interesting about this result?

96. T ◆ Use the result of Exercise 95 and technology to compute a table of values for $x = 1, 2, 3$ for an antiderivative $A(x)$ of e^{-x^2} with the property that $A(0) = 0$. (Round answers to two decimal places.)

CHAPTER 6 REVIEW

KEY CONCEPTS

Website www.WanerMath.com
Go to the Website at www.WanerMath.com to find a comprehensive and interactive Web-based summary of Chapter 6.

6.1 The Indefinite Integral

An antiderivative of a function f is a function F such that $F' = f$. *p. 452*

Indefinite integral $\int f(x)\,dx$ *p. 452*

Power rule for the indefinite integral:

$$\int x^n\,dx = \frac{x^{n+1}}{n+1} + C \quad (\text{if } n \neq -1) \quad p.\ 454$$

$$\int x^{-1}\,dx = \ln|x| + C \quad p.\ 454$$

Indefinite integral of e^x and b^x:

$$\int e^x\,dx = e^x + C$$

$$\int b^x\,dx = \frac{b^x}{\ln b} + C \quad p.\ 455$$

Indefinite integral of $|x|$:

$$\int |x|\,dx = \frac{x|x|}{2} + C \quad p.\ 455$$

Sums, differences, and constant multiples:

$$\int [f(x) \pm g(x)]\,dx = \int f(x)\,dx \pm \int g(x)\,dx$$

$$\int kf(x)\,dx = k\int f(x)\,dx \quad (k \text{ constant}) \quad p.\ 455$$

Combining the rules *p. 457*

Position, velocity, and acceleration:

$$v = \frac{ds}{dt} \qquad s(t) = \int v(t)\,dt$$

$$a = \frac{dv}{dt} \qquad v(t) = \int a(t)\,dt$$

pp. 460–461

Motion in a straight line *p. 461*

Vertical motion under gravity *p. 463*

6.2 Substitution

Substitution rule:

$$\int f\,dx = \int \left(\frac{f}{du/dx}\right) du \quad p.\ 468$$

Using the substitution rule *p. 469*

Shortcuts: integrals of expressions involving $(ax + b)$:

$$\int (ax+b)^n\,dx = \frac{(ax+b)^{n+1}}{a(n+1)} + C \quad (\text{if } n \neq -1)$$

$$\int (ax+b)^{-1}\,dx = \frac{1}{a}\ln|ax+b| + C$$

$$\int e^{ax+b}\,dx = \frac{1}{a}e^{ax+b} + C$$

$$\int c^{ax+b}\,dx = \frac{1}{a\ln c}c^{ax+b} + C$$

$$\int |ax+b|\,dx = \frac{1}{2a}(ax+b)|ax+b| + C \quad p.\ 474$$

Mike's shortcut rule:

If $\int f(x)\,dx = F(x) + C$ and g and u are differentiable functions of x, then

$$\int g \cdot f(u)\,dx = \frac{g}{u'} \cdot F(u) + C$$

provided that $\frac{g}{u'}$ is constant. *p. 475*

6.3 The Definite Integral: Numerical and Graphical Viewpoints

Left Riemann sum:

$$\sum_{k=0}^{n-1} f(x_k)\Delta x = [f(x_0) + f(x_1) + \cdots + f(x_{n-1})]\Delta x \quad p.\ 484$$

Computing the Riemann sum from a formula *p. 486*

Computing the Riemann sum from a graph *p. 486*

Definite integral of f from a to b:

$$\int_a^b f(x)\,dx = \lim_{n\to\infty}\sum_{k=0}^{n-1} f(x_k)\Delta x. \quad p.\ 487$$

Estimating the definite integral from a graph *p. 489*

Estimating the definite integral using technology *p. 491*

Application to motion in a straight line *p. 491*

6.4 The Definite Integral: Algebraic Viewpoint and the Fundamental Theorem of Calculus

Computing total cost from marginal cost *p. 499*

The Fundamental Theorem of Calculus (FTC) *p. 500*

Using the FTC to compute definite integrals *p. 501*

Using the FTC with substitution *p. 502*

Computing area *p. 503*

REVIEW EXERCISES

Evaluate the indefinite integrals in Exercises 1–18.

1. $\int (x^2 - 10x + 2)\,dx$

2. $\int (e^x + \sqrt{x})\,dx$

3. $\int \left(\frac{4x^2}{5} - \frac{4}{5x^2}\right) dx$

4. $\int \left(\frac{3x}{5} - \frac{3}{5x}\right) dx$

5. $\int (2x)^{-1}\,dx$

6. $\int (-2x+2)^{-2}\,dx$

7. $\int e^{-2x+11}\,dx$

8. $\int \frac{dx}{(4x-3)^2}$

9. $\int x(x^2+1)^{1.3}\,dx$

10. $\int x(x^2+4)^{10}\,dx$

11. $\int \frac{4x}{(x^2-7)}\,dx$

12. $\int \frac{x}{(3x^2-1)^{0.4}}\,dx$

13. $\int (x^3-1)\sqrt{x^4-4x+1}\,dx$

14. $\int \frac{x^2+1}{(x^3+3x+2)^2}\,dx$ **15.** $\int (-xe^{x^2/2})dx$

16. $\int xe^{-x^2/2}\,dx$ **17.** $\int \frac{x+1}{x+2}\,dx$

18. $\int x\sqrt{x-1}\,dx$

In Exercises 19 and 20, use the given graph to estimate the left Riemann sum for the given interval with the stated number of subdivisions.

19. $[0, 3]$, $n = 6$ **20.** $[1, 3]$, $n = 4$

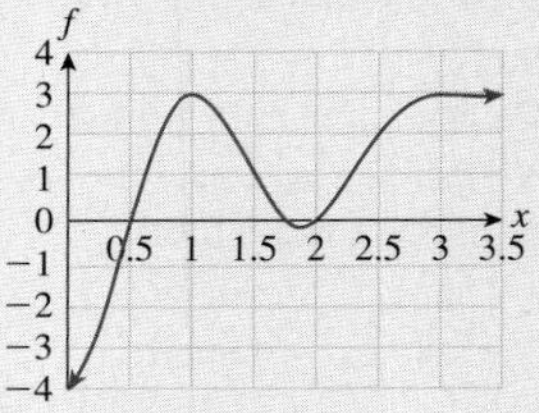

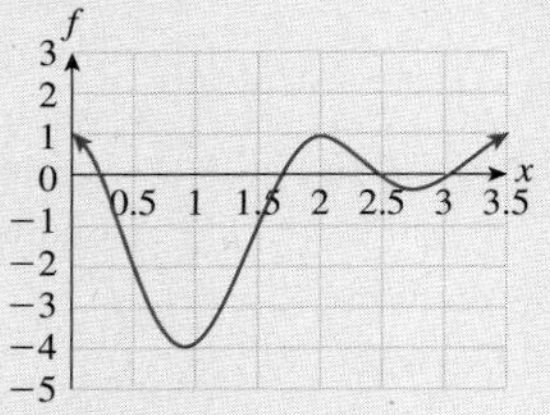

Calculate the left Riemann sums for the given functions over the given interval in Exercises 21–24, using the given values of n. (When rounding, round answers to four decimal places.)

21. $f(x) = x^2 + 1$ over $[-1, 1]$, $n = 4$

22. $f(x) = (x-1)(x-2) - 2$ over $[0, 4]$, $n = 4$

23. $f(x) = x(x^2 - 1)$ over $[0, 1]$, $n = 5$

24. $f(x) = \frac{x-1}{x-2}$ over $[0, 1.5]$, $n = 3$

T *In Exercises 25 and 26, use technology to approximate the given definite integrals using left Riemann sums with $n = 10$, 100, and 1,000. (Round answers to four decimal places.)*

25. $\int_0^1 e^{-x^2}\,dx$ **26.** $\int_1^3 x^{-x}\,dx$

In Exercises 27 and 28, the graph of the derivative $f'(x)$ of $f(x)$ is shown. Compute the total change of $f(x)$ over the given interval.

27. $[-1, 2]$ **28.** $[0, 2]$

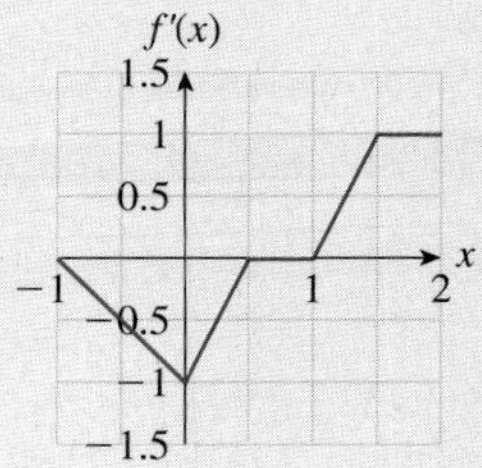

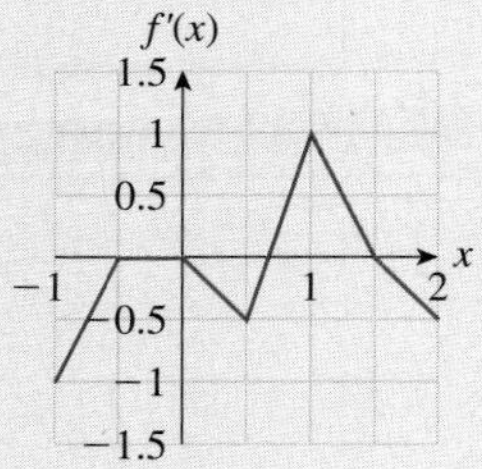

Evaluate the definite integrals in Exercises 29–38, using the Fundamental Theorem of Calculus.

29. $\int_{-1}^{1} (x - x^3 + |x|)\,dx$ **30.** $\int_0^9 (x + \sqrt{x})\,dx$

31. $\int_{-1}^{1} \frac{3}{(2x-5)^2}\,dx$ **32.** $\int_0^9 \frac{1}{x+1}\,dx$

33. $\int_0^{50} e^{-0.02x-1}\,dx$ **34.** $\int_{-20}^{0} 3e^{2.2x}\,dx$

35. $\int_0^2 x^2\sqrt{x^3+1}\,dx$ **36.** $\int_0^2 \frac{x^2}{\sqrt{x^3+1}}\,dx$

37. $\int_0^{\ln 2} \frac{e^{-2x}}{1+4e^{-2x}}\,dx$ **38.** $\int_0^{\ln 3} e^{2x}(1-3e^{2x})^2\,dx$

In Exercises 39–42, find the areas of the specified regions. (Do not count area below the x-axis as negative.)

39. The area bounded by $y = 4 - x^2$, the x-axis, and the lines $x = -2$ and $x = 2$

40. The area bounded by $y = 4 - x^2$, the x-axis, and the lines $x = 0$ and $x = 5$

41. The area bounded by $y = xe^{-x^2}$, the x-axis, and the lines $x = 0$ and $x = 5$

42. The area bounded by $y = |2x|$, the x-axis, and the lines $x = -1$ and $x = 1$

APPLICATIONS: OHaganBooks.com

43. ***Sales*** The rate of net sales (sales minus returns) of *The Secret Loves of John O*, a romance novel by Margó Dufón, can be approximated by

$$n(t) = 196 + t^2 - 0.16t^5 \text{ copies per week}$$

t weeks since its release.

a. Find the total net sales N as a function of time t.

b. How many books are still held by customers after 6 weeks? (Round your answer to the nearest book.)

44. ***Demand*** If OHaganBooks.com were to give away its latest bestseller, *A River Burns through It*, the demand q would be 100,000 books. The marginal demand (dq/dp) for the book is $-20p$ at a price of p dollars.

a. What is the demand function for this book?

b. At what price does demand drop to zero?

45. ***Motion under Gravity*** Billy-Sean O'Hagan's friend Juan (Billy-Sean is John O'Hagan's son, currently a senior in college) says he can throw a baseball vertically upward at 100 feet per second. Assuming Juan's claim is true,

a. Where would the baseball be at time t seconds?

b. How high would the ball go?

c. When would it return to Juan's hand?

46. ***Motion under Gravity*** An overworked employee at OHaganBooks.com goes to the top of the company's 100-foot-tall headquarters building and flings a book up into the air at a speed of 60 feet per second.

a. When will the book hit the ground 100 feet below? (Neglect air resistance.)

b. How fast will it be traveling when it hits the ground?

c. How high will the book go?

47. *Sales* Sales at the OHaganBooks.com Web site of *Larry Potter and the Riemann Sum* fluctuated rather wildly in the first 5 months of last year as the following graph shows:

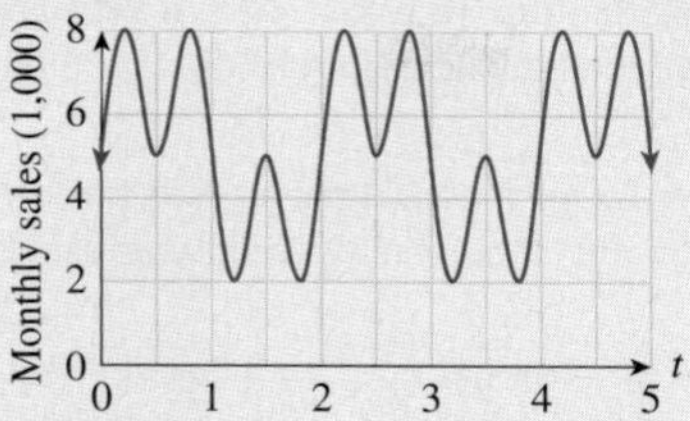

Puzzled by the graph, CEO John O'Hagan asks Jimmy Duffin[60] to estimate the total sales over the entire 5-month period shown. Jimmy decides to use a left Riemann sum with 10 partitions to estimate the total sales. What does he find?

48. *Sales* The following graph shows the approximate rate of change $s(t)$ of the total value, in thousands of dollars, of Spanish books sold online at OHaganBooks.com (t is the number of months since January 1):

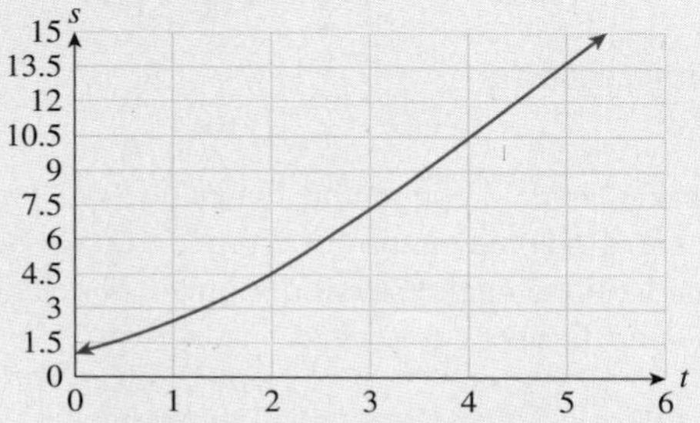

Use the graph to estimate the total value of Spanish books sold from March 1 through June 1. (Use a left Riemann sum with three subdivisions.)

49. *Promotions* Unlike sales of *Larry Potter and the Riemann Sum*, sales at OHaganBooks.com of the special leather-bound gift editions of *Calculus for Vampires* have been suffering lately, as shown in the following graph (negative sales indicate returns by dissatisfied customers; t is time in months since January 1 of this year):

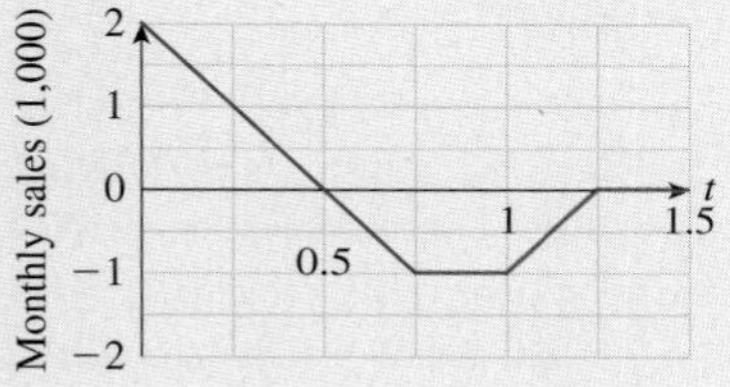

Use the graph to compute the total (net) sales over the period shown.

50. *Sales* Even worse than with the leather-bound *Calculus for Vampires*, sales of *Real Estate for Werewolves* have been dismal, as shown in the following graph (negative sales indicate returns by dissatisfied customers; t is time in months since January 1 of this year):

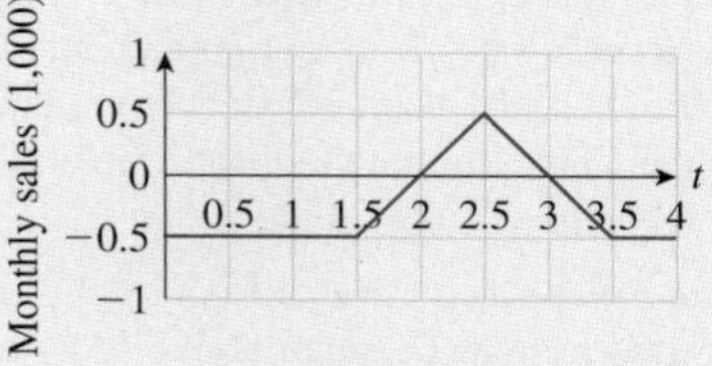

Use the graph to compute the total (net) sales over the period shown.

51. *Web Site Activity* The number of "hits" on the OHaganBooks.com Web site has been steadily increasing over the past month in response to recent publicity over a software glitch that caused the company to pay customers for buying books online. The activity can be modeled by

$$n(t) = 1{,}000t - 10t^2 + t^3 \text{ hits per day,}$$

where t is time in days since news about the software glitch was first publicized on GrungeReport.com. Use a left Riemann sum with five partitions to estimate the total number of hits during the first 10 days of the period.

52. *Web Site Crashes* The latest DoorsXL servers OHaganBooks.com has been using for its Web site have been crashing with increasing frequency lately. One of the student summer interns has estimated the number of crashes to be

$$q(t) = 0.05t^2 + 0.4t + 9 \text{ crashes per week} \quad (0 \le t \le 10),$$

where t is the number of weeks since the DoorsXL system was first installed. Use a Riemann sum with five partitions to estimate the total number of crashes from the start of week 5 to the start of week 10. (Round your answer to the nearest crash.)

53. *Student Intern Costs* The marginal monthly cost of maintaining a group of summer student interns at OHaganBooks .com is calculated to be

$$c(x) = \frac{1{,}000(x+3)^2}{(8 + (x+3)^3)^{3/2}} \text{ thousand dollars per additional student.}$$

Compute, to the nearest \$100, the total monthly cost if O'HaganBooks increases the size of the student intern program from five students to seven students.

54. *Legal Costs* The legal team maintained by OHaganBooks .com to handle the numerous lawsuits brought against the company by disgruntled clients may have to be expanded. The marginal monthly cost to maintain a team of x lawyers is estimated (by a method too complicated to explain) as

$$c(x) = (x-2)^2[8 - (x-2)^3]^{3/2} \text{ thousand dollars per additional lawyer.}$$

Compute, to the nearest \$1,000, the total monthly cost if O'HaganBooks goes ahead with a proposal to increase the size of the legal team from two to four.

[60]Marjory Duffin's nephew, currently at OHaganBooks.com on a summer internship.

55. ***Projected Sales*** When OHaganBooks.com was about to go online, it estimated that its weekly sales would begin at about 6,400 books per week, with sales increasing at such a rate that weekly sales would double about every 2 weeks. If these estimates had been correct, how many books would the company have sold in the first 5 weeks? (Round your answer to the nearest 1,000 books.)

56. ***Projected Sales*** Once OHaganBooks.com actually went online, its weekly sales began at about 7,500 books per week, with weekly sales doubling every 3 weeks. How many books did the company actually sell in the first 5 weeks? (Round your answer to the nearest 1,000 books.)

57. ***Actual Sales*** OHaganBooks.com modeled its revised weekly sales over a period of time after it went online with the function

$$s(t) = 6{,}053 + \frac{4{,}474e^{0.55t}}{e^{0.55t} + 14.01},$$

where t is the time in weeks after it went online. According to this model, how many books did it actually sell in the first 5 weeks?

58. ***Computer Usage*** A consultant recently hired by OHaganBooks.com estimates total weekly computer usage as

$$w(t) = 620 + \frac{900e^{0.25t}}{3 + e^{0.25t}} \text{ hours} \quad (0 \le t \le 20),$$

where t is time in weeks since January 1 of this year. Use the model to estimate the total computer usage during the first 14 weeks of the year.

Case Study Spending on Housing Construction

Bill Varie/Flirt/Corbis

It is March 2007, and *Time* magazine, in its latest edition, is asking "Will the Housing Bubble Burst in 2007?"[61] You are a summer intern at *Ronald Ramp Real Estate Development, Inc.*, which is considering a major luxury condominium development in Tampa, Florida nicknamed the "Ramp Towers Tampa."

Yesterday, you received the following memo from your supervisor:

> **DATE:** March 15, 2007
> **TO:** SW@EnormousStateU.edu
> **FROM:** SC@RonaldRampDev.com (Junior VP Development)
> **CC:** SGLombardoVP@RonaldRampDev.com (S. G. Lombardo, Senior VP Development)
> **SUBJECT:** Residential Construction Trends. Urgent!
>
> Help! There is a management meeting in two hours and Michelle Homestead, who, as you know, is spearheading the latest Ramp Towers Tampa feasibility study, must report to "the Ronald" by tomorrow and has asked me to immediately produce some mathematical formulas to (1) model the trend in residential construction spending since January 2006, when it was \$618.7 billion, and (2) estimate the average spent per month on residential construction over a specified period of time. All I have on hand so far is data giving the month-over-month percentage changes (attached). Do you have any ideas?

[61] *Time,* February, 2007 (www.time.com/time/business/article/0,8599,1592751,00.html).

ATTACHMENT*

Month	% Change	Month	% Change
1	1.16	16	−1.59
2	1.17	17	−1.62
3	1.33	18	−1.58
4	0.67	19	−1.67
5	0.42	20	−1.77
6	−0.04	21	−1.92
7	−0.24	22	−2.06
8	−0.44	23	−2.19
9	−0.70	24	−2.45
10	−0.94	25	−2.50
11	−1.31	26	−2.65
12	−1.34	27	−2.85
13	−1.49	28	−2.65
14	−1.75	29	−2.66
15	−1.74	30	−2.66

*Based on 12-month moving average; Source for data: U.S. Census Bureau: Manufacturing, Mining and Construction Statistics, Data 360 (www.data360.org/dataset.aspx?Data_Set_Id=3627).

Getting to work, you decide that the first thing to do is fit these data to a mathematical curve that you can use to project future changes in construction spending. You graph the data to get a sense of what mathematical models might be appropriate (Figure 24).

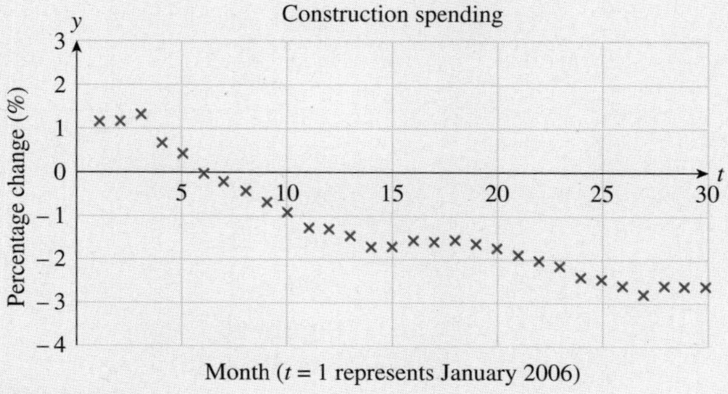

Figure 24

The graph suggests a decreasing trend, possibly concave up. You recall that there are a variety of curves that can behave this way, one of the simplest being

$$y = at^c + b \quad (t > 0),$$

where a, b, and c are constants.

You convert all the percentages to decimals, giving the following table of data:

t	y	t	y
1	0.0116	16	−0.0159
2	0.0117	17	−0.0162
3	0.0133	18	−0.0158
4	0.0067	19	−0.0167
5	0.0042	20	−0.0177
6	−0.0004	21	−0.0192
7	−0.0024	22	−0.0206
8	−0.0044	23	−0.0219
9	−0.0070	24	−0.0245
10	−0.0094	25	−0.0250
11	−0.0131	26	−0.0265
12	−0.0134	27	−0.0285
13	−0.0149	28	−0.0265
14	−0.0175	29	−0.0266
15	−0.0174	30	−0.0266

* To do this, you can use Excel's Solver or the Website function evaluator and grapher with model `$1*x^$2+$3`.

You then find the values of a, b, and c that best fit the given data:*

$$a = -0.0200974, b = 0.0365316, c = 0.345051.$$

These values give you the following model for construction spending (with figures rounded to five significant digits):

$$y = -0.020097t^{0.34505} + 0.036532.$$

Figure 25 shows the graph of y superimposed on the data.

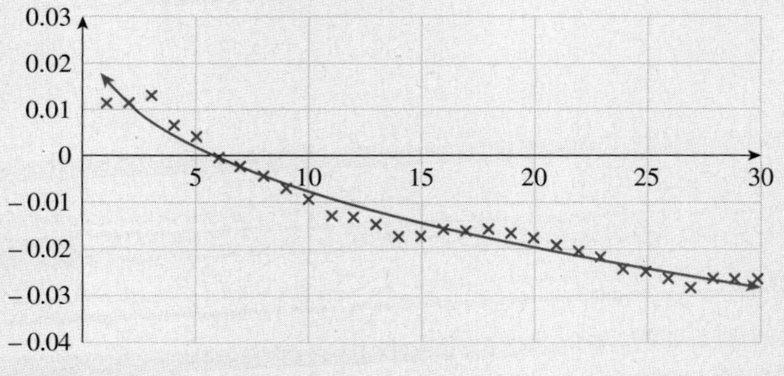

Figure 25

Now that you have a model for the month-over-month change in construction spending, you must use it to find the actual spending on construction. First, you realize that the model gives the *fractional rate of increase* of construction spending (because it is specified as a percentage, or fraction, of the total spending). In other words, if $p(t)$ represents the construction cost in month t, then

$$y = \frac{dp/dt}{p} = \frac{d}{dt}(\ln p). \qquad \text{By the chain rule for derivatives}$$

You find an equation for actual monthly construction cost at time t by solving for p:

$$\begin{aligned}\ln p &= \int y\,dt \\ &= \int (at^c + b)\,dt \\ &= \frac{at^{c+1}}{c+1} + bt + K \\ &= dt^{c+1} + bt + K,\end{aligned}$$

where

$$d = \frac{a}{c+1} = \frac{-0.020097}{0.34505 + 1} \approx -0.014941,$$

b and c are as above, and K is the constant of integration. So

$$p(t) = e^{dt^{c+1}+bt+K}.$$

To compute K, you substitute the initial data from the memo: $p(1) = 618.7$. Thus,

$$618.7 = e^{d+b+K} = e^{-0.014941+0.036532+K} = e^{0.021591+K}.$$

Thus,

$$\ln(618.7) = 0.021591 + K,$$

which gives

$$K = \ln(618.7) - 0.021591 \approx 6.4060 \text{ (to five significant digits).}$$

Now you can write down the following formula for the monthly spending on residential construction as a function of t, the number of months since the beginning of 2006:

$$p(t) = e^{dt^{c+1}+bt+K} = e^{-0.014941t^{0.34505+1}+0.036532t+6.4060}.$$

What remains is the calculation of the average spent per month over a specified period $[r, s]$. Since p is the rate of change of the total spent, the total spent on housing construction over this period is

$$P = \int_r^s p(t)\,dt$$

and so the average spent per month is

$$\bar{P} = \frac{1}{s-r}\int_r^s p(t)\,dt. \qquad \frac{1}{\text{Number of months}} \times \text{Total spent}$$

Substituting the formula for $p(t)$ gives

$$\bar{P} = \frac{1}{s-r}\int_r^s e^{-0.014941t^{0.34505+1}+0.036532t+6.4060}\,dt.$$

You cannot find an explicit antiderivative for the integrand, so you decide that the only way to compute it is numerically. You send the following memo to SC.

DATE: March 15, 2007
TO: SC@RonaldRampDev.com (Junior VP Development)
FROM: SW@EnormousStateU.edu
CC: SGLombardoVP@RonaldRampDev.com (S. G. Lombardo, Senior VP Development)
SUBJECT: The formula you wanted

Spending in the U.S. on housing construction in the tth month of 2006 can be modeled by

$$p(t) = e^{-0.014941t^{0.34505+1}+0.036532t+6.4060} \text{ million dollars.}$$

Further, the average spent per month from month r to month s (since the start of January 2006) can be computed as

$$\bar{P} = \frac{1}{s-r}\int_r^s e^{-0.014941t^{0.34505+1}+0.036532t+6.4060}\,dt$$

To calculate it easily (and impress the subcommittee members), I suggest you have a graphing calculator on hand and enter the following on your graphing calculator (watch the parentheses!):

```
Y1=1/(S-R)*fnInt(e^(-0.014941T^(0.34505+1)+0.036532T+6.4060),T,R,S)
```

Then suppose, for example, you need to estimate the average for the period March 1, 2006 ($t = 3$) to February 1, 2007 ($t = 14$). All you do is enter

```
3→R
14→S
Y1
```

and your calculator will give you the result: The average spending was $628 million per month.

Good luck with the meeting!

EXERCISES

1. Use the actual January 2006 spending figure of $618.7 million and the percentage changes in the table to compute the actual spending in February, March, and April of that year. Also use the model of monthly spending to estimate those figures, and compare the predicted values with the actual figures. Is it unacceptable that the April figures agree to only one significant digit? Explain.
2. Use the model developed above to estimate the average monthly spending on residential construction over the 12-month period beginning June 1, 2006. (Round your answer to the nearest $1 million.)
3. What (if any) advantages are there to using a model for residential construction spending when the actual residential construction spending figures are available?
4. The formulas for $p(t)$ and $\bar{P}$ were based on the January 2006 spending figure of $618.7 million. Change the models to allow for a possibly revised January 2006 spending figure of $\$p_0$ million.
5. If we had used quadratic regression to model the construction spending data, we would have obtained

$$y = 0.00005t^2 - 0.0028t + 0.0158.$$

(See the graph.)

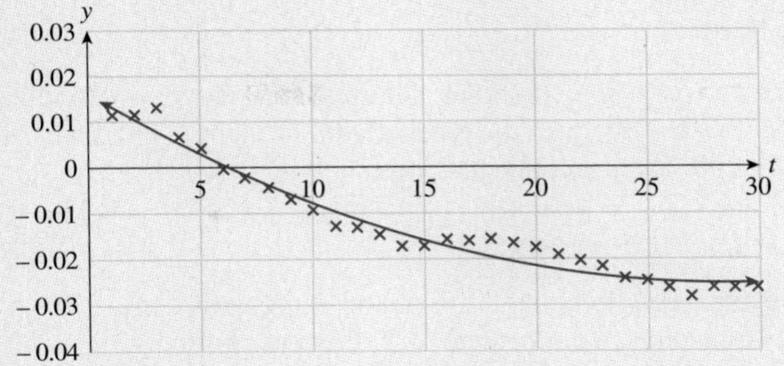

Use this formula and the given January 2006 spending figure to obtain corresponding models for $p(t)$ and $\bar{P}$.

6. Compare the model in the text with the quadratic model in Exercise 5 in terms of both short- and long-term predictions; in particular, when does the quadratic model predict construction spending will have reached its biggest monthly decrease? Are either of these models realistic in the near term? in the long term?

TI-83/84 Plus Technology Guide

Section 6.3

Example 5 (page 491) Estimate the area under the graph of $f(x) = 1 - x^2$ over the interval [0, 1] using $n = 100$, $n = 200$, and $n = 500$ partitions.

Solution with Technology

There are several ways to compute Riemann sums with a graphing calculator. We illustrate one method. For $n = 100$, we need to compute the sum

$$\sum_{k=0}^{99} f(x_k)\Delta x = [f(0) + f(0.01) + \cdots + f(0.99)](0.01).$$

See discussion in Example 5.

Thus, we first need to calculate the numbers $f(0)$, $f(0.01)$, and so on, and add them up. The TI-83/84 Plus has a built-in `sum` function (available in the LIST MATH menu), which, like the SUM function in a spreadsheet, sums the entries in a list.

1. To generate a list that contains the numbers we want to add together, use the `seq` function (available in the LIST OPS menu). If we enter

   `seq(1-X^2,X,0,0.99,0.01)`

   seq: [2ND] [LIST] OPS [5]

   the calculator will calculate a list by evaluating `1-X^2` for values of `X` from 0 to 0.99 in steps of 0.01.
2. To take the sum of all these numbers, we wrap the `seq` function in a call to `sum`:

   `sum(seq(1-X^2,X,0,0.99,0.01))`

   sum: [2ND] [LIST] MATH [5]

   This gives the sum

   $$f(0) + f(0.01) + \cdots + f(0.99) = 67.165.$$
3. To obtain the Riemann sum, we need to multiply this sum by $\Delta x = 0.01$, and we obtain the estimate of $67.165 \times 0.01 = 0.67165$ for the Riemann sum:

We obtain the other Riemann sums similarly, as shown here:

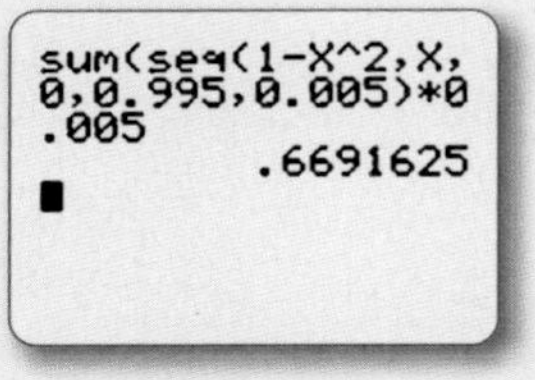

$n = 200$

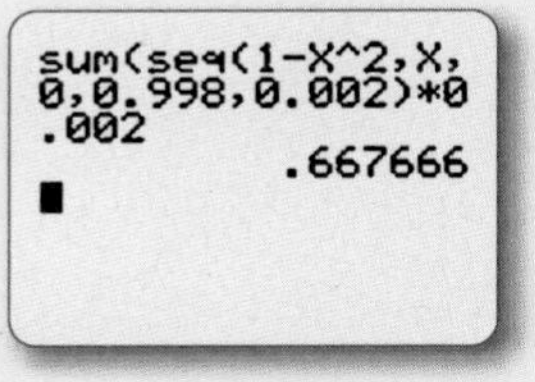

$n = 500$

One disadvantage of this method is that the TI-83/84 Plus can generate and sum a list of at most 999 entries. The LEFTSUM program below calculates left Riemann sums for any n. The TI-83/84 Plus also has a built-in function `fnInt`, which finds a very accurate approximation of a definite integral, using a more sophisticated technique than the one we are discussing here.

The LEFTSUM program for the TI-83/84 Plus

The following program calculates (left) Riemann sums for any n. The latest version of this program (and others) is available at the Website.

```
PROGRAM: LEFTSUM
:Input "LEFT ENDPOINT? ",A          Prompts for the left endpoint a
:Input "RIGHT ENDPOINT? ",B         Prompts for the right endpoint b
:Input "N? ",N                      Prompts for the number of rectangles
:(B-A)/N→D                          D is Δx = (b − a)/n.
:Ø→L                                L will eventually be the left sum.
:A→X                                X is the current x-coordinate.
:For(I,1,N)                         Start of a loop—recall the sigma notation.
:L+Y1→L                             Add f(x_{i−1}) to L.
:A+I*D→X                            Uses formula x_i = a + iΔx
:End                                End of loop
:L*D→L                              Multiply by Δx.
:Disp "LEFT SUM IS ",L
:Stop
```

SPREADSHEET Technology Guide

Section 6.3

Example 5 (page 491) Estimate the area under the graph of $f(x) = 1 - x^2$ over the interval [0, 1] using $n = 100$, $n = 200$, and $n = 500$ partitions.

Solution with Technology

We need to compute various sums.

$$\sum_{k=0}^{99} f(x_k)\Delta x = [f(0) + f(0.01) + \cdots + f(0.99)](0.01)$$

See discussion in Example 5.

$$\sum_{k=0}^{199} f(x_k)\Delta x = [f(0) + f(0.005) + \cdots + f(0.995)](0.005)$$

$$\sum_{k=0}^{499} f(x_k)\Delta x = [f(0) + f(0.002) + \cdots + f(0.998)](0.002).$$

Here is how you can compute them all on the same spreadsheet.

1. Enter the values for the endpoints a and b, the number of subdivisions n, and the formula $\Delta x = (b - a)/n$:

	A	B	C	D
1	x	f(x)	a	0
2			b	1
3			n	100
4			Delta x	=(D2-D1)/D3

2. Next, we compute all the x-values we might need in column A. Because the largest value of n that we will be using is 500, we will need a total of 501 values of x. Note that the value in each cell below A3 is obtained from the one above by adding Δx.

	A	B	C	D
1	x	f(x)	a	0
2	=D1		b	1
3	=A2+$D$4		n	100
4			Delta x	0.01
501				
502				

	A	B	C	D
1	x	f(x)	a	0
2	0		b	1
3	0.01		n	100
4	0.02		Delta x	0.01
501	4.99			
502	5			

(The fact that the values of x currently go too far will be corrected in the next step.)

3. We need to calculate the numbers $f(0)$, $f(0.01)$, and so on, but only those for which the corresponding x-value is less than b. To do this, we use a logical formula like we did with piecewise-defined functions in Chapter 1:

	A	B	C	D
1	x	f(x)	a	0
2	0	=(1-A2^2)*(A2<$D$2)	b	1
3	0.01		n	100
4	0.02		Delta x	0.01
501	4.99			
502	5			

When the value of x is b or above, the function will evaluate to zero, because we do not want to count it.

4. Finally, we compute the Riemann sum by adding up everything in column B and multiplying by Δx:

	A	B	C	D
1	x	f(x)	a	0
2	0	1	b	1
3	0.01	0.9999	n	100
4	0.02	0.9996	Delta x	0.01
5	0.03	0.9991	Left Sum	=SUM(B:B)*D4
6	0.04	0.9984		

↓

	A	B	C	D
1	x	f(x)	a	0
2	0	1	b	1
3	0.01	0.9999	n	100
4	0.02	0.9996	Delta x	0.01
5	0.03	0.9991	Left Sum	0.67165
6	0.04	0.9984		

Now it is easy to obtain the sums for $n = 200$ and $n = 500$: Simply change the value of n in cell D3:

	A	B	C	D
1	x	f(x)	a	0
2	0	1	b	1
3	0.005	0.999975	n	200
4	0.01	0.9999	Delta x	0.005
5	0.015	0.999775	Left Sum	0.6691625
6	0.02	0.9996		

	A	B	C	D
1	x	f(x)	a	0
2	0	1	b	1
3	0.002	0.999996	n	500
4	0.004	0.999984	Delta x	0.002
5	0.006	0.999964	Left Sum	0.667666
6	0.008	0.999936		

7

Further Integration Techniques and Applications of the Integral

Website

www.WanerMath.com

At the Website you will find:

- A detailed chapter summary
- A true/false quiz
- Additional review exercises
- A numerical integration utility
- Graphing calculator programs for numerical integration
- Graphers, Excel tutorials, and other resources

Case Study Estimating Tax Revenues

You have just been hired by the incoming administration to coordinate national tax policy, and the so-called experts on your staff can't seem to agree on which of two tax proposals will result in more revenue for the government. The data you have are the two income tax proposals (graphs of tax vs. income) and the distribution of incomes in the country. **How do you use this information to decide which tax policy will result in more revenue?**

Dmitriy Shironosov/Shutterstock.com

Introduction

In the preceding chapter, we learned how to compute many integrals and saw some of the applications of the integral. In this chapter, we look at some further techniques for computing integrals and then at more applications of the integral. We also see how to extend the definition of the definite integral to include integrals over infinite intervals, and show how such integrals can be used for long-term forecasting. Finally, we introduce the beautiful theory of differential equations and some of its numerous applications.

7.1 Integration by Parts

Integration by parts is an integration technique that comes from the product rule for derivatives. The tabular method we present here has been around for some time and makes integration by parts quite simple, particularly in problems where it has to be used several times.*

* The version of the tabular method we use was developed and taught to us by Dan Rosen at Hofstra University.

We start with a little notation to simplify things while we introduce integration by parts. (We use this notation only in the next few pages.) If u is a function, denote its derivative by $D(u)$ and an antiderivative by $I(u)$. Thus, for example, if $u = 2x^2$, then

$$D(u) = 4x$$

and

$$I(u) = \frac{2x^3}{3}.$$

[If we wished, we could instead take $I(u) = \frac{2x^3}{3} + 46$, but we usually opt to take the simplest antiderivative.]

Integration by Parts

If u and v are continuous functions of x, and u has a continuous derivative, then

$$\int u \cdot v\,dx = u \cdot I(v) - \int D(u)I(v)\,dx.$$

Quick Example

(Discussed more fully in Example 1 below)

$$\int x \cdot e^x dx = xI(e^x) - \int D(x)I(e^x)\,dx$$

$$= xe^x - \int 1 \cdot e^x\,dx \qquad I(e^x) = e^x;\ D(x) = 1$$

$$= xe^x - e^x + C. \qquad \int e^x\,dx = e^x + C$$

As the Quick Example shows, although we could not immediately integrate $u \cdot v = x \cdot e^x$, we could easily integrate $D(u)I(v) = 1 \cdot e^x = e^x$.

Derivation of Integration-by-Parts Formula

As we mentioned, the integration-by-parts formula comes from the product rule for derivatives. We apply the product rule to the function $uI(v)$

$$\begin{aligned} D[u \cdot I(v)] &= D(u)I(v) + uD(I(v)) \\ &= D(u)I(v) + uv \end{aligned}$$

because $D(I(v))$ is the derivative of an antiderivative of v, which is v. Integrating both sides gives

$$u \cdot I(v) = \int D(u)I(v)\,dx + \int uv\,dx.$$

A simple rearrangement of the terms now gives us the integration-by-parts formula.

The integration-by-parts formula is easiest to use via the tabular method illustrated in the following example, where we repeat the calculation we did in the Quick Example above.

EXAMPLE 1 Integration by Parts: Tabular Method

Calculate $\int xe^x\,dx$.

Solution First, the reason we *need* to use integration by parts to evaluate this integral is that none of the other techniques of integration that we've talked about up to now will help us. Furthermore, we cannot simply find antiderivatives of x and e^x and multiply them together. [You should check that $(x^2/2)e^x$ is *not* an antiderivative of xe^x.] However, as we saw above, this integral can be found by integration by parts. We want to find the integral of the *product* of x and e^x. We must make a decision: Which function will play the role of u and which will play the role of v in the integration-by-parts formula? Because the derivative of x is just 1, differentiating makes it simpler, so we try letting x be u and letting e^x be v. We need to calculate $D(u)$ and $I(v)$, which we record in the following table.

	D	***I***
$+$	x ↘	e^x
$-\int$	$1 \longrightarrow$	e^x

The table is read as $+x \cdot e^x - \int 1 \cdot e^x\,dx$.

Below x in the D column, we put $D(x) = 1$; below e^x in the I column, we put $I(e^x) = e^x$. The arrow at an angle connecting x and $I(e^x)$ reminds us that the product $xI(e^x)$ will appear in the answer; the plus sign on the left of the table reminds us that it is $+xI(e^x)$ that appears. The integral sign and the horizontal arrow connecting $D(x)$ and $I(e^x)$ remind us that the *integral* of the product $D(x)I(e^x)$ also appears in the answer; the minus sign on the left reminds us that we need to subtract this integral. Combining these two contributions, we get

$$\int xe^x\,dx = xe^x - \int e^x\,dx.$$

The integral that appears on the right is much easier than the one we began with, so we can complete the problem:

$$\int xe^x\,dx = xe^x - \int e^x\,dx = xe^x - e^x + C.$$

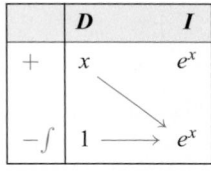

➡ **Before we go on...** In Example 1, what if we had made the opposite decision and put e^x in the D column and x in the I column? Then we would have had the following table:

	D	I
$+$	e^x	x
$-\int$	e^x	$x^2/2$

This gives

$$\int xe^x\,dx = \frac{x^2}{2}e^x - \int \frac{x^2}{2}e^x\,dx.$$

The integral on the right is harder than the one we started with, not easier! How do we know beforehand which way to go? We don't. We have to be willing to do a little trial and error: We try it one way, and if it doesn't make things simpler, we try it another way. *Remember, though, that the function we put in the I column must be one that we can integrate.* ■

EXAMPLE 2 Repeated Integration by Parts

Calculate $\int x^2e^{-x}\,dx$.

Solution Again, we have a product—the integrand is the product of x^2 and e^{-x}. Because differentiating x^2 makes it simpler, we put it in the D column and get the following table:

	D	I
$+$	x^2	e^{-x}
$-\int$	$2x$	$-e^{-x}$

This table gives us

$$\int x^2e^{-x}\,dx = x^2(-e^{-x}) - \int 2x(-e^{-x})\,dx.$$

The last integral is simpler than the one we started with, but it still involves a product. It's a good candidate for another integration by parts. The table we would use would start with $2x$ in the D column and $-e^{-x}$ in the I column, which is exactly what we see in the last row of the table we've already made. Therefore, we *continue the process*, elongating the table above:

	D	I
$+$	x^2	e^{-x}
$-$	$2x$	$-e^{-x}$
$+\int$	2	e^{-x}

(Notice how the signs on the left alternate. Here's why: To compute $-\int 2x(-e^{-x})\,dx$ we use the negative of the following table:

	D	I
$+$	$2x$	$-e^{-x}$
$-\int$	2	e^{-x}

so we reverse all the signs.)

Now, we still have to compute an integral (the integral of the product of the functions in the bottom row) to complete the computation. But why stop here? Let's continue the process one more step:

	D	I
$+$	x^2	e^{-x}
$-$	$2x$	$-e^{-x}$
$+$	2	e^{-x}
$-\int$	0	$-e^{-x}$

In the bottom line we see that all that is left to integrate is $0(-e^{-x}) = 0$. Because the indefinite integral of 0 is C, we can read the answer from the table as

$$\begin{aligned}\int x^2e^{-x}\,dx &= x^2(-e^{-x}) - 2x(e^{-x}) + 2(-e^{-x}) + C\\ &= -x^2e^{-x} - 2xe^{-x} - 2e^{-x} + C\\ &= -e^{-x}(x^2 + 2x + 2) + C.\end{aligned}$$

In Example 2 we saw a technique that we can summarize as follows:

Integrating a Polynomial Times a Function

If one of the factors in the integrand is a polynomial and the other factor is a function that can be integrated repeatedly, put the polynomial in the D column and keep differentiating until you get zero. Then complete the I column to the same depth, and read off the answer.

For practice, redo Example 1 using this technique.

It is not always the case that the integrand is a polynomial times something easy to integrate, so we can't always expect to end up with a zero in the D column. In that case we hope that at some point we will be able to integrate the product of the functions in the last row. Here are some examples.

EXAMPLE 3 Polynomial Times a Logarithm

Calculate: **a.** $\int x \ln x \, dx$ **b.** $\int (x^2 - x) \ln x \, dx$ **c.** $\int \ln x \, dx$

Solution

a. This is a product and therefore a good candidate for integration by parts. Our first impulse is to differentiate x, but that would mean integrating $\ln x$, and we do not (yet) know how to do that. So we try it the other way around and hope for the best.

	D	*I*
$+$	$\ln x$	x
$-\int$	$\frac{1}{x}$	$\frac{x^2}{2}$

Why did we stop? If we continued the table, both columns would get more complicated. However, if we stop here we get

$$\begin{aligned}\int x \ln x \, dx &= (\ln x)\left(\frac{x^2}{2}\right) - \int \left(\frac{1}{x}\right)\left(\frac{x^2}{2}\right) dx \\ &= \frac{x^2}{2} \ln x - \frac{1}{2} \int x \, dx \\ &= \frac{x^2}{2} \ln x - \frac{x^2}{4} + C.\end{aligned}$$

b. We can use the same technique we used in part (a) to integrate any polynomial times the logarithm of x:

	D	*I*
$+$	$\ln x$	$x^2 - x$
$-\int$	$\frac{1}{x}$	$\frac{x^3}{3} - \frac{x^2}{2}$

$$\begin{aligned}\int (x^2 - x) \ln x \, dx &= (\ln x)\left(\frac{x^3}{3} - \frac{x^2}{2}\right) - \int \left(\frac{1}{x}\right)\left(\frac{x^3}{3} - \frac{x^2}{2}\right) dx \\ &= \left(\frac{x^3}{3} - \frac{x^2}{2}\right) \ln x - \int \left(\frac{x^2}{3} - \frac{x}{2}\right) dx \\ &= \left(\frac{x^3}{3} - \frac{x^2}{2}\right) \ln x - \frac{x^3}{9} + \frac{x^2}{4} + C.\end{aligned}$$

c. The integrand $\ln x$ is not a product. We can, however, *make* it into a product by thinking of it as $1 \cdot \ln x$. Because this is a polynomial times $\ln x$, we proceed as in parts (a) and (b):

	D	*I*
$+$	$\ln x$	1
$-\int$	$1/x$	x

We notice that the product of $1/x$ and x is just 1, which we know how to integrate, so we can stop here:

$$\begin{aligned}\int \ln x\,dx &= x\ln x - \int\left(\frac{1}{x}\right)x\,dx\\ &= x\ln x - \int 1\,dx\\ &= x\ln x - x + C.\end{aligned}$$

FAQs

Whether to Use Integration by Parts, and What Goes in the *D* and *I* Columns

Q: *Will integration by parts always work to integrate a product?*

A: No. Although integration by parts often works for products in which one factor is a polynomial, it will almost *never* work in the examples of products we saw when discussing substitution in Section 6.2. For example, although integration by parts can be used to compute $\int(x^2 - x)e^{2x-1}\,dx$ (put $x^2 - x$ in the *D* column and e^{2x-1} in the *I* column), it *cannot* be used to compute $\int(2x - 1)e^{x^2-x}\,dx$ (put $u = x^2 - x$). Recognizing when to use integration by parts is best learned by experience.

Q: *When using integration by parts, which expression goes in the D column, and which in the I column?*

A: Although there is no general rule, the following guidelines are useful:

- To integrate a product in which one factor is a polynomial and the other can be integrated several times, put the polynomial in the *D* column and the other factor in the *I* column. Then differentiate the polynomial until you get zero.
- If one of the factors is a polynomial but the other factor cannot be integrated easily, put the polynomial in the *I* column and the other factor in the *D* column. Stop when the product of the functions in the bottom row can be integrated.
- If neither factor is a polynomial, put the factor that seems easier to integrate in the *I* column and the other factor in the *D* column. Again, stop the table as soon as the product of the functions in the bottom row can be integrated.
- If your method doesn't work, try switching the functions in the *D* and *I* columns or try breaking the integrand into a product in a different way. If none of this works, maybe integration by parts isn't the technique to use on this problem.

7.1 EXERCISES

▼ more advanced ◆ challenging

T indicates exercises that should be solved using technology

Evaluate the integrals in Exercises 1–40 using integration by parts where possible. HINT [See the Examples in the text.]

1. $\int 2xe^x\,dx$

2. $\int 3xe^{-x}\,dx$

3. $\int (3x - 1)e^{-x}\,dx$

4. $\int (1 - x)e^x\,dx$

5. $\int (x^2 - 1)e^{2x}\,dx$

6. $\int (x^2 + 1)e^{-2x}\,dx$

7. $\int (x^2 + 1)e^{-2x+4}\,dx$

8. $\int (x^2 + 1)e^{3x+1}\,dx$

9. $\int (2-x)2^x\,dx$ **10.** $\int (3x-2)4^x\,dx$

11. $\int (x^2-1)3^{-x}\,dx$ **12.** $\int (1-x^2)2^{-x}\,dx$

13. ▼ $\int \frac{x^2-x}{e^x}\,dx$ **14.** ▼ $\int \frac{2x+1}{e^{3x}}\,dx$

15. $\int x(x+2)^6\,dx$ (See note.[1]) **16.** $\int x^2(x-1)^6\,dx$ (See note.[1])

17. ▼ $\int \frac{x}{(x-2)^3}\,dx$ **18.** ▼ $\int \frac{x}{(x-1)^2}\,dx$

19. $\int x^3 \ln x\,dx$ **20.** $\int x^2 \ln x\,dx$

21. $\int (t^2+1)\ln(2t)\,dt$ **22.** $\int (t^2-t)\ln(-t)\,dt$

23. $\int t^{1/3}\ln t\,dt$ **24.** $\int t^{-1/2}\ln t\,dt$

25. $\int \log_3 x\,dx$ **26.** $\int x\log_2 x\,dx$

27. ▼ $\int (xe^{2x}-4e^{3x})\,dx$ **28.** ▼ $\int (x^2e^{-x}+2e^{-x+1})\,dx$

29. ▼ $\int \left(x^2e^x - xe^{x^2}\right)dx$

30. ▼ $\int \left[(2x+1)\,e^{x^2+x} - x^2e^{2x+1}\right]dx$

31. ▼ $\int (3x-4)\sqrt{2x-1}\,dx$ (See note.[1])

32. ▼ $\int \frac{2x+1}{\sqrt{3x-2}}\,dx$ (See note.[1])

33. $\int_0^1 (x+1)e^x\,dx$ **34.** $\int_{-1}^1 (x^2+x)e^{-x}\,dx$

35. $\int_0^1 x^2(x+1)^{10}\,dx$ **36.** $\int_0^1 x^3(x+1)^{10}\,dx$

37. $\int_1^2 x\ln(2x)\,dx$ **38.** $\int_1^2 x^2\ln(3x)\,dx$

39. $\int_0^1 x\ln(x+1)\,dx$ **40.** $\int_0^1 x^2\ln(x+1)\,dx$

41. Find the area bounded by the curve $y = xe^{-x}$, the x-axis, and the lines $x = 0$ and $x = 10$.

42. Find the area bounded by the curve $y = x\ln x$, the x-axis, and the lines $x = 1$ and $x = e$.

43. Find the area bounded by the curve $y = (x+1)\ln x$, the x-axis, and the lines $x = 1$ and $x = 2$.

44. Find the area bounded by the curve $y = (x-1)e^x$, the x-axis, and the lines $x = 0$ and $x = 2$.

[1] Several exercises, including these, can also be done using substitution, although integration by parts is easier and should be used instead.

Integrals of Functions Involving Absolute Values *In Exercises 45–52, use integration by parts to evaluate the given integral using the following integral formulas where necessary. (You have seen some of these before; all can be checked by differentiating.)*

Integral Formula	Shortcut Version
$\int \frac{\|x\|}{x}\,dx = \|x\| + C$	$\int \frac{\|ax+b\|}{ax+b}\,dx = \frac{1}{a}\|ax+b\| + C$ Because $\frac{d}{dx}\|x\| = \frac{\|x\|}{x}$.
$\int \|x\|\,dx = \frac{1}{2}x\|x\| + C$	$\int \|ax+b\|\,dx$ $= \frac{1}{2a}(ax+b)\|ax+b\| + C$
$\int x\|x\|\,dx = \frac{1}{3}x^2\|x\| + C$	$\int (ax+b)\|ax+b\|\,dx$ $= \frac{1}{3a}(ax+b)^2\|ax+b\| + C$
$\int x^2\|x\|\,dx = \frac{1}{4}x^3\|x\| + C$	$\int (ax+b)^2\|ax+b\|\,dx$ $= \frac{1}{4a}(ax+b)^3\|ax+b\| + C$

45. $\int x|x-3|\,dx$ **46.** $\int x|x+4|\,dx$

47. $\int 2x\frac{|x-3|}{x-3}\,dx$ **48.** $\int 3x\frac{|x+4|}{x+4}\,dx$

49. ▼ $\int 2x^2|-x+4|\,dx$ **50.** ▼ $\int 3x^2|2x-3|\,dx$

51. ▼ $\int (x^2-2x+3)|x-4|\,dx$

52. ▼ $\int (x^2-x+1)|2x-4|\,dx$

APPLICATIONS

53. ***Displacement*** A rocket rising from the ground has a velocity of $2{,}000te^{-t/120}$ ft/sec, after t seconds. How far does it rise in the first two minutes?

54. ***Sales*** Weekly sales of graphing calculators can be modeled by the equation

$$s(t) = 10 - te^{-t/20},$$

where s is the number of calculators sold per week after t weeks. How many graphing calculators (to the nearest unit) will be sold in the first 20 weeks?

55. ***Total Cost*** The marginal cost of the xth box of light bulbs is $10 + [\ln(x+1)]/(x+1)^2$, and the fixed cost is \$5,000. Find the total cost to make x boxes of bulbs.

56. ***Total Revenue*** The marginal revenue for selling the xth box of light bulbs is $10 + 0.001x^2e^{-x/100}$. Find the total revenue generated by selling 200 boxes of bulbs.

57. ***Spending on Gasoline*** During 2000–2008, the United States consumed gasoline at a rate of about

$$q(t) = -3.5t + 280 \text{ billion gallons per year.} \quad (0 \le t \le 8)$$

(t is the number of years since 2000.)[2] During the same period, the price of gasoline was approximately

$$p(t) = 1.2e^{0.12t} \text{ dollars per gallon.}$$

Use an integral to estimate, to the nearest billion dollars, the total spent on gasoline during the given period. HINT [Rate of spending $= p(t)q(t)$.]

58. ***Spending on Gasoline*** During 1992–2000, the United States consumed gasoline at a rate of about

$$q(t) = 3.2t + 240 \text{ billion gallons per year.} \quad (0 \le t \le 8)$$

(t is the number of years since 1992.)[3] During the same period, the price of gasoline was approximately

$$p(t) = 1.0e^{0.02t} \text{ dollars per gallon.}$$

Use an integral to estimate, to the nearest billion dollars, the total spent on gasoline during the given period. HINT [Rate of spending $= p(t)q(t)$.]

59. ***Housing*** The following graph shows the annual number of housing starts in the United States during 2000–2008 together with a quadratic approximating model:

$$s(t) = -30t^2 + 240t + 800 \text{ thousand homes per year} \quad (0 \le t \le 8).$$

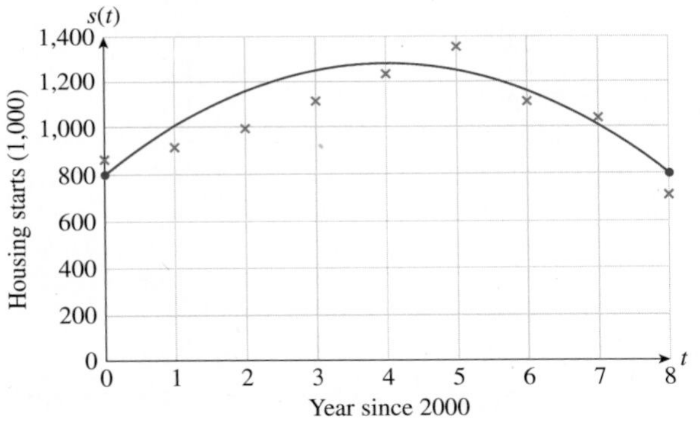

(t is the time in years since 2000.)[4] At the same time, the homes being built were getting larger: The average area per home was approximately

$$a(t) = 40t + 2{,}000 \text{ square feet.}$$

Use the given models to estimate the total housing area under construction over the given period. (Use integration by parts to evaluate the integral and round your answer to the nearest billion square feet.) HINT [Rate of change of area under construction $= s(t)a(t)$.]

60. ***Housing for Sale*** The following graph shows the number of housing starts for sale purposes in the United States during 2000–2008 together with a quadratic approximating model:

$$s(t) = -33t^2 + 240t + 700 \text{ thousand homes per year} \quad (0 \le t \le 8).$$

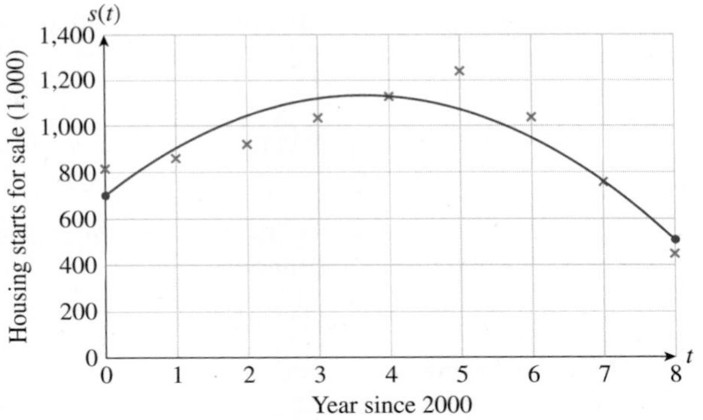

(t is the time in years since 2000.)[5] At the same time, the homes being built were getting larger: The average area per home was approximately

$$a(t) = 40t + 2{,}000 \text{ square feet.}$$

Use the given models to estimate the total housing area under construction for sale purposes over the given period. (Use integration by parts to evaluate the integral and round your answer to the nearest billion square feet.) HINT [Rate of change of area under construction $= s(t)a(t)$.]

61. ▼ ***Bottled Water Sales*** The rate of U.S. sales of bottled water for the period 2000–2010 can be approximated by

$$s(t) = -45t^2 + 900t + 4{,}200 \text{ million gallons per year} \quad (0 \le t \le 10),$$

where t is time in years since the start of 2000.[6] After conducting a survey of sales in your town, you estimate that consumption in gyms accounts for a fraction

$$f(t) = \sqrt{0.1 + 0.02t}$$

of all bottled water sold in year t. Assuming your model is correct, estimate, to the nearest hundred million gallons, the total amount of bottled water consumed in gyms from the start of 2005 to the start of 2010. HINT [Rate of consumption $= s(t)f(t)$. Also see Exercise 31.]

62. ***Bottled Water Sales*** The rate of U.S. per capita sales of bottled water for the period 2000–2010 can be approximated by

$$s(t) = -0.18t^2 + 3t + 15 \text{ gallons per year} \quad (0 \le t \le 10),$$

where t is the time in years since the start of 2000.[7] After conducting a survey of sales in your state, you estimate that consumption in gyms accounts for a fraction

$$f(t) = \sqrt{0.2 + 0.04t}$$

[2] Source for data: Energy Information Administration (Department of Energy) (www.eia.gov).

[3] *Ibid.*

[4] Source for data: U.S. Census Bureau (www.census.gov).

[5] *Ibid.*

[6] Source for data: Beverage Marketing Corporation/ www.bottledwater.org.

[7] *Ibid.*

of all bottled water consumed in year t. Assuming your model is correct, estimate, to the nearest gallon, the total amount of bottled water consumed per capita in gyms from the start of 2005 to the start of 2010. HINT [Rate of consumption $= s(t)f(t)$. Also see Exercise 31.]

63. ▼ ***Oil Production in Mexico:*** **Pemex** The rate of oil production by Pemex, Mexico's national oil company, can be approximated by

$$q(t) = -8t^2 + 70t + 1{,}000 \text{ million barrels per year} \quad (0 \le t \le 9),$$

where t is time in years since the start of 2000.[8] During that time, the price of oil was approximately[9]

$$p(t) = 25e^{0.1t} \text{ dollars per barrel.}$$

Obtain an expression for Pemex's total oil revenue $R(x)$ since the start of 2000 to the start of year x as a function of x. (Do not simplify the answer.) HINT [Rate of revenue $= p(t)q(t)$.]

64. ▼ ***Oil Imports from Mexico*** The rate of oil imports to the United States from Mexico can be approximated by

$$r(t) = -5t^2 + 40t + 500 \text{ million barrels per year} \quad (0 \le t \le 8),$$

where t is time in years since the start of 2000.[10] During that time, the price of oil was approximately[11]

$$p(t) = 25e^{0.1t} \text{ dollars per barrel.}$$

Obtain an expression for the total oil revenue $R(x)$ Mexico earned from the United States since the start of 2000 to the start of year x as a function of x. (Do not simplify the answer.) HINT [Rate of revenue $= p(t)r(t)$.]

65. ▼ ***Revenue*** You have been raising the price of your *Lord of the Fields* T-shirts by 50¢ per week, and sales have been falling continuously at a rate of 2% per week. Assuming you are now selling 50 T-shirts per week and charging \$10 per T-shirt, how much revenue will you generate during the coming year? (Round your answer to the nearest dollar.) HINT [Weekly revenue = weekly sales × price per T-shirt.]

66. ▼ ***Revenue*** Luckily, sales of your *Star Wars and Piece* T-shirts are now 50 T-shirts per week and increasing continuously at a rate of 5% per week. You are now charging \$10 per T-shirt and are decreasing the price by 50¢ per week. How much revenue will you generate during the next six weeks?

Integrals of Piecewise-Linear Functions *Exercises 67 and 68 are based on the following formula that can be used to represent a piecewise linear function as a closed-form function:*

$$\begin{cases} p(x) & \text{if } x < a \\ q(x) & \text{if } x > a \end{cases} = p(x) + \frac{1}{2}[q(x) - p(x)]\left[1 + \frac{|x-a|}{x-a}\right]$$

Such functions can then be integrated using the technique of Exercises 45–52.

67. ◆ ***Population: Mexico*** The rate of change of population in Mexico over 1990–2010 was approximately

$$r(t) = \begin{cases} -0.1t + 3 & \text{if } 0 \le t \le 10 \\ -0.05t + 2.5 & \text{if } 10 \le t \le 20 \end{cases} \text{ million people per year,}$$

where t is time in years since 1990.

a. Use the formula given before the exercise to represent $r(t)$ as a closed-form function. HINT [Use the formula with $a = 10$.]

b. Use the result of part (a) and a definite integral to estimate the total increase in population over the given 20-year period. HINT [Break up the integral into two, and use the technique of Exercises 45–52 to evaluate one of them.]

68. ◆ ***Population: Mexico*** The rate of change of population in Mexico over 1950–1990 was approximately

$$r(t) = \begin{cases} 0.05t + 2.5 & \text{if } 0 \le t \le 20 \\ -0.075t + 5 & \text{if } 20 \le t \le 40 \end{cases} \text{ million people per year,}$$

where t is time in years since 1950.

a. Use the formula given before the exercise to represent $r(t)$ as a closed-form function. HINT [Use the formula with $a = 20$.]

b. Use the result of part (a) and a definite integral to estimate the total increase in population over the given 40-year period. HINT [Break up the integral into two, and use the technique of Exercises 45–52 to evaluate one of them.]

COMMUNICATION AND REASONING EXERCISES

69. Your friend Janice claims that integration by parts allows one to integrate any product of two functions. Prove her wrong by giving an example of a product of two functions that cannot be integrated using integration by parts.

70. Complete the following sentence in words: The integral of u v is the first times the integral of the second minus the integral of _____.

71. Give an example of an integral that can be computed in two ways: by substitution or integration by parts.

72. Give an example of an integral that can be computed by substitution but not by integration by parts. (You need not compute the integral.)

In Exercises 73–80, indicate whether the given integral calls for integration by parts or substitution.

73. $\int (6x - 1)e^{3x^2 - x}\,dx$

74. $\int \frac{x^2 - 3x + 1}{e^{2x-3}}\,dx$

---

[8] Source for data: Energy Information Administration/Pemex (www.eia.gov).

[9] Source for data: BP Statistical Review of World Energy (www.bp.com/statisticalreview).

[10] Source for data: Energy Information Administration/Pemex (www.eia.gov).

[11] Source for data: BP Statistical Review of World Energy (www.bp.com/statisticalreview).

75. $\int (3x^2 - x)e^{6x-1}\,dx$

76. $\int \frac{2x - 3}{e^{x^2-3x+1}}\,dx$

77. $\int \frac{1}{(x+1)\ln(x+1)}\,dx$

78. $\int \frac{\ln(x+1)}{x+1}\,dx$

79. $\int \ln(x^2)\,dx$

80. $\int (x+1)\ln(x+1)\,dx$

81. ▼ If $p(x)$ is a polynomial of degree n and $f(x)$ is some function of x, how many times do we generally have to integrate $f(x)$ to compute $\int p(x)f(x)\,dx$?

82. ▼ Use integration by parts to show that $\int (\ln x)^2\,dx = x(\ln x)^2 - 2x\ln x + 2x + C$.

83. ◆ ***Hermite's Identity*** If $f(x)$ is a polynomial of degree n, show that

$$\int_0^b f(x)e^{-x}\,dx = F(0) - F(b)e^{-b},$$

where $F(x) = f(x) + f'(x) + f''(x) + \cdots + f^{(n)}(x)$. (This is the sum of f and all of its derivatives.)

84. ◆ Write down a formula similar to Hermite's identity for $\int_0^b f(x)e^x\,dx$ when $f(x)$ is a polynomial of degree n.

7.2 Area between Two Curves and Applications

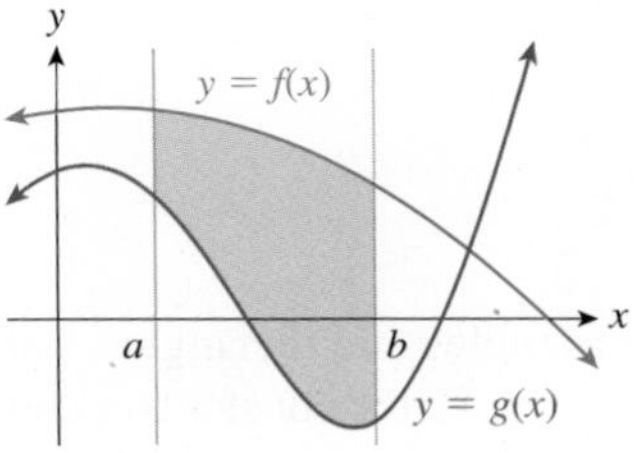

Figure 1

As we saw in the preceding chapter, we can use the definite integral to calculate the area between the graph of a function and the x-axis. With only a little more work, we can use it to calculate the area between two graphs. Figure 1 shows the graphs of two functions, $f(x)$ and $g(x)$, with $f(x) \geq g(x)$ for every x in the interval $[a, b]$.

To find the shaded area between the graphs of the two functions, we use the following formula.

Area between Two Graphs

If $f(x) \geq g(x)$ for all x in $[a, b]$ (so that the graph of f does not move below that of g), then the area of the region between the graphs of f and g and between $x = a$ and $x = b$ is given by

$$A = \int_a^b [f(x) - g(x)]\,dx. \quad \text{Integral of (Top – Bottom)}$$

Caution If the graphs of f and g cross in the interval, the above formula does not hold; for instance, if $f(x) = x$ and $g(x) = -x$, then the total area shown in the figure is 2 square units, whereas $\int_{-1}^{1} [f(x) - g(x)]\,dx = 0$.

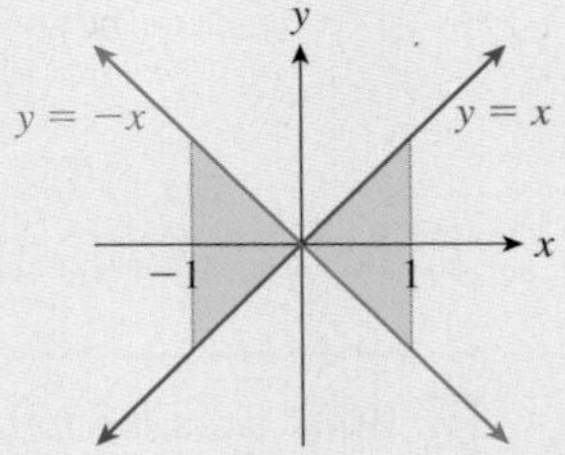

Let's look at an example and then discuss why the formula works.

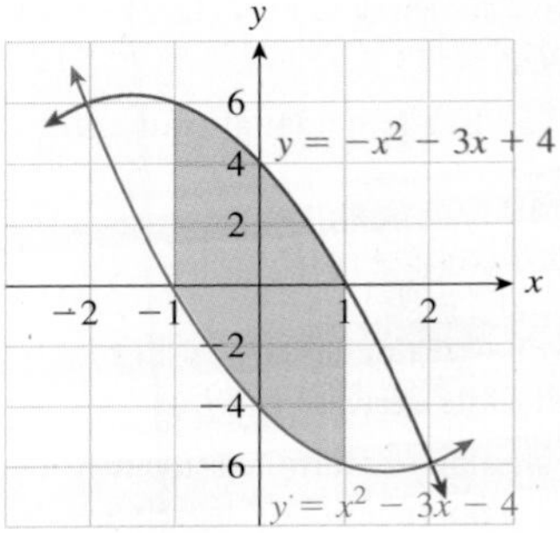

Figure 2

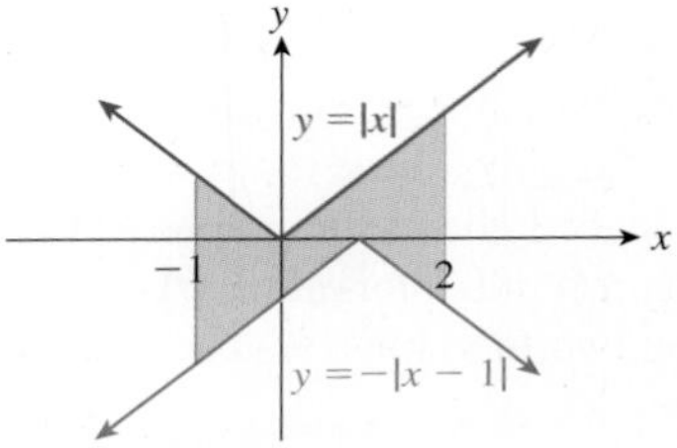

Figure 3

EXAMPLE 1 The Area between Two Curves

Find the areas of the following regions:

a. Between $f(x) = -x^2 - 3x + 4$ and $g(x) = x^2 - 3x - 4$ and between $x = -1$ and $x = 1$

b. Between $f(x) = |x|$ and $g(x) = -|x - 1|$ over $[-1, 2]$

Solution

a. The area in question is shown in Figure 2. Because the graph of f lies above the graph of g in the interval $[-1, 1]$, we have $f(x) \geq g(x)$ for all x in $[-1, 1]$. Therefore, we can use the formula given above and calculate the area as follows:

$$A = \int_{-1}^{1} [f(x) - g(x)]\, dx$$

$$= \int_{-1}^{1} [(-x^2 - 3x + 4) - (x^2 - 3x - 4)]\, dx$$

$$= \int_{-1}^{1} (8 - 2x^2)\, dx$$

$$= \left[8x - \frac{2}{3}x^3\right]_{-1}^{1}$$

$$= \frac{44}{3}.$$

b. The given area (see Figure 3) can be broken up into triangles and rectangles, but we already know a formula for the antiderivative of $|ax + b|$ for constants a and b, so we can use calculus instead:

$$A = \int_{-1}^{2} [f(x) - g(x)]\, dx$$

$$= \int_{-1}^{2} [|x| - (-|x - 1|)]\, dx$$

$$= \int_{-1}^{2} [|x| + |x - 1|]\, dx$$

$$= \frac{1}{2}[x|x| + (x - 1)|x - 1|]_{-1}^{2} \qquad \int |ax + b|\, dx = \frac{1}{2a}(ax + b)|ax + b| + C$$

$$= \frac{1}{2}[(4 + 1) - (-1 - 4)]$$

$$= \frac{1}{2}(10) = 5.$$

Q: *Why does the formula for the area between two curves work?*

A: Let's go back once again to the general case illustrated in Figure 1, where we were given two functions f and g with $f(x) \geq g(x)$ for every x in the interval $[a, b]$. To avoid complicating the argument by the fact that the graph of g, or f, or both may dip below the x-axis in the interval $[a, b]$ (as occurs in Figure 1 and also in Example 1), we shift both graphs vertically upward by adding a big enough constant M to lift them both above the x-axis in the interval $[a, b]$, as shown in Figure 4.

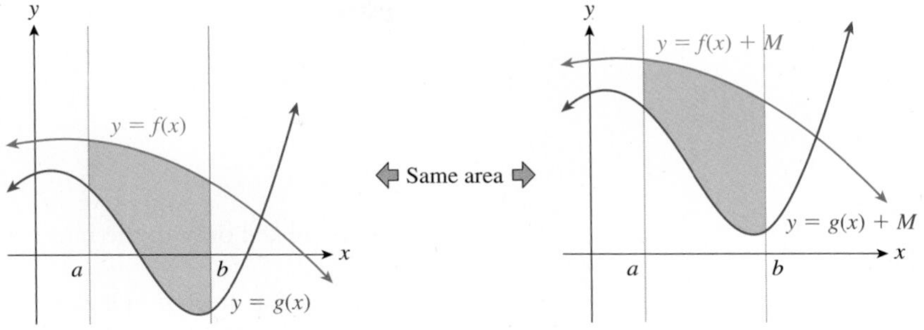

Figure 4

As the figure illustrates, the area of the region between the graphs is not affected, so we will calculate the area of the region shown on the right of Figure 4. That calculation is shown in Figure 5.

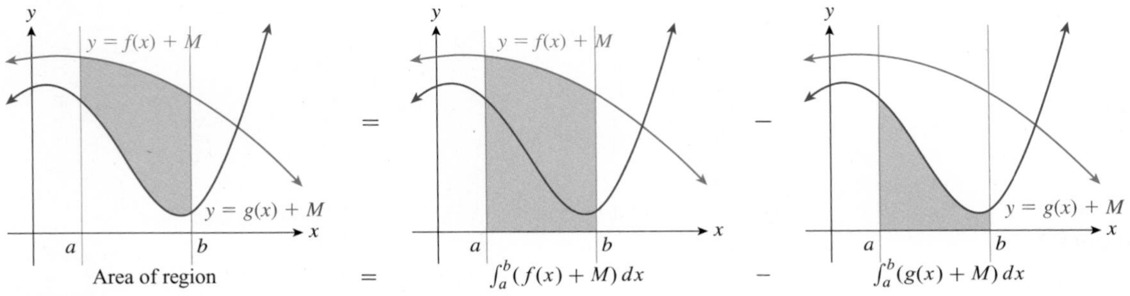

Figure 5

From the figure, the area we want is

$$\int_a^b (f(x) + M)\,dx - \int_a^b (g(x) + M)\,dx = \int_a^b [(f(x) + M) - (g(x) + M)]\,dx$$

$$= \int_a^b [f(x) - g(x)]\,dx,$$

which is the formula we gave originally.

So far, we've been assuming that $f(x) \geq g(x)$, so that the graph of f never dips below the graph of g and so the graphs cannot cross (although they can touch). Example 2 shows how we compute the area between graphs that *do* cross.

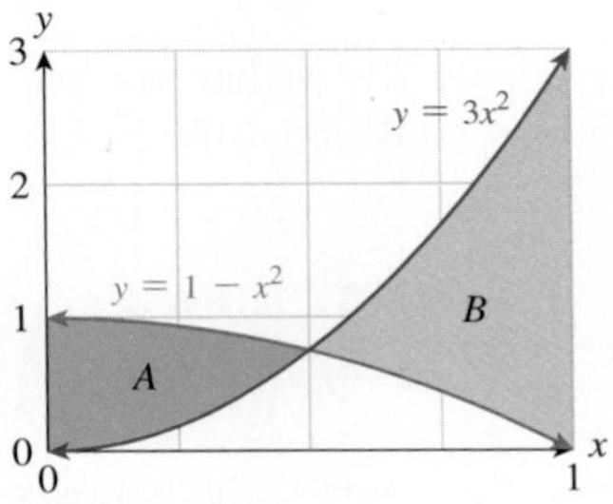

Figure 6

EXAMPLE 2 Regions Enclosed by Crossing Curves

Find the area of the region between $y = 3x^2$ and $y = 1 - x^2$ and between $x = 0$ and $x = 1$.

Solution The area we wish to calculate is shown in Figure 6. From the figure, we can see that neither graph lies above the other over the whole interval. To get around this, we break the area into the two pieces on either side of the point at which the graphs cross and then compute each area separately. To do this, we need to know exactly where that crossing point is. The crossing point is where $3x^2 = 1 - x^2$, so we solve for x:

$$\begin{aligned} 3x^2 &= 1 - x^2 \\ 4x^2 &= 1 \\ x^2 &= \frac{1}{4} \\ x &= \pm\frac{1}{2}. \end{aligned}$$

Because we are interested only in the interval [0, 1], the crossing point we're interested in is at $x = 1/2$.

Now, to compute the areas A and B, we need to know which graph is on top in each of these areas. We can see that from the figure, but what if the functions were more complicated and we could not easily draw the graphs? To be sure, we can test the values of the two functions at some point in each region. But we really need not worry. If we make the wrong choice for the top function, the integral will yield the negative of the area (why?), so we can simply take the absolute value of the integral to get the area of the region in question. For this example, we have

$$\begin{aligned} A &= \int_0^{1/2} [(1 - x^2) - 3x^2]\,dx = \int_0^{1/2} (1 - 4x^2)\,dx \\ &= \left[x - \frac{4x^3}{3}\right]_0^{1/2} \\ &= \left(\frac{1}{2} - \frac{1}{6}\right) - (0 - 0) = \frac{1}{3} \end{aligned}$$

and

$$\begin{aligned} B &= \int_{1/2}^{1} [3x^2 - (1 - x^2)]\,dx = \int_{1/2}^{1} (4x^2 - 1)\,dx \\ &= \left[\frac{4x^3}{3} - x\right]_{1/2}^{1} \\ &= \left(\frac{4}{3} - 1\right) - \left(\frac{1}{6} - \frac{1}{2}\right) = \frac{2}{3}. \end{aligned}$$

This gives a total area of $A + B = \frac{1}{3} + \frac{2}{3} = 1$.

➡ **Before we go on...** What would have happened in Example 2 if we had not broken the area into two pieces but had just calculated the integral of the difference of the two functions? We would have calculated

$$\int_0^1 [(1 - x^2) - 3x^2]\,dx = \int_0^1 [1 - 4x^2]\,dx = \left[x - \frac{4x^3}{3}\right]_0^1 = -\frac{1}{3},$$

which is not even close to the right answer. What this integral calculated was actually $A - B$ rather than $A + B$. Why? ■

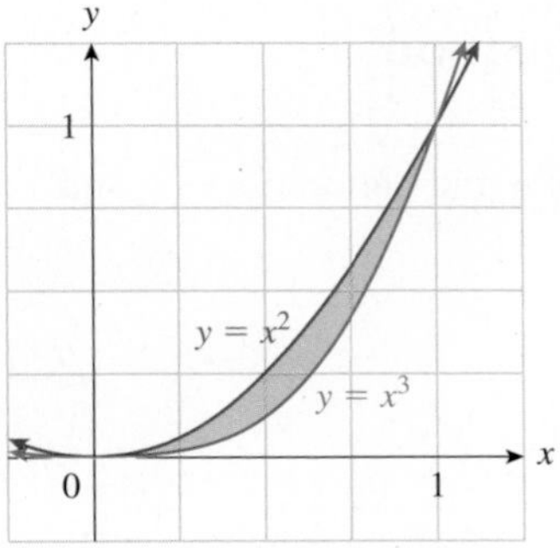

Figure 7

EXAMPLE 3 The Area Enclosed by Two Curves

Find the area enclosed by $y = x^2$ and $y = x^3$.

Solution This example has a new wrinkle: We are not told what interval to use for x. However, if we look at the graph in Figure 7, we see that the question can have only one meaning.

We are being asked to find the area of the shaded sliver, which is the only region that is actually *enclosed* by the two graphs. This sliver is bounded on either side by the two points where the graphs cross, so our first task is to find those points. They are the points where $x^2 = x^3$, so we solve for x:

$$\begin{aligned} x^2 &= x^3 \\ x^3 - x^2 &= 0 \\ x^2(x-1) &= 0 \\ x = 0 \quad &\text{or} \quad x = 1 \end{aligned}$$

Thus, we must integrate over the interval [0, 1]. Although we see from the diagram (or by substituting $x = 1/2$) that the graph of $y = x^2$ is above that of $y = x^3$, if we didn't notice that we might calculate

$$\int_0^1 (x^3 - x^2)\,dx = \left[\frac{x^4}{4} - \frac{x^3}{3}\right]_0^1 = -\frac{1}{12}.$$

This tells us that the required area is $1/12$ square units and also that we had our integral reversed. Had we calculated $\int_0^1 (x^2 - x^3)\,dx$ instead, we would have found the correct answer, $1/12$.

We can summarize the procedure we used in the preceding two examples.

Finding the Area between the Graphs of $f(x)$ and $g(x)$

1. Find all points of intersection by solving $f(x) = g(x)$ for x. This either determines the interval over which you will integrate or breaks up a given interval into regions between the intersection points.
2. Determine the area of each region you found by integrating the difference of the larger and the smaller function. (If you accidentally take the smaller minus the larger, the integral will give the negative of the area, so just take the absolute value.)
3. Add together the areas you found in step 2 to get the total area.

Q: *Is there any quick and easy method to find the area between two graphs without having to find all points of intersection? What if it is hard or impossible to find out where the curves intersect?*

A: We can use technology to give the approximate area between two graphs. First recall that, if $f(x) \geq g(x)$ for all x in $[a, b]$, then the area between their graphs over $[a, b]$ is given by $\int_a^b [f(x) - g(x)]\,dx$, whereas if $g(x) \geq f(x)$, the area is given by $\int_a^b [g(x) - f(x)]\,dx$. Notice that both expressions are equal to

$$\int_a^b |f(x) - g(x)|\,dx$$

telling us that we can use this same formula in both cases.

T Area between Two Graphs: Approximation Using Technology

The area of the region between the graphs of f and g and between $x = a$ and $x = b$ is given by

$$A = \int_a^b |f(x) - g(x)|\, dx.$$

Quick Example

To approximate the area of the region between $y = 3x^2$ and $y = 1 - x^2$ and between $x = 0$ and $x = 1$ we calculated in Example 2, use technology to compute

$$\int_0^1 |3x^2 - (1 - x^2)|\, dx = 1.$$

TI-83/84 Plus: Enter `fnInt(abs(3x^2-(1-x^2)),X,0,1)`

Website: Online Utilities → Numerical Integration Utility
Enter `abs(3x^2-(1-x^2))` for $f(x)$ and 0 and 1 for the lower and upper limits, and press "Integral". (See Figure 8.)

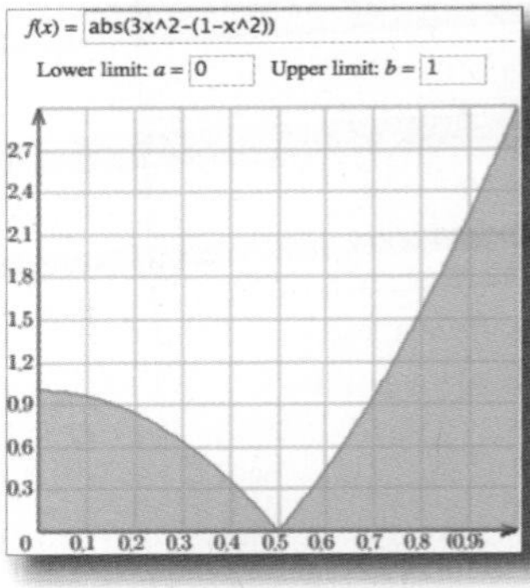

Figure 8

7.2 EXERCISES

▼ more advanced ◆ challenging

T indicates exercises that should be solved using technology

Find the area of the shaded region in Exercises 1–8. (We suggest you use technology to check your answers.)

1.

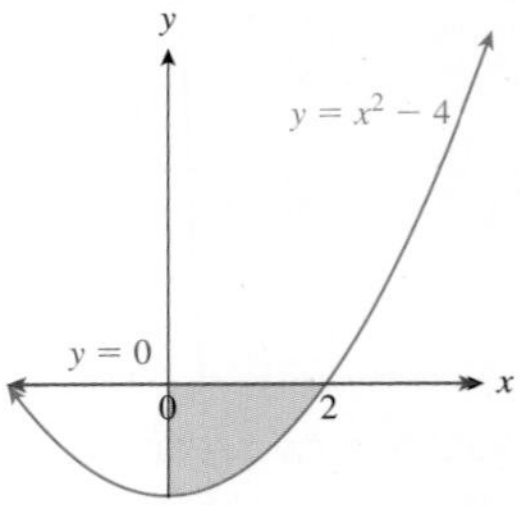

2.

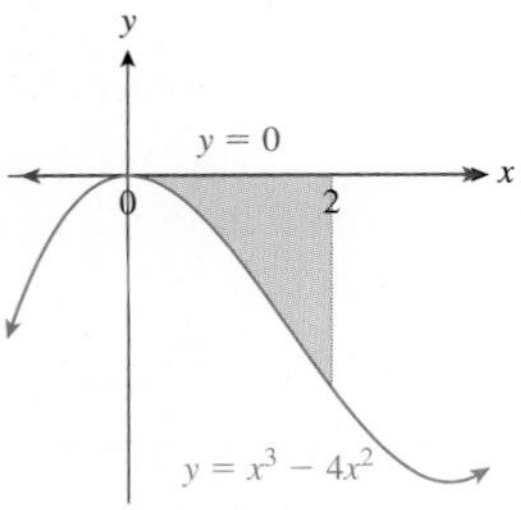

3.

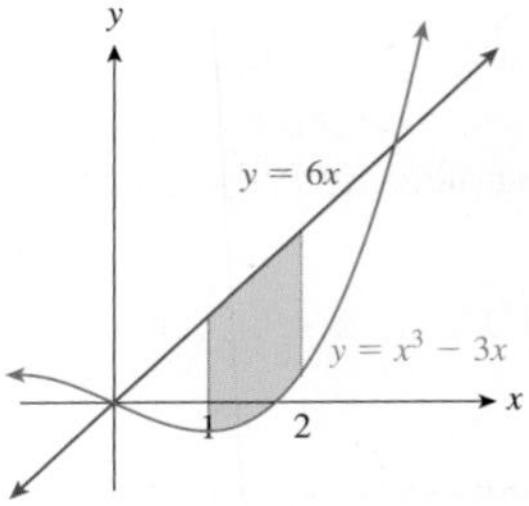

4.

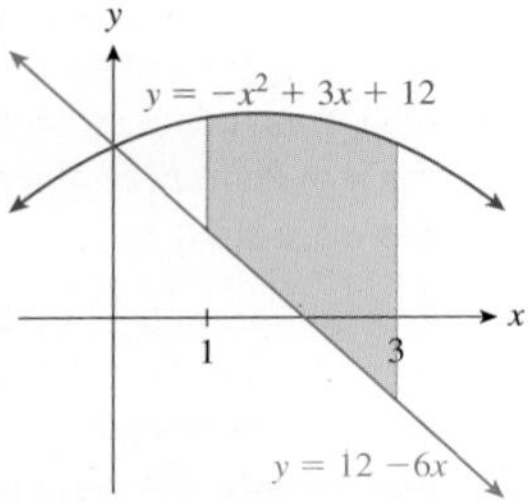

5.

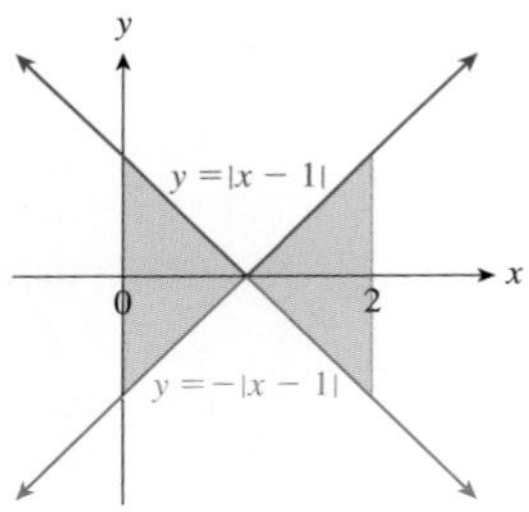

6.

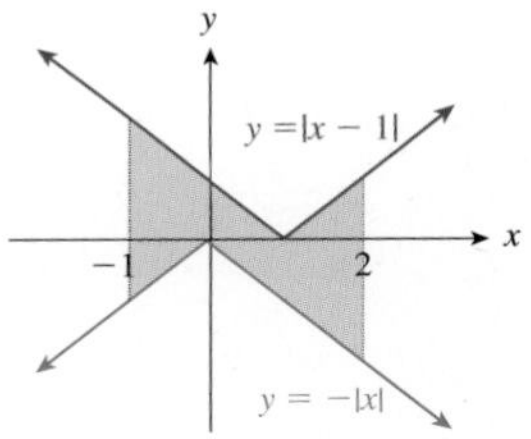

7. ▼

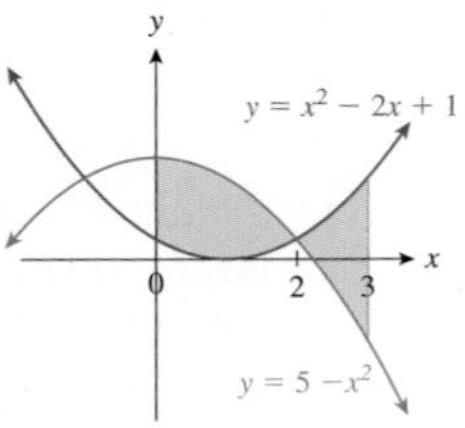

8. ▼

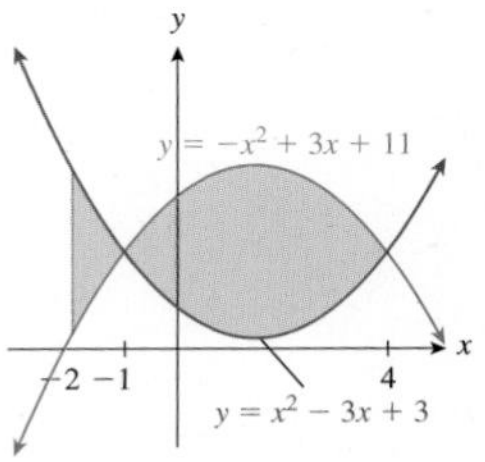

Find the area of the indicated region in Exercises 9–42. We suggest you graph the curves to check whether one is above the other or whether they cross, and that you use technology to check your answers.

9. Between $y = x^2$ and $y = -1$ for x in $[-1, 1]$ HINT [See Example 1.]

10. Between $y = x^3$ and $y = -1$ for x in $[-1, 1]$ HINT [See Example 1.]

11. Between $y = -x$ and $y = x$ for x in $[0, 2]$

12. Between $y = -x$ and $y = x/2$ for x in $[0, 2]$

13. Between $y = |x|$ and $y = x^2$ in $[-1, 1]$

14. Between $y = -|x|$ and $y = x^2 - 2$ in $[-1, 1]$

15. Between $y = x$ and $y = x^2$ for x in $[-1, 1]$ HINT [See Example 2.]

16. Between $y = x$ and $y = x^3$ for x in $[-1, 1]$ HINT [See Example 2.]

17. Between $y = x^2 - 2x$ and $y = -x^2 + 4x - 4$ for x in $[0, 2]$

18. Between $y = x^2 - 4x + 2$ and $y = -x^2 + 4x - 4$ for x in $[0, 3]$

19. Between $y = 2x^2 + 10x - 5$ and $y = -x^2 + 4x + 4$ for x in $[-3, 2]$

20. Between $y = 2x^2 + 7x - 2$ and $y = -x^2 + 4x + 4$ for x in $[-2, 2]$

21. Between $y = e^x$ and $y = x$ for x in $[0, 1]$

22. Between $y = e^{-x}$ and $y = -x$ for x in $[0, 1]$

23. Between $y = (x - 1)^2$ and $y = -(x - 1)^2$ for x in $[0, 1]$

24. Between $y = x^2(x^3 + 1)^{10}$ and $y = -x(x^2 + 1)^{10}$ for x in $[0, 1]$

25. Enclosed by $y = x$ and $y = x^4$ HINT [See Example 3.]

26. Enclosed by $y = x$ and $y = -x^4$ HINT [See Example 3.]

27. Enclosed by $y = x^3$ and $y = x^4$

28. Enclosed by $y = x$ and $y = x^3$

29. Enclosed by $y = x^2$ and $y = x^4$

30. Enclosed by $y = x^4 - x^2$ and $y = x^2 - x^4$

31. Enclosed by $y = x^2 - 2x$ and $y = -x^2 + 4x - 4$

32. Enclosed by $y = x^2 - 4x + 2$ and $y = -x^2 + 4x - 4$

33. Enclosed by $y = 2x^2 + 10x - 5$ and $y = -x^2 + 4x + 4$

34. Enclosed by $y = 2x^2 + 7x - 2$ and $y = -x^2 + 4x + 4$

35. Enclosed by $y = e^x$, $y = 2$, and the y-axis

36. Enclosed by $y = e^{-x}$, $y = 3$, and the y-axis

37. Enclosed by $y = \ln x$, $y = 2 - \ln x$, and $x = 4$

38. Enclosed by $y = \ln x$, $y = 1 - \ln x$, and $x = 4$

39. T Enclosed by $y = e^x$, $y = 2x + 1$, $x = -1$, and $x = 1$ (Round answer to four significant digits.) HINT [See Quick Example page 536.]

40. T Enclosed by $y = 2^x$, $y = x + 2$, $x = -2$, and $x = 2$ (Round answer to four significant digits.) HINT [See Quick Example page 536.]

41. T Enclosed by $y = \ln x$ and $y = \frac{x}{2} - \frac{1}{2}$ (Round answer to four significant digits.) [First use technology to determine approximately where the graphs cross.]

42. T Enclosed by $y = \ln x$ and $y = x - 2$ (Round answer to four significant digits.) [First use technology to determine approximately where the graphs cross.]

APPLICATIONS

43. ***Revenue and Cost*** Suppose your daily revenue from selling used DVDs is

$$R(t) = 100 + 10t \quad (0 \le t \le 5)$$

dollars per day, where t represents days from the beginning of the week, while your daily costs are

$$C(t) = 90 + 5t \quad (0 \le t \le 5)$$

dollars per day. Find the area between the graphs of $R(t)$ and $C(t)$ for $0 \le t \le 5$. What does your answer represent?

44. ***Income and Expenses*** Suppose your annual income is

$$I(t) = 50{,}000 + 2{,}000t \quad (0 \le t \le 3)$$

dollars per year, where t represents the number of years since you began your job, while your annual expenses are

$$E(t) = 45{,}000 + 1{,}500t \quad (0 \le t \le 3)$$

dollars per year. Find the area between the graphs of $I(t)$ and $E(t)$ for $0 \le t \le 3$. What does your answer represent?

45. ***Housing*** The total number of housing starts in the United States during 2000–2008 was approximately

$$h(t) = -30t^2 + 240t + 800 \text{ thousand homes per year} \quad (0 \le t \le 8),$$

where t is time in years since the start of 2000.[12] During that time, the number of housing starts for sale purposes in the United States was approximately

$$s(t) = -33t^2 + 240t + 700 \text{ thousand homes per year} \quad (0 \le t \le 8).$$

Compute the area shown in the graph, and interpret the answer.

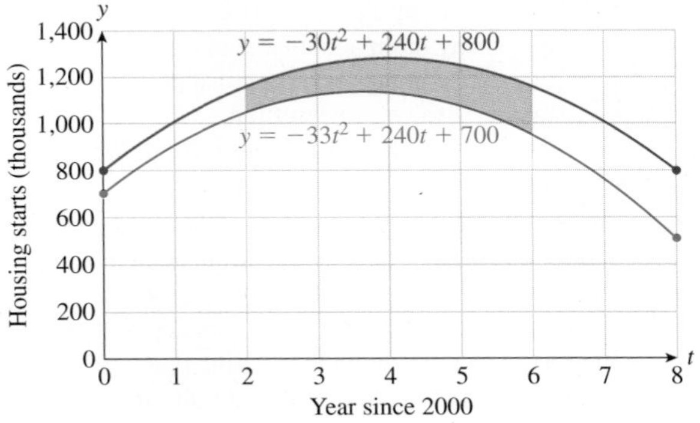

46. ***Oil Production in Mexico:*** **Pemex** The rate of oil production by Pemex, Mexico's national oil company, can be approximated by

$$q(t) = -8t^2 + 70t + 1{,}000 \text{ million barrels per year} \quad (0 \le t \le 9),$$

[12] Source for data: U.S. Census Bureau (www.census.gov).

where t is time in years since the start of 2000.[13] During that time, Mexico exported oil to the United States at a rate of

$$r(t) = -5t^2 + 40t + 500 \text{ million barrels per year}$$
$$(0 \leq t \leq 8).$$

Compute the area shown in the graph, and interpret the answer.

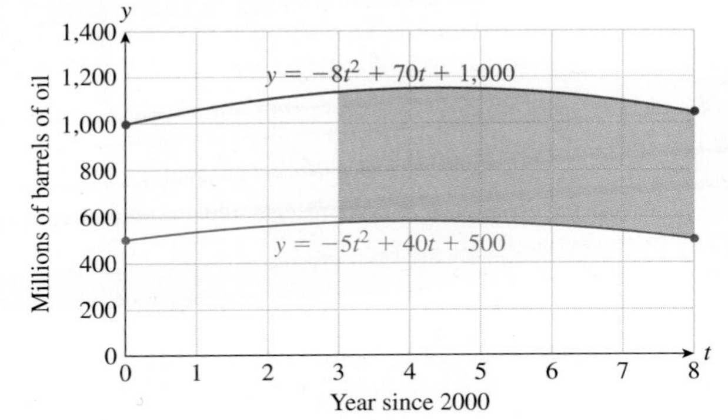

MySpace _and_ Facebook *Exercises 47 and 48 are based on the following models, which show the rate at which new members joined Facebook and MySpace in the period from 2005 to the middle of 2008:*

Facebook:[14] $f(t) = 12t^2 - 20t + 10$ *million members per year* $(0 \leq t \leq 3.5)$

MySpace:[15] $m(t) = 10.5t^2 + 25t + 18.5$ *million members per year* $(0 \leq t \leq 3.5)$

(t is time in years since the start of 2005.)

47. a. Use a graph to determine which of the two Internet sites was experiencing a larger influx of new members from June 2005 to the start of 2007. Use an integral to estimate how many more people joined that Internet site than joined its competitor during that period. (Round your answer to the nearest million.)
 b. To what area does the integral used in part (a) correspond?

48. a. Use a graph to determine which of the two Internet sites was experiencing a larger influx of new members from the start of 2007 to June 2008. Use an integral to estimate how many more people joined that Internet site than joined its competitor during that period. (Round your answer to the nearest million.)
 b. To what area does the integral used in part (a) correspond?

Big Brother *Exercises 49 and 50 are based on the following models, which show the total number of wiretaps authorized per year by all state and federal courts in the United States and the number authorized by state courts.*

State and federal courts: $a(t) = 820e^{0.051t}$ $(0 \leq t \leq 20)$
State courts: $s(t) = 440e^{0.06t}$ $(0 \leq t \leq 20)$

(t is time in years since the start of 1990*.)*[16]

49. ▼ Estimate the area between the graphs of the two functions over the interval $[0, t]$. Interpret your answer.

50. ▼ Estimate the area between the graphs of the two functions over the interval $[t, 20]$. Interpret your answer.

COMMUNICATION AND REASONING EXERCISES

51. If f and g are continuous functions with $\int_a^b [f(x) - g(x)]\, dx = 0$, it follows that the area between the graphs of f and g is zero, right?

52. You know that f and g are continuous and their graphs do not cross on the interval $[a, b]$, so you calculate $\int_a^b [f(x) - g(x)]\, dx$ and find that the answer is -40. Why is it negative, and what is the area between the curves?

53. The following graph shows annual U.S. exports and imports for the period 1960–2007.[17]

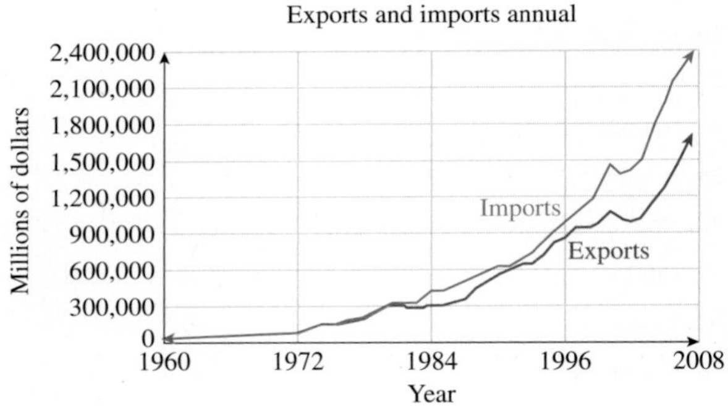

What does the area between the export and import curves represent?

54. The following graph shows a fictitious country's monthly exports and imports for the period 1997–2001.

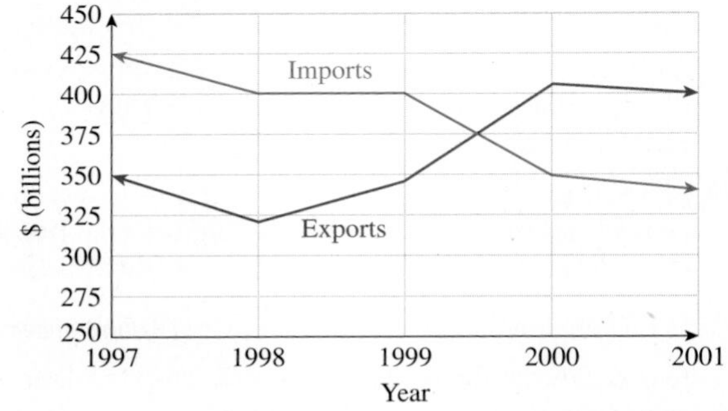

[13] Source for data: Energy Information Administration/Pemex (www.eia.gov).

[14] Sources for data: Some data are interpolated (www.facebook.com/, www.insidehighered.com).

[15] Source for data: www.swivel.com/data_sets.

[16] Source for data: Wiretap Reports, Administrative Office of the United States Courts (www.uscourts.gov/Statistics/WiretapReports.aspx).

[17] Source: Data 360 (www.data360.org).

What does the total area enclosed by the export and import curves represent, and what does the definite integral of the difference, Exports − Imports, represent?

55. ▼ The following graph shows the daily revenue and cost in your *Adopt-a-Chia* operation t days from its inception.

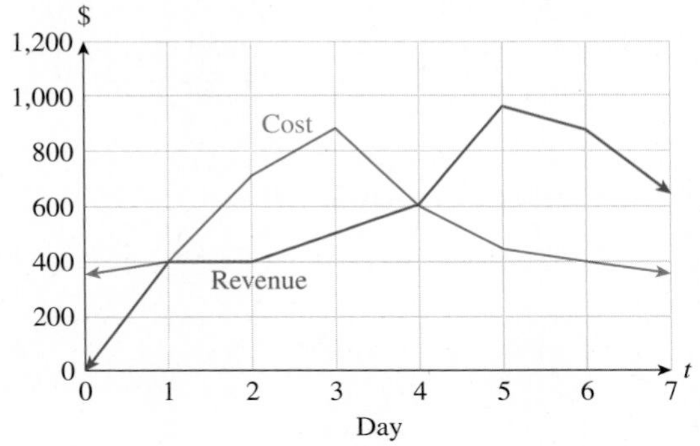

Multiple choice: The area between the cost and revenue curves represents:

(A) the accumulated loss through day 4 plus the accumulated profit for days 5 through 7.
(B) the accumulated profit for the week.
(C) the accumulated loss for the week.
(D) the accumulated cost through day 4 plus the accumulated revenue for days 5 through 7.

56. ▼ The following graph shows daily orders and inventory (stock on hand) for your *Jackson Pollock Paint by Number* sets t days into last week.

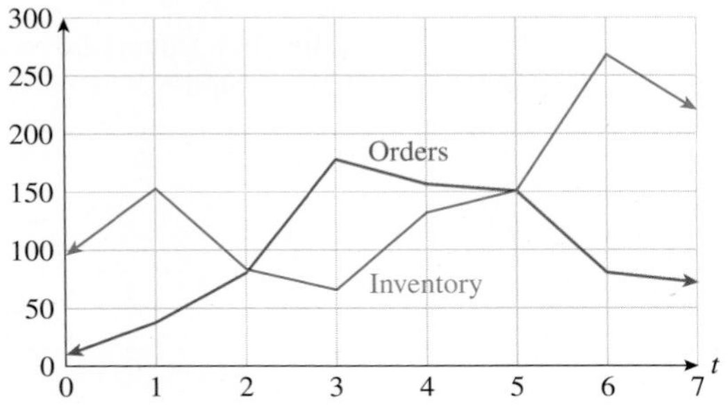

a. Multiple choice: Which is greatest?

(A) $\int_0^7 (\text{Orders} - \text{Inventory})\,dt$

(B) $\int_0^7 (\text{Inventory} - \text{Orders})\,dt$

(C) The area between the Orders and Inventory curves

b. Multiple choice: The answer to part (a) measures

(A) the accumulated gap between orders and inventory.
(B) the accumulated surplus through day 3 minus the accumulated shortage for days 3 through 5 plus the accumulated surplus through days 6 through 7.
(C) the total net surplus.
(D) the total net loss.

57. ▼ What is wrong with the following claim? "I purchased Novartis AG shares for \$50 at the beginning of March 2008. My total profit per share from this investment from March through August is represented by the area between the stock price curve and the purchase price curve as shown on the following graph, where t is time in months since March 1, 2008."[18]

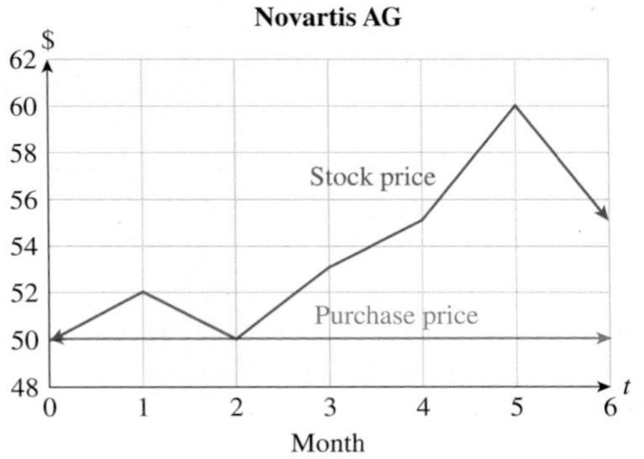

58. ▼ Your pharmaceutical company monitors the amount of medication in successive batches of 100 mg tetracycline capsules, and obtains the following graph.

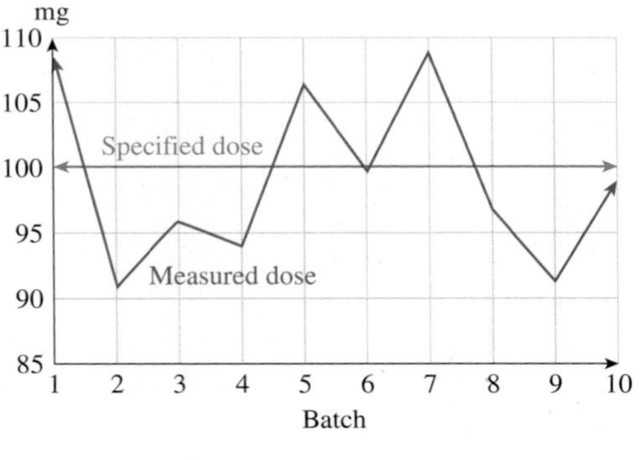

Your production manager claims that the batches of tetracycline conform to the exact dosage requirement because half of the area between the graphs is above the Specified dose line and half is below it. Comment on this reasoning.

[18] Source: www.finance.google.com.

7.3 Averages and Moving Averages

Averages

To find the average of, say, 20 numbers, we simply add them up and divide by 20. More generally, if we want to find the **average**, or **mean**, of the n numbers $y_1, y_2, y_3, \ldots y_n$, we add them up and divide by n. We write this average as $\bar{y}$ ("y-bar").

Average, or Mean, of a Collection of Values

$$\bar{y} = \frac{y_1 + y_2 + \cdots + y_n}{n}$$

Quick Example

The average of $\{0, 2, -1, 5\}$ is $\bar{y} = \dfrac{0 + 2 - 1 + 5}{4} = \dfrac{6}{4} = 1.5$.

But, we also use the word *average* in other senses. For example, we speak of the average speed of a car during a trip.

EXAMPLE 1 Average Speed

Over the course of 2 hours, my speed varied from 50 miles per hour to 60 miles per hour, following the function $v(t) = 50 + 2.5t^2$, $0 \le t \le 2$. What was my average speed over those 2 hours?

Solution Recall that average speed is simply the total distance traveled divided by the time it took. Recall, also, that we can find the distance traveled by integrating the speed:

$$\begin{aligned}\text{Distance traveled} &= \int_0^2 v(t)\,dt \\ &= \int_0^2 (50 + 2.5t^2)\,dt \\ &= \left[50t + \frac{2.5}{3}t^3\right]_0^2 \\ &= 100 + \frac{20}{3} \\ &\approx 106.67 \text{ miles.}\end{aligned}$$

It took 2 hours to travel this distance, so the average speed was

$$\text{Average speed} \approx \frac{106.67}{2} \approx 53.3 \text{ mph.}$$

In general, if we travel with velocity $v(t)$ from time $t = a$ to time $t = b$, we will travel a distance of $\int_a^b v(t)\,dt$ in time $b - a$, which gives an average velocity of

$$\text{Average velocity} = \frac{1}{b-a}\int_a^b v(t)\,dt.$$

Thinking of this calculation as finding the average value of the velocity function, we generalize and make the following definition.

Average Value of a Function

The **average**, or **mean**, of a function $f(x)$ on an interval $[a, b]$ is

$$\bar{f} = \frac{1}{b-a}\int_a^b f(x)\,dx.$$

Quick Example

The average of $f(x) = x$ on $[1, 5]$ is

$$\bar{f} = \frac{1}{b-a}\int_a^b f(x)\,dx$$

$$= \frac{1}{5-1}\int_1^5 x\,dx$$

$$= \frac{1}{4}\left[\frac{x^2}{2}\right]_1^5 = \frac{1}{4}\left(\frac{25}{2} - \frac{1}{2}\right) = 3.$$

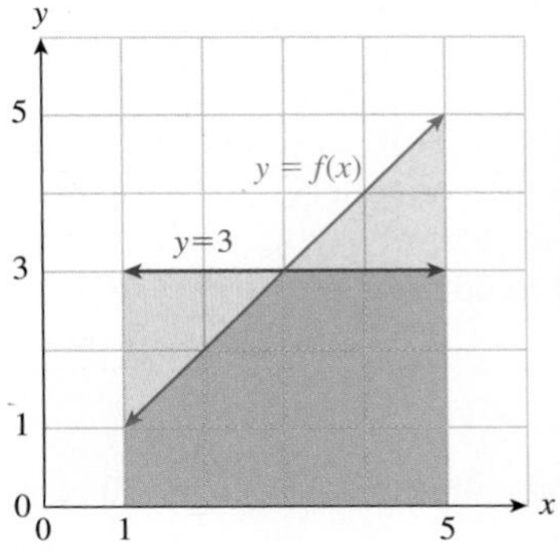

Figure 9

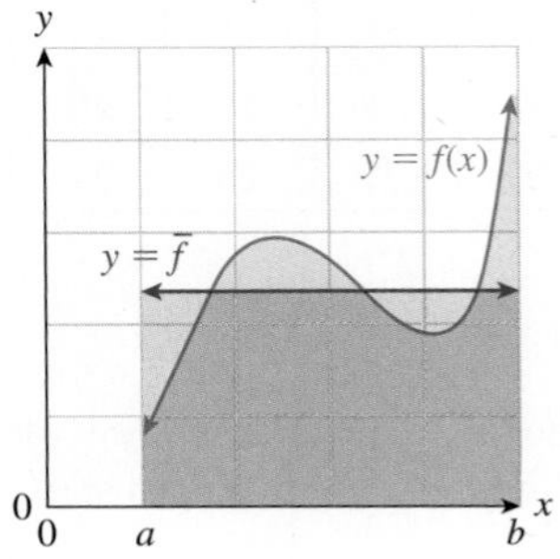

Figure 10

Interpreting the Average of a Function Geometrically

The average of a function has a geometric interpretation. Referring to the Quick Example above, we can compare the graph of $y = f(x)$ with the graph of $y = 3$, both over the interval $[1, 5]$ (Figure 9). We can find the area under the graph of $f(x) = x$ by geometry or by calculus; it is 12. The area in the rectangle under $y = 3$ is also 12.

In general, the average $\bar{f}$ of a positive function over the interval $[a, b]$ gives the height of the rectangle over the interval $[a, b]$ that has the same area as the area under the graph of $f(x)$ as illustrated in Figure 10. The equality of these areas follows from the equation

$$(b-a)\bar{f} = \int_a^b f(x)\,dx.$$

EXAMPLE 2 Average Balance

A savings account at the People's Credit Union pays 3% interest, compounded continuously, and at the end of the year you get a bonus of 1% of the average balance in the account during the year. If you deposit \$10,000 at the beginning of the year, how much interest and how large a bonus will you get?

Solution We can use the continuous compound interest formula to calculate the amount of money you have in the account at time t:

$$A(t) = 10{,}000e^{0.03t},$$

where t is measured in years. At the end of 1 year, the account will have

$$A(1) = \$10{,}304.55$$

so you will have earned $304.55 interest. To compute the bonus, we need to find the average amount in the account, which is the average of $A(t)$ over the interval [0, 1]. Thus,

$$\begin{aligned}\bar{A} &= \frac{1}{b-a}\int_a^b A(t)\,dt \\ &= \frac{1}{1-0}\int_0^1 10{,}000e^{0.03t}\,dt = \frac{10{,}000}{0.03}\left[e^{0.03t}\right]_0^1 \\ &\approx \$10{,}151.51.\end{aligned}$$

The bonus is 1% of this, or $101.52.

➡ **Before we go on...** The 1% bonus in Example 2 was one third of the total interest. Why did this happen? What fraction of the total interest would the bonus be if the interest rate was 4%, 5%, or 10%? ■

Moving Averages

Suppose you follow the performance of a company's stock by recording the daily closing prices. The graph of these prices may seem jagged or "jittery" due to random day-to-day fluctuations. To see any trends, you would like a way to "smooth out" these data. The **moving average** is one common way to do that.

EXAMPLE 3 Stock Prices

The following table shows Colossal Conglomerate's closing stock prices for 20 consecutive trading days.

Day	1	2	3	4	5	6	7	8	9	10
Price	20	22	21	24	24	23	25	26	20	24
Day	11	12	13	14	15	16	17	18	19	20
Price	26	26	25	27	28	27	29	27	25	24

Plot these prices and the 5-day moving average.

Solution The 5-day moving average is the average of each day's price together with the prices of the preceding 4 days. We can compute the 5-day moving averages starting on the fifth day. We get these numbers:

Day	1	2	3	4	5	6	7	8	9	10
Moving Average					22.2	22.8	23.4	24.4	23.6	23.6
Day	11	12	13	14	15	16	17	18	19	20
Moving Average	24.2	24.4	24.2	25.6	26.4	26.6	27.2	27.6	27.2	26.4

using Technology

See the Technology Guides at the end of the chapter to find out how to tabulate and graph moving averages using a graphing calculator or a spreadsheet. Outline:

TI-83/84 Plus

STAT EDIT; days in L1, prices in L2.

Home screen:

```
seq((L2(X)+L2(X-1)
+L2(X-2)+L2(X-3)
+L2(X-4))/5,X,5,20)
→L3
```

[More details on page 585.]

Spreadsheet

Day data in A2–A21

Price data in B2–B21

Enter `=AVERAGE(B2:B6)` in C6, copy down to C21.

Graph the data in columns A–C.

[More details on page 586.]

The closing stock prices and moving averages are plotted in Figure 11.

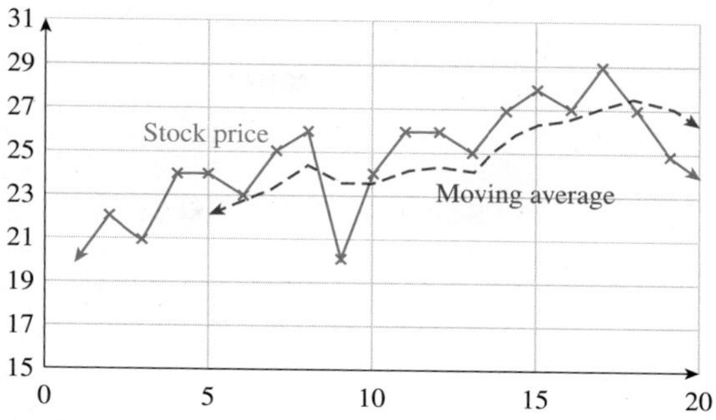

Figure 11

As you can see, the moving average is less volatile than the closing price. Because the moving average incorporates the stock's performance over 5 days at a time, a single day's fluctuation is smoothed out. Look at day 9 in particular. The moving average also tends to lag behind the actual performance because it takes past performance into account. Look at the downturns at days 6 and 18 in particular.

The period of 5 days for a moving average, as used in Example 3, is arbitrary. Using a longer period of time would smooth the data more but increase the lag. For data used as economic indicators, such as housing prices or retail sales, it is common to compute the four-quarter moving average to smooth out seasonal variations.

It is also sometimes useful to compute moving averages of continuous functions. We may want to do this if we use a mathematical model of a large collection of data. Also, some physical systems have the effect of converting an input function (an electrical signal, for example) into its moving average. By an ***n*-unit moving average** of a function $f(x)$ we mean the function $\bar{f}$ for which $\bar{f}(x)$ is the average of the value of $f(x)$ on $[x-n, x]$. Using the formula for the average of a function, we get the following formula.

n-Unit Moving Average of a Function

The n-unit moving average of a function f is

$$\bar{f}(x) = \frac{1}{n}\int_{x-n}^{x} f(t)\,dt.$$

Quick Example

The 2-unit moving average of $f(x) = x^2$ is

$$\bar{f}(x) = \frac{1}{2}\int_{x-2}^{x} t^2\,dt = \frac{1}{6}\left[t^3\right]_{x-2}^{x} = x^2 - 2x + \frac{4}{3}.$$

The graphs of $f(x)$ and $\bar{f}(x)$ are shown in Figure 12.

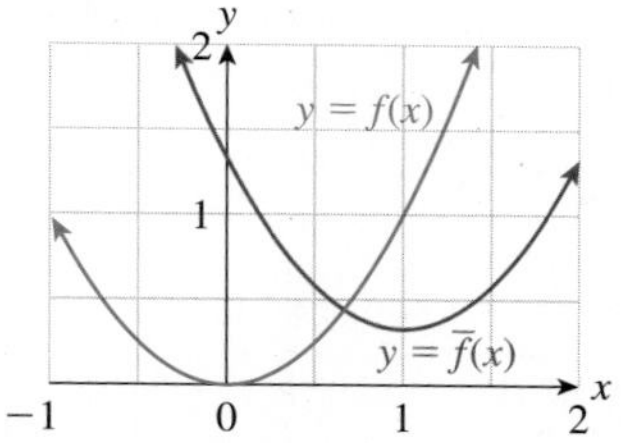

Figure 12

EXAMPLE 4 Moving Averages: Sawtooth and Step Functions

Graph the following functions, and then compute and graph their 1-unit moving averages.

$$f(x) = |x| - |x-1| + |x-2| \qquad \text{Sawtooth}$$

$$g(x) = \frac{1}{2}\left[1 + \frac{|x-1|}{x-1}\right] \qquad \text{Unit step at } x = 1$$

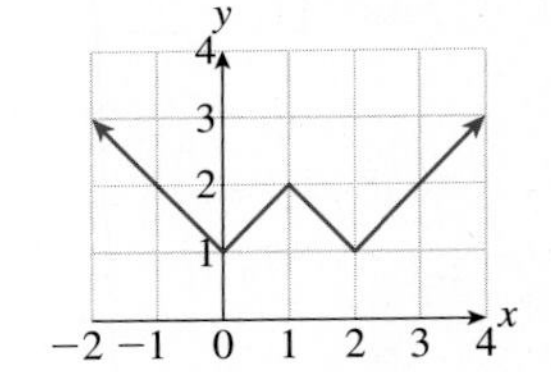

$f(x) = |x| - |x-1| + |x-2|$

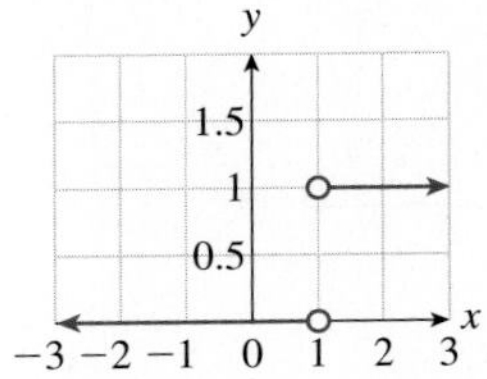

$g(x) = \frac{1}{2}\left[1 + \frac{|x-1|}{x-1}\right]$

Figure 13

Solution The graphs of f and g are shown in Figure 13. (Notice that the step function is not defined at $x = 1$. Most graphers will show the step function as an actual step by connecting the points (1, 0) and (1, 1) with a vertical line.)

The 1-step moving averages are:

$$\bar{f}(x) = \int_{x-1}^{x} f(t)\,dt = \int_{x-1}^{x} [|t| - |t-1| + |t-2|]\,dt$$

$$= \frac{1}{2}[t|t| - (t-1)|t-1| + (t-2)|t-2|]_{x-1}^{x}$$

$$= \frac{1}{2}([x|x| - (x-1)|x-1| + (x-2)|x-2|]$$
$$- [(x-1)|x-1| - (x-2)|x-2| + (x-3)|x-3|])$$

$$= \frac{1}{2}[x|x| - 2(x-1)|x-1| + 2(x-2)|x-2| - (x-3)|x-3|].$$

$$\bar{g}(x) = \int_{x-1}^{x} g(t)\,dt = \int_{x-1}^{x} \frac{1}{2}\left[1 + \frac{|t-1|}{t-1}\right]dt$$

$$= \frac{1}{2}[t + |t-1|]_{x-1}^{x}$$

$$= \frac{1}{2}[(x + |x-1|) - (x - 1 + |x-2|)]$$

$$= \frac{1}{2}[1 + |x-1| - |x-2|]$$

The graphs of $\bar{f}$ and $\bar{g}$ are shown in Figure 14.

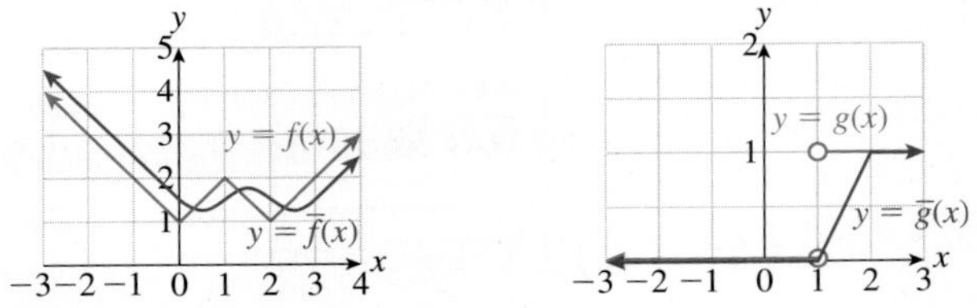

Figure 14

Notice how the graph of $\bar{f}$ smooths out the zig-zags of the sawtooth function.

using Technology

TI-83/84 Plus

We can graph the moving average of f in Example 4 on a TI-83/84 Plus as follows:

```
Y1=abs(X)-abs(X-1)
+abs(X-2)
Y2=fnInt(Y1(T),T,
X-1,X)
[ZOOM] [0]
```

For g, change Y_1 to

```
Y1=.5*(1+abs(X-1)/
(X-1))
```

Before we go on... Figure 15 shows the 2-unit moving average of f in Example 4,

$$\bar{f}(x) = \frac{1}{2}\int_{x-2}^{x} f(t)\,dt$$

$$= \frac{1}{4}(x|x| - (x-1)|x-1| + (x-3)|x-3| - (x-4)|x-4|).$$

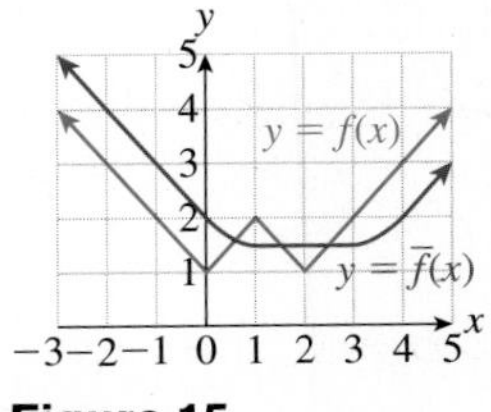

Figure 15

Notice how the 2-point moving average has completely eliminated the zig-zags, illustrating how moving averages can be used to remove seasonal fluctuations in real-life situations. ■

7.3 EXERCISES

▼ more advanced ◆ challenging

T indicates exercises that should be solved using technology

Find the averages of the functions in Exercises 1–8 over the given intervals. Plot each function and its average on the same graph (as in Figure 8). HINT [See Quick Example page 541.]

1. $f(x) = x^3$ over $[0, 2]$ **2.** $f(x) = x^3$ over $[-1, 1]$

3. $f(x) = x^3 - x$ over $[0, 2]$ **4.** $f(x) = x^3 - x$ over $[0, 1]$

5. $f(x) = e^{-x}$ over $[0, 2]$ **6.** $f(x) = e^x$ over $[-1, 1]$

7. $f(x) = |2x - 5|$ over $[0, 4]$

8. $f(x) = |-x + 2|$ over $[-1, 3]$

In Exercises 9 and 10, complete the given table with the values of the 3-unit moving average of the given function. HINT [See Example 3.]

9.

x	0	1	2	3	4	5	6	7
$r(x)$	3	5	10	3	2	5	6	7
$\bar{r}(x)$								

10.

x	0	1	2	3	4	5	6	7
$s(x)$	2	9	7	3	2	5	7	1
$\bar{s}(x)$								

In Exercises 11 and 12, some values of a function and its 3-unit moving average are given. Supply the missing information.

11.

x	0	1	2	3	4	5	6	7
$r(x)$	1	2			11		10	2
$\bar{r}(x)$			3	5		11		

12.

x	0	1	2	3	4	5	6	7
$s(x)$	1	5		1				
$\bar{s}(x)$			5		5	2	3	2

Calculate the 5-unit moving average of each function in Exercises 13–24. Plot each function and its moving average on the same graph, as in Example 4. (You may use graphing technology for these plots, but you should compute the moving averages analytically.) HINT [See Quick Example page 543, and Example 4.]

13. $f(x) = x^3$ **14.** $f(x) = x^3 - x$

15. $f(x) = x^{2/3}$ **16.** $f(x) = x^{2/3} + x$

17. $f(x) = e^{0.5x}$ **18.** $f(x) = e^{-0.02x}$

19. $f(x) = \sqrt{x}$ **20.** $f(x) = x^{1/3}$

21. $f(x) = 1 - \dfrac{|2x - 1|}{2x - 1}$ **22.** $f(x) = 2 + \dfrac{|3x + 1|}{3x + 1}$

23. ▼ $f(x) = 2 - |x + 1| + |x|$ [Do not simplify the answer.]

24. ▼ $f(x) = |2x + 1| - |2x| - 2$ [Do not simplify the answer.]

T *In Exercises 25–34, use graphing technology to plot the given functions together with their 3-unit moving averages.* HINT [See Technology Note for Example 4.]

25. $f(x) = \dfrac{10x}{1 + 5|x|}$ **26.** $f(x) = \dfrac{1}{1 + e^x}$

27. $f(x) = \ln(1 + x^2)$ **28.** $f(x) = e^{1-x^2}$

29. $f(x) = |x| - |x - 1| + |x - 2| - |x - 3| + |x - 4|$

30. $f(x) = |x| - 2|x - 1| + 2|x - 2| - 2|x - 3| + |x - 4|$

31. $f(x) = \dfrac{|x|}{x} - \dfrac{|x - 1|}{x - 1} + \dfrac{|x - 2|}{x - 2} - \dfrac{|x - 3|}{x - 3}$

32. $f(x) = \dfrac{|x|}{x} - 2\dfrac{|x - 1|}{x - 1} + 2\dfrac{|x - 2|}{x - 2} - \dfrac{|x - 3|}{x - 3}$

33. $f(x) = \dfrac{|x|}{x} + \dfrac{|x - 1|}{x - 1} + \dfrac{|x - 2|}{x - 2} + \dfrac{|x - 3|}{x - 3}$

34. $f(x) = 4 - \dfrac{|x|}{x} - \dfrac{|x - 1|}{x - 1} - \dfrac{|x - 2|}{x - 2} - \dfrac{|x - 3|}{x - 3}$

APPLICATIONS

35. ***Television Advertising*** The cost, in millions of dollars, of a 30-second television ad during the Super Bowl in the years 2000 to 2010 can be approximated by

$$C(t) = 0.14t + 1.1 \text{ million dollars} \quad (0 \le t \le 10)$$

($t = 0$ represents 2000).[19] What was the average cost of a Super Bowl ad during the given period? HINT [See Example 1.]

36. ***Television Advertising*** The cost, in millions of dollars, of a 30-second television ad during the Super Bowl in the years 1980 to 2000 can be approximated by

$$C(t) = 0.044t + 0.222 \text{ million dollars} \quad (0 \le t \le 20)$$

($t = 0$ represents 1980).[20] What was the average cost of a Super Bowl ad during the given period? HINT [See Example 1.]

37. ***Membership:*** **Facebook** The number of new members joining Facebook each year in the period from 2005 to the middle of 2008 can be modeled by

$$m(t) = 12t^2 - 20t + 10 \text{ million members per year} \quad (0 \le t \le 3.5),$$

[19] Source for data: en.wikipedia.org/wiki/Super_Bowl_advertising.

[20] *Ibid.*

where t is time in years since the start of 2005.[21] What was the average number of new members joining Facebook each year from the start of 2005 to the start of 2008?

38. ***Membership:* MySpace** The number of new members joining Myspace each year in the period from 2004 to the middle of 2007 can be modeled by

$$m(t) = 10.5t^2 + 14t - 6 \text{ million members per year} \quad (0 \le t \le 3.5),$$

where t is time in years since the start of 2004.[22] What was the average number of new members joining MySpace each year from the start of 2004 to the start of 2007?

39. ***Freon Production*** Annual production of ozone-layer-damaging Freon 22 (chlorodifluoromethane) in developing countries from 2000 to 2010 can be modeled by

$$F(t) = 97.2(1.20)^t \text{ million tons} \quad (0 \le t \le 10)$$

(t is the number of years since 2000).[23] What was the average annual production over the period shown? (Round your answer to the nearest million tons.) HINT [See Example 2.]

40. ***Health Expenditures*** Annual expenditures on health in the United States from 1980 to 2010 could be modeled by

$$F(t) = 296(1.08)^t \text{ billion dollars} \quad (0 \le t \le 30)$$

($t = 0$ represents 1980).[24] What was the average annual expenditure over the period shown? (Round your answer to the nearest billion dollars.) HINT [See Example 2.]

41. ***Investments*** If you invest \$10,000 at 8% interest compounded continuously, what is the average amount in your account over one year?

42. ***Investments*** If you invest \$10,000 at 12% interest compounded continuously, what is the average amount in your account over one year?

43. ▼ ***Average Balance*** Suppose you have an account (paying no interest) into which you deposit \$3,000 at the beginning of each month. You withdraw money continuously so that the amount in the account decreases linearly to 0 by the end of the month. Find the average amount in the account over a period of several months. (Assume that the account starts at \$0 at $t = 0$ months.)

44. ▼ ***Average Balance*** Suppose you have an account (paying no interest) into which you deposit \$4,000 at the beginning of each month. You withdraw \$3,000 during the course of each month, in such a way that the amount decreases linearly. Find the average amount in the account in the first two months. (Assume that the account starts at \$0 at $t = 0$ months.)

[21] Sources for data: www.facebook.com, insidehighered.com. (Some data are interpolated.)

[22] Source for data: www.swivel.com/data_sets.

[23] Figures are approximate. Source: Lampert Kuijpers (Panel of the Montreal Protocol), National Bureau of Statistics in China, via CEIC Data/*New York Times*, February 23, 2007, p. C1.

[24] Source for data: U.S. Department of Health & Human Services/Centers for Medicare & Medicaid Services, National Health Expenditure Data, downloaded April 2011 from www.cms.gov.

45. T ***Online Vehicle Sales*** The value of vehicle transactions on **eBay** each quarter from the first quarter of 2008 through the last quarter of 2010 could be approximated by

$$v(t) = -0.002x^3 + 0.06x^2 - 0.55x + 3.9 \text{ billion dollars per quarter} \quad (1 \le t \le 13)$$

(t is time in quarters; $t = 1$ represents the first quarter of 2008).[25] Use technology to estimate the average quarterly value of vehicle transactions on eBay during the given period. (Round your answer to the nearest hundred million dollars.)

46. T ***Online Auctions*** The net number of new active **eBay** users each quarter from the first quarter of 2008 through the last quarter of 2010 could be approximated by

$$n(t) = -0.002x^4 + 0.06x^3 - 0.55x^2 + 1.9x - 1 \text{ million users per quarter} \quad (1 \le t \le 13)$$

(t is time in quarters; $t = 1$ represents the first quarter of 2008).[26] Use technology to estimate the average number of new active eBay users each quarter during the given period. (Round your answer to the nearest hundred thousand users.)

47. ***Stock Prices:* Exxon Mobil** The following table shows the approximate price of Exxon Mobil stock in December of each year from 2001 through 2010.[27] Complete the table by computing the 4-year moving averages. (Note the peak in 2007 and the drop in subsequent years.) Round each average to the nearest dollar.

Year t	2001	2002	2003	2004	2005	2006	2007	2008	2009	2010
Stock Price	39	35	41	51	56	77	94	80	68	73
Moving Average (rounded)										

The stock price spiked in 2007 and then dropped steeply in 2008. What happened to the corresponding moving average? HINT [See Example 3.]

48. ***Stock Prices:* Nokia** The following table shows the approximate price of Nokia stock in December of each year from 2001 through 2010.[28] Complete the table by computing the 4-year moving averages. (Note the peak in 2007 and the drop in subsequent years.) Round each average to the nearest dollar.

Year t	2001	2002	2003	2004	2005	2006	2007	2008	2009	2010
Stock Price	25	16	17	16	18	20	38	16	13	10
Moving Average (rounded)										

[25] Source for data: eBay company reports http://investor.ebay.com/.

[26] *Ibid.*

[27] Source: finance.yahoo.com.

[28] *Ibid.*

How does the average year-by-year change in the moving average compare with the average year-by-year change in the stock price? HINT [See Example 3.]

49. ▼ ***Cancun*** The *Playa Loca Hotel* in Cancun has an advertising brochure with the following chart, showing the year-round temperature.[29]

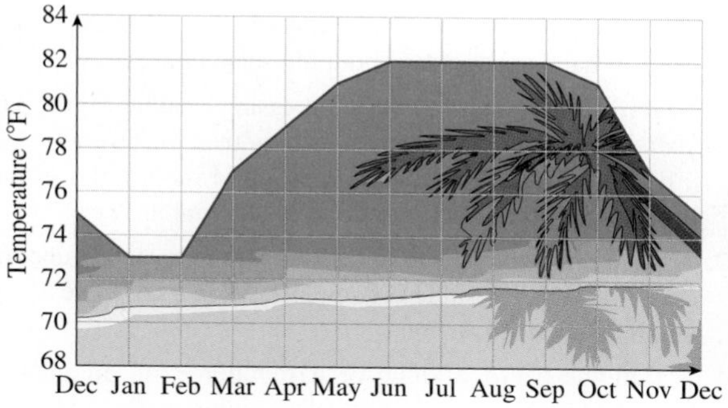

a. Estimate and plot the year-round 6-month moving average. (Use graphing technology, if available, to check your graph.)

b. What can you say about the 12-month moving average?

50. ▼ ***Reykjavik*** Repeat the preceding exercise, using the following data from the brochure of the *Tough Traveler Lodge* in Reykjavik.[30]

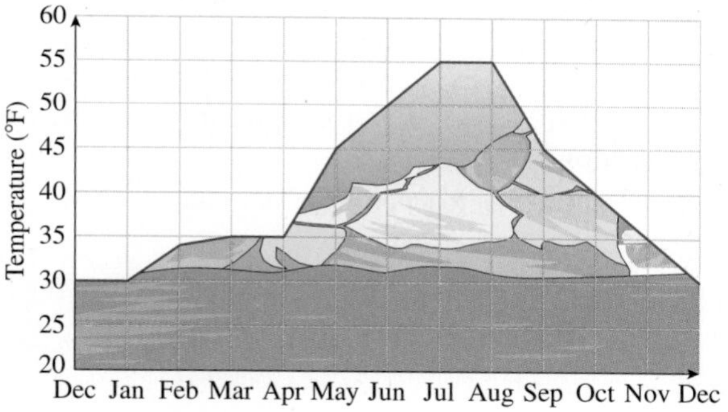

51. T ▼ ***Sales:* Apple** The following table shows approximate quarterly sales of iPods in millions of units, starting in the first quarter of 2006.[31]

Quarter	2006 Q1	2006 Q2	2006 Q3	2006 Q4	2007 Q1	2007 Q2	2007 Q3	2007 Q4	2008 Q1	2008 Q2
Sales (millions)	8.5	8.1	8.7	21.1	10.5	9.8	10.2	22.1	10.6	11.0
Quarter	**2008 Q3**	**2008 Q4**	**2009 Q1**	**2009 Q2**	**2009 Q3**	**2009 Q4**	**2010 Q1**	**2010 Q2**	**2010 Q3**	**2010 Q4**
Sales (millions)	11.1	22.7	11.0	10.2	10.2	21.0	10.9	9.4	9.1	19.5

a. Use technology to compute and plot the four-quarter moving average of these data.

b. The graph of the moving average for the last eight quarters will appear almost linear during 2009 and 2010. Use the 2009 Q1 and 2010 Q4 figures of the moving average to give an estimate (to the nearest 0.1 million units) of the rate of change of iPod sales during 2009–2010.

52. T ▼ ***Housing Starts*** The following table shows the number of housing starts for one-family units, in thousands of units, starting in the first quarter of 2006.[32]

Quarter	2006 Q1	2006 Q2	2006 Q3	2006 Q4	2007 Q1	2007 Q2	2007 Q3	2007 Q4	2008 Q1	2008 Q2
Housing Starts (1,000)	382	433	372	278	260	333	265	188	162	194
Quarter	**2008 Q3**	**2008 Q4**	**2009 Q1**	**2009 Q2**	**2009 Q3**	**2009 Q4**	**2010 Q1**	**2010 Q2**	**2010 Q3**	**2010 Q4**
Housing Starts (1,000)	163	103	78	124	138	105	114	142	119	96

a. Use technology to compute and plot the four-quarter moving average of these data.

b. The graph of the moving average for the eight quarters in 2007 and 2008 will appear almost linear. Use the 2007 Q1 and 2008 Q4 figures of the moving average to give an estimate (to the nearest thousand units) of the rate of change of housing starts during 2007–2008.

53. ***Bottled Water Sales*** The rate of U.S. sales of bottled water for the period 2000–2010 could be approximated by

$$s(t) = -45t^2 + 900t + 4{,}200 \text{ million gallons per year} \quad (0 \le t \le 10),$$

where t is time in years since the start of 2000.[33]

a. Estimate the average annual sales of bottled water over the period 2000–2010, to the nearest 100 million gallons per year. HINT [See Quick Example page 541.]

b. Compute the two-year moving average of s. (You need not simplify the answer.) HINT [See Quick Example page 543.]

c. Without simplifying the answer in part (b), say what kind of function the moving average is.

54. ***Bottled Water Sales*** The rate of U.S. per capita sales of bottled water for the period 2000–2010 coud be approximated by

$$s(t) = -0.18t^2 + 3t + 15 \text{ gallons per year} \quad (0 \le t \le 10),$$

where t is the time in years since the start of 2000.[34] Repeat the preceding exercise as applied to per capita sales. (Give your answer to (a) to the nearest gallon per year.)

[29] Source: www.holiday-weather.com. (Temperatures are rounded.)

[30] *Ibid.*

[31] Source: Apple quarterly press releases, www.apple.com/investor.

[32] Source: U.S. Census Bureau, www.census.gov/const/www/newresconstindex.html.

[33] Source for data: Beverage Marketing Corporation/www.bottledwater.org.

[34] *Ibid.*

55. ***Medicare Spending*** Annual spending on Medicare was projected to increase from \$526 billion in 2010 to around \$977 billion in 2021.[35]
    a. Use this information to express s, the annual spending on Medicare (in billions of dollars), as a linear function of t, the number of years since 2010.
    b. Find the 4-year moving average of your model.
    c. What can you say about the slope of the moving average?

56. ***Pasta Imports in the 1990s*** In 1990, the United States imported 290 million pounds of pasta. From 1990 to 2000 imports increased by an average of 40 million pounds per year.[36]
    a. Use these data to express q, the annual U.S. imports of pasta (in millions of pounds), as a linear function of t, the number of years since 1990.
    b. Find the 4-year moving average of your model.
    c. What can you say about the slope of the moving average?

57. ▼ ***Moving Average of a Linear Function*** Find a formula for the a-unit moving average of a general linear function $f(x) = mx + b$.

58. ▼ ***Moving Average of an Exponential Function*** Find a formula for the a-unit moving average of a general exponential function $f(x) = Ae^{kx}$.

[35]Source: Congressional Budget Office, *March 2011 Medicare Baseline* (www.cbo.gov).

[36]Data are rounded. Sources: Department of Commerce/*New York Times*, September 5, 1995, p. D4, International Trade Administration (www.ita.doc.gov) March 31, 2002.

COMMUNICATION AND REASONING EXERCISES

59. Explain why it is sometimes more useful to consider the moving average of a stock price rather than the stock price itself.

60. Sales this month were sharply lower than they were last month, but the 12-unit moving average this month was higher than it was last month. How can that be?

61. Your company's 6-month moving average of sales is constant. What does that say about the sales figures?

62. Your monthly salary has been increasing steadily for the past year, and your average monthly salary over the past year was x dollars. Would you have earned more money if you had been paid x dollars per month? Explain your answer.

63. ▼ What property does the graph of a (nonconstant) function have if its average value over an interval is zero? Give an example of such a function.

64. ▼ Can the average value of a function f on an interval be greater than its value at every point in that interval? Explain.

65. ▼ Criticize the following claim: The average value of a function on an interval is midway between its highest and lowest value.

66. ▼ Your manager tells you that 12-month moving averages give at least as much information as shorter-term moving averages and very often more. How would you argue that he is wrong?

67. ▼ Which of the following most closely approximates the original function: (A) its 10-unit moving average, (B) its 1-unit moving average, or (C) its 0.8-unit moving average? Explain your answer.

68. ▼ Is an increasing function larger or smaller than its 1-unit moving average? Explain.

7.4 Applications to Business and Economics: Consumers' and Producers' Surplus and Continuous Income Streams

Consumers' Surplus

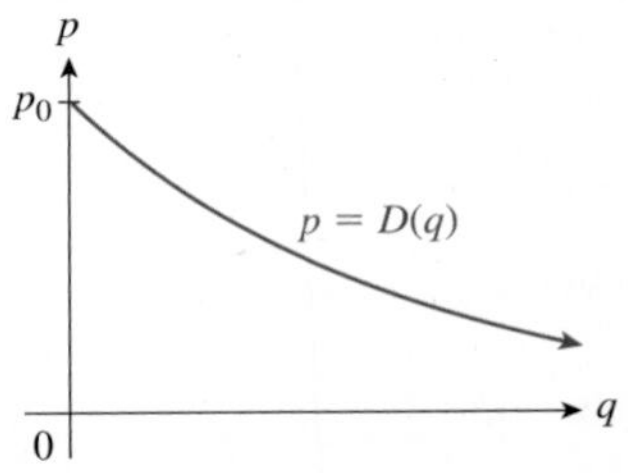

Figure 16

Consider a general demand curve presented, as is traditional in economics, as $p = D(q)$, where p is unit price and q is demand measured, say, in annual sales (Figure 16). Thus, $D(q)$ is the price at which the demand will be q units per year. The price p_0 shown on the graph is the highest price that customers are willing to pay.

Suppose, for example, that the graph in Figure 16 is the demand curve for a particular new model of computer. When the computer first comes out and supplies are low (q is small), "early adopters" will be willing to pay a high price. This is the part of the graph on the left, near the p-axis. As supplies increase and the price drops, more consumers will be willing to pay and more computers will be sold. We can ask the following question: How much are consumers willing to spend for the first $\bar{q}$ units?

Consumers' Willingness to Spend

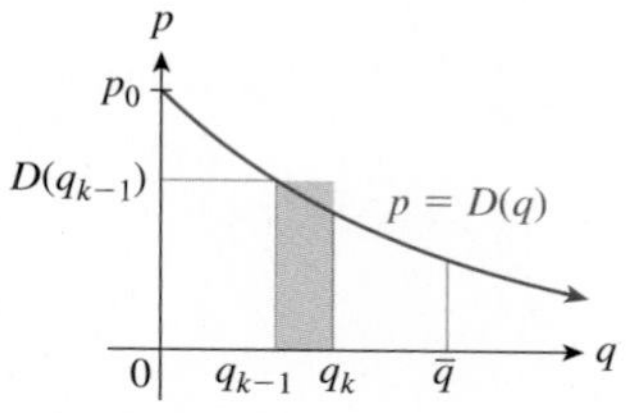

Figure 17

We can approximate consumers' willingness to spend on the first $\bar{q}$ units as follows. We partition the interval $[0, \bar{q}]$ into n subintervals of equal length, as we did when discussing Riemann sums. Figure 17 shows a typical subinterval, $[q_{k-1}, q_k]$.

The price consumers are willing to pay for each of units q_{k-1} through q_k is approximately $D(q_{k-1})$, so the total that consumers are willing to spend for these units is approximately $D(q_{k-1})(q_k - q_{k-1}) = D(q_{k-1})\Delta q$, the area of the shaded region in Figure 17. Thus, the total amount that consumers are willing to spend for items 0 through $\bar{q}$ is

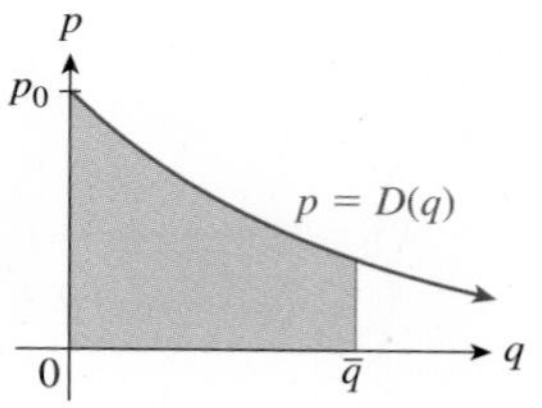

Figure 18

$$W \approx D(q_0)\Delta q + D(q_1)\Delta q + \cdots + D(q_{n-1})\Delta q = \sum_{k=0}^{n-1} D(q_k)\Delta q,$$

which is a Riemann sum. The approximation becomes better the larger n becomes, and in the limit the Riemann sums converge to the integral

$$W = \int_0^{\bar{q}} D(q)\,dq.$$

This quantity, the area shaded in Figure 18, is the total consumers' willingness to spend to buy the first $\bar{q}$ units.

Consumers' Expenditure

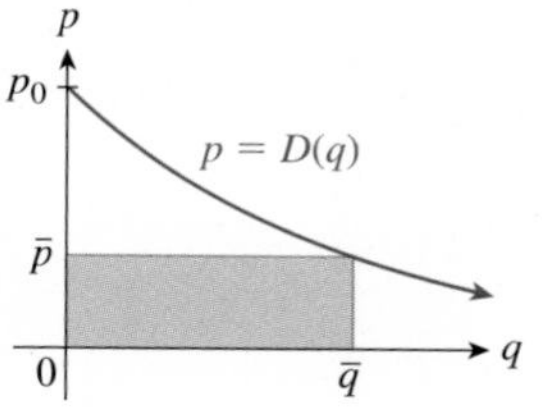

Figure 19

Now suppose that the manufacturer simply sets the price at $\bar{p}$, with a corresponding demand of $\bar{q}$, so $D(\bar{q}) = \bar{p}$. Then the amount that consumers will actually spend to buy these $\bar{q}$ is $\bar{p}\,\bar{q}$, the product of the unit price and the quantity sold. This is the area of the rectangle shown in Figure 19. Notice that we can write $\bar{p}\bar{q} = \int_0^{\bar{q}} \bar{p}\,dq$, as suggested by the figure.

The difference between what consumers are willing to pay and what they actually pay is money in their pockets and is called the **consumers' surplus**.

Consumers' Surplus

If demand for an item is given by $p = D(q)$, the selling price is $\bar{p}$, and $\bar{q}$ is the corresponding demand [so that $D(\bar{q}) = \bar{p}$], then the **consumers' surplus** is the difference between willingness to spend and actual expenditure:*

$$CS = \int_0^{\bar{q}} D(q)\,dq - \bar{p}\bar{q} = \int_0^{\bar{q}} (D(q) - \bar{p})\,dq.$$

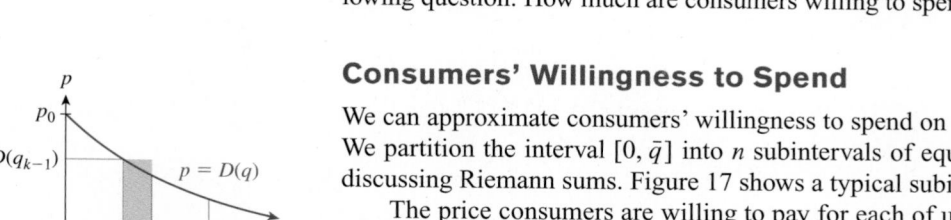

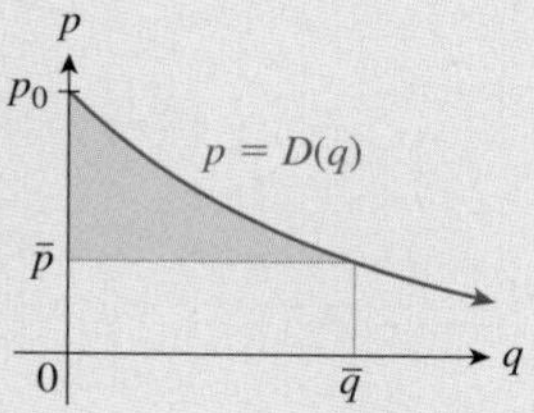

Graphically, it is the area between the graphs of $p = D(q)$ and $p = \bar{p}$, as shown in the figure.

* Multiletter variables like *CS* used here may be unusual in a math textbook but are traditional in the math of finance. In particular, the notations *PV* and *FV* used later in this section are almost universally used in finance textbooks, calculators (such as the TI-83/84 Plus), and such places as study guides for the finance portion of the Society of Actuaries exams.

EXAMPLE 1 Consumers' Surplus

Your used-CD store has an exponential demand equation of the form

$$p = 15e^{-0.01q}$$

where q represents daily sales of used CDs and p is the price you charge per CD. Calculate the daily consumers' surplus if you sell your used CDs at \$5 each.

Solution We are given $D(q) = 15e^{-0.01q}$ and $\bar{p} = 5$. We also need $\bar{q}$. By definition,

$$D(\bar{q}) = \bar{p}$$

or $$15e^{-0.01\bar{q}} = 5,$$

which we must solve for $\bar{q}$:

$$e^{-0.01\bar{q}} = \frac{1}{3}$$

$$-0.01\bar{q} = \ln\left(\frac{1}{3}\right) = -\ln 3$$

$$\bar{q} = \frac{\ln 3}{0.01} \approx 109.8612.$$

We now have

$$\begin{aligned} CS &= \int_0^{\bar{q}} (D(q) - \bar{p})\, dq \\ &= \int_0^{109.8612} (15e^{-0.01q} - 5)\, dq \\ &= \left[\frac{15}{-0.01}e^{-0.01q} - 5q\right]_0^{109.8612} \\ &\approx (-500 - 549.31) - (-1{,}500 - 0) \\ &= \$450.69 \text{ per day.} \end{aligned}$$

Producers' Surplus

We can also calculate extra income earned by producers. Consider a supply equation of the form $p = S(q)$, where $S(q)$ is the price at which a supplier is willing to supply q items (per time period). Because a producer is generally willing to supply more units at a higher price per unit, a supply curve usually has a positive slope, as shown in Figure 20. The price p_0 is the lowest price that a producer is willing to charge.

Figure 20

Arguing as before, we see that the minimum amount of money producers are willing to receive in exchange for $\bar{q}$ items is $\int_0^{\bar{q}} S(q)\, dq$. On the other hand, if the producers charge $\bar{p}$ per item for $\bar{q}$ items, their actual revenue is $\bar{p}\bar{q} = \int_0^{\bar{q}} \bar{p}\, dq$.

The difference between the producers' actual revenue and the minimum they would have been willing to receive is the **producers' surplus**.

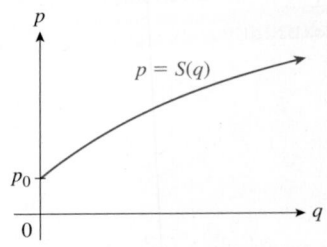

Producers' Surplus

The **producers' surplus** is the extra amount earned by producers who were willing to charge less than the selling price of $\bar{p}$ per unit and is given by

$$PS = \int_0^{\bar{q}} [\bar{p} - S(q)]\, dq,$$

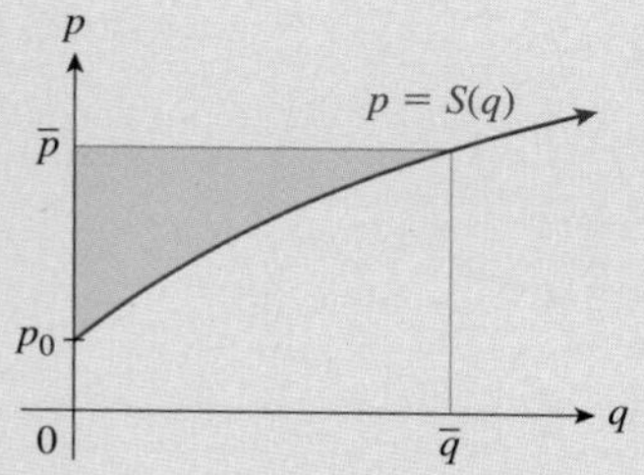

where $S(\bar{q}) = \bar{p}$. Graphically, it is the area of the region between the graphs of $p = \bar{p}$ and $p = S(q)$ for $0 \le q \le \bar{q}$, as in the figure.

EXAMPLE 2 Producers' Surplus

My tie-dye T-shirt enterprise has grown to the extent that I am now able to produce T-shirts in bulk, and several campus groups have begun placing orders. I have informed one group that I am prepared to supply $20\sqrt{p-4}$ T-shirts at a price of p dollars per shirt. What is my total surplus if I sell T-shirts to the group at \$8 each?

Solution We need to calculate the producers' surplus when $\bar{p} = 8$. The supply equation is

$$q = 20\sqrt{p-4}$$

but in order to use the formula for producers' surplus, we need to express p as a function of q. First, we square both sides to remove the radical sign:

$$q^2 = 400(p-4)$$

so

$$p - 4 = \frac{q^2}{400}$$

giving

$$p = S(q) = \frac{q^2}{400} + 4.$$

We now need the value of $\bar{q}$ corresponding to $\bar{p} = 8$. Substituting $p = 8$ in the original equation gives

$$\bar{q} = 20\sqrt{8-4} = 20\sqrt{4} = 40.$$

Thus,

$$\begin{aligned} PS &= \int_0^{\bar{q}} (\bar{p} - S(q))\, dq \\ &= \int_0^{40} \left[8 - \left(\frac{q^2}{400} + 4\right)\right] dq \\ &= \int_0^{40} \left(4 - \frac{q^2}{400}\right) dq \\ &= \left[4q - \frac{q^3}{1{,}200}\right]_0^{40} \approx \$106.67. \end{aligned}$$

Thus, I earn a surplus of \$106.67 if I sell T-shirts to the group at \$8 each.

EXAMPLE 3 Equilibrium

To continue the preceding example: A representative informs me that the campus group is prepared to order only $\sqrt{200(16-p)}$ T-shirts at p dollars each. I would like to produce as many T-shirts for them as possible but avoid being left with unsold T-shirts. Given the supply curve from the preceding example, what price should I charge per T-shirt, and what are the consumers' and producers' surpluses at that price?

Solution The price that guarantees neither a shortage nor a surplus of T-shirts is the **equilibrium price**, the price where supply equals demand. We have

$$\text{Supply:} \quad q = 20\sqrt{p-4}.$$

$$\text{Demand:} \quad q = \sqrt{200(16-p)}.$$

Equating these gives

$$20\sqrt{p-4} = \sqrt{200(16-p)}$$

$$400(p-4) = 200(16-p),$$

$$400p - 1{,}600 = 3{,}200 - 200p$$

$$600p = 4{,}800$$

$$p = \$8 \text{ per T-shirt.}$$

We therefore take $\bar{p} = 8$ (which happens to be the price we used in the preceding example). We get the corresponding value for q by substituting $p = 8$ into either the demand or supply equation:

$$\bar{q} = 20\sqrt{8-4} = 40.$$

Thus, $\bar{p} = 8$ and $\bar{q} = 40$.

We must now calculate the consumers' surplus and the producers' surplus. We calculated the producers' surplus for $\bar{p} = 8$ in the preceding example:

$$PS = \$106.67.$$

For the consumers' surplus, we must first express p as a function of q for the demand equation. Thus, we solve the demand equation for p as we did for the supply equation and we obtain

$$\text{Demand:} \quad D(q) = 16 - \frac{q^2}{200}.$$

Therefore,

$$CS = \int_0^{\bar{q}} (D(q) - \bar{p})\, dq$$

$$= \int_0^{40} \left[\left(16 - \frac{q^2}{200}\right) - 8\right] dq$$

$$= \int_0^{40} \left(8 - \frac{q^2}{200}\right) dq$$

$$= \left[8q - \frac{q^3}{600}\right]_0^{40} \approx \$213.33.$$

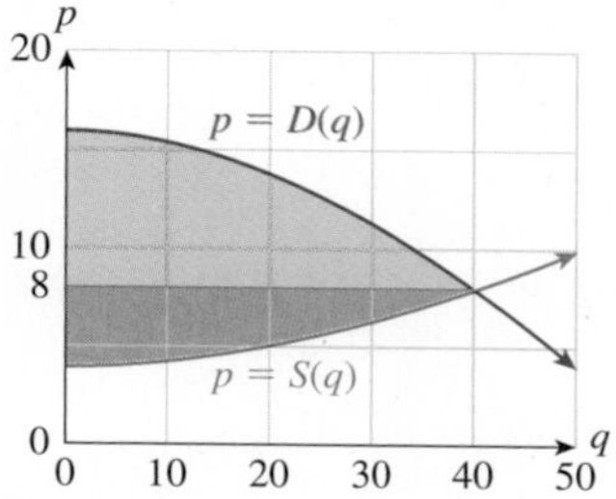

Figure 21

➡ **Before we go on...** Figure 21 shows both the consumers' surplus (top portion) and the producers' surplus (bottom portion) from Example 3. Because extra money in people's pockets is a good thing, the total of the consumers' and the producers' surpluses is called the **total social gain**. In this case it is

$$\text{Social gain} = CS + PS = 213.33 + 106.67 = \$320.00.$$

As you can see from the figure, the total social gain is also the area between two curves and equals

$$\int_0^{40} (D(q) - S(q))\,dq.$$

■

Continuous Income Streams

For purposes of calculation, it is often convenient to assume that a company with a high sales volume receives money continuously. In such a case, we have a function $R(t)$ that represents the rate at which money is being received by the company at time t.

Jim West/PhotoEdit

EXAMPLE 4 Continuous Income

An ice cream store's business peaks in late summer; the store's summer revenue is approximated by

$$R(t) = 300 + 4.5t - 0.05t^2 \text{ dollars per day} \quad (0 \le t \le 92),$$

where t is measured in days after June 1. What is its total revenue for the months of June, July, and August?

Solution Let's approximate the total revenue by breaking up the interval [0, 92] representing the three months into n subintervals $[t_{k-1}, t_k]$, each with length Δt. In the interval $[t_{k-1}, t_k]$ the store receives money at a rate of approximately $R(t_{k-1})$ dollars per day for Δt days, so it will receive a total of $R(t_{k-1})\Delta t$ dollars. Over the whole summer, then, the store will receive approximately

$$R(t_0)\Delta t + R(t_1)\Delta t + \cdots + R(t_{n-1})\Delta t \text{ dollars.}$$

As we let n become large to better approximate the total revenue, this Riemann sum approaches the integral

$$\text{Total revenue} = \int_0^{92} R(t)\,dt.$$

Substituting the function we were given, we get

$$\begin{aligned}\text{Total revenue} &= \int_0^{92} (300 + 4.5t - 0.05t^2)\,dt \\ &= \left[300t + 2.25t^2 - \frac{0.05}{3}t^3\right]_0^{92} \\ &\approx \$33,666.\end{aligned}$$

➡ **Before we go on...** We could approach the calculation in Example 4 another way: $R(t) = S'(t)$, where $S(t)$ is the total revenue earned up to day t. By the Fundamental Theorem of Calculus,

$$\text{Total revenue} = S(92) - S(0) = \int_0^{92} R(t)\,dt.$$

We did the calculation using Riemann sums mainly as practice for the next example. ■

Generalizing Example 4, we can say the following:

Total Value of a Continuous Income Stream

If the rate of receipt of income is $R(t)$ dollars per unit of time, then the total income received from time $t = a$ to $t = b$ is

$$\text{Total value} = TV = \int_a^b R(t)\,dt.$$

EXAMPLE 5 Future Value

Suppose the ice cream store in the preceding example deposits its receipts in an account paying 5% interest per year compounded continuously. How much money will it have in its account at the end of August?

Solution Now we have to take into account not only the revenue but also the interest it earns in the account. Again, we break the interval [0, 92] into n subintervals. During the interval $[t_{k-1}, t_k]$, approximately $R(t_{k-1})\Delta t$ dollars are deposited in the account. That money will earn interest until the end of August, a period of $92 - t_{k-1}$ days, or $(92 - t_{k-1})/365$ years. The formula for continuous compounding tells us that by the end of August, those $R(t_{k-1})\Delta t$ dollars will have turned into

$$R(t_{k-1})\Delta t e^{0.05(92-t_{k-1})/365} = R(t_{k-1})e^{0.05(92-t_{k-1})/365}\Delta t \text{ dollars.}$$

(Recall that 5% is the *annual* interest rate.) Adding up the contributions from each subinterval, we see that the total in the account at the end of August will be approximately

$$R(t_0)e^{0.05(92-t_0)/365}\Delta t + R(t_1)e^{0.05(92-t_1)/365}\Delta t + \cdots + R(t_{n-1})e^{0.05(92-t_{n-1})/365}\Delta t.$$

This is a Riemann sum; as n gets large the sum approaches the integral

$$\text{Future value} = FV = \int_0^{92} R(t)e^{0.05(92-t)/365}\,dt.$$

Substituting $R(t) = 300 + 4.5t - 0.05t^2$, we obtain

$$FV = \int_0^{92} (300 + 4.5t - 0.05t^2)e^{0.05(92-t)/365}\,dt$$

$$\approx \$33{,}880. \qquad \text{Using technology or integration by parts}$$

➡ **Before we go on...** The interest earned in the account in Example 5 was fairly small. (Compare this answer to that in Example 4.) Not only was the money in the account for only three months, but much of it was put in the account toward the end of that period, so had very little time to earn interest. ■

Generalizing again, we have the following:

Future Value of a Continuous Income Stream

If the rate of receipt of income from time $t = a$ to $t = b$ is $R(t)$ dollars per unit of time and the income is deposited as it is received in an account paying interest at rate r per unit of time, compounded continuously, then the amount of money in the account at time $t = b$ is

$$\text{Future value} = FV = \int_a^b R(t)e^{r(b-t)}dt.$$

EXAMPLE 6 Present Value

You are thinking of buying the ice cream store discussed in the preceding two examples. What is its income stream worth to you on June 1? Assume that you have access to the same account paying 5% per year compounded continuously.

Solution The value of the income stream on June 1 is the amount of money that, if deposited June 1, would give you the same future value as the income stream will. If we let PV denote this "present value," its value after 92 days will be

$$PVe^{0.05\times92/365}.$$

We equate this with the future value of the income stream to get

$$PVe^{0.05\times92/365} = \int_0^{92} R(t)e^{0.05(92-t)/365}\,dt$$

so

$$PV = \int_0^{92} R(t)e^{-0.05t/365}\,dt.$$

Substituting the formula for $R(t)$ and integrating using technology or integration by parts, we get

$$PV \approx \$33{,}455.$$

The general formula is the following:

Present Value of a Continuous Income Stream

If the rate of receipt of income from time $t = a$ to $t = b$ is $R(t)$ dollars per unit of time and the income is deposited as it is received in an account paying interest at rate r per unit of time, compounded continuously, then the value of the income stream at time $t = a$ is

$$\text{Present value} = PV = \int_a^b R(t)e^{r(a-t)}dt.$$

We can derive this formula from the relation

$$FV = PVe^{r(b-a)}$$

because the present value is the amount that would have to be deposited at time $t = a$ to give a future value of FV at time $t = b$.

Note These formulas are more general than we've said. They still work when $R(t) < 0$ if we interpret negative values as money flowing *out* rather than in. That is, we can use these formulas for income we receive or for payments that we make, or for situations where we sometimes receive money and sometimes pay it out. These formulas can also be used for flows of quantities other than money. For example, if we use an exponential model for population growth and we let $R(t)$ represent the rate of immigration $[R(t) > 0]$ or emigration $[R(t) < 0]$, then the future value formula gives the future population. ■

7.4 EXERCISES

▼ more advanced ◆ challenging

T indicates exercises that should be solved using technology

Calculate the consumers' surplus at the indicated unit price $\bar{p}$ for each of the demand equations in Exercises 1–12. HINT [See Example 1.]

1. $p = 10 - 2q$; $\bar{p} = 5$

2. $p = 100 - q$; $\bar{p} = 20$

3. $p = 100 - 3\sqrt{q}$; $\bar{p} = 76$

4. $p = 10 - 2q^{1/3}$; $\bar{p} = 6$

5. $p = 500e^{-2q}$; $\bar{p} = 100$

6. $p = 100 - e^{0.1q}$; $\bar{p} = 50$

7. $q = 100 - 2p$; $\bar{p} = 20$

8. $q = 50 - 3p$; $\bar{p} = 10$

9. $q = 100 - 0.25p^2$; $\bar{p} = 10$

10. $q = 20 - 0.05p^2$; $\bar{p} = 5$

11. $q = 500e^{-0.5p} - 50$; $\bar{p} = 1$

12. $q = 100 - e^{0.1p}$; $\bar{p} = 20$

Calculate the producers' surplus for each of the supply equations in Exercises 13–24 at the indicated unit price $\bar{p}$. HINT [See Example 2.]

13. $p = 10 + 2q$; $\bar{p} = 20$

14. $p = 100 + q$; $\bar{p} = 200$

15. $p = 10 + 2q^{1/3}$; $\bar{p} = 12$

16. $p = 100 + 3\sqrt{q}$; $\bar{p} = 124$

17. $p = 500e^{0.5q}$; $\bar{p} = 1{,}000$

18. $p = 100 + e^{0.01q}$; $\bar{p} = 120$

19. $q = 2p - 50$; $\bar{p} = 40$

20. $q = 4p - 1{,}000$; $\bar{p} = 1{,}000$

21. $q = 0.25p^2 - 10$; $\bar{p} = 10$

22. $q = 0.05p^2 - 20$; $\bar{p} = 50$

23. $q = 500e^{0.05p} - 50$; $\bar{p} = 10$

24. $q = 10(e^{0.1p} - 1)$; $\bar{p} = 5$

In Exercises 25–30, find the total value of the given income stream and also find its future value (at the end of the given interval) using the given interest rate. HINT [See Examples 4 and 5.]

25. $R(t) = 30{,}000$, $0 \le t \le 10$, at 7%

26. $R(t) = 40{,}000$, $0 \le t \le 5$, at 10%

27. $R(t) = 30{,}000 + 1{,}000t$, $0 \le t \le 10$, at 7%

28. $R(t) = 40{,}000 + 2{,}000t$, $0 \le t \le 5$, at 10%

29. $R(t) = 30{,}000e^{0.05t}$, $0 \le t \le 10$, at 7%

30. $R(t) = 40{,}000e^{0.04t}$, $0 \le t \le 5$, at 10%

In Exercises 31–36, find the total value of the given income stream and also find its present value (at the beginning of the given interval) using the given interest rate. HINT [See Examples 4 and 6.]

31. $R(t) = 20{,}000$, $0 \le t \le 5$, at 8%

32. $R(t) = 50{,}000$, $0 \le t \le 10$, at 5%

33. $R(t) = 20{,}000 + 1{,}000t$, $0 \le t \le 5$, at 8%

34. $R(t) = 50{,}000 + 2{,}000t$, $0 \le t \le 10$, at 5%

35. $R(t) = 20{,}000e^{0.03t}$, $0 \le t \le 5$, at 8%

36. $R(t) = 50{,}000e^{0.06t}$, $0 \le t \le 10$, at 5%

APPLICATIONS

37. ***College Tuition*** A study of U.S. colleges and universities resulted in the demand equation $q = 20{,}000 - 2p$, where q is the enrollment at a public college or university and p is the average annual tuition (plus fees) it charges.[37] Officials at Enormous State University have developed a policy whereby the number of students it will accept per year at a tuition level of p dollars is given by $q = 7{,}500 + 0.5p$. Find the equilibrium tuition price $\bar{p}$ and the consumers' and producers' surpluses at this tuition level. What is the total social gain at the equilibrium price? HINT [See Example 3.]

38. ***Fast Food*** A fast-food outlet finds that the demand equation for its new side dish, "Sweetdough Tidbit," is given by

$$p = \frac{128}{(q+1)^2},$$

where p is the price (in cents) per serving and q is the number of servings that can be sold per hour at this price. At the same time, the franchise is prepared to sell $q = 0.5p - 1$ servings per hour at a price of p cents. Find the equilibrium price $\bar{p}$ and the consumers' and producers' surpluses at this price level. What is the total social gain at the equilibrium price? HINT [See Example 3.]

39. ***Revenue:*** **Nokia** The annual net sales (revenue) earned by Nokia in the years January 2004 to January 2010 can be approximated by

$$R(t) = -1.75t^2 + 12.5t + 30 \text{ billion euros per year} \quad (0 \le t \le 6),$$

where t is time in years ($t = 0$ represents January 2004).[38] Estimate, to the nearest €10 billion, Nokia's total revenue from January 2006 to January 2010. HINT [See Example 4.]

40. ***Revenue:*** **Nintendo** The annual net sales (revenue) earned by Nintendo Co., Ltd., in the fiscal years from April 1, 2004, to April 1, 2010, can be approximated by

$$R(t) = -14.5t^3 + 38t^2 + 380t + 510 \text{ billion yen per year} \quad (0 \le t \le 6),$$

where t is time in years ($t = 0$ represents April 1, 2004).[39] Estimate, to the nearest ¥100 billion, Nintendo's total revenue from April 1, 2006, to April 1, 2010. HINT [See Example 4.]

41. ***Revenue:*** **Walmart** The annual revenue earned by Walmart in the years from January 2004 to January 2010 can be approximated by

$$R(t) = 242e^{0.098t} \text{ billion dollars per year} \quad (0 \le t \le 6),$$

where t is time in years ($t = 0$ represents January 2004).[40] Estimate, to the nearest \$10 billion, Wal-Mart's total revenue from January 2004 to January 2008.

42. ***Revenue:*** **Target** The annual revenue earned by Target for fiscal years 2004 through 2010 can be approximated by

$$R(t) = 41e^{0.094t} \text{ billion dollars per year} \quad (0 \le t \le 6),$$

where t is time in years ($t = 0$ represents the beginning of fiscal year 2004).[41] Estimate, to the nearest \$10 billion, Target's total revenue from the beginning of fiscal year 2006 to the beginning of fiscal year 2010.

43. ▼ ***Revenue*** Refer back to Exercise 39. Suppose that, from January 2004 on, **Nokia** invested its revenue in an investment yielding 4% compounded continuously. What, to the nearest €10 billion, would the total value of Nokia's revenue from January 2006 to January 2010 have been in January 2010? HINT [See Example 5.]

44. ▼ ***Revenue*** Refer back to Exercise 40. Suppose that, from April 2004 on, **Nintendo** invested its revenue in an investment yielding 5% compounded continuously. What, to the nearest ¥100 billion, would the total value of Nintendo's revenue from April 1, 2006, to April 1, 2010, have been in April 2010? HINT [See Example 5.]

45. ▼ ***Revenue*** Refer back to Exercise 41. Suppose that, from January 2004 on, **Walmart** invested its revenue in an investment that depreciated continuously at a rate of 5% per year. What, to the nearest \$10 billion, would the total value of Walmart's revenues from January 2004 to January 2008 have been in January 2008?

46. ▼ ***Revenue*** Refer back to Exercise 42. Suppose that, from the start of fiscal year 2004 on, **Target** invested its revenue in an investment that depreciated continuously at a rate of 3% per year. What, to the nearest \$10 billion, would the total value of Target's revenue from the beginning of fiscal year 2006 to the beginning of fiscal year 2010 have been at the beginning of fiscal year 2010?

[37] Idea based on a study by A. L. Ostrosky, Jr. and J. V. Koch, as cited in their book *Introduction to Mathematical Economics* (Waveland Press, Illinois, 1979, p. 133). The data used here are fictitious, however.

[38] Source for data: Nokia financial statements (www.investors.nokia.com).

[39] Source for data: Nintendo annual reports (www.nintendo.com/corp).

[40] Source for data: Wal-Mart annual reports (www.Walmartstores.com/Investors).

[41] Source for data: Target annual reports (investors.target.com).

47. ▼ ***Saving for Retirement*** You are saving for your retirement by investing $700 per month in an annuity with a guaranteed interest rate of 6% per year. With a continuous stream of investment and continuous compounding, how much will you have accumulated in the annuity by the time you retire in 45 years?

48. ▼ ***Saving for College*** When your first child is born, you begin to save for college by depositing $400 per month in an account paying 12% interest per year. With a continuous stream of investment and continuous compounding, how much will you have accumulated in the account by the time your child enters college 18 years later?

49. ▼ ***Saving for Retirement*** You begin saving for your retirement by investing $700 per month in an annuity with a guaranteed interest rate of 6% per year. You increase the amount you invest at the rate of 3% per year. With continuous investment and compounding, how much will you have accumulated in the annuity by the time you retire in 45 years?

50. ▼ ***Saving for College*** When your first child is born, you begin to save for college by depositing $400 per month in an account paying 12% interest per year. You increase the amount you save by 2% per year. With continuous investment and compounding, how much will have accumulated in the account by the time your child enters college 18 years later?

51. ▼ ***Bonds*** The U.S. Treasury issued a 30-year bond on February 10, 2011, paying 4.750% interest.[42] Thus, if you bought $100,000 worth of these bonds you would receive $4,750 per year in interest for 30 years. An investor wishes to buy the rights to receive the interest on $100,000 worth of these bonds. The amount the investor is willing to pay is the present value of the interest payments, assuming a 5% rate of return. Assuming (incorrectly, but approximately) that the interest payments are made continuously, what will the investor pay? HINT [See Example 6.]

52. ▼ ***Bonds*** The Megabucks Corporation is issuing a 20-year bond paying 7% interest. (See the preceding exercise.) An investor wishes to buy the rights to receive the interest on $50,000 worth of these bonds, and seeks a 6% rate of return. Assuming that the interest payments are made continuously, what will the investor pay? HINT [See Example 6.]

53. ▼ ***Valuing Future Income*** Inga was injured and can no longer work. As a result of a lawsuit, she is to be awarded the present value of the income she would have received over the next 20 years. Her income at the time she was injured was $100,000 per year, increasing by $5,000 per year. What will be the amount of her award, assuming continuous income and a 5% interest rate?

54. ▼ ***Valuing Future Income*** Max was injured and can no longer work. As a result of a lawsuit, he is to be awarded the present value of the income he would have received over the next 30 years. His income at the time he was injured was $30,000 per year, increasing by $1,500 per year. What will be the amount of his award, assuming continuous income and a 6% interest rate?

COMMUNICATION AND REASONING EXERCISES

55. Complete the following: The future value of a continuous income stream earning 0% interest is the same as the ______ value.

56. Complete the following: The present value of a continuous income stream earning 0% interest is the same as the ______ value.

57. ▼ ***Linear Demand*** Given a linear demand equation $q = -mp + b$ $(m > 0)$, find a formula for the consumers' surplus at a price level of $\bar{p}$ per unit.

58. ▼ ***Linear Supply*** Given a linear supply equation of the form $q = mp + b$ $(m > 0)$, find a formula for the producers' surplus at a price level of $\bar{p}$ per unit.

59. ▼ Your study group friend says that the future value of a continuous stream of income is always greater than the total value, assuming a positive rate of return. Is she correct? Why?

60. ▼ Your other study group friend says that the present value of a continuous stream of income can sometimes be greater than the total value, depending on the (positive) interest rate. Is he correct? Explain.

61. ▼ Arrange from smallest to largest: Total Value, Future Value, Present Value of a continuous stream of income (assuming a positive income and positive rate of return).

62. ▼ **a.** Arrange the following functions from smallest to largest $R(t)$, $R(t)e^{r(b-t)}$, $R(t)e^{r(a-t)}$, where $a \le t \le b$, and r and $R(t)$ are positive.
b. Use the result from part (a) to justify your answers in Exercises 59–61.

[42]Source: The Bureau of the Public Debt (www.publicdebt.treas.gov).

7.5 Improper Integrals and Applications

All the definite integrals we have seen so far have had the form $\int_a^b f(x)\,dx$, with a and b finite and $f(x)$ piecewise continuous on the closed interval $[a, b]$. If we relax one or both of these requirements somewhat, we obtain what are called **improper integrals**. There are various types of improper integrals.

Integrals in Which a Limit of Integration Is Infinite

Integrals in which one or more limits of integration are infinite can be written as

$$\int_a^{+\infty} f(x)\,dx,\quad \int_{-\infty}^{b} f(x)\,dx,\quad \text{or}\quad \int_{-\infty}^{+\infty} f(x)\,dx.$$

Let's concentrate for a moment on the first form, $\int_a^{+\infty} f(x)\,dx$. What does the $+\infty$ mean here? As it often does, it means that we are to take a limit as something gets large. Specifically, it means the limit as the upper bound of integration gets large.

Improper Integral with an Infinite Limit of Integration

We define

$$\int_a^{+\infty} f(x)\,dx = \lim_{M\to+\infty} \int_a^{M} f(x)\,dx,$$

provided the limit exists. If the limit exists, we say that $\int_a^{+\infty} f(x)\,dx$ **converges**. Otherwise, we say that $\int_a^{+\infty} f(x)\,dx$ **diverges**. Similarly, we define

$$\int_{-\infty}^{b} f(x)\,dx = \lim_{M\to-\infty} \int_M^{b} f(x)\,dx,$$

provided the limit exists. Finally, we define

$$\int_{-\infty}^{+\infty} f(x)\,dx = \int_{-\infty}^{a} f(x)\,dx + \int_a^{+\infty} f(x)\,dx$$

for some convenient a, provided *both* integrals on the right converge.

Quick Examples

1. $\displaystyle\int_1^{+\infty} \frac{dx}{x^2} = \lim_{M\to+\infty} \int_1^{M} \frac{dx}{x^2} = \lim_{M\to+\infty} \left[-\frac{1}{x}\right]_1^M = \lim_{M\to+\infty} \left(-\frac{1}{M}+1\right) = 1$

   Converges

2. $\displaystyle\int_1^{+\infty} \frac{dx}{x} = \lim_{M\to+\infty} \int_1^{M} \frac{dx}{x} = \lim_{M\to+\infty} [\ln|x|]_1^M = \lim_{M\to+\infty} (\ln M - \ln 1) = +\infty$

   Diverges

3. $\displaystyle\int_{-\infty}^{-1} \frac{dx}{x^2} = \lim_{M\to-\infty} \int_M^{-1} \frac{dx}{x^2} = \lim_{M\to-\infty} \left[-\frac{1}{x}\right]_M^{-1} = \lim_{M\to-\infty} \left(1+\frac{1}{M}\right) = 1$

   Converges

4. $$\int_{-\infty}^{+\infty} e^{-x}\,dx = \int_{-\infty}^{0} e^{-x}\,dx + \int_{0}^{+\infty} e^{-x}\,dx$$
$$= \lim_{M\to-\infty}\int_{M}^{0} e^{-x}\,dx + \lim_{M\to+\infty}\int_{0}^{M} e^{-x}\,dx$$
$$= \lim_{M\to-\infty} -[e^{-x}]_M^0 + \lim_{M\to+\infty} -[e^{-x}]_0^M$$
$$= \lim_{M\to-\infty}(e^{-M}-1) + \lim_{M\to+\infty}(1-e^{-M})$$
$$= +\infty + 1$$
Diverges

5. $$\int_{-\infty}^{+\infty} xe^{-x^2}\,dx = \int_{-\infty}^{0} xe^{-x^2}\,dx + \int_{0}^{+\infty} xe^{-x^2}\,dx$$
$$= \lim_{M\to-\infty}\int_{M}^{0} xe^{-x^2}\,dx + \lim_{M\to+\infty}\int_{0}^{M} xe^{-x^2}\,dx$$
$$= \lim_{M\to-\infty}\left[-\frac{1}{2}e^{-x^2}\right]_M^0 + \lim_{M\to+\infty}\left[-\frac{1}{2}e^{-x^2}\right]_0^M$$
$$= \lim_{M\to-\infty}\left(-\frac{1}{2}+\frac{1}{2}e^{-M^2}\right) + \lim_{M\to+\infty}\left(-\frac{1}{2}e^{-M^2}+\frac{1}{2}\right)$$
$$= -\frac{1}{2}+\frac{1}{2} = 0$$
Converges

Q: *We learned that the integral can be interpreted as the area under the curve. Is this still true for improper integrals?*

A: Yes. Figure 22 illustrates how we can represent an improper integral as the area of an infinite region.

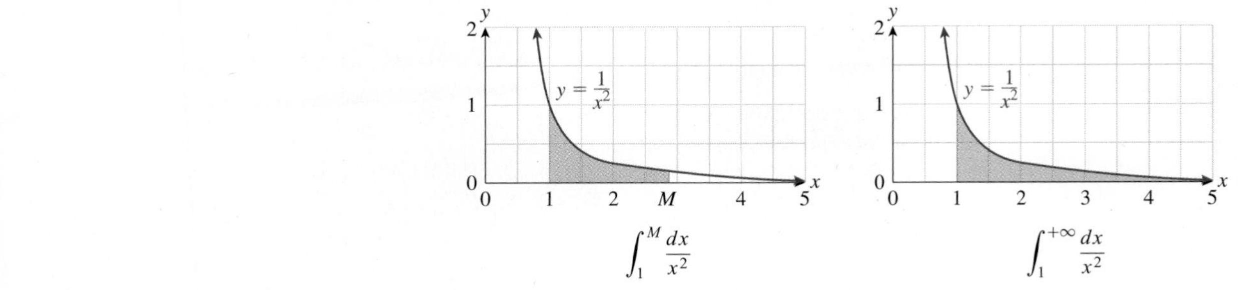

Figure 22

On the left we see the area represented by $\int_1^M dx/x^2$. As M gets larger, the integral approaches $\int_1^{+\infty} dx/x^2$. In the picture, think of M being moved farther and farther along the x-axis in the direction of increasing x, resulting in the region shown on the right.

Q: *Wait! We calculated $\int_1^{+\infty} dx/x^2 = 1$. Does this mean that the infinitely long area in Figure 22 has an area of only 1 square unit?*

A: That is exactly what it means. If you had enough paint to cover 1 square unit, you would never run out of paint while painting the region in Figure 22. This is one of the places where mathematics seems to contradict common sense. But common sense is notoriously unreliable when dealing with infinities.

Andy Crawford/Dorling Kindersley/ Getty Images

EXAMPLE 1 Future Sales of CDs

By 2009, music downloads were making serious inroads into the sales of physical CDs. Approximately 290 million CD albums were sold in 2009 and sales declined by about 23% per year the following year.[43] Suppose that this rate of decrease were to continue indefinitely and continuously. How many CD albums, total, would be sold from 2009 on?

Solution Recall that the total sales between two dates can be computed as the definite integral of the rate of sales. So, if we wanted the sales between 2009 and a time far in the future, we would compute $\int_0^M s(t)\,dt$ with a large M, where $s(t)$ is the annual sales t years after 2009. Because we want to know the *total* number of CD albums sold from 2009 on, we let $M \to +\infty$; that is, we compute $\int_0^{+\infty} s(t)\,dt$.

Because sales of CD albums are decreasing by 23% per year, we can model $s(t)$ by

$$s(t) = 290(0.77)^t \text{ million CD albums per year,}$$

where t is the number of years since 2009.

$$\begin{aligned}
\text{Total sales from 2009 on} &= \int_0^{+\infty} 290(0.77)^t\,dt \\
&= \lim_{M\to+\infty} \int_0^M 290(0.77)^t\,dt \\
&= \frac{290}{\ln 0.77} \lim_{M\to+\infty} [(0.77)^t]_0^M \\
&= \frac{290}{\ln 0.77} \lim_{M\to+\infty} (0.77^M - 0.77^0) \\
&= \frac{290}{\ln 0.77}(-1) \\
&\approx 1{,}110 \text{ million CD albums}
\end{aligned}$$

using Technology

You can estimate the integral in Example 1 with technology by computing $\int_0^M 290(0.77)^t\,dt$ for $M = 10, 100, 1000, \ldots$. You will find that the resulting values appear to converge to about 1,110. (Stop when the effect of further increases of M has no effect at this level of accuracy.)

TI-83/84 Plus

```
Y1=290*0.77^X
```

Home screen:

```
fnInt(Y1,X,0,10)
fnInt(Y1,X,0,100)
fnInt(Y1,X,0,1000)
```

Website

www.WanerMath.org:

On-Line Utilities

→ Numerical Integration Utility and Grapher

Enter

```
290*0.77^X
```

for $f(x)$. Enter 0 and 10 for the lower and upper limits and press "Integral" for the most accurate estimate of the integral.

Repeat with the upper limit set to 100, 1000, and higher.

Integrals in Which the Integrand Becomes Infinite

We can sometimes compute integrals $\int_a^b f(x)\,dx$ in which $f(x)$ becomes infinite. As we'll see in Example 4, the Fundamental Theorem of Calculus does not work for such integrals. The first case to consider is when $f(x)$ approaches $\pm\infty$ at either a or b.

[43]Source: *2010 Year-End Shipment Statistics*, Recording Industry Association of America (www.riaa.com).

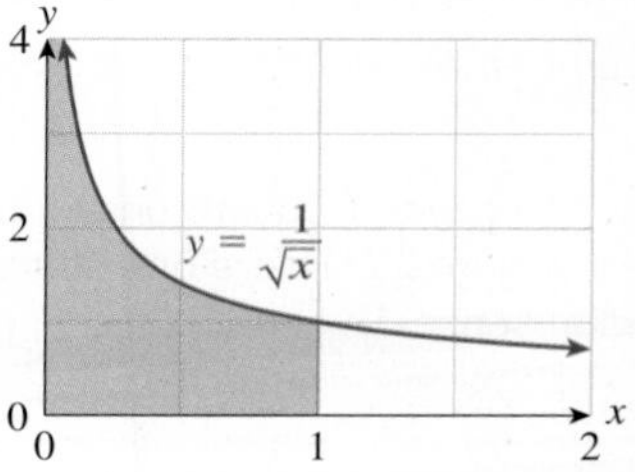

Figure 23

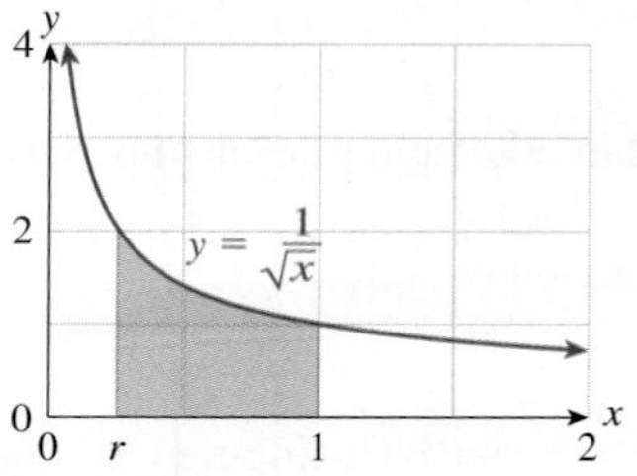

Figure 24

EXAMPLE 2 Integrand Infinite at One Endpoint

Calculate $\displaystyle\int_0^1 \frac{1}{\sqrt{x}}\,dx.$

Solution Notice that the integrand approaches $+\infty$ as x approaches 0 from the right and is not defined at 0. This makes the integral an improper integral. Figure 23 shows the region whose area we are trying to calculate; it extends infinitely vertically rather than horizontally.

Now, if $0 < r < 1$, the integral $\int_r^1 (1/\sqrt{x})\,dx$ is a proper integral because we avoid the bad behavior at 0. This integral gives the area shown in Figure 24. If we let r approach 0 from the right, the area in Figure 24 will approach the area in Figure 23. So, we calculate

$$\begin{aligned}\int_0^1 \frac{1}{\sqrt{x}}\,dx &= \lim_{r\to 0^+}\int_r^1 \frac{1}{\sqrt{x}}\,dx\\ &= \lim_{r\to 0^+}[2\sqrt{x}]_r^1\\ &= \lim_{r\to 0^+}(2-2\sqrt{r})\\ &= 2.\end{aligned}$$

Thus, we again have an infinitely long region with finite area.

Generalizing, we make the following definition.

Improper Integral in Which the Integrand Becomes Infinite

If $f(x)$ is defined for all x with $a < x \le b$ but approaches $\pm\infty$ as x approaches a, we define

$$\int_a^b f(x)\,dx = \lim_{r\to a^+}\int_r^b f(x)\,dx$$

provided the limit exists. Similarly, if $f(x)$ is defined for all x with $a \le x < b$ but approaches $\pm\infty$ as x approaches b, we define

$$\int_a^b f(x)\,dx = \lim_{r\to b^-}\int_a^r f(x)\,dx$$

provided the limit exists. In either case, if the limit exists, we say that $\int_a^b f(x)\,dx$ **converges**. Otherwise, we say that $\int_a^b f(x)\,dx$ **diverges**.

Note We saw in Chapter 6 that the Fundamental Theorem of Calculus applies to piecewise continuous functions as well as continuous ones. Examples are $f(x) = |x|/x$ and $(x^2-1)/(x-1)$. The integrals of such functions are not improper, and we can use the Fundamental Theorem of Calculus to evaluate such integrals in the usual way. ■

EXAMPLE 3 Testing for Convergence

Does $\int_{-1}^{3} \frac{x}{x^2-9}\,dx$ converge? If so, to what?

Solution We first check to see where, if anywhere, the integrand approaches $\pm\infty$. That will happen where the denominator becomes 0, so we solve $x^2 - 9 = 0$.

$$\begin{aligned} x^2 - 9 &= 0 \\ x^2 &= 9 \\ x &= \pm 3 \end{aligned}$$

The solution $x = -3$ is outside of the range of integration, so we ignore it. The solution $x = 3$ is, however, the right endpoint of the range of integration, so the integral is improper. We need to investigate the following limit:

$$\int_{-1}^{3} \frac{x}{x^2-9}\,dx = \lim_{r\to 3^-} \int_{-1}^{r} \frac{x}{x^2-9}\,dx.$$

Now, to calculate the integral we use a substitution:

$$\begin{aligned} u &= x^2 - 9 \\ \frac{du}{dx} &= 2x \\ dx &= \frac{1}{2x}\,du \end{aligned}$$
when $x = r$, $u = r^2 - 9$
when $x = -1$, $u = (-1)^2 - 9 = -8$

Thus,

$$\begin{aligned} \int_{-1}^{r} \frac{x}{x^2-9}\,dx &= \int_{-8}^{r^2-9} \frac{1}{2u}\,du \\ &= \frac{1}{2}[\ln|u|]_{-8}^{r^2-9} \\ &= \frac{1}{2}(\ln|r^2-9| - \ln 8). \end{aligned}$$

Now we take the limit:

$$\begin{aligned} \int_{-1}^{3} \frac{x}{x^2-9}\,dx &= \lim_{r\to 3^-} \int_{-1}^{r} \frac{x}{x^2-9}\,dx \\ &= \lim_{r\to 3^-} \frac{1}{2}(\ln|r^2-9| - \ln 8) \\ &= -\infty \end{aligned}$$

because, as $r \to 3$, $r^2 - 9 \to 0$, and so $\ln|r^2-9| \to -\infty$. Thus, this integral diverges.

EXAMPLE 4 Integrand Infinite between the Endpoints

Does $\int_{-2}^{3} \frac{1}{x^2}\,dx$ converge? If so, to what?

Solution Again we check to see if there are any points at which the integrand approaches $\pm\infty$. There is such a point, at $x = 0$. This is between the endpoints of the range of integration. To deal with this we break the integral into two integrals:

$$\int_{-2}^{3} \frac{1}{x^2}\,dx = \int_{-2}^{0} \frac{1}{x^2}\,dx + \int_{0}^{3} \frac{1}{x^2}\,dx.$$

Each integral on the right is an improper integral with the integrand approaching $\pm\infty$ at an endpoint. If both of the integrals on the right converge, we take the sum as the value of the integral on the left. So now we compute

$$\begin{aligned}\int_{-2}^{0} \frac{1}{x^2}\,dx &= \lim_{r\to 0^-} \int_{-2}^{r} \frac{1}{x^2}\,dx \\ &= \lim_{r\to 0^-} \left[-\frac{1}{x}\right]_{-2}^{r} \\ &= \lim_{r\to 0^-} \left(-\frac{1}{r} - \frac{1}{2}\right),\end{aligned}$$

which diverges to $+\infty$. There is no need now to check $\int_0^3 (1/x^2)\,dx$; because one of the two pieces of the integral diverges, we simply say that $\int_{-2}^{3} (1/x^2)\,dx$ diverges.

➡ **Before we go on...** What if we had been sloppy in Example 4 and had not checked first whether the integrand approached $\pm\infty$ somewhere? Then we probably would have applied the Fundamental Theorem of Calculus and done the following:

$$\int_{-2}^{3} \frac{1}{x^2}\,dx = \left(-\frac{1}{x}\right)_{-2}^{3} = \left(-\frac{1}{3} - \frac{1}{2}\right) = -\frac{5}{6}. \qquad ✗ \textit{ WRONG!}$$

Notice that the answer this "calculation" gives is patently ridiculous. Because $1/x^2 > 0$ for all x for which it is defined, any definite integral of $1/x^2$ must give a positive answer. *Moral:* Always check to see whether the integrand blows up anywhere in the range of integration. If it does, the FTC does not apply, and we must use the methods of this example. ■

We end with an example of what to do if an integral is improper for more than one reason.

EXAMPLE 5 An Integral Improper in Two Ways

Does $\int_{0}^{+\infty} \frac{1}{\sqrt{x}}\,dx$ converge? If so, to what?

Solution This integral is improper for two reasons. First, the range of integration is infinite. Second, the integrand blows up at the endpoint 0. In order to separate these two problems, we break up the integral at some convenient point:

$$\int_0^{+\infty} \frac{1}{\sqrt{x}}\,dx = \int_0^1 \frac{1}{\sqrt{x}}\,dx + \int_1^{+\infty} \frac{1}{\sqrt{x}}\,dx$$

We chose to break the integral at 1. Any positive number would have sufficed, but 1 is generally easier to use in calculations.

The first piece, $\int_0^1 (1/\sqrt{x})\,dx$, we discussed in Example 2; it converges to 2. For the second piece we have

$$\begin{aligned}\int_1^{+\infty} \frac{1}{\sqrt{x}}\,dx &= \lim_{M\to+\infty} \int_1^M \frac{1}{\sqrt{x}}\,dx \\ &= \lim_{M\to+\infty} [2\sqrt{x}]_1^M \\ &= \lim_{M\to+\infty} (2\sqrt{M} - 2),\end{aligned}$$

which diverges to $+\infty$. Because the second piece of the integral diverges, we conclude that $\int_0^{+\infty}(1/\sqrt{x})\,dx$ diverges.

7.5 EXERCISES

▼ more advanced ◆ challenging

T indicates exercises that should be solved using technology

Note: For some of the exercises in this section you need to assume the fact that $\lim_{M\to+\infty} M^n e^{-M} = 0$ for all $n \geq 0$. (See Exercises 59 and 60 in Section 3.1 and Exercise 103 in Section 3.3.)

In Exercises 1–26, decide whether or not the given integral converges. If the integral converges, compute its value. HINT [See Quick Examples page 559.]

1. $\int_1^{+\infty} x\,dx$

2. $\int_0^{+\infty} e^{-x}\,dx$

3. $\int_{-2}^{+\infty} e^{-0.5x}\,dx$

4. $\int_1^{+\infty} \frac{1}{x^{1.5}}\,dx$

5. $\int_{-\infty}^{2} e^x\,dx$

6. $\int_{-\infty}^{-1} \frac{1}{x^{1/3}}\,dx$

7. $\int_{-\infty}^{-2} \frac{1}{x^2}\,dx$

8. $\int_{-\infty}^{0} e^{-x}\,dx$

9. $\int_0^{+\infty} x^2 e^{-6x}\,dx$

10. $\int_0^{+\infty} (2x-4)e^{-x}\,dx$

11. $\int_0^5 \frac{2}{x^{1/3}}\,dx$ HINT [See Example 2.]

12. $\int_0^2 \frac{1}{x^2}\,dx$

13. $\int_{-1}^2 \frac{3}{(x+1)^2}\,dx$ HINT [See Example 3.]

14. $\int_{-1}^2 \frac{3}{(x+1)^{1/2}}\,dx$

15. $\int_{-1}^2 \frac{3x}{x^2-1}\,dx$ HINT [See Example 4.]

16. $\int_{-1}^2 \frac{3}{x^{1/3}}\,dx$

17. $\int_{-2}^2 \frac{1}{(x+1)^{1/5}}\,dx$

18. $\int_{-2}^2 \frac{2x}{\sqrt{4-x^2}}\,dx$

19. $\int_{-1}^1 \frac{2x}{x^2-1}\,dx$

20. $\int_{-1}^2 \frac{2x}{x^2-1}\,dx$

21. $\int_{-\infty}^{+\infty} xe^{-x^2}\,dx$

22. $\int_{-\infty}^{\infty} xe^{1-x^2}\,dx$

23. $\int_0^{+\infty} \frac{1}{x\ln x}\,dx$ HINT [See Example 5.]

24. $\int_0^{+\infty} \ln x\,dx$

25. ▼ $\int_0^{+\infty} \frac{2x}{x^2-1}\,dx$

26. ▼ $\int_{-\infty}^{0} \frac{2x}{x^2-1}\,dx$

T *In Exercises 27–34, use technology to approximate the given integrals with $M = 10, 100, 1{,}000, \ldots$ and hence decide whether the associated improper integral converges and estimate its value to four significant digits if it does.* HINT [See the Technology Note for Example 1.]

27. $\int_1^M \frac{1}{x^2}\,dx$

28. $\int_0^M e^{-x^2}\,dx$

29. $\int_0^M \frac{x}{1+x}\,dx$

30. $\int_{1/M}^1 \frac{1}{\sqrt{x}}\,dx$

31. $\int_{1+1/M}^2 \frac{1}{\sqrt{x-1}}\,dx$

32. $\int_1^M \frac{1}{x}\,dx$

33. $\int_0^{1-1/M} \frac{1}{(1-x)^2}\,dx$

34. $\int_0^{2-1/M} \frac{1}{(2-x)^3}\,dx$

APPLICATIONS

35. ***New Home Sales*** Sales of new homes in the United States decreased dramatically from 2005 to 2010 as shown in the model

$$n(t) = 1.33e^{-0.299t} \text{ million homes per year} \quad (0 \le t \le 5),$$

where t is the year since 2005.[44] If this trend were to have continued into the indefinite future, estimate the total number of new homes that would have been sold in the United States from 2005 on. HINT [See Example 1.]

36. ***Revenue from New Home Sales*** Revenue from the sale of new homes in the United States decreased dramatically from 2005 to 2010 as shown in the model

$$r(t) = 412e^{-0.323t} \text{ billion dollars per year} \quad (0 \le t \le 5),$$

where t is the year since 2005.[45] If this trend were to have continued into the indefinite future, estimate the total revenue from the sale of new homes in the United States from 2005 on. HINT [See Example 1.]

37. ***Cigarette Sales*** According to data published by the Federal Trade Commission, the number of cigarettes sold domestically has been decreasing by about 3% per year from the 2000 total of about 415 billion.[46] Use an exponential model to forecast the total number of cigarettes sold from 2000 on. (Round your answer to the nearest 100 billion cigarettes.) HINT [Use a model of the form Ab^t.]

38. ***Sales*** Sales of the text *Calculus and You* have been declining continuously at a rate of 5% per year. Assuming that *Calculus and You* currently sells 5,000 copies per year and that sales will continue this pattern of decline, calculate total future sales of the text. HINT [Use a model of the form Ae^{rt}.]

39. ▼ ***Sales*** My financial adviser has predicted that annual sales of Frodo T-shirts will continue to decline by 10% each year. At the moment, I have 3,200 of the shirts in stock and am selling them at a rate of 200 per year. Will I ever sell them all?

40. ▼ ***Revenue*** Alarmed about the sales prospects for my Frodo T-shirts (see the preceding exercise), I will try to make up lost revenues by increasing the price by \$1 each year. I now charge \$10 per shirt. What is the total amount of revenue I can expect to earn from sales of my T-shirts, assuming the sales levels described in the previous exercise? (Give your answer to the nearest \$1,000.)

41. ▼ ***Education*** Let $N(t)$ be the number of high school students graduated in the United States in year t. This number has been changing at a rate of about

$$N'(t) = 0.22t^{-0.91} \text{ million graduates per year} \quad (2 \le t \le 9),$$

where t is time in years since 2000.[47] In 2002, there were about 2.7 million high school students graduated. By extrapolating the model, what can you say about the number of high school students graduated in a year far in the future?

42. ▼ ***Education, Martian*** Let $M(t)$ be the number of high school students graduated in the Republic of Mars in year t. This number is projected to change at a rate of about

$$M'(t) = 0.321t^{-1.10} \text{ thousand graduates per year} \quad (1 \le t \le 50),$$

where t is time in years since 2020. In 2021, there were about 1,300 high school students graduated. By extrapolating the model, what can you say about the number of high school students graduated in a year far in the future?

43. ▼ ***Cellphone Revenues*** The number of cellphone subscribers in China in the early 2000s was projected to follow the equation,[48]

$$N(t) = 39t + 68 \text{ million subscribers}$$

in year t ($t = 0$ represents 2000). The average annual revenue per cellphone user was \$350 in 2000.

a. Assuming that, due to competition, the revenue per cellphone user decreases continuously at an annual rate of 10%, give a formula for the annual revenue in year t.

b. Using the model you obtained in part (a) as an estimate of the rate of change of total revenue, estimate the total revenue from 2000 into the indefinite future.

---

[44] Based on new home sales data from the U.S. Census Bureau (www.census.gov/const/www/newressalesindex.html).

[45] *Ibid.*

[46] Source for data: Federal Trade Commission Cigarette Report for 2007 and 2008, issued July 2011 (www.ftc.gov).

[47] Based on a regression model. Source for Data: U.S. Department of Education, National Center for Education Statistics, *Digest of Education Statistics: 2010,* April 2011 (nces.ed.gov).

[48] Based on a regression of projected figures (coefficients are rounded). Source: Intrinsic Technology/*New York Times*, Nov. 24, 2000, p. C1.

44. ▼ ***Vidphone Revenues*** The number of vidphone subscribers in the Republic of Mars for the period 2200–2300 was projected to follow the equation

$$N(t) = 18t - 10 \text{ thousand subscribers}$$

in year t ($t = 0$ represents 2200). The average annual revenue per vidphone user was Z40 in 2200.[49]

a. Assuming that, due to competition, the revenue per vidphone user decreases continuously at an annual rate of 20%, give a formula for the annual revenue in year t.

b. Using the model you obtained in part (a) as an estimate of the rate of change of total revenue, estimate the total revenue from 2200 into the indefinite future.

45. T ***Development Assistance*** According to data published by the World Bank, development assistance to low-income countries from 2000 through 2008 was approximately

$$q(t) = 0.2t^2 + 3.5t + 60 \text{ billion dollars per year}$$

where t is time in years since 2000.[50] Assuming a worldwide inflation rate of 3% per year, and that the above model remains accurate into the indefinite future, find the value of all development assistance to low-income countries from 2000 on in constant dollars. (The constant dollar value of $q(t)$ dollars t years from now is given by $q(t)e^{-rt}$, where r is the fractional rate of inflation. Give your answer to the nearest \$100 billion.) HINT [See Technology Note for Example 1.]

46. T ***Humanitarian Aid*** Repeat the preceding exercise, using the following model for humanitarian aid.[51]

$$q(t) = 0.07t^2 + 0.3t + 5 \text{ billion dollars per year}$$

47. ▼ ***Hair Mousse Sales*** The amount of extremely popular hair mousse sold online at your Web site can be approximated by

$$N(t) = \frac{80(7)^t}{20 + 7^t} \text{ million gallons per year.}$$

($t = 0$ represents the current year.) Investigate the integrals $\int_0^{+\infty} N(t)\,dt$ and $\int_{-\infty}^0 N(t)\,dt$ and interpret your answers.

48. ▼ ***Chocolate Mousse Sales*** The weekly demand for your company's *Lo-Cal Chocolate Mousse* is modeled by the equation

$$q(t) = \frac{50e^{2t-1}}{1 + e^{2t-1}} \text{ gallons per week,}$$

where t is time from now in weeks. Investigate the integrals $\int_0^{+\infty} q(t)\,dt$ and $\int_{-\infty}^0 q(t)\,dt$ and interpret your answers.

T ***The Normal Curve*** *Exercises 49–52 require the use of a graphing calculator or computer programmed to do numerical integration. The normal distribution curve, which models the distributions of data in a wide range of applications, is given by the function*

$$p(x) = \frac{1}{\sqrt{2\pi}\sigma} e^{-(x-\mu)^2/2\sigma^2},$$

where $\pi = 3.14159265\ldots$ *and* σ *and* μ *are constants called the standard deviation and the mean, respectively. Its graph (for* $\sigma = 1$ *and* $\mu = 2$*) is shown in the figure.*

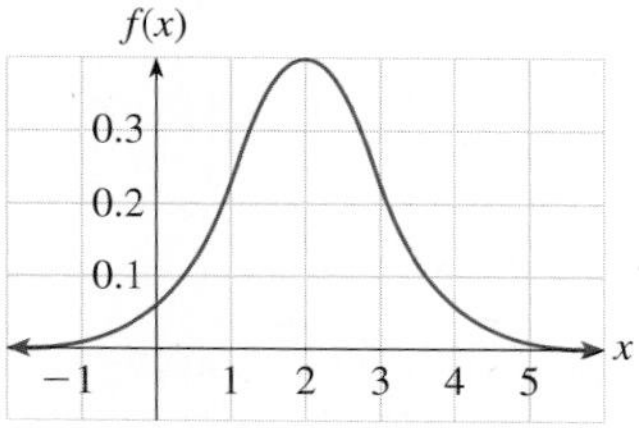

49. ▼ With $\sigma = 4$ and $\mu = 1$, approximate $\int_{-\infty}^{+\infty} p(x)\,dx$. HINT [See Example 5 and Technology Note for Example 1.]

50. ▼ With $\sigma = 1$ and $\mu = 0$, approximate $\int_0^{+\infty} p(x)\,dx$.

51. ▼ With $\sigma = 1$ and $\mu = 0$, approximate $\int_1^{+\infty} p(x)\,dx$.

52. ▼ With $\sigma = 1$ and $\mu = 0$, approximate $\int_{-\infty}^{1} p(x)\,dx$.

53. ◆ ***Variable Sales*** The value of your Chateau Petit Mont Blanc 1963 vintage burgundy is increasing continuously at an annual rate of 40%, and you have a supply of 1,000 bottles worth \$85 each at today's prices. In order to ensure a steady income, you have decided to sell your wine at a diminishing rate—starting at 500 bottles per year, and then decreasing this figure continuously at a fractional rate of 100% per year. How much income (to the nearest dollar) can you expect to generate by this scheme? HINT [Use the formula for continuously compounded interest.]

54. ◆ ***Panic Sales*** Unfortunately, your large supply of Chateau Petit Mont Blanc is continuously turning to vinegar at a fractional rate of 60% per year! You have thus decided to sell off your Petit Mont Blanc at \$50 per bottle, but the market is a little thin, and you can only sell 400 bottles per year. Because you have no way of knowing which bottles now contain vinegar until they are opened, you shall have to give refunds for all the bottles of vinegar. What will your net income be before all the wine turns to vinegar?

55. ◆ ***Meteor Impacts*** The frequency of meteor impacts on Earth can be modeled by

$$n(k) = \frac{1}{5.6997k^{1.081}}$$

where $n(k) = N'(k)$, and $N(k)$ is the average number of meteors of energy less than or equal to k megatons that will

---

[49] The zonar (Z) is the official currency in the city-state of Utarek, Mars. Source: www.Marsnext.com, a now extinct virtual society.

[50] The authors' approximation, based on data from the World Bank, obtained from www.worldbank.org.

[51] *Ibid.*

hit the Earth in one year.[52] (A small nuclear bomb releases on the order of one megaton of energy.)

a. How many meteors of energy at least $k = 0.2$ hit the Earth each year?

b. Investigate and interpret the integral $\int_0^1 n(k)\,dk$.

56. ◆ ***Meteor Impacts*** (continuing the previous exercise)

a. Explain why the integral

$$\int_a^b kn(k)\,dk$$

computes the total energy released each year by meteors with energies between a and b megatons.

b. Compute and interpret

$$\int_0^1 kn(k)\,dk.$$

c. Compute and interpret

$$\int_1^{+\infty} kn(k)\,dk.$$

57. ◆ ***The Gamma Function*** The gamma function is defined by the formula

$$\Gamma(x) = \int_0^{+\infty} t^{x-1}e^{-t}\,dt.$$

a. Find $\Gamma(1)$ and $\Gamma(2)$.

b. Use integration by parts to show that for every positive integer n, $\Gamma(n+1) = n\Gamma(n)$.

c. Deduce that $\Gamma(n) = (n-1)!\,[= (n-1)(n-2)\cdots 2\cdot 1]$ for every positive integer n.

58. ◆ ***Laplace Transforms*** The Laplace transform $F(x)$ of a function $f(t)$ is given by the formula

$$F(x) = \int_0^{+\infty} f(t)e^{-xt}\,dt \quad (x > 0).$$

a. Find $F(x)$ for $f(t) = 1$ and for $f(t) = t$.

b. Find a formula for $F(x)$ if $f(t) = t^n$ $(n = 1, 2, 3, \ldots)$.

c. Find a formula for $F(x)$ if $f(t) = e^{at}$ (a constant).

[52]The authors' model, based on data published by NASA International Near-Earth-Object Detection Workshop (*The New York Times*, Jan. 25, 1994, p. C1).

COMMUNICATION AND REASONING EXERCISES

59. Why can't the Fundamental Theorem of Calculus be used to evaluate $\displaystyle\int_{-1}^{1} \frac{1}{x}\,dx$?

60. Why can't the Fundamental Theorem of Calculus be used to evaluate $\displaystyle\int_{1}^{+\infty} \frac{1}{x^2}\,dx$?

61. It sometimes happens that the Fundamental Theorem of Calculus gives the correct answer for an improper integral. Does the FTC give the correct answer for improper integrals of the form

$$\int_{-a}^{a} \frac{1}{x^{1/r}}\,dx$$

if $r = 3, 5, 7, \ldots$?

62. Does the FTC give the correct answer for improper integrals of the form

$$\int_{-a}^{a} \frac{1}{x^r}\,dx$$

if $r = 3, 5, 7, \ldots$?

63. Which of the following integrals are improper, and why? (Do not evaluate any of them.)

a. $\displaystyle\int_{-1}^{1} \frac{|x|}{x}\,dx$ **b.** $\displaystyle\int_{-1}^{1} x^{-1/3}\,dx$

c. $\displaystyle\int_{0}^{2} \frac{x-2}{x^2-4x+4}\,dx$

64. Which of the following integrals are improper, and why? (Do not evaluate any of them.)

a. $\displaystyle\int_{-1}^{1} \frac{|x-1|}{x-1}\,dx$ **b.** $\displaystyle\int_{0}^{1} \frac{1}{x^{2/3}}\,dx$

c. $\displaystyle\int_{0}^{2} \frac{x^2-4x+4}{x-2}\,dx$

65. T ▼ How could you use technology to approximate improper integrals? (Your discussion should refer to each type of improper integral.)

66. T ▼ Use technology to approximate the integrals $\int_0^M e^{-(x-10)^2}\,dx$ for larger and larger values of M, using Riemann sums with 500 subdivisions. What do you find? Comment on the answer.

67. ▼ Make up an interesting application whose solution is $\int_{10}^{+\infty} 100te^{-0.2t}dt = \$1{,}015.01$.

68. ▼ Make up an interesting application whose solution is $\int_{100}^{+\infty} \frac{1}{r^2}\,dr = 0.01$.

7.6 Differential Equations and Applications

A **differential equation** is an equation that involves a derivative of an unknown function. A **first-order differential equation** involves only the first derivative of the unknown function. A **second-order differential equation** involves the second derivative of the unknown function (and possibly the first derivative). Higher order differential equations are defined similarly. In this book, we will deal only with first-order differential equations.

To **solve** a differential equation means to find the unknown function. Many of the laws of science and other fields describe how things change. When expressed mathematically, these laws take the form of equations involving derivatives—that is, differential equations. The field of differential equations is a large and very active area of study in mathematics, and we shall see only a small part of it in this section.

EXAMPLE 1 Motion

A dragster accelerates from a stop so that its speed t seconds after starting is $40t$ ft/sec. How far will the car go in 8 seconds?

Solution We wish to find the car's position function $s(t)$. We are told about its speed, which is ds/dt. Precisely, we are told that

$$\frac{ds}{dt} = 40t.$$

This is the differential equation we have to solve to find $s(t)$. But we already know how to solve this kind of differential equation; we integrate:

$$s(t) = \int 40t\ dt = 20t^2 + C.$$

We now have the **general solution** to the differential equation. By letting C take on different values, we get all the possible solutions. We can specify the one **particular solution** that gives the answer to our problem by imposing the **initial condition** that $s(0) = 0$. Substituting into $s(t) = 20t^2 + C$, we get

$$0 = s(0) = 20(0)^2 + C = C$$

so $C = 0$ and $s(t) = 20t^2$. To answer the question, the car travels $20(8)^2 = 1{,}280$ feet in 8 seconds.

We did not have to work hard to solve the differential equation in Example 1. In fact, any differential equation of the form $dy/dx = f(x)$ can (in theory) be solved by integrating. (Whether we can actually carry out the integration is another matter!)

Simple Differential Equations

A **simple** differential equation has the form

$$\frac{dy}{dx} = f(x).$$

Its general solution is

$$y = \int f(x)\,dx.$$

Quick Example

The differential equation

$$\frac{dy}{dx} = 2x^2 - 4x^3$$

is simple and has general solution

$$y = \int f(x)\,dx = \frac{2x^3}{3} - x^4 + C.$$

Not all differential equations are simple, as the next example shows.

EXAMPLE 2 Separable Differential Equation

Consider the differential equation $\dfrac{dy}{dx} = \dfrac{x}{y^2}$.

a. Find the general solution.

b. Find the particular solution that satisfies the initial condition $y(0) = 2$.

Solution

a. This is not a simple differential equation because the right-hand side is a function of both x and y. We cannot solve this equation by just integrating; the solution to this problem is to "separate" the variables.

Step 1: *Separate the variables algebraically.* We rewrite the equation as

$$y^2\,dy = x\,dx.$$

Step 2: *Integrate both sides.*

$$\int y^2\,dy = \int x\,dx$$

giving

$$\frac{y^3}{3} = \frac{x^2}{2} + C$$

Step 3: *Solve for the dependent variable.* We solve for y:

$$y^3 = \frac{3}{2}x^2 + 3C = \frac{3}{2}x^2 + D$$

(Rewriting $3C$ as D, an equally arbitrary constant), so

$$y = \left(\frac{3}{2}x^2 + D\right)^{1/3}.$$

This is the general solution of the differential equation.

b. We now need to find the value for D that will give us the solution satisfying the condition $y(0) = 2$. Substituting 0 for x and 2 for y in the general solution, we get

$$2 = \left(\frac{3}{2}(0)^2 + D\right)^{1/3} = D^{1/3}$$

so

$$D = 2^3 = 8.$$

Thus, the particular solution we are looking for is

$$y = \left(\frac{3}{2}x^2 + 8\right)^{1/3}.$$

➡ **Before we go on...** We can check the general solution in Example 2 by calculating both sides of the differential equation and comparing.

$$\frac{dy}{dx} = \frac{d}{dx}\left(\frac{3}{2}x^2 + D\right)^{1/3} = x\left(\frac{3}{2}x^2 + D\right)^{-2/3}$$

$$\frac{x}{y^2} = \frac{x}{\left(\frac{3}{2}x^2 + 8\right)^{2/3}} = x\left(\frac{3}{2}x^2 + D\right)^{-2/3} \quad ✔$$

■

Q: *In Example 2, we wrote $y^2\,dy$ and $x\,dx$. What do they mean?*

A: Although it is possible to give meaning to these symbols, for us they are just a notational convenience. We could have done the following instead:

$$y^2\frac{dy}{dx} = x.$$

Now we integrate both sides with respect to x.

$$\int y^2\frac{dy}{dx}\,dx = \int x\,dx$$

We can use substitution to rewrite the left-hand side:

$$\int y^2\frac{dy}{dx}\,dx = \int y^2\,dy,$$

which brings us back to the equation

$$\int y^2\,dy = \int x\,dx.$$

We were able to separate the variables in the preceding example because the right-hand side, x/y^2, was a *product* of a function of x and a function of y—namely,

$$\frac{x}{y^2} = x\left(\frac{1}{y^2}\right).$$

In general, we can say the following:

Separable Differential Equation

A **separable** differential equation has the form

$$\frac{dy}{dx} = f(x)g(y).$$

We solve a separable differential equation by separating the xs and the ys algebraically, writing

$$\frac{1}{g(y)}\,dy = f(x)\,dx$$

and then integrating:

$$\int \frac{1}{g(y)}\,dy = \int f(x)\,dx.$$

EXAMPLE 3 Rising Medical Costs

Spending on Medicare from 2010 to 2021 was projected to rise continuously at an instantaneous rate of 5.6% per year.[53] Find a formula for Medicare spending y as a function of time t in years since 2010.

Solution When we say that Medicare spending y was going up continuously at an instantaneous rate of 5.6% per year, we mean that

the instantaneous rate of increase of y was 5.6% of its value

or
$$\frac{dy}{dt} = 0.056y.$$

This is a separable differential equation. Separating the variables gives

$$\frac{1}{y}dy = 0.056\,dt.$$

Integrating both sides, we get

$$\int \frac{1}{y}\,dy = \int 0.056\,dt$$

so
$$\ln y = 0.056t + C.$$

(We should write $\ln|y|$, but we know that the medical costs are positive.) We now solve for y.

$$y = e^{0.056t+C} = e^{C}e^{0.056t} = Ae^{0.056t},$$

where A is a positive constant. This is the formula we used before for continuous percentage growth.

[53]Spending is in constant 2010 dollars. Source for projected data: Congressional Budget Office, *March 2011 Medicare Baseline* (www.cbo.gov).

➡ **Before we go on...** To determine A in Example 3 we need to know, for example, Medicare spending at time $t = 0$ (the initial condition). The source cited gives Medicare spending as \$525.6 billion in 2010. Substituting $t = 0$ in the equation above gives

$$525.6 = Ae^0 = A.$$

Thus, projected Medicare spending is

$$y = 525.6e^{0.056t} \text{ billion dollars}$$

t years after 2010. ■

EXAMPLE 4 Newton's Law of Cooling

Newton's Law of Cooling states that a hot object cools at a rate proportional to the difference between its temperature and the temperature of the surrounding environment (the **ambient temperature**). If a hot cup of coffee, at 170°F, is left to sit in a room at 70°F, how will the temperature of the coffee change over time?

Solution We let $H(t)$ denote the temperature of the coffee at time t. Newton's Law of Cooling tells us that $H(t)$ *decreases* at a rate proportional to the difference between $H(t)$ and 70°F, the ambient temperature. In other words,

$$\frac{dH}{dt} = -k(H - 70),$$

where k is some positive constant.* Note that $H \geq 70$: The coffee will never cool to less than the ambient temperature.

* When we say that a quantity Q is *proportional* to a quantity R, we mean that $Q = kR$ for some constant k. The constant k is referred to as the **constant of proportionality**.

The variables here are H and t, which we can separate as follows:

$$\frac{dH}{H - 70} = -k\,dt.$$

Integrating, we get

$$\int \frac{dH}{H - 70} = \int (-k)\,dt$$

so $\quad \ln(H - 70) = -kt + C.$

(Note that $H - 70$ is positive, so we don't need absolute values.) We now solve for H:

$$H - 70 = e^{-kt+C}$$
$$= e^C e^{-kt}$$
$$= Ae^{-kt}$$

so

$$H(t) = 70 + Ae^{-kt},$$

where A is some positive constant. We can determine the constant A using the initial condition $H(0) = 170$:

$$170 = 70 + Ae^0 = 70 + A$$

so $\quad A = 100.$

Therefore,

$$H(t) = 70 + 100e^{-kt}.$$

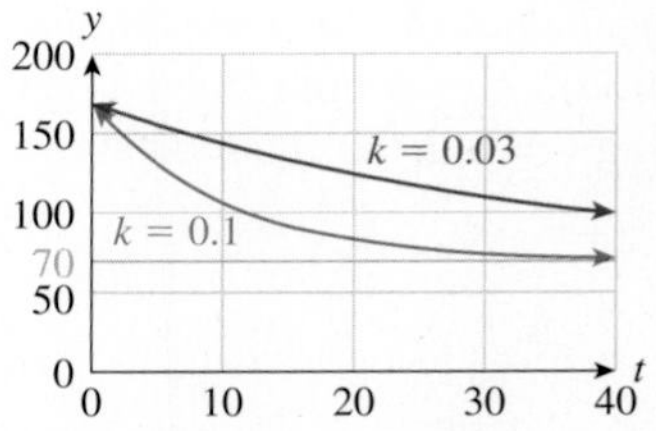

Figure 25

Q: *But what is k?*

A: The constant k determines the rate of cooling. Its value depends on the units of time we are using, on the substance cooling—in this case the coffee—and on its container. Because k depends so heavily on the particular circumstances, it's usually easiest to determine it experimentally. Figure 25 shows two possible graphs, one with $k = 0.1$ and the other with $k = 0.03$ ($k \approx 0.03$ would be reasonable for a cup of coffee in a polystyrene container with t measured in minutes).

In any case, we can see from the graph or the formula for $H(t)$ that the temperature of the coffee will approach the ambient temperature exponentially.

Before we go on... Notice that the calculation in Example 4 shows that the temperature of an object cooling according to Newton's Law is given in general by

$$H(t) = T_a + (T_0 - T_a)e^{-kt},$$

where T_a is the ambient temperature (70° in the example) and T_0 is the initial temperature (170° in the example). The formula also holds if the ambient temperature is higher than the initial temperature ("Newton's Law of Heating"). ■

7.6 EXERCISES

▼ more advanced ◆ challenging

T indicates exercises that should be solved using technology

Find the general solution of each differential equation in Exercises 1–10. Where possible, solve for y as a function of x.

1. $\dfrac{dy}{dx} = x^2 + \sqrt{x}$ HINT [See Quick Example page 570.]
2. $\dfrac{dy}{dx} = \dfrac{1}{x} + 3$ HINT [See Quick Example page 570.]
3. $\dfrac{dy}{dx} = \dfrac{x}{y}$ HINT [See Example 2(a).]
4. $\dfrac{dy}{dx} = \dfrac{y}{x}$ HINT [See Example 2(a).]
5. $\dfrac{dy}{dx} = xy$
6. $\dfrac{dy}{dx} = x^2y$
7. $\dfrac{dy}{dx} = (x+1)y^2$
8. $\dfrac{dy}{dx} = \dfrac{1}{(x+1)y^2}$
9. $x\dfrac{dy}{dx} = \dfrac{1}{y}\ln x$
10. $\dfrac{1}{x}\dfrac{dy}{dx} = \dfrac{1}{y}\ln x$

For each differential equation in Exercises 11–20, find the particular solution indicated. HINT [See Example 2(b).]

11. $\dfrac{dy}{dx} = x^3 - 2x;\ y = 1$ when $x = 0$
12. $\dfrac{dy}{dx} = 2 - e^{-x};\ y = 0$ when $x = 0$
13. $\dfrac{dy}{dx} = \dfrac{x^2}{y^2};\ y = 2$ when $x = 0$
14. $\dfrac{dy}{dx} = \dfrac{y^2}{x^2};\ y = \dfrac{1}{2}$ when $x = 1$
15. $x\dfrac{dy}{dx} = y;\ y(1) = 2$
16. $x^2\dfrac{dy}{dx} = y;\ y(1) = 1$
17. $\dfrac{dy}{dx} = x(y+1);\ y(0) = 0$
18. $\dfrac{dy}{dx} = \dfrac{y+1}{x};\ y(1) = 2$
19. $\dfrac{dy}{dx} = \dfrac{xy^2}{x^2+1};\ y(0) = -1$
20. $\dfrac{dy}{dx} = \dfrac{xy}{(x^2+1)^2};\ y(0) = 1$

APPLICATIONS

21. ***Sales*** Your monthly sales of Green Tea Ice Cream are falling at an instantaneous rate of 5% per month. If you currently sell 1,000 quarts per month, find the differential equation describing your change in sales, and then solve it to predict your monthly sales. HINT [See Example 3.]
22. ***Profit*** Your monthly profit on sales of Avocado Ice Cream is rising at an instantaneous rate of 10% per month. If you currently make a profit of $15,000 per month, find the differential equation describing your change in profit, and solve it to predict your monthly profits. HINT [See Example 3.]
23. ***Newton's Law of Cooling*** For coffee in a ceramic cup, suppose $k \approx 0.05$ with time measured in minutes. **(a)** Use Newton's Law of Cooling to predict the temperature of the coffee, initially at a temperature of 200°F, that is left to sit in a room at 75°F. **(b)** When will the coffee have cooled to 80°F? HINT [See Example 4.]

24. ***Newton's Law of Cooling*** For coffee in a paper cup, suppose $k \approx 0.08$ with time measured in minutes. **(a)** Use Newton's Law of Cooling to predict the temperature of the coffee, initially at a temperature of 210°F, that is left to sit in a room at 60°F. **(b)** When will the coffee have cooled to 70°F? HINT [See Example 4.]

25. ***Cooling*** A bowl of clam chowder at 190°F is placed in a room whose air temperature is 75°F. After 10 minutes, the soup has cooled to 150°F. Find the value of k in Newton's Law of Cooling, and hence find the temperature of the chowder as a function of time.

26. ***Heating*** Suppose that a pie, at 20°F, is put in an oven at 350°F. After 15 minutes, its temperature has risen to 80°F. Find the value of k in Newton's Law of Heating (see the note after Example 4), and hence find the temperature of the pie as a function of time.

27. ***Market Saturation*** You have just introduced a new 3D monitor to the market. You predict that you will eventually sell 100,000 monitors and that your monthly rate of sales will be 10% of the difference between the saturation value of 100,000 and the total number you have sold up to that point. Find a differential equation for your total sales (as a function of the month) and solve. (What are your total sales at the moment when you first introduce the monitor?)

28. ***Market Saturation*** Repeat the preceding exercise, assuming that monthly sales will be 5% of the difference between the saturation value (of 100,000 monitors) and the total sales to that point, and assuming that you sell 5,000 monitors to corporate customers before placing the monitor on the open market.

29. ***Determining Demand*** *Nancy's Chocolates* estimates that the elasticity of demand for its dark chocolate truffles is $E = 0.05p - 1.5$ where p is the price per pound. Nancy's sells 20 pounds of truffles per week when the price is \$20 per pound. Find the formula expressing the demand q as a function of p. Recall that the elasticity of demand is given by

$$E = -\frac{dq}{dp} \times \frac{p}{q}.$$

30. ***Determining Demand*** *Nancy's Chocolates* estimates that the elasticity of demand for its chocolate strawberries is $E = 0.02p - 0.5$ where p is the price per pound. It sells 30 pounds of chocolate strawberries per week when the price is \$30 per pound. Find the formula expressing the demand q as a function of p. Recall that the elasticity of demand is given by

$$E = -\frac{dq}{dp} \times \frac{p}{q}.$$

Linear Differential Equations *Exercises 31–36 are based on* ***first-order linear differential equations with constant coefficients****. These have the form*

$$\frac{dy}{dt} + py = f(t) \quad (p \text{ constant})$$

and the general solution is

$$y = e^{-pt} \int f(t)e^{pt}\, dt. \quad \textit{(Check this by substituting!)}$$

31. Solve the linear differential equation

$$\frac{dy}{dt} + y = e^{-t};\ y = 1 \text{ when } t = 0.$$

32. Solve the linear differential equation

$$\frac{dy}{dt} - y = e^{2t};\ y = 2 \text{ when } t = 0.$$

33. Solve the linear differential equation

$$2\frac{dy}{dt} - y = 2t;\ y = 1 \text{ when } t = 0.$$

HINT [First rewrite the differential equation in the form $\frac{dy}{dt} + py = f(t)$.]

34. Solve the linear differential equation

$$2\frac{dy}{dt} + y = -t. \quad y = 1 \text{ when } t = 0$$

HINT [First rewrite the differential equation in the form $\frac{dy}{dt} + py = f(t)$.]

35. ▼ ***Electric Circuits*** The flow of current $i(t)$ in an electric circuit without capacitance satisfies the linear differential equation

$$L\frac{di}{dt} + Ri = V(t),$$

where L and R are constants (the *inductance* and *resistance,* respectively) and $V(t)$ is the applied voltage. (See figure.)

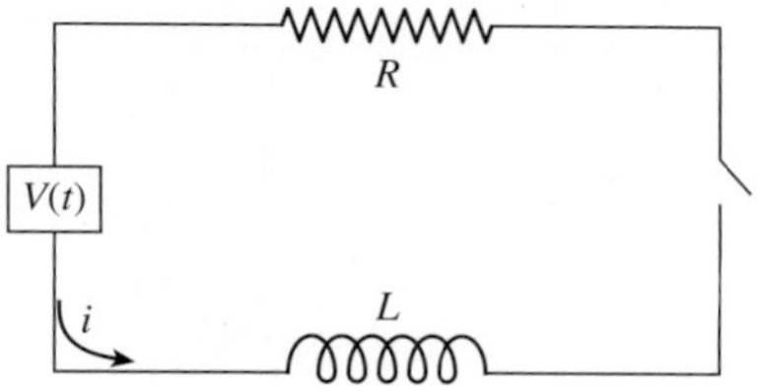

If the voltage is supplied by a 10-volt battery and the switch is turned on at time $t = 1$, then the voltage V is a step function that jumps from 0 to 10 at $t = 1$: $V(t) = 5\left[1 + \frac{|t-1|}{t-1}\right]$. Find the current as a function of time for $L = R = 1$. Use a grapher to plot the resulting current as a function of time. (Assume there is no current flowing at time $t = 0$.) [Use the following integral formula: $\int \left[1 + \frac{|t-1|}{t-1}\right] e^t\, dt = \left[1 + \frac{|t-1|}{t-1}\right](e^t - e) + C$.]

36. ▼ ***Electric Circuits*** Repeat Exercise 35 for $L = 1$, $R = 5$, and $V(t) = 5\left[1 + \frac{|t-2|}{t-2}\right]$. (The switch flipped on at time $t = 2$.) [Use the following integral formula: $\int \left[1 + \frac{|t-2|}{t-2}\right] e^{5t}\, dt = \left(1 + \frac{|t-2|}{t-2}\right)\left(\frac{e^{5t} - e^{10}}{5}\right) + C$.]

37. ▼ ***Approach to Equilibrium*** The *Extrasoft Toy Co.* has just released its latest creation, a plush platypus named "Eggbert." The demand function for Eggbert dolls is $D(p) = 50{,}000 - 500p$ dolls per month when the price is p dollars. The supply function is $S(p) = 30{,}000 + 500p$ dolls per month when the price is p dollars. This makes the equilibrium price \$20. The **Evans price adjustment model** assumes that if the price is set at a value other than the equilibrium price, it will change over time in such a way that its rate of change is proportional to the shortage $D(p) - S(p)$.

   a. Write the differential equation given by the Evans price adjustment model for the price p as a function of time.

   b. Find the general solution of the differential equation you wrote in (a). (You will have two unknown constants, one being the constant of proportionality.)

   c. Find the particular solution in which Eggbert dolls are initially priced at \$10 and the price rises to \$12 after one month.

38. ▼ ***Approach to Equilibrium*** *Spacely Sprockets* has just released its latest model, the Dominator. The demand function is $D(p) = 10{,}000 - 1{,}000p$ sprockets per year when the price is p dollars. The supply function is $S(p) = 8{,}000 + 1{,}000p$ sprockets per year when the price is p dollars.

   a. Using the Evans price adjustment model described in the preceding exercise, write the differential equation for the price $p(t)$ as a function of time.

   b. Find the general solution of the differential equation you wrote in (a).

   c. Find the particular solution in which Dominator sprockets are initially priced at \$5 each but fall to \$3 each after one year.

39. ▼ ***Logistic Equation*** There are many examples of growth in which the rate of growth is slow at first, becomes faster, and then slows again as a limit is reached. This pattern can be described by the differential equation

$$\frac{dy}{dt} = ay(L - y),$$

where a is a constant and L is the limit of y. Show by substitution that

$$y = \frac{CL}{e^{-aLt} + C}$$

is a solution of this equation, where C is an arbitrary constant.

40. ▼ ***Logistic Equation*** Using separation of variables and integration with a table of integrals or a symbolic algebra program, solve the differential equation in the preceding exercise to derive the solution given there.

T *Exercises 41–44 require the use of technology.*

41. ▼ ***Market Saturation*** You have just introduced a new model of Blu-ray disc player. You predict that the market will saturate at 2,000,000 Blu-ray disc players and that your total sales will be governed by the equation

$$\frac{dS}{dt} = \frac{1}{4}S(2 - S),$$

where S is the total sales in millions of Blu-ray disc players and t is measured in months. If you give away 1,000 Blu-ray disc players when you first introduce them, what will S be? Sketch the graph of S as a function of t. About how long will it take to saturate the market? (See Exercise 39.)

42. ▼ ***Epidemics*** A certain epidemic of influenza is predicted to follow the function defined by

$$\frac{dA}{dt} = \frac{1}{10}A(20 - A),$$

where A is the number of people infected in millions and t is the number of months after the epidemic starts. If 20,000 cases are reported initially, find $A(t)$ and sketch its graph. When is A growing fastest? How many people will eventually be affected? (See Exercise 39.)

43. ▼ ***Growth of Tumors*** The growth of tumors in animals can be modeled by the Gompertz equation:

$$\frac{dy}{dt} = -ay\ln\left(\frac{y}{b}\right),$$

where y is the size of a tumor, t is time, and a and b are constants that depend on the type of tumor and the units of measurement.

   a. Solve for y as a function of t.

   b. If $a = 1, b = 10$, and $y(0) = 5$ cm^3 (with t measured in days), find the specific solution and graph it.

44. ▼ ***Growth of Tumors*** Refer back to the preceding exercise. Suppose that $a = 1$, $b = 10$, and $y(0) = 15$ cm^3. Find the specific solution and graph it. Comparing its graph to the one obtained in the preceding exercise, what can you say about tumor growth in these instances?

COMMUNICATION AND REASONING EXERCISES

45. What is the difference between a particular solution and the general solution of a differential equation? How do we get a particular solution from the general solution?

46. Why is there always an arbitrary constant in the general solution of a differential equation? Why are there not two or more arbitrary constants in a first-order differential equation?

47. ▼ Show by example that a **second-order** differential equation, one involving the second derivative y'', usually has two arbitrary constants in its general solution.

48. ▼ Find a differential equation that is not separable.

49. ▼ Find a differential equation whose general solution is $y = 4e^{-x} + 3x + C$.

50. ▼ Explain how, knowing the elasticity of demand as a function of either price or demand, you may find the demand equation. (See Exercise 29.)

CHAPTER 7 REVIEW

KEY CONCEPTS

Website www.WanerMath.com

Go to the Website at www.WanerMath.com to find a comprehensive and interactive Web-based summary of Chapter 7.

7.1 Integration by Parts

Integration-by-parts formula:

$$\int u \cdot v\,dx = u \cdot I(v) - \int D(u)I(v)\,dx$$ *p. 522*

Tabular method for integration by parts *p. 523*

Integrating a polynomial times a logarithm *p. 526*

7.2 Area between Two Curves and Applications

If $f(x) \geq g(x)$ for all x in $[a, b]$, then the area of the region between the graphs of f and g and between $x = a$ and $x = b$ is given by

$$A = \int_a^b [f(x) - g(x)]\,dx$$ *p. 531*

Regions enclosed by crossing curves *p. 533*

Area enclosed by two curves *p. 535*

General instructions for finding the area between the graphs of $f(x)$ and $g(x)$ *p. 535*

Approximating the area between two curves using technology:

$$A = \int_a^b |f(x) - g(x)|\,dx$$ *p. 536*

7.3 Averages and Moving Averages

Average, or mean, of a collection of values

$$\bar{y} = \frac{y_1 + y_2 + \cdots + y_n}{n}$$ *p. 540*

The *average*, or *mean*, of a function $f(x)$ on an interval $[a, b]$ is

$$\bar{f} = \frac{1}{b-a}\int_a^b f(x)\,dx.$$ *p. 541*

Average balance *p. 541*

Computing the moving average of a set of data *p. 542*

n-Unit moving average of a function:

$$\bar{f}(x) = \frac{1}{n}\int_{x-n}^{x} f(t)\,dt$$ *p. 543*

Computing moving averages of sawtooth and step functions *p. 544*

7.4 Applications to Business and Economics: Consumers' and Producers' Surplus and Continuous Income Streams

Consumers' surplus:

$$CS = \int_0^{\bar{q}} [D(q) - \bar{p}]\,dq$$ *p. 549*

Producers' surplus:

$$PS = \int_0^{\bar{q}} [\bar{p} - S(q)]\,dq$$ *p. 551*

Equilibrium price *p. 552*

Social gain $= CS + PS$ *p. 553*

Total value of a continuous income stream: $TV = \int_a^b R(t)\,dt$ *p. 554*

Future value of a continuous income stream: $FV = \int_a^b R(t)e^{r(b-t)}\,dt$ *p. 555*

Present value of a continuous income stream: $PV = \int_a^b R(t)e^{r(a-t)}\,dt$ *p. 555*

7.5 Improper Integrals and Applications

Improper integral with an infinite limit of integration:

$$\int_a^{+\infty} f(x)\,dx,\ \int_{-\infty}^{b} f(x)\,dx,$$

$$\int_{-\infty}^{+\infty} f(x)\,dx$$ *p. 559*

Improper integral in which the integrand becomes infinite *p. 562*

Testing for convergence *p. 563*

Integrand infinite between the endpoints *p. 564*

Integral improper in two ways *p. 564*

7.6 Differential Equations and Applications

Simple differential equations:

$$\frac{dy}{dx} = f(x)$$ *p. 569*

Separable differential equations:

$$\frac{dy}{dx} = f(x)g(y)$$ *p. 572*

Newton's Law of Cooling *p. 573*

REVIEW EXERCISES

Evaluate the integrals in Exercises 1–10.

1. $\int (x^2 + 2)e^x\,dx$
2. $\int (x^2 - x)e^{-3x+1}\,dx$
3. $\int x^2 \ln(2x)\,dx$
4. $\int \log_5 x\,dx$
5. $\int 2x|2x + 1|\,dx$
6. $\int 3x|-x + 5|\,dx$
7. $\int 5x\frac{|-x+3|}{-x+3}\,dx$
8. $\int 2x\frac{|3x+1|}{3x+1}\,dx$
9. $\int_{-2}^{2} (x^3 + 1)e^{-x}\,dx$
10. $\int_1^e x^2 \ln x\,dx$

In Exercises 11–14, find the areas of the given regions.

11. Between $y = x^3$ and $y = 1 - x^3$ for x in $[0, 1]$
12. Between $y = e^x$ and $y = e^{-x}$ for x in $[0, 2]$
13. Enclosed by $y = 1 - x^2$ and $y = x^2$
14. Between $y = x$ and $y = xe^{-x}$ for x in $[0, 2]$

In Exercises 15–18, find the average value of the given function over the indicated interval.

15. $f(x) = x^3 - 1$ over $[-2, 2]$
16. $f(x) = \frac{x}{x^2 + 1}$ over $[0, 1]$
17. $f(x) = x^2 e^x$ over $[0, 1]$
18. $f(x) = (x + 1)\ln x$ over $[1, 2e]$

In Exercises 19–22, find the 2-unit moving averages of the given function.

19. $f(x) = 3x + 1$

20. $f(x) = 6x^2 + 12$

21. $f(x) = x^{4/3}$

22. $f(x) = \ln x$

In Exercises 23 and 24, calculate the consumers' surplus at the indicated unit price $\bar{p}$ for the given demand equation.

23. $p = 50 - \frac{1}{2}q;\ \bar{p} = 10$

24. $p = 10 - q^{1/2};\ \bar{p} = 4$

In Exercises 25 and 26, calculate the producers' surplus at the indicated unit price $\bar{p}$ for the given supply equation.

25. $p = 50 + \frac{1}{2}q;\ \bar{p} = 100$

26. $p = 10 + q^{1/2};\ \bar{p} = 40$

In Exercises 27–32, decide whether the given integral converges. If the integral converges, compute its value.

27. $\int_1^{\infty} \frac{1}{x^5}\,dx$

28. $\int_0^1 \frac{1}{x^5}\,dx$

29. $\int_{-1}^{1} \frac{x}{(x^2-1)^{5/3}}\,dx$

30. $\int_0^2 \frac{x}{(x^2-1)^{1/3}}\,dx$

31. $\int_0^{+\infty} 2xe^{-x^2}\,dx$

32. $\int_0^{+\infty} x^2 e^{-6x^3}\,dx$

Solve the differential equations in Exercises 33–36.

33. $\frac{dy}{dx} = x^2y^2$

34. $\frac{dy}{dx} = xy + 2x$

35. $xy\frac{dy}{dx} = 1;\ y(1) = 1$

36. $y(x^2+1)\frac{dy}{dx} = xy^2;\ y(0) = 2$

APPLICATIONS: OHaganBooks.com

37. *Spending on Stationery* Alarmed by the volume of pointless memos and reports being copied and circulated by management at OHaganBooks.com, John O'Hagan ordered a 5-month audit of paper usage at the company. He found that management consumed paper at a rate of

$$q(t) = 45t + 200 \text{ thousand sheets per month} \quad (0 \le t \le 5)$$

(t is the time in months since the audit began). During the same period, the price of paper was escalating; the company was charged approximately

$$p(t) = 9e^{0.09t} \text{ dollars per thousand sheets.}$$

Use an integral to estimate, to the nearest hundred dollars, the total spent on paper for management during the given period.

38. *Spending on Shipping* During the past 10 months, OHaganBooks.com shipped orders at a rate of about

$$q(t) = 25t + 3{,}200 \text{ packages per month} \quad (0 \le t \le 10)$$

(t is the time in months since the beginning of the year). During the same period, the cost of shipping a package averaged approximately

$$p(t) = 4e^{0.04t} \text{ dollars per package.}$$

Use an integral to estimate, to the nearest thousand dollars, the total spent on shipping orders during the given period.

39. *Education Costs* Billy-Sean O'Hagan, having graduated *summa cum laude* from college, has been accepted by the doctoral program in biophysics at Oxford. John O'Hagan estimates that the total cost (minus scholarships) he will need to pay is \$2,000 per month, but that this cost will escalate at a continuous compounding rate of 1% per month.

a. What, to the nearest dollar, is the average monthly cost over the course of two years?

b. Find the four-month moving average of the monthly cost.

40. *Investments* OHaganBooks.com keeps its cash reserves in a hedge fund paying 6% compounded continuously. It starts a year with \$1 million in reserves and does not withdraw or deposit any money.

a. What is the average amount it will have in the fund over the course of two years?

b. Find the one-month moving average of the amount it has in the fund.

41. *Consumers' and Producers' Surplus* Currently, the hottest selling item at OHaganBooks.com is *Mensa for Dummies*[54] with a demand curve of $q = 20{,}000(28 - p)^{1/3}$ books per week, and a supply curve of $q = 40{,}000(p - 19)^{1/3}$ books per week.

a. Find the equilibrium price and demand.

b. Find the consumers' and producers' surpluses at the equilibrium price.

42. *Consumers' and Producers' Surplus* OHaganBooks.com is about to start selling a new coffee table book, *Computer Designs of the Late Twentieth Century*. It estimates the demand curve to be $q = 1{,}000\sqrt{200 - 2p}$, and its willingness to order books from the publisher is given by the supply curve $q = 1{,}000\sqrt{10p - 400}$.

a. Find the equilibrium price and demand.

b. Find the consumers' and producers' surpluses at the equilibrium price.

43. *Revenue* Sales of the bestseller *A River Burns through It* are dropping at OHaganBooks.com. To try to bolster sales, the company is dropping the price of the book, now \$40, at a rate of \$2 per week. As a result, this week OHaganBooks.com will sell 5,000 copies, and it estimates that sales will fall continuously at a rate of 10% per week. How much revenue will it earn on sales of this book over the next 8 weeks?

44. *Foreign Investments* Panicked by the performance of the U.S. stock market, Marjory Duffin is investing her 401(k) money in a Russian hedge fund at a rate of approximately

$$q(t) = 1.7t^2 - 0.5t + 8 \text{ thousand shares per month,}$$

[54] The actual title is: *Let Us Just Have A Ball! Mensa for Dummies,* by Wendu Mekbib, Silhouette Publishing Corporation.

where t is time in months since the stock market began to plummet. At the time she started making the investments, the hedge fund was selling for \$1 per share, but subsequently declined in value at a continuous rate of 5% per month. What was the total amount of money Marjory Duffin invested after one year? (Answer to the nearest \$1,000.)

45. ***Investments*** OHaganBooks.com CEO John O'Hagan has started a gift account for the Marjory Duffin Foundation. The account pays 6% compounded continuously and is initially empty. OHaganBooks.com deposits money continuously into it, starting at the rate of \$100,000 per month and increasing continuously by \$10,000 per month.

a. How much money will the company have in the account at the end of two years?

b. How much of the amount you found in part (a) was principal deposited and how much was interest earned? (Round answers to the nearest \$1,000.)

46. ***Savings*** John O'Hagan had been saving money for Billy-Sean's education since he had been a wee lad. O'Hagan began depositing money at the rate of \$1,000 per month and increased his deposits continuously by \$50 per month. If the account earned 5% compounded continuously and O'Hagan continued these deposits for 15 years,

a. How much money did he accumulate?

b. How much was money deposited and how much was interest?

47. ***Acquisitions*** The Megabucks Corporation is considering buying OHaganBooks.com. It estimates OHaganBooks.com's revenue stream at \$50 million per year, growing continuously at a 10% rate. Assuming interest rates of 6%, how much is OHaganBooks.com's revenue for the next year worth now?

48. ***More Acquisitions*** OHaganBooks.com is thinking of buying JungleBooks and would like to recoup its investment after three years. The estimated net profit for JungleBooks is \$40 million per year, growing linearly by \$5 million per year. Assuming interest rates of 4%, how much should OHaganBooks.com pay for JungleBooks?

49. ***Incompetence*** OHaganBooks.com is shopping around for a new bank. A junior executive at one bank offers it the following interesting deal: The bank will pay OHaganBooks.com interest continuously at a rate numerically equal to 0.01% of the square of the amount of money it has in the account at any time. By considering what would happen if \$10,000 was deposited in such an account, explain why the junior executive was fired shortly after this offer was made.

50. ***Shrewd Bankers*** The new junior officer at the bank (who replaced the one fired in the preceding exercise) offers OHaganBook.com the following deal for the \$800,000 they plan to deposit: While the amount in the account is less than \$1 million, the bank will pay interest continuously at a rate equal to 10% of the difference between \$1 million and the amount of money in the account. When it rises over \$1 million, the bank will pay interest of 20%. Why should OHaganBooks.com not take this offer?

Case Study

Estimating Tax Revenues

Dmitriy Shironosov/Shutterstock.com

You have just been hired by the incoming administration of your country as chief consultant for national tax policy, and you have been getting conflicting advice from the finance experts on your staff. Several of them have come up with plausible suggestions for new tax structures, and your job is to choose the plan that results in more revenue for the government.

Before you can evaluate their plans, you realize that it is essential to know your country's income distribution—that is, how many people earn how much money.* You might think that the most useful way of specifying income distribution would be to use a function that gives the exact number $f(x)$ of people who earn a given salary x. This would necessarily be a discrete function—it makes sense only if x happens to be a whole number of cents. There is, after all, no one earning a salary of exactly \$22,000.142567! Furthermore, this function would behave rather erratically, because there are, for example, probably many more people making a salary of exactly \$30,000 than exactly \$30,000.01. Given these problems, it is far more convenient to start with the function defined by

$N(x) =$ *the total number of people earning between* 0 *and* x *dollars.*

* To simplify our discussion, we are assuming that (1) all tax revenues are based on earned income and that (2) everyone in the population we consider earns some income.

Actually, you would want a "smoothed" version of this function. The graph of $N(x)$ might look like the one shown in Figure 26.

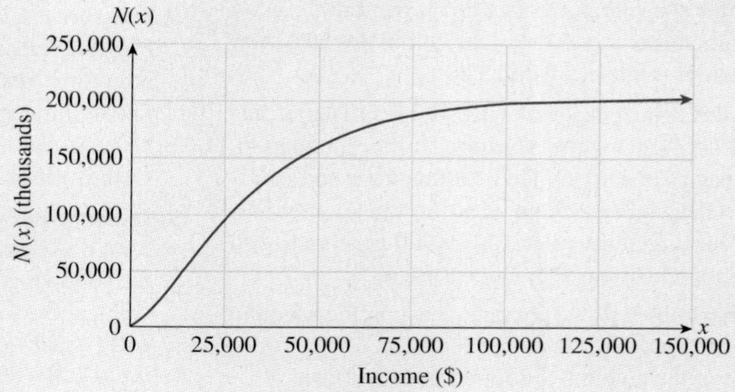

Figure 26

If we take the *derivative* of $N(x)$, we get an income distribution function. Its graph might look like the one shown in Figure 27.

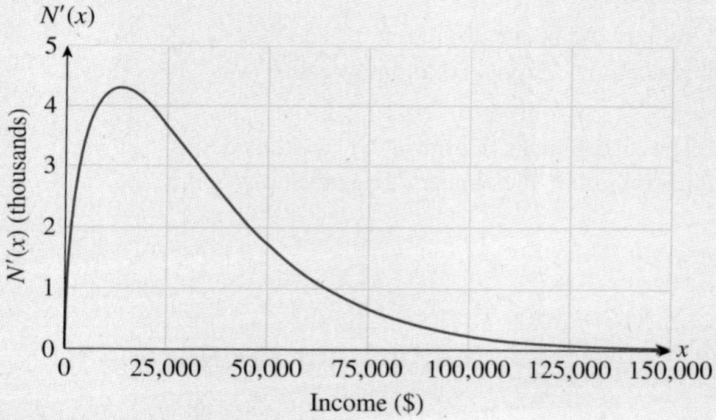

Figure 27

Because the derivative measures the rate of change, its value at x is the additional number of taxpayers per $1 increase in salary. Thus, the fact that $N'(25{,}000) \approx 3{,}700$ tells us that approximately 3,700 people are earning a salary of between $25,000 and $25,001. In other words, N' shows the distribution of incomes among the population—hence, the name "distribution function."*

You thus send a memo to your experts requesting the income distribution function for the nation. After much collection of data, they tell you that the income distribution function is

$$N'(x) = 14x^{0.672}e^{-x/20{,}400}.$$

This is in fact the function whose graph is shown in Figure 27 and is an example of a **gamma distribution**.† (You might find it odd that you weren't given the original function N, but it will turn out that you don't need it. How would you compute it?)

Given this income distribution, your financial experts have come up with the two possible tax policies illustrated in Figures 28 and 29.

* A very similar idea is used in probability. See the optional chapter "Calculus Applied to Probability and Statistics" on the Website.

† Gamma distributions are often good models for income distributions. The one used in the text is the authors' approximation of the income distribution in the United States in 2009. Source for data: U.S. Census Bureau, Current Population Survey, 2010 Annual Social and Economic Supplement. (www.census.gov).

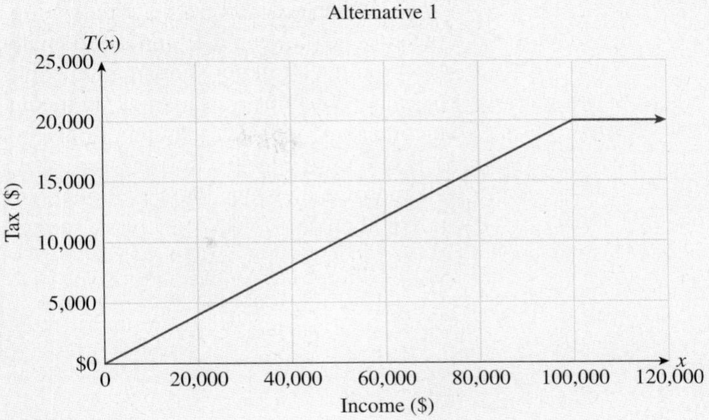

Figure 28

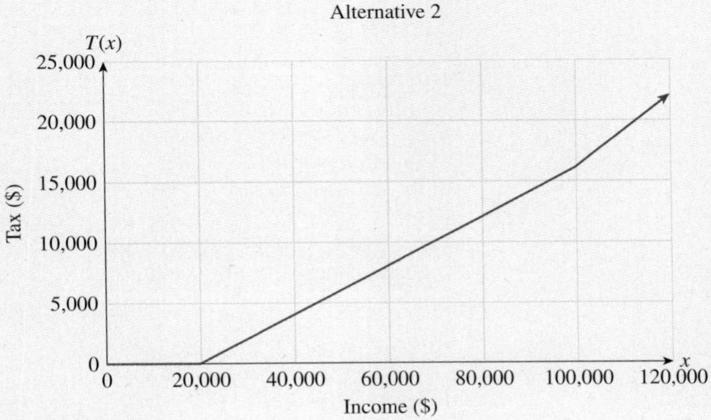

Figure 29

In the first alternative, all taxpayers pay 20% of their income in taxes, except that no one pays more than \$20,000 in taxes. In the second alternative, there are three tax brackets, described by the following table:

Income	*Marginal tax rate*
\$0–20,000	0%
\$20,000–100,000	20%
Above \$100,000	30%

Now you must determine which alternative will generate more annual tax revenue.

Each of Figures 28 and 29 is the graph of a function, T. Rather than using the formulas for these particular functions, you begin by working with the general situation. You have an income distribution function N' and a tax function T, both functions of annual income. You need to find a formula for total tax revenues. First you decide to use a cutoff so that you need to work only with incomes in some finite interval $[0, M]$; you might use, for example, $M = \$10$ million. (Later you will let M approach $+\infty$.) Next, you subdivide the interval $[0, M]$ into a large number of intervals of small width, Δx. If $[x_{k-1}, x_k]$ is a typical such interval, you wish to calculate the approximate tax revenue from people whose total incomes lie between x_{k-1} and x_k. You will then sum over k to get the total revenue.

You need to know how many people are making incomes between x_{k-1} and x_k. Because $N(x_k)$ people are making incomes *up to* x_k and $N(x_{k-1})$ people are making incomes up to x_{k-1}, the number of people making incomes between x_{k-1} and x_k is $N(x_k) - N(x_{k-1})$. Because x_k is very close to x_{k-1}, the incomes of these people are all approximately equal to x_{k-1} dollars, so each of these taxpayers is paying an annual tax of about $T(x_{k-1})$. This gives a tax revenue of

$$[N(x_k) - N(x_{k-1})]T(x_{k-1}).$$

Now you do a clever thing. You write $x_k - x_{k-1} = \Delta x$ and replace $N(x_k) - N(x_{k-1})$ by

$$\frac{N(x_k) - N(x_{k-1})}{\Delta x}\Delta x.$$

This gives you a tax revenue of about

$$\frac{N(x_k) - N(x_{k-1})}{\Delta x}T(x_{k-1})\Delta x$$

from wage-earners in the bracket $[x_{k-1}, x_k]$. Summing over k gives an approximate total revenue of

$$\sum_{k=1}^{n}\frac{N(x_k) - N(x_{k-1})}{\Delta x}T(x_{k-1})\Delta x,$$

where n is the number of subintervals. The larger n is, the more accurate your estimate will be, so you take the limit of the sum as $n \to \infty$. When you do this, two things happen. First, the quantity

$$\frac{N(x_k) - N(x_{k-1})}{\Delta x}$$

approaches the derivative, $N'(x_{k-1})$. Second, the sum, which you recognize as a Riemann sum, approaches the integral

$$\int_0^M N'(x)T(x)\,dx.$$

You now take the limit as $M \to +\infty$ to get

$$\text{Total tax revenue} = \int_0^{+\infty} N'(x)T(x)\,dx.$$

This improper integral is fine in theory, but the actual calculation will have to be done numerically, so you stick with the upper limit of \$10 million for now. You will have to check that it is reasonable at the end. (Notice that, by the graph of N', it appears that extremely few, if any, people earn that much.) Now you already have a formula for $N'(x)$, but you still need to write formulas for the tax functions $T(x)$ for both alternatives.

Alternative 1 The graph in Figure 28 rises linearly from 0 to 20,000 as x ranges from 0 to 100,000, and then stays constant at 20,000. The slope of the first part is $20{,}000/100{,}000 = 0.2$. The taxation function is therefore

$$T_1(x) = \begin{cases} 0.2x & \text{if } 0 \le x < 100{,}000 \\ 20{,}000 & \text{if } x \ge 100{,}000 \end{cases}.$$

For use of technology, it's convenient to express this in closed form using absolute values:*

* To see how to obtain the formula, consult the introduction to Exercises 67–68 in Section 7.1.

$$T_1(x) = 0.2x + \frac{1}{2}\left(1 + \frac{|x - 100{,}000|}{x - 100{,}000}\right)(20{,}000 - 0.2x).$$

The total revenue generated by this tax scheme is, therefore,

$$R_1 = \int_0^{10{,}000{,}000} (14x^{0.672}e^{-x/20{,}400}) \times \left[0.2x + \frac{1}{2}\left(1 + \frac{|x - 100{,}000|}{x - 100{,}000}\right)(20{,}000 - 0.2x)\right] dx.$$

You decide not to attempt this by hand! You use numerical integration software to obtain a grand total of $R_1 = \$1{,}360{,}990{,}000{,}000$, or \$1.36099 trillion (rounded to six significant digits).

(If you use the Numerical Integration utility on the Website, enter

```
14x^(0.672)*exp(-x/20400)*(0.2x+0.5*(20000-0.2x)*
        (1+abs(x-100000)/(x-100000)))
```

for $f(x)$, and 0 and 10000000 for a and b respectively, and press "Integral".)

Alternative 2 The graph in Figure 29 rises with a slope of 0.2 from 0 to 16,000 as x ranges from 20,000 to 100,000, then rises from that point on with a slope of 0.3. (This is why we say that the *marginal* tax rates are 20% and 30%, respectively.) The taxation function is therefore

$$T_2(x) = \begin{cases} 0 & \text{if } 0 \le x < 20{,}000 \\ 0.2(x - 20{,}000) & \text{if } 20{,}000 \le x < 100{,}000 \\ 16{,}000 + 0.3(x - 100{,}000) & \text{if } x \ge 100{,}000 \end{cases}.$$

Again, you express this in closed form using absolute values:

$$\begin{aligned} T_2(x) &= [0.2(x - 20{,}000)]\frac{1}{2}\left(\frac{|x - 20{,}000|}{x - 20{,}000} - \frac{|x - 100{,}000|}{x - 100{,}000}\right) \\ &\quad + [16{,}000 + 0.3(x - 100{,}000)]\frac{1}{2}\left(1 + \frac{|x - 100{,}000|}{x - 100{,}000}\right) \\ &= 0.1(x - 20{,}000)\left(\frac{|x - 20{,}000|}{x - 20{,}000} - \frac{|x - 100{,}000|}{x - 100{,}000}\right) \\ &\quad + [8{,}000 + 0.15(x - 100{,}000)]\left(1 + \frac{|x - 100{,}000|}{x - 100{,}000}\right). \end{aligned}$$

Values of x between 0 and 20,000 do not contribute to the integral, so

$$R_2 = \int_{20{,}000}^{10{,}000{,}000} 14x^{0.672}e^{-x/20{,}400}\, T_2(x)\, dx$$

with $T_2(x)$ as above. Numerical integration software gives $R_2 = \$0.713465$ trillion—considerably less than Alternative 1. Thus, even though Alternative 2 taxes the wealthy more heavily, it yields less total revenue.

Now what about the cutoff at \$10 million annual income? If you try either integral again with an upper limit of \$100 million, you will see no change in either result to six significant digits. There simply are not enough taxpayers earning an income above \$10,000,000 to make a difference. You conclude that your answers are sufficiently accurate and that the first alternative provides more tax revenue.

EXERCISES

In Exercises 1–4, calculate the total tax revenue for a country with the given income distribution and tax policies (all currency in dollars).

1. T $N'(x) = 100x^{0.466}e^{-x/23,000}$; 25% tax on all income
2. T $N'(x) = 100x^{0.4}e^{-x/30,000}$; 45% tax on all income
3. T $N'(x) = 100x^{0.466}e^{-x/23,000}$; tax brackets as in the following tax table:

Income	*Marginal Tax Rate*
\$0–30,000	0%
\$30,000–250,000	10%
Above \$250,000	80%

4. T $N'(x) = 100x^{0.4}e^{-x/30,000}$; no tax on any income below \$250,000, 100% marginal tax rate on any income above \$250,000
5. Let $N'(x)$ be an income distribution function.
   a. If $0 \le a < b$, what does $\int_a^b N'(x)\,dx$ represent? HINT [Use the Fundamental Theorem of Calculus.]
   b. What does $\int_0^{+\infty} N'(x)\,dx$ represent?
6. Let $N'(x)$ be an income distribution function. What does $\int_0^{+\infty} xN'(x)\,dx$ represent? HINT [Argue as in the text.]
7. Let $P(x)$ be the number of people earning more than x dollars.
   a. What is $N(x) + P(x)$?
   b. Show that $P'(x) = -N'(x)$.
   c. Use integration by parts to show that, if $T(0) = 0$, then the total tax revenue is
   $$\int_0^{+\infty} P(x)T'(x)\,dx.$$
   [Note: You may assume that $T'(x)$ is continuous, but the result is still true if we assume only that $T(x)$ is continuous and piecewise continuously differentiable.]
8. Income tax functions T are most often described, as in the text, by tax brackets and marginal tax rates.
   a. If one tax bracket is $a < x \le b$, show that $\int_a^b P(x)\,dx$ is the total income earned in the country that falls into that bracket (P as in the preceding exercise).
   b. Use (a) to explain directly why $\int_0^{+\infty} P(x)T'(x)\,dx$ gives the total tax revenue in the case where T is described by tax brackets and constant marginal tax rates in each bracket.

TI-83/84 Plus Technology Guide

Section 7.3

Example 3 (page 542) The following table shows Colossal Conglomerate's closing stock prices for 20 consecutive trading days:

Day	1	2	3	4	5	6	7	8	9	10
Price	20	22	21	24	24	23	25	26	20	24
Day	11	12	13	14	15	16	17	18	19	20
Price	26	26	25	27	28	27	29	27	25	24

Plot these prices and the 5-day moving average.

Solution with Technology

Here is how to automate this calculation on a TI-83/84 Plus.

1. Use

`seq(X,X,1,20)→L₁` 2ND STAT → OPS → 5
STO 2ND STAT → L₁

to enter the sequence of numbers 1 through 20 into the list L_1, representing the trading days.

2. Using the list editor accessible through the STAT menu, enter the daily stock prices in list L_2.

3. Calculate the list of 5-day moving averages by using the following command:

```
seq((L2(X)+L2(X-1)+L2(X-2)+L2(X-3)
  +L2(X-4))/5,X,5,20)→L3
```

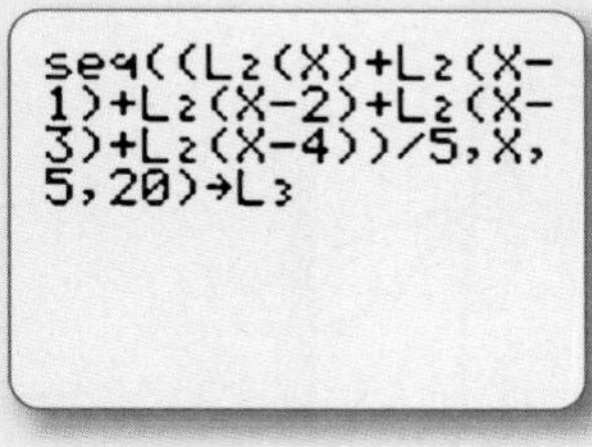

This has the effect of putting the moving averages into elements 1 through 15 of list L_3.

4. If you wish to plot the moving average on the same graph as the daily prices, you will want the averages in L_3 to match up with the prices in L_2. One way to do this is to put four more entries at the beginning of L_3—say, copies of the first four entries of L_2. The following command accomplishes this:

```
augment(seq(L2(X),X,1,4),L3)→L3
```
2ND STAT → OPS → 9

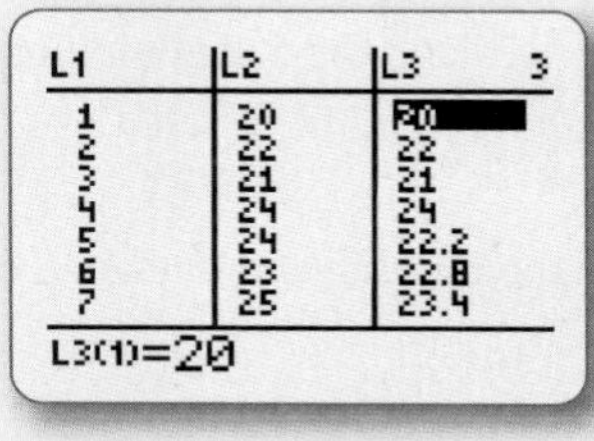

5. You can now graph the prices and moving averages by creating an xyLine scatter plot through the STAT PLOT menu, with L_1 being the Xlist and L_2 being the Ylist for `Plot1`, and L_1 being the Xlist and L_3 the Ylist for `Plot2`:

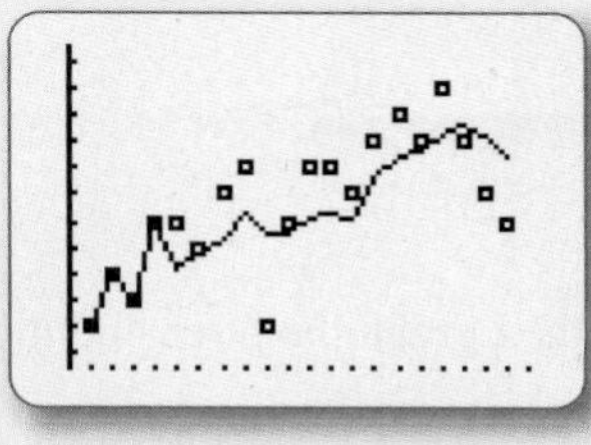

SPREADSHEET Technology Guide

Section 7.3

Example 3 (page 542) The following table shows Colossal Conglomerate's closing stock prices for 20 consecutive trading days:

Day	1	2	3	4	5	6	7	8	9	10
Price	20	22	21	24	24	23	25	26	20	24
Day	11	12	13	14	15	16	17	18	19	20
Price	26	26	25	27	28	27	29	27	25	24

Plot these prices and the 5-day moving average.

Solution with Technology

1. Compute the moving averages in a column next to the daily prices, as shown here:

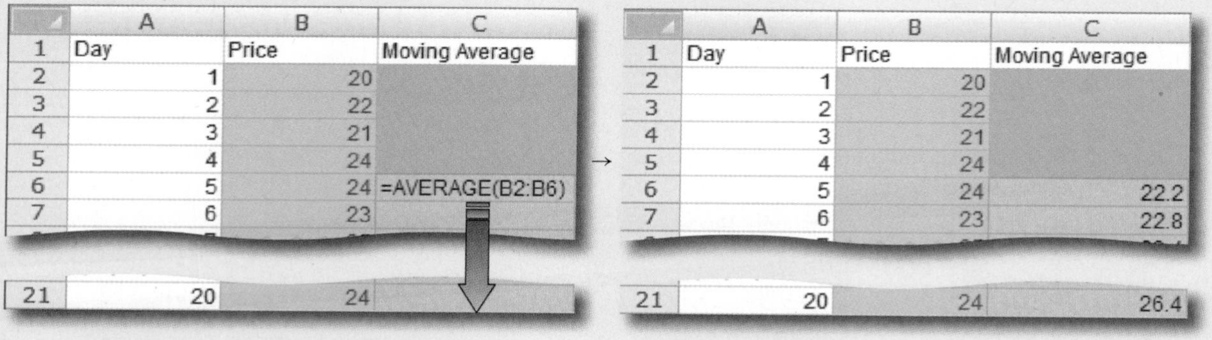

2. You can then graph the price and moving average using a scatter plot.

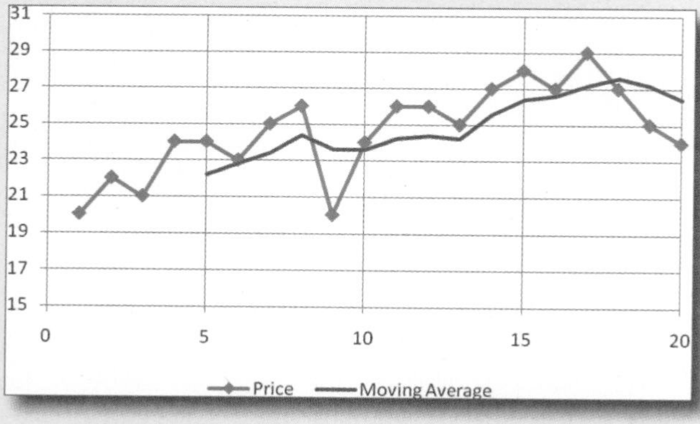

8

Functions of Several Variables

Website
www.WanerMath.com
At the Website you will find:

- A detailed chapter summary
- A true/false quiz
- A surface grapher
- An Excel surface grapher
- A linear multiple regression utility
- The following optional extra sections:

  Maxima and Minima: Boundaries and the Extreme Value Theorem

  The Chain Rule for Functions of Several Variables

Case Study Modeling College Population

College Malls, Inc. is planning to build a national chain of shopping malls in college neighborhoods. The company is planning to lease only to stores that target the specific age demographics of the national college student population. To decide which age brackets to target, the company has asked you, a paid consultant, for an analysis of the college population by student age, and of its trends over time. **How can you analyze the relevant data?**

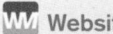

david pearson/Alamy

Introduction

We have studied functions of a single variable extensively. But not every useful function is a function of only one variable. In fact, most are not. For example, if you operate an online bookstore in competition with Amazon.com, BN.com, and BooksAMillion.com, your sales may depend on those of your competitors. Your company's daily revenue might be modeled by a function such as

$$R(x, y, z) = 10{,}000 - 0.01x - 0.02y - 0.01z + 0.00001yz,$$

where x, y, and z are the online daily revenues of Amazon.com, BN.com, and BooksAMillion.com, respectively. Here, R is a function of three variables because it *depends on* x, y, and z. As we shall see, the techniques of calculus extend readily to such functions. Among the applications we shall look at is optimization: finding, where possible, the maximum or minimum of a function of two or more variables.

8.1 Functions of Several Variables from the Numerical, Algebraic, and Graphical Viewpoints

Numerical and Algebraic Viewpoints

Recall that a function of one variable is a rule for manufacturing a new number $f(x)$ from a single independent variable x. A function of two or more variables is similar, but the new number now depends on more than one independent variable.

Function of Several Variables

A **real-valued function,** f, **of** $x, y, z, \ldots$ is a rule for manufacturing a new number, written $f(x, y, z, \ldots)$, from the values of a sequence of independent variables $(x, y, z, \ldots)$. The function f is called a **real-valued function of two variables** if there are two independent variables, a **real-valued function of three variables** if there are three independent variables, and so on.

Quick Examples

1. $f(x, y) = x - y$ — Function of two variables
   $f(1, 2) = 1 - 2 = -1$ — Substitute 1 for x and 2 for y.
   $f(2, -1) = 2 - (-1) = 3$ — Substitute 2 for x and -1 for y.
   $f(y, x) = y - x$ — Substitute y for x and x for y.
2. $g(x, y) = x^2 + y^2$ — Function of two variables
   $g(-1, 3) = (-1)^2 + 3^2 = 10$ — Substitute -1 for x and 3 for y.
3. $h(x, y, z) = x + y + xz$ — Function of three variables
   $h(2, 2, -2) = 2 + 2 + 2(-2) = 0$ — Substitute 2 for x, 2 for y, and -2 for z.

Note It is often convenient to use $x_1, x_2, x_3, \ldots$ for the independent variables, so that, for instance, the third example above would be $h(x_1, x_2, x_3) = x_1 + x_2 + x_1x_3$. ■

Figure 1 illustrates the concept of a function of two variables: In goes a pair of numbers and out comes a single number.

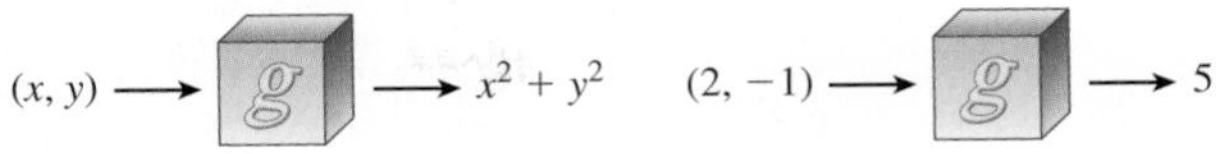

Figure 1

As with functions of one variable, functions of several variables can be represented numerically (using a table of values), algebraically (using a formula as in the above examples), and sometimes graphically (using a graph).

Let's now look at a number of examples of interesting functions of several variables.

EXAMPLE 1 Cost Function

You own a company that makes two models of speakers: the Ultra Mini and the Big Stack. Your total monthly cost (in dollars) to make x Ultra Minis and y Big Stacks is given by

$$C(x, y) = 10{,}000 + 20x + 40y.$$

What is the significance of each term in this formula?

Roy Mehta/The Image Bank/Getty Images

Solution The terms have meanings similar to those we saw for linear cost functions of a single variable. Let us look at the terms one at a time.

Constant Term Consider the monthly cost of making no speakers at all ($x = y = 0$). We find

$$C(0, 0) = 10{,}000. \quad \text{Cost of making no speakers is \$10,000.}$$

Thus, the constant term 10,000 is the **fixed cost**, the amount you have to pay each month even if you make no speakers.

Coefficients of x and y Suppose you make a certain number of Ultra Minis and Big Stacks one month and the next month you increase production by one Ultra Mini. The costs are

$$\begin{aligned} C(x, y) &= 10{,}000 + 20x + 40y && \text{First month} \\ C(x+1, y) &= 10{,}000 + 20(x+1) + 40y && \text{Second month} \\ &= 10{,}000 + 20x + 20 + 40y \\ &= C(x, y) + 20. \end{aligned}$$

Thus, each Ultra Mini adds \$20 to the total cost. We say that \$20 is the **marginal cost** of each Ultra Mini. Similarly, because of the term $40y$, each Big Stack adds \$40 to the total cost. The marginal cost of each Big Stack is \$40.

This cost function is an example of a *linear function of two variables*. The coefficients of x and y play roles similar to that of the slope of a line. In particular, they give the rates of change of the function as each variable increases while the other stays constant (think about it). We shall say more about linear functions below.

using Technology

See the Technology Guides at the end of the chapter to see how you can use a TI-83/84 Plus and a spreadsheet to display various values of $C(x, y)$ in Example 1. Here is an outline:

TI-83/84 Plus

Y_1=10000+20X+40Y

To evaluate C(10, 30):

10 → X

30 → Y

Y_1 [More details on page 653.]

Spreadsheet

x-values down column A starting in A2

y-values down column B starting in B2

=10000+20*A2+40*B2

in C2; copy down column C. [More details on page 653.]

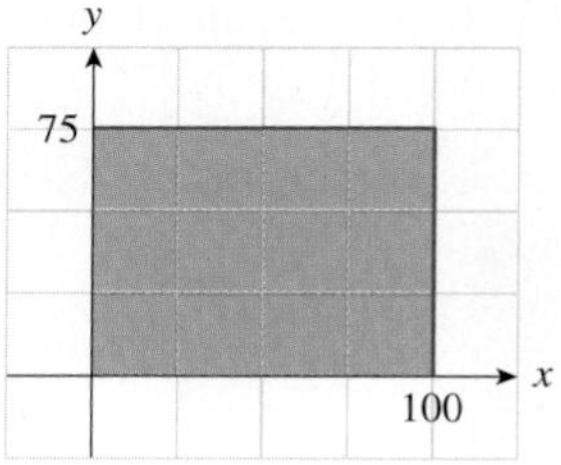

Figure 2

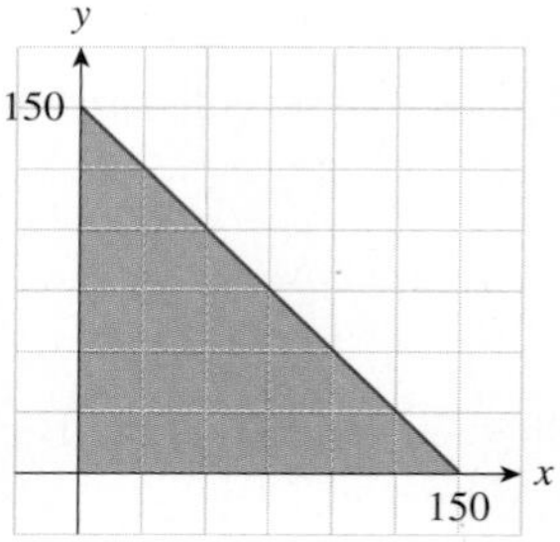

Figure 3

➡ **Before we go on...** In Example 1 which values of x and y may we substitute into $C(x, y)$? Certainly we must have $x \geq 0$ and $y \geq 0$ because it makes no sense to speak of manufacturing a negative number of speakers. Also, there is certainly some upper bound to the number of speakers that can be made in a month. The bound might take one of several forms. The number of each model may be bounded—say $x \leq 100$ and $y \leq 75$. The inequalities $0 \leq x \leq 100$ and $0 \leq y \leq 75$ describe the region in the plane shaded in Figure 2.

Another possibility is that the *total* number of speakers is bounded—say, $x + y \leq 150$. This, together with $x \geq 0$ and $y \geq 0$, describes the region shaded in Figure 3.

In either case, the region shown represents the pairs (x, y) for which $C(x, y)$ is defined. Just as with a function of one variable, we call this region the **domain** of the function. As before, when the domain is not given explicitly, we agree to take the largest domain possible. ■

EXAMPLE 2 Faculty Salaries

David Katz came up with the following function for the salary of a professor with 10 years of teaching experience in a large university.

$$S(x, y, z) = 13{,}005 + 230x + 18y + 102z$$

Here, S is the salary in 1969–1970 in dollars per year, x is the number of books the professor has published, y is the number of articles published, and z is the number of "excellent" articles published.[1] What salary do you expect that a professor with 10 years' experience earned in 1969–1970 if she published 2 books, 20 articles, and 3 "excellent" articles?

Solution All we need to do is calculate

$$\begin{aligned} S(2, 20, 3) &= 13{,}005 + 230(2) + 18(20) + 102(3) \\ &= \$14{,}131. \end{aligned}$$

➡ **Before we go on...** In Example 1, we gave a linear function of two variables. In Example 2 we have a linear function of three variables. Katz came up with his model by surveying a large number of faculty members and then finding the linear function "best" fitting the data. Such models are called **multiple linear regression** models. In the Case Study at the end of this chapter, we shall see a spreadsheet method of finding the coefficients of a multiple regression model from a set of observed data.

What does this model say about the value of a single book or a single article? If a book takes 15 times as long to write as an article, how would you recommend that a professor spend her writing time? ■

Here are two simple kinds of functions of several variables.

Linear Function

A function f of n variables is **linear** if f has the property that

$$f(x_1, x_2, \ldots, x_n) = a_0 + a_1x_1 + \cdots + a_nx_n \qquad (a_0, a_1, a_2, \ldots, a_n \text{ constants}).$$

[1] David A. Katz, "Faculty Salaries, Promotions and Productivity at a Large University," *American Economic Review*, June 1973, pp. 469–477. Prof. Katz's equation actually included other variables, such as the number of dissertations supervised; our equation assumes that all of these are zero.

Quick Examples

1. $f(x, y) = 3x - 5y$ — Linear function of x and y
2. $C(x, y) = 10{,}000 + 20x + 40y$ — Example 1
3. $S(x_1, x_2, x_3) = 13{,}005 + 230x_1 + 18x_2 + 102x_3$ — Example 2

Interaction Function

If we add to a linear function one or more terms of the form bx_ix_j (b a nonzero constant and $i \neq j$), we get a **second-order interaction function.**

Quick Examples

1. $C(x, y) = 10{,}000 + 20x + 40y + 0.1xy$
2. $R(x_1, x_2, x_3) = 10{,}000 - 0.01x_1 - 0.02x_2 - 0.01x_3 + 0.00001x_2x_3$

So far, we have been specifying functions of several variables **algebraically**—by using algebraic formulas. If you have ever studied statistics, you are probably familiar with statistical tables. These tables may also be viewed as representing functions **numerically**, as the next example shows.

EXAMPLE 3 Function Represented Numerically: Body Mass Index

The following table lists some values of the "body mass index," which gives a measure of the massiveness of your body, taking height into account.* The variable w represents your weight in pounds, and h represents your height in inches. An individual with a body mass index of 25 or above is generally considered overweight.

* It is interesting that weight-lifting competitions are usually based on weight, rather than body mass index. As a consequence, taller people are at a significant disadvantage in these competitions because they must compete with shorter, stockier people of the same weight. (An extremely thin, very tall person can weigh as much as a muscular short person, although his body mass index would be significantly lower.)

$h \downarrow$ / $w \rightarrow$	130	140	150	160	170	180	190	200	210
60	25.2	27.1	29.1	31.0	32.9	34.9	36.8	38.8	40.7
61	24.4	26.2	28.1	30.0	31.9	33.7	35.6	37.5	39.4
62	23.6	25.4	27.2	29.0	30.8	32.7	34.5	36.3	38.1
63	22.8	24.6	26.4	28.1	29.9	31.6	33.4	35.1	36.9
64	22.1	23.8	25.5	27.2	28.9	30.7	32.4	34.1	35.8
65	21.5	23.1	24.8	26.4	28.1	29.7	31.4	33.0	34.7
66	20.8	22.4	24.0	25.6	27.2	28.8	30.4	32.0	33.6
67	20.2	21.8	23.3	24.9	26.4	28.0	29.5	31.1	32.6
68	19.6	21.1	22.6	24.1	25.6	27.2	28.7	30.2	31.7
69	19.0	20.5	22.0	23.4	24.9	26.4	27.8	29.3	30.8
70	18.5	19.9	21.4	22.8	24.2	25.6	27.0	28.5	29.9
71	18.0	19.4	20.8	22.1	23.5	24.9	26.3	27.7	29.1
72	17.5	18.8	20.2	21.5	22.9	24.2	25.6	26.9	28.3
73	17.0	18.3	19.6	20.9	22.3	23.6	24.9	26.2	27.5
74	16.6	17.8	19.1	20.4	21.7	22.9	24.2	25.5	26.7
75	16.1	17.4	18.6	19.8	21.1	22.3	23.6	24.8	26.0
76	15.7	16.9	18.1	19.3	20.5	21.7	22.9	24.2	25.4

using Technology

See the Technology Guides at the end of the chapter to see how to use a spreadsheet to create the table in Example 3. Here is an outline:

Spreadsheet

w-values 130 to 210 in B1–J1

h-values 60 to 76 in A2–A18

```
=0.45*B$1/
(0.0254*$A2)^2
```

in B2; copy down and across through J18. [More details on page 653.]

As the table shows, the value of the body mass index depends on two quantities: w and h. Let us write $M(w, h)$ for the body mass index function. What are $M(140, 62)$ and $M(210, 63)$?

Solution We can read the answers from the table:

$$M(140, 62) = 25.4 \qquad w = 140 \text{ lb}, h = 62 \text{ in}$$

and

$$M(210, 63) = 36.9. \qquad w = 210 \text{ lb}, h = 63 \text{ in}$$

The function $M(w, h)$ is actually given by the formula

$$M(w, h) = \frac{0.45w}{(0.0254h)^2}.$$

[The factor 0.45 converts the weight to kilograms, and 0.0254 converts the height to meters. If w is in kilograms and h is in meters, the formula is simpler: $M(w, h) = w/h^2$.]

Geometric Viewpoint: Three-Dimensional Space and the Graph of a Function of Two Variables

Just as functions of a single variable have graphs, so do functions of two or more variables. Recall that the graph of $f(x)$ consists of all points $(x, f(x))$ in the xy-plane. By analogy, we would like to say that the graph of a function of *two* variables, $f(x, y)$, consists of all points of the form $(x, y, f(x, y))$. Thus, we need three axes: the x-, y-, and z-axes. In other words, our graph will live in **three-dimensional space**, or **3-space**.*

* If we were dealing instead with a function of *three* variables, then we would need to go to *four-dimensional* space. Here we run into visualization problems (to say the least!) so we won't discuss the graphs of functions of three or more variables in this text.

Just as we had two mutually perpendicular axes in two-dimensional space (the xy-plane; see Figure 4(a)), so we have three mutually perpendicular axes in three-dimensional space (Figure 4(b)).

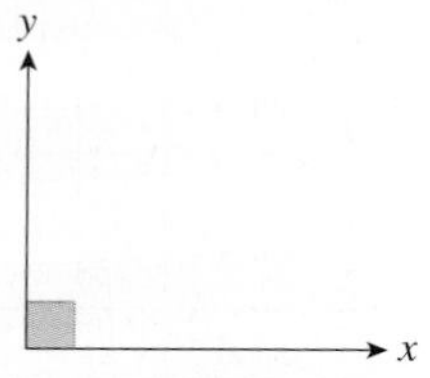

Two-dimensional space

Figure 4(a)

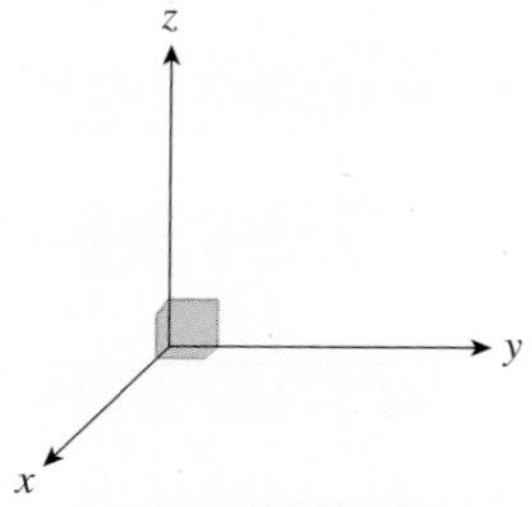

Three-dimensional space

Figure 4(b)

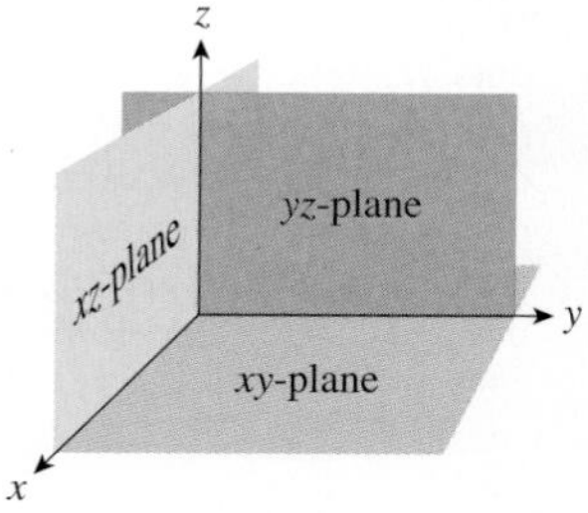

Figure 5

In both 2-space and 3-space, the axis labeled with the last letter goes up. Thus, the z-direction is the "up" direction in 3-space, rather than the y-direction.

Three important planes are associated with these axes: the xy-plane, the yz-plane, and the xz-plane. These planes are shown in Figure 5. Any two of these planes intersect in one of the axes (for example, the xy- and xz-planes intersect in the x-axis) and all three meet at the origin. Notice that the xy-plane consists of all points with z-coordinate zero, the xz-plane consists of all points with $y = 0$, and the yz-plane consists of all points with $x = 0$.

In 3-space, each point has *three* coordinates, as you might expect: the x-coordinate, the y-coordinate, and the z-coordinate. To see how this works, look at the following examples.

EXAMPLE 4 Plotting Points in Three Dimensions

Locate the points $P(1, 2, 3)$, $Q(-1, 2, 3)$, $R(1, -1, 0)$, and $S(1, 2, -2)$ in 3-space.

Solution To locate P, the procedure is similar to the one we used in 2-space: Start at the origin, proceed 1 unit in the x direction, then proceed 2 units in the y direction, and finally, proceed 3 units in the z direction. We wind up at the point P shown in Figures 6(a) and 6(b).

Here is another, extremely useful way of thinking about the location of P. First, look at the x- and y-coordinates, obtaining the point $(1, 2)$ in the xy-plane. The point we want is then 3 units vertically above the point $(1, 2)$ because the z-coordinate of a point is just its height above the xy-plane. This strategy is shown in Figure 6(c).

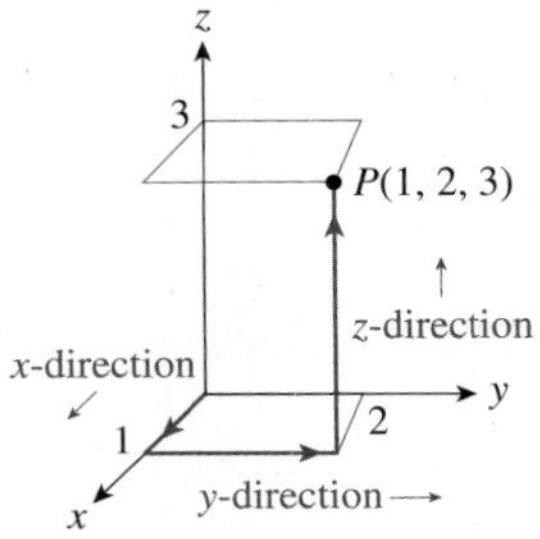

Figure 6(a)

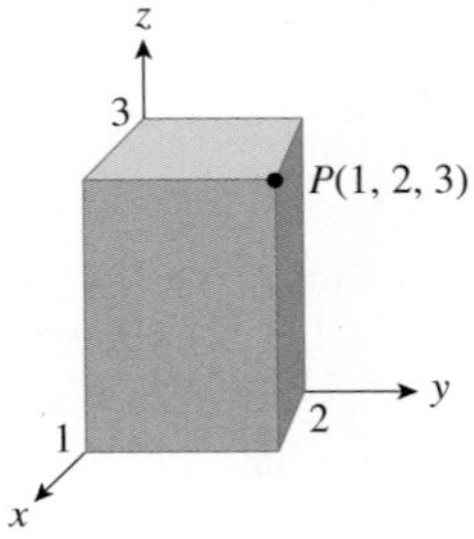

Figure 6(b)

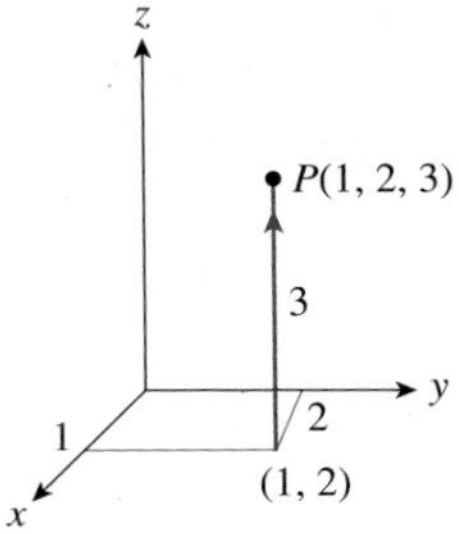

Figure 6(c)

Plotting the points Q, R, and S is similar, using the convention that negative coordinates correspond to moves back, left, or down. (See Figure 7.)

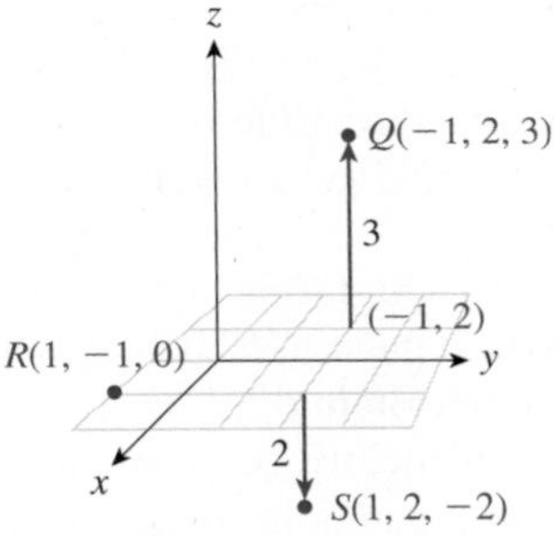

Figure 7

Our next task is to describe the graph of a function $f(x, y)$ of two variables.

Graph of a Function of Two Variables

The **graph of the function f of two variables** is the set of all points $(x, y, f(x, y))$ in three-dimensional space, where we restrict the values of (x, y) to lie in the domain of f. In other words, the graph is the set of all the points (x, y, z) with $z = f(x, y)$.

Note For *every* point (x, y) in the domain of f, the z-coordinate of the corresponding point on the graph is given by evaluating the function at (x, y). Thus, there will be a point of the graph on the vertical line through *every* point in the domain of f, so that the graph is usually a *surface* of some sort (see the figure).

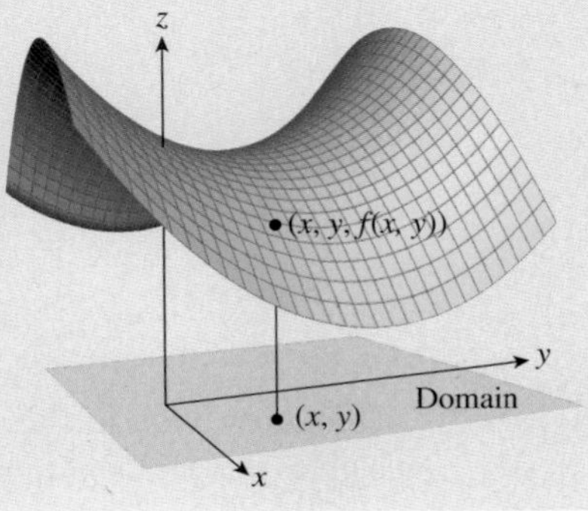

EXAMPLE 5 Graph of a Function of Two Variables

Describe the graph of $f(x, y) = x^2 + y^2$.

Solution Your first thought might be to make a table of values. You could choose some values for x and y and then, for each such pair, calculate $z = x^2 + y^2$. For example, you might get the following table:

$y \downarrow$ \ $x \rightarrow$	**−1**	**0**	**1**
−1	2	1	2
0	1	0	1
1	2	1	2

$f(x, y) = x^2 + y^2$

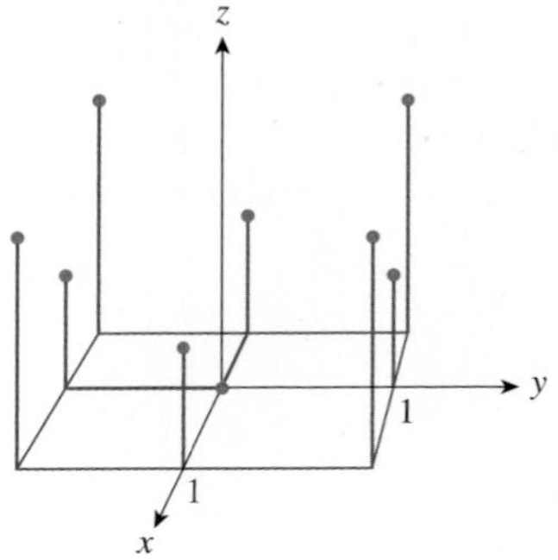

Figure 8

This gives the following nine points on the graph of f: $(-1, -1, 2)$, $(-1, 0, 1)$, $(-1, 1, 2)$, $(0, -1, 1)$, $(0, 0, 0)$, $(0, 1, 1)$, $(1, -1, 2)$, $(1, 0, 1)$, and $(1, 1, 2)$. These points are shown in Figure 8.

The points on the xy-plane we chose for our table are the grid points in the xy-plane, and the corresponding points on the graph are marked with solid dots. The problem is that this small number of points hardly tells us what the surface looks like, and even if we plotted more points, it is not clear that we would get anything more than a mass of dots on the page.

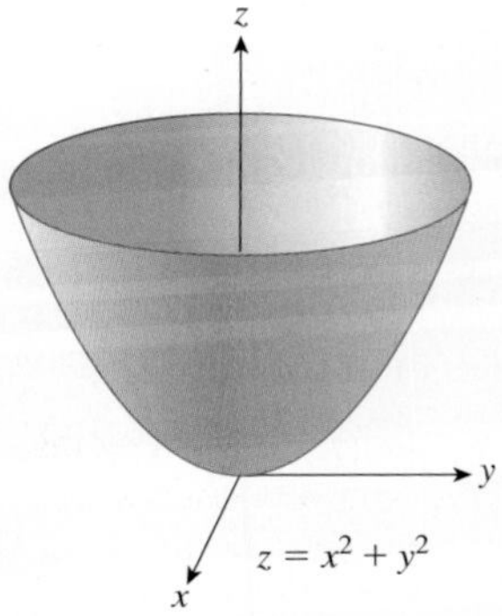

Figure 9

What can we do? There are several alternatives. One place to start is to use technology to draw the graph. (See the technology note on the next page.) We then obtain something like Figure 9. This particular surface is called a **paraboloid**.

If we slice vertically through this surface along the yz-plane, we get the picture in Figure 10. The shape of the front edge, where we cut, is a parabola. To see why, note that the yz-plane is the set of points where $x = 0$. To get the intersection of $x = 0$ and $z = x^2 + y^2$, we substitute $x = 0$ in the second equation, getting $z = y^2$. This is the equation of a parabola in the yz-plane.

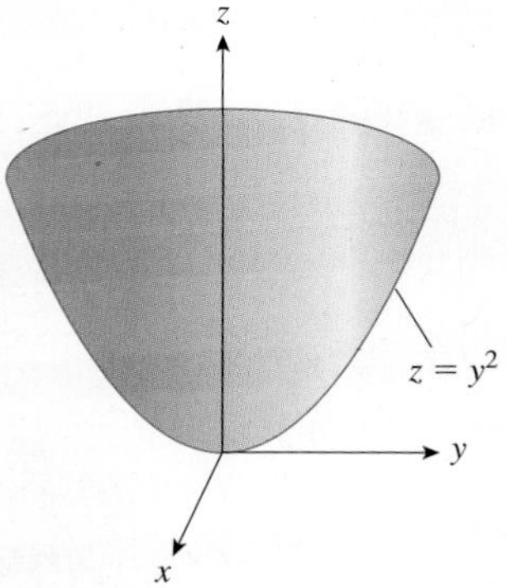

Figure 10

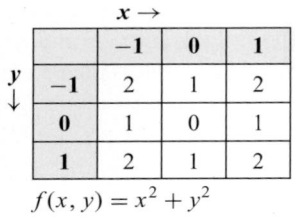

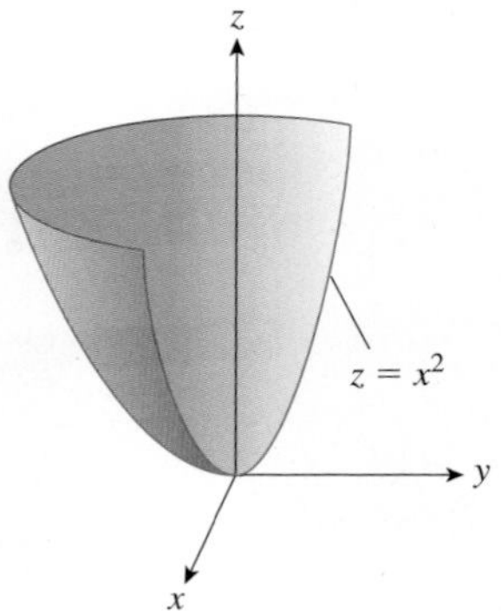

Figure 11

Similarly, we can slice through the surface with the xz-plane by setting $y = 0$. This gives the parabola $z = x^2$ in the xz-plane (Figure 11).

We can also look at horizontal slices through the surface, that is, slices by planes parallel to the xy-plane. These are given by setting $z = c$ for various numbers c. For example, if we set $z = 1$, we will see only the points with height 1. Substituting in the equation $z = x^2 + y^2$ gives the equation

$$1 = x^2 + y^2,$$

which is the equation of a circle of radius 1.* If we set $z = 4$, we get the equation of a circle of radius 2:

* See Section 0.7 for a discussion of equations of circles.

$$4 = x^2 + y^2.$$

In general, if we slice through the surface at height $z = c$, we get a circle (of radius $\sqrt{c}$). Figure 12 shows several of these circles.

using Technology

We can use technology to obtain the graph of the function in Example 5:

Spreadsheet

Table of values:
x-values −3 to 3 in B1–H1
y-values −3 to 3 in A2–A8
`=B$1^2+$A2^2`
in B2; copy down and across through H8.
Graph: Highlight A1 through H8 and insert a Surface chart. [More details on page 654.]

Website

www.WanerMath.com
Online Utilities
→ Surface Graphing Utility
Enter `x^2+y^2` for $f(x, y)$
Set xMin = −3, xMax = 3, yMin = −3, yMax = 3
Press "Graph".

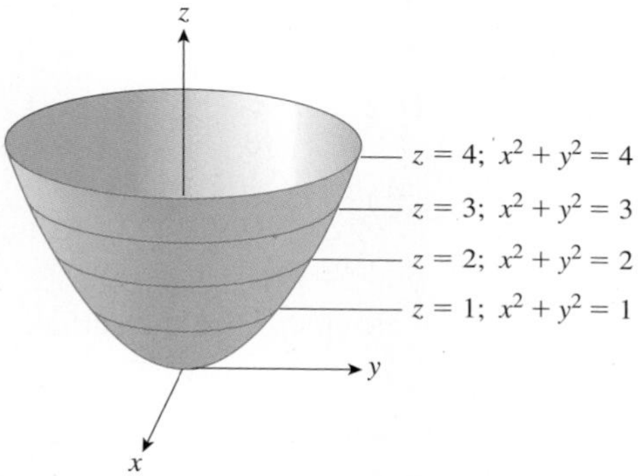

Figure 12

Looking at these circular slices, we see that this surface is the one we get by taking the parabola $z = x^2$ and spinning it around the z-axis. This is an example of what is known as a **surface of revolution**.

➡ **Before we go on...** The graph of any function of the form $f(x, y) = Ax^2 + By^2 + Cxy + Dx + Ey + F$ ($A, B, \ldots, F$ constants), with $4AB - C^2$ positive, can be shown to be a paraboloid of the same general shape as that in Example 5 if A and B are positive, or upside-down if A and B are negative. If $A \neq B$, the horizontal slices will be ellipses rather than circles.

Notice that each horizontal slice through the surface in Example 5 was obtained by putting $z = \textit{constant}$. This gave us an equation in x and y that described a curve. These curves are called the **level curves** of the surface $z = f(x, y)$ (see the discussion on the next page). In Example 5, the equations are of the form $x^2 + y^2 = c$ (c constant), and so the level curves are circles. Figure 13 shows the level curves for $c = 0$, 1, 2, 3, and 4.

The level curves give a contour map or topographical map of the surface. Each curve shows all of the points on the surface at a particular height c. You can use this contour map to visualize the shape of the surface. Imagine moving the contour at $c = 1$ to a height of 1 unit above the xy-plane, the contour at $c = 2$ to a height of 2 units above the xy-plane, and so on. You will end up with something like Figure 12. ■

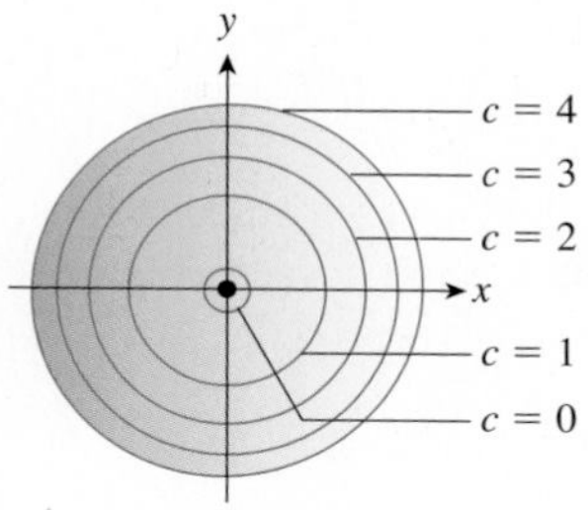

Level curves of the paraboloid $z = x^2 + y^2$

Figure 13

The following summary includes the techniques we have just used plus some additional ones:

Analyzing the Graph of a Function of Two Variables

If possible, use technology to render the graph $z = f(x, y)$ of a given function f of two variables. You can analyze its graph as follows:

Step 1 Obtain the **x-, y-, and z-intercepts** (the places where the surface crosses the coordinate axes).

x-Intercept(s): Set $y = 0$ and $z = 0$ and solve for x.

y-Intercept(s): Set $x = 0$ and $z = 0$ and solve for y.

z-Intercept: Set $x = 0$ and $y = 0$ and compute z.

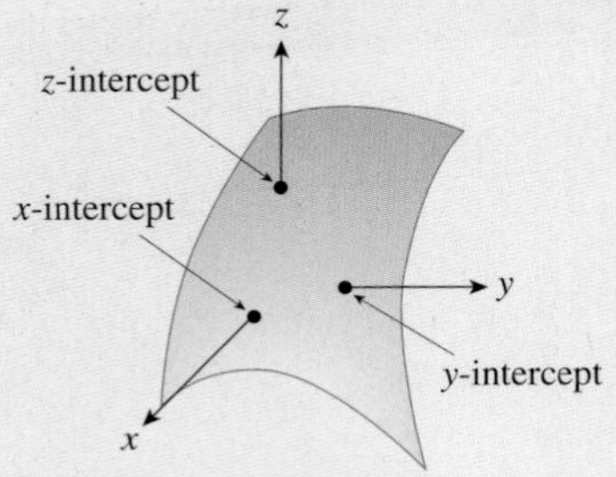

Step 2 Slice the surface along planes parallel to the xy-, yz-, and xz-planes.

z* = *constant Set $z = constant$ and analyze the resulting curves. These are the curves resulting from horizontal slices, and are called the **level curves** (see below).

x* = *constant Set $x = constant$ and analyze the resulting curves. These are the curves resulting from slices parallel to the yz-plane.

y* = *constant Set $y = constant$ and analyze the resulting curves. These are the curves resulting from slices parallel to the xz-plane.

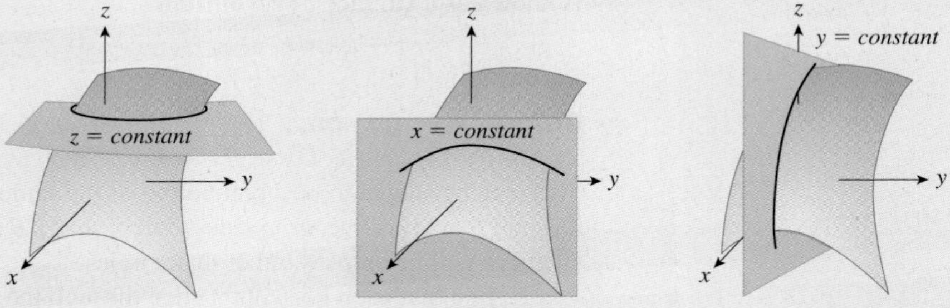

Level Curves

The **level curves** of a function f of two variables are the curves with equations of the form $f(x, y) = c$, where c is constant. These are the curves obtained from the graph of f by slicing it horizontally as above.

Quick Examples

1. Figure 13 above shows some level curves of $f(x, y) = x^2 + y^2$. The ones shown have equations $f(x, y) = 0, 1, 2, 3$, and 4.

2. Let $f(x, y) = y - x^2 + 4$. Its level curves have the form $y - x^2 + 4 = c$ (c constant). If we solve this equation for y, we see that $y = x^2 + c - 4$, the equation of a parabola with its vertex on the y-axis at the point $c - 4$. The following figure shows a portion of the graph of f and some of its level curves.

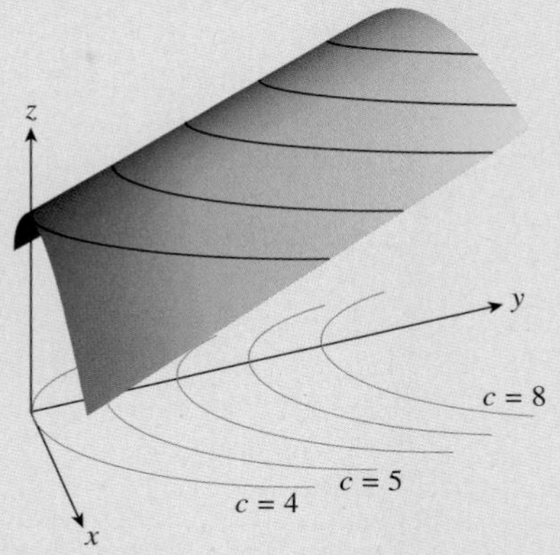

Spreadsheets often have built-in features to render surfaces such as the paraboloid in Example 5. In the following example, we use Excel to graph another surface and then analyze it as above.

EXAMPLE 6 Analyzing a Surface

Describe the graph of $f(x, y) = x^2 - y^2$.

Solution First we obtain a picture of the graph using technology. Figure 14 shows two graphs obtained using resources at the Website.

Chapter 8 → Math Tools for Chapter 8 → Surface Graphing Utility

Chapter 8 → Math Tools for Chapter 8 → Excel Surface Graphing Utility

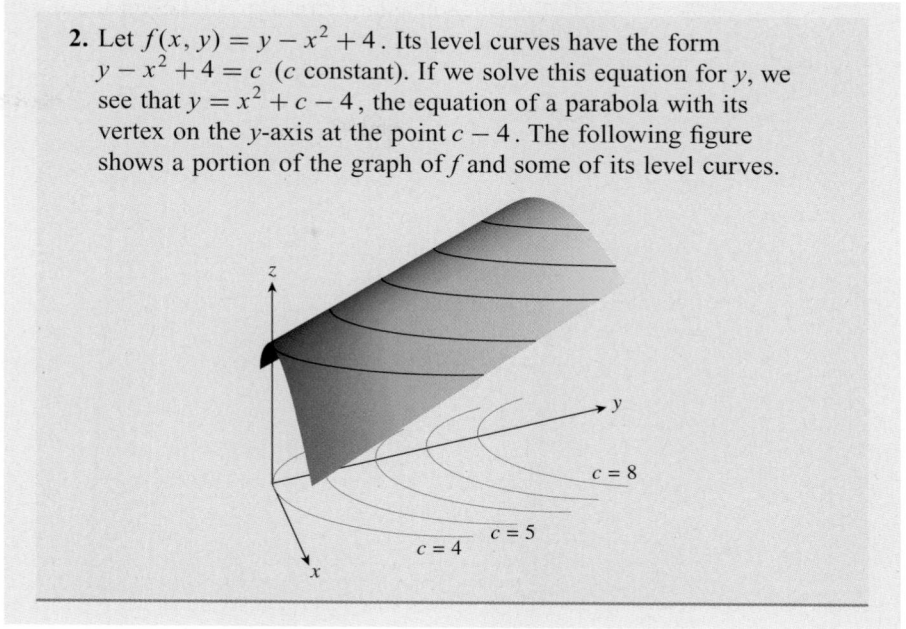

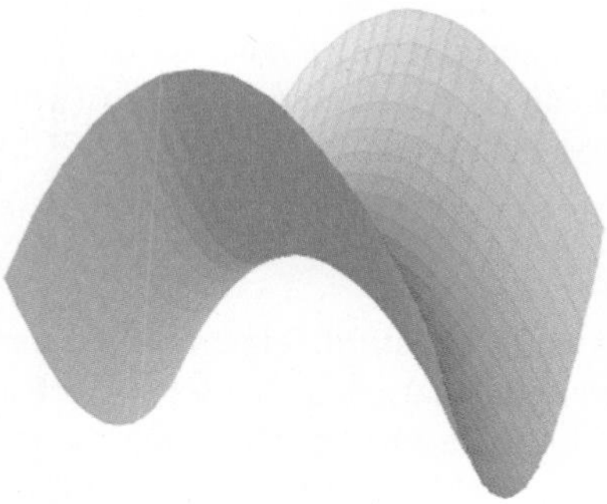

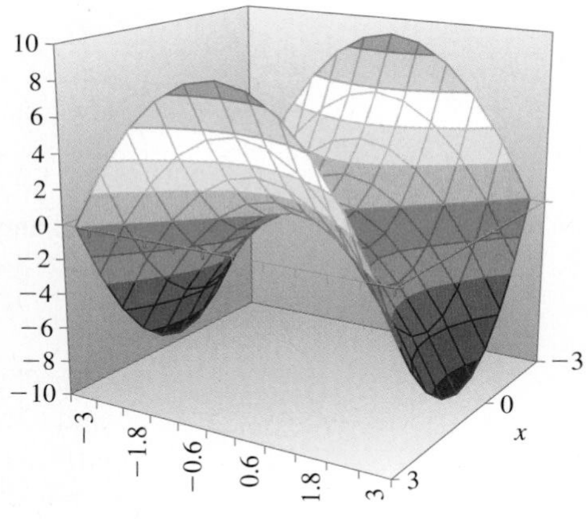

Figure 14

See the Technology Guides at the end of the chapter to find out how to obtain a similar graph from scratch using a spreadsheet.

The graph shows an example of a "saddle point" at the origin. (We return to this idea in Section 8.3.) To analyze the graph for the features shown in the box above, replace $f(x, y)$ by z to obtain

$$z = x^2 - y^2.$$

Step 1: *Intercepts* Setting any two of the variables x, y, and z equal to zero results in the third also being zero, so the x-, y-, and z-intercepts are all 0. In other words, the surface touches all three axes in exactly one point, the origin.

Step 2: *Slices* Slices in various directions show more interesting features.

Slice by $x = c$ This gives $z = c^2 - y^2$, which is the equation of a parabola that opens downward. You can see two of these slices ($c = -3, c = 3$) as the front and back edges of the surface in Figure 14. (More are shown in Figure 15(a).)

Slice by $y = c$ This gives $z = x^2 - c^2$, which is the equation of a parabola once again—this time, opening upward. You can see two of these slices ($c = -3, c = 3$) as the left and right edges of the surface in Figure 14. (More are shown in Figure 15(b).)

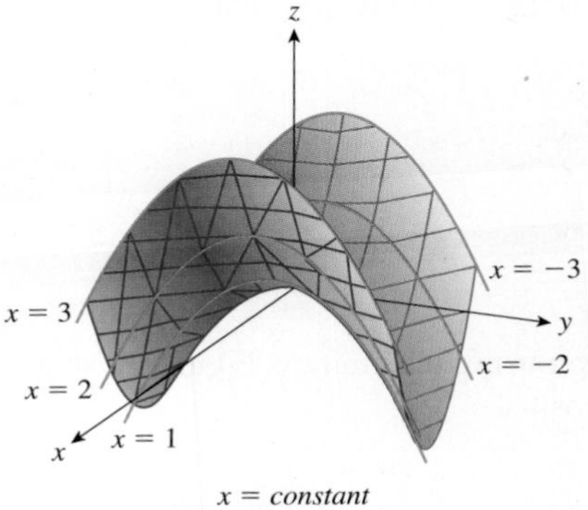

Figure 15(a)

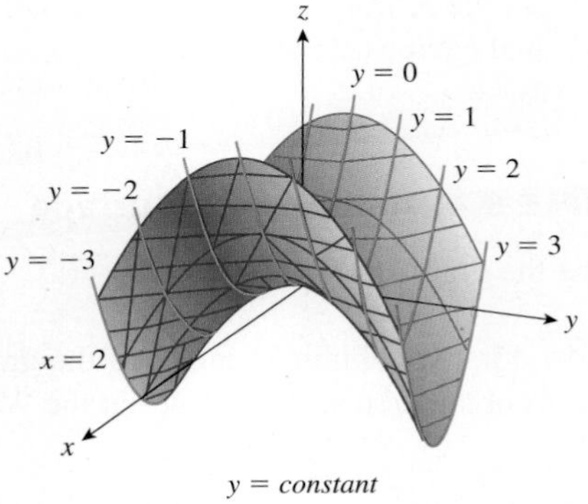

Figure 15(b)

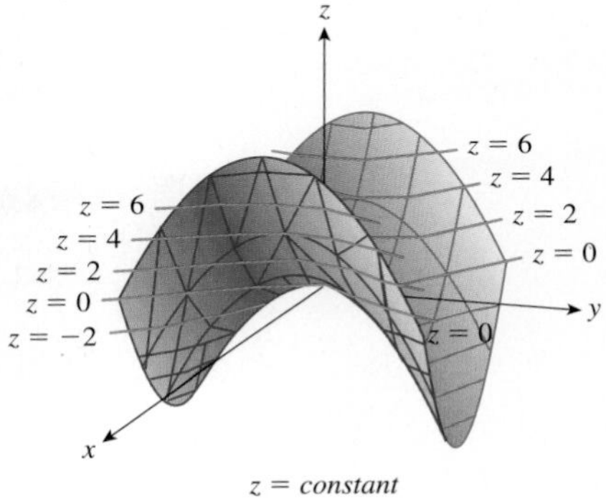

Figure 15(c)

Level Curves: Slice by $z = c$ This gives $x^2 - y^2 = c$, which is a hyperbola. The level curves for various values of c are visible in Figure 14 as the horizontal slices. (See Figure 15(c).) The case $c = 0$ is interesting: The equation $x^2 - y^2 = 0$ can be rewritten as $x = \pm y$ (why?), which represents two lines at right angles to each other.

To obtain really beautiful renderings of surfaces, you could use one of the commercial computer algebra software packages, such as Mathematica® or Maple®, or, if you use a Mac, the built-in grapher (grapher.app located in the Utilities folder).

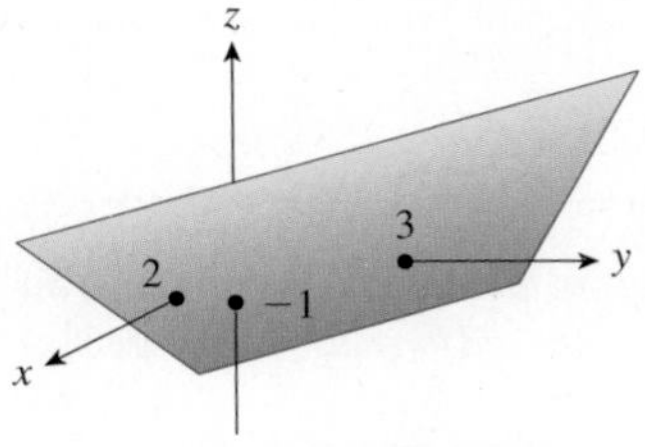

$z = \frac{1}{2}x + \frac{1}{3}y - 1$

Figure 16

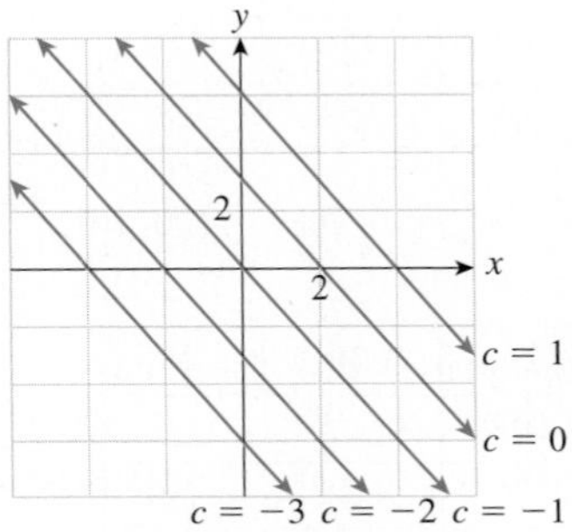

Level curves: $3x + 2y = 12$

Figure 17

* Think about what happens when the function is constant.

EXAMPLE 7 Graph and Level Curves of a Linear Function

Describe the graph of $g(x, y) = \dfrac{1}{2}x + \dfrac{1}{3}y - 1$.

Solution Notice first that g is a linear function of x and y. Figure 16 shows a portion of the graph, which is a plane.

We can get a good idea of what plane this is by looking at the x-, y-, and z-intercepts.

x-intercept Set $y = z = 0$, which gives $x = 2$.

y-intercept Set $x = z = 0$, which gives $y = 3$.

z-intercept Set $x = y = 0$, which gives $z = -1$.

Three points are enough to define a plane, so we can say that the plane is the one passing through the three points (2, 0, 0), (0, 3, 0), and (0, 0, −1). It can be shown that the graph of every linear function of two variables is a plane.

Level curves: Set $g(x, y) = c$ to obtain $\frac{1}{2}x + \frac{1}{3}y - 1 = c$, or $\frac{1}{2}x + \frac{1}{3}y = c + 1$. We can rewrite this equation as $3x + 2y = 6(c + 1)$, which is the equation of a straight line. Choosing different values of c gives us a family of parallel lines as shown in Figure 17. (For example, the line corresponding to $c = 1$ has equation $3x + 2y = 6(1 + 1) = 12$.) In general, the set of level curves of every non-constant linear function is a set of parallel straight lines.*

EXAMPLE 8 Using Level Curves

A certain function f of two variables has level curves $f(x, y) = c$ for $c = -2, -1, 0, 1$, and 2, as shown in Figure 18. (Each grid square is 1×1.)

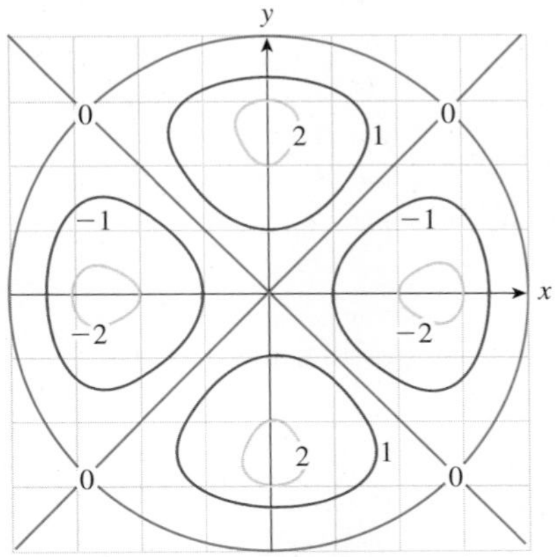

Level curves of f

Figure 18

Estimate the following: $f(1, 1)$, $f(1.5, -2)$, $f(1.5, 0)$, and $f(1, 2)$.

Solution The point (1, 1) appears to lie exactly on the red level curve $c = 0$, so $f(1, 1) \approx 0$. Similarly, the point $(1.5, -2)$ appears to lie exactly on the blue level curve $c = 1$, so $f(1.5, -2) \approx 1$. The point (1.5, 0) appears to lie midway between the level curves $c = -1$ and $c = -2$, so we estimate $f(1.5, 2) \approx -1.5$. Finally, the point (1, 2) lies between the level curves $c = 1$ and $c = 2$, but closer to $c = 1$, so we can estimate $f(1, 2)$ at around 1.3.

8.1 EXERCISES

▼ more advanced ◆ challenging

T indicates exercises that should be solved using technology

*For each function in Exercises 1–4, evaluate **(a)** $f(0, 0)$; **(b)** $f(1, 0)$; **(c)** $f(0, -1)$; **(d)** $f(a, 2)$; **(e)** $f(y, x)$; **(f)** $f(x+h, y+k)$* HINT [See Quick Examples page 588.]

1. $f(x, y) = x^2 + y^2 - x + 1$

2. $f(x, y) = x^2 - y - xy + 1$

3. $f(x, y) = 0.2x + 0.1y - 0.01xy$

4. $f(x, y) = 0.4x - 0.5y - 0.05xy$

*For each function in Exercises 5–8, evaluate **(a)** $g(0, 0, 0)$; **(b)** $g(1, 0, 0)$; **(c)** $g(0, 1, 0)$; **(d)** $g(z, x, y)$; **(e)** $g(x+h, y+k, z+l)$, provided such a value exists.*

5. $g(x, y, z) = e^{x+y+z}$

6. $g(x, y, z) = \ln(x + y + z)$

7. $g(x, y, z) = \dfrac{xyz}{x^2 + y^2 + z^2}$

8. $g(x, y, z) = \dfrac{e^{xyz}}{x + y + z}$

9. Let $f(x, y, z) = 1.5 + 2.3x - 1.4y - 2.5z$. Complete the following sentences. HINT [See Example 1.]

a. f ___ by ___ units for every 1 unit of increase in x.
b. f ___ by ___ units for every 1 unit of increase in y.
c. _______ by 2.5 units for every _______.

10. Let $g(x, y, z) = 0.01x + 0.02y - 0.03z - 0.05$. Complete the following sentences.

a. g ___ by ___ units for every 1 unit of increase in z.
b. g ___ by ___ units for every 1 unit of increase in x.
c. _______ by 0.02 units for every _______.

In Exercises 11–18, classify each function as linear, interaction, or neither. HINT [See Quick Examples page 591.]

11. $L(x, y) = 3x - 2y + 6xy - 4y^2$

12. $L(x, y, z) = 3x - 2y + 6xz$

13. $P(x_1, x_2, x_3) = 0.4 + 2x_1 - x_3$

14. $Q(x_1, x_2) = 4x_2 - 0.5x_1 - x_1^2$

15. $f(x, y, z) = \dfrac{x + y - z}{3}$

16. $g(x, y, z) = \dfrac{xz - 3yz + z^2}{4z} \quad (z \neq 0)$

17. $g(x, y, z) = \dfrac{xz - 3yz + z^2y}{4z} \quad (z \neq 0)$

18. $f(x, y) = x + y + xy + x^2y$

In Exercises 19 and 20, use the given tabular representation of the function f to compute the quantities asked for. HINT [See Example 3.]

19.

$y \downarrow$ \ $x \rightarrow$	10	20	30	40
10	−1	107	162	−3
20	−6	194	294	−14
30	−11	281	426	−25
40	−16	368	558	−36

a. $f(20, 10)$ **b.** $f(40, 20)$ **c.** $f(10, 20) - f(20, 10)$

20.

$y \downarrow$ \ $x \rightarrow$	10	20	30	40
10	162	107	−5	−7
20	294	194	−22	−30
30	426	281	−39	−53
40	558	368	−56	−76

a. $f(10, 30)$ **b.** $f(20, 10)$ **c.** $f(10, 40) + f(10, 20)$

T *In Exercises 21 and 22, use a spreadsheet or some other method to complete the given tables.*

21. $P(x, y) = x - 0.3y + 0.45xy$

$y \downarrow$ \ $x \rightarrow$	10	20	30	40
10				
20				
30				
40				

22. $Q(x, y) = 0.4x + 0.1y - 0.06xy$

$y \downarrow$ \ $x \rightarrow$	10	20	30	40
10				
20				
30				
40				

23. T ▼ The following statistical table lists some values of the "Inverse F distribution" ($\alpha = 0.5$):

$n \rightarrow$ (columns), $d \downarrow$ (rows)

	1	2	3	4	5	6	7	8	9	10
1	161.4	199.5	215.7	224.6	230.2	234.0	236.8	238.9	240.5	241.9
2	18.51	19.00	19.16	19.25	19.30	19.33	19.35	19.37	19.39	19.40
3	10.13	9.552	9.277	9.117	9.013	8.941	8.887	8.812	8.812	8.785
4	7.709	6.944	6.591	6.388	6.256	6.163	6.094	5.999	5.999	5.964
5	6.608	5.786	5.409	5.192	5.050	4.950	4.876	4.772	4.772	4.735
6	5.987	5.143	4.757	4.534	4.387	4.284	4.207	4.099	4.099	4.060
7	5.591	4.737	4.347	4.120	3.972	3.866	3.787	3.677	3.677	3.637
8	5.318	4.459	4.066	3.838	3.688	3.581	3.500	3.388	3.388	3.347
9	5.117	4.256	3.863	3.633	3.482	3.374	3.293	3.179	3.179	3.137
10	4.965	4.103	3.708	3.478	3.326	3.217	3.135	3.020	3.020	2.978

In a spreadsheet, you can compute the value of this function at (n, d) by the formula

`=FINV(0.05, n, d)` The 0.05 is the value of alpha (α).

Use a spreadsheet to re-create this table.

24. T ▼ The formula for body mass index $M(w, h)$, if w is given in kilograms and h is given in meters, is

$$M(w, h) = \frac{w}{h^2}.$$ See Example 3.

Use this formula to complete the following table in a spreadsheet:

$w \rightarrow$ (columns), $h \downarrow$ (rows)

	70	80	90	100	110	120	130
1.8							
1.85							
1.9							
1.95							
2							
2.05							
2.1							
2.15							
2.2							
2.25							
2.3							

T *In Exercises 25–28, use either a graphing calculator or a spreadsheet to complete each table. Express all your answers as decimals rounded to four decimal places.*

25.

x	y	$f(x, y) = x^2\sqrt{1 + xy}$
3	1	
1	15	
0.3	0.5	
56	4	

26.

x	y	$f(x, y) = x^2e^y$
0	2	
−1	5	
1.4	2.5	
11	9	

27.

x	y	$f(x, y) = x\ln(x^2 + y^2)$
3	1	
1.4	−1	
e	0	
0	e	

28.

x	y	$f(x, y) = \dfrac{x}{x^2 - y^2}$
−1	2	
0	0.2	
0.4	2.5	
10	0	

29. ▼ Brand Z's annual sales are affected by the sales of related products X and Y as follows: Each \$1 million increase in sales of brand X causes a \$2.1 million decline in sales of brand Z, whereas each \$1 million increase in sales of brand Y results in an increase of \$0.4 million in sales of brand Z. Currently, brands X, Y, and Z are each selling \$6 million per year. Model the sales of brand Z using a linear function.

30. ▼ Brand Z's annual sales are affected by the sales of related products X and Y as follows: Each \$1 million increase in sales of brand X causes a \$2.5 million decline in sales of brand Z, whereas each \$2 million increase in sales of brand Y results in an increase of \$23 million in sales of brand Z. Currently, brands X and Y are each selling \$2 million per year and brand Z is selling \$62 million per year. Model the sales of brand Z using a linear function.

31. Sketch the cube with vertices (0, 0, 0), (1, 0, 0), (0, 1, 0), (0, 0, 1), (1, 1, 0), (1, 0, 1), (0, 1, 1), and (1, 1, 1). HINT [See Example 4.]

32. Sketch the cube with vertices $(-1, -1, -1)$, $(1, -1, -1)$, $(-1, 1, -1)$, $(-1, -1, 1)$, $(1, 1, -1)$, $(1, -1, 1)$, $(-1, 1, 1)$, and $(1, 1, 1)$. HINT [See Example 4.]

33. Sketch the pyramid with vertices $(1, 1, 0)$, $(1, -1, 0)$, $(-1, 1, 0)$, $(-1, -1, 0)$, and $(0, 0, 2)$.

34. Sketch the solid with vertices $(1, 1, 0)$, $(1, -1, 0)$, $(-1, 1, 0)$, $(-1, -1, 0)$, $(0, 0, -1)$, and $(0, 0, 1)$.

Sketch the planes in Exercises 35–40.

35. $z = -2$

36. $z = 4$

37. $y = 2$

38. $y = -3$

39. $x = -3$

40. $x = 2$

Match each equation in Exercises 41–48 with one of the graphs below. (If necessary, use technology to render the surfaces.) HINT [See Examples 5, 6, and 7.]

41. $f(x, y) = 1 - 3x + 2y$

42. $f(x, y) = 1 - \sqrt{x^2 + y^2}$

43. $f(x, y) = 1 - (x^2 + y^2)$

44. $f(x, y) = y^2 - x^2$

45. $f(x, y) = -\sqrt{1 - (x^2 + y^2)}$

46. $f(x, y) = 1 + (x^2 + y^2)$

47. $f(x, y) = \dfrac{1}{x^2 + y^2}$

48. $f(x, y) = 3x - 2y + 1$

(A)

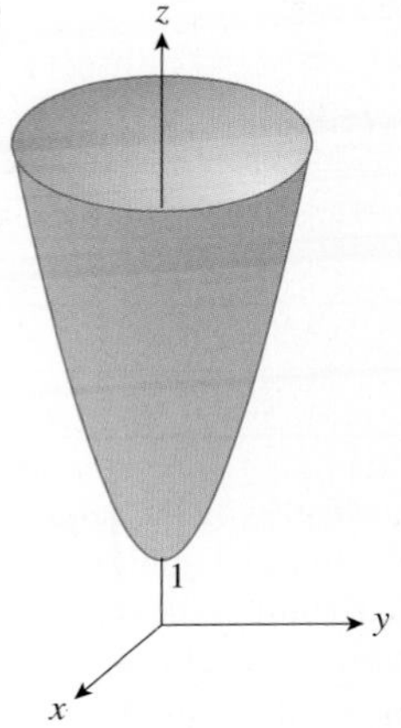

(B)

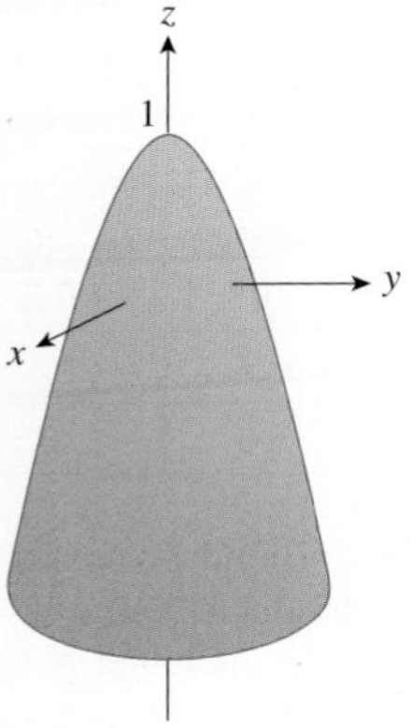

(C)

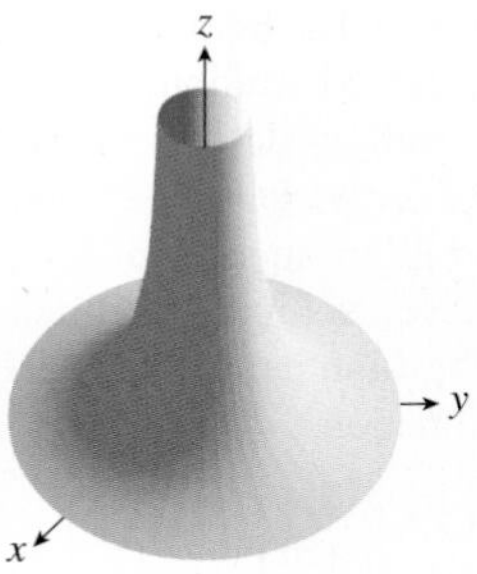

(D)

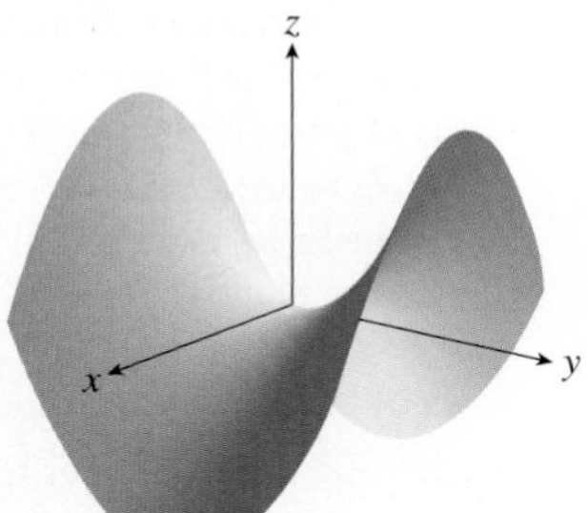

(E)

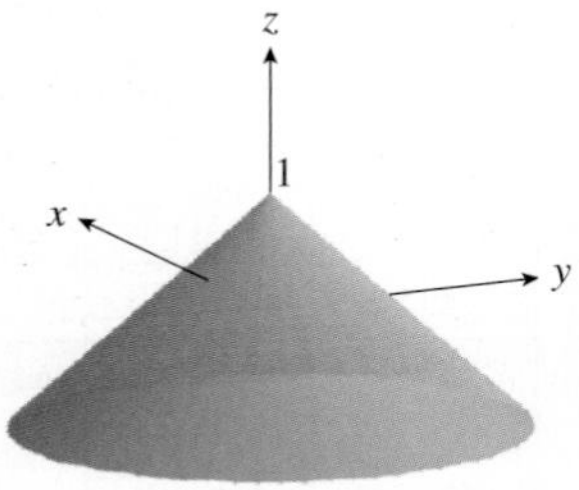

(F)

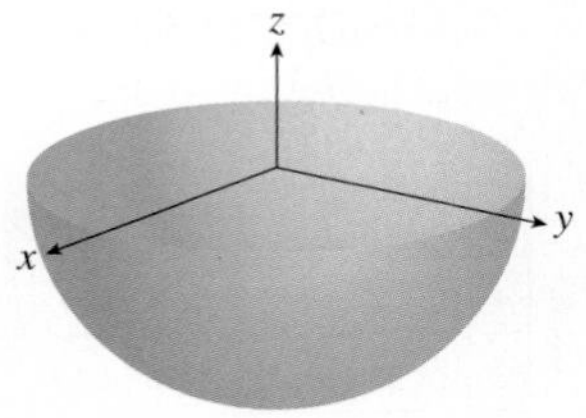

(G)

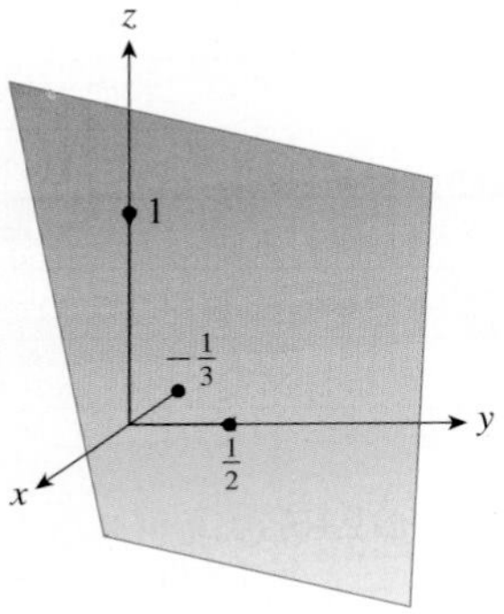

(H)

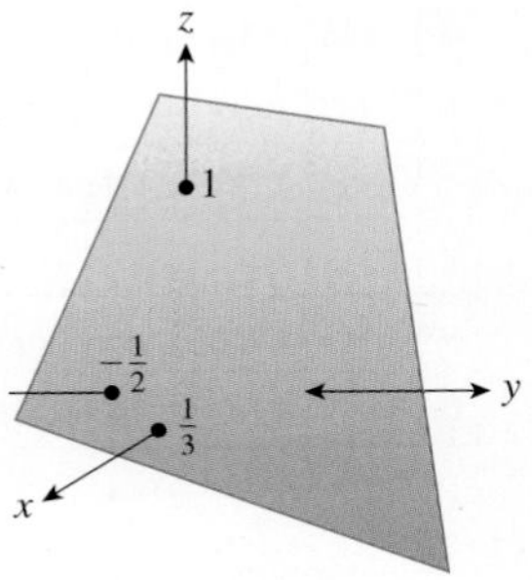

In Exercises 49–54, sketch the level curves $f(x, y) = c$ for the given function and values of c. HINT [See Example 5.]

49. $f(x, y) = 2x^2 + 2y^2$; $c = 0, 2, 18$

50. $f(x, y) = 3x^2 + 3y^2$; $c = 0, 3, 27$

51. $f(x, y) = y + 2x^2$; $c = -2, 0, 2$

52. $f(x, y) = 2y - x^2$; $c = -2, 0, 2$

53. $f(x, y) = 2xy - 1$; $c = -1, 0, 1$

54. $f(x, y) = 2 + xy$; $c = -2, 0, 2$

Exercises 55–58 refer to the following plot of some level curves of $f(x, y) = c$ for $c = -2, 0, 2, 4,$ and 6. (Each grid square is 1 unit × 1 unit.) HINT [See Example 8.]

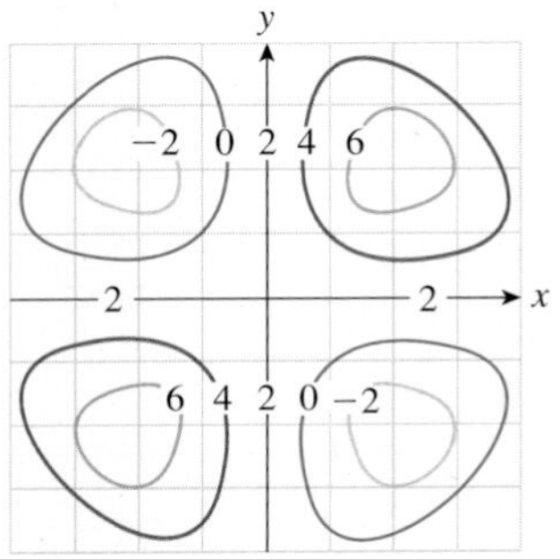

55. Estimate: **a.** $f(1, 1)$ **b.** $f(-2, -1)$ **c.** $f(3, -2.5)$

56. Estimate: **a.** $f(0, 1)$ **b.** $f(-1, -0.5)$ **c.** $f(-2, 1)$

57. At approximately which point or points does f appear to attain a maximum value?

58. At approximately which point or points does f appear to attain a minimum value?

Sketch the graphs of the functions in Exercises 59–74. HINT [See Example 7.]

59. $f(x, y) = 1 - x - y$
60. $f(x, y) = x + y - 2$
61. $g(x, y) = 2x + y - 2$
62. $g(x, y) = 3 - x + 2y$
63. $h(x, y) = x + 2$
64. $h(x, y) = 3 - y$

T *Use of technology is suggested in Exercises 65–74.* HINT [See Example 6.]

65. $s(x, y) = 2x^2 + 2y^2$. Show cross sections at $z = 1$ and $z = 2$.

66. $s(x, y) = -(x^2 + y^2)$. Show cross sections at $z = -1$ and $z = -2$.

67. $f(x, y) = 2 + \sqrt{x^2 + y^2}$. Show cross sections at $z = 3$ and $y = 0$.

68. $f(x, y) = 2 - \sqrt{x^2 + y^2}$. Show cross sections at $z = 0$ and $y = 0$.

69. $f(x, y) = y^2$
70. $g(x, y) = x^2$
71. $h(x, y) = \frac{1}{y}$
72. $k(x, y) = e^y$
73. $f(x, y) = e^{-(x^2+y^2)}$
74. $g(x, y) = \frac{1}{\sqrt{x^2 + y^2}}$

APPLICATIONS

75. ***Cost*** Your weekly cost (in dollars) to manufacture x cars and y trucks is

$$C(x, y) = 240{,}000 + 6{,}000x + 4{,}000y.$$

a. What is the marginal cost of a car? Of a truck? HINT [See Example 1.]
b. Describe the graph of the cost function C. HINT [See Example 7.]
c. Describe the slice $x = 10$. What cost function does this slice describe?
d. Describe the level curve $z = 480{,}000$. What does this curve tell you about costs?

76. ***Cost*** Your weekly cost (in dollars) to manufacture x bicycles and y tricycles is

$$C(x, y) = 24{,}000 + 60x + 20y.$$

a. What is the marginal cost of a bicycle? Of a tricycle? HINT [See Example 1.]
b. Describe the graph of the cost function C. HINT [See Example 7.]
c. Describe the slice by $y = 100$. What cost function does this slice describe?
d. Describe the level curve $z = 72{,}000$. What does this curve tell you about costs?

77. ***Cost*** Your sales of online video and audio clips are booming. Your Internet provider, Moneydrain.com, wants to get in on the action and has offered you unlimited technical assistance and consulting if you agree to pay Moneydrain 3¢ for every video clip and 4¢ for every audio clip you sell on the site. Further, Moneydrain agrees to charge you only \$10 per month to host your site. Set up a (monthly) cost function for the scenario, and describe each variable.

78. ***Cost*** Your Cabaret nightspot "Jazz on Jupiter" has become an expensive proposition: You are paying monthly costs of \$50,000 just to keep the place running. On top of that, your regular cabaret artist is charging you \$3,000 per performance, and your jazz ensemble is charging \$1,000 per hour. Set up a (monthly) cost function for the scenario, and describe each variable.

79. ***Scientific Research*** In each year from 1983 to 2003, the percentage y of research articles in *Physical Review* written by researchers in the United States can be approximated by

$$y = 82 - 0.78t - 1.02x \text{ percentage points} \quad (0 \le t \le 20),$$

where t is the year since 1983 and x is the percentage of articles written by researchers in Europe.[2]

a. In 2003, researchers in Europe wrote 38% of the articles published by the journal that year. What percentage was written by researchers in the United States?
b. In 1983, researchers in the United States wrote 61% of the articles published that year. What percentage was written by researchers in Europe?
c. What are the units of measurement of the coefficient of t?

80. ***Scientific Research*** The number z of research articles in *Physical Review* that were written by researchers in the United States from 1993 through 2003 can be approximated by

$$z = 5{,}960 - 0.71x + 0.50y \quad (3{,}000 \le x, y \le 6{,}000)$$

articles each year, where x is the number of articles written by researchers in Europe and y is the number written by researchers in other countries (excluding Europe and the United States).[3]

a. In 2000, approximately 5,500 articles were written by researchers in Europe, and 4,500 by researchers in other countries. How many (to the nearest 100) were written by researchers in the United States?
b. According to the model, if 5,000 articles were written in Europe and an equal number by researchers in the United States and other countries, what would that number be?
c. What is the significance of the fact that the coefficient of x is negative?

---

[2] Based on a linear regression. Source for data: The American Physical Society/*New York Times*, May 3, 2003, p. A1.
[3] *Ibid.*

81. ***Market Share in the 1990s: Chrysler, Ford, General Motors*** In the late 1990s, the relationship between the domestic market shares of three major U.S. manufacturers of cars and light trucks could be modeled by

$$x_3 = 0.66 - 2.2x_1 - 0.02x_2,$$

where x_1, x_2, and x_3 are, respectively, the fractions of the market held by Chrysler, Ford, and General Motors.[4] Thinking of General Motors' market share as a function of the shares of the other two manufacturers, describe the graph of the resulting function. How are the different slices by $x_1 = constant$ related to one another? What does this say about market share?

82. ***Market Share in the 1990s: Kellogg, General Mills, General Foods*** In the late 1990s, the relationship among the domestic market shares of three major manufacturers of breakfast cereal was

$$x_1 = -0.4 + 1.2x_2 + 2x_3,$$

where x_1, x_2, and x_3 are, respectively, the fractions of the market held by Kellogg, General Mills, and General Foods.[5] Thinking of Kellogg's market share as a function of the shares of the other two manufacturers, describe the graph of the resulting function. How are the different slices by $x_2 = constant$ related to one another? What does this say about market share?

83. ***Prison Population*** The number of prisoners in federal prisons in the United States can be approximated by

$$N(x, y) = 27 - 0.08x + 0.08y + 0.0002xy \text{ thousand inmates},$$

where x is the number, in thousands, in state prisons, and y is the number, in thousands, in local jails.[6]

a. In 2007 there were approximately 1.3 million in state prisons and 781 thousand in local jails. Estimate, to the nearest thousand, the number of prisoners in federal prisons that year.

b. Obtain N as a function of x for $y = 300$, and again for $y = 500$. Interpret the slopes of the resulting linear functions.

84. ***Prison Population*** The number of prisoners in state prisons in the United States can be approximated by

$$N(x, y) = -260 + 7x + 2y - 0.009xy \text{ thousand inmates},$$

where x is the number, in thousands, in federal prisons, and y is the number, in thousands, in local jails.[7]

a. In 2007 there were approximately 189 thousand in federal prisons and 781 thousand in local jails. Estimate, to the nearest 0.1 million, the number of prisoners in state prisons that year.

b. Obtain N as a function of y for $x = 80$, and again for $x = 100$. Interpret the slopes of the resulting linear functions.

85. ***Marginal Cost (Interaction Model)*** Your weekly cost (in dollars) to manufacture x cars and y trucks is

$$C(x, y) = 240{,}000 + 6{,}000x + 4{,}000y - 20xy.$$

(Compare with Exercise 75.)

a. Describe the slices $x = $ constant and $y = $ constant.

b. Is the graph of the cost function a plane? How does your answer relate to part (a)?

c. What are the slopes of the slices $x = 10$ and $x = 20$? What does this say about cost?

86. ***Marginal Cost (Interaction Model)*** Repeat the preceding exercise using the weekly cost to manufacture x bicycles and y tricycles given by

$$C(x, y) = 24{,}000 + 60x + 20y + 0.3xy.$$

(Compare with Exercise 76.)

87. ▼ ***Online Revenue*** Your major online bookstore is in direct competition with Amazon.com, BN.com, and BooksAMillion.com. Your company's daily revenue in dollars is given by

$$R(x, y, z) = 10{,}000 - 0.01x - 0.02y - 0.01z + 0.00001yz,$$

where x, y, and z are the online daily revenues of Amazon.com, BN.com, and BooksAMillion.com, respectively.

a. If, on a certain day, Amazon.com shows revenue of \$12,000, while BN.com and BooksAMillion.com each show \$5,000, what does the model predict for your company's revenue that day?

b. If Amazon.com and BN.com each show daily revenue of \$5,000, give an equation showing how your daily revenue depends on that of BooksAMillion.com.

88. ▼ ***Online Revenue*** Repeat the preceding exercise, using the revised revenue function

$$R(x, y, z) = 20{,}000 - 0.02x - 0.04y - 0.01z + 0.00001yz.$$

89. ▼ ***Sales: Walmart, Target*** The following table shows the approximate net sales, in billions of dollars, of Walmart and Target in 2004, 2008, and 2010.[8]

	2004	2008	2010
Walmart	250	370	420
Target	42	62	68

Model Walmart's net earnings as a function of Target's net earnings and time, using a linear function of the form

$$f(x, t) = Ax + Bt + C \quad (A, B, C \text{ constants}),$$

where f is Walmart's net earnings (in billions of dollars), x is Target's net earnings (in billions of dollars), and t is time in years since 2004. In 2006 Target's net earnings were about \$52.5 billion. What, to the nearest billion dollars, does your model estimate as Walmart's net earnings that year?

[4] Based on a linear regression. Source of data: Ward's AutoInfoBank/*New York Times*, July 29, 1998, p. D6.

[5] Based on a linear regression. Source of data: Bloomberg Financial Markets/*New York Times*, November 28, 1998, p. C1.

[6] Source for data: Sourcebook of Criminal Justice Statistics Online (www.albany.edu/sourcebook/wk1/t6132007.wk1).

[7] *Ibid.*

[8] Sources: http://walmartstores.com/Investors, http://investors.target.com, www.wikinvest.com.

90. ▼ ***Sales: Nintendo, Nokia*** The following table shows the approximate net sales of Nintendo (in billions of yen) and Nokia (in billions of euro) in 2000, 2004, and 2008.[9]

	2004	2008	2010
Nintendo	510	1,700	1,010
Nokia	30	52	42

Model Nintendo's net earnings as a function of Nokia's net earnings and time, using a linear function of the form

$$f(x, t) = Ax + Bt + C \quad (A, B, C \text{ constants}),$$

where f is Nintendo's net earnings (in billions of yen), x is Nokia's net earnings (in billions of euro), and t is time in years since 2004. In 2007 Nokia's net earnings were about €50 billion. What, to the nearest billion yen, does your model estimate as Nintendo's net earnings that year?

91. ▼ ***Utility*** Suppose your newspaper is trying to decide between two competing desktop publishing software packages, Macro Publish and Turbo Publish. You estimate that if you purchase x copies of Macro Publish and y copies of Turbo Publish, your company's daily productivity will be

$$U(x, y) = 6x^{0.8}y^{0.2} + x,$$

where $U(x, y)$ is measured in pages per day (U is called a *utility function*). If $x = y = 10$, calculate the effect of increasing x by one unit, and interpret the result.

92. ▼ ***Housing Costs***[10] The cost C (in dollars) of building a house is related to the number k of carpenters used and the number e of electricians used by

$$C(k, e) = 15{,}000 + 50k^2 + 60e^2.$$

If $k = e = 10$, compare the effects of increasing k by one unit and of increasing e by one unit. Interpret the result.

93. ▼ ***Volume*** The volume of an ellipsoid with cross-sectional radii a, b, and c is $V(a, b, c) = \frac{4}{3}\pi abc$.

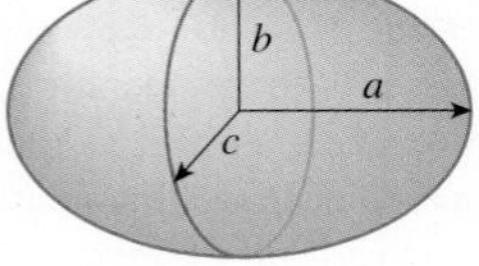

a. Find at least two sets of values for a, b, and c such that $V(a, b, c) = 1$.

b. Find the value of a such that $V(a, a, a) = 1$, and describe the resulting ellipsoid.

94. ▼ ***Volume*** The volume of a right elliptical cone with height h and radii a and b of its base is $V(a, b, h) = \frac{1}{3}\pi abh$.

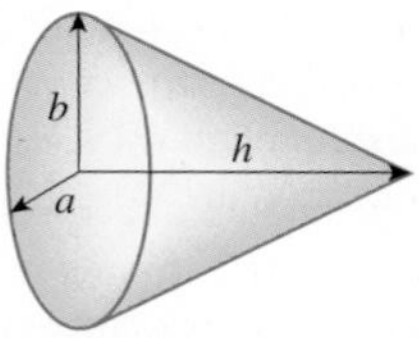

a. Find at least two sets of values for a, b, and h such that $V(a, b, h) = 1$.

b. Find the value of a such that $V(a, a, a) = 1$, and describe the resulting cone.

Exercises 95–98 involve "Cobb-Douglas" productivity functions. These functions have the form

$$P(x, y) = Kx^a y^{1-a},$$

where P stands for the number of items produced per year, x is the number of employees, and y is the annual operating budget. (The numbers K and a are constants that depend on the situation we are looking at, with $0 \le a \le 1$.*)*

95. ***Productivity*** How many items will be produced per year by a company with 100 employees and an annual operating budget of \$500,000 if $K = 1{,}000$ and $a = 0.5$? (Round your answer to one significant digit.)

96. ***Productivity*** How many items will be produced per year by a company with 50 employees and an annual operating budget of \$1,000,000 if $K = 1{,}000$ and $a = 0.5$? (Round your answer to one significant digit.)

97. ▼ ***Modeling Production with Cobb-Douglas*** Two years ago my piano manufacturing plant employed 1,000 workers, had an operating budget of \$1 million, and turned out 100 pianos. Last year, I slashed the operating budget to \$10,000, and production dropped to 10 pianos.

a. Use the data for each of the two years and the Cobb-Douglas formula to obtain two equations in K and a.

b. Take logs of both sides in each equation and obtain two linear equations in a and $\log K$.

c. Solve these equations to obtain values for a and K.

d. Use these values in the Cobb-Douglas formula to predict production if I increase the operating budget back to \$1 million but lay off half the work force.

98. ▼ ***Modeling Production with Cobb-Douglas*** Repeat the preceding exercise using the following data: Two years ago—1,000 employees, \$1 million operating budget, 100 pianos; last year—1,000 employees, \$100,000 operating budget, 10 pianos.

99. ▼ ***Pollution*** The burden of human-made aerosol sulfate in the Earth's atmosphere, in grams per square meter, is

$$B(x, n) = \frac{xn}{A},$$

where x is the total weight of aerosol sulfate emitted into the atmosphere per year and n is the number of years it remains in the atmosphere. A is the surface area of the Earth, approximately 5.1×10^{14} square meters.[11]

[9] Sources: www.nintendo.com/corp, http://investors.nokia.com, www.wikinvest.com.

[10] Based on an Exercise in *Introduction to Mathematical Economics* by A. L. Ostrosky Jr. and J. V. Koch (Waveland Press, Illinois, 1979).

[11] Source: Robert J. Charlson and Tom M. L. Wigley, "Sulfate Aerosol and Climatic Change," *Scientific American*, February, 1994, pp. 48–57.

a. Calculate the burden, given the 1995 estimated values of $x = 1.5 \times 10^{14}$ grams per year, and $n = 5$ days.

b. What does the function $W(x, n) = xn$ measure?

100. ▼ ***Pollution*** The amount of aerosol sulfate (in grams) was approximately 45×10^{12} grams in 1940 and has been increasing exponentially ever since, with a doubling time of approximately 20 years.[12] Use the model from the preceding exercise to give a formula for the atmospheric burden of aerosol sulfate as a function of the time t in years since 1940 and the number of years n it remains in the atmosphere.

101. ▼ ***Alien Intelligence*** Frank Drake, an astronomer at the University of California at Santa Cruz, devised the following equation to estimate the number of planet-based civilizations in our Milky Way galaxy willing and able to communicate with Earth:[13]

$$N(R, f_p, n_e, f_l, f_i, f_c, L) = R f_p n_e f_l f_i f_c L$$

R = the number of new stars formed in our galaxy each year

f_p = the fraction of those stars that have planetary systems

n_e = the average number of planets in each such system that can support life

f_l = the fraction of such planets on which life actually evolves

f_i = the fraction of life-sustaining planets on which intelligent life evolves

f_c = the fraction of intelligent-life-bearing planets on which the intelligent beings develop the means and the will to communicate over interstellar distances

L = the average lifetime of such technological civilizations (in years)

a. What would be the effect on N if any one of the variables were doubled?

b. How would you modify the formula if you were interested only in the number of intelligent-life-bearing planets in the galaxy?

c. How could one convert this function into a linear function?

d. (For discussion) Try to come up with an estimate of N.

102. ▼ ***More Alien Intelligence*** The formula given in the preceding exercise restricts attention to planet-based civilizations in our galaxy. Give a formula that includes intelligent planet-based aliens from the galaxy Andromeda. (Assume that all the variables used in the formula for the Milky Way have the same values for Andromeda.)

COMMUNICATION AND REASONING EXERCISES

103. Let $f(x, y) = \dfrac{x}{y}$. How are $f(x, y)$ and $f(y, x)$ related?

104. Let $f(x, y) = x^2y^3$. How are $f(x, y)$ and $f(-x, -y)$ related?

105. Give an example of a function of the two variables x and y with the property that interchanging x and y has no effect.

106. Give an example of a function f of the two variables x and y with the property that $f(x, y) = -f(y, x)$.

107. Give an example of a function f of the three variables x, y, and z with the property that $f(x, y, z) = f(y, x, z)$ and $f(-x, -y, -z) = -f(x, y, z)$.

108. Give an example of a function f of the three variables x, y, and z with the property that $f(x, y, z) = f(y, x, z)$ and $f(-x, -y, -z) = f(x, y, z)$.

109. Illustrate by means of an example how a real-valued function of the two variables x and y gives different real-valued functions of one variable when we restrict y to be different constants.

110. Illustrate by means of an example how a real-valued function of one variable x gives different real-valued functions of the two variables y and z when we substitute for x suitable functions of y and z.

111. ▼ If f is a linear function of x and y, show that if we restrict y to be a fixed constant, then the resulting function of x is linear. Does the slope of this linear function depend on the choice of y?

112. ▼ If f is an interaction function of x and y, show that if we restrict y to be a fixed constant, then the resulting function of x is linear. Does the slope of this linear function depend on the choice of y?

113. ▼ Suppose that $C(x, y)$ represents the cost of x CDs and y cassettes. If $C(x, y + 1) < C(x + 1, y)$ for every $x \geq 0$ and $y \geq 0$, what does this tell you about the cost of CDs and cassettes?

114. ▼ Suppose that $C(x, y)$ represents the cost of renting x DVDs and y video games. If $C(x + 2, y) < C(x, y + 1)$ for every $x \geq 0$ and $y \geq 0$, what does this tell you about the cost of renting DVDs and video games?

115. Complete the following: The graph of a linear function of two variables is a _____ .

116. Complete the following: The level curves of a linear function of two variables are ____ .

117. ▼ ***Heat-Seeking Missiles*** The following diagram shows some level curves of the temperature, in degrees Fahrenheit, of a region in space, as well as the location, on the 100-degree curve, of a heat-seeking missile moving through the region. (These level curves are called **isotherms**.) In which of the three directions shown should the missile be traveling so as to experience the fastest rate of increase in temperature at the given point? Explain your answer.

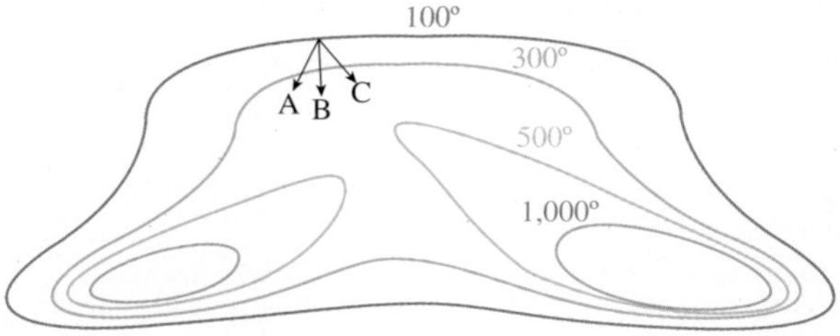

[12]Source: Robert J. Charlson and Tom M. L. Wigley, "Sulfate Aerosol and Climatic Change," *Scientific American*, February, 1994, pp. 48–57.

[13]Source: "First Contact" (Plume Books/Penguin Group)/*New York Times*, October 6, 1992, p. C1.

118. ▼ ***Hiking*** The following diagram shows some level curves of the altitude of a mountain valley, as well as the location, on the 2,000-ft curve, of a hiker. The hiker is currently moving at the greatest possible rate of descent. In which of the three directions shown is he moving? Explain your answer.

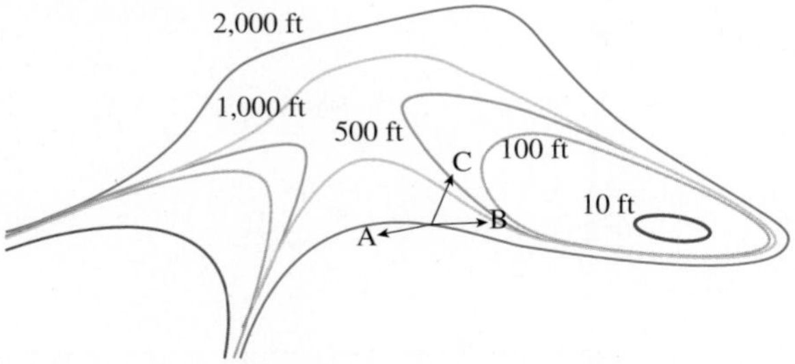

119. Your study partner Slim claims that because the surface $z = f(x, y)$ you have been studying is a plane, it follows that all the slices $x =$ *constant* and $y =$ *constant* are straight lines. Do you agree or disagree? Explain.

120. Your other study partner Shady just told you that the surface $z = xy$ you have been trying to graph must be a plane because you've already found that the slices $x =$ *constant* and $y =$ *constant* are all straight lines. Do you agree or disagree? Explain.

121. Why do we not sketch the graphs of functions of three or more variables?

122. The surface of a mountain can be thought of as the graph of what function?

123. Why is three-dimensional space used to represent the graph of a function of two variables?

124. Why is it that we can sketch the graphs of functions of two variables on the two-dimensional flat surfaces of these pages?

8.2 Partial Derivatives

Recall that if f is a function of x, then the derivative df/dx measures how fast f changes as x increases. If f is a function of two or more variables, we can ask how fast f changes as each variable increases while the others remain fixed. These rates of change are called the "partial derivatives of f," and they measure how each variable contributes to the change in f. Here is a more precise definition.

Partial Derivatives

The **partial derivative of *f* with respect to *x*** is the derivative of f with respect to x, when all other variables are treated as constant. Similarly, the **partial derivative of *f* with respect to *y*** is the derivative of f with respect to y, with all other variables treated as constant, and so on for other variables. The partial derivatives are written as $\frac{\partial f}{\partial x}, \frac{\partial f}{\partial y}$, and so on. The symbol ∂ is used (instead of d) to remind us that there is more than one variable and that we are holding the other variables fixed.

Quick Examples

1. Let $f(x, y) = x^2 + y^2$.

$$\frac{\partial f}{\partial x} = 2x + 0 = 2x$$ Because y^2 is treated as a constant

$$\frac{\partial f}{\partial y} = 0 + 2y = 2y$$ Because x^2 is treated as a constant

2. Let $z = x^2 + xy$.

$$\frac{\partial z}{\partial x} = 2x + y \qquad \frac{\partial}{\partial x}(xy) = \frac{\partial}{\partial x}(x \cdot \text{constant}) = \text{constant} = y$$

$$\frac{\partial z}{\partial y} = 0 + x \qquad \frac{\partial}{\partial y}(xy) = \frac{\partial}{\partial y}(\text{constant} \cdot y) = \text{constant} = x$$

3. Let $f(x, y) = x^2y + y^2x - xy + y$.

$$\frac{\partial f}{\partial x} = 2xy + y^2 - y \qquad y \text{ is treated as a constant.}$$

$$\frac{\partial f}{\partial y} = x^2 + 2xy - x + 1 \qquad x \text{ is treated as a constant.}$$

Interpretation

$\frac{\partial f}{\partial x}$ is the rate at which f changes as x changes, for a fixed (constant) y.

$\frac{\partial f}{\partial y}$ is the rate at which f changes as y changes, for a fixed (constant) x.

EXAMPLE 1 Marginal Cost: Linear Model

We return to Example 1 from Section 8.1. Suppose that you own a company that makes two models of speakers, the Ultra Mini and the Big Stack. Your total monthly cost (in dollars) to make x Ultra Minis and y Big Stacks is given by

$$C(x, y) = 10{,}000 + 20x + 40y.$$

What is the significance of $\frac{\partial C}{\partial x}$ and of $\frac{\partial C}{\partial y}$?

Solution First we compute these partial derivatives:

$$\frac{\partial C}{\partial x} = 20$$

$$\frac{\partial C}{\partial y} = 40.$$

We interpret the results as follows: $\frac{\partial C}{\partial x} = 20$ means that the cost is increasing at a rate of \$20 per additional Ultra Mini (if production of Big Stacks is held constant); $\frac{\partial C}{\partial y} = 40$ means that the cost is increasing at a rate of \$40 per additional Big Stack (if production of Ultra Minis is held constant). In other words, these are the **marginal costs** of each model of speaker.

Before we go on... How much does the cost rise if you increase x by Δx and y by Δy? In Example 1, the change in cost is given by

$$\Delta C = 20\Delta x + 40\Delta y = \frac{\partial C}{\partial x}\Delta x + \frac{\partial C}{\partial y}\Delta y.$$

This suggests the **chain rule for several variables**. Part of this rule says that if x and y are both functions of t, then C is a function of t through them, and the rate of change of C with respect to t can be calculated as

$$\frac{dC}{dt} = \frac{\partial C}{\partial x}\cdot\frac{dx}{dt} + \frac{\partial C}{\partial y}\cdot\frac{dy}{dt}.$$

See the optional section on the chain rule for several variables for further discussion and applications of this interesting result. ■

EXAMPLE 2 Marginal Cost: Interaction Model

Another possibility for the cost function in the preceding example is an interaction model

$$C(x, y) = 10{,}000 + 20x + 40y + 0.1xy.$$

a. *Now* what are the marginal costs of the two models of speakers?

b. What is the marginal cost of manufacturing Big Stacks at a production level of 100 Ultra Minis and 50 Big Stacks per month?

Solution

a. We compute the partial derivatives:

$$\frac{\partial C}{\partial x} = 20 + 0.1y$$

$$\frac{\partial C}{\partial y} = 40 + 0.1x.$$

Thus, the marginal cost of manufacturing Ultra Minis increases by \$0.1 or 10¢ for each Big Stack that is manufactured. Similarly, the marginal cost of manufacturing Big Stacks increases by 10¢ for each Ultra Mini that is manufactured.

b. From part (a), the marginal cost of manufacturing Big Stacks is

$$\frac{\partial C}{\partial y} = 40 + 0.1x.$$

At a production level of 100 Ultra Minis and 50 Big Stacks per month, we have $x = 100$ and $y = 50$. Thus, the marginal cost of manufacturing Big Stacks at these production levels is

$$\left.\frac{\partial C}{\partial y}\right|_{(100,50)} = 40 + 0.1(100) = \$50 \text{ per Big Stack.}$$

Partial derivatives of functions of three variables are obtained in the same way as those for functions of two variables, as the following example shows.

EXAMPLE 3 Function of Three Variables

Calculate $\dfrac{\partial f}{\partial x}$, $\dfrac{\partial f}{\partial y}$, and $\dfrac{\partial f}{\partial z}$ if $f(x, y, z) = xy^2z^3 - xy$.

Solution Although we now have three variables, the calculation remains the same: $\partial f/\partial x$ is the derivative of f with respect to x, with *both* other variables, y and z, held constant:

$$\frac{\partial f}{\partial x} = y^2z^3 - y.$$

Similarly, $\partial f/\partial y$ is the derivative of f with respect to y, with both x and z held constant:

$$\frac{\partial f}{\partial y} = 2xyz^3 - x.$$

Finally, to find $\partial f/\partial z$, we hold both x and y constant and take the derivative with respect to z.

$$\frac{\partial f}{\partial z} = 3xy^2z^2.$$

Note The procedure for finding a partial derivative is the same for any number of variables: To get the partial derivative with respect to any one variable, we treat all the others as constants. ■

Geometric Interpretation of Partial Derivatives

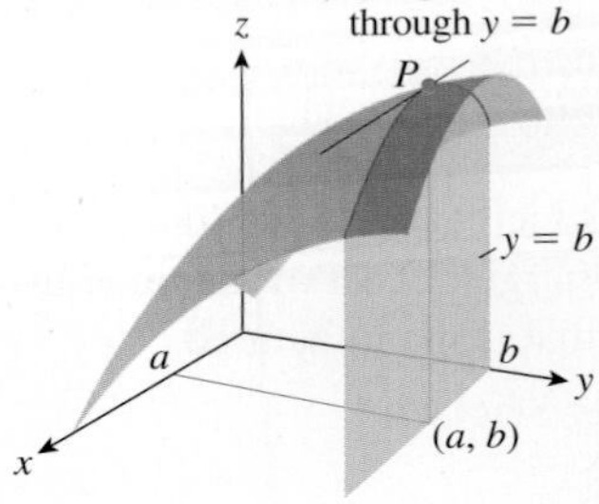

$\left.\dfrac{\partial f}{\partial x}\right|_{(a,b)}$ is the slope of the tangent line at the point $P(a, b, f(a, b))$ along the slice through $y = b$.

Figure 19

Recall that if f is a function of one variable x, then the derivative df/dx gives the slopes of the tangent lines to its graph. Now, suppose that f is a function of x and y. By definition, $\partial f/\partial x$ is the derivative of the function of x we get by holding y fixed. If we evaluate this derivative at the point (a, b), we are holding y fixed at the value b, taking the ordinary derivative of the resulting function of x, and evaluating this at $x = a$. Now, holding y fixed at b amounts to slicing through the graph of f along the plane $y = b$, resulting in a curve. Thus, the partial derivative is the slope of the tangent line to this curve at the point where $x = a$ and $y = b$, along the plane $y = b$ (Figure 19). This fits with our interpretation of $\partial f/\partial x$ as the rate of increase of f with increasing x when y is held fixed at b.

The other partial derivative, $\partial f/\partial y|_{(a,b)}$, is, similarly, the slope of the tangent line at the same point $P(a, b, f(a, b))$ but along the slice by the plane $x = a$. You should draw the corresponding picture for this on your own.

EXAMPLE 4 Marginal Cost

Referring to the interactive cost function $C(x, y) = 10{,}000 + 20x + 40y + 0.1xy$ in Example 2, we can identify the marginal costs $\partial C/\partial x$ and $\partial C/\partial y$ of manufacturing Ultra Minis and Big Stacks at a production level of 100 Ultra Minis and 50 Big Stacks per month as the slopes of the tangent lines to the two slices by $y = 50$ and $x = 100$ at the point on the graph where $(x, y) = (100, 50)$ as seen in Figure 20.

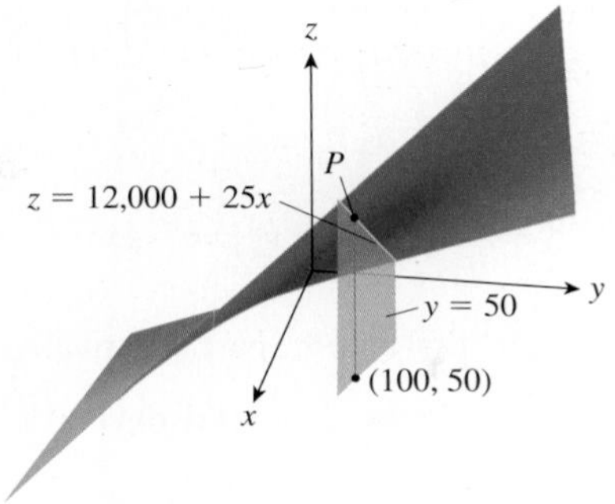

Figure 20(a)

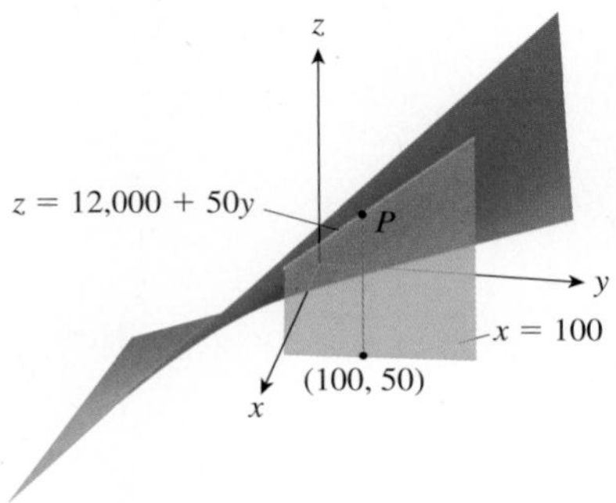

Figure 20(b)

Figure 20(a) shows the slice at $y = 50$ through the point $P = (100, 50, C(100, 50)) = (100, 50, 14{,}500)$. The equation of that slice is given by substituting $y = 50$ in the cost equation:

$$C(x, 50) = 10{,}000 + 20x + 40(50) + 0.1x(50) = 12{,}000 + 25x. \quad \text{A line of slope 25}$$

Because the slice is already a line, it coincides with the tangent line through P as depicted in Figure 19. This slope is equal to $\partial C/\partial x|_{(100,50)}$:

$$\frac{\partial C}{\partial x} = 20 + 0.1y \qquad \text{See Example 2.}$$

so $$\left.\frac{\partial C}{\partial x}\right|_{(100,50)} = 20 + 0.1(50) = 25.$$

Similarly, Figure 20(b) shows the slice at $x = 100$ through the same point P. The equation of that slice is given by substituting $x = 100$ in the cost equation:

$$C(100, y) = 10{,}000 + 20(100) + 40y + 0.1(100)y = 12{,}000 + 50y. \quad \text{A line of slope 50}$$

This slope is equal to $\partial C/\partial y|_{(100,50)} = 50$ as we calculated in Example 2.

Second-Order Partial Derivatives

Just as for functions of a single variable, we can calculate second derivatives. Suppose, for example, that we have a function of x and y, say, $f(x, y) = x^2 - x^2y^2$. We know that

$$\frac{\partial f}{\partial x} = 2x - 2xy^2.$$

If we take the partial derivative with respect to x once again, we obtain

$$\frac{\partial}{\partial x}\left(\frac{\partial f}{\partial x}\right) = 2 - 2y^2. \qquad \text{Take } \frac{\partial}{\partial x} \text{ of } \frac{\partial f}{\partial x}.$$

(The symbol $\partial/\partial x$ means "the partial derivative with respect to x," just as d/dx stands for "the derivative with respect to x.") This is called the **second-order partial derivative** and is written $\frac{\partial^2 f}{\partial x^2}$. We get the following derivatives similarly:

$$\frac{\partial f}{\partial y} = -2x^2y$$

$$\frac{\partial^2 f}{\partial y^2} = -2x^2. \qquad \text{Take } \frac{\partial}{\partial y} \text{ of } \frac{\partial f}{\partial y}.$$

Now what if we instead take the partial derivative with respect to y of $\partial f/\partial x$?

$$\frac{\partial^2 f}{\partial y \partial x} = \frac{\partial}{\partial y}\left(\frac{\partial f}{\partial x}\right) \qquad \text{Take } \frac{\partial}{\partial y} \text{ of } \frac{\partial f}{\partial x}.$$

$$= \frac{\partial}{\partial y}[2x - 2xy^2] = -4xy$$

Here, $\frac{\partial^2 f}{\partial y \partial x}$ means "first take the partial derivative with respect to x and then with respect to y" and is called a **mixed partial derivative**. If we differentiate in the opposite order, we get

$$\frac{\partial^2 f}{\partial x \partial y} = \frac{\partial}{\partial x}\left(\frac{\partial f}{\partial y}\right) = \frac{\partial}{\partial x}[-2x^2 y] = -4xy,$$

the same expression as $\frac{\partial^2 f}{\partial y \partial x}$. This is no coincidence: The mixed partial derivatives $\frac{\partial^2 f}{\partial x \partial y}$ and $\frac{\partial^2 f}{\partial y \partial x}$ are always the same as long as the first partial derivatives are both differentiable functions of x and y and the mixed partial derivatives are continuous. Because all the functions we shall use are of this type, we can take the derivatives in any order we like when calculating mixed derivatives.

Here is another notation for partial derivatives that is especially convenient for second-order partial derivatives:

f_x means $\frac{\partial f}{\partial x}$

f_y means $\frac{\partial f}{\partial y}$

f_{xy} means $(f_x)_y = \frac{\partial^2 f}{\partial y \partial x}$ (Note the order in which the derivatives are taken.)

f_{yx} means $(f_y)_x = \frac{\partial^2 f}{\partial x \partial y}$.

8.2 EXERCISES

▼ more advanced ◆ challenging

T indicates exercises that should be solved using technology

In Exercises 1–18, calculate $\frac{\partial f}{\partial x}, \frac{\partial f}{\partial y}, \left.\frac{\partial f}{\partial x}\right|_{(1,-1)}$, *and* $\left.\frac{\partial f}{\partial y}\right|_{(1,-1)}$ *when defined.* HINT [See Quick Examples pages 607–608.]

1. $f(x, y) = 10{,}000 - 40x + 20y$
2. $f(x, y) = 1{,}000 + 5x - 4y$
3. $f(x, y) = 3x^2 - y^3 + x - 1$
4. $f(x, y) = x^{1/2} - 2y^4 + y + 6$
5. $f(x, y) = 10{,}000 - 40x + 20y + 10xy$
6. $f(x, y) = 1{,}000 + 5x - 4y - 3xy$
7. $f(x, y) = 3x^2 y$
8. $f(x, y) = x^4 y^2 - x$
9. $f(x, y) = x^2 y^3 - x^3 y^2 - xy$
10. $f(x, y) = x^{-1} y^2 + xy^2 + xy$
11. $f(x, y) = (2xy + 1)^3$
12. $f(x, y) = \frac{1}{(xy + 1)^2}$
13. ▼ $f(x, y) = e^{x+y}$
14. ▼ $f(x, y) = e^{2x+y}$
15. ▼ $f(x, y) = 5x^{0.6} y^{0.4}$
16. ▼ $f(x, y) = -2x^{0.1} y^{0.9}$
17. ▼ $f(x, y) = e^{0.2xy}$
18. ▼ $f(x, y) = xe^{xy}$

In Exercises 19–28, find $\frac{\partial^2 f}{\partial x^2}, \frac{\partial^2 f}{\partial y^2}, \frac{\partial^2 f}{\partial x \partial y}$, *and* $\frac{\partial^2 f}{\partial y \partial x}$, *and evaluate them all at* $(1, -1)$ *if possible.* HINT [See discussion on pages 611–612.]

19. $f(x, y) = 10{,}000 - 40x + 20y$
20. $f(x, y) = 1{,}000 + 5x - 4y$
21. $f(x, y) = 10{,}000 - 40x + 20y + 10xy$

22. $f(x, y) = 1{,}000 + 5x - 4y - 3xy$

23. $f(x, y) = 3x^2y$

24. $f(x, y) = x^4y^2 - x$

25. ▼ $f(x, y) = e^{x+y}$

26. ▼ $f(x, y) = e^{2x+y}$

27. ▼ $f(x, y) = 5x^{0.6}y^{0.4}$

28. ▼ $f(x, y) = -2x^{0.1}y^{0.9}$

In Exercises 29–40, find $\frac{\partial f}{\partial x}, \frac{\partial f}{\partial y}, \frac{\partial f}{\partial z}$, *and their values at* $(0, -1, 1)$ *if possible.* HINT [See Example 3.]

29. $f(x, y, z) = xyz$

30. $f(x, y, z) = xy + xz - yz$

31. ▼ $f(x, y, z) = -\dfrac{4}{x + y + z^2}$

32. ▼ $f(x, y, z) = \dfrac{6}{x^2 + y^2 + z^2}$

33. ▼ $f(x, y, z) = xe^{yz} + ye^{xz}$

34. ▼ $f(x, y, z) = xye^z + xe^{yz} + e^{xyz}$

35. ▼ $f(x, y, z) = x^{0.1}y^{0.4}z^{0.5}$

36. ▼ $f(x, y, z) = 2x^{0.2}y^{0.8} + z^2$

37. ▼ $f(x, y, z) = e^{xyz}$

38. ▼ $f(x, y, z) = \ln(x + y + z)$

39. ▼ $f(x, y, z) = \dfrac{2{,}000z}{1 + y^{0.3}}$

40. ▼ $f(x, y, z) = \dfrac{e^{0.2x}}{1 + e^{-0.1y}}$

APPLICATIONS

41. ***Marginal Cost (Linear Model)*** Your weekly cost (in dollars) to manufacture x cars and y trucks is

$$C(x, y) = 240{,}000 + 6{,}000x + 4{,}000y.$$

Calculate and interpret $\frac{\partial C}{\partial x}$ and $\frac{\partial C}{\partial y}$. HINT [See Example 1.]

42. ***Marginal Cost (Linear Model)*** Your weekly cost (in dollars) to manufacture x bicycles and y tricycles is

$$C(x, y) = 24{,}000 + 60x + 20y.$$

Calculate and interpret $\frac{\partial C}{\partial x}$ and $\frac{\partial C}{\partial y}$.

43. ***Scientific Research*** In each year from 1983 to 2003, the percentage y of research articles in *Physical Review* written by researchers in the United States can be approximated by

$$y = 82 - 0.78t - 1.02x \text{ percentage points} \quad (0 \le t \le 20),$$

where t is the year since 1983 and x is the percentage of articles written by researchers in Europe.[14] Calculate and interpret $\frac{\partial y}{\partial t}$ and $\frac{\partial y}{\partial x}$.

[14]Based on a linear regression. Source for data: The American Physical Society/*New York Times*, May 3, 2003, p. A1.

44. ***Scientific Research*** The number z of research articles in *Physical Review* that were written by researchers in the United States from 1993 through 2003 can be approximated by

$$z = 5{,}960 - 0.71x + 0.50y \quad (3{,}000 \le x, y \le 6{,}000)$$

articles each year, where x is the number of articles written by researchers in Europe and y is the number written by researchers in other countries (excluding Europe and the United States).[15] Calculate and interpret $\frac{\partial z}{\partial x}$ and $\frac{\partial z}{\partial y}$.

45. ***Marginal Cost (Interaction Model)*** Your weekly cost (in dollars) to manufacture x cars and y trucks is

$$C(x, y) = 240{,}000 + 6{,}000x + 4{,}000y - 20xy.$$

(Compare with Exercise 41.) Compute the marginal cost of manufacturing cars at a production level of 10 cars and 20 trucks. HINT [See Example 2.]

46. ***Marginal Cost (Interaction Model)*** Your weekly cost (in dollars) to manufacture x bicycles and y tricycles is

$$C(x, y) = 24{,}000 + 60x + 20y + 0.3xy.$$

(Compare with Exercise 42.) Compute the marginal cost of manufacturing tricycles at a production level of 10 bicycles and 20 tricycles. HINT [See Example 2.]

47. ***Brand Loyalty*** The fraction of Mazda car owners who chose another new Mazda can be modeled by the following function:[16]

$$M(c, f, g, h, t) = 1.1 - 3.8c + 2.2f + 1.9g - 1.7h - 1.3t.$$

Here, c is the fraction of Chrysler car owners who remained loyal to Chrysler, f is the fraction of Ford car owners remaining loyal to Ford, g the corresponding figure for General Motors, h the corresponding figure for Honda, and t for Toyota.

a. Calculate $\frac{\partial M}{\partial c}$ and $\frac{\partial M}{\partial f}$ and interpret the answers.

b. One year it was observed that $c = 0.56$, $f = 0.56$, $g = 0.72$, $h = 0.50$, and $t = 0.43$. According to the model, what percentage of Mazda owners remained loyal to Mazda? (Round your answer to the nearest percentage point.)

48. ***Brand Loyalty*** The fraction of Mazda car owners who chose another new Mazda can be modeled by the following function:[17]

$$M(c, f) = 9.4 + 7.8c + 3.6c^2 - 38f - 22cf + 43f^2,$$

[15]*Ibid.*

[16]The model is an approximation of a linear regression based on data from the period 1988–1995. Source for data: Chrysler, Maritz Market Research, Consumer Attitude Research, and Strategic Vision/*New York Times*, November 3, 1995, p. D2.

[17]The model is an approximation of a second-order regression based on data from the period 1988–1995. Source for data: Chrysler, Maritz Market Research, Consumer Attitude Research, and Strategic Vision/*New York Times*, November 3, 1995, p. D2.

where c is the fraction of **Chrysler** car owners who remained loyal to Chrysler and f is the fraction of **Ford** car owners remaining loyal to Ford.

a. Calculate $\frac{\partial M}{\partial c}$ and $\frac{\partial M}{\partial f}$ evaluated at the point (0.7, 0.7), and interpret the answers.

b. One year it was observed that $c = 0.56$, and $f = 0.56$. According to the model, what percentage of Mazda owners remained loyal to Mazda? (Round your answer to the nearest percentage point.)

49. ***Marginal Cost*** Your weekly cost (in dollars) to manufacture x cars and y trucks is

$$C(x, y) = 200{,}000 + 6{,}000x + 4{,}000y - 100{,}000e^{-0.01(x+y)}.$$

What is the marginal cost of a car? Of a truck? How do these marginal costs behave as total production increases?

50. ***Marginal Cost*** Your weekly cost (in dollars) to manufacture x bicycles and y tricycles is

$$C(x, y) = 20{,}000 + 60x + 20y + 50\sqrt{xy}.$$

What is the marginal cost of a bicycle? Of a tricycle? How do these marginal costs behave as x and y increase?

51. ▼ ***Income Gap*** The following model is based on data on the median family incomes of Hispanic and white families in the United States for the period 1980–2008:[18]

$$z(t, x) = 31{,}200 + 270t + 13{,}500x + 140xt,$$

where

$$z(t, x) = \text{median family income}$$
$$t = \text{year } (t = 0 \text{ represents } 1980)$$
$$x = \begin{cases} 0 & \text{if the income was for a Hispanic family} \\ 1 & \text{if the income was for a white family} \end{cases}.$$

a. Use the model to estimate the median income of a Hispanic family and of a white family in 2000.

b. According to the model, how fast was the median income for a Hispanic family increasing in 2000? How fast was the median income for a white family increasing in 2000?

c. Do the answers in part (b) suggest that the income gap between white and Hispanic families was widening or narrowing during the given period?

d. What does the coefficient of xt in the formula for $z(t, x)$ represent in terms of the income gap?

52. ▼ ***Income Gap*** The following model is based on data on the median family incomes of black and white families in the United States for the period 1980–2008:[19]

$$z(t, x) = 24{,}500 + 390t + 20{,}200x + 20xt,$$

where

$$z(t, x) = \text{median family income}$$
$$t = \text{year } (t = 0 \text{ represents } 1980)$$
$$x = \begin{cases} 0 & \text{if the income was for a black family} \\ 1 & \text{if the income was for a white family} \end{cases}.$$

a. Use the model to estimate the median income of a black family and of a white family in 2000.

b. According to the model, how fast was the median income for a black family increasing in 2000? How fast was the median income for a white family increasing in 2000?

c. Do the answers in part (b) suggest that the income gap between white and black families was widening or narrowing during the given period?

d. What does the coefficient of xt in the formula for $z(t, x)$ represent in terms of the income gap?

53. ▼ ***Average Cost*** If you average your costs over your total production, you get the **average cost**, written $\bar{C}$:

$$\bar{C}(x, y) = \frac{C(x, y)}{x + y}.$$

Find the average cost for the cost function in Exercise 49. Then find the marginal average cost of a car and the marginal average cost of a truck at a production level of 50 cars and 50 trucks. Interpret your answers.

54. ▼ ***Average Cost*** Find the average cost for the cost function in Exercise 50. (See the preceding exercise.) Then find the marginal average cost of a bicycle and the marginal average cost of a tricycle at a production level of five bicycles and five tricycles. Interpret your answers.

55. ▼ ***Marginal Revenue*** As manager of an auto dealership, you offer a car rental company the following deal: You will charge \$15,000 per car and \$10,000 per truck, but you will then give the company a discount of \$5,000 times the square root of the total number of vehicles it buys from you. Looking at your marginal revenue, is this a good deal for the rental company?

56. ▼ ***Marginal Revenue*** As marketing director for a bicycle manufacturer, you come up with the following scheme: You will offer to sell a dealer x bicycles and y tricycles for

$$R(x, y) = 3{,}500 - 3{,}500e^{-0.02x-0.01y} \text{ dollars.}$$

Find your marginal revenue for bicycles and for tricycles. Are you likely to be fired for your suggestion?

57. ▼ ***Research Productivity*** Here we apply a variant of the Cobb-Douglas function to the modeling of research productivity. A mathematical model of research productivity at a particular physics laboratory is

$$P = 0.04x^{0.4}y^{0.2}z^{0.4},$$

where P is the annual number of groundbreaking research papers produced by the staff, x is the number of physicists on the research team, y is the laboratory's annual research budget, and z is the annual National Science Foundation subsidy to the laboratory. Find the rate of increase of research papers per government-subsidy dollar at a subsidy level of \$1,000,000 per year and a staff level of 10 physicists if the annual budget is \$100,000.

[18] Incomes are in 2007 dollars. Source for data: U.S. Census Bureau (www.census.gov).
[19] *Ibid.*

58. ▼ ***Research Productivity*** A major drug company estimates that the annual number P of patents for new drugs developed by its research team is best modeled by the formula

$$P = 0.3x^{0.3}y^{0.4}z^{0.3},$$

where x is the number of research biochemists on the payroll, y is the annual research budget, and z is the size of the bonus awarded to discoverers of new drugs. Assuming that the company has 12 biochemists on the staff, has an annual research budget of \$500,000, and pays \$40,000 bonuses to developers of new drugs, calculate the rate of growth in the annual number of patents per new research staff member.

59. ▼ ***Utility*** Your newspaper is trying to decide between two competing desktop publishing software packages, Macro Publish and Turbo Publish. You estimate that if you purchase x copies of Macro Publish and y copies of Turbo Publish, your company's daily productivity will be

$$U(x, y) = 6x^{0.8}y^{0.2} + x \text{ pages per day.}$$

a. Calculate $U_x(10, 5)$ and $U_y(10, 5)$ to two decimal places, and interpret the results.

b. What does the ratio $\dfrac{U_x(10, 5)}{U_y(10, 5)}$ tell about the usefulness of these products?

60. ▼ ***Grades***[20] A production formula for a student's performance on a difficult English examination is given by

$$g(t, x) = 4tx - 0.2t^2 - x^2,$$

where g is the grade the student can expect to get, t is the number of hours of study for the examination, and x is the student's grade-point average.

a. Calculate $g_t(10, 3)$ and $g_x(10, 3)$ and interpret the results.

b. What does the ratio $\dfrac{g_t(10, 3)}{g_x(10, 3)}$ tell about the relative merits of study and grade-point average?

61. ▼ ***Electrostatic Repulsion*** If positive electric charges of Q and q coulombs are situated at positions (a, b, c) and (x, y, z), respectively, then the force of repulsion they experience is given by

$$F = K\frac{Qq}{(x-a)^2 + (y-b)^2 + (z-c)^2},$$

where $K \approx 9 \times 10^9$, F is given in newtons, and all positions are measured in meters. Assume that a charge of 10 coulombs is situated at the origin, and that a second charge of 5 coulombs is situated at (2, 3, 3) and moving in the y-direction at one meter per second. How fast is the electrostatic force it experiences decreasing? (Round the answer to one significant digit.)

62. ▼ ***Electrostatic Repulsion*** Repeat the preceding exercise, assuming that a charge of 10 coulombs is situated at the origin and that a second charge of 5 coulombs is situated at (2, 3, 3) and moving in the negative z direction at one meter per second. (Round the answer to one significant digit.)

63. ▼ ***Investments*** Recall that the compound interest formula for annual compounding is

$$A(P, r, t) = P(1 + r)^t,$$

where A is the future value of an investment of P dollars after t years at an interest rate of r.

a. Calculate $\dfrac{\partial A}{\partial P}$, $\dfrac{\partial A}{\partial r}$, and $\dfrac{\partial A}{\partial t}$, all evaluated at (100, 0.10, 10). (Round your answers to two decimal places.) Interpret your answers.

b. What does the function $\left.\dfrac{\partial A}{\partial P}\right|_{(100,0.10,t)}$ of t tell about your investment?

64. ▼ ***Investments*** Repeat the preceding exercise, using the formula for continuous compounding:

$$A(P, r, t) = Pe^{rt}.$$

65. ▼ ***Modeling with the Cobb-Douglas Production Formula*** Assume you are given a production formula of the form

$$P(x, y) = Kx^a y^b \quad (a + b = 1).$$

a. Obtain formulas for $\dfrac{\partial P}{\partial x}$ and $\dfrac{\partial P}{\partial y}$, and show that $\dfrac{\partial P}{\partial x} = \dfrac{\partial P}{\partial y}$ precisely when $x/y = a/b$.

b. Let x be the number of workers a firm employs and let y be its monthly operating budget in thousands of dollars. Assume that the firm currently employs 100 workers and has a monthly operating budget of \$200,000. If each additional worker contributes as much to productivity as each additional \$1,000 per month, find values of a and b that model the firm's productivity.

66. ▼ ***Housing Costs***[21] The cost C of building a house is related to the number k of carpenters used and the number e of electricians used by

$$C(k, e) = 15{,}000 + 50k^2 + 60e^2.$$

If three electricians are currently employed in building your new house and the marginal cost per additional electrician is the same as the marginal cost per additional carpenter, how many carpenters are being used? (Round your answer to the nearest carpenter.)

67. ▼ ***Nutrient Diffusion*** Suppose that one cubic centimeter of nutrient is placed at the center of a circular petri dish filled with water. We might wonder how the nutrient is distributed after a time of t seconds. According to the classical theory of diffusion, the concentration of nutrient (in parts of nutrient per part of water) after a time t is given by

$$u(r, t) = \frac{1}{4\pi Dt}e^{-\frac{r^2}{4Dt}}.$$

Here D is the *diffusivity*, which we will take to be 1, and r is the distance from the center in centimeters. How fast is the concentration increasing at a distance of 1 cm from the center 3 seconds after the nutrient is introduced?

[20] Based on an Exercise in *Introduction to Mathematical Economics* by A. L. Ostrosky Jr. and J. V. Koch (Waveland Press, Illinois, 1979).

[21] *Ibid.*

68. ▼ ***Nutrient Diffusion*** Refer back to the preceding exercise. How fast is the concentration increasing at a distance of 4 cm from the center 4 seconds after the nutrient is introduced?

COMMUNICATION AND REASONING EXERCISES

69. Given that $f(a, b) = r$, $f_x(a, b) = s$, and $f_y(a, b) = t$, complete the following: _____ is increasing at a rate of _____ units per unit of x, _____ is increasing at a rate of _____ units per unit of y, and the value of _____ is _____ when $x =$ _____ and $y =$ _____.

70. A firm's productivity depends on two variables, x and y. Currently, $x = a$ and $y = b$, and the firm's productivity is 4,000 units. Productivity is increasing at a rate of 400 units per unit *decrease* in x, and is decreasing at a rate of 300 units per unit increase in y. What does all of this information tell you about the firm's productivity function $g(x, y)$?

71. Complete the following: Let $f(x, y, z)$ be the cost to build a development of x cypods (one-bedroom units) in the city-state of Utarek, Mars, y argaats (two-bedroom units), and z orbici (singular: orbicus; three-bedroom units) in $\overline{\overline{Z}}$ (zonars, the designated currency in Utarek). Then $\frac{\partial f}{\partial z}$ measures _____ and has units _____ .

72. Complete the following: Let $f(t, x, y)$ be the projected number of citizens of the Principality State of Voodice, Luna in year t since its founding, assuming the presence of x lunar vehicle factories and y domed settlements. Then $\frac{\partial f}{\partial x}$ measures _____ and has units _____ .

73. Give an example of a function $f(x, y)$ with $f_x(1, 1) = -2$ and $f_y(1, 1) = 3$.

74. Give an example of a function $f(x, y, z)$ that has all of its partial derivatives equal to nonzero constants.

75. ▼ The graph of $z = b + mx + ny$ (b, m, and n constants) is a plane.
    a. Explain the geometric significance of the numbers b, m, and n.
    b. Show that the equation of the plane passing through (h, k, l) with slope m in the x direction (in the sense of $\partial/\partial x$) and slope n in the y direction is
    $$z = l + m(x - h) + n(y - k).$$

76. ▼ The **tangent plane** to the graph of $f(x, y)$ at $P(a, b, f(a, b))$ is the plane containing the lines tangent to the slice through the graph by $y = b$ (as in Figure 19) and the slice through the graph by $x = a$. Use the result of the preceding exercise to show that the equation of the tangent plane is
$$z = f(a, b) + f_x(a, b)(x - a) + f_y(a, b)(y - b).$$

8.3 Maxima and Minima

In Chapter 5, on applications of the derivative, we saw how to locate relative extrema of a function of a single variable. In this section we extend our methods to functions of two variables. Similar techniques work for functions of three or more variables.

Figure 21 shows a portion of the graph of the function

$$f(x, y) = 2(x^2 + y^2) - (x^4 + y^4) + 1.$$

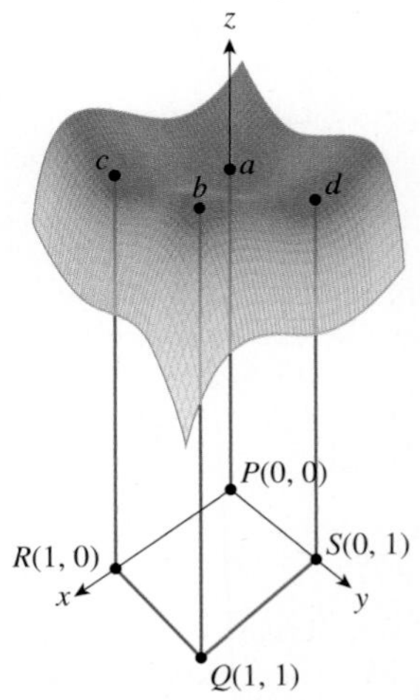

Figure 21

The graph in Figure 21 resembles a "flying carpet," and several interesting points, marked a, b, c, and d, are shown.

1. The point a has coordinates $(0, 0, f(0, 0))$, is directly above the origin $(0, 0)$, and is the lowest point in its vicinity; water would puddle there. We say that f has a **relative minimum** at $(0, 0)$ because $f(0, 0)$ is smaller than $f(x, y)$ for any (x, y) near $(0, 0)$.
2. Similarly, the point b is higher than any point in its vicinity. Thus, we say that f has a **relative maximum** at $(1, 1)$.
3. The points c and d represent a new phenomenon and are called **saddle points**. They are neither relative maxima nor relative minima but seem to be a little of both.

To see more clearly what features a saddle point has, look at Figure 22, which shows a portion of the graph near the point d.

If we slice through the graph along $y = 1$, we get a curve on which d is the *lowest* point. Thus, d looks like a relative minimum along this slice. On the other hand, if we slice through the graph along $x = 0$, we get another curve, on which d is the *highest*

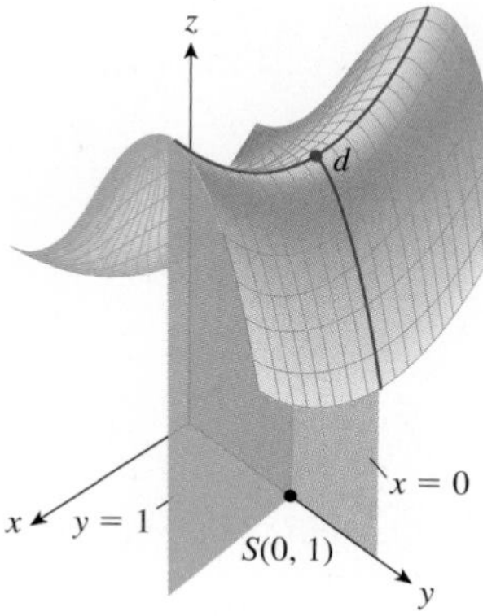

Figure 22

point, so d looks like a relative maximum along this slice. This kind of behavior characterizes a saddle point: f has a **saddle point** at (r, s) if f has a relative minimum at (r, s) along some slice through that point and a relative maximum along another slice through that point. If you look at the other saddle point, c, in Figure 21, you see the same characteristics.

While numerical information can help us locate the approximate positions of relative extrema and saddle points, calculus permits us to locate these points accurately, as we did for functions of a single variable. Look once again at Figure 21, and notice the following:

- The points P, Q, R, and S are all in the **interior** of the domain of f; that is, none lie on the boundary of the domain. Said another way, we can move some distance in any direction from any of these points without leaving the domain of f.
- The tangent lines along the slices through these points parallel to the x- and y-axes are *horizontal*. Thus, the partial derivatives $\partial f/\partial x$ and $\partial f/\partial y$ are zero when evaluated at any of the points P, Q, R, and S. This gives us a way of locating candidates for relative extrema and saddle points.

The following summary generalizes and also expands on some of what we have just said:

Relative and Absolute Maxima and Minima

The function f of n variables has a **relative maximum** at $(x_1, x_2, \ldots, x_n) = (r_1, r_2, \ldots, r_n)$ if $f(r_1, r_2, \ldots, r_n) \geq f(x_1, x_2, \ldots, x_n)$ for every point $(x_1, x_2, \ldots, x_n)$ near* $(r_1, r_2, \ldots, r_n)$ in the domain of f. We say that f has an **absolute maximum** at $(r_1, r_2, \ldots, r_n)$ if $f(r_1, r_2, \ldots, r_n) \geq f(x_1, x_2, \ldots, x_n)$ for every point $(x_1, x_2, \ldots, x_n)$ in the domain of f. The terms **relative minimum** and **absolute minimum** are defined in a similar way. Note that, as with functions of a single variable, absolute extrema are special kinds of relative extrema.

Locating Candidates for Extrema and Saddle Points in the Interior of the Domain of *f*

- Set $\dfrac{\partial f}{\partial x_1} = 0, \dfrac{\partial f}{\partial x_2} = 0, \ldots, \dfrac{\partial f}{\partial x_n} = 0$, simultaneously, and solve for $x_1, x_2, \ldots, x_n$.
- Check that the resulting points $(x_1, x_2, \ldots, x_n)$ are in the interior of the domain of f.

Points at which all the partial derivatives of f are zero are called **critical points**. The critical points are the only candidates for extrema and saddle points in the interior of the domain of f, assuming that its partial derivatives are defined at every point.†

Quick Examples

In each of the following Quick Examples, the domain is the whole Cartesian plane, and the partial derivatives are defined at every point, so the critical points give us the only candidates for extrema and saddle points:

1. Let $f(x, y) = x^3 + (y - 1)^2$. Then $\dfrac{\partial f}{\partial x} = 3x^2$ and $\dfrac{\partial f}{\partial y} = 2(y - 1)$.

Thus, we solve the system

$$3x^2 = 0 \quad \text{and} \quad 2(y - 1) = 0.$$

* For $(x_1, x_2, \ldots, x_n)$ to be near $(r_1, r_2, \ldots, r_n)$ we mean that x_1 is in some open interval centered at r_1, x_2 is in some open interval centered at r_2, and so on.

† One can use the techniques of the next section to find extrema on the *boundary* of the domain of a function; for a complete discussion, see the optional extra section: *Maxima and Minima: Boundaries and the Extreme Value Theorem.* (We shall not consider the analogs of the singular points.)

The first equation gives $x = 0$, and the second gives $y = 1$. Thus, the only critical point is (0, 1).

2. Let $f(x, y) = x^2 - 4xy + 8y$. Then $\frac{\partial f}{\partial x} = 2x - 4y$ and $\frac{\partial f}{\partial y} = -4x + 8$. Thus, we solve

$$2x - 4y = 0 \quad \text{and} \quad -4x + 8 = 0.$$

The second equation gives $x = 2$, and the first then gives $y = 1$. Thus, the only critical point is (2, 1).

3. Let $f(x, y) = e^{-(x^2+y^2)}$. Taking partial derivatives and setting them equal to zero gives

$$-2xe^{-(x^2+y^2)} = 0 \qquad \text{We set } \frac{\partial f}{\partial x} = 0.$$

$$-2ye^{-(x^2+y^2)} = 0. \qquad \text{We set } \frac{\partial f}{\partial y} = 0.$$

The first equation implies that $x = 0$,* and the second implies that $y = 0$. Thus, the only critical point is (0, 0).

* Recall that if a product of two numbers is zero, then one or the other must be zero. In this case the number $e^{-(x^2+y^2)}$ can't be zero (because e^u is never zero), which gives the result claimed.

In the remainder of this section we will be interested in locating all critical points of a given function and then classifying each one as a relative maximum, minimum, saddle point, or none of these. Whether or not any relative extrema we find are in fact absolute is a subject we discuss in the next section.†

† In some of the applications in the exercises you will, however, need to consider whether the extrema you find are absolute.

EXAMPLE 1 Locating and Classifying Critical Points

Locate all critical points of $f(x, y) = x^2y - x^2 - 2y^2$. Graph the function to classify the critical points as relative maxima, minima, saddle points, or none of these.

Solution The partial derivatives are

$$f_x = 2xy - 2x = 2x(y - 1)$$
$$f_y = x^2 - 4y.$$

Setting these equal to zero gives

$$x = 0 \text{ or } y = 1$$
$$x^2 = 4y.$$

We get a solution by choosing either $x = 0$ or $y = 1$ and substituting into $x^2 = 4y$.

***Case 1:* $x = 0$** Substituting into $x^2 = 4y$ gives $0 = 4y$ and hence $y = 0$. Thus, the critical point for this case is $(x, y) = (0, 0)$.

***Case 2:* $y = 1$** Substituting into $x^2 = 4y$ gives $x^2 = 4$ and hence $x = \pm 2$. Thus, we get two critical points for this case: (2, 1) and (−2, 1).

We now have three critical points altogether: (0, 0), (2, 1), and (−2, 1). Because the domain of f is the whole Cartesian plane and the partial derivatives are defined at every point, these critical points are the only candidates for relative extrema and saddle points. We get the corresponding points on the graph by substituting for x and y in the equation for f to get the z-coordinates. The points are (0, 0, 0), (2, 1, −2), and (−2, 1, −2).

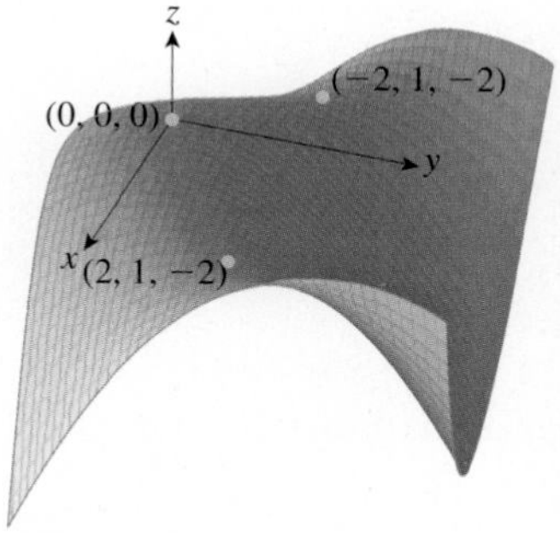

Figure 23

Classifying the Critical Points Graphically To classify the critical points graphically, we look at the graph of f shown in Figure 23.

Examining the graph carefully, we see that the point (0, 0, 0) is a relative maximum. As for the other two critical points, are they saddle points or are they relative maxima? They are relative maxima along the y-direction, but they are relative minima along the lines $y = \pm x$ (see the top edge of the picture, which shows a dip at (−2, 1, 2)) and so they are saddle points. If you don't believe this, we will get more evidence following and in a later example.

Classifying the Critical Points Numerically We can use a tabular representation of the function to classify the critical points numerically. The following tabular representation of the function can be obtained using a spreadsheet. (See the Spreadsheet Technology Guide discussion of Section 8.1 Example 3 at the end of the chapter for information on using a spreadsheet to generate such a table.)

$x \rightarrow$, $y \downarrow$

	−3	**−2**	**−1**	**0**	**1**	**2**	**3**
−3	−54	−34	−22	−18	−22	−34	−54
−2	−35	−20	−11	−8	−11	−20	−35
−1	−20	−10	−4	−2	−4	−10	−20
0	−9	−4	−1	**0**	−1	−4	−9
1	−2	**−2**	−2	−2	−2	**−2**	−2
2	1	−4	−7	−8	−7	−4	1
3	0	−10	−16	−18	−16	−10	0

The shaded and colored cells show rectangular neighborhoods of the three critical points (0, 0), (2, 1), and (−2, 1). (Notice that they overlap.) The values of f at the critical points are at the centers of these rectangles. Looking at the gray neighborhood of $(x, y) = (0, 0)$, we see that $f(0, 0) = 0$ is the largest value of f in the shaded cells, suggesting that f has a maximum at (0, 0). The shaded neighborhood of (2, 1) on the right shows $f(2, 1) = -2$ as the maximum along some slices (e.g., the vertical slice), and a minimum along the diagonal slice from top left to bottom right. This is what results in a saddle point on the graph. The point (−2, 1) is similar, and thus f also has a saddle point at (−2, 1).

Q: *Is there an algebraic way of deciding whether a given point is a relative maximum, relative minimum, or saddle point?*

A: There is a "second derivative test" for functions of two variables, stated as follows.

Second Derivative Test for Functions of Two Variables

Suppose (a, b) is a critical point in the interior of the domain of the function f of two variables. Let H be the quantity

$$H = f_{xx}(a, b) f_{yy}(a, b) - [f_{xy}(a, b)]^2. \qquad H \text{ is called the } \textit{Hessian}.$$

Then, if H is *positive*,

- f has a relative minimum at (a, b) if $f_{xx}(a, b) > 0$.
- f has a relative maximum at (a, b) if $f_{xx}(a, b) < 0$.

If H is *negative*,

- f has a saddle point at (a, b).

If $H = 0$, the test tells us nothing, so we need to look at the graph or a numerical table to see what is going on.

Quick Examples

1. Let $f(x, y) = x^2 - y^2$. Then

$$f_x = 2x \quad \text{and} \quad f_y = -2y,$$

which gives (0, 0) as the only critical point. Also,

$$f_{xx} = 2,\ f_{xy} = 0, \quad \text{and} \quad f_{yy} = -2,$$ Note that these are constant.

which gives $H = (2)(-2) - 0^2 = -4$. Because H is negative, we have a saddle point at (0, 0).

2. Let $f(x, y) = x^2 + 2y^2 + 2xy + 4x$. Then

$$f_x = 2x + 2y + 4 \quad \text{and} \quad f_y = 2x + 4y.$$

Setting these equal to zero gives a system of two linear equations in two unknowns:

$$x + y = -2$$
$$x + 2y = 0.$$

This system has solution (−4, 2), so this is our only critical point. The second partial derivatives are $f_{xx} = 2$, $f_{xy} = 2$, and $f_{yy} = 4$, so $H = (2)(4) - 2^2 = 4$. Because $H > 0$ and $f_{xx} > 0$, we have a relative minimum at (−4, 2).

Note There is a second derivative test for functions of three or more variables, but it is considerably more complicated. We stick with functions of two variables for the most part in this book. The justification of the second derivative test is beyond the scope of this book. ■

EXAMPLE 2 Using the Second Derivative Test

Use the second derivative test to analyze the function $f(x, y) = x^2y - x^2 - 2y^2$ discussed in Example 1, and confirm the results we got there.

Solution We saw in Example 1 that the first-order derivatives are

$$f_x = 2xy - 2x = 2x(y - 1)$$
$$f_y = x^2 - 4y$$

and the critical points are (0, 0), (2, 1), and (−2, 1). We also need the second derivatives:

$$f_{xx} = 2y - 2$$
$$f_{xy} = 2x$$
$$f_{yy} = -4.$$

The point (0, 0): $f_{xx}(0, 0) = -2$, $f_{xy}(0, 0) = 0$, $f_{yy}(0, 0) = -4$, so $H = 8$. Because $H > 0$ and $f_{xx}(0, 0) < 0$, the second derivative test tells us that f has a relative maximum at (0, 0).

The point (2, 1): $f_{xx}(2, 1) = 0$, $f_{xy}(2, 1) = 4$ and $f_{yy}(2, 1) = -4$, so $H = -16$. Because $H < 0$, we know that f has a saddle point at (2, 1).

The point (−2, 1): $f_{xx}(-2, 1) = 0$, $f_{xy}(-2, 1) = -4$ and $f_{yy}(-2, 1) = -4$, so once again $H = -16$, and f has a saddle point at $(-2, 1)$.

Deriving the Formulas for Linear Regression

Back in Section 1.4, we presented the following set of formulas for the **regression** or **best-fit** line associated with a given set of data points $(x_1, y_1), (x_2, y_2), \ldots, (x_n, y_n)$.

Regression Line

The line that best fits the n data points $(x_1, y_1), (x_2, y_2), \ldots, (x_n, y_n)$ has the form

$$y = mx + b,$$

where

$$m = \frac{n(\sum xy) - (\sum x)(\sum y)}{n(\sum x^2) - (\sum x)^2}$$

$$b = \frac{\sum y - m(\sum x)}{n}$$

n = number of data points.

Derivation of the Regression Line Formulas

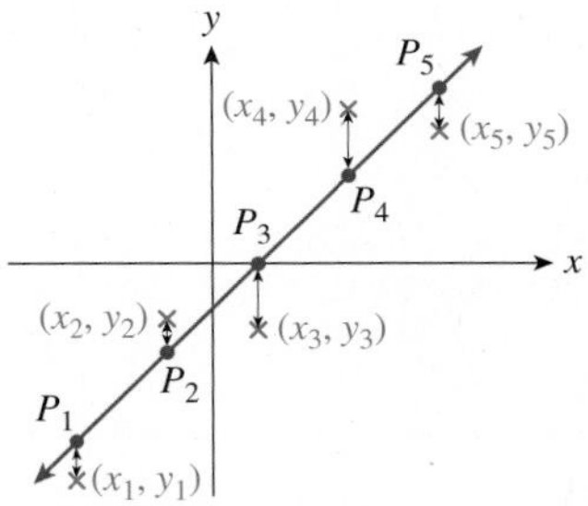

Figure 24

Recall that the regression line is defined to be the line that minimizes the sum of the squares of the **residuals**, measured by the vertical distances shown in Figure 24, which shows a regression line associated with $n = 5$ data points. In the figure, the points $P_1, \ldots, P_n$ on the regression line have coordinates $(x_1, mx_1 + b), (x_2, mx_2 + b), \ldots, (x_n, mx_n + b)$. The residuals are the quantities $y_{\text{Observed}} - y_{\text{Predicted}}$:

$$y_1 - (mx_1 + b), y_2 - (mx_2 + b), \ldots, y_n - (mx_n + b).$$

The sum of the squares of the residuals is therefore

$$S(m, b) = [y_1 - (mx_1 + b)]^2 + [y_2 - (mx_2 + b)]^2 + \cdots + [y_n - (mx_n + b)]^2$$

and this is the quantity we must minimize by choosing m and b. Because we reason that there is a line that minimizes this quantity, there must be a relative minimum at that point. We shall see in a moment that the function S has at most one critical point, which must therefore be the desired absolute minimum. To obtain the critical points of S, we set the partial derivatives equal to zero and solve:

$$S_m = 0: \quad -2x_1[y_1 - (mx_1 + b)] - \cdots - 2x_n[y_n - (mx_n + b)] = 0$$

$$S_b = 0: \quad -2[y_1 - (mx_1 + b)] - \cdots - 2[y_n - (mx_n + b)] = 0.$$

Dividing by -2 and gathering terms allows us to rewrite the equations as

$$m(x_1^2 + \cdots + x_n^2) + b(x_1 + \cdots + x_n) = x_1y_1 + \cdots + x_ny_n$$

$$m(x_1 + \cdots + x_n) + nb = y_1 + \cdots + y_n.$$

We can rewrite these equations more neatly using $\sum$-notation:

$$\begin{aligned} m\left(\sum x^2\right) + b\left(\sum x\right) &= \sum xy \\ m\left(\sum x\right) + nb &= \sum y. \end{aligned}$$

This is a system of two linear equations in the two unknowns m and b. It may or may not have a unique solution. When there is a unique solution, we can conclude that the best-fit line is given by solving these two equations for m and b. Alternatively, there is a general formula for the solution of any system of two equations in two unknowns, and if we apply this formula to our two equations, we get the regression formulas above.

8.3 EXERCISES

▼ more advanced ◆ challenging

T indicates exercises that should be solved using technology

In Exercises 1–4, classify each labeled point on the graph as one of the following:

Relative maximum
Relative minimum
Saddle point
Critical point but neither a relative extremum nor a saddle point
None of the above HINT [See Example 1.]

1.

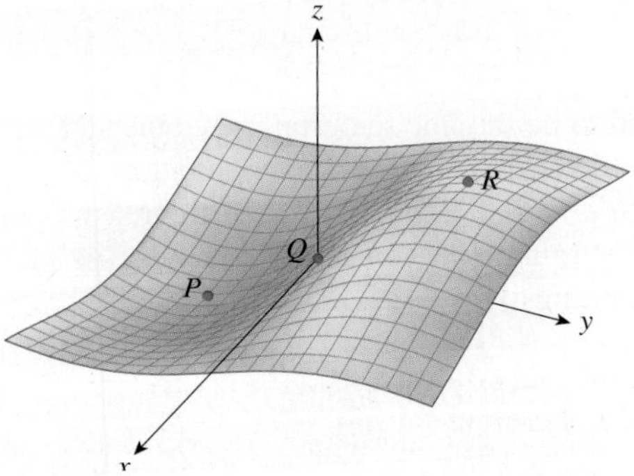

2.

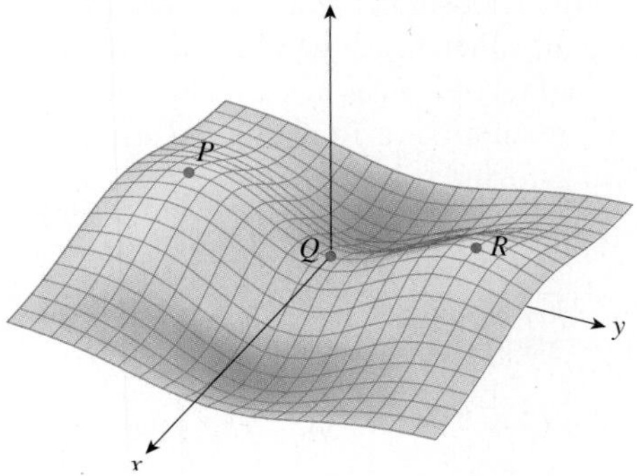

3.

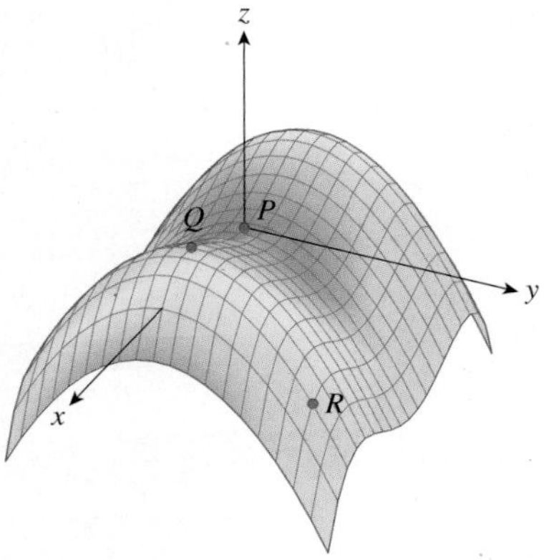

4.

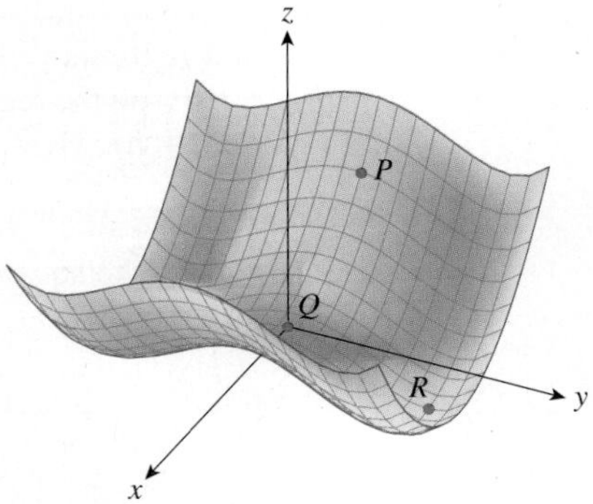

In Exercises 5–10, classify the shaded value in each table as one of the following:

Relative maximum
Relative minimum
Saddle point
Neither a relative extremum nor a saddle point

Assume that the shaded value represents a critical point.

5. $x \rightarrow$ ($y \downarrow$)

	−3	−2	−1	0	1	2
−3	10	5	2	1	2	5
−2	9	4	1	0	1	4
−1	10	5	2	1	2	5
0	13	8	5	4	5	8
1	18	13	10	9	10	13
2	25	20	17	16	17	20
3	34	29	26	25	26	29

6. $x \rightarrow$ ($y \downarrow$)

	−3	−2	−1	0	1	2
−3	5	0	−3	−4	−3	0
−2	8	3	0	−1	0	3
−1	9	4	1	0	1	4
0	8	3	0	−1	0	3
1	5	0	−3	−4	−3	0
2	0	−5	−8	−9	−8	−5
3	−7	−12	−15	−16	−15	−12

7. $x \rightarrow$ ($y \downarrow$)

	−3	−2	−1	0	1	2
−3	5	0	−3	−4	−3	0
−2	8	3	0	−1	0	3
−1	9	4	1	0	1	4
0	8	3	0	−1	0	3
1	5	0	−3	−4	−3	0
2	0	−5	−8	−9	−8	−5
3	−7	−12	−15	−16	−15	−12

8. $x \rightarrow$ ($y \downarrow$)

	−3	−2	−1	0	1	2
−3	2	3	2	−1	−6	−13
−2	3	4	3	0	−5	−12
−1	2	3	2	−1	−6	−13
0	−1	0	−1	−4	−9	−16
1	−6	−5	−6	−9	−14	−21
2	−13	−12	−13	−16	−21	−28
3	−22	−21	−22	−25	−30	−37

9. $x \rightarrow$ ($y \downarrow$)

	−3	−2	−1	0	1	2
−3	4	5	4	1	−4	−11
−2	3	4	3	0	−5	−12
−1	4	5	4	1	−4	−11
0	7	8	7	4	−1	−8
1	12	13	12	9	4	−3
2	19	20	19	16	11	4
3	28	29	28	25	20	13

10. $x \rightarrow$ ($y \downarrow$)

	−3	−2	−1	0	1	2
−3	100	101	100	97	92	85
−2	99	100	99	96	91	84
−1	98	99	98	95	90	83
0	91	92	91	88	83	76
1	72	73	72	69	64	57
2	35	36	35	32	27	20
3	−26	−25	−26	−29	−34	−41

Locate and classify all the critical points of the functions in Exercises 11–36. HINT [See Example 2.]

11. $f(x, y) = x^2 + y^2 + 1$

12. $f(x, y) = 4 - (x^2 + y^2)$

13. $g(x, y) = 1 - x^2 - x - y^2 + y$

14. $g(x, y) = x^2 + x + y^2 - y - 1$

15. $k(x, y) = x^2 - 3xy + y^2$

16. $k(x, y) = x^2 - xy + 2y^2$

17. $f(x, y) = x^2 + 2xy + 2y^2 - 2x + 4y$

18. $f(x, y) = x^2 + xy - y^2 + 3x - y$

19. $g(x, y) = -x^2 - 2xy - 3y^2 - 3x - 2y$

20. $g(x, y) = -x^2 - 2xy + y^2 + x - 4y$

21. $h(x, y) = x^2y - 2x^2 - 4y^2$

22. $h(x, y) = x^2 + y^2 - y^2x - 4$

23. $f(x, y) = x^2 + 2xy^2 + 2y^2$

24. $f(x, y) = x^2 + x^2y + y^2$

25. $s(x, y) = e^{x^2+y^2}$

26. $s(x, y) = e^{-(x^2+y^2)}$

27. $t(x, y) = x^4 + 8xy^2 + 2y^4$

28. $t(x, y) = x^3 - 3xy + y^3$

29. $f(x, y) = x^2 + y - e^y$

30. $f(x, y) = xe^y$

31. $f(x, y) = e^{-(x^2+y^2+2x)}$

32. $f(x, y) = e^{-(x^2+y^2-2x)}$

33. ▼ $f(x, y) = xy + \dfrac{2}{x} + \dfrac{2}{y}$

34. ▼ $f(x, y) = xy + \dfrac{4}{x} + \dfrac{2}{y}$

35. ▼ $g(x, y) = x^2 + y^2 + \frac{2}{xy}$

36. ▼ $g(x, y) = x^3 + y^3 + \frac{3}{xy}$

37. ▼ Refer back to Exercise 11. Which (if any) of the critical points of $f(x, y) = x^2 + y^2 + 1$ are absolute extrema?

38. ▼ Refer back to Exercise 12. Which (if any) of the critical points of $f(x, y) = 4 - (x^2 + y^2)$ are absolute extrema?

39. T ▼ Refer back to Exercise 21. Which (if any) of the critical points of $h(x, y) = x^2y - 2x^2 - 4y^2$ are absolute extrema?

40. T ▼ Refer back to Exercise 22. Which (if any) of the critical points of $h(x, y) = x^2 + y^2 - y^2x - 4$ are absolute extrema?

APPLICATIONS

41. ***Brand Loyalty*** Suppose the fraction of Mazda car owners who chose another new Mazda can be modeled by the following function:[22]

$$M(c, f) = 11 + 8c + 4c^2 - 40f - 20cf + 40f^2,$$

where c is the fraction of Chrysler car owners who remained loyal to Chrysler and f is the fraction of Ford car owners remaining loyal to Ford. Locate and classify all the critical points and interpret your answer. HINT [See Example 2.]

42. ***Brand Loyalty*** Repeat the preceding exercise using the function:

$$M(c, f) = -10 - 8f - 4f^2 + 40c + 20fc - 40c^2.$$

HINT [See Example 2.]

43. ▼ ***Pollution Control*** The cost of controlling emissions at a firm goes up rapidly as the amount of emissions reduced goes up. Here is a possible model:

$$C(x, y) = 4{,}000 + 100x^2 + 50y^2,$$

where x is the reduction in sulfur emissions, y is the reduction in lead emissions (in pounds of pollutant per day), and C is the daily cost to the firm (in dollars) of this reduction. Government clean-air subsidies amount to \$500 per pound of sulfur and \$100 per pound of lead removed. How many pounds of pollutant should the firm remove each day in order to minimize *net* cost (cost minus subsidy)?

44. ▼ ***Pollution Control*** Repeat the preceding exercise using the following information:

$$C(x, y) = 2{,}000 + 200x^2 + 100y^2$$

with government subsidies amounting to \$100 per pound of sulfur and \$500 per pound of lead removed per day.

45. ▼ ***Revenue*** Your company manufactures two models of speakers, the Ultra Mini and the Big Stack. Demand for each depends partly on the price of the other. If one is expensive, then more people will buy the other. If p_1 is the price of the Ultra Mini, and p_2 is the price of the Big Stack, demand for the Ultra Mini is given by

$$q_1(p_1, p_2) = 100{,}000 - 100p_1 + 10p_2,$$

where q_1 represents the number of Ultra Minis that will be sold in a year. The demand for the Big Stack is given by

$$q_2(p_1, p_2) = 150{,}000 + 10p_1 - 100p_2.$$

Find the prices for the Ultra Mini and the Big Stack that will maximize your total revenue.

46. ▼ ***Revenue*** Repeat the preceding exercise, using the following demand functions:

$$q_1(p_1, p_2) = 100{,}000 - 100p_1 + p_2$$
$$q_2(p_1, p_2) = 150{,}000 + p_1 - 100p_2.$$

47. ▼ ***Luggage Dimensions: American Airlines*** American Airlines requires that the total outside dimensions (length + width + height) of a checked bag not exceed 62 inches.[23] What are the dimensions of the largest volume bag that you can check on an American flight?

48. ▼ ***Carry-on Bag Dimensions: American Airlines*** American Airlines requires that the total outside dimensions (length + width + height) of a carry-on bag not exceed 45 inches.[24] What are the dimensions of the largest volume bag that you can carry on an American flight?

49. ▼ ***Package Dimensions: USPS*** The U.S. Postal Service (USPS) will accept only packages with a length plus girth no more than 108 inches.[25] (See the figure.)

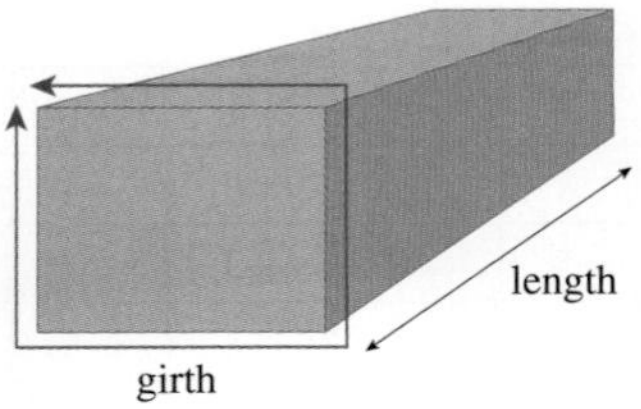

What are the dimensions of the largest volume package that the USPS will accept? What is its volume?

50. ▼ ***Package Dimensions: UPS*** United Parcel Service (UPS) will accept only packages with length no more than 108 inches and length plus girth no more than 165 inches.[26] (See figure for the preceding exercise.) What are the dimensions of the largest volume package that UPS will accept? What is its volume?

[22] This model is not accurate, although it was inspired by an approximation of a second-order regression based on data from the period 1988–1995. Source for original data: Chrysler, Maritz Market Research, Consumer Attitude Research, and Strategic Vision/ *New York Times*, November 3, 1995, p. D2.

[23] According to information on its Web site (www.aa.com).

[24] *Ibid.*

[25] The requirement for packages sent other than Parcel Post, as of August 2011 (www.usps.com).

[26] The requirement as of August 2011 (www.ups.com).

COMMUNICATION AND REASONING EXERCISES

51. Sketch the graph of a function that has one extremum and no saddle points.

52. Sketch the graph of a function that has one saddle point and one extremum.

53. ▼ Sketch the graph of a function that has one relative extremum, no absolute extrema, and no saddle points.

54. ▼ Sketch the graph of a function that has infinitely many absolute maxima.

55. Let $H = f_{xx}(a, b)f_{yy}(a, b) - f_{xy}(a, b)^2$. What condition on H guarantees that f has a relative extremum at the point (a, b)?

56. Let H be as in the preceding exercise. Give an example to show that it is possible to have $H = 0$ and a relative minimum at (a, b).

57. ▼ Suppose that when the graph of $f(x, y)$ is sliced by a vertical plane through (a, b) parallel to either the xz-plane or the yz-plane, the resulting curve has a relative maximum at (a, b). Does this mean that f has a relative maximum at (a, b)? Explain your answer.

58. ▼ Suppose that f has a relative maximum at (a, b). Does it follow that, if the graph of f is sliced by a vertical plane parallel to either the xz-plane or the yz-plane, the resulting curve has a relative maximum at (a, b)? Explain your answer.

59. ▼ ***Average Cost*** Let $C(x, y)$ be any cost function. Show that when the average cost is minimized, the marginal costs C_x and C_y both equal the average cost. Explain why this is reasonable.

60. ▼ ***Average Profit*** Let $P(x, y)$ be any profit function. Show that when the average profit is maximized, the marginal profits P_x and P_y both equal the average profit. Explain why this is reasonable.

61. ◆ The tangent plane to a graph was introduced in Exercise 76 in the preceding section. Use the equation of the tangent plane given there to explain why the tangent plane is parallel to the xy-plane at a relative maximum or minimum of $f(x, y)$.

62. ◆ Use the equation of the tangent plane given in Exercise 76 in the preceding section to explain why the tangent plane is parallel to the xy-plane at a saddle point of $f(x, y)$.

8.4 Constrained Maxima and Minima and Applications

So far we have looked only at the relative extrema of functions with no constraints. However, in Section 5.2 we saw examples in which we needed to find the maximum or minimum of an objective function subject to one or more constraints on the independent variables. For instance, consider the following problem:

$$\text{Minimize } S = xy + 2xz + 2yz \quad \text{subject to } xyz = 4 \text{ with } x > 0, y > 0, z > 0.$$

One strategy for solving such problems is essentially the same as the strategy we used earlier: Solve the constraint equation for one of the variables, substitute into the objective function, and then optimize the resulting function using the methods of the preceding section. We will call this the *substitution method.** An alternative method, called the *method of Lagrange multipliers*, is useful when it is difficult or impossible to solve the constraint equation for one of the variables, and even when it is possible to do so.

* Although often the method of choice, the substitution method is not infallible (see Exercises 19 and 20).

Substitution Method

EXAMPLE 1 Using Substitution

Minimize $S = xy + 2xz + 2yz$ subject to $xyz = 4$ with $x > 0, y > 0, z > 0$.

Solution As suggested in the above discussion, we proceed as follows:

Solve the constraint equation for one of the variables and then substitute in the objective function. The constraint equation is $xyz = 4$. Solving for z gives

$$z = \frac{4}{xy}.$$

The objective function is $S = xy + 2xz + 2yz$, so substituting $z = 4/xy$ gives

$$S = xy + 2x\frac{4}{xy} + 2y\frac{4}{xy}$$
$$= xy + \frac{8}{y} + \frac{8}{x}.$$

Minimize the resulting function of two variables. We use the method in Section 8.4 to find the minimum of $S = xy + \frac{8}{y} + \frac{8}{x}$ for $x > 0$ and $y > 0$. We look for critical points:

$$S_x = y - \frac{8}{x^2} \qquad S_y = x - \frac{8}{y^2}$$
$$S_{xx} = \frac{16}{x^3} \qquad S_{xy} = 1 \qquad S_{yy} = \frac{16}{y^3}.$$

We now equate the first partial derivatives to zero:

$$y = \frac{8}{x^2} \qquad \text{and} \qquad x = \frac{8}{y^2}.$$

To solve for x and y, we substitute the first of these equations in the second, getting

$$x = \frac{x^4}{8}$$
$$x^4 - 8x = 0$$
$$x(x^3 - 8) = 0.$$

The two solutions are $x = 0$, which we reject because x cannot be zero, and $x = 2$. Substituting $x = 2$ in $y = 8/x^2$ gives $y = 2$ also. Thus, the only critical point is $(2, 2)$. To apply the second derivative test, we compute

$$S_{xx}(2, 2) = 2 \qquad S_{xy}(2, 2) = 1 \qquad S_{yy}(2, 2) = 2$$

and find that $H = 3 > 0$ and $S_{xx}(2, 2) > 0$, so we have a relative minimum at $(2, 2)$.

The corresponding value of z is given by the constraint equation:

$$z = \frac{4}{xy} = \frac{4}{4} = 1.$$

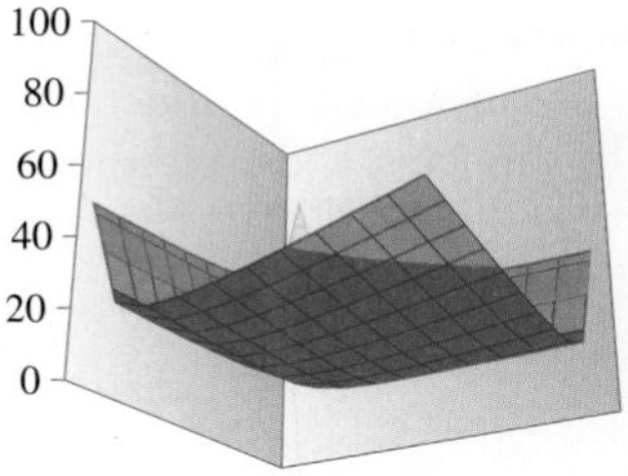

Graph of $S = xy + \frac{8}{y} + \frac{8}{x}$
$(0.2 \le x \le 5, 0.2 \le y \le 5)$
Figure 25

The corresponding value of the objective function is

$$S = xy + \frac{8}{y} + \frac{8}{x} = 4 + \frac{8}{2} + \frac{8}{2} = 12.$$

Figure 25 shows a portion of the graph of $S = xy + \frac{8}{y} + \frac{8}{x}$ for positive x and y (drawn using the Excel Surface Grapher in the Chapter 8 utilities at the Website) and suggests that there is a single absolute minimum, which must be at our only candidate point $(2, 2)$.

We conclude that the minimum of S is 12 and occurs at $(2, 2, 1)$.

The Method of Lagrange Multipliers

As we mentioned above, the method of Lagrange multipliers has the advantage that it can be used in constrained optimization problems when it is difficult or impossible to solve a constraint equation for one of the variables. We restrict attention to the case of a single constraint equation, although the method also generalizes to any number of constraint equations.

Locating Relative Extrema Using the Method of Lagrange Multipliers

To locate the candidates for relative extrema of a function $f(x, y, \ldots)$ subject to the constraint $g(x, y, \ldots) = 0$:

1. Construct the **Lagrangian function**

$$L(x, y, \ldots) = f(x, y, \ldots) - \lambda g(x, y, \ldots)$$

where λ is a new unknown called a **Lagrange multiplier.**

2. The candidates for the relative extrema occur at the critical points of $L(x, y, \ldots)$. To find them, set all the partial derivatives of $L(x, y, \ldots)$ equal to zero and solve the resulting system, together with the constraint equation $g(x, y, \ldots) = 0$, for the unknowns $x, y, \ldots$ and λ.

The points $(x, y, \ldots)$ that occur in solutions are then the candidates for the relative extrema of f subject to $g = 0$.

Although the justification for the method of Lagrange multipliers is beyond the scope of this text (a derivation can be found in many vector calculus textbooks), we will demonstrate by example how it is used.

EXAMPLE 2 Using Lagrange Multipliers

Use the method of Lagrange multipliers to find the maximum value of $f(x, y) = 2xy$ subject to $x^2 + 4y^2 = 32$.

Solution We start by rewriting the problem with the constraint in the form $g(x, y) = 0$:

$$\text{Maximize } f(x, y) = 2xy \text{ subject to } x^2 + 4y^2 - 32 = 0.$$

Here, $g(x, y) = x^2 + 4y^2 - 32$, and the Lagrangian function is

$$\begin{aligned} L(x, y) &= f(x, y) - \lambda g(x, y) \\ &= 2xy - \lambda(x^2 + 4y^2 - 32). \end{aligned}$$

The system of equations we need to solve is thus

$$\begin{aligned} L_x = 0: &\quad 2y - 2\lambda x = 0 \\ L_y = 0: &\quad 2x - 8\lambda y = 0 \\ g = 0: &\quad x^2 + 4y^2 - 32 = 0. \end{aligned}$$

It is often convenient to solve such a system by first solving one of the equations for λ and then substituting in the remaining equations. Thus, we start by solving the first equation to obtain

$$\lambda = \frac{y}{x}.$$

(A word of caution: Because we divided by x, we made the implicit assumption that $x \neq 0$, so before continuing we should check what happens if $x = 0$. But if $x = 0$, then the first equation, $2y = 2\lambda x$, tells us that $y = 0$ as well, and this contradicts the third equation: $x^2 + 4y^2 - 32 = 0$. Thus, we can rule out the possibility that $x = 0$.) Substituting the value of λ in the second equation gives

$$2x - 8\left(\frac{y}{x}\right)y = 0 \quad \text{or} \quad x^2 = 4y^2.$$

We can now substitute $x^2 = 4y^2$ in the constraint equation, obtaining

$$\begin{aligned} 4y^2 + 4y^2 - 32 &= 0 \\ 8y^2 &= 32 \\ y &= \pm 2. \end{aligned}$$

We now substitute back to obtain

$$x^2 = 4y^2 = 16,$$

or

$$x = \pm 4.$$

We don't need the value of λ, so we won't solve for it. Thus, the candidates for relative extrema are given by $x = \pm 4$ and $y = \pm 2$; that is, the four points $(-4, -2)$, $(-4, 2)$, $(4, -2)$, and $(4, 2)$. Recall that we are seeking the values of x and y that give the maximum value for $f(x, y) = 2xy$. Because we now have only four points to choose from, we compare the values of f at these four points and conclude that the maximum value of f occurs when $(x, y) = (-4, -2)$ or $(4, 2)$.

Something is suspicious in Example 2. We didn't check to see whether these candidates were relative extrema to begin with, let alone absolute extrema! How do we justify this omission? One of the difficulties with using the method of Lagrange multipliers is that it does not provide us with a test analogous to the second derivative test for functions of several variables. However, if you grant that the function in question does have an absolute maximum, then we require no test, because one of the candidates must give this maximum.

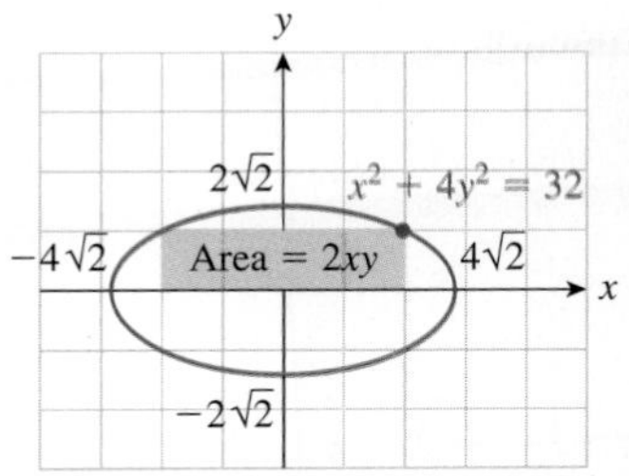

Figure 26

Q: *But how do we know that the given function has an absolute maximum?*

A: The best way to see this is by giving a geometric interpretation. The constraint $x^2 + 4y^2 = 32$ tells us that the point (x, y) must lie on the ellipse shown in Figure 26. The function $f(x, y) = 2xy$ gives the area of the rectangle shaded in the figure. There must be a *largest* such rectangle, because the area varies continuously from 0 when (x, y) is on the x-axis, to positive when (x, y) is in the first quadrant, to 0 again when (x, y) is on the y-axis, so f must have an absolute maximum for at least one pair of coordinates (x, y).

We now show how to use Lagrange multipliers to solve the minimization problem in Example 1:

EXAMPLE 3 Using Lagrange Multipliers: Function of Three Variables

Use the method of Lagrange multipliers to find the minimum value of $S = xy + 2xz + 2yz$ subject to $xyz = 4$ with $x > 0, y > 0, z > 0$.

Solution We start by rewriting the problem in standard form:

$$\text{Maximize } f(x, y, z) = xy + 2xz + 2yz$$
$$\text{subject to } xyz - 4 = 0 \text{ (with } x > 0, y > 0, z > 0).$$

Here, $g(x, y, z) = xyz - 4$, and the Lagrangian function is

$$L(x, y, z) = f(x, y, z) - \lambda g(x, y, z)$$
$$= xy + 2xz + 2yz - \lambda(xyz - 4).$$

The system of equations we need to solve is thus

$$L_x = 0: \quad y + 2z - \lambda yz = 0$$
$$L_y = 0: \quad x + 2z - \lambda xz = 0$$
$$L_z = 0: \quad 2x + 2y - \lambda xy = 0$$
$$g = 0: \quad xyz - 4 = 0.$$

As in the last example, we solve one of the equations for λ and substitute in the others. The first equation gives

$$\lambda = \frac{1}{z} + \frac{2}{y}.$$

Substituting this into the second equation gives

$$x + 2z = x + \frac{2xz}{y}$$

or $$2 = \frac{2x}{y},$$ Subtract x from both sides and then divide by z.

giving $$y = x.$$

Substituting the expression for λ into the third equation gives

$$2x + 2y = \frac{xy}{z} + 2x$$

or $$2 = \frac{x}{z},$$ Subtract $2x$ from both sides and then divide by y.

giving $$z = \frac{x}{2}.$$

Now we have both y and z in terms of x. We substitute these values in the last (constraint) equation:

$$x(x)\left(\frac{x}{2}\right) - 4 = 0$$
$$x^3 = 8$$
$$x = 2.$$

Thus, $y = x = 2$, and $z = \frac{x}{2} = 1$. Therefore, the only critical point occurs at (2, 2, 1), as we found in Example 1, and the corresponding value of S is

$$S = xy + 2xz + 2yz = (2)(2) + 2(2)(1) + 2(2)(1) = 12.$$

➡ **Before we go on...** Again, the method of Lagrange multipliers does not tell us whether the critical point in Example 3 is a maximum, minimum, or neither. However, if you grant that the function in question does have an absolute minimum, then the values we found must give this minimum value. ■

APPLICATIONS

EXAMPLE 4 Minimizing Area

Find the dimensions of an open-top rectangular box that has a volume of 4 cubic feet and the smallest possible surface area.

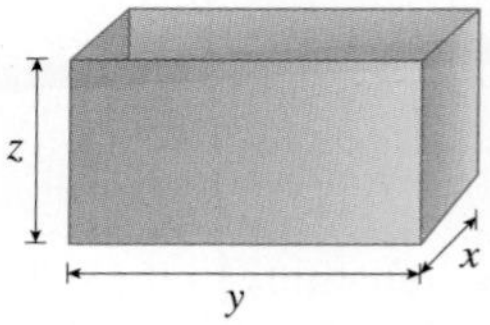

Figure 27

Solution Our first task is to rephrase this request as a mathematical optimization problem. Figure 27 shows a picture of the box with dimensions x, y, and z. We want to minimize the total surface area, which is given by

$$S = xy + 2xz + 2yz. \quad \text{Base + Sides + Front and Back}$$

This is our objective function. We can't simply choose x, y, and z to all be zero, however, because the enclosed volume must be 4 cubic feet. So,

$$xyz = 4. \quad \text{Constraint}$$

This is our constraint equation. Other unstated constraints are $x > 0$, $y > 0$, and $z > 0$, because the dimensions of the box must be positive. We now restate the problem as follows:

$$\text{Minimize } S = xy + 2xz + 2yz \quad \text{subject to } xyz = 4, x > 0, y > 0, z > 0.$$

But this is exactly the problem in Examples 1 and 3, and has a solution $x = 2$, $y = 2$, $z = 1$, $S = 12$. Thus, the required dimensions of the box are

$$x = 2 \text{ ft}, y = 2 \text{ ft}, z = 1 \text{ ft},$$

requiring a total surface area of 12 ft^2.

Q: *In Example 1 we checked that we had a relative minimum at $(x, y) = (2, 2)$ and we were persuaded graphically that this was probably an absolute minimum. Can we be sure that this relative minimum is an absolute minimum?*

A: Yes. There must be a least surface area among all boxes that hold 4 cubic feet. (Why?) Because this would give a relative minimum of S and because the only possible relative minimum of S occurs at (2, 2), this is the absolute minimum.

EXAMPLE 5 Maximizing productivity

An electric motor manufacturer uses workers and robots on its assembly line and has a Cobb-Douglas productivity function* of the form

$$P(x, y) = 10x^{0.2}y^{0.8} \text{ motors manufactured per day,}$$

where x is the number of assembly-line workers and y is the number of robots. Daily operating costs amount to \$100 per worker and \$16 per robot. How many workers and robots should be used to maximize productivity if the manufacturer has a daily budget of \$4,000?

* Cobb-Douglas production formulas were discussed in Section 4.6.

Solution Our objective function is the productivity $P(x, y)$, and the constraint is

$$100x + 16y = 4{,}000.$$

So, the optimization problem is:

$$\text{Maximize } P(x, y) = 10x^{0.2}y^{0.8} \text{ subject to } 100x + 16y = 4{,}000 \ (x \geq 0, y \geq 0).$$

Here, $g(x, y) = 100x + 16y - 4{,}000$, and the Lagrangian function is

$$\begin{aligned} L(x, y) &= P(x, y) - \lambda g(x, y) \\ &= 10x^{0.2}y^{0.8} - \lambda(100x + 16y - 4{,}000). \end{aligned}$$

The system of equations we need to solve is thus

$$\begin{aligned} L_x = 0&: \quad 2x^{-0.8}y^{0.8} - 100\lambda = 0 \\ L_y = 0&: \quad 8x^{0.2}y^{-0.2} - 16\lambda = 0 \\ g = 0&: \quad 100x + 16y = 4{,}000. \end{aligned}$$

We can rewrite the first two equations as:

$$2\left(\frac{y}{x}\right)^{0.8} = 100\lambda \qquad 8\left(\frac{x}{y}\right)^{0.2} = 16\lambda.$$

Dividing the first by the second to eliminate λ gives

$$\frac{1}{4}\left(\frac{y}{x}\right)^{0.8}\left(\frac{y}{x}\right)^{0.2} = \frac{100}{16}$$

that is, $$\frac{1}{4}\frac{y}{x} = \frac{25}{4},$$

giving $$y = 25x.$$

Substituting this result into the constraint equation gives

$$\begin{aligned} &100x + 16(25x) = 4{,}000 \\ &500x = 4{,}000 \end{aligned}$$

so $x = 8$ workers, $y = 25x = 200$ robots

for a productivity of

$$P(8{,}200) = 10(8)^{0.2}(200)^{0.8} \approx 1{,}051 \text{ motors manufactured per day.}$$

FAQ

When to Use Lagrange Multipliers

Q: *When can I use the method of Lagrange multipliers? When should I use it?*

A: We have discussed the method only when there is a single equality constraint. There is a generalization, which we have not discussed, that works when there are more equality constraints (we need to introduce one multiplier for each constraint). So, if you have a problem with more than one equality constraint, or with any inequality constraints, you must use the substitution method. On the other hand, if you have one equality constraint, and it would be difficult to solve it for one of the variables, then you should use Lagrange multipliers.

8.4 EXERCISES

▼ more advanced ◆ challenging

T indicates exercises that should be solved using technology

In Exercises 1–6, solve the given optimization problem by using substitution. HINT [See Example 1.]

1. Find the maximum value of $f(x, y, z) = 1 - x^2 - y^2 - z^2$ subject to $z = 2y$. Also find the corresponding point(s) (x, y, z).
2. Find the minimum value of $f(x, y, z) = x^2 + y^2 + z^2 - 2$ subject to $x = y$. Also find the corresponding point(s) (x, y, z).
3. Find the maximum value of $f(x, y, z) = 1 - x^2 - x - y^2 + y - z^2 + z$ subject to $3x = y$. Also find the corresponding point(s) (x, y, z).
4. Find the maximum value of $f(x, y, z) = 2x^2 + 2x + y^2 - y + z^2 - z - 1$ subject to $z = 2y$. Also find the corresponding point(s) (x, y, z).
5. Minimize $S = xy + 4xz + 2yz$ subject to $xyz = 1$ with $x > 0, y > 0, z > 0$.
6. Minimize $S = xy + xz + yz$ subject to $xyz = 2$ with $x > 0, y > 0, z > 0$.

In Exercises 7–18, use Lagrange multipliers to solve the given optimization problem. HINT [See Example 2.]

7. Find the maximum value of $f(x, y) = xy$ subject to $x + 2y = 40$. Also find the corresponding point(s) (x, y).
8. Find the maximum value of $f(x, y) = xy$ subject to $3x + y = 60$. Also find the corresponding point(s) (x, y).
9. Find the maximum value of $f(x, y) = 4xy$ subject to $x^2 + y^2 = 8$. Also find the corresponding point(s) (x, y).
10. Find the maximum value of $f(x, y) = xy$ subject to $y = 3 - x^2$. Also find the corresponding point(s) (x, y).
11. Find the minimum value of $f(x, y) = x^2 + y^2$ subject to $x + 2y = 10$. Also find the corresponding point(s) (x, y).
12. Find the minimum value of $f(x, y) = x^2 + y^2$ subject to $xy^2 = 16$. Also find the corresponding point(s) (x, y).
13. The problem in Exercise 1. HINT [See Example 3.]
14. The problem in Exercise 2. HINT [See Example 3.]
15. The problem in Exercise 3.
16. The problem in Exercise 4.
17. The problem in Exercise 5.
18. The problem in Exercise 6.
19. ◆ Consider the following constrained optimization problem:

$$\text{Minimize } f(x, y, z) = (x - 3)^2 + y^2 + z^2$$
$$\text{subject to } x^2 + y^2 - z = 0.$$

   a. Explain why this minimization problem must have a solution, and solve it using the method of Lagrange multipliers.
   b. Solve it again using the substitution method by solving the constraint equation for z.
   c. Now try to solve it using the substitution method by solving the constraint equation for y.
   d. Explain what goes wrong in part (c).

20. ◆ Consider the following constrained optimization problem:

$$\text{Minimize } f(x, y, z) = x^2 + (y + 3)^2 + (z - 4)^2$$
$$\text{subject to } 4 - x^2 - y^2 - z = 0.$$

   a. Explain why this minimization problem must have a solution, and solve it using the method of Lagrange multipliers.
   b. Solve it again using the substitution method by solving the constraint equation for z.
   c. Now try to solve it using the substitution method by solving the constraint equation for x.
   d. Explain what goes wrong in part (c).

APPLICATIONS

Exercises 21–24 were solved in Section 5.2. This time, use the method of Lagrange multipliers to solve them.

21. ***Fences*** I want to fence in a rectangular vegetable patch. The fencing for the east and west sides costs $4 per foot, and the fencing for the north and south sides costs only $2 per foot. I have a budget of $80 for the project. What is the largest area I can enclose?

22. ***Fences*** My orchid garden abuts my house so that the house itself forms the northern boundary. The fencing for the southern boundary costs $4 per foot, and the fencing for the east and west sides costs $2 per foot. If I have a budget of $80 for the project, what is the largest area I can enclose?

23. ***Revenue*** *Hercules Films* is deciding on the price of the video release of its film *Son of Frankenstein*. Its marketing people estimate that at a price of p dollars, it can sell a total of $q = 200{,}000 - 10{,}000p$ copies. What price will bring in the greatest revenue?

24. ***Profit*** *Hercules Films* is also deciding on the price of the video release of its film *Bride of the Son of Frankenstein*. Again, marketing estimates that at a price of p dollars it can sell $q = 200{,}000 - 10{,}000p$ copies, but each copy costs $4 to make. What price will give the greatest *profit*?

25. ***Geometry*** At what points on the sphere $x^2 + y^2 + z^2 = 1$ is the product xyz a maximum? (The method of Lagrange multipliers can be used.)

26. ***Geometry*** At what point on the surface $z = (x^2 + x + y^2 + 4)^{1/2}$ is the quantity $x^2 + y^2 + z^2$ a minimum? (The method of Lagrange multipliers can be used.)

27. ▼ ***Geometry*** What point on the surface $z = x^2 + y - 1$ is closest to the origin? HINT [Minimize the square of the distance from (x, y, z) to the origin.]

28. ▼ ***Geometry*** What point on the surface $z = x + y^2 - 3$ is closest to the origin? HINT [Minimize the square of the distance from (x, y, z) to the origin.]

29. ▼ ***Geometry*** Find the point on the plane $-2x + 2y + z - 5 = 0$ closest to $(-1, 1, 3)$. HINT [Minimize the square of the distance from the given point to a general point on the plane.]

30. ▼ ***Geometry*** Find the point on the plane $2x - 2y - z + 1 = 0$ closest to $(1, 1, 0)$. HINT [Minimize the square of the distance from the given point to a general point on the plane.]

31. ***Construction Cost*** A closed rectangular box is made with two kinds of materials. The top and bottom are made with heavy-duty cardboard costing 20¢ per square foot, and the sides are made with lightweight cardboard costing 10¢ per square foot. Given that the box is to have a capacity of 2 cubic feet, what should its dimensions be if the cost is to be minimized? HINT [See Example 4.]

32. ***Construction Cost*** Repeat the preceding exercise assuming that the heavy-duty cardboard costs 30¢ per square foot, the lightweight cardboard costs 5¢ per square foot, and the box is to have a capacity of 6 cubic feet. HINT [See Example 4.]

33. ***Package Dimensions: USPS*** The U.S. Postal Service (USPS) will accept only packages with a length plus girth no more than 108 inches.[27] (See the figure.)

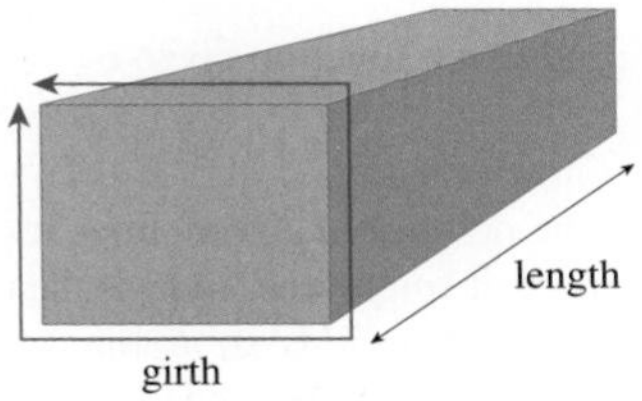

What are the dimensions of the largest volume package that the USPS will accept? What is its volume? (This exercise is the same as Exercise 49 in the preceding section. This time, solve it using Lagrange multipliers.)

34. ***Package Dimensions: UPS*** United Parcel Service (UPS) will accept only packages with length no more than 108 inches and length plus girth no more than 165 inches.[28] (See figure for the preceding exercise.) What are the dimensions of the largest volume package that UPS will accept? What is its volume? (This exercise is the same as Exercise 50 in the preceding section. This time, solve it using Lagrange multipliers.)

35. ▼ ***Construction Cost*** My company wishes to manufacture boxes similar to those described in Exercise 31 as cheaply as possible, but unfortunately the company that manufactures the cardboard is unable to give me price quotes for the heavy-duty and lightweight cardboard. Find formulas for the dimensions of the box in terms of the price per square foot of heavy-duty and lightweight cardboard.

36. ▼ ***Construction Cost*** Repeat the preceding exercise, assuming that only the bottoms of the boxes are to be made using heavy-duty cardboard.

37. ▼ ***Geometry*** Find the dimensions of the rectangular box with largest volume that can be inscribed above the xy-plane and under the paraboloid $z = 1 - (x^2 + y^2)$.

38. ▼ ***Geometry*** Find the dimensions of the rectangular box with largest volume that can be inscribed above the xy-plane and under the paraboloid $z = 2 - (2x^2 + y^2)$.

39. ***Productivity*** The Gym Shirt Company manufactures cotton socks. Production is partially automated through the use of robots. Daily operating costs amount to $150 per laborer and $60 per robot. The number of pairs of socks the company can manufacture in a day is given by a Cobb-Douglas production formula

$$q = 50n^{0.6}r^{0.4},$$

where q is the number of pairs of socks that can be manufactured by n laborers and r robots. Assuming that the company has a daily operating budget of $1,500 and

[27] The requirement for packages sent other than Parcel Post, as of August 2011 (www.usps.com).

[28] The requirement as of August 2011 (www.ups.com).

wishes to maximize productivity, how many laborers and how many robots should it use? What is the productivity at these levels? HINT [See Example 5.]

40. ***Productivity*** Your automobile assembly plant has a Cobb-Douglas production function given by

$$q = 100x^{0.3}y^{0.7},$$

where q is the number of automobiles it produces per year, x is the number of employees, and y is the monthly assembly-line budget (in thousands of dollars). Annual operating costs amount to an average of \$60 thousand per employee plus the operating budget of \$12y thousand. Your annual budget is \$1,200,000. How many employees should you hire and what should your assembly-line budget be to maximize productivity? What is the productivity at these levels? HINT [See Example 5.]

COMMUNICATION AND REASONING EXERCISES

41. Outline two methods of solution of the problem "*Maximize* $f(x, y, z)$ *subject to* $g(x, y, z) = 0$" and give an advantage and disadvantage of each.

42. Suppose we know that $f(x, y)$ has both partial derivatives in its domain D: $x > 0$, $y > 0$, and that (a, b) is the only point in D such that $f_x(a, b) = f_y(a, b) = 0$. Must it be the case that, if f has an absolute maximum, it occurs at (a, b)? Explain.

43. Under what circumstances would it be necessary to use the method of Lagrange multipliers?

44. Under what circumstances would the method of Lagrange multipliers not apply?

45. Restate the following problem as a maximization problem of the form "*Maximize* $f(x, y)$ *subject to* $g(x, y) = 0$":

Find the maximum value of $h(x) = 1 - 2x^2$.

46. Restate the following problem as a maximization problem of the form "*Maximize* $f(x, y, z)$ *subject to* $g(x, y, z) = 0$":

Find the maximum value of $h(x, y) = 1 - 2(x^2 + y^2)$.

47. ▼ If the partial derivatives of a function of several variables are always defined and never 0, is it possible for the function to have relative extrema when restricted to some domain? Explain your answer.

48. ▼ Give an example of a function f of three variables with an absolute maximum at (0, 0, 0) but where the partial derivatives of f are never zero wherever they are defined.

49. ◆ A **linear programming problem in two variables** is a problem of the form: *Maximize (or minimize)* $f(x, y)$ *subject to constraints of the form* $C(x, y) \geq 0$ *or* $C(x, y) \leq 0$. Here, the objective function f and the constraints C are linear functions. There may be several linear constraints in one problem. Explain why the solution cannot occur in the interior of the domain of f.

50. ◆ Refer back to Exercise 49. Explain why the solution will actually be at a corner of the domain of f (where two or more of the line segments that make up the boundary meet). This result—or rather a slight generalization of it—is known as the Fundamental Theorem of Linear Programming.

8.5 Double Integrals and Applications

When discussing functions of one variable, we computed the area under a graph by integration. The analog for the graph of a function of two variables is the *volume* V under the graph, as in Figure 28. Think of the region R in the xy-plane as the "shadow" under the portion of the surface $z = f(x, y)$ shown.

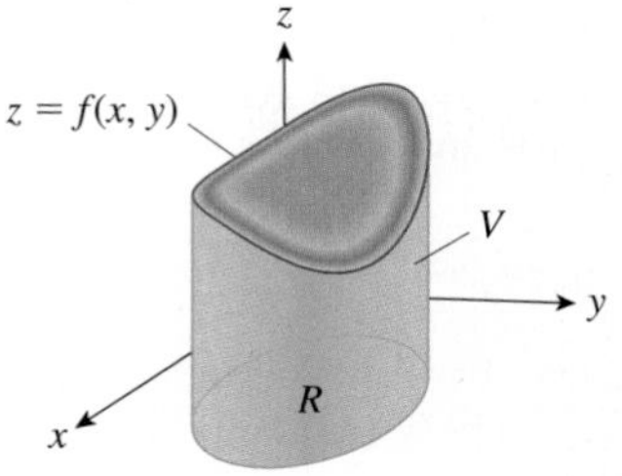

Figure 28

By analogy with the definite integral of a function of one variable, we make the following definition:

Geometric Definition of the Double Integral

The **double integral of $f(x, y)$ over the region R in the xy-plane** is defined as

(Volume *above* the region R and under the graph of f)
− (Volume *below* the region R and above the graph of f).

We denote the double integral of $f(x, y)$ over the region R by $\iint_R f(x, y)\,dx\,dy$.

Quick Example

Take $f(x, y) = 2$ and take R to be the rectangle $0 \le x \le 1, 0 \le y \le 1$. Then the graph of f is a flat horizontal surface $z = 2$, and

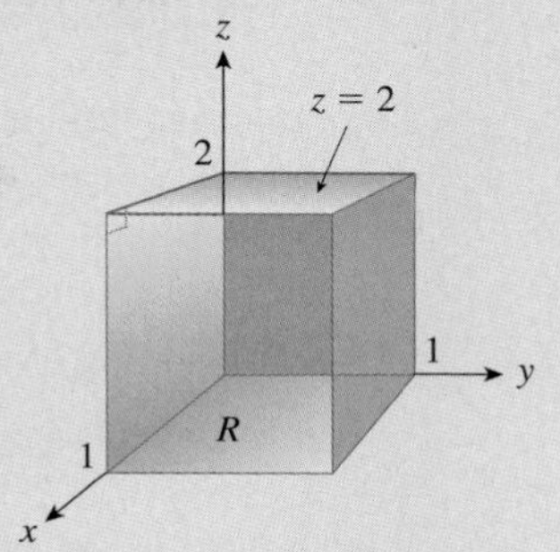

$$\iint_R f(x, y)\, dx\, dy = \text{Volume of box}$$
$$= \text{Width} \times \text{Length} \times \text{Height} = 1 \times 1 \times 2 = 2.$$

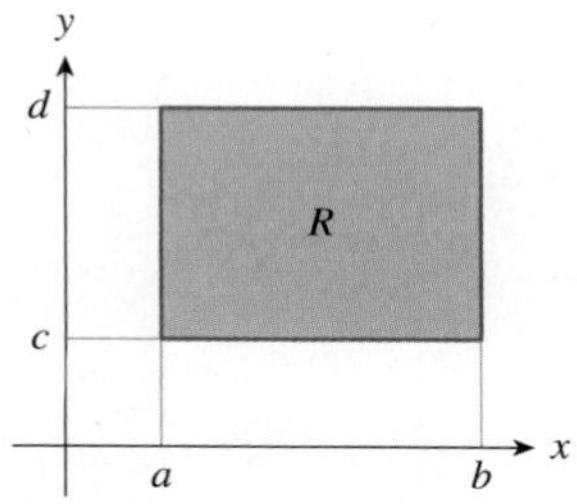

Figure 29

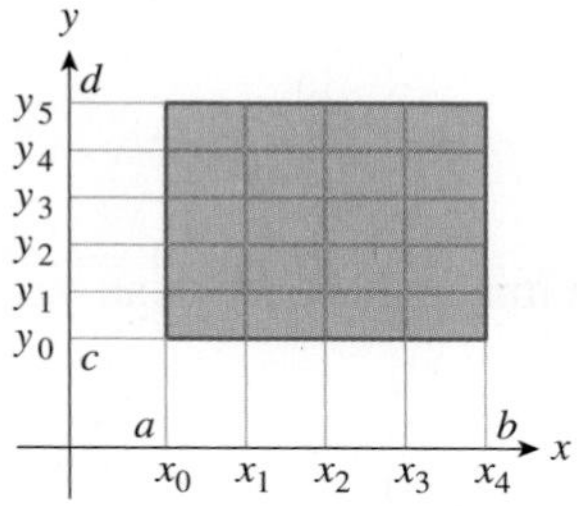

Figure 30

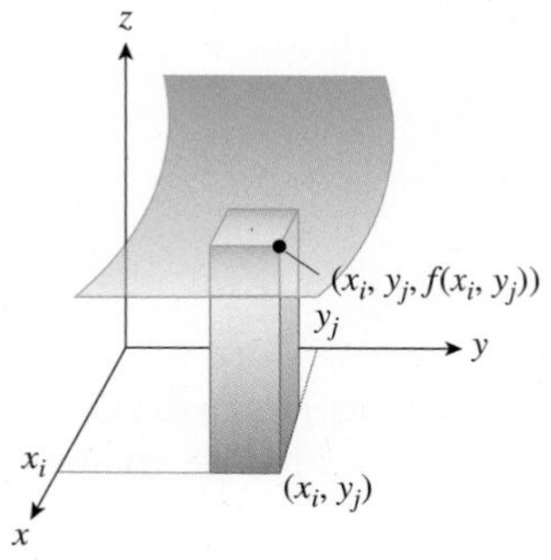

Figure 31

As we saw in the case of the definite integral of a function of one variable, we also desire *numerical* and *algebraic* definitions for two reasons: (1) to make the mathematical definition more precise, so as not to rely on the notion of "volume," and (2) for direct computation of the integral using technology or analytical tools.

We start with the simplest case, when the region R is a rectangle $a \le x \le b$ and $c \le y \le d$. (See Figure 29.) To compute the volume over R, we mimic what we did to find the area under the graph of a function of one variable. We break up the interval $[a, b]$ into m intervals all of width $\Delta x = (b - a)/m$, and we break up $[c, d]$ into n intervals all of width $\Delta y = (d - c)/n$. Figure 30 shows an example with $m = 4$ and $n = 5$.

This gives us mn rectangles defined by $x_{i-1} \le x \le x_i$ and $y_{j-1} \le y \le y_j$. Over one of these rectangles, f is approximately equal to its value at one corner—say $f(x_i, y_j)$. The volume under f over this small rectangle is then approximately the volume of the rectangular brick (size exaggerated) shown in Figure 31. This brick has height $f(x_i, y_j)$, and its base is Δx by Δy. Its volume is therefore $f(x_i, y_j)\Delta x \Delta y$. Adding together the volumes of all of the bricks over the small rectangles in R, we get

$$\iint_R f(x, y)\, dx\, dy \approx \sum_{j=1}^{n} \sum_{i=1}^{m} f(x_i, y_j)\Delta x\, \Delta y.$$

This double sum is called a **double Riemann sum**. We define the double integral to be the limit of the Riemann sums as m and n go to infinity.

Algebraic Definition of the Double Integral

$$\iint_R f(x, y)\, dx\, dy = \lim_{n \to \infty} \lim_{m \to \infty} \sum_{j=1}^{n} \sum_{i=1}^{m} f(x_i, y_j)\Delta x\, \Delta y$$

Note This definition is adequate (the limit exists) when f is continuous. More elaborate definitions are needed for general functions. ■

This definition also gives us a clue about how to compute a double integral. The innermost sum is $\sum_{i=1}^{m} f(x_i, y_j)\Delta x$, which is a Riemann sum for $\int_a^b f(x, y_j)\, dx$. The innermost limit is therefore

$$\lim_{m\to\infty} \sum_{i=1}^{m} f(x_i, y_j)\Delta x = \int_a^b f(x, y_j)\, dx.$$

The outermost limit is then also a Riemann sum, and we get the following way of calculating double integrals:

Computing the Double Integral over a Rectangle

If R is the rectangle $a \le x \le b$ and $c \le y \le d$, then

$$\iint_R f(x, y)\, dx\, dy = \int_c^d \left(\int_a^b f(x, y)\, dx \right) dy = \int_a^b \left(\int_c^d f(x, y)\, dy \right) dx.$$

The second formula comes from switching the order of summation in the double sum.

Quick Example

If R is the rectangle $1 \le x \le 2$ and $1 \le y \le 3$, then

$$\iint_R 1\, dx\, dy = \int_1^3 \left(\int_1^2 1\, dx \right) dy$$

$$= \int_1^3 [x]_{x=1}^{2}\, dy \qquad \text{Evaluate the inner integral.}$$

$$= \int_1^3 1\, dy \qquad [x]_{x=1}^{2} = 2 - 1 = 1.$$

$$= [y]_{y=1}^{3} = 3 - 1 = 2.$$

The Quick Example used a constant function for the integrand. Here is an example in which the integrand is not constant.

EXAMPLE 1 Double Integral over a Rectangle

Let R be the rectangle $0 \le x \le 1$ and $0 \le y \le 2$. Compute $\iint_R xy\, dx\, dy$. This integral gives the volume of the part of the boxed region under the surface $z = xy$ shown in Figure 32.

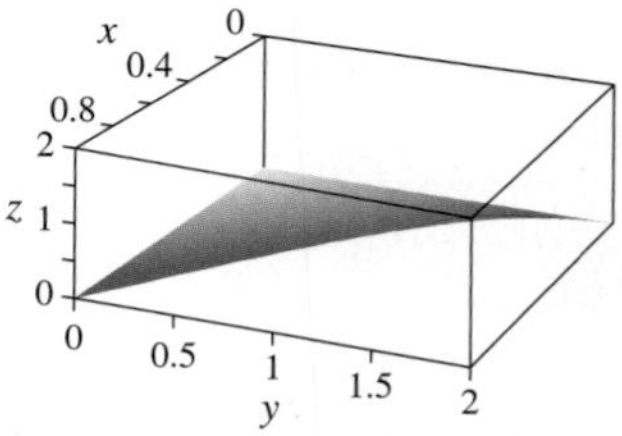

$z = xy$, $0 \le x \le 1$ and $0 \le y \le 2$

Figure 32

Solution

$$\iint_R xy\, dx\, dy = \int_0^2 \int_0^1 xy\, dx\, dy$$

(We usually drop the parentheses around the inner integral like this.) As in the Quick Example, we compute this **iterated integral** from the inside out. First we compute

$$\int_0^1 xy\, dx.$$

To do this computation, we do as we did when finding partial derivatives: We treat y as a constant. This gives

$$\int_0^1 xy\,dx = \left[\frac{x^2}{2}\cdot y\right]_{x=0}^1 = \frac{1}{2}y - 0 = \frac{y}{2}.$$

We can now calculate the outer integral.

$$\int_0^2\int_0^1 xy\,dx\,dy = \int_0^2 \frac{y}{2}\,dy = \left[\frac{y^2}{4}\right]_0^2 = 1$$

Before we go on... We could also reverse the order of integration in Example 1:

$$\int_0^1\int_0^2 xy\,dy\,dx = \int_0^1 \left[x\cdot\frac{y^2}{2}\right]_{y=0}^2 = \int_0^1 2x\,dx = \left[x^2\right]_0^1 = 1.$$

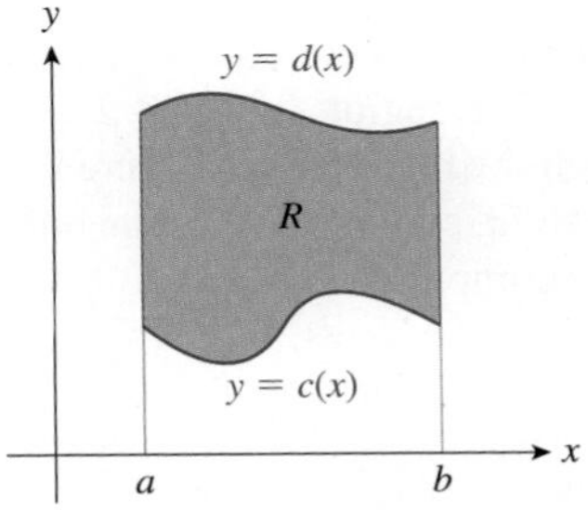

Figure 33

Often we need to integrate over regions R that are not rectangular. There are two cases that come up. The first is a region like the one shown in Figure 33. In this region, the bottom and top sides are defined by functions $y = c(x)$ and $y = d(x)$, respectively, so that the whole region can be described by the inequalities $a \le x \le b$ and $c(x) \le y \le d(x)$. To evaluate a double integral over such a region, we have the following formula:

Computing the Double Integral over a Nonrectangular Region

If R is the region $a \le x \le b$ and $c(x) \le y \le d(x)$ (Figure 33), then we integrate over R according to the following equation:

$$\iint_R f(x, y)\,dx\,dy = \int_a^b\int_{c(x)}^{d(x)} f(x, y)\,dy\,dx.$$

EXAMPLE 2 Double Integral over a Nonrectangular Region

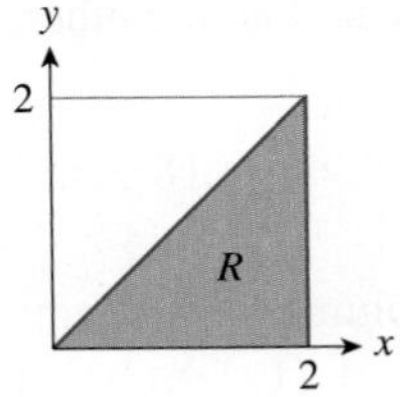

Figure 34

R is the triangle shown in Figure 34. Compute $\iint_R x\,dx\,dy$.

Solution R is the region described by $0 \le x \le 2$, $0 \le y \le x$. We have

$$\begin{aligned}\iint_R x\,dx\,dy &= \int_0^2\int_0^x x\,dy\,dx \\ &= \int_0^2 \left[xy\right]_{y=0}^x\,dx \\ &= \int_0^2 x^2\,dx \\ &= \left[\frac{x^3}{3}\right]_0^2 = \frac{8}{3}.\end{aligned}$$

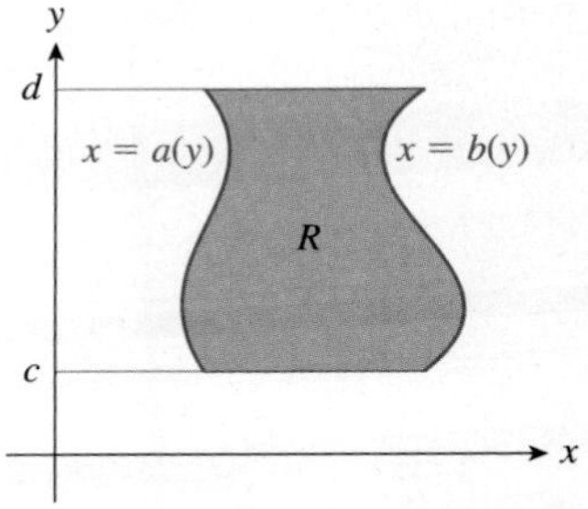

Figure 35

The second type of region is shown in Figure 35. This is the region described by $c \le y \le d$ and $a(y) \le x \le b(y)$. To evaluate a double integral over such a region, we have the following formula:

Double Integral over a Nonrectangular Region (continued)

If R is the region $c \le y \le d$ and $a(y) \le x \le b(y)$ (Figure 35), then we integrate over R according to the following equation:

$$\iint_R f(x, y)\, dx\, dy = \int_c^d \int_{a(y)}^{b(y)} f(x, y)\, dx\, dy.$$

EXAMPLE 3 Double Integral over a Nonrectangular Region

Redo Example 2, integrating in the opposite order.

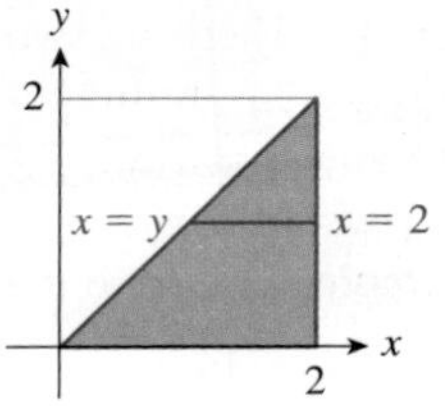

Figure 36

Solution We can integrate in the opposite order if we can describe the region in Figure 34 in the way shown in Figure 35. In fact, it is the region $0 \le y \le 2$ and $y \le x \le 2$. To see this, we draw a horizontal line through the region, as in Figure 36. The line extends from $x = y$ on the left to $x = 2$ on the right, so $y \le x \le 2$. The possible heights for such a line are $0 \le y \le 2$. We can now compute the integral:

$$\iint_R x\, dx\, dy = \int_0^2 \int_y^2 x\, dx\, dy$$

$$= \int_0^2 \left[\frac{x^2}{2}\right]_{x=y}^{2} dy$$

$$= \int_0^2 \left(2 - \frac{y^2}{2}\right) dy$$

$$= \left[2y - \frac{y^3}{6}\right]_0^2 = \frac{8}{3}.$$

Note Many regions can be described in two different ways, as we saw in Examples 2 and 3. Sometimes one description will be much easier to work with than the other, so it pays to consider both. ■

APPLICATIONS

There are many applications of double integrals besides finding volumes. For example, we can use them to find *averages*. Remember that the average of $f(x)$ on $[a, b]$ is given by $\int_a^b f(x)\, dx$ divided by $(b - a)$, the length of the interval.

Average of a Function of Two Variables

The average of $f(x, y)$ on the region R is

$$\bar{f} = \frac{1}{A} \iint_R f(x, y)\, dx\, dy.$$

Here, A is the area of R. We can compute the area A geometrically, or by using the techniques from the chapter on applications of the integral, or by computing

$$A = \iint_R 1\, dx\, dy.$$

Quick Example

The average value of $f(x, y) = xy$ on the rectangle given by $0 \le x \le 1$ and $0 \le y \le 2$ is

$$\bar{f} = \frac{1}{2}\iint_R xy\, dx\, dy \qquad \text{The area of the rectangle is 2.}$$

$$= \frac{1}{2}\int_0^2\int_0^1 xy\, dx\, dy$$

$$= \frac{1}{2}\cdot 1 = \frac{1}{2}. \qquad \text{We calculated the integral in Example 1.}$$

EXAMPLE 4 Average Revenue

Your company is planning to price its new line of subcompact cars at between \$10,000 and \$15,000. The marketing department reports that if the company prices the cars at p dollars per car, the demand will be between $q = 20{,}000 - p$ and $q = 25{,}000 - p$ cars sold in the first year. What is the average of all the possible revenues your company could expect in the first year?

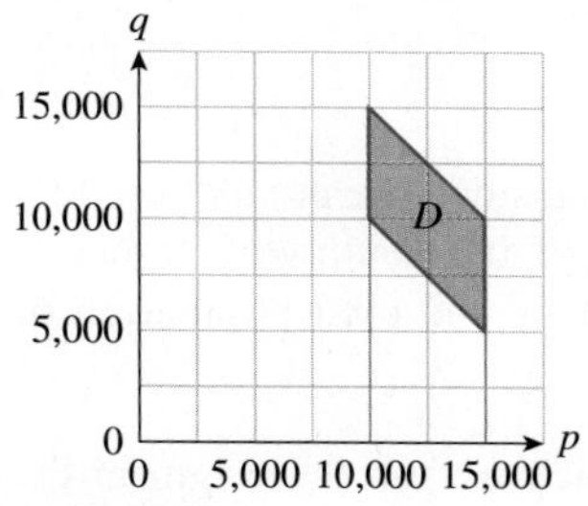

Figure 37

Solution Revenue is given by $R = pq$ as usual, and we are told that

$$10{,}000 \le p \le 15{,}000$$

and $$20{,}000 - p \le q \le 25{,}000 - p.$$

This domain D of prices and demands is shown in Figure 37.

To average the revenue R over the domain D, we need to compute the area A of D. Using either calculus or geometry, we get $A = 25{,}000{,}000$. We then need to integrate R over D:

$$\iint_D pq\, dp\, dq = \int_{10{,}000}^{15{,}000}\int_{20{,}000-p}^{25{,}000-p} pq\, dq\, dp$$

$$= \int_{10{,}000}^{15{,}000}\left[\frac{pq^2}{2}\right]_{q=20{,}000-p}^{25{,}000-p} dp$$

$$= \frac{1}{2}\int_{10{,}000}^{15{,}000}[p(25{,}000-p)^2 - p(20{,}000-p)^2]\, dp$$

$$= \frac{1}{2}\int_{10{,}000}^{15{,}000}[225{,}000{,}000p - 10{,}000p^2]\, dp$$

$$\approx 3{,}072{,}900{,}000{,}000{,}000.$$

The average of all the possible revenues your company could expect in the first year is therefore

$$\bar{R} = \frac{3{,}072{,}900{,}000{,}000{,}000}{25{,}000{,}000} \approx \$122{,}900{,}000.$$

Before we go on... To check that the answer obtained in Example 4 is reasonable, notice that the revenues at the corners of the domain are \$100,000,000 per year, \$150,000,000 per year (at two corners), and \$75,000,000 per year. Some of these are smaller than the average and some larger, as we would expect. ■

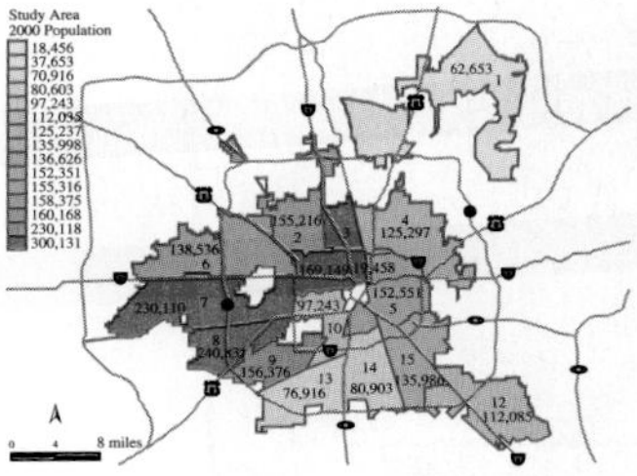

Darker regions have higher population density

Figure 38

Another useful application of the double integral comes about when we consider density. For example, suppose that $P(x, y)$ represents the population density (in people per square mile, say) in the city of Houston, shown in Figure 38.

If we break the city up into small rectangles (for example, city blocks), then the population in the small rectangle $x_{i-1} \le x \le x_i$ and $y_{j-1} \le y \le y_j$ is approximately $P(x_i, y_j)\Delta x \Delta y$. Adding up all of these population estimates, we get

$$\text{Total population} \approx \sum_{j=1}^{n} \sum_{i=1}^{m} P(x_i, y_j)\, \Delta x\, \Delta y.$$

Because this is a double Riemann sum, when we take the limit as m and n go to infinity, we get the following calculation of the population of the city:

$$\text{Total population} = \iint_{\text{City}} P(x, y)\, dx\, dy.$$

EXAMPLE 5 Population

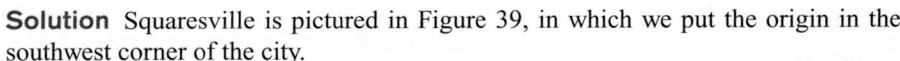

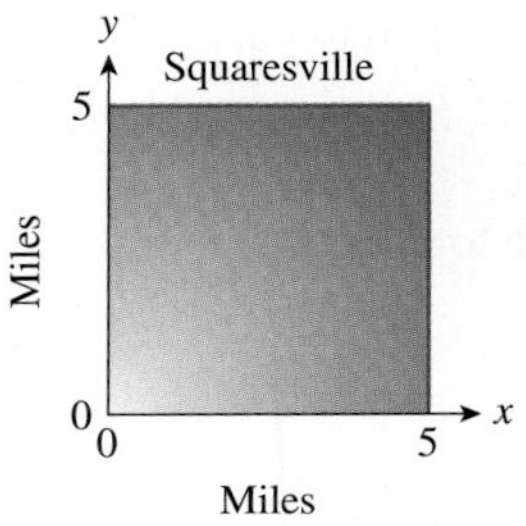

Figure 39

Squaresville is a city in the shape of a square 5 miles on a side. The population density at a distance of x miles east and y miles north of the southwest corner is $P(x, y) = x^2 + y^2$ thousand people per square mile. Find the total population of Squaresville.

Solution Squaresville is pictured in Figure 39, in which we put the origin in the southwest corner of the city.

To compute the total population, we integrate the population density over the city S.

$$\begin{aligned}
\text{Total population} &= \iint_{\text{Squaresville}} P(x, y)\, dx\, dy \\
&= \int_0^5 \int_0^5 (x^2 + y^2)\, dx\, dy \\
&= \int_0^5 \left[\frac{x^3}{3} + xy^2\right]_{x=0}^{5} dy \\
&= \int_0^5 \left[\frac{125}{3} + 5y^2\right] dy \\
&= \frac{1{,}250}{3} \approx 417 \text{ thousand people}
\end{aligned}$$

Before we go on... Note that the average population density is the total population divided by the area of the city, which is about 17,000 people per square mile. Compare this calculation with the calculations of averages in the previous two examples. ■

8.5 EXERCISES

▼ more advanced ◆ challenging

T indicates exercises that should be solved using technology

Compute the integrals in Exercises 1–16. HINT [See Example 1.]

1. $\int_0^1 \int_0^1 (x - 2y)\,dx\,dy$

2. $\int_{-1}^1 \int_0^2 (2x + 3y)\,dx\,dy$

3. $\int_0^1 \int_0^2 (ye^x - x - y)\,dx\,dy$

4. $\int_1^2 \int_2^3 \left(\frac{1}{x} + \frac{1}{y}\right) dx\,dy$

5. $\int_0^2 \int_0^3 e^{x+y}\,dx\,dy$

6. $\int_0^1 \int_0^1 e^{x-y}\,dx\,dy$

7. $\int_0^1 \int_0^{2-y} x\,dx\,dy$

8. $\int_0^1 \int_0^{2-y} y\,dx\,dy$

9. $\int_{-1}^1 \int_{y-1}^{y+1} e^{x+y}\,dx\,dy$ HINT [See Example 2.]

10. $\int_0^1 \int_y^{y+2} \frac{1}{\sqrt{x+y}}\,dx\,dy$ HINT [See Example 2.]

11. $\int_0^1 \int_{-x^2}^{x^2} x\,dy\,dx$

12. $\int_1^4 \int_{-\sqrt{x}}^{\sqrt{x}} \frac{1}{x}\,dy\,dx$

13. $\int_0^1 \int_0^x e^{x^2}\,dy\,dx$

14. $\int_0^1 \int_0^{x^2} e^{x^3+1}\,dy\,dx$

15. $\int_0^2 \int_{1-x}^{8-x} (x+y)^{1/3}\,dy\,dx$

16. $\int_1^2 \int_{1-2x}^{x^2} \frac{x+1}{(2x+y)^3}\,dy\,dx$

In Exercises 17–24, find $\iint_R f(x, y)\,dx\,dy$, where R is the indicated domain. (Remember that you often have a choice as to the order of integration.) HINT [See Example 2.]

17. $f(x, y) = 2$

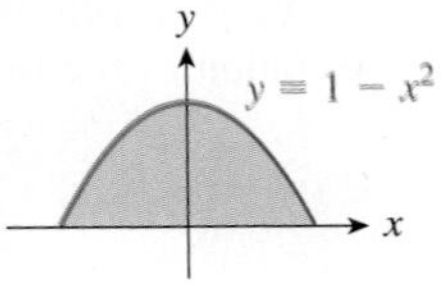

18. $f(x, y) = x$

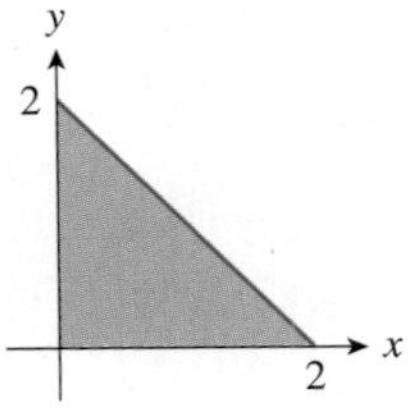

19. $f(x, y) = 1 + y$ HINT [See Example 3.]

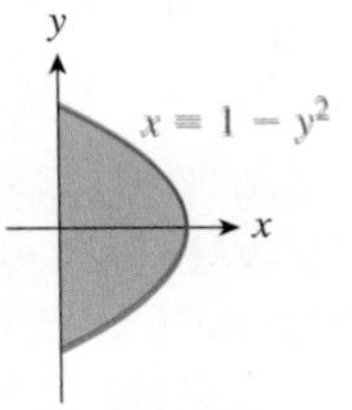

20. $f(x, y) = e^{x+y}$ HINT [See Example 3.]

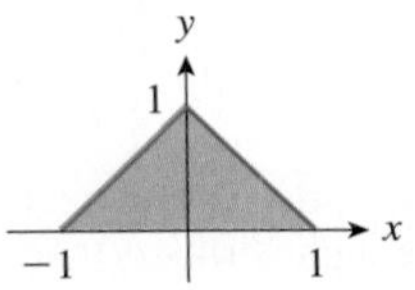

21. $f(x, y) = xy^2$

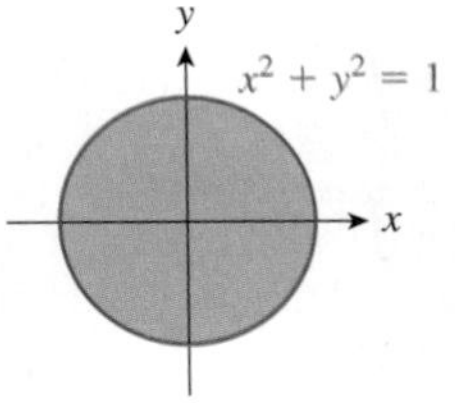

22. $f(x, y) = xy^2$

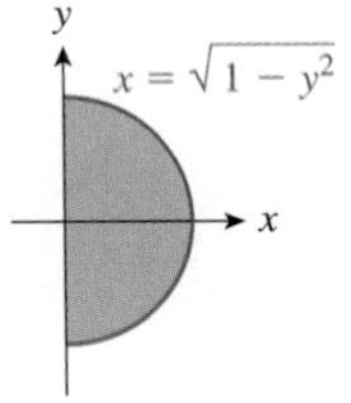

23. $f(x, y) = x^2 + y^2$

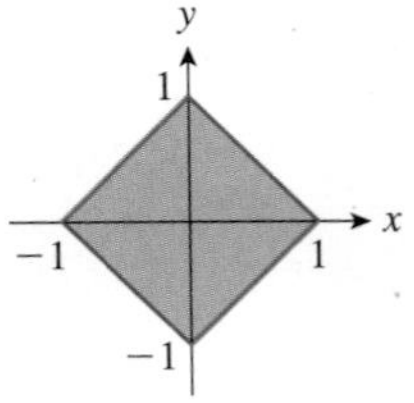

24. $f(x, y) = x^2$

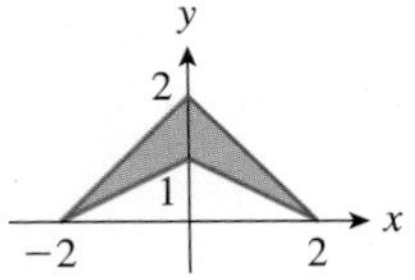

In Exercises 25–30, find the average value of the given function over the indicated domain. HINT [See Quick Example page 639.]

25. $f(x, y) = y$

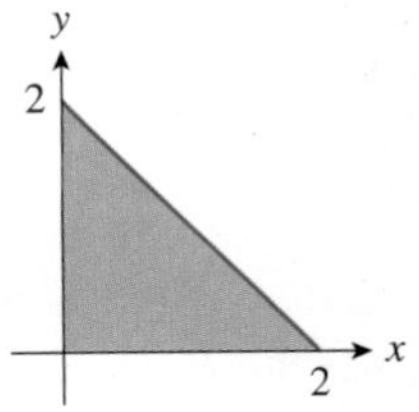

26. $f(x, y) = 2 + x$

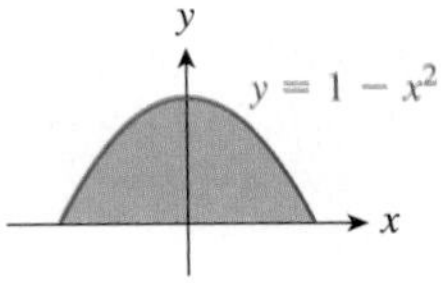

27. $f(x, y) = e^y$

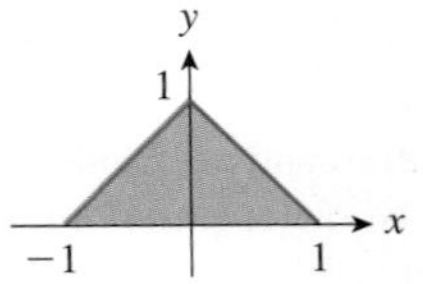

28. $f(x, y) = y$

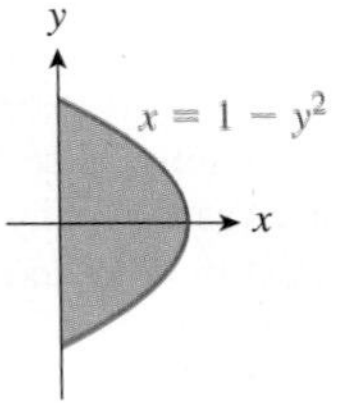

29. $f(x, y) = x^2 + y^2$

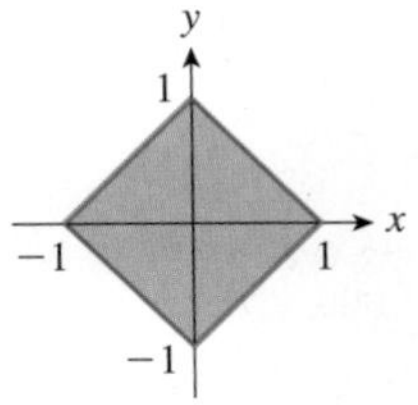

30. $f(x, y) = x^2$

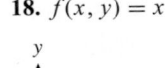

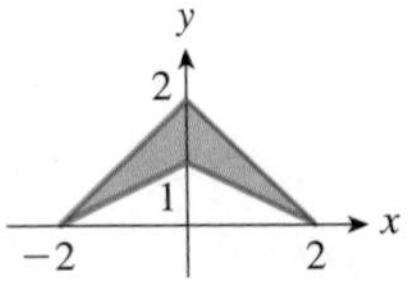

In Exercises 31–36, sketch the region over which you are integrating, and then write down the integral with the order of integration reversed (changing the limits of integration as necessary).

31. ▼ $\int_0^1 \int_0^{1-y} f(x, y)\, dx\, dy$ **32.** ▼ $\int_{-1}^1 \int_0^{1+y} f(x, y)\, dx\, dy$

33. ▼ $\int_{-1}^1 \int_0^{\sqrt{1+y}} f(x, y)\, dx\, dy$ **34.** ▼ $\int_{-1}^1 \int_0^{\sqrt{1-y}} f(x, y)\, dx\, dy$

35. ▼ $\int_1^2 \int_1^{4/x^2} f(x, y)\, dy\, dx$ **36.** ▼ $\int_1^{e^2} \int_0^{\ln x} f(x, y)\, dy\, dx$

37. Find the volume under the graph of $z = 1 - x^2$ over the region $0 \le x \le 1$ and $0 \le y \le 2$.

38. Find the volume under the graph of $z = 1 - x^2$ over the triangle $0 \le x \le 1$ and $0 \le y \le 1 - x$.

39. ▼ Find the volume of the tetrahedron shown in the figure. Its corners are $(0, 0, 0)$, $(1, 0, 0)$, $(0, 1, 0)$, and $(0, 0, 1)$.

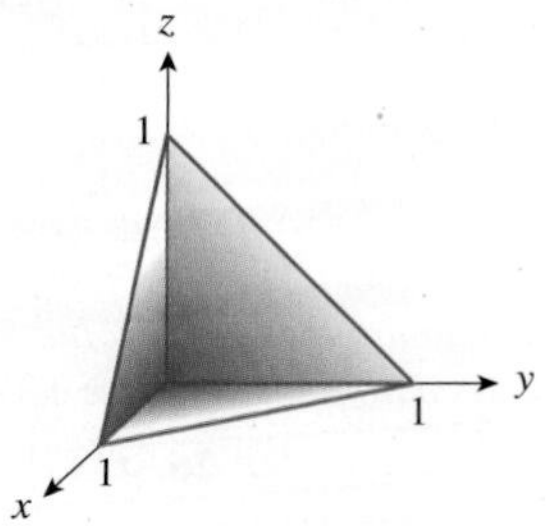

40. ▼ Find the volume of the tetrahedron with corners at $(0, 0, 0)$, $(a, 0, 0)$, $(0, b, 0)$, and $(0, 0, c)$.

APPLICATIONS

41. *Productivity* A productivity model at the *Handy Gadget Company* is

$$P = 10{,}000x^{0.3}y^{0.7},$$

where P is the number of gadgets the company turns out per month, x is the number of employees at the company, and y is the monthly operating budget in thousands of dollars. Because the company hires part-time workers, it uses anywhere between 45 and 55 workers each month, and its operating budget varies from \$8,000 to \$12,000 per month. What is the average of the possible numbers of gadgets it can turn out per month? (Round the answer to the nearest 1,000 gadgets.) HINT [See Quick Example page 639.]

42. *Productivity* Repeat the preceding exercise using the productivity model

$$P = 10{,}000x^{0.7}y^{0.3}.$$

43. *Revenue* Your latest CD-ROM of clip art is expected to sell between $q = 8{,}000 - p^2$ and $q = 10{,}000 - p^2$ copies if priced at p dollars. You plan to set the price between \$40 and

\$50. What is the average of all the possible revenues you can make? HINT [See Example 4.]

44. *Revenue* Your latest DVD drive is expected to sell between $q = 180{,}000 - p^2$ and $q = 200{,}000 - p^2$ units if priced at p dollars. You plan to set the price between \$300 and \$400. What is the average of all the possible revenues you can make? HINT [See Example 4.]

45. *Revenue* Your self-published novel has demand curves between $p = 15{,}000/q$ and $p = 20{,}000/q$. You expect to sell between 500 and 1,000 copies. What is the average of all the possible revenues you can make?

46. *Revenue* Your self-published book of poetry has demand curves between $p = 80{,}000/q^2$ and $p = 100{,}000/q^2$. You expect to sell between 50 and 100 copies. What is the average of all the possible revenues you can make?

47. *Population Density* The town of West Podunk is shaped like a rectangle 20 miles from west to east and 30 miles from north to south. (See the figure.) It has a population density of $P(x, y) = e^{-0.1(x+y)}$ hundred people per square mile x miles east and y miles north of the southwest corner of town. What is the total population of the town? HINT [See Example 5.]

30 miles West Podunk

←— 20 miles —→

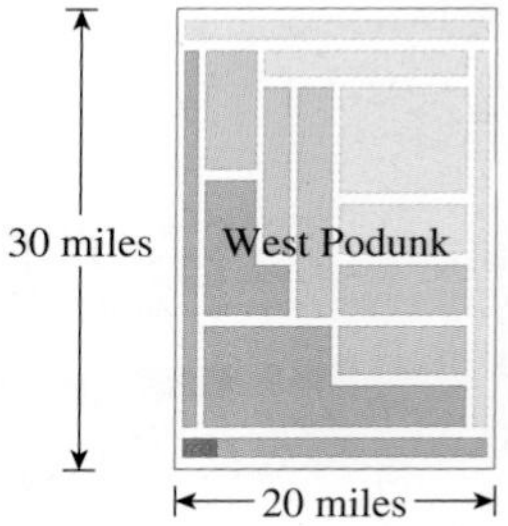

48. *Population Density* The town of East Podunk is shaped like a triangle with an east-west base of 20 miles and a north-south height of 30 miles. (See the figure.) It has a population density of $P(x, y) = e^{-0.1(x+y)}$ hundred people per square mile x miles east and y miles north of the southwest corner of town. What is the total population of the town? HINT [See Example 5.]

30 miles East Podunk

←— 20 miles —→

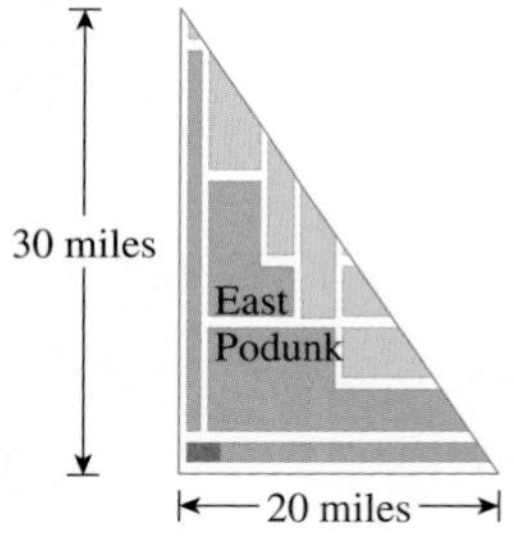

49. *Temperature* The temperature at the point (x, y) on the square with vertices $(0, 0)$, $(0, 1)$, $(1, 0)$, and $(1, 1)$ is given by $T(x, y) = x^2 + 2y^2$. Find the average temperature on the square.

50. ***Temperature*** The temperature at the point (x, y) on the square with vertices (0, 0), (0, 1), (1, 0), and (1, 1) is given by $T(x, y) = x^2 + 2y^2 - x$. Find the average temperature on the square.

COMMUNICATION AND REASONING EXERCISES

51. Explain how double integrals can be used to compute the area between two curves in the xy plane.

52. Explain how double integrals can be used to compute the volume of solids in 3-space.

53. Complete the following: The first step in calculating an integral of the form $\int_a^b \int_{r(x)}^{s(x)} f(x, y)\,dy\,dx$ is to evaluate the integral ______, obtained by holding ___ constant and integrating with respect to ___.

54. If the units of $f(x, y)$ are zonars per square meter, and x and y are given in meters, what are the units of $\int_a^b \int_{r(x)}^{s(x)} f(x, y)\,dy\,dx$?

55. If the units of $\int_a^b \int_{r(x)}^{s(x)} f(x, y)\,dy\,dx$ are paintings, the units of x are picassos, and the units of y are dalis, what are the units of $f(x, y)$?

56. Complete the following: If the region R is bounded on the left and right by vertical lines and on the top and bottom by the graphs of functions of x, then we integrate over R by first integrating with respect to ____ and then with respect to ___.

57. ▼ Show that if a, b, c, and d are constant, then $\int_a^b \int_c^d f(x)\, g(y)\,dx\,dy = \int_c^d f(x)\,dx \int_a^b g(y)\,dy$. Test this result on the integral $\int_0^1 \int_1^2 ye^x\,dx\,dy$.

58. ▼ Refer to Exercise 57. If a, b, c, and d are constants, can $\displaystyle\int_a^b \int_c^d \frac{f(x)}{g(y)}\,dx\,dy$ be expressed as a product of two integrals? Explain.

CHAPTER 8 REVIEW

KEY CONCEPTS

Website www.WanerMath.com
Go to the Website at www.WanerMath.com to find a comprehensive and interactive Web-based summary of Chapter 8.

8.1 Functions of Several Variables from the Numerical, Algebraic, and Graphical Viewpoints

A real-valued function, f, of $x, y, z, \dots$ *p. 588*
Cost functions *p. 589*
A linear function of the variables $x_1, x_2, \dots, x_n$ is a function of the form $f(x_1, x_2, \dots, x_n) = a_0 + a_1x_1 + \cdots + a_nx_n$ ($a_0, a_1, \dots, a_n$ constants) *p. 590*
Representing functions of two variables numerically *p. 591*
Using a spreadsheet to represent a function of two variables *p. 592*
Plotting points in three dimensions *p. 592*
Graph of a function of two variables *p. 593*
Analyzing the graph of a function of two variables *p. 596*
Graph of a linear function *p. 599*

8.2 Partial Derivatives

Definition of partial derivatives *p. 607*
Application to marginal cost: linear cost function *p. 608*
Application to marginal cost: interaction cost function *p. 609*
Geometric interpretation of partial derivatives *p. 610*
Second-order partial derivatives *p. 611*

8.3 Maxima and Minima

Definition of relative maximum and minimum *p. 617*
Locating candidates for relative maxima and minima *p. 618*
Classifying critical points graphically *p. 619*
Classifying critical points numerically *p. 619*
Second derivative test for a function of two variables *p. 619*
Using the second derivative test *p. 620*
Formulas for Linear Regression

$$m = \frac{n\left(\sum xy\right) - \left(\sum x\right)\left(\sum y\right)}{n\left(\sum x^2\right) - \left(\sum x\right)^2}$$

$$b = \frac{\sum y - m\left(\sum x\right)}{n}$$

n = number of data points *p. 621*

8.4 Constrained Maxima and Minima and Applications

Constrained maximum and minimum problem *p. 625*
Solving constrained maxima and minima problems using substitution *p. 626*
The method of Lagrange multipliers *p. 627*
Using Lagrange multipliers *p. 627*

8.5 Double Integrals and Applications

Geometric definition of the double integral *p. 634*
Algebraic definition of the double integral

$$\iint_R f(x, y)\,dx\,dy = \lim_{n\to\infty}\lim_{m\to\infty}\sum_{j=1}^{n}\sum_{i=1}^{m} f(x_i, y_j)\Delta x\,\Delta y$$

p. 635
Computing the double integral over a rectangle *p. 636*
Computing the double integral over nonrectangular regions *p. 637*
Average of $f(x, y)$ on the region R:

$$\bar{f} = \frac{1}{A}\iint_R f(x, y)\,dx\,dy \quad p.\ 638$$

REVIEW EXERCISES

1. Let $f(x, y, z) = \dfrac{x}{y + xz} + x^2y$. Evaluate $f(0, 1, 1)$, $f(2, 1, 1)$, $f(-1, 1, -1)$, $f(z, z, z)$, and $f(x + h, y + k, z + l)$.

2. Let $g(x, y, z) = xy(x + y - z) + x^2$. Evaluate $g(0, 0, 0)$, $g(1, 0, 0)$, $g(0, 1, 0)$, $g(x, x, x)$, and $g(x, y + k, z)$.

3. Let $f(x, y, z) = 2.72 - 0.32x - 3.21y + 12.5z$. Complete the following: f___ by ___ units for every 1 unit of increase in x, and ___ by ___ units for every unit of increase in z.

4. Let $g(x, y, z) = 2.16x + 11y - 1.53z + 31.4$. Complete the following: g___ by ___ units for every 1 unit of increase in y, and ___ by ___ units for every unit of increase in z.

In Exercises 5–6 complete the given table for values for $h(x, y) = 2x^2 + xy - x$.

5.

$y \downarrow$ \ $x \rightarrow$	−1	0	1
−1			
0			
1			

6.

$y \downarrow$ \ $x \rightarrow$	−2	2	3
−2			
2			
3			

7. Give a formula for a (single) function f with the property that $f(x, y) = -f(y, x)$ and $f(1, -1) = 3$.

8. Let $f(x, y) = x^2 + (y + 1)^2$. Show that $f(y, x) = f(x + 1, y - 1)$.

Sketch the graphs of the functions in Exercises 9–14.

9. $r(x, y) = x + y$

10. $r(x, y) = x - y$

11. $t(x, y) = x^2 + 2y^2$. Show cross sections at $x = 0$ and $z = 1$.

12. $t(x, y) = \dfrac{1}{2}x^2 + y^2$. Show cross sections at $x = 0$ and $z = 1$.

13. $f(x, y) = -2\sqrt{x^2 + y^2}$. Show cross sections at $z = -4$ and $y = 1$.

14. $f(x, y) = 2 + 2\sqrt{x^2 + y^2}$. Show cross sections at $z = 4$ and $y = 1$.

In Exercises 15–20, compute the partial derivatives shown for the given function.

15. $f(x, y) = x^2 + xy$; find f_x, f_y, and f_{yy}

16. $f(x, y) = \dfrac{6}{xy} + \dfrac{xy}{6}$; find f_x, f_y, and f_{yy}

17. $f(x, y) = 4x + 5y - 6xy$; find $f_{xx}(1, 0) - f_{xx}(3, 2)$

18. $f(x, y) = e^{xy} + e^{3x^2 - y^2}$; find $\dfrac{\partial f}{\partial x}$ and $\dfrac{\partial^2 f}{\partial x \partial y}$

19. $f(x, y, z) = \dfrac{x}{x^2 + y^2 + z^2}$; find $\dfrac{\partial f}{\partial x}, \dfrac{\partial f}{\partial y}, \dfrac{\partial f}{\partial z}$, and $\left.\dfrac{\partial f}{\partial x}\right|_{(0,1,0)}$.

20. $f(x, y, z) = x^2 + y^2 + z^2 + xyz$; find $f_{xx} + f_{yy} + f_{zz}$

In Exercises 21–26, locate and classify all critical points.

21. $f(x, y) = (x - 1)^2 + (2y - 3)^2$

22. $g(x, y) = (x - 1)^2 - 3y^2 + 9$

23. $k(x, y) = x^2y - x^2 - y^2$

24. $j(x, y) = xy + x^2$

25. $h(x, y) = e^{xy}$

26. $f(x, y) = \ln(x^2 + y^2) - (x^2 + y^2)$

In Exercises 27–30, solve the given constrained optimization problem by using substitution to eliminate a variable. (Do not use Lagrange multipliers.)

27. Find the largest value of xyz subject to $x + y + z = 1$ with $x > 0, y > 0, z > 0$. Also find the corresponding point(s) (x, y, z).

28. Find the minimum value of $f(x, y, z) = x^2 + y^2 + z^2 - 1$ subject to $x = y + z$. Also find the corresponding point(s) (x, y, z).

29. Find the point on the surface $z = \sqrt{x^2 + 2(y - 3)^2}$ closest to the origin.

30. Minimize $S = xy + x^2z^2 + 4yz$ subject to $xyz = 1$ with $x > 0, y > 0, z > 0$.

In Exercises 31–34, use Lagrange multipliers to solve the given optimization problem.

31. Find the minimum value of $f(x, y) = x^2 + y^2$ subject to $xy = 2$. Also find the corresponding point(s) (x, y).

32. The problem in Exercise 28.

33. The problem in Exercise 29.

34. The problem in Exercise 30.

In Exercises 35–40, compute the given quantities.

35. $\displaystyle\int_0^1 \int_0^2 (2xy)\, dx\, dy$

36. $\displaystyle\int_1^2 \int_0^1 xye^{x+y}\, dx\, dy$

37. $\displaystyle\int_0^2 \int_0^{2x} \frac{1}{x^2 + 1}\, dy\, dx$

38. The average value of xye^{x+y} over the rectangle $0 \le x \le 1$, $1 \le y \le 2$

39. $\iint_R (x^2 - y^2)\, dx\, dy$, where R is the region shown in the figure

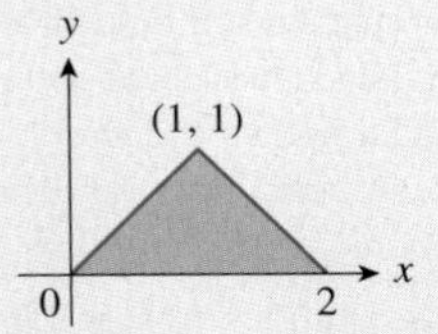

40. The volume under the graph of $z = 1 - y$ over the region in the xy plane between the parabola $y = 1 - x^2$ and the x-axis

APPLICATIONS: OHaganBooks.com

41. ***Web Site Traffic*** OHaganBooks.com has two principal competitors: JungleBooks.com and FarmerBooks.com. Current Web site traffic at OHaganBooks.com is estimated at 5,000 hits per day. This number is predicted to decrease by 0.8 for every new customer of JungleBooks.com and by 0.6 for every new customer of FarmerBooks.com.

a. Use this information to model the daily Website traffic at OHaganBooks.com as a linear function of the new customers of its two competitors.

b. According to the model, if Junglebooks.com gets 100 new customers and OHaganBooks.com traffic drops to 4,770 hits per day, how many new customers has FarmerBooks.com obtained?

c. The model in part (a) did not take into account the growth of the total online consumer base. OHaganBooks .com expects to get approximately one additional hit per day for every 10,000 new Internet shoppers. Modify your model in part (a) so as to include this information using a new independent variable.

d. How many new Internet shoppers would it take to offset the effects on traffic at OHaganBooks.com of 100 new customers at each of its competitor sites?

42. ***Productivity*** Billy-Sean O'Hagan is writing up his Ph.D. thesis in biophysics but finds that his productivity is affected by the temperature and the number of text messages he receives per hour. On a brisk winter's day when the temperature is 0°C and there are no text messages, Billy-Sean can produce 15 pages of his thesis. His productivity goes down by 0.3 pages per degree Celsius increase in the temperature and by 1.2 pages for each additional text message per hour.

a. Use this information to model Billy-Sean's productivity p as a function of the temperature and the hourly rate of text messages.

b. The other day the temperature was 20°C and Billy-Sean managed to produce only three pages of his thesis. What was the hourly rate of incoming text messages?

c. Billy-Sean reasons that each cup of coffee he drinks per hour can counter the effect on his productivity of two text messages per hour. Modify the model in part (a) to take consumption of coffee into account.

d. What would the domain of your function look like to ensure that p is never negative?

43. ***Internet Advertising*** To increase business at OHaganBooks.com, you have purchased banner ads at well-known Internet portals and have advertised on television. The following interaction model shows the average number h of hits per day as a function of monthly expenditures x on banner ads and y on television advertising (x and y are in dollars).

$$h(x, y) = 1{,}800 + 0.05x + 0.08y + 0.00003xy$$

a. Based on your model, how much traffic can you anticipate if you spend \$2,000 per month for banner ads and \$3,000 per month on television advertising?

b. Evaluate $\frac{\partial h}{\partial y}$, specify its units of measurement, and indicate whether it increases or decreases with increasing x.

c. How much should the company spend on banner ads to obtain 1 hit per day for each \$5 spent per month on television advertising?

44. ***Company Retreats*** Their companies having recently been bailed out by the government at taxpayer expense, Marjory Duffin and John O'Hagan are planning a joint winter business retreat in Cancun, but they are not sure how many sales reps to take along. The following interaction model shows the estimated cost C to their companies (in dollars) as a function of the number of sales reps x and the length of time t in days.

$$C(x, t) = 20{,}000 - 100x + 600t + 300xt$$

a. Based on the model, how much would it cost to take five sales reps along for a 10-day retreat?

b. Evaluate $\frac{\partial C}{\partial t}$, specify its units of measurement, and indicate whether it increases or decreases with increasing x.

c. How many reps should they take along if they wish to limit the marginal daily cost to \$1,200?

45. ***Internet Advertising*** Refer to the model in Exercise 43. One or more of the following statements is correct. Identify which one(s).

(A) If nothing is spent on television advertising, one more dollar spent per month in banner ads will buy approximately 0.05 hits per day at OHaganBooks.com.

(B) If nothing is spent on television advertising, one more hit per day at OHaganBooks.com will cost the company about 5¢ per month in banner ads.

(C) If nothing is spent on banner ads, one more hit per day at OHaganBooks.com will cost the company about 5¢ per month in banner ads.

(D) If nothing is spent on banner ads, one more dollar spent per month in banner ads will buy approximately 0.05 hits per day at OHaganBooks.com.

(E) Hits at OHaganBooks.com cost approximately 5¢ per month spent on banner ads, and this cost increases at a rate of 0.003¢ per month, per hit.

46. ***Company Retreats*** Refer to the model in Exercise 44. One or more of the following statements is correct. Identify which one(s).

(A) If the retreat lasts for 10 days, the daily cost per sales rep is \$400.

(B) If the retreat lasts for 10 days, each additional day will cost the company \$2,900.

(C) If the retreat lasts for 10 days, each additional sales rep will cost the company \$800.

(D) If the retreat lasts for 10 days, the daily cost per sales rep is \$2,900.

(E) If the retreat lasts for 10 days, each additional sales rep will cost the company \$2,900.

47. ***Productivity*** The holiday season is now at its peak and OHaganBooks.com has been understaffed and swamped with orders. The current backlog (orders unshipped for two or more days) has grown to a staggering 50,000, and new orders are coming in at a rate of 5,000 per day. Research based on productivity data at OHaganBooks.com results in the following model:

$$P(x, y) = 1{,}000x^{0.9}y^{0.1} \text{ additional orders filled per day,}$$

where x is the number of additional personnel hired and y is the daily budget (excluding salaries) allocated to eliminating the backlog.

a. How many additional orders will be filled per day if the company hires 10 additional employees and budgets an additional \$1,000 per day? (Round the answer to the nearest 100.)

b. In addition to the daily budget, extra staffing costs the company \$150 per day for every new staff member hired. In order to fill at least 15,000 additional orders per day at a minimum total daily cost, how many new staff members should the company hire? (Use the method of Lagrange multipliers.)

48. ***Productivity*** The holiday season has now ended, and orders at OHaganBooks.com have plummeted, leaving staff members in the shipping department with little to do besides spend their time on their Facebook pages, so the company is considering laying off a number of personnel and slashing the shipping budget. Research based on productivity data at OHaganBooks.com results in the following model:

$$C(x, y) = 1{,}000x^{0.8}y^{0.2} \text{ fewer orders filled per day,}$$

where x is the number of personnel laid off and y is the cut in the shipping budget (excluding salaries).

a. How many fewer orders will be filled per day if the company lays off 15 additional employees and cuts the budget by an additional \$2,000 per day? (Round the answer to the nearest 100.)

b. In addition to the cut in the shipping budget, the layoffs will save the company \$200 per day for every new staff member laid off. The company needs to meet a target of 20,000 fewer orders per day but, for tax reasons, it must minimize the total resulting savings. How many new staff members should the company lay off? (Use the method of Lagrange multipliers.)

49. ***Profit*** If OHaganBooks.com sells x paperback books and y hardcover books per week, it will make an average weekly profit of

$$P(x, y) = 3x + 10y \text{ dollars.}$$

If it sells between 1,200 and 1,500 paperback books and between 1,800 and 2,000 hardcover books per week, what is the average of all its possible weekly profits?

50. ***Cost*** It costs Duffin House

$$C(x, y) = x^2 + 2y \text{ dollars}$$

to produce x coffee table art books and y paperback books per week. If it produces between 100 and 120 art books and between 800 and 1,000 paperbacks per week, what is the average of all its possible weekly costs?

Case Study

Modeling College Population

david pearson/Alamy

College Malls, Inc. is planning to build a national chain of shopping malls in college neighborhoods. However, malls in general have been experiencing large numbers of store closings due to, among other things, misjudgments of the shopper demographics. As a result, the company is planning to lease only to stores that target the specific age demographics of the national college student population.

As a marketing consultant to College Malls, you will be providing the company with a report that addresses the following specific issues:

- A quick way of estimating the number of students of any specified age and in any particular year, and the effect of increasing age on the college population
- The ages that correspond to relatively high and low college populations
- How fast the 20-year old and 25-year old student populations are increasing
- Some near-term projections of the student population trend

You decide that a good place to start would be with a visit to the Census Bureau's Web site at www.census.gov. After some time battling with search engines, all you can find is some data on college enrollment for three age brackets for the period 1980–2009, as shown in the following table:[29]

College Enrollment (Thousands)

Year	1980	1985	1990	1995	2000	2001	2002	2003	2004	2005	2006	2007	2008	2009
18–24	7,229	7,537	7,964	8,541	9,451	9,629	10,033	10,365	10,611	10,834	10,587	11,161	11,466	12,072
25–34	2,703	3,063	3,161	3,349	3,207	3,422	3,401	3,494	3,690	3,600	3,658	3,838	4,013	6,141
35–44	700	963	1,344	1,548	1,454	1,557	1,678	1,526	1,615	1,657	1,548	1,520	1,672	1,848

The data are inadequate for several reasons: The data are given only for certain years, and in age brackets rather than year-by-year; nor is it obvious as to how you would project the figures. However, you notice that the table is actually a numerical representation of a function of two variables: year and age. Since the age brackets are of different sizes, you "normalize" the data by dividing each figure by the number of years represented in the corresponding age bracket; for instance, you divide the 1980 figure for the first age group by 7 in order to obtain the average enrollment for each year of age in that group. You then rewrite the resulting table representing the years by values of t and each age bracket by the (rounded) age x at its center (enrollment values are rounded):

[29] Source: Census Bureau (www.census.gov/population/www/socdemo/school.html).

$x \downarrow$ \ $t \rightarrow$	0	5	10	15	20	21	22	23	24	25	26	27	28	29
21	1,033	1,077	1,138	1,220	1,350	1,376	1,433	1,481	1,516	1,548	1,512	1,594	1,638	1,725
30	270	306	316	335	321	342	340	349	369	360	366	384	401	614
40	70	96	134	155	145	156	168	153	162	166	155	152	167	185

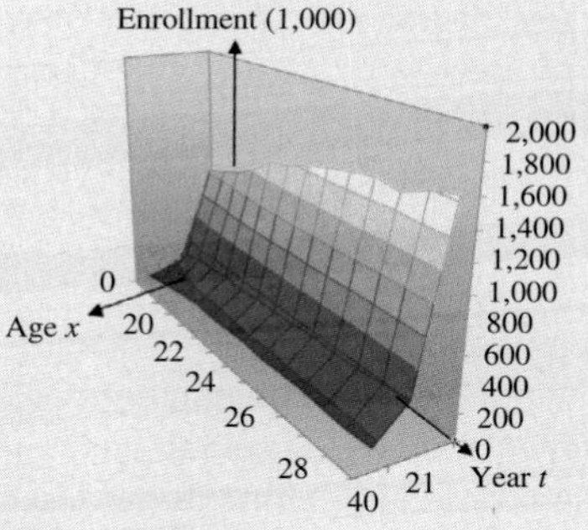

Figure 40

In order to see a visual representation of what the data are saying, you use Excel to graph the data as a surface (Figure 40). It is important to notice that Excel does not scale the t-axis as you would expect: It uses one subdivision for each year shown in the chart, and the result is an uneven scaling of the t-axis. Despite this drawback, you do see two trends after looking at views of the graph from various angles. First, enrollment of 21-year olds (the back edge of the graph) seems to be increasing faster than enrollment of other age groups. Second, the enrollment for all ages seem to be increasing approximately linearly with time, although at different rates for different age groups; for instance, the front and rear edges rise more-or-less linearly, but do not seem to be parallel.

At this point you realize that a mathematical model of these data would be useful; not only would it "smooth out the bumps" but it would give you a way to estimate enrollment N at each specific age, project the enrollments, and thereby complete the project for College Malls. Although technology can give you a regression model for data such as this, it is up to you to decide on the form of the model. It is in choosing an appropriate model that your analysis of the graph comes in handy. Because N should vary linearly with time t for each value of x, you would like

$$N = mt + k$$

for each value of x. Also, because there are three values of x for every value of time, you try a quadratic model for N as a function of x:

$$N = a + bx + cx^2.$$

Putting these together, you get the following candidate model:

$$N(t, x) = a_1 + a_2t + a_3x + a_4x^2,$$

where a_1, a_2, a_3, and a_4 are constants. However, for each specific age $x = k$, you get

$$N(t, k) = a_1 + a_2t + a_3k + a_4k^2 = \text{Constant} + a_2t$$

with the same slope a_2 for every choice of the age k, contrary to your observation that enrollment for different age groups is rising at different rates, so you will need a more elaborate model. You recall from your applied calculus course that interaction functions give a way to model the effect of one variable on the rate of change of another, so, as an experiment, you try adding interaction terms to your model:

Model 1: $N(t, x) = a_1 + a_2t + a_3x + a_4x^2 + a_5xt$ — Second-order model

Model 2: $N(t, x) = a_1 + a_2t + a_3x + a_4x^2 + a_5xt + a_6x^2t.$ — Third-order model

(Model 1 is referred to as a second-order model because it contains no products of more than two independent variables, whereas Model 2 contains the third-order term $x^2t = x \cdot x \cdot t$.) If you study these two models for specific values k of x you get:

Model 1: $N = \text{Constant} + (a_2 + a_5k)t$ — Slope depends linearly on age.

Model 2: $N = \text{Constant} + (a_2 + a_5k + a_6k^2)t.$ — Slope depends quadratically on age.

◇	A	B	C
1	N	t	x
2	1033	0	21
3	1077	5	21
4	1138	10	21
5	1220	15	21
6	1350	20	21
7	1376	21	21
8	1433	22	21
9	1481	23	21
10	1516	24	21
11	1548	25	21
12	1512	26	21
13	1594	27	21
14	1638	28	21
15	1725	29	21
16	270	0	30
17	306	5	30
18	316	10	30
19	335	15	30
20	321	20	30
21	342	21	30
22	340	22	30
23	349	23	30
24	369	24	30
25	360	25	30
26	366	26	30
27	384	27	30
28	401	28	30
29	614	29	30
30	70	0	40
31	96	5	40
32	134	10	40
33	155	15	40
34	145	20	40
35	156	21	40
36	168	22	40
37	153	23	40
38	162	24	40
39	166	25	40
40	155	26	40
41	152	27	40
42	167	28	40
43	185	29	40

Figure 41

This is encouraging: Both models show different slopes for different ages. Model 1 would predict that the slope either increases with increasing age (a_5 positive) or decreases with increasing age (a_5 negative). However, the graph suggests that the slope is larger for both younger and older students, but smaller for students of intermediate age, contrary to what Model 1 predicts, so you decide to go with the more flexible Model 2, which permits the slope to decrease and then increase with increasing age, which is exactly what you observe on the graph, and so you decide to go ahead with Model 2.

You decide to use Excel to generate your model. However, the data as shown in the table are not in a form Excel can use for regression; the data need to be organized into columns; Column A for the dependent variable N and Columns B–C for the independent variables, as shown in Figure 41.

You then add columns for the higher order terms x^2, xt, and x^2t as shown below:

◇	A	B	C	D	E	F
1	N	t	x	x^2	x*t	x^2*t
2	1033	0	21	=C2^2	=C2*B2	=C2^2*B2
3	1077	5	21			
4	1138	10	21			
5	1220	15	21			
6	1350	20	21			
7	1376	21	21			
8	1433	22	21			
9	1481	23	21			

Figure 42

◇	A	B	C	D	E	F
1	N	t	x	x^2	x*t	x^2*t
2	1033	0	21	441	0	0
3	1077	5	21	441	105	2205
4	1138	10	21	441	210	4410
5	1220	15	21	441	315	6615
6	1350	20	21	441	420	8820
7	1376	21	21	441	441	9261
8	1433	22	21	441	462	9702
9	1481	23	21	441	483	10143

Figure 43

Next, highlight a vacant 5×6 block (the block A46:F50 say), type the formula =LINEST(A2:A43,B2:F43,,TRUE), and press Ctrl+Shift+Enter (not just Enter!). You will see a table of statistics like the following:

42						
43	185	29	40	1600	1160	46400
44						
45						
46	=LINEST(A2:A43,B2:F43,,TRUE)					
47						
48						
49						
50						

Figure 44

42						
43	185	29	40	1600	1160	46400
44						
45						
46	0.088570354	-6.46546922	3.21423521	-241.273271	120.009278	4594.62978
47	0.02096866	1.28767845	0.44955302	27.6069027	18.6958148	400.824866
48	0.99337478	49.506512	#N/A	#N/A	#N/A	#N/A
49	1079.5571	36	#N/A	#N/A	#N/A	#N/A
50	13229404.1	88232.2104	#N/A	#N/A	#N/A	#N/A

Figure 45

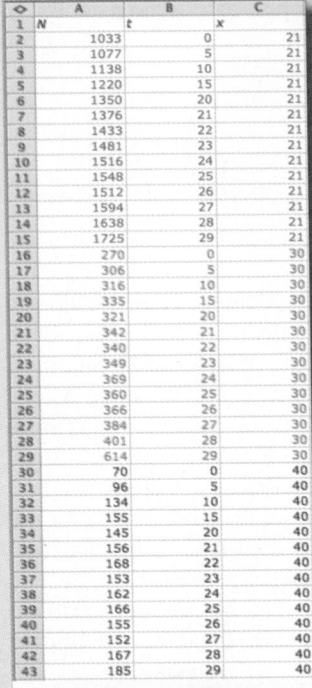

The desired constants $a_1, a_2, a_3, a_4, a_5, a_6$ appear in the first row of the data, but in *reverse order*. Thus, if we round to 5 significant digits, we have

$$a_1 = 4{,}594.6 \quad a_2 = 120.01 \quad a_3 = -241.27$$
$$a_4 = 3.2142 \quad a_5 = -6.4655 \quad a_6 = 0.088570,$$

which gives our regression model:

$$N(t, x) = 4{,}594.6 + 120.01t - 241.27x + 3.2142x^2 - 6.4655xt + 0.088570x^2t.$$

Fine, you say to yourself, now you have the model, but how good a fit is it to the data? That is where rest of the data shown in the output comes in: In the second row are the "standard errors" corresponding to the corresponding coefficients. Notice that each of the standard errors is small compared with the magnitude of the coefficient above it; for instance, 0.021 is only around 1/4 of the magnitude of $a_6 \approx 0.088$ and indicates that the dependence of N on x^2t is statistically significant. (What we do not want to see are standard errors of magnitudes comparable to the coefficients, as those could indicate the wrong choice of independent variables.) The third figure in the left column, 0.99337478, is R^2, where R generalizes the coefficient of correlation discussed in the section on regression in Chapter 1: The closer R is to 1, the better the fit. We can interpret R^2 as indicating that approximately 99.3% of the variation in college enrollment is explained by the regression model, indicating an excellent fit. The figure 1,079.5571 beneath R^2 is called the "F-statistic." The higher the F-statistic (typically, anything above 4 or so would be considered "high"), the more confident we can be that N does depend on the independent variables we are using.*

* We are being deliberately vague about the exact meaning of these statistics, which are discussed fully in many applied statistics texts.

As comforting as these statistics are, nothing can be quite as persuasive as a graph. You turn to the graphing software of your choice and notice that the graph of the model appears to be a faithful representation of the data. (See Figure 46.)

Now you get to work, using the model to address the questions posed by College Malls.

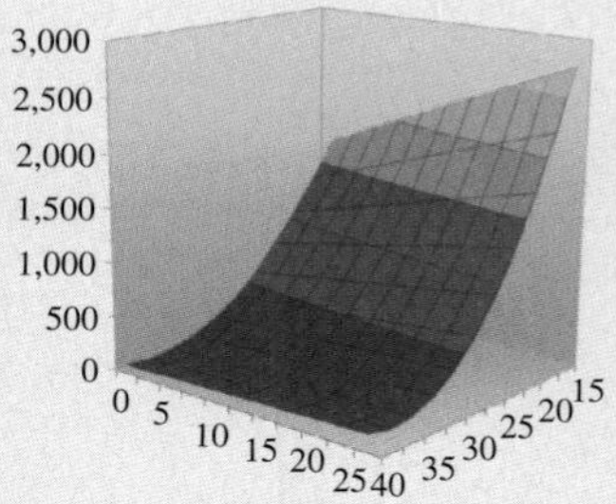

Figure 46

1. *A quick way of estimating the number of students of any specified age and in any particular year, and the effect of increasing age on the college population.* You already have a quantitative relationship in the form of the regression model. As for the second part of the question, the rate of change of college enrollment with respect to age is given by the partial derivative:

$$\frac{\partial N}{\partial x} = -241.27 + 6.4284x - 6.4655t + 0.17714xt$$ thousand students per additional year of age.

Thus, for example, with $x = 20$ in 2004 ($t = 24$), we have

$$\frac{\partial N}{\partial x} = -241.27 + 6.4284(20) - 6.4655(24) + 0.17714(20)(24)$$
$$\approx -183 \text{ thousand students per additional year of age,}$$

so there were about 183,000 fewer students of age 21 than age 20 in 2004.

On the other hand, when $x = 38$ in the same year, we have

$$\frac{\partial N}{\partial x} = -241.27 + 6.4284(38) - 6.4655(24) + 0.17714(38)(24)$$
$$\approx 9.4 \text{ thousand students per additional year of age,}$$

so there were about 9,400 more students of age 39 than age 38 that year.

2. *The ages that correspond to relatively high and low college populations.* Although a glance at the graph shows you that there are no relative maxima, holding t constant (that is, on any given year) gives a parabola along the corresponding slice and hence a minimum somewhere along the slice.

$$\frac{\partial N}{\partial x} = 0$$

when $$-241.27 + 6.4284x - 6.4655t + 0.17714xt = 0,$$

which gives $x = \dfrac{241.27 + 6.4655t}{6.4284 + 0.17714t}$ years of age

For instance, in 2010 ($t = 30$; we are extrapolating the model slightly), the age at which there were fewest students (in the given range) is 37 years of age. The relative maxima for each slice occur at the front and back edges of the surface, meaning that there are relatively more students of the lowest and highest ages represented. The absolute maximum for each slice occurs, as expected, at the lowest age. In short, a mall catering to college students in 2010 should have focused mostly on freshman age students, least on 37-year-olds, and somewhat more on people around age 40.

3. *How fast the 20-year-old and 25-year-old student populations are increasing.* The rate of change of student population with respect to time is

$$\frac{\partial N}{\partial t} = 120.01 - 6.4655x + 0.088570x^2 \text{ thousand students per year.}$$

For the two age groups in question, we obtain

$$x = 20\text{: } 120.01 - 6.4655(20) + 0.088570(20)^2 \approx 26.1 \text{ thousand students/year}$$

$$x = 25\text{: } 120.01 - 6.4655(25) + 0.088570(25)^2 \approx 13.7 \text{ thousand students/year.}$$

(Note that these rates of change are independent of time as we chose a model that is linear in time.)

4. *Some near-term projections of the student population trend.* As we have seen throughout the book, extrapolation can be a risky venture; however, near-term extrapolation from a good model can be reasonable. You enter the model in an Excel spreadsheet to obtain the following predicted college enrollments (in thousands) for the years 2010–2015:

$x \downarrow$ / $t \rightarrow$	30	31	32	33	34	35
21	1,644	1,668	1,691	1,714	1,737	1,761
30	422	428	434	439	445	451
40	180	183	186	189	192	195

EXERCISES

1. Use a spreadsheet to obtain Model 1:

$$N(t, x) = a_1 + a_2t + a_3x + a_4x^2 + a_5xt.$$

Compare the fit of this model with that of the quadratic model above. Comment on the result.

2. Obtain Model 2 using only the data through 2005, and also obtain the projections for 2010–2015 using the resulting model. Compare the projections with those based on the more complete set of data in the text.

3. Compute and interpret $\left.\frac{\partial N}{\partial t}\right|_{(10,18)}$ and $\left.\frac{\partial^2 N}{\partial t \partial x}\right|_{(10,18)}$ for the model in the text. What are their units of measurement?

4. Notice that the derivatives in the preceding exercise do not depend on time. What additional polynomial term(s) would make both $\partial N/\partial t$ and $\partial^2 N/\partial t \partial x$ depend on time? (Write down the entire model.) Of what order is your model?

5. Test the model you constructed in the preceding question by inspecting the standard errors associated with the additional coefficients.

TI-83/84 Plus Technology Guide

Section 8.1

Example 1 (page 589) You own a company that makes two models of speakers: the Ultra Mini and the Big Stack. Your total monthly cost (in dollars) to make x Ultra Minis and y Big Stacks is given by

$$C(x, y) = 10{,}000 + 20x + 40y.$$

Compute several values of this function.

Solution with Technology

You can have a TI-83/84 Plus compute $C(x, y)$ numerically as follows:

1. In the "Y=" screen, enter

```
Y1=10000+20X+40Y
```

2. To evaluate, say, $C(10, 30)$ (the cost to make 10 Ultra Minis and 30 Big Stacks), enter

```
10→X
30→Y
Y1
```

```
10→X
                 10
30→Y
                 30
Y1
              11400
■
```

and the calculator will evaluate the function and give the answer $C(10, 30) = 11{,}400$.

This procedure is too laborious if you want to calculate $f(x, y)$ for a large number of different values of x and y.

SPREADSHEET Technology Guide

Section 8.1

Example 1 (page 589) You own a company that makes two models of speakers: the Ultra Mini and the Big Stack. Your total monthly cost (in dollars) to make x Ultra Minis and y Big Stacks is given by

$$C(x, y) = 10{,}000 + 20x + 40y.$$

Compute several values of this function.

Solution with Technology

Spreadsheets handle functions of several variables easily. The following setup shows how a table of values of C can be created, using values of x and y you enter:

	A	B	C
1	x	y	C(x, y)
2	10	30	=10000+20*A2+40*B2
3	20	30	
4	15	0	
5	0	30	
6	30	30	

↓

	A	B	C
1	x	y	C(x, y)
2	10	30	11400
3	20	30	11600
4	15	0	10300
5	0	30	11200
6	30	30	11800

A disadvantage of this layout is that it's not easy to enter values of x and y systematically in two columns. Can you find a way to remedy this? (See Example 3 for one method.)

Example 3 (page 591) Use technology to create a table of values of the body mass index

$$M(w, h) = \frac{0.45w}{(0.0254h)^2}.$$

Solution with Technology

We can use this formula to recreate a table in a spreadsheet, as follows:

	A	B	C	D
1		130	140	150
2	60	=0.45*B$1/(0.0254*$A2)^2		
3	61			
4	62			
5	63			
6	64			
7	65			
8	66			
9	67			

In the formula in cell B2 we have used B$1 instead of B1 for the w-coordinate because we want all references to w to use the same row (1). Similarly, we want all references to h to refer to the same column (A), so we used $A2 instead of A2.

We copy the formula in cell B2 to all of the red shaded area to obtain the desired table:

	A	B	C	D	
1		130	140	150	
2	60	25.18755038	27.12505425	29.06255813	3
3	61	24.36849808	26.24299793	28.11749778	29.9
4	62	23.58875685	25.40327661	27.21779637	29.0
5	63	22.84585068	24.60322381	26.36059694	28.1
6	64	22.13749545	23.84037971	25.54326398	27.2
7	65	21.46158138	23.11247226	24.76336314	26.4
8	66	20.81615733	22.41740021	24.01864308	25.6
9	67	20.19941665	21.75321793	23.30701921	24.8

Example 5 (page 594) Obtain the graph of $f(x, y) = x^2 + y^2$.

Solution with Technology

1. Set up a table showing a range of values of x and y and the corresponding values of the function (see Example 3):

	A	B	C	D	E	F	G	H
1		-3	-2	-1	0	1	2	3
2	-3	=B1^2+A2^2						
3	-2							
4	-1							
5	0							
6	1							
7	2							
8	3							

↓

	A	B	C	D	E	F	G	H
1		-3	-2	-1	0	1	2	3
2	-3	18	13	10	9	10	13	18
3	-2	13	8	5	4	5	8	13
4	-1	10	5	2	1	2	5	10
5	0	9	4	1	0	1	4	9
6	1	10	5	2	1	2	5	10
7	2	13	8	5	4	5	8	13
8	3	18	13	10	9	10	13	18

2. Select the cells with the values (B2: H8) and insert a chart, with the "Surface" option selected and "Series in Columns" selected as the data option, to obtain a graph like the following:

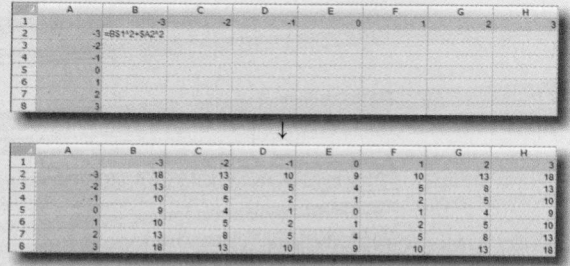

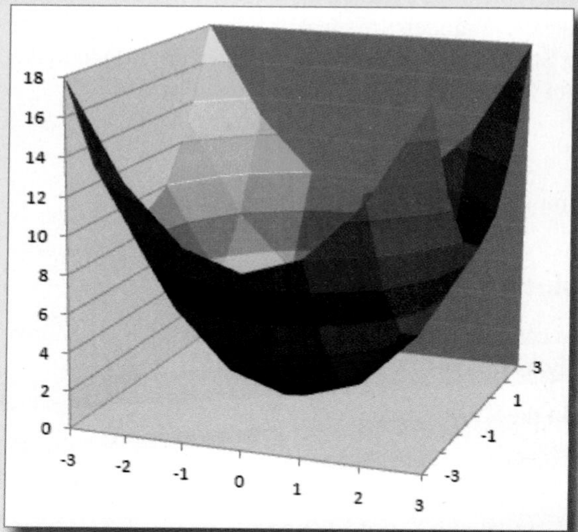

9

Trigonometric Models

Website
www.WanerMath.com
At the Website you will find:

- A detailed chapter summary
- A true/false quiz
- Graphers, Excel tutorials, and other resources

Case Study Predicting Airline Empty Seat Volume

You are a consultant to the Department of Transportation's Special Task Force on Air Traffic Congestion and have been asked to model the volume of empty seats on U.S. airline flights, to make short-term projections of this volume, and to give a formula that estimates the accumulated volume over a specified period of time. You have data from the Bureau of Transportation Statistics on the number of seats and passengers each month starting with January 2002. **How will you analyze these data to prepare your report?**

Lawrence Manning/Flirt/Corbis

Introduction

Cyclical behavior is common in the business world: There are seasonal fluctuations in the demand for surfing equipment, swim wear, snow shovels, and many other items. The nonlinear functions we have studied up to now cannot model this kind of behavior. To model cyclical behavior, we need the **trigonometric** functions.

In the first section, we study the basic trigonometric functions—especially the **sine** and **cosine** functions from which all the trigonometric functions are built—and see how to model various kinds of periodic behavior using these functions. The rest of the chapter is devoted to the calculus of the trigonometric functions—their derivatives and integrals—and to its numerous applications.

9.1 Trigonometric Functions, Models, and Regression

The Sine Function

Figure 1 shows the approximate average daily high temperatures in New York's Central Park.[1] If we draw the graph for several years, we get the repeating pattern shown in Figure 2, where the x-coordinate represents time in years, with $x = 0$ corresponding to August 1, and where the y-coordinate represents the temperature in degrees F. This is an example of **cyclical** or **periodic** behavior.

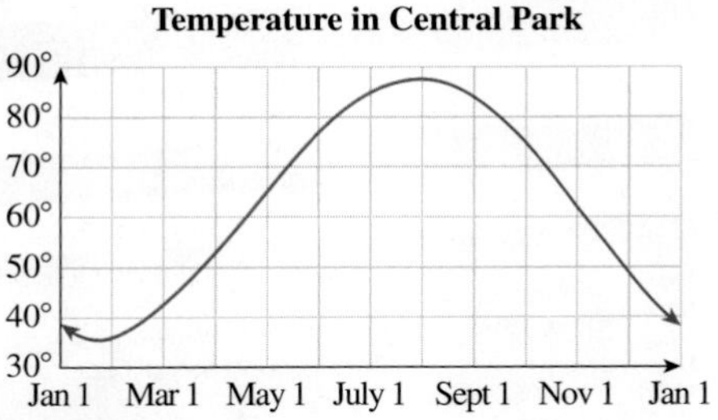

Figure 1

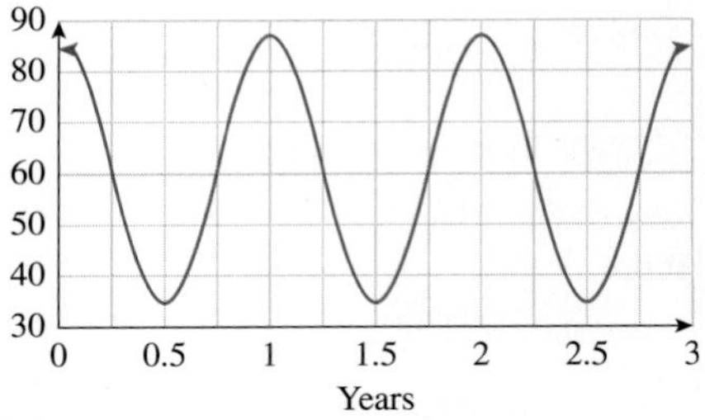

Figure 2

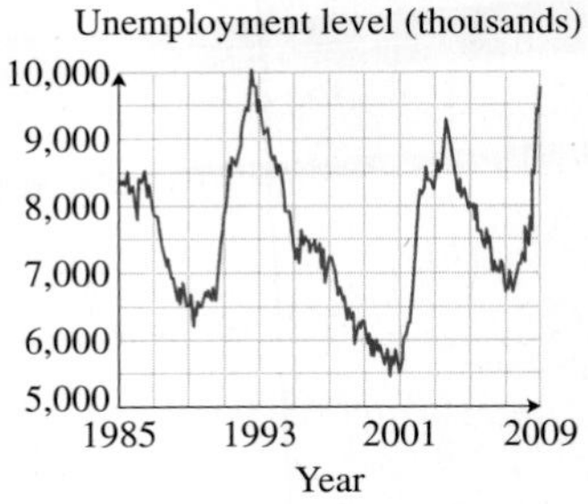

Source: Bureau of Labor Statistics, December 2008 (www.data.bls.gov).

Figure 3

Cyclical behavior is also common in the business world. The graph in Figure 3 suggests cyclical behavior in the U.S. unemployment level.

From a mathematical point of view, the simplest models of cyclical behavior are the **sine** and **cosine** functions. An easy way to describe these functions is as follows. Imagine a bicycle wheel whose radius is one unit, with a marker attached to the rim of the rear wheel, as shown in Figure 4.

[1] Source: National Weather Service/*New York Times*, January 7, 1996, p. 36.

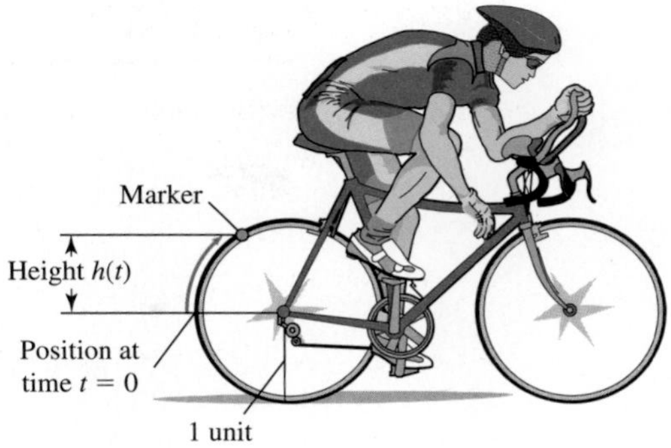

Figure 4

Now, we can measure the height $h(t)$ of the marker above the center of the wheel. As the wheel rotates, $h(t)$ fluctuates between -1 and $+1$. Suppose that, at time $t = 0$, the marker was at height zero as shown in the diagram, so $h(0) = 0$. Because the wheel has a radius of 1 unit, its circumference (the distance all around) is 2π, where $\pi = 3.14159265\ldots$. If the cyclist happens to be moving at a speed of 1 unit per second, it will take the bicycle wheel 2π seconds to make one complete revolution. During the time interval $[0, 2\pi]$, the marker will first rise to a maximum height of $+1$, drop to a low point of -1, and then return to the starting position of 0 at $t = 2\pi$. This function $h(t)$ is called the **sine function**, denoted by $\sin(t)$. Figure 5 shows its graph.

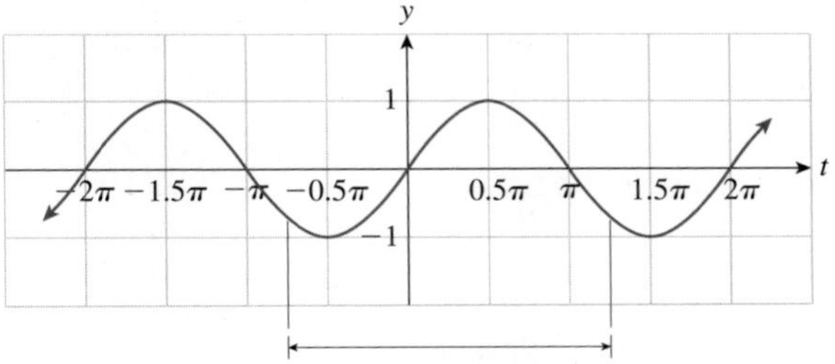

2π units = One complete revolution

Graph of $y = \sin(t)$

Technology formula: `sin(t)`

Figure 5

Sine Function

"Bicycle Wheel" Definition

If a wheel of radius 1 unit rolls forward at a speed of 1 unit per second, then $\sin(t)$ is the height after t seconds of a marker on the rim of the wheel, starting in the position shown in Figure 4.

Geometric Definition

The **sine** of a real number t is the y-coordinate (height) of the point P in the following diagram, where $|t|$ is the length of the arc shown.

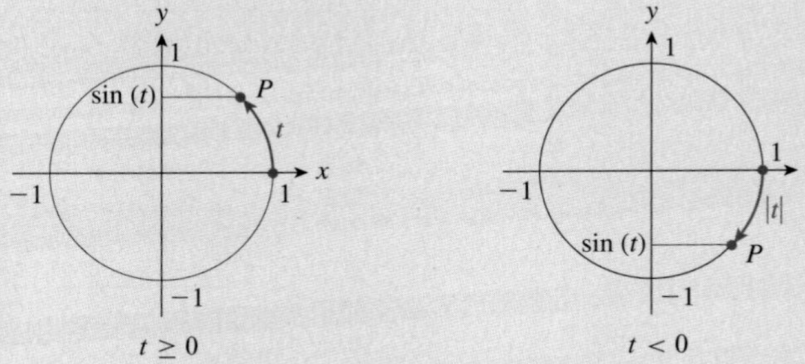

sin(t) = y-coordinate of the point P

Quick Examples

From the graph, we see that

1. $\sin(\pi) = 0$ Graphing Calculator: `sin(π)` Spreadsheet: `sin(PI())`

2. $\sin\left(\frac{\pi}{2}\right) = 1$ Graphing Calculator: `sin(π/2)` Spreadsheet: `sin(PI()/2)`

3. $\sin\left(\frac{3\pi}{2}\right) = -1.$ Graphing Calculator: `sin(3π/2)` Spreadsheet: `sin(3*PI()/2)`

Note We shall often write "sin x" without the parentheses to mean $\sin(x)$; for instance, we may write $\sin(\pi)$ above as $\sin \pi$. Remember, however, that this does *not* mean we are "multiplying" sin by π (which makes no sense). *Always read* sin x as "*the sine **of** x*." ■

EXAMPLE 1 Some Trigonometric Functions

Use technology to plot the following pairs of graphs on the same set of axes.

a. $f(x) = \sin x$; $g(x) = 2\sin x$

b. $f(x) = \sin x$; $g(x) = \sin(x + 1)$

c. $f(x) = \sin x$; $g(x) = \sin(2x)$

Solution

a. (Important note: If you are using a calculator, make sure it is set to *radian mode*, not degree mode.) We enter these functions as `sin(x)` and `2*sin(x)`, respectively. We use the range $-2\pi \le x \le 2\pi$ (approximately $-6.28 \le x \le 6.28$) for x suggested by the graph in Figure 5, but with larger range of y-coordinates (why?): $-3 \le y \le 3$. The graphs are shown in Figure 6. Here, $f(x) = \sin x$ is shown in red, and $g(x) = 2\sin x$ in blue. Notice that multiplication by 2 has doubled the **amplitude**, or *distance it oscillates up and down*. Where the original sine curve oscillates between −1 and 1, the new curve oscillates between −2 and 2. In general:

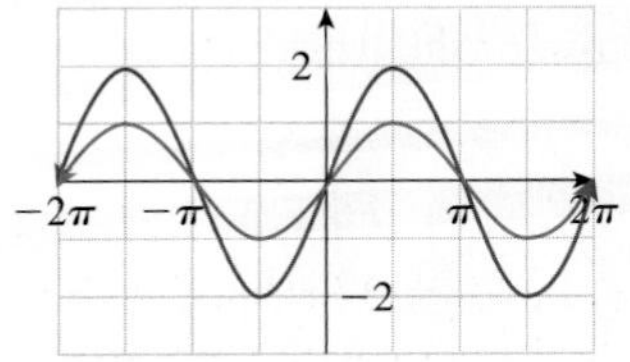

Figure 6

The graph of A sin(x) *has amplitude* A.

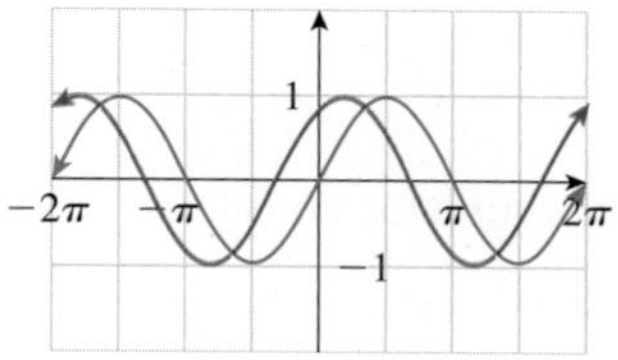

Figure 7

b. We enter these functions as `sin(x)` and `sin(x+1)`, respectively, and we get Figure 7. Once again, $f(x) = \sin x$ is shown in red and $g(x) = \sin(x + 1)$ is in blue. The addition of 1 to the argument has shifted the graph to the left by 1 unit. In general:

Replacing x by x + c shifts the graph to the left c units.

(How would we shift the graph to the *right* 1 unit?)

c. We enter these functions as `sin(x)` and `sin(2*x)`, respectively, and get the graph in Figure 8. The graph of $\sin(2x)$ oscillates twice as fast as the graph of $\sin x$. In other words, the graph of $\sin(2x)$ makes two complete cycles on the interval $[0, 2\pi]$ whereas the graph of $\sin x$ completes only one cycle. In general:

Replacing x by bx multiplies the rate of oscillation by b.

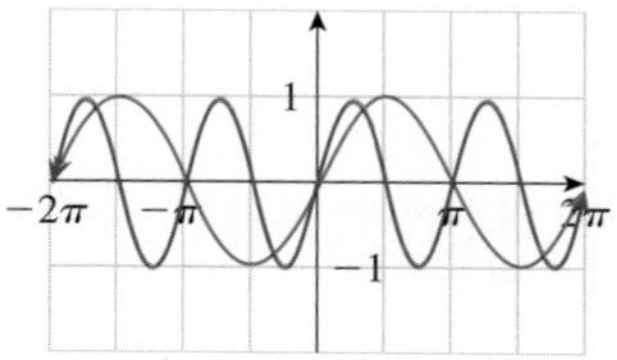

Figure 8

We can combine the operations in Example 1, and a vertical shift as well, to obtain the following.

Website
www.WanerMath.com
At the Website you will find the following optional online interactive section:

Internet Topic: New Functions from Old: Scaled and Shifted Functions

The General Sine Function

The general sine function is

$$f(x) = A\sin[\omega(x - \alpha)] + C.$$

Its graph is shown here.

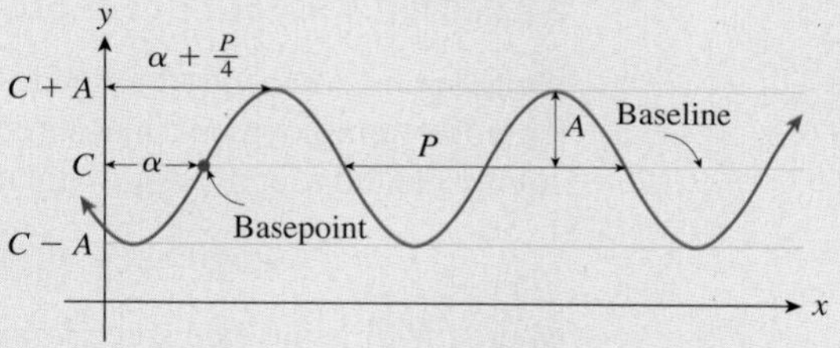

- A is the **amplitude** (the height of each peak above the baseline).
- C is the **vertical offset** (height of the baseline).
- P is the **period** or **wavelength** (the length of each cycle) and is related to ω by

$$P = 2\pi/\omega \quad \text{or} \quad \omega = 2\pi/P.$$

- ω is the **angular frequency** (the number of cycles in every interval of length 2π).
- α is the **phase shift.**

EXAMPLE 2 Electrical Current

The typical voltage V supplied by an electrical outlet in the United States is a sinusoidal function that oscillates between −165 volts and +165 volts with a frequency of 60 cycles per second. Find an equation for the voltage as a function of time t.

Solution What we are looking for is a function of the form

$$V(t) = A\sin[\omega(t-\alpha)] + C.$$

Referring to the figure on the preceding page, we can determine the constants.

Amplitude A and Vertical Offset C: Because the voltage oscillates between -165 volts and $+165$ volts, we see that $A = 165$ and $C = 0$.

Period P: The electric current completes 60 cycles in one second, so the length of time it takes to complete one cycle is $1/60$ second. Thus, the period is $P = 1/60$.

Angular Frequency ω: This is given by the formula

$$\omega = \frac{2\pi}{P} = 2\pi(60) = 120\pi.$$

Phase Shift α: The phase shift α tells us when the curve first crosses the t-axis as it ascends. As we are free to specify what time $t = 0$ represents, let us say that the curve crosses 0 when $t = 0$, so $\alpha = 0$.

Thus, the equation for the voltage at time t is

$$\begin{aligned} V(t) &= A\sin[\omega(t-\alpha)] + C \\ &= 165\sin(120\pi t) \end{aligned}$$

where t is time in seconds.

EXAMPLE 3 Cyclical Employment Patterns

An economist consulted by your employment agency indicates that the demand for temporary employment (measured in thousands of job applications per week) in your county can be roughly approximated by the function

$$d = 4.3\sin(0.82t - 0.3) + 7.3,$$

where t is time in years since January 2000. Calculate the amplitude, the vertical offset, the phase shift, the angular frequency, and the period, and interpret the results.

Solution To calculate these constants, we write

$$\begin{aligned} d = A\sin[\omega(t-\alpha)] + C &= A\sin[\omega t - \omega\alpha] + C \\ &= 4.3\sin(0.82t - 0.3) + 7.3 \end{aligned}$$

and we see right away that $A = 4.3$ (the amplitude), $C = 7.3$ (vertical offset), and $\omega = 0.82$ (angular frequency). We also have

$$\omega\alpha = 0.3$$

so that $$\alpha = \frac{0.3}{\omega} = \frac{0.3}{0.82} \approx 0.37$$

(rounding to two significant digits; notice that all the constants are given to two digits). Finally, we get the period using the formula

$$P = \frac{2\pi}{\omega} = \frac{2\pi}{0.82} \approx 7.7.$$

We can interpret these numbers as follows: The demand for temporary employment fluctuates in cycles of 7.7 years about a baseline of 7,300 job applications per week. Every cycle, the demand peaks at 11,600 applications per week (4,300 above the baseline) and dips to a low of 3,000. In May 2000 ($t = 0.37$) the demand for employment was at the baseline level and rising.

Note The generalized sine function in Example 3 was given in the form

$$f(x) = A \sin(\omega t + d) + C$$

for some constant d. Every generalized sine function can be written in this form:

$$A \sin[\omega(t - \alpha)] + C = A \sin(\omega t - \omega\alpha) + C. \qquad d = -\omega\alpha$$

Generalized sine functions are often written in this form. ■

The Cosine Function

Closely related to the sine function is the cosine function, defined as follows. (Refer to the definition of the sine function for comparison.)

Cosine Function

Geometric Definition

The **cosine** of a real number t is the x-coordinate of the point P in the following diagram, in which $|t|$ is the length of the arc shown.

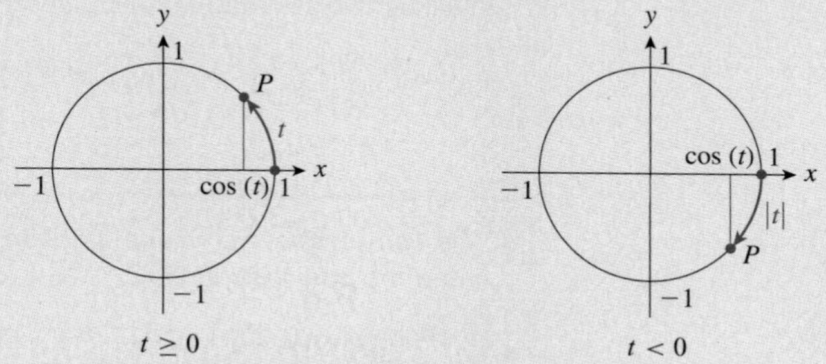

$\cos(t) = x$-coordinate of the point P

Graph of the Cosine Function

The graph of the cosine function is identical to the graph of the sine function, except that it is shifted $\pi/2$ units to the left.

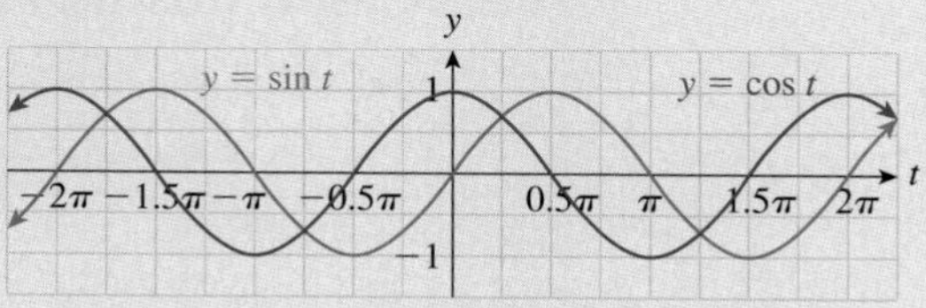

Technology formula: `cos(t)`

Notice that the coordinates of the point P in the diagram above are $(\cos t, \sin t)$ and that the distance from P to the origin is 1 unit. It follows from the Pythagorean theorem that the distance from a point (x, y) to the origin is $\sqrt{x^2 + y^2}$. Thus:

$$\text{Square of the distance from } P \text{ to } (0, 0) = 1$$

$$(\sin t)^2 + (\cos t)^2 = 1.$$

We often write $(\sin t)^2$ as $\sin^2 t$ and similarly for the cosine, so we can rewrite the equation as

$$\sin^2 t + \cos^2 t = 1.$$

This equation is one of the important relationships between the sine and cosine functions.

Fundamental Trigonometric Identities: Relationships between Sine and Cosine

The sine and cosine of a number t are related by

$$\sin^2 t + \cos^2 t = 1.$$

We can obtain the cosine curve by shifting the sine curve to the left a distance of $\pi/2$. [See Example 1(b) for a shifted sine function.] Conversely, we can obtain the sine curve from the cosine curve by shifting it $\pi/2$ units to the right. These facts can be expressed as

$$\cos t = \sin(t + \pi/2)$$
$$\sin t = \cos(t - \pi/2).$$

Alternative Formulation

We can also obtain the cosine curve by first inverting the sine curve horizontally (replace t by $-t$) and then shifting to the *right* a distance of $\pi/2$. This gives us two alternative formulas (which are easier to remember):

$$\cos t = \sin(\pi/2 - t)$$ Cosine is the sine of the complementary angle.
$$\sin t = \cos(\pi/2 - t).$$

Q: *We can rewrite the cosine function in terms of the sine function, so do we really need the cosine function?*

A: Technically, we don't need the cosine function and could get by with only the sine function. On the other hand, it is convenient to have the cosine function because it starts at its highest point rather than at zero. These two functions and their relationship play important roles throughout mathematics.

The General Cosine Function

The general cosine function is

$$f(x) = A\cos[\omega(x - \beta)] + C.$$

Its graph is as follows.

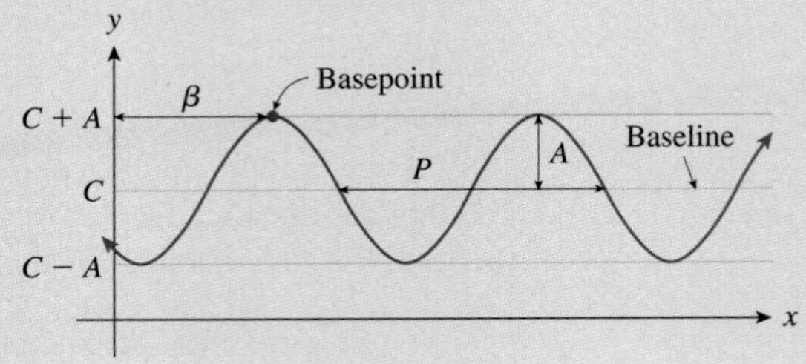

Note that the basepoint of the cosine curve is at the highest point of the curve. All the constants have the same meaning as for the general sine curve:

- A is the **amplitude** (the height of each peak above the baseline).
- C is the **vertical offset** (height of the baseline).
- P is the **period** or **wavelength** (the length of each cycle) and is related to ω by
$$P = 2\pi/\omega \quad \text{or} \quad \omega = 2\pi/P.$$
- ω is the **angular frequency** (the number of cycles in every interval of length 2π).
- β is the phase shift.

Notes

1. We can also describe the above curve as a generalized sine function: Observe by comparing the picture on the preceding page to the one on page 659 that $\beta = \alpha + P/4$. Thus, $\alpha = \beta - P/4$, and the above curve is also
$$f(x) = A \sin[\omega(x - \beta + P/4)] + C.$$
2. As is the case with the generalized sine function, the cosine function above can be written in the form
$$f(x) = A \cos(\omega t + d) + C. \qquad d = -\omega\beta$$

■

EXAMPLE 4 Cash Flows into Stock Funds

The annual cash flow into stock funds (measured as a percentage of total assets) has fluctuated in cycles of approximately 40 years since 1955, when it was at a high point. The highs were roughly +15% of total assets, whereas the lows were roughly −10% of total assets.[2]

a. Model this cash flow with a cosine function of the time t in years, with $t = 0$ representing 1955.

b. Convert the answer in part (a) to a sine function model.

Solution

a. Cosine modeling is similar to sine modeling; we are seeking a function of the form
$$P(t) = A \cos[\omega(t - \beta)] + C.$$

Amplitude A and Vertical Offset C: The cash flow fluctuates between −10% and +15%. We can express this as a fluctuation of $A = 12.5$ about the average $C = 2.5$.

Period P: This is given as $P = 40$.

Angular Frequency ω: We find ω from the formula
$$\omega = \frac{2\pi}{P} = \frac{2\pi}{40} = \frac{\pi}{20} \approx 0.157.$$

[2]Source: Investment Company Institute/*New York Times*, February 2, 1997, p. F8.

Phase Shift β: The basepoint is at the high point of the curve, and we are told that cash flow was at its high point at $t = 0$. Therefore, the basepoint occurs at $t = 0$, and so $\beta = 0$.

Putting the model together gives

$$\begin{aligned} P(t) &= A \cos [\omega(t - \beta)] + C \\ &\approx 12.5 \cos (0.157t) + 2.5, \end{aligned}$$

where t is time in years since 1955.

b. To convert between a sine and cosine model, we can use one of the relationships given earlier. Let us use the formula

$$\cos x = \sin (x + \pi/2).$$

Therefore,

$$\begin{aligned} P(t) &\approx 12.5 \cos (0.157t) + 2.5 \\ &= 12.5 \sin (0.157t + \pi/2) + 2.5. \end{aligned}$$

The Other Trigonometric Functions

The ratios and reciprocals of sine and cosine are given their own names.

Tangent, Cotangent, Secant, Cosecant

Tangent: $\tan x = \dfrac{\sin x}{\cos x}$

Cotangent: $\cot x = \operatorname{cotan} x = \dfrac{\cos x}{\sin x} = \dfrac{1}{\tan x}$

Secant: $\sec x = \dfrac{1}{\cos x}$

Cosecant: $\csc x = \operatorname{cosec} x = \dfrac{1}{\sin x}$

Trigonometric Regression

In the examples so far, we were given enough information to obtain a sine (or cosine) model directly. Often, however, we are given data that only *suggest* a sine curve. In such cases we can use regression to find the best-fit generalized sine (or cosine) curve.

EXAMPLE 5 Spam

The authors of this book tend to get inundated with spam email. One of us systematically documented the number of spam emails arriving at his email account, and noticed a curious cyclical pattern in the average number of emails arriving each week.[3] Figure 9 shows the daily spam for a 16-week period[4] (each point is a one-week average):

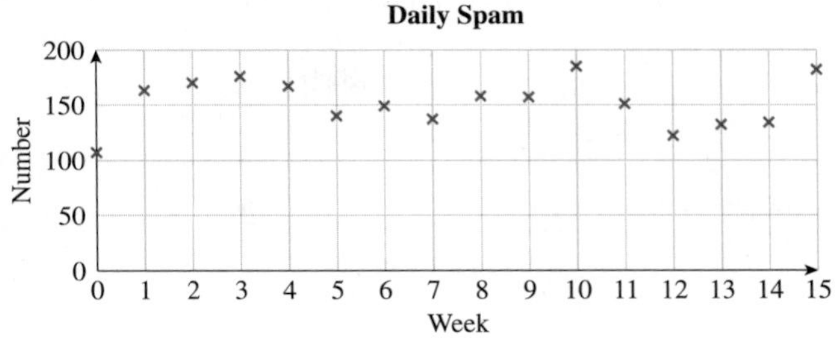

Figure 9

Week	0	1	2	3	4	5	6	7	8	9	10	11	12	13	14	15
Number	107	163	170	176	167	140	149	137	158	157	185	151	122	132	134	182

a. Use technology to find the best-fit sine curve of the form $S(t) = A\sin[\omega(t-\alpha)] + C$.

b. Use your model to estimate the period of the cyclical pattern in spam mail, and also to predict the daily spam average for week 23.

Solution

a. Following are the models obtained by using the TI-83/84 Plus, Excel with Solver, and the Function Evaluator and Grapher on the Website. (See the Technology Guides at the end of the chapter to find out how to obtain these models. For the Website utility, we used the initial guess $A = 50$, $\omega = 1$, $\alpha = 0$, and $C = 150$.)

TI-83/84 Plus: $S(t) \approx 11.6\sin[0.910(t-1.63)] + 155$

Excel and Website grapher: $S(t) \approx 25.8\sin[0.96(t-1.22)] + 153$

Q: *Why do the models from the TI-83/84 Plus differ so drastically from the Solver and Website model?*

A: Not all regression algorithms are identical, and it seems that the TI-83/84 Plus's algorithm is not very efficient at finding the best-fit sine curve. Indeed, the value for the sum-of-squares error (SSE) for the TI-83/84 Plus regression curve is around 5,030, whereas it is around 2,148 for the Excel curve, indicating a far better fit.* Notice another thing: The sine curve does not appear to fit the data well in either graph. In general, we can expect better agreement between the different forms of technology for data that follow a sine curve more closely.

* This comparison is actually unfair: The method using Excel's Solver or the Website grapher starts with an initial guess of the coefficients, so the TI-83/84 Plus algorithm, which does not require an initial guess, is starting at a significant disadvantage. An initial guess that is way off can result in Solver or the Website grapher coming up with a very different result! On the other hand, the TI-83/84 Plus algorithm seems problematic and tends to fail (giving an error message) on many sets of data.

b. This model gives a period of approximately

TI-83/84 Plus: $P = \frac{2\pi}{\omega} \approx \frac{2\pi}{0.910} \approx 6.9$ weeks

Excel and Website grapher: $P = \frac{2\pi}{\omega} \approx \frac{2\pi}{0.96} \approx 6.5$ weeks.

So, both models predict a very similar period.

[3]Confirming the notion that academics have little else to do but fritter away their time in pointless pursuits.

[4]Beginning June 6, 2005.

Website
www.WanerMath.com
At the Website you will find the following optional online interactive section, in which you can find further discussion of the graphs of the trigonometric functions and their relationship to right triangles:
Internet Topic: Trigonometric Functions and Calculus
→ The Six Trigonometric Functions.

In week 23, we obtain the following predictions:

TI-83/84 Plus: $S(23) \approx 11.6 \sin[0.910(23 - 1.63)] + 155$
≈ 162 spam emails per day

Excel and Website grapher: $S(23) \approx 25.8 \sin[0.96(23 - 1.22)] + 153$
≈ 176 spam emails per day.

Note The actual figure for week 23 was 213 spam emails per day. The discrepancy illustrates the danger of using regression models to extrapolate. ■

9.1 EXERCISES

▼ more advanced ◆ challenging
T indicates exercises that should be solved using technology

In Exercises 1–12, graph the given functions or pairs of functions on the same set of axes.

a. *Sketch the curves without any technological help by consulting the discussion in Example* 1.

b. T *Use technology to check your sketches.* HINT [See Example 1.]

1. $f(t) = \sin(t)$; $g(t) = 3\sin(t)$
2. $f(t) = \sin(t)$; $g(t) = 2.2\sin(t)$
3. $f(t) = \sin(t)$; $g(t) = \sin(t - \pi/4)$
4. $f(t) = \sin(t)$; $g(t) = \sin(t + \pi)$
5. $f(t) = \sin(t)$; $g(t) = \sin(2t)$
6. $f(t) = \sin(t)$; $g(t) = \sin(-t)$
7. $f(t) = 2\sin[3\pi(t - 0.5)] - 3$
8. $f(t) = 2\sin[3\pi(t + 1.5)] + 1.5$
9. $f(t) = \cos(t)$; $g(t) = 5\cos[3(t - 1.5\pi)]$
10. $f(t) = \cos(t)$; $g(t) = 3.1\cos(3t)$
11. $f(t) = \cos(t)$; $g(t) = -2.5\cos(t)$
12. $f(t) = \cos(t)$; $g(t) = 2\cos(t - \pi)$

In Exercises 13–18, model each curve with a sine function. (Note that not all are drawn with the same scale on the two axes.) HINT [See Example 2.]

13.

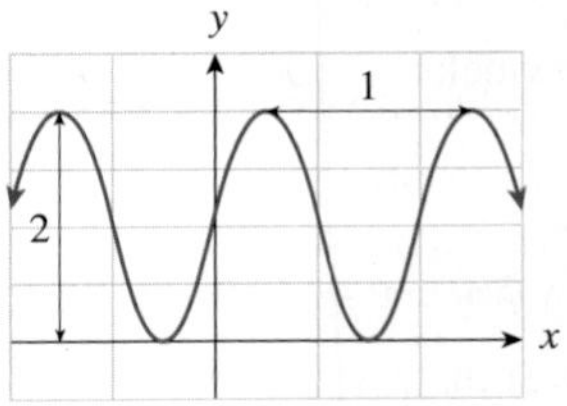

14.

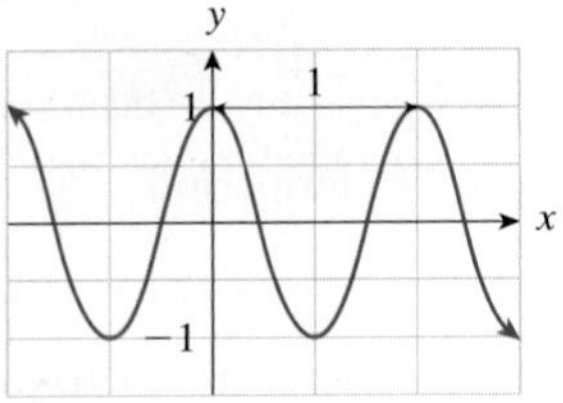

15.

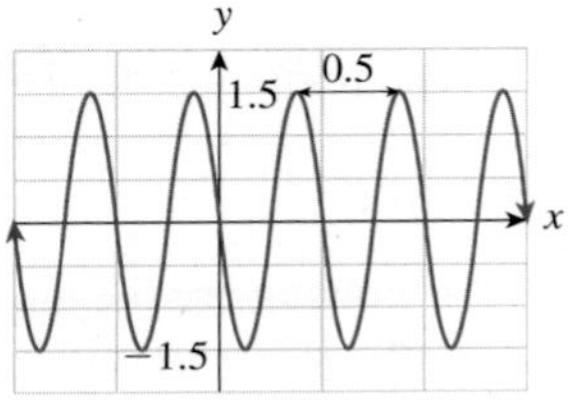

16.

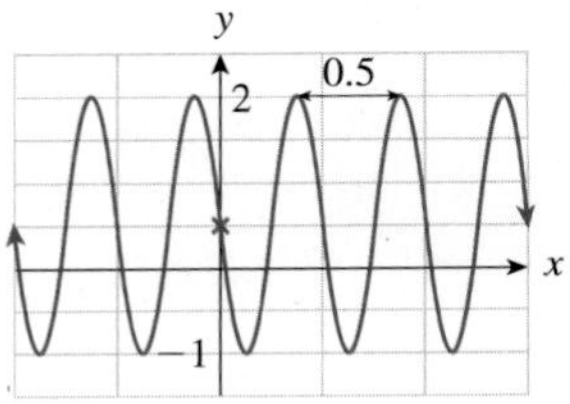

17.

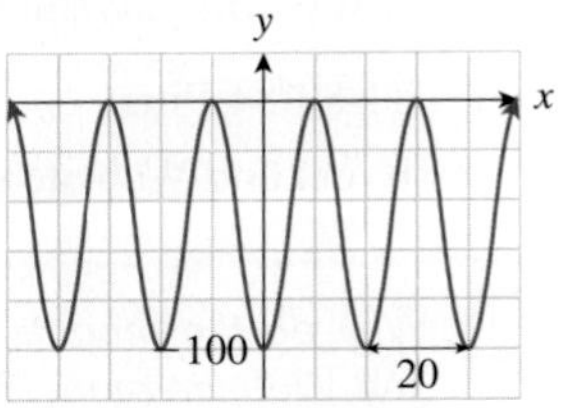

18.

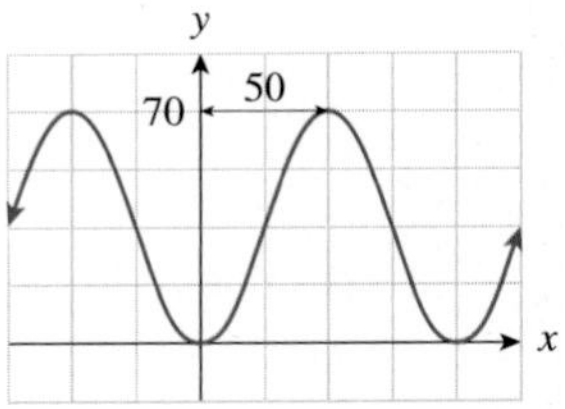

In Exercises 19–24, model each curve with a cosine function. (Note that not all are drawn with the same scale on the two axes.) HINT [See Example 2.]

19.

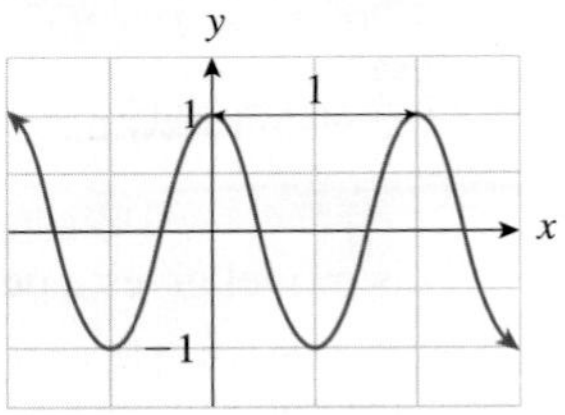

20.

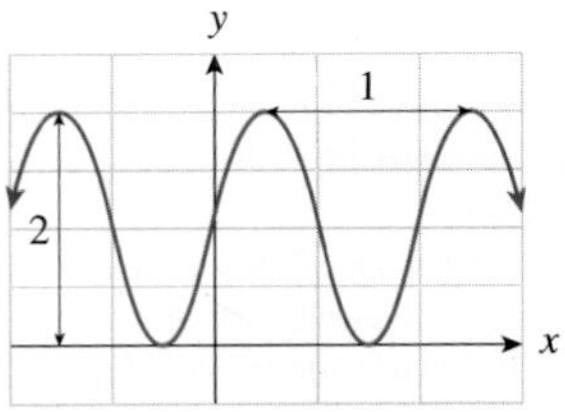

21.

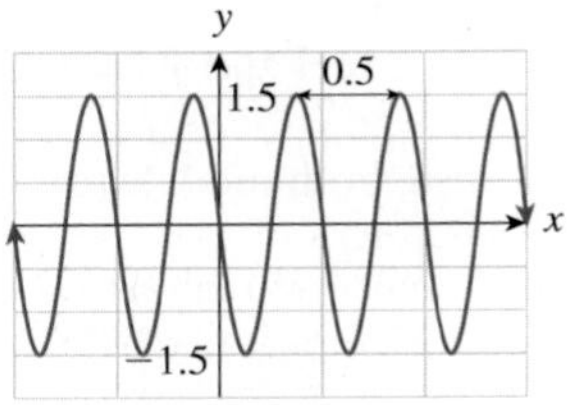

22.

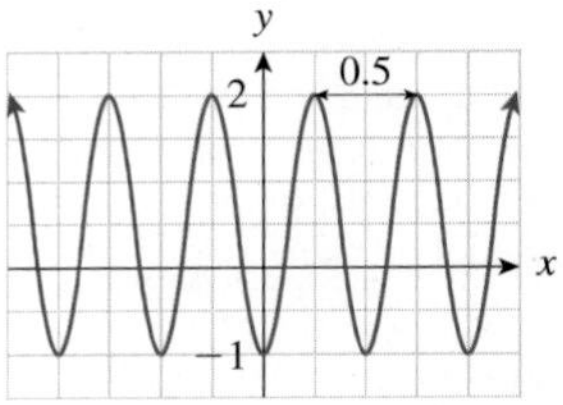

23.

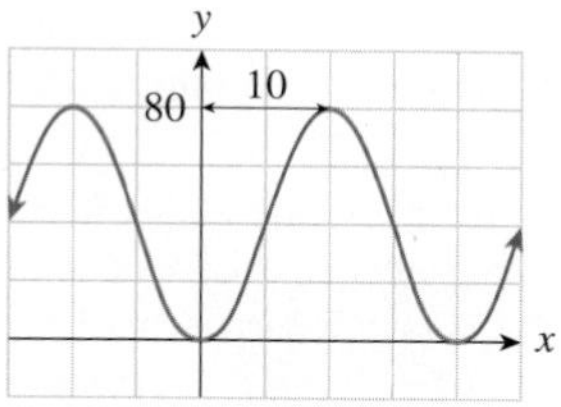

24.

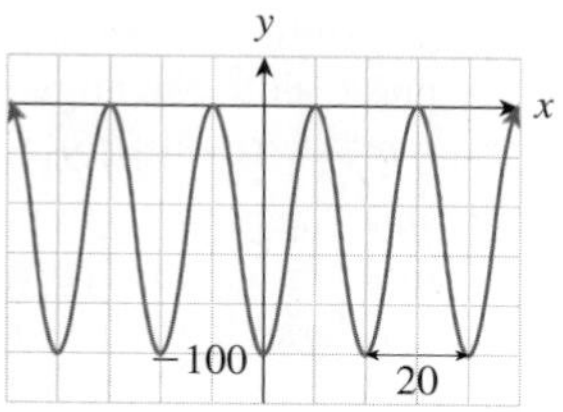

In Exercises 25–28, use the conversion formula $\cos x = \sin(\pi/2 - x)$ *to replace each expression by a sine function.*

25. ▼ $f(t) = 4.2 \cos(2\pi t) + 3$

26. ▼ $f(t) = 3 - \cos(t - 4)$

27. ▼ $g(x) = 4 - 1.3 \cos[2.3(x - 4)]$

28. ▼ $g(x) = 4.5 \cos[2\pi(3x - 1)] + 7$

Some Identities *Starting with the identity* $\sin^2 x + \cos^2 x = 1$ *and then dividing both sides of the equation by a suitable trigonometric function, derive the trigonometric identities in Exercises 29 and 30.*

29. ▼ $\sec^2 x = 1 + \tan^2 x$ **30.** ▼ $\csc^2 x = 1 + \cot^2 x$

Exercises 31–38 are based on the ***addition formulas:***

$$\sin(x + y) = \sin x \cos y + \cos x \sin y$$
$$\sin(x - y) = \sin x \cos y - \cos x \sin y$$
$$\cos(x + y) = \cos x \cos y - \sin x \sin y$$
$$\cos(x - y) = \cos x \cos y + \sin x \sin y$$

31. ▼ Calculate $\sin(\pi/3)$, given that $\sin(\pi/6) = 1/2$ and $\cos(\pi/6) = \sqrt{3}/2$.

32. ▼ Calculate $\cos(\pi/3)$, given that $\sin(\pi/6) = 1/2$ and $\cos(\pi/6) = \sqrt{3}/2$.

33. ▼ Use the formula for $\sin(x + y)$ to obtain the identity $\sin(t + \pi/2) = \cos t$.

34. ▼ Use the formula for $\cos(x + y)$ to obtain the identity $\cos(t - \pi/2) = \sin t$.

35. ▼ Show that $\sin(\pi - x) = \sin x$.

36. ▼ Show that $\cos(\pi - x) = -\cos x$.

37. ▼ Use the addition formulas to express $\tan(x + \pi)$ in terms of $\tan x$.

38. ▼ Use the addition formulas to express $\cot(x + \pi)$ in terms of $\cot x$.

APPLICATIONS

39. ***Sunspot Activity*** The activity of the sun (sunspots, solar flares, and coronal mass ejection) fluctuates in cycles of around 10–11 years. Sunspot activity can be modeled by the following function:[5]

$$N(t) = 57.7 \sin[0.602(t - 1.43)] + 58.8,$$

where t is the number of years since January 1, 1997, and $N(t)$ is the number of sunspots observed at time t. HINT [See Example 3.]

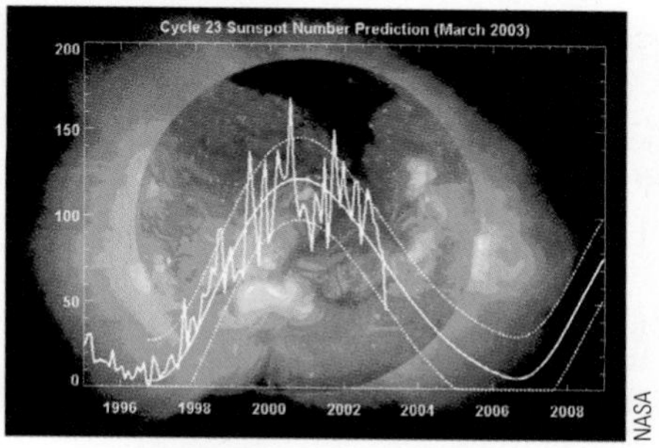

Cycle 23 Sunspot Number Prediction (March 2003)

a. What is the period of sunspot activity according to this model? (Round your answer to the nearest 0.1 year.)

b. What is the maximum number of sunspots observed? What is the minimum number? (Round your answers to the nearest sunspot.)

c. When, to the nearest year, is sunspot activity expected to reach the first high point beyond 2012?

40. ***Solar Emissions*** The following model gives the flux of radio emission from the sun:

$$F(t) = 49.6 \sin[0.602(t - 1.48)] + 111,$$

where t is the number of years since January 1, 1997, and $F(t)$ is the flux of solar emissions of a specified wavelength at time t.[6] HINT [See Example 3.]

a. What is the period of radio activity according to this model? (Round your answer to the nearest 0.1 year.)

b. What is the maximum flux of radio emissions? What is the minimum flux? (Round your answers to the nearest whole number.)

c. When, to the nearest year, is radio activity expected to reach the first low point beyond 2012?

[5]The model is based on a regression obtained from predicted data for 1997–2006 and the mean historical period of sunspot activity from 1755 to 1995. Source: NASA Science Directorate; Marshall Space Flight Center, August 2002 (http://science.nasa.gov/ssl/pad/solar/predict.htm).

[6]*Ibid.* Flux is measured at a wavelength of 10.7 cm.

41. **iPod Sales** Sales of personal electronic devices like Apple's iPods are subject to seasonal fluctuations. Apple's sales of iPods in 2008 through 2010 can be approximated by the function

$$s(t) = 6.00 \sin(1.51t + 1.85) + 15 \text{ million iPods per quarter} \quad (0 \le t \le 12),$$

where t is time in quarters ($t = 0$ represents the start of the first quarter of 2008).[7]

a. Use technology to plot sales versus time from the beginning of 2008 through the end of 2010. Then use your graph to estimate the value of t and the quarters during which sales were lowest and highest.

b. Estimate Apple's maximum and minimum quarterly sales of iPods.

c. Indicate how the answers to part (b) can be obtained directly from the equation for $s(t)$.

42. **Housing Starts** Housing construction is subject to seasonal fluctuations. The number of housing starts (number of new privately owned housing units started) from 2009 through mid-2011 can be approximated by the function

$$s(t) = 10.2 \sin(0.537t - 1.46) + 47.6 \text{ thousand housing starts per month} \quad (0 \le t \le 30),$$

where t is time in months ($t = 0$ represents the start of January 2009).[8]

a. Use technology to plot housing starts versus time from the beginning of 2009 through the end of June 2011. Then use your graph to estimate the value of t and the months during which housing starts were lowest and highest.

b. Estimate the maximum and minimum number of housing starts.

c. Indicate how the answers to part (b) can be obtained directly from the equation for $s(t)$.

43. **iPod Sales** (Based on Exercise 41, but no technology required) Apple's sales of iPods in 2008 through 2010 can be approximated by the function

$$s(t) = 6.00 \sin(1.51t + 1.85) + 15 \text{ million iPods per quarter} \quad (0 \le t \le 12),$$

where t is time in quarters ($t = 0$ represents the start of the first quarter of 2008). Calculate the amplitude, the vertical offset, the phase shift, the angular frequency, and the period, and interpret the results.

44. **Housing Starts** (Based on Exercise 42, but no technology required) The number of housing starts (number of new privately owned housing units started) from 2009 through mid-2011 can be approximated by the function

$$s(t) = 10.2 \sin(0.537t - 1.46) + 47.6 \text{ thousand housing starts per month} \quad (0 \le t \le 30),$$

where t is time in months ($t = 0$ represents the start of January 2009). Calculate the amplitude, the vertical offset, the phase shift, the angular frequency, and the period, and interpret the results.

45. **Biology** Sigatoka leaf spot is a plant disease that affects bananas. In an infected plant, the percentage of leaf area affected varies from a low of around 5% at the start of each year to a high of around 20% at the middle of each year.[9] Use the sine function to model the percentage of leaf area affected by Sigatoka leaf spot t weeks since the start of a year. HINT [See Example 2.]

46. **Biology** Apple powdery mildew is an epidemic that affects apple shoots. In a new infection, the percentage of apple shoots infected varies from a low of around 10% at the start of May to a high of around 60% 6 months later.[10] Use the sine function to model the percentage of apple shoots affected by apple powdery mildew t months since the start of a year.

47. **Cancun** The *Playa Loca Hotel* in Cancun has an advertising brochure with a chart showing the year-round temperature.[11] The added curve is an approximate 5-month moving average.

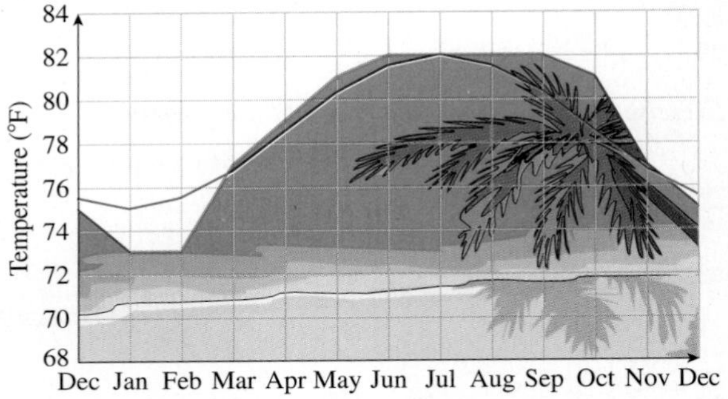

Use a cosine function to model the temperature (moving average) in Cancun as a function of time t in months since December.

48. **Reykjavik** Repeat the preceding exercise, using the following data from the brochure of the *Tough Traveler Lodge* in Reykjavik.[12]

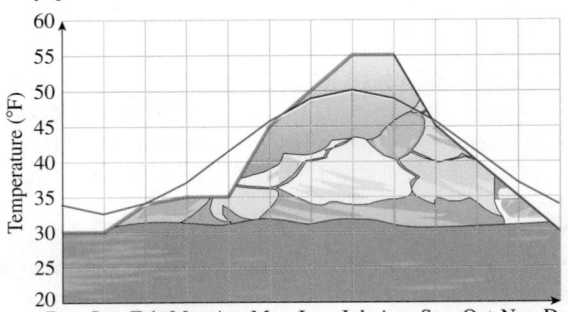

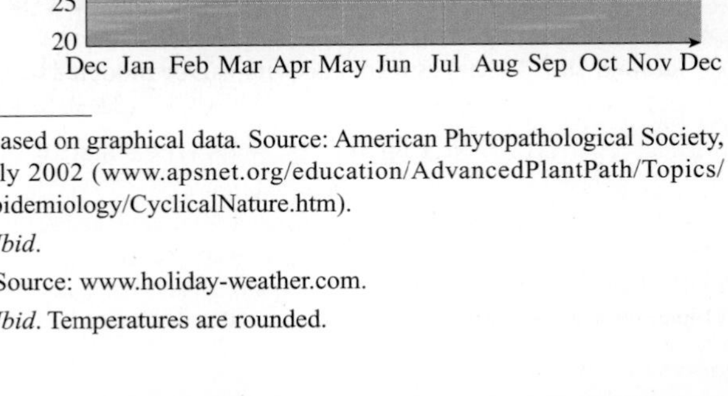

[7] Authors' model. Source for data: Apple quarterly press releases (www.apple.com/investor).

[8] Authors' regression model. Source for data: U.S. Census Bureau (www.census.gov/const/www/newresconstindex.html).

[9] Based on graphical data. Source: American Phytopathological Society, July 2002 (www.apsnet.org/education/AdvancedPlantPath/Topics/Epidemiology/CyclicalNature.htm).

[10] *Ibid.*

[11] Source: www.holiday-weather.com.

[12] *Ibid.* Temperatures are rounded.

49. ***Net Income Fluctuations: General Electric*** General Electric's quarterly net income $n(t)$ fluctuated from a low of \$4.5 billion in Quarter 1 of 2007 ($t = 0$) to a high of \$7 billion, and then back down to \$4.5 billion in Quarter 1 of 2008 ($t = 4$).[13] Use a sine function to model General Electric's quarterly net income $n(t)$, where t is time in quarters.

50. ***Sales Fluctuations*** Sales of cypods (one-bedroom units) in the city-state of Utarek, Mars[14] fluctuate from a low of 5 units per week each February 1 ($t = 1$) to a high of 35 units per week each August 1 ($t = 7$). Use a sine function to model the weekly sales $s(t)$ of cypods, where t is time in months.

51. ***Net Income Fluctuations*** Repeat Exercise 49, but this time use a cosine function for your model. HINT [See Example 4.]

52. ***Sales Fluctuations*** Repeat Exercise 50, but this time use a cosine function for your model.

53. ***Tides*** The depth of water at my favorite surfing spot varies from 5 to 15 feet, depending on the time. Last Sunday, high tide occurred at 5:00 am and the next high tide occurred at 6:30 pm. Use a sine function model to describe the depth of water as a function of time t in hours since midnight on Sunday morning.

54. ***Tides*** Repeat Exercise 53 using data from the depth of water at my second favorite surfing spot, where the tide last Sunday varied from a low of 6 feet at 4:00 am to a high of 10 feet at noon.

55. ▼ ***Inflation*** The uninflated cost of *Dugout* brand snow shovels currently varies from a high of \$10 on January 1 ($t = 0$) to a low of \$5 on July 1 ($t = 0.5$).

a. Assuming this trend continues indefinitely, calculate the uninflated cost $u(t)$ of Dugout snow shovels as a function of time t in years. (Use a sine function.)

b. Assuming a 4% annual rate of inflation in the cost of snow shovels, the cost of a snow shovel t years from now, adjusted for inflation, will be 1.04^t times the uninflated cost. Find the cost $c(t)$ of Dugout snow shovels as a function of time t.

56. ▼ ***Deflation*** Sales of my exclusive 2010 vintage *Chateau Petit Mont Blanc* vary from a high of 10 bottles per day on April 1 ($t = 0.25$) to a low of 4 bottles per day on October 1.

a. Assuming this trend continues indefinitely, find the undeflated sales $u(t)$ of Chateau Petit Mont Blanc as a function of time t in years. (Use a sine function.)

b. Regrettably, ever since that undercover exposé of my wine-making process, sales of Chateau Petit Mont Blanc have been declining at an annual rate of 12%. Using the preceding exercise as a guide, write down a model for the deflated sales $s(t)$ of Chateau Petit Mont Blanc t years from now.

57. T ***Air Travel: Domestic*** The following table shows total domestic air travel on U.S. air carriers in specified months from January 2006 to July 2008 ($t = 0$ represents January 2006):[15]

t	0	3	6	9	12	15	18	21	24	27	30
Revenue Passenger Miles (billions)	43	49	55	47	44	50	57	49	45	48	55

a. Plot the data and *roughly* estimate the period P and the parameters C, A, and β for a cosine model.

b. Find the best-fit cosine curve approximating the given data. [You may have to use your estimates from part (a) as initial guesses if you are using Solver.] Plot the given data together with the regression curve (round coefficients to three decimal places).

c. Complete the following: Based on the regression model, domestic air travel on U.S. air carriers showed a pattern that repeats itself every ___ months, from a low of ___ to a high of ___ billion revenue passenger miles. (Round answers to the nearest whole number.) HINT [See Example 5.]

58. T ***Air Travel: International*** The following table shows total international travel on U.S. air carriers in specified months from January 2006 to July 2008 ($t = 0$ represents January 2006):[16]

t	0	3	6	9	12	15	18	21	24	27	30
Revenue Passenger Miles (billions)	18	19	23	19	19	20	24	20	25	20	25

a. Plot the data and *roughly* estimate the period P and the parameters C, A, and β for a cosine model.

b. Find the best-fit cosine curve approximating the given data. [You may have to use your estimates from part (a) as initial guesses if you are using Solver.] Plot the given data together with the regression curve (round coefficients to three decimal places).

c. Complete the following: Based on the regression model, international travel on U.S. air carriers showed a pattern that repeats itself every ___ months, from a low of ___ to a high of ___ billion revenue passenger miles. (Round answers to the nearest whole number.) HINT [See Example 5.]

---

[13] Source: Company reports (www.ge.com/investors).

[14] Based on www.Marsnext.com, a now extinct virtual society.

[15] Source: Bureau of Transportation Statistics (www.bts.gov).

[16] *Ibid.*

Music *Musical sounds exhibit the same kind of periodic behavior as the trigonometric functions. High-pitched notes have short periods (less than 1/1,000 second) while the lowest audible notes have periods of about 1/100 second. Some electronic synthesizers work by superimposing (adding) sinusoidal functions of different frequencies to create different textures. Exercises 59–62 show some examples of how superposition can be used to create interesting periodic functions.*

59. T ▼ ***Sawtooth Wave***

a. Graph the following functions in a window with $-7 \le x \le 7$ and $-1.5 \le y \le 1.5$.

$$y_1 = \frac{2}{\pi}\cos x$$

$$y_3 = \frac{2}{\pi}\cos x + \frac{2}{3\pi}\cos 3x$$

$$y_5 = \frac{2}{\pi}\cos x + \frac{2}{3\pi}\cos 3x + \frac{2}{5\pi}\cos 5x$$

b. Following the pattern established above, give a formula for y_{11} and graph it.

c. How would you modify y_{11} to approximate a sawtooth wave with an amplitude of 3 and a period of 4π?

60. T ▼ ***Square Wave*** Repeat the preceding exercise using sine functions in place of cosine functions (which results in an approximation of a square wave).

61. T ▼ ***Harmony*** If we add two sinusoidal functions with frequencies that are simple ratios of each other, the result is a pleasing sound. The following function models two notes an octave apart together with the intermediate fifth:

$$y = \cos(x) + \cos(1.5x) + \cos(2x).$$

Graph this function in the window $0 \le x \le 20$ and $-3 \le y \le 3$ and estimate the period of the resulting wave.

62. T ▼ ***Discord*** If we add two sinusoidal functions with similar, but unequal, frequencies, the result is a function that "pulsates," or exhibits "beats." (Piano tuners and guitar players use this phenomenon to help them tune an instrument.) Graph the function

$$y = \cos(x) + \cos(0.9x)$$

in the window $-50 \le x \le 50$ and $-2 \le y \le 2$ and estimate the period of the resulting wave.

COMMUNICATION AND REASONING EXERCISES

63. What are the highs and lows for sales of a commodity modeled by a function of the form $s(t) = A\sin(2\pi t) + B$ (A, B constants)?

64. Your friend has come up with the following model for choral society Tupperware stock inventory: $r(t) = 4\sin(2\pi(t-2)/3) + 2.3$, where t is time in weeks and $r(t)$ is the number of items in stock. Why is the model not realistic?

65. Your friend is telling everybody that all six trigonometric functions can be obtained from the single function $\sin x$. Is he correct? Explain your answer.

66. Another friend claims that all six trigonometric functions can be obtained from the single function $\cos x$. Is she correct? Explain your answer.

67. If weekly sales of sodas at a movie theater are given by $s(t) = A + B\cos(\omega t)$, what is the largest B can be? Explain your answer.

68. Complete the following: If the cost of an item is given by $c(t) = A + B\cos[\omega(t-\alpha)]$, then the cost fluctuates by ____ with a period of ____ about a base of ____, peaking at time $t =$ ____.

9.2 Derivatives of Trigonometric Functions and Applications

We start with the derivatives of the sine and cosine functions.

Theorem Derivatives of the Sine and Cosine Functions

The sine and cosine functions are differentiable with

$$\frac{d}{dx}\sin x = \cos x$$

$$\frac{d}{dx}\cos x = -\sin x$$

Notice the sign change.

Quick Examples

1. $\frac{d}{dx}(x \cos x) = 1 \cdot \cos x + x \cdot (-\sin x)$ — Product rule: $x \cos x$ is a product.*

$= \cos x - x \sin x$

2. $\frac{d}{dx}\left(\frac{x^2 + x}{\sin x}\right) = \frac{(2x+1)(\sin x) - (x^2 + x)(\cos x)}{\sin^2 x}$ — Quotient rule

* Apply the calculation thought experiment: If we were to compute x cos x, the last operation we would perform is the multiplication of x and cos x. Hence, x cos x is a product.

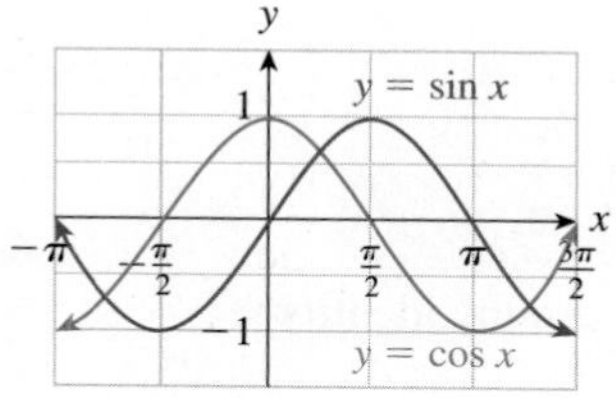

Figure 10(a)

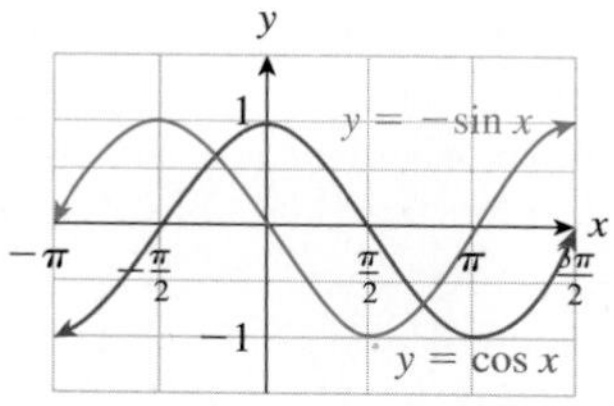

Figure 10(b)

Before deriving these formulas, we can see right away that they are plausible by examining Figure 10, which shows the graphs of the sine and cosine functions together with their derivatives. Notice, for instance, that in Figure 10(a) the graph of $\sin x$ is rising most rapidly when $x = 0$, corresponding to the maximum value of its derivative, $\cos x$. When $x = \pi/2$, the graph of $\sin x$ levels off, so that its derivative, $\cos x$, is 0. Another point to notice: Because periodic functions (such as sine and cosine) repeat their behavior, their derivatives must also be periodic.

Derivation of Formulas for Derivatives of the Sine and Cosine Functions

We first calculate the derivative of $\sin x$ from scratch, using the definition of the derivative:

$$\frac{d}{dx} f(x) = \lim_{h \to 0} \frac{f(x+h) - f(x)}{h}.$$

Thus,

$$\frac{d}{dx} \sin x = \lim_{h \to 0} \frac{\sin(x+h) - \sin x}{h}.$$

We now use the addition formula given in Exercise Set 9.1:

$$\sin(x+h) = \sin x \cos h + \cos x \sin h.$$

Substituting this expression for $\sin(x+h)$ gives

$$\frac{d}{dx} \sin x = \lim_{h \to 0} \frac{\sin x \cos h + \cos x \sin h - \sin x}{h}.$$

Grouping the first and third terms together and factoring out the term $\sin x$ gives

$$\frac{d}{dx} \sin x = \lim_{h \to 0} \frac{\sin x (\cos h - 1) + \cos x \sin h}{h}$$

$$= \lim_{h \to 0} \frac{\sin x (\cos h - 1)}{h} + \lim_{h \to 0} \frac{\cos x \sin h}{h} \quad \text{Limit of a sum}$$

$$= \sin x \lim_{h \to 0} \frac{\cos h - 1}{h} + \cos x \lim_{h \to 0} \frac{\sin h}{h}.$$

and we are left with two limits to evaluate. Calculating these limits analytically requires a little trigonometry.† Alternatively, we can get a good idea of what these two

† You can find these calculations on the Website by following the path:

Website
→ Everything for Calculus
→ Chapter 9
→ Proof of Some Trigonometric Limits

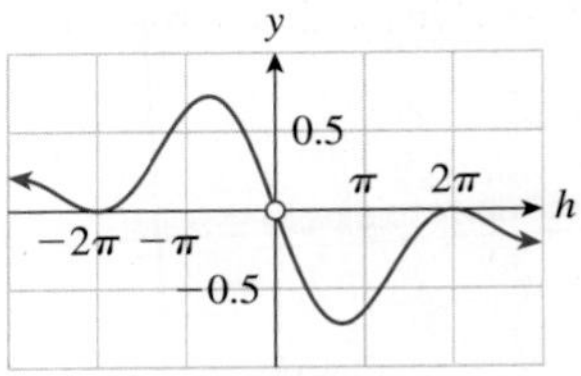

$y = \frac{\cos h - 1}{h}$

Figure 11

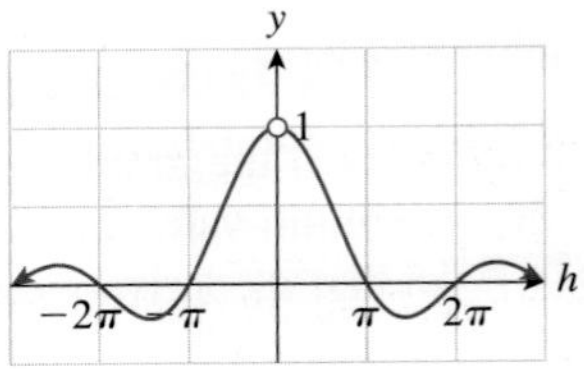

$y = \frac{\sin h}{h}$

Figure 12

limits are by estimating them numerically or graphically. Figures 11 and 12 show the graphs of $(\cos h - 1)/h$ and $(\sin h)/h$, respectively.

We find that:

$$\lim_{h \to 0} \frac{\cos h - 1}{h} = 0$$

and

$$\lim_{h \to 0} \frac{\sin h}{h} = 1.$$

Therefore,

$$\frac{d}{dx} \sin x = (\sin x)(0) + (\cos x)(1) = \cos x.$$

This is the required formula for the derivative of $\sin x$.

Turning to the derivative of the cosine function, we use the identity

$$\cos x = \sin(\pi/2 - x)$$

from Section 9.1. If $y = \cos x = \sin(\pi/2 - x)$, then, using the chain rule, we have

$$\begin{aligned} \frac{dy}{dx} &= \cos(\pi/2 - x)\frac{d}{dx}(\pi/2 - x) \\ &= (-1)\cos(\pi/2 - x) \\ &= -\sin x. \end{aligned}$$

Using the identity $\cos(\pi/2 - x) = \sin x$

This is the required formula for the derivative of $\cos x$.

Just as with logarithmic and exponential functions, the chain rule can be used to find more general derivatives.

Derivatives of Sines and Cosines of Functions

Original Rule	*Generalized Rule*	*In Words*
$\frac{d}{dx}\sin x = \cos x$	$\frac{d}{dx}\sin u = \cos u \frac{du}{dx}$	*The derivative of the sine of a quantity is the cosine of that quantity, times the derivative of that quantity.*
$\frac{d}{dx}\cos x = -\sin x$	$\frac{d}{dx}\cos u = -\sin u \frac{du}{dx}$	*The derivative of the cosine of a quantity is negative sine of that quantity, times the derivative of that quantity.*

Quick Examples

1. $\frac{d}{dx}\sin(3x^2 - 1) = \cos(3x^2 - 1)\frac{d}{dx}(3x^2 - 1)$ $\quad u = 3x^2 - 1$ (See margin note*)

$= 6x \cos(3x^2 - 1)$ $\quad$ We placed the $6x$ in front—see Note below.

2. $\frac{d}{dx}\cos(x^3 + x) = -\sin(x^3 + x)\frac{d}{dx}(x^3 + x)$ $\quad u = x^3 + x$

$= -(3x^2 + 1)\sin(x^3 + x)$

* If we were to evaluate $\sin(3x^2 - 1)$, the last operation we would perform is taking the sine of a quantity. Thus, the calculation thought experiment tells us that we are dealing with the *sine of a quantity*, and we use the generalized rule.

Note Avoid writing ambiguous expressions like $\cos(3x^2-1)(6x)$. Does this mean

$$\cos[(3x^2-1)(6x)]? \qquad \text{The cosine of the quantity } (3x^2-1)(6x)$$

Or does it mean

$$[\cos(3x^2-1)](6x)? \qquad \text{The product of } \cos(3x^2-1) \text{ and } 6x$$

To avoid the ambiguity, use parentheses or brackets and write $\cos[(3x^2-1)(6x)]$ if you mean the former. If you mean the latter, place the $6x$ in front of the cosine expression and write

$$6x\cos(3x^2-1). \qquad \text{The product of } 6x \text{ and } \cos(3x^2-1)$$

■

EXAMPLE 1 Derivatives of Trigonometric Functions

Find the derivatives of the following functions.

a. $f(x)=\sin^2 x$ **b.** $g(x)=\sin^2(x^2)$ **c.** $h(x)=e^{-x}\cos(2x)$

Solution

a. Recall that $\sin^2 x=(\sin x)^2$. The calculation thought experiment tells us that $f(x)$ is the square of a quantity.* Therefore, we use the chain rule (or generalized power rule) for differentiating the square of a quantity:

$$\frac{d}{dx}(u^2)=2u\frac{du}{dx}$$

$$\frac{d}{dx}(\sin x)^2=2(\sin x)\frac{d(\sin x)}{dx} \qquad u=\sin x$$

$$=2\sin x\cos x.$$

Thus, $f'(x)=2\sin x\cos x$.

* Notice the difference between $\sin^2 x$ and $\sin(x^2)$. The first is the square of $\sin x$, whereas the second is the sine of the quantity x^2.

b. We rewrite the function $g(x)=\sin^2(x^2)$ as $[\sin(x^2)]^2$. Because $g(x)$ is the square of a quantity, we have

$$\frac{d}{dx}\sin^2(x^2)=\frac{d}{dx}[\sin(x^2)]^2 \qquad \text{Rewrite } \sin^2(-) \text{ as } [\sin(-)]^2.$$

$$=2\sin(x^2)\frac{d[\sin(x^2)]}{dx} \qquad \frac{d}{dx}[u^2]=2u\frac{du}{dx} \text{ with } u=\sin(x^2)$$

$$=2\sin(x^2)\cdot\cos(x^2)\cdot 2x. \qquad \frac{d}{dx}\sin u=\cos u\frac{du}{dx} \text{ with } u=x^2$$

Thus, $g'(x)=4x\sin(x^2)\cos(x^2)$.

c. Because $h(x)$ is the product of e^{-x} and $\cos(2x)$, we use the product rule:

$$h'(x)=(-e^{-x})\cos(2x)+e^{-x}\frac{d}{dx}[\cos(2x)]$$

$$=(-e^{-x})\cos(2x)-e^{-x}\sin(2x)\frac{d}{dx}[2x] \qquad \frac{d}{dx}\cos u=-\sin u\frac{du}{dx}$$

$$=-e^{-x}\cos(2x)-2e^{-x}\sin(2x)$$

$$=-e^{-x}[\cos(2x)+2\sin(2x)].$$

Derivatives of Other Trigonometric Functions

Because the remaining trigonometric functions are ratios of sines and cosines, we can use the quotient rule to find their derivatives. For example, we can find the derivative of tan as follows:

$$\begin{aligned}\frac{d}{dx}\tan x &= \frac{d}{dx}\left(\frac{\sin x}{\cos x}\right)\\ &= \frac{(\cos x)(\cos x) - (\sin x)(-\sin x)}{\cos^2 x}\\ &= \frac{\cos^2 x + \sin^2 x}{\cos^2 x}\\ &= \frac{1}{\cos^2 x}\\ &= \sec^2 x.\end{aligned}$$

We ask you to derive the other three derivatives in the exercises. Here is a list of the derivatives of all six trigonometric functions and their chain rule variants.

Derivatives of the Trigonometric Functions

Original Rule	*Generalized Rule*
$\frac{d}{dx}\sin x = \cos x$	$\frac{d}{dx}\sin u = \cos u\frac{du}{dx}$
$\frac{d}{dx}\cos x = -\sin x$	$\frac{d}{dx}\cos u = -\sin u\frac{du}{dx}$
$\frac{d}{dx}\tan x = \sec^2 x$	$\frac{d}{dx}\tan u = \sec^2 u\frac{du}{dx}$
$\frac{d}{dx}\cot x = -\csc^2 x$	$\frac{d}{dx}\cot u = -\csc^2 u\frac{du}{dx}$
$\frac{d}{dx}\sec x = \sec x\tan x$	$\frac{d}{dx}\sec u = \sec u\tan u\frac{du}{dx}$
$\frac{d}{dx}\csc x = -\csc x\cot x$	$\frac{d}{dx}\csc u = -\csc u\cot u\frac{du}{dx}$

Quick Examples

1. $\frac{d}{dx}\tan v(x^2-1) = \sec^2(x^2-1)\frac{d(x^2-1)}{dx}$ $\quad u = x^2 - 1$

$= 2x\sec^2(x^2-1)$

2. $\frac{d}{dx}\csc(e^{3x}) = -\csc(e^{3x})\cot(e^{3x})\frac{d(e^{3x})}{dx}$ $\quad u = e^{3x}$

$= -3e^{3x}\csc(e^{3x})\cot(e^{3x})$ $\quad$ The derivative of e^{3x} is $3e^{3x}$.

EXAMPLE 2 Gas Heating Demand

In the preceding section we saw that seasonal fluctuations in temperature suggested a sine function. For instance, we can use the function

$$T = 60 + 25\sin\left[\frac{\pi}{6}(x-4)\right]$$ T = temperature in °F; x = months since Jan 1

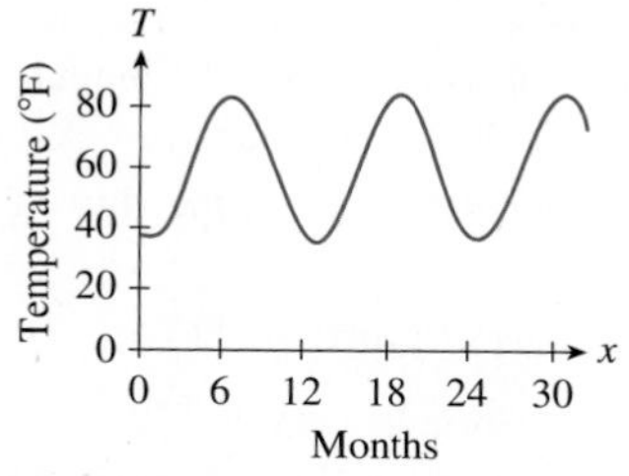

Figure 13

to model a temperature that fluctuates between 35°F on Feb. 1 ($x = 1$) and 85°F on Aug. 1 ($x = 7$). (See Figure 13.)

The demand for gas at a utility company can be expected to fluctuate in a similar way because demand grows with increased heating requirements. A reasonable model might therefore be

$$G = 400 - 100 \sin\left[\frac{\pi}{6}(x - 4)\right], \quad \text{Why did we subtract the sine term?}$$

where G is the demand for gas in cubic yards per day. Find and interpret $G'(10)$.

Solution First, we take the derivative of G:

$$G'(x) = -100 \cos\left[\frac{\pi}{6}(x - 4)\right] \cdot \frac{\pi}{6}$$

$$= -\frac{50\pi}{3} \cos\left[\frac{\pi}{6}(x - 4)\right] \text{ cubic yards per day, per month.}$$

Thus,

$$G'(10) = -\frac{50\pi}{3} \cos\left[\frac{\pi}{6}(10 - 4)\right]$$

$$= -\frac{50\pi}{3} \cos(\pi) = \frac{50\pi}{3}. \quad \text{Because } \cos\pi = -1$$

The units of $G'(10)$ are cubic yards per day per month, so we interpret the result as follows: On November 1 ($x = 10$) the daily demand for gas is increasing at a rate of $50\pi/3 \approx 52$ cubic yards per day, per month. This is consistent with Figure 13, which shows the temperature decreasing on that date.

9.2 EXERCISES

▼ more advanced ◆ challenging

T indicates exercises that should be solved using technology

In Exercises 1–32, find the derivatives of the given functions. HINT [See Quick Examples pages 671, 672, and 674.]

1. $f(x) = \sin x - \cos x$ **2.** $f(x) = \tan x - \sin x$

3. $g(x) = (\sin x)(\tan x)$ **4.** $g(x) = (\cos x)(\cot x)$

5. $h(x) = 2\csc x - \sec x + 3x$

6. $h(x) = 2\sec x + 3\tan x + 3x$

7. $r(x) = x\cos x + x^2 + 1$ **8.** $r(x) = 2x\sin x - x^2$

9. $s(x) = (x^2 - x + 1)\tan x$ **10.** $s(x) = \dfrac{\tan x}{x^2 - 1}$

11. $t(x) = \dfrac{\cot x}{1 + \sec x}$

12. $t(x) = (1 + \sec x)(1 - \cos x)$

13. $k(x) = \cos^2 x$ **14.** $k(x) = \tan^2 x$

15. $j(x) = \sec^2 x$ **16.** $j(x) = \csc^2 x$

17. $f(x) = \sin(3x - 5)$ **18.** $f(x) = \cos(2x + 7)$

19. $f(x) = \cos(-2x + 5)$ **20.** $f(x) = \sin(-4x - 5)$

21. $p(x) = 2 + 5\sin\left[\frac{\pi}{5}(x - 4)\right]$

22. $p(x) = 10 - 3\cos\left[\frac{\pi}{6}(x + 3)\right]$

23. $u(x) = \cos(x^2 - x)$ **24.** $u(x) = \sin(3x^2 + x - 1)$

25. $v(x) = \sec(x^{2.2} + 1.2x - 1)$

26. $v(x) = \tan(x^{2.2} + 1.2x - 1)$

27. $w(x) = \sec x \tan(x^2 - 1)$ **28.** $w(x) = \cos x \sec(x^2 - 1)$

29. $y(x) = \cos(e^x) + e^x \cos x$ **30.** $y(x) = \sec(e^x)$

31. $z(x) = \ln|\sec x + \tan x|$ **32.** $z(x) = \ln|\csc x + \cot x|$

In Exercises 33–36, derive the given formulas from the derivatives of sine and cosine. HINT [See discussion starting at the bottom of page 673.]

33. ▼ $\dfrac{d}{dx}\sec x = \sec x \tan x$ **34.** ▼ $\dfrac{d}{dx}\cot x = -\csc^2 x$

35. ▼ $\dfrac{d}{dx}\csc x = -\csc x \cot x$ **36.** ▼ $\dfrac{d}{dx}\ln|\sec x| = \tan x$

Calculate the derivatives in Exercises 37–44.

37. ▼ $\frac{d}{dx}[e^{-2x}\sin(3\pi x)]$ **38.** ▼ $\frac{d}{dx}[e^{5x}\sin(-4\pi x)]$

39. ▼ $\frac{d}{dx}[\sin(3x)]^{0.5}$ **40.** ▼ $\frac{d}{dx}\cos\left(\frac{x^2}{x-1}\right)$

41. ▼ $\frac{d}{dx}\sec\left(\frac{x^3}{x^2-1}\right)$ **42.** ▼ $\frac{d}{dx}\left(\frac{\tan x}{2+e^x}\right)^2$

43. ▼ $\frac{d}{dx}([\ln|x|][\cot(2x-1)])$ **44.** ▼ $\frac{d}{dx}\ln|\sin x - 2xe^{-x}|$

In Exercises 45 and 46, investigate the differentiability of the given functions at the given points. If $f'(a)$ exists, give its approximate value.

45. ▼ $f(x) = |\sin x|$ **a.** $a = 0$ **b.** $a = 1$

46. ▼ $f(x) = |\sin(1-x)|$ **a.** $a = 0$ **b.** $a = 1$

*Estimate the limits in Exercises 47–52 **(a)** numerically and **(b)** using l'Hospital's rule.*

47. ▼ $\lim_{x\to 0}\frac{\sin^2 x}{x}$ **48.** ▼ $\lim_{x\to 0}\frac{\sin x}{x^2}$

49. ▼ $\lim_{x\to 0}\frac{\sin(2x)}{x}$ **50.** ▼ $\lim_{x\to 0}\frac{\sin x}{\tan x}$

51. ▼ $\lim_{x\to 0}\frac{\cos x - 1}{x^3}$ **52.** ▼ $\lim_{x\to 0}\frac{\cos x - 1}{x^2}$

In Exercises 53–56, find the indicated derivative using implicit differentiation.

53. ▼ $x = \tan y$; find $\frac{dy}{dx}$ **54.** ▼ $x = \cos y$; find $\frac{dy}{dx}$

55. ▼ $x + y + \sin(xy) = 1$; find $\frac{dy}{dx}$

56. ▼ $xy + x\cos y = x$; find $\frac{dy}{dx}$

APPLICATIONS

57. ***Cost*** The cost in dollars of *Dig-It* brand snow shovels is given by

$$c(t) = 3.5\sin[2\pi(t - 0.75)],$$

where t is time in years since January 1, 2010. How fast, in dollars per week, is the cost increasing each October 1? HINT [See Example 2.]

58. ***Sales*** Daily sales of *Doggy* brand cookies can be modeled by

$$s(t) = 400\cos[2\pi(t-2)/7]$$

cartons, where t is time in days since Monday morning. How fast are sales changing on Thursday morning? HINT [See Example 2.]

59. ***Sunspot Activity*** The activity of the sun can be approximated by the following model of sunspot activity:[17]

$$N(t) = 57.7\sin[0.602(t - 1.43)] + 58.8,$$

where t is the number of years since January 1, 1997, and $N(t)$ is the number of sunspots observed at time t. Compute and interpret $N'(6)$.

60. ***Solar Emissions*** The following model gives the flux of radio emission from the sun:

$$F(t) = 49.6\sin[0.602(t - 1.48)] + 111,$$

where t is the number of years since January 1, 1997, and $F(t)$ is the average flux of solar emissions of a specified wavelength at time t.[18] Compute and interpret $F'(5.5)$.

61. ***Inflation*** Taking a 3.5% rate of inflation into account, the cost of *DigIn* brand snow shovels is given by

$$c(t) = 1.035^t[0.8\sin(2\pi t) + 10.2],$$

where t is time in years since January 1, 2010. How fast, in dollars per week, is the cost of DigIn shovels increasing on January 1, 2011?

62. ***Deflation*** Sales, in bottles per day, of my exclusive mass-produced 2010 vintage *Chateau Petit Mont Blanc* follow the function

$$s(t) = 4.5e^{-0.2t}\sin(2\pi t),$$

where t is time in years since January 1, 2010. How fast were sales rising or falling on January 1, 2011?

63. ***Tides*** The depth of water at my favorite surfing spot varies from 5 to 15 feet, depending on the time. Last Sunday high tide occurred at 5:00 am and the next high tide occurred at 6:30 pm.

a. Obtain a cosine model describing the depth of water as a function of time t in hours since 5:00 am on Sunday morning.

b. How fast was the tide rising (or falling) at noon on Sunday?

64. ***Tides*** Repeat Exercise 63 using data from the depth of water at my other favorite surfing spot, where the tide last Sunday varied from a low of 6 feet at 4:00 am to a high of 10 feet at noon. (As in Exercise 63, take t as time in hours since 5:00 am.)

65. ▼ ***Full-Wave Rectifier*** A *rectifier* is a circuit that converts alternating current to direct current. A *full-wave rectifier* does so by effectively converting the voltage to its absolute value as a function of time. A 110-volt 50 cycles per second AC current would be converted to a voltage as shown:

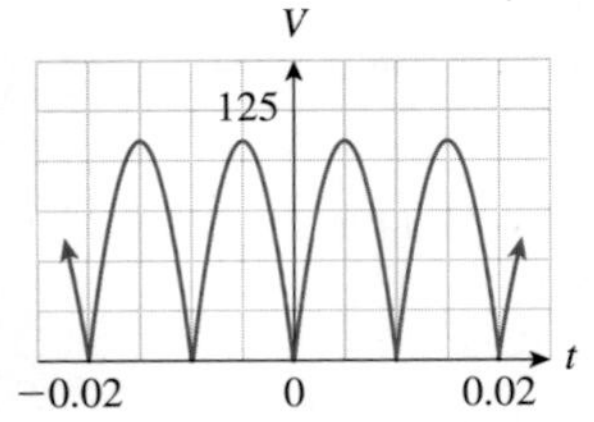

Full rectified wave
$V(t) = 110\,|\sin(100\pi t)|$

[17]The model is based on a regression obtained from predicted data for 1997–2006 and the mean historical period of sunspot activity from 1755 to 1995. Source: NASA Science Directorate; Marshall Space Flight Center, August 2002 (www.science.nasa.gov/ssl/pad/solar/predict.htm).

[18]*Ibid.* Flux measured at a wavelength of 10.7 cm.

Compute and graph $\frac{dV}{dt}$, and explain the sudden jumps you see in the graph of the derivative.

66. ▼ ***Half-Wave Rectifier*** (See the preceding exercise.) In a *half-wave rectifier* the negative voltage is "zeroed out" while the positive voltage is untouched. A 110-volt 50 cycles per second AC current would be converted to a voltage as shown:

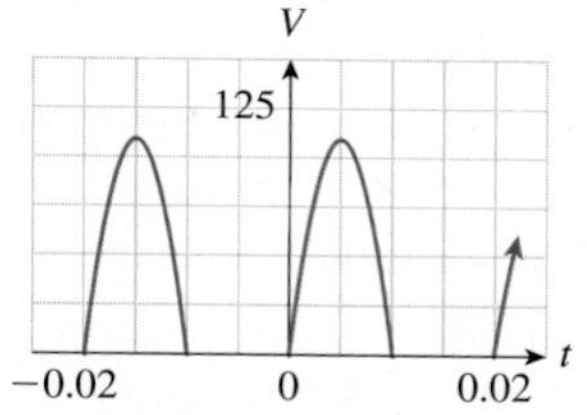

Half rectified wave
$V(t) = 55[\,|\sin(100\pi t)| + \sin(100\pi t)$

Compute and graph $\frac{dV}{dt}$, and explain the sudden jumps you see in the graph of the derivative.

Simple Harmonic Motion and Damped Harmonic Motion *In mechanics, an object whose position relative to a rest position is given by a generalized cosine (or sine) function*

$$p(t) = A\cos(\omega t + d)$$

is called a simple harmonic oscillator. *Examples of simple harmonic oscillators are a mass suspended from a spring and a pendulum swinging through a small angle, in the absence of frictional damping forces. When we take damping forces into account, we obtain a* damped harmonic oscillator*:*

$$p(t) = Ae^{-bt}\cos(\omega t + d)$$

(assuming the damping forces are not so large as to prevent the system from oscillating entirely). Exercises 67–70 are based on these concepts.

67. ▼ A mass on a spring is undergoing simple harmonic motion so that its vertical position at time t seconds is given by

$$p(t) = 1.2\cos(5\pi t + \pi) \text{ cm below the rest position.}$$

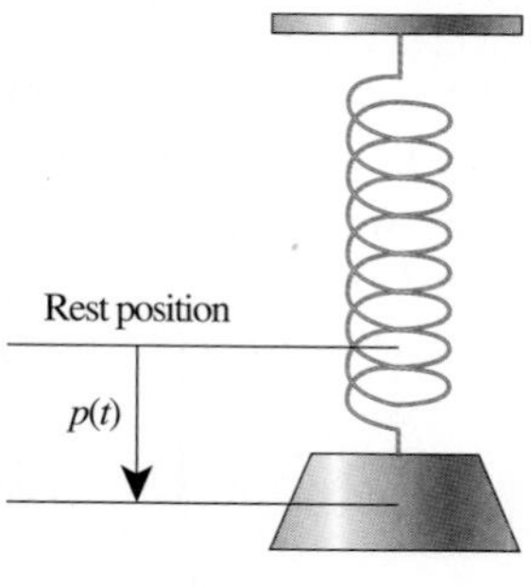

a. What is its vertical position at time $t = 0$?
b. How fast is the mass moving, and in what direction, at times $t = 0$ and $t = 0.1$?
c. The *frequency* of oscillation is defined as the reciprocal of the period. What is the frequency of oscillation of the spring?

68. ▼ A worn shock absorber on a car undergoes simple harmonic motion so that the height of the car frame after t seconds is

$$p(t) = 4.2\sin(2\pi t + \pi/2) \text{ cm above the rest position.}$$

a. What is its vertical position at time $t = 0$?
b. How fast is the height of the car changing, and in what direction, at times $t = 0$ and $t = 0.25$?
c. The *frequency* of oscillation is defined as the reciprocal of the period. What is the frequency of oscillation of the car frame?

69. ▼ A mass on a spring is undergoing damped harmonic motion so that its vertical position at time t seconds is given by

$$p(t) = 1.2e^{-0.1t}\cos(5\pi t + \pi) \text{ cm below the rest position.}$$

a. How fast is the mass moving, and in what direction, at times $t = 0$ and $t = 0.1$?
b. T Graph p and p' as functions of t for $0 \le t \le 10$ and also for $0 \le t \le 1$ and use your graphs and graphing technology to estimate, to the nearest tenth of a second, the time at which the (downward) velocity of the mass is greatest.

70. ▼ A worn shock absorber on a car undergoes damped harmonic motion so that the height of the car frame after t seconds is

$$p(t) = 4.2e^{-0.5t}\sin(2\pi t + \pi/2) \text{ cm above the rest position.}$$

a. How fast is the top of the car moving, and in what direction, at times $t = 0$ and $t = 0.25$?
b. T Graph p and p' as functions of t for $0 \le t \le 10$ and also for $0 \le t \le 2$ and use your graphs and graphing technology to estimate, to the nearest hundredth of a second, the time at which the (upward) velocity of the car is greatest.

71. ▼ ***Tilt of the Earth's Axis*** The tilt of the Earth's axis from its plane of rotation about the sun oscillates between approximately 22.5° and 24.5° with a period of approximately 40,000 years.[19] We know that 500,000 years ago, the tilt of the Earth's axis was 24.5°.

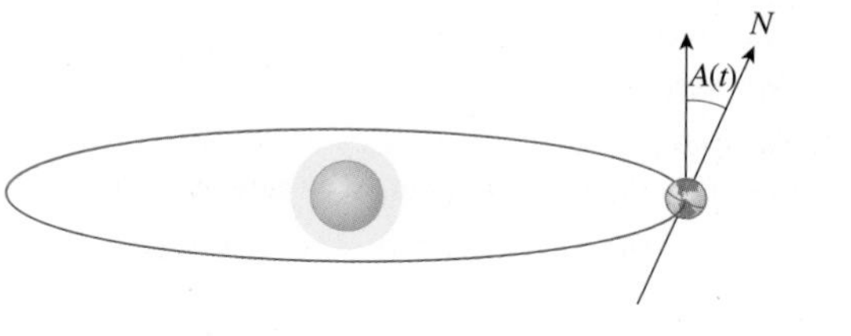

[19]Source: Dr. David Hodell, University of Florida/Juan Valesco/ *New York Times*, February 16, 1999, p. F1.

a. Which of the following functions best models the tilt of the Earth's axis?

(I) $A(t) = 23.5 + 2\sin\left(\frac{2\pi t + 500}{40}\right)$

(II) $A(t) = 23.5 + \cos\left(\frac{t + 500}{80\pi}\right)$

(III) $A(t) = 23.5 + \cos\left(\frac{2\pi(t + 500)}{40}\right)$

where $A(t)$ is the tilt in degrees and t is time in thousands of years, with $t = 0$ being the present time.

b. Use the model you selected in part (a) to estimate the rate at which the tilt was changing 150,000 years ago. (Round your answer to three decimal places, and be sure to give the units of measurement.)

72. ▼ ***Eccentricity of the Earth's Orbit*** The eccentricity of the Earth's orbit (that is, the deviation of the Earth's orbit from a perfect circle) can be modeled by[20]

$$E(t) = 0.025\left[\cos\left(\frac{2\pi(t + 200)}{400}\right) + \cos\left(\frac{2\pi(t + 200)}{100}\right)\right],$$

where $E(t)$ is the eccentricity and t is time in thousands of years, with $t = 0$ being the present time. What was the value of the eccentricity 200,000 years ago, and how fast was it changing?

[20] *Ibid.* This is a rough model based on the actual data.

COMMUNICATION AND REASONING EXERCISES

73. Complete the following: The rate of change of $f(x) = 3\sin(2x - 1) + 3$ oscillates between ___ and ___.

74. Complete the following: The rate of change of $g(x) = -3\cos(-x + 2) + 2x$ oscillates between ___ and ___.

75. Give two examples of a function $f(x)$ with the property that $f''(x) = -f(x)$.

76. Give two examples of a function $f(x)$ with the property that $f''(x) = -4f(x)$.

77. Give two examples of a function $f(x)$ with the property that $f'(x) = -f(x)$.

78. Give four examples of a function $f(x)$ with the property that $f^{(4)}(x) = f(x)$.

79. ▼ By referring to the graph of $f(x) = \cos x$, explain why $f'(x) = -\sin x$, rather than $\sin x$.

80. ▼ If A and B are constants, what is the relationship between $f(x) = A\cos x + B\sin x$ and its second derivative?

81. ▼ If the value of a stock price is given by $p(t) = A\sin(\omega t + d)$ above yesterday's close for constants $A \neq 0$, $\omega \neq 0$, and d, where t is time, explain why the stock price is moving the fastest when it is at yesterday's close.

82. ▼ If the value of a stock price is given by $p(t) = A\cos(\omega t + d)$ above yesterday's close for positive constants A, ω, and d, where t is time, explain why its acceleration is greatest when its value is the lowest.

83. ▼ At what angle does the graph of $f(x) = \sin x$ depart from the origin?

84. ▼ At what angle does the graph of $f(x) = \cos x$ depart from the point (0, 1)?

9.3 Integrals of Trigonometric Functions and Applications

We saw in Section 6.1 that every calculation of a derivative also gives us a calculation of an antiderivative. For instance, because we know that $\cos x$ is the derivative of $\sin x$, we can say that an antiderivative of $\cos x$ is $\sin x$:

$$\int \cos x\, dx = \sin x + C. \qquad \text{An antiderivative of } \cos x \text{ is } \sin x.$$

The rules for the derivatives of sine, cosine, and tangent give us the following antiderivatives.

Indefinite Integrals of Some Trig Functions

$$\int \cos x\, dx = \sin x + C \qquad \text{Because } \frac{d}{dx}(\sin x) = \cos x$$

$$\int \sin x\, dx = -\cos x + C \qquad \text{Because } \frac{d}{dx}(-\cos x) = \sin x$$

$$\int \sec^2 x\, dx = \tan x + C \qquad \text{Because } \frac{d}{dx}(\tan x) = \sec^2 x$$

Quick Examples

1. $\int(\sin x + \cos x)\, dx = -\cos x + \sin x + C$ Integral of sum = Sum of integrals
2. $\int(4\sin x - \cos x)\, dx = -4\cos x - \sin x + C$ Integral of constant multiple
3. $\int(e^x - \sin x + \cos x)\, dx = e^x + \cos x + \sin x + C$

EXAMPLE 1 Substitution

Evaluate $\int(x+3)\sin(x^2+6x)\, dx$.

Solution There are two parenthetical expressions that we might replace with u. Notice, however, that the derivative of the expression (x^2+6x) is $2x+6$, which is twice the term $(x+3)$ in front of the sine. Recall that we would like the derivative of u to appear as a factor. Thus, let us take $u = x^2 + 6x$.

$$u = x^2 + 6x$$
$$\frac{du}{dx} = 2x + 6 = 2(x+3)$$
$$dx = \frac{1}{2(x+3)}\, du$$

Substituting into the integral, we get

$$\int (x+3)\sin(x^2+6x)\, dx = \int (x+3)\sin u \left(\frac{1}{2(x+3)}\right) du = \int \frac{1}{2}\sin u\, du$$
$$= -\frac{1}{2}\cos u + C = -\frac{1}{2}\cos(x^2+6x) + C.$$

EXAMPLE 2 Definite Integrals

Compute the following.

a. $\int_0^{\pi} \sin x\, dx$ **b.** $\int_0^{\pi} x\sin(x^2)\, dx$

Solution

a. $\int_0^{\pi} \sin x\, dx = \left[-\cos x\right]_0^{\pi} = (-\cos \pi) - (-\cos 0) = -(-1) - (-1) = 2$

Thus, the area under one "arch" of the sine curve is exactly two square units!

b. $$\int_0^{\pi} x \sin(x^2)\,dx = \int_0^{\pi^2} \frac{1}{2}\sin u\,du \qquad \text{After substituting } u = x^2$$

$$= \left[-\frac{1}{2}\cos u\right]_0^{\pi^2}$$

$$= \left[-\frac{1}{2}\cos(\pi^2)\right] - \left[-\frac{1}{2}\cos(0)\right]$$

$$= -\frac{1}{2}\cos(\pi^2) + \frac{1}{2} \qquad \cos(0) = 1$$

We can approximate $\frac{1}{2}\cos(\pi^2)$ by a decimal or leave it in the above form, depending on what we want to do with the answer.

Antiderivatives of the Six Trigonometric Functions

The following table gives the indefinite integrals of the six trigonometric functions. (The first two we have already seen.)

Integrals of the Trigonometric Functions

$$\int \sin x\,dx = -\cos x + C$$

$$\int \cos x\,dx = \sin x + C$$

$$\int \tan x\,dx = -\ln|\cos x| + C \qquad \text{Shown below.}$$

$$\int \cot x\,dx = \ln|\sin x| + C \qquad \text{See the Exercise Set.}$$

$$\int \sec x\,dx = \ln|\sec x + \tan x| + C \qquad \text{Shown below.}$$

$$\int \csc x\,dx = -\ln|\csc x + \cot x| + C \qquad \text{See the Exercise Set.}$$

Derivations of Formulas for Antiderivatives of Trigonometic Functions

To show that $\int \tan x\,dx = -\ln|\cos x| + C$, we first write $\tan x$ as $\dfrac{\sin x}{\cos x}$ and put $u = \cos x$ in the integral:

$$\int \tan x\,dx = \int \frac{\sin x}{\cos x}\,dx$$

$$= -\int \frac{\sin x}{u}\frac{du}{\sin x}$$

$$= -\int \frac{du}{u}$$

$$= -\ln|u| + C$$

$$= -\ln|\cos x| + C.$$

$$u = \cos x$$

$$\frac{du}{dx} = -\sin x$$

$$dx = -\frac{du}{\sin x}$$

To show that $\int \sec x\,dx = \ln|\sec x + \tan x| + C$, first use a little "trick": Write $\sec x$ as $\sec x\left(\frac{\sec x + \tan x}{\sec x + \tan x}\right)$ and put u equal to the denominator:

$$\begin{aligned}\int \sec x\,dx &= \int \sec x\left(\frac{\sec x + \tan x}{\sec x + \tan x}\right) dx \\ &= \int \sec x \frac{\sec x + \tan x}{u} \frac{du}{\sec x(\tan x + \sec x)} \\ &= \int \frac{du}{u} \\ &= \ln|u| + C \\ &= \ln|\sec x + \tan x| + C.\end{aligned}$$

$$\begin{aligned}u &= \sec x + \tan x \\ \frac{du}{dx} &= \sec x \tan x + \sec^2 x \\ &= \sec x\,(\tan x + \sec x) \\ dx &= \frac{du}{\sec x\,(\tan x + \sec x)}\end{aligned}$$

Shortcuts

If a and b are constants with $a \neq 0$, then we have the following formulas. (All of them can be obtained using the substitution $u = ax + b$. They will appear in the exercises.)

Shortcuts: Integrals of Expressions Involving $(ax + b)$

Rule	Quick Example
$\int \sin(ax+b)\,dx = -\frac{1}{a}\cos(ax+b) + C$	$\int \sin(-4x)\,dx = \frac{1}{4}\cos(-4x) + C$
$\int \cos(ax+b)\,dx = \frac{1}{a}\sin(ax+b) + C$	$\int \cos(x+1)\,dx = \sin(x+1) + C$
$\int \tan(ax+b)\,dx = -\frac{1}{a}\ln\lvert\cos(ax+b)\rvert + C$	$\int \tan(-2x)\,dx = \frac{1}{2}\ln\lvert\cos(-2x)\rvert + C$
$\int \cot(ax+b)\,dx = \frac{1}{a}\ln\lvert\sin(ax+b)\rvert + C$	$\int \cot(3x-1)\,dx = \frac{1}{3}\ln\lvert\sin(3x-1)\rvert + C$
$\int \sec(ax+b)\,dx = \frac{1}{a}\ln\lvert\sec(ax+b) + \tan(ax+b)\rvert + C$	$\int \sec(9x)\,dx = \frac{1}{9}\ln\lvert\sec(9x) + \tan(9x)\rvert + C$
$\int \csc(ax+b)\,dx = -\frac{1}{a}\ln\lvert\csc(ax+b) + \cot(ax+b)\rvert + C$	$\int \csc(x+7)\,dx = -\ln\lvert\csc(x+7) + \cot(x+7)\rvert + C$

EXAMPLE 3 Sales

The rate of sales of cypods (one-bedroom living units) in the city-state of Utarek, Mars[21] can be modeled by

$$s(t) = 7.5\cos(\pi t/6) + 87.5 \text{ units per month,}$$

where t is time in months since January 1. How many cypods are sold in a calendar year?

Solution Total sales over one calendar year are given by

$$\begin{aligned}
\int_0^{12} s(t)\,dt &= \int_0^{12} [7.5\cos(\pi t/6) + 87.5]\,dt \\
&= \left[7.5\frac{6}{\pi}\sin(\pi t/6) + 87.5t\right]_0^{12} && \text{We used a shortcut on the first term.} \\
&= \left[7.5\frac{6}{\pi}\sin(2\pi) + 87.5(12)\right] - \left[7.5\frac{6}{\pi}\sin(0) + 87.5(0)\right] \\
&= 87.5(12) && \sin(2\pi) = \sin(0) = 0. \\
&= 1{,}050 \text{ cypods.}
\end{aligned}$$

➡ **Before we go on...** Would it have made any difference in Example 3 if we had computed total sales over the period [12, 24], [6, 18], or any interval of the form $[a, a + 12]$? ■

Using Integration by Parts with Trig Functions

EXAMPLE 4 Integrating a Polynomial Times Sine or Cosine

Calculate $\int (x^2 + 1)\sin(x + 1)\,dx$.

Solution We use the column method of integration by parts described in Section 7.1. Because differentiating $x^2 + 1$ makes it simpler, we put it in the D column and get the following table:

	D	I
$+$	$x^2 + 1$	$\sin(x + 1)$
$-$	$2x$	$-\cos(x + 1)$
$+$	2	$-\sin(x + 1)$
$-\int$	0 →	$\cos(x + 1)$

[21]Based on www.Marsnext.com, a now extinct virtual society.

[Notice that we used the shortcut formulas to repeatedly integrate $\sin(x+1)$.] We can now read the answer from the table:

$$\begin{aligned}\int (x^2+1)\sin(x+1)\,dx &= (x^2+1)[-\cos(x+1)] - 2x[-\sin(x+1)] \\ &\quad + 2[\cos(x+1)] + C \\ &= (-x^2-1+2)\cos(x+1) + 2x\sin(x+1) + C \\ &= (-x^2+1)\cos(x+1) + 2x\sin(x+1) + C.\end{aligned}$$

EXAMPLE 5 Integrating an Exponential Times Sine or Cosine

Calculate $\int e^x \sin x\,dx$.

Solution The integrand is the product of e^x and $\sin x$, so we put one in the D column and the other in the I column. For this example, it doesn't matter much which we put where.

	D	I
$+$	$\sin x$	e^x
$-$	$\cos x$	e^x
$+\int$	$-\sin x \longrightarrow$	e^x

It looks like we're just spinning our wheels. Let's stop and see what we have:

$$\int e^x \sin x\,dx = e^x \sin x - e^x \cos x - \int e^x \sin x\,dx.$$

At first glance, it appears that we are back where we started, still having to evaluate $\int e^x \sin x\,dx$. However, if we add this integral to both sides of the equation above, we can solve for it:

$$2\int e^x \sin x\,dx = e^x \sin x - e^x \cos x + C.$$

(Why $+\ C$?) So,

$$\int e^x \sin x\,dx = \frac{1}{2}e^x \sin x - \frac{1}{2}e^x \cos x + \frac{C}{2}.$$

Because $C/2$ is just as arbitrary as C, we write C instead of $C/2$, and obtain

$$\int e^x \sin x\,dx = \frac{1}{2}e^x \sin x - \frac{1}{2}e^x \cos x + C.$$

9.3 EXERCISES

▼ more advanced ◆ challenging
T indicates exercises that should be solved using technology

Evaluate the integrals in Exercises 1–28. HINT [See Quick Examples page 679.]

1. $\int (\sin x - 2\cos x)\, dx$

2. $\int (\cos x - \sin x)\, dx$

3. $\int (2\cos x - 4.3\sin x - 9.33)\, dx$

4. $\int (4.1\sin x + \cos x - 9.33/x)\, dx$

5. $\int \left(3.4\sec^2 x + \frac{\cos x}{1.3} - 3.2e^x\right) dx$

6. $\int \left(\frac{3\sec^2 x}{2} + 1.3\sin x - \frac{e^x}{3.2}\right) dx$

7. $\int 7.6\cos(3x - 4)\, dx$ HINT [See Example 1.]

8. $\int 4.4\sin(-3x + 4)\, dx$ HINT [See Example 1.]

9. $\int x\sin(3x^2 - 4)\, dx$

10. $\int x\cos(-3x^2 + 4)\, dx$

11. $\int (4x + 2)\sin(x^2 + x)\, dx$

12. $\int (x + 1)[\cos(x^2 + 2x) + (x^2 + 2x)]\, dx$

13. $\int (x + x^2)\sec^2(3x^2 + 2x^3)\, dx$

14. $\int (4x + 2)\sec^2(x^2 + x)\, dx$

15. $\int (x^2)\tan(2x^3)\, dx$

16. $\int (4x)\tan(x^2)\, dx$

17. $\int 6\sec(2x - 4)\, dx$

18. $\int 3\csc(3x)\, dx$

19. $\int e^{2x}\cos(e^{2x} + 1)\, dx$

20. $\int e^{-x}\sin(e^{-x})\, dx$

21. $\int_{-\pi}^{0} \sin x\, dx$ HINT [See Example 2.]

22. $\int_{\pi/2}^{\pi} \cos x\, dx$ HINT [See Example 2.]

23. $\int_0^{\pi/3} \tan x\, dx$

24. $\int_{\pi/6}^{\pi/2} \cot x\, dx$

25. $\int_1^{\sqrt{\pi+1}} x\cos(x^2 - 1)\, dx$

26. $\int_{0.5}^{(\pi+1)/2} \sin(2x - 1)\, dx$

27. ▼ $\int_{1/\pi}^{2/\pi} \frac{\sin(1/x)}{x^2}\, dx$

28. ▼ $\int_0^{\pi/3} \frac{\sin x}{\cos^2 x}\, dx$

In Exercises 29–32, derive each equation, where a and b are constants with $a \neq 0$.

29. ▼ $\int \cos(ax + b)\, dx = \frac{1}{a}\sin(ax + b) + C$

30. ▼ $\int \sin(ax + b)\, dx = -\frac{1}{a}\cos(ax + b) + C$

31. ▼ $\int \cot x\, dx = \ln|\sin x| + C$

32. ▼ $\int \csc x\, dx = -\ln|\csc x + \cot x| + C$

Use the shortcut formulas on page 681 to calculate the integrals in Exercises 33–40 mentally.

33. $\int \sin(4x)\, dx$

34. $\int \cos(5x)\, dx$

35. $\int \cos(-x + 1)\, dx$

36. $\int \sin\left(\frac{1}{2}x\right) dx$

37. $\int \sin(-1.1x - 1)\, dx$

38. $\int \cos(4.2x - 1)\, dx$

39. $\int \cot(-4x)\, dx$

40. $\int \tan(6x)\, dx$

Use geometry (not antiderivatives) to compute the integrals in Exercises 41–44. HINT [First draw the graph.]

41. $\int_{-\pi/2}^{\pi/2} \sin x\, dx$

42. $\int_0^{\pi} \cos x\, dx$

43. ▼ $\int_0^{2\pi} (1 + \sin x)\, dx$

44. ▼ $\int_0^{2\pi} (1 + \cos x)\, dx$

Use integration by parts to evaluate the integrals in Exercises 45–52. HINT [See Example 4.]

45. $\int x\sin x\, dx$

46. $\int x^2\cos x\, dx$

47. $\int x^2\cos(2x)\, dx$

48. $\int (2x + 1)\sin(2x - 1)\, dx$

49. ▼ $\int e^{-x}\sin x\, dx$

50. ▼ $\int e^{2x}\cos x\, dx$

51. ▼ $\int_0^{\pi} x^2\sin x\, dx$

52. ▼ $\int_0^{\pi/2} x\cos x\, dx$

Recall from Section 7.3 that the average of a function $f(x)$ on an interval $[a, b]$ is

$$\bar{f} = \frac{1}{b - a}\int_a^b f(x)\, dx.$$

Find the averages of the functions in Exercises 53 and 54 over the given intervals. Plot each function and its average on the same graph.

53. ▼ $f(x) = \sin x$ over $[0, \pi]$

54. ▼ $f(x) = \cos(2x)$ over $[0, \pi/4]$

Decide whether each integral in Exercises 55–58 converges. (See Section 7.5.) If the integral converges, compute its value.

55. $\int_0^{+\infty} \sin x\, dx$

56. $\int_0^{+\infty} \cos x\, dx$

57. ▼ $\int_0^{+\infty} e^{-x} \cos x\, dx$

58. ▼ $\int_0^{+\infty} e^{-x} \sin x\, dx$

APPLICATIONS

59. ***Varying Cost*** The cost of producing a bottle of suntan lotion is changing at a rate of $0.04 - 0.1 \sin\left[\frac{\pi}{26}(t - 25)\right]$ dollars per week, t weeks after January 1. If it cost \$1.50 to produce a bottle 12 weeks into the year, find the cost $C(t)$ at time t.

60. ***Varying Cost*** The cost of producing a box of holiday tree decorations is changing at a rate of $0.05 + 0.4 \cos\left[\frac{\pi}{6}(t - 11)\right]$ dollars per month, t months after January 1. If it cost \$5 to produce a box on June 1, find the cost $C(t)$ at time t.

61. ▼ ***Pets*** My dog Miranda is running back and forth along a 12-foot stretch of garden in such a way that her velocity t seconds after she began is

$$v(t) = 3\pi \cos\left[\frac{\pi}{2}(t - 1)\right] \text{ feet per second.}$$

How far is she from where she began 10 seconds after starting the run? HINT [See Example 3.]

62. ▼ ***Pets*** My cat, Prince Sadar, is pacing back and forth along his favorite window ledge in such a way that his velocity t seconds after he began is

$$v(t) = -\frac{\pi}{2} \sin\left[\frac{\pi}{4}(t - 2)\right] \text{ feet per second.}$$

How far is he from where he began 10 seconds after starting to pace? HINT [See Example 3.]

For Exercises 63–68, recall from Section 7.3 that the average of a function $f(x)$ on an interval $[a, b]$ is

$$\bar{f} = \frac{1}{b - a} \int_a^b f(x)\, dx.$$

63. ***Sunspot Activity*** The activity of the sun (sunspots, solar flares, and coronal mass ejection) fluctuates in cycles of around 10–11 years. Sunspot activity can be modeled by the following function:[22]

$$N(t) = 57.7 \sin[0.602(t - 1.43)] + 58.8,$$

where t is the number of years since January 1, 1997, and $N(t)$ is the number of sunspots observed at time t. Estimate the average number of sunspots visible over the 2-year period beginning January 1, 2002. (Round your answer to the nearest whole number.)

64. ***Solar Emissions*** The following model gives the flux of radio emission from the sun:

$$F(t) = 49.6 \sin[0.602(t - 1.48)] + 111,$$

where t is the number of years since January 1, 1997, and $F(t)$ is the flux of solar emissions of a specified wavelength at time t.[23] Estimate the average flux of radio emission over the 5-year period beginning January 1, 2001. (Round your answer to the nearest whole number.)

65. ▼ ***Biology*** Sigatoka leaf spot is a plant disease that affects bananas. In an infected plant, the percentage of leaf area affected varies from a low of around 5% at the start of each year to a high of around 20% at the middle of each year.[24] Use a sine function model of the percentage of leaf area affected by Sigatoka leaf spot t weeks since the start of a year to estimate, to the nearest 0.1%, the average percentage of leaf area affected in the first quarter (13 weeks) of a year.

66. ▼ ***Biology*** Apple powdery mildew is an epidemic that affects apple shoots. In a new infection, the percentage of apple shoots infected varies from a low of around 10% at the start of May to a high of around 60% 6 months later.[25] Use a sine function model of the percentage of apple shoots affected by apple powdery mildew t months since the start of a year to estimate, to the nearest 0.1%, the average percentage of apple shoots affected in the first 2 months of a year.

67. T ▼ ***Electrical Current*** The typical voltage V supplied by an electrical outlet in the United States is given by

$$V(t) = 165 \cos(120\pi t),$$

where t is time in seconds.

[22] The model is based on a regression obtained from predicted data for 1997–2006 and the mean historical period of sunspot activity from 1755 to 1995. Source: NASA Science Directorate; Marshall Space Flight Center, August, 2002 (www.science.nasa.gov/ssl/pad/solar/predict.htm).

[23] *Ibid.* Flux measured at a wavelength of 10.7 cm.

[24] Based on graphical data. Source: American Phytopathological Society (www.apsnet.org/education/AdvancedPlantPath/Topics/Epidemiology/CyclicalNature.htm).

[25] *Ibid.*

a. Find the average voltage over the interval [0, 1/6]. How many times does the voltage reach a maximum in one second? (This is referred to as the number of **cycles per second**.)

b. Plot the function $S(t) = (V(t))^2$ over the interval [0, 1/6].

c. The **root mean square (RMS)** voltage is given by the formula

$$V_{\text{rms}} = \sqrt{\bar{S}},$$

where $\bar{S}$ is the average value of $S(t)$ over one cycle. Estimate V_{rms}.

68. ▼ ***Tides*** The depth of water at my favorite surfing spot varies from 5 to 15 feet, depending on the time. Last Sunday, high tide occurred at 5:00 am and the next high tide occurred at 6:30 pm. Use the cosine function to model the depth of water as a function of time t in hours since midnight on Sunday morning. What was the average depth of the water between 10:00 am and 2:00 pm?

Income Streams *Recall from Section 7.4 that the total income received from time* $t = a$ *to time* $t = b$ *from a continuous income stream of* $R(t)$ *dollars per year is*

$$\text{Total value} = TV = \int_a^b R(t)\,dt.$$

In Exercises 69 and 70, find the total value of the given income stream over the given period.

69. $R(t) = 50{,}000 + 2{,}000\pi \sin(2\pi t),\ 0 \le t \le 1$

70. $R(t) = 100{,}000 - 2{,}000\pi \sin(\pi t),\ 0 \le t \le 1.5$

COMMUNICATION AND REASONING EXERCISES

71. What can you say about the definite integral of a sine or cosine function over a whole number of periods?

72. How are the derivative and antiderivative of $\sin x$ related?

73. ▼ What is the average value of $1 + 2\cos x$ over a large interval?

74. ▼ What is the average value of $3 - \cos x$ over a large interval?

75. ▼ The acceleration of an object is given by $a = K \sin(\omega t - \alpha)$. What can you say about its displacement at time t?

76. ▼ Write down a function whose derivative is -2 times its antiderivative.

CHAPTER 9 REVIEW

KEY CONCEPTS

WW Website www.WanerMath.com

Go to the Website at www.WanerMath.com to find a comprehensive and interactive Web-based summary of Chapter 9.

9.1 Trigonometric Functions, Models, and Regression

The **sine** of a real number *p. 657*

Plotting the graphs of functions based on $\sin x$ *p. 658*

The general sine function:

$f(x) = A\sin[\omega(x-\alpha)] + C$

A is the **amplitude**.

C is the **vertical offset** or height of the **baseline**.

ω is the **angular frequency**.

$P = 2\pi/\omega$ is the **period** or **wavelength**.

α is the **phase shift**. *p. 659*

Modeling with the general sine function *p. 660*

The **cosine** of a real number *p. 661*

Fundamental trigonometric identities:

$\sin^2 t + \cos^2 t = 1$

$\cos t = \sin(t + \pi/2)$

$\cos t = \sin(\pi/2 - t)$

$\sin t = \cos(t - \pi/2)$

$\sin t = \cos(\pi/2 - t)$ *p. 662*

The general cosine function:

$f(x) = A\cos[\omega(x-\beta)] + C$ *p. 662*

Modeling with the general cosine function *p. 663*

Other trig functions:

$$\tan x = \frac{\sin x}{\cos x}$$

$$\cot x = \operatorname{cotan} x = \frac{\cos x}{\sin x} = \frac{1}{\tan x}$$

$$\sec x = \frac{1}{\cos x}$$

$$\csc x = \operatorname{cosec} x = \frac{1}{\sin x} \quad p.\ 664$$

9.2 Derivatives of Trigonometric Functions and Applications

Derivatives of sine and cosine:

$$\frac{d}{dx}\sin x = \cos x$$

$$\frac{d}{dx}\cos x = -\sin x \quad p.\ 670$$

Some trigonometric limits:

$$\lim_{h\to 0}\frac{\sin h}{h} = 1$$

$$\lim_{h\to 0}\frac{\cos h - 1}{h} = 0 \quad p.\ 671$$

Derivatives of sines and cosines of functions:

$$\frac{d}{dx}\sin u = \cos u\frac{du}{dx}$$

$$\frac{d}{dx}\cos u = -\sin u\frac{du}{dx} \quad p.\ 672$$

Derivatives of the other trigonometric functions:

$$\frac{d}{dx}\tan x = \sec^2 x$$

$$\frac{d}{dx}\cot x = -\csc^2 x$$

$$\frac{d}{dx}\sec x = \sec x\tan x$$

$$\frac{d}{dx}\csc x = -\csc x\cot x \quad p.\ 674$$

9.3 Integrals of Trigonometric Functions and Applications

$$\int \cos x\,dx = \sin x + C$$

$$\int \sin x\,dx = -\cos x + C$$

$$\int \sec^2 x\,dx = \tan x + C \quad p.\ 679$$

Substitution in integrals involving trig functions *p. 679*

Definite integrals involving trig functions *p. 679*

Antiderivatives of the other trigonometric functions:

$$\int \tan x\,dx = -\ln|\cos x| + C$$

$$\int \cot x\,dx = \ln|\sin x| + C$$

$$\int \sec x\,dx = \ln|\sec x + \tan x| + C$$

$$\int \csc x\,dx = -\ln|\csc x + \cot x| + C$$

p. 680

Shortcuts: Integrals of expressions involving $(ax+b)$ *p. 681*

Using integration by parts with trig functions *p. 682*

REVIEW EXERCISES

In Exercises 1–4, model the given curve with a sine function. (The scales on the two axes may not be the same.)

1.

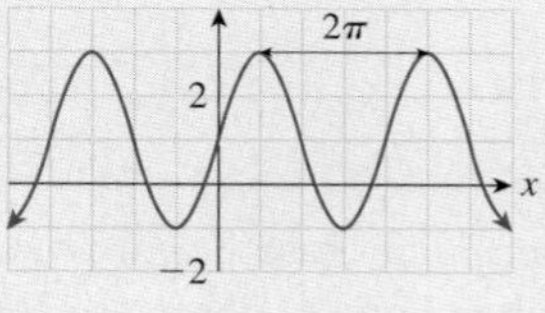

2.

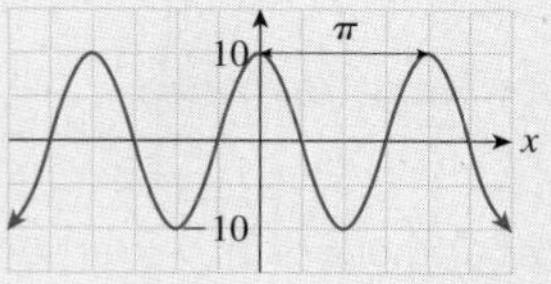

3.

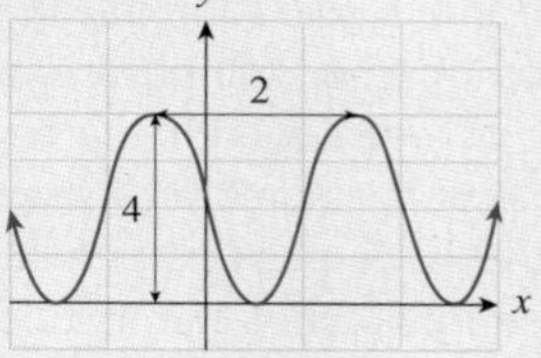

4.

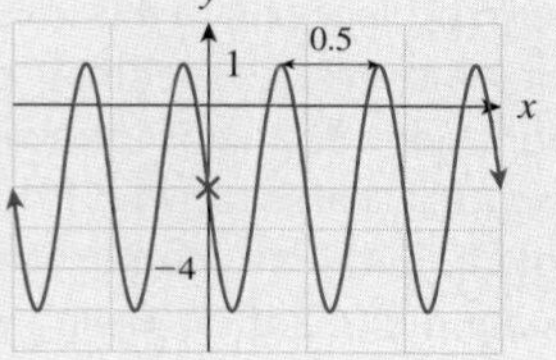

In Exercises 5–8, model the curves in Exercises 1–4 with cosine functions.

5. The curve in Exercise 1 **6.** The curve in Exercise 2

7. The curve in Exercise 3 **8.** The curve in Exercise 4

In Exercises 9–14, find the derivative of the given function.

9. $f(x) = \cos(x^2 - 1)$

10. $f(x) = \sin(x^2+1)\cos(x^2-1)$

11. $f(x) = \tan(2e^x - 1)$ **12.** $f(x) = \sec\sqrt{x^2 - x}$

13. $f(x) = \sin^2(x^2)$ **14.** $f(x) = \cos^2[1 - \sin(2x)]$

In Exercises 15–22, evaluate the given integral.

15. $\int 4\cos(2x-1)\,dx$

16. $\int (x-1)\sin(x^2 - 2x + 1)\,dx$

17. $\int 4x \sec^2(2x^2 - 1)\,dx$ **18.** $\int \dfrac{\cos\left(\frac{1}{x}\right)}{x^2 \sin\left(\frac{1}{x}\right)}\,dx$

19. $\int x \tan(x^2 + 1)\,dx$ **20.** $\int_0^{\pi} \cos(x + \pi/2)\,dx$

21. $\int_{\ln(\pi/2)}^{\ln(\pi)} e^x \sin(e^x)\,dx$ **22.** $\int_{\pi}^{2\pi} \tan(x/6)\,dx$

Use integration by parts to evaluate the integrals in Exercises 23 and 24.

23. $\int x^2 \sin x\,dx$ **24.** $\int e^x \sin 2x\,dx$

APPLICATIONS: OHaganBooks.com

25. ***Sales*** After several years in the business, OHaganBooks.com noticed that its sales showed seasonal fluctuations, so that weekly sales oscillated in a sine wave from a low of 9,000 books per week to a high of 12,000 books per week, with the high point of the year being three quarters of the way through the year, in October. Model OHaganBooks.com's weekly sales as a generalized sine function of t, the number of weeks into the year.

26. ***Mood Swings*** The shipping personnel at OHaganBooks.com are under considerable pressure to cope with the large volume of orders, and periodic emotional outbursts are commonplace. The human resources department has been logging these outbursts over the course of several years, and has noticed a peak of 50 outbursts a week during the holiday season each December and a low point of 15 per week each June (probably attributable to the mild June weather). Model the weekly number of outbursts as a generalized cosine function of t, the number of months into the year ($t = 1$ represents January).

27. ***Precalculus for Geniuses*** The "For Geniuses" series of books has really been taking off since Duffin House first gained exclusive rights to the series 6 months ago, and revenues from *Precalculus for Geniuses* are expected to follow the curve

$$R(t) = 100{,}000 + 20{,}000e^{-0.05t} \sin\left[\frac{\pi}{6}(t-2)\right] \text{ dollars} \quad (0 \le t \le 72),$$

where t is time in months from now and $R(t)$ is the monthly revenue. How fast, to the nearest dollar, will the revenue be changing 20 months from now?

28. ***Elvish for Dummies*** The sales department at OHagan-Books.com predicts that the revenue from sales of the latest blockbuster *Elvish for Dummies* will vary in accordance with annual releases of episodes of the movie series "Lord of the Rings Episodes 9–12." It has come up with the following model (which includes the effect of diminishing sales):

$$R(t) = 20{,}000 + 15{,}000e^{-0.12t} \cos\left[\frac{\pi}{6}(t-4)\right] \text{ dollars} \quad (0 \le t \le 72),$$

where t is time in months from now and $R(t)$ is the monthly revenue. How fast, to the nearest dollar, will the revenue be changing 10 months from now?

29. ***Revenue*** Refer back to Question 27. Use technology or integration by parts to estimate, to the nearest \$100, the total revenue from sales of *Precalculus for Geniuses* over the next 20 months.

30. ***Revenue*** Refer back to Question 28. Use technology or integration by parts to estimate, to the nearest \$100, the total revenue from sales of *Elvish for Dummies* over the next 10 months.

31. ***Mars Missions*** Having completed his doctorate in biophysics, Billy-Sean O'Hagan will be accompanying the first manned mission to Mars. For reasons too complicated to explain (but having to do with the continuation of his doctoral research project and the timing of messages from his fiancée), during the voyage he will be consuming protein at a rate of

$$P(t) = 150 + 50 \sin\left[\frac{\pi}{2}(t-1)\right] \text{ grams per day}$$

t days into the voyage. Find the total amount of protein he will consume as a function of time t.

32. ***Utilities*** Expenditure for utilities at OHaganBooks.com fluctuated from a high of \$9,500 in October ($t = 0$) to a low of \$8,000 in April ($t = 6$). Construct a sinusoidal model for the monthly expenditure on utilities and use your model to estimate the total annual cost.

Case Study

Predicting Airline Empty Seat Volume

Lawrence Manning/Flirt/Corbis

You are a consultant to the Department of Transportation's Special Task Force on Air Traffic Congestion and have been asked to model the volume of empty seats on U.S. airline flights, to make short-term projections of this volume, and to give a formula that estimates the accumulated volume over a specified period of time. You have data from the Bureau of Transportation Statistics showing, for each month starting January 2002, the number of available seat-miles (the total of the number of seats times the number of miles flown), and also the number of revenue passenger-miles (the total of the number of seats occupied by paying passengers times the number of miles flown), so their difference (if you ignore nonpaying passengers) measures the number of empty seat-miles. (The data can be downloaded at the Website by following Everything for Calculus → Chapter 9 Case Study.)[26]

Month	Empty Seat-Miles (billions)	Month	Empty Seat-Miles (billions)	Month	Empty Seat-Miles (billions)	Month	Empty Seat-Miles (billions)
1	25	21	23	41	20	61	23
2	21	22	22	42	16	62	20
3	18	23	21	43	15	63	17
4	21	24	21	44	18	64	17
5	21	25	26	45	21	65	18
6	18	26	23	46	21	66	13
7	19	27	20	47	19	67	14
8	19	28	19	48	20	68	15
9	25	29	21	49	22	69	21
10	24	30	16	50	19	70	19
11	24	31	16	51	17	71	19
12	21	32	19	52	17	72	21
13	26	33	22	53	17	73	23
14	22	34	21	54	14	74	21
15	22	35	22	55	14	75	17
16	22	36	23	56	18	76	18
17	19	37	24	57	21	77	18
18	16	38	22	58	20	78	15
19	15	39	18	59	19	79	15
20	17	40	20	60	20	80	16

On the graph (Figure 14) you notice two trends: A 12-month cyclical pattern, and also an overall declining trend. This overall trend is often referred to as the *secular trend* and can be seen more clearly using the 12-month moving average (Figure 15).

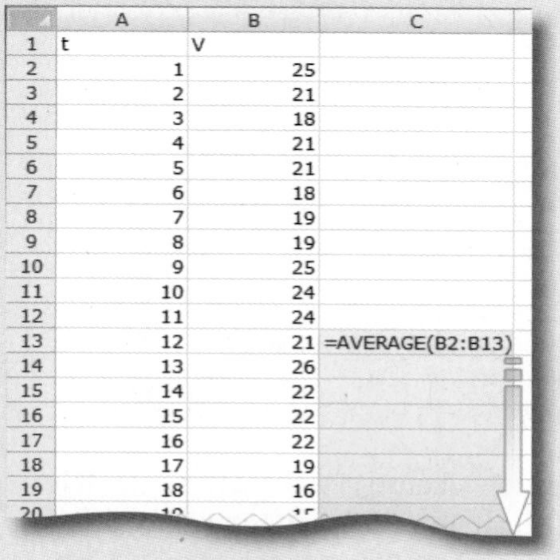

	A	B	C
1	t	V	
2	1	25	
3	2	21	
4	3	18	
5	4	21	
6	5	21	
7	6	18	
8	7	19	
9	8	19	
10	9	25	
11	10	24	
12	11	24	
13	12	21	=AVERAGE(B2:B13)
14	13	26	
15	14	22	
16	15	22	
17	16	22	
18	17	19	
19	18	16	

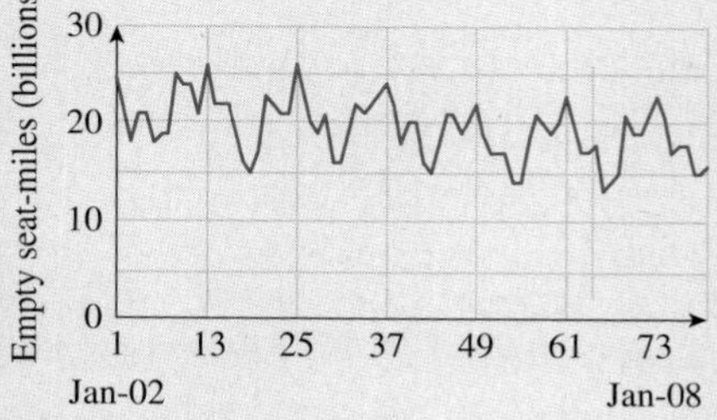

Figure 14

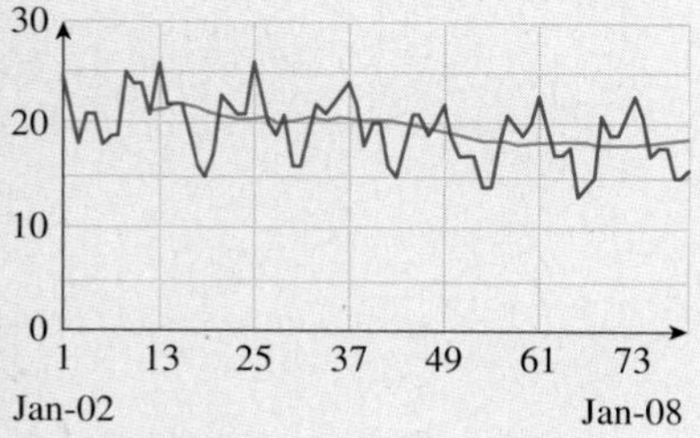

Figure 15

[26]Source: Bureau of Transportation Statistics (www.bts.gov).

You notice that the secular trend appears more-or-less linear. The simplest model of a cyclical term with 12-month period added to a linear secular trend has the form

$$V(t) = \underbrace{A\sin(\pi t/6 + d)}_{\text{Cyclical term}} + \underbrace{Bt + C}_{\text{Secular trend}}. \qquad \omega = 2\pi/12 = \pi/6$$

You are about to use Solver to construct the model when you discover that your copy of Excel has mysteriously lost its Solver, so you wonder whether there is an alternative way to construct the model. After consulting various statistics textbooks, you discover that there is: You can use the addition formula to write

$$A\sin(\pi t/6 + d) = A[\sin(\pi t/6)\cos d + \cos(\pi t/6)\sin d]$$
$$= P\sin(\pi t/6) + Q\cos(\pi t/6)$$

for constants $P = A\cos d$ and $Q = A\sin d$, so instead you could use an equivalent model of the form

$$V(t) = P\sin(\pi t/6) + Q\cos(\pi t/6) + Bt + C.$$

Note that the equations $P = A\cos d$ and $Q = A\sin d$ give

$$P^2 + Q^2 = A^2\cos^2 d + A^2\sin^2 d = A^2(\cos^2 d + \sin^2 d) = A^2,$$

so $\quad A = \sqrt{P^2 + Q^2},$

giving the amplitude in terms of P and Q.

But what has all of this to do with avoiding Solver? The point is that, now, *V is a linear function of the variables* $\sin(\pi t/6)$, $\cos(\pi t/6)$, and t, meaning that you can model y using ordinary linear regression along the lines of the Case Study in Chapter 8: First you rearrange the data so that the V column is first, and add columns to calculate $\sin(\pi t/6)$ and $\cos(\pi t/6)$:

	A	B	C	D
1	V	t	sin(πt/6)	cos(πt/6)
2	25	1	=sin(PI()*B2/6)	=cos(PI()*B2/6)
3	21	2		
4	18	3		
5	21	4		
6	21	5		
7	18	6		
8	19	7		
9	19	8		

↓

	A	B	C	D
1	V	t	sin(πt/6)	cos(πt/6)
2	25	1	0.5	0.866025404
3	21	2	0.866025404	0.5
4	18	3	1	6.12574E-17
5	21	4	0.866025404	-0.5
6	21	5	0.5	-0.866025404
7	18	6	1.22515E-16	-1
8	19	7	-0.5	-0.866025404
9	19	8	-0.866025404	-0.5

Next, in the "Analysis" section of the Data tab, choose "Data analysis." (If this command is not available, you will need to load the Analysis ToolPak add-in.) Choose "Regression" from the list that appears, and in the resulting dialogue box enter the location of the data and where you want to put the results as shown on the left in Figure 16; identify where the dependent and independent variables are (A1–A81 for the Y range, and B1–D81 for the X range), check "Labels", and click "OK".

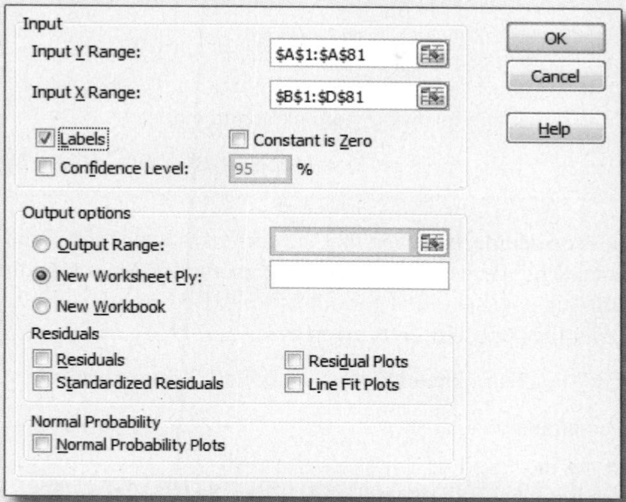

ANOVA	
	df
Regression	3
Residual	76
Total	79
	Coefficients
Intercept	21.6833363
t	-0.051345
sin(πt/6)	0.2044244
cos(πt/6)	2.87103179

Figure 16

A portion of the output is shown above on the right, with the coefficients highlighted. You use the output to write down the regression equation (with coefficients rounded to four significant digits):

$$V(t) = 0.2044 \sin(\pi t/6) + 2.871 \cos(\pi t/6) - 0.05135t + 21.68.$$

Figure 17 shows the original data with the graph of V superimposed.

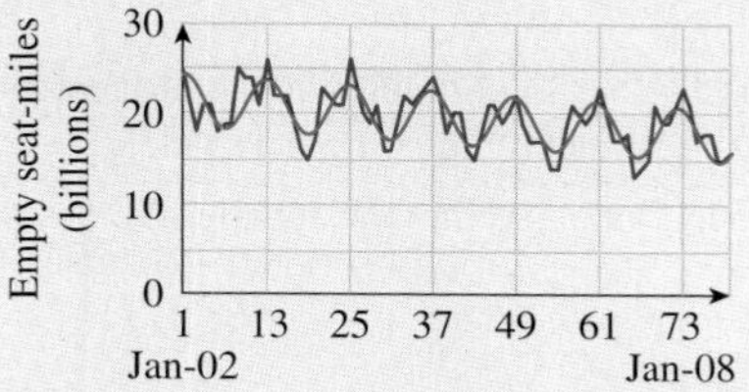

Excel Formula:
`0.2044*sin(PI()*t/6)+2.871*cos(PI()*t/6)-0.05135*t+21.68`

Figure 17

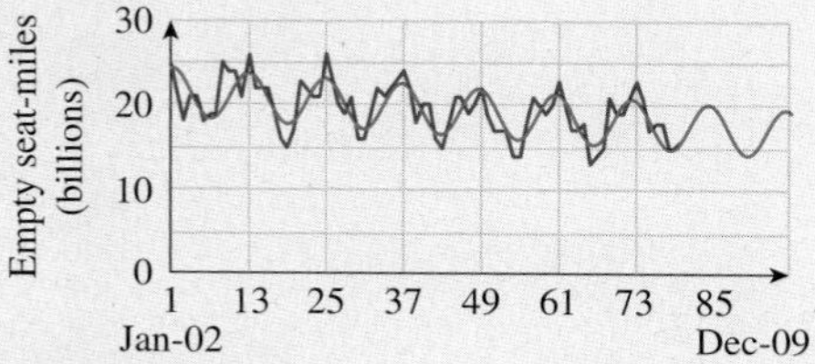

Figure 18

Although the graph does not give a perfect fit, the model captures the behavior quite accurately. Figure 18 shows the 1-year projection of the model.

Q: *How would one alter the model to capture the sharp upward spike every November and the downward spike every June-July?*

A: One could add additional terms, called *seasonal variables:*

$$x_1 = \begin{cases} 1 & \text{if } t = 11, 23, 35, \ldots \\ 0 & \text{if not} \end{cases} \qquad x_1 = 1 \text{ every November}$$

$$x_2 = \begin{cases} 1 & \text{if } t = 6, 7, 18, 19, \ldots \\ 0 & \text{if not} \end{cases} \qquad x_2 = 1 \text{ every June and July}$$

to obtain the following more elaborate model:

$$V(t) = P\sin(\pi t/6) + Q\cos(\pi t/6) + Bt + Cx_1 + Dx_2 + E.$$

You decide, however, that the current model is satisfactory for your purposes, and proceed to address the second task: estimating the total volume of empty seats accumulating over specified periods of time. Because the total accumulation of a function V over the period $[a, b]$ is given by

$$\text{Total Accumulated Empty Seat-Miles} = \text{Total Accumulation of } V = \int_a^b V(t)\,dt,$$

you calculate

$$\begin{aligned}\int_a^b V(t)\,dt &= \int_a^b [P\sin(\pi t/6) + Q\cos(\pi t/6) + Bt + C]\,dt \\ &= \frac{6P}{\pi}[\cos(\pi a/6) - \cos(\pi b/6)] + \frac{6Q}{\pi}[\sin(\pi b/6) - \sin(\pi a/6)] \\ &\quad + \frac{B(b^2 - a^2)}{2} + C(b - a)\end{aligned}$$

billion empty seat-miles.

This is a formula which, on plugging in the values of P, Q, B, and C calculated above together with the values for a and b defining the period you're interested in, gives you the total accumulated empty seat-miles over that period.

EXERCISES

1. According to the regression model, the volume of empty seat-miles fluctuates by ____ billion seat-miles below the secular line to ____ billion miles above it.
2. Use the observed data to compute the actual accumulated empty seat-miles for 2007 and compare it to the value predicted by the model.
3. **T** Graph the accumulated empty seat-miles from January 2002 to month t as a function of t and use your graph to project when, to the nearest month, the accumulated total will pass 1,900 billion empty seat-miles.
4. Use regression on the original data to obtain a model of the form
$$V(t) = P\sin(\pi t/6) + Q\cos(\pi t/6) + Bt + Cx_1 + Dx_2 + E,$$
where $x_1 = \begin{cases} 1 & \text{if } t = 11, 23, 35, \ldots \\ 0 & \text{if not} \end{cases}$ and $x_2 = \begin{cases} 1 & \text{if } t = 6, 7, 18, 19, \ldots \\ 0 & \text{if not} \end{cases}$
as discussed in the text. Graph the resulting model together with the original data. (Round model coefficients to four significant digits.) (Use two additional columns for the independent variables, one showing the values of x_1 and the other x_2.)
5. Redo the model of the text, but using instead available seat-miles (in billions). For the data, go to the Website and follow Everything for Calculus → Chapter 9 Case Study. Note that the data are in thousands of seat-miles, so you would first need to divide by 1,000,000.

TI-83/84 Plus Technology Guide

Section 9.1

Example 5(a) (page 664) The following data show the daily spam for a 16-week period (each figure is a one-week average):

Week	0	1	2	3	4	5	6	7	8	9	10	11	12	13	14	15
Number	107	163	170	176	167	140	149	137	158	157	185	151	122	132	134	182

Use technology to find the best-fit sine curve of the form $S(t) = A\sin[\omega(t-\alpha)] + C$.

Solution with Technology The TI-83/84 Plus has a built-in sine regression utility.

1. As with the other forms of regression discussed in Chapter 2, we start by entering the coordinates of the data points in the lists L_1 and L_2, as shown below on the left:

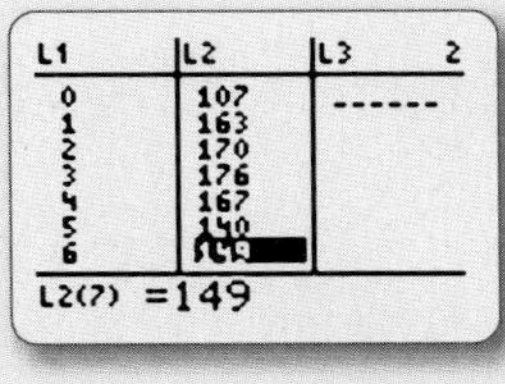

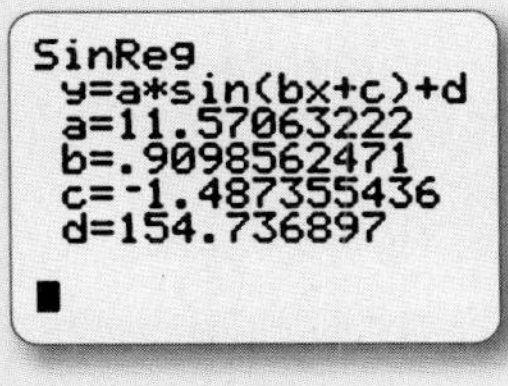

2. Press STAT, select CALC, and choose option #C: `SinReg`.
3. Pressing ENTER gives the sine regression equation in the home screen as seen above right (we have rounded the coefficients):

$$S(t) \approx 11.57\sin(0.9099t - 1.487) + 154.7.$$

Although this is not exactly in the form we want, we can rewrite it:

$$S(t) \approx 11.57\sin\left[0.9099\left(t - \frac{1.487}{0.9099}\right)\right] + 154.7$$
$$\approx 11.6\sin[0.910(t-1.63)] + 155.$$

4. To graph the points and regression line in the same window, turn Stat Plot on by pressing 2nd STAT PLOT, selecting `1`, and turning `Plot1` on, as shown below on the left:

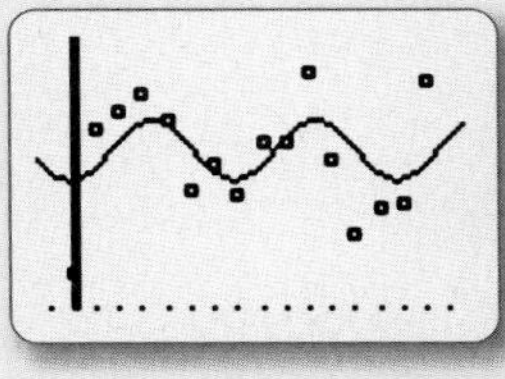

5. Enter the regression equation in the Y= screen by pressing Y=, clearing out whatever function is there, and pressing VARS 5 and selecting `EQ` option #1: `RegEq`.
6. To obtain a convenient window showing all the points and the lines, press ZOOM and choose option #9: `ZoomStat`, and you will obtain the output shown above on the right.

SPREADSHEET Technology Guide

Section 9.1

Example 5(a) (page 664) The following data show the daily spam for a 16-week period (each figure is a one-week average):

Week	0	1	2	3	4	5	6	7	8	9	10	11	12	13	14	15
Number	107	163	170	176	167	140	149	137	158	157	185	151	122	132	134	182

Use technology to find the best-fit sine curve of the form $S(t) = A\sin[\omega(t - \alpha)] + C$.

Solution with Technology We set up our worksheet, shown below, as we did for logistic regression in Section 2.4.

1. For our initial guesses, let us roughly estimate the parameters from the graph. The amplitude is around $A = 30$, and the vertical offset is roughly $C = 150$. The period seems to be around 7 weeks, so let us choose $P = 7$. This gives $\omega = 2\pi/P \approx 0.9$. Finally, let us take $\alpha = 0$ to begin with.

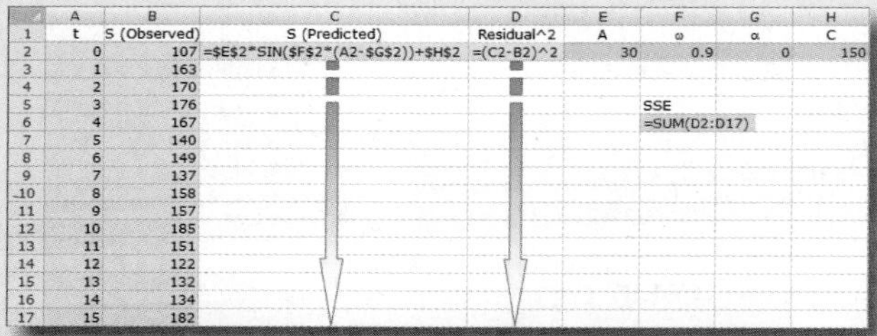

	A	B	C	D	E	F	G	H
1	t	S (Observed)	S (Predicted)	Residual^2	A	ω	α	C
2	0	107	=$E$2*SIN($F$2*(A2-$G$2))+$H$2	=(C2-B2)^2	30	0.9	0	150
3	1	163						
4	2	170						
5	3	176				SSE		
6	4	167				=SUM(D2:D17)		
7	5	140						
8	6	149						
9	7	137						
10	8	158						
11	9	157						
12	10	185						
13	11	151						
14	12	122						
15	13	132						
16	14	134						
17	15	182						

2. We then use Solver to minimize SSE by changing cells E2 through H2 as in Section 2.4 (see the setup below on the left). We obtain the following model (we have rounded the coefficients to three decimal places):

$$S(t) = 25.8\sin[0.96(t - 1.22)] + 153$$

with SSE $\approx$ 2,148. Plotting the observed and predicted values of S gives the graph shown on the right:

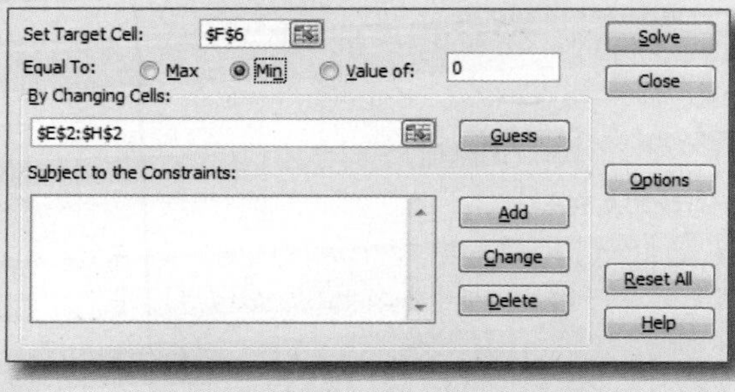

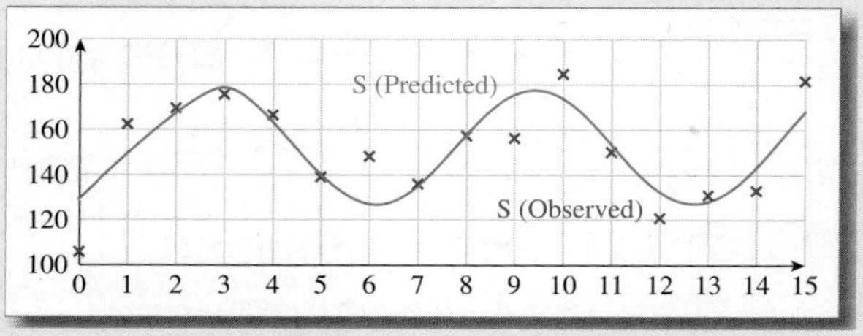

Note that Solver estimated the period for us. However, in many situations, we know what to use for the period beforehand: For example, we expect sales of snow shovels to fluctuate according to an annual cycle. Thus, if we were using regression to fit a regression sine or cosine curve to snow shovel sales data, we would set $P = 1$ year, compute ω, and have Solver estimate only the remaining coefficients: A, C, and α.

Answers to Selected Exercises

Chapter 0

Section 0.1

1. -48 **3.** $2/3$ **5.** -1 **7.** 9 **9.** 1 **11.** 33 **13.** 14 **15.** $5/18$ **17.** 13.31 **19.** 6 **21.** $43/16$ **23.** 0 **25.** `3*(2-5)` **27.** `3/(2-5)` **29.** `(3-1)/(8+6)` **31.** `3-(4+7)/8` **33.** `2/(3+x)-x*y^2` **35.** `3.1x^3-4x^(-2)-60/(x^2-1)` **37.** `(2/3)/5` **39.** `3^(4-5)*6` **41.** `3*(1+4/100)^(-3)` **43.** `3^(2*x-1)+4^x-1` **45.** `2^(2x^2-x+1)` **47.** `4*e^(-2*x)/(2-3e^(-2*x))` or `4(*e^(-2*x))/(2-3e^(-2*x))` **49.** `3(1-(-1/2)^2)^2+1`

Section 0.2

1. 27 **3.** -36 **5.** $4/9$ **7.** $-1/8$ **9.** 16 **11.** 2 **13.** 32 **15.** 2 **17.** x^5 **19.** $-\dfrac{y}{x}$ **21.** $\dfrac{1}{x}$ **23.** x^3y **25.** $\dfrac{z^4}{y^3}$ **27.** $\dfrac{x^6}{y^6}$ **29.** $\dfrac{x^4y^6}{z^4}$ **31.** $\dfrac{3}{x^4}$ **33.** $\dfrac{3}{4x^{2/3}}$ **35.** $1-0.3x^2-\dfrac{6}{5x}$ **37.** 2 **39.** $1/2$ **41.** $4/3$ **43.** $2/5$ **45.** 7 **47.** 5 **49.** -2.668 **51.** $3/2$ **53.** 2 **55.** 2 **57.** ab **59.** $x+9$ **61.** $x\sqrt[3]{a^3+b^3}$ **63.** $\dfrac{2y}{\sqrt{x}}$ **65.** $3^{1/2}$ **67.** $x^{3/2}$ **69.** $(xy^2)^{1/3}$ **71.** $x^{3/2}$ **73.** $\dfrac{3}{5}x^{-2}$ **75.** $\dfrac{3}{2}x^{-1.2}-\dfrac{1}{3}x^{-2.1}$ **77.** $\dfrac{2}{3}x-\dfrac{1}{2}x^{0.1}+\dfrac{4}{3}x^{-1.1}$ **79.** $\dfrac{3}{4}x^{1/2}-\dfrac{5}{3}x^{-1/2}+\dfrac{4}{3}x^{-3/2}$ **81.** $\dfrac{3}{4}x^{2/5}-\dfrac{7}{2}x^{-3/2}$ **83.** $(x^2+1)^{-3}-\dfrac{3}{4}(x^2+1)^{-1/3}$ **85.** $\sqrt[3]{2^2}$ **87.** $\sqrt[3]{x^4}$ **89.** $\sqrt[5]{\sqrt{x}\,\sqrt[3]{y}}$ **91.** $-\dfrac{3}{2\sqrt[4]{x}}$ **93.** $\dfrac{0.2}{\sqrt[3]{x^2}}+\dfrac{3\sqrt{x}}{7}$ **95.** $\dfrac{3}{4\sqrt{(1-x)^5}}$ **97.** 64 **99.** $\sqrt{3}$ **101.** $1/x$ **103.** xy **105.** $\left(\dfrac{y}{x}\right)^{1/3}$ **107.** ±4 **109.** $\pm2/3$ **111.** $-1, -1/3$ **113.** -2 **115.** 16 **117.** ±1 **119.** $33/8$

Section 0.3

1. $4x^2+6x$ **3.** $2xy-y^2$ **5.** x^2-2x-3 **7.** $2y^2+13y+15$ **9.** $4x^2-12x+9$ **11.** x^2+2+1/x^2 **13.** $4x^2-9$ **15.** y^2-1/y^2 **17.** $2x^3+6x^2+2x-4$ **19.** $x^4-4x^3+6x^2-4x+1$ **21.** $y^5+4y^4+4y^3-y$ **23.** $(x+1)(2x+5)$ **25.** $(x^2+1)^5(x+3)^3(x^2+x+4)$ **27.** $-x^3(x^3+1)\sqrt{x+1}$ **29.** $(x+2)\sqrt{(x+1)^3}$ **31. a.** $x(2+3x)$ **b.** $x=0, -2/3$ **33. a.** $2x^2(3x-1)$ **b.** $x=0, 1/3$ **35. a.** $(x-1)(x-7)$ **b.** $x=1, 7$ **37. a.** $(x-3)(x+4)$ **b.** $x=3, -4$ **39. a.** $(2x+1)(x-2)$ **b.** $x=-1/2, 2$ **41. a.** $(2x+3)(3x+2)$ **b.** $x=-3/2, -2/3$ **43. a.** $(3x-2)(4x+3)$ **b.** $x=2/3, -3/4$ **45. a.** $(x+2y)^2$ **b.** $x=-2y$ **47. a.** $(x^2-1)(x^2-4)$ **b.** $x=\pm1, \pm2$

Section 0.4

1. $\dfrac{2x^2-7x-4}{x^2-1}$ **3.** $\dfrac{3x^2-2x+5}{x^2-1}$ **5.** $\dfrac{x^2-x+1}{x+1}$ **7.** $\dfrac{x^2-1}{x}$ **9.** $\dfrac{2x-3}{x^2y}$ **11.** $\dfrac{(x+1)^2}{(x+2)^4}$ **13.** $\dfrac{-1}{\sqrt{(x^2+1)^3}}$ **15.** $\dfrac{-(2x+y)}{x^2(x+y)^2}$

Section 0.5

1. -1 **3.** 5 **5.** $13/4$ **7.** $43/7$ **9.** -1 **11.** $(c-b)/a$ **13.** $x=-4, 1/2$ **15.** No solutions **17.** $\pm\sqrt{\dfrac{5}{2}}$ **19.** -1 **21.** $-1, 3$ **23.** $\dfrac{1\pm\sqrt{5}}{2}$ **25.** 1 **27.** $\pm1, \pm3$ **29.** $\pm\sqrt{\dfrac{-1\pm\sqrt{5}}{2}}$ **31.** $-1, -2, -3$ **33.** -3 **35.** 1 **37.** -2 **39.** $1, \pm\sqrt{5}$ **41.** $\pm1, \pm\dfrac{1}{\sqrt{2}}$ **43.** $-2, -1, 2, 3$

Section 0.6

1. 0, 3 **3.** $\pm\sqrt{2}$ **5.** $-1, -5/2$ **7.** -3 **9.** $0, -1, 1$ **11.** $x=-1$ ($x=-2$ is not a solution.) **13.** $-2, -3/2, -1$ **15.** -1 **17.** $\pm\sqrt[4]{2}$ **19.** ±1 **21.** ±3 **23.** $2/3$ **25.** $-4, -1/4$

Section 0.7

1. $P(0, 2)$, $Q(4, -2)$, $R(-2, 3)$, $S(-3.5, -1.5)$, $T(-2.5, 0)$, $U(2, 2.5)$

3.

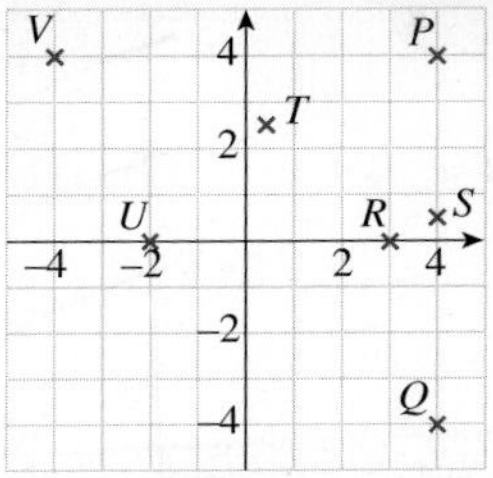

5.

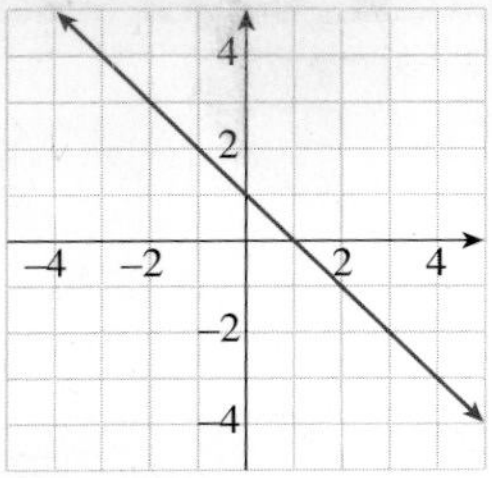

7.

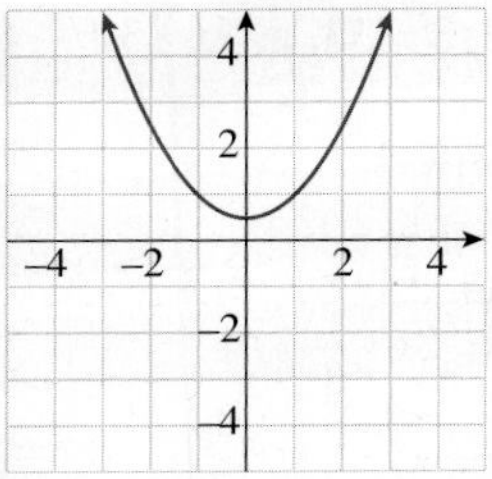

9.

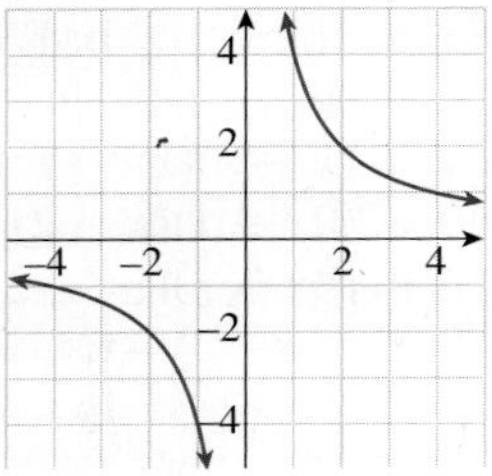

11.

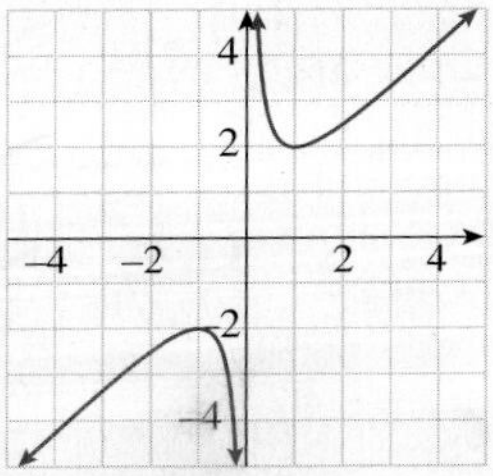

13. $\sqrt{2}$

15. $\sqrt{a^2 + b^2}$

17. 1/2

19. Circle with center (0, 0) and radius 3

Chapter 1

Section 1.1

1. a. 2 **b.** 0.5 **3. a.** −1.5 **b.** 8 **c.** −8 **5. a.** 20 **b.** 30 **c.** 30 **d.** 20 **e.** 0 **7. a.** −1 **b.** 1.25 **c.** 0 **d.** 1 **e.** 1 **9. a.** Yes; $f(4) = 63/16$ **b.** Not defined **c.** Not defined **11. a.** Not defined **b.** Not defined **c.** Yes, $f(-10) = 0$ **13. a.** −7 **b.** −3 **c.** 1 **d.** $4y - 3$ **e.** $4(a + b) - 3$ **15. a.** 3 **b.** 6 **c.** 2 **d.** 6 **e.** $a^2 + 2a + 3$ **f.** $(x + h)^2 + 2(x + h) + 3$ **17. a.** 2 **b.** 0 **c.** 65/4 **d.** $x^2 + 1/x$ **e.** $(s + h)^2 + 1/(s + h)$ **f.** $(s + h)^2 + 1/(s + h) - (s^2 + 1/s)$

19.

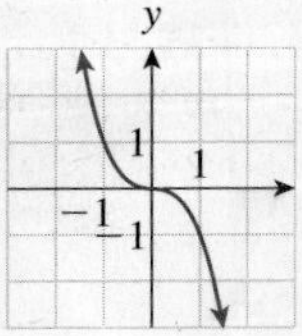

-(x^3)

21.

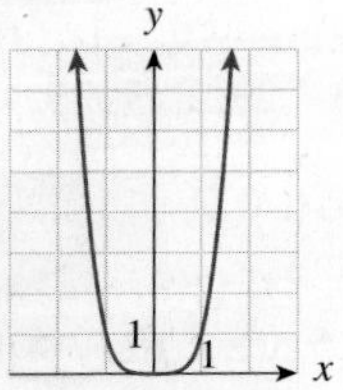

x^4

23.

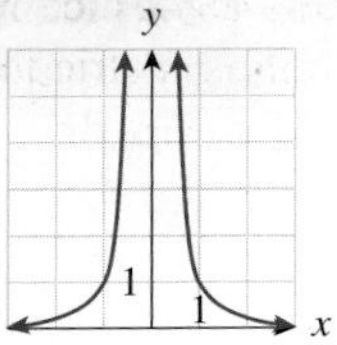

1/x^2

25. a. (I) **b.** (IV) **c.** (V) **d.** (VI) **e.** (III) **f.** (II)

27. 0.1*x^2-4*x+5

x	0	1	2	3
***f*(*x*)**	5	1.1	−2.6	−6.1
x	4	5	6	7
***f*(*x*)**	−9.4	−12.5	−15.4	−18.1
x	8	9	10	
***f*(*x*)**	−20.6	−22.9	−25	

29. (x^2-1)/(x^2+1)

x	0.5	1.5	2.5	3.5
***h*(*x*)**	−0.6000	0.3846	0.7241	0.8491
x	4.5	5.5	6.5	7.5
***h*(*x*)**	0.9059	0.9360	0.9538	0.9651
x	8.5	9.5	10.5	
***h*(*x*)**	0.9727	0.9781	0.9820	

31. a. −1 **b.** 2 **c.** 2

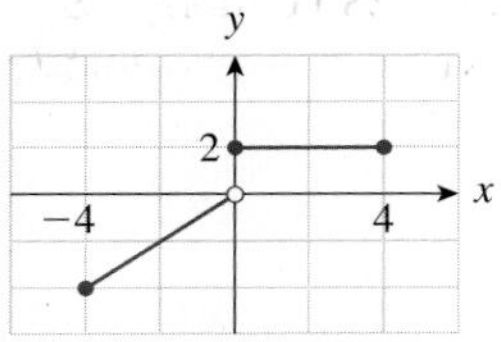

x*(x<0)+2*(x>=0)

33. a. 1 **b.** 0 **c.** 1

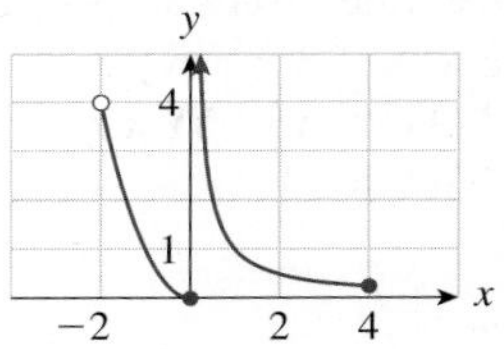

(x^2)*(x<=0)+(1/x)*(0<x)

35. a. 0 **b.** 2 **c.** 3 **d.** 3

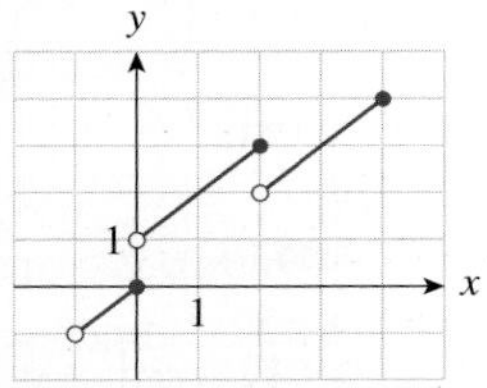

x*(x<=0)+(x+1)*(0<x)*(x<=2)+x*(2<x)

37. a. $h(2x + h)$ **b.** $2x + h$ **39. a.** $-h(2x + h)$ **b.** $-(2x + h)$ **41. a.** $s(1) = 3.8$. In 2006, Pemex sold 3.8 billion metric tons of petrochemicals domestically (i.e., in Mexico). $s(4) = 4.0$. In 2009, Pemex sold

4.0 billion metric tons of petrochemicals domestically. $s(5) = 4.1$. In 2010, Pemex sold 4.1 billion metric tons of petrochemicals domestically. **b.** [0, 5] **c.** Graph:

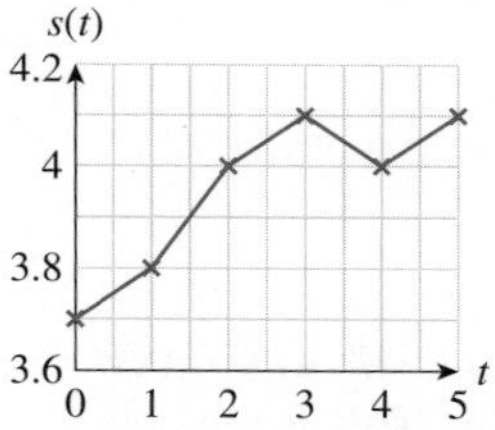

$s(1.5) \approx 3.9$. Pemex sold about 3.9 billion metric tons of petrochemicals domestically in the year ending June 30, 2007. **43.** $f(4) \approx 1{,}600$, $f(5) \approx 1{,}700$, $f(7.5) \approx 800$. There were 1.6 million housing starts in 2004, 1.7 million housing starts in 2005, and 800,000 housing starts in the year beginning July 2007.
45. $f(8) - f(0)$. The change in the number of housing starts from 2000 to 2008 was larger in magnitude than the change from 2000 to 2005.
47. a. $P(0) \approx -100$; $P(4) \approx -400$; $P(1.5) \approx 400$. Continental Airlines lost about \$100 million in 2005, lost about \$400 million in 2009, and made a profit of about \$400 million in the year starting July 1, 2006. **b.** 0; Continental's net income was increasing most rapidly in 2005. **c.** 2.5; Continental's net income was decreasing most rapidly midway through 2007.
49. a. [0, 10]. $t \geq 0$ is not an appropriate domain because it would predict U.S. trade with China into the indefinite future with no basis. **b.** \$280 billion; U.S. trade with China in 2004 was valued at approximately \$280 billion. **51. a.** `100*(1-12200/t^4.48)`
b. Graph:

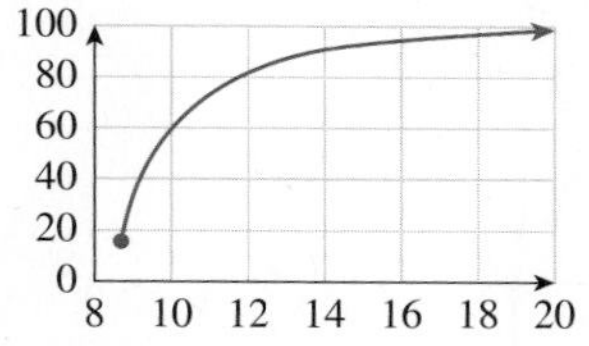

c. Table:

t	9	10	11	12	13	14
p(t)	35.2	59.6	73.6	82.2	87.5	91.1
t	15	16	17	18	19	20
p(t)	93.4	95.1	96.3	97.1	97.7	98.2

d. 82.2% **e.** 14 months
53. a. $v(10) \approx 58$, $v(16) = 200$, $v(28) = 3{,}800$. Processor speeds were about 58 MHz in 1990, 200 MHz in 1996, and 3,800 MHz in 2008.
b. `(8*(1.22)^x)*(x<16)+(400*x-6200)*(x>=16)*(x<25)+3800*(x>=25)`

c. Graph:

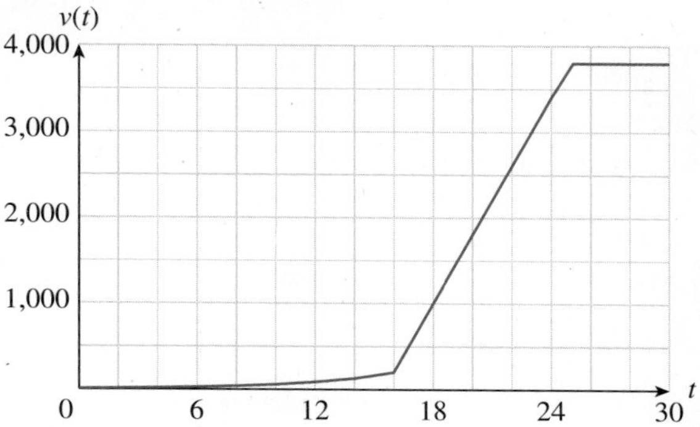

Table:

t	0	2	4	6	8	10
v(t)	8.0	12	18	26	39	58
t	12	14	16	18	20	22
v(t)	87	130	200	1,000	1,800	2,600
t	24	26	28	30		
v(t)	3,400	3,800	3,800	3,800		

d. 2003
55. a.

$$T(x) = \begin{cases} 0.10x & \text{if } 0 < x \leq 8{,}375 \\ 837.50 + 0.15(x - 8{,}375) & \text{if } 8{,}375 < x \leq 34{,}000 \\ 4{,}663.25 + 0.25(x - 34{,}000) & \text{if } 34{,}000 < x \leq 82{,}400 \\ 16{,}763.25 + 0.28(x - 82{,}400) & \text{if } 82{,}400 < x \leq 171{,}850 \\ 41{,}809.25 + 0.33(x - 171{,}850) & \text{if } 171{,}850 < x \leq 373{,}650 \\ 108{,}403.25 + 0.35(x - 373{,}650) & \text{if } 373{,}650 < x \end{cases}$$

b. \$5,163.25 **57.** *t*; *m* **59.** $y(x) = 4x^2 - 2$ (or $f(x) = 4x^2 - 2$) **61.** False. A graph usually gives infinitely many values of the function while a numerical table will give only a finite number of values.
63. False. In a numerically specified function, only certain values of the function are specified so we cannot know its value on every real number in [0, 10], whereas an algebraically specified function would give values for every real number in [0, 10]. **65.** False: Functions with infinitely many points in their domain (such as $f(x) = x^2$) cannot be specified numerically. **67.** As the text reminds us: to evaluate *f* of a quantity (such as $x + h$) replace x everywhere by the *whole quantity* $x + h$, getting $f(x + h) = (x + h)^2 - 1$.
69. They are different portions of the graph of the associated equation $y = f(x)$. **71.** The graph of *g* is the same as the graph of *f*, but shifted 5 units to the right.

Section 1.2

1. a. $s(x) = x^2 + x$ **b.** Domain: All real numbers **c.** 6 **3. a.** $p(x) = (x-1)\sqrt{x+10}$ **b.** Domain: $[-10, 0)$ **c.** -14 **5. a.** $q(x) = \frac{\sqrt{10-x}}{x-1}$ **b.** Domain: $0 \le x \le 10;\ x \ne 1$ **c.** Undefined **7. a.** $m(x) = 5(x^2+1)$ **b.** Domain: All real numbers **c.** 10 **9.** $N(t) = 200 + 10t$ (N = number of music files, t = time in days) **11.** $A(x) = x^2/2$ **13.** $C(x) = 12x$

15. $h(n) = \begin{cases} 4 & \text{if } 1 \le n \le 5 \\ 0 & \text{if } n > 5 \end{cases}$

17. $C(x) = 1{,}500x + 1{,}200$ per day **a.** \$5,700 **b.** \$1,500 **c.** \$1,500 **d.** Variable cost = \$1,500x; Fixed cost = \$1,200; Marginal cost = \$1,500 per piano **e.** Graph:

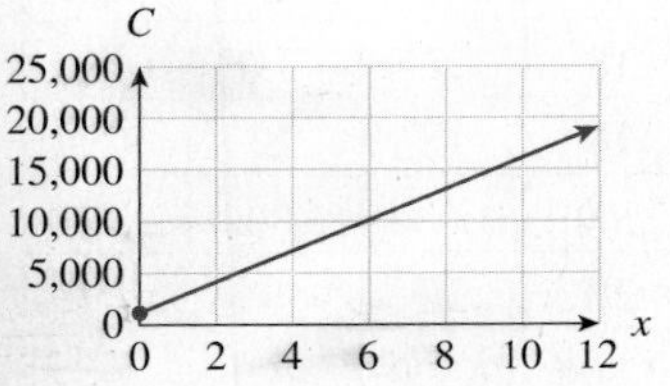

19. a. $C(x) = 0.4x + 70,\ R(x) = 0.5x,\ P(x) = 0.1x - 70$ **b.** $P(500) = -20$; a loss of \$20 **c.** 700 copies **21.** $R(x) = 100x,\ P(x) = -2{,}000 + 90x - 0.2x^2$; at least 24 jerseys. **23.** $P(x) = -1.7 - 0.02x + 0.0001x^2$; approximately 264 thousand square feet **25.** $P(x) = 100x - 5{,}132$, with domain [0, 405]. For profit, $x \ge 52$ **27.** 5,000 units **29.** $FC/(SP - VC)$ **31.** $P(x) = 579.7x - 20{,}000$, with domain $x \ge 0$; $x = 34.50$ g per day for breakeven **33. a.** Graph:

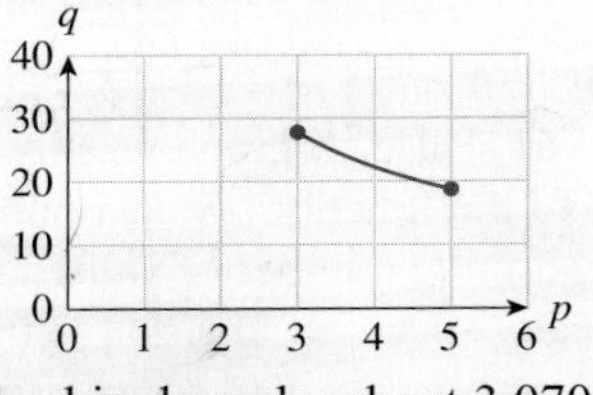

b. Ridership drops by about 3,070 rides per day. **35. a.** Graph:

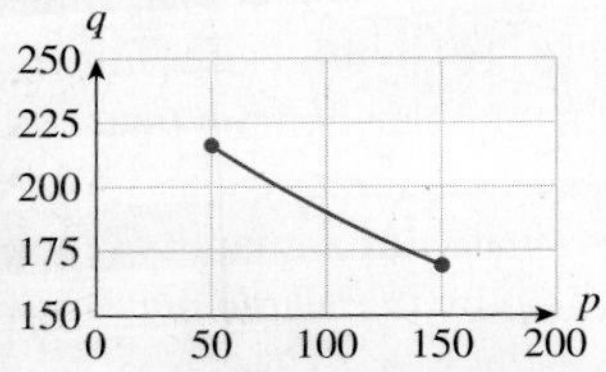

b. 210 million units **c.** 233 million units **d.** $R(p) = 0.0009p^3 - 0.63p^2 + 245p$ million dollars/year; \$13 billion/year **37.** \$240 per skateboard. **39. a.** \$110 per phone. **b.** Shortage of 25 million phones

41. a. \$3.50 per ride. Graph:

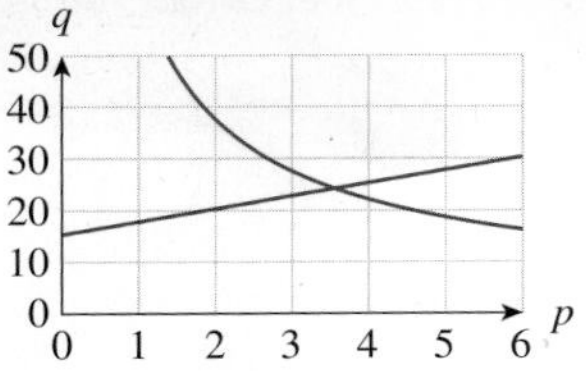

b. A surplus of around 9,170 rides. **43. a.** \$12,000 **b.** $N(q) = 2{,}000 + 100q^2 - 500q$; This is the cost of removing q pounds of PCPs per day after the subsidy is taken into account. **c.** $N(20) = \$32{,}000$; The net cost of removing 20 pounds of PCPs per day is \$32,000. **45. a.** **(B)** **b.** \$36.8 billion **47. a.** **(C)** **b.** \$20.80 per shirt if the team buys 70 shirts Graph:

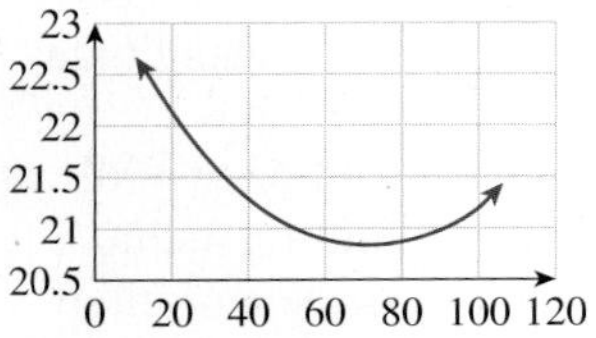

49. a. Graph:

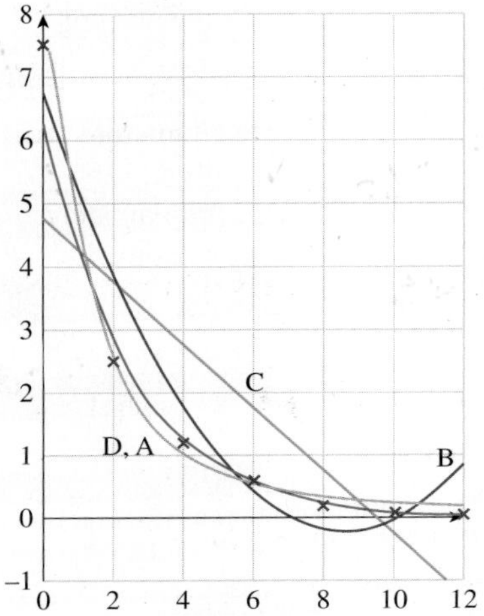

(A), (D) **b.** Model (A); Approximately \$0.0021 **51.** A linear model (A) is the best choice; a plot of the given points gives a straight line. **53.** Model (D) is the best choice; the exponential models predict either perpetually increasing or perpetually decreasing sales, and Model (C) would give a concave-up parabola. **55.** $A(t) = 5{,}000(1 + 0.003/12)^{12t}$; \$5,106 **57.** 2024 **59.** 31.0 grams, 9.25 grams, 2.76 grams **61.** 20,000 years **63. a.** 1,000 years: 65%, 2,000 years: 42%, 3,000 years: 27% **b.** 1,600 years **65.** 30 **67.** Curve fitting. The model is based on fitting a curve to a given set of observed data.

69. The cost of downloading a movie was \$4 in January and is decreasing by 20¢ per month. **71.** Variable; marginal. **73.** Yes, as long as the supply is going up at a faster rate, as illustrated by the following graph:

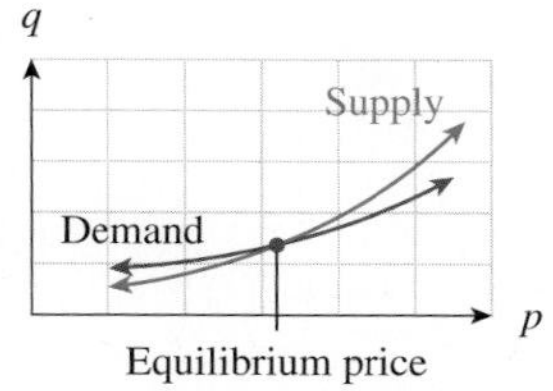

75. Extrapolate both models and choose the one that gives the most reasonable predictions.
77. They are ≥ 0. **79.** Books per person

Section 1.3

1. 11; $m = 3$ **3.** -4; $m = -1$ **5.** 7; $m = 3/2$
7. $f(x) = -x/2 - 2$ **9.** $f(0) = -5$, $f(x) = -x - 5$
11. f is linear: $f(x) = 4x + 6$ **13.** g is linear: $g(x) = 2x - 1$ **15.** $-3/2$ **17.** $1/6$ **19.** Undefined
21. 0 **23.** $-4/3$

25.

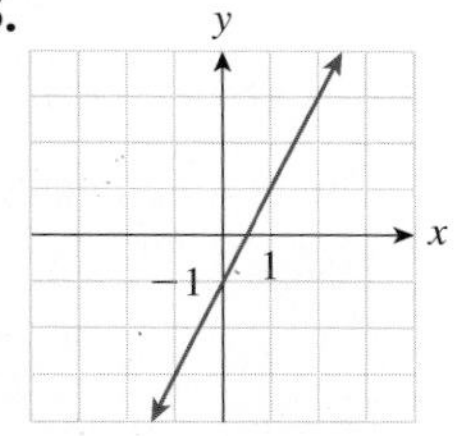

27.

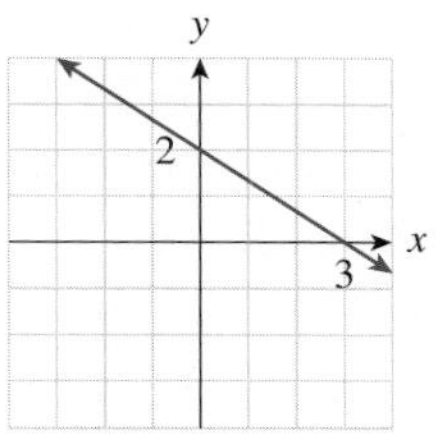

29.

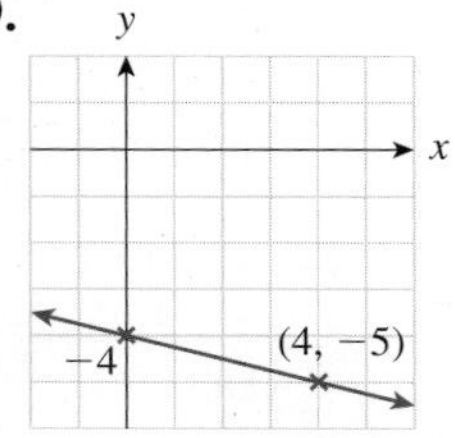

31.

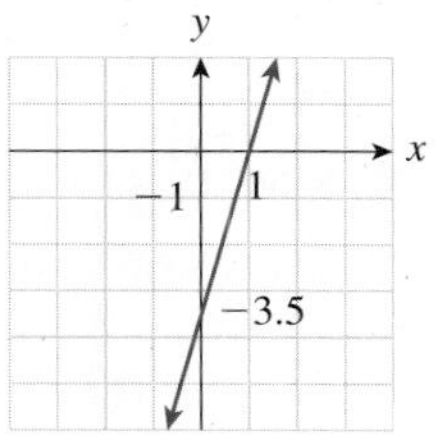

33.

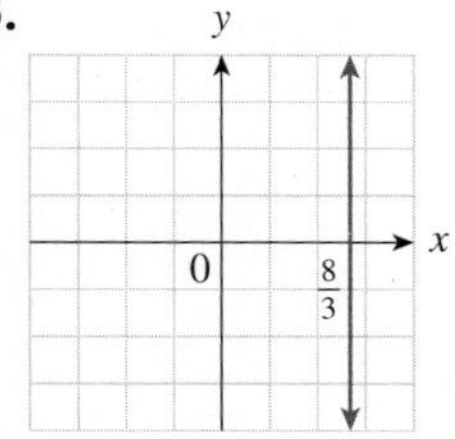

35.

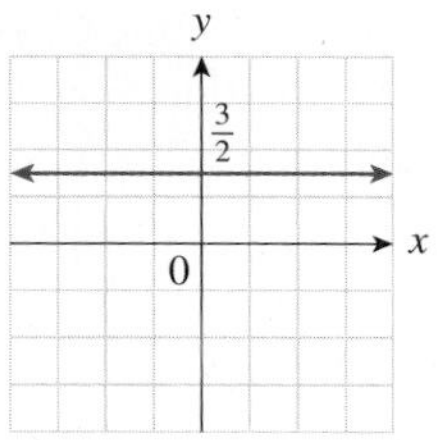

37.

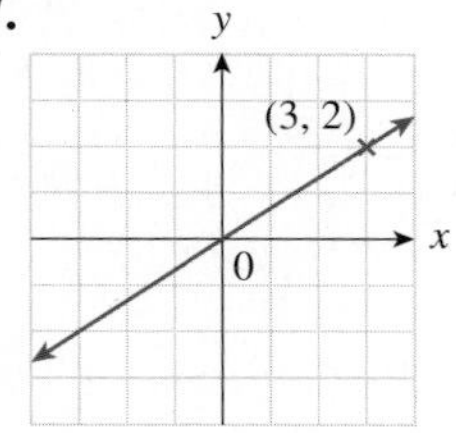

39. 2 **41.** 2 **43.** -2 **45.** Undefined **47.** 1.5
49. -0.09 **51.** $1/2$ **53.** $(d - b)/(c - a)$
55. Undefined **57.** $-b/a$ **59. a.** 1 **b.** $1/2$ **c.** 0
d. 3 **e.** $-1/3$ **f.** -1 **g.** Undefined **h.** $-1/4$ **i.** -2

61. $y = 3x$ **63.** $y = \frac{1}{4}x - 1$

65. $y = 10x - 203.5$ **67.** $y = -5x + 6$
69. $y = -3x + 2.25$ **71.** $y = -x + 12$
73. $y = 2x + 4$ **75.** $y = \frac{q}{p}x$ **77.** $y = q$
79. Fixed cost = \$8,000, marginal cost = \$25 per bicycle **81.** $C = 188x + 20$; \$188 per iPhone; \$7,540
83. $q = -40p + 2{,}000$ **85. a.** $q = -2p + 273$; 123 million phones **b.** \$1; 2 million
87. a. $q = -4{,}500p + 41{,}500$ **b.** Rides/day per \$1 increase in the fare; ridership decreases by 4,500 rides per day for every \$1 increase in the fare.
c. 14,500 rides/day **89. a.** $y = 40t + 290$ million pounds of pasta **b.** 890 million pounds
91. a. $N = 5t - 20$ **b.** Billions of dollars per year; Amazon's net income grew at a rate of \$5 billion per year. **c.** \$20 billion **93. a.** 2.5 ft/sec **b.** 20 feet along the track **c.** after 6 seconds **95. a.** 130 miles per hour **b.** $s = 130t - 1{,}300$ **97. a.** $L = 55n + 475$
b. Pages per edition; *Applied Calculus* is growing at a rate of 55 pages per edition. **c.** 19th edition
99. $F = 1.8C + 32$; 86°F; 72°F; 14°F; 7°F
101. a. $A = 2.4C - 730$ **b.** \$100 million lower than the actual \$450 million net income American earned in 2007 **c.** Millions of dollars of American's net income per million dollars of Continental's net income; American earned an additional net income of \$2.40 per \$1 additional net income earned by Continental.
103. $I(N) = 0.05N + 50{,}000$; $N = \$1{,}000{,}000$; marginal income is $m = 5¢$ per dollar of net profit
105. Increasing at 400 MHz per year
107. a. $y = 31.1t + 78$ **b.** $y = 90t - 1{,}100$

c. $y = \begin{cases} 31.1t + 78 & \text{if } 0 \leq t < 20 \\ 90t - 1{,}100 & \text{if } 20 \leq t \leq 40 \end{cases}$ or

$y = \begin{cases} 31.1t + 78 & \text{if } 0 \leq t \leq 20 \\ 90t - 1{,}100 & \text{if } 20 < t \leq 40 \end{cases}$

d. \$1,960,000, considerably lower than the actual shown on the graph. The actual cost is not linear in the range 1990–2010.

109. $N = \begin{cases} 0.22t + 3 & \text{if } 0 \leq t \leq 5 \\ -0.15t + 4.85 & \text{if } 5 < t \leq 9 \end{cases}$

3.8 million jobs

111. Compute the corresponding successive changes Δx in x and Δy in y, and compute the ratios $\Delta y/\Delta x$. If the answer is always the same number, then the values in the table come from a linear function.

113. $f(x) = -\frac{a}{b}x + \frac{c}{b}$. If $b = 0$, then $\frac{a}{b}$ is undefined, and y cannot be specified as a function of x. (The graph of the resulting equation would be a vertical line.) **115.** slope, 3. **117.** If m is positive, then y will increase as x increases; if m is negative, then y will decrease as x increases; if m is zero, then y will not change as x changes. **119.** The slope increases, because an increase in the y-coordinate of the second point increases Δy while leaving Δx fixed. **121.** Bootlags per zonar; bootlags **123.** It must increase by 10 units each day, including the third. **125.** (B) **127.** It is linear with slope $m + n$. **129.** Answers may vary. For example, $f(x) = x^{1/3}$, $g(x) = x^{2/3}$ **131.** Increasing the number of items from the break-even number results in a profit: Because the slope of the revenue graph is larger than the slope of the cost graph, it is higher than the cost graph to the right of the point of intersection, and hence corresponds to a profit.

Section 1.4

1. 6 **3.** 86 **5. a.** 0.5 (better fit) **b.** 0.75
7. a. 27.42 **b.** 27.16 (better fit)
9. $y = 1.5x - 0.6667$
Graph:

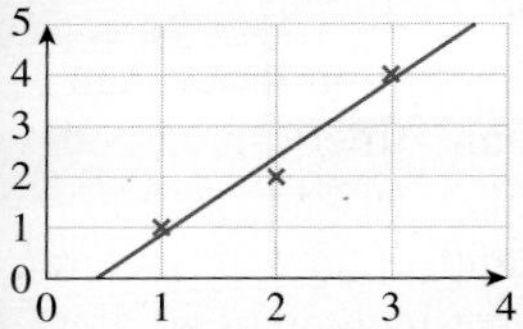

11. $y = 0.7x + 0.85$
Graph:

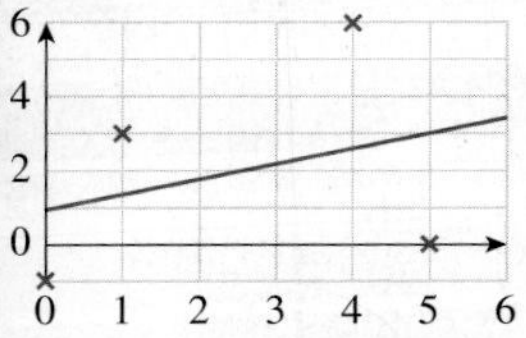

13. a. $r = 0.9959$ (best, not perfect) **b.** $r = 0.9538$
c. $r = 0.3273$ (worst)

15.

x	y	xy	x^2
2	0	0	4
6	70	420	36
10	900	9,000	100
18	970	9,420	140

$y = 112.5x - 351.7$; 998.3 million

17. $y = 3.4t + 5$; \$25.4 billion **19.** $y = 0.135x + 0.15$; 6.9 million jobs **21. a.** $I = 44S - 220$ **b.** Amazon.com earned \$44 million in net income per billion dollars in net sales. **c.** \$28 billion
d. Graph:

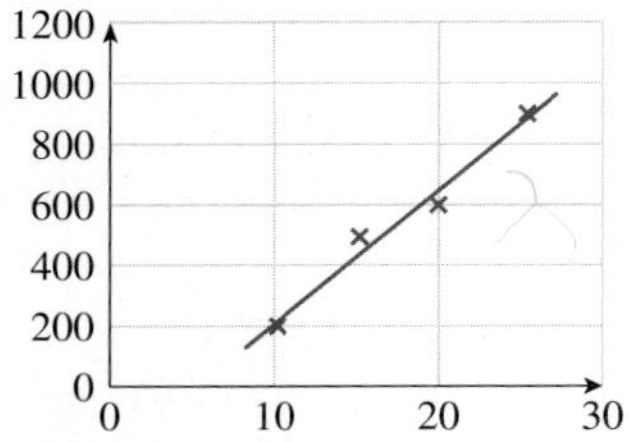

The graph shows a close fit, so the linear model seems reasonable. **23. a.** $L = 52.70n + 486.30$
Graph:

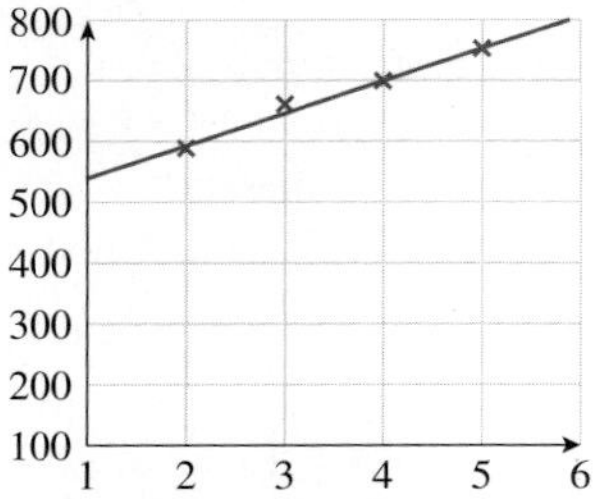

b. *Applied Calculus* is growing at a rate of 52.7 pages per edition. **25. a.** $y = 1.62x - 23.87$.
Graph:

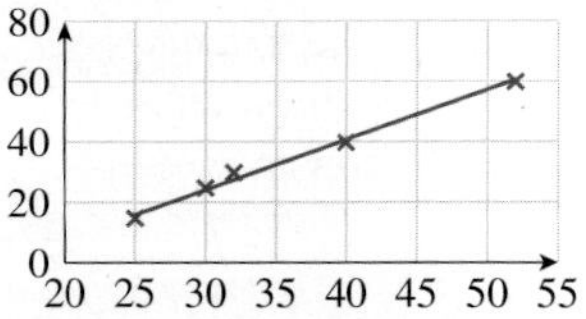

b. Each acre of cultivated land produces about 1.62 tons of soybeans.
27. a. $y = -11.85x + 797.71$; $r \approx -0.414$
b. Continental's net income is not correlated to the price of oil. **c.** The points are nowhere near the regression line, confirming the conclusion in (b).
Graph:

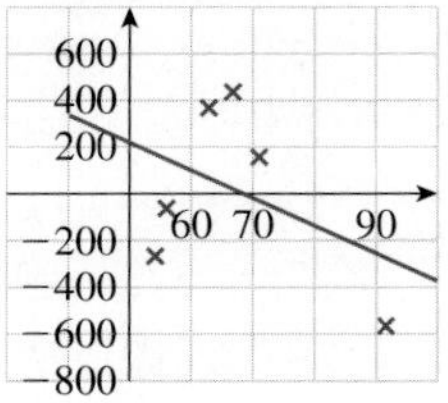

29. a. Regression line: $y = 0.582x + 35.4$ Graph:

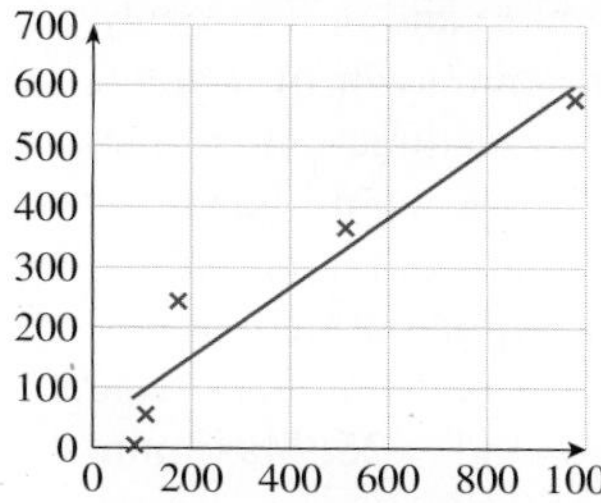

b. There are about 582 additional doctorates in engineering per additional 1,000 doctorates in the natural sciences. **c.** $r \approx 0.949$; a strong correlation. **d.** No, the data points suggest a concave down curve rather than a straight line. **31. a.** $y = 44.0t - 67.8$; $r \approx 0.912$
Graph:

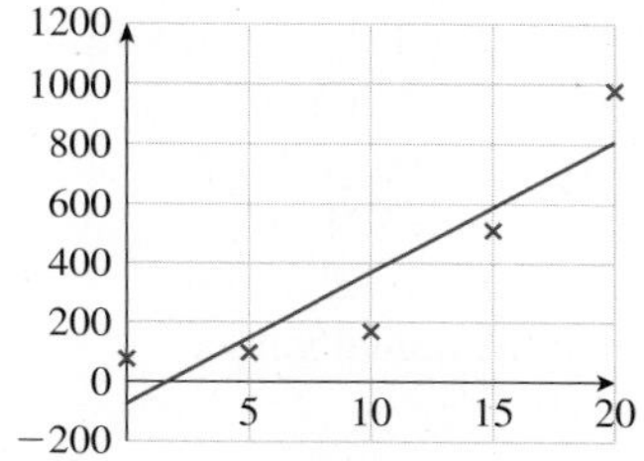

b. The number of natural science doctorates has been increasing at a rate of about 44 per year. **c.** Faster and faster rate; the slopes of successive pairs of points increase as we go from left to right. **d.** No; If r had been equal to 1, then the points would lie exactly on the regression line, which would indicate that the number of doctorates is growing at a constant rate.
33. a. $p = 0.13t + 0.22$; $r \approx 0.97$
Graph:

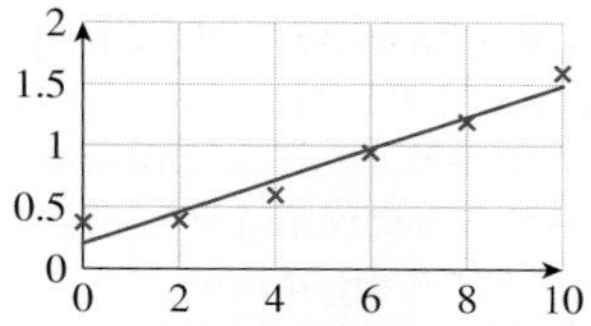

b. Yes; the first and last points lie above the regression line, while the central points lie below it, suggesting a curve.
c.

	A	B	C	D
1	t	p (Observed)	p (predicted)	Residual
2	0	0.38	0.22	0.16
3	2	0.4	0.48	-0.08
4	4	0.6	0.74	-0.14
5	6	0.95	1	-0.05
6	8	1.2	1.26	-0.06
7	10	1.6	1.52	0.08
8				

Notice that the residuals are positive at first, then become negative, and then become positive, confirming the impression from the graph.

35. The line that passes through (a, b) and (c, d) gives a sum-of-squares error SSE $= 0$, which is the smallest value possible. **37.** The regression line is the line passing through the given points. **39.** 0 **41.** No. The regression line through $(-1, 1)$, $(0, 0)$, and $(1, 1)$ passes through none of these points. **43.** (Answers may vary.) The data in Exercise 33 give $r \approx 0.97$, yet the plotted points suggest a curve, not a straight line.

Chapter 1 Review

1. a. 1 **b.** −2 **c.** 0 **d.** −1 **3. a.** 1 **b.** 0 **c.** 0 **d.** −1
5.

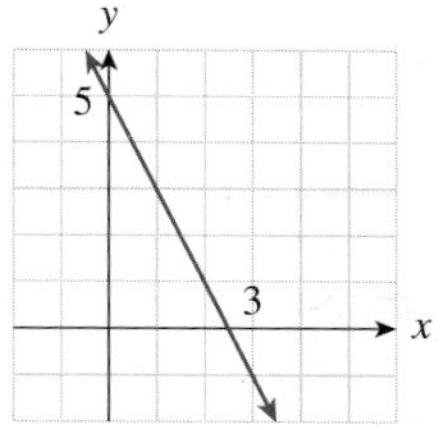

7.

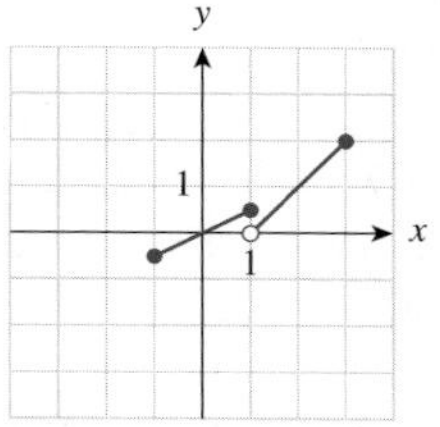

9. Absolute value **11.** Linear **13.** Quadratic
15. $y = -3x + 11$ **17.** $y = 1.25x - 4.25$
19. $y = (1/2)x + 3/2$ **21.** $y = 4x - 12$
23. $y = -x/4 + 1$ **25.** $y = -0.214x + 1.14$, $r \approx -0.33$
27. a. Exponential. Graph:

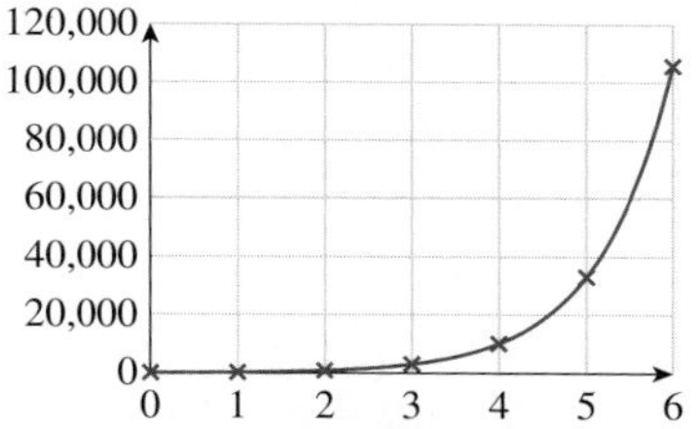

b. The ratios (rounded to 1 decimal place) are:

$V(1)/V(0)$	$V(2)/V(1)$	$V(3)/V(2)$	$V(4)/V(3)$	$V(5)/V(4)$	$V(6)/V(5)$
3	3.3	3.3	3.2	3.2	3.2

They are close to 3.2. **c.** About 343,700 visits/day
29. a. 2.3; 3.5; 6 **b.** For Web site traffic of up to 50,000 visits per day, the number of crashes is increasing by 0.03 per additional thousand visits. **c.** 140,000 **31. a.** (A) **b.** (A) Leveling off (B) Rising (C) Rising; begins to fall after 7 months (D) Rising **33. a.** The number of visits would increase by 30 per day. **b.** No; it would increase at a slower and slower rate and then begin to decrease. **c.** Probably not. This model predicts that Web site popularity will start to decrease as advertising increases beyond \$8,500 per month, and then drop toward zero. **35. a.** $v = 0.05c + 1{,}800$ **b.** 2,150 new visits per day **c.** \$14,000 per month **37.** $d = 0.95w + 8$; 86 kg **39. a.** Cost: $C = 5.5x + 500$; Revenue: $R = 9.5x$; Profit $P = 4x - 500$ **b.** More than 125 albums per week **c.** More than 200 albums per week

41. a. $q = -80p + 1{,}060$ **b.** 100 albums per week **c.** \$9.50, for a weekly profit of \$700
43. a. $q = -74p + 1{,}015.5$ **b.** 239 albums per week

Chapter 2

Section 2.1

1. Vertex: $(-3/2, -1/4)$, y-intercept: 2, x-intercepts: $-2, -1$

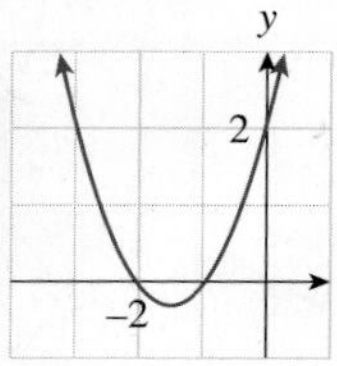

3. Vertex: (2,0), y-intercept: -4, x-intercept: 2

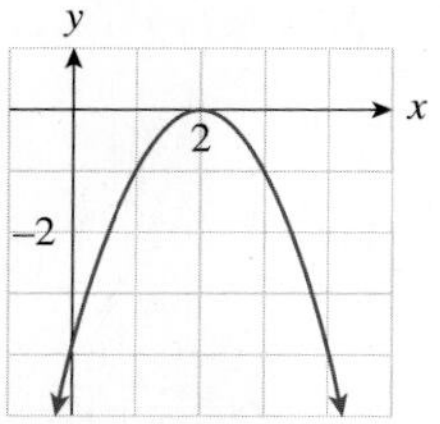

5. Vertex: $(-20, 900)$, y-intercept: 500, x-intercepts: -50, 10

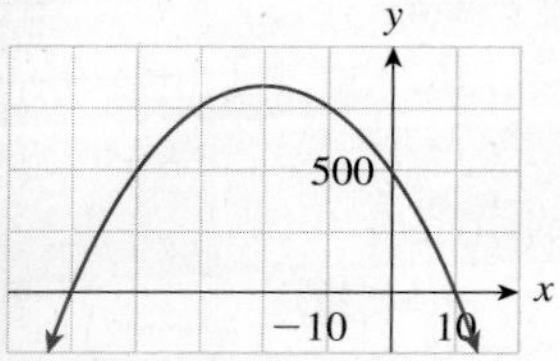

7. Vertex: $(-1/2, -5/4)$, y-intercept: -1, x-intercepts: $-1/2 \pm \sqrt{5}/2$

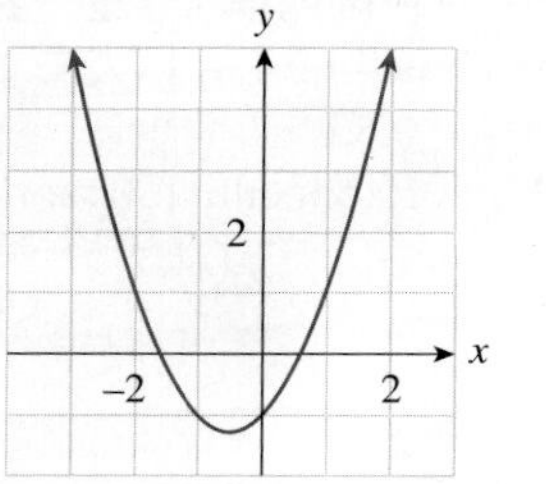

9. Vertex: (0, 1), y-intercept: 1, no x-intercepts

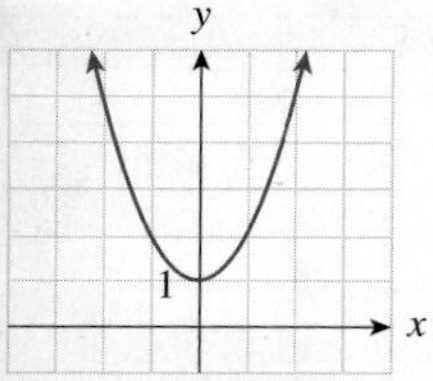

11. $R = -4p^2 + 100p$; Maximum revenue when $p = \$12.50$

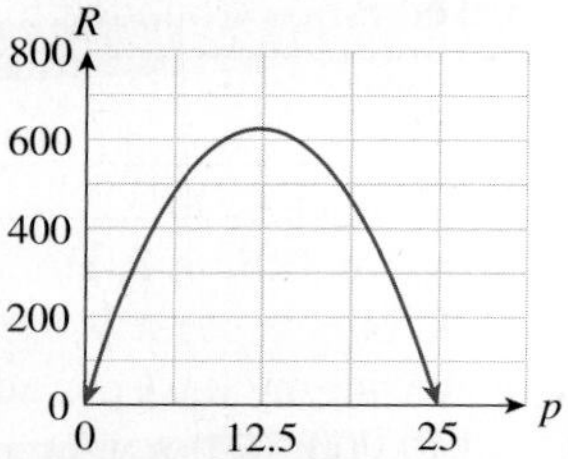

13. $R = -2p^2 + 400p$; Maximum revenue when $p = \$100$

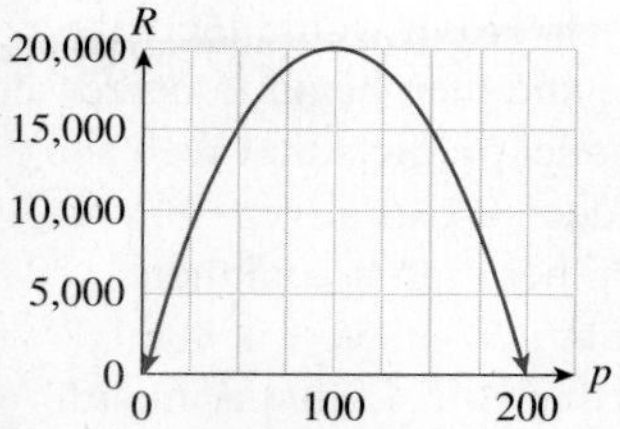

15. $y = -0.7955x^2 + 4.4591x - 1.6000$
17. $y = -1.1667x^2 - 6.1667x - 3.0000$
19. a. Positive because the data suggest a curve that is concave up. **b.** (C) **c.** 1998. Extrapolating in the positive direction leads one to predict more and more steeply rising military expenditure, which may or may not occur; extrapolating in the negative direction predicts continually more an more steeply rising military expenditure as we go back in time, contradicting history. **21.** 2003; about 1.6 million barrels/day
23. 2006; About \$21 billion; No, as the model predicts net income dropping without bound. **25.** Maximum revenue when $p = \$140$, $R = \$9{,}800$
27. Maximum revenue with 70 houses, $R = \$9{,}800{,}000$
29. a. $q = -4{,}500p + 41{,}500$ **b.** \$4.61 for a daily revenue of \$95,680.55 **c.** No
31. a. $q = -560x + 1{,}400$; $R = -560x^2 + 1{,}400x$ **b.** $P = -560x^2 + 1{,}400x - 30$; $x = \$1.25$; $P = \$845$ per month **33.** $C = -200x + 620$; $P = -400x^2 + 1{,}400x - 620$; $x = \$1.75$ per log-on; $P = \$605$ per month **35. a.** $q = -10p + 400$ **b.** $R = -10p^2 + 400p$ **c.** $C = -30p + 4{,}200$ **d.** $P = -10p^2 + 430p - 4{,}200$; $p = \$21.50$
37. $f(t) = 6.25t^2 - 100t + 1{,}200$; \$1,425 billion, which is \$25 billion lower than the actual value.
39. a. $S(t) = 3.0t^2 - 37t + 120$;
Graph:

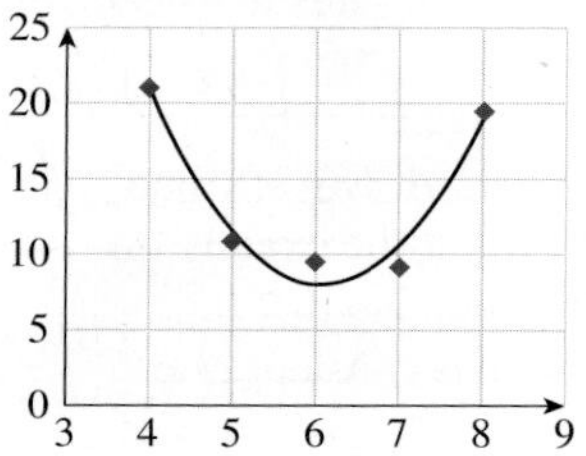

b. 30 million units. If we look at more historical data, we see that iPod sales were highly seasonal, with sales in the last quarter of each year being significantly higher than in other quarters. The model's figure of 30 million units for the first quarter of 2011 is therefore probably much too high. **41.** The graph is a straight line.
43. (C) **45.** Positive; the x coordinate of the vertex is negative, so $-b/(2a)$ must be negative. Because a is positive (the parabola is concave up), this means that b must also be positive to make $-b/(2a)$ negative. **47.** The x-coordinate of the vertex represents the unit price that leads to the maximum revenue, the y-coordinate of the vertex gives the maximum possible revenue, the x-intercepts give the unit prices that result in zero revenue, and the y-intercept gives the revenue resulting from zero unit price (which is obviously zero).
49. Graph the data to see whether the points suggest a curve rather than a straight line. It the curve suggested by the graph is concave up or concave down, then a quadratic model would be a likely candidate.

51. No; the graph of a quadratic function is a parabola. In the case of a concave-up parabola, the curve would unrealistically predict sales increasing without bound in the future. In the case of a concave-down parabola, the curve would predict "negative" sales from some point on. **53.** If $q = mp + b$ (with $m < 0$), then the revenue is given by $R = pq = mp^2 + bp$. This is the equation of a parabola with $a = m < 0$, and so is concave down. Thus, the vertex is the highest point on the parabola, showing that there is a single highest value for R, namely, the y-coordinate of the vertex.
55. Since $R = pq$, the demand must be given by

$$q = \frac{R}{p} = \frac{-50p^2 + 60p}{p} = -50p + 60.$$

Section 2.2

1. `4^x`

x	−3	−2	−1	0	1	2	3
$f(x)$	$\frac{1}{64}$	$\frac{1}{16}$	$\frac{1}{4}$	1	4	16	64

3. `3^(-x)`

x	−3	−2	−1	0	1	2	3
$f(x)$	27	9	3	1	$\frac{1}{3}$	$\frac{1}{9}$	$\frac{1}{27}$

5. `2*2^x or 2*(2^x)`

x	−3	−2	−1	0	1	2	3
$f(x)$	$\frac{1}{4}$	$\frac{1}{2}$	1	2	4	8	16

7. `-3*2^(-x)`

x	−3	−2	−1	0	1	2	3
$f(x)$	−24	−12	−6	−3	$-\frac{3}{2}$	$-\frac{3}{4}$	$-\frac{3}{8}$

9. `2^x-1`

x	−3	−2	−1	0	1	2	3
$f(x)$	$-\frac{7}{8}$	$-\frac{3}{4}$	$-\frac{1}{2}$	0	1	3	7

11. `2^(x-1)`

x	−3	−2	−1	0	1	2	3
$f(x)$	$\frac{1}{16}$	$\frac{1}{8}$	$\frac{1}{4}$	$\frac{1}{2}$	1	2	4

13.

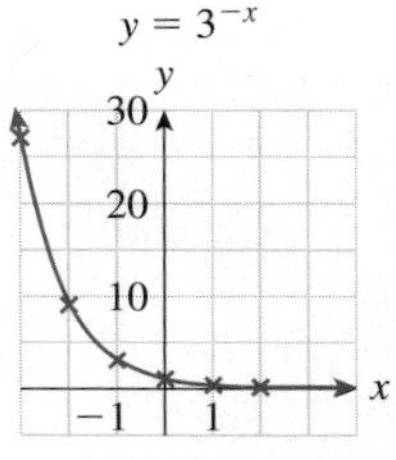

15.

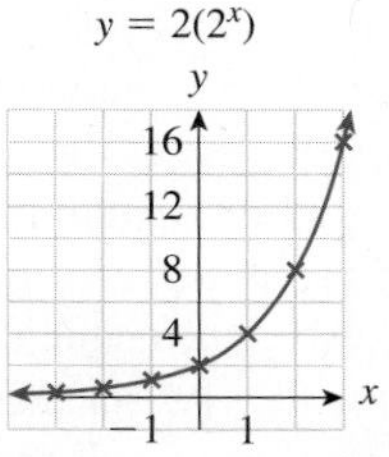

17.

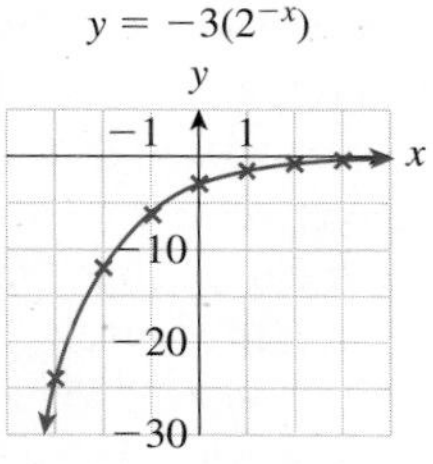

19. Both; $f(x) = 4.5(3^x)$. $g(x) = 2(1/2)^x$, or $2(2^{-x})$
21. Neither **23.** g; $g(x) = 4(0.2)^x$

25. `e^(-2*x)` or `EXP(-2*x)`

x	-3	-2	-1	0	1	2	3
$f(x)$	403.4	54.60	7.389	1	0.1353	0.01832	0.002479

27. `1.01*2.02^(-4*x)`

x	-3	-2	-1	0	1	2	3
$f(x)$	4662	280.0	16.82	1.01	0.06066	0.003643	0.0002188

29. `50*(1+1/3.2)^(2*x)`

x	-3	-2	-1	0	1	2	3
$f(x)$	9.781	16.85	29.02	50	86.13	148.4	255.6

31. `2^(x-1)` *not* `2^x-1` **33.** `2/(1-2^(-4*x))` *not* `2/1-2^-4*x` *and not* `2/1-2^(-4*x)`
35. `(3+x)^(3*x)/(x+1)` or `((3+x)^(3*x))/(x+1)` *not* `(3+x)^(3*x)/x+1` *and not* `(3+x^(3*x))/(x+1)`
37. `2*e^((1+x)/x)` or `2*EXP((1+x)/x)` *not* `2*e^1+x/x` *and not* `2*e^(1+x)/x` *and not* `2*EXP(1+x)/x`

39.

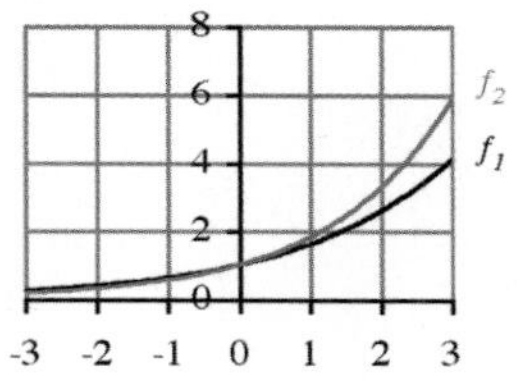

`y1 = 1.6^x   y2 = 1.8^x`

41.

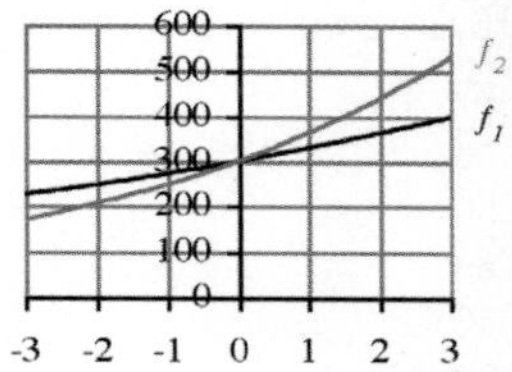

`y1 = 300*1.1^x`
`y2 = 300*1.1^(2*x)`

43.

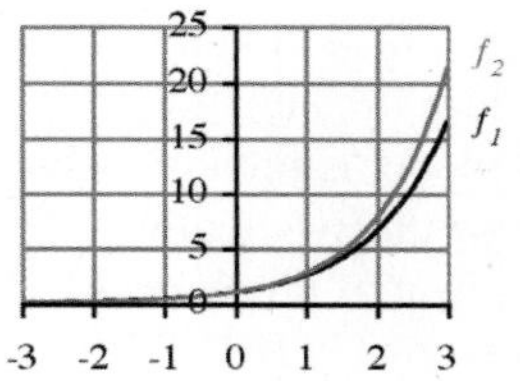

`y1 = 2.5^(1.02*x)`
`y2 = e^(1.02*x)`
`or exp(1.02*x)`

45.

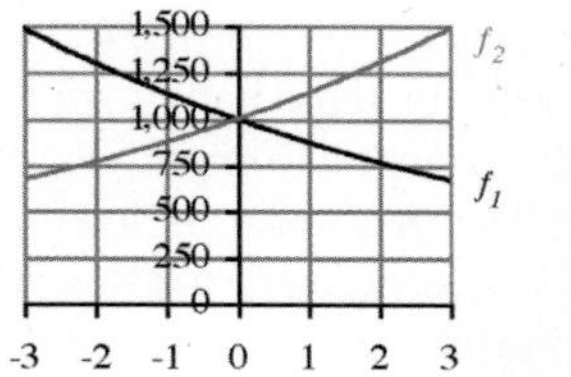

`y1 = 1000*1.045^(-3*x)`
`y2 = 1000*1.045^(3*x)`

47. $f(x) = 500(0.5)^x$ **49.** $f(x) = 10(3)^x$
51. $f(x) = 500(0.45)^x$ **53.** $f(x) = -100(1.1)^x$
55. $y = 4(3^x)$ **57.** $y = -1(0.2^x)$
59. $y = 2.1213(1.4142^x)$ **61.** $y = 3.6742(0.9036^x)$
63. $f(t) = 5{,}000e^{0.10t}$ **65.** $f(t) = 1{,}000e^{-0.063t}$
67. $y = 1.0442(1.7564)^x$ **69.** $y = 15.1735(1.4822)^x$
71. $f(t) = 300(0.5)^t$; 9.375 mg **73. a.** Linear model: $F = 65t - 60$. Exponential model: $F = 97.2(1.20)^t$. The exponential model is more appropriate. **b.** 418 tons, not too far off the projected figure

75. a. $P = 180(1.01087)^t$ million **b.** 6 significant digits **c.** 344 million **77. a.** $y = 50{,}000(1.5^{t/2})$, t = time in years since two years ago **b.** 91,856 tags **79.** $y = 1{,}000(2^{t/3})$; 65,536,000 bacteria after 2 days **81.** $A(t) = 167(1.18)^t$; 1,695 cases **83.** $A(t) = 5{,}000(1 + 0.003/12)^{12t}$; \$5,106 **85.** 2024 **87.** 491.82 **89.** $A(t) = 4.9e^{0.032t}$ million homes; 2010: 5.2 million homes; 2012: 5.6 million homes **91. a.**

Year	1950	2000	2050	2100
$C(t)$ parts per million	355	377	400	425

b. 2030 **93. a.** $P(t) = 0.339(1.169)^t$.
Graph:

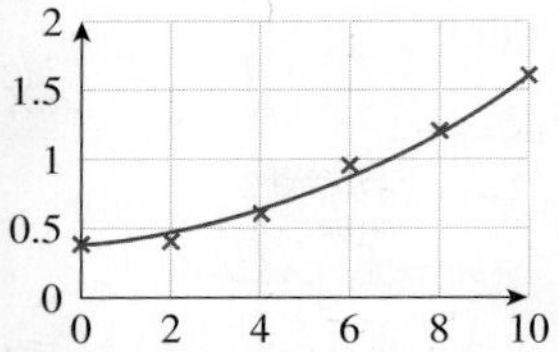

b. \$1.9 million
95. a. $n = 1.127(3.544)^t$
Graph:

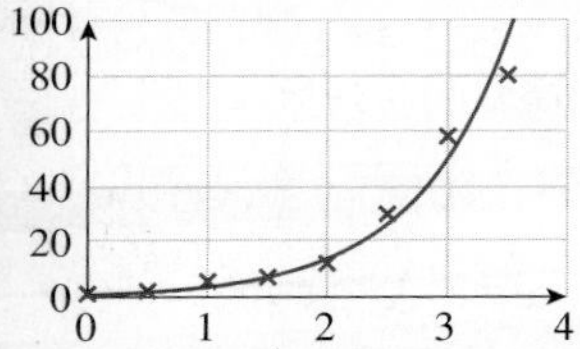

b. 3.544 **c.** 178 million **97.** (B) **99.** Exponential functions of the form $f(x) = Ab^x$ $(b > 1)$ increase rapidly for large values of x. In real-life situations, such as population growth, this model is reliable only for relatively short periods of growth. Eventually, population growth tapers off because of pressures such as limited resources and overcrowding. **101.** The article was published about a year before the "housing bubble" burst in 2006, whereupon house prices started to fall, contrary to the prediction of the graph—they continued to drop for several years, as documented in Exercise 90. This shows the danger of using any mathematical model to extrapolate. The blogger was, however, cautious in the choice of words, claiming only to be estimating what the future U.S. median house price "might be." **103.** Linear functions better: cost models where there is a fixed cost and a variable cost; simple interest, where interest is paid on the original amount invested. Exponential models better: compound interest, population growth. (In both of these, the rate of growth depends on the present number of items, rather than on some fixed quantity.) **105.** Take the ratios y_2/y_1 and y_3/y_2. If they are the same, the points fit on an exponential curve. **107.** This reasoning is suspect—the bank need not use its computer resources to update all the accounts every minute, but can instead use the continuous compounding formula to calculate the balance in any account at any time.

Section 2.3

1.

Logarithmic Form	$\log_{10} 10{,}000 = 4$	$\log_4 16 = 2$	$\log_3 27 = 3$	$\log_5 5 = 1$	$\log_7 1 = 0$	$\log_4 \frac{1}{16} = -2$

3.

Exponential Form	$(0.5)^2 = 0.25$	$5^0 = 1$	$10^{-1} = 0.1$	$4^3 = 64$	$2^8 = 256$	$2^{-2} = \frac{1}{4}$

5. 1.4650 **7.** −1.1460 **9.** −0.7324 **11.** 6.2657
13.

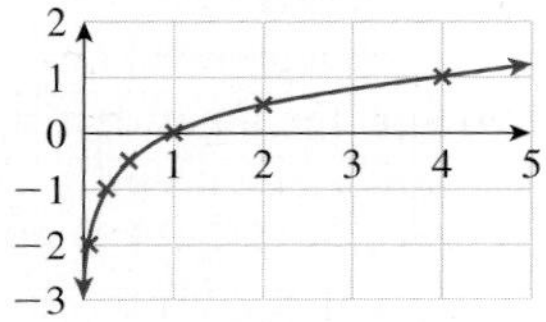

15.

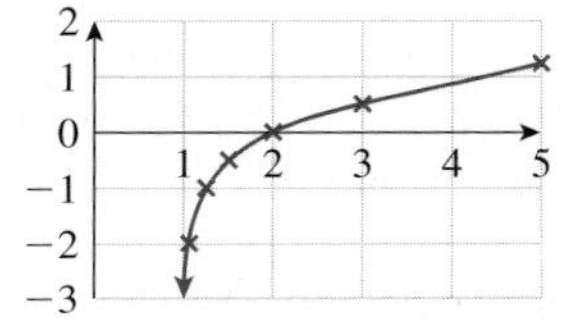

17.

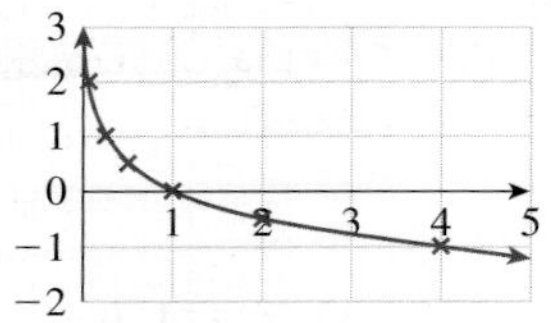

19. $Q = 1{,}000e^{-t\ln 2}$ **21.** $Q = 1{,}000e^{t(\ln 2)/2}$ **23.** Doubling time = 2 ln 2 **25.** Half-life = (ln 2)/4 **27.** $f(x) = 4(7.389)^x$ **29.** $f(t) = 2.1e^{0.000\,9995t}$ **31.** $f(t) = 10e^{-0.01309t}$. **33.** 3.36 years **35.** 11 years **37.** 23.1% **39.** 63,000 years old **41.** 12 years **43.** 238 months **45.** 13 years **47.** 20.39 years **49.** 1,600 years **51. a.** $b = 3^{1/6} \approx 1.20$ **b.** 3.8 months **53. a.** $Q(t) = Q_0e^{-0.139t}$ **b.** 3 years **55.** 2,360 million years **57.** 3.2 hours **59.** 3.89 days **61. a.** $P(t) = 6.591\ln(t) - 17.69$ **b.** 1 digit **c.** (A) **63.** $S(t) = 55.49\ln t + 39.67$
Graph:

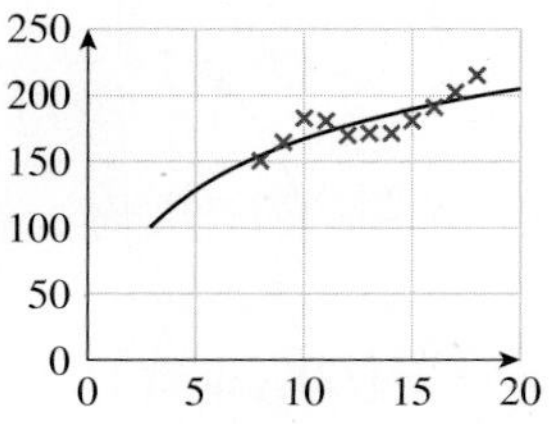

Positive direction; extrapolating in the negative direction eventually leads to negative values, which do not model reality.
65. a. About 4.467×10^{23} ergs **b.** About 2.24% **c.** $E = 10^{1.5R+11.8}$ **d.** Proof **e.** 1,000 **67. a.** 75 dB, 69 dB, 61 dB **b.** $D = 95 - 20\log r$ **c.** 57,000 feet
69. Graph:

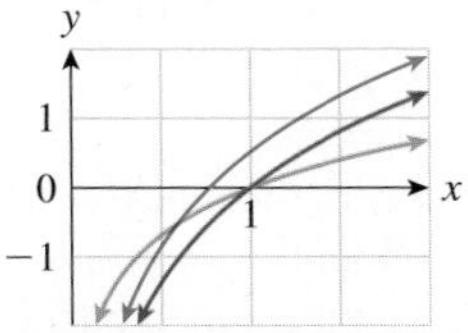

The green curve is $y = \ln x$. The blue curve is $y = 2\ln x$, and the red curve is $y = 2\ln x + 0.5$. Multiplying by A stretches the graph in the y-direction by a factor of A. Adding C moves the graph C units vertically up. **71.** The logarithm of a negative number, were it defined, would be the power to which a base must be raised to give that negative number. But raising a base to a power never results in a negative number, so there can be no such number as the logarithm of a negative number. **73.** Any logarithmic curve $y = \log_b t + C$ will eventually surpass 100%, and hence not be suitable as a long-term predictor of market share. **75.** $\log_4 y$ **77.** 8 **79.** x **81.** Time is increasing logarithmically with population; solving $P = Ab^t$ for t gives $t = \log_b(P/A) = \log_b P - \log_b A$, which is of the form $t = \log_b P + C$. **83.** (Proof)

Section 2.4

1. $N = 7, A = 6, b = 2$;

`7/(1+6*2^-x)`

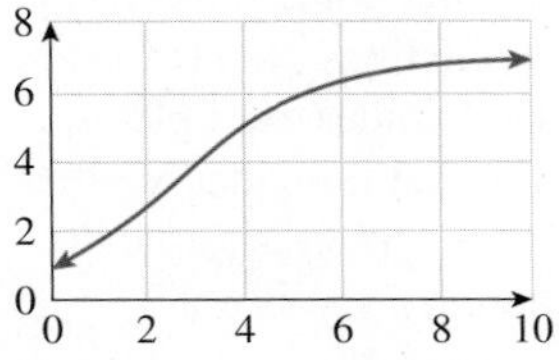

3. $N = 10, A = 4, b = 0.3$;

`10/(1+4*0.3^-x)`

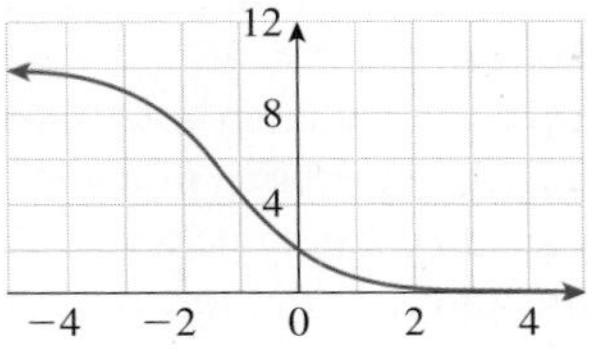

5. $N = 4, A = 7, b = 1.5$;

`4/(1+7*1.5^-x)`

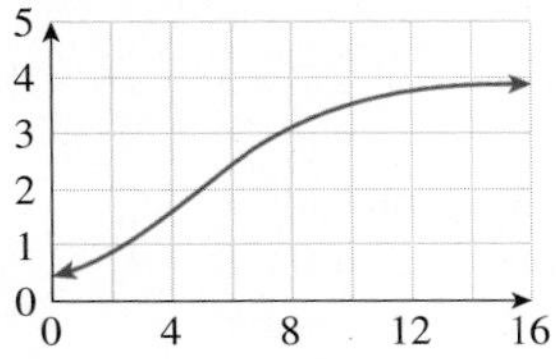

7. $f(x) = \dfrac{200}{1 + 19(2^{-x})}$ **9.** $f(x) = \dfrac{6}{1 + 2^{-x}}$

11. (B) **13.** (B) **15.** (C)

17. $y = \dfrac{7.2}{1 + 2.4(1.04)^{-x}}$

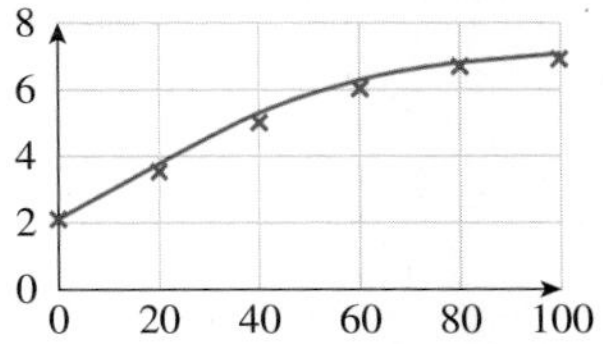

19. $y = \dfrac{97}{1 + 2.2(0.942)^{-x}}$

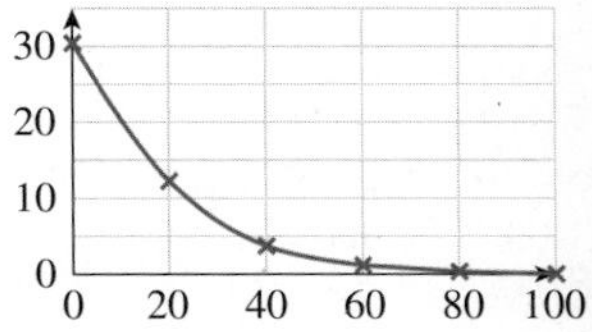

21. a. (A) **b.** 2003 **23. a.** (A) **b.** 20% per year **25. a.** 95.0% **b.** $P(x) \approx 25.13(1.064)^x$ **c.** \$18,000

27. $N(t) = \dfrac{10{,}000}{1 + 9(1.25)^{-t}}$; $N(7) \approx 3{,}463$ cases

29. $N(t) = \dfrac{3{,}000}{1 + 29(2^{1/5})^{-t}}$; $t = 16$ days

31. a. $A(t) = \dfrac{6.3}{1 + 4.8(1.2)^{-t}}$; 6,300 articles **b.** 5,200 articles **33. a.** $B(t) = \dfrac{1{,}090}{1 + 0.410(1.09)^{-t}}$; 1,090 teams **b.** $t \approx -10.3$. According to the model, the number of teams was rising fastest about 10.3 years *prior* to 1990; that is, sometime during 1979. **c.** The number of men's basketball teams was growing by about 9% per year in the past, well before 1979.

35. $y = \dfrac{4{,}500}{1 + 1.1466(1.0357)^{-t}}$; 2013 **37.** Just as diseases are communicated via the spread of a pathogen (such as a virus), new technology is communicated via the spread of information (such as advertising and publicity). Further, just as the spread of a disease is ultimately limited by the number of susceptible individuals, so the spread of a new technology is ultimately limited by the size of the potential market. **39.** It can be used to predict where the sales of a new commodity might level off. **41.** The curve is still a logistic curve, but decreases when $b > 1$ and increases when $b < 1$. **43.** (Proof)

Chapter 2 Review

1.

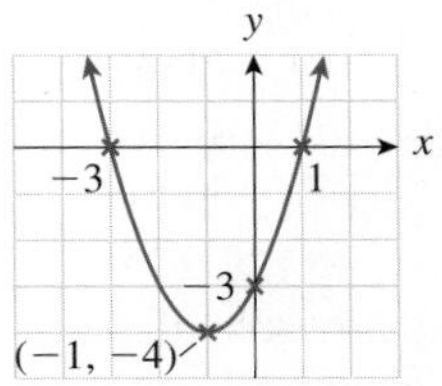

3. f: $f(x) = 5(1/2)^x$, or $5(2^{-x})$

5.

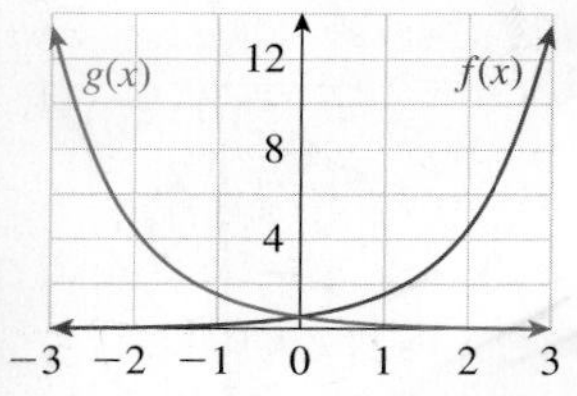

7.

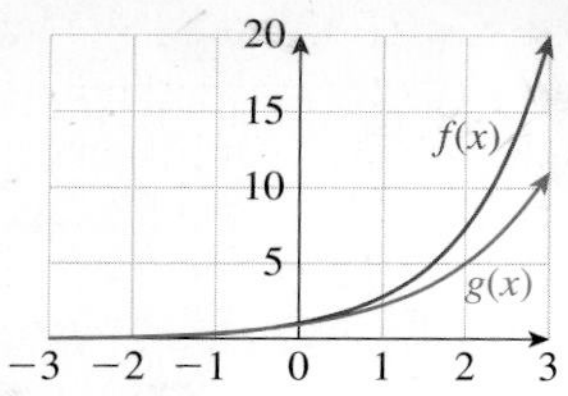

9. \$3,484.85 **11.** \$3,705.48 **13.** \$3,485.50

15. $f(x) = 4.5(9^x)$ **17.** $f(x) = \frac{2}{3}3^x$ **19.** $-\frac{1}{2}\log_3 4$

21. $\frac{1}{3}\log 1.05$

23.

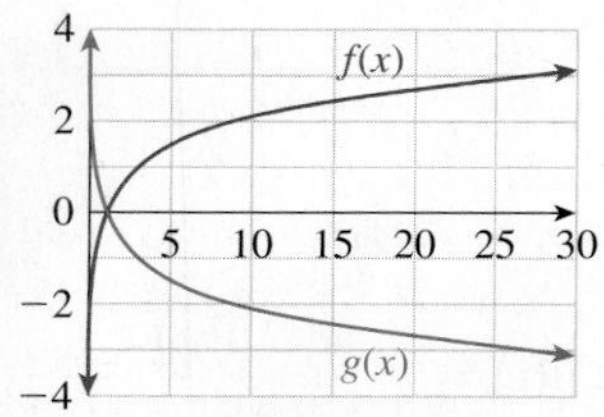

25. $Q = 5e^{-0.00693t}$ **27.** $Q = 2.5e^{0.347t}$
29. 10.2 years **31.** 10.8 years
33. $f(x) = \dfrac{900}{1 + 8(1.5)^{-x}}$

35. $f(x) = \dfrac{20}{1 + 3(0.8)^{-x}}$ **37. a.** \$8,500 per month; an average of approximately 2,100 hits per day **b.** \$29,049 per month **c.** The fact that -0.000005, the coefficient of c^2, is negative.
39. a. $R = -60p^2 + 950p$; $p = \$7.92$ per novel, Monthly revenue = \$3,760.42
b. $P = -60p^2 + 1{,}190p - 4{,}700$; $p = \$9.92$ per novel, Monthly profit = \$1,200.42 **41. a.** 9.1, 19
b. About 310,000 pounds **43.** 2016
45. 1.12 million pounds **47.** $n(t) = 9.6(0.80^t)$ million pounds of lobster **49.** (C)

Chapter 3

Section 3.1

1. 0 **3.** 4 **5.** Does not exist **7.** 1.5 **9.** 0.5
11. Diverges to $+\infty$ **13.** 0 **15.** 1 **17.** 0 **19.** 0
21. a. -2 **b.** -1 **23. a.** 2 **b.** 1 **c.** 0 **d.** $+\infty$
25. a. 0 **b.** 2 **c.** -1 **d.** Does not exist **e.** 2 **f.** $+\infty$
27. a. 1 **b.** 1 **c.** 2 **d.** Does not exist **e.** 1 **f.** 2
29. a. 1 **b.** Does not exist **c.** Does not exist **d.** 1
31. a. 1 **b.** $+\infty$ **c.** $+\infty$ **d.** $+\infty$ **e.** not defined **f.** -1
33. a. -1 **b.** $+\infty$ **c.** $-\infty$ **d.** Does not exist **e.** 2 **f.** 1
35. 210 trillion pesos per month. In the long term, the model predicts that the value of sold goods in Mexico will approach 210 trillion pesos per month. **37.** $+\infty$; In the long term, Amazon's revenue will grow without bound. **39.** 7.0; In the long term, the number of research articles in *Physical Review* written by researchers in Europe approaches 7,000 per year.
41. 573. This suggests that students with an exceptionally large household income earn an average of 573 on the math SAT test. **43. a.** $\lim_{t\to 14.75^-} r(t) = 21$, $\lim_{t\to 14.75^+} r(t) = 21$, $\lim_{t\to 14.75} r(t) = 21$, $r(14.75) = 0.01$ **b.** Just prior to 2:45 pm, the stock was approaching \$21, but then fell suddenly to a penny (\$0.01) at 2:45 exactly, after which time it jumped back to values close to \$21. **45.** 100; In the long term, the home price index will level off at 100 points.
47. $\lim_{t\to 1^-} C(t) = 0.06$, $\lim_{t\to 1^+} C(t) = 0.08$, so $\lim_{t\to 1} C(t)$ does not exist. **49.** $\lim_{t\to +\infty} I(t) = +\infty$, $\lim_{t\to +\infty}(I(t)/E(t)) \approx 2.5$. In the long term, U.S. imports from China will rise without bound and be 2.5 times U.S. exports to China. In the real world, imports and exports cannot rise without bound. Thus, the given models should not be extrapolated far into the future.
51. To approximate $\lim_{x\to a} f(x)$ numerically, choose values of x closer and closer to, and on either side of $x = a$, and evaluate $f(x)$ for each of them. The limit (if it exists) is then the number that these values of $f(x)$ approach. A disadvantage of this method is that it may never give the exact value of the limit, but only an approximation. (However, we can make this as accurate as we like.) **53.** Any situation in which there is a sudden change can be modeled by a function in which $\lim_{t\to a^+} f(t)$ is not the same as $\lim_{t\to a^-} f(t)$. One example is the value of a stock market index before and after a crash: $\lim_{t\to a^-} f(t)$ is the value immediately before the crash at time $t = a$, while $\lim_{t\to a^+} f(t)$ is the value immediately after the crash. Another example might be the price of a commodity that is suddenly increased from one level to another. **55.** It is possible for $\lim_{x\to a} f(x)$ to exist even though $f(a)$ is not defined. An example is $\lim\limits_{x\to 1} \dfrac{x^2 - 3x + 2}{x - 1}$.
57. An example is $f(x) = (x - 1)(x - 2)$.
59. These limits are all 0.

Section 3.2

1. Continuous on its domain **3.** Continuous on its domain **5.** Discontinuous at $x = 0$
7. Discontinuous at $x = -1$ **9.** Continuous on its domain **11.** Continuous on its domain
13. Discontinuous at $x = -1$ and 0 **15.** (A), (B), (D), (E) **17.** 0 **19.** -1 **21.** No value possible
23. -1 **25.** Continuous on its domain

27. Continuous on its domain **29.** Discontinuity at $x = 0$ **31.** Discontinuity at $x = 0$ **33.** Continuous on its domain **35.** Not unless the domain of the function consists of all real numbers. (It is impossible for a function to be continuous at points not in its domain.) For example, $f(x) = 1/x$ is continuous on its domain—the set of nonzero real numbers—but not at $x = 0$. **37.** True. If the graph of a function has a break in its graph at any point a, then it cannot be continuous at the point a. **39.** Answers may vary. $f(x) = 1/[(x-1)(x-2)(x-3)]$ is such a function; it is undefined at $x = 1, 2, 3$ and so its graph consists of three distinct curves. **41.** Answers may vary.

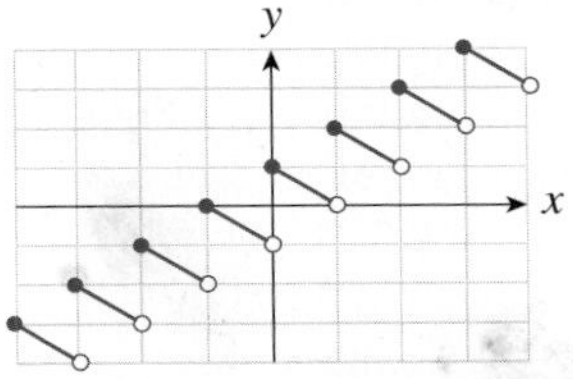

43. Answers may vary. The price of OHaganBooks.com stocks suddenly drops by $10 as news spreads of a government investigation. Let *f*(*x*) = Price of OHaganBooks.com stocks.

Section 3.3

1. $x = 1$ **3.** 2 **5.** Determinate; diverges to $+\infty$ **7.** Determinate; does not exist **9.** Determinate; diverges to $-\infty$ **11.** Determinate; 0 **13.** Indeterminate; $-1/3$ **15.** Indeterminate; 0 **17.** Determinate; 0 **19.** Determinate; -60 **21.** 1 **23.** 2 **25.** 0 **27.** 6 **29.** 4 **31.** 2 **33.** 0 **35.** 0 **37.** 12 **39.** $+\infty$ **41.** Does not exist; left and right (infinite) limits differ. **43.** $-\infty$ **45.** Does not exist **47.** $+\infty$ **49.** 0 **51.** 1/6 **53.** 3/2 **55.** 1/2 **57.** $+\infty$ **59.** 3/2 **61.** 1/2 **63.** $-\infty$ **65.** 0 **67.** 12 **69.** 0 **71.** $+\infty$ **73.** 0 **75.** Discontinuity at $x = 0$ **77.** Continuous everywhere **79.** Discontinuity at $x = 0$ **81.** Discontinuity at $x = 0$ **83. a.** $\lim_{t\to 15^-} v(t) = 3{,}800$, $\lim_{t\to 15^+} v(t) = 3{,}800$; Shortly before 2005 the speed of Intel processors was approaching 3,800 MHz. Shortly after 2005 the speed of Intel processors was close to 3,800 MHz **b.** Continuous at $t = 15$; No abrupt changes. **85. a.** 0.49, 1.16. Shortly before 1999 annual advertising expenditures were close to $0.49 billion. Shortly after 1999 annual advertising expenditures were close to $1.16 billion. **b.** Not continuous; movie advertising expenditures jumped suddenly in 1999. **87.** 1.59; if the trend continued indefinitely, the annual spending on police would be 1.59 times the annual spending on courts in the long run. **89.** 573. This suggests that students with an exceptionally large household income earn an average of 573 on the math SAT test. **91.** $\lim_{t\to+\infty} I(t) = +\infty$, $\lim_{t\to+\infty}(I(t)/E(t)) = 2.5$. In the long term, U.S. imports from China will rise without bound and be 2.5 times U.S. exports to China. In the real world, imports and exports cannot rise without bound. Thus, the given models should not be extrapolated far into the future. **93.** $\lim_{t\to+\infty} p(t) = 100$. The percentage of children who learn to speak approaches 100% as their age increases. **95.** To evaluate $\lim_{x\to a} f(x)$ algebraically, first check whether $f(x)$ is a closed-form function. Then check whether $x = a$ is in its domain. If so, the limit is just $f(a)$; that is, it is obtained by substituting $x = a$. If not, then try to first simplify $f(x)$ in such a way as to transform it into a new function such that $x = a$ is in its domain, and then substitute. A disadvantage of this method is that it is sometimes extremely difficult to evaluate limits algebraically, and rather sophisticated methods are often needed. **97.** $x = 3$ is not in the domain of the given function *f*, so, yes, the *function* is undefined at $x = 3$. However, the *limit* may well be defined. In this case, it leads to the indeterminate form $0/0$, telling us that we need to try to simplify, and that leads us to the correct limit of 27. **99.** She is wrong. Closed-form functions are continuous only at points in their domains, and $x = 2$ is not in the domain of the closed-form function $f(x) = 1/(x-2)^2$. **101.** Answers may vary. (1) See Example 1(b): $\lim_{x\to 2} \frac{x^3 - 8}{x - 2}$, which leads to the indeterminate form $0/0$ but the limit is 12. (2) $\lim_{x\to+\infty} \frac{60x}{2x}$, which leads to the indeterminate form ∞/∞, but where the limit exists and equals 30. **103.** $\pm\infty/\infty$; The limits are zero. This suggests that limits resulting in $\frac{p(\infty)}{e^{\infty}}$ are zero. **105.** The statement may not be true, for instance, if $f(x) = \begin{cases} x+2 & \text{if } x < 0 \\ 2x - 1 & \text{if } x \ge 0 \end{cases}$, then $f(0)$ is defined and equals -1, and yet $\lim_{x\to 0} f(x)$ does not exist. The statement can be corrected by requiring that *f* be a closed-form function: "If *f* is a closed-form function, and $f(a)$ is defined, then $\lim_{x\to a} f(x)$ exists and equals $f(a)$." **107.** Answers may vary, for example

$$f(x) = \begin{cases} 0 & \text{if } x \text{ is any number other than 1 or 2} \\ 1 & \text{if } x = 1 \text{ or } 2 \end{cases}$$

109. Answers may vary.

(1) $\lim_{x\to+\infty} [(x+5) - x] = \lim_{x\to+\infty} 5 = 5$

(2) $\lim_{x\to+\infty} [x^2 - x] = \lim_{x\to+\infty} x(x-1) = +\infty$

(3) $\lim_{x\to+\infty} [(x-5) - x] = \lim_{x\to+\infty} -5 = -5$

Section 3.4

1. −3 **3.** 0.3 **5.** −$25,000 per month **7.** −200 items per dollar **9.** $1.33 per month **11.** 0.75 percentage point increase in unemployment per 1 percentage point increase in the deficit **13.** 4 **15.** 2 **17.** 7/3

19.

h	Ave. Rate of Change
1	2
0.1	0.2
0.01	0.02
0.001	0.002
0.0001	0.0002

21.

h	Ave. Rate of Change
1	−0.1667
0.1	−0.2381
0.01	−0.2488
0.001	−0.2499
0.0001	−0.24999

23.

h	Ave. Rate of Change
1	9
0.1	8.1
0.01	8.01
0.001	8.001
0.0001	8.0001

25. a. $60 billion per year; World military expenditure increased at an average rate of $60 billion per year during 2005–2010. **b.** $50 billion per year; World military expenditure increased at an average rate of $50 billion per year during 2000–2010. **27. a.** −20,000 barrels/year; during 2002–2007, daily oil production by Pemex was decreasing at an average rate of 20,000 barrels of oil per year. **b.** (C) **29. a.** 1.7; the percentage of mortgages classified as subprime was increasing at an average rate of around 1.7 percentage points per year between 2000 and 2006. **b.** 2004–2006
31. a. 2007–2009; During 2007–2009 immigration to Ireland was decreasing at an average rate of 22,500 people per year. **b.** 2008–2010; During 2008–2010 immigration to Ireland was decreasing at an average rate of 7,500 people per year. **33. a.** [3, 5]; −0.25 thousand articles per year. During the period 1993–1995, the number of articles authored by U.S. researchers decreased at an average rate of 250 articles per year. **b.** Percentage rate ≈ −0.1765; Average rate = −0.09 thousand articles/year. Over the period 1993–2003, the number of articles authored by U.S. researchers decreased at an average rate of 90 per year, representing a 17.65% decrease over that period.
35. a. 12 teams per year **b.** Decreased **37. a.** (A) **b.** (C) **c.** (B) **d.** Approximately −$0.088 per year (if we round to two significant digits). This is less than the slope of the regression line, about −$0.063 per year.

39. Answers may vary. Graph:

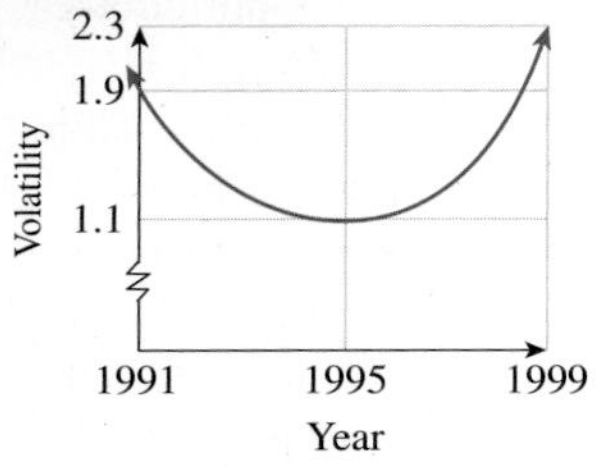

41. The index was increasing at an average rate of 300 points per day. **43. a.** $0.15 per year **b.** No; according to the model, during that 25-year period the price of oil went down from around $93 to a low of around $25 in 1993 before climbing back up.
45. a. 47.3 new cases per day; the number of SARS cases was growing at an average rate of 47.3 new cases per day over the period March 17 to March 23. **b.** (A) **47. a.** 8.85 manatee deaths per 100,000 boats; 23.05 manatee deaths per 100,000 boats **b.** More boats result in more manatee deaths per additional boat. **49. a.** The average rates of change are shown in the following table

Interval	[0, 40]	[40, 80]	[80, 120]	[120, 160]	[160, 200]
Average Rate of Change of *S*	1.35	0.80	0.48	0.28	0.17

b. For household incomes between $40,000 and $80,000, a student's math SAT increases at an average rate of 0.80 points per $1,000 of additional income. **c.** (A) **d.** (B) **51.** The average rate of change of *f* over an interval [*a*, *b*] can be determined numerically, using a table of values, graphically, by measuring the slope of the corresponding line segment through two points on the graph, or algebraically, using an algebraic formula for the function. Of these, the least precise is the graphical method, because it relies on reading coordinates of points on a graph. **53.** No, the formula for the average rate of a function *f* over [*a*, *b*] depends only on $f(a)$ and $f(b)$, and not on any values of *f* between *a* and *b*. **55.** Answers will vary. Graph:

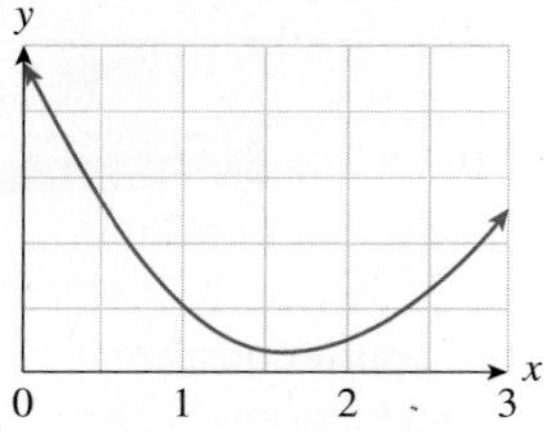

57. 6 units of quantity A per unit of quantity C
59. (A)

61. Yes. Here is an example:

Year	2000	2001	2002	2003
Revenue ($ billion)	$10	$20	$30	$5

63. (A)

Section 3.5

1. 6 **3.** -5.5

5.

h	1	0.1	0.01
Ave. rate	39	39.9	39.99

Instantaneous rate $=$ \$40 per day

7.

h	1	0.1	0.01
Ave. Rate	140	66.2	60.602

Instantaneous rate $=$ \$60 per day

9.

h	10	1
C_{ave}	4.799	4.7999

11.

h	10	1
C_{ave}	99.91	99.90

$C'(1{,}000) = \$4.80$ per item $C'(100) = \$99.90$ per item
13. 1/2 **15.** 0 **17. a.** R **b.** P **19. a.** P **b.** R
21. a. Q **b.** P **23. a.** Q **b.** R **c.** P **25. a.** R
b. Q **c.** P **27. a.** $(1, 0)$ **b.** None **c.** $(-2, 1)$
29. a. $(-2, 0.3)$, $(0, 0)$, $(2, -0.3)$ **b.** None **c.** None
31. $(a, f(a))$; $f'(a)$ **33.** (B) **35. a.** (A) **b.** (C)
c. (B) **d.** (B) **e.** (C) **37.** -2 **39.** -1.5 **41.** -5
43. 16 **45.** 0 **47.** -0.0025

49. a. 3 **b.** $y = 3x + 2$ **51. a.** $\frac{3}{4}$ **b.** $y = \frac{3}{4}x + 1$

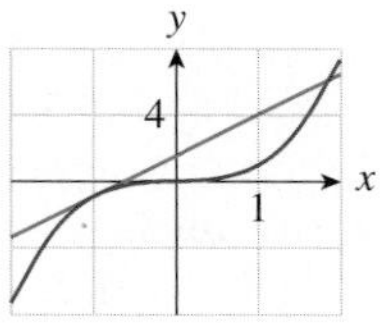

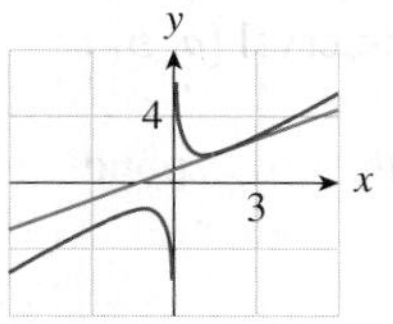

53. a. $\frac{1}{4}$ **b.** $y = \frac{1}{4}x + 1$

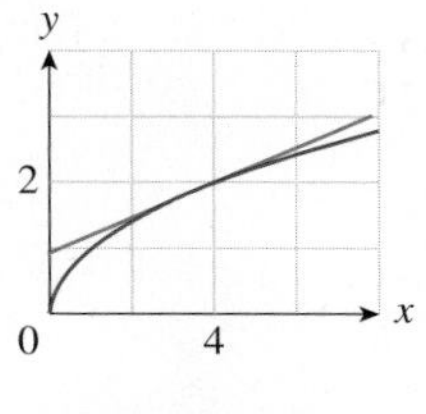

55. 1.000 **57.** 1.000 **59.** (C) **61.** (A) **63.** (F)
65. Increasing for $x < 0$; decreasing for $x > 0$.
67. Increasing for $x < -1$ and $x > 1$; decreasing for $-1 < x < 1$ **69.** Increasing for $x > 1$; decreasing for $x < 1$. **71.** Increasing for $x < 0$; decreasing for $x > 0$.

73. $x = -1.5$, $x = 0$
Graph:

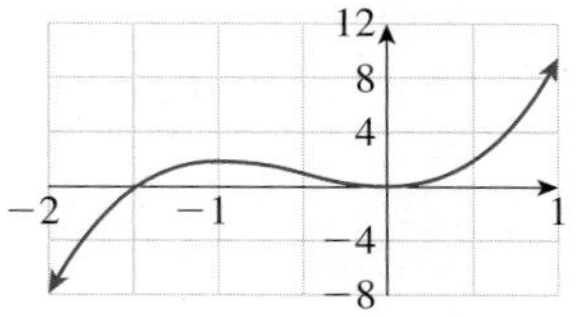

75. Note: Answers depend on the form of technology used. Excel ($h = 0.1$):

	A	B	C	D	E	F
1	x	f(x)	f'(x)	xmin	4	
2	4	6	-4.545454545	h	0.1	
3	4.1	5.545454545	-3.787878788			
4	4.2	5.166666667	-3.205128205			
5	4.3	4.846153846	-2.747252747			
6	4.4	4.571428571	-2.380952381			
7	4.5	4.333333333	-2.083333333			
8	4.6	4.125	-1.838235294			
9	4.7	3.941176471	-1.633986928			
10	4.8	3.777777778	-1.461988304			
11	4.9	3.631578947	-1.315789474			
12	5	3.5				
13						
14						

Graphs:

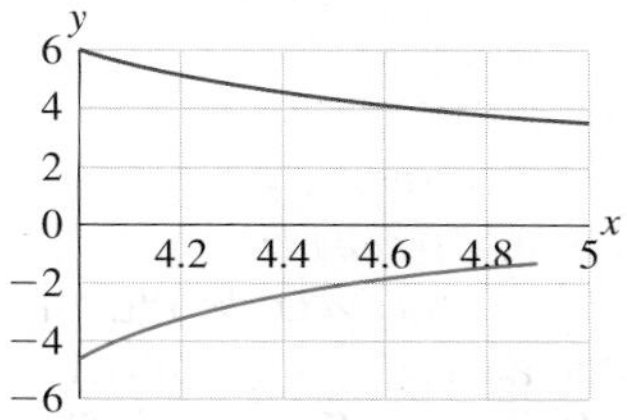

77. $q(100) = 50{,}000$, $q'(100) = -500$. A total of 50,000 pairs of sneakers can be sold at a price of \$100, but the demand is decreasing at a rate of 500 pairs per \$1 increase in the price. **79. a.** -0.05; daily oil imports from Mexico in 2005 were 1.6 million barrels and declining at a rate of 0.05 million barrels (or 50,000 barrels) per year. **b.** Decreasing **81. a.** (B) **b.** (B) **c.** (A) **d.** 2004 **e.** 0.033; in 2004 the U.S. prison population was increasing at a rate of 0.033 million prisoners (33,000 prisoners) per year. **83. a.** -96 ft/sec **b.** -128 ft/sec **85. a.** \$0.60 per year; the price per barrel of crude oil in constant 2008 dollars was growing at an average rate of about 60¢ per year over the 28-year period beginning at the start of 1980.
b. $-\$12$ per year; the price per barrel of crude oil in constant 2008 dollars was dropping at an instantaneous rate of about \$12 per year at the start of 1980.
c. The price of oil was decreasing in January 1980, but eventually began to increase (making the average rate of change in part (a) positive). **87. a.** 144.7 new cases per day; the number of SARS cases was growing at a rate of about 144.7 new cases per day on March 27.
b. (A)

89. $S(5) \approx 109, \left.\frac{dS}{dt}\right|_{t=5} \approx 9.1$. After 5 weeks, sales are 109 pairs of sneakers per week, and sales are increasing at a rate of 9.1 pairs per week each week. **91.** $A(0) = 4.5$ million; $A'(0) = 60{,}000$ subscribers/week **93. a.** 60% of children can speak at the age of 10 months. At the age of 10 months, this percentage is increasing by 18.2 percentage points per month. **b.** As t increases, p approaches 100 percentage points (all children eventually learn to speak), and dp/dt approaches zero because the percentage stops increasing. **95. a.** $A(6) \approx 12.0$; $A'(6) \approx 1.4$; at the start of 2006, about 12% of U.S. mortgages were subprime, and this percentage was increasing at a rate of about 1.4 percentage points per year **b.** Graphs:

Graph of A:

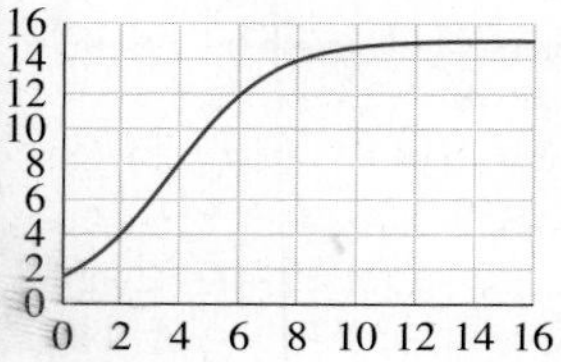

Graph of A':

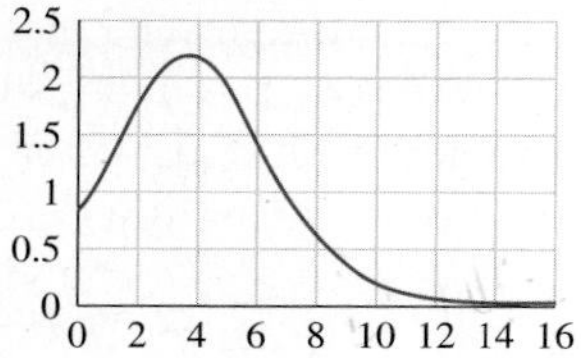

From the graphs, $A(t)$ approaches 15 as t becomes large (in terms of limits, $\lim_{x \to +\infty} A(t) = 15$) and $A'(t)$ approaches 0 as t becomes large (in terms of limits, $\lim_{x \to +\infty} A'(t) = 0$). Interpretation: If the trend modeled by the function A had continued indefinitely, in the long term 15% of U.S. mortgages would have been subprime, and this percentage would not be changing. **97. a.** (D) **b.** 33 days after the egg was laid **c.** 50 days after the egg was laid. Graph:

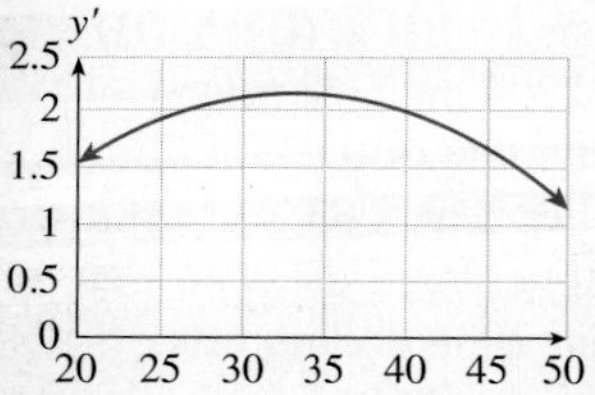

99. $L(.95) \approx 31.2$ meters and $L'(.95) \approx -304.2$ meters/warp. Thus, at a speed of warp 0.95, the spaceship has an observed length of 31.2 meters and its length is decreasing at a rate of 304.2 meters per unit warp, or 3.042 meters per increase in speed of 0.01 warp. **101.** The difference quotient is not defined when $h = 0$ because there is no such number as $0/0$. **103.** (D) **105.** The derivative is positive and decreasing toward zero. **107.** Company B. Although the company is currently losing money, the derivative is positive, showing that the profit is increasing. Company A, on the other hand, has profits that are declining. **109.** (C) is the only graph in which the instantaneous rate of change on January 1 is greater than the one-month average rate of change. **111.** The tangent to the graph is horizontal at that point, and so the graph is almost horizontal near that point. **113.** Answers may vary.

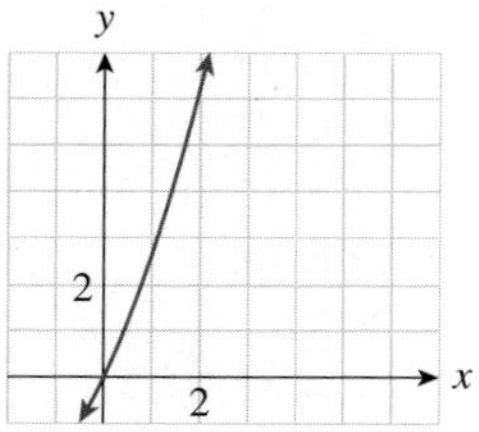

115. If $f(x) = mx + b$, then its average rate of change over any interval $[x, x + h]$ is $\frac{m(x + h) + b - (mx + b)}{h} = m$. Because this does not depend on h, the instantaneous rate is also equal to m. **117.** Increasing because the average rate of change appears to be rising as we get closer to 5 from the left. (See the bottom row.) **119.** Answers may vary.

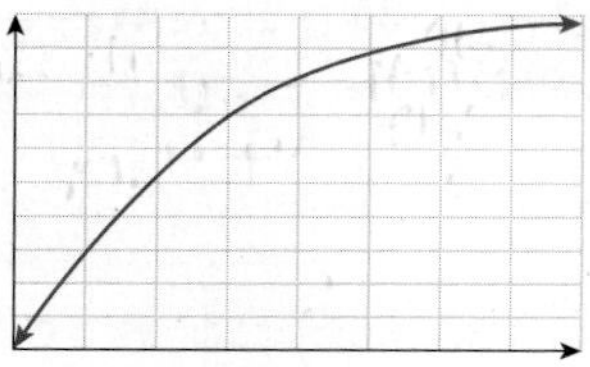

121. Answers may vary.

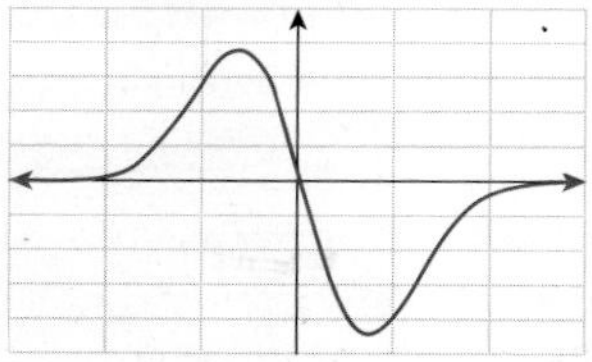

123. (B) **125.** Answers will vary.

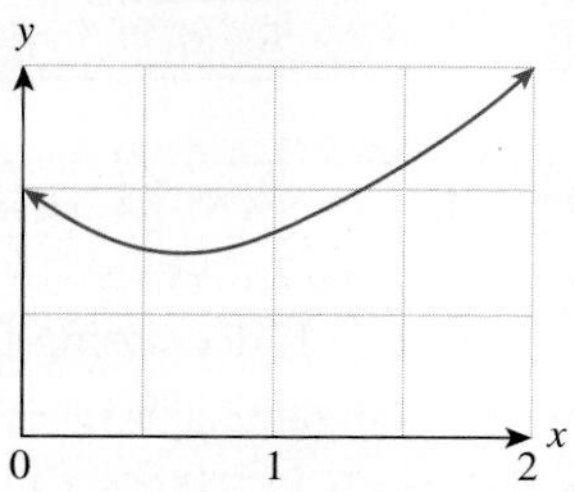

Section 3.6

1. 4 **3.** 3 **5.** 7 **7.** 4 **9.** 14 **11.** 1 **13.** m **15.** $2x$ **17.** 3 **19.** $6x+1$ **21.** $2-2x$ **23.** $3x^2+2$ **25.** $1/x^2$ **27.** m **29.** -1.2 **31.** 30.6 **33.** -7.1 **35.** 4.25 **37.** -0.6 **39.** $y=4x-7$ **41.** $y=-2x-4$ **43.** $y=-3x-1$ **45.** $s'(t)=-32t$; $s'(4)=-128$ ft/sec **47.** $dI/dt=-0.030t+0.1$; daily oil imports were decreasing at a rate of 0.11 million barrels per year. **49.** $R'(t)=-90t+900$; Increasing at a rate of 450 million gallons per year **51.** $f'(8)=26.6$ manatee deaths per 100,000 boats. At a level of 800,000 boats, the number of manatee deaths is increasing at a rate of 26.6 manatees per 100,000 additional boats. **53.** Yes; $\lim_{t\to 20^-} C(t) = \lim_{t\to 20^+} C(t) = 700 = C(20)$. **b.** No; $\lim_{t\to 20^-} C'(t) = 31.1$ while $\lim_{t\to 20^+} C'(t) = 90$. Until 1990, the cost of a Super Bowl ad was increasing at a rate of \$31,100 per year. Immediately thereafter, it was increasing at a rate of \$90,000 per year. **55.** The algebraic method because it gives the exact value of the derivative. The other two approaches give only approximate values (except in some special cases). **57.** The error is in the second line: $f(x+h)$ is *not* equal to $f(x)+h$. For instance, if $f(x)=x^2$, then $f(x+h)=(x+h)^2$, whereas $f(x)+h=x^2+h$. **59.** The error is in the second line: One could only cancel the h if it were a *factor* of both the numerator and denominator; it is not a factor of the numerator. **61.** Because the algebraic computation of $f'(a)$ is exact and not an approximation, it makes no difference whether one uses the balanced difference quotient or the ordinary difference quotient in the algebraic computation. **63.** The computation results in a limit that cannot be evaluated.

Chapter 3 Review

1. 5 **3.** Does not exist **5. a.** -1 **b.** 3 **c.** Does not exist **7.** $-4/5$ **9.** -1 **11.** -1 **13.** Does not exist **15.** $10/7$ **17.** Does not exist **19.** $+\infty$ **21.** 0 **23.** Diverges to $-\infty$ **25.** 0 **27.** 2/5 **29.** 1

31.

h	1	0.01	0.001
Ave. Rate of Change	-0.5	-0.9901	-0.9990

Slope ≈ -1

33.

h	1	0.01	0.001
Avg. Rate of Change	6.3891	2.0201	2.0020

Slope ≈ 2

35. a. P **b.** Q **c.** R **d.** S **37. a.** Q **b.** None **c.** None **d.** None **39. a.** (B) **b.** (B) **c.** (B) **d.** (A) **e.** (C) **41.** $2x+1$ **43.** $2/x^2$

45.

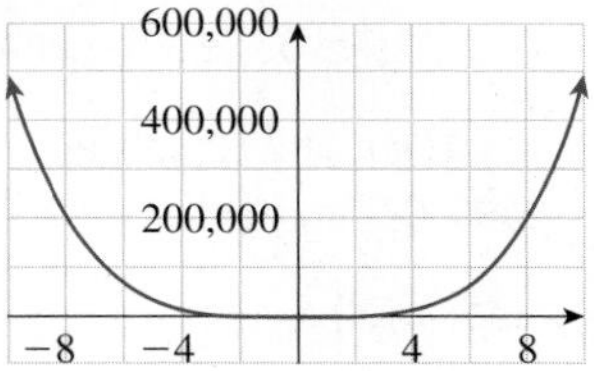

47.

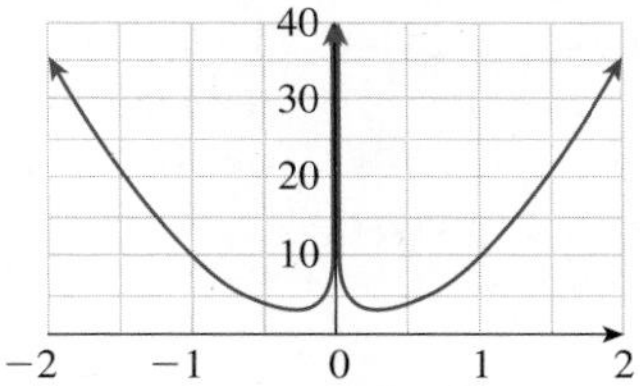

49. a. $P(3)=25$: O'Hagan purchased the stock at \$25. $\lim_{t\to 3^-} P(t) = 25$: The value of the stock had been approaching \$25 up to the time he bought it. $\lim_{t\to 3^+} P(t)=10$: The value of the stock dropped to \$10 immediately after he bought it. **b.** Continuous but not differentiable. Interpretation: the stock price changed continuously but suddenly reversed direction (and started to go up) the instant O'Hagan sold it. **51. a.** $\lim_{t\to 3} p(t) \approx 40$; $\lim_{t\to +\infty} p(t) = +\infty$. Close to 2007 ($t=3$), the home price index was about 40. In the long term, the home price index will rise without bound. **b.** 10 (The slope of the linear portion of the curve is 10.) In the long term, the home price index will rise about 10 points per year. **53. a.** 500 books per week **b.** [3, 4], [4, 5] **c.** [3, 5]; 650 books per week **55. a.** 3 percentage points per year **b.** 0 percentage points per year **c.** (D) **57. a.** $72t+250$ **b.** 322 books per week **c.** 754 books per week.

Chapter 4

Section 4.1

1. $5x^4$ **3.** $-4x^{-3}$ **5.** $-0.25x^{-0.75}$ **7.** $8x^3+9x^2$ **9.** $-1-1/x^2$ **11.** $\frac{dy}{dx}=10(0)=0$ (constant multiple and power rule) **13.** $\frac{dy}{dx}=\frac{d}{dx}(x^2)+\frac{d}{dx}(x)$ (sum rule) $=2x+1$ (power rule) **15.** $\frac{dy}{dx}=\frac{d}{dx}(4x^3)+\frac{d}{dx}(2x)-\frac{d}{dx}(1)$ (sum and difference) $=4\frac{d}{dx}(x^3)+2\frac{d}{dx}(x)-\frac{d}{dx}(1)$ (constant multiples) $=12x^2+2$ (power rule) **17.** $f'(x)=2x-3$ **19.** $f'(x)=1+0.5x^{-0.5}$ **21.** $g'(x)=-2x^{-3}+3x^{-2}$ **23.** $g'(x)=-\frac{1}{x^2}+\frac{2}{x^3}$ **25.** $h'(x)=-\frac{0.8}{x^{1.4}}$ **27.** $h'(x)=-\frac{2}{x^3}-\frac{6}{x^4}$

29. $r'(x) = -\dfrac{2}{3x^2} + \dfrac{0.1}{2x^{1.1}}$

31. $r'(x) = \dfrac{2}{3} - \dfrac{0.1}{2x^{0.9}} - \dfrac{4.4}{3x^{2.1}}$

33. $t'(x) = |x|/x - 1/x^2$ **35.** $s'(x) = \dfrac{1}{2\sqrt{x}} - \dfrac{1}{2x\sqrt{x}}$

37. $s'(x) = 3x^2$ **39.** $t'(x) = 1 - 4x$

41. $2.6x^{0.3} + 1.2x^{-2.2}$ **43.** $1.2(1 - |x|/x)$

45. $3at^2 - 4a$ **47.** $5.15x^{9.3} - 99x^{-2}$

49. $-\dfrac{2.31}{t^{2.1}} - \dfrac{0.3}{t^{0.4}}$ **51.** $4\pi r^2$ **53.** 3 **55.** −2 **57.** −5

59. $y = 3x + 2$

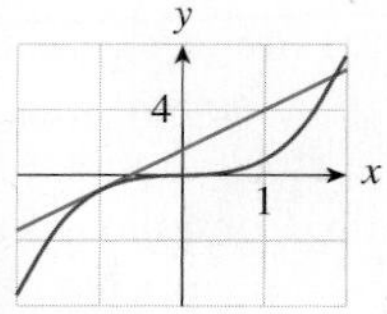

61. $y = \dfrac{3}{4}x + 1$

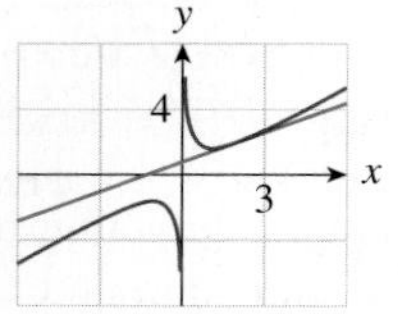

63. $y = \dfrac{1}{4}x + 1$

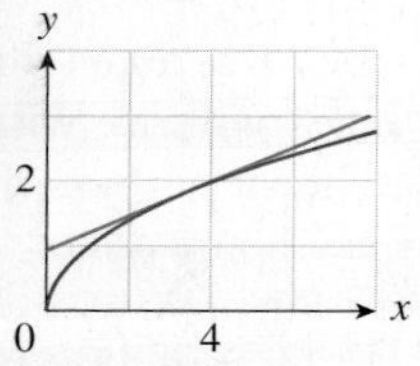

65. $x = -3/4$
67. No such values
69. $x = 1, -1$
71. See Solutions Manual.
73. a. 2/3 **b.** Not differentiable at 0
75. a. 5/2 **b.** Not differentiable at 0

77. Yes; 0 **79.** Yes; 12 **81.** No; 3 **83.** Yes; 3/2 **85.** Yes; diverges to $-\infty$ **87.** Yes; diverges to $-\infty$ **89.** $P'(t) = 0.9t - 12$; $P'(20) = 6$; the price of a barrel of crude oil was increasing at a rate of \$6 per year in 2000. **91.** 0.55 **93. a.** $s'(t) = -32t$; $0, -32, -64, -96, -128$ ft/s **b.** 5 seconds; downward at 160 ft/s **95. a.** $P'(t) = -4.0t + 6.6$; Decreasing at a rate of \$5.4 billion per year **b.** (B) **97. a.** $f'(x) = 7.1x - 30.2$; $f'(8) = 26.6$ manatees per 100,000 boats; At a level of 800,000 boats, manatee deaths are increasing at a rate of 26.6 deaths each year per 100,000 additional boats. **b.** Increasing; the number of manatees killed per additional 100,000 boats increases as the number of boats increases. **99. a.** $I - A$ measures the amount by which the iPhone market share exceeds the Android market share. $(I - A)'$ measures the rate at which this difference is changing. **b.** (B) **c.** $-0.2t + 0.5$ percentage points per month; (C); The vertical distance between the graphs at first increases, and then decreases; the iPhone increases its advantage over the Android share at first, but then the Android begins to catch up. **d.** −0.3 percentage points per month; In May 2009, the iPhone's advantage over Android was decreasing at a rate of 0.3 percentage points per month. **101.** After graphing the curve $y = 3x^2$, draw the line passing through $(-1, 3)$ with slope −6. **103.** The slope of the tangent line of g is twice the slope of the tangent line of f. **105.** $g'(x) = -f'(x)$ **107.** The left-hand side is not equal to the right-hand side. The *derivative* of the left-hand side is equal to the right-hand side, so your friend should have written $\dfrac{d}{dx}\left(3x^4 + 11x^5\right) = 12x^3 + 55x^4$. **109.** $\dfrac{1}{2x}$ is not equal to $2x^{-1}$. Your friend should have written $y = \dfrac{1}{2x} = \dfrac{1}{2}x^{-1}$, so $\dfrac{dy}{dx} = -\dfrac{1}{2}x^{-2}$. **111.** The derivative of a constant times a function is the constant times the derivative of the function, so that $f'(x) = (2)(2x) = 4x$. Your enemy mistakenly computed the *derivative* of the constant times the derivative of the function. (The derivative of a product of two functions is not the product of the derivative of the two functions. The rule for taking the derivative of a product is discussed later in the chapter.). **113.** For a general function f, the derivative of f is defined to be $f'(x) = \lim_{h\to 0} \dfrac{f(x+h) - f(x)}{h}$. One then finds by calculation that the derivative of the specific function x^n is nx^{n-1}. In short, nx^{n-1} is the derivative of a specific function: $f(x) = x^n$, it is not the *definition* of the derivative of a general function or even the definition of the derivative of the function $f(x) = x^n$. **115.** Answers may vary.

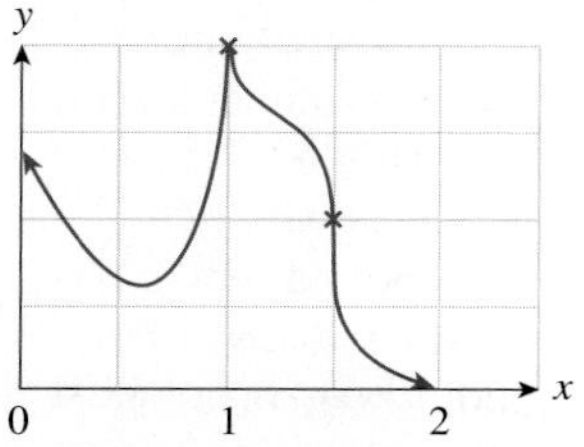

Section 4.2

1. $C'(1{,}000) = \$4.80$ per item **3.** $C'(100) = \$99.90$ per item **5.** $C'(x) = 4$; $R'(x) = 8 - 0.002$; $P'(x) = 4 - 0.002x$; $P'(x) = 0$ when $x = 2{,}000$. Thus, at a production level of 2,000, the profit is stationary (neither increasing nor decreasing) with respect to the production level. This may indicate a maximum profit at a production level of 2,000. **7. a.** (B) **b.** (C) **c.** (C) **9. a.** $C'(x) = 2{,}500 - 0.04x$; The cost is going up at a rate of \$2,499,840 per television commercial. The exact cost of airing the fifth television commercial is \$2,499,820. **b.** $\overline{C}(x) = 150/x + 2{,}500 - 0.02x$; $\overline{C}(4) = 2{,}537.42$ thousand dollars. The average cost of airing the first four television commercials is \$2,537,420. **11. a.** $R'(x) = 0.90$, $P'(x) = 0.80 - 0.002x$ **b.** Revenue: \$450, Profit: \$80, Marginal revenue: \$0.90, Marginal profit: −\$0.20. The total revenue from the sale of 500 copies is \$450. The profit from the production and sale of 500 copies is \$80. Approximate revenue from the sale of the 501st copy is 90¢. Approximate loss from the sale of the 501st copy is 20¢. **c.** $x = 400$. The profit is a maximum when you produce and sell 400 copies. **13.** The profit on the sale of 1,000 DVDs is \$3,000, and is decreasing at a rate of \$3 per additional DVD sold. **15.** Profit ≈ \$257.07; Marginal profit ≈ 5.07. Your current profit is \$257.07 per month, and this would increase at a rate of \$5.07 per additional magazine sold. **17. a.** \$2.50 per pound **b.** $R(q) = 20{,}000/q^{0.5}$ **c.** $R(400) = \$1{,}000$. This is the monthly revenue that will result from setting the price at \$2.50 per pound. $R'(400) = -\$1.25$ per pound of tuna. Thus, at a demand level of 400 pounds per month, the revenue is decreasing at a rate of \$1.25 per pound. **d.** The fishery should raise the price (to reduce the demand). **19.** $P'(50) = \$350$. This means that, at an employment level of 50 workers, the firm's daily profit will increase at a rate of \$350 per additional worker it hires. **21. a.** (B) **b.** (B) **c.** (C)

23. a. $C(x) = 500{,}000 + 1{,}600{,}000x - 100{,}000\sqrt{x}$;

$$C'(x) = 1{,}600{,}000 - \frac{50{,}000}{\sqrt{x}};$$

$$\overline{C}(x) = \frac{500{,}000}{x} + 1{,}600{,}000 - \frac{100{,}000}{\sqrt{x}}$$

b. $C'(3) \approx \$1{,}570{,}000$ per spot, $\bar{C}(3) \approx \$1{,}710{,}000$ per spot. The average cost will decrease as x increases. **25. a.** \$2,000 per one-pound reduction in emissions. **b.** 2.5 pounds per day reduction. **c.** $N(q) = 100q^2 - 500q + 4{,}000$; 2.5 pounds per day reduction. The value of q is the same as that for part (b). The net cost to the firm is minimized at the reduction level for which the cost of controlling emissions begins to increase faster than the subsidy. This is why we get the answer by setting these two rates of increase equal to each other. **27.** $M'(10) \approx 0.0002557$ mpg/mph. This means that, at a speed of 10 mph, the fuel economy is increasing at a rate of 0.0002557 miles per gallon per 1-mph increase in speed. $M'(60) = 0$ mpg/mph. This means that, at a speed of 60 mph, the fuel economy is neither increasing nor decreasing with increasing speed. $M'(70) \approx -0.00001799$. This means that, at 70 mph, the fuel economy is decreasing at a rate of 0.00001799 miles per gallon per 1-mph increase in speed. Thus 60 mph is the most fuel-efficient speed for the car. **29.** (C) **31.** (D) **33.** (B) **35.** Cost is often measured as a function of the number of items x. Thus, $C(x)$ is the cost of producing (or purchasing, as the case may be) x items. **a.** The average cost function $\overline{C}(x)$ is given by $\overline{C}(x) = C(x)/x$. The marginal cost function is the derivative, $C'(x)$, of the cost function. **b.** The average cost $\overline{C}(r)$ is the slope of the line through the origin and the point on the graph where $x = r$. The marginal cost of the rth unit is the slope of the tangent to the graph of the cost function at the point where $x = r$. **c.** The average cost function $\overline{C}(x)$ gives the average cost of producing the first x items. The marginal cost function $C'(x)$ is the rate at which cost is changing with respect to the number of items x, or the incremental cost per item, and approximates the cost of producing the $(x + 1)$st item. **37.** Answers may vary. An example is $C(x) = 300x$. **39.** The marginal cost **41.** Not necessarily. For example, it may be the case that the marginal cost of the 101st item is larger than the average cost of the first 100 items (even though the marginal cost is decreasing). Thus, adding this additional item will *raise* the average cost. **43.** The circumstances described suggest that the average cost function is at a relatively low point at the current production level, and so it would be appropriate to advise the company to maintain current production levels; raising or lowering the production level will result in increasing average costs.

Section 4.3

1. 3 **3.** $3x^2$ **5.** $2x + 3$ **7.** $210x^{1.1}$ **9.** $-2/x^2$ **11.** $2x/3$ **13.** $36x^2 - 3$ **15.** $3x^2 - 5x^4$ **17.** $8x + 12$ **19.** $-8/(5x - 2)^2$ **21.** $-14/(3x - 1)^2$ **23.** 0 **25.** $-|x|/x^3$ **27.** $3\sqrt{x}/2$ **29.** $(x^2 - 1) + 2x(x + 1) = (x + 1)(3x - 1)$ **31.** $(x^{-0.5} + 4)(x - x^{-1}) + (2x^{0.5} + 4x - 5)(1 + x^{-2})$ **33.** $8(2x^2 - 4x + 1)(x - 1)$ **35.** $(1/3.2 - 3.2/x^2)(x^2 + 1) + 2x(x/3.2 + 3.2/x)$ **37.** $2x(2x + 3)(7x + 2) + 2x^2(7x + 2) + 7x^2(2x + 3)$ **39.** $5.3(1 - x^{2.1})(x^{-2.3} - 3.4) - 2.1x^{1.1}(5.3x - 1)(x^{-2.3} - 3.4) - 2.3x - 3.3(5.3x - 1)(1 - x^{2.1})$ **41.** $\frac{1}{2\sqrt{x}}\left(\sqrt{x} + \frac{1}{x^2}\right) + (\sqrt{x} + 1)\left(\frac{1}{2\sqrt{x}} - \frac{2}{x^3}\right)$

43. $\dfrac{(4x+4)(3x-1)-3(2x^2+4x+1)}{(3x-1)^2} = (6x^2-4x-7)/(3x-1)^2$

45. $\dfrac{(2x-4)(x^2+x+1)-(x^2-4x+1)(2x+1)}{(x^2+x+1)^2} = (5x^2-5)/(x^2+x+1)^2$

47. $\dfrac{(0.23x^{-0.77}-5.7)(1-x^{-2.9})-2.9x^{-3.9}(x^{0.23}-5.7x)}{(1-x^{-2.9})^2}$

49. $\dfrac{\frac{1}{2}x^{-1/2}(x^{1/2}-1)-\frac{1}{2}x^{-1/2}(x^{1/2}+1)}{(x^{1/2}-1)^2} = \dfrac{-1}{\sqrt{x}\left(\sqrt{x}-1\right)^2}$ **51.** $-3/x^4$

53. $\dfrac{[(x+1)+(x+3)](3x-1)-3(x+3)(x+1)}{(3x-1)^2} = (3x^2-2x-13)/(3x-1)^2$

55. $\dfrac{[(x+1)(x+2)+(x+3)(x+2)+(x+3)(x+1)](3x-1)-3(x+3)(x+1)(x+2)}{(3x-1)^2}$

57. $4x^3-2x$ **59.** 64 **61.** 3 **63.** Difference; $4x^3-12x^2+2x-480$ **65.** Sum; $1+2/(x+1)^2$ **67.** Product; $\left[\dfrac{x}{x+1}\right]+(x+2)\dfrac{1}{(x+1)^2}$ **69.** Difference; $2x-1-2/(x+1)^2$ **71.** $y=12x-8$ **73.** $y=x/4+1/2$ **75.** $y=-2$ **77.** $q'(5)=1{,}000$ units/month (sales are increasing at a rate of 1,000 units per month); $p'(5)=-\$10$/month (the price of a sound system is dropping at a rate of \$10 per month); $R'(5)=900{,}000$ (revenue is increasing at a rate of \$900,000 per month). **79.** \$703 million; increasing at a rate of \$67 million per year **81.** Decreasing at a rate of \$1 per day **83.** Decreasing at a rate of approximately \$0.10 per month **85.** $M'(x)=\dfrac{3{,}000(3{,}600x^{-2}-1)}{(x+3{,}600x^{-1})^2}$; $M'(10)\approx 0.7670$ mpg/mph. This means that, at a speed of 10 mph, the fuel economy is increasing at a rate of 0.7670 miles per gallon per one mph increase in speed. $M'(60)=0$ mpg/mph. This means that, at a speed of 60 mph, the fuel economy is neither increasing nor decreasing with increasing speed. $M'(70)\approx -0.0540$. This means that, at 70 mph, the fuel economy is decreasing at a rate of 0.0540 miles per gallon per one mph increase in speed. 60 mph is the most fuel-efficient speed for the car. (In the next chapter we shall discuss how to locate largest values in general.) **87. a.** $P(t)-I(t)$ represents the daily production of oil in Mexico that was not exported to the United States. $I(t)/P(t)$ represents U.S. imports of oil from Mexico as a fraction of the total produced there. **b.** -0.023 per year; at the start of 2008, the fraction of oil produced in Mexico that was imported by the United States was decreasing at a rate of 0.023 (or 2.3 percentage points) per year. **89.** Increasing at a rate of about \$3,420 million per year. **91.** $R'(p)=-\dfrac{5.625}{(1+0.125p)^2}$; $R'(4)=-2.5$ thousand organisms per hour, per 1,000 organisms. This means that the reproduction rate of organisms in a culture containing 4,000 organisms is declining at a rate of 2,500 organisms per hour, per 1,000 additional organisms. **93.** Oxygen consumption is decreasing at a rate of 1,600 milliliters per day. This is due to the fact that the number of eggs is decreasing, because $C'(25)$ is positive. **95.** 20; 33 **97.** $5/4$; $-17/16$ **99.** The analysis is suspect, as it seems to be asserting that the annual increase in revenue, which we can think of as dR/dt, is the product of the annual increases, dp/dt in price, and dq/dt in sales. However, because $R=pq$, the product rule implies that dR/dt is not the product of dp/dt and dq/dt, but is instead $\dfrac{dR}{dt}=\dfrac{dp}{dt}\cdot q+p\cdot\dfrac{dq}{dt}$. **101.** Answers will vary $q=-p+1{,}000$ is one example. **103.** Mine; it is increasing twice as fast as yours. The rate of change of revenue is given by $R'(t)=p'(t)q(t)$ because $q'(t)=0$. Thus, $R'(t)$ does not depend on the selling price $p(t)$. **105.** (A)

Section 4.4

1. $4(2x+1)$ **3.** $-(x-1)^{-2}$ **5.** $2(2-x)^{-3}$ **7.** $(2x+1)^{-0.5}$ **9.** $-3/(3x-1)^2$

11. $4(x^2+2x)^3(2x+2)$ **13.** $-4x(2x^2-2)^{-2}$
15. $-5(2x-3)(x^2-3x-1)^{-6}$ **17.** $-6x/(x^2+1)^4$
19. $1.5(0.2x-4.2)(0.1x^2-4.2x+9.5)^{0.5}$
21. $4(2s-0.5s^{-0.5})(s^2-s^{0.5})^3$ **23.** $-x/\sqrt{1-x^2}$
25. $\frac{3|3x-6|}{3x-6}$ **27.** $\frac{(-3x^2+5)|-x^3+5x|}{-x^3+5x}$
29. $-[(x+1)(x^2-1)]^{-3/2}(3x-1)(x+1)$
31. $6.2(3.1x-2)+6.2/(3.1x-2)^3$
33. $2[(6.4x-1)^2+(5.4x-2)^3]\times[12.8(6.4x-1)+16.2(5.4x-2)^2]$
35. $-2(x^2-3x)^{-3}(2x-3)(1-x^2)^{0.5}-x(x^2-3x)^{-2}(1-x^2)^{-0.5}$
37. $-56(x+2)/(3x-1)^3$ **39.** $3z^2(1-z^2)/(1+z^2)^4$
41. $3[(1+2x)^4-(1-x)^2]^2[8(1+2x)^3+2(1-x)]$
43. $6|3x-1|$ **45.** $\frac{|x-(2x-3)^{1/2}|}{x-(2x-3)^{1/2}}[1-(2x-3)^{-1/2}]$
47. $-\frac{\left(\frac{1}{\sqrt{2x+1}}-2x\right)}{\left(\sqrt{2x+1}-x^2\right)^2}$
49. $54(1+2x)^2(1+(1+2x)^3)^2(1+(1+(1+2x)^3)^3)^2$
51. $(100x^{99}-99x^{-2})\,dx/dt$
53. $(-3r^{-4}+0.5r^{-0.5})\,dr/dt$ **55.** $4\pi r^2 dr/dt$
57. $-47/4$ **59.** $1/3$ **61.** $-5/3$ **63.** $1/4$
65. $\left.\frac{dP}{dn}\right|_{n=10}=146{,}454.9$. At an employment level of 10 engineers, Paramount will increase its profit at a rate of \$146,454.90 per additional engineer hired. **67.** $y=35(7+0.2t)^{-0.25}$; -0.11 percentage points per month. **69.** −\$30 per additional ruby sold. The revenue is decreasing at a rate of \$30 per additional ruby sold.
71. $\frac{dy}{dt}=\frac{dy}{dx}\frac{dx}{dt}=(1.5)(-2)=-3$ murders per 100,000 residents/yr each year. **73.** $5/6\approx 0.833$; relative to the 2003 levels, home sales were changing at a rate of about 0.833 percentage points per percentage point change in price. (Equivalently, home sales in 2008 were dropping at a rate of about 0.833 percentage points per percentage point drop in price.) **75.** 12π mi²/h **77.** \$200,000π/week ≈ \$628,000/week **79. a.** $q'(4)\approx 333$ units per month **b.** dR/dq = \$800/unit **c.** $dR/dt\approx$ \$267,000 per month **81.** 3% per year **83.** 8% per year **85.** The glob squared, times the derivative of the glob. **87.** The derivative of a quantity cubed is three times the *original quantity* squared, times the derivative of the quantity, not three times the derivative of the quantity squared. Thus, the correct answer is $3(3x^3-x)^2(9x^2-1)$.

89. First, the derivative of a quantity cubed is three times the *original quantity* squared times the derivative of the quantity, not three times the derivative of the quantity squared. Second, the derivative of a quotient is not the quotient of the derivatives; the quotient rule needs to be used in calculating the derivative of $\frac{3x^2-1}{2x-2}$. Thus, the correct result (before simplifying) is $3\left(\frac{3x^2-1}{2x-2}\right)^2\left(\frac{6x(2x-2)-(3x^2-1)(2)}{(2x-2)^2}\right)$.
91. Following the calculation thought experiment, pretend that you were evaluating the function at a specific value of x. If the last operation you would perform is addition or subtraction, look at each summand separately. If the last operation is multiplication, use the product rule first; if it is division, use the quotient rule first; if it is any other operation (such as raising a quantity to a power or taking a radical of a quantity) then use the chain rule first. **93.** An example is $f(x)=\sqrt{x+\sqrt{x+\sqrt{x+\sqrt{x+\sqrt{x+1}}}}}$.

Section 4.5

1. $1/(x-1)$ **3.** $1/(x\ln 2)$ **5.** $2x/(x^2+3)$
7. e^{x+3} **9.** $-e^{-x}$ **11.** $4^x\ln 4$ **13.** $2^{x^2-1}2x\ln 2$
15. $1+\ln x$ **17.** $2x\ln x+(x^2+1)/x$
19. $10x(x^2+1)^4\ln x+(x^2+1)^5/x$
21. $3/(3x-1)$ **23.** $4x/(2x^2+1)$
25. $(2x-0.63x^{-0.7})/(x^2-2.1x^{0.3})$
27. $-2/(-2x+1)+1/(x+1)$
29. $3/(3x+1)-4/(4x-2)$
31. $1/(x+1)+1/(x-3)-2/(2x+9)$
33. $5.2/(4x-2)$
35. $2/(x+1)-9/(3x-4)-1/(x-9)$
37. $\frac{1}{(x+1)\ln 2}$ **39.** $\frac{1-1/t^2}{(t+1/t)\ln 3}$ **41.** $\frac{2\ln|x|}{x}$
43. $\frac{2}{x}-\frac{2\ln(x-1)}{x-1}$ **45.** $e^x(1+x)$
47. $1/(x+1)+3e^x(x^3+3x^2)$ **49.** $e^x(\ln|x|+1/x)$
51. $2e^{2x+1}$ **53.** $(2x-1)e^{x^2-x+1}$ **55.** $2xe^{2x-1}(1+x)$
57. $4(e^{2x-1})^2$ **59.** $2\cdot 3^{2x-4}\ln 3$
61. $2\cdot 3^{2x+1}\ln 3+3e^{3x+1}$
63. $\frac{2x3^{x^2}[(x^2+1)\ln 3-1]}{(x^2+1)^2}$
65. $-4/(e^x-e^{-x})^2$

67. $5e^{5x-3}$ **69.** $-\frac{\ln x + 1}{(x\ln x)^2}$ **71.** $2(x-1)$ **73.** $\frac{1}{x\ln x}$ **75.** $\frac{1}{2x\ln x}$ **77.** $y = (e/\ln 2)(x-1) \approx 3.92(x-1)$ **79.** $y = x$ **81.** $y = -[1/(2e)](x-1) + e$ **83.** $163 billion and increasing at a rate of $5.75 billion per year **85.** $163 billion and increasing at a rate of $5.75 billion per year. **87.** −1,653 years per gram; the age of the specimen is decreasing at a rate of about 1,653 years per additional one gram of carbon 14 present in the sample. (Equivalently, the age of the specimen is increasing at a rate of about 1,653 years per additional one gram less of carbon 14 in the sample.) **89.** Average price: $1.4 million; increasing at a rate of about $220,000 per year. **91. a.** $N(15) \approx 1{,}762 \approx 1{,}800$ (rounded to 2 significant digits) wiretap orders; $N'(15) \approx 89.87 \approx 90$ wiretap orders per year (rounded to 2 significant digits). The constants in the model are specified to 2 significant digits, so we cannot expect the answer to be accurate to more than 2 digits. **b.** In 2005, the number of people whose communications were intercepted was about 180,000 and increasing at a rate of about 9,000 people per year. **c.** (C) **93.** $451.00 per year **95.** $446.02 per year **97.** $A(t) = 167(1.18)^t$; 280 new cases per day **99. a.** (A) **b.** The math SAT increases by approximately 0.97 points. **c.** $S'(x)$ decreases with increasing x, so that as parental income increases, the effect on math SAT scores decreases. **101. a.** −6.25 years/child; when the fertility rate is 2 children per woman, the average age of a population is dropping at a rate of 6.25 years per one-child increase in the fertility rate. **b.** 0.160 **103.** 3,300,000 cases/week; 11,000,000 cases/week; 640,000 cases/week **105.** 2.1 percentage points per year; the rate of change is the slope of the tangent at $t = 3$. This is also approximately the average rate of change over [2, 4], which is about $4/2 = 2$, in approximate agreement with the answer. **107. a.** 2.1 percentage points per year **b.** $\lim_{t\to+\infty} A(t) = 15$; Had the trend continued indefinitely, the percentage of mortgages that were subprime would have approached 15% in the long term. $\lim_{t\to+\infty} A'(t) = 0$; Had the trend continued indefinitely, the rate of change of the percentage of mortgages that were subprime would have approached 0 percentage points per year in the long term. **109.** 277,000 people per year **111.** 0.000283 g/yr **113.** $R(t) = 350e^{-0.1t}(39t + 68)$ million dollars; $R(2) \approx \$42$ billion; $R'(2) \approx \$7$ billion per year

115. e raised to the glob, times the derivative of the glob. **117.** 2 raised to the glob, times the derivative of the glob, times the natural logarithm of 2. **119.** The derivative of $\ln|u|$ is not $\frac{1}{|u|}\frac{du}{dx}$; it is $\frac{1}{u}\frac{du}{dx}$. Thus, the correct derivative is $\frac{3}{3x+1}$. **121.** The power rule does not apply when the exponent is not constant. The derivative of 3 raised to a quantity is 3 raised to the quantity, times the derivative of the quantity, times ln 3. Thus, the correct answer is $3^{2x}\, 2 \ln 3$. **123.** No. If $N(t)$ is exponential, so is its derivative. **125.** If $f(x) = e^{kx}$, then the fractional rate of change is $\frac{f'(x)}{f(x)} = \frac{ke^{kx}}{e^{kx}} = k$, the fractional growth rate. **127.** If $A(t)$ is growing exponentially, then $A(t) = A_0e^{kt}$ for constants A_0 and k. Its percentage rate of change is then $\frac{A'(t)}{A(t)} = \frac{kA_0e^{kt}}{A_0e^{kt}} = k$, a constant.

Section 4.6

1. $-2/3$ **3.** x **5.** $(y-2)/(3-x)$ **7.** $-y$ **9.** $-\frac{y}{x(1+\ln x)}$ **11.** $-x/y$ **13.** $-2xy/(x^2-2y)$ **15.** $-(6+9x^2y)/(9x^3-x^2)$ **17.** $3y/x$ **19.** $(p+10p^2q)/(2p-q-10pq^2)$ **21.** $(ye^x - e^y)/(xe^y - e^x)$ **23.** $se^{st}/(2s - te^{st})$ **25.** $ye^x/(2e^x + y^3e^y)$ **27.** $(y-y^2)/(-1+3y-y^2)$ **29.** $-y/(x+2y-xye^y-y^2e^y)$ **31. a.** 1 **b.** $y = x - 3$ **33. a.** −2 **b.** $y = -2x$ **35. a.** −1 **b.** $y = -x + 1$ **37. a.** −2,000 **b.** $y = -2{,}000x + 6{,}000$ **39. a.** 0 **b.** $y = 1$ **41. a.** −0.1898 **b.** $y = -0.1898x + 1.4721$

43. $\frac{2x+1}{4x-2}\left[\frac{2}{2x+1} - \frac{4}{4x-2}\right]$

45. $\frac{(3x+1)^2}{4x(2x-1)^3}\left[\frac{6}{3x+1} - \frac{1}{x} - \frac{6}{2x-1}\right]$

47. $(8x-1)^{1/3}(x-1)\left[\frac{8}{3(8x-1)} + \frac{1}{x-1}\right]$

49. $(x^3+x)\sqrt{x^3+2}\left[\frac{3x^2+1}{x^3+x} + \frac{1}{2}\frac{3x^2}{x^3+2}\right]$

51. $x^x(1+\ln x)$ **53.** −$3,000 per worker. The monthly budget to maintain production at the fixed level P is decreasing by approximately $3,000 per additional worker at an employment level of 100 workers and a monthly operating budget of $200,000.

55. −125 T-shirts per dollar; when the price is set at \$5, the demand is dropping by 125 T-shirts per \$1 increase in price. **57.** $\left.\frac{dk}{de}\right|_{e=15} = -0.307$ carpenters per electrician. This means that, for a \$200,000 house whose construction employs 15 electricians, adding one more electrician would cost as much as approximately 0.307 additional carpenters. In other words, one electrician is worth approximately 0.307 carpenters. **59. a.** 22.93 hours. (The other root is rejected because it is larger than 30.) **b.** $\frac{dt}{dx} = \frac{4t - 20x}{0.4t - 4x}$; $\left.\frac{dt}{dx}\right|_{x=3.0} \approx$ −11.2 hours per grade point. This means that, for a 3.0 student who scores 80 on the examination, 1 grade point is worth approximately 11.2 hours. **61.** $\frac{dr}{dy} = 2\frac{r}{y}$, so $\frac{dr}{dt} = 2\frac{r}{y}\frac{dy}{dt}$ by the chain rule. **63.** x, y, y, x **65.** Let $y = f(x)g(x)$. Then $\ln y = \ln f(x) + \ln g(x)$, and

$$\frac{1}{y}\frac{dy}{dx} = \frac{f'(x)}{f(x)} + \frac{g'(x)}{g(x)},$$

so $$\frac{dy}{dx} = y\left(\frac{f'(x)}{f(x)} + \frac{g'(x)}{g(x)}\right) =$$

$$f(x)g(x)\left(\frac{f'(x)}{f(x)} + \frac{g'(x)}{g(x)}\right) = f'(x)g(x) + f(x)g'(x).$$

67. Writing $y = f(x)$ specifies y as an explicit function of x. This can be regarded as an equation giving y as an *implicit* function of x. The procedure of finding dy/dx by implicit differentiation is then the same as finding the derivative of y as an explicit function of x: We take d/dx of both sides. **69.** Differentiate both sides of the equation $y = f(x)$ with respect to y to get $1 = f'(x) \cdot \frac{dx}{dy}$, giving $\frac{dx}{dy} = \frac{1}{f'(x)} = \frac{1}{dy/dx}$.

Chapter 4 Review

1. $50x^4 + 2x^3 - 1$ **3.** $9x^2 + x^{-2/3}$ **5.** $1 - 2/x^3$ **7.** $-\frac{4}{3x^2} + \frac{0.2}{x^{1.1}} + \frac{1.1x^{0.1}}{3.2}$ **9.** $e^x(x^2 + 2x - 1)$ **11.** $(-3x|x| + |x|/x - 6x)/(3x^2 + 1)^2$ **13.** $-4(4x - 1)^{-2}$ **15.** $20x(x^2 - 1)^9$ **17.** $-0.43(x + 1)^{-1.1}[2 + (x + 1)^{-0.1}]^{3.3}$ **19.** $e^x(x^2 + 1)^9(x^2 + 20x + 1)$ **21.** $3^x[(x - 1)\ln 3 - 1]/(x - 1)^2$ **23.** $2xe^{x^2-1}$ **25.** $2x/(x^2 - 1)$ **27.** $x = 7/6$ **29.** $x = \pm 2$ **31.** $x = (1 - \ln 2)/2$ **33.** None **35.** $\frac{2x - 1}{2y}$ **37.** $-y/x$ **39.** $\frac{(2x - 1)^4(3x + 4)}{(x + 1)(3x - 1)^3} \times \left[\frac{8}{2x - 1} + \frac{3}{3x + 4} - \frac{1}{x + 1} - \frac{9}{3x - 1}\right]$ **41.** $y = -x/4 + 1/2$ **43.** $y = -3ex - 2e$ **45.** $y = x + 2$ **47. a.** 274 books per week **b.** 636 books per week **c.** The function w begins to decrease more and more rapidly after $t = 14$ Graph:

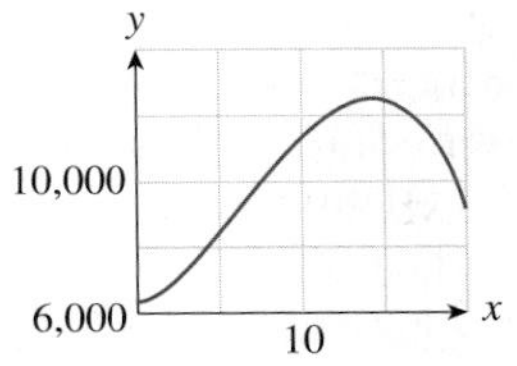

d. Because the data suggest an upward curving parabola, the long-term prediction of sales for a quadratic model would be that sales will increase without bound, in sharp contrast to (c) **49. a.** \$2.88 per book **b.** \$3.715 per book **c.** Approximately −\$0.000104 per book, per additional book sold. **d.** At a sales level of 8,000 books per week, the cost is increasing at a rate of \$2.88 per book (so that the 8,001st book costs approximately \$2.88 to sell), and it costs an average of \$3.715 per book to sell the first 8,000 books. Moreover, the average cost is decreasing at a rate of \$0.000104 per book, per additional book sold. **51. a.** \$3,000 per week (rising) **b.** 300 books per week **53.** $R = pq$ gives $R' = p'q + pq'$. Thus, $R'/R = R'/(pq) = (p'q + pq')/pq = p'/p + q'/q$ **55.** \$110 per year **57. a.** $s'(t) = \frac{2{,}475e^{-0.55(t-4.8)}}{(1 + e^{-0.55(t-4.8)})^2}$; 556 books per week **b.** 0; In the long term, the rate of increase of weekly sales slows to zero. **59.** 616.8 hits per day per week. **61. a.** −17.24 copies per \$1. The demand for the gift edition of *The Complete Larry Potter* is dropping at a rate of about 17.24 copies per \$1 increase in the price. **b.** \$138 per dollar is positive, so the price should be raised.

Chapter 5

Section 5.1

1. Absolute min: (−3, −1), relative max: (−1, 1), relative min: (1, 0), absolute max: (3, 2) **3.** Absolute min: (3, −1) and (−3, −1), absolute max: (1, 2) **5.** Absolute min: (−3, 0) and (1, 0), absolute max: (−1, 2) and (3, 2) **7.** Relative min: (−1, 1) **9.** Absolute min: (−3, −1), relative max: (−2, 2), relative min: (1, 0), absolute max: (3, 3)

11. Relative max: $(-3, 0)$, absolute min: $(-2, -1)$, stationary nonextreme point: $(1, 1)$ **13.** Absolute max: $(0, 1)$, absolute min: $(2, -3)$, relative max: $(3, -2)$ **15.** Absolute min: $(-4, -16)$, absolute max: $(-2, 16)$, absolute min: $(2, -16)$, absolute max: $(4, 16)$ **17.** Absolute min: $(-2, -10)$, absolute max: $(2, 10)$ **19.** Absolute min: $(-2, -4)$, relative max: $(-1, 1)$, relative min: $(0, 0)$ **21.** Relative max: $(-1, 5)$, absolute min: $(3, -27)$ **23.** Absolute min: $(0, 0)$ **25.** Absolute maxima at $(0, 1)$ and $(2, 1)$, absolute min at $(1, 0)$ **27.** Relative maximum at $(-2, -1/3)$, relative minimum at $(-1, -2/3)$, absolute maximum at $(0, 1)$ **29.** Relative min: $(-2, 5/3)$, relative max: $(0, -1)$, relative min: $(2, 5/3)$ **31.** Relative max: $(0, 0)$; absolute min: $(1/3, -2\sqrt{3}/9)$ **33.** Relative max: $(0, 0)$, absolute min: $(1, -3)$ **35.** No relative extrema **37.** Absolute min: $(1, 1)$ **39.** Relative max: $(-1, 1 + 1/e)$, absolute min: $(0, 1)$, absolute max: $(1, e - 1)$ **41.** Relative max: $(-6, -24)$, relative min: $(-2, -8)$ **43.** Absolute max $(1/\sqrt{2}, \sqrt{e/2})$, absolute min: $(-1/\sqrt{2}, -\sqrt{e/2})$ **45.** Relative min at $(0.15, -0.52)$ and $(2.45, 8.22)$, relative max at $(1.40, 0.29)$ **47.** Absolute max at $(-5, 700)$, relative max at $(3.10, 28.19)$ and $(6, 40)$, absolute min at $(-2.10, -392.69)$ and relative min at $(5, 0)$. **49.** Stationary minimum at $x = -1$ **51.** Stationary minima at $x = -2$ and $x = 2$, stationary maximum at $x = 0$ **53.** Singular minimum at $x = 0$, stationary nonextreme point at $x = 1$ **55.** Stationary minimum at $x = -2$, singular nonextreme points at $x = -1$ and $x = 1$, stationary maximum at $x = 2$

57. Answers will vary.

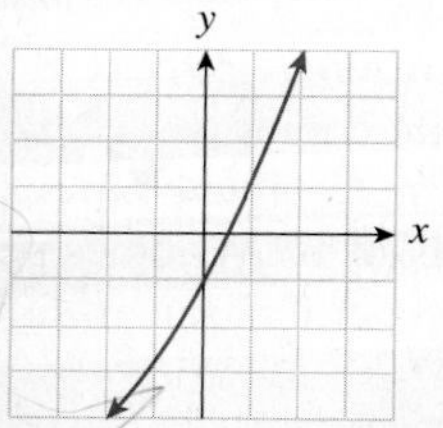

59. Answers will vary.

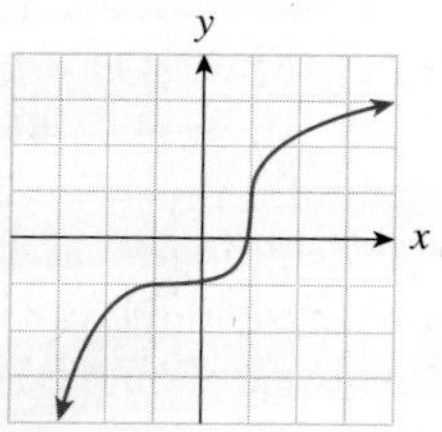

61. Not necessarily; it could be neither a relative maximum nor a relative minimum, as in the graph of $y = x^3$ at the origin.

63. Answers will vary.

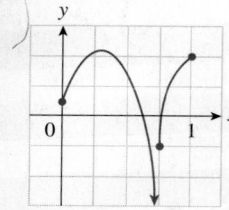

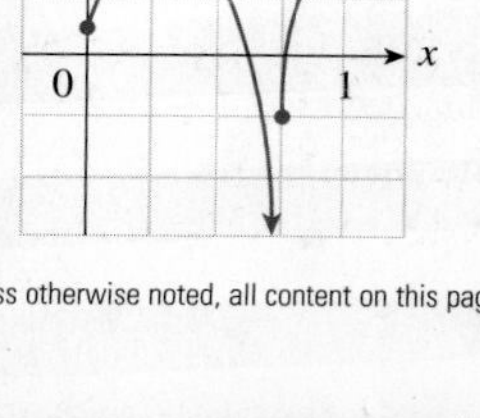

65. The graph oscillates faster and faster above and below zero as it approaches the end-point at 0, so 0 cannot be either a relative minimum or maximum.

Section 5.2

1. $x = y = 5$; $P = 25$ **3.** $x = y = 3$; $S = 6$ **5.** $x = 2$, $y = 4$; $F = 20$ **7.** $x = 20$, $y = 10$, $z = 20$; $P = 4{,}000$ **9.** 5×5 **11.** 1,500 per day for an average cost of \$130 per iPod **13.** $\sqrt{40} \approx 6.32$ pounds of pollutant per day, for an average cost of about \$1,265 per pound **15.** 2.5 lb **17.** 5×10 **19.** 50×10 for an area of 250 sq. ft. **21.** 11×22 **23.** \$10 **25.** \$78 for a quarterly revenue of \$6,084 million, or \$6.084 billion **27.** \$4.61 for a daily revenue of \$95,680.55 **29. a.** \$1.41 per pound **b.** 5,000 pounds **c.** \$7,071.07 per month **31.** 34.5¢ per pound, for an annual (per capita) revenue of \$5.95 **33.** \$98 for an annual profit of \$3,364 million, or \$3.364 billion **35. a.** 656 headsets, for a profit of \$28,120 **b.** \$143 per headset **37.** Height = Radius of base ≈ 20.48 cm. **39.** Height ≈ 10.84 cm; Radius ≈ 2.71 cm; Height/Radius = 4 **41.** $13\frac{1}{3}$ in × $3\frac{1}{3}$ in × $1\frac{1}{3}$ in for a volume of $1{,}600/27 \approx 59$ cubic inches **43.** $5 \times 5 \times 5$ cm **45.** $l = w = h \approx 20.67$ in, volume ≈ 8,827 in^3 **47.** $l = 30$ in, $w = 15$ in, $h = 30$ in **49.** $l = 36$ in, $w = h = 18$ in, $V = 11{,}664$ in^3 **51. a.** 1.6 years, or year 2001.6; **b.** $R_{max} =$ \$28,241 million **53.** $t = 2.5$ or midway through 1972; $D(2.5)/S(2.5) \approx 4.09$. The number of new (approved) drugs per \$1 billion of spending on research and development reached a high of around four approved drugs per \$1 billion midway through 1972. **55.** 30 years from now **57.** 55 days **59.** 1,600 copies. At this value of x, average profit equals marginal profit; beyond this the marginal profit is smaller than the average. **61.** 40 laborers and 250 robots **63.** 71 employees **65.** Increasing most rapidly in 1990; increasing least rapidly in 2007 **67.** Maximum when $t = 17$ days. This means that the embryo's oxygen consumption is increasing most rapidly 17 days after the egg is laid.

69. Graph of derivative:

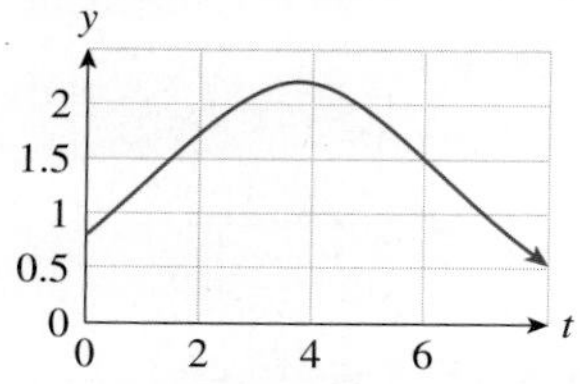

The absolute maximum occurs at approximately (3.7, 2.2) during the year 2003. The percentage of mortgages that were subprime was increasing most rapidly during 2003, when it increased at a rate of around 2.2 percentage points per year. **71.** You should sell them in 17 years' time, when they will be worth approximately \$3,960. **73.** 25 additional trees **75.** (D) **77.** (A); (B) **79.** The problem is uninteresting because the company can accomplish the objective by cutting away the entire sheet of cardboard, resulting in a box with surface area zero. **81.** Not all absolute extrema occur at stationary points; some may occur at an endpoint or singular point of the domain, as in Exercises 29, 30, 65, and 66. **83.** The minimum of dq/dp is the fastest that the demand is dropping in response to increasing price.

Section 5.3

1. 6 **3.** $4/x^3$ **5.** $-0.96x^{-1.6}$ **7.** $e^{-(x-1)}$ **9.** $2/x^3 + 1/x^2$ **11. a.** $a = -32$ ft/sec^2 **b.** $a = -32$ ft/sec^2 **13. a.** $a = 2/t^3 + 6/t^4$ ft/sec^2 **b.** $a = 8$ ft/sec^2 **15. a.** $a = -1/(4t^{3/2}) + 2$ ft/sec^2 **b.** $a = 63/32$ ft/sec^2 **17.** (1, 0) **19.** (1, 0) **21.** None **23.** $(-1, 0)$, $(1, 1)$ **25.** Points of inflection at $x = -1$ and $x = 1$ **27.** One point of inflection, at $x = -2$ **29.** Points of inflection at $x = -2$, $x = 0$, $x = 2$ **31.** Points of inflection at $x = -2$ and $x = 2$ **33.** $x = 2$; minimum **35.** Maximum at $x = -2$, minimum at $x = 2$ **37.** Maximum at $t = -1/\sqrt{3}$, minimum at $t = 1/\sqrt{3}$ **39.** Nonextreme stationary point at $x = 0$ minimum at $x = 3$ **41.** Maximum at $x = 0$ **43.** Minimum at $x = -1/\sqrt{2}$; maximum at $x = 1/\sqrt{2}$ **45.** $f'(x) = 8x - 1$; $f''(x) = 8$; $f'''(x) = f^{(4)}(x) = \ldots = f^{(n)}(x) = 0$ **47.** $f'(x) = -4x^3 + 6x$; $f''(x) = -12x^2 + 6$; $f'''(x) = -24x$; $f^{(4)}(x) = -24$; $f^{(5)}(x) = f^{(6)}(x) = \ldots = f^{(n)}(x) = 0$ **49.** $f'(x) = 8(2x + 1)^3$; $f''(x) = 48(2x + 1)^2$; $f'''(x) = 192(2x + 1)$; $f^{(4)}(x) = 384$; $f^{(5)}(x) = f^{(6)}(x) = \ldots = f^{(n)}(x) = 0$ **51.** $f'(x) = -e^{-x}$; $f''(x) = e^{-x}$; $f'''(x) = -e^{-x}$; $f^{(4)}(x) = e^{-x}$; $f^{(n)}(x) = (-1)^n e^{-x}$ **53.** $f'(x) = 3e^{3x-1}$; $f''(x) = 9e^{3x-1}$; $f'''(x) = 27e^{3x-1}$; $f^{(4)}(x) = 81e^{3x-1}$; $f^{(n)}(x) = 3^n e^{3x-1}$ **55.** -3.8 m/s^2 **57.** $6t - 2$ ft/s^2; increasing **59.** Decelerating by 90 million gals/yr^2 **61. a.** 400 ml **b.** 36 ml/day **c.** -1 ml/day^2 **63. a.** 0.6% **b.** Speeding up **c.** Speeding up for $t < 3.33$ (prior to 1/3 of the way through March) and slowing for $t > 3.33$ (after that time) **65. a.** December 2005: -0.202% (deflation rate of 0.202%) February 2006: 0.363% **b.** Speeding up **c.** Speeding up for $t > 4.44$ (after mid-November) and decreasing for $t < 4.44$ (prior to that time). **67.** Concave up for $8 < t < 20$, concave down for $0 < t < 8$, point of inflection around $t = 8$. The percentage of articles written by researchers in the United States was decreasing most rapidly at around $t = 8$ (1991). **69. a.** (B) **b.** (B) **c.** (A) **71.** Graphs:

$A(t)$:

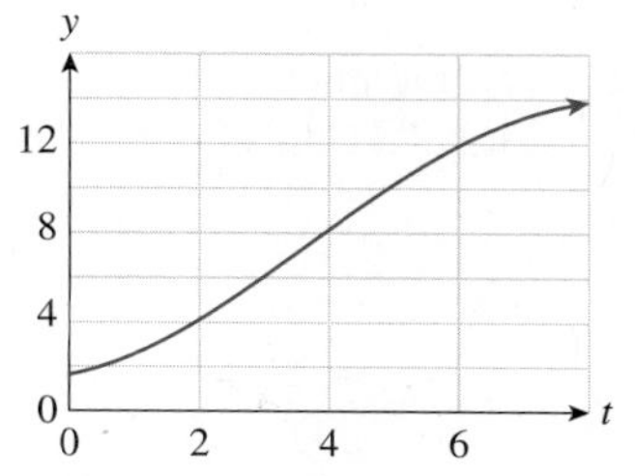

$A'(t)$:

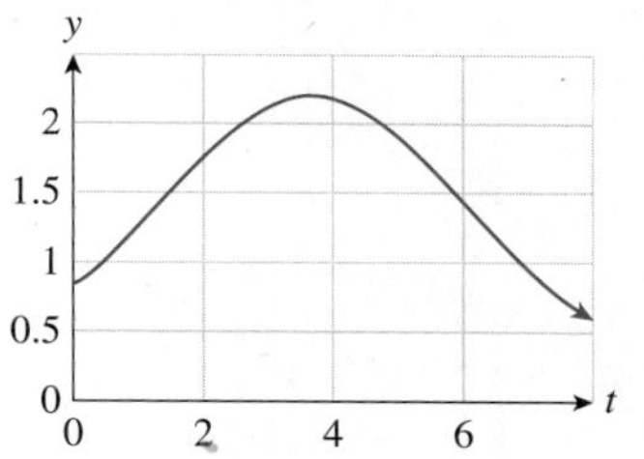

$A''(t)$:

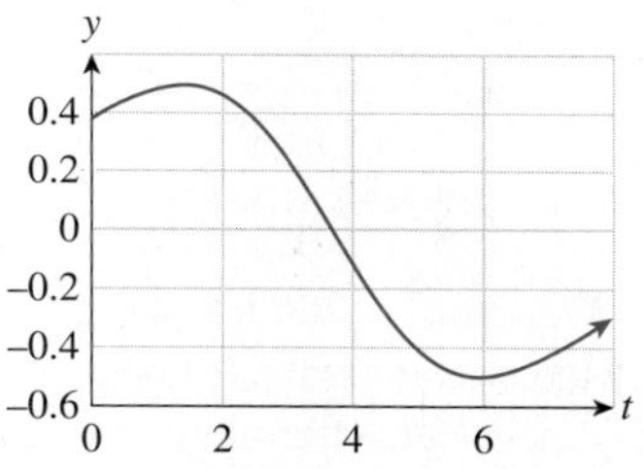

Concave up when $t < 4$; concave down when $t > 4$; point of inflection when $t \approx 4$. The percentage of U.S. mortgages that were subprime was increasing fastest at the beginning of 2004. **73. a.** 2 years into the epidemic **b.** 2 years into the epidemic **75. a.** 2024 **b.** 2026 **c.** 2022; (A) **77. a.** There are no points of inflection in the graph of S. **b.** Because the graph is concave up, the derivative of S is increasing, and so the rate of *decrease* of SAT scores with increasing numbers of prisoners was diminishing. In other words, the apparent effect of more prisoners on SAT scores was diminishing. **79. a.** $\left.\frac{d^2n}{ds^2}\right|_{s=3} = -21.494$. Thus, for a firm with annual sales of \$3 million, the rate at which new patents are produced decreases with

increasing firm size. This means that the returns (as measured in the number of new patents per increase of \$1 million in sales) are diminishing as the firm size increases. **b.** $\left.\frac{d^2n}{ds^2}\right|_{s=7} = 13.474$. Thus, for a firm with annual sales of \$7 million, the rate at which new patents are produced increases with increasing firm size by 13.474 new patents per \$1 million increase in annual sales. **c.** There is a point of inflection when $s \approx 5.4587$, so that in a firm with sales of \$5,458,700 per year, the number of new patents produced per additional \$1 million in sales is a minimum.
81. Graphs:

$I(t)/P(t)$:

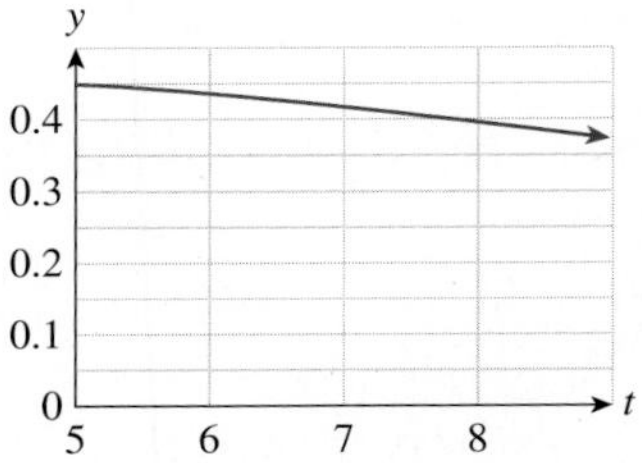

$[I(t)/P(t)]'$:

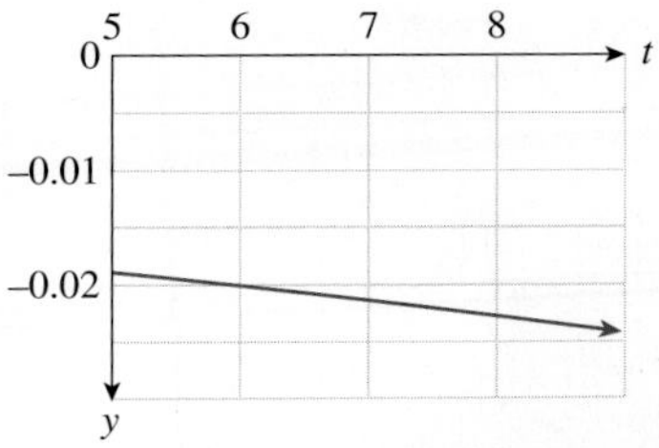

Concave down; (D) **83.** (Proof) **85.** $t \approx 4$; the population of Puerto Rico was increasing fastest in 1954. **87.** About \$570 per year, after about 12 years **89.** Increasing most rapidly in 17.64 years, decreasing most rapidly now (at $t = 0$) **91.** Non-negative **93.** Daily sales were decreasing most rapidly in June 2002.

95.

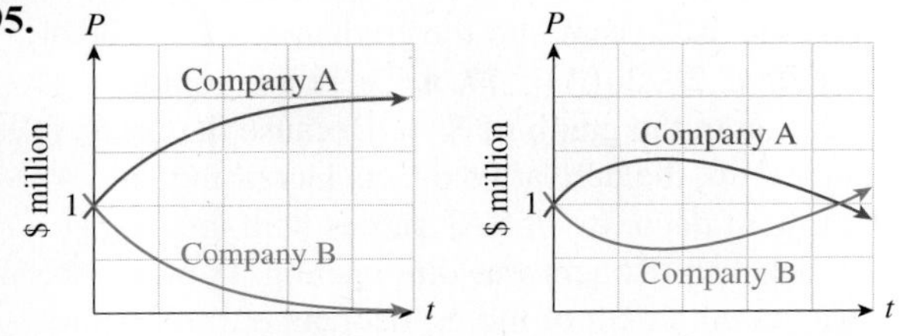

97. At a point of inflection, the graph of a function changes either from concave up to concave down, or vice versa. If it changes from concave up to concave down, then the derivative changes from increasing to decreasing, and hence has a relative maximum. Similarly, if it changes from concave down to concave up, the derivative has a relative minimum.

Section 5.4

1. a. x-intercept: -1; y-intercept: 1 **b.** Absolute min at $(-1, 0)$ **c.** None **d.** None **e.** $y \to +\infty$ as $x \to \pm\infty$
Graph:

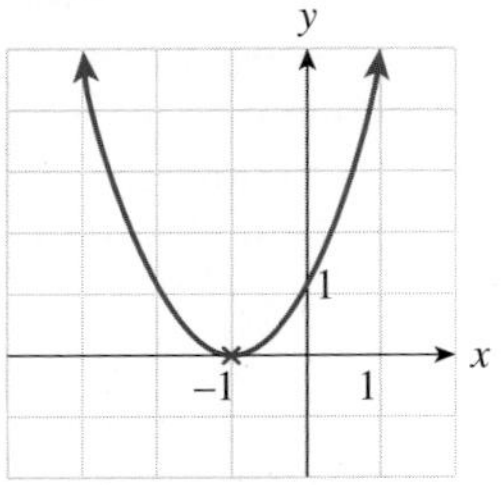

3. a. x-intercepts: $-\sqrt{12}, 0, \sqrt{12}$; y-intercept: 0
b. Absolute min at $(-4, -16)$ and $(2, -16)$, absolute max at $(-2, 16)$ and $(4, 16)$ **c.** $(0, 0)$ **d.** None
e. None
Graph:

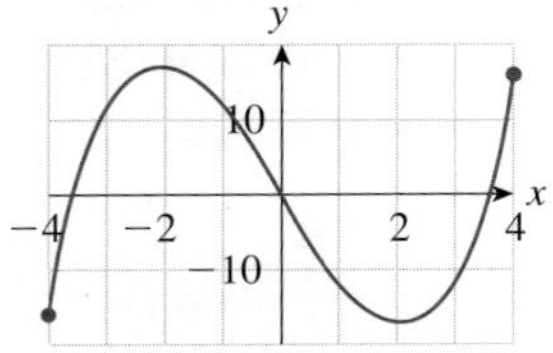

5. a. x-intercepts: $-3.6, 0, 5.1$; y-intercept: 0
b. Relative max at $(-2, 44)$, relative min at $(3, -81)$
c. $(0.5, -18.5)$ **d.** None **e.** $y \to -\infty$ as $x \to -\infty$; $y \to +\infty$ as $x \to +\infty$
Graph:

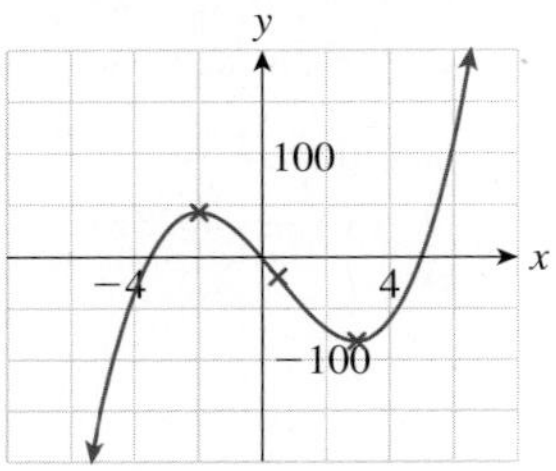

7. a. x-intercepts: $-3.3, 0.1, 1.8$; y-intercept: 1
b. Relative max at $(-2, 21)$, relative min at $(1, -6)$
c. $(-1/2, 15/2)$ **d.** None **e.** $y \to -\infty$ as $x \to -\infty$; $y \to +\infty$ as $x \to +\infty$

Graph:

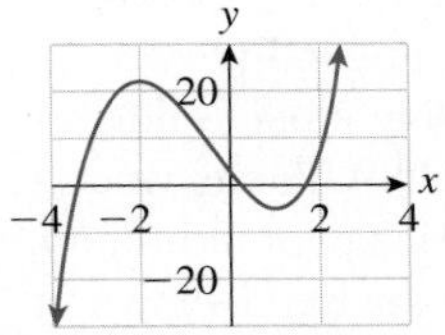

9. a. x-intercepts: $-2.9, 4.2$; y-intercept: 10
b. Relative max at $(-2, 74)$, relative min at $(0, 10)$, absolute max at $(3, 199)$ **c.** $(-1.12, 44.8)$, $(1.79, 117.3)$
d. None **e.** $y \to -\infty$ as $x \to -\infty$; $y \to -\infty$ as $x \to +\infty$
Graph:

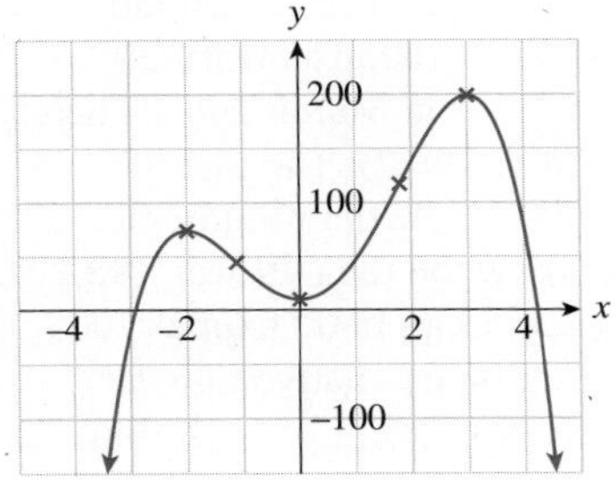

11. a. t-intercepts: $t = 0$; y-intercept: 0 **b.** Absolute min at $(0, 0)$ **c.** $(1/3, 11/324)$ and $(1, 1/12)$ **d.** None
e. $y \to +\infty$ as $t \to -\infty$; $y \to +\infty$ as $t \to +\infty$
Graph:

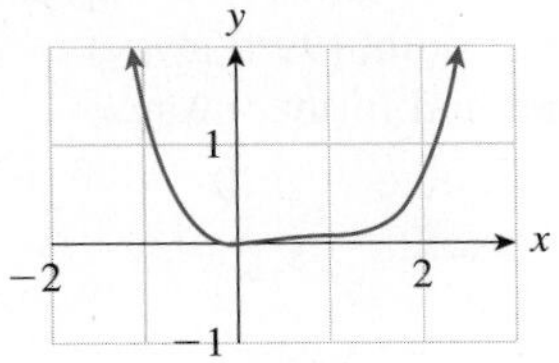

13. a. x-intercepts: None; y-intercept: None
b. Relative min at $(1, 2)$, relative max at $(-1, -2)$
c. None **d.** $y \to -\infty$ as $x \to 0^-$; $y \to +\infty$ as $x \to 0^+$, so there is a vertical asymptote at $x = 0$. **e.** $y \to -\infty$ as $x \to -\infty$; $y \to +\infty$ as $x \to +\infty$
Graph:

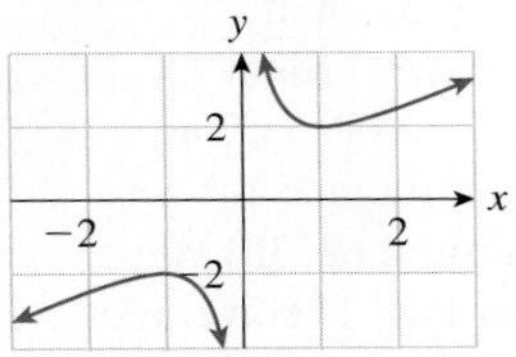

15. a. x-intercept: 0; y-intercept: 0 **b.** None **c.** $(0, 0)$, $(-3, -9/4)$, and $(3, 9/4)$ **d.** None **e.** $y \to -\infty$ as $x \to -\infty$; $y \to +\infty$ as $x \to +\infty$

Graph:

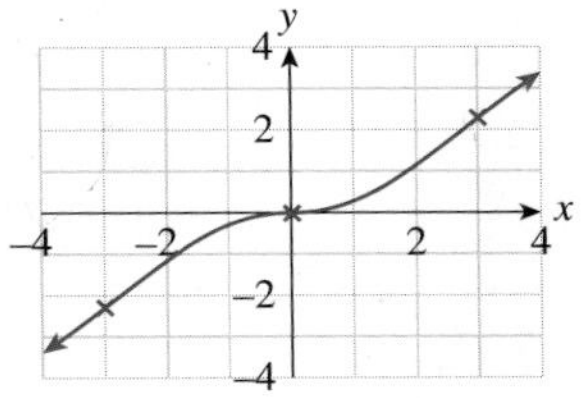

17. a. t-intercepts: None; y-intercept: -1 **b.** Relative min at $(-2, 5/3)$ and $(2, 5/3)$, relative max at $(0, -1)$ **c.** None **d.** $y \to +\infty$ as $t \to -1^-$; $y \to -\infty$ as $t \to -1^+$; $y \to -\infty$ as $t \to 1^-$; $y \to +\infty$ as $t \to 1^+$; so there are vertical asymptotes at $t = \pm 1$. **e.** None
Graph:

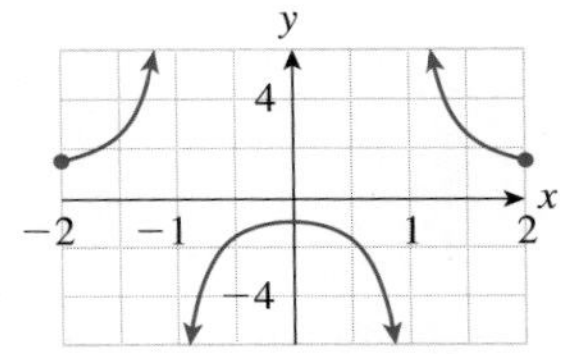

19. a. x-intercepts: -0.6; y-intercept: 1 **b.** Relative maximum at $(-2, -1/3)$, relative minimum at $(-1, -2/3)$ **c.** None **d.** None. **e.** $y \to -\infty$ as $x \to -\infty$; $y \to +\infty$ as $x \to +\infty$
Graph:

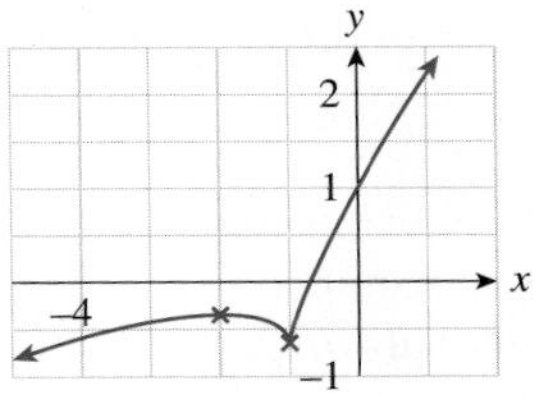

21. a. x-intercepts: None; y-intercept: None
b. Absolute min at $(1, 1)$ **c.** None **d.** Vertical asymptote at $x = 0$ **e.** $y \to +\infty$ as $x \to +\infty$
Graph:

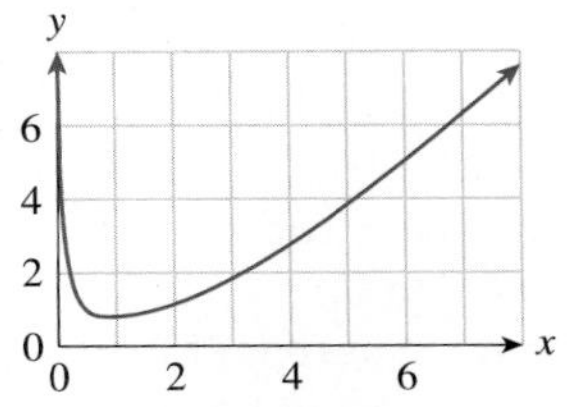

23. a. x-intercepts: ± 0.8; x-intercept: None **b.** None **c.** $(1,1)$ and $(-1, 1)$ **d.** $y \to -\infty$ as $x \to 0$; vertical asymptote at $x = 0$ **e.** $y \to +\infty$ as $x \to \pm\infty$

Graph:

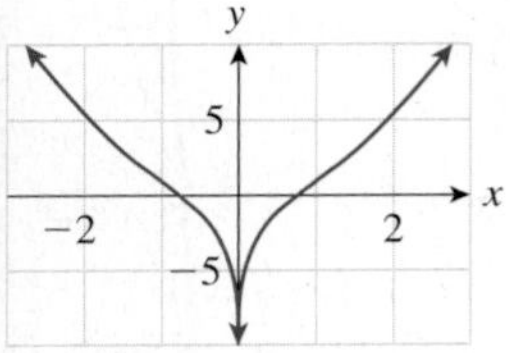

25. a. t-intercepts: None; y-intercept: 1 **b.** Absolute min at (0, 1). Absolute max at $(1, e - 1)$, relative max at $(-1, e^{-1} + 1)$. **c.** None **d.** None **e.** None
Graph:

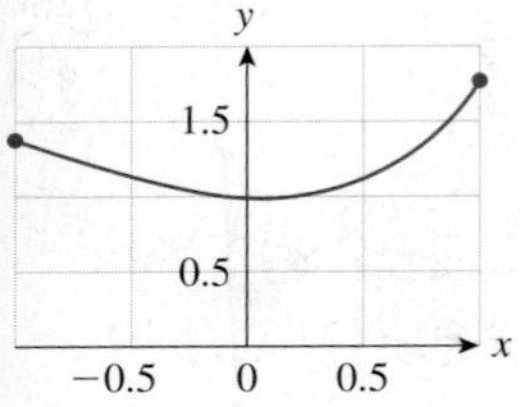

27. Absolute min at (1.40, −1.49); points of inflection: (0.21, 0.61), (0.79, −0.55)
Graph:

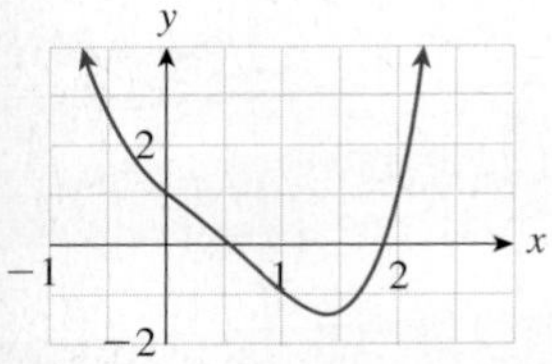

29. $f(x) = e^x - x^3$. Relative min at (−0.46, 0.73), relative max at (0.91, 1.73), absolute min at (3.73, −10.22); points of inflection at (0.20, 1.22) and (2.83, −5.74)
Graph:

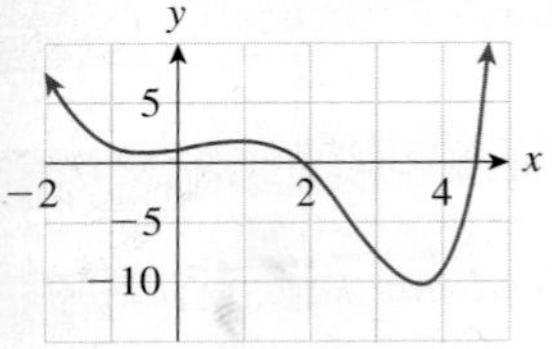

31. y-intercept: 125; t-intercepts: None. The median home price was about \$125,000 at the start of 2000 ($t = 0$). Extrema: Absolute minimum at (0, 125); absolute maximum at (6, 225). The median home price was lowest in 2000 ($t = 0$) when it stood at \$125,000; the median home price was at its highest at the start of 2006 ($t = 6$) at \$225,000. Points of inflection at (3, 175) and (10, 200). The median home price was increasing most rapidly at the start of 2003 ($t = 3$) when it was \$175,000, and decreasing most rapidly at the start of 2010 when it was \$200,000. Points where the function is not defined: None. Behavior at infinity: As $t \to +\infty$, $y \to 175$. Assuming the trend shown in the graph continues indefinitely, the median home price will approach a value of \$175,000 in the long term. **33. a.** Intercepts: No t-intercept; y-intercept at $I(0) = 195$. The CPI was never zero during the given period; in July 2005 the CPI was 195. Absolute min at (0, 195), absolute max at (8, 199.3), relative max at (2.9, 198.7), relative min at (6.0, 197.8). The CPI was at a low of 195 in July 2005, rose to 198.7 around October 2005, dipped to 197.8 around January 2006, and then rose to a high of 199.3 in March 2006. There is a point of inflection at (4.4, 198.2). The rate of change of the CPI (inflation) reached a minimum around mid-November 2005 when the CPI was 198.2. **b.** The inflation rate was zero at around October 2005 and January 2006. **35.** Extrema: Relative max at (0, 100), absolute min at (1, 99); point of inflection (0.5, 99.5); $s \to +\infty$ as $t \to +\infty$. At time $t = 0$ seconds, the UFO is 100 ft away from the observer, and begins to move closer. At time $t = 0.5$ seconds, when the UFO is 99.5 feet away, its distance is decreasing most rapidly (it is moving toward the observer most rapidly). It then slows down to a stop at $t = 1$ sec when it is at its closest point (99 ft away) and then begins to move further and further away.
Graph:

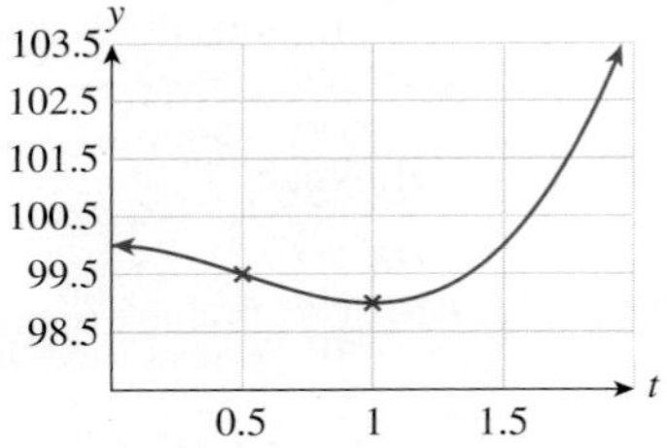

37. Intercepts: None; Absolute minimum at (1,500, 130); No points of inflection; vertical asymptote at $x = 0$. As $x \to +\infty$, $y \to +\infty$. The average cost is never zero, nor is it defined for zero iPods. The average cost is a minimum (\$130) when 1,500 iPods are manufactured per day. The average cost becomes extremely large for very small or very large numbers of iPods.

Graph:

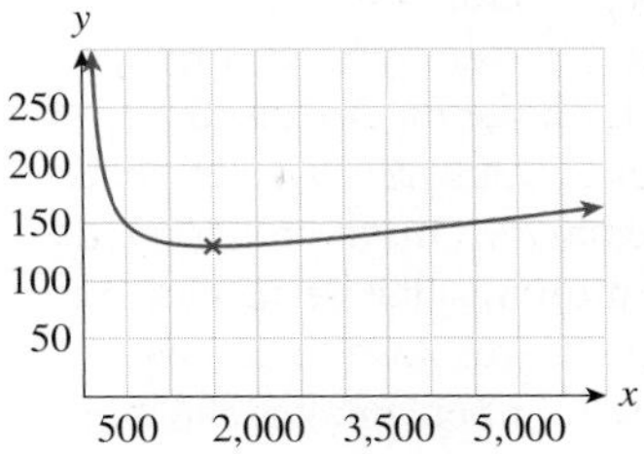

39. Graph of derivative:

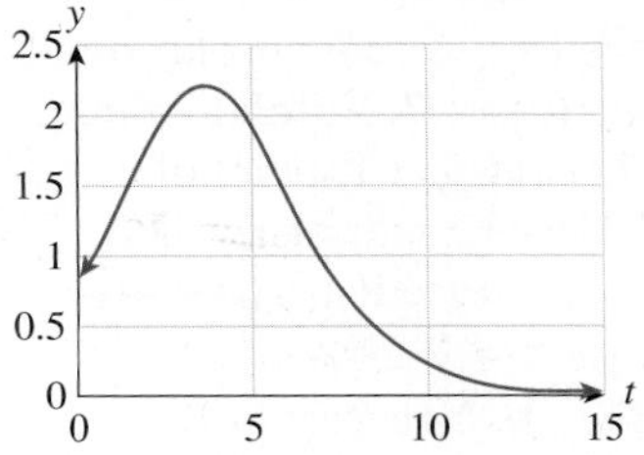

The absolute maximum occurs at approximately (3.7, 2.2); during the year 2003. The percentage of mortgages that were subprime was increasing most rapidly during 2003, when it increased at a rate of around 2.2 percentage points per year. As $t \to +\infty$, $A'(t) \to 0$; In the long term, assuming the trend shown in the model continues, the rate of change of the percentage of mortgages that were subprime approaches zero; that is, the percentage of mortgages that were subprime approaches a constant value. **41.** No; yes. Near a vertical asymptote the value of y increases without bound, and so the graph could not be included between two horizontal lines; hence, no vertical asymptotes are possible. Horizontal asymptotes are possible, as for instance in the graph in Exercise 31. **43.** It too has a vertical asymptote at $x = a$; the magnitude of the derivative increases without bound as $x \to a$. **45.** No. If the leftmost critical point is a relative maximum, the function will decrease from there until it reaches the rightmost critical point, so can't have a relative maximum there. **47.** Between every pair of zeros of $f(x)$ there must be a local extremum, which must be a stationary point of $f(x)$, hence a zero of $f'(x)$.

Section 5.5

1. $P = 10{,}000$; $\dfrac{dP}{dt} = 1{,}000$ **3.** Let R be the annual revenue of my company, and let q be annual sales. $R = 7{,}000$ and $\dfrac{dR}{dt} = -700$. Find $\dfrac{dq}{dt}$. **5.** Let p be the price of a pair of shoes, and let q be the demand for shoes. $\dfrac{dp}{dt} = 5$. Find $\dfrac{dq}{dt}$. **7.** Let T be the average global temperature, and let q be the number of Bermuda shorts sold per year. $T = 60$ and $\dfrac{dT}{dt} = 0.1$. Find $\dfrac{dq}{dt}$. **9. a.** $6/(100\pi) \approx 0.019$ km/sec **b.** $6/(8\sqrt{\pi}\,) \approx 0.4231$ km/sec **11.** $3/(4\pi) \approx 0.24$ ft/min **13.** 7.5 ft/sec **15.** Decreasing at a rate of \$1.66 per player per week **17.** Monthly sales will drop at a rate of 26 T-shirts per month. **19.** Raise the price by 3¢ per week. **21.** Increasing at a rate of \$233.68 million per year **23.** 1 laborer per month **25.** Dropping at a rate of \$2.40 per year. **27.** The price is decreasing at a rate of approximately 31¢ per pound per month. **29.** $2{,}300/\sqrt{4{,}100} \approx 36$ miles/hour. **31.** About 10.7 ft/sec **33.** The y coordinate is decreasing at a rate of 16 units per second. **35.** \$534 per year **37.** Their prior experience must increase at a rate of approximately 0.97 years every year. **39.** $\dfrac{2{,}500}{9\pi}\left(\dfrac{3}{5{,}000}\right)^{2/3} \approx 0.63$ m/sec **41.** $\dfrac{\sqrt{1+128\pi}}{4\pi} \approx 1.6$ cm/sec **43.** 0.5137 computers per household, and increasing at a rate of 0.0230 computers per household per year. **45.** The average SAT score was 904.71 and decreasing at a rate of 0.11 per year. **47.** Decreasing by 2 percentage points per year **49.** The section is called "related rates" because the goal is to compute the rate of change of a quantity based on a knowledge of the rate of change of a related quantity. **51.** Answers may vary: A rectangular solid has dimensions 2 cm × 5 cm × 10 cm, and each side is expanding at a rate of 3 cm/second. How fast is the volume increasing? **53.** (Proof) **55.** Linear **57.** Let x = my grades and y = your grades. If $dx/dt = 2\,dy/dt$, then $dy/dt = (1/2)\,dx/dt$.

Section 5.6

1. $E = 1.5$; the demand is going down 1.5% per 1% increase in price at that price level; revenue is maximized when $p = \$25$; weekly revenue at that price is \$12,500. **3. a.** $E = 6/7$; the demand is going down 6% per 7% increase in price at that price level; thus, a price increase is in order. **b.** Revenue is maximized when $p = 100/3 \approx \$33.33$ **c.** 4,444 cases per week **5. a.** $E = (4p - 33)/(-2p + 33)$ **b.** 0.54; the demand for $E = mc^2$ T-shirts is going down by about 0.54% per 1% increase in the price. **c.** \$11 per shirt for a daily revenue of \$1,331 **7. a.** $E = 1.81$. Thus, the demand is elastic at the given tuition level, showing that a decrease in tuition will result in an increase in revenue. **b.** They should charge an average of \$2,250 per student, and this will result in an enrollment of about 4,950 students, giving a revenue of about \$11,137,500. **9. a.** $E = 51$; the demand is going down 51% per 1% increase in price at that price level; thus, a large price decrease is advised. **b.** ¥50 **c.** About 78 paint-by-number sets per month **11. a.** $E = -\dfrac{mp}{mp+b}$ **b.** $p = -\dfrac{b}{2m}$ **13. a.** $E = r$ **b.** E is independent of p. **c.** If $r = 1$, then the revenue is not affected by the price. If $r > 1$, then the revenue is always elastic, while if $r < 1$, the revenue is always inelastic. This is an unrealistic model because there should always be a price at which the revenue is a maximum. **15. a.** $q = -1{,}500p + 6{,}000$. **b.** \$2 per hamburger, giving a total weekly revenue of \$6,000 **17.** $E \approx 0.77$. At a family income level of \$20,000, the fraction of children attending a live theatrical performance is increasing by 0.77% per 1% increase in household income. **19. a.** $E = \dfrac{1.554xe^{-0.021x}}{-74e^{-0.021x} + 92}$; $E(100) \approx 0.23$: At a household income level of \$100,000, the percentage of people using broadband in 2010 was increasing by 0.23% per 1% increase in household income. **b.** The model predicts elasticity approaching zero for households with large incomes. **21. a.** $E \approx 0.46$. The demand for computers is increasing by 0.46% per 1% increase in household income. **b.** E decreases as income increases. **c.** Unreliable; it predicts a likelihood greater than 1 at incomes of \$123,000 and above. In a more appropriate model, we would expect the curve to level off at or below 1. **d.** $E \approx 0$

23. The income elasticity of demand is

$$\frac{dQ}{dY} \cdot \frac{Y}{Q} = a\beta P^{\alpha} Y^{\beta-1} \frac{Y}{aP^{\alpha}Y^{\beta}} = \beta.$$

25. a. $q = 1{,}000e^{-0.30p}$ **b.** At $p = \$3$, $E = 0.9$; at $p = \$4$, $E = 1.2$; at $p = \$5$, $E = 1.5$ **c.** $p = \$3.33$ **d.** $p = \$5.36$. Selling at a lower price would increase demand, but you cannot sell more than 200 pounds anyway. You should charge as much as you can and still be able to sell all 200 pounds. **27.** The price is lowered. **29.** Start with $R = pq$, and differentiate with respect to p to obtain $\dfrac{dR}{dp} = q + p\dfrac{dq}{dp}$. For a stationary point, $dR/dp = 0$, and so $q + p\dfrac{dq}{dp} = 0$. Rearranging this result gives $p\dfrac{dq}{dp} = -q$, and hence $-\dfrac{dq}{dp} \cdot \dfrac{p}{q} = 1$, or $E = 1$, showing that stationary points of R correspond to points of unit elasticity. **31.** The distinction is best illustrated by an example. Suppose that q is measured in weekly sales and p is the unit price in dollars. Then the quantity $-dq/dp$ measures the drop in weekly sales per \$1 increase in price. The elasticity of demand E, on the other hand, measures the *percentage* drop in sales per 1% increase in price. Thus, $-dq/dp$ measures absolute change, while E measures fractional, or percentage, change.

Chapter 5 Review

1. Relative max: $(-1, 5)$, absolute min: $(-2, -3)$ and $(1, -3)$ **3.** Absolute max: $(-1, 5)$, absolute min: $(1, -3)$ **5.** Absolute min: $(1, 0)$ **7.** Absolute min: $(-2, -1/4)$ **9.** Relative max at $x = 1$, point of inflection at $x = -1$ **11.** Relative max at $x = -2$, relative min at $x = 1$, point of inflection at $x = -1$ **13.** One point of inflection, at $x = 0$ **15. a.** $a = 4/t^4 - 2/t^3$ m/sec^2 **b.** 2 m/sec^2 **17.** Relative max: $(-2, 16)$; absolute min: $(2, -16)$; point of inflection: $(0, 0)$; no horizontal or vertical asymptotes

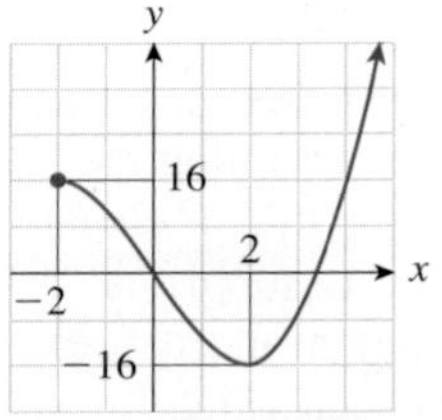

19. Relative min: $(-3, -2/9)$; relative max: $(3, 2/9)$; inflection: $(-3\sqrt{2}, -5\sqrt{2}/36)$, $(3\sqrt{2}, 5\sqrt{2}/36)$; vertical asymptote: $x = 0$; horizontal asymptote: $y = 0$

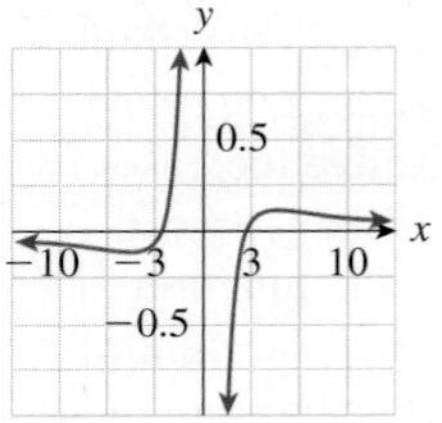

21. Relative max at $(0, 0)$, absolute min at $(1, -2)$, no asymptotes

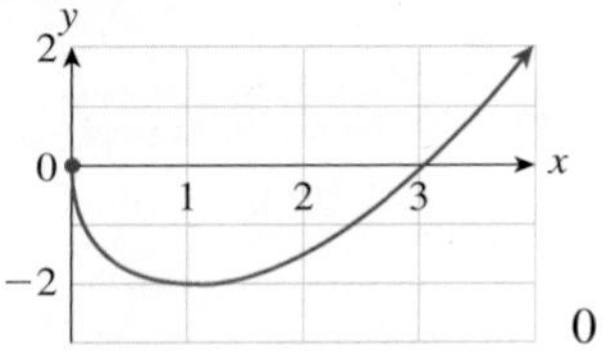

23. \$22.14 per book **25. a.** Profit $= -p^3 + 42p^2 - 288p - 181$ **b.** \$24 per copy; \$3,275 **c.** For

maximum revenue, the company should charge \$22.14 per copy. At this price, the cost per book is decreasing with increasing price, while the revenue is not decreasing (its derivative is zero). Thus, the profit is increasing with increasing price, suggesting that the maximum profit will occur at a higher price.
27. 12 in × 12 in × 6 in, for a volume of 864 in^3
29. a. $E = \dfrac{2p^2 - 33p}{-p^2 + 33p + 9}$ **b.** 0.52, 2.03; when the price is \$20, demand is dropping at a rate of 0.52% per 1% increase in the price; when the price is \$25, demand is dropping at a rate of 2.03% per 1% increase in the price. **c.** \$22.14 per book **31. a.** $E = 2p^2 - p$ **b.** 6; the demand is dropping at a rate of 6% per 1% increase in the price. **c.** \$1.00, for a monthly revenue of \$1,000 **33. a.** Week 5 **b.** Point of inflection on the graph of s; maximum on the graph of s', t-intercept in the graph of s''. **c.** 10,500; if weekly sales continue as predicted by the model, they will level off at around 10,500 books per week in the long term. **d.** 0; if weekly sales continue as predicted by the model, the rate of change of sales approaches zero in the long term. **35. a.–d.** $10/\sqrt{2}$ ft/sec

Chapter 6

Section 6.1

1. $x^6/6 + C$ **3.** $6x + C$ **5.** $x^2/2 + C$
7. $x^3/3 - x^2/2 + C$ **9.** $x + x^2/2 + C$
11. $-x^{-4}/4 + C$
13. $x^{3.3}/3.3 - x^{-0.3}/0.3 + C$ **15.** $u^3/3 - \ln|u| + C$
17. $\dfrac{4x^{5/4}}{5} + C$ **19.** $3x^5/5 + 2x^{-1} - x^{-4}/4 + 4x + C$
21. $2\ln|u| + u^2/8 + C$ **23.** $\ln|x| - \dfrac{2}{x} + \dfrac{1}{2x^2} + C$
25. $3x^{1.1}/1.1 - x^{5.3}/5.3 - 4.1x + C$
27. $\dfrac{x^{0.9}}{0.3} + \dfrac{40}{x^{0.1}} + C$
29. $2.55t^2 - 1.2\ln|t| - \dfrac{15}{t^{0.2}} + C$
31. $2e^x + 5x|x|/2 + x/4 + C$
33. $12.2x^{0.5} + x^{1.5}/9 - e^x + C$ **35.** $\dfrac{2^x}{\ln 2} - \dfrac{3^x}{\ln 3} + C$
37. $\dfrac{100(1.1^x)}{\ln(1.1)} - \dfrac{x|x|}{3} + C$ **39.** $x^3/3 + 3x^{-5}/10 + C$
41. $1/x - 1/x^2 + C$ **43.** $f(x) = x^2/2 + 1$
45. $f(x) = e^x - x - 1$
47. $C(x) = 5x - x^2/20{,}000 + 20{,}000$
49. $C(x) = 5x + x^2 + \ln x + 994$

51. a. $M(t) = 0.8t^4 - 6t^2 + 10t + 1$
b. 83 million members
53. $I(t) = 42{,}000 + 1200t$; \$48,000
55. $S(t) = -15t^3 + 450t^2 + 4{,}200t$; 54,720 million gallons **57. a.** $H'(t) = 3.5t + 65$ billion dollars per year **b.** $H(t) = 1.75t^2 + 65t + 700$ billion dollars
59. a. $-0.4t + 1$ percentage points per year
b. $-0.2t^2 + t + 13$; 13.8 **61. a.** $s = t^3/3 + t + C$
b. $C = 1$; $s = t^3/3 + t + 1$ **63.** 320 ft/sec downward **65. a.** $v(t) = -32t + 16$ **b.** $s(t) = -16t^2 + 16t + 185$; zenith at $t = 0.5$ sec $s = 189$ feet, 4 feet above the top of the tower.
67. a. $s = 525t + 25t^2$ **b.** 3 hours **c.** The negative solution indicates that, at time $t = -24$, the tail wind would have been large and negative, causing the plane to be moving backward through that position 24 hours prior to departure and arrive at the starting point of the flight at time 0! **69.** (Proof) **71.** $(1{,}280)^{1/2} \approx$ 35.78 ft/sec **73. a.** 80 ft/sec **b.** 60 ft/sec
c. 1.25 seconds **75.** $\sqrt{2} \approx 1.414$ times as fast
77. The term *indefinite* refers to the arbitrary constant term in the indefinite integral; we do not obtain a definite value for C and hence the integral is "not definite." **79.** Constant; because the derivative of a linear function is constant, linear functions are antiderivatives of constant functions. **81.** No; there are infinitely many antiderivatives of a given function, each pair of them differing by a constant. Knowing the value of the function at a specific point suffices.
83. They differ by a constant, $G(x) - F(x) =$ Constant **85.** Antiderivative, marginal **87.** Up to a constant, $\int f(x)\,dx$ represents the total cost of manufacturing x items. The units of $\int f(x)\,dx$ are the product of the units of $f(x)$ and the units of x.
89. The indefinite integral of the constant 1 is not zero; it is x (+ constant). Correct answer: $3x^2/2 + x + C$
91. There should be no integral sign ($\int$) in the answer. Correct answer: $2x^6 - 2x^2 + C$ **93.** The integral of a constant times a function is the constant times the integral of the function; not the *integral* of the constant times the integral of the function. (In general, the integral of a product is *not* the product of the integrals.) Correct answer: $4(e^x - x^2) + C$ **95.** It is the *integral* of $1/x$ that equals $\ln|x| + C$, and not $1/x$ itself. Correct answer: $\int \frac{1}{x}dx = \ln|x| + C$
97. $\int (f(x) + g(x))\,dx$ is, by definition, an antiderivative of $f(x) + g(x)$. Let $F(x)$ be an antiderivative of $f(x)$ and let $G(x)$ be an antiderivative of $g(x)$. Then, because the derivative of $F(x) + G(x)$ is $f(x) + g(x)$ (by the rule for sums of derivatives), this means that $F(x) + G(x)$ is an antiderivative of $f(x) + g(x)$. In

symbols, $\int(f(x) + g(x))\,dx = F(x) + G(x) + C = \int f(x)\,dx + \int g(x)\,dx$, the sum of the indefinite integrals. **99.** Answers will vary. $\int x \cdot 1\,dx = \int x\,dx = x^2/2 + C$, whereas $\int x\,dx \cdot \int 1\,dx = (x^2/2 + D) \cdot (x + E)$, which is not the same as $x^2/2 + C$, no matter what values we choose for the constants C, D, and E. **101.** Derivative; indefinite integral; indefinite integral; derivative

Section 6.2

1. $(3x - 5)^4/12 + C$ **3.** $(3x - 5)^4/12 + C$
5. $-e^{-x} + C$ **7.** $-e^{-x} + C$ **9.** $\frac{1}{2}e^{(x+1)^2} + C$
11. $(3x + 1)^6/18 + C$ **13.** $1.6(3x - 4)^{3/2} + C$
15. $2e^{(0.6x+2)} + C$ **17.** $(3x^2 + 3)^4/24 + C$
19. $2(3x^2 - 1)^{3/2}/9 + C$ **21.** $-(x^2 + 1)^{-0.3}/0.6 + C$
23. $(4x^2 - 1)|4x^2 - 1|/16 + C$ **25.** $x + 3e^{3.1x-2} + C$
27. $-(1/2)e^{-x^2+1} + C$ **29.** $-(1/2)e^{-(x^2+2x)} + C$
31. $(x^2 + x + 1)^{-2}/2 + C$
33. $(2x^3 + x^6 - 5)^{1/2}/3 + C$
35. $(x - 2)^7/7 + (x - 2)^6/3 + C$
37. $4[(x + 1)^{5/2}/5 - (x + 1)^{3/2}/3] + C$
39. $20 \ln|1 - e^{-0.05x}| + C$ **41.** $3e^{-1/x} + C$
43. $-\dfrac{(4 + 1/x^2)^4}{8} + C$ **45.** $(e^x - e^{-x})/2 + C$
47. $\ln(e^x + e^{-x}) + C$
49. $(1 - e^{3x-1})|1 - e^{3x-1}|/6 + C$
51. $(e^{2x^2-2x} + e^{x^2})/2 + C$ **53.** Derivation
55. Derivation **57.** $-e^{-x} + C$ **59.** $(1/2)e^{2x-1} + C$
61. $(2x + 4)^3/6 + C$ **63.** $(1/5) \ln|5x - 1| + C$
65. $(1.5x)^4/6 + C$ **67.** $\dfrac{1.5^{3x}}{3 \ln(1.5)} + C$
69. $\frac{1}{4}(2x + 4)|2x + 4| + C$ **71.** $\dfrac{2^{3x+4} - 2^{-3x+4}}{3 \ln 2} + C$
73. $f(x) = (x^2 + 1)^4/8 - 1/8$
75. $f(x) = (1/2)e^{x^2-1}$ **77.** $(5x^2 - 3)^7/70 + C$
79. $2(3e^x - 1)^{1/2}/3 + C$ **81.** $e^{(x^4-8)}/4 + C$
83. $\frac{1}{6} \ln|1 + 2e^{3x}| + C$
85. $210t + 1{,}240e^{-0.05t} - 1{,}240$
87. $8e^{0.25t} - 35.854$; $62 billion
89. $C(x) = 5x - 1/(x + 1) + 995.5$
91. a. $N(t) = 35 \ln(5 + e^{0.2t}) - 63$ **b.** 80,000 articles
93. $S(t) = 3{,}600[\ln(3 + e^{0.25t}) - \ln 4]$; 6,310 sets
95. a. $s = (t^2 + 1)^5/10 + t^2/2 + C$ **b.** $C = 9/10$; $s = (t^2 + 1)^5/10 + t^2/2 + 9/10$
97. a. $S(t) = -15(t - 2{,}000)^3 + 450(t - 2{,}000)^2 + 4{,}200(t - 2{,}000) - 16{,}245$ million gallons **b.** 38,475 million gallons **99.** None; the substitution $u = x$ simply replaces the letter x throughout by the letter u, and thus does not change the integral at all. For instance, the integral $\int x(3x^2 + 1)\,dx$ becomes $\int u(3u^2 + 1)\,du$ if we substitute $u = x$. **101.** It may mean that, but it may not; see Example 4. **103.** (D); to compute the integral, first break it up into a sum of two integrals: $\displaystyle\int \frac{x}{x^2 - 1}\,dx + \int \frac{3x}{x^2 + 1}\,dx$, and then compute the first using $u = x^2 - 1$ and the second using $u = x^2 + 1$. **105.** There are several errors: First, the term "dx" is missing in the integral, and this affects all the subsequent steps (since we must substitute for dx when changing to the variable u). Second, when there is a noncanceling x in the integrand, we cannot treat it as a constant. Correct answer: $3(x^2 - 1)^2/4 + C$ **107.** In the fourth step, u was substituted back for x before the integral was taken and du was just changed to dx; they're not equal. Correct answer: $(x^3 - 1)^2/6 + C$ **109.** Proof

Section 6.3

1. 4 **3.** 6 **5.** 0.7456 **7.** 2.3129 **9.** 2.5048 **11.** 30 **13.** 22 **15.** −2 **17.** 0 **19.** 1 **21.** 1/2 **23.** 1/4 **25.** 2 **27.** 0 **29.** 6 **31.** 0 **33.** 0.5 **35.** 3.3045, 3.1604, 3.1436 **37.** 0.0275, 0.0258, 0.0256 **39.** 15.76 liters **41.** $99.95 **43.** 41 billion gallons **45.** $19 billion **47. a.** Left sum: about 46,000 articles, right sum: about 55,000 articles **b.** 50.5; a total of about 50,500 articles in *Physical Review* were written by researchers in Europe in the 16-year period beginning 1983. **49.** 118,750 degrees **51.** 54,000 students **53.** Left sum: 76; right sum: 71; Left sum, as it is the sum of the annual net incomes for the given years. **55. a.** Left sum = 15.6; right sum = 15.9 **b.** Pemex sold a total of 15.9 billion tons of petrochemicals in the period 2006 through 2009. **57.** −84.8; after 4 seconds, the stone is about 84.8 ft below where it started. **59.** 91.2 ft **61.** 394; A total of about 394 million members joined Facebook from the start of 2005 to the start of 2010. **63.** 18,400; a total of 18,400 wiretaps were authorized by U.S. state and federal courts during the 15-year period starting January 1990. **65.** Yes. The Riemann sum gives an estimated area of 420 square feet.
67. a. Graph:

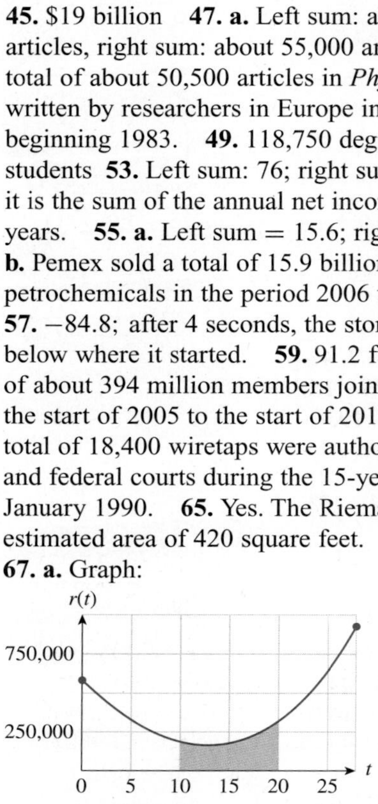

Total expenditure on oil in the United States from 1990 to 2000. **b.** 2,010,000; a total of \$2,010,000 million, or \$2.01 trillion, was spent on oil in the U.S. from 1990 to 2000. **69. a.** 99.4% **b.** 0 (to at least 15 decimal places) **71.** Stays the same **73.** Increases **75.** The area under the curve and above the x axis equals the area above the curve and below the x axis. **77.** Answers will vary. One example: Let $r(t)$ be the rate of change of net income at time t. If $r(t)$ is negative, then the net income is decreasing, so the change in net income, represented by the definite integral of $r(t)$, is negative.
79. Answers may vary.

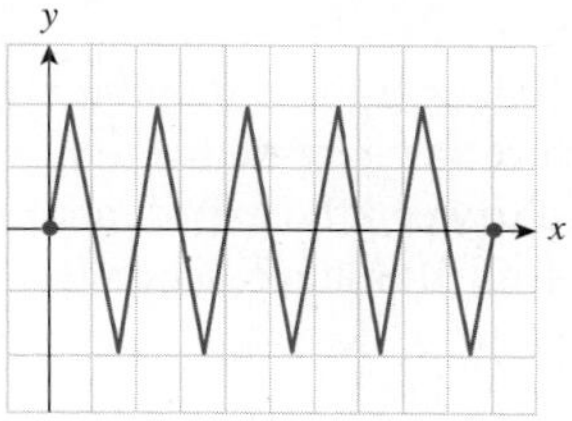

81. The total cost is $c(1) + c(2) + \cdots + c(60)$, which is represented by the Riemann sum approximation of $\int_1^{61} c(t)\,dt$ with $n = 60$. **83.** $[f(x_1) + f(x_2) + \cdots + f(x_n)]\Delta x = \sum_{k=1}^{n} f(x_k)\Delta x$
85. Answers may vary:

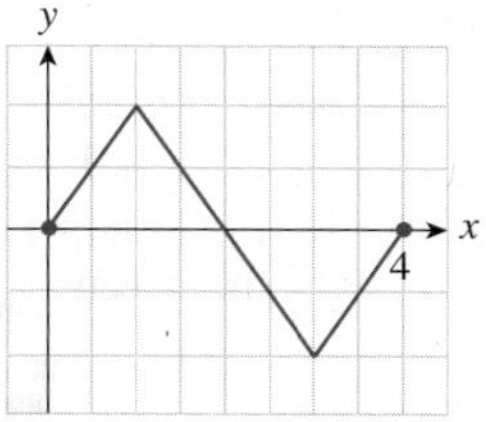

Section 6.4

1. $14/3$ **3.** 5 **5.** 0 **7.** $40/3$ **9.** -0.9045
11. $2(e-1)$ **13.** $2/3$ **15.** $1/\ln 2$
17. $4^6 - 1 = 4{,}095$ **19.** $(e^1 - e^{-3})/2$ **21.** $3/(2\ln 2)$
23. $40/3$ **25.** $5/4$ **27.** 0 **29.** $(5/2)(e^3 - e^2)$
31. $(1/3)[\ln 26 - \ln 7]$ **33.** $\dfrac{0.1}{2.2\ln(1.1)}$
35. $e - e^{1/2}$ **37.** 0.2221 **39.** $2 - \ln 3$ **41.** $-4/21$
43. $3^{5/2}/10 - 3^{3/2}/6 + 1/15$ **45.** $1/2$ **47.** $16/3$
49. $9/2$ **51.** $56/3$ **53.** $1/2$ **55.** \$783
57. 296 miles **59.** 260 ft **61.** 54,720 million gallons
63. 391.2 million members **65.** 18,470; a total of about 18,470 wiretaps were authorized by U.S. state and federal courts during the 15-year period starting January 1990. **67.** $210t + 1{,}240e^{-0.05t} - 1{,}240$
69. 9 gallons **71.** 907 T-shirts **73.** 68 milliliters
75. 20.48; The total value of vehicle transactions on eBay during 2008 and 2009 was about \$20.48 billion. **77.** Change in cost $= \int_0^x m(t)\,dt = C(x) - C(0)$ by the FTC, so $C(x) = C(0) + \int_0^x m(t)\,dt$. $C(0)$ is the *fixed cost.* **79.** 80,000 articles **81. a., b.** (Proofs) **c.** 2,401 thousand students **85.** They are related by the Fundamental Theorem of Calculus, which (briefly) states that the definite integral of a suitable function can be calculated by evaluating the indefinite integral at the two endpoints and subtracting.
87. Computing its definite integral from a to b.
89. Calculate definite integrals by using antiderivatives. **91.** An example is $v(t) = t - 5$.
93. An example is $f(x) = e^{-x}$. **95.** By the FTC, $\int_a^x f(t)\,dt = G(x) - G(a)$, where G is an antiderivative of f. Hence, $F(x) = G(x) - G(a)$. Taking derivatives of both sides, $F'(x) = G'(x) + 0 = f(x)$, as required. The result gives us a formula, in terms of area, for an antiderivative of any continuous function.

Chapter 6 Review

1. $x^3/3 - 5x^2 + 2x + C$ **3.** $4x^3/15 + 4/(5x) + C$
5. $(1/2)\ln|2x| + C$ or $(1/2)\ln|x| + C$
7. $-e^{-2x+11}/2 + C$ **9.** $(x^2+1)^{2.3}/4.6 + C$
11. $2\ln|x^2 - 7| + C$ **13.** $\frac{1}{6}(x^4 - 4x + 1)^{3/2} + C$
15. $-e^{x^2/2} + C$ **17.** $(x+2) - \ln|x+2| + C$ or $x - \ln|x+2| + C$ **19.** 1 **21.** 2.75
23. -0.24 **25.** 0.7778, 0.7500, 0.7471
27. 0 **29.** 1 **31.** $2/7$ **33.** $50(e^{-1} - e^{-2})$
35. $52/9$ **37.** $[\ln 5 - \ln 2]/8 = \ln(2.5)/8$
39. $32/3$ **41.** $(1 - e^{-25})/2$
43. a. $N(t) = 196t + t^2/2 - 0.16t^6/6$ **b.** 4 books
45. a. At a height of $-16t^2 + 100t$ ft **b.** 156.25 ft **c.** After 6.25 seconds **47.** 25,000 copies. **49.** 0 books
51. 39,200 hits **53.** \$8,200 **55.** About 86,000 books
57. About 35,800 books

Chapter 7

Section 7.1

1. $2e^x(x-1) + C$ **3.** $-e^{-x}(2+3x) + C$
5. $e^{2x}(2x^2 - 2x - 1)/4 + C$
7. $-e^{-2x+4}(2x^2 + 2x + 3)/4 + C$
9. $2^x[(2-x)/\ln 2 + 1/(\ln 2)^2] + C$
11. $-3^{-x}[(x^2-1)/\ln 3 + 2x/(\ln 3)^2 + 2/(\ln 3)^3] + C$
13. $-e^{-x}(x^2 + x + 1) + C$
15. $\frac{1}{7}x(x+2)^7 - \frac{1}{56}(x+2)^8 + C$

17. $-\dfrac{x}{2(x-2)^2} - \dfrac{1}{2(x-2)} + C$
19. $(x^4 \ln x)/4 - x^4/16 + C$
21. $(t^3/3 + t)\ln(2t) - t^3/9 - t + C$
23. $(3/4)t^{4/3}(\ln t - 3/4) + C$
25. $x \log_3 x - x/\ln 3 + C$
27. $e^{2x}(x/2 - 1/4) - 4e^{3x}/3 + C$
29. $e^x(x^2 - 2x + 2) - e^{x^2}/2 + C$
31. $\dfrac{1}{3}(3x-4)(2x-1)^{3/2} - \dfrac{1}{5}(2x-1)^{5/2} + C$
33. e **35.** 38,229/286
37. $(7/2)\ln 2 - 3/4$ **39.** 1/4
41. $1 - 11e^{-10}$ **43.** $4\ln 2 - 7/4$
45. $\dfrac{1}{2}x(x-3)|x-3| - \dfrac{1}{6}(x-3)^2|x-3| + C$
47. $2x|x-3| - (x-3)|x-3| + C$
49. $-x^2(-x+4)|-x+4| - \dfrac{2}{3}x(-x+4)^2|-x+4| - \dfrac{1}{6}(-x+4)^3|-x+4| + C$
51. $\dfrac{1}{2}(x^2-2x+3)(x-4)|x-4| - \dfrac{1}{3}(x-1)(x-4)^2|x-4| + \dfrac{1}{12}(x-4)^3|x-4| + C$
53. $28{,}800{,}000(1 - 2e^{-1})$ ft
55. $5{,}001 + 10x - 1/(x+1) - [\ln(x+1)]/(x+1)$
57. \$4,252 billion **59.** 19 billion square feet
61. 20,800 million gallons
63. $e^{0.1x}(250[-8x^2 + 70x + 1{,}000] - 2{,}500[-16x + 70] - 400{,}000) + 325{,}000$ **65.** 33,598
67. a. $r(t) = -0.075t + 2.75 + [0.025t - 0.25]\dfrac{|t-10|}{t-10}$
b. 42.5 million people **69.** Answers will vary. Examples are xe^{x^2} and $e^{x^2} = 1 \cdot e^{x^2}$. **71.** Answers will vary. Examples are Exercises 31 and 32, or, more simply, integrals like $\int x(x+1)^5\,dx$.
73. Substitution **75.** Parts **77.** Substitution
79. Parts **81.** $n + 1$ times **83.** Proof.

Section 7.2

1. 16/3 **3.** 9.75 **5.** 2 **7.** 31/3 **9.** 8/3 **11.** 4
13. 1/3 **15.** 1 **17.** 2 **19.** 39 **21.** $e - 3/2$ **23.** 2/3
25. 3/10 **27.** 1/20 **29.** 4/15 **31.** 1/3 **33.** 32
35. $2\ln 2 - 1$ **37.** $8\ln 4 + 2e - 16$ **39.** 0.9138
41. 0.3222 **43.** 112.5. This represents your total profit for the week, \$112.50. **45.** 608; there were approximately 608,000 housing starts from the start of 2002 to the start of 2006 not for sale purposes.

47. a. Graph: (The upper curve is **Myspace**.)

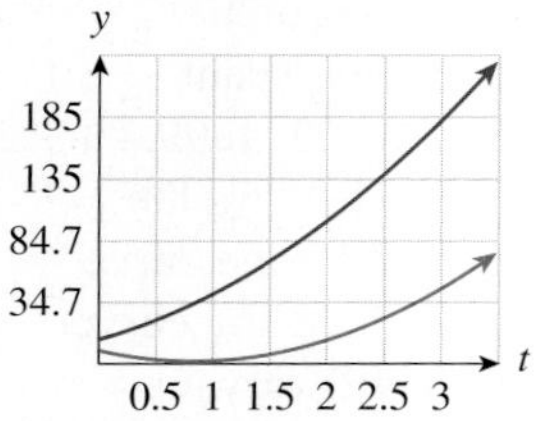

Myspace; about 93 million members **b.** The area between the curves $y = f(t)$ and $y = m(t)$ over [0.5, 2]
49. $16{,}078(e^{0.051t} - 1) - 7{,}333.3(e^{0.06t} - 1)$; the total number of wiretaps authorized by federal courts from the start of 1990 up to time t was about $16{,}078(e^{0.051t} - 1) - 7{,}333.3(e^{0.06t} - 1)$.
51. Wrong: It could mean that the graphs of f and g cross, as shown in the caution at the start of this topic in the textbook. **53.** The area between the export and import curves represents the United States's accumulated trade deficit (that is, the total excess of imports over exports) from 1960 to 2007. **55.** (A) **57.** The claim is wrong because the area under a curve can only represent income if the curve is a graph of income *per unit time*. The value of a stock price is not income per unit time—the income can be realized only when the stock is sold, and it amounts to the current market price. The total net income (per share) from the given investment would be the stock price on the date of sale minus the purchase price of \$50.

Section 7.3

1. Average = 2

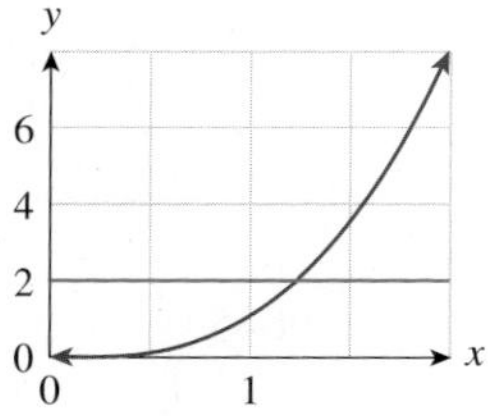

3. Average = 1

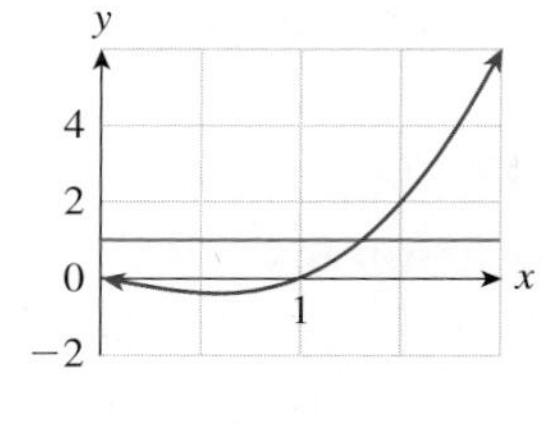

5. Average = $(1 - e^{-2})/2$

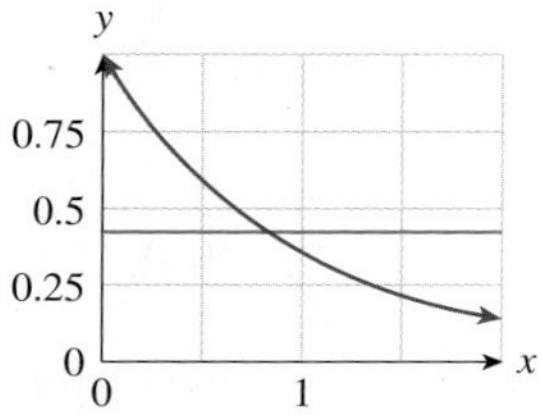

7. Average = 17/8

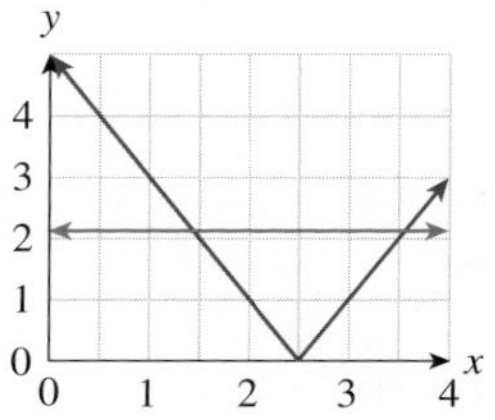

9.

x	0	1	2	3	4	5	6	7
$r(x)$	3	5	10	3	2	5	6	7
$\bar{r}(x)$			6	6	5	10/3	13/3	6

11.

x	0	1	2	3	4	5	6	7
$r(x)$	1	2	6	7	11	15	10	2
$\bar{r}(x)$			3	5	8	11	12	9

13. Moving average:

$\bar{f}(x) = x^3 - (15/2)x^2 + 25x - 125/4$

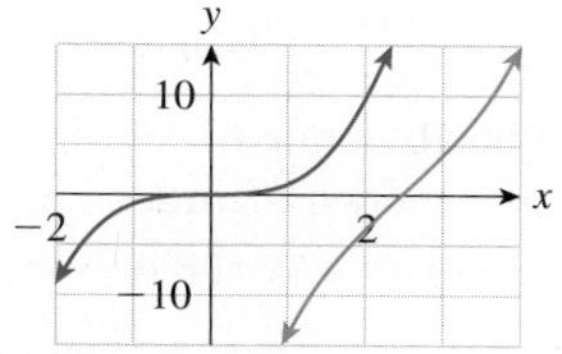

15. Moving average:

$\bar{f}(x) = (3/25)[x^{5/3} - (x-5)^{5/3}]$

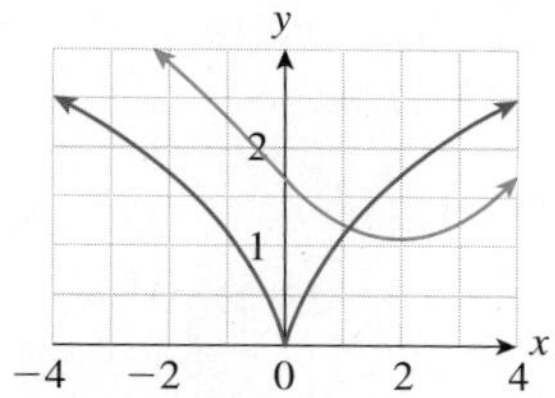

17. $\bar{f}(x) = \frac{2}{5}(e^{0.5x} - e^{0.5(x-5)})$

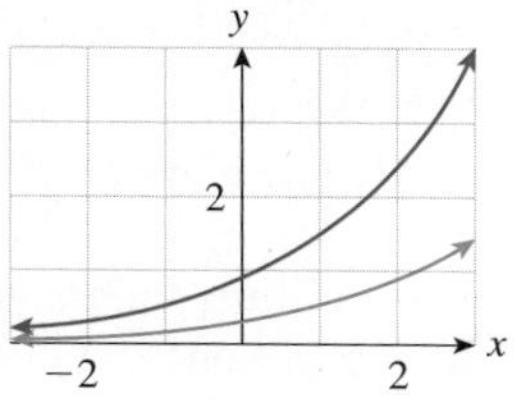

19. $\bar{f}(x) = \frac{2}{15}(x^{3/2} - (x-5)^{3/2})$

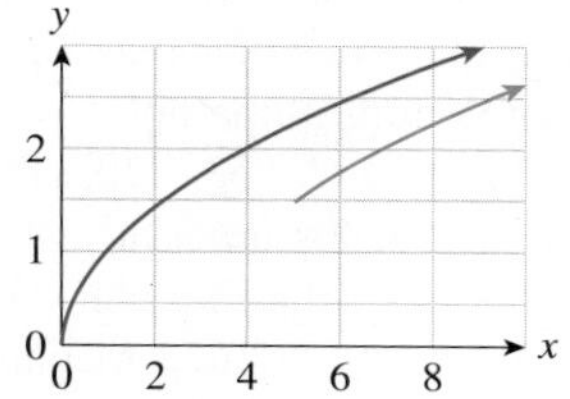

21. $\bar{f}(x) = \frac{1}{5}\left[5 - \frac{1}{2}|2x-1| + \frac{1}{2}|2x-11|\right]$

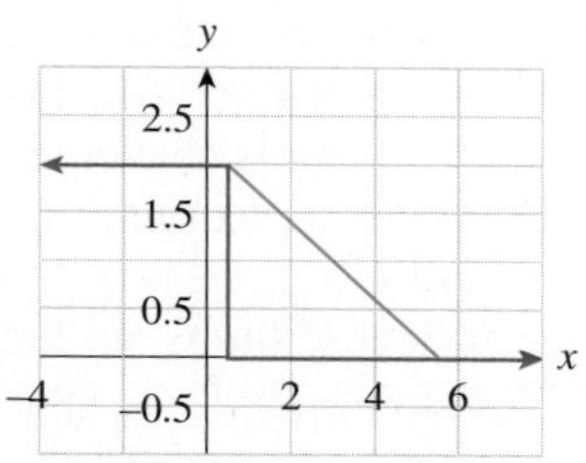

23. $\bar{f}(x) = \frac{1}{5}\Big[2x - \frac{1}{2}(x+1)|x+1| + \frac{1}{2}x|x| - 2(x-5) + \frac{1}{2}(x-4)|x-4| - \frac{1}{2}(x-5)|x-5|\Big]$

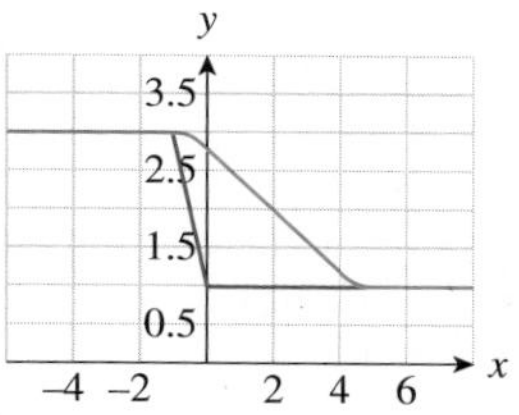

25.

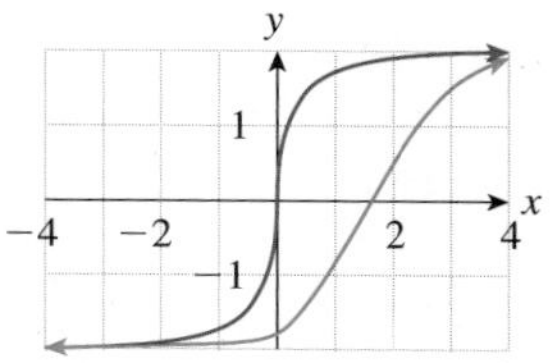

27.

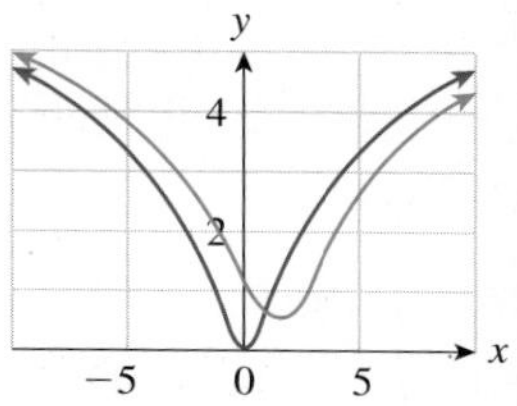

29.

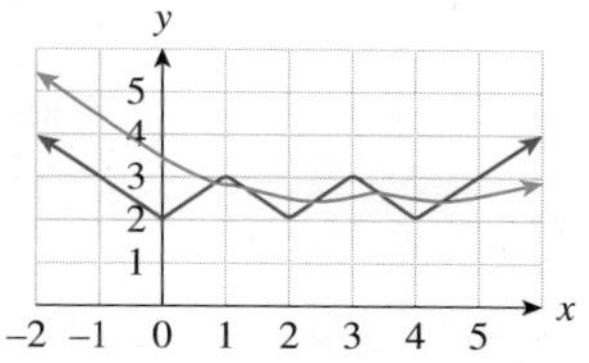

31.

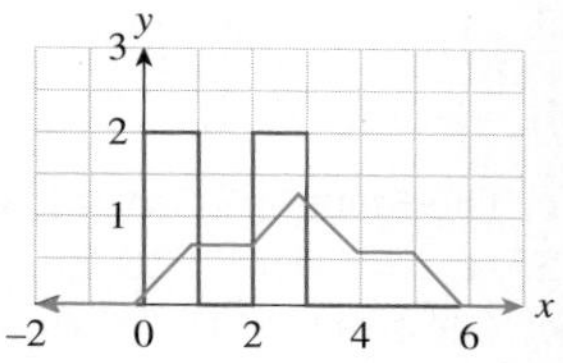

33.

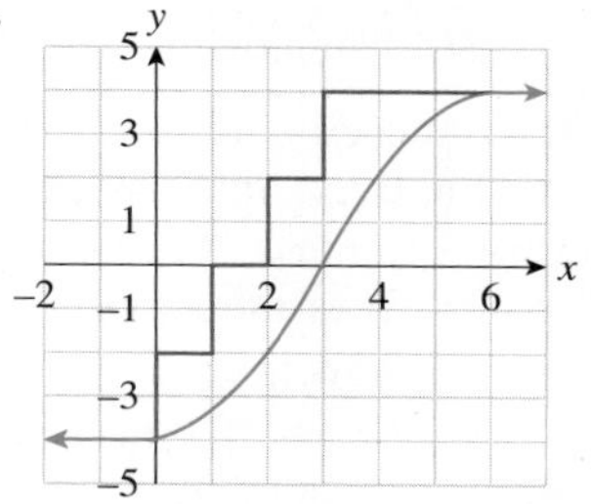

35. \$1.8 million **37.** 16 million members per year **39.** 277 million tons **41.** \$10,410.88 **43.** \$1,500 **45.** \$2.5 billion per quarter

47.

Year t	2001	2002	2003	2004	2005	2006	2007	2008	2009	2010
Stock Price	39	35	41	51	56	77	94	80	68	73
Moving Average (rounded)				42	46	56	70	77	80	79

The moving average continued to rise, at a lower rate, until it began to fall in 2010.

49. a. To obtain the moving averages from January to June, use the fact that the data repeats every 12 months.

Graph:

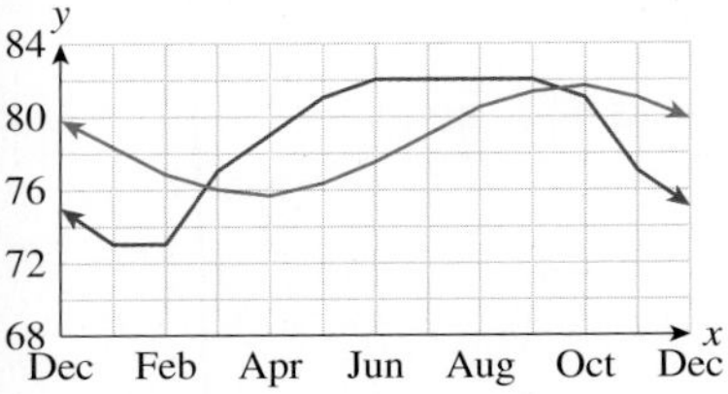

b. The 12-month moving average is constant and equal to the year-long average of approximately 79°.
51. a. Graph:

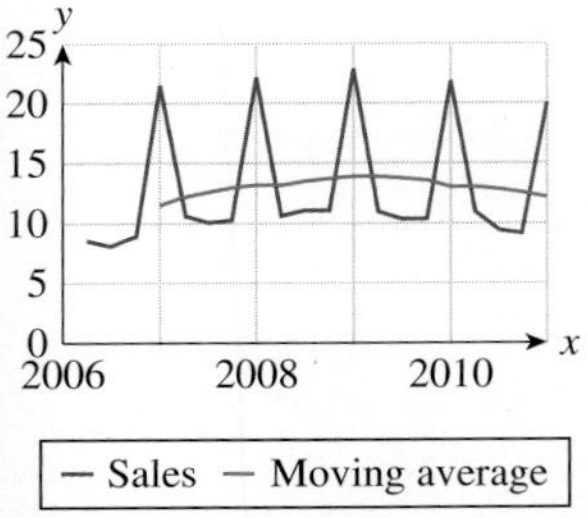

b. Approximately −0.2 million iPods per quarter
53. a. 7,200 million gallons per year
b. $\frac{1}{2}[-15[t^3 - (t-2)^3] + 450[t^2 - (t-2)^2] + 8{,}400]$
c. The function is quadratic because the t^3 terms cancel.
55. a. $s = 41t + 526$ **b.** $\bar{s}(t) = 41t + 444$
c. The slope of the moving average is the same as the slope of the original function.
57. $\bar{f}(x) = mx + b - \frac{ma}{2}$ **59.** The moving average "blurs" the effects of short-term oscillations in the price and shows the longer-term trend of the stock price. **61.** They repeat every 6 months. **63.** The area above the x-axis equals the area below the x-axis. Example: $y = x$ on $[-1,1]$ **65.** This need not be the case; for instance, the function $f(x) = x^2$ on [0, 1] has average value 1/3, whereas the value midway between the maximum and minimum is 1/2.
67. (C) A shorter-term moving average most closely approximates the original function because it averages the function over a shorter period, and continuous functions change by only a small amount over a small period.

Section 7.4

1. \$6.25 **3.** \$512 **5.** \$119.53 **7.** \$900 **9.** \$416.67 **11.** \$326.27 **13.** \$25 **15.** \$0.50 **17.** \$386.29 **19.** \$225 **21.** \$25.50 **23.** \$12,684.63
25. $TV = \$300{,}000$, $FV = \$434{,}465.45$
27. $TV = \$350{,}000$, $FV = \$498{,}496.61$
29. $TV = \$389{,}232.76$, $FV = \$547{,}547.16$
31. $TV = \$100{,}000$, $PV = \$82{,}419.99$
33. $TV = \$112{,}500$, $PV = \$92{,}037.48$
35. $TV = \$107{,}889.50$, $PV = \$88{,}479.69$
37. $\bar{p} = \$5{,}000$, $\bar{q} = 10{,}000$, $CS = \$25$ million, $PS = \$100$ million. The total social gain is \$125 million. **39.** €200 billion **41.** \$1,190 billion **43.** €220 billion **45.** \$1,080 billion **47.** \$1,943,162.44 **49.** \$3,086,245.73 **51.** \$73,802.63 **53.** \$1,792,723.35
55. total **57.** $CS = \frac{1}{2m}(b - m\bar{p})^2$ **59.** She is correct, provided there is a positive rate of return, in which case the future value (which includes interest) is greater than the total value (which does not). **61.** $PV < TV < FV$

Section 7.5

1. Diverges **3.** Converges to $2e$ **5.** Converges to e^2
7. Converges to ½ **9.** Converges to 1/108
11. Converges to $3 \times 5^{2/3}$ **13.** Diverges
15. Diverges **17.** Converges to $\frac{5}{4}(3^{4/5} - 1)$
19. Diverges **21.** Converges to 0 **23.** Diverges
25. Diverges **27.** 0.9, 0.99, 0.999, . . . ; converges to 1. **29.** 7.602, 95.38, 993.1, . . . ; diverges.
31. 1.368, 1.800, 1.937, 1.980, 1.994, 1.998, 1.999, 2.000, . . . ; converges to 2. **33.** 9.000, 99.00, 999.0, . . . ; diverges to $+\infty$. **35.** 4.45 million homes
37. 13,600 billion cigarettes **39.** No; you will not sell more than 2,000 of them. **41.** The number of graduates each year will rise without bound.
43. a. $R(t) = 350e^{-0.1t}(39t + 68)$ million dollars/yr; **b.** \$1,603,000 million **45.** \$20,700 billion
47. $\int_0^{+\infty} N(t)\,dt$ diverges, indicating that there is no bound to the expected future total online sales of mousse. $\int_{-\infty}^{0} N(t)\,dt$ converges to approximately 2.006, indicating that total online sales of mousse prior to the current year amounted to approximately 2 million gallons. **49.** 1 **51.** 0.1587 **53.** \$70,833
55. a. 2.468 meteors on average **b.** The integral diverges. We can interpret this as saying that the number of impacts by meteors smaller than 1 megaton is very large. (This makes sense because, for example, this number includes meteors no larger than a grain of dust.) **57. a.** $\Gamma(1) = 1$; $\Gamma(2) = 1$ **59.** The integrand is neither continuous nor piecewise continuous on the interval $[-1, 1]$, so the FTC does not apply (the integral is improper). **61.** Yes; the integrals converge to 0, and the FTC also gives 0. **63. a.** Not improper. $|x|/x$ is not defined at zero, but $\lim_{x\to 0^-} |x|/x = -1$ and $\lim_{x\to 0^+} |x|/x = 1$. Because these limits are finite, the integrand is piecewise continuous on $[-1, 1]$ and

so the integral is not improper. **b.** Improper, because $x^{-1/3}$ has infinite left and right limits at 0. **c.** Improper, since $(x-2)/(x^2-4x+4) = 1/(x-2)$, which has an infinite left limit at 2. **65.** In all cases, you need to rewrite the improper integral as a limit and use technology to evaluate the integral of which you are taking the limit. Evaluate for several values of the endpoint approaching the limit. In the case of an integral in which one of the limits of integration is infinite, you may have to instruct the calculator or computer to use more subdivisions as you approach $+\infty$.
67. Answers will vary.

Section 7.6

1. $y = \dfrac{x^3}{3} + \dfrac{2x^{3/2}}{3} + C$ **3.** $\dfrac{y^2}{2} = \dfrac{x^2}{2} + C$

5. $y = Ae^{x^2/2}$ **7.** $y = -\dfrac{2}{(x+1)^2 + C}$

9. $y = \pm\sqrt{(\ln x)^2 + C}$ **11.** $y = \dfrac{x^4}{4} - x^2 + 1$

13. $y = (x^3+8)^{1/3}$ **15.** $y = 2x$ **17.** $y = e^{x^2/2} - 1$

19. $y = -\dfrac{2}{\ln(x^2+1)+2}$ **21.** With $s(t)$ = monthly sales after t months, $\dfrac{ds}{dt} = -0.05s$; $s = 1{,}000$ when $t = 0$. Solution: $s = 1{,}000e^{-0.05t}$ quarts per month

23. a. $75 + 125e^{-0.05t}$ **b.** 64.4 minutes

25. $k \approx 0.04274$; $H(t) = 75 + 115e^{-0.04274t}$ degrees Fahrenheit after t minutes **27.** With $S(t)$ = total sales after t months, $\dfrac{ds}{dt} = 0.1(100{,}000 - S)$; $S(0) = 0$. Solution: $S = 100{,}000(1 - e^{-0.1t})$ monitors after t months. **29.** $q = 0.6078e^{-0.05p}p^{1.5}$

31. $y = e^{-t}(t+1)$

33. $y = e^{t/2}\left[-2te^{-t/2} - 4e^{-t/2} + 5\right]$

35. $i = 5e^{-t}(e^t - e)\left[1 + \dfrac{|t-1|}{t-1}\right]$

Graph:

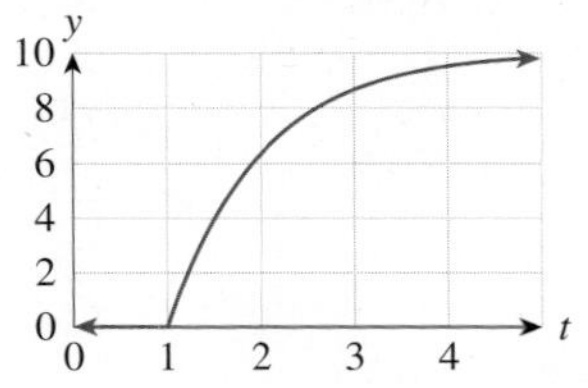

37. a. $\dfrac{dp}{dt} = k(D(p) - S(p)) = k(20{,}000 - 1{,}000p)$

b. $p = 20 - Ae^{-kt}$ **c.** $p = 20 - 10e^{-0.2231t}$ dollars after t months **39.** Verification

41. $S = \dfrac{2/1{,}999}{e^{-0.5t} + 1/1{,}999}$

Graph:

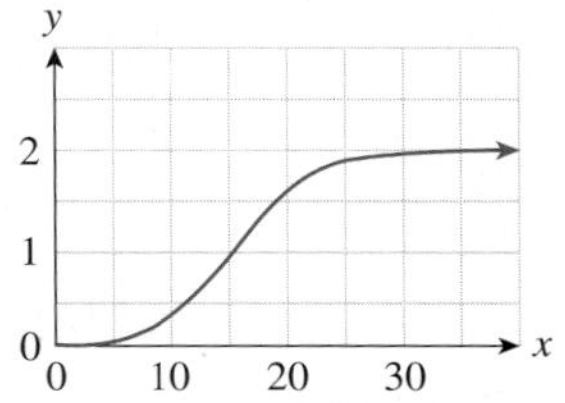

It will take about 27 months to saturate the market.

43. a. $y = be^{Ae^{-at}}$, A = constant **b.** $y = 10e^{-0.69315e^{-t}}$

Graph:

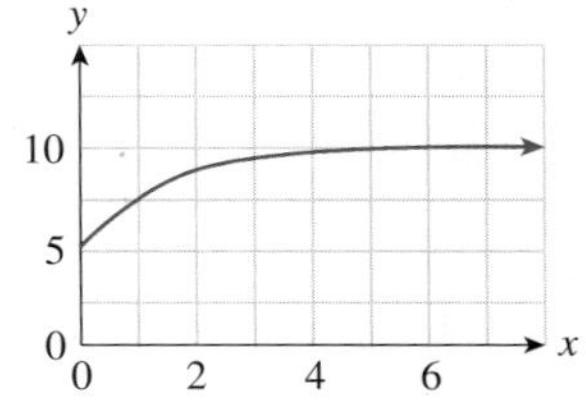

45. A general solution gives all possible solutions to the equation, using at least one arbitrary constant. A particular solution is one specific function that satisfies the equation. We obtain a particular solution by substituting specific values for any arbitrary constants in the general solution. **47.** Example: $y'' = x$ has general solution $y = \frac{1}{6}x^3 + Cx + D$ (integrate twice). **49.** $y' = -4e^{-x} + 3$

Chapter 7 Review

1. $(x^2 - 2x + 4)e^x + C$ **3.** $(1/3)x^3 \ln 2x - x^3/9 + C$

5. $\dfrac{1}{2}x(2x+1)|2x+1| - \dfrac{1}{12}(2x+1)^2|2x+1| + C$

7. $-5x|-x+3| - \dfrac{5}{2}(-x+3)|-x+3| + C$

9. $-e^2 - 39/e^2$ **11.** $\dfrac{3}{2\cdot 2^{1/3}} - \dfrac{1}{2}$ **13.** $\dfrac{2\sqrt{2}}{3}$ **15.** -1

17. $e - 2$ **19.** $3x - 2$ **21.** $\dfrac{3}{14}[x^{7/3} - (x-2)^{7/3}]$

23. \$1,600 **25.** \$2,500 **27.** 1/4 **29.** Diverges **31.** 1

33. $y = -\dfrac{3}{x^3 + C}$ **35.** $y = \sqrt{2\ln|x| + 1}$

37. \$18,200 **39. a.** \$2,260 **b.** $50{,}000e^{0.01t}(1 - e^{-0.04}) \approx 1{,}960.53e^{0.01t}$

41. a. $\bar{p} = 20$, $\bar{q} = 40{,}000$ **b.** CS = \$240,000, PS = \$30,000 **43.** Approximately \$910,000

45. a. \$5,549,000 **b.** Principal: \$5,280,000, interest: \$269,000 **47.** \$51 million **49.** The amount in the account would be given by $y = 10{,}000/(1-t)$, where t is time in years, so would approach infinity 1 year after the deposit.

Chapter 8

Section 8.1

1. a. 1 **b.** 1 **c.** 2 **d.** $a^2 - a + 5$ **e.** $y^2 + x^2 - y + 1$ **f.** $(x+h)^2 + (y+k)^2 - (x+h) + 1$ **3. a.** 0 **b.** 0.2 **c.** -0.1 **d.** $0.18a + 0.2$ **e.** $0.1x + 0.2y - 0.01xy$ **f.** $0.2(x+h) + 0.1(y+k) - 0.01(x+h)(y+k)$ **5. a.** 1 **b.** e **c.** e **d.** e^{x+y+z} **e.** $e^{x+h+y+k+z+l}$ **7. a.** Does not exist **b.** 0 **c.** 0 **d.** $xyz/(x^2+y^2+z^2)$ **e.** $(x+h)(y+k)(z+l)/[(x+h)^2+(y+k)^2+(z+l)^2]$ **9. a.** Increases; 2.3 **b.** Decreases; 1.4 **c.** Decreases; 1 unit increase in z **11.** Neither **13.** Linear **15.** Linear **17.** Interaction **19. a.** 107 **b.** -14 **c.** -113

21.

$y \downarrow$ / $x \rightarrow$	**10**	**20**	**30**	**40**
10	52	107	162	217
20	94	194	294	394
30	136	281	426	571
40	178	368	558	748

25. 18, 4, 0.0965, 47,040 **27.** 6.9078, 1.5193, 5.4366, 0 **29.** Let z = annual sales of Z (in millions of dollars), x = annual sales of X, and y = annual sales of Y. The model is $z = -2.1x + 0.4y + 16.2$.

31.

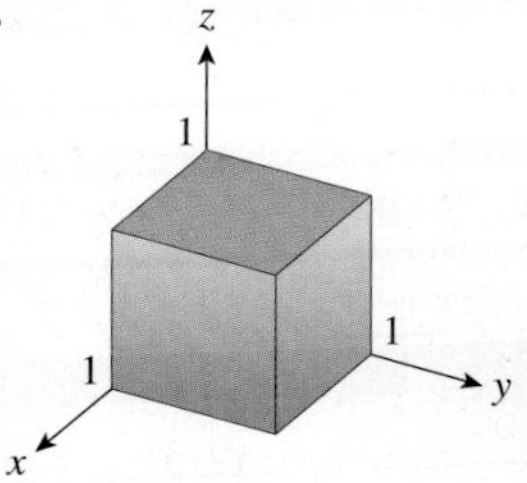

33.

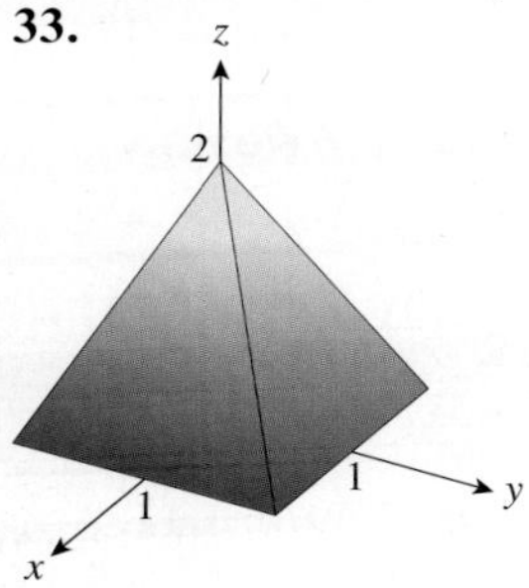

35.

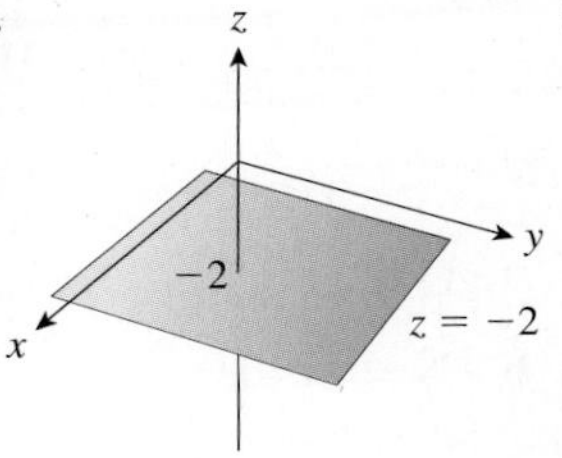

37.

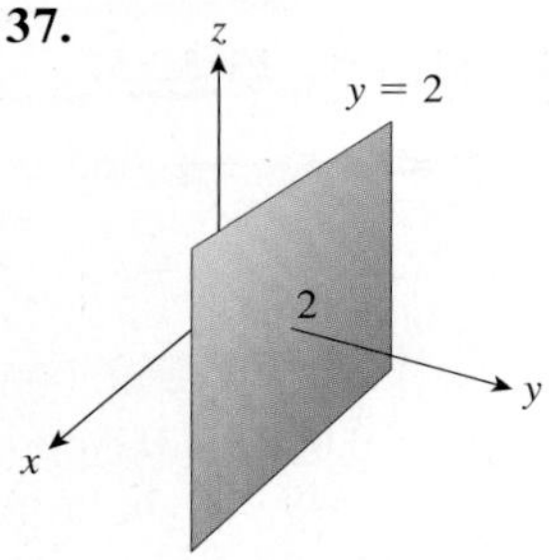

39.

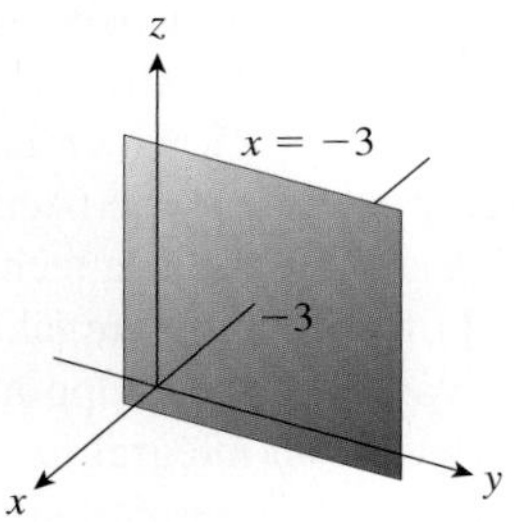

41. (H) **43.** (B) **45.** (F) **47.** (C)

49.

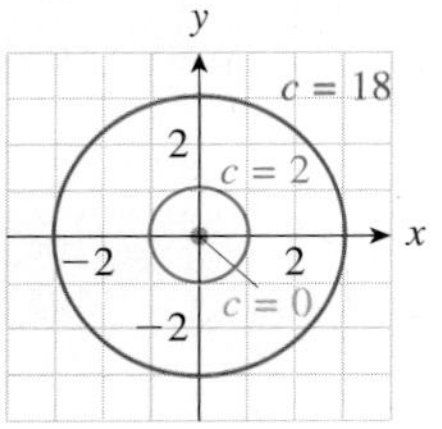

51.

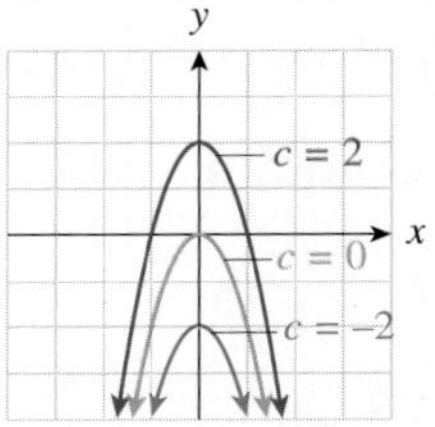

53.

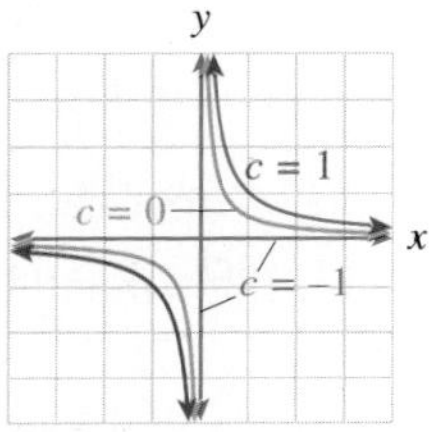

55. a. 4 **b.** 5 **c.** -1 **57.** (2, 2) and $(-2, -2)$

59.

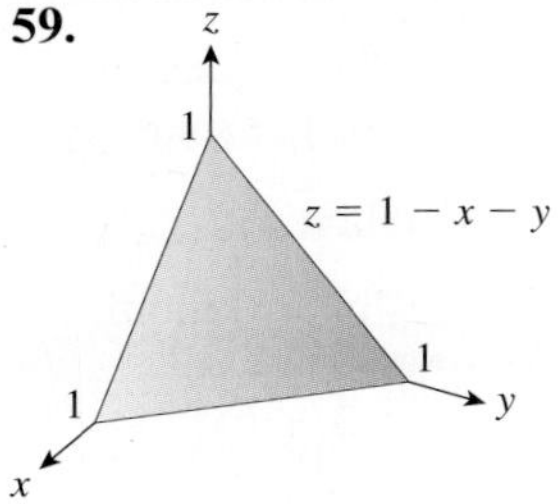

61.

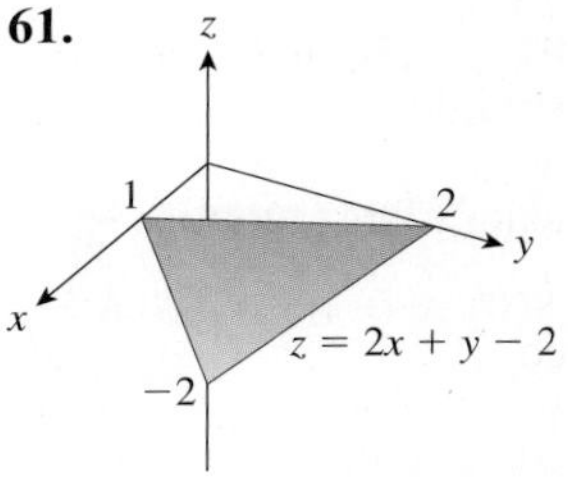

63.

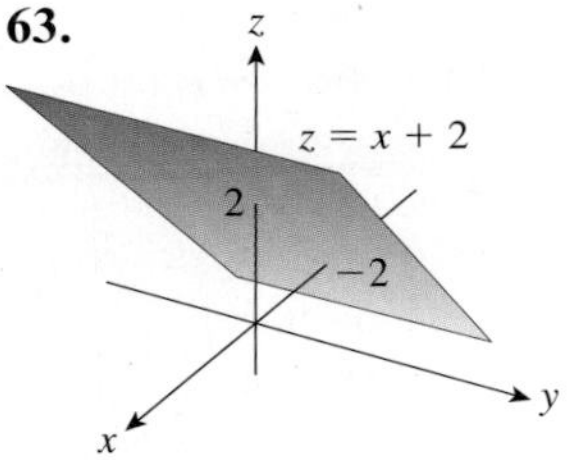

65.

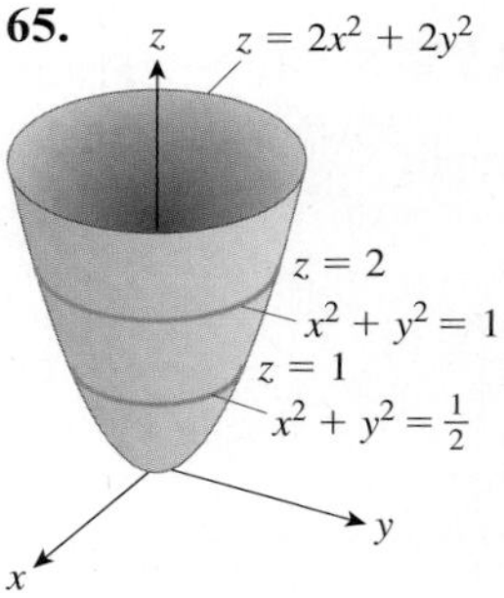

67.

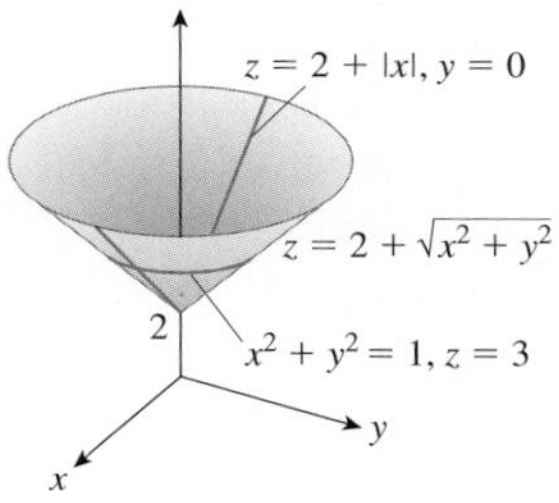

69.

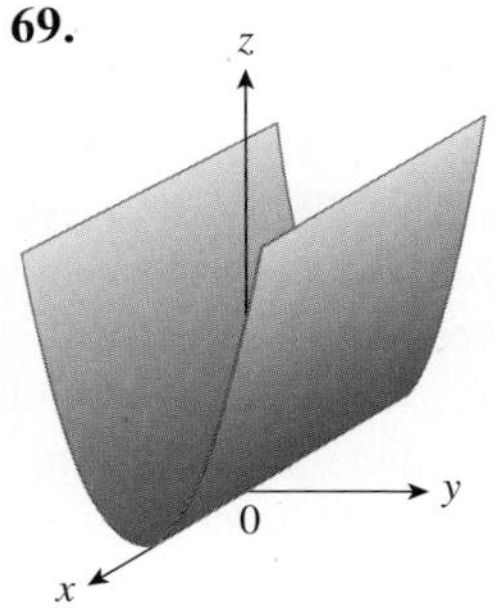

71.

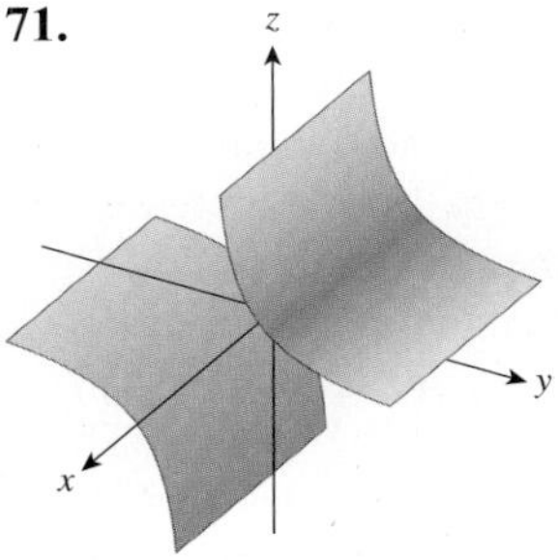

73.

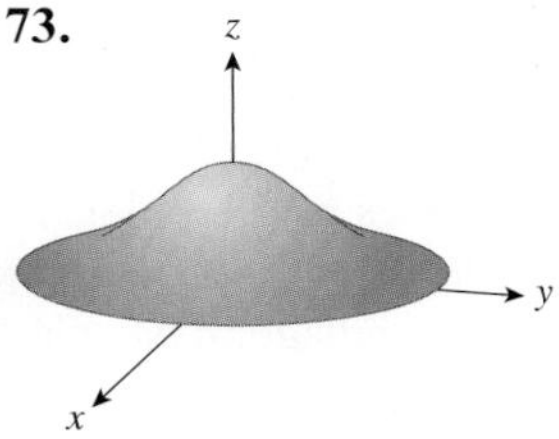

75. a. The marginal cost of cars is \$6,000 per car. The marginal cost of trucks is \$4,000 per truck. **b.** The graph is a plane with x-intercept -40, y-intercept -60, and z-intercept 240,000. **c.** The slice $x = 10$ is the straight line with equation $z = 300{,}000 + 4{,}000y$. It describes the cost function for the manufacture of trucks if car production is held fixed at 10 cars per week. **d.** The level curve $z = 480{,}000$ is the straight line $6{,}000x + 4{,}000y = 240{,}000$. It describes the number of cars and trucks you can manufacture to maintain weekly costs at \$480,000. **77.** $C(x, y) = 10 + 0.03x + 0.04y$, where C is the cost in dollars, $x = \#$ video clips sold per month, $y = \#$ audio clips sold per month **79. a.** 28% **b.** 21% **c.** Percentage points per year **81.** The graph is a plane with x_1-intercept 0.3, x_2-intercept 33, and x_3-intercept 0.66. The slices by $x_1 =$ constant are straight lines that are parallel to each other. Thus, the rate of change of General Motors' share as a function of Ford's share does not depend on Chrysler's share. Specifically, GM's share decreases by 0.02 percentage points per one percentage-point increase in Ford's market share, regardless of Chrysler's share. **83. a.** 189 thousand prisoners **b.** $y = 300$: $N = -0.02x + 51$; $y = 500$: $N = 0.02x + 67$; when there are 300,000 prisoners in local jails, the number in federal prisons decreases by 20 per 1,000 additional prisoners in state prisons. When there are 500,000 prisoners in local jails, the number in federal prisons increases by 20 per 1,000 additional prisoners in state prisons. **85. a.** The slices $x =$ constant and $y =$ constant are straight lines. **b.** No. Even though the slices $x =$ constant and $y =$ constant are straight lines, the level curves are not, and so the surface is not a plane. **c.** The slice $x = 10$ has a slope of 3,800. The slice $x = 20$ has a slope of 3,600. Manufacturing more cars lowers the marginal cost of manufacturing trucks. **87. a.** \$9,980 **b.** $R(z) = 9{,}850 + 0.04z$ **89.** $f(x, t) = 2.5x + 17.5t + 145$; \$311 billion **91.** $U(11, 10) - U(10, 10) \approx 5.75$. This means that, if your company now has 10 copies of Macro Publish and 10 copies of Turbo Publish, then the purchase of one additional copy of Macro Publish will result in a productivity increase of approximately 5.75 pages per day. **93. a.** Answers will vary. $(a, b, c) = (3, 1/4, 1/\pi)$; $(a, b, c) = (1/\pi, 3, 1/4)$. **b.** $a = \left(\frac{3}{4\pi}\right)^{1/3}$. The resulting ellipsoid is a sphere with radius a. **95.** 7,000,000 **97. a.** $100 = K(1{,}000)^a(1{,}000{,}000)^{1-a}$; $10 = K(1{,}000)^a(10{,}000)^{1-a}$ **b.** $\log K - 3a = -4$; $\log K - a = -3$ **c.** $a = 0.5$, $K \approx 0.003162$ **d.** $P = 71$ pianos (to the nearest piano) **99. a.** 4×10^{-3} gram per square meter **b.** The total weight of sulfates in the Earth's atmosphere **101. a.** The value of N would be doubled. **b.** $N(R, f_p, n_e, f_l, f_i, L) = R\, f_p\, n_e\, f_l\, f_i\, L$, where L is the average lifetime of an intelligent civilization **c.** Take the logarithm of both sides, since this would yield the linear function $\ln(N) = \ln(R) + \ln(f_p) + \ln(n_e) + \ln(f_l) + \ln(f_i) + \ln(f_c) + \ln(L)$. **103.** They are reciprocals of each other. **105.** For example, $f(x, y) = x^2 + y^2$. **107.** For example, $f(x, y, z) = xyz$. **109.** For example, take $f(x, y) = x + y$. Then setting $y = 3$ gives $f(x, 3) = x + 3$. This can be viewed as a function of the single variable x. Choosing other values for y gives other functions of x. **111.** The slope is independent of the choice of $y = k$. **113.** That CDs cost more than cassettes **115.** plane **117. (B)** Traveling in the direction B results in the shortest trip to nearby isotherms, and hence the fastest rate of increase in temperature. **119.** Agree: Any slice through a plane is a straight line. **121.** The graph of a function of three or more variables lives in four-dimensional (or higher) space, which makes it difficult to draw and visualize. **123.** We need one dimension for each of the variables plus one dimension for the value of the function.

Section 8.2

1. $f_x(x, y) = -40$; $f_y(x, y) = 20$; $f_x(1, -1) = -40$; $f_y(1, -1) = 20$ **3.** $f_x(x, y) = 6x + 1$; $f_y(x, y) = -3y^2$; $f_x(1, -1) = 7$; $f_y(1, -1) = -3$ **5.** $f_x(x, y) = -40 + 10y$; $f_y(x, y) = 20 + 10x$; $f_x(1, -1) = -50$; $f_y(1, -1) = 30$ **7.** $f_x(x, y) = 6xy$; $f_y(x, y) = 3x^2$; $f_x(1, -1) = -6$; $f_y(1, -1) = 3$ **9.** $f_x(x, y) = 2xy^3 - 3x^2y^2 - y$; $f_y(x, y) = 3x^2y^2 - 2x^3y - x$; $f_x(1, -1) = -4$; $f_y(1, -1) = 4$ **11.** $f_x(x, y) = 6y(2xy + 1)^2$; $f_y(x, y) = 6x(2xy + 1)^2$; $f_x(1, -1) = -6$; $f_y(1, -1) = 6$ **13.** $f_x(x, y) = e^{x+y}$; $f_y(x, y) = e^{x+y}$; $f_x(1, -1) = 1$; $f_y(1, -1) = 1$ **15.** $f_x(x, y) = 3x^{-0.4}y^{0.4}$; $f_y(x, y) = 2x^{0.6}y^{-0.6}$; $f_x(1, -1)$ undefined; $f_y(1, -1)$ undefined **17.** $f_x(x, y) = 0.2ye^{0.2xy}$; $f_y(x, y) = 0.2xe^{0.2xy}$; $f_x(1, -1) = -0.2e^{-0.2}$; $f_y(1, -1) = 0.2e^{-0.2}$ **19.** $f_{xx}(x, y) = 0$; $f_{yy}(x, y) = 0$; $f_{xy}(x, y) = f_{yx}(x, y) = 0$; $f_{xx}(1, -1) = 0$; $f_{yy}(1, -1) = 0$; $f_{xy}(1, -1) = f_{yx}(1, -1) = 0$ **21.** $f_{xx}(x, y) = 0$; $f_{yy}(x, y) = 0$; $f_{xy}(x, y) = f_{yx}(x, y) = 10$; $f_{xx}(1, -1) = 0$; $f_{yy}(1, -1) = 0$; $f_{xy}(1, -1) = f_{yx}(1, -1) = 10$ **23.** $f_{xx}(x, y) = 6y$; $f_{yy}(x, y) = 0$; $f_{xy}(x, y) = f_{yx}(x, y) = 6x$; $f_{xx}(1, -1) = -6$; $f_{yy}(1, -1) = 0$; $f_{xy}(1, -1) = f_{yx}(1, -1) = 6$ **25.** $f_{xx}(x, y) = e^{x+y}$; $f_{yy}(x, y) = e^{x+y}$; $f_{xy}(x, y) = f_{yx}(x, y) = e^{x+y}$; $f_{xx}(1, -1) = 1$; $f_{yy}(1, -1) = 1$; $f_{xy}(1, -1) = f_{yx}(1, -1) = 1$ **27.** $f_{xx}(x, y) = -1.2x^{-1.4}y^{0.4}$; $f_{yy}(x, y) = -1.2x^{0.6}y^{-1.6}$; $f_{xy}(x, y) = f_{yx}(x, y) = 1.2x^{-0.4}y^{-0.6}$; $f_{xx}(1, -1)$ undefined; $f_{yy}(1, -1)$ undefined; $f_{xy}(1, -1)$ & $f_{yx}(1, -1)$ undefined **29.** $f_x(x, y, z) = yz$; $f_y(x, y, z) = xz$; $f_z(x, y, z) = xy$; $f_x(0, -1, 1) = -1$; $f_y(0, -1, 1) = 0$; $f_z(0, -1, 1) = 0$ **31.** $f_x(x, y, z) = 4/(x + y + z^2)^2$; $f_y(x, y, z) = 4/(x + y + z^2)^2$; $f_z(x, y, z) = 8z/(x + y + z^2)^2$; $f_x(0, -1, 1)$ undefined; $f_y(0, -1, 1)$ undefined; $f_z(0, -1, 1)$ undefined **33.** $f_x(x, y, z) = e^{yz} + yze^{xz}$; $f_y(x, y, z) = xze^{yz} + e^{xz}$; $f_z(x, y, z) = xy(e^{yz} + e^{xz})$; $f_x(0, -1, 1) = e^{-1} - 1$; $f_y(0, -1, 1) = 1$; $f_z(0, -1, 1) = 0$ **35.** $f_x(x, y, z) = 0.1x^{-0.9}y^{0.4}z^{0.5}$; $f_y(x, y, z) = 0.4x^{0.1}y^{-0.6}z^{0.5}$; $f_z(x, y, z) = 0.5x^{0.1}y^{0.4}z^{-0.5}$; $f_x(0, -1, 1)$ undefined; $f_y(0, -1, 1)$ undefined, $f_z(0, -1, 1)$ undefined **37.** $f_x(x, y, z) = yze^{xyz}$, $f_y(x, y, z) = xze^{xyz}$, $f_z(x, y, z) = xye^{xyz}$; $f_x(0, -1, 1) = -1$; $f_y(0, -1, 1) = f_z(0, -1, 1) = 0$ **39.** $f_x(x, y, z) = 0$; $f_y(x, y, z) = -\dfrac{600z}{y^{0.7}(1 + y^{0.3})^2}$; $f_z(x, y, z) = \dfrac{2{,}000}{1 + y^{0.3}}$; $f_x(0, -1, 1)$ undefined; $f_y(0, -1, 1)$ undefined; $f_z(0, -1, 1)$ undefined **41.** $\partial C/\partial x = 6{,}000$, the marginal cost to manufacture each car is \$6,000. $\partial C/\partial y = 4{,}000$, the marginal cost to manufacture each truck is \$4,000. **43.** $\partial y/\partial t = -0.78$. The number of articles written by researchers in the United States was decreasing at a rate of 0.78 percentage points per year. $\partial y/\partial x = -1.02$. The number of articles written by researchers in the United States was decreasing at a rate of 1.02 percentage points per one percentage-point increase in articles written in Europe. **45.** \$5,600 per car **47. a.** $\partial M/\partial c = -3.8$, $\partial M/\partial f = 2.2$. For every 1 point increase in the percentage of Chrysler owners who remain loyal, the percentage of Mazda owners who remain loyal decreases by 3.8 points. For every 1 point increase in the percentage of Ford owners who remain loyal, the percentage of Mazda owners who remain loyal increases by 2.2 points. **b.** 16% **49.** The marginal cost of cars is $\$6{,}000 + 1{,}000e^{-0.01(x+y)}$ per car. The marginal cost of trucks is $\$4{,}000 + 1{,}000e^{-0.01(x+y)}$ per truck. Both marginal costs decrease as production rises. **51. a.** \$36,600; \$52,900 **b.** \$270 per year; \$410 per year **c.** Widening **d.** The rate at which the income gap is widening
53. $\bar{C}(x, y) = \dfrac{200{,}000 + 6{,}000x + 4{,}000y - 100{,}000e^{-0.01(x+y)}}{x + y}$; $\bar{C}_x(50, 50) = -\$2.64$ per car. This means that at a production level of 50 cars and 50 trucks per week, the average cost per vehicle is decreasing by \$2.64 for each additional car manufactured. $\bar{C}_y(50, 50) = -\$22.64$ per truck. This means that at a production level of 50 cars and 50 trucks per week, the average cost per vehicle is decreasing by \$22.64 for each additional truck manufactured.
55. No; your marginal revenue from the sale of cars is $\$15{,}000 - \dfrac{2{,}500}{\sqrt{x + y}}$ per car and $\$10{,}000 - \dfrac{2{,}500}{\sqrt{x + y}}$ per truck from the sale of trucks. These increase with increasing x and y. In other words, you will earn more revenue per vehicle with increasing sales, and so the rental company will pay more for each additional vehicle it buys.
57. $P_z(10, 100{,}000, 1{,}000{,}000) \approx 0.0001010$ papers/\$
59. a. $U_x(10, 5) = 5.18$, $U_y(10, 5) = 2.09$. This means that if 10 copies of Macro Publish and 5 copies of Turbo Publish are purchased, the company's daily productivity is increasing at a rate of 5.18 pages per day for each additional copy of Macro purchased and by 2.09 pages per day for each additional copy of Turbo purchased. **b.** $\dfrac{U_x(10, 5)}{U_y(10, 5)} \approx 2.48$ is the ratio

of the usefulness of one additional copy of Macro to one of Turbo. Thus, with 10 copies of Macro and 5 copies of Turbo, the company can expect approximately 2.48 times the productivity per additional copy of Macro compared to Turbo. **61.** 6×10^9 N/sec **63. a.** $A_P(100, 0.1, 10) = 2.59$; $A_r(100, 0.1, 10) = 2{,}357.95$; $A_t(100, 0.1, 10) = 24.72$. Thus, for a \$100 investment at 10% interest, after 10 years the accumulated amount is increasing at a rate of \$2.59 per \$1 of principal, at a rate of \$2,357.95 per increase of 1 in r (note that this would correspond to an increase in the interest rate of 100%), and at a rate of \$24.72 per year. **b.** $A_P(100, 0.1, t)$ tells you the rate at which the accumulated amount in an account bearing 10% interest with a principal of \$100 is growing per \$1 increase in the principal, t years after the investment. **65. a.** $P_x = Ka\left(\frac{y}{x}\right)^b$ and $P_y = Kb\left(\frac{x}{y}\right)^a$. They are equal precisely when $\frac{a}{b} = \left(\frac{x}{y}\right)^b\left(\frac{x}{y}\right)^a$. Substituting $b = 1 - a$ now gives $\frac{a}{b} = \frac{x}{y}$. **b.** The given information implies that $P_x(100, 200) = P_y(100, 200)$. By part (a), this occurs precisely when $a/b = x/y = 100/200 = 1/2$. But $b = 1 - a$, so $a/(1 - a) = 1/2$, giving $a = 1/3$ and $b = 2/3$. **67.** Decreasing at 0.0075 parts of nutrient per part of water/sec **69.** _f_ is increasing at a rate of _s_ units per unit of x, _f_ is increasing at a rate of _t_ units per unit of y, and the value of _f_ is _r_ when $x =$ _a_ and $y =$ _b_ **71.** the marginal cost of building an additional orbicus; zonars per unit. **73.** Answers will vary. One example is $f(x, y) = -2x + 3y$. Others are $f(x, y) = -2x + 3y + 9$ and $f(x, y) = xy - 3x + 2y + 10$. **75. a.** b is the z-intercept of the plane. m is the slope of the intersection of the plane with the xz-plane. n is the slope of the intersection of the plane with the yz-plane. **b.** Write $z = b + rx + sy$. We are told that $\partial z/\partial x = m$, so $r = m$. Similarly, $s = n$. Thus, $z = b + mx + ny$. We are also told that the plane passes through (h, k, l). Substituting gives $l = b + mh + nk$. This gives b as $l - mh - nk$. Substituting in the equation for z therefore gives $z = l - mh - nk + mx + ny = l + m(x - h) + n(y - k)$, as required.

Section 8.3

1. P: relative minimum; Q: none of the above; R: relative maximum **3.** P: saddle point; Q: relative maximum; R: none of the above **5.** Relative minimum **7.** Neither **9.** Saddle point **11.** Relative minimum at (0, 0, 1) **13.** Relative maximum at $(-1/2, 1/2, 3/2)$ **15.** Saddle point at (0, 0, 0) **17.** Minimum at $(4, -3, -10)$ **19.** Maximum at $(-7/4, 1/4, 19/8)$ **21.** Relative maximum at (0, 0, 0), saddle points at $(\pm 4, 2, -16)$ **23.** Relative minimum at (0, 0, 0), saddle points at $(-1, \pm 1, 1)$ **25.** Relative minimum at (0, 0, 1) **27.** Relative minimum at $(-2, \pm 2, -16)$, (0, 0) a critical point that is not a relative extremum **29.** Saddle point at $(0, 0, -1)$ **31.** Relative maximum at $(-1, 0, e)$ **33.** Relative minimum at $(2^{1/3}, 2^{1/3}, 3(2^{2/3}))$ **35.** Relative minimum at (1, 1, 4) and $(-1, -1, 4)$ **37.** Absolute minimum at (0, 0, 1) **39.** None; the relative maximum at (0, 0, 0) is not absolute. **41.** Minimum of 1/3 at $(c, f) = (2/3, 2/3)$. Thus, at least 1/3 of all Mazda owners would choose another new Mazda, and this lowest loyalty occurs when 2/3 of Chrysler and Ford owners remain loyal to their brands. **43.** It should remove 2.5 pounds of sulfur and 1 pound of lead per day. **45.** You should charge \$580.81 for the Ultra Mini and \$808.08 for the Big Stack. **47.** $l = w = h \approx 20.67$ in, volume $\approx$ 8,827 cubic inches **49.** 18 in × 18 in × 36 in, volume = 11,664 cubic inches

51.

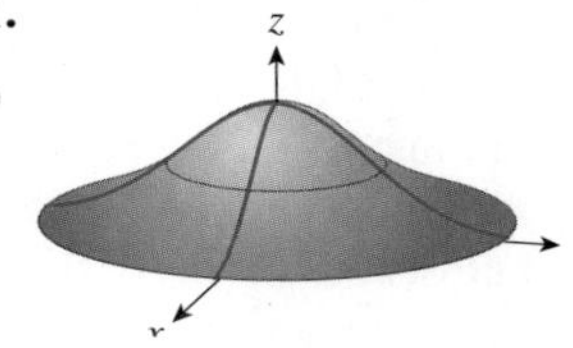

53.

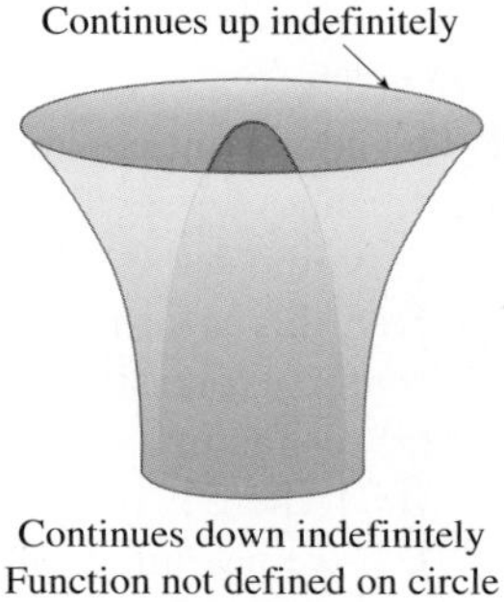

55. H must be positive. **57.** No. In order for there to be a relative maximum at (a, b), *all* vertical planes through (a, b) should yield a curve with a relative maximum at (a, b). It could happen that a slice by another vertical plane through (a, b) (such as $x - a = y - b$) does not yield a curve with a relative maximum at (a, b). [An example is $f(x, y) = x^2 + y^2 - \sqrt{xy}$, at the point (0, 0). Look at the slices through $x = 0$, $y = 0$ and $y = x$.]

59. $\bar{C}_x = \frac{\partial}{\partial x}\left(\frac{C}{x+y}\right) = \frac{(x+y)C_x - C}{(x+y)^2}$. If this is zero, then $(x+y)C_x = C$, or $C_x = \frac{C}{x+y} = \bar{C}$. Similarly, if $\bar{C}_y = 0$, then $C_y = \bar{C}$. This is reasonable because if the average cost is decreasing with increasing x, then the average cost is greater than the marginal cost C_x. Similarly, if the average cost is increasing with increasing x, then the average cost is less than the marginal cost C_x. Thus, if the average cost is stationary with increasing x, then the average cost equals the marginal cost C_x. (The situation is similar for the case of increasing y.) **61.** The equation of the tangent plane at the point (a, b) is $z = f(a, b) + f_x(a, b)(x - a) + f_y(a, b)(y - b)$. If f has a relative extremum at (a, b), then $f_x(a, b) = 0 = f_y(a, b)$. Substituting these into the equation of the tangent plane gives $z = f(a, b)$, a constant. But the graph of $z =$ *constant* is a plane parallel to the xy-plane.

Section 8.4

1. 1; (0, 0, 0) **3.** 1.35; (1/10, 3/10, 1/2) **5.** Minimum value = 6 at (1, 2, 1/2) **7.** 200; (20, 10) **9.** 16; (2, 2) and (−2, −2) **11.** 20; (2, 4) **13.** 1; (0, 0, 0) **15.** 1.35; (1/10, 3/10, 1/2) **17.** Minimum value = 6 at (1, 2, 1/2) **19. a.** $f(x, y, z)$ is the square of the distance from the point (x, y, z) to (3, 0, 0), and the constraint tells us that (x, y, z) must lie on the paraboloid $z = x^2 + y^2$. Because there must be such a point (or points) on the paraboloid closest to (3, 0, 0), the given problem must have at least one solution. Solution: $(x, y, z) = (1, 0, 1)$ for a minimum value of 5. **b.** Same solution as part (a) **c.** There are no critical points using this method. **d.** The constraint equation $y^2 = z - x^2$ tells us that $z - x^2$ cannot be negative, and thus restricts the domain of f to the set of points (x, y, z) with $z - x^2 \geq 0$. However, this information is lost when $z - x^2$ is substituted in the expression for f, and so the substitution in part (c) results in a different optimization problem; one in which there is no requirement that $z - x^2$ be ≥ 0. If we pay attention to this constraint we can see that the minimum will occur when $z = x^2$, which will then lead us to the correct solution. **21.** 5 × 10 = 50 sq. ft. **23.** \$10 **25.** $(1/\sqrt{3}, 1/\sqrt{3}, 1/\sqrt{3})$, $(-1/\sqrt{3}, -1/\sqrt{3}, 1/\sqrt{3})$, $(1/\sqrt{3}, -1/\sqrt{3}, -1/\sqrt{3})$, $(-1/\sqrt{3}, 1/\sqrt{3}, -1/\sqrt{3})$ **27.** (0, 1/2, −1/2) **29.** (−5/9, 5/9, 25/9) **31.** $l \times w \times h = 1 \times 1 \times 2$ **33.** 18 in × 18 in × 36 in, volume = 11,664 cubic inches **35.** $(2l/h)^{1/3} \times (2l/h)^{1/3} \times 2^{1/3}(h/l)^{2/3}$, where l = cost of lightweight cardboard and h = cost of heavy-duty cardboard per square foot **37.** 1 × 1 × 1/2 **39.** 6 laborers, 10 robots for a productivity of 368 pairs of socks per day **41.** Method 1: Solve $g(x, y, z) = 0$ for one of the variables and substitute in $f(x, y, z)$. Then find the maximum value of the resulting function of two variables. Advantage (answers may vary): We can use the second derivative test to check whether the resulting critical points are maxima, minima, saddle points, or none of these. Disadvantage (answers may vary): We may not be able to solve $g(x, y, z) = 0$ for one of the variables. Method 2: Use the method of Lagrange multipliers. Advantage (answers may vary): We do not need to solve the constraint equation for one of the variables. Disadvantage (answers may vary): The method does not tell us whether the critical points obtained are maxima, minima, points of inflection, or none of these. **43.** If the only constraint is an equality constraint, and if it is impossible to eliminate one of the variables in the objective function by substitution (solving the constraint equation for a variable or some other method). **45.** Answers may vary: Maximize $f(x, y) = 1 - x^2 - y^2$ subject to $x = y$. **47.** Yes. There may be relative extrema at points on the boundary of the domain. The partial derivatives of the function need not be 0 at such points. **49.** In a linear programming problem, the objective function is linear, and so the partial derivatives can never all be zero. (We are ignoring the simple case in which the objective function is constant.) It follows that the extrema cannot occur in the interior of the domain (since the partial derivatives must be zero at such points).

Section 8.5

1. −1/2 **3.** $e^2/2 - 7/2$ **5.** $(e^3 - 1)(e^2 - 1)$ **7.** 7/6 **9.** $[e^3 - e - e^{-1} + e^{-3}]/2$ **11.** 1/2 **13.** $(e - 1)/2$ **15.** 45/2 **17.** 8/3 **19.** 4/3 **21.** 0 **23.** 2/3 **25.** 2/3 **27.** $2(e - 2)$ **29.** 1/3

31. $\int_0^1 \int_0^{1-x} f(x, y)\,dy\,dx$

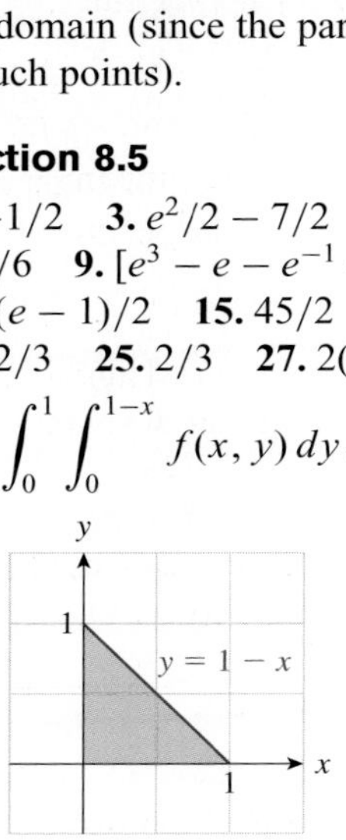

33. $\int_0^1 \int_0^{1-x} f(x, y)\,dy\,dx$

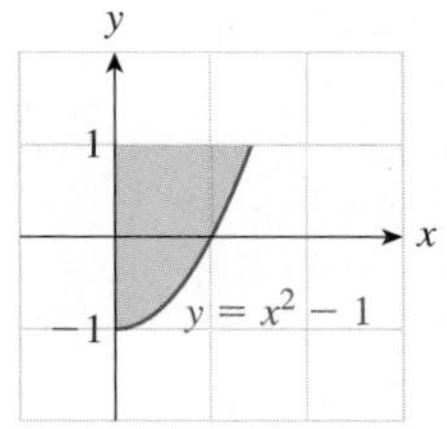

35. $\int_1^4 \int_1^{2/\sqrt{y}} f(x, y)\,dx\,dy$

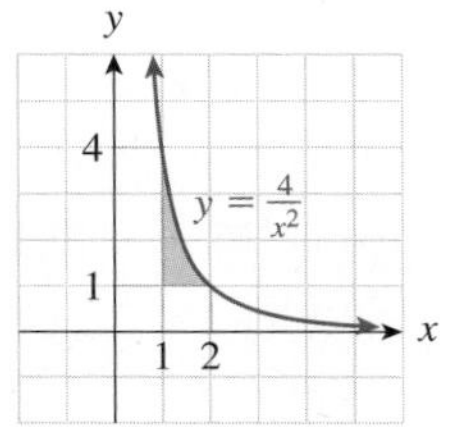

37. 4/3 **39.** 1/6 **41.** 162,000 gadgets **43.** \$312,750 **45.** \$17,500 **47.** 8,216 **49.** 1 degree **51.** The area between the curves $y = r(x)$ and $y = s(x)$ and the vertical lines $x = a$ and $x = b$ is given by $\int_a^b \int_{r(x)}^{s(x)} dy\,dx$ assuming that $r(x) \le s(x)$ for $a \le x \le b$. **53.** The first step in calculating an integral of the form $\int_a^b \int_{r(x)}^{s(x)} f(x, y)\,dy\,dx$ is to evaluate the integral $\int_{r(x)}^{s(x)} f(x, y)\,dy$, obtained by holding x constant and integrating with respect to y. **55.** Paintings per picasso per dali **57.** Left-hand side is $\int_a^b \int_c^d f(x)\,g(y)\,dx\,dy = \int_a^b \left(g(y) \int_c^d f(x)\,dx\right) dy$ (because $g(y)$ is treated as a constant in the inner integral) $= \left(\int_c^d f(x)\,dx\right) \int_a^b g(y)\,dy$ (because $\int_c^d f(x)\,dx$ is a constant and can therefore be taken outside the integral). $\int_0^1 \int_1^2 ye^x\,dx\,dy = \frac{1}{2}(e^2 - e)$ no matter how we compute it.

Chapter 8 Review

1. 0; 14/3; 1/2; $\frac{1}{1+z} + z^3$; $\frac{x+h}{y+k+(x+h)(z+l)} + (x+h)^2(y+k)$ **3.** Decreases by 0.32 units; increases by 12.5 units **5.** Reading left to right, starting at the top: 4, 0, 0, 3, 0, 1, 2, 0, 2 **7.** Answers may vary; two examples are $f(x, y) = 3(x - y)/2$ and $f(x, y) = 3(x - y)^3/8$.

9.

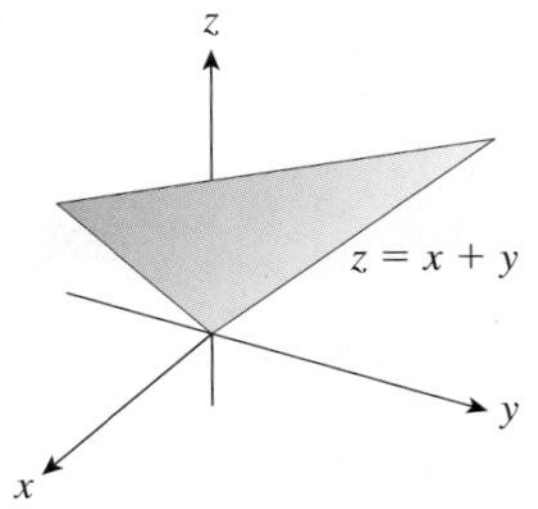

11.

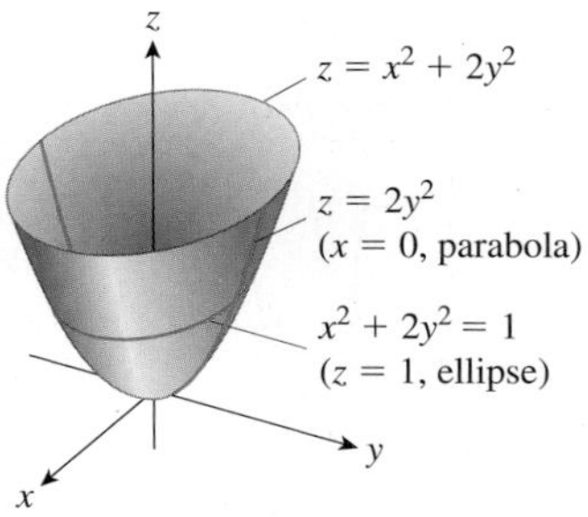

13.

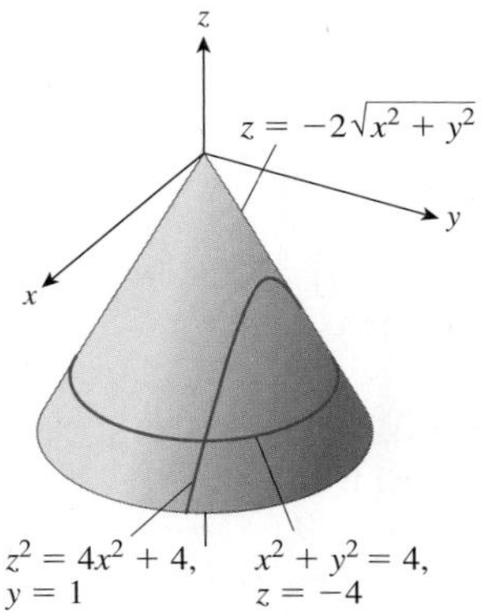

15. $f_x = 2x + y$, $f_y = x$, $f_{yy} = 0$ **17.** 0

19. $\frac{\partial f}{\partial x} = \frac{-x^2 + y^2 + z^2}{(x^2 + y^2 + z^2)^2}$, $\frac{\partial f}{\partial y} = \frac{2xy}{(x^2 + y^2 + z^2)^2}$, $\frac{\partial f}{\partial z} = -\frac{2xz}{(x^2 + y^2 + z^2)^2}$, $\left.\frac{\partial f}{\partial x}\right|_{(0,1,0)} = 1$

21. Absolute minimum at (1, 3/2) **23.** Maximum at (0, 0), saddle points at $(\pm\sqrt{2}, 1)$ **25.** Saddle point at (0, 0) **27.** 1/27 at (1/3, 1/3, 1/3) **29.** $(0, 2, \sqrt{2})$ **31.** 4; $(\sqrt{2}, \sqrt{2})$ and $(-\sqrt{2}, -\sqrt{2})$ **33.** $(0, 2, \sqrt{2})$ **35.** 2 **37.** ln 5 **39.** 1 **41. a.** $h(x, y) = 5{,}000 - 0.8x - 0.6y$ hits per day (x = number of new customers at JungleBooks.com, y = number of new customers at FarmerBooks.com) **b.** 250 **c.** $h(x, y, z) = 5{,}000 - 0.8x - 0.6y + 0.0001z$ (z = number of new Internet shoppers) **d.** 1.4 million **43. a.** 2,320 hits per day **b.** $0.08 + 0.00003x$ hits (daily) per dollar spent on television advertising per month; increases with increasing x **c.** \$4,000 per month **45.** (A) **47. a.** About 15,800 additional orders per day **b.** 11 **49.** \$23,050

Chapter 9

Section 9.1

1.

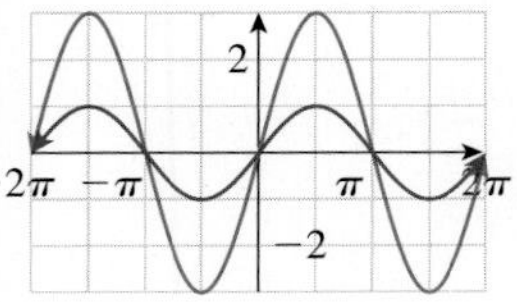

3.

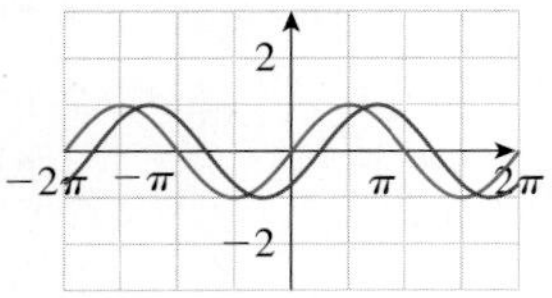

5.

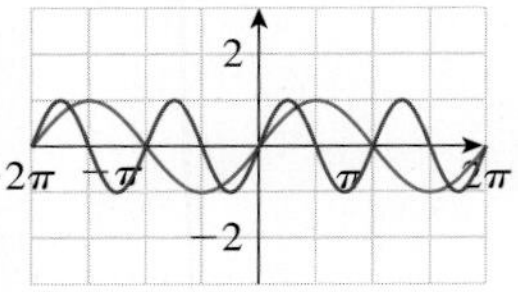

7.

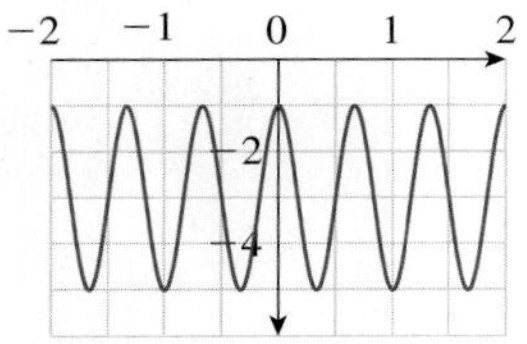

9.

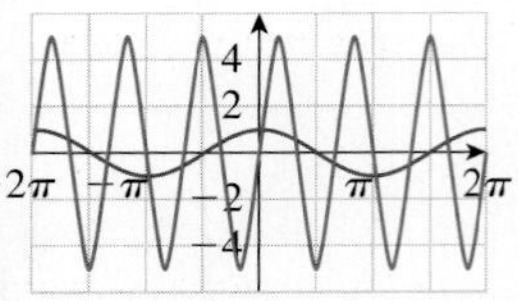

11.

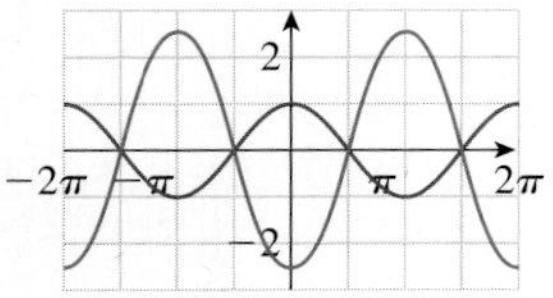

13. $f(x) = \sin(2\pi x) + 1$
15. $f(x) = 1.5\sin(4\pi(x - 0.25))$
17. $f(x) = 50\sin(\pi(x - 5)/10) - 50$
19. $f(x) = \cos(2\pi x)$
21. $f(x) = 1.5\cos(4\pi(x - 0.375))$
23. $f(x) = 40\cos(\pi(x - 10)/10) + 40$
25. $f(t) = 4.2\sin(\pi/2 - 2\pi t) + 3$
27. $g(x) = 4 - 1.3\sin[\pi/2 - 2.3(x - 4)]$ **31.** $\sqrt{3}/2$
37. $\tan(x + \pi) = \tan(x)$ **39. a.** $2\pi/0.602 \approx 10.4$ years. **b.** Maximum: $58.8 + 57.7 = 116.5 \approx 117$; minimum: $58.8 - 57.7 = 1.1 \approx 1$
c. $1.43 + P/4 + 2P = 1.43 + 23.48 \approx 25$ years, or about the beginning of 2022 **41. a.** Sales were highest when $t \approx 0, 4, 8$, and 12, which correspond to the end of the last quarter or beginning of the first quarter of each year. Sales were lowest when $t \approx 2, 6$, and 10, which correspond to the beginning of the third quarter of each year. **b.** The maximum quarterly sales were approximately 21 million iPods per quarter; minimum quarterly sales were approximately 9 million iPods per quarter. **c.** Maximum: $15 + 6 = 21$; minimum: $15 - 6 = 9$ **43.** Amplitude $= 6.00$, vertical offset $= 15$, phase shift $= -1.85/1.51 \approx -1.23$, angular frequency $= 1.51$, period ≈ 4.16. From 2008 through 2010, Apple's sales of iPods fluctuated in cycles of 4.16 quarters about a baseline of 15 million iPods per quarter. Every cycle, sales peaked at $15 + 6 = 21$ million iPods per quarter and dipped to a low of $15 - 6 = 9$ million iPods per quarter. Sales first peaked at $t = -1.23 + (5/4) \times 4.16 = 3.97$, the end of 2008. **45.** $P(t) = 7.5\sin[\pi(t - 13)/26] + 12.5$
47. $T(t) = 3.5\cos[\pi(t - 7)/6] + 78.5$
49. $n(t) = 1.25\sin[\pi(t - 1)/2] + 5.75$
51. $n(t) = 1.25\cos[\pi(t - 2)/2] + 5.75$
53. $d(t) = 5\sin(2\pi(t - 1.625)/13.5) + 10$
55. a. $u(t) = 2.5\sin(2\pi(t - 0.75)) + 7.5$
b. $c(t) = 1.04^t[2.5\sin(2\pi(t - 0.75)) + 7.5]$
57. a. $C \approx 50$, $A \approx 8$, $P \approx 12$, $\beta \approx 6$

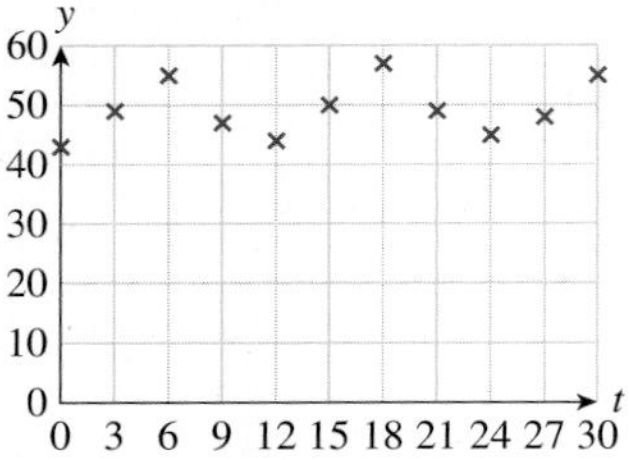

b. $f(t) = 5.882\cos[2\pi(t - 5.696)/12.263] + 49.238$

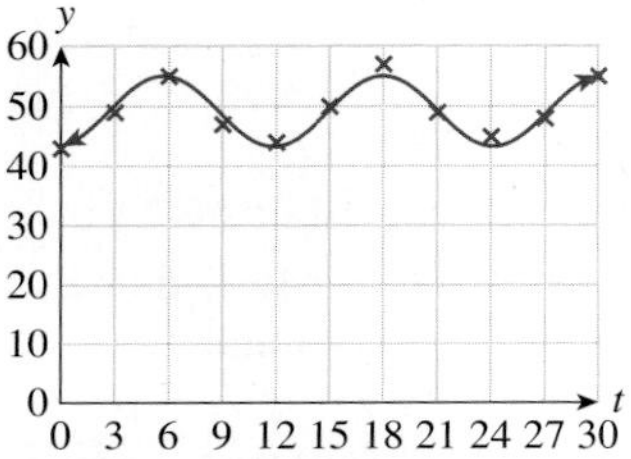

c. 12; 43; 55

59. a.

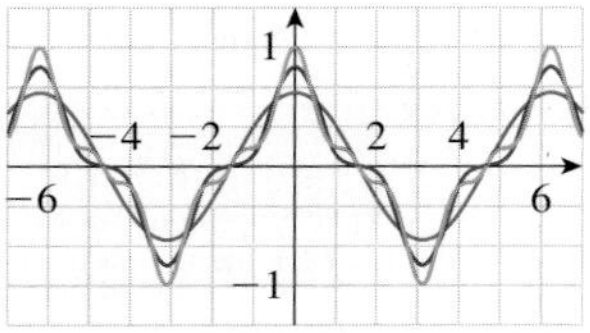

b. $$y_{11} = \frac{2}{\pi}\cos x + \frac{2}{3\pi}\cos 3x + \frac{2}{5\pi}\cos 5x + \frac{2}{7\pi}\cos 7x + \frac{2}{9\pi}\cos 9x + \frac{2}{11\pi}\cos 11x$$

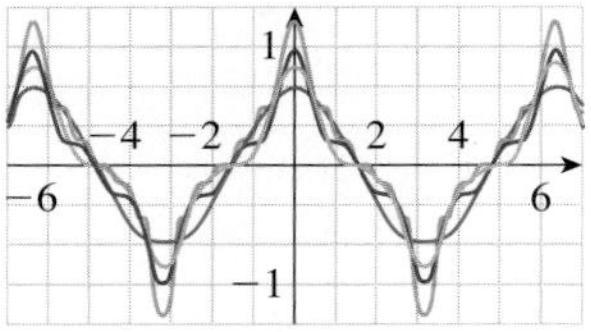

c. Multiply the amplitudes by 3 and change ω to 1/2:

$$y_{11} = \frac{6}{\pi}\cos\frac{x}{2} + \frac{6}{3\pi}\cos\frac{3x}{2} + \frac{6}{5\pi}\cos\frac{5x}{2} + \frac{6}{7\pi}\cos\frac{7x}{2} + \frac{6}{9\pi}\cos\frac{9x}{2} + \frac{6}{11\pi}\cos\frac{11x}{2}.$$

61. The period is approximately 12.6 units.

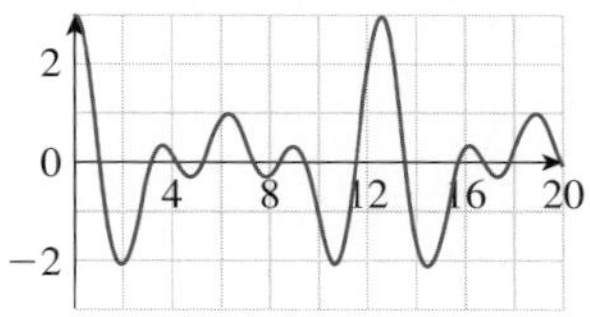

63. Lows: $B - A$; highs: $B + A$. **65.** He is correct. The other trig functions can be obtained from the sine function by first using the formula $\cos x = \sin(x + \pi/2)$ to obtain cosine, and then using the formulas

$$\tan x = \frac{\sin x}{\cos x},\ \cot x = \frac{\cos x}{\sin x},\ \sec x = \frac{1}{\cos x},$$

$\csc x = \dfrac{1}{\sin x}$ to obtain the rest **67.** The largest B can be is A. Otherwise, if B is larger than A, the low figure for sales would have the negative value of $A - B$.

Section 9.2

1. $\cos x + \sin x$ **3.** $(\cos x)(\tan x) + (\sin x)(\sec^2 x)$
5. $-2\csc x \cot x - \sec x \tan x + 3$
7. $\cos x - x \sin x + 2x$
9. $(2x - 1)\tan x + (x^2 - x + 1)\sec^2 x$
11. $-[\csc^2 x(1 + \sec x) + \cot x \sec x \tan x]/(1 + \sec x)^2$
13. $-2\cos x \sin x$ **15.** $2\sec^2 x \tan x$
17. $3\cos(3x - 5)$ **19.** $2\sin(-2x + 5)$
21. $\pi \cos\left[\frac{\pi}{5}(x - 4)\right]$ **23.** $-(2x - 1)\sin(x^2 - x)$
25. $(2.2x^{1.2} + 1.2)\sec(x^{2.2} + 1.2x - 1)\tan(x^{2.2} + 1.2x - 1)$ **27.** $\sec x \tan x \tan(x^2 - 1) + 2x \sec x \sec^2(x^2 - 1)$ **29.** $e^x[-\sin(e^x) + \cos x - \sin x]$
31. $\sec x$ **37.** $e^{-2x}[-2\sin(3\pi x) + 3\pi\cos(3\pi x)]$
39. $1.5[\sin(3x)]^{-0.5}\cos(3x)$

41. $\dfrac{x^4 - 3x^2}{(x^2 - 1)^2}\sec\left(\dfrac{x^3}{x^2 - 1}\right)\tan\left(\dfrac{x^3}{x^2 - 1}\right)$

43. $\dfrac{\cot(2x - 1)}{x} - 2\ln|x|\csc^2(2x - 1)$

45. a. Not differentiable at 0 **b.** $f'(1) \approx 0.5403$
47. 0 **49.** 2 **51.** Does not exist **53.** $1/\sec^2 y$
55. $-[1 + y\cos(xy)]/[1 + x\cos(xy)]$
57. $c'(t) = 7\pi\cos[2\pi(t - 0.75)]$; $c'(0.75) \approx \$21.99$ per *year* $\approx \$0.42$ per week **59.** $N'(6) \approx -32.12$ On January 1, 2003, the number of sunspots was decreasing at a rate of 32.12 sunspots per year.
61. $c'(t) = 1.035^t \times [\ln(1.035)(0.8\sin(2\pi t) + 10.2) + 1.6\pi\cos(2\pi t)]$; $c'(1) = 1.035[10.2\ln|1.035| + 1.6\pi] \approx \$5.57$ per year, or \$0.11 per week.
63. a. $d(t) = 5\cos(2\pi t/13.5) + 10$ **b.** $d'(t) = -(10\pi/13.5)\sin(2\pi t/13.5)$; $d'(7) \approx 0.270$. At noon, the tide was rising at a rate of 0.270 feet per hour.

65. $\dfrac{dV}{dt} = 11{,}000\pi\dfrac{|\sin(100\pi t)|}{\sin(100\pi t)}\cos(100\pi t)$
Graph:

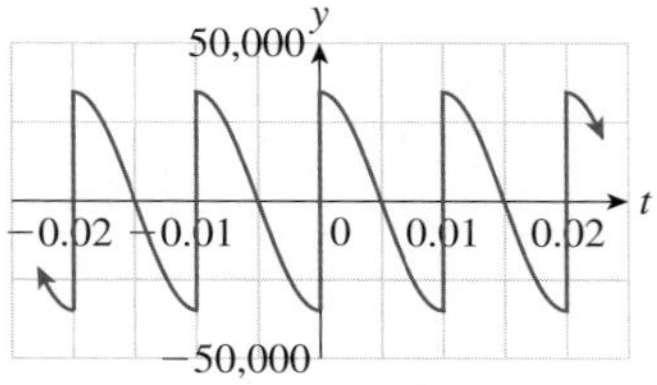

The sudden jumps in the graph are due to the nondifferentiability of V at the times 0, ± 0.01, ± 0.02, ... The derivative is negative immediately to the left and positive immediately to the right of these points. **67. a.** 1.2 cm above the rest position **b.** 0 cm/sec; not moving; moving downward at 18.85 cm/sec **c.** 2.5 cycles per second **69. a.** Moving downward at 0.12 cm/sec; moving downward at 18.66 cm/sec **b.** 0.1 sec
Graphs: of p:

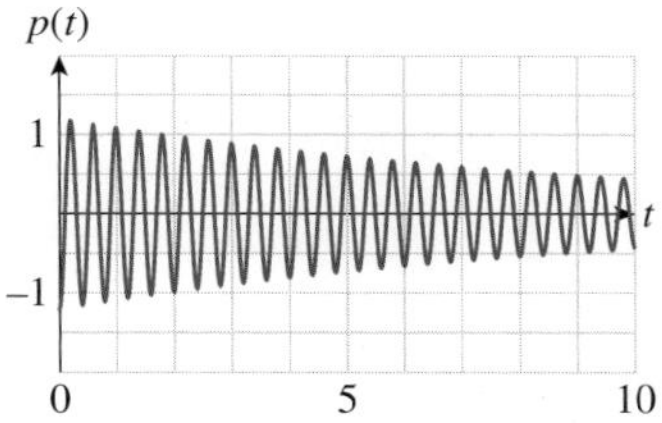

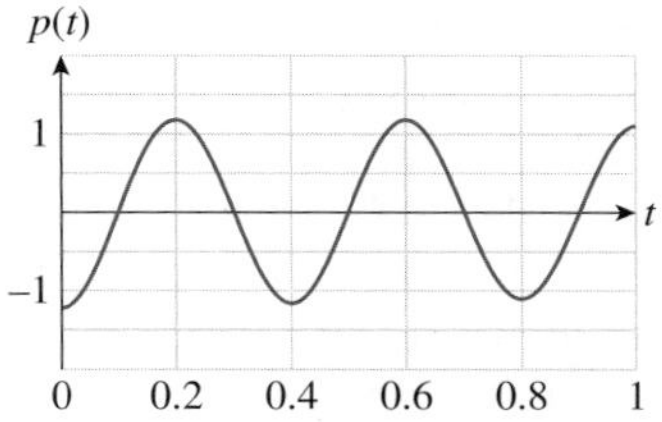

Graphs of p':

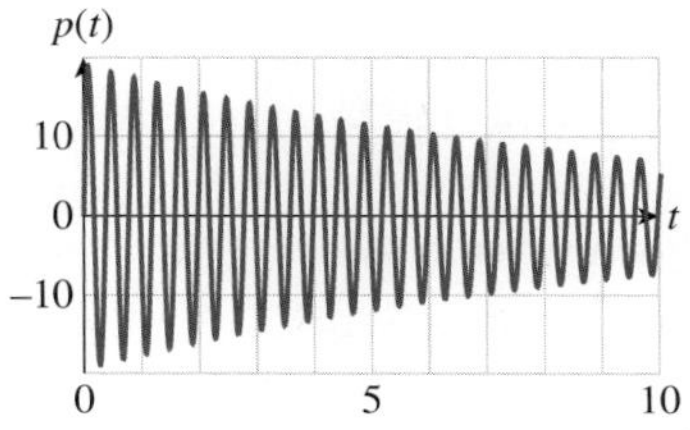

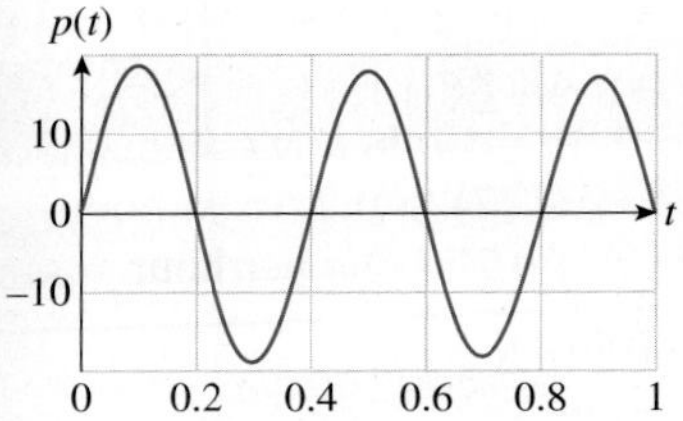

71. a. (III) **b.** Increasing at a rate of 0.157 degrees per thousand years **73.** −6; 6 **75.** Answers will vary. Examples: $f(x) = \sin x$; $f(x) = \cos x$ **77.** Answers will vary. Examples: $f(x) = e^{-x}$; $f(x) = -2e^{-x}$
79. The graph of $\cos x$ slopes down over the interval $(0, \pi)$, so that its derivative is negative over that interval. The function $-\sin x$, and not $\sin x$, has this property. **81.** The velocity is $p'(t) = A\omega \cos(\omega t + d)$, which is a maximum when its derivative, $p''(t) = -A\omega^2 \sin(\omega t + d)$, is zero. But this occurs when $\sin(\omega t + d) = 0$, so that $p(t)$ is zero as well, meaning that the stock is at yesterday's close.
83. The derivative of $\sin x$ is $\cos x$. When $x = 0$, this is $\cos(0) = 1$. Thus, the tangent to the graph of $\sin x$ at the point (0, 0) has slope 1, which means it slopes upward at 45°.

Section 9.3

1. $-\cos x - 2\sin x + C$
3. $2\sin x + 4.3\cos x - 9.33x + C$
5. $3.4\tan x + (\sin x)/1.3 - 3.2e^x + C$
7. $(7.6/3)\sin(3x - 4) + C$
9. $-(1/6)\cos(3x^2 - 4) + C$
11. $-2\cos(x^2 + x) + C$
13. $(1/6)\tan(3x^2 + 2x^3) + C$
15. $-(1/6)\ln|\cos(2x^3)| + C$
17. $3\ln|\sec(2x - 4) + \tan(2x - 4)| + C$
19. $(1/2)\sin(e^{2x} + 1) + C$ **21.** −2 **23.** ln(2)
25. 0 **27.** 1 **33.** $-\frac{1}{4}\cos(4x) + C$
35. $-\sin(-x + 1) + C$
37. $[\cos(-1.1x - 1)]/1.1 + C$
39. $-\frac{1}{4}\ln|\sin(-4x)| + C$
41. 0 **43.** 2π **45.** $-x\cos x + \sin x + C$
47. $\left[\frac{x^2}{2} - \frac{1}{4}\right]\sin(2x) + \frac{x}{2}\cos(2x) + C$
49. $-\frac{1}{2}e^{-x}\cos x - \frac{1}{2}e^{-x}\sin x + C$ **51.** $\pi^2 - 4$
53. Average $= 2/\pi$

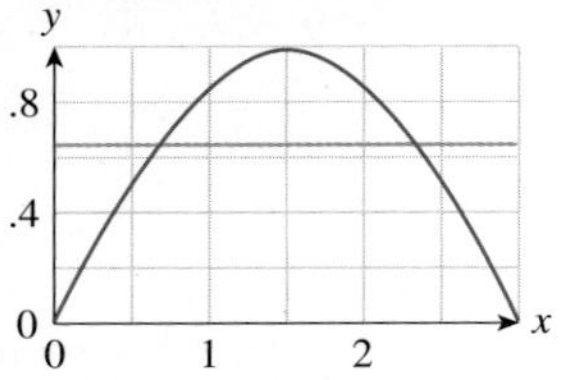

55. Diverges **57.** Converges to 1/2
59. $C(t) = 0.04t + \frac{2.6}{\pi}\cos\left[\frac{\pi}{26}(t - 25)\right] + 1.02$
61. 12 feet **63.** 79 sunspots
65. $P(t) = 7.5\sin[(\pi/26(t - 13)] + 12.5$; 7.7%
67. a. Average voltage over [0, 1/6] is zero; 60 cycles per second.
b.

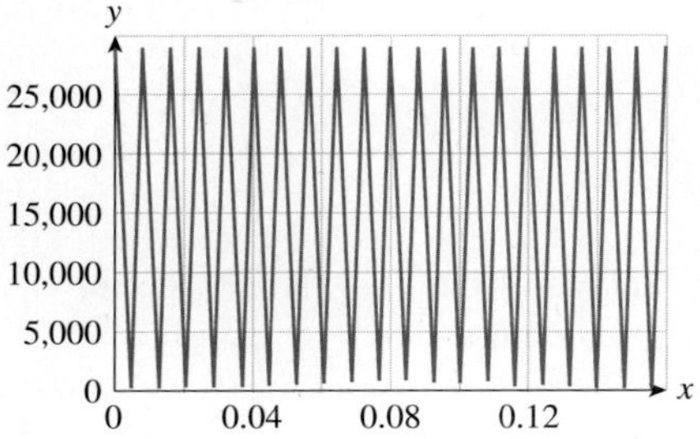

c. 116.673 volts **69.** \$50,000 **71.** It is always zero.
73. 1 **75.** $s = -\frac{K}{\omega^2}\sin(\omega t - \alpha) + Lt + M$ for constants L and M

Chapter 9 Review

1. $f(x) = 1 + 2\sin x$
3. $f(x) = 2 + 2\sin[\pi(x - 1)] = 2 + 2\sin[\pi(x + 1)]$
5. $f(x) = 1 + 2\cos(x - \pi/2)$
7. $f(x) = 2 + 2\cos[\pi(x + 1/2)] =$ $2 + 2\cos[\pi(x - 3/2)]$ **9.** $-2x\sin(x^2 - 1)$
11. $2e^x\sec^2(2e^x - 1)$ **13.** $4x\sin(x^2)\cos(x^2)$
15. $2\sin(2x - 1) + C$ **17.** $\tan(2x^2 - 1) + C$
19. $-\frac{1}{2}\ln|(\cos(x^2 + 1)| + C$ **21.** 1
23. $-x^2\cos x + 2x\sin x + 2\cos x + C$
25. $s(t) = 10{,}500 + 1{,}500\sin[(2\pi/52)t - \pi] =$ $10{,}500 + 1{,}500\sin(0.12083t - 3.14159)$
27. Decreasing at a rate of \$3,852 per month
29. \$2,029,700
31. $150t - \frac{100}{\pi}\cos\left[\frac{\pi}{2}(t - 1)\right]$ grams

Index